D0026637

LIBERTY, EQUALITY, POWER

William Gropper, *Automobile Industry*, 1940–1941 The Works Progress Administration of the U.S. Government commissioned the artist, William Gropper, to paint this mural on interior walls of the Northwestern Branch of the Detroit, Michigan Post Office in 1940 and 1941. Gropper's mural conveys the dynamism of America's most important industry—automobile manufacturing—then headquartered in Detroit and nearby Dearborn and Flint. It also conveys Gropper's admiration for the automobile workers themselves who are drawn as strong, purposive, and working in harmony with each other and with their machines. In its emphasis on working-class themes, this mural is representative of an important artistic trend during the New Deal era (1933–1945). When this Detroit post office was demolished in 1971, the mural was preserved and moved to the Student Center Lounge of Wayne State University (Detroit), where it is still on display.

LIBERTY, EQUALITY, POWER

A HISTORY OF THE AMERICAN PEOPLE

Enhanced Seventh Edition

John M. Murrin
Princeton University, Emeritus

Pekka Hämäläinen
University of Oxford

Paul E. Johnson
University of South Carolina, Emeritus

Denver Brunsman
George Washington University

James M. McPherson
Princeton University, Emeritus

Alice Fahs
University of California, Irvine, Emeritus

Gary Gerstle
University of Cambridge

Emily S. Rosenberg
University of California, Irvine, Emeritus

Norman L. Rosenberg
Macalester College, Emeritus

Australia • Brazil • Mexico • Singapore • United Kingdom • United States

***Liberty, Equality, Power: A History of the American People*, Enhanced Seventh Edition**
John M. Murrin, Pekka Hämäläinen, Paul E. Johnson, Denver Brunsman, James M. McPherson, Alice Fahs, Gary Gerstle, Emily S. Rosenberg, and Norman L. Rosenberg

Product Manager: Joseph Potvin

Product Assistant: Haley Gaudreau

Marketing Manager: Valerie Hartman

Content Manager: Claire Branman

Senior IP Analyst: Alexandra Ricciardi

IP Project Manager: Kelli Besse

Production Service/Compositor: SPi Global

Text Designer: Diane Beaseley

Cover Designer: Sarah Cole

Cover Image: Smithsonian American Art Museum, Washington, DC/Art Resource, NY

Library of Congress Control Number: 2018951021

Student Edition:
ISBN: 978-1-337-69974-7

Loose-leaf Edition:
ISBN: 978-0-357-02074-6

Cengage
20 Channel Center Street
Boston, MA 02210
USA

Printed in the United States of America
Print Number: 01 Print Year: 2018

About the Authors

JOHN M. MURRIN
Princeton University, Emeritus

John M. Murrin studies American colonial and revolutionary history and the early republic. He has edited one multivolume series and five books, including two essay collections, *Colonial America: Essays in Politics and Social Development*, Sixth Edition (2011), and *Saints and Revolutionaries: Essays in Early American History* (1984). His own essay topics range from ethnic tensions, the early history of trial by jury, the emergence of the legal profession, the Salem witch trials, and the political culture of the colonies and the new nation to the rise of professional baseball and college football in the 19th century. He served as president of the Society for Historians of the Early American Republic in 1998–1999.

PEKKA HÄMÄLÄINEN
University of Oxford

Pekka Hämäläinen is the Rhodes Professor of American History at the University of Oxford. A specialist in early American, Native American, borderlands, and environmental history, he is the author of *The Comanche Empire* (2008), which won multiple awards, including the Bancroft Prize, the Merle Curti Award, the Norris and Hundley Award, the William P. Clements Prize, and the Caughey Western History Association Prize. His writings have appeared in the *American Historical Review*; the *Journal of American History; History and Theory*; the *William and Mary Quarterly*; and the *Western Historical Quarterly*. He is currently working on a project on nomadic empires in world history, which is funded by the European Research Council. His new book, *Iktómi's People: The Lakota Age in America*, will be published by Yale University Press in 2019.

PAUL E. JOHNSON
University of South Carolina, Distinguished Professor Emeritus

A specialist in early national social and cultural history, Paul E. Johnson is the author of *The Early American Republic, 1789–1829* (2006); *Sam Patch, the Famous Jumper* (2003); and *A Shopkeeper's Millennium: Society and Revivals in Rochester, New York, 1815–1837*, 25th Anniversary Edition (2004). He is coauthor (with Sean Wilentz) of *The Kingdom of Matthias: Sex and Salvation in 19th-Century America* (1994) and editor of *African-American Christianity: Essays in History* (1994). He has been awarded the Merle Curti Award of the Organization of American Historians (1980), the Richard P. McCormick Prize of the New Jersey Historical Association (1989), and fellowships from the National Endowment for the Humanities (1985–1986), the John Simon Guggenheim Foundation (1995), the Gilder Lehrman Institute (2001), and the National Endowment for the Humanities (2006–2007).

DENVER BRUNSMAN
George Washington University

Denver Brunsman writes on the politics and social history of the American Revolution, the early American republic, and the British Atlantic world. His book, *The Evil Necessity: British Naval Impressment in the Eighteenth-Century Atlantic World* (2013), received the Walker Cowen Memorial Prize for an outstanding work in 18th-century studies in the Americas and Atlantic world. He is also a coauthor of *Leading Change: George Washington and Establishing the Presidency* (2017) and an editor of *The American Revolution Reader* (2013) and *Colonial America: Essays in Politics and Social Development*, Sixth Edition (2011), among other works. The recipient of numerous teaching awards, he was inducted into the George Washington University Academy of Distinguished Teachers in 2016.

JAMES M. MCPHERSON
Princeton University, Emeritus

James M. McPherson is a distinguished Civil War historian and was president of the American Historical Association in 2003. He won the 1989 Pulitzer Prize for his book *Battle Cry of Freedom: The Civil War Era*. His other publications include *Marching Toward Freedom: Blacks in the Civil War*, Second Edition (1991); *Ordeal by Fire: The Civil War and Reconstruction*, Third Edition (2001); *Abraham Lincoln and the Second American Revolution* (1991);

For Cause and Comrades: Why Men Fought in the Civil War which won the Lincoln Prize in 1998; *Crossroads of Freedom: Antietam* (2002); and *Tried by War: Abraham Lincoln as Commander in Chief* (2008), which won the Lincoln Prize for 2009.

ALICE FAHS

University of California, Irvine, Emeritus

Alice Fahs is a specialist in American cultural history of the 19th and 20th centuries. Her 2001 *The Imagined Civil War: Popular Literature of the North and South, 1861–1865* was a finalist in 2002 for the Lincoln Prize. Together with Joan Waugh, she published the edited collection *The Memory of the Civil War in American Culture* in 2004; she also edited Louisa May Alcott's *Hospital Sketches* (2004), an account of Alcott's nursing experiences during the Civil War first published in 1863. Her most recent book is *Out on Assignment: Newspaper Women and the Making of Modern Public Space* (2011). Her honors include an American Council of Learned Societies Fellowship and a Gilder Lehrman Fellowship, as well as fellowships from the American Antiquarian Society, the Newberry Library, and the Huntington Library.

GARY GERSTLE

University of Cambridge

Gary Gerstle is the Paul Mellon Professor of American History at the University of Cambridge. He previously taught at Princeton University, the Catholic University of America, the University of Maryland, and Vanderbilt University. A historian of the 20th-century United States, he is the author, coauthor, and coeditor of eight books and the author of nearly 40 articles. His books include *Working-Class Americanism: The Politics of Labor in a Textile City, 1914–1960* (1989); *American Crucible: Race and Nation in the Twentieth Century* (2001 winner of the Saloutos Prize for outstanding work in immigration and ethnic history (republished in 2017 with a new chapter on race and nation in the age of Obama); *The Rise and Fall of the New Deal Order, 1930–1980* (1989); *Ruling America: Wealth and Power in a Democracy* (2005); and *Liberty and Coercion: The Paradox of American Government from the Founding to the Present*, winner of the Organization of American Historians' Hawley Prize for the best book in American political history. He is the creator, writer, and narrator of a four-part radio series, "America: Laboratory of Democracy," that aired on BBC World Service in 2017 and on multiple National Public Radio stations in 2018. Gerstle has served on the board of editors of the *Journal of American History*, the *American Historical Review*, *Modern American History*, and *Past and Present*. He is a Fellow of the British Academy and a member of the Society of American Historians. Gerstle's other honors include a National Endowment for the Humanities Fellowship, a John Simon Guggenheim Memorial Fellowship, the Harmsworth Visiting Professorship of American History at the University of Oxford, and the 2013 Jeffrey Nordhaus Award for Excellence in Undergraduate Teaching at Vanderbilt University.

EMILY S. ROSENBERG

University of California, Irvine, Emeritus

Emily S. Rosenberg specializes in U.S. international relations in the 20th century and is the author of *Spreading the American Dream: American Economic and Cultural Expansion, 1890–1945* (1982); *Financial Missionaries to the World: The Politics and Culture of Dollar Diplomacy* (1999), which won the Ferrell Book Award; *A Date Which Will Live: Pearl Harbor in American Memory* (2004); and *Transnational Currents in a Shrinking World, 1870–1945* (2014). Her other publications include (with Norman L. Rosenberg) *In Our Times: America Since 1945*, Seventh Edition (2003), and numerous articles dealing with foreign relations in the context of international finance, American culture, and gender ideology. She has served on the board of the Organization of American Historians, on the board of editors of the *American Historical Review*, and as president of the Society for Historians of American Foreign Relations.

NORMAN L. ROSENBERG

Macalester College, Emeritus

Norman L. Rosenberg is DeWitt Wallace Professor of History and Legal Studies. His books include *Protecting the "Best Men": An Interpretive History of the Law of Libel* (1990) and (with Emily S. Rosenberg) *In Our Times: America Since 1945*, Seventh Edition (2003). He has published articles in the *Rutgers Law Review*, *UCLA Law Review*, *Constitutional Commentary*, *Law & History Review*, and many other journals and law-related anthologies.

Brief Contents

Contents in Detail

Maps and Features

MAPS

FEATURES

History Through Film

What They Said

Interpreting the Visual Past

To the Student

Why Study History?

Why take a course in American history? This is a question that many college and university students ask. In many respects, students today are like the generations of Americans who have gone before them: optimistic and forward looking, far more eager to imagine where we as a nation might be going than to reflect on where we have been. If anything, this tendency has become more pronounced in recent years, as the Internet revolution has accelerated the pace and excitement of change and made even the recent past seem at best quaint, at worst uninteresting and irrelevant.

But it is precisely in these moments of change that a sense of the past can be indispensable in terms of guiding our actions in the present and future. We can find in other periods of American history moments, like this one, of dizzying technological change, rapid alterations in the concentration of wealth and power, and basic changes in patterns of work, residence, and play. How did Americans at those times create, embrace, and resist these changes? In earlier periods of American history, the United States was home, as it is today, to a broad array of ethnic and racial groups. How did earlier generations of Americans respond to the cultural conflicts and misunderstandings that often arise from conditions of diversity? How did immigrants of the early 1900s perceive their new land? How and when did they integrate themselves into American society? To study how ordinary Americans of the past struggled with these issues is to gain perspective on the opportunities and problems that Americans face today.

History also provides an important guide to affairs of state. What role should America assume in world affairs? Should it participate in international bodies such as the United Nations, or insist on its ability to act autonomously and without the consent of other nations? What is the proper role of government in economic and social life? Should the government regulate the economy? To what extent should the government promote morality regarding religion, sexual practices, drinking and drugs, movies, TV, and other forms of mass culture? And what responsibilities do Americans as citizens owe to each other and to their nation? Americans of past generations debated these issues with verve and conviction. Learning about these debates and how they were resolved will strengthen our grasp of the policy possibilities for today and tomorrow.

History, finally, is about stories—stories that people tell about themselves; their families; their communities; their ethnicity, race, region, and religion; and their nation. They are stories of triumph and tragedy, of engagement and flight, and of high ideals and high comedy. When Americans tell these stories, "American history" may be the furthest thing from their minds. But, often, an implicit sense of the past informs what people say about grandparents who immigrated many years ago; the suburb in which they live; the church, synagogue, or mosque at which they worship; or the ethnic or racial group to which they belong. How well, we might ask, do we really understand these individuals, institutions, and groups? Do our stories about them capture their history and complexity? Or do our stories wittingly or unwittingly simplify or alter what these individuals and groups experienced? A study of American history helps us first to ask these questions and then to answer them. In the process, students can embark on a journey of intellectual and personal discovery and situate themselves more firmly than they had thought possible in relation to those who came before them. They can gain a firmer self-knowledge and a greater appreciation for the richness of the American nation and its history.

Analyzing Historical Sources

Astronomers investigate the universe through telescopes. Biologists study the natural world by collecting plants and animals in the field and then examining them with microscopes. Sociologists and psychologists study human behavior through observation and controlled laboratory experiments.

Historians study the past by examining historical "evidence" or "source" materials: government documents; the records of private institutions ranging from religious and charitable organizations to labor unions, corporations, and lobbying groups; letters, advertisements, paintings, music, literature, movies, and cartoons; buildings, clothing, farm implements, industrial machinery, and landscapes: anything and everything written or created by our ancestors that give clues about their lives and the times in which they lived.

Historians refer to written material as "documents." Excerpts of dozens of documents appear throughout the textbook. Each chapter also includes many visual representations of the American past as expressed in paintings, murals, cartoons, sculptures, photographs of buildings and individuals, and other kinds of historical evidence. The more you examine this "evidence," the more you will understand the main ideas of this book and of the U.S. history course you are taking. More generally, encounters with this evidence will enhance your ability to interpret the past.

Source Material Comes in Two Main Types: Primary and Secondary

"Primary" evidence is material that comes to us exactly as it was spoken, written, or drawn by the person who created it. The easiest way to locate examples of primary evidence in this textbook is to sample several *What They Said* features, each of which contains two or more primary documents. Each document introduces you to a point of view expressed by a past American in his or her own words, as he or she spoke them at the time. See, for example, "Virginians Debate the Constitution" in Chapter 6 (p. 195); "The Senate Debates the Compromise of 1850" in Chapter 13 (p. 368); "Differing Visions of Black Progress" in Chapter 18 (p. 515); or "Civil Liberties in Wartime" in Chapter 26 (p. 741).

"Secondary" evidence is an account constructed by an individual, usually a historian, about an event, organization, idea, or personality of historical significance. Stories about Abraham Lincoln recorded by his secretary of war would give us primary source information about Lincoln by someone who knew him. But imagine an account about Lincoln's performance as president written by someone who did not know Lincoln and who was born 50 or 100 years after Lincoln had lived. This individual would have to consult all the available primary sources he or she could find: Lincoln's own writings, letters, memos, and speeches; the accounts of Lincoln's presidency appearing in newspapers and magazines of the time; the writings and speeches of Lincoln's allies and enemies in civilian and military life; letters to Lincoln written by his supporters and opponents; documents pertaining to the performance of various government departments during Lincoln's presidency; and so on. Typically, someone studying Lincoln in such detail would do so with the ambition of writing a book about the man and his presidency. That book would be considered a secondary source of information about Lincoln.

In this textbook, we include lists of secondary sources at the end of each chapter under the heading, "Suggested Readings." These are books by historians pertinent to important issues discussed in that chapter. If you turn to the suggested readings for Chapter 17, for example, you will notice that two books listed there examine Reconstruction, the project begun during Lincoln's presidency to emancipate the slaves, establish racial equality in the South, and determine the circumstances under which the Confederate states would be readmitted to the Union. These books, Eric Foner, *Reconstruction: America's Unfinished Revolution, 1863–1877*, and Kenneth M. Stampp, *The Era of Reconstruction, 1865–1877*, are examples of secondary sources.

"Reading" and Studying Photographs, Artwork, and Movies

Your experience of this textbook will be enriched, we believe, if you take the time to study the artwork, photography, movies, and other forms of visual representation that are integral to it. For an example of what the textbook offers in its art program, and how you might study the art, consult the *Interpreting the Visual Past* feature in Chapter 23, "Turning the German Enemy into a Beast," (p. 640), reproduced below. This feature asks you, the student, to examine a U.S. Army recruiting poster from World War I that depicts the German enemy as a "mad brute" who must be destroyed. Take a close look at this poster. Among the questions you might ask about this poster are the following:

1. Why did the U.S. government choose to encourage support for the war by depicting the Germans as apes running amok in the land?
2. Why depict this beast as a sexual predator? Does the power of the poster stem in part from the contrast between the beast's dark brutishness and the light skin of the captive woman—a contrast that would have reminded early 20th century Americans of unresolved black–white tensions in their own society?
3. What do you think the consequences of representing Germans as beasts might have been for the millions of German immigrants and their descendants living in the United States?

Interpreting the Visual Past **Turning the German Enemy into a Beast**

By 1918, the government's campaign to engender support for the war focused as much on fear as on hope. In this poster, the German enemy is represented as a terrifying brute who violates Columbia—the Athena-like woman who was thought to embody America's highest aspirations to liberty, fairness, and wisdom. Many Americans had long admired Germany for the quality of its culture and of the immigrants it had sent to America. But Germany's lack of democracy and perceived militarism had also generated suspicions that pro-war propagandists now sought to use to strengthen sentiment in America for war.

The poster is notable, too, for its imagery of sexual violence. Fantasies of black brutes using their force to overpower and deflower chaste white women were common in America at this time; they became part of the rationale for segregating blacks from whites and for justifying the lynching of African American men. Here these fantasies are being deployed for foreign rather than domestic purposes.

Q *Compare this depiction of Columbia with the one in the Interpreting the Visual Past feature in Chapter 21 (see Image 21.8). What are the similarities? What are the differences? Why did Columbia become such a popular symbol of America?*

Q *Do you think that the artist who created this poster was correct in thinking that the sexualized images at the heart of this design would be effective in influencing attitudes toward Germany?*

HIP/Art Resource, NY

23.9 **Harry R. Hopps, *Destroy This Mad Brute, Enlist*, 1918.**

Most of you will not be able to answer these questions simply by studying the poster. You will need to acquire knowledge of relevant historical background and context—knowledge that the pages that surround this poster provide. But a good part of historical understanding comes not simply from finding answers but from being able to ask the right questions. Examining a piece of artwork may lead you to ask a series of queries that are potentially full of insight and that otherwise might not have occurred to you. So, as you read through the chapters, please pause to study the posters, portraits, cartoons, and photographs that grace its pages. To facilitate such learning in this seventh enhanced edition, we have added questions to hundreds of images appearing throughout the book. Have a look at these questions, which can be found in the captions that appear underneath many images; pause to answer them, and to share answers with your professor or teacher and fellow students. Raise questions about the textbook images that we have not thought to ask. Questions of this sort—and the discussions that arise from them—spur the learning process.

Reading and Studying Maps

Historical events happen in specific places. It is important to learn all you can about those places, and good maps can help you do this.

Your textbook includes many different kinds of maps, including those that show political boundaries, election results, population, topography, military battles, and irrigation and transportation networks. To study maps effectively, you should first take the time to identify and study map labels. Take a look at the foldout insert inside the front cover, which includes territorial growth and elevation maps of the United States. These maps provide four kinds of basic labels. They do the following:

1. Identify the states within and the countries bordering the United States
2. Identify the state capitals and major cities
3. Identify the rivers, large lakes, major bays, gulfs, and oceans
4. Identify the mountain ranges, important individual mountains, plateaus, plains, and deserts

In addition, these maps contain a distance scale in miles and kilometers. The scales appear in the lower right-hand corner of each map. The scales permit a reader to determine the actual size of different parts of U.S. territory and the distances between them. These maps also contain insets to show parts of the United States that are either too far from the mainland to be drawn to scale (Alaska and Hawaii) or too small to show up clearly on the map (Puerto Rico and the Virgin Islands).

Many of the maps in this book contain legends that use colors and other forms of coding to convey important information without cluttering up the map with words. Most maps in this book also have captions written by the textbook authors. Each caption is meant to describe the basic purpose of the map and to draw readers' attention to particular details. For this edition, we have added critical thinking questions to each of the map captions.

Below are three examples of the kinds of historical information that maps can communicate.

Example #1: Using Maps to Study Geographic-Political Change Across the 240 years of U.S. history, the political boundaries of the country and the number of states belonging to the United States have changed a great deal. Maps can help us to see and study those changes. Compare these two maps: Map 3.7 (this notation refers to the seventh map in the third chapter, p. 92), which shows how small the area of English settlement was in 1700; and Map 6.5 (p. 188), which shows the original 13 states at the time of independence as well as their claims to western land. Can you identify which new states were added to the United States out of the western lands that the original 13 states ceded to the national government between 1784 and 1802?

Example #2: Using Maps to Study Battles Maps can convey a wealth of knowledge about military battles in a compressed and efficient way. Take a look at Map 16.2 (p. 449), which charts the progress of the Battle of Chancellorsville (and Fredericksburg) during the Civil War. The boxed legend defines the 10 different kinds of bars

▲ MAP 3.7

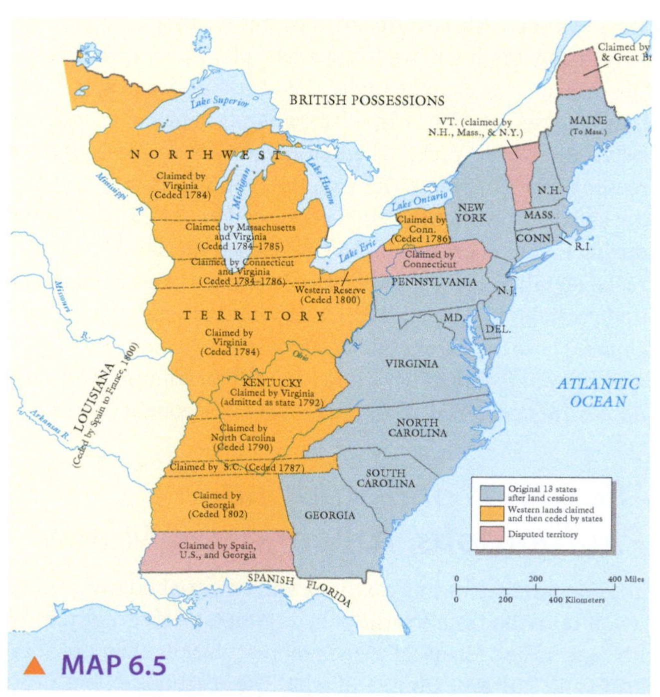

▲ MAP 6.5

and arrows that are used on the map to show the position of the Union and Confederate forces on the five different days of the battle and to demonstrate how the two armies conducted their advances and retreats. From studying the map itself, can you determine which side won the Battle of Chancellorsville? What information in the map led you to that conclusion?

Example #3: Using Maps to Study the American Economy The most detailed legend in the book is attached to Map 19.1 (p. 525), which shows the distribution of industries across America in the years 1900–1920. Twenty-two industries are identified by icons in the legend, and those icons, in turn, demonstrate where those industries were concentrated in the 48 states. A second legend to the right of the first uses color coding to identify the scale of manufacturing (measured in the dollars of factory production generated in each state in 1919). After examining this map, answer these questions:

1. In what states were the meatpacking, textile, and petroleum-refining industries concentrated?
2. Which state had no significant industrial output of any sort?
3. Which seven states had the highest factory output, as measured in dollars? Which six states had the lowest factory output? Were the states with the highest and lowest factory outputs clustered in particular regions? If so, which ones? Do you think that the uneven distribution of industry in the United States shaped American politics and culture in the 20th century?

We invite you to explore the maps mentioned in this guide as well as the many others offered in the textbook.

Preface

We are pleased to present the Enhanced Seventh Edition of *Liberty, Equality, Power.* Like the previous seven editions, this one captures the drama and excitement of America's past, from the pre-Columbian era through our own time. It integrates social and cultural history into a political story that is organized around the themes of liberty, equality, and power, and synthesizes the finest historical scholarship to create a narrative that is balanced, lively, and accessible to a broad range of students.

The *Liberty, Equality, Power* Approach

In this book, we tell many small stories, and one large one: how America transformed itself, in a relatively brief period of world history, from a land inhabited by hunter–gatherer and agricultural Native American societies into the most powerful industrial nation on earth. This story has been told many times before, and those who have told it in the past have usually emphasized the political experiment in liberty and equality that took root in North America in the 18th century.

We, too, stress the extraordinary and transformative impact that the ideals of liberty and equality exerted on American politics, society, and economics during the American Revolution and after. We show how the creation of a free economic environment—one in which entrepreneurial spirit, technological innovation, and manufacturing have flourished—underpinned American industrial might. We have also emphasized the successful struggles for freedom that, over the course of the country's 240 plus years of existence, have brought rights and opportunities—first to all white men, then to men of color, then to women—that they had not previously known.

But we have also identified a third factor in this pantheon of American ideals—that of power. We examine power in many forms: the accumulation of vast economic fortunes and their influence on the economy and on politics; the dispossession of American Indians from land that they regarded as their home; the enslavement of millions of Africans and their African-American descendants for a period of almost 250 years; the relegation of women and of racial, ethnic, and religious minorities to subordinate places in American society; and the extension of American control over foreign peoples, such as Latin Americans and Filipinos, who would have preferred to have been free and self-governing. We do not mean to suggest that American power has always been turned to these negative purposes. Subordinate groups have also marshaled power to combat oppression, as in the abolitionist and civil rights crusades, the campaign for woman suffrage, and the labor movement. The government has at times used its power to moderate poverty and to manage the economy in the interests of general prosperity. And it has used its military power to defeat Nazi Germany, World War II Japan, the cold war Soviet Union, and other enemies of freedom.

The invocation of power as a variable in American history impels us to widen the lens through which we look at the past and to enrich the stories we tell. Ours has been a history of freedom and domination; of progress toward realizing a broadly democratic polity and of delays and reverses; of abundance and poverty; of wars for freedom and justice and for control of foreign markets. In complicating our master narrative in this way, we think we have rendered American history more exciting and intriguing. Progress has not been automatic, but the product of ongoing struggles.

In this book, we have tried to capture the diversity of the American past, both in terms of outcomes and in terms of the variety of groups who have participated in America's making. American Indians are not presented simply as the victims of European aggression but as peoples diverse in their own ranks, with a variety of systems of social organization and cultural expression. We give equal treatment to the industrial titans of American history—the likes of Andrew Carnegie and John D. Rockefeller—and to those, such as small farmers and ordinary workers, who resisted the corporate reorganization of economic life. We examine the major advances of 1863, when African Americans were freed from slavery, and of 1868, when they were made full citizens of the United States. But we also note how a majority of African Americans had to wait another 100 years, until the civil rights movement of the 1960s, to gain full access to American freedoms. We tell similarly complex stories about women, Latinos, and other groups of ethnic Americans.

Political issues are only part of America's story. Americans have always loved their leisure and have created the world's most vibrant popular culture. They have embraced technological innovations, especially those promising to make their lives easier and more fun. We have, therefore, devoted considerable space to a discussion of American popular culture, from the founding of the first newspapers in the 18th century and the rise of movies, jazz, and the comics in the early 20th century to the cable television and Internet revolutions in recent years. We have also analyzed how American industry has periodically altered home and personal life by making new products—such as clothing, cars, refrigerators, and computers—available to consumers. In such ways, we hope to give our readers a rich portrait of how Americans lived at various points in our history.

New to the Enhanced Seventh Edition

We wish to take note of two major changes to the last edition that are still heavily influencing this one: first, the addition of two new authors, Pekka Hämäläinen and Denver Brunsman, and, second, a dramatic expansion of our primary source program. Pekka and Denver, specialists in the history of early America and the early Republic, have enabled us to preserve our textbook's robust history of British America while also enhancing its coverage of Spanish America, French America, and Native America. Pekka and Denver have worked very closely with each other and the rest of the authors both to introduce new material and perspectives and to maintain the great strengths of earlier editions. They have enhanced the book's continental perspective, including far more on the early history of North American territory that would become California, New Mexico, and Texas. They have expanded significantly the attention to environmental history, and revised Chapters 4–10 to bring the latest scholarship to bear on these subjects: the role of women in 18th-century transatlantic consumer society; loyalists in the American revolutionary era; slavery and the Atlantic slave trade; the international threats faced by the United States in the early decades of the 19th century; and the relations among European empires, Native Americans, and the United States in the first half of the 19th century. We are delighted that Pekka and Denver have joined the *Liberty, Equality, Power* team.

We also chose to preserve in the enhanced seventh edition the major revision and expansion of the primary source program undertaken in the last edition. The most important change in that program was the introduction of a new feature, ***What They Said***, which appears in every one of the textbook's 32 chapters. Each *What They Said* feature focuses on a controversial issue pertinent to the time period covered in that chapter and presents two or more sides of that issue in the words of individuals who were actual participants in the debates. The response to this feature has been very positive, which has impelled us to maintain it as a central feature of this new edition.

What They Said, in combination with two other primary document features, ***Interpreting the Visual Past*** and the much admired ***History Through Film***, endow *Liberty, Equality, Power* with one of the most comprehensive, diverse, and intriguing programs of primary sources available in any U.S. history textbook. To keep our *History Through Film* series up-to-date, we have selected for this edition five new films to examine: *Even the Rain* (2010); *Hamilton's America* (2016); *Lincoln* (2012); *The Immigrant* (2013); and *Selma* (2014). We hope you will share our excitement about the inclusion of these new movies.

As in past editions, we have continued to make sure that the textbook's last chapter (Chapter 32) is up to date and gives adequate attention to the important developments in politics, economics, and culture of the 21st century. The revised Chapter 32 offers discussion of George W. Bush's victories in 2000 and 2004; the destruction of the World Trade Center towers on September 11, 2001; the resulting wars on terrorism and on Saddam Hussein in Iraq and the Taliban in Afghanistan; Barack Obama's victories in 2008 and 2012; the financial crash of 2008–2009; the passage of the Affordable Care Act and the rise of the Tea Party; and the 2016 election of Donald J. Trump.

In preparing for this revision, we solicited feedback from professors and scholars throughout the country, many of whom have used the seventh edition of *Liberty, Equality, Power* in their classrooms. Their comments proved most helpful, and many of their suggestions have been incorporated into this edition.

We have carried over and, in some cases, enhanced pedagogical changes that we made to earlier editions and that have proved popular with professors and students. Each chapter now begins with a set of **learning objectives**. **Chapter outlines** and **chronology boxes** continue to appear at the beginning of each chapter, and **focus questions** at the beginning of each major section and at each chapter's end, where they appear alongside ***Critical Thinking*** questions. We have updated our ***Identifications*** (boldfaced terms that appear throughout the text) and supply the definitions for these terms in a comprehensive ***Glossary*** appearing at the end of the book. Each map in our outstanding map program comes equipped with a brief caption instructing students about how to interpret the geographical and topographical data it contains. For the first time, we have inserted questions into each map caption to encourage students to engage with the material that the maps contain. For the first time as well, we have added student-focused questions to hundreds of images appearing throughout the text. In order to keep the art program fresh, we have replaced about 10 percent of the images. Finally, we have updated our ***Suggested Readings*** for each chapter while keeping the lists brief.

We believe that both instructors and students will find these aids to be useful and well-placed tools for reviewing what they have learned and for pushing outward the frontiers of their knowledge.

Finally, we have scrutinized each page of this textbook, making sure our prose is clear, the historical issues well presented, and the scholarship up to date and accurate.

Specific Revisions to Content and Coverage

Chapter 1 New History Through Film Feature, *Even the Rain* (2010).

Chapter 3 Expanded the discussion of the early 18th-century Indigenous Southwest as well as Indian women and gender dynamics.

Chapter 6 Updated material to highlight the role of loyalists and enslaved African Americans in the American Revolutionary War; added new section on "Violence and Attrition" that draws on growing scholarship that emphasizes the American Revolution as a violent event; new History Through Film feature, *Hamilton's America* (2016); streamlined discussion of state constitutions and American constitutionalism.

Chapter 9 Provided new section on "Slavery and Capitalism" and updated other sections to reflect emerging literature that links slavery to the development of American and global capitalism; consolidated content on southern families and the place of mastery and honor in southern culture.

Chapter 15 Updated History Through Film feature, *Glory* (1989).

Chapter 16 New History Through Film feature, *Lincoln* (2012).

Chapter 17 Updated "Education" section to "Churches and Schools" and provided additional information on the educational opportunities that were created for African American children by African Americans during Reconstruction. Revised "Blacks in Office" section to lend more focus to accomplishments of African Americans in this time.

Chapter 18 Updated sections to bring the focus to the specific Indian tribes, especially the sections "Conflict with the Dakota Sioux" and "Suppression of Central Plains Indians."

Chapter 19 New Interpreting the Visual Past feature "Women and Bicycles."

Chapter 20 Took two sections on middle-class women's lives that in previous editions had appeared in Chapter 19 and incorporated them into a new section, "The 'New Woman' and the Rise of Feminism" in this chapter. The result is a much more robust section on gender and the history of sexuality.

Chapter 21 Took two sections on middle-class women's lives previously appearing in Chapter 19 and incorporated them into an expanded section, "Settlement Houses and Clubwomen," in this chapter. The result is a significantly enhanced section on women's history.

Chapter 24 New History Through Film Feature, *The Immigrant* (2013).

Chapter 28 New section titles and updates to "Policies toward the Third World," "The New Conservative Critique," "Foreign Policy, 1960-1963," "Domestic Policy, 1960-1963," and "The Cold War Eases—and Ends."

Chapter 30 New section titles and updates to "Debating Economic Policies," and "Debating Welfare and Energy Policies."

Chapter 32 Revised and updated entire chapter, especially on economic issues associated with the Great Recession and on the political volatility that led to the election of Donald Trump in 2016. New History Through Film feature, *Selma* (2014).

Supplements

Instructor Resources

MindTap for *Liberty, Equality, Power: A History of the American People*, Enhanced Seventh Edition is a flexible online learning platform that provides students with a relevant and engaging learning experience that builds their critical thinking skills and fosters their argumentation and analysis skills. Through a carefully designed chapter-based learning path, MindTap supports students as they develop historical understanding, improve their reading and writing skills, and practice critical thinking by making connections between ideas.

Students read sections of the ebook and take Check Your Understanding quizzes that test their reading comprehension. They put higher-level critical thinking skills into practice to complete chapter tests. They also use these skills to analyze textual and visual primary sources in each chapter through an autograded image primary source activity and a manually graded short essay in which students write comparatively about multiple primary sources.

Beyond the chapter-level content, students can increase their comfort in analyzing primary sources through thematically-organized primary source autograded activities that span the text. They also practice synthesizing their knowledge and articulating what they have learned through responding to essay prompts that span broader themes in the book.

MindTap also allows instructors to customize their content, providing tools that seamlessly integrate YouTube clips, outside websites, and personal content directly into the learning path. Instructors can assign additional primary source content through the Instructor Resource Center and Questia, primary- and secondary-source databases located on the MindTap app dock that house thousands of peer-reviewed journals, newspapers, magazines, and books.

The additional content available in MindTap mirrors and complements the authors' narrative, but also includes primary-source content and assessments not found in the printed text. To learn more, ask your Cengage Learning sales representative to demo it for you—or go to www.cengage.com/mindtap.

Instructor's Companion Website The Instructor's Companion Website, accessed through the Instructor Resource Center (login.cengage.com), houses all of the supplemental materials you can use for your course. This includes a Test Bank, Instructor's Manual, and PowerPoint Lecture Presentations. The Test Bank contains multiple-choice and true-or-false questions for each chapter. The Instructor's Resource Manual includes chapter outlines, chronologies, thematic topics for enrichment, suggested essay topics, lecture outlines, and teaching resources. Finally, the PowerPoint Lectures are ADA-compliant slides that collate the key takeaways from the chapter in concise visual formats perfect for in-class presentations or student review.

Cengage.com/student Save your students time and money. Direct them to www.cengage.com/student for a choice in formats and savings and a better chance to succeed in your class. Cengage.com/student, Cengage Learning's online store, is a single destination for more than 10,000 new textbooks, ebooks, study tools, and audio supplements. Students have the freedom to purchase à la carte exactly what they need when they need it. Students can save up to 70% on the ebook electronic textbook.

CENGAGE UNLIMITED

The first-of-its-kind digital subscription designed specially to lower costs. Students get total access to everything Cengage has to offer on demand—in one place. That's 20,000 eBooks, 2,300 digital learning products, and dozens of study tools across 70 disciplines and over 675 courses. Currently available in select markets. Details at **www.cengage.com/unlimited**

Learn more at Cengage.com about books that build skills in doing history including:

- *Doing History: Research and Writing in the Digital Age*, 2e ISBN: 9781133587880 Prepared by Michael J. Galgano, J. Chris Arndt, and Raymond M. Hyser of James Madison University.
- *Writing for College History*, 1e ISBN: 9780618306039 Prepared by Robert M. Frakes of Clarion University.
- *The Modern Researcher*, 6e ISBN: 9780495318705 Prepared by Jacques Barzun and Henry F. Graff of Columbia University.

Reader Program. Cengage Learning publishes a number of readers. Some contain exclusively primary sources, others are devoted to essays and secondary sources, and still others provide a combination of primary and secondary sources. All of these readers are designed to guide students through the process of historical inquiry. Visit www.cengage.com/history for a complete list of readers.

Custom Options. Nobody knows your students like you, so why not give them a text that is tailor-fit to their needs? Cengage Learning offers custom solutions for your course—whether it's making a small modification to *Liberty, Equality, Power* Enhanced 7e, to match your syllabus or combining multiple sources to create something truly unique. Contact your Cengage Learning representative to explore custom solutions for your course.

Acknowledgments

We recognize the contributions of reviewers who read portions of the manuscript in various stages:

Sam Abrams, The Beacon School
William Allison, Weber State University
Angie Anderson, Southeastern Louisiana University
Kenneth G. Anthony, University of North Carolina, Greensboro
Rick Ascheman, Rochester Community and Technical College
Paul R. Beezley, Texas Tech University
David Bernstein, California State University at Long Beach
Sue Blanchette, Hillcrest High School
Jeff Bloodworth, Ohio University
Michael R. Bradley, Motlow College
Betty Brandon, University of South Alabama
Daniel Patrick Brown, Moorpark College
Ronald G. Brown, College of Southern Maryland
Susan Burch, Gallaudet University
Vanessa M. Camacho, El Paso Community College
Thomas M. Cangiano, The Lawrenceville School
Edward V. Carroll, Heartland Community College
Jeffrey W. Coker, Belmont University
Phil Crow, North Harris College
Lorenzo M. Crowell, Mississippi State University
Amy E. N. Darty, University of Central Florida
Thomas M. Deaton, Dalton State College
Norman C. Delaney, Del Mar College
Ted Delaney, Washington and Lee University
Andrew J. DeRoche, Front Range Community College
Rebecca de Schweinitz, Brigham Young University
Bruce Dierenfield, Canisius College
Brian R. Dirck, Anderson University
Maura Doherty, Illinois State University
R. Blake Dunnavent, Lubbock Christian University
Eileen Eagan, University of Southern Maine
Derek Elliott, Tennessee State University
B. Jane England, North Central Texas College
Joe Escobar, Lane Community College
William B. Feis, Buena Vista University
David J. Fitzpatrick, Washtenaw Community College
Van Forsyth, Clark College
Michael P. Gabriel, Kutztown University of Pennsylvania
Gary Gallagher, Pennsylvania State University
Kevin M. Gannon, Grand View University
Gerald Ghelfi, Santa Ana College
Michael Goldberg, University of Washington, Bothell
Kathleen Gorman, Minnesota State University, Mankato
David E. Hamilton, University of Kentucky
Michael J. Haridopolos, Brevard Community College
Mark Harvey, North Dakota State University
Brenda Hasterok, Spain Park High School
Kurt Hohenstein, Hampden Sydney College
Mark Huddle, University of Georgia
Samuel C. Hyde Jr., Southeastern Louisiana University

Thomas N. Ingersoll, Ohio State University
J. Michael Jeffries, Northeastern Technical College
Frank Karpiel, Ramapo College of New Jersey
Anthony E. Kaye, Pennsylvania State University
Michael Kazin, Georgetown University
Michael King, Moraine Valley Community College
Greg Kiser, Northwest Arkansas Community College
Michael Krenn, Appalachian State
Matthew Kruer, University of Oklahoma
Donna Kumler, Grayson College
Frank Lambert, Purdue University
Pat Ledbetter, North Central Texas College
Michelle LeMaster, Eastern Illinois University
Jan Leone, Middle Tennessee State University
Craig Livingston, Montgomery College
Robert F. Marcom, San Antonio College
Suzanne Marshall, Jacksonville State University
Brenda Taylor Matthews, Texas Wesleyan University
Joanne Maypole, Front Range Community College
Christopher McColm, Aims Community College
Jimmie McGee, South Plains College
Nora E. McMillan, San Antonio College
Jerry Mills, Midland College
Charlene Mires, Villanova University
Nancy Mitchell, North Carolina State University
Brock Mislan, Watchung Hills Regional High School
Rick Moniz, Chabot College
Rick Murray, Los Angeles Valley College
Caryn Neumann, Miami University of Ohio
James Nichols, Queensborough Community College
Michael R. Nichols, Tarrant County College, Northwest
Linda Noel, Morgan State University
Christy Olsen, Skyline High School
Richard B. Partain, Bakersfield College
William Pencak, Pennsylvania State University
Jaakko Puisto, Scottsdale Community College
Teresa Thomas Perrin, Austin Community College
David Poteet, New River Community College
Donald Rakestraw, Winthrop University
Howard Reed, University of Bridgeport
Jonathan Rees, Colorado State University–Pueblo
Thomas S. Reid, Valencia Community College
Anne Richardson, Texas Christian University
Lelia M. Roeckell, Molloy College
Thomas J. Rowland, University of Wisconsin, Oshkosh
Mark Sattler, Rockingham Community College
Roy Scott, Mississippi State University
Reynolds J. Scott-Childress, State University of New York at New Paltz
Katherine A. S. Sibley, St. Joseph's University
Herb Sloan, Barnard College
M. Todd Smallwood, Manatee Community College
John Smolenski, University of California, Davis
Steve Stein, University of Memphis
Michael J. Steiner, Northwest Missouri State University
Jennifer Stollman, University of Mississippi
Siegfried H. Sutterlin, Indian Hills Community College
Richard O. Swanson, Duxbury High School
John Wood Sweet, The University of North Carolina at Chapel Hill
Teresa Fava Thomas, Fitchburg State College
Xiansheng Tian, Metro State College of Denver
Jamie Underwood, Montana State University Northern
Juan Valenzuela, Kennesaw State University
Vincent Vinikas, University of Arkansas, Little Rock
Vernon Volpe, University of Nebraska
Harry L. Watson, The University of North Carolina at Chapel Hill
Thomas Weyant, University of Akron
William Benton Whisenhunt, College of DuPage
David K. White, McHenry County College
Laura Matysek Wood, Tarrant County College, Northwest

We wish to thank the members of the Cengage staff, many of them new to the project, for embracing our textbook wholeheartedly and for expertly guiding the production of this seventh enhanced edition. Special thanks to Joseph Potvin, Product Manager; Claire Branman and Erika Hayden, Content Managers; Kate MacLean, Learning Designer; and Hannah Whitcher, Project Manager at SPiGlobal. We wish to thank as well these members of the Cengage team: Sarah Cole, Senior Designer; Robert Alper, Senior In-House, SME; Valerie Hartman, Senior Marketing Manager; and Haley Gaudreau, Product Assistant. A big thanks, finally, to Cengage's marketing department and to the sales representatives who have worked hard and creatively to generate interest in our book among university, college, and high school teachers across America.

No project of this scope is completely error free. If you find any errors, please let us know what they are. Feel free as well to send queries and suggestions our way. The book will be enriched by such feedback. Please send comments to our product manager, Joseph Potvin at joseph.potvin@cengage.com.

Finally, each of us would like to offer particular thanks to those historians, friends, and family members who helped to bring this project to a successful conclusion.

Personal Acknowledgments

JOHN M. MURRIN Mary R. Murrin has provided the kind of moral and personal support that made completion of this project possible. James Axtell and Gregory Evans Dowd saved me from many mistakes, mostly about Indians. John E. Selby and Eugene R. Sheridan were particularly helpful on the Revolution. Fred Anderson and Virginia DeJohns Anderson offered acute suggestions. Several former colleagues and graduate students have also contributed in various ways, especially Stephen Aron, Andrew Isenberg, Ignacio Gallup-Diaz, Evan P. Haefeli, Beth Lewis-Pardoe, Geoffrey Plank, Nathaniel J. Sheidley, and Jeremy Stern.

PEKKA HÄMÄLÄINEN I would like to thank Gary Gerstle and the other authors for welcoming me so warmly to the team. Gary was an inexhaustible source of knowledge and guidance, and Denver Brunsman was an absolute delight to work with. I also want to express my gratitude to John Murrin and Paul Johnson for the opportunity to continue and build on their work. I am grateful to Margaret Beasley for her remarkable proficiency, support, and patience.

PAUL E. JOHNSON My greatest debt is to the community of scholars who write about the United States between the Revolution and the Civil War. Closer to home, I owe thanks to the other writers of this book, particularly to John Murrin. The Department of History at the University of South Carolina provided time to work, while my wife, Kasey Grier, and stray dogs named Lucy, Bill, Buddy, and Patty provided the right kinds of interruptions.

DENVER BRUNSMAN I thank my fellow authors, particularly Gary Gerstle for steering the good ship *LEP* into port. As always, it was a joy to collaborate with Pekka Hämäläinen. We all appreciate the editorial team at Cengage for their vision in committing to a new edition of the textbook in an industry experiencing massive changes. Without the dedicated work of countless scholars, a new edition would not be necessary. Moreover, without students, there would be no need for this book. At George Washington University, I am lucky to have the best students imaginable to help develop ideas and serve as my first test audience. Finally, I continue to draw on the boundless support and inspiration of my wife, Taryn, and our children, Gavin and Sanne, for this and all projects.

JAMES M. MCPHERSON My family provided an environment of affection and stability that contributed immeasurably to the writing of my chapters, while undergraduate students at Princeton University who have taken my courses over the years provided feedback, questions, and insights that helped me to understand what students know and don't know, and what they need to know.

ALICE FAHS Thanks are due to Gary Gerstle, whose keen editorial eye and judgment helped greatly with revisions of Chapter 19. Our "team leader" among the authors, Gary has given generously of his time to the rest of us, providing constant support. Margaret Beasley was a crucial resource of intelligence and good cheer during her years as development editor; we all know we are very lucky. I am grateful as well to Ann West, our former editor at Cengage, for her exceptional leadership and commitment to excellence; and to James M. McPherson for the initial invitation to become part of *Liberty, Equality, Power.* At the University of California, Irvine, David Igler was an important resource for past revisions of Chapter 18. My students, both undergraduate and graduate, have continued to be a source of inspiration to me in conceptualizing this textbook. Finally, my family continues to listen patiently to history anecdotes over breakfasts, lunches, and dinners—whether in California or Texas. To Charlie and to Mimi, many thanks.

GARY GERSTLE A long time ago, Jerald Podair, Thomas Knock, and the late Roy Rosenzweig gave me exceptionally thorough, thoughtful, and insightful critiques on early drafts of my chapters. This textbook still benefits from their good and generous work. Former graduate students Kathleen Trainor, Reynolds Scott-Childress, Linda Noel, Kelly Ryan, Robert Chase, Marcy Wilson, Thomas Castillo, and Katarina Keane offered skillful research assistance on earlier editions. At Vanderbilt, research assistants Monte Holman and William Bishop made many indispensable and timely contributions to the sixth and seventh editions. My undergraduate students at the University of Maryland and at Vanderbilt University kept me young, and on my toes. Teaching modern American history abroad to Cambridge University undergraduates in the age of Brexit and Trump has been a privilege, and a source of new perspectives on my native land. A special thanks both to my original coauthors for their intelligence, wit, and deep commitment to this project, and to my new coauthors, who have helped me to imagine what a textbook for this new century ought to look like.

EMILY AND NORMAN ROSENBERG would like to thank our children—Sarah, Molly, Ruth, and Joe—for all of the wisdom and good cheer they provided while the six of us were moving through the period of history related in the final chapters of this book. Successive generations of students at Macalester College, some now academics themselves, offered pointed critiques of our classes, and these inspired (and provoked) us continually to revise our approach toward teaching and writing about the recent past. Our former colleagues at Macalester merit a similar kind of thanks. (Here, we note, with deep sadness and fond memories, the recent passing of one them, Jerry K. Fisher, a keen, inside observer of electronic and digital media as well as a professor who excelled in moving student learning beyond the classroom.) More recently, Emily Rosenberg's graduate students at the University of California, Irvine, helped clarify how our chapters might better reach out to students who may be using this enhanced seventh edition. We also thank the historians who offered both supportive and helpfully critical comments on earlier versions of *Liberty, Equality, Power.* We have not always followed their advice, but this enhanced seventh edition is much the better for their assistance.

John M. Murrin, Pekka Hämäläinen, Paul E. Johnson, Denver Brunsman, James M. McPherson, Alice Fahs, Gary Gerstle, Emily S. Rosenberg, Norman L. Rosenberg

1 When Old Worlds Collide: Encounters in the Atlantic World to 1600

Source: Wikipedia.org

1.1 Sebastian Münster's Map of the New World, 1540 When overseas exploration brought the hemispheres together, Native Americans and European newcomers saw one another as strange and alien. Europeans struggled to make sense of the worlds they discovered, and Indians struggled to make sense of the motives and demands of the colonists. The encounters between natives and colonists in the Western Hemisphere resulted both in violent conquests and complex exchanges of technology, foods, pathogens, ideas, and styles. Indians and Europeans fought and killed one another, but, over time, they also found ways to cooperate and accommodate one another.

WHEN CHRISTOPHER COLUMBUS crossed the Atlantic, he did not know where he was going, and he died without realizing where he had been. Yet, he altered the history of the world. In two generations after 1492, European navigators mastered the oceans of the world, joining together societies that had lived in isolation for thousands of years. European invaders colonized the Americas, not just with sails, gunpowder, and steel, but also with their crops and livestock and, most of all, their diseases. They brought slavery with them as well. By 1600, they had created the first global economy in the history of humankind and had inflicted upon the native peoples of the Americas—unintentionally, for the most part—the greatest known catastrophe that human societies have ever experienced.

In the 15th century, when all of this started, the Americas were in some ways a more ancient world than Western Europe. For example, the Portuguese, Spanish, French, and English languages were only beginning to assume their modern forms during the century or two before and after Columbus's voyage. Centuries earlier, when Rome was falling into ruins and Paris and London were little more than hamlets, huge cities were thriving in the Andes and Mesoamerica (the area embracing Central America and southern and central Mexico). Which world was old and which was new is a matter of perspective. Each already had its own distinctive past. ■

1-1 Peoples in Motion

Q *How did the extinction of megafauna shape human history in the Americas?*

Like all other countries of North and South America, the United States is a nation of immigrants. Even the native peoples were once migrants who settled a strange new land.

Long before Europeans discovered and explored the wide world around them, many different peoples had migrated thousands of miles over thousands of years across oceans and continents. Before Christopher Columbus sailed west from Spain in 1492, several waves of immigrants had already swept over the Americas. The earliest came from Asia. The last, from northern Europe, did not stay.

1-1a *From Beringia to the Americas*

During the most recent Ice Age, glaciers covered huge portions of the Americas, Europe, and Asia. The ice captured so much of the world's water that sea level fell drastically and created a land bridge 600 miles wide across the Bering Strait between Siberia and Alaska. For thousands of years, this exposed area—Beringia—was dry land on which plants, animals, and humans could live. Starting about 15,000 years ago, people drifted in small bands from Asia to North America, probably following steppe bison, caribou, musk oxen, and other large prey animals (see Map 1.1). Slowly they moved southward, some following a narrow ice-free corridor that emerged on the eastern flank of the Rocky Mountains as the Ice Age drew to a close and the glaciers melted into oceans. Others may have moved down the Pacific coastline on small fishing vessels, subsisting on the rich sea life that flourished in an offshore kelp "forest" that stretched from Alaska to Baja California.

The numbers of these first Americans were, in all likelihood, quite small. They were distinctly healthy, for their long migrations across cold Beringia had destroyed many of the pathogens they might have carried. They were also highly mobile and their nomadic communities spread rapidly throughout the hemisphere. By 8000 BCE, they had reached all the way to Tierra del Fuego at the southern tip of South America. Near the eastern coast of North America, the Thunderbird dig in Virginia's Shenandoah Valley shows signs of continuous human occupation from before 9000 BCE until the arrival of Europeans.

Not everyone pushed to the south, however. The ancestors of the Inuits (called Eskimos by other Indians) crossed after 7000 BCE, when Beringia was again under water. Around 2000 BCE, these people began to migrate from the Aleutian Islands and Alaska to roughly their present sites in the Americas. Unlike their predecessors, they found the arctic environment to their liking and migrated across the northern rim of North America and then across the north Atlantic to Greenland.

1-1b *The Great Extinction and the Rise of Agriculture*

As the glaciers receded and the climate warmed, the people who had moved south and east found an attractive environment teeming with game. Imperial mammoths, huge mastodons, woolly rhinoceroses, a species of enormous bison, and giant ground sloths roamed the plains and forests, along with camels and herds of small horses, which could not be ridden and were valued only as food. These animals had thrived in a frigid climate but they had trouble adjusting to hot weather. They also had no instinctive fear of the two-legged intruders, who became ever more skillful at hunting them. A superior spear point, the fluted **Clovis tip**, appeared in the area of present-day New Mexico and Texas around 13,000 BCE, and its use spread rapidly throughout North and South America. As human families fanned out across the hemisphere, however, the big game began to disappear. Overhunting pushed the megafauna toward extinction, but the impact of human predation was vastly amplified by shifting environmental conditions. The warming climate reduced the available water and forage, debilitating the massive beasts. Most large animals of the Americas disappeared about 9,000 years ago.

Their passing left the hemisphere with a severely depleted number of animal species. Nothing as big as the elephant survived. The largest beasts left were bears, bison, and moose; the biggest cat was the jaguar. The extinction of these animal species probably led to a decline in human population as people struggled to cope with the diminished biodiversity and searched for new sources of food. Some Native Americans raised guinea pigs, turkeys, and ducks, but apart from dogs on both continents, they domesticated no large animals except in South America, where they used llamas to haul light loads in mountainous terrain and raised alpacas for wool. In Eurasia, with its numerous domesticated animals, the killer diseases such as smallpox and bubonic plague took hold first among domestic animals and then spread among humans. Disease by disease, over a long period of time, survivors developed some immunities. No comparable process occurred in the Americas, where few animals could be domesticated.

Some native peoples settled down without becoming farmers. Those in the Pacific Northwest sustained themselves through fishing, hunting, and the gathering of nuts, berries, and other edible plants. Men fished and hunted; women gathered. California peoples maintained some of the densest populations north of Mexico by collecting acorns and processing them into meal, which they baked into cakes. In the rain forests of Brazil, in south and central Florida, and in the cold woodlands of northern New England, hunter-gatherers also prospered without becoming farmers. In the Great Plains, the modern bison, a greatly dwarfed adaptation of the cold-climate bison, numbered in the millions, supporting numerous nomadic hunting societies for thousands of years.

CHRONOLOGY

30,000–13,000 BCE	Bering land bridge open • Migrations to the Americas begin
9000 BCE	Shenandoah Valley occupied
9000–7000 BCE	Most large American mammals become extinct
500 BCE–400 CE	Adena-Hopewell mound builders thrive in Ohio River valley
200–900	Mayan civilization flourishes in Mesoamerica
900–1250	Medieval Warm Period • Toltecs dominate the Valley of Mexico • Maize becomes a major food source in North America • Mogollon, Hohokam, and Anasazi cultures thrive in American Southwest • Cahokia becomes the largest Mississippian mound builders' city
1001–1014	Norse find Vinland on Newfoundland
1200s–1300s	Little Ice Age begins • Original inhabitants abandon Cahokia • Mogollon, Hohokam, and Anasazi cultures decline
1400s	Incas begin to dominate the Andes; Aztecs begin to dominate Mesoamerica (1400–1450) • Cheng Ho makes voyages of exploration for China (1405–1434) • Portuguese begin to master the Atlantic coast of Africa (1434) • First Portuguese slave factory established on African coast (1448) • Dias reaches Cape of Good Hope (1487) • Columbus reaches the Caribbean (1492) • Treaty of Tordesillas divides non-Christian world between Portugal and Spain (1494) • da Gama rounds Cape of Good Hope and reaches India (1497–1499)
1500s	Portuguese discover Brazil (1500) • Balboa crosses Isthmus of Panama to the Pacific (1513) • Magellan's fleet circumnavigates the globe; Cortés conquers the Aztec Empire (1519–1522) • de Vaca makes overland journey from Florida to Mexico (1528–1536) • Pizarro conquers the Inca Empire (1531–1532) • de Soto's expedition explores the American Southeast (1539–1543) • Coronado explores the American Southwest (1540–1542) • Jesuit mission established at Chesapeake Bay (1570–1571) • Philip II issues Royal Order for New Discoveries (1573) • Philip II unites Spanish and Portuguese empires (1580)

Most communities could not depend solely on hunting and gathering food, however. In a few places, some of them, almost certainly women, began to plant and harvest crops instead of simply gathering and eating what they found. In Asia and Africa, this practice—closely linked to the domestication of animals—happened quickly enough to be called the **Neolithic** (new or late Stone Age) revolution. But in the Americas the rise of farming had little to do with animals, occurred gradually, and might better be termed the Neolithic *evolution*. For millennia, farming supplemented diets that still depended mostly on fishing and hunting, now of smaller animals. In many regions, the main agricultural technique was the slash-and-burn system in which farmers cleared small patches of trees, burned away the underbrush, and planted seeds in an ashy soil that was rich with heat-released nutrients. Because this system gradually depleted the soil, communities had to move to new fields after a decade or two, often because accessible firewood had been exhausted. In this semisedentary way of life, few Indians acquired more personal property than the women could carry from one place to another, either during the annual hunt or when the whole community had to move. This limited interest in consumption would profoundly condition their response to capitalism after contact with Europeans.

Between 4000 and 1500 BCE, permanent farm villages developed in the Valley of Mexico, Central America, and the Andes. Their crops were different from those of the agricultural centers of Europe, the Middle East, and East Asia. The first American farmers grew manioc, chili peppers, pumpkins, potatoes, tomatoes, and several varieties of beans. Experimenting with different mutations of teosinte, a wild mountain grass, they transformed that modest plant into nutrient-rich maize, or Indian corn, which helped launch a population surge that was great enough to support cities.

1-2 The Emergence of Complex Societies in the Americas

What were the major similarities and differences between the histories of the Andes and Mesoamerica during the first and early second millennia?

Despite their feats of plant manipulation and their soaring populations, even the most complex societies in the Americas faced daunting technological constraints. Indigenous Americans made use of metals, but more for decorative than practical purposes. Most metalworking skills originated in South America and spread to Mesoamerica during the early second millennium CE. Societies across the hemisphere fashioned copper into fishing tools and art objects, but they did not make bronze (a compound of copper and tin), nor did they find any use for iron. Nearly all of their tools were made of stone or bone, and their sharpest weapons were made from obsidian, a hard, glassy, volcanic rock. Some knew how to make a wheel—they had wheeled toys—but they did not seek practical purposes for this invention, apparently because North America had no draft animals, and South Americans used llamas mostly in steep, mountainous areas where wheeled vehicles would have been of no use.

▲ **MAP 1.1 Indian Settlement of America** The probable routes that people followed after they left Beringia and spread throughout the Americas.

Q *Why did people follow several different routes into the Americas?*

Q *What factors may have encouraged people to stop and settle down?*

1-2a *The Andes: Cycles of Complex Cultures*

Despite these technological limitations, indigenous Americans profoundly reshaped their worlds and built enduring civilizations. During the second millennium BCE, elaborate urban societies took shape in the Andes, where engineers devised highly productive agricultural systems at 12,000 feet above sea level, far above the altitude at which anyone else has ever been able to raise crops. In the 1980s, when archaeologists rebuilt part of the prehistoric Andean irrigation system according to ancient specifications, they discovered that it was far more productive than a system using modern fertilizers and machines. Some Andean peoples could produce 10 metric tons of potatoes per hectare (about 2.4 acres), as opposed to 1 to 4 tons on nearby modern fields. Lands using the Andean canal system never had to lie fallow.

This type of irrigation took hold around Lake Titicaca about 1000 BCE and spread throughout the Andes. Monumental architecture and urbanization appeared in the

Slowbird/Dreamstime.com

1.2 **Petroglyph Canyon, Valley of Fire, near Las Vegas, Nevada**
People lived in the Valley of Fire since c. 2,000 BCE, recording important events and carving symbols into sandstone.

Q *What different meanings might the carvings have served and what different purposes might they have had?*

interior mountains and along the Peruvian coast. The coastal societies produced finely detailed pottery, much of it erotic, and built pyramids as centers of worship. In the highlands, people grew a great variety of food plants both tropical and temperate. Terraces, laid out at various altitudes on the mountainside, enabled communities to raise crops from different climatic zones, all a few hours distant from one another. At the lowest levels, they planted cotton in the hot, humid air. Farther up the mountain, they raised maize and other crops suitable to a temperate zone. At still higher elevations, they grew potatoes and grazed their alpacas and llamas. Taking advantage of the frost that formed most nights of the year, they invented freeze-dried food by carrying it far up the mountains. These classic Andean cultures collapsed by the 11th century, debilitated by prolonged droughts and intergroup rivalries. But the disruption that followed was temporary because new complex societies rose to reign over the region.

1-2b *Inca Civilization*

Around 1400 CE, the **Incas** emerged as the dominant imperial power in the Andes. They built their capital at Cuzco, high in the mountains. From that upland center, the Incas—the word applied both to the ruler and to the empire's dominant nation—forged an empire that eventually extended more than 2,000 miles from south to north. Narrow and long, the Inca Empire was the world's fastest-growing empire in the late 15th century. It was also one of the most ecologically diverse, covering steep mountains and deep valleys and extending from coastal lowlands to interior forests. The Incas bound their expanding realm together with an efficient network of roads and suspension bridges. Along these roads, the Incas maintained numerous storehouses for grain. They had no written language, but high-altitude runners, who memorized the Inca's oral commands, raced along the roads to relay their ruler's decrees over vast distances. They extracted resources from a variety of ecological niches, safeguarding themselves against climate shifts and crop failures, and they invented a decimal system that they used to keep records of the tribute they levied upon subject peoples. They used a device called a *quipu*, knotting variously colored strings in particular ways to encode information. By 1500, the Inca Empire ruled perhaps 8 to 12 million people. No other nonliterate culture has ever matched that feat.

1-2c *Mesoamerica: Cycles of Complex Cultures*

Mesoamerica experienced a similar cycle of change, but over a somewhat shorter period. Its successive cultures also comprised both upland and lowland societies. The **Olmecs**, who flourished in the hot and humid lowlands along the Gulf Coast between 1200 and 400 BCE, became the parent culture for the region. Theirs was the first urban culture in the Americas—it centered on three cities, San Lorenzo,

iStock.com/poladamonte

1.3 **Terraces of Winay Wayna**
Terraced agriculture was one of the most impressive achievements of pre-Columbian culture in the Andes. This terrace is located at the center of Inca power, near Cuzco and Machu Picchu.

Q *What were the advantages of terraced farming?*

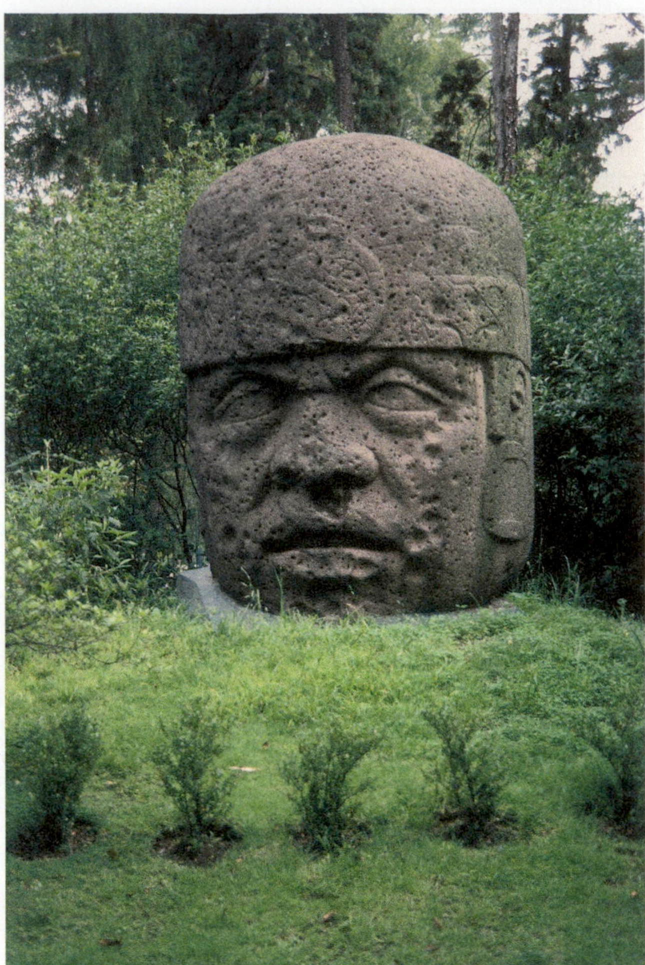

1.4 **Olmec Stone Head** This giant head is eight feet eight inches tall.

La Venta, and Tres Zapotes—which featured colossal stone heads that honored Olmec rulers. Aspects of Olmec culture became widely diffused throughout Mesoamerica. The Olmecs built the first pyramids and the first ballparks in the region. Their game, played with a heavy rubber ball, spread as far as what is now the southwestern United States. They developed a writing system and a dual calendar system that endured through the Aztec era. At the end of a 52-year cycle, the first day of the "short" calendar would again coincide with the first day of the "long" one. Olmecs faced the closing days of each cycle with dread, lest the gods allow the sun and all life on earth to be destroyed—something that, Olmecs warned, had already happened several times. They believed that the sacrifice of a god had been necessary to set the sun in motion in each new creation cycle and that only the blood of human sacrifice could placate the gods and keep the sun moving. These beliefs endured in Mesoamerica for millennia, regardless of the rise and fall of empires and cities. The arrival of the Spaniards in 1519 would create a religious as well as a political crisis, because that year marked the end of a 52-year cycle.

The Olmecs were succeeded by the city and empire of Teotihuacan, which emerged in the mountains not far from modern Mexico City (see Map 1.2). By the 4th century CE, Teotihuacan was already a city of 200,000 inhabitants, enormous temple pyramids, and brightly painted murals. Teotihuacan invested resources in comfortable apartment dwellings for ordinary people, not in monuments or inscriptions to rulers. It probably had a form of senate government, not a monarchy. The rapidly growing city extended its influence in all directions, founding new colonies across Mesoamerica to extract maize, beans, and other supplies. It remained a powerful force until its sudden destruction in the mid-8th century, apparently by conquest, because its shrines were toppled and the city was abandoned. Teotihuacan's growth may also have so depleted the resources of its core area that the city could not have sustained itself much longer.

In the tropical lowlands of Central America and the dry and hilly plateau of Yucatán, the **Mayan** culture went through a similar cycle from expansion to ecological crisis. It was also urban but less centralized than that of Teotihuacan, although some Mayan temples were just as monumental. For more than 1,000 years, Mayan culture rested on a network of competing city-states, which, as in ancient Greece, shared similar values. One of the largest Mayan cities, Tikal, arose on the plateau separating rivers flowing into the Caribbean from those emptying into the Gulf of Mexico. It controlled commerce with Teotihuacan and housed 100,000 people at its peak in the 8th century. Twenty other cities, most about one-fourth the size of Tikal, flourished throughout the region. Mayan engineers built canals to water the crops needed to support this urban system.

Mayans developed an expressive writing system that utilized stone carvings and they recorded their history in great detail. Scholars have deciphered most Mayan inscriptions, and Mayan texts are now studied much like those of Europe. Mayan art and writings reveal, for example, their preoccupation with astronomical computations, timekeeping, and a royal ritual of bloodletting, which facilitated communication with ancestors and gods. They also reveal the long reign of Pacal the Great, king (or "Great Sun") of the elegant city of Palenque, who was born on March 26, 603, and died on August 31, 683. His sarcophagus lists his ancestors through six generations. Other monuments tell of the Great Suns of other cities whom Pacal vanquished and sacrificed to the gods.

The classic Mayan civilization began to weaken after the fall of Teotihuacan, which disrupted Mayan trade with the Valley of Mexico. The crisis spread rapidly. Palenque, Tikal, and other prominent cities decayed in the 9th and 10th centuries when prolonged droughts destabilized their intensive farming system. The center of Mayan population and civilization shifted from the lowlands to the Yucatán plateau. Chichén Itzá, a city that had existed for centuries, preserved many distinctive Mayan traits but merged them with new influences from the Valley of Mexico, where the Toltecs had become dominant.

The Toltecs were a military society whose capital at Tula, with 40,000 people, was one-fifth the size of Teotihuacan at its peak. They prospered from the cocoa trade with tropical lowlands and extended their influence over surrounding societies. They controlled the Valley of Mexico until about 1200 CE, when they too declined. They left a legacy of conquest to later rulers in the valley, who all claimed descent from Toltec kings.

▲ **MAP 1.2 The Major Empires and Cities of the Andes and Mesoamerica from the 10th to the Early 15th Century** Both the Andes and Mesoamerica saw the rise and fall of numerous powerful regimes and cultural centers before the arrival of Europeans.

Q *Why did empires rise where they did between the 10th and early-15th centuries?*

Q *What were the main similarities and differences between the Aztec and Inca empires?*

1.5 ***El Caracol*, a Late Mayan Observatory at Chichén Itzá** Astronomy was well developed in all of the pre-Columbian high cultures of Mesoamerica; however, if the Mayans used any specialized instruments to study the heavens, we do not know what they were.

1-2d *The Aztecs and Tenochtitlán*

By 1400, power in the Valley of Mexico was passing to the **Aztecs**, who had migrated from the north about two centuries earlier and had settled, with the bare sufferance of their neighbors, on the shore of Lake Texcoco. They built a great city, **Tenochtitlán**, out on the lake. Its only connection with the mainland was by several broad causeways. Lake Texcoco was 5,000 feet above sea level, and the lands around it were swampy, offering little cultivable soil. The Aztecs compensated by creating highly productive *chinampas*, floating gardens made of sediment and decaying vegetation, on swampy parts of the lake. Yet, their mounting population strained the food supply. In the 1450s, the threat of famine was severe (see Map 1.3).

Tenochtitlán, with a population exceeding 200,000, had forged an alliance with Texcoco and Tlacopan, two smaller lakeside cities. Together they dominated the area, but by the second quarter of the 15th century leadership was clearly passing to the Aztecs. As newcomers to the region, the Aztecs needed to prove themselves worthy heirs to Tula and Teotihuacan. They adopted the old religion and built and constantly rebuilt and enlarged their Great Pyramid of the Sun. They waged nearly constant wars to gain captives and to subdue bordering groups. Unlike the Incas, the Aztecs sought to extort rather than control others. By the late 15th century, Tenochtitlán held hundreds of tributary communities in its orbit, extracting massive amounts of maize, beans, cocoa, cotton, and luxuries from them. The Aztecs also acquired, through war and tribute, large numbers of captives, whose sacrifice they believed appeased the gods and empowered the empire.

Human sacrifice was an ancient ritual in Mesoamerica, but the Aztecs practiced it on an unprecedented scale. Although neighboring peoples shared the religious beliefs of the Aztecs, they nevertheless hated these conquerors from the north. After 1519, many Indians in Mesoamerica would help the Spaniards bring down the Aztecs. By contrast, the Spaniards would find few allies in the Andes, where resistance in the name of the Inca would persist for most of the 16th century and would even revive in the late 18th century—250 years after the conquest.

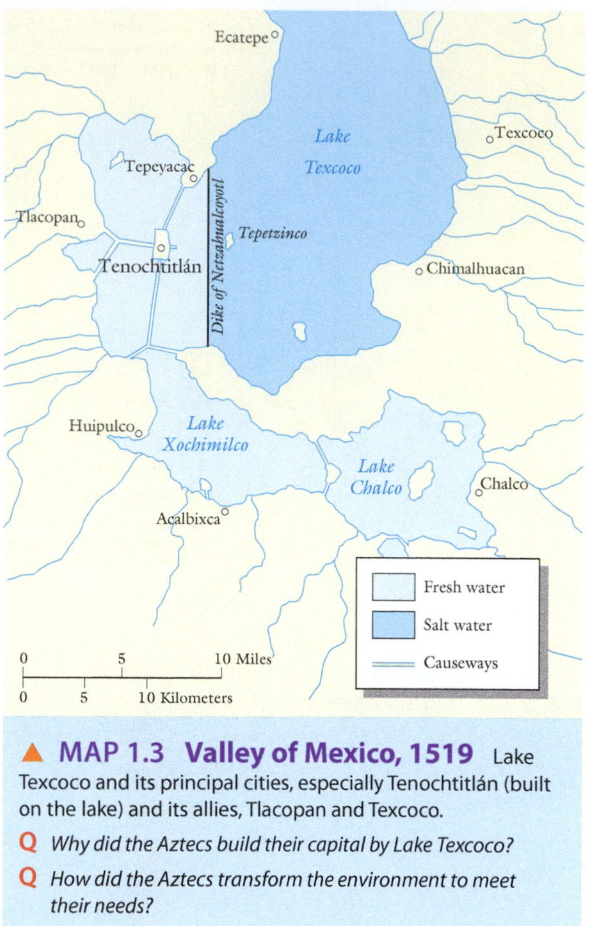

▲ **MAP 1.3 Valley of Mexico, 1519** Lake Texcoco and its principal cities, especially Tenochtitlán (built on the lake) and its allies, Tlacopan and Texcoco.

Q *Why did the Aztecs build their capital by Lake Texcoco?*

Q *How did the Aztecs transform the environment to meet their needs?*

1-3 Agricultural Take Off in North America

Q *How did maize cultivation change human history in North America?*

Mesoamerica was for North America what the Fertile Crescent was for Western Europe: a source of seeds and crops that would alter the parameters of human existence. The human-engineered maize was a life-transforming plant that could launch population explosions and prop up civilizations, but it was hard to transplant. A subtropical crop, it required warmth and long growing seasons, and it took centuries for people to develop new strains that could withstand the colder climates and drier soils in the north. Maize arrived in the semiarid highlands of the American Southwest around 2000 BCE, but it took several more centuries to turn it into a staple. Gradually, through trial and error, the region's farmers developed a new form of maize, *maiz de ocho*, a highly nutritious and adaptable eight-rowed flint corn that required a relatively short growing season. And when they began to plant squash and beans with maize, they produced a triad of crops that revolutionized food production in North America. Maize stalks provided structure for bean vines; beans restored nitrogen—which maize depleted—to the soil; and squash, spreading along the ground,

© Boltin Picture Library/ The Bridgeman Art Library

1.6 **The Temple of the Sun at Teotihuacan** The giant, stepped pyramid shown here is one of pre-Columbian America's most elegant pyramids.

Q *Why did the Aztecs build their capital by Lake Texcoco?*

Q *How did the Aztecs transform the environment to meet their needs?*

retained moisture in the soil and lessened weed growth. The three crops also complemented each other nutritionally. Maize is rich in carbohydrates, dried beans in protein, and together the three crops contain most essential vitamins and amino acids.

1-3a *Urban Cultures of the Southwest*

With the improved food production, complex societies emerged in the Southwest. The last century of the first millennium saw the onset of a warmer climate cycle—the Medieval Warm Period—which allowed the Mogollon and the Hohokam peoples to integrate farming firmly into their hunting and gathering economies. Both lived in villages and towns that featured multiroom adobe houses and public plazas, produced exquisitely painted pottery, and relied on canalirrigation farming. The Hohokams' irrigation system consisted of several hundred miles of canals and produced two harvests per year (see Map 1.4). They wove cotton cloth and traded with places as distant as California and Mesoamerica, circulating marine shells, turquoise, copper bells, and mirrors across vast distances. They imported a version of the Mesoamerican ball game and staged large public tournaments. Perhaps because of massive floods or because irrigation increased the salinity of the soil, their culture, after enduring for centuries, went into irreversible decline in the 14th century.

Even more tantalizing and mysterious is the brief flowering of the **Anasazi** (a Navajo word meaning "the ancient ones"), a cliff-dwelling people who have left behind some remarkable artifacts at Chaco Canyon in New Mexico,

RGB Ventures LLC dba SuperStock/Alamy Stock Photo

1.7 **Aztec Skull Rack Altar** Displaying the skulls of sacrificial victims, such racks alienated native societies from the Aztecs and shocked the invading Spaniards.

Q *What do skull racks tell us about the Aztec society and culture?*

Courtesy of the John Carter Brown Library at Brown University

1.8 **Indian Women as Farmers**
In this illustration, a French artist depicted 16th-century Indian women in southeastern North America.

at Mesa Verde in Colorado, and at other sites. In their caves and cliffs, they constructed apartment houses five stories high with hundreds of dwellings and with elegant and spacious kivas, meeting rooms for religious functions. The Anasazi were superb astronomers. Through an arrangement of rock slabs, open to the sun and moon at the mouth of a cave, and of spirals on the interior wall that plotted the movement of the sun and moon, they created a calendar that could track the summer and winter solstices and even the 19-year cycles of the moon, an astronomical refinement Europeans had not yet achieved. They traveled to their fields and brought in lumber and other distant supplies on a network of roads that ran for scores of miles in several directions. They achieved most of these feats over a period of about two centuries, although Anasazi pottery has been found that dates from much earlier times. In the late 13th century, apparently overwhelmed by a prolonged drought and by hostile invaders, they abandoned their principal sites. Pueblo architecture is a direct successor of that of the Anasazi, and the Pueblo Indians are descended from them.

1-3b *North American Mound Builders*

Another North American center of cultural innovation and social complexity emerged in the Eastern Woodlands, where distinct cultures of "mound builders" exerted a powerful influence over the interior. Named for the huge earthen mounds they erected, these cultures arose near the Mississippi and Ohio rivers and their tributaries. The earliest mound builders became semisedentary even before learning to grow crops. Fish, game, and the lush vegetation of the river valleys sustained them for most of the year and enabled them to erect permanent dwellings.

The first mound-building culture, the Adena-Hopewell, flourished between 500 BCE and 400 CE in the Ohio River valley (see Map 1.5). Its mounds were increasingly elaborate burial sites, suggesting belief in an afterlife and social stratification into elites and commoners. Mound-building communities participated in a commerce that spanned most of the continent between the Appalachians and the Rockies, the Great Lakes and the Gulf of Mexico. Obsidian from the Yellowstone Valley in the West, copper from the Great Lakes basin, and shells from the Gulf of Mexico have all been found buried in the Adena-Hopewell mounds. Both the mound building and the long-distance trade largely ceased after 400 CE, for reasons that remain unclear. Yet, the mounds were so impressive that when American settlers found them after the Revolution, they refused to believe that "savages" could have built them.

Adena-Hopewell culture had relied on casual cultivation of various crops. When the companion planting of squash, beans, and maiz de ocho spread into the Eastern Woodlands around 1000 CE, mound building revived, producing a dramatic epoch known as the Mississippian culture. This culture dominated the Mississippi River valley from modern St. Louis to Natchez, with the largest center at Cahokia in present-day Illinois. Ordinary people became "stinkards" in this culture, while some families had elite status. The "Great Sun" ruled with authority and was transported by litter from place to place. When he died, some of his wives, relatives, and retainers were sacrificed at his funeral to join him in the afterlife. Burial mounds thus became much grander in Mississippian communities. Atop the mounds in which their

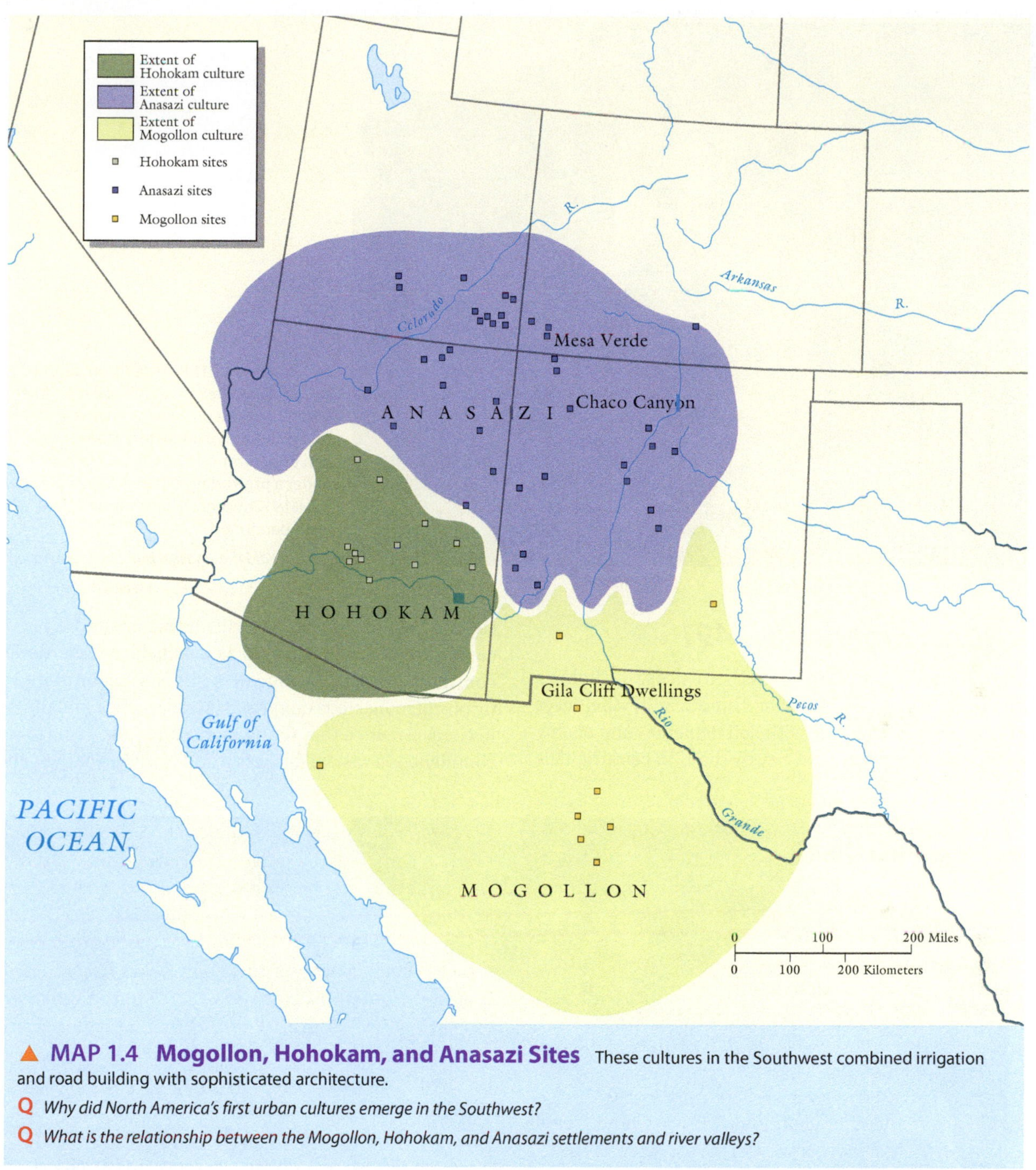

▲ **MAP 1.4 Mogollon, Hohokam, and Anasazi Sites** These cultures in the Southwest combined irrigation and road building with sophisticated architecture.

Q *Why did North America's first urban cultures emerge in the Southwest?*

Q *What is the relationship between the Mogollon, Hohokam, and Anasazi settlements and river valleys?*

rulers were interred, the Indians built elaborate places of worship and residences for the priests and Great Suns of their highly stratified society.

The city of **Cahokia**, near modern St. Louis, flourished from 900 to 1200 CE and may have had 20,000 or more residents at its peak, making it the largest city north of Mexico and half as populous as the contemporary Toltec capital at Tula. As was typical for many North American urban centers, a large portion of Cahokia's population consisted of captives and slaves, taken by war or via trade from other societies. Slaves added to Cahokia's labor force as well as its prestige. In North America control of people was more important than control of territory, and slaves were a tangible manifestation of Cahokia's power over others.

Sitting on the American Bottom, a broad floodplain at the juncture of the Mississippi and Missouri rivers, Cahokia was a bustling metropolis with an extensive hinterland. It had a grid pattern of rectangular plazas and platform mounds and it was surrounded by suburbs, auxiliary villages, and vast cornfields that stretched into the horizon. It was a center of continent-spanning trade networks and a seat of political power. Its enormous central mound, 100-foot-high Monks Mound, is the world's largest earthen work, and it speaks of the city's paramount status in the Mississippian world.

Source: National Park Service

1.9 **Anasazi Cliff Palace in Mesa Verde** This building complex in what is today southern Colorado was a prominent Anasazi cliff dwelling that consisted of multistory stone rooms, towers, and underground kivas. It sat in a high alcove under a protruding cliff and was inhabited from the late 12th century until around 1300, when it was abandoned.

Q *Why did the Anasazi build their houses on cliffs?*

1-3c *North America in 1491*

Like the Hohokam and Anasazi cultures, Cahokia's preeminence did not last. Another climate shift, the onset of the Little Ice Age, together with soil depletion and enemy attacks brought down the great city by the 13th century. This sudden collapse of urban civilizations created a persisting caricature of North America as a somehow underdeveloped continent. Where European colonists encountered awe-inspiring indigenous empires in Mesoamerica and the Andes, in North America they found mere ruins, and came to see the continent as a vast wilderness world of savage natives and lost

© Richard A. Cooke/Encyclopedia/Corbis

1.10 **The Great Serpent Mound** Located near Chillicothe, Ohio, this mound is about 1,200 feet long and is one of the most spectacular mounds to survive from the Adena-Hopewell era.

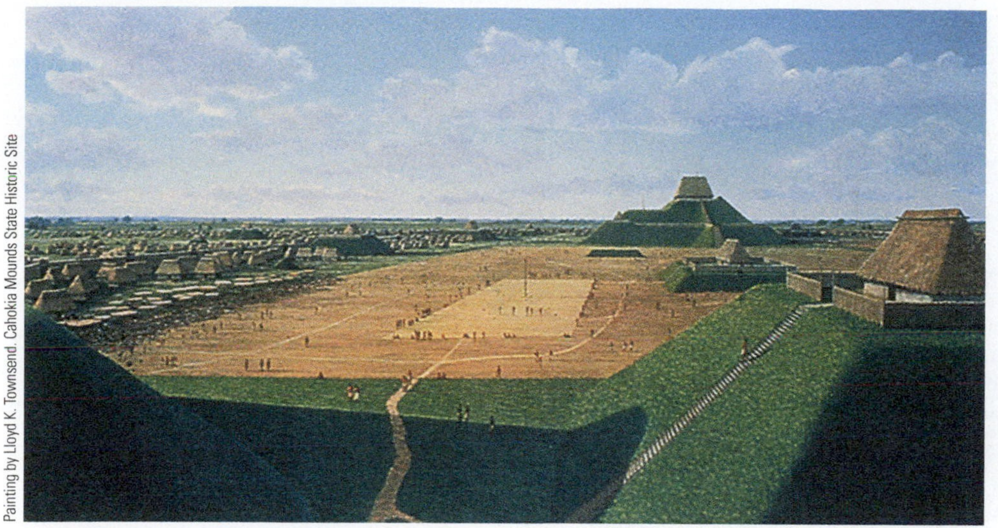
Painting by Lloyd K. Townsend. Cahokia Mounds State Historic Site

1.11 **Cahokia** The largest Mississippian mound-building site was Cahokia, in Illinois, near St. Louis, Missouri. Depicted here is the city's sacred ceremonial center facing toward Monks Mound in the distance.

Q *How did Cahokia become so central and influential?*

cultural opportunities. Recent scholarship has overturned this image, showing how North America was culturally dynamic, covered with trade networks, and filled with people. In the late 15th century, North America was home to perhaps as many as 10 million people (the estimates for the entire hemisphere range from 50 million to more than 100 million) who spoke hundreds of languages, pursued diverse economic strategies, believed in numerous gods, and envisioned widely different ways of organizing the social worlds in which they lived. Some lived in locally oriented communities, while others—such as the Iroquois and the Hurons in the Northeast—formed powerful confederacies that dominated large areas. North America on the eve of European contact was an old and complex world in motion.

1-3d *The Norse Connection*

The Medieval Warm Period that had facilitated the agricultural take off and the rise of such urban centers as Chaco Canyon and Cahokia in North America also facilitated the movement of Europeans over long distances. The Norse, a Germanic people in Scandinavia, began to extend their excursions beyond the British Isles and France into the Atlantic. Challenging the contrary currents of the north Atlantic with their sleek, sail- and oar-powered longboats, Viking warriors occupied Iceland in the late 9th century; a century later they reached and settled in Greenland (then much greener than today), encountering the Inuits.

In 1001, Leif Ericsson sailed west from Greenland and began to explore the coast of North America. He made three more voyages and started a colony that he called "Vinland" on the northern coast of Newfoundland. The local Indians (called "Skrellings" by the Norse, which means "barbarians" or "weaklings") resisted vigorously, but the Norse soon quarreled among themselves and abandoned the colony by 1014. The Norse left Vinland, but they continued to visit North America for another century, probably to get wood. A 12th-century Norse coin, recovered from an Indian site in Maine, provides proof of their continuing contact with North America.

In the late 15th century, the Norse also lost Greenland. There, not long before Columbus sailed in 1492, the last Norse settler died a lonely death. In the chaos that followed the Black Death in Europe and Greenland after 1350 and the onset of the Little Ice Age, the colony suffered a severe population decline and slowly withered away. Despite their spectacular exploits, the Norse had no impact on the later course of American history. They had reached a dead end.

1-4 Europe and the World by the 15th Century

Q *What enabled relatively backward European societies to establish dominance over the oceans of the world?*

Nobody in the year 1400 could have foreseen the course of European expansion that was about to begin. Europe stood at the edge, not the center, of world commerce. It desired much that others possessed but made little that those others wished to acquire.

1-4a *China: The Rejection of Overseas Expansion*

By just about every standard, China under the Ming dynasty was the world's most complex culture. In the 15th century, the government of China, staffed by well-educated bureaucrats, ruled 100 million people, a total half again as large as the combined populations of all the European states west of Russia. The Chinese had invented the compass, gunpowder, and early forms of printing and paper money. Foreigners coveted the silks, teas, and other fine products available in China, but they had little to offer in exchange. China's capital

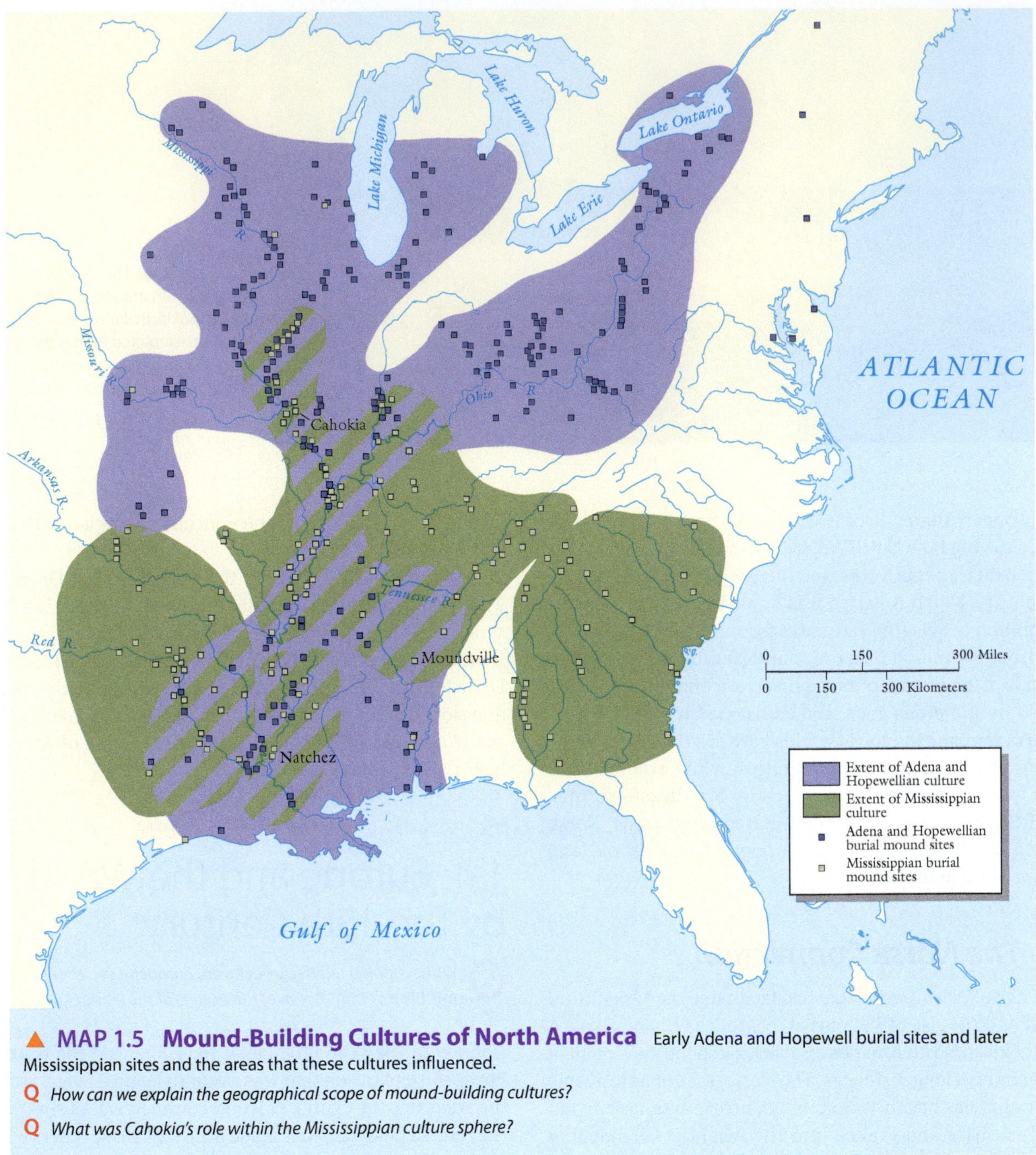

▲ **MAP 1.5 Mound-Building Cultures of North America** Early Adena and Hopewell burial sites and later Mississippian sites and the areas that these cultures influenced.

Q *How can we explain the geographical scope of mound-building cultures?*

Q *What was Cahokia's role within the Mississippian culture sphere?*

city (today's Beijing) was the world's largest and grandest, insisted the Venetian merchant-traveler Marco Polo; it received 1,000 cartloads of silk a day. China, he maintained, outshone Europe and all other cultures.

The Chinese agreed. Between 1405 and 1434, a royal eunuch, Cheng Ho, led six large fleets from China to the East Indies and the coast of East Africa, trading and exploring along the way. Had China thrown its resources and talents into overseas expansion, the subsequent history of the world would have been vastly different, but most of what the Chinese learned about the outside world merely confirmed their belief that other cultures had little to offer their Celestial Kingdom. No one followed Cheng Ho's lead after he died. Instead, the emperor banned the construction of oceangoing ships and later forbade anyone to own a vessel with more than two masts. China turned inward.

1-4b *Christian Europe Challenges Islam*

Western Europe was, by global standards, a backward place in 1400. Compared with China or the Islamic world, it suffered severe disadvantages. Europeans desired China's

© SF photo/Shutterstock.com

© North Wind Picture Archives

© Historical Picture Archive/CORBIS

1.12a (top left), 1.12b (top right), and 1.12c (bottom left) **Longhouse, Wigwam, and Tepee** The longhouse (top left), made from bark or mats stretched over a wooden frame, was the standard communal dwelling of the Iroquois and Huron peoples. Most Algonquian peoples of the Eastern Woodlands lived in wigwams (top right) like this undated example. Wigwams were made by bending the boughs of trees into a frame to be covered with animal skins. West of the Mississippi, most Plains Indians lived in small but strong tepees (bottom left), which were usually made from poles covered with buffalo hides. All of these dwellings were constructed by women.

Q *Identify the similarities and differences among the three different dwelling styles. What might explain them?*

silks and coveted East Indian spices to enliven their food and help preserve it through long winters. But because Europeans produced little that Asians wished to buy, they had to pay for these imports with silver or gold, both of which were scarce. Moreover, Europe's location on the Atlantic rim of the Eurasian continent had always made access to Asian trade difficult and costly. Islamic societies controlled overland trade with Asia and the only known seaborne route to Asia through the Persian Gulf. As of 1400, Arab mariners were the world's best.

In fact, while Europe's sphere of influence was shrinking, and while China seemed content with what it already had, Islamic states embarked on another great phase of expansion. Europe's mounted knights in heavy armor failed to stop the Ottoman Turks, who took Constantinople in 1453, overran the Balkans by the 1520s, and even threatened Vienna. The Safavid Empire in Iran (Persia) rose to new splendor at the same time. Other Muslims carried the Koran to Indonesia and northern India, where they erected the powerful Mughal Empire (see Map 1.6).

Yet, Europe had its own advantages. Its economy had made impressive gains in the Middle Ages, primarily because of agricultural advances, such as improved plows and crop rotation, which fostered population growth. By 1300, more than 100 million people were living in Europe. Europe's farms could not sustain further growth, however. As the climate cooled, lean years and famines ensued, leaving people undernourished. In the late 1340s, the Black Death (bubonic plague) reduced the population by more than one-third. Recurring bouts of plague kept population low until about 1500, when vigorous growth resumed. The long decline during the 15th century had allowed overworked soils to regain their fertility, and per capita income rose dramatically among people who now had stronger immunities to disease.

By then, European metallurgy and architecture were quite advanced. The Renaissance, which revived interest in the literature and art of ancient Greece and Rome, also gave a new impetus to European culture, especially after Johannes Gutenberg invented the printing press and movable type in the 1430s. Soon information began to circulate more rapidly in Europe than anywhere else in the world. This revolution in communications permitted improvements in ship design and navigational techniques to become a self-reinforcing process. The Arabs, by contrast, borrowed block printing from China in the 10th century but gave it up by 1400.

Unlike China, none of Europe's kingdoms was a self-contained economy. All states had to trade with one another and with the non-Christian world. Although in 1400 this need was a handicap, it slowly became an asset. No single state had a monopoly on the manufacture of firearms or on the flow of capital, and European states began to compete with one another to gain access to these resources and master new maritime and military techniques. The ensuing rivalries and wars increased rather than undermined state power. States

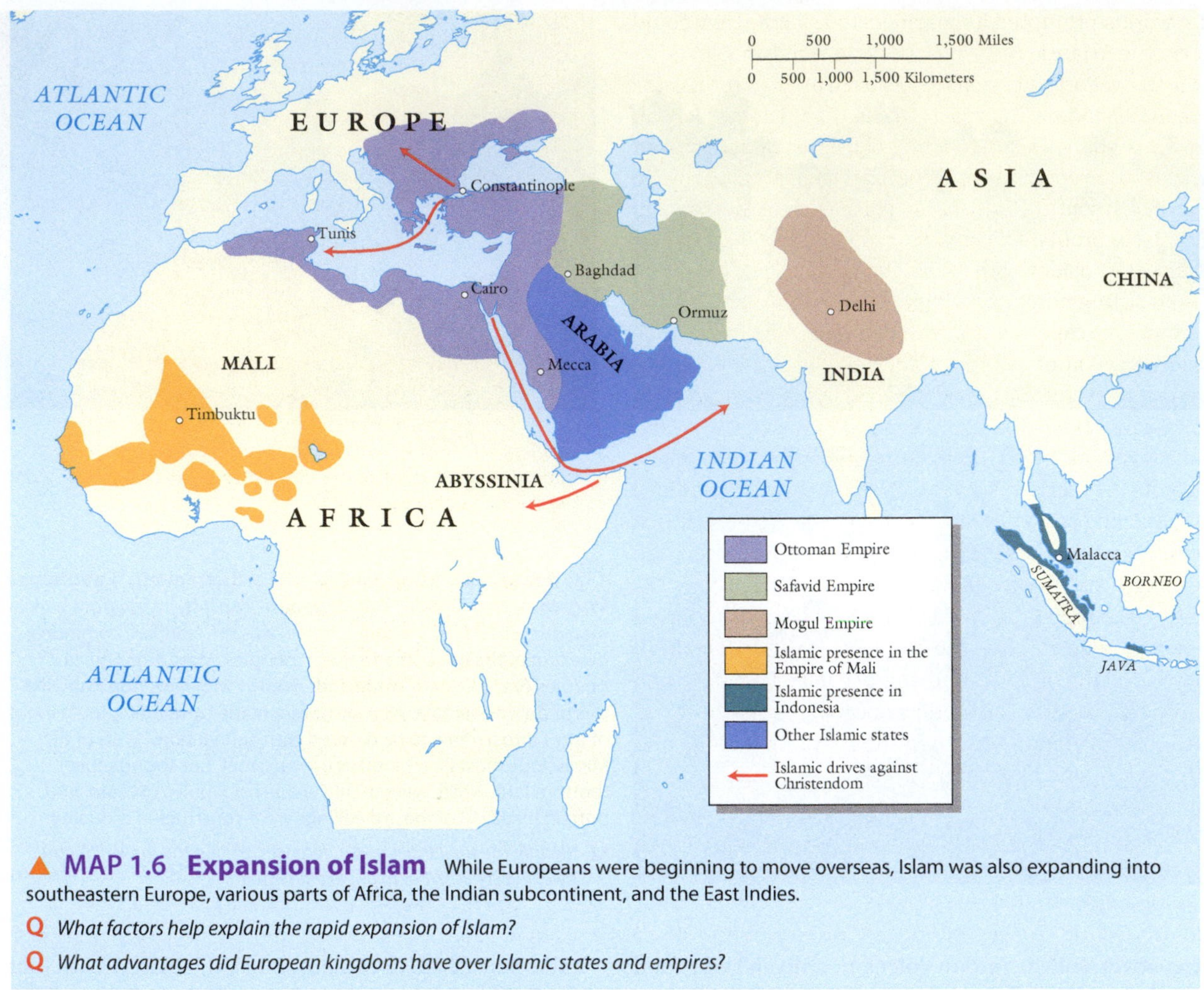

▲ **MAP 1.6 Expansion of Islam** While Europeans were beginning to move overseas, Islam was also expanding into southeastern Europe, various parts of Africa, the Indian subcontinent, and the East Indies.

Q *What factors help explain the rapid expansion of Islam?*

Q *What advantages did European kingdoms have over Islamic states and empires?*

extracted the means of war—money, men, weapons—from their subjects, growing increasingly powerful in the process. European armies grew more formidable, and European fleets started to outsail and outfight their rivals.

1-4c *The Legacy of the Crusades*

Much earlier historical experiences helped turn Europe's growing power into overseas expansion. In the early second millennium, Europeans organized several crusades to conquer the Holy Land from Islam. Crusaders established their own Kingdom of Jerusalem, which survived for more than a century but was finally retaken in 1244. During the next 250 years, while a new wave of Islamic expansion seemed about to engulf much of the world, Christian Europe gained only a few Mediterranean and Atlantic islands but learned some important lessons in the process. To make Palestine profitable, the crusaders had taken over sugar plantations already there and had worked them with a combination of free and slave labor. After they were driven from the Holy Land, the crusaders retreated to the Mediterranean islands of Cyprus, Malta, Crete, and Rhodes, where they used slaves to raise sugar cane or grapevines.

Long before Columbus, these planters had created the economic components of overseas expansion. They assumed that colonies should produce a **staple crop**, at least partly through **slave labor**, for sale in Europe. The first slaves were Muslim captives. In the 14th and 15th centuries, planters turned to pagan Slavs (hence the word *slave*) from the Black Sea area and the Adriatic. Some black Africans were also acquired from Arab merchants who controlled the caravan trade across the Sahara Desert, but these early plantations did not exploit their laborers with the intensity that later became routine in the Americas.

1-4d *The Unlikely Pioneer: Portugal*

It seemed highly improbable in 1400 that Europe was standing on the threshold of a dramatic expansion. That Portugal would lead the way seemed even less likely. A small kingdom of fewer than a million people, Portugal had been united for less than a century. Lisbon, with 40,000 people, was the only city of any size. Portugal's maritime traditions lagged well behind those of the Italian states, France, and England. Its merchant class was tiny, and it had little capital.

But Portugal also had significant advantages. It enjoyed internal peace and an efficient government at a time when its neighbors were beset by war and internal upheaval. Moreover, its location at the intersection of the Mediterranean and

Atlantic worlds prompted its mariners to ask how they could transform the Atlantic from a barrier into a highway.

At first, the Portuguese were interested in short-term gains rather than in some all-water route to Asia. They knew that Arab caravans crossed the Sahara to bring gold, slaves, and ivory from black Africa to Europe, and they believed that an Atlantic voyage to coastal points south of the Sahara would undercut Arab traders and bring large profits. The greatest problem they faced in this quest was Cape Bojador, with its treacherous shallows, awesome waves, and strong northerly winds. Several bold captains had sailed around the cape, but none had returned. A member of the Portuguese royal family, Prince Henry, challenged this barrier by sponsoring several voyages along the African coast. In 1434, an expedition passed the cape, explored the coastline, and then sailed west into the Atlantic until it met favorable winds and currents that carried it back to Europe. Other expeditions followed, opening sea-lanes into the resource-rich West Africa below Sahara, where the Portuguese found the wealth they had been seeking—gold, ivory, and slaves.

During the following decades, Portugal vaulted past all rivals in two major areas—the ability to navigate the high seas beyond sight of land, and the capacity to defeat any non-European fleet on the world's oceans. Portuguese (and later Spanish) navigators mapped the prevailing winds and currents on the high seas over most of the globe. They collected geographic information from classical sources, foreigners, and modern navigators. They studied the superior designs of Arab vessels, copied them, and improved on them. They increased the ratio of length to beam (width at the broadest point of the hull) from 2:1 to 3:1, borrowed the lateen (triangular) sail from the Arabs, and combined it with square rigging in the right proportion to produce a superb oceangoing vessel, the caravel. A **caravel** could achieve speeds from 3 to 12 knots and could beat closer to a headwind than any other sailing ship. Portuguese captains also used the compass and adopted the Arabs' astrolabe, a device that permits accurate calculation of latitude, or distances north and south. (The calculation of longitude—distances east and west—is much more difficult and was not mastered until the 18th century.) As they skirted the African coast, these Portuguese sailors made precise charts and maps that later mariners could follow.

The Portuguese also learned how to mount heavy cannon on the decks of their ships—a formidable advantage in an age when others fought naval battles by grappling and boarding enemy vessels. Portuguese ships were able to stand farther off and literally blow their opponents out of the water. As the 15th century advanced, Portuguese mariners explored ever farther along the African coast, looking for wealth and eventually a direct, cheap route to Asia.

1-4e *Africa, Colonies, and the Slave Trade*

The mostly agricultural population that inhabited West Africa also included skilled craftsmen. West Africans probably learned how to use iron long before Europeans did, and they

1.13 ***The Caravel:* A Swift Oceangoing Vessel** This caravel is a modern reconstruction of the 15th-century *Niña*, which crossed the Atlantic with Columbus in 1492.

had been supplying Europe with most of its gold for hundreds of years through indirect trade across the desert. West Africa's political history had been marked by the rise and fall of a series of large inland states. The most recent of these, the empire of Mali, was already in decline by 1450. As the Portuguese advanced past the Sahara, their commerce began to pull trade away from the desert caravans, which further weakened Mali and other interior states. By 1550, the empire had fallen apart.

The Portuguese also founded offshore colonies along the way. They began to settle the uninhabited Madeira Islands in 1418, took possession of the Azores between 1427 and 1450, occupied the Cape Verde group in the 1450s, and took over São Tomé in 1470. Like exploration, colonization turned a profit. Lacking investment capital and experience in overseas settlement, the Portuguese drew on Italian merchants for both. In this way, the plantation complex of staple crops and slavery migrated from the Mediterranean to the Atlantic. Beginning in the 1440s, Portuguese island planters produced sugar or wine, increasingly with slave labor imported from nearby Africa. Some plantations, particularly on São Tomé, kept several hundred slaves at work growing and processing sugar (see Map 1.7).

At first, the Portuguese acquired their slaves by landing on the African coast, attacking agricultural villages, and carrying off everyone they could catch; but these raids enraged coastal peoples and made other forms of trade more difficult. In the decades after 1450, the slave trade assumed its classic form. The Portuguese established small posts, or **factories**, along the coast—or ideally, on small offshore islands, such as Arguin Island near Cape Blanco, where they built their first African fort in 1448. Operating out of these bases, traders would buy slaves from the local rulers, who usually acquired their victims by waging war. During the long history of the **Atlantic slave trade**, nearly every African shipped overseas had first been enslaved by other Africans.

Slavery had long existed in Africa. African societies raided their neighbors for slaves, which were a significant form of personal wealth, and Muslim traders may have transported more than 10 million people out of Africa between 750 and

▲ **MAP 1.7 Africa and the Mediterranean in the 15th Century** The Mediterranean islands held by Europeans in the late Middle Ages, the Atlantic islands colonized by Portugal and Spain in the 15th century, the part of West Africa from Cape Blanco to Angola that provided the main suppliers of the Atlantic slave trade, and the Portuguese all-water route to India after 1497.

Q *What factors explain the rapid rise of Portugal's empire?*

Q *Why did the Portuguese not build settler colonies in Africa and Asia?*

1500. Yet, the slavery that Europeans imposed marked a major departure. When the Atlantic slave trade began, no African middleman could have foreseen how the enslavement of Africans by Europeans would differ from the enslavement of Africans by Africans. In Africa, slaves were not forced to toil endlessly to produce staple crops, and their descendants often became fully assimilated into the captors' society. Slaves were not isolated as a separate caste. By the time African middlemen learned about the cruel conditions of slavery under European rule, the trade had become too lucrative to stop, although several African societies tried. They discovered, moreover, that those who refused to participate in the trade were likely

1.14 **The Portuguese Slave-Trading Fortress of Elmina** Located on the Gold Coast of West Africa, the fortress was built in 1481.

Q *How did slave-trading fortresses like Elmina shape world history?*

to become its victims. When the rulers of the Kongo embraced Catholicism in the 16th century, they protested against the Atlantic slave trade, only to see their own people become vulnerable to enslavement by others. The non-Christian kingdom of Benin learned the same lesson.

The Portuguese made the slave trade profitable by exploiting rivalries among the more than 200 small states of West and Central Africa, an area that was divided into more languages and small states than Europeans would find anywhere else in the world. Despite many cultural similarities among these groups, West Africans had never thought of themselves as a single people. Nor did they share a universal religion that might have restrained them from selling other Africans into slavery. Muslims believed it sinful to enslave a fellow believer. Western Europeans, although quite capable of waging destructive wars against one another, believed that enslaving fellow Christians was immoral. Enslaving pagan or Muslim Africans was another matter. Some Europeans even believed that they were doing these people a favor by making their souls eligible for salvation.

1-4f *Portugal's Asian Empire*

Portuguese exploration continued, paying for itself through gold, ivory, and slaves. The government finally decided to support the quest for an all-water route to Asia. In 1487, Bartolomeu Dias reached the Cape of Good Hope at the southern tip of Africa and headed east toward the Indian Ocean, but his crew rebelled in those stormy waters, and he turned back. Ten years later, Vasco da Gama led a small fleet around the Cape of Good Hope and sailed on to the southwestern coast of India. In a voyage that lasted more than two years (1497–1499), da Gama bargained and fought for spices that yielded a 20-to-1 profit.

Da Gama opened the way for Portugal's empire in the East. To secure their Asian trade, the Portuguese established a chain of naval bases that extended from East Africa to the mouth of the Persian Gulf, then to Goa on the west coast of India, and from there to the Moluccas, or East Indies. Portuguese missionaries penetrated Japan. The Moluccas became the Asian center of the Portuguese seaborne empire, with their spices yielding most of the wealth that Portugal extracted from its eastern holdings. In the early 16th century, African and Asian trade was providing two-thirds of Portugal's state revenues. Beyond ensuring its continued access to spices, Portugal made little effort to govern its holdings, and its eastern empire never became colonies of settlement. In all of their Asian outposts, the Portuguese remained heavily outnumbered by native peoples.

1-4g *Early Lessons*

As the Norse failure showed, the ability to navigate the high seas gave no guarantee of lasting success. Sustained expansion overseas required the support of a home government and ready access to what other states had learned. The Portuguese drew on Italian capital and maritime skills, as well as on Arab learning and technology, in launching their ventures. The Spaniards, in turn, would learn much from the Portuguese. The French, Dutch, and English would borrow from the Italians, Portuguese, and Spaniards.

The economic impulse behind colonization was thus in place long before Columbus sailed west. The desire for precious metals provided the initial stimulus, but staple crops and slavery kept that impetus alive. Before the 19th century, more than two-thirds of the people who crossed the Atlantic were slaves who were brought to America to grow sugar or other staples. The Atlantic slave trade was not some unfortunate exception to a larger story of liberty. For three and a half centuries, it was the norm.

1.15 **The City of Benin (1668)** By both European and African standards, Benin, a center of the slave trade, was a very large city in the 17th century.

1-5 Spain, Columbus, and the Americas

Q *What kinds of different motives shaped early Spanish colonialism in the Americas?*

While the Portuguese surged east, Spaniards more sluggishly moved west. Shortly after 1400, as Portugal gained experience by colonizing Madeira and the Azores, the Spanish kingdom of Castile sent its first settlers to the Canary Islands. The Spaniards spent the last third of the 15th century conquering the local inhabitants, the Guanches, who had left North Africa before the rise of Islam and had been living almost completely cut off from Africa and Europe for a thousand years. By the 1490s, the Spanish had all but exterminated them, the first people to face virtual extinction in the wake of European expansion.

Except for seizing the Canaries, the Spaniards devoted little attention to exploration or colonization. Instead, for most of the 15th century, the Iberian kingdoms of Aragon and Castile warred against other powers, quarreled with each other, or dealt with internal unrest. But in 1469 Prince Ferdinand of Aragon married Princess Isabella of Castile. They soon inherited their respective thrones to form the kingdom of Spain, which had a population of about 4.9 million by 1500. Together, Aragon and Castile formed a powerful, expansionist realm. Aragon, a Mediterranean society, had made good on an old claim to the Kingdom of Naples and Sicily and thus possessed an imperial bureaucracy with experience in administering overseas possessions. Castile had turned over much of its overseas trade to merchants and mariners from Genoa in northern Italy, who had settled in the port of Seville, imbuing the city with commercial ambition. Castilians had also taken the lead in expelling the Moors from the Iberian Peninsula, developing in the process a dynamic culture of expansion, violence, and fervent Catholicism.

In January 1492, Isabella and Ferdinand completed the reconquest of Spain by taking Granada, the last outpost of Islam on the Iberian Peninsula. Flush with victory, they gave unconverted Jews six months to become Christians or be expelled from Spain. More than half of Spain's 80,000 Jews fled. A decade later, Ferdinand and Isabella also evicted all unconverted Moors. Castile entered the 16th century as an expanding and fiercely Catholic society, and this attitude accompanied the Spanish overseas.

1-5a *Columbus*

A talented navigator from Genoa named Christopher Columbus sought to benefit from the victory at Granada. He had served the Portuguese Crown for several years, engaged in the slave trade between Africa and the Atlantic islands, married the daughter of a prominent Madeira planter, and may even have sailed to Iceland. He had been pleading for years with the courts of Portugal, England, France, and Spain to give him the ships and men to attempt an unprecedented feat: He planned to reach East Asia by sailing west across the Atlantic.

Columbus's proposed voyage was controversial, but not because he assumed the earth was round. Learned men agreed on that point, but they disagreed about the earth's size. Columbus put its circumference at only 16,000 miles. He proposed to reach Japan or China by sailing west a mere 3,000 miles. The Portuguese scoffed at his reasoning. They put the planet's circumference at about 26,000 miles, and they warned Columbus that he would perish on the vast ocean if he tried his mad scheme. Their calculations were, of course, far more accurate than those of Columbus; the circumference of the earth is about 25,000 miles at the equator. Even so, the fall of Granada gave Columbus another chance to plead his case. Isabella, who now had men and resources to spare, grew more receptive to his request. She put him in charge of a fleet of two caravels, the *Niña* and the *Pinta*, together with a larger, square-rigged vessel, the ***Santa María***, which Columbus made his flagship.

Columbus's motives were both religious and practical. Like many contemporaries, he believed that the world was going to end soon but that God would make the Gospel available to all humankind before the last days. As the "Christ-bearer" (the literal meaning of his first name), Columbus was convinced that he had a role to play in bringing on the Millennium, the period at the end of history when Jesus would return and rule with his saints for 1,000 years; however, he was not at all averse to acquiring wealth and glory along the way.

Embarking in August 1492, Columbus headed south to the Canaries, picked up provisions, and sailed west across the Atlantic. He promised a prize to the first sailor to sight land. Despite his assurances that they had not sailed far, the crews grew restless in early October. Columbus pushed on. When land was spotted, on October 12, he claimed the prize for himself. He said he had seen a light in the distance the previous night (see Map 1.8).

The Spaniards splashed ashore on San Salvador, now Watling's Island in the Bahamas. Convinced that he was somewhere in the East Indies, near Japan or China, Columbus called the local inhabitants "Indians," a word that meant nothing to them but one that has endured. When the peaceful Tainos (or Arawaks) claimed that the Carib Indians on nearby islands were cannibals, Columbus interpreted their word for "Carib" to mean the great "Khan" or emperor of China, known to him through Marco Polo's account of his travels to China in the 1270s. Searching for the Caribs, Columbus poked about the coasts of Cuba and Hispaniola. Then, on Christmas, the *Santa María* ran onto rocks and had to be abandoned. A few weeks later, Columbus sailed for Spain on the *Niña*, leaving some of his crew to occupy Hispaniola. By then the Tainos had seen enough. Before Columbus returned on his second voyage in late 1493, they had killed all of them.

The voyage had immediate consequences. In 1493, Pope Alexander VI (a Spaniard) issued a bull, *Inter Caeteras*, which divided all non-Christian lands between Spain and Portugal. A year later, in the Treaty of Tordesillas, the two kingdoms adjusted the dividing line, with Spain eventually claiming most of the Western Hemisphere, plus the Philippines, and Portugal most of the Eastern Hemisphere, including the African coast, plus Brazil. As a result, Spain never acquired direct access to the African slave trade.

Columbus made three more voyages in quest of China and served as governor of the Spanish Indies. He made concerted efforts to plant colonies and Christianity in the new lands, but his efforts were frustrated by the kind of deep cultural misunderstandings that would complicate the relations between Europeans and Indians for centuries. On his second voyage, Columbus brought the first missionaries to the Americas. After one of them preached to a group of Tainos and presented them with some holy images, the Indians "left the chapel, ... flung the images to the ground, covered them with a heap of earth, and pissed upon it." The governor, a brother of Columbus, had them burned alive. The Indians may have seen this punishment as a form of human sacrifice to a vengeful god. They had no context for understanding the Christian distinction between human sacrifice and punishment for desecration.

Columbus also faced resistance back in Spain. Castilians never really trusted this Genoese opportunist, who spoke their language with a foreign accent and was a weak and cruel administrator to boot. The colonists often defied him and in 1500, after his third voyage, they shipped him back to Spain in chains. Although later restored to royal favor, he died in 1506 a bitter, disappointed man.

1-5b *Spain and the Caribbean*

By then, overseas settlement had acquired a momentum of its own as thousands of ex-soldiers, frustrated hidalgos (minor nobles with little wealth), and assorted adventurers drifted across the Atlantic. They carried with them seeds for Europe's cereal crops and livestock, including horses, cows, sheep, goats, and pigs. On islands without fences, the animals roamed freely, eating everything in sight, and soon threatened the Tainos' food supply. Unconcerned, the Spaniards forced the increasingly malnourished Indians to work for them, mostly panning for gold. Under these pressures, the native population fell catastrophically throughout the Caribbean. By 1514, only 22,000 able-bodied adults remained on Hispaniola, from an initial population of perhaps 1 million. The native people died even more rapidly than the meager supply of placer gold disappeared. This story was soon repeated on Cuba, Jamaica, and other islands. A whole way of life all but vanished from the earth to be replaced by sugar, slaves, and livestock as the Spaniards despaired of finding other forms of wealth. African slaves, acquired from the Portuguese, soon arrived to replace the dead Indians as a labor force.

The Spaniards continued their New World explorations. Juan Ponce de León tramped through Florida in quest of a legendary fountain of youth, calculating that such an elixir would bring a handsome price in Europe. Vasco Núñez de Balboa became the first European to reach the Pacific Ocean after he crossed the Isthmus of Panama in 1513. Even so, a full generation after Columbus's first voyage, Spain had gained little wealth from these new possessions, whatever and wherever they turned out to be. One geographer concluded that Spain had found a whole new continent, which he named "America" in honor of his informant, the explorer Amerigo Vespucci. For those who doubted this claim, Ferdinand Magellan, a Portuguese mariner serving the king of Spain, settled the issue when his fleet sailed around the world between 1519 and 1522.

Interpreting the Visual Past

How to Understand Columbus's Landing?

When printed books became more affordable and common during the 16th century, Europeans increasingly learned about the Western Hemisphere—its indigenous habitants and its colonization—through images. One of the most prolific and influential illustrators of the age was Theodor de Bry, who produced several books based on firsthand observations by European explorers, each lavishly illustrated with engravings. This engraving, published in 1594, depicts Columbus's landing in San Salvador in 1492 and his first encounter with the Taino Indians. Produced and published more than a century after the actual event, de Bry's image captures how many Europeans had come to understand Columbus's landing and the subsequent colonization of the Americas. It is, therefore, both a portrayal and an interpretation of a seminal historical event. For historians, it is a value-laden document that invites critical scrutiny.

Q *By the late 16th century, the subjugation and enslavement of Native Americans had become an intensely debated question in Europe. How do you think images like this have shaped contemporary European understandings of New World encounters and the history of colonialism?*

Q *Consider how de Bry depicts different actors and the landscape. Does his image promote a particular political agenda? How do you think the advocates and opponents of Indian slavery might have reacted to the image?*

1.16 **Theodor de Bry, Christopher Columbus (1451–1506) Welcomed by the Natives, 1594.**

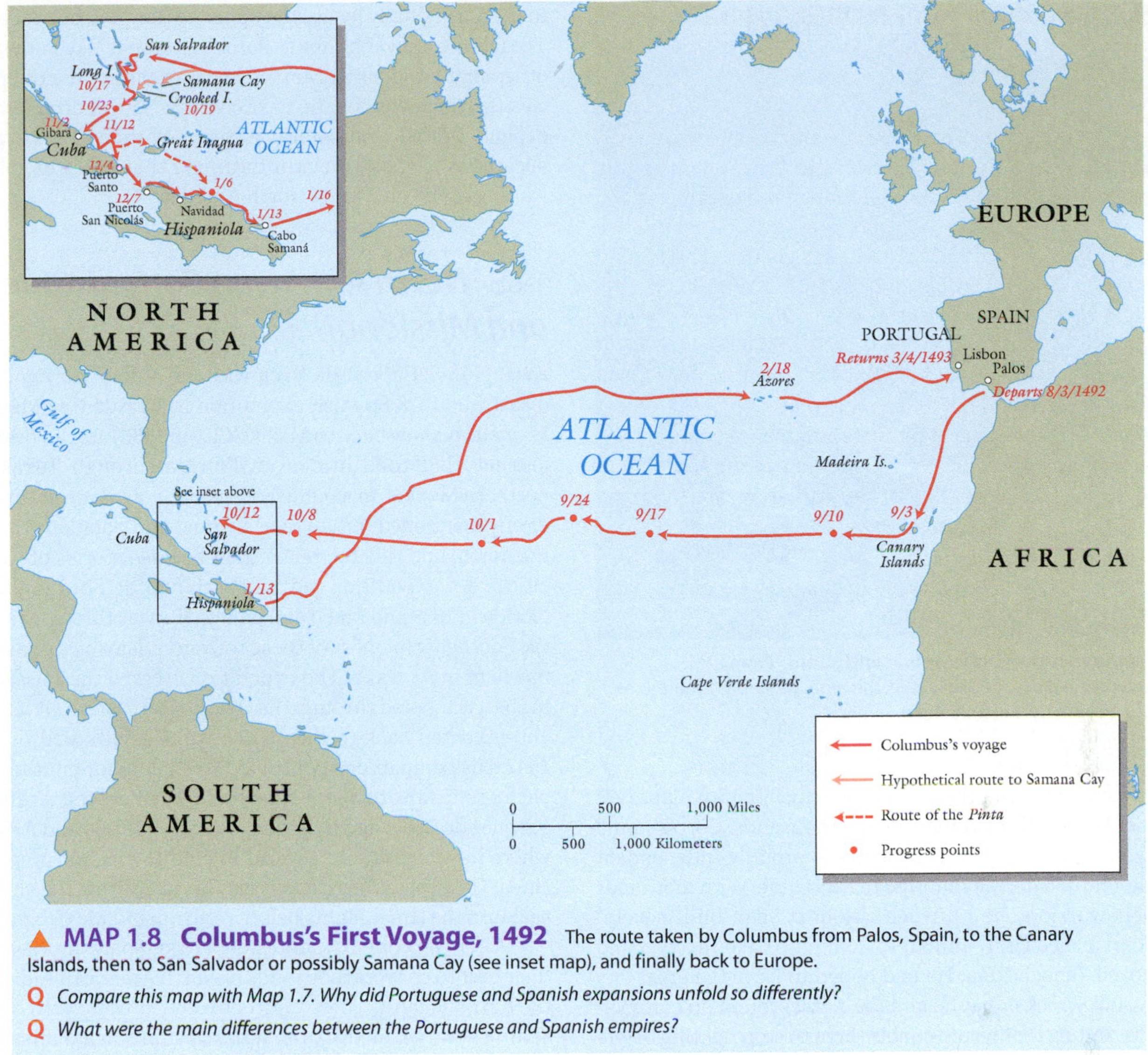

▲ **MAP 1.8 Columbus's First Voyage, 1492** The route taken by Columbus from Palos, Spain, to the Canary Islands, then to San Salvador or possibly Samana Cay (see inset map), and finally back to Europe.

Q *Compare this map with Map 1.7. Why did Portuguese and Spanish expansions unfold so differently?*

Q *What were the main differences between the Portuguese and Spanish empires?*

1-6 Conquest and Catastrophe

Q *What enabled relatively few Spanish conquerors to subjugate the powerful empires of the Aztecs and the Incas?*

A generation after Columbus's landing on San Salvador, Spanish ***conquistadores***, or conquerors, shifted their sights from the Caribbean islands to the American mainland. There, in the highlands of Mexico and Peru, they stumbled upon a different kind of Native America, one of ancient civilizations and vast empires. They found this Native America both daunting and irresistible.

1-6a *The Conquest of Mexico and Peru*

During the three years when Ferdinand Magellan's fleet was circumnavigating the globe, **Hernán Cortés** sailed from Cuba, invaded Mexico, and found the treasure that Spaniards had been seeking. In 1519, he landed at a place he named Veracruz (The True Cross), and over the next several months he succeeded in tracking down the fabulous empire of the Aztecs high in the Valley of Mexico. When his small army of 400 men first laid eyes on the Aztec capital of Tenochtitlán, they wondered if they were dreaming, but they marched on. Moctezuma (or Montezuma II), the Aztec "speaker," or ruler, sent rich presents to persuade the Spaniards to leave, but the gesture had the opposite effect. "They picked up the gold and fingered it like monkeys," an Aztec later recalled. "Their bodies swelled with greed, and their hunger was ravenous... . They snatched at the golden ensigns, waved them from side to side and examined every inch of them."

Ecstatic, Cortés led his army into Tenochtitlán and seized Moctezuma, the Aztec ruler, as prisoner and hostage. Although overwhelmingly outnumbered, Cortés and his men began to destroy Aztec religious objects, replacing them with images of the Virgin Mary or other Catholic saints. In response, while Cortés was away, the Aztecs rose against the intruders. Moctezuma was killed, and the Spaniards were driven out

Haitian School/Musee de l'Homme, Paris, France/The Bridgeman Art Library

1.17 **Wooden Stool (Duho) Inlaid with Gold** From the late pre-Columbian era in the Caribbean, this stool probably honored the deities and ancestors of a chieftain.

with heavy losses. But then smallpox, which the Spaniards left behind, began killing Aztecs by the thousands. Cortés found refuge with the nearby Tlaxcalans, a proudly independent people who had never submitted to Aztec rule. With thousands of their warriors, he returned the next year, built several warships armed with cannons to dominate Lake Texcoco, and destroyed Tenochtitlán. He had hoped to leave the great city intact, not wreck it, but he and the Aztecs found no common understanding that would enable them to stop fighting before the city lay in ruins. With royal support from Spain, the conquistadores established themselves as new imperial rulers in Mesoamerica, looted all the silver and gold they could find, and built Mexico City on the ruins of Tenochtitlán.

Rumors abounded about an even richer civilization far to the south, and in 1531 and 1532 Francisco Pizarro finally located the Inca Empire high in the Andes. Smallpox had preceded him and killed the reigning Inca. In the civil war that followed, Atahualpa had defeated his brother to become the new Inca. Pizarro captured Atahualpa, held him hostage, and massacred many of his followers. Some of the Inca's recent enemies allied with Pizarro and the Spaniards. Atahualpa filled his throne room with precious metals as a truly royal ransom, but Pizarro had him strangled anyway. Tens of thousands of angry Indians besieged the Spaniards for months in Cuzco, the Inca capital, but Pizarro, although vastly outnumbered, managed to hold out and finally prevailed. After subduing the insurgents, the Spanish established a new capital at Lima on the coast.

In the course of a few years, some hundreds of Spanish soldiers with thousands of Indian allies had conquered two enormous empires with a combined population perhaps five times greater than that of all Spain. But only in the 1540s did the Spanish finally locate the bonanza they had been seeking. The fabulous silver mines at Potosí in present-day Bolivia and other smaller lodes in Mexico became the source of Spain's wealth and power for the next century. So wondrous did the exploits of the conquistadores seem by then that anything became believable, including rumors that cities of gold lay waiting in the interior of North America.

1-6b *North American Conquistadores and Missionaries*

Alvar Núñez Cabeza de Vaca was one of four survivors of a disastrous 1528 Spanish expedition to Florida (see Map 1.9). He made his way back to Mexico City in 1536 after an overland journey that took him from Florida through Texas and northern Mexico. In a published account of his adventures, he briefly mentioned Indian tales of great and populous cities to the north, and this reference soon became stories of "golden cities." An expedition led by Hernando de Soto landed in Florida in 1539 and raped and pillaged its way through much of the Southeast in quest of these treasures, leaving disease and mayhem in its wake. The expedition crossed the Mississippi in 1541, wandered through the Ozarks and eastern Oklahoma, and marched back to the great river. De Soto died there in 1542. His companions continued to explore for another year before returning to Spanish territory. Farther west, Francisco Vasquez de Coronado marched into New Mexico and Arizona, where he encountered several Pueblo towns but no golden cities. The expedition reached the Grand Canyon, then headed east into the Great Plains before returning to Mexico in 1542.

After the conquistadores departed, Spanish priests did their best to convert thousands of North American Indians to the Catholic faith. These efforts extended well north of New Spain (Mexico). In 1570, the Jesuits established a mission in what is now Virginia, but local Indians soon wiped it out. After the failure of the Jesuit mission, Spain tried to treat the Indians of Florida and New Mexico with decency and later came to rely on the missions to protect its holdings against English and French intruders. The Jesuits withdrew and Franciscans took their place. In 1573, King Philip II (1556–1598) issued the Royal Orders for New Discoveries, which prohibited the military conquest of the Indians and set limitations on labor coercion. Unarmed priests were to bring Indians together in missions and convert them into peaceful Catholic subjects of Spain. The Franciscans quickly discovered that, without military support, they were more likely to win martyrdom than converts. They reluctantly accepted military protection, but they tried, not always successfully, to make sure that none of the few soldiers who accompanied them behaved like conquistadores.

Franciscans built their missions within the permanent Indian villages of northern Florida and New Mexico's Pueblo communities along the upper Rio Grande Valley (see Map 1.10). The Spanish incursion into New Mexico began violently with the slaughter of some 800 Acoma Indian men, women, and children in 1599, and the imperial authorities in Mexico nearly aborted the project. New Mexico became a royal colony,

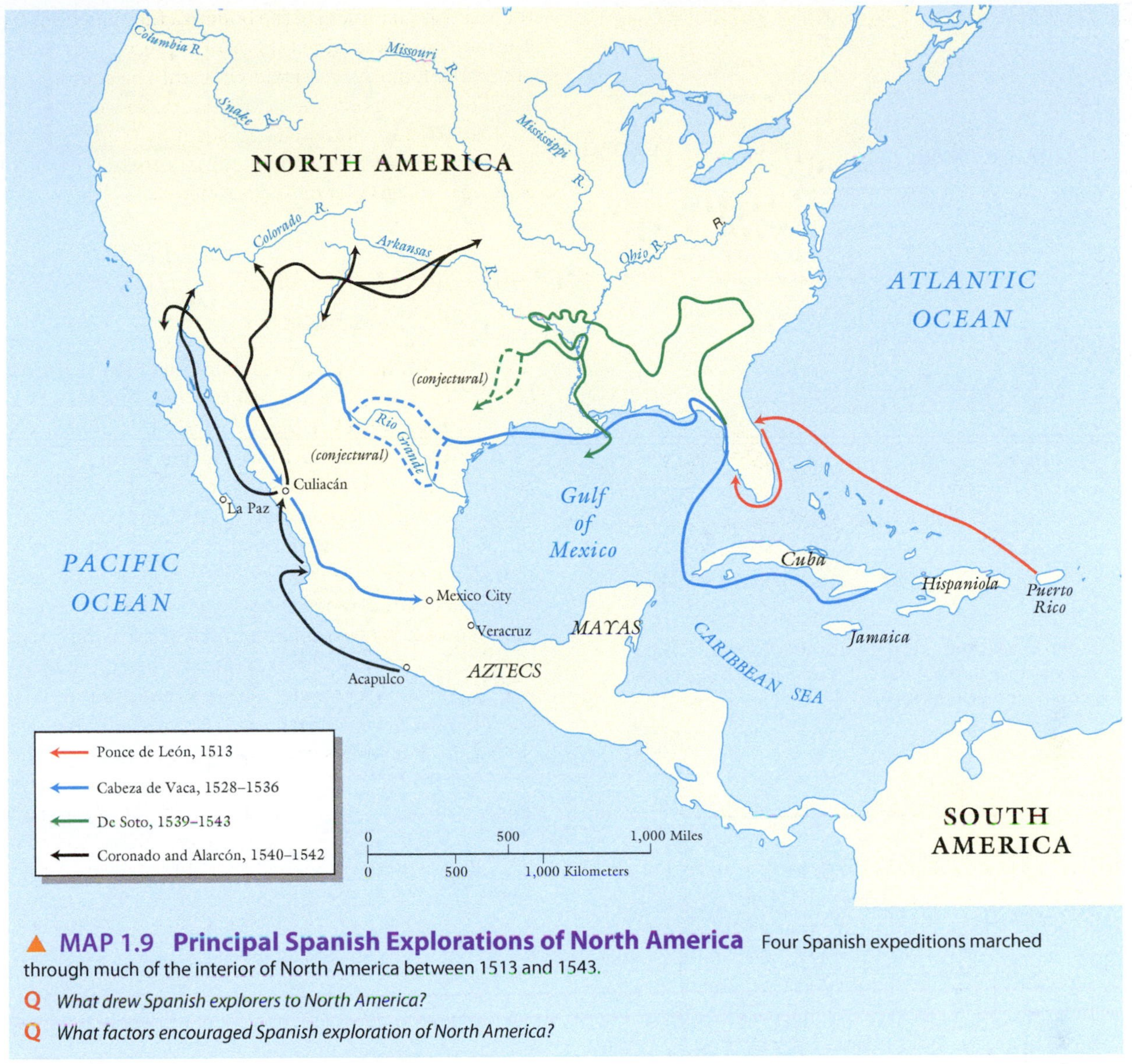

▲ **MAP 1.9 Principal Spanish Explorations of North America** Four Spanish expeditions marched through much of the interior of North America between 1513 and 1543.

Q *What drew Spanish explorers to North America?*

Q *What factors encouraged Spanish exploration of North America?*

and Franciscans continued to convert the Pueblos. By 1630, Pueblo Indian women, under the priests' supervision, had built more than 50 churches in New Mexico, and some 86,000 Pueblo, Apache, and Navajo Indians had accepted baptism. In Florida, 30 missions boasted about 26,000 baptized Indians by midcentury, covering an area that extended some 250 miles from the Atlantic coast of what is now Georgia westward into the Florida Panhandle.

The missions were not merely sites of religious conversion; they were also institutions of cultural modification. Many aspects of native social organization confounded the Europeans—that they were often **matrilineal**, tracing descent through the maternal line, and polygamous; that women did most of the farming, could own considerable property, and often had a say in such political matters as starting a war—and they tried to change them after their own image. The Franciscans pushed their converts to wear European clothing, give up their sacred dances and songs, abandon polygamy for monogamy, and provide labor for the missions. They also pressured the Indians to modify their labor and gender conventions to comply with European mores, forcing native men to take up such traditionally women's tasks as building construction and farming.

Many Indians converted to Christianity, but that did not necessarily mean that they became the kind of Christians the missionaries hoped for. Franciscan dreams of a spiritual paradise in the Americas remained elusive. Indians adopted the Christian doctrine selectively, mixing elements of it with their own religious traditions; often, Jesus, Mary, and various saints joined, rather than replaced, teeming indigenous pantheons. Native men refused to become farmers, protesting that it would turn them into women. A vast cultural gap between Europeans and Indians undermined the missionary work. Missionaries eagerly brought news of the Christ and of how he had died to save humankind from sin. Catholic worship, then as now, centered on the Mass and the Eucharist, in which a priest transforms bread and wine into the literal body and blood of Christ. To Indians, Christians seemed to be people

▲ **MAP 1.10 Spanish Missions in Florida and New Mexico circa 1675** Franciscan friars established missions in Florida from the Atlantic to the Gulf of Mexico and in New Mexico along the Rio Grande Valley and, in a few cases, farther inland.

Q *Consult Map 1.9. Why did the early Spanish outposts in North America cluster in Florida and New Mexico?*

Q *What were the similarities and differences between the Spanish mission systems in Florida and New Mexico?*

who ate their god but grew outraged at such lesser matters as serving multiple gods or having multiple wives. Neither side fully recognized such obstacles to mutual understanding. Although early missionaries converted thousands of Indians, the results were mixed at best. As Christianization and Hispanicization proceeded across the Americas, so too did indigenous resentment and resistance.

1-6c *The Spanish Empire and Demographic Catastrophe*

Spanish conquistadores had led small armies that rarely exceeded 1,000 men. Yet, because they were also able to raise large Indian armies as allies, they managed to subdue two indigenous empires much larger than Spain. Spain's core

What They Said

Two Spanish Scholars Debate Indian Slavery

Spanish colonization of the Americas became a highly charged, fiercely debated issue on both sides of the Atlantic. At the heart of the controversy was an uncertainty about the roles and rights the Indians would have in the emerging colonial societies. Was their subjugation and dispossession justified and, if so, on what grounds? In these selections from the mid-16th century, two Spanish scholars debate whether Indians were natural slaves.

Juan Ginés de Sepúlveda

The man rules over the woman, the adult over the child, the father over his children. That is to say, the most powerful and most perfect rule over the weakest and most imperfect. This same relationship exists among men, there being some who by nature are masters and others who by nature are slaves. Those who surpass the rest in prudence and intelligence, although not in physical strength, are by nature the masters. On the other hand, those who are dim-witted and mentally lazy, although they may be physically strong enough to fulfill all the necessary tasks, are by nature slaves. . . . It will always be just and in conformity with natural law that such people submit to the rule of more cultured and humane princes and nations. . . .

These people [Indians] possess neither science nor even an alphabet, nor do they preserve any monuments of their history except for some obscure and vague reminiscences depicted in certain paintings, nor do they have written laws, but barbarous institutions and customs. In regard to their virtues, how much restraint or gentleness are you to expect of men who are devoted to all kinds of intemperate acts and abominable lewdness, including the eating of human flesh? And you must realize that prior to the arrival of the Christians, they did not live in that peaceful kingdom of Saturn that the poets imagine, but on the contrary they made war against one another continually and fiercely, with such fury that victory was of no meaning if they did not satiate their monstrous hunger with the flesh of their enemies. . . .

For numerous and grave reasons these barbarians are obligated to accept the rule of the Spaniards according to natural law. For them it ought to be even more advantageous than for the Spaniards, since virtue, humanity, and the true religion are more valuable than gold or silver.

Bartolomé de las Casas

Let us now speak about the unbelievers who live in kingdoms ruled by non-Christians, such as the Moors of Africa, the Turks, the Scythians, the Persians, and those with whom the present controversy is concerned, the Indians. Surely, no matter how despicable the crimes they may commit against God, or even against religion among themselves or within their territories, neither the Church nor Christian rulers can take cognizance of them or punish them for these. For there is no jurisdiction, which is the necessary basis for all juridical acts, especially for punishing a person. Therefore, in this case, the emperor, the prince, or the king has no jurisdiction but is the same as a private citizen, and whatever he does has no force.

...this is proved, first, by the fact that unbelievers who have never accepted the faith of Christ are not actually subject to Christ and therefore not to the Church or its authority.

...Sepulveda claims that the Supreme Pontiff Alexander VI advised the kings of Castile to subjugate the Indians by war and that he condoned the war by which those peoples have been brought under our rule. This is absolutely false. The Pope granted the kings of Castile the right to set themselves over the Indian rulers whom they had converted to the faith of Christ and keep them as subjects under their protection and jurisdiction. But the Pope never commanded or permitted them to subjugate these rulers by war. For how would he permit something that conflicts with Christ's precept and instruction and produces hatred of the name of Christ in the hearts of unbelievers, and is utterly irreligious? For the will of a ruler is always judged to be in conformity with the law.

...the Pope praises the Kings and precisely because they wanted to seek new regions, unknown in former centuries, with the intention of spreading the Christian religion ... [the kings] subjugate (that is, dispose) them [the Indians] for the faith in a way in which one should subjugate a most civilized, sincere, naked, docile, decent, and peaceful people who are very ready to serve, that is, mildly, in a Christian and humane way. As a result, after they first know the true God through belief in the gospel, they may at last freely subject themselves to the king of Castile (from whom they have received such a benefit) as to their supreme prince and emperor, while the rights of their natural lords are retained. . . .

What are the key similarities and differences in these arguments? How do their notions of law, religion, and culture differ from each other? Which do you think was more successful in persuading the contemporary Spanish policymakers? How do you think contemporary Native Americans might have understood such a debate?

Sources: (top) Juan Ginés de Sepúlveda speech from 1547 reprinted in John H. Parry and Robert G. Keith, eds. New Iberian World: A Documentary History of the Discovery and Settlement of Latin America to the Early 17th Century (New York: Times Books: Hector & Rose, 1984), 1: 324–26. (bottom) Bartolomé de Las Casas speech from 1547 reprinted in John H. Parry and Robert G. Keith, eds. New Iberian World: A Documentary History of the Discovery and Settlement of Latin America to the Early 17th Century (New York: Times Books: Hector & Rose, 1984), 1: 324–26.

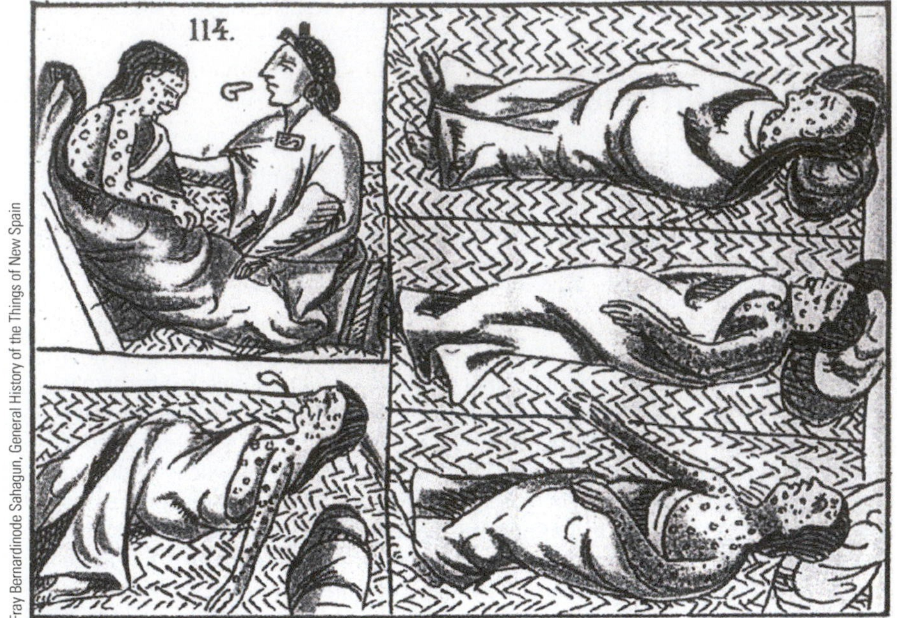

Fray Bernardinode Sahagun, General History of the Things of New Spain

1.18 **The Ravages of Smallpox** These drawings show the devastation of smallpox among the Aztecs, as depicted in the Aztec Codex, one of the few surviving collections of Aztec writing.

Q *What might the image reveal about how Native Americans understood the spread of such viral diseases like smallpox?*

American holdings in Peru and Mexico were protected by a strong defensive perimeter in the Caribbean and surrounded by a series of frontier missions, extending in the north into Florida and New Mexico. There, the Spaniards looked around for more worlds to conquer, but failed to replicate their triumphs in the south. The success of Spanish colonialism in the Americas depended on the exploitation and co-option of existing urban populations, agricultural economies, and social hierarchies. Beyond great indigenous empires, Spanish colonial expansion tended to slow down and falter.

By the late 16th century, the Spanish Empire had developed into a system of direct colonial rule in Mexico and Peru. Spanish conquistadores had targeted the largest and richest of the Americas' indigenous empires and placed themselves on top of them as masters. Leaving large parts of these empires' political and social structures intact, they took over their existing systems of tribute. The Spaniards also brought new systems of labor and new religious institutions to their overseas colonies, although in time both were altered by local conditions.

In the course of the 16th century, the Spanish Crown enacted a series of laws that specifically prohibited the buying, selling, and owning of Indian slaves. These laws were widely contested in the Americas, where the colonists employed other, formally legal methods of extracting and coercing native labor. For much of the 16th century, Spanish rulers in Mexico, Peru, and New Mexico relied on a form of labor tribute called ***encomienda***. This system permitted the holder, or *encomendero*, to claim labor from an Indian district for a stated period of time. *Encomienda* worked because it resembled the way the Aztecs and the Incas had routinely levied labor for their own massive public buildings and irrigation projects. In time, the king intervened to correct abuses and limit labor tribute to Crown projects, such as mining and the construction of churches or other public buildings. Spanish settlers resisted the reforms at first but slowly shifted from demanding labor to claiming land. In the countryside, the ***hacienda***, a large estate with its own crops and herds, became a familiar institution.

Although the Church never had enough clergy to meet its needs, it became a massive presence during the 16th century. Yet, America changed it, too. As missionaries acquired land and labor, they began to exhibit less zeal for Indian souls. The Franciscans—in Europe, the gentlest of Catholic religious orders—brutally and systematically tortured their Mayan converts in the 1560s whenever they caught them worshiping their old gods. To the Franciscans, the slightest lapse could signal a reversion to Satan worship, with human sacrifice a likely consequence. They did not dare to be kind.

Most important, the Spaniards brought deadly microbes with them. Smallpox, measles, typhus, cholera, and other crowd diseases, often spreading in successive pandemics, devastated the Indians. The reasons for the Indians' vulnerability to European diseases are not clear, but the evidence points to certain features in their immunological makeup. Having lived for millennia in relatively disease-free environments, the Indians, unlike the Europeans, may not have been genetically selected to resist infectious diseases. It is also possible that their immune systems were relatively homogenous—they had descended from a rather small sample of the total gene pool of Asia—making it easier for viruses to jump bodies. What is clear, however, is that the destructiveness of European diseases was greatly magnified by colonialism itself. The social turmoil, environmental stress, malnutrition, and psychological trauma caused by colonial expansion sapped the strength of indigenous societies, rendering them vulnerable to alien pathogens.

The result was an unprecedented population collapse. When Cortés arrived in 1519, the native population of Mexico probably exceeded 15 million. In the 1620s, after waves of killing epidemics, it bottomed out at 700,000 and did not regain its pre-Spanish level until the 1950s. Peru suffered nearly as horribly. Its population fell from about 10 million in 1525 to 600,000 a century later. For the hemisphere as a whole, any given region probably lost 90 to 95 percent of its population within a century of sustained contact with Europeans. Lowland tropical areas usually suffered the heaviest casualties; in some of these places, all of the Indians died. Highland areas and sparsely settled regions often fared better.

The Spanish Crown spent much of the 16th century trying to keep abreast of these changes, but eventually it imposed administrative order on the unruly conquistadores and brought peace to its colonies. At the center of the imperial bureaucracy, in Seville, stood the Council of the Indies. The council administered the three American viceroyalties of New Spain, Peru, and eventually New Granada, which were further subdivided into smaller *audiencias*, executive and judicial jurisdictions supervised by the viceroys. The Council of the Indies appointed the viceroys and other major officials, who ruled from the new cities that the Spaniards built with local labor at Havana, Mexico City, Lima, and elsewhere. Although centralized and autocratic in theory, the Spanish Empire allowed local officials a fair degree of initiative, if only because years could elapse in trying to communicate across its immense distances. "If death came from Spain," mused one official, "we should all live long lives."

1-6d *Brazil*

Pedro Álvares Cabral discovered Brazil for Portugal in 1500, when he was blown off course while trying to round the Cape of Good Hope. Like Spanish America, Portuguese Brazil became a colony with a strong autocratic streak, but it was divided into 14 "captaincies," or provinces, and so was far less centralized. The Portuguese invasion did not lead to direct rule over native societies but to their displacement or enslavement. After the colonists on the northeast coast turned to raising sugar in the late 16th century, Brazilian frontiersmen, or *bandeirantes*, foraged deep into the continent to enslave more Indians. They even raided remote Spanish Andean missions, rounded up the converts, and dragged them thousands of miles across mountains and through jungles to be worked to death on plantations. On several occasions, while Brazil was ruled by Spain (see below), missionaries persuaded the king to abolish slavery. Not even absolutism could achieve that goal. Slavery continued without pause, and Africans gradually replaced Indians as the dominant labor force. Brazil was the major market for African slaves until the 1640s, when Caribbean demand became even greater.

1-7 Global Colossus, Global Economy

In what ways did American silver both bolster and weaken the Spanish Empire?

American silver made the king of Spain the most powerful monarch in Christendom. Philip II commanded the largest army in Europe, held the Turks in check in the Mediterranean, and tried to crush the Protestant Reformation in northern Europe (see Chapter 2). In 1580, after the king of Portugal died with no direct heir, Philip claimed that throne, thus uniting under his own rule Portugal's Asian empire, Brazil, Spain's American possessions, and the Philippines. This colossus was the greatest empire the world had ever seen. It also sustained the first truly global economy, because the Portuguese used Spain's American silver to pay for the spices and silks they imported from Asia. The union of Spain and Portugal lasted until the 1640s, when Portugal revolted and regained its independence.

The Spanish colossus became part of an even broader economic pattern. **Serfdom**, which tied peasants to their lords and to the land, had been Europe's predominant labor system in the early Middle Ages. Although peasants could not move, neither could they be sold; they were not slaves. Serfdom had been declining in Western Europe since the 12th century and was nearly gone by 1500. A system of free labor gradually arose in its place, and overseas expansion strengthened that trend within Western Europe. Although free labor prevailed in the Western European homeland, unfree labor systems took root all around Europe's periphery, both overseas and in Eastern Europe, and the two systems were structurally linked. In general, free labor reigned where populations were dense and still growing. Large pools of labor kept wages low, but around the periphery of Western Europe, where land was cheap and labor expensive, coercive systems became the only efficient way for Europeans to extract from those areas the products they desired (see Map 1.11).

The forms of unfree labor varied greatly across space and time, from slavery to less brutal systems. In New Spain, as the native population dwindled, the practice of *encomienda* slowly yielded to debt peonage. Unpayable debts kept Indians tied to the ***haciendas*** of the countryside. The mining of precious metals, on the other hand, was so dangerous and unpleasant that it almost always required a large degree of physical coercion. In the Andes the Spaniards instituted a system of labor draft called *mita*, which forced communities to provide one-seventh of their male labor force for Spanish overlords. Similarly, any colonial region that devoted itself to the production of staple crops for sale in Europe also turned to unfree labor and eventually to overt slavery. Sugar production first reduced Indians to bondage in Brazil and the Caribbean and later, as they died off, led to the importation of African slaves by the millions. Other staples—tobacco, rice, coffee, cotton—later followed similar patterns. At first these crops were considered luxuries and commanded high prices, but as they became widely available on the world market, their prices fell steeply, profit margins contracted, and planters turned overwhelmingly to coerced labor. Even in Eastern Europe, which began to specialize in producing cereal crops for sale in the more diversified West, serfdom revived. In Russia, where the Orthodox Church never condemned the enslavement of fellow Christians, the condition of a serf came to resemble that of a slave in one of the Atlantic empires. Some serfs were even bought and sold.

Spain's rise had been spectacular, but its empire was vulnerable. Although silver from the Americas vastly enhanced the Crown's ability to wage war, the costs of continuous conflict, the inflation generated by a steady influx of silver, and

History Through Film Even the Rain (2010)

Directed by Icíar Bollaín.
Starring Gael García Bernal (Sebastián), Luis Tosar (Costa), Juan Carlos Aduviri (Daniel), Karra Ejalade (Anton/Christopher Columbus).

Even the Rain opens in Cochabamba, the third largest city in Bolivia, in 2000. A movie crew has arrived to shoot a revisionist film about Christopher Columbus, and Cochabamba is to stand in for Hispaniola. Costa (Luis Tosar), the producer, has chosen Cochabamba less for authenticity than finances: The local Indians can be hired as manual laborers and extras for $2 per day. The pay is meager, but vast numbers line up for auditions; the queue of indigenous people vanishes into the horizon.

Things soon spin out of control. Pressured by the World Bank, the Bolivian government has sold the country's water rights to a multinational water consortium, which suddenly closes local wells, aiming to raise prices. Catching rainwater is about to become illegal; even the rain will belong to someone else. The poor, the country's vast majority, are in danger of being denied clean water. People start protesting, and the film crew finds itself in the midst of a populist uprising.

These real-life events are the setting for the director, Icíar Bollaín, to examine colonialism, imperialism, globalization, and exploitation over a long time span, from Columbus to the cusp of the 21st century. The film is steeped in irony. Costa and his idealistic director Sebastián (Gael García Bernal) want to make a film that exposes the brutality and callousness of European colonialism in the Americas, but end up, as embodiments of globalization, exploiting the Indians for their own purposes—not entirely unlike what Columbus did. Where Columbus was fixated on securing slaves, souls, and precious metals for the Spanish Crown, the filmmakers seem to have few scruples as they exploit the native people for their high-minded artistic ends. In keeping with true Hollywood mythology, Sebastián is an obsessive visionary determined to make the film he feels he needs to make.

Enter Daniel (Juan Carlos Aduviri), a passionate young Indian who not only is cast in the film's leading role but is also one of the leaders of the water-rights movement. Daniel's activism draws police attention to the film set, and the escalating unrest threatens to bring the production to a grinding halt. Confronted by the contemporary South American political struggles, the filmmakers find themselves grappling with the legacies of colonialism as they witness how their indigenous workers suffer under global inequalities. Daniel is the moral touchstone against which Costa and Sebastián must define their actions. They react in contrasting ways: Costa experiences an awakening of social conscience and seeks to help the protestors, while Sebastián remains committed only to his film, coldly ignoring the suffering around him.

Everett Collection Inc/Alamy Stock Photo

1.19 Gael García Bernal (Sebastián) and Luis Tosar (Costa), play leading roles in *Even the Rain*.

Even the Rain is a highly self-conscious movie. It is a film within a film, and it pulls no punches in drawing parallels between 16th-century colonialism and modern-day globalization. The movie shifts from showing the film crew shooting scenes of Columbus burning Taino Indians alive; to Daniel being brutalized by the police; to the filmmakers inserting themselves into Bolivian politics; to Anton, a boozy actor playing Columbus (Karra Ejalade), reading Columbus's real letters to Ferdinand and Isabella. Fiction and reality and the past and present blur together, inviting the viewer to contemplate how oppression, exploitation, and inequality, in different forms, echo through the centuries. ■

the need to defend a much greater perimeter absorbed Spain's new resources and a great deal more. Between 1492 and 1580, Spain's population grew from 4.9 million to 8 million, but over the course of the following century, it fell by 20 percent, mostly because of the escalating costs, both financial and human, of Spain's wars. As population declined, taxes rose. Castile grew poorer, not richer, in its century and a half of imperial glory. Much of the wealth of the Indies went elsewhere to pay for goods or services that Spain failed to provide for itself: to merchants in Genoa, to manufacturers in Lombardy and the Low Countries, and to bankers in Augsburg.

1-8 Explanations: Patterns of Conquest, Submission, and Resistance

Q *What is the Columbian Exchange and how has it shaped world history?*

By the middle of the 18th century, Europeans who thought seriously about the discovery of America and its global implications generally agreed that the whole process had been

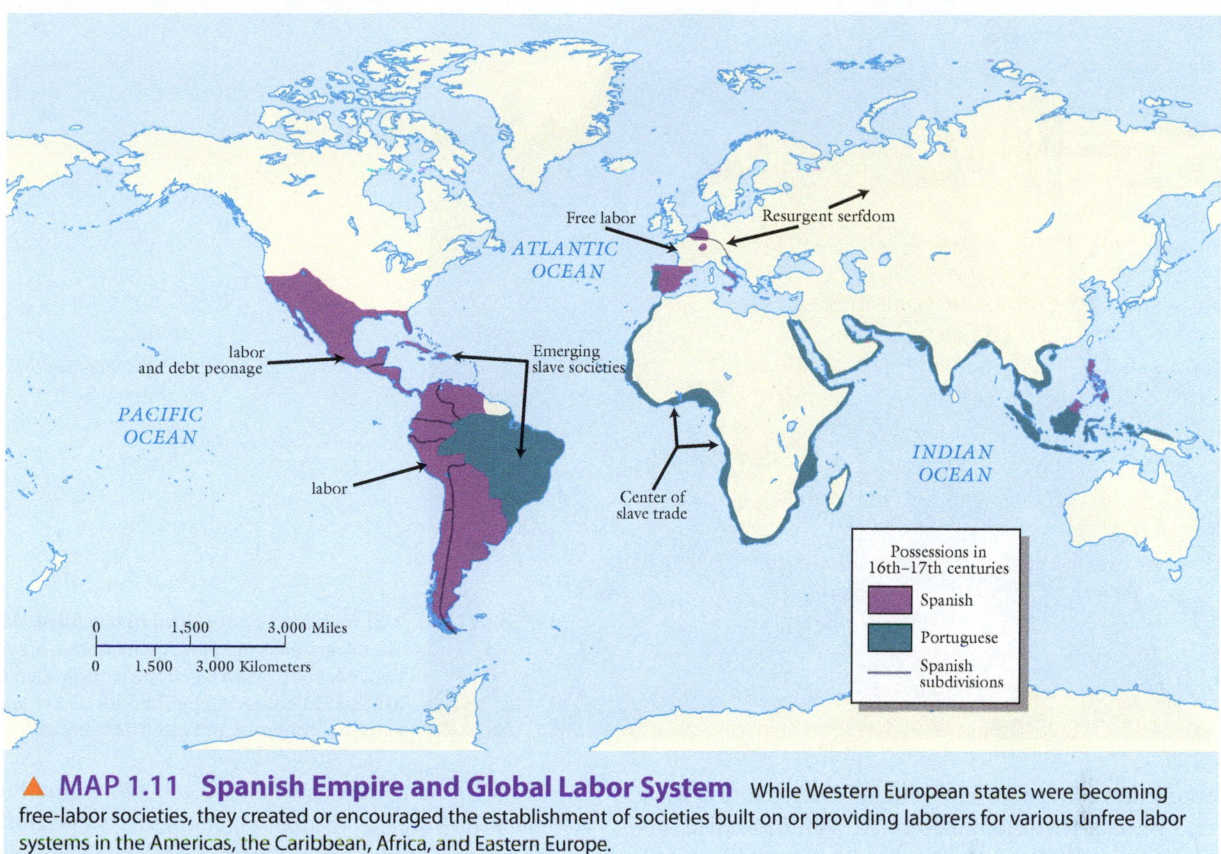

▲ **MAP 1.11 Spanish Empire and Global Labor System** While Western European states were becoming free-labor societies, they created or encouraged the establishment of societies built on or providing laborers for various unfree labor systems in the Americas, the Caribbean, Africa, and Eastern Europe.

Q *Why did slave societies emerge where they did?*

Q *How can the Columbian Exchange help explain the different patterns of colonial expansion in the two hemispheres?*

a moral outrage, possibly the worst in history. Conquest and settlement had killed millions of Indians, enslaved millions of Africans, and degraded Europeans. By comparison, the benefits to humanity seemed small even though economic gains by 1750 were large. If the cruelest of the conquerors had foreseen the results of this process, asked the Abbé Raynal, would he have proceeded? "Is it to be imagined that there exists a being infernal enough to answer this question in the affirmative?" The success of the American Revolution, with its message of freedom and human rights, quieted such thinking for a time, but the critique has revived in recent years, especially in the developing world.

Modern historians, less moralistic than Raynal, also realize that he considerably underestimated the death toll. Even so, they are more interested in asking how and why these things happened. One major reason is geographical. The Eurasian landmass, the world's largest, follows an east-west axis that permits life-forms and human inventions to travel immense distances without going through forbidding changes of climate. Domesticated plants and animals spread quickly from the Fertile Crescent across Eurasia in roughly similar climate zones. The intensifying food production fueled rapid population growth, which in turn stimulated rivalries and exchanges among societies. People learned from one another, and innovations moved from region to region. The use of iron spread gradually throughout most of Afro-Eurasia, and even though Europeans knew little about China, they slowly acquired Chinese inventions such as paper, the compass, and gunpowder. Steel, far more than firearms or even horses, made European colonialism possible. Steel weapons became common in Europe in the early second millennium, giving its states a decisive technological edge. European armor stopped enemy spears and arrows, and European swords killed opponents swiftly without any need to reload. By contrast, the Americas lie along north-south axes, which frustrated intercultural exchanges and the spread of innovations. Separated by chasms of climate, human societies in the Americas remained more isolated than those in Eurasia and could not learn as easily from one another.

The biological consequences of isolation were even more momentous than the technological barriers. The devastation that European microbes inflicted upon the Indian population is the greatest tragedy in the history of humankind. European plants also thrived at the expense of native vegetation. For example, when British settlers first crossed the Appalachians, they marveled at the lush Kentucky bluegrass. They did not realize that they were looking at an accidental European import that had conquered the landscape even faster than they had. European animals also prevailed over potential American rivals. Horses spread north from Mexico with Spanish settlement, transforming the way of life of the Apaches, Comanches, and other Plains Indians. The lowly sparrow never had it so good until someone turned a few loose in North America. But other life-forms moved in the opposite direction, from the Americas to Europe, Asia, and Africa. Corn, potatoes, and tomatoes enriched the diets in Europe, supporting growing

1.20 **Tribute Labor (*Mita*) in the Silver Mines** The silver mines of Potosí, in the Andes, are about two miles above sea level. The work, as depicted in this 1603 engraving by Theodor de Bry, was extremely onerous and often dangerous.

populations that could afford to send more and more of their numbers overseas. Historian Alfred W. Crosby has called this larger process the "**Columbian Exchange**." One of the most important historical transformations, it created a worldwide network of ecological exchanges, recast the biology of both hemispheres, bolstered and destabilized human societies, and paved the way for Europe's expansion into the Americas.

Conclusion

Americans like to believe that their history is a story of progress. They are right about its European phase. After its tragic beginnings in conquest, depopulation, and enslavement, some things finally did improve.

For thousands of years, the Americas had been cut off from the rest of the world. The major cultures of Eurasia and Africa had existed in relative isolation, engaging in direct contact with only their immediate neighbors. Islamic societies that shared borders with India, the East Indies, black Africa, and Europe had been the principal mediators among these cultures and, in that era, were more tolerant than most Christian societies.

In just 40 years, daring European navigators, supported by the crowns of Portugal and Spain, joined the world together and challenged Islam's mediating role in Afro-Eurasia. Between 1492 and 1532, Europe, Africa, Asia, the Spice Islands, the Philippines, the Caribbean, Aztec Mexico, Inca Peru, and other parts of the Americas came into intense and often violent contact with one another. The Atlantic Ocean transformed from a barrier into a communication conduit that linked together the continents around it. A few individuals gained much from these new connections, and Spain acquired a military advantage within Europe that endured into the 1640s. Nearly everybody else suffered, millions horribly, especially in the Americas and Africa. And Spain spent the rest of the 16th century trying to create an imperial system that could impose order on this turbulent reality. But Spain had many enemies. They too would find the lure of wealth and land overseas irresistible.

CHAPTER REVIEW

Review

1. How did the extinction of megafauna shape human history in the Americas?
2. What were the major similarities and differences between the histories of the Andes and Mesoamerica during the first and early second millennia?
3. How did maize cultivation change human history in North America?
4. What enabled relatively backward European societies to establish dominance over the oceans of the world?
5. What kinds of different motives shaped early Spanish colonialism in the Americas?

6. What enabled relatively few Spanish conquistadores to subjugate the powerful empires of the Aztecs and the Incas?
7. In what ways did American silver both bolster and weaken the Spanish Empire?
8. What is the Columbian Exchange and how has it shaped world history?

Critical Thinking

1. European expansion inflicted enormous destruction upon the peoples of sub-Saharan Africa and the Americas. Is there any way that this vast projection of European power overseas also contributed to an eventual expansion of liberty?
2. Why did the free-labor societies of Western Europe generate unfree labor systems in their colonies?

Identifications

Review your understanding of the following key terms, people, and events for this chapter (terms in bold in text are included in the Glossary).

Clovis tip, p. 4
Neolithic, p. 5
Incas, p. 7
Olmecs, p. 7
Mayan, p. 8
Aztecs, p. 10
Tenochtitlán, p. 10
Anasazi, p. 11
Cahokia, p. 13
staple crop, p. 18
slave labor, p. 18
caravel, p. 19
factories, p. 19
Atlantic slave trade, p. 19
Santa María, p. 23
conquistadores, p. 25
Hernán Cortés, p. 25
matrilineal, p. 27
encomienda, p. 30
hacienda, p. 30
serfdom, p. 31
Columbian Exchange, p. 34

Suggested Readings

Three recent general surveys of early American history provide excellent coverage up to U.S. independence: **Alan Taylor**, ***American Colonies*** (2001); **Richard Middleton**, ***Colonial America: A History, 1565–1776***, 3rd ed. (2002); and **Daniel K. Richter**, ***Before the Revolution: America's Ancient Pasts*** (2011). For a useful collection of essays, see **Stanley N. Katz, John M. Murrin, Douglas Greenberg, Denver Brunsman, and David Silverman, eds.**, ***Colonial America: Essays in Politics and Social Development***, 6th ed. (2010).

Brian M. Fagan, ***The Great Journey: The Peopling of Ancient America*** (1987) is a fine introduction to pre-Columbian America. See also **David Webster**, ***The Fall of the Ancient Maya: Solving the Mystery of the Collapse*** (2002). ***Jared Diamond, Guns, Germs, and Steel: The Fates of Human Societies*** (1997) is provocative and challenging in its global perspective. For the age of explorations, see **G. V. Scammell**, ***The First Imperial Age: European Overseas Expansion c. 1400–1715*** (1989); and **Alfred W. Crosby's** classic synthesis, ***The Columbian Exchange: Biological and Cultural Consequences of 1492*** (1972). **Charles C. Mann's** ***1491: New Revelations of the Americas Before Columbus*** (2005) and ***1493: Uncovering the World Columbus Created*** (2011) have helped popularize Crosby's work. For the slave trade, see **John Thornton**, ***Africa and Africans in the Making of the Modern World, 1400–1800***, 2nd ed. (1998), which insists that Africans retained control of their affairs, including the slave trade, through the 17th century. For authoritative overviews of slavery in the Americas, see **David Brion Davis**, ***Inhuman Bondage: The Rise and Fall of Slavery in the New World*** (2006) and **Ira Berlin**, ***Many Thousands Gone: The First Two Centuries of Slavery in North America*** (1998). **Andres Reséndez's** ***The Other Slavery: The Uncovered Story of Indian Enslavement in America*** (2016) is an eye-opening study that reveals a long history of mass Indian enslavement in the Americas and argues that slavery was the key cause to indigenous depopulation.

James Lockhart and Stuart B. Schwartz, ***Early Latin America: A History of Colonial Latin America and Brazil*** (1983) is an outstanding introduction to the Iberian empires. **David J. Weber's**, ***The Spanish Frontier in North America*** (1992) is the best introduction to its subject. For Brazil, see **John Hemming**, ***Red Gold: The Conquest of the Brazilian Indians, 1500–1760*** (1978).

2 Colonization in North America, 1600–1680

The Cataract of NIAGARA, some make
this Water-Fall to be half a League while
others reckon it no more than
a hundred Fathom.

2.1 **Working Beavers** Detail from Herman Moll, *A New Exact Map of the Dominions of the King of Great Britain* (1715). One of the earliest depictions of Niagara Falls consigns that site to the background, with beavers dominating the foreground. Although Europeans valued beavers primarily for their pelts and hunted them almost to extinction, they also admired their industry and their skill at building dams.

CATHOLIC FRANCE and two Protestant countries, the Dutch Republic and England, challenged Spanish power in Europe and overseas. None of them planted a permanent settlement in North America before 1600. In the quarter-century after 1600, they all did. Europeans, Indians, and Africans interacted in contrasting ways in this strange "New World." Spain's rivals created colonies of different kinds. Some, such as Virginia and Barbados, grew staple crops with indentured servants and African slaves. New France and New Netherland developed a prosperous trade with the Indians and forged close political ties with them. In New England, the Puritans relied on free labor provided mostly by family members. After 1660, England conquered New Netherland, and English Quakers created another free-labor society in the Delaware Valley. ■

2-1 The Protestant Reformation and the Challenge to Spain

Q *How did Europe's political and religious landscape change in the 16th century?*

By the time its enemies felt strong enough to challenge Spain overseas, the Protestant Reformation had shattered the religious unity of Europe. In November 1517, not long before Cortés landed in Mexico, Martin Luther nailed his 95 Theses to the cathedral door at Wittenberg in Saxony and touched off the Reformation. Salvation, he insisted, comes through faith alone, and God grants saving faith only to those who hear his Word preached to them, struggle to understand it, and admit that, without God's grace, they are damned. Within a generation, the states of northern Germany and Scandinavia had embraced Lutheranism.

John Calvin, a French Protestant, also embraced justification by faith alone and put his own militant principles into practice in the Swiss canton of Geneva. The Huguenot movement in France, the Dutch Reformed Church in the Netherlands, and the Presbyterian Kirk (or Church) of Scotland all embraced Calvin's principles. In England, the Anglican Church adopted Calvinist doctrines but kept much Catholic liturgy, a compromise that prompted the Puritan reform movement toward a more thoroughly Calvinist Church of England. After 1620, Puritans carried their religious vision across the Atlantic to New England.

Calvinists rejected the pope, all Catholic sacraments except baptism and the Lord's Supper, clerical celibacy, veneration of the saints, and the pious rituals by which Catholics strove to win salvation. They denounced these rites as "work righteousness." Calvin gave central importance to **predestination**. According to that doctrine, God has already decreed who will be saved and who will be damned. Christ died, not for all humankind, but only for God's elect. Because salvation and damnation were beyond human power to alter, Calvinists—especially English Puritans—felt a compelling need to find out whether they were saved. They struggled to recognize in themselves a conversion experience, the process by which God's elect discovered that they had received saving grace.

France, the Netherlands, and England, all with powerful Protestant movements, challenged Spanish power in Europe. Until 1559, France was the main threat, with Italy as the battleground, but Spain won that phase. In the 1560s, with France embroiled in its own Wars of Religion, a new challenge came from the 17 provinces of the Netherlands, which Spain ruled. The Dutch rebelled against the heavy taxes and severe Catholic orthodoxy imposed by Philip II. As Spanish armies put down the rebellion in the 10 southern provinces (modern Belgium), merchants and Protestants fled north. Many went to Amsterdam, which replaced Spanish-controlled Antwerp as the economic center of northern Europe. The seven northern provinces gradually took shape as the Dutch Republic, or the United Provinces of the Netherlands. The Dutch turned their resistance into a war for independence from Catholic Spain. The conflict lasted 80 years, drained Spanish resources, and spread to Asia, Africa, and America. England long remained on the edges of this struggle, only to emerge in the end as the biggest winner overseas.

2-2 New France and the Iroquois League

What were the main similarities and differences between French and Spanish colonial projects in North America?

In 1500, France had three times the population of Spain. The French made a few stabs at overseas expansion before 1600, but with little success.

2-2a *Early French Explorers*

In 1524, King Francis I sent Giovanni da Verrazano, an Italian, to America in search of a northwest passage to Asia. Verrazano explored the North American coast from the Carolinas to Nova Scotia and noted Manhattan's superb potential as a harbor but found no passage to Asia. Between 1534 and 1543, Jacques Cartier made three voyages to North America. He explored the St. Lawrence Valley without finding any fabulous wealth. Severe Canadian winters made him give up. For the rest of the century, the French ignored Canada, except for a few fur traders and for fishermen who descended on Newfoundland each year in growing numbers. By the 1580s, the Canadian fisheries rivaled New Spain in the volume of shipping they sustained.

After 1550, the French turned to warmer climates. **Huguenots** sacked Havana, prompting Spain to turn it into a fortified, year-round naval base under the command of Admiral **Pedro Menéndez de Avilés**. Others planted a settlement on the Atlantic coast of Florida. Menéndez attacked them in 1565, talked them into surrendering, and then executed adult males who refused to accept the Catholic faith.

France's Wars of Religion blocked further efforts for the rest of the 16th century. King Henry IV (1589–1610), a Protestant, converted to Catholicism and granted limited toleration to Huguenots through the Edict of Nantes in 1598, thus ending the civil wars for the rest of his reign. Henry was a *politique*; he insisted that the survival of the state take precedence over religious differences. Moreover, he believed in toleration for its own sake. Another *politique* was the Catholic soldier and explorer Samuel de Champlain.

2-2b *Missions and Furs*

Champlain believed that Catholics and Huguenots could work together, Europeanize the Indians, convert them, and even marry them. Before his death in 1635, he made 11 voyages to Canada. During his second trip (1604–1606), he planted a predominantly Huguenot settlement in Acadia (Nova Scotia). In 1608, he sailed up the St. Lawrence River, established friendly

CHRONOLOGY

1517	Luther begins the Protestant Reformation
1580s	Gilbert claims Newfoundland for England (1583) • Raleigh twice fails to colonize Roanoke Island (1585–1587) • England repels attack by the Spanish armada (1588)
1607	English settlement established at Jamestown
1608	Champlain founds Quebec
1609	Virginia receives sea-to-sea charter
1613–1614	Rolfe grows tobacco, marries Pocahontas
1619	First Africans arrive in Virginia • House of Burgesses and headright system created
1620s	Pilgrims adopt Mayflower Compact, land at Plymouth (1620) • Dutch West India Company chartered (1621) • Opechancanough launches war of extermination in Virginia (1622) • James I assumes direct control of Virginia (1624) • Minuit founds New Amsterdam (1626)
1630s	Puritans settle Massachusetts Bay (1630) • Maryland chartered (1632) • Williams founds Providence; Hooker founds Hartford (1636) • Anne Hutchinson banished to Rhode Island; Minuit founds New Sweden (1638) • New Haven Colony founded (1639)
1640s	Massachusetts "Body of Liberties" (1641) • English civil wars begin (1642) • Virginia subjugates Powhatans (1646) • Charles I beheaded (1649)
Mid-1650s	New Netherland conquers New Sweden • Quakers invade New England
1660s	Charles II restored to English throne (1660) • Puritans institute Half-Way Covenant (1662) • First Carolina charter granted (1663) • New France becomes Crown colony (1663) • New Netherland surrenders to the English (1664) • New Jersey becomes a separate colony (1665) • Carolina's Fundamental Constitutions proposed (1669) • Virginia laws stipulate that children of slaves inherit their mother's status
1670s	First permanent English settlement in South Carolina (1670) • Dutch retake New York (1673–1674)
1680s	Charleston founded (1680) • Pennsylvania charter granted (1681) • New York and Pennsylvania each adopt a Charter of Liberties (1683)
1662–1664	Charles II grants Rhode Island and Connecticut charters • England conquers New Netherland

relations with the Hurons, Montagnais, and Algonquins, and founded Quebec. "Our sons shall wed your daughters," he told them, "and we shall be one people." Many Frenchmen cohabited with Indian women, but only 15 formal marriages took place between them in the 17th century. Champlain's ties to the Indians of the St. Lawrence Valley also drew him into their wars against the Haudenosaunee, the five confederated Iroquois nations—Senecas, Cayugas, Onondagas, Oneidas,

2.2 **Spaniards Torturing Indians, as Depicted by Theodor de Bry, Late 16th Century** Among Protestants in northern Europe, images such as this one merged into a "black legend" of Spanish cruelty, which in turn helped justify their own challenge to Spanish power overseas. But in practice, the behavior of Protestant settlers toward Indians was often as harsh as anything the Spaniards had done.

and Mohawks—who dominated the lands farther south. In the course of the 17th century, Iroquois power politics would almost destroy New France.

Champlain failed to unite Catholics and Protestants in mutual harmony. Huguenots in France were eager to trade with Canada, but few settled there. Their ministers showed no interest in converting the Indians, whereas Catholic priests became zealous missionaries. In 1625, the French Crown declared that only the Catholic faith could be practiced in New France, thus ending Champlain's dream of a colony that was more tolerant than France. Acadia soon became Catholic as well. As dreams of religious harmony faded, economic aspirations came to the fore. Itinerant traders, ***coureurs de bois*** (runners of the woods), pushed into the woodlands around the St. Lawrence Valley, where they traded metal utensils, beads, and brandy for beaver, otter, and other pelts with the Indians. The fur trade became New France's economic lifeline, providing exports that fetched high prices in Europe, where furbearing animals were becoming scarce.

But the fur trade also entangled New France in Indian politics. Champlain nurtured a close alliance with the Huron Confederacy, which competed with the powerful Iroquois Confederacy over hunting territories. Both confederacies were armed with European weapons—the Hurons by the French, the Iroquois by the Dutch—and both needed beaver pelts to fuel their arms trade. When beaver populations began to decline in their homelands in the 1640s, the Iroquois pushed to the north and the west, clashing with the Hurons and the French. In these attacks, they took large numbers of native captives whom they incorporated into their ranks to compensate for the losses they suffered to recurring outbreaks

Interpreting the Visual Past French-Huron Alliance Takes Shape

The engraving below, "The Defeat of the Iroquois at Lake Champlain," depicts a battle that took place in 1609 between some 200 Mohawk Iroquois and 60 or so allied French, Hurons, Montagnais, and Algonquins. Fought near a Mohawk fort (depicted in the upper right corner), the battle marked a clash between Native American and European styles of warfare and it ended in a resounding defeat for the Mohawks. The battle helped solidify a long-lasting French-Huron alliance that contended with the Iroquois Confederacy for supremacy in the Northeast. The engraving is based on Samuel de Champlain's sketch that has been lost. The source and the key character of the image are therefore one and the same person, which makes it an interpretive challenge for historians.

Q *Who do you think was the engraving's intended audience? What was its desired effect?*

Q *Historians have pointed out numerous factual inaccuracies in the engraving, including palm trees in Canada and Indian canoes that look like French ones. How do such inaccuracies affect the engraving's value as a historical source?*

Q *How does the engraving depict the relations between Champlain (at center, holding a costly arquebus and donning a high-crowned helmet usually worn by noblemen) and his Indian allies? Should we judge the image simply as Champlain's unabashed self-promotion or does it allow more nuanced interpretations?*

Q *Compare this engraving to the 1596 engraving of Columbus's landing in San Salvador in Chapter 1 (see page 24). What do the similarities and differences between the two images suggest about how the contemporaries understood Spanish and French colonial projects in the Americas?*

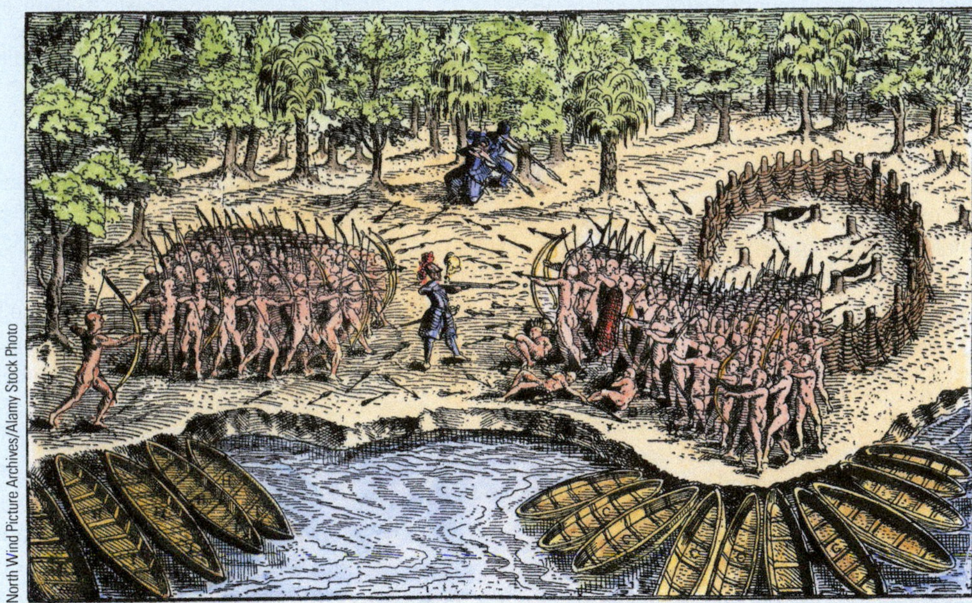

North Wind Picture Archives/Alamy Stock Photo

2.3 **Engraving based on Samuel de Champlain's Original Drawing, The Defeat of the Iroquois at Lake Champlain, circa 1885.**

of smallpox and other diseases. The Iroquois wars were both "beaver wars" and "**mourning wars**." They were often initiated by grieving clan matriarchs who commanded warriors to go on raids and bring back enemy captives, who would be absorbed into Iroquois families. The captives took the social place of deceased loved ones, assuaging the emotional pain of loss and repairing fractured clans. By the mid-17th century, as much as one-half of the Iroquois population may have been captives.

While becoming embroiled with indigenous politics, the French worked to reshape Indian cultures. Jesuit missionaries made concerted efforts to bring Christ to the Indians. The Society of Jesus, or Jesuits, emerged in the 16th century as the Catholic Church's best-educated and most militant religious order. Uncompromising in their opposition to Protestants, Jesuits proved remarkably flexible in dealing with non-Christian peoples, from China to North America. Other missionaries insisted that Indians must be Europeanized before they could be converted, but the Jesuits were comfortable with a nation of Christians that retained most of its Indian culture.

The Jesuits mastered Indian languages, lived in Indian villages, accepted many Indian customs, and converted 10,000 Indians in 40 years, most of them members of the Huron Confederacy, but this success antagonized Indians who were still attached to their own rituals (see Map 2.1). When smallpox devastated the Hurons in the 1640s, Jesuits baptized hundreds

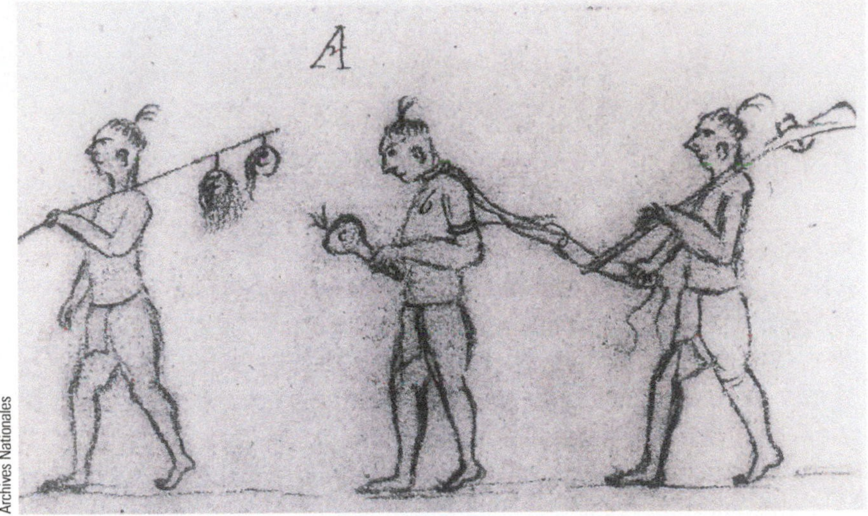

Archives Nationales

2.4 **Iroquois Warriors Leading an Indian Prisoner into Captivity, 1660s** Because Indian populations had been depleted by war and disease, the survival of the Iroquois became dependent on their ability to assimilate captives. This is a French copy of an Iroquois pictograph.

Q *What does this image reveal and perhaps miss about Iroquois slave raids and captivity?*

of dying victims to ensure their salvation. The Hurons split into pro-French Catholics and those who rejected the Jesuits and their faith. Factionalized and weakened, the Huron Confederacy disintegrated under Iroquois attacks. Without it, New France sat exposed to Iroquois raids, which nearly wiped out the colony. By the 1660s, the Iroquois Confederacy was the dominant power in the northern woodlands. In an emergency measure, the French Crown assumed the control of the exposed and depleted New France.

2-2c *New France under Louis XIV*

Royal intervention transformed Canada. Louis XIV and his minister, Jean-Baptiste Colbert, took charge of the colony and tried to turn it into a model absolutist society—peaceful, orderly, and deferential. Government was in the hands of two appointive officials: a governor-general responsible for military and diplomatic affairs, and an ***intendant*** who administered affordable justice, partly by banning lawyers. The people paid few taxes, and the church tithe, or tax, was set at half its rate in France. The governor appointed all militia officers and granted promotion through merit, not by selling commissions.

Colbert also sent 774 young women to the St. Lawrence Valley, to provide brides for settlers and soldiers. He offered bonuses to couples that produced large families and fined fathers whose children failed to marry while still in their teens, and the colony's population began to grow. Between 1665 and 1667, New France negotiated peace treaties with the Five Nations, granting them trading privileges along the St. Lawrence Valley. The cessation of Iroquois attacks allowed cities to grow, and Quebec, Montreal, and Three Rivers started to instill New France with an urban flavor. Farming took hold in the St. Lawrence Valley, and by the 1690s Canada was growing enough wheat to feed itself and to provide its *habitants*, or settlers, a level of comfort about equal to that of contemporary New Englanders. A new class of *seigneurs*, or gentry, claimed most of the land between Quebec and Montreal, but they had few feudal privileges and never exercised the kind of power wielded by aristocrats in France. Yet, when the Church was also the *seigneur*, as often happened near Quebec and Montreal, the obligations imposed on farmers could be heavy.

But Canada did not long remain the center of French overseas activity. Most of the French who crossed the Atlantic preferred the warmer climes and greater economic prospects of the Caribbean. At first, the French in the West Indies joined with other enemies of Spain to prey upon Spanish colonies and ships, contributing the word "buccaneer" (*boucanier*) to the English language. Then they transformed the island colonies of Saint Domingue (modern Haiti), Guadeloupe, and Martinique into centers of sugar or coffee production, where a small planter class prospered from the labor of thousands of slaves. The sugar islands were worth far more than Canada. By the late 18th century, Saint Domingue was generating more wealth than any other colony in the world.

2-3 New Netherland

Q *What key motivations drove Dutch colonialism in North America?*

For most of the 17th century, the Dutch were more active overseas than the French. The Dutch Republic, whose 2 million people inhabited the most densely populated part of Europe, surpassed all rivals in finance, shipping, and trade. It offered an ideological as well as a political challenge to Spanish absolutism. In contrast to Spain, which stood for Catholic orthodoxy and the centralizing tendencies of Europe's "new monarchies," Dutch republicanism emphasized local liberties, prosperity, and, in major centers such as Amsterdam, religious toleration. Political power was decentralized to the cities and their wealthy merchants, who favored informal toleration, tried to keep trade as free as possible, and resisted the monarchical ambitions of the House of Orange. The Prince of Orange usually served as *stadholder* (captain general) of Holland, the richest province, and commanded its armies, and often those of other Dutch provinces as well.

The Dutch Republic—with Protestant dissenters from many countries, a sizable Jewish community, and a Catholic minority that exceeded 30 percent of the population—was

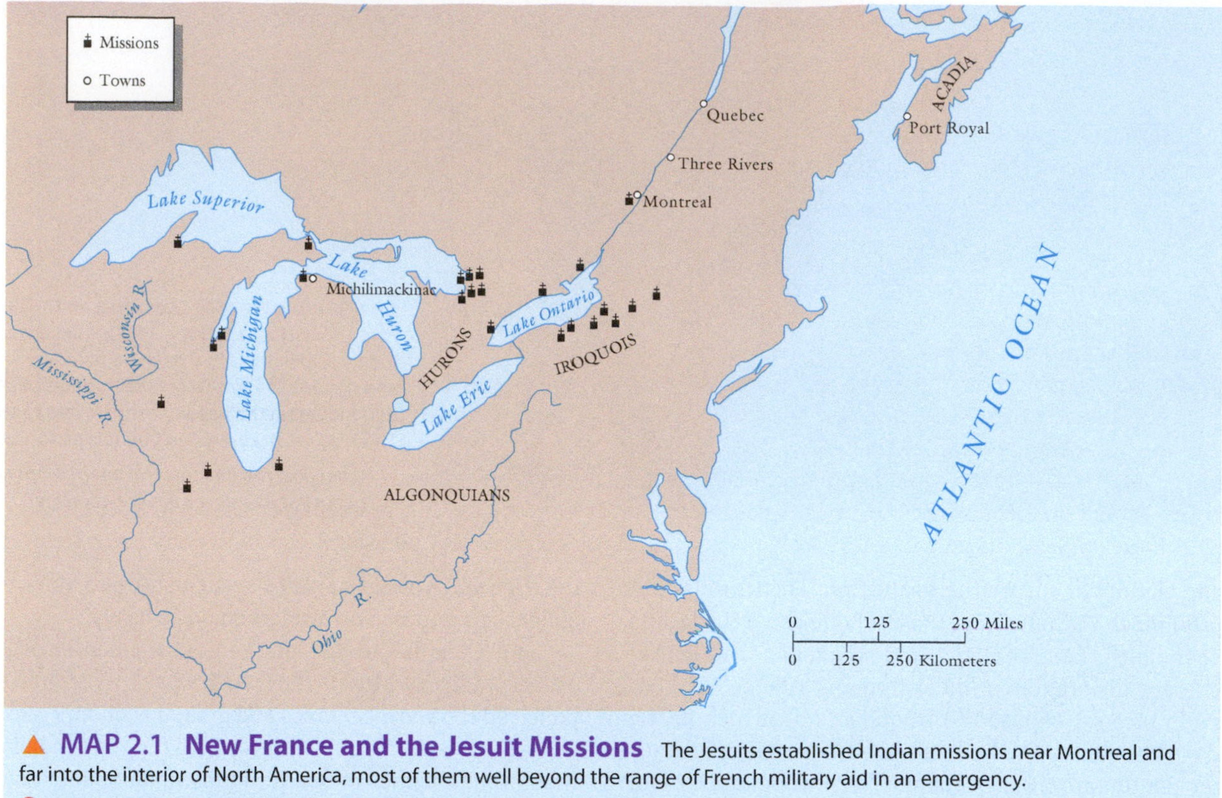

▲ **MAP 2.1 New France and the Jesuit Missions** The Jesuits established Indian missions near Montreal and far into the interior of North America, most of them well beyond the range of French military aid in an emergency.

Q *What factors help explain the location of French missions?*

Q *Why did the French Jesuits keep pushing deeper and deeper to the interior?*

actually a polyglot confederation. Amsterdam's merchant republicanism competed with the Calvinist Dutch Reformed Church for the allegiance of the people. The States General, to which each province sent representatives, became a weak central government for the republic. The broader public did not vote or participate actively in public life. The tension between tolerant merchant republicanism and Calvinist orthodoxy carried over into New Netherland.

2-3a *The East and West India Companies*

In 1602, the States General chartered the Dutch East India Company, the richest corporation the world had yet seen. It elbowed the Portuguese out of the Spice Islands and even out of Nagasaki in Japan, and the Dutch set up their own capital at Batavia (now Jakarta) on the island of Java. In the 17th century, Dutch merchants dominated Europe's trade in Asia.

The Atlantic and the Americas also attracted the Dutch. During their long wars with Spain, they forced the Spaniards to use expensive convoys to protect the silver fleets crossing the Atlantic, critically weakening their rival. In 1621, the States General chartered the Dutch West India Company and granted it jurisdiction over the African slave trade and commerce in the Americas. The company captured Portugal's slave-trading posts in West Africa and occupied the richest sugar-producing region of Brazil until the Portuguese took it back.

In 1609, Henry Hudson, an Englishman in Dutch service, sailed up what the Dutch called the North River (the English later renamed it the Hudson) and claimed the area for the Dutch Republic. The first permanent settlers arrived in 1624. Two years later, Deacon Pierre Minuit, leading a group of Protestant refugee families, bought, according to his own understanding, Manhattan Island from the Indians, and founded the port of New Amsterdam. The Dutch established Fort Orange (modern Albany) 150 miles upriver for trade with the Iroquois. Much like New France, New Netherland depended on the goodwill of nearby Indians, and the fur trade gave the colony a similar urban flavor. But unlike New France, few Dutchmen ventured into the deep woods. There were no *coureurs de bois* and hardly any missionary efforts. The Indians brought their furs to Fort Orange and exchanged them for firearms and other goods that the Dutch sold more cheaply than anyone else. The Dutch sold muskets to the Iroquois to win a larger share of the lucrative interior fur trade. By arming the Iroquois, they were effectively fighting the French by proxy, buttressing the military might of an indigenous confederacy that soon threatened the very existence of New France.

2-3b *New Netherland as a Pluralistic Society*

New Netherland became North America's first experiment in ethnic and religious pluralism. Primarily a commercial venture, the colony was ruled by autocratic governors. It

History Through Film *Black Robe* (1991)

Directed by Bruce Beresford.
Starring Lothaire Bluteau (Father Laforgue), Aden Young (Daniel), Jean Brusseau (Samuel de Champlain), and Sandrine Holt (Annuka).

In *Black Robe*, director Bruce Beresford has given us the most believable film portrayal of 17th-century North America—both the landscape and its peoples—yet produced. This Canada–Australia co-production won six Genie Awards (Canada's equivalent of the Oscar), including best picture, best director, and best cinematography. The film is based on Brian Moore's novel of the same title, and Moore wrote the screenplay. It was filmed on location amid the spectacular scenery in the Lac St. Jean/ Saguenay region of Quebec.

In New France in the 1630s, Father Laforgue (Lothaire Bluteau), a young Jesuit, and Daniel (Aden Young), his teenaged assistant and translator, leave on Laforgue's first mission assignment. Samuel de Champlain (Jean Brusseau), the governor of the colony, has persuaded the Algonquin tribe to convey the two to their mission site among the Hurons, far in the interior. Before long, Daniel falls in love with Annuka (Sandrine Holt), the beautiful daughter of Algonquin chief Chomina (August Schellenberg). When the priest inadvertently watches the young couple make love, he realizes that he has committed a mortal sin. From that point, his journey into the North American heartland almost becomes a descent into hell.

The Algonquins, guided by a dream quest, pursue a logic that makes no sense to the priest. Conversely, his religious message baffles them. Even so, when Chomina is wounded and Laforgue and Daniel are captured by the Iroquois, Annuka seduces the lone Iroquois guard, kills him, and enables all four of them to escape. Chomina dies of his wounds, politely but firmly rejecting baptism until the end. What Indian, he asks, would want to go to the Christian heaven, populated by many black robes but none of his own ancestors?

With the priest's approval, Daniel and Annuka go off by themselves. Laforgue reaches the mission, only to find many of the Indians dead or dying from some European disease. As the film closes, we learn that smallpox would devastate the mission in the following decade, and the Jesuits would abandon it in 1649.

Brian Moore's realism romanticizes nobody but treats both the Jesuits and the Algonquins with great respect. The screenplay drew criticism for its harsh depiction of the Iroquois, but it portrayed them through the eyes of the people they planned to torture. A smaller criticism is that Laforgue is the lone priest on the journey, during which he commits the sin of watching Daniel and Annuka make love. Jesuits, however, traveled in pairs precisely so they would always be accompanied by someone who could hear their confessions. Bruce Beresford, an Australian, directed *Breaker Morant* (1979), a highly acclaimed film set in the Boer War a century ago, and also *Driving Miss Daisy* (1989). ■

ALLIANCE/GOLDWYN/THE KOBAL COLLECTION/Picture Desk

2.5 *Black Robe*, based on Brian Moore's novel of the same title, is set in 17th-century North America.

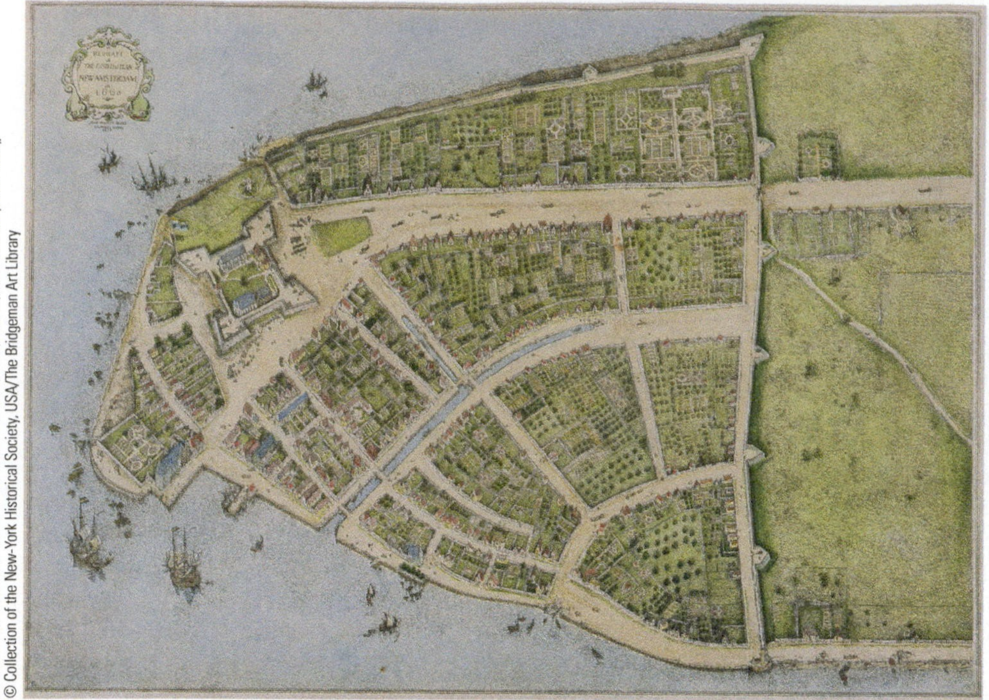

2.6 **New Amsterdam in 1660** This illustration, discovered in Florence about a century ago, is one of the finest city maps in all of early American history. It depicts 342 distinct structures, nearly all of them behind the wall that would later become Wall Street. At right angles to the wall, the broadest thoroughfare between it and the fort at the tip of Manhattan is what would later become Broadway. A census taken at the same time identifies the occupants of all 342 structures.

had no assembly and it attracted few immigrants. Only one settler, Killian Van Rensselaer, managed to build a thriving agricultural community on his gigantic personal estate, known as a **patroonship**, on the Hudson above and below Fort Orange.

But those who did immigrate to New Netherland were a diverse lot: Dutch-speaking Flemish and French-speaking Walloons from the Netherlands would intermingle with Danes, Swedes, Finns, Germans, and Scots. The government of the colony tried to utilize this diversity by drawing on two conflicting precedents from the Netherlands. On the one hand, it appealed to religious refugees by emphasizing the company's Protestant role in the struggle against Spain. On the other hand, the West India Company recognized that religious diversity could stimulate trade. After all, the pursuit of prosperity through toleration was the normal role of Amsterdam in Dutch politics.

Dutch toleration had its limits, though. In 1631, Pierre Minuit returned to Europe, where he organized another refugee project, this one for Flemings who had been uprooted by the war with Spain. When Dutch authorities refused to back him, he looked for support to the Lutheran kingdom of Sweden. Financed by private Dutch capital, he returned to America in 1638 with Flemish and Swedish settlers to found New Sweden, with its capital at Fort Christina (modern Wilmington) near the mouth of the Delaware River, on land claimed by New Netherland. Alarmed, Amsterdam sent troops to take over all of New Sweden, followed by settlers whose presence guaranteed Dutch control. Lutherans were persecuted in New Amsterdam, but they fared better in the Delaware Valley, where they became a majority.

2-3c *English Encroachments*

The English, already entrenched around Chesapeake Bay to the south and New England to the east (see the illustration of New Amsterdam in 1660), threatened to overwhelm the few thousand Dutch as they moved from New England onto Long Island. New Netherland welcomed them in the 1640s and gave them local privileges greater than those enjoyed by the Dutch, in the hope that their farms and herds would give the colony valuable exports. Governor Pieter Stuyvesant regarded these **Yankees** (a Dutch word that probably meant "land pirates") as good Calvinists, English-speaking equivalents of his Dutch Reformed settlers. They agitated for a more active role in government, but their loyalty was questionable. If England attacked the colony, would these Puritans side with the Dutch Calvinists or the Anglican invaders? Which ran deeper, their religious or their ethnic loyalties? Stuyvesant would learn the answer when England attacked him in 1664.

2-4 English Colonization Begins

Q *What kinds of ambitions and historical developments committed England to overseas colonization?*

England's interest in America emerged slowly. In 1497, Henry VII (1485–1509) sent Giovanni Cabato (John Cabot), an Italian mariner who had moved to Bristol, to search for a northwest passage to Asia. Cabot's two expeditions probably took him to Newfoundland, which he found teeming with cod. His report encouraged French, Spanish, and Portuguese fishermen to expand their operations on the north Atlantic coast. England itself would not develop interest in Newfoundland fisheries until the late 16th century, but Cabot's voyages did give it a vague claim to parts of the North American coast.

2-4a *The English Reformation*

When interest in America revived in the late 16th century, England was rapidly becoming a Protestant kingdom. Henry VIII (1509–1547), desperate for a male heir, had cut ties with the pope in order to divorce the queen and marry Anne Boleyn. He proclaimed himself the "Only Supreme Head" of the Church of England, confiscated monastic lands, and opened the way for serious Protestant reformers. Henry's oldest daughter, Mary I (1553–1558), reimposed Catholicism, burned hundreds of Protestants at the stake, and drove thousands into exile. Many of them became Calvinists. However, Elizabeth I, the daughter of Henry VIII and Anne Boleyn, accepted Protestantism, and the exiles returned. The Church of England became Calvinist in doctrine and theology but remained largely Catholic in structure, liturgy, and ritual. By the time of Elizabeth's death, England's Catholics were a tiny, fitfully persecuted minority, but they had powerful allies abroad, especially in Spain.

Some Protestants demanded the eradication of Catholic vestiges and the replacement of the Anglican Book of Common Prayer with sermons and psalms as the dominant mode of worship. These Puritans, also called **Non-Separatists**, insisted they were loyal to the true Church of England and resisted any relaxation of Calvinist rigor. They would play a major role in English expansion overseas. More extreme Protestants, called **Separatists**, denied that the Church of England was a true church and began to set up independent congregations of their own. Some of them would found the small colony of Plymouth.

2-4b *From Plundering to Colonization*

In the mid-16th century, England was a rather backward country of some 3 million people, but its population was growing rapidly. The country's chief export was woolen cloth, which found ready markets in continental Europe, fueling the growth of sheep farms. Increasingly, people and sheep competed for the same land. When farms were enclosed for sheep pasture, laborers were set adrift and often faced bleak prospects, creating the impression that England was overpopulated. Thousands headed for London, lifting the city's population from 50,000 in 1500 to 375,000 by 1650. As England's population and wealth grew, so too did its ambitions. English merchants and policymakers wanted their country to stake a claim in the contest for American riches. Sir Francis Drake, Sir Walter Raleigh, and other English "sea dogs" tried to break into Spain and Portugal's American markets, plundered Spanish colonies and treasure fleets, and explored America's Pacific side—often with Queen Elizabeth's approval. Although such exploits could be highly profitable, they could not sustain permanent colonization.

The English had two models for successful colonization. The conquistador model, based on coerced exploitation of native populations, had yielded Spain massive profits and possessions with moderate investments. Many English policy advocates urged the Court to follow the Spanish example in order to challenge Spanish preeminence in the Americas. The most prominent of them was Richard Hakluyt, who published accounts of England's overseas exploits and offered advice on how to make future colonization efforts more successful.

Another colonization model was closer at hand in Ireland, which the English Court had claimed for centuries. In the mid-16th century, the English tried to impose their agriculture, language, local government, legal system, aristocracy, and religion upon the Irish, who responded by becoming more intensely Roman Catholic than ever. England's colonization efforts in Ireland took the form of war, terror, and ethnic replacement with Protestants. A few decades later, English conquistadors would carry that colonization model across the Atlantic into their dealings with Native Americans. The English formed their preconceptions about American Indians largely from contact with the Irish, who, claimed one Elizabethan, are "more uncivil, more uncleanly, more barbarous and more brutish in their customs and demeanors, than in any part of the world that is known."

One such conquistador was Sir Humphrey Gilbert, a well-educated humanist and a veteran of the Irish wars, who proposed that England grab control of the Newfoundland fisheries, a nursery of seamen and naval power. In 1583, he took a fleet across the Atlantic north to claim the region. The crews of 22 Spanish and Portuguese fishing vessels and 18 French and English ships listened in wonder as he read his royal patent to them, divided up the land among them, assigned them rents, and established the Church of England for this mostly Catholic group. He then sailed away to explore more of the American coast. His own ship went under during a storm. Another ambitious English conquistador, Sir Walter Raleigh, Gilbert's half-brother, received a patent from Queen Elizabeth to colonize North America in more southern latitudes. In 1587, after a failed attempt two years earlier, Raleigh sent a large expedition to Roanoke Island, off the coast of North Carolina. The expedition included a few women, a sign that the English envisioned a permanent colony. When John White, the colony's governor, sailed back to England for more supplies, his return to Roanoke was delayed by the assault of the Spanish armada on England. By the time he reached Roanoke in 1590, the settlers had vanished, leaving a cryptic message—"CROATOAN"—carved on a tree (see Map 2.2). The colonists may have settled among the Chesapeake nation of Indians near the entrance to Chesapeake Bay. Sketchy evidence suggests that the Powhatans, the region's most powerful Indians, destroyed the Chesapeakes, along with any English living with them, in spring 1607, just as the first Jamestown settlers were arriving in the bay.

The Spanish Armada touched off a war that lasted until 1604 and strained the resources of England. The loss of the Armada, first to nimbler English ships in the English Channel and then to fierce storms off the Irish coast, crippled Spain, which had already begun to weaken due to a declining population and decreasing tax revenues. Sensing an opening, London became intensely involved in American affairs by launching **privateering** fleets against Spain. Even though London merchants remained more interested in trade with India, the Mediterranean, and Muscovy than in North American projects, the city's growing involvement with Atlantic privateering marked a significant shift: England had turned toward the Atlantic.

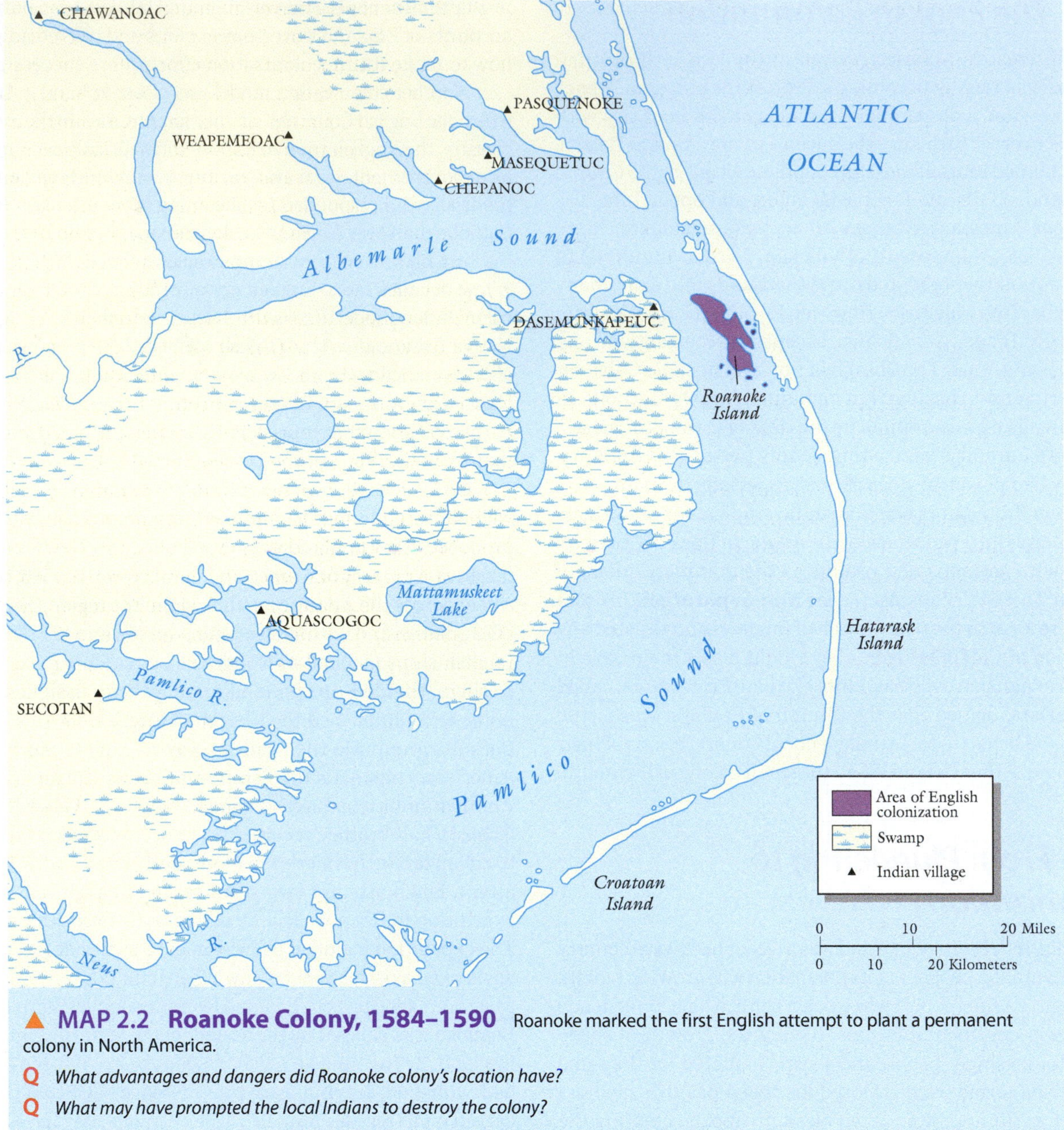

▲ **MAP 2.2 Roanoke Colony, 1584–1590** Roanoke marked the first English attempt to plant a permanent colony in North America.

Q *What advantages and dangers did Roanoke colony's location have?*

Q *What may have prompted the local Indians to destroy the colony?*

2-4c *The Swarming of the English*

In the 17th century, more than 700,000 people crossed the Atlantic to the English colonies in North America and the Caribbean. Most European migrants were single young men who arrived as servants. At first even some Africans were treated as servants, not slaves.

The Europeans who settled in New England or the Hudson or Delaware valleys were the most fortunate. Because Puritans and Quakers migrated as families into healthy regions, their population expanded at a rate far beyond anything known in Europe. The descendants of this small, idealistic minority soon became a substantial part of the total population, and they played a role in American history far out of proportion to their original numbers. As Table 2.1 shows, the New England and Middle Atlantic colonies together attracted only 5.4 percent of the immigrants, but by 1700 they contained 37 percent of all the newcomers' descendants in the English colonies and 55 percent of the Europeans' offspring.

2-5 The Chesapeake and West Indian Colonies

Q *Why did the English, crossing the Atlantic at roughly the same time, create such radically different societies in the Chesapeake, the West Indies, and New England?*

In 1606, King James I of England (1603–1625) chartered the Virginia Company with authority to colonize North America between the 34th and 45th parallels. A **joint-stock company** of numerous small investors, the Virginia Company had two branches: the Plymouth Company, which received jurisdiction over the northern portion of the grant, and the London Company, which received the southern portion (see Map 2.3). In 1607, the Plymouth Company established a settlement at Sagadahoc on the coast of Maine, but the settlers abandoned the venture within a year, having failed to open trade with the region's Abenaki Indians. In that same year, the London Company sent out three ships with 104 colonists, who landed at a defensible peninsula on what they called the James River. They built a fort and other crude buildings and named their settlement Jamestown. Investors hoped to find gold or silver, a northwest passage to Asia, a cure for syphilis, or other valuable products for sale in Europe. The settlers expected to persuade local Indians to work for them, much as Spain had done. If the Indians proved hostile, the settlers were told to form alliances with more distant Indians and subdue those who resisted. Company officials did not realize that a chief named Powhatan ruled more than 30 villages across a vast domain, **Tsenacommacah** ("our land"), below the **fall line**. He had no rival within striking distance. The company's other expectations proved equally skewed.

2-5a *The Jamestown Disaster*

The colony was a deathtrap. Every summer, the river became contaminated around Jamestown and sent out killing waves of dysentery and typhoid fever. Before long, malaria also set in. Only 38 colonists survived the first year. The survivors owed their good fortune to the resourcefulness of Captain John Smith, a soldier and adventurer who outmaneuvered the other leaders of the colony. When his explorations uncovered neither gold or silver nor any quick route to Asia, he concentrated on sheer survival. He visited Powhatan's village, hoping to awe the chief and convince him to sell corn. For his part, Powhatan sought to embrace Jamestown as a new tributary village for his confederacy. He staged a ritual performance in which Smith was symbolically clubbed to death and then reawakened as Powhatan's kin. The chief's ten-year-old daughter, Pocahontas, played a role in the ritual as a giver of life. The event was probably carefully scripted, something that Smith missed.

For a while, friendly relations prevailed between the settlers and the Powhatans, and Virginia's prospects seemed bright. A new royal charter extended its boundaries to the Pacific, and the London Company sent in more than 700 new settlers. But an intense drought failed the crops, and the colonists starved again. They survived by eating horses, rats, cats, and the leather of their boots. Some resorted to cannibalism, and many pushed into native villages, demanding and stealing corn, taking hostages, and killing Indians. Smith, who had been wounded in an explosion, sailed back to England. Only 60 colonists survived the winter of 1609–1610.

At this low point, a new governor arrived with 300 new soldier-settlers, who set out to establish English power in the region. Open warfare with Indians broke out. Powhatan's warriors picked off any settlers who strayed far from Jamestown. The English retaliated by slaughtering whole villages and destroying crops, as they had in Ireland. The war finally ended after the English captured Pocahontas and used her as a hostage to negotiate peace. She converted to Christianity and married John Rolfe, a widower. In 1614, Powhatan accepted the colonists' peace offer. Demoralized, he passed on leadership of the confederacy to his brother Opechancanough.

Despite the Indian war, the colony's prospects improved. The governors imposed martial law on the settlers and sent some of them to healthier locations, such as Henrico, 50 miles upstream. Through Rolfe's efforts, the colony began to produce a cash crop. He imported from the West Indies a mild, sweet-scented strain of tobacco, which swiftly took over English markets. The king, who had insisted no one could build a colony "upon smoke," was proved wrong, and soon the settlers were growing tobacco in the streets of Jamestown.

2-5b *Reorganization, Reform, and Crisis*

The London Company adopted an ambitious reform program for the colony. It encouraged economic diversification, such as glass-blowing, the planting of grapevines, and the raising of silkworms. English common law replaced martial law. The settlers were allowed to elect their own assembly, the **House of Burgesses**, to meet with the governor and his council and make local laws. Finally, the most popular reform permitted settlers to own land. Under this **headright** system, a colonist received

Table 2.1 THE PATTERN OF SETTLEMENT IN THE ENGLISH COLONIES TO 1700

	Immigrants (or Settlers) (in thousands)				Population in 1700 (in thousands)			
Region	**Europeans**		**Africans**		**European Americans**		**African Americans**	
West Indies	220	(29.6%)	316	(42.5%)	33	(8.3%)	115	(28.8%)
South	135	(18.1%)	30	(4.0%)	82	(20.5%)	22	(5.5%)
Mid-Atlantic	20	(2.7%)	2	(0.3%)	51	(12.8%)	3	(0.8%)
New England	20	(2.7%)	1	(0.1%)	91	(22.8%)	2	(0.5%)
Total	395	(53.1%)	349	(46.9%)	257	(64.4%)	142	(35.6%)

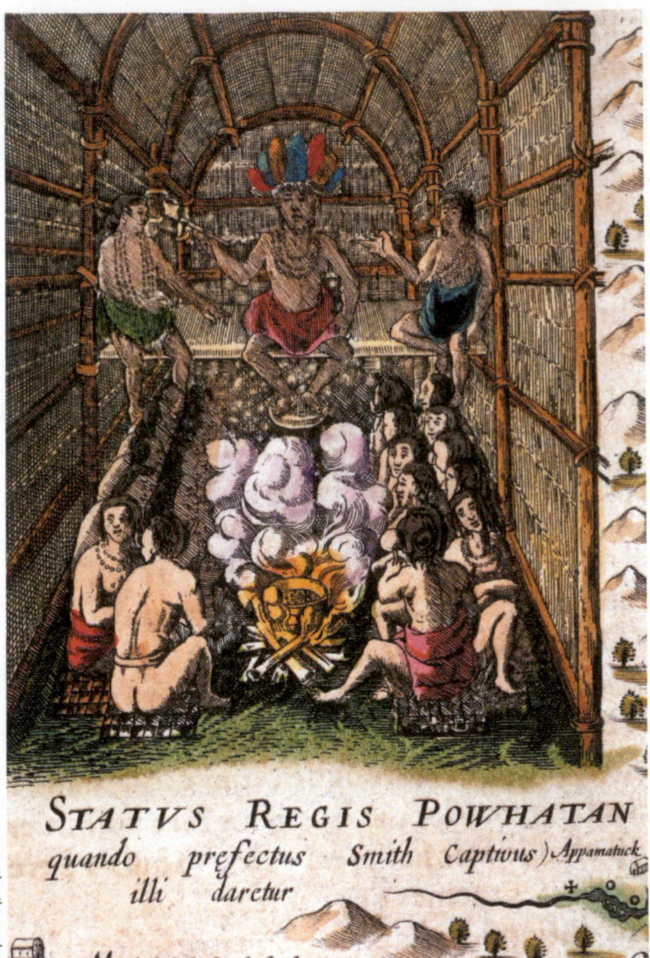

Newberry Library/SuperStock

2.7 **Regal State** Illustration of Powhatan with tobacco pipe enthroned in his lodge, from vignette embellishing Smith's map of Virginia, first published in 1612.

Q *What does the image tell us about how the English understood Powhatan as a chief?*

50 acres for each person whose passage to Virginia he financed. By 1623, the company had shipped 4,000 settlers to Virginia, but the economic diversification program failed. Only tobacco found a market. Corn still provided most of the food. Instead of growing silkworms and grapes, Virginians raised Indian crops with Indian methods, which meant using hoes instead of plows.

The flood of newcomers strained the food supply and soured relations with the Indians. In March 1622, Opechancanough launched an attack to wipe out the colony. Without a last-minute warning from a friendly Indian, Jamestown might not have survived. Still, 347 settlers were killed that day, and most of the outlying settlements were destroyed. Newcomers who arrived in subsequent months had nowhere to go, and with food again scarce, hundreds died over the winter.

Back in London, several stockholders withdrew their capital and asked the king to intervene. In 1624, the king declared the London Company bankrupt and assumed direct control of Virginia, making it the first royal colony, with a governor and council appointed by the Crown. The London Company had invested some £200,000 in the enterprise, equal to more than £150 for every surviving settler, at a time when skilled English craftsmen were lucky to earn £50 per year. Such extravagance guaranteed that future colonies would be organized in different ways.

2-5c *Tobacco, Servants, and Survival*

During the two decades following Opechancanough's 1622 attack, Virginia proved that it could survive. Despite an appalling death rate, about a thousand new settlers came each year, raising the population above 8,000 by 1640. The export of tobacco financed the importation of indentured servants, even after oversupply plummeted the price of tobacco in the 1630s. Most servants were young men who agreed to work for a term of years in exchange for the cost of passage, plus bed and board during their years of service, and modest freedom dues when their terms expired. Those signing indentures in England usually had valuable skills and negotiated terms of four or five years. Those men arriving without an indenture, most of whom were younger and less skilled, were sold by the ship captain to a planter. Those older than age 19 served five years, whereas those younger than 19 served until age 24. The system turned servants into freemen, who then hoped to prosper on their own. Most former servants became tenants for several years while they tried to save enough to buy their own land.

Better tobacco prices enabled many to succeed between 1640 and 1660, but those who imported the servants were always in a stronger economic position, collecting the headright of 50 acres for each one. When tobacco prices fell again after 1660, upward mobility became even more difficult. Political offices usually went to the richest 15 percent of the settlers, and eventually their descendants monopolized the posts of justice

Bettmann/Corbis

2.8 **Pocahontas** After her conversion, Pocahontas went to England, where she was widely celebrated. The inscription around the portrait says "Matoaka [one of her Indian names] alias Rebecca [her baptismal name] daughter of the powerful Prince Powhatan, Emperor of Virginia."

The massacre of the settlers in 1622, plate VII, from 'America, Part XIII', German edition, 1628 (coloured engraving), Merian, Matthaus, the Elder (1593–1650)/Virginia Historical Society, Richmond, Virginia, USA/ The Bridgeman Art Library

2.9 **The Opechancanough Massacre of 1622** This famous event, as portrayed in an engraving from the workshop of Theodor de Bry, depicts the warriors as treacherous, bloodthirsty savages and the settlers as innocent victims.

Q *Images like this one were highly popular across Europe. Why?*

of the peace (who presided over county courts), the pool from which the members of the House of Burgesses were normally chosen. Virginia, a prospering colony with a long history of local self-government, was becoming a class-based society.

2-5d *The Collapse of Tsenacommacah*

Because tobacco plants quickly wore out the soil, the settlers pushed steadily up the James, York, and Potomac rivers, attacking Powhatan villages, converting native fields into plantations, and fencing off hunting grounds into headrights. Pigs and cattle crowded Indian lands and diseases ravaged Indian communities. In 1644, Opechancanough made a desperate bid to push back the settlers. His warriors killed more than 400 colonists, but soon lost the upper hand. English militia subjugated Powhatan villages and captured the chief. Nearly 100 years old, Opechancanough was shot in captivity. Two years later, the remaining Powhatans became subjects of the king of England. Indians continued to occupy small pockets of land in Virginia, but Tsenacommacah as a political entity was no more.

2-5e *Maryland*

Maryland arose from the social and religious vision of Sir George Calvert, baron of Baltimore, and his son Cecilius, who both became Catholics and looked to America as a refuge for persecuted English and Irish Catholics. The colony was named after Henrietta Maria, the French Catholic queen of Charles I (1629–1649). The Maryland charter of 1632 made Baltimore "lord proprietor" of the colony. The most sweeping delegation of power that the Crown could make, it came close to making Baltimore king within Maryland. After 1630, most new colonial projects were **proprietary colonies**, often with the Maryland charter as a model. Many of them embodied the distinctive social ideals of their founders (see Map 2.4).

Like Champlain, the Calverts believed that Catholics and Protestants could live in harmony in a single colony. Cecilius Calvert, second lord of Baltimore, extended religious tolerance to all Maryland's Christians, but he also expected servants, who were mostly Protestants, to continue to serve Catholic gentlemen even after their indentures expired. This turned the gentlemen into manor lords, with the power to preside over feudal courts that were nearly obsolete in England. However, the conditions for Catholics improved in England during the reign of Charles I, which meant that fewer of them immigrated to Maryland. A small minority in a largely Protestant colony, Maryland's Catholic elite failed to preserve the manorial system. Protestant servants acquired their own land, and the Maryland assembly, the House of Delegates, became more forceful than Virginia's House of Burgesses in demanding the liberties of Englishmen. Like Virginia, Maryland became a rural colony of independent-minded tobacco planters, who strove to better their futures by raising their crop for Atlantic markets. Religion provided the biggest difference between the two colonies. Virginia was determinedly Anglican, while Maryland had no established church.

2-5f Chesapeake Family Life

At first, European men outnumbered women in Virginia by at least 5 to 1. Among new immigrant servants as late as the 1690s, the ratio was still 5 to 2. Population became self-sustaining about 1680, when live births finally began to outnumber deaths. Among adults, this transition was felt after 1700. Until then, most prominent people were immigrants.

Life expectancy improved as the colonists planted orchards to provide wholesome cider to drink, but it still remained much lower than in England, where those who reached puberty could expect to live into their 50s. Chesapeake immigrants had survived childhood diseases in Europe, but men at age 20 typically lived only to about 45, with 70 percent dead by age 50. Women died at even younger ages, especially in areas

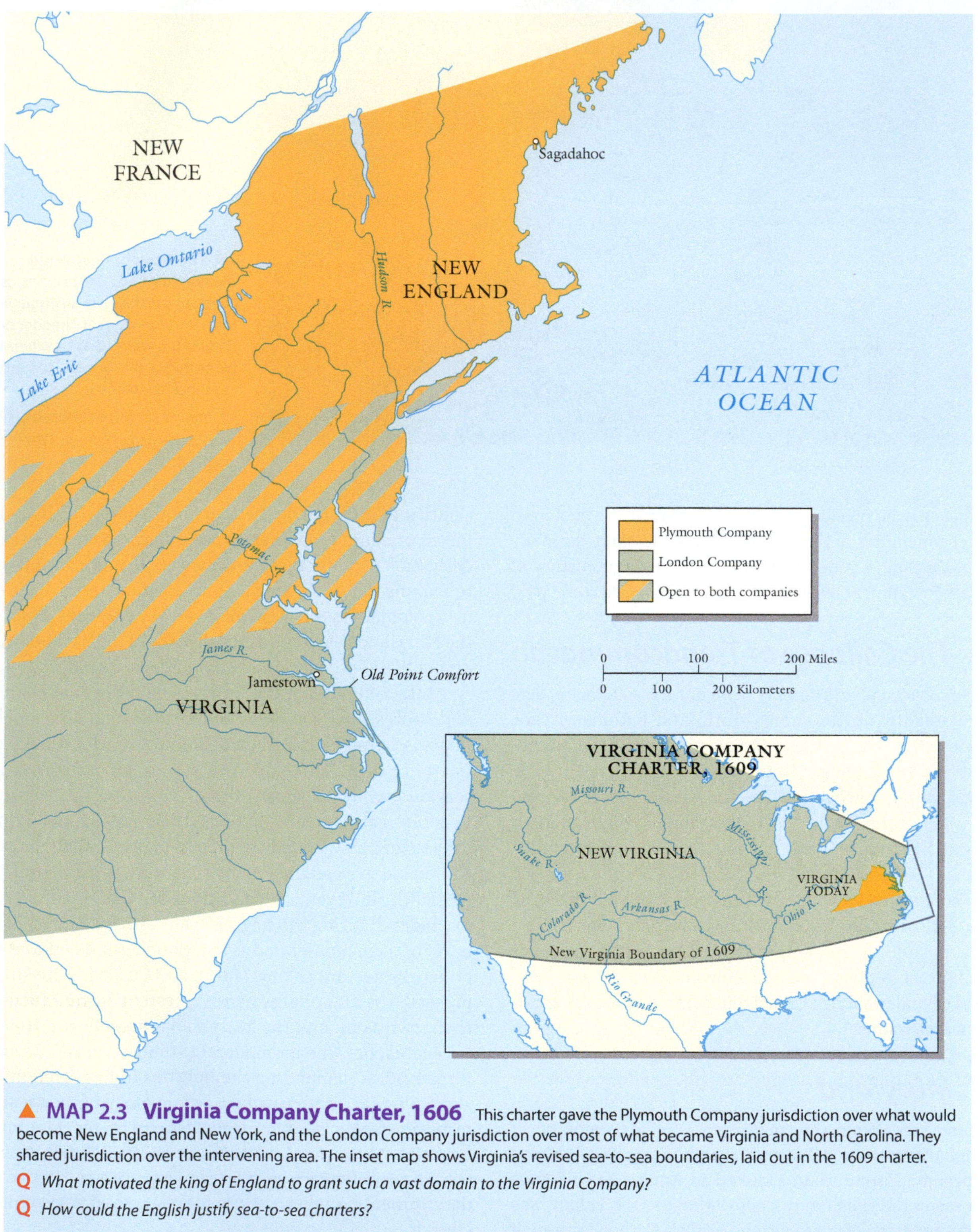

▲ **MAP 2.3 Virginia Company Charter, 1606** This charter gave the Plymouth Company jurisdiction over what would become New England and New York, and the London Company jurisdiction over most of what became Virginia and North Carolina. They shared jurisdiction over the intervening area. The inset map shows Virginia's revised sea-to-sea boundaries, laid out in the 1609 charter.

Q *What motivated the king of England to grant such a vast domain to the Virginia Company?*

Q *How could the English justify sea-to-sea charters?*

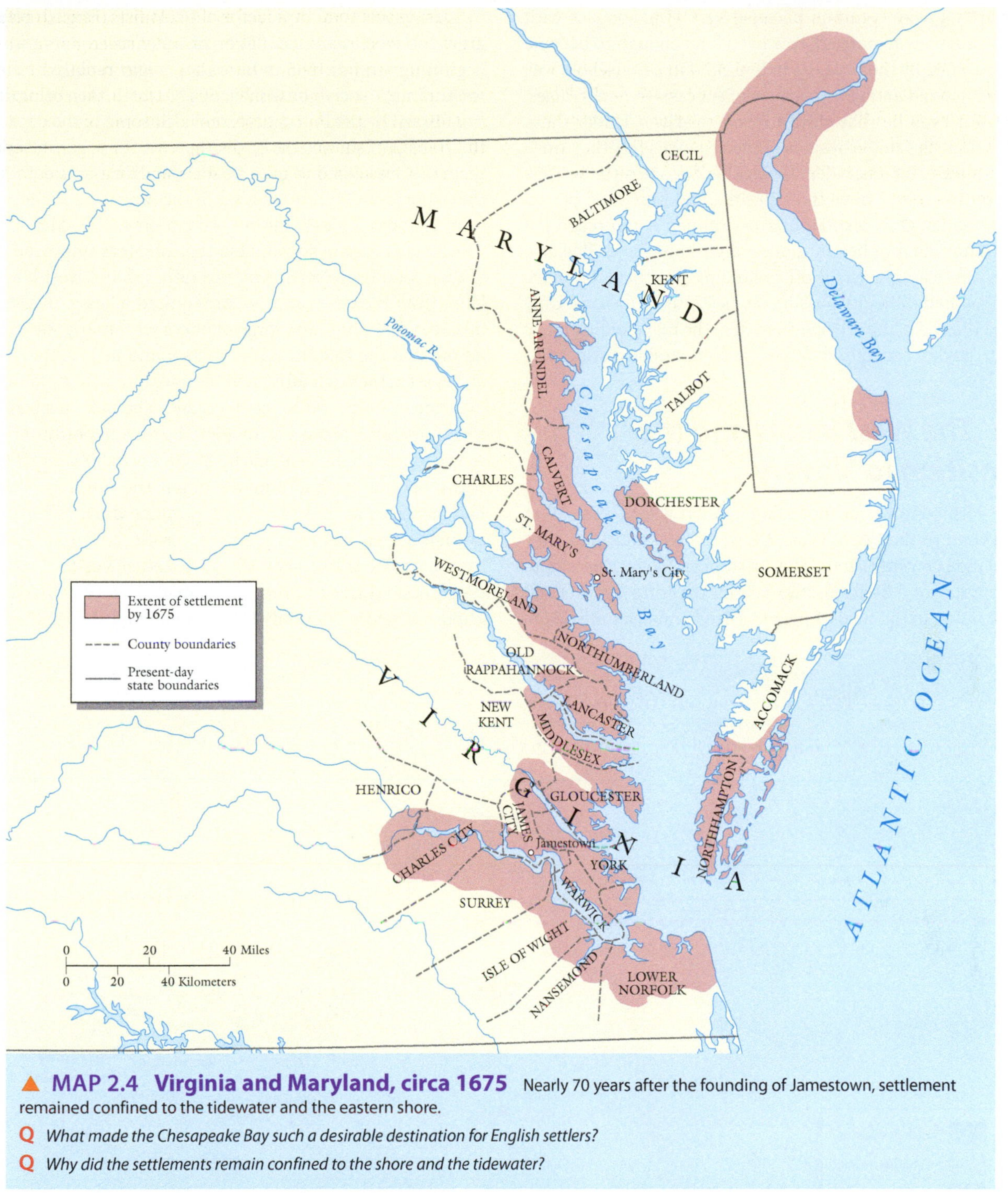

▲ **MAP 2.4 Virginia and Maryland, circa 1675** Nearly 70 years after the founding of Jamestown, settlement remained confined to the tidewater and the eastern shore.

Q *What made the Chesapeake Bay such a desirable destination for English settlers?*

Q *Why did the settlements remain confined to the shore and the tidewater?*

ravaged by malaria, a dangerous disease during pregnancy. In those places, women rarely lived to age 40. For many, marriage became unattainable. About 70 percent of the men never married or, if they did, fathered no children. Most men had to wait years after completing their service before they could marry. Because women could not marry until they had fulfilled their indentures, most spent a good part of their childbearing years unwed. Despite severe legal penalties, about one-fifth of the women had illegitimate children and roughly one-third were pregnant on their wedding day. Virtually all women married, most as soon as they could, usually to a landowner. In short, upward mobility for women exceeded that for men.

In a typical Chesapeake marriage, the groom was in his 30s and the bride eight or ten years younger. Although men outlived women, this age gap meant that the husband usually died before his wife, who then quickly remarried. In one Virginia county, three-fourths of all children lost a parent, and one-third lost both. Native-born settlers married at a much earlier age than immigrants; women were often in their middle to late teens when they wed. Orphans were a major community problem.

Stepparents were common because surviving spouses with property usually remarried. Few lived long enough to become grandparents. By the time the oldest child in a household was 20, the husband and wife, because of successive remarriages, might not even be that child's blood relatives. Under these circumstances, family loyalties tended to focus on other kin—uncles, aunts, cousins, older stepbrothers or stepsisters—thus contributing to the value that Virginia and Maryland placed on hospitality. Only a small number of men could reach the patriarchal ideal of heading one's own household. Because fathers died young, even the office-holding elite that took shape after 1650 had difficulty passing on its status to its sons. Only toward the end of the 17th century were the men holding office likely to be descended from fathers of comparable distinction.

2-5g *The West Indies and the Transition to Slavery*

In the 17th century, far more Englishmen went to the West Indies than to the Chesapeake. Between 1624 and 1640, they settled the Leeward Islands (St. Christopher, Nevis, Montserrat, and Antigua) and Barbados, tiny islands covering just over 400 square miles. In the 1650s, England seized Jamaica from Spain, increasing this total by a factor of 10. At first, English planters grew tobacco, using the labor of indentured servants, but beginning around 1645 in Barbados, sugar replaced tobacco, with dramatic social consequences. The Dutch, then being driven from Brazil by the Portuguese, provided some of the capital for this transition, showed the English how to raise sugar, introduced them to slave labor on a massive scale, and for a time dominated the exportation and marketing of the crop. The French built small island colonies in the eastern Caribbean (see Map 2.5).

Sugar became so valuable that planters imported most of their food from North America rather than divert land and labor from the cash crop. Sugar required a heavy investment in slaves and mills, and large planters with many slaves soon dominated the islands. Ex-servants found little employment, and most of them left after their terms expired. Many joined the buccaneers or moved to the mainland. Their exodus hastened the transition to slavery. In 1660, Europeans outnumbered slaves in the English islands by 33,000 to 22,000. By 1700, the white population had stagnated, but the number of slaves had increased sixfold. Planters appropriated about 80 percent of their slaves' labor for their own profit, an unprecedented rate of exploitation. They often worked slaves to death and then bought others to replace them. Of the 316,000 Africans imported before 1700, only 115,000 remained alive in that year.

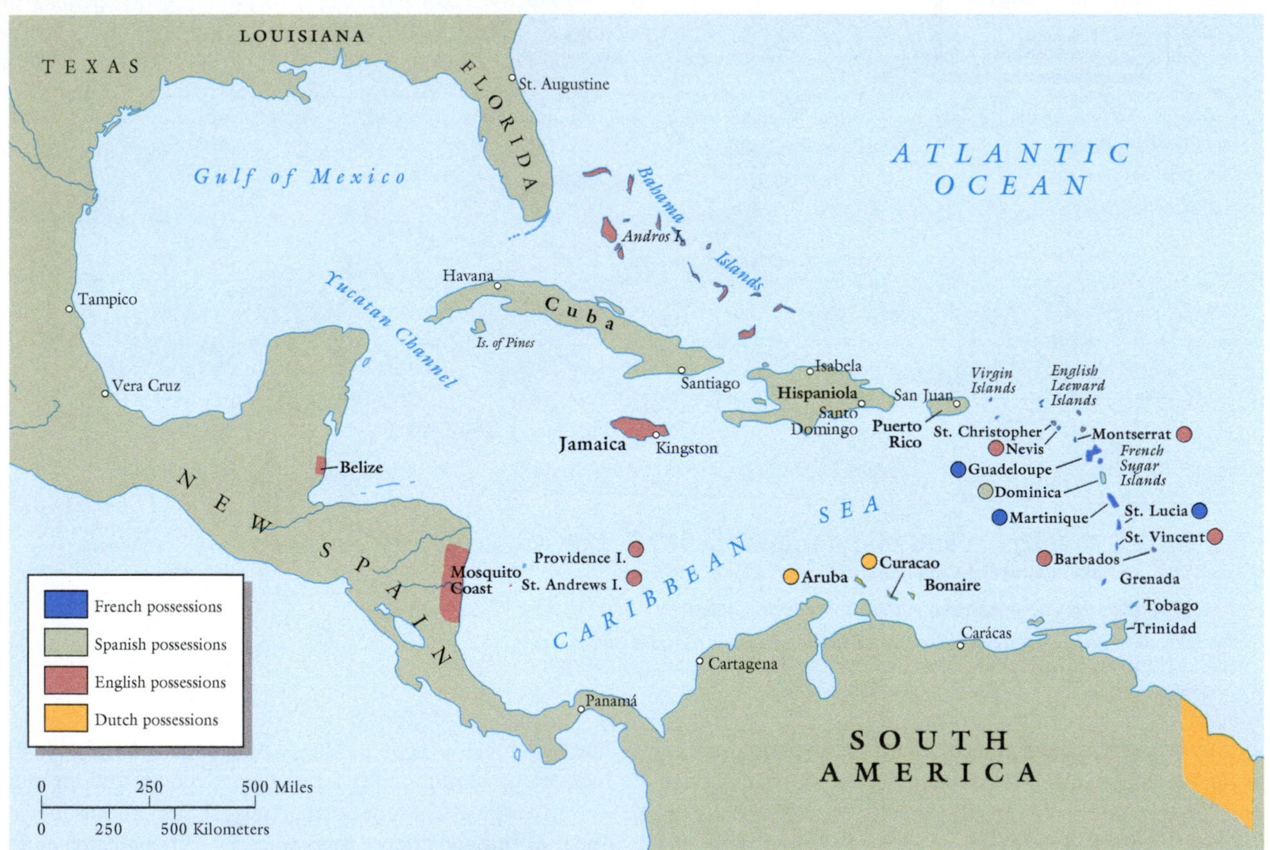

▲ **MAP 2.5 Principal West Indian Colonies in the 17th Century** Spain retained control of the large islands of Cuba, Hispaniola, and Puerto Rico, while its English, French, and Dutch rivals settled the smaller but fertile islands east of Puerto Rico and south of Cuba.

Q *How can we explain the fact that four European empires managed to simultaneously hold colonies in the Caribbean in the 17th century?*

Q *Which of the four empires was best positioned to exploit the Caribbean resources, and why?*

2.10 **Slaves on a Sugar Plantation in Antigua** Sugar was an even more demanding crop than tobacco, partly because workers could easily cut themselves on the sharp edges of the cane stalks, and because planters tried to compel workers to toil almost around the clock at harvest time so that the cane could be crushed in a mill and the juice boiled before it could spoil. A weary slave could easily lose fingers or an arm while trying to feed the mill.

Q *Is the painting idealized and romanticized? How and why?*

Observers were depressed by the moral climate on the islands, where underworked and overfed planters arrogantly dominated their overworked and underfed slaves. Yet, the islands generated enormous wealth for the British Empire, far more than the mainland colonies. Around 1700, the islands sent sugar worth £710,000 per year to England at a time when Chesapeake planters were getting only £230,000 for their tobacco.

2-5h *The Rise of Slavery in North America*

Africans reached Virginia in 1619 when, as John Rolfe reported, a Dutch ship "sold us twenty Negars." Their status was ambiguous for decades after slavery had been sharply defined in the West Indies. In the Chesapeake, many of the first Africans were Creoles with a great deal of intercultural experience around the Atlantic world and were in a stronger position to negotiate with their masters than later comers would be. Some Africans were treated as servants and won their freedom after several years.

Because the English had no experience with slavery at home, a rigid caste system took time to crystallize. When Hugh Davis was whipped in 1630 "for abusing himself to the dishonor of God and shame of Christians, by defiling his body in lying with a negro," his offense may have been sodomy rather than miscegenation. The record is unclear. The case of Elizabeth Key, a mulatto, a Christian, and the bastard daughter of Thomas Key, shows similar ambiguity. In 1655, when she claimed her freedom, her new owner fought to keep her enslaved. William Greensted, who had fathered two children by her, sued on her behalf, won, and then married her. He had probably fallen in love with her.

In the late 17th century, the caste structure of the Chesapeake colonies began to consolidate. Fewer indentured servants reached the Chesapeake from England, as the Delaware Valley and the expanding English army and navy competed more successfully for the same young men. Slaves, many of them imported from Barbados, took their place. Some of the emerging great planters deliberately chose to replace indentured servants with enslaved Africans. In Virginia, a series of laws in the 1660s began to institutionalize slavery by solidifying the blurred and shifting lines between freedom and unfreedom and servitude and slavery. Most importantly, the laws stipulated that the children of slaves inherited the status of their mother, which reversed the common-law practice and meant that a mulatto child of a slave woman inherited the mother's status of unfreedom. Virginia was turning from temporary servitude toward lifelong and hereditary slavery.

2-6 The New England Colonies

Q *How did religious concerns shape the colonization of New England?*

In New England, unlike the Chesapeake colonies, settlers reproduced the mixed economy of old England, with minor variations. Their quarrel with England was over religion, not economics. They came to America, they insisted, to worship as God commanded, not as the Church of England required.

2-6a *The Pilgrims and Plymouth*

The Pilgrims were Separatists who left England for the Netherlands between 1607 and 1609, convinced that the Church of England was no true daughter of the Reformation. They hoped to worship freely in the Netherlands. After a decade there, they became disillusioned by Dutch religious pluralism, which prompted a minority of the congregation to seek religious fulfillment in America. In 1620, the *Mayflower* sailed for Virginia with 102 passengers, roughly one-third of them Pilgrims, but the ship was blown off course in late 1620, landing first on Cape Cod and then on the mainland well north of the charter boundaries of Virginia, at a place they named Plymouth. Before landing, the passengers agreed to the Mayflower Compact, which bound them all to obey the decisions of the majority, a sound precaution in a colony with uncertain legal status.

Short on supplies, the colonists suffered keenly during the first winter. Half of them died, including the governor and all but three of the married women. William Bradford became governor, and he would be reelected annually for all but five years until his death in 1656.

The settlers fared much better when spring came. During the previous three years, the Indian communities of the area had been ravaged by diseases spread by European traders. As much as 90 percent of the region's Indians may have died. The much-diminished Wampanoags sought an alliance with the settlers, hoping to recruit their support against rival Narragansetts. Mediated by Samoset and Squanto, Patuxet Indians who spoke broken English, the settlers met with a powerful Wampanoag **sachem** (or chief), Massasoit. Massasoit promised to regulate the relations between the Indians and the colonists, believing that the arrangement had bound the newcomers to him as tributary dependents. The English, in turn, believed that Massasoit had submitted his people under English sovereignty. Despite such misunderstandings, relative peace prevailed for several years, allowing the Plymouth Bay colony to survive. By 1630, the settlers numbered about 300. They founded several new towns and sold their surplus crops to the colonists flooding into Massachusetts Bay.

2-6b *Massachusetts Bay*

In 1629, several English Puritans obtained a charter for the Massachusetts Bay Company, a typical joint-stock corporation except for one feature: The charter did not specify where the company was to be located. Led by John Winthrop, the Puritans decided to carry the charter to New England, beyond the gaze of Charles I, who had become impatient with Puritan demands for reforming the Church of England. Charles expected obedience from the Puritans, who came to realize that church reform would have better prospects across the Atlantic. Rather than using the charter to organize a business corporation in England, they used it to found a colony of pure Christianity in New England, far away from state control. Puritan colonists came from the broad middle range of English society, and most of them owned property. When they sold it to go to America, they probably liquidated far more capital than the London Company had invested in the Chesapeake Bay. A godly haven was expensive to build.

An advance party that sailed in 1629 took over a fishing village on the coast and renamed it Salem. The next year, more than 1,000 colonists arrived. In small groups, they scattered around Massachusetts Bay, founding towns and appointing a minister and a magistrate for each. Church and state were closely bound from the start. The local congregation was the first institution to take shape, and from it evolved the town meeting. The colonists planted corn and English grains, but one-third of them perished during the first winter. Then conditions rapidly improved, as they had at Plymouth a decade earlier. About 13,000 settlers came to Massachusetts by 1641, most as families—a unique event in Atlantic empires to that time. They raised sheep, produced woolen textiles, and embarked on active shipbuilding. The colony began to prosper after 1650, when Boston merchants opened up West Indian markets for New England grain, lumber, and fish.

The very existence of colonies committed to free labor was odd. To sustain free labor, towns severely restricted inward migration, thus guaranteeing a home market to their own craftsmen and other laborers. But towns also imposed strict discipline upon the settlers: New England magistrates whipped more freemen than any other English colonies. And to prosper, the New England colonies had to trade with more typical colonies, the societies elsewhere in the hemisphere that raised tobacco and sugar with unfree labor.

2-6c *Covenant Theology*

Puritans embraced what they called covenant theology. According to this system, God had made two biblical covenants with humans: the covenant of works and the covenant of grace. In the covenant of works, God had promised Adam that if he kept God's law he would never die, but Adam disobeyed, was expelled from the Garden of Eden, and died. All of Adam's descendants remain under the same covenant, but because of his fall can never be capable of keeping the law; they *deserve* damnation. But God was merciful and answered sin with the covenant of grace. God will save his chosen people; everyone else will be damned. Even though the covenant of works can no longer bring eternal life, it remains in force and establishes the strict moral standards that every Christian must strive to follow, before and after conversion. A Christian's inability to

What They Said

English Colonists and Huron Indians Enter New Worlds

Europeans and Native Americans both encountered a "new world" in the Americas from the 16th century onward. Europeans had discovered an entire hemisphere that seemed drastically different from Europe. Native Americans found their lifeways so fundamentally transformed by European colonialism that the Americas became a new and often alien world for them. That much was common to both, but what exactly was new to each could be strikingly different. The two documents here illuminate these complexities. The first, an excerpt from William Bradford's history of the Plymouth colony, describes the Pilgrims' views of the landscape after their landing. The second is a French Jesuit's description of Huron Indians' reaction to a smallpox epidemic. Both documents are alive with anxiety, but what are its causes and consequences? What role does knowledge—or its lack—play in both cases? How do the colonists and Indians try to cope in their respective new worlds?

William Bradford, 1620

It is recorded in scripture as a mercie to the apostle & his shipwraked company, that the barbarians shewed them no smale kindness in refreshing them, but these savage barbarians, when they mette with them (as after will appeare) were readier to fill their sids full of arrows then otherwise. And for the season it was winter, and they that know the winters of the cuntrie, know them to be sharp & violent, & subjecte to cruell & feirce stormes, deangerous to travill to known places, much more to serch an unknown coast. Besids, what could they see but a hideous & desolate wildernes, full of wild beasts & willd men? and what multituds ther might be of them they knew not. Nether could they, as it were, goe up to the tope of Pisgah, to vew from this willdernes a more goodly cuntrie to feed their hops; for which way soever they turnd their eys (save upward to the heavens) they could have litle solace or content in respecte of any outward objects. For sumer being done, all things stand upon them with a wetherbeaten face; and the whole countrie, full of woods & thickets, represented a wild & savage heiw. If they looked behind them, ther was the mighty ocean which they had passed, and was now as a maine barr & goulfe to separate them from all the civill parts of the world. . . . What could now sustaine them but the spirite of God & his grace? May not & ought not the children of these fathers rightly say: *Our faithers were Englishmen which came over this great ocean, and were ready to perish in this willdernes. . . .*

Jérôme Lalemant, 1640

They observed, with some sort of reason, that, since our arrival in these lands, those who had been the nearest to us, had happened to be the most ruined by the diseases, and that the whole villages of those who had received us now appeared utterly exterminated; and certainly, they said, the same would be the fate of all the others if the course of this misfortune were not stopped by the massacre of those who were the cause of it. This was a common opinion, not only in private conversation but in the general councils held on this account, where the plurality of the votes went for our death, — there being only a few elders, who thought they greatly obliged us by resolving upon banishment.

What powerfully confirmed this false imagination was that, at the same time, they saw us dispersed throughout the country, — seeking all sorts of ways to enter the cabins, instructing and baptizing those most ill with a care which they had never seen. No doubt, they said, it must needs be that we had a secret understanding with the disease (for they believe that it is a demon), since we alone were all full of life and health, although we constantly breathed nothing but a totally infected air, — staying whole days close by the side of the most foul-smelling patients, for whom every one felt horror; no doubt we carried the trouble with us, since, wherever we set foot, either death or disease followed us. In consequence of all these sayings, many had us in abomination; they expelled us from their cabins, and did not allow us to approach their sick, and especially children: not even to lay eyes on them, — in a word, we were dreaded as the greatest sorcerers on earth.

Wherein truly it must be acknowledged that these poor people are in some sense excusable. For it has happened very often, and has been remarked more than a hundred times, that where we were most welcome, where we baptized most people, there it was in fact where they died the most; and, on the contrary, in the cabins to which we were denied entrance, although they were sometimes sick to extremity, at the end of a few days one saw every person prosperously cured. We shall see in heaven the secret, but ever adorable, judgments of God therein.

Sources: (top) William Bradford, "Of Plimoth Plantation" (Boston: Wright and Potter, 1900), pp. 95–126. (bottom) Reuben Gold Thwaites, ed., *The Jesuit Relations and Allied Documents: Travels and Explorations of the Jesuit Missionaries in New France 1610–1791*, Vol. XIX (Cleveland, The Burrows Brothers Company Publishers, 1899), 91–93.

keep the law usually triggered the conversion experience by demonstrating that only faith, not works, could save.

At this level, covenant theology merely restated Calvinist orthodoxy, but the Puritans gave it a novel social dimension by pairing each personal covenant with a communal counterpart. Each congregation organized itself into a church, a community of the elect. The founders of each church, after satisfying one another of their own conversions, agreed that within their church the Gospel would be properly preached and discipline would be strictly maintained. God, in turn, promised to bestow saving grace within that church—not to everyone, but presumably to most of the children of the elect. This communal covenant determined not who was saved or damned, but the rise and fall of nations or peoples. As a people, New Englanders agreed to obey the law, and God promised to prosper them. If magistrates enforced God's law and the people supported these efforts, God would not punish the whole community for the misdeeds of individuals. But if sinners escaped public account, God's anger would be terrible toward his chosen people of New England. God gave them much and demanded much in return. In England, the government had refused to assume a godly role. Puritans fleeing to America hoped to escape the divine wrath that threatened England and to create in America the kind of churches that God demanded.

2-6d *Puritan Family Life*

In rural areas, New Englanders soon observed a remarkable fact. After the first winter, deaths were rare. The place was undeniably healthy, and families grew rapidly as unprecedented numbers of children reached maturity. The settlers had left most European diseases behind and had encountered no new ones in the bracing climate. For the founders and their children, life expectancy far exceeded the European norm. More than one-fifth of the men who founded Andover lived past age 80. Infant mortality fell, and few mothers died in childbirth. Because people lived so long, New England families became intensely patriarchal. Many fathers refused to grant land titles to their sons before their own deaths. In the early years, settlers often moved, looking for the richest soil, the best neighbors, and the most inspiring minister. By the mid-1640s, most of them had found what they sought. Migration into or out of country towns became much lower than in England, and the New England town settled into a tight community that slowly became an intricate web of cousins. Once the settlers had formed a typical farming town, they grew reluctant to admit "strangers" to their midst. New Englanders largely avoided slavery, not out of sympathy for Africans or hatred of the institution, but to keep outsiders from contaminating their religion.

2-6e *Conversion, Dissent, and Expansion*

The vital force behind Puritanism was the quest for conversion. Probably because of John Cotton's stirring sermons in Boston, the settlers crossed an invisible boundary in the mid-1630s. As Cotton's converts described their religious experiences, their neighbors turned from analyzing the legitimacy of their own conversions to assessing the validity of someone else's. Churches began to impose tests for regeneracy, and the standards of acceptance escalated rapidly.

The conversion experience was deeply ambiguous to a Puritan. Anyone who found no inner trace of saving grace was damned. It began with the discovery that one could not keep God's law because all people were sinners. It progressed through despair to hope, which always arose from passages of scripture that spoke to that person's condition. A "saint" at last found reason to believe that God had saved him or her. The whole process involved a painful balance between assurance and doubt. A saint was sure of salvation, but never too sure.

This quest for conversion generated dissent and new colonies. In the mid-1630s, Reverend Thomas Hooker, alarmed by Cotton's preaching, led his congregation west from Massachusetts, where a new colony emerged along the Connecticut River. In 1639, an affluent group planted the New Haven Colony on Long Island Sound. Their spiritual leader, Reverend John Davenport, imposed the strictest requirements for church membership in New England. While the founders of Connecticut Colony feared that Massachusetts was becoming too severe in certifying church membership, the New Haveners worried that the Bay colony was too lenient.

The residents of most towns agreed on the kind of worship they preferred, but some settlers, such as Roger Williams and **Anne Hutchinson**, made greater demands. Williams was a Separatist who refused to worship with anyone who did

Robert Gibbs at 4 1/2 Years, 1670 (oil on canvas), Freake-Gibbs Painter (fl. 1670–80)/Museum of Fine Arts, Boston, Massachusetts, USA/M. and M. Karolik Fund/Photograph (c) 2016 Museum of Fine Arts, Boston

2.11 **Portrait of Robert Gibbs (1670)** New Englanders did not provide distinctive garments for small boys and girls. They wore the same clothes.

Q *What does the image reveal about childhood in 17th-century New England?*

not explicitly repudiate the Church of England. Nearly all Massachusetts Puritans were Non-Separatists who claimed only to be reforming the Anglican Church. In 1636, after Williams challenged the king's right as a Christian to grant Indian lands to anyone at all, the colony banished him. He fled to Narragansett Bay with a few disciples and founded Providence. He developed eloquent arguments for religious liberty and the complete separation of church and state.

Anne Hutchinson, an admirer of John Cotton, claimed that virtually all other ministers were preaching only the covenant of works, not the covenant of grace, and were leading their people to hell. In Boston, she won a large following, many of them women. At her trial there, she claimed to have received direct messages from God (the Antinomian heresy). By forcefully defending her beliefs, Hutchinson also challenged the patriarchal Puritan gender order. She was banished in 1638 and fled with followers to Narragansett Bay, where they founded Newport and Portsmouth. These towns united with Providence to form the colony of Rhode Island and accepted both the religious liberty and the separation of church and state that Williams advocated.

This territorial expansion was fast, mostly unplanned, and locally driven. None of the new Puritan colonies—Connecticut, New Haven, and Rhode Island—sprang into existence with royal charters (see Map 2.6). The expansion stemmed not only from religious idealism, but also from a need for more land to accommodate a steady stream of transatlantic migration. Puritans spread to interior New England with their fields and fences, disturbing deer and other wildlife and disrupting native hunting economies. Pushed into poor lands, the Pequot Indians forged trade relations with the Dutch along the Hudson River to secure weapons and military support. In 1637, the Puritans launched a war against the Pequots, attacking them with their Narragansett and Mohegan allies. In May, New Englanders faced a choice of two Pequot villages to attack—one held by warriors, the other inhabited by women, children, and elderly. They chose the latter, set it on fire, and with their Narragansett and Mohegan allies shot anyone who tried to flee. More than 400 died. Many of the surviving Pequots were sold into slavery in the West Indies.

Fearful of renewed Indian wars, the factious New England colonies tightened their binds. Massachusetts, Plymouth, Connecticut, and New Haven formed a defensive alliance, the New England Confederation (the religiously unorthodox Rhode Island was not invited to join). The confederation nurtured ties with the Mohegans, who had clashed with the Narragansetts over the vacated Pequot lands, hoping to gain access to new lands through a native proxy.

2-6f *Puritan Indian Missions*

The Puritans coveted the Indians' lands, but they also coveted their souls. Building the perfect Christian community in the New World required, in the minds of some Puritans, extending God's grace to the natives. Serious efforts to convert Indians to Protestantism began in the 1640s on Martha's Vineyard under Thomas Mayhew, Sr., and Thomas Mayhew, Jr. The Mayhews worked with local sachems and challenged only the powwaws (tribal medicine men) in their efforts to spread Christianity. They encouraged Indian men to teach the settlers how to hunt whales, an activity that made them a vital part of the settlers' economy without threatening their identity as men. John Eliot, pastor of the Roxbury church, focused his efforts on the Massachusett Indians. He translated the Bible into the Massachusett language and gave sermons in that language. In contrast to the Mayhews, he attacked the authority of the sachems as well as the powwaws, challenged the traditional tribal structure, and insisted on turning Indian men into farmers, a female role in these native societies.

Both methods—Eliot's assertive approach and the Mayhews' more measured one—brought results among the New England Indians who struggled to explain the success of English colonization and their own weakened condition. By the 1670s, a string of 14 "praying towns" extended from Massachusetts to Connecticut, and more than 2,000 Indians were in various stages of conversion. Yet, only a few natives would achieve the kind of conversion experience that Puritans required for full membership in a church. Few Indians shared the Puritan sense of sin. They could not grasp why their best deeds should stink in the nostrils of the Lord. The praying towns provided the beleaguered Indians some means to cope with the consequences of colonialism—disease, death, land loss, alcoholism—but they also caused fear and resentment, further deepening the chasm between the natives and the newcomers.

2-6g *Congregations, Towns, and Colony Governments*

By the mid-17th century, life in the New England colonies began to fall into distinctive and broadly similar patterns. Congregations abandoned the Anglican Book of Common Prayer, vestments, incense, church courts, and the need to be ordained by a bishop. The sermon became the dominant rite, and each congregation chose and ordained its own minister. No singing was permitted, except of psalms. A 1648 synod issued the Cambridge Platform, which defined "Congregationalist" worship and church organization.

By then the town had become something distinct from the congregation. Town meetings decided who got how much land. It was distributed broadly but never equally. In Springfield, at one extreme, the Pynchon family controlled most of the land and most of the labor as well. In other towns, such as Dedham, the distribution was much more equitable. In some villages, town meetings occurred often, made most of the decisions, and left only the details to a board of elected "selectmen." In others, the selectmen did most of the governing. Usually, all adult males participated in local decisions, but Massachusetts and New Haven restricted the vote for colony-wide offices to only those men who were full church members, a decision that greatly narrowed the electorate.

Massachusetts had a bicameral legislature by the 1640s. Voters in each town chose representatives who met as the Chamber of Deputies, or lower house. Voters also elected the governor and the magistrates, or upper house. Massachusetts defined its legal system in the "Body of Liberties" of 1641 (which may actually be history's first bill of rights) and in a

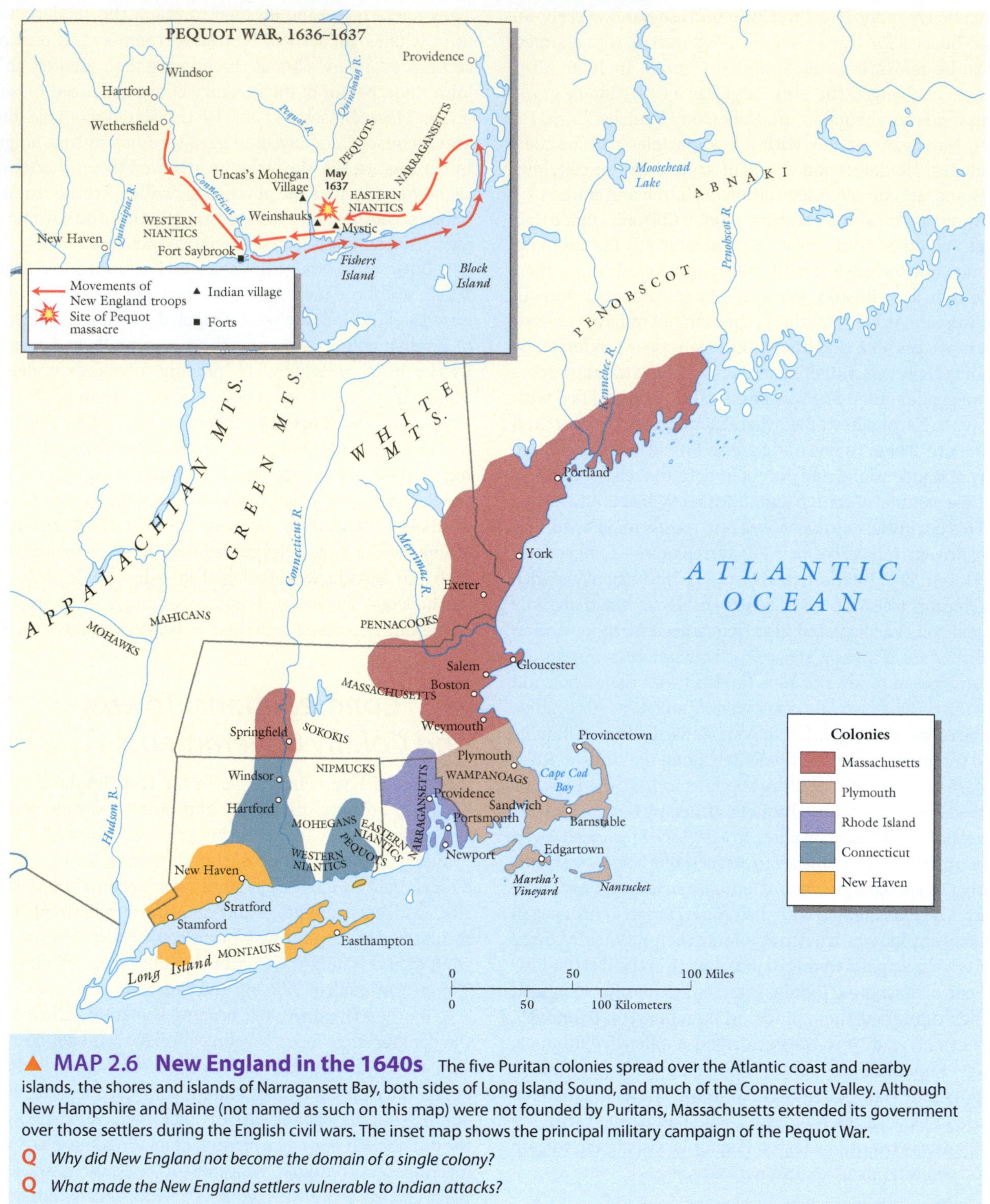

▲ **MAP 2.6 New England in the 1640s** The five Puritan colonies spread over the Atlantic coast and nearby islands, the shores and islands of Narragansett Bay, both sides of Long Island Sound, and much of the Connecticut Valley. Although New Hampshire and Maine (not named as such on this map) were not founded by Puritans, Massachusetts extended its government over those settlers during the English civil wars. The inset map shows the principal military campaign of the Pequot War.

Q *Why did New England not become the domain of a single colony?*

Q *What made the New England settlers vulnerable to Indian attacks?*

comprehensive law code of 1648 that was widely imitated in other colonies. Massachusetts sharply reduced the number of capital offenses under English law and listed them in the order of the Ten Commandments. Unlike England, Massachusetts seldom executed anyone for a crime against property. Other distinctive features of the legal system included an explicit recognition of the liberties of women, children, servants, foreigners, and even "the Bruite Creature," or animals; a serious effort to ban professional lawyers; and the swift punishment of crime.

New England also transformed the traditional English jury system. New Haven abolished juries altogether because the Bible does not mention them, but the other colonies vastly expanded the role of civil (noncriminal) juries, using them even to decide appeals, something that never happened in England. Except in capital trials, however, the criminal jury—a fixture of English justice—almost disappeared in New England. The punishment of sin involved fidelity to the covenant and was too important to leave to 12 ordinary men. This system worked

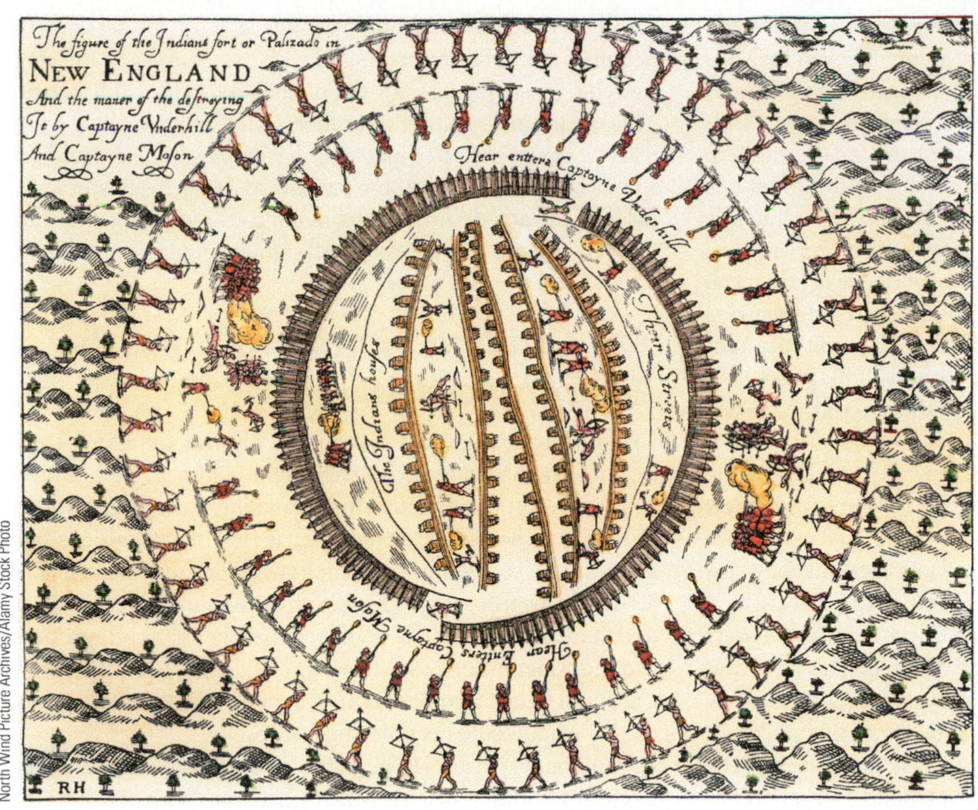

2.12 **The Puritan Massacre of the Pequot Indians, 1637** The massacre took place at what is now Mystic, Connecticut. Most of the victims were women and children. The Indians shown in the outer circle were Narragansett allies of the settlers and were appalled by the carnage.

well because even sinners shared its values. Most offenders appeared in court and accepted their punishments. Acquittals were rare, almost unheard of in New Haven. Yet, hardly anyone ran away to avoid trial or punishment.

2-6h *Infant Baptism and New Dissent*

Although most of the founders of the New England colonies became church members during the fervor of the 1630s, their children had trouble achieving conversion. They had never lived as part of a persecuted minority in England, nor had they experienced the joy of joining with other holy refugees in founding their own church. They had to find God on their own and then persuade their elders—who were on guard because leniency had let Williams, Hutchinson, and other deviants through—that their conversions were authentic. Most failed. They grew up, married, and requested baptism for their children. The Cambridge Platform declared that only "saints" (the converted) and their children could be baptized, which excluded increasing numbers from the church's full embrace. By the mid-17th century, this problem was becoming acute.

Dissenters offered two answers, and the ministers a third. Some colonists became Baptists, who argued that only converted adults (and no children) should receive baptism. Quakers, who arrived in New England in the 1650s, taught that salvation was available to all those who would allow their Inner Light, God's presence within a person, to shine forth—a blasphemous notion to Puritans, who believed in predestination. The clergy's answer to the lack of conversions became known as the Half-Way Covenant. Parents who had been baptized but had not experienced conversion could bring their children before the church, "own the covenant with God," and have their children baptized. Aging church members resisted the Half-Way Covenant, but as the founders died off in the 1670s and 1680s, it took hold and soon led to something like universal baptism.

Yet, dissent and tension persisted. The orthodox colonies were divided over whether to persecute or to ignore their Baptist and Quaker minorities. Ministers preached "jeremiads," shrill warnings against any backsliding from the standards of the founding generation. The new partial church members could have their children baptized but could not accept communion or vote.

2-7 From Civil War to the First Restoration Colonies

Q *In what ways did the Restoration colonies differ from those founded earlier in the Chesapeake and New England?*

England's first American colonies had emerged during a period of overall stability in the mother country. In the 1640s, however, England fell apart. Tensions mounted during the reign of Charles I, who, like Spanish and French monarchs, aspired to build a centralized realm of religious uniformity and personal rule. After governing without Parliament from 1629 to 1640, Charles I tried to impose the Anglican Book of Common Prayer upon Presbyterian Scotland. The Scots revolted and invaded England. Charles had to summon Parliament, which in 1642 rose against the authoritarian king. Parliament won the military struggle.

In 1649, it executed the king, abolished the House of Lords, and proclaimed England a commonwealth (or republic). In 1653, the army named its most successful general, Oliver Cromwell, lord protector of England. When the protectorate collapsed after Cromwell's death in 1658, part of the army invited Charles II to return from exile and accept the throne, but with limitations to his authority. By then the Church of England had nearly disintegrated. The new Restoration government worked hard to restore the old order. It brought back the House of Lords and reestablished the Church of England. The English state, denying any right of dissent, persecuted both Catholics and Protestant dissenters: Presbyterians, Congregationalists, Baptists, and Quakers. This persecution would drive thousands of Quakers to the Delaware Valley in the 1670s.

The disorder of the English civil wars spread into the American colonies as well. In Maryland, Protestants overthrew Lord Baltimore's regime, but the Puritan-dominated parliament sided with him. To appease Maryland's Protestant majority, Baltimore responded with the Toleration Act of 1649, which granted the freedom of worship to all Christians. In the West Indies, the colonists took advantage of the collapse of royal power by demanding and receiving elective assemblies. The new assemblies of Barbados and the Leeward Islands diverted their trade from England to the Dutch, who took over much of the English West Indies and Chesapeake sugar and tobacco trade.

If the Restoration reestablished much of the old order in England, it ushered in a new era in the colonies. The Crown took control of the governments of Barbados, Jamaica, and the Leeward Islands and imposed restrictions on their recently granted assemblies. The Crown insisted that it had created and granted the constitutional structure for each colony, a view that few settlers accepted, believing that they had an inherent right to constitutional rule. Charles II envisioned England as a centralized imperial state embodied in the person of the monarch and he saw the colonies as a means to fulfill his vision. He bestowed vast landholdings in the North American mainland on the noblemen who had supported the Stuart cause during the civil wars. The king owed the loyal elite something, and a colonial charter cost him nothing. New colonies, moreover, would yield the state much-needed revenue through trade and taxes. During the Restoration era (1660–1688), six new colonies were founded, doubling the number of England's mainland colonies.

Most of the new colonies shared certain common features and also differed in some respects from earlier settlements. All were proprietary in form, which empowered the organizers to pursue daring social experiments. Except for Pennsylvania, the Restoration colonies were all founded by men with big ideas and small purses. The proprietors tried to attract settlers from the older colonies because importing them from Europe was expensive. The most readily available prospects were servants completing their indentures in the West Indies and being driven out by the sugar revolution. Many went to Carolina. The most prized settlers, however, were New Englanders. Proprietors distrusted both their piety and their politics, but New Englanders had built the most thriving colonies in North America. However, few of them would go farther south than New Jersey.

The Restoration colonies made it easy for settlers to acquire land, and they competed with one another by offering newcomers strong guarantees of civil and political liberties. They all promised either toleration or full religious liberty, at least for Christians. Whereas Virginia and New England (except Rhode Island) were still homogeneous societies, the Restoration colonies attracted a mix of religious and ethnic groups. They all found it difficult to create political stability out of this diversity.

2-7a *Carolina, Harrington, and the Aristocratic Ideal*

In 1663, eight courtiers obtained a charter by which they became the board of proprietors for a colony to be founded south of Virginia. Calling their province Carolina in honor of the king, they tried to colonize the region in the 1660s but achieved no success until the following decade. Most of the settlers came from two sources. Former servants from Virginia and Maryland, many in debt, hoped that they could claim land around Albemarle Sound in what eventually became North Carolina. Other former servants came from Barbados. They settled what would become South Carolina.

To the proprietors in England, these scattered settlements made up a single colony called Carolina. With the help of the philosopher John Locke, they drafted the Fundamental Constitutions of Carolina, an incredibly complex plan for organizing a colony. The document drew on the work of Commonwealth England's most prominent republican thinker, James Harrington, author of *Oceana* (1656). He aspired to design a republic that could endure—unlike ancient Athens or Rome, which had finally become despotic states. Harrington argued that widespread ownership of land was the best guarantee against absolute government. He also proposed several other republican devices, such as frequent rotation of officeholders (called "term limits" today), the secret ballot, and a bicameral legislature, with the smaller, upper house proposing laws and the larger one approving or rejecting them. Harrington had greater impact on colonial governments than any other thinker of his time.

The Carolina proprietors had set out to create in a distant land a model aristocratic society founded on an elaborate distribution of privileges and responsibilities. The Fundamental Constitutions proposed a government that was far more complex than any colony could sustain. For example, England had three supreme courts; Carolina would have eight. The document envisioned a class of lowly whites, "leetmen," who would live on small tracts and serve the great landlords. The document accepted slavery. "Every Freeman of Carolina shall have absolute Power and Authority over his Negro Slaves," declared Article 110. Carolina presented its organizers with unanticipated obstacles to these aristocratic goals. The proprietors assumed that landownership would be the key to everything else, including wealth and status, but many settlers prospered in other ways. The ex-servants from overcrowded Barbados who settled in Carolina resisted the hierarchical Fundamental Constitutions. They were also disappointed in the prospects of sugar cultivation in Carolina and instead began to raise cattle and hogs, letting them run free on open land. Some of their African slaves were probably America's first cowboys. In the Albemarle region, settlers from Virginia moved in to exploit the thick forests to produce masts, turpentine, tar, and pitch for sale for English shipbuilders. They channeled the bulk of their commerce through Virginia's ports. The settlers also traded with the Indians, usually for deerskins, often acquired from the Cherokees and Creeks west of the Appalachians. As in New France and New Netherland, the Indian trade sustained a genuine city, Charleston, founded in 1670. Charleston traders sold their Indian clients guns, clothing, and liquor, stirring competition among different groups. The Westos and Yamasees won favored status by offering an alluring commodity: Indian slaves, captured from Spanish Florida and the interior. The Indian slave trade would become the colony's biggest business and it would profoundly shape the geopolitics of the Southeast.

2-7b *New York: An Experiment in Absolutism*

In 1664, James, Duke of York, obtained a charter from his royal brother for a colony between the Delaware and Connecticut rivers. Charles II claimed that New Netherland was rightfully English territory because it was included in the Virginia charter of 1606 (see Map 2.7). James sent a fleet to Manhattan, and the English settlers on Long Island rose to support his claim. Reluctantly, Stuyvesant surrendered without resistance. The English renamed the province New York. New Amsterdam became New York City, and Fort Orange became Albany. The Dutch ceded New Netherland with few regrets, never having been able to turn a profit with it. New York took over all of Long Island. It also inherited New Netherland's role as mediator between the settlers and the Iroquois Confederacy. In effect, the Duke of York's autocratic colony assumed most of the burdens of this relationship while unintentionally conferring most of the benefits on the Quakers who would begin to settle the Delaware Valley a decade later. The shield provided by New York and the Iroquois would make the Quaker experiment in pacifism a viable option.

Although English soldiers abused many Dutch civilians, official policy toward the Dutch was conciliatory. Those who chose to leave could take their property with them. Those who stayed retained their property and were assured of religious toleration. Most stayed. Except in New York City and the small Dutch portion of Long Island, Dutch settlers still lived under Dutch law. Dutch inheritance practices, which were far more generous to women than English law, survived in New York well into the 18th century. Against the hopes of England's merchants, New York continued to trade with Amsterdam. The Duke boldly tried to do in New York what he and the king did not dare attempt in England—to govern without an elective assembly. A 1665 legal code, the Duke's Laws, shifted power to the governor and his council, upsetting English settlers far more that the Dutch, who had no experience with representative government. This made it difficult to attract English colonists, a problem that became aggravated when the Duke of York granted the area west of the lower Hudson River as a separate colony of New Jersey to two Carolina proprietors, Sir George Carteret and Baron John Berkeley. New Jersey granted settlers the right to elect an assembly, which made that colony far more attractive to English settlers than New York. The creation of New Jersey also slowed the flow of Dutch settlers across the Hudson and thus helped to keep New York Dutch.

The transition from a Dutch to an English colony did not go smoothly. James expected his English invaders to assimilate the conquered Dutch, but the reverse was more common for a generation or so. Most Englishmen who settled in New York after the conquest married Dutch women (few unmarried English women were available) and sent their children to the Dutch Reformed Church. In effect, the Dutch were assimilating the English. Nor did the Dutch give up their loyalty to the Netherlands. When the Netherlands recaptured the colony in 1672 during an Anglo-Dutch War, the Dutch settlers refused to assist New York's war effort. New York City became New Orange after William III of Nassau, the military leader of the Dutch Republic. The Dutch again concluded that the colony was not worth what it cost and ceded it permanently to England in 1674. The new governor, Major Edmund Andros, established an autocratic rule that alienated the colony's English and Dutch settlers alike. He arrested prominent Dutch merchants who, threatened with the confiscation of their property, relented and swore an oath of loyalty to England. He also helped secure bilingual ministers for the Dutch Reformist pulpits, which caused alarm among ordinary Dutch Protestants. New York's English merchants harbored their own grievances. They resented the Dutch elite's staying power and insisted that the colony had to become more English and less autocratic to attract newcomers. The merchants refused to pay duties not accepted by an elective assembly, and the court of assize, New York's circuit court that had been under the governor's control, supported the tax strike. English towns on Long Island joined the demands for an elective assembly, an urgent matter now that William Penn's much freer Quaker colony on the Delaware threatened to drain away New York's English population.

The Duke finally relented and conceded an assembly. In 1683, it adopted a Charter of Liberties that proclaimed government by consent. It also imposed English law on the Dutch parts of the province. However, New York remained in the shadow of Philadelphia, which drew far more immigrants and absorbed a growing share of the Atlantic trade.

2-8 Brotherly Love: The Quakers and America

Q *How did Pennsylvania's policy toward the Native Americans differ from the Indian policies of New England and the Chesapeake colonies? What explains those differences?*

The most fascinating social experiment of the Restoration era took place in the Delaware Valley, where Quakers led another family-based, religiously motivated migration of more than 10,000 people between 1675 and 1690. Founded by George Fox during England's civil wars, the Society of

▲ **MAP 2.7 The Duke of York's Colonial Charter** This map shows the boundary of New York as set forth in the charter of 1664, the compromise boundary the first English governor negotiated with Connecticut, and the principal manors created in the 17th century.

Q *How was Charles II able to grant such a massive colonial charter to his brother James, Duke of York?*

Q *What threats and challenges did New York face during its early years?*

Friends expanded dramatically in the ensuing years as it went through a heroic phase of missionaries and martyrs, including four who were executed in Massachusetts. After the Restoration, persecution in England finally prompted Quakers to seek refuge in America. Like the Puritans in New England, the Roman Catholic Calverts in Maryland, and the aristocratic proprietors in Carolina, the Quakers saw America as a haven for a kind of ideal society that could no longer be achieved in Europe.

2-8a *Quaker Beliefs*

Quakers were radically different from other Christians. They insisted that God, in the form of the Inner Light, is present in all people, who can become good—even perfect—if only they will let that light shine forth. They took literally Jesus' advice to "Turn the other cheek." They became pacifists, enraging Catholics and most other Protestants, nearly all of whom had found ways to justify war. Quakers also obeyed Jesus' command to "swear not."

They denounced oaths as sinful. Again, other Christians reacted with horror because their judicial systems rested on oaths.

Although orderly and peaceful, Quakers struck others as dangerous radicals whose beliefs would bring anarchy. For instance, slavery made the Friends uncomfortable, although they did not embrace abolitionism until a century later (see Chapter 5). Also, in what they called "the Lamb's war" against human pride, Quakers refused to doff their hats to social superiors. Hats symbolized the social hierarchy of Europe. Every man knew his place so long as he understood whom to doff to, and who should doff to him. And Quakers refused to accept or to confer titles. They called everyone "thee" or "thou," familiar terms used by superiors when addressing inferiors, especially servants.

The implications of Quaker beliefs appalled other Christians. The Inner Light seemed to obliterate predestination, original sin, maybe even the Trinity. Quakers had no sacraments, not even an organized clergy. They denounced Protestant ministers as "hireling priests." Quakers also held distinctive views about revelation. If God speaks directly to Friends, that Word must be as inspired as anything in the Bible. Quakers compiled books of their "sufferings," which they thought were the equal of the Acts of the Apostles in the New Testament, a claim that seemed blasphemous to others.

While allowing each member to follow the Light in some unique way, Quakers found ways to deal with discord. The heart of Quaker worship was the "weekly meeting" of the local congregation. There was no sermon or liturgy. People spoke whenever the Light inspired them. The few men and women who spoke often and with great effect became recognized as **public Friends**, the closest the Quakers came to having a clergy. Public Friends occupied special, elevated seats in some meetinghouses, and many went on missionary tours in Europe or America. The weekly meetings within a region sent representatives to a "monthly meeting," which resolved questions of policy and discipline. The monthly meetings sent delegates to the "yearly meeting" in London. At every level, decisions had to be unanimous. There is only one Inner Light, and it must convey the same message to every believer. This insistence on unanimity provided strong safeguards against schism.

2.13 **Quaker Meeting House in Philadelphia, early 18th century** Hooded women are seen seated in rows opposite men in a Quaker meeting house.

Q *In what ways does the image capture some of the central Quaker beliefs and practices?*

Q *Why might have those practices been repugnant to other denominations?*

2-8b Quaker Families

Quakers transformed the traditional family as well. Women enjoyed almost full equality, and some of them, such as Mary Dyer, became exceptional preachers, even martyrs. Women held their own formal meetings and made important decisions about discipline and betrothals. Quaker reforms also affected children, whom most Protestants saw as tiny sinners whose wills must be broken by severe discipline. Quakers, who did not worry about original sin, saw children as innocents in whom the Light would shine if only they could be protected from worldly corruption. In America, Quakers created affectionate families, built larger houses than non-Quakers with equivalent resources, and worked hard to acquire land for all of their children. Earlier than other Christians, they began to limit family size to give more love to the children they did have. Once the missionary impulse faded, they seldom associated with non-Quakers. To marry an outsider meant expulsion from the Society, a fate more likely to befall poor Friends than rich ones.

2-8c West New Jersey

In 1674, the New Jersey proprietors split their holding into two colonies. Sir George Carteret claimed what he now called East New Jersey, a province near New York City with half a dozen towns populated by Baptist, Quaker, Puritan, and Dutch Reformed settlers. Lord Berkeley claimed West New Jersey. Soon, Quakers bought all of West New Jersey and parts of East New Jersey, positioning themselves between Maryland and New York. West New Jersey Quakers launched an unprecedented political experiment—the most radical in America before the Revolution—by envisioning a religiously tolerant society of godly people, who would live in harmony without internal conflict or lawyers, keep the government close to the people, and make land easily available. But as

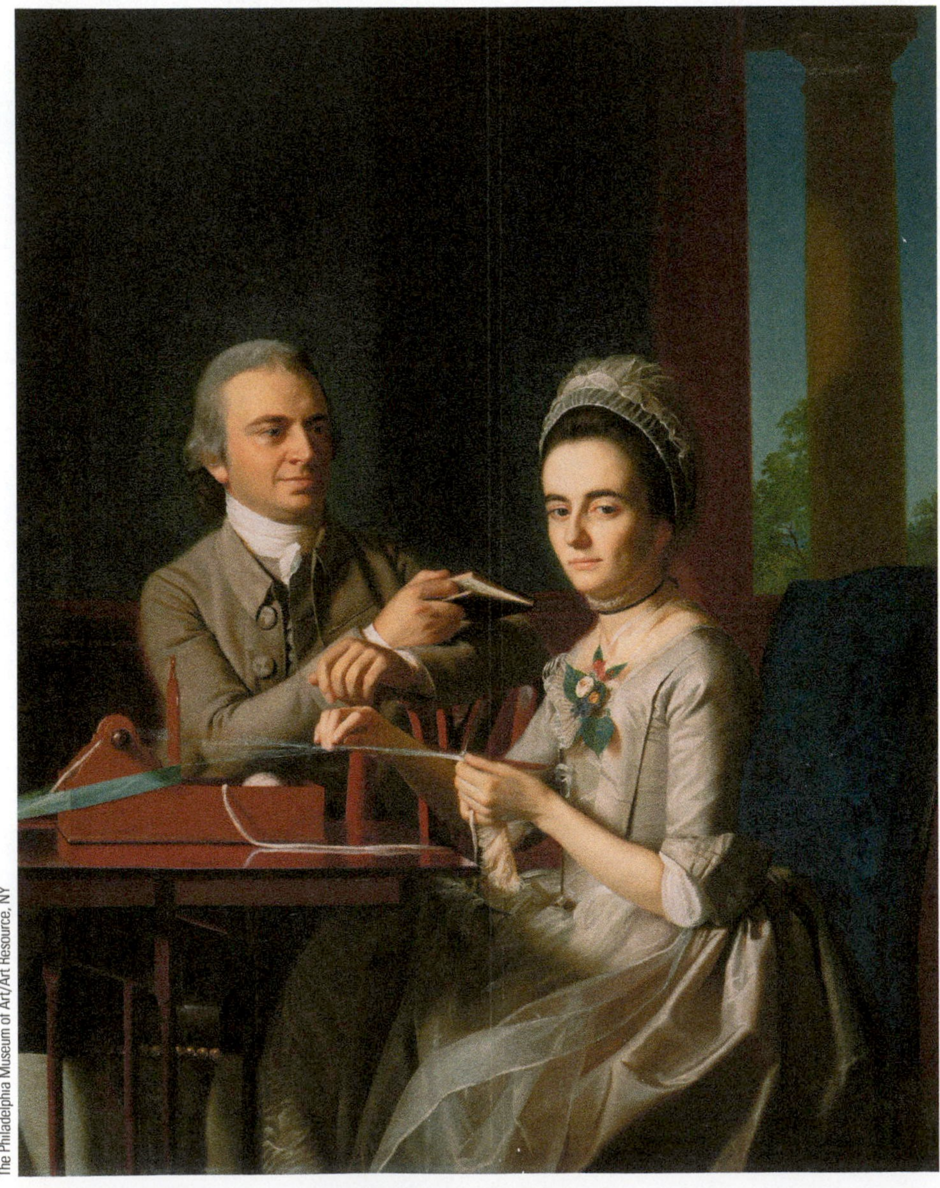

2.14 **Mr. and Mrs. Thomas Mifflin, Oil Painting by John Singleton Copley (1773)** Traditional family portraits emphasized the patriarch's superiority. Quakers stressed the equality of husbands and wives.

The Gallery Collection/Fine Art/Corbis

2.15 **Penn's Treaty with the Indians, by Benjamin West** This 1771 painting celebrates William Penn's efforts, nearly a century earlier, to establish peaceful relations with the Delaware Indians.

Q *How does the painting idealize the relations between the Quakers and the Indians?*

Q *What Christian motives can you find in the painting?*

non-Quaker immigration increased, the system broke down. Quaker rule collapsed, and the Crown took over the colony in 1702.

2-8d *Pennsylvania*

By then, Quaker attention had already shifted to the west bank of the Delaware River. There, William Penn launched a much larger, if rather more cautious, "holy experiment" in brotherly love. The son of a Commonwealth admiral, Penn grew up surrounded by privilege. He knew well both Charles II and the Duke of York, attended Oxford, went on the grand tour of Europe, and began to manage his father's Irish estates. Then something happened that embarrassed his family. "Mr. William Pen," reported a neighbor in December 1667, "is a Quaker again, or some very melancholy thing." Penn often traveled to the continent on behalf of the Society of Friends, winning converts and recruiting settlers in the Netherlands and Germany.

A gentleman and a Quaker, Penn was no ordinary colonizer. In 1681, using his contacts at court, he secured a royal charter for a proprietary colony, Pennsylvania. More thought went into planning Pennsylvania than any other colony. Twenty drafts survive of Penn's constitution for the province, which, like Carolina's first constitution, was inspired by the ideas of James Harrington. But as in Carolina, lofty ideas for a perfect government proved too complex for a new society of transatlantic migrants who were more concerned with mere survival in a new environment. Many of the first settlers had to live in caves and dugouts along river valleys and fend off aggravated Indians. Yet, Penn's ideas of representative government, religious liberty, and ready availability of land through a **quitrent** system of annual fees survived to shape Pennsylvania's future.

In England, persecution had kept Quaker antiauthoritarianism in check. In the colony, these attitudes soon became public. Penn envisioned that Pennsylvania would rely on tightly regulated trade with England, but the colony's transatlantic commerce was soon eclipsed by a trade with the Caribbean colonies, which was dominated by Quakers from Barbados, Jamaica, New York, and Boston. These wealthy men became the opposition faction in the colony, demanding more land and resisting Penn's quitrents. The legislature became divided. Pennsylvania became a haven for all religions, but its politics remained turbulent into the 1720s.

Despite these controversies, Pennsylvania quickly became an economic success, well established in the Caribbean trade as an exporter of wheat and flour. Philadelphia along the Delaware quickly grew into a major Atlantic port city. Quaker families thrived, and the colony's policy of religious liberty attracted thousands of outsiders. Quakers from other English colonies flocked in, as too did German pacifists, who shared the ideals of the Society of Friends. But among the immigrants were also Anglicans and Presbyterians who warned that the Quakers were unfit to rule—anywhere.

Pennsylvania owed its success to its Atlantic and Caribbean connections that provided a steady inflow of goods and people. But Pennsylvania also owed its success to its creative and, among English colonies, unique Indian policy. Unlike any other colonists, the Quakers entered America unarmed. Egalitarian-minded pacifists, they wanted to treat Native Americans fairly and integrate them into their "peaceful kingdom." The Delawares, an ethnically diverse native society of farmers and hunters, controlled the lands around the Delaware River. Penn recognized the Delawares' sovereignty over their territory and negotiated treaties with payments for land transactions. Although there were clashes between Indians and settlers over land, for a few decades a mutual accommodation was possible on Pennsylvania's borderlands. Native refugees from near and distant war zones gravitated to the region. With its diverse colonial and native population, the mid-Atlantic had become North America's most heterogeneous region.

Conclusion

In the 16th century, France, the Netherlands, and England all challenged Spanish power in Europe and across the ocean. After 1600, all three founded their own colonies in North America and the Caribbean. New France became a land of missionaries and traders and fashioned close ties of cooperation with most nearby Indians. New Netherland also was founded to participate in the fur trade. Both colonies slowly acquired an agricultural base.

The English, by contrast, desired the land itself. They founded colonies of settlement and did not seek to incorporate Indians into their political, legal, and social communities. English colonialism posed a direct challenge to indigenous power and sovereignty across the eastern seaboard, except in the Delaware Valley, where Quakers maintained relative peace. England's southern mainland and Caribbean colonies produced staple crops for sale in Europe, first with the labor of indentured servants and then with enslaved Africans. The Puritan and Quaker colonies became smaller versions of England's mixed economy, with an emphasis on family farms. Maintaining the fervor of the founders was a problem for both. After conquering New Netherland, England controlled the Atlantic coastline from Maine to South Carolina.

Yet, in the late 17th century, the European presence and power in North America were still limited. Three colonial empires—Spain, France, and England—possessed viable outposts on the continent, but those outposts were confined to the margins. All three empires claimed vast portions of the continent in legal documents and on maps, but on the ground Native Americans controlled most of its shores and all of its vast interior. New France along the St. Lawrence Valley and the Spanish settlements in Florida and along the Rio Grande Valley were small enclaves bounded by powerful independent native societies. The more populous English colonies were expanding on the Atlantic lowlands and up its major river valleys, but this expansion unfolded without a centralized imperial plan, and it fragmented England's colonial realm as much as it extended it. Rivalries and disputes among England's North American colonies were rife throughout the 17th century. Moreover, the western frontiers of the English colonies brushed against native societies that were determined to protect their lands and lifestyles. Overseas colonialism had become entrenched in North America, but the continent's future remained undetermined. No one people yet had a decisive advantage.

CHAPTER REVIEW

Review

1. How did Europe's political and religious landscape change in the 16th century?
2. What were the main similarities and differences between French and Spanish colonial projects in North America?
3. What key motivations drove Dutch colonialism in North America?
4. What kinds of ambitions and historical developments committed England to overseas colonization?
5. Why did the English, crossing the Atlantic at roughly the same time, create such radically different societies in the Chesapeake, the West Indies, and New England?
6. How did religious concerns shape the colonization of New England?
7. In what ways did the Restoration colonies differ from those founded earlier in the Chesapeake and New England?
8. How did Pennsylvania's policy toward the Native Americans differ from the Indian policies of New England and the Chesapeake colonies? What explains those differences?

Critical Thinking

1. Does the splintering of New England into multiple colonies, each with a somewhat different vision of the Puritan mission, indicate that religious uniformity could be maintained only under the strong government of a single state?
2. In the 17th century, Quakers came closer than any other settler group to affirming equality as a positive value. Does their experience in England and America suggest how difficult it might be to persuade an entire society to embrace that value?

Identifications

Review your understanding of the following key terms, people, and events for this chapter (terms in bold in text are included in the Glossary).

predestination, p. 38
Huguenots, p. 38
Pedro Menéndez de Avilés, p. 38
coureurs de bois, p. 39
mourning wars, p. 40
intendant, p. 41
patroonship, p. 44
Yankees, p. 44
Non-Separatists, p. 45
Separatists, p. 45
privateer, p. 45
joint-stock company, p. 46
Tsenacommacah, p. 47
fall line, p. 47
House of Burgesses, p. 47
headright, p. 47
proprietary colonies, p. 49
sachem, p. 54
Anne Hutchinson, p. 56
public Friends, p. 63
quitrent, p. 65

Suggested Readings

W. J. Eccles, ***The French in North America, 1500–1783***, rev. ed. (1998) is a concise and authoritative survey. **Bruce Trigger**, ***The Children of Aataentsic: A History of the Huron People to 1660*** (1976), and **Daniel Richter**, ***The Ordeal of the Longhouse: The Peoples of the Iroquois League in the Era of European Colonization*** (1992) detail the fates of Huron and Iroquois Confederacies. For the Dutch republic and overseas empire, see **C. R. Boxer**, ***The Dutch Seaborne Empire, 1600–1800*** (1965) and **Jonathan I. Israel**, ***The Dutch Republic: Its Rise, Greatness, and Fall, 1477–1806*** (1995). **Karen O. Kupperman**, ***Indians and English: Facing Off in Early America*** (2000) is an effort to keep Indians and the settlers of early Virginia and New England within a common focus. **J. H. Elliott**, ***Empires of the Atlantic World: Britain and Spain in America, 1492–1830*** (2006) offers a penetrating comparison of the two empires. **Colin G. Calloway**, ***New Worlds for All: Indians, Europeans, and the Remaking of Early America*** (1997), and **Daniel K. Richter**, ***Facing East from Indian Country: A Native History of Early America*** (2001) reexamine early America from a native perspective.

Edmund S. Morgan's ***American Slavery, American Freedom: The Ordeal of Colonial Virginia*** (1975) is a classic study of class struggle and the rise of chattel slavery in Virginia. **Kathleen M. Brown's** ***Good Wives, Nasty Wenches, and Anxious Patriarchs: Gender, Race, and Power in Colonial Virginia*** (1996) is essential for understanding gender and race relations in colonial Virginia. **David Hall**, ***Days of Wonder, Days of Judgment: Popular Religious Belief in Early New England*** (1989) offers a fascinating view into the beliefs and mindset of 17th-century New England colonists. **Daniel Vickers**, ***Farmers and Fishermen: Two Centuries of Work in Essex County, Massachusetts, 1630–1850*** (1994) is an outstanding introduction to the New England economy. For the West Indies, **Richard S. Dunn**, ***Sugar and Slaves: The Rise of the Planter Class in the English West Indies, 1624–1713*** (1972) remains indispensable. For the Restoration colonies, see especially **Peter H. Wood**, ***Black Majority: Negroes in Colonial South Carolina from 1670 through the Stono Rebellion*** (1974); and **Alan Gallay**, ***The Indian Slave Trade: The Rise of the English Empire in the American South, 1670–1717*** (2002). **Evan Haefeli's** ***New Netherland and the Dutch Origins of American Religious Liberty*** (2012) traces Dutch influences in American religious and cultural life.

3 Empires, Indians, and the Struggle for Power in North America, 1670–1720

3.1 ***The Kingfisher* Engaging the Barbary Pirates on 22 May, 1681, by Willem van de Velde the Younger** By the end of the 17th century, England had become the greatest naval power in the world, a position that it would maintain until overtaken by the United States in the Second World War.

THE HALF-CENTURY BETWEEN 1670 AND 1720 was a period of intensifying imperial rivalry and accelerating colonization in North America. The small and scattered European colonies transformed into imperial realms with expanding spheres of influence, and their growing ambitions provoked violent native resistance and bitter imperial wars that destabilized large parts of the continent. The turmoil triggered internal reforms that only accelerated imperial expansion. By the 1720s, Spain, France, and Britain had entrenched themselves in North America, each possessing its distinctive vision for empire.

Everyday life in North America also changed dramatically. As the European presence magnified, more and more native societies had to either relocate or learn to live with the newcomers. Relatively few in number, the French and Spaniards built societies that offered multiple places for Native Americans and Africans. In English America, most changes emanated from the mother country, which emerged in the 18th century as the dominant Atlantic power, survived a revolution that disposed a king, and adopted a unique constitution that rested on parliamentary supremacy and responsible government under the Crown. By 1700, England and the colonies had begun to converge around the newly defined principles of English constitutionalism. The colonies formed a spectrum of settlement with contrasting economies, social relationships, and institutions, which daunted the English government. Yet by 1700, England had created a system of regulation that respected colonial liberties while asserting imperial power. ■

3-1 Indians, Settlers, Upheaval: The Cataclysmic 1670s and 1680s

Q *Why did violence erupt between Indians and Europeans in different parts of North America in roughly the same period?*

In 1670, after three generations of sustained colonization, Europeans possessed scattered settlements on North America's eastern seaboard and along a few of its major rivers. No sharp boundaries separated Indian lands from colonial settlements. Boston, the largest city north of Mexico, was only 15 miles from an Indian village. The English settlements on the James, Susquehannock, Hudson, and Connecticut rivers and the Spanish settlements along the upper Rio Grande Valley amounted to little more than narrow ribbons in Indian worlds. New France along the St. Lawrence Valley brushed against the powerful and expanding Iroquois confederacy. In the event of war, nearly every European settlement was open to attack.

With time, the commercial possibilities of North America had become much clearer. The French mastered the fur trade because they controlled the St. Lawrence system, the critical all-water route from the Atlantic to the interior. South Carolinians went around the southern extreme of the Appalachians. The Spaniards sought to expand their commercial reach to the interior from bases in New Mexico and Florida. All of them needed Indian trading partners.

In some ways, America had become as much a new world for Indians as it had for colonists. European cloth, muskets, hatchets, knives, and pots appealed to Indians and spread far into the interior, and many Indians who used them gradually abandoned traditional skills and became increasingly dependent on European goods. They became consumers whose economies and societies depended on imported commodities. Drunkenness, a by-product of European trade, became a major, if intermittent, social problem. Aggressive proselytism disrupted existing social hierarchies in Indian societies and created deep internal conflicts. Diseases spread from European outposts into Indian lands, devastating many coastal societies. The increasing death toll magnified the depleted Indians' need for captives, greatly increasing the intensity of wars among native societies. In the 1670s and 1680s, almost simultaneously in different parts of the continent, the mounting tensions erupted into violent revolts and war.

CHRONOLOGY

1673	Dutch retake New York for 15 months
1675	Lords of Trade established • Metacom's War breaks out in New England
1676	Bacon's Rebellion begins in Virginia
1680	Pueblo Revolt in New Mexico
1683	New France invades Iroquoia
1684	Massachusetts charter revoked
1685	Louis XIV revokes Edict of Nantes
1686	Dominion of New England established
1688–1689	Glorious Revolution in England
1689	Anglo-French wars begin • Glorious Revolution spreads to Massachusetts, New York, and Maryland
1691	Leisler executed in New York
1692	Nineteen people hanged for witchcraft in Salem • Spaniards retake New Mexico
1696	Parliament passes comprehensive Navigation Act • Board of Trade replaces Lords of Trade
1699	French establish Louisiana • Woolens Act passed
1701	Iroquois make peace with New France
1702–1704	Carolina slavers destroy Florida missions
1707	Anglo-Scottish union creates kingdom of Great Britain
1713–1714	Britain and France make peace • George I ascends British throne
1715	Yamasee War devastates South Carolina
1716–1720	Spain establishes missions and military forts in Texas
1722	New Orleans becomes the capital of Louisiana

3-1a *The Pueblo Revolt*

In the late 17th century, the Spanish missions of North America entered a period of crisis. Franciscan zeal began to slacken, and fewer priests took the trouble to master Indian languages, insisting instead that the Indians learn Spanish. For all of their good intentions, the missionaries regarded Indians as children and savage inferiors and often whipped or shackled them for minor infractions. Disease also took its toll. Indian population loss led to pressing labor demands by missionaries and *encomenderos*, holders of tributary native labor. Despite strong prohibitions, settlers enslaved Indians in Florida and New Mexico.

The greatest challenge to the Spanish arose in New Mexico, where the Pueblo population had fallen from 80,000 in 1598 to 17,000 in 1679. A prolonged drought, together with Apache and Navajo attacks, prompted many Pueblos to abandon Christianity and resume their old forms of worship. The Spanish responded by whipping 47 medicine men for sorcery and by hanging three of them in 1675. A fourth committed suicide. Popé, a San Juan Pueblo medicine man, was one of those whipped for his beliefs. He moved north to Taos Pueblo, where he organized the most successful Indian revolt in American history. In 1680, in a carefully timed uprising, the Pueblos killed 200 of the 1,000 Spaniards in New Mexico and destroyed or raided every Spanish building in the province. They desecrated every church and killed 21 of New Mexico's 40 priests (see Map. 3.1). "Now," they declared, "the God of the Spaniards, who was their father, is dead," but the Pueblos' own god, whom they obeyed, "[had] never died." Spanish survivors fled from Santa Fe down the Rio Grande to El Paso.

Popé lost his influence when traditional Pueblo rites failed to end the drought or stop the attacks of hostile Indians. Many also struggled with Popé's extreme vision for a Spanish-free Pueblo world, which involved annulling Franciscan-sanctioned marriages and rejecting the new crops the Spanish had introduced. When the Spanish returned in 1692, the Pueblos were badly divided. Most villages yielded without much resistance, and Spain accepted their submission, but Santa Fe held out until December 1693. When it fell, the Spanish executed 70 men and gave 400 women and children to the returning settlers as their slaves. The Spanish failed to bring the Hopi Indians in the west under their rule, but New Mexico's core area along the upper Rio Grande Valley they once again controlled.

However, the Spaniards soon realized that restoring the old colonial order in New Mexico would be difficult. During their 12-year absence, the region had changed profoundly. Pueblo rebels had confiscated the horse herds of the fleeing Spaniards, and most of the animals had spread among the neighboring native societies through trading and raiding. In the Great Plains, the Apaches developed a dynamic culture of horseback hunting and warfare and expanded their settlements at the expense of other native groups. In the Great Basin north of New Mexico, the Ute Indians staged mounted raids into Pueblo villages, taking horses and captives with their new allies, the Comanches, recent

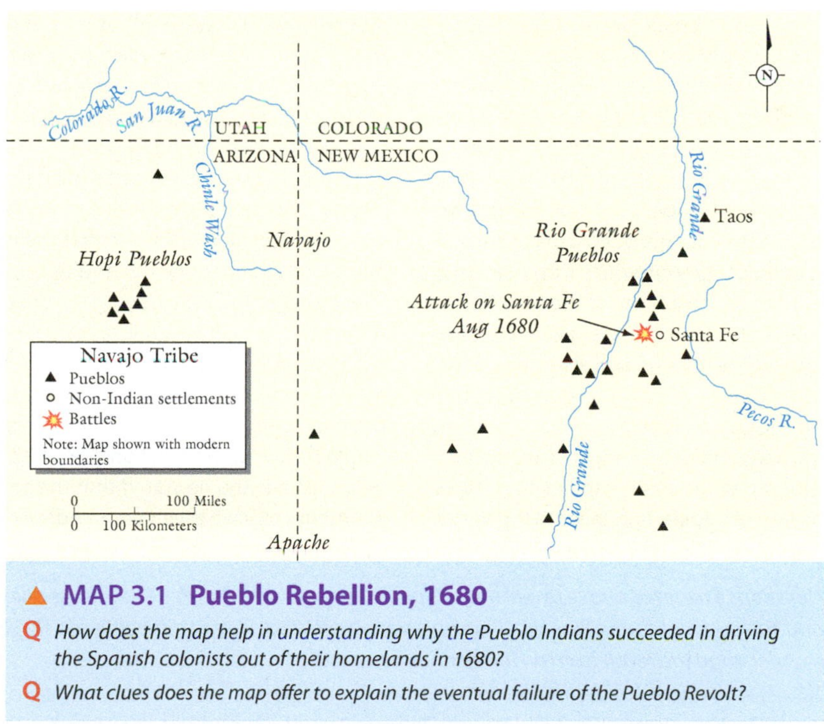

MAP 3.1 Pueblo Rebellion, 1680

Q *How does the map help in understanding why the Pueblo Indians succeeded in driving the Spanish colonists out of their homelands in 1680?*

Q *What clues does the map offer to explain the eventual failure of the Pueblo Revolt?*

What They Said

Why Did the Pueblo Indians Revolt against the Spaniards in 1680?

The Pueblo Revolt of 1680 was the most successful indigenous rebellion against European colonialism in North America, and it shocked the Spanish imperial administration to the core. Desperate to understand what had happened, the Spaniards interrogated numerous captured Pueblo Indians, asking them to divulge what they knew about the causes, goals, and organization of the revolt.

Declaration of Josephe, Spanish-speaking Indian

...he said that he ... has heard it generally stated that while they were besieging the villa the rebellious traitors burned the church and shouted in loud voices, "Now the God of the Spaniards, who was their father, is dead, and Santa Maria, who was their mother, and the saints, who were pieces of rotten wood," saying that only their god lived.... The captains and chiefs ordered that the names of Jesus and of Mary should nowhere be uttered, and that they should discard their baptismal names, and abandon the wives whom God had given them in matrimony, and take the ones that they pleased. He saw that as soon as the remaining Spaniards had left, they ordered all the estufas erected, which are their houses of idolatry, and danced throughout the kingdom the dance of the cazina, making many masks for it in the image of the devil.

Declaration of Lucas, Píro Indian

...he said that of everything contained in the question he knows only that the temples and images, crosses and rosaries were burned generally by all the Indians of the districts, and he also heard it said that each one was to live according to such law as he wished, forsaking that of the Spaniards, which was not good, and that these commands came from the jurisdictions above here; he does not know who gave them nor does he understand the languages, or any other except his own, which is Pira.

Declaration of Pedro Naranjo of the Queres Nation

...in the past years, at the summons of an Indian named Popé who is said to have communication with the devil, it happened that in an estufa of the pueblo of Los Taos there appeared to the said Popé three figures of Indians who never came out of the estufa. They gave the said Popé to understand that they were going underground to the lake of Copala. He saw these figures emit fire from all the extremities of their bodies, and that one of them was called Caudi, another Tilini, and the other Tleume; and these three beings spoke to the said Popé, who was in hiding from the secretary, Francisco Xavier, who wished to punish him as a sorcerer....

...he stated that the said Indian, Popé, came down in person and with him El Saca and El Chato from the pueblo of Los Taos ... and he ordered in all the pueblos through which he passed that they instantly break up and burn the images of the holy Christ, the Virgin Mary and the other saints, the crosses, and everything pertaining to Christianity.... They did this, and also many other things which he does not recall, given to understand that this mandate had come from the Caydi [Caudi] and the other two who emitted fire from their extremities in the said estufa of Taos, and that they thereby returned to the state of their antiquity, as when they came from the lake of Copala; that this was the better life and the one they desired, because the God of the Spaniards was worth nothing and theirs was very strong, the Spaniard's God being rotten wood. These things were observed and obeyed by all except some who, moved by the zeal of Christians, opposed it, and such persons the said Popé caused to be killed immediately. He saw to it that they at once erected and rebuilt their houses of idolatry which they call estufas, and made very ugly masks in imitation of the devil in order to dance the dance of the cacina; and he said likewise that the devil had given them to understand that living thus in accordance with the law of their ancestors, they would harvest a great deal of maize, many beans, a great abundance of cotton, calabashes, and very large watermelons and cantaloupes; and that they could erect their houses and enjoy abundant health and leisure.... Following what has already been stated, in order to terrorize them further and cause them to observe the diabolical commands, there came to them a pronouncement from the three demons already described, and from El Popé, to the effect that he who might still keep in his heart a regard for the priests, the governor, and the Spaniards would be known from his unclean face and clothes, and would be punished. And he stated that the said four persons stopped at nothing to have their commands obeyed.

Q *What do the three declarations excerpted above reveal about Pueblo motives? Could such declarations allow the Spaniards to construct a coherent and conclusive picture of the rebellion and its causes? What kind of difficulties do these documents pose to a historian who seeks to understand the revolt from an indigenous perspective?*

Sources: (top) "Declaration of Josephe, Spanish-speaking Indian," in Charles W. Hackett, ed. *Revolt of the Pueblo Indians of New Mexico and Otermin's Attempted Reconquest, 1680–1682* (Albuquerque: University of New Mexico Press, 1942), 2: 238–240. (middle) "Declaration of Lucas, Piro Indian," in Charles W. Hackett, ed. *Revolt of the Pueblo Indians of New Mexico and Otermin's Attempted Reconquest, 1680–1682* (Albuquerque: University of New Mexico Press, 1942), 2: 243–274. (bottom) "Declaration of Pedro Naranjo of the Queres Nation," in Charles W. Hackett, ed. *Revolt of the Pueblo Indians of New Mexico and Otermin's Attempted Reconquest, 1680–1682* (Albuquerque: University of New Mexico Press, 1942), 2: 245–248.

migrants from the north. Powerful equestrian Indians were converging around New Mexico, and the future of the Spanish colonial venture seemed far from certain.

3-1b *Metacom's War*

In 1675, five years before the Pueblo Revolt began, violence erupted between Indians and English settlers in New England. As in New Mexico, the conflict had been brewing for years. Indians and colonists clashed over borders and proper ways of using the land. The colonists' growing settlements shrank the Indians' land base, and their free-running hogs and cows wrecked the Indians' cornfields. The settlers wanted clear pastures and fenced farms, while Indians needed extensive forests for hunting. English efforts to convert Indians and bring them into praying towns only increased the tension. Many New England families had also become heavily involved in Indian slave trade, sending captured Native Americans—men, women, and children—to sugar plantations in the Caribbean on the ships that coursed through Boston and other New England ports.

The pressure of English colonialism was particularly hard on the Wampanoags, whose lands around the Narragansett Bay were invaded by colonists from Plymouth, Rhode Island, and Massachusetts. Led by Metacom (the English called him King Philip), the Wampanoags began to prepare for war. Metacom was a sachem and the son of Massasoit, who had maintained an alliance with the Pilgrims from the 1620s through the 1650s. English missionaries tried repeatedly to convert the influential sachem, but Metacom became convinced that accommodation with the colonists would weaken and destroy his people. With only 1,000 Wampanoags left and half of them living in praying towns, Metacom denounced the English. "If I be a praying sachem," he declared, "I shall be a poor and weak one, and easily be trod upon by others."

War broke out after Plymouth executed three Wampanoags for murdering John Sassamon, a Harvard-educated Indian preacher who may have been spying on Metacom. The fighting began in the frontier town of Swansea in June 1675 after settlers killed an Indian they found looting an abandoned house. When the Indians demanded satisfaction, the settlers laughed in their faces. The Indians took revenge, and the violence escalated into war (see Map 3.2).

The settlers, recalling their easy triumph over the Pequots a generation earlier (see Chapter 2), were confident of victory. But since then, the Indians had acquired flintlock muskets. They had built forges to make musket balls and repair their weapons. They had become marksmen with the smoothbore musket by firing several smaller bullets, instead of a single shot, with each charge. Settlers, who seldom hunted, were often armed with older firelocks and were terrible shots. In the tradition of European armies, they discharged volleys without aiming. To the shock of the colonists, Metacom won several engagements against Plymouth militia, usually by ambushing the noisy intruders. He then moved northwest to the upper Connecticut Valley, where local Indians, after being ordered to disarm, joined him instead. Together they burned five towns in three months.

Massachusetts and Connecticut joined the fray. As winter approached, rather than attack Metacom's Wampanoags, they went after the Narragansetts, who had welcomed some Wampanoag refugees while trying to remain neutral. Many prominent settlers dreamed of acquiring their fertile lands. In the Great Swamp Fight of December 1675, a Puritan army, with the aid of Indian guides, attacked an unfinished Narragansett fort during a blizzard and massacred hundreds of Indians, most of them women and children, but not before Indian snipers picked off a high percentage of the officers. The surviving warriors joined Metacom's confederacy and showed that they too could use terror. They torched more towns. During the war, about 2,000 settlers were killed and two dozen towns, more than half of New England's colonial settlements, were destroyed. The colonists abandoned the interior and retreated to the coast.

Terrified settlers demanded the annihilation of all nearby Indians, even Christian converts. The Massachusetts government, shocked to realize that it could not win the war without Indian allies, did what it could to protect the **praying Indians**. The magistrates evacuated them to a bleak island in Boston Harbor and broke up an attempt to massacre them. Despite a miserable winter, many agreed to fight Metacom in the spring campaign. The struggle against the colonists turned into a civil war among the Indians.

The war nearly tore New England apart. Increase Mather, a prominent Boston minister, saw the conflict as God's judgment on a sinful people and warned that no victory would come until New England repented and reformed. Many settlers agreed, interpreting the war and its unprecedented cruelty as a sign of moral corruption, the New Englanders' degeneration from civilization into savagery. By slaughtering Indians for their savage cruelty, the colonists feared that they had become savages themselves. Quakers saw the war as divine punishment for their persecution by the Puritans. The settlers finally turned the tide in 1676. Governor Andros of New York persuaded the powerful Mohawks to attack Metacom's winter camp and disperse his people, who by then were short of gunpowder. The New Englanders, working closely with Mohegan and Christian Indian allies, adopted Indian tactics to attack Metacom's war parties and killed hundreds of Indians, including Metacom. A total of 5,000 Indians died, and hundreds of survivors were sold into slavery in the West Indies. Some of those enslaved had not been party to the conflict and had requested asylum from it. The settlers put Metacom's severed head on display in Plymouth to mark the end of a war that, in proportion to population, has proved the most fatal in American history.

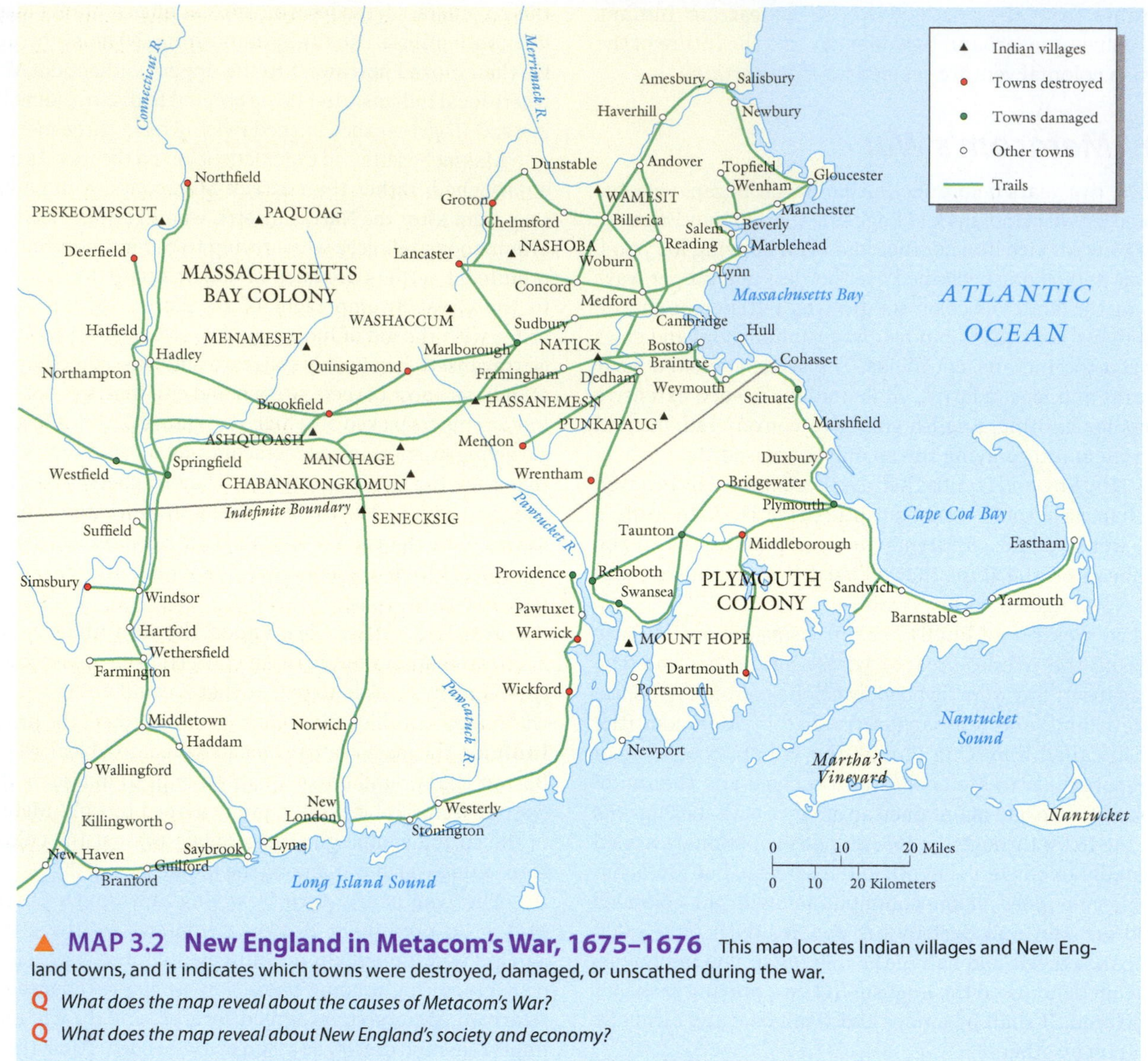

▲ **MAP 3.2 New England in Metacom's War, 1675–1676** This map locates Indian villages and New England towns, and it indicates which towns were destroyed, damaged, or unscathed during the war.

Q *What does the map reveal about the causes of Metacom's War?*

Q *What does the map reveal about New England's society and economy?*

3-1c *Virginia's Indian War*

In Virginia, Governor Sir William Berkeley, who had defeated Opechancanough 30 years earlier, rejoiced in the New Englanders' woes. Metacom's War was the least they deserved for the way the Puritans had dismantled England and executed Charles I during the civil wars. Then Virginia began to have its own troubles.

In 1675, the Doegs, Algonquian-speaking people who had fled Virginia to seek safety in the Potomac Valley, demanded payment of an old debt from a Virginia planter. When he refused, they ran off some of his livestock. After his overseer killed one of the Doegs, the others fled but later returned to ambush and kill the man. The county militia mustered and followed the Doegs across the Potomac into Maryland. At a fork in the trail, the militia split into two parties. Each party found a group of Indians in a shack a few hundred yards up the path it was following. Both parties fired at point-blank range, killing 11 at one cabin and 14 at the other. One of the bands was indeed Doeg, but the other was not: "Susquehannock friends," blurted one Indian as he fled.

The Susquehannocks were a strong Iroquoian-speaking people with firearms. They had moved south to escape Iroquois attacks, and Maryland had invited them to occupy lands north of the Potomac, hoping to build a buffer of loyal Indians against the Five Nations. Berkeley, eager to avoid war, sent John Washington (ancestor of George) with Virginia militia to investigate the killings and, if possible, to set things right. But Washington preferred vengeance. His Virginia militia joined with a Maryland force, and together they besieged a formidable Susquehannock fort on the north bank of the Potomac, too strong to take without artillery. When the Indians sent out five or six sachems to negotiate, the militia murdered them and then laid siege to the fort for six weeks. The Indians, short of provisions, finally broke out one night with all of their people, killing several militiamen. After hurling taunts of defiance

Darley
THE KING PHILIP WAR—A RAID ON THE SETTLERS.

Source: Wikimedia Commons

3.2 Engraving from The Providence Plantations for 250 Years, 1886 A depiction of a Native American raid on the settlers in New England during King Philip's War.

Q *Engravings like this became wildly popular in New England after the Metacom's War. Why?*

and promises of vengeance, they disappeared into the forest. In January 1676 they killed 36 Virginians. The colonists began to panic.

Berkeley favored a defensive strategy against the Indians; most settlers wanted to attack. In March 1676, the governor summoned a special session of the Virginia legislature to approve the creation of a string of forts above the fall line of the major rivers, with companies of "rangers" to patrol the stretches between them. Berkeley also hoped to maintain a distinction between the clearly hostile Susquehannocks and other Indians who might still be neutral or friendly. Frontier settlers, mostly former servants frustrated by low tobacco prices and unable to acquire tidewater lands because speculators had bought them up, demanded war against all Indians. Finally, to avoid further provocation, Berkeley restricted the fur trade to a few close associates. To the men excluded from that circle, his actions looked like favoritism. To settlers in frontier counties, whose access to new lands was blocked by Indians and who now had to pay higher taxes, Berkeley's strategy seemed intolerable.

Colonists denounced the building of any more forts and demanded an offensive campaign waged by unpaid volunteers, who would take their rewards by plundering and enslaving Indians. In April, the frontiersmen found a reckless leader in Nathaniel Bacon, a young newcomer to the colony with a scandalous past and £1,800 to invest. Using his political connections (he was the governor's cousin by marriage), he managed an appointment to the council soon after his arrival in the colony in 1674. Bacon, the owner of a trading post in Henrico County at the falls of the James River (now Richmond), was one of those excluded from the Indian trade under Berkeley's new rules.

3-1d *Bacon's Rebellion*

Against Berkeley's orders, Bacon led his men south in search of the elusive Susquehannocks. After several days, the weary force reached a village of friendly Occaneechees, who offered them shelter, announced that they knew where to find a Susquehannock camp, and volunteered to attack it. They surprised and defeated the Susquehannocks and returned with their captives to celebrate the victory with Bacon. But after the Occaneechees fell asleep, Bacon's men massacred them, seized their furs and prisoners, and then boasted of their prowess as Indian killers.

By then Berkeley had outlawed Bacon, dissolved the legislature, and called the first general election since 1661. The old assembly had recently imposed a property requirement for voting, but Berkeley suspended it and asked the burgesses to bring their grievances to the June assembly for redress. "How miserable that man is," he complained, "that Governes a People where six parts of seaven at least are Poore Endebted Discontented and Armed."

To show their resentment against elite planters, voters elected a fair number of burgesses who were not justices of the peace; since midcentury, justices of the peace had dominated the House of Burgesses and other political offices (see Chapter 2). The voters of Henrico elected Bacon to the assembly. Berkeley had Bacon arrested when he reached Jamestown, and made Bacon kneel before him and the council and apologize for his disobedience. Berkeley pardoned Bacon and restored him to his seat on the council. By then, even Governor Berkeley had abandoned the effort to distinguish between hostile and friendly Indians, but he still favored a defensive war. While the burgesses were passing laws to reform the county courts, the vestries, and the tax system, Bacon slipped away to Henrico, summoned his followers again, and marched on Jamestown. At gunpoint, he forced Berkeley to commission him as general of volunteers and compelled the legislature to authorize another expedition against the Indians.

Berkeley retreated downriver to Gloucester County and mustered its militia, but they refused to follow him against Bacon. They would fight only Indians. Mortified, Berkeley fled to the eastern shore, the only part of the colony that was safe from Indian attack and thus still loyal to him. Bacon hastened to Jamestown, summoned a meeting of planters at the governor's Green Spring mansion, made them swear an oath of loyalty to him, and ordered the confiscation of the estates of Berkeley's major supporters, who were men in the process of becoming great planters. Meanwhile, Berkeley raised his own force on the eastern shore by promising the men an exemption from taxes for 21 years and the right to plunder Bacon's supporters.

Beyond New England, few Indians killed other Indians in 1676. Virginia settlers fought one another during this civil

Wendell Metzen/Bruce Coleman Inc./Photoshot, Inc.

3.3 Crude Housing for Settlers in North America When the first settlers came to North America, their living quarters were anything but luxurious. The crude housing shown in this modern reconstruction of Jamestown remained typical of Virginia and Maryland throughout the 17th century.

Q *Why did the first settlers not build larger and more comfortable homes for themselves?*

war, and royal government collapsed under the strain. During that summer, hundreds of settlers tried to make their fortunes by plundering Indians, other colonists, or both. Fueled by simmering class resentments, Bacon's Rebellion was the largest colonial upheaval before 1775 (see Map 3.3).

Bacon never did kill a hostile Indian. While he was slaughtering and enslaving the unresisting Pamunkeys along the frontier, Berkeley assembled a small fleet and retook Jamestown in August. Bacon rushed east and laid siege to Jamestown, exhibiting his Indian captives along the way as a demonstration of his ability to protect the colonists against the natives. He captured the wives of prominent Berkeley supporters and forced them to stand in the line of fire as he dug his trenches closer to the capital. After suffering only a few casualties, the governor's men grew discouraged and in early September the whole force returned to the eastern shore. Bacon burned Jamestown to the ground. He also boasted of his ability to hold off an English army, unite Virginia with Maryland, and win Dutch support for setting up an independent Chesapeake republic.

Instead, Bacon died of dysentery in October, and Berkeley soon regained control of Virginia. Using the ships of the London tobacco fleet, he overpowered the plantations that Bacon had fortified. Then, in January 1677, a force of 1,000 redcoats arrived, too late to help but in time to strain the colony's depleted resources. Ignoring royal orders to show clemency, Berkeley hanged 23 of the rebels. A new assembly repudiated the reforms of 1676, and in many counties the governor's men used their control of the courts to continue plundering the Baconians through confiscations and fines.

The rebellion had brought a festering class conflict to the surface, awakening Virginians to the need of social reform. In its aftermath many of the emerging great planters deliberately chose to replace their indentured servants with enslaved Africans whom they could dominate without legal restraint. Virginia's whites became increasingly fixated on racial difference. New legislation outlawed marriages between blacks and whites, forbade planters from freeing slaves unless they paid for their transportation beyond the colony, and prohibited free blacks from voting, bearing arms, or employing white servants. Skin color became the primary marker of identity, and dark skin became associated with slavery. As the colony gradually developed its system of racial slavery, class tensions among its white settlers diminished. Finding a bond in their shared sense of racial superiority, the commoners and the elite disregarded the vast distinctions of wealth and power among themselves and united in an alliance based on racial solidarity and white supremacy.

3-1e *New France Besieged*

Like Spain and England, France faced a serious crisis in the late 17th century. New France had established peace with the powerful **Iroquois League** in the 1660s, which had given the colony a much-needed respite from war. The peace allowed the fur trade, New France's economic engine, to flourish, but it collapsed in the early 1680s. Epidemics had devastated the Iroquois, reigniting their mourning wars against neighboring Indians, many of whom were allied with the French (see Chapter 2). In the 1670s, the Iroquois had also established an alliance, the **Covenant Chain of Peace**, with New York, which pulled them away from the French orbit. New York's autocratic governor, Edmond Andros, urged the Iroquois to push the French out of the Great Lakes. Armed by New York, the Iroquois attacked French traders, and soon open warfare raged across the Iroquois-French borderlands. Both sides suffered enormous losses. The Five Nations raided St. Lawrence settlements, attacked Montreal, and forced the French to abandon all their forts in the western Great Lakes. The French and their Indian allies retaliated by burning Iroquois villages and their food caches. They opened

Fort Stafford
SUSQUEHANNOCK
DOEG
Rappahannock R.
Potomac R.
Chesapeake Bay
Pamunkey R.
Fort Royal
Great Dragon Swamp
Fort James
NEW KENT CO.
ORAPAX
James R.
PAMUNKEY
Fort Charles
Bacon's Quarter
GLOUCESTER CO.
HENRICO CO.
ARROHATECK
Henrico
Varina
York R.
Powhatan
Bermuda Hundred
Shirley Hundred
APPAMATUCK
PASPAHEGH
Appomattox R.
Fort Henry
Flowerdew Hundred
Martin's Brandon
Jamestown
Martin's Hundred
Smith's Fort
KECOUGHTAN
Fort Algernon
James R.
EASTERN SHORE
NORTHAMPTON CO.
Dale's Gift
ATLANTIC OCEAN
Nottoway R.
Roanoke R.
OCCANEECHEE

0 10 20 Miles
0 10 20 Kilometers

Settled areas
English settlements
Indian village
English fort
Bacon's campaigns

▲ **MAP 3.3 Bacon's Rebellion in Virginia, 1676** Settlement had just reached the fall line by the 1670s. The map also shows Bacon's two military campaigns, against the Occaneechees and the Pamunkeys.

Q *What clues does the map offer to explain the causes of Bacon's Rebellion?*

Q *What factors led to the failure of Bacon's Rebellion?*

The Virginia Journals of Benjamin Henry Latrobe (2 vols., New Haven, 1977) I, 181–182, 247, plate 21

3.4 **Henry Latrobe's Sketch of Green Spring, the Home of Governor Sir William Berkeley, at the Time of Bacon's Rebellion** Green Spring was one of the first great houses built in Virginia. Latrobe made this drawing in the 1790s.

Iroquois graves to steal burial items, depriving Iroquois lands of their spiritual power. The Iroquois lost one-fourth of their population of 8,000.

While fighting the English-allied Iroquois in the south and the west, the French faced another threat from the north. In 1670, the English Crown chartered the Hudson's Bay Company, which soon established trading posts on James Bay, challenging France's monopoly on the Canadian fur trade. The French launched attacks on the English posts, and New France became entangled in warfare on multiple fronts. Unlike in New England and Virginia where the violence soon exhausted itself, in New France the crisis persisted.

3-2 Converging Empires: Spain and France in North America

Q *How did negotiation, conciliation, and alliance-making shape France's and Spain's Indian policies?*

The wars and crises of the 1670s and 1680s shocked the Spanish, French, and English colonists. Settlers and colonial administrators responded to the upheavals with systematic violence, seeking to punish and vanquish the enemies who threatened their existence. Bloodshed washed over Virginia, New England, New Mexico, and New France. But the chaos also triggered critical self-reflection and reforms. In the late 17th century, Spain, France, and England implemented new policies and practices that secured their battered realms and reinvigorated their imperial projects. By the early 18th century, all three were expanding again, each claiming an ever-greater portion of the continent and its resources.

Spanish, French, and English colonists shared the desire to expand their holdings, but they employed increasingly divergent strategies to achieve their goals. The English maintained alliances with powerful native confederacies like the Iroquois, but, growing rapidly in number, began to rely increasingly on raw force in their dealings with Indians. Lacking England's demographic power, the Spaniards and French attempted to expand their spheres *through* Indians, by keeping as many native societies as possible in their orbit. Both tried coercing and dictating to Indians, but soon realized that diplomacy and mediation brought more enduring results. While England's North American realm was turning into a settler empire—self-sufficient, land-hungry, and intolerant of native presence—Spain and France built negotiated empires that offered distinctive places for native peoples.

3-2a *Spanish New Mexico*

By the mid-1690s, Spain had reestablished colonial rule in New Mexico. The Pueblo Revolt had been suppressed, the Franciscans were rebuilding destroyed missions, and soldiers reasserted Spanish control over the Pueblo communities. The Spaniards were determined to turn New Mexico into a robust colony that would anchor Spanish power in western North America. But the presence of powerful horse-riding native societies on New Mexico's borders made the Spanish position precarious. Horse and captive raids by the Apaches, Utes, and Comanches threatened the colony from without, while the prospect of another Pueblo uprising threatened it from within. In 1696, the Pueblos revolted again. Although the Spaniards rapidly suppressed the uprising, they realized that their old strategies were no longer feasible.

The Spanish colonists adopted a more conciliatory policy toward the Pueblos. The settlers accepted smaller landholdings and reduced their demands on Pueblo labor. Officers implemented new laws that protected the Pueblos against colonial exploitation and secured their landholdings. Franciscans adopted a more pragmatic attitude toward religious indoctrination and allowed previously prohibited Pueblo ceremonies. To appease the priests, Pueblos accepted Catholic sacraments but performed their traditional rituals in underground *kivas*. The Spaniards and Pueblos remained distinct peoples within a colonial society that was based on unequal access to power, but gradually the social distance between them narrowed. They forged kinship relationships through the Catholic institution of godparenthood, and intermarriages became more common. Mixed Spanish-Pueblo settlements emerged along the upper Rio Grande Valley, and cultural blending deepened.

Such accommodations did not erase political antagonisms and cultural differences between the Spaniards and the Pueblos, but they did help to sustain a viable multicultural society in the upper Rio Grande Valley. The Pueblos never launched another major revolt against the Spaniards, and the two groups combined forces against Ute, Comanche, and Navajo raiders. New Mexico mounted punitive expeditions against native raiders and formed diplomatic ties with the plains Apaches, who were pressured by the Comanche-Ute coalition. Spanish officials invited Apache groups to relocate near New Mexico, hoping to turn them into a bulwark against the expanding nomads. Desperate to secure Spanish support, many Apaches pledged to accept Christianity and build permanent villages on New Mexico's borderlands.

3-2b *French and Indians on the Middle Ground*

New France was also undergoing transformation. In the 1680s, New France was in a perilous situation, fighting the English-allied Iroquois in the south and west, and the English Hudson's Bay Company in the north. More a financial liability than an asset to the French Crown, the colony received limited support from the mother country, and seemed to be dissipating. Yet, only a generation later, France's North American empire was secure and expanding. It boasted a vast interior fur trade system and its territorial claims arched from the St. Lawrence Valley across the Great Lakes basin down the Mississippi Valley to the Gulf Coast.

The French success was grounded in a new Indian policy that gradually took shape in the late 17th century in the Great Lakes region (see Map 3.4). There the Iroquois expansion made possible an unusual accommodation between the colonists and the Indians. The survival of the Iroquois Five Nations depended on their ability to assimilate captives seized from other nations through incessant warfare. Iroquois raiders, armed with English muskets, terrorized western Indians and carried away thousands of captives. The Iroquois wars depopulated nearly all of what is now the state of Ohio and much of the Ontario peninsula. The Indians around lakes Erie and Huron either fled west to escape these horrors or were absorbed by the Iroquois. The refugees, mostly Algonquian-speaking nations, founded new communities farther west. Most of these villages contained families from several different nations, and village loyalties gradually supplanted older political or ethnic loyalties. When refugees disagreed with one another, the collapse of traditional political structures made it difficult to resolve conflicts. Over time, French officials, soldiers, and missionaries began to mediate.

French policymakers were eager to bring these Indians into an alliance network that would shield the fragile New France against the Iroquois and contain the English east of the Appalachians. They began by easing tensions among the Great Lakes Indians, while supplying them with firearms, metal utensils, and other European goods. Threatened by common enemies, the French and the Indians recognized their mutual dependency and the necessity of adapting to each other's expectations. Little by little, they crafted an alliance that rested on creative compromises that transformed the Great Lakes basin into a middle ground where the two peoples accommodated one another in ways that benefited both.

French officials who gave orders rather than listened only alienated the Indians, who were accustomed to making decisions by consensus. Vastly outnumbered, the French knew that they could not impose their will on the Indians. The

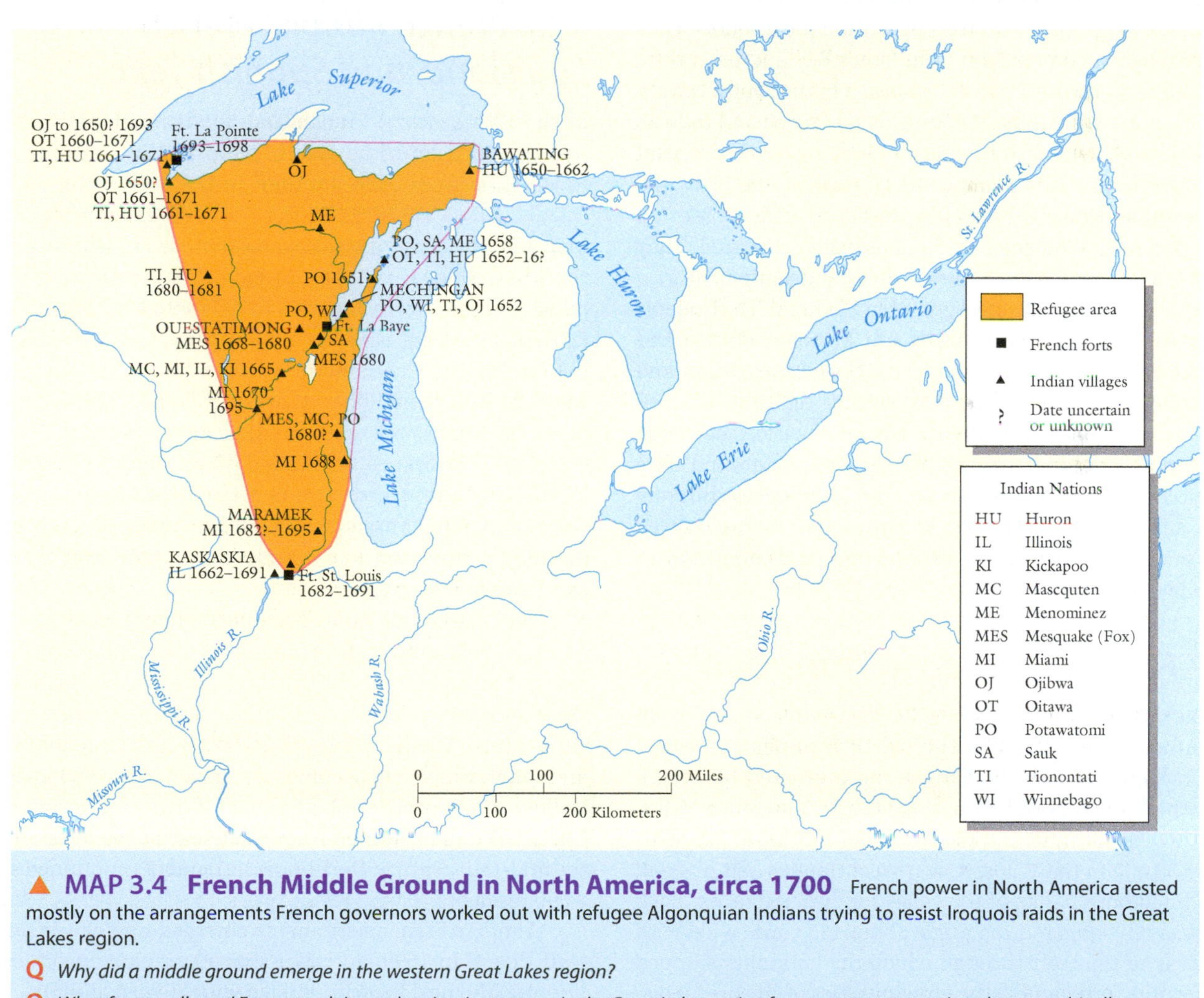

▲ **MAP 3.4 French Middle Ground in North America, circa 1700** French power in North America rested mostly on the arrangements French governors worked out with refugee Algonquian Indians trying to resist Iroquois raids in the Great Lakes region.

Q *Why did a middle ground emerge in the western Great Lakes region?*

Q *What factors allowed France to claim and maintain presence in the Great Lakes region for over a century against demographically superior English colonies?*

governor of New France became a version of a traditional Indian chief. Algonquians called him **Onontio** ("Great Mountain"), the supreme alliance chief who won cooperation through persuasion and generosity. Gift exchanges became central to the middle ground diplomacy, the French customarily showing more generosity as an acknowledgment of their dependency on the Algonquians' military support. Cultural differences between the two peoples did not disappear, but both learned to negotiate around them. For example, the murders of French traders by Indians required careful balancing between two legal traditions. The French demanded the perpetrator to be identified, tried, and executed; the Indians wanted to appease the victim's kin by "covering" the death with presents or by "raising the dead" with a slave who took the victim's vacated social place. The solution of the middle ground was a cultural hybrid that allowed both sides to maintain face. Indians surrendered murderers to French authorities, who condemned them to death, only to quietly allow them to escape to freedom. Both sides detested such compromises but, desperate for support, accepted them nonetheless. By doing so, they sustained their alliance and held the interior.

Backed by their Indian allies, the French gained an upper hand in their struggles with the English and the Iroquois. They blocked English competition from James Bay and used their Indian allies to thwart English expansion in the south. During King William's War (1689–1697), the allied French and Indians raided across the English frontier, devastating most of coastal Maine and parts of New Hampshire. Throughout the 1690s, the French–Indian coalition also kept inflicting heavy losses on the Iroquois. By 1701, the Five Nations were exhausted. They negotiated a peace treaty known as the Grand Settlement with the French and some 30 native groups in Montreal. The Iroquois agreed to remain neutral in any war between France and England. They stopped their raids in the Great Lakes region, and the English pledged to protect their hunting rights in the west. France's Indian allies, supported by a new French fort erected at Detroit in 1701, began returning to the fertile lands around lakes Erie and Huron. By the 1710s, the interior fur trade was thriving again, supplying Indians with much-needed manufactured goods and sustaining France's expanding inland empire.

3-2c *French Canada in Transition*

The lucrative fur trade kept the cost-conscious French government committed to the North American imperial project. Supported by the Crown and protected by Indian allies, the French population along the St. Lawrence Valley grew, through natural increase, from about 10,000 in the 1680s to over 30,000 in the 1720s. A nearly continuous belt of small farms lined both banks of the valley for over 150 miles. Each farm was an elongated rectangle about 165 yards wide with an access to the river through which the habitants shipped their farming products to the growing cities of Quebec, Trois-Rivières, and Montreal, the center of the western fur trade. The population was intensely Catholic, and a seminary (now Laval University) in Quebec served its spiritual needs.

New France attracted few non-French immigrants and remained for a long time ethnically homogenous. It was in many ways as French as New England was English. This started to change with the creation of the Great Lakes middle ground, which alerted French policymakers to the value of captives and slaves in Indian diplomacy. France's western allies brought captives taken from enemy Indians for sale or offered them as ceremonial gifts that cemented bonds between allies. Louis XIV had expressly forbidden the enslavement of Indians, but the command became a dead letter and was officially rescinded in 1709. By the 1720s, up to 5 percent of New France's population consisted of Indian slaves, who labored as field hands, domestic servants, dock loaders, and millers. Some women became wives and concubines of the settlers. As in Spanish New Mexico and Florida, the incorporated Indians were exposed to intense religious indoctrination. Arriving from distant interior places—many were Apaches from the Great Plains—the captive-slaves were highly vulnerable to European microbes and died in vast numbers. Few survived in bondage longer than a decade.

3-2d *French Illinois, French Louisiana, and Spanish Texas*

In the 17th century, French and Spanish colonial projects had unfolded on the opposite sides of the continent and in isolation from each another; in the early 18th century, they began to converge in the heart of the continent (see Map 3.5). The convergence began when the French discovered the Mississippi River. The French dreamt about a water passage across North America to Asia into the 1670s, only to learn that the Mississippi River flowed into the Gulf of Mexico, not the Pacific. Their ambitions turned from the west to the south. In 1682, René-Robert Cavelier, *sieur* de La Salle, traveled down the Mississippi to its mouth, claimed possession of the entire area for France, and called it Louisiana for Louis XIV. When La Salle returned to the Gulf two years later, he overshot the mouth of the Mississippi, landed in Texas, and wandered around for three years in search of the great river until his exasperated men murdered him.

The Mississippi Valley became a magnet for the French. Around 1700, several disgruntled Frenchmen established a new settlement around the town of Kaskaskia in what became the Illinois Country near the confluence of the Mississippi and Ohio rivers. The habitants rejected seigneurs, feudal dues, and tithes, which had become established in the St. Lawrence Valley. Most prospered as wheat farmers and married Christian Indian women from the Great Lakes missions. By the mid-18th century, the Illinois settlements contained some 3,000 residents.

Another French settlement emerged downriver on the Gulf Coast. In 1699, a Crown-sponsored expedition led by Pierre le Moyne d'Iberville landed with 80 men at Biloxi, built a fort, and began trading with the Indians. Soon, he moved his headquarters to Mobile, closer to the more populous nations of the interior, especially the Choctaws, who were looking

The Art Archive/Picture Desk

3.5 La Salle and Father Hennepin on the Mississippi After La Salle and his party traveled down the Mississippi to its mouth, he claimed possession of the entire area for France. Father Louis Hennepin made this drawing in about 1683.

Q *How could Hennepin's drawing reinforce France's right to claim the Mississippi Valley and the lands around it?*

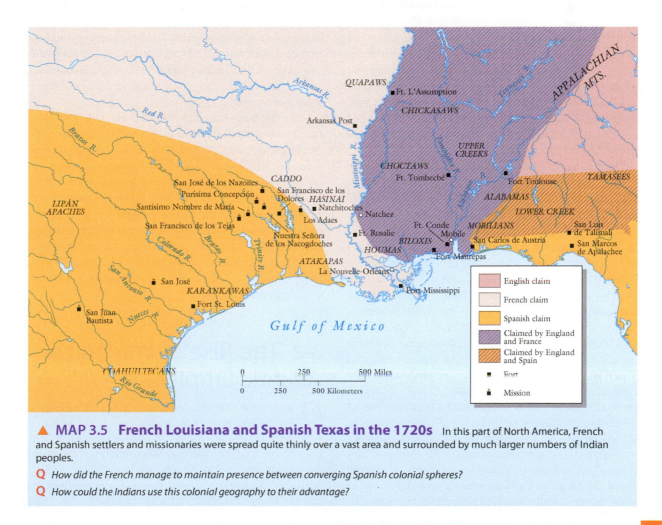

▲ MAP 3.5 French Louisiana and Spanish Texas in the 1720s In this part of North America, French and Spanish settlers and missionaries were spread quite thinly over a vast area and surrounded by much larger numbers of Indian peoples.

Q *How did the French manage to maintain presence between converging Spanish colonial spheres?*

Q *How could the Indians use this colonial geography to their advantage?*

for allies against the English. The Choctaws could still field 5,000 warriors but had suffered heavy losses from slaving raids organized by South Carolinians and carried out mostly by that colony's Chickasaw and Creek allies. About 1,800 Choctaws had been killed and 500 enslaved during the preceding decade.

Using the Choctaws as an anchor, the French integrated themselves into the southern Indian trade system, which had been oriented toward English Carolina and Virginia. West of the lower Mississippi Valley, the French established ties with the powerful Osages and Caddos, who controlled access to the hide, food, and slave trades of the Great Plains. A thick exchange network emerged around French Louisiana. As in the Great Lakes, this frontier exchange economy was based on close, face-to-face interactions between the French and several, often competing native societies. This fluid and multiethnic exchange system allowed the French to carve out a colonial niche in the midst of powerful indigenous societies. Although European diseases had been ravaging the area since the 16th century, the Indians around the lower Mississippi Valley still numbered about 70,000. In 1708, the French settlers numbered fewer than 300, including 80 Indian slaves. They were lucky to survive at all.

French ventures into the lower Mississippi Valley galvanized the Spaniards, who correctly saw French settlements as a potential threat to their mines in northern Mexico and their shipping lines on the Gulf. French ministers specifically planned Louisiana as a springboard for an invasion into northern New Spain. In 1690, alarmed by rumors of La Salle's expedition, Spain sent missionaries into eastern Texas; they brought smallpox with them. Their explanation that the epidemic was God's "holy will" did not mollify the Tejas Indians, who soon banished them. In 1698, the Spaniards tried to make inroads by sea and built a garrison in Pensacola Bay to establish a foothold on the Gulf Coast between the Florida missions and French Louisiana.

In 1716, Spain tried again in Texas by sending missionaries and soldiers among the powerful Caddos, who lived in several populous agricultural villages east of the Mississippi and north of the Gulf Coast. Before its disintegration, the Caddos had been linked to the Cahokia-centric trading and ceremonial network (see Chapter 1), but now their villages had become commercial and cultural centers in their own right. Their widely dispersed local villages united into three confederacies, commanding a vast domain. The Caddo society was matrilineal—it traced descent through the maternal line—and women organized the all-important agricultural work. Male chiefs, caddis, led the local villages, and each confederacy was headed by a xinesí, a paramount religious leader, but all elite men depended on the guidance of the female heads of households.

The Spaniards struggled to understand the Caddo world, and the Caddos struggled to understand the newcomers. Unlike the French, the Spaniards did not seek to establish trade or marry Indian women. Instead of kinship ties, they offered religious education. Franciscan priests, who lived in celibacy, baffled the Caddos, who expected visitors to travel with women, which signaled peaceful intentions. The Spaniards did build two forts and six missions in east Texas among the Caddos, but the Franciscans won few converts. The forts suffered frequent depredations by Indians carrying French muskets, and eventually the soldiers and priests fled west to the San Antonio River, which became the nucleus of Spanish Texas. By 1720, a small colony with ranches, missions, and a presidio (military garrison) had risen along the river. In response, France bolstered its hold on the Gulf Coast. It created the Company of the Indies, which shipped 7,000 settlers and 2,000 African slaves to Louisiana and founded New Orleans, which became the capital in 1722. Settlers died in staggering numbers in the humid subtropical climate where mosquitoes and yellow fever thrived, but the colony persisted.

Policymakers had envisioned Spanish Texas and French Louisiana as imperial outposts that would transform critical parts of North America into Spanish and French spaces, but both projects evolved into something quite different. The low mid-continent became a complex world marked by imperial rivalries, colonial compromises, and flexible allegiances. In Louisiana, a growing black population carved out a distinct place in the frontier exchange economy that sustained the colony. Although most of them were slaves, the Africans enjoyed considerable economic autonomy in the colony. Laboring as herders, hunters, woodcutters, and boatmen, they moved freely around Louisiana and marketed their garden products in frequent small transactions. Many sold their labor as militiamen, eventually winning their freedom. In Spanish Texas, seminomadic Indians incorporated missions into their seasonal migrations as resource depots where they could subsist on Spanish resources during lean months; come spring, they left the missions, ignoring the objections of the Franciscan priests.

On the borderlands between them, the Spaniards and the French competed for the loyalties of the Caddos and other native groups, who traded with both, keeping their options open. But the Spaniards and the French also cooperated in unexpected ways. To prevent smuggling, the Spanish Crown refused to open a seaport on the Gulf Coast, which left Texas isolated from the empire's supply lines. Los Adaes, the easternmost settlement and the capital of Spanish Texas, was established to contain French encroachments, but it became dependent on the nearby French town of Natchitoches for food. Here, imperial visions and colonial realities were becoming startlingly disconnected.

3-3 The Rise of England's Atlantic Empire

Q *What was the Glorious Revolution and how did it change England's North American colonies?*

Like Spain and France, England redefined its goals and position in North America in the late 17th and early 18th centuries. While Spanish and French realms were expanding and colliding in the interior and the Gulf Coast, England's fragmented and divided mainland colonies began to coalesce into a coherent, centrally governed Atlantic empire. This was a long and convoluted process that was rooted in rapidly changing conditions in the mother country.

In the late 17th century, as England gradually recovered from the chaos of its civil wars, the Stuart monarchs and Parliament realized that the overseas colonies were slipping out of their control. The Caribbean colonies were under royal administration, but they were trading much of their sugar to Dutch merchants who dominated the world's oceanic trade. The Chesapeake colonies were doing the same with their tobacco. Alarmed, England turned toward the Atlantic once again. In a sense, it now first realized just how important colonies were to its prosperity, power, and prestige.

3-3a *The Foundations of Empire: Mercantilism and the Navigation Acts*

During the 17th century, most European powers followed a set of policies now usually called **mercantilism**. According to mercantilist theory, power derived ultimately from the wealth of a country. The world's wealth, however, was thought to be finite, which meant that each nation should organize itself in a way that allowed it to carve out the largest possible slice of the global wealth. Competing for the fixed pool of riches, nations were thought to be either growing richer or poorer, and to augment their power, they had to expropriate the resources of their rivals. The key means to achieve this was a positive **balance of trade** with other nations; a healthy nation imported less than it exported, and most of its exports were luxuries. Colonies were considered essential, for they provided the mother country with raw materials and bought its manufactured commodities. Clearly, a nation had to control the commerce of its colonies, but mercantilists disagreed over the best ways to promote growth. The Dutch favored virtual free trade within Europe, whereas England came to prefer stronger state regulation of the domestic and imperial economy.

In line with mercantilist principles, the English Parliament passed three Navigation Acts between 1651 and 1673. Primarily aimed at removing the Dutch from England's colonial markets and dislodging the Netherlands from its dominant position in world trade, the acts established three major regulations: All colonial trade was to be carried on English ships; **enumerated commodities**, of which sugar and tobacco were most important, could be shipped from the colony of origin only to England or to another colony, the intent being to give England a monopoly over the export of major staples from every English colony to Europe and the rest of the world; and products from Europe and Asia had to land and be levied in England before they could be delivered to colonies.

England intended nothing less than a revolution in Atlantic trade. In 1675, the Crown created a new agency, the Lords of Trade, to enforce the Navigation Acts and administer the colonies. Custom officers were sent to the colonies to collect duties and vice-royalty courts, tribunals without juries, were established to prosecute violators. Gradually, England dislodged the Dutch and established hegemony over its Atlantic trade. By the early 18th century, the Royal Navy was the largest in the Atlantic world, and nearly all British colonial trade was carried on English ships. Colonial commerce accounted for a rapidly growing share of Britain's overseas trade. Sugar, tobacco, and other staple crops all passed through Britain on their way to their ultimate destination. Nearly all of the manufactured goods consumed in the colonies were made in Britain.

The Navigation Acts reordered England's Atlantic trade, but they also redefined England's relationship with its overseas colonies: Tobacco- and sugar-producing colonies in the Chesapeake and the Caribbean found their market outlets and profits diminished. Beneath the surface of tightly regulated trade, smuggling persisted, sustaining long-standing traditions of colonial freedom from imperial supervision. Building an empire would take time.

3-3b *Crisis in England and the Expansion of Royal Authority*

England's tightening control of its American colonies sprang from mercantilist thinking, but it also reflected autocratic aspirations of the Stuart monarchs, who hoped to rule without parliamentary restrictions. In 1676, when Bacon's Rebellion caused both Virginia's tobacco production and England's customs revenues to plummet, King Charles II was obliged to ask Parliament for more money. Headed by a growing opposition that was soon named the **Whigs**, Parliament demanded an amendment to royal succession. Charles II had no legitimate children, which made his brother James, duke of York, heir to the throne. James had become a Catholic, and the Whigs, terrified by the prospect of a Catholic king, demanded his exclusion from the throne in favor of his Protestant daughters by his first marriage. Charles, after getting secret financial support from King Louis XIV of France, dissolved Parliament in 1681 and ruled without it until he died in 1685.

The prolonged struggles between the Stuart court and the Whig opposition had a profound impact on the colonies. Supported by the **Tories**, Stuart followers who favored legitimate succession, the monarchy set out to reinforce royal power, both in England and in the colonies. Although the Navigation Acts now regulated their Atlantic commerce, the colonies enjoyed considerable freedom from direct imperial control. Local autonomy, embodied in representative assemblies, had become an expected part of colonial life. Most colonists believed that they had an inherent right to government by consent. Stuart reforms challenged that autonomy head-on. The Stuarts issued strict instructions to royal governors and they imposed new revenue acts on Virginia, New York, and Jamaica, England's key sugar colony in the Caribbean. The acts obliged the colonies to pay for their own government in exchange for the right to have elected assemblies.

The Stuarts deplored the eclectic nature of the colonial system. In the late 1670s, there was only one royal colony, Virginia,

Mary Evans Picture Library/The Image Works

3.6 **Gillis van Schendel, *Tobacco* (1628)** This scene from an Amsterdam public house associates tobacco with dissipation. Note the man in the lower right throwing up on the floor and the animal above him enjoying a pipe while dancing with humans. Because no Dutch colony adopted tobacco as a staple crop, the source of tobacco could have been Virginia, in violation of English trade policy.

on the mainland. Only Virginia had royally appointed governors, who could veto laws passed by its representative assembly. New England colonies were corporate colonies, where legislatures or property-holding men elected all officials, including governors. The rest of the mainland colonies were proprietary in form, chartered by the king to individuals or groups who held full governing rights. The Lords of the Trade viewed all New England and proprietary colonies with deep suspicion. Seen from London, they were dangerously autonomous entities that engaged in smuggling, violated the Navigation Acts, and practiced religious policies that contradicted English laws. The Stuarts aspired to a more uniform and centralized administration of the colonies. The possibility of authoritarian rule suddenly emerged in English America.

3-3c *The Dominion of New England*

Charles II died and his brother became King James II in early 1685. James II focused on New England in his endeavor to assert royal authority in America. Absolutist New York now became the king's model for reorganizing New England. James disallowed the New York Charter of Liberties of 1683 that proclaimed government by consent (see Chapter 2) and sent Sir Edmund Andros, the autocratic governor of New York from 1674 to 1680, to Massachusetts to take over a new sprawling administrative domain called the Dominion of New England. All colonies north of Pennsylvania lost their charters as New Hampshire, Plymouth, Rhode Island, Connecticut, New York, and both Jerseys were lumped together in the Dominion. Andros disbanded elected assemblies and governed the supercolony through an appointive council and a superior court that rode the circuit, dispensing justice. He imposed religious toleration and tied voting rights to property rather than church membership, trying to dissolve the close relationship between the church and the state that characterized the Puritan order.

At first, Andros won support from merchants who had been excluded from politics by the Puritan requirement that they be full church members, but his rigorous enforcement of the Navigation Acts soon alienated them too. When he tried to compel New England farmers to take out new land titles that included annual quitrents (land taxes), he enraged the whole countryside. His suppression of a tax revolt in Essex County, Massachusetts, started many people thinking more highly of their rights as Englishmen than of their peculiar liberties as Puritans. By 1688, government by consent seemed more valuable than ever.

The Trustees of the British Museum/Art Resource, NY

3.7 **A London Coffeehouse** The first coffeehouses dated from the 1650s, and by the 18th century merchants routinely met in such specialized establishments as the Virginia Coffeehouse or the New England Coffeehouse to transact their colonial business. England's rapidly growing consumption of coffee, tea, and chocolate stimulated most of the demand for sugar, which in turn sustained the Atlantic slave trade.

Q *How and why did coffeehouses emerge as popular places of political debate from the 17th century onward?*

3-3d *The Glorious Revolution in England and America*

The Dominion of New England was the most drastic of the Stuart experiments in imperial reform. It was also the last. In 1688, the birth of a son to James II raised the prospect of a Catholic *dynasty* in England. A cadre of Whig and Tory leaders swallowed their mutual hatred and invited William of Orange, the *stadholder* (governor) of the Netherlands, to England. William, the husband of the king's older Protestant daughter Mary by the king's first marriage, had become the most prominent Protestant soldier in Europe during a long war against Louis XIV. William landed in England with 21,000 soldiers, forcing James II to flee to France. Parliament elected William and Mary to the throne, completing an elite-engineered bloodless coup against "popery" and arbitrary power. The Glorious Revolution preserved the institution of the monarchy, but profoundly changed its character. It secured Protestant succession to the throne, reaffirmed Parliament's right to control taxation and legislation, and confirmed English liberties and the rule of law.

The Glorious Revolution reverberated across English North America, revealing deep fractures within colonial societies. The Boston militia overthrew Andros, and all New England colonies reestablished their old governments. In New York City, most of the active rebels were Dutch Calvinists, and their leader, Jacob Leisler, took over the government. Fearing conquest by Catholics from New France, Leisler acted like a Dutch *stadholder* in a nominally English colony. He jailed many of his English opponents without a trial, only to be outmaneuvered by powerful groups in England who persuaded the Dutch king of England to destroy Leisler. William appointed a new governor, Henry Sloughter, who arrested Leisler and his son-in-law, tried both for treason, and had them hanged, drawn (disemboweled), and quartered. A new assembly restored a modified version of the abolished Charter of Liberties of 1683, this time denying toleration to Catholics. Bitter struggles between Leislerians and Anti-Leislerians raged for decades in New York.

In Maryland, Protestant rebels overthrew the Catholic government of Lord Baltimore, who had refused to proclaim William and Mary even after all the other colonies had done so. The proprietary charter of Lord Baltimore and the Calvert family was withdrawn, and the Protestants set up a new government. The Calverts regained their proprietary power in 1715 when they converted to Anglicanism, and Maryland remained under Protestant control. The Protestant majority established the Church of England as Maryland's official church and barred Catholics from voting and holding public office. The colony's experiment in religious toleration was over.

Massachusetts also was transformed. Unlike other New England colonies, Massachusetts failed to restore its original charter. A new charter, issued in 1691, retained traces of the dissolved Dominion of New England. Massachusetts remained a royal colony and absorbed Plymouth and Maine. The colony's traditional town meetings survived and the General Court continued to control land distribution, but its governors and justices were now appointed in London. In accordance with English law, Massachusetts was required to grant toleration to other Protestant denominations, which the Puritan clergy deemed as heretic. Rather than church membership, voting rights were now based on property qualifications, and Puritan "saints" lost their control over the colony's politics. Liberty and property had triumphed over godliness. John Winthrop's vision of a "city upon a hill" had been replaced by a different kind of order emanating out of London.

3-3e *The Salem Witch Trials*

A year later, Massachusetts was gripped by a witchcraft crisis. Witchcraft accusations arose in Salem Village (modern Danvers) among a group of girls that included a young daughter and a niece of the local minister, Samuel Parris. They then spread to older girls, some of whom had been orphaned during the Indian wars. The girls howled, barked, and stretched themselves into frightful contortions. At first, Parris treated the outbursts as cases of demonic possession, but after weeks of prayer sessions brought no improvement, he accepted a diagnosis of witchcraft. With adult encouragement, the girls accused many village residents of witchcraft, mostly people who did not approve of Parris. The number of the accused escalated sharply, and the crisis spread far beyond the village after 14-year-old Abigail Hobbs confessed in April that she had made a compact with the devil in Maine at age 10 just before the outbreak of the Indian war that had since devastated northern New England. Altogether about 150 people were accused in Essex County and beyond. Satan, supported by Indian warriors on the frontier and by witches within the colony, seemed determined to destroy Massachusetts.

The trials began in Salem Town in June. The court, which included judges badly compromised by their willing service to the Andros regime, hung 19 people, pressed one man to death because he refused to stand trial, and allowed several other people to die in jail. All of those executed insisted on their innocence. Of 50 who confessed, none was hanged. Many of the victims were grandmothers, several quite conspicuous for their piety. One was a former minister at Salem Village who had become a Baptist. The governor finally halted the trials after someone accused his wife of witchcraft. By then, public support for the trials was collapsing. The Salem witch trials provided a bitter finale to the era of political uncertainty that had afflicted Massachusetts during the Stuarts' imperial reforms. Along with the new charter of 1691, the trials brought the Puritan era to a close.

Thomas B. Macaulay, *History of England from the Accession of James II*, ed. Charles H. Firth (London: Macmillan, 1914)

Thomas B. Macaulay, History of England from the Accession of James II, ed. by Charles H. Firth (London: Macmillan, 1914)

3.8a (left) and 3.8b (right) ***Calvinism on Its Deathbed* and *Le Roy de France*** Louis XIV's persecution of the Huguenots led his supporters to hope that France would soon be rid of all Protestants. Le Roy de France, a Dutch Protestant response to the persecution, depicts Louis, the "Sun King," as death.

3-3f *The New Imperial Order*

The Glorious Revolution killed ambitions for unrestricted governing power and absolute rule in English America and guaranteed that royal colonies would have representative governments. Royal colonies became the norm, and by 1730 there were seven of them: Virginia, New York, Massachusetts, New Hampshire, New Jersey, North Carolina, and South Carolina. The monarch administered these colonies through governors, but both Crown and colonists now took it for granted that royal colonies would have representative governments. The monarch would appoint governors and (except in Massachusetts) their councils, but settlers would elect an assembly to vote on taxes and local laws. Connecticut and Rhode Island continued to elect their governors, retaining their corporate form of government. Maryland and Pennsylvania (along with Delaware, which became a separate colony under the Penn proprietorship in 1704) were the only surviving proprietary provinces on the mainland, and their proprietors were usually careful to abide by London's imperial regulations and representatives.

Such careful compromises between the Crown and the colonies were fraught with tension, however, for the Glorious Revolution had a complex legacy in English America. The consolidation of royal power under King William established the principle of limited constitutional monarchy in England, which in turn allowed for greater self-governance in the colonies. But the Glorious Revolution also emboldened England to tighten its hold on the colonies. Enjoying internal stability at long last under King William, England grew stronger and more confident, which reignited the vision of a more integrated, wealth-producing empire. Underneath the liberal reforms of the Glorious Revolution, the process of imperial centralization began by the Stuarts thus continued.

In 1696, then, England passed two major pieces of commercial legislation that aimed to consolidate its imperial system. First, Parliament passed a new, comprehensive Navigation Act that plugged several loopholes in earlier laws and extended to America the English system of vice-admiralty courts, which dispensed quick justice without juries. When the new courts settled routine maritime disputes or condemned enemy merchant ships captured by colonial privateers, their services were welcomed, but when the courts tried to assume jurisdiction over the Navigation Acts, they aroused controversy. Sometimes the common-law courts intervened and took over these cases. William also replaced the Lords of Trade in 1696 with a new agency, the Board of Trade. Its powers were almost purely advisory. It corresponded with governors and other officials in the colonies, listened to lobbyists in England, and made policy recommendations to appropriate governmental bodies. The board tried to collect information on complex questions and offer helpful advice. It was, in short, an early attempt at government by experts. John Locke, England's foremost philosopher and an able economist, was one of the board's first members. Together with the new Navigation Act, the Board of Trade helped create a secure and thriving commercial zone that connected England to its American colonies.

Another difficult problem was resolved in 1707 when England and Scotland agreed to merge their separate parliaments and become the single kingdom of Great Britain. At a stroke, the Act of Union placed Scotland inside the Navigation Act system, legalized Scottish participation in the tobacco trade, and opened numerous colonial offices to ambitious Scots. By the mid-18th century, Scotland owed its growing prosperity to its colonial trade.

The transformations that took place between 1689 and 1707 defined the structure of the British Empire until the American Revolution. Although Parliament claimed full power over the colonies, in practice it seldom regulated anything except Atlantic commerce. By the early 18th century, London was the center of a secure transatlantic empire united around commerce and Protestantism and against Catholicism and arbitrary power. Crown officials pulled back from Stuart autocracy and allowed the colonies considerable freedom in their internal affairs. The empire had stumbled into a system of de facto federalism, an arrangement that no one could quite explain or justify. Parliament exercised only limited powers, and the colonies controlled the rest. What seemed an arrangement of convenience in London soon acquired overtones of right in America, the right to consent to all taxes and local laws. Yet, the colonists were committed to England and the Atlantic empire. "It is no little blessing of God," Cotton Mather wrote in 1700, "that we are part of the English nation." A few years earlier, Mather had struggled, and failed, to preserve Puritan rule in New England, but the consolidation of England's imperial power compelled the colonists to align with the distant mother country.

The relationship, moreover, was starting to yield unforeseen benefits. A wildly unstable nation for a half-century, England emerged by the early 18th century as the most stable and dynamic among European powers. The key to England's success, nearly everyone agreed, lay in its "mixed and balanced" constitution. Government by the king, the House of Lords, and the House of Commons mirrored society itself—the monarchy, aristocracy, and commonality—and literally embodied all three in its structure. Each checked the power of the others, and as long as each placed the public good ahead of its own interests, English liberty would be secure. The prospect that corrupt Crown ministers could manipulate and undermine the House of Commons fueled anxiety and endless debates during the 18th century, but the English on both sides of the Atlantic believed that they were the freest people in history. The English empire, they believed, would be an empire of liberty.

It would also be, they realized, an empire of unprecedented prosperity and power. From the 1690s on, England raised larger fleets and armies than it had ever mobilized before. To support them, the kingdom created for the first time a **funded national debt**, in which the state agreed to pay the interest due to its creditors ahead of all other obligations.

History Through Film — *Three Sovereigns for Sarah* (1986)

Directed by Philip Leacock.
Starring Vanessa Redgrave (Sarah Cloyse), Phyllis Thaxter (Rebecca Nurse), and Kim Hunter (Mary Easty).

This film, originally a PBS American Playhouse miniseries, is the most powerful and effective dramatization ever made of the Salem witch trials of 1692. The three principal actresses were all previous Academy Award winners. When this series appeared, British director Philip Leacock was perhaps best known in the United States for *The War Lover* (1962) and *The Daughters of Joshua Cabe* (1972).

The screenplay by Victor Pisano, who also produced the film, concentrates on the three Towne sisters: Sarah Cloyse (Vanessa Redgrave), Rebecca Nurse (Phyllis Thaxter), and Mary Easty (Kim Hunter). Rebecca Nurse's ordeal became a major turning point in the Salem tragedy. Hers was one of the early trials, and at first the jury acquitted her, only to be urged by the judges to reconsider the verdict. They did, and she was hanged. After this reversal, no one else was acquitted. Mary Easty, after she too had been convicted, sent a petition to the magistrates, one of the most eloquent documents ever written in colonial America. As a committed Christian, she accepted her own death, but she urged the judges to reconsider their procedures because she knew that she was innocent, and so must be many of the other condemned witches. She was hanged. Of the three sisters, only Sarah Cloyse survived the trials. The film focuses on Cloyse's lifelong efforts to vindicate the reputations of her older sisters. Vanessa Redgrave's portrayal of her suffering and her resistance to the whole appalling affair is one of the most compelling performances of her acting career.

3.9 The witch crisis of 1692 began in the parsonage of Reverend Samuel Parris (shown above), then spread throughout Salem Village and to other towns, mostly in Essex County.

The screenplay, by concentrating on the three sisters and their families, brings home the human tragedy that the trials became. This emphasis forced Pisano to leave out other important victims. For example, the Reverend George Burroughs, the only minister executed in the trials (or in any New England colony in the 17th century, for that matter), is not even mentioned. In addition, Pisano never explains that Sarah Cloyse survived because the grand jury refused to indict her. Grand juries were exempt from explaining their decisions to anyone else, and so we do not know why she became an exception, but evidently the jurors believed that she was too dedicated a Christian woman to sell her soul to the devil. Finally, the screenplay attributes the onset of the crisis to fortune telling in the Samuel Parris household by Tituba, an Indian slave from South America who reached the village via Barbados. Guilt for indulging in this occult activity presumably triggered the seizures of the afflicted girls. Several historians have demolished this interpretation since the film appeared. We do not know what provoked the girls' fits.

Three Sovereigns for Sarah is a compelling, relentless drama. It romanticizes nothing and makes clear, unlike some Hollywood depictions of these events, that nothing about the trials was sexy. The accusation scenes, dominated by girls, convey the madness of the whole affair. Most of those accused and executed were grandmothers. When they are turned off the ladder, their bodies bounce as the nooses take hold. This film is a cinematic triumph. ■

This simple device gave Britain enormous borrowing power. The government created the Bank of England to facilitate its own finances, and the London Stock Exchange emerged. Parliament levied a heavy land tax on the gentry and excises on ordinary people to meet wartime expenses. Together, debt, bank, stock market, and new sources of revenue added up to a financial revolution that enabled England to outspend France, despite having only one-fourth of France's population. Sustained by taxes and loans, the English state was able to organize large-scale military campaigns to protect its interests in Europe and across the Atlantic. If in the 17th century the colonists had often sought distance from England and its control, they now began to look to it for protection.

3-4 An Empire of Settlement: The Growth of British America

Q *Why was the colonial household such an engine of British expansion? Did it give Britain an advantage over its imperial rivals in North America? What limits did Indians impose on the European colonies in the 18th century?*

By 1700, when 250,000 settlers and slaves were already living in England's mainland colonies, the population was doubling every 25 years. New France matched that pace, but with only

14,000 people in 1700, it could not close the gap. The population of Spanish New Mexico was beginning to grow, but Spanish Texas had only a few hundred settlers, and Florida's mission belt was rapidly declining. In the struggle for empire, a growing population became England's greatest asset. If Spain and France were building North American empires on trade, missions, and Indian diplomacy, England was building one on settlement.

3-4a *The Atlantic Prism and the Spectrum of Settlement*

In 1700, English America was an amalgam of two connected but distinctive parts. Facing east from the Atlantic coast, it was part of a vast transoceanic commercial empire that linked it to England's ports, merchants, government, and culture. Facing west from the coast, English America was a sprawling empire of settlers, who were growing explosively in number and pushing their frontiers inland. If the colonies' Atlantic linkages had become increasingly structured in the late 17th century, giving them a measure of unity, the colonies themselves were anything but (see Map 3.6).

America had divided the English. Moving across the Atlantic for a range of religious, political, and economic reasons, the colonists had sorted themselves out along a vast arc from the cold North to the subtropical Caribbean. If we imagine England as a source of white light, and the Atlantic as a prism refracting that light, English America becomes a spectrum of settlement, with each color merging imperceptibly into the shade next to it. Each province had much in common with its neighbors but shared few traits with more distant colonies (see Table 3.1).

The most pronounced differences involved life expectancy, the sex ratio (the ratio of men to women in any society), and family structure. At one extreme were buccaneers, the all-male, multiethnic societies in the Caribbean that lived only for plunder. In the sugar colonies, European men often died by age 40, and slaves even sooner. Despite the appalling death rate in the sugar and tobacco colonies, most young men remained optimistic and upbeat, as they looked forward to challenging the world and making their fortunes. Female settlers were scarce in the islands at first; families hardly existed. Even when the sex ratio became more equal, couples had few children. Life expectancy in early Carolina was slightly better than in the islands, slightly lower than in the Chesapeake colonies. In Virginia and Maryland, men who survived childhood diseases lived to an average age of about 45 years during the last half of the 17th century, still less than in England, where life expectancy exceeded 50. Then, as natural increase replaced immigration as the main source of population growth after 1680, women became more numerous, married much earlier, and raised larger families.

The northern colonies were much healthier. In the Delaware and Hudson valleys, a man who reached adulthood could expect to live past 60. On Long Island in the 1680s, one woman claimed that she had more than 300 living descendants. New England was one of the healthiest places in the world. Because the sex ratio rapidly approached equality and because the economy permitted couples to marry perhaps two years earlier than in England, population exploded.

These demographic differences had major consequences. For example, the Caribbean and southern colonies were youthful societies in which men with good connections could expect to achieve high office while in their 30s, or even 20s. By contrast, the New England colonies gradually became dominated by grandfathers. A man rarely became even a selectman by age 40.

The degree of racial and ethnic mixture also varied from region to region, along with economic priorities. The West Indies already had a large slave majority by 1700, when English settlers were still a clear majority in the southern mainland colonies, but African slaves became a majority in Carolina in the 1710s. They would comprise 40 percent of Virginia's population by the 1730s. Africans were less numerous in the Delaware and Hudson valleys, although slavery became deeply entrenched in New York City and parts of northern New Jersey. Most colonies had large numbers of Indians living among the settlers. In the southern colonies, most Indians were slaves, seized from the interior by English and native slave raiders. In the northern colonies, most Indians were nominally free people who had stayed behind as their nations retreated or dissolved in the face of expanding settlements. They struggled to blend in by dressing, speaking, farming, and drinking like the colonists, while quietly trying to preserve their customs and identities. In the Middle Atlantic region, settlers from all over northwestern Europe were creating a new ethnic mosaic. English colonists were probably always a minority, outnumbered at first by the Dutch, and later by Germans, Scots, and Irish. New England was in every sense the most English of the colonies. The farther south one went, the more diverse the population—the farther north, the more uniform (see Map 3.7).

Slavery and staple crops went together. Slave societies raised sugar, rice, or tobacco for sale in Europe. General farming and family labor also went together. By 1700, the mid-Atlantic was the wheat belt of North America and commercially oriented. New Englanders farmed primarily for local consumption, but many coastal towns exported fish, livestock, and lumber to the West Indies. Patterns of ecological change reflected the different regional economies. New Englanders cut timber for sale at such a rate that it created climatic change: moister air, drier hillsides, and more winds. The numbers of several species of birds and mammals declined drastically, reducing the region's biodiversity. In the south, intensive tobacco cultivation depleted the soil of minerals and nutrients, causing crop failures and forcing the settlers to rotate tobacco with corn, wheat, and other crops.

Cultural patterns also varied among the colonies. Settlers lived in local and regional communities that followed their distinctive forms of civic life and worship. The intensity of religious observance differed immensely across the spectrum of settlement, ranging from irreverence and indifference in the West Indies to intense piety in Pennsylvania and New England. Literacy followed a similar pattern. Colonists everywhere tried to prevent slaves from learning to read, and low literacy

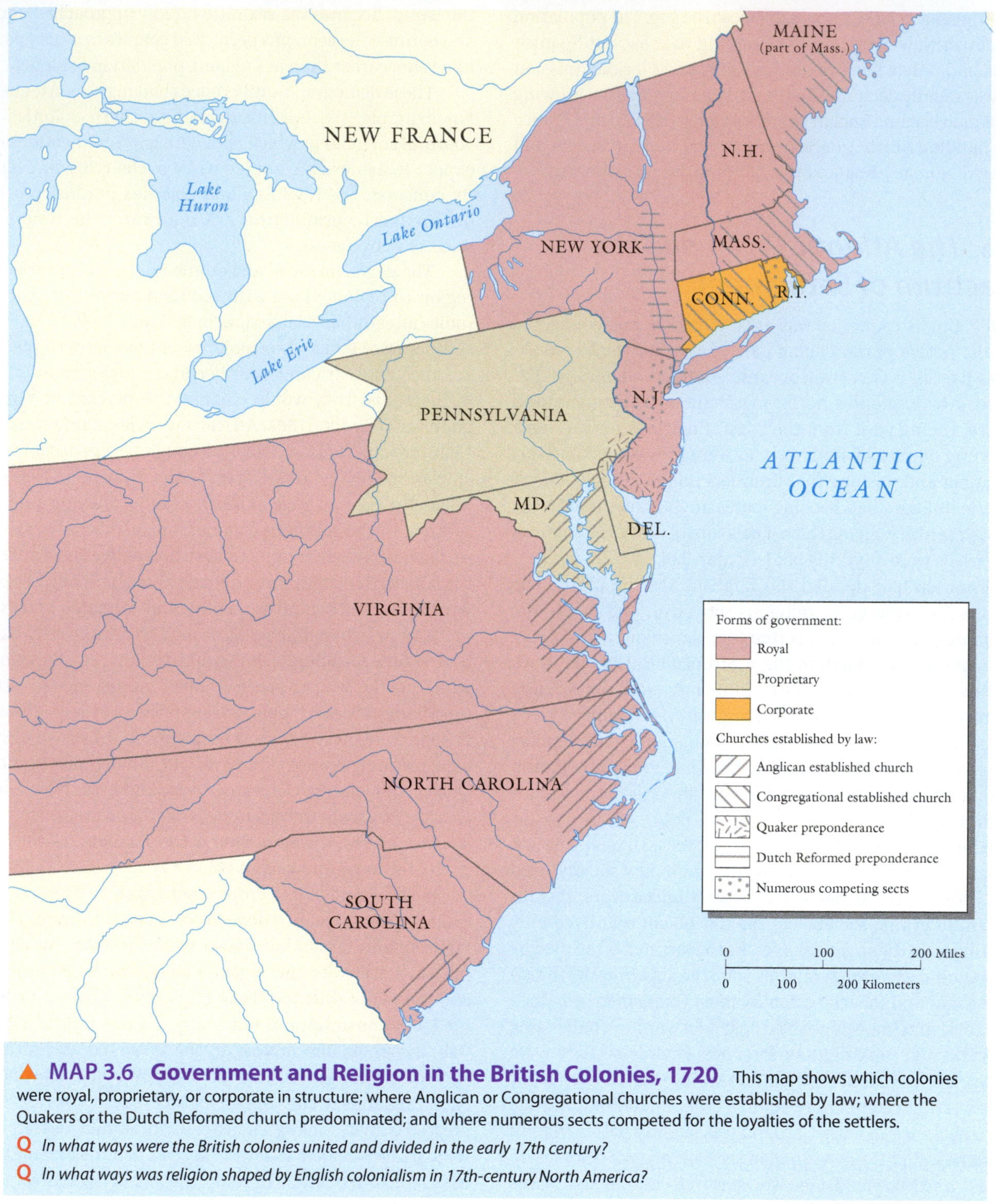

▲ **MAP 3.6 Government and Religion in the British Colonies, 1720** This map shows which colonies were royal, proprietary, or corporate in structure; where Anglican or Congregational churches were established by law; where the Quakers or the Dutch Reformed church predominated; and where numerous sects competed for the loyalties of the settlers.

Q *In what ways were the British colonies united and divided in the early 17th century?*

Q *In what ways was religion shaped by English colonialism in 17th-century North America?*

prevailed wherever slavery predominated. Chesapeake settlers provided almost no formal schooling for their children before the 1690s. Massachusetts founded Harvard College in 1636, and in 1642 required every town to have a writing school, and larger towns to support a Latin grammar school. Along the spectrum, piety, literacy, and education grew stronger from south to north. Public support for the clergy, and hence the proportion of ministers, followed the same pattern. Both were much greater in the north.

3-4b *The Engine of British Expansion: The Colonial Household*

Diverse as they were, the English colonies shared a key characteristic: They were all growing rapidly in number. The engine of that expansion was the colonial household. Ordinary northern farmers and southern great planters shared something in common that distinguished their households from those in England. With few exceptions, colonial families

Eileen Tweedy/The Art Archive/Picture Desk

3.10 **George III (1760–1820) Going into His Palace by a Side Entrance** In court culture, even everyday events, such as the king entering or leaving his palace by a side gate, had to display the honor, splendor, and hierarchy surrounding the monarch.

rejected the English customs of entail and primogeniture. **Entail** prohibited a landowner, or his heir, from dividing up his landed estate (i.e., selling part of it) during his lifetime. **Primogeniture** obliged him to leave all of his land to his eldest surviving son. Primogeniture and entail became more common in the 18th-century colonies than they had been before, but they never came to structure social relations the way they did in England. A Virginia planter, for example, might entail his home estate (the site of his big house) and bequeath it to his oldest son, but he would also leave land and slaves, and sometimes whole plantations, to his other sons. The primacy of the eldest son was far more sentimental than structural. The patriarchs of colonial households tried to pass on their status to all of their sons and to provide dowries that would enable all of their daughters to marry men of equal status. Until 1750 or so, these goals were usually realistic. For younger sons, then, the colonies presented unique opportunities. They could marry earlier (especially in regions with relatively balanced sex ratios) and have more children than their counterparts in Europe. Benjamin Franklin's *Autobiography*, colonial America's greatest success story, boasted that he was "the youngest Son of the youngest Son for 5 Generations back." Some women were able to acquire property, usually by inheritance from a deceased husband, particularly in the Chesapeake colonies during the long period when men greatly outnumbered women. Single women who crossed the Atlantic as servants

Table 3.1 THE SPECTRUM OF SETTLEMENT: DEMOGRAPHY, ETHNICITY, ECONOMY, 1650–1700

Category	West Indies	Lower South	Chesapeake	Mid-Atlantic	New England
Life expectancy for men, at age 20	40	42	45	60+	Late 60s
Family size	Below replacement rate	About two children	Rising after 1680	Very large	Very large
Race and ethnicity	Black majority by circa 1670s	Black majority by circa 1710	Growing black minority	Ethnic mix, N.W. Europe, English a minority	Almost all English
Economy	Sugar	Rice	Tobacco	Furs, farms	Farms, fishing, shipbuilding

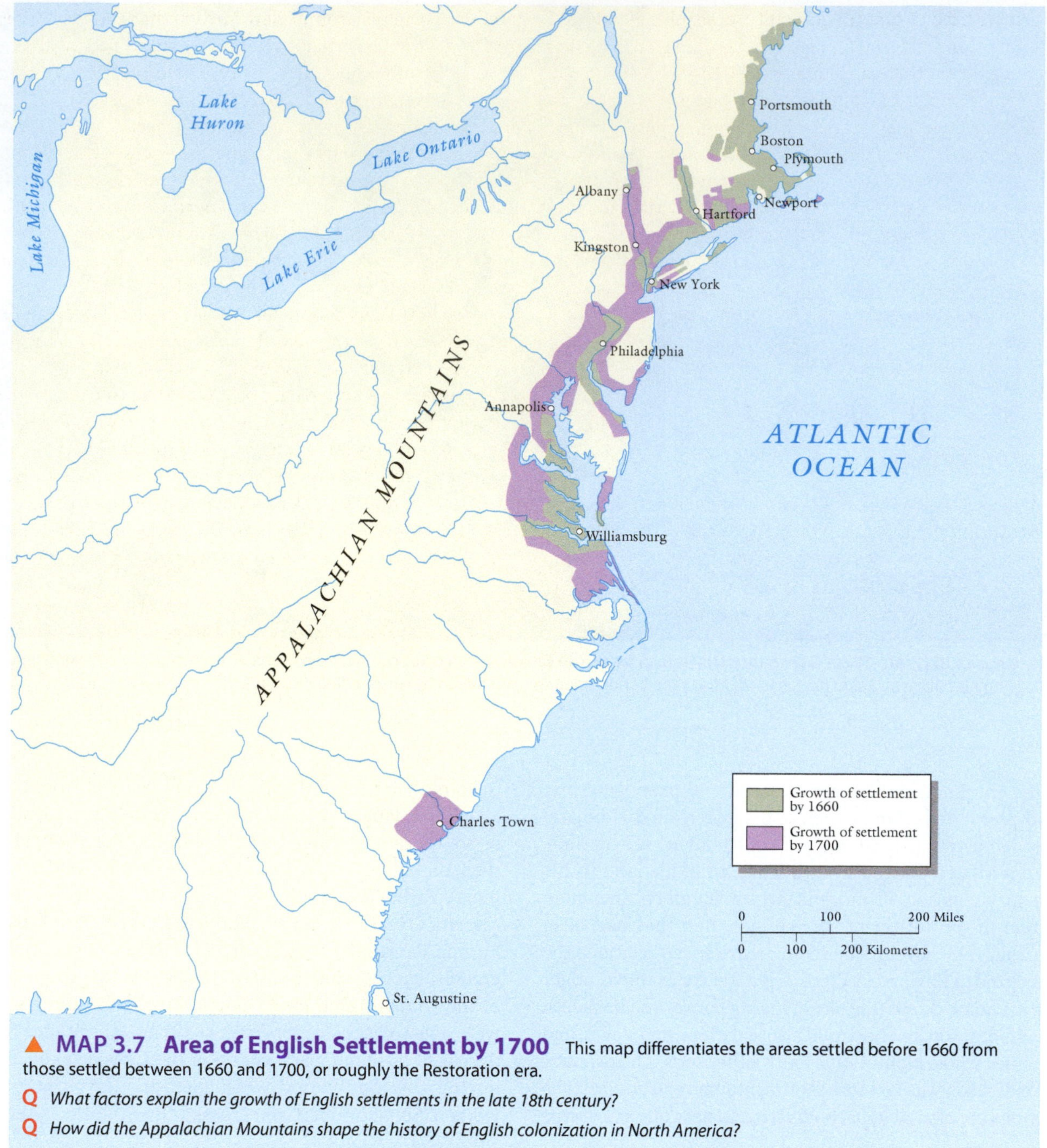

▲ **MAP 3.7 Area of English Settlement by 1700** This map differentiates the areas settled before 1660 from those settled between 1660 and 1700, or roughly the Restoration era.

Q *What factors explain the growth of English settlements in the late 18th century?*

Q *How did the Appalachian Mountains shape the history of English colonization in North America?*

were desperate people who had hit bottom in England. Those who survived in the colonies enjoyed a fantastic chance at upward mobility. By marrying landowners, many won a respectability that was never available to them in England.

English households had become Americanized in the colonies during the earliest years of settlement, as soon as Virginia and Plymouth made land available to nearly all male settlers. By the mid-18th century, the question was whether that system could survive the pressures of a rising population. Social change began to drive households toward English practices. Only expansion onto new lands might enable colonial households to provide equal opportunity for all sons, but probably not for all daughters.

Colonial households were patriarchal. The father protected and cared for his family and hoped to be loved and revered by his wife and children but insisted on being obeyed. A man's local standing depended on his success as a master at home. A mature male was expected to be the master of others. In New England and Pennsylvania, most householders probably thought they were the rough equals of other householders. Above all, a patriarch strove to perpetuate his household into the next generation and to preserve his own independence, or autonomy. Of course, complete independence was impossible. Every household owed small debts or favors to its neighbors, but these temporary obligations seldom compromised a family's standing in the community.

Farmers tried to grow an agricultural surplus, if only as a hedge against drought, storms, and other unpredictable events. Farmers marketed their surplus and used the proceeds to pay taxes or their ministers' salaries and to buy British imports. These arrangements sometimes placed families in short-term debt to merchants, but most farmers and artisans avoided long-term debt. Settlers accepted temporary dependency among freemen—of sons on their parents, indentured servants on their masters, or apprentices and journeymen on master craftsmen. Sons often worked as laborers on local farms, as sailors, or as journeymen craftsmen, provided that such dependence was temporary. A man who became permanently dependent on others lost the respect of his community.

3-4c *The Voluntaristic Ethic, Public Life, and War*

Householders carried their quest for independence into public life. In entering politics and in waging war, their autonomy became an ethic of voluntarism. Few freemen could be coerced into doing something of which they disapproved. Local officials serving without pay frequently ignored orders contrary to their own interests or the interests of their community. Colonists waged wars with short-term volunteers for whom terror against Indian women and children was often the tactic of choice. While Europe was moving toward professional armies and limited wars, the colonists demanded quick and total victories.

Most young men accepted military service only if it suited their future plans. They would serve only under officers they knew, and then for only a single campaign. Few reenlisted. To the exasperation of professional British soldiers, provincials, like Indians, regarded blind obedience to commands as slavery. They did not enlist in order to become soldiers for life. After serving, they used their bonus and their pay, and often the promise of a land grant, to speed their way to becoming householders themselves. Military service, for those who survived, could lead to landownership and an earlier marriage.

3-4d *Spanish and French Counterpoints*

British households—independent, patriarchal, sizable, and often geographically mobile—did not have equivalents elsewhere in North America. In Spanish America, a substantial settler society emerged only in New Mexico, whereas Florida and California were essentially missionary enterprises. As in British America, New Mexico's colonial families were patriarchal and often large, but they were not self-reliant or mobile in the way the British households were. The centralized and urban-oriented Spanish imperial system discouraged the dispersal of population in the countryside—and beyond effective Crown control. Moreover, many Spanish men had both Spanish and native wives, and such intimate ties bound the families to local communities. Finally, the rise of powerful Indian societies around New Mexico made any attempts to extend Spanish settlements into the interior dangerous and virtually impossible. As a result, Spain's settlement frontier never moved far beyond the Rio Grande Valley.

Households in French North America mirrored their British counterparts in some respects; they too were patriarchal and growing. In New France and Louisiana, however, reliance on river transportation and the presence of powerful native societies nearby placed strong constraints on household mobility. This was particularly the case in the St. Lawrence Valley, where the British threat, the seigneurial system, and a centralized imperial administration helped keep the settlers fixed in place. A typical St. Lawrence household had an established relationship with a seigneur through annual charges and obligations, was loyal to the Crown and the governor-general, relied on its local parish as a source for spiritual and social guidance, and provided men to militia companies that protected a shared riverine world against British and Indian attacks. Individual Frenchmen pushed deep into the interior, whereas French families had deep roots in particular places and tended to stay put.

3-4e *Queen Anne's War and the Yamasee War*

The land appetite of the colonial household rather than royal officials drove the expansion of British North America. In the early 18th century, more and more families pushed farther west, looking for cheap land and new economic opportunities. Sons of growing families sought unclaimed farmland and the patriarchal independence it conveyed. Life in the frontier was hard—most farmsteads were far from roads, and isolated—but diminishing prospects in the old communities lured settlers westward. Crown-sponsored exploration and royal charters had launched England's North American empire; locally driven settlement would build it.

The expansion of English settlement did not go unchallenged. The French in the north, the Spaniards in the south, and native peoples across the western frontier monitored the growing English ambitions with alarm (see Map 3.8). When another war broke out in Europe (War of the Spanish Succession) in 1702, English colonists clashed with France, Spain, and Indians from Massachusetts to Florida in a series of conflicts that came to be known as Queen Anne's War.

In 1704, the French and Indians destroyed Deerfield, Massachusetts, in a winter attack and marched most of its people into captivity in Canada. Hundreds of New Englanders from Deerfield and other towns spent months or even years as captives. One of them was Eunice Williams, young daughter of John Williams, the pastor of Deerfield. Refusing to return to New England when the town's captives were released, she remained in Canada, became a Catholic, and married an Indian. Another New England woman who refused to return was Esther Wheelwright, daughter of a prominent Maine family. Captured by the Abenakis, she was taken to New France, where she also refused repatriation, converted to Catholicism, became a nun

(Esther Marie Joseph de L'Enfant Jésus), and finally emerged as mother superior of the Ursuline order in Canada—surely an unlikely career for a Puritan girl.

As the war dragged on, New Englanders twice failed to take Port Royal in Acadia, but a combined British and colonial force finally succeeded in 1710, renaming the colony Nova Scotia. An effort to subdue Quebec the following year met with disaster when many of the British ships ran aground in a treacherous stretch of the St. Lawrence River.

Farther south, the imperial struggle was grimmer and even more tragic (see Map 3.9). The Franciscan missions of Florida were already in decline, but Carolina slavers still targeted mission Indians. Between 1702 and 1704, James Moore, the governor of Carolina, devastated Florida with a large force of Indian allies. The invaders failed to take the Spanish fort of St. Augustine, but wrecked missions, dragged 4,000 women and children into slavery, and drove 9,000 Indians from their homes. Other raiders—British, Creeks, and Yamasees—followed, destroying the remaining Spanish missions in Florida. By the mid-1710s, much of Florida was nearly empty of Indians, and the Spanish presence in the region was confined to St. Augustine and two Gulf Coast outposts, San Marcos and Pensacola.

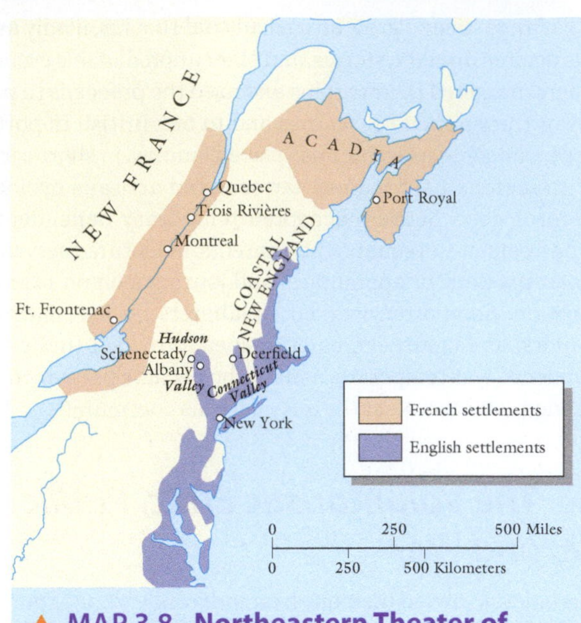

▲ **MAP 3.8 Northeastern Theater of War, 1689–1713** For a quarter of a century, starting with King William's War, the colonies north of the Quaker settlements in the Delaware Valley were locked in a brutal and costly struggle against the French and Indians to their north and west.

Q *Why did the Franco-English wars become so protracted in the Northeast?*

Q *What kind of dangers and opportunities did the colonial wars between England and France introduce to the Indians?*

Esther Wheelwright, c.1763 (oil on canvas), American School, (18th century) / © Massachusetts Historical Society, Boston, MA, USA/ The Bridgeman Art Library

3.11 **Portrait of Esther Wheelwright** Esther Wheelwright (1696–1780), an English Puritan who was captured by the French and Indians during Queen Anne's War, converted to Catholicism and became Sister Esther Marie Joseph de L'Enfant Jésus and eventually mother superior of the Ursuline nuns in the province of Quebec.

Q *What can Esther Wheelwright's life and career teach us about race, gender, identity, and belonging in early 18th-century North America?*

Carolina's greed for Indian slaves and other abuses finally alienated the colony's strongest Indian allies, the Yamasees. Traders frequently abused Indian women, including some of high status, an offense almost unknown within Indian communities. Moreover, the chaos and destruction of the ongoing wars among the British, Spaniards, and their Indian allies undermined the Yamasees' ability to bring slaves and deerskins to Carolina markets, threatening to leave them impoverished and isolated. In 1707, to resolve disputes between traders and Indians, Carolina created the office of Indian agent, which was held first by John Wright and then Thomas Nairne. They belonged to rival factions of Indian traders, and their controversies paralyzed the colony's government. In late 1714, Wright's bloc filed so many lawsuits against Nairne that for six months he could not leave Charleston to address Yamasee grievances. When the exasperated Indians threatened war, the government sent both Nairne and Wright to resolve the crisis in April 1715. Nairne brought a message of peace; Wright privately threatened war, which would most likely lead to enslavement. Appalled and angered, the Yamasees killed both men and all the other traders who had just arrived to collect their debts. Throughout the Southeast, most Indian nations trading with Carolina followed the Yamasees' example, killing nearly all of the colony's experienced traders and launching attacks that almost wrecked the colony. The loose native coalition disintegrated soon, however, allowing South Carolina to organize itself for a counteroffensive. The Yamasees were thrust back and nearly destroyed. Carolina made peace with most of the Indians, and the Yamasees fled as refugees to Florida.

The Yamasee War profoundly changed the Southeast. Carolina split into two separate colonies with their own governments, and both South and North Carolina became royal colonies in 1729, when the disillusioned proprietors sold their interests to the Crown. South and North Carolina also diverged economically and socially. North Carolina's economy continued to revolve around the naval stores industry and small farms, while South Carolina developed a profitable plantation economy. The turmoil of the Yamasee War forced Carolinians to abandon the Indian slave trade that had supported their colonial project for four decades by providing bodies for the lucrative Caribbean slave trade. South Carolina shifted increasingly to rice cultivation and African slavery, deepening its links to the Caribbean colonies that supplied it with slaves. Rice became the colony's mainstay, produced by African slaves who dried tidewater swamps and provided the planters with the technical knowledge of West African rice cultivation. The Yamasee War thus marked the birth of a new economic regime of African slavery and cash crops that would dominate the South until the Civil War. By the 1730s, two-thirds of South Carolina's 30,000 people were African slaves, most toiling on rice plantations.

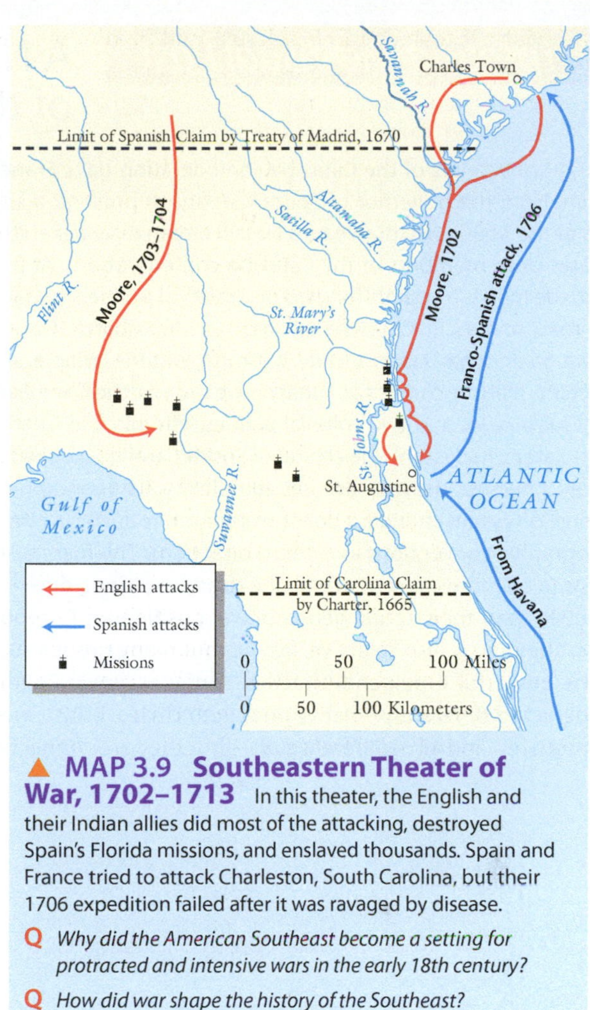

▲ **MAP 3.9 Southeastern Theater of War, 1702–1713** In this theater, the English and their Indian allies did most of the attacking, destroyed Spain's Florida missions, and enslaved thousands. Spain and France tried to attack Charleston, South Carolina, but their 1706 expedition failed after it was ravaged by disease.

Q *Why did the American Southeast become a setting for protracted and intensive wars in the early 18th century?*

Q *How did war shape the history of the Southeast?*

Illustrated London News

3.12 **South Carolina Colonists Enslaving an Indian** The colony enslaved thousands of Indians from 1680 through 1715, a practice that was finally abandoned after the Yamasee War nearly destroyed the colony.

3-4f *The Colonial Rim and the Indigenous Interior*

The wars and their chaotic violence halted the movement of British settlers onto new lands in New England and the Carolinas in the early 18th century. In the wars' aftermath, Maine had only four towns left, while South Carolina struggled to adjust to the rice economy that forced settlers to live in humid, swampy lowlands where malaria, yellow fever, and smallpox were rampant. By 1720, after half a century of existence, South Carolina still had only 5,200 settlers (and 11,800 slaves). In Pennsylvania, Maryland, and Virginia—colonies that had not been deeply involved in the wars—the expansive thrust continued.

Queen Anne's War and the Yamasee War removed some of the major causes of animosity among the rival North American powers, ushering in a "Long Peace" that lasted into the early 1740s. The Yamasee War had ended the highly destabilizing Indian slave trade in the Southeast, while in the Northeast the 1701 Grand Settlement and the ensuing Iroquois neutrality stabilized relations among the French, English, and native nations. Imperial claims over the continent seemed

Interpreting the Visual Past

A Native American Representation of the Colonial Southeast

In 1721, the chiefs of the Catawba confederation gave Francis Nicholson, the governor of South Carolina, a present: a skin map of the Southeast, drawn by a Nasaw Indian mapmaker (the Nasaws were members of the Catawba confederation). At first sight, the map is a straightforward depiction of polities in space. The map names 11 Catawba villages: Casuie, Charra, Nasaw, Nustie, Saxippaha, Succa, Suttirie, Wasmisa, Waterie, Wiapie, and Youchine. It also includes two other native groups, the Cherokees and Chickasaws, and two colonial polities, Virginia and Charles Town (later Charleston), the capital of South Carolina. Looked at closely, however, the map accrues complexity. Its geographical proportions seem strange; it does not conform to such European cartographic conventions as cardinal directions. The mapmaker seems to be more concerned with the relations among different societies than their actual geographical position and proportions. The map is also selective, leaving out many groups such as the powerful Creek and Choctaw confederations. Polities are depicted differently—native ones with circles, British ones with squares, and all in different sizes—but they are connected with a complex web of pathways. There are also three animate entities—two humans and a deer—that may convey symbolic meaning. A caption identifies the smaller human figure as "An Indian a Hunting."

Q *Study carefully what kinds of things this map emphasizes and how it depicts space and the relationships among different societies. Consider each item separately, but also think about how it contributes to the mapmaker's overall message. For example, how does the deer-hunting, musket-carrying Indian embody the interactions between native and colonial societies in the Southeast? And what is the symbol in the lower left corner? Why might the native mapmaker have thought it important to include it?*

Q *The map was probably meant to serve as a social manual that would educate the British on how to behave on the frontier. How do you think the Catawbas expected the British to see and treat native societies?*

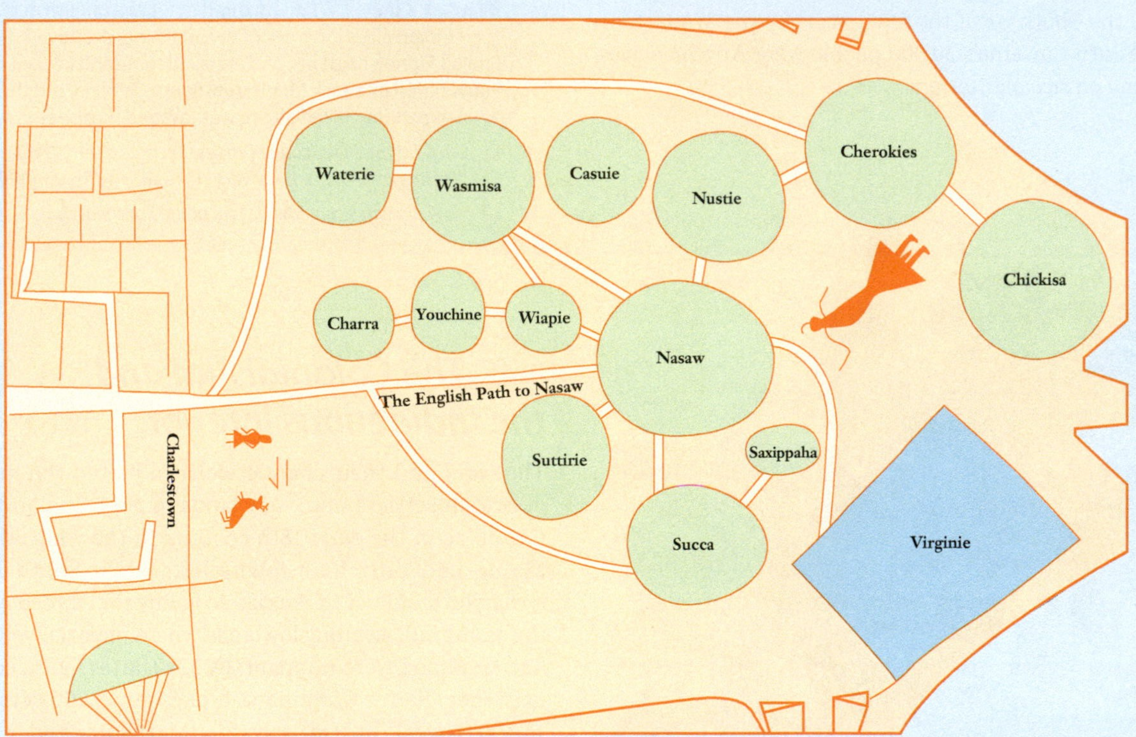

Figure 3.1 **Nasaw Map of the Southeast, 1721.**

to have reached a rough balance. France claimed a massive, triangle-shaped domain that extended from the Mississippi Delta northeastward to Newfoundland and northwestward to the Canadian plains. Spain clung to its Florida bases, but focused increasingly on fortifying its defensive outposts in the Southwest. Britain disputed France's vast claims in the interior, but since its settlements were still confined east of the Appalachians, the issue was yet pressing.

The tidy blocks and lines on European maps concealed a more complex reality, however. In 1720, the Indians still controlled more than 90 percent of the continent and most of the lands claimed by France, Spain, and Britain. In fact, beyond shores and key interior places, Europeans knew very little of North America's geography, and everywhere native nations contested European pretensions of dominance with their presence, borders, and power. French and Spanish outposts were like small islands in oceans of Indians. French Louisiana was deeply dependent on the trade and military support of the many small and large native nations around it. "We can do nothing by ourselves," Louisiana's frustrated French governor would complain as late as 1750, after half a century of colonization. In New Mexico and Texas, the Apaches, Comanches, and other horse-mounted societies raided with virtual impunity the missions and villages that were supposed to denote Spain's imperial authority in the region.

Despite their overwhelming numbers, the British too had to acknowledge the native presence on their western frontiers. The still-powerful Iroquois employed careful play-off politics to check France and Britain's meddling and territorial aspirations, threatening to side with one empire to restrain the other. The Creeks, Cherokees, and Choctaws did the same in the Southeast, pitting the British colonies against French Louisiana and Spain's Florida bases. Less populous and weaker nations relied on smaller-scale political maneuvering to contain European ambitions. They cultivated personal ties with colonial leaders and used cultural brokers to enhance mutual understanding and preserve peaceful relations. Groups like the Catawbas, a small, multiethnic confederation living in the North Carolina Piedmont, mixed deft diplomacy, persuasion, and closely regulated trade to preserve their autonomy and land base. They called the British "nothings," people who lacked kinship ties with native peoples and should therefore rely on the Catawbas to survive. The Catawbas managed to retain a fraction of their ancient homelands, on which they live to this day.

Conclusion

Although much of North America was still under native control in the early 18th century, Spain, France, and Britain had entrenched themselves on the continent. The three imperial powers wanted roughly similar things in North America—territory, prosperity, freedom, opportunities to serve their god better—and they held roughly similar views of the land and its peoples, pronouncing them both wild and in need of improvement. If challenged by natives who refused to submit, the three powers were quick to use violence, as the suppression of a series of Indian rebellions in the 1670s and 1680s demonstrated. But there were also differences, which became increasingly pronounced in the late 17th and early 18th centuries as rivalries over dominance in North America intensified.

Few in number and unable to subdue the Indians, the Spaniards and French both found it necessary to mediate and coexist with native peoples in order to extend their imperial reach. Their settlements remained concentrated along river valleys—Spain's in the upper Rio Grande, France's in the St. Lawrence and the Mississippi—and both strove to expand their spheres of influence into the interior through Indian alliances. By the early 18th century, France was becoming dominant, having erected a sprawling commercial inland empire built on creative Indian diplomacy. Spain's influence in Florida was faltering, and its outposts in the Southwest were surrounded by expanding independent Indians. The Spanish Empire adopted an increasingly defensive stance in North America and began to treat New Mexico and Texas as buffers that would shield the empire's crucial silver-mining districts in northern Mexico against foreign encroachments.

While Spain and France were jockeying for position in the interior, a different kind of empire emerged in the east: The disparate English colonies coalesced into a flourishing, Atlantic-spanning British Empire. The British saw their enterprise as a modern empire of commerce, constitutional liberalism, and Protestantism, which it was. Outsiders—Indians, Africans, and Catholics—saw it as an aggressive settler empire and a vicious racial regime. Increasingly, they also deemed it overwhelming. By 1720, with more than 400,000 settlers in the mainland colonies, the British Empire started to appear uncontainable.

Such ascendancy would have been difficult to imagine half a century earlier, when English America had been a collection of diverse, disagreeing, and autonomous colonies. From the 1670s onward, however, the English government found ways to regulate colonial trade, mostly for the mutual benefit of England and the colonies. Once the Crown gave up its claims to absolute power, both sides discovered much on which they could agree.

Political values in England and the colonies began to converge during and after the Glorious Revolution. Englishmen throughout the empire insisted that the right to property was sacred, that without it liberty could never be secure. They celebrated liberty under law, government by consent, and the toleration of all Protestants. They barred Catholics from succession to the throne and loaded them with severe disabilities of other kinds. In an empire dedicated to "liberty, property, and no popery," Catholics became big losers.

So did Indians and Africans. Racism directed against Indians mostly welled up from below, taking root among ordinary settlers who competed with Indians for land and other resources, and then bore the brunt of Indian reprisals. Colonial elites tried, often ineffectually, to contain this popular rage at Indians that nearly tore apart both New England and Virginia in 1675–1676. By contrast, racism directed against enslaved Africans was typically imposed from above and increasingly enforced by law. Ordinary settlers and Africans knew one another by name, made love, sometimes even married, stole hogs together, ran away together, and even fought together under Nathaniel Bacon's leadership. Class, more than race, separated people from one another. This changed during the late 17th and early 18th centuries when Chesapeake planters replaced indentured servitude with African slavery, brushed aside inequalities among themselves, and erected a new regime of racial slavery and white supremacy.

By the 18th century, the British colonists, despite or perhaps even because of their growing racism, had come to believe they were the freest people on earth. They attributed this fortune to their widespread ownership of land and to the English constitutional principles they had incorporated into their own governments. When George I became king in 1714, they proudly proclaimed their loyalty to the Hanoverian dynasty, which guaranteed a Protestant succession to the British throne. In their minds, the British Empire had become the world's last bastion of liberty.

CHAPTER REVIEW

Review

1. Why did violence erupt between Indians and Europeans in different parts of North America in roughly the same period?
2. How did negotiation, conciliation, and alliance-making shape France's and Spain's Indian policies?
3. What was the Glorious Revolution and how did it change England's North American colonies?
4. Why was the colonial household such an engine of British expansion? Did it give Britain an advantage over its imperial rivals in North America? What limits did Indians impose on the European colonies in the 18th century?

Critical Thinking

1. From the Restoration era to the American Revolution, most Englishmen and colonists understood politics as a perpetual struggle between power and liberty, one in which victory had almost always gone to power. How then was the English empire able to increase both its power and its commitment to liberty over that period?
2. Discuss the changing forms of racism and the role they played in the English colonies between their founding and the Yamasee War.
3. What enabled sparsely settled New France to resist British expansion for more than half a century, whereas Spanish Florida seemed almost helpless against a similar threat?

Identifications

Review your understanding of the following key terms, people, and events for this chapter (terms in bold in text are included in the Glossary).

praying Indians, p. 73
Iroquois League, p. 76
Covenant Chain of Peace, p. 76
Onontio, p. 80
mercantilism, p. 83
balance of trade, p. 83
enumerated commodities, p. 83
Whigs, p. 83
Tories, p. 83
funded national debt, p. 87
entail, p. 91
primogeniture, p. 91

Suggested Readings

Jill Lepore's ***The Name of War: King Philip's War and the Origins of American Identity*** (1998); **Andrew L. Knaut's** ***The Pueblo Revolt of 1680*** (1995); and **Wilcomb Washburn's,** ***The Governor and the Rebel: A History of Bacon's Rebellion in Virginia*** (1957) are all essential to understanding the crisis of the 1670s and 1680s. For the transition to slavery after Bacon's Rebellion, see **Anthony S. Parent, Jr.,** ***Foul Means: The Formation of a Slave Society in Virginia, 1660–1740*** (2003). For a superb study of Native Americans in the English backcountry, see **James H. Merrell,** ***The Indians' New World: The Catawbas and Their Neighbors from European Contact through the Era of Removal*** (1989).

Ian K. Steele, ***The English Atlantic, 1675–1740: An Exploration of Communication and Community*** (1986) is a careful, imaginative, and original analysis of the tumultuous period. For the Dominion of New England and the Glorious Revolution in the colonies, see **Richard R. Johnson,** ***Adjustment to Empire: The New England Colonies, 1675–1715*** (1981); and **John M. Murrin,** "The Menacing Shadow of Louis XIV and the Rage of Jacob Leisler: The Constitutional Ordeal of Seventeenth-Century New York," in **Stephen L. Schechter and Richard B. Bernstein, eds.,** ***New York and the Union: Contributions to the American Constitutional Experience*** (1990), pp. 29–71. The best study of Salem witchcraft, which is also a superb introduction to the Indian wars in northern New England, is **Mary Beth Norton,** ***In the Devil's Snare: The Salem Witchcraft Crisis of 1692*** (2002).

For the French and Spanish colonies and their relations with Native Americans in these critical decades, see especially **Richard White,** ***The Middle Ground: Indians, Empires, and Republics in the Great Lakes Region, 1650–1815*** (1991); **Ramón Gutiérrez,** ***When Jesus Came, the Corn Mothers Went Away: Marriage, Sexuality, and Power in New Mexico, 1500–1846*** (1991); **Daniel H. Usner, Jr.,** ***Indians, Settlers, & Slaves in a Frontier Exchange Economy: The Lower Mississippi Valley before 1783*** (1992); **Alan Gallay,** ***The Indian Slave Trade: The Rise of the English Empire in the American South, 1670–1717*** (2002); **Juliana Barr,** ***Peace Came in the Form of a Woman:***

Indians and Spaniards in the Texas Borderlands (2007); **Ned Blackhawk,** ***Violence over the Land: Indian and Empires in the early American West*** (2007); **Michael Witgen,** ***An Infinity of Nations: How the Native New World Shaped Early North America*** (2012); and **Brett Rushforth,** ***The Bonds of Alliance: Indigenous and Atlantic Slaveries in New France*** (2012). For a ground-breaking study of New England's involvement in Indian slave trade, see **Wendy Warren,** ***New England Bound: Slavery and Colonization in Early America*** (2016).

On the householder economy in English North America, see **Laurel Thatcher Ulrich's** ***Good Wives: Images and Reality in the Lives of Women in Northern New England*** (1982), and **Mary M. Schweitzer,** ***Custom and Contract: Household, Government, and the Economy in Colonial Pennsylvania*** (1987).

4 Provincial America and the Struggle for a Continent, 1720–1763

B Christopher/Alamy Stock Photo

4.1 **George Washington in the Uniform of a Colonel of the Virginia Regiment** Charles Willson Peale's 1772 portrait is the earliest recorded image of Washington. It is telling that, amidst the American revolutionary crisis, he chose to be painted in the uniform that he wore as a provincial officer in the French and Indian War more than a decade earlier. Like other American colonists, Washington took great pride in his British identity by the mid-18th century.

THE BRITISH COLONISTS, who thought they were the freest people on earth, faced a growing dilemma in the 18th century. To maintain the opportunity that settlers had come to expect, the colonies had to expand onto new lands. But provincial society also emulated the cultural values of Great Britain—its architecture, polite learning, religion, and politics. Relentless expansion made this commitment difficult because new settlements were not genteel. The two goals often worked at cross-purposes. An anglicized province would become more hierarchical than the colonies had been so far and might not even try to provide a rough equality of opportunity. The settlers hoped to sustain both goals, an effort that brought renewed conflict with their neighbors—the Indians, the Spanish, and the French.

When the British again went to war against Spain and France after 1739, the settlers joined in the struggle and declared that liberty itself was at stake. Less fortunate people among them disagreed. Slaves in the southern colonies saw Spain, not Britain, as their hope for liberty. In the eastern woodlands, most Indians identified France, not Britain, as the one possible ally that might remain committed to their survival and independence. ■

4-1 Expansion versus Anglicization

Q *In what ways did American colonists attempt to imitate British society in the 18th century?*

In the 18th century, as the British colonists sought to emulate their homeland, many of the institutions and material goods they had left behind in the 17th century began to reappear, a process known to historians today as **anglicization**. After 1740, for example, imports of British goods grew spectacularly. The gentry, merchants, and professionals dressed in the latest London fashions and embraced the capital's standards of taste and elegance. Southern planters erected "big houses," such as Mount Vernon, built by Lawrence Washington and bequeathed to his half-brother George. In Boston, on Beacon Hill, the merchant Thomas Hancock erected a stylish residence that later passed to his nephew John. Newspapers and learned professions based on English models proliferated after 1700, and colonial seaports began to resemble Bristol and other provincial ports in England.

But the population of British North America doubled every 25 years. Each generation required as many new colleges, ministers, lawyers, physicians, craftsmen, printers, sailors, and unskilled laborers as all the preceding generations combined. Without them, standards of "civility" would decline. Colonial institutions had to grow to meet these needs. As the 18th century progressed, the colonies became the scene of a contest between the unrelenting pace of raw expansion and these newer, anglicizing tendencies.

The southern colonies, which looked to England to satisfy their needs for skilled talent, could no longer attract as many people as they needed. In 1700, for example, Oxford and Cambridge universities in England had managed to meet the colonies' demand for Anglican clergymen, most of whom went to the southern provinces. By 1750, the colonial demand far exceeded what stagnant Oxford and Cambridge could supply, and the colonies were also importing Scottish and Irish clergy. Before long, those sources also proved inadequate. By contrast, northern colonies trained their own ministers, lawyers, and doctors in their own colleges, as well as their own skilled craftsmen through apprenticeships. Although still colonies, they were becoming America's first modernizing societies. They learned to do for themselves what Britain did for the southern colonies.

Much of this change occurred during prolonged periods of warfare. By midcentury, the wars were becoming a titanic struggle for control of the North American continent. Indians gradually realized that they would be the ultimate victims of British victory. Constant expansion for the settlers meant unending retreat for them.

4-1a *Threats to Householder Autonomy*

As population rose, some families acquired more prestige than others. Before 1700, farmers and small planters often sat in colonial assemblies. After 1700, the assemblies grew much more slowly than the overall population. In the five colonies from New York to Maryland, their size remained almost unchanged despite enormous population growth. Those active in public life above the local level were likely to be gentlemen who performed no manual labor. They had greater wealth, a more impressive lineage, and a better education than farmers or craftsmen. But unlike members of Parliament, few of them enjoyed a patron–client relationship with the voters. In England, one or two families dominated each of the "pocket boroughs" that elected most members. In the colonies, most voters remained independent.

By midcentury, despite the high value that colonists placed on householder autonomy, patterns of dependency were beginning to emerge. In tidewater Virginia by 1760, about 80 percent of the land was entailed. That is, the landowner could not divide or sell the estate but had to bequeath it intact to his heir. Younger sons had to look west for a landed inheritance. In one Maryland county, 27 percent of the householders were tenants who worked small tracts of land without slaves, or were men who owned a slave or two but had no claim to land. Such families could not satisfy the ambitions of all their children. In Pennsylvania's Chester County, a new class of married farm laborers arose. Their employers, without granting them

CHRONOLOGY

1690	Massachusetts invents fiat money
1704	*Boston News-Letter founded*
1712	Slaves revolt in New York City
1716	Spanish begin to settle in Texas
1718	Beginning of Scots-Irish emigration to North America
1721	Boylston introduces smallpox inoculation in Boston
1730	Three hundred slaves revolt in Virginia, and 29 are hanged
1732	Georgia charter granted by Parliament
1733	Molasses Act passed
1734	Edwards launches massive religious revival in the Connecticut Valley
1735	Zenger acquitted of seditious libel in New York
1738	Spanish found Mose in Florida
1739	Slaves revolt in Stono, South Carolina
1739–1741	Whitefield launches Great Awakening
1741	New York slave conspiracy trials lead to 35 executions
1745	New England volunteers take Louisbourg
1747	Ohio Company of Virginia founded • Anti-impressment rioters in Boston resist Royal Navy
1750	Massachusetts converts from paper money to silver
1754	Washington attacks French patrol near the forks of the Ohio River • Albany Congress proposes plan for colonial union
1755	Braddock suffers disaster near Fort Duquesne • British expel Acadians from Nova Scotia
1756–1757	Loudoun antagonizes the colonies as commander in chief
1756	French take Oswego
1757	French take Fort William Henry • Pitt becomes Britain's war minister
1758	British take Fort Duquesne, Louisbourg, and Fort Frontenac • French repel British at Ticonderoga
1759	British take Ticonderoga and Crown Point • Wolfe dies taking Quebec; Montcalm also killed
1760	Montreal falls; Canada surrenders to the British
1760–1761	Cherokee War devastates South Carolina backcountry
1762	Spain enters war, loses Havana and Manila
1763	Peace of Paris ends Seven Years' War

title or lease, let them use a small patch of land on which they could build a cottage and raise some food. Called "inmates" in Chester County records (or "cottagers" in England), such people made up 25 percent of the county population. Tenants on New York manors had to accept higher rents and shorter leases after 1750. In one parish in Ipswich, Massachusetts, half the farmers had land enough for only some of their sons by 1760.

Families that could not provide for all of their children reverted toward English social norms. In Connecticut, from the 1750s to the 1770s, about 75 percent of eligible sons inherited some land, but for daughters the rate fell from 44 percent to 34 percent. When a father could not support all his sons, he favored the eldest over younger sons. The younger sons, in turn, took up a trade or headed for the frontier. To increase their resources and sustain family autonomy, many New England farmers added a craft or two to the household. The 300 families of Haverhill, Massachusetts, supported 44 workshops and 19 mills by 1767. In Northampton, more than one-third of all farming families also practiced a craft. The goal of independence continued to exercise great power, but it was under siege.

4-1b *Anglicizing the Role of Women*

The changing role of women provides a striking example of the anglicizing tendencies of the 18th century. When they married, most women received a **dowry** from their father, usually in cash or goods, not land. Under the common-law doctrine of **coverture**, the legal personality of the husband "covered" his wife, and he made all legally binding decisions. If he died first, his widow was entitled to **dower rights**, usually one-third of the estate.

Women in many, perhaps most, households had to work harder to maintain the family's status—at the spinning wheel, for example. New England women did virtually all of the region's weaving, which was a male occupation in Britain and in other colonies. Yet, women were becoming more English in other ways, thus reversing some earlier trends. Until 1700, many Chesapeake widows inherited all of their husbands' property and administered their own estates. After 1700, such arrangements were rare. In the Hudson Valley, Dutch law had been much more generous than English common law in bestowing property rights on women, but during the 18th century, English law gradually prevailed. In New England, too, as Puritan intensity waned, women suffered losses. Before 1700, courts often punished men for sexual offenses, such as fornication, and many men pleaded guilty and accepted their sentences. After 1700, almost no man would plead guilty, except to making love to his wife before their wedding day. But to avoid a small fine, some husbands humiliated their wives by denying that charge, even if their wives had already pleaded guilty after giving birth to a child that had obviously been conceived before marriage. Courts rarely convicted men of sex offenses, not even serious crimes such as rape. The European double standard of sexual behavior, which punished women for their indiscretions while tolerating male infractions, had been in some jeopardy under the Puritan regime. It now revived.

4-2 Expansion, Immigration, and Regional Differentiation

Q *What were the principal differences between the populations and economies of the three major colonial regions, the South, the mid-Atlantic, and New England?*

After 1715, settled portions of North America enjoyed their longest era of peace since their founding. Until midcentury, people poured into these areas, usually without provoking the strong Indian nations of the interior. As the colonies expanded, they evolved into distinct regions, but only New Englanders acquired a self-conscious sense of regional identity before independence.

Renewed immigration, particularly of unfree migrants, drove much of the postwar expansion. After 1730, the flow became enormous. In that year, about 630,000 settlers and slaves lived in the mainland colonies. By 1775, another 248,000 Africans and 284,000 Europeans had landed, including 50,000 British convicts, shipped mostly to Maryland and Virginia, where they served long indentures. All told, by the onset of the American Revolutionary War in 1775, approximately three-fourths of all immigrants to the 13 mainland colonies arrived as slaves, servants, convicts, or in some other unfree status. During this period, the African slave trade to North America reached its peak. European migration decisively outweighed the influx of slaves only after 1763.

4-2a *Emergence of the Old South*

The forced migration of enslaved Africans to North America grew out of the larger Atlantic slave trade. Between 1519 and 1867, the dates of the first and last known transatlantic slave voyages directly from Africa, Europeans enslaved and carried upwards of 12.5 million Africans to the Western Hemisphere. (More than 1 million slaves perished during the **Middle Passage** across the Atlantic Ocean.) During the colonial era, the vast majority of slaves—about 90 percent—were taken to Brazil or the West Indies, both sugar-producing regions. Although each of Britain's 13 mainland colonies had slavery, only the southern colonies bore some resemblance to the slave societies of Brazil and the Caribbean sugar islands.

Almost 90 percent of the slaves in British North America went to the southern colonies. At least 84,000 went to Charleston, 70,000 to Virginia, and 25,000 to Maryland. One-eighth of the slaves went to northern colonies. About 80 percent of the slaves arrived from Africa on overcrowded, stinking British-owned vessels. Most of the rest came, a few at a time, from the West Indies on smaller New England ships.

This massive influx created the Old South, a society consisting of wealthy slaveholding planters, a much larger class of small planters, and tens of thousands of slaves. By 1720, slaves made up 70 percent of South Carolina's population. By 1740, they were 40 percent of Virginia's and 30 percent of Maryland's. (In comparison, slaves comprised 90 percent of Jamaica's population.) Slaves did most of the manual labor in the southern colonies, and their arrival transformed the social structure. In 1700, most members of Virginia's House of Burgesses were small planters who raised tobacco with a few indentured servants and perhaps a slave or two. After 1730, the typical burgess was a great planter who owned at least 20 slaves. And by 1750, the rice planters of South Carolina were richer than any other group in British North America. Tobacco and rice planters had few contacts with each other, except in North Carolina, where they did not get along. They did not yet think of themselves as "southerners."

The life of slaves in the upper South (Maryland, Virginia, and the Albemarle region of North Carolina) differed considerably from that of slaves in the lower South (from Cape Fear in North Carolina through South Carolina and eventually Georgia). Chesapeake tobacco planters organized their enslaved labor into a **gang system**, groups of slaves closely supervised and disciplined by a white overseer. Weather permitting, owners kept their slaves in the fields all day. To make their plantations more self-sufficient, they also trained perhaps 10 percent of them as skilled artisans. The planters, who saw themselves as benevolent paternalists, encouraged family life among their slaves, who by the 1720s were achieving a rate of reproduction almost equal to that of the settlers. Slaveholders justified brutal whippings as fatherly corrections of members of their household.

Paternalism even extended to religion. In the 1720s, for the first time on any significant scale, many Virginia planters began to urge their slaves to convert to Christianity. At first, only adults who had a good command of the catechism, which they had to memorize because literacy for them was illegal, were accepted into the church, but by the 1730s, growing numbers of infants were baptized. These efforts expanded despite a massive slave uprising. A rumor spread that the British government had promised freedom to any slave who converted but that the colony was suppressing the news. In September 1730, about 300 slaves tried to escape through the Great Dismal Swamp. The planters hired Indians to track them, crushed the rebels, and hanged 29 of them. Yet, the conversions continued to gain momentum, mostly, it seems, because planters hoped that Christianized slaves would be more dutiful.

South Carolina planters also began with paternalistic goals, but the rice swamps and mosquitoes defeated them. Whites supervising slave gangs in rice fields usually caught malaria. Although seldom fatal, malaria left its victims vulnerable to other diseases that often did kill them. Many planters relocated their big houses to higher ground, at a safe distance from the fields. With few exceptions, they made no efforts to Christianize their laborers.

Africans fared much better than whites in marshy rice fields. (Modern medicine has shown that many Africans possess a **sickle cell** in their blood that protects against malaria, but it can expose their children to a deadly form of inherited anemia.) As the ability of Africans to resist malaria became evident, Carolina planters seldom ventured into the rice fields and became less paternalistic than their Virginia counterparts except toward their household servants. After midcentury, many chose to spend their summers in Charleston or in

The Granger Collection, NYC

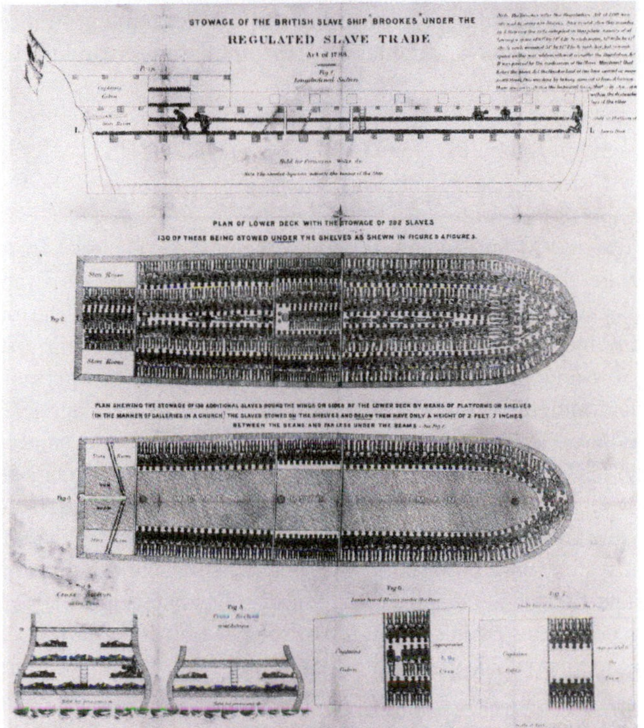

Snark/Art Resource, NY

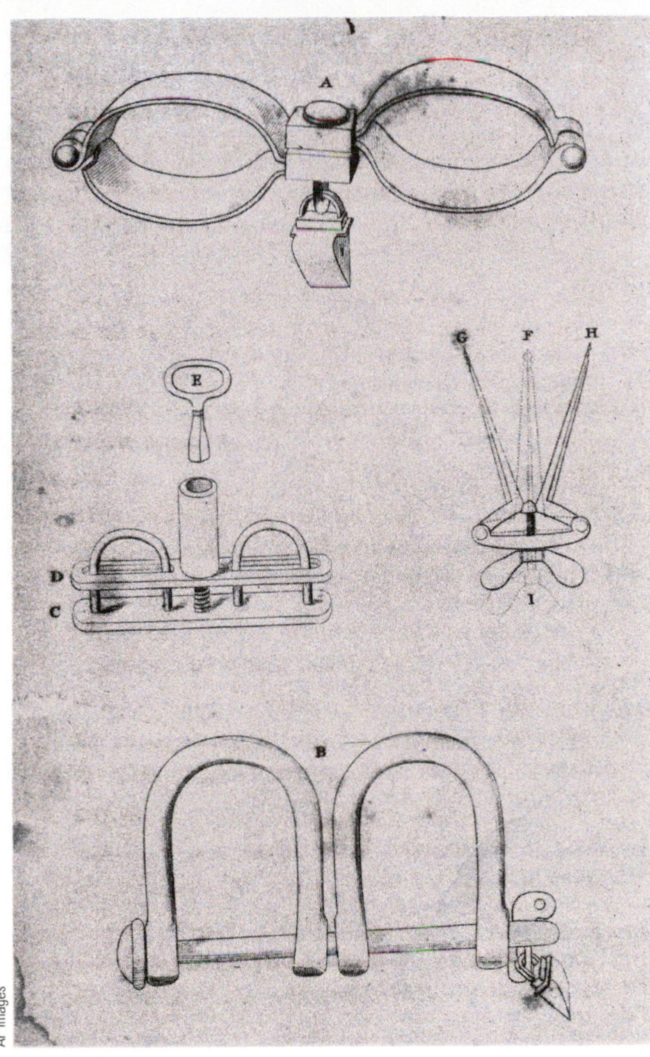

AP Images

4.2a (top left), 4.2b (bottom left), and 4.2c (right) **Britain's African Slave Trade at Its Peak** **(a)** African middlemen on the coast launched expeditions ever deeper into the interior to capture slaves, preferably young men, usually yoked together in a coffle, and marched often hundreds of miles to ships going to America. Many died along the way. **(b)** The captives were packed aboard slave ships, often so tightly that they could scarcely move and had to inhale the stench and humiliation of their own human waste. The most famous illustration of such a ship, the *Brooks* of Liverpool, was published by antislavery advocates in London in 1789 and gave a tremendous boost to what became Britain's abolitionist movement. **(c)** Cruel Instruments of Restraint. Aboard ship, the captives' wrists (top) and ankles (bottom) were shackled. The thumbscrew (middle, left) was used to torture rebellious slaves, and the speculum oris (middle, right) to force open the mouths of slaves who refused to eat. Slaves who died were dumped at sea. Some living slaves who jumped overboard to escape their fate in America were eaten by sharks, which had learned to follow slave ships.

Q *How did the cruel methods and tools of the slave trade and Middle Passage begin to define enslaved Africans as property and not people even before they reached the western hemisphere?*

homes on high ground in the interior. Some even sailed off to Newport, Rhode Island.

This situation altered work patterns. To get local manufactures, planters relied on white artisans in Charleston, many of whom bought or leased slaves, who then did most of the actual work. To produce rice, planters devised the **task system**. Slaves had to finish certain assignments each day, but then their time was their own. They used this free time to raise crops, hunt, or fish, activities that enabled them to create their own largely invisible economy.

Thus, while many Chesapeake slaves were becoming skilled artisans, South Carolina's plantation slaves were heading in the other direction. Before rice became the colony's staple, they had performed numerous tasks, but the huge profits from rice now condemned nearly all of them to extremely unpleasant labor in the marshes, although it, in turn, freed them from direct oversight by their masters. Rice culture produced low rates of African reproduction. Yet, slaves preferred it to gang labor. It gave them more control over their own lives.

The task system also slowed assimilation into the British world. African words and customs survived longer in South Carolina than in the Chesapeake colonies. Newly imported slaves spoke **Gullah**, originally a pidgin language (that is, a simple second language that enabled people from different cultures to communicate). Gullah began with phrases common to many West African languages, gradually added English words, and became the natural language of later generations.

South Carolina's enslaved population failed to grow by natural increase until perhaps the 1770s, a half-century later than in the tobacco colonies. Even South Carolina planters had difficulty replacing themselves before 1760. But by the Revolution, the American South was becoming the world's only self-sustaining slave society. Nowhere else could colonies with staple crops reproduce their enslaved labor force without continuous imports from Africa.

Slavery required brute force to sustain everywhere it took hold. Slaves convicted of arson were often burned at the stake, an unthinkable punishment for a white person. Whippings were frequent, with the master or overseer setting the number of stripes. In South Carolina, one overseer killed five slaves in two or three years before 1712. When one slave fell asleep and lost a parcel of rice in the river, the overseer chained him, whipped him twice a day, refused to give him food, and confined him at night in a "hellish Machine contrived by him into the Shape of a Coffin where [he] could not stir." The victim finally killed himself.

If such extreme cruelty was rare, random acts of violence were common and, from a slave's perspective, unpredictable. In Virginia, William Byrd II was one of the most refined settlers in the colony. His diary reveals that when he and his wife Lucy disagreed, the slaves could suffer. "My wife and I had a terrible quarrel about whipping Eugene while Mr. Mumford was there but she had a mind to show her authority before company but I would not suffer it, which she took very ill." This time Eugene was spared, but slaves were not always so lucky. On another occasion, "My wife caused Prue to be whipped violently notwithstanding I desired not, which provoked me to have Anaka whipped likewise who had deserved it much more, on which my wife flew into such a passion she hoped she would be revenged of me." This time both slaves were whipped. House servants must have dreaded days that Byrd spent in Williamsburg, leaving Lucy in charge of the plantation.

The southern colonies prospered in the 18th century by exchanging their staple crops for British imports. By midcentury, much of this trade had been taken over by Scots. Glasgow became the leading tobacco port of the Atlantic. Tobacco profits remained precarious before 1730 but then improved in later decades, partly because Virginia guaranteed a high-quality leaf by passing an inspection law in 1730 (Maryland followed suit in 1747), and partly because a tobacco contract between Britain and France brought lucrative revenues to both governments and opened up a vast continental market for Chesapeake planters. By 1770, more than 90 percent of their tobacco was reexported to Europe from Britain.

Other exports and new crafts also contributed to rising prosperity. South Carolina continued to export provisions to the sugar islands and deerskins to Britain. Indigo, used as a dye by the British textile industry, received a cash bounty from Parliament and emerged at midcentury as a second staple crop, pioneered by a woman planter, Eliza Lucas Pinckney. North Carolina, where the population increased fivefold between 1720 and 1760 and more than doubled again by 1775, sold naval stores (pitch, resin, turpentine) to British shipbuilders. Many Chesapeake planters turned to wheat as a second cash crop. It required mills to grind it into flour, barrels in which to pack it, and ships to carry it away. It did for the Chesapeake what tobacco had failed to do: It created cities. Norfolk and Baltimore had nearly 10,000 people by 1775, and smaller cities, such as Alexandria and Georgetown, also thrived. Shipbuilding, linked to the export of wheat, became a major Chesapeake industry.

4-2b *The Mid-Atlantic Colonies: The "Best Poor Man's Country"*

The mid-Atlantic colonies had been pluralistic societies from the start. Immigration added to this ethnic and religious diversity after 1700. The region had the most prosperous family farms in America and, by 1760, the two largest cities, Philadelphia and New York. Pennsylvania outpaced New York in the competition for immigrants. In the 1680s and 1690s, New York governors had granted some political supporters enormous manorial estates in the Hudson Valley that discouraged immigration. As late as 1750, the small colony of New Jersey had as many settlers as New York but fewer slaves. Pennsylvania's growth exploded, driven by both natural increase and the surge of immigration. The 12th of 13 colonies to be founded, Pennsylvania was the second most populous by 1770, surpassed only by Virginia.

After 1720, Ireland and Germany replaced England as the main source of voluntary immigrants. About 70 percent of Ireland's emigrants came from Ulster. They were Presbyterians whose forebears had come to Ireland from Scotland in the 17th century. (Historians now call them the Scots-Irish, a term seldom used at the time.) Most left Ireland to avoid an increase in rents and to enjoy greater trading privileges than Parliament had allowed them. Most Ulster immigrants headed for the Delaware Valley. Maybe 30 percent of Irish immigrants came from southern Ireland. Most were Catholics, but perhaps one-fourth were Anglicans. Roughly 80,000 Catholic and Protestant Irish reached the Delaware Valley before 1776.

Nearly 85,000 free and unfree immigrants were Germans. Many arrived as **redemptioners**, a new form of indentured service attractive to married couples because it allowed families to find and bind themselves to the same master. After completing their service, most streamed into the interior of Pennsylvania, where by 1750 Germans outnumbered the original English and Welsh settlers. Others moved on to the southern backcountry with the Irish.

These colonies grew excellent wheat and built their own ships to carry it abroad. At first, New York flour outsold

Pennsylvania's, but Pennsylvania gained the edge in the 1720s after it instituted a system of public inspection and quality control. When Europe's population surged after 1740, the middle colonies shipped flour across the Atlantic. Around 1760, both Philadelphia and New York City overtook Boston's stagnant population of 15,000. Philadelphia, with 32,000 people, was the largest city in British North America by 1775.

4-2c *The Backcountry*

Many Scots-Irish, and some Germans, pushed west into the mountains and up the river valleys into the interior parts of Virginia and the Carolinas. In South Carolina, about 100 miles of pine barrens separated these backcountry settlements from the coastal plantations. Most English-speaking colonists were immigrants from Ulster, northern England, or lowland Scotland, who brought their folkways with them and soon gave the region its own distinctive culture. Although most of them farmed, many hunted or raised cattle. Unlike the coastal settlements, the backcountry had no newspapers, few clergymen or other professionals, and little elegance. South Carolina's backcountry had almost no government. A visiting Anglican clergyman bemoaned "the abandon'd Morals and profligate Principles" of the settlers. Refined easterners found the backcountry frightening. Clannish and violent, backcountry settlers drank heavily and hated Indians. By the 1750s, the situation grew tense in Pennsylvania, where the Quaker assembly insisted on handling differences with the Indians through peaceful negotiations. Once war broke out, most backcountry men demanded their extermination. Virginia and South Carolina faced similar tensions.

4-2d *New England: A Faltering Economy and Paper Money*

New England, a land of farmers, fishermen, lumberjacks, shipwrights, and merchants, still considered itself more pious than the rest of the British Empire, but the region faced serious problems. Few immigrants went there. In fact, since about 1660, more people had been leaving the region, mostly for New York and New Jersey, than had been arriving.

New England's relative isolation in the 17th century began to have negative consequences after 1700. Life expectancy declined as diseases from Europe, especially smallpox and diphtheria, invaded the region. The first settlers had left them behind, but lack of exposure in childhood made later generations vulnerable. When smallpox threatened to devastate Boston in 1721, Zabdiel Boylston, a self-taught doctor who drew on Muslim examples, began inoculating people with the disease, believing that healthy ones would survive the injection and become immune. Although the city's leading physicians opposed the experiment as too risky, it worked and soon became a regular feature of public health in many colonies. Even so, a diphtheria epidemic in the 1730s and high military losses after 1740 took their toll. New England's rate of population growth fell behind that of other regions.

After peace returned in 1713, New England's economy weakened. The region had prospered in the 17th century, mostly by exporting cod, grain, cattle, and barrel staves to the West Indies. But after 1700, declining wheat yields left the Yankees struggling to feed themselves, much less others. They compensated by opening new markets in the lucrative French sugar islands, sending fish and forest products to the islands in exchange for molasses, which they used as a sweetener (cheaper than sugar) or distilled into rum. British West Indian planters, alarmed by the flood of French molasses, urged Parliament to stamp out New England's trade with the French islands. Parliament passed the Molasses Act of 1733, which placed a prohibitive duty on all foreign molasses. Strictly enforced, the act would have strangled New England trade; instead, bribery and smuggling kept the molasses flowing.

Shipbuilding gave New England most of its leverage in the Atlantic economy. Yankees built more ships than all of the other colonies combined. New England ships earned enough from freight in most years to offset trade losses, but Boston merchants often had to scramble to pay for their imports. New England ran unfavorable balances with nearly every trading partner, especially England. Yankees imported many British products but produced little that Britain cared to buy. Whale oil, used in lamps, was an exception. A thriving whaling industry emerged on the island of Nantucket, but trade with the mid-Atlantic and Chesapeake colonies was not profitable. Settlers there eagerly bought rum and a few slaves from Yankee vessels that stopped on their way back from the West Indies. Newport became deeply involved in slave trading along the African coast. That traffic never supplied a large percentage of North America's slaves, but it contributed greatly to Newport's growth.

New England's experience with paper money illustrates these economic difficulties. In response to a military emergency in 1690, Massachusetts invented **fiat money**—that is, paper money backed, not by silver or gold, but only by the government's promise to accept it in payment of taxes. This system worked well enough to prompt most other colonies to do likewise, but serious depreciation set in after the Treaty of Utrecht in 1713.

The declining value of money touched off a fierce debate that raged from 1714 until 1750. Creditors and members of Parliament attacked paper money as fraudulent: Only gold and silver, they claimed, had real value. Defenders retorted that, in most other colonies, paper was holding its value. The problem, they insisted, lay with the New England economy, which could not generate enough exports to pay for the region's imports. The elimination of paper, they warned, would only deepen the region's problems. War disrupted shipping in the 1740s, and military expenditures sent New England currency to a new low. In 1748, Parliament agreed to reimburse Massachusetts for these expenses, but at an earlier exchange rate. Governor William Shirley and House Speaker Thomas Hutchinson, an outspoken opponent of paper money, persuaded a skeptical legislature to use the grant to retire all paper and convert to silver money.

That decision was a drastic example of anglicization. Although fiat money was the colony's invention, Massachusetts repudiated its offspring in 1750 in favor of

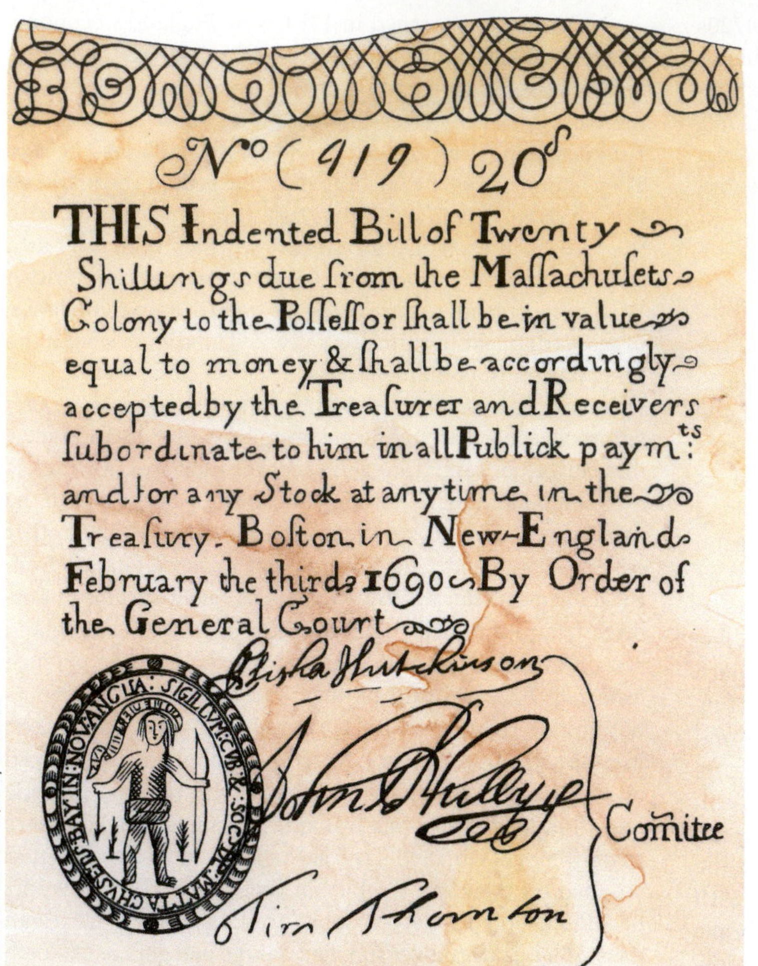

No (919) 20s

THIS Indented Bill of Twenty Shillings due from the Maſſachuſets Colony to the Poſſeſſor ſhall be in value equal to money & ſhall be accordingly accepted by the Treaſurer and Receivers ſubordinate to him in all Publick paym[ts]: and for any Stock at any time in the Treaſury. Boſton in New-England February the third 1690 By Order of the General Court

Eliſha Hutchinſon
John Phillips } Comitee
Tim Thornton

North Wind Picture Archives/Alamy Stock Photo

4.3 **First American Paper Money, Massachusetts (1690)** Facing daunting military costs during King William's War, Massachusetts issued the first paper money in the western world in 1690. Other colonies soon followed suit, creating a challenge for Parliament that lasted until American independence.

British methods of public finance. But as Hutchinson's critics had warned, silver gravitated to Boston and then to London to pay for imports. Lacking sufficient currency, New England's economy fell into a deep recession in 1750. It did not revive until the next French war.

4-3 Anglicizing Provincial America

What was the Enlightenment and how did it shape the 18th-century colonies?

Forms of production had made American colonial regions diverse. They became more alike through what they imported from Britain. Although each region exported its own distinctive products, patterns of consumption became quite similar throughout the colonies. In the mid-1740s, the mainland colonies and the West Indies consumed almost identical amounts of British imports. A decade later, the mainland provinces had forged ahead by a margin of 2 to 1. Their ability to consume ever-larger quantities of British goods was making the mainland colonies more valuable than the sugar islands to the empire. The mainland also welcomed English revivalists and absorbed much of Britain's intellectual and political culture.

4-3a *The World of Print*

Few 17th-century American settlers owned books and, except in New England, even fewer engaged in the intellectual debates of the day. For most of the century, only Massachusetts had printing presses, first in Cambridge to serve Harvard College, the clergy, and the government, and then in Boston beginning in 1674. For the next century, Boston remained the print capital of North America. In the 1680s, William Bradford became Philadelphia's first printer, but he soon moved to New York. By 1740, Boston had eight printers; Philadelphia and New York had two apiece. No other community had more than one.

Not surprisingly, Boston also led the way in newspaper publishing. John Campbell, the city's postmaster, established the *Boston News-Letter* in 1704. By the early 1720s, two more papers had opened in Boston. Philadelphia and New York City had each acquired one. The *South Carolina Gazette* was founded in Charleston in 1732 and the *Virginia Gazette* in Williamsburg in 1736. Benjamin Franklin took charge of the *Pennsylvania Gazette* in 1729, and **John Peter Zenger** launched the controversial *New York Weekly Journal* in 1733 and won a major victory for freedom of the press when a jury acquitted him of seditious libel, the common-law crime of criticizing government officials.

Newspapers helped spread the **Enlightenment**—a broad intellectual movement that applied reason to a wide range

Bettmann/Corbis

4.4 An 18th-Century Printing Press This printing press resembles the one that James Franklin brought to Boston from London in 1717. Benjamin, his younger brother and apprentice, used the press to learn the trade of a printer.

Q *Despite its clear connection to the Enlightenment, why was printing still considered an artisanal (ungenteel) craft in the 18th century?*

of human affairs—from Europe to North America. Colonial papers were weeklies that devoted their space to European matters. Before midcentury, they rarely reported local news because they assumed their readers already knew it. At first, they merely reprinted items from the *London Gazette.* Beginning in the 1720s, however, the *New England Courant,* under James Franklin, began to reprint Richard Steele's essays from the *Spectator;* Joseph Addison's pieces from the *Tatler;* and the angry, polemical writings, mostly aimed at religious bigotry and political and financial corruption, of "Cato," a pen name used jointly by John Trenchard and Thomas Gordon. *Cato's Letters* became immensely popular among colonists.

Benjamin Franklin personified the Enlightenment values that the newspapers were spreading. As a boy, although raised in Puritan Boston, he skipped church on Sundays to read Addison and Steele and to perfect his prose style. As a young printer with his brother's *New England Courant* in the 1720s, he helped publish the writings of John Checkley, an Anglican apologist whom the courts twice prosecuted in vain attempts to silence him. Franklin joined the Church of England after moving to Philadelphia. After 1729, he made his *Pennsylvania Gazette* the best edited and most widely read paper in America.

Franklin always sought ways to improve society. In 1727, he helped found the Junto, a workingman's debating society that met weekly to discuss literary and philosophical questions. It later evolved into the American Philosophical Society, which still thrives near Independence Hall. He was also a founder of North America's first Masonic lodge in 1730, the Library Company of Philadelphia a year later, the Union Fire Company in 1736, the Philadelphia Hospital in 1751, and an academy that became the College of Philadelphia (now the University of Pennsylvania) in the 1750s. But his greatest fame arose from his ingenious electrical experiments. He also invented the Franklin stove (much more efficient than a fireplace) and the lightning rod. He became the most celebrated North American in the world.

4-3b *The Enlightenment in America*

Aside from a common emphasis on rational thought, the Enlightenment varied among European nations. The English Enlightenment, which rejected a wrathful God and exalted man's capacity for knowledge and social improvement, had the greatest impact in America. It grew out of the rational and benevolent piety favored by Low Church (or latitudinarian) Anglicans in Restoration England. They disliked rigid doctrine, scoffed at conversion experiences, attacked superstition, and rejected all "fanaticism," whether that of High Church Laudians, who had brought on England's great crisis of

1640–1642, or that of the Puritans, who had executed Charles I. High Church men, a small group after 1689, still stood for orthodoxy, ritual, and liturgy.

Enlightened writers celebrated Sir Isaac Newton's laws of motion as one of the greatest intellectual achievements of all time, joined the philosopher John Locke in looking for ways to improve society, and began to suspect that moderns had surpassed the ancients in learning and wisdom. John Tillotson, archbishop of Canterbury until his death in 1694, embodied this "polite and Catholick [that is, universal] spirit." He preached morality rather than dogma and had a way of defending the doctrine of eternal damnation that left his listeners wondering how a merciful God could possibly have ordained such a cruel punishment.

Enlightened ideas won an elite constituency in the mainland colonies even before newspapers began circulating these new views. Tillotson had a huge impact on America. His sermons appeared in numerous southern libraries and made a deep impression on tutors at Harvard College, including John Leverett, Jr. After Leverett became Harvard's president in 1708, Tillotson's ideas became entrenched in the curriculum. For the rest of the century, most Harvard-trained ministers, although still nominal Calvinists, embraced latitudinarian piety. They stressed the similarities, not the differences, between Congregationalists and Anglicans and favored broad religious toleration. After 1800, most Harvard-educated ministers became Unitarians who no longer believed in hell or the divinity of Jesus.

In 1701, largely in reaction against this trend at Harvard, a new college was founded as a bastion of orthodoxy and finally settled in New Haven, Connecticut. It was named Yale College in honor of a wealthy English benefactor, Elihu Yale, who gave his library to the school. Ironically, these Anglican books helped to convert the Yale faculty to the rational religion of the English Enlightenment that the institution had been founded in protest against. In 1722, the entire faculty, except for 19-year-old Jonathan Edwards, converted to the Church of England and sailed for England to be ordained by the bishop of London. Their leader, Timothy Cutler, became the principal Anglican spokesman in Boston.

The rise of the legal and medical professions further spread Enlightenment ideas. Early colonists despised lawyers as men who took advantage of the misery of others and who deliberately stirred up discord. By the mid-18th century, however, lawyers emerged, particularly in New England, as a new learned elite.

Medicine also became an enlightened profession, with Philadelphia setting the pace. William Shippen

iStock.com/wynnter

4.5 **Robert Feke's Portrait of Benjamin Franklin as a Gentleman** This portrait, painted at about the time that Franklin retired as a printer in 1747, announced his coming out as a gentleman. Note the wig and ruffled cuffs, indicating that Franklin would no longer be working with his hands.

earned degrees at Princeton and Edinburgh, the best medical school in the world at the time, before returning to Philadelphia in 1762, where he became the first American to lecture on medicine, publish a treatise on chemistry, and dissect human cadavers, a practice that shocked the unenlightened. His student, John Morgan, became the first professor of medicine in North America when the College of Philadelphia established a medical faculty a few years later. Benjamin Rush, who also studied at Princeton and Edinburgh, brought the latest Scottish techniques to the newly founded Philadelphia Hospital. He too became an enlightened reformer, attacking slavery and alcohol and supporting the American Revolution.

4-3c Women and the Consumer Revolution

By the 1730s and 1740s, consumption of British products joined learning as a key measure of refinement and social class in the American colonies. The period witnessed the birth of an Anglo-American **consumer society**. Small manufacturing concerns scattered throughout England produced huge quantities of consumer goods, including cloth, ceramics, glassware, paper, and cutlery, which colonists purchased at a dizzying pace. Each succeeding generation of colonial Americans owned more British imports than the previous generation. By one measure, the American market for imported goods rose 120 percent between 1750 and 1773.

The explosion in British goods contributed to the process of anglicization in the American colonies. Items manufactured in England quickly replaced locally made goods, resulting in a more homogenous British material culture in America. In 1751 Benjamin Franklin boasted, "A vast Demand is growing for British Manufacturers, a glorious market wholly in the Power of Britain."

The emerging consumer society provided new opportunities for colonial American women, particularly in port cities. Women participated in a commercial urban economy in which they enjoyed broad influence through their consumption patterns. The exercise of choice in the marketplace could be liberating at a time when other public venues, particularly politics, remained closed to their participation.

Products related to tea and clothing became especially feminized by the mid-18th century. Imported from South Asia by English merchants, tea began to appear in the homes of wealthier American colonists in the early 1700s. By the 1740s, taking tea had become a common afternoon practice for refined ladies and gentlemen. The ritual provided women with a social space where they exercised a measure of control due in part to their mastery of the pots, cups, saucers, spoons, strainers, and sugar tongs that made up a proper tea service. A New York newspaper declared the young men of the city "utterly ignorant in the Ceremony of the Tea-Table" and advised employing a knowledgeable woman "to teach them the Laws, Rules, Customs, Phrases and Names of the Tea Utensils."

By midcentury, colonial women also embraced clothing fashions imported from London. The expanded production and availability of cloth made purchasing fabric preferable to investing the time and energy necessary to create homespun. Women learned of the latest fashions from British periodical literature, such as the *Spectator*, as well as from advertisements by merchants and shopkeepers in American newspapers. Events such as balls and tea parties served as arenas for women to display the newest fashions as evidence of their social distinction.

For their part, colonial men did not escape the lure of British fashion. In 1759, the Reverend Jonathan Boucher relocated from the north of England to Port Royal, Virginia, a small tobacco community on the Rappahannock River. The move left him feeling underdressed. "I'm noth'g amongst the Lace and Lac'd fellows that are here," Boucher reported. Wigs, increasingly of a shorter length, helped to define masculine gentility in the colonies. As with other products, male colonists desired the most authentically British wigs available—those made with English human hair.

4-3d Georgia: The Failure of an Enlightenment Utopia

In the 1730s, Anglican humanitarianism and the Enlightenment belief in the possibility of social improvement converged in Britain to provide support for the founding of Georgia. The sponsors of this project hoped to create a society that could make productive use of England's "worthy" poor (but not the lazy or criminal poor). They also intended to shield South Carolina's slave society from Spanish Florida by populating Georgia with disciplined, armed freemen. Appalled by what cheap English gin was doing to the sobriety and industry of England's working people, Georgia's sponsors prohibited hard liquor as well as slavery. Slaves would make Georgia just like South Carolina, with all of that colony's vulnerabilities.

A distinguished group of trustees set themselves up as a nonprofit corporation and announced that they would give land away, not sell it. Led by James Oglethorpe, they got a 20-year charter from Parliament in 1732, raised money from Anglican friends, and launched the colony on land claimed by both Spain and Britain. They interviewed many prospective settlers to distinguish the worthy poor from the unworthy. They engaged silk and wine experts to produce staples that no English colony had yet made profitable, and recruited Scottish Highlanders as soldiers.

In 1733, the first settlers laid out Savannah, a town with spacious streets. Within 10 years, 1,800 charity cases and just over 1,000 self-supporting colonists reached Georgia. The trustees refused to consult the settlers on what might be good for Georgia. As refined men, they believed they knew what the colony needed. They created no elective assembly, nor did they give the British government much chance to supervise them. Because, under its charter, Georgia's laws had to be approved by the British Privy Council, the trustees passed only three "laws" during their 20 years of rule. One laid out the land system, and the others prohibited slavery and hard liquor.

Interpreting the Visual Past A Display of Consumer Goods

This portrait by an unknown artist shows a young girl, Susanna Truax, of Dutch descent, at home in Albany, New York. Truax, only four at the time of the portrait in 1730, displays several of the material goods that had started to flood into the colonies from Britain. She wears a bright, striped dress, typical of the fabric then sought after by American consumers. On the table sit a teapot, sugar cubes, and a cup and saucer, while Truax holds a lump of sugar in her spoon. Apparently at ease with the consumer revolution of the mid-18th century, Truax lived until 1805, long enough to witness a few more revolutions.

Q *The portrait in colonial America offered an opportunity to display one's possessions and social status. What can we learn about the standing of Truax's family from the painting? Why might a girl so young have been placed with material goods normally associated with adults?*

Q *How does the portrait illustrate the process of anglicization in the colonies? Does it matter that Truax belonged to a Dutch family? What does her ancestry tell us about the competing forces of cultural diversity and consolidation in the 18th century?*

Atlas Archive/The Image Works

4.6 **Artist Unknown, Susanna Truax, 1730.**

They governed through "regulations" instead of laws. An elective assembly, they promised, would come once Georgia's character had been firmly set.

The land system never worked as intended. The trustees gave 50 acres to every male settler whose passage was paid for out of charitable funds. Those who paid their own way could claim up to 500 acres. Ordinary farmers did poorly; they could not support a family on 50 acres of the sandy soil around Savannah. Because the trustees envisioned every landowner as a soldier, women could not inherit land, nor could landowners sell their plots.

The settlers could not grow grapes or persuade the sickly worms that survived the Atlantic crossing to make silk out of mulberry leaves. They clamored for rum, smuggled it into the colony when they could, and insisted that Georgia would never thrive without slaves. By the mid-1740s, enough people had died or left to reduce the population by more than half, and by 1752, it had fallen below the 2,800 who had first settled the colony. Between 1750 and 1752, the trustees dropped their ban on alcohol, allowed the importation of slaves, called an elective assembly (only to consult, not legislate), and finally surrendered their charter. The establishment of royal government in 1752 gave Georgia an elective assembly with full powers of legislation, and the colony became what it was never meant to be, a smaller version of South Carolina, producing rice and indigo with slave labor. By then, ironically, it had done more to spread religious revivalism than to vindicate Enlightenment ideals.

4-4 The Great Awakening

Q *What was the Great Awakening and how did it change religion in the American colonies in the 18th century?*

Between the mid-1730s and the early 1740s, an immense religious revival swept across the Protestant world. Within the British Empire, it affected some areas more intensely than others. England, Scotland, Ulster, New England, the mid-Atlantic colonies, and, for a time, South Carolina responded warmly to emotional calls for a spiritual rebirth. Southern Ireland, the West Indies, and the Chesapeake colonies remained on the margins until Virginia and Maryland were drawn into a later phase of the movement in the 1760s and 1770s. This "Great Awakening" shattered some denominational loyalties in the colonies and enabled the Methodists and the Baptists to surge ahead of all Protestant rivals after 1780.

4-4a *Origins of the Revivals*

Some of the earliest revivals originated in the colonies. Around 1720, Theodorus Jacobus Frelinghuysen of the Dutch Reformed Church sparked several of them in New Brunswick, New Jersey. Gilbert Tennent, the local Presbyterian pastor, watched and learned. Tennent was a younger son of William Tennent, Sr., an Anglican-turned-Presbyterian minister who had moved from Ulster to America. At Neshaminy, Pennsylvania, he set up his Log College, where he trained his sons and other young men as **evangelical** preachers. Evangelicals were committed to spreading the teachings of the Bible in an emotional style that resulted in conversion experiences among their listeners. The Tennent family dominated the **Presbytery** (a regional body) of New Brunswick, used it to ordain ministers, and sent them off to congregations that requested one, even in other presbyteries. These intrusions angered the Philadelphia **Synod**, the overall governing body of the Presbyterian Church in the colonies (see Figure 4.1). Most of its ministers emphasized orthodoxy over a personal conversion experience. In a 1740 sermon, *The Dangers of an Unconverted Ministry,* Gilbert Tennent warned that those preachers were leading their people to hell. His attack split the church. In 1741, the outnumbered revivalists withdrew and founded their own Synod of New York.

In New England, Solomon Stoddard of Northampton, between the 1670s and his death in 1729, presided over six revivals. Jonathan Edwards, his grandson and successor, touched off a revival in 1734 and 1735 that rocked dozens of Connecticut Valley towns. Edwards's *A Faithful Narrative of the Surprising Work of God* (1737) explained what a **revival** was—an emotional response to God's Word that brought sudden conversions to scores of people. He described these conversions in acute detail and won admirers even in Britain.

In England, John Wesley and George Whitefield set the pace. At worldly Oxford University, Wesley and his brother Charles founded the Holy Club, a High Church society whose members fasted until they could barely walk. These methodical practices prompted scoffers to call them "Methodists." In 1735, Wesley went to Georgia as a missionary, but the settlers rejected his ascetic piety. In 1737, on the return voyage to England, some Moravians convinced him that, for all his zeal, he had never grasped the central Protestant message, justification by faith alone. Some months later, he was deeply moved by Edwards's *Faithful Narrative.* Soon Wesley found his life's mission, the conversion of sinners, and it launched him on an extraordinary preaching career for the next half-century.

George Whitefield, a talented amateur actor in his youth, joined the Holy Club at Oxford and became an Anglican minister. He followed Wesley to Georgia, founded an orphanage, then returned to England and preached all over the kingdom to raise money for it. He had the power to move masses of people through a single sermon, and he too began to preach the "new birth"—the necessity of a conversion experience. When many pastors banned him from their pulpits, he began preaching in open fields to anyone who would listen. Newspapers reported the controversy, and soon his admirers told the press where he would be on any given day. Colonial newspapers, keenly sensitive to the English press, followed his career.

4-4b *Whitefield Launches the Transatlantic Revival*

In 1739, Whitefield made his second trip to America, and thousands flocked to hear him preach. After landing in Delaware, he preached his way northward through Philadelphia, New Jersey, and New York City, and then headed south through the Chesapeake colonies and into South Carolina. In September 1740, he sailed to Newport and for two months toured New England. During his travels, he met Benjamin Franklin, Gilbert Tennent, and Jonathan Edwards. In the cities he sometimes attracted as many as 30,000 people, twice Boston's population. His voice was so musical, claimed one observer, that he could seduce a crowd just by the way he pronounced "Mesopotamia." Using his acting skills, he imitated Christ on the cross, shedding "pious tears" for poor sinners. Or he became God at the Last Judgment, thundering: "Depart from me ye accursed into everlasting fire!" When he wept, so did his audience. When he condemned them, they fell to the ground in agony.

Although Whitefield wore the surplice of an Anglican minister and carried the *Book of Common Prayer* when he preached, Anglican ministers distrusted him. In Charleston and New York City, the official spokesmen for the bishop of London denounced him, but Presbyterians, Congregationalists, and Baptists embraced him, at least until some of them began

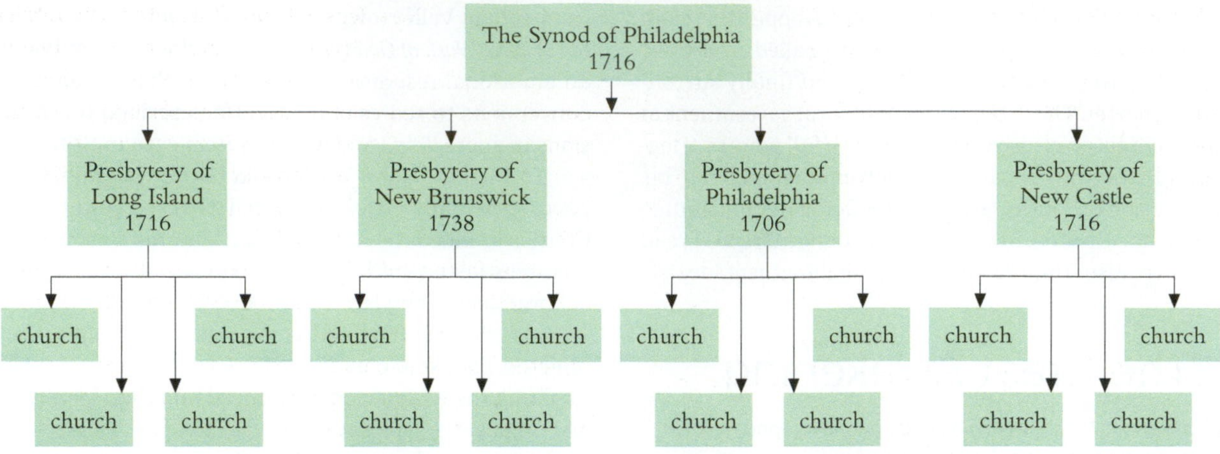

Fig. 4.1 **The Synod of Philadelphia by 1738** The chart shows the organization of the Presbyterian Church in the colonies. In actuality, some presbyteries had more churches than others. Arrows indicate descending lines of authority.

to fear that he was doing more harm than good. To many he embodied the old Non-Separatist ideal that all English Protestants were somehow members of the same church.

4-4c *Disruptions*

After Whitefield departed, other preachers tried to assume his role, but they aroused fierce controversy. In South Carolina, Hugh Bryan, a wealthy planter, began preaching the evangelical message to his slaves. In 1742, when memories of a major slave revolt were still fresh (see later section), he denounced slavery as a sin and warned that God would pour out his wrath on the colony unless it repented. Proclaiming himself an American Moses, he tried to part the waters of the Savannah River and lead the slaves to freedom in Georgia. He almost drowned and had to be rescued. He then confessed publicly that he had been deluded. Bryan discredited evangelicalism among the planters of the lower South for another generation, but he and his family continued to convert their own slaves. African American evangelical piety, including some of the first black preachers, took root from these efforts.

Whitefield's successors also disrupted New England. Gilbert Tennent, who lacked Whitefield's musical voice and Oxford diction, spoke with a Scottish burr and specialized in "Holy Laughter," the scornful peals of a triumphant God as sinners tumble into hell. He abandoned the usual garb of a minister for a robe and sandals and let his hair grow long, thereby proclaiming himself a new John the Baptist heralding the Second Coming of Christ.

James Davenport succeeded Tennent. He denounced unregenerate ministers by name. He liked to preach by eerie candlelight, roaring damnation at his listeners, even grabbing Satan and wrestling him back to hell. He advised admirers to drink rat poison rather than listen to another lifeless sermon. In 1743, he established the Shepherd's Tent in New London to train awakened preachers. This outdoor school abandoned the classical curriculum of colleges and insisted only on a valid conversion experience. He organized a book burning, in which titles by Increase Mather and other New England dignitaries went up in flames, and he threw his britches on the fire, declaring them a mark of human vanity. A grand jury, asked to indict him, proclaimed him mad instead. He too repented, and the Shepherd's Tent collapsed.

4-4d *Long-Term Consequences of the Revivals*

The revivals had dramatic consequences. Amid the enthusiasm of Whitefield's tour, more men than usual joined a church, but after another year or two, men became hard to convert. The number of women church members soared, however, until by 1800 they often formed a majority of 3 or 4 to 1 in evangelical churches, and in some congregations they acquired an informal veto over the choice of the minister. Partly in reaction to the revivals, thousands of men became **Freemasons**, often instead of joining a church. They very nearly turned these voluntary associations into a religion of manliness, complete with mysterious rituals that extolled sobriety, industry, brotherhood, benevolence, and citizenship. The movement peaked during the American Revolution and for a few decades after it.

The revivals shattered the unity of New England's Congregational Church. Evangelicals seceded from dozens of congregations to form their own "Separate" churches. Many of those that survived went Baptist by the 1760s, thereby gaining protection under the toleration statutes of the New England colonies. In the middle colonies, the revivals strengthened denominational loyalties and energized the clergy. In the 1730s, most people in the region, particularly in New Jersey and Pennsylvania, had never joined a church. The revivals prompted many of them to become **New Side** (evangelical) Presbyterians, **Old Side** (antirevival) Presbyterians, or nonevangelical Anglicans. Similar cleavages ran through the German population. The southern colonies were less affected, although evangelical Presbyterians made modest gains in the Virginia piedmont after 1740. Finally, in the 1760s, the Baptists began to win thousands of converts in Virginia,

HIP/Art Resource, NY

4.7 **William Hogarth's *Credulity, Superstition, and Fanaticism* (1762)** Opponents of the revivals condemned their excessive emotionalism.

Q *How does the artist use various forms of exaggeration in the church scene to register his opposition to religious revivalism?*

as did the Methodists after 1776. Their numbers surpassed the Baptists' within a few decades.

The revivals created new cosmopolitan links with Britain and between colonies. Whitefield ran the most efficient publicity machine in the Atlantic world. In London, Glasgow, and Boston, periodicals called *The Christian History* carried news of revivals occurring all over the empire. For years, London evangelicals held regular "Letter Days" at which they read accounts of revivals in progress. When fervor declined in New England, Edwards organized a Concert of Prayer with his Scottish correspondents, setting regular times for them all to beseech the Lord to pour out his grace once more. As Anglicans split into Methodists and Latitudinarians, Congregationalists into pro-revival **New Lights** and antirevival **Old Lights**, and Presbyterians into comparable New Side and Old Side synods, evangelicals discovered that they had more in common with revivalists in other denominations than with antirevivalists in their own.

4-4e *New Colleges*

The Great Awakening created several new colleges. In 1740, North America had only three: Harvard, William and Mary, and Yale. Although Yale eventually embraced the revivals, all three opposed them at first. In 1746, middle colony evangelicals, eager to show their commitment to classical learning after the fiasco of the Shepherd's Tent, founded the College of New Jersey (now Princeton University). It graduated its first class in 1748 and settled in Princeton in 1756. Unlike the older colleges, it drew students from all 13 colonies and sent its graduates throughout America, especially to the middle and southern colonies. It also reshaped the Presbyterian Church. When Presbyterians healed their schism and reunited in 1758, the New Siders set the terms. Outnumbered in 1741, they held a large majority of ministers by 1758. Through control of Princeton, their numbers had increased rapidly. The Old Side, still dependent on the University of Glasgow in Scotland, could barely replace those who died.

New Light Baptists founded the College of Rhode Island (now Brown University) in the 1760s. Dutch Reformed revivalists set up Queens College (now Rutgers University) in New Jersey. Eleazer Wheelock opened an evangelical school for Indians in Lebanon, Connecticut. After his first graduate, Samson Occum, raised £12,000 for the school in England, Wheelock moved to New Hampshire and used most of the money to found Dartmouth College instead, although Dartmouth occasionally admitted an Indian. By 1790, Dartmouth was turning out more graduates, and far more ministers, than any other American college.

In the 1750s, Anglicans countered with two new colleges of their own: the College of Philadelphia (now the University of Pennsylvania), which had Old Side Presbyterian support, and King's College in New York (now Columbia University). Their undergraduate programs remained small, however, and few of their students chose a ministerial career. In the competition for student loyalties, nonevangelicals could not yet compete effectively with revivalists.

4-4f *The Denominational Realignment*

The revivals transformed American religious life. In 1700, the three strongest denominations had been the Congregationalists in New England, the Quakers in the Delaware Valley, and the Anglicans in the South. By 1800, all three had lost ground to newcomers: the Methodists, who grew at an astonishing rate as heirs of the collapsing Church of England during and after the Revolution; the Baptists, who leaped into second place; and the Presbyterians. Methodists and Baptists, who did not expect their preachers to attend college, recruited them from a much broader segment of the population than their rivals could tap. Although they never created their own Shepherd's Tent, they embraced similar principles, demanding only a conversion experience, integrity, knowledge of the Bible, and a talent for preaching.

Anti-revivalist denominations, especially Anglicans and Quakers, suffered heavy losses. New Light Congregationalists made few gains because, when their people left the established churches of New England to move west, they usually joined a Presbyterian church, which gave them a support structure that isolated congregations in a pluralistic society could not sustain.

What They Said

The Controversy over Religious Revivals

The feud between New Lights and Old Lights in New England sparked a public debate between the revivalist minister Jonathan Edwards and the antirevivalist clergyman Charles Chauncy in the early 1740s. A man of the Enlightenment, Chauncy attacked the revivals as frauds because of their emotional excess. Edwards agreed that no emotional response, however intense, could itself prove the presence of God in a person's soul. Yet, he insisted that intense feeling must always accompany the reception of divine grace. In effect, Edwards countered Chauncy's emotional defense of reason with his own rational defense of emotion.

Charles Chauncy

...that *Terror* so many have been the Subjects of; Expressing itself in *strange Effects* upon the *Body*, such as *swooning away* and *falling to the Ground*, where Persons have lain, for a Time, speechless and motionless; bitter *Shriekings* and *Screamings; Convulsion-like Tremblings* and *Agitations, Strugglings,* and *Tumblings* which, in some Instances, have been attended with Indecencies I shan't mention ... I am not against the *Preaching of Terror*; but whenever this is done, it ought to be in a Way that may enlighten the Mind, as well as to alarm the Passions: And I am greatly mistaken, if this has been the Practice, among some Sort of Preachers, so much as it ought to be. And to this it may be owing, that Religion, of late, has been *more a Commotion in the Passions* than a *Change* in the *Temper* of the *Mind*.

Jonathan Edwards

Now if such things are enthusiasm, and the fruits of a distempered brain, let my brain be evermore possessed of that happy distemper! If this be distraction, I pray God that the world of mankind may be all seized with this benign, meek, beneficent, beatifical, glorious distraction! ...there is that uniformity observable, that it is easy to be seen that in general it is the same spirit from whence the work in all parts of the land has originated. And what notions have they of religion, that reject what has been described, as not true religion!

As there is the clearest evidence, from those things that have been observed, that this is the work of God; so it is evident that it is a very great and wonderful and exceeding glorious work of God. This is certain, that it is a great and wonderful event, a strange revolution, an unexpected, surprising overturning of things, suddenly brought to pass; such as never has been seen in New England, and scarce ever has been heard of in any land.

Q *How did Chauncy use vivid descriptive language to discredit the religious revivals? What was his explanation for the physical manifestations of religious conversion displayed during the Great Awakening?*

Q *How did Edwards use the Enlightenment principle of logical reasoning to counter the argument that the revivals were not authentic? Are there points of agreement between him and Chauncy?*

Sources: (top) From a sermon/pamphlet by Charles Chauncy, *Seasonable Thoughts on the State of Religion in New-England, a Treatise in Five Parts* (Boston: Printed by Rogers and Fowle, for Samuel Eliot in Cornhill, 1743), 76–77, 109. Accessed via Google Books. https://goo.gl/fTr2EK; (bottom) From sermon/pamphlet by Jonathan Edwards, *Edwards on Revivals: Containing a Faithful Narrative of the Surprising Work of God in the Conversion of Many Hundred Souls in Northhampton, Massachusetts, A.D. 1735: Also Thoughts on the Revival of Religion in New England, 1742, and the Way in which It Ought to be Acknowledged and Promoted* (New York: Dunning & Spalding, 1832), 174–177.

4-5 Political Culture in the Colonies

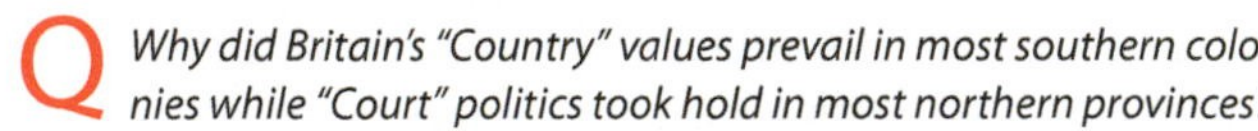

Q *Why did Britain's "Country" values prevail in most southern colonies while "Court" politics took hold in most northern provinces?*

In politics as in other activities, the colonies became more like Britain in the 18th century. A quarter-century of warfare after 1689 convinced the settlers that they needed Britain's protection and strengthened their admiration for its parliamentary system. Colonists agreed that they were free because they were British—and Protestants—who also had mixed constitutions that united monarchy, aristocracy, and democracy in almost perfect balance. In the colonies, the governor stood for monarchy; the council, or upper house, for aristocracy (the House of Lords in Britain); and the assembly for democracy (the House of Commons).

By the 1720s, the Crown appointed the governor for every colony except Connecticut and Rhode Island, which kept the power granted by their 17th-century charters to select their own governors. The two New England colonies, along with their neighbor Massachusetts, also elected their councils (although Massachusetts did so indirectly, through its assembly). The Crown appointed the council in every other colony. In all 13 colonies, once the Crown took over Georgia, the settlers elected the assembly.

As with the structure, the style of colonial politics increasingly resembled that of Britain. Since the Glorious Revolution of 1688, the dominant pattern of politics in England had pitted the Court, or ruling government, against the Country, or party out of power. Court statesmen favored policies that strengthened central ministerial control, particularly in the waging of war. The Country opposition stood for liberty by denouncing patronage and institutions such as standing armies as engines of corruption. The colonies reproduced the dynamic, yet with an important twist. Whereas the Country party, by definition, never came into power in Britain, Country principles, especially in the southern colonies, often came to dominate politics in British North America.

4-5a *The Rise of the Assembly and the Governor*

The rise of the assembly was a major political trend of the era. The right to vote in the colonies was more widely shared than in England, where two-thirds of adult males were disfranchised. By contrast, something like three-fourths of free adult white men in the colonies became potential voters for assembly representatives by some point in their adult lives. The frequency of elections varied—from every seven years in New York (by the 1740s) and Virginia, as well as in Britain, to at least once a year in five colonies. As the century advanced, legislatures sat longer and passed more laws. The lower house—the assembly—began to initiate most major bills. It made most of its gains at the expense of the council, not the governor.

Every royal colony except New York and Georgia already had an assembly with a strong sense of its own privileges when the first royal governor arrived, yet governors also grew more powerful. Because the governor's instructions usually challenged some existing practices, clashes occurred. The first royal governors never got all of their demands, but they often won concessions and became more adept over the years. In royal colonies, between 1730 and 1765, most governors learned that their success depended less on their prerogatives (royal powers embodied in their commissions) than on their ability to win the assembly's cooperation through persuasion or patronage.

Early in the century, conflicts between governor and assembly tended to be legalistic. Each cited technical precedents to justify the governor's prerogatives or the assembly's privileges. Later on, when conflict spilled over into pamphlets and newspapers, it often pitted an aggrieved minority (unable to win a majority in the assembly) against both governor and assembly. These contests were ideological. The opposition accused the governor of corrupting the assembly, and he in turn denounced his critics as a "faction." Everyone condemned factions, embryonic political parties, as self-interested and destructive. Hardly anyone claimed to be a party member; the other side was the faction.

4-5b *Court and Country Politics*

The joint rise of the assembly and the governor produced different political cultures in the southern and northern colonies (see Table 4.1). In most southern colonies, the "Country" principles of the British opposition became the common assumptions of public life, acceptable to both governor and assembly, typically after a failed attempt by a governor to impose the "Court" alternative. In Britain, despite vociferous protests from the Country opposition, ruling governments built legislative majorities through **placemen**, members of Parliament who received financial inducements and often owed their seats to supporting the government. Yet, when Virginia's Governor Alexander Spotswood (served 1710–1722) used patronage to fill the assembly with his own placemen, the voters turned nearly all of them out at the next election. Then, just as Spotswood had learned that he could not dominate the house through patronage, so the assembly discovered that it could not coerce a governor who controlled a permanent revenue from the Crown.

Wangkun Jia/Dreamstime

4.8 The Governor's Palace at Williamsburg, Virginia
The governor's palace was finished during the term of Governor Alexander Spotswood (1710–1722) and restored in the 20th century. For Spotswood, the palace was an extension of royal might and splendor across the ocean. He set a standard of elegance that many planters imitated when they built their own great houses in the second quarter of the 18th century.

Q *How did the governor's palace express through architecture the principles of anglicization and the Enlightenment?*

Table 4.1 THE SPECTRUM OF COLONIAL POLITICS

Constitutional Type	Successful	Unsuccessful
Northern "Court"	New York, circa 1710–1728 New Hampshire after 1741 Massachusetts after 1741 New Jersey after 1750	New York after 1728 Pennsylvania (successful in peace, ineffective in war)
Southern "Country"	Virginia after 1720 South Carolina after 1730 Georgia after 1752	Maryland North Carolina

Connecticut and Rhode Island never really belonged to either system.

Accordingly, Virginia and South Carolina cultivated a **politics of harmony**, a system of ritualized mutual flattery. Governors found that they could accomplish more through persuasion than through patronage, and the assemblies openly showed their appreciation. The planters of Virginia and South Carolina concluded that their societies embodied almost exactly what British opposition writers had been demanding. Factions disappeared, allowing the governor and the assembly to pursue the "common good" in an atmosphere free of rancor or corruption. Georgia adopted similar practices in the 1750s.

This system worked because the planters were doing what Britain wanted them to do: growing staple crops and shipping them to Britain or other destinations allowed by Parliament. Both sides could agree on measures that would make this process more efficient, such as the Virginia Tobacco Inspection Act of 1730. In Virginia, public controversy all but ceased. Between 1720 and 1765, particularly during the able administration of Sir William Gooch (1727–1749), the governor and House of Burgesses engaged in only one public quarrel, an unparalleled record of political harmony. South Carolina's politics became almost as placid from the 1730s into the 1760s, but harmony there masked serious social problems that were beginning to emerge in the unrepresented backcountry. By contrast, the politics of harmony never took hold in Maryland, where the lord proprietor always tried to seduce assemblymen with his lavish patronage, nor in factional North Carolina, where the tobacco and rice planters in some years paralyzed the government with their fierce wrangling, while disgusting the growing backcountry in the process.

The northern colonies never produced a politics of harmony. Instead, with many economic interests and ethnic and religious groups to satisfy, northern colonial governors often resorted to a Court-style politics to control and offset the multiple factions. The long ministry of Sir Robert Walpole (1721–1742), recognized by some as Britain's first prime minister, provided a model for savvy colonial governors when using patronage for rewarding some groups and disciplining others. William Shirley, governor of Massachusetts from 1741 to 1756, used judicial and militia appointments and war contracts to sustain a majority in the assembly. Like Walpole, he was a master of Court politics. In New Hampshire, Benning Wentworth created a political machine that rewarded just about every assemblyman from the 1750s to 1767. Ineffective oppositions in both colonies accused their governor of corrupting the assembly, but Shirley and Wentworth each claimed that his actions were essential to his colony's needs. Both governors remained in control.

The opposition, although seldom able to implement its demands at the provincial level, was important nonetheless. It kept settlers alert to any infringements on their liberties, and it usually dominated the Boston town meeting from 1720 on. Boston artisans engaged in ritualized mob activities with a sharp political edge. Every year on November 5, Guy Fawkes Day, a North End mob and a South End mob bloodied each other for the privilege of burning, on Beacon Hill, effigies of the pope, the devil, and the Stuart pretender to the British throne. These men were raucously celebrating liberty, property, and no popery—the British constitution, as they understood it. The violence made many wealthy merchants nervous, and by 1765 some of them would become its victims.

In both north and south, colonists embraced Country political ideals with more enthusiasm than British subjects in England ever had. In particular, colonists absorbed the warnings of the British opposition—that men in power nearly always tried to destroy liberty and that corruption was power's most dangerous weapon. By 1776, that view would justify independence and the repudiation of a "corrupt" king and Parliament.

4-6 The Renewal of Imperial Conflict

Q *How did Indians and African slaves take advantage of opportunities presented by a new round of European wars starting in 1739?*

A new era of imperial war began in 1739 and continued, with only a brief interruption, until 1763. The British colonies, New Spain, New France, and the Indians of the Eastern Woodlands all became involved in a war to determine who would dominate North America.

4-6a *Challenges to French Power*

By the second quarter of the 18th century, the French colonial project in North America remained land rich but settlement poor. Although France claimed more territory than Britain, it had far fewer white colonists and continued to depend on

Indian alliances for military strength. The French hold on the interior also began to weaken, both north and south. Indians returned to the Ohio Valley, mostly to trade with pacifist Pennsylvania or with Fort Oswego, a new British post on Lake Ontario. Compared with the French, the British were often clumsy in their dealings with Indians, but they had one advantage: cheaper trade goods. Many Indians created what the French disparagingly called **republics**, villages outside the French alliance system that were eager for British trade. The chiefs at Venango, Logstown, and other republics accepted people from all tribes—Delawares from the east, Shawnees from the south and east, Mingoes (Iroquois who had left their homeland) from the north, and other Algonquian peoples of the Great Lakes region to the west. Because inhabitants of each new village had blood relatives among all of the nearby nations, the chiefs welcomed colonial traders and hoped that none of their Indian neighbors would endanger their own relatives by attacking these communities.

Sometimes the French system of mediation broke down. For instance, an arrogant French officer decided to take over the lands of the Natchez Indians (the last of the Mississippian mound builders) and ordered them to leave. While pretending to comply, the Natchez planned a counterstroke and on November 28, 1729, killed every French male in the vicinity. In the war that followed, the French and their Choctaw allies destroyed the Natchez as a distinct people, although some refugees found homes among the Chickasaws or the Creeks.

In 1730, the French barely averted a massive slave uprising in New Orleans. To stir up hatred between Indians and Africans, they turned over some of the African leaders of the revolt to the Choctaws to be burned alive. Unable to afford enough gifts to sustain alliances with both Choctaws and Chickasaws, they encouraged hostilities between the two nations. This policy seriously damaged the French. Instead of weakening the pro-British Chickasaws, it touched off a civil war among the Choctaws, and France lost both influence and prestige.

4-6b *The Danger of Slave Revolts and War with Spain*

In the immediate term, the Spanish presence in Florida proved more troublesome to the British, particularly in South Carolina. In the 16th century, Francis Drake had proclaimed himself a liberator when he attacked St. Augustine and promised freedom to Indians and Africans who, he assumed, were groaning under Spanish tyranny (see Chapter 3). By the 1730s, these roles had been reversed. On several occasions after 1680, Spanish Florida had promised freedom to any slaves who escaped from Carolina and were willing to accept Catholicism. In 1738, the governor established, just north of St. Augustine, a new town, Gracia Real de Santa Teresa de Mose (or Mose for short, pronounced "Moe-shah"), and made it the first community of free blacks in what is now the United States. The very existence of Mose acted as a magnet for Carolina slaves.

In 1739, Florida's governor offered liberty to any slaves from the British colonies who could make their way to Florida. This manifesto, and rumors about Mose, touched off the Stono Rebellion in South Carolina, the most violent slave revolt in the history of the 13 colonies. Some of the rebellion's leaders were Catholics from the African Kingdom of the Kongo, where Portuguese missionaries had made numerous converts since the 16th century.

On September 9, 1739, 20 slaves attacked a store at Stono (south of Charleston), killed the owner, seized weapons, and moved on to assault other houses and win new recruits. Heading toward Florida, they killed another 25 settlers that day. At the Edisto River, they stopped, raised banners, and shouted "Liberty!" hoping to begin a general uprising. There the militia caught them and killed about two-thirds of the growing force. In the weeks that followed, the settlers killed another 60. No rebels reached Florida, but, as the founders of Georgia had foreseen, South Carolina was indeed vulnerable in any conflict with Spain.

4.9 ***Savages of Several Nations, New Orleans, 1735*** This painting by Alexandre de Batz depicts a multiethnic Indian village near New Orleans. The woman at lower left was a Fox Indian who had been captured and enslaved. The African boy was an adoptee.

At that moment, the War of Jenkins's Ear broke out between Britain and Spain, derisively named for a ship captain and smuggler who had displayed his severed ear to Parliament as proof of Spanish cruelty. The war cost Britain dearly because Spanish defenses held everywhere. Some 3,000 men from the 13 colonies, eager for plunder, joined expeditions in 1741 and 1742 against the seaport of Cartagena in New Granada (now Colombia), and against Cuba and Panama (see Map 4.1). All were British disasters. Most of the men died of disease; only 10 percent of the volunteers returned home. But one survivor, Lawrence Washington, so admired the British naval commander, Edward Vernon, that he named his Virginia plantation after him. Britain also experienced a surge of patriotic fervor from the war. Both "God Save the King" and "Rule Britannia" were written during the struggle.

Georgia was supposed to protect South Carolina. General Oglethorpe, its governor, retaliated against the Spanish by invading Florida in 1740. He dispersed the black residents of Mose and occupied the site, but the Spaniards mauled his garrison in a surprise counterattack (see Map 4.2). Oglethorpe retreated without taking St. Augustine and returned to Georgia with disturbing reports. Spain, he said, was sending blacks into the British colonies to start slave uprisings, and Spanish priests in disguise were mingling with the black conspirators. This news set off panics in the rice and tobacco colonies, but it had its biggest impact in New York City.

Back in 1712, a slave revolt had shaken New York. After setting fire to a barn one night, slaves had shot 15 settlers who rushed to put out the blaze, killing nine. Twenty-one slaves were executed, some after gruesome tortures. By 1741, New York City's 2,000 slaves were the largest concentration of blacks in British North America outside of Charleston. On March 18, Fort George burned down in what was probably an accident, but when a series of other suspicious fires broke out, the settlers grew nervous. New York's racial tensions combined with the supposed threat of Spanish Catholics, evident in Oglethorpe's warning, led to widespread fears of a "popish plot" to murder the city's whites and free the slaves. The number of individuals accused in the conspiracy escalated throughout the spring. The New York conspiracy trials, which proceeded from May into August of 1741, reminded one observer that the testimony of several girls in the Salem witch trials of 1692 had led to 19 hangings. The toll in New York was worse. Four whites and 18 slaves were hanged, 13 slaves were burned alive, and 70 banished to the West Indies. The judges spoke pompously about the sacred rights of Englishmen, again in danger from popish conspirators, and grew enraged at any African who dared to imperil what the colony would not let him share.

In 1742, King Philip V of Spain nearly accomplished what Oglethorpe and the New York judges dreaded. He sent 36 ships and 2,000 soldiers from Cuba with orders to devastate Georgia and South Carolina, "sacking and burning all the towns, posts, plantations, and settlements" and freeing the slaves. Although the invaders probably outnumbered the entire population of Georgia, Oglethorpe carried out an ingenious bluff to mask the weakness of his forces. The Spanish departed in haste, leaving British North America as a safe haven once more for liberty, property, no popery—and slavery.

▲ MAP 4.1 Caribbean Theater of War, 1739–1742 Spanish defenses held up remarkably well against repeated and very costly British attacks.

Q *In terms of geography, what made attacks on coastal defenses so difficult?*

Q *Given that Britain lost most battles in the War of Jenkins's Ear, what might have contributed to the surge of British nationalism in the war?*

4-6c *France versus Britain: King George's War*

In 1744, when France joined Spain in the war against Britain, the main action shifted to the north. After the French laid siege to Annapolis Royal, the capital of Nova Scotia, Governor Shirley of Massachusetts intervened to save the small garrison, and the French withdrew. Shirley then planned a rash attack on Louisbourg, the French fortress on Cape Breton Island. The Massachusetts governor, with a force of untrained Yankees and timely assistance from the British navy, subdued the mightiest fortress in America.

After that nothing went right. Hundreds of volunteers died before regular troops arrived to garrison Louisbourg. Plans to attack Quebec by sea in 1746 and 1747 came to nothing because no British fleet appeared. French and Indian raiders assaulted the weakly defended frontier. Bristol County farmers rioted against high taxes, and four towns in western Massachusetts seceded to join Connecticut.

When the Royal Navy finally docked at Boston in late 1747, its commander, Admiral Charles Knowles, sent bands of men known as **press gangs** on merchant ships in the harbor and ashore to force anyone they could seize into serving with the fleet. Angry locals descended on the sailors, took some officers hostage, and controlled the streets of Boston for three days. The Knowles Riot, as it has become known, signified the largest protest against imperial officials in the colonies between the Glorious Revolution of 1688 and the Stamp Act Riots of 1765 (see Chapter 5). Knowles soon relented and released all of the Massachusetts men he had impressed. (The rioters let him keep outsiders.) After the disturbance, the strongest defender

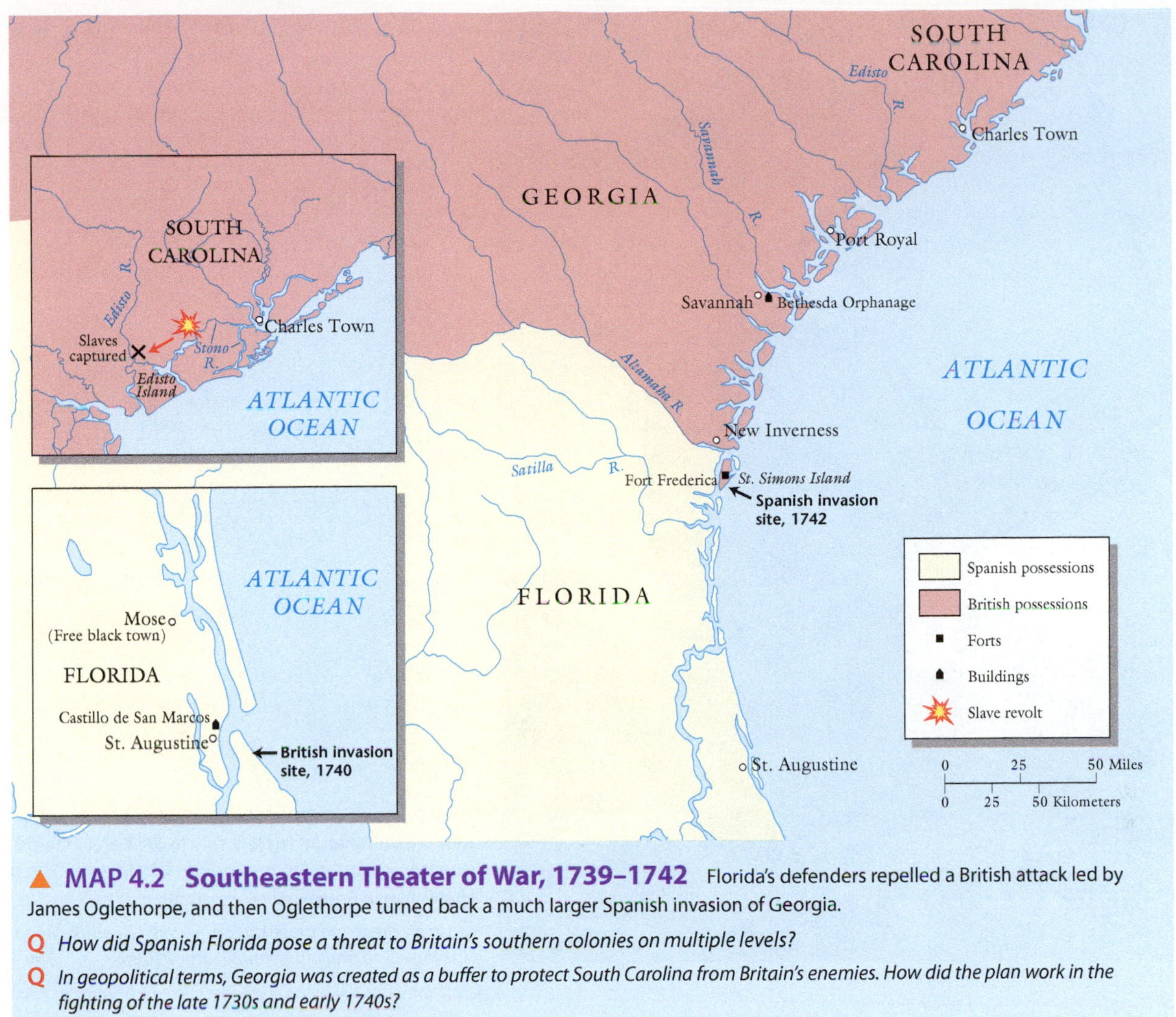

▲ **MAP 4.2 Southeastern Theater of War, 1739–1742** Florida's defenders repelled a British attack led by James Oglethorpe, and then Oglethorpe turned back a much larger Spanish invasion of Georgia.

Q *How did Spanish Florida pose a threat to Britain's southern colonies on multiple levels?*

Q *In geopolitical terms, Georgia was created as a buffer to protect South Carolina from Britain's enemies. How did the plan work in the fighting of the late 1730s and early 1740s?*

of Boston's crowd action was the young Samuel Adams, fresh out of Harvard, where his master's thesis explored when it was legitimate to resist civil government.

Ultimately, to offset losses in Europe, Britain returned Louisbourg to France under the peace settlement that ended the war in 1748. Enormous sacrifices gained Yankees nothing except pride.

4-6d *The Impending Storm*

The war drove back the frontiers of British settlement, but the colonies had promised postwar land grants to many volunteers for their service. Thus, peace touched off a frenzy of expansion that alarmed Indians and French alike. The British, aware that their hold on Nova Scotia was feeble, sent four regiments of redcoats and recruited 2,500 Protestants from the continent of Europe to populate the colony. In 1749, they founded Halifax as the new capital of Nova Scotia.

In the 13 colonies, settlers eagerly pressed on to new lands. Yankees swarmed into Maine and New Hampshire and west into the middle colonies, creating serious tensions. By refusing to pay rent to the manor lords of the Hudson Valley, they sparked a tenant revolt in 1753 that was subdued only with difficulty. A year later, Connecticut's delegation to the Albany Congress (see next section) bribed Iroquois chiefs to acquire title to all of northern Pennsylvania, which Connecticut claimed on the basis of its sea-to-sea charter of 1663. Various controversies with the Mohawks west of Albany so infuriated Chief Hendrik that he bluntly told the governor of New York in 1753, "The Covenant Chain is broken between you and us [the Iroquois League]. So brother you are not to hear of me any more, and Brother we desire to hear no more of you." New York, Pennsylvania, and Virginia competed for trade with the new Indian republics between Lake Erie and the Ohio River. Expansion pitted colony against colony, as well as settler against Indian, and British against French. Virginians, whom the Indians called "long knives," were particularly aggressive. Citing their own 1609 sea-to-sea charter (see Map 2.3, p. 50), they organized the Ohio Company of Virginia in 1747 to settle the Ohio Valley and established their first outpost where the Monongahela and Allegheny rivers converge to form the Ohio River (the site of modern Pittsburgh). The company hired George Washington as a surveyor. Farther south, encroachments upon the Cherokees nearly provoked war with South Carolina in 1750.

Mary Evans/The Image Works

4.10 **Portrait of Chief Hendrik of the Mohawks** Hendrik's ultimatum to New York in 1753 precipitated the summoning of the Albany Congress a year later. This print shows him in British military clothing.

Q *In his dress and presentation, how did Hendrik integrate anglicized and indigenous cultural forms?*

The French began to panic. The fall of Louisbourg had interrupted the flow of French trade goods to the Ohio Country for several years, and the men who had long been conducting Indian diplomacy had either died or left office by the late 1740s. Authoritarian newcomers from France replaced them and began giving orders to western Indians instead of negotiating with them. But the French did make some constructive moves. They repaired Louisbourg and built Fort Beauséjour on the neck connecting mainland Canada to Nova Scotia. In 1755, they erected Fort Carillon (Ticonderoga to the British) on Lake Champlain to protect Crown Point (see Map 4.3).

The French clearly intended to prevent British settlement west of the Alleghenies. Marquis Duquesne sent 2,000 Canadians, with almost no Indian support, to erect a line of posts from Lake Erie to Fort Duquesne (now Pittsburgh). Duquesne thought this policy so beneficial to the Indians that it needed no explanation. Yet, the Mingoes warned him not to build a fort in their territory, and a delegation of Delawares and Shawnees asked the Virginians if they would be willing to expel the French from the Ohio Country and then go back home.

The Indians did not like the response. In 1753, Virginia sent Washington to the Ohio Country to warn Duquesne to withdraw, and a small Virginia force further threatened Indian control of the territory by beginning to build its own fort at the forks of the Ohio. Duquesne ignored Washington, advanced toward the Ohio, expelled the Virginians, took over their site, and finished building what now became Fort Duquesne. Virginia sent Washington back to the Ohio in 1754. On May 28, after discovering a French patrol nearby, he launched an attack. That order set off a world war.

4-7 The War for North America

Q *What made the War for North America (1754–1763) so much more decisive than the three earlier Anglo-French wars?*

In spring 1754, both New France and Virginia expected a limited clash at the forks of the Ohio River. Neither anticipated the titanic struggle that encounter would set off, nor did the French and British governments, which hoped to limit any conflict to a few strategic points in North America. New Englanders, however, saw an apocalyptic struggle in the making between "Protestant freedom" and "popish slavery,"

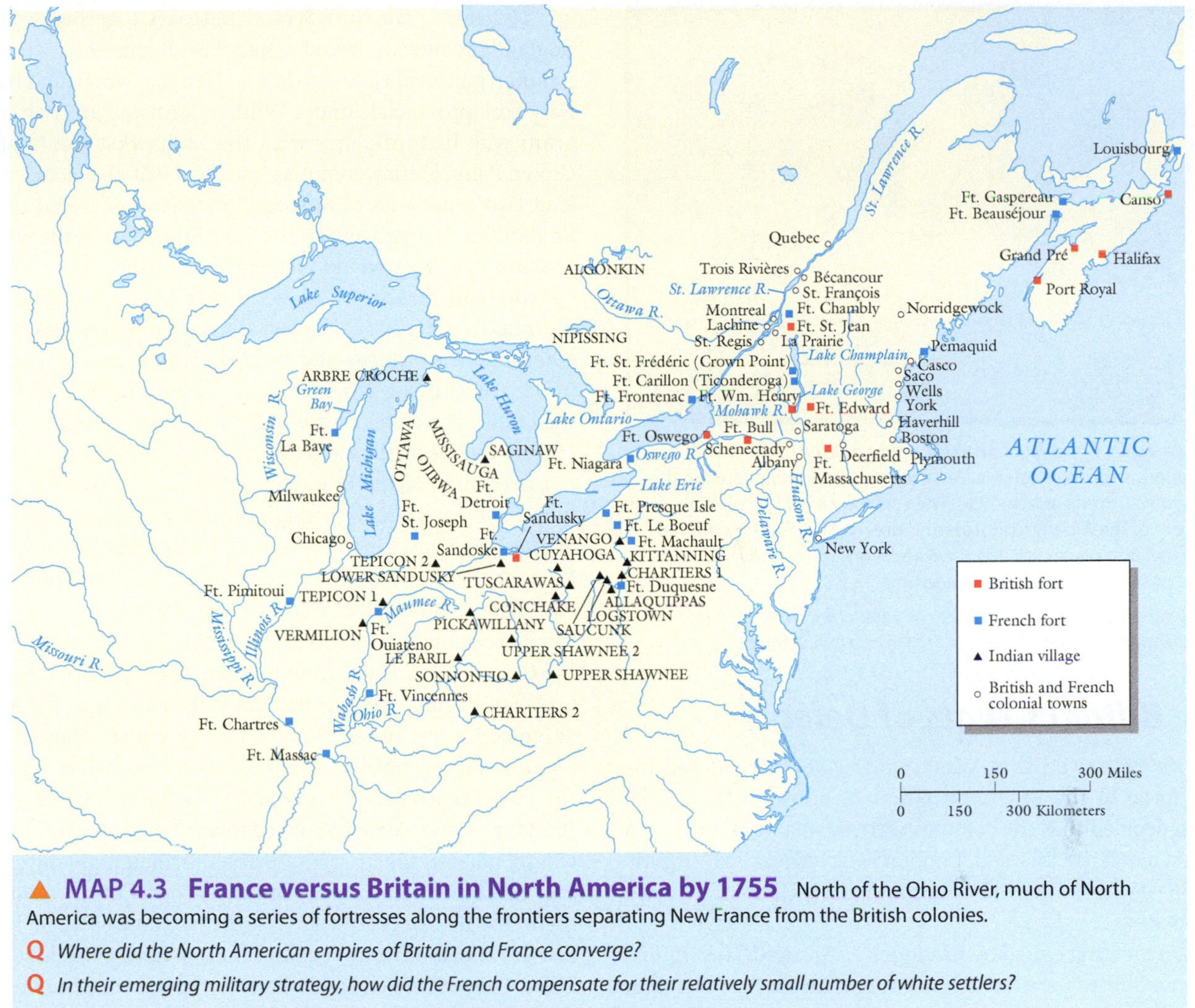

▲ **MAP 4.3 France versus Britain in North America by 1755** North of the Ohio River, much of North America was becoming a series of fortresses along the frontiers separating New France from the British colonies.

Q *Where did the North American empires of Britain and France converge?*

Q *In their emerging military strategy, how did the French compensate for their relatively small number of white settlers?*

with the North American continent as the battleground. "The continent is not wide enough for us both," declared one preacher, "and they [the French] intend to have the whole." Thus began the French and Indian War, pitting France against Britain for the control of North America.

4-7a *The Albany Congress and the Onset of War*

Britain, fearful that the Six Nations (the Tuscaroras had joined the original Five Nations by the 1720s) might side with New France, ordered New York to host an intercolonial congress at Albany to redress Iroquois grievances. The governor invited every colony as far south as Virginia, except nonroyal Connecticut and Rhode Island. Virginia and New Jersey declined to attend. Governor Shirley of Massachusetts, on his own initiative, invited Connecticut and Rhode Island to participate, and the Massachusetts legislature asked its delegates to work for a plan of intercolonial union.

In Philadelphia, Benjamin Franklin too was thinking about colonial union. On May 9, 1754, his *Pennsylvania Gazette* printed one of the first political cartoons in American history, with the caption "JOIN, or DIE." A month later, he drafted his "Short Hints towards a Scheme for Uniting the Northern Colonies," which he presented to the **Albany Congress** in June. His plan called for a "President General" to be appointed by the Crown as commander in chief and to administer the laws of the union, and for a "Grand Council" to be elected for three-year terms by the lower houses of each colony. To take effect, the plan would require approval by the Crown and each colonial legislature, and presentation to Parliament for its consent. The Albany Congress adopted an amended version of Franklin's proposal.

Shirley and Franklin were far ahead of public opinion. Newspapers ignored the Albany Plan. Every colony rejected it, most with little debate, some unanimously. The voting was close only in Massachusetts, which had borne the heaviest burden in the earlier French wars. As Franklin later explained, the colonies feared that the president general might become too powerful. But they also distrusted each other. Despite the French threat, they were not ready to put aside their differences and unite. They did not yet see themselves as "Americans."

4.11 Benjamin Franklin's Snake Cartoon One of the first newspaper cartoons in colonial America, this device appeared in the *Pennsylvania Gazette* in May 1754. The cartoon called for colonial union on the eve of the Albany Congress and drew on the folk legend that a snake, cut into pieces, could revive and live if it somehow joined its severed parts together before sundown.

Q *Why was it so difficult to convince the various British colonies to cooperate in the face of the clear French and Indian threat?*

4-7b *Britain's Years of Defeat*

After news arrived that Washington had surrendered his small force to the French at Great Meadows in July 1754, Britain decided that the colonies were incapable of uniting in their own defense. Instead, London sent redcoats to Virginia in 1755—two regiments, commanded by General Edward Braddock.

At a meeting called by Braddock at Alexandria, Virginia, Governor Shirley persuaded him to accept a much bolder plan for battling the French than what London had authorized. Instead of a single expedition aimed at one fort, to be followed by others if time permitted, the campaign of 1755 became four distinct offensives designed to crush the outer defenses of New France and leave it open to British invasion (see Map 4.4). Braddock was so impressed with Shirley that he named him second in command of the British army in North America, not bad for an English lawyer with no military training who had arrived in Boston almost penniless 25 years earlier.

Braddock and Shirley tried to make maximum use of both redcoats and provincials. The redcoats were disciplined, long-term professional soldiers trained to fight other professional armies. Irregular war in the forests of North America made them uneasy. Provincials, by contrast, were recruited by individual colonies. They were volunteers, often quite young, who enlisted for a single campaign. The Americans knew little about military drill, expected to serve under the officers who had recruited them, and sometimes disobeyed orders that they disliked. They admired the courage of the redcoats but were shocked by their irreverent speech, which included too much swearing for Yankee tastes, and by the brutal discipline that professional soldiers had to endure. Yet, thousands of colonists, mostly immigrants, enlisted in the British army, providing up to 40 percent of its strength in North America by 1760.

Under the plan, Nova Scotia's redcoats, together with New England provincials, would assault Fort Beauséjour, where the Acadian peninsula joins mainland Canada. New England and New York provincials under William Johnson, an Irish immigrant who had influence with the Mohawks, would attack Crown Point. Shirley, commissioned as a British colonel, would lead two regiments of redcoats (recently recruited in New England) to Niagara and cut off New France from the western Indians. Braddock would take Fort Duquesne.

Instead, Braddock erred in his Indian strategy and marched to disaster. The western Delawares asked him whether their villages and hunting rights would be secure under the British. "No Savage," he sneered, "Should Inherit the Land." The chiefs responded, "That if they might not have Liberty To Live on the Land they would not Fight for it." He "did not need their Help," Braddock retorted. It took him several months to hack a road through the forest wide enough for his artillery. Taking care to prevent ambushes at two fords of the Monongahela, he crossed that stream on July 9 and pushed on, confident that he had overcome all obstacles.

Fort Duquesne's commander could muster only 72 French, 146 Canadians, and 637 Indians against 1,400 British regulars and 450 Virginia provincials. The French ran into the British vanguard a few miles southeast of the fort. They clashed along a narrow path with thick forest and brush on either side. The French and Indians took cover on the British flanks. Braddock's rear elements rushed toward the sound of the guns where, massed together, the British formed a gigantic bull's eye. The French and Indians poured round after round into them; the British fired wild volleys into the trees. The British lost 977 killed or wounded, and their artillery. Braddock was killed. Only 39 French and Indians were killed or wounded. The redcoats finally broke and ran. Washington, who had fought as a Virginia volunteer on Braddock's staff, reported that, for the rest of the year, offensive operations would be impossible. Braddock's road through the wilderness became a highway for the enemy. For the first time in their history, Pennsylvania's settlers faced the horrors of a frontier war.

In Nova Scotia, Fort Beauséjour fell on June 17, 1755. Then the commanders did something to indicate that this war would not be a conventional, limited struggle. When the Acadians refused to take an oath that might have obliged them to bear arms against other Frenchmen, the British and Yankees responded with an 18th-century version of ethnic cleansing. They rounded up between 6,000 and 7,000 Acadians, forced them aboard ships, and expelled them from the province, to be scattered among the 13 colonies, none of which was prepared for the influx. A second roundup in 1759 caught most of the families that had evaded the first one. The officers who organized these expulsions insisted that they had found a humane way of compelling French Catholics to assimilate with the Protestant majority. Reasoning also that the Acadians were not British subjects because they had not taken the oath, and that only British subjects could own land in a British colony, the government of Nova Scotia confiscated the land the Acadians had farmed for generations

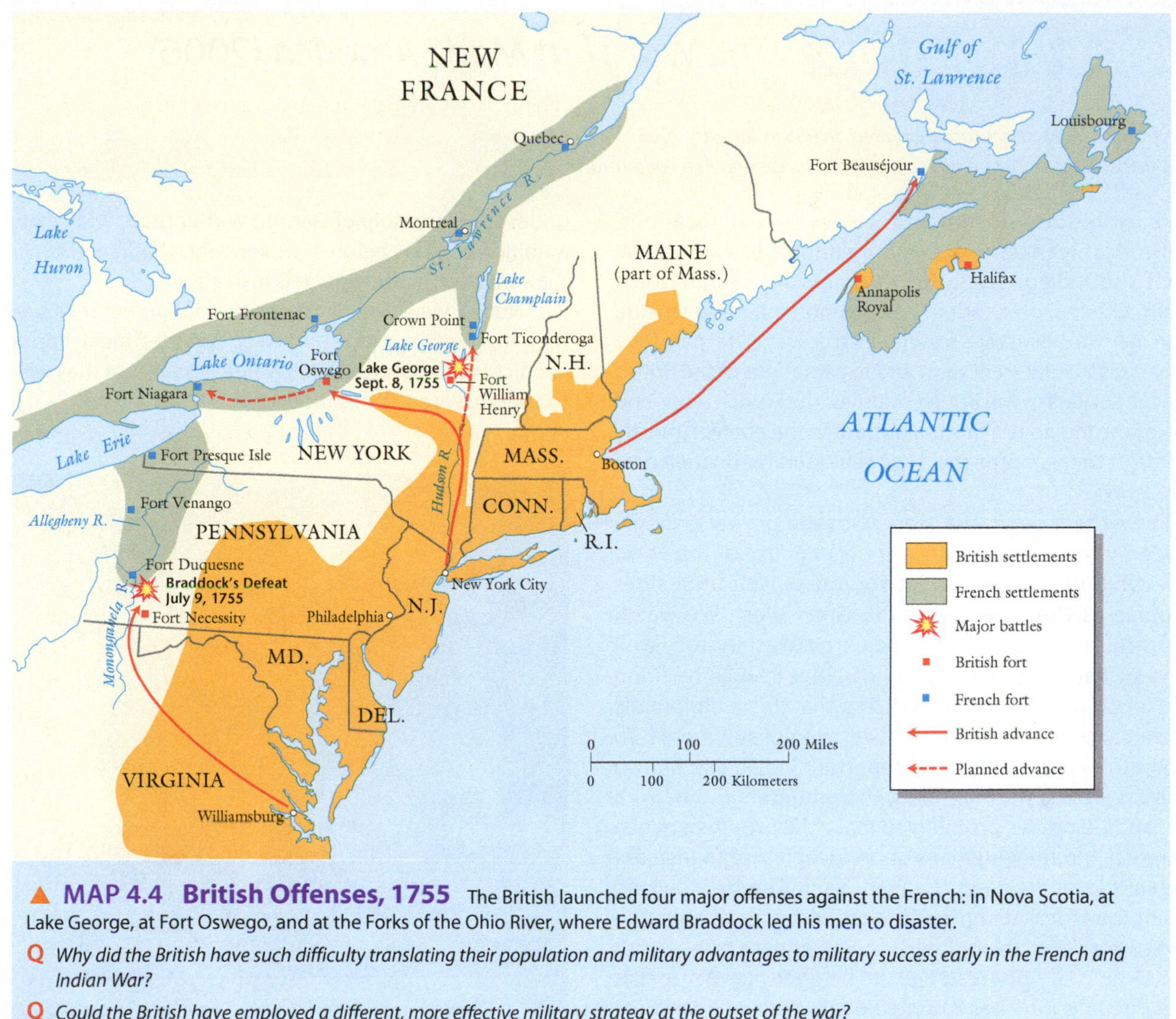

▲ **MAP 4.4 British Offenses, 1755** The British launched four major offenses against the French: in Nova Scotia, at Lake George, at Fort Oswego, and at the Forks of the Ohio River, where Edward Braddock led his men to disaster.

Q *Why did the British have such difficulty translating their population and military advantages to military success early in the French and Indian War?*

Q *Could the British have employed a different, more effective military strategy at the outset of the war?*

and redistributed it to Protestant settlers, mostly from New England. About 3,000 Acadian refugees, after spending miserable years as unwanted Catholic exiles in a Protestant world, finally made it to French Louisiana, where their descendants became known as Cajuns. Others went to France, and some even made their way back to Nova Scotia or what later became New Brunswick. Few remained in the 13 colonies.

In the major northern theater of war in 1755, Johnson led his provincials against Crown Point. The French commander, Jean-Armand, Baron Dieskau, hoping to repeat the French success against Braddock, attacked a body of provincials on September 8 and drove it back in panic to its base camp at Fort William Henry near Lake George. French regulars assailed the fort but were driven off with heavy losses in a six-hour struggle. Colonial newspapers proclaimed the battle a great victory because the provincials had not only held the field but had also wounded and captured Dieskau. Johnson probably could have taken poorly defended Crown Point, but he too had been wounded and was content to hold Fort William Henry and nearby Fort Edward at the headwaters of the Hudson.

Farther west, Shirley's Niagara campaign reached Oswego on Lake Ontario and then stopped for the winter, checked by the French at Fort Frontenac on the lake's northern shore. Heavy snows soon cut off Oswego. Malnutrition and disease ravaged the garrison.

4-7c *A World War*

With the death of Braddock and the capture of Dieskau, military amateurs took over both armies: Shirley in the British colonies and Governor-General Pierre de Rigaud de Vaudreuil in New France. Vaudreuil, a Canadian, understood his colony's weakness without Indian support. The white population of the 13 colonies outnumbered that of New France by 13 to 1; Massachusetts alone had nearly three times as many settlers as New France. Vaudreuil also knew that if the redcoats and the British colonies concentrated their resources in a few critical places, they might well overwhelm New France. Thus, Vaudreuil sought allies among the Indians and sought to

History Through Film *The War That Made America* (2006)

A four-hour documentary that aired on PBS in January 2006. Written, produced, and directed by Eric Stange and Ben Loeterman.

This ambitious documentary uses actual locations, historical reenactments, and a narrator to explore the French and Indian War in North America. The narrator is Graham Greene, an Academy Award nominee and Oneida Indian whose ancestors fought in the war. The narrative emphasizes the different roles and expectations of the British army, the settlers in the British colonies, the French army, and many of the Indian nations that fought in the conflict, mostly in an effort to guarantee that they could survive on their own native lands.

The writers begin the story with the prewar struggle between Virginia and New France for control of the Forks of the Ohio River (modern Pittsburgh), which both sides recognize as the gateway to the Great West. We watch a youthful and inexperienced George Washington, well played by Larry Nehring, open hostilities in 1754 by firing on a French patrol without realizing that it is a diplomatic mission carrying a message to the governor of Virginia. To Washington's horror, his most important Indian ally, known to the English as the Half King, then murders the patrol's commanding officer, probably to make the breach between the French and the Virginians unbridgeable and to increase the chief's local prestige. The French retaliate by attacking Washington's force at improvised Fort Necessity. Washington has to surrender to the murdered commander's brother, but because he could not read French, he does not realize that in the document he has to sign, he takes full responsibility for the killing.

Viewers then witness General Edward Braddock's disastrous defeat in 1755, the ravaging of the frontiers of Pennsylvania and Virginia, the serious quarrels between Lord Loudoun (the new British commander) and the colonists, the resurgence of British power under the leadership of William Pitt, and the fall of New France after defeats at Quebec and Montreal. Pontiac's War of 1763–1764 and the atrocities committed by the Paxton Boys get major attention. The final episode argues that Britain's victory left the army and the home government so arrogant and confident of their power that they alienated the North American colonists. Ironically, Greene tells us, the unintended consequences of the struggle prove far more important than the intended ones. The victory lessened Britain's power in America by provoking a revolution that led to the creation of the United States of America under the leadership of George Washington, whose highest ambition 20 years before independence had been to acquire a commission in the regular British army.

Not all viewers will accept the documentary's premise that the French and Indian War was the most important conflict ever fought on North American soil, but they will have to take that argument seriously. ■

North Wind Picture Archives/Alamy Stock Photo

4.12 In July 1755, a combined French and Indian force killed British General Edward Braddock and soundly defeated his army at the Battle of the Monongahela, events depicted in *The War That Made America*.

engage British settlers, most of whom had little redcoat support, along a broad front. A horrible frontier war ensued.

As long as Vaudreuil was in charge, New France kept winning. Indian attacks devastated frontier settlements, especially in Pennsylvania, a pacifist colony without a militia or any forts when the war began. Even so, the French government decided that New France needed a professional general and sent Louis-Joseph, Marquis de Montcalm, in 1756. Shocked and repelled by the brutality of frontier warfare, Montcalm tried to turn the conflict into a traditional European struggle of sieges and battles in which the advantage (as Vaudreuil well understood) would pass to the British. Nevertheless, Montcalm won several major successes. Oswego fell in summer 1756. When Fort William Henry surrendered to him a year later, he promised the garrison the honors of war, which meant that it could keep its property and march unmolested to Fort Edward. But France's Indian allies considered this agreement a betrayal of their customs. They killed or carried off 308 of the 2,400 prisoners, an event that colonial newspapers called the Massacre of Fort William Henry. Most of those killed were trying to save their property, which the Indians considered their rightful plunder. Montcalm lost heavily at Fort William Henry. He was never again able to raise sizable bodies of western Indians, and because the British blamed him for the "massacre," they refused to grant the honors of war to any French force for the rest of the conflict.

Meanwhile, Braddock's defeat, combined with the British loss of Minorca in the Mediterranean, convinced London that the struggle with France could not be limited to a few outposts. Britain declared war in 1756, and the French and Indian War in the colonies merged with a general European struggle—the Seven Years' War (1756–1763)—involving France, Austria, and Russia against Prussia, which was heavily subsidized by Britain. Although religion had little to do with the war in Europe, the Seven Years' War aligned coalitions of Protestant states against Catholic states in a way not seen for a century. To many colonial clergymen, a Protestant victory might herald the onset of the Millennium. The conflict spread even to India, where British forces expelled the French from nearly the whole subcontinent.

Reluctant to antagonize Britain, Spain remained neutral for most of the war, a choice with huge implications in North America. In the previous war, Spain had been able to turn the slaves of South Carolina against their masters and create unrest even in New York. Spanish hostilities early in the war would have opened another theater of conflict. Instead, Spain's neutrality permitted Britain to concentrate an overwhelming force against New France.

4-7d *Imperial Tensions: From Loudoun to Pitt*

When London realized in 1755 that the amateur Shirley had taken command of the British army in North America, it dispatched an irascible Scot, John Campbell, earl of Loudoun, to replace him. Loudoun had a special talent for infuriating provincials. Colonial units did not care to serve under his command and sometimes bluntly rejected his orders. Provincials believed they had a contractual relationship with *their* officers; they had never agreed to serve under Loudoun's professionals. They refused to serve beyond their term of enlistment, which expired on November 1 or December 1 of each year. When ordered to stay longer, many of them defiantly marched home.

Many British officers despised the provincials. "The Americans are in general the dirtiest most contemptible cowardly dogs that you can conceive," snarled General James Wolfe. "They fall down dead in their own dirt and desert by battalions, officers and all." General John Forbes was usually more positive, but he too once suggested "shooting dead a Dozen of their cowardly Officers at the Head of the Line." Some British officers held more favorable opinions. Horatio Gates, Richard Montgomery, Hugh Mercer, and Arthur St. Clair all remained in America after the war and became generals in the American army during the Revolution. In the House of Commons in 1765, Colonel Isaac Barré praised the courage of America's "Sons of Liberty"—a label soon adopted by men resisting Britain's postwar policies.

As the new commander in chief, Loudoun faced other problems: the quartering (or housing) of British soldiers, the relative rank of British and provincial officers, military discipline, revenue, and smuggling. He tried to impose authoritarian solutions on them all. When he sent redcoats into a city, he demanded that the assembly pay to quarter them, or else he would take over buildings by force. He tried to make any British senior captain superior in rank to any provincial officer, a rule that angered such experienced New England officers as General John Winslow and his six colonels. Loudoun ordered New England troops to serve directly under British officers and to accept the harsh discipline of the British army, an arrangement that, New Englanders insisted, violated their enlistment terms. They refused to cooperate. If a colonial assembly refused to vote adequate supplies, Loudoun urged Parliament to tax the colonies directly.

In 1757, William Pitt came to power as Britain's war minister and found workable solutions using voluntaristic principles to the problems that had defeated Loudoun's authoritarian methods. Pitt understood that consent worked better than coercion in the colonies. Colonial assemblies built barracks to house British soldiers. Pitt declared that every provincial officer would rank immediately behind the equivalent British rank but above all lesser officers, British or provincial. He then promoted every British lieutenant colonel to the rank of "colonel in America only." That decision left only about 30 British majors vulnerable to being ordered about by a provincial colonel, but few of them had independent commands anyway. Provincial units under the command of their own officers cooperated with the British army, and the officers began to impose something close to British discipline on them, including hundreds of lashes for routine offenses. Quite a few men began to reenlist.

Rather than impose a parliamentary tax, Pitt set aside £200,000 beginning in 1758 (later reduced to £133,000)

Hulton Archive/Stringer/Hulton Archive/Getty Images

4.13 **"The English Lion Dismember'd" (1756)** This striking cartoon reflects British consternation during the first half of the Seven Years' War. France had just taken the Mediterranean island of Minorca from the British.

and told the colonies that they could claim a share of it in proportion to their contribution to the war effort. In effect, he gave the colonies incentive to compete voluntarily in support of the war. The subsidies covered something less than half of the cost of fielding 20,000 provincials each year from 1758 to 1760, and rather smaller numbers in 1761 and 1762 as operations shifted to the Caribbean. By then, Canada, Martinique, and Guadeloupe, as well as Spanish Havana, were all in British hands.

Pitt had no patience with military failure. After Loudoun failed to attack Louisbourg in 1757, Pitt replaced him with James Abercrombie. He also put Jeffrey Amherst in charge of a new Louisbourg expedition, with James Wolfe as one of his brigadiers. By 1758, the British Empire had put together a military force capable of overwhelming New France and knew how to use it. Cooperation between redcoats and provincials became devastatingly effective.

4-7e *The Years of British Victory*

By 1758, the Royal Navy had cut off reinforcements and supplies to Canada. Britain had sent a large navy and more than 30 regiments to North America. Combined with 20,000 provincials, thousands of bateau men rowing supplies into the interior, and swarms of **privateers** (private ships with government authorization to take enemy prizes) preying on French commerce, Britain had mustered perhaps 60,000 men in North America and nearby waters. Most of them now closed in on the 75,000 people of New France. Montcalm, who was running out of goods for the Indian trade, refused to encourage more Indian attacks on the frontier and prepared to defend the approaches to Canada at Forts Duquesne, Niagara, Frontenac, Ticonderoga, Crown Point, and Louisbourg.

Spurred on by Quaker mediators, the British and colonial governments came to terms with the western Indians in 1758, arranging an uneasy peace mostly by promising not to seize their lands after the war. Few settlers or officials had yet noticed a new trend that was emerging during the conflict. Before the 1750s, Indian nations had often waged terrible wars against one another. Now, however, few Indians in the northeastern woodlands were willing to attack others. In 1755, for example, some Senecas fought with New France and some Mohawks with the British, but they carefully avoided confronting each other. This Iroquois sense of solidarity was spreading. Iroquois and western Algonquians, once deadly enemies, saw real advantages in cooperation. A pan-Indian identity was beginning to emerge.

Peace with the western Indians in 1758 permitted the British to revive the grand military plan of 1755, except that this time the overall goal was the conquest of New France (see Map 4.5). Amherst and Wolfe, with 9,000 regulars and 500 provincials, besieged Louisbourg, and it fell in September, enabling Nova Scotia to annex Cape Breton Island. Colonel John Bradstreet's 3,000 provincials advanced to Lake Ontario, took Fort Frontenac, and began building a fleet. This victory cut off the French in the Ohio Valley from their supplies. A powerful force of regulars under John Forbes and provincials under Washington marched west, this time through Pennsylvania, to attack Fort Duquesne, but the French blew up the fort and retreated north just before they arrived. The British erected Fort Pitt on the ruins.

The only British defeat in 1758 occurred in northern New York when Abercrombie ordered a costly frontal assault against a heavily fortified position at Ticonderoga (Carillon). When Pitt heard the news, he sacked Abercrombie, put Amherst in charge of the New York theater of war, and left Wolfe at Louisbourg to plan an attack up the St. Lawrence River against Quebec.

In 1759, while the provincials on Lake Ontario took Niagara, Amherst spent the summer cautiously reducing Ticonderoga and Crown Point. (Pitt expected him to

▲ **MAP 4.5 Conquest of Canada, 1758–1760** In three campaigns, the British, with strong colonial support, first subdued the outer defenses of New France, then took Quebec in 1759 and Montreal in 1760.

Q *Compare this map with Map 4.4, which details the British offensive of 1755. What similarities and differences do you notice? What made the offensive of 1758–1760 more successful?*

Q *Dating to the seventeenth century, the Saint Lawrence River Valley had signified the heart of New France. How did the British finally manage to conquer the region?*

reach Montreal.) The most dramatic campaign occurred farther east. In June, Wolfe ascended the St. Lawrence with 8,000 redcoats and colonial rangers and laid siege to Quebec, defended by Montcalm with 16,000 regulars, Canadian militia, and Indians. When an attack below the city failed, Wolfe mounted howitzers on high ground across the river from Quebec and began reducing the city to rubble. Frustrated by the French refusal to come out and fight, he turned loose his American rangers ("the worst soldiers in the universe," he boasted), who burned more than 1,400 farms. Anyone who resisted was shot and scalped. Still the French held out.

By September, both Wolfe and Montcalm realized that the British fleet would soon have to depart or risk being frozen in during the long winter. Wolfe made a last desperate effort, preferring to die rather than fail. His men silently sailed up the river, climbed a formidable cliff above the city in darkness, and on the morning of September 13, 1759, deployed on the Plains of Abraham behind Quebec. Montcalm panicked. Instead of using his artillery to defend the walls from inside (Wolfe's force had been able to drag only two small guns with them), he marched out of Quebec onto the plains. Both generals now got what they craved most, a set piece but brief European battle. Wolfe and Montcalm were mortally wounded, but the British swept the field and took Quebec. Montreal fell in 1760, and Canada surrendered.

Only later, in January 1762, after France had been defeated, did Spain finally enter the war. British forces quickly took Havana and even Manila in the distant Philippines. France and Spain sued for peace.

World History Archive/Image Asset Management Ltd/Alamy Stock Photo

4.14 ***Death of General Wolfe* (1771)** Benjamin West, who was born in Pennsylvania, taught himself to paint, opened a studio in Philadelphia, and then went to Europe. He studied the great Italian masters for several years and then settled in London, where he became the first American artist to have an enormous impact. Contemporary heroes had been displayed in classical attire, but West used their actual uniforms. George III was so impressed that he made West the history painter to the royal court.

Q *Although sentiment and nationalism are usually more associated with the 19th century than the 18th century, how does West use each sensation to produce feeling in the painting?*

4-7f *The Peace of Paris*

In 1763, the Peace of Paris ended the war. Britain returned Martinique and Guadeloupe to France. France gave Britain several minor West Indian islands and all of North America east of the Mississippi, except New Orleans. In exchange for Havana, Spain ceded Florida to the British and agreed to pay a large ransom for Manila. To compensate its Spanish ally, France gave New Orleans and Louisiana west of the Mississippi to Spain. Most Spanish and African occupants of Florida withdrew to other parts of the Spanish Empire, but nearly all of the French settlers remained in Canada, the Illinois Country, and what was now Spanish Louisiana.

British colonists were jubilant. The age of warfare and frontier carnage seemed over at last. Britain and the colonies could now develop their vast resources in an imperial partnership that would bring unprecedented prosperity. But western Indians angrily rejected the peace settlement. No one had conquered them, and they denied the right of France to surrender their lands to Great Britain. They began to plan their own war of liberation.

Conclusion

Between 1713 and 1754, expansion and renewed immigration pushed North American settlement ever farther into the interior (see Map 4.6). With a population that doubled every 25 years, many householders could no longer give all of their sons and daughters the level of economic success that they were enjoying. By midcentury, many family members took up a trade or looked westward for what their fathers could not provide. Women worked harder just to sustain opportunity for their households. Many families had to favor sons over daughters and the eldest son over his younger brothers, reluctantly following practices used in England.

The colonies anglicized in other ways as well. Newspapers and the learned professions spread the Enlightenment to the colonies. Male and female colonists rapidly consumed British goods. English revivalists, especially George Whitefield, had a huge impact in North America. Northern colonies borrowed Court politics from Walpole's Britain, while most southern colonies favored politics as envisioned by Britain's Country opposition. Both considered themselves the freest people on earth. When imperial rivalries again led to war after 1739, the colonists discovered that African slaves associated Spain with liberty, while most Eastern Woodland Indians still looked to New France for support. The threat of internal upheaval kept King George's War indecisive in the 1740s. Taking advantage of Spain's neutral position when Britain and France went to war in 1755, the British Empire concentrated its resources and conquered New France.

The French and Indian War left behind vivid memories. Provincials admired the courage of the redcoats and the victories they won but hated their brutal discipline and arrogant officers. British officials greatly exaggerated what military force alone could accomplish and underestimated colonial contributions to the imperial cause. The concord and prosperity that were supposed to follow the empire's great triumph yielded instead to bitter strife.

▲ **MAP 4.6 Growth of Population to 1760** Between 1700 and 1760, the population of the British colonies had increased by more than a factor of six, from 250,000 to almost 1.6 million. Settlement had filled the piedmont in most areas and was beginning to cross the Appalachian watershed into the Ohio Valley.

Q *What factors contributed to the greater population growth and territorial expansion in the mid-Atlantic and southern regions compared to the north?*

Q *From a British imperialistic perspective, what were the advantages and disadvantages of America's prodigious population growth?*

CHAPTER REVIEW

Review

1. In what ways did American colonists attempt to imitate British society in the 18th century?
2. What were the principal differences between the populations and economies of the three major colonial regions, the South, the mid-Atlantic, and New England?
3. What was the Enlightenment and how did it shape the 18th-century colonies?
4. What was the Great Awakening and how did it change religion in the American colonies in the 18th century?
5. Why did Britain's "Country" values prevail in most southern colonies while "Court" politics took hold in most northern provinces?
6. How did Indians and African slaves take advantage of opportunities presented by a new round of European wars starting in 1739?
7. What made the War for North America (1754–1763) so much more decisive than the three earlier Anglo-French wars?

Critical Thinking

1. "How is it that we hear the loudest yelps for liberty among the drivers of Negroes?" asked Dr. Samuel Johnson, a towering literary figure in 18th-century England, on the eve of the Revolutionary War. Thomas Jefferson, George Washington, Patrick Henry, James Madison, and many other prominent spokesmen for the American cause owned dozens, even hundreds, of slaves. Is there any way that being a large slaveholder might have increased a planter's commitment to liberty as it had come to be understood in England and the colonies by that time? Did Johnson have a point?
2. The Duc de Choiseul, who negotiated the Treaty of Paris that ended the Seven Years' War in 1763, and the Comte de Vergennes, who negotiated the Franco-American alliance of 1778, both claimed that France's decision to cede Canada to Great Britain in 1763 was a master stroke of French policy because, with no enemy to fear on their borders, the colonies would no longer need British protection and would soon move toward complete independence. By contrast, the leaders of colonial resistance after 1763 always insisted that Britain's postwar policies provoked both the resistance and independence. Who was right?

Identifications

Review your understanding of the following key terms, people, and events for this chapter (terms in bold in text are included in the Glossary).

anglicization, p. 102
dowry, p. 103
coverture, p. 103
dower rights, p. 103
Middle Passage, p. 104
gang system, p. 104
sickle cell, p. 104
task system, p. 105
Gullah, p. 106
redemptioners, p. 106
fiat money, p. 107
John Peter Zenger, p. 108
Enlightenment, p. 108
consumer society, p. 111
evangelical, p. 113
Presbytery, p. 113
Synod, p. 113
revival, p. 113
Freemasons, p. 114
New Side, p. 114
Old Side, p. 114
New Lights, p. 115
Old Lights, p. 115
placemen, p. 117
politics of harmony, p. 118
republics, p. 119
press gangs, p. 120
Albany Congress, p. 123
privateers, p. 128

Suggested Readings

The most important study of immigration in the 18th century is ***Marianne S. Wokeck, Trade in Strangers: The Beginnings of Mass Migration to North America*** (1999). The ***Trans-Atlantic Slave Trade Database***, available at www.slavevoyages.org, provides updated figures on the Atlantic slave trade and information on every documented slave ship voyage in the early modern Atlantic world. For the nature of slave life in colonial North America, see **Philip D. Morgan's** ***Slave Counterpoint: Black Culture in the Eighteenth-Century Chesapeake & Lowcountry*** (1998). For gentility and the Enlightenment, excellent studies include **Richard L. Bushman,** ***The Refinement of America: Persons, Houses, Cities*** (1992); and **Ned Landsman,** ***From Colonials to Provincials: Thought and Culture in America, 1680–1760*** (1998). **Jennifer L. Anderson,** ***Mahogany: The Costs of Luxury in Early America*** (2012) explores the human and environmental impact of an important luxury good. For women and the consumer revolution, see **Zara Anishanslin,** ***Portrait of a Woman in Silk: Hidden Histories of the British Atlantic World*** (2016). ***Mark A. Noll, The Rise of Evangelical Religion: The Age of Edwards, Whitefield, and the Wesleys*** (2003), provides a comprehensive overview of the Great Awakening. **Richard R. Beeman's** ***Varieties of Political Experience in Eighteenth-Century America*** (2004); and

Brendan McConville's ***The King's Three Faces: The Rise & Fall of Royal America, 1688–1776*** (2006), are ambitious studies of politics in the British colonies.

For the renewal of imperial conflict after 1739, see **Jill Lepore,** ***New York Burning: Liberty, Slavery, and Conspiracy in Eighteenth-Century Manhattan*** (2005); **Denver Brunsman,** ***The Evil Necessity: British Naval Impressment in the Eighteenth-Century Atlantic World*** (2013); **Fred Anderson,** ***Crucible of War: The Seven Years War and the Fate of Empire in British North America, 1754–1766*** (2000); **Timothy J. Shannon,** ***Indians and Colonists at the Crossroads of Empire: The Albany Congress of 1754*** (2000); and **Christopher Hodson,** ***The Acadian Diaspora: An Eighteenth-Century History*** (2012).

5 Reform, Resistance, Revolution, 1763–1776

5-1 Imperial Reform

Learning Objective: *Describe how Britain's victory in the Seven Years' War led to controversial imperial reforms for its American colonies.*

Impetus for Reform
Indian Policy and Pontiac's War
The Sugar Act
The Currency Act and the Quartering Act
The Stamp Act

5-2 The Stamp Act Crisis

Learning Objective: *Explain how Parliament resolved the Stamp Act crisis without fully surrendering its right to tax the American colonies.*

Nullification
Repeal

5-3 The Townshend Crisis

Learning Objective: *Identify what made the resolution of the Townshend crisis less satisfying for American colonists than the end to the Stamp Act crisis.*

The Townshend Program
Resistance: The Politics of Escalation
The Wilkes Crisis
The Boston Massacre
Partial Repeal
Disaffection

5-4 Internal Cleavages: The Contagion of Liberty

Learning Objective: *Trace how the British imperial crisis helped to expose tensions within American society among the following groups: patriots and loyalists (and loyal colonies); artisans and gentlemen; tenants and landlords; settlers and proprietors; women and men; and slaves and masters.*

Divided Loyalties
Urban and Rural Discontent
Slaves and Women

5-5 The Last Imperial Crisis

Learning Objective: *Analyze why the colonists started a revolution after the Tea Act lowered the price of tea.*

The Tea Crisis
Britain's Response: The Coercive Acts
The Radical Explosion
The First Continental Congress
Toward War

5-6 The Improvised War

Learning Objective: *Detail how the onset of war with Britain influenced America's decision to declare independence and the language in the Declaration of Independence.*

The Second Continental Congress
War and Legitimacy, 1775–1776
Independence

5.1 **Engagement at the North Bridge in Concord, April 19, 1775** This 1775 painting by Ralph Earl is quite accurate in its details. It shows the first American military victory in the war when the militia drove the British back from Concord Bridge and eventually through Lexington and all the way to Boston.

BRITAIN LEFT AN ARMY IN NORTH AMERICA after 1763 and taxed the colonies to pay part of its cost. The colonists agreed that they should contribute to their own defense but insisted that taxation without representation violated their rights as Englishmen. Three successive crises, provoked by parliamentary taxation, shattered Britain's North American empire by 1776.

In the Stamp Act crisis, the colonists first petitioned Parliament for a redress of grievances. When that effort failed, they nullified the Stamp Act and continued their resistance until Parliament repealed the tax in 1766. The settlers joyfully celebrated their victory. In the Townshend crisis of 1767–1770, Parliament imposed new taxes on certain imported goods. The colonists petitioned and resisted simultaneously, mostly through an intercolonial nonimportation movement. The British sent troops to Boston. After several violent confrontations, the soldiers withdrew, while Parliament modified but did not repeal the Townshend Revenue Act. The duty on tea remained. Repeal of the other duties broke the back of the nonimportation movement. Nobody celebrated. The Tea Act of 1773 launched the third crisis, and it quickly escalated. Boston destroyed British tea without bothering to petition first. When Parliament responded with the

Coercive Acts of 1774, the colonists created the Continental Congress to organize further resistance. Neither side dared back down, and the confrontation careened toward military violence. War broke out in April 1775. Fifteen months later, the colonies declared their independence. ■

5-1 Imperial Reform

Q *How did Britain's victory in the Seven Years' War lead to controversial imperial reforms for its American colonies?*

In 1760, George III (1760–1820) inherited the British throne at the age of 22. The king's pronouncements on behalf of religion and virtue at first won him many admirers in North America, but the political coalition leading Britain to victory over France fell apart. The king's new ministers set out to reform the empire.

5-1a *Impetus for Reform*

At the start of his reign, George feared that the Seven Years' War would bankrupt Britain. He had cause for concern. By the Treaty of Paris in 1763, Britain's national debt had nearly doubled from its prewar levels and stood at more than £130 million. Interest alone absorbed more than half of annual revenues, and Britain was already one of the most heavily taxed societies in the world.

Adding to the challenge, the war was not a one-time cost. The sheer scale of Britain's victory required more revenue just to police its new conquests. In April 1763, George Grenville became first lord of the treasury and the king's leading minister. Grenville pursued a policy of leaving 20 battalions (about 7,000) men in America, mostly in Canada and Florida, with small garrisons scattered throughout Indian territory. Because the colonists would receive the benefit of this protection, Grenville argued, they ought to pay a reasonable portion of the cost, and eventually all of it. He never asked the settlers to contribute anything to Britain's national debt or to urgent domestic needs, but he insisted that they contribute to their own defense.

The king's **Proclamation of 1763** further outlined Britain's approach to governing its expanded American empire. The measure set up governments in Canada, Florida, and other conquered colonies, and it created the so-called Proclamation Line along the Appalachian watershed to regulate the pace of western expansion (see Map 5.1). No settlements could be planted west of that line unless Britain first purchased the land from the Indians. Settlers would be encouraged to move instead to Nova Scotia, northern New England, Georgia, or Florida.

For colonists, many of whom had fought against France to open western lands to settlement, Britain's initial policies after the Seven Years' War were troubling. A more skillful approach to reforming the empire might have built on the voluntaristic measures that William Pitt had used to win the war. Instead, Grenville reverted to the demands for coercive reforms that had crisscrossed the Atlantic during Britain's years of defeat from 1755 to 1757. In his mind, Britain had won the war, not with the cooperation of the colonies, but despite their obstruction. London, he believed, had to act quickly to establish its authority before the colonies, with their astonishing rate of growth, slipped completely out of control. In effect, he set in motion a self-fulfilling prophecy in which the British government brought about precisely what it was trying to prevent. Nearly every step it took undermined the colonies' loyalty to Britain.

5-1b *Indian Policy and Pontiac's War*

Initially, at least, events on the ground seemed to support Grenville's reasoning that Britain needed a residual force to keep the peace in North America. In 1760, upon the British defeat of the French, General Jeffery Amherst had made a fateful decision to stop distributing Indian gifts. His contempt for Indian customs deprived the government of most of its leverage with natives just when their ability to unite had become stronger than ever.

In 1761, Neolin, a western Delaware, reported a vision in which God commanded Indians to return to their ancestral ways. Neolin's call for an end to Indian dependence on European goods, especially rum, resonated with his followers, who were dismayed by the British decision to end gifts. He stopped short of condemning the French still living in the Great Lakes region. Many of his followers even hoped that their fierce resolve would attract the support of King Louis XV of France (1715–1774), restore the friendly relations of the past, and halt British expansion.

With unprecedented unity, the Indians struck in 1763. **Pontiac's War**, named for an Ottawa chief and follower of Neolin, combined Seneca, Mingo, Delaware, Shawnee,

CHRONOLOGY

1759–1761	Cherokee War devastates South Carolina backcountry
1760	George III becomes king of Great Britain
1763	Grenville ministry takes power • Wilkes publishes *North Briton* No. 45 • Pontiac's War begins • King issues Proclamation of 1763
1764	Parliament passes Currency Act and Sugar Act
1765	Parliament passes Quartering Act • Stamp Act passed and nullified • Rockingham replaces Grenville as prime minister
1766	Parliament repeals Stamp Act, passes Declaratory Act and Revenue Act of 1766 • Chatham (Pitt) ministry takes power
1767	Parliament passes New York Restraining Act and Townshend Revenue Act
1768	Massachusetts assembly dispatches Circular Letter • Wilkes elected to Parliament • Massacre of St. George's Fields in England • Massachusetts refuses to rescind Circular Letter • *Liberty* riot in Boston • Assemblies supporting Circular Letter are dissolved • Redcoats sent to Boston
1769	Nonimportation becomes effective • Regulators achieve major goals in South Carolina
1770	North becomes prime minister • Boston Massacre • Townshend Revenue Act partially repealed • Nonimportation collapses
1771	North Carolina regulators defeated at Alamance Creek
1772–1773	*Gaspée* affair • Twelve colonies create committees of correspondence
1773	Tea Act passed • Boston Tea Party • Wheatley's poetry published
1774	American Quakers prohibit slaveholding • Parliament passes Coercive Acts and Quebec Act • First Continental Congress convenes
1775	Revolutionary War begins at Lexington and Concord • Second Continental Congress creates Continental army • Olive Branch Petition fails • George III issues Proclamation of Rebellion
1775–1776	Americans invade Canada
1776	Paine publishes *Common Sense* • British evacuate Boston • Continental Congress approves Declaration of Independence

Wyandot, Miami, Ottawa, and other warriors. They attacked 13 British posts in the West. Between May 16 and June 20, all of the forts fell except Niagara, Pitt, Detroit, and a tiny outpost on Green Bay that the Indians did not bother to attack. For months, the Indians kept Detroit and Pitt under close siege, something Indians were supposed to be incapable of doing. They hoped to drive British settlers back to the eastern seaboard.

Enraged by these successes, Amherst ordered Colonel Henry Bouquet, commander at Fort Pitt, to distribute smallpox-infested blankets among the western nations, contributing to a lethal epidemic in 1763 and 1764. "You will do well to try to Inoculate the Indians by means of Blankets," he wrote to Bouquet, "as well as to Try Every other Method that can serve to Extirpate this Execrable Race." In 1764, British and provincial forces ended resistance, restored peace, and compelled the Indians to return their hundreds of captives, many of whom preferred to stay. The British then reluctantly accepted the role that the French had played in the Great Lakes region by distributing gifts and mediating differences. On that question, the Indians won an important victory.

Still, Britain's reversal on gifts and other imperial reforms failed to keep the peace between settlers and Indians. Perhaps sensing the Indians' growing unity, many settlers began to assume that all Indians must be the enemies of all whites. In December 1763, the Scots-Irish of Paxton Township, Pennsylvania, murdered six unarmed Christian Indians—two old men, three women, and a child—at nearby Conestoga. Two weeks later, the "Paxton Boys" slaughtered 14 more Christian Indians who had been brought to Lancaster for protection. After Governor John Penn removed 140 Moravian mission Indians to Philadelphia for safety, the Paxton Boys marched on the capital, determined to kill them all.

Denouncing the Paxton Boys as "Christian white Savages," Benjamin Franklin led a delegation from the assembly that met the marchers at Germantown and persuaded them to go home after they presented a list of their grievances. The Moravian Indians had been spared. But efforts to bring the murderers to justice failed, and Pennsylvania and Virginia frontiersmen virtually declared an open season on Indians that continued for years. Settlers in Augusta County, Virginia, slaughtered nine Shawnees in 1765. Frederick Stump murdered 10 more in Pennsylvania in 1768 but could not be convicted in his frontier county. Such atrocities kept western Indians smoldering. London had hoped that its officials would bring evenhanded justice to the frontier. Indians had won real benefits from Britain's postwar policies, such as protection from land speculators, but otherwise they found no good option between Amherst's smallpox blankets and the murderous rage of the Paxton Boys.

5-1c *The Sugar Act*

In a step that settlers found ominous, Grenville's Sugar Act of 1764 proclaimed it "just and necessary, that a revenue be raised ... in America for defraying the expenses of defending, protecting, and securing" the colonies. The act placed duties on Madeira wine, coffee, and other products, but Grenville expected the greatest revenue to come from the molasses duty of three pence per gallon. The Molasses Act of 1733 had been designed to keep French molasses out of North America by

▲ **MAP 5.1 Pontiac's War and the Proclamation Line of 1763** Britain claimed possession of North America east of the Mississippi only to face an extraordinary challenge from the Indians of the interior, who wiped out eight garrisons but could not take Detroit, Niagara, or Fort Pitt.

Q *Why did Pontiac and his coalition target former French forts that had only become British as a result of the Seven Years' War?*

Q *How did Pontiac's War reinforce the logic of Britain's imperial reforms, such as the Proclamation of 1763?*

imposing a prohibitive duty of six pence per gallon. Instead, by paying a bribe of about a penny per gallon, merchants got French molasses certified as British. By 1760, more than 90 percent of all molasses imported into New England came from the French islands. Planters in the British islands gave up, lost interest in New England markets, and turned their molasses into quality rum for sale in Britain and Ireland. Nobody, in short, had any interest in stopping the trade in French molasses. New England merchants said they were willing to pay a duty of one penny (the current cost of bribes), but Grenville insisted on three. He hoped to raise £100,000 per year from the molasses duty, although in public he seldom put the figure above £40,000.

The Sugar Act also launched Grenville's war against smugglers. It vastly increased the amount of paperwork required of ship captains and permitted seizures of ships for what owners considered to be mere technicalities. In effect, Grenville tried to make it more profitable for customs officers to hound the merchants than to accept bribes from them. The Sugar Act encouraged them to prosecute violators in vice-admiralty courts, which did not use juries, rather than in common-law courts, which did. Prosecutors were virtually immune from any suit for damages, even when the merchant won an acquittal, so long as the judge certified "probable cause" for the seizure.

5-1d *The Currency Act and the Quartering Act*

Grenville passed several other imperial measures. The Currency Act of 1764 responded to wartime protests of London merchants against Virginia's paper money, which had lost almost 15 percent of its value between 1759 and 1764. The act forbade the colonies to issue any paper money as legal tender. The money question was urgent because the Sugar Act (and, later, the Stamp Act) required that all duties be paid in specie (silver or gold). Supporters of those taxes argued that the new duties would keep the specie in America to pay the army, but the colonists replied that the drain of specie from some colonies would put impossible constraints on trade. Boston and Newport, for instance, would pay most of the molasses tax, but specie collected there would follow the army to Quebec, New York, the Great Lakes, and Florida. Grenville saw "America" as a single region in which specie would circulate to the benefit of all. The colonists knew better. As of 1765, "America" existed only in British minds, not yet in colonial hearts.

Another reform measure was the Quartering Act of 1765, requested by Sir Thomas Gage, Amherst's successor as army commander. Gage asked for parliamentary authority to quarter soldiers in private homes, if necessary, when on the march and away from their barracks. Parliament ordered colonial assemblies to vote specific supplies, such as beer and candles, for the troops, which the assemblies were willingly doing already. But it also required the army to quarter its soldiers only in public buildings, such as taverns (which existed in large numbers only in cities) and not in private homes. The Quartering Act solved no problems, but it created several new ones.

5-1e *The Stamp Act*

In early 1764, when Parliament passed the Sugar Act, Grenville announced that a stamp tax on legal documents and on publications might also be needed. No one in the House of Commons, he declared, doubted Parliament's right to impose such a tax. Because Parliament had never levied a direct tax on the colonies, however, he also knew that he must persuade the settlers that a stamp tax would not be a constitutional innovation. This measure, his supporters insisted, did not violate the principle of no taxation without representation. The colonists were no different from the large nonvoting majority of subjects within Great Britain. They all shared **virtual representation** in Parliament. Each member of Parliament represented the entire empire, not just his constituency. Grenville also denied that there was any legal difference between external taxes (port duties, such as that on molasses) and internal (or inland) taxes, such as the proposed stamp tax.

Grenville put off passage of the Stamp Act while he collected more complete information about legal forms in the colonies. He also indicated that, if the colonies could devise a revenue plan better than a stamp tax, he would listen. His offer created confusion and became a public relations disaster for the government. All 13 colonial assemblies drafted petitions objecting to the Stamp Act as a form of taxation without representation. Most of them also attacked the duties imposed by the Sugar Act because they went beyond the regulation of trade. With few exceptions, they too rejected the distinction between internal and external taxes. Both, they declared, violated the British constitution. While agreeing that they ought to contribute to their own defense, they urged the government to return to the traditional method of requisitions, in which the Crown asked a colony for a specific sum, and the assembly decided how (or whether) to raise it. Colonists feared that taxation by Parliament might tempt Britain to rule them without consulting their assemblies.

As these petitions reached London, Parliament refused to receive them, citing a standing rule that prohibited petitions against money bills and declaring that any challenge to Parliament's right to pass such a tax was inadmissible. To Grenville, requisitions were not a better idea. They had often been tried, had never worked efficiently, and never would. He rejected the petitions with a clear conscience. But to the colonists, he seemed to have acted in bad faith all along. He had asked their advice and had then refused even to consider it.

The Stamp Act passed in February 1765, to go into effect on November 1. All contracts, licenses, commissions, and most other legal documents would be void unless they were executed on officially stamped paper. Law courts would not recognize any document that lacked the proper stamp, and the colonists would quietly, if grudgingly, accept Parliament's power to tax them. The act would almost enforce itself. A stamp duty was also put on all newspapers and pamphlets, a requirement likely to anger every printer in the colonies. Playing cards and dice were also taxed.

When the Stamp Act became law, most colonial leaders resigned themselves to a situation that seemed beyond their power to change. Daniel Dulany, a Maryland lawyer who did more than any other colonist to refute the argument for virtual representation, drew a line short of overt resistance. "I am upon a Question of *Propriety* not of Power," he wrote; "...at the same Time that I invalidate the Claim upon which [the Stamp Act] is founded, I may very consistently recommend a Submission to the Law, whilst it endures." But ordinary settlers recognized that direct action, and nothing else, might prevent implementation of the act.

5.2 **This is the Place to Affix the Stamp** This haunting image appeared in a Philadelphia newspaper in October 1765, reflecting deep colonial anger at the Stamp Act. A skull and crossbones replaced the symbol of the Crown that appeared on official stamps required by the act.

5-2 The Stamp Act Crisis

Q *How did Parliament resolve the Stamp Act crisis without fully surrendering its right to tax the American colonies?*

Resistance to the Stamp Act began in spring 1765 and continued for nearly a year, until it was repealed. Patrick Henry, a newcomer to the Virginia House of Burgesses, launched the first wave by introducing five resolutions on May 30 and 31. His resolves passed by margins ranging between 22 to 17 and 20 to 19; one was rescinded and expunged from the record the next day. Henry had two more in his pocket that he decided not to introduce. But over the summer, the *Newport Mercury* printed six of Henry's seven resolutions, and the *Maryland Gazette* published all of them. Neither paper reported that some of the seven had not passed. To other colonies, Virginia seemed to have taken a far more radical position than it actually had. The last resolve printed in the *Maryland Gazette* claimed that anyone defending Parliament's right to tax Virginia "shall be Deemed, an Enemy to this his Majesty's Colony."

In their fall or winter sessions, eight colonial legislatures passed new resolutions condemning the Stamp Act. Nine colonies sent delegates to the Stamp Act Congress, which met in New York in October. It passed resolutions affirming colonial loyalty to the king and "all due subordination" to Parliament but condemned the Stamp Act and Sugar Act. By 1765, nearly all colonial spokesmen agreed that the Stamp Act was unconstitutional, that colonial representation in Parliament (urged by a few writers) was impractical because of the distance and the huge expense, and thus that the Stamp Act had to be repealed. They accepted the idea of virtual representation *within* the colonies—their assemblies, they said, represented both voters and nonvoters in each colony—but the colonists ridiculed the argument when it was applied across the Atlantic. A disfranchised Englishman who acquired sufficient property could become a voter, pointed out Daniel Dulany, in a pamphlet that was widely admired, even in Britain. But, Dulany explained, no colonist, no matter how wealthy he became, could vote for a member of Parliament. Members of Parliament paid the taxes that they levied on others within Britain, but they would never pay any tax imposed on the colonies.

5-2a *Nullification*

No matter how eloquent, resolutions and pamphlets alone could not defeat the Stamp Act. Street violence might, however, and Boston showed the way, led by men calling themselves Sons of Liberty. On August 14, the town awoke to find an effigy of Andrew Oliver, the stamp distributor, hanging on what became the town's Liberty Tree (a gallows for hanging enemies of the people). The sheriff dared not remove the effigy. After dark, a crowd of men roamed the streets, shouted defiance at the governor and council, demolished a new building Oliver was erecting that "they called the Stamp Office," beheaded and burned Oliver's effigy, and finally invaded Oliver's home, "declaring they would kill Him." He had already fled to a neighbor's home. Thoroughly cowed, he resigned.

On August 26, another crowd all but demolished the elegant mansion of Lt. Governor Thomas Hutchinson. Most Bostonians believed that, in letters to British friends, he had defended and even helped to draft the Stamp Act. In fact, he had opposed it. Shocked by the destruction of property, the militia finally appeared to police the streets, but when Governor Francis Bernard tried to arrest those responsible for the first riot, he got nowhere. Bostonians deplored the events of August 26 but approved those of August 14. No one was punished for either event, although the whole city knew that Ebenezer McIntosh, a shoemaker and an organizer of the annual Pope's Day (Guy Fawkes Day) processions, led both riots.

Everywhere except in Georgia, the stamp master was forced to resign before the law took effect on November 1. With no one to distribute stamps, the act could not be implemented. Merchants adopted **nonimportation agreements** (boycotts of British goods) to pressure the British into repeal. In other cities the Sons of Liberty followed Boston's lead and took control of the streets. After November 1, they agitated to open the ports and courts, which had closed down rather than operate without stamps. Neither the courts nor the customs officers had any stamps to use because nobody dared distribute them. As winter gave way to spring, most ports and some courts resumed business. Only Newport matched Boston's level of violence, but in New York City a clash between the Sons of Liberty and the British garrison grew ugly and almost escalated into an armed encounter. Violent resistance worked. The Stamp Act was nullified—even in Georgia, eventually.

5-2b *Repeal*

The next move was up to Britain. For reasons that had nothing to do with the colonies, the king dismissed Grenville in summer 1765 and replaced his ministry with a narrow coalition organized primarily by William Augustus, duke of Cumberland, the king's uncle. An untested young nobleman, Charles Watson-Wentworth, Marquess of Rockingham, took over the treasury. This "Old Whig" ministry had to deal with the riots in America. Cumberland—the man who had sent Braddock to America in the winter of 1754–1755—may have favored a similar use of force in late 1765. If so, he never had a chance to issue the order. On October 31, minutes before an emergency cabinet meeting to address the American crisis, he died of a heart attack, leaving Rockingham in charge of the government. At first, Rockingham favored amending the Stamp Act, but by December he had decided on repeal. To win over the other ministers, the king, and Parliament, he would need great skill.

To Rockingham, the only alternative to repeal seemed to be a ruinous civil war in America, but as the king's chief minister, he could hardly tell Parliament that the world's greatest empire must yield to unruly mobs. He needed a better reason for repeal. Even before the first American nonimportation agreements reached London on December 12 (New York City's) and December 26 (Philadelphia's), he began to mobilize British merchants and manufacturers who traded with America. They petitioned Parliament to repeal the Stamp Act. They condemned the Grenville program as an economic disaster, and their arguments gave Rockingham the leverage he needed.

He won the concurrence of the other ministers only by promising to support a Declaratory Act affirming Parliament's sovereignty over the colonies. Rockingham still faced resistance from the king, who favored "modification" rather than repeal. George III appeared willing to repeal all of the stamp duties except those on dice and playing cards, the two levies most difficult to enforce. Only Grenville, however, was ready to use the army to enforce even an amended Stamp Act. Rockingham brought the king around by threatening to resign, which would have forced the king to bring back Grenville, whom he hated. Many pro-American witnesses appeared before Parliament to urge repeal, including Benjamin Franklin, who gave a masterful performance. Slowly, Rockingham put together his majority.

Three pieces of legislation ended the crisis. The first, the Declaratory Act, affirmed that Parliament had "full power and authority to make laws and statutes of sufficient force and validity to bind the colonies and people of America ... in all cases whatsoever." Rockingham resisted pressure to insert the word "taxes" along with "laws and statutes." That omission permitted the colonists, who drew a sharp distinction between legislation (which, they conceded, Parliament had a right to pass) and taxation (which it could not), to interpret the act as an affirmation of their position, while nearly everyone in Britain read precisely the opposite meaning into the phrase "laws and statutes." Old Whigs hoped that Parliament would never again insist on its sovereign power over America. Like the royal veto of an act of Parliament, that power existed, explained Edmund Burke; and like the veto, which had not been used for almost 60 years, it should never again be invoked. The colonists agreed. They read the Declaratory Act as a face-saving gesture that made repeal of the Stamp Act possible.

The second measure repealed the Stamp Act as "greatly detrimental to the commercial interests" of the empire. The third, which modern historians call the Revenue Act of 1766 even though its preamble described it as a regulation of trade, reduced the duty on molasses from three pence per gallon to one penny, but imposed it on all molasses, British or foreign, imported into the mainland colonies. Although the act was more favorable to the molasses trade than any other

The Library Company of Philadelphia

The Library Company of Philadelphia

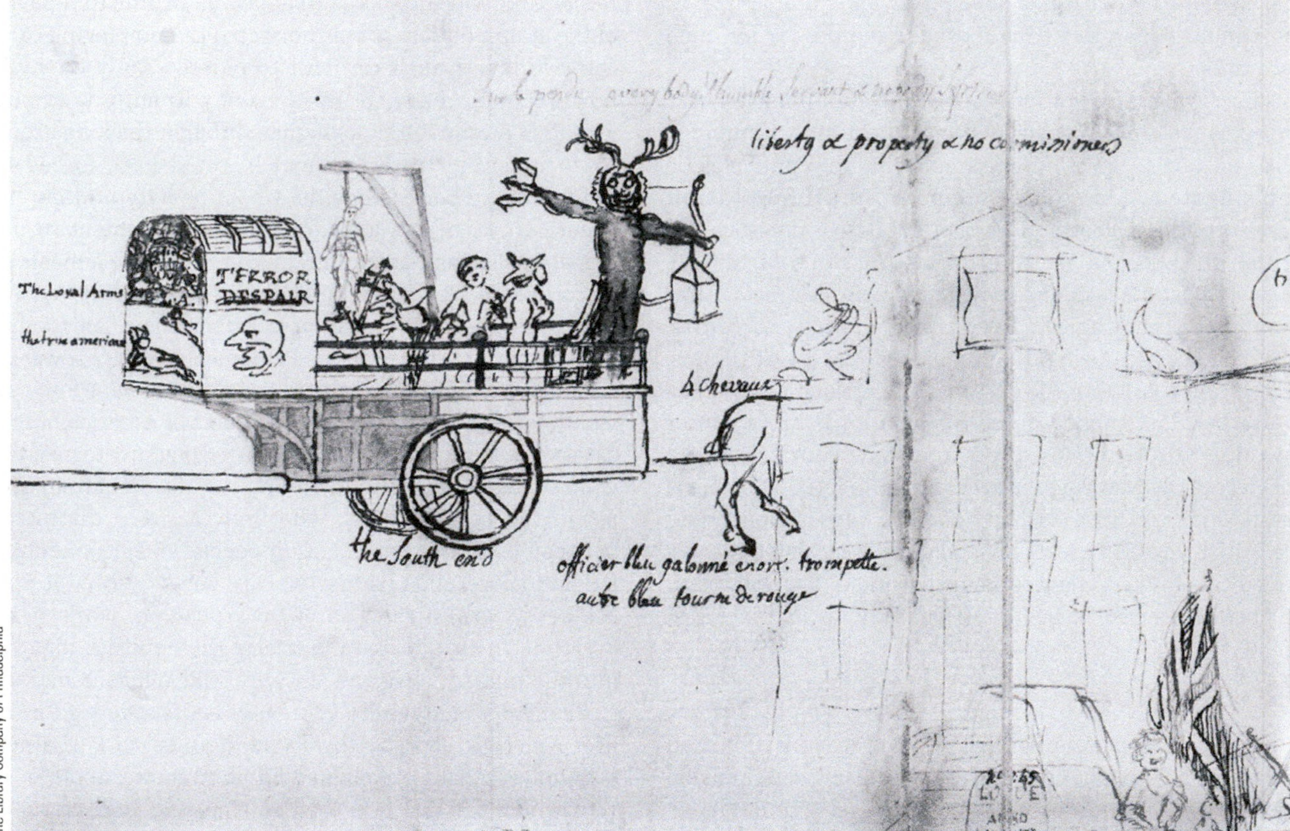

5.3a (top) and 5.3b (bottom) **Du Simitière, *Boston Affairs* (1765) and *Boston Affairs* (1767)** Boston's Pope's Day processions into 1765 had raucously applauded the king's role as protector of Europe's Protestants, but in 1767 they sided with the political opposition in England, especially John Wilkes.

Q *How did colonists adapt existing forms of public celebrations and protests to oppose Britain's imperial reforms in the 1760s?*

measure yet passed by Parliament, it clearly was also a revenue measure, and it generated more income for the empire than any other colonial tax. Few colonists attacked it for violating the principle of no taxation without representation. In Britain, it seemed that the colonists objected only to internal taxes but would accept external duties.

Against the advice of British friends, the colonists greeted repeal with wild celebrations. Over the next decade, many communities observed March 18 as the anniversary of the Stamp Act's repeal. Neither side fully appreciated the misunderstandings that had made repeal possible or their significance. In the course of the struggle, both sides, British and colonial, had rejected the distinction between internal and external taxes. They could find no legal or philosophical basis for condemning the one while approving the other. Hardly anyone except Franklin noticed in 1766 that the difference was quite real and that the crisis had in fact been resolved according to that distinction. Parliament had tried to extend its authority over the internal affairs of the colonies and had failed, but it continued to collect port duties in the colonies, some to regulate trade, others for revenue. No one could justify this division of authority, but the external–internal cleavage marked, even defined, the power axis of the empire, the boundary between what Parliament could do on its own and what, internally, only the Crown could do, and then only with the consent of the colonists.

Another misunderstanding was equally grave. Only the riots had created a crisis severe enough to push Parliament into repeal. Both sides, however, preferred to believe that economic pressure had been decisive. For the colonies, this conviction set the pattern of resistance for the next two imperial crises.

5-3 The Townshend Crisis

Q *What made the resolution of the Townshend crisis less satisfying for American colonists than the end to the Stamp Act crisis?*

The good will created by repeal did not last. In 1766, the king again replaced his ministry. This time he persuaded William Pitt to form a government. Pitt's ministry, which included many former supporters of Grenville, faced serious opposition within Parliament. Pitt compounded that problem by accepting a peerage as Earl of Chatham, a decision that removed his compelling oratory from the House of Commons and left Charles Townshend, the chancellor of the exchequer (treasury), as his spokesman in that chamber. A witty, extemporaneous speaker, Townshend had betrayed every leader he ever served. The only consistent policy in his political career had been his hard-line attitude toward the colonies.

5-3a *The Townshend Program*

Chatham learned that he could not control the House of Commons from his position in the House of Lords. During the Christmas recess of 1766–1767, he saw the extent of his failure and began to slip into an acute depression that lasted more than two years. He refused to communicate with other ministers or even with the king. The colonists, who admired him more than any other Englishman of the day, expected sympathy from his administration. Instead, they got Townshend, who took charge of colonial policy in spring 1767.

The Townshend Revenue Act of 1767 imposed new duties in colonial ports on certain imports that colonists could legally buy only from Britain: tea, paper, glass, red and white lead, and painter's colors. But Townshend also removed more duties on tea within Britain than he could offset with the new revenue to be collected in the colonies. Revenue, clearly, was not his main object. The statute's preamble stated his real goal: to use the new American revenues to pay the salaries of governors and judges in the colonies, thereby freeing them from dependence on the assemblies. This devious strategy aroused suspicions of conspiracy in the colonies. Even sober provincials began to fear that, in the bowels of the British government, men were plotting against their liberties.

Other measures gave appellate powers to the vice-admiralty courts in Boston, Philadelphia, and Charleston and created a separate American Board of Customs Commissioners to enforce the trade and revenue laws in the colonies. The board was placed in Boston, where resistance to the Stamp Act had been fiercest, rather than in Philadelphia, which had been rather quiet in 1765 and would have been a much more convenient location. Townshend was eager for confrontation.

The British army also began to withdraw from nearly all frontier posts and concentrate near the coast. Although the primary motive was to save money, the implications were striking. An army in America to guard the frontier, partially supported by the colonists, was one thing, but an army far distant from the frontier presumably existed to police the colonists. Why should they pay costs to enforce policies that would deprive them of their liberties?

Townshend ridiculed the distinction between internal and external taxes, which he attributed to Chatham and the colonists, but he declared that he would honor it anyway. After winning approval for his program, he died suddenly in September 1767 and passed on to others the dilemmas he had created. Frederick, Lord North, replaced him as chancellor of the exchequer. Chatham resigned, and the Duke of Grafton became prime minister.

5-3b *Resistance: The Politics of Escalation*

The external–internal distinction perplexed the colonists. Since 1765, they had objected to all taxes for revenue, but in 1766, they had accepted the penny duty on molasses with few complaints. Defeating the Townshend Revenue Act would prove tougher than nullifying the Stamp Act. Parliament had never been able to impose its will on the internal affairs of the colonies, as the Stamp Act fiasco demonstrated, but it did control the seas. Goods subject to duties might arrive on any of hundreds of ships from Britain each year, but screening the cargo of every vessel threatened to impose an enormous, perhaps impossible burden on the Sons of Liberty. General nonimportation would be easier to implement, but British trade played a bigger role in the colonial economy than North American trade did in Britain's. To hurt Britain a little, the colonies would have to harm themselves a lot.

The colonists divided over strategies of resistance. The radical *Boston Gazette* called for complete nonimportation of all British goods. The merchants' paper, the *Boston Evening Post,* disagreed. In October, the Boston town meeting

Interpreting the Visual Past

A British Cartoon of the Stamp Act Repeal

"The Repeal or the Funeral of Miss Americ-Stamp." This London cartoon, published on March 18, 1766, the day Parliament repealed the Stamp Act, became one of the most popular satirical prints of the 18th century. The print's artist, Benjamin Wilson, had close ties to the Marquess of Rockingham, who orchestrated the repeal. The main focus is a funeral procession of the Stamp Act's supporters carrying the act to a burial vault. George Grenville has the dubious honor of holding the coffin (note the child size, as the act "died" at just over four months old). The text above the vault indicates that it holds other taxes and legislation "which tended to alienate the Affections of Englishmen to their Country."

In the background, three ships, labeled "Conway," "Rockingham," and "Grafton" after the parliamentary leaders responsible for the repeal of the Stamp Act, prepare to carry the large unshipped cargoes destined for America that have accumulated on the dock. Stamps just returned from America are also stacked on the wharf.

Q *The cartoon sacrifices subtlety (note the action of the dog toward the Stamp Act's supporters) to deliver a clear political message. How might the scene have been different had Wilson tried to incorporate the other key components of the repeal, the Declaratory Act and the Revenue Act of 1766?*

Q *Despite the somber tone of the cartoon, how does it express optimism about the future relationship between Britain and its American colonies?*

Q *How might the cartoon have reinforced Americans' perception that their nonimportation agreements had forced the British to repeal the Stamp Act?*

5.4 **Benjamin Wilson, "The Repeal or the Funeral of Miss Americ-Stamp," 1766.**

encouraged greater use of home manufactures and urged voluntary nonconsumption of British goods, but no organized resistance developed and the Townshend duties became operative in November 1767 with little opposition. A month later, John Dickinson, a Philadelphia lawyer, tried to rouse his fellow colonists through 12 urgent letters printed in nearly every colonial newspaper. These *Letters from a Farmer in Pennsylvania* denied the distinction between internal and external taxes, insisted that all parliamentary taxes for revenue violated the colonists' rights, and speculated darkly about Townshend's motives.

Massachusetts again set the pace of resistance. In February 1768, its assembly petitioned the king, not Parliament, against the new measures. Without waiting for a reply, it also sent a Circular Letter to the other assemblies, urging them to pursue "constitutional measures" of resistance against the Quartering Act, the new taxes, and the use of Townshend revenues to pay the salaries of governors and judges. The implication was that, because Britain responded only to resistance, the colonies had better work together. By the spring of 1768, nonimportation also finally began to take hold in Boston and New York, although Philadelphia held out until early 1769.

The British ministry got the point. Wills Hill, earl of Hillsborough and secretary of state for the American colonies (an office created in 1768), responded so sharply that he turned tepid opposition into serious resistance. He ordered the Massachusetts assembly to rescind the Circular Letter and instructed all governors to dissolve any assembly that accepted it. In June 1768, the Massachusetts House voted 92 to 17 not to rescind. Most other assemblies had shown little interest in the Townshend program, particularly in the southern colonies, where governors already had fixed salaries. Even so, they bristled at being told what they could or could not debate. They took up the Circular Letter or began to draft their own. One by one, their assemblies were dissolved until government by consent seemed in serious peril.

The next escalation again came from Boston. On March 18, 1768, the town's celebration of the anniversary of the Stamp Act's repeal grew so raucous that the governor and the new American Board of Customs Commissioners asked Hillsborough for troops. He ordered General Gage, based in New York, to send two regiments from Nova Scotia to Boston. On June 10, before Gage could respond, a riot broke out in Boston after customs collectors seized John Hancock's sloop *Liberty* for having smuggled Madeira wine (taxed under the Sugar Act) on its *previous* voyage. By waiting until the ship had a new cargo, informers and customs officials could split larger shares when the sloop was condemned. Terrified by the fury of the popular response, the commissioners fled to Castle William in Boston Harbor and again petitioned Hillsborough for troops. He sent two more regiments from Ireland.

In early October 1768, the British fleet entered Boston Harbor in battle array and landed 1,000 soldiers, sent by Gage from Nova Scotia. The regiments from Ireland joined them later. To warn the public against the dangers posed by a standing army in time of peace, the patriots compiled a "Journal of the Times," describing how British soldiers were undermining public order in Boston—clashing with the town watch, endangering the virtue of young women, disturbing church services, and picking fights. The "journal" always appeared first as a newspaper column in some other city, usually New York. Only later was it reprinted in Boston, after memories of any specific incident had grown hazy.

Though detested, Britain's initial experiment in military coercion managed to halt violence against customs officers in Boston for several months. London was satisfied enough to withdraw half the soldiers in summer 1769. As Boston calmed, the town started winning sympathy among the southern colonies, which had not been deeply involved in resistance to the Townshend duties. Virginia, Maryland, and South Carolina each adopted nonimportation agreements. In the Chesapeake, the movement had more support among planters than among tobacco merchants, who were mostly Scots loyal to their parent firms. No enforcement mechanism was ever put in place. Charleston, however, took nonimportation seriously. Up and down the continent, the feeble resistance of mid-1768 became formidable in 1769.

5-3c The Wilkes Crisis

John Wilkes, a member of Parliament and a radical opposition journalist, had fled into exile in 1763 and had been outlawed for publishing an attack on the king in his newspaper, *The North Briton* No. 45. In 1768, just as the Townshend crisis was brewing, George III dissolved Parliament and issued writs for the usual septennial elections. Wilkes returned from France and won a seat for the English county of Middlesex. He then received a one-year sentence in King's Bench Prison. Hundreds of supporters gathered to chant "Wilkes and Liberty!" or even "No Wilkes? No King!" On May 10, 1768, as the new Parliament convened, Wilkites just outside the prison clashed with soldiers who fired into the crowd, killing six and wounding 15. Wilkes denounced "the massacre of St. George's Fields." The House of Commons expelled Wilkes and ordered a new election, but the voters chose him again. Two more expulsions and two more elections took place the next year, until April 1769 when, after Wilkes won again by 1,143 votes to 296, the House voted to seat the loser. Wilkes had created a constitutional crisis. His adherents founded "the Society of Gentlemen Supporters of the Bill of Rights," which raised money to pay off his huge debts and organized a national campaign on his behalf. About one-fourth of the voters of the entire kingdom signed petitions demanding a new general election. Wilkites called for a reduction of royal patronage and major reforms of the electoral system. They also began the regular publication of parliamentary debates and sympathized openly with North American protests. Colonial Sons of Liberty applauded Wilkes. If he lost, they warned, their own liberties would be in danger. Boston even printed a parody of the Apostles' Creed. It began: "I believe in Wilkes, the firm patriot, maker of number 45. Who was born for our good. Suffered under arbitrary power. Was banished and imprisoned." It ended with a hope for "the resurrection of liberty, and the life of universal freedom forever. Amen." In 1769, South Carolina's assembly borrowed £1,500 sterling from the colony's treasurer and donated it to Wilkes. When the assembly passed an appropriation to cover the gift, the council rejected the bill. Because neither side would yield, the assembly voted no taxes after 1769 and passed no laws after 1771. Royal government broke down over the Wilkes question.

The Townshend crisis and the Wilkite movement became an explosive combination. Many colonists began to question the British government's commitment to liberty. That a conspiracy existed to destroy British and colonial liberty began to seem quite plausible.

5-3d The Boston Massacre

By late 1769, the redcoats had intimidated Boston for nearly a year. The Sons of Liberty finally reciprocated. The town watch clashed with the army's guard posts because the watch, when challenged by the redcoats' call "Who goes there?" refused to give the required answer: "Friends." Under English common law, soldiers could not fire on civilians without an order from

5.5 **Paul Revere's Engraving of the British Army Landing in Boston, 1768** The navy approached the city in battle array, a sight familiar to veterans of the French wars. To emphasize the peaceful, Christian character of Boston, Revere exaggerated the height of the church steeples.

Q *How does the engraving by Revere, which is presented as a factual representation, actually make a political argument?*

a civil magistrate, except in self-defense when their lives were in danger. By the fall of 1769, no magistrate dared issue such a command. Clashes between soldiers and civilians grew frequent, and justices of the peace singled out the soldiers for punishment.

By 1770, the soldiers often felt under siege. The Sons of Liberty also freely intimidated merchants who violated nonimportation. They nearly lynched Ebenezer Richardson, a customs informer who fired a musket from his home into a stone-throwing crowd and killed an 11-year-old boy. The lad's funeral on February 26, 1770, became an enormous display of public mourning. And although Richardson was convicted of murder, George III pardoned him.

After the funeral, tensions between soldiers and citizens reached a fatal climax. Off-duty soldiers often supplemented their meager wages with part-time employment, a practice that angered local artisans, who resented competition in the city's depressed economy. On Friday, March 2, 1770, three soldiers visited John Hancock's wharf. "Soldier, will you work?" asked Samuel Gray, a rope maker. "Yes," replied one. "Then go and clean my shit house," sneered Gray. After an ugly brawl, won by the workers despite reinforcements for the redcoats, Gray's employer persuaded their colonel to confine his men to barracks. Peace prevailed through the Puritan Sabbath that ran from Saturday night to sunrise on Monday, but everyone expected trouble on Monday, March 5.

After dark on Monday, fire bells began ringing throughout the town, and civilians and soldiers clashed at several places. A crowd hurling snowballs and rocks closed in on the lone sentinel guarding the hated customs house that stored the king's revenue. The guard called for help. Eight soldiers, including two who had been in the wharf brawl, rushed to his aid and loaded their weapons. Captain Thomas Preston took command and ordered the soldiers to drive the attackers slowly back with fixed bayonets. The crowd taunted the soldiers, daring them to fire. One soldier apparently slipped, discharging his musket into the air as he fell. The others then fired into the crowd, killing five and wounding six. One of the victims was Samuel Gray; another was Crispus Attucks, a man of African and Indian ancestry.

With the whole town turning out, the soldiers were withdrawn to Castle William. Preston and six of his men stood trial for murder and were defended, brilliantly, by two radical patriot lawyers, John Adams and Josiah Quincy, Jr., who believed that every accused person deserved to have a proper defense. Preston and four of the soldiers were acquitted. The other two were convicted only of manslaughter, which permitted them to plead a legal technicality called "benefit of clergy." They were branded on the thumb and released. The **Boston Massacre**, as the Sons of Liberty called this encounter, became the colonial counterpart to the Massacre of St. George's Fields in England. It marked the failure of Britain's first attempt at military coercion.

History Through Film *John Adams* (2008)

A seven-part miniseries that aired on HBO in the spring of 2008. Directed by TomHooper.
Starring Paul Giamatti (John Adams), Laura Linney (Abigail Adams), Stephen Dillane (Thomas Jefferson), David Morse (George Washington), Tom Wilkinson (Benjamin Franklin).

Based on David McCullough's Pulitzer Prize–winning biography, *John Adams* traces the political career of its title character (Paul Giamatti) in seven episodes, each approximately an hour. The net effect delivers to Adams something that the vainglorious Massachusetts lawyer and politician could have only dreamed of: a starring role in the founding of the United States, from the movement for independence in the 1770s through his work in President George Washington's administration as vice president and his own presidency in the 1790s to his busy retirement in the early 1800s.

The first episode, "Join or Die," centers on Adams's legal defense of the British soldiers accused of murdering five colonists on March 5, 1770, in the Boston Massacre (for background, see the text in this section). Adams agreed to defend the soldiers and their commanding officer, Captain Thomas Preston (Ritchie Coster), on the principle that all men deserve a fair trial. After Adams's successful defense in the trial, the last part of the episode compresses time to depict the deteriorating relations between Britain and America due to the Tea Act of 1773 and the Coercive Acts of 1774. The episode ends with Adams riding to Philadelphia (purposefully on his own horse rather than in an ornate carriage) to represent Massachusetts in the First Continental Congress.

Unfortunately, the episode is riddled with historical errors, starting in its first scenes. From home, Adams responds to ringing church bells, usually an indication of fire, to discover a scene of confusion on King Street with crowds running, Captain Preston yelling at his men not to fire, and freshly wounded men and boys dying in the snow. Actually, Adams was at a friend's house in South Boston and missed the whole commotion. "When We arrived We saw nothing," Adams wrote in his autobiography. The episode never introduces Adams's legal partner, Josiah Quincy, Jr., and it combines the prosecution of Preston and his men into one trial when they were actually separate. Adams's key witness, Richard Palmes (John Bedford Lloyd), was not a disheveled rope maker, as the film suggests, but a prominent merchant. Finally, the program exaggerates Adams's legal achievement by having the jury declare all the soldiers "not guilty." In fact, two of Preston's men were found guilty of the lesser charge of manslaughter.

The end of "Join or Die" includes a chilling portrayal of the tarring and feathering of a British customs official around the time of the Boston Tea Party in December 1773. John Hancock (Justin Theroux) orders the punishment and John Adams's cousin, Samuel Adams (Danny Huston), approves, to the dismay of John. The problem is that the incident never took place. Moreover, Hancock and Samuel Adams were never documented at any tarring and feathering, which happened infrequently. Similar errors persist throughout the remaining six episodes of *John Adams*.

Why bother then to watch the miniseries? *John Adams* is visually stunning, with some of the most ambitious sets of colonial and early national America ever realized (much of it was filmed in Colonial Williamsburg, Virginia). The first episode invites viewers to feel the bustle of the Boston waterfront, complete with teams of maritime workers and towering ships' masts. In addition, the series features a realistic, engaging portrayal of the storied marriage of John and Abigail Adams (Laura Linney, who, like Giamatti, won an Emmy Award for her role). As in real life, Abigail serves as John's moral anchor. She warns him before his closing statement in the Boston Massacre trial to avoid his cardinal sin of vanity. "Vanity?" asks John. To which Abigail replies, "You have overburdened your argument with ostentatious erudition."

Adams would go on to remind the Boston jury that "facts are stubborn things" (which he truly said). We must take the same message to heart when viewing *John Adams*. The series forces us both to appreciate the wonder of early America and to take in our history, regardless of the medium, with a critical eye.

HBO Films/High noon productions/ Playtone/Album/Newscom

5.6 *John Adams* includes a convincing portrayal of the storied marriage between John and Abigail Adams.

5-3e *Partial Repeal*

The day of the massacre marked a turning point in Britain too, for on March 5, Lord North asked Parliament to repeal the Townshend duties, except the one on tea. North wanted all of them repealed, but the cabinet had rejected complete repeal by a 5-to-4 margin. As with the Stamp Act, Britain had three choices: enforcement, repeal, or modification. Force having failed, North chose the middle ground that had been rejected in 1766—modification. He claimed to be retaining only a preamble without a statute, a vestige of the Townshend Revenue Act, while repealing the substance. In fact, he did the opposite. Tea provided nearly three-fourths of the revenue under the act. North kept the substance but gave up the shadow.

This news reached the colonies just after nonimportation had achieved its greatest success in 1769 (see Table 5.1). The colonies reduced imports by about one-third from what they had been in 1768, but the impact on Britain was slight, partly because Britain had found a lucrative market for textiles by selling new uniforms to the huge Russian army. North had hoped that partial repeal, although it would not placate all of the colonists, would at least divide them. It did. Most merchants favored renewed importation of everything but tea, while the Sons of Liberty, most of whom were artisans, still supported broad nonimportation to sustain increased demand for their own manufactures.

Resistance collapsed first in Newport, where smuggling had always been the preferred method of challenging British authority. It spread to New York City, where the boycott on imports had been most effective. Soon Philadelphia caved in, followed by Boston in October 1770. By contrast, nonimportation had not caused a ripple in the import trade of the Chesapeake colonies. North's repeal was followed by an orgy of importation of British goods, setting record highs everywhere.

5-3f *Disaffection*

Repeal in 1770 lacked the impact that it had in 1766. There was no public rejoicing, not even when Lord North's government (he had replaced Grafton as prime minister in January 1770) took further steps to reduce tensions. The Quartering Act expired quietly in 1770, some of the more objectionable features of the vice-admiralty courts were softened, and the Currency Act of 1764 was repealed in stages between 1770 and 1773, as even London began to recognize that it was harming trade. Yet, North failed to restore confidence in the justice and decency of the British government. To a degree now difficult to appreciate, the empire ran on trust, or voluntarism, what people at the time called "affection." Its opposite, disaffection, had a more literal and dangerous meaning to them than it does today.

That fear sometimes broke through the surface calm between 1770 and 1773. Rhode Islanders had often clashed with customs officers and had even fired on the king's ships once or twice without stirring much interest in other colonies. Then in 1772, a predatory customs vessel, the *Gaspée,* ran aground near Providence while pursuing some peaceful coastal ships. After dark, men with blackened faces boarded the *Gaspée,* wounded its captain, and burned the ship. Britain sent a panel of dignitaries to the colony with instructions to send the perpetrators to England for trial. The inquiry failed because no one would talk.

Twelve colonial assemblies considered this threat so ominous that they created permanent **committees of correspondence** to keep in touch with each other and *anticipate* new threats to their liberties. Even colonial moderates now believed that British officials were conspiring to destroy liberty in America. When Governor Hutchinson announced in 1773 that, under the Townshend Act, Massachusetts Superior Court justices would receive their salaries from the imperial treasury, Boston created its own committee of correspondence and urged other towns to do the same. Boston's role in the "patriot" cause had grown dramatically since the convention of 1768, and such Bostonians as John Adams had become major spokesmen for colonial resistance. A plot to destroy their liberties now seemed plausible to many colonials. Hutchinson, amused at first, grew alarmed when most towns of any size followed Boston's lead. That there was a plot to destroy their liberties seemed obvious to them.

The Boston Massacre trials and the *Gaspée* affair convinced London that it was pointless to prosecute individuals for politically motivated crimes. Whole

Table 5.1 **EXPORTS IN £000 STERLING FROM ENGLAND AND SCOTLAND TO THE AMERICAN COLONIES, 1766–1775**

Colony	1766	1767	1768	1769	1770	1771	1772	1773	1774	1775
New England	419	416	431	224	417	1,436*	844	543	577	85.0
New York	333	424	491	76	480	655*	349	296	460	1.5
Pennsylvania	334	383	442	205	140	747*	526	436	646	1.4
Chesapeake†	520	653	670	715	997*	1,224*	1,016	589	690	1.9
Lower South‡	376	292	357	385*	228	515*	1,016	448	471	130.5
Totals	1,982	2,168	2,391	1,605	2,262	4,577*	3,310	2,312	2,844	220.3

Average total exports, 1766–1768 = £2,180; 1769 = 73.6% of that average, or 67.1% of 1768 exports; 1770 = 103.8% of that average, or 94.6% of 1768 exports.

*These totals surpassed all previous highs.

†Chesapeake = Maryland and Virginia.

‡Lower South = Carolinas and Georgia.

communities would have to be punished. That choice brought the government to the edge of a precipice. Was the empire held together by law and consent, or only by force? The use of force against entire communities could lead to outright war, and war is not and cannot be a system of justice. The spread of committees of correspondence within Massachusetts and throughout the colonies suggested that settlers who had been unable to unite against New France at Albany in 1754 now deemed unity against Britain essential to their liberties. By 1773, several New England newspapers were calling on the colonies to create a formal union.

In effect, the Townshend crisis never ended. With the tea duty standing as a symbol of Parliament's right to tax the colonies without their consent, genuine imperial harmony was becoming impossible. North's decision to retain the tea tax in 1770 did not guarantee that armed resistance would break out five years later, but it severely narrowed the ground on which any compromise could be built. The price of miscalculation had grown enormously.

5-4 Internal Cleavages: The Contagion of Liberty

Q *How did the British imperial crisis help to expose tensions within American society among the following groups: patriots and loyalists (and loyal colonies); artisans and gentlemen; tenants and landlords; settlers and proprietors; women and men; and slaves and masters?*

In his reply to his wife Abigail Adams's call to "Remember the Ladies" at the Second Continental Congress (see following sections), John Adams claimed to but laugh. "We have been told that our Struggle has loosened the bands of Government everywhere," he acknowledged. "That Children and Apprentices were disobedient—that schools and Colledges were grown turbulent—that Indians slighted their Guardians and Negroes grew insolent to their Masters." Indeed, American resistance to British imperial policies in the 1760s and 1770s opened new divisions and exposed existing cleavages in colonial American society. The imperial crisis encouraged a wide range of groups—including slaves, women, artisans, tenants, and even those who remained loyal to the Crown—to conceive of liberty in new ways.

5-4a *Divided Loyalties*

The imperial crisis divided Americans most obviously according to political allegiance. After American independence, it became common to characterize **loyalists**, those who remained committed to the king and to the British Empire, as backward, cowardly, and conservative to a fault. For the radical Thomas Paine, loyalists operated according to a "servile, slavish, self-interested fear" that kept them in Britain's corner. The early historian of the American Revolution Mercy Otis Warren called loyalists "Blockheads." Despite these stereotypes, loyalism was far from a marginal position. Between one-fifth and one-third of all Americans remained loyal to the Crown during the imperial crisis (still others were disaffected and avoided choosing a side, unless forced).

The terms "loyalist" and "patriot" (describing an American revolutionary) did not apply until the Revolutionary War, but the divisions were already becoming apparent by the late 1760s. The Townshend crisis was a far more accurate predictor of future behavior than response to the Stamp Act had been. Nearly everyone had denounced the Stamp Act, including such future loyalists as Daniel Dulany. By contrast, most merchants and lawyers who resisted nonimportation in 1768 became loyalists by 1775. Artisans, merchants, and lawyers who supported the boycotts, especially those who favored continuing them past 1770, became patriots.

In other respects, few differences distinguished the supporters and opponents of American resistance to British policies. The two sides shared a common appreciation for British liberties and the rule of law. Many loyalists also resented London's efforts to tax the American colonies. Still, for some, particularly in official government positions, the cost of supporting resistance proved too high. For others, a cautious cast of mind or temperament impeded radical action. The longtime Massachusetts colonial official Thomas Hutchinson fit both cases. "My Temper Does Not Incline to Enthusiasm," he once stated. For a generation, Hutchinson had been the most reliable public opponent of British navy press gangs in Boston and had privately opposed the Stamp Act. Yet, in June 1774, upon being relieved of his duties as Massachusetts governor, he sailed for England, never to return. In London, Hutchinson connected with other American-born British subjects exiled from their home. The group included the celebrated artists Benjamin West and John Singleton Copley, who reported in August that he "dined with Gov'r Hutchinson, and I think there was 12 of us altoge[the]r, all Bostonians, and we had Choice Salt Fish for Dinner."

Besides high colonial officials, northern Anglican clergymen constituted the most loyal group to the Crown. From 1760, the Massachusetts native Jacob Bailey served as an Anglican missionary on the Maine frontier. A Harvard classmate of John Adams, Bailey faced increasing pressure in the 1760s and 1770s to violate his sacred oath to the king, the head of his church, in favor of supporting the American resistance movement. Bailey endured numerous public threats and the slaughter of his livestock before fleeing to Nova Scotia in 1779. The war would turn other religious groups, most notably Quakers and German pietists in Pennsylvania, into de facto loyalists for abiding by their spiritual belief in pacifism and refusing to take sides in the imperial conflict.

The tactics of American resistance produced further divisions in the colonial population. The Sons of Liberty censured those who did not support resistance as "Tories," after the one of Britain's two traditional parties most associated with monarchism. As nonimportation emerged as a leading tactic for resisting British policies, committees formed in the colonies to monitor consumption behavior. Individuals signaled their political allegiance by the beverages they drank and the garments they wore. The consequences of violating nonimportation agreements ranged from forced confessions and apologies to acts of violence and public humiliation, such as tarring and feathering.

The aggressive efforts to enforce compliance often backfired. Sixteen-year-old Kezia Coffin, a member of a wealthy whaling family in Nantucket, Massachusetts, denounced the American rebels in her diary: "It is Liberty which they pretend they are fighting for yet don't allow others liberty to think as they please." The loyalism of Coffin's family concerned her cousins Benjamin Franklin and his sister Jane Mecom. The break with Britain proved especially personal for Franklin. He disowned his son William, the colonial governor of New Jersey, for remaining loyal to the British Crown.

As with families, the imperial crisis divided entire British colonies and Atlantic regions from one another. By the early 1770s, Britain had 26 imperial units in the Western Hemisphere; half would remain loyal. Events during the Stamp Act crisis of 1765–1766 and Townshend crisis of 1767–1770 anticipated this divergence within the British Atlantic community. Leaders of the American resistance hoped for support in British Canada, particularly Nova Scotia. Despite an influx of New England settlers and some street protests against the Stamp Act, the Nova Scotia assembly never objected to the British taxes. London-based business interests and the Royal Navy's primary North American base at Halifax dominated the colony's politics.

Nova Scotia joined Quebec, Florida, Bermuda, Grenada, Barbados, Jamaica, and Georgia (briefly) as British colonial territories where the Stamp Act went into effect. As the two largest, most populous, and most lucrative Caribbean colonies, Jamaica and Barbados also represented the most disappointing losses for the American resistance movement. The British West Indies as a whole paid 78 percent of total stamp revenues before the law's repeal. With their large slave populations (and fear of slave rebellions) and close political and economic ties to Britain, the sugar islands objected to what the Barbados assembly called the "violent spirit" of American protests. The response opened a rift in the formerly close relationship between the mainland colonies and the West Indies. Upon learning of the Barbadian position, John Dickinson defended colonial resistance in declaring, "I am a North-American." By the First Continental Congress in 1774, American leaders still held out some hope (in vain) of Canadian participation, but did not bother to court the West Indian colonies.

5-4b *Urban and Rural Discontent*

Patriot leaders also faced challenges from within their own ranks. Urban artisans, who had mobilized to resist Britain in 1765 and 1769, demanded more power. In Boston, where the economy had been faltering since the 1740s while taxes remained high, Britain's policies bore hard on the town and gave an angry edge to its protests. Boston's radical artisans set the pace of resistance in every imperial crisis. In New York City, Philadelphia, and Charleston, artisans began to play a much more assertive role in public affairs.

Tensions increased in the countryside as well as in the cities. Three processes intensified discontent in rural areas: a revival of old proprietary claims, massive foreign immigration, and settlement of the backcountry.

Between about 1730 and 1750, the men who owned 17th-century proprietary charters or manorial patents finally began to see prospects for huge profits by enforcing these old legal claims. Taken together, the claims of New York's manor lords, the East Jersey proprietors, and the Penn (Pennsylvania), Baltimore (Maryland), Fairfax (Virginia), and Granville (North Carolina) families blanketed the colonies from New York to North Carolina. They were the biggest winners in America's **feudal revival**, the use of old charters to pry income from the settlers (see Map 5.2).

In the charged atmosphere created by the imperial crisis, the attempt to raise land rents and leases produced unrest in several rural areas. Some of the largest disturbances took place on the great estates of the Hudson Valley in New York. As leases became more restrictive and as Yankees swarmed into New York, discontent increased. In 1753, the proprietor of Livingston Manor had difficulty putting down Yankee rioters, and tension spread throughout the Hudson Valley over the next decade.

In 1766, several thousand angry farmers, inspired by the Stamp Act riots, took to the fields and the roads to protest the terms of their leases. They threatened to kill the lord of Livingston Manor or to pull down the New York City mansions of absentee landlords. Supported by some of the city's most prominent Sons of Liberty, the colony called in redcoats to suppress the riots. New York's experience exposed the difficulties of uniting urban and rural radicals in a common cause. But when New York landlords tried to make good their claims to the upper Connecticut Valley, the settlers defied them, set up their own government, and, after a long struggle, ultimately became the independent state of Vermont.

Massive immigration from Europe, mostly through Philadelphia, and the settlement of the backcountry added to rural social tensions. Most immigrants were Scottish or Scots-Irish Presbyterians, Lutherans, or German Reformed Protestants. They were dissenters from the prevailing faith in the colonies they entered, whether it was the Quaker religion in Pennsylvania or the Church of England from Maryland to Georgia. They angered Indians by squatting on their land and, often, by murdering those in their way—behavior that the Paxton Boys' 1763 uprising attempted to justify. In the Carolina backcountry, the newcomers provoked the Cherokee War of 1759–1761, which brutalized and demoralized the whole region.

After the Cherokee War, bands of outlaws, men dislocated by the war, began roaming the countryside, plundering the more prosperous farmers and often raping their wives and daughters. As the violence peaked between 1765 and 1767, the more respectable settlers organized themselves as "regulators" (a later generation would call them "vigilantes") to impose order in the absence of organized government. South Carolina claimed jurisdiction over the backcountry, but the colony's law courts were in Charleston, more than 100 miles to the east.

▲ **MAP 5.2 Feudal Revival: Great Estates of Late Colonial America** On the eve of the Revolution, more than half of the land between the Hudson Valley and North Carolina was claimed by men who had inherited or acquired various kinds of 17th-century charters or patents.

Q *Although they were generally separate from Britain's imperial reforms of the 1760s and 1770s, how did the attempts by proprietors and other large landowners to raise rents resemble official British policies?*

Q *How did the feudal revival, in which a small number of people held vast amounts of land, clash with the spirit of the emerging American Revolution?*

Even though most white settlers now lived in the backcountry, they elected only two of the 48 members of South Carolina's assembly. They had no local government.

The regulators in South Carolina soon caused as many disturbances as they put down. By 1769, civil war was only averted when the governor promised to create a circuit court system for the colony that would finally bring government to the backcountry. Violence ebbed, but tensions remained severe.

In the North Carolina backcountry, a separate regulator movement emerged to address abuses and corruption in the colony's government. The backcountry contained over half the colony's population but elected only 17 of 78 assemblymen. By 1770, after first trying to work within the assembly, the regulators openly challenged the authority of the colonial government. In early 1771, North Carolina governor William Tryon responded by marching 1,000 militiamen westward. They defeated a force of more than 2,000 poorly armed regulators at the battle of Alamance Creek. Seven regulators were hanged, and many fled the colony. North Carolina entered the Revolution as a bitterly divided society.

5-4c *Slaves and Women*

In Charleston, South Carolina, in 1765, the Sons of Liberty marched through the streets chanting "Liberty and No Stamps." To their amazement, slaves organized a parade of their own, shouting, "Liberty! Liberty!" Merchant Henry Laurens tried to convince himself that they probably did not understand the meaning of the word.

Around the middle of the 18th century, slavery came under serious attack for the first time. An antislavery movement arose on both sides of the Atlantic and attracted both future patriots and loyalists. In the 1740s and 1750s, Benjamin Lay, John Woolman, and Anthony Benezet urged fellow Quakers to free their slaves. In the 1750s, the Quaker Yearly Meeting placed the slave trade off-limits and finally, in 1774, forbade slaveholding altogether. Any Friend not complying by 1779 would be disowned. Britain's Methodist leader, John Wesley, in most other respects a social conservative, also attacked slavery, as did several colonial disciples of Jonathan Edwards. A few decades after the Great Awakening, many evangelicals were beginning to agree with South Carolina's Hugh Bryan in 1742, that slavery was a sin.

By the 1760s, supporters of slavery found that they now had to defend the institution. Hardly anyone had bothered to do so earlier, because a social hierarchy seemed necessary and inevitable, and slavery simply marked the bottom extreme. As equal rights became a popular topic, however, some suggested that *all* people could claim these rights, and slavery came under attack. In Scotland, Adam Smith, the most original economist of the age, praised African slaves for their "magnanimity," which, he claimed, "the soul of the sordid master is scarce capable of conceiving." Arthur Lee, a Virginian, defended the character of his fellow planters against Smith's charge but discovered that he could not justify slavery, "always the deadly enemy to virtue and science." Patrick Henry agreed. Slavery, he wrote, "is as repugnant to humanity as it is inconsistent with the Bible and destructive of liberty." He did keep slaves, but only because of "the general inconvenience of living without them. I will not, I cannot justify it." Granville Sharp, an early abolitionist, brought the Somerset case before the Court of King's Bench in 1771 and compelled Chief Justice William Murray, baron Mansfield, to declare slavery incompatible with the "free air" of England. That reluctant decision enabled many of England's 10,000 or 15,000 blacks to claim their freedom.

New Englanders began to head in similar directions. Two women, Sarah Osborn and **Phillis Wheatley**, played leading roles in the movement. Osborn, an English immigrant to Newport, Rhode Island, and a widow, opened a school in 1744 to support her family. A friend of revivalist George Whitefield, she also taught women and blacks and began holding evening religious meetings, which turned into a big local revival. At one point in the 1760s, about one-sixth of Newport's Africans were attending her school. That made them the most literate African population in the colonies, even though they were living in the colonial city with the highest percentage of its merchants deeply involved in the African slave trade. Osborn's students supported abolition of the slave trade and, later, of slavery itself.

In 1761, an eight-year-old girl who would become known as Phillis Wheatley arrived in Boston from Africa and was purchased by wealthy John Wheatley as a servant for his wife, Susannah, who treated her more like a daughter than a slave and taught her to read and write. In 1767, Phillis published her first poem in Boston, and she visited London as a celebrity in 1773 after a volume of her poetry was published there. Her poems deplored slavery but rejoiced in the Christianization of Africans. Some of them supported the patriot cause against Britain, but she withheld those from the London edition.

Soon many of Boston's blacks sensed an opportunity for emancipation. On several occasions in 1773 and 1774, they petitioned the legislature or the governor for freedom, arguing that, although they had never forfeited their natural rights, they were being "held in slavery in the bowels of a free and Christian Country." When the legislature passed a bill on their behalf, Governor Hutchinson vetoed it. Boston slaves made it clear to Hutchinson's successor General Gage that they would serve him as a loyal militia in exchange for their freedom. In short, they offered allegiance to whichever side supported their emancipation. Many patriots began to rally to their cause. "If we would look for Liberty ourselves," the town of Medfield declared in 1773, "...we ought not to continue to enslave others but immediately set about some effectual method to prevent it for the future."

The patriots could look to another group of allies as well. Many women became indispensable to the broader resistance movement. Although they could not vote or hold office, nonimportation, without their willing support, would have been not just a failure, but a fiasco. In thousands of households, women joined the intense discussions about liberty and agreed to make homespun clothing to take the place of imported British textiles. Moreover, women made a disproportionate sacrifice by giving up tea, which they mostly consumed, while men kept drinking rum (which escaped the first rounds of nonimportation).

5.7 **Phillis Wheatley** Portrait of Phillis Wheatley by Scipio Moorhead, a black artist, appeared opposite the title page of her collected poems, published in 1773.

Freedom's ferment made a heady wine. After 1773, further challenges to British power would continue to trigger enormous social changes within the colonies.

5-5 The Last Imperial Crisis

Q *Why did the colonists start a revolution after the Tea Act* lowered *the price of tea?*

The surface calm between 1770 and 1773 ended when Lord North moved to save the East India Company, Britain's largest corporation, from bankruptcy. It was being undersold in southeastern England and the colonies by low-priced, smuggled Dutch tea, which left the company's warehouses bulging with millions of unsold pounds of its own. North's main concern was the company, not colonial resistance to Townshend's tea duty. He failed on both fronts, creating a colonial crisis too big for Britain to handle without solving the company's problems.

5-5a *The Tea Crisis*

Lord North tried to rescue the company by empowering it to undersell its Dutch rivals. Franklin, in London as a colonial agent, reminded North that he could achieve that goal, for sound economic reasons, by repealing the Townshend duty in the colonies. North rejected that idea. The settlers would hardly revolt if he somehow managed to give them cheap tea! His Tea Act of 1773 repealed import duties on tea in England but retained the Townshend duty in the colonies. In both places, legal tea would be cheaper than anyone else's. The company would be saved, and the settlers, to get cheap tea, would accept Parliament's power to tax them.

Another aspect of the Tea Act antagonized most merchants in the colonies. The company sold tea to all comers at public auctions in London, but the Tea Act gave it a monopoly on the shipping and distribution of tea in the colonies. Only company ships could carry it, and a few consignees in each port would have the exclusive right to sell it. The combined dangers of taxation and monopoly again forged the coalition of artisans and merchants that had helped defeat the Stamp Act by 1766 and resist the Townshend Act by 1769. Patriots saw the Tea Act as a Trojan horse that would destroy liberty by seducing the settlers into accepting parliamentary sovereignty. North also unintentionally gave a tremendous advantage to those determined to resist the Tea Act. He had devised an oceanic, or external, measure that the colonists could actually nullify despite British control of the seas. No one would have to police the entire waterfront, looking for tea importers. The patriots had only to wait for the specially chartered tea ships and prevent their cargoes from landing.

GL Archive/Alamy Stock Photo

5.8 **"The Bostonians Paying the Excise-Man, or Tarring and Feathering"** This London cartoon of 1774 satirized the Sons of Liberty.

Q *How does the cartoon use powerful imagery to remove America from the moral high ground in the imperial crisis?*

Direct threats usually did the job. Most tea ships quickly departed—except in Boston. There, Governor Hutchinson, whose sons were the local tea consignees, decided to face down the radicals. He refused to grant clearance papers to three tea ships that, under the law, had to pay the Townshend duty within 21 days of arrival or face seizure. Hutchinson meant to force them to land the tea and pay the duty. This deadline led to urgent mass meetings for several weeks and, finally, a major crisis. Convinced that they had no other way to block the landing of the tea, the radicals organized the **Boston Tea Party**. Disguised as Indians, they threw 342 chests of tea, worth about £11,000 sterling (the equivalent of more than $1 million in current dollars), into Boston Harbor on the night of December 16, 1773.

5-5b *Britain's Response: The Coercive Acts*

This willful destruction of private property shocked both Britain and America. Convinced that severe punishment was essential to British credibility, Parliament passed four **Coercive Acts** during spring 1774. The Boston Port Act closed the city's port until the town paid for the tea. A new Quartering Act allowed the army to quarter soldiers among civilians, if necessary. In response to the Boston Massacre trials, the Administration of Justice Act permitted a British soldier or official, charged with a crime while carrying out his duties, to be tried in another colony or in England. Most controversial of all was the Massachusetts Government Act. It modified the Massachusetts charter of 1691, made its elected council appointive, and restricted town meetings. In effect, it made Massachusetts like other royal colonies. Before it passed, the king named General Gage, already the commander of the British army in North America, as the new governor of Massachusetts, with the understanding that he could use military force against civilians.

Parliament passed a fifth law, unrelated to the Coercive Acts but significant nonetheless. The Quebec Act established French civil law and the Roman Catholic Church in the Province of Quebec, provided for trial by jury in criminal but not in civil cases, gave legislative but not taxing power to an appointive governor and council, and extended Quebec's administrative boundaries to the area between the Great Lakes and the Ohio River, saving the legitimate charter claims of other colonies. Historians now regard the act as a farsighted measure that gave French Catholics the toleration that the empire had denied to Acadians 20 years earlier, but settlers from New England to Georgia were appalled. Instead of leniency and toleration, they saw a deliberate revival of the power of New

Library of Congress Prints and Photographs Division [LC-DIG-ppmsca-19467]

5.9 **"The Able Doctor, or America Swallowing the Bitter Draught"** This 1774 engraving by Paul Revere used "The Bostonians Paying the Excise-Man" as a model but turned it into a patriot statement. In Revere's version, the British are forcing tea down the throat of America (represented by a ravished lady, Liberty). The British are also imposing martial law in Boston.

France and the Catholic Church on their northern border, now bolstered by Britain's naval and military might. The Quebec Act intensified the fear that evil ministers in London were conspiring to destroy British and colonial liberties. Many colonists suspected that the autocratic government of Quebec might become a model for restructuring their own provinces. Settlers lumped the Quebec Act with the Coercive Acts and coined their own name for all of them—the Intolerable Acts.

5-5c *The Radical Explosion*

The interval between passage of the Port Act in March and the Massachusetts Government Act in May permits us to compare the response that each provoked. The Port Act was quite enforceable and immune to nullification by the colonists. It led to the summoning of the First Continental Congress and another round of nonimportation; but the colonists *did* nullify the Government Act. This resistance led to war. The redcoats marching to Concord on April 19, 1775 were trying to enforce that act against settlers who absolutely refused to obey it.

Gage took over as governor of Massachusetts in May 1774, before passage of the Massachusetts Government Act. In June, he closed the ports of Boston and Charlestown, just north of Boston. The navy gave him that power. While Boston split over the proper response, a mass meeting in New York City rejected immediate nonimportation in favor of an intercolonial congress. Philadelphia followed New York's lead. In both cities, cautious merchants hoped that a congress might postpone or prevent radical measures of resistance.

North assumed that the Coercive Acts would isolate Boston from the rest of the province, Massachusetts from the rest of New England, and New England from the other colonies, a goal that Britain would pursue through 1777. Instead, contributions began pouring in from all of the colonies to help Boston survive. The Stamp Act crisis and the Townshend crisis had been largely urban affairs. The Intolerable Acts politicized the countryside on a scale never seen before. When royal governors outside Massachusetts dismissed their assemblies to prevent them from joining the resistance movement, colonists elected **provincial congresses**, or conventions, to organize resistance. These bodies were larger than the legal assemblies they displaced, and they mobilized far more people. As the congresses took hold, royal government began to collapse almost everywhere. Numerous calls for a continental congress made the movement irresistible. By June, it was also obvious that any congress would adopt nonimportation. Except for some details, that issue had been settled, even before the congress met, by mandates that the delegates brought with them.

Yet, Gage remained optimistic well into the summer. Then news of the Massachusetts Government Act arrived on August 6. Gage's authority disintegrated when he tried to enforce the act, which marked the most dramatic attempt yet made by Parliament to control any colony's internal affairs. The councilors that Gage appointed to the new upper house either resigned their seats or fled to Boston to seek the army's protection. The Superior Court could not hold its sessions, even in Boston under the guns of the army, because jurors refused to take an oath under the new act. At the county level (the real center of royal power in the colony), popular conventions closed the courts and took charge of law enforcement in August and September. Gage began to realize that none of his major objectives was achievable.

Before this explosion of radical activity, Gage had called for a new General Court to meet in Salem in October. Many towns sent representatives, but others followed the lead of the Worcester County Convention, which urged all towns to elect delegates to a provincial congress in Concord, 17 miles inland, out of range of the navy. Although Gage revoked his call for a General Court, about 90 representatives met at Salem anyway. When Gage refused to recognize them, they adjourned to Concord in early October and joined the 200 delegates already gathered there as the Massachusetts Provincial Congress. That body became the de facto government of the colony and adopted the radical demands of the Suffolk Convention (representing Boston and its hinterland), which included a purge of unreliable militia officers, the creation of a special force of armed "minutemen" able to respond rapidly to any crisis, and the payment of taxes to the congress in Concord, not to Gage in Boston. The Provincial Congress collected military stores at Concord and created an executive arm, the Committee of Public Safety.

Library of Congress Prints and Photographs Division Washington, D.C.[LC-USZC4-5280]

5.10 "The Alternative of Williams-burg" (1775)
Published in London, this cartoon highlights the violence and intimidation faced by loyalists. A Virginia loyalist is forced to sign a patriot document by a mob of club-wielding "liberty men." On the left, a man is led toward a gallows in the background from which hangs a sack of feathers and a barrel of tar.

North assumed that Gage's army would uphold the new Massachusetts government. Instead, Gage's government survived only where the army could protect it. Thoroughly frustrated, he wrote North on October 30 that "a small Force rather encourages Resistance than terrifys." Gage then stunned London by asking for 20,000 redcoats, nearly as many as had been needed to conquer Canada.

5-5d *The First Continental Congress*

Into 1774, colonial patriots had looked to John Wilkes in London for leadership. At the **First Continental Congress**, they began relying on themselves. Twelve colonies (all but Georgia) sent delegates. In September 1774, they met at Philadelphia's Carpenters' Hall, a center of artisan strength. They scarcely even debated nonimportation. The southern colonies insisted, and the New Englanders agreed, that nonimportation finally be extended to molasses, which still generated revenue under the penny duty of 1766. The delegates were almost unanimous in adopting nonexportation if Britain did not redress colonial grievances by September 1775. Nonexportation was much more radical than nonimportation because it raised the threat of repudiating debts to British merchants, which colonial exports normally paid for.

Joseph Galloway, a Pennsylvania loyalist, submitted a plan of imperial union that would have required all laws affecting the colonies to be passed by both Parliament and an intercolonial congress, but his proposal was tabled by a vote of six colonies to five. The Congress spent three weeks trying to define colonial rights. Everyone insisted that the Coercive Acts, the Quebec Act, and all surviving revenue acts had to be repealed, and that all infringements on trial by jury had to be rejected. The delegates generally agreed on what would break the impasse, but they had trouble finding the precise language for their demands. They finally accepted the new principle of no *legislation* without consent—but added a saving clause that affirmed colonial assent to existing acts of Parliament that *only* regulated their trade.

Congress petitioned the king, not Parliament, because patriots no longer recognized it as a legitimate legislature for the colonies. Congress explained its position in separate addresses to the people of the 13 colonies, the people of Quebec, and the people of Great Britain. It took two other radical steps: It agreed to meet again in May 1775 if the British response was inadequate, and it created **the Association**—with citizen committees in every community—to enforce its trade sanctions against Britain. Most towns and counties heartily embraced the idea, and perhaps 7,000 men served on such committees during the winter of 1774–1775. In approving the Association, Congress began to act as a central government for the United Colonies.

5-5e *Toward War*

The news from Boston and Philadelphia shook the North ministry. "The New England Governments are in a State of Rebellion," George III wrote North, "blows must decide whether they are to be subject to this Country or independent." Although Franklin kept assuring the British that Congress meant exactly what it said, both North and the opposition assumed that conciliation could be achieved on lesser terms. Edmund Burke, out of office since 1766, urged a return to pre-1763 understandings without explaining how to restore the loyalty that had made them workable. "A great empire and little minds go ill together," he cautioned in an eloquent speech urging conciliation. Lord Chatham (William Pitt) introduced a bill to prohibit Parliament from taxing the colonies, to recognize Congress, and even to ask it to provide revenue for North American defense and to help pay down the national debt. When a government spokesman challenged him, Chatham retorted that his plan, if implemented, "must annihilate your power ... and at once reduce you to that state of insignificance for which God and nature designed you." Neither plan passed.

The initiative lay with Lord North, who still hoped for a peaceful solution, but in January 1775, he made war inevitable. He ordered Gage to send troops to Concord, destroy the arms stored there, and arrest John Hancock and Samuel Adams. Only after sending this dispatch did he introduce his own Conciliatory Proposition. Parliament pledged that it would tax no colony that paid its share for imperial defense and gave proper salaries to its royal officials, but Britain would use force against delinquent colonies. To assure hard-liners that he was not turning soft, he introduced his New England Restraining Act on the same day. It barred Yankees from the Atlantic fisheries and prohibited commerce between New England and any place except Britain and the British West Indies, precisely the trade routes that Congress was blocking through nonimportation. Both sides were now committed to economic sanctions.

North's orders to Gage arrived before his Conciliatory Proposition reached America, and Gage obeyed. He hoped to surprise Concord with a predawn march, but Boston radicals knew about the expedition almost as soon as the orders were written. They had already made careful preparations to alert the whole countryside. Their informant, in all likelihood, was Gage's wife, Margaret Kemble Gage, a New Jerseyan by birth. At 2:00 a.m. on the night of April 18–19, about 700 elite troops began their march toward Concord. Paul Revere, a Boston silversmith who had done as much as anyone to create the information network that he now set in motion, galloped west with the news that "The redcoats are coming!" When he was captured past Lexington by a British patrol, Dr. Samuel Prescott, who was returning from a lady friend's house at the awkward hour of 1:00 a.m., managed to get the message through to Concord. As the British approached Lexington Green at dawn, they found 60 or 70 minutemen drawn up to face them. The outnumbered militia began to withdraw. Then somebody—probably a colonial bystander but possibly a British soldier—fired the first shot in what became the Battle of Lexington. The British line fired, killing eight and wounding nine. From every direction, like angry hornets, the countryside surged toward them. Secrecy had become pointless, and the British broke out their regimental fifes and drums. Cheered by the tunes, they marched to Concord and into another world war.

Mrs. Thomas Gage, 1771 (oil on canvas), Copley, John Singleton (1738–1815) / The Putnam Foundation, Timken Museum of Art, San Diego, USA / The Bridgeman Art Library

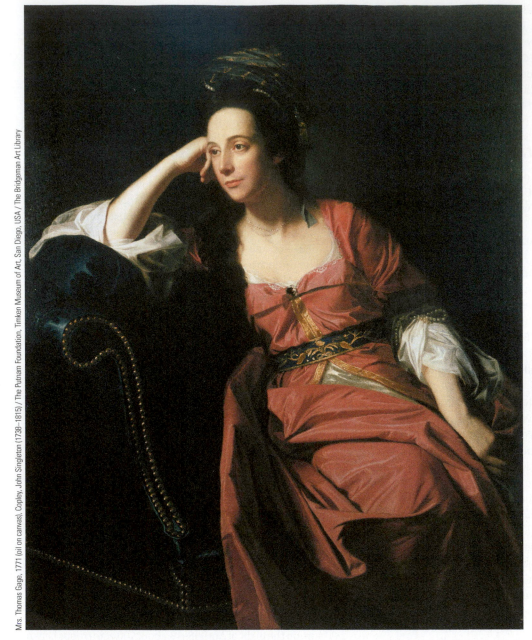

5.11 **John Singleton Copley's 1771 Portrait of Margaret Kemble Gage, the New Jersey Woman Who Married General Sir Thomas Gage** Pro-American in her sympathies, she was, in all probability, the highest-ranking informant that the Sons of Liberty ever acquired. Although no surviving document proves her involvement, Gage shipped her to England after Lexington and Concord, and the couple never again cohabited.

Q *How did the possible intelligence supplied by Margaret Kemble Gage to the patriot side both resemble and expand upon the actions of other women in the American resistance movement?*

5-6 The Improvised War

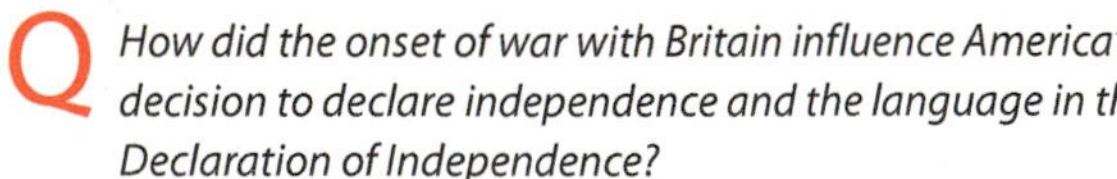

Q *How did the onset of war with Britain influence America's decision to declare independence and the language in the Declaration of Independence?*

In April 1775, neither side had a plan for winning a major war. Gage sent soldiers to enforce acts of Parliament. The militia fought for a political regime that Parliament was determined to change. They drove the British from Concord Bridge and pursued them all the way to Boston. Suffering only 95 casualties, they inflicted 273 on the British. Had a relief force not met the battered British survivors near Lexington, all of them might have been lost (see Map 5.3).

Even though no adequate command or supply structure existed, the colonists besieged Boston. After two months, Gage finally declared that all settlers bearing arms, and those who aided them, were rebels and traitors. He offered to pardon anyone who returned to his allegiance, except John Hancock and Samuel Adams. Instead of complying, the besiegers escalated the struggle two days later. They fortified the high ground on Breed's Hill (next to Bunker Hill) near Charlestown and overlooking Boston. The British sent 2,400 men, one-fifth of the garrison, to take the hills on June 17. Merely by seizing Charlestown Neck, a smaller force could have cut off the Yankee militia at low risk to itself. Instead, to prove that civilians had no chance against a regular army, General William Howe launched three frontal attacks. Secure behind their defenses, the settlers shot more than 1,000 of the attackers, killing 92 officers (about one-sixth of those lost in the entire war), before they ran out of ammunition and withdrew. The defenders suffered about 370 casualties, nearly all during the retreat. A few more such victories, reflected one officer, and no one would be left alive to carry the news to London.

Well into 1776, both sides fought an improvised war. In May 1775, Vermont and Massachusetts militia took Fort Ticonderoga on Lake Champlain and seized the artillery and gunpowder that would be used months later to end the siege of Boston. Crown Point also fell. With nearly all of their forces in Boston, the British were too weak to defend other positions or to intervene in the short Indian conflict—Lord Dunmore's War—that broke out in the upper Ohio Valley in 1774. The collapse of royal government meant that the rebels now controlled the militia and most of the royal powder houses.

The militia became the key to political allegiance. Compulsory service with the militia politicized many waverers, who decided that they really were patriots only when a redcoat shot at them or when they drove a loyalist into exile. The militia kept the countryside committed to the Revolution wherever the British army was too weak to overwhelm them.

5-6a *The Second Continental Congress*

When the **Second Continental Congress** met in May 1775, it inherited the war. For months it pursued conflicting strategies of resistance and conciliation. It voted to turn the undisciplined men besieging Boston into a Continental army. As in earlier wars, the soldiers were volunteers willing to serve for only a few months, or a single campaign. In the absence of royal authority, they elected their officers, who tried to win obedience through persuasion, not command. Supplying them with food and munitions became a huge problem.

5.12 **The Battle of Lexington, April 19, 1775** Ralph Earl's painting, which was engraved by Amos Doolittle in 1775, accurately portrays the opening shots of the Revolutionary War. The British are firing a volley into the Lexington militia, who are trying to leave the field without offering resistance. In fact, the first British soldiers who fired did so without orders, possibly in response to a shot from a colonial bystander. The militia was indeed trying to withdraw.

Q *How did the image reflect the differences in experience and training between the British regulars and the American militia?*

Most of the men were Yankees who would have preferred to serve under their own officers, but Congress realized that a successful war effort would have to engage the other colonies as well. On June 15, at the urging of John Adams of Massachusetts, Congress made George Washington of Virginia commanding general. When Washington took charge of the Continental army, he was appalled at the poor discipline among the soldiers and their casual familiarity with their officers. He insisted that officers behave with dignity and instill obedience. As the months passed, most of them won his respect. At year's end, however, nearly all of the men went home, and Washington had to train a new army for 1776. But enthusiasm for the cause remained strong, and fresh volunteers soon filled his camp.

In June 1775, Congress authorized an invasion of Canada to win over the French before they could side with the British and attack New York or New England. Two forces moved northward. One, under General Richard Montgomery, took Montreal. The other, commanded by Colonel Benedict Arnold, advanced on Quebec through the Maine forests and laid siege to the city, where Montgomery joined Arnold in December. With enlistments about to expire, they decided to assault the city, partly to get maximum service out of their men and partly to inspire some to reenlist. Their attack in a blizzard on December 31 was a disaster. Nearly half of the 900 men still with them were killed, wounded, or captured. Montgomery was killed and Arnold wounded. Both were hailed as American heroes.

The colonial objective in this fighting was still to restore government by consent under the Crown. After rejecting Lord North's Conciliatory Proposition out of hand, Congress approved an Olive Branch Petition to George III on July 5, 1775, in the hope of ending the bloodshed. Moderates, led by Dickinson, strongly favored the measure. The petition affirmed the colonists' loyalty to the Crown, did not even mention "rights," and implored the king to take the initiative in devising "a happy and permanent reconciliation." Another document written mostly by Virginia's Thomas Jefferson, "The Declaration of the Causes and Necessities of Taking Up Arms," set forth the colonies' grievances and justified their armed resistance. "We have counted the cost of this contest," Jefferson proclaimed, "and find nothing so dreadful as voluntary slavery." Like the Olive Branch, the declaration assured the British people "that we mean not to dissolve that Union which has so long and so happily subsisted between us." It reached London along with news of Bunker (Breed's) Hill. George III replied with a formal proclamation of rebellion on August 23. Predictably, the king's refusal to receive this moderate petition strengthened colonial radicals.

Congress began to function increasingly like a government, but with few exceptions, it assumed royal rather than parliamentary powers, which were taken over by the individual colonies. Congress did not tax or regulate trade, beyond encouraging nonimportation. It passed no laws. It took command of the Continental army, printed paper money, opened diplomatic relations with Indian nations, took over the postal service, and decided which government was legitimate in individual colonies—all functions previously performed by the Crown. In short, Congress thought of itself as a temporary plural executive for the continent, not as a legislature.

5-6b *War and Legitimacy, 1775–1776*

Into 1776, the British reacted with fitful displays of violence and grim threats of turning slaves and Indians against the settlers. When the weak British forces could neither restore order nor make good on their threats, they conciliated no one, enraged thousands, and undermined British claims to legitimacy. The navy burned Falmouth (now Portland), Maine, in October 1775. On November 7, John Murray, Earl of Dunmore and governor of Virginia, offered freedom to any slaves of rebel planters who would join his 200 redcoats. About 800 mustered under his banner only to fall victim to smallpox after the Virginia militia defeated them in a single action. **Dunmore's Proclamation**, as it became known, had a more immediate political influence, as the prospect of a mass slave emancipation pushed planters in Virginia and neighboring southern colonies toward independence.

In a separate action, Dunmore bombarded Norfolk, setting several buildings ablaze. The patriots, who considered Norfolk a loyalist bastion, burned the rest of the city and then blamed Dunmore for its destruction. Overall, his campaign undermined whatever loyalist sentiment survived among Virginia planters beyond Norfolk.

British efforts suffered other disasters in Boston and the Carolinas. The greatest colonial victory came at Boston, where most of the British army lay virtually imprisoned. On March 17, 1776, after Washington fortified Dorchester Heights south of the city and brought heavy artillery (from Ticonderoga) to bear on it, the British pulled out and sailed for Nova Scotia. A loyalist uprising by Highland Scots in North Carolina was crushed at Moore's Creek Bridge on February 27, and a British naval expedition sent to take Charleston was repulsed with heavy losses in June. Cherokee attacks against Virginia failed in 1776 because they occurred after Dunmore had left and did not fit into any larger general strategy. Before spring turned to summer, patriot forces had won control of the territory of all 13 colonies. Except in East and West Florida, Quebec, and Nova Scotia, the British had been driven from the continent.

5-6c *Independence*

Dismissal by George III of the Olive Branch Petition left moderates no option but to yield or fight. In late 1775, Congress created a committee to correspond with foreign powers. By early 1776, delegates from New England, Virginia, and Georgia already favored independence, but they knew that unless they won over all 13 colonies, the British would be able to divide them. The British attack on Charleston in June nudged the Carolinas toward independence.

Resistance to independence came mostly from the mid-Atlantic colonies, from New York through Maryland. Elsewhere, provincial congresses had supplanted the colonial assemblies in 1774 and 1775. In the middle colonies, however, both assemblies and congresses met and competed for the loyalties of the people. None of the five legal assemblies in the mid-Atlantic region ever repudiated the Crown. All of them had to be overthrown along with royal (or proprietary) government itself. The last royal governor to be driven from his post was New Jersey's William Franklin (Benjamin's son), who was arrested on June 19, 1776, to prevent him from summoning a new session of the regular assembly.

In the struggle for middle colony loyalties, Thomas Paine's pamphlet *Common Sense* became a huge success. Published in Philadelphia in January 1776, it sold more than 100,000 copies within a few months and reached more people than any other colonial tract ever had. Paine, a recent immigrant from England, wasted no reverence on Britain's mixed and balanced constitution. To him, George III was "the Pharaoh of England" and "the Royal Brute of Great Britain." Paine attacked monarchy and aristocracy as degenerate institutions and urged Americans to unite under a simple republican government of their own. "Reconciliation and ruin are nearly related," he insisted. "There is something very absurd, in supposing a Continent to be perpetually governed by an island."

The British continued to alienate the colonists. The king named Lord George Germain, a hard-liner, as secretary of state for the American colonies, and thus as war minister. Germain tried to hire 20,000 Russian mercenaries, who, smirked one British official, would make "charming visitors at New York and civilize that part of America wonderfully." When that effort failed, the British bought the services of 17,000 soldiers from Hesse and other north German states.

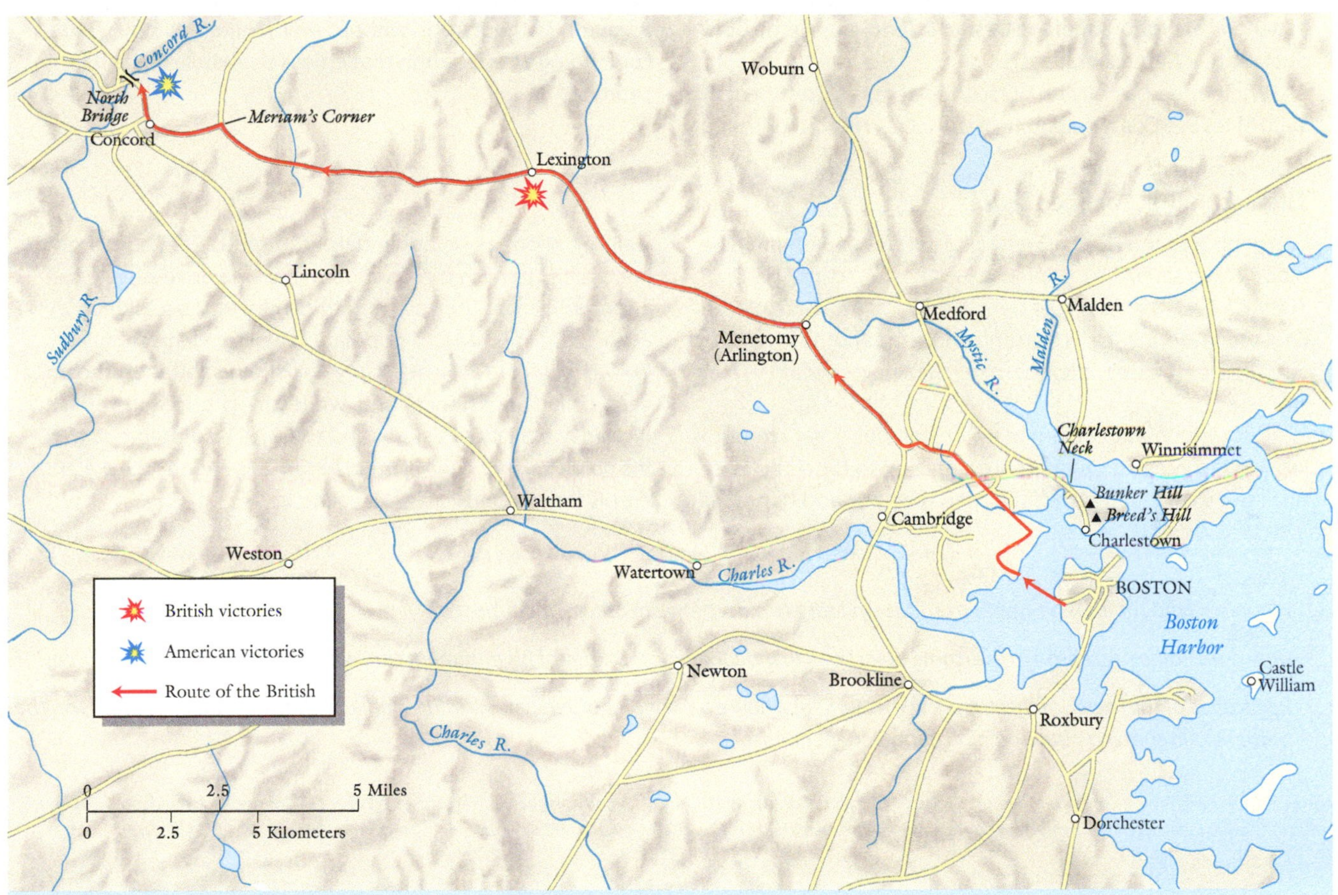

▲ **MAP 5.3 Lexington, Concord, and Boston, 1775** The British march to Lexington and Concord on April 19, 1775, touched off the Revolutionary War. The colonists drove the redcoats back to Boston and then besieged the city for 11 months until the British withdrew.

Q *How did the geography of the Massachusetts countryside and the improvised nature of the opening battles of the American Revolutionary War tend to favor the patriot side and its militia forces?*

Q *How might the outcome of the opening battles of the Revolutionary War gone differently had the Americans declared independence before the war started?*

What They Said

Contrasting Views of American Independence

In January 1776, with war continuing between Britain and its American colonies, the idea of American independence gained currency for the first time. In a remarkable coincidence, on January 9, the same day that Thomas Paine's pamphlet *Common Sense* calling for independence was first published, an anonymous loyalist writing under the name "Junius" argued against independence in a letter printed in the *New-Hampshire Gazette*. Whereas Paine's pamphlet helped to ignite a revolution, Junius's letter ultimately failed in its attempt to keep New Hampshire's rebellious assembly (known as the Provincial Congress) from supporting independence. On January 9, however, this outcome was far from clear. These two works, published on the same day, indicate the wide spectrum of political views that existed in America on the eve of independence.

Junius, "To the Congress at Exeter"

We began the Controversy on this Principle, to seek *Redress of Grievances*: since, we have lost Sight of the Object, and are in Quest of what will terminate most certainly in our Ruin, & Destruction: I mean INDEPENDENCY upon Great Britain; a Step that the Public are exceedingly averse to; but the Public in general are ignorant of the Design & Tendency of the Conduct of their Representatives. . . .

[W]e depend wholly on ourselves—that is a Continent of 1000 Miles Sea Coast defending themselves without one Ship of War against 310 Battle Ships compleatly manned and fitted. A Country that can pay but 30 Thousand Men, at War with a Nation that has paid, and can pay 150 thousand. A Country of three Millions of Inhabitants, fighting with a Nation of 15 Millions. A Country that can raise but 1 Mil[lion] in Specie. A Country without Arms, without Ammunition, without Trade, contending with a Nation that enjoys the whole in the fullest Latitude.

Thomas Paine, *Common Sense*

Every thing that is right or natural pleads for separation. The blood of the slain, the weeping voice of nature cries, 'TIS TIME TO PART. Even the distance at which the Almighty hath placed England and America, is a strong and natural proof, that the authority of the one, over the other, was never the design of Heaven. . . .

It is not in numbers, but in unity, that our great strength lies; yet our present numbers are sufficient to repel the force of all the world. . . . Youth is the seed time of good habits, as well in nations as in individuals. It might be difficult, if not impossible, to form the Continent into one government half a century hence. The vast variety of interests, occasioned by an increase of trade and population would create confusion. Colony would be against colony. Each being able might scorn each other's assistance: and while the proud and foolish gloried in their little distinctions, the wise would lament, that the union had not been formed before. Wherefore, the *present time* is the *true time* for establishing it.

Q *What fears did Junius have about a broader military conflict between Britain and America?*

Q *How does Paine use reason to overcome objections to independence? Do any of his arguments answer the fears expressed by Junius?*

Q *Regardless of the merits of their respective arguments, how do the works of Junius and Paine highlight the importance of events on the battlefield in shaping public opinion about independence?*

Sources: (top) Junius, "To the Congress at Exeter," *The New-Hampshire Gazette, and Historical Chronicle*, January 9, 1776, page 1; Library of Congress microfilm no. sv97017977; (bottom) Thomas Paine, *Common Sense*, originally published Philadelphia, 1776. Au. cited: Dover Thrift Edition, Mineola, New York, 1997, pp. 22, 25, 34, & 40.

(The colonists called them all **Hessians**.) To Jefferson, this action was "the last stab to [the] agonizing affection" that had once bound together the people of Britain and North America. Disturbing (but false) rumors suggested that Britain and France were about to sign a "partition treaty," dividing the eastern half of North America between them. Many congressmen concluded, some of them sadly, that only independence could counter these dangers by engaging Britain's European enemies on America's side. As long as conciliation was the goal, France would not participate, because American success would mean restoring the British Empire to its former glory. But Louis XVI (1774–1793) might well help the colonies win their independence if that meant crippling Britain.

From April to June, about 90 communities issued calls for independence. Most of them looked no further back than 1775 to justify their demand. The king had placed the colonists outside his protection, was waging war against them, and had hired foreigners to kill them. Self-defense demanded a permanent separation.

Congress finally broke the stalemate. On May 15, 1776, it voted to suppress "every kind of authority" under the British Crown, thus giving radicals an opportunity to seize power in Pennsylvania and New Jersey. Moderates still controlled New York, Delaware, and Maryland, but they reluctantly accepted independence as inevitable. In early June, Congress named a committee of five, including Jefferson, John Adams, and Franklin, to prepare a declaration that would vindicate America's decision to the whole world once independence had actually been decided upon.

On July 2, with the necessary votes in place, Congress passed Richard Henry Lee's resolution "that these United colonies are, and of right, ought to be, Free and Independent States; ... and that all political connexion between them, and the state of Great Britain, is, and ought to be, totally dissolved." Two days later, 12 colonies, with New York abstaining for the time being, unanimously approved Jefferson's Declaration of Independence, as amended by Congress. "We hold these truths to be self-evident, that all men are created equal, that they are endowed by their Creator with certain unalienable Rights, that among these are Life, Liberty, and the pursuit of Happiness," Congress proclaimed in what is perhaps the most famous statement ever made in American public life. Whenever "any Form of Government becomes destructive of these ends, it is the Right of the People to alter or to abolish it, and to institute new Government, laying its foundation on such principles ... as to them shall seem most likely to effect their Safety and Happiness."

Years later, Jefferson claimed that the Declaration "was intended to be an expression of the American mind." Rather than a product of any single philosophical tradition, it is a masterpiece of intellectual synthesis. Jefferson drew on several Enlightenment influences, including the natural rights theories of John Locke, the English opposition tradition, the moral sense philosophy of leading Scottish thinkers, and the universalist message of French *philosophes*. In turn, the Declaration itself became embraced as an Enlightenment text that contributed immediately to the law of nations, particularly for defining statehood, independence, and the recognition of new states.

After its opening rhetorical flourishes, the longest section of the Declaration listed 27 grievances indicting George III as a tyrant. The charges were crucial for justifying political separation from Britain and for enlisting support—both at home and abroad—for the American cause. As with the dozens of community declarations that preceded it, the Declaration emphasized the war as the key reason for independence. The indictment against the king builds to the final five most severe charges, all of which highlight war crimes committed by George III. The 27th and last grievance blames him for exciting "domestic insurrections amongst us," a veiled reference to Dunmore's Proclamation offering freedom to slaves who left their masters for the British war effort.

As if on cue, during the three days that Congress spent proclaiming American independence, the first ships of the largest armada yet sent across the Atlantic began landing British soldiers on Staten Island. Americans celebrated the creation of their new republic at the very moment that they faced a military challenge more ominous than any they had ever confronted before.

Conclusion

Between 1763 and 1776, Britain and the colonies became trapped in a series of self-fulfilling prophecies. Britain feared that without major reforms to guarantee Parliament's control of the empire, the colonies would drift toward independence. Colonial resistance to the new policies convinced the British that a movement for independence was already under way, a perception that led to sterner measures. Until a few months before it happened, nearly all colonists denied that they desired independence, but they began to fear that the British government was determined to deprive them of their rights as Englishmen. Britain's policy drove them toward a closer union with one another and finally provoked armed resistance. With the onset of war, both sides felt vindicated. The thousands of redcoats heading toward America did not bode well for colonial liberties. When the colonists did leave the empire, British ministers believed that their predictions had finally come true.

Both sides were wrong. The British had no systematic plan to destroy liberty in North America, and until the winter of 1775–1776, hardly any colonists favored independence. But the three imperial crises undermined mutual confidence and brought about what no one had desired in 1765, or even 1774—an independent American nation. Unable to govern North America, Britain now faced the grim task of conquering it instead.

CHAPTER REVIEW

Review

1. How did Britain's victory in the Seven Years' War lead to controversial imperial reforms for its American colonies?
2. How did Parliament resolve the Stamp Act crisis without fully surrendering its right to tax the American colonies?
3. What made the resolution of the Townshend crisis less satisfying for American colonists than the end to the Stamp Act crisis?
4. How did the British imperial crisis help to expose tensions within American society among the following groups: patriots and loyalists (and loyal colonies); artisans and gentlemen; tenants and landlords; settlers and proprietors; women and men; and slaves and masters?
5. Why did the colonists start a revolution after the Tea Act *lowered* the price of tea?
6. How did the onset of war with Britain influence America's decision to declare independence and the language in the Declaration of Independence?

Critical Thinking

1. The colonists insisted that the right to property was essential to the preservation of liberty. Taxation without representation was unconstitutional precisely because it deprived them of their property without their consent. How then could they find it appropriate and legitimate to resist British policies by destroying the property of stamp distributors, Thomas Hutchinson, and the East India Company?
2. In 1775, Lord North promised that Parliament would not tax any colony that paid its share of the costs of imperial defense and gave adequate salaries to its civil officers, but Congress rejected the proposal out of hand. Had George Grenville offered something of the kind between 1763 and 1765, might Britain have averted the Revolution? Specifically, if he had praised New Englanders and Virginians for their vigorous cooperation with the empire during the French and Indian War while censuring colonies such as Maryland and North Carolina for their lack of cooperation, would Boston have rioted and Patrick Henry have urged resistance?

Identifications

Review your understanding of the following key terms, people, and events for this chapter (terms in bold in text are included in the Glossary).

Proclamation of 1763, p. 136
Pontiac's War, p. 136
virtual representation, p. 139
nonimportation agreements, p. 141
Boston Massacre, p. 146
committees of correspondence, p. 148
loyalists, p. 149
feudal revival, p. 150
Phillis Wheatley, p. 152
Boston Tea Party, p. 155
Coercive Acts, p. 155
provincial congress, p. 156
First Continental Congress, p. 157
(the) Association, p. 157
Second Continental Congress, p. 159
Dunmore's Proclamation, p. 160
Hessians, p. 163

Suggested Readings

The best one-volume narrative history of the coming of the Revolution remains **Merrill Jensen's *The Founding of a Nation: A History of the American Revolution, 1763–1776*** (1968). **Bernard Bailyn's *The Ideological Origins of the American Revolution*** (1967) is necessary for understanding the ideological context for American protests. **Alan Taylor's *American Revolutions: A Continental History, 1750–1804*** (2016) is an ambitious attempt to explain the Revolution from the perspective of multiple groups and geographical vantages.

On the three imperial crises, **Edmund S. Morgan** and **Helen M. Morgan's *The Stamp Act Crisis, Prologue to Revolution***, 3rd ed. (1953, 1995) has lost none of its saliency. **Pauline Maier's *From Resistance to Revolution: Colonial Radicals and the Development of American Opposition to Britain, 1765–1776*** (1972); **Richard D. Brown's *Revolutionary Politics in Massachusetts: The Boston Committee of Correspondence and the Towns*** (1970); and **Eric Hinderaker, Boston's Massacre** (2017) are all excellent on the process of disaffection. Important studies of America's internal tensions and urban protests include **Gary B. Nash's *The Urban Crucible: Social Change, Political Consciousness, and the Origins of the American Revolution*** (1979); and **Benjamin L. Carp's *Rebels Rising: Cities and the American Revolution*** (2007).

For engaging treatments of the imperial crisis from the British perspective, see **S. Max Edelson**, ***The New Map of Empire: How Britain Imagined America before Independence*** (2017); and **Eliga H. Gould**, ***The Persistence of Empire: British Political Culture in the Age of the American Revolution*** (2000).

David Hackett Fischer's *Paul Revere's Ride* (1994) and **Woody Holton's *Forced Founders: Indians, Debtors, Slaves and the Making of the American Revolution in Virginia*** (1999) trace the opening of the improvised war in Massachusetts and Virginia, respectively. **Pauline Maier's *American Scripture: Making the Declaration of Independence*** (1997) uses 90 local declarations of independence issued in spring 1776 to give context to Jefferson's famous text. Inversely, **David Armitage's *The Declaration of Independence: A Global History*** (2009) explores the broad global influences and impact of the document.

 MINDTAP is a fully online personalized learning experience built upon Cengage Learning content. MindTap® combines student learning tools—readings, multimedia, activities, and assessments—into a singular Learning Path that guides students through the course and helps students develop the critical thinking, analysis, and communication skills that are essential to academic and professional success.

6 The Revolutionary Republic, 1776–1789

6-1 Hearts and Minds: The Northern War, 1776–1777

Learning Objective: *Explain how the British decision to allow Washington's army to escape New York in August 1776 came back to haunt them in the battles of Trenton and Princeton.*

The British Offensive

The Trenton-Princeton Campaign

6-2 The Campaigns of 1777 and Foreign Intervention

Learning Objective: *Identify what led France to intervene on the American side in the war.*

The Loss of Philadelphia

Saratoga

French Intervention

Spanish Expansion and Intervention

6-3 The Crisis of the Revolution, 1778–1783

Learning Objective: *List the different considerations that drove loyalists, African Americans, and Indians to join the British war effort.*

Loyalists, Black and White

The Indian Struggle for Unity and Survival

Violence and Attrition

Mutiny and Reform

6-4 The British Offensive in the South

Learning Objective: *Determine the factors that contributed to American victory in the south after the initial success of Britain's southern campaign.*

Britain's Southern Strategy

The Partisan War

From the Ravaging of Virginia to Yorktown and Peace

6-5 A Revolutionary Society

Learning Objective: *Analyze the social changes that came about in the United States either directly or indirectly as a result of the American Revolution.*

Religious Transformations

The First Emancipation

The Challenge to Patriarchy

Western Expansion, Discontent, and Conflict with Indians

The Northwest Ordinance

6-6 American Constitutionalism

Learning Objective: *Detail ways that state constitutions advanced American constitutional thinking during the revolutionary era.*

John Adams and the Separation of Powers

Early State Constitutions

Massachusetts Redefines Constitutionalism

Articles of Confederation

6-7 The Constitution: A More Perfect Union

Learning Objective: *Examine how conditions in the United States in the 1780s influenced the outcome of the Constitution.*

Commerce, Debt, and Shays's Rebellion

Cosmopolitans versus Localists

The Philadelphia Convention

Ratification

The Art Archive/Alamy Stock Photo

6.1 ***The Surrender of Lord Cornwallis*** This painting by John Trumbull, completed in 1820, celebrates the American victory over the British in the last major battle of the Revolutionary War, at Yorktown, Virginia, in October 1781. Claiming illness, the British commanding officer, General Lord Cornwallis, did not attend the ceremony, sending in his place General Charles O'Hara. General George Washington followed suit, directing his second-in-command, General Benjamin Lincoln, to accept the symbolic sword of surrender from O'Hara. Washington, to the right, looks on with his American forces, while their French allies observe to the left.

THE REVOLUTIONARY WAR killed a higher percentage of Americans who fought in it than any other American conflict except the Civil War. It too was a civil war. People were more likely to fight neighbors during the Revolution than they were between 1861 and 1865, when the geographical line separating the two sides would be much sharper. Twice, in 1776 and 1780, the British might have won, but in both campaigns the Americans somehow rallied. They won only by bringing in France as an ally. France brought in Spain.

During the war, Americans began to think, more than before, in crude racial categories. Ideas about racial inferiority clashed sharply with claims of universal rights and human equality. As whites, blacks, and Indians redefined their differences, they often resorted to racial stereotypes. Most Indians and enslaved Africans hoped that Britain would win the war.

Even as the war raged and the economy disintegrated, Americans drafted state constitutions and eloquent bills of rights that reached far beyond the racism many of them felt. They knew they were attempting something daring—the creation of a stable, enduring republic. Some European monarchies were 1,000 years old. No republic had lasted that long. Educated people knew a great deal about the city-states of classical Greece and about republican Rome—how they had called forth the noblest sentiments of patriotism for a time and then decayed into despotisms. Still, once Americans broke with Britain, they warmly embraced republicanism and never looked back. They were able to build viable republican governments because they grasped the voluntaristic dynamics of their society. They knew they had to restructure their governments through persuasive means. The use of force against armed fellow citizens would be self-defeating.

The war demonstrated how weak Congress was, even after ratification of the Articles of Confederation in 1781. Congress could not pay its bills. It could not expel the British from their western military posts or defeat the Indians of the Ohio Country. Yet in the Northwest Ordinance of 1787, Congress announced plans to create new states and admit them to the Union as equals of the original 13. Also in 1787, the Philadelphia Convention drafted a new Constitution for the United States. After ratification by 11 states, it went into effect in April 1789. The federal system it created became the most distinctive achievement of the revolutionary generation. ■

6-1 Hearts and Minds: The Northern War, 1776–1777

Q *How did the British decision to allow Washington's army to escape New York in August 1776 come back to haunt them in the battles of Trenton and Princeton?*

The price of patriotism escalated once independence became America's goal. The men ruling Britain believed the loss of the colonies would be fatal to British power. As a result, Britain raised more soldiers and larger fleets than ever before and more than doubled its national debt. Americans, too confident after their early successes, staggered initially under the onslaught before later recovering.

6-1a *The British Offensive*

The first setback came in Canada. In May 1776, when a fresh British force sailed up the St. Lawrence River, the Americans, weakened by smallpox, had to retreat. By July, Sir Guy Carleton drove them back into northern New York, to Fort Ticonderoga on Lake Champlain. Both sides built ships to control that strategic waterway. Largely through Benedict Arnold's efforts, the Americans held, and Carleton returned to Canada for the winter.

Farther south, Richard, Viscount Howe, admiral of the British fleet, and his brother General William Howe prepared an awesome striking force on Staten Island. They also acted as peace commissioners, with power to restore whole colonies to the king's peace and to pardon individual rebels. They hoped to avoid using their huge army, but when they wrote George Washington to open negotiations, he refused to accept the letter because it did not address him as "General." To do so would have recognized the legitimacy of his appointment. Unable to negotiate, the Howes had to fight.

Washington had moved his army from Boston to New York City, where he had about 19,000 men to face more than 30,000 redcoats and Hessians. Early successes had kept morale high among American forces and helped sustain the *rage militaire* (warlike enthusiasm) that had prompted thousands to volunteer in 1775 and 1776, including 4,000 veterans of 1775 who reenlisted for 1776. Although some men served in the Continental army and others with state militia units, the difference between them was still minimal. Neither had formal military training, and the men in both served only for short terms.

Washington was reluctant to abandon any large city. Against conventional military wisdom, he divided his inferior force and sent half of it from Manhattan to Long Island. Most of the men dug in on Brooklyn Heights, just two miles from lower Manhattan, and waited for a frontal attack. The British

CHRONOLOGY

1769	Spanish found San Diego
1775	Settlement of Kentucky begins
1776	Virginia becomes first state to adopt a permanent constitution and bill of rights • British forces land on Staten Island • Declaration of Independence • Pennsylvania constitution creates unicameral legislature • British win battle of Long Island; New York City falls • Washington wins at Trenton
1777	Washington wins at Princeton • Howe takes Philadelphia • Burgoyne surrenders at Saratoga • Congress completes Articles of Confederation
1778	Franco-American alliance
1779	Indians form alliances from the Gulf to the Great Lakes • Spain declares war on Britain • Continental dollar collapses
1780	Massachusetts constitution approved • Pennsylvania adopts gradual emancipation • British take Charleston, overrun South Carolina • Gordon riots in London • Arnold's treason exposed • Americans win at King's Mountain
1781	Continental army mutinies • Americans win at Cowpens • Congress creates executive departments • Articles of Confederation ratified • Cornwallis surrenders at Yorktown
1782	Americans massacre 100 unarmed Indians at Gnadenhutten
1783	Peace of Paris recognizes American independence
1785	Congress passes Land Ordinance
1786	Virginia passes Statute for Religious Freedom • Annapolis Convention
1786–1787	Shays's Rebellion in Massachusetts
1787	Northwest Ordinance • Philadelphia Convention drafts federal Constitution
1787–1788	Eleven states ratify the Constitution
1789	First federal Congress sends Bill of Rights to the states for ratification
1799	New York adopts gradual emancipation
1804	New Jersey adopts gradual emancipation

invaded Long Island, a loyalist stronghold, and on August 27, 1776, sent a force around the American left flank through unguarded Jamaica Pass. While Hessians feinted a frontal assault, the flanking force crushed the American left and rear and sent the survivors reeling.

The Howes did nothing to prevent the evacuation of the rest of the American army to Manhattan, which occurred under the cover of a fierce nor'easter storm. Instead, on September 11 the British opened informal talks with several members of Congress on Staten Island. The talks collapsed when the Americans insisted that the British recognize their independence before discussing other issues. Washington evacuated lower Manhattan. The British took New York City, much of which was destroyed on September 21 by fire, most likely set by Americans. The Howes then appealed directly to the people to lay down their arms and return to British allegiance within 60 days in exchange for a full pardon. In southern New York State, several thousand complied.

In October, the Howes drove Washington's remaining forces from Manhattan and Westchester. Although the brothers could have destroyed Washington's army on Long Island or Manhattan, they probably knew what they were doing. British victories and the American reliance on short-term volunteers were destroying Washington's army. British success seemed to prove that no American force could stand before a properly organized British army. But to capture Washington's entire army would have been a political embarrassment, leading to massive treason trials, executions, and great bitterness. Instead, Britain's impressive victories demoralized Americans and encouraged them to go home, many taking their muskets with them. In September, 27,000 Americans stood fit for duty in the northern theater (including the Canadian border); by December, only 6,000 remained, most of whom intended to leave when their enlistments expired on December 31.

The Howes' strategy nearly worked. In December, British forces swept across New Jersey as far south as Burlington. They captured Charles Lee, next in command after Washington, and Richard Stockton, a signer of the Declaration of Independence. Several thousand New Jersey residents, including Stockton, took the king's oath. To seal off Long Island Sound from both ends, the Howes also captured Newport, Rhode Island. Many observers thought the war was all but over as sad remnants of the Continental army crossed the Delaware River into Pennsylvania, confiscating all boats along the way so that the British could not follow them. One general believed that the time had come to "bargain away the Bubble of Independency for British Liberty well secured." Even Jefferson began to think about terms on which a restoration of the monarchy might be acceptable.

6-1b *The Trenton-Princeton Campaign*

Washington knew he had to do something dramatic to restore morale and encourage his soldiers to reenlist. In mid-December, the New Jersey militia, which had been silent for weeks, showed him how by harassing British outposts and patrols in the Delaware Valley, pushing the Hessian garrison at Trenton toward exhaustion. On Christmas night 1776, Washington crossed the ice-choked Delaware and marched south, surprising the Trenton garrison at dawn, which was nearly blinded by another nor'easter (see Map 6.1). At small cost to the attackers, nearly 1,000 Hessians surrendered.

The British sent their most energetic general, Charles, Earl Cornwallis, south with 8,000 men to "bag the fox"—Washington and the 5,000 Continentals and militia still with him. Cornwallis caught him at Trenton near sunset on January 2 but decided to wait until dawn before attacking. British patrols watched the Delaware to prevent another escape across the river, but Washington tried nothing of the kind. With his campfires burning, he muffled the wheels of his wagons and guns and stole around the British left flank, heading north. At dawn, he met a British regiment beginning its march from Princeton to Trenton. In the Battle of Princeton, the Americans, with a 5-to-1 edge in numbers, mauled yet another garrison.

Washington's two quick victories had an enormous impact on the war, although they inspired few reenlistments. The Howes, who had seemed to possess a firm grasp of revolutionary warfare, blundered in not hounding Washington's remnant of an army to its destruction after Princeton, if that was still possible. As the British departed, the New Jersey militia returned, asking who had sworn oaths to the king. Those who had taken the oath now groveled, as the price of acceptance, or fled to British lines. The Howes had encouraged loyalists to expose themselves and then abandoned them to the king's enemies. Together, the British and Hessians had lost the hearts and minds of the settlers. In 1777, few would be willing to declare for the Crown. The Revolution survived.

6-2 The Campaigns of 1777 and Foreign Intervention

Q *What led France to intervene on the American side in the war?*

Britain's thoughtful strategy of 1776 gave way to incoherence in 1777. The Howes again had a plan for winning the war, but it required 20,000 reinforcements that did not exist. Instead, Lord George Germain, Britain's war minister, ordered the Howes to take Philadelphia. He also sent John Burgoyne, a poet and playwright as well as a general, to Canada with orders to march his army south and link up with the garrison of New York City, commanded by Sir Henry Clinton.

The British aimed to control the Hudson River and isolate New England, where they still believed the rebellion to be strongest. Yet, without a firm commitment from the Howes to send men to support Burgoyne's march, the campaign made little sense. Instead, the Howes kept their forces together, rejected an overland march to Philadelphia as too risky, and decided to invade by sea—decisions that allowed Washington to shift men north to oppose Burgoyne.

6-2a *The Loss of Philadelphia*

After Trenton and Princeton, Washington demanded stricter discipline and longer terms of enlistment. Congress responded by raising the number of lashes a soldier could receive from 39 to 100 and by promising a cash bonus to anyone enlisting for three years, and a land bounty to anyone serving for the duration. Congress never came close to raising the 75,000 men it hoped for, but these new policies did create a solid foundation for a more experienced army. Longer terms made military training a real possibility, which in turn made the Continentals much more professional than the militia.

The Continental army acquired its own distinctive character. The men who signed up were often poor. About half of the New Jersey Line came from families that were not on the tax rolls. Some recruits were British deserters. Short-term militiamen, by contrast, usually held a secure place in their communities and were more likely than the Continentals to be church members. As the 1777 recruits came in, the two northern armies, swelled by militia, grew to about 28,000 men fit for duty—17,000 in northern New York and 11,000 under Washington.

In July 1777, the Howes sailed south from New York with 13,000 men. After his experience in New York, Washington was wary of being trapped in a city. Instead of trying to hold Philadelphia, he took up strong positions at Brandywine Creek along the British marching route but left open a line of retreat. On September 11, Howe again outmaneuvered him, drove in his right flank, and forced him to retreat. Congress fled to Lancaster. The British occupied Philadelphia on September 26.

After failing to destroy a British outpost at Germantown, Washington headed west to Valley Forge, where the army endured a miserable winter. There, Frederich Wilhelm, Baron von Steuben, a Prussian serving with the Continental army who would soon become a major general, devised a drill manual for Americans based on Prussian standards. (Known informally as the "blue book," the manual influences drill and ceremony in the U.S. Army to this day.) Through Steuben's efforts, the Continentals became far more soldierly. Other European volunteers also helped. From France came the Marquis de Lafayette and Johann, Baron de Kalb. The Poles sent Thaddeus Kosciuszko (a talented engineer) and Casimir, Count Pulaski. De Kalb and Pulaski were killed in American service. By the last years of the war, perhaps one-fifth of all Continental officers were professional soldiers from Europe, who gave the American officer corps an aristocratic tone that sometimes alarmed civilians.

6-2b *Saratoga*

In northern New York, Fort Ticonderoga fell to Burgoyne on June 2, 1777, but little went right for the British after that. Without support from the Howes, Burgoyne's army of 7,800, advancing from Ticonderoga toward Albany, was overwhelmed in the upper Hudson Valley. As his supply line to Canada grew longer, American militia swarmed behind him to cut it. By the time Burgoyne's surviving soldiers reached the Hudson and started toward Albany, the Americans under Horatio Gates outnumbered them 3 to 1. The British got as far as Bemis Heights, 30 miles north of Albany, but failed to break through in two costly battles, with Benedict Arnold distinguishing himself. Burgoyne retreated 10 miles to **Saratoga**, where he surrendered his entire army on October 17.

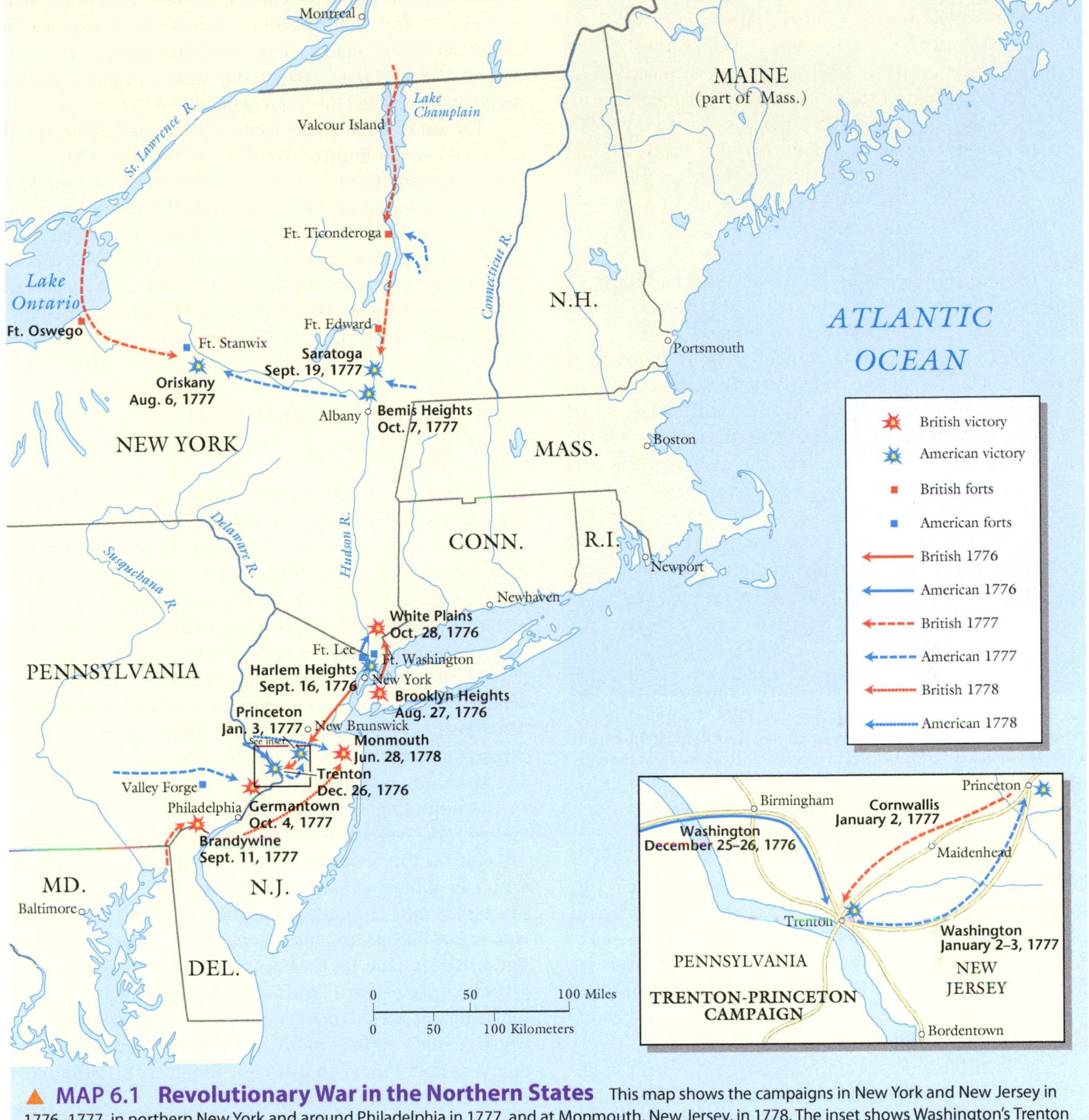

▲ **MAP 6.1 Revolutionary War in the Northern States** This map shows the campaigns in New York and New Jersey in 1776–1777, in northern New York and around Philadelphia in 1777, and at Monmouth, New Jersey, in 1778. The inset shows Washington's Trenton and Princeton campaigns after Christmas 1776.

Q *In a typical European conflict, Britain would have been the victor after winning major battles and occupying large American seaports, including New York and Philadelphia. Why was this not the case in the American Revolutionary War?*

Q *How did George Washington adjust his strategy after suffering a major defeat at New York in the summer of 1776?*

6-2c *French Intervention*

If Trenton and Princeton restored American morale, Saratoga won French hearts and minds. Since May 1776, Louis XVI had authorized secret aid to the American rebels. A French dramatist, Pierre-Augustin Caron de Beaumarchais, author of *The Barber of Seville* (1775) and later *The Marriage of Figaro* (1784), set up a fake firm to smuggle supplies through Britain's weak blockade of the American coast. (The British navy had committed most of its ships to transport and supply the army.) Without this aid, the Americans could not have continued the war.

In December 1776, Benjamin Franklin arrived in France as an agent of Congress. Although the French court could not officially receive him without risking a declaration of war

Library of Congress Prints and Photographs Division

6.2 **Benjamin Franklin as Noble Savage, 1777** Franklin charmed the French court and polite society by playing the role of an American rustic. His diplomatic skill helped to secure France as an ally in the war against Britain.

Q *How did Franklin's appearance help to define the new American character?*

by Britain, the 70-year-old Franklin took Parisian society by storm. He adopted simple clothes, replaced his wig with a fur cap, and played to perfection the role of an innocent man of nature that French philosophes associated with Pennsylvania. Through Beaumarchais, he kept the supplies flowing and organized privateering raids on British commerce, which the French court claimed it could not stop.

The fall of Philadelphia alarmed Foreign Minister Charles Gravier, Comte de Vergennes. He feared that Congress might give up unless France entered the war. But Burgoyne's defeat at Saratoga convinced Louis that the Americans could win and that intervention was a good risk. Franklin and Vergennes signed two treaties in February 1778. One, a commercial agreement, granted Americans generous trading terms with France. In the other, France made a perpetual alliance with the United States, recognized American independence, agreed to fight until Britain conceded independence, and disavowed all territorial ambitions on the North American continent. Americans could not have hoped for more. Vergennes also brought Spain into the war a year later.

Franklin's treaties stunned London. Lord North proposed a plan of conciliation that conceded virtually everything but independence and sent a distinguished group of commissioners under Frederick Howard, Earl of Carlisle, to present it to Congress and block the French alliance. In 1775, such terms would have resolved the imperial crisis, but in June 1778, Congress, recognizing them as signs of British desperation, rejected them out of hand.

The war now transformed into a global conflict. George III declared war on France, recalled the Howe brothers, and ordered General Clinton to abandon Philadelphia. Fearing a French invasion of the British Isles while most of the Royal Navy was in American waters, the British redeployed their forces on a global scale. They stood on the defensive in America through most of 1778 and 1779 and even evacuated Newport, but loyalists, based in New York City or Long Island, often raided Connecticut and New Jersey.

6-2d *Spanish Expansion and Intervention*

Like France, Spain was eager to avenge old defeats against Britain. The Spanish king, Charles III (1759–1788), had endured the loss of Florida shortly after ascending the throne but had received Louisiana from France in compensation. Spanish rule there did not begin well. In 1769, Spain suppressed a small revolt against its restrictions on trade, but in later years, when its trade policy became more favorable, Louisiana enjoyed a level of prosperity it had never known before. The province attracted 2,000 immigrants from the Canary Islands, perhaps 3,000 Acadian refugees, and other French settlers from the Illinois Country.

Spaniards also moved into California, partly in response to the migration of Russian hunters into Alaska. Spain founded San Diego in 1769. In the next few years, Spaniards explored the Pacific coastline as far north as southern Alaska, set up an outpost at San Francisco Bay, and built a series of Franciscan missions under Junípero Serra. With little danger from other Europeans, Spain sent relatively few soldiers to California. In fact, its California frontier embodied many aspects of the earlier Florida missions. For the last time in the history of North America, missionaries set the tone for a whole province. As in Florida earlier, Indians died in appalling numbers from European diseases, and many bristled under the severe discipline of the missions.

Charles III saw the danger of one imperial power urging the subjects of another to revolt and never made an alliance with the United States, but in 1779 he joined France's war against Britain, hoping to retake Gibraltar and stabilize Spain's North American borders. Britain held Gibraltar, but Spain took West Florida. In 1783, Britain ceded East Florida as well, giving Spain, for the first time in a century, control of the entire coastline of the Gulf of Mexico. The treaty did not specify the northern boundary for Spanish West Florida, which resulted in a prolonged and bitter dispute between the United States and Spain. The Americans insisted that the boundary ran along the 31st parallel, while the Spanish claimed the east flank of the Mississippi River all the way up to the Ohio and Tennessee rivers.

History Through Film *Hamilton's America* (2016)

Documentary that aired for the PBS series Great Performances *in the fall of 2016. Directed by Alex Horwitz.*
Starring Lin-Manuel Miranda, Thomas Kail, Alex Lacamoire, Ron Chernow, Leslie Odom, Jr., Christopher Jackson, Phillipa Soo, Barack Obama, George W. Bush.

Arguably the most celebrated American cultural phenomenon of the early 21st century, the musical *Hamilton* has introduced a new generation to the American founders through rap lyrics and multiethnic casting. *Hamilton's America* provides a behind-the-scenes look at the musical, while also telling the biography of the musical's creator, Lin-Manuel Miranda, and its protagonist, Alexander Hamilton, America's first treasury secretary.

The documentary follows Miranda with footage dating to 2008, when he first started penning the opening number to the musical (then envisioned as *The Hamilton Mixtape*), shortly after returning from a vacation during which he read historian Ron Chernow's biography *Alexander Hamilton*. In 2009, Miranda performed the song before President Barack Obama and First Lady Michelle Obama at the White House Evening of Poetry, Music and the Spoken Word. The performance went viral, providing momentum for Miranda and his principle collaborators, musician Alex Lacamoire and director Thomas Kail, to complete the full musical. In early 2015, it debuted to rave reviews off Broadway at the Public Theater before soon moving to the Richard Rogers Theater on Broadway. *Hamilton's America* carries the story through the 2016 Tony Awards, in which *Hamilton* received a record-setting 16 nominations, winning 11 (including best musical), and Miranda's triumphant return to the White House to perform again, this time with his full cast, and to interview President Obama.

With *Hamilton*, Miranda accomplished something improbable in the eyes of most historians: transform Hamilton, "the ten-dollar Founding Father," from a conservative icon to a liberal hero. The musical emphasizes Hamilton's humble origins as a penniless, orphaned immigrant from the Caribbean who came to America to help found a country that was, like him, "young, scrappy, and hungry." The show's biggest applause line comes from a scene at the Battle of Yorktown at the close of the Revolutionary War in which Hamilton and the French aristocrat and general, the Marquis de Lafayette, declare: "Immigrants: We get the job done." The show further sells Hamilton to a contemporary audience by stressing his antislavery views in contrast to the slaveholding of his rival Thomas Jefferson.

Despite its popularity, the revisionism of *Hamilton* has not escaped criticism. Historians point out, immigrant or not, Hamilton became one of the most elitist founders and a fervent critic of democracy, arguing at the Constitutional Convention that the president and senators should serve for life. Moreover, while Miranda may have cast black and Latino actors as the founders, he includes few actual nonwhite characters in his story. The musical's celebratory tone is representative of "Founders Chic," a genre defined by uncritical salutes to the genius of the founders.

The documentary format of *Hamilton's America* allows for more nuance. The musical's actors visit historic and contemporary sites associated with their historical subjects. Miranda's trip to Wall Street and the New York Stock Exchange, as well as an interview with Senator Elizabeth Warren, provides the opportunity to explore Hamilton's mixed legacy of American financial success and economic inequality. The actor Christopher Jackson, who played George Washington in the musical's original production, makes a moving visit to Mount Vernon, Washington's estate, and discusses the challenge as an African American of playing a white slaveholder. The program even complicates common perceptions of Aaron Burr, who killed Hamilton in a duel and serves as the musical's chief villain. As a result, even without seeing *Hamilton* on stage, viewers of the documentary will engage deeply with the musical's parting question about how history is made and the past is remembered: "Who lives, who dies, who tells your story?" ■

6.3 Lin-Manuel Miranda as Alexander Hamilton in the musical *Hamilton*. In the background, Aaron Burr (to the left, Leslie Odom, Jr.) and George Washington (to the right, Christopher Jackson), applaud the musical's hero.

Richard Cummins/Encyclopedia/Corbis

6.4 **San Diego de Alcala** This mission, the first California mission established by Spain, was founded on July 16, 1769.

6-3 The Crisis of the Revolution, 1778–1783

Q *What different considerations drove loyalists, African Americans, and Indians to join the British war effort?*

Americans expected a quick victory under the French alliance. Instead, the struggle turned into a grim war of attrition, testing which side would first exhaust its resources or lose the will to fight. The longer the war dragged on, the more it split each of America's broad cultural groups: whites, African Americans, and Indians. At times, America's revolutionaries even turned on one another.

The British sought to capitalize on American disunity. Loyalists became much more important to the British war effort, both as a source of manpower and as a major justification for continuing the war. The British also welcomed increasing numbers of Indians and African Americans to their side. Even as the imperial conflict between Britain and America turned into a global war, American society fractured into civil war and discord.

6-3a *Loyalists, Black and White*

Loyalists continued to embrace English ideas of liberty. They thought that creating a new American union was a far riskier venture than remaining part of the British Empire. Still, many waited until the fighting reached their door before deciding which soldiers to join. The British, in turn, were slow to take advantage of the loyalists. At first, British officers regarded loyalist military potential with the same disdain that they bestowed on the patriots. But after Saratoga, loyalists, who stood to lose everything in an American victory, showed that they could be impressive soldiers.

As much as a third of the white population chose the British side, and another third or more remained neutral or disaffected at different junctures of the war. 19,000 men joined one of some 40-odd loyalist military units, mostly after 1778, when Britain grew desperate for soldiers. Unlike most patriots, loyalists served long terms, even for the duration. They could not go home unless they won. By 1780, the number of loyalists under arms may have exceeded the number of Continentals by almost 2 to 1. American states retaliated by banishing prominent loyalists under pain of death and by confiscating their property.

When given the choice, most slaves south of New England also sided with Britain. In New England, they sensed that they could gain freedom by joining the rebels; many volunteered for service. Elsewhere, although some fought for the Revolution, they realized that their best chance of emancipation lay with the British army. During the war, at least 50,000 and as many as 100,000 slaves fled their owners amidst the commotion of the conflict; of that total, the British evacuated about 20,000 at the end of the war.

The decision to flee carried risks. In South Carolina during Clinton's 1776 invasion, hundreds reached the Sea Islands to join the British, only to face their owners' wrath when the British failed to rescue them. Some approached British units only to be treated as contraband (property). They faced possible resale. But most slaves who reached British lines won their freedom, even though the British army never became an instrument of systematic emancipation. When the British withdrew after the war, blacks went with them, many to Jamaica, some to Nova Scotia, others to London. In the 1780s, the British created a colony for former slaves at Sierra Leone in West Africa. A few even ended up in Australia.

The war, in short, created an enormous stream of refugees, black and white. In addition to 20,000 former slaves, some 60,000 to 70,000 colonists left for other parts of the British Empire. The American Revolution created 30 refugees for every 1,000 people, compared with 5 per 1,000 created by the French Revolution in the 1790s. About 35,000 settlers found their way to the Maritime Provinces. Another 6,000 to 10,000 fled to Quebec, settled upriver from the older French population, and in 1791 became the new province of Upper Canada (later Ontario).

After 1783, loyalist refugees helped to reinvigorate the British Empire. In Canada, low taxes and a generous land policy, which required an oath of allegiance to George III, attracted thousands of loyalist immigrants from the United States (known as "late loyalists" because they fled after the Revolutionary War). By the War of 1812, four-fifths of Upper Canada's 100,000 people were American-born. Although only one-fifth of them could be traced to the loyalist emigration, these settlers supported Britain in that war. In a real sense, the American Revolution laid the foundation for two new nations—the United States and Canada—and competition between them for settlers and their loyalties continued long after the fighting stopped.

6-3b *The Indian Struggle for Unity and Survival*

As the war persisted, Indians also increasingly joined the British. Most Indians saw that an American victory would threaten their survival as a people on their ancestral lands. They supported Britain in the hope that a British victory might stem the flood of western expansion, and they achieved a level of unity without precedent in their history (see Map 6.2).

At first, most Indians tried to remain neutral. The British were rebuffed when they asked the Iroquois to fight against the colonists. Delawares and Shawnees, defeated in Dunmore's War in 1774, also stood neutral. Only the Cherokees took up arms in 1776. Short on British supplies, they took heavy losses before making peace and accepting neutrality—although a splinter group, the Chickamaugas, continued to resist. In the Deep South, only the Catawbas—by now much reduced in number—fought on the American side.

Burgoyne's invasion brought the Iroquois into the war. Mohawks in the east and Senecas in the west sided with Britain under the leadership of **Joseph Brant**, a literate, educated Mohawk and a Freemason. His sister, Mary Brant, emerged as a skillful diplomat in the alliance between the Iroquois and the loyalists. A minority of Oneidas and Tuscaroras fought with the Americans. Most were becoming Christians under a patriot Presbyterian missionary, Samuel Kirkland. Despite severe strains during the Revolution, the Iroquois League did not dissolve until after the war, when those who fought for Britain migrated to Canada.

A minority of Shawnees, led by Cornstalk, and of Delawares, led by White Eyes and Killbuck, desired friendly relations with the Americans. They provided intelligence to American forces and served as wilderness guides, but they refused to fight other Indians and did their best to preserve peace along the frontier. Christian Moravian Indians in the Ohio Country took a similar stance. The reluctance of Indians to kill other Indians, already becoming evident during the Seven Years' War, grew even more obvious during the Revolution. Loyalists and patriots were far more willing than Indians to kill one another.

Frontier racism, already conspicuous in Pontiac's War, intensified and made Indian neutrality all but impossible. Backcountry settlers from Carolina through New York refused to accept the neutrals on their own terms. Indian warriors, especially young men influenced by nativist prophets, increasingly believed that the Great Spirit had created whites, Indians, and blacks as separate peoples who ought to remain apart. Their militancy further enraged the settlers. White hunters, disdained by easterners as "near savages," secured their identity as "whites" (a fairly new term) by killing Indians.

Hatred of Indians grew so extreme that it threatened to undercut the American war effort. In 1777, American militia murdered Cornstalk, and in 1778 militiamen killed White Eyes. Four years later, Americans massacred 100 unarmed Moravian mission Indians at Gnadenhutten, Ohio. Nearly all of them were women and children who knelt in prayer as, one by one, their skulls were crushed with mallets. This atrocity brutalized Indians as well as settlers. Until then, most Indians had refrained from the ritual torture of prisoners, but after Gnadenhutten they resumed the custom—selectively. They burned alive any known leaders of the massacre whom they captured.

Faced with hatred, Indians united to protect their lands. They won the frontier war north of the Ohio River. The Iroquois ravaged the Wyoming Valley of Pennsylvania in 1778. When an American army devastated Iroquoia in 1779 and committed many atrocities along the way, the Indians fell back on the British post at Niagara and continued the struggle. In 1779, nearly all Indians, from the Creeks on the Gulf Coast to the nations of the Great Lakes, exchanged emissaries and planned an all-out war along the frontier. George Rogers Clark of Virginia thwarted their offensive with a daring winter raid in which he captured Vincennes and cut off the western nations from British supplies, but the Indians regrouped, and by 1782 drove the Virginia "long knives" out of the Ohio Country.

6-3c *Violence and Attrition*

The escalating costs of war, both human and financial, ravaged Britain and the United States. After 1778, George III's determination to continue the war bitterly divided his kingdom. Much of the British public doubted that the war could be won. Trade was disrupted, thousands of ships were lost to privateers, taxes and the national debt soared, military recruits became harder to find, and a French invasion became a serious threat. Political dissent rose and included widespread demand for the reduction of royal patronage and for electoral reforms. By several measures, the American Revolutionary War was one of the least popular wars in British history.

Art Fleury/Alamy Stock Photo

6.5 **Joseph Brant, Portrait by Gilbert Stuart (1786)** Brant, a Mohawk and a Freemason, was one of Britain's most effective commanders of loyalist and Indian forces. After the war, he led most of the Six Nations to Canada for resettlement.

Desperate for men, the British army had been quietly recruiting Irish Catholics, and North supported a modest degree of toleration for English and Scottish Catholics. This leniency produced a surge of Protestant violence culminating in the Gordon riots, named for an eccentric agitator, Lord George Gordon. For a week in June 1780, crowds roared through London, smashing Catholic chapels attached to foreign embassies, liberating prisoners from city jails, and finally attacking the Bank of England. The army, supported by Lord Mayor John Wilkes, put down the rioters. This spectacular violence discredited the reformers and gave North one more chance to win the war.

In America, shocking acts of violence became commonplace. In May 1777, a British-Hessian unit in New Jersey ambushed a Continental Army patrol and hacked to death an American officer, William Martin, and several of his men, apparently in retaliation for an earlier American attack. Martin's body was so badly mutilated that Washington had it delivered in a makeshift coffin to the nearby British headquarters of General Cornwallis with a cover letter complaining that the officer was "unnecessarily murdered with the most aggravated circumstances of barbarity." Cornwallis responded matter-of-factly, "When a man is kill'd in that manner [with sabers], his body must of course be mangled."

Prisoners of war suffered perhaps the harshest treatment in the war. From 1776 to 1783, British forces occupying New York City converted abandoned or decommissioned warships anchored just off shore into floating prisons. The most notorious of these ships, the *Jersey*, exposed American prisoners to inhuman crowding, poor ventilation, and severe want of food and clothing. In total, about 18,000 men languished on British prison ships during the war, and at least 8,500 died—a nearly 50 percent mortality rate. A former prisoner, the writer Philip Freneau accused the British of purposefully killing Americans in his narrative poem "The British Prison-Ship" (1781): "ungenerous Britons, you/Conspire to murder those you can't subdue." By the end of the war, Congress sponsored squalid and brutal prisons of its own, but they never equaled the mortality rates on the British prison vessels.

Over time, the twin forces of violence and attrition impacted America's full population. Indian raids reduced harvests, and military levies kept thousands of men away from productive work. Loyalist raids into Connecticut and New Jersey wore down the defenders and destroyed a great deal of property. A 1779 raid on Virginia carried off or destroyed property worth £2 million. Merchants lost most of their European and West Indian markets, although a few of them made huge profits through blockade running or

▲ **MAP 6.2 War on the Frontier, 1777–1782** Indian unity strengthened during the Revolution beyond what had been achieved in Pontiac's War.

Q *Given Indian unity and strength in the trans-Appalachian West during the Revolutionary War, should the British Proclamation Line of 1763 be determined a success?*

Q *Would Native Americans have experienced a different long-term fate had Britain defeated America and stopped independence?*

privateering. Average household income plunged by more than 40 percent. Even major American triumphs came at a high price. Burgoyne's surrender left Americans with the burden of feeding his army for the rest of the war. Provisioning a French fleet in American waters, and later a French army, put huge strains on American resources.

These heavy demands led to the collapse of the Continental dollar in 1779–1780. Congress had been printing money to pay its bills, using the Spanish dollar as its basic monetary unit. With French support bolstering American credit, this practice worked reasonably well into 1778. The money depreciated, but without causing widespread dissatisfaction. As the war

The Granger Collection, NYC

6.6 **Nineteenth-Century Representation of British Prison Ship in New York Harbor** The British regarded American prisoners as loathsome traitors and treated them accordingly. Far more Americans died as POWs than in combat. Thousands died on hulks or prison ships in the harbor.

ground on, though, the value of Continental money fell to less than a penny on the dollar in 1779. Congress agreed to stop the printing presses and to rely instead on requisitions from the states and on foreign and domestic loans, but without paper money it could not even pay the army. Congress and the army had to requisition supplies directly from farmers in exchange for certificates geared to an inflation rate of 40 to 1, well below its true rate. Many farmers, rather than lose money on their crops, simply cut back production. William Beadle, a Connecticut shopkeeper, tried to fight inflation by accepting Continental money at face value until he saw the consequences. Rather than leave his wife and children impoverished, he slit their throats and shot himself.

6-3d *Mutiny and Reform*

America's national government, consisting solely of Congress, struggled to meet the war's many challenges. The makeshift structure of Congress remained largely unchanged since the First Continental Congress in 1774, with each state having one vote. The formal expression of this arrangement, the Articles of Confederation, was not ratified by the states until March 1, 1781, only months before the major fighting of the war ended. The Articles did not change the most glaring weakness of the national government, the inability to tax.

Congress might have limped through the war without any significant reforms, except for one dire threat: Continental soldiers—unpaid, ill clothed, and often poorly fed—grew mutinous. As Continentals became more professional through frequent drill, they also became more contemptuous of civilians. The winter of 1779–1780, the worst of the century, marked a low point in morale among the main force of Continentals snowed in with Washington at Morristown, New Jersey. Many deserted. In May 1780, two Connecticut regiments of the Continental Line, without food for three days, threatened to go home, raising the danger that the whole army might dissolve. Their officers barely managed to restore control. On paper, Washington had 16,000 men. His real strength was 3,600 and not even enough horses to move his artillery.

Charles Allen Munn Collection, Fordham University Library, Bronx, New York

6.7 **John Trumbull, "American Prisoners"** Conditions on British prison ships almost reached the horrors of the Middle Passage from Africa but lasted longer.

Q *What, if any, risks did the British incur by treating American prisoners so poorly?*

Discontent again erupted in the army on New Year's Day 1781. Insisting that their three-year enlistments had expired, 1,500 men of the Pennsylvania Line got drunk, killed three officers, and marched out of their winter quarters at Morristown. General Clinton sent agents from New York to promise these men a pardon and their back pay if they defected to the British, but instead the mutineers marched south toward Princeton and turned Clinton's agents over to Pennsylvania authorities, who then executed the agents. Congress, reassured, negotiated with the soldiers. More than half of them accepted discharges, and those who reenlisted got furloughs and bonuses. Encouraged by this treatment, 200 New Jersey soldiers at Pompton also mutinied, but Washington used New England units to disarm them and executed two of the leaders.

Congress saw these outbursts as calls for national reforms. While armed partisans were making the war more radical, politics became more conservative, moving toward the creation of European state forms, such as executive departments and a bank. Congress abandoned its cumbersome committee system and created executive departments of foreign affairs, finance, war, and marine. Robert Morris, a Philadelphia merchant, became secretary of finance, helped organize the Bank of North America (the first in America), and made certain that the Continental army was clothed and well fed, although it still was not paid. Congress began to requisition more revenue from the states to support its reforms, but efforts to amend the Articles of Confederation to allow for a direct national tax failed. The reforms of 1781 were barely sufficient to keep a smaller army in the field for the rest of the war.

6-4 The British Offensive in the South

Q *After the initial success of Britain's southern campaign, what factors contributed to American victory in the south?*

In 1780, the British attacked in the Deep South with great success. The Revolution entered its most critical phase and nearly collapsed. "I have almost ceased to hope," Washington confessed. In December 1778, a small British amphibious force had taken Savannah and had held it through 1779. The British even restored royal government with an elective assembly in Georgia between 1780 and 1782. By early 1780, they were ready to launch a major offensive. General Clinton had finally devised a strategy for winning the war (see Map 6.3).

6-4a *Britain's Southern Strategy*

Much of Clinton's New York army would sail to Charleston, take it, and dispatch loyalists to pacify the countryside. Clinton's plan reflected a change of thinking in London since France entered the war. Rather than snuff out the American rebellion in the north, where it was strongest, the British would concentrate on the south, where it was weakest. The strategy would capitalize on the Deep South as the likeliest recruiting ground for armed loyalists. Having pacified the region, Clinton would then attempt to destroy Washington's army and consolidate Britain's gains in the north and south.

iStock.com/smartstock

6.8 **Gadsden Flag** Americans experimented with many different flags during the Revolution. One of the most popular motifs was a snake paired with the motto "Don't tread on me!" as in this flag designed by the South Carolina soldier and statesman Christopher Gadsden.

Clinton's invasion of South Carolina began with awesome successes. While the British navy sealed off Charleston from the sea, an army of 10,000 closed off the land approaches to the city and forced Benjamin Lincoln and 5,000 defenders to surrender on May 12, 1780. Loyalists under Banastre Tarleton caught the 350 remaining Continentals at the Waxhaws near the North Carolina border on May 29 and, in what became infamous as "Tarleton's quarter," killed them all. This calculated brutality was designed to terrorize civilians into submission. It worked for a time, but Thomas Sumter began to retaliate after loyalists burned his plantation. His mounted raiders attacked British outposts and terrorized loyalists. At Hanging Rock on August 6, Sumter's 800 men scattered 500 loyalists, killing or wounding nearly half of them. All participants on both sides were colonists. Civil war consumed the Deep South.

Confident of British control of South Carolina, Clinton left Cornwallis in command of 8,300 men and sailed north to confront Washington. Yet to Clinton's dismay, New Jersey militia and the state's regiments of the Continental Line blocked British advances in June 1780. The stout defense forced the British to withdraw to New York. With Washington's army intact, Clinton ignored the French when they took Newport.

The British commander also failed in his attempt to take over the American base at West Point. For months, Clinton had negotiated secretly with a disgruntled Benedict Arnold (he had won little recognition for his heroics in the Saratoga campaign) for the surrender of West Point, which would have opened the Hudson to British ships as far north as Albany. But in September 1780 the Americans captured Clinton's agent, John André, with documents detailing the treason. André was hanged, and Arnold fled to British lines and became a general in the British army.

The developments in the north forced the British to pin all their hopes on the southern campaign. Despite Sumter's harassment, Cornwallis's conquest of the Carolinas proceeded rapidly. Congress scraped together 900 tough Maryland and Delaware Continentals, put Horatio Gates, the victor at Saratoga, in command, and sent them south against Cornwallis. Bolstered by 2,000 Virginia and North Carolina militia, Gates rashly offered battle at Camden on August 16,

Library of Congress Rare Book and Special Collections Division [LC-USZ62-45487]

6.9 **Banastre Tarleton (1782)** During the British southern campaign of 1780 and 1781, Tarleton gained notoriety for his ruthless treatment of Americans while commanding a unit of loyalist soldiers popularly known as "Tarleton's Raiders."

even though many of his men suffered from diarrhea after eating half-baked bread. The militia, who lacked bayonets, fled in panic at the first British charge. The exposed Continentals fought bravely but were crushed.

Two days after Camden, Tarleton surprised Sumter's camp at Fishing Creek, near the Waxhaws, killing 150 men and wounding 300. In four months, the British had destroyed all of the Continental forces in the Deep South, mauled Sumter's partisans, and opened North Carolina to invasion. These victories seemed to fulfill Cornwallis's boast that he would strip "three stripes ... from the detestable thirteen." He unleashed his loyalists to pacify South Carolina and marched confidently on to "liberate" North Carolina.

6-4b *The Partisan War*

But resistance continued. In the west, frontier riflemen, led by Daniel Morgan and enraged by Britain's support for Indians, crossed the Blue Ridge 1,800 strong to challenge Patrick Ferguson's loyalists at King's Mountain near the North Carolina border. On October 7, 1780, Morgan lost only 88 men as his marksmen picked off many defenders. He overwhelmed

Library of Congress Prints and Photographs Division [LC-USZ62-45442]

6.10 **"The Present State of Great Britain" (1779), Probably by James Gillray** The war is going badly for weary John Bull (England). America, the Indian, is stealing liberty; the Dutch are lifting Britain's purse; and the French are attacking. Only a surly Scot is defending John Bull, and he may lose his dagger.

Q *How does the cartoon reflect Britain's global challenges in the second half of the Revolutionary War?*

the loyalists, killing 160 men, including Ferguson, and capturing 860. They shot many prisoners and hanged a dozen, their answer to "Tarleton's quarter." This victory, the first major British setback in the Deep South, stung Cornwallis, who halted his drive into North Carolina.

In October 1780, Congress sent General **Nathanael Greene**, a Rhode Islander, to the Carolinas with a small Continental force. After Sumter withdrew to nurse a wound, Francis Marion took his place. A much abler leader, Marion (who became known as the Swamp Fox) operated from remote bases in the marshy low country. Greene's prospects still seemed desperate. The ugliness of the partisan war—the mutilation of corpses, killing of prisoners, and wanton destruction of property—and the condition of his soldiers appalled him. Yet Greene and Marion devised a masterful strategy of partisan warfare that finally wore out the British.

In the face of a greatly superior enemy, Greene ignored a maxim of war and split up his force of 1,800 Continentals. He sent 300 men east to bolster Marion and ordered Daniel Morgan and 300 riflemen west to threaten the British outpost of Ninety-Six. Cornwallis, worried that after King's Mountain, Morgan might raise the entire backcountry against the British, divided his own army. He sent Tarleton with a mixed force of 1,100 British and loyalists after Morgan, who decided to stand with his back to a river at Cowpens, where a loyalist kept cattle. Including militia, Morgan had 1,040 men.

Tarleton attacked at Cowpens on January 17, 1781. In another unorthodox move, Morgan sent his militia out front as skirmishers. He ordered them to fire two rounds and then redeploy in his rear. Relieved of their fear of a bayonet charge, they obeyed. As they pulled back, the British rushed forward into the Continentals, who also retreated at first, then wheeled and fired a lethal volley. After Morgan's cavalry charged into the British left flank, the militia returned to the fray. Although Tarleton escaped, Morgan annihilated his army.

As Morgan rejoined Greene, Cornwallis staked everything on his ability to find Greene and crush him, precisely what he had failed to do to Washington after Trenton and Princeton. But Greene proved elusive and lured Cornwallis into a march of exhaustion into North Carolina. In March 1781, nearly three months after the last major engagement at Cowpens, Greene judged that Cornwallis was so weak that the Americans could offer battle at Guilford Court House. With militia he outnumbered Cornwallis 4,400 to 1,900. On March 15, even though the British retained possession of the battlefield, they lost one-quarter of their force and the strategic initiative. Cornwallis retreated to Wilmington to refit.

Throughout the southern campaign, the British had confronted an enemy far deadlier than the Americans—mosquitoes. Malaria, the mosquito-borne disease that American colonists had long known, ravaged Cornwallis's army. In April 1781, with another hot disease season looming, Cornwallis explained to Clinton that he would have to get "to the upper parts of the Country, where alone I can hope to preserve the troops from fatal sickness, which has so nearly ruined the Army last autumn." Cornwallis decided to march north to Virginia in search of healthier conditions and better battlefield results.

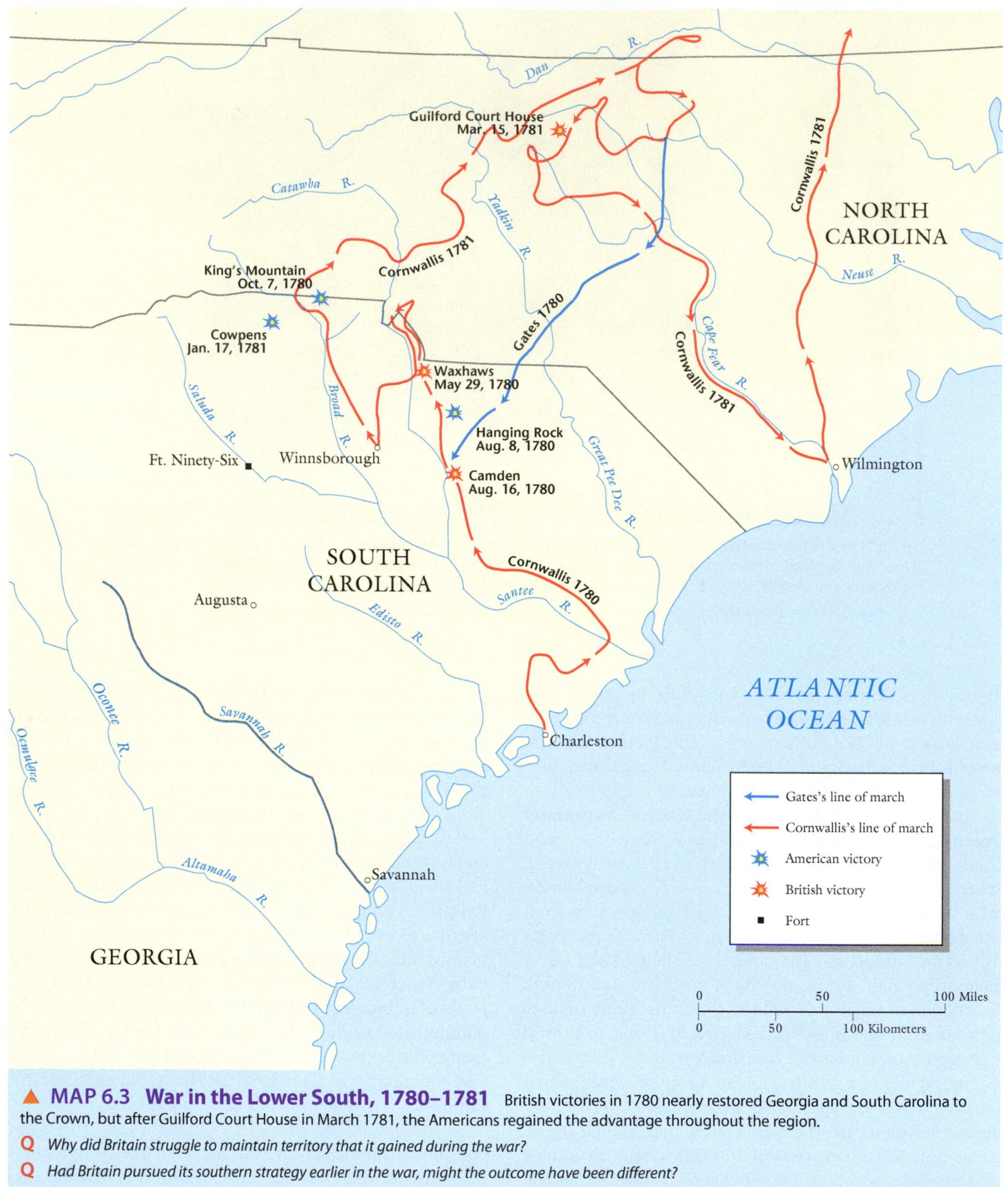

▲ **MAP 6.3 War in the Lower South, 1780–1781** British victories in 1780 nearly restored Georgia and South Carolina to the Crown, but after Guilford Court House in March 1781, the Americans regained the advantage throughout the region.

Q *Why did Britain struggle to maintain territory that it gained during the war?*

Q *Had Britain pursued its southern strategy earlier in the war, might the outcome have been different?*

Instead of following him, Greene returned to South Carolina, where he and Marion took the surviving British outposts one by one. After the British evacuated Ninety-Six on July 1, 1781, they held only Savannah and Charleston in the Deep South. Against heavy odds, Greene had reclaimed the region for the Revolution.

6-4c *From the Ravaging of Virginia to Yorktown and Peace*

Both Cornwallis and Washington believed that events in Virginia would decide the war. When a large British force

Interpreting the Visual Past A French View of Yorktown

An unknown artist completed this hand-colored copper engraving after news of the American-French allied victory at Yorktown reached Paris in the fall of 1781. Without the benefit of witnessing the event, the artist made several factual errors. The coloring of the American and French uniforms in the foreground is inexact, and imaginary mountains dot the countryside. Most fancifully, European-style castles in the background are meant to represent the settlement at Yorktown.

Still, the image is valuable for providing a rare French perspective on the Revolutionary War. Note especially the prominent place of the French naval fleet in the engraving. The artist used imagination to suggest what historians now accept as fact: Without French assistance, it is doubtful that America could have won its independence.

Q *Compare the French image with the painting of Yorktown by the American artist John Trumbull at the opening of this chapter. What differences do you notice?*

Q *Trumbull's version of the British surrender at Yorktown has more accurate details. Yet, like the artist of the French engraving, Trumbull was not present at Yorktown. Moreover, he completed his painting nearly 40 years later. Does this information change your interpretation of the two works? Does the French engraving have any claim to providing a more honest account of Yorktown?*

6.11 **French Engraving of the Battle of Yorktown, 1781.**

raided the state in late 1780, Governor Thomas Jefferson called up enough militia to keep the British bottled up in Portsmouth, while he continued to ship men and supplies to Greene in the Carolinas. Thereafter, the state's ability to raise men and supplies almost collapsed.

In January 1781, Clinton sent Arnold by sea from New York with 1,600 men, mostly loyalists. They sailed up the James and gutted the new capital of Richmond. When Jefferson called out the militia, few responded. Most Virginia freemen had already done service, if only as short-term militia, thousands in response to the 1780 raid. Cornwallis took command in April, and Arnold departed for New York. But the raids continued into summer, sweeping as far west as Charlottesville, where Tarleton, who had recruited a new legion since Cowpens, scattered the Virginia legislature and almost captured Jefferson. Many of Jefferson's slaves greeted the British as liberators. Washington sent Lafayette with 1,200 northern Continentals to contain the damage. On Clinton's orders, Cornwallis withdrew to **Yorktown**—a small settlement on a peninsula surrounded by the James and York rivers and Chesapeake Bay—to await reinforcements from the Royal Navy (see Map 6.4).

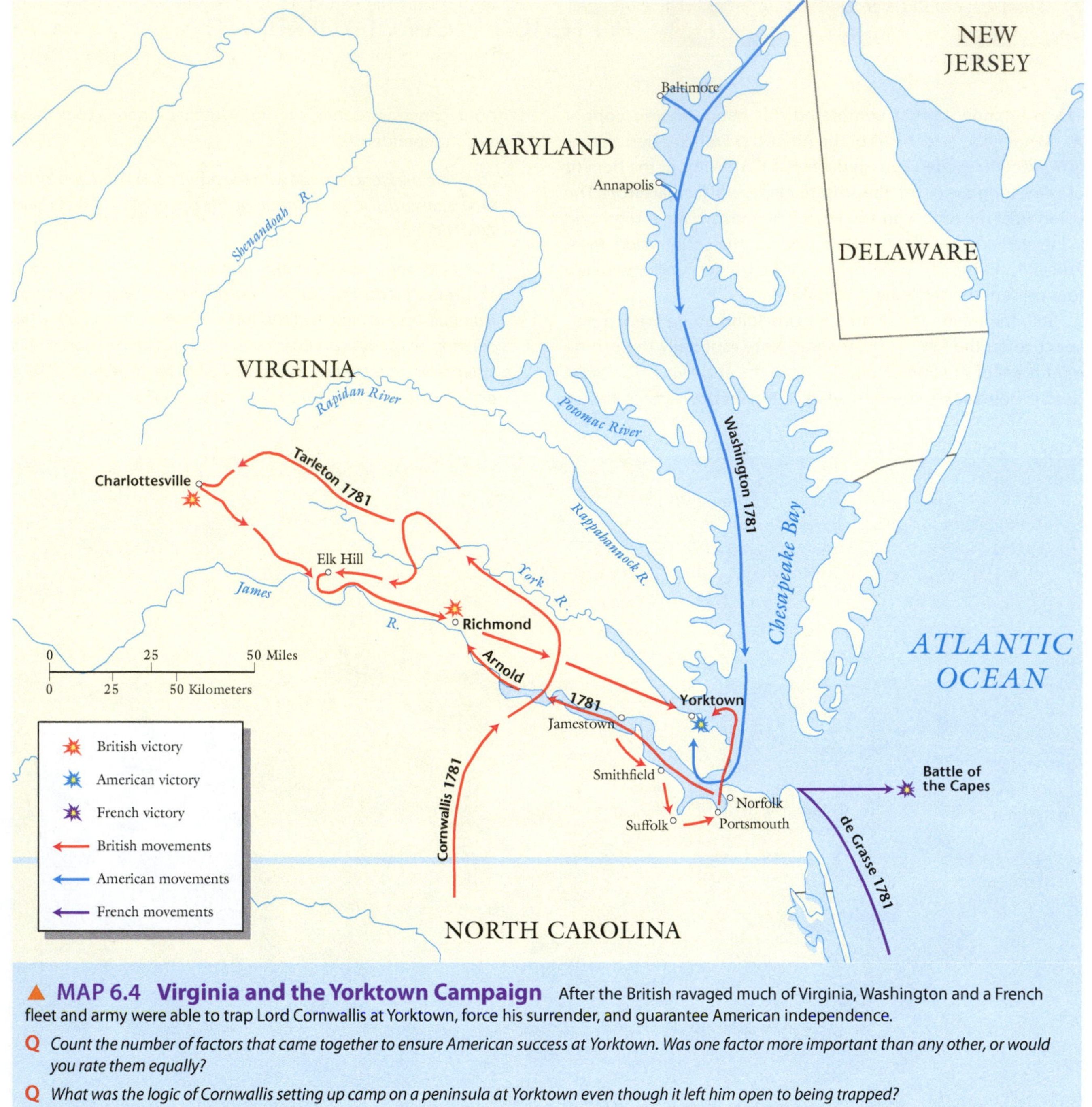

▲ **MAP 6.4 Virginia and the Yorktown Campaign** After the British ravaged much of Virginia, Washington and a French fleet and army were able to trap Lord Cornwallis at Yorktown, force his surrender, and guarantee American independence.

Q *Count the number of factors that came together to ensure American success at Yorktown. Was one factor more important than any other, or would you rate them equally?*

Q *What was the logic of Cornwallis setting up camp on a peninsula at Yorktown even though it left him open to being trapped?*

At last, Washington saw an opportunity to launch a major strike. He learned that a powerful French fleet under Francois, Comte de Grasse, with 3,000 soldiers would sail from Saint-Domingue for Chesapeake Bay on August 13. Cooperating closely with the French army commander, Jean Baptiste Donatien, Comte de Rochambeau, Washington sprang his trap. Rochambeau led his 5,000 soldiers from Newport to the outskirts of New York, where they joined Washington's 5,000 Continentals.

After feinting an attack to freeze Clinton in place, Washington led the combined French and American armies 400 miles south to tidewater Virginia, where they linked up with Lafayette's Americans and the other French army brought by de Grasse. Once de Grasse's fleet beat off a British relief force at the Battle of the Capes on September 5, Washington cut off all retreat routes and besieged Yorktown. On October 19, 1781, Cornwallis surrendered his army of 8,000 men. Many escaped slaves died during the siege, most from smallpox, but planters hovered nearby to reclaim survivors.

Yorktown brought down the British government in March 1782. Lord North resigned, and George III even drafted an abdication message but never released it. The new ministry, committed to American independence as the price of peace, continued to fight the French in the Caribbean and the Spanish at Gibraltar, but the British evacuated Savannah and Charleston to concentrate their remaining forces in New York City.

The Treaty of Paris ended the war in 1783. The American diplomatic commission of John Jay, John Adams, and Benjamin Franklin won British recognition of territory east of the Mississippi, with the river (absent New Orleans) marking the western boundary of the new republic. New Englanders retained the right to fish off Newfoundland. The treaty recognized the validity of prewar transatlantic debts, and Congress promised to urge the states to restore confiscated loyalist property.

These terms gave American diplomats almost everything they could have desired. Western Indians, by contrast, were appalled to learn that the treaty gave their lands to the United States. They had not been conquered, whatever European diplomats might say. Their war for survival continued with few breaks into 1795.

Congress still faced ominous problems. In March 1783, many Continental officers threatened a coup d'état unless Congress granted them generous pensions. Washington, confronting them at their encampment at Newburgh, New York, fumbled for his glasses and remarked, "I have grown gray in your service, and now find myself growing blind." Tears filled the eyes of his comrades in arms, and the threat of a coup vanished.

In Philadelphia two months later, unpaid Pennsylvania soldiers marched on the statehouse, where both Congress and the state's executive council sat. Ignoring Congress, they demanded that Pennsylvania redress their grievances. Congress felt insulted and left the city for Princeton, where it reconvened in Nassau Hall. Its archives and administrative departments remained in Philadelphia. "I confess I have great apprehensions for the union of the states," wrote Charles Thomson, secretary to Congress since 1774. The British threat, Thomson knew, had created the American Union. He feared that the Union would dissolve with the return of peace. Congress moved on from Princeton to Annapolis and eventually settled in New York, but the Union's survival remained uncertain.

6-5 A Revolutionary Society

Q *What social changes came about in the United States either directly or indirectly as a result of the American Revolution?*

Independence transformed America. The biggest winners were free householders, who gained enormous benefits from the democratization of politics and the chance to colonize the West. Besides loyalists, the biggest losers were Indians, determined to resist settler expansion. Many slaves won freedom, and women struggled for greater dignity. Both succeeded only when their goals proved compatible with the ambitions of white householders.

6-5a *Religious Transformations*

Independence left the Anglican Church vulnerable, if only because George III was its "supreme head." Although most Anglican clergymen supported the Revolution or remained neutral, an aggressive loyalist minority stirred the wrath of patriots. Religious dissenters disestablished the Anglican Church in every southern state. They deprived it of its tax support and other privileges, such as the sole right to perform marriages. In 1786, Virginia passed Jefferson's Statute for Religious Freedom, which declared that efforts to use coercion

NPS/Alamy Stock Photo

6.12 **Interior of Touro Synagogue in Newport, Rhode Island** The synagogue shown here presents the best surviving example of Jewish artistic taste in 18th-century America.

in matters of religion "tend only to beget habits of hypocrisy and meanness." In Virginia, church attendance and the support of ministers became voluntary activities.

Other states moved more slowly. In New England, Congregational churches supported the Revolution and were less vulnerable to attack. Ministers' salaries continued to be paid out of public taxes, although lawful dissenters, such as Baptists, could insist that their church taxes go to their own clergy. The Congregational Church exercised other public or quasi-public functions, especially on thanksgiving, fast, and election days. Disestablishment did not become complete until 1818 in Connecticut and 1833 in Massachusetts.

Although most states still restricted the holding of office to Christians or Protestants, many people were coming to regard the coercion of anyone's conscience as morally wrong. Jews and Catholics both gained from the new atmosphere of tolerance. When Britain recognized the Catholic Church in the Quebec Act of 1774, most Protestants had shuddered with dread, but in 1790, when John Carroll of Maryland became the first Roman Catholic bishop in the United States, hardly anyone protested. Before independence, an Anglican bishop had become an explosive issue, but in the 1780s, the Church of England reorganized itself as the Protestant Episcopal Church and began to consecrate its own bishops. Both Episcopalians and Presbyterians paid homage to republican values by adopting written constitutions.

6-5b *The First Emancipation*

The Revolution freed tens of thousands of slaves, but it also gave new vitality to slavery in the region that people were beginning to call "the South." Within a generation, slavery was abolished in the emerging "North." Race became a defining factor in both regions. In the South, most blacks remained slaves. In the North, they became free but not equal. The independent householder and his voluntaristic ethic remained almost a white monopoly.

Many slaves freed themselves. The British army enabled more than half the slaves of Georgia and a significant fraction in South Carolina to choose freedom. A similar process was under way in Virginia in 1781, only to be cut short at Yorktown. Hundreds of New England slaves won freedom through military service. Many revealed what they were fighting for in the surnames they chose. Jeffrey Liberty, Cuff Liberty, Dick Freeman, and Jube Freeman served in one Connecticut regiment. After the Massachusetts bill of rights proclaimed that all people were "born free and equal," Elizabeth (Bett) Freeman sued her master in 1781 and won her liberty. Thereafter, most of the slaves in Massachusetts and New Hampshire simply walked away from their masters.

Elsewhere, legislative action was necessary. Pennsylvania led the way in 1780 with the modern world's first **gradual emancipation** statute. Rather than emancipate, or free, slaves immediately, it declared that children born to slaves after a given date would become free at age 28. The slaves, not masters or taxpayers, thus bore the costs of their own emancipation. This requirement left them unable to compete on equal terms with free white men, who usually entered adult life with inherited property. Some masters shipped their slaves south shortly before emancipation, and some whites kidnapped freedmen and carried them south. The Pennsylvania Abolition Society existed largely to fight these abuses. By 1800, Philadelphia had America's largest community of free blacks, with their own churches and other voluntary societies.

The Pennsylvania pattern took hold, with variations, in most other northern states until all of them had made provision for emancipation. Where slaves constituted more than 10 percent of the population, as in southern New York and northeastern New Jersey, slaveholders' resistance delayed legislation for years. New York yielded in 1799, New Jersey in 1804.

In the upper South, many Methodists and Baptists opposed slavery in the 1780s, only to retreat in later years. Maryland and Virginia authorized the **manumission**, or freeing, of individual slaves by their owners. By 1810, more than one-fifth of Maryland's slaves had been freed, as had 10,000 of Virginia's 300,000 slaves, including more than 123 freed under Washington's will after he died in 1799. But slaves were essential to the plantation economy and were usually their masters' most valuable asset. In the South, emancipation would have amounted to a social revolution and the impoverishment of the planter class. Planters supported such humane reforms as the Christianization of their slaves, but they resisted emancipation, especially with the rise of cotton as a new cash crop after the war. Cut off from British textiles during the war, South Carolina slaves insisted on growing cotton as a substitute. Their owners saw the huge potential of that crop which, in effect, condemned the children and grandchildren of those slaves to indefinite bondage.

Maryland and Virginia, where population growth among the slaves exceeded what the tobacco economy could absorb, banned the Atlantic slave trade, as had all other states outside the Deep South. Georgia and South Carolina, to make good their losses during the war and to meet the demand for cotton after 1790, reopened the Atlantic slave trade. South Carolina imported almost 60,000 more Africans before Congress prohibited that traffic in 1808.

6-5c *The Challenge to Patriarchy*

Nothing as dramatic as emancipation altered relations between the sexes. With the men away fighting, many women were left in charge of the household, sometimes with interesting consequences. "I hope you will not consider yourself as commander in chief of your own house," Lucy Knox warned her soldier husband, Henry, in 1777, "but be convinced ... that there is such a thing as equal command." Although some women acquired new authority, nearly all of them had to work harder to keep their households functioning. The war cut them off from most European consumer goods. Household manufactures, largely the task of women, filled the gap. Women accepted these duties without demanding broader legal or political rights, but soaring food prices made many of them assertive. In numerous food riots, women tried to force merchants to lower prices or stop hoarding grain.

Attitudes toward marriage were also changing. The common-law rule of coverture still denied wives any legal personality, but a few persuaded state governments not to impoverish them by confiscating the property of their loyalist husbands. Many writers insisted that good marriages rested on mutual affection, not on property settlements. In portraits of wealthy northeastern families, husbands and wives were beginning to appear as equals. Parents were urged to respect the personalities of their children and to avoid severe discipline. Traditional reverence for the elderly was yielding to an idealization of youth and energy.

In 1780, to relieve the sufferings of Continental soldiers, Esther de Berdt Reed organized the Philadelphia Ladies Association, the first women's society in American history to take on a public role. Although few women yet demanded equal political rights, the New Jersey Constitution of 1776 let them vote if they headed a household (usually as a widow) and paid taxes. This right was revoked in 1807.

Especially in the Northeast, more women learned to read and write. Philosophers, clergymen, and even popular writers were beginning to treat women as morally superior to men, a sharp reversal of earlier teachings. The first female academies were founded in the 1790s. By 1830, nearly all native-born women in the Northeast had become literate. The ideal of the "**republican wife**" and the "**republican mother**" took hold, giving wives and mothers an expanding educational role within the family. They encouraged diligence in their husbands and patriotism in their sons. The novel became a major cultural form in the United States. Its main audience was female, as were many of the authors. Novels cast women as central characters and warned young women to beware of suitors motivated only by greed or lust.

6-5d *Western Expansion, Discontent, and Conflict with Indians*

Westward expansion continued during the Revolutionary War. With 30 axmen, Daniel Boone, a North Carolina hunter, hacked out the Wilderness Road from Cumberland Gap to the

FIRST in WAR,
FIRST in PEACE,
&
FIRST in the HEARTS
OF HIS
COUNTRYMEN.

Source: Fenimore Art Museum

6.13 **Liberty and Washington (c. 1800)** This example of folk art shows how women came to personify liberty in the early American republic. While placing a laurel on a bust of George Washington, the female figure stomps on a crown that represents monarchy.

Kentucky bluegrass country in early 1775. The first settlers called Kentucky "the best poor man's country" and claimed it should belong to those who tilled its soil, not to speculators in the Transylvania Company, which claimed ownership. Few Indians lived in Kentucky, but it was the favorite hunting ground of the Shawnees and other nations. Their raids often prevented settlers from planting crops. Instead they hunted and put up log cabins against the inside walls of large rectangular stockades, 10 feet high and built from oak logs. At each corner, a blockhouse with a protruding second story permitted the defenders to fire along the outside walls. Three of these "Kentucky stations" were built—at Boonesborough, St. Asaph, and Harrodsburg (see Map 6.2).

Because of the constant danger, settlement grew slowly at first. Kentucky lived up to its old Indian reputation as the "dark and bloody ground." Only a few thousand settlers stuck it out until the war ended, when they were joined by swarms of newcomers. Speculators and absentees were already trying to claim the best bluegrass land. The Federal Census of 1790 listed 74,000 settlers and slaves in Kentucky and about half that many in Tennessee, where the Cherokees had ceded a large tract after their defeat in 1776. Those settlers thrived

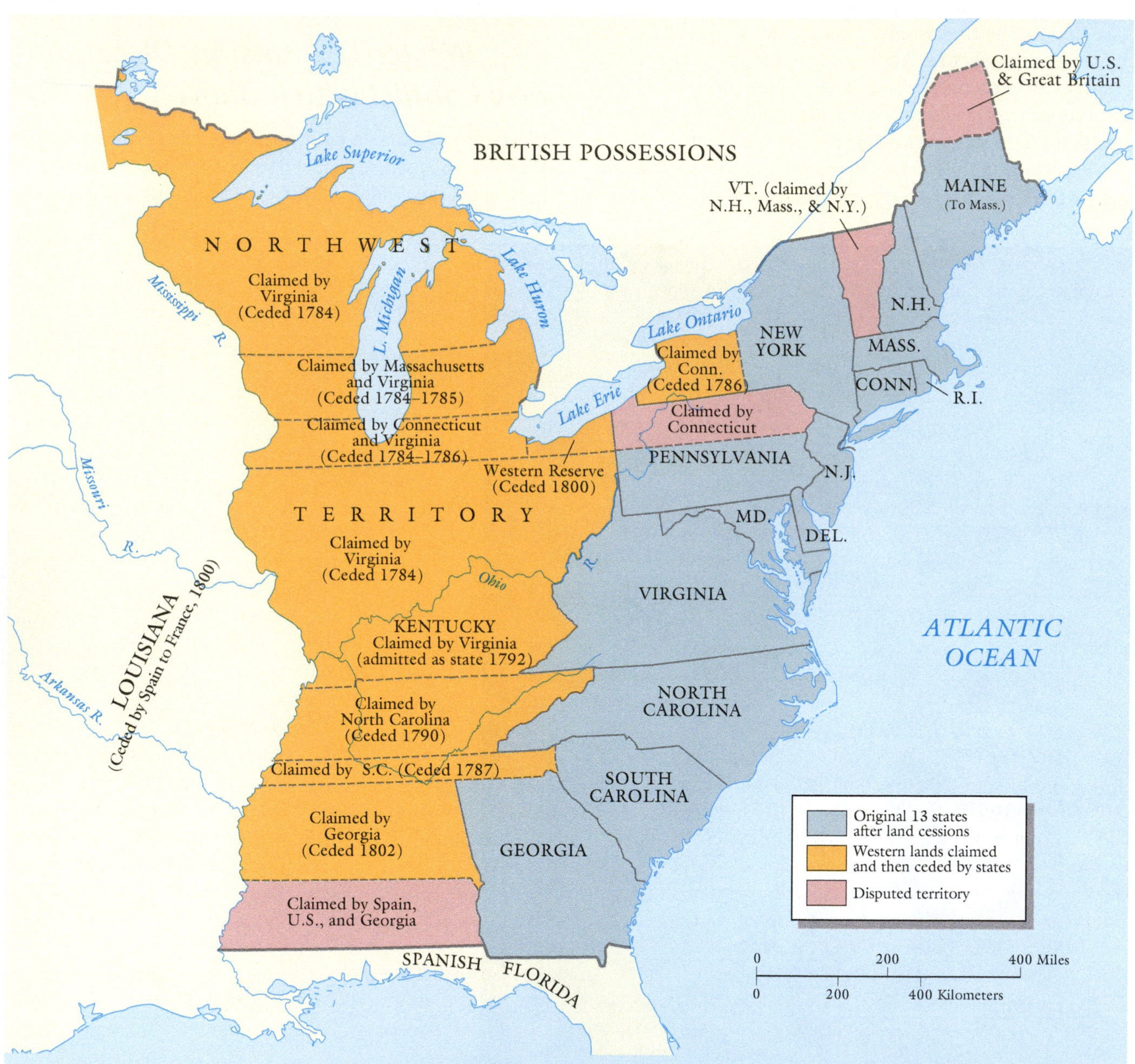

▲ **MAP 6.5 Western Land Claims during the Revolution** One of the most difficult questions that Congress faced was the competing western land claims of several states. After Virginia ceded its claims north of the Ohio to Congress, other states followed suit, creating the national domain and what soon became the Northwest Territory.

Q *How did the creation of the Northwest Territory end the possibility that the United States would formally establish new colonies in western lands?*

Q *What assumption did the Northwest Territory make about Native American claims to land west of the Mississippi River?*

both because few Indians lived there and because British and Spanish raiders found it hard to reach them.

To the south and north of this bulge, settlement was much riskier. After the war, Spain supplied arms and trade goods to Creeks, Cherokees, Choctaws, and Chickasaws who were willing to resist Georgia's attempt to settle its western lands. North of the Ohio River, Britain refused to withdraw its garrisons and traders from Niagara, Detroit, and a few other posts, even though, according to the Treaty of Paris, those forts now lay within the boundaries of the United States. To justify their refusal, the British cited Congress's failure to honor treaty obligations to loyalists and British creditors. When small groups of Indians sold large tracts of land to Georgia, Pennsylvania, and New York, as well as to Congress, the Indian nations repudiated those sales and, supported by either Spain or Britain, continued to resist.

During the Revolutionary War, Americans had recruited soldiers with promises of land after the war, and now they needed Indian lands to fulfill these pledges. The Indian nations that supported the United States suffered the most. In the 1780s, after Joseph Brant led most of the Iroquois north to Canada, New York confiscated much of the land of the friendly Iroquois who stayed. South Carolina dispossessed the Catawbas of most of their lands. The states had a harder time seizing the land of hostile Indians who had Spanish or British aid.

Secessionist movements arose in the 1780s when neither Congress nor eastern state governments seemed able to solve western problems. Some Tennessee settlers seceded from North Carolina to maintain, briefly, a separate state of Franklin. Separatist sentiment also ran strong in Kentucky. Settlers in western Pennsylvania thought of setting up on their own after Spain closed the Mississippi to American traffic in 1784. When Congress refused to accept Vermont's independence from New York, even the radical Green Mountain Boys sounded out Canadian officials about readmission to the British Empire as a separate province.

6-5e *The Northwest Ordinance*

After Virginia ceded its land claims north of the Ohio River to Congress in 1781, other states followed suit. Jefferson offered a resolution in 1784 that would have created 10 or more new states in this Northwest Territory. In the Land Ordinance of 1785, Congress authorized the survey of the Northwest Territory and its division into townships six miles square, each composed of 36 "sections" of 640 acres. Surveyed land would be sold at auction starting at a dollar per acre. Alternate townships would be sold in sections or as a whole, to satisfy settlers and speculators, respectively.

In July 1787, while the Constitutional Convention met in Philadelphia, Congress (in New York) returned to the problems of the Northwest Territory and passed the **Northwest Ordinance** (see Map 6.5). It authorized the creation of from 3 to 5 states, to be admitted to the Union as equals of the original 13. The ordinance thus rejected colonialism among white people except as a temporary phase through which a "territory" would pass on its way to statehood. Congress would appoint a governor and a council to rule until population reached 5,000. At that point, the settlers could elect an assembly empowered to pass laws, although the governor (modeled on earlier royal governors) had an absolute veto. When population reached 60,000, the settlers could adopt their own constitution and petition Congress for statehood. The ordinance protected civil liberties, provided for public education, and prohibited slavery in the territory.

Southern delegates all voted for the Northwest Ordinance despite its antislavery clause. The clause may have been part of a larger Compromise of 1787, involving both the ordinance and the clauses on slavery in the federal Constitution. The Philadelphia Convention permitted states to count three-fifths of their slaves for purposes of representation and direct taxation. The antislavery concession to northerners in the ordinance was made at the same time that southern states won this concession in Philadelphia. Several congressmen were also delegates to the Constitutional Convention and traveled back and forth between the two cities while these decisions were being made. They may have struck a deal.

6-6 American Constitutionalism

In what ways did state constitutions advance American constitutional thinking during the revolutionary era?

Another major preoccupation of Americans both during and following the Revolutionary War centered on a basic question: Having disposed of British authority, how would they create new governments? The first wave of constitutionalism focused on the states. In 1776, the prospect of independence touched off intense debate among Americans about how best to reconstitute authority. They agreed that every state needed a written constitution to limit the powers of government in terms more explicit than the precedents, statutes, and customs that made up Britain's unwritten constitution. That constitution had resulted in parliamentary sovereignty, the idea that Parliament held **sovereign power** (or ultimate control) over Britain and its overseas empire. Americans disagreed and instead maintained that their individual colonial (and later state) assemblies were sovereign within their respective borders. In essence, the American reply to Britain's sovereign Parliament was 13 sovereign state legislatures. After 1776, Americans moved from embracing state sovereignty and the European notion that sovereignty must be lodged in government toward ever-fuller expressions of **popular sovereignty**—the theory that all power must be derived from the people. This learning process at the state level would have profound influence on the U.S. Constitution.

6-6a *John Adams and the Separation of Powers*

No one influenced the development of state constitutions more than John Adams. By the spring of 1776, when he wrote

Thoughts on Government, Adams was already moving away from the British notion of a "mixed and balanced" constitution, in which government by King, Lords, and Commons embodied the distinct social orders of British society. He was groping toward quite a different notion, the **separation of powers**. Government, he affirmed, should be divided into three branches—an executive armed with veto power, a legislature, and a judiciary independent of both. The legislature, he insisted, must be bicameral, so that each house could expose the failings of the other. **Unicameral legislatures** (those with a single legislative body), which Thomas Paine advocated and Georgia, Pennsylvania, and Vermont all adopted, risked having one interest dominate the government.

Governments exist to promote the happiness of the people, Adams declared. Happiness depends on "virtue," both public and private. **Public virtue** meant "patriotism," the willingness of citizens to value the common good above their personal interests and even to die for their country. The form of government that rests entirely on virtue, Adams argued, is a republic. Americans must elect legislatures that would mirror society. Britain had put the nobility in one house and the commoners in another, but in America, everyone was a commoner. America had no social orders. A free government did not embody distinctly social orders to be stable. It could uphold republican values through virtue and by being properly balanced within itself.

6-6b *Early State Constitutions*

In June 1776, Virginia became the first state to adopt a permanent, republican constitution. The provincial congress (called a "convention" in Virginia), which had assumed full legislative powers, affirmed "that the legislative and executive powers ... should be separate and distinct from the judiciary," but then wrote a constitution that made the legislature supreme. It chose the governor, the governor's council, and all judges above the level of justice of the peace. The governor had no veto and hardly any patronage. The lower house faced annual elections, but members of the upper house served four-year terms.

George Mason drafted a declaration of rights that the Virginia delegates passed before approving the constitution, on the theory that the people should define their rights before empowering the government. The convention's amended text affirmed human equality but, unlike Mason's original version, was carefully worded to exclude enslaved people. Mason upheld the right to life, liberty, property, and the pursuit of happiness, condemned hereditary privilege, called for rotation in office, provided guarantees for trial by jury and due process, and extolled religious liberty. Legally, Virginia's bill of rights was merely a statute, with no more authority than any other law, but it was eloquent, and many states copied it.

Other states adopted variations of the Virginia model. Because America had no aristocracy, uncertainty about the proper makeup of the upper house was widespread. Some states imposed higher property qualifications on "senators" than on "representatives." In three states, the lower house elected the upper house, but most states created separate election districts for senators. Most states also increased the number of representatives in the lower house. Inland counties, which were underrepresented in most colonial assemblies, became better represented, and men of moderate wealth won a majority of seats in most states, displacing the rich, who had won most late colonial elections. Most states also stripped the governor of patronage and of such royal prerogatives as the power to dissolve the legislature. At this stage, only New York empowered the governor—in conjunction with a Council of Revision—to veto bills.

Pennsylvania crafted the most radical state constitution. In June 1776, radicals overthrew the British colonial government, rejected the leadership of both the old Quaker and Proprietary parties, and elected artisans to office in Philadelphia and ordinary farmers in rural areas. The radicals summoned a special convention whose only task was to write a constitution. That document established a unicameral assembly and a plural executive of 12 men, one of whom would preside and thus be called "president." All freemen who paid taxes, and their adult sons living at home, could vote. Elections were annual, voting was by secret ballot, legislative sessions were open to the public, and no representative could serve for more than four years out of any seven. All bills were to be offered to the public for discussion before passage. Only at the next legislative session could they be passed into law, except in emergencies.

The Pennsylvania constitution, however revolutionary, generated intense conflict. Many residents condemned it as illegitimate because such a small group had produced the constitution. In 1790, it was replaced with a new state constitution that created a bicameral legislature and an elective governor with a veto that could be overridden.

6-6c *Massachusetts Redefines Constitutionalism*

Pennsylvania's experience exposed the dangers of resting sovereignty solely in the government. Another bitter struggle occurred in Massachusetts. After four years of intense debate, Massachusetts found a way to lodge sovereignty with the people and not with government—that is, a way to distinguish a constitution from simple laws. This achievement became the hallmark of American constitutionalism.

The breakthrough did not come easily. After the British withdrew from Boston in March 1776, the General Court (still the name for the assembly) reformed. But rather than follow the old system in which most towns elected a single representative, the legislature reapportioned its representatives in proportion to population. The new system rewarded the older, populous eastern towns like Boston at the expense of lightly settled western towns. In response, the western Massachusetts counties exploded in protest.

In fall 1776, the General Court responded to growing unrest by asking the towns to authorize it to draft a constitution. By a 2-to-1 margin, the voters agreed, a result that

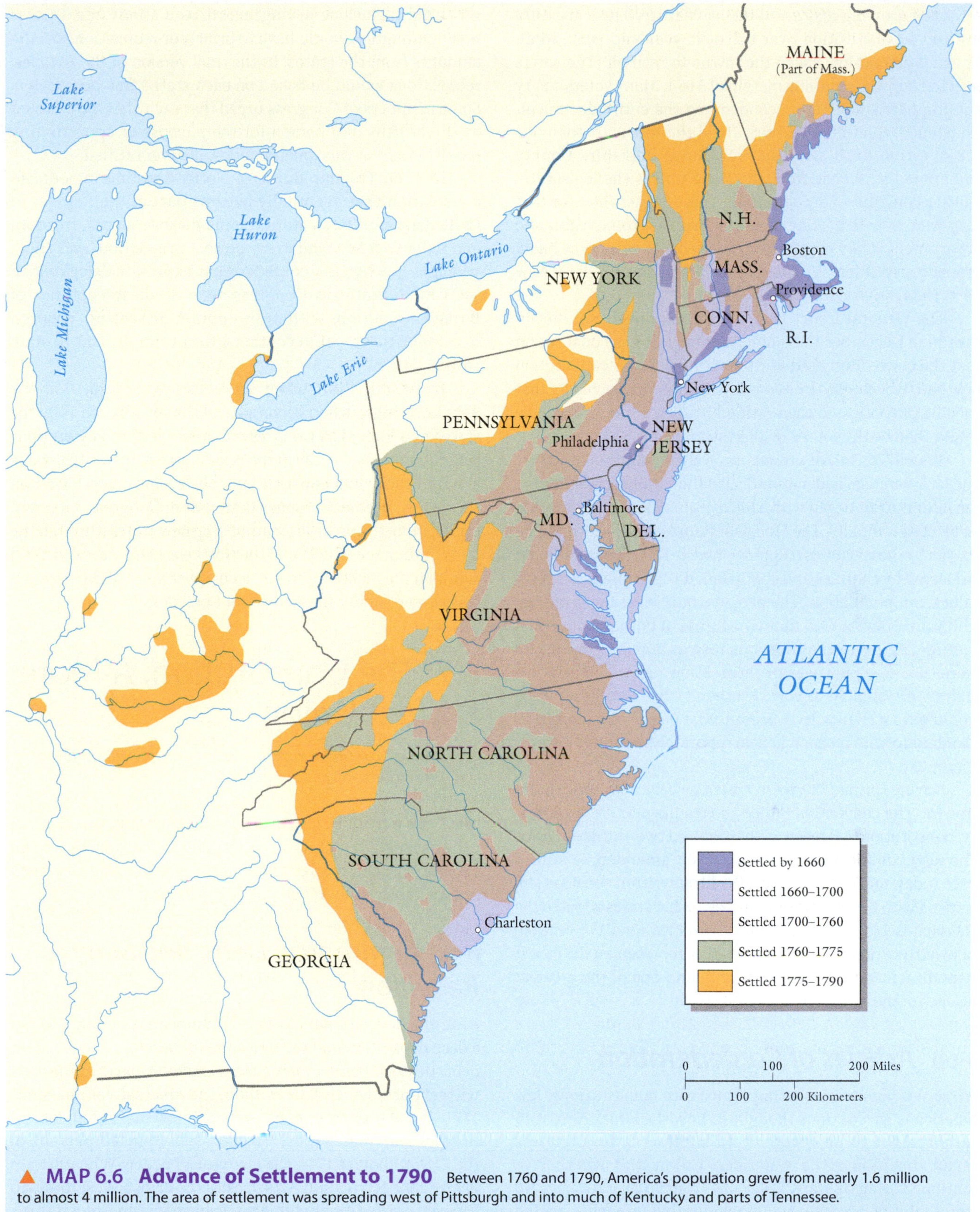

▲ **MAP 6.6 Advance of Settlement to 1790** Between 1760 and 1790, America's population grew from nearly 1.6 million to almost 4 million. The area of settlement was spreading west of Pittsburgh and into much of Kentucky and parts of Tennessee.

Q *Until 1790, most population growth still took place within existing states. What were the political implications of these population increases, particularly in western areas, at the state level?*

Q *How did America's population growth and advancing settlement help to drive national policies in the 1780s?*

reflected growing *distrust* of the legislature. The legislature drafted a constitution over the next year and then, in an unusual precaution, asked the towns to ratify it. The voters rejected it by the stunning margin of 5 to 1. Many voters, angry about a particular clause, condemned the entire document. Chastened, the General Court urged the towns to postpone the question until after the war. Rural Berkshire County threatened to secede from the state unless the legislature called a constitutional convention. These farmers insisted that they were now in a "state of nature," subject to no legitimate government. They might even join another state that had a proper constitution. With Vermont already seceding from New York, theirs was no idle threat.

The General Court gave in, and a convention met in Boston in December 1779. John Adams drafted a constitution that the convention used as its starting point. A constitution now had to be drafted by a convention that was elected for that specific purpose, and then ratified by the people. The people would then be the source of all legitimate authority.

Since 1776, Adams's thoughts on the separation of powers and bicameralism had matured. Like the Virginia constitution, the Adams draft began with a bill of rights. Both houses would be elected annually. The House of Representatives would be chosen by the towns, as reapportioned in 1776. Senators would be elected by counties and apportioned according to property values, not population. The people would elect the governor, who would have a veto that two-thirds of both houses could override. Property qualifications rose as a man's civic duties increased. For purposes of ratification only, all free adult males were eligible to vote. Everyone (that is, all free men) would have a chance to consent to the basic social compact. Men had to vote on each article separately, not on the whole document.

During spring 1780, town meetings began the ratification process. The convention tallied the results and declared that the constitution had received the required two-thirds majority. The new constitution, although often amended, is still in force today, making it the world's oldest written constitution. Starting with New Hampshire in 1784, other states adopted the Massachusetts model. Its separate constitutional convention, followed by a popular ratifying process, represented the purest embodiment of popular sovereignty and one of the greatest legacies of the revolutionary era.

6-6d *Articles of Confederation*

While passionately debating their state constitutions, few Americans gave serious thought to how the larger American nation ought to be governed. In summer 1776, Congress began discussing the American union and whether to continue voting by state. Delegates from large states favored representation according to population, but no census existed to give precise numbers, and the small states insisted on being treated as equals.

In an early draft of the Articles of Confederation, John Dickinson rejected proportional representation in favor of state equality. He also enumerated the powers of Congress, which did not include levying taxes or regulating trade. To raise money, Congress would have to print it or requisition specific amounts from the states. In the final version of the Articles, requisitions would be based on each state's free population. Some members of Congress urged that each slave be counted as three-fifths of a person for the purpose of apportioning requisitions, but this amendment was never ratified.

In 1777, Thomas Burke of North Carolina introduced a resolution that eventually became part of the Articles of Confederation: "Each state retains its sovereignty, freedom and independence, and every power, jurisdiction, and right, which is not by this confederation expressly delegated to the United States in Congress assembled." Acceptance of Burke's resolution, with only Virginia dissenting, ensured that the Articles would contain a firm commitment to state sovereignty.

By March 1781, when the states finally ratified the Articles, Congress had become a weak institution. In 1776, the states had looked to Congress to confer legitimacy on their governments, especially in the middle states, but as the states adopted their own constitutions, their legitimacy, based on the people, became stronger than that of Congress. Fittingly, establishing the process for admitting new states (through the Land Ordinance of 1785 and the Northwest Ordinance of 1787) signified the most important accomplishment of the national government under the Articles of Confederation.

6-7 The Constitution: A More Perfect Union

Q *How did conditions in the United States in the 1780s influence the outcome of the Constitution?*

The 1780s were difficult times. The economy failed to rebound, debtors fought creditors, and state politics became bitter and contentious. Out of this ferment arose the demand to amend or even replace the Articles of Confederation.

6-7a *Commerce, Debt, and Shays's Rebellion*

After the Revolutionary War, the American economy entered a deep depression marked by a large trade deficit and rampant debt. In 1784, British merchants flooded American markets with exports worth £3.7 million, the greatest volume since 1771, but Americans could not pay for them. Exports to Britain that year were £750,000—less than 40 percent of the £1.9 million of 1774, the last year of peace. When Britain invoked the Navigation Acts to close the British West Indies to American ships (but not to American goods), indirect returns through this once-profitable channel also faltered. Trade with France closed some of the gap, but because the French could not offer the long-term credit that the British had provided, it remained disappointing. Exports rose to almost £900,000 by 1785, still far below prewar levels.

Individuals suffered in the postwar economy. Private debts became a huge social problem that the states, buried under their own war debts, could not easily mitigate. Merchants, dunned by British creditors, sued their customers, many of whom could not even pay their taxes. Farmers, many faced with the loss of their crops and even their farms, resisted foreclosures and looked to their states for relief.

About half of the states issued paper money in the 1780s, and many passed **stay laws** to postpone the date on which a debt would come due. Massachusetts rejected both options and raised taxes to new heights. In 1786, many farmers in Hampshire County took matters into their own hands. Crowds gathered to prevent the courts from conducting business, much as patriots had done against the British in 1774. Governor James Bowdoin insisted that acts of resistance once appropriate against a tyrannical monarch were unacceptable in a government elected by the people. But in early 1787, the protestors, loosely organized under a Continental army veteran, Captain Daniel Shays, threatened the federal arsenal at Springfield. An army of volunteers under Benjamin Lincoln marched west with artillery and scattered the protestors. Yet Shaysites won enough seats in the May assembly elections to pass a stay law. In Massachusetts, **Shays's Rebellion** converted into nationalists many gentlemen and artisans who until then had opposed strengthening the central government.

6-7b *Cosmopolitans versus Localists*

The tensions racking Massachusetts surfaced elsewhere as well. Angry debtors in other states closed law courts or even besieged the legislature. State politics reflected a persistent rift between "cosmopolitan" and "localist" coalitions (see Map 6.6). Merchants, professional men, urban artisans, commercial farmers, southern planters, and former Continental army officers made up the cosmopolitan bloc. They favored aggressive trade policies, hard money, payment of public debts, good salaries for executive officials and judges, and leniency to returning loyalists. Localists were farmers, rural artisans, and militia veterans who distrusted those policies. They demanded paper money, debtor relief, and generous salaries for representatives so that ordinary men could afford to serve. In most states, localists used these issues to control legislatures.

Congress also faced severe fiscal problems. Between October 1781 and February 1786, it requisitioned $15.7 million from the states but received only $2.4 million. Its annual income had fallen to $400,000 at a time when interest on its debt neared $2.5 million and the principal on the foreign debt was about to come due. Requisitions were beginning to seem as inefficient as George Grenville had predicted when he proposed the Stamp Act.

Foreign relations took an ominous turn. Without British protection, American ships that entered the Mediterranean risked capture by Barbary pirates and the enslavement of their crews. In 1786, Foreign Secretary John Jay negotiated a treaty with Don Diego de Gardoqui, Spanish minister to the United States. It offered northern merchants trading privileges with Spanish colonies in exchange for closure of the Mississippi River to American traffic for 25 years. Seven northern states voted for the treaty, but all five southern states in Congress rejected these terms, thus defeating the treaty, which needed nine votes for ratification under the Articles of Confederation. Angry talk of disbanding the Union filled Congress. Delegates began haggling over which state would join what union after a breakup. The quarrel became public in early 1787 when a Boston newspaper called for dissolution of the Union.

By the mid-1780s, many cosmopolitans were becoming nationalists eager to strengthen the Union. Many of them had served long, frustrating years in the army or in Congress, unable to carry out measures that they considered vital to the Confederation. In 1785, some of them tried to see what could be done outside Congress. To resolve disputes about navigation rights on the Potomac River, Washington invited Virginia and Maryland delegates to a conference at Mount Vernon,

ArtPix/Alamy Stock Photo

6.14 **Daniel Shays and Job Shattuck** Veterans of the Revolutionary War, Shays and Shattuck helped to lead the farmers' revolt in western Massachusetts known as Shays's Rebellion. This woodcut from a Boston almanac in 1787 exaggerates the organization of the uprising by giving the men uniforms, a flag, and artillery.

Q *How did the image both overestimate and underestimate the potential power of Shays's Rebellion?*

where they drafted an agreement acceptable to both states and to Congress. Prompted by James Madison, the Virginia legislature urged all states to participate in a convention at Annapolis to explore ways to improve American trade.

Four states, including Maryland, ignored the call, and the New Englanders had not yet arrived when, in September 1786, the delegates from the four middle states and Virginia accepted a report drafted by Alexander Hamilton of New York. It asked all of the states to send delegates to a convention at Philadelphia the next May "to devise such further provisions as shall appear to them necessary to render the constitution of the Federal Government adequate to the exigencies of the Union." Seven states responded positively before Congress endorsed the convention on February 21, 1787, and five accepted later. Rhode Island refused to participate. Madison used the winter months to study the defects of classical and European confederacies and to draft his own plan for a stronger union.

6-7c *The Philadelphia Convention*

The convention opened in May 1787 with a plan similar to the Virginia constitution of 1776. It proposed an almost sovereign Parliament for the United States. By September, the delegates had produced a document much closer to the Massachusetts constitution of 1780, with a clear separation of powers. The delegates, in four months of secret sessions, repeated the constitutional learning process that had taken four years at the state level after 1776.

Most Virginia and Pennsylvania delegates, who arrived early, formed a nationalist bloc. With Washington presiding, Governor Edmund Randolph proposed the **Virginia Plan** (also known as the "large state" plan). Drafted by Madison, it proposed a bicameral legislature, with representation in both houses apportioned according to population. The legislature would choose the executive and the judiciary. It would possess all powers currently lodged in Congress and the power "to legislate in all cases to which the separate States are incompetent." It could "negate all laws passed by the several States, contravening in [its] opinion ... the articles of Union." Remarkably, the plan did not include specific powers to tax or regulate trade, although Madison intended to add them later on. His plan also required ratification by state conventions, not by state legislatures. Within two weeks, the delegates agreed on three-year terms for members of the lower house and seven-year terms for the upper house. The legislature would choose the executive for a single term of seven years.

In mid-June, delegates from the small states struck back. William Paterson proposed the **New Jersey Plan**, which kept the system under the Articles with each state having one vote. The plan also gave the existing Congress power to levy import duties and a stamp tax (as in Grenville's imperial reforms of 1764 and 1765), to regulate trade, and to use force to collect delinquent requisitions from the states (as in North's Conciliatory Proposition of 1775). In another alternative, perhaps designed to terrify the small states into accepting the Virginia Plan, Hamilton suggested a government in which both the senate and the executive would serve "on good behavior"—that is, for life! To him, the British constitution still seemed the best in the world, but he never formally proposed his plan. No other New York delegate would have supported it.

All of the options before the convention at that point seemed counterrevolutionary. Madison's Parliament for America, Paterson's emulation of Grenville and North, and Hamilton's enthusiasm for the British Empire all challenged in major ways the principles of 1776. But as the summer progressed, the delegates asked themselves what the voters would or would not accept and relearned the hard lessons of popular sovereignty that the state constitutions had taught. The result was a federal Constitution that was, in its own way, revolutionary.

Before the Constitution took its final shape, however, the debate grew as hot as the summer weather. The small states warned that their voters would never accept a constitution that let the large states swallow them. The large states insisted on proportional representation in both houses. "The Large States dare not dissolve the Confederation," retorted Delaware's Gunning Bedford in the most inflammatory outburst of the convention. "If they do, the small ones will find some foreign ally of more honor and good faith, who will take them by the hand and do them justice." Then the Connecticut delegates announced that they would be happy with proportional representation in one house and state equality in the other.

In July, the delegates accepted this **Connecticut Compromise** and then completed the document by September. They finally realized that they were creating a government of laws, to be enforced on individuals through federal courts, and were not propping up a system of congressional resolutions to be carried out (or ignored) by the states. Terms for representatives were reduced to two years, and terms for senators to six, with each state legislature choosing two senators. The president would serve four years, could be reelected, and would be chosen by an **Electoral College** (an idea borrowed from the system for choosing state senators in Maryland's 1776 state constitution). Each state received as many electors as it had congressmen and senators combined, and the states were free to decide how to choose their electors. Each elector had to vote for two candidates for president, of whom one had to be from another state. This provision reflected a fear that localist impulses might block a majority for anyone. Washington would surely be the first president, but there was no obvious choice after him.

In other provisions, free and slave states agreed to count only three-fifths of the slaves in apportioning both representation and direct taxes. The enumeration of congressional powers became lengthy and explicit and included taxation, the regulation of foreign and interstate commerce, and the catchall "necessary and proper" clause. Madison's negative on state laws yielded to the gentler "supreme law of the land" clause. Over George Mason's last-minute objection, the delegates refused to include a bill of rights.

What They Said

Virginians Debate the Constitution

The Constitution has served as the framework of the United States government for more than 225 years, making it difficult today to conceive of any alternative. Yet, when first proposed, the Constitution faced passionate opposition in many states. Nowhere was ratification more contentious than in Virginia. For most of June 1788, the Virginia Ratifying Convention met and debated in Richmond. Supporters of the Constitution, such as James Madison and John Marshall, faced off against their neighbors and fellow revolutionaries, including Patrick Henry, George Mason, and James Monroe.

Below are excerpts of speeches from the debate by Henry and Madison. For Anti-Federalists like Henry, the proposed new government threatened liberty on at least two levels, by not protecting individual liberties and by removing sovereignty from the states. Henry argued that the true design of the Constitution was to create "consolidated" government—that is, a purely centralized governing authority. In response, Madison claimed that the Constitution provided for federal, or shared, authority between the national and state governments. Ultimately, Madison's argument carried the day, but just barely. On June 25, the Virginia convention ratified the Constitution by a vote of 89 to 79.

Patrick Henry

Mr. Chairman, the public mind, as well as my own, is extremely uneasy at the proposed change of government... . A year ago, the minds of our citizens were at perfect repose. Before the meeting of the late Federal Constitution at Philadelphia, a general peace and a universal tranquillity prevailed in this country; but since that period, they are exceedingly uneasy and disquieted... .

I would make this inquiry of those worthy characters who composed a part of the late Federal Constitution. I am sure they were full impressed with the necessity of forming a great consolidated government, instead of a confederation. That this is a consolidated government is demonstrably clear; and the danger of such a government is, to my mind, very striking... . Who authorized them to speak the language of, *We, the People*, instead of, *We, the States*? States are the characteristics and the soul of a confederation. If the States be not the agents of this compact, it must be one great consolidated National Government, of the people of all the States... . The people gave them no power to use their name. That they exceeded their power is perfectly clear.

James Madison

He [Henry] informs us that the people of this country are at perfect repose, that every man enjoys the fruits of his labor peaceably and securely, and that everything is in perfect tranquillity and safety. I wish sincerely, sir, this were true. If this be their happy situation, why has every State acknowledged the contrary?

The principal question is, whether it be a federal or consolidated government... . I conceived myself that it is of a mixed nature; it is in a manner unprecedented. We cannot find one express example in the experience of the world: it stands by itself. In some respects it is a government of a federal nature; in others it is of a consolidated nature. Even if we attend to the manner in which the Constitution is investigated, ratified, and made the act of the people of America, I can say, notwithstanding what the honorable gentleman has alleged, that this government is not completely consolidated, nor is it entirely federal. Who are parties to it? The people—but not the people as composing one great body; but the people as composing thirteen sovereignties... . Should all the States adopt it, it will be then a government established by the Thirteen States of America.

Q *How did Henry and Madison interpret conditions under the Articles of Confederation differently?*

Q *Are you surprised that Henry valued the power of the states more than that of the people? How might Virginia's long colonial experience and Britain's imperial reforms of the 1760s and 1770s help to explain his veneration for state sovereignty?*

Q *How did Madison attempt to minimize his differences with Henry and other Anti-Federalists? Do you think his rhetoric was effective?*

Sources: (top) From speech delivered by Patrick Henry, June 1788. From *Debates and other Proceedings of the Convention of Virginia, Convened at Richmond, on Monday the 2nd day of June 1788, for the purpose of deliberating on the Constitution recommended by the Grand Federal Convention*, 3 vols. (Petersburg, VA., 1788-1789). Reprinted in Samuel Eliot Morison, ed., *Sources and Documents Illustrating the American Revolution, 1764–1788, and the Formation of the Federal Constitution*, 1st ed. (New York: Oxford University Press, 1923) pp. 307–310; (bottom) From speech delivered by James Madison, June 1788. From *Debates and other Proceedings of the Convention of Virginia, Convened at Richmond, on Monday the 2nd day of June 1788, for the purpose of deliberating on the Constitution recommended by the Grand Federal Convention*, 3 vols. (Petersburg, VA., 1788–1789). Reprinted in Samuel Eliot Morison, ed., *Sources and Documents Illustrating the American Revolution, 1764–1788, and the Formation of the Federal Constitution*, 1st ed. (New York: Oxford University Press, 1923) pp. 332, 333 & 337.

With little debate, the convention approved a revolutionary proposal for ratifying the Constitution. This clause called for special conventions in each state and declared that the Constitution would go into force as soon as any nine states had accepted it, even though the Articles of Confederation required unanimous approval for all amendments. The delegates understood that they were proposing an illegal but peaceful overthrow of the existing legal order—that is, a revolution. They hoped that once nine or more states accepted the Constitution, the others would follow their example after the new government got under way and would make ratification unanimous. At that point, their revolution would become both peaceful and legal. The Constitution would then rest on popular sovereignty in a way that the Articles never had. The **Federalists**, as supporters of the Constitution now called themselves, were willing to risk destroying the Union in order to save and strengthen it, but they knew that they would have to use persuasion, not force, to win approval.

6-7d *Ratification*

Back home, Federalist delegates made a powerful case for the Constitution in newspapers, most of which favored a stronger central government. Most Anti-Federalists, or opponents of the Constitution, were localists with few interstate contacts and limited access to the press. Federalists gave them little time to organize. The first ratifying conventions met in December. Delaware ratified unanimously on December 7, Pennsylvania by a 46-to-23 vote five days later, and New Jersey unanimously on December 18. Georgia ratified unanimously on January 2, and then Connecticut approved by a lopsided margin.

Except in Pennsylvania, these victories were in small states. Ironically, although the Constitution was mostly a "large state" document, small states embraced it while large states hesitated. Small states, once they had equality in the senate, saw advantages in a strong central government. Under the Articles, for example, New Jerseyans had to pay duties to neighboring states on foreign goods imported through New York City or Philadelphia. Under the Constitution, import duties would go to the federal government, a clear gain for every small state but Rhode Island, which stood to lose revenue at both Providence and Newport.

Pennsylvania was the only large state with a solid majority for ratification. But Anti-Federalists there demanded a federal bill of rights and major changes in the structure of the new government. Large states could think of going it alone; small states could not—except Rhode Island, with its two cities and its long history of defying its neighbors.

The first hotly contested state was Massachusetts, which set a pattern for struggles in other divided states. Federalists there won by a slim margin (187 to 168) in February 1788. They blocked Anti-Federalist attempts to make ratification conditional on the adoption of specific amendments. Instead, they won their slim majority by promising to support a bill of rights by constitutional amendment *after* ratification. The Rhode Island legislature voted overwhelmingly against summoning a ratifying convention. Maryland and South Carolina ratified easily in April and May, bringing the total to eight of the nine states required. Then conventions met almost simultaneously in New Hampshire, Virginia, New York, and North Carolina. In each, a majority at first opposed ratification.

As resistance stiffened, the ratification controversy turned into the first great debate about the American Union, over what kind of national government the United States ought to have. Anti-Federalists argued that the new government would be too remote from the people to be trusted with the broad powers specified in the Constitution. They warned that in a House of Representatives divided into districts of 30,000 people (twice the size of Boston), only very prominent men would be elected. The absence of a bill of rights also troubled them.

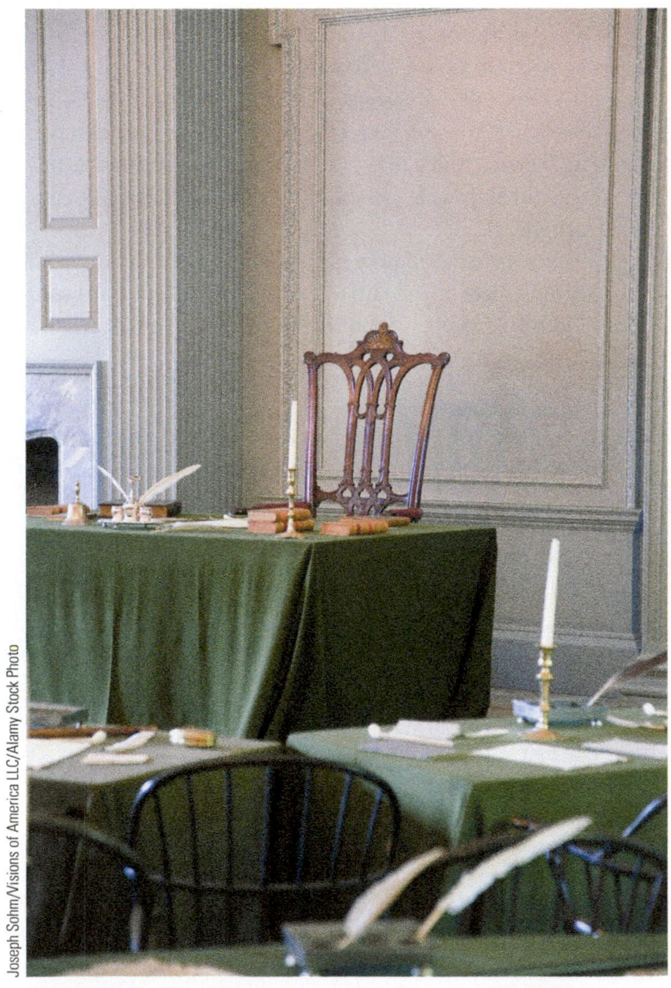

Joseph Sohm/Visions of America LLC/Alamy Stock Photo

6.15 Restored Assembly Room with "Rising Sun" Chair of George Washington, Independence Hall, Philadelphia
Washington sat in this chair in his role as president of the Constitutional Convention in 1787. Benjamin Franklin confessed that during the difficult days of the Convention he could not tell whether the sun on the chair's back was rising or setting. By the end of the Convention, however, Franklin was confident that the sun, like America, was rising.

During the struggle over ratification, Hamilton, Madison, and Jay wrote a series of 85 essays, published first in New York newspapers, and then widely reprinted elsewhere. They defended the Constitution almost clause by clause. Signing themselves "Publius," they later published the collected essays as *The Federalist Papers*, the most comprehensive body of political thought produced by the revolutionary generation. In *Federalist, no. 10*, Madison challenged 2,000 years of received wisdom when he argued that a large republic would be more stable than a small one. Small republics were unstable, he insisted, because majority factions could easily gain power within them, crush the rights of minorities, and ignore the common good. But in a huge republic as diverse as the United States, factions would seldom be able to forge a majority. "Publius" hoped that the new government would draw on the talents of the wisest and best-educated citizens. To those who accused him of trying to erect an American aristocracy, he noted that the Constitution forbade titles and hereditary rule.

Federalists won a narrow majority (57 to 46) in New Hampshire on June 21, and Madison guided Virginia to ratification (89 to 79) five days later (see the "What They Said" feature). New York approved, by 30 votes to 27, one month later, bringing 11 states into the Union, enough to launch the new government. North Carolina rejected the Constitution in July 1788 but finally ratified in November 1789 after the first Congress had drafted the Bill of Rights and sent it to the states. Rhode Island, after refusing seven times to call a ratifying convention, finally summoned one that ratified by a vote of only 34 to 32 in May 1790. The Bill of Rights was ratified a year later.

Conclusion

Americans survived the most devastating war they had yet fought and won independence, but only with massive aid from France. Most Indians and blacks, free to do so, sided with Britain. During the struggle, white Americans affirmed liberty and equality for themselves in their new state constitutions and bills of rights, but they rarely applied these values to blacks or Indians, even though every northern state adopted either immediate or gradual emancipation. The discontent of the postwar years created the Federalist coalition, which drafted and ratified a new national Constitution to replace the Articles of Confederation. Federalists endowed the new central government with more power than Parliament had ever successfully exercised over the colonies but insisted that the Constitution was fully compatible with the liberty and equality proclaimed during the Revolution. Nothing resembling American federalism had ever been tried before. Under this new system, sovereignty was removed from government and bestowed on the people, who then empowered separate levels of government through their state and federal constitutions. As the Great Seal of the United States proclaimed, it was a *novus ordo seclorum*, a new order for the ages.

CHAPTER REVIEW

Review

1. How did the British decision to allow Washington's army to escape New York in August 1776 come back to haunt them in the battles of Trenton and Princeton?
2. What led France to intervene on the American side in the war?
3. What different considerations drove loyalists, African Americans, and Indians to join the British war effort?
4. After the initial success of Britain's southern campaign, what factors contributed to American victory in the south?
5. What social changes came about in the United States either directly or indirectly as a result of the American Revolution?
6. In what ways did state constitutions advance American constitutional thinking during the revolutionary era?
7. How did conditions in the United States in the 1780s influence the outcome of the Constitution?

Critical Thinking

1. Americans today often forget that, among other things, the American Revolution was a war. How did the war affect the character of the Revolution? Had the war not turned so bitter or continued for so long, is it possible that American society might have developed differently? If so, how?
2. For the past century, American historians have passionately debated whether the federal Constitution fulfilled or undermined the revolutionary principles of 1776. Which side do you support?

Identifications

Review your understanding of the following key terms, people, and events for this chapter (terms in bold in text are included in the Glossary).

Saratoga, p. 170
Joseph Brant, p. 175

Nathanael Greene, p. 181
Yorktown, p. 183
gradual emancipation, p. 186
manumission, p. 186
republican wife/mother, p. 187
Northwest Ordinance, p. 189
sovereign power, p. 189
popular sovereignty, p. 189
separation of powers, p. 190
unicameral legislature, p. 190
public virtue, p. 190
stay laws, p. 193
Shays's Rebellion, p. 193
Virginia Plan, p. 194
New Jersey Plan, p. 194
Connecticut Compromise, p. 194
Electoral College, p. 194
Federalists, p. 196

Suggested Reading

John Ferling's ***Almost a Victory: The American Victory in the War of Independence*** (2007) is the best single volume on the war. **Holger Hoock's** ***Scars of Independence: America's Violent Birth*** (2017) emphasizes violence in reframing the American Revolution. The essays in **John Shy's** ***A People Numerous and Armed: Reflections on the Military Struggle for American Independence***, rev. ed. (1990), have had a tremendous influence on other historians. **David Hackett Fischer's** ***Washington's Crossing*** (2004) introduces important insights on Trenton and Princeton. **Andrew Jackson O'Shaughnessy**, ***The Men Who Lost America: British Leadership, the American Revolution, and the Fate of Empire*** (2014), tells the war from the British perspective. **J.R. McNeil's** chapter on Yorktown in ***Mosquito Empires: Ecology and War in the Greater Caribbean, 1620–1914*** (2010) has changed how scholars understand Cornwallis's defeat.

Maya Jasanoff's ***Liberty's Exiles: American Loyalists in the Revolutionary World*** (2011) has quickly become the standard work on loyalists. For the war's impact on slavery, see **Cassandra Pybus**, ***Epic Journeys of Freedom: Runaway Slaves of the American Revolution and their Global Quest for Liberty*** (2006), and **Simon Schama**, ***Rough Crossings: Britain, the Slaves, and the American Revolution*** (2006). For the Indian experience, see **Colin G. Calloway**, ***The American Revolution in Indian Country: Crisis and Diversity in Native American Communities*** (1995). **Rosemarie Zagarri's** ***Revolutionary Backlash: Women and Politics in the Early American Republic*** (2007) analyzes what women gained from the Revolution.

The single most important book on emerging American constitutionalism remains **Gordon S. Wood**, ***The Creation of the American Republic, 1776–1787*** (1969). The most recent thorough study of the Philadelphia Convention is **Richard Beeman**, ***Plain, Honest Men: The Making of the American Constitution*** (2009). **Saul Cornell** provides a thoughtful approach to ***The Other Founders: Anti-Federalism and the Dissenting Tradition in America*** (1999). **Woody Holton's** ***Unruly Americans and the Origins of the Constitution*** (2008) also highlights opponents of the Constitution.

7 Completing the Revolution, 1789–1815

7.1 **View of the City of New Orleans, Celebrating the Louisiana Purchase, 1803** The early United States grew rapidly both in population and size, nearly doubling with the Louisiana Purchase in 1803. The image here captures the dynamism of the new nation that now stretched from the Mississippi River to the Rocky Mountains. At the same time, white settlers would use slave labor in much of this new western territory, and New Orleans would become a leading departure point in the domestic slave trade.

ALMOST BY ACCLAMATION, George Washington became the first president under the Constitution. Washington and his closest advisers (they would soon call themselves Federalists) believed that the balance between power and liberty had tipped toward anarchy after the Revolution. "Local mischiefs," they said, had nearly destroyed the union of the states that had made independence possible. Federalists wanted the Constitution to counter democratic excesses. They were determined to make the national government powerful enough to command respect abroad and to impose order at home. For the most part, they succeeded, but in the process, they aroused a determined opposition that feared the Federalists' consolidation of central power at the expense of the states and the citizenry. These self-styled Democratic Republicans (led almost from the beginning by Thomas Jefferson) were as firmly tied to revolutionary ideals of limited government and a citizenry of independent farmers as the Federalists were to visions of an orderly commercial republic with a powerful national state. The fight between Federalists and Democratic Republicans echoed the revolutionary contest between liberty and power—conducted this time against an ominous backdrop of international intrigue and war between France (which entered a republican revolution of its own in 1789) and Britain. Only when this Age of Democratic Revolution ended in 1815 could Americans survey the kind of society and government that their own Revolution had made. ■

7-1 Establishing the National Government

Q *What was the Federalist plan for organizing the national government and its finances?*

George Washington left Mount Vernon for the temporary capital in New York City in April 1789. The way was lined with the grateful citizens of the new republic. Militia companies and local dignitaries escorted him from town to town, crowds cheered, church bells marked his progress, and lines of girls in white dresses waved demurely as he passed. At Newark Bay, he boarded a flower-bedecked barge and, surrounded by scores of boats, crossed to New York City. He arrived on April 23 and was inaugurated seven days later.

7-1a *The "Republican Court"*

Reporting for work, President Washington found the new government embroiled in its first controversy—an argument over the dignity that would attach to his own office. Vice President John Adams had asked the Senate to create a title of honor for the president. Adams and others wanted a title that would reflect the power of the new executive. They rejected "His Excellency" because that was the term used for ambassadors, colonial governors, and other minor officials. Among the other titles they considered were "His Highness," "His Mightiness," "His Elective Highness," "His Most Benign Highness," "His Majesty," and "His Highness, the President of the United States, and Protector of Their Liberties." The Senate debated the question for a full month, and then gave up when it became clear that the more democratic House of Representatives disliked titles. They settled on the literal description in the Constitution of "President of the United States of America," which later became expressed informally as "Mr. President." A senator from Pennsylvania expressed relief that the "silly business" was over. Thomas Jefferson pronounced the whole affair "the most superlatively ridiculous thing I ever heard of."

Jefferson would learn, however, that much was at stake in the argument over titles. The Constitution provided a blueprint for the republic. George Washington's administration would translate the blueprint into a working state. It mattered very much how citizens addressed their president, for that was part of the huge constellation of laws, customs, and forms of etiquette that would give the new government either a republican or a courtly tone. Many Federalists wanted to bolster presidential power against the localism and democracy that, they believed, had nearly killed the republic in the 1780s. Washington's stately inaugural tour, the high salaries paid to executive appointees, the endless round of formal balls and presidential dinners, the public celebration of the president's birthday (an English royal custom), the appearance of Washington's profile on some of the nation's coins—all dramatized the power and grandeur of the new government, particularly of its executive. When Jefferson became secretary of state and attended official social functions, he often found that aristocratic sentiments prevailed, "unless there chanced to be some [democrat] from the legislative Houses." Thus, the battle over presidential titles was not "silly business." It was a revealing episode in the argument over how questions of power and liberty that Americans had debated since the 1760s would finally be answered.

7-1b *The First Congress*

Leadership of the First Congress fell to James Madison, the Virginia congressman who had helped write the Constitution. Under his guidance, Congress strengthened the new national government at every turn. First it passed a **tariff**, or tax, on imports, which would be the government's chief source of income. Next, it turned to amendments to the Constitution demanded by the state ratifying conventions.

Madison proposed 19 constitutional amendments to the House. The 10 that survived congressional scrutiny and ratification by the states became the **Bill of Rights**. They reflected fears that were raised by a generation of struggle with centralized power. The First Amendment guaranteed the freedoms of speech, press, and religion against federal interference. The Second and Third Amendments, prompted by old fears of a standing army, guaranteed the continuation of a militia of armed citizens and stated the specific conditions under which soldiers could be quartered in citizens' households. The Fourth through Eighth Amendments defined a citizen's rights in court and when under arrest—rights that had been central to the Revolution's list of grievances. The Ninth Amendment stated that the enumeration of specific rights in the first eight amendments did not imply a denial of other rights. Finally, the Tenth Amendment stated that powers not assigned to the national government by the Constitution remained with the states and the citizenry, though the intentional omission of the word "expressly" left room for argument.

Madison, a committed nationalist, had performed skillfully. Many doubters at the ratifying conventions had called for amendments that would weaken the national government. By channeling their fears into the area of civil liberties, Madison soothed popular fears while preserving governmental power.

To fill out the framework of government outlined in the Constitution, Congress created the executive departments of war, state, and treasury and guaranteed that the president would appoint the heads of those departments (and their assistants), thus removing them from congressional control. Congress next created the federal courts, which were demanded by but not specified in the Constitution. The Judiciary Act of 1789 established a Supreme Court with six members, along with 13 district courts and three **circuit courts** of appeal. The act allowed certain cases to be appealed from state courts to these federal circuit courts presided over by traveling Supreme Court justices, thus dramatizing

CHRONOLOGY

1789	George Washington inaugurated as first president of the United States • Judiciary Act establishes the Supreme Court and federal circuit courts
1790	Hamilton delivers his Report on Public Credit to Congress • Congress drafts the Bill of Rights
1794	Federalists' excise tax triggers Whiskey Rebellion • The Battle of Fallen Timbers
1796	Jay's Treaty and Pinckney's Treaty ratified
1798	XYZ Affair results in undeclared war with France • Alien and Sedition Acts passed by Congress
1801	Thomas Jefferson inaugurated as third president of the United States
1803	United States purchases Louisiana Territory from France • *Marbury v. Madison* establishes the doctrine of judicial review
1804–1806	Lewis and Clark explore the Louisiana Purchase and the Columbia River basin
1807	*Chesapeake-Leopard* Affair ignites anti-British sentiment • Congress passes Embargo Act
1810	Henry Clay elected Speaker of the House
1812	War with England begins
1813	The Battle of the Thames
1814	Federalists convene the Hartford Convention • Treaty of Ghent ends the War of 1812
1815	American victory at the Battle of New Orleans

National Portrait Gallery, Smithsonian Institution/Art Resource, NY

7.2 **George Washington in 1796, Near the End of His Presidency** The artist captured the formal dignity of the first president and surrounded him with gold, red velvet, a presidential throne, and other emblems of kingly power.

Q *What republican features of the painting help to balance its monarchical character?*

federal power. As James Madison and other members of the intensely nationalist First Congress surveyed their handiwork, they could congratulate themselves on having strengthened national authority at every opportunity.

7-1c *Hamiltonian Economics: The National Debt*

Washington filled posts in his cabinet with familiar faces. As secretary of war, he chose Henry Knox, an old comrade from the Revolution. The State Department went to his fellow Virginian, Thomas Jefferson. He chose Alexander Hamilton of New York, his trusted aide-de-camp during the Revolution, to head the Department of the Treasury.

Hamilton was the most single-minded nationalist in the new government. He was a brilliant economic thinker, an admirer of the British system of centralized government and finance, and a supremely arrogant and ambitious man. More than any other cabinet member, and perhaps even more than Washington (he later referred to Washington's presidency as "my administration"), Hamilton directed the making of a national government.

In 1789, Congress asked Secretary of the Treasury Hamilton to report on the public debt. The debt fell into three categories, Hamilton reported. The first was the $11 million owed to foreigners—primarily debts to France incurred during the Revolution. The second and third—roughly $24 million each—were debts owed by the national and state governments to American citizens who had supplied food, arms, and other resources to the revolutionary cause. Congress agreed that both justice and the credibility of the new government dictated that the foreign debts be paid in full, but the domestic debts raised troublesome questions. Those debts consisted of notes issued during the Revolution to soldiers, and to merchants, farmers, and others who had helped the war effort. Over the years, speculators had purchased many of these notes at a fraction of their face value; when word spread that the Constitution would create a government likely to pay its debts, speculators and their agents fanned out across the countryside, buying all the notes they could find. By 1790, the government debt was concentrated in the hands of businessmen and speculators—most of them northeasterners—who had bought notes at prices only 10 percent to 30 percent of their original value. Full payment would bring them enormous windfall profits.

The Revolutionary War debt of the individual states was another source of contention. Nationalists, with Hamilton at their head, wanted to assume the states' debts as part of a national debt. The states' debts also had been bought up by speculators, and they posed another problem as well: Many states, including all of the southern states with the exception of South Carolina, had paid off most of their notes in the 1780s; the other states still had significant outstanding debts. If the federal government assumed the states' debts, money would flow out of the southern, middle, and western states into the Northeast, whose citizens would hold fully four-fifths of the combined national debt.

That is precisely what Hamilton proposed in his Report on Public Credit, issued in January 1790. He urged Congress to assume the states' debts and combine them with the federal government's foreign and domestic debts into a consolidated national debt. He agreed that the foreign debt should be paid promptly, a move that would announce to the international community that the government of the United States would pay its bills. But he insisted that debts owed to Americans be a permanent, tax-supported fixture of government. Under his plan, the government would issue securities to its creditors and would pay an annual rate of interest of 4 percent. A permanent debt would encourage wealthy financiers to invest in government securities, thus allying them with the national state. Servicing the debt would also require a significant enlargement of the federal civil service, national financial institutions, and federal taxes. The national debt, in short, was at the center of Alexander Hamilton's plan for a powerful national state.

7-1d *Hamiltonian Economics: The Bank and the Excise*

As part of that plan, Hamilton asked Congress to charter a Bank of the United States. The government would store its funds in the bank and would supervise its operations, but directors representing private stockholders would control the bank. The Bank of the United States would print and back the national currency and would regulate other banks. Hamilton's proposal also made stock in the bank payable in government securities, thus (1) adding to the value of the securities, (2) giving the bank a powerful interest in the fiscal stability of the government, and (3) binding the holders of the securities even closer to the national government. Those who looked closely saw that Hamilton's Bank of the United States was a carbon copy of the Bank of England.

To fund the national debt, Hamilton called for a federal **excise tax** (a tax on goods) on wines, coffee, tea, and spirits. The tax on spirits would fall most heavily on the whiskey produced in abundance on the frontier. Its purpose, stated openly by Hamilton, was not only to produce revenue but also to establish the government's power to create an internal tax and to collect it in the most remote regions of the republic.

Passed in April 1791, the national bank and the federal excise measures completed Hamilton's organization of government finances. Taken separately, the consolidated government debt, the national bank, and the federal excise tax ably solved discrete problems of government finance. Taken together, however, they constituted a full-scale replica of the treasury-driven government of Britain.

7-1e *The Rise of Jeffersonian Opposition*

In 1789, nearly every federal officeholder wanted to make the new government work. In particular, Alexander Hamilton at Treasury and James Madison in the House of Representatives expected to continue the political partnership that had helped them write the Constitution and get it ratified. Yet, in the debate over the national debt, Madison led congressional opposition to Hamilton. In 1792, Thomas Jefferson joined the opposition, insisting that Hamilton's schemes would dismantle the Revolution. Within a few short years, the consensus of 1789 had degenerated into an angry argument over what sort of government would finally result from the American Revolution.

Hamilton's proposal for a national debt provided the last major compromise between the two sides. Madison and other southerners opposed the debt because they did not want northern speculators to reap fortunes from notes bought at rock-bottom prices from soldiers, widows, and orphans. He branded Hamilton's plan "public plunder." But at the urging of Jefferson, Madison and the congressional opposition compromised with Hamilton. In exchange for accepting his proposals on the debt, they won his promise to locate the permanent capital of the United States at a site on the Potomac River (which would become Washington, D.C.). The compromise went to the heart of American revolutionary republicanism. Hamilton intended to tie northeastern commercial interests to the federal government. If New York or Philadelphia became the permanent capital, political and economic power might be concentrated there as it was in Paris and London—court cities in which power, wealth, and every kind of excellence were in league against the countryside. The compromise would distance the commercial power of the cities from the federal government and would put an end to the "republican court" that had formed around President Washington.

Hamilton's proposed Bank of the United States split the nation's political elites and their followers into permanent factions, Hamilton's Federalists and Jefferson and Madison's Democratic Republicans, or Republicans for short (not to be confused with the modern Republican Party founded in the 1850s; see Chapter 14). Jefferson argued that Congress had no constitutional right to charter a bank, and that allowing Congress to do so would revive the popular fears of centralized despotism that had nearly defeated ratification of the Constitution. Hamilton responded with the first

What They Said

Washington, Jefferson, and the Image of the President

For American politics in the 1790s, style was substance. George Washington surrounded the office of the presidency with formality, which became characteristic of Federalist style. Below is a description of President Washington at a formal reception near the end of his presidency by the Massachusetts writer and public official William Sullivan, who at the time was a young lawyer.

More democratic members of the new government, including Secretary of State Thomas Jefferson, considered the Federalist style reminiscent of European court society. When he became president in 1801, Jefferson introduced a less formal tone for his administration. In 1804, Sir John Augustus Foster took over his duties as Secretary of the British Legation in Washington. He described President Thomas Jefferson's unassuming Democratic Republican style at an official government function.

Description of George Washington

On entering, he [the visitor] saw the tall manly figure of Washington clad in black velvet; his hair in full dress, powdered and gathered behind in a large silk bag; yellow gloves on his hands; holding a cocked hat with cockade in it, and the edges adorned with a black feather about an inch deep. He wore knee and shoe buckles; and a long sword, with a finely wrought and polished steel hilt, which appeared at the left hip; the coat worn over the sword, so that the hilt, and the part below the folds of the coat behind, were in view. The scabbard was white polished leather.

He stood always in front of the fire-place, with his face towards the door of entrance. . . . He received his visitor with a dignified bow, while his hands were so disposed of as to indicate, that the salutation was not to be accompanied with shaking hands. This ceremony never occurred in these visits, even with his most near friends.

Description of Thomas Jefferson

Having mentioned Mr. Jefferson, it may be interesting to the reader to have the following description of his person as he appeared to me on my arrival in the United States in the year 1804. He was a tall man with a very red freckled face and grey neglected hair; his manners goodnatured, frank and rather friendly though he had somewhat of a cynical expression of countenance. He wore a blue coat, a thick grey-coloured hairy waistcoat, with a red under-waistcoat lapped over it, green velveteen breeches with pearl buttons, yarn stockings, and slippers down at the heels; his appearance being very much like that of a tall large-boned farmer. He said he washed his feet as often as he did his hands in order to keep off cold, and appeared to think himself unique in so doing.

Q *How did the public presentation of Washington and Jefferson differ? How did their images relate to what the two men wanted to accomplish as president of the United States?*

Q *Why do you think Washington avoided shaking hands with his guests? Why do you think Jefferson felt free to talk about washing his feet?*

Sources: (top) William Sullivan, *The Public Men of the Revolution* (Philadelphia: Carey and Hart, 1847), p. 120; (bottom) *The Quarterly Review* Vol. LXVIII (London: John Murray, 1841), p. 24.

argument for expanded federal power under the clause in the Constitution empowering Congress "to make all laws which shall be necessary and proper" to the performance of its duties. President Washington and a majority in Congress sided with Hamilton.

Jefferson's strict constructionism (his insistence that the government had no powers beyond those specified in the Constitution) revealed his fears of the de facto constitution that Hamilton was making. Jefferson argued that the federal bank was unconstitutional, that a federal excise tax was certain to arouse public opposition, and that funding the debt would reward speculators and penalize ordinary citizens. More important, Jefferson argued, Hamilton used government securities and stock in the Bank of the United States to buy the loyalty not only of merchants and speculators but also of members of Congress. "The ultimate object of all this," insisted Jefferson, "is to prepare the way for a change, from the present republican form of government, to that of a monarchy, of which the English constitution is to be the model."

7.3 **Portrait of Alexander Hamilton by John Trumbull, 1804** Washington's brilliant, ambitious, and slippery secretary of the treasury, he almost single-handedly designed the fiscal structure of the new United States.

For their part, Hamilton and his Federalist supporters insisted that centralization of power and a strong executive were necessary to the survival of the republic. The alternative was a return to the localism and public disorder of the 1780s and, ultimately, the failure of the Revolution. The argument drew its urgency from the understanding of both Hamilton and his detractors that the United States was a weak republic in a world governed by kings and aristocrats, and that republics had a long history of failure. They all knew that Americans might yet lose their Revolution. As both sides began to mobilize popular support, events in Europe came to make that fear all too real. The combination of external threats and internal discord placed the American republican experiment in jeopardy.

7-2 The American Republic in a Changing World

Q *What were the principal foreign and internal threats to the newly independent United States in the late 18th century?*

The American Revolution and the creation of the United States dominate the historical accounts of late 18th-century North America. The year 1776 is a hinge around which the history of the continent—indeed, the hemisphere—seems to turn. Yet, the rise of the United States was only one of many sweeping developments that shaped American history during this period. The Spaniards reorganized their colonial system and forged a transcontinental empire in North America. The French remained a powerful presence in the Caribbean, the British strove to turn Canada into a seat of imperial resurgence, and both harbored ambitions to reclaim their lost North American empires. The Native Americans, who still controlled most of the continent, continued to live according to their own traditions and challenged European pretensions to continental dominance.

7-2a *New Spain and the Bourbon Reforms*

In the mid-18th century, Spain and its American empire were in a spiraling crisis. A declining population, fiscal inefficiency, and the ascendancy of its rivals had relegated the once formidable empire to a secondary status. To reverse the trend, Spain's Bourbon kings, who had held the Spanish Crown since 1700, implemented sweeping reforms to restore the empire to its former glory. Aspiring to build a more secular and modern Spain, they reorganized the justice system, reformed taxation, simplified the top-heavy mercantilist bureaucracy, and limited the Church's role in the government. The reforms had far-reaching consequences in North America, where the Bourbons meant to thwart the rising might of the newly independent United States.

The late 18th century witnessed a resurgence of Spanish power and influence in North America. Spain had claimed an unbroken, transcontinental zone across the lower continent since 1783, when Britain ceded East and West Florida to it (see Chapter 6). In the following decades, the Bourbon Court made a concerted effort to turn those claims into an imperial realm. In California, Franciscan missionaries built 21 missions on the coastal lowlands, bringing tens of thousands of Indians into the Catholic fold—and into a colonial regime of religious indoctrination, coerced labor, and social surveillance. The Indians were incorporated into mission communities in which they were exposed to new marital and sexual norms, new foods, and new lethal microbes. The result was a demographic and cultural catastrophe. The mission Indians "fatten, sicken, and die," one Franciscan noted. The Indian population of coastal California collapsed roughly by half in a generation, but the missions survived, entrenching Spanish power in California. In 1821, some 3,200 Hispanics—missionaries, soldiers, colonists—lived there, frustrating competing colonization efforts. Russian trappers and traders, advancing down the Pacific coast, established a foothold in northern California but failed to push farther south. British merchants as well operated along the Pacific coast, and a 1795 treaty between Spain and Britain established the Pacific Northwest as a free zone. California, however, remained beyond Britain's reach.

Spanish administrators also managed to secure New Mexico and Texas, which in the early 18th century had been exposed to devastating raids by the equestrian Apaches and Comanches (see Chapter 3). A sprawling, continent-wide smallpox epidemic ravaged the powerful Comanches in the early 1780s, opening the door for Spanish diplomats. Spanish New Mexico and Texas formed alliances with the temporarily weakened Comanches, and the new allies launched a joint war against the Apaches. By 1800, most Apaches had retreated in the mountains and desert shrublands south and west of the Rio Grande, where many of them moved into Spanish-monitored "peace establishments," which foreshadowed the 19th-century Indian reservations in the United States.

Spain's main ambition, however, was to contain the United States in Louisiana (which it had won from France in 1762) and in the Floridas. Again, the Spaniards relied on Indian diplomacy. The Spanish Crown considered Louisiana primarily as a buffer colony and made little effort to change its French and African character (see Chapter 3). Instead, they focused on building a network of loyal Indians—Chickasaws, Choctaws, Creeks, and Cherokees—who would block the westward-pushing American settlers. The strategy was a striking success, allowing Spain to operate far above its demographic weight. The Gulf of Mexico, with Spain in control of its northern shore, was essentially a "Spanish lake." Moreover, by sponsoring an anti-U.S. Indian alliance system on both sides of the Mississippi Valley, the Spaniards blocked the Americans from the great river, cutting off Ohio and other booming western territories from ocean access. Through the 1780s and 1790s, American settlers in the trans-Appalachian West felt oppressed and victimized by Spain. Increasingly, they blamed the Federalist elite for their blight, accusing it of disinterest in western affairs.

7-2b *Americans and the French Revolution*

At the same time, shifts in transatlantic geopolitics also imperiled the new republic. Late in 1792, French revolutionaries rejected monarchy and proclaimed the French Republic. They beheaded Louis XVI in January 1793. Eleven days later, the French, who were already at war with Austria and Prussia, declared war on conservative Britain, thus launching a war that, with periodic outbreaks of peace, would embroil the Atlantic world until the defeat of France in 1815.

Americans could not have escaped involvement even if they wanted to. Treaties signed in 1778 allied the United States with France, although Federalists and Jeffersonians would argue whether those treaties applied to the French Republic that had killed the king who made them. Americans had overwhelmingly supported the French Revolution of 1789 and had applauded the progress of French republicanism during its first three years. Their gratitude for French help during the American Revolution and hopes for international republicanism faced severe tests in 1793, when the French Republic began to execute thousands of aristocrats, priests, and other "counterrevolutionaries," and when the French threatened the sovereignty of nations by declaring a war of all peoples against all monarchies. The argument between Jeffersonian republicanism and Hamiltonian centralization was no longer a squabble within the U.S. government. National politics was now caught up and subsumed within the struggle over international republicanism.

As Britain and France went to war in 1793, President Washington declared American neutrality, thereby abrogating the 1778 treaties with the French. Washington and most of his advisers realized that the United States was in no condition to fight a war. They also wanted to stay on good terms with Britain. Ninety percent of American imports came from Britain, and 90 percent of the federal revenue came from customs duties on those imports. Thus, both the nation's commerce and the financial health of the government depended on good relations with Britain. Moreover, Federalists genuinely sympathized with the British in the war with France. They regarded the United States as a "perfected" England and viewed Britain as the defender of hierarchical society and ordered liberty against the homicidal anarchy of the French.

Jefferson and his friends saw things differently. They applauded the French for carrying on the republican revolution Americans had begun in 1776, and they had no affection for the monarchical politics of the Federalists or for Americans' continued neocolonial dependence on British trade. Although the Jeffersonians agreed that the United States should stay out of the war, they sympathized as openly with the French as the Federalists did with the British. Common people formed Democratic-Republican societies to raise toasts, organize parades, and otherwise celebrate the spread of republican ideas throughout the Atlantic world.

7-2c *Citizen Genêt*

Throughout the war years from 1793 to 1815, both Britain and France, by intervening freely in the internal affairs of the United States, made American isolationism impossible.

In April 1793, the French sent Citizen Edmond Genêt as minister to the United States. Genêt's ruling Girondists were the revolutionary faction that had declared the war on all monarchies; they ordered Genêt to enlist American aid with or without the Washington administration's consent. After the president's proclamation of neutrality, Genêt openly commissioned American privateers to harass British shipping and enlisted Americans in intrigues against the Spanish outpost of New Orleans. Genêt then opened France's Caribbean colonies to American shipping, providing American shippers a choice between French free trade and British mercantilism. Genêt's mission ended abruptly in summer 1793, when Robespierre and the infamous Terror drove the Girondists from power.

The British answered Genêt's free-trade declaration with a promise to seize any ship trading with French colonies in the Caribbean. Under these Orders in Council, the British seized 250 American ships. Royal Navy press gangs also searched American ships for British sailors who had deserted or who had switched to safer, better-paying work in the American merchant marine. Under British law, the Royal Navy could impress any British seafaring subject into service during wartime. Inevitably, American sailors were also impressed into the British navy in a contemptuous and infuriating assault on American sovereignty. Meanwhile, the British, operating from Canada and from their still-garrisoned forts in the Northwest, began promising military aid to the Indians north of the Ohio River. Thus, while the French ignored the neutrality of the United States, the British engaged in both overt and covert acts of war.

7-2d *Western Troubles*

The problems with France and on the high seas were accompanied by an intensified threat from British and Indian forces in the west, as well as from settlers in that region. The situation came to a head in summer and fall 1794. The Shawnee and their allies plotted with the British and talked of driving all settlers out of their territory. At the same time, frontier whites, sometimes with the encouragement of English and Spanish officials, grew increasingly contemptuous of a national government that could neither pacify the Indians nor guarantee their free use of the Mississippi River. President Washington heard that 2,000 Kentuckians were armed and ready to attack New Orleans—a move that would have started a war between the United States and Spain. Settlers in Georgia were making unauthorized forays against the Creeks, and settlers up and down the frontier refused to pay the Federalists' excise tax on whiskey—a direct challenge to federal authority known as the **Whiskey Rebellion**. In western Pennsylvania, mobs tarred and feathered excise officers and burned the property of distillers who paid the tax. In July 1794, near Pittsburgh, 500 militiamen marched on the house of the unpopular federal excise collector General John Neville. Neville, his family, and a few federal soldiers fought the militiamen, killing two and wounding six before they abandoned the house to be looted and burned. Two weeks later, 6,000 "Whiskey Rebels" met at Braddock's Field near Pittsburgh, threatening to attack the town. Sectional tensions between eastern elites and western settlers threatened to dismantle the infant republic.

Faced with serious international and domestic threats to his new government, Washington determined to defeat the Indians and the Whiskey Rebels by force, thus securing American control of the Northwest. He sent General "Mad Anthony" Wayne against the northwestern Indians. Wayne's decisive victory at Fallen Timbers in August 1794—fought almost in the shadow of a British fort—ended the Indian–British challenge in the Northwest for many years. In September, Washington ordered 12,000 federalized militiamen from eastern Pennsylvania, Maryland, Virginia, and New Jersey to quell the Whiskey Rebellion. The president promised amnesty to rebels who pledged to support the government and prison terms to those who did not. As the army marched west from Carlisle, they found defiant liberty poles but no armed resistance. Arriving at Pittsburgh, the army arrested 20 suspected rebels—none of them leaders—and marched them back to Philadelphia for trial. In the end, only two "rebels," both of them feebleminded, were convicted. President Washington pardoned them, and the Whiskey Rebellion was over.

7-2e *The Collapse of the Miami Confederacy*

Although the territories of many of the woodland Indians were still intact in 1790, they were in serious trouble. The Iroquois had been restricted to reservations in New York and Pennsylvania, and many had fled to Canada. In the Northwest, a multitribal Miami Confederacy led by Blue Jacket and Little Turtle—with the help of the British, who still occupied seven forts within what was formally the United States—continued to trade furs and to impede white settlement. Skirmishes with settlers, however, brought reprisals, and the Indians now faced not only hostile pioneers but the U.S. Army as well. In the Ohio Country, punitive expeditions led by General Josiah Harmar and General Arthur St. Clair failed in 1790 and 1791—the second ending in an Indian victory in which 630 soldiers died.

Source: metmuseum.org

7.4 **Washington Reviewing the Western Army at Fort Cumberland, Maryland** In fall 1794, in his effort to suppress the Whiskey Rebellion, Washington became the first and last sitting president to lead troops in the field. After reviewing the militiamen at Fort Cumberland and at Bedford, Pennsylvania, the president left the army in charge of subordinates, including Alexander Hamilton, to march to Pittsburgh.

In 1794, the U.S. finally succeeded in defeating the Miami Confederacy with General Wayne's victory at Fallen Timbers, near present-day Toledo. The Treaty of Greenville forced the Native Americans to cede two-thirds of what are now Ohio and southeastern Indiana (see Map 7.1). As compensation, the U.S. government agreed to dispense annuity payments, which soon became a standard practice in treaty negotiations between the United States and Indians. The government also began to distribute cattle, pigs, and hoes, hoping to transform the Indians from hunters and warriors into farmers. This practice rapidly evolved into a sweeping "civilization" program that would frame U.S. Indian policy for well over a century.

Following their victory at Fallen Timbers, whites filtered into what remained of Indian lands. In 1796, President Washington threw up his hands and announced that "I believe scarcely any thing, short of a Chinese Wall, or a line of troops, will restrain Land Jobbers and the encroachment of settlers upon the Indian Territory." Five years later, Governor William Henry Harrison of the Indiana Territory admitted that frontier whites "consider the murdering of the Indians in the highest degree meritorious."

7-2f *The Jay Treaty*

While he sent armies against Indians and frontiersmen, President Washington capitulated to the British on the high seas. In 1794, he sent John Jay, chief justice of the Supreme Court, to negotiate the conflicts between the United States and Britain. Armed with news of Wayne's victory, Jay extracted a promise from the British to remove their troops from American territory in the Northwest. On every other point of dispute, however, he agreed to British terms. Jay's Treaty made no mention of British navy impresses or other violations of American maritime rights, nor did it refer to the old issue of British payment for slaves carried off during the Revolution. The treaty did allow small American ships back into the West Indies, but only on terms that the Senate would reject. In short, Jay's Treaty granted British trade a most-favored-nation status in exchange for the agreement of the British to abandon their northwestern forts. Given the power of Britain, it was the best that Americans could expect. Washington, obliged to choose between an unpopular treaty and an unwinnable war, passed Jay's Treaty on to the Senate, which, in June 1795, ratified it by a bare two-thirds majority.

During the fight over Jay's Treaty, dissension within the government was first aired in public. The seaport cities and much of the Northeast reacted favorably to the treaty. It ruled out war with England and cemented an Anglo-American trade relationship that strengthened both Hamilton's national state and the established commercial interests that supported it. The South, on the other hand, saw Jay's Treaty as a blatant sign of the designs of Britain and the Federalists to subvert republicanism in both France and the United States. The Virginia legislature branded the treaty as unconstitutional,

▲ **MAP 7.1 The West, 1790–1796** In 1790, the United States "owned" nearly all of its present territory east of the Mississippi River, but white Americans remained concentrated east of the Appalachians (see Map 8.1 on page 228) and independent Indian peoples controlled the rest of the country, their territorial sovereignty recognized by the treaties they had formed with the U.S. government. The Battle of Fallen Timbers and the resultant Treaty of Greenville pushed white settlement across Ohio and into Indiana, but the Indians of the Northwest remained intact, determined, and in touch with the British in Canada. Native Americans also controlled nearly the entire Southwest, and Florida and the Gulf Coast—including all outlets from the interior to the Caribbean—remained in Spanish hands. The American West was very far from secure in the 1790s.

Q *What was the primary obstacle to western settlement in the early 1790s?*

Q *Why was the Battle of Fallen Timbers in 1794 so integral to the future expansion of the United States?*

and Republican congressmen demanded to see all documents relating to Jay's negotiations. Washington responded by telling them that their request could be legitimate only if the House was planning to initiate **impeachment** proceedings, thus tying approval of the treaty to his enormous personal prestige.

Meanwhile, on March 3, 1796, Washington released the details of a treaty that Thomas Pinckney had negotiated with Spain. In this treaty, Spain recognized American neutrality and set the border between the United States and Spanish Florida on American terms. Most important, Pinckney's Treaty ended Spanish claims to the Ohio Valley and gave Americans the unrestricted right to navigate the Mississippi River and to transship produce at the Spanish port of New Orleans. Combined with the victory at Fallen Timbers, the British promise to abandon their posts in the Northwest, and Washington's personal popularity, Pinckney's Treaty helped turn the tide in favor of the unpopular Jay's Treaty. Dissension in the trans-Appalachian West abated. With a diminishing number of hotheads willing to oppose Washington, western representatives joined the Northeast and growing numbers of southerners to ratify Jay's Treaty. Spain and its native allies now faced an increasingly united and expansionist republic on their borders.

7-2g *The Election of 1796*

George Washington refused to run for reelection in 1796, thus setting a two-term limit observed by every president until Franklin Roosevelt (see Chapter 25). Washington could be proud of his accomplishments. He had presided over the creation of a national government. He had secured American control over the western settlements by ending British, Spanish, and Indian military threats and by securing free use of the Mississippi River for western produce. Those policies, together with the federal invasion of western Pennsylvania, had made it evident that the government could control its most distant regions. Washington had also avoided war with Britain, although not without overlooking assaults on American sovereignty. As he was about to leave government, he wrote, with substantial help from Hamilton, his Farewell Address. In it he warned against "permanent alliances with any portion of the foreign world." America, he said, should act independently in international affairs—an ideal that many felt had been betrayed in Jay's Treaty. Washington also warned against internal political divisions.

Washington's retirement opened the way to the very competition for public office that he warned against. In 1796, Americans experienced their first contested presidential election. The Federalists chose as their candidate John Adams of Massachusetts, who had served as vice president. The Democratic Republicans nominated Thomas Jefferson. According to the gentlemanly custom of the day, the candidates did not campaign in person, but friends of the candidates, the newspaper editors who enjoyed their patronage, and even European governments ensured that the election would be hotly contested.

Adams won a close election. The distribution of electoral votes revealed the sectional bases of Federalist and Republican support: Adams received only 2 electoral votes south of the Potomac, and Jefferson received only 18 (all but 5 of them in Pennsylvania) north of the Potomac. Behind the outcome, there was considerable intrigue. Alexander Hamilton, who had retired from the Treasury in 1795, knew that he could not manipulate the independent and almost perversely upright John Adams. So, he secretly instructed South Carolina's Federalist electors to withhold their votes from Adams. That would have given the presidency to Adams's running mate, Thomas Pinckney. (Before the ratification of the Twelfth Amendment in 1804, the candidate with a majority of the electoral votes became president, and the second-place candidate became vice president.) Like some of Hamilton's other schemes, this one backfired. New England electors heard of the plan and angrily withheld their votes from Pinckney. As a result, Adams was elected president and his opponent Thomas Jefferson became vice president. Adams took office with a justifiable mistrust of many members of his own party and with the head of the opposition party as his second in command. It was not an auspicious beginning.

7-2h *Troubles with France, 1796–1800*

As Adams entered office, an international crisis was already in full swing. France, regarding Jay's Treaty as an Anglo-American alliance, broke off relations with the United States. The French hinted that they intended to overthrow the reactionary government of the United States but would postpone taking action in the hope that a friendlier Thomas Jefferson would replace "old man Washington" in 1797. When the election went to John Adams, the French gave up on the United States and set about denying Britain its new de facto ally. In 1797, the French ordered that American ships carrying "so much as a handkerchief" made in England be confiscated without compensation; in the same vein, they announced that American seamen serving in the British navy (most of whom were impressed and had no choice) would be summarily hanged if captured.

President Adams wanted to protect American commerce from French depredations, but he knew that the United States might not survive a war with France. He also knew that French grievances (including Jay's Treaty and the abrogation of the French-American treaties of 1778) were legitimate. He decided to send a mission to France, made up of three respected statesmen: Charles Cotesworth Pinckney of South Carolina, John Marshall of Virginia, and Elbridge Gerry of Massachusetts. When the delegates reached Paris, however, they were left cooling their heels in the outer offices of the Directory—the revolutionary committee of five that had replaced France's beheaded king. At last, three French officials (the correspondence identified them only as "X, Y, and Z," and the incident later became known as the **XYZ Affair**) discreetly hinted that France would receive them if they paid a bribe of $250,000, arranged for the United States to loan $12 million to the French government, and apologized for unpleasant remarks that John Adams had made about France. The delegates refused, saying "No, not a sixpence," and returned home. There a journalist transformed their remark into "Millions for defense, but not one cent for tribute."

President Adams asked Congress to prepare for war, and the French responded by seizing more American ships. Thus began, in April 1798, an undeclared war between France and the United States in the Caribbean, known today as the Quasi War. While the French navy dealt with the British in the north Atlantic, French privateers inflicted costly blows on American shipping. But after nearly a year of fighting, with the British providing powder and shot for American guns, the U.S. Navy chased the French privateers out of the Caribbean. Fearful of losing their American possessions entirely, French policymakers began to seek for a foothold in the North American mainland.

7-2i *The Crisis at Home, 1798–1800*

The troubles with France precipitated a crisis at home. Disclosure of the XYZ correspondence, together with the Quasi War in the Caribbean, produced a surge of public hostility toward the French and their Republican friends in the United States. Many Federalists, led by Alexander Hamilton, wanted to use the crisis to destroy their political opponents.

Without consulting President Adams, the Federalist-dominated Congress passed several wartime measures. The first was a federal property tax—graduated, spread equally between sections of the country, and justified by military necessity, but a direct federal tax nonetheless. Congress then passed four laws known as the **Alien and Sedition Acts**. The first three were directed at immigrants: They extended the naturalization period to become citizens from 5 to 14 years and empowered the president to detain enemy aliens during wartime and to deport those he deemed dangerous to the United States. The fourth law—the Sedition Act—set jail terms and fines for persons who advocated disobedience to federal law or who wrote, printed, or spoke "false, scandalous, and malicious" statements against "the government of the United States, or the President of the United States [note that Vice President Jefferson was not included], with intent to defame . . . or to bring them or either of them, into contempt or disrepute."

President Adams never used the powers granted under the Alien Acts, but the Sedition Act resulted in the prosecution of 14 Republicans, most of them journalists. William Duane, editor of the Philadelphia *Aurora* newspaper, was indicted when he and two Irish friends circulated a petition against the Alien Act on the grounds of a Catholic church. Another prominent Republican went to jail for statements made in a private letter. Matthew Lyon, a scurrilous Republican congressman from Vermont, had brawled with a Federalist representative in the House chamber; he went to jail for his criticisms of President Adams, Federalist militarism, and what he called the "ridiculous pomp" of the national administration.

Republicans charged that the Alien and Sedition Acts violated the First Amendment, and they turned to the states for help. Southern states, which had provided only 4 of the 44 congressional votes for the Sedition Act, took the lead. Jefferson provided the Kentucky legislature with draft resolutions, and Madison did the same for the Virginia legislature. These so-called **Virginia and Kentucky Resolves** restated the constitutional fundamentalism that had guided Republican opposition from the beginning. Jefferson's Kentucky Resolves reminded Congress that the Alien and Sedition Acts gave the national government powers not mentioned in the Constitution and that the Tenth Amendment reserved such powers to the states. He also argued that the Constitution was a "compact" between sovereign states and that state legislatures could "nullify" federal laws they deemed unconstitutional, thus anticipating constitutional theories that states'-rights southerners would use after 1830.

Federalists took another ominous step when President Adams asked Congress to create a military prepared for war. Adams wanted a stronger navy, both because the undeclared war with France was being fought on the ocean and because he agreed with other Federalists that America's future as a commercial nation required a respectable navy. Hamilton and his followers, who were becoming known as "**High Federalists**" for their strident views, preferred a standing army. At the urging of Washington and against his own judgment, Adams appointed Hamilton inspector general. As such, Hamilton would be the de facto commander of the U.S. Army. Congress authorized a 20,000-man army, and Hamilton proceeded to raise it. Congress also provided for a much larger army to be called up in the event of a declaration of war. When Hamilton expanded the officer corps in anticipation of such an army, he excluded Republicans and commissioned only his political friends. High Federalists wanted a standing army to enforce the Alien and Sedition Acts and to put down an impending rebellion in the South. Beyond that, there was little need for such a force. The war was being fought at sea, and most Americans believed that the citizen militia could hold off any land invasion until an army was raised. The Republicans, President Adams, and many other Federalists now became convinced that Hamilton and his High Federalists were determined to destroy their political opponents, enter into an alliance with Britain, and impose Hamilton's statist designs by force.

Adams was angry. First the Hamiltonians had tried to rob him of the presidency. Then they had passed the Alien and Sedition Acts, the direct tax, and plans for a standing army without consulting him. None of this would have been possible if not for the crisis with France.

Adams, who had resisted calls for a declaration of war, began looking for ways to declare peace. He opened negotiations with France and stalled the creation of Hamilton's army while the talks took place. In the agreement that followed, the French canceled the obligations that the United States had assumed under the treaties of 1778. But they refused to pay reparations for attacks on American shipping since 1793—the very point over which many Federalists had wanted war. Peace with France cut the ground from under the militaristic High Federalists. Hamilton would campaign against Adams in 1800, damaging the president's chances for reelection.

7-2j *The Election of 1800*

Thomas Jefferson and his Democratic Republicans approached the election of 1800 better organized and more determined than they had four years earlier. Moreover, events in the months preceding the election worked in their favor. The Alien and Sedition Acts, the direct tax of 1798, and the Federalist military buildup were never popular. Taken together, these events gave credence to the Republicans' allegation that the Federalists were using the crisis with France to consolidate their power, destroy liberty and the opposition, and overthrow the American republic. The Federalists countered by warning that the election of Jefferson and his radical allies would release the worst horrors of the French Revolution onto the streets of American towns. Each side believed that its defeat in 1800 would mean the end of the republic.

The Democratic Republicans were strong in the South and weak in the Northeast. Jefferson knew that he had to win New York, the state that had cost him the 1796 election. Jefferson's running mate, the New Yorker **Aaron Burr**, arranged a truce between New York's Republican factions and chose candidates for the state legislature who were both locally respected and committed to Jefferson. The strategy succeeded. The Republicans carried New York City and won a slight majority in the legislature. New York's electoral votes belonged to Jefferson. Jefferson and Burr won the election with 73 votes each. Adams had 65 votes, and his running mate Charles Cotesworth Pinckney had 64 (see Map 7.2). (In order to distinguish between their presidential and vice-presidential candidates—and thus thwart yet another of Hamilton's attempts to rig the election—the Federalists of Rhode Island had withheld 1 vote from Pinckney.) Jefferson and Burr had tied, though everyone knew that Jefferson was the presidential candidate. But under the Constitution, a lame-duck Federalist Congress decided the outcome. Federalists supported Burr to keep Jefferson from becoming president, prompting talk of civil war in Republican strongholds.

After six quarrelsome days and 35 ballots on which most Federalist congressmen voted for Burr (whose part in these proceedings has never been fully uncovered), a compromise was reached: Many Federalists abandoned Burr but turned in blank ballots and thus avoided voting for the hated (but victorious) Jefferson. With that, the "Revolution of 1800" had won its first round.

7-3 The Jeffersonians in Power

Q *What were the principal reforms of the national government during Thomas Jefferson's administration?*

On the first Tuesday of March 1801, Thomas Jefferson left his rooms at Conrad and McMunn's boardinghouse in Washington and walked up Pennsylvania Avenue. Jefferson received military salutes along the way, but he forbade the pomp and ceremony that had ushered Washington into office. Accompanied by a few friends and a company of artillery from the Maryland militia (and not by Hamilton's regulars), Jefferson walked (no carriages) up the street and into the unfinished Capitol building. The central tower and the wing that would house Congress were only half completed. Jefferson joined Vice President Burr, other members of the government, and a few foreign diplomats in the newly finished Senate chamber.

7-3a *The Republican Program*

Jefferson took the oath of office from Chief Justice John Marshall, a distant relative and political opponent from Virginia. Then, in a small voice that was almost inaudible to those at a distance, he delivered his inaugural address. Referring to the political discord that had brought him into office, he began with a

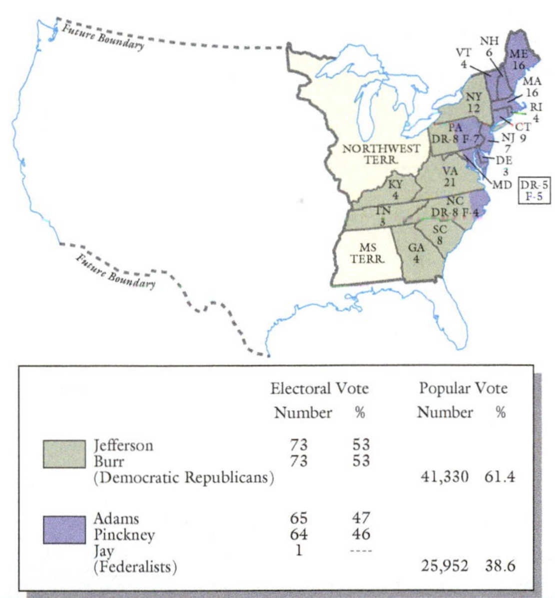

	Electoral Vote Number	Electoral Vote %	Popular Vote Number	Popular Vote %
Jefferson	73	53		
Burr	73	53		
(Democratic Republicans)			41,330	61.4
Adams	65	47		
Pinckney	64	46		
Jay	1	----		
(Federalists)			25,952	38.6

▲ **MAP 7.2 Presidential Election, 1800** The electoral votes in 1800 split along starkly sectional lines. The South voted for Jefferson, New England voted for Adams, and the election was decided by close contests in Pennsylvania and New York.

Q *Why was New York so crucial to Jefferson's winning coalition of states?*

Q *What conclusions could be drawn about the future of the Federalist Party based on this electoral map?*

plea for unity, insisting that "every difference of opinion is not a difference of principle. We have called by different names brethren of the same principle. We are all Republicans, we are all Federalists." Jefferson did not mean that he and his opponents should forget their ideological differences. He meant only to invite moderate Federalists into a broad Republican coalition in which there was no room for the statist designs of Alexander Hamilton and his High Federalist friends.

Jefferson went on to outline the kind of government a republic should have. A "wise and frugal" government would respect the powers of the states and preserve the liberties ensured by the Bill of Rights. It would be small, and it would pay its debts without incurring new ones, thus ending the need for taxation and cutting the ground from beneath the burgeoning Federalist state. It would rely for defense on "a disciplined militia" that would fight invaders while regulars were being trained, thus eliminating Hamilton's standing army. It would protect republican liberties from enemies at home and from the nations of Europe. And, Jefferson promised, it would ensure "the encouragement of agriculture, and of commerce as its handmaiden." Beyond the fostering of an agrarian republic and the maintenance of limited government, Jefferson promised little. Blessed with peace abroad and the defeat of the High Federalists at home, he believed that the United States could at last enter into its experiment with truly republican government.

The simplicity of Jefferson's inauguration set the social tone of his administration. The new president reduced the number and grandeur of formal balls, levees, and dinners. He sent his annual messages to Congress to be read by a clerk, rather than delivering them in person in the manner of English kings and Federalist presidents. He refused to ride about Washington in a carriage, preferring to carry out his errands on horseback. Abandoning grand banquets, Jefferson entertained senators and congressmen at small dinners, which were served at a round table without formal seating, thus ending the fine-tuned hierarchy of the Federalists' old arrangements. Jefferson presided over the meals without wearing a wig and dressed in old homespun clothes and a pair of worn bedroom slippers. The casualness (slovenliness, said some of his critics) did not extend to what was served at dinner, however. The food was prepared by expert chefs and accompanied by fine wines, and it was followed by brilliant conversation perfected by Jefferson while he was a diplomat and a visitor to the salons of Paris.

Bettmann/Corbis

7.5 **Portrait of Jefferson by Rembrandt Peale, 1805** A self-consciously plain President Jefferson posed for this portrait in January 1805, near the end of his first term. He wears an unadorned fur-collared coat, is surrounded by no emblems of office, and gazes calmly and directly at the viewer.

Jefferson's first order of business was to reduce the size and expense of government. The Federalists, despite their big government dispositions, had left a surprisingly small federal establishment. Jefferson found only 316 employees who were subject to presidential appointment and removal. Those employees, together with 700 clerks and assistants and 3,000 post office workers, made up the entire federal civil service. Jefferson reduced the diplomatic corps and replaced officeholders who were incompetent, corrupt, or avowedly antirepublican. Even so, the rate of turnover was only about 50 percent during his first term. The replacements were not the violent revolutionaries that Federalists had warned against but Republican gentlemen who matched the social status of the departing Federalists. Jefferson altered the politics of the civil service, but he left its size and shape intact.

Jefferson made more substantial cuts in the military. The Federalists had built a sizable army and navy to prepare for war and, if necessary, to put down opposition at home. Legislation passed in March 1802 reduced the army to two regiments of infantry and one of artillery—a total of 3,350 officers and men, most of whom were assigned to western posts far from the centers of white population. Similar cutbacks reduced the navy. The goal, Jefferson explained, was to rely mainly on the militia for national defense but to maintain a small, well-trained professional army as well. (The same legislation that reduced the army created the military academy at West Point.) At Jefferson's urging, Congress also abolished the direct tax of 1798 and repealed the parts of the Alien and Sedition Acts that had not already expired. Jefferson personally pardoned the 10 victims of those acts who were still in jail and repaid their fines with interest.

Thus, with a few strokes, Jefferson dismantled the repressive apparatus of the Federalist state. By reducing government expenditures, he reduced the government's debt and the army of civil servants and papermen gathered around it. During Jefferson's administration, the national debt fell from $80 million to $57 million, and the government built up a treasury surplus, even after paying $15 million in cash for the **Louisiana Purchase** (discussed later in this chapter). Although some doubted the wisdom of such stringent economy, no one questioned Jefferson's frugality.

7-3b *The Jeffersonians and the Courts*

Jefferson next turned his attention to the federal courts. The Constitution had created the Supreme Court but had left the creation of lesser federal courts to Congress. The First Congress had created circuit courts presided over by the justices of the Supreme Court. Only Federalists served on the Supreme Court under Washington and Adams, and Federalists on the circuit courts had extended federal authority into the hinterland—a fact that prosecutions under the Alien and Sedition Acts had made abundantly clear. Jeffersonian mistrust of the federal courts intensified when the lame-duck Federalist Congress passed a Judiciary Act early in 1801. The act reduced the number of associate justices of the Supreme Court from six to five when the next vacancy occurred, thus reducing Jefferson's chances of appointing a new member to the Court. The Judiciary Act also took Supreme Court justices off circuit and created a new system of circuit courts. This allowed Adams to appoint 16 new judges, along with marshals, federal attorneys, clerks, and justices of the peace. Adams worked until nine o'clock on his last night in office signing commissions for these "**midnight judges**." All of them were staunch Federalists. Coupled with President Adams's appointment of Federalist John Marshall as chief justice in January, the Judiciary Act ensured long-term Federalist domination of the federal courts.

Republicans disagreed on what to do about the Federalists' packing of the courts. Some distrusted the whole idea of an independent judiciary and wanted judges elected by popular vote. Jefferson and most in his party wanted the courts shielded from democratic control, but they deeply resented the Federalist "midnight judges" created by the Judiciary Act of 1801. Jefferson replaced the new federal marshals and attorneys with Republicans and dismissed some of the federal justices of the peace, but judges were appointed for life and could be removed only through impeachment. The Jeffersonians hit on a simple solution: They got rid of the new judges by abolishing their jobs. Early in 1802, with some of Jefferson's supporters questioning the constitutionality of what they were doing, Congress repealed the Judiciary Act of 1801 and thus did away with the midnight appointees.

With the federal courts scaled back to their original size, Republicans in Congress went after High Federalists who were still acting as judges. As a first test of impeachment, they chose John Pickering, a federal attorney with the circuit court of New Hampshire. Pickering was a highly partisan Federalist and a notorious alcoholic. The Federalists who had appointed him had long considered him an embarrassment. The House drew up articles of impeachment, and the senate removed Pickering by a strict party vote.

On the same day, Congress went after bigger game: It voted to impeach Supreme Court Justice Samuel Chase.

7.6 **A Federalist Attack upon Jefferson** From the beginning, Federalists branded Jefferson as a friend to a French Revolution that had promised liberty and equality, then degenerated into violence and dictatorship. Here Jefferson worships at the altar of Gallic Despotism in a political cartoon.

Q *What is the symbolism of the eagle holding the Constitution in the cartoon?*

He hated the Jeffersonians, but his faults did not add up to the "high crimes and misdemeanors" that are the constitutional grounds for impeachment. Moderate Republicans doubted the wisdom of impeaching Chase. Their uneasiness grew when John Randolph took over the prosecution. Randolph led a radical states'-rights faction of the Republican Congress. As Randolph led the prosecution of Samuel Chase, he lectured in his high-pitched voice that Jefferson was double-crossing southern Republicans in an effort to win support in the Northeast. (There was some truth to the accusation: Jefferson envisioned a national Republican coalition, sometimes at the expense of radical states'-rights southerners.) Most Republican senators sided with Jefferson. With Jefferson's approval, many Republicans in the Senate joined the Federalists in voting to acquit Samuel Chase, thus isolating and humiliating Randolph and his states'-rights friends.

7-3c *Justice Marshall's Court*

Chief Justice John Marshall probably cheered the acquittal of Justice Chase because it was clear that Marshall was next on the list. Secretary of state under John Adams, Marshall was committed to Federalist ideas of national power, as he demonstrated with his decision in the case of ***Marbury v. Madison***. William Marbury was one of the justices of the peace whom Jefferson had eliminated in his first few days in office. He sued Jefferson's secretary of state, James Madison, for his commission. Although Marbury never got his job, Marshall used the case to hand down important rulings that laid the basis for the practice of **judicial review**—the Supreme Court's power to rule on the constitutionality of acts of Congress. In arguing that Congress could not alter the jurisdiction of the Supreme Court, Marshall stated that the Constitution is "fundamental and paramount law" and that it is "emphatically the province and duty of the judicial department to say what law is."

Some Republicans saw Marshall's ruling as an attempt to arrogate power to the Court, but Jefferson and other moderates noted that Marshall was less interested in the power of the judiciary than in its independence. Ultimately, they decided they trusted Marshall more than they trusted the radicals in their own party. With the acquittal of Justice Chase, Jeffersonian attacks on the federal courts ceased.

Justice Marshall confirmed his independence in the treason trial of former vice president Aaron Burr in 1807. Following his failed attempt at the presidency in 1801, Burr's relations with northern Federalists so declined that he killed Alexander Hamilton in a duel in 1804. The disgraced Burr headed west and organized a cloudy conspiracy that may have involved (according to varying testimonies) an invasion of Mexico or Florida or the secession of Louisiana. President Jefferson ordered his arrest. Burr was tried for treason at Richmond, Virginia, with the chief justice, who was riding circuit, on the bench. Kings had frequently used the charge of treason to silence dissent. Marshall stopped what he and other Federalists considered Jefferson's attempt to do the same thing by limiting the definition of treason to overt acts of war against the United States or to adhering to the republic's foreign enemies—and by requiring two witnesses to an overt act of treason. Under these guidelines, Burr went free. At the same time, the United States had formally separated internal dissent from treason.

7-3d *Louisiana*

It was Jefferson's good fortune that Europe remained at peace and stayed out of American affairs for the early part of his first term. The one development that posed an international threat to the United States turned into a grand triumph: the purchase of the Louisiana Territory from France (see Map 7.3).

By 1801, half a million Americans lived west of the Appalachians, and Republicans saw westward expansion as the best hope for the survival of the republic. Social inequality and the erosion of yeoman independence would almost inevitably take root in the East, but in the vast lands west of the mountains, the republic could renew itself for many generations to come. To serve that purpose, however, the West needed ready access to markets through the river system that emptied into the Gulf of Mexico at New Orleans. "There is on the globe," wrote President Jefferson, "one single spot, the possessor of which is our natural and habitual enemy. It is New Orleans."

In 1801, under Pinckney's Treaty, Spain allowed Americans to transship produce from the interior via the Mississippi River and New Orleans. The year before, however, Spain had secretly ceded the Louisiana Territory (roughly, all the land west of the Mississippi drained by the Missouri and Arkansas rivers) to France, having concluded that the United States' westward thrust could not be stalled. Napoleon Bonaparte had plans for a new French empire in America with the sugar island of Hispaniola (present-day Haiti and the Dominican Republic) at its center, and with mainland colonies feeding the islands and thus making the empire self-sufficient. Late in 1802, the Spanish, who had retained control of New Orleans, closed the port to American commerce, creating rumors that they would soon transfer the city to France, which would have threatened the very existence of American settlements west of the Appalachians. President Jefferson sent a delegation to Paris early in 1803 with authorization to buy New Orleans for the United States.

By the time the delegates reached Paris, events had dissolved French plans for a new American empire. The slaves of Saint-Domingue (the French colony on Hispaniola) had revolted and had defeated French attempts to regain control of the island. At the same time, another war between Britain and France seemed imminent. Napoleon—reputedly chanting, "Damn sugar, damn coffee, damn colonies"—decided to bail out of America and concentrate his resources in Europe. He astonished Jefferson's delegation by offering to sell not only New Orleans but the whole Louisiana Territory—which would double the size of the United States—for the bargain price of $15 million.

Jefferson, who had criticized Federalists when they violated the letter of the Constitution, faced a dilemma: The

National Portrait Gallery, Smithsonian Institution/Resource, NY

7.7 **John Marshall** A Virginian and distant relative of Thomas Jefferson, John Marshall became chief justice of the Supreme Court in the last months of John Adams's administration. He used the Court as a conservative, centralizing force until his death in 1835.

president lacked the constitutional power to buy territory, but the chance to buy Louisiana was too good to refuse. It would ensure Americans access to the rivers of the interior; it would eliminate a serious foreign threat on America's western border; and it would give American farmers enough land to sustain the agrarian republic for a long time to come. Swallowing his constitutional scruples (and at the same time half-heartedly asking for a constitutional amendment to legalize the purchase), Jefferson told the American delegates to buy Louisiana. Republican senators quickly ratified the Louisiana treaty over Federalist objections that the purchase would encourage rapid settlement and add to backcountry barbarism and Republican strength. For his part, Jefferson was certain that the republic had gained the means of renewing itself through time. As he claimed in his second inaugural address, he had bought a great "empire of liberty."

7-3e *Lewis and Clark*

The Americans knew almost nothing about the land they had bought. Only a few French trappers and traders had traveled the plains between the Mississippi and the Rocky Mountains, and no white person had seen the territory drained by the Columbia River. In 1804, Jefferson sent an expedition under Meriwether Lewis, his private secretary, and William Clark, brother of the Indian fighter George Rogers Clark, to explore the new land. To prepare for the expedition, Lewis studied astronomy, zoology, and botany; Clark was already an accomplished mapmaker. The two explorers kept meticulous journals about one of the epic adventures in American history.

In May 1804, Lewis and Clark and 41 companions boarded a keelboat and two large canoes at the village of St. Louis. They poled and paddled 1,600 miles up the Missouri River, passing through rolling plains dotted by the farm villages of the Pawnee, Oto, Missouri, Crow, Omaha, Hidatsa, and Mandan peoples. The villages of the lower Missouri had been cut off from the western buffalo herds and reduced to dependence by mounted Sioux warriors, who had begun to establish their hegemony over the northern plains.

Lewis and Clark traveled through Sioux territory and stopped for the winter at the heavily fortified Mandan villages at the big bend of the Missouri River in Dakota Country. In the spring they hired Toussaint Charbonneau, a French fur trader, to guide them to the Pacific. Charbonneau was useless, but his wife, a teenaged Shoshone girl named Sacajawea, was an indispensable guide, interpreter, and diplomat. With her help, Lewis and Clark navigated the upper Missouri, crossed the

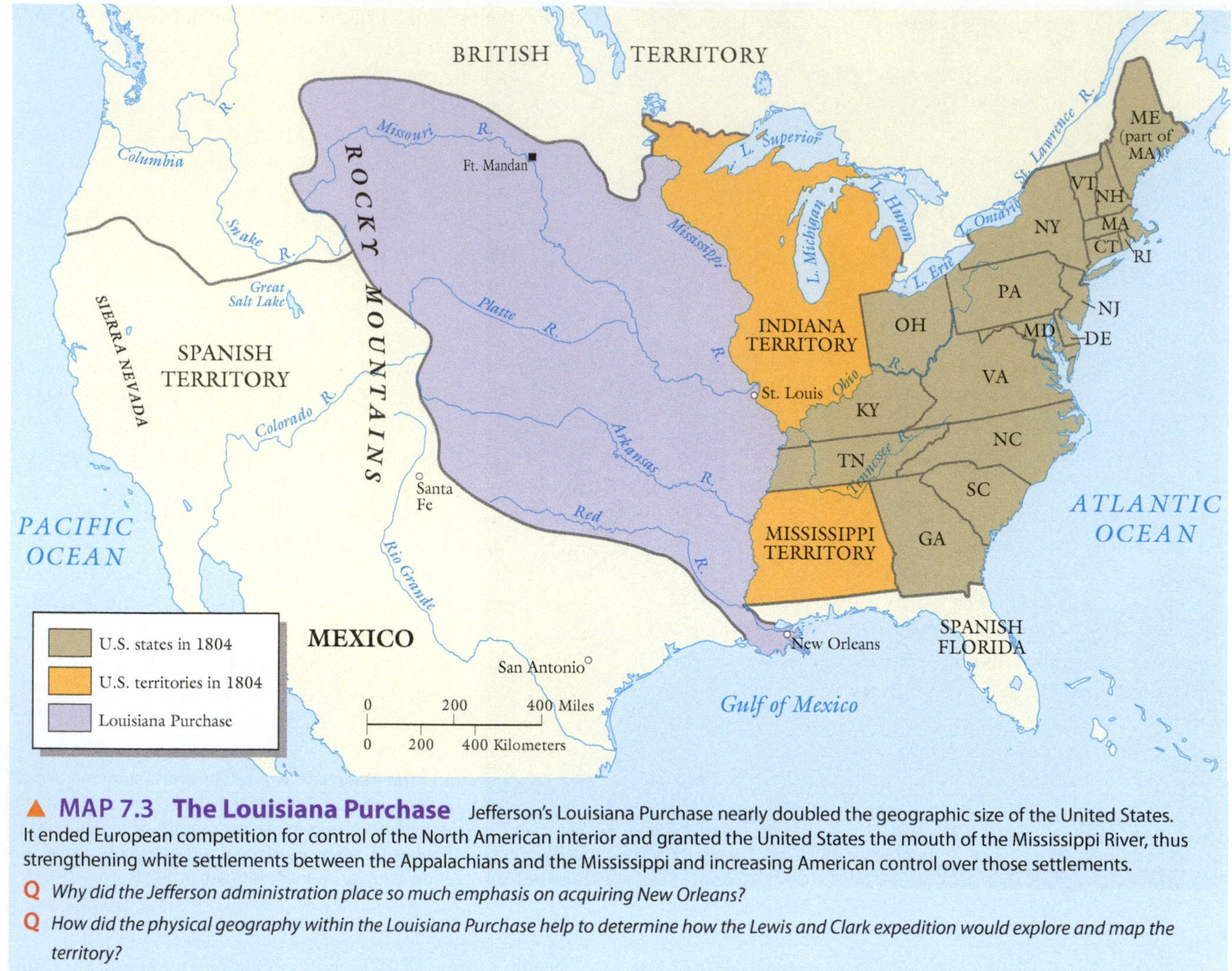

▲ **MAP 7.3 The Louisiana Purchase** Jefferson's Louisiana Purchase nearly doubled the geographic size of the United States. It ended European competition for control of the North American interior and granted the United States the mouth of the Mississippi River, thus strengthening white settlements between the Appalachians and the Mississippi and increasing American control over those settlements.

Q *Why did the Jefferson administration place so much emphasis on acquiring New Orleans?*

Q *How did the physical geography within the Louisiana Purchase help to determine how the Lewis and Clark expedition would explore and map the territory?*

Rockies to the Snake River, and followed that stream to the Columbia River. They reached the Pacific in November 1805 and spent the winter at what is now Astoria, Oregon. Retracing their steps the following spring and summer, they returned to St. Louis in September 1806. They brought with them many volumes of drawings and notes, along with assurances that the Louisiana Purchase had been worth many, many times its price.

As Jefferson stood for reelection in 1804, he could look back on an astonishingly successful first term. He had dismantled the government's power to coerce its citizens, and he had begun to wipe out the national debt. The Louisiana Purchase had doubled the size of the republic at remarkably little cost. Moreover, by eliminating France from North America, it had strengthened the argument for reducing the military and the debts and taxes that went with it. Jefferson was more certain than ever that the republic could preserve itself through peaceful expansion. The "wise and frugal" government he had promised in 1801 was becoming a reality.

The combination of international peace, territorial expansion, and inexpensive, unobtrusive government left the Federalists without an issue in the 1804 election. They nominated Charles Cotesworth Pinckney of South Carolina as their presidential candidate and then watched Jefferson capture the electoral votes of every state but Delaware and Connecticut. As he began his second term in 1805, Jefferson could assume that he had ended the Federalist threat to the republic.

7-4 The Republic and the Napoleonic Wars, 1803–1815

Q *What was the place of the United States within the changing international politics between 1803 and 1815?*

In spring 1803, a few weeks after closing the deal for Louisiana, Napoleon declared war on Britain. This 11-year war, like the wars of the 1790s, dominated the national politics of the United States. Most Americans wanted to remain neutral. Few Republicans supported Bonaparte as they had supported the French revolutionaries of 1789, and none but the most rabid Federalists wanted to intervene on the side of Britain. Neither France nor Britain, however, would permit American neutrality.

7-4a *The Dilemmas of Neutrality*

At the beginning, both Britain and France, whose rural economies were disrupted by war, encouraged the Americans to resume their role as neutral carriers and suppliers of food. For a time, Americans made huge profits. Between 1803 and 1807, U.S. exports—mostly foodstuffs and plantation staples—rose from $66.5 million to $102.2 million. Reexports—goods produced in the British, Spanish, and French islands of the Caribbean, picked up by American vessels, and then reloaded in American ports onto American ships bound for Europe—rose even faster, from $13.5 million to $58.4 million.

In 1805, the Royal Navy under Admiral Lord Horatio Nelson destroyed the French and Spanish fleets at the Battle of Trafalgar. Later that year, Napoleon's armies won a decisive victory over Austria and Russia at the Battle of Austerlitz and won effective control of Europe. The war reached a stalemate: Napoleon's army occupied Europe, and the British navy controlled the seas.

Britain decided to use its naval supremacy to blockade Europe and starve the French into submission. The Essex Decision of 1805 empowered the Royal Navy to seize American ships engaged in the reexport trade with France. Then Britain blockaded long stretches of the European coast. Napoleon responded with the Berlin Decree, outlawing all trade with the British Isles. The British answered with an Order in Council, which demanded that neutral ships trading with Europe stop first for inspection and licensing in a British port. Napoleon responded with the Milan Decree, which stated that any vessel that obeyed the British decrees or allowed itself to be searched by the Royal Navy was subject to seizure by France. Beginning in 1805 and ending with the Milan Decree in December 1807, the barrage of European decrees and counter-decrees meant that one or the other of the warring powers would outlaw virtually all American commerce with Europe.

7-4b *Trouble on the High Seas*

Given British naval supremacy, France had few opportunities to harass American shipping. The Royal Navy, on the other hand, maintained a loose blockade of the North American coast and stopped and searched American ships as they left the major seaports. Hundreds of ships were seized, along with their cargoes and crews. Many British sailors, including legions of deserters from the Royal Navy, continued to hide in the American merchant marine, where they avoided the danger, low pay, bad food, and draconian discipline of the British navy. British ships commandeered those men. They also took British subjects who had taken out U.S. citizenship (an act the British did not recognize) and native-born Americans, particularly those who still bore a cultural resemblance to the British in their dress, speech, and manners. An estimated 10,000 American citizens were impressed into the Royal Navy between 1793 and 1812, more than 6,000 of them after the resumption of the Anglo-French wars in 1803. American diplomats and newspapers protested the practice by using the menacing term "**impressment**," as opposed to the more common British terms "press" or "impress," to describe the systematic violation of U.S. sovereignty.

The kidnapping of American sailors enraged Americans and brought the country close to war in summer 1807. In June, the American naval frigate *Chesapeake* signed on four English deserters from the British navy, along with some Americans who had joined the British navy, and then deserted. Some of the deserters spotted their old officers from HMS *Leopard* in Norfolk, Virginia, and taunted them on the streets. The *Leopard* left port and resumed its patrol of the American coast. On June 21, the *Leopard* caught the *Chesapeake* off Hampton Roads and demanded the return of the British deserters. When the American captain refused, the British fired on the *Chesapeake*, killing three Americans and wounding 18. The British then boarded the *Chesapeake*, seized the four deserters, and later hanged one of them.

The *Chesapeake* affair set off huge anti-British demonstrations in the seaport towns and angry cries for war throughout the country. President Jefferson responded by barring British ships from American ports and American territorial waters and by ordering state governors to prepare to call up as many as 100,000 militiamen. The United States in 1807 stood at the brink of full-scale war with the most powerful nation in the world.

7-4c *Embargo*

Jefferson wanted to avoid war, which would inevitably bring high taxes, government debt, a bloated military and civil service, and the repression of dissent—precisely the evils that Jefferson had vowed to eliminate. Worse, war carried the danger of defeat and thus the possible failure of the United States.

Jefferson had one more card to play: He could suspend trade with Europe altogether and thus keep American ships out of harm's way. Jefferson assumed that U.S. farm products and the U.S. market for imported goods were crucial to the European economies. He could use trade as a means of "peaceable coercion" to enforce respect for American neutral rights and keep the country out of war. Convinced that America's yeoman republic could survive without European luxuries more easily than Europe could survive without American food, Jefferson decided to give "peaceable coercion" a serious test. Late in 1807, he asked Congress to suspend all U.S. trade with foreign countries.

Congress passed the **Embargo Act** on December 22. Within a few months, it was clear that it would not work. The British found other markets and other sources of food. The embargo most hurt American commerce. Its 1807 exports of $108 million dropped to $22 million in 1808. The economy slowed in every section of the country, but it ground to a halt in the cities of the Northeast. While much of the oceangoing merchant fleet rotted at anchor, unemployed sailors, dockworkers, and other maritime workers and their families sank to levels of economic despair seldom seen in British North America. Federalists accused Jefferson of plotting an end to commerce and a reversion to rural barbarism, and they often took the lead in trying to subvert the embargo through smuggling and other means.

Interpreting the Visual Past

Capturing the World: The Illustrations of the Journals of Lewis and Clark

President Thomas Jefferson had several goals for the Lewis and Clark expedition, ranging from geographical discovery to the establishment of trade with Native Americans and the consolidation of U.S. sovereignty over the newly acquired lands. He also instructed the team to observe and record the region's indigenous habitants, flora, fauna, minerals, soil, topography, and climate. As the expedition's naturalist, Lewis drew several detailed illustrations of animals, including this one of the eulachon (*Thaleichthys pacificus*), a small migratory ocean fish that lives along the Pacific coast. The drawings are interesting in their own right as artifacts of one of the most influential expeditions in American history, but a historian might want to probe their broader political and cultural implications. A straightforward drawing of a fish can prompt questions that illuminate an entire society and epoch.

Q *What do drawings like this one suggest about early 19th-century American views of nature and the environment? How was the Lewis and Clark expedition as a scientific endeavor a product of its time?*

Q *How did the geopolitical, commercial, and scientific goals of the expedition support one another? In what ways can describing, naming, and classifying nature be a political act?*

The Granger Collection, NYC

7.8 **Meriwether Lewis, Drawing of an Eulachon from the Journals of the Lewis and Clark Expedition, 1806.**

The Federalists gained ground in the elections of 1808. James Madison, Jefferson's old ally and chosen successor, was elected president with 122 electoral votes to 47 for his Federalist opponent, Charles Cotesworth Pinckney. Although Republicans retained control of both houses of Congress, Federalists made significant gains in Congress and won control of several state legislatures. Federalist opposition to the embargo, and to the supposed southern, agrarian stranglehold on national power, was gaining ground.

7-4d *The Road to War*

When President Madison took office in spring 1809, it was clear that the embargo had failed. It created misery in the seaport cities, choked off the imports that provided 90 percent of federal revenue, and revived Federalist opposition to Republican dominance. Early in 1809, Congress passed the Non-Intercourse Act, which retained the ban on trade with Britain and France but reopened trade with other nations. It also gave President Madison the power to reopen trade with either Britain or France once one of the countries agreed to respect American rights. Neither complied, and the Non-Intercourse Act proved nearly as ineffective as the embargo.

In 1810, Congress passed Macon's Bill No. 2, a complex piece of legislation that rescinded the ban on trade with France and Britain but also authorized the president to reimpose the Non-Intercourse Act on either belligerent if the other agreed to end its restrictions on U.S. trade. Napoleon decided to test the Americans. In September 1810, the French promised, with vague conditions, that France would repeal the Berlin and Milan Decrees. Although the proposal was a clear attempt to lead the United States into conflict with Great Britain, Madison saw no choice but to go along with it. He accepted the French promise and proclaimed in November 1810 that the British had three months to follow suit.

In the end, Madison's proclamation led to war. The French repealed only those sections of the Berlin and Milan Decrees that applied to the neutral rights of the United States. The British refused to revoke their Orders in Council and told the Americans to withdraw their restrictions on British trade until the French had repealed theirs. The United States would either have to obey British orders (thus making American exports and the American merchant marine a part of the British war effort—a neocolonial situation that was utterly repugnant to most Americans) or go to war. When Congress reconvened in November 1811, it voted military measures in preparation for war with Great Britain.

7-4e *The War Hawk Congress, 1811–1812*

Republicans controlled both houses of Congress in 1811–1812; they made up 75 percent of the House and 82 percent of the Senate, but they were a divided majority. The Federalist minority was united in opposition to Madison. The Federalists were often joined by northeastern Republicans who followed the pro-British, Federalist line on international trade, and by Republicans who wanted a more powerful military than other Republicans would allow. Also opposed to Madison were the self-styled Old Republicans of the South, led by John Randolph. It was a deeply divided Congress that met the war crisis.

In this confused situation, a group of talented young congressmen took control. Nearly all of them were Republicans from the South or the West: Richard M. Johnson and Henry Clay of Kentucky, John C. Calhoun and William Lowndes of South Carolina, George M. Troup of Georgia, Peter B. Porter from the Niagara district of New York, and others. Called the **War Hawks**, these ardent nationalists wanted to declare war on England to protect U.S. rights. Through their organizational, oratorical, and intellectual power, they won control of Congress. Henry Clay, only 34 years old and serving his first term in Congress, was elected Speaker of the House. More vigorous than his predecessors, Clay controlled debate, packed key committees, worked tirelessly behind the scenes, and imposed order on his fellow congressmen.

In the winter and spring of 1811–1812, the War Hawks led Congress into a declaration of war. In November they voted military preparations, and in April they enacted a 90-day embargo—not to coerce the British but to return American ships safely to port before war began. On June 1, Madison sent a war message to Congress. This was to be the first war declared under the Constitution, and the president stayed out of congressional territory by not asking explicitly for a declaration of war. He did, however, present a list of British crimes that could be interpreted in no other way: (1) the enforcement of the Orders in Council, even within the territorial waters of the United States; (2) the impressment of American seamen; (3) the use of spies and provocateurs within the United States; and (4) the wielding of "a malicious influence over the Indians of the Northwest Territory."

Congress declared war on June 18. The vote was far from unanimous: 79 to 49 in the House of Representatives, 19 to 13 in the Senate. All 30 Federalists voted against the declaration, as did one in five Republicans, nearly all of them from the Northeast. Thus, the war was declared by the Democratic

North Wind/North Wind Picture Archives

7.9 **Henry Clay** This portrait of Henry Clay was engraved at about the time the brilliant first-term congressman from Kentucky, as Speaker of the House, helped his fellow War Hawks steer the United States into the War of 1812.

Republican Party, more particularly by the Republicans of the South and the West. The Northeast, whose commercial rights were supposedly the issue at stake, opposed the declaration.

7-4f *American Strategy in 1812*

The War Hawks declared a war to defend the sovereignty, the western territory, and the maritime rights of the United States. The war they planned and fought, however, bore the stamp of southern and western Republicanism. Federalists and many northeastern Republicans expected a naval war. After all, the British had committed their atrocities on the ocean, and some, remembering U.S. naval successes against France in the Quasi War of 1798–1800, predicted similar successes against Great Britain. Yet, when Madison asked Congress to prepare for war, the War Hawks led a majority that strengthened the U.S. Army and left the navy weak. Reasoning that no U.S. naval force could challenge British control of the seas, they prepared instead for a land invasion of British Canada.

The decision to invade Canada led the Federalists, along with many of Randolph's Old Republicans, to accuse Madison and the congressional majority of planning a war of territorial aggression. Some members of Congress did want to annex Canada to the United States, but most saw the decision to invade Canada as a matter of strategy. Lightly garrisoned and with a population of only half a million (many of them French, and most of the others American émigrés of doubtful loyalties), Canada seemed the easiest and most logical place in which to damage the British. It was also from bases in Canada that the British armed the Indians of the Northwest, and western Republicans were determined to end that threat decisively. Indeed, many Republicans saw Canada as a counterrevolutionary monarchist regime that was posed to roll back American republicanism and pull the United States back into Britain's imperial fold. Finally, Canada was a valuable colony of Britain. The American embargoes, coupled with Napoleon's control of Europe, had impaired Britain's ability to supply its plantation colonies in the West Indies, and Canadian farmers had begun to fill the gap. Thus, Canada was both valuable and vulnerable, and American policymakers reasoned that they could take it and hold it hostage while demanding that the British back down on other issues. Although U.S. military strategy focused on Canada, maritime rights and national honor, along with the British-fed Indian threat west of the Appalachians, were the central issues in 1812.

7-4g *The Rise of Tecumseh*

Native peoples east of the Mississippi River recognized alliances with Britain as a final chance to hold back American settlers. Northwestern Indians had lost much of their land at the Battle of Fallen Timbers and the Treaty of Greenville. Relegated to smaller territory but still dependent on the European fur trade, they fell into competition with settlers and other Indians for the diminishing supply of game. The Creeks, Choctaws, and other nations of the Southeast faced the same problem: Even when they chased settlers out of their territory, the settlers managed to kill or scare off the deer and other wildlife, thus ruining the old hunting grounds. When the Shawnee sent hunting parties farther west, they met irate western Indians. The Choctaws also sent hunters across the Mississippi, where they found both new sources of furs and angry warriors of the Osage and other peoples of Louisiana and Arkansas. The Indians of the interior now realized that the days of the fur trade, on which they depended for survival, were numbered.

Faced with shrinking territories, the disappearance of wildlife, and diminished opportunities to be traditional hunters and warriors, many Indian societies sank into despair. Epidemics of European diseases (smallpox, influenza, measles) attacked peoples who were increasingly sedentary and vulnerable. Old internal frictions grew nastier. In the Southeast, full-blooded Indians came into conflict with mixed-blood Indians, who often no longer spoke the native language and who wanted their people to adopt white ways. Murder and clan revenge plagued native communities, and depression and suicide became more common. The use of alcohol, which had been a scourge on Indian societies for two centuries, increased. Indian males spent more time in their villages and less on the hunt, and by most accounts they drank more and grew more violent when they drank.

Out of this cultural wreckage emerged visionary leaders who spoke of a regenerated native society and the expulsion of all whites from the old tribal lands. The prophet who came closest to military success was Tenskwatawa, a Shawnee who had failed as a warrior and medicine man. He went into a deep trance in 1805 and awoke with a prophetic vision not unlike Neolin's in the early 1760s (see Chapter 5). First, all Indians must stop drinking and fighting among themselves. They must also return to their traditional food, clothing, tools, and hairstyles, and must extinguish all of their fires and start new ones without using European tools. All who opposed the new order (including local chiefs, medicine men, shamans, and witches) must be put down by force. When all of that had been done, God (a monotheistic, punishing God borrowed from the Christians) would restore the world that Indians had known before the whites came over the mountains.

Tenskwatawa's message soon found its way to the Delawares (who attacked the Christians among their people as witches) and other native peoples of the Northeast. Several native leaders who had embraced the United States' civilization program were executed. When converts flooded into the prophet's home village, he moved to Prophetstown (Tippecanoe) in what is now Indiana. There, with the help of his brother Tecumseh, he created an army estimated by the whites at anywhere between 650 and 3,000. Tecumseh, who took control of the movement, announced to the whites that he was the sole chief of all the Indians north of the Ohio River. Land cessions by anyone else would be invalid. Tenskwatawa's prophecy and Tecumseh's leadership had united the Indians of the Northwest in an unprecedented stand against white encroachment.

Tecumseh's confederacy posed a threat to the United States. A second war with England was looming, and Tecumseh was receiving supplies and encouragement from the British in Canada. He was also planning to visit the southern Indians in an attempt to bring them into his confederacy. The prospect of unified resistance by the western tribes in league with the British jeopardized every settler west of the Appalachians. In 1811, William Henry Harrison led an army toward Prophetstown. With Tecumseh away in the South, Tenskwatawa ordered a risky attack on Harrison's army and was beaten at the Battle of Tippecanoe. But Tecumseh's confederacy remained a formidable opponent of the United States.

7-4h *The War with Canada, 1812–1813*

The United States attacked Canada in 1812, with disastrous results (see Map 7.4). The plan was to invade Upper Canada (Ontario) from the Northwest, thus cutting off the Shawnee, Potawatomi, and other pro-British Indian tribes from their British support. When General William Hull, governor of Michigan Territory, took a poorly supplied, badly led army of militiamen and volunteers into Canada from a base in Detroit, he found that the British had outguessed him. The area was crawling with British troops and their Indian allies. With detachments of his army overrun and his supply lines cut, he retreated to the garrison at Detroit. Under siege, he heard that Indian forces had captured the garrison at Fort Dearborn (Chicago) and sacked Fort Mackinac in northern Michigan Territory. British general Isaac Brock, who knew that Hull was afraid of Indians, sent a note into the fort telling him, "the numerous body of Indians who have attached themselves to my troops, will be beyond my controul the moment the contest commences." Without consulting his officers, Hull surrendered his army of 2,000 to the smaller British force. Hull was later court-martialed for cowardice, but the damage was done: The British and Indians transformed the American invasion of Upper Canada into a British occupation of much of the Northwest—the largest surrender of U.S. territory in history.

The invasion of Canada from the east went no better. In October a U.S. force of 6,000 faced 2,000 British and Indians across the Niagara River separating Ontario from western New York. The U.S. regular army crossed the river, surprised the British, and established a toehold at Queenston Heights. While the British prepared a counterattack, New York militiamen refused to cross the river to reinforce the regulars. Ohio militiamen had behaved the same way when Hull invaded Canada, and similar problems had arisen with the New York militia near Lake Champlain. Throughout the war, citizen-soldiers proved that Jefferson's confidence in the militia could not be extended to the invasion of other countries. The British regrouped and slaughtered the outnumbered, exhausted U.S. regulars at Queenston Heights.

As winter set in, it was clear that Canada would not fall as easily as the Americans had assumed. The invasion, which U.S. commanders had thought would knife through an apathetic Canadian population, had the opposite effect: The attacks by the United States turned the ragtag assortment of American loyalist émigrés discharged British soldiers, and American-born settlers into a self-consciously British Canadian people.

7-4i *Tecumseh's Last Stand*

Tecumseh's confederacy, bruised but not broken in the Battle of Tippecanoe, allied itself with the British in 1812. On a trip to the southern tribes, Tecumseh found the traditionalist wing of the Creeks—led by medicine men who called themselves Red Sticks—willing to join him. The augmented confederacy provided stiff resistance to the United States throughout the war. The Red Sticks chased settlers from much of Tennessee. They then attacked a group of settlers who had taken refuge in a stockade surrounding the house of an Alabama trader named George Mims. In what whites called the Massacre at Fort Mims, the Red Sticks (reputedly in collusion with the black slaves within the fort) killed at least 247 men, women, and children. In the Northwest, Tecumseh's warriors, fighting alongside the British, spread terror throughout the white settlements.

A wiser U.S. Army returned to Canada in 1813. It raided and burned the Canadian capital at York (Toronto) in April, and then fought inconclusively throughout the summer. An autumn offensive toward Montreal failed, but the Americans had better luck on Lake Erie. The barrier of Niagara Falls kept Britain's saltwater navy out of the upper Great Lakes, and on Lake Erie, the British and Americans engaged in a frenzied shipbuilding contest throughout the first year of the war. The Americans won. In September 1813, Commodore Oliver Hazard Perry destroyed the British fleet off the American anchorage at Put-in-Bay, after which he reported triumphantly to General William Henry Harrison: "We have met the enemy and they are ours."

Control of Lake Erie enabled the United States to cut off supplies to the British in the Northwest, and Harrison's army retook the area and continued on into Canada. On October 5, Harrison caught up with a force of British and Indians at the Thames River and beat them badly. In the course of that battle, Richard M. Johnson, a War Hawk congressman acting as commander of the Kentucky militia, was credited with killing Tecumseh. Proud militiamen returned to Kentucky with pieces of hair and clothing and even swatches of skin torn from Tecumseh's corpse. Their officers reaped huge political rewards: The Battle of the Thames would produce a president of the United States (Harrison), a vice president (Johnson), three governors of Kentucky, three lieutenant governors, four U.S. senators, and about 20 congressmen—telling evidence of how seriously the settlers of the interior had taken Tecumseh.

The following spring, General Andrew Jackson's Tennessee militia, aided by Choctaw, Creek, and Cherokee allies, attacked and slaughtered the Red Sticks, who had fortified themselves at Horseshoe Bend in Alabama. Jackson enforced a treaty on the Creeks, who ceded 22 million acres of land in the Mississippi Territory. With the Battle of the Thames and the Battle of Horseshoe Bend, the military power of the Indian peoples east of the Mississippi River was broken.

7-4j *The British Offensive, 1814*

The British defeated Napoleon in April 1814, thus ending the war in Europe. They then turned their attention to the American war and went on the offensive. They had already blockaded

▲ **MAP 7.4 War of 1812** Early in the war, Americans chose to fight the British in Canada, with costly and inconclusive results. Later, the British determined to blockade the whole coast of the United States and, late in the war, to raid important coastal towns. The results were equally inconclusive: Both sides could inflict serious damage, but neither could conquer the other. The one clear military outcome—one that the Americans were determined to accomplish—was the destruction of Indian resistance east of the Mississippi.

Q *What options did the Americans have for attacking the British in the War of 1812?*

Q *Despite the United States having a far greater population in North America, what important tactical advantage did the British establish in the war?*

much of the American coast from Georgia to Maine. During summer 1814, they raided Chesapeake Bay and marched on Washington, D.C. They chased the army and politicians out of town and burned down the Capitol building and the president's mansion. In September, the British attacked Baltimore, but could not blast their way past the determined garrison that commanded the harbor from Fort McHenry. This was the battle that inspired Francis Scott Key to write the lyrics of "The Star-Spangled Banner," which was set to the tune of an old English drinking song ("To Anacreon in Heaven," music by John

Stafford Smith). It became the national anthem in the 1930s. When a British offensive on Lake Champlain stalled during the autumn, the war reached a stalemate: Britain had turned back the invasion of Canada and had blockaded the American coast, but neither side could take and hold the other's territory.

The British now shifted their attention to the Gulf Coast, particularly to New Orleans, a city of vital importance to U.S. trans-Appalachian trade and communications. Peace negotiations had begun in August, and the British wanted to capture and hold New Orleans as a bargaining chip. A large British force landed eight miles south of New Orleans. There they met an American army made up of U.S. regulars, Kentucky and Tennessee militiamen, clerks, workingmen, free blacks from the city, and about a thousand French pirates—all under the command of Andrew Jackson of Tennessee. Throughout late December and early January, unaware that a peace treaty had been signed on December 24, the armies exchanged artillery barrages and the British probed and attacked American lines. On January 8, they launched a frontal assault. A formation of 6,000 British soldiers marched across open ground toward 4,000 Americans concealed behind breastworks. With the first American volley, it was clear that the British had made a mistake. Veterans of the bloodiest battles of the Napoleonic wars swore that they had never seen such withering fire; soldiers in the front ranks who were not cut down threw themselves to the ground and surrendered when the shooting stopped. The charge lasted half an hour. At the end, 2,000 British soldiers lay dead or wounded. American casualties numbered only 70. Fought nearly two weeks after the peace treaty, the Battle of New Orleans had no effect on the outcome of the war or on the peace terms, but it salved the injured pride of

Library of Congress, Prints and Photographs Division

7.10 **Death of Tecumseh** The Battle of the Thames relieved the Northwest of the British and Indian threat. Through prints like this, Richard M. Johnson gained the reputation for killing Tecumseh.

Americans, fostered a potent and unifying patriotism, and made a national hero and a political power of Andrew Jackson.

7-4k The Hartford Convention

While most of the nation celebrated Jackson's victory, events in Federalist New England went differently. New Englanders had disliked Republican trade policies, and their congressmen had voted overwhelmingly against going to war. The New England states seldom met their quotas of militiamen for the war effort, and some Federalist leaders had openly urged resistance to the war. The British had encouraged that resistance by not extending their naval blockade to the New England coast, and throughout the first two years of the war, New England merchants and farmers had traded freely with the enemy. In 1814, after the Royal Navy had extended its blockade northward and had begun to raid the towns of coastal Maine, some Federalists talked openly about seceding and making a separate peace with Britain.

In an attempt to undercut the secessionists, moderate Federalists called a convention at Hartford to air the region's grievances. The Hartford Convention, which met in late December 1814, proposed amendments to the Constitution that indicated New England's position as a self-conscious minority within the Union. First, the convention delegates wanted the "three-fifths" clause, which led to overrepresentation of the South in Congress, and the Electoral College (see Chapter 6) stricken from the Constitution. They also wanted to deny naturalized citizens—who were strongly Republican—the right to hold office. They wanted to make it more difficult for new states, all of which sided with the Republicans and their southern leadership, to enter the Union. Finally, they wanted to require a two-thirds majority of both houses for a declaration of war—a requirement that would have prevented the War of 1812.

Leaders of the Hartford Convention, satisfied that they had headed off the secessionists, took their proposals to Washington in mid-January. They arrived to find the capital celebrating news of the peace treaty and Jackson's victory at New Orleans. When they aired their sectional complaints, they were branded as traitors. Although Federalists continued for a few years to wield power in southern New England, the Hartford debacle ruined any chance of a nationwide Federalist resurgence after the war. Andrew Jackson had stolen control of American history from New England. He would do so again in the years ahead.

7-4l The Treaty of Ghent

Britain's defeat of Napoleon had spurred British and American efforts to end a war that neither wanted. In August 1814, they opened peace talks in the Belgian city of Ghent. Perhaps waiting for the results of their 1814 offensive, the British opened with proposals that the Americans were certain to reject. They demanded the right to navigate the Mississippi. Moreover, they wanted territorial concessions and the creation of the permanent, independent Indian buffer state in the Northwest that they had promised their Indian allies. The Americans ignored these proposals and talked instead about impressment and maritime rights. As the autumn wore on and the war reached stalemate, both sides began to compromise. The British knew that the Americans would grant concessions in the interior only if they were thoroughly defeated, an outcome that British commanders thought impossible. For their part, the Americans realized that British maritime depredations were by-products of the struggle with Napoleonic France. Faced with peace in Europe and a senseless military stalemate in North America, negotiators on both sides began to withdraw their demands. The Treaty of Ghent, signed on Christmas Eve

7.11 ***The Taking of the City of Washington* (1814)** The United States suffered one of its greatest military embarrassments in 1814, when the British raided Washington, D.C., brushed off the opposition, and burned most government buildings, including the president's house and the Capitol building.

Q *Are there any clues that this print was produced in London rather than in America?*

History Through Film

Master and Commander: The Far Side of the World (2003)

Directed by Peter Weir.
Starring Russell Crowe (Capt. Jack Aubrey), Paul Bettany (Dr. Stephen Maturin), James D'Arcy (1st Lt. Tom Pullings), Max Pirkis (Blakeney, midshipman), Billy Boyd (Barrett Bonden, coxswain).

Peter Weir directed this epic historical drama based on the acclaimed Aubrey-Maturin sea novel series by Patrick O'Brian. The year is 1805. As Britain and France duel for global supremacy during the Napoleonic Wars, British navy captain "Lucky" Jack Aubrey (Russell Crowe) receives orders off the northern coast of Brazil to "intercept French Privateer Acheron en route to Pacific intent on carrying the war into those waters . . . Sink, Burn or take her a Prize." The film's action follows Aubrey's frigate, HMS *Surprise*, south in pursuit of Acheron around Cape Horn and into the Pacific. Aubrey's close friend, the naval surgeon Stephen Maturin (Paul Bettany), joins him throughout this adventure to "the far side of the world."

The film borrows scenes and dialogue from more than a dozen of the twenty novels in O'Brian's series. The movie title comes from the first book in the series, *Master and Commander*, and refers to an officer rank in the British navy that Aubrey received upon getting his first ship command in 1800 (by 1805, he has been promoted to post-captain). The subtitle comes from the tenth novel, *The Far Side of the World*, from which the film also gets its plot, with a crucial difference: The enemy in the novel is not a French privateer but an American navy frigate, USS *Norfolk*, during the War of 1812. The film's producers changed the villain, worrying that American audiences would not cheer the sinking of the Stars and Stripes, especially so close to the terrorist attacks of September 11 (the film was released in 2003).

The decision kept the War of 1812 from providing the backdrop for at least one truly great film. Yet, the war still has an indirect influence on the movie. In *The Far Side of the World*, O'Brian based the fictional *Norfolk* on the actual American frigate USS *Essex*. Commanded by Captain David Porter, *Essex* wreaked havoc on Britain's Pacific whaling fleet in 1813, before being decimated by the British navy off the coast of Valparaiso, Chile, in 1814. In the film, *Acheron's* French captain (Thierry Segall) channels Porter's mischievous spirit. Moreover, as a 44-gun "super frigate" with a heavy, reinforced hull, *Acheron* overmatches the 28-gun *Surprise*, much like USS *Constitution* (nicknamed "Old Ironsides") and other oversized American frigates dominated their British counterparts in the War of 1812. If *Acheron* seems like *Constitution* in French sheathing, it is no accident. The film's special-effects team created computer models of the French privateer based on digital images of "Old Ironsides."

Regardless of Britain's enemy, the *Master and Commander* film, like the book series, provides insight into how the Royal Navy became the supreme fighting force of its time, on sea or land. The wooden world of a sailing vessel reproduced the social hierarchy and inequities of British society. It required teams of skilled seafarers, many of them pressed into service, to keep a British naval vessel afloat. At the same time, the navy produced real-life Aubreys, officers who used shipboard discipline, skilled leadership, and superior seamanship to keep their large, diverse crews working in unison. Through the magic of cinema, viewers appreciate how these men braved storms, tedium, and the horrific violence of naval warfare.

Master and Commander delights with other historical details and references. Without physically appearing, Britain's greatest naval hero, Admiral Nelson, has a presence in the film, both through Aubrey's firsthand accounts and as an inspiration to the young midshipman Blakeney (Max Pirkis). Like Nelson, Blakeney loses his arm in battle. By incorporating the Galapagos Islands from O'Brian's storyline, Weir also makes clever allusions to Charles Darwin. Maturin, a naturalist as well as a physician, collects many of the same specimens that Darwin later used to conceive of the idea of evolution through natural selection. Maturin is denied the achievement because he has to abandon his discoveries in the name of duty.

Weir and Crowe had aspirations of turning *Master and Commander* into a series, but its box office returns did not justify a sequel. Instead, another maritime saga released in 2003, *Pirates of the Caribbean*, based on the Disneyland theme park attraction, would become a franchise. This is unfortunate. Not simply the lesser of two evils (or "lesser of two weevils," as Jack Aubrey might say), *Master and Commander* is the finest film on the Age of Sail ever made. ■

Everett Collection/Glow images

7.12 Russell Crowe stars as the fictional British navy captain Jack Aubrey in *Master and Commander: The Far Side of the World.*

The New York Public Library/Art Resource, NY

7.13 ***A View of the Bombardment of Fort McHenry* by J. Bower, 1816** The British attack on Baltimore depended upon getting past Fort McHenry, which guarded the approach to the harbor. The Americans strengthened the garrison and blocked the narrow inlet with sunken ships. British ships fired as many as 1,800 exploding shells at the fort, to no avail. Baltimore's Francis Scott Key was aboard a British vessel (he was trying to negotiate the release of a prisoner). He witnessed the bombardment and wrote a poem entitled "The Defense of Fort McHenry," which eventually became the national anthem.

1814, simply ended the war. The border between Canada and the United States remained where it had been in 1812; Indians south of that border—defeated and without allies—were left to the mercy of the United States; and British maritime violations were not mentioned. The makers of the treaty stopped a war that neither side could win, trusting that a period of peace would resolve the problems created by two decades of world war.

Conclusion

In 1816, Thomas Jefferson was in retirement at Monticello, satisfied that he had defended liberty against the Federalists' love of power. The High Federalists' attempt to consolidate power, militarize government, and jail their opposition had failed. Their direct taxes were repealed. Their debt and their national bank remained in place, but only under the watchful eyes of true republicans. And their attempt to ally the United States with the antirepublican designs of Britain had ended in what many called the Second War of American Independence. American independence was truly won, and Jefferson's vision of a union of independent republican states seemed to have been realized.

Yet, for all his successes, Jefferson saw that he must sacrifice some of his longest-held dreams. Jefferson's republican ideal was grounded in farmer-citizens whose vision was local and who wanted nothing more from government than protection of their property and rights. Jefferson's imagined yeomen traded farm surpluses for European manufactured goods—a system that encouraged rural prosperity, prevented the growth of cities and factories (the much-feared nurseries of corruption and dependence), and thus sustained the landed independence on which republican citizenship rested. Westward expansion, Jefferson had believed, would ensure the yeoman republic for generations to come. By 1816, that dream was ended. The British and French had "cover[ed] the earth and sea with robberies and piracies," disrupting America's vital export economy whenever it suited their whims. Arguing as Hamilton had argued in 1790, Jefferson insisted, "we must now place the manufacturer by the side of the agriculturalist."

CHAPTER REVIEW

Review

1. What was the Federalist plan for organizing the national government and its finances?
2. What were the principal foreign and internal threats to the newly independent United States in the late 18th century?
3. What were the principal reforms of the national government during Thomas Jefferson's administration?
4. What was the place of the United States within the changing international politics between 1803 and 1815?

Critical Thinking

1. In the 1790s, Federalists and Democratic Republicans argued about the nature of the new national government. On what specific issues was this argument conducted? Was there a larger argument underlying these specifics?
2. Thomas Jefferson had a vision of the American republic and of the role of the national government within it. In what ways did his presidency succeed in realizing that vision? In what ways did it fail?

Identifications

Review your understanding of the following key terms, people, and events for this chapter (terms in bold in text are included in the Glossary).

tariff, p. 202
Bill of Rights, p. 202
circuit court, p. 202
excise tax, p. 204
Whiskey Rebellion, p. 208
impeachment, p. 211
XYZ Affair, p. 211
Alien and Sedition Acts, p. 212
Virginia and Kentucky Resolves, p. 212
High Federalists, p. 212
Aaron Burr, p. 213
Louisiana Purchase, p. 214
midnight judges, p. 215
Marbury v. Madison, p. 216
judicial review, p. 216
impressment, p. 219
Embargo Act, p. 219
War Hawks, p. 221

Suggested Readings

Stanley Elkins and Eric McKitrick, ***The Age of Federalism: The Early American Republic, 1788–1800*** (1993); and **Gordon S. Wood**, ***Empire of Liberty: A History of the American Republic, 1789–1815*** (2009) are definitive surveys of these years. For the politics of the founding generation, see **Stuart Leibiger**, ***Founding Friendship: George Washington, James Madison, and the Creation of the American Republic*** (1999); **Joanne B. Freeman**, ***Affairs of Honor: National Politics in the New Republic*** (2001); and **James Roger Sharp**, ***American Politics in the Early Republic: The New Nation in Crisis*** (1993). **Lance Banning**, ***The Jeffersonian Persuasion: Evolution of a Party Ideology*** (1980); **Drew R. McCoy**, ***The Elusive Republic: Political Economy in Jeffersonian America*** (1980); and **Annette Gordon-Reed and Peter S. Onuf**, ***"Most Blessed of Patriarchs": Thomas Jefferson and the Empire of the Imagination*** (2016) are insightful studies of Jeffersonianism.

Alan Taylor's ***The Civil War of 1812: American Citizens, British Subjects, Irish Rebels, and Indian Allies*** (2010) offers a penetrating look into the complex divisions, anxieties, and ambitions behind the War of 1812. For other perspectives on the crises leading to the war, see **R. David Edmunds**, ***Tecumseh and the Quest for Indian Leadership*** (2006); **Francis D. Cogliano**, ***Emperor of Liberty: Thomas Jefferson's Foreign Policy*** (2014); and **Paul A. Gilje**, ***Free Trade and Sailors' Rights in the War of 1812*** (2013). For an effective survey of the war, see **Donald R. Hickey**, ***The War of 1812: A Forgotten Conflict*** (1989). **Nicole Eustace's** ***1812: War and the Passions of Patriotism*** (2012) explores the American patriotic legacy of the conflict, while **Troy Bickham**, ***The Weight of Vengeance: The United States, the British Empire, and the War of 1812*** **(2012)** details its implications for Britain and Canada.

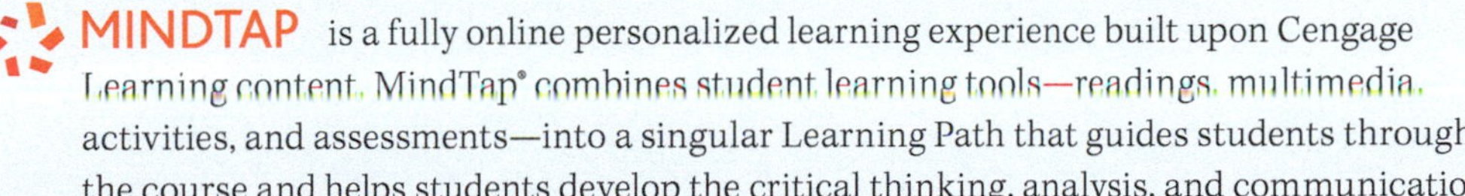

MINDTAP is a fully online personalized learning experience built upon Cengage Learning content. MindTap® combines student learning tools—readings, multimedia, activities, and assessments—into a singular Learning Path that guides students through the course and helps students develop the critical thinking, analysis, and communication skills that are essential to academic and professional success.

8 Northern Transformations, 1790–1850

8-1 Postcolonial Society, 1790–1815

Learning Objective: *Determine the nature of the northern agricultural economy and of agricultural society in the years 1790 to 1815.*

- Farms
- Neighbors
- Standards of Living
- Inheritance
- The Seaport Cities

8-2 The Northwest: From Backcountry to Frontier

Learning Objective: *Detail how eastern opinion of the Northwest and of its settlers changed between 1790 and 1820.*

- The Backcountry, 1790–1815
- Settlement

8-3 Transportation Revolution, 1815–1850

Learning Objective: *List improvements in transportation that channeled commerce within and between regions.*

- Transportation in 1815
- Internal Improvements
- Time, Money, and New Markets

8-4 Northeastern Farms, 1815–1850

Learning Objective: *Analyze how northern farm families experienced the transition into commercial agriculture between 1815 and 1850.*

- The New England Livestock Economy
- New Farm Households
- The Landscape of Privacy

8-5 The Northwest in Transition

Learning Objective: *Describe how northern and southern settlers flooding into the Northwest after 1815 viewed the new market economy differently.*

- Southern Settlers
- Northern Farmers

8-6 The Beginnings of the Industrial Revolution

Learning Objective: *Explain why America's first factories started in the northern countryside.*

- Factory Towns: The Rhode Island System
- Factory Towns: The Waltham-Lowell System
- Cities
- Metropolitan Industrialization

8.1 **A Bird's-Eye View of New York City, 1850** After 1825, prints and lithographs such as this were printed in New York and sent through the new channels of trade to help decorate parlor walls throughout the North and West. This one depicts New York City. The ships surrounding Manhattan Island are testimony to New York's dominance of both coastal and international trade. But maritime occupations were far outnumbered by men and women who manufactured goods and did the paperwork for an expanding market that was transforming the North.

IN 1790, AMERICAN SOCIETY approximated Jefferson's ideal: The United States was a nation of farmers who provided for themselves and sent surpluses overseas to be traded for manufactured goods. To put it in a less bucolic way, Americans remained on the colonial periphery of North Atlantic capitalism. They sent timber, cured fish, wheat, tobacco, rice, and money to Europe (primarily Britain), and Europe (again, Britain was the big player) sent manufactured goods—along with bills for shipping, insurance, banking, and tariff duties—back to America. In the 25 years following adoption of the Constitution, this old relationship fed significant economic growth in the United States, as European wars increased the demand for American produce and American shipping. Americans sent growing mountains of food and raw materials overseas, and they decorated their homes with comforts and small luxuries produced in British factories.

Beginning in the 1790s and accelerating dramatically with the peace of 1815, northern farmers changed that relationship: By 1830, the primary engine of northern economic development was no longer the North Atlantic trade; it was the self-sustained internal development of the northern United States. Northeastern businessmen noted that rural markets were expanding, that imports were unreliable, and that a crowded countryside produced people eager to work for wages.

They began to invest in factories. New factory towns, together with the old seaports and new inland towns that served a commercializing agriculture, provided the country's first significant domestic market for food. Governments of the northern states built roads and canals that linked farmers to distant markets, and farmers turned to cash-crop agriculture and bought necessary goods (and paid mortgages and crop loans) with the money they made. By 1830, a large and growing portion of New England, the mid-Atlantic, and the Northwest had transcended colonial economics to become an interdependent, self-sustaining market society.

The pioneering sociologist Max Weber made a distinction between capitalism and the *spirit* of capitalism. Economic exchange and the desire for profit, Weber noted, have existed in all societies. Only a few, however, have organized capitalism into an everyday culture. Historians have coined the term "**Market Revolution**" to describe the transformation of the North from a society with markets to a market society—a society in which the market was implicated in the ways in which northerners saw the world and dealt with it. This chapter describes that revolution in the North up to 1850. The succeeding chapter describes the very different patterns of change in the South in the same years. ■

8-1 Postcolonial Society, 1790–1815

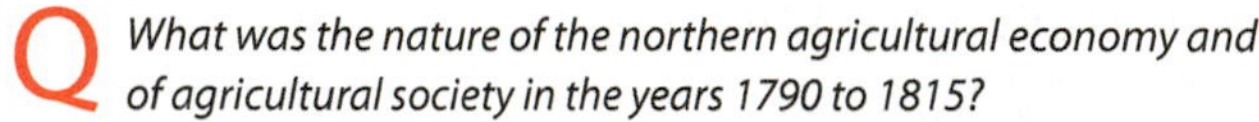

What was the nature of the northern agricultural economy and of agricultural society in the years 1790 to 1815?

In 1782, J. Hector St. John de Crèvecoeur, a French soldier who had settled in rural New York, explained America's agrarian republic through the words of a fictionalized farmer. First of all, he said, the American farmer owns his own land and bases his claim to dignity and citizenship on that fact. Second, according to the farmer, landownership endows the American farmer with the powers and responsibilities of fatherhood. "Often when I plant my low ground," he said, "I place my little boy on a chair which screws to the beam of the plough—its motion and that of the horses please him; he is perfectly happy and begins to chat. As I lean over the handle, various are the thoughts which crowd into my mind. I am now doing for him, I say, what my father did for me; may God enable him to live that he may perform the same operations for the same purposes when I am worn out and old!"

8-1a *Farms*

Crèvecoeur's farmer, musing on liberty and property, working the ancestral fields with his male heir strapped to the plough, was concerned with proprietorship and fatherhood, not with making money. He shared those concerns with most northern farmers. Their first concern was to provide food and common comforts for their households. Their second was to achieve long-term security and the ability to pass their farms on to their sons. The goal was to create what rural folks called a "**competence**": the ability to live up to neighborhood standards of material decency while protecting the long-term independence of the household. Farmers thought of themselves first as fathers, neighbors, and stewards of family resources, and they avoided financial risk. Weather, bad crop years, pests, and unexpected injuries or deaths provided enough of that without adding the uncertainties of cash-crop agriculture and international commodity prices.

In this situation, most farmers played it safe. They raised a variety of animals and plants and did not concentrate on a single cash crop. Most farms in New England and the middle states were divided into corn and grain fields, pasturage for

CHRONOLOGY

1790	Samuel Slater builds his first Arkwright spinning mill at Pawtucket, Rhode Island
1791	Vermont enters the union as the 14th state
1793	Beginning of Anglo-French War • Ohio enters the union as the 17th state
1807	Robert Fulton launches first steamboat
1812	Second war with Britain begins
1813	Boston Associates erect their first textile mill at Waltham, Massachusetts
1815	War of 1812 ends
1818	National Road completed to Ohio River at Wheeling, Virginia
1822	President Monroe vetoes National Road reparations bill
1825	New York completes the Erie Canal between Buffalo and Albany
1828	Baltimore and Ohio Railroad (America's first) completed
1835	Main Line Canal connects Philadelphia and Pittsburgh

animals, woodlands for fuel, a vegetable garden, with perhaps a dairy cow. The multifarious configurations of these farms provided a hedge against the uncertainties of rural life. Farm families ate most of what they grew, bartered much of the rest within their neighborhoods, and gambled surpluses on long-distance trade.

West Indian and European markets for American meat, grain, and corn had been growing since the mid-18th century. They expanded dramatically between 1793 and 1815, when war disrupted farming in Europe. Many northern farmers, particularly in the mid-Atlantic states, expanded production to take advantage of these overseas markets (see Map 8.1). The prosperity and aspirations of hundreds of thousands of farmers rose, and their houses were sprinkled with tokens of comfort and gentility. The same markets, however, sustained traditions of household independence and neighborly cooperation. Farmers continued to provide for their families from their own farms and neighborhoods, and they risked little by increasing their surpluses and sending them overseas. They profited from world markets without becoming dependent on them.

Production for overseas markets after 1790 did, however, alter relationships within farm families—usually in ways that reinforced the independence of the household and the power of its male head. Farm labor in post-revolutionary America was carefully divided by sex. Men worked in the fields, and production for markets both intensified that labor and made it more exclusively male. In the grain fields of the middle states, for instance, the long-handled scythe was replacing the sickle as the principal harvest tool. Women could use the sickle efficiently, but because of its length and weight, men were better able to wield the scythe. At the same time, farmers completed the substitution of ploughs for hoes as the principal cultivating tools—not only because ploughs worked better, but also because rural Americans had developed a prejudice against women working in the fields, and ploughs were male tools. By the early 19th century, visitors to the long-settled farming areas (with the exception of some mid-Atlantic German communities) seldom saw women in the fields. In his travels throughout France, Thomas Jefferson spoke harshly of peasant communities where he saw women doing field labor.

At the same time, household responsibilities multiplied and fell more exclusively to women. Farm women's labor and ingenuity helped create a more varied and nutritious rural diet in these years. Bread and salted meat were still the staples. The bread was the old mix of Indian corn and coarse wheat ("Rye and Injun," the farmers called it), with crust so thick that it was used as a scoop for soups and stews. Though improved brines and pickling techniques augmented the supply of salt meat, farmers' palates doubtless told them it was the same old salt meat.

But by the 1790s, improved winter feeding for cattle and better techniques for making and storing butter and cheese kept dairy products on the tables of the more prosperous farm families throughout the year. Chickens became more common, and farmwomen began to fence and manure their kitchen gardens, planting them with potatoes, turnips, cabbages, squashes, beans, and other vegetables that could be stored in the root cellars that were becoming standard features of farmhouses.

8-1b *Neighbors*

Rural communities were far more than accumulations of independent farm-owning households. The struggle to maintain household independence involved most farm families in elaborate networks of neighborly cooperation, and long-term, give-and-take relationships with neighbors were essential economic and social assets. Few farmers possessed the tools, the labor, and the food they would have needed to be truly self-sufficient. They regularly worked for one another, borrowed oxen and plows, and swapped one kind of food crop for another. Women traded ashes, herbs, butter and eggs, vegetables, seedlings, baby chicks, goose feathers, and the products of their spinning wheels and looms. The regular exchange of such goods and services was crucial to the workings of rural neighborhoods. Some undertakings—house and barn raisings and husking bees, for example—brought the whole neighborhood together, transforming a necessary chore into a pleasant social event. The gossip, drinking, and dancing that took place on such occasions were fun. They were also—like the exchanges of goods and labor—social rituals that strengthened the neighborly relations within which farmers created a livelihood and passed it on to their sons.

Few of these neighborhood transactions involved money. In 1790, no paper money had yet been issued by the states or the federal government, and the widespread use of Spanish, English, and French coins testified to the shortage of specie. In New England, farmers kept careful accounts of neighborhood debts. In the South and West, farmers used a **"changing system"** in which they simply remembered what

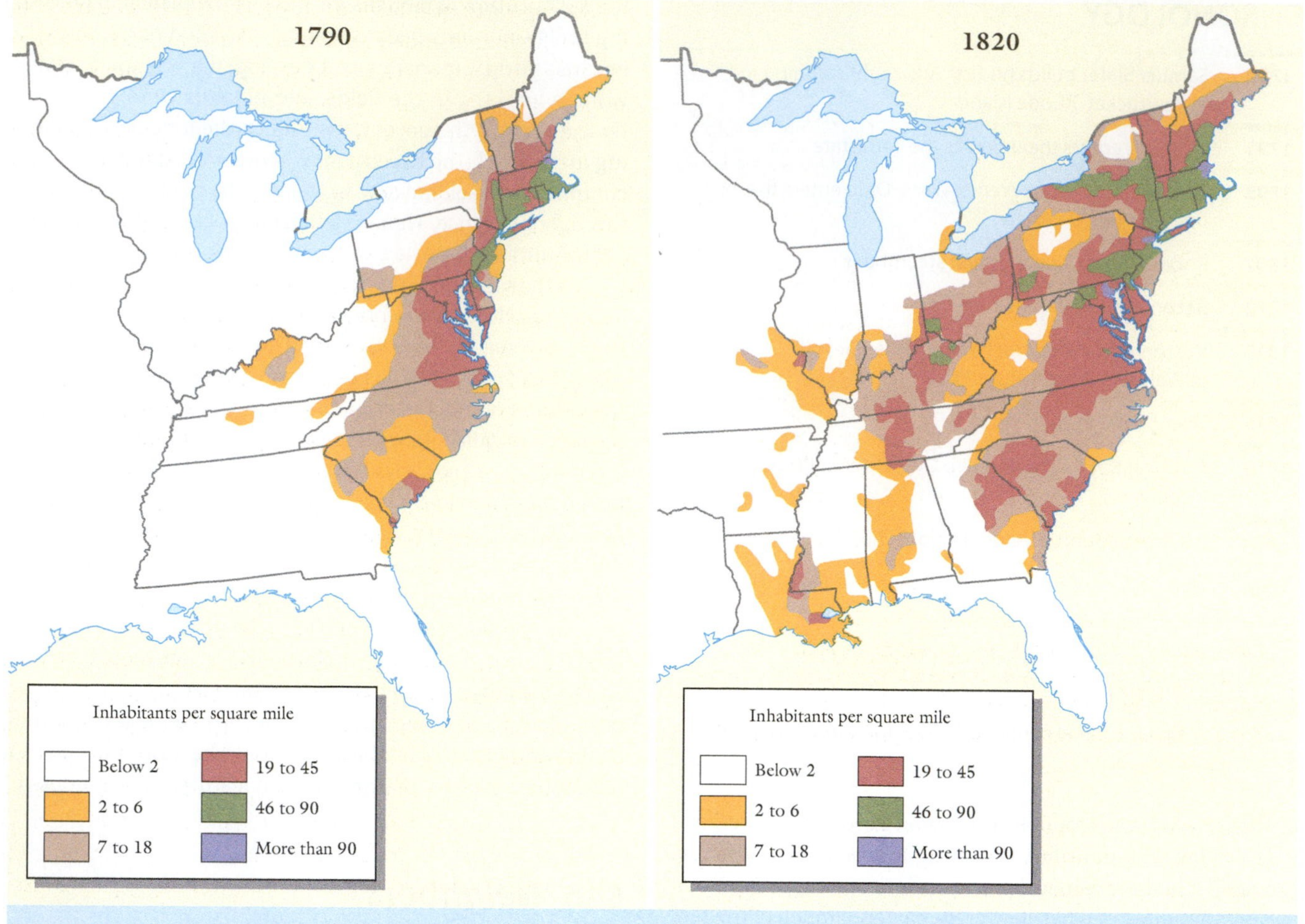

▲ **MAP 8.1 Population Density, 1790–1820** The population of the United States nearly doubled between 1790 and 1820, growing from 5.2 million to 9.6 million persons. In the South, an overwhelmingly rural population spread rapidly across space. The population of the Northeast and mid-Atlantic also occupied new territory over these years, but the rise of seaport towns and intensely commercialized (and often overcrowded) farming areas was turning the North into a much more densely settled region.

Q *How did different economic ideologies in the North and South affect the pace of economic development and population density?*

Q *What other factors might have encouraged more sprawling development in the South and West?*

they owed; they regarded the New England practice as a sign of Yankee greed and lack of character. Yet, farmers everywhere relied more on barter than on cash.

Country storekeepers and village merchants handled relationships between farmers and long-distance markets, and they were as much a part of their neighborhoods as of the wider world. In most areas, farmers brought produce—often a mixed batch of grain, vegetables, ashes, goose down, and so on—to the storekeeper, who arranged its shipment to a seaport town. Some paid cash for produce, but most simply credited the farmer's account. Farmers also bought store goods on credit, and when bad crop years or bad luck made them unable to pay, storekeepers tended to wait for payment without charging interest.

In many instances, the store was incorporated into the relations of local exchange. Hudson River merchants paid the same prices for local goods that were to be sold locally over long periods of time—a price that reflected their relative value within the local barter economy. When sent to New York City, the prices of the same goods rose and fell with their value on international markets. Storekeepers also played a role in local networks of debt, for it was common for farmers to bring their grain, ashes, butter, and eggs to the store, and to have them credited to the accounts of neighbors to whom they were in debt, thus turning the storekeeper into a broker within the complicated web of neighborhood obligations.

8-1c *Standards of Living*

In 1790, most farmhouses in the older rural areas were small, one-story structures, and few farmers bothered to keep their surroundings clean or attractive. They repaired their fences only when they became too dilapidated to function. They rarely planted trees or shrubs, and housewives threw out garbage for chickens and pigs that foraged near the house.

Inside, there were few rooms and many people. Beds stood in every room, and few family members slept alone. Growing up in Bethel, Connecticut, the future show-business entrepreneur P. T. Barnum shared a bed with his brother and an Irish servant. Guests shared beds in New England taverns

8.2 **Venerate the Plough** This image, celebrating America's independent yeoman farmer, was engraved for the *Columbian Magazine* and used for a medal of the Philadelphia Society for the Promotion of Agriculture starting in 1786.

Q *What features of the image reinforce the perception of agriculture as a virtuous pursuit?*

until the 1820s. The hearth remained the source of heat and light in most farmhouses. Between 1790 and 1810, over half the households in central Massachusetts, an old and relatively prosperous area, owned only one or two candlesticks, suggesting that one of the great disparities between wealthy families and their less affluent neighbors was that the wealthy could light their houses at night. Another disparity was in the outward appearance of houses.

Increased income from foreign markets did result in improvement. Farmers bought traditional necessities such as salt and pepper, gunpowder, tools, and coffee and tea, but these were now supplemented with an increasingly alluring array of little luxuries such as crockery, flatware, finished cloth, mirrors, clocks and watches, wallpaper, and the occasional book. At mealtimes, only the poorest families continued to eat with their fingers or with spoons from a common bowl. By 1800, individual place settings with knives and forks and china plates, along with individual chairs instead of benches, had become common in rural America.

8-1d *Inheritance*

Northern farmers between 1790 and 1815 were remarkably like Jefferson's yeoman-citizen ideal: prosperous, independent, living in rough equality with neighbors who shared the same status. Yet, even as rural Americans acted out that vision, its social base was disintegrating. Overcrowding and the growth of markets caused the price of good farmland to rise sharply throughout the older settlements. Most young men could expect to inherit only a few acres of exhausted land, or to move to wilderness land. Failing that, they could expect to quit farming altogether. Crèvecoeur's baby boy—who in fact ended up living in Boston—was in a more precarious position than his seat on his father's plough might have indicated.

In revolutionary America, fathers had been judged by their ability to support and govern their households, to serve as good neighbors, and to pass land on to their sons. After the war, fewer farm fathers were able to do that. Those in the old settlements had small farms and large families, which made it impossible for them to provide a competence for all of their offspring. Fathers felt that they had failed as fathers, and their sons, with no prospect of an adequate inheritance, were obliged to leave home. Most fathers tried to provide for all of their heirs (generally by leaving land to their sons and personal property to their daughters). Few left all of their land to one son, and many stated in their wills that the sons to whom they left the land must share barns and cider mills—even houses—on farms that could be subdivided no further. Such provisions indicated a social system that had reached the end of the line.

Outside New England, farm **tenancy** was on the increase. In parts of Pennsylvania and other areas, farmers often bought farms when they became available in the neighborhood, rented them to tenants to augment the household income, and gave them to their sons when they reached adulthood. The sons of poorer farmers often rented a farm in the hope of saving enough money to buy it. Some fathers bought tracts of unimproved land in the backcountry —sometimes on speculation, more often to provide their sons with land they could make into a farm. Others paid to have their sons educated, or arranged an apprenticeship to provide them with an avenue of escape from a crowded countryside. As a result, more and more young men left home. The populations of the old farming communities grew older and more female, while the populations of the rising frontier settlements and seaport cities became younger and more male. The young men who stayed home often had nothing to look forward to but a lifetime as tenants or hired hands.

8-1e *The Seaport Cities*

When the first federal census takers made their rounds in 1790, they found 94 percent of Americans living on farms and in rural villages. The remaining 6 percent lived in 24 towns with a population of more than 2,500 (a census definition of "urban" that included many communities that were, by modern standards, very small). Only five places had populations over 10,000: Boston (18,038), New York (33,131), Philadelphia (42,444), Baltimore (13,503), and Charleston (16,359). All five were seaports, which is testimony to the key role of international commerce in the economy of the early republic.

The little streams of produce that left farm neighborhoods joined with others on the rivers and the coastal shipping lanes, and they piled up as a significant national surplus on the docks of the seaport towns. When war broke out between Britain and France in 1793, the overseas demand for American foodstuffs, and thus the production of American farms, increased. The warring European powers also needed shipping to carry products from the Caribbean islands to Europe. America's

Old Dartmouth Historical Society/New Bedford Whaling Museum

8.3 **The Dining Room of Dr. Whitbridge, a Rhode Island Country Doctor, circa 1815**
It is a comfortable, neatly furnished room, but with little decoration. The doctor must sit near the fire in layered clothing to ward off the morning chill.

saltwater merchants, free from the old colonial restrictions, responded by building one of the great merchant fleets in the world, and American overseas trade entered a period of unprecedented growth. Ocean trade during these years was risky and uneven, subject to the tides of war and the strategies of the belligerents. But by 1815, wartime commerce had transformed the seaports and the institutions of American business. New York City had become the nation's largest city, with a population that grew to 96,373 in 1810. Philadelphia's population had risen to 53,722 by 1810; Boston's to 34,322; and Baltimore's to 46,555. Economic growth in the years 1790 to 1815 was most palpably concentrated in these cities.

Seaport merchants in these years amassed the private fortunes and built the financial infrastructure that would soon take up the task of commercializing and industrializing the northern United States. Old merchants like the Brown brothers of Providence and Elias Hasket Darby of Salem grew richer, and newcomers like the immigrant John Jacob Astor of New York City built huge personal fortunes. To manage those fortunes, new institutions emerged. Docking and warehousing facilities improved dramatically. Bookkeepers were replaced by accountants, who were familiar with the new double-entry system of accounting, and insurance and banking companies were formed to handle the risks and rewards of wartime commerce.

The cities prospered in these years. The main thoroughfares and a few of the side streets were paved with cobblestones and lined with fine shops and townhouses. But in other parts of the cities, visitors learned that the boom was creating poverty as well as wealth. There had been poor people and depressed neighborhoods in the 18th-century seaports, but not on the scale that prevailed between 1790 and 1820. A few steps off the handsome avenues were narrow streets crowded with ragged children, browsing dogs and pigs, with garbage and waste filling the open sewers.

The slums were evidence that money created by commerce was being distributed in undemocratic ways. Per capita wealth in New York rose 60 percent between 1790 and 1825, but the wealthiest 4 percent of the population owned over half of that wealth. The wages of skilled and unskilled labor rose in these years, but the increase in seasonal and temporary employment, together with the recurring interruptions of foreign commerce, cut deeply into the security and prosperity of ordinary women and men. Added to the old insecurities of sickness, fire, accident, aging, and any number of personal misfortunes, these ate up the gains made by laborers, sailors, and most artisans and their families.

Meanwhile, the status of artisans in the big cities was undergoing change. In 1790, artisans were the self-proclaimed "middling classes" of the towns. They demanded and usually received the respect of their fellow citizens. Skilled manual workers constituted about half the male workforce of the seaport cities, and their respectability and usefulness, together with the role they had played in the Revolution, had earned them an honorable status.

That status rested in large part on their independence. In 1790, most artisan workshops were household operations with at most one or two apprentices and hired **journeymen**—wage earners who looked forward to owning their own shops one day. Most master craftsmen lived modestly (on the borderline of poverty in many cases) and aspired only to support their household in security and decency, and to do so by performing useful work. They identified their way of life with republican virtue. Jefferson proclaimed them "the yeomen of the cities."

The patriarchal base of that republicanism, however, was eroding. With the growth of the maritime economy, the nature of construction work, shipbuilding, the clothing trades, and other specialized crafts changed. Artisans were being replaced by cheaper labor and undercut by subcontracted "slop work" performed by semiskilled rural outworkers. Perhaps one in five master craftsmen entered the newly emerging business class. The others took work as laborers or wage-earning craftsmen. By 1815, most young craftsmen in the seaports could not hope to own their own shops. The world of artisans like Paul Revere, Benjamin Franklin, and Thomas Paine was passing out of existence. Wage labor was taking its place.

History Through Film A *Midwife's Tale* (1998)

Directed by Richard D. Rodgers (PBS).

The historian Laurel Thatcher Ulrich's *A Midwife's Tale* won the Pulitzer Prize for history and biography in 1991. Shortly thereafter, the Public Broadcasting System (PBS) turned the book into a documentary movie—a close and imaginative analysis of the diary of Martha Ballard, a Maine farmwoman and midwife of the late 18th and early 19th centuries. Events are acted out on screen, and period modes of dress, housing, gardening, washing, coffin making, spinning and weaving, and other details are reconstructed with labored accuracy.

The viewer hears the sounds of footfalls, horses, handlooms, and dishes, but the only human sounds are an occasional cough, exclamation, or drinking song. The principal narrative is carried by an actress who reads passages from the diary, and Thatcher occasionally breaks in to explain her own experiences with the diary and its interpretation. The result is a documentary film that knows the difference between dramatizing history and making it up. It also dramatizes the ways in which a skilled and sensitive historian goes about her work.

Martha Ballard was a midwife in a town on the Kennebec River. She began keeping a daily diary at the age of 50 in 1785, and continued until 1812. Most of the film is about her daily life: delivering babies, nursing the sick, helping neighbors, keeping house, raising and supervising the labor of her daughters and niece, gardening, and tending cattle and turkeys. In both the book and the film, the busyness of an ordinary woman's days—and a sense of her possibilities and limits—in the early republic come through in exhausting detail. The dailiness of her life is interrupted only occasionally by an event: a fire at her husband's sawmill, an epidemic of scarlet fever, a parade organized to honor the death of George Washington, the rape of a minister's wife by his enemies (including the local judge, who is set free), and a neighbor's inexplicable murder of his wife and six children.

There is also the process of getting old. At the beginning, Martha Ballard is the busy wife in a well-run household. As she ages and her children leave to set up households of their own, Ballard hires local girls who—perhaps because an increasingly democratic culture has made them less subservient than Ballard would like, perhaps because Ballard is growing old and impatient, perhaps both—tend to be surly. Her husband, a surveyor who works for merchants speculating in local land, is attacked twice in the woods by squatters and spends a year and a half in debtor's jail—not for his own debts but because, as tax collector, he failed to collect enough. While the husband is in jail and his aging wife struggles to keep the house going, their son moves his own family into the house and Martha is moved into a single room and is made to feel unwanted—a poignant and unsentimental case of the strained relations between generations that historians have discovered in the early republic.

A *Midwife's Tale* is a modest film that comes as close as a thorough and imaginative historian and a good filmmaker can to recreating the texture of lived experience in the northeastern countryside at the beginning of the 19th century. Students who enjoy the movie should go immediately to the book. ■

Blueberry Hill Productions, photo by Glenn D. Ross

8.4 The midwife and farm woman Martha Ballard (portrayed by Kaiulani Lee) writes in her diary, the primary source for the book and film, *A Midwife's Tale*.

8.5 **Procession of Victuallers, 1815**
The frequent and festive parades in the seaport cities included militia companies, political officials, clergymen, and artisans organized by trade. In this Philadelphia parade celebrating the end of the War of 1812, the victuallers, preceded by militia cavalrymen, carry a penned steer and a craft flag high atop a wagon, while butchers in top hats and clean aprons ride below. Behind them, shipbuilders drag a ship through the streets.

Q *How did the organization of the parade communicate the place of artisans within early northeastern urban society?*

8-2 The Northwest: From Backcountry to Frontier

Q *How did eastern opinion of the Northwest and its settlers change between 1790 and 1820?*

The United States was a huge country in 1790, at least on paper. In the treaty that ended the War of Independence in 1783, the British ignored Indian claims and ceded all of the land from the Atlantic Ocean to the Mississippi River to the new republic, with the exceptions of Spanish Florida and New Orleans. The states then surrendered their individual claims to the federal government, and in 1790 George Washington became president of a nation that stretched nearly 1,500 miles inland. Still, most white Americans lived on thin strips of settlement on the Atlantic coast and along the few navigable rivers that emptied into the Atlantic. Some were pushing their way into the wilds of Maine and northern Vermont, and in New York others set up communities as far west as the Mohawk Valley. Pittsburgh was a struggling new settlement, and two outposts had been established on the Ohio River: at Marietta and at what would become Cincinnati.

8-2a *The Backcountry, 1790–1815*

To easterners, the backcountry whites, who were displacing the Indians, seemed no different from the defeated aborigines. In fact, in accommodating themselves to a borderless forest used by both Indians and whites, many settlers—like many Indians—had melded Indian and white ways. To clear the land, backcountry farmers simply girdled the trees and left them to die and fall down by themselves. They plowed the land by navigating between the stumps. To easterners' minds, the worst offense was that women often worked the fields, particularly while their men, as did Indians, spent long periods away on hunting trips for food game and animal skins for trade. The arch-pioneer Daniel Boone, for instance, braided his hair, dressed himself in Indian leggings, and, with only his dogs for company, disappeared for months at a time on "long hunts." When easterners began to "civilize" his neighborhood, Boone moved farther west.

Eastern visitors were appalled not only by the poverty, lice, and filth of frontier life but also by the drunkenness and violence of the frontiersmen. Americans everywhere drank heavily in the early years of the 19th century, but everyone agreed that westerners drank more and were more violent when drunk than men anywhere else. Stories arose of half-legendary heroes such as Davy Crockett of Tennessee, who wrestled bears and alligators and had a recipe for Indian stew, and Mike Fink, a Pennsylvania boatman who brawled and drank his way along the rivers of the interior until he was shot and killed in a drunken episode that none of the participants could clearly remember. Samuel Holden Parsons, a New Englander serving as a judge in the Northwest Territory, called the frontiersmen "our white savages." Massachusetts conservative Timothy Pickering branded them "the least worthy subjects of the United States. They are little less savage than the Indians."

8-2b *Settlement*

After 1789, settlers of the backcountry made two demands of the new national government: protection from Indians and a guarantee of the right to navigate the Ohio and Mississippi rivers. The Indians were pushed back in the 1790s and removed as a threat in the War of 1812; in 1803, Jefferson's Louisiana Purchase ended the European presence on the rivers and at the crucial chokepoint at New Orleans. Over these years, the pace of settlement quickened. In 1790, only 10,000 settlers lived west of the Appalachians—about one American in 40. By 1800, the number of settlers had risen to nearly 1 million. By 1820, 2 million Americans were westerners—one in five.

The new settlers bought land from speculators who had acquired tracts under the Northwest Ordinance in the Northwest; from English, Dutch, and American land companies in western New York; and from land dealers in western areas of the Southeast and in northern New England. They built frame

8.6 **Colonel Crockett 1839** The frontiersman Davy Crockett, pictured here as a colonel in the Tennessee militia, helped to cement the reputation of the early American backcountry as wild, dangerous, and uncivilized.

Q *Although Crockett was clearly white, how did race factor into the eastern critique of western frontiersmen?*

houses surrounded by cleared fields, planted marketable crops, and settled into the struggle to make farms out of the wilderness and to meet mortgage payments along the way. Ohio entered the union in 1803, followed by Indiana (1816) and Illinois (1818). As time passed, the term *backcountry*, which easterners had used to refer to the wilderness and the dangerous misfits who lived in it, fell into disuse. By 1820, the term **frontier** had replaced it. The new western settlements no longer represented the backwash of American civilization. They were its cutting edge.

8-3 Transportation Revolution, 1815–1850

Q *How did improvements in transportation channel commerce within and between regions?*

After 1815, dramatic **internal improvements** in transportation—more and better roads, canals, and railroads—tied old communities together and penetrated previously isolated neighborhoods and transformed them. Most of these projects were the work of state governments. Together, the improvements produced a **transportation revolution** that made the transition to a market society physically possible by drastically reducing the cost of shipping surplus crops and goods (see Map 8.2).

8-3a *Transportation in 1815*

In 1815, the United States was a rural nation stretching from the old settlements on the Atlantic coast to the trans-Appalachian west, with transportation facilities that ranged from primitive to nonexistent. Americans despaired of communicating, to say nothing of doing business on a national scale. In 1816, a Senate committee reported that $9 would move a ton of goods across the 3,000-mile expanse of the North Atlantic. The same $9 would move the same ton of goods only 30 miles inland. A year later, the cost of transporting wheat from the new settlement of Buffalo to New York City was three times higher than the selling price of wheat in New York. Farming for profit made sense only for farmers near urban markets or with easy river access to the coast.

Transporting goods into the western settlements was even more difficult. Keelboatmen like Mike Fink could navigate upstream—using eddies and back currents, sailing when the wind was right, but usually poling their boats against the current. Skilled crews averaged only 15 miles a day, and the trip from New Orleans to Louisville took three to four months. Looking for better routes, some merchants dragged finished goods across Pennsylvania and into the West at Pittsburgh, but transport costs made these goods prohibitively expensive. Consequently, the trans-Appalachian settlements—home to one in five Americans by 1820—remained marginal to the market economy.

8-3b *Internal Improvements*

In 1816, Congress resumed construction of the **National Road** (first authorized in 1802) that linked the Potomac River with the Ohio River at Wheeling, Virginia (now West Virginia)—an attempt to link west and east through the Chesapeake. The smooth, crushed-rock thoroughfare reached Wheeling in 1818. At about the same time, Pennsylvania extended the Lancaster Turnpike to make it run from Philadelphia to the Ohio River at Pittsburgh. These ambitious roads into the West, however, had limited effects. The National Road made it easier for settlers and a few merchants' wagons to reach the West, but the cost of moving bulky farm produce over the road remained high. Eastbound traffic on the National Road consisted largely of cattle and pigs, which carried themselves to market. Farmers continued to float their corn, cotton, wheat, salt pork, and whiskey south by riverboat and from there to eastern markets.

It was the steamboat that first made commercial agriculture feasible in the Northwest. Tinkerers and mechanics had been experimenting with steam-powered boats for a generation or more when an entrepreneur named **Robert Fulton** launched the first commercial steamboat, the *Clermont*, on an upriver trip from New York City to Albany in 1807. Over the next few years, Americans developed flat-bottomed steamboats that could navigate rivers even at low water. The first steamboat reached Louisville from New Orleans in 1815. Two years later, with 17 steamboats already working western rivers, the *Washington* made the New Orleans–Louisville run in 25 days, a feat that convinced westerners that two-way river trade was possible. By 1820, 69 steamboats were operating on western rivers. The 60,000 tons of produce that farmers and planters had shipped out of the interior in 1810 grew to 500,000 tons in 1840. The steamboat had transformed the interior from an isolated frontier into a busy commercial region that traded farm and plantation products for manufactured goods.

In the East, state governments created rivers where nature had made none. In 1817, Governor DeWitt Clinton, after failing to get federal support, talked the New York legislature into building a canal linking the Hudson River to Lake Erie, thus opening a continuous water route between the Northwest and New York City. The **Erie Canal** was a visionary feat of engineering. Designed by self-taught engineers and built by gangs of Irish immigrants, local farm boys, and convict laborers, it stretched 364 miles from Albany to Buffalo. Although "Clinton's Ditch" passed through carefully chosen level ground, it required a complex system of 83 locks, and it passed over 18 rivers on stone aqueducts. Construction began in 1819, and the canal reached Buffalo in 1825. It was clear even before then that the canal would repay New York State's investment of $7.5 million many times over, and that it would transform the territory that it served.

The Erie Canal would direct the trade of the whole Great Lakes watershed into New York City, but its first and most powerful effects were on western New York, which had been a raw frontier accessible to the East only over a notoriously bad state road. By 1830, the New York corridor of the Erie Canal, settled largely from hill-country New England, was one of the world's great grain-growing regions, dotted with market towns and new cities like Syracuse, Rochester, and Buffalo.

The Erie Canal was an immense success, and legislators and entrepreneurs in other states joined a canal boom that lasted for 20 years. When construction began on the Erie Canal, there were fewer than 100 miles of canal in the United States. By 1840, there were 3,300 miles, nearly all of them in the Northeast and Northwest. Northwestern states, Ohio in particular, built ambitious canal systems that linked isolated areas to the Great Lakes and thus to the Erie Canal. Northeastern states followed suit. A canal between Worcester and Providence linked the farms of central Massachusetts with Narragansett Bay. Another canal linked the coal mines of northeastern Pennsylvania with the Hudson River at Kingston, New York. In 1835, Pennsylvania completed a canal from Philadelphia to Pittsburgh.

The canal boom was followed quickly by a boom in railroads. The first of them connected burgeoning cities to rivers and canals. The Baltimore and Ohio Railroad, for example, linked Baltimore to the rivers of the West. Although the approximately 3,000 miles of railroads built between the late 1820s and 1840 helped the market positions of some cities, they did not constitute a national or even a regional rail network. A national system developed with the 5,000 miles of track laid in the 1840s and with the flurry of railroad building that by 1860 gave the United States a rail network of 30,000 miles—a continuous, integrated system that created numerous links between the East and the Northwest and threatened to put canals out of business (see Maps 8.3 and 8.4). In fact, the New York Central, which paralleled the Erie Canal, rendered that canal obsolete. Other railroads, particularly in the northwestern states, replaced canal and river transport almost completely, even though water transport remained cheaper. By 1860, few farmers in the North and West lived more than 20 road miles from railroads, canals, or rivers that could deliver their produce to regional, national, and international markets.

8-3c *Time, Money, and New Markets*

The transportation revolution brought a dramatic reduction in the time and money that it took to move heavy goods. Turnpikes cut the cost of wagon transport, but goods traveled most cheaply on water. In 1816, freight rates on the Ohio–Mississippi system had been 1.3 cents per ton-mile for downriver travel and 5.8 cents for upriver travel. Steamboats cut both costs to a bit more than a third of a cent. The Erie Canal and the Ohio canals reduced the distance between East and West and carried goods at about one cent per ton-mile. By 1830, farmers in the Northwest and western New York could grow wheat and sell it at a profit on the New York market.

Interpreting the Visual Past

Transportation before the Market Revolution

The Russian artist Pavel Petrovich Svinin completed this watercolor painting, *Travel by Stage Coach near Trenton, New Jersey,* between 1811 and 1813, when he traveled up and down the East Coast sketching and taking notes. It captures the state of transportation in America before the Market Revolution. The coach is small and open to the weather, the passengers are crowded and uncomfortable (one of them has lost his hat), and the road is a dirt path with a steep incline—difficult when going uphill, dangerous when going down. The driver, like many of the people who worked with horses, is black.

Q *Considering that Trenton was one of the most developed parts of the country in the early 1810s, what does this image tell us about the state of early American transportation? Despite the obvious drawbacks, what advantages are apparent compared to travel in other, less developed parts of the country?*

Q *Reflect on how a historian might use this painting as evidence. What does it show about the relationship between transportation and the Market Revolution? What does the painting illustrate about early American social relations?*

8.7 **Pavel Petrovich Svinin, *Travel by Stage Coach near Trenton, New Jersey,* 1811–1813.**

Improvements in speed were nearly as dramatic. The overland trip from Cincinnati to New York in 1815 (by keelboat upriver to Pittsburgh, then by wagon the rest of the way) had taken a minimum of 52 days. Steamboats traveled from Cincinnati to New Orleans, and then passed goods on to coasting ships that finished the trip to New York City in a total of 28 days. By 1840, the Ohio canal system enabled Cincinnati to send goods north through Ohio, across Lake Erie, over the Erie Canal, and down the Hudson to New York City—an all-water route that reduced costs and made the trip in 18 days. Similar improvements occurred in the densely settled and increasingly urbanized Northeast. By 1840, travel time between the big northeastern cities had been reduced from one-fourth to one-eleventh of what it had been in 1790. These improvements in speed and economy made a northern market economy possible.

Improved transportation helped to bring together previously isolated markets—the final step of the Market Revolution. Foreign trade, which had driven American economic growth up until 1815, continued to expand. The value of American exports in 1815 had stood at $52.6 million, while imports totaled $113 million. Both rose dramatically in the years of the Market Revolution: Exports (now consisting more of southern cotton than of northern food crops) continued to increase, and the flow of imported manufactured goods increased as well. Yet, foreign trade now accounted for a smaller proportion of American—particularly northern—market activity. Before 1815, Americans had exported about 15 percent of their total national product. By 1830, exports accounted for only 6 percent of a vastly increased national production. The reason for this shift was that after 1815, the United States developed self-sustaining domestic markets for farm produce and manufactured goods. The great engine of economic growth in the North and West was not the old colonial relationship with Europe but a self-sustaining domestic market.

8.8 The Erie Canal at Lockport, New York, in 1839 The canal stretched for 364 miles between Albany and Buffalo, linking New York City to the Great Lakes through the Hudson River. It required complex engineering, including locks (pictured here), which raised or lowered boats to navigate water at different elevation levels.

Until 1840, the Market Revolution produced greater results within regions than between them. The farmers of New England traded food for finished goods from Boston, Lynn, Lowell, and other towns in what was becoming an urban, industrial region. Philadelphia traded manufactures for food from the farmers of the Delaware Valley. The Erie Canal created a huge potential for interregional trade, but until 1839 most of its westbound tonnage originated in western New York. In the West, market-oriented farmers fed such rapidly growing cities as Rochester, Pittsburgh, and Cincinnati, which in turn supplied the farmers with locally manufactured farm tools, furniture, shoes, and other goods. Thus, although the Market Revolution was initially more a regional than an interregional phenomenon, it was clear to anyone who looked at a map that the New England, mid-Atlantic, and Northwestern states were on their way to becoming an integrated market society—one that did not include southern plantations that grew for export (see Chapter 9).

8-4 Northeastern Farms, 1815–1850

Q *How did northern farm families experience the transition into commercial agriculture between 1815 and 1850?*

In the old farming communities of the Northeast, the transformations of the early 19th century sent many young people off to cities and factory towns and others to the West. Those who remained at home engaged in new forms of agriculture on a transformed rural landscape, while their cousins in the Northwest turned a wilderness into cash-producing farms. In both regions, farmers abandoned the old mixed, safety-first agriculture and began to raise a single crop intended for distant markets. That decision committed them to buying things that their forebears had grown or made, participating as both producers and consumers in a new market economy.

8-4a *The New England Livestock Economy*

New Englanders who tried to grow grain on their rocky, worn-out soil could not compete with the farmers of western New York and the Northwest. At the same time, however, the new factories and growing cities of the Northeast provided Yankee farmers with a market for meat and other perishables. Beef became the great New England cash crop. Dairy products were not far behind, and the proximity to city markets encouraged the spread of poultry and egg farms, fruit orchards, and truck gardens. The burgeoning shoe industry bought leather from the farmers, and woolen mills created a demand for wool, and thus for great flocks of New England sheep. As a result, millions of trees were stripped from the New England landscape to make way for pastureland.

The rise of livestock specialization reduced the amount of land under cultivation. Early in the century, New Englanders still tilled their few acres in the old three-year rotation: corn the first year, rye the second, fallow the third. By the 1820s and 1830s, as farmers raised more livestock and less grain, the land that remained in cultivation was farmed more intensively. Farmers saved manure and ashes for fertilizer, plowed more deeply and systematically, and tended their crops more carefully. These improved techniques, along with cash from the sale of their livestock and the availability of food at stores, encouraged Yankee farmers to allocate less and less land to the growing of food crops. In Concord, Massachusetts—the hometown of the agrarian republic—the portion of town land in tillage dropped from 20 to 7 percent between 1771 and 1850.

The transition to livestock-raising transformed woodlands into open pastures. As farmers leveled the forests, they

▲ **MAP 8.2 Rivers, Roads, and Canals, 1825–1860** In the second quarter of the 19th century, transportation projects linked the North and Northwest into an integrated economic and social system. There were fewer improvements in the South: Farm produce traveled down navigable rivers from bottomland plantations to river and seaport towns, thence to New York for shipment overseas. Southern legislatures and entrepreneurs saw little use for further improvements.

Q *Compare this map with Map 8.1. How did new transportation networks linking the North and Northwest help to make possible greater population density in northeastern cities?*

Q *What might have been some of the social, economic, and political consequences of the relative isolation of southern communities?*

sold the wood to fuel-hungry cities. It was a lucrative, although short-term, market. In the 1820s, manufacturers began marketing cast-iron stoves that heated houses more cheaply and more efficiently than open hearths, and canals brought cheap Pennsylvania anthracite to the Northeast. The shift came too late to prevent massive deforestation. In 1790, in the central Massachusetts town of Petersham, forest covered 85 percent of the town lands. By 1830, the creation of pastureland through commercial woodcutting had reduced the forested area to 30 percent. (By 1850, woods covered only 10 percent of the town, the pasturelands were overgrazed and ruined, and the landscape was dotted with abandoned farms.)

With the shift to specialized market agriculture, New England farmers became customers for necessities that their forebears had produced themselves or had acquired through barter. The turning point came in the 1820s. Farm families heated their houses with coal dug by Pennsylvania miners. They wore cotton cloth made by the factory women at Lowell. New Hampshire farm girls made straw hats for them, and the craftsmen of Lynn made their shoes. By 1830

The Granger Collection, NYC

8.9 **View of the First American Railway Train** The first locomotives were simply steam engines mounted on wheeled platforms, and the first coaches were stagecoaches on metal wheels. Within a few years, both engines and coaches had taken on their familiar 19th-century designs.

Q *What can the passengers and their dress tell us about early railway travel in America?*

or so, many farmers were even buying food. The Erie Canal and the western grain belt sent flour from Rochester into eastern neighborhoods where grain was no longer grown. Many farmers found it easier to produce specialized crops for market, and to buy butter, cheese, eggs, and vegetables at country stores.

As a result, spinning wheels and handlooms disappeared from the farmhouses of New England. Farm families that bought the new cast-iron stoves enjoyed pies and bread baked from western white flour; the old "Rye and Injun" disappeared. All of these things cost money and committed farm families to increasing their cash incomes. Standards of living rose dramatically. At the same time, northeastern farmers depended on markets in ways that their fathers and grandfathers would have considered dangerous not only to family welfare but to the welfare of the republic itself.

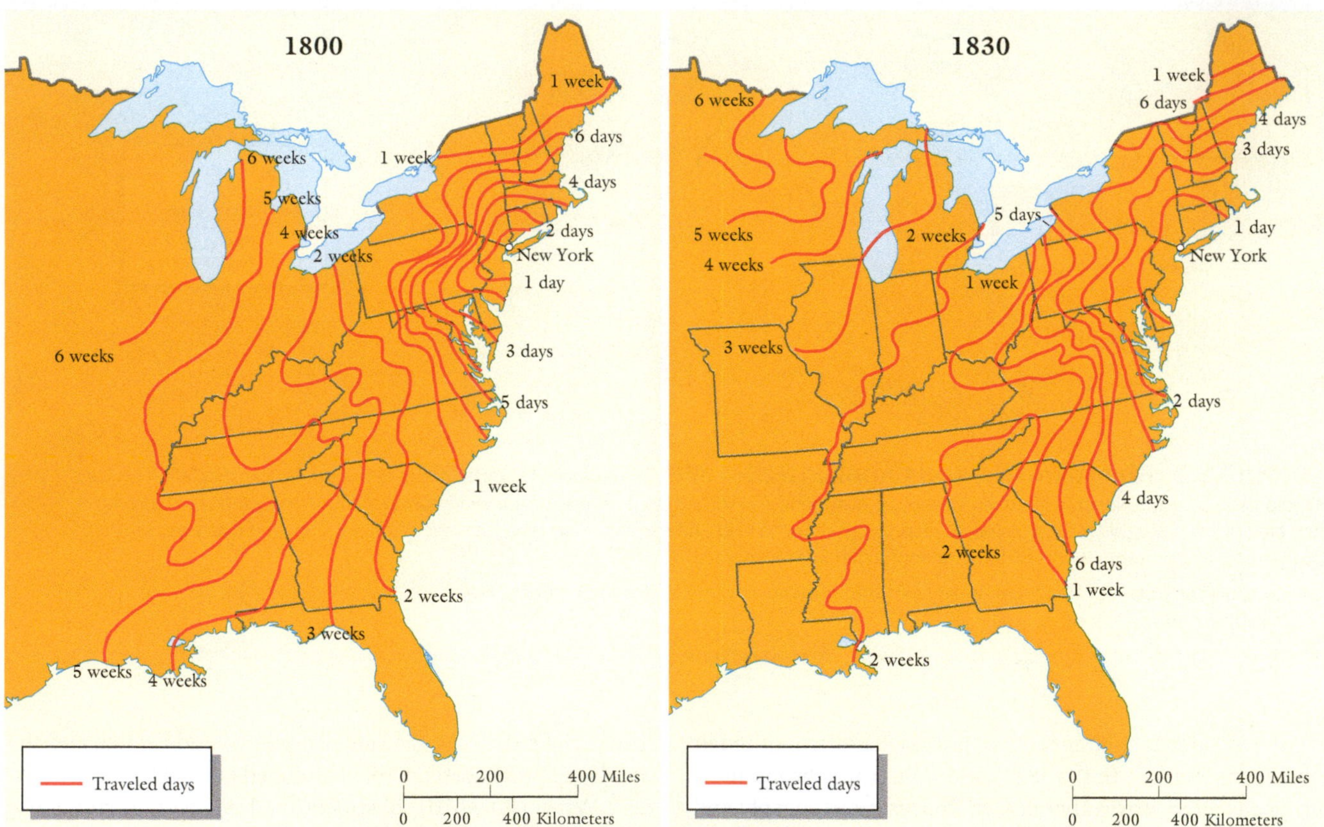

▲ **MAP 8.3 Time Required to Travel from New York City, 1800 and 1830** These maps illustrate the increasing ease of travel in the first third of the 19th century. In general, travelers could cover nearly twice as much territory in a day in 1830 as in 1800, although in both cases travel became more difficult as one left the densely settled East.

Q *Which areas had the most dramatic change in travel time between 1800 and 1830? Which areas had the least change?*

Q *How did the factor of travel time influence major economic decisions and trends?*

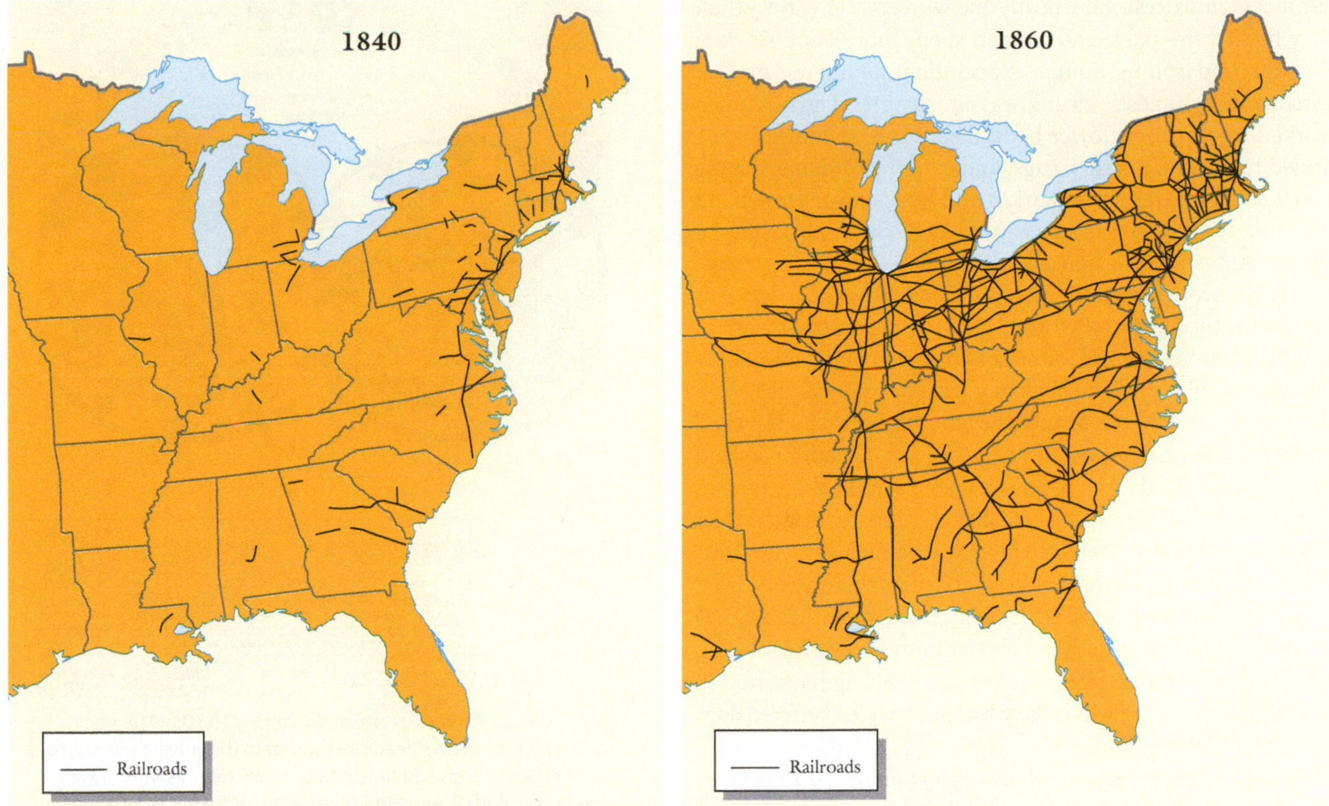

▲ **MAP 8.4 Railroads in the United States, 1840 and 1860** In these 20 years, both the North and South built railway systems. Northerners built rail lines that integrated the market economies of the Midwest and the East—both within sections and between them. For the most part, southern railroads linked the plantation belt with the ocean. Revealingly, only a few lines connected the North and South.

Q *Compare these maps with Map 8.2. Why did the pattern of railroad development so closely follow existing transportation networks created by canals and roads?*

Q *Why did railroads run from East to West but not from North to South? What might have been some of the social and political consequences of this pattern?*

8-4b *New Farm Households*

The Market Revolution had an equally dramatic impact on the relations within households. For one thing, Americans began to limit the size of their families. White women who married in 1800 had given birth to an average of 6.4 children. Those who married between 1800 and 1849 averaged 4.9 children. The decline was most pronounced in the North, particularly in commercialized areas.

Rural birthrates remained at 18th-century levels in the southern uplands, in the poorest and most isolated communities of the North, and on the frontier. (As New Yorker Washington Irving passed through the Northwest in the 1830s, he noted in his journal: "Illinois—famous for children and dogs—in house with nineteen children and thirty-seven dogs.") These communities practiced the old labor-intensive agriculture and relied on the labor of large families. For farmers who used newer techniques or switched to livestock or grain, large families made less sense. Moreover, large broods hampered the ability of future-minded parents to provide for their children and conflicted with new notions of privacy and domesticity that were taking shape among an emerging rural **middle class**—a social group that, like its urban counterpart, defined itself against poorer laborers and those who did not adapt to the new market society.

Before 1815, farmwives had labored in the house, the barnyard, and the garden while their husbands and sons worked in the fields. With the Market Revolution came a sharper distinction between male work that was part of the cash economy and female work that was not. Even such traditional women's tasks as dairying, vegetable gardening, and poultry raising became men's work once they became cash-producing specialties. A Pennsylvanian who lived among businesslike New Englanders in the Northwest was appalled at such tampering with hallowed gender roles and wrote the Yankees off as "a shrewd, selfish, enterprising, cow-milking set of men."

At the same time, new kinds of women's work emerged within households. Though there were fewer children to care for, the culture began to demand forms of child rearing that were more intensive, individualized, and mother-centered. Store-bought white flour, butter, and eggs and the new iron stoves eased the burdens of food preparation, but they also created demands for pies, cakes, and other fancy foods that earlier generations had only dreamed of. And while farm women no longer spun and wove their own cloth, the availability of manufactured cloth created the expectation that their families would dress more neatly and with greater variety than they had in the past, and women spent more time sewing, washing, and ironing. Similar expectations demanded greater personal and domestic cleanliness and taste, and farm women worked at planting flower beds; cleaning and maintaining prized furniture, mirrors, rugs, and ceramics; and scrubbing floors and children. The market and housework grew hand in hand: Among the first mass-produced commodities in the United States was the household broom.

Housework was tied to new notions of privacy, decency, and domestic comfort. Before 1820, farmers cared little about how their houses looked, often tossing trash and garbage out the door for pigs and chickens that foraged near the house. In the 1820s and 1830s, as farmers began to grow cash crops and adopt middle-class ways, they began to plant shade trees and to keep their yards free of trash. They painted their houses and sometimes their fences and outbuildings, arranged their woodpiles into neat stacks, surrounded their houses with flowers and ornamental shrubs, and tried to hide their privies from view. The new sense of refinement extended into other aspects of country life. The practice of chewing (and spitting) tobacco was gradually banned in churches and meeting halls, and in 1823 the minister in Shrewsbury, Massachusetts, ordered dogs out of the meetinghouse.

Inside, prosperous farmhouses took on an air of privacy and comfort. As separate kitchens and iron stoves replaced open hearths, many families used a set of matched dishes for individual place settings. The availability of finished cloth also permitted the regular use of tablecloths, napkins, doilies, curtains, bedspreads, and quilts. Oil lamps replaced homemade candles, and the more prosperous families began to decorate their homes with wallpaper and upholstered furniture. Farm couples moved their beds away from the hearth and (along with the children's beds that had been scattered throughout the house) put them into spaces designated as bedrooms. They took washstands and basins out of the kitchen and put them into the bedroom, thus making sleeping, bathing, and sex more private than they had been in the past. At the center of this new house stood the farmwife, apart from the bustling world of commerce but decorating and caring for the amenities that commerce bought, and demanding that men respect the new domestic world that commerce had made possible.

Historical/Corbis

8.10 **A Soap Advertisement from the 1850s** The rigors of "Old Washing Day" lead the mother in this advertisement to abuse the children and house pets, while her husband leaves the house. With American Cream Soap, domestic bliss returns: The children and cats are happy, the husband returns, and the wife has time to sew.

Q *Consider the advertisement in relation to advertising today. What, if anything, has changed in the use of psychology to influence consumer behavior?*

8-4c *The Landscape of Privacy*

By 1830, the Market Revolution was transforming the rural landscape of the North. The forests had been reduced, the swamps had been drained, and most of the streams and rivers were interrupted by mill dams. Bears, panthers, and wolves had disappeared, along with the beaver and many of the fish. Now there were extensive pastures where English cattle and sheep browsed on English grasses dotted with English wildflowers like buttercups, daisies, and dandelions. Next to the pastures were neatly cultivated croplands that were regularly fertilized and seldom allowed to lie fallow. And at the center stood painted houses and outbuildings surrounded by flowers and shrubs and vegetable gardens. Many towns, particularly in New England, had planted shade trees along the country roads, completing a rural landscape of straight lines and human cultivation—a landscape that looked both settled and comfortable, and that made it easy to think of nature as a commodity to be altered and controlled.

Within that landscape, old practices and old forms of neighborliness fell into disuse. Neighbors continued to exchange goods and labor and to contract debts that might be left unpaid for years, but debts were more likely to be owed to profit-minded storekeepers and creditors, and even debts between neighbors were often paid in cash. Traditionally, storekeepers had allowed farmers to bring in produce and have it credited to a neighbor/creditor's account—a practice that made the storekeeper an agent of neighborhood bartering. In 1830, half of all the stores in rural New England still carried accounts of this sort, but storekeepers increasingly demanded cash payment or charged lower prices to those who paid cash.

The farm newspapers that appeared in these years urged farmers to keep careful records of the amount of fertilizer used, labor costs, and per-acre yields, and discouraged them from relying on the old system of neighboring. Neighborly rituals like parties, husking bees, and barn raisings—with their drinking and socializing—were scorned as inefficient and morally suspect wastes of time. *The Farmer's Almanac* of 1833 warned New England farmers: "If you love fun, frolic, and waste and slovenliness more than economy and profit, then make a husking."

8.11 **McCormick Reaper** This advertisement, for a farm machinery company in Ohio, illustrates how mechanized agriculture helped to revolutionize the American economy. Patented in the 1830s, the McCormick reaper used a wheel frame pulled by horses to reap (cut) crops at harvest. Two young men look on, holding respectively a sickle and a scythe, the instruments displaced by the new technology.

By 1830, the efficient northern farmer concentrated on producing commodities that could be marketed outside the neighborhood, and used his cash income to buy material comforts for his family, pay debts, and provide a cash inheritance for his children. Maintaining economic independence in the North now required unprecedented levels of dependence on the outside world.

8-5 The Northwest in Transition

Q *How did northern and southern settlers flooding into the Northwest after 1815 view the new market economy differently?*

One reason the Market Revolution in the Northeast went as smoothly as it did was that young people with little hope of inheriting land in the old settlements moved to towns and cities or to the new farmlands of the Northwest. Between 1815 and 1840—precisely the years in which northeastern agriculture became a cash-crop business—migrants from the older areas transformed the Northwest Territory into a working agricultural landscape. The region became the meeting ground of market-conscious northerners and southerners still more accustomed to older forms of subsistence farming and neighbor-to-neighbor exchange.

8-5a *Southern Settlers*

In the Northwest until the 1820s, most settlers were yeomen from Kentucky and Tennessee, usually a generation removed from Virginia, the Carolinas, and western Maryland. They moved along the Ohio and up the Muskingum, Miami, Scioto, Wabash, and Illinois rivers to set up farms in the southern and central counties of Ohio, Indiana, and Illinois. When southerners moved north of the Ohio River into territory that banned slavery, they often did so saying that slavery blocked opportunities for poor whites. The Methodist preacher Peter Cartwright left Kentucky thinking, "I would get entirely clear of the evil of slavery," and "could raise my children to work where work was not thought a degradation." Similar hopes drew thousands of other southern yeomen north of the Ohio.

But even those who rejected slavery seldom rejected southern folkways. Like their kinfolk in Kentucky and Tennessee, the farmers of southern and central Ohio, Indiana, and Illinois remained tied to the river trade and to a mode of agriculture that favored free-ranging livestock over cultivated fields. The typical farmer fenced in a few acres of corn and left the rest of his land in woods to be roamed by hogs known as "razorbacks" and "land sharks." These animals were thin and tough (they seldom grew to over 200 pounds), and they could run long distances, leap fences, and fend for themselves in the woods. They were notoriously fierce: More settlers were injured by their own hogs than by wild animals. When it was time to gather the hogs for slaughter, many settlers played it safe and hunted them with guns.

The southern-born pioneers of the Northwest, like their cousins across the Ohio River, depended more on their families and neighbors than on distant markets. Newcomers found that they could neither rent tools from their southern neighbors nor present them with "gifts" during hard times. Southerners insisted on repaying debts in kind and on lending tools rather than renting them, thus engaging outsiders in the elaborate network of "neighboring" through which transplanted southerners made their livings. As late as the 1840s, in the bustling town of Springfield, Illinois, barter was the preferred system of exchange. "In no part of the world," said a Scotsman in southern Illinois, "is good neighborship found in greater perfection than in the western territory."

8-5b *Northern Farmers*

In the 1820s, with improved transportation and with the wars with Indians and Canadians at an end, northeastern migrants entered the Northwest. They settled near the Great Lakes, filling the new lands of Michigan and the northern counties of the older northwestern states. Most of them were New Englanders who had spent a generation in western New York (such settlers accounted for three-fourths of the early population of Michigan). The rest came directly from New England. Arriving in the Northwest along the market's busiest arteries, they practiced an intensive, market-oriented agriculture. They penned their cattle and hogs and fattened them up, making them bigger and worth more than those farther south. They planted their land in grain and transformed the region—beginning with western New York's Genesee County in the 1820s and rolling through the Northwest—into one of the world's great wheat-producing regions. In 1820, the Northwest had exported only 12 percent of its agricultural produce. By 1840, that figure had risen to 27 percent, and it stood much higher among northern-born grain farmers.

The new settlers were notably receptive to improvements in farming techniques. While there were plenty of southern proponents of progress and plenty of backward northerners, the line between new and old agricultural ways separated northern grain farmers from southern settlers. In breaking new land, for instance, southerners still used the old shovel plow, which dug a shallow furrow and skipped over roots. Northerners preferred newer, more expensive cast-iron plows, which cut cleanly through oak roots four inches thick. By the 1830s, the efficient, expensive grain cradle had replaced the age-old sickle as the principal harvest tool in northwestern wheat fields. Instead of threshing their grain by driving cattle and horses over it, farmers bought new horse-powered and treadmill threshers and used hand-cranked fanning mills to speed the process of cleaning the grain.

Most agricultural improvements were tailored to grain and dairy farming and were taken up most avidly by the northern farmers. Others rejected them as expensive and unnatural. They thought that cast-iron plows poisoned the soil and that fanning mills made a "wind contrary to nater," and thus offended God. John Chapman, an eccentric Yankee who earned the nickname "Johnny Appleseed" by planting apple tree cuttings in southern Ohio and Indiana before the settlers arrived, planted only low-yield, common trees. He regarded grafting, which farmers farther north and east were using to improve the quality of their apples, as "against nature." Southerners scoffed at the Yankee fondness for mechanical improvements, the systematic breeding of animals and plants, careful bookkeeping, and farm techniques learned from books. "I reckon," said one, "I know as much about farming as the printers do."

8-6 The Beginnings of the Industrial Revolution

Q *Why did America's first factories start in the northern countryside?*

In the 50 years following 1820, American cities grew faster than ever before or since. The old seaports—New York City in particular—grew rapidly in these years, but the fastest growth was in new cities that served commercial agriculture and in factory towns that produced for a largely rural domestic market. Even in the seaports, growth derived more from commerce with the hinterland than from international trade. Paradoxically, the Market Revolution in the countryside had produced the beginnings of industry and the greatest period of urban growth in U.S. history.

8-6a *Factory Towns: The Rhode Island System*

Jeffersonians held that the United States must always remain rural. Americans, they insisted, could expand into the West, trade their farm surpluses for European finished goods, and thus avoid creating cities with their dependent social classes. Proponents of domestic manufactures argued that Americans could enjoy the benefits of factory production without the troublesome blight of industrial cities. They assured Americans that abundant waterpower—particularly the fast-running streams of the Northeast—would enable Americans to build their factories in the countryside. Such a decentralized factory system would provide employment for country women and children and thus subsidize the independence of struggling farmers. It was on those premises that the first American factories were built.

The American textile industry originated in industrial espionage. The key to the mass production of cotton and woolen textiles was a water-powered machine that spun yarn and thread. The machine had been invented and patented by the Englishman Richard Arkwright in 1769, and the British government forbade the machinery and the people who worked with it to leave the country. Scores of textile workers, however, defied the law and made their way to North America. One of them was Samuel Slater, who had served an apprenticeship under Jedediah Strutt, a partner of Arkwright who had improved on the original machine. Working from memory while employed by Moses Brown, a Providence merchant, Slater built the first Arkwright spinning mill in America at Pawtucket, Rhode Island, in 1790.

Slater's first mill was a small frame building tucked among the town's houses and craftsmen's shops. Although its capacity was limited to the spinning of cotton yarn, it provided work for children in the mill and for women who wove yarn into cloth in their homes. Thus this first mill satisfied American requirements: It did not require the creation of a factory town, and it supplemented the household incomes of farmers and artisans. As his business grew and he advertised for widows with children, however, Slater was greeted by families headed by landless, impoverished men. Slater's use of children from these families prompted respectable farmers and craftsmen to pull their children out of Slater's growing complex of mills. More poor families arrived to take their places, and during the first years of the 19th century, Pawtucket became a disorderly mill town.

Soon Slater and other mill owners built factory villages in the countryside where they could exert better control over their operations and their workers. The practice became known as the **Rhode Island System** (or "family" system). At Slatersville, Rhode Island, Oxford, Massachusetts, and other locations in southern New England, mill owners built whole villages surrounded by company-owned farmland that they rented to the husbands and fathers of their mill workers. The workplace was closely supervised, and drinking and other troublesome practices were forbidden in the villages. Fathers and older sons worked either on rented farms or as laborers at the mills. By the late 1820s, Slater and most of the other owners were getting rid of the outworkers and were buying power looms, thus transforming the villages into self-contained factory towns that turned raw cotton into finished cloth, but at great cost to old forms of household independence. When President Andrew Jackson visited Pawtucket in 1829, he remarked to Samuel Slater, "I understand you taught us how to spin, so as to rival Great Britain in her manufactures; you set all these thousands of spindles to work, which I have been delighted in viewing, and which have made so many happy, by a lucrative employment." "Yes sir," replied Slater. "I suppose that I gave out the psalm and they have been singing to the tune ever since."

The New York Public Library/Art Resource, NY

8.12 **Pawtucket in 1817** Here is America's first textile milling town. It is set beside a waterfall that provides power for the mills. A bridge runs directly over the brink of the falls, and men and boys fish and play in the pool below them.

Q *Consider how factories violated the Jeffersonian ideal of yeoman farming. How might have this pastoral scene helped to ease the transition from agriculture to industrialization?*

8-6b *Factory Towns: The Waltham-Lowell System*

A second act of industrial espionage was committed by a Boston merchant named Francis Cabot Lowell. Touring English factory districts in 1811, Lowell asked questions and made secret drawings of the machines. He also experienced a genteel distaste for the squalor of the English textile towns. Returning home, Lowell joined with wealthy friends to form the Boston Manufacturing Company—soon known as the Boston Associates. In 1813, they built their first mill at Waltham, Massachusetts, and then expanded into Lowell, Lawrence, and other new towns near Boston during the 1820s.

The company built mills according to the **Waltham-Lowell System**, which differed from the early Rhode Island mills in two ways: (1) They were heavily capitalized and as fully mechanized as possible, turning raw cotton into finished cloth with little need for skilled workers; and (2) their workers were young, single women recruited from the farms of northern New England—farms that were switching to livestock raising, and thus had little need for the labor of daughters. The company provided boardinghouses for them and enforced rules of conduct both on and off the job. The young women, soon to become known as **Lowell mill girls**, worked steadily, never drank, seldom stayed out late, and attended church faithfully. They dressed neatly—often stylishly—and read newspapers and attended lectures. They impressed visitors, particularly those who had seen factory workers in other places, as a dignified and self-respecting workforce.

The brick mills and prim boardinghouses set within landscaped towns and occupied by the sober, well-behaved Lowell girls signified the Boston Associates' desire to build a profitable textile industry without creating a permanent working class. According to the plan, the young farm women would work for a few years in a carefully controlled environment, send their wages back to their families, and return home to live as country housewives. They did in fact form an efficient, decorous workforce, but the decorum was imposed less by the owners than by the women themselves. In order to protect their own reputations, they punished transgressions and shunned fellow workers who misbehaved. Nor did most of the Lowell women send their wages home or, as was popularly believed, use them to pay for their brothers' college educations. Some saved their money to use as dowries that their fathers could not afford. More, however, spent their wages on themselves, particularly on clothes and books.

The owners of the factories expected that the young women's sojourn would reinforce their own paternalism and that of the girls' fathers. Instead, it produced a self-respecting sisterhood of wage-earning women. Twice in the 1830s, the women of Lowell went on strike, proclaiming that they were not wage slaves but "the daughters of freemen." The women survived as a labor force into the late 1840s, when new waves of immigrants, particularly from Ireland, displaced them from northern factories (see Chapter 10). By then, the majority of Lowell mill girls had become housewives, but not on the terms their mothers had known. One in three of them married Lowell men and became city dwellers. Those who returned home remained unmarried longer than their sisters who had stayed on the farm, and then married men about their own age who worked at something other than farming. Thus the Boston Associates kept their promise to produce cotton cloth profitably without creating a permanent working class, but they did not succeed in shuttling young women between rural and urban paternalism and back again. Wage labor, the ultimate degradation for agrarian-republican men, opened a road to independence for thousands of young women.

8-6c *Cities*

The Market Revolution hit American cities—the old seaports as well as the new marketing and manufacturing towns—with particular force. Here there was little concern for creating a classless industrial society: Vastly wealthy men of finance, a new middle class that bought and sold an ever-growing variety of consumer goods, and the impoverished women and men who made those goods lived together in communities that unabashedly recognized the reality of social class.

The richest men were seaport merchants who had survived and prospered during the world wars that ended in 1815. They carried on as importers and exporters, took control of banks and insurance companies, and made great fortunes in urban real estate. Those in Boston constituted an urbane and responsible cluster of old Protestant families known as the **Boston Brahmins**. The elite class of Philadelphia was less unified and perhaps less responsible, and that of New York even

North Wind Picture Archives/Alamy Stock Photo

8.13 **Lowell Mill Girls** Early cotton textile factories in New England employed young farm women as wage laborers, a role customarily filled by men in Europe.

Q *How did the appearance of the Lowell mill girls attempt to counter the stereotype of wage labor as demeaning and potentially corrupting?*

less. These families continued in international commerce, profiting mainly from cotton exports and from a vastly expanded range of imports. They speculated in urban real estate, and they sometimes invested in manufacturing ventures.

Below the old mercantile elite (or, in the case of the new cities of the interior, at the top of society) stood a growing middle class of wholesale and retail merchants, small manufacturers, and an army of lawyers, salesmen, auctioneers, clerks, bookkeepers, and accountants who handled the paperwork for a new market society. At the head of this new middle class were the wholesale merchants of the seaports who bought hardware, crockery, and other commodities from importers (and increasingly from American manufacturers) and then sold them in smaller lots to storekeepers from the interior. The greatest concentration of wholesale firms was on Pearl Street in New York City. Slightly below them were the large processors of farm products, including the meat packers of Cincinnati and the flour millers of Rochester, and large merchants and real estate dealers in the new inland cities.

Another step down were specialized retail merchants who dealt in books, furniture, crockery, and other consumer goods. Alongside the merchants stood master craftsmen who had become manufacturers. With their workers busy in backrooms or in household workshops, they now called themselves shoe dealers and merchant tailors. At the bottom of this new commercial world were hordes of clerks, most of them young men who hoped to rise in the world. Many of them—one study puts the figure at between 25 percent and 38 percent—did move up in society. Both in numbers and in the nature of the work, this white-collar army formed a new class created by the Market Revolution, particularly by the emergence of a huge consumer market in the countryside.

In the 1820s and 1830s, the commercial classes transformed the look and feel of American cities. As retailing and manufacturing became separate activities (even in firms that did both), the merchants, salesmen, and clerks now worked in quiet offices on downtown business streets. The seaport merchants built counting rooms and decorated their warehouses in the "new counting house style." Both in the seaports and the new towns of the interior, impressive brick-and-glass storefronts appeared on the main streets. Perhaps the most telling monuments of the new business society were the handsome retail arcades that began going up in the 1820s. Boston's Quincy Market (1825), a two-story arcade on Philadelphia's Chestnut Street (1827), and Rochester's four-story Reynolds Arcade (1828) provided consumers with comfortable, gracious spaces in which to shop.

8-6d *Metropolitan Industrialization*

While businessmen were developing a new middle-class ethos, and their families were flocking to the new retail stores to buy emblems of their status, the people who made the consumer goods were growing more numerous and disappearing from view. With the exception of textiles and a few other commodities, few goods were made in mechanized factories before the 1850s. Most of the clothes and shoes, brooms, hats, books, furniture, candy, and other goods available in country stores and city shops were made by hand. City merchants and master craftsmen met the growing demand by hiring more workers. The largest handicrafts—shoemaking, tailoring, and the building trades—were divided into skilled and semiskilled segments and farmed out to subcontractors who could turn a profit only by cutting labor costs. The result was the creation of an urban working class, not only in the big seaports and factory towns but in scores of milling and manufacturing towns throughout the North and West as well.

The rise of New York City's ready-made clothing trade provides an example. In 1815, wealthy Americans wore tailor-made clothing. Everyone else wore clothes sewn by women at home. In the 1820s, the availability of cheap manufactured cloth and an expanding pool of cheap—largely female—labor, along with the creation of the southern and western markets, transformed New York City into the center of a national market in ready-made clothes. The first big market was in "Negro cottons"—graceless shirts, pants, and sack dresses in which southern planters clothed their slaves. Within a few years, New York manufacturers were sending dungarees and hickory shirts to western farmers and supplying inexpensive clothing to urban workers. By the 1830s, many New York tailoring houses, including the storied Brooks Brothers, offered fancier ready-made clothes to the new middle class.

High rents and costly real estate, together with the absence of waterpower, prohibited locating large factories in cities, but the nature of the clothing trade and the availability of cheap labor gave rise to a system of subcontracting that transformed

What They Said

The Lowell Mill Girls

A distinctive feature of the early Industrial Revolution in America was that women, not men, supplied the majority of factory labor. The use of young farm women in the Waltham-Lowell factory system responded to both a demographic challenge—a shortage of young working men because of new opportunities in western areas—and the Jeffersonian ideological bias against wage labor as a demeaning, corrupting influence.

As the following documents suggest, however, the use of women in factories did not silence all critics of wage labor. In 1840, the New England intellectual Orestes Brownson applied old fears about the moral depravity of wages to the Lowell mill girls, who he claimed would be so tarnished by their experience that they would never marry. In fact, after finishing their stint in the textile mills, most Lowell women did marry and many entered public life as reformers, including the author of the other document selection, Lucy Larcom. A successful poet, Larcom wrote a memoir of her childhood in the 1880s that upheld the dignity of the work by her and other Lowell girls against critics like Brownson.

Orestes Brownson

We pass through our manufacturing villages; most of them appear neat and flourishing. The operatives are well dressed, and we are told, well paid. They are said to be healthy, contented, and happy. This is the fair side of the picture; the side exhibited to distinguished visitors. There is a dark side, moral as well as physical. Of the common operatives, few, if any, by their wages, acquire a competence … the great many mass wear out their health, spirits, and morals, without becoming one whit better off than when they commenced labor. The bills of mortality in these factory villages are not striking, we admit, for the poor girls when they can toil no longer go home to die. The average life, working life we mean, of the girls that come to Lowell, for instance, from Maine, New Hampshire, and Vermont, we have been assured, is only about three years. What becomes of them then? Few of them ever marry; fewer still ever return to their native places with reputations unimpaired. "She has worked in a Factory," is almost enough to damn to infamy the most worthy and virtuous girl.

Lucy Larcom

I do not believe that any Lowell mill-girl was ever absurd enough to wish to be known as a "factory-lady," although most of them knew that "factory-girl" did not represent a high type of womanhood in the Old World. But they themselves belonged to the New World, not to the Old; and they were making their own traditions, to hand down to their Republican descendants,—one of which was and is that honest work has no need to assert itself or to humble itself in a nation like ours, but simply to take its place as one of the foundation stones of the Republic.

The young women who worked at Lowell had the advantage of living in a community where character alone commanded respect. They never, at their work or away from it, heard themselves contemptuously spoken of on account of their occupation, except by the ignorant or weak-minded, whose comments they were of course too sensible to heed.

Q *What does Brownson seem to most oppose: wage labor, or the notion of working women—or both? How might his critique have been different if only men had worked in early factories?*

Q *How does Larcom respond to the charge that work, especially by women, violated republican principles?*

Q *Although Larcom claims that the Lowell mill girls were largely immune from outside criticism, what evidence suggests that Brownson won at least a partial victory in the debate about the probity of working women?*

Sources: (top) Orestes A. Brownson, "The Laboring Classes," an Article from the Boston *Quarterly Review* (Boston: Benjamin H. Greene, 1840), p. 11; (bottom) Lucy Larcom, *A New England Girlhood, Outlined from Memory* (Boston: Houghton Mifflin Company, 1889), pp. 201–202.

8.14 **Charles Oakford's Hat Store in Philadelphia, circa 1855** Such specialized retail establishments (unlike the craftsmen's shops that preceded them) hid the process of manufacturing from customers' view.

needlework into the first "sweated" trade in America. Merchants kept a few skilled male tailors to take care of the custom trade and to cut cloth into patterned pieces for ready-made clothing. The pieces were sent out, often by way of subcontractors, to needleworkers who sewed them together in a process known as the **putting-out system**, or cottage industry, because the work was done in homes or small workshops. Male tailors continued to do the finishing work on men's suits, but most of the work—on cheap goods destined for the countryside—was done by women who worked for piece rates that ranged from 75 cents to $1.50 per week. Along with clothing, women in garrets and tenements manufactured the items with which the middle class decorated itself and its homes: embroidery, doilies, artificial flowers, fringe, tassels, fancy-bound books, and parasols. All provided work for ill-paid legions of female workers in the putting-out system.

Other trades followed similar patterns. For example, northeastern shoes were made in uniform sizes and sent in barrels all over the country. Like tailoring, shoemaking was divided into skilled operations and time-consuming unskilled tasks. Men performed the skilled work of cutting and shaping the uppers. The drudgery of sewing the pieces together went tolow-paid women. In the shops of Lynn, Massachusetts, in the shoemakers' boardinghouses in Rochester and other new manufacturing cities of the interior, and in the cellars and garrets of New York City, skilled shoemakers performed the most difficult work for taskmasters who passed the work along to subcontractors who controlled poorly paid, unskilled workers. Skilled craftsmen could earn as much as $2 per day making custom boots and shoes. Men shaping uppers in boardinghouses earned a little more than half of that. Women binders could work a full week and earn as little as 50 cents. In this as in other trades, wage rates and gendered tasks reflected the old family division of labor, which was based on the assumption that female workers lived with an income-earning husband or father. In fact, increasing numbers of them were young women living alone or older women who had been widowed, divorced, or abandoned—often with small children.

In their shops and counting rooms, the new middle class entertained notions of gentility based on the distinction between manual and nonmanual work. Lowly clerks and wealthy merchants prided themselves on the fact that they worked with their heads and not their hands. They fancied that their entrepreneurial and managerial skills were making the Market Revolution happen, while manual workers simply performed tasks thought up by the middle class. The old distinction between proprietorship and dependence, which had placed master craftsmen and independent tradesmen, along with farm-owning yeomen, among the respectable "middling sort," disappeared. The men and women of an emerging working class struggled to find dignity and a sense of public worth in a society that hid them from view and defined them as "hands."

Conclusion

In the first half of the 19th century, northern society became based in buying and selling. The Northeast—New York City in particular—sloughed off its old colonial status and moved from the periphery to the industrial and financial core of the world market economy. Britain was the first country to make this industrial transition, yet it deemphasized agriculture, drew its populations into cities, and relied on the export of manufactured goods as its principal source of income. The American North, on the other hand, built factories and commercial farms at the same time and as parts of the same process. The market for American manufactures was in the American countryside. (Industrial exports from the United States were insignificant until the end of the 19th century.) The principal market for American food was in American towns and cities, and even on farms whose proprietors were too busy with staple crops to grow the old array of food. The result was a massive commercialization of the northwestern, mid-Atlantic, and New England states and the beginnings of their integration into a unified northern capitalist democracy.

CHAPTER REVIEW

Review

1. What was the nature of the northern agricultural economy and of agricultural society in the years 1790 to 1820?
2. How did eastern opinion of the Northwest and its settlers change between 1790 and 1820?
3. How did improvements in transportation channel commerce within and between regions?
4. How did northern farm families experience the transition into commercial agriculture between 1815 and 1850?
5. How did northern and southern settlers flooding into the Northwest after 1815 view the new market economy differently?
6. Why did America's first factories start in the northern countryside?

Critical Thinking

1. The economic changes associated with the Market Revolution did not take hold until the 1820s. Why? What were the constraints upon growth before then, and how did those constraints help shape earlier economic development?
2. How did America's new market economy impact women? To what extent did the experience of women differ according to their social class? Even as the economic lives of women changed, sometimes dramatically, why did attitudes about them remain mostly unchanged?

Identifications

Review your understanding of the following key terms, people, and events for this chapter (terms in bold in text are included in the Glossary).

Market Revolution, p. 232
competence, p. 232
changing system, p. 233
tenancy, p. 235
journeyman, p. 236
frontier, p. 239
internal improvements, p. 239
transportation revolution, p. 239
National Road, p. 240
Robert Fulton, p. 240
Erie Canal, p. 240
middle class, p. 245
Rhode Island System, p. 248
Waltham-Lowell System, p. 249
Lowell mill girls, p. 249
Boston Brahmins, p. 249
putting-out system, p. 252

Suggested Readings

For the Market Revolution, see **Charles Sellers**, ***The Market Revolution: Jacksonian America, 1815–1846*** (1994); and **John L. Larson**, ***The Market Revolution in America: Liberty, Ambition, and the Eclipse of the Common Good*** (2010). **Christopher Clark's *Social Change in America: From the Revolution through the Civil War*** (2006) surveys social development in these years. An essential treatment of social and cultural results of transportation improvement is **Carol Sheriff**, ***The Artificial River: The Erie Canal and the Paradox of Progress*** (1997). Studies of rural society include **Christopher Clark**, ***The Roots of Rural Capitalism: Western Massachusetts, 1780–1860*** (1990); **Laurel Thatcher Ulrich**, ***A Midwife's Tale: The Life of Martha Ballard, Based on Her Diary, 1785–1812*** (1990); **Martin Bruegel**, ***Farm, Shop, Landing: The Rise of a Market Society in the Hudson Valley, 1780–1860*** (2002); and **Carolyn Merchant**, ***Ecological Revolutions: Nature, Gender, and Science in New England*** (1989).

David R. Meyer's *The Roots of American Industrialization* (2003) surveys urban-industrial development. Specialized studies include **Thomas Dublin**, ***Women at Work: The Transformation of Work and Community in Lowell, Massachusetts, 1810–1860*** (1979); **Michael Zakim**, ***Ready-Made Democracy: A History of Men's Dress in the American Republic, 1760–1860*** (2003); and **Brian P. Luskey**, ***On the Make: Clerks and the Quest for Capital in Nineteenth-Century America*** (2011). For the emergence of social-economic classes, see **Sean Wilentz**, ***Chants Democratic: New York City and the Rise of the American Working Class*** (1984); **Christine Stansell**, ***City of Women: Sex and Class in New York, 1789–1860*** (1986); and **Richard Stott**, ***Workers in the Metropolis: Class, Ethnicity and Youth in Antebellum New York City*** (1990).

MINDTAP is a fully online personalized learning experience built upon Cengage Learning content. MindTap® combines student learning tools—readings, multimedia, activities, and assessments—into a singular Learning Path that guides students through the course and helps students develop the critical thinking, analysis, and communication skills that are essential to academic and professional success.

9 The Old South, 1790–1850

9-1 **Old Farms: The Southeast**

Learning Objective: *List the principal differences between the slave economies of the Chesapeake and the South Carolina–Georgia lowcountry.*

The Chesapeake, 1790–1820

Flirting with Emancipation

The Lowcountry, 1790–1820

9-2 **New Farms: The Rise of the Deep South**

Learning Objective: *Describe the ways that the economy and society of the Cotton Belt differed from that of older plantation regions.*

Slavery and Capitalism

The Interstate Slave Trade

Cotton and Slave Labor

Mastery as a Way of Life

9-3 **The Southern Yeomanry**

Learning Objective: *Assess how southern yeoman farmers differed from planters who presided over much larger plantations.*

Yeomen and Planters

Yeoman Neighborhoods

9-4 **Slave Culture**

Learning Objective: *Identify the prominent features of the cultural life that slaves made for themselves within the limits of slavery.*

Slave Families and the Slave Trade

Slave Theology

Religion and Revolt

Gabriel's Rebellion

Denmark Vesey

Nat Turner

9-5 **A Southern Market Revolution?**

Learning Objective: *Determine the nature and limits of the Market Revolution in the South.*

Abby Aldrich Rockefeller Folk Art Museum

9.1 ***The Old Plantation*** In the late 18th century, the South Carolina slaveholder John Rose most likely painted this scene of slaves dancing and playing musical instruments. The painting offers a rare glimpse into early plantation life and shows that, within the considerable oppression of slavery, individual slaves managed to keep their own cultural ways.

THE SOUTHERN STATES experienced a parallel Market Revolution, but it was transacted on southern terms. From the 1790s onward, international markets and technological innovation encouraged planters to grow cotton. Cotton became the great southern cash crop, and the plantation spread across an expanding Deep South. The planters sent mountains of cotton (along with tobacco from the Upper South, rice from the Georgia–Carolina coast, and sugar from Louisiana) to Britain. They made a lot of money, and they bought a lot of nice things. Other southerners, however, were not as fortunate. Enslaved workers experienced longer hours and tighter discipline than in the past. They lost their families and friends to a soulless interstate slave trade, and they watched their masters' commitment to slavery harden into an unmovable political axiom. In addition, most white farmers moved to the edges of the commercial economy. They continued in the old-style mixed agriculture, and traded relatively little beyond their neighborhoods. In the North, country people became the great consumer market that drove regional economic development. In the South, slaves and most whites bought little, and what they bought was made outside of the region.

The South experienced stupendous economic growth between 1790 and 1850, but most southern investment and entrepreneurial talent went into producing plantation staples for export, an activity that produced wealth for the planters, but that strengthened the South's neocolonial dependence upon Britain and, increasingly, the northeastern United States. It put the South in the peculiar position of helping to fuel the capitalist transformation of the North and Europe while not realizing the full commercial benefits of the economic changes. ■

9-1 Old Farms: The Southeast

Q *What were the principal differences between the slave economies of the Chesapeake and the South Carolina–Georgia lowcountry?*

In 1790, the planters of Virginia and South Carolina were among the richest men in the new republic. But international markets for their tobacco and rice were declining, and they faced uncertain futures.

9-1a *The Chesapeake, 1790–1820*

In 1790, the future of plantation agriculture in the Chesapeake (the states of Virginia, Maryland, and Delaware) was precarious. The market for tobacco, its principal crop, had been falling since before the Revolution, and it continued to decline after 1790. Tobacco also depleted the soil, and by the late 18th century, tidewater farms and plantations were giving out. As lands west of the Appalachians opened to settlement, white tenants, laborers, and small farmers left the Chesapeake in droves. Many of them moved to Kentucky, Tennessee, or the western reaches of Virginia. Many others found new homes in nonslave states north of the Ohio River. Faced with declining opportunities within the slave societies of the Chesapeake, thousands of the poorer whites voted with their feet.

With tobacco profits falling, many Chesapeake planters were switching to wheat, corn, and livestock. They did it on a large scale. In many parts of the region, the old tobacco lands gave way to grain fields and pastures, and by 1830, Richmond rivaled Rochester, New York, as the nation's leading flour-milling center. It was a sensible move, but it left the Chesapeake with a huge investment in slaves who were less and less necessary. Grazing animals and raising wheat required less labor than tobacco. Enslaved workers planted individual tobacco plants and then pruned, weeded, and picked worms off of them by hand. At harvest time they picked the leaves one at a time, then hung them to cure, packed them, and shipped them off to market. In sharp contrast, grain and livestock took care of themselves through most of the year. Planters with large numbers of slaves had to think up new uses for them. Some divided their land into small plots and rented both the plots and their slaves to white tenant farmers; others, particularly in Maryland, recruited tenants from the growing ranks of free blacks; still others hired out their slaves as artisans and urban laborers.

The increasing diversification of the Chesapeake economy assigned new chores to slave women and men. Wheat cultivation, for example, meant a switch from the hoes used for tobacco to the plow and grain cradle, both of which called for the upper-body strength of adult men. The grain economy also required carts, wagons, mills, and good roads, and thus created a need for greater numbers of slave artisans, who were nearly all men. Many of these artisans were hired out to urban employers and lived as a semifree caste in cities and towns. In the new economy of the Chesapeake, male slaves did the plowing, mowing, sowing, ditching, and carting and performed most of the tasks requiring artisanal skills. All of this work demanded high levels of training and could be performed by someone working either alone or in a small group with little need for supervision.

Slave women were left with the lesser tasks. Contrary to legend, few slave women in the Chesapeake worked as domestic servants in the planters' houses. Some were assigned to such chores as cloth manufacture, sewing, candle molding, and the preparation of salt meat, but most female slaves still did farmwork—hoeing, weeding, spreading manure, cleaning stables—that was monotonous, unskilled, and closely supervised. This new division of labor was clearly evident during the wheat harvest. On George Washington's farm, for example, male slaves, often working beside temporary white laborers, moved in a broad line as they mowed the grain. Following them came a gang of children and women on their hands and knees binding wheat

CHRONOLOGY

1791–1803	Slave revolt in French colony of Saint-Domingue (Haiti)
1792	Kentucky enters the union as the 15th state
1793	Eli Whitney invents the cotton gin
1796	Tennessee enters the union as the 16th state
1800	Gabriel's Rebellion in Virginia
1803	Jefferson purchases the Louisiana Territory from France
1804	Haiti becomes an independent republic
1808	International slave trade ends
1812	Second war with Britain begins
1817	Mississippi enters the union
1819	Alabama enters the union • Adams-Onis Treaty conveys Florida and the Gulf Coast to the United States
1822	Denmark Vesey's slave conspiracy in South Carolina
1831	Nat Turner's rebellion in Virginia

into shocks. Thomas Jefferson, who had been startled to see French women working in the fields, abandoned his concern for female delicacy when his own slaves were involved. At the grain harvest, he instructed his overseers to organize "gangs of half men and half women."

9-1b *Flirting with Emancipation*

Neither new crops nor new employments, however, erased the growing fact that Chesapeake proprietors needed less slave labor than they had in the past—or the parallel fact that their slaves reproduced at a higher rate than almost any other Americans. Nothing, it seemed, could employ the great mass of enslaved people or repay the planters' huge investment in them. In this situation, some Chesapeake planters (who had, after all, fought a revolution in the name of natural rights) began to manumit their slaves. The farmers of Maryland and Delaware in particular set their slaves free. By 1810, 76 percent of Delaware blacks and 23 percent of Maryland blacks were free. (In 1790, these figures had stood at 31 percent and 7 percent, respectively.) Virginia's economic and cultural commitment to the plantation was stronger, but even in the Old Dominion there was a movement to manumit slaves. George Washington stated that he wished "to liberate a certain species of property," and manumitted his slaves by will. Robert Carter, reputedly the largest slaveholder in Virginia, also freed his slaves, as did many others. The free black population of Virginia stood at 3,000 in 1782, when the state passed a law permitting manumission. The number of free blacks rose to 12,766 in 1790, to 20,124 in 1800, and to 30,570 in 1810. These were impressive numbers, but the birthrate of Virginia slaves erased them. Between 1780 and 1810, the slave population of the state rose from 250,000 to 400,000.

Emancipation moved slowly in Virginia for several reasons. First, few Virginia planters could afford to free their slaves without compensation. Second, white Virginians feared the social consequences of black freedom. Thomas Jefferson, for instance, owned 175 slaves when he penned the phrase that "all men are created equal." He lived off their labor, sold them to pay his debts, gave them away as gifts, sold them away from their families as a punishment, and kept one of them, a woman named Sally Hemings, as a mistress and fathered several children by her. Through it all he insisted that slavery was wrong. He could not imagine emancipation, however, without sending freed slaves far from Virginia. A society of free blacks and whites, Jefferson insisted, would end in disaster with "the extermination of the one or the other race."

9-1c *The Lowcountry, 1790–1820*

The other center of plantation slavery in 1790 was lowcountry South Carolina and Georgia. Here the principal crop was rice, which, along with other American foodstuffs, enjoyed a rise in international demand during the European wars between 1793 and 1815. But lowcountry planters faced increasing competition from rice farmers in India, Java, Burma, and Europe. The rice coast—one of the great sources of American wealth in the 18th century—remained profitable, but it was losing relative position to faster-growing regions. The planters of the lowcountry, like those in Virginia, remained wealthy men. Their long-term future, however, was in doubt.

The Library of Virginia

9.2 Blacks Working on the James River, 1798–1799 In the Chesapeake, enslaved and free black watermen provided transportation in a region that had poor roads and good rivers. They performed skilled, often hazardous work, and they lived for days and weeks at a time without white supervision.

Q *How did the diversification of the Chesapeake economy make this and other new kinds of work possible for free and enslaved black men?*

Thousands of slaves in this region had either run away or been carried off by the British in the Revolution, and planters knew that the African slave trade was scheduled to end in 1808 (the earliest date allowed by the Constitution). Lowcountry planters, unlike their Chesapeake counterparts, could not imagine emancipating their slaves. They rushed to import as many Africans as they could in the time remaining. From 1783 to 1808, between 100,000 and 190,000 captive people were brought directly from Africa to the United States, nearly all of them to Charleston and Savannah. It was the busiest period in the history of the slave trade in North America.

In the plantation counties of coastal South Carolina and Georgia, slaves made up 80 percent of the population, and more than 90 percent in many parishes. Farms and slave labor forces were big, and rice cultivation demanded intensive labor, often performed by workers who stood knee-deep in water. The work and the hot, sticky climate encouraged deadly summer diseases, which kept white owners and overseers out of the fields. Many of the wealthiest planters built homes in Charleston and Savannah and hired others to manage their plantations. Both they and planters who stayed on their farms organized enslaved workers according to the task system, as they had since the early 18th century (see Chapter 4). Each morning the owner or manager assigned a specific task to each slave. When the task was done, the rest of the day belonged to the slave. Slaves who did not finish their task were punished, and when too many slaves finished early, the owners assigned heavier tasks. In the 18th century, each slave had been expected to tend three to four acres of rice each day. In the early 19th century, with the growth of a competitive rice market, the assignment was raised to five acres.

Slaves under the task system won the right to cultivate land as **private fields**, not the little garden plots common in the Chesapeake but farms of up to five acres on which they grew produce and raised livestock for market. There was a lively trade in slave-produced goods, and eventually slaves in the lowcountry not only produced and exchanged property but also passed it on to their children. The owners tolerated such activity because slaves on the task system worked hard, required minimal supervision, produced much of their own food, and made money for their owners. The rice planters in South Carolina and Georgia were among the richest men in the United States.

9-2 New Farms: The Rise of the Deep South

Q *In what ways did the economy and society of the Cotton Belt differ from that of older plantation regions?*

While the old centers of slavery and southern power stagnated or declined, planters discovered a new and promising cash crop. British textile factories had been buying raw cotton since the mid-18th century. Southern planters knew they could sell all of the cotton they could grow. But long-staple cotton, the only variety that could be profitably grown, was a delicate plant that thrived only on the Sea Islands off the coasts of Georgia and South Carolina. The short-staple variety was hardier, but its sticky seeds had to be removed by hand before the cotton could be milled. It took a full day for an adult slave to clean a single pound of short-staple cotton—an expenditure of labor that took the profit out of cotton. In 1790, the United States produced only 3,000 bales of cotton, nearly all of it on the long-staple plantations of the Sea Islands.

Scores of tinkerers tried to devise a mechanical cotton-cleaner, but it was **Eli Whitney**, a Connecticut Yankee who had come south to work as a tutor, who made a model of a **cotton gin** (a southern contraction of "engine") that combed the seeds from the fiber with metal pins fitted into rollers. Working with Whitney's machine, a slave could clean 50 pounds of short-staple cotton in a day. Others quickly developed improved models, and amid a storm of patent disputes and litigation, cotton became the great southern cash crop and contributed to the development of global capitalism.

9-2a *Slavery and Capitalism*

Along with the profitability of short-staple cotton, it was the national government that made possible the southern **Cotton Belt**—a region specializing in cotton production that stretched south from South Carolina into Florida and west to eastern Texas by the mid-19th century (see Map 9.1). Planters did not take their money and slaves into the interior until the government had ended Indian resistance in the War of 1812. Jefferson's Louisiana Purchase of 1803 had secured free navigation of the Mississippi Valley, and the United States gained Florida and the Gulf Coast under the Adams-Onis Treaty of 1819. Given military security and access to markets, the greater South was safe for slavery.

Planters and their slaves had moved into upland South Carolina and Georgia in the 1790s, transforming a sparsely settled farm country into the first great short-staple cotton region. With the end of war in 1815, the plantation rolled west into a Cotton Belt that stretched beyond the Mississippi River. By 1834, the new states of Alabama, Mississippi, and Louisiana grew more than half of a vastly increased U.S. cotton crop. In 1810, the South produced 178,000 bales of ginned cotton, more than 59 times the 3,000 bales it had produced in 1790. With the opening of new cotton lands, production jumped to 334,000 bales in 1820 and to 1,350,000 bales in 1840. In these years, cotton made up from one-half to two-thirds of the value of all U.S. exports. The South produced three-fourths of the world supply of cotton—a commodity that, more than any other, was the raw material of industrialization in Britain and Europe and, increasingly, in the northeastern United States. Cotton, in short, was a very big business.

Without the labor of enslaved African Americans, cotton could not have become the world's most widely traded commodity and fueled the Industrial Revolution. Indeed, though a premodern institution, slavery was integral to the development of American and global

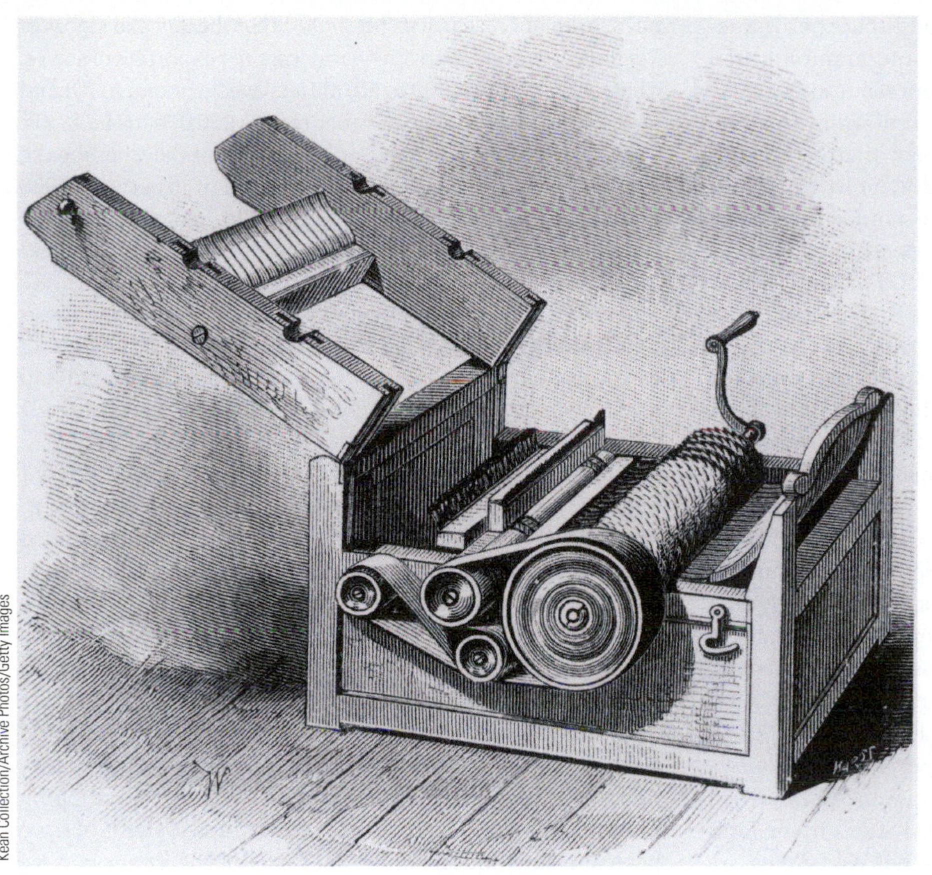
Kean Collection/Archive Photos/Getty Images

9.3 **Cotton Gin** With the turn of a handle, Eli Whitney's cotton gin eased the removal of seeds from short-staple cotton. But, far from eliminating the need for slave labor, the 1793 invention created a new task for enslaved workers and led to the expansion of cotton plantations in the Deep South.

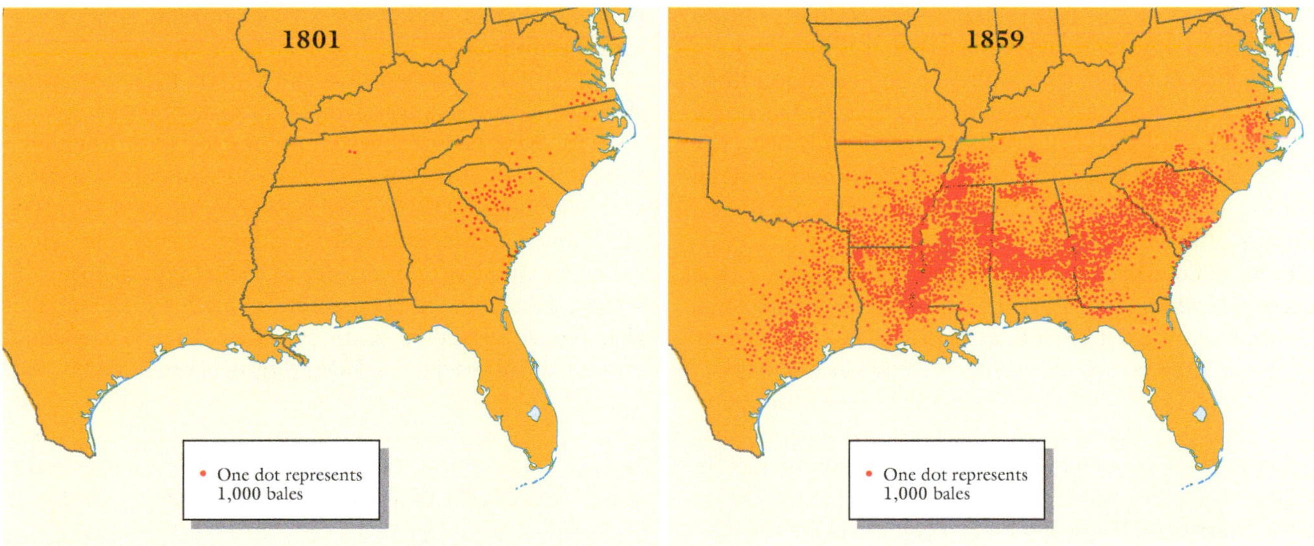

▲ **MAP 9.1 Cotton Production, 1801 and 1859** Short-staple cotton thrived wherever there was fertile soil, heat and humidity, low altitude, and a long growing season. As a result, a great belt of cotton and slavery took shape in the Lower South, from the midlands of South Carolina through eastern Texas.

Q *Aside from climate, what other factors came together in the first half of the 19th century to support such rapid expansion of cotton production in the Lower South?*

Q *What were the economic costs for the South in placing so much emphasis in producing a single commodity?*

capitalism. The U.S. was unique among all other industrializing nations in that it both grew and manufactured its own cotton. The work of slaves represented the first step in what emerged as the most dynamic and far-reaching production complex in human history to that point. Creating and maintaining the Cotton Belt involved banks that capitalized on the slave trade, insurance companies that underwrote the trade, riverboat operators who transported cotton and slaves, cotton traders in New Orleans known as "factors," textile mills in Britain and the northern U.S., merchant houses in New York and Liverpool, and slave traders who secured the labor necessary to keep the cotton flowing. In New Orleans alone, there were about twenty separate establishments whose sole business was the buying and selling of enslaved people.

The Deep South also required massive flows of capital to make the Cotton Belt possible. In the 1820s and into the early 1830s, the Second Bank of the United States and its affiliate state branches lent southern borrowers, mostly elite planters, millions of dollars. This money helped to fuel the ongoing cycle of land and slavery expansion: The more land and slave purchases planters could finance, the more cotton they could produce; the more cotton, the more profits and ability to repay debts before starting the cycle anew. Planters could only borrow such high amounts because they owned the biggest pool of collateral in the United States in the form of enslaved African Americans. By the Civil War, America's nearly four million slaves were worth more than $3 billion, or about 20 percent of all the wealth owned by U.S. citizens.

Over time, southerners developed more complex global financial innovations to meet the insatiable demand for land, slaves, and cotton. In 1827, the Louisiana state legislature chartered the Consolidated Association of the Planters of Louisiana (C.A.P.L.). The organization pioneered efforts at using slaves as collateral to raise capital overseas to then reinvest in more slaves and land in the Cotton Belt. The C.A.P.L. did this by selling bonds—backed by slaves—on the financial markets of the Western world. Banks like Baring Brothers of London, which had helped to finance the U.S. purchase of Louisiana in 1803, sold the bonds to investors in London, Hamburg, Amsterdam, Paris, Philadelphia, Boston, New York, and other financial centers. After President Andrew Jackson vetoed the recharter of the Second Bank of the United States in 1832 (see Chapter 11), several southern states filled the lending vacuum by replicating the C.A.P.L. innovations to raise global capital in their own banks. In the mid-1830s, a visitor to former Chickasaw Indian land in northeastern Mississippi observed: "People here are run mad with speculation. They do business in ... a kind of phrenzy. [Gold] is scarce, but credit is plenty."

9-2b *The Interstate Slave Trade*

With the international slave trade abolished in 1808, the source of slaves for the Cotton Belt was the old seaboard states—states with a huge population of slaves and a shrinking need for them. As early as the 1790s, the Chesapeake states of Virginia, Delaware, and Maryland were net exporters of slaves. Those states sent 40,000 to 50,000 enslaved workers south and west in that decade. The number rose to 120,000 in the 1810s. The slave families and slave communities of the Chesapeake lost 1 in 12 of their members in the 1790s, 1 in 10 between 1800 and 1810, and 1 in 5 between 1810 and 1820. In the 1820s, South Carolina and Kentucky joined the slave-exporting states, and 150,000 slaves left their homes and crossed state lines. In total, around 1 million slaves were moved from the older slave states westward by 1860. The trade in slaves reordered the human geography of the South. In 1790, Virginia and Maryland had held 56 percent of all American slaves. By 1860, they held only 15 percent (see Map 9.2).

Masters or masters' sons carried as many as 30 percent of enslaved migrants to the new lands of the Cotton Belt. These slaves made new plantations and new lives surrounded by some of the people they had known at home. But most were sold and resold as individuals in the **interstate slave trade**. Soon after the Revolution, men known as "Georgia Traders" appeared in the Upper South, buying slaves on speculation and selling them farther south. By 1820, the slave trade had become an organized business with sophisticated financing, sellers who had an accurate knowledge of slave prices in various southern markets, a well-traveled shipping route between Norfolk and New Orleans, and systems of slave pens and safe houses along the roads of the interior. With the exception of the plantation itself, the domestic slave trade was the biggest and most modern business in the South. The centrality of that trade advertised the nature of southern economic development: While northerners exchanged wheat, furniture, books, and shoes with each other, southerners exchanged slaves.

Most slaves moved into the Cotton Belt with other slaves who were strangers, under the temporary ownership of traders who knew them only as merchandise. Those who were transported by ship experienced some of the horrors of the old Middle Passage from Africa: cramped quarters, minimal food, discipline at the hands of nervous white crewmen, and the odd murder or casual rape. Those who walked west from the old plantations along the Cotton Belt experienced their own share of terrors. The journey could take as long as seven weeks, and traders organized it with military precision.

9-2c *Cotton and Slave Labor*

The cotton plantations operated more efficiently than the old estates on the Chesapeake and in the lowcountry. First, cotton planters exerted a more disciplined and direct control over their enslaved workers. Masters on the seaboard had hired their slaves out, given them time and land with which to grow their own food, and worked them by the task system or under slave overseers—all of which reduced the costs of supervising and providing for slaves. On the cotton frontier, good land and slave labor were too valuable to be worked

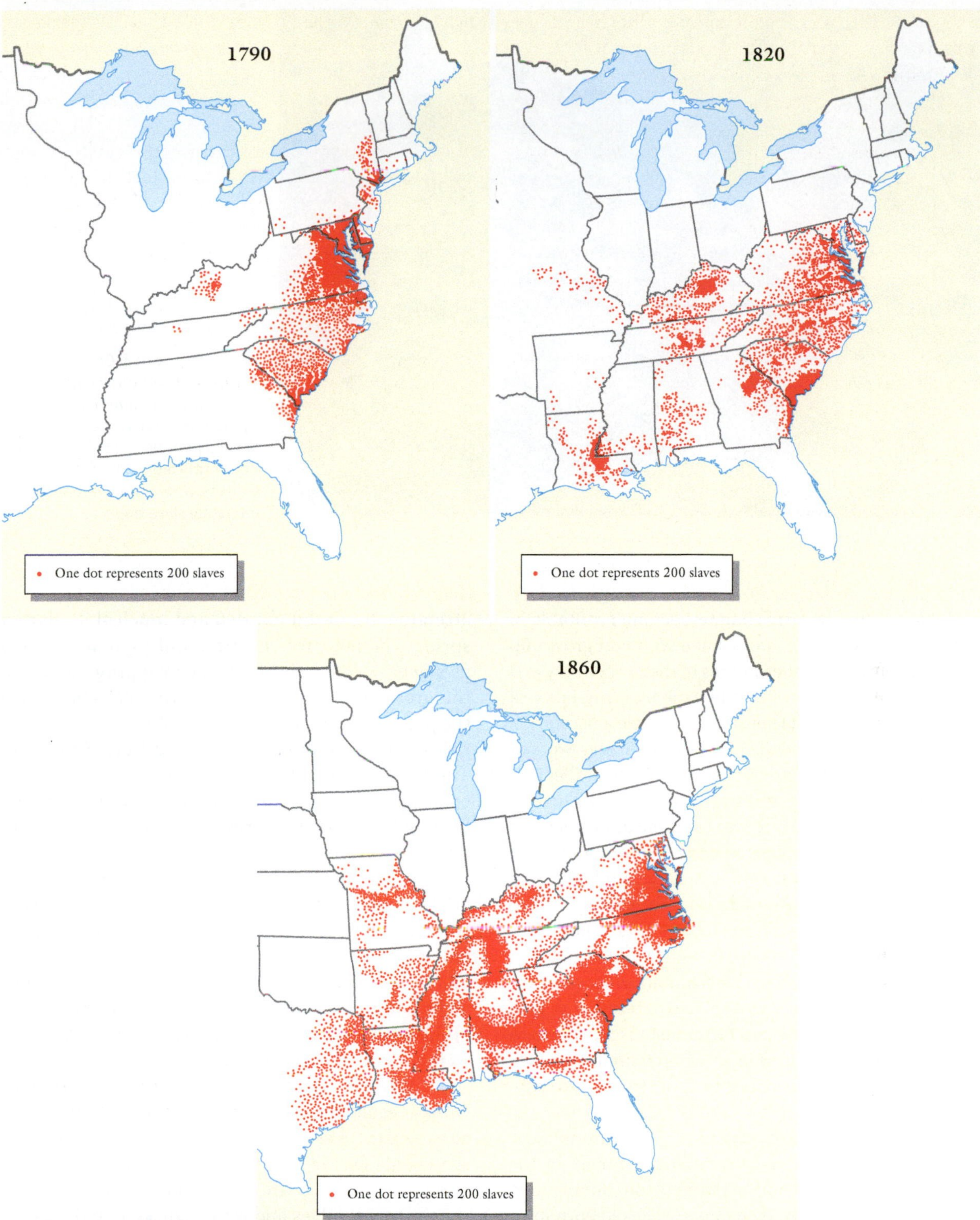

▲ **MAP 9.2 Distribution of Slave Population, 1790, 1820, and 1860** In 1790, slaves were concentrated in the Chesapeake and in the South Carolina and Georgia low country. Over the next 70 years, Chesapeake planters put thousands of slaves into the interstate trade, which sold them into the Cotton Belt stretching from the interior of the Carolinas to eastern Texas.

Q *How did economic and demographic conditions in the Chesapeake make possible the interstate slave trade?*

Q *How does the interstate slave trade challenge popular conceptions of western expansion as a march of democracy and liberty?*

9.4 **Price, Birch & Co., Alexandria, Virginia** From this location, marked openly with the sign "Dealers in Slaves," thousands of slaves were kept in squalid pens before being auctioned or transported, most often to New Orleans, where they were sold within the interstate slave trade.

in casual ways, and new farms had to become profitable in a short time. Enslaved men and women who had grown up with the relatively loose work routines of the lowcountry and the Chesapeake now performed the backbreaking labor of turning forests into farms. (They had to "whittle a plantation right out of the woods," recalled one slave.) Slaves worked in gangs, usually under white owners or overseers. Clearing trees, rolling logs, pulling stumps, clearing and burning brush, and building cabins, fences, and outbuildings was hard labor. The planters preferred crews of young men for these tasks, but such slaves were expensive, and everyone was put to work. A teenage boy sold from the Chesapeake to Mississippi saw women clearing brush from new land, and remarked that "such work was not done by women slaves in Virginia." Another slave recalled that her mother drove a two-horse plow "when she warn't cleanin' new ground or diggin' ditches." The labor of making new farms lasted from dawn to dusk, and enslaved men and women worked under the eyes of owners who knew that they must turn the forest into cash-producing farms or go broke.

Once established, these southern plantations were among the most intensely commercialized farms in the world. Many of them grew nothing but cotton, buying food from their neighbors or from merchants who sold corn meal and salt pork in bulk. Others grew supplementary crops and produced their own food. But nearly all of the plantation owners, from the proudest grandee to the ambitious farmer with a few slaves, organized labor in ways that maximized production and reinforced the dominance of the white men who owned the farms.

Slaves from the Chesapeake and the rice coast experienced cotton cultivation as a difficult step down. Cotton required a long growing season and a lot of attention, but it did not demand much skill. Early in the spring, the land was cleared and ploughed, and gangs of slaves walked the furrows dropping seeds. During the growing season, black laborers constantly thinned the plants and cleared the fields of weeds, "chopping" the fields with hoes in the hot, humid Deep South summer. The cotton ripened unevenly. In a harvest season that could last long past Christmas, pickers swept through the fields selecting only the ripe bolls, then repeated the task until the full crop was harvested. Slaves in the diversifying Chesapeake had made barrels and crates, boats, wagons, barns, and storage sheds; slaves on the rice coast farther south had built complex systems of dikes and levees and had mastered the science of moving and controlling large amounts of water. In the Cotton Belt, they gave up those skills and went to work with axes, hoes, and their hands. (Tobacco and sugar, the other western plantation crops, were no less labor intensive.)

The work was relentless. Planters in the East had found it economical to allow slaves to work at varied tasks, at irregular times, or under the tasking system. They gave slaves only part of their food (often cornmeal and nothing else), then provided time and land with which slaves grew their own vegetables and raised chickens and pigs. Planters on the cotton frontier did away with all that. Only a few Cotton Belt planters retained the task system, and these were looked upon as eccentrics by their neighbors, who worked their slaves in gangs from dawn to dusk six days a week. Cotton land was too valuable to permit large slave gardens. It made more sense to keep the slaves constantly at cotton cultivation and to supply them with all of their food. It was a more efficient and productive way of growing cotton. It was also a way of reducing the slaves' customary privileges within

Abby Aldrich Rockefeller Folk Art Museum, The Colonial Williamsburg Foundation, Williamsburg, VA

9.5 **Going to Tennessee** The Pennsylvanian Lewis Miller met with this group of slaves near Staunton, Virginia, in 1853. They were being sent from their old farms in Virginia to the slave markets of Tennessee and from there to the cotton fields of the newer southern states. In the years after 1820, hundreds of thousands of Upper South slaves suffered this migration.

Q *In what ways did the interstate slave trade resemble the Middle Passage? How were the two forced migrations different?*

slavery, and of enforcing the master's role as the giver and taker of all things. Even slaves who grew their own food did so in white-supervised fields and not in family plots. In order to create "a perfect dependence," an Alabama planter insisted that "my Negroes have no time whatever."

The masters set harsher working conditions and longer hours than slaves had known in their old homes. Slaves could not hope to reinstitute the task system, the family gardens and little farms, the varied tasks, or the uneven hours of labor that they had known on the coast. Yet, slaves were able to force some concessions from their masters. Gardens reappeared in many new slave quarters, and some slaves found that they could hold masters to agreed-upon standards of time and work. Masters who demanded extra hours of labor on Sunday found the work particularly slow going. In the 1840s, a Mississippi planter noted that slaves had adapted to the long hours, close supervision, and pace of work under the gang system, but would perform the new customary workload and nothing more: "All of them know what their duty is upon a plantation, and that they are generally willing to do, and nothing more." When asked to work harder or longer "they will not submit to it, but become turbulent and impatient of control, and all the whips in Christendom cannot drive them to perform more than they think they ought to do, or have been in the long habit of doing."

On the whole, the exploitation of slave labor after 1820 became more rigorous, with a humane veneer. Planters imposed a new and more total control over their slaves, but they clothed it within a larger attempt to make North American slavery paternalistic and humane, and to portray themselves as gentlemen and not as heartless slave drivers. Food and clothing seem to have improved, and individual cabins for slave families became standard. State laws often forbade the more brutal forms of discipline, and they uniformly demanded that slaves be given Sunday off.

By some measures, material standards rose. Slaves suffered greater infant mortality than whites, but those who survived infancy lived out "normal" life spans. Brazil, Cuba, and other slave societies had to import Africans to make up for the deaths of slaves, but the slave population of the southern states increased threefold—from 657,000 to 1,981,000—between 1790 and 1830. With the importation of new Africans banned after 1808 (and with runaways outnumbering new Africans who were smuggled into the country), the increase was due entirely to the fact that—alone among the slave societies of the Western Hemisphere—the American slave population was healthy enough to reproduce itself.

Material conditions on the plantations sprang from both planter self-interest and an attempt to exert a kindly, paternal control over slaves, whom planters often called "our people" or "our family, black and white." But humane treatment came at a high price. At the same time that they granted slaves protection from the worst kinds of brutality, Cotton Belt states enacted slave codes that defined slaves as persons without rights. The Louisiana code of 1824, for instance, stated that "[The slave] is incapable of making any kind of contract... . They can transmit nothing by succession.... The slave is incapable of exercising any public office, or private trust... . He cannot be a party in any civil action.... Slaves cannot marry without the consent of their masters, and their marriages do not produce any of the civil effects which result from such contract." It was the exact opposite of the rights enjoyed by the white men who owned the plantations, controlled the slaves, and wrote the laws.

9-2d *Mastery as a Way of Life*

Plantation masters, both the old southeastern nabobs and the cotton planters of newer regions, were the acknowledged economic, social, cultural, and political elite of the South. Their authority rested on economic power and on their connections—often family relationships—with each other. But they dressed their power in gentility and an aura of mastery, a visible "right to rule" that few others, North or South, could match. That power and authority were tied intimately to the ownership of slaves. When assessing a planter's standing, contemporaries seldom added up his acreage or his money. Instead, they counted slaves. In the most common calculation, the ownership of 20 slaves separated planters from yeoman farmers.

It was a good enough measure, for the planter class made itself out of slaves. Slave labor bought the carpets, chandeliers, fine clothes, English chivalric novels, and racehorses with which planters displayed their social mastery. Just as important, slaves enabled planters and their ladies to distinguish themselves as gentlefolk who did not work. An observer of one plantation mistress noted that "She has a faithful nurse (Negro) to whose care she abandons her babes entirely, only when she has a fancy to caress them does she see them. Eight children and cannot lay to their charge the loss of a single night's rest." The ownership of slaves transformed a harried housewife into a lady.

Southern farmers without slaves tended to sire very large families and to keep their children in the fields. The women worked outdoors as well. Southerners who owned slaves had fewer children, sent them to school, and moved their wives indoors. The skin of farmwomen was weathered, cracked, and darkened by the sun; plantation mistresses were less exhausted, and their skin was smoother and literally whiter.

The opposite of gentility was the South Carolina farmer who, according to a neighbor, "used to work [his daughters] in the fields like Negroes." According to northern visitors, this association of labor with slavery encouraged laziness among southern whites and robbed work of the dignity it enjoyed in other parts of the country. Most southern white yeoman farmers would have disagreed, but the association of black labor, white leisure, and white gentility was central to the plantation regime.

The exercise of mastery by plantation owners extended to patriarchal control over their own families. Among southern white men, wealth generally counted for less than did maintaining one's personal and family honor and thus winning membership in the democracy of honorable males. Children learned early that their first duty was to their family's reputation. As John Horry Dent, an Alabama slaveholder and bad amateur poet, put it:

> Honor and shame from all conditions rise;
> Act well your part and there the honor lies.

In particular, women and girls who misbehaved—with transgressions ranging from simple gossip to poor housekeeping to adultery—damaged not only their own reputations but also the honor of the fathers or husbands who could not control them. Such a charge could mean social death in a rural community made up of patriarchal households and watchful neighbors. Mastery and honor came to define the South's identity.

9-3 The Southern Yeomanry

Q *How did southern yeoman farmers differ from planters who presided over much larger plantations?*

Some southern boosters advertised cotton as a "democratic" crop that could be cultivated at a profit by almost any southern farmer, but that is not how it worked. Cotton, like other

The Olivier Plantation, 1861 (w/conpaper), Persac, Adrien (1823–73)/ Louisiana State Museum, USA/The Bridgeman Art Library

9.6 **Olivier Plantation in 1861** The artist Marie Adrien Persac portrayed this southern Louisiana plantation as a site of white gentility, not of slavery and sugar production. The smoking chimneys of the processing plant at right tell us that work is going on. But the fields, the slave quarters, and the slaves themselves are hidden from view.

Q *What role did the ideology of southern gentility, as portrayed in this image, play in perpetuating slavery?*

Interpreting the Visual Past — A View of Slavery as Benevolent

Here is a representation of plantation society by a northern apologist for slavery, Edward Williams Clay, in 1841. The white family is genteel: a well-dressed, relaxed, and subdued father and mother, two well-dressed and well-behaved children, and a well-bred dog. In the text to the right, the master/father assures us that he has inherited his slaves (he does not buy or sell them) and that he is devoting his fortune to their welfare and happiness.

For their part, the slaves are content. They live in whitewashed houses, they are nicely dressed, they play and dance, and healthy, contented old folks look on with pleasure. The wording to the left voices the slaves' devotion to their master: "God Bless you massa! you feed and clothe us. When we are sick you nurse us, and when too old to work, you provide for us!"

Q *How is slavery portrayed in this picture? What is missing? Aside from the text, how do the postures and facial expressions of whites and blacks advance a particular interpretation of slavery?*

Q *The print advances a view of slavery more common to the South than to the North. Are you surprised that a northern artist completed the print and that it was first printed in New York? What does this tell us about northern society by the early 1840s and how some Americans, in the North and South, understood slavery?*

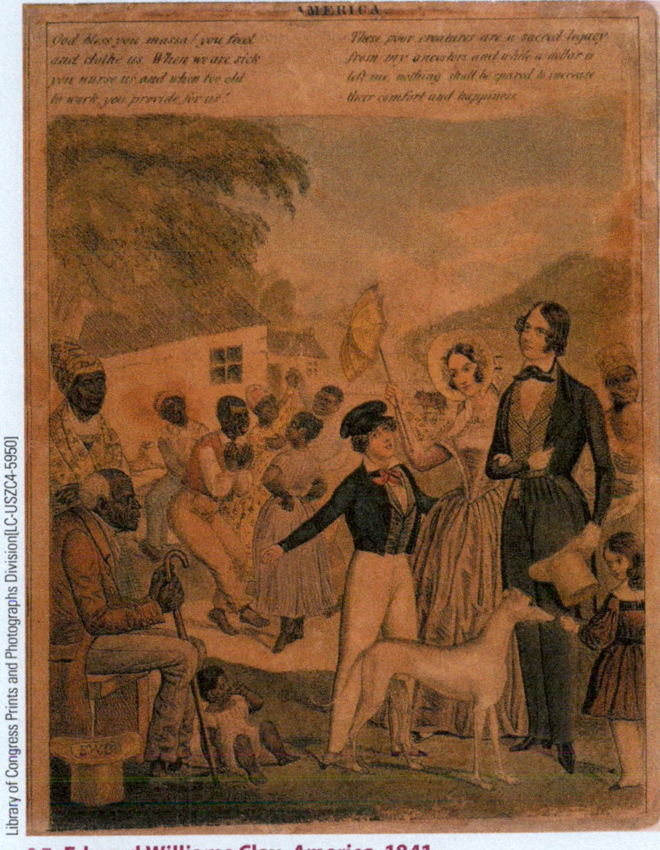

9.7 Edward Williams Clay, *America*, 1841.

plantation crops, rewarded economies of scale: Planters with big farms and many slaves operated more efficiently and more profitably than farmers with fewer resources. The wealthier planter families bought up good cotton land with ready access to markets. They also bought up the majority of slaves. Only 30 percent to 35 percent of southern white families owned at least one slave in 1830, and that percentage dropped as time passed. On the eve of the Civil War, only one white family in four owned a slave. Among the minority of southerners who were slave owners, half owned fewer than five, and less than 5 percent owned 20 or more slaves—the roughly agreed-upon number that separated planters from yeoman farmers. Cotton, it turned out, was not democratic. Among southern whites it produced not only an unequal distribution of wealth but a dual economy: plantations at the commercial center and a marginally commercial yeomanry on the fringes.

9-3a *Yeomen and Planters*

As land prices and local taxes rose in the plantation counties, many of the poorer whites moved out. Those who stayed subsisted on poor, hilly land far from navigable rivers. They tended to be commercial farmers, growing a few bales of cotton with family labor and perhaps a slave or two. Many of them were poor relatives of prosperous plantation owners. They voted the great planters into office and used their cotton gins and tapped into their marketing networks. Some of them worked as overseers for their wealthy neighbors, sold them food, and served on local slave patrols. Economic disparities between planters and farmers in the plantation belt continued to widen, but the farmers remained tied to the cotton economy and its economic and social imperatives.

Most yeomen, however, lived away from the plantations in neighborhoods with few slaves and limited commercial activities. Large numbers of them moved into nonslave territory north of the Ohio River, but most stayed in the South: in the upcountry and the eastern slopes of the Appalachians from the Chesapeake through Georgia, the western slopes of the mountains in Kentucky and Tennessee, the pine-covered hill country of northern Mississippi and Alabama, and in swampy, hilly, heavily wooded lands throughout the southern states. All of these areas were unsuitable for plantation crops. Here the farmers built a yeoman society that retained many of the characteristics of the 18th-century countryside, North and South. But while northern farmers commercialized in the 19th century, their southern cousins continued in a

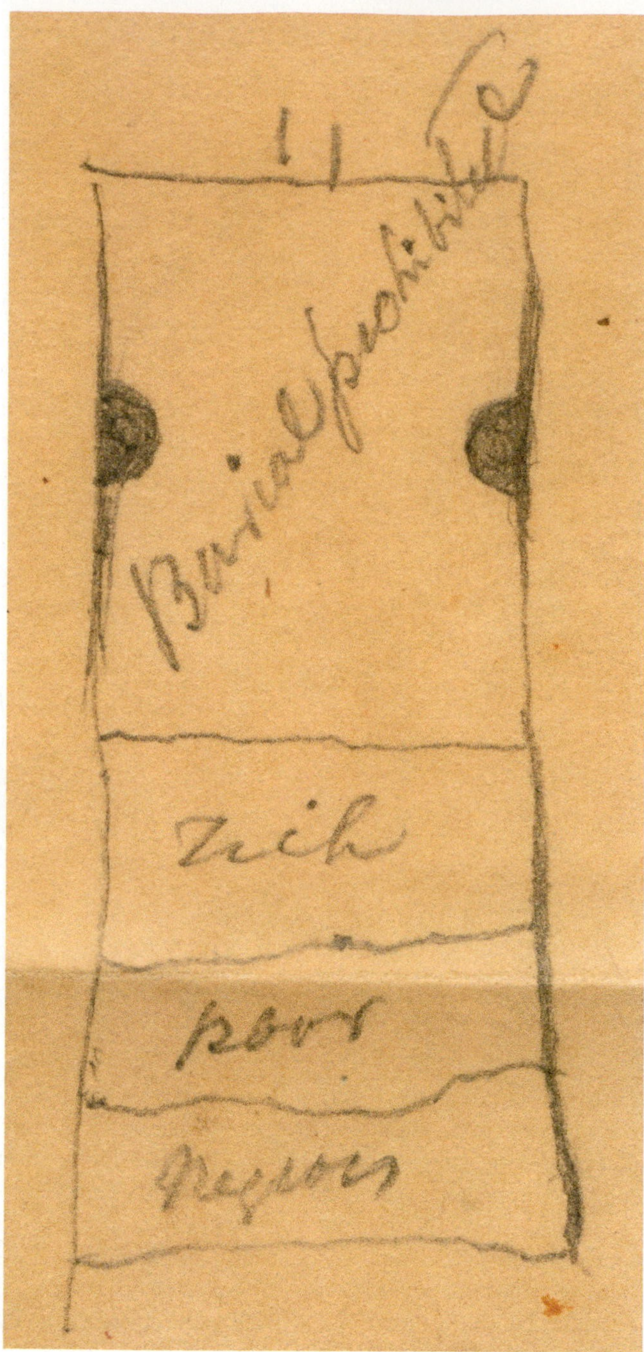

The Library of Virginia

9.8 A Map of the Burial Ground in Farmville, Virginia In 1840, a lawyer sketched the map of a graveyard in slaveholding country near the Appomattox River to make a point in a court case. It was a map of the living as well: rich whites at the top, poor whites in the middle, blacks at the bottom, yet all occupying the same ground.

household- and neighborhood-centered agriculture until the Civil War and beyond.

Many southern farmers stayed outside the market almost entirely. The mountaineers of the southern Appalachians sent a trickle of livestock and timber out of their neighborhoods, but the mountains remained largely outside the market until the coming of big-business coal mines in the late 19th century. Moreover, farmers in large parts of the upcountry South preferred raising livestock to growing cotton or tobacco. They planted cornfields and let their pigs run loose in the woods and on unfenced private land. In late summer and fall, they rounded up the animals and sold them to drovers who herded them cross-country and sold them to flatland merchants and planters. Thus, these hill-country yeomen lived off a market with which they had little firsthand experience. It was a way of life that sustained some of the most fiercely independent neighborhoods in the country.

A larger group of southern yeomen practiced mixed farming for household subsistence and neighborhood exchange, with the surplus sent to market. Most of them owned their own land. The settlement of new lands in the old backcountry and the southwestern states reversed the 18th-century drift toward white tenancy. Few of these farmers kept slaves. In the counties of upland Georgia, for instance, between seven and nine out of 10 households were without slaves. These farmers practiced a mixed agriculture that was complicated by the nature of southern cash crops. Northern yeomen before 1815 had grown grain and livestock with which they fed their families and traded with neighbors. Whatever was left over, they sent to market. But cotton, like tobacco and other southern cash crops, was not a food. It was useful only as a market crop. Most middling and poor southern farmers played it safe: They put their improved land into corn and sweet potatoes, and set pigs and cattle loose to browse the remaining land. The more substantial and ambitious of them cultivated a few acres of cotton. They grew more cotton as transportation made markets more accessible, but few southern yeomen became wholly dependent on the market. With the income from a few bales of cotton, they could pay their debts and taxes and buy coffee, tea, sugar, tobacco, cloth, and shoes. But they continued to enter and leave the market at will, and to retain the ability to subsist within their neighborhoods. In the yeoman neighborhoods of the southern states, the economic and social practices of the 18th century were alive and well.

9-3b *Yeoman Neighborhoods*

The way of life in most southern farm neighborhoods discouraged businesslike farming and individual ambition. Because few farms were self-sufficient, farmers routinely traded labor and goods with each other. In the plantation counties, such cooperation tended to reinforce the power of planters, who put some of their resources at the disposal of their poorer neighbors. In the upcountry, cooperation reinforced neighborliness. As one upland Georgian remarked, "Borrowing ... was neighboring." Debts contracted within the network of kin and neighbors were generally paid in kind or in labor, and creditors often allowed their neighbors' debts to go unpaid for years.

Among southern neighborly restraints on entrepreneurialism, none was more distinctive than the region's attitude toward fences. Northerners never tired of comparing their neatly fenced farms with the dilapidated or absent fences of the South. In the capitalist North, well-maintained fences were a sign of ambitious, hardworking farmers. The poorly maintained fences of the South, they said, were a sign of laziness. Actually, the scarcity of fences in most southern neighborhoods was the result of local custom and state law. Georgia, for instance, required farmers to fence their planted fields but not the rest of their land. In country neighborhoods where families fished and hunted for food, and where livestock roamed freely, fences conflicted with a local economy that required neighborhood use of privately owned land. In this sense, the northerners were right: The absence of fences in the South reflected neighborhood constraints on the private use of private property, and thus on individual acquisitiveness and ambition. Such constraints, however, were necessary to the subsistence of families and neighborhoods as they were organized in the upland South.

Southern farmers marketed their cotton and food surpluses at country stores, and again the patterns of the 18th and early 19th centuries persisted. Northern stores, particularly in the more commercializing regions, were stocking their shelves with a wider variety of imported and domestic goods to serve farm families that no longer produced for themselves and that had money to spend. Southern yeomen, on the other hand, bought very little. A relatively prosperous backwoods farmer in South Carolina recalled that "My farm gave me and my whole family a good living on the produce of it, and left me, one year after another, one hundred and fifty silver dollars, *for I never spent more than ten dollars a year,* which was for salt, nails and the like. Nothing to wear, eat or drink was purchased, as my farm provided all."

Families such as these continued to live without carpets or curtains, to eat homegrown food from wooden or pewter plates, and to wear everyday cloth spun and woven by the women of the family, although many who could afford it wore clothing fashioned from machine-made cloth on Sunday. And like the rest of their transactions, yeomen seldom bought items or settled debts in cash. The store of Leach Carrigan and Samuel Carrigan in South Carolina, for instance, traded 85 percent of its merchandise for cotton. While the northern countryside and the lowland plantation districts functioned in businesslike ways, the old barter economy—and the forms of family independence and neighborly cooperation on which it rested—persisted in the southern upcountry.

Unlike the plantations, the farm neighborhoods of the South were places in which white people worked. Most farmers relied solely on family labor. They sired many children and put them to work at an early age. Farmwives often labored in the fields, particularly at peak times. Even those who were spared from fieldwork took up heavy burdens. A southern yeoman remembered that his mother worked "in the house sutch as cooking carding spinning and weaving and washing. Thare [were] 14 in the family," and "she did not have any servant to help her." Poor whites occupied a social space in the South at odds with the planter class above them, yet enjoyed rights and privileges unknown to the slaves below them.

9-4 Slave Culture

Q *What were prominent features of the cultural life that slaves made for themselves within the limits of slavery?*

In 1790, slaves in the Chesapeake had lived for generations in the same neighborhoods—old communities filled with kinfolk, ancestral graveyards, family gardens, and familiarity with each other and with local whites. They had made a distinctively African American way of life within the boundaries of slavery. Slaves along the South Carolina–Georgia rice coast, living and working in large groups under minimal white supervision, had made their own African American ways. In the early decades of the 19th century, hundreds of thousands of these people were torn from their communities and sold into the cotton states. It began a period of cultural destruction and reconstruction equaled only by the process of enslavement itself. We can view that process intimately by looking into the most vital of slave institutions: the slave family and slave religion.

9-4a *Slave Families and the Slave Trade*

In law, in the census, and in the minds of planters, slaves were members of a plantation household over which the owner exercised absolute authority as owner, paternal protector, and lawgiver. Yet, both slaveholders and slaves knew that slaves could not be treated like farm animals or little children. Wise masters learned that the success of a plantation depended less on terror and draconian discipline (though whippings—and worse—were common) than on the accommodations by which slaves traded labor and obedience for privileges and some measure of autonomy within the bonds of slavery. These privileges included holidays, garden plots, friendships and social gatherings both on and off the plantation, hunting and fishing rights, the right to trade slave-made goods, and—most vitally—the right to make their own families. These hard-won privileges provided some of the ground on which slaves in the old plantation states had made their own lives within slavery. The domestic slave trade and movement onto the cotton frontier cut that ground from beneath them. Slaves learned painfully that they were not members of families or communities—either the masters' or their own. They were property, and they could be bought and sold.

The most precious privilege on Chesapeake plantations had been the right to live in families. As early as the revolutionary era, most Chesapeake slaves lived in units consisting of a mother, a father, and their small children. On Charles Carroll's Maryland farms in 1773, for example, 325 of the 400 slaves lived in such families. At Thomas Jefferson's Monticello, most slave marriages were for life, and small children almost always lived with both parents. The most common exceptions were fathers who had married away from their own plantations and who visited "broad wives" and children during their off hours. Owners encouraged stable marriages because they made farms more peaceful and productive and because they flattered the owners' own religious and paternalistic sensibilities. For their part, slaves demanded families as part of the price of their labor.

Yet, slave families had always been vulnerable. Many slaveholders coerced sex from female slaves. Some kept slaves as mistresses. The planters tended, however, to keep these liaisons within bounds. While the slave community seldom punished sex before marriage, it took adultery seriously. Slaveholders knew that violations of married slave women could be enormously disruptive and strongly discouraged them. Slave sales also threatened families, but most sales before 1800 or so took place within neighborhoods, damaging slave families and communities without destroying them. The most serious threat was the death or bankruptcy of the slaveholder, which led to the division of property among heirs. Yet even these events, in comparison to what came later, tended to keep slaves in the same extended neighborhood.

This all changed with the growth of the Cotton Belt and the interstate slave trade. Masters in the seaboard states claimed (often truthfully) that they tried to keep slave families together and that they sold slaves to traders only out of dire necessity or as a means of getting rid of troublesome individuals. The latter category could be used as a threat. One slave remembered: "Slaves usually got scared when it became clear that Negro-Trader [John] White was in the community. The owners used White's name as a threat to scare the slaves when they had violated some rule." "If a man did anything out of the way," recalled another slave, "he was in more danger of being sold than being whipped."

Chesapeake planters and slaves knew, however, that the slave trade was more than a means of settling debts or punishing individuals. It had become an important source of income. The children of slaves in the exporting states could expect to be sold into long-distance markets when they came of age. The systematic selling of teenaged and young adult slaves, who commanded the highest prices, became a standard way in which Chesapeake gentlemen maintained their status. John Randolph of Roanoke, one of the great planter-politicians of Virginia, routinely translated younger members of his "plantation family" into cash. In 1823, he traveled to New York to see the great match race between the northern horse American Eclipse and the southern horse Henry. In a moment of pride and exuberance, he shouted from the grandstand that he would bet "a year's crop of negroes" on the southern champion.

Professional slave traders made no effort to hide their willingness to break slave families. Neither did the frontier planters who bought slaves from the older states. One planter insisted that "it is better to buy *none in families,* but *to select only choice, first rate, young hands from 14 to 25 years of age* (buying no children or aged negroes)." Seaboard planters, trying to convince themselves and anyone who would listen that they were responsible paternalists, made a sharp division between the plantation "family" and the well-known horrors of the domestic slave trade, but the slaves knew better. A Virginia slave woman had this to say of the planter who had sold her daughters: "he was a mean dirty slave trader."

Separated from their kinfolk and communities, Cotton Belt slaves began the old process of negotiation with their masters, and they reconstructed families. Cotton planters preferred young men for the labor of clearing the land, but they soon began importing nearly equal numbers of women, encouraging marriage, and providing cabins for slave families. Families made for greater peace and quiet on the plantations,

9.9 **Five Generations of a Slave Family on a South Carolina Sea Island Plantation, 1862** Complex family ties such as those of the family shown here were among the most hard-won and vulnerable cultural accomplishments of enslaved blacks.

Q *Nearly all successful human societies place some value on the family unit defined broadly, but what particular conditions and threats made enslaved African Americans particularly cherish families?*

and they were a good long-term investment in the production of new slaves. The slaves grasped the opportunity. From the 1820s, 51 percent of rural Louisiana slaves lived in families composed of two parents and their children. That figure was smaller than it had been on the old farms, but in view of what the slaves had been through, it was surprisingly large.

Slaveholders who encouraged slave marriages—perhaps even solemnizing them with a religious ceremony—knew that marriage implied a form of self-ownership that conflicted with the slaves' status as property. Some conducted ceremonies in which couples "married" by jumping over a broomstick. Others had the preacher omit the phrases "let no man put asunder" and "till death do you part" from the ceremony. Slaves knew that such ceremonies had no legal force. A Virginia slave remarked, "We slaves knowed that them words wasn't bindin'. Don't mean nothin' lessen you say, 'What God has jined, caint no man pull asunder.' But dey never would say dat. Jus' say 'Now you married.'" A South Carolina slave preacher routinely ended the ceremony with "Till death or buckra [whites] part you."

Slaves built their sense of family and kinship around such uncertainties. Because separation from father or mother was common, children spread their affection among adult relatives, treating grandparents, aunts, and uncles almost as though they were parents. In fact, slaves often referred to all of their adult relatives as "parents." They also called nonrelatives "brother," "sister," "aunt," and "uncle," thus extending a sense of kinship to the slave community at large. Slaves chose as surnames for themselves the names of former owners, Anglicized versions of African names, or names that simply sounded good. They rarely chose the name of their current owner. Families tended to use the same given names over and over, naming boys after their father or grandfather, perhaps to preserve the memory of fathers who might be taken away. They seldom named girls after their mothers, however. Unlike southern whites, slaves never married a first cousin, even though many members of their community were close relatives. Slaves practiced these customs consistently, often without the knowledge of slaveholders.

9-4b *Slave Theology*

Until the mid-18th century, neither enslaved Africans nor their masters showed much interest in Christianizing slaves. That changed with the rise of evangelical Christianity in the South (see Chapter 10). Blacks participated in the revivals of the southern Great Awakening, and the number of Christian slaves increased steadily in the second half of the 18th century. In the slave communities of the Upper South, as well as the burgeoning free and semifree black populations in the towns, the evangelical revivals of the late 18th and early 19th centuries appealed powerfully to African Americans, who sensed that the bonds of slavery were loosening. By 1820, most blacks in the Chesapeake considered themselves Christians. They would take their religion with them when they went farther south.

Between the Revolution and 1820, Chesapeake slaves embraced Christianity and began to turn it into a religion of their own. Slaves attended camp meetings, listened to **itinerant preachers** (those who usually lacked their own parish and therefore traveled from place to place), and joined the Baptist and Methodist congregations of the southern revival. The revivalists, in turn, welcomed slaves and free blacks to their meetings and sometimes recruited them as preachers. Evangelical preaching, singing, and spiritual exercises were much more attractive than the cold, high-toned lectures of the Anglicans. So were the humility and suffering of evangelical whites, most of whom were poor men and outsiders. Finally, the slaves gloried in the evangelicals' assault on the slaveholders' culture and in the antislavery sentiments of many white evangelicals. The result was a huge increase in the number of African American Christians. Methodists, who counted converts more carefully than some others, claimed 20,000 black members in 1800—one in three American Methodists.

The integrated congregations, however, did not last. There were exceptions, but most congregations were in fact internally segregated, with blacks sitting in the back of the church or upstairs in the gallery, and with only whites serving in positions of authority. Blacks, with both positive and negative encouragement from whites, organized independent churches in Baltimore, Wilmington, Richmond, Norfolk, and the scattered villages that had risen to serve the Chesapeake's new mixed economy. Even Charleston boasted an independent Methodist conference made up of 4,000 slaves and free blacks in 1815. By 1820, roughly 700 independent black churches operated in the United States. There had been none at all 30 years earlier. And on the plantations, slaves met informally—sometimes with the masters' permission, sometimes without it—to preach and pray.

Slaves understood and used the message of Christianity in their own ways. The biblical notion that slavery could be punishment for sin and the white southern notion that God intended blacks to be slaves never took root among enslaved Christians. Hannah Scott, a slave in Arkansas, remarked on what she heard a white preacher say: "But all he say is 'bedience to de white folks, and we hears 'nough of dat without him telling us." One slave asked a white preacher, "Is us slaves gonna be free in heaven?" The preacher had no answer. As one maid boldly told her mistress, "God never made us to be slaves for white people."

Another way in which slave religion differed from what was preached to them by whites was in the practice of conjuring, folk magic, root medicine, and other occult knowledge, most of it passed down from West Africa. Such practices provided help in areas in which Christianity was useless. They could reputedly cure illnesses, make people fall in love, ensure a good day's fishing, or bring harm to one's enemies. Sometimes African magic was in competition with plantation Christianity. Just as often, however, slaves combined the two. For instance, slaves sometimes determined the guilt or innocence of a person accused of stealing by hanging a Bible by a thread, then watching the way it turned. The form was West African; the Bible was not.

What They Said

The Treatment of Slave Families

The separation of families constituted one of the principal tragedies of slavery. In 1852, a slave mother, Maria Perkins, was caught up in the domestic slave trade. She wrote from Charlottesville, Virginia, to her husband about the sale of their son, Albert. At the same time, George Fitzhugh, also in Virginia, was a leading defender of slavery. In his view, the institution protected slaves, especially compared to the condition of northern workers, by adopting them as members of a slave master's own family.

Maria Perkins

Charlottesville, Oct 8th, 1852

Dear Husband I write you a letter to let you know of my distress my master has sold albert to a trader on Monday court day and myself and other child is for sale also and I want you to let [me] hear from you very soon before next cort if you can I don't know when I don't want you to wait till Christmas I want you to tell dr Hamelton and your master if either will buy me they can attend to it know and then I can go afterwards. I don't want a trader to get me they asked me if I had got any person to buy me and I told them no they took me to the court houste too they never put me up a man buy the name of brady bought albert and is gone I don't know where they say he lives in Scottesville my things is in several places some is in staunton and if I should be sold I don't know what will become of them I don't expect to meet with the luck to get that way till I am quite heartsick nothing more I am and ever will be your kind wife Maria Perkins.

George Fitzhugh

The slaves are all well fed, well clad, have plenty of fuel, and are happy. They have no dread of the future–no fear of want. A state of dependence is the only condition in which reciprocal affection can exist among human beings–the only situation in which the war of competition ceases, and peace, amity and good will arise. A state of independence always begets more or less of jealous rivalry and hostility. A man loves his children because they are weak, helpless and dependent; he loves his wife for similar reasons. When his children grow up and assert their independence, he is apt to transfer his affection to his grand-children. He ceases to love his wife when she becomes masculine or rebellious; but slaves are always dependent, never the rivals of their master. Hence, though men are often found at variance with wife or children, we never saw one who did not like his slaves, and rarely a slave who was not devoted to his master.

Q *Slaves uniformly feared the unpredictability and destructiveness of the domestic slave trade. Within Perkins's brief letter, how many social and personal injuries can you count?*

Q *How does the experience of the Perkins family counter the benign depiction of slavery presented by Fitzhugh?*

Q *Given Fitzhugh's patriarchal definition of family, which depended on the unequal status of women and children, is it possible that he and other slave masters truly viewed slaves as members of their families? Put another way, were slaves simply at the bottom of a larger patriarchal structure on plantations?*

Sources: (top) From a letter written in 1852 by Maria Perkins, a slave mother, reproduced in Ulrich B. Phillips, *Life and Labor in the Old South* (Boston: Little, Brown, and Company, 1929), p. 212; (bottom) From George Fitzhugh, *Sociology for the South, or the Failure of Free Society* (Richmond: A. Morris, 1854), pp. 246–247.

While Christianity could not cure sick babies or identify thieves, it gave slaves something more important: a sense that they were a historical people with a role to play in God's cosmic drama. In slave Christianity, Moses the liberator (and not the slaveholders' Abraham) stood beside Jesus. The slaves' appropriation of the book of Exodus denied the smug assumption of the whites that they were God's chosen people who had escaped the bondage of despotic Europe to enter the promised land of America. To the slaves, America was Egypt, they were the chosen people, and the slaveholders were Pharaoh. Thomas Wentworth Higginson, a Boston abolitionist who went south during the Civil War to lead a Union regiment of freed South Carolina slaves, wrote that his men knew the Old Testament books of Moses and the New Testament book of Revelation. "All that lies between," he said, "even the life of Jesus, they hardly cared to read or to hear." He found their minds "a vast bewildered chaos of Jewish history and biography; and most of the events of the past, down to the period of the American Revolution, they instinctively attribute to Moses."

The slaves' religious songs, which became known as spirituals, told of God's people, their travails, and their ultimate deliverance. In songs and sermons, the figures

Library of Congress, Prints and Photographs Division

9.10 **Slave Cabins on a Plantation in Northern Florida** Consisting of one room and set exactly 12 feet apart, this was minimal housing indeed. Yet, it provided slaves with a place to live in families and the rudimentary sense of proprietorship exercised by these black workers sitting in front of their "own" houses.

The Granger Collection, NYC

9.11 **A Secret Slave Prayer Meeting** Many masters encouraged or overlooked the religious life that slaves made for themselves. But others opposed it. Their slaves often met in secret, praying and singing in a whisper, far enough from whites so that their meetings could not be heard.

Q *For slaveholders, what were the potential risks of allowing slaves to pursue their own spiritual and religious practices?*

of Jesus and Moses were often blurred, and it was not always clear whether deliverance—accompanied by divine retribution—would take place in this world or the next. But deliverance always meant an end to black slavery, often with a reversal of relations between slaves and masters. "The idea of a revolution in the conditions of the whites and blacks," said the escaped slave Charles Ball, "is the cornerstone of the religion of the latter."

9-4c *Religion and Revolt*

In comparison with slaves in Cuba, Jamaica, Brazil, and other New World plantation societies, North American slaves seldom went into organized, armed revolt. The environment of the United States was unfriendly to such events. American plantations were relatively small and dispersed, and the southern white population was large, vigilant, and very well armed. Whites also enjoyed—until the cataclysm of the Civil War—internal political stability. There were thus few situations in which slaves could hope to win their freedom by violent means. Thousands of slaves demonstrated their hatred of the system by running away. Others fought masters or overseers, sabotaged equipment and animals, stole from planters, and found other ways to oppose slavery, but most knew that open revolt was suicide.

Christianity convinced slaves that history was headed toward an apocalypse that would result in divine justice and their own deliverance. It thus contained the possibility of revolt. But slave preachers seldom indulged in prophecy and almost never told their congregations to become actively engaged in God's divine plan, for they knew that open resistance was hopeless. Slave Christians believed that God hated slavery and would end it, but that their role was to have faith in God, to take care of one another, to preserve their identity as a people, and to await deliverance. Only occasionally did slaves take retribution and deliverance into their own hands. Each time, they were armed with some mix of republican equalitarianism and evangelical Christianity.

9-4d *Gabriel's Rebellion*

Masters who talked of liberty, natural rights, and equality before God sometimes worried that slaves might imagine that such language could apply to them. The long slave revolt in the French Caribbean colony of Saint-Domingue, which resulted in the independent black republic of Haiti in 1804, gave American slave masters reason to fear. Southern slaves from the 1790s onward whispered of natural rights and imagined themselves as part of a larger democratic revolution. In 1800, a conservative Virginia white complained: "Liberty and Equality has been infused into the minds of the negroes." A South Carolina congressman agreed that "this newfangled French philosophy of liberty and equality" was stirring up the slaves. Even Thomas Jefferson, who applauded the spread of French republicanism, conceded, "the West Indies appears to have given considerable impulse to the minds of the slaves ... in the United States."

This covert republic of the slaves sometimes came into the open. In Richmond in 1800, a slave blacksmith named Gabriel hatched a conspiracy, which became known as **Gabriel's Rebellion**, to overthrow Virginia's slave regime. Gabriel had been hired out to Richmond employers for most of his adult life; he was shaped less by plantation slavery than by the democratic, loosely interracial underworld of urban artisans. In the late 1790s, the repressive acts of the

Federalist national government and the angry responses of the Jeffersonian opposition (see Chapter 7), along with the news from Haiti, drove the democratic sensibilities of that world to new heights.

Gabriel, working with his brother and other hired-out slave artisans, planned his revolt with meticulous attention to detail. Working at religious meetings, barbecues, and the grog shops of Richmond, they recruited soldiers among slave artisans, adding plantation slaves only at the last moment. Gabriel planned to march an army of 1,000 men on Richmond in three columns. The outside columns would set diversionary fires in the warehouse district and prevent the militia from entering the town. The center would seize Capitol Square, including the treasury, the arsenal, and Governor James Monroe.

Although his army would be made up of slaves, and although his victory would end slavery in Virginia, Gabriel hoped to make a republican revolution, not a slave revolt. His chosen enemies were the Richmond "merchants" who had controlled his labor. Gabriel expected "the poor white people" and "the most redoubtable republicans" to join him. He in fact had the shadowy support of two Frenchmen, and rumors indicated that other whites were involved, although never at levels that matched the delusions of the conspirators or of worried whites. Gabriel planned to kill anyone who opposed him, but he would spare Quakers, Methodists, and Frenchmen, for they were "friendly to liberty." Unlike earlier slave insurgents, Gabriel did not plot violent retribution or a return to or reconstruction of West Africa. He was an American revolutionary, and he dreamed of a truly democratic republic for Virginia. His army would march into Richmond under the banner "Death or Liberty."

Gabriel recruited at least 150 soldiers who agreed to gather near Richmond on August 30, 1800. The leaders expected 500 to 600 more to join them as they marched upon the town. On the appointed day, however, it rained heavily, washing out bridges and making roads impassable. Rebels could not reach the meeting point, and amid white terror and black betrayals, Gabriel and his henchmen were hunted down, tried, and sentenced to death. In all, the state hanged 27 supposed conspirators, while others were sold and transported out of Virginia. The condemned carried their republican dreams to their graves. When asked to explain the revolt, one condemned man replied in terms that could only have disturbed the white republicans of Virginia: "I have nothing more to offer than what General Washington would have had to offer, had he been taken by the British and put to trial by them. I have adventured my life in endeavoring to obtain the liberty of my countrymen, and am a willing sacrifice in their cause."

9-4e *Denmark Vesey*

A second major slave conspiracy may not have been a conspiracy at all. In 1822, **Denmark Vesey**, a free black of Charleston, South Carolina (he had won a lottery and bought himself), stood trial for plotting rebellion. Vesey was a leading member of an African Methodist congregation that had seceded from the white Methodists and had been independent from 1817 to 1821. Vesey and some of the other members read widely in political tracts, including the antislavery arguments in the Missouri debates (see Chapter 11). They also read the Bible, and talked openly of their delivery out of Egypt. According to testimony coerced from slaves who wanted to avoid prosecution themselves, Vesey and his coconspirators planned the destruction of Charleston in 1822. A few dozen Charleston blacks would take the state armory, the story went, then arm rural slaves who would rise up to help them. They would kill the whites and commandeer ships in the harbor and make their getaway to black-controlled Haiti.

We cannot know how much of that was true. But Charleston's white authorities pulled the story out of terrified blacks, believed it, and hanged Vesey and 35 other accused conspirators—22 of them on one day. For many years afterwards, frightened whites "knew" that most of the conspirators (estimates ranged from 600 to 9,000) remained at large and lived among them.

9-4f *Nat Turner*

There is no doubt that the revolt in Southampton County, Virginia, in August 1831 was real. It was led by **Nat Turner**, a Baptist lay preacher, not a republican visionary like Gabriel or Denmark Vesey. Turner was, he told his captors, a Christian prophet and an instrument of God's wrath. Around 1830, he received visions of the final battle in Revelation, recast as a war between white and black spirits. He saw Christ crucified against the night sky, and the next morning he saw Christ's blood in a cornfield. Convinced by a solar eclipse in February 1831 that the time had come, Turner began telling other slaves about his visions, recruited his force, and launched his bloody revolt. Turner and his followers hacked to death 55 white men, women, and children before they were stopped. In the aftermath, Virginia executed at least 40 blacks, including Turner, who managed to hide in the woods for two months. White mobs also responded to the revolt by killing dozens more blacks in Virginia.

The revolts of Gabriel, Turner, and Vesey, along with scores of more limited conspiracies, deeply troubled southern whites. Slaveholders were committed to a paternalism that was increasingly tied to the South's attempt to make slavery both domestic and Christian. For their part, slaves recognized that they could receive decent treatment and pockets of autonomy in return for outward docility. Gabriel, Vesey, and Turner opened wide cracks in that mutual charade. During the Turner revolt, slaves whose masters had been murdered joined the rebels without a second thought. A plantation mistress who survived by hiding in a closet listened to the murders of her husband and children, and then heard her house servants arguing over possession of her clothes. A Charleston grandee named Elias Horry, upon finding that his coachman was among the Vesey conspirators, asked him, "What were your

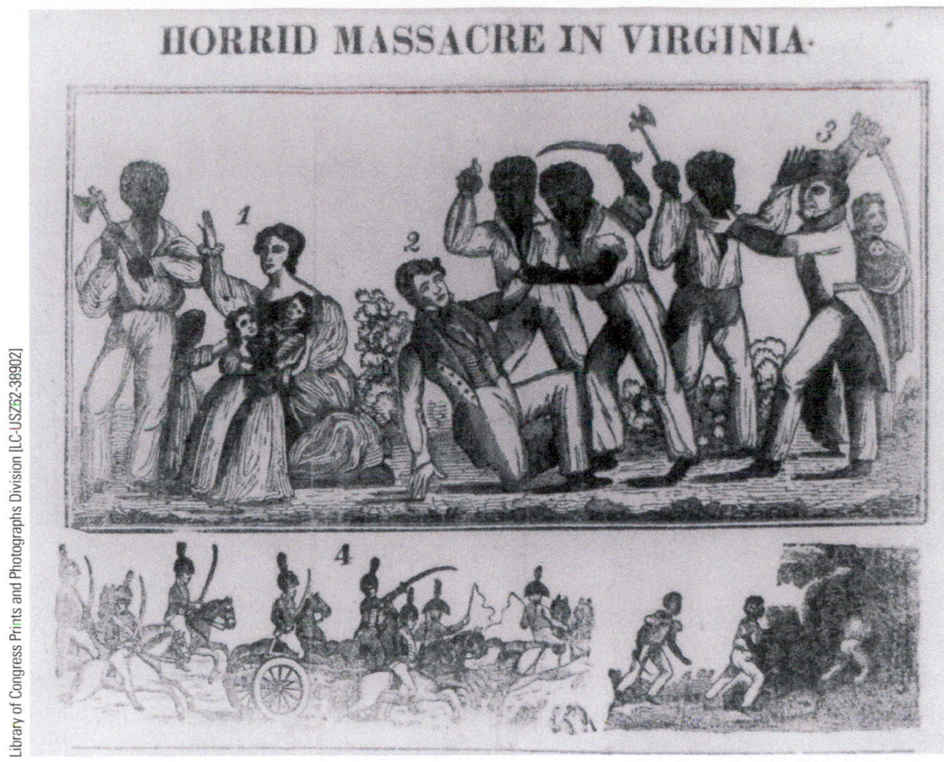

Library of Congress Prints and Photographs Division [LC-USZ62-38902]

9.12 **Nat Turner** This contemporary woodcut depicts scenes from Nat Turner's rebellion. In this bloodiest of all North American slave revolts, 55 whites, most of them women and children, were hacked to death.

intentions?" The formerly docile slave replied that he had intended "to kill you, rip open your belly, and throw your guts in your face."

9-5 A Southern Market Revolution?

Q *What were the nature and limits of the Market Revolution in the South?*

The South experienced explosive economic growth between 1790 and 1860 that constituted a Market Revolution, but in different ways and with different results than in the North. The plantation was a profitable business, and it was big. In 1860 the cash value of the southern slave population was $3 billion. That was more than the value of investments in banking, railroads, and manufacturing combined. The annual rate of return on the larger plantations stood at 10 percent—higher than that of factories or banks.

Southern expansion, however, had its limits. Economic growth was concentrated on the largest farms, and prosperity and change did not reach far beyond those farms. Planters invested their profits in more slaves and more land. The result was a lack of diversification and an increasing concentration of resources in the hands of the planter class. The South was a poor market for manufactured goods, outside of finery purchased by the larger planters. Most white farmers relied on the production of their households and neighbors, and they remained marginal to the market economy. They bought finished goods from the outside, but at a far lower rate than their northern counterparts. Slaves wore shoes and cheap cloth made in the Northeast and bought by their masters. Overall, the South continued to export its plantation staples and to pay outsiders for shipping, financial services, and finished goods. In contrast, the commercialization of northern farms created a rural demand for credit, banking facilities, farm tools, clothing, and other consumer goods and services—most of them provided by other northerners—and thus made a Market Revolution that included most northern families. In the South, economic growth produced more cotton and more slavery and comparatively little else.

Not that the South neglected technological change and agricultural improvement. Southerners developed the early cotton gin into big milling machines. They also improved steamboat design, making flat-bottomed boats that could travel far up shallow rivers. They also developed, among others, a machine with a huge wooden screw powered by horses or mules to press ginned cotton into tight bales for shipping. Jordan Goree, a slave craftsman in Huntsville, Texas, won a reputation for being able to carve whole trees into perfect screws for these machines. There were, however, few such innovations, and they had to do with the processing and shipping of cotton. Despite the experiments of a few gentleman-planters, there were almost no improvements in the *cultivation* of cotton aside from the ever crueller treatment of slaves. The truth is that cotton was a labor-intensive crop that discouraged innovation. Moreover, slaves often resisted "progress." They sabotaged tools and draft animals, scattered

History Through Film 12 *Years a Slave* (2013)

Directed by Steve McQueen.
Starring Chiwetel Ejiofor (Solomon Northup), Lupita Nyong'o (Patsey), Michael Fassbender (Edwin Epps), Brad Pitt (Bass).

Upon its release in 2013, *12 Years a Slave* was instantly hailed by critics and historians as the most accurate, powerful film depiction of slavery ever made, helping it to win the Academy Award for Best Picture. Unlike other films that explore the issues of race, slavery, and freedom in 19th-century America, including such strong productions as *Amistad* (1997) and *Glory* (1989), *12 Years* is told entirely from the slave's perspective. There are no scenes between whites without slaves present. The effect is to immerse the viewer in the horrific world of American slavery before the Civil War, when the interstate slave trade meant that no person with dark skin could rest easy, regardless of his or her whereabouts or legal status.

The film follows the true story of Solomon Northup (played brilliantly by Chiwetel Ejiofor), a free black violinist and family man in Saratoga, New York. In 1841, Northup accepts a job playing violin in a circus with a pair of white men traveling to Washington, D.C. After enjoying a night out with the men, Northup wakes up drugged and shackled in a slave pen in the shadow of the Capitol Building. He is beaten senseless and shipped south to New Orleans, where he is forced to adopt the name and persona of a slave, "Platt," as he is passed from master to master in Louisiana.

12 Years hews closely to Northup's own narrative written and published in 1853, the subtitle of which summarizes his saga: "Narrative of Solomon Northup, a Citizen of New-York, Kidnapped in Washington City in 1841, and Rescued in 1853, From a Cotton Plantation Near the Red River, in Louisiana." With few exceptions, director Steve McQueen found no need to deviate from Northup's narrative (something that mars an earlier film adaptation, *Solomon Northup's Odyssey*, made for public television in 1984 by the pioneering African American photographer Gordon Parks). As the noted abolitionist and escaped slave Frederick Douglass commented on Northup's story, "its truth is stranger than fiction."

The majority of the film centers on Northup's enslavement on different plantations in the Louisiana Cotton Belt. He quickly learns the mix of violence and negotiation that characterized slavery in the American South. Depending on his master, Northup can win small rewards, including a new fiddle, yet he also faces and witnesses constant acts of cruelty. The experience of women, both slaves and slave mistresses, gets special attention. An enslaved mother, Eliza (Adepero Oduye), never recovers from the tragedy of being torn from her two children. Another slave woman, Patsey (Lupita Nyong'o, in an Academy Award-winning performance), must confront the sexual advances of a sadistic slave master, Edwin Epps (Michael Fassbender), and the malicious jealousy of his wife, Mary (Sarah Paulson).

Ultimately, *12 Years* triumphs most by capturing the hopelessness of slavery without denying the agency, or free will, of individual slaves. Northup faces dehumanizing circumstances, but he never surrenders his humanity. Whether plotting an escape or making the calculated decision to comply with his masters, Northup retains some control over his actions (sadly, the same is not always true for the female slaves, particularly Patsey). His resilience finally pays off when a journeyman Canadian carpenter, Bass (Brad Pitt), helps to set in motion his release.

But there is no happy ending. Although Northup reunites with his wife and children, his brothers and sisters on the plantation remain trapped in slavery and his abductors escape punishment (Northup brought his kidnappers to trial, but they went free on legal technicalities). If the audience feels uncomfortable watching *12 Years*, that is the point. American viewers are also left to consider why the most redeeming white character was Canadian and why it took a British director (McQueen) and a largely international, non-American cast to bring this most American of stories fully to light.

AF archive/Alamy Stock Photo

9.13 *12 Years a Slave*, released to critical acclaim in 2013, tells the true story of Solomon Northup, a free black man who was kidnapped and sold into slavery before the Civil War.

manure in haphazard ways, and passively resisted innovations that would have added to their drudgery. The cotton fields continued to be cultivated by enslaved people working with clumsy, mule-drawn plows that barely scratched the soil, by women wielding heavy hoes, and by gangs who harvested the crop by hand.

Southern state governments spent comparatively little on internal improvements—there was no southern transportation revolution. A Virginia canal linked the flour mills at Richmond with inland grain fields, and another would connect Chesapeake Bay with the National Road, thus realizing—too late—Washington's and Jefferson's dreams of a thoroughfare between the Chesapeake and the Ohio Valley. But planters built their farms on alluvial land with access to the South's magnificent system of navigable rivers. They had little interest in expensive, state-supported internal improvements that their own neighborhoods did not need. Upcountry whites, particularly in the Upper South, sometimes campaigned for roads and canals, but they seldom got such measures through planter-dominated legislatures.

Nor did the South build cities, much less a regional *system* of cities. In 1800, about 82 percent of the southern workforce and about 70 percent of the northern workforce were employed in agriculture. By 1860, only 40 percent of the northern workforce was so employed. In the South, the proportion had risen to 84 percent. The old northern seaports grew dramatically in the early 19th century, and they extended their sway over systems of satellite cities. New York, which became America's great city in the first third of the 19th century, exercised commercial and cultural power over the old capital at Albany, as well as new Erie Canal cities such as Utica, Syracuse, Rochester, and Buffalo. Between 1800 and 1840, the urban population of New York State rose from 12.7 percent to 19.4 percent, despite the settlement of huge tracts of new agricultural land. In Massachusetts, the urban population rose from 15.4 percent to 37.9 percent in these years. By 1840, every northeastern and mid-Atlantic state with the exceptions of Maine and Vermont had at least 10 percent of its people living in cities. No southern state urbanized at that level. Virginia, at 6.9 percent, had the largest urban population of any of the future Confederate states.

Commercial and manufacturing cities sprouted up throughout the interior of the North. The few southern cities were located on the periphery of the region and served as transportation depots for plantation crops. River cities like Louisville, Memphis, and St. Louis were little more than stopping places for steamboats. The great seaports of New Orleans, Charleston, and Baltimore had in the past shipped plantation staples directly to British and European markets. But as the 19th century progressed, they sent more and more of their goods by coasting vessel to New York City to be shipped to foreign ports. In turn, Europe's manufactured goods were funneled into New York, and then sold off to the southern (and northern) countryside. The commercial metropolis of the southern United States was becoming less London and more New York. What had *not* changed was the colonial status of the South.

Thus while the North and the Northwest developed towns and cities throughout their regions, southern cities continued to be few and to perform the colonial functions of 18th-century seaport towns. Southern businessmen turned to New York City for credit, insurance, coastal and export shipping, and finished goods. *De Bow's Review,* the principal business journal of the South, reported that South Carolina storekeepers who bought goods from Charleston wholesalers claimed they had bought them directly from New York City, for it was well known that New York provided better goods at lower prices than any supplier in the South. De Bow testified to the superior skill and diversification of the North when, after trying several New Orleans sources, he awarded the publishing contract for his *Review* to a northern printer. That was not surprising in any case, because De Bow received three-fourths of his income from northern advertisers.

Conclusion

On the eve of the Civil War, James H. Hammond, a slaveholding senator from South Carolina, asked, "What would happen if no cotton was furnished for three years.... England would topple headlong and carry the whole civilized world with her save the south. No, you dare not make war on cotton. No power on earth dares to make war on cotton. Cotton is king." Hammond was arguing, as Jefferson had argued in 1807, that farmers at the fringes of the world market economy could coerce the commercial-industrial center. He was wrong. The commitment to cotton and slavery had isolated the South politically. It had also deepened the South's dependence on the world's financial and industrial centers. Ironically, slavery and cotton, each critical to the growth of global capitalism, left the South itself with uneven market and industrial development. The North transformed its role as a part of the old colonial periphery (the suppliers of food and raw materials) into a part of the core (the suppliers of manufactured goods and financing) of the world market economy, while the South continued to export plantation staples in exchange for imported goods. In the process, the South worked itself deeper and deeper into dependence, now as much upon the American Northeast as upon the old colonial rulers in London.

CHAPTER REVIEW

Review

1. What were the principal differences between the slave economies of the Chesapeake and the South Carolina—Georgia lowcountry?
2. In what ways did the economy and society of the Cotton Belt differ from that of older plantation regions?
3. How did southern yeoman farmers differ from planters who presided over much larger plantations?
4. What were prominent features of the cultural life that slaves made for themselves within the limits of slavery?
5. What were the nature and limits of the Market Revolution in the South?

Critical Thinking

1. The central institutions of slave culture were the family and religion. Some have argued that these institutions helped slaves accommodate to slavery, whereas others have argued that they helped them resist it, and still others have argued that they did both. What is your position on this question?
2. Historians have long debated how to characterize the southern economy and society. Some contend that it was stridently capitalist, while others argue that this is impossible because the southern economy depended on slavery, a primitive, pre-capital form of labor. Where do you stand in this debate? Does it matter whether the South was capitalist or not? Why or why not?

Identifications

Review your understanding of the following key terms, people, and events for this chapter (terms in bold in text are included in the Glossary).

private fields, p. 258
Eli Whitney, p. 258
cotton gin, p. 258
Cotton Belt, p. 258
interstate slave trade, p. 260
itinerant preachers, p. 269
Gabriel's Rebellion, p. 271
Denmark Vesey, p. 272
Nat Turner, p. 272

Suggested Readings

In recent years, several works have transformed our understanding of the Deep South and its place in the national and global economy. For leading examples, see **Walter Johnson**, ***River of Dark Dreams: Slavery and Empire in the Cotton Kingdom*** (2013); **Edward E. Baptist**, ***The Half Has Never Been Told: Slavery and the Making of American Capitalism*** (2014); and **Sven Beckert**, ***Empire of Cotton: A Global History*** (2014). On planter culture, see **Bertram Wyatt-Brown**, ***Honor and Violence in the Old South*** (1986); ***Kenneth S. Greenberg***, ***Honor & Slavery*** (1997); and **Elizabeth Fox Genovese and Eugene D. Genovese**, ***The Mind of the Master Class: History and Faith in the Southern Slaveholders' Worldview*** (2005). **Walter Johnson's** ***Soul by Soul: Life Inside the Antebellum Slave Market*** (1999) brilliantly undermines the myth of slaveholder paternalism. For the domestic slave trade, see also **Steven Deyle**, ***Carry Me Back: The Domestic Slave Trade in American Life*** (2005); and **Adam Rothman**, ***Slave Country: American Expansion and the Origins of the Deep South*** (2005).

On the southern yeomanry, see **Stephanie McCurry**, ***Masters of Small Worlds: Yeoman Households, Gender Relations, & the Political Culture of the South Carolina Lowcountry*** (1995); and **Steven Hahn**, ***The Roots of Southern Populism: Yeoman Farmers and the Transformation of the Georgia Upcountry, 1850–1890*** (1983). Two classic works on slave culture are **Eugene D. Genovese**, ***Roll, Jordan, Roll: The World the Slaves Made*** (1974); and **Lawrence W. Levine**, ***Black Culture and Black Consciousness: Afro-American Folk Thought from Slavery to Freedom*** (1977). **Charles Joyner**, ***Down by the Riverside: A South Carolina Slave Community*** (1986); **Mark M. Smith**, ***Mastered by the Clock: Time, Slavery and Freedom in the American South*** (1986); and **Albert J. Raboteau**, ***Canaan Land: A Religious History of African Americans*** (2001) are also essential.

10 Toward an American Culture, 1815–1850

National Portrait Gallery, Smithsonian Institution/Art Resource, NY

10.1 **P.T. Barnum and Tom Thumb, circa 1850** Here is Phineas Taylor Barnum, America's greatest showman, together with the sprightly midget Tom Thumb, his first hugely successful attraction. The photograph conveys the combination of chicanery, farce, strangeness, and straight-faced respectability that made Barnum (but not Tom Thumb) a rich man.

AMERICANS AFTER 1815 experienced wave after wave of social and cultural change. Territorial expansion, the growth of the market, and the spread of plantation slavery broke old social patterns. Americans in these years reinvented family life. They created American forms of popular literature and art. They flocked to evangelical churches that expanded and remade American religious life. They began, in short, to make a distinctively American culture.

The emerging American culture was more or less uniformly republican, capitalist, and Protestant. But different kinds of Americans made different cultures out of the revolutionary inheritance, market expansion, and revival religion. Southern farmers and their northern cousins thought differently about fatherhood and the proper way to make a family. Northeastern businessmen and southern planters agreed that economic progress was indeed progress, but they differed radically on its moral implications. Slaveholders, factory hands, rich and poor farmers, and middle-class women all heard the same Bible stories and learned different lessons. The result, visible from the 1830s onward, was an American national culture that was (and is) less an accepted body of rules than an ongoing conversation. This chapter identifies the varying ways in which Americans thought about four of the hot spots in that conversation: family life and personal identity, the Christian inheritance, the question of race, and the nature of republican citizenship. ■

10-1 The Democratization of Culture

Q *In what ways did literacy and print help to democratize American culture?*

The weakening of traditional authority created spaces that Americans filled in their own ways. Important pillars of old cultures remained: The Bible and revolutionary ideas of liberty and equality were fundamental. But the transportation network that carried wheat and cotton out of rural neighborhoods brought new things in: furniture and ways of arranging it, new clothing styles, new forms of entertainment, new information, new aspirations. In part, Americans made new ways of thinking and living as consumers of these cultural goods.

Among the items reaching Americans was information—newspapers, books, magazines, business communications, personal letters, and travelers who carried news. The information circulated among a public that was remarkably literate and well informed. The literacy rate in the preindustrial United States was among the highest ever recorded. In 1790, approximately 85 percent of adult men in New England and 60 percent of those in Pennsylvania and the Chesapeake could read and write. The literacy rate among women was lower—about 45 percent in New England—but on the rise. By 1820, all but the poorest white Americans, particularly in the North, could read and write. The United States, more than perhaps any other country, was a nation of readers.

10-1a *A Revolution in Print*

The rise of a reading public was accompanied by a print revolution: Enterprising men (and a few women) learned how to make their livings by providing cheap Bibles and English novels, almanacs, newspapers, and other printed matter. People were encouraged to read by their republican governments. The states provided schools, and the national government helped the flow of print in ways that were unprecedented.

The governments of Great Britain and the European powers tried to control the circulation of information; they established few post offices, taxed newspapers, monitored what was said in the newspapers and even in the mail, and prosecuted people who said the wrong things in print. There were attempts to do such things in America. The Stamp Tax of 1765 had included a tax on newspapers, and in 1798 Federalists had jailed editors with whom they disagreed. Americans defeated both of these attempts. The First Amendment guaranteed freedom of the press, and the U.S. government (with that brief Federalist exception) did not interfere with newspapers. Just the opposite: Newspapers enjoyed discounted postal rates and circulated far beyond their points of publication. A law of 1792 allowed newspapers to mail copies to each other without cost, and the editors of country weeklies cut national and international news from the New York, Baltimore, and Philadelphia papers, combined it with local advertising and legal notices, and provided their readers with cheap sources of information that were remarkably uniform throughout the North and West and much of the South. In effect, then, government directly and knowingly subsidized the rise of a democratic and national reading public.

Newspapers were the most widely distributed form of print in the new republic. In 1790, 106 newspapers were being published in the United States. In 1835, 1,258 were in publication, 90 of which were dailies. In the latter year, the number of newspapers per capita in the United States was two to three times greater than in Great Britain. Though only about one household in 10 subscribed to a newspaper, the democratic public knew what was in them, for the papers were passed from hand to hand, read aloud in groups, and made available at taverns and public houses.

CHRONOLOGY

1825	Charles Grandison Finney begins religious revival meetings in upstate New York
1830	Joseph Smith founds the Church of Jesus Christ of Latter-Day Saints
1831	First minstrel show is presented
1843	William Miller's Adventists expect the world to end
1845	George Lippard's lurid novel *The Quaker City* becomes a best seller
1849	Astor Place theater riot in New York City leaves 20 dead
1852	Harriet Beecher Stowe publishes *Uncle Tom's Cabin*

Improvements in distribution and printing technology encouraged other forms of popular literature as well. The emerging evangelical crusade made innovative use of print. Sunday school tracts, temperance pamphlets, and other religious materials were printed in New York and distributed efficiently and cheaply through the mails, while the American Bible Society devised a realistic plan to provide every household in America with a free Bible. Newspapers were men's reading, but the religious tracts tended to find their way into the hands of women. Women also were the principal readers of novels, a new form of reading matter that Thomas Jefferson and other authorities denounced as frivolous and aberrant. Novels were seen as dangerous not only because they contained questionable subject matter but also because girls and women read them silently and in private. Printed matter provided information and opinion for the men who exercised power and conducted the public life of democracy, but it could also provide sustenance for the spirits and imaginations of Americans who were excluded from power and the public.

The increase in literacy and in printed matter accelerated both the market and democratic individualism. Books and newspapers were scarce in the 18th century, and most Americans had experienced the written word only as it was read aloud by fathers, ministers, or teachers. After 1790, private, silent reading of new kinds of texts became common. No longer were adult male authorities the sole interpreters of the world for families and neighborhoods. The new print culture encouraged Americans to read, think, and interpret information for themselves.

10-2 The Northern Middle Class

What were the central cultural maxims of the emerging northern middle class?

"The most valuable class in any community," declared the poet-journalist Walt Whitman in 1858, "is the **middle class**." At that time, the term *middle class* (and the social group that it described) had been in use no more than 30 or 40 years. The Market Revolution had created new towns and cities and transformed the old ones, and it had turned the rural North into a landscape of family-owned commercial farms. Those who claimed the title "middle class" were largely the new kinds of proprietors made in that transformation—city and country merchants, master craftsmen who had turned themselves into manufacturers, and the mass of market-oriented farmers. They lived at the centers of the new marketing and communications networks, and they developed a self-conscious middle-class identity that was remarkably uniform throughout the North.

10-2a *A New Middle Class*

New England played a disproportionate role in the making of middle-class culture. The region was the first center of factory production, and southern New England farms were thoroughly commercialized by the 1830s. Yankee migrants dominated the commercial heartland of western New York and the northern regions of the Northwest. Even in the seaport cities (New York's Pearl Street wholesale houses are a prime example), businessmen from New England were often at the center of economic innovation. This Yankee middle class invented cultural forms that became the core of an emerging business civilization. Liberty for them meant self-ownership and the freedom of action and ambition. Equality meant equality of opportunity. They upheld the autonomous and morally accountable individual against the claims of traditional neighborhoods and traditional families. They devised an intensely private, mother-centered domestic life. Most of all they adhered to a reformed Yankee Protestantism whose moral imperatives became the foundation of American middle-class culture.

10-2b *The Evangelical Base*

Religion helped to define the new middle-class culture. From the 1790s, a series of intense religious revivals took place on the western frontier. By the mid-1820s and 1830s, these revivals, together known as the **Second Great Awakening**, reached the emerging middle class of the North and continued in areas throughout the country into the 1850s. The evangelist Charles Grandison Finney, who led his first revival in 1825, was most responsible for bringing the awakening to the northern middle class. So fiery were the revivals in and around Finney's base of Rochester, New York, and other towns along the Erie Canal that people began to call the area the "Burned-Over District." The revivals had much in common with the First Great Awakening of the 1730s and 1740s (see Chapter 4). Transplanted New Englanders, the heirs of what was left of Yankee Calvinism, composed much of Finney's audience and would have easily recognized his vivid warnings of hell for the sinful and unconverted.

Yet, the message of the Second Great Awakening also differed from the First in significant ways. Finney and other preachers reached beyond the traditional Puritan themes of original sin, innate sinfulness, and predestination. Those living through the economic changes associated with the Market Revolution had witnessed firsthand the ability of humans to

Bettmann/Corbis

10.2 **Charles Finney** The evangelist, pictured here at the height of his preaching power in the 1830s, was remarkably successful at organizing the new middle-class culture into a millennial crusade.

shape their environment. And as middle-class Christians improved the material and social worlds, the doctrines of human inability and natural depravity, along with faith in divine providence, made less sense.

To such an audience, Finney preached the organizing principle of northern middle-class evangelicalism: "God," he insisted, "has made man a moral free agent." Neither the social order, the troubles of this world, nor the spiritual state of individuals was divinely ordained. People would make themselves and the world better by choosing right over wrong—though they would choose right only after submitting their rebellious wills to the will of God. It was a religion that valued individual holiness over a permanent and sacred social order. It made the spiritual nature of individuals a matter of prayer, submission, and choice. Thus, it gave Christians the means—through the spread of revivals—to bring on the thousand-year reign of Christianity that they believed would precede the Second Coming of Christ. As Charles Finney told his Rochester audience, "If [Christians] were united all over the world the Millennium might be brought about in three months."

Yankee evangelists had been moving toward Finney's formulation since the turn of the 19th century. Like Finney, they borrowed revival techniques from the Methodists (weeklong meetings in which women prayed in public, and an "**anxious bench**"—a space reserved in meetings for the most likely converts), but toned them down for their own more "respectable" audience. At the same time, middle-class evangelicals retained the Puritans' Old Testament sense of cosmic history. They enlisted personal holiness in a fight to the finish between the forces of good and evil in this world. Building on these imperatives, the entrepreneurial families of the East and Northwest constructed an American middle-class culture after 1825. It was based, paradoxically, on an intensely private and emotionally loaded family life and an aggressively reformist stance toward the world at large.

10-2c *Domesticity*

The message of the Second Great Awakening had application in both the home and workplace, where qualities such as industry, sobriety, and self-discipline (all freely chosen moral behaviors) led to success in the new market culture. At the same time, the Yankee middle class made crucial distinctions between the home and the world—distinctions that grew from the disintegration of the old patriarchal household economy.

Men in cities and towns now went off to work, leaving wives and children to spend the day at home. Even commercializing farmers made a distinction between (male) work that was oriented toward markets and (female) work that was tied to household maintenance (see Chapter 8). The new middle-class evangelicalism encouraged this division of domestic labor. The public world of politics and economic exchange, said the preachers, was the proper sphere of men; women, on the other hand, were to exercise new kinds of moral influence within households. As one evangelical put it, "Each has a distinct sphere of duty—the husband to go out into the world—the wife to superintend the house-hold. ... Man profits from connection with the world, but women never; their constituents [sic] of mind are different. The one is raised and exalted by mingled association. The purity of the other is maintained in silence and seclusion."

The result was a feminization of domestic life. In the old yeoman-artisan republic, fathers were God's delegated authorities on earth, assigned the task of governing women, children, and other underlings. Middle-class evangelicals raised new spiritual possibilities for women and children. Mothers replaced fathers as the principal rearers of children, and they enlisted the doctrines of free agency and individual moral responsibility in that task. Middle-class mothers raised their children with love and reason, not fear. They sought to develop the children's conscience and their capacity to love, to teach them to make good moral choices, and to help them to prepare for conversion and a lifetime of Christian service.

Middle-class mothers could take up these tasks because they could concentrate their efforts on household duties and because they had fewer children than their mothers or grandmothers had had. In Utica, New York, for example, women who entered their childbearing years in the 1830s averaged only 3.6 births apiece; those who had started families only 10 years earlier averaged 5.1 births. Housewives also spaced their pregnancies differently. Unlike their forebears, who gave birth to a child about once every two years throughout their childbearing years, Utica's middle-class housewives had their children at five-year intervals, which meant that they could give each child close attention. As a result, households were quieter and less crowded; children learned from their mothers how to govern themselves and seldom experienced the rigors of patriarchal family government. Thus, mothers assumed responsibility for nurturing the children who would be carriers of the new middle-class culture, and male authorities recognized the importance of that job. Edward Kirk, a minister in Albany, insisted that "the hopes of human society are to be found in the character, in the views, and in the conduct of mothers."

Middle-class women and girls became a huge market for new forms of popular literature. There were cookbooks, etiquette books, manuals on housekeeping, sermons, and sentimental novels, many of them written and most of them read by women. The works of popular religious writers such as Lydia Sigourney, Lydia Maria Child, and Timothy Shay Arthur found their way into thousands of middle-class homes. **Sarah Josepha Hale**, whose *Godey's Lady's Book* was the first mass-circulation magazine for women, acted as an arbiter of taste not only in furniture, clothing, and food but also in sentiments and ideas. Upon reviewing the sentimental literature read in middle-class homes, Nathaniel Hawthorne was not the only "serious" writer to deplore a literary marketplace dominated by "a damned mob of scribbling women."

Hawthorne certainly had economic reason for complaint. Sentimental novels written by women outsold by wide margins his *Scarlet Letter* and *House of Seven Gables*; Ralph Waldo Emerson's essays; Henry David Thoreau's *Walden*; Herman Melville's *Moby Dick*; Walt Whitman's *Leaves of Grass*; and other works of the American Renaissance of the 1850s. Susan Warner's *The Wide, Wide World* broke all sales records when it appeared in 1850. Harriet Beecher Stowe's *Uncle Tom's Cabin* (1852) broke the records set by Warner. In 1854, Maria Cummins's *The Lamplighter* (the direct target of Hawthorne's lament about scribbling women) took its place as the third of the monster best sellers of the early 1850s.

These sentimental novels upheld the new middle-class domesticity. They sacralized the middle-class home and the trials and triumphs of Christian women. In sentimental **domestic fiction**, women assume the role of evangelical ministers, demonstrating Christian living by precept, example, and moral persuasion. Female moral influence, wielded by women who had given themselves to God, is at war with the male world of politics and the marketplace—areas of power, greed, and moral compromise. Although few sentimental writers shared the views of the feminist Margaret Fuller, they would have agreed with her on the place of religion in women's lives. "I wish women to live first for God's sake," she wrote. "Then she will not make an imperfect man her God, and thus sink to idolatry."

Popular sentimental novels were not, as Hawthorne and his friends believed, frivolous fairy tales into which house-wives retreated from the real world. They were subversive depictions of a higher spiritual reality that would move the feminine ethos of the Christian home to the center of civilization. That vision drove an organized public assault on irreligion, drunkenness, prostitution, slavery, and other practices and institutions that substituted passion and force for Christian love (see Chapter 12), an assault that tried to "domesticate" the world and shape it in the image of the middle-class evangelical home.

10-3 The Plain People of the North

Q *Within the North, what were the alternatives to middle-class culture?*

From the 1830s onward, northern middle-class reformers proposed their religious and domestic values as a national culture for the United States. Even in their own region, however, most people rejected their cultural leadership. The

10.3 **"The Polka Fashions" from *Godey's Lady's Book*, 1845** The popular magazine acted as an arbiter of taste in nearly all things for women, including formal dancing attire.

Q *What were the distinguishing features of upper-class women's fashion in the 1840s?*

plain folk of the North were a varied lot: settlers in the lower Northwest who remained culturally southern; hill-country northerners who had experienced little of what their middle-class cousins called "progress"; refugees from the countryside who had taken up urban wage labor; and increasing thousands of Irish and German immigrants. They did share a cultural conservatism—often grounded in the traditional, father-centered family—that rejected sentimentalism and reformist religion out of hand. As often as not, that conservatism was grounded in religious values that were very different from those of the new middle class.

10-3a *The Rise of Democratic Sects*

During the American revolutionary era, state constitutions withdrew government support from religion, and the First Amendment to the U.S. Constitution clearly prescribed the separation of church and the national state. Reduced to their own sources of support, the established churches—Congregationalism in New England, the Church of England (renamed Episcopalianism) in the South and much of the mid-Atlantic—went into decline. In 1780, nearly all of the 750 Congregational churches in the United States were in New England. In the next 40 years, although the nation's population rose from 4 million to 10 million, the number of Congregational churches rose only to 1,100. Ordinary women and men were leaving the churches that had dominated the religious life of colonial America, sometimes ridiculing the learned clergy as they departed. To many elites in the former established churches, it seemed that the republic was plunging into atheism.

They were wrong. The collapse of the established churches, the social dislocations of the post-revolutionary years, and the increasingly antiauthoritarian, democratic sensibilities of ordinary northerners provided fertile ground for the growth of new democratic sects. These were the years of camp meeting revivalism, years in which Methodists and Baptists grew from small, half-organized sects into the great popular denominations they have been ever since (see Map 10.1). They were also years in which fiercely independent dropouts from older churches were putting together a loosely organized movement that would become the Disciples of Christ. At the same time, ragged, half-educated preachers were spreading the Universalist and Freewill Baptist messages in upcountry New England, while in western New York young **Joseph Smith** was receiving the visions that would lead to Mormonism.

The result was, first of all, a vast increase in the variety of choices on the northern religious landscape, but within that welter of new churches, the fastest-growing sects shared a roughly uniform democratic style. First, they renounced the need for an educated, formally authorized clergy. Religion was now a matter of the heart and not the head. **Crisis conversion** (understood in most churches as spiritual transformation that resulted from direct experience of the Holy Ghost) was a necessary credential for preachers; a college degree was not. The new preachers substituted emotionalism and storytelling for Episcopal ritual and Congregational theological lectures. Stories attracted listeners, and they were harder for the learned clergy to refute. The new churches also held up the Bible as the one source of religious knowledge, thus undercutting all theological knowledge and placing every literate Christian on a level with the best-educated minister. These tendencies often ended in **Restorationism**—the belief that all theological and institutional changes since the end of biblical times were man-made mistakes, and that religious organizations must restore themselves to the purity and simplicity of the church of the Apostles. In sum, this loose democratic creed rejected learning and tradition and raised up the priesthood of all believers.

Baptists and Methodists were by far the most successful at preaching to the new democratic audience. The United States had only 50 Methodist churches in 1783; by 1820 it had 2,700. Over those same years, the number of Baptist churches rose from 400 to 2,700. Together, in 1820, these two denominations outnumbered Episcopalians and Congregationalists by three to one, almost a reversal of their relative standings 40 years earlier. Baptists based much of their appeal on localism and congregational democracy. Methodist success, on the other hand, entailed skillful national organization. Bishop Francis Asbury, the head of the church in its fastest-growing years, built an episcopal bureaucracy that seeded churches throughout the republic and sent **circuit-riding preachers** to places that had none. These early Methodist missions were grounded in self-sacrifice to the point of martyrdom. Asbury demanded much of his itinerant preachers, and until 1810, he strongly suggested that they remain celibate. "To marry," he said, "is to locate." Asbury also knew that married circuit riders would leave many widows and orphans behind, for hundreds of them worked themselves to death. Of the men who served as Methodist itinerants before 1819, at least 60 percent died before the age of 40.

From seaport cities to frontier settlements, few Americans escaped the sound of Methodist preaching in the early 19th century. The Methodist preachers were common men who spoke plainly, listened carefully to others, and carried hymnbooks with simple tunes that anyone could sing. They also, particularly in the early years, shared traditional folk beliefs with their humble flocks. Some of the early circuit riders relied heavily on dreams; some could predict the future; many visited heaven and hell and returned with full descriptions.

In the end, however, it was the hopefulness and simplicity of the Methodist message that attracted ordinary Americans. Even more than Finney (a Presbyterian), the Methodists rejected the old terrors of Calvinist determinism and taught that although salvation comes only through God, men and women can open themselves to divine grace and thus play a decisive role in their own salvation. They also taught that a godly life is a gradual, lifetime growth in grace, thus allowing for repentance for minor, and sometimes even major, lapses of faith and behavior. By granting responsibility (one might say sovereignty) to the individual believer, the Methodists established their democratic credentials and drew hundreds of thousands of Americans into their fold.

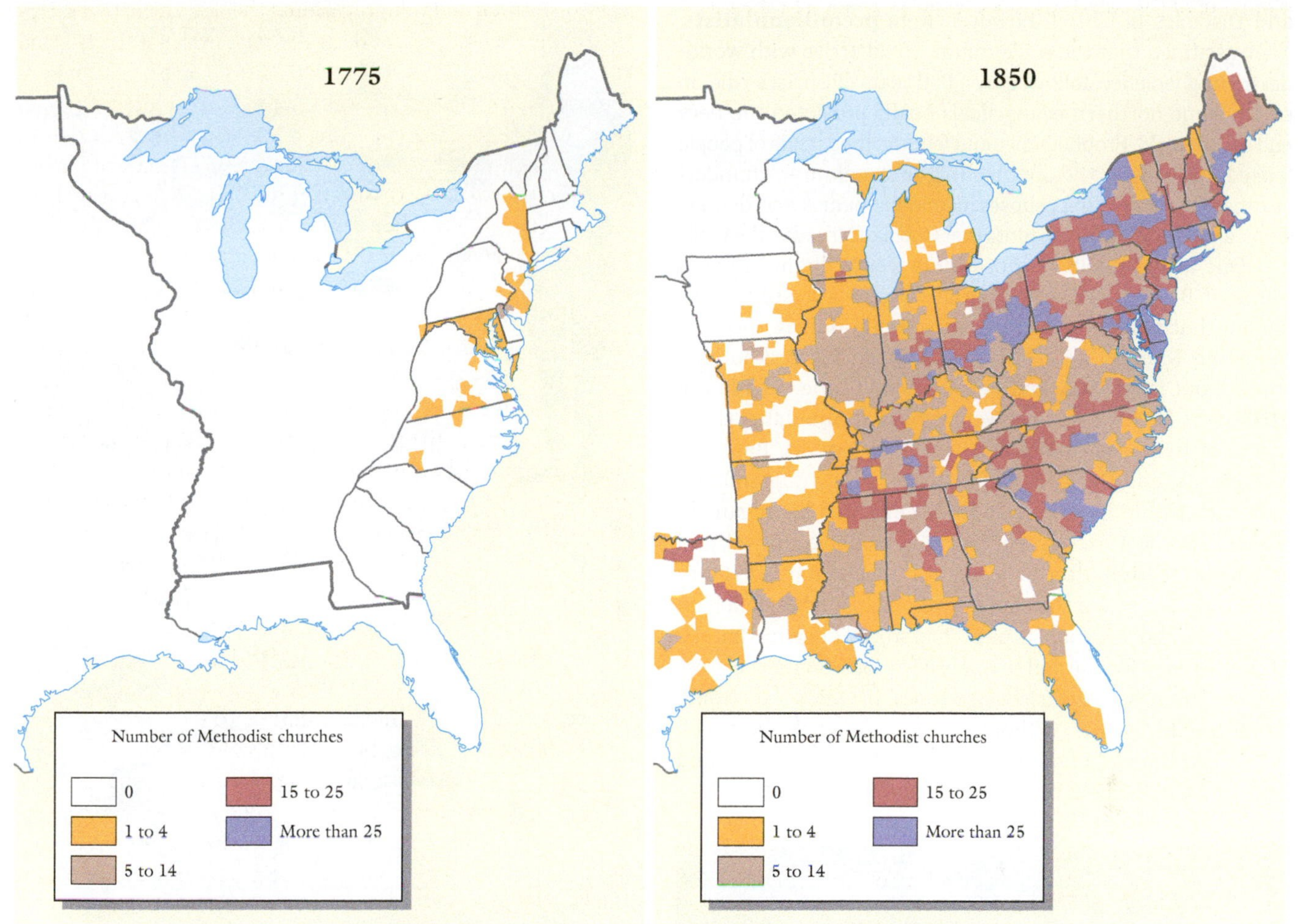

▲ **MAP 10.1 Growth of American Methodism, 1775–1850** This is a county-by-county map of the rise of American Methodism from the Revolution through the eve of the Civil War. In 1775, Methodism was almost nonexistent in British North America. By 1850, the Methodists were the largest Protestant denomination in the United States. They were truly a national faith: There were Methodist churches in almost every county in the country.

Q *What factors help explain the growth of American Methodism?*

Q *How can we explain the regional variations in American Methodism in 1850?*

10-3b *The Providential Worldview*

Northern plain folk favored churches as doctrinally varied as the people themselves. These ranged from the voluntaristic "free grace" doctrines of the Methodists to the iron-bound Calvinism of most Baptists, from the fine-tuned hierarchy of the Mormons to the near-anarchy of the Disciples of Christ. They included the most popular faiths (Baptists and Methodists came to contain two-thirds of America's professing Protestants), as well as such smaller sects as Hicksite Quakers, Universalists, Adventists, Moravians, and Freewill Baptists. Yet for all their diversity, these churches had important points in common. Most shared an evangelical emphasis on individual experience over churchly authority. Most favored democratic, local control of religious life and distrusted outside organization and religious professionalism. They also rejected middle-class optimism and reformism, even as several of the groups emerged in the same Burned-Over District of upstate New York as Finney and other preachers of the Second Great Awakening.

The most pervasive strain was a belief in providence—the conviction that human history is part of God's vast and unknowable plan, and that all events are willed or allowed by God. Middle-class evangelicals spoke of providence, too, but they seemed to assume that God's plan was manifest in the progress of market society and middle-class religion. Humbler evangelicals held to the older notion that providence is immediate, mysterious, and unknowable. They believed that the events of everyday life are parts of a vast blueprint that exists only in the mind of God—and not in the vain aspirations of women and men. When making plans, they added the caveat "the Lord willing," and they learned to accept misfortune with fortitude. They responded to epidemics, bad crop years, aches and pains, illness, and early death by praying for the strength to endure.

Such providentialism lent itself to millennial thinking. Middle-class evangelicals were **postmillennialists**. They believed that Christ's Second Coming would occur at the end of 1,000 years of social perfection brought about by the missionary conversion of the world. Ordinary Baptists, Methodists, and Disciples of Christ, however, were **premillennialists**. They assumed that the millennium would arrive with world-destroying violence, followed by 1,000 years of Christ's rule on earth. Some northern evangelicals boldly predicted the fiery end of the world. Prophets rose and fell, and thousands of people looked for signs of the approaching millennium in thunderstorms, shooting stars, eclipses, economic panics and depressions, and—especially—in hints that God had placed in the Bible.

One avid student of those hints was William Miller, a Vermont Baptist who, after years of systematic study, concluded that God would destroy the world during the year following March 1843. Miller publicized his predictions throughout the 1830s, and near the end of the decade the **Millerites** (as his followers were called) accumulated thousands of believers—most of them conservative Baptists, Methodists, and Disciples in hill-country New England and in poor neighborhoods in New York, Ohio, and Michigan. As the end approached, the believers read the Bible, prayed, and attended meeting after meeting. A publicist named Henry Jones reported that a shower of meat and blood had fallen on Jersey City, and newspapers published stories alleging that the Millerites were insane and sexually licentious. Some, the press reported, were sewing "ascension robes" in which they would rise straight to heaven without passing through death.

When the end of the year—March 23, 1844—came and went, most of the believers quietly returned to their churches.

Source: Wikipedia Commons

10.4 **Joseph Smith, 1842** Smith founded the Mormon Church in 1830 and attracted thousands of followers before being killed in Carthage, Illinois, in 1844.

Courtesy, American Antiquarian Society

10.5 **Prophetic Chart** A fixture at Millerite Adventist meetings, prophetic charts such as the one shown here displayed the succession of biblical kingdoms and the prophecies of Daniel and John. Millerites revised their charts when the world failed to end in 1843.

A committed remnant, however, kept the faith, and by the 1860s founded the Seventh-Day Adventist Church. The Millerite movement was a reminder that hundreds of thousands of northern Protestants continued to believe that the God of the Old Testament governed everything from bee stings to the course of human history, and that one day he would destroy the world in fire and blood.

10-3c *Family and Society*

Baptists, Methodists, Disciples of Christ, and the smaller popular sects evangelized primarily among persons who had been bypassed or hurt by the Market Revolution. Many had been reduced to dependent, wage-earning status. Others had become market farmers or urban storekeepers or master workmen; few had become rich. Their churches taught them that the temptations of market society were at the center of the world they must reject.

Often their rhetoric turned to criticism of market society, its institutions, and its centers of power. The Quaker schismatic Elias Hicks, a Long Island farmer who fought the worldliness and pride of wealthy urban Quakers, listed the following among the mistakes of the early 19th century: railroads, the Erie Canal, fancy food and other luxuries, banks and the credit system, the city of Philadelphia, and the study of chemistry. The Baptist millenarian William Miller expressed his hatred of banks, insurance companies, stock jobbing, chartered monopolies, personal greed, and the city of New York. In short, what the evangelical middle class identified as the march of progress, poorer and more conservative evangelicals often condemned as a descent into worldliness that would almost certainly provoke God's wrath.

Members of the popular sects often held to the patriarchal family form in which they had been raised, and with which both the Market Revolution and middle-class domesticity seemed at war. Hundreds of thousands of northern Protestants considered the erosion of domestic patriarchy a profound cultural loss and not, as it seemed to the middle class, an avenue to personal liberation. Their cultural conservatism was apparent in their efforts to sustain the father-centered family of the old rural North or to revive it in new forms.

For some, religious conversion came at a point of crisis in the traditional family. William Miller, for example, had a strict Calvinist upbringing in a family in which his father, an uncle, and his grandfather were all Baptist ministers. As a young man he rejected his family, set about making money, and became a deist—actions that deeply wounded his parents. When his father died, Miller was stricken with guilt. He moved back to his hometown, took up his family duties, became a leader of the Baptist church, and (after reading a sermon entitled "Parental Duties") began the years of Bible study that resulted in his world-ending prophecies. Alexander Campbell, one of the founders of the Disciples of Christ, dramatized his filial piety when he debated the freethinking socialist Robert Owen before a large audience in the Methodist meetinghouse in Cincinnati in 1828. He insisted that his white-haired father (a Scots Presbyterian minister) stand in the pulpit above the debaters.

10-3d *The Emergence of Mormonism*

Over the long term, the most successful religious group to emerge from the Burned-Over District was the Church of Jesus Christ of Latter-Day Saints (also known as the Mormon Church). In 1827, according to the group's founder and prophet, Joseph Smith, the Angel Moroni led him to golden plates near his family's farm outside Palmyra, New York. Smith translated the plates into *The Book of Mormon*, which, together with the Old and New Testaments, became the basis of a new faith. *The Book of Mormon* tells the story of a light-skinned people, descendants of the Hebrews, who had sailed to North America long before Columbus. They had an epic, violent history and a covenanted relationship with God, and Jesus had visited them following his crucifixion and resurrection.

In 1830, Smith printed 5,000 copies of *The Book of Mormon* and founded the Mormon Church. Like other religious groups of the era, its organization countered the weakening of patriarchal authority and other social disruptions connected to the Market Revolution. The church was ruled, not by professional clergy, but by an elaborate lay hierarchy of adult males. On top sat the father of Joseph Smith, who was appointed Patriarch of the Church. Below him were Joseph Smith and his brother Hyrum, who were called First and Second Elders. The hierarchy descended through a succession of male authorities that finally reached the fathers of households. Smith claimed that this hierarchy restored the ancient priesthood that had disappeared over the 18 centuries of greed and error that he labeled the Great Apostasy of the Christian churches.

The Mormon Church grew rapidly, claiming 8,000 members by the mid-1830s. But its inclusiveness and new theology aroused suspicion and intense hostility among mainstream Protestant denominations. The Mormons faced persecution that drove them from western New York to Ohio, Missouri, Illinois, and ultimately Utah (see Chapter 13).

10-4 A New Popular Culture

Q *The amusements of common folk were varied, but they exhibited a few common themes. What were those themes?*

Not all of the northern plain folk spent their time in church. Particularly in cities and towns, they became both producers and consumers of a nonreligious (sometimes irreligious) commercial popular culture. The sports and shows attended by northern plain folk, like the churches they attended, were often grounded in an antisentimental view of the world and in traditional forms of patriarchy and masculinity.

10-4a *Blood Sports*

Urban working-class neighborhoods were particularly fertile ground for popular amusements. Young workingmen formed a bachelor subculture that contrasted with the piety and self-restraint of the middle class. They organized volunteer fire companies and militia units that spent more time drinking and fighting rival groups than drilling or putting out fires. Gathering at firehouses, saloons, and street corners, they drank, joked, boasted, and nurtured notions of manliness based on physical prowess and coolness under pressure.

They also engaged in such "**blood sports**" as cock fighting, ratting, and dog fighting, even though many states had laws forbidding such activities. Such contests grew increasingly popular during the 1850s and often were staged by saloonkeepers doubling as sports impresarios. One of the best known was Kit Burns of New York City, who ran Sportsman Hall, a saloon frequented by prizefighters, criminals, and their hangers-on. Behind the saloon was a space—reached through a narrow doorway that could be defended against the police—with animal pits and a small amphitheater that seated 250 but that regularly held 400 yelling spectators. Although workingmen dominated the audiences, a few members of the old aristocracy who rejected middle-class ways also attended these

History Through Film *Gangs of New York* (2002)

Directed by Martin Scorsese.
Starring Leonardo DiCaprio (Amsterdam Vallon), Daniel Day-Lewis (Bill "The Butcher" Cutting), and Cameron Diaz (Jenny Everdeane).

This is Martin Scorsese's movie about the Five Points of New York—a dangerous neighborhood that was home to the working-class world that sustained the new forms of urban popular culture. The film is an operatic tragedy about an Irish boy (Leonardo DiCaprio) whose father, the leader of a gang called the Dead Rabbits, is killed by a nativist chieftain (Daniel Day-Lewis) in a gang fight. He grows up in an orphanage and returns to the neighborhood to take revenge. He becomes part of the criminal entourage of his father's killer, falls in love with a beautiful and talented female thief (Cameron Diaz) who was raised (and used) by the same gang boss, and bides his time—tortured all the while by the prospect of killing a second father figure. In the end, the Irish boy resurrects his father's gang and challenges the nativists to a battle for control of the Five Points. The battle coincides with the Draft Riots of 1863, and the film ends (as it began) in a horrendous bloodbath. The Irish thug kills the nativist thug and the film ends with U2 singing "We Who Built America."

For those who can stomach close-up fights with clubs and hatchets, it is a good enough melodrama. Unhappily, Scorsese casts his story against real history and gets much of it wrong. The film takes pains to "reconstruct" Manhattan's Five Points, but our first view of the neighborhood is taken from a painting of a Brooklyn street made 50 years earlier. The oppressive noise and overcrowding that contemporary visitors describe are obliterated by a large public space at the center of the Points—historically nonexistent, but a fine field for the gang fights that begin and end the movie. Scorsese does cast the nativist leader as a butcher, a trade that was in fact dominated by nonimmigrant workers who were at the center of street gangs, prizefighting, and other low activities. He also reconstructs a theatrical performance—complete with actors in blackface—that rings true. But he puts his characters into too many fictional places. Historically, the gangs were headquartered at saloons, firehouses, and stables. Scorsese's operatic sensibilities, however, move the Dead Rabbits into catacombs beneath the Old Brewery—complete with torchlight, a crude armory, and an untidy pyramid of skulls. The nativists, on the other hand, prefer an Asian motif, holding their get-togethers in an ornate Chinese theater and social house that lends an air of orientalist extravaganza to a neighborhood that knew nothing of such things. The catalog of crimes against history could go on and on: The Dead Rabbits did not follow the cross into battle (Irish street gangs were not particularly religious), Irish priests did not look like Peter the Hermit, and Leonardo DiCaprio does not have a convincing Irish accent.

The "reformers" who minister to the Five Points receive equally silly treatment. Chief among the reformers are the aristocratic Schermerhorns. In fact, most Five Points missionaries were middle-class evangelicals who had little to do with the Schermerhorns or the other old families of New York. The movie reformers hold a dance for the neighborhood; in fact, the evangelicals hated dancing and parties. The reformers also attend a public hanging, cheering as four innocent men are put to death. But New York had outlawed public executions a generation earlier; felons were now hanged within prison walls before small invited audiences. Even if public hangings had persisted, reformers would not have attended them (they had stopped going to such spectacles soon after 1815), and had they been dragged out of their parlors to witness an execution, they would not have cheered. There is also an appearance by P. T. Barnum. Barnum had made his museum the premier middle-class entertainment spot in New York by eschewing low theater, cockfights, and other raucous and violent shows. Yet, the movie has Barnum sponsoring a bare-knuckle prizefight—an act that would have cost him his reputation and his livelihood. The climactic riot includes another Barnum fabrication: Barnum's museum is set on fire; his menagerie escapes, and a terrified elephant romps through the burning streets. It almost certainly did not happen, but even the most fact-bound historian must bow to Scorsese's artistic license on that one. ■

Mario Tursi/Miramax/Dimension Films/The Kobal Collection/Picture Desk

10.6 Daniel Day-Lewis (playing Bill "The Butcher" Cutting) and his Five Points gang.

events. In 1861, for instance, 250 spectators paid as much as $3 each to witness a fight between roosters belonging to the prizefighter John Morrissey and Mr. Genet, president of the New York City board of aldermen. A newspaper estimated bets on the event at $50,000.

10-4b *Boxing*

Prizefighting emerged from the same subterranean culture that sustained cockfights and other blood sports. This sport, imported from Britain, called for an enclosed ring, clear rules, cornermen, a referee, and a paying audience. Boxing's popularity rose during the 1840s and 1850s, a time of increasing immigration and violence in poor city neighborhoods. Many of the fighters had close ties with ethnic-based saloons, militia units, fire companies, and street gangs such as New York's (Irish) Dead Rabbits and (native) Bowery B'hoys, and many labored at occupations with a peculiarly ethnic base. Some of the best American-born fighters were New York City butchers—a licensed, privileged trade from which cheap immigrant labor was systematically excluded. Butchers usually finished work by 10 a.m. They could then spend the rest of the day idling at a firehouse or a bar and often were prominent figures in neighborhood gangs. A prizefight between an American-born butcher and an Irish day laborer would attract a spirited audience that understood its class and ethnic meaning.

10-4c *An American Theater*

In the 18th and early 19th centuries, all American theaters were in the large seaport cities. Those who attended were members of the urban elite, and nearly all of the plays, managers, and actors were English. After 1815, new theaters sprang up not only in New York and Philadelphia but also in dozens of other new towns, while traveling troupes carried theatrical performances to the smallest hamlets. The new theaters catered to male, largely plebeian audiences. Before 1830, the poorer theatergoers—nearly all of them men—occupied the cheap balcony seats (with the exception of the second balcony, which was reserved for prostitutes); artisans and other workingmen filled benches in the ground-floor area known as "the pit"; wealthier and more genteel patrons sat in the boxes. Those sitting in the pit and balcony joined in the performance: They ate and drank, talked, and shouted encouragement and threats to the actors. The genteel New Yorker Washington Irving lamented the "discharge of apples, nuts, and gingerbread" flying out of the balconies.

Library of Congress Prints and Photographs Division Washington, D.C.[LC-USZ62-920]

Bob Thomas/Popperfoto/Getty Images

10.7a (left) and 10.7b (right) **Prizefighters** The Irishman James "Yankee" Sullivan (left) and the nativeborn Tom Hyer (right) were immensely popular heroes of Irish and native workingmen, as well as of the street gangs and political factions of their respective ethnic groups.

Q *What explains the rapid rise of boxing as a popular sport in the mid-19th-century United States?*

What They Said

A Fatal Prizefight, 1842

In 1842, in Hastings, New York, the English boxer Chris Lilly beat the Irishman Tom McCoy to death in a 119-round prizefight. A crowd of more than 2,000 attended the contest. The respectable press denounced the fight as an affront to humanity and civilization. A sportswriter, while he regretted that the fight had not been stopped, admired the male beauty of the losing fighter and the bravery and dignity with which he died. Following are three editorials.

The Sun (Baltimore), 17 September 1842

In connection with [prize-fighting] we now present … a terrible illustration of the consequences of this imbruting and pernicious vice; a detail of scenes enacted in a civilized country, calculated to summon the blush of shame to the cheek of manhood for such voluntary degradation of our race. It will be seen that in a matter of "sport"—to gratify the devilish taste of a certain class of the community—and for a purse of a few dollars, a wretched man has been beaten to death—in the presence of a crowd of spectators bearing the human form… . As a civilized people, we shudder at the contemplation of the scenes familiar to the old Gladiatorial arena, but in comparison with those witnessed the other day in New York, and in view of "the enlightened age in which we live," the former are elevated in their character and become a virtue in our eyes. Let us earnestly hope, that while we import the virtues, many of the foibles, and some of the vices of the old world, we may be able to avoid the diabolical iniquity and savage barbarity of its blood-stained "ring."

Public Ledger (Philadelphia), 15 September 1842

Beauties of the Ring—A Foul Murder—; A foul murder was committed in New York on Tuesday, which, for brutality and shocking barbarity, exceeds the most atrocious act of the kind recently recorded. It was the more atrocious from the fact that it was committed in the presence of thousands, who stood coolly looking on, enjoying the sport and encouraging it by approbative cries. That such an act should be committed in the presence of thousands of pleased spectators, in the nineteenth century, shows that we have begun too soon to boast of our civilization—that there still exists a low brutality of feeling in a large portion of the public, which could not be exceeded in the most debased condition of any former age, or among the most abject of its people.

Excerpts from the Sportswriter's Account

If Lilly's appearance was fine, *McCoy's* was beautiful. His skin had a warmer glow than the former's; his form was more elegantly proportioned, and his air and style more graceful and manlike. His swelling breast curved out like a cuirass; his shoulders were deep, with a bold curved blade, and the muscular development of the arms large and finely brought out. His head was rather large and long, yet it indicated courage and a love for strife, and the manner in which it was set betokened strength.

*Round 28*th—Lilly cool as a cucumber, and wary as an Indian—McCoy, on the contrary, too free, and too ready to fight… . McCoy, game as a pebble, and fearless as a lion, rushed wildly in, caught two or three more before he could clinch, and then was badly thrown.

Round 103d. McCoy suffering very much, scarcely able to breathe, and spitting [blood] from his mouth… . He came up bravely (the noble boy!), without the slightest indication of a desire to shrink, got in a good body blow, but in the close was badly thrown.

*Round 120*th—[McCoy] was led slowly to the mark, and took his position—a dying man—but as erect, as dignified, as game as ever. Lilly was also much fatigued, and enduring considerable suffering from the heavy body blows he had received.

Q *The newspapers condemned prizefighting in the name of civilization, religion, and a proper sense of manhood. Look closely at the language that they applied to the boxing community. How did they characterize those people and what they did? How did that characterization buttress their own conceptions of "civilization?"*

Q *The sportswriter described the aesthetics of the male body and the bravery, dignity, and sense of honor with which the doomed fighter conducted himself. In what fundamental ways did this description conflict with the world that the editorialists were making and defending?*

Sources: (top) *The Sun* (Baltimore newspaper), 17 September 1842; (middle) *Public Ledger* (Philadelphia newspaper), 15 September 1842; (bottom) *The American Fistiana: Containing a History of Prize Fighting in the United States, with all the Principal Battles for the Last Forty Years* (New York: H. Johnson, 1849), pp. 15–21.

As time passed, rowdyism turned into violence. Working-class theatergoers protested the elegant speech, gentlemanly bearing, and understated performances of the English actors, which happened to match the speech, manners, and bearing of the American urban elite. Protests were directed not only at the English actors but also at the ladies and gentlemen in the orchestra who were seen as adherents of an aristocratic English culture unsuitable in a democratic republic.

The first theater riot occurred in 1817, when the English actor Charles Incledon refused a New York audience's demand that he stop what he was doing and sing "Black-Eyed Susan." Such assaults grew more common even though separate theaters began to offer separate kinds of performances for rich and poor. The violence culminated in the rivalry between the American actor Edwin Forrest and the English actor William Charles Macready in the 1840s (see "Interpreting the Visual Past").

Playhouses that catered to working-class audiences continued to feature Shakespearean tragedies (*Richard III*, played broadly and with a lot of swordplay, was the favorite), but they soon shared the stage with works written in the American vernacular. The stage "Yankee," rustic but shrewd, appeared at this time, and so did Mose the Bowery B'hoy, a New York volunteer fireman who performed feats of derring-do. Both frequently appeared in opposition to well-dressed characters with English accents. The Yankee outsmarted them; Mose beat them up.

10.8 **Jim Crow** Thomas D. Rice wearing the costume of his character "Jim Crow," in 1833.

Q *What contemporary racial stereotypes was Thomas Rice channeling and reinforcing?*

Q *Why did minstrelsy shows appeal to white audiences in the North?*

10-4d *Minstrelsy*

The most popular form of theater was the blackface **minstrel show**. These shows were blatantly racist, and they were the preferred entertainment of workingmen in northern cities from 1840 to 1880. The first minstrel show was presented in 1831 when a white showman named Thomas Rice blacked his face and "jumped Jim Crow," imitating a black shuffle-dance he had seen on the Cincinnati docks.

Minstrel shows developed a form that every theatergoer knew by heart. The shows lasted an hour and a half and were presented in three sections. The first consisted of songs and dances performed in a walkaround, in which the audience was encouraged to clap and sing along. This was followed by a longer middle section in which the company sat in a row with a character named Tambo at one end and a character named Bones at the other (named for the tambourine and bones, the instruments they played), with an interlocutor in the middle. The Tambo character, often called Uncle Ned, was a simple-minded plantation slave dressed in plain clothing. The Bones character, usually called Zip Coon, was a dandified, oversexed free black dressed in top hat and tails. The interlocutor was the straight man—fashionably dressed, slightly pretentious, with an English accent. This middle portion of the show consisted of a conversation among the three, which included pointed political satire, skits ridiculing the wealthy and the educated, and sexual jokes that bordered on obscenity. The third section featured songs, dances, and jokes, most of them familiar enough so that the audience could sing along and laugh at the right places.

The minstrel shows introduced African American song and dance—in toned-down, Europeanized form—to audiences who would not have permitted black performers on the stage. They also reinforced racial stereotypes that were near the center of American popular culture. Finally, hiding behind black masks, minstrel performers dealt broadly with aspects of social and political life that other performers avoided.

10-4e *Novels and the Penny Press*

Few of the commodities made widely available by the Market Revolution were more ubiquitous than newspapers and inexpensive books. Improvements in printing and papermaking enabled entrepreneurs to sell daily newspapers for a penny. Cheap "story papers" became available in the 1830s, "yellowback" fiction in the 1840s, and dime novels from the 1850s onward. Although these offerings were distributed throughout the North and the West, they found their first and largest audience among city workers.

Interpreting the Visual Past

The Actors' War: Forrest and Macready

Edwin Forrest was America's great native-born actor. He was a democratic-nationalist hero, with a voice (according to the democratic press) like the roar of Niagara Falls and a body "carved out of the American forest." He played Shakespeare as American melodrama filled with bombast and physicality. Forrest's great international rival was the British actor William Charles Macready. Macready was engaged, both as an actor and a theater manager, in a campaign to rescue the theater from democracy. He insisted that acting demanded study and formal training, and that plays be performed with fidelity to the text (Shakespeare the way Shakespeare wrote it) before knowledgeable audiences that rewarded the best actors and the best plays. Macready condemned Forrest's extravagant acting style and his working-class audiences as the opposite of high culture and good taste. Their rivalry began during Forrest's tour of Great Britain in 1846, and culminated in Macready's visit to America three years later. Macready was hissed in Boston and showered with rotten potatoes in New York, and he had to dodge a sheep carcass that was thrown onto the stage in Cincinnati. The attacks on Macready came to a head when he played the elite Astor Place Opera House in New York. Handbills told American democrats to descend on the "English Aristocratic Opera House," and the militia was called out to protect Macready, the theater, and its genteel audience. The result was the worst theater riot in American history, which left 20 dead.

These pictures portray Forrest and Macready as Shakespeare's Macbeth. They are similar, but the differences are telling. Macready stands beneath a vast sky in an open countryside. His body is composed, his toes are properly pointed, and he gazes meaningfully into the heavens. Forrest, on the other hand, stands before a gothic/melodramatic backdrop that features a witch's cauldron, threatening rocks, and broken trees. His body is less elegant and more powerful than Macready's, he stares forcefully off-stage, and his weapon is bigger than Macready's. Macready is prepared for a classical performance. Forrest is ready for physical melodrama.

Q *Look closely at these pictures. Find as many differences in dress, demeanor, and surroundings as you can. What do these differences say to you about these two men?*

Q *Edwin Forrest was often hailed as a model of a new kind of American manhood. What were the components of that model, and how do they relate to the themes of this chapter?*

The New York Public Library/Art Resource, NY

Mr Macready as Macbeth, Act I Scene 3, in the play by William Shakespeare (1564-1616) (engraving), English School, (19th century)/ Private Collection/The Stapleton Collection/The Bridgeman Art Library

10.9a (left) and 10.9b (right) **Augustus Robin, Edwin Forrest as Macbeth, mid 19th century (left). Thomas Sherratt, William Charles Macready as Macbeth, mid 19th century (right).**

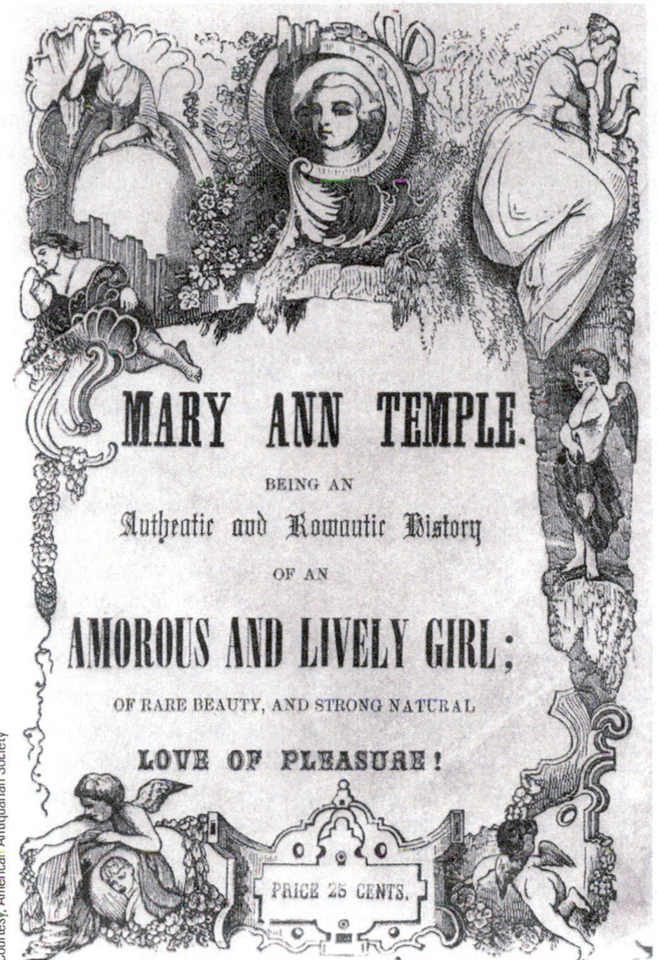

MARY ANN TEMPLE.

BEING AN

Authentic and Romantic History

OF AN

AMOROUS AND LIVELY GIRL;

OF RARE BEAUTY, AND STRONG NATURAL

LOVE OF PLEASURE!

PRICE 25 CENTS.

Courtesy, American Antiquarian Society

THE

FEMALE LAND PIRATE;

OR

AWFUL, MYSTERIOUS, AND HORRIBLE DISCLOSURES

OF

AMANDA BANNORRIS,

WIFE AND ACCOMPLICE OF RICHARD BANNORRIS, A LEADER IN THAT TERRIBLE BAND OF ROBBERS AND MURDERERS, KNOWN FAR AND WIDE AS THE

MURRELL MEN.

At length the door opened, and two large fellows, with masks on their faces, carrying a dark lantern, entered, and in a gruff voice said I must go with them. Their first operation was to blindfold me—which done, one of them seized me in his brawny arms, bore me out, mounted me on a horse, and rode swiftly away—the other following. (*See page* 17.)

CINCINNATI.

PRINTED FOR, AND PUBLISHED BY E. E. BARCLAY.

1847.

Courtesy, American Antiquarian Society

10.10a (left) and 10.10b (right) **Yellow-Back Novels** Here are two pulp fiction hits of the 1840s: an erotic novel about the "amorous and lively" Mary Ann Temple (left) and a crime story about robberies and murders committed by the "Female Land Pirate" (right)—not the kinds of women encountered in middle-class sentimental fiction.

Q *What social and cultural developments explain the wide popularity of such sensational novels as* Mary Ann Temple *and* The Female Land Pirate?

Mass-audience newspapers were heavily spiced with sensationalism. The *Philadelphia Gazette* in late summer 1829, for instance, treated its eager readers to the following: "Female Child with Two Heads," "Bats," "Another Shark," "More Stabbing," "Fishes Travelling on Land," "Dreadful Steam Boat Disaster," "Raffling for Babies," "Combat with a Bear," "Lake Serpent," "Atrocious Murder," and much more. Henry David Thoreau commented on the "startling and monstrous events as fill the daily papers," while his friend Ralph Waldo Emerson reported that Americans were "reading all day murders & railroad accidents." These sensational stories portrayed a haunted, often demonic nature that regularly produced monstrosities and ruined the works of humankind, as well as a human nature that, despite appearances, was often deceptive and depraved.

Working-class readers discovered a similarly untrustworthy world in cheap fiction. George Lippard's *The Quaker City* (1845) sold more than 200,000 copies in six years, making it the best-selling American book before the sentimental blockbusters of the 1850s. *The Quaker City* was a fictional exposé of the hypocrisy, lust, and cruelty of Philadelphia's outwardly genteel and Christian elite. Lippard and other adventure writers (whose works accounted for 60 percent of all American fiction titles published between 1831 and 1860) indulged in a pornography of violence that included cannibalism, blood drinking, and murder by every imaginable means. They also dealt with sex in unprecedentedly explicit ways, introducing readers not only to seduction and rape but also to transvestitism, child pornography, necrophilia, miscegenation, group sex, homosexuality, and—perhaps most shocking of all—women with criminal minds and insatiable sexual appetites. The scenes of gore and sexual depravity were presented voyeuristically—as self-righteous exposés of the perversions of the rich and powerful and stories of the Founders' Republic trampled upon by a vicious elite that pretended virtue but lived only for its appetites.

Popular fictions—like most popular plays and much of what went on in blood sports, the prize ring, and the penny press—were melodramatic contests between good and evil. Evil was described in terms reminiscent of original sin: It provided the background of all human action, and heroes met a demonic world with courage and guile without hoping to change it. Melodramatic heroes frequently acknowledged evil in themselves while claiming moral superiority over the hypocrites and frauds that governed the world. A murderer in Ned Buntline's *G'hals of New York* (1850) remarks, "There isn't no *real* witue [virtue] and honesty nowhere, 'cept among the perfessional dishonest." By contrast, in middle-class sentimental novels, the universe was benign; good could be nurtured, and evil could be defeated and transformed. Harriet Beecher Stowe's slave driver Simon Legree—the best-known villain in American literature—is evil not because of a natural disposition toward evil, but because he had been deprived of a mother's love during childhood. The world, in Stowe's view, could be nurtured into being good. Most northern plain folk (whether they favored church or popular entertainments) did not want to fix an imperfect and often chaotic world. They wanted only to live decently and bravely within it.

10-5 Family, Church, and Neighborhood: The White South

Q *In what specific ways did evangelical Protestantism act as a conservative force within southern culture?*

The southern states experienced cultural transformations of a more conservative nature—transformations grounded in persistent localism, in the father-centered family, and in the pervasive influence of a traditionalist evangelical Christianity.

10-5a *The Beginnings of the Bible Belt*

In the first third of the 19th century, evangelical Protestantism and revivalism of the Second Great Awakening transformed the South into what it has been ever since: the Bible Belt. That transformation began when poor and middling whites found spiritual alternatives to the culture of the gentry—to their formalistic Episcopalianism, their love of luxury and display, and their enjoyment of money and power. Early southern Baptists and Methodists demanded a crisis conversion followed by a life of piety and a rejection of what they called "the world." To no small degree, the world was the economic, cultural, and political world controlled by the planters. James McGready, who preached in rural North Carolina in the 1790s, openly condemned the gentry: "The world is in all their thoughts day and night. All their talk is of corn and tobacco, of land and stock. The price of merchandise and negroes are inexhaustible themes of conversation. But for them, the name of Jesus has no charms; it is rarely mentioned unless to be profaned." This was dangerous talk, as McGready learned when young rakes rode their horses through one of his outdoor meetings, tipped over the benches, set the altar on fire, and threatened to kill McGready.

Southern Baptists, Methodists, and Presbyterians spread their message during the awakening through the **camp meeting**, and this too was subversive of southern social distinctions. Though its origins stretched back into the 18th century, the first full-blown camp meeting took place at Cane Ridge, Kentucky, in 1801. Here the annual "Holy Feast," a three-day communion service of Scots-Irish Presbyterians, was transformed into an outdoor revival at which hundreds experienced conversion under Presbyterian, Methodist, and Baptist preaching. Estimates of the crowd at Cane Ridge ranged from 10,000 to 20,000 persons. Some converts fainted, others jerked uncontrollably, and a few barked like dogs, all of them visibly taken by the Holy Spirit. These exercises fell upon women and men, whites and blacks, rich and poor, momentarily blurring social hierarchy in moments of profound and very public religious ecstasy. A witness to a later camp meeting recounted that "to see a bold and courageous Kentuckian (undaunted by the horrors of war) turn pale and tremble at the reproof of a weak woman, a little boy, or a poor African; to see him sink down in deep remorse, roll and toss, and gnash his teeth, till black in the face, entreat the prayers of those he came to devour ... who can say the change was not supernatural?" Southern white men, even when under religious conviction, sometimes resisted this loss of mastery and self-control. One preacher remembered a "fine, strong, good-looking young man" who felt himself giving in to camp meeting preaching. He "found no relief until he drew a large pistole out of his pocket, with which he intended to defend himself if any one should offer to speak to him on the subject of religion."

The early southern evangelicals irritated and angered the elite and white men generally, for they seemed to question not only worldliness but also the white male dominance that held the southern world together. The conversion of wives and children (not to mention slaves) could trouble southern families; the conversion of white men could render them "womanish." The governors of southern farms and southern families, however, had little to worry about. The Baptists, Methodists, and Presbyterians of the South, though they never stopped railing against greed and pride, found that they could conquer the South and live comfortably with a system of fixed hierarchy and God-given social roles—with slavery and father-dominated families in particular.

10-5b *Slavery and Southern Evangelicals*

Slavery became a major case in point. For a brief period after the Revolution, evangelicals joined with an elite minority of slaveholders to oppose slavery. Methodists and Baptists preached to slaves as well as to whites, and Bishop Francis Asbury, the principal architect of American Methodism, admired John Wesley's statement that slavery was against "all the laws of Justice, Mercy, and Truth." In 1780, a conference of Methodist preachers ordered circuit riders to free their slaves and advised all Methodists to do the same. In 1784, the Methodists declared that they would excommunicate members who failed to free their slaves within two years. Many lay Methodists took the order seriously. On the Delmarva Peninsula (Delaware and the Eastern Shore of Maryland and Virginia), for instance, Methodist converts freed thousands of slaves in the late 18th century.

The period of greatest evangelical growth, however, came during the years in which the South committed irrevocably to plantation slavery. As increasing numbers of both slaves and slave owners came within the evangelical fold, the southern churches had to rethink their position on human bondage. The Methodists never carried out their threat to excommunicate slaveholders, and in 1816 confessed, "little can be done to abolish the practice so contrary to moral justice." Similarly, the Baptists and Presbyterians never translated their antislavery rhetoric into action. By 1820, evangelicals were coming to terms with slavery. Instead of demanding freedom for slaves, they suggested, as the Methodist James O'Kelly put it, that slave owners treat slaves as "dear brethren in Christ." After 1830, with much of the planter elite converted to evangelicalism, this would evolve into a full-scale effort to Christianize the institution of slavery.

10-5c *Gender, Power, and the Evangelicals*

Southern white men, yeomen as well as planters, distrusted the early evangelicals for more than their views on slavery. The preachers seemed even more grievously mistaken about white manhood and the integrity of white families. Southerners were localistic and culturally conservative. They distrusted outsiders and defended rural neighborhoods grounded in the sovereignty of fathers.

The early evangelicals threatened southern patriarchy. They preached individual salvation to women, children, and slaves—often hinting that the "family" of believers could replace blood ties. Churches sometimes intervened in family disputes or disciplined family members in ways that subverted patriarchal control. Perhaps worse, many of the preachers failed to act out the standards of southern manhood in their own lives. James McGready and other camp meeting preachers often faced hecklers and rowdies and quietly took their beatings, which violated the southern notions of male honor.

As they had with slavery, southern evangelicals came to terms with the notions of manhood and the father-centered families of the South. The preachers learned to assert traditional forms of manhood. Their fathers and often themselves, they said, had fought the British and Indians heroically. They revealed that they had often been great drinkers, gamblers, fighters, and fornicators before submitting to God, and they also began fighting back when attacked. Peter Cartwright, who conquered much of Kentucky and southern Illinois for Methodism, walked on many occasions out of the pulpit to confront hecklers, and punched more than a few of them. The preachers also made it clear that they would pose no threat to the authority of fathers. They discouraged the excesses of female and juvenile piety. At the same time, church disciplinary cases involving adultery, wife beating, private drunkenness, and other offenses committed within families became more and more rare.

10-5d *Religious Conservatism*

More fundamentally, evangelicals upheld the southern world of fixed hierarchy and God-given social roles, and their churches reinforced localistic neighborhoods and the patriarchal family. Some southern communities began when a whole congregation moved onto new land. Others were settled by the chain migration of brothers and cousins, and subsequent revivals spread through family networks. Rural isolation limited most households to their own company during the week, but on Sundays church meetings united the neighborhood's cluster

10.11 **Colonel and Mrs. Whiteside** Colonel and Mrs. James Whiteside are pictured at home in their mansion on the heights above Chattanooga, Tennessee, with their infant son and their slaves. The colonel, Bible in hand, looks directly at his wife, while she looks shyly and indirectly back at him.

Q *What does this carefully constructed painting reveal about the southern genteel ideal?*

of extended families into a community of believers. In most neighborhoods, social connections seldom extended beyond that. The word "church" referred ultimately to the worldwide community of Christians, and the war between the "church" and the "world" referred to a cosmic history that would end in millennial fire. But in the day-to-day understandings of southern evangelicals, the church was the local congregation and the world was local sins and local sinners. Churches disciplined members for such worldly practices as drinking, gambling, dancing, swearing, fornication, and adultery.

Southern evangelicalism rested on the sovereignty of God, a conviction of human imperfection, and an acceptance of disappointment and pain as part of God's grand and unknowable design. When the young son of a planter family died, his mother was certain that he died because his parents had loved him more than God: "But God took him for he saw he was our idol." Francis Pickens of South Carolina lost his wife and child, and wrote, "I had almost forgot there was a God, and now I stand the scattered ... and blasted monument of his just wrath." It was a far cry from the middle-class North's sentimentalism and the romantic, redemptive deaths of children in sentimental fiction.

Within this flawed and dangerous world, patriarchal social relations were crucial to Christian living. Southerners revered the patriarch and slaveholder Abraham more than any other figure in the Bible, and John C. Calhoun would proclaim "Hebrew Theocracy" the best government ever experienced by humankind. The father must—like Abraham—govern and protect his household, the mother must assist the father, and the women, children, and slaves must faithfully act out the duties of their stations. Eternal salvation was possible for everyone, but the saved lived out their godliness by striving to be good mothers, good fathers, good slaves. By the same token, a Christian never questioned his or her God-given social role.

10-5e *Pro-Slavery Christianity*

In revolutionary and early national America, white southerners had been the most radical of republicans. Jeffersonian planter-politicians led the fights for equal rights and the absolute separation of church and state, and southern evangelicals were the early republic's staunchest opponents of slavery. By 1830, however, the South was an increasingly conscious minority within a democratic and capitalist nation. The northern middle classes proclaimed a link between material and moral progress, identifying both with individual autonomy and universal rights. A radical northern minority was agitating for the immediate abolition of slavery (Chapter 12).

Southerners met this challenge with an "intellectual blockade" against outside publications and ideas and with a moral and religious defense of slavery. The Bible provided plenty of ammunition. Southerners preached that the Chosen People of the Old Testament had been patriarchs and slaveholders, and that Jesus had lived in a society that sanctioned slavery and never criticized the institution. Some ministers claimed that blacks were the descendants of Ham and thus deserved enslavement. The most common religious argument, however, was that slavery had given millions of heathen Africans the priceless opportunity to become Christians and to live in a Christian society. Thornton Stringfellow, a Virginia Baptist minister, insisted that "their condition . . . is now better than that of any equal number of laborers on earth, and is daily improving."

Like their northern counterparts, southern clergymen applauded the material improvements of the age, but they insisted that moral improvement occurred only when people embraced the timeless truths of the Bible. The South Carolinian William F. Hutson put it simply: "In religion and morals, we doubt all improvements, not known to certain fishermen who lived eighteen hundred years ago." Northern notions of progress through individual liberation, equal rights, and universal Christian love were wrongheaded and dangerous. The Presbyterian John Adger asserted that relations of dominance and submission (and not "barbarism and personal savage independence") were utterly necessary to both social and individual fulfillment, and that the distribution of rights and responsibilities was unequal and God-given. "The rights of the father are natural, but they belong only to the fathers. Rights of property are natural, but they belong only to those who have property," and such natural rights were coupled with the awesome duties of fatherhood and proprietorship. In the end, southern pro-slavery intellectuals rejected Jefferson's "self-evident" equality of man; Edmund Ruffin, for instance, branded that passage of the Declaration of Independence as "indefensible" as well as "false and foolish."

10-5f *The Mission to the Slaves*

By the 1820s, southern evangelicalism had long since abandoned its hostility toward slavery, and slaveholders commonly attended camp meetings and revivals. These prosperous converts faced conflicting duties. Their churches taught them that slaves had immortal souls and that planters were responsible for their spiritual welfare. A planter on his deathbed told his children that humane treatment and religious instruction for slaves was the duty of slave owners; if these were neglected, "we will have to answer for the loss of their souls." After Nat Turner's bloody slave revolt in 1831 (Chapter 9), missions to the slaves took on new urgency: If the churches were to create a Christian society in the South, that society would have to include the slaves. The result after 1830 was a concerted attempt to Christianize the slaves.

To this end, Charles Colcock Jones, a Presbyterian minister from Georgia, wrote manuals on how to preach to slaves. He taught that no necessary connection linked social position and spiritual worth: There were good and bad slaveholders and good and bad slaves. He also taught, preaching from the Epistles of Paul ("Servants, obey your masters"), that slaves must accept the master's authority as God's, and that obedience was their prime religious virtue. Jones warned white preachers never to become personally involved with their slave listeners—to pay no attention to their quarrels, their complaints about their master or about their fellow slaves, or about working conditions on the plantation. "We separate entirely their religious from their civil condition," he said, "and contend that one may be attended to without interfering with the other." The catechism Jones prepared for slaves included the question, "What did God make you for?" The answer was, "To make a crop."

The evangelical mission to the slaves was not as completely self-serving as it may seem. For to accept one's worldly station, to be obedient and dutiful within that station, and to seek salvation outside of this world were precisely what the planters demanded of themselves and their own families. An important goal of plantation missions was to create safe and profitable plantations. Yet that goal was to be achieved by Christianizing both slaveholders and slaves—a lesson that some slaveholders learned when they were expelled from their churches for mistreating their slaves. As for the slaves, we have seen that they listened selectively to what white missionaries preached, and turned evangelical Christianity into a religion of their own (see Chapter 9). This continued throughout the Second Great Awakening, which drew thousands of slaves into Methodist and Baptist churches. The slaves responded to the awakening's democratizing message even as they continued to adapt Christianity to African practices, often organizing their own services beyond white oversight.

10-6 Race

Q *In what ways did the racial order of the North change in the first half of the 19th century?*

Americans in the first half of the 19th century revised the racial order as well as the religious and domestic order of their society. White Americans had long assumed that Africans belonged at the bottom of society, but they assumed that others belonged there as well. In a colonial world in which many whites were indentured servants, tenants, apprentices, and workers who lived in their employers' homes, where increasing numbers of blacks were formally free and many others were hired out as semifree, few Americans made rigid distinctions concerning the "natural" independence of whites and the "natural" dependence of blacks. (All Americans, after all, were colonial dependents of the British king.) The language of colonial social division separated gentlemen from the "middling sort," and relegated the propertyless and dependent to the "lower orders" or the "lower sort." While the better-off whites were far from color blind, they wrote off poverty, disorder, drunkenness, and rioting as the work not of blacks but of an undifferentiated substratum of "Negroes, sailors, servants, and boys."

Modern racism—the notion that blacks were a separate and hopelessly inferior order of humankind—emerged from developments in the early 19th century: national independence and the crucial new distinction between Americans who were citizens and those who were not, the recommitment to slavery in the South, and the making of what would be called "free labor" in the North. Whites who faced lifetimes of wage labor and dependence struggled to make dignity out of that situation. At the same time, freed slaves entered the bottom of a newly defined "free labor" society and tried to do the same. With plenty of help from the wealthy and powerful, whites succeeded in making white democracy out of the rubble of the old patriarchal republic. In the process, they defined nonwhites as constitutionally incapable of self-discipline, personal independence, and political participation.

10-6a *Free Blacks*

There had been sizable pockets of slavery in the northern colonies, but revolutionary idealism, coupled with the growing belief that slavery was inefficient, led one northern state after another to abolish it. Vermont, where there were almost no slaves, outlawed slavery in its revolutionary constitution. By 1804, every northern state had taken some action, usually by passing laws that mandated gradual emancipation. The first of such laws, and the model for others, was passed in Pennsylvania in 1780. This law freed slaves born after 1780 when they reached their 28th birthday. Slaves born before 1780 would remain slaves, and slave children would remain slaves through their prime working years. By 1830, only a handful of aging blacks remained slaves in the North.

Gradual emancipation did not stop at the Mason-Dixon Line. We have seen (Chapter 9) that thousands of Chesapeake slaveholders freed their slaves in the decades following the Revolution. Virginia seriously considered abolishing slavery outright. In 1832, a Virginia constitutional convention argued the question of immediate emancipation by state law. With the western counties supporting abolition (but insisting that freed blacks be transported from the state) and some of the eastern, slaveholding counties threatening to secede from the state if abolition won, the convention rejected emancipation by a vote of 73–58. In the Deep South, where slavery was a big and growing business, whites did not talk about emancipation. They assumed that slavery was permanent, and that the only proper status for blacks was bondage and submission to whites.

From Virginia on north, the rising population of free blacks gravitated to the cities and towns. Despite the flood of white immigrants from Europe and the American countryside, African Americans constituted a sizable minority in the rapidly expanding cities. New York City's black population, 10.5 percent in 1800, was still 8.8 percent in 1820. Philadelphia, the haven of thousands of southern refugees, was 10.3 percent African American in 1800, 11.9 percent in 1820.

Blacks in the seaports tended to take stable, low-paying jobs. A few became successful (occasionally wealthy) entrepreneurs, while some others practiced skilled trades. Many took jobs as waiters or porters in hotels, as merchant seamen, as barbers, and as servants in wealthy families. Others worked as dockworkers and laborers. Still others became dealers in used clothing, or draymen with their own carts and horses, or food vendors in the streets and in basement shops. (In New York, oysters were a black monopoly.) As never before, free black faces and voices became parts of the landscape and soundscape of cities and towns—hawking buttermilk, hot corn, and oysters, talking and laughing in the streets, jostling their way through

Heritage Images/Hulton Fine Art Collection/Getty Images

10.12 **Portrait of a Sailor, c. 1800** In the early 19th century, free African Americans in the North found new opportunities in a variety of occupations, including sailing. By 1820, about 20 percent of all American seamen were black

city crowds. More than a few whites were disturbed. The New York journalist Mordecai Noah, like many other elite whites, had expected freed slaves to be grateful and deferential to their former masters, but "instead of thankfulness for their redemption, they have become impudent and offensive beyond all precedent."

African Americans with money established businesses and institutions of their own. At one end were black-owned gambling houses, saloons, brothels, oyster cellars, and dance halls, which often served a mixed clientele. At the other end were institutions built by self-consciously "respectable" free blacks. Most prominent among these were churches, which sprang up wherever African Americans lived. In Philadelphia, black preachers Richard Allen and Absalom Jones rebelled against segregated seating in St. George's Methodist Church and, in 1794, founded two separate black congregations. The African Methodist Episcopal Church grew from Allen's church, and established itself as a national denomination in 1816. Sustained by the evangelical fervor of the Second Great Awakening, black evangelical churches proliferated in the North, promoting a liberating faith and the abolition of slavery. The membership of the African Methodist Episcopal Church reached 20,000 by the 1850s. Schools and relief societies, usually associated with churches, also grew quickly. Black Masonic lodges attracted hundreds of members. Many of the churches and social organizations took names that proudly called up the blacks' African origins. In Philadelphia, for instance, there were African Methodists, Abyssinian Baptists, the Daughters of Ethiopia, the African Dorcas Society—to name only a few. Not only their names and activities but their presence as black-owned buildings filled with respectable former slaves caught the attention of their white and black neighbors. It was from this matrix of black businesses and institutions that black abolitionists—David Walker in Boston, Frederick Douglass in New Bedford and Rochester, the itinerant Sojourner Truth, and many others—would emerge to demand abolition of slavery and equal rights for black citizens.

10-6b *The Beginnings of Modern Racism*

In post-revolutionary America, the most important social and political distinction was not between black and white or rich and poor. It was between the heads of independent households and the women, slaves, servants, apprentices, and others who were their dependents. Wage labor and tenancy reduced the number of northern whites who were, by traditional measures, independent. They fought that threat in a number of ways: Their skills and labor, they said, constituted a kind of property; their manhood conferred judgment and strength and thus independence. These were assertions of worth and independence that had little to do with the ownership of property. In ways that were sometimes subtle but just as often brutal, they often made those assertions at the expense of African Americans. Along with the value of their labor and their manhood, white men discovered the decisive value of white skin.

Whites in the early 19th century began refusing to work alongside blacks, and some of the earliest and most decisive racist assaults came when whites asserted their control over some occupations and relegated blacks to others. They chased blacks out of skilled jobs by pressuring employers to discriminate, and often by outright violence. As a result, African Americans disappeared from the skilled trades, while many unskilled and semiskilled blacks lost their jobs on the docks and in warehouses. In 1834, a Philadelphian reported that "colored persons, when engaged in their usual occupations, were repeatedly assailed and maltreated, usually on the [waterfront]. Parties of white men have insisted that no blacks shall be employed in certain departments of labor." And as their old jobs disappeared, blacks were systematically excluded from the new jobs that were opening up in factories.

Even whites who remained in positions of personal dependence (servants, waiters, and other jobs that were coming to be defined as "black" work) refused the signs and language of servility. White servants refused to wear livery, which became the uniform of black servants of the rich. Whites also refused to be called "servants." As early as 1807, when an English visitor asked a New England servant for her master, the woman replied that she had no master. "I am Mr.___'s *help*," she said. "I'd have you know, *man*, that I am no *sarvant*; none but *negars* are *sarvants*." There was trouble off the job as well. As early as the 1790s, whites had disrupted African American church meetings, and they frequently attacked black celebrations of northern emancipation and Haitian independence. Black neighborhoods and institutions came under increasing attack. In the late 1820s and early 1830s, every northern city experienced antiblack rioting. In 1829, white mobs destroyed black homes and businesses in Cincinnati. Hundreds of blacks fled that city for Canada; many others sought refuge in slaveholding Kentucky. Between 1828 and 1849 in Philadelphia, simmering racial tensions between blacks and working-class whites erupted into five sprawling race riots that wrecked black churches, businesses, and homes.

Above all, white populists pronounced blacks unfit to be citizens of the republic. Federalists and other upper-class whites had often supported various forms of black suffrage; less-privileged whites opposed it. The insistence that blacks were incapable of citizenship reinforced an equally natural white male political capacity. The most vicious racist assaults were often carried out beneath symbols of the revolutionary republic. Antiblack mobs in Baltimore, Cincinnati, and Toledo called themselves Minute Men and Sons of Liberty. Philadelphia blacks who gathered to hear the reading of the Declaration of Independence on the Fourth of July were attacked for "defiling the government." The more respectable and powerful whites had long been worried about the mixed-race underclass of the cities and towns. Now, as the disorder that they expected of the lower orders took the form of race riots, the authorities responded. But rather than protect the jobs, churches, schools, businesses, friends, and political rights of African Americans from criminal attack, they determined to stop the trouble by removing black people—from employment, from public festivities, from their already-limited citizenship, and, ultimately, from the United States. Cities either excluded black children from public schools or set up segregated schools. In 1845, when Massachusetts passed a law declaring that all children had the right to attend neighborhood schools, the Boston School Committee blithely ruled that the law did not apply to blacks. Blacks were also excluded from white churches or sat in segregated pews. Even the Quakers seated blacks and whites separately.

10-7 Citizenship

Q *How did American voting rights change between the adoption of the Constitution and the Civil War?*

The transition from republic to democracy—and the relation of that transition to the decline of patriarchy and efforts to shore up white manhood—took on legal, institutional shape in a redefinition of republican citizenship. The revolutionary constitutions of most states retained colonial freehold (property) qualifications for voting. In the yeoman societies of the late 18th century, freehold qualifications granted the vote to between one-half and three-quarters of adult white men. Many of the disfranchised were dependent sons who expected to inherit citizenship along with land. Some states dropped the freehold clause and gave the vote to all adult men who paid taxes, but with little effect on the voting population. Both the freehold and taxpaying qualifications tended to give political rights to heads of households, granting active citizenship to independent fathers and not to their dependents. Arthur St. Clair, the territorial governor of Ohio, argued for retention of the Northwest Ordinance's 50-acre freehold qualification for voting in territorial elections in set-piece republican language: "I do not count independence and wealth always together," he said, "but I pronounce poverty and dependence inseparable." When Nathaniel Macon, a respected old revolutionary from North Carolina, saw that his state would abolish property qualifications in 1802, he suggested that the suffrage be limited to married men. Like St. Clair's proposition, it was an attempt to maintain the old distinction between citizen-householders and disfranchised dependents.

Between 1790 and 1820, citizenship grounded in fatherhood and proprietorship gave way to a democratic insistence on equal rights for all white men. There were several reasons for that development. First, the proportion of adult white men who could not meet property qualifications multiplied at an alarming rate. In the new towns and cities, artisans and laborers and even many merchants and professionals did not own real estate. And in the West, new farms were often valued below property qualifications. This became particularly troublesome after the War of 1812, when a large proportion of veterans could not vote. In Shenandoah County, Virginia,

Library of Congress, Prints and Photographs Division

10.13 "The People" from John Latrobe, *The Juvenile National Calendar* (1824) Here is a page from a children's book published in 1824. It depicts The People engaged in democratic politics. Some are shouting, shoving, and turning politics into raucous play. Others, in more genteel postures, look on with amusement and disdain. All are white men. In democratic America, children learn that The People include "each of the men who are aged twenty-one." There are no women or nonwhites in the picture. They are not part of The People.

for instance, 700 of 1,000 men at a militia muster could not vote. In 1829, the "Non-Freeholders of the City of Richmond" petitioned for the right to vote, arguing that the ownership of property did not make a man "wiser and better." "Virtue" and "intelligence," they insisted, were "not among the products of the soil." Even the aging Thomas Jefferson had come to believe, by 1824, that property restrictions violated "the principal of equal political rights."

In the early 19th century, state after state extended the vote to all adult white men. In 1790, only Vermont granted the vote to all free men. Kentucky entered the Union in 1792 without property or taxpaying qualifications. Tennessee followed with a freehold qualification, but only for newcomers who had resided in their counties for less than six months. The federal government dropped the 50-acre freehold qualification in the territories in 1812. Of the eight territories that became states between 1796 and 1821, none kept a property qualification, only three maintained a taxpaying qualification, and five explicitly granted the vote to all white men. In the same years, one eastern state after another widened the franchise. By 1840, only Rhode Island retained a propertied electorate, primarily because Yankee farmers in that state wanted to retain power in a society made up increasingly of urban, immigrant wage earners. (When Rhode Island finally reformed the franchise in 1843, the new law included a freehold requirement that applied only to the foreign-born, and explicitly withheld the franchise from blacks.) With that exception, the white men of every state held the vote.

Suffrage reform gave political rights to propertyless men, and thus took a long step away from the Founders' republic and toward mass democracy. At the same time, however, reformers explicitly restricted the vote to those who were white and male. New Jersey's revolutionary constitution, for instance, had granted the vote to "persons" who met a freehold qualification. This loophole enfranchised property-holding widows, many of whom exercised their rights. A law of 1807 abolished property restrictions and gave the vote to all white men. The same law ended female voting. The question of woman suffrage would not be considered again until women raised it in 1848. It would not be settled until well into the 20th century.

New restrictions also applied to blacks. The revolutionary constitutions of Massachusetts, New Hampshire, Vermont, and Maine—northeastern states with tiny black minorities—granted the vote to free blacks. New York and North Carolina laws gave the vote to "all men" who met the qualifications, and propertied African Americans (a tiny but symbolically crucial minority) routinely exercised the vote. Post-revolutionary laws that extended voting rights to all white men often specifically excluded or severely restricted votes for blacks. Free blacks lost the suffrage in New York, New Jersey, Pennsylvania, Connecticut, Maryland, Tennessee, and North Carolina—all states in which they had previously voted. By 1840, fully 93 percent of blacks in the North lived in states that either banned or severely restricted their right to vote, and the restrictions were explicitly about race. A delegate to the New York constitutional convention of 1821, noting the movement of freed slaves into New York City, argued against allowing them to vote: "The whole host of Africans that now deluge our city (already too impertinent to be borne), would be placed upon an equal with the citizens." At the Tennessee convention that eliminated property and residence requirements for whites while it stripped the vote from free blacks in 1834, delegate G. W. L. Marr declared: "We the People" meant "we the free white people of the United States and the free white people only." The convention declared blacks "outside the social compact." A year later, Nathaniel Macon told a North Carolina convention that in 1776, free blacks had been "no part of the then political family."

Thus, the "universal" suffrage of which many Americans boasted was far from universal. New laws dissolved the ties between political rights and property, and thus saved the citizenship of thousands who were becoming propertyless tenants and wage earners. The same laws that gave the vote to all white men, however, explicitly barred other Americans from political participation. Faced with the disintegration of Jefferson's republic of proprietor-patriarchs, the wielders of power had chosen to blur the emerging distinctions of social class while they hardened the boundaries of sex and race. In 1790, citizenship had belonged to men who were fathers and farm owners. Forty years later, the citizenry was made up of those who were (the phrase came into use at this time) "free, white, and twenty-one." Much more explicitly and completely than had been the case at the founding, America in 1830 was a white man's republic.

Conclusion

By the second quarter of the 19th century, Americans had made a patchwork of regional, class, and ethnic cultures. The new middle classes of the North and West compounded their Protestant and republican inheritance with a new entrepreneurial faith in progress. The result was a way of life grounded in the self-made and morally accountable individual and the sentimentalized (often feminized) domestic unit.

Most Americans, however, did not live and think like the middle class. The poorer urban dwellers and farmers of the North remained grimly loyal to the unsentimental, male-dominated families of their fathers and grandfathers, to new and old religious sects that preached human depravity and the mysterious workings of providence, and to the suspicion that perfidy and disorder lurked behind the smiling moral order of market economics and middle-class culture.

In the South, most white farmers persisted in a neighborhood-based, intensely evangelical, and socially conservative way of life; when asked their opinions, they often talked like classic Jeffersonian yeomen. Southern planters, although they shared in the northern elite's belief in material progress and the magic of the market, were bound by family values, a system of slave labor, and a code of honor that was strikingly at variance with middle-class faith in an orderly universe and perfectible individuals. And we have seen (Chapter 9) that slaves in these years continued to make cultural forms of their own. Despite their exclusion from the white world of liberty and equality, they tied their aspirations to the family, to an evangelical Protestant God, and to the individual and collective dignity that republics promise to their citizens.

CHAPTER REVIEW

Review

1. In what ways did literacy and print help to democratize American culture?
2. What were the central cultural maxims of the emerging northern middle class?
3. Within the North, what were the alternatives to middle-class culture?
4. The amusements of common folk were varied, but they exhibited a few common themes. What were those themes?
5. In what specific ways did evangelical Protestantism act as a conservative force within southern culture?
6. In what ways did the racial order of the North change in the first half of the 19th century?
7. How did American voting rights change between the adoption of the Constitution and the Civil War?

Critical Thinking

1. Compare and contrast the domestic lives and family values of the northern middle class and the southern planter elite.
2. Compare and contrast the racial orders of the North and South in 1850. How do you explain the similarities and differences?

Identifications

Review your understanding of the following key terms, people, and events for this chapter (terms in bold in text are included in the Glossary).

middle class, p. 281
Second Great Awakening, p. 281
anxious bench, p. 282
Sarah Josepha Hale, p. 283
domestic fiction, p. 283
Joseph Smith, p. 284
crisis conversion, p. 284
Restorationism, p. 284
circuit-riding preachers, p. 284
postmillennialists, p. 285
premillennialists, p. 286
Millerites, p. 286
blood sports, p. 287
minstrel show, p. 291
camp meeting, p. 294

Suggested Readings

Daniel Walker Howe's ***What Hath God Wrought: The Transformation of America, 1815–1848*** (2007) emphasizes the communications revolution as an important catalyst for social changes during the era. **Stuart M. Blumin**, ***The Emergence of the Middle Class: Social Experience in the American City, 1760–1900*** (1989) is a thorough study of work and material life among the urban middle class. Studies that treat middle-class religion, family, and sentimental culture include **Paul E. Johnson**, ***A Shopkeeper's Millennium: Society and Revivals in Rochester, New York, 1815–1837*** (1978); **Mary P. Ryan**, ***Cradle of the Middle Class: The Family in Oneida County, New York, 1790–1865*** (1981); and **Jane Tompkins**, ***Sensational Designs: The Cultural Work of American Fiction, 1790–1860*** (1985). **Nathan O. Hatch**, ***The Democratization of American Christianity*** (1989) is a good introduction to plain-folk religion in these years. **Paul C. Gutjahr's** ***The Book of Mormon: A Biography*** (2012) provides a balanced history and analysis of the influential book.

Studies of popular literature and entertainments include **Elliott J. Gorn**, ***The Manly Art: Bare-Knuckle Prize Fighting in America*** (1986); **Eric Lott**, ***Love & Theft: Blackface Minstrelsy and the American Working Class*** (1993); and **David S. Reynolds**, ***Beneath the American Renaissance: The Subversive Imagination in the Age of Emerson and Melville*** (1988). Essential books on the culture of southern whites are cited in the Suggested Readings for Chapter 9. Students should also consult **Christine Leigh Heyerman**, ***Southern Cross: The Beginnings of the Bible Belt*** (1997); **Elizabeth Fox Genovese and Eugene D. Genovese**, ***Slavery in White and Black: Class and Race in the Southern Slaveholders' New World Order*** (2008); and **Lacy K. Ford**, ***Deliver Us from Evil: The Slavery Question in the Old South*** (2009). On the racial order of the North, see **David R. Roediger**, ***The Wages of Whiteness: Race and the Making of the American Working Class*** (revised edition, 2007); and **John Wood Sweet**, ***Bodies Politic: Negotiating Race in the American North, 1730–1830*** (2007).

11 Whigs and Democrats, 1815–1840

National Portrait Gallery, Smithsonian Institution/Art Resource, NY

11.1 **Jackson as Democracy Incarnate** Andrew Jackson struck a romantic military pose for this portrait painted in 1820. Posing as the embodiment of democracy and as an extravagantly melodramatic hero, Jackson imposed himself on his times as few Americans have done.

NATIONAL POLITICAL LEADERS from the 1820s until the outbreak of the Civil War faced two persistent problems. First, economic development and territorial expansion made new demands on government—demands that involved federal participation in state and local affairs. Second, a deepening rift between slave and free states rendered such involvement contested and dangerous.

The Whig Party proposed the **American System** as the answer to both questions. The national government, said the Whigs, should subsidize roads and canals, foster industry with protective tariffs, and maintain a national bank to control credit and currency. The result would be a peaceful, prosperous, and truly national market society. If the South, the West, and the Northeast profited by doing business with each other, the argument went, sectional jealousies would quiet down. Jacksonian Democrats, on the other hand, argued that the American System was unconstitutional, that it violated the rights of states and localities, and that it taxed honest citizens to benefit corrupt and wealthy insiders. Most dangerous of all, argued the Democrats, Whigs would create an activist, interventionist national government that would anger the slaveholding South. To counter both threats, the Jacksonians resurrected Thomas Jefferson's rhetoric of states' rights and inactive, inexpensive government—all of it deeply inflected in the code of white male equality, domestic patriarchy, and racial slavery. ■

11-1 The American System

Q *What were the components of the "American System"? What did the American System promise to accomplish?*

President James Madison delivered his annual message to the Fourteenth Congress in December 1815. He asked for legislation to create a new national bank, a tariff to protect American manufacturers, and congressional support for canals and roads. Congress agreed. Made up overwhelmingly of Jeffersonian Republicans and led by the young southern and western nationalists who had favored the war with Britain, this Congress reversed many of the positions taken by Jefferson's old party. It chartered a national bank, enacted a protective tariff, and debated a national system of roads and canals at federal expense. Most prewar Republicans had viewed such programs as heresy. But by 1815, the Republican majority in Congress accepted them as orthodox and necessary. Secretary of the Treasury Albert Gallatin explained: "The War has renewed and reinstated the national feelings which the Revolution had given and which were daily lessened. The people have now more general objects of attachment with which their pride and political opinions are connected. They are more American."

Even as they convinced themselves that they had won the war, Republicans were painfully aware of the weaknesses that the war had displayed. Put simply, the United States had been unable to coordinate a national fiscal and military effort: Bad roads, local jealousies, and a bankrupt treasury had nearly lost the war. In addition, the war and the years leading up to it convinced many Republicans, including Jefferson and Madison, that the export economy rendered the United States dangerously dependent on Europe (and especially Great Britain). Finally, many of the younger Republicans in Congress were interested less in ideological purity than in bringing commerce into new regions. The nation, they said, must abandon Jefferson's export-oriented agrarianism and encourage prosperity and national independence through subsidies to commerce, manufactures, and internal improvements.

11-1a *National Republicans*

Henry Clay of Kentucky, retaining his power in the postwar Congress, headed the drive for protective tariffs, the bank, and internal improvements. He called his program the "American System," arguing that it would foster national economic growth and harmony between geographic sections, thus a happy and prosperous republic.

In 1816, Congress chartered a Second Bank of the United States, headquartered in Philadelphia and empowered to establish branches wherever it saw fit. The government agreed to deposit its funds in the Bank; to accept the Bank's notes as payment for government land, taxes, and other transactions; and to buy one-fifth of the Bank's stock. The Bank of the United States was more powerful than the one that had been rejected (by one vote) by a Republican Congress in 1811. The fiscal horrors of the War of 1812, however, had convinced most representatives to support a national currency and centralized control of money and credit. The alternative was to allow state banks—which had increased in number from 88 to 208 between 1813 and 1815—to issue the unregulated and grossly inflated notes that had weakened the war effort and promised to throw the anticipated postwar boom into chaos.

With no discussion of the constitutionality of what it was doing, Congress chartered the Bank of the United States as the sole banking institution empowered to do business throughout the country. Notes issued by the Bank would be the first semblance of a national currency (they would soon constitute from one-tenth to one-third of the value of notes in circulation). Moreover, the Bank could regulate the currency by demanding that state bank notes used in transactions with the federal government be redeemable in gold. In 1816, the Bank set up shop in Philadelphia's Carpenter's Hall, and in 1824, it moved around the corner to a Greek Revival edifice modeled after the Parthenon—a marble embodiment of the republican conservatism that directors of the Bank of the United States promised as their fiscal stance. From that vantage point they would fight (with a few huge lapses)

CHRONOLOGY

1816	Congress charters a Second Bank of the United States and the first avowedly protective tariff • *Dartmouth College v. Woodward* defines a private charter as a contract that cannot be altered by a state legislature
1819	Controversy arises over Missouri's admission to the Union as a slave state • Panic of 1819 marks the first failure of the national market economy
1820	Missouri Compromise adopted
1823	Monroe Doctrine written by Secretary of State John Quincy Adams
1824	*Gibbons v. Ogden* asserts federal control of interstate commerce
1824–1825	Adams wins the presidency over Andrew Jackson • Adams appoints Henry Clay as secretary of state • Jacksonians charge a "Corrupt Bargain" between Adams and Clay
1827	Cherokees in Georgia declare themselves a republic
1828	Jackson defeats Adams for the presidency • "Tariff of Abominations" passed by Congress • John C. Calhoun's *Exposition and Protest* presents doctrine of nullification
1830	Congress passes the Indian Removal Act
1832	Jackson reelected over Henry Clay • *Worcester v. Georgia* exempts the Cherokees from Georgia law • Jackson vetoes recharter of the Bank of the United States
1833	Force Bill and Tariff of 1833 end the nullification crisis
1834	Whig Party formed in opposition to Jacksonians
1835	Treaty of New Echota
1836	Congress adopts "gag rule" to table antislavery petitions • Van Buren elected president
1837	Financial panic ushers in a severe economic depression
1838	U.S. Army marches the remaining Cherokees to Indian Territory
1840	Whig William Henry Harrison defeats Van Buren for presidency

a running battle with state banks and local interests in an effort to impose fiscal discipline and centralized control over an exploding market economy.

The same Congress drew up the nation's first overtly protective tariff in 1816. Shut off from British imports during the war, the Americans had built their first factories, almost entirely in southern New England and the mid-Atlantic. The British planned to flood the postwar market with cheap goods and kill American manufactures, and Congress determined to stop them. Shepherded through the House by Clay and his fellow nationalist John C. Calhoun of South Carolina, the Tariff of 1816 raised import duties an average of 25 percent, protecting American manufactures at the expense of consumers and foreign trade. Again, wartime difficulties and wartime nationalism had paved the way: Since Americans could not depend on imported manufactures, Congress saw domestic manufactures as a patriotic necessity and a spur to commerce between the sections. The Northeast and the West supported the tariff, and it had enough southern support to ensure its passage. Tariffs would rise and fall between 1816 and the Civil War, but the principle of protectionism would persist.

Many of the Founders had seen a national transportation system as essential to the prosperity and safety of the union. George Washington had urged roads and canals linking the Atlantic states with the interior—providing western farmers with the civilizing benefits of commerce and securing their loyalty to the United States. Thomas Jefferson shared Washington's views and, like his fellow Virginian, he favored improvements that would link the Potomac River with the Ohio. In 1802, President Jefferson signed a bill that began construction of the Cumberland Road (often called the National Road) from Cumberland, Maryland, to the Ohio River at Wheeling.

These early dreams and projects served the postcolonial economy: They would deliver farm produce to the coast and then to international markets; the coastal towns would receive imported goods and ship them back into the countryside. As early as 1770, George Washington had dreamed of making the Potomac River a busy "Channel of Commerce between Great Britain" and the farmers of the interior. Others dreamed of other routes and rivers, but nearly all proponents of transportation into the West shared the great assumption of Washington's early vision: The export economy would remain dominant; the United States would be an independent, unified, and prosperous economic colony of the Old World.

Henry Clay's American System grew into a new vision: a national transportation network that would make the United States economically independent of Europe and interdependent within itself. The Bank of the United States would supply fiscal stability and a uniform, trustworthy currency. The tariff would encourage northeasterners to build factories and citizens in other parts of the country to buy what American manufacturers made, and farmers would enjoy expanded domestic markets. The West would sell food to the cities and to the plantation South, and the South would supply the burgeoning textile industry with cotton. The system would not deny international trade, but it would make the United States an economically integrated and independent nation.

Bills for transportation projects, however, did not get through Congress. Internal improvements were subject to local ambitions: Canals and roads that helped one place hurt another. Some areas—southern New England and eastern Pennsylvania are examples—had already built good roads and did not want to subsidize the competition. There were also objections based on old Republican ideals. Roads and canals were big public works projects with scores of contractors and subcontractors—all dependent on government subsidies, with the potential for becoming a system of corruption that was impossible to stop. Finally, federally sponsored improvements, however beneficial, were constitutionally doubtful. In the Constitutional Convention, Benjamin Franklin had proposed that the power to build roads and cut canals within the

The Granger Collection, NYC

11.2 **The Second Bank of the United States** Located in downtown Philadelphia and modeled on the Parthenon in classical Athens, the new bank building was intended to be both republican and awesome. It was from here that gentleman-directors attempted to impose their kind of order on the exploding monetary and credit systems of the 1820s and 1830s.

states be written into the Constitution, and his proposal had been voted down. National support for internal improvements could be justified only by the "necessary and proper" and "general welfare" clauses. The Republicans could charter a Second Bank of the United States because Hamilton's bank had established the precedent. Roads and canals—extensive local projects at national expense—would stretch those clauses much further, worrying many Republicans (most of them southern) that future legislatures would justify whatever struck them as necessary and proper at any given time.

When Congress agreed to complete the National Road—the one federal internal improvement already under way—President Madison and his Republican successor James Monroe vetoed the bills, refusing to support further internal improvements without a constitutional amendment. In 1822, Monroe even vetoed a bill authorizing repairs on the National Road, stating once again that the Constitution did not empower the federal government to build roads within the states. As a result, the financing and construction of roads and canals fell to the states, overwhelmingly the *northern* states. Henry Clay watched his vision of transportation as a nationalizing force turn into northern regionalization and southern isolation, a dangerous trend that continued throughout his long political life.

11-1b *Commerce and the Law*

The courts after 1815 played an important nationalizing and commercializing role. John Marshall, who presided over the Supreme Court from 1801 to 1835, took the lead. From the beginning he saw the Court as a conservative hedge against the excesses of provincial democratic legislatures. His early decisions protected the independence of the courts and their right to review legislation (see Chapter 7). From 1816 onward, his decisions encouraged business and strengthened the national government at the expense of the states. His most important decisions protected the sanctity of contracts and corporate charters against state legislatures. In ***Dartmouth College v. Woodward*** (1819), he overturned New Hampshire's decision to turn the college into a public institution by upholding its original corporate charter from 1769. With this, corporate charters acquired the legal status of contracts, beyond the reach of democratic politics, which helped protect business corporations operating under charters granted by state governments.

Two weeks after deciding the *Dartmouth* case, Marshall handed down the majority decision in ***McCulloch v. Maryland***. The Maryland legislature, nurturing old Jeffersonian doubts about the constitutionality of the Bank of the United States, had attempted to tax the Bank's Baltimore branch, which in fact was a corrupt and ruinous institution (see later section). The Bank had challenged the legislature's right to do so, and the Court decided in favor of the Bank. Marshall stated, first, that the Constitution granted the federal government "implied powers" that included chartering the Bank, and he denied Maryland's right to tax the Bank or any other federal agency: "The power to tax," he said, "involves the power to destroy." It was Marshall's most explicit blow against Jeffersonian strict construction. Americans, he said, "did not design to make their government dependent on the states." And yet there were many, particularly in Marshall's native South, who remained certain that that was precisely what the Founders had intended.

In *Gibbons v. Ogden* (1824), the Marshall Court broke a state-granted steamship monopoly in New York Harbor. The monopoly, Marshall argued, interfered with federal jurisdiction over interstate commerce. Like the *Dartmouth* case and *McCulloch v. Maryland*, this decision empowered the national government in relation to the states, and like them, it encouraged private entrepreneurs. As surely as congressmen who supported the American System, John Marshall's Supreme Court assumed a natural and beneficial link between federal power and market society.

Meanwhile, the state courts were working on quieter but equally profound transformations of American law. In the early republic, state courts had often viewed property not only as a private possession but also as part of a neighborhood. Thus, when a miller built a dam that flooded upriver farms or impaired the fishery, the courts might make him take those interests into account, often in ways that reduced the business uses of his property. By 1830, New England courts routinely granted the owners of industrial mill sites unrestricted water rights, even when the exercise of those rights inflicted damage on their neighbors. In the courts of northern and western states, what was coming to be called "progress" demanded legal protection for the business uses of private property, even when such uses conflicted with old common-law restraints.

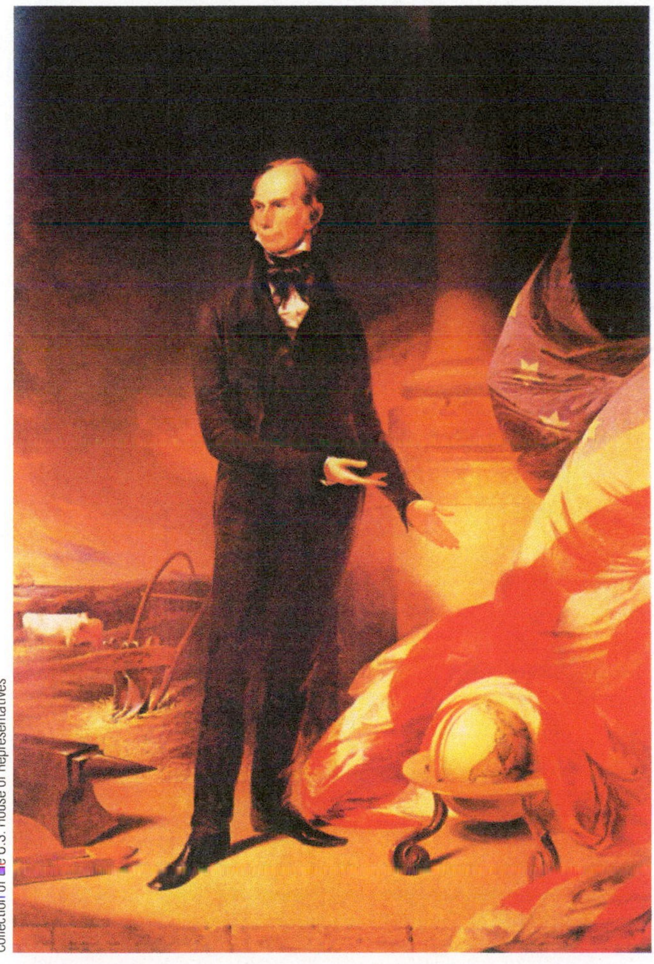

Collection of the U.S. House of Representatives

11.3 **Henry Clay** Clay was the most consistent and eloquent spokesman for the American System. His supposed participation in the "Corrupt Bargain" of 1825 severely hurt his chances of becoming president.

Q *In what ways does the painting portray Clay as a champion of the American System?*

11-2 1819

Q *What enduring political issues were raised by the Missouri controversy and the Panic of 1819?*

Many traditionalist Jeffersonians disliked these developments, but they could not stop them. That changed in 1819. First, the debate that surrounded Missouri's admission as a slave state revealed the centrality and vulnerability of slavery within the national Union. Second, a severe financial collapse led many Americans to doubt the Market Revolution's compatibility with the Jeffersonian republic. By 1820, politicians were determined to reconstruct the limited-government, states'-rights coalition that had elected Thomas Jefferson.

11-2a *The Argument over Missouri*

Early in 1819, slaveholding Missouri applied for admission to the Union as the first new state to be carved out of the Louisiana Purchase. New York congressman James Tallmadge, Jr., quickly proposed two amendments to the Missouri statehood bill. The first would bar additional slaves from being brought into Missouri (16 percent of Missouri's people were already slaves). The second would emancipate Missouri slaves born after admission when they reached their 25th birthday. Put simply, the **Tallmadge Amendments** would admit Missouri only if Missouri agreed to become a free state.

The congressional debates on the Missouri question had little to do with humanitarian objections to slavery and everything to do with political power. Rufus King of New York, an old Federalist who led the northerners in the Senate, insisted that he opposed the admission of a new slave state "solely in its bearing and effects upon great political interests, and upon the just and equal rights of the freemen of the nation." Northerners had long chafed at the added representation in Congress and in the Electoral College that the "three-fifths" rule granted to the slave states (see Chapter 6). The rule had, in fact, added significantly to southern power: In 1790, the South, with 40 percent of the white population, controlled 47 percent of the votes in Congress—enough to decide close votes both in Congress and in presidential elections. Federalists pointed out that of the 12 additional electoral votes the three-fifths rule gave to the South, 10 had gone to Thomas Jefferson in 1800 and had given him the election. Without the bogus votes provided by slavery, they argued, Virginia's stranglehold on the presidency would have been broken with Washington's departure in 1796.

In 1819, the North held a majority in the House of Representatives. The South, thanks to the recent admissions of Alabama and southern-oriented Illinois, controlled a bare majority in the Senate. The Tallmadge Amendments passed in the House of Representatives by a starkly sectional vote, then went on to the Senate. There, a unanimous South defeated the Tallmadge Amendments with the help of the two Illinois senators and three northerners. Deadlocked between a Senate in favor of admitting Missouri as a slave state and a House dead set against it, Congress broke off one of the angriest sessions in its history and went home.

11-2b *The Missouri Compromise*

The new Congress that convened in the winter of 1819–1820 passed the legislative package that became known as the **Missouri Compromise** (see Map 11.1). Massachusetts offered its northern counties as the new free state of Maine, thus neutralizing fears that the South would gain votes in the Senate with the admission of Missouri. Senator Jesse Thomas of Illinois proposed the so-called Thomas Proviso: If the North would admit Missouri as a slave state, the South would agree to outlaw slavery in territories above 36° 30'N latitude—a line extending from the southern border of Missouri to Spanish (within a year, Mexican) territory. That line would open Arkansas Territory (present-day Arkansas and Oklahoma) to slavery and would ban slavery from the remainder of the Louisiana Territory—land that would subsequently become all or part of nine states.

Congress admitted Maine with little debate, but the Thomas Proviso met northern opposition. Finally, a joint Senate-House committee decided to separate the two bills. With half of the southern representatives and nearly all of the northerners supporting it, the Thomas Proviso passed. Congress next took up the admission of Missouri. With the votes of a solid South and 14 compromise-minded northerners,

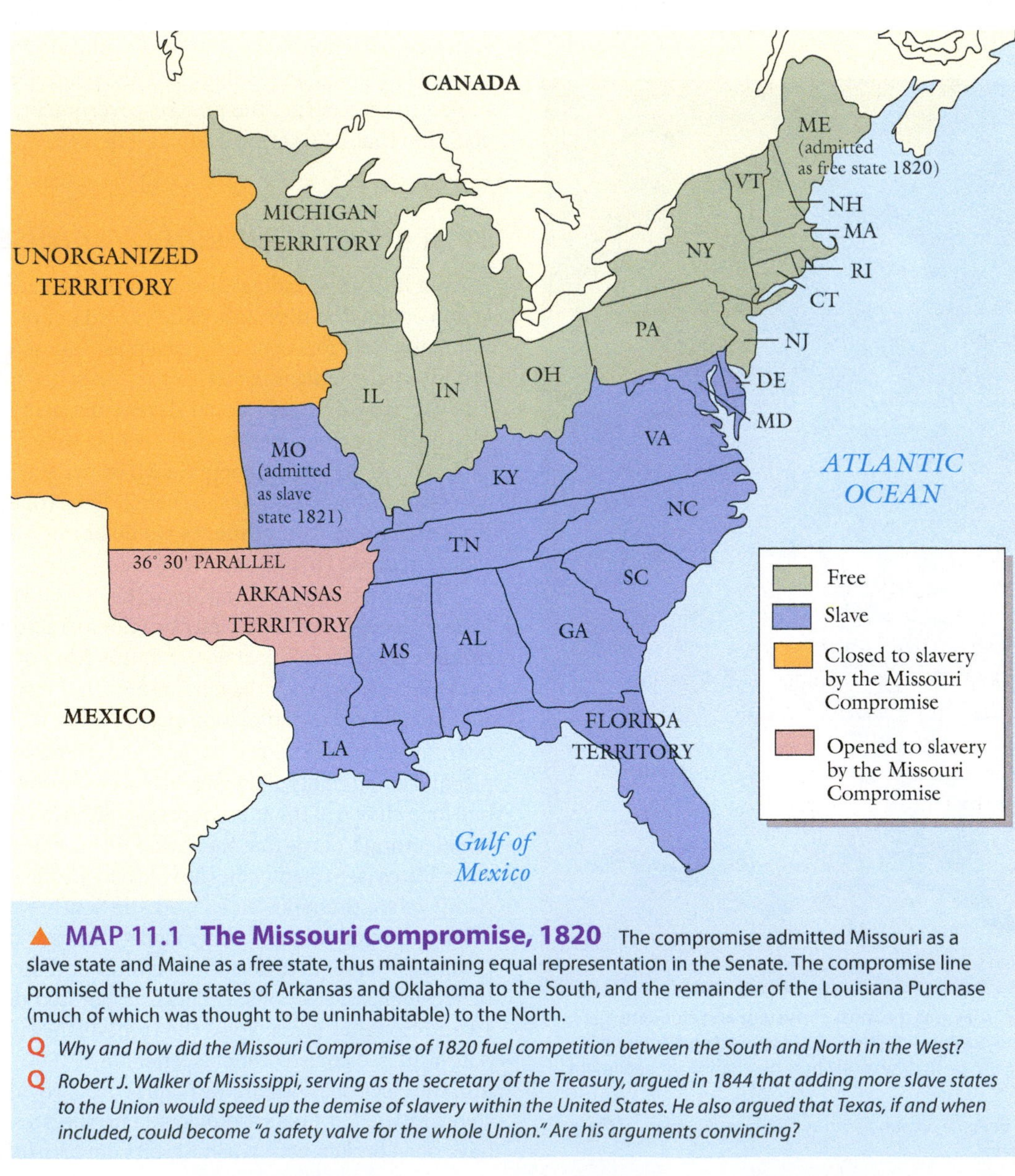

▲ **MAP 11.1 The Missouri Compromise, 1820** The compromise admitted Missouri as a slave state and Maine as a free state, thus maintaining equal representation in the Senate. The compromise line promised the future states of Arkansas and Oklahoma to the South, and the remainder of the Louisiana Purchase (much of which was thought to be uninhabitable) to the North.

Q *Why and how did the Missouri Compromise of 1820 fuel competition between the South and North in the West?*

Q *Robert J. Walker of Mississippi, serving as the secretary of the Treasury, argued in 1844 that adding more slave states to the Union would speed up the demise of slavery within the United States. He also argued that Texas, if and when included, could become "a safety valve for the whole Union." Are his arguments convincing?*

Missouri entered the Union as a slave state. President James Monroe applauded the "patriotic devotion" of the northern representatives "who preferr'd the sacrifice of themselves at home" to endangering the Union. His words were prophetic: Nearly all of the 14 were voted out of office in the next election.

The Missouri crisis brought the South's commitment to slavery and the North's resentment of southern political power into collision. While northerners vowed to relinquish no more territory to slavery, southerners talked openly of disunion and civil war. A Georgia politician announced that the Missouri debates had lit a fire that "seas of blood can only extinguish." President Monroe's secretary of state, John Quincy Adams, saw the debates as an omen: Northerners would unanimously oppose the extension of slavery whenever the question came to a vote. Viewing the crisis from Monticello, the aging Thomas Jefferson was distraught: "A geographical line, coinciding with a marked principle, moral and political, once conceived and held up to the angry passions of men, will never be obliterated; every new irritation will mark it deeper and deeper... . This momentous question, like a fire-bell in the night, awakened and filled me with terror. I considered it at once the knell of the Union." The Missouri question underlined a basic fact of American national politics: If politicians argued about slavery, they would split along North–South lines and the Union would be endangered.

11-2c *The Panic of 1819*

Politicians debated the Missouri question against a darkening backdrop of economic depression. The origins of the Panic of 1819 were international and numerous. European agriculture was recovering from the Napoleonic wars, thereby reducing the demand for American foodstuffs, while revolutionary wars in Latin America cut off the supply of precious metals, the base of the international money supply. American bankers and businessmen met the situation by expanding credit and issuing banknotes that were mere dreams of real money, thereby creating an inflationary bubble. When the price of cotton collapsed in 1819, the bubble burst.

The president of the Second Bank of the United States, Langdon Cheves of South Carolina, responded to the crisis by curtailing credit and demanding that state banknotes received by the Bank of the United States be redeemed in specie (silver and gold). By doing so, Cheves rescued the Bank from the paper economy created by state-chartered banks, but at huge expense: When the state banks were forced to redeem their notes in specie, they demanded payment from their own borrowers, and the national money and credit system collapsed.

The depression that followed the Panic of 1819 was the first failure of the market economy. Local ups and downs had occurred since the 1790s, but this collapse was nationwide. Employers who could not meet their debts went out of business, and hundreds of thousands of workers lost their jobs. In Philadelphia, unemployment reached 75 percent. A tent city of the unemployed sprang up on the outskirts of Baltimore. Other cities and towns were hit as hard, and the situation was no better in the countryside. Thomas Jefferson reported that farms in his neighborhood were selling for what had earlier been a year's rent.

Faced with a collapse that none could control and that few understood, many Americans directed their resentment onto the Bank of the United States. John Jacob Astor, a New York merchant and reputedly the richest man in America, admitted that "there has been too much Speculation and too much assumption of Power on the Part of the Bank Directors which has caused [sic] the institution to become unpopular." William Gouge, who would become the Jacksonian Democrats' favorite economist, put it more bluntly: When the Bank demanded that state banknotes be redeemed in specie, he said, "the Bank was saved and the people were ruined." By the end of 1819, the Bank of the United States had won the name that it would carry to its death in the 1830s: the Monster.

11-3 Republican Revival

What were the events and political motives that contributed to the republican revival that formed around Andrew Jackson?

The crises during 1819 and 1820 prompted demands for a return to Jeffersonian principles. President Monroe's happily proclaimed Era of Good Feelings—a new era of partyless politics created by the collapse of Federalism—was, according to worried Republicans, a disaster. Without opposition, Jefferson's dominant Republican Party had lost its way. The nationalist Congress of 1816 had enacted much of the Federalist program under the name of Republicanism. The result, said the old Republicans, was an aggressive government that helped bring on the Panic of 1819. At the same time, the collapse of Republican Party unity in Congress had allowed the Missouri question to divide Congress along dangerous sectional lines. By 1820, many Republicans were calling for a Jeffersonian revival that would limit government power and guarantee southern rights within the Union.

11-3a *Martin Van Buren Leads the Way*

The busiest and the most astute of those Republicans was Martin Van Buren of New York. An immensely talented man without family connections (his father was a Hudson Valley tavern keeper) or formal education, Van Buren built his political career out of a commitment to Jeffersonian principles, personal charm, and party discipline. He and his colleagues in New York had begun to invent the modern political party. The Founders had denounced parties, claiming that republics rested on civic virtue, not competition. Van Buren's New York experience, however, along with his reading of national politics, told him that disciplined political parties were necessary democratic tools. Van Buren insisted that competition and party divisions were inevitable and good, but that they must be made to serve the republic. He wrote: "We must always have party distinctions, and the old ones are the best... If the old ones are suppressed, geographical differences founded on local instincts or what is worse, prejudices between free & slave holding states will inevitably take their place." Van Buren claimed that the one-party politics of the Era of Good Feelings had allowed privileged insiders to create a big national state and to reorganize politics along sectional lines. Arriving in Washington in the aftermath of the Missouri debates and the Panic of 1819, he hoped to apply his new politics to what he perceived as a dangerous turning point in national public life.

Working with like-minded politicians, Van Buren reconstructed the coalition of northern and southern agriculturalists that had elected Thomas Jefferson. The result was the Democratic Party and, ultimately, a national two-party system that persisted until the eve of the Civil War.

11-3b *The Election of 1824*

With the approach of the 1824 presidential election, Van Buren and his friends supported William H. Crawford, Monroe's secretary of war and a staunch Georgia Republican. The Van Burenites controlled the Republican **congressional caucus**, the body that traditionally chose the party's presidential candidates. The public distrusted the caucus as undemocratic because it represented the only party in government and thus could dictate the choice of a president. Van Buren, however, continued to regard it as a necessary tool of party discipline. With most congressmen fearing their constituents, only a minority showed up for the caucus vote. They dutifully nominated Crawford.

With Republican Party unity broken, the list of sectional candidates grew. John Quincy Adams was the son of a Federalist president, successful secretary of state under Monroe, and one of the northeastern Federalist converts to Republicanism who, according to people like Van Buren and Crawford, had blunted the republican thrust of Jefferson's old party. Adams entered the contest as New England's favorite son. Henry Clay of Kentucky, chief proponent of the American System, expected to carry the West. John C. Calhoun of South Carolina announced his candidacy, but when he saw the swarm of candidates, he dropped out and put himself up as the sole candidate for vice president.

The wild card was Andrew Jackson of Tennessee, who in 1824 was known only as a military hero—scourge of the southern Indians and victor over the British at New Orleans (see Chapter 7). He was also a frontier nabob with a reputation for violence: He had killed a rival in a duel, had engaged in a shootout in a Nashville tavern, and had reputedly stolen his wife from her estranged husband. According to Jackson's detractors, such impetuosity marked his public life as well. As commander of U.S. military forces in the South in 1818, Jackson had led an unauthorized invasion of Spanish Florida, claiming that it was a hideout for Seminole warriors who raided into the United States and a sanctuary for runaway Georgia slaves. During the action, he had occupied Spanish forts, summarily executed Seminoles, and hanged two British subjects. Secretary of State John Quincy Adams had belatedly approved the raid, knowing that the show of American force would encourage the Spanish to sell Florida to the United States. After serving briefly as the governor of newly acquired Florida in 1821, Jackson retired from public life. It was a short retirement because only two years later Tennessee voters elected him to the U.S. Senate. In 1824, eastern politicians knew Jackson only as a "military chieftain," "the Napoleon of the woods," a frontier hothead, and, possibly, a robber-bridegroom.

11.4 John Quincy Adams Adams enjoyed a remarkably productive career as Monroe's secretary of state, then rode into the presidency in the conflicted and controversial election of 1824. The intelligence and erudition that the picture projects had served him well as a diplomat. As president, they marked him as aloof, aristocratic, and incapable of governing a democratic nation.

Jackson may have been all of those things, but he was immensely popular, particularly in the new states of the South and West. In the election of 1824, in the 16 states that chose presidential electors by popular vote (six states still left the choice to their legislatures), Jackson polled 152,901 votes to Adams's 114,023 and Clay's 47,217. Crawford, who suffered a crippling stroke during the campaign, won 46,979 votes. Jackson's support was not only larger but also more nearly national than that of his opponents. Adams carried only his native New England and a portion of New York. Clay's meager support was limited to the Northwest, and Crawford's to the Southeast and to the portions of New York that Van Buren was able to deliver. Jackson carried 84 percent of the votes of his own Southwest, won victories in Pennsylvania, New Jersey, North Carolina, Indiana, and Illinois, and ran a close second in several other states (see Map 11.2).

11-3c "A Corrupt Bargain"

Jackson assumed that he had won the election: He had received 42 percent of the popular vote to his nearest rival's 33 percent, and he was clearly the nation's choice, but his 99 electoral votes were 32 shy of the plurality demanded by the Constitution. And so, acting under the Twelfth Amendment, the House of Representatives selected a president from among the top three candidates. As the candidate with the fewest electoral votes, Henry Clay was eliminated, but he remained Speaker of the House and had enough support to throw the election to either Jackson or Adams. Years later, Jackson told a dinner guest that Clay had offered to support him in exchange for Clay's appointment as secretary of state—an office that traditionally led to the presidency. When Jackson turned him down, according to Jacksonian legend, Clay went to Adams and made the same offer. Adams accepted what became known as the **"Corrupt Bargain"** in January 1825. During the House vote, Clay's supporters, joined by several old Federalists, switched to Adams, giving him a one-vote victory. The new president appointed Henry Clay as his secretary of state.

Reaction to the alleged Corrupt Bargain dominated the Adams administration and created a rhetoric of intrigue and betrayal that nourished a rising democratic movement. After the vote in the House of Representatives, Jackson declared, "The rights of the people have been bartered for promises of office." He continued, "So you see, the *Judas* of the West has closed the contract and will receive the thirty pieces of silver. His end will be the same." Others in Washington agreed, denouncing the Clay-Adams union as "unnatural & preposterous" and "monstrous." The charge of corruption would follow Clay for the rest of his political life.

Library of Congress Prints and Photographs Division[LC-DIG-ds-00856]

11.5 **"The Symptoms of a Locked Jaw"** In 1827, Henry Clay published a rebuttal of Jacksonian charges that he had participated in a Corrupt Bargain to deliver the presidency to John Quincy Adams. Here, a pro-Clay cartoonist displays Clay as a tailor in the act of sewing Andrew Jackson's mouth shut. Neither the rebuttal nor the cartoon worked: The long-term suspicions of the bargain with Adams ruined Clay's chances to become president.

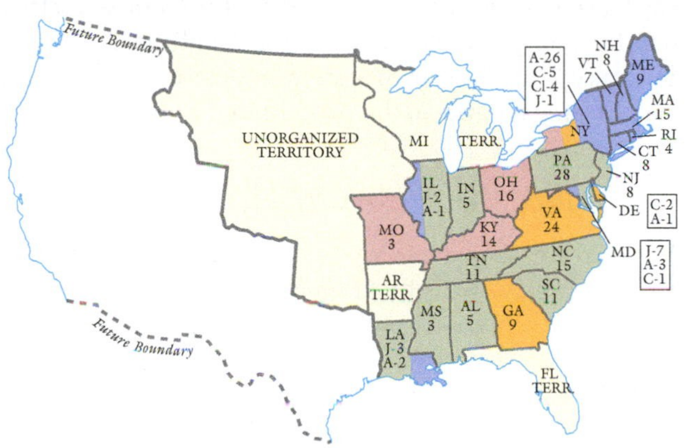

	Electoral Vote		Popular Vote	
	Number	%	Number	%
Jackson (Democratic Republican)	99	37.9	152,901	42.3
J. Q. Adams (Democratic Republican)	84	32.2	114,023	31.6
Crawford (Democratic Republican)	41	15.7	46,979	13
Clay (Democratic Republican)	37	14.2	47,217	13.1

▲ **MAP 11.2 Presidential Election, 1824**

Voting in the four-cornered contest of 1824 was starkly sectional. John Quincy Adams carried his native New England, while Crawford and Clay carried only a few states in their own sections. Only Andrew Jackson enjoyed national support: He carried states in every section but New England, and he ran a strong second in many of the states that were awarded to other candidates.

Q *In what ways did the election of 1824 pave the way for modern American politics?*

Q *Was Andrew Jackson's claim that he was robbed of presidency justified?*

11-3d *Jacksonian Melodrama*

Andrew Jackson regarded the intrigues that robbed him of the presidency in 1825 as the culmination of a long train of corruption that the nation had suffered over the previous decade. Although his campaign had made only vague policy statements, he had firm ideas of what had gone wrong with the republic, and he made his views known in what he called "memorandums." (This was the kind of gaffe that appalled his educated eastern opponents and pleased nearly everyone else.)

A frontier planter with a deep distrust of banks, Jackson claimed that self-serving miscreants in the Bank of the United States brought on the Panic of 1819. The national debt, he insisted, was another source of corruption. It must be paid off and never allowed to recur. The federal government under

James Monroe was filled with swindlers, and in the name of a vague nationalism they were taking power for themselves and scheming against the liberties of the people. The politicians had been bought off, said Jackson, and had attempted—through "King Caucus"—to select a president by backstairs deals rather than by popular election. Finally, in 1825, they had stolen the presidency outright.

Like hundreds of thousands of other Americans, Jackson sensed that something had gone wrong with the republic—that selfishness and intrigue had corrupted the government. In the language of revolutionary republicanism, which Jackson had learned as a boy in the Carolina backwoods and would speak throughout his life, a corrupt power once again threatened to snuff out liberty.

In his memorandums, Jackson set against the designs of that power the classic republican safeguard: a virtuous citizenry. Unlike most of his revolutionary forebears, however, he believed that government should follow the will of popular majorities. An aroused public, he said, was the republic's best hope: "My fervent prayers are that our republican government may be perpetual, and the people alone by their virtue, and independent exercise of their free suffrage can make it perpetual."

More completely than any of his rivals, Jackson had captured the rhetoric of the revolutionary republic. And, with his fixation on secrecy, corruption, and intrigues, he transformed both that rhetoric and his own biography into popular melodrama. Finally, with a political alchemy that his rivals never understood, Jackson submerged old notions of republican citizenship into a firm faith in majoritarian democracy: Individuals might become selfish and corrupt, he believed, but a democratic majority was, by its very nature, opposed to corruption and governmental excess. Thus, the republic was safe only when governed by the will of the majority. The Corrupt Bargain of 1825 had made that clear: Either the people or political schemers would rule.

11-4 Adams versus Jackson

Q *What were the principal events of the John Quincy Adams administration, and how did they contribute to his defeat in 1828?*

While Jackson plotted revenge, John Quincy Adams assumed the duties of the presidency. He was well prepared. The son of a Federalist president, he had been an extraordinarily successful secretary of state under Monroe, guiding American diplomacy in the postwar world.

11-4a *Nationalism in an International Arena*

In the Rush-Bagot Treaty of 1817 and the British-American Convention of 1818, Secretary of State John Quincy Adams helped pacify the Great Lakes, restore American fishing rights off the coast of Canada, and draw the U.S.-Canadian boundary west to the Rocky Mountains—actions that transformed the Canadian-American frontier from a battleground into the peaceful border that it has been ever since. He pacified the southern border as well. In 1819, following Jackson's raid into Florida, the Adams-Onís Treaty procured Florida for the United States and defined the U.S.-Spanish border west of the Mississippi in ways that gave the Americans claims to the Pacific Northwest.

Trickier problems had arisen when Spanish colonies in the Americas declared their independence. Spain could not prevent this, and the powers of Europe, victorious over Napoleon and determined to roll back the republican revolution, talked openly of helping Spain or of annexing South American territory for themselves. Both the Americans and the British opposed such a move, and the British proposed a joint statement outlawing the interference of any outside power (including themselves) in Latin America. Adams had thought it better for the United States to make its own policy than to "come in as cock-boat in the wake of the British man-of-war." In 1823, he wrote what became known as the **Monroe Doctrine**. Propounded at the same time that the United States recognized the new Latin American republics, it declared American opposition to any European attempt at colonization in the New World without (as the British had wanted) denying the right of the United States to annex new territory. Although the international community knew that the British navy, and not the Monroe Doctrine, kept the European powers out of the Americas, Adams had announced that the United States was determined to become the preeminent power in the Western Hemisphere.

11-4b *Nationalism at Home*

As president, Adams translated his fervent nationalism into domestic policy. In his first annual message to Congress, he outlined an ambitious program for national development under the auspices of the federal government: roads, canals, a national university, a national astronomical observatory ("lighthouses of the skies"), and other costly initiatives:

> The spirit of improvement is abroad upon the earth... . While foreign nations less blessed with ... freedom ... than ourselves are advancing with gigantic strides in the career of public improvement, were we to slumber in indolence or fold up our arms and proclaim to the world that we are palsied by the will of our constituents, would it not ... doom ourselves to perpetual inferiority?

Congressmen could not believe their ears. Here was a president who had received only one in three votes and who had entered office accused of intrigues against the democratic will. And yet at the first opportunity he told Congress to pass an ambitious program and not to be "palsied" by the will of the electorate. Hostile politicians and journalists never tired of joking about Adams's "lighthouses of the skies." More lasting, however, was the connection they drew between federal public works projects and high taxes, intrusive government, the denial of democratic majorities, and expanded opportunities for corruption, secret deals, and special favors. Even members of Congress who favored Adams's program were afraid to vote for it. Congress never acted on the president's proposals, and the Adams administration emerged as little more than a long prelude to the election of 1828.

11-4c *The Birth of the Democratic Party*

As early as 1825, it was clear that the election of 1828 would pit Adams against Andrew Jackson. Van Buren and like-minded Republicans, with their candidate Crawford hopelessly incapacitated, switched their allegiance to Jackson. They wanted Jackson elected, however, not only as a popular hero but as head of a disciplined and committed Democratic Party that would continue the states'-rights, limited-government positions of the old Jeffersonian Republicans.

The new Democratic Party linked white democracy with the defense of southern slavery. Van Buren began preparations for 1828 with a visit to John C. Calhoun of South Carolina. Calhoun was moving along the road from postwar nationalism to states'-rights conservatism. He also wanted to stay on as vice president and thus keep his presidential hopes alive. After convincing Calhoun to support Jackson, Van Buren embarked on reviving the alliance of "the planters of the South and the plain Republicans of the North" that had elected Jefferson. Thus, a new Democratic Party, committed to states' rights and minimal government and dependent on the votes of both slaveholding and nonslaveholding states, would ensure white democracy, the continuation of slavery, and the preservation of the Union. The alternative, Van Buren argued, was an expensive and invasive national state (Adams's "lighthouses of the skies"), the isolation of the slaveholding South, and mortal danger to the republic.

11-4d *The Election of 1828*

The presidential campaign of 1828 was an exercise in slander rather than a debate on public issues. Adhering to custom, neither Adams nor Jackson campaigned directly, but their henchmen viciously personalized the campaign. Jacksonians hammered away at the Corrupt Bargain of 1825, while the Adams forces attacked Jackson's character. They reminded voters of his duels and tavern brawls and circulated a "coffin handbill" describing Jackson's execution of militiamen during the Creek War. The most egregious slander centered on Andrew Jackson's marriage. In 1790, Jackson had married Rachel Donelson, probably aware that she was estranged but not divorced from a man named Robards. Branding the marriage an "abduction," the Adams team screamed that Jackson had "torn from a husband the wife of his bosom," and had lived with her in a state of "open and notorious lewdness." They branded Rachel Jackson (now a deeply pious plantation housewife) an "American Jezebel," a "profligate woman," and a "convicted adulteress" whose ungoverned passions made her unfit to be First Lady of a "Christian nation."

The Adams strategy backfired. Many voters did agree that only a man who strictly obeyed the law was fit to be president and that Jackson's "passionate" nature disqualified him. But others criticized Adams for making Jackson's private life a public issue and claimed that his rigid legalism left no room for privacy or for local notions of justice. Whatever the legality of their marriage, Andrew and Rachel Jackson had lived as models of fidelity for nearly 40 years. Their neighbors had long ago forgiven whatever transgressions they may have committed. Thus, Jackson's supporters accused the Adams campaign of a gross violation of privacy and defended Jackson's marriage—and his duels, brawls, executions, and unauthorized military forays—as a triumph of what was honorable and just over what was narrowly legal. The attempt to brand Jackson as a lawless man, in fact, enhanced his image as a melodramatic hero who battled shrewd, unscrupulous, legalistic enemies by drawing on his natural nobility and force of will.

The campaign caught the public imagination. Voter turnout was double what it had been in 1824, totaling 56.3 percent. Jackson won with 56 percent of the popular vote (a landslide unmatched until the 20th century) and with a margin of 178 to 83 in electoral votes. Adams carried New England, Delaware, and most of Maryland, and took 16 of New York's 36 electoral votes. Jackson carried every other state (see Map 11.3). It was a clear triumph of democracy over genteel statesmanship, of limited government over expansive nationalism, and of the South and the West over New England. Just as clearly, it was a victory of popular melodrama over old forms of cultural gentility.

Everett Collection Inc/Age Fotostock

11.6 **Rachel Donelson Jackson as a Mature Plantation Mistress** Andrew Jackson supposedly wore this miniature portrait of his beloved Rachel over his heart after her death in 1828.

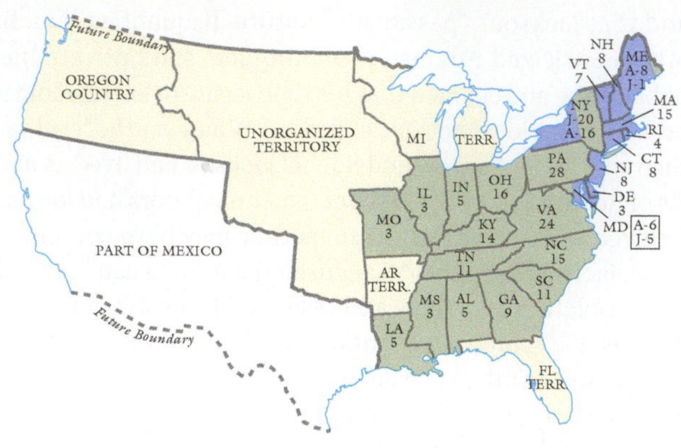

	Electoral Vote Number	%	Popular Vote Number	%
Jackson (Jacksonian Democrat)	178	68.2	647,276	56
J. Q. Adams (National Republican)	83	31.8	508,064	44

▲ **MAP 11.3 Presidential Election, 1828**

The 1828 presidential contest was a clear result of the organizing efforts that were building a national Democratic Party under the name of Andrew Jackson. Jackson picked up all of the states that had gone for Crawford or Clay in 1824, leaving only New England and small portions of the mid-Atlantic for John Quincy Adams.

Q *In what ways were Martin Van Buren's efforts critical to Jackson's victory?*

Q *How do changes in voting participation explain Jackson's victory?*

11-4e *A People's Inauguration*

Newspapers estimated that from 15,000 to 30,000 citizens came to Washington to witness Jackson's inauguration on March 4, 1829. They were "like the inundation of the northern barbarians into Rome," remarked Senator Daniel Webster. Many had traveled as much as 500 miles, and "they really seem to think that the country is rescued from some dreadful danger." As members of the Washington establishment watched uneasily, the crowd filled the open spaces and the streets near the east portico of the Capitol Building, where Jackson was to deliver his inaugural address.

Jackson arrived at the Capitol in mourning. In December, his wife Rachel had gone to Nashville to shop and had stopped to rest in a newspaper office. There, for the first time, she read the accusations that had been made against her. She fainted on the spot. Although she had been in poor health, no one would ever convince Jackson that her death in January was not caused by his political enemies. He assumed the presidency wearing a black suit and black tie, a black armband, and a black hatband that trailed down his neck in what was called a weeper.

Jackson's inaugural address was vague. He promised "proper respect" for states' rights, a reform of the civil service, and the retirement of the national debt through "a strict and faithful economy." Beyond that, he said little, although he took every opportunity to flatter the popular majority. He had been elected "by the choice of a free people" (and not by King Caucus or Corrupt Bargains), and he pledged "the zealous dedication of my humble abilities to their service and their good." He finished—as he often finished an important statement—by reminding Americans that a benign providence looked over them. He then looked up to a roar of applause.

The crowd followed Jackson from the Capitol to the White House, invading the mansion, muddying the carpets, tipping things over, breaking dishes, and standing in dirty boots on upholstered chairs. Jackson had to retreat to avoid being crushed. The White House staff lured much of the crowd outside by moving the punch bowls and liquor to the lawn. A wealthy Washington matron who had admired the well-behaved crowd at the inaugural address exclaimed, "What a scene did we witness! *The Majesty of the People* had disappeared, and a rabble, a mob, of boys, negros, women, children, scrambling, fighting, romping. What a pity, what a pity." A Democratic newspaper reported more favorably: "General Jackson is *their own* President.... He was greeted by them with an enthusiasm which bespoke him the Hero of a popular triumph."

11-4f *The Spoils System*

Jackson had begun to assemble his administration months before he took office. Martin Van Buren, who had mobilized much of the support Jackson gained between 1824 and 1828, was the new secretary of state—positioned to succeed Jackson as president. He became Jackson's most valued adviser. Other appointments were less promising, for Jackson filled cabinet posts with old friends and political supporters who, in many cases, proved unfit for their jobs. A critic looked at Jackson's cabinet and pronounced it—with the exception of Van Buren—"the Millennium of the Minnows."

Others were more concerned about what Jackson would do to the civil service than about whom he named to his cabinet. During the campaign, Jackson had vowed to fire corrupt officeholders—a term he applied to grafters, incompetents, long-term officeholders who considered their jobs personal property, and those who supported John Quincy Adams. Opponents soon complained that Jackson was replacing able public servants with political hacks who had been promised government posts in return for political support. They soon had convincing evidence: Samuel Swarthout, whom Jackson had appointed collector of the Port of New York (an office that handled $15 million in tariff revenue annually), stole $1.2 million and took off for Europe. Jackson insisted that he merely intended to end the long tenures that, he said, turned the civil service into "support of the few at the expense of the many," but the furor over his **"spoils system"** raged on. Jackson removed about 1 in 10 executive appointees during his eight years in office, and his replacements were most decidedly *political* appointees. Acting out of his own need for personal loyalty and on the advice of Van Buren and other architects of the Democratic Party, Jackson filled vacancies—down to postmasters in the smallest towns—with Democrats who had worked for his election.

In resorting to patronage to build the party, Jackson gave his opponents an important issue. Revolutionary republicans feared a government of lackeys dependent on a powerful executive,

Library of Congress Prints and Photographs Division [LC-USZC4-970]

11.7 **The President's Levee** Robert Cruikshank drew Jackson's inaugural reception with men and women of all classes, children, dogs, and bucking horses celebrating the Old General's victory. Cruikshank subtitled his lithograph "All Creation Going to the White House."

Q *What does the picture reveal about how citizens saw and related to the institution of presidency in the 1830s?*

and congressional opponents argued that Jackson was using appointments to "convert the entire body of those in office into corrupt and supple instruments of power." "A standing army," railed Henry Clay in the Senate, "has been, in all free countries, a just object of jealousy and suspicion. But is not a corps of one hundred thousand dependents upon government, actuated by one spirit, obeying one will, and aiming at one end, more dangerous than a standing army?" It became an anti-Jacksonian axiom that Jackson had made the federal civil service an arm of the Democratic Party and of despotic executive power.

11-5 Jacksonian Democracy and the South

At the national level, how did Jacksonian Democrats and their rivals deal with widening differences between the North and South?

Andrew Jackson was a national figure, but his base of support was in the South, where he won 8 of every 10 votes in 1828. Southerners had grown wary of an activist government in which they were in the minority. They looked to Jackson not only as a military hero but also as a Tennessee planter who talked about returning to republican fundamentals. Although southerners expected Jackson to look after southern interests, disagreement arose within the administration about how those interests should be protected. Some sided with Vice President Calhoun, who argued that states had the right to veto federal legislation and in extreme cases to secede from the Union. Others agreed with Secretary of State Van Buren that the Union was inviolable and that the South's best safeguard was in a political party committed to states' rights within the Union. The differences were fought out in the contest between Calhoun and Van Buren for the right to succeed Jackson as president, a contest that shaped every major issue of Jackson's first term.

11-5a *Southerners and Indians*

When Jackson entered office, a final crisis between frontier whites and the native peoples of the Eastern Woodlands was under way. Many earlier policymakers had believed that the American agrarian republic could assimilate Native Americans through civilization programs that transformed tribespeople into yeoman farmers who would voluntarily give up their hunting grounds for white settlement (see Chapter 7). But Indians' continuing resistance and white Americans' deep-seated beliefs in native savagery frustrated such scenarios.

In 1818, President James Monroe declared that "experience has clearly demonstrated that independent Savage communities cannot long exist within the limits of a civilized population... . it seems indispensable that their independence as communities should cease, and that the control of the United States over them should be complete and undisputed." The architects of the new American nation claimed sovereignty over Indian-occupied territories east of the Mississippi River and imagined westward expansion as a legitimate, indeed providential, undertaking that turned undeveloped native lands into flourishing, privately owned farms. By the 1820s, few Indians remained east of the Appalachians. The Iroquois of New York were penned into tiny reservations, and the tribes of the Great Lakes region were broken and scattered.

Yet, in the early 1820s, more than 120,000 Indians still lived between the Appalachians and the Mississippi River. Cherokees, Creeks, Choctaws, Chickasaws, and Seminoles in the South comprised half of them, living on their ancestral lands with tenure guaranteed by federal treaties that, at least implicitly, recognized them as sovereign peoples. Congress had appropriated funds for schools, tools, seeds, and training to help these populous peoples make the transition to farming. Some government officials assumed that the tribes would eventually trade their old lands and use their farming skills on new land west of the Mississippi. In contrast, many southern Indians embraced the United States' civilization program as a means to build stronger governments and economies and ultimately protect their lands as sovereign nations. They became **Civilized Tribes** with schools, roads, mills, individual property rights, cotton plantations, and large numbers of black slaves. The lives of their propertied, slaveholding elite families did not differ much from those of their wealthy white neighbors in Georgia, Alabama, and Mississippi.

Southern whites resented federal Indian policy as an affront to both white democracy and states' rights. The poorer farmers coveted the Indians' land, and states'-rights southerners denied the federal government's authority to make treaties or to recognize sovereign peoples within their states. Resistance centered in Georgia, where Governor George Troup brought native lands under the state's jurisdiction and then turned them over to poor whites by way of lotteries, thus tying states' rights to white hunger for Indian land. At one point, Troup sent state surveyors onto Creek territory before federal purchase from the Indians was complete, telling President Adams that if he resisted state authority he would be considered a "public enemy."

The Cherokees in Georgia pressed the issue in 1827 by declaring themselves a republic with its own written constitution, legislature, courts, police, and appointed principal leader—a sovereign indigenous nation within the state of Georgia. The Georgia legislature promptly declared Cherokee law null and void, extended Georgia's authority into Cherokee country, and began surveying the lands for sale. Hinting at the old connection between state sovereignty and the protection of slavery, Governor Troup warned that the federal "jurisdiction claimed over one portion of our population may very soon be asserted over *another*." Alabama and Mississippi quickly followed Georgia's lead by extending state authority over Indian lands and denying federal jurisdiction.

11-5b *Indian Removal*

President Jackson agreed that the federal government lacked the authority to recognize native sovereignty within a state and declared that he could not protect the Cherokees and the other Civilized Tribes from state governments. Instead, he offered to remove them to federal land west of the Mississippi, where they would be under the authority of the benevolent federal government. Congress made that offer official in the **Indian Removal Act** of 1830.

The Cherokees, with the help of New England missionaries, had taken their claims of sovereignty to court in the late 1820s. In 1831, John Marshall's Supreme Court ruled in *Cherokee Nation v. Georgia* that the Cherokees could not sue Georgia because they were not a foreign nation but a "domestic dependent nation"—a dependent of the federal government, and not of the state of Georgia. In a consequential formulation, Marshall noted that the relationship between the tribes and the United States "resembles that of a ward to his guardian." Cherokees understood the decision as an affirmation of their sovereignty and initiated another federal court case against Georgia. The Court's decision in *Worcester v. Georgia* (1832) declared that Georgia's extension of state law over Cherokee land was unconstitutional. Marshall's ruling, which was strongly motivated by his desire to assert the precedence of federal power over states' power in Indian affairs, was a victory for the Cherokees—although, as it turned out, a hollow one. President Jackson ignored the decision, reportedly telling a congressman, "John Marshall has made his decision: Now let him enforce it!"

The prolonged struggles with Georgia and the rapid economic and social changes among the Cherokees had split their nation into traditionalists who persistently opposed removal and those who favored accommodation with the whites. In 1835, a small minority group signed a Treaty of New Echota with the U.S. government, hoping to secure tolerable terms for the removal that seemed inevitable to its members. The vast majority of the Cherokees denounced the treaty, but to no avail. In 1838, Jackson's successor, Martin Van Buren, sent the army to march the 15,000 remaining Cherokees to a new Indian Territory in today's Oklahoma. At least four thousand of them died along this Trail of Tears of exposure, disease, starvation, and white depredation. Their suffering continued in the West. The Cherokees had brought their pre-existing internal divisions and disputes to Indian Territory, where bloodshed and instability plagued their lives for decades. They also clashed with the Comanches, Osages, and other powerful Plains Indians, who resented the newcomers on their borders. The Cherokee removal was but one of many cases of ethnic cleansing in the early 19th-century United States. Numerous native groups were moved to the West from Ohio, Michigan, Wisconsin, Illinois, and across the South, where westward-pushing settlers demanded more land for farms and plantations. In total, some 80,000 Native Americans were removed from the eastern United States during the 1820s and 1830s. Some, like the Seminoles in the Florida Everglades and Black Hawk's Sauks, Fox, and Kickapoos, fought back, but eventually they too had to go.

What They Said

President Andrew Jackson and the Cherokee Nation Debate Indian Removal

First introduced by Thomas Jefferson as an idea in 1803, the removal of eastern Indians west of the Mississippi River became one of the most contested issues in the early republic. The first selection below is Andrew Jackson's second State of the Union address on December 6, 1830, in which the president discusses the recently passed Indian Removal Act. The second is a memorial of the Cherokee Nation to the U.S. Congress.

Andrew Jackson, State of the Union Address, December 6, 1830

What good man would prefer a country covered with forests and ranged by a few thousand savages to our extensive Republic, studded with cities, towns, and prosperous farms, embellished with all the improvements which art can devise or industry execute, occupied by more than 12,000,000 happy people, and filled with all the blessings of liberty, civilization, and religion?

...to better their condition in an unknown land our forefathers left all that was dear in earthly objects. Our children by thousands yearly leave the land of their birth to seek new homes in distant regions. Does Humanity weep at these painful separations from every thing, animate and inanimate, with which the young heart has become entwined? Far from it. It is rather a source of joy that our country affords scope where our young population may range unconstrained in body or in mind, developing the power and faculties of man in their highest perfection.

...can it be cruel in this Government when, by events which it can not control, the Indian is made discontented in his ancient home to purchase his lands, to give him a new and extensive territory, to pay the expense of his removal, and support him a year in his new abode? How many thousands of our own people would gladly embrace the opportunity of removing to the West on such conditions! If the offers made to the Indians were extended to them, they would be hailed with gratitude and joy.

And is it supposed that the wandering savage has a stronger attachment to his home than the settled, civilized Christian? Is it more afflicting to him to leave the graves of his fathers than it is to our brothers and children? Rightly considered, the policy of the General Government toward the red man is not only liberal, but generous. He is unwilling to submit to the laws of the States and mingle with their population. To save him from this alternative, or perhaps utter annihilation, the General Government kindly offers him a new home, and proposes to pay the whole expense of his removal and settlement.

Memorial of the Cherokee Nation, 1830

We are aware that some persons suppose it will be for our advantage to remove beyond the Mississippi. We think otherwise. Our people universally think otherwise. Thinking that it would be fatal to their interests, they have almost to a man sent their memorial to Congress, deprecating the necessity of a removal....

We wish to remain on the land of our fathers. We have a perfect and original right to remain without interruption or molestation. The treaties with us, and laws of the United States made in pursuance of treaties, guaranty our residence and our privileges, and secure us against intruders. Our only request is, that these treaties may be fulfilled, and these laws executed.

But if we are compelled to leave our country, we see nothing but ruin before us. The country west of the Arkansas territory is unknown to us. From what we can learn of it, we have no prepossessions in its favor. All the inviting parts of it, as we believe, are preoccupied by various Indian nations, to which it has been assigned. They would regard us as intruders...

...the far greater part of that region is, beyond all controversy, badly supplied with wood and water; and no Indian tribe can live as agriculturists without these articles. All our neighbors ... would speak a language totally different from ours, and practice different customs. The original possessors of that region are now wandering savages lurking for prey in the neighborhood.... Were the country to which we are urged much better than it is represented to be ... still it is not the land of our birth, nor of our affections. It contains neither the scenes of our childhood, nor the graves of our fathers.

...there is not a man within our limits so ignorant as not to know that he has a right to live on the land of his fathers, in the possession of his immemorial privileges, and that this right has been acknowledged by the United States; nor is there a man so degraded as not to feel a keen sense of injury, on being deprived of his right and driven into exile....

Q *What sorts of similarities can you detect in the tone and style of the two documents? How does each use notions of law, history, and civilization to bolster its case? How does each depict Native Americans' relationship to land? By1830, the Cherokees had developed a deep understanding of the United States and its ambitions, legal system, and self-understanding. They had interacted with its political agents, traders, and missionaries for more than three generations, and many of them were literate mixed-bloods (people with both white and Indian ancestry) who knew the American value system intimately. How effective, do you think, was the Cherokee Nation's memorial in soliciting a sympathetic emotional response among the American audience?*

Sources: (top) *Andrew Jackson*, State of the Union Address, December 6, 1830; (bottom) *Memorial of the Cherokee Nation*, 1830.

Picture History/Newscom

11.8 **Trail of Tears** In 1838, the U.S. Army marched some 15,000 Cherokee men, women, and children, along with their animals and whatever they could carry, out of their home territory and into Oklahoma. At least 4,000—most of them old or very young—died during the march.

Q *Does the painting commemorate the suffering of Cherokees under forced relocation or sanitize the history of Indian Removal?*

Indian removal also had profound political consequences in the United States. It violated Supreme Court decisions and thus strengthened Jackson's reputation as an enemy of the rule of law and a friend of local, "democratic" solutions. At the same time, it reaffirmed the link between racism and white democracy in the South and announced Jackson's commitment to state sovereignty and limited federal authority.

11-5c *Southerners and the Tariff*

In 1828, a Democratic Congress passed a tariff, hoping to win votes for Jackson in the upcoming presidential election. Assured of support in the South, they fished for votes in the mid-Atlantic states and the Northwest by protecting raw wool, flax, molasses, hemp, and distilled spirits. The result was a patchwork tariff that pleased northern and western farmers but that worried the South and violated Jackson's own ideas of what a "judicious" tariff should be. Protective tariffs hurt the South by diminishing exports of cotton and other staples and by raising the price of manufactured goods. More ominous, they demonstrated the power of other sections to write laws that helped them and hurt the outnumbered South. Calling the new bill a **"Tariff of Abominations,"** the legislature of one southern state after another denounced it as unconstitutional, unjust, and oppressive.

South Carolina, guided by Vice President Calhoun, led the opposition to the Tariff of 1828. During the War of 1812 and the ensuing Era of Good Feelings, Calhoun's South Carolina—confident of its future and deeply engaged in international markets for its rice and cotton—had favored the economic nationalism of the American System. Then the Missouri debates and the Denmark Vesey slave conspiracy of 1822 (see Chapter 9) sent South Carolinians looking for ways to safeguard slavery. Their fears grew more intense when federal courts shot down a state law forbidding black merchant seamen from moving about freely while their ships were docked at Charleston. Carolinians were disturbed too by persistent talk of gradual emancipation—at a time when their own commitment to slavery was growing stronger. Finally, southerners noted that in the congressional logrolling that made the Tariff of 1828, many western representatives had abandoned their old Jeffersonian alliance with the South to trade favors with the Northeast.

With the growth in the Northeast of urban markets for western produce, the American System's promise of interdependence among regions was beginning to work, but in ways that united the northern states against the export-oriented South. The Tariff of 1828 was the last straw: It benefited the city and commercial food producers at the expense of the plantation, and it demonstrated that the South could do nothing to block the passage of such laws.

11-5d *Nullification*

As early as 1827, Calhoun concluded that southern states could protect themselves from national majorities only if they possessed the power to veto federal legislation within their boundaries. In 1828, in his anonymously published essay *Exposition and Protest*, he argued that the Constitution was a contract between sovereign states and that the states (not the federal courts) could decide the constitutionality of federal laws. A state convention (like the conventions that had ratified the Constitution) could nullify any federal law within state borders. "Constitutional government and the government of a majority," Calhoun argued, "are utterly incompatible." *Exposition and Protest* echoed the Virginia and Kentucky Resolves of 1798 and 1799 and anticipated the secessionist arguments of 1861: The Union was a voluntary compact between sovereign states, states were the ultimate judges of the validity of federal law, and states could break the compact if they wished.

Nullification was extreme, and Calhoun and his friends tried to avoid using it. They knew that President Jackson was a states'-rights slaveholder who disliked the Tariff of 1828, and they assumed that Vice President Calhoun would succeed to the presidency and would protect southern interests. They were wrong on both counts. Jackson favored states' rights, but only within a perpetual and inviolable union. A tariff was ultimately a matter of foreign policy, clearly within the jurisdiction of the federal government. To allow a state to veto a tariff would be to deny the legal existence of the United States.

Jackson revealed his views at a celebration of Jefferson's birthday on April 13, 1830. Calhoun's southern friends dominated the speechmaking, and Jackson listened quietly as speaker after speaker defended the extreme states'-rights position. After the formal speeches were over, the president rose to propose an after-dinner toast. "Our Federal Union: *It must be preserved*," he said. Isaac Hill, a New Hampshire Democrat and a supporter of Van Buren, reported, "an order to arrest Calhoun where he sat would not have come with more blinding, staggering force." Dumbstruck, the southerners looked to Calhoun, who as vice president was to propose the second toast. Shaken by Jackson's unqualified defense of the Union, Calhoun offered this toast: "The Union. Next to our liberties the most dear." They were strong words, but they had little meaning after Jackson's affirmation of the Union. A few days later, a South Carolina congressman on his way home asked the president if he had any message for him to take back. "Yes, I have," replied Jackson. "Please give my compliments to my friends in your state, and say to them, that if a single drop of blood shall be shed there in opposition to the laws of the United States, I will hang the first man I can lay my hand on engaged in such treasonable conduct, upon the first tree I can reach."

Having reaffirmed the Union and rejected nullification, Jackson asked Congress to reduce the tariff rates in the hope that he could isolate the nullifiers from southerners who simply hated the tariff. The resulting Tariff of 1832 lowered the rates on many items but still affirmed the principle of protectionism. That, along with Boston abolitionist William Lloyd Garrison's declaration of war on slavery in 1831, followed by Nat Turner's bloody slave uprising in Virginia that same year (see Chapter 9), led the whites of South Carolina and Georgia to intensify their distrust of outside authority and their insistence on the right to govern their own neighborhoods. South Carolina, now with Calhoun's open leadership and support, called a state convention that nullified the Tariffs of 1828 and 1832.

In Washington, President Jackson raged that nullification (not to mention the right of secession that followed logically from it) was illegal. Insisting that "disunion ... is *treason*," he asked Congress for a Force Bill empowering him to personally lead a federal army into South Carolina. At the same time, however, he supported the rapid reduction of tariffs. When Democratic attempts at reduction bogged down, Henry Clay, who was now back in the Senate, took on the tricky legislative task of rescuing his beloved protective tariff while quieting southern fears. The result was the Compromise Tariff of 1833, which, by lowering tariffs over the course of several years, gave southern planters the relief they demanded while maintaining moderate protectionism and allowing northern manufacturers time to adjust to the lower rates. Congress also passed the Force Bill. Jackson signed both into law on March 2, 1833.

With that, the nullification crisis came to a quiet end. No other southern state had joined South Carolina in nullifying the tariff, although some states had made vague pledges of support in the event that Jackson led his army to Charleston. The Compromise Tariff of 1833 isolated the South Carolina nullifiers. Deprived of their issue and most of their support, they declared victory and disbanded their convention, but not before nullifying the Force Bill. Jackson chose to overlook that last defiant gesture because he had accomplished what he wanted: He had asserted a perpetual Union, and he had protected southern interests within it.

11-5e *The "Petticoat Wars"*

The spoils system, Indian removal, nullification, and other heated questions of Jackson's first term were fought out against a backdrop of gossip, intrigue, and angry division within the inner circles of Jackson's government. The talk centered on Peggy O'Neal Timberlake, a Washington tavern keeper's daughter who, in January 1829, had married John Henry Eaton, Jackson's old friend and his soon-to-be secretary of war. Eaton was middle-aged; his bride was 29, pretty, flirtatious, and, according to Washington gossip, "frivolous, wayward, [and] passionate." Knowing that his marriage might cause trouble for the new administration, Eaton had asked for and received Jackson's blessing—and, by strong implication, his protection.

The marriage of John and Peggy Eaton came at a turning point in the history of both Washington society and elite sexual mores. Until the 1820s, most officeholders had left their families at home. They took lodgings at taverns and boardinghouses and lived in a bachelor world of shirtsleeves, tobacco, card playing, and occasional liaisons with local women. But in the 1820s, the boardinghouse world was giving way to high society. Cabinet members, senators, congressmen, and other officials moved into Washington houses, and their wives presided over the round of dinner parties through which much

Universal History Archive/Getty Images

11.9 President Andrew Jackson's Celestial Cabinet, 1836 This lithograph cartoon satirizes Andrew Jackson's cabinet meeting on the uproar over Peggy Eaton.

Q *What do the controversies around Peggy Eaton reveal about American values, morals, and politics of the time?*

Q *What does the controversy tell us about women's status and agency in society?*

of the government's business was done. As in other wealthy families, political wives imposed new forms of gentility and politeness on these affairs, and they assumed the responsibility of drawing up the guest lists. Many of them determined to exclude Peggy Eaton from polite society.

The shunning of Peggy Eaton split the Jackson administration in two. Jackson was committed to protecting her. He had met his own beloved Rachel while boarding at her father's Nashville tavern, and their grand romance (as well as the gossip that surrounded it) was a striking parallel to the affair of John and Peggy Eaton. That, coupled with Jackson's honor-bound agreement to the Eaton marriage, ensured that he would protect the Eatons to the bitter end. Always suspicious of intrigues, Jackson labeled the "dark and sly insinuations" about Peggy Eaton part of a "conspiracy" against his presidency. Before long, his suspicions centered on Vice President Calhoun, whose wife, Floride Bonneau Calhoun, a powerful Washington matron, was a leader of the assault on Peggy Eaton. Sensing that Jackson was losing his patience with Calhoun, fellow Democrats, soon after the Jefferson birthday banquet in spring 1830, showed Jackson a letter from William H. Crawford revealing that while serving in Monroe's cabinet, Calhoun, contrary to his protestations, had favored censuring Jackson for his unauthorized invasion of Florida in 1818. An open break with Calhoun became inevitable.

11-5f *The Fall of Calhoun*

Jackson resolved the Peggy Eaton controversy, as he would resolve nullification, in ways that favored Van Buren in his contest with Calhoun. He pointedly made Peggy Eaton the official hostess at the White House. Then, in spring 1831, Van Buren gave Jackson a free hand to reconstruct his tangled administration. He offered to resign his cabinet post and engineered the resignations of nearly all other members of the cabinet, thus allowing Jackson to remake his administration without firing anyone. Many of those who left were southern supporters of Calhoun. Jackson replaced them with a mixed cabinet that included political allies of Van Buren. Also at this time, President Jackson began to consult with an informal Kitchen Cabinet that included journalists Amos Kendall and Francis Preston Blair, along with Van Buren and a few others. The Peggy Eaton controversy and the resulting shakeup in the administration were contributing mightily to the success of Van Buren's southern strategy.

Van Buren's victory over Calhoun came to a quick conclusion. As part of his cabinet reorganization, Jackson appointed Van Buren minister to Great Britain—an important post that would temporarily remove him from the heat of Washington politics. Vice President Calhoun, sitting as president of the Senate, rigged the confirmation so that he cast the deciding vote against Van Buren's appointment—a petty act that turned out to be his last exercise of national power. Jackson replaced Calhoun with Van Buren as the vice presidential candidate in 1832 and let it be known that he wanted Van Buren to succeed him as president.

11-5g *Petitions, the Gag Rule, and the Southern Mails*

The Democratic Party's rigid party discipline and its commitment to slavery and states' rights antagonized many northerners and evangelical Protestants who advocated abolition, energetic government, and social and moral reforms. The antagonism came to a head in 1835, when abolitionists launched a "postal campaign," flooding the mail—in the North and South—with antislavery tracts that condemned slavery in the federal territories, the interstate slave trade, and the admission of new slave states. The southerners and most northerners considered such tactics incendiary.

Some Jacksonians, including Jackson, wanted to stop the postal campaign with a federal censorship law. Calhoun and other southerners, however, argued that the states had the right to censor mail crossing their borders. Knowing that state censorship of the mail was unconstitutional and that federal censorship of the mail would be a political disaster, Jackson's administration devised an informal solution. Without changing the law, the general postmaster simply looked the other way as local postmasters removed abolitionist materials from the mail. Calhoun and his supporters continued to demand state censorship, but the Democrats had no intention of relinquishing federal control over the federal mail. They made it clear, however, that no abolitionist literature would reach the South as long as Democrats controlled the U.S. Post Office.

The Democrats dealt in similar ways with antislavery petitions to Congress. With their postal campaign disabled, abolitionists began to bombard Congress with petitions to abolish slavery and the slave trade in the District of Columbia (where Congress had undisputed authority) and to deny the slaveholding Republic of Texas admission to the Union. Pressured by irritated pro-slavery representatives to resolve the matter, Congress conceived an unusual procedure: It simply voted at each session to table the petitions without reading them, thus acknowledging that they had been received but sidestepping any debate on them. This procedure, which became known as the **"gag rule,"** was passed by the support of southern representatives and the vast majority of northern Democrats. Increasingly, abolitionists sent their petitions to ex-president John Quincy Adams, who had returned to Washington as a congressman from Massachusetts. Adams spoke forcefully against slavery and the violations of civil liberties in Congress, evading the gag rule, which was rescinded in 1844, after eight years in effect. Thus, the Jacksonians answered the question that had arisen with the Missouri debates: how to protect the slaveholding South within the federal Union. Whereas Calhoun and other southern radicals found the answer in nullification and other forms of state sovereignty, Jackson and the Democratic coalition insisted that the Union was inviolable and that any attempt to dissolve it would be met with force. At the same time, a disciplined Democratic Party uniting northern and southern agrarians into a states'-rights, limited-government majority could guarantee southern rights within the Union. This answer to the southern question stayed in place until the breakup of the Democratic Party on the eve of the Civil War.

11-6 Jacksonian Democracy and the Market Revolution

Q *How did Democrats and Whigs in the national government argue questions raised by economic development?*

Jacksonian Democrats cherished the simplicity of Jefferson's agrarian republic. They assumed power at the height of the Market Revolution, and they spent much of the 1830s and 1840s trying to reconcile the market and the republic. Like the Jeffersonians before them, Democrats welcomed commerce as long as it served the liberty and rough equality of white men, but paper currency and the dependence on credit that came with the Market Revolution posed problems. The so-called paper economy separated wealth from "real work" and encouraged an unrepublican spirit of luxury and greed. Worst of all, the new paper economy required government-granted privileges that the Jacksonians, still speaking the language of revolutionary republicanism, branded "corruption." For the same reasons, the protective tariffs and government-sponsored roads and canals of the American System were unacceptable. The Jackson presidency aimed to curtail government involvement in the economy, to end special privilege, and thus to rescue the republic from the Money Power.

Jackson's policies met with growing opposition, which coalesced into a new party, the Whigs, in 1834. The Whigs favored an activist central government that would encourage orderly economic development through the American System of protective tariffs, a federally subsidized transportation network, and a national bank. This system, they argued, would encourage national prosperity. At the same time, it would create a truly national market economy that would soften sectional divisions. Jacksonian rhetoric about the Money Power and the Old Republic, they argued, was little more than the demagoguery of unqualified, self-seeking politicians.

11-6a *The Second Bank of the United States*

The argument between Jacksonians and their detractors came to focus on the Second Bank of the United States that Congress had chartered in 1816. The national government deposited its revenue in the bank, thus giving it an enormous capital base. The government deposits also included state banknotes that had been used to pay customs duties or to buy public land; the Bank of the United States had the power to demand redemption of these notes in specie, thus discouraging state banks from issuing inflationary notes that they could not back up. The bank also issued notes of its own, which served as the beginnings of a national paper currency. Thus, with powers granted under its federal charter, the Bank of the United States exercised central control over the nation's monetary and credit systems.

Most members of the business community valued the Bank of the United States because it promised a stable, uniform paper currency and competent, centralized control over the banking system. But millions of Americans resented and distrusted the national bank, citing its role in the Panic of 1819 as evidence of the dangers posed by privileged, powerful institutions. President Jackson agreed with the latter opinion. A southwestern agrarian who had lost money in an early speculation, he was leery of paper money, banks, and the credit system. He insisted that both the bank and paper money were unconstitutional and that the only safe, natural, republican currencies were gold and silver. Above all, Jackson saw the Bank of the United States as a government-sponsored concentration of power that threatened American liberty.

History Through Film *Amistad* (1997)

Directed by Steven Spielberg.
Starring Matthew McConaughey (Roger Baldwin), Morgan Freeman (Theodore Joadson), Anthony Hopkins (John Quincy Adams), Djimon Hounsou (Cinque).

In 1839, an American cruiser seized the Cuban slave ship Amistad off the shore of Long Island. The ship carried 41 Africans who had revolted, killed the captain and crew, and commandeered the ship—along with two Spanish slave dealers who bargained for their lives by promising to sail the ship east to Africa, then steered for North America. The Africans were imprisoned at New Haven and tried for piracy and murder in federal court. The government of Spain demanded their return, and southern leaders pressured President Van Buren for a "friendly" decision. The legal case centered on whether the Africans were Cuban slaves or kidnapped Africans. (The international slave trade was by then illegal.) The New Haven court acquitted them, the federal government appealed the case, and the Supreme Court freed them again. The Africans were returned to Sierra Leone.

The Africans spend most of the movie in a dark jail or in court, and the film centers on them and their experiences with two groups of Americans: the abolitionists who are trying to free them, and the political and legal officials who want to hang them—largely to keep their own political system intact. Spielberg's abolitionists are Lewis Tappan, a black activist (Morgan Freeman), an obscure young white lawyer (Matthew McConaughey), and, in the grand finale, congressman and former president John Quincy Adams (played wonderfully by Anthony Hopkins). In the historical case, the defense was handled by veteran abolitionists or by persons who had been working with abolitionists for a long time. Spielberg shaped this group to tell his own story, beginning with reluctant and confused reformers and politicians who, along with the audience, gradually realize the moral imperatives of the case.

Andrew Cooper/Dreamworks LLC/The Kobal Collection/Picture Desk

11.10 *Amistad* (1997) tells the story of 41 Africans who stage a revolt on the slave ship carrying them to Cuba and the trial that follows.

In one of the film's more powerful sequences, the Africans' leader, Cinque (Djimon Hounsou), through a translator, tells his story to the lawyer: his village life in Sierra Leone (the one scene filmed in bright sunlight), his capture by Africans, his transportation to the slave fort of Lomboko, the horrors of the passage on the Portuguese slaver *Tecora*, the slave market in Havana, and the bloody revolt on the *Amistad*—all of it portrayed wrenchingly on the screen. The Africans' story continues in jail, as they study pictures in a Bible and try to figure out the American legal, political, and moral system. In court, they finally cut through the mumbo jumbo by standing and chanting "Give Us Free!"

In a fictive interview on the eve of the Supreme Court case, Cinque tells Adams that he is optimistic because he has called on the spirits of his ancestors to join him in court. This moment, he says, is the whole reason for their having existed at all. Adams, whose own father had helped lead the Revolution, speaks for his and Cinque's ancestors before the Supreme Court: To the prosecution's argument that the Africans are pirates and murderers and to southern arguments that slavery is a natural state, he answers that America is founded on the "self-evident truth" that one's natural state is freedom. It is a fine Hollywood courtroom speech: Adams has honored his ancestors, the justices and the audience see the moral rightness of his case, and the Africans are returned to Sierra Leone. (In a subscript, Spielberg tells us that Cinque returns to a village that had been destroyed in civil war, but the final ironic note is overwhelmed by the moral triumphalism of the rest of the movie.) ■

11-6b *The Bank War*

The charter of the Bank of the United States ran through 1836, but Senators Henry Clay and Daniel Webster encouraged Nicholas Biddle, the Bank's brilliant, aristocratic president, to apply for recharter in 1832. Clay planned to oppose Jackson in the presidential election later that year, and he knew that Jackson hated the bank. He and his friends hoped to provoke the hot-tempered Jackson into a response they could use against him in the election. The Bank applied for recharter in January 1832, and Congress passed the bill in early July and sent it on to the president. Jackson understood the early request for recharter as a political ploy. On July 4, Van Buren visited the White House and found Jackson sick in bed; Jackson took Van Buren's hand and said, "The bank, Mr. Van Buren, is trying to kill me, *but I will kill it!*" Jackson vetoed the bill.

Jackson's Bank Veto Message was a manifesto of Jacksonian democracy. It combined Jeffersonian verities with appeals to the public's prejudice and declared that the bank was "unauthorized by the Constitution, subversive of the rights of the states, and dangerous to the liberties of the people." Its charter, Jackson complained, bestowed special privilege on the bank and its stockholders, who were almost all northeastern businessmen or, worse, British investors. Having made most of its loans to southerners and westerners, the bank was a huge monster that sucked resources out of the agrarian South and West and poured them into the pockets of northeastern gentlemen and their English friends. The Bank Veto Message was a long, rambling attack that, in the opinion of the Bank's supporters, demonstrated Jackson's unfitness for office. "It has all the fury of a chained panther biting the bars of its cage," said Nicholas Biddle. "It really is," he concluded, "a manifesto of anarchy." So certain were they that the public shared their views that Clay's supporters distributed Jackson's Bank Veto Message as *anti*-Jackson propaganda during the 1832 campaign. They were wrong. Most voters shared Jackson's attachment to a society of virtuous, independent producers and to pristine republican government. They also agreed that the republic was being subverted by parasites, who grew rich by manipulating credit, prices, paper money, and government-bestowed privileges. Jackson portrayed himself as both the protector of the Old Republic and a melodramatic hero contending with illegitimate, aristocratic, privileged, secretive powers. With the bank and Jackson's veto as the principal issues, Jackson won reelection by a landslide in 1832 (see Map 11.4).

Jackson began his second term determined to kill the Bank of the United States before Congress could reverse his veto. The bank would be able to operate under its old charter until 1836, but Jackson hurried its death by withdrawing government deposits as they were needed and by depositing new government revenues in carefully selected state banks—soon to be called "Pet Banks" by the opposition. By law, the decision to remove the deposits had to be made by the secretary of the treasury. Two successive treasury secretaries refused to do so; Jackson removed both from office and appointed Roger B. Taney, a loyal Democrat who promptly withdrew the deposits. Without the deposits, the Second Bank withered away.

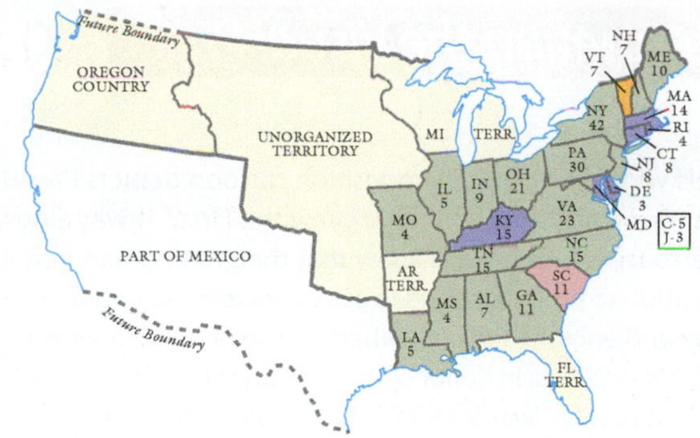

	Electoral Vote		Popular Vote	
	Number	%	Number	%
Jackson (Democratic)	219	76.6	701,780	54.5
Clay (National Republican)	49	17.1	484,205	37.6
Wirt (Anti-Masonic)	7	2.5	100,715	7.8
Floyd (Independent Democrat)	11	3.8	----------	----

▲ MAP 11.4 Presidential Election, 1832

The election of 1832 was a landslide victory for Andrew Jackson. The National Republican Henry Clay carried only his native Kentucky, along with Delaware and southern New England. A defeated and resentful South Carolina ran its own candidate. Jackson, on the other hand, won in the regions in which he had been strong in 1828 and added support in New York and northern New England.

Q *In what ways did the debates over the national bank shape the outcome of the election of 1832?*

Q *Was Andrew Jackson's 1832 campaign an anti-establishment campaign?*

11-6c *The Beginnings of the Whig Party*

Conflict over deposit removal and related questions of presidential power united anti-Jacksonians—most of them committed advocates of the American System—into the Whig Party. The name of the party, as everyone who understood the language of the republic knew, stood for legislative opposition to a power-mad executive. Jackson, argued the Whigs, had transformed himself from the limited executive described in the Constitution into King Andrew I. They listed the spoils systems and frequent vetoes of congressional legislation as his principal offenses. While earlier presidents had exercised the veto only nine times, Jackson alone used it 12 times during his two terms. According to his critics, the president used his veto power in particular to restrain the growth of the markets, the American System, and federal spending. The bank veto conveyed the same position, and the withdrawal of the government deposits brought the question of "executive usurpation" to a head, causing uneasiness even among the president's supporters,

Henry Clay, who had watched as Jackson denied one component after another of his American System, joined with Daniel Webster to lead the old National Republican coalition (the name that anti-Jacksonians had assumed since 1824) into the new Whig Party. They were joined by southerners (including Calhoun) who resented Jackson's treatment of the South Carolina nullifiers and Biddle's bank, and who distrusted his assurances on slavery. Jackson's war on the Bank of the United States chased lukewarm supporters into the opposition, enabling Democrats to point to an increasingly sharp division between the Money Power and the Old Republic.

The dismantling of the Second Bank of the United States had left a federal surplus of $5 million (produced by tariff proceeds and sales of public lands) without a depository. Jackson wanted to prevent the surplus money from being redistributed to the states, fearing that it would bolster the hated paper economy and encourage Congress to keep land prices and tariff rates high. Whigs, who by now despaired of ever creating a

Interpreting the Visual Past King Andrew the First

This widely distributed opposition cartoon depicts President Andrew Jackson as "King Andrew the First." It was a powerful cartoon, for Americans knew that their nation had begun in opposition to monarchy, and to a royal government that usurped power and encroached upon liberty. Jackson's opponents called themselves Whigs, in honor of the parliamentary faction that had opposed royal power in Britain. In fact, Jackson favored a small, inactive national government and used (abused, said his critics) presidential power to limit the powers of the government in Washington, largely by vetoing bills passed by the Whig legislatures that he faced throughout his presidency.

In the cartoon, King Andrew holds his scepter in one hand and a vetoed bill in the other. Internal improvements, the Bank of the United States, and the Constitution lie in ruins at his feet. The small print lists his crimes in detail: He had appointed federal officials that Whigs did not like, he had ignored Supreme Court decisions (on Indian removal in particular), and he had vetoed a lot of legislation—all of it in violation of "the will of the people."

Q *Andrew Jackson has traditionally been known as a "powerful" president. What was the nature of his power, and to what ends did he use it?*

Q *The cartoon refers repeatedly to "the People." In the language and context of the cartoon, who were they?*

KING

ANDREW

THE FIRST,

"Born to Command."

A KING who, possessing as much power as his Gracious Brother *William IV.*, makes a worse use of it.

A KING who has placed himself above the laws, as he has shown by his contempt of our judges.

A KING who would destroy our currency, and substitute *Old Rags*, payable by no one knows who, and no one knows where, instead of *good Silver Dollars*.

A KING born to command, as he has shown himself by appointing men to office contrary to the will of the People.

A KING who, while he was feeding his favourites out of the public money, denied a pittance to the *Old Soldiers* who fought and bled for our independence.

A KING whose *Prime Minister* and *Heir Apparent*, was thought unfit for the office of ambassador by the people:

Shall he reign over us,

Or shall the PEOPLE RULE?

New-York Historical Society

11.11 **"King Andrew the First", circa 1833.**

federally subsidized, coordinated transportation system, picked up the idea of redistribution. With help from the like-minded Democrats, they passed the Deposit Act of 1836, which increased the number of banks receiving federal deposits (thus removing power from Jackson's Pet Banks) and distributed the federal surplus to the states to be spent on roads, canals, and other internal improvements. Jackson, who distrusted state-chartered banks as much as he distrusted the Bank of the United States, planned to veto the bill, but faced an overwhelming congressional coalition of Whigs and Democrats. He demanded a provision limiting the state banks' right to print banknotes. With that provision, he reluctantly signed the Deposit Act.

Jackson and many members of his administration had deep fiscal and moral concerns about the inflationary boom that accompanied the rapid growth of commerce, credit, roads, canals, new farms, and the other manifestations of the Market Revolution in the 1830s. After insisting that his hard-money, anti-inflationary provision be added to the Deposit Act, Jackson issued a **Specie Circular** in 1836. This provided that speculators could only buy large parcels of public land with silver and gold coins, while settlers could continue to buy farm-sized plots with banknotes. Henceforth, speculators would have to bring wagonloads of coins from eastern banks to frontier land offices. With this provision, Jackson hoped to curtail speculation and to reverse the flow of specie out of the South and West. The Specie Circular was Jackson's final assault on the paper economy. It repeated familiar themes: It favored hard currency over paper, settlers over speculators, and the South and West over the Northeast.

11-7 The Second American Party System

Q *What was peculiarly national about the Second Party System?*

In his farewell address in 1837, Jackson spoke once again of the incompatibility between the republic and the Money Power. He warned against a revival of the Bank of the United States and against all banks, paper money, the spirit of speculation, and every aspect of the "paper system." That system encouraged greed and luxury, which were at odds with republican virtue, he said. Worse, it thrived on special privilege, creating a world in which insiders meeting in "secret conclaves" could buy and sell elections. The solution, as always, was a society of small producers, a vigilant democratic electorate, and a chaste republican government that granted no special privileges.

11-7a *"Martin Van Ruin"*

Sitting beside Jackson as he delivered his farewell address was his chosen successor, Martin Van Buren. In the election of 1836, the Whigs had acknowledged that Henry Clay, the leader of their party, could not win a national election. Instead, they ran three sectional candidates: Daniel Webster in the Northeast, the old Indian fighter William Henry Harrison in the West, and Hugh Lawson White of Tennessee, a turncoat Jacksonian, in the South. With this ploy, the Whigs hoped to deprive Van Buren of a majority and throw the election into the Whig-controlled House of Representatives.

The strategy failed. Van Buren had engineered a national Democratic Party that could avert the dangers of sectionalism, and he questioned the patriotism of the Whigs and their sectional candidates, asserting, "True republicans can never lend their aid and influence in creating geographical parties." That, along with his association with Jackson's popular presidency, won him the election. Van Buren carried 15 of the 26 states and received 170 electoral votes against 124 for his combined opposition. His popular plurality, however, was less than 51 percent (see Map 11.5).

Van Buren had barely taken office when the inflationary boom of the mid-1830s collapsed. Economic historians ascribe the Panic of 1837 and the ensuing depression largely to events outside the country. The Bank of England, concerned over the flow of British gold to American speculators, cut off credit to firms that did business in the United States. As a result, British demand for American cotton fell sharply, and the price of cotton dropped by half. With much of the speculative boom tied to cotton grown in the South, the economy collapsed. The first business failures came in March 1837, just as Van Buren took office. By May, New York banks, unable to accommodate

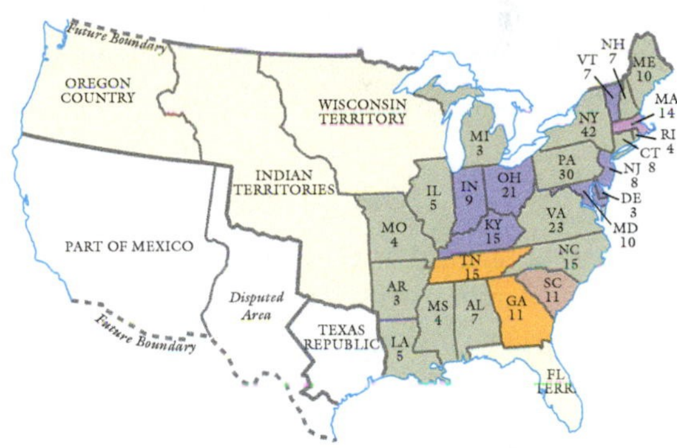

	Electoral Vote		Popular Vote	
	Number	%	Number	%
Van Buren (Democrat)	170	57.8	764,176	50.9
Harrison (Whig)	73	24.8	550,816	36.7
White (Whig)	26	8.8	146,107	9.7
Webster (Whig)	14	4.8	41,201	2.7
Mangum (Independent Democrat)	11	3.7	---------	----

▲ **MAP 11.5 Presidential Election, 1836**

In 1836, the Whigs tried to beat the Democrats' national organization with an array of sectional candidates, hoping to throw the election into the House of Representatives. The strategy failed. Martin Van Buren, with significant support in every section of the country, defeated the three Whig candidates combined.

Q *Is it fair to say that the Whigs lost the election of 1836 rather than the Democrats winning it?*

Q *In what ways was the election of 1832 different from previous elections?*

people who were demanding hard coin for their notes, suspended specie payments. Other banks followed suit, and soon banks all over the country went out of business. The financial and export sectors of the economy suffered most. In the seaport cities, one firm after another closed its doors, and about one-third of the workforce was unemployed. For those who kept their jobs, wages declined by 30 to 50 percent. It was the deepest, most widespread, and longest economic depression Americans had ever faced.

Whigs blamed the depression on Jackson's hard-money policies, particularly his destruction of the Bank of the United States and his Specie Circular. With economic distress the main issue, Whigs scored huge gains in the midterm elections of 1838, even winning control of Van Buren's New York with a campaign that castigated the president as "Martin Van Ruin." Democrats blamed the crash on speculation, luxury, and Whig paper money. Whigs demanded a new national bank, but Van Buren proposed the complete divorce of government from the banking system. Under his plan, the federal government would simply hold and dispense its money without depositing it in banks. He also required that customs and land purchases be paid in gold and silver coins or in notes from specie-paying banks, a provision that allowed government to regulate state banknotes without resorting to a central bank. Van Buren asked Congress to set up the Independent Treasury in 1837, and Congress spent the rest of Van Buren's time in office arguing about it. The **Independent Treasury Bill** finally passed in 1840, completing the Jacksonian separation of bank and state.

11-7b *The Election of 1840*

Whigs were confident that they could take the presidency away from Van Buren in 1840. Trying to offend as few voters as possible, they passed over their best-known leaders, Senators Henry Clay and Daniel Webster, and nominated William Henry Harrison of Ohio as their presidential candidate. Harrison was the hero of the Battle of Tippecanoe (see Chapter 7) and a westerner whose Virginia origins made him palatable in the South. He was also a proven vote-getter: As the Whigs' "western" candidate in 1836, he had carried seven states scattered across the Northwest, the mid-Atlantic, New England, and the Upper South. Best of all, he was a military hero who had expressed few opinions on national issues and who had no political record to defend. As his running mate, the Whigs chose John Tyler, a states'-rights Virginian who had joined the Whigs out of hatred for Jackson. To promote this baldly pragmatic ticket, the Whigs came up with a catchy slogan: "Tippecanoe and Tyler Too." One wealthy New York City Whig admitted that the slogan (and the ticket) had "rhyme, but no reason in it."

Early in the campaign, a Democratic journalist, commenting on Harrison's political inexperience and alleged unfitness for the presidency, wrote, "Give [Harrison] a barrel of hard cider, and settle a pension of two thousand a year on him, and my word for it, he will sit out the remainder of his days in his log cabin." Whigs, who had been trying to shake their elitist image, seized on the statement and launched what was known as the Log Cabin Campaign. The log cabin, the cider barrel, and Harrison's folksiness and heroism constituted the entire Whig campaign, while Van Buren was pictured as living in luxury at the public's expense. The Whigs conjured up an image of a nattily dressed President "Van Ruin" sitting on silk chairs and dining on gold and silver dishes while farmers and workingmen struggled to make ends meet. Whig doggerel contrasted Harrison the hero with Van Buren the professional politician:

> The knapsack pillow'd Harry's head
> The hard ground eas'd his toils;
> while Martin on his downy bed
> Could dream of naught but spoils.

Democrats howled that Whigs were peddling lies and refusing to discuss issues, but they knew they had been beaten at their own game. Harrison won only a narrow majority of the popular vote, but a landslide of 234 to 60 votes in the Electoral College (see Map 11.6).

The election of 1840 signaled the completion of the Second Party System—the most fully national alignment of parties in U.S. history. Andrew Jackson had won in 1828 with Jefferson's old southern and western agrarian constituency; in 1832, he had carried his old voters and had won added support in the mid-Atlantic states and in northern New England. In 1836, Whigs capitalized

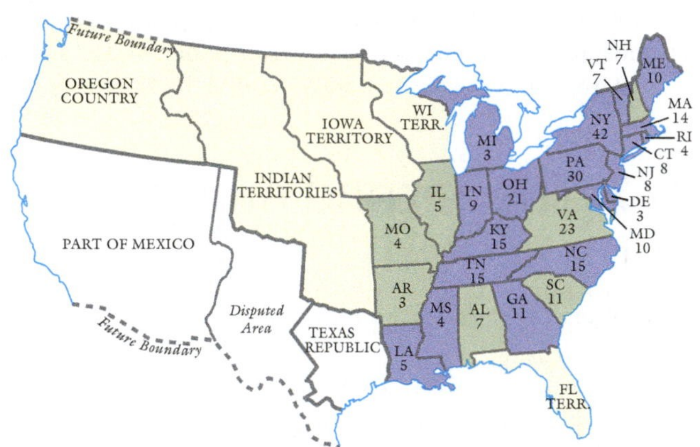

	Electoral Vote		Popular Vote	
	Number	%	Number	%
Harrison (Whig)	234	79.6	1,275,612	53
Van Buren (Democrat)	60	20.4	1,130,033	47
* Birney (Liberty)	----	----	7,053	----

▲ **MAP 11.6 Presidential Election, 1840** In 1840, the Whigs united under William Henry Harrison, the one Whig candidate who had won national support four years earlier. Borrowing campaign tactics from the Democrats and inventing many of their own, Whigs campaigned hard in every state. The result was a Whig victory and a truly national two-party system.

Q *Why did Harrison win the election of 1840?*

Q *It what ways did the election of 1840 break new ground in American politics?*

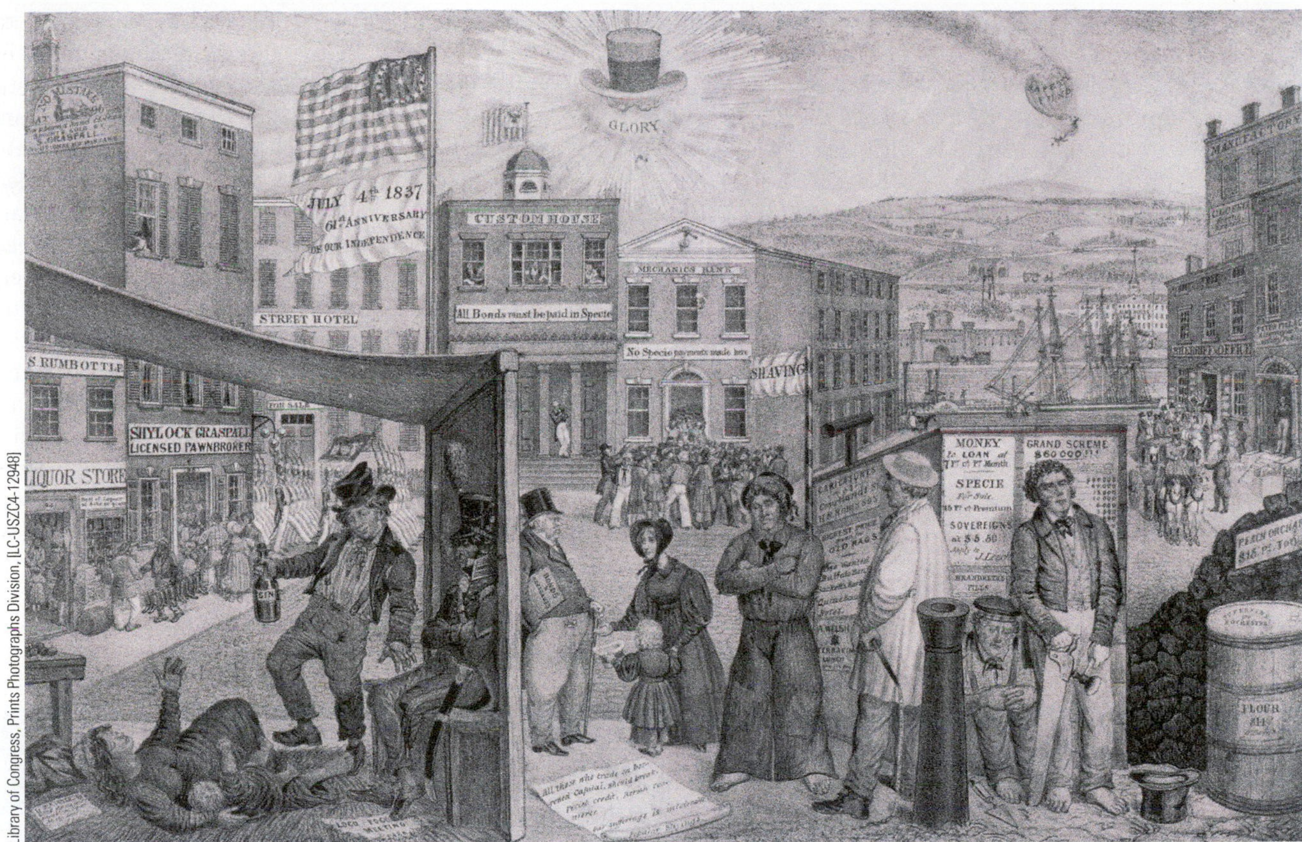

11.12 **The Times** This Whig cartoon from the 1840 campaign blames the Panic of 1837 on the Democrats. The factories are closed, the bank has suspended specie payments, and sailors and craftsmen are out of work, but the sheriff, the prison, the pawnbroker, and the liquor store are doing a booming business.

on southern resentment of Jackson's defeat of nullification and on southern mistrust of the New Yorker Van Buren. They broke the Democratic hold on the South, carrying Kentucky, Georgia, South Carolina, and even Jackson's Tennessee. Jackson had won 8 in 10 southern votes; Van Buren carried barely half. The election of 1840 completed the transition: Harrison and Van Buren contested the election in nearly every state and they received nearly equal levels of support in the slave and free states. Van Buren's dream of a national party system that transcended sectional differences was realized. Ironically, the final pieces fell into place in an election that cost him the presidency.

The election of 1840 also witnessed the high-water mark of voter turnout. Whig and Democratic organizations focused on presidential elections, and prospective voters met a quadrennial avalanche of oratory, door-to-door canvassing, torchlight parades, and party propaganda. Neither Democrats nor Whigs could take any state in the Union for granted. (In 1828, winning candidates carried individual states by an average of 36 percent; by 1840, that figure had dropped to 11 percent.) Whigs and Democrats maintained organizations and contested elections in nearly every neighborhood in the country, and the result was increased popular interest in politics. In 1824, about one in four adult white men had voted in the presidential election. Jackson's vengeful campaign of 1828 lifted the turnout to 56.3 percent, and it stayed at about that level in 1832 and 1836. The campaign of 1840 brought out 78 percent of eligible voters, and the turnout remained at that high level for the rest of the 19th century.

In every part of the country, Whigs presented themselves as the party of active government and economic progress. They promised good roads, public schools, stable currency, and social harmony. In the North, the wealthiest men were Whigs (8 in 10 of the merchant elites in New York and Boston, for example). But the Whig Party received its core northern support among the market farmers, local merchants, and manufacturers created by the new market economy and the fires of middle-class revivals—supporters not only of Whig nationalism but of roads and canals and a wide array of reforms in their own neighborhoods. In the South, Whigs ran well in plantation districts and in county-seat towns—the centers of southern wealth, commerce, and gentility. Many southern leaders came to dislike Jackson, and they took their personal followings into the Whig Party. Whigs also won votes in areas—eastern Tennessee and western North Carolina are examples—where farmers *wanted* to be brought into the flow of commerce. Put very simply, Whigs tended to be persons who were or wanted to be beneficiaries of the Market Revolution, and who embraced its attendant social and cultural transformations. They saw themselves as "improvers."

The Democrats, on the other hand, posed as defenders of the common (white) man and the Old Republic. They tended to be persons who had been hurt or bypassed by the Market Revolution; who belonged to conservative, otherworldly churches; and who distrusted Whigs who talked about progress, big government, and social homogeneity. In the South, Democrats were strong in districts with small farms, few slaves, and limited market activity. The northern Democrats were a coalition of small farmers, working people, and small businessmen, along with cultural minorities (Irish immigrants, for instance, were almost unanimously Democratic). North and South, Democrats were localists. They argued for the limited national government that since Jefferson's day had been a bulwark of the revolutionary republic, of white male democracy, and of chattel slavery.

Conclusion

Thus, the party system answered the questions of slavery and economic development that had helped bring it into being. Nationally, Democrats stopped the American System. They dismantled the Bank of the United States, refused federal support for roads and canals, and revised the tariff in ways that mollified the export-oriented South. As a result, the stupendous growth of the American economy between 1830 and 1860 became a question of state and local—not national—government action. Neither the national commercial society envisioned by the Whigs nor the return to Jeffersonian agrarianism favored by many Democrats came into being. Instead, the United States experienced an almost inadvertent experiment in laissez-faire capitalism, with results that reflected the aims of the most ambitious states. Trade and transportation networks linked the North and mid-Atlantic and isolated the export economy of the South—a result that few politicians had intended. Regarding the political problems surrounding slavery, the two-party system did what Van Buren had hoped it would do: Because both Whigs and Democrats needed both northern and southern support, they focused national political debates on economic development and stayed away from the questions of sectionalism and slavery. It worked that way until the party system disintegrated on the eve of the Civil War.

CHAPTER REVIEW

Review

1. What were the components of the "American System"? What did the American System promise to accomplish?
2. What enduring political issues were raised by the Missouri controversy and the Panic of 1819?
3. What were the events and political motives that contributed to the republican revival that formed around Andrew Jackson?
4. What were the principal events of the John Quincy Adams administration, and how did they contribute to his defeat in 1828?
5. At the national level, how did Jacksonian Democrats and their rivals deal with widening differences between North and South?
6. How did Democrats and Whigs in the national government argue questions raised by economic development?
7. What was peculiarly national about the Second Party System?

Critical Thinking

1. Jacksonian Democrats represented themselves as a revival of Jeffersonian democracy. In what ways was that representation accurate? In what ways was it not?
2. Whigs claimed to be the party of economic progress. Yet, unlike modern pro-growth politicians, they demanded a powerful, interventionist national government. How did they argue that position?

Identifications

Review your understanding of the following key terms, people, and events for this chapter (terms in bold in text are included in the Glossary).

American System, p. 303
Dartmouth College v. Woodward, p. 306
McCulloch v. Maryland, p. 306
Tallmadge Amendments, p. 307
Missouri Compromise, p. 308
congressional caucus, p. 310
"Corrupt Bargain," p. 311
Monroe Doctrine, p. 312
"spoils system," p. 314
Civilized Tribes, p. 316
Indian Removal Act, p. 316
"Tariff of Abominations," p. 318
nullification, p. 319
"gag rule," p. 321
Specie Circular, p. 325
Independent Treasury Bill, p. 326

Suggested Readings

Sean Wilentz, ***The Rise of American Democracy: Jefferson to Lincoln (2006)*** is a comprehensive political history. **Harry L. Watson**, ***Liberty and Power: The Politics of Jacksonian America*** (1990) is an excellent shorter synthesis. **Mathew**

Mason, *Slavery & Politics in the Early American Republic* **(2006)** and **Don E. Fehrenbacher**, *The Slaveholding Republic: An Account of the United States Government's Relations to Slavery* (2001) document the centrality of slavery through all these years. On southern Indians and the Indian removal, see **Claudio Saunt**, *A New Order of Things: Property, Power, and the Transformation of the Creek Indians, 1733–1816* (1999) and **Theda Perdue and Michael Green**, *The Cherokee Removal: A Brief History with Documents* (2005). On specific issues, see **John Lauritz Larson**, *Internal Improvement: National Public Works and the Promise of Popular Government in the Early United States* (2001); **A.F.C. Wallace**, *The Long, Bitter Trail: Andrew Jackson and the Indians* (1993); **R. Kent Newmeyer**, *The Supreme Court under Marshall and Taney* (1968); **Morton J. Horwitz**, *The Transformation of American Law, 1780–1860* (1977); **Robert Pierce Forbes**, *The Missouri Compromise and Its Aftermath: Slavery and the Meaning of America* (2007); **William W. Freehling**, *Prelude to Civil War: The Nullification Controversy in South Carolina, 1816–1836* (1965); **Richard E. Ellis**, *The Union at Risk: Jacksonian Democracy, States' Rights and the Nullification Crisis* (1987); and **Catherine Allgor**, *Parlor Politics: In Which the Ladies of Washington Help Build a City and a Government* (2000). **Steve Inskeep**, *Jacksonland: President Andrew Jackson, Cherokee Chief John Ross, and a Great American Land Grab* (2015), is an incisive and highly readable study of President Jackson and the Indian Removal. For Indian Removal as ethnic cleansing, see **Gary Clayton Anderson**, *Ethnic Cleansing: The Crime That Should Haunt America* (2014).

MINDTAP is a fully online personalized learning experience built upon Cengage Learning content. MindTap® combines student learning tools—readings, multimedia, activities, and assessments—into a singular Learning Path that guides students through the course and helps students develop the critical thinking, analysis, and communication skills that are essential to academic and professional success.

12 Antebellum Reform, 1820–1860

Library of Congress Prints and Photographs Division [LC-USZ62-11212]

12.1 **Harriet Beecher Stowe** Harriet Beecher Stowe was a daughter of Rev. Lyman Beecher, an evangelist who helped start the temperance movement in the United States. Her sister, Catharine Beecher, was a prominent reformer of housekeeping and domestic life. Her brother, Henry Ward Beecher, was an ardent antislavery advocate and a nationally famous preacher, and her husband, Calvin Stowe, designed the public school system for the state of Ohio. Harriet wrote *Uncle Tom's Cabin*, a huge best seller and the most powerful of antislavery tracts. She filled her book with the well-documented horrors of slavery, but she grounded it in the reform culture in which she grew up and which she helped to shape. Stowe and her family and coworkers wanted more than the end of slavery and alcohol abuse. They wanted to shape America in the image of northern evangelicalism and the middle-class home.

BETWEEN 1820 AND 1845, Thomas Jefferson's agrarian republic became Andrew Jackson's mass democracy. Politicians who built the Whig and Democratic parties participated in the economic and social transformations of those years. They were also consumers and producers of the new forms of popular culture. In making their political appeals, they tapped skillfully into the national patchwork of aspiration, fear, and resentment. John Quincy Adams, Henry Clay, and their National Republican and Whig allies envisioned smooth-running, government-sponsored transportation and financial systems. Such visions echoed the faith in cosmic order, material progress, and moral improvement that had become cultural axioms for the more prosperous and cosmopolitan Americans. Democrats, on the other hand, defended Jefferson's republic of limited government and white liberty and equality. They portrayed a haunted political universe in which trickery, deceit, and special privilege—the old signs of encroaching power—lurked behind the promises of the Whigs.

Whigs and Democrats constructed their coalitions largely at the neighborhood and state levels. Their arguments for and against state-supported internal improvements and state-chartered banks and corporations mirrored the national debate, and thus strengthened and nationalized party loyalties. Local cultural battles—arguments over alcohol, sexual morality, education, crime, and much more—also sharpened Democratic and Whig attitudes.

In the North, the churchgoing middle class provided the Whig Party with a political culture, a reform-oriented social agenda, and most of its electoral support. Whig evangelicals believed that with God's help they could improve the world by improving the individuals within it, and they enlisted the Whig Party in that campaign. On a variety of issues, including prostitution, temperance, public education, and state-supported insane asylums and penitentiaries, Whigs used government to improve individual morality and discipline. Democrats argued that attempts to legislate morality were anti-republican and wrong. Questions of social reform provoked the angriest differences between Democrats and Whigs, particularly in the North. Not all reform movements, however, strengthened the party system. When some whiggish northerners insisted upon women's rights and the immediate emancipation of all slaves, they attacked the foundations of the white republic and the party system, opening important questions that the political parties wanted to ignore. ■

12-1 The Politics of Progress

What were Whig and Democratic conceptions of the duties and limits of government?

Whigs assumed that both markets and government were agents of progress. Democrats, locally as well as nationally, preached that markets were good and governments were necessary, but that collaboration between the two produced corruption.

12-1a *Markets and Governments*

Whigs praised the new market economy as more than a means of producing national wealth. The market was, they insisted, an engine of social and moral progress. Markets created opportunities, and individuals who developed good work habits and moral discipline would prosper. Thus, the market would discourage laziness and ignorance and encourage social harmony, good manners, and disciplined ambition. At the same time, it would fill American homes with comfortable furniture and moral housewives. William H. Seward, the Whig governor of New York, supported transportation projects because they broke down neighborhood isolation and hastened the emergence of a market society, with "all the consequent advantages of morality, piety, and knowledge." The market, in short, produced moral progress.

Whigs believed that Americans enjoyed a harmony of class interests and an equality of opportunity that every virtuous person would recognize and that only the

CHRONOLOGY

1819 New York State builds the first prison under the Auburn system

1826 Reformers found the American Society for the Promotion of Temperance

1831 William Lloyd Garrison begins publication of the antislavery *Liberator* • New York Magdalen Society publishes its first annual report

1883 Abolitionists found the American Anti-Slavery Society

1840 Working-class drinkers found the Washington Temperance Society

1848 First Women's Rights Convention held in Seneca Falls, New York

1851 Maine becomes the first of 17 states to enact statewide prohibition

1860 New York enacts the Married Women's Property Act

resentful, the mean-spirited, and the unworthy would doubt. (Almost as much as the Democrats, Whigs excluded racial minorities from the "Americans.") To poor farmers and city workers who believed that the Market Revolution undermined traditional forms of independence, Whigs promised social mobility within a new system of interdependence, but only to deserving individuals. Pointing to self-made Whigs such as Daniel Webster and Abraham Lincoln, Whigs promised national prosperity in a world that rewarded virtue.

As they did nationally, Whigs at the state and local levels wanted government to subsidize economic development and the moral improvement that would come along with it. Government should build roads, establish public schools, and create and oversee a stable, reliable currency. It should also foster virtue. "The government," remarked a New York City Whig in 1848, "is not merely a machine for making wars and punishing felons, but is bound to do all that is within its power to promote the welfare of the People." *The American Review*, a Whig periodical, went further: "Forms of government are instituted for the protection and fostering of virtue, and are valuable only as they accomplish this."

Democrats saw things differently. Few of them condemned market society, but they argued forcefully against activist government, high taxes, and government partnerships with private interests. In contrast to Whig optimism, they tended to view human nature through a grim combination of classical republicanism and gothic romance and saw government not as a tool of progress but as a potential evil—a concentration of power in the hands of imperfect, self-interested men. The only safe course was to limit its power. In 1837, the *United States Magazine and Democratic Review* declared: "The best government is that which governs least," and went on to denounce the "natural imperfection, both in wisdom and judgment and purity of purpose, of all human legislation, exposed constantly to the pressure of partial interest; interests which, at the same time that they are essentially selfish and tyrannical, are ever vigilant, persevering, and subtle in all the arts of deception and corruption." It was a lot like what Democrats saw in stage melodramas, read in cheap fiction, and heard in their conservative churches. Most of all, Democrats insisted that Whig governments would create privilege and inequality. Corporate charters, banks, and subsidies to turnpike, canal, and railroad companies, they said, benefited insiders and transformed republican government into an engine of corruption and inequality.

Jackson himself acknowledged that varying levels of talent and energy (not to mention inheritance and social connections) create inequalities of power and wealth. He and other Democrats never talked of economic leveling. But they constantly accused Whigs of using government to make the rich richer. The granting of government privileges, warned one Democrat, was sure "to break up that social equality which is the legitimate foundation of our institutions, and the destruction of which would render our boasted freedom a mere phantom." By contrast, the government favored by the Whigs would enrich a favored few. Democrats demanded limited government that was deaf to the demands of special interests. Neither government nor the market, they said, should be allowed to subvert the democracy of white men on which the republic rested.

12-1b *Banks, Roads, Canals*

Andrew Jackson's national administration destroyed the Bank of the United States (see Chapter 11). As a result, regulation of banking, credit, and currency fell to the state governments. Banks emerged as a central political issue in nearly every state, particularly after the widespread bank failures following the crash of 1837. Whigs defended banks as agents of economic progress, arguing that they provided credit for roads and canals, loans to businessmen and commercial farmers, and the banknotes that served as the chief medium of exchange. Democrats branded banks as government-protected agents of inequality dominated by insiders who controlled artificial concentrations of money, who enjoyed chartered privileges, and who issued banknotes and expanded or contracted credit to suit their own advantage.

In state legislatures, Whigs defended what had become a roughly standard system of private banks chartered by state governments. They had the right to circulate banknotes and had **limited liability** to protect directors and stockholders from debts incurred by the bank. Many Democrats proposed abolishing all banks—"a set of swindling machines," said one western Democrat. Others proposed reforms, demanding, for example, a high ratio of specie reserves to banknotes as a guard against inflationary paper money. Democrats also wanted to hold bank directors and stockholders responsible for corporate debts and bankruptcies. Some proposed banning corporate charters altogether.

By these and other means, Democrats in the states protected currency and credit from the government favoritism, dishonesty, and elitism that, they argued, enriched Whig insiders and impoverished honest Democrats. Whigs responded that corporate privileges and immunities and an abundant, elastic currency were keys to economic development, and they fought Democrats every step of the way.

Democrats in Congress and the White House blocked federally funded roads and canals (see Chapter 11). In response, the states launched the transportation revolution themselves, either by taking direct action or by chartering private corporations to do the work. State legislatures everywhere debated the wisdom of direct state action, of corporate privileges, of subsidies to canals and railroads, and of government debt. Predictably, Whigs favored direct action by state governments. Democrats often supported internal improvements, but they opposed "partial" legislation that would benefit part of a state at the expense of the rest. They also opposed projects that would lead to higher taxes and put state governments into debt. They made the same argument in every state: Beneath Whig plans for extensive improvements lay schemes to create special privilege, inequality, debt, and corruption—all at the expense of a hoodwinked people.

The argument about government and economic development in the states mirrored the national debate. Whigs wanted to use government and the market to make an economically and morally progressive—albeit hierarchical—republic. Democrats viewed both government and the new institutions of market society with suspicion and vowed not to subvert the equal rights and rough equality of condition that were, in their view, the preconditions of republican citizenship. In language that echoed their Jeffersonian forebears, Jacksonian Democrats demanded that the market remain subservient to the republic. These state-level debates helped to cement party loyalties and make them national. Whig and Democratic arguments about banks and internal improvement were essentially the same in every state. In arguing their cases in Alabama or Pennsylvania, legislators and voters strengthened their identities as Democrats or Whigs and their ties with like-minded people throughout the republic. Thus, these state-level fights bolstered a national two-party system that did its best to ignore regional differences.

12-2 The Politics of Social Reform: Schools and Asylums

Q *What were Whig and Democratic positions on the issues of public schools, prisons, and asylums?*

The establishment of public schools and institutions for criminals and the insane worked the same way. Whigs and Democrats agreed that such state-supported institutions had become necessary. But Whigs wanted them to improve the character and morals of their inmates, and were willing to spend money for that purpose. Democrats wanted to educate children and incarcerate criminals and the insane, but they wanted to do it cheaply. The debates over state-run institutions, in short, gave Americans another opportunity to behave like Democrats and Whigs.

12-2a *Public Schools*

During the second quarter of the 19th century, local and state governments built systems of tax-supported public schools, known as **common schools**. Before that time, most children learned reading, writing, and arithmetic at home, in poorly staffed town schools, in private schools, or in charity schools run by churches or other benevolent organizations. Despite the lack of any system of education, most children learned to read and write. That was, however, more likely among boys than among girls, among whites than among blacks, and among northeasterners than among westerners or southerners.

By the 1830s, Whigs and Democrats agreed that providing common schools was a proper function of government, and Democrats often agreed with Whigs that schools could equalize opportunity. Massachusetts Democrat Robert Rantoul, for example, believed that rich and poor children should "be brought equally and together up to the starting point at the public expense; after that we must shift for ourselves." More radical Democrats, however, wanted public schooling that would erase snobbery. Marcus Morton, Democratic governor of Massachusetts, wrote that it was the job of the common schools to democratize children "before the pride of family or wealth, or other adventitious distinction has taken a deep root in the young heart."

The reformers who created the most advanced, expensive, and centralized state school systems were Whigs: Horace Mann of Massachusetts, Henry Barnard of Connecticut, Calvin Stowe (husband of Harriet Beecher) of Ohio, and others. These reformers talked more about character building and Whig Protestant culture than about the three R's. They wanted schools that would downplay class divisions, but they were interested less in democratizing wealthy children than in civilizing the poor. Calvin H. Wiley, the Whig superintendent of schools in North Carolina, promised that proper schools would make Americans "homogeneous ... intelligent, eminently republican, sober, calculating, moral and conservative." William Seward, the Whig governor of New York, insisted that "education tends to produce equality, not by leveling all to the condition of the base, but by elevating all to the association of the wise and good."

The schools taught a basic Whig axiom: that social questions could be reduced to questions of individual character. A textbook entitled *The Thinker, A Moral Reader* (1855) told children to "remember that all the ignorance, degradation, and misery in the world, is the result of indolence and vice." To teach that lesson, the schools had children read from the King James Bible and recite prayers acceptable to all of the Protestant sects. Such texts reaffirmed a common Protestant morality while avoiding divisive doctrinal matters. Until the arrival of significant numbers of Catholic immigrants in the 1840s and 1850s, few parents complained about Protestant religious instruction in the public schools.

North Wind Picture Archives

12.2 **The Eureka Schoolhouse in Springfield, Vermont** Mandated by state law and supported by local taxes, such one-room schools taught generations of American children the three R's.

Political arguments centered less on curriculum than on organization. Whigs wanted state-level centralization and proposed state superintendents and state boards of education, **normal schools** (state teachers' colleges), texts chosen at the state level, and uniform school terms. They also (often with the help of economy-minded Democrats) recruited young women as teachers. In addition to fostering civility and Protestant morality in the schools, these women were a source of cheap labor. Salaries for female teachers in the northern states ranged from 40 percent to 60 percent lower than the salaries of their male coworkers. Largely as a result, the proportion of women among Massachusetts teachers rose from 56 percent in 1834 to 78 percent in 1860.

Democrats objected to the Whigs' insistence on centralization as elitist, intrusive, and expensive. They gave power to individual school districts, thus enabling local school committees to shape the curriculum, the length of the school year, and the choice of teachers and texts to local needs and preferences. Centralization, they argued, would create a metropolitan educational culture that served the purposes of the rich but ignored the preferences of farmers and working people. It was standard Democratic social policy: inexpensive government and local control. Henry Barnard, Connecticut's superintendent of schools, denounced his Democratic opponents as "ignorant demagogues" and "a set of blockheads."

12-2b *Ethnicity, Religion, and the Schools*

The argument between Whig centralism and Democratic parsimony dominated the debate over public education until the children of Irish and German immigrants entered schools by the thousands in the mid-1840s. Most immigrant families were poor and relied on their children to work and supplement the family income. Consequently, their children's attendance at school was irregular at best. Moreover, most immigrants were Catholics. The Irish regarded Protestant prayers and the King James Bible as heresies and as hated tools of British oppression. Some of the textbooks were worse. Olney's *Practical System of Modern Geography*, a standard textbook, declared that "the Irish in general are quick of apprehension, active, brave and hospitable; but passionate, ignorant, vain, and superstitious." A nun in Connecticut complained that Irish children in the public schools "see their parents looked upon as an inferior race." Whigs, joined by many native-born Democrats, saw Catholic complaints as popish assaults on the Protestantism that they insisted was at the heart of American republicanism.

Some school districts, particularly in the rural areas to which many Scandinavian and German immigrants found their way, created foreign-language schools and provided bilingual instruction. In other places, state support for church-run charity schools persisted. New York City supported both Catholic and Protestant schools until 1825. So did Lowell, Massachusetts; Hartford and Middletown, Connecticut; and Milwaukee, Wisconsin, at various times from the 1830s through the 1860s. New Jersey provided state support to Catholic as well as other church schools until 1866. In northeastern cities, however, where immigrant Catholics often formed militant local majorities, such demands led to violence and to organized nativist (anti-immigrant) politics. In 1844, the Native American Party, with the endorsement of the Whigs, won the New York City elections. That same year in Philadelphia, riots that pitted avowedly Whig Protestants against Catholic immigrants, ostensibly over the issue of Bible reading in schools, killed 13 people. Such conflicts would severely damage the northern Democratic coalition in the 1850s.

12-2c *Prisons*

From the 1820s onward, state governments built institutions to house orphans, the dependent poor, the insane, and criminals. The Market Revolution increased the numbers of

Prisoners at the State Prison at Auburn.

The Granger Collection, NYC

12.3 **Auburn Prison** Inmates at New York's Auburn Prison were forbidden to speak and were marched in lockstep between workshops, dining halls, and their cells.

North Wind/North Wind Picture Archives

12.4 **The Whipping Post and Pillory at New Castle, Delaware** Delaware was a slave state that continued to inflict public, corporal punishment on lawbreakers. One criminal is tied to the post, while another, up above, is held in a pillory.

Q *Punishment in early and mid-19th-century United States was often a public spectacle. Why? What clues does the painting offer as to the contemporary thinking and sensibilities?*

such persons and made them more visible, more anonymous, and more separated from family and community resources. Americans in the 18th century (and many in the 19th century as well) had assumed that poverty, crime, insanity, and other social ills were among God's ways of punishing sin and testing the human capacity for both suffering and charity. By the 1820s, however, reformers were arguing that deviance was the result of childhood deprivation. "Normal" people, they argued, learned discipline and respect for work, property, laws, and other people from their parents. Deviants were the products of brutal, often drunken households devoid of parental love and discipline. The cure was to place them in a controlled setting, teach them work and discipline, and turn them into useful citizens.

In state legislatures, Whigs favored putting deviants into institutions for rehabilitation. Democrats, although they agreed that the states should incarcerate criminals and deviants, regarded attempts at rehabilitation as wrongheaded and expensive. They favored institutions that isolated the insane, warehoused the dependent poor, and punished criminals. Most state systems were a compromise between the two positions.

Pennsylvania built prisons at Pittsburgh (1826) and Philadelphia (1829) that put solitary prisoners into cells to contemplate their misdeeds and to plot a new life. The results of such solitary confinement included few reformations and numerous attempts at suicide. Only New Jersey imitated the Pennsylvania system. Far more common were institutions based on the model developed in New York at Auburn (1819) and Sing Sing (1825). In the **Auburn system**, prisoners slept in solitary cells and marched in military formation to meals and workshops. They were forbidden to speak to one another at any time. The rule of silence, it was believed, encouraged both discipline and contemplation. The French writer Alexis de Tocqueville, visiting a New York prison in 1830, remarked that "the silence within these vast walls ... is that of death... . There were a thousand living beings, and yet it was a vast desert solitude."

The Auburn system was designed both to reform criminals and to reduce expenses, for the prisons sold workshop products to the outside. Between these two goals, Whigs favored rehabilitation. Democrats favored profit-making workshops, and thus lower operating costs and lower taxes. Robert Wiltse, named by the Democrats to run Sing Sing prison in the 1830s, used harsh punishments (including flogging and starving), sparse meals, and forced labor to punish criminals and make the prison pay for itself. In 1839, William Seward, as the newly elected Whig governor of New York, fired Wiltse and appointed administrators who substituted privileges and rewards for punishment and emphasized rehabilitation over profit making. They provided religious instruction; they improved food and working conditions; and they cut back on the use of flogging. When Democrats took back the statehouse in the 1842 elections, they discovered that the Whigs' brief experiment in kindness had produced a $50,000 deficit, so they swiftly reinstated the old regime.

12-2d *Asylums*

The leading advocate of humane treatment of the insane was **Dorothea Dix**, a Boston humanitarian who was shocked by the incarceration and abuse of the insane in common jails. She traveled throughout the country, urging citizens to pressure their state legislatures into building asylums committed to what reformers called "moral treatment." The asylums were to be clean and pleasant places, preferably outside the cities, and the inmates were to be treated humanely. Attendants were not to beat inmates or tie them up, although they could use cold showers as a form of discipline. Dix and other reformers wanted the asylums to be safe, nurturing environments in which the insane could be made well.

By 1860, the legislatures of 28 of the 33 states had established state-run insane asylums. Whig legislators, with minimal support from Democrats, approved appropriations for the more expensive and humane moral treatment facilities. Occasionally, however, Dorothea Dix won Democratic support as well. In North Carolina, she befriended the wife of a powerful Democratic legislator as the woman lay on her deathbed. The dying woman convinced her husband to support building an asylum. His impassioned speech won the approval of the lower house for a state asylum to be named Dix Hill. In the North Carolina senate, however, the proposal won the votes of 91 percent of the Whigs and only 14 percent of the Democrats—a partisan division that held in state after state.

12-3 The Politics of Alcohol

Q *Trace the history of alcohol as a social and political question from the 1820s through the 1840s. Which Americans favored temperance? Which opposed it?*

Central to party formation in the North was the fight between evangelical Whigs who demanded that government regulate public (and often private) morality and Democrats who feared both big government and the Whig cultural agenda. The most persistent issue in that argument was the question of alcohol—so much so that in many places the temperance question defined the differences between Democrats and Whigs.

Niday Picture Library/Alamy Stock Photo

12.5 **Barroom Dancing, circa 1820** Inns, taverns, saloons, and bars were important public places in 19th-century United States, fostering a particular kind of public sphere.

Q *Based on the painting, what are some of the defining features of that sphere?*

12-3a *The Alcoholic Republic*

The years 1790 to 1830 witnessed a dramatic rise in alcohol consumption. Americans had been drinking alcohol since the time of the first settlements. (The Puritan flagship *Arabella* had carried three times as much beer as water.) But drinking, like all other "normal" behaviors, took place within a structure of paternal authority. Americans tippled every day in the course of their ordinary activities: at family meals and around the fireside, at work, and at barn raisings, militia musters, dances, court days (even judges and juries passed the bottle), weddings, funerals, corn huskings—even at the ordinations of ministers. Under such circumstances, drinking—even drunkenness—seldom posed a threat to authority or to the social order.

That old pattern of communal drinking persisted into the 19th century, but during the 50 years following the Revolution, it gradually gave way to a new pattern. Farmers, particularly those in newly settled areas, regularly produced a surplus of grain that they turned into whiskey. In Washington County in western Pennsylvania, for example, 1 family in 10 operated a distillery in the 1790s. Whiskey was safer than water and milk, which were often tainted, and it was cheaper than coffee or tea. It was also cheaper than imported rum, so Americans embraced whiskey as their national drink and consumed extraordinary quantities of it. Per capita consumption of pure alcohol in all its forms increased from three to nearly four gallons annually between 1790 and 1830, and most of the increase was in the form of cheap and potent whiskey. By 1830, per capita consumption of distilled spirits was more than five gallons per year—the highest it has ever been, and three times what it is in the United States today. The United States had become, as one historian has said, an "alcoholic republic."

The nation's growing thirst was driven not by conviviality or neighborliness but by a desire to get drunk. Most Americans drank regularly, although with wide variations. Men drank far more than women, the poor and the rich drank more than the emerging middle class, city dwellers drank more than farmers, westerners drank more than easterners, and southerners drank a bit more than northerners. Throughout the nation, the heaviest drinking took place among the increasing numbers of young men who lived away from their families and outside the old social controls: soldiers and sailors, boatmen and other transport workers, lumberjacks, schoolmasters, journeyman craftsmen, college students. Among such men, the controlled tippling of the 18th century gave way to the binge and to solitary drinking. By the 1820s, American physicians were learning to diagnose delirium tremens—the trembling and the paranoid delusions brought on by withdrawal from physical addiction to alcohol. By that decade, social reformers branded alcohol as a threat to individual well-being, domestic peace, public order, and the republic itself.

12-3b *Temperance Movement*

Drinking had been a part of social life since the beginnings of English settlement, but the withering of authority during the Market Revolution led to increased consumption, increased public drunkenness, and a perceived increase in alcohol-fed violence and social problems. After repeated false starts, the temperance crusade began in earnest in 1826, when northeastern evangelicals founded the American Society for the Promotion of Temperance, soon renamed the **American Temperance Society**. The movement's manifesto was Lyman Beecher's *Six Sermons on the Nature, Occasions, Signs, Evils, and Remedy of Intemperance* (1826). Addressing the churchgoing middle class, Beecher declared alcohol an addictive drug and warned that even moderate drinkers risked becoming hopeless drunkards. Thus, temperance, like other evangelical reforms, was presented as a contest between self-control and slavery to one's appetites. By encouraging total abstinence, reformers hoped to stop the creation of new drunkards while the old ones died out. Even though Beecher pinned his hopes on self-discipline, he wanted middle-class abstainers to spread reform through both example and coercion. As middle-class evangelicals eliminated alcohol from their own lives, they also ceased to offer it to their guests, buy or sell it, or provide it to their employees, and they encouraged their friends to do the same.

Beecher's crusade gathered strength in the middle-class revivals of the 1820s and 1830s. Charles Grandison Finney (see Chapter 10), in his revival at Rochester, made total abstinence a condition of conversion. Many other ministers and churches followed suit, and by the mid-1830s, the evangelical middle class had largely disengaged from alcohol and the people who drank it. Following a temperance lecture by Finney's coworker Theodore Dwight Weld, Rochester grocers Elijah and Albert Smith rolled their stock of whiskey out on the sidewalk, smashed the barrels, and let the liquor spill into the street. Other Rochester merchants threw their liquor into the Erie Canal or sold it off at cost. Hundreds of evangelical businessmen pledged that they would refuse to rent to merchants who sold liquor, sell grain to distillers, or enter a store that sold alcohol. Many of them made abstinence a condition of employment, placing ads that carried the line "None But Temperate Men Need Apply." Abstinence and opposition to the use of distilled spirits (people continued to argue about wine and beer) had become a badge of middle-class respectability.

Among themselves, the reformers achieved considerable success. By 1835, the American Temperance Society claimed 1.5 million members and estimated that 2 million Americans had renounced ardent spirits (whiskey, rum, and other distilled liquors); 250,000 had formally pledged to completely abstain from alcohol. The society further estimated that 4,000 distilleries had gone out of business, and that many of the survivors had cut back their production. Many politicians stopped buying drinks to win votes. The Kentucky Whig Henry Clay, once known for keeping late hours, began to serve only cold water when he entertained, and in 1833 members of Congress formed the American Congressional Temperance Society. The U.S. Army put an end to the age-old liquor ration in 1832, and increasing numbers of militia officers stopped supplying their men with whiskey. The annual consumption of alcohol, which had reached an all-time high in the 1820s, dropped by more than half in the 1830s (from 3.9 gallons of pure alcohol per adult in 1830 to 1.8 gallons in 1840).

12.6 **"Death on the Striped Pig," 1839** This cartoon, portraying the Massachusetts tavern keepers' famous striped pig. In the upper-left corner, the devil says, "Go it, Stripes. You are the best servant I ever sent into the field."

Q *What or who does the striped pig represent?*

Q *What is the cartoon's message?*

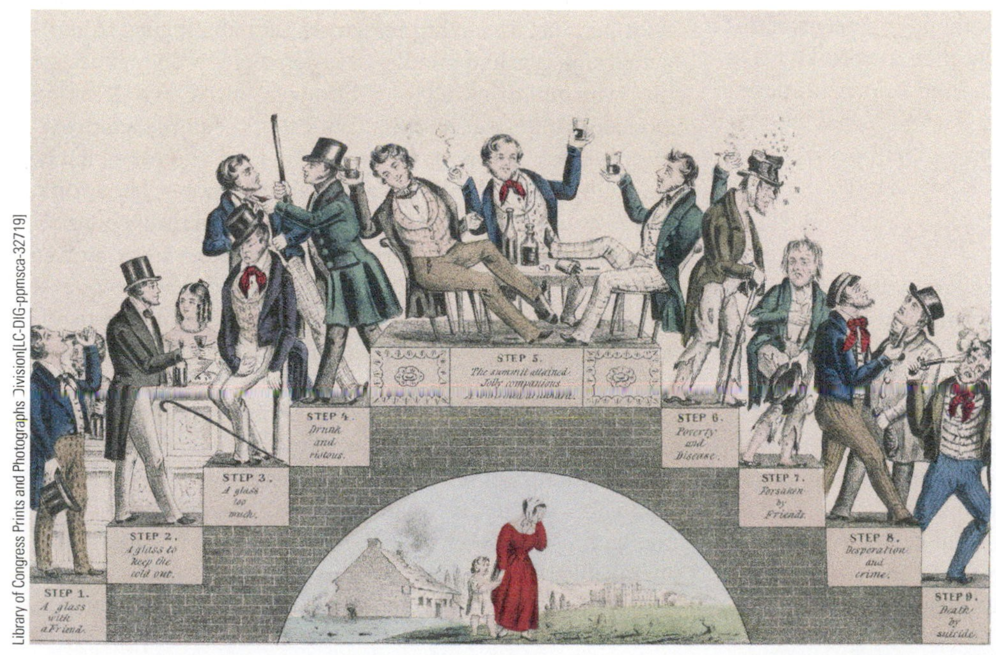

12.7 **"The Drunkard's Progress"** This popular print describes the drunkard's progression from social drinking to alcoholism, isolation, crime, and death by suicide. His desolate wife and daughter and his burning house are at bottom.

12-3c *The Origins of Prohibition*

In the middle 1830s, Whigs made temperance a political issue. Realizing that voluntary abstinence would not end drunkenness, Whig evangelicals drafted coercive, prohibitionist legislation. First, they attacked the licenses granting grocery stores and taverns the right to sell liquor by the drink and to permit it to be consumed on the premises. The licenses were important sources of revenue for local governments. They also gave local authorities the power to cancel the licenses of troublesome establishments. Militant temperance advocates, usually in association with local Whigs, demanded that the authorities use that power to outlaw all public drinking places. In communities throughout the North, the licensing issue, always freighted with divisions over religion and social class, became the issue around which local parties organized. The question first reached the state level in Massachusetts, when in 1838 a Whig legislature passed the Fifteen-Gallon Law, which decreed that merchants could sell ardent spirits only in quantities of 15 gallons or more, thus outlawing every public drinking place in the state. In 1839, Massachusetts voters sent enough Democrats to the legislature to rescind the law.

The Whig attempt to cancel tavern licenses proved unenforceable because proprietors simply operated without licenses or found ways to get around the laws. While the Massachusetts Fifteen-Gallon Law was in effect, one Boston tavern keeper painted stripes on a pig and charged patrons an admission fee of six cents (the old price of a drink) to view the "exhibition." He then provided customers—who paid over and over to see the pig—with a "complimentary" glass of whiskey.

Leading Democrats agreed with Whigs that Americans drank too much, but whereas Whigs insisted that regulating morality was a proper function of government, Democrats warned that coercive government intrusion into areas of private choice would violate republican liberties. In many communities, alcohol became the defining difference between Democrats and Whigs. In 1834, for instance, a Whig campaign worker ventured into a poor neighborhood in Rochester and asked a woman how her husband planned to vote. "Why, he has always been Jackson," she said, "and I don't think he's joined the Cold Water."

12-3d *The Washingtonians*

Not all temperance movements sprang from organized political and evangelical action. One evening in 1840—in the depths of a devastating economic depression—six craftsmen were drinking at Chase's Tavern in Baltimore. More or less as a joke, they sent one of their number to a nearby temperance lecture. He came back a teetotaler and converted the others. They then drew up a total abstinence pledge and promised to devote themselves to the reform of other drinkers. Within months, from this beginning a national movement had emerged, called the **Washington Temperance Society**. With a core membership of men who had opposed temperance in the 1830s, the Washingtonians differed from older temperance societies in several ways. First, they identified themselves as members of the laboring classes. Second, they were separated from the churches. Although many of them were churchgoers (usually Methodist or Baptist), many were not, and the Washingtonians avoided religious controversy by avoiding religion. Third, the Washingtonians—at least those who called themselves True Washingtonians—rejected recourse to politics and legislation and concentrated instead on the conversion of drinkers through compassion and persuasion. Finally, they welcomed "hopeless" drunkards—who accounted for about 10 percent of the membership—and hailed them as heroes when they sobered up.

Whig reformers welcomed the Washingtonians at first, but they soon had second thoughts. The nonreligious character of the movement disturbed those who saw temperance as an arm of evangelical reform. Previous advocates of temperance had assumed that sobriety would be accompanied by evangelical decorum. Instead, the meetings, picnics, and parades held by the Washingtonians were continuous with a popular culture that Whig evangelicals opposed. While the temperance regulars read pamphlets and listened to lectures by clergymen, lawyers, and doctors, the Washingtonians enjoyed raucous sing-alongs, comedy routines, barnyard imitations, dramatic skits, and even full-dress minstrel shows geared to temperance themes. Meetings featured experience speeches by reformed drunkards. Speaking extemporaneously, they omitted none of the horrors of an alcoholic life—attempts at suicide, friendships betrayed, fathers and mothers desolated, wives beaten and abandoned, children dead of starvation. Although Washingtonians had given up alcohol, their melodramatic tales, street parades, songbooks, and minstrel shows—even when presented with a Methodist or Baptist accent—were not the temperance reformation that Lyman Beecher and the Whigs had had in mind.

Nowhere did the Washingtonians differ more sharply from the temperance regulars than in their visions of the reformed life. The Whig reformers tied abstinence to individual ambition and middle-class domesticity. They expected men who quit drinking to withdraw from the male drinking world and to retreat into the comfort of the newly feminized middle-class family. Washingtonians, on the other hand, translated traditional male sociability into sober forms. Moreover, they called former drinkers back to the responsibilities of traditional fatherhood. Their experience stories began with the hurt drunkards had caused their wives and children and ended with their transformation into dependable providers and authoritative fathers. While the Whig temperance regulars tried to extend the ethos of individual ambition and the new middle-class domesticity into society at large, Washingtonians sought to rescue the self-respect and moral authority of working-class fathers.

The Washington Temperance Society collapsed toward the end of the 1840s, but its legacy survived. Among former drinkers in the North, it had introduced a new sense of domestic responsibility and a healthy fear of drunkenness.

Consumption of pure alcohol dropped from 1.8 to 1.0 gallons annually in the 1840s. Along the way, the Washingtonians and related groups created a self-consciously respectable native Protestant working class in American cities.

12-3e *Ethnicity and Alcohol*

In the 1840s and 1850s, millions of Irish and German immigrants poured into neighborhoods recently stirred by working-class revivals and temperance agitation. The newcomers had their own time-honored relations to alcohol. The Germans introduced lager beer to the United States, thus providing a wholesome alternative for Americans who wished to give up spirits without joining the teetotalers. The Germans also built old-country beer halls in American cities, complete with sausage counters, oompah bands, group singing, and other family attractions. For their part, the Irish reaffirmed their love of whiskey—a love forged in colonial oppression and in a culture that accepted trouble with resignation—a love that legitimized levels of male drunkenness and violence that Americans, particularly the temperance forces, found appalling. Differences in immigrant drinking were given architectural expression. German beer halls provided seating arrangements for whole families. Irish bars, on the other hand, provided a bar but no tables or chairs. If a drinker had to sit down, they reasoned, it was time for him to go home.

In the 1850s, native resentment of Catholic immigrants drove thousands of Baptist and Methodist "respectables" out of the Democratic coalition and into nativist Whig majorities that—beginning with Maine in 1851—established legal prohibition in several northern and mid-Atlantic states. Many of these Democrats became part of the North's Republican majority on the eve of the Civil War.

12-3f *The South and Social Reform*

On economic issues, southern state legislatures divided along the same lines as northern legislatures: Whigs wanted government participation in the economy, Democrats did not. On social questions, however, southern Whigs and Democrats both opposed moralizing legislation. The South was a rural, conservative region of father-dominated households. Southern voters, Whigs as well as Democrats, perceived attempts at "social improvement" as intrusive, wrongheaded assaults on the autonomy of neighborhoods and families.

The southern states enacted school laws and drew up blueprints for state school systems, but the white South had little need for schools to enforce a common culture. Moreover, the South had less money and less faith in government. Consequently, southern schools tended to be locally controlled, to be infused with southern evangelical culture, and to have a limited curriculum and a short school year. In 1860, northern children attended school for an average of more than 50 days a year; white children in the South attended school for an average of 10 days annually.

By 1860, every slave state except Florida and the Carolinas had built prisons modeled on the Auburn system. Southern prisons, however, stressed punishment and profits over rehabilitation. Some southern Whigs favored northern-style reforms, but they knew that voters would reject them. Popular votes in Alabama in 1834 and in North Carolina in 1846 brought in resounding defeats for proposals to build or reform penitentiaries in those states. While northern evangelicals preached that criminals could be reformed, southern preachers demanded Old Testament vengeance, arguing that hanging, whipping, and branding were inexpensive, more effective than mere incarceration, and sanctioned by the Bible. Other southerners, defending the code of honor, charged that victims and their relatives would be denied vengeance if criminals were hidden away in prisons. Some southern prisons leased convict labor (and sometimes whole prisons) to private entrepreneurs, and the dream of reforming criminals was never taken seriously in the South.

The South did participate in temperance. By the 1820s, Baptists and Methodists had made deep inroads into southern society. Southern ministers preached against alcohol, while churchgoing women discouraged their husbands, sons, and suitors from drinking. (An Alabama man complained that "the women our way seem determined to deprive us of all of our privileges; if I offer to take a drink of whiskey as I used to do, my wife tells me of the *Temperation Society*, and says its mean, and low, and sinful.") Many southern men either stopped or reduced their drinking, and the South contributed its share to the national drop in alcohol consumption. During the 1840s, the Washington Temperance Society and other voluntary temperance groups won a solid footing in southern cities and county-seat towns, with leaders who included Whigs and Democrats alike. But legal prohibition, which became dominant in the North, got nowhere in the South. In the 1850s, while 17 northern legislatures passed statewide prohibition, the only slave state to follow was tiny, northern-oriented Delaware.

At bottom, southern resistance to social reform stemmed from a conservative, Bible-based acceptance of suffering and human imperfection and a commitment to the power and independence of white men who headed families—"families" that included their slaves as well as their wives and children. Any proposal that sounded like social tinkering or the invasion of paternal rights was doomed to failure. Moreover, many reforms—public schools, Sunday schools, reform-oriented prisons, prohibition, humane asylums—were seen as the work of well-funded missionaries from the Northeast who wanted to shape society in their own image. The Virginian John Randolph spoke for many southerners when he warned against the Yankees' "meddling, obtrusive, intrusive, restless, self-dissatisfied spirit," exhibited in "Sunday schools, Missionary Societies, subscriptions to Colonization Societies—taking care of the Sandwich Islanders, free negroes, and God knows who." The southern distrust of reform was powerfully reinforced after 1830, when northern reformers began to call for the abolition of slavery and equality of the sexes—reforms that most white southerners found unthinkable.

12-4 The Politics of Slavery and Race

Q *How did Whigs and Democrats differ on questions of slavery and race?*

Most whites in antebellum America believed in "natural" differences based on sex and race. God, they said, had given women and men and whites and blacks different mental, emotional, and physical capacities. Because humankind (female and nonwhite more than others) was innately sinful and prone to disorder, God ordained a fixed social hierarchy in which white men exercised power over others. Slaves and free blacks accepted their subordinate status only as a fact of life, not as something that was natural and just. Some women also opposed patriarchy, but before 1830, hierarchy based on sex and race was seldom questioned in public, particularly by persons who were in a position to change it.

In the antebellum years, as southerners and most northerners stiffened their defense of white supremacy (see Chapter 10), a radical minority of Whig evangelicals began to envision a world based on Christian love and individual worth and accomplishment, not "natural" differences. They also questioned the more virulent forms of racism. While conservative Christians insisted that relations based on dominance and submission were the lot of a sinful humankind, reformers argued that such relations interposed human power, too often in the form of brute force, between God and the individual spirit. They called for a world that substituted spiritual freedom and Christian love for every form of worldly domination. The result was a community of uncompromising radical reformers who attacked slavery as America's great national sin. In doing so, they assaulted the white republic and the core compromise of the American political system.

12-4a *Democratic Racism*

Whigs and Democrats both wanted to keep slavery and race out of politics, and neither encouraged the aspirations of slaves or free blacks. But it was the Democrats who incorporated racism into their political agenda. Minstrel shows, for example, often reflected the Democratic line on current events, and Democratic cartoonists featured minstrelsy's bug-eyed, woolly-haired caricatures of blacks. By the time of the Civil War, Democrats mobilized voters almost solely with threats of "amalgamation" and "Negro rule." Meanwhile, educated Democrats learned to think in racist terms. Among most scientists, biological determinism replaced historical and environmental explanations of racial differences; many argued that whites and blacks were separate species. Democrats welcomed that "discovery." John Van Evrie, a New York doctor and Democratic pamphleteer, declared that "it is a palpable and unavoidable fact that Negroes are a different species," and that the story of Adam and Eve referred only to the origin of *white* people. In 1850, the *Democratic Review* confided, "Few or none now seriously adhere to the theory of the unity of the races. The whole state of the science at this moment seems to indicate that there are several distinct races of men on the earth, with entirely different capacities, physical and mental."

As whites came to perceive racial differences as God-given and immutable, they changed the nature of those differences as well. In the 18th and early 19th centuries, whites had stereotyped blacks as ignorant and prone to drunkenness and thievery, but they had also maintained a parallel stereotype of blacks as loyal and self-sacrificing servants. From the 1820s onward, racists continued to regard blacks as incompetent, but they found it harder to distinguish mere carelessness from dishonesty. Now they saw blacks as treacherous, shrewd, and secretive—individuals who only *pretended* to feel loyalty to white families and affection for the white children they took care of, while awaiting the chance to steal from them or poison them. The writer Herman Melville, a lifelong Democrat who shared little of his compatriots' racism but who helped codify their fascination with duplicity and deceit, dramatized these fears in *Benito Cereno*, a novel about slaves who commandeer a sailing ship and its captain and crew, then (with knives secretly at the throats of their captives) act out a servile charade for unsuspecting visitors who come aboard.

12-4b *Antislavery before 1830*

Before 1830, few whites opposed slavery politically. Quakers had condemned both the slave trade and slavery in the 1750s, and Methodists and some Baptists had done the same late in the century. Washington, Jefferson, and other Chesapeake gentlemen doubted the wisdom, if not the morality, of holding slaves. New England Federalists had condemned slavery in the course of condemning southern Jeffersonians. But there were too few Quakers to make a difference, and the movement to free slaves in the Upper South and the antislavery sentiments of southern evangelicals both died out early in the 19th century. Southerners and most northerners—when they bothered to think about it at all—tended to accept slavery as an unchangeable institution that they had inherited, an institution grounded, ultimately, in human (read "black") depravity and God's unknowable plan. The New England and mid-Atlantic states freed (and then shunned) their slaves but seldom argued that the South should do the same.

The biggest organization that addressed questions of slavery and race before 1830 was the **American Colonization Society**, founded in 1816. This elite organization of white men never attacked slavery. The rising population of free blacks was their principal concern. "The rapid increase of the black population in some parts of our country," said a Boston colonizationist in 1822, "is becoming every year more serious." Their answer was to colonize free blacks (but not slaves) in Liberia, on the west coast of Africa. The society held its first meeting in the chamber of the House of Representatives, with Bushrod Washington, stepson of George Washington, as president. Early members included Henry Clay, John Taylor of Caroline,

Andrew Jackson, and other political leaders of the West, the middle states, and the Upper South. Blacks, they said, would continue to suffer from white prejudice and their own deficiencies as long as they stayed in the United States. They would exercise freedom and learn Christian and republican ways only if exported to Liberia. Among the favored fundraising sites for the ACS were July 4 celebrations—festivities from which blacks were excluded.

Free blacks had agitated against slavery and legal racism for many years, demanding both abolition and equal rights. While a few sailed to Liberia, most insisted that colonization was not an offer of freedom but an attempt to round up black people and make them disappear. The black abolitionist James Forten spoke for many when he insisted that colonization "originated more immediately from prejudice than from philanthropy." Opposition to colonization created an immediatist, confrontational black antislavery movement—a movement that decisively shaped the later abolition crusade.

12-4c *Abolitionists*

Few white Americans actively opposed slavery before 1830, but the writing was on the wall. Emancipation in the North constituted an implicit condemnation of slavery in the South. So did events outside the United States. Toussaint L'Ouverture's successful slave revolution in Saint-Domingue threatened slavery everywhere (see Chapter 7). Mexico, Peru, Chile, Gran Colombia (present-day Colombia, Venezuela, Ecuador, and Panama), and other new republics carved out of the Spanish mainland empire emancipated their slaves. The British, whose navy could enforce their dictates at sea, outlawed the Atlantic slave trade in 1808, and the United States followed suit. The most powerful blow came in 1830, when the British Parliament emancipated the slaves of Jamaica, Bermuda, and other Caribbean islands ruled by Britain.

Historians usually date American **abolitionism** from 1831, when the veteran reformer **William Lloyd Garrison** published the first issue of the *Liberator* in Boston. Garrison condemned slavery not simply as a social problem or a bad idea but as America's great national sin. He demanded immediate emancipation and equal citizenship for African Americans. "I am in earnest," he declared in his first editorial. "I will not equivocate—I will not excuse—I will not retreat a single inch—and I will be heard!" Garrison opposed discrimination as well as slavery, thus coupling southern slavery with the national question of race. From the beginning, he enjoyed the support and influence of northern free blacks. In its first year fully three-fourths of the *Liberator*'s subscribers and one-fifth of its writers were black, and when Garrison and his coworkers formed the New England Anti-Slavery Society in 1832 blacks made up one-fourth of the membership. Black orators such as Frederick Douglass and Sojourner Truth became stars of a well-organized abolitionist lecture circuit, and the heartfelt autobiographies of escaped slaves (many of them "as told to" white abolitionists) were mainstays of abolitionist literature, steering the movement away from the legalism of the colonizationists and toward personal, emotional appeals. When the wealthy abolitionist Gerrit Smith harbored the fugitive slave Harriet Powell on his estate, he invited his friends to meet her. He told Powell to "make good abolitionists of them by telling them the story of your life."

Abolitionists proposed not only emancipation but also racial equality. Assuming that God had created blacks and whites as members of one human family, they opposed the "scientific" racism spouted by Democrats and many Whigs. Moderates and latecomers to the movement spoke of inherent racial characteristics, but still tended to view blacks in benign (if condescending) ways. Harriet Beecher Stowe, for instance, portrayed blacks as simple, innocent, loving people who possessed a capacity for sentiment and emotionalism that most whites had lost. In 1852, Horace Mann told an audience

12.8 **The Resurrection of Henry Box Brown** One of the most resourceful of escaped slaves was Henry Brown of Richmond. Distraught at the sale of his wife and children, in 1849 he paid a white storekeeper to ship him as "dry goods" to James Miller McKim, a well-known abolitionist in Philadelphia. Brown was nailed into a small shipping crate and, after moving by two freight wagons, two trains, and a steamboat on which he was packed upside down, he arrived at McKim's house in free territory. He became a hero to abolitionists, who renamed him "Box" Brown. Afraid of recapture, he moved to England.

Interpreting the Visual Past

An Abolitionist View of Southern Society

This provocative woodcut appeared in the *Anti-Slavery Almanac for 1840* (Boston, 1839). At the center, a southern mob lynches slaves and their abolitionist allies. Surrounding the hanging tree are men (there are no women in the picture) engaged in other activities that northern reformers insisted grew from the brutality and despotism of southern society. Men duel with pistols and knives, others engage in a no-holds-barred wrestling match, others gamble and get drunk, and still others cheer for (and bet on) cockfights and horse races. At one corner of the picture, a white man tortures a slave by drawing a cat's claws down his back. At the other corner, a white master whips a slave child. The enemy here is not simply slavery but the debauchery and unbridled passions that abolitionists associated with it.

Q *Compare this with the photo on page 258. Both pictures are extreme overstatements, but they overstate their cases in different ways. Why do you think a southern apologist and a northern abolitionist chose these specific ways to portray the same society? Why do white women and children appear in the southern picture? Why are they absent in the abolitionist portrayal? Why is the southern picture set in a domestic environment? Why are all traces of family life absent from the abolitionist portrayal?*

12.9 **Anti-Slavery Almanac for 1840, "The peculiar Domestic Institutions of our Southern brethren," Boston, 1839.**

of blacks in Ohio that "in intellect, the blacks are inferior to the whites, while in sentiment and affections, the whites are inferior to the blacks." Radical abolitionists, however, remained committed to racial equality. Lydia Maria Child of New York City declared, "In the United States, colored persons have scarcely any chance to rise. But if colored persons are well treated, and have the same inducements to industry as others, they [will] work as well and behave as well." The abolitionists backed up their equalitarian rhetoric with successful campaigns against segregation in Boston's schools and public transportation, and against legal bans on miscegenation. Most of their fellow citizens disliked the abolitionists—not only because their attack upon slavery threatened the Union and the party system that held it together, but because their integrated movement and their anti-racist campaigns undermined the white republic.

The radicalized abolitionists were a combination of old and new reformers. Some of them—Wendell Phillips, Thomas Wentworth Higginson, Theodore Parker—were cultivated Bostonians who opposed slavery as an affront to reason and humanity. Others were Quakers—the poet John Greenleaf Whittier, the lay minister Lucretia Mott, and many more—who added their antislavery experience and convictions to the cause. Abolitionists found their greatest support, however, in southern New England, western New York, northern Ohio, and among the new middle classes of the cities—ground that Yankee settlement, the Market Revolution, and Finneyite revivals had turned into the heartland of the northern Whig Party.

It was also the center of the new evangelical domesticity, and of the questioning of traditional roles for women and men. Women from evangelical families participated in church affairs and in the temperance movement, and the more radical of them moved into abolitionism. The American Colonization Society and other early antislavery societies were largely elite and entirely male and they made male arguments: Slavery, they said, was economically and socially irrational and dangerous. Abolitionists, on the other hand, enrolled blacks, women, and white men who questioned the old rigidities of gender and race. They attacked slavery on moral grounds, and their appeals were unabashedly emotional. Abolitionist speeches, pamphlets, and escaped-slave narratives attacked slavery less for its supposed irrationality as a labor system than for what it did to slaves. The crucial argument, repeated over and over, was that slavery crushed the family, and particularly the sentimental relation between mothers and small children.

This argument reached its culmination in Harriet Beecher Stowe's *Uncle Tom's Cabin*, which was first published in installments in an antislavery newspaper. When published as a book in 1852, it became the most powerful antislavery tract, in part because it successfully dramatized the moral and political imperatives of the northern middle class. At its core, **Uncle Tom's Cabin** indicts slavery as a system of absolute power at odds with domesticity and Christian love. The novel reverses the power relations of this world: In it, the home, and particularly the kitchen, is the ultimate locus of good, whereas law, politics, and the marketplace—the whole realm of white men—are moved to the periphery and defined as unfeeling destroyers. Based solidly in revival Christianity, the novel lambasts the rational calculation, greed, and power-hunger of the "real world" that was made and governed by white men and upholds the domestic space filled with women, slaves, and children who gain spiritual power through submission to Christ. The two most telling scenes—the deaths of the Christian slave Uncle Tom and the perfect child Eva St. Claire—reenact the crucifixion of Jesus. Uncle Tom prays for his tormentors as he is beaten to death, and little Eva extracts promises of Christian behavior from her deathbed. Both are powerless, submissive characters who die in order to redeem a fallen humankind. Their deaths are thus Christian triumphs that convert the powerful and hasten the millennial day when the world will be governed by a feminized Christian love and not by male power.

12-4d *Agitation*

Antislavery, unlike other reforms, was a radical attack on one of the nation's central institutions, and the movement attracted a minority even among middle-class evangelicals. Both Lyman Beecher and Charles Finney opposed the abolitionists in the 1830s, arguing that emancipation would come about sooner or later through the religious conversion of slave owners; antislavery agitation and the denunciation of slaveholders, they argued, would divide Christians, slow the revival movement, and thus actually delay emancipation. Finney warned his abolitionist friend Theodore Dwight Weld that the logical end of antislavery was civil war. Other opponents, including some within the antislavery ranks, were outraged that blacks and whites and men and women met, organized, and socialized together, and that women and blacks delivered speeches to mixed audiences. When the American Antislavery Society held an organizing convention in Philadelphia in 1833, the city's hotels, churches, and meeting halls refused to admit its members, and the police announced that they could not protect "the amalgamationist conclave." Most of the delegates boarded in black households, and they met in a black-owned hall next door to Philadelphia's oldest black church.

Radical abolitionists knew that they were a small, despised minority, and that government and most citizens wanted to ignore the question of slavery. The abolitionists staged a series of campaigns to force government and the public to face the South's "peculiar institution." In 1835, the society launched its **Postal Campaign** and then deluged Congress with petitions to curtail slavery (see Chapter 11). Two-thirds of the signers of these petitions were women, prompting a Mississippi senator to declare that there would be less trouble "if the ladies and Sunday school children would let us alone."

From the beginnings of antislavery agitation, the public response was often violent. Riots aimed at blacks and their white friends exploded in nearly every northern city. Mobs destroyed black neighborhoods in New York and Philadelphia. A mob surrounded a convention of the Boston Female Anti-slavery Society in 1835, forced the women to leave, then went looking for Garrison. Garrison was roughed up, but then he escaped the mob by going

The Granger Collection, NYC

12.10 **Woman and a Sister** For many years, the British antislavery forces had used the iconic image of a male slave, kneeling and holding up his chains, with the words "Am I not a man and a brother?" American abolitionists used that image as well, but added a similar image of a supplicant female slave, underlining the participation of women and the emerging centrality of women's issues in the American antislavery movement.

into police custody, where he was charged with disturbing the peace. In July 1834, a New York City mob sacked the house of the white abolitionist merchant Lewis Tappan; moved on to the Reverend Charles Finney's Chatham Street Chapel, where abolitionists were said to be meeting, and finished the evening by attacking a British (and thus supposedly aristocratic) actor at the Bowery theater. The manager saved his theater by waving two American flags and ordering an American actor to perform popular minstrel routines for the mob. Democracy and working-class aspirations—not to mention local authorities—were in league with racism.

Southern whites had fewer free blacks or abolitionists to attack, but they found their own ways to respond. A crowd in Charleston rushed the post office, removed anti-slavery literature that was held there, and made a bonfire at the center of town. A committee in Mississippi invited Garrison and other antislavery leaders to come south and be hanged. In Congress, southerners and their northern friends forced President Jackson to permit southern postal workers to censor the mails. They also forced Democrats and southern Whigs to adopt the gag rule, abridging the right of petition to avoid discussion of slavery in Congress (see Chapter 11).

In these ways, abolitionists demonstrated the complicity of the party system (and the Democrats in particular) in the institution of slavery. They brought the slavery question to public attention and tied it to questions of civil liberties in the North and political power nationally. They thus threw light on the compromises with slavery that made the United States possible, and they undermined the white republic at its foundations. Moreover, they did all that with an active, public membership that included prominent women and blacks. The abolitionists were a dangerous minority indeed.

12-5 The Politics of Gender and Sex

How did Democrats and Whigs differ on questions of gender and sex? Knowing what you know about the political cultures of the two parties, how do you explain those differences?

Whigs valued a reformed masculinity that was lived out in the sentimentalized homes of the northern business classes or in the Christian gentility of the Whig plantation and farm. Jacksonian voters defended domestic patriarchy. Whereas most were unimaginative paternalists, Democrats often made heroes of men whose flamboyant, rakish lives directly challenged Whig domesticity. Whigs denounced Andrew Jackson for allegedly stealing his wife from her lawful husband; Democrats often admired him for the same reason. Richard M. Johnson of Kentucky, who was vice president under Martin Van Buren, openly kept a mulatto mistress and had two daughters by her; with his pistols always at hand, he accompanied her around Washington, D.C. "Prince" John Van Buren, the president's son and a prominent New York Democrat, met a "dark-eyed, well-formed Italian lady," who called herself Amerigo Vespucci and claimed to be a direct descendant of the man for whom America was named. She became young Van Buren's "fancy lady," remaining with him until he lost her in a high-stakes card game.

Whigs made Democratic contempt for sentimental domesticity a political issue. William Crane, a Michigan Whig, claimed that Democrats "despised no man for his sins," and went on to say that "brothel-haunters flocked to this party, because here in all political circles, and political movements, they were treated as nobility." Much of the Whig cultural agenda (and much of Democratic hatred of that agenda) was rooted in contests between Whig and Democratic masculine styles.

12-5a *Moral Reform*

Sexual self-control became a badge of middle-class status. Men supposedly had the greatest difficulty taming their appetites. The old image—beginning with Eve and including Delilah and Jezebel and other dangerous women of the Old Testament—of woman as seductress persisted in the more traditionalist churches and in the pulp fiction from which middle-class mothers tried to protect their sons (see Chapter 10). Whig evangelicals, on the other hand, believed that women were naturally free of desire and that only men were subject to the animal passions. "What terrible temptations lie in the way of your sex," wrote Harriet Beecher Stowe to her husband. "Tho I did love you with an almost insane love before I married you, I never knew yet or felt the pulsation which showed me that I could be tempted in that way. I loved you as I now love God." The middle-class ideal combined female purity and male self-control. For the most part, it was a private reform, contained within the home. Sometimes, however, evangelical domesticity produced moral crusades to impose that ethos on the world at large. Many of these crusades were led by women from Whig families.

In 1828, a band of Sunday school teachers, most of them women, initiated an informal mission to prostitutes that grew into the **New York Magdalen Society**. Taking a novel approach to an age-old question, the society argued that prostitution was created by brutal fathers and husbands who abandoned their young daughters or wives, by dandies who seduced them and turned them into prostitutes, and by lustful men who bought their services. Prostitution, in other words, was not the result of the innate sinfulness of prostitutes; it was the result of the brutality and lust of men. The solution was to separate prostitutes from bad male power, pray with them, and convert them to middle-class morality.

The Magdalen Society's *First Annual Report* (1831) inveighed against male lust and printed shocking life histories of prostitutes. Some men, however, read it as pornography. Others used it as a guidebook to the seamier side of New York City. The wealthy male evangelicals who had bankrolled the Magdalen Society withdrew their support, and the organization fell apart. Thereupon many of the women reformers set up the Female Moral Reform Society, with a House of Industry in which prostitutes were taught morality and household skills to prepare them for new lives as domestic servants in pious middle-class homes. This effort also failed, largely because few prostitutes were interested in domestic service or evangelical religion. That fact became distressingly clear when in 1836 the society was obliged to close its House of Industry after the residents had taken it over during the caretaker's absence.

The Female Moral Reform Society was more successful with members of its own class. Its newspaper, the *Advocate of Moral Reform*, circulated throughout the evangelical North, eventually reaching 555 auxiliary societies with 20,000 readers. Now evangelical women fought prostitution by publishing the names of customers. They campaigned against pornography, obscenity, lewdness, and seduction and taught their sons to be pure, even when it meant dragging them out of brothels. Occasionally, they prosecuted men who took advantage of servant girls. They also publicized the names of adulterers, and they had seducers brought into court. In the process, women reformers fought the sexual double standard and assumed the power to define what was respectable and what was not.

12-5b *Women's Rights*

From the late 1820s onward, middle-class women in the North assumed roles that would have been unthinkable to their mothers and grandmothers. Evangelical domesticity made loving mothers (and not stern fathers) the principal rearers of children. Housewives saw themselves as missionaries to their families, influencing the moral choices their children and husbands made. In that role, women became arbiters of fashion, diet, and sexual behavior. Many joined the temperance movement and moral reform societies, where they became public reformers while posing as mothers protecting their sons from rum sellers and seducers. They gained a sense of spiritual empowerment that led some to question their own subordinate status within a system of gendered social roles. Lydia Maria Child, a writer of sentimental fiction and manuals on household economy as well as a leading abolitionist and moral reformer, proclaimed, "Those who urged women to become missionaries and form tract societies ... have changed the household utensil to a living, energetic being, and they have no spell to turn it into a broom again."

Nearly all early feminists, like Child, were veterans of the antislavery crusade. Abolitionists, following the perfectionist implications of Whig evangelicalism to their logical ends, called for absolute human equality and a near-anarchist rejection of impersonal institutions and prescribed social roles. It became clear to some female abolitionists that the critique of slavery (a root-and-branch denunciation of patriarchy and prescribed hierarchy) applied as well to inequality based on sex.

Radical female abolitionists reached the conclusion that they were human beings first and women second. In 1837, **Sarah Grimke** announced, "The Lord Jesus defines the duties of his followers in his Sermon on the Mount ... without any reference to sex or condition ... never even referring to the distinction now so strenuously insisted upon between masculine and feminine virtues... . Men and women are CREATED EQUAL! They are both moral and accountable beings, and whatever is right for a man to do is right for woman."

Such talk—and worse, the fact that women were delivering such speeches in public—aroused opposition even among abolitionists. In 1840, the American Antislavery Society sent a delegation to an international convention in London—with women delegates and the woman abolitionist Abbey Kelley on the business committee. The convention voted to exclude women, and the Americans came home angry and divided. Garrison and the radicals supported full rights for women and published their speeches and writings in the *Liberator*. Others wished to win public favor for antislavery issues and argued that the woman question was at best a distraction. The result was a split in the antislavery crusade, largely over the question of women's rights, and intensification of the feminist movement.

Beginning about 1840, women lobbied state legislatures against the common-law custom that women and children were under the protection and authority of their husbands and fathers, and thus had limited rights to property and over themselves. The reformers won significant changes in the laws governing women's rights to own and inherit property, to keep the wages of their own labor, and to retain custody of children in cases of divorce. Fourteen northern states passed such legislation, culminating in New York's wide-ranging Married Women's Property Act in 1860.

The first Woman's Rights Convention met in Seneca Falls, New York, in 1848. The busiest organizer of the convention was **Elizabeth Cady Stanton**, wife of the abolitionist Henry B. Stanton and an attendee at the London convention of 1840. Stanton was a lukewarm abolitionist, but the argument over women in the movement drove her into full-time feminism. Along with other feminist abolitionists, she organized the **Seneca Falls Convention**. The only male delegate was the black abolitionist Frederick Douglass. Sojourner Truth, another prominent black opponent of slavery, also attended. Nearly all of the other delegates were white women abolitionists. Both as abolitionists and as feminists, they based their demands for equality not only on legal and moral arguments but also on the spirit of republican institutions. The principal formal document issued by the convention, a Declaration of Sentiments and Resolutions based on the Declaration of Independence, denounced "the repeated injuries and usurpations on the part of man toward woman."

Most of those "injuries and usurpations" were political. The central issue was the right to vote. Lucretia Mott and other Quaker delegates, along with many Garrisonian abolitionists, did not want a *political* movement. ("Lizzy," Mott chided Stanton, "thee will make us ridiculous.") But Stanton believed

History Through Film *Not for Ourselves Alone* (1999)

Directed by Ken Burns (PBS).

In 1999, Ken Burns made a documentary film on the women's rights movement. Part One tells the story from about 1840 through the Civil War. It is vintage Ken Burns: old photographs scanned to give them the appearance of movies, period documents read over the pictures by actors (in this case, Sally Kellerman), modern-day experts speaking with authority, the same period music that Burns used in *The Civil War* and his other forays into the 19th century, and the same undercurrent of sentimentality. The film focuses on the collaboration and friendship between Susan B. Anthony and Elizabeth Cady Stanton, and through that medium and within its limits, it tells its story well.

Elizabeth Cady Stanton was descended, on her mother's side, from one of the great landholding families of colonial New York. Her father was a prosperous lawyer and judge. Young Elizabeth hungered for education, but no American college admitted women. She enrolled at Emma Willard's Female Seminary in Troy, New York, and shared her family's interest in the temperance and antislavery movements. She met lawyer and well-known antislavery speaker Henry B. Stanton through her cousin, wealthy abolitionist Gerrit Smith, and married Stanton in 1840. (Elizabeth excised the word "obey" from the ceremony.) The Stantons honeymooned at an antislavery convention in London that year. Organizers of the convention segregated women and men and forbade the women to speak. Stanton realized—as legions of women would realize—that the logic of antislavery applied to women as well as slaves, and that rights reform that was less than universal was badly flawed. The Stantons took up housekeeping in Boston, then moved to Seneca Falls in western New York. Henry Stanton was frequently away on lecture tours, and Elizabeth stayed at home, had babies, and grew weary of housework.

In 1848, after a visit with her friend and fellow activist Lucretia Mott, she helped organize the first Woman's Rights Convention in Seneca Falls. She authored the declaration demanding civil and legal equality for women, including the demand (truly shocking to contemporaries) that women be allowed to vote. Shortly after the Seneca Falls Convention, Stanton met Susan B. Anthony, another veteran reformer. Anthony, a Quaker, had been born into much humbler circumstances than Stanton, remained unmarried, and often upbraided other women reformers for marrying and having children. The differences between Stanton and Anthony added up to a lifelong collaboration: The educated and housebound Stanton wrote the manifestos, and the brave and unencumbered Anthony took them into lecture halls and the state legislature. They and their coworkers won some battles (in the area of women's property rights in particular), but could do little more than publicize their radical demands for the legal reform of marriage and for civil and political equality. This limitation became painfully clear during the Civil War, when their fellow reformers told Stanton and Anthony to delay women's rights while slaves were freed and given the same rights for which the women's movement had fought. At the close of Part One, women's civil and legal equality remain far from realization.

Not For Ourselves Alone tells a familiar story clearly and entertainingly. Along the way, it portrays a friendship between women within the antebellum reform community and (intermittently) throws light on the workings of a reform culture that enlisted much of the zeal and intellect of the antebellum North. ■

12.11 *Not For Ourselves Alone* focuses on the long friendship between Elizabeth Cady Stanton and Susan B. Anthony to tell the story of the early women's rights movement.

What They Said

Making Fun of Women's Rights

In 1848, delegates to the first women's rights convention issued a Declaration of Sentiments modeled on the Declaration of Independence. Here is their list of demands (as reported in the *New York Herald*, 30 July 1848):

The history of mankind is a history of repeated injuries and usurpations on the part of man toward woman, having in direct object the establishment of an absolute tyranny over her. To prove this, let fact be submitted to a candid world.

He has never permitted her to exercise her ... right to the elective franchise.

He has compelled her to submit to laws in the formation of which she has had no voice.

...having deprived her of this first right of citizens, the elective franchise, thereby leaving her without representation in the halls of legislation, he has oppressed her on all sides.

He has made her, if married, in the eyes of the law, civilly dead.

He has taken from her all right in property, even to the wages she earns.

...in the covenant of marriage, she is compelled to promise obedience to her husband—he becoming, to all intents and purposes, her master—the law giving him power to deprive her of her liberty, and to administer chastisement.

...he has monopolized nearly all the means of profitable employment, and from those she is permitted to follow, she receives but a paltry remuneration.

He closes against her all the avenues to wealth and distinction which he considers most honorable to himself. As a teacher of theology, medicine or law, she is not known.

He has denied her the facilities for obtaining a thorough education—all colleges being closed against her.

...he has created a false public sentiment by giving to the world a different code of morals for men and women, by which moral delinquencies which exclude woman from society are not only tolerated but deemed of little account in men.

He has usurped the prerogative of Jehovah himself, claiming it as his right to assign for her a sphere of action, when that belongs to her conscience and her God.

In 1856, the New York legislature received petitions making the same complaints and demanding the same rights. Here is the legislature's response (as reported in the Plattsburgh Republican, 29 March 1856):

Judge Foote, of Ontario, the learned chairman of the Assembly Judiciary Committee, last week made a report on "Women's Rights" that set the whole House in roars of laughter.... [The committee has] left the subject pretty much to the married gentlemen. They have considered it with the aid of the ... experience married life has given them. Thus, aided they are enabled to state, that ladies always have the best piece, and choicest titbit at table—They have the best seat in the cars, carriages and sleighs; the warmest place in winter and the coolest place in summer. They have their choice on which side of the bed they will lie.... A lady's dress costs three times as much as that of a gentleman; and at the present time, with the prevailing fashion, one lady occupies three times as much space in the world as a gentleman. It has thus appeared to the married gentlemen of our committee ... that if there is any inequality or oppression in the case, the gentlemen are the sufferers. They, however, have presented no petitions for redress, having doubtless made up their minds to yield to an inevitable destiny.

On the whole, the committee have concluded to recommend no measure, except, that as they have observed several instances in which husband and wife have both signed the same petition. In such case, they would recommend the party to apply for a law authorizing them to change dresses, so that the husband may wear the petty coats, and, the wife the breeches, and thus indicate to their neighbors, and the public the true relation in which they stand to each other.

Q *Why did the women use the Declaration of Independence as a model, and why did they begin their list of demands with the rights of citizenship?*

Q *At this time the idea of political, legal, and civil equality between women and men was, for the great majority of Americans, unthinkable. This was grounded in the cultural axiom that there were separate spheres of activity prescribed for the sexes by nature and God. Can you explain the antics of the legislature in terms of that cultural axiom?*

Q *How would the women of Seneca Falls have responded to the legislature's statements?*

Sources: (top) *New York Herald*, 30 July 1848; (bottom) *Plattsburgh Republican*, 29 March 1856.

12.12 **Elizabeth Cady Stanton with Two of Her Three Sons** Suffragist, social activist, and abolitionist, Stanton wrote, "The prejudice against color, of which we hear so much, is no stronger than that against sex. It is produced by the same cause, and manifested very much the same way. The negro's skin and the woman's sex are *prima facie* evidence that they were intended to be in subjection to the white Saxon man."

Q *Why did Stanton juxtapose racial slavery and women's status and abolitionist and suffragist movements?*

that political rights—voting in particular—were crucial. Voting was central to the "democratic" pattern that granted liberty and equality to white men regardless of class and excluded Americans who were not white and male. Thus, female participation in politics was a direct challenge to a male-ordained women's place. A distraught New York legislator agreed: "It is well known that the object of these unsexed women is to overthrow the most sacred of our institutions... . Are we to put the stamp of truth upon the libel here set forth, that men and women, in the matrimonial relation, are to be equal?" Later, Elizabeth Cady Stanton recalled such reactions: "Political rights," she said, "involving in their last results equality everywhere, roused all the antagonism of a dominant power, against the self-assertion of a class hitherto subservient."

Conclusion

By the 1830s, most citizens firmly identified with either the Whig or Democratic Party, so much so that party affiliation was a big part of personal identity. In the states and neighborhoods, Whigs embraced commerce and activist government, arguing that both would foster prosperity, social harmony, and moral progress. Faith in progress and improvement led northern and western Whigs, primarily the more radical evangelicals among them, to imagine that liberty and equality might apply to women and blacks as well as white men. The Democratic response to this was grounded in a defense of white patriarchy and the Old Republic. Like the Whigs, they did not doubt the value of commerce. But they worried that the market and its infrastructure of banking, credit, and paper money—all of it subsidized by government—forced inequality upon the white male citizenry and corrupted the republic. Democrats also looked with angry disbelief at attempts of Whigs (and rebellious members of Whig families) to govern private and public behavior, and sometimes even to attack the "natural" and fundamental distinctions of sex and race.

Whigs reformulated the revolutionary legacy of liberty and equality, moving away from classical notions of citizenship and toward liberty of conscience and equality of opportunity within a market-driven democracy. They often attempted to civilize that new world by using government power to encourage commerce, social interdependence, cultural homogeneity, and moral uplift. Democrats trusted none of that. Theirs was a Jeffersonian formulation grounded in a fierce defense of the liberty and equality of white men, and in a minimal, inexpensive, decentralized government that protected the liberties of those men without threatening their independence or their power over their households and within their neighborhoods. That was the fundamental political argument in the United States from the 1820s to the 1850s, and, for all its noise and uproar, it underwrote a party system that was outwardly stable and safe. But with the rise of antislavery and the acquisition of new territory, the political system was forced to address questions that the parties could not control.

CHAPTER REVIEW

Review

1. What were Whig and Democratic conceptions of the duties and limits of government?
2. What were Whig and Democratic positions on the issues of public schools, prisons, and asylums?
3. Trace the history of alcohol as a social and political question from the 1820s through the 1840s. Which Americans favored temperance? Which opposed it?

4. How did Whigs and Democrats differ on questions of slavery and race?
5. How did Democrats and Whigs differ on questions of gender and sex? Knowing what you know about the political cultures of the two parties, how do you explain those differences?

Critical Thinking

1. Choose a position either defending or attacking this statement: "Differences between Whigs and Democrats on economic policy, social reform, race, and gender boil down to differences in Whig and Democratic conceptions of white manhood."
2. What were the goals and assumptions that drove the movements for public schools, humane prisons and asylums, and temperance? Were those primarily Democratic or Whig assumptions?

Identifications

Review your understanding of the following key terms, people, and events for this chapter (terms in bold in text are included in the Glossary).

limited liability, p. 333
common schools, p. 334
normal schools, p. 335
Auburn system, p. 336
Dorothea Dix, p. 337
American Temperance Society, p. 338
Washington Temperance Society, p. 340
American Colonization Society, p. 342
abolitionism, p. 343
William Lloyd Garrison, p. 343
Uncle Tom's Cabin, p. 345
Postal Campaign, p. 345
New York Magdalen Society, p. 346
Sarah Grimke, p. 347
Elizabeth Cady Stanton, p. 347
Seneca Falls Convention, p. 347

Suggested Readings

On state-level internal improvements, see **John Majewski,** ***A House Divided: Economic Development in Pennsylvania and Virginia before the Civil War*** (2000). An entertaining introduction to money and banking is **Stephen Mihm,** ***A Nation of Counterfeiters: Capitalists, Con Men, and the Making of the United States*** (2007). **Carl F. Kaestle,** ***Pillars of the Republic: Common Schools and American Society, 1780–1860*** (1983), surveys the politics of schools. Influential studies of prisons and asylums include **David J. Rothman,** ***The Discovery of the Asylum: Social Order and Disorder in the New Republic*** (1971); **Michael Meranze,** ***Laboratories of Virtue: Punishment, Revolution, and Authority in Philadelphia, 1760–1835*** (1996); and **Thomas J. Brown,** ***Dorothea Dix: New England Reformer*** (1998). Drinking and temperance are the subjects of **W. J. Rorabaugh,** ***The Alcoholic Republic: An American Tradition*** (1979). **Christine Sismondo's** ***America Walks into a Bar: A Spirited History of Taverns and Saloons, Speakeasies and Grog Shops*** (2011) traces the centrality of bars and taverns in American social and political life. The literature on reform movements is synthesized in **Steven Mintz,** ***Moralists & Modernizers: America's Pre-Civil War Reformers*** (1995), which can be supplemented by **Bruce Dorsey,** ***Reforming Men & Women: Gender in the Antebellum City*** (2002) and **Richard S. Newman,** ***The Transformation of American Abolitionism: Fighting Slavery in the Early Republic*** (2002). See also **Robert H. Abzug,** ***Cosmos Crumbling: American Reform and the Religious Imagination*** (1994); **John W. Quist,** ***Restless Visionaries: The Social Roots of Antebellum Reform in Alabama and Michigan*** (1998); **Lori D. Ginzberg,** ***Women and the Work of Benevolence: Morality, Politics, and Class in the 19th-Century United States*** (1990); and **Ginzberg,** ***Elizabeth Cady Stanton: An American Life*** (2009). The cultural and moral underpinnings of reform are a subtext of **Karen Halttunen's** subtle and important ***Murder Most Foul: The Killer and the American Gothic Imagination*** (1998). **Sally G. McMillen's** ***Seneca Falls and the Origins of the Women's Rights Movement*** (2008) is an incisive and accessible study of the Seneca Falls convention, and **Jean H. Baker's** ***Sisters: The Lives of America Suffragists*** (2005) traces the rise of women's rights movement through the lives and experiences of individual women.

13 Manifest Destiny: An Empire for Liberty—or Slavery? 1845–1860

AP Images/National Portrait Gallery

13.1 ***War News from Mexico*** Richard Caton Woodville's 1848 painting captures the excitement felt by some Americans as they read newspaper accounts of the Mexican War (1846–1848). But notice that the African American man and child, dressed in rags, are not part of the celebratory group gathered on the porch of the allegorical "American Hotel," although they appear interested in the war news. The painting reminds us that an underlying question of the Mexican War was whether slavery would be extended into new territory; it also reminds us that African Americans were not equal members of the American nation. At the far right we can see that an old woman peers out the window to see what is going on; she, too, is not part of the main group at the heart of the painting—just as women were not yet voting citizens of the American republic. The strong narrative thrust of Woodville's painting marks it as one of many "genre paintings" that in the 1830s, 1840s, and 1850s depicted ordinary Americans and often told allegorical stories of daily life and politics.

THE UNITED STATES became a transcontinental nation between 1845 and 1848, increasing in size by 50 percent. Through annexation, negotiation, and war, the United States gained more than 1 million square miles, with western migration and settlement playing an important role in making this territorial acquisition desirable. Many Americans enthusiastically supported expansionism and celebrated the creation of an American empire. But expansionism aroused opposition as well. On both sides of the debate, the nation's politicians and citizens worried over an increasingly fraught question: Was this new empire for liberty—or for slavery? The acquisition of vast new stretches of land reopened the issue of slavery's expansion and planted the bitter seeds of civil war. ■

CHRONOLOGY

1844	Senate rejects Texas annexation • James K. Polk elected president
1845	Congress annexes Texas • Mexico spurns U.S. bid to buy California and New Mexico
1846	United States declares war on Mexico • United States and Britain settle Oregon boundary dispute • United States occupies California and New Mexico • House passes Wilmot Proviso • U.S. forces under Zachary Taylor capture Monterrey, Mexico
1847	Americans win Battle of Buena Vista • U.S. Army under Winfield Scott lands at Veracruz • Mexico City falls
1848	Treaty of Guadalupe Hidalgo ends Mexican War, fixes Rio Grande as border, cedes New Mexico and California to United States • Gold discovered in California • Spain spurns Polk's offer of $100 million for Cuba • Zachary Taylor elected president
1849	John C. Calhoun pens "Address of the Southern Delegates" • California seeks admission as a free state
1850	Taylor dies; Millard Fillmore becomes president • Bitter sectional debate culminates in Compromise of 1850 • Fugitive Slave Law empowers federal commissioners to recover escaped slaves
1851	Fugitive Slave Law provokes rescues and violent conflict in North • American filibusters executed in Cuba
1852	*Uncle Tom's Cabin* becomes best seller • Franklin Pierce elected president
1854	Anthony Burns returned from Boston to slavery • William Walker's filibusters invade Nicaragua • Pierce tries to buy Cuba • Ostend Manifesto issued
1856	William Walker legalizes slavery in Nicaragua
1860	William Walker executed in Honduras

13-1 Growth as the American Way

What impulses lay behind the "Manifest Destiny" of America's westward expansion?

By 1850, older Americans had seen the area of the United States quadruple in their lifetime. Since the Louisiana Purchase of 1803, the American population had also quadrupled. Many Americans in 1850 considered this evidence of God's beneficence to this virtuous republic. During the 1840s, a group of expansionists affiliated with the Democratic Party began to call themselves the **Young America movement**. They proclaimed that it was the **Manifest Destiny** of the United States "to overspread and to possess the whole of the continent which Providence has given us for the development of the great experiment of liberty," as John L. O'Sullivan, editor of the *Democratic Review*, wrote in 1845.

For Native Americans, however, Manifest Destiny was a story of defeat and contraction. By 1850, the diseases and guns first introduced by whites had reduced the Indian population north of the Rio Grande to fewer than half a million, a fraction of the population of two or three centuries earlier. The relentless westward march of white settlements had pushed all but a few thousand Indians beyond the Mississippi. In the 1840s, the U.S. government decided to create a "permanent Indian frontier" at about the 95th meridian (roughly the western borders of Iowa, Missouri, and Arkansas). But white emigrants were already violating that frontier on the overland trails to the Pacific, and settlers were pressing against the borders of Indian Territory. In little more than a decade, the idea of "one big reservation" in the West would give way to the policy of forcing Indians onto small reservations. The government "negotiated" with Indian chiefs for vast cessions of land in return for annuity payments that were often extracted by shrewd or corrupt traders. Many Indians perished of disease, malnutrition, and alcohol—first introduced by whites—and in futile efforts to break out of the reservations and regain their land.

13-1a *Manifest Destiny and Slavery*

By 1846, the empire for liberty that Thomas Jefferson had envisioned for the Louisiana Purchase seemed more an empire for slavery. Territorial acquisitions since 1803 had brought into the republic the slave states of Louisiana, Missouri, Arkansas, Florida, Texas, and parts of Alabama and Mississippi. Only Iowa, admitted in 1846, had joined the ranks of the free states.

Although the division between slavery and freedom in the rest of the Louisiana Purchase had supposedly been settled by the Compromise of 1820, the expansion of slavery into new territories instead became an explosive issue (see Map 13.1). The issue first arose with the annexation of Texas, which helped provoke war with Mexico in 1846—a war that many antislavery northerners considered an ugly effort to expand slavery.

13-1b *The Expansionist Impulse*

Many Americans of European descent saw their future in the West. In the 1840s, newspaper editor Horace Greeley urged, "Go west, young man." And to the West they went in unprecedented numbers, driven in part by the depression of 1837–1843 that prompted thousands to search for cheap land and better opportunity.

An earlier wave of migration had populated the region between the Appalachians and the Missouri River, bringing a new state into the Union on an average of every three years. Reports from explorers, fur traders, missionaries, and sailors filtered back from California and the Pacific Northwest, describing the bounteous resources and benign climates of those wondrous regions. Guidebooks rolled off the presses describing the boundless prospects that awaited settlers who

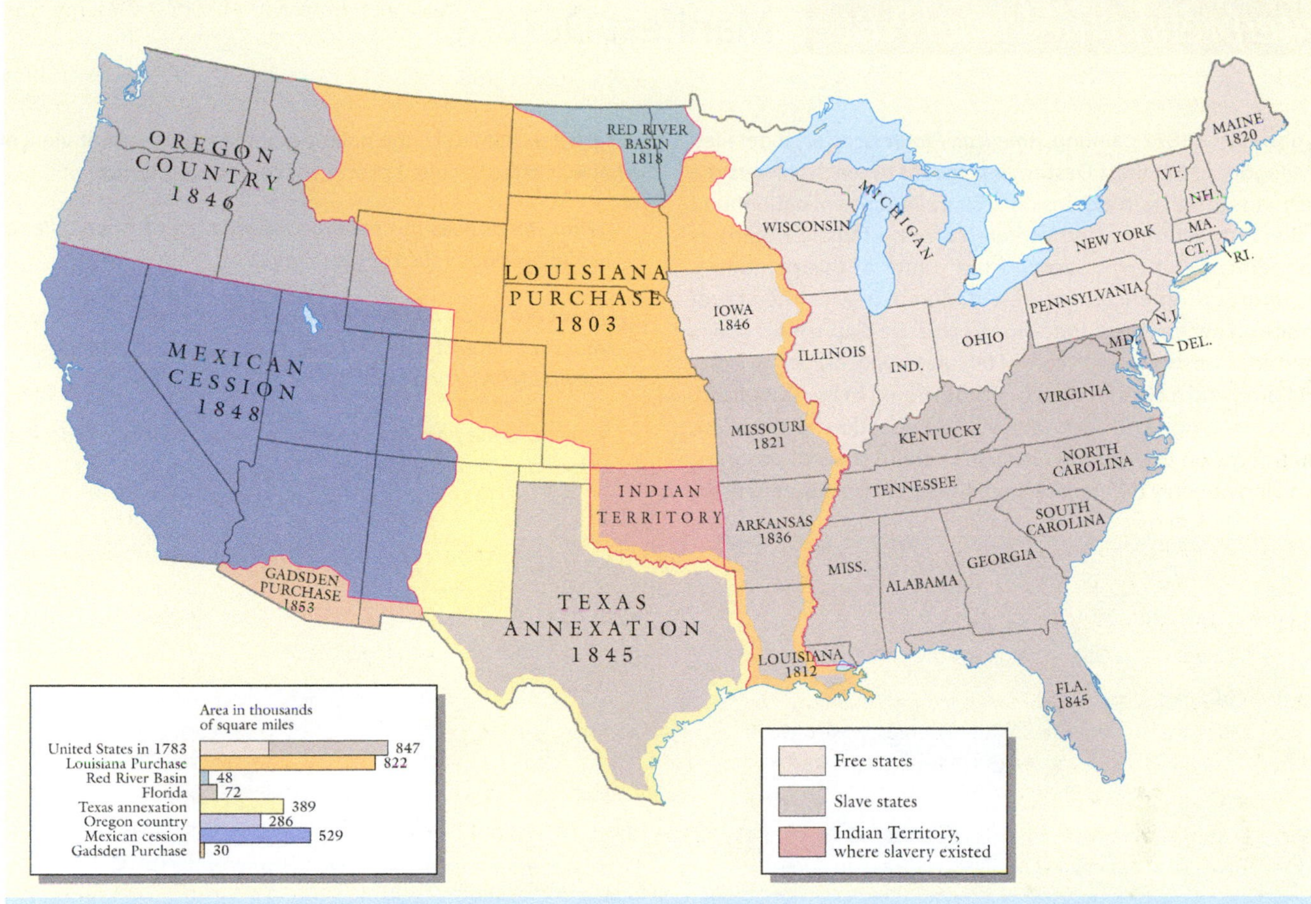

▲ **MAP 13.1 Free and Slave States and Territories, 1848** This map illustrates the larger number of slave than free states entering the Union from the territories acquired from France (Louisiana Purchase) and Spain (Florida). It also shows the huge amount of new territory added by the acquisition of Texas and the Southwest from Mexico and the settlement of the Oregon boundary in the 1840s.

Q *How does this map reveal the critical importance of the territory that would become the states of Kansas and Nebraska in the controversy over the expansion of slavery?*

Q *Does this map reveal that slavery threatened to become a national phenomenon?*

would turn "those wild forests, trackless plains, untrodden valleys" into "one grand scene of continuous improvements, universal enterprise, and unparalleled commerce."

13-1c *New Mexico and California*

By the time Mexico won its independence from Spain in 1821, some 80,000 Mexicans lived in portions of the region west of the 98th meridian. Three-fourths of them had settled in the Rio Grande Valley of New Mexico and most of the rest in California. Centuries earlier, the Spaniards had introduced horses, cattle, and sheep to the New World. These animals became the economic mainstay of Hispanic society along New Spain's northern frontier. Later, Anglo-Americans would adopt Hispanic ranching methods to invade and subdue the lands of the arid western plains. Spanish words still describe the tools of the trade and the land: *bronco, mustang, lasso, rodeo, stampede, canyon, arroyo, mesa.*

Colonial society on New Spain's northern frontier had centered on the **missions** and the ***presidios***. Intended to Christianize Indians, the missions also became an instrument to exploit their labor, while the presidios (military posts) protected the settlers from hostile Indians. By the late 18th century, the mission system had fallen into decline, and 15 years after Mexican independence in 1821, it collapsed entirely. The presidios, underfunded and understaffed, also declined, so that the defense of Mexico's far northern provinces increasingly fell to the residents. But by the 1830s, many residents of New Mexico and California were more interested in bringing American traders in than in keeping American settlers out. A flourishing trade over the Santa Fe Trail from Independence, Missouri, brought American manufactured goods to Santa Fe, New Mexico (and points south), in exchange for Mexican horses, mules, beaver pelts, and silver (see Map 13.2). New England ships carried American goods all the way around the horn of South America to San Francisco and other California ports in exchange for tallow and hides produced by *californio* ranchers. This trade linked the economies of New Mexico and California more closely to the United States than to the Mexican heartland.

Interpreting the Visual Past Manifest Destiny

John Gast's 1872 painting, *American Progress*, offers a detailed allegory of Manifest Destiny: It is meant to teach viewers the meanings of western expansion. Visual allegories of nationhood in the 19th century often centered around female figures as embodiments of civilization: At the center of this painting is the figure of American Progress (Columbia), with the star of empire on her forehead. Precariously clad in a diaphanous gown, she strides westward, with coils of telegraph wire draped over her right arm, and a clearly labeled "School Book" in her right hand: She is bringing both technology and education to the West. The figures on the ground also tell a careful story of progress, involving not only different technologies but also different types of settlers. Ultimately, the painting offers a benevolent view of what was often a violent process of conquering territory.

Q *What stories does this painting tell regarding technologies of white civilization such as the railroad?*

Q *How does the painting organize a visual narrative of settlement moving from east to west? Does it represent such settlement as inevitable? Why or why not?*

Q *How does the painting view Native Americans? How do they respond to "American Progress"?*

13.2 **John Gast, *American Progress*, 1872.**

13-1d *The Oregon and California Trails*

At the depth of the economic depression in 1842 and 1843, Oregon fever swept the Mississippi Valley. Thousands of farm families sold their land, packed their worldly goods in covered wagons along with supplies for five or six months on the trail, hitched up their oxen, and headed out from Independence or St. Joseph, Missouri, for the trek of almost 2,000 miles to the river valleys of Oregon or California. From 1840 to 1869, an estimated 50,000 emigrants made the trek to Oregon (see Map 13.2).

Adult men outnumbered women by more than 2 to 1 on the western trails before the gold rush. Many women

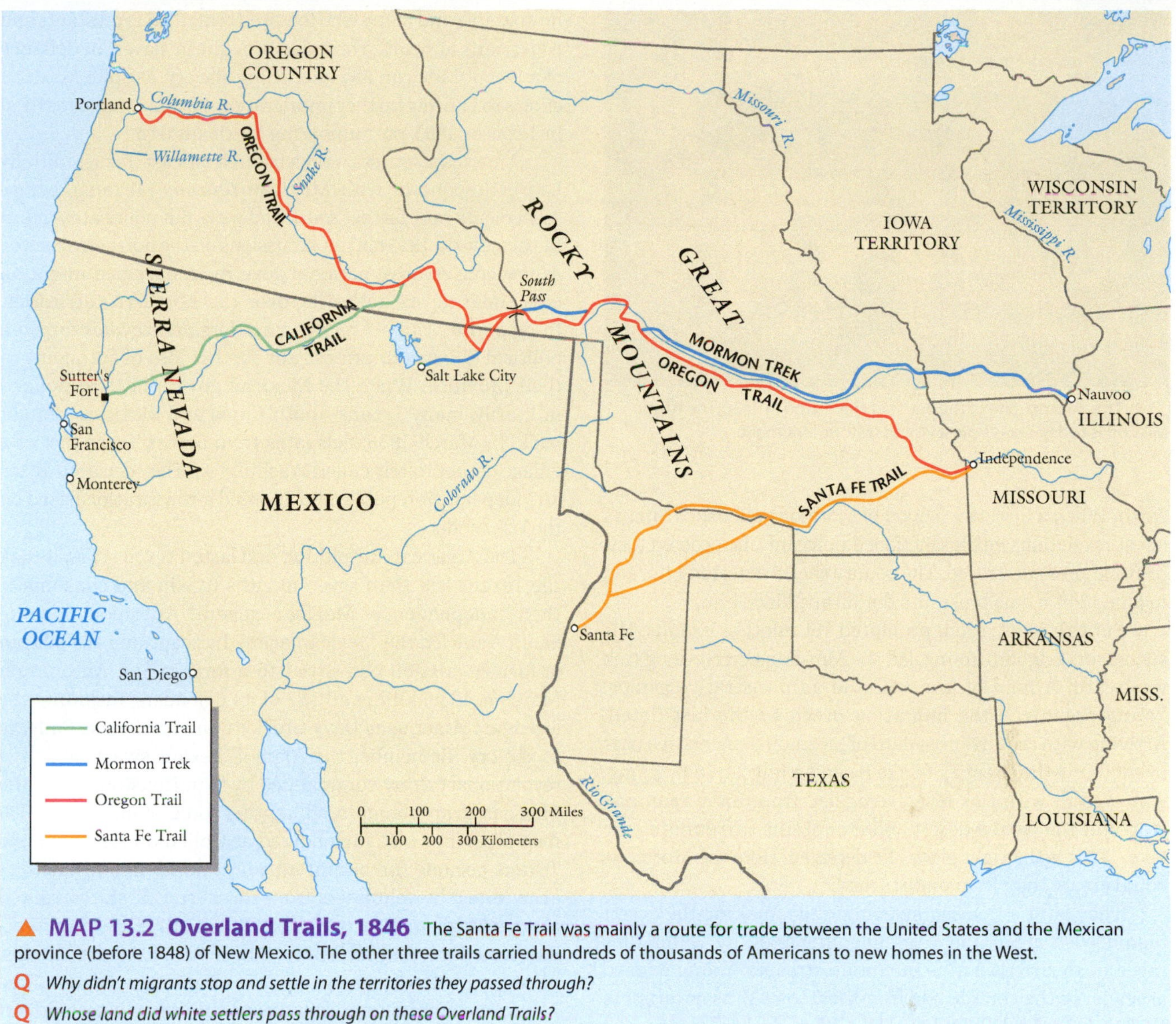

▲ **MAP 13.2 Overland Trails, 1846** The Santa Fe Trail was mainly a route for trade between the United States and the Mexican province (before 1848) of New Mexico. The other three trails carried hundreds of thousands of Americans to new homes in the West.

Q *Why didn't migrants stop and settle in the territories they passed through?*

Q *Whose land did white settlers pass through on these Overland Trails?*

were reluctant emigrants, and their diaries testified to their unhappiness: "What had possessed my husband, anyway, that he should have thought of bringing us away out through this God-forsaken country?" wrote one woman. She was sorry she had ever consented "to take this wild goose chase." For some families it did turn out to be a wild goose chase, but for many of those who stayed the course and settled in the far West, it was a success story in which women were critical in transforming settlements into communities.

On the way west, migrants passed through regions claimed by three nations—the United States, Mexico, and Britain—and they settled on land owned by Mexico (California) or claimed jointly by the United States and Britain (Oregon, which then stretched north to the border of Russian Alaska). But no matter who claimed it, the land was inhabited mostly by Indians. Few emigrants thought about settling down along the way, for this vast reach of arid plains, forbidding mountains, and burning wastelands was then known as the **Great American Desert**. Whites considered it suitable only for Indians and a disappearing breed of fur trappers. But one group did find its new home at the edge of the Great Salt Lake.

13-1e *The Mormon Migration*

Subjected to persecution that drove them from their original home in western New York to Ohio, Missouri, and eventually to Illinois, the **Mormons** established Nauvoo, Illinois, a thriving community of 15,000 souls, based on collective economic effort and theocratic discipline imposed by their founder and prophet, Joseph Smith. But the people of Illinois proved no more hospitable to the Mormons than the sect's previous neighbors. Smith provoked hostility with his insistence that God spoke through him, his autocratic suppression of dissent, and his assertion that the Mormons were the only true Christians and would inherit the

Dean Fikar/Shutterstock.com

13.3 **The Alamo** Site of the Battle of the Alamo in 1836, the Alamo Mission is today Texas's most visited historic landmark.

earth. When a dissident faction of Mormons published Smith's latest revelation, which sanctioned polygamy, he ordered their printing press destroyed. The county sheriff arrested him, and in June 1844, a mob broke into the jail and killed him.

Smith's martyrdom prompted yet another exodus. His successor, Brigham Young, led the Mormons on the long trek westward. A man of iron will and administrative genius, Young organized the migration down to the last detail. Arriving with the advance guard of Mormon pioneers at a pass overlooking the Great Salt Lake Basin on July 24, 1847, Young, who was ill with tick fever, struggled from his wagon and stared at the barren desert and mountains surrounding the lake. "This is the right place," he declared. Here the Mormons could create their Zion undisturbed.

They built a flourishing community, making the desert bloom with grain and vegetables irrigated by water they ingeniously diverted from mountain streams. Young reigned as leader of the church, and from 1850 to 1857 as governor of the newly created Utah Territory.

Zion, however, did not remain undisturbed. Relations with the government in Washington, D.C., and with territorial officials were never smooth, especially after Young's proclamation in 1852 authorizing polygamy. When conflict between the Mormons and the U.S. Army broke out in 1857, Young surrendered his civil authority and made an uneasy peace with the government.

13-1f *The Republic of Texas*

As the Mormons were starting west, a crisis between Mexico and the United States was coming to a boil. The United States had renounced any claim to Texas in a treaty with Spain negotiated in 1819. By the time the treaty was ratified in 1821, Mexico had won its independence from Spain. The new Republic of Mexico, seeking to develop its northern borderlands in Texas, gave Stephen F. Austin, a Missouri businessman, a large land grant to settle 300 American families there. Despite their pledge to become Roman Catholics and Mexican citizens, these immigrants and many who followed remained Protestants and Americans at heart. They also brought in slaves, in defiance of a recent Mexican law abolishing slavery. Despite Mexican efforts to ban any further immigration, 30,000 Americans lived in Texas by 1835, outnumbering Mexicans 6 to 1.

American settlers, concentrated in east Texas, initially had little contact with Mexican ***tejanos*** (Texans), whose settlements were farther south and west. But political events in Mexico City in 1835 had repercussions on the northern frontier. A new conservative national government seemed intent on consolidating its authority over the northern territories. In response, Anglo-American settlers and *tejanos* forged a political alliance to protest any further loss of autonomy in their province. When the Mexican government responded militarily, many Texans—both Anglo and Mexican—fought back. In March 1836, delegates from across Texas met at a village appropriately called Washington. They declared Texas an independent republic and adopted a constitution based on the U.S. model.

The American Revolution had lasted seven years; it took the Texans less than seven months to win and consolidate their independence. Mexican general Antonio López de Santa Anna led the Mexican army that captured the **Alamo** (a former mission converted to a fort) in San Antonio on March 6, 1836, killing all 187 of its defenders, including the legendary Americans Davy Crockett and Jim Bowie. Rallying to the cry "Remember the Alamo!" Texans swarmed to the revolutionary army commanded by Sam Houston. When the Mexican army slaughtered another force of more than 300 men after they had surrendered at Goliad on March 19, the Texans became further inflamed. A month later, Houston's army, aided by volunteers from southern U.S. states, routed a larger Mexican force on the San Jacinto River (near present-day Houston) and captured Santa Anna. Under duress, he signed a treaty granting Texas its independence. The Mexican congress later repudiated the treaty but could not muster enough strength to reestablish its authority north of the Nueces River. The victorious Texans elected Sam Houston president of their new republic and petitioned for annexation to the United States.

13-1g *The Annexation Controversy*

President Andrew Jackson, wary of provoking war with Mexico or quarrels with antislavery northerners, rebuffed the annexationists. So did his successor, Martin Van Buren. Although disappointed, the Texans turned their energies to building their republic. The British government encouraged the Texans, in the hope that they would stand as a buffer against further U.S. expansion. Texas leaders made friendly responses to some of the British overtures, probably in the hope of provoking American annexationists to take action. They did.

Vice President John Tyler had unexpectedly become president after the death of President William Henry Harrison from pneumonia in 1841, only weeks after his inauguration as the first Whig president. Tyler was nominally a Whig—but he soon broke with the Whig Party that had elected him. A states-rights Virginian who sought to create a new coalition to reelect him in 1844, Tyler seized on the annexation of Texas as "the only matter that will take sufficient hold of the feelings of the South to rally it on a southern candidate."

Tyler's secretary of state, John C. Calhoun, negotiated a treaty of annexation with the eager Texans, but then he made a mistake: He released to the press his letter informing the British minister to the United States that, together with other reasons, Americans wanted to annex Texas in order to protect slavery. This seemed to confirm abolitionist charges that annexation was a pro-slavery plot. Northern senators of both parties defeated the treaty in June 1844.

By then, Texas had become the main issue in the forthcoming presidential election. Whig candidate Henry Clay had come out against annexation, as had the leading contender for the Democratic nomination, former president Martin Van Buren. Van Buren's stand ran counter to the rising tide of Manifest Destiny sentiment within the Democratic Party. It also angered southern Democrats, who were determined to have Texas. Through eight ballots at the Democratic National Convention, they blocked Van Buren's nomination; on the ninth, the southerners broke the stalemate by nominating one of their own, James K. Polk of Tennessee. Polk's nomination undercut President Tyler's forlorn hope of being reelected on the Texas issue, so he bowed out of the race.

Polk ran on a platform that called for not only the annexation of Texas but also the acquisition of all of Oregon up to 50°40′ (the Alaskan border) (see Map 13.3). That demand was aimed at voters in the western free states, who believed that bringing Oregon into the Union would balance the expansion of slavery into Texas. Polk was more than comfortable with this platform. In fact, he wanted not only Texas and Oregon, but California and New Mexico as well.

Texas fever swept the South during the campaign. So powerful was the issue that Clay began to waver, stating that he would support annexation if it could be done without starting a war with Mexico. This concession won him a few southern votes but angered northern antislavery Whigs. Many of them voted for James G. Birney, candidate of the Liberty Party, which opposed adding any more slave territory. Birney probably took enough Whig votes from Clay in New York to give Polk victory there and in the Electoral College.

13-1h *Acquisition of Texas and Oregon*

Although the election was extremely close (Polk won only a plurality of 49.5 percent of the popular vote), Democrats regarded it as a mandate for annexation. Congress passed a joint resolution of annexation in March 1845, and Texas became the 15th slave state. Backed now by the United States, Texans claimed a southern and western border beyond the Nueces River all the way to the Rio Grande, which nearly tripled the area that Mexico had formerly defined as Texas. Mexico responded by breaking off diplomatic relations with the United States.

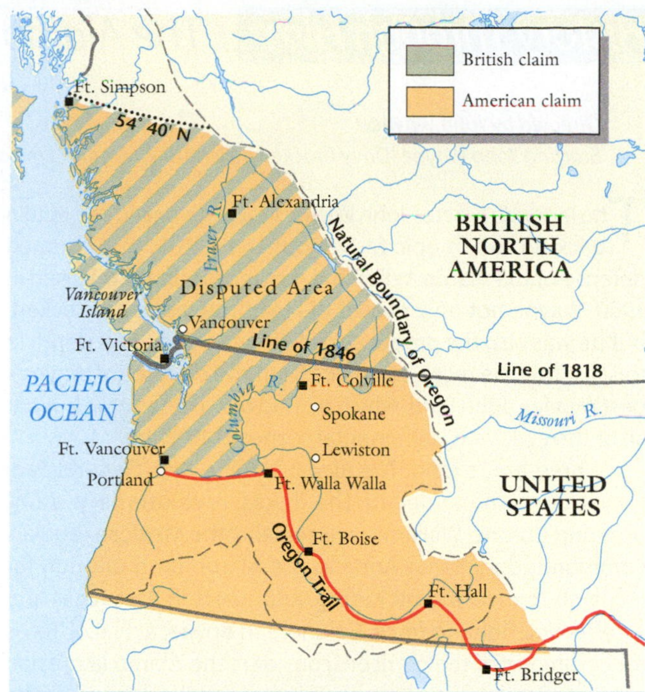

▲ **MAP 13.3 Settlement of the Oregon Boundary Dispute, 1846** Before the 1840s, the only white residents of the Oregon Country were fur traders and missionaries. Migration of Americans over the Oregon Trail created pressures to make all of Oregon part of the United States, but President Polk was not willing to go to war for the boundary of 50°40′.

Q *What does this map show about British and American tensions in the 19th century?*

Q *Why wasn't President Polk willing to go to war over the disputed area of the map?*

Meanwhile, Polk lost no time in addressing his promise to annex Oregon. "Our title to the country of the Oregon is 'clear and unquestionable,'" he said in his inaugural address. The problem was to persuade Britain to recognize the title. Both countries had jointly "occupied" Oregon since 1818, overseeing the fur trade carried on by British and American companies. Chanting the slogan "Fifty-four forty or fight!" many Americans in 1845 demanded all of Oregon, as pledged in the Democratic platform. But Polk proved unwilling to fight for 50°40′. So far, Americans had settled only in the region south of the Columbia River, at roughly the 46th parallel. In June 1846, Polk accepted a compromise treaty that split the Oregon country between the United States and Britain at the 49th parallel. Several Democratic senators from the Old Northwest accused Polk of betrayal and voted against the treaty. They had supported Texas to the Rio Grande, and they had expected Polk to support Oregon to 50°40′. A sectional breach had opened in the Democratic Party that would soon grow wider.

History Through Film The Alamo (1960)

Directed by John Wayne.
Starring John Wayne (Davy Crockett), Richard Widmark (Jim Bowie), Laurence Harvey (William Travis).

The legendary actor John Wayne worked a decade to obtain backing for an epic film about the heroic but doomed defense of the Alamo. When the movie was finally released in 1960, Wayne not only played the lead role as Davy Crockett, but he was also the producer and director. Out of his depth in this last role, he received advice from the director of Wayne's best movies, John Ford, which helped overcome some but not all of the awkward, sentimental scenes in the film.

Three hours long, *The Alamo* begins with General Sam Houston, commander of the Texas revolutionary army, ordering Colonel William Travis to delay the Mexican regulars commanded by Santa Anna at the Alamo long enough for Houston to organize his ragtag volunteers in east Texas into an effective fighting force. Colonel Jim Bowie, a rival of Travis for command of the garrison, considers the Alamo (a mission converted into a fort) a trap and wants to pull out, because the Mexican army outnumbers the Texans 20 to 1.

Right away, Hollywood departs from historical reality. Houston had actually ordered Bowie to blow up the Alamo and retreat to join him, but Bowie and Travis agreed to stay and fight, supported by Davy Crockett and his fellow Tennessee volunteers who had come to Texas looking for excitement. The tension between Travis and Bowie (with Crockett as a mediator) was real and is vividly portrayed, if sometimes overdramatized, in the film, but the tension concerned their relative authority, not strategy.

In wide-screen splendor, the film depicts the approach of the Mexican army, the artillery duels between the garrison and the Mexicans, and the infantry assaults that finally overpower the garrison after 13 days of resistance, killing them to the last man, sparing only the wife and child of a Texas lieutenant. The combat footage in the final attack is spectacular. Mexican artillery bombards the Alamo; infantrymen move forward, taking heavy casualties, swarm over the wall, and overwhelm the doomed defenders. Bowie is wounded early in the fight and sent to an improvised hospital in the chapel, where he dies fighting from his bed. Travis is killed at the gate after dispatching several Mexicans with his sword. Crockett fights with fury until he is impaled by a Mexican lancer, but lives long enough to throw a torch into the powder magazine, blowing up the fort and hundreds of Mexicans.

In reality, none of it happened this way. Bowie had gone to bed with typhoid fever early in the siege; Travis was killed early in the final assault with a bullet through his head; and Crockett, along with a few others, surrendered but were executed on Santa Anna's orders. For Hollywood, and perhaps for most Americans, however, history is less important than legend. The Alamo became a heroic legend, a rallying cry for Texans in 1836, and a powerful symbol ever since. The film version dramatizes the legend better than an accurate version could have done.

The movie also reflects the cold-war mentality of the 1950s and Wayne's own full-blooded anti-communist stance. Crockett's windy speeches about freedom and individual rights evoke the 1950s rhetoric of "better dead than red." Ironically, the Texans were fighting for an independent republic with slavery, in defiance of Mexico's recent abolition of the institution—an issue that the film virtually ignores.

Although *The Alamo* might have carried more punch if it had been edited down to two hours, it nevertheless is visually powerful. It received seven Academy Award nominations, including one for Best Picture, but received only one Oscar—for sound. ■

Everett Collection

13.4 John Wayne in a Poster Advertising *The Alamo*.

13-2 The Mexican War

What were the causes and consequences of the Mexican War?

Having avoided a war with Britain, Polk provoked one with Mexico. In 1845, he sent a special envoy to Mexico City with an offer to buy California and New Mexico for $30 million. To help Mexico make the right response, he ordered federal troops to the disputed border area between Mexico and Texas, dispatched a naval squadron to patrol the Gulf Coast of Mexico, and instructed the American consul at Monterey (the Mexican capital of California) to stir up annexation sentiment among settlers there. These strong-arm tactics provoked a political revolt in Mexico City that brought a militant anti-American regime to power.

Polk responded in January 1846 by ordering 4,000 soldiers under General Zachary Taylor to advance all the way to the Rio Grande. Recognizing that he could achieve his goals only through armed conflict, Polk waited for news from Texas that would justify a declaration of war. Finally, on May 9, 1846, word arrived that two weeks earlier Mexican troops had crossed the Rio Grande and attacked an American patrol, killing 11 soldiers. Polk had what he wanted and sent a war message to Congress on May 11. Most Whigs opposed war with Mexico, but in the end, not wanting to be branded unpatriotic, all but a handful of them voted for what they called "Mr. Polk's War."

The United States went to war with a tiny regular army of fewer than 8,000 men, supplemented by 60,000 volunteers in state regiments, and an efficient navy that quickly established domination of the sea-lanes. Mexican soldiers outnumbered American in most of the battles, but the Americans had higher morale, better leadership, better weapons (especially artillery), and the backing of a more determined, stable government and a far stronger economy. The U.S. forces won every battle—and the war—in a fashion that humiliated Mexico and left a legacy of national hostility and border violence.

13.5 **American Forces in Saltillo, Mexico** This posed photograph of General John E. Wool and his staff, members of Zachary Taylor's army on its march southward from Monterrey through Saltillo in November 1846, is the earliest known photograph of an American military force. Photography had recently been invented, and pictures such as this one were extremely rare before the 1850s.

13-2a *Military Campaigns of 1846*

The Mexican War's first phase was carried out by Zachary Taylor, whose 4,000 regulars routed numerically superior Mexican forces on the Rio Grande in early May, even before Congress had declared war. Those victories made "Old Rough and Ready" Taylor a hero, a reputation he rode to the presidency two years later. Reinforced by several thousand volunteers, Taylor pursued the retreating Mexicans 100 miles south of the Rio Grande to the heavily fortified Mexican city of Monterrey, and took the city after four days of fighting in September 1846. Mexican resistance in the area crumbled, and Taylor's force settled down as an army of occupation.

Meanwhile, the second phase of American strategy had gone forward in New Mexico and California. In June 1846, General Stephen Watts Kearny led an army of 1,500 tough frontiersmen and regulars west from Fort Leavenworth toward Santa Fe. Kearny's army occupied Santa Fe on August 18 without firing a shot. With closer economic ties to the United States than to their own country, which taxed them well but governed them poorly, many New Mexicans seemed willing to accept American rule.

After receiving reinforcements, Kearny sent part of his army into the Mexican province of Chihuahua. In the most extraordinary campaign of the war, these troops marched 1,500 miles, foraging supplies along the way; fought and beat two much larger enemy forces; and finally linked up with Zachary Taylor's army near Monterrey in spring 1847 (see Map 13.4).

Kearny led another contingent across deserts and mountains to California. Events there had anticipated his arrival. In June 1846, a group of American settlers backed by Captain John C. Frémont, a renowned western explorer with the army topographical corps, captured Sonoma and raised the flag of an independent California, displaying the silhouette of a grizzly bear. This "bear-flag revolt" paved the way for the conquest of California by the *americanos*. The U.S. Pacific Fleet seized California's ports and the capital at Monterey; sailors from the fleet and volunteer soldiers under Frémont subdued Mexican resistance. Kearny's weary and battered force arrived in December 1846, barely in time to help with the mopping up.

13-2b *Military Campaigns of 1847*

The Mexican government refused to admit that the war was lost. Early in 1847, Santa Anna raised new levies and marched north to attack Taylor's army near Monterrey. Taylor, 62 years old, was still rough but not as ready to withstand a counteroffensive as he had been a few weeks earlier. After capturing Monterrey in September 1846, he had let the defeated Mexican army go and had granted an eight-week armistice in the hope that it would allow time for peace negotiations. Angry at Taylor's presumption in making such a decision and suspicious of the general's political ambitions, Polk canceled the armistice and named General-in-Chief Winfield Scott to command the third phase of the war. A large, punctilious man, Scott acquired the nickname "Old Fuss and Feathers" for a military professionalism that contrasted with the homespun manner of "Rough and Ready" Zach Taylor. Scott decided to invade Mexico from a beachhead at Veracruz and in January 1847 ordered the transfer of more than half of Taylor's troops to his own expeditionary force (see Map 13.4).

Left with fewer than 5,000 men, most of them untried volunteers, Taylor complained bitterly of political intrigue and military favoritism. Nevertheless, he marched out to meet Santa Anna's army of 18,000. In a two-day battle on

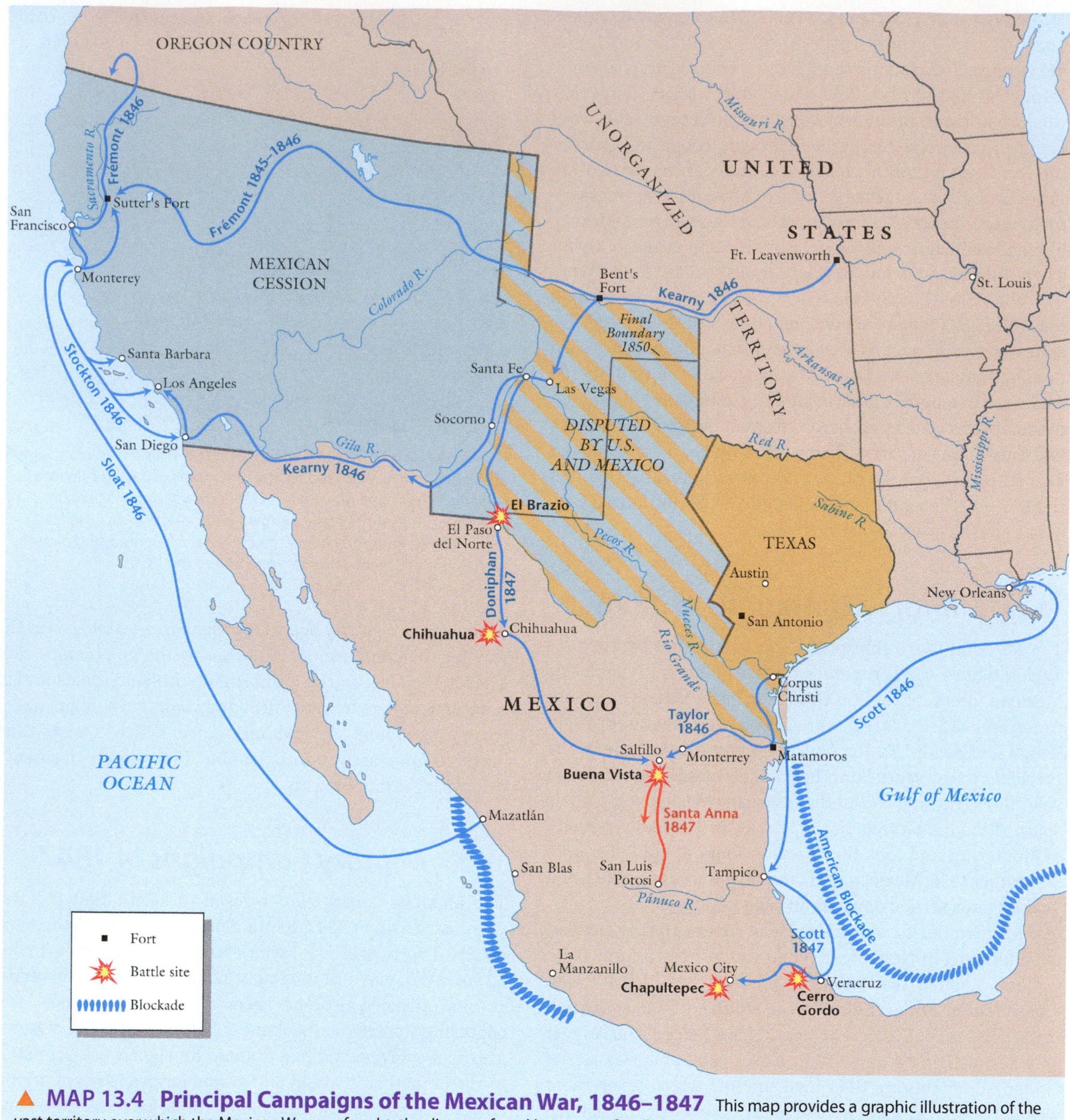

▲ **MAP 13.4 Principal Campaigns of the Mexican War, 1846–1847** This map provides a graphic illustration of the vast territory over which the Mexican War was fought; the distance from Veracruz to San Francisco is 2,500 miles.

Q *Does this map show that the Mexican War was primarily a land war or a naval war?*

Q *What strategies for winning the war does this map reveal?*

February 22 and 23 at Buena Vista, Taylor's force inflicted twice as many casualties as they suffered in a fierce struggle highlighted by the brilliant counterattack of a Mississippi regiment commanded by Jefferson Davis. The bloodied Mexican army retreated toward the capital. When news of the victory reached the East, Taylor's popularity soared to new heights. If Polk had wanted to quash a political rival by taking away most of his troops—as Taylor believed—he had achieved just the opposite.

But it was General Scott who actually won the war. With a combined army–navy force, he took the coastal fortress at Veracruz in March 1847. Over the next five months, his army, which never totaled more than 14,000 men, marched and fought its way over more than 200 miles of mountains and plains to Mexico City. Scott's outnumbered forces captured Mexico City on September 14, after fierce hand-to-hand combat in the battles of Contreras, Churubusco, Molino del Rey, and Chapultepec.

13-2c *Antiwar Sentiment*

The war had enthusiastic support in the South and West and among Democrats, but Whigs and many people in the Northeast, especially in New England, considered it "a wicked and disgraceful war." Democrats and Whigs had different notions of progress. Democrats believed in expanding American institutions over *space*—in particular, the space occupied by Mexicans and Indians. Whigs, on the other hand, believed in improving American institutions over *time*. "Opposed to the instinct of boundless acquisition stands that of Internal Improvement," said Horace Greeley. "A nation cannot simultaneously devote its energies to the absorption of others' territories and the improvement of its own."

Antislavery people raised their eyebrows when they heard Manifest Destiny rhetoric about "extending the blessings of American liberty" to benighted regions. They suspected that the real reason was the desire to extend slavery. Hosea Biglow, the rustic Yankee philosopher created by the abolitionist poet James Russell Lowell, observed:

> They jest want this Californy
> So's to lug new slave-states in
> To abuse ye an' to scorn ye,
> And to plunder ye like sin

13-2d *The Wilmot Proviso*

The slavery issue overshadowed all others in the debate over the Mexican War. President Polk could not understand the reason for the fuss. "There is no probability," he wrote in his diary, "that any territory will ever be acquired from Mexico in which slavery would ever exist." But other Americans were less sure. Many southerners hoped that slavery would spread into the fertile lowlands of Mexican territory. Many northerners feared that it might. The issue came to a head early in the war. On August 8, 1846, Pennsylvania Democratic congressman David Wilmot offered an amendment to an army appropriations bill: "...that, as an express and fundamental condition of the acquisition of any territory from the Republic of Mexico ... neither slavery nor involuntary servitude shall ever exist in any part of said territory."

This famous **Wilmot Proviso** framed the national debate over slavery for the next 15 years. The House passed the amendment. Nearly all northern Democrats joined all northern Whigs in the majority, while southern Democrats and southern Whigs voted almost unanimously against it. In the Senate, greater southern strength defeated the proviso. This outcome marked an ominous wrenching of the party division between Whigs and Democrats into a *sectional* division between free and slave states. It was a sign that the two-party system might not successfully contain the convulsive question of slavery expansion.

Several factors underlay the split of northern Democrats from their own president on this issue. Ever since southern Democrats had blocked Van Buren's nomination in 1844, resentment had been growing in the party's northern wing. Polk's acceptance of 49° latitude for Oregon's northern boundary exacerbated this feeling. "Our rights to Oregon have been shamefully compromised," fumed an Ohio Democrat. "The administration is Southern, Southern, Southern! ... Since the South have fixed boundaries for free territory, let the North fix boundaries for slave territories." The reduced rates

$200 Reward.

RANAWAY from the subscriber, on the night of Thursday, the 30th of Sepember,

FIVE NEGRO SLAVES,

To-wit: one Negro man, his wife, and three children.

The man is a black negro, full height, very erect, his face a little thin. He is about forty years of age, and calls himself *Washington Reed*, and is known by the name of Washington. He is probably well dressed, possibly takes with him an ivory headed cane, and is of good address. Several of his teeth are gone.

Mary, his wife, is about thirty years of age, a bright mulatto woman, and quite stout and strong.

The oldest of the children is a boy, of the name of FIELDING, twelve years of age, a dark mulatto, with heavy eyelids. He probably wore a new cloth cap.

MATILDA, the second child, is a girl, six years of age, rather a dark mulatto, but a bright and smart looking child.

MALCOLM, the youngest, is a boy, four years old, a lighter mulatto than the last, and about equally as bright. He probably also wore a cloth cap. If examined, he will be found to have a swelling at the navel.

Washington and Mary have lived at or near St. Louis, with the subscriber, for about 15 years.

It is supposed that they are making their way to Chicago, and that a white man accompanies them, that they will travel chiefly at night, and most probably in a covered wagon.

A reward of $150 will be paid for their apprehension, so that I can get them, if taken within one hundred miles of St. Louis, and $200 if taken beyond that, and secured so that I can get them, and other reasonable additional charges, if delivered to the subscriber, or to THOMAS ALLEN, Esq., at St. Louis, Mo. The above negroes, for the last few years, have been in possession of Thomas Allen, Esq., of St. Louis.

WM. RUSSELL.

ST. LOUIS, Oct. 1, 1847.

Library of Congress Prints and Photograph Division [LC-USZ62-62797]

13.6 Runaway Slave Advertisement, 1847 This 1847 advertisement by a slave owner near St. Louis, Missouri reveals the desperate attempt of a family of five slaves–a husband, wife, and three children–to free themselves by escaping north. The slave owner assumes that they are on their way to Chicago, located in a "free state."

Q *Under federal law, would this family be safe from slave catchers once they arrived there?*

of the Walker tariff in 1846 (sponsored by Robert J. Walker of Mississippi, Polk's secretary of the treasury) dismayed Democrats from Pennsylvania's industrial districts. Polk further angered Democrats from the Old Northwest by vetoing a rivers and harbors bill that would have provided federal aid for transportation improvements in their districts. The Wilmot Proviso was in part the product of these pent-up frustrations over what northerners were increasingly calling "the slave power." "The time has come," said a Democratic congressman in 1846, "when the Northern Democracy should make a stand. Every thing has taken a Southern shape and been controlled by Southern caprice for years.... We must satisfy the Northern people ... that we are not to extend the institution of slavery as a result of this war."

The slavery issue hung like the sword of Damocles over Polk's efforts to negotiate peace with Mexico. Polk also came under pressure from expansionist Democrats who, excited by military victory, wanted more Mexican territory, perhaps even "all Mexico." Polk had sent diplomat Nicholas Trist with Scott's army to negotiate the terms of Mexican surrender. Authorized to pay Mexico $15 million for California, New Mexico, and a Texas border on the Rio Grande, Trist worked out such a treaty. In the meantime, though, Polk had succumbed to the "all Mexico" clamor. He ordered Trist back to Washington, intending to replace him with someone who would exact greater concessions from Mexico. Trist ignored the recall, signed the **Treaty of Guadalupe Hidalgo** on February 2, 1848, and sent it to Washington. Although angered by Trist's defiance, Polk nonetheless decided to end the controversy by submitting the treaty to the Senate, which approved it on March 10 by a vote of 38 to 14. Half the opposition came from Democrats who wanted more Mexican territory and half from Whigs who wanted none. As it was, the treaty sheared off half of Mexico and increased the size of the United States by one-fourth.

13-3 The Election of 1848

 *How did the question of slavery affect the election of 1848?*

The treaty did nothing to settle the question of slavery in the new territory, however. Mexico had abolished the institution two decades earlier; would the United States reintroduce it? Many Americans looked to the election of 1848 to decide the matter. Four positions on the issue emerged, each identified with a candidate for the presidential nomination.

The Wilmot Proviso represented the position of those determined to bar slavery from all territories. The Liberty Party endorsed the proviso and nominated Senator John P. Hale of New Hampshire for president. Southern Democrat John C. Calhoun formulated the "southern-rights" position. Directly challenging the Wilmot Proviso, Calhoun introduced resolutions in the Senate in February 1847 affirming the right of slave owners to take their human property into any territory. The Constitution protected the right of property, Calhoun pointed out; Congress could no more prevent a settler from taking his slaves to California than it could prevent him from taking his horses there.

Although most southerners agreed with Calhoun, the Democratic Party sought a middle ground. The Polk administration endorsed the idea of extending the old Missouri Compromise line of 36°30′ to the Pacific. This would have excluded slavery from present-day Washington, Oregon, Idaho, Utah, Nevada, and the northern half of California, but would have allowed it in present-day New Mexico, Arizona, and southern California. Secretary of State James Buchanan, also a candidate for the Democratic presidential nomination (Polk did not seek renomination), embraced this position.

Another compromise position became known as **"popular sovereignty."** Identified with Senator Lewis Cass of Michigan, yet another contender for the Democratic nomination, this concept proposed to let the settlers of each territory decide for themselves whether to permit slavery. This solution contained a crucial ambiguity: It did not specify *at what stage* the settlers of a territory could decide on slavery. Most northern Democrats assumed that a territorial legislature would make that decision as soon as it was organized. Most southerners assumed that the decision would not be made until the settlers had drawn up a state constitution. That would normally happen only after several years as a territory, during which time slavery might well have taken deep enough root to be implanted in the state constitution. So long as neither assumption was tested, each faction could support popular sovereignty.

The Democratic convention nominated Cass for president, thereby seeming to endorse popular sovereignty. In an attempt to maintain party unity, however, the platform made no mention of the matter. The attempt was not entirely successful: Two Alabama delegates walked out when the convention refused to endorse Calhoun's southern-rights position, and an antislavery faction from New York walked out when it failed to win a credentials fight.

The Whig convention tried to avoid a similar schism by adopting no platform at all, but the slavery issue would not die. In the eyes of many antislavery delegates who styled themselves **Conscience Whigs**, the party made itself ridiculous by nominating Zachary Taylor for president. Desperate for victory, the Whigs chose a hero from a war that most of them had opposed. But the fact that Taylor was also a large slaveholder who owned several plantations in Louisiana and Mississippi was too much for the Conscience Whigs. They bolted from the party and formed a coalition with the Liberty Party and antislavery Democrats.

13-3a *The Free Soil Party*

These **Free-Soilers** met in convention in August 1848 and nominated former president Martin Van Buren. The meeting resembled a religious camp meeting more than a political gathering. Speakers proclaimed slavery "a great moral, social, and political evil—a relic of barbarism which must necessarily be swept away in the progress of Christian civilization." The convention did not say how that would be done, but it did adopt a platform calling for "no more Slave States and no more Slave Territories."

The campaign was marked by the futile efforts of both major parties to bury the slavery issue. Free Soil pressure compelled both northern Democrats and Whigs to take a stand against slavery in the territories. Whigs pointed to their earlier support of the Wilmot Proviso, while Democrats said popular sovereignty would keep the territories free. In the South, though, the two parties presented other faces. There, the Democrats pointed with pride to their expansionist record that had brought to the nation hundreds of thousands of square miles of territory—into which slavery might expand. But Taylor proved the strongest candidate in the South because he was a southerner and a slaveholder. "Will the people of [the South] vote for a Southern President or a Northern one?" asked southern newspapers. "We prefer Old Zack with his sugar and cotton plantations and four hundred negroes to all their compromises."

Taylor carried 8 of the 15 slave states and increased the Whig vote in the South by 10 percent over 1844, while the Democratic vote declined by 4 percent. Although he did less well in the North, he carried New York and enough other states to win the election. The Free-Soilers won no electoral votes but polled 14 percent of the popular vote in the North. They also elected nine congressmen along with two senators who would be heard from in the future: Salmon P. Chase of Ohio, architect of the Free Soil coalition in 1848, and Charles Sumner of Massachusetts, leader of the Conscience Whigs.

13-3b *The Gold Rush and California Statehood*

In 1848, workers building a sawmill on the American River near Sacramento discovered flecks of gold in the riverbed. The word gradually leaked out, reaching the East in August 1848, where a public that had been surfeited with tall tales out of the West greeted this news with skepticism. But in December, Polk's final message to Congress confirmed the "extraordinary" discoveries of gold. Two days later, a tea caddy containing 320 ounces of pure gold from California arrived in Washington. Now all doubts disappeared. By spring 1849, 100,000 gold-seekers were poised to take off by foot on the overland trail or by ship—either around Cape Horn or to the isthmus of Central America, where, after a land crossing, they could board another ship to take them up the Pacific Coast. Eighty thousand actually made it that first year (5,000 succumbed to a cholera epidemic).

San Francisco became a boomtown and a new center of Pacific trade, with ships arriving filled with cargos of wheat, coffee, sugar, rice, and other commodities from Chile, Australia, China, and Alaska. Men and women (outnumbered 10 to 1 by men) rushed to California from Chile, Mexico, Peru, France, Belgium, and China. African Americans and Miwok Indians also worked as miners—although they were quickly pushed aside by land-hungry Anglo-Americans, who in 1850 instituted discriminatory laws that not only privileged whites but forced the expulsion of Mexicans—many of whom were American citizens under the Treaty of Guadalupe Hidalgo. While a few miners struck it rich, most instead earned a bare pittance—and soon raced off to new gold rushes in British Columbia, Colorado, and Nevada.

The population increase meant that the political organization of California could not be postponed: Miners needed law and order; settlers needed courts, land and water laws, mail service, and other amenities of established government. In New Mexico, the 60,000 former Mexican citizens, now Americans, also needed a governmental structure for their new allegiance. Nor could the growing Mormon community at Salt Lake be ignored.

Still, the slavery question paralyzed Congress. In December 1848, lame-duck president Polk recommended extension of the Missouri Compromise 36°30′ line to the Pacific. The Whig-controlled House defied him, reaffirmed the Wilmot Proviso, drafted a bill to organize California as a free territory, and debated abolishing the slave trade and even slavery itself in the District of Columbia. Fistfights flared in Congress; southerners declared that they would secede if any of those measures became law; the Democratic Senate quashed all the bills. A southern caucus asked Calhoun to draft an address setting forth its position. He eagerly complied, producing in January 1849 a document that breathed fire against "unconstitutional" northern efforts to keep slavery out of the territories. Calhoun reminded southerners that their "property, prosperity, equality, liberty, and safety" were at stake and prophesied secession if the South did not prevail.

But Calhoun's firebomb fizzled. Only two-fifths of the southern congressmen and senators signed it. Southern Whigs wanted nothing to do with it. They looked forward to good times in the Taylor administration and opposed rocking the boat.

They were in for a rude shock. Taylor viewed matters as a nationalist, not as a southerner. He proposed to admit California and New Mexico (the latter comprising present-day New Mexico, Arizona, Nevada, Utah, and part of Colorado) immediately as *states*, skipping the territorial stage.

From the South came cries of outrage. Immediate admission would bring in two more free states because slavery had not existed under Mexican law, and most of the 49ers were Free Soil in sentiment. With the administration's support, Californians held a convention in October 1849, drew up a constitution excluding slavery, and applied to Congress for admission as a state. Taylor's end run would tip the existing balance of 15 slave and 15 free states in favor of the North, probably forever. The South would lose its de facto veto in the Senate. "For the first time," said freshman senator Jefferson Davis of Mississippi, "we are about permanently to destroy the balance of power between the sections." Davis insisted that slave labor was suitable to mining and that slavery should be permitted in California. Southerners vowed never to "consent to be thus degraded and enslaved" by such a "monstrous trick and injustice" as admission of California as a free state.

Courtesy of the California History Room, California State Library, Sacramento, California.

13.7 **The California Gold Rush** Prospectors for gold in the foothills of California's Sierra Nevada came from all over the world, including China. This photograph shows American-born and Chinese miners near Auburn, California, a year or two after the initial gold rush of 1849. It illustrates the original technology of separating gravel from gold by panning or by washing the gravel away in a sluice box, leaving the heavier gold flakes behind.

13-4 The Compromise of 1850

Q *What issues were at stake in the congressional debates that led to the Compromise of 1850? How successfully did the compromise resolve these issues?*

California and New Mexico became the focal points of a cluster of slavery issues that faced the Congress of 1849–1850. An earlier Supreme Court decision (*Prigg v. Pennsylvania*, 1842) had relieved state officials of any obligation to enforce the return of **fugitive slaves** who had escaped into free states, declaring that this was a federal responsibility. Southerners therefore demanded a strong national fugitive slave law (in utter disregard of their oft-stated commitment to states' rights); antislavery northerners, on the other hand, were calling for an end to the disgraceful buying and selling of slaves in the national capital; and in the Southwest, a shooting war threatened to break out between Texas and New Mexico. Having won the Rio Grande as their southern border with Mexico, Texans insisted that the river must also mark their western border with New Mexico. (That would have given Texas more than half of the present state of New Mexico.) This dispute also involved slavery because the terms of Texas's annexation authorized the state to split into as many as five states, and the territory it carved out of New Mexico would create the potential for still another slave state.

These problems produced both a crisis and an opportunity. The crisis lay in the threat to break up the Union. Southern states agreed to meet at Nashville in June 1850 "to devise and adopt some mode of resistance to northern aggression." Few doubted that the mode would be secession unless Congress met southern demands at least halfway, but Congress got off to an unpromising start. Sectional disputes prevented either major party from commanding a majority in electing a Speaker of the House. Through three weeks and 62 ballots, the contest went on while tempers shortened. Northerners and southerners shouted insults at each other, fistfights broke out, and a Mississippian drew a revolver during one heated debate. Southern warnings of secession became a litany: "If, by your legislation, you seek to drive us from the territories of California and New Mexico," thundered Robert Toombs of Georgia, *"I am for disunion."* On the 63rd ballot, the exhausted legislators finally elected Howell Cobb of Georgia as Speaker by a plurality rather than a majority.

13-4a *The Senate Debates*

As he had in 1820 and 1833, Henry Clay hoped to turn the crisis into an opportunity. Seventy-two years old, a veteran of 30 years in Congress, three times an unsuccessful candidate for president, Clay was the most respected and still the most magnetic figure in the Senate. A nationalist from the border state of Kentucky, he hoped to unite North and South in a compromise. On January 29, 1850, he presented eight proposals to the Senate and supported them with an eloquent speech, the first of many to be heard in that body during what turned out to be the most famous congressional debate in U.S. history. Clay grouped the first six of his proposals into three pairs, each pair offering one concession to the North and one to the South. The first pair would admit California as a free state but would organize the rest of the Mexican cession without restrictions against slavery. The second would settle the Texas boundary dispute in favor of New Mexico but would compensate Texas to enable the state to pay off bonds it had sold when it was an independent republic. (Many holders of the Texas bonds were southerners.) The third pair of proposals would abolish the slave trade in the District of Columbia but would guarantee the continued existence of slavery there unless both Maryland and Virginia consented to abolition. Of Clay's final two proposals, one affirmed that Congress had no jurisdiction over the interstate slave trade; the other called for a strong national fugitive slave law.

At the end of a long, grueling bargaining process, the final shape of the **Compromise of 1850** closely resembled Clay's package. The public face of this process featured set speeches in the Senate, the most notable of which were those of John C. Calhoun, Daniel Webster, and William H. Seward, a rising star of the new generation. Each spoke for one of the three principal viewpoints on the issues.

On March 4, Calhoun, suffering from consumption (he would die within a month), sat shrouded in flannel as a colleague read his speech to a rapt audience. Unless northerners returned fugitive slaves in good faith, Calhoun warned, unless they consented to the expansion of slavery into the territories, the South might not remain in the Union.

Webster's speech three days later was both a reply to Calhoun and an appeal to the North for compromise. "I wish to speak today, not as a Massachusetts man, nor as a Northern man, but as an American," he said. "I speak to-day for the preservation of the Union. Hear me for my cause." Although Webster had voted for the Wilmot Proviso, he now urged Yankees not to insist upon it. Nature would exclude slavery from New Mexico. He even endorsed a fugitive slave law.

On March 11, Seward expressed the antislavery position. Both slavery and compromise were "radically wrong and essentially vicious," he said. In reply to Calhoun's arguments for the constitutional protection of slavery in the territories, he invoked the law of God in whose sight all persons were equal. Instead of legislating the expansion of slavery or the return of fugitive slaves, he said, the country should be considering how to bring slavery peacefully to an end, for "you cannot roll back the tide of social progress."

13-4b *Passage of the Compromise*

While these speeches were being delivered, committee members worked ceaselessly behind the scenes to fashion compromise legislation. But in reaching for a compromise, Clay chose what turned out to be the wrong tactic. He lumped most of his proposals together in a single bill, hoping that supporters of any given part of the compromise would vote for the whole in order to win the part they liked. Instead, most senators and representatives voted against the package in order to defeat the parts they disliked. President Taylor continued to insist on the immediate admission of California (and New Mexico, when it was ready) with no quid pro quo for the South. Exhausted and discouraged, Clay fled Washington's summer heat, leaving a young senator from Illinois, Stephen A. Douglas, to lead the forces of compromise.

Another rising star of the new generation, Douglas reversed Clay's tactics. Starting with a core of supporters made up of Democrats from the Old Northwest and Whigs from the upper South, he built a majority for each part of the compromise by submitting it separately and adding its supporters to his core: northerners for a free California, southerners for a fugitive slave law, and so on. This effort benefited from Taylor's sudden death on July 9 (of gastroenteritis, after consuming large quantities of iced milk and cherries on a hot Fourth of July). The new president, Millard Fillmore, was a conservative Whig from New York who gave his support to the compromise. One after another, in August and September, the separate measures became law: the admission of California as a free state; the organization of the rest of the Mexican cession into the two territories of New Mexico and Utah without restrictions against slavery; the settlement of the Texas–New Mexico border dispute in favor of New Mexico and the compensation of Texas with $10 million; the abolition of the slave trade in the District of Columbia and the guarantee of slavery there; and the passage of a new fugitive slave law. When it was over, most Americans breathed a sigh of relief, and President Fillmore christened the Compromise of 1850 "a final settlement" of all sectional problems. Calhounites in the South and antislavery activists in the North branded the compromise a betrayal of principle, but for the time being they seemed to be in a minority.

The compromise produced consequences different from what many anticipated. California came in as the 16th free state, but its senators during the 1850s were in fact conservative Democrats who voted with the South on most issues. California law even allowed slave owners to keep their slaves while sojourning in the state. The territorial legislatures of Utah and New Mexico legalized slavery, but few slaves were brought there. And the fugitive slave law generated more trouble and controversy than all the other parts of this final settlement combined.

13-4c *The Fugitive Slave Law*

The Constitution required that a slave who escaped into a free state must be returned to his or her owner, but it failed to specify how that should be done. Under a 1793 law, slave owners

What They Said

The Senate Debates the Compromise of 1850

Two of the most notable Senate speeches during the debates over the Compromise of 1850 were delivered by Daniel Webster and William H. Seward. Many of Webster's former antislavery admirers repudiated him after his much-anticipated speech. Seward, by contrast, was catapulted into renown because of what became known as his "higher law" speech. In these selections Webster and Seward reveal their differences regarding a fugitive slave law as part of the compromise.

Daniel Webster

But I will state ... one complaint of the South, which has in my opinion just foundation; and that is, that there has been found at the North, among individuals and among the Legislatures of the North, a disinclination to perform, fully, their constitutional duties, in regard to the return of persons bound to service, who have escaped into the free States. In that respect, it is my judgement that the South is right, and the North is wrong. Every member of every northern Legislature is bound, by oath, like every other officer in the country, to support the Constitution of the United States; and this article of the Constitution, which says to these States, they shall deliver up fugitives from service, is as binding in honor and conscience as any other article. No man fulfills his duty in any Legislature who sets himself to find excuses, evasions, escapes from the constitutional obligation...

I say that the South has been injured in this respect, and has a right to complain. Then, sir, there are those abolition societies, of which I am unwilling to speak, but in regard to which I have very clear notions and opinions. I do not think them useful. I think their operations for the last twenty years have produced nothing good or valuable ... I cannot but see what mischiefs their interference with the South has produced. And is it not plain to every man?

William H. Seward

We deem the principle of the law for the recapture of fugitives ... unjust, unconstitutional, and immoral ... Your Constitution and laws convert hospitality to the refugee, from the most degrading oppression on earth, into a crime, but all mankind except you esteem that hospitality a virtue. The right of extradition of a fugitive from justice, is not admitted by the law of nature and of nations, but rests in voluntary compacts...

I know that there are laws of various sorts which regulate the conduct of men. There are constitutions and statutes, codes mercantile and codes civil; but when we are legislating for States, especially when we are founding States, all these laws must be brought to the standard of the laws of God, and must be tried by that standard, and must stand or fall by it...

The Constitution regulates our stewardship; the Constitution devotes the domain to union, to justice, to defence, to welfare, and to liberty.

But there is a higher law than the Constitution, which regulates our authority over the domain, and devotes it to the same noble purposes. The territory is a part—no inconsiderable part—of the common heritage of mankind, bestowed upon them by the Creator of the Universe. We are his stewards, and must so discharge our trust so as to secure, in the highest attainable degree, their happiness....

Q *How do Webster's and Seward's views of the Constitution differ? How does Webster justify returning fugitive slaves to slavery? On what grounds does Seward justify not enforcing a fugitive slave law?*

Sources: (top) Daniel Webster's congressional speech March 7, 1850. From *Appendix* to the Congressional Globe, 31st Congress, 1st Session, vol. XXII, pt. 1 (1850), 269, 274–276; (bottom) William H. Seward's congressional speech March 11, 1850. From *Appendix* to the Congressional Globe, 31st Congress, 1st Session, vol. XXII, pt. 1 (1850), 262, 263, 265, 266, 268.

could take their recaptured property before any state or federal court to prove ownership. This procedure worked well enough so long as officials in free states were willing to cooperate. But as the antislavery movement gained momentum in the 1830s, some officials proved uncooperative. And professional slave-catchers sometimes went too far—kidnapping free blacks, forging false affidavits to "prove" they were slaves, and selling them south into bondage. Several northern states responded by passing antikidnapping laws that gave alleged fugitives the right of trial by jury. The laws also prescribed criminal penalties for kidnapping. The U.S. Supreme Court declared Pennsylvania's anti-kidnapping law unconstitutional. But the Court also ruled that enforcing the Constitution's fugitive slave clause was entirely a federal responsibility, thereby absolving the states of any need to cooperate in enforcing it. Nine northern states thereupon passed **personal liberty laws** prohibiting the use of state facilities (courts, jails, police or sheriffs, and so on) in the recapture of fugitives.

Fugitive slaves vividly dramatized the poignancy and cruelties of bondage. A man or woman risking all for freedom was not an abstract issue but a real human being whose plight invited sympathy and help. Consequently, many northerners who were not necessarily opposed to slavery in the South nonetheless felt outrage at the idea of fugitives being seized in a land of freedom and returned to slavery. The **"underground railroad"** that helped spirit slaves out of bondage took on legendary status. Stories of secret chambers where fugitives were hidden, dramatic trips at night between stations on the underground, and clever or heroic measures to foil pursuing bloodhounds exaggerated the legend.

Probably fewer than 1,000 of a total 3 million slaves actually escaped to freedom each year. But to southerners the return of those fugitives—like the question of the legality of slavery in California or New Mexico—was a matter of *honor* and *rights*. "Although the loss of property is felt," said Senator James Mason of Virginia, sponsor of the Fugitive Slave Act, "the loss of honor is felt still more." The fugitive slave law, said another southern politician, was "the only measure of the Compromise [of 1850] calculated to secure the rights of the South." Southerners therefore regarded obedience to the fugitive slave law as a test of the North's good faith in carrying out the compromise.

The provisions of that law were extraordinary. It created federal commissioners who could issue warrants for arrests of fugitives and before whom a slaveholder would bring a captured fugitive to prove ownership. All the slaveholder needed for proof was an affidavit from a slave-state court or the testimony of white witnesses. The fugitive had no right to testify on his or her own behalf. The commissioner received a fee of $10 if he found the owner's claim valid, but only $5 if he let the fugitive go. (The difference was supposedly justified by the larger amount of paperwork required to return the fugitive to slavery.) The federal treasury would pay all costs of enforcement. The commissioner could call on federal marshals to apprehend fugitives, and the marshals in turn could deputize any citizen to help. A citizen who refused could be fined up to $1,000, and anyone who harbored a fugitive or obstructed his or her capture would be subject to imprisonment.

13-4d *The Slave-Catchers*

Abolitionists denounced the law as draconian, immoral, and unconstitutional. They vowed to resist it. Opportunities soon came, as slave owners sent agents north to recapture fugitives, some of whom had escaped years earlier (the act set no statute of limitations). In February 1851, slave-catchers arrested a black man living with his family in Indiana and returned him to an owner who said he had run away 19 years before. A Maryland man tried to claim ownership of a Philadelphia woman who he said had escaped 22 years earlier; he also wanted her six children, all of whom were born in Philadelphia. In this case, the commissioner disallowed his claim to both mother and children, but statistics show that the law was rigged in favor of the claimants. In the first 15 months of its operation, 84 fugitives were returned to slavery and only 5 were released. (For the entire decade of the 1850s, the ratio was 332 to 11.)

Two of the most famous of these fugitive slaves were William and Ellen Craft, whose successful struggle for liberty inspired other slaves and abolitionists on both sides of the Atlantic. Both born in slavery, William and Ellen were married in Georgia in 1846. Unwilling to give birth to children who might be sold away from her, Ellen plotted with her husband to escape to the North. Light enough to pass for white (she was the daughter of her master and his light-skinned concubine), Ellen sewed herself a pair of trousers and posed as a deaf-mute invalid young man traveling to Philadelphia for medical treatment attended by "his" slave William. After some close calls, they made it to Philadelphia at the end of 1848 and moved on to Boston in 1849.

After passage of the Fugitive Slave Law in 1850, however, two agents from Georgia appeared in Boston to recapture the Crafts. Local abolitionists spirited them away to Canada and then to England, where the Crafts lived for the next 19 years and had five children.

Unable to protect their freedom through legal means, many other blacks, with the support of white allies, also resorted to flight and resistance. Thousands of northern blacks fled to Canada—3,000 in the last three months of 1850 alone. In February 1851, slave-catchers arrested a fugitive who had taken the name Shadrach when he escaped from Virginia a year earlier. They rushed him to the federal courthouse, where a few deputy marshals held him, pending a hearing. But a group of black men broke into the courtroom, overpowered the deputies, and spirited Shadrach out of the country to Canada. This was too much for the Fillmore administration. In April 1851, another fugitive, Thomas Sims, was arrested in Boston, and the president sent 250 soldiers to help 300 armed deputies enforce the law and return Sims to slavery.

Continued rescues and escapes kept matters at a fever pitch for the rest of the decade. In the fall of 1851, a Maryland slave owner and his son accompanied federal marshals to Christiana, Pennsylvania, a Quaker village, where two of the man's slaves had taken refuge. The hunters ran into a fusillade of gunfire from a house where a dozen black men were protecting the fugitives. When the shooting stopped, the slave owner was dead and his son was seriously wounded. Three of the blacks fled to Canada. This time Fillmore sent in the marines. They helped marshals arrest 30 black men and half a dozen whites who were indicted for treason. But the U.S. attorney dropped charges after a jury acquitted the first defendant, a Quaker.

Two of the most famous fugitive slave cases of the 1850s ended in tragedy. In spring 1854, federal marshals in Boston arrested a Virginia fugitive, Anthony Burns. Angry abolitionists poured into Boston to save him. Some of them tried to attack the federal courthouse, where a deputy was killed in an exchange of gunfire. But the new president, Franklin Pierce, was determined not to back down. "Incur any expense," he wired the district attorney in Boston, "to enforce the law." After every legal move to free Burns had failed, Pierce sent federal troops. While thousands of angry Yankees lined the streets under American flags hanging upside down to signify the loss of liberty in the cradle of the Revolution, 200 marines and soldiers marched this lone black man back into bondage.

Two years later, Margaret Garner escaped from Kentucky to Ohio with her husband and four children. When a posse of marshals and deputies caught up with them, Margaret seized a kitchen knife and tried to kill her children and herself rather than return to slavery. She managed to cut her three-year-old daughter's throat before she was overpowered. After complicated legal maneuvers, the federal commissioner remanded the fugitives to their Kentucky owner. He promptly sold them down the river to Arkansas, and, in a steamboat accident along the way, one of Margaret Garner's sons drowned in the Mississippi.

Such events had a profound impact on public emotions. Most northerners were not abolitionists, and few of them regarded black people as equals, but millions of them moved closer to an antislavery—or perhaps it would be more accurate to say anti-southern—position in response to the shock of seeing armed slave-catchers on their streets. "When it was all over," agreed two previously conservative Whigs in Boston after the Anthony Burns affair, "I put my face in my hands and wept I could do nothing less.... We went to bed one night old-fashioned, conservative, compromise Union Whigs and waked up stark mad Abolitionists."

Several northern states passed new personal liberty laws in defiance of the South. Although those laws did not make it impossible to recover fugitives, they made it so difficult, expensive, and time consuming that many slave owners gave up trying. The failure of the North to honor the Fugitive Slave Law, part of the Compromise of 1850, was one of the South's bitter grievances in the 1850s. Several southern states cited it as one of their reasons for seceding in 1861.

13-4e *Uncle Tom's Cabin*

A novel inspired by the plight of fugitive slaves further intensified public sentiment. Harriet Beecher Stowe was a member of a prominent New England family of clergymen and writers, and was herself a short story writer. In the 1840s, while living in Cincinnati with her husband, a minister, she became acquainted with fugitive slaves who had escaped across the Ohio River. Outraged by the Fugitive Slave Act of 1850, in 1851 she began to write a new piece of fiction—managing to write a chapter a week after she had put her children to bed.

Uncle Tom's Cabin became a runaway best seller, and was eventually translated into 20 languages. The novel's powerful central theme was the tragedy of the breakup of families by slavery—dramatized in scenes that would become an important part of American popular culture, such as the slave Eliza's escape across the ice-choked Ohio River to save her son from a slave trader. Throughout the novel Stowe spoke directly to white women readers, asking them to imagine being torn from their own children. Yet, it was not just women who responded to her calls to end slavery: Men, too, wrote of being deeply affected by the tragic story she told.

Although banned in some parts of the South, *Uncle Tom's Cabin* found a wide but hostile readership there. Pro-slavery authors rushed into print with more than a dozen novels challenging Stowe's themes, but all of them together made nothing like the impact of *Uncle Tom's Cabin*. The book helped shape a whole generation's view of slavery.

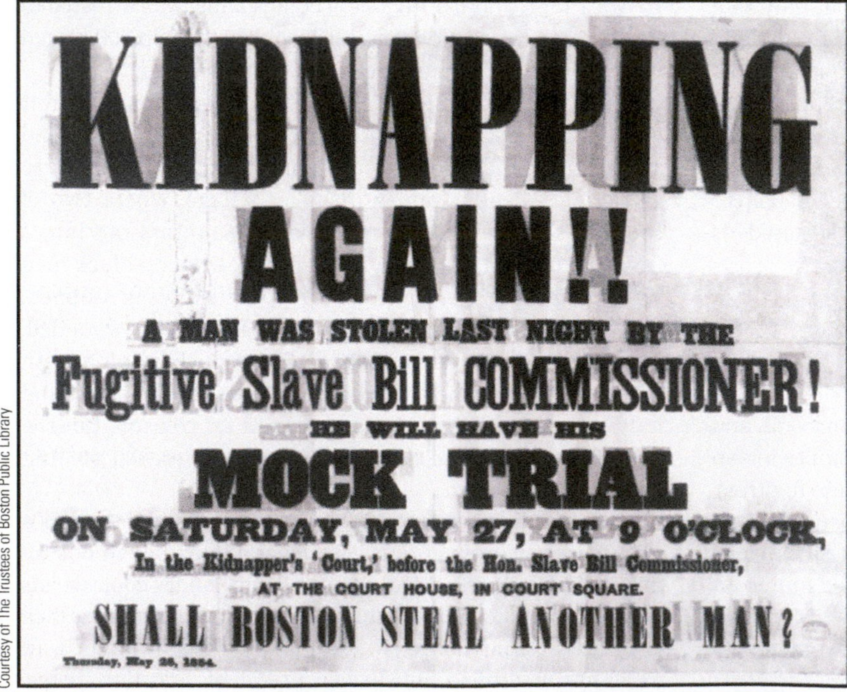
KIDNAPPING
AGAIN!!
A MAN WAS STOLEN LAST NIGHT BY THE
Fugitive Slave Bill COMMISSIONER!
HE WILL HAVE HIS
MOCK TRIAL
ON SATURDAY, MAY 27, AT 9 O'CLOCK,
In the Kidnapper's 'Court,' before the Hon. Slave Bill Commissioner,
AT THE COURT HOUSE, IN COURT SQUARE.
SHALL BOSTON STEAL ANOTHER MAN?
Thursday, May 26, 1854.

13.8 **Kidnapping Again!** This is a typical poster printed by abolitionist opponents of the Fugitive Slave Law. It was intended to rally the citizens of Boston against the recapture and reenslavement of Anthony Burns, a fugitive slave from Virginia seized in Boston in May 1854.

Q *How does this poster attempt to arouse the reader's outrage?*

Historical/Corbis

13.9 **Harriet Tubman** Born into slavery in Maryland around 1822, Harriet Tubman escaped to freedom in 1849, settling at first in Philadelphia. Despite the many dangers she faced, Tubman returned to the South over and over in the years before the Civil War, helping her own relatives as well as dozens of other slaves to escape north. Wanted posters throughout the upper South described this "Moses," as Tubman was called, but she eluded capture. During the Civil War the intrepid Tubman worked for the Union army as a nurse and cook, as well as a scout and spy in Confederate territory. Tubman was also active in the woman suffrage movement late in the century. Working by necessity in secret before the Civil War, today Tubman is remembered, along with Frederick Douglass, as one of the most prominent abolitionists of the 19th century.

13-5 Filibustering

Q *How was filibustering related to demands for the expansion of slavery?*

If the prospects for slavery in New Mexico appeared unpromising, southerners could contemplate a closer region where slavery already existed—Cuba. Enjoying an economic boom based on slave-grown sugar, this Spanish colony only 90 miles from American shores had nearly 400,000 slaves in 1850—more than any American state except Virginia. President Polk, his appetite for territory not yet sated by the acquisition of Texas, Oregon, and half of Mexico, offered Spain $100 million for Cuba in 1848. The Spanish foreign minister spurned the offer, stating that he would rather see the island sunk in the sea than sold.

13-5a *Cuba*

If money did not work, revolution might. Cuban planters, restive under Spanish rule, intrigued with American expansionists in the hope of fomenting an uprising on the island. Their leader was Narciso López, a Venezuelan-born Cuban soldier of fortune. In 1849, López recruited several hundred American adventurers for the first **"filibustering"** expedition against Cuba (from the Spanish *filibustero*, a freebooter or pirate). When President Taylor ordered the navy to prevent López's ships from leaving New York, López shifted his operations to the friendlier environs of New Orleans, where he raised a new force of filibusters, many of them Mexican War veterans. Port officials in New Orleans looked the other way when the expedition sailed in May 1850, but Spanish troops

Bettmann/Historical/Corbis

13.10 **Harriet Beecher Stowe and Family** Harriet Beecher Stowe, the author of *Uncle Tom's Cabin*, was part of a large and influential family. In this formal 1850 photograph, Stowe is seated on the far right in the first row; her father, Lyman Beecher, one of the most prominent ministers in American history, is seated in the middle of the row. Left of Lyman Beecher is Harriet Beecher Stowe's sister Catherine Beecher, famous both as an educator and for her books on household management that expounded the national importance of women in their domestic roles. In the back row, on the right, stands Stowe's brother Henry Ward Beecher, widely regarded as the most inspiring preacher of the post–Civil War era. While Harriet's father Lyman had been a stern, Calvinist-inspired minister demanding individual repentance during numerous religious revivals before the Civil War, his son Henry instead emphasized the importance of the heart and individual responsibility in his own preaching. We can see that same emphasis on the central importance of emotion and "right feeling" in Harriet Beecher Stowe's abolitionist writings.

Q *What does this formal photograph reveal about middle-class family relationships in the mid-19th century?*

drove the filibusters into the sea after they had established a beachhead in Cuba.

Undaunted, López escaped and returned to a hero's welcome in the South, where he raised men and money for a third try in 1851. This time, William Crittenden of Kentucky, nephew of the U.S. attorney general, commanded the 420 Americans in the expedition, but the invasion ended in fiasco and tragedy. Spanish soldiers suppressed a local uprising timed to coincide with the invasion and then defeated the filibusters, killing 200 and capturing the rest. López was garroted in the public square of Havana. Then 50 American prisoners, including Crittenden, were lined up and executed by firing squad.

These events dampened southerners' enthusiasm for Cuba, but only for a time. "Cuba must be ours," declared Jefferson Davis, in order to "increase the number of slave-holding constituencies." In 1852, the Democrats nominated Franklin Pierce of New Hampshire for president. Although a Yankee, Pierce had a reputation as a "doughface"—a northern man with southern principles. Southern Democrats were delighted with his nomination. Pierce was "as reliable as Calhoun himself," wrote one, while another said that "a nomination so favorable to the South had not been anticipated." Especially gratifying was Pierce's support for annexing Cuba, which he made one of the top priorities of his new administration after winning a landslide victory over a demoralized Whig Party weakened by schism between its northern and southern wings.

Pierce covertly encouraged a new filibustering expedition to Cuba. This one was to be led by former governor John Quitman of Mississippi. While Quitman was recruiting hundreds of volunteers, southerners in Congress introduced a resolution to suspend the neutrality law that prohibited American interference in the internal affairs of other countries. But at the last moment Pierce backed off, fearful of political damage in the North if his administration became openly identified with filibustering. The Quitman expedition never sailed.

Pierce again tried to buy Cuba, instructing the American minister in Madrid to offer Spain $130 million. The minister was Pierre Soulé, a flamboyant Louisianan who managed to alienate most Spaniards by his clumsy intriguing. Soulé's crowning act came in October 1854 at a meeting with the American ministers to Britain and France in Ostend, Belgium. He persuaded them to sign what came to be known as the Ostend Manifesto. "Cuba is as necessary to the North American republic as any of its present ... family of states," declared this document. If Spain persisted in refusing to sell, then "by every law, human and divine, we shall be justified in wresting it from Spain."

This "manifesto of the brigands," as antislavery Americans called it, caused an international uproar. The administration repudiated the Ostend Manifesto and recalled Soulé. Nevertheless, acquisition of Cuba remained an objective of the Democratic Party. The issue played a role in both the 1860 presidential election and the secession controversy during 1860 and 1861. Meanwhile, American filibustering shifted its focus 750 miles south of Havana to Nicaragua. There, the most remarkable of the *filibusteros*, William Walker, had proclaimed himself president and restored the institution of slavery.

13-5b *The Gray-Eyed Man of Destiny*

A native of Tennessee and a brilliant, restless man, Walker had earned a medical degree from the University of Pennsylvania and studied and practiced law in New Orleans before joining the 1849 rush to California. Weighing less than 120 pounds, Walker seemed an unlikely fighter or leader of men, but he fought three duels, and his luminous eyes, which seemed to transfix his fellows, won him the sobriquet "gray-eyed man of destiny."

Walker found his true calling in filibustering. At the time, numerous raids were taking place back and forth across the border with Mexico, some of them staged to seize more of that country for the United States. In 1853, Walker led a ragged "army" of footloose 49ers into Baja California and Sonora and declared the region an independent republic. Exhaustion and desertion depleted his troops, however, and the Mexicans drove the survivors back to California.

Walker decided to try again, with another goal. Many southerners eyed Nicaragua's potential for growing cotton, sugar, coffee, and other crops. The unstable Nicaraguan government offered a tempting target. In 1854, Walker signed a contract with rebel leaders in the civil war of the moment. The following spring, he led an advance guard of filibusters to Nicaragua and proclaimed himself commander-in-chief of the rebel forces. At the head of 2,000 American volunteers, he gained control of the country and named himself president in 1856. The Pierce administration extended diplomatic recognition to Walker's regime.

The other Central American republics soon formed an alliance to invade Nicaragua and overthrow Walker. To win greater support from the southern states, Walker issued a decree in September 1856 reinstituting slavery in Nicaragua. A convention of southern economic promoters meeting in Savannah praised Walker's efforts "to introduce civilization in the States of Central America, and to develop these rich and productive regions by slave labor." Boatloads of new recruits arrived in Nicaragua from New Orleans, but in spring 1857, they succumbed to disease and to the Central American armies.

Walker escaped to New Orleans, where he was welcomed as a hero. He had no trouble recruiting men for another attempt, but the navy stopped him in November 1857. Southern congressmen condemned the naval commander and encouraged Walker to try again. He did, in December 1858, after a New Orleans jury refused to convict him of violating the neutrality law. On this third expedition, Walker's ship struck a reef and sank. Undaunted, he tried yet again. He wrote a book to raise funds for another invasion of Nicaragua, urging "the hearts of Southern youth to answer the call of honor... . The true field for the expansion of slavery is in tropical America." A few more southern youths answered the call, but they were stopped in Honduras. There, on September 12, 1860, the gray-eyed man met his destiny before a firing squad.

Conclusion

Within the three-year period from 1845 to 1848, the annexation of Texas, the settlement of the Oregon boundary dispute with Britain, and the acquisition by force of New Mexico and California from Mexico added 1,150,000 square miles to the United States. This expansion was America's "Manifest Destiny," according to Senator Stephen A. Douglas of Illinois. He further proclaimed:

> Increase, and multiply, and expand, is the law of this nation's existence. You cannot limit this great republic by mere boundary lines. Any one of you gentlemen might as well say to a son twelve years old that he is big enough, and must not grow any larger, and in order to prevent his growth put a hoop around him and keep him to his present size. Either the hoop must burst and be rent asunder, or the child must die. So it would be with this great nation.

But other Americans feared that the country could not absorb such rapid growth without strains that might break it apart. At the outbreak of the war with Mexico, Ralph Waldo Emerson predicted that "the United States will conquer Mexico, but it will be as the man swallows the arsenic, which brings him down in turn. Mexico will poison us." Emerson proved correct. The poison was the reopening of the question of slavery's expansion, which had supposedly been settled by the Missouri Compromise in 1820. The admission of Texas as a huge new slave state and the possibility that more slave states might be carved out of the territory acquired from Mexico provoked northern congressmen to pass the Wilmot Proviso. Southerners bristled at this attempt to prevent the further expansion of slavery. Threats of secession and civil war poisoned the atmosphere in 1849 and 1850.

The Compromise of 1850 defused the crisis and appeared to settle the issue once again, but events would soon prove that this compromise had merely postponed the crisis. The fugitive slave issue and filibustering expeditions to acquire more slave territory kept sectional controversies smoldering. In 1854, the Kansas-Nebraska Act would cause them to burst into a hotter flame than ever.

CHAPTER REVIEW

Review

1. What impulses lay behind the "Manifest Destiny" of America's westward expansion?
2. What were the causes and consequences of the Mexican War?
3. How did the question of slavery affect the election of 1848?
4. What issues were at stake in the congressional debates that led to the Compromise of 1850? How successfully did the compromise resolve these issues?
5. How was filibustering related to demands for the expansion of slavery?

Critical Thinking

1. Between 1803 and 1845, the territorial size of the United States increased by only 5 percent (with the acquisition of Florida in 1819). Yet, in the three years from 1845 to 1848, the size of the United States mushroomed by another 50 percent. How do you explain this remarkable phenomenon?
2. Why was the issue of slavery in the territories so important and controversial in the 1840s and 1850s when slavery already existed in half of the states?

Identifications

Review your understanding of the following key terms, people, and events for this chapter (terms in bold in text are included in the Glossary).

Young America movement, p. 354
Manifest Destiny, p. 354
missions, p. 355
presidios, p. 355
Great American Desert, p. 357
Mormons, p. 357
tejanos, p. 358
Alamo, p. 358
Wilmot Proviso, p. 363
Treaty of Guadalupe Hidalgo, p. 364
popular sovereignty, p. 364
Conscience Whigs, p. 364
Free-Soilers, p. 364
fugitive slaves, p. 366
Compromise of 1850, p. 367
personal liberty laws, p. 369
underground railroad, p. 369
filibustering, p. 371

Suggested Readings

On Manifest Destiny and filibustering, see **Amy S. Greenberg**, ***Manifest Manhood and the Antebellum American Empire*** (2005). For an excellent account of the history of the West, see **Robert V. Hine** and **John Mack Faragher**, ***The American West: An Interpretive History*** (2000). On the rise of a Native American empire that resisted European colonization, see **Pekka Hämäläinen**, ***The Comanche Empire*** (2009). The political polarization produced by the controversy over the annexation of Texas is clearly laid out by **Joel H. Silbey**,

Storm over Texas: The Annexation Controversy and the Road to Civil War (2005). For the Mexican War, see **Amy Greenberg**, ***A Wicked War: Polk, Clay, Lincoln and the 1846 U.S. Invasion of Mexico*** (2012). On the gold rush, see **Malcolm J. Rohrbough**, ***Days of Gold: The California Gold Rush and the American Nation*** (1997); **Susan Lee Johnson**, ***Roaring Camp: The Social World of The California Gold Rush*** (2000); and **David Igler**, ***The Great Ocean: Pacific Worlds from Captain Cook to the Gold Rush*** (2013). For the conflict provoked by the issue of slavery's expansion into territory acquired from Mexico, a classic is **David M. Potter**, ***The Impending Crisis 1848–1861*** (1976); see also **Michael A. Morrison**, ***Slavery and the American West: The Eclipse of Manifest Destiny and the Coming of the Civil War*** (1997); and **Leonard D. Richards**, ***The Slave Power: The Free North and Southern Domination, 1780–1860*** (2000). The partisan roots of sectional conflict are emphasized in **Michael F. Holt**, ***The Fate of Their Country: Politicians, Slavery Extension, and the Coming of the Civil War*** (2004). On filibustering, see **Robert E. May**, ***Manifest Destiny's Underworld: Filibustering in Antebellum America*** (2004).

14 The Gathering Tempest, 1853–1860

Stump Speaking (oil on canvas), Bingham, George Caleb (1811-79)/Private Collection/The Bridgeman Art Library

14.1 **Stump Speaking** George Caleb Bingham's 1853–1854 genre painting *Stump Speaking* captures the cultural importance of politics in American life in the pre–Civil War era. Here a diverse rural audience listens to an open-air speaker. We can see plainly dressed men and women sitting on the ground and listening intently, a bored child, and well-fed and well-dressed gentlemen seated on chairs. The standing man in the foreground, wearing hat and coat, seems about to interrupt the speaker—or perhaps is just listening especially closely. This portrait of political engagement reminds us that oratory was a central part of the practice of politics in mid-19th-century America.

THE WOUNDS caused by the 1850 battle over slavery in the territories had barely healed when they were reopened. This time the strife concerned the question of slavery in the Louisiana Purchase territory, an issue presumably settled 34 years earlier by the Missouri Compromise of 1820.

The Compromise of 1820 had admitted Missouri as a slave state but had banned slavery from the rest of the Purchase north of 36°30". To obtain southern support for the organization of Kansas and Nebraska as territories, Senator Stephen Douglas consented to the repeal of this provision. Northern outrage at this repudiation of a "sacred contract" killed the Whig Party and gave birth to the antislavery Republican Party. In 1857, the Supreme Court added insult to injury with the **Dred Scott** decision, which denied Congress the power to restrict slavery from the territories. The ominous reorientation of national politics along sectional lines was accompanied by a bloody civil war in Kansas and a raid on the federal arsenal at **Harpers Ferry**, Virginia, by **John Brown** and his followers. ■

CHRONOLOGY

1852	Plenary Council of Catholic Church seeks tax support for parochial schools
1853	American Party ("Know-Nothings") emerges
1854	Crimean War begins • Congress passes Kansas-Nebraska Act • Republican Party organized • Antebellum immigration reaches peak
1855	Ethnic riots in several cities • "Border ruffian" legislature in Kansas legalizes slavery
1856	Civil war in Kansas • Preston Brooks canes Charles Sumner on Senate floor • Crimean War ends • Buchanan wins three-way presidential election
1857	Supreme Court issues Dred Scott decision • Lecompton constitution written in Kansas • Congress enacts lower tariff • Panic of 1857 • Helper's *Impending Crisis* published
1858	Kansas voters reject Lecompton constitution • Lincoln-Douglas debates
1859	Congress defeats federal slave code for territories • John Brown's raid at Harpers Ferry
1860	Shoemakers' strike in New England • Buchanan vetoes Homestead Act

14-1 Kansas and the Rise of the Republican Party

Q *Why did the Whig Party die, and why did the Republican Party emerge as the new majority party in the North?*

By 1853, land-hungry settlers had pushed up the Missouri River to its confluence with the Kansas and Platte rivers, and entrepreneurs were talking about a railroad across the continent to San Francisco. But settlement west of Missouri and land surveys for a railroad required the organization of this region as a territory. Accordingly, in 1853 the House passed a bill creating the Nebraska Territory, embracing the area north of Indian Territory (present-day Oklahoma) up to the Canadian border. But the House bill ran into trouble in the Senate. Under the Missouri Compromise, slavery would be excluded from the new territory. Having lost California, the pro-slavery forces were determined to salvage something from Nebraska. Missourians were particularly adamant, because a free Nebraska would leave them almost surrounded on three sides by free soil.

The sponsor of the Senate bill was Stephen A. Douglas, chairman of the Senate Committee on Territories. Only 5 feet 4 inches tall, Douglas had earned the nickname Little Giant for his parliamentary skill, which he had demonstrated most dramatically in helping pass the Compromise of 1850 through Congress. In Douglas's opinion, the application of popular sovereignty to the slavery question in New Mexico and Utah had been the centerpiece of the compromise. The initial draft of his Nebraska bill merely repeated the language used for those territories, specifying that when any portion of the Nebraska Territory came in as a state, it could do so "with or without slavery, as its constitution may provide."

This was not good enough for southern congressmen, who insisted on an explicit repeal of the Missouri Compromise. Sighing that this would "raise a hell of a storm," Douglas nevertheless agreed. He further agreed to divide the area in question into two territories: Kansas west of Missouri and Nebraska west of Iowa and Minnesota. To many northerners this looked suspiciously like a scheme to mark Kansas out for slavery and Nebraska for freedom.

14-1a *The Kansas-Nebraska Act*

The **Kansas-Nebraska Act** did "raise a hell of a storm." Contemporaries and historians have speculated endlessly on Douglas's motives. Some thought he wanted to win southern support for the presidential nomination in 1856. Perhaps, but he risked losing northern support. Others point out that Douglas's real estate holdings in Illinois would have increased in value if a transcontinental railroad were to traverse the Nebraska Territory and that southern opposition could block this route. The most likely reason, however, was Douglas's passionate belief in Manifest Destiny, in filling up the continent with American settlers and institutions. For this, he was willing to pay the South's price for support of his Kansas-Nebraska bill. But he failed to recognize the depth of northern opposition to the "slave power" and to the expansion of slavery. Douglas had no firm moral convictions about slavery. He said that he cared not whether the settlers voted slavery up or down; the important thing was to give them a chance to vote.

But many Americans did care. They regarded the expansion of slavery as a national question, and one that was too important to be left to territorial voters. One of them was an old acquaintance of Douglas, **Abraham Lincoln**. An antislavery Whig who had served four terms in the Illinois legislature and one term in Congress, Lincoln was propelled back into politics by the shock of the Kansas-Nebraska bill. He acknowledged the constitutional right to hold slave property in the states where it already existed, but he believed slavery was "an unqualified evil to the negro, the white man, and to the state.... There can be no moral right in connection with one man's making a slave of another." Lincoln admitted he did not know how to bring this deeply entrenched institution to an end. He understood that race prejudice was a powerful obstacle to emancipation. Still, he believed that the country must face up to the problem. It must stop any further expansion of slavery as the first step on the long road to its "ultimate extinction."

Lincoln excoriated Douglas's "care not" attitude toward whether slavery was voted up or down. He branded Douglas's assertion that slavery would never be imported into Kansas because of the region's supposedly unsuitable climate a "LULLABY argument." The climate of eastern Kansas was similar to that of the Missouri River valley in Missouri, where slaves were busily raising hemp and tobacco. Missouri slaveholders were already poised to take their slaves into the

Adoc-photos/Art Resource, NY

14.2 **Abraham Lincoln** Nominated to oppose Stephen A. Douglas's reelection to the Senate from Illinois in 1858, Abraham Lincoln was not yet a national figure. But his status would change dramatically with the Lincoln-Douglas debates of 1858, which focused on the issue of slavery. Lincoln's eloquence in this series of debates propelled him into national prominence.

Kansas River valley. "Climate will not ... keep slavery out of these territories," said Lincoln. "Nothing in *nature* will." Many of the Founding Fathers had looked forward to the day when slavery would no longer exist in republican America. Instead, the United States had become the world's largest slaveholding society, and Douglas's bill would permit slavery to expand even further. In a political speech at Peoria, Illinois, in October 1854, Lincoln insisted:

> The monstrous injustice of slavery deprives our republican example of its just influence in the world—enables the enemies of free institutions, with plausibility, to taunt us as hypocrites... . Let us re-adopt the Declaration of Independence, and with it, the practices, and policy, which harmonize with it... . If we do this, we shall not only have saved the Union; but we shall have so saved it, as to make, and to keep it, forever worthy of the saving.

With these eloquent words, Lincoln gave voice to the feelings rising up against the Kansas-Nebraska bill. Abolitionists, Free-Soilers, northern Whigs, and even many northern Democrats held impassioned meetings to form anti-Nebraska coalitions, but they could not stop passage of the bill. It cleared the Senate easily, supported by a solid South and 15 of the 20 northern Democrats. In the House, it passed by a vote of 113 to 100.

14-1b *Death of the Whig Party*

These proceedings completed the destruction of the Whigs as a national party. Southern Whigs had been disappearing ever since Zachary Taylor had "betrayed" them on the issue of a free California. After the presidential election of 1852, few Whigs remained in the cotton South. In that year, the Whig Party nominated General Winfield Scott for president. Although he was a Virginian, Scott, like Taylor, took a national rather than a southern view. He was the candidate of the northern Whigs in the national convention, which nominated him on the 53rd ballot after a bitter contest between the northern and southern wings of the party. A mass exodus of southern Whigs into the Democratic Party enabled Franklin Pierce to carry all but two slave states in the election. The unanimous vote of northern Whigs in Congress against the Kansas-Nebraska bill was the final straw. The Whig Party never recovered its influence in the South.

Whig strength seemed to be on its last legs in the North as well. Antislavery Whig leaders, such as William H. Seward and Lincoln, hoped to channel the flood of anti-Nebraska sentiment through the Whig Party, an effort akin to containing Niagara Falls. Free-Soilers and antislavery Democrats spurned the Whig label. Political coalitions arose spontaneously in the North under various names: anti-Nebraska, Fusion, People's, Independent. The name that caught on evoked memories of America's first fight for freedom in 1776: Republican. The first use of this name seems to have occurred at an anti-Nebraska rally in a Congregational church at Ripon, Wisconsin, in May 1854. Soon, most of the congressional candidates fielded by anti-Nebraska coalitions ran their campaigns under the Republican banner.

The 1854 elections were disastrous for northern Democrats. One-fourth of Democratic voters deserted the party. The Democrats lost control of the House of Representatives when 66 of 91 incumbent free-state Democratic congressmen went down to defeat. Combined with the increase in the number of Democratic congressmen from the South, where the party had picked up the pieces of the shattered Whig organization, this rout brought the party under southern domination more than ever.

But who would pick up the pieces of old parties in the North? The new Republican Party hoped to do so, but it suffered a shock in urban areas of the Northeast. Hostility toward immigrants created a tidal wave of **nativism** that threatened to swamp the anti-Nebraska movement. "Nearly everybody appears to have gone deranged on Nativism," reported a Pennsylvania Democrat, while a Whig in upstate New York warned that his district was "very badly infected with Know-nothingism." Described as a "tornado," a "hurricane," a "freak of political insanity," the **Know-Nothings** won landslide victories in Massachusetts and Delaware, polled an estimated 40 percent of the vote in Pennsylvania, and did well elsewhere in the Northeast and border states. Who were these mysterious Know-Nothings? What did they stand for?

Library of Congress Prints and Photographs Division

14.3 **Stephen A. Douglas** The Little Giant began his meteoric rise to leadership of the Democratic Party with his successful effort to have the Compromise of 1850 enacted by Congress. Having forestalled sectional schism in 1850, he drove a wedge more deeply than ever between North and South with the Kansas-Nebraska bill of 1854. Six years later, Douglas became a victim of sectional schism when the Democratic Party split into northern and southern factions and thereby ruined his chance of winning the presidency.

Q *Why did Douglas sponsor a bill in 1854 that he knew would "raise a hell of a storm"?*

14-2 Immigration and Nativism

Q *What were the origins of nativism? How did this movement relate to the slavery issue?*

During the early 19th century, immigration was less pronounced than in most other periods of U.S. history. The volume of immigration (the number of new immigrants in proportion to the whole population) was little more than 1 percent in the 1820s, increasing to 4 percent in the 1830s. Three-quarters of the newcomers were Protestants, mainly from Britain. Most of them were skilled workers, farmers, or members of white-collar occupations.

In the 1840s, a combination of factors abruptly quadrupled the volume of immigration and changed its ethnic and occupational makeup. The pressure of expanding population on limited land in Germany and successive failures of the potato crop in Ireland impelled millions of German and Irish peasants to emigrate (see Figure 14.1). A majority came to the United States, where recovery from the depression of the early 1840s brought an economic boom and an insatiable demand for labor. During the decade after 1845, 3 million immigrants entered the United States—15 percent of the total American population in 1845, the highest proportional volume of immigration in American history. Many of them, especially the Irish, joined the unskilled and semiskilled labor force in the rapidly growing eastern cities.

Most of the new arrivals were Roman Catholics. Anti-Catholicism had centuries-deep roots in Anglo-American Protestantism. Fear of the pope and of the Roman Church as autocratic and anti-republican was never far below the surface of American political culture, and scurrilous anti-Catholic literature circulated during the 1830s. Several ethnic riots between Protestant and Catholic workers over the years culminated in pitched battles and numerous deaths in Philadelphia in 1844. In several eastern cities nativist political parties sprang up in the early 1840s with the intent of curbing the political rights of immigrants.

Nativism appeared to subside with the revival of prosperity after 1844, but the decline was temporary. Established Americans perceived more recent arrivals as responsible for an increase of crime and poverty in the cities. They also viewed immigrant culture with suspicion. The social and political life of both the Irish and the Germans revolved around taverns and beer parlors at a time when the temperance crusade had sharply curtailed drinking among native-born Protestants (see Chapter 12).

14-2a *Immigrants in Politics*

The growing political power of immigrants became a bone of contention. Most of the immigrants became Democrats, because that party welcomed or at least tolerated them and many Whigs did not. Foreign-born voters leaned toward the pro-slavery wing of the Democratic Party, even though seven-eighths of them settled in free states. Mostly working-class and poor, they rubbed shoulders against the small northern black population; Irish American mobs sometimes attacked black neighborhoods and rioted against black workers. They supported the Democratic Party as the best means of keeping blacks in slavery and out of the North. These attitudes sparked hostility toward immigrants among many antislavery people.

Attitudes toward immigrants had political repercussions. Two of the hottest issues in state and local politics during the early 1850s were temperance and schools. The temperance crusaders had grown confident and aggressive enough to go into politics. The drunkenness and rowdiness they associated with Irish immigrants became one of their particular targets. Beginning with Maine in 1851, 12 states had enacted prohibition laws by 1855. Although several of the laws were soon weakened by the courts or repealed by legislatures, they exacerbated ethnic tensions.

So too did battles over public schools versus parochial schools. Catholics resented the Protestant domination of public

RALLY

SPIRITS OF '76!

ALL CITIZENS OF

LEOMINSTER,

without distinction of party, who disapprove of the

"Nebraska Iniquity,"

are requested to meet at the

TOWN HALL,

Monday Evening, July 10th,

AT 7 O'CLOCK,

to choose delegates to meet in a

Mass Convention,

at Worcester, the 20th inst., to teach the "South" we have a "North," and will maintain our CONSTITUTIONAL RIGHTS.

CALEB C. FIELD, LEONARD BURRAGE, MERRITT WOOD.

Leominster, July 8, 1854.

14.4 Birth of the Republican Party The Kansas-Nebraska Act galvanized antislavery northerners of all parties into new anti-Nebraska organizations opposed to the repeal of the Missouri Compromise's ban on slavery in Louisiana Purchase territories north of 36°30". Appealing to the "spirit of '76," these organizations coalesced into the Republican Party, which held its first convention at Pittsburgh on Washington's birthday in 1856 to organize a national party in preparation for the presidential nominating convention later that year.

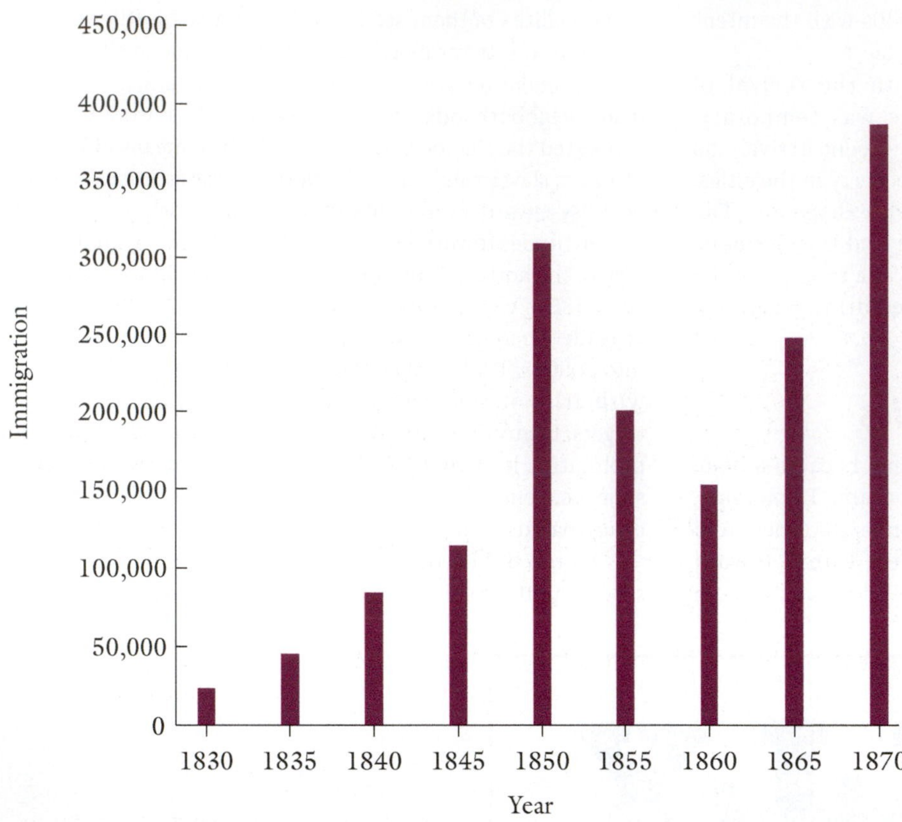

Figure 14.1 **Immigration to the United States** Revolution in Germany and potato famine in Ireland were significant factors behind the dramatic rise in immigration to the United States between 1845 and 1850. Another surge in immigration occurred after the Civil War ended in 1865.

Source: Data from *Historical Statistics of the United States, Millennial Online Addition*, "U.S. Immigrants and Emigrants: 1820–1998" [Table Ad1-2].

education and the reading of the King James Bible in schools. The Catholic Church began to build parochial schools for the faithful, and in 1852, the first Plenary Council of American bishops decided to seek tax support for these schools or tax relief for Catholic parents who sent their children to them. This effort set off heated election contests in numerous northern cities and states. Anti-Catholic "free school" tickets won most of these elections on a platform of defending public schools against the "bold effort" of this "despotic faith" to "uproot the tree of Liberty."

14-2b *The Rise of the Know-Nothings*

It was in this context that the Know-Nothings (their formal name was the American Party) burst onto the political scene. This party was the result of the merger in 1852 of two secret fraternal societies that limited their membership to native-born Protestants: the Order of the Star-Spangled Banner and the Order of United Americans. Recruiting mainly young men in skilled blue-collar and lower white-collar occupations, the merged order had a membership of 1 million or more by 1854. The order supported temperance and opposed tax support for parochial schools. Members wanted public office restricted to native-born men and sought to lengthen the naturalization period before immigrants could become citizens. Members were also pledged to secrecy; if asked about the order, they were to reply, "I know nothing."

This was the tornado that swept through the Northeast in the 1854 elections. Although the American Party drew voters from both major parties, it cut more heavily into the Whig constituency. Northern Whigs who had not already gone over to the Republicans flocked to the Know-Nothings.

When the dust of the 1854 elections settled, it was clear that those who opposed the Democrats would control the next House of Representatives. But who would control the opposition—antislavery Republicans or nativist Americans?

Some northern voters adhered to both political faiths. But many Republicans warned against flirting with religious bigotry. In a letter to a friend, Abraham Lincoln asked:

> How can any one who abhors the oppression of negroes, be in favor of degrading classes of white people? ... As a nation, we began by declaring that "all men are created equal." We now practically read it "all men are created equal, except negroes." When the Know Nothings get control, it will read "all men are created equal, except negroes, and foreigners, and Catholics." When it comes to this I should prefer emigrating to some country where they make no pretense of loving liberty—to Russia, for instance, where despotism can be taken pure, and without the base alloy of hypocrisy.

14-2c *The Decline of Nativism*

In 1855, Republican leaders maneuvered skillfully to divert the energies of northern Know-Nothings from their crusade against the pope to a crusade against the slave power. Two developments helped them. The first was turmoil in Kansas, which convinced many northerners that the slave power was a greater threat than the pope. The second was an increase of nativist sentiment in the South. The American Party won elections in Maryland,

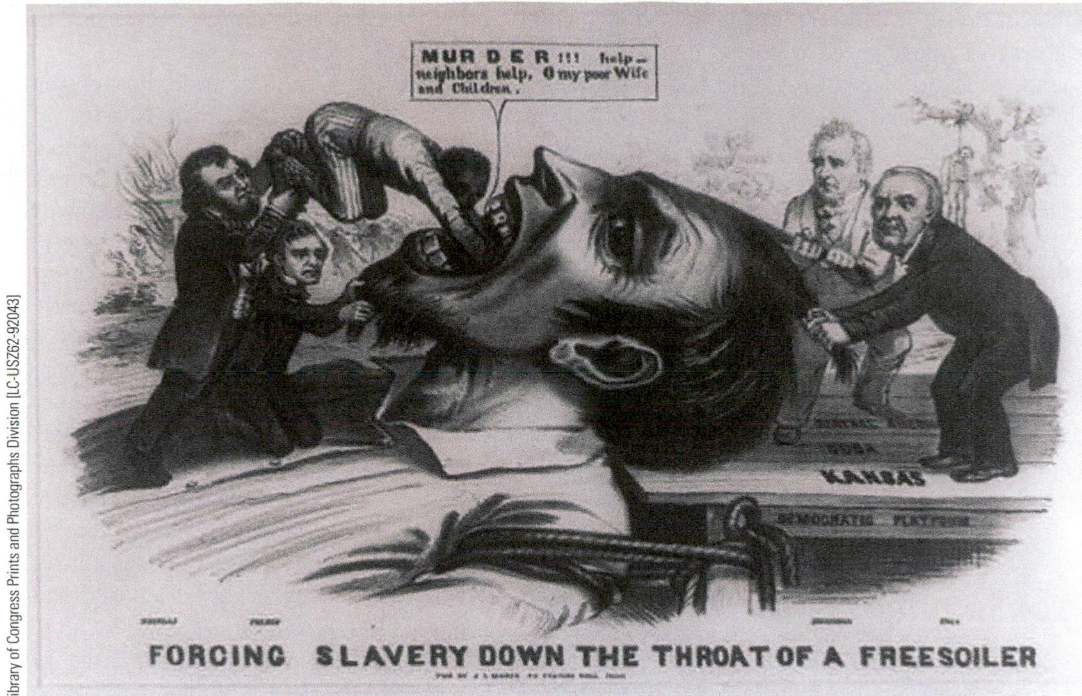

14.5 **"Forcing Slavery Down the Throat of a Freesoiler"** This striking 1856 political cartoon shows a Freesoiler bound against his will to the Democratic Platform. Four of the small figures are prominent Democrats, including Stephen Douglas, who are attempting to force the Freesoiler to swallow the issue of slavery.

Q *How would you interpret the portrayal of the fifth small figure here, the African American man?*

Q *Is this antislavery image also pro-black?*

Kentucky, and Tennessee and polled at least 45 percent of the votes in five other southern states. Violence in several southern cities with large immigrant populations revealed a significant streak of nativism in the South.

These developments had important implications at the national level. Southern Know-Nothings were pro-slavery, whereas many of their Yankee counterparts were antislavery. Just as the national Whig Party had floundered on the slavery issue, so did the American Party during 1855 and 1856. At the party's first national council in June 1855, most of the northern delegates walked out when southerners and northern conservatives joined forces to pass a resolution endorsing the Kansas-Nebraska Act. A similar scene occurred at an American Party convention in 1856. By that time, most northern members of the party had, in effect, become Republicans.

Nativism faded. The volume of immigration suddenly dropped by more than half in 1855 and stayed low for the next several years. Ethnic tensions eased, and cultural issues such as temperance and schools receded. But there was no easing of the conflict between North and South over the extension of slavery. That conflict led to civil war—and the war seemed already to have begun in the territory of Kansas.

14-3 Violent Conflict in the 1850s

Q *How was violence in Kansas related to the issue of slavery?*

When it became clear that southerners had enough votes to pass the Kansas-Nebraska Act, the stage was set for conflict. At first, Missouri settlers in Kansas posted the stronger numbers. As the year 1854 progressed, however, settlers from the North came pouring in. Alarmed by this influx, bands of Missourians, labeled **"border ruffians"** by the Republican press, rode into Kansas prepared to vote as many times as necessary to install a pro-slavery government. In fall 1854, they cast at least 1,700 illegal ballots and sent a pro-slavery territorial delegate to Congress.

When the time came for the election of a territorial legislature the following spring, David Rice Atchison led a contingent of border ruffians to Kansas for the election. "There are eleven hundred coming over from Platte County to vote," he told his followers, "and if that ain't enough, we can send five thousand—enough to kill every God-damned abolitionist in the Territory."

His count was accurate. Nearly 5,000 came and voted illegally to elect a pro-slavery territorial legislature. The territorial governor pleaded with President Pierce to nullify the election, but Pierce listened to Atchison and removed the governor. Meanwhile, the new territorial legislature legalized slavery and adopted a slave code that even authorized the death penalty for helping a slave to escape.

Members of the so-called Free State Party, outraged by these proceedings, had no intention of obeying laws enacted by this "bogus legislature." By fall 1855, they constituted a majority of bona fide settlers in Kansas. They called a convention, adopted a free-state constitution, and elected their own legislature and governor. By January 1856, two territorial governments in Kansas stood with their hands at each other's throats.

14-3a *Bleeding Kansas*

Kansas now became the leading issue in national politics (see Map 14.1). The Democratic Senate and President Pierce recognized the pro-slavery legislature meeting in the town of

Lecompton, while the Republican House of Representatives recognized the antislavery legislature in the town of Lawrence. Southerners saw the struggle as crucial to their future. "The admission of Kansas into the Union as a slave state is now a point of honor," wrote Congressman Preston Brooks of South Carolina. "The fate of the South is to be decided with the Kansas issue." On the other side, Charles Sumner of Massachusetts gave a well-publicized speech in the Senate on May 19 and 20 entitled "The Crime against Kansas." "Murderous robbers from Missouri," charged Sumner, "from the drunken spew and vomit of an uneasy civilization" had committed the "rape of a virgin territory, compelling it to the hateful embrace of slavery." Among the southern senators Sumner singled out for special condemnation and ridicule was a cousin of Congressman Brooks, Andrew Butler of South Carolina. Butler was a "Don Quixote," said Sumner, "who had chosen a mistress to whom he has made his vows ... the harlot, Slavery."

14-3b *The Caning of Sumner*

Sumner's speech incensed southerners, none more than Preston Brooks, who decided to avenge his cousin. Two days after the speech, Brooks walked into the Senate chamber and began beating Sumner with a heavy cane. His legs trapped beneath the desk that was bolted to the floor, Sumner wrenched the desk loose as he stood up to try to defend himself, whereupon Brooks clubbed him so ferociously that Sumner slumped forward, bloody and unconscious.

News of the incident sent a thrill of pride through the South and a rush of rage through the North. Charleston newspapers praised Brooks for "standing forth so nobly in defense of ... the honor of South Carolinians." Brooks resigned from Congress after censure by the House and was unanimously reelected. From all over the South came gifts of new canes, some inscribed with such mottoes as "Hit Him Again" and "Use Knock-Down Arguments." But in the North, the Republicans gained thousands of voters as a result of the affair. It seemed to prove their contentions about "the barbarism of slavery." "Has it come to this," asked the poet William Cullen Bryant, editor of the *New York Evening Post*, "that we must speak with bated breath in the presence of our Southern masters? ... Are we to be chastised as they chastise their slaves?" A veteran New York politician reported that he had "never before seen anything at all like the present state of deep, determined, & desperate feelings of hatred, & hostility to the further extension of slavery, & its political power."

Republicans were soon able to add "Bleeding Kansas" to "Bleeding Sumner" in their repertoire of winning issues. Even as Sumner was delivering his speech in Washington, an "army" of pro-slavery Missourians, complete with artillery, marched on the free-state capital of Lawrence, Kansas. On May 21, they shelled and sacked the town, burning several buildings.

14.6 **Free-State Men Ready to Defend Lawrence, Kansas, in 1856** After pro-slavery forces sacked the free-state capital of Lawrence in 1856, northern settlers decided they needed more firepower to defend themselves. Somehow they got hold of a six-pound howitzer. This cannon did not fire a shot in anger during the Kansas troubles, but its existence may have deterred the "border ruffians."

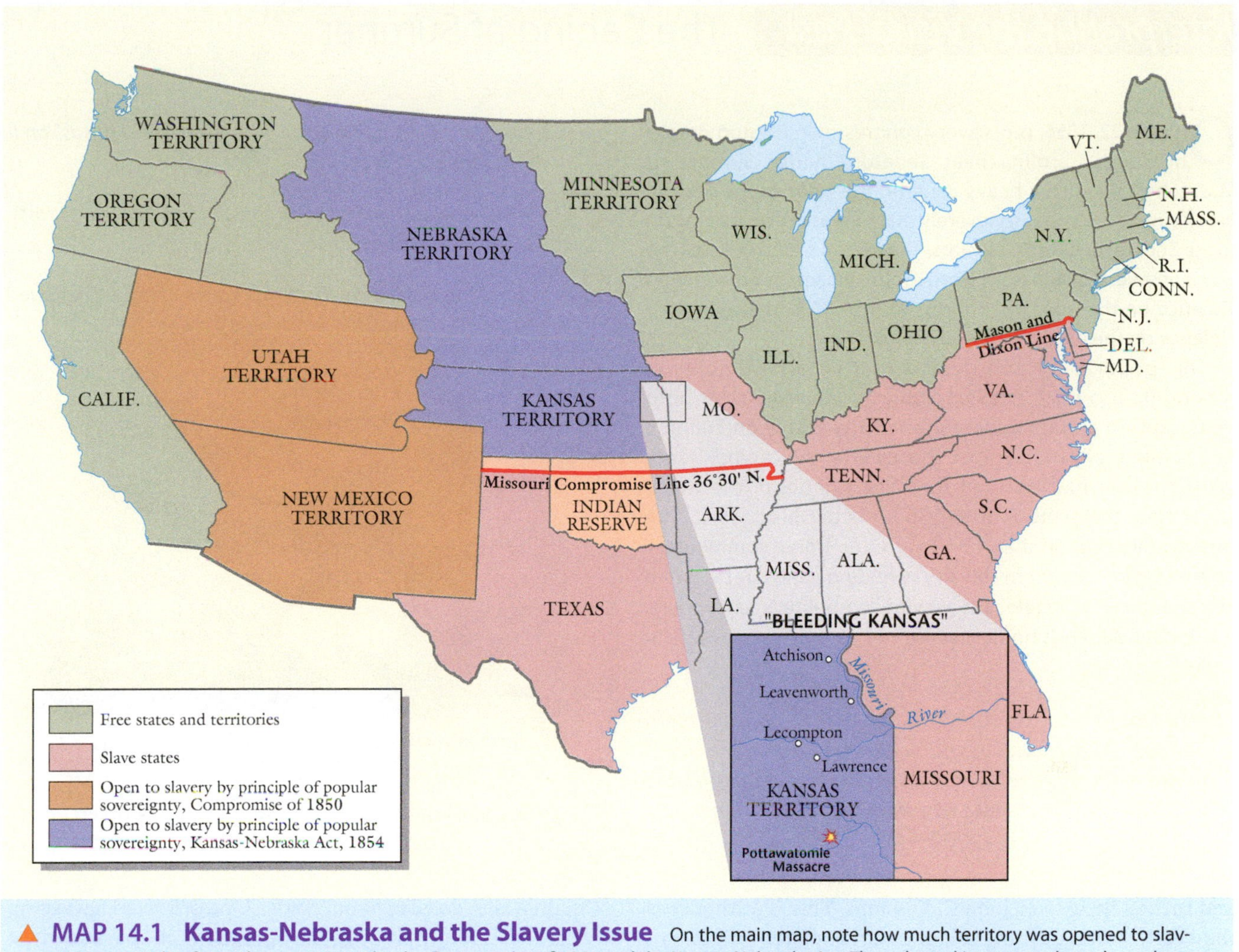

▲ **MAP 14.1 Kansas-Nebraska and the Slavery Issue** On the main map, note how much territory was opened to slavery on the principle of popular sovereignty by the Compromise of 1850 and the Kansas-Nebraska Act. The enlarged inset map shows how close together were the centers of Free Soil and pro-slavery forces in Lawrence and Lecompton, respectively.

Q *Why did Southerners believe that the "fate of the South" was to be decided with the Kansas issue?*

Q *Why was Nebraska Territory less hotly contested?*

A rival force of free-state men arrived too late to intercept them. One of the free-state "captains" was John Brown, an abolitionist zealot who considered himself anointed by the Lord to avenge the sins of slaveholders. When he learned of the murder of several free-state settlers and the sack of Lawrence, he "went crazy—crazy," according to one of his followers. We must "fight fire with fire," Brown declared. "Something must be done to show these barbarians that we, too, have rights." Leading four of his sons and three other men to a pro-slavery settlement at Pottawatomie Creek on the night of May 24–25, 1856, Brown dragged five men from their cabins and split open their heads with broadswords.

Brown's murderous act set off a veritable civil war in Kansas. One of Brown's sons was among the estimated 200 men killed in bushwhacker raids. Not until President Pierce sent a tough new territorial governor and 1,300 federal troops to Kansas in September 1856 did the violence subside—just in time to save the Democrats from possible defeat in the presidential election.

14-4 The Election of 1856

Q *What role did the issue of slavery play in the election of 1856?*

By 1856, the Republicans had become the largest party in the North. They were also the first truly sectional party in American history, for they had little prospect of carrying a single county in the slave states. At their first national convention, the Republicans wrote a platform that focused mainly on that "relic of barbarism," slavery. The platform also incorporated the old Whig program of federal aid to internal improvements, including a railroad to California. For its presidential nominee, the party steered away from its most prominent leaders, who were identified with the old parties,

Interpreting the Visual Past The Caning of Sumner

On May 22, 1856, pro-slavery congressman Preston Brooks of South Carolina beat Senator Charles Sumner of Massachusetts with a heavy cane on the floor of the Senate. Brooks injured Sumner so severely that he was not able to return to the Senate for over three years. The caning of Sumner was the worst of several instances of North-South violence or threatened violence on the floor of Congress in the 1850s, presaging the violence on the battlefields of the 1860s.

This political cartoon depicts that notorious violence, making its pro-northern sympathies graphically clear both in its caption and its visualization of the attack on Sumner. At a Sumner rally in New York shortly after the caning, Henry Ward Beecher had asserted that "the symbol of the North is the pen; the symbol of the South is the bludgeon." The caption picks up on that theme, offering ironic commentary on a thuggish "Southern chivalry" wielding "clubs" rather than argument in the Senate. But as with any political cartoon, its full impact depends not just on words but also on a powerful image.

Q *How does the artist visually emphasize his pro-northern position? What choices has he made in positioning the bodies of the two men here? How does he visually emphasize the viciousness of the attack? Why does the fallen Sumner hold a quill in one hand and a scroll with the word "Kansas" on it in the other?*

Q *The artist has hidden the face of Brooks. Is this an effective artistic choice? Why or why not?*

Q *Why does the artist show cartoon figures in the background smiling at the violence? What message does he convey?*

SOUTHERN CHIVALRY— ARGUMENT VERSUS CLUB'S.

The New York Public Library/Art Resvource, NY

14.7 **Lithograph Depicting The Caning of Charles Sumner, 1856.**

and turned instead to John C. Frémont. This "Pathfinder of the West" had a dashing image as an explorer and for his role in the acquisition of California. With little political experience, he had few political enemies, and his antislavery credentials were satisfactory.

The Democrats chose as their candidate James Buchanan, a veteran of 30 years in various public offices. The Democratic platform endorsed popular sovereignty and condemned the Republicans as a "sectional party" that incited "treason and armed resistance in the Territories."

This would be a three-party election because the American Party was still in the field. Having become mainly a way station for former southern Whigs, the party nominated ex-Whig Millard Fillmore. The three-party campaign sifted out into a pair of two-party contests: Democrats versus Americans in the South and Democrats versus Republicans in the North. Fillmore, despite a good showing of 44 percent of the popular vote in the South, carried only Maryland. Considering Buchanan colorless but safe, the rest of the South gave him three-fourths of the electoral votes he needed for victory (see Table 14.1).

The real excitement in this election showed itself in the North. For many Republicans, the campaign was a moral cause, an evangelical crusade against the sin of slavery. Republican "Wide Awake" clubs marched in torchlight parades chanting "Free Soil, Free Speech, Free Men, Frémont!" A veteran politician in Indiana marveled: "Men, Women & Children all seemed to be out, with a kind of fervor I have never witnessed before in six Pres. Elections in which I have taken an active part." The turnout of eligible voters in the North was a remarkable 83 percent. One awestruck journalist, anticipating a Republican victory, wrote that "the process now going on in the United States is a *Revolution*."

Not quite. Although the Republicans swept New England and the upper parts of New York State and the Old Northwest—both settled by New Englanders, where evangelical and antislavery reform movements had taken hold—the contest in the lower North was close. Buchanan needed only to carry Pennsylvania and either Indiana or Illinois to win the presidency, and the campaign focused on those states. The immigrant and working-class voters of the eastern cities and the rural voters of the lower Midwest, descendants of upland southerners who had settled there, were antiblack and anti-abolitionist in sentiment. They were ripe for Democratic propaganda that accused Republicans of favoring racial equality. "**Black Republicans**," declared an Ohio Democratic newspaper, intended to "turn loose ... millions of negroes, to elbow you in the workshops, and compete with you in fields of honest labor." A Democrat in Pennsylvania told voters that "the one aim" of the Republicans was "to elevate the African race in this country to complete equality of political and economic condition with the whiteman." Indiana Democrats organized parades with young girls in white dresses carrying banners inscribed: "Fathers, save us from nigger husbands."

Table 14.1 POPULAR AND ELECTORAL VOTES IN THE 1856 PRESIDENTIAL ELECTION

	Free States		Slave States		Total	
Candidate	Popular	Electoral	Popular	Electoral	Popular	Electoral
Buchanan (Democrat)	1,227,000	62	607,000	112	1,833,000	174
Frémont (Republican)	1,338,000	114	0	0	1,338,000	114
Fillmore (American)	396,000	0	476,000	8	872,000	8

The Republicans in these areas denied that they favored racial equality. They insisted that the main reason for keeping slavery out of the territories was to enable white farmers and workers to make a living there without competition from black labor. But their denials were in vain. Support for the Republican Party by prominent black leaders, including Frederick Douglass, convinced hundreds of thousands of voters that the Black Republicans were racial egalitarians. For the next two decades, that sentiment would be one of the most potent weapons in the Democratic arsenal.

The charge that a Republican victory would destroy the Union was even more effective. Buchanan set the tone in his instructions to Democratic Party leaders: "The Black Republicans must be ... boldly assailed as disunionists, and the charge must be re-iterated again and again." It was. And southerners helped the cause by threatening to secede if Frémont won. Fears of disruption caused many conservative ex-Whigs in the North to support Buchanan, who carried Pennsylvania, New Jersey, Indiana, Illinois, and California and won the presidency (see Map 14.2).

But southerners did not intend to let Buchanan forget that he owed his election mainly to the South. "Mr. Buchanan and the Northern Democracy are dependent on the South," wrote a Virginian after the election. "If we can succeed in Kansas ... and add a little more slave territory, we may yet live free men under the Stars and Stripes."

14-4a *The Dred Scott Case*

The South took the offensive at the outset of the Buchanan administration. Its instrument was the Supreme Court, which had a majority of five justices from slave states, led by Chief Justice Roger B. Taney of Maryland. Those justices saw the Dred Scott case as an opportunity to settle once and for all the question of slavery in the territories.

Dred Scott was a slave whose owner, an army surgeon, had kept him at military posts in Illinois and in Wisconsin Territory for several years before taking him back to Missouri. After the owner's death, Scott sued for his freedom on the grounds of his prolonged stay in the Wisconsin Territory, where slavery had been outlawed by the Missouri Compromise. The case worked its way up from Missouri courts through a federal circuit court to the U.S. Supreme Court. There it attracted attention as a test case of Congress's power to prohibit slavery in the territories.

The southern Supreme Court justices decided to declare that the Missouri Compromise ban on slavery in the territories was unconstitutional. To avoid the appearance of a purely sectional decision, they sought the concurrence of a northern Democratic justice, Robert Grier of Pennsylvania. President-elect Buchanan played an improper role by pressing his fellow Pennsylvanian to go along with the southern majority. Having obtained Justice Grier's concurrence, Chief Justice Taney issued the Court's ruling stating that Congress lacked the power to keep slavery out of a territory, because slaves were property and the Constitution protects the right of property. For good measure, Taney also wrote that the circuit court should not have accepted the Scott case in the first place because black men were not citizens of the United States and therefore had no standing in its courts. The two non-Democratic northern justices dissented vigorously. They stated that blacks were legal citizens in several northern states and were therefore citizens of the United States. To buttress their opinion that Congress could prohibit slavery in the territories, they cited Congress's constitutional power to make "all needful rules and regulations" for the territories. Modern scholars agree with the dissenters. In 1857, however, Taney had a majority, and his ruling became law.

Republicans denounced Taney's decision as a "gross perversion" of the Constitution. Several Republican state legislatures resolved that the ruling was "not binding in law and conscience." They looked forward to the election of a Republican president who could "reconstitute" the Court and secure a reversal of the decision. "The remedy," said the *Chicago Tribune*, "is the ballot box.... Let the next President be Republican, and 1860 will mark an era kindred with that of 1776."

14-4b *The Lecompton Constitution*

Instead of settling the slavery controversy, the Dred Scott decision intensified it. Meanwhile, pro-slavery advocates, having won legalization of slavery in the territories, moved to ensure that it would remain legal when Kansas became a state. That required deft maneuvering, because legitimate antislavery settlers outnumbered pro-slavery settlers by more than two to one. In 1857, the pro-slavery legislature (elected by the fraudulent votes of border ruffians two years earlier) called for a constitutional convention at Lecompton to prepare Kansas for statehood. Because the election for delegates was rigged, Free Soil voters refused to participate. One-fifth of the

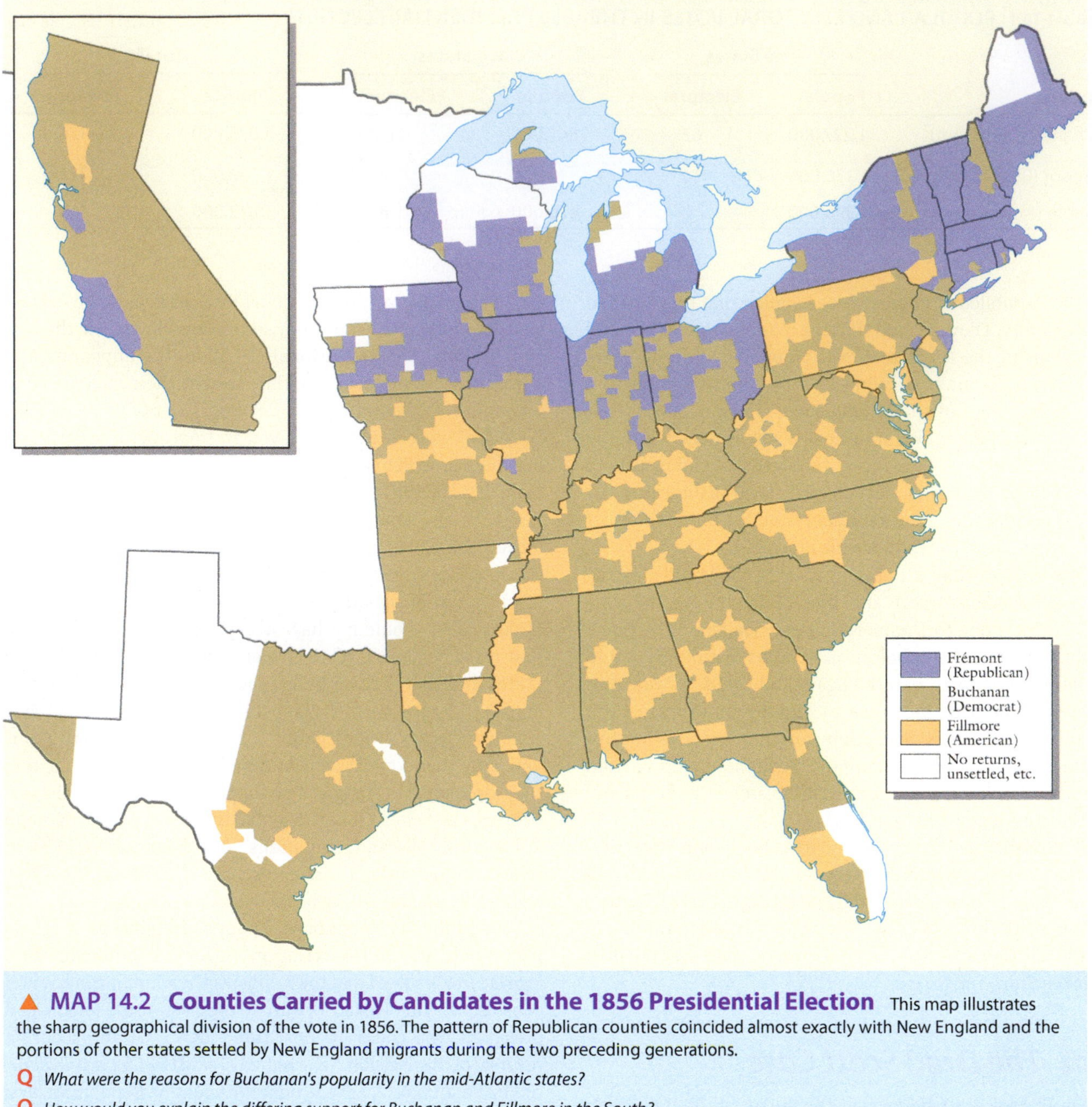

▲ **MAP 14.2 Counties Carried by Candidates in the 1856 Presidential Election** This map illustrates the sharp geographical division of the vote in 1856. The pattern of Republican counties coincided almost exactly with New England and the portions of other states settled by New England migrants during the two preceding generations.

Q *What were the reasons for Buchanan's popularity in the mid-Atlantic states?*

Q *How would you explain the differing support for Buchanan and Fillmore in the South?*

registered voters thereupon elected convention delegates, who met at Lecompton and wrote a state constitution that made slavery legal.

Then a nagging problem arose. Buchanan had promised that the Lecompton constitution would be presented to voters in a fair referendum. The problem was how to pass the pro-slavery constitution, given the antislavery majority of voters. The convention came up with an ingenious solution. Instead of a referendum on the whole constitution, it would allow the voters to choose between a constitution "with slavery" and one "with no slavery." The catch was that the constitution "with no slavery" guaranteed slave owners' "inviolable" right of property in the 200 slaves already in Kansas and their progeny. It also did nothing to prevent future smuggling of slaves across the 200-mile border with Missouri. Once in Kansas, they, too, would become "inviolable" property.

Free-state voters branded the referendum a farce and boycotted it. One-quarter of the eligible voters went to the polls in December 1857 and approved the constitution "with slavery." Meanwhile, in a fair election policed by federal troops, the antislavery party won control of the new territorial legislature and promptly submitted both constitutions to a referendum that was boycotted by pro-slavery voters. This time, 70 percent of the eligible voters went to the polls and overwhelmingly rejected both constitutions.

Which referendum would the federal government recognize? That question proved even more divisive than the Kansas-Nebraska debate four years earlier. President Buchanan faced a dilemma. He had promised a fair referendum. But southerners, who dominated both the Democratic Party and the administration, threatened secession if Kansas was not admitted to statehood under the Lecompton constitution "with slavery." "If Kansas is *driven out of the Union for being a Slave State*," thundered Senator James Hammond of South Carolina, "can any Slave State remain in it with honor?" Buchanan caved in. He explained to a shocked northern Democrat that if he did not accept the Lecompton constitution, southern states would "secede from the Union or take up arms against us." Buchanan sent the Lecompton constitution to Congress with a message recommending statehood. Kansas, said the president, "is at this moment as much a slave state as Georgia or South Carolina."

What would Stephen Douglas do? If he endorsed the Lecompton constitution, he would undoubtedly be defeated in his bid for reelection to the Senate in 1858. And he regarded the Lecompton constitution as a travesty of popular sovereignty. He broke with the administration on the issue. He could not vote to "force this constitution down the throats of the people of Kansas," he told the Senate, "in opposition to their wishes and in violation of our pledges."

The fight in Congress was long and bitter. The South and the administration had the votes they needed in the Senate and won handily there, but the Democratic majority in the House was so small that the defection of even a few northern Democrats would defeat the Lecompton constitution. The House debate at one point got out of hand, and a wild fistfight erupted between Republicans and southern Democrats. "There were some fifty middle-aged and elderly gentlemen pitching into each other," wrote a bemused reporter, "most of them incapable, from want of wind and muscle, from doing each other any serious harm."

When the vote was finally taken, two dozen northern Democrats defected, providing enough votes to defeat Lecompton. Both sides then accepted a compromise proposal to resubmit the constitution to Kansas voters, who decisively rejected it. This meant that while Kansas would not come in as a slave state, neither would it come in as a free state for some time yet. Nevertheless, the Lecompton debate had split the Democratic Party, leaving a legacy of undying enmity between southerners and Douglas. The election of a Republican president in 1860 was now all but assured.

14-5 The Economy in the 1850s

Q *How did economic developments in the 1840s and 1850s widen the breach between North and South?*

Beginning in the mid-1840s, the American economy enjoyed a dozen years of unprecedented growth and prosperity, particularly for the railroads. The number of miles in operation quintupled. Railroad construction provided employment for many immigrants and spurred growth in industries that produced rails, rolling stock, and other railroad equipment. Most railroad construction took place in the Old Northwest, linking the region more closely to the Northeast and continuing the reorientation of transportation networks from a north-south river pattern to an east-west canal and rail pattern. By the mid-1850s, the east-west rail and water routes carried more than twice as much freight tonnage as the north-south river routes (see Map 14.3). This closer binding of the western and eastern states reinforced the effect of slavery in creating a self-conscious "North" and "South."

Although the Old Northwest remained predominantly agricultural, rapid expansion of railroads there laid the basis for its industrialization. During the 1850s, industrial output in the free states west of Pennsylvania grew at twice the rate of Northeast industrial output and three times the rate in the South. The Northwest urban growth rate tripled that of the Northeast and quadrupled that of the South. Chicago became the terminus for 15 rail lines in the 1850s, during which its population grew by 375 percent. In 1847, two companies that contributed to the rapid growth of agriculture during this era built their plants in Illinois: the McCormick reaper works at Chicago and the John Deere steel-plow works at Moline.

Economic expansion considerably outstripped even the prodigious pace of population increase. While the number of Americans grew by 44 percent during these 12 years (1844–1856), the value of both exports and imports increased by 200 percent; mined coal tonnage by 270 percent; banking capital, industrial capital, and industrial output by approximately 100 percent; farmland value by 100 percent; and cotton, wheat, and corn harvests by about 70 percent. These advances meant a significant increase of per capita production and income, although the distance between rich and poor was widening—a phenomenon that has characterized all capitalist economies during stages of rapid industrial growth.

By the later 1850s, the United States had forged ahead of most other countries to become the second-biggest industrial producer in the world, behind only Britain. But the country was still in the early stages of industrial development. Agricultural product processing and raw materials still played the dominant role. By 1860, the four leading industries, measured by value added in manufacturing, were cotton textiles, lumber products, boots and shoes, and flour milling. Iron and machinery, industries typical of a more mature manufacturing economy, ranked sixth and seventh.

14-5a *"The American System of Manufactures"*

The United States had pioneered in one crucial feature of modern industry: the mass production of **interchangeable parts**. This revolutionary concept had begun with the manufacture of firearms earlier in the 19th century and had spread to many products by the 1850s. High wages and

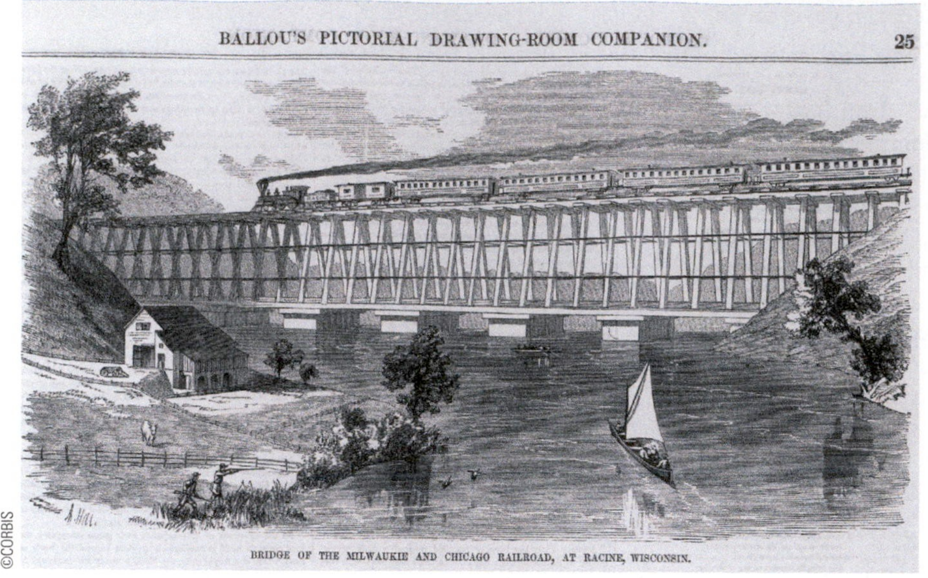

BALLOU'S PICTORIAL DRAWING-ROOM COMPANION.
25
BRIDGE OF THE MILWAUKIE AND CHICAGO RAILROAD, AT RACINE, WISCONSIN.

14.8 **Bridge of the Milwaukee and Chicago Railroad at Racine, Wisconsin** By the 1850s, Chicago had become the hub for a dozen or more railroads that tied the fast-growing Midwest to the older South and East. This illustration shows the railroad bridge over the Root River between Chicago and Milwaukee.

a shortage of the skilled craftsmen who had traditionally fashioned guns, furniture, locks, watches, and other products had compelled American entrepreneurs to seek alternative methods. "Yankee ingenuity," already world-famous, came up with an answer: special-purpose machine tools that would cut and shape an endless number of parts that could be fitted together to make whole guns, locks, clocks, and sewing machines in mass quantities. These products were less elegant and less durable than products made by skilled craftsmen, but they were also less expensive and thus more widely available to the "middling classes."

Such American-made products were the hit of the first World's Fair, the Crystal Palace Exhibition at London in 1851. British manufacturers were so impressed by Yankee techniques, which they dubbed "the American system of manufactures," that they sent two commissions to the United States to study them. The British also invited Samuel Colt of Connecticut, inventor of the famous six-shooting revolver, to set up a factory in England stocked with machinery from Connecticut. In testimony before a parliamentary committee in 1854, Colt summed up the American system of manufactures in a single sentence: "There is nothing that cannot be produced by machinery." Although the British had a half-century head start over Americans in the Industrial Revolution, Colt's testimony expressed a philosophy that would enable the United States to surpass Britain as the leading industrial nation by 1880.

The British industrial commissions cited the American educational system as an important reason for the country's technological proficiency. "Educated up to a far higher standard than those of a much superior grade in the Old World," reported the 1854 commission, "every [American] workman seems to be continually devising some new thing to assist him in his work, and there is a strong desire ... to be 'posted up' in every new improvement." By contrast, the British workman, trained by long apprenticeship "in the trade," rather than in school, lacked "the ductility of mind and the readiness of apprehension for a new thing" and was therefore "unwilling to change the methods he has been used to."

Whether this British commission was right in its belief that American schooling encouraged the "adaptative versatility" of Yankee workers, it was certainly true that public education and literacy were more widespread in the United States than in Europe. Almost 95 percent of adults in the free states were literate in 1860, compared with 65 percent in England and 55 percent in France. The standardization and expansion of public school systems that had begun earlier in New England had spread to the mid-Atlantic states and into the Old Northwest by the 1850s. Nearly all children received a few years of schooling, and most completed at least six or seven years.

This improvement in education coincided with the feminization of the teaching profession, which opened up new career opportunities for young women. By the 1850s, nearly three-quarters of the public school teachers in New England were women (who worked for lower salaries than male teachers), a trend that was spreading to the mid-Atlantic states and the Old Northwest as well.

14-5b *The Southern Economy*

In the South, 80 percent of the free population and only 10 percent of the slaves were literate. This was one of several differences between North and South that antislavery people pointed to as evidence of the backward, repressive, and pernicious nature of a slave society.

Still, the South shared in the economy's rapid growth following recovery from the depression of 1837–1843. Cotton prices and production both doubled between 1845 and 1855. Similar increases in price and output emerged in tobacco and sugar. The price of slaves also doubled during this decade. Southern crops provided three-fifths of all U.S. exports, with cotton alone supplying more than half.

▲ **MAP 14.3 Main Transportation Routes in the 1850s** These maps illustrate how the transportation networks by natural waterways (rivers and the Atlantic coastal waters) oriented commerce north and south while the canals and railroads linked east and west. By 1860, railroads tied the midwestern states economically to the Northeast.

Q *Why was railroad development so different in North and South?*

Q *How important were transportation networks to patterns of settlement?*

Library of Congress Prints and Photographs Division[LC-USZ62-19431]

14.9 **Colt Arms Plant in Hartford, Connecticut** Samuel Colt's factory for manufacturing firearms was a showpiece for the American system of manufactures in the 1850s. All of the processes for production of the famous Colt revolver were housed under one roof, with power-driven machinery cutting the metal and shaping the interchangeable parts. Hand filing was necessary, however, for a perfect fit of the parts, because the tolerances of machine tools were not yet as finely calibrated as they later became.

© Francis G. Mayer/Corbis

14.10 **The Country School** This famous painting by Winslow Homer portrays the typical one-room rural schoolhouse in which millions of American children learned the "three R's" (reading, 'riting, and 'rithmetic) in the 19th century. By the 1850s, teaching elementary school was a profession increasingly dominated by women, an important change from earlier generations.

But a growing number of southerners deplored the fact that the **colonial economy** of the South was so dependent on the export of agricultural products and the import of manufactured goods. Northern or British firms owned the ships that carried southern cotton; Yankees or Englishmen provided most of the financial and commercial services. In the years of rising sectional tensions around 1850, many southerners began calling for economic independence from the North. How could they obtain their rights, they asked, if they were "financially more enslaved than our negroes?" Yankees "abuse and denounce slavery and slaveholders," declared a southern newspaper in 1851, yet "we purchase all our luxuries and necessaries from the North.... Our slaves are clothed with Northern manufactured goods and work with Northern hoes, ploughs, and other implements.... The slaveholder dresses in Northern goods ... and on Northern-made paper, with a Northern pen, with Northern ink, he resolves and re-resolves in regard to his rights."

Southerners must "throw off this humiliating dependence," declared James D. B. De Bow, the young champion of economic diversification in the South. In 1846, De Bow had founded in New Orleans a periodical eventually known as *De Bow's Review*. Proclaiming on its cover that "Commerce is King," the *Review* set out to make this slogan a southern reality. De Bow took the lead in organizing annual commercial conventions that met in various southern cities during the 1850s. In its early years, this movement encouraged southerners to invest in shipping lines, railroads, textile mills ("bring the spindles to the cotton"), and other enterprises. "Give us factories, machine shops, work shops," declared southern proponents of King Commerce, "and we shall be able ere long to assert our rights."

Economic diversification in the South did make headway during the 1850s. The slave states quadrupled their railroad mileage, increased the amount of capital invested in manufacturing by 77 percent, and boosted their output of cotton textiles by 44 percent. But northern industry was growing even faster. In 1860, the North had five times more industrial output per capita than the South, and it had three times the railroad capital and mileage per capita and per thousand square miles. Southerners had a larger percentage of their capital invested in land and slaves in 1860 than they had had 10 years earlier. Some 80 percent of the South's labor force worked in agriculture—the same as 60 years earlier. By contrast, while farming remained, at 40 percent, the largest single occupation in the North, the northern economy developed a strong manufacturing and commercial sector whose combined labor force almost equaled that of agriculture by 1860.

14-5c *The Sovereignty of King Cotton*

A good many southerners preferred to keep it that way. "That the North does our trading and manufacturing mostly is true," wrote an Alabama planter in 1858. "We are willing that they should. Ours is an agricultural people, and God grant that we may continue so. It is the freest, happiest, most independent, and with us, the most powerful condition on earth." In the later 1850s, the drive for economic diversification in the South lost steam. King Cotton reasserted its primacy over King Commerce as cotton output *and* prices continued to rise, suffusing the South in a glow of prosperity. "Our Cotton is the most wonderful talisman on earth," declared a planter. "By its power we are transmuting whatever we choose into whatever we want." In a speech that became famous, James Hammond of South Carolina told his fellow senators in 1858 that "the slaveholding South is now the controlling power of the world.... No power on earth dares to make war on cotton. Cotton *is* king."

Even the commercial conventions in the South seem to have embraced this gospel. By the later 1850s, one of the main goals of these conventions was to reopen the African slave trade, prohibited by law since 1808. The conventions also lobbied for the annexation of Cuba, which would bring a productive agricultural economy and 400,000 more slaves into the United States.

Nowhere in the South, said defenders of slavery, did one see such "scenes of beggary, squalid poverty, and wretchedness" as one could find in any northern city. Slaves, they insisted, enjoyed a higher standard of living than white "wage slaves" in northern factories. Slaves never suffered from unemployment or wage cuts, they received free medical care, and they were taken care of in old age.

This argument reached its fullest development in the writings of George Fitzhugh, a Virginia farmer-lawyer whose newspaper articles were gathered into two books published in 1854 and 1857, *Sociology for the South and Cannibals All.* Free-labor capitalism, said Fitzhugh, was a competition in which the strong exploited and starved the weak. Slavery, by contrast, was a paternal institution that guaranteed protection of the workers. "Capital exercises a more perfect compulsion over free laborers than human masters over slaves," wrote Fitzhugh, "for free laborers must at all times work or starve, and slaves are supported whether they work or not.... What a glorious thing is slavery, when want, misfortune, old age, debility, and sickness overtake [the slave]."

14-5d *Labor Conditions in the North*

How true was this portrait of poverty and starvation among northern workers? Some northern labor leaders did complain that the "slavery" of the wage system gave "bosses" control over the hours, conditions, and compensation of labor. But there is no evidence that a northern workingman ever offered to change places with a southern slave. Average per capita income was about 40 percent higher in the North than in the South. Although that average masked large disparities between rich and poor—even between the middle class and the poor—those disparities were no greater, and probably smaller, in the North than in the South.

To be sure, substantial numbers of recent immigrants, day laborers, and young single women in large northern cities lived on the edge of poverty—or slipped over the edge. Many women seamstresses, shoe binders, milliners, and the like, who worked 60 or 70 hours per week in the outwork system, earned less than a living wage. Some of them resorted to prostitution in order to survive. The widespread adoption of the newly invented sewing machine in the 1850s did nothing to make life easier for seamstresses; it only lowered their per-unit piecework wages and forced them to turn out more shirts and trousers than before. Many urban working-class families could not survive on the wages of an unskilled or semiskilled man. Women had to take in laundry, boarders, or outwork, and one or more children also had to work. Much employment was seasonal or intermittent, leaving workers without wages for long periods, especially during the winter. The poverty, overcrowding, and disease in the tenement districts of a few large cities—especially New York City—seemed to lend substance to pro-slavery claims that slaves were better off.

But they were not—even apart from the psychological contrast between being free and being a slave. New York City's poverty, although highly concentrated and visible, was exceptional. In the North, only one fourth of the people lived in cities or towns of more than 2,500 people. Wages and opportunities for workers were greater in the North than anywhere else in the world, including the South. That was why 4 million immigrants came to the United States from 1845 to 1860 and why seven-eighths of them settled in free states. It was also why twice as many white residents of slave states migrated to free states than vice versa.

Library of Congress Prints and Photographs Division

© The Granger Collection, New York

14.11a (top) and 14.10b (bottom) **Southern Portraits of Slavery and Free Labor** Romanticized images of happy, well-fed slaves enjoying their work picking cotton were common in pro-slavery literature (top). Such images were often contrasted with the supposed harshness of life in northern tenement districts, as in this illustration of a communal pump that has run dry on a hot summer day in an immigrant neighborhood on New York's Lower East Side (bottom).

14-5e *The Panic of 1857*

In fall 1857, the relative prosperity of the North was interrupted by a financial panic that caused a short-lived but intense depression. When the Crimean War in Europe (1854–1856) cut off Russian grain from the European market, U.S. exports had mushroomed to meet the deficiency. After the Crimean War ended, U.S. grain exports slumped. The sharp rise in interest rates in Britain and France, caused by the war, spread to U.S. financial markets in 1857 and dried up sources of credit. Meanwhile, the economic boom of the preceding years had caused the American economy to overheat: Land prices had soared, railroads had built beyond the capacity of earnings to service their debts, and banks had made too many risky loans.

This speculative house of cards came crashing down in September 1857. The failure of one banking house sent a wave of panic through the financial community. Banks suspended specie payments, businesses failed, railroads went bankrupt, construction halted, and factories shut down. Hundreds of thousands of workers were laid off, and others went on part-time schedules or took wage cuts, just as the cold winter months were arriving. The specter of class conflict similar to the European revolutions of 1848 haunted the public. Unemployed workers in several northern cities marched in parades carrying banners demanding work or bread. A mob broke into the shops of flour merchants in New York City. On November 10, a crowd gathered on Wall Street and threatened to break into the U.S. customs house and sub-treasury vaults, where $20 million was stored. Soldiers and marines had to be called out to disperse the mob.

But the country got through the winter with little violence. No one was killed in the demonstrations—in contrast to the dozens who had been killed in ethnic riots a few years earlier and the hundreds killed in the guerrilla war in Kansas. Class conflict turned out to be the least threatening of the various discords that endangered society in the 1850s. Charity and public works helped tide the poor over the winter, and the panic inspired a vigorous religious revival. Spontaneous prayer meetings arose in many northern cities, bringing together bankers and seamstresses, brokers and street sweepers. They asked God's forgiveness for the greed and materialism that, in a self-flagellating mood, they believed had caused the panic.

The depression was short-lived. By early 1858, banks had resumed specie payments; the stock market rebounded in the spring; factories reopened; railroad construction resumed; and by spring 1859, recovery was complete. The modest labor union activities of the 1850s revived after the depression, as workers in some industries went on strike to bring wages back to pre-panic levels. In February 1860, the shoemakers of Lynn, Massachusetts, began the largest strike in U.S. history up to that time, eventually involving 20,000 workers in the New England shoe industry. Despite the organization of several national unions of skilled workers during the 1850s, however, less than 1 percent of the labor force was unionized in 1860.

14-5f *Sectionalism and the Panic*

The Panic of 1857 intensified sectional animosities. The South largely escaped the depression. Its export-driven economy seemed insulated from domestic downturns. After a brief dip, cotton and tobacco prices returned to high levels and production continued to increase: The cotton crop set new records in 1858 and 1859 (see Map 14.4). Southern boasts about the superiority of the region's economic and labor systems took on added bravado. "Who can doubt, that has looked at recent events, that cotton is supreme?" asked Senator James Hammond in March 1858. "When thousands of the strongest commercial houses in the world were coming down," he told Yankees, "what brought you up? ... We have poured in upon you one million six hundred thousand bales of cotton... . We have sold it for $65,000,000, and saved you."

Northerners were not grateful. In fact, many blamed southern congressmen for blocking measures, especially higher tariffs, that would have eased the effects of the depression and helped not only manufacturers but also unemployed workers. In each session of Congress from 1858 through 1860, a combination of southerners and about half of the northern Democrats blocked Republican efforts to raise tariffs. In the words of one bitter Pennsylvania Republican, this was proof that Congress remained "shamelessly prostituted, in a base subserviency to the Slave Power."

Three other measures acquired additional significance after the Panic of 1857. Republicans supported each of them as a means to promote economic health and to aid farmers and workers, but southerners perceived all of them as aimed at helping *northern* farmers and workers and used their power to defeat them. One was a homestead act to grant 160 acres of public land to each farmer who settled and worked the land. Believing that this bill "would prove a most efficient ally for Abolition by encouraging and stimulating the settlement of free farms with Yankees," southern senators defeated it after the House had passed it in 1859. The following year both houses passed the Homestead Act, but Buchanan vetoed it and southern senators blocked an effort to pass it over his veto. A similar fate befell bills for land grants to a transcontinental railroad and for building agricultural and mechanical colleges to educate farmers and workers. In the Old Northwest, where these measures were popular, Republican prospects for 1860 were enhanced by southern and Democratic opposition to them.

14-5g *Free-Labor Ideology*

By the later 1850s, the Republican antislavery argument had become a finely honed philosophy that historians have labeled a **free-labor ideology**. It held that all work in a free society was honorable, but that slavery degraded the calling of manual labor by equating it with bondage. Slaves worked inefficiently, by compulsion; free men were stimulated to work hard and efficiently by the desire to get ahead. Social mobility was central to the free-labor ideology. Free workers who practiced the virtues of industry, thrift, self-discipline, and sobriety could move up the ladder of success. "I am not ashamed to confess," Abraham Lincoln told a working-class audience in 1860, "that twenty-five years ago I was a hired laborer, mauling rails, at work on a flat-boat—just what might happen to any poor man's son!" But in the free states, said Lincoln, a man knows that "he can better his condition... . The free labor system opens the way for all—gives hope to all, and energy, and progress, and improvement of condition to all."

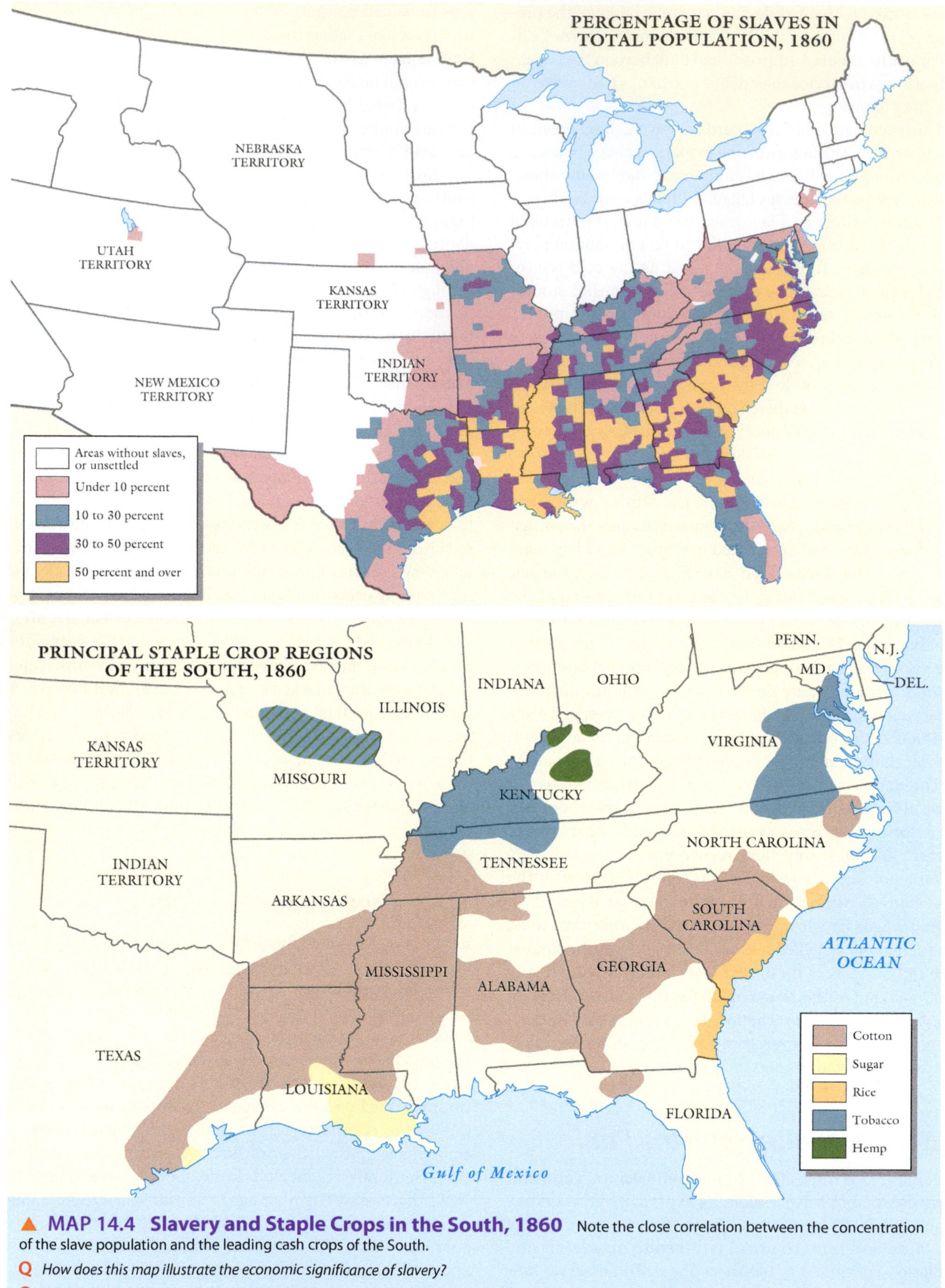

▲ **MAP 14.4 Slavery and Staple Crops in the South, 1860** Note the close correlation between the concentration of the slave population and the leading cash crops of the South.

Q *How does this map illustrate the economic significance of slavery?*

Q *Why did cotton become dominant as a cash crop across the lower South?*

14.12 **The Panic on Wall Street** This October 1857 *Harper's Weekly* cartoon pictures the consternation among New York investors and financiers when banks and businesses crashed in autumn 1857, leading to a short but sharp recession in 1857 and 1858. Notice the frantic men in the background pounding on the doors of a failed bank, while in the foreground one man looks at us and smirks, having likely made a profit from others' disasters.

Q *What attitude towards the 1857 Panic does this cartoon reveal?*

Lincoln drew a rosy picture of northern reality, for large numbers of workers in the North had little hope of advancing beyond the status of wage laborer. Still, he expressed a belief that was widely shared in the antebellum North. "There is not a working boy of average ability in the New England states, at least," observed a visiting British industrialist in 1854, "who has not an idea of some mechanical invention or improvement in manufactures, by which, in good time, he hopes to better his condition, or rise to fortune and social distinction." Americans could point to numerous examples of men who had achieved dramatic upward mobility. Belief in this "American dream" was most strongly held by Protestant farmers, skilled workers, and white-collar workers who had some real hope of getting ahead. These men tended to support the Republican Party and its goal of excluding slavery from the territories.

For slavery was the antithesis of upward mobility. Bondsmen were "fatally fixed in that condition for life," as Lincoln noted. Slaves could not hope to move up the ladder of success, nor could free men who lived in a society where they had to compete with slave labor. "Slavery withers and blights all it touches," declared an Iowa Republican. "It is a curse upon the poor, free, laboring white men." In the United States, social mobility often depended on geographic mobility. The main reason so many families moved into new territories was to make a new start, to get ahead. But, declared a Republican editor, if slavery goes into the territories, "the free labor of all the states will not. If the free labor of the states goes there, the slave labor of the southern states will not, and in a few years the country will teem with an active and energetic population."

Southerners contended that free labor was prone to unrest and strikes. Of course it was, said Lincoln in a speech to a New England audience during the shoemakers' strike of 1860. "I am glad to see that a system prevails in New England under which laborers *can* strike when they want to *(Cheers)*.... I like the system which lets a man quit when he wants to, and wish it might prevail everywhere *(Tremendous applause)*." Strikes were one of the ways in which free workers could try to improve their prospects. "I want every man," said Lincoln, "to have the chance—and I believe a black man is entitled to it—in which he can better his condition." That was why Republicans were determined to contain the expansion of slavery, because if the South got its way in the territories, "free labor that can strike will give way to slave labor that cannot!"

14-5h *The Impending Crisis*

From the South came a maverick voice that echoed the Republicans. Hinton Rowan Helper considered himself a spokesman for the nonslaveholding whites of the South. Living in upcountry North Carolina, a region of small farms and few slaves, he had brooded for years over slavery's retarding influence on southern development. In 1857, he poured out his bitterness in a book entitled *The Impending Crisis of the South.* Using selective statistics from the 1850 census, he pictured a South mired in economic backwardness, widespread illiteracy, poverty for the masses, and great wealth for the elite. He contrasted this dismal situation with the bustling, prosperous northern economy and its near-universal literacy, neat farms, and progressive institutions. What caused this startling contrast? "Slavery lies at the root of all the shame, poverty, ignorance, tyranny, and imbecility of the South," he wrote. Slavery monopolized the best land, degraded all labor to the level of bond labor, denied schools to the poor, and impoverished all but "the lords of the lash [who] are not only absolute masters of the blacks [but] of all nonslaveholding whites, whose freedom is merely nominal, and whose unparalleled illiteracy and degradation is purposely and fiendishly perpetrated." The remedy? Nonslaveholding whites must organize and use their votes to overthrow "this entire system of oligarchical despotism."

North Wind Picture Archives

14.13 A Southern Yeoman Farmer's Home This modest log cabin on the edge of a small clearing, with the farmer's wife drawing water from a well in the foreground, was typical of nonslaveholders' farms in the backcountry of the South. Often stigmatized as poor whites, many of these families were in fact comfortable by the standards of the day. They did not feel the sense of oppression by the planter class that Hinton Rowan Helper believed they should feel.

No southern publisher dared touch this book. Helper lugged his bulky manuscript to New York City, where a printer brought it out in summer 1857. *The Impending Crisis* was virtually banned in the South, and few southern whites read it, but it made a huge impact in the North. Republicans welcomed it as confirmation of all they had been saying about the evils of slavery and the virtues of free labor. The Republican Party subsidized an abridged edition and distributed thousands of copies as campaign documents. During the late 1850s, a war of books (Helper's *Impending Crisis* versus Fitzhugh's *Cannibals All*) exacerbated sectional tensions. Fitzhugh's book circulated freely in the North, whereas the sale or possession of Helper's book was a criminal offense in many parts of the South. Northern spokesmen did not hesitate to point out the moral: A free society could tolerate free speech and a free press, but a slave society could not.

14-5i *Southern Nonslaveholders*

How accurate was Helper's portrayal of southern poor whites degraded by slavery and ready to revolt against it? The touchy response of many southern leaders suggested that the planters felt uneasy about that question. After all, slaveholding families constituted less than one-third of the white population in slave states, and the proportion was declining as the price of slaves continued to rise. Open hostility to the planters' domination of society and politics was evident in the mountainous and upcountry regions of the South. These would become areas of Unionist sentiment during the Civil War and of Republican strength after it.

But Helper surely exaggerated the disaffection of most nonslaveholders in the South. Three bonds held them to the system: kinship, economic interest, and race. In the Piedmont and the low-country regions of the South, nearly half of the whites lived in slaveholding families. Many of the rest were cousins or nephews or in-laws of slaveholders in the South's extensive and tightly knit kinship network. Moreover, many young, ambitious nonslaveholders hoped to buy slaves eventually. Some of them *rented* slaves. And because slaves could be made to do the menial, unskilled labor in the South—the "mudsill" tasks, in Senator Hammond's language—white workers monopolized the more skilled, higher-paying jobs.

Even if they did not own slaves, white people owned the most important asset of all—white skin. White supremacy was an article of faith in the South (and in most of the North, for that matter). Race was a more important social distinction than class. Southern law, politics, and social ideology were based on the concept of domination by the "master race" of whites. Subordination was the Negro's fate, and slavery was the best means of subordination. Emancipation would loose a flood of free blacks on society and would undermine the foundations of white supremacy. Thus many of the poor whites in the South and immigrant workers or poorer farmers in the North supported slavery.

Racist themes permeated pro-slavery rhetoric. "With us," said John C. Calhoun in 1848, "the two great divisions of society are not the rich and the poor, but white and black; and all the former, the poor as well as the rich, belong to the upper class, and are respected and treated as equals." True freedom, as Americans understood it, required equality of rights and status (although not of wealth or income). Slavery ensured such freedom for all whites by putting a floor under them, a mudsill of black slaves that kept whites from falling into the mud of inequality. "Break down slavery," said a Virginia congressman, "and you would with the same blow destroy the great Democratic principle of equality among men."

14-6 The Lincoln-Douglas Debates

Q *What were the major issues of the Lincoln-Douglas debates?*

Abraham Lincoln believed the opposite. For him, slavery and freedom were incompatible; the one must die that the other might live. This became the central theme of a memorable series of debates between Lincoln and Douglas in 1858, which came to be known as the **Lincoln-Douglas debates** and turned out to be a dress rehearsal for the presidential election of 1860.

The debates were arranged after Lincoln was nominated to oppose Douglas's reelection to the Senate. State legislatures elected U.S. senators at that time, so the campaign was technically for election by the Illinois legislature. The real issue, however, was the senatorship, and Douglas's prominence gave the contest national significance. Lincoln launched his bid with one of his most notable speeches. "'A house divided against itself cannot stand,'" he said. "I believe this government cannot endure, permanently half slave and half free... . It will become all one thing, or all the other." Under the Dred Scott decision, which Douglas had endorsed, slavery was legal in all of the territories. And what, asked Lincoln, would prevent the Supreme Court, using the same reasoning that had led it to interpret the Constitution as protecting property in slaves, from legalizing slavery in free states? (A case based on this question was then before the New York courts.) The advocates of slavery, charged Lincoln, were trying to "push it forward, till it shall become lawful in all the States." But Republicans intended to keep slavery out of the territories, thus stopping its growth and placing it "where the public mind shall rest in the belief that it is in the course of ultimate extinction."

The seven open-air debates between Douglas and Lincoln focused almost entirely on the issue of slavery. Douglas asked: Why could the country not continue to exist half slave and half free as it had for 70 years? Lincoln's talk about the "ultimate extinction" of slavery would provoke the South to secession. Douglas professed himself no friend of slavery, but if people in the southern states or in the territories wanted it, they had the right to have it. Douglas did not want black people—either slave or free—in Illinois. Lincoln's policy would not only free the slaves but would also grant them equality. "Are you in favor of conferring upon the negro the rights and privileges of citizenship?" Douglas called out to supporters in the crowd. "No, no!" they shouted back. He continued:

> Do you desire to strike out of our State Constitution that clause which keeps slaves and free negroes out of the State ... in order that when Missouri abolishes slavery she can send one hundred thousand emancipated slaves into Illinois, to become citizens and voters on an equality with yourselves? *("Never," "no.")*. ...if you desire to allow them to come into the State and settle with the white man, if you desire them to vote ... then support Mr. Lincoln and the Black Republican party, who are in favor of the citizenship of the negro. *("Never, never.")*

Douglas's demagoguery put Lincoln on the defensive. He responded with cautious denials that he favored "social and political equality" of the races. The "ultimate extinction" of slavery might take a century. It would require the voluntary cooperation of the South and would perhaps be contingent on the emigration of some freed slaves from the country. But come what may, freedom must prevail. Americans must reaffirm the principles of the Founding Fathers. In Lincoln's words, a black person was

> entitled to all the natural rights enumerated in the Declaration of Independence, the right to life, liberty and the pursuit of happiness. *(Loud cheers.)* I hold that he is as much entitled to these as the white man. I agree with Judge Douglas he is not my equal in many respects... . But in the right to eat the bread, without leave of anybody else, which his own hand earns, he is my equal and the equal of Judge Douglas, and the equal of every living man. *(Great applause.)*

Lincoln deplored Douglas's "care not" attitude about whether slavery was voted up or down. He "looks to no end of the institution of slavery," said Lincoln. By endorsing the Dred Scott decision, Lincoln claimed, Douglas looks to its "perpetuity and nationalization." Douglas was thus "eradicating the light of reason and liberty in this American people." That was the real issue in the election, insisted Lincoln:

> That is the issue that will continue in this country when these poor tongues of Judge Douglas and myself shall be silent. It is the eternal struggle between these two principles—right and wrong—throughout the world... . The one is the common right of humanity and the other the divine right of kings... . No matter in what shape it comes, whether from a king who seeks to bestride the people of his own nation and live by the fruit of their labor, or from one race of men as an apology for enslaving another race, it is the same tyrannical principle.

Old Paper Studios/Alamy Stock Photo

14.14 **The Lincoln-Douglas Debates** The Lincoln-Douglas contest for the Senate in 1858 produced the most famous—and fateful—political debates in American history. At stake was nothing less than the future of the nation. Thousands of people crowded into seven towns to listen to these three-hour debates that took place outdoors from August to October in weather ranging from stifling heat to cold rain.

Q *What are the similarities and differences between this portrayal of the Lincoln-Douglas Debates and George Caleb Bingham's painting* Stump Speaking *(this chapter's opening image)?*

Q *What do these idealized images reveal about the practice of politics in American life?*

14-6a *The Freeport Doctrine*

The popular vote for Republican and Democratic state legislators in Illinois was virtually even in 1858, but because apportionment favored the Democrats, they won a majority of seats and reelected Douglas. But Lincoln was the ultimate victor, for his performance in the debates lifted him from political obscurity, while Douglas further alienated southern Democrats. In the Freeport debate, Lincoln had asked Douglas how he reconciled his support for the Dred Scott decision with his policy of popular sovereignty, which supposedly gave residents of a territory the power to vote slavery down. Douglas replied that even though the Court had legalized slavery in the territories, the enforcement of that right would depend on the people who lived there. This was a popular answer in the North, but it gave added impetus to southern demands for congressional passage of a federal slave code in territories such as Kansas, where the Free-Soil majority had by 1859 made slavery virtually null. In the next two sessions of Congress after the 1858 elections, southern Democrats, led by **Jefferson Davis**, tried to pass a federal slave code for all territories. Douglas and northern Democrats joined with Republicans to defeat it. Consequently, southern hostility toward Douglas mounted as the presidential election of 1860 approached.

History Through Film *Abe Lincoln in Illinois* (1940)

Directed by John Cromwell.
Starring Raymond Massey (Abraham Lincoln), Gene Lockhard (Stephen Douglas), Ruth Gordon (Mary Todd Lincoln).

Raymond Massey's portrayal of Abraham Lincoln in Robert Sherwood's Broadway play, which opened in 1938 and was made into a movie in 1940, launched this Canadian-born actor as the image and voice of Lincoln on stage, screen, and radio for a generation. More people saw or heard Massey as Lincoln than ever saw or heard the real Lincoln. Perhaps that was appropriate because Sherwood's Lincoln spoke more to the generation of the Second World War than to the generation of the Civil War.

In one of the film's most dramatic scenes of the Lincoln-Douglas debates, Massey/Lincoln delivers a speech against slavery that applied equally to fascist totalitarianism and defended democracy in language resonant with the four freedoms that the Allies fought for in the Second World War. In an interview, Massey said, "If you substitute the word *dictatorship* for the word *slavery* throughout Sherwood's script, it becomes electric for our time." In the final scene, as Lincoln departs from Springfield to take up the burdens of the presidency, Massey's Lincoln sees beyond the challenge of disunion to the challenge to democracy in a world at war.

14.15 Raymond Massey as the 23-year-old Abraham Lincoln just elected captain of a New Salem militia company in the Black Hawk War of 1832.

Sherwood skillfully wove together Lincoln's words with his own script to portray Lincoln's growth from the gawky youth of 1831 to the champion of freedom and democracy in 1861. Sherwood took many liberties, but what scriptwriter does not? He combined bits and pieces of several Lincoln speeches into one; he invented incidents and wrenched chronology in some of the 12 scenes from these 30 years of Lincoln's life.

Perhaps the film's sharpest departure from reality is the tension it depicts between "politics," which is bad, and "democracy," which is good. Sherwood's Lincoln doesn't want to play the dirty game of politics; early in the film, the homespun youth declares: "I don't want to be no politician." It is Mary Todd Lincoln who is ambitious for her husband and pushes a reluctant Abraham toward his destiny. The real Lincoln loved the game of politics and played it masterfully. He was also as ambitious in his own right as Mary was for him; Lincoln's law partner William Herndon said that Abraham's ambition was "a little engine that knew no rest." Sherwood's Lincoln who transcends politics to become a great statesman could not have existed without the real Lincoln, the ambitious politician. ■

14-6b *John Brown at Harpers Ferry*

Southern tempers were already frayed at the start of the 1859–1860 session of Congress because of what had happened at **Harpers Ferry**, Virginia, in the previous October. After his exploits in Kansas, John Brown had disappeared from public view. But he had not been idle. Like the Old Testament warriors he admired, Brown intended to carry his war against slavery into Babylon—the South. His favorite New Testament passage was Hebrews 9:22: "Without shedding of blood there is no remission of sin." Brown worked up a plan to capture the federal arsenal at Harpers Ferry, arm slaves with the muskets he seized there, and move southward along the Appalachian Mountains, attracting more slaves to his army along the way until the "whole accursed system of bondage" collapsed.

Brown recruited 5 black men and 17 whites, including three of his sons, for this reckless scheme. He also had the secret support of a half-dozen Massachusetts and New York abolitionists, who had helped him to raise funds. On the night of October 16, 1859, Brown led his men across the Potomac River and occupied the sleeping town of Harpers Ferry without resistance. Few slaves flocked to his banner, but the next day, state militia units poured into town and drove Brown's band into the fire-engine house. At dawn on October 18, a company of U.S. Marines commanded by Colonel Robert E. Lee and Lieutenant J. E. B. Stuart stormed the engine house and captured the surviving members of Brown's party. Four townsmen, one marine, and ten of Brown's men (including two of his sons) were killed; not a single slave was liberated.

John Brown's raid lasted 36 hours, but its repercussions resounded for years. Brown and six of his followers were promptly tried by the state of Virginia, convicted, and hanged. This scarcely ended matters. The raid sent a wave of revulsion and alarm through the South. Although no slaves had risen in revolt, it revived fears of slave insurrection that were never far beneath the surface of southern consciousness. Exaggerated reports of Brown's network of abolitionist supporters confirmed southern suspicions that a widespread northern conspiracy was afoot, determined to destroy their society. Although Republican leaders denied any connection with Brown and disavowed his actions, few southerners believed them. Had not Lincoln talked of the extinction of slavery? And had not William H. Seward, who was expected to be the next Republican presidential nominee, given a campaign speech in 1858 in which he predicted an irrepressible conflict between the free and slave societies?

Many northerners, impressed by Brown's dignified bearing and eloquence during his trial, considered him a martyr to freedom. In his final statement to the court, Brown said:

> I see a book kissed, which I suppose to be the Bible, which teaches me that all things whatsoever I would that men should do to me, I should do even so to them. It teaches me, further, to remember them that are in bonds as bound with them. I endeavored to act up to that instruction… . Now, if it is deemed necessary that I should forfeit my life for the furtherance of the ends of justice, and mingle my blood further with the blood of my children and with the blood of millions in this slave country whose rights are disregarded by wicked, cruel, and unjust enactments, I say, let it be done.

On the day of Brown's execution, bells tolled in hundreds of northern towns, guns fired salutes, and ministers preached sermons of commemoration. "The death of no man in America has ever produced so profound a sensation," commented one northerner. Ralph Waldo Emerson declared that Brown had made "the gallows as glorious as the cross."

This outpouring of northern sympathy for Brown shocked and enraged southerners and weakened the already frayed threads of the Union. "The Harper's Ferry invasion has advanced the cause of disunion more than any event that has happened since the formation of the government," observed a Richmond, Virginia, newspaper. "I have always been a fervid Union man," wrote a North Carolinian, but "the endorsement of the Harper's Ferry outrage … has shaken my fidelity… . I am willing to take the chances of every possible evil that may arise from disunion, sooner than submit any longer to Northern insolence."

14.16 **The Last Moments of John Brown** This famous 1882–1884 painting of John Brown by Thomas Hovenden reminds us that the memory of Brown's 1859 attack on Harpers Ferry resonated deeply in American culture. Here, a sentimental portrait of Brown portrays him about to kiss a baby, while the soldiers who will escort him to his death are positioned as an honor guard. Depicting Brown as a gentle hero and martyr to the cause of antislavery, this genre painting avoids grappling with the ferocity and violence of Brown's actions, whether in Kansas or at Harpers Ferry.

Q *How would you explain the importance of John Brown in American political history?*

Something approaching a reign of terror now gripped the South. Every Yankee seemed to be another John Brown; every slave who acted suspiciously seemed to be an insurrectionist. Hundreds of northerners were run out of the South in 1860, some wearing a coat of tar and feathers. Several "incendiaries," both white and black, were lynched. "Defend yourselves!" Senator Robert Toombs cried out to the southern people. "The enemy is at your door … meet him at the doorsill, and drive him from the temple of liberty, or pull down its pillars and involve him in a common ruin."

Conclusion

Few decades in American history witnessed a greater disjunction between economic well-being and political upheaval than the 1850s. Despite the recession following the Panic of 1857, the total output of the American economy grew by 62 percent during the decade. Railroad mileage more than

What They Said

Reactions to John Brown

The October 1859 attack on Harpers Ferry by John Brown electrified the nation and hardened sectional loyalties. These two newspaper editorials reveal the deep differences in northern and southern interpretations of Brown.

Wilmington, North Carolina, *Daily Herald*, December 5, 1859

It is useless to disguise the fact, that the entire North and Northwest are hopelessly abolitionized. We want no better evidence than that presented to us by their course in this Harper's affair. With the exception of a few papers … that have had the manliness to denounce the act as it deserved, the great majority have either sympathized with the offenders, or maintained an ominous silence.

Let us look calmly at the case: A sovereign State, in the peaceful employment of the rights guaranteed by the Constitution, has been invaded by an armed force, not foreign mercenaries, but citizens of the same Confederacy, and her people shot down in the public highways. The question is a natural one—Why is this thing done? Why is murder and rapine committed?—And who are the perpetrators? The answer is found in the fact that the State whose territory has thus been invaded, is a Southern State in which the institution of slavery exists according to the law and the gospel; and the actors in the terrible drama were but carrying out the precepts and teachings of our *Northern brethren*. The "irrepressible conflict" between the North and the South then, has already commenced; to this complexion it must come at last. It is useless to talk of the conservatism of the North. Where has there been any evidence of it? Meetings upon meetings have been held for the purpose of expressing sympathy for murderers and traitors; but none, no, not one solitary expression of horror, or disapprobation even, for the crime committed, have we yet seen from any State North of Mason & Dixon's line.

Horace Greeley, *New-York Tribune*, December 3, 1859

We are not those who say, "if slavery is wrong, then John Brown was wholly right." There are fit and unfit modes of combating a great evil; we think Brown at Harper's Ferry pursued the latter. . . . And, while we heartily wish every slave in the world would run away from his master tomorrow and never be retaken, we should not feel justified in entering a slave state to incite them to do so, even if we were sure to succeed in the enterprise. Of course, we regard Brown's raid as utterly mistaken and, in its direct consequences, pernicious.

But his are the errors of a fanatic, not the crimes of a felon. It were absurd to apply to him opprobrious epithets or wholesale denunciations. The essence of crime is the pursuit of selfish gratification in disregard of others' good; and that is the precise opposite of Old Brown's impulse and deed. He periled and sacrificed not merely his own life—that were, perhaps, a moderate stake—but the lives of his beloved sons, the earthly happiness of his family and theirs, to benefit a despised and downtrodden race—to deliver from bitter bondage and degradation those whom he had never seen.

Unwise, the world will pronounce him. Reckless of artificial yet palpable obligations he certainly was, but his very errors were heroic—the faults of a brave, impulsive, truthful nature, impatient of wrong, and only too conscious that "resistance to tyrants is obedience to God." Let whoever would first cast a stone ask himself whether his own noblest act was equal in grandeur and nobility to that for which John Brown pays the penalty of death on the gallows.

Q *The Wilmington, North Carolina, editorial writer accuses the entire North of being "abolitionized." Is this a fair accusation? Why or why not?*

Q *Would southerners have been reassured by Greeley's assertion that Brown's raid was "utterly mistaken"? Why or why not? What does Greeley argue in the rest of his editorial?*

Sources: (top) From an editorial in the newspaper: Wilmington, North Carolina, *Daily Herald*, December 5, 1859. (bottom) From an editorial by Horace Greeley in the newspaper *New-York Tribune*, December 3, 1859.

tripled, value added by manufacturing nearly doubled, and gross farm product grew by 40 percent. Americans were more prosperous than ever before.

Yet a profound malaise gripped the country. Riots between immigrants and nativists in the mid-1850s left more than 50 people dead. Fighting in Kansas between pro-slavery and antislavery forces killed at least 200. Fistfights broke out on the floor of Congress. A South Carolina congressman bludgeoned a Massachusetts senator to unconsciousness with a heavy cane. Representatives and senators came to congressional sessions armed with weapons as well as with violent words.

The nation proved capable of absorbing the large influx of immigrants despite the tensions and turmoil of the mid-1850s. It might also have been able to absorb the huge territorial expansion of the late 1840s had not the slavery issue been reopened in an earlier territorial acquisition, the Louisiana Purchase, by the Kansas-Nebraska Act of 1854. This legislation, followed by the Dred Scott decision in 1857, seemed to authorize the unlimited expansion of slavery. Within two years of its founding in 1854, however, the Republican Party emerged as the largest party in the North on a platform of preventing all future expansion of slavery. By 1860, the United States had reached a fateful crossroads. As Lincoln had said, it could not endure permanently half-slave and half-free. The presidential election of 1860 would decide which road America would take into the future.

CHAPTER REVIEW

Review

1. Why did the Whig Party die, and why did the Republican Party emerge as the new majority party in the North?
2. What were the origins of nativism? How did this movement relate to the slavery issue?
3. How was violence in Kansas related to the issue of slavery?
4. What role did the issue of slavery play in the election of 1856?
5. How did economic developments in the 1840s and 1850s widen the breach between North and South?
6. What were the major issues of the Lincoln-Douglas debates?

Critical Thinking

1. Why did the northern and southern economic systems develop in such different directions? Why did the effort by some southerners to escape from their "colonial" economic relationship fail?
2. One of the main points of contention in the Lincoln-Douglas debates was the question of whether the country could continue to endure half-slave and half-free. Why did Lincoln challenge Douglas's position that because the nation had so endured for 70 years, there was no reason why it could not continue to do so?

Identifications

Review your understanding of the following key terms, people, and events for this chapter (terms in bold in text are included in the Glossary).

Dred Scott, p. 377
Harpers Ferry, p. 377
John Brown, p. 377
Kansas-Nebraska Act, p. 378
Abraham Lincoln, p. 378
nativism, p. 379
Know-Nothings, p. 379
"border ruffians", p. 383
Black Republicans, p. 386
interchangeable parts, p. 389
colonial economy, p. 392
free-labor ideology, p. 395
Lincoln-Douglas debates, p. 399
Jefferson Davis, p. 400

Suggested Readings

For an overview of the 1850s, see **James M. McPherson**, ***Battle Cry of Freedom: The Civil War Era*** (1988). The Kansas-Nebraska Act and its political consequences are treated in **Gerald W. Wolff**, ***The Kansas-Nebraska Bill: Party, Section, and the Coming of the Civil War*** (1977). The conflict in Kansas is treated in **Nicole Etcheson**, ***Bleeding Kansas: Contested Liberty in the Civil War Era*** (2004). For the cross-cutting issue of nativism and the Know-Nothings, see **William E. Gienapp**, ***The Origins of the Republican Party, 1852–1856*** (1987), and **Tyler Anbinder**, ***Nativism and Politics: The Know Nothing Party in the Northern United States*** (1992). Two excellent studies of the role of Abraham Lincoln in the rise of the Republican Party are **Don E. Fehrenbacher**, ***Prelude to Greatness: Lincoln in the 1850s*** (1962), and **Kenneth Winkle**, ***The Young Eagle: The Rise of Abraham Lincoln*** (2003). The southern response to the growth of antislavery political sentiment in the North is the theme of **William J. Cooper, Jr.**, ***The South and the Politics of Slavery 1828–1856*** (1978).

The year 1857 witnessed a convergence of many crucial events; for a stimulating book that pulls together the threads of that year of crisis, see **Kenneth M. Stampp**, ***America in***

1857: A Nation on the Brink (1990). For economic developments during the era, an older classic is still the best introduction: **George Rogers Taylor**, ***The Transportation Revolution, 1815–1860*** (1951). An important dimension of the southern economy is elucidated in **Fred Bateman and Thomas Weiss**, ***A Deplorable Scarcity: The Failure of Industrialization in the Slave Economy*** (1981). The political impact of the Panic of 1857 is the subject of **James L. Huston**, ***The Panic of 1857 and the Coming of the Civil War*** (1987). Still the best study of Republican free-labor ideology is **Eric Foner**, ***Free Soil, Free Labor, Free Men: The Ideology of the Republican Party before the Civil War*** (2nd ed., 1995). For southern yeoman farmers, a good study is **Stephanie McCurry**, ***Masters of Small Worlds: Yeoman Households, Gender Relations, and the Political Culture of the Antebellum South Carolina Low Country*** (1995). The best single study of the Dred Scott case is **Don E. Fehrenbacher**, ***The Dred Scott Case: Its Significance in American Law and Politics*** (1978), which was published in an abridged version with the title ***Slavery, Law, and Politics: The Dred Scott Case in Historical Perspective*** (1981). A thought-provoking biography of John Brown is **David S. Reynolds**, ***John Brown: Abolitionist*** (2005). On Harper's Ferry see also **Tony Horwitz**, ***Midnight Rising: John Brown and the Raid that Sparked the Civil War*** (2011).

15 Secession and Civil War, 1860–1862

Library of Congress Prints and Photographs Division [LC-DIG-cwpb-01663]

15.1 **Tent Life of the 31st Pennsylvania Infantry Regiment** This posed photograph, taken in camp near Washington, D.C. in 1861, shows us the home created by one ordinary soldier and his family in the midst of war. In the background several soldiers and an African American man watch the photographic process with interest. Many women followed their husbands to war in 1861 and 1862, when men in the Army of the Potomac spent long months in camp. But families were left behind when military campaigns began and men marched away.

AS 1860 BEGAN, THE DEMOCRATIC PARTY was one of the few national institutions left in the country. The Whig Party and the nativist American Party had been shattered by sectional antagonism in the mid-1850s. In April 1860, even the Democratic Party, at its national convention in Charleston, South Carolina, split into northern and southern camps. This virtually ensured the election of a Republican president. Such a prospect aroused deep fears among southern whites that a Republican administration might use its power to bring liberty and perhaps even equality to the slaves.

When Abraham Lincoln was elected president, the lower-South states seceded from the Union. When Lincoln refused to remove U.S. troops from **Fort Sumter**, South Carolina, the new Confederate States army opened fire on the fort. Lincoln called out the militia to suppress the insurrection. Four more slave states seceded. In 1861, the country drifted into a civil war whose immense consequences no one could foresee. ■

CHRONOLOGY

1860	Lincoln elected president (November 6) • South Carolina secedes (December 20) • Federal troops transfer from Fort Moultrie to Fort Sumter (December 26)
1861	Rest of lower South secedes (January–February) • Crittenden Compromise rejected (February) • Jefferson Davis inaugurated as provisional president of new Confederate States of America (February 18) • Abraham Lincoln inaugurated as president of the United States (March 4) • Fort Sumter falls; Lincoln calls out troops, proclaims blockade (April) • Four more states secede to join Confederacy (April–May) • Battle of Bull Run (Manassas) (July 21) • Battle of Wilson's Creek (August 10) • The *Trent* Affair (November–December)
1862	Union captures Forts Henry and Donelson (February 6 and 16) • Congress passes Legal Tender Act (February 25) •Battle of Pea Ridge (March 7–8) • Battle of the *Monitor* and *Merrimac* (*Virginia*) (March 9) • Battle of Glorieta Pass (March 26–28) • Battle of Shiloh (April 6–7) • Union navy captures New Orleans (April 25) • Stonewall Jackson's Shenandoah Valley campaign (May–June) • Seven Days' battles (June 25–July 1) • Second Battle of Manassas (Bull Run) (August 29–30) • Lee invades Maryland (September) • Battle of Corinth (October 3–4) • Battle of Perryville (October 8)
1863	Congress passes National Banking Act (February 25)

15-1 The Election of 1860

Q *Why did the Republican Party choose Abraham Lincoln as its candidate in 1860?*

A hotbed of southern-rights radicalism, Charleston, South Carolina, turned out to be the worst possible place for the Democrats to hold their national convention. Sectional confrontations took place inside the convention hall and on the streets. Since 1836, the Democratic Party had required a two-thirds majority of delegates for a presidential nomination, a rule that in effect gave southerners veto power. Although Stephen A. Douglas had the backing of a simple majority of the delegates, southern Democrats were determined to deny him the nomination. His opposition to the Lecompton constitution in Kansas had convinced pro-slavery southerners that they would be unable to control a Douglas administration.

The first test came in the debate on the platform. Southern delegates insisted on a plank favoring a federal slave code for the territories. Douglas could not run on a platform that contained such a plank, and if the party adopted it, Democrats were sure to lose every state in the North. By a slim majority, the convention rejected the plank and reaffirmed the 1856 platform endorsing popular sovereignty. Fifty southern delegates thereupon walked out of the convention. Even after they left, Douglas could not muster a two-thirds majority, nor could any other candidate. After 57 futile ballots, the convention adjourned to meet in Baltimore 6 weeks later to try again.

By then the party was too badly shattered to be put back together. That pleased some pro-slavery radicals. The election of a "Black Republican" president, they believed, would provide the shock necessary to mobilize a southern majority for **secession**. Two of the most prominent secessionists were William L. Yancey and Edmund Ruffin. In 1858, they founded the League of United Southerners to "fire the Southern heart ... and at the proper moment, by one organized, concerted action, we can precipitate the Cotton States into a revolution." After walking out of the Democratic convention, the eloquent Yancey inspired a huge crowd in Charleston's moonlit courthouse square to give three cheers "for an Independent Southern Republic."

In Baltimore, an even larger number of delegates from southern states walked out. They formed their own Southern Rights Democratic Party and nominated John C. Breckinridge of Kentucky (the incumbent vice president) for president on a slave-code platform. When regular Democrats nominated Douglas, the stage was set for what would become a four-party election. A coalition of former southern Whigs, who could not bring themselves to vote Democratic, and northern Whigs, who considered the Republican Party too radical, formed the Constitutional Union Party, which nominated John Bell of Tennessee for president. Bell had no chance of winning; the party's purpose was to exercise a conservative influence on a campaign that threatened to polarize the country.

15-1a *The Republicans Nominate Lincoln*

From the moment the Democratic Party broke apart, it became clear that 1860 could be the year when the dynamic young Republican Party elected its first president. The Republicans could expect no electoral votes from the 15 slave states. In 1856, however, they had won all but five northern states, and with only two or three of those five they could win the presidency. The crucial states were Pennsylvania, Illinois, and Indiana. Douglas might still carry them and throw the presidential election into the House, where anything could happen. Thus the Republicans had to carry at least two of the swing states to win.

As the Republican delegates poured into Chicago for their convention, their leading presidential prospect was William H. Seward of New York. An experienced politician who had served as governor and senator, Seward was by all odds the most prominent Republican, but in his long career he had made many enemies. His antinativist policies had alienated some former members of the American Party, whose support he would need to carry Pennsylvania. His "Higher Law" speech against the Compromise of 1850 and

Inauguration of Abraham Lincoln - March 4, 1861.

15.2 **The Inauguration of President Lincoln on March 4, 1861** Only distant photographic views survive of Abraham Lincoln's fist inauguration. Here Lincoln is just visible standing under the wood canopy in the center of the photograph as he delivers his inaugural address to a large crowd. While his face is in shadow, we can see his white shirt front. Above him, the scaffolding reminds us that the Capitol Dome was unfinished at the time.

his "Irrepressible Conflict" speech in 1858, predicting the ultimate overthrow of slavery, had given him a reputation for radicalism that might drive away voters in the vital swing states of the lower North.

Several of the delegates, uneasy about that reputation, staged a stop-Seward movement. The next candidate to the fore was Abraham Lincoln. Although he too had opposed nativism, he had done so less prominently than Seward. His "House Divided" speech had made essentially the same point as Seward's "Irrepressible Conflict" speech, but his reputation was still that of a more moderate man. He was from one of the lower-North states where the election would be close, and his rise from a poor farm boy and rail-splitter to successful lawyer and political leader perfectly reflected the free-labor theme of social mobility extolled by the Republican Party. By picking up second-choice votes from states that switched from their favorite sons, Lincoln overtook Seward and won the nomination on the third ballot. Seward accepted the outcome gracefully, and the Republicans headed into the campaign as a united, confident party.

The Republican platform appealed to many groups in the North. Its main plank pledged exclusion of slavery from the territories. Other planks called for a higher tariff (especially popular in Pennsylvania), a homestead act (popular in the Northwest), and federal aid for construction of a transcontinental railroad and for improvement of river navigation. This program was designed for a future in which the "house divided" would become a free-labor society modeled on northern capitalism. Its blend of idealism and materialism proved especially attractive to young people; a large majority of first-time voters in the North voted Republican in 1860.

15-1b *Southern Fears*

Militant enthusiasm in the North was matched by fear and rage in the South. Few people there could see any difference between Lincoln and Seward—or for that matter between Lincoln and William Lloyd Garrison. They were all Black Republicans and abolitionists. Had not Lincoln branded slavery a moral, social, and political evil? Had he not said that the Declaration of Independence applied to blacks as well as whites? Had he not expressed a hope that excluding slavery from the territories would put it on the road to ultimate extinction? To southerners, the Republican pledge not to interfere with slavery in the states was meaningless.

A Republican victory in the presidential election would put an end to the South's political control of its destiny. Two-thirds of the time from 1789 to 1860, southerners (all slaveholders) had been president of the United States. Two-thirds of the Speakers of the House and presidents pro tem of the Senate had been southerners. Southern justices had been a majority on the Supreme Court since 1791. Lincoln's election would mark an irreversible turning away from this southern ascendancy. Even southern moderates warned that the South could not remain in the Union if Lincoln won. "This Government and Black Republicanism cannot live together," said one of them.

Most whites in the South voted for Breckinridge, who carried 11 slave states (see Map 15.1). Bell won the upper South states of Virginia, Kentucky, and Tennessee. Missouri went to Douglas—the only state he carried, although he came in second in the popular vote. Although Lincoln received less than 40 percent of the popular vote, he won every free state and swept the presidency by a substantial margin in the Electoral College (see Table 15.1).

15.3 **Wide-Awake Parade in New York, October 5, 1860** The Wide-Awakes were an organization of young Republicans who roused political enthusiasm by marching in huge torchlight parades during the political campaign of 1860. A year later, many of these same men would march down the same streets in army uniforms carrying rifles instead of torches on their way to the front.

Table 15.1 **VOTING IN THE 1860 ELECTION**

	All States		Free States (18)		Slave States (15)	
Candidate	**Popular**	**Electoral**	**Popular**	**Electoral**	**Popular**	**Electoral**
Lincoln	1,864,735	180	1,838,347	180	26,388	0
Opposition to Lincoln	2,821,157	123	1,572,637	3	1,248,520	120
"Fusion" Tickets*	595,846	—	580,426	—	15,420	—
Douglas	979,425	12	815,857	3	163,568	9
Breckinridge	669,472	72	99,381	0	570,091	72
Bell	576,414	39	76,973	0	499,441	39

*In several states, the two Democratic parties and the Constitutional Union Party arranged a single anti-Lincoln ballot. These "fusion" tickets carried several counties but failed to win any state.

15-2 The Lower South Secedes

Why did political leaders in the lower South think that Lincoln's election made secession imperative?

Lincoln's victory provided the shock that southern fire-eaters had craved. The tension that had been building up for years suddenly exploded like a string of firecrackers, as seven states seceded one after another. According to the theory of secession, when each state ratified the Constitution and joined the Union, it authorized the national government to act as its agent in the exercise of certain functions of sovereignty, but the states had never given away their fundamental underlying sovereignty. Any state, then, by the act of its own convention, could withdraw from its "compact" with the other states and reassert its individual sovereignty. Therefore, the South Carolina legislature called for such a convention and ordered an election of delegates to consider withdrawing from the United States. On December 20, 1860, the South Carolina convention did withdraw, by a vote of 169 to 0.

The outcome was closer in other lower-South states. Unconditional unionism was rare, but many conservatives and former Whigs shrank from the drastic step of secession. At the conventions in each of the next six states to secede, some delegates tried to delay matters with vague proposals for "cooperation" among all southern states, or even with proposals to wait until after Lincoln's inauguration on March 4, 1861, to see what course he would pursue. Nonetheless, proponents of immediate secession overrode those minority factions. The conventions followed the example of South Carolina and voted to take their states out of the Union: Mississippi on January 9, 1861; Florida on the 10th; Alabama

15.4 **Banner of the South Carolina Secession Convention**
With its banner featuring a palmetto tree and a snake reminiscent of the American Revolution's "Don't Tread on Me" slogan, the South Carolina secession convention in 1860 looked forward to a grand new southern republic composed of all 15 slave states and built on the ruins of the old Union. Note the large South Carolina keystone of the arch and the stones of free states lying cracked and broken on the ground.

on the 11th; Georgia on the 19th; Louisiana on the 26th; and Texas on February 1. In those six states as a whole, 20 percent of the delegates voted against secession, but most of these "went with their states" after the final votes had been tallied. Delegates from the seven seceding states met in Montgomery, Alabama, in February to create a new nation to be called the Confederate States of America.

15-2a *Northerners Affirm the Union*

Most people in the North considered secession unconstitutional and treasonable. In his final annual message to Congress, on December 3, 1860, President Buchanan insisted that the Union was not "a mere voluntary association of States, to be dissolved at pleasure by any one of the contracting parties." If secession were consummated, Buchanan warned, it would create a disastrous precedent that would make the United States government "a rope of sand." He continued:

> Our thirty-three States may resolve themselves into as many petty, jarring, and hostile republics ... . By such a dread catastrophe ... our example for more than eighty years would not only be lost, but it would be quoted as proof that man is unfit for self-government.

European monarchists and conservatives were already expressing smug satisfaction at "the great smashup" of the republic in North America. They predicted that other disaffected minorities would also secede and that the United States would ultimately collapse into anarchy and revolution. That was precisely what northerners and even some upper-South **Unionists** feared. "The doctrine of secession is anarchy," declared a Cincinnati newspaper. "If any minority have the right to break up the Government at pleasure, because they have not had their way, there is an end of all government." Lincoln denied that the states had ever possessed independent sovereignty before becoming part of the United States. Rather, they had been colonies or territories that never would have become part of the United States had they not accepted unconditional sovereignty of the national government. "No State, upon its own mere motion, can lawfully get out of the Union ... . They can only do so against law, and by revolution."

In that case, answered many southerners, we invoke the right of revolution to justify secession. After all, the United States was born of revolution. The secessionists maintained that they were merely following the example of their forefathers in declaring independence from a government that threatened their rights and liberties. An Alabaman asked rhetorically: "[Were not] the men of 1776, who withdrew their allegiance from George III and set up for themselves ... Secessionists?"

Northerners could scarcely deny the right of revolution: They too were heirs of 1776. But "the right of revolution, is never a legal right," said Lincoln. "At most, it is but a moral right, when exercised for a morally justifiable cause. When exercised without such a cause revolution is no right, but simply a wicked exercise of physical power." The South, in Lincoln's view, had no morally justifiable cause. In fact, the event that had precipitated secession was his very election by a constitutional majority. For southerners to cast themselves in the mold of 1776 was "a libel upon the whole character and conduct" of the Founding Fathers, said the antislavery poet and journalist William Cullen Bryant. They rebelled "to establish the rights of man ... and principles of universal liberty," whereas southerners in 1861 were rebelling to protect "a domestic despotism ... . Their motto is not liberty, but slavery."

15-2b *Compromise Proposals*

Bryant conveniently overlooked the fact that slavery had existed in most parts of the republic founded by the revolutionaries of 1776. In any event, most people in the North agreed with Lincoln that secession was a "wicked exercise of physical power." The question was what to do about it. All kinds of compromise proposals came before Congress when it met in December 1860. To sort them out, the Senate and the House each set up a special committee. The Senate committee came up with a package of compromises sponsored by Senator John J. Crittenden of Kentucky. The Crittenden Compromise consisted of a series of proposed constitutional amendments: to guarantee slavery in the states perpetually against federal interference; to prohibit Congress from abolishing slavery in the

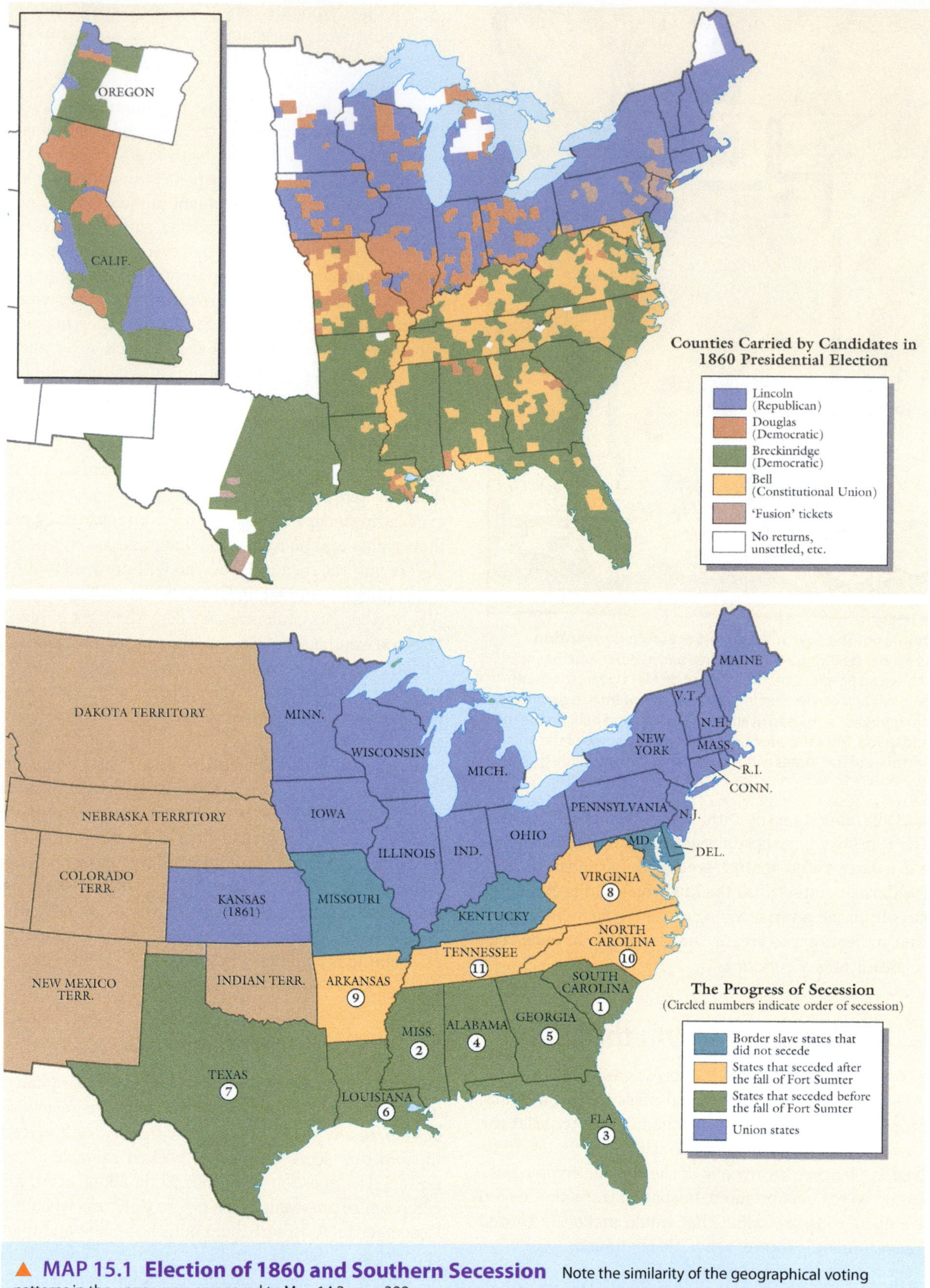

▲ **MAP 15.1 Election of 1860 and Southern Secession** Note the similarity of the geographical voting patterns in the upper map compared to Map 14.2 on p. 388.

Q *Can you explain the correlation between the vote for Breckinridge (upper map) and the first seven states to secede (lower map)?*

Q *Why didn't Douglas have more support in the South?*

District of Columbia or on any federal property (forts, arsenals, naval bases, and so on); to deny Congress the power to interfere with the interstate slave trade; to compensate slaveholders who were prevented from recovering fugitive slaves who had escaped to the North; and, most important, to protect slavery south of latitude 36° 30″ in all territories "now held *or hereafter acquired*."

Given the appetite of the South for more slave territory in the Caribbean and Central America, that italicized phrase, in the view of most Republicans, might turn the United States into "a great slavebreeding and slavetrading empire." But even though endorsement of the territorial clause in the Crittenden Compromise would require Republicans to repudiate the platform on which they had just won the election, some conservatives in the party were willing to accept it in the interest of peace and conciliation. Their votes, together with those of Democrats and upper-South Unionists whose states had not seceded, might have gotten the compromise through Congress. In any case, word came from Springfield, Illinois, where president-elect Lincoln was preparing for his inaugural trip to Washington, telling key Republican senators and congressmen to stand firm against compromise on the territorial issue. "Entertain no proposition for a compromise in regard to the *extension* of slavery," wrote Lincoln.

> We have just carried an election on principles fairly stated to the people. Now we are told in advance, the government shall be broken up, unless we surrender to those we have beaten .... If we surrender, it is the end of us. They will repeat the experiment upon us *ad libitum*. A year will not pass, till we shall have to take Cuba as a condition upon which they will stay in the Union.

Lincoln's advice was decisive. The Republicans voted against the Crittenden Compromise, which therefore failed in Congress. Most Republicans, though, went along with a proposal by Virginia for a "peace convention" of all the states to be held in Washington in February 1861. In the end, however, the peace convention produced nothing better than a modified version of the Crittenden Compromise, which suffered the same fate as the original.

Nothing that happened in Washington would have made any difference to the seven states that had seceded. No compromise could bring them back. "We spit upon every plan to compromise," said one secessionist. No power could "stem the wild torrent of passion that is carrying everything before it," wrote former U.S. senator Judah P. Benjamin of Louisiana. Secession "is a revolution [that] can no more be checked by human effort ... than a prairie fire by a gardener's watering pot."

15-2c *Establishment of the Confederacy*

While the peace convention deliberated in Washington, the seceded states focused on a convention in Montgomery, Alabama, that drew up a constitution and established a government for the new Confederate States of America. The Confederate constitution contained clauses that guaranteed slavery in both the states and the territories, strengthened the principle of state sovereignty, and prohibited its Congress from enacting a protective (as distinguished from a revenue) tariff. It limited the president to a single 6-year term. The convention delegates constituted themselves a provisional Congress for the new nation until regular elections could be held in November 1861. For provisional president and vice president, the convention turned away from radical secessionists, such as Yancey, and elected Jefferson Davis, a moderate secessionist, and Alexander Stephens, who had originally opposed Georgia's secession but ultimately had supported it.

Davis and Stephens were two of the most able men in the South, with 25 years of service in the U.S. Congress between them. A West Point graduate, Davis had commanded a regiment in the Mexican War and had been secretary of war in the Pierce administration—a useful fund of experience if civil war became a reality. But perhaps the main reason they were elected was to present an image of moderation and respectability to the eight upper-South states that remained in the Union. The Confederacy needed those states—at least some of them—if it was to be a viable nation, especially if war came. Without the upper South, the Confederate states would have less than one-fifth of the population (and barely one-tenth of the free population) and only one-twentieth of the industrial capacity of the Union states.

Confederate leaders appealed to the upper South to join them because of the "common origin, pursuits, tastes, manners and customs [that] bind together in one brotherhood the ... slaveholding states." Residents of the upper South were indeed concerned about preserving slavery, but the issue was less salient there (see Table 15.2). A strong heritage of Unionism competed with the commitment to slavery. Virginia had contributed more men to the pantheon of Founding Fathers than any other state. Tennessee took pride in being the state of Andrew Jackson, who was famous for his stern warning to John C. Calhoun: "Our Federal Union—It must be preserved." Kentucky was the home of Henry Clay, the Great Pacificator, who had put together compromises to save the Union on three occasions. These states would not leave the Union without greater cause.

15-3 The Fort Sumter Issue

Q *Why did compromise efforts to forestall secession fail, and why did war break out at Fort Sumter?*

As each state seceded, it seized the forts, arsenals, customs houses, and other federal property within its borders. Still in federal hands, however, were two remote forts in the Florida Keys, another on an island off Pensacola, and Fort Moultrie in the Charleston harbor. Moultrie quickly became a bone of contention. In December 1860, the self-proclaimed republic of South Carolina demanded its evacuation by the 84-man garrison of the U.S. Army. Moultrie was vulnerable to attack by the South Carolina militia that swarmed into the area. On the day after Christmas 1860, Major Robert Anderson, commander at Moultrie, moved his men to Fort Sumter, an uncompleted but immensely strong bastion on an artificial island in the

What They Said

Cornerstone of the Confederacy

Alexander H. Stephens of Georgia had opposed the secession of his state in January 1861. But when Georgia seceded anyway, he "went with his state," as did so many other southerners who had initially counseled against secession. Stephens was subsequently elected vice president of the Confederate States of America. On March 21, 1861, he gave an address in Savannah, Georgia, which became known as the Cornerstone Speech, in which he proclaimed slavery to be the cornerstone of the new Confederacy.

After the Civil War, however, Stephens wrote a two-volume history titled *The War Between the States*, in which he maintained that slavery was not the cornerstone of the Confederacy or the reason for secession. Instead, he argued that in seceding from the Union, southerners had defended a "great right, which lies at the foundation of the federative system"—what Stephens saw as a fundamental constitutional right of independence and state sovereignty.

Alexander H. Stephens, "The Cornerstone of the Confederacy," 1861

The new Constitution [of the Confederate States] has put at rest forever all the agitating questions relating to our peculiar institution—African slavery as it exists among us—the proper status of the negro in our form of civilization. This was the immediate cause of the late rupture and present revolution.

[Thomas] Jefferson, in his forecast, had anticipated this, as the "rock upon which the old Union would split." He was right . . . . But whether he fully comprehended the great truth upon which that rock stood and stands, may be doubted. The prevailing ideas entertained by him and most of the leading statesmen at the time of the formation of the old Constitution were, that the enslavement of the African was in violation of the laws of nature; that it was wrong in principle, socially, morally, and politically. It was an evil they knew not well how to deal with; but the general opinion of the men of that day was, that, somehow or other, in the order of Providence, the institution would be evanescent and pass away . . . . Those ideas, however, were fundamentally wrong . . . .

Our new Government is founded upon exactly the opposite ideas; its foundations are laid, its cornerstone rests, upon the great truth that the negro is not equal to the white man; that slavery, subordination to the superior race, is his natural and moral condition. This, our new Government, is the first, in the history of the world, based upon this great physical, philosophical, and moral truth.

Alexander H. Stephens, *The War Between the States*, 1868

The matter of Slavery, so-called ... was of infinitely less importance to the Seceding States, than the recognition of this great principle [the right of withdrawal on the part of the seceding States]. I say Slavery, so-called, because there was with us no such thing as Slavery in the full and proper sense of that word. No people ever lived more devoted to the principles of liberty, secured by free democratic institutions, than were the people of the South. None had ever given stronger proofs of this than they had done, from the day that Virginia moved in behalf of the assailed rights of Massachusetts, in 1774, to the firing of the first gun in Charleston Harbor, in 1861. What was called Slavery amongst us, was but a legal subordination of the African to the Caucasian race. This relation was so regulated by law as to promote, according to the intent and design of the system, the best interests of both races, the Black as well as the White, the Inferior, as well as the Superior. Both had rights secured, and both had duties imposed. It was a system of reciprocal service, and mutual bonds. But even the two thousand million dollars invested in the relation thus established, between private capital and the labor of this class of population, under the system, was but as the dust in the balance, compared with the vital attributes of the rights of Independence and Sovereignty on the part of the several States.

Q *Why did Stephens deny the central importance of slavery to the seceding states in his 1868 history? How had his views changed from 1861, and why?*

Q *Did Stephens's justifications for slavery change at all between 1861 and 1868?*

Sources: (top) From speech by Alexander H. Stephens, "The Cornerstone of the Confederacy," 1861 reprinted in Alexander H. Stephens in *Public and Private with Letters and Speeches Before, During, and After the War*, ed. Henry Cleveland, Philadelphia (National Publishing Company, 1866), p. 721. (bottom) From Alexander H. Stephens, *A Constitutional View of the Late War Between the States*, (National Publishing Company, 1868).

channel leading into Charleston Bay. A Kentuckian married to a Georgian, Anderson sympathized with the South but remained loyal to the United States. He deplored the possibility of war and hoped that moving the garrison to Sumter would ease tensions by reducing the possibility of an attack. Instead, it lit a fuse that eventually set off the war.

South Carolina sent a delegation to President Buchanan to negotiate the withdrawal of the federal troops. Buchanan surprised them by saying no. He even tried to reinforce the garrison. On January 9, the unarmed merchant ship *Star of the West*, carrying 200 soldiers for Sumter, tried to enter the bay but was driven away by South Carolina artillery. Loath to start a war, Major Anderson refused to return fire with Sumter's guns. Matters then settled into an uneasy truce. The Confederate government sent General Pierre G. T. Beauregard to take command of the troops ringing Charleston Bay with their cannons pointed at Fort Sumter, and waited to see what the incoming Lincoln administration would do.

When Abraham Lincoln took the oath of office as the 16th—and, some speculated, the last—president of the United States, he knew that his inaugural address would be the most important in American history. On his words would hang the issues of union or disunion, peace or war. His goal was to keep the upper South in the Union while cooling passions in the lower South, hoping that, in time, southern loyalty to the Union would reassert itself. In his address, he demonstrated firmness in purpose to preserve the Union and forbearance in the means of doing so. He repeated his pledge not "to interfere with the institution of slavery where it exists." He assured the Confederate states, "the government will not assail *you*." His first draft had also included the phrase "unless you *first* assail it," but William H. Seward, whom Lincoln had appointed secretary of state, persuaded him to drop those words as too provocative. Lincoln's first draft had also stated his intention to use "all the powers at my disposal [to] reclaim the public property and places which have fallen." He deleted that statement as too warlike and said only that he would "hold, occupy, and possess the property, and places belonging to the government," without defining exactly what he meant or how he would do it. In his eloquent peroration, Lincoln appealed to southerners as Americans who shared with other Americans four score and five years of national history. "We are not enemies, but friends," he said.

> Though passion may have strained, it must not break, our bonds of affection. The mystic chords of memory, stretching from every battlefield and patriot grave to every living heart and hearthstone all over this broad land, will yet swell the chorus of the Union when again touched, as surely they will be, by the better angels of our nature.

Lincoln hoped to buy time with his inaugural address—time to demonstrate his peaceful intentions and to enable southern Unionists (whose numbers Republicans overestimated) to regain the upper hand. But the day after his inauguration, Lincoln learned that time was running out. A dispatch from Major Anderson informed him that provisions for the soldiers at Fort Sumter would soon be exhausted. The garrison must either be resupplied or evacuated. Any attempt to send in supplies by force would undoubtedly provoke a response from Confederate guns at Charleston. And by putting the onus of starting a war on Lincoln's shoulders, such an action would undoubtedly divide the North and unite the South, driving at least four more states into the Confederacy. Thus, most members of Lincoln's cabinet, along with the army's general-in-chief Winfield Scott, advised Lincoln to withdraw the troops from Sumter. That, however, would bestow a great moral victory on the Confederacy. It would confer legitimacy on the Confederate government and would probably lead to diplomatic recognition by foreign powers. Having pledged to "hold, occupy, and possess" national property, could Lincoln afford to abandon that policy during his first month in office?

Bettmann/Getty Images

15.5 The Bombardment of Fort Sumter, April 12, 1861 This *Harper's Weekly* illustration shows Confederate guns at Fort Johnson firing on Fort Sumter on April 13, 1861. During the war *Harper's Weekly* became immensely popular, reaching hundreds of thousands of readers, in large part because it provided detailed illustrations that satisfied Americans' intense desire to visualize the war. But this illustration is not strictly accurate: there were no Northern photographers or artists at Fort Johnson to record the bombardment, so the artists at *Harper's Weekly* simply provided a dramatic representation of their own.

The pressures from all sides caused Lincoln many sleepless nights. Finally, he hit upon a solution that evidenced the mastery that would mark his presidency. He decided to send in unarmed ships with supplies but to hold troops and warships outside the harbor with authorization to go into action only if the Confederates used force to stop the supply ships. And he would give South Carolina officials advance notice of his intention. This stroke of genius shifted the decision for war or peace to Jefferson Davis. If Confederate troops fired on the supply ships, the South would stand convicted of starting a war by attacking "a mission of humanity" bringing "food for hungry men." If Davis allowed the supplies to go in peacefully, the U.S. flag would continue to fly over Fort Sumter. The Confederacy would lose face at home and abroad, and southern Unionists would take courage.

Davis did not hesitate. He ordered General Beauregard to compel Sumter's surrender before the supply ships got there. At 4:30 a.m. on April 12, 1861, Confederate guns set off the Civil War by firing on Fort Sumter. After a 33-hour bombardment, the burning fort lowered the U.S. flag in surrender.

15-4 Choosing Sides

Q *Why did the border states remain in the Union?*

News of the attack triggered an outburst of anger and war fever in the North. "The town is in a wild state of excitement," wrote a Philadelphia diarist. "The American flag is to be seen everywhere .... Men are enlisting as fast as possible." A New York woman wrote that the "time before Sumter" seemed like another century. "It seems as if we were never alive till now; never had a country till now."

Because the tiny U.S. Army—most of whose 16,000 soldiers were stationed at remote frontier posts—was inadequate to quell the "insurrection," Lincoln called on the states for 75,000 militia. The free states filled their quotas immediately. More than twice as many men volunteered as Lincoln had requested. Recognizing that the 90 days' service to which the militia were limited by law would be too short a time, on May 3 Lincoln issued a call for three-year volunteers. Before the war was over, more than 2 million men would serve in the Union army and navy.

The eight slave states still in the Union rejected Lincoln's call for troops. Four of them—Virginia, Arkansas, Tennessee, and North Carolina—soon seceded and joined the Confederacy. As a former Unionist in North Carolina remarked, "The division must be made on the line of slavery. The South must go with the South .... Blood is thicker than Water."

Few found the choice harder to make than **Robert E. Lee** of Virginia. One of the most promising officers in the U.S. Army, Lee believed that southern states had no legal right to secede. Still, he felt compelled to resign after the Virginia convention passed an ordinance of secession on April 17. "I must side either with or against my section," Lee told a northern friend. "I cannot raise my hand against my birthplace, my home, my children."

Most southern whites embraced war against the Yankees with more enthusiasm. When news of Sumter's surrender reached Richmond, crowds poured into the state capitol square and ran up the Confederate flag. "Everyone is in favor of secession [and] perfectly frantic with delight," wrote a participant. "I never in all my life witnessed such excitement." No one in the cheering crowds could know that before the war ended, at least 260,000 Confederate soldiers would lose their lives (along with 365,000 Union soldiers) and that the slave South they fought to defend would be utterly destroyed.

15-4a *The Border States*

Except for Delaware, which remained firmly in the Union, the slave states that bordered free states were sharply divided by the outbreak of war. Leaders in these states talked vaguely of neutrality, but they were to be denied that luxury.

The first blood was shed in Maryland on April 19, 1861, when a mob attacked Massachusetts troops traveling through Baltimore to Washington. The soldiers fired back, leaving 12 Baltimoreans and 4 soldiers dead. Confederate partisans burned bridges and tore down telegraph wires, cutting Washington off from the North for nearly a week until additional troops from Massachusetts and New York reopened communications and seized key points in Maryland. The troops also arrested many Confederate sympathizers. To prevent Washington from becoming surrounded by enemy territory, federal forces turned Maryland into an occupied state. Although thousands of Marylanders slipped into Virginia to join the Confederate army, a substantial majority of Maryland residents remained loyal to the Union.

Table 15.2 SLAVERY AND SECESSION

The higher the proportion of slaves and slaveholders in the population of a southern state, the greater the intensity of secessionist sentiment

	Population Who Were Slaves	White Population in Slaveholding Families
Seven states that seceded December 1860–February 1861 (South Carolina, Mississippi, Florida, Alabama, Georgia, Louisiana, Texas)	47%	38%
Four states that seceded after the firing on Fort Sumter (Virginia, Arkansas, Tennessee, North Carolina)	32%	24%
Four border slave states remaining in Union (Maryland, Delaware, Kentucky, Missouri)	14%	15%

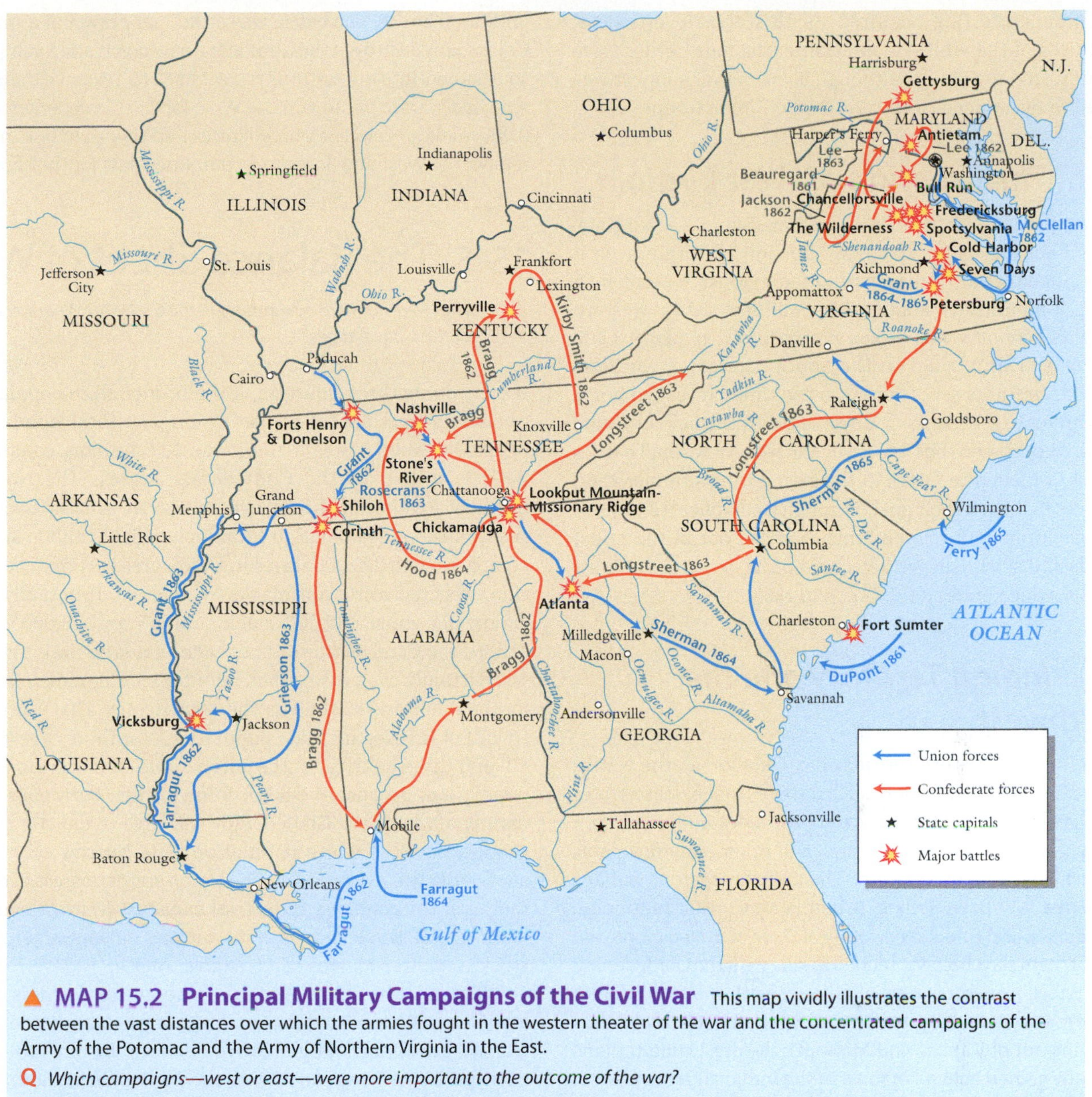

▲ **MAP 15.2 Principal Military Campaigns of the Civil War** This map vividly illustrates the contrast between the vast distances over which the armies fought in the western theater of the war and the concentrated campaigns of the Army of the Potomac and the Army of Northern Virginia in the East.

Q *Which campaigns—west or east—were more important to the outcome of the war?*

Q *What were the relative advantages of South and North in conducting war over this vast terrain?*

The same was true of Missouri. Aggressive action by Union commander Nathaniel Lyon provoked a showdown between Unionist and pro-Confederate militia that turned into a riot in St. Louis on May 10 and 11, 1861, in which 36 people died. Lyon then led his troops in a summer campaign that drove the Confederate militia, along with the governor and pro-southern legislators, into Arkansas, where they formed a Missouri Confederate government in exile. Reinforced by Arkansas regiments, these rebel Missourians invaded their home state, and on August 10 defeated Lyon (who was killed) in the bloody battle of Wilson's Creek in the southwest corner of Missouri. The victorious Confederates marched northward all the way to the Missouri River, capturing a Union garrison at Lexington 40 miles east of Kansas City on September 20. Union forces then regrouped and drove the ragged Missouri Confederates back into Arkansas.

From then until the war's end, Unionists maintained political control of Missouri through military power. Even so, continued guerrilla attacks by Confederate "**bushwhackers**" and counterinsurgency tactics by Unionist "jayhawkers" turned large areas of the state into a no-man's-land of hit-and-run raids, arson, ambush, and murder. During these years, the famous postwar outlaws Jesse and Frank James and Cole and Jim Younger rode with the notorious rebel guerrilla chieftains William Quantrill and "Bloody Bill" Anderson. More than any other state, Missouri suffered from a civil war within the Civil War, and its bitter legacy persisted for generations.

In elections held during summer and fall 1861, Unionists gained firm control of the Kentucky and Maryland legislatures. Kentucky Confederates, like those of Missouri, formed a state government in exile. When the Confederate Congress admitted both Kentucky and Missouri to full representation, the Confederate flag acquired its 13 stars. Nevertheless, two-thirds of the white population in the four border slave states favored the Union, although some of that support was undoubtedly induced by the presence of Union troops.

15-4b *The Creation of West Virginia*

The war produced a fifth Union border state: West Virginia. Most of the delegates from the portion of Virginia west of the Shenandoah Valley had voted against secession. A region of mountains, small farms, and few slaves, western Virginia's economy was linked more closely to nearby Ohio and Pennsylvania than to the South. Delegates who had opposed Virginia's secession from the Union returned home determined to secede from Virginia. With the help of Union troops, who crossed the Ohio River and won a few small battles against Confederate forces in the area during summer 1861, they accomplished their goal. Through a complicated process of conventions and referendums—carried out in the midst of raids and skirmishes—they created the new state of West Virginia, which entered the Union in 1863.

15-4c *Indian Territory and the Southwest*

In the Indian Territory (present-day Oklahoma), the Native Americans, who had been resettled there from eastern states in the generation before the war, chose sides and carried on bloody guerrilla warfare against each other as ferocious as the bushwhacking in Missouri. The more prosperous Indians of the five "Civilized Tribes" (Cherokees, Creeks, Seminoles, Chickasaws, and Choctaws), many of them of mixed blood and some of them slaveholders, tended to side with the Confederacy. Some tribes signed treaties of alliance with the Confederate government. Aided by white and black Union regiments operating out of Kansas and Missouri, the pro-Union Indians gradually gained control of most of the Indian Territory.

In the meantime, Confederates had made their boldest bid to fulfill antebellum southern ambitions to win the Southwest. A small army composed mostly of Texans pushed up the Rio Grande Valley into New Mexico in 1861. The following February, they launched a deeper strike to capture Santa Fe. They hoped to push even farther westward and northward to gain the mineral wealth of California and Colorado gold mines, whose millions were already helping to finance the Union war effort and could do wonders for Confederate finances. A good many southerners lived in these western territories and in California.

At first, the Confederate drive up the Rio Grande went well. The Texans won a victory over the Unionist New Mexico militia and a handful of regulars at the battle of Valverde, 100 miles south of Albuquerque, on February 21, 1862. They continued up the valley, occupied Albuquerque and Santa Fe, and pushed on toward Fort Union near Santa Fe. But Colorado miners who had organized themselves into Union regiments and had carried out the greatest march of the war, over the rugged Rockies in winter, met the Texans in the battle of Glorieta Pass on March 26–28. The battle was a tactical draw, but a unit of Coloradans destroyed the Confederate wagon train, forcing the southerners into a disastrous retreat back to Texas. Of the 3,700 who had started out to win the West for the Confederacy, only 2,000 made it back. The Confederates had shot their bolt in this region; the West and Southwest remained safe for the Union.

15-5 The Balance Sheet of War

Q *What were northern advantages in the Civil War? What were southern advantages?*

If one counts three-quarters of the border state population (including free blacks) as pro-Union, the total number of people in Union states in 1861 was 22.5 million, compared with 9 million in the Confederate states. The North's military manpower advantage was even greater because the Confederate population total included 3.7 million slaves, compared with 300,000 slaves in Union areas. At first, neither side expected to recruit blacks as soldiers. Eventually, the Union did enlist 180,000 black soldiers and 18,000 black sailors; the Confederacy did not take that step until the war was virtually over. Altogether, about 2.1 million men fought for the Union and 850,000 for the Confederacy. That was close to half of the North's male population of military age (18 to 40) and three-quarters of the comparable Confederate white population. Because the labor force of the South consisted mainly of slaves, the Confederacy was able to enlist a larger proportion of its white population. The North's economic superiority was even greater. The Union states possessed nine-tenths of the country's industrial capacity, four-fifths of its bank capital, three-fourths of its railroad mileage and rolling stock, and three-fourths of its taxable wealth.

These statistics gave pause to some southerners. In a long war that mobilized the total resources of both sides, the North's advantages might prove decisive. But in 1861, few anticipated how long and intense the war would be. Both sides expected a short and victorious conflict. Confederates seemed especially confident, partly because of their vaunted sense of martial superiority over the "bluebellied" Yankee nation of shopkeepers. Many southerners really did believe that one of their own could lick three Yankees. "Let brave men advance with flintlocks and old-fashioned bayonets, on the popinjays of Northern cities," said ex-governor Henry Wise of Virginia, now a Confederate general, and "the Yankees would break and run."

Although this turned out to be a grievous miscalculation, the South did have some reason to believe that its martial qualities were superior. A higher proportion of southerners than northerners had attended West Point and other military schools, had fought in the Mexican War, or had served as officers in the regular army. Volunteer military companies were more prevalent in the antebellum South than in the North. As a rural people, southerners were proficient in hunting, riding, and other outdoor skills useful in military operations. Moreover, the South had begun to prepare for war earlier than the North. As each state seceded, it mobilized

History Through Film Glory (1989)

Directed by Edward Zwick.
Starring Matthew Broderick (Robert Gould Shaw), Denzel Washington (Trip), Morgan Freeman (Rawlins).

In 1862 some Union commanders began to organize black regiments in occupied portions of Louisiana, South Carolina, and Missouri. But despite passionate advocacy of black soldiering by Frederick Douglass and other black leaders, official enlistment of African American soldiers into the Union Army began only after Lincoln issued the Emancipation Proclamation on January 1, 1863 (see Chapter 16). *Glory* is the first feature film to treat the role of black soldiers in the Civil War. It tells the story of the 54th Massachusetts Volunteer Infantry from its organization in early 1863 through its climactic assault on Fort Wagner six months later. When the 54th moved out at dusk on July 18 to lead the attack, the idea of black combat troops still seemed a risky experiment. The *New York Tribune*, a strong supporter of black enlistment, had nevertheless observed in May 1863 that many northern whites "have no faith" that black soldiers would stand and fight southern whites who considered themselves a master race. The unflinching behavior of the regiment in the face of an overwhelming hail of lead and iron and its casualties of some 50 percent settled the matter. "Who now asks in doubt and derision 'Will the Negro fight?'" commented one abolitionist. "The answer comes to us from those graves beneath Fort Wagner's walls, which the American people will surely never forget."

Many did forget, but *Glory* revived their collective memory. Its combat scenes, climaxed by the assault on Fort Wagner, are among the most realistic and effective in any war movie. Morgan Freeman and Denzel Washington give memorable performances as a fatherly sergeant and a rebellious private who nevertheless picks up the flag when the color-bearer falls and carries it to the ramparts of Fort Wagner, where he too is killed. Matthew Broderick's portrayal of Colonel Robert Gould Shaw is less memorable because the real Shaw was more assertive and mature than Broderick's Shaw.

Except for Shaw, the principal characters in the film are fictional. There was no real Major Cabot Forbes; no tough Irish Sergeant Mulcahy; no black Sergeant John Rawlins; no brash, hardened Private Trip. A larger fiction is involved here. The movie gives the impression that most of the 54th's soldiers were former slaves. In fact, this atypical black regiment was recruited mainly in the North, so most of the men had always been free. The story that screenwriter Kevin Jarre and director Edward Zwick chose to tell is not simply about the 54th Massachusetts but about black soldiers in the Civil War. Most of the 179,000 African Americans in the Union army (and 16,000 in the navy) were slaves until a few months, even days, before they joined up. Fighting for the Union bestowed upon former slaves a new dignity, self-respect, and militancy, which helped them achieve equal citizenship and political rights—for a time—after the war.

Many of the events dramatized in *Glory* are also fictional: the incident of the racist quartermaster who initially refuses to distribute shoes to Shaw's men; the whipping Trip receives as punishment for going AWOL; Shaw's threat to expose his superior officer's corruption as a way of securing a combat assignment for the 54th; and the religious meeting the night before the assault on Fort Wagner. All of these scenes point toward a larger truth, however, most vividly portrayed symbolically in a surreal, and at first glance, irrelevant scene. During a training exercise, Shaw gallops his horse along a path flanked by stakes, each holding aloft a watermelon. Shaw slashes right and left with his sword, slicing and smashing every melon. The point becomes clear when we recall the identification of watermelons with the racist "darky" stereotype. The image of smashed melons drives home the essential message of *Glory*. ■

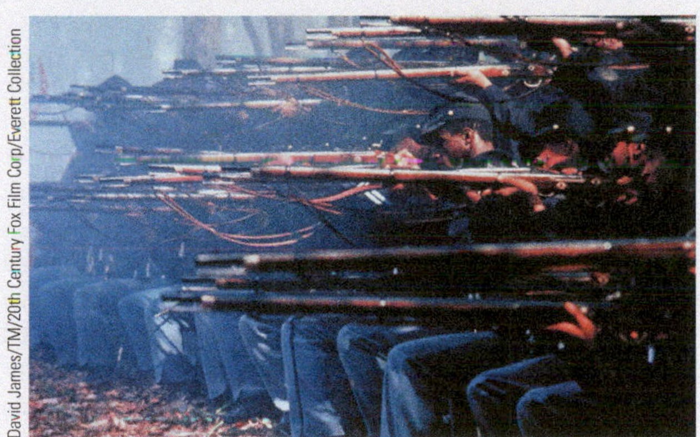
David James/TM/20th Century Fox Film Corp/Everett Collection

15-6 A scene from *Glory* showing black soldiers of the 54th Massachusetts ready to fire at the enemy.

militia and volunteer military companies. Not until summer 1861 would the North's greater manpower manifest itself in the form of a larger army.

15-5a *Strategy and Morale*

Even when fully mobilized, the North's superior resources did not guarantee success. Its military task was much more difficult than that of the South. The Confederacy had come into being in firm control of 750,000 square miles—a vast territory larger than all of Western Europe and twice as large as the 13 colonies in 1776. To win the war, Union forces would have to invade, conquer, and occupy much of that territory, cripple its people's ability to sustain a war of independence, and destroy its armies (see Map 15.2). Britain had been unable to accomplish a similar task in the war for independence, even though it enjoyed a far greater superiority of resources over the United States in 1776 than the Union enjoyed over the Confederacy in 1861. Victory does not always ride with the heaviest battalions.

To "win" the war, the Confederacy did not need to invade or conquer the Union or even to destroy its armies; it needed only to hold out long enough to convince northerners that the cost of victory was too high. Most Confederates were confident in 1861 that they were more than equal to the task. Most European military experts agreed.

The important factor of morale also seemed to favor the Confederacy. To be sure, Union soldiers fought for powerful symbols: nation, flag, Constitution. "We are fighting to maintain the best government on earth" was a common phrase in their letters and diaries. It is a "grate [sic] struggle for Union, Constitution, and law," wrote a New Jersey soldier. A Chicago newspaper declared that the South had "outraged the Constitution, set at defiance all law, and trampled under foot that flag which has been the glorious and consecrated symbol of American Liberty."

But Confederates, too, fought for nation, flag, constitution, and liberty—of whites. In addition, they fought to defend their land, homes, and families against invading "Yankee vandals," who many southern whites quite literally believed were coming to "free the negroes and force amalgamation between them and the children of the poor men of the South." An army fighting in defense of its homeland generally has the edge in morale. "We shall have the enormous advantage of fighting on our own territory and for our very existence," wrote a Confederate leader.

15-5b *Mobilizing for War*

More than four-fifths of the soldiers on both sides were volunteers. The Confederacy passed a conscription law in April 1862, and the Union followed suit in March 1863, but even afterward, most recruits were volunteers. In both North and South, patriotic rallies with martial music and speeches motivated local men to enlist in a company (100 men) organized by the area's leading citizens. The recruits elected their own company officers (a captain and two lieutenants), who received their commissions from the state governor. A regiment consisted of 10 infantry companies, and each regiment was commanded by a colonel, with a lieutenant colonel and a major as second and third in command—all of them appointed by the governor. Cavalry regiments were organized in a similar manner. Field artillery units were known as batteries.

Volunteer units received a state designation and number in the order of their completion—the Second Massachusetts Volunteer Infantry, the Fifth Virginia Cavalry, and so on. In most regiments, the men in each company generally came from the same town or locality. Some Union regiments were composed of men of a particular ethnic group. By the end of the war, the Union army had raised about 2,000 infantry and cavalry regiments and 700 batteries; the Confederates had organized just under half as many. As the war went on, the original thousand-man complement of a regiment was usually whittled down to half or less by disease, casualties, desertions, and detachments. The states generally preferred to organize new regiments rather than keep the old ones up to full strength.

These were citizen-soldiers, not professionals. They carried their peacetime notions of democracy and discipline into the army. That is why, in the tradition of the citizen militia, the men elected their company officers and sometimes their field officers (colonel, lieutenant colonel, and major) as well. Professional military men deplored the egalitarianism and slack discipline that resulted. Political influence often counted for more than military training in the election and appointment of officers. These civilians in uniform were extremely awkward and unmilitary at first, and some regiments suffered battlefield disasters because of inadequate training, discipline, and leadership. In time, however, raw recruits became battle-hardened veterans commanded by experienced officers.

As the two sides organized their field armies, both grouped four or more regiments into brigades and three or more brigades into divisions. By 1862, they began grouping two or more divisions into corps and two or more corps into armies. Each of these larger units was commanded by a general appointed by the president. Most of the higher-ranking generals on both sides were West Point graduates, but others were appointed because they represented an important political, regional, or (in the North) ethnic constituency whose support Lincoln or Davis wished to solidify. Some of these "political" generals, like elected regimental officers, were incompetent, but as the war went on, they too either learned their trade or were weeded out. Some outstanding generals emerged from civilian life and were promoted up the ranks during the war. In both the Union and the Confederate armies, the best officers (including generals) *led* their men by example as much as by precept; they commanded from the front, not the rear. Combat casualties were higher among officers than among privates, and highest of all among generals, who died in action at a rate 50 percent higher than enlisted men.

15-5c *Weapons and Tactics*

In Civil War battles, the infantry rifle was the most lethal weapon. Muskets and rifles caused 80–90 percent of the combat casualties. From 1862 on, most of these weapons were "rifled"—that is, they had spiral grooves cut in the barrel to impart a spin to the bullet. This innovation was only a decade old, dating to the perfection in the 1850s of the "minié ball" (named after French army captain Claude Minié, its principal inventor), a cone-shaped lead bullet with a base that expanded on firing to "take" the **rifling** of the barrel. This made it possible to load and fire a muzzle-loading rifle as rapidly (two or three times per minute) as the old smoothbore musket. Moreover, the rifle had greater accuracy and at least four times the effective range (400 yards or more) of the smoothbore.

Civil War infantry tactics adjusted only gradually to the greater lethal range and accuracy of the new rifle, however,

The Art Archive/Culver Pictures

15.7 **The Richmond Grays** This photograph depicts a typical volunteer military unit that joined the Confederate army in 1861. Note the determined and confident appearance of these young men. By 1865, one-third of them would be dead and several others maimed for life.

for the prescribed massed formations had emerged from experience with the smoothbore musket. Close-order assaults against defenders equipped with rifles resulted in enormous casualties. The defensive power of the rifle became even greater when troops began digging into trenches. Massed frontal assaults became almost suicidal. Soldiers and their officers learned the hard way to adopt skirmishing tactics, taking advantage of cover and working around the enemy flank.

Interpreting the Visual Past The Soldier's Dream of Home

The Civil War was a home-front war, requiring the support of the civilian population at home—including women. This popular Currier & Ives print works to allay some of the uneasiness northerners on the home front might have felt as their husbands, sons, and brothers left home to become soldiers. It pictures a Union soldier asleep on the ground, with a palm tree above him to his left indicating that he is deployed in the South. Rather than portraying a soldier in battle, this image instead presents a soothing vision of an unbroken link between soldier and home. Part of an extensive visual propaganda produced during the war, it reassures viewers that men have not fundamentally changed by becoming trained killers.

Q *Think of this image as a story with several parts to be "read." Why is the soldier shown with a letter next to him on the ground? What is he dreaming, as shown in the "bubble" above him? Would this image be equally effective in your view if the soldier were shown thinking of home while awake?*

Q *How does the image allude to the violence of war? How might this scene offer comfort to those on the home front?*

15.8 **Currier & Ives, The Soldier's Dream of Home, c. 1862.**

15-5d *Logistics*

Wars are fought not only by men and weapons but also by the logistical apparatus that supports and supplies them. The Civil War is often called the world's first modern war because of the role played by railroads, steam-powered ships, and the telegraph, which did not exist in earlier wars fought on a similar scale (those of the French Revolution and Napoleon). Railroads and steamboats transported supplies and soldiers with unprecedented speed and efficiency; the telegraph provided rapid communication between army headquarters and field commanders.

Yet these modern forms of transport and communications were extremely vulnerable. Cavalry raiders and guerrillas could cut telegraph wires, burn railroad bridges, and tear up the tracks. Confederate cavalry became particularly skillful at sundering the supply lines of invading Union armies and thereby neutralizing forces several times larger than their own. The more deeply the Union armies penetrated into the South, the more men they had to detach to guard bridges, depots, and supply bases.

Once the campaigning armies had moved away from their railhead or wharf-side supply base, they returned to dependence on animal-powered transport. Depending on terrain, road conditions, length of supply line, and proportion of artillery and cavalry, Union armies required one horse or mule for every two or three men. Thus a large invading Union army of 100,000 men (the approximate number in Virginia from 1862 to 1865 and in Georgia in 1864) would need about 40,000 draft animals. Confederate armies, operating mostly in friendly territory closer to their bases, needed fewer. The poorly drained dirt roads typical of much of the South turned into a morass of mud in the frequently wet weather. These logistical problems did much to offset the industrial supremacy of the North, particularly during the first year of the war when bottlenecks, shortages, and inefficiency marked the logistical effort on both sides. By 1862, though, the North's economy had fully geared up for war, making the Union army the best-supplied army in history up to that time.

Confederate officials accomplished impressive feats of improvisation in creating war industries, especially munitions and gunpowder, but the southern industrial base was too slender to sustain adequate production. Particularly troublesome for the Confederacy was its inability to replace rails and rolling stock for its railroads. Although the South produced plenty of food, the railroads deteriorated to the point that food could not reach soldiers or civilians. As the war went into its third and fourth years, the northern economy grew stronger and the southern economy grew weaker.

15-5e *Financing the War*

One of the greatest defects of the Confederate economy was finance. The Confederate Congress, wary of dampening patriotic ardor, was slow to raise taxes. And because most capital in the South was tied up in land and slaves, little was available for buying war bonds. So, expecting a short war, the Confederate Congress authorized a limited issue of **treasury notes** in 1861, to be redeemable in **specie** (gold or silver) within two years after the end of the war. The first modest issue was followed by many more because the notes declined in value from the outset. The rate of decline increased during periods of Confederate military reverses, when people wondered whether the government would survive. By early 1863 it took eight dollars to buy what one dollar had bought two years earlier; just before the war's end, the Confederate dollar was worth one U.S. cent.

In 1863 the Confederate Congress tried to stem runaway inflation by passing a comprehensive law that taxed income, consumer purchases, and business transactions and included a "tax in kind" on agricultural products, allowing tax officials to seize 10 percent of a farmer's crops. This tax was extremely unpopular among farmers, many of whom hid their crops and livestock or refused to plant, thereby worsening the Confederacy's food shortages. The tax legislation was too little and too late to remedy the South's fiscal chaos. The Confederate government raised less than 5 percent of its revenue by taxes and less than 40 percent by loans, leaving 60 percent to be created by the printing press. That turned out to be a recipe for disaster.

In contrast, the Union government raised 66 percent of its revenue by selling war bonds, 21 percent by taxes, and only 13 percent by printing treasury notes. The Legal Tender Act authorizing these notes—the famous "greenbacks," the origin of modern paper money in the United States—passed in February 1862. Congress had enacted new taxes in 1861, including the first income tax in American history, and had authorized the sale of war bonds. By early 1862, however, these measures had not yet raised enough revenue to pay for the rapid military buildup. To avert a crisis, Congress created the greenbacks. Instead of promising to redeem them

Library of Congress Prints and Photographs Division [LC-DIG-ppmsca-20497]

15.9 **Crossing a River** This woodcut drawing portrays part of the Army of the Potomac crossing the Rapidan River in Virginia on May 4, 1864, at the beginning of what came to be called the Overland Campaign, which ended almost a year later with the surrender of the Army of Northern Virginia at Appomattox. The infantry is crossing on a pontoon bridge—planks laid over anchored boats—while supply wagons are fording the shallow river. This scene was typical of hundreds of river crossings by armies during the Civil War.

Q *What does this drawing reveal about the logistical difficulties of fighting the Civil War?*

in specie at some future date, as the South had done, Congress made them **legal tender**—that is, it required everyone to accept them as real money at face value. The North's economy suffered inflation during the war—about 80 percent over four years—but that was mild compared with the 9,000 percent inflation in the Confederacy. The greater strength and diversity of the North's economy, together with wiser fiscal legislation, accounted for the contrast.

The Union Congress also passed the National Banking Act of 1863. Before the war, the principal form of money had been notes issued by state-chartered banks. After Andrew Jackson's destruction of the Second Bank of the United States (Chapter 11), the number and variety of **banknotes** had skyrocketed until 7,000 different kinds of state banknotes were circulating in 1860. Some were virtually worthless. The National Banking Act of 1863 resulted from the desire of Republicans to resurrect the centralized banking system and create a more stable banknote currency, as well as to finance the war. Under the act, chartered national banks could issue banknotes up to 90 percent of the value of the U.S. bonds they held. This provision created a market for the bonds and, in combination with the greenbacks, replaced the glut of state banknotes with a more uniform national currency.

National banknotes would be an important form of money for the next half-century. They had two defects, however: First, because the number of notes that could be issued was tied to each bank's holdings of U.S. bonds, the volume of currency available depended on the amount of federal debt rather than on the economic needs of the country. Second, the banknotes tended to concentrate in the Northeast, where most of the large national banks were located, leaving the South and West short. The creation of the Federal Reserve System in 1913 (Chapter 21) largely remedied these defects, but Civil War legislation established the principle of a uniform national currency issued and regulated by the federal government.

15-6 Navies, the Blockade, and Foreign Relations

Q *Why did Confederate foreign policy fail to win diplomatic recognition from other nations?*

To sustain its war effort, the Confederacy needed to import large quantities of material from abroad. To shut off these imports and the exports of cotton that paid for them, on April 19, 1861, Lincoln proclaimed a **blockade** of Confederate ports. At first, the blockade was more a policy than a reality because the navy had only a few ships on hand to enforce it. The task was formidable; the Confederate coastline stretched for 3,500 miles, with two dozen major ports and another 150 bays and coves where cargo could be landed. The U.S. Navy, which since the 1840s had been converting from sail to steam, recalled its ships from distant seas, took old sailing vessels out of mothballs, and bought or chartered merchant ships and armed them. Eventually, the navy placed several hundred warships on blockade duty. But in 1861, the blockade was so thin that 9 of every 10 vessels slipped through it on their way to or from Confederate ports.

15-6a *King Cotton Diplomacy*

The Confederacy, however, inadvertently contributed to the blockade's success when it adopted King Cotton diplomacy. Cotton was vital to the British economy because textiles were at the heart of British industry, and three-fourths of Britain's supply of raw cotton came from the South. If that supply was cut off, southerners reasoned, British factories would shut down, unemployed workers would starve, and Britain would face the prospect of revolution. Rather than risk such a consequence, people in the South believed that Britain (and other powers) would recognize the Confederacy's independence and then use the powerful British navy to break the blockade.

Southerners were so firmly convinced of cotton's importance to the British economy that they kept the 1861 cotton crop at home rather than try to export it through the blockade, hoping thereby to compel the British to intervene. But the strategy backfired. Bumper crops in 1859 and 1860 had piled up a surplus of cotton in British warehouses and delayed the anticipated "cotton famine" until 1862. In the end, the South's voluntary embargo of cotton cost it dearly. The Confederacy missed its chance to ship out its cotton and store it abroad, where it could be used as collateral for loans to purchase war material.

Moreover, the Confederacy's King Cotton diplomacy contradicted its own foreign policy objective: to persuade the British and French governments to refuse to recognize the legality of the blockade. Under international law, a blockade must be "physically effective" to be respected by neutral nations. Confederate diplomats claimed that the Union effort was a mere "paper blockade," yet the dearth of cotton reaching European ports as a result of the South's embargo suggested to British and French diplomats that the blockade was at least partly effective. And by 1862 it was. Slow-sailing ships with large cargo capacity rarely tried to run the blockade, and the sleek, fast, steam-powered "**blockade runners**" that became increasingly prominent had a smaller cargo capacity and charged high rates because of the growing risk of capture or sinking by the Union navy. Although most blockade runners got through, by 1862 the blockade had reduced the Confederacy's seaborne commerce enough to convince the British government to recognize it as legitimate. The blockade was also squeezing the South's economy. After lifting its cotton embargo in 1862, the Confederacy had increasing difficulty exporting enough cotton through the blockade to pay for needed imports.

Confederate foreign policy also failed to win diplomatic recognition by other nations. That recognition would have conferred international legitimacy on the Confederacy and might even have led to treaties of alliance or of foreign aid. The French emperor Napoleon III expressed sympathy for the Confederacy, as did influential groups in the British Parliament. But Prime Minister Lord Palmerston and Foreign

Library of Congress Prints and Photographs Division

15.10 The Confederate Blockade Runner *Robert E. Lee* Confederate armies depended heavily on supplies brought in from abroad on blockade runners, paid for by cotton smuggled out through the Union naval cordon by these same blockade runners. The sleek, narrow-beamed ships with raked masts and smokestacks (which could be telescoped to deck level) were designed for speed and deception to elude the blockade—a feat successfully accomplished on four-fifths of their voyages during the war. One of the most successful runners was the *Robert E. Lee*, photographed here after it had run the blockade 14 times before being captured on the 15th attempt.

Q *How successful was the Union blockade of Confederate ports?*

Minister John Russell refused to recognize the Confederacy while it was engaged in a war it might lose, especially if recognition might jeopardize relations with the United States. The Union foreign policy team of Secretary of State Seward and Minister to England Charles Francis Adams did a superb job. Seward issued blunt warnings against recognizing the Confederacy; Adams softened them with the velvet glove of diplomacy. Other nations followed Britain's lead; by 1862, it had become clear that Britain would withhold recognition until the Confederacy had virtually won its independence, but such recognition would have come too late to help the Confederacy win.

15-6b *The* Trent *Affair*

If anything illustrated the frustrations of Confederate diplomacy, it was the *Trent* Affair. In October 1861, southern envoys James Mason and John Slidell slipped through the blockade. Mason hoped to represent the Confederacy in London and Slidell in Paris. On November 8, Captain Charles Wilkes of the U.S.S. *San Jacinto* stopped the British mail steamer *Trent* with Mason and Slidell on board, near Cuba. Wilkes arrested the two southerners, took them to Boston, and became an instant hero in the North. When the news reached England, the British government and public were outraged by Wilkes's "highhanded" action. Britain demanded an apology and the release of Mason and Slidell. The popular press on both sides of the Atlantic stirred up war fever. Soon, however, good sense prevailed and Britain softened its demands. With a philosophy of "one war at a time," the Lincoln administration released Mason and Slidell the day after Christmas 1861, declaring that Captain Wilkes had acted "without instructions." The British accepted this statement in lieu of an apology, and the crisis ended.

15-6c *The Confederate Navy*

Lacking the capacity to build a naval force at home, the Confederacy hoped to use British shipyards for the purpose. Through a loophole in the British neutrality law, two fast commerce raiders built in Liverpool made their way into Confederate hands in 1862. Named the *Florida* and the *Alabama*, they roamed the seas for the next two years, capturing or sinking Union merchant ships and whalers. The *Alabama* was the most feared raider. She sank 62 merchant vessels plus a Union warship before another warship, the U.S.S. *Kearsarge*, sank the *Alabama* off Cherbourg, France, on June 19, 1864. Altogether, Confederate privateers and commerce raiders destroyed or captured 257 Union merchant vessels and drove at least 700 others to foreign registry. This Confederate achievement, although spectacular, made only a tiny dent in the Union war effort, especially when compared with the 1,500 blockade runners captured or destroyed by the Union navy.

15-6d *The* Monitor *and the* Virginia

Though plagued by shortages on every hand, the Confederate navy department demonstrated great skill at innovation. Southern engineers developed "torpedoes" (mines) that sank or damaged 43 Union warships in southern bays and rivers. The South also constructed the world's first combat submarine, the *H. L. Hunley*, which sank a blockade ship off Charleston in 1864 but then went down before she could return to shore. Another important innovation was the building of ironclad "rams" to sink the blockade ships. The idea of iron armor for warships was not new—the British and French navies had prototype ironclads in 1861—but the Confederacy built the first one to see action. It was the C.S.S. *Virginia*, commonly called (even in the South) the *Merrimac* because it was rebuilt from the steam frigate U.S.S. *Merrimack*. Ready for its trial-by-combat on March 8, 1862, the *Virginia* steamed out to attack the blockade squadron at Hampton Roads. She sank one warship with her iron ram and another with her 10 guns. Other Union ships ran aground trying to escape, to be finished off (Confederates expected) the next day. Union shot and shells bounced off the *Virginia's* armor plate. It was the worst day the U.S. Navy would have until December 7, 1941.

Panic seized Washington and the whole northeastern seaboard. In almost Hollywood fashion, however, the Union's

15.11a (top) and 15.11b (bottom) ***The Monitor and Merrimac*** The above black-and-white photograph shows the crew of the Union ironclad *Monitor* standing in front of its revolving two-gun turret. In action, the sun canopy above the turret would be taken down, and all sailors would be at their stations inside the turret or the hull, as shown in the color painting of the famed battle, on March 9, 1862, between the *Monitor* and the Confederate *Virginia* (informally called the *Merrimac* because it had been converted from the captured U.S. frigate *Merrimack*). There is no photograph of the *Virginia*, which was blown up by its crew two months later when the Confederates retreated toward Richmond because its draft was too deep to go up the James River.

Q *How did the Civil War stimulate changes in the technology used to fight war?*

own ironclad sailed into Hampton Roads in the nick of time and saved the rest of the fleet. This was the U.S.S. *Monitor*, completed just days earlier at the Brooklyn navy yard. Much smaller than the *Virginia*, with two 11-inch guns in a **revolving turret** (an innovation) set on a deck almost flush with the water, the *Monitor* looked like a "tin can on a shingle." It presented a small target and was capable of concentrating considerable firepower in a given direction with its revolving turret. The next day, the *Monitor* fought the *Virginia* in history's first battle between ironclads. It was a draw, but the *Virginia* limped home to Norfolk never again to menace the Union fleet. Although the Confederacy built other ironclad rams, none achieved the initial success of the *Virginia*. By the war's end, the Union navy had built or started 58 ships of the *Monitor* class, launching a new age in naval history.

15-7 Campaigns and Battles, 1861–1862

Q *How did the Union's and Confederacy's respective military advantages manifest themselves in the campaigns and battles of 1861 and 1862?*

Wars can be won only by hard fighting. Some leaders on both sides overlooked this truth. One of them was Winfield Scott, general-in-chief of the U.S. Army. Scott, a Virginian who had remained loyal to the Union, evolved a military strategy based on his conviction that a great many southerners were willing to be won back to the Union. The main elements of his strategy were a naval blockade and a combined army-navy expedition to take control of the Mississippi, thus sealing off the Confederacy on all sides and enabling the Union to "bring them to terms with less bloodshed than by any other plan." The northern press labeled Scott's strategy the Anaconda Plan, after the South American snake that squeezes its prey to death.

15-7a *The Battle of Bull Run*

Most northerners believed that the South could be overcome only by victory in battle. Virginia emerged as the most likely battleground, especially after the Confederate government moved its capital to Richmond in May 1861. "Forward to Richmond," clamored northern newspapers. And forward toward Richmond moved a Union army of 35,000 men in July, despite Scott's misgivings and those of the army's field commander, Irvin McDowell. McDowell believed his raw, 90-day Union militiamen were not ready to fight a real battle. They got no farther than Bull Run, a sluggish stream 25 miles southwest of Washington, where a Confederate army commanded by Beauregard had been deployed to defend a key rail junction at Manassas.

Another small Confederate army in the Shenandoah Valley under General Joseph E. Johnston had given a Union force the slip and had traveled to Manassas by rail to reinforce Beauregard. On July 21, the attacking Federals forded Bull Run and hit the rebels on the left flank, driving them back (see Map 15.3). By early afternoon, the Federals seemed to be on the verge of victory, but a Virginia brigade commanded by **Thomas J. Jackson** stood "like a stone wall," earning Jackson the nickname he carried ever after. By midafternoon, Confederate reinforcements, including one brigade just off the train from the Shenandoah Valley, had grouped for a screaming counterattack (the famed "rebel yell" was first heard here). They drove the exhausted and disorganized Yankees back across Bull Run in a retreat that turned into a rout.

Although the Battle of Manassas (or Bull Run, as northerners called it) was small by later Civil War standards, it made a profound impression on both sides. Of the 18,000 soldiers actually engaged on each side, Union casualties (killed, wounded, and captured) were about 2,800 and Confederate casualties 2,000. The victory exhilarated Confederates and confirmed their belief in their martial superiority. It also gave them a morale advantage in the Virginia theater that persisted for two years. And yet, Manassas also bred overconfidence. Some in the South thought the war was won. Northerners, by contrast, were jolted out of their expectations of a short war. A new mood of reality and grim determination gripped the North. Congress authorized the enlistment of up to 1 million three-year volunteers. Hundreds of thousands flocked to recruiting offices in the next few months. Lincoln called General **George B. McClellan** to Washington to organize the new troops into the Army of the Potomac.

An energetic, talented officer who was only 34 years old, McClellan soon won the nickname "The Young Napoleon." He had commanded the Union forces that gained control of West Virginia, and he took firm control in Washington during summer and fall 1861. He organized and trained the Army of the Potomac into a large, well-disciplined, and well-equipped fighting force. He was just what the North needed after its dispiriting defeat at Bull Run. When Scott stepped down as general-in-chief on November 1, McClellan took his place.

As winter approached, however, and McClellan did nothing to advance against the smaller Confederate army whose outposts stood only a few miles from Washington, his failings as a commander began to show. McClellan was afraid to take risks; he never learned the military lesson that no victory can be won without risking defeat. He consistently overestimated the strength of enemy forces facing him and used these faulty estimates as a reason for inaction until he could increase his own force. When Republicans in Congress and in the press began to criticize him (he was a Democrat), he accused his critics of political motives. Having built a fine fighting machine, he was afraid to start it up for fear it might break. The caution that McClellan instilled in the Army of the Potomac's officer corps persisted for more than a year after Lincoln removed him from command in November 1862.

15-7b *Naval Operations*

Because of McClellan, no significant action occurred in the Virginia theater after the Battle of Bull Run until spring 1862. Meanwhile, the Union navy won a series of victories over Confederate coastal forts at Hatteras Inlet on the North

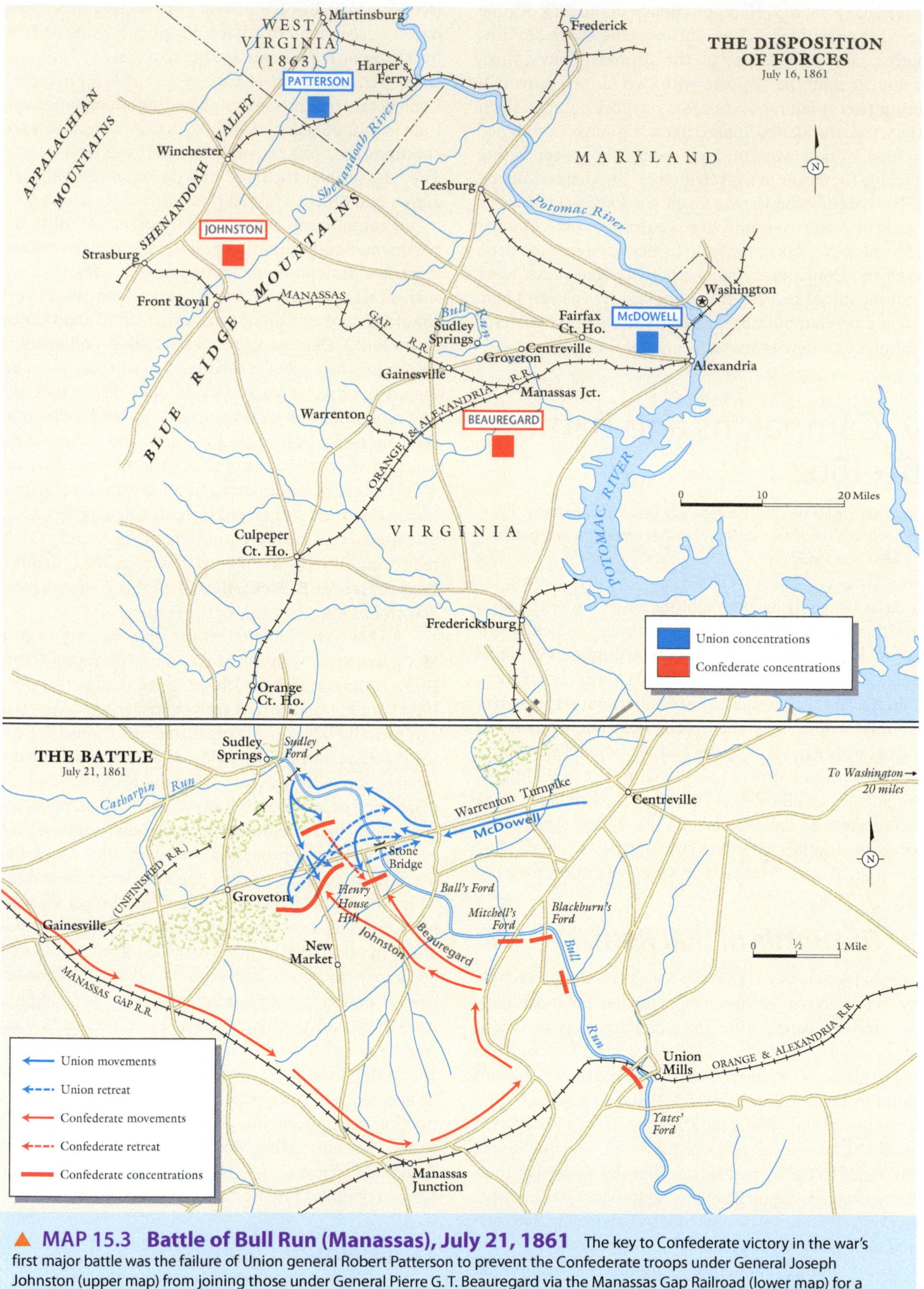

▲ **MAP 15.3 Battle of Bull Run (Manassas), July 21, 1861** The key to Confederate victory in the war's first major battle was the failure of Union general Robert Patterson to prevent the Confederate troops under General Joseph Johnston (upper map) from joining those under General Pierre G. T. Beauregard via the Manassas Gap Railroad (lower map) for a counterattack that won the battle.

Q *How important was the railroad to Confederate victory at Bull Run?*

Q *Did the South or the North appear to have a greater advantage at the outset of battle?*

Carolina coast, Port Royal Sound in South Carolina, and other points along the Atlantic and Gulf coasts. These successes provided new bases from which to expand and tighten the blockade. They also provided small Union armies with takeoff points for operations along the southern coast. In February and March 1862, an expeditionary force under General Ambrose Burnside won a string of victories and occupied several crucial ports on the North Carolina sounds. Another Union force captured Fort Pulaski at the mouth of the Savannah River, cutting off that important Confederate port from the sea.

One of the Union navy's most impressive achievements was the capture in April 1862 of New Orleans, the Confederacy's largest city and principal port. Most Confederate troops in the area had been called up the Mississippi to confront a Union invasion of Tennessee, leaving only some militia, an assortment of steamboats converted into gunboats, and two strong forts flanking the river 70 miles below New Orleans. In a daring action on April 24, 1862, Union naval commander David Farragut led his fleet upriver past the forts, losing one ship but scattering or destroying the Confederate gunboats. The Union fleet compelled the surrender of New Orleans with nine-inch naval guns trained on its streets.

15-7c Fort Henry and Fort Donelson

These victories demonstrated the importance of sea power even in a civil war. Even more important were Union victories won by the combined efforts of the army and fleets of river gunboats on the Tennessee and Cumberland rivers, which flow through Tennessee and Kentucky and empty into the Ohio River just before it joins the Mississippi. The unlikely hero of these victories was Ulysses S. Grant, who had failed in several civilian occupations after resigning from the peacetime military in 1854. Grant rejoined when war broke out. His quiet efficiency and determined will won him promotion from Illinois colonel to brigadier general. When Confederate units entered Kentucky in September, Grant moved quickly to occupy the mouths of the Cumberland and Tennessee rivers.

Military strategists on both sides understood the importance of these navigable rivers as highways of invasion into the South's heartland. The Confederacy had built forts at strategic points along the rivers and had begun to convert a few steamboats into gunboats and rams to back up the forts. The Union also converted steamboats into "timberclad" gunboats and built a new class of ironclad gunboats designed for river warfare.

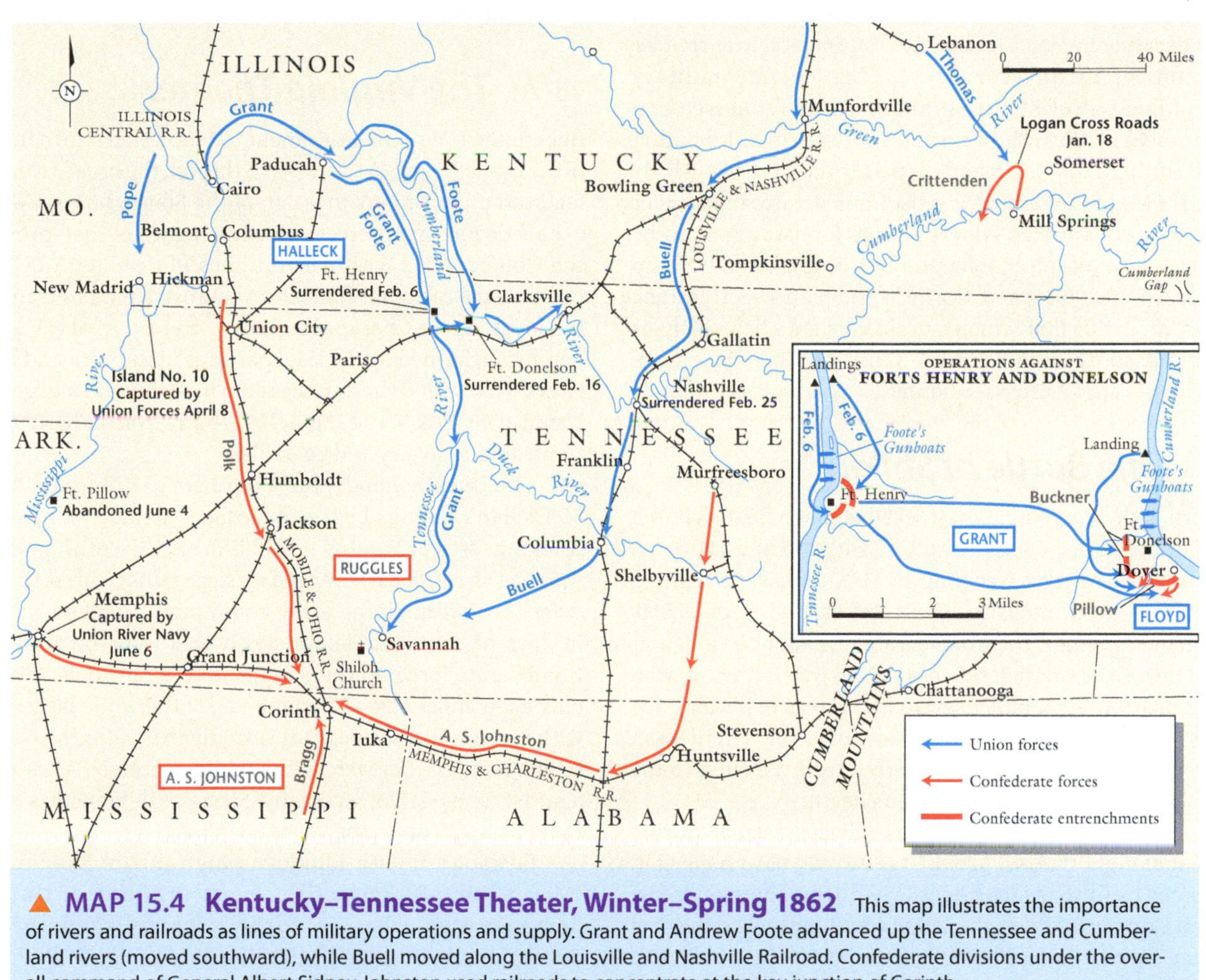

▲ **MAP 15.4 Kentucky–Tennessee Theater, Winter–Spring 1862** This map illustrates the importance of rivers and railroads as lines of military operations and supply. Grant and Andrew Foote advanced up the Tennessee and Cumberland rivers (moved southward), while Buell moved along the Louisville and Nashville Railroad. Confederate divisions under the overall command of General Albert Sidney Johnston used railroads to concentrate at the key junction of Corinth.

Q *How important was control of rivers to Union victory?*

Q *How important was the war in the West to the ultimate outcome of the Civil War?*

With the help of these strange-looking but formidable craft, Grant struck in February 1862. His objectives were Forts Henry and Donelson on the Tennessee and Cumberland rivers just south of the Kentucky-Tennessee border (see Map 15.4). The gunboats knocked out Fort Henry on February 6. Fort Donelson proved a tougher nut to crack. Its guns repulsed a gunboat attack on February 14. The next day, the 17,000-man Confederate army attacked Grant's besieging army, which had been reinforced to 27,000 men. With the calm decisiveness that became his trademark, Grant directed a counterattack that penned the defenders back up in their fort. Cut off from support by either land or river, the Confederate commander asked for surrender terms on February 16. Grant's reply made him instantly famous when it was published in the North: "No terms except an immediate and unconditional surrender can be accepted. I propose to move immediately upon your works." With no choice, the 13,000 surviving Confederates surrendered (some had escaped), giving Grant the most striking victory in the war thus far.

These victories had far-reaching strategic consequences. Union gunboats now ranged all the way up the Tennessee River to northern Alabama, enabling a Union division to occupy the region, and up the Cumberland to Nashville, which became the first Confederate state capital to surrender to Union forces on February 25. Confederate military units pulled out of Kentucky and most of Tennessee and reassembled at Corinth in northern Mississippi. Jubilation spread through the North and despair through the South. By the end of March 1862, however, the Confederate commander in the western theater, Albert Sidney Johnston (not to be confused with Joseph E. Johnston in Virginia), had built up an army of 40,000 men at Corinth. His plan was to attack Grant's force of 35,000, which had established a base 20 miles away at Pittsburg Landing on the Tennessee River just north of the Mississippi-Tennessee border.

15-7d *The Battle of Shiloh*

On April 6, the Confederates attacked at dawn near a church called Shiloh. They caught Grant by surprise and drove his army toward the river (see Map 15.5). After a day's fighting of unprecedented intensity, with total casualties of 15,000, Grant's men brought the Confederate onslaught to a halt at dusk. One of the Confederate casualties was Johnston, who bled to death when a bullet severed an artery in his leg—the highest-ranking general on either side to be killed in the war. Beauregard, who had been transferred from Virginia to the West, took command after Johnston's death.

Some of Grant's subordinates advised retreat during the dismal night of April 6, but Grant would have none of it. Reinforced by fresh troops from a Union army commanded by General Don Carlos Buell, the Union counterattacked the next morning (April 7) and, after 9,000 more casualties to the two sides, drove the Confederates back to Corinth. Although Grant had snatched victory from the jaws of defeat, his reputation suffered a decline for a time because of the heavy Union casualties (13,000) and the suspicion that he had been caught napping the first day.

Union triumphs in the western theater continued. The combined armies of Grant and Buell, under the overall command of the top-ranking Union general in the West, Henry W. Halleck, drove the Confederates out of Corinth at the end of May. Meanwhile, the Union gunboat fleet fought its way down the Mississippi to Vicksburg, virtually wiping out the Confederate fleet in a spectacular battle at Memphis on June 6. At Vicksburg, the Union gunboats from the north connected with part of Farragut's fleet that had come up from New Orleans, taking Baton Rouge and Natchez along the way. The heavily fortified Confederate bastion at Vicksburg, however, proved too strong for Union naval firepower to subdue. Nevertheless, the dramatic succession of Union triumphs in the West from February to June, including a decisive victory at the battle of Pea Ridge in northwest Arkansas on March 7 and 8, convinced the North that the war was nearly won. "Every blow tells fearfully against the rebellion," boasted the leading northern newspaper, the New York *Tribune*. "The rebels themselves are panic-stricken, or despondent. It now requires no very far reaching prophet to predict the end of this struggle."

15-7e *The Virginia Theater*

But affairs in Virginia were about to take a sharp turn in favor of the Confederacy. In the western theater, the broad rivers had facilitated the Union's invasion of the South, but in Virginia a half-dozen small rivers flowing west to east provided the Confederates with natural lines of defense. McClellan persuaded a reluctant Lincoln to approve a plan to transport his army down Chesapeake Bay to the tip of the Virginia peninsula, formed by the tidal portions of the York and James rivers. That would shorten the route to Richmond and give the Union army a seaborne supply line secure from harassment by Confederate cavalry and guerrillas.

This was a good plan—in theory. But once again, McClellan's failings began to surface. A small Confederate blocking force at Yorktown held him for the entire month of April, as he cautiously dragged up siege guns to blast through defenses that his large army could have punched through in days on foot. McClellan slowly followed the retreating Confederate force up the peninsula to a new defensive line only a few miles east of Richmond. All the while he bickered with Lincoln and Secretary of War Edwin M. Stanton over the reinforcements they were withholding to protect Washington against a possible strike by Stonewall Jackson's small Confederate army in the Shenandoah Valley.

Jackson's month-long campaign in the Shenandoah (May 8–June 9), one of the most brilliant of the war, demonstrated what could be accomplished through deception, daring, and mobility. With only 17,000 men, Jackson moved by forced marches so swift that his infantry earned the nickname "Jackson's foot cavalry." Darting here and there through the valley, they marched 350 miles in the

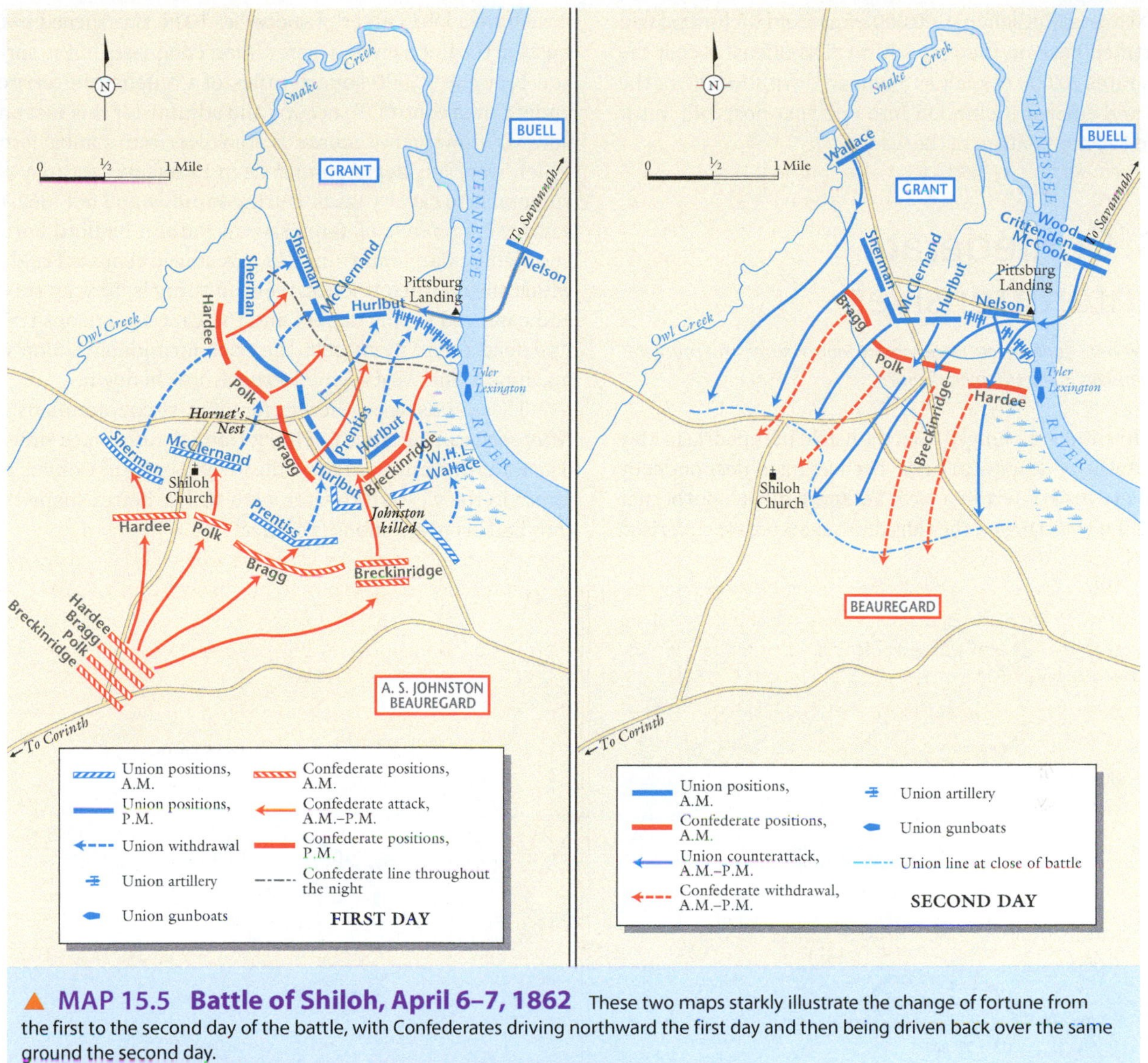

▲ **MAP 15.5 Battle of Shiloh, April 6–7, 1862** These two maps starkly illustrate the change of fortune from the first to the second day of the battle, with Confederates driving northward the first day and then being driven back over the same ground the second day.

Q *Do you see any evidence of Union retreat after the losses of the first day of battle?*

Q *Why did Grant's reputation decline for a while after the Battle of Shiloh?*

course of one month; won four battles against three separate Union armies, whose combined numbers surpassed Jackson's by more than 2 to 1 (but which Jackson's force always outnumbered at the point of contact); and compelled Lincoln to divert to the valley some of the reinforcements McClellan demanded.

Even without those reinforcements, McClellan's army substantially outnumbered the Confederate force defending Richmond, commanded by Joseph E. Johnston. McClellan overestimated Johnston's strength at double what it was and acted accordingly. Even so, by the last week of May, McClellan's army was within six miles of Richmond (see Map 15.6). A botched Confederate counterattack on May 31 and June 1 (the battle of Seven Pines) produced no result except 6,000 Confederate and 5,000 Union casualties. One of those casualties was Johnston, who was wounded in the shoulder. Jefferson Davis named Robert E. Lee to replace him.

15-7f *The Seven Days' Battles*

That appointment marked a major turning point in the campaign. Lee had done little so far to earn a wartime reputation, having failed in his only field command to dislodge Union forces from control of West Virginia. His qualities as a commander began to manifest when he took over what he renamed the Army of Northern Virginia. Those qualities were boldness, a willingness to take great risks, an almost uncanny ability to read the enemy commander's mind, and a charisma that won the devotion of his men. While McClellan continued to dawdle, Lee sent his dashing cavalry commander, J. E. B. "Jeb" Stuart, to lead a reconnaissance around the Union army to discover its weak points. Lee also brought Jackson's army in from the Shenandoah Valley and launched a June 26 attack on McClellan's right flank in what became known as the Seven Days' battles (see Map 15.6). Constantly attacking, Lee's army of 90,000 drove McClellan's 100,000 away from Richmond to a new fortified base on the James River. The offensive cost the Confederates 20,000 casualties (compared with 16,000 for the Union) and turned Richmond into one vast hospital, but it reversed the momentum of the war.

15-8 Confederate Counteroffensives

Q *Why were Confederate forces able to launch successful counteroffensives in the summer of 1862?*

Northern sentiment plunged from the height of euphoria in May to the depths of despair in July. "The feeling of despondency here is very great," wrote a New Yorker, while a southerner exulted, "Lee has turned the tide, and I shall not be surprised if we have a long career of successes." The tide turned in the western theater as well, where Union conquests in the spring had brought 50,000 square miles of Confederate territory under Union control. To occupy and administer this vast area, however, drew many thousands of soldiers from combat forces, which were left depleted and deep in enemy territory and vulnerable to cavalry raids. During summer and fall 1862, the cavalry commands of Tennesseean Nathan Bedford Forrest and Kentuckian John Hunt Morgan staged repeated raids in which they burned bridges, blew up tunnels, tore up tracks, and captured supply depots and the Union garrisons trying to defend them. By August the once-formidable Union war machine in the West seemed to have broken down.

These raids paved the way for infantry counteroffensives. After recapturing some territory, Confederate forces suffered defeats at Corinth and Perryville in October. But Confederate forces in the western theater were still in better shape than they had been four months earlier.

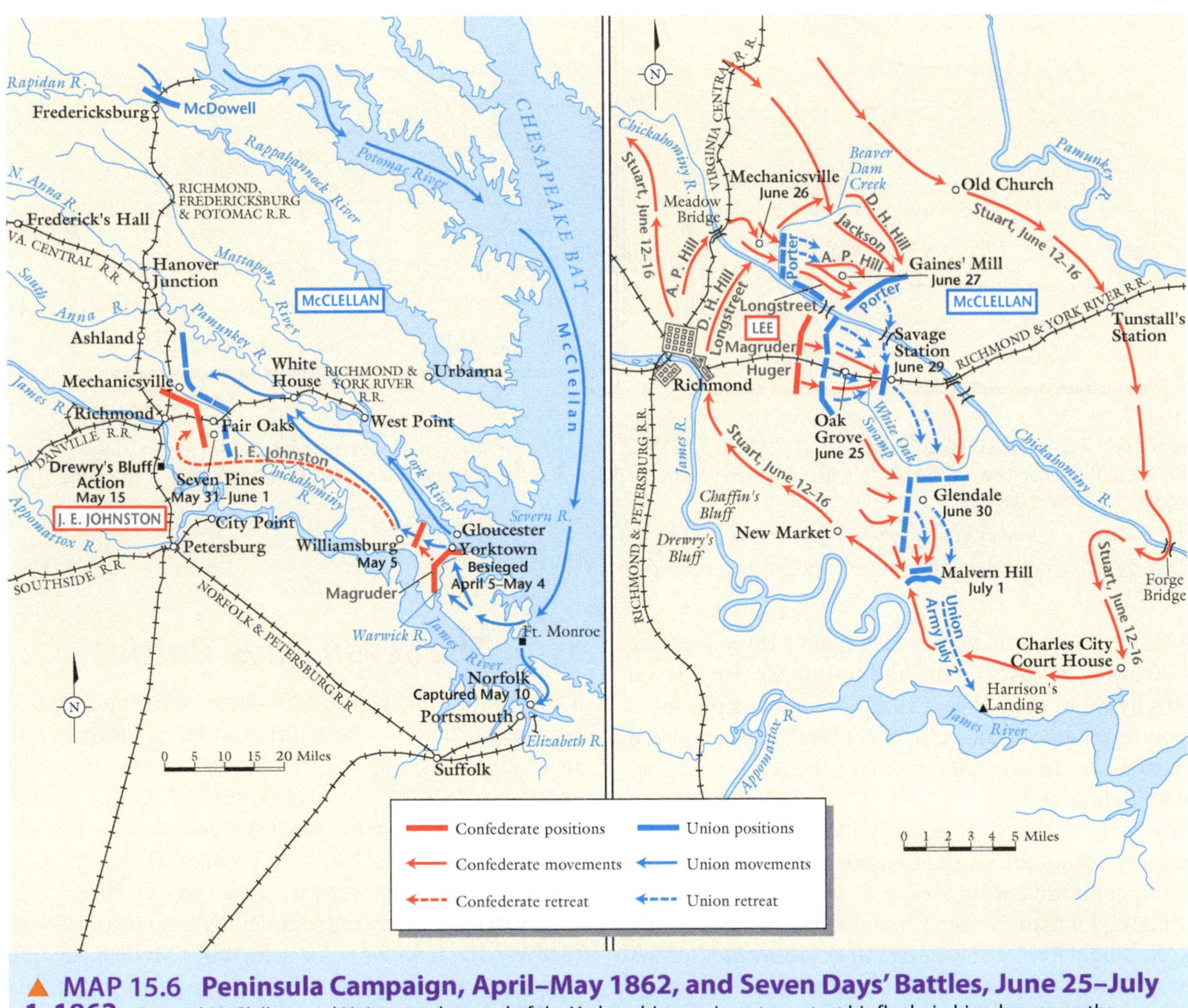

▲ **MAP 15.6 Peninsula Campaign, April–May 1862, and Seven Days' Battles, June 25–July 1, 1862** General McClellan used Union naval control of the York and James rivers to protect his flanks in his advance up the peninsula formed by these rivers (left map). When Robert E. Lee's Army of Northern Virginia counterattacked in the Seven Days' battles (right map), McClellan was forced back to the James River at Harrison's Landing.

Q *How would you compare Lee's and McClellan's differing approaches to command?*

Q *What are the chief reasons why McClellan failed to reach Richmond during the spring and summer of 1862, despite being within six miles of the city?*

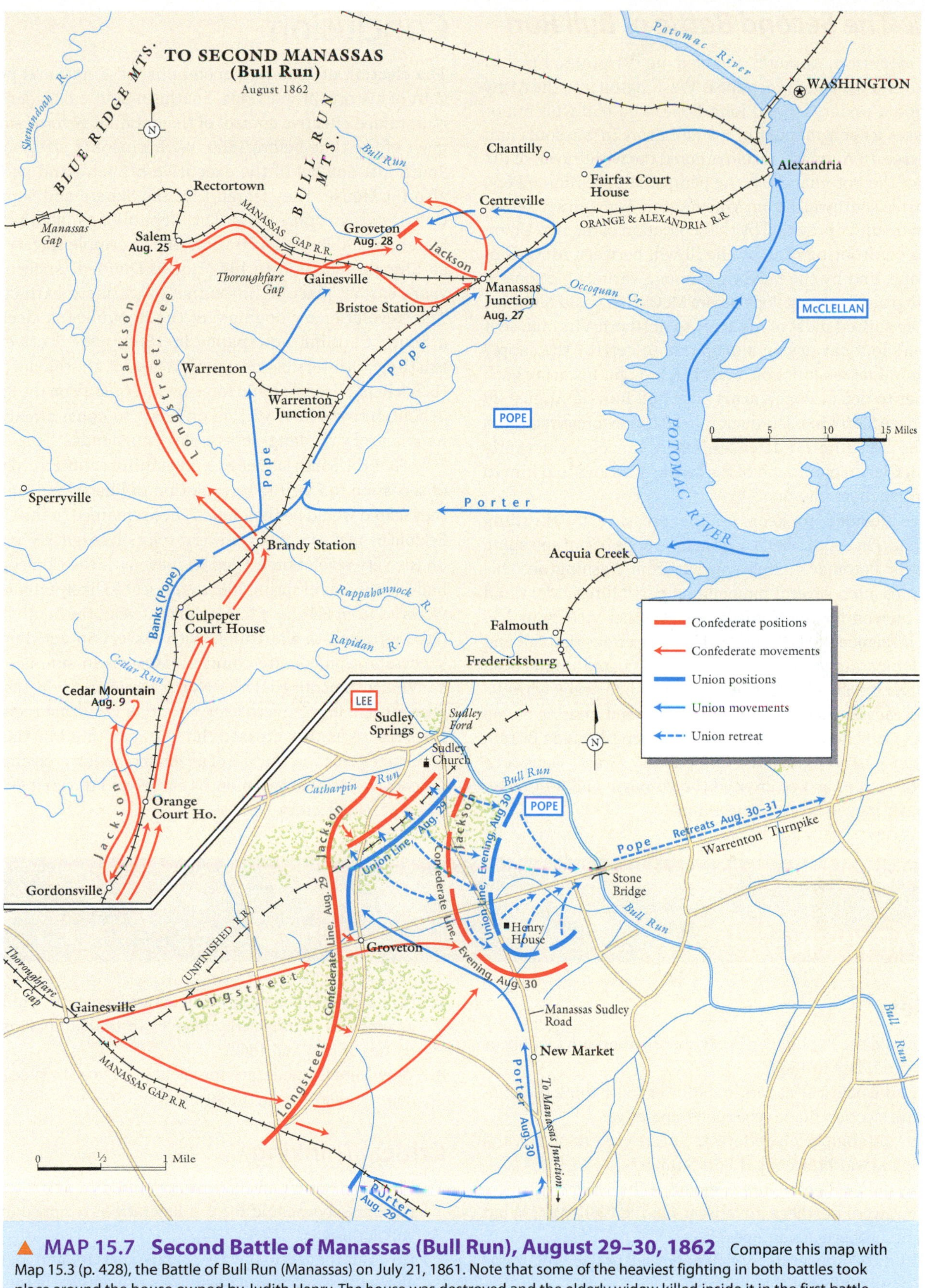

▲ **MAP 15.7 Second Battle of Manassas (Bull Run), August 29–30, 1862** Compare this map with Map 15.3 (p. 428), the Battle of Bull Run (Manassas) on July 21, 1861. Note that some of the heaviest fighting in both battles took place around the house owned by Judith Henry. The house was destroyed and the elderly widow killed inside it in the first battle.

Q *What were the reasons behind a second Confederate victory at Bull Run?*

Q *What political and military issues were a barrier to Union victory at Second Bull Run?*

15-8a *The Second Battle of Bull Run*

Most attention, though, focused on Virginia. Lincoln reorganized the Union corps near Washington into the Army of Virginia under General John Pope, who had won minor successes as commander of a small army in Missouri and Tennessee. In August, Lincoln ordered the withdrawal of the Army of the Potomac from the peninsula to reinforce Pope for a drive southward from Washington. Lee quickly seized the opportunity provided by the separation of the two Union armies confronting him, by the ill will between McClellan and Pope, and by the bickering among various factions in Washington. To attack Pope before McClellan could reinforce him, Lee shifted most of his army to northern Virginia, sent Jackson's foot cavalry on a deep raid to destroy the supply base at Manassas Junction, and then brought his army back together to defeat Pope's army near Bull Run on August 29 and 30 (see Map 15.7). The demoralized Union forces retreated into the Washington defenses, where Lincoln reluctantly gave McClellan command of the two armies and told him to reorganize them into one.

Lee decided to keep up the pressure by invading Maryland. On September 4, his weary troops began splashing across the Potomac 40 miles upriver from Washington. This move presented several momentous possibilities: Maryland might be won for the Confederacy. Another victory by Lee might influence the U.S. congressional elections that fall and help Democrats gain control of Congress, and might even force the Lincoln administration to negotiate peace with the Confederacy. Successful invasion of Maryland, coming on top of other Confederate successes, might even persuade Britain and France to recognize the Confederacy. Great issues rode with the armies as Lee crossed the Potomac and McClellan cautiously moved north to meet him.

Conclusion

The election of 1860 had accomplished a national power shift of historic proportions. Southern political leaders had maintained effective control of the national government for most of the time before 1860. With Lincoln's election, the South lost control of the executive branch—and perhaps also the House. They feared that the Senate and Supreme Court would soon follow. The Republicans, southerners feared, would launch a "revolution" to cripple slavery and, as Lincoln had said in his "House Divided" speech two years earlier, place it "in course of ultimate extinction." The "revolutionary dogmas" of the Republicans, declared a South Carolina newspaper in 1860, were "active and bristling with terrible designs." Worst of all, the northern "Black Republicans" would force racial equality on the South: "Abolition preachers will be on hand to consummate the marriage of your daughters to black husbands."

Thus the South launched a preemptive counterrevolution of secession to forestall a revolution of liberty and equality they feared would be their fate if they remained in the Union. Seldom has a preemptive counterrevolution so quickly brought on the very revolution it tried to prevent. If the Confederacy had lost the war in spring 1862, as appeared likely after Union victories from February to May of that year, the South might have returned to the Union with slavery intact. Instead, successful Confederate counteroffensives in summer 1862 convinced Lincoln that the North could not win the war without striking against slavery. Another issue that rode with Lee's troops as they crossed the Potomac into Maryland in September 1862 was the fate of an emancipation proclamation Lincoln had drafted two months earlier and then put aside to await a Union victory.

CHAPTER REVIEW

Review

1. Why did the Republican Party choose Abraham Lincoln as its candidate in 1860?
2. Why did political leaders in the lower South think that Lincoln's election made secession imperative?
3. Why did compromise efforts to forestall secession fail, and why did war break out at Fort Sumter?
4. Why did the border states remain in the Union?
5. What were northern advantages in the Civil War? What were southern advantages?
6. Why did Confederate foreign policy fail to win diplomatic recognition from other nations?
7. How did the Union's and Confederacy's respective military advantages manifest themselves in the campaigns and battles of 1861 and 1862?
8. Why were Confederate forces able to launch successful counteroffensives in the summer of 1862?

Critical Thinking

1. Given the North's advantages in population and economic resources, how could the Confederacy have hoped to prevail in the war?
2. How did the factors of geography, terrain, and logistics shape the strategy and operations of each side in the war?

Identifications

Review your understanding of the following key terms, people, and events for this chapter (terms in bold in text are included in the Glossary).

Fort Sumter, p. 407
secession, p. 408
Unionists, p. 411
Robert E. Lee, p. 416
bushwhackers, p. 417
rifling, p. 420
treasury notes, p. 423
specie, p. 423
legal tender, p. 424
banknotes, p. 424
blockade, p. 424
blockade runner, p. 424
revolving turret, p. 427
Thomas J. ("Stonewall") Jackson, p. 427
George B. McClellan, p. 427

Suggested Readings

The most comprehensive one-volume study of the Civil War years is **James M. McPherson**, ***Battle Cry of Freedom: The Civil War Era*** (1988). For the perspective of the soldiers and sailors who fought the battles, see **Bell I. Wiley's** classic ***The Life of Johnny Reb*** (1943) and ***The Life of Billy Yank*** (1952). On the terrible costs of battle, see **Drew Gilpin Faust**, ***This Republic of Suffering*** (2008). For the naval war, see **James M. McPherson**, ***War on the Waters: The Union and Confederate Navies, 1861–1865*** (2012).

For the home front in North and South, see **Phillip Shaw Paludan**, ***"A People's Contest": The Union and Civil War, 1861–1865*** (1988), and **Emory Thomas**, ***The Confederate Nation, 1861–1865*** (1979). For women and children, see **Nina Silber**, ***Daughters of the Union: Northern Women Fight the Civil War*** (2005); and **George C. Rable**, ***Civil Wars: Women and the Crisis of Southern Nationalism*** (1989).

For the commanders in chief and their principal generals, consult **James M. McPherson**, ***Tried by War: Abraham Lincoln as Commander in Chief*** (2007); **William C. Cooper**, ***Jefferson Davis, American*** (2000); **Stephen W. Sears**, ***George B. McClellan: The Young Napoleon*** (1988); **Ron Chernow**, ***Ulysses S. Grant*** (2017); and **Emory M. Thomas**, ***Robert E. Lee*** (1995). A superb study of Lincoln and his cabinet is **Doris Kearns Goodwin**, ***Team of Rivals: The Political Genius of Abraham Lincoln*** (2005). For the guerrilla war, the most useful of several books is **Daniel E. Sutherland**, ***A Savage Conflict: The Decisive Role of Guerrillas in the American Civil War*** (2009). Of the many studies of diplomacy during the war, the most useful is **David P. Crook**, ***The North, The South, and the Powers 1861–1865*** (1974), an abridged version of which was published with the title ***Diplomacy during the Civil War*** (1975). On the international dimensions of the war, see **Don H. Doyle**, ***The Cause of All Nations: An International History of the American Civil War*** (2015).

16 A New Birth of Freedom, 1862–1865

A Ride for Liberty (oil on board), Johnson, Eastman (1824–1906)/Brooklyn Museum of Art, New York, USA/ Gift of Gwendolyn O.L. Conkling/The Bridgeman Art Library International

16.1 ***A Ride for Liberty*** This splendid painting by Eastman Johnson of a slave family escaping to Union lines during the Civil War dramatizes the experiences of thousands of slaves who thereby became "contrabands" and gained their freedom. Most of them came on foot, but this enterprising family is instead shown stealing a horse as well as themselves from their master.

Q *Most critics agree that this painting makes an argument against slavery. Why?*

ONE OF THE GREAT issues awaiting resolution as the armies moved into Maryland in September 1862 was emancipation of the slaves. The war had moved beyond the effort to restore the old Union. It now required the North to mobilize every resource that might bring victory or to destroy any enemy resource that might inflict defeat. To abolish slavery would strike at a vital Confederate resource (slave labor) and mobilize that resource for the Union along with the moral power of fighting for freedom. Slaves had already made clear their choice by escaping to Union lines by the tens of thousands. Lincoln had made up his mind to issue an emancipation proclamation and was waiting for a Union victory to give it credibility and potency.

This momentous decision would radically enlarge the scope and purpose of the Union war effort. It would also polarize northern public opinion and political parties. So long as the North fought simply for restoration of the Union, northern unity was impressive, but the events of 1862 and 1863 raised the divisive question of what kind of Union was to be restored. Would it be a Union without slavery, as abolitionists and radical Republicans hoped? Or "the Union as it was, the Constitution as it is," as Democrats desired? The answer to this question would determine not only the course of the war but also the future of the United States. ■

16-1 Slavery and the War

Q *What factors led Lincoln to his decision to issue the Emancipation Proclamation?*

In the North, the issue of emancipation was deeply divisive. Lincoln had been elected on a platform pledged to contain the expansion of slavery, but that pledge had provoked most of the southern states to quit the Union. For the administration to take action against slavery in 1861 would be to risk the breakup of the fragile coalition Lincoln had stitched together to fight the war: Republicans, Democrats, and border-state Unionists. Spokesmen for the latter two groups served notice that, although they supported a war for the Union, they would not support a war against slavery. In July 1861, with Lincoln's endorsement, Congress passed a resolution affirming that northern war aims included no intention "of overthrowing or interfering with the rights or established institutions of the States"—in plain words, slavery—but intended only "to defend and maintain the supremacy of the Constitution and to preserve the Union."

Many northerners saw matters differently. They insisted that a rebellion sustained *by* slavery in defense *of* slavery could be suppressed only by striking *against* slavery. As Frederick Douglass stated, "War for the destruction of liberty must be met with war for the destruction of slavery."

Wars tend to develop a logic and momentum that go beyond their original purposes. When northerners discovered at Bull Run in July 1861 that they were not going to win an easy victory, many of them began to take a harder look at slavery. Slaves constituted the principal labor force in the South. They raised most of the food and fiber, built most of the military fortifications, worked on the railroads and in mines and munitions factories. Southern newspapers boasted that slavery was "a tower of strength to the Confederacy" because it enabled the South "to place in the field a force so much larger in proportion to her white population than the North." So why not convert this Confederate asset to a Union advantage by confiscating slaves as enemy property and using them to help the northern war effort?

16-1a *The "Contrabands"*

The slaves entered this debate in a dramatic fashion. As Union armies penetrated the South, a growing number of slaves voted for freedom with their feet. By twos and threes, by families, and eventually by scores, they escaped from their masters and came over to the Union lines. By obliging Union officers either to return them to slavery or accept them, these escaped slaves began to make the conflict a war for freedom.

Although some commanders returned escaped slaves to their masters or prevented them from entering Union camps, increasingly, most did not. When three slaves who had been working for the Confederate army escaped to General Benjamin Butler's lines near Fortress Monroe in May 1861, Butler refused to return them on the grounds that they were **contraband of war**. The phrase caught on in the North. For the rest of the war, slaves who came within Union lines were known as "contrabands"—a term that blacks disliked and that, ironically, continued to define human beings as property. On August 6, 1861, Congress passed a confiscation act that authorized the seizure of all property that was being used for Confederate military purposes, including slaves. The following March, Congress forbade the return of slaves who entered Union lines.

16-1b *The Border States*

The problem of slavery in the loyal border states preoccupied Lincoln. On August 30, 1861, John C. Frémont, whose political influence had won him a commission as major general and command of Union forces in Missouri, issued an order freeing the slaves of all Confederate sympathizers in Missouri. This caused such a backlash among border-state Unionists, who feared it was a prelude to a general abolition edict, that Lincoln revoked the order, lest it "alarm our Southern Union friends, and turn them against us."

In spring 1862, Lincoln tried persuasion instead of force in the border states. At his urging, Congress passed a resolution offering federal compensation to states that

CHRONOLOGY

1862	Confederacy enacts conscription (April 16) • Lincoln informs the cabinet of intention to issue Emancipation Proclamation (July 22) • Battle of Antietam (September 17) • Lincoln issues preliminary Emancipation Proclamation (September 22) • Battle of Fredericksburg (December 13) • Battle of Stones River (December 31–January 2)
1863	Lincoln issues final Emancipation Proclamation (January 1) • Union enacts conscription (March 3) • Richmond bread riot (April 2) • Battle of Chancellorsville (May 1–5) • Battle of Gettysburg (July 1–3) • Vicksburg surrenders (July 4) • Port Hudson surrenders (July 9) • New York draft riot (July 13–16) • Assault on Fort Wagner (July 18) • Battle of Chickamauga (September 19–20) • Battles of Chattanooga (November 24–25)
1864	Battle of the Wilderness (May 5–6) • Battle of Spotsylvania (May 8–19) • Fighting at Petersburg (June 15–18) leads to nine-month siege • Fall of Atlanta (September 1) • Reelection of Lincoln (November 8) • Battle of Nashville (December 15–16)
1865	Capture of Fort Fisher (January 15) • Confederates evacuate Richmond (April 2) • Lee surrenders at Appomattox (April 9) • Booth assassinates Lincoln (April 14) • Last Confederate army surrenders (June 23) • Thirteenth Amendment abolishing slavery ratified (December 6)

voluntarily abolished slavery. Three times, from March to July 1862, Lincoln urged border-state congressmen to accept the offer. He told them that the Confederate hope that their states might join the rebellion was helping to keep the war alive. Adopt the proposal for **compensated emancipation**, he pleaded, and that hope would die. The pressure for a bold antislavery policy was growing stronger, he warned them in May. Another Union general had issued an emancipation order; Lincoln had suspended it, but "you cannot," Lincoln told the border-state congressmen, "be blind to the signs of the times."

They did seem to be blind. They complained of being coerced, bickered about the amount of compensation, and wrung their hands over the prospects of economic ruin and race war, even if emancipation were to take place gradually over a 30-year period, as Lincoln had suggested. At a final meeting on July 12, Lincoln warned them, "If the war continue long ... the institution in your states will be extinguished by mere friction and abrasion." Again they failed to see the light, and by a vote of 20 to 9, they rejected the proposal for compensated emancipation.

16-1c *The Decision for Emancipation*

That very evening, Lincoln decided to issue an emancipation proclamation in his capacity as commander in chief with power to order the seizure of enemy property. Several factors, in addition to the recalcitrance of the border states, impelled

Library of Congress Prints and Photographs Division

16.2 **African Americans Coming into Union Lines** This photograph taken in 1862 or 1863 shows slaves fording the Rappahannock River in Virginia in order to reach freedom. Note the family groups of men, women, and children, as well as the goods that they had struggled to bring with them to their new life.

Lincoln to this fateful decision. One was a growing demand from his own party for bolder action. Another was rising sentiment in the army to "take off the kid gloves" when dealing with "traitors." Finally, Lincoln's decision reflected his sentiments about the "unqualified evil" and "monstrous injustice" of slavery.

The military situation, however, rather than his moral convictions, determined the timing and scope of Lincoln's emancipation policy. Northern hopes that the war would soon end had risen after the victories of early 1862 but had then plummeted amid the reverses of that summer.

Three courses of action seemed possible. One, favored by the so-called Peace Democrats, urged an armistice and peace negotiations to patch together some kind of Union, but that would have been tantamount to conceding Confederate victory. Republicans therefore reviled the Peace Democrats as traitorous **Copperheads**, after the poisonous snake. A second alternative was to keep on fighting—in the hope that with a few more Union victories, the rebels would lay down their arms and the Union could be restored. Such a policy would leave slavery intact. The third alternative was to mobilize all the resources of the North and to destroy all the resources of the South, including slavery—a war not to restore the old Union but to build a new one.

On July 22, a week after his meeting with the border-state representatives convinced him there could be no compromise, Lincoln notified the cabinet of his intention to issue an emancipation proclamation. It was "a military necessity, absolutely essential to the preservation of the Union," said Lincoln. "We must free the slaves or be ourselves subdued. The slaves [are] undeniably an element of strength to those who [have] their service, and we must decide whether that element should be with us or against us."

The cabinet agreed, except for Postmaster General Montgomery Blair, a resident of Maryland and a former Democrat, who warned that the border states and the Democrats would rebel against the proclamation and perhaps cost the administration the fall congressional elections as well as vital support for the war. Lincoln might have agreed two months earlier. Now he believed that the strength gained from an emancipation policy—from the slaves themselves, from the dynamic Republican segment of northern opinion, and in the eyes of foreign nations—would more than compensate for the hostility of Democrats and border-state Unionists. Lincoln did, however, accept the advice of Secretary of State Seward to delay the proclamation "until you can give it to the country supported by military success." Otherwise, Seward argued, it might be viewed "as the last measure of an exhausted government, a cry for help ... our last *shriek*, on the retreat." Lincoln slipped his proclamation into a desk drawer and waited for a military victory.

16-1d *New Calls for Troops*

Meanwhile, Lincoln issued a call for 300,000 new three-year volunteers for the army. In July, Congress passed a militia act giving the president greater powers to mobilize the state militias into federal service and to draft men into the militia if the states failed to do so. Although not a national draft law, this was a step in that direction. In August, Lincoln called up 300,000 militia for nine months of service, in addition to the 300,000 three-year volunteers. (These calls eventually yielded 421,000 three-year volunteers and 88,000 nine-month militia.) The Peace Democrats railed against these measures and provoked antidraft riots in some localities. The government responded by arresting rioters and antiwar activists under the president's suspension of the writ of habeas corpus.[1]

Democrats denounced these "arbitrary arrests" as unconstitutional violations of civil liberties and added this issue to others on which they hoped to gain control of the next House of Representatives in the fall elections. With the decline in northern morale following the defeat at Second Bull Run, prospects for a Democratic triumph seemed bright. One more military victory by Lee's Army of Northern Virginia might crack the North's will to continue the fight. It might bring diplomatic recognition of the Confederacy by Britain and France. Lee's legions began crossing the Potomac into Maryland on September 4, 1862.

16-1e *The Battle of Antietam*

The Confederate invasion ran into difficulties from the start. Western Marylanders responded impassively to Lee's proclamation that he had come "to aid you in throwing off this foreign yoke" of Yankee rule. Lee split his army into five parts. Three of them, under the overall command of Stonewall Jackson, occupied the heights surrounding the Union garrison at Harpers Ferry, which lay athwart the Confederate supply route from the Shenandoah Valley (see Map 16.1). The other two remained on watch in the South Mountain passes west of Frederick. Then, on September 13, Union commander George B. McClellan had an extraordinary stroke of luck. In a field near Frederick, two of his soldiers found a copy of Lee's orders for these deployments. Wrapped around three cigars, they had apparently been dropped by a careless southern officer when the Confederate army passed through Frederick four days earlier. With this new information, McClellan planned to pounce on the separated segments of Lee's army before they could reunite.

But McClellan moved so cautiously that he lost much of his advantage. Although Union troops overwhelmed the Confederate defenders of the South Mountain passes on September 14, they advanced too slowly to save the garrison at Harpers Ferry, which surrendered 12,000 men to Jackson on September 15. Lee then managed to reunite most

[1]A writ of habeas corpus is an order issued by a judge to law enforcement officers requiring them to bring an arrested person before the court to be charged with a crime so that the accused can have a fair trial. The U.S. Constitution permits the suspension of this writ "in cases of rebellion or invasion," so that the government can arrest enemy agents, saboteurs, or any individual who might hinder the defense of the country, and hold such individuals without trial. Lincoln had suspended the writ, but political opponents charged him with usurping a power possessed only by Congress in order to curb freedom of speech of antiwar opponents and political critics guilty of nothing more than speaking out against the war.

Interpreting the Visual Past Photographs of the Dead at Antietam

In October 1862, the Matthew Brady studio in New York City held an exhibition of photographs from the battlefield at Antietam. Photography as a technology came into its own during the Civil War; these photographs, taken two days after the battle, were the first images of battlefield dead most Americans had ever seen. The palpable shock many viewers felt was captured by an anonymous reviewer for the *New York Times*, who said that the photographs "bring home to us the terrible reality and earnestness of war." He commented on the "terrible fascination" that "draws one near these pictures, and makes him loth to leave them." Such photographs changed the way in which Americans saw and imagined war.

Q *Why, when Americans already understood that men were killed in battle, would these photographs have brought home the "terrible reality" of war? What was it about photography as a medium of representation that changed Americans' perceptions of the human costs of war?*

Library of Congress, Prints and Photographs Division

16.3a **Alexander Gardner, Antietam, MD. Confederate Dead by a Fence on the Hagerstown Road, September—October 1862.**

Bettmann/Corbis

16.3b **Some of the Casualties from the Civil War Battle of Antietam, September 17, 1862.**

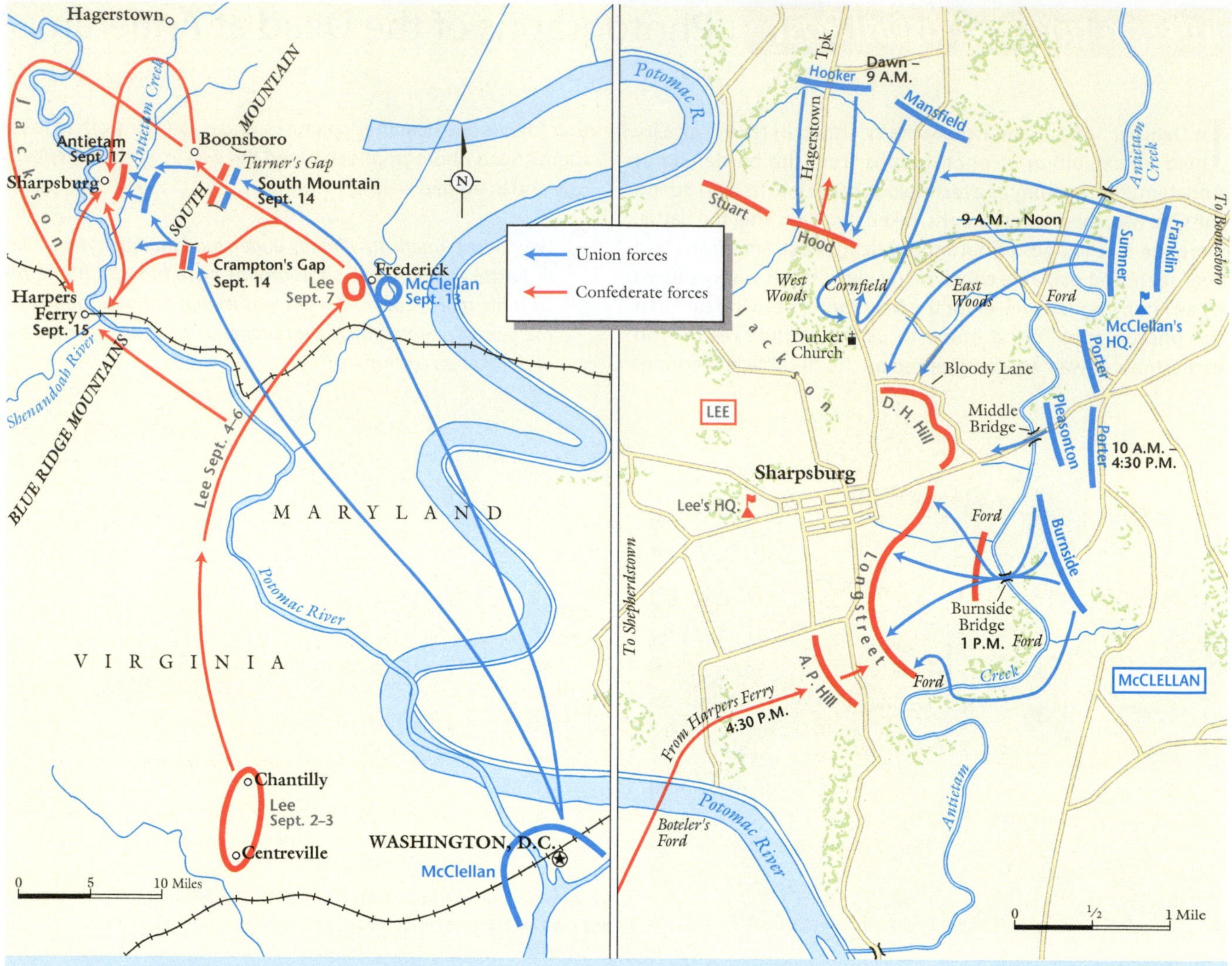

▲ **MAP 16.1 Lee's Invasion of Maryland, 1862, and the Battle of Antietam, September 17, 1862**
Both the advantages and disadvantages of Lee's defensive position in this battle are illustrated by the right-hand map. The Confederate flanks were protected by water barriers (the Potomac River on the left and Antietam Creek on the right), but the Confederates fought with their back to the Potomac and only Boteler's Ford as the single line of retreat across the river. If Burnside's attack on the Confederate right had succeeded before A. P. Hill's division arrived, Lee's forces could have been trapped north of the river.

Q *What advantages and disadvantages did McClellan have at Antietam?*

Q *Why is Antietam considered one of the most important battles of the Civil War?*

of his army near the village of Sharpsburg by September 17, when McClellan finally crossed Antietam Creek to attack. Even so, the Union forces outnumbered the Confederates by 2 to 1 (80,000 to 40,000 men), but McClellan, as usual, believed that the enemy outnumbered him. Thus, he missed several opportunities to inflict a truly crippling defeat on the Confederacy. The battle of Antietam (called Sharpsburg by the Confederates) nevertheless proved to be the single bloodiest day in American history, with more than 23,000 casualties (killed, wounded, and captured) in the two armies.

Attacking from right to left on a four-mile front, McClellan's Army of the Potomac achieved potential breakthroughs at a sunken road northeast of Sharpsburg (known ever after as Bloody Lane) and in the rolling fields southeast of town. But fearing counterattacks from phantom reserves that he was sure Lee possessed, McClellan held back 20,000 of his troops and failed to follow through. Thus, the battle ended in a draw. The battered Confederates still clung to their precarious line, with the Potomac at their back, at the end of a day in which more than 6,000 men on both sides were killed or mortally wounded—almost as many Americans as were killed or mortally wounded in combat during the entire seven years of the Revolutionary War.

Even though he received reinforcements the next day, McClellan did not renew the attack. Nor did he follow up vigorously when the Confederates finally retreated across the Potomac on the night of September 18.

16-1f *The Emancipation Proclamation*

Lincoln was not happy with this equivocal Union victory, despite its important consequences. Britain and France decided to withhold diplomatic recognition of the

MPI/Getty Images

16.4 **The Emancipation Proclamation** This famous contemporary painting by Francis Carpenter portrays Lincoln and his cabinet discussing the Emancipation Proclamation, which lies on the desk before Lincoln. The other members of the cabinet, from left to right, are Secretary of War Edwin M. Stanton, Secretary of the Treasury Salmon P. Chase, Secretary of the Navy Gideon Welles, Secretary of the Interior Caleb B. Smith, Secretary of State William H. Seward (seated facing Lincoln), Postmaster General Montgomery Blair, and Attorney General Edward Bates.

Confederacy. Northern Democrats failed to gain control of the House in the fall elections. And most significant of all, on September 22, Lincoln seized the occasion to issue his preliminary emancipation proclamation. It did not come as a total surprise. A month earlier, after Horace Greeley had written a strong editorial in the *New York Tribune* calling for action against slavery, Lincoln had responded with a public letter to Greeley (much as a president today might use a televised news conference). "My paramount object in this struggle," wrote Lincoln, "*is* to save the Union… . If I could save the Union without freeing *any* slave I would do it, and if I could save it by freeing *all* the slaves I would do it; and if I could save it by freeing some and leaving others alone I would also do that." Lincoln had crafted these phrases carefully to maximize public support for his anticipated proclamation. He portrayed emancipation not as an end in itself—despite his personal convictions to that effect—but only as an instrument, a *means* toward saving the Union.

Lincoln's proclamation of September 22 did not go into effect immediately. Rather, it stipulated that if any state, or part of a state, was still in rebellion on January 1, 1863, the president would proclaim the slaves therein "forever free." Confederate leaders scorned this warning, and by January 1st no southern state had returned to the Union. After hosting a New Year's Day reception at the White House, Lincoln signed the final proclamation as an "act of justice" as well as "a fit and necessary war measure for suppressing said rebellion."

The Emancipation Proclamation exempted the border states, plus Tennessee and those portions of Louisiana and Virginia already under Union occupation because these areas were deemed not to be in rebellion, and Lincoln's constitutional authority for the proclamation derived from his power as commander in chief to confiscate enemy property. Although the proclamation did not immediately liberate slaves in areas under Confederate control, it essentially made the northern soldiers an army of liberation, however reluctant many of them were to risk their lives for that purpose. If the North won the war, slavery would die. But in the winter and spring of 1862–1863, victory was far from assured.

16-2 A Winter of Discontent

What were the sources of internal dissent and dissension in the Confederacy? In the Union?

Although Lee's retreat from Maryland suggested that the Confederate tide might be ebbing, the tide soon turned. The Union could never win the war simply by turning back Confederate invasions. Northern armies would have to invade the South, defeat its armies, and destroy its ability to fight.

Displeased by McClellan's "slows" after Antietam, Lincoln replaced him on November 7 with General Ambrose E. Burnside. An imposing man whose mutton-chop whiskers gave the anagram "sideburns" to the language, Burnside proposed to cross the Rappahannock River at Fredericksburg for a move on Richmond before bad weather forced both sides into winter quarters. Although Lee put his men into a strong defensive position on the heights behind Fredericksburg, Burnside nevertheless attacked on December 13. He was repulsed with heavy casualties that shook the morale of both the army and the public.

News from the western theater did little to dispel the gloom. The Confederates had fortified Vicksburg on bluffs commanding the Mississippi River. This bastion gave them control of an important stretch of the river and preserved transportation links between the states to the east and west. To sever those links, in November 1862 General Ulysses S. Grant launched a two-pronged drive against Vicksburg. With 40,000 men, he marched 50 miles southward from Memphis by land, while his principal subordinate William T. Sherman came down the river with 32,000 men accompanied by a gunboat fleet. But Confederate cavalry raids destroyed the railroads and supply depots in Grant's rear, forcing him to retreat to Memphis. Meanwhile, Sherman attacked the Confederates at Chickasaw Bluffs in December, with no more success than Burnside had enjoyed at Fredericksburg.

Union forces under William S. Rosecrans did score a victory by driving the Confederates to retreat at the Battle of Stones River in Tennessee, but elsewhere matters went from bad to worse. Renewing the campaign against Vicksburg, Grant bogged down in the swamps and rivers that protected that Confederate bastion on three sides. Only on the east, away from the river, did he find high ground suitable for an assault on Vicksburg's defenses. Grant's problem was to get his army across the Mississippi to that high ground. For three months, he floundered in the Mississippi-Yazoo bottomlands, while disease and exposure depleted his troops. False rumors of excessive drinking that had dogged Grant for years broke out anew, but Lincoln resisted pressures to remove him from command. "What I want," Lincoln said, "is generals who will fight battles and win victories. Grant has done this, and I propose to stand by him."

16-2a *The Rise of the Copperheads*

During the winter of 1863, the Copperhead faction of the Democratic Party found a ready audience for its message that the war was a failure and should be abandoned. Ohio congressman Clement L. Vallandigham, who planned to run for governor, asked northern audiences what this "wicked" war had accomplished: "Let the dead at Fredericksburg and Vicksburg answer." The Confederacy could never be conquered; the only trophies of the war were "debt, defeat, sepulchres." The solution was to "stop the fighting. Make an armistice. Withdraw your army from the seceded states." Above all, give up the unconstitutional effort to abolish slavery.

Vallandigham and other Copperhead spokesmen had a powerful effect on northern morale. Alarmed by a wave of desertions, the army commander in Ohio had Vallandigham arrested in May 1863. A military court convicted him of treason for aiding and abetting the enemy. The court's action raised serious questions of civil liberties. Was the conviction a violation of Vallandigham's First Amendment right of free speech? Could a military court try a civilian under **martial law** in a state such as Ohio where civil courts were functioning?

Lincoln was embarrassed by the swift arrest and trial of Vallandigham, which he learned about from the newspapers. To keep Vallandigham from becoming a martyr, Lincoln commuted his sentence from imprisonment to banishment—to the Confederacy! On May 15, Union cavalry escorted Vallandigham under a flag of truce to Confederate lines in Tennessee, where the southerners reluctantly accepted their uninvited guest. He soon escaped to Canada on a blockade runner. There, from exile, Vallandigham conducted his campaign for governor of Ohio—an election he lost in October 1863, after the military fortunes of the Union had improved.

16-2b *Economic Problems in the South*

Southerners were buoyed by their military success but were suffering from food shortages and hyperinflation. The tightening Union blockade, the weaknesses and imbalances of the Confederate economy, the escape of slaves to Union lines, and enemy occupation of some of the South's prime agricultural areas made it increasingly difficult to produce both guns and butter. Despite the conversion of hundreds of thousands of acres from cotton to food production, the deterioration of southern railroads and the priority given to army shipments made food scarce in some areas. Prices rose

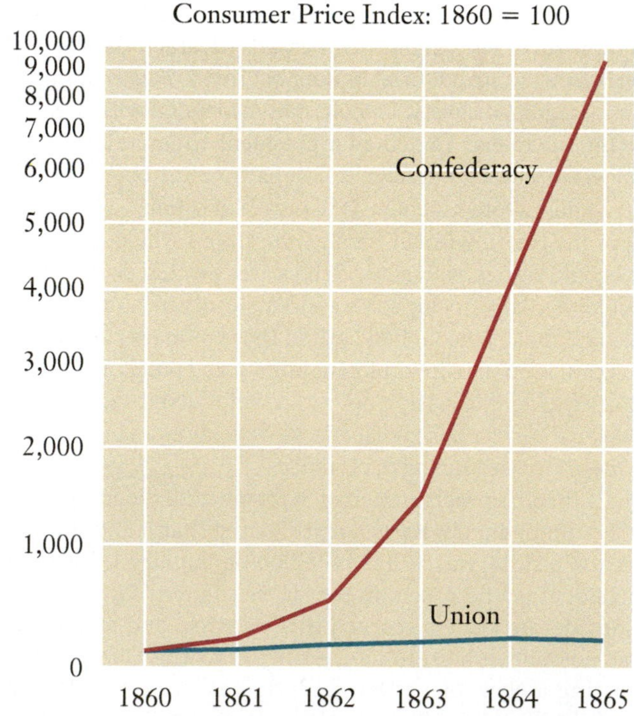

Figure 16.1 **Wartime Inflation in the Confederacy and the Union**

much faster than wages (see Figure 16.1). Even the middle class suffered, especially in Richmond, whose population had more than doubled since 1861. "The shadow of the gaunt form of famine is upon us," wrote a war department clerk in March 1863.

Poor people were worse off, especially the wives and children of nonslaveholders away in the army. By spring 1863, food supplies were virtually gone. Some women took matters into their own hands. Denouncing "speculators" who allegedly hoarded goods to drive up prices, they marched to stores, asked the price of bacon or cornmeal or salt, denounced such "extortion," and took what they wanted without paying. On April 2, 1863, a crowd of more than 1,000 women and boys looted several shops in Richmond before the militia forced them to disperse. The Confederate government subsequently released some emergency food stocks to civilians, and state and county governments aided the families of soldiers. Better crops in 1863 helped alleviate the worst shortages, but serious problems persisted.

Library of Congress Prints and Photographs Division [LC-USZ62-42028]

16.5 **The Richmond Bread Riot** Illustrating the economic problems of the Confederacy and the suffering of poor civilians in overcrowded cities, the bread riot in Richmond involved 1,000 women and boys who broke into shops to take food and other goods on April 2, 1863. This image from a popular northern illustrated newspaper, *Frank Leslie's Illustrated Weekly*, depicted the plight of Confederate civilians and undercut popular notions of genteel Southern womanhood propaganda.

Q *How does this illustration work as northern propaganda?*

16-2c *The Wartime Draft and Class Tensions*

In both South and North, the draft intensified social unrest and turned it in the direction of class conflict. In April 1862, the Confederacy enacted a draft that made all white men (with certain occupational exemptions) ages 18 to 35 liable to conscription. A drafted man could hire a substitute, but the price of substitutes soon rose beyond the means of the average southern farmer or worker, giving rise to the bitter cry that it was "a rich man's war and a poor man's fight."

The cry grew louder in October 1862 when the Confederate Congress raised the draft age to 45 and added a clause exempting one white man from the draft on every plantation with 20 or more slaves. The purpose of this "overseer exemption" was to keep up production and prevent slave uprisings. It had been prompted by the complaints of planters' wives, who had been left alone to manage the slaves after the departure of husbands, sons, and overseers for the army. The so-called **Twenty Negro Law** was regarded as blatant discrimination by nonslaveholding farm families whose men were also at the front. The law provoked widespread draft dodging and desertions.

Similar discontent greeted the enactment of a conscription law in the North. In summer 1863, some 30,000 Union soldiers would be leaving military service, along with 80,000 of the nine-month militia called into service the preceding autumn. To meet the looming shortfall of men, Congress decreed in March that all male citizens ages 20 to 45 must enroll for the draft. Not all of them would necessarily be called (administrative policy exempted married men over 35), but all would be liable.

The law was intended more to encourage volunteers to come forward than to draft men directly. The War Department set a quota for every congressional district and allowed 50 days for the quota to be met with volunteers before resorting to a draft lottery. Some districts avoided drafting anyone by offering large bounties to volunteers. The bounty system produced glaring abuses, including **bounty jumpers** who enlisted and then deserted as soon as they got their money—often to enlist again under another name somewhere else.

The drafting process was also open to abuse. Like the Confederate law, the Union law permitted hiring substitutes. To keep the price from skyrocketing as it had in the Confederacy, the law allowed a drafted man the alternative of paying a **commutation fee** of $300 that exempted him from the current draft call (but not necessarily from the next one). That provision raised the cry of "rich man's war, poor man's fight" in the North as well. The Democratic Party nurtured this sense of class resentment, and racism intensified it. Democratic newspapers told white workers, especially the large Irish American population, that the draft would force them to fight a war to free the slaves, who would then come north to take their jobs. This volatile issue sparked widespread violence when the northern draft got

THE RIOTS IN NEW YORK: DESTRUCTION OF THE COLOURED ORPHAN ASYLUM.

16.6 **The Antidraft Riots** The worst urban violence in American history occurred July 13–16, 1863, in New York City. Thousands of rioters attacked draft offices, homes, businesses, and individuals. Black residents of the city were among the mob's victims because they symbolized labor competition to Irish Americans, who constituted most of the rioters and who believed they would be drafted to fight a war to free the slaves. This illustration shows the burning of the Colored Orphan Asylum, a home for black orphans. More than 100 people were killed during those four days, most of them rioters shot down by police and soldiers.

Q *How does this anti-Irish illustration portray rioters in a negative light?*

under way in summer 1863. The worst riot occurred in July in New York City, where huge mobs consisting mostly of Irish Americans demolished draft offices, lynched several blacks, and destroyed huge areas of the city in four days of looting and burning.

16-2d *A Poor Man's Fight?*

The grievance that it was a rich man's war and a poor man's fight was more apparent than real. Property, excise, and income taxes to sustain the war bore proportionately more heavily on the wealthy than on the poor. In the South, wealthy property owners suffered greater damage and confiscation losses than did nonslaveholders. The war liberated 4 million slaves, the poorest class in America. Both the Union and Confederate armies fielded men from all strata of society in proportion to their percentage of the population. If anything, among those who volunteered in 1861 and 1862, the planter class was overrepresented in the Confederate army and the middle class in the Union forces because those privileged groups believed they had more at stake in the war and joined up in larger numbers during the early months of enthusiasm. Those volunteers—especially the officers—suffered the highest percentage of combat casualties.

Nor did conscription fall much more heavily on the poor than on the rich. Those who escaped the draft by decamping to the woods, the territories, or Canada were mostly poor. The Confederacy abolished substitution in December 1863 and made men who had previously sent substitutes liable to the draft. In the North, several city councils, political machines, and businesses contributed funds to pay the commutation fees of drafted men who were too poor to pay out of their own pockets. In the end, it was neither a rich man's war nor a poor man's fight. It was an American war.

16-3 Blueprint for Modern America

Q *How did wartime legislation transform American society? How did women contribute to the war effort?*

The Thirty-seventh Congress (1861–1863)—the Congress that enacted conscription, passed measures for confiscation and emancipation, and created the greenbacks and the national banking system (see Chapter 15)—also enacted three laws that, together with the war legislation, provided what one historian has called "a blueprint for modern America": the Homestead Act, the Morrill Land-Grant College Act, and the Pacific Railroad Act. For several years before the war, Republicans and some northern Democrats had tried to pass these laws to provide social benefits and to promote economic growth, only to see them defeated by southern opposition or by President Buchanan's veto. The secession of southern states, ironically, enabled Congress to pass all three laws in 1862.

The Homestead Act granted 160 acres of land to a farmer virtually free after he had lived on the land for five years and had made improvements on it. The Morrill Land-Grant College Act gave each state thousands of acres to fund the establishment of colleges to teach "agricultural and mechanical arts." The Pacific Railroad Act granted land and loans to railroad companies to spur the building of a transcontinental railroad from Omaha to Sacramento. Despite waste, corruption, and exploitation of the original Indian owners of this land, these laws helped farmers settle some of the most fertile land in the world, studded the land with state colleges, and spanned it with steel rails in a manner that altered the landscape of the western half of the country.

16-3a *Women and the War*

The war advanced many other social changes, particularly with respect to women. In factories and on farms, women replaced men who had gone off to war. Explosions in ordnance plants and arsenals killed at least 100 women, who were as surely war casualties as men killed in battle. The war accelerated the entry of women into the teaching profession, a trend that had already begun in the Northeast and now spread to other parts of the country. It also brought significant numbers of women into the civil service. During the 1850s, a few women had worked briefly in the U.S. Patent Office (including Clara Barton, who became a famous wartime nurse and founded the American Red Cross). The huge expansion of government bureaucracies after 1861 and the departure of male clerks to the army provided openings that were filled partly by women. After the war, the private sector began hiring women as clerks, bookkeepers, "typewriters" (the machine was invented in the 1870s), and telephone operators (the telephone was another postwar invention).

Library of Congress, Prints and Photographs Division

16.7 **Union Army Hospital** The Armory Square military hospital in Washington, with its clean, cheerful wards apparently decorated for the Christmas holidays, showed Union medical care at its best.

16-3b *Women as Aid Workers and Nurses*

Women's most visible impact was in the field of medicine. The outbreak of war prompted the organization of soldiers' aid societies, hospital societies, and other voluntary associations in which women played a leading role. Their most important function was to help—and sometimes to prod—the medical branches of the Union and Confederate armies to provide more efficient, humane care for sick and wounded soldiers. Dr. Elizabeth Blackwell, the first American woman to earn an MD (1849), organized a meeting of 3,000 women in New York City on April 29, 1861. They put together the Women's Central Association for Relief, which became the nucleus for the most powerful voluntary association of the war, the U.S. Sanitary Commission.

Eventually embracing 7,000 local auxiliaries, the Sanitary Commission was an essential adjunct of the Union army's medical bureau. Most of its local volunteers were women, as were most of the nurses it provided to army hospitals. Nursing was not a new profession for women, but it had lacked respect as a wartime profession. The fame won by Florence Nightingale of Britain during the Crimean War a half-dozen years earlier had begun to change that perception. As thousands of middle- and even upper-class women volunteers flocked to army hospitals, nursing began its transformation from a menial occupation to a respected profession.

The nurses had to overcome the deeply ingrained suspicions of army surgeons and the opposition of husbands and fathers who shared the cultural sentiment that the shocking, embarrassingly physical atmosphere of an army hospital was no place for a respectable woman. Many thousands of women went to work, winning grudging and then enthusiastic admiration.

16.8a (left) and 16.8b (right) **Female Spies and Soldiers** In addition to working in war industries and serving as army nurses, some women pursued traditionally male wartime careers as spies and soldiers. One of the most famous Confederate spies was Rose O'Neal Greenhow, a Washington widow and socialite who fed information to officials in Richmond. Federal officers arrested her in August 1861 and deported her to Richmond in spring 1862. She was photographed (left) with her daughter in the Old Capitol prison in Washington, D.C., while awaiting trial. In October 1864, she drowned in a lifeboat off Wilmington, North Carolina, after a blockade runner carrying her back from a European mission was run aground by a Union warship. The second photograph (right) shows a Union soldier who enlisted in the 95th Illinois Infantry under the name of Albert Cashier and fought through the war. A farm accident in 1911 revealed Albert Cashier to be a woman, whose real name was Jennie Hodgers. Most of the other estimated 400 women who evaded the superficial physical exams and passed as men to enlist in the Union and Confederate armies were more quickly discovered and discharged. A few, however, served long enough to be killed in action.

16-4 The Confederate Tide Crests and Recedes

Q *How did the Union army achieve a victory at Gettysburg?*

The Army of Northern Virginia and the Army of the Potomac spent the winter of 1862–1863 on opposite banks of the Rappahannock River. With the coming of spring, Union commander Joe Hooker resumed the offensive with hopes of redeeming the December disaster at Fredericksburg. On April 30, instead of charging straight across the river, Hooker crossed his men several miles upriver and came in on Lee's rear. Lee quickly faced most of his troops about and confronted the enemy in dense woods, known locally as the Wilderness, near the crossroads mansion of Chancellorsville. Nonplussed, Hooker lost the initiative.

16-4a *The Battle of Chancellorsville*

Even though Union forces outnumbered the Confederates by almost two to one, Lee boldly went over to the offensive. On May 2, Stonewall Jackson led 28,000 men on a stealthy march through the woods to attack the Union right flank late in the afternoon (see Map 16.2). The surprise was complete. Jackson's assault crumpled the Union flank as the sun set. Jackson then rode out to scout the terrain for a moonlight attack but was wounded on his return by jittery Confederates who mistook him and his staff for Union cavalry. Nevertheless, Lee resumed the attack the next day. In three more days of fighting that caused 12,800 Confederate and 16,800 Union casualties (the largest number for a single battle in the war so far), Lee drove the Union troops back across the Rappahannock. It was a brilliant victory.

In the North, the gloom grew deeper. Southern elation, however, was tempered by grief at the death on May 10 of Jackson, who had contracted pneumonia after amputation of his arm. Nevertheless, Lee decided to parlay his tactical victory at Chancellorsville into a strategic offensive by again invading the North. A victory on Union soil would convince northerners and foreigners alike that the Confederacy was invincible. As his army moved north in June 1863, Lee was confident of success. "There never were such men in an army before," he wrote of his troops. "They will go anywhere and do anything if properly led."

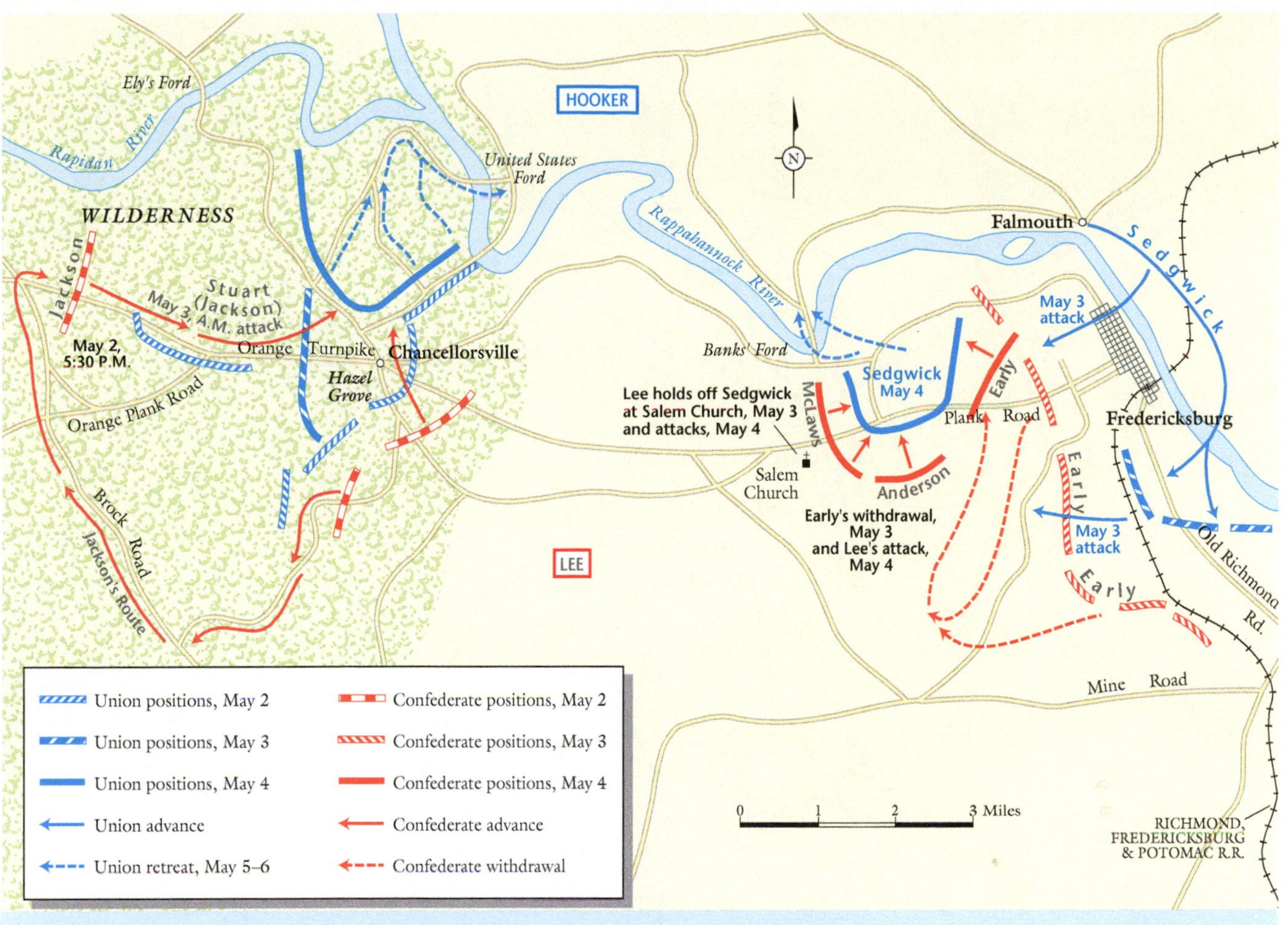

▲ **MAP 16.2 Battle of Chancellorsville, May 2–6, 1863** This map demonstrates the advantage of holding "interior lines," which enabled General Lee to shift troops back and forth to and from the Chancellorsville and Fredericksburg fronts over the course of three days while the two parts of the Union army remained separated.

Q *What other reasons for Confederate victory are visible on this map?*

Q *What effect did victory at Chancellorsville have on Confederate strategy?*

16-4b *The Gettysburg Campaign*

At first, all went well. The Confederates brushed aside or captured Union forces in the northern Shenandoah Valley and in Pennsylvania. Stuart's cavalry threw a scare into Washington by raiding behind Union lines into Maryland and Pennsylvania. That very success led to trouble. With Stuart's cavalry separated from the rest of the army, Lee lost the vital intelligence that the cavalry garnered as the army's eyes. By June 28, several detachments of Lee's forces were scattered about Pennsylvania, far from their base and vulnerable.

At this point, Lee learned that the Army of the Potomac was moving toward him, now under the command of George Gordon Meade. Lee immediately ordered his own army to reassemble in the vicinity of Gettysburg, an agricultural and college town at the hub of a dozen roads leading in from all directions. There, on the morning of July 1, the vanguard of the two armies met in a clash that grew into the greatest battle in American history (see Map 16.3).

As the fighting spread west and north of town, couriers pounded up the roads to summon reinforcements to both sides. The Confederates fielded more men and broke the Union lines late that afternoon, driving the survivors to a defensive position on Cemetery Hill south of town. General Richard Ewell, Jackson's successor as commander of the Confederate Second Corps, judging this position too strong to take with his own troops, chose not to press the attack as the sun went down on what he presumed would be another Confederate victory.

When the sun rose the next morning, however, the reinforced Union army was holding a superb defensive position from Culp's Hill and Cemetery Hill south to Little Round Top. Lee's principal subordinate, First Corps commander James Longstreet, advised against attack, urging instead a maneuver to the south, toward Washington, to force the Federals to attack Lee in a strong defensive position. But Lee believed his army invincible. After its victory on July 1, a move to the south might look like a retreat. Pointing to the Union lines, he said: "The enemy is there, and I am going to attack him there." Longstreet reluctantly led the attack on the Union left. Once committed, his men fought with fury. The Union troops fought back with equal fury. As the afternoon passed, peaceful areas

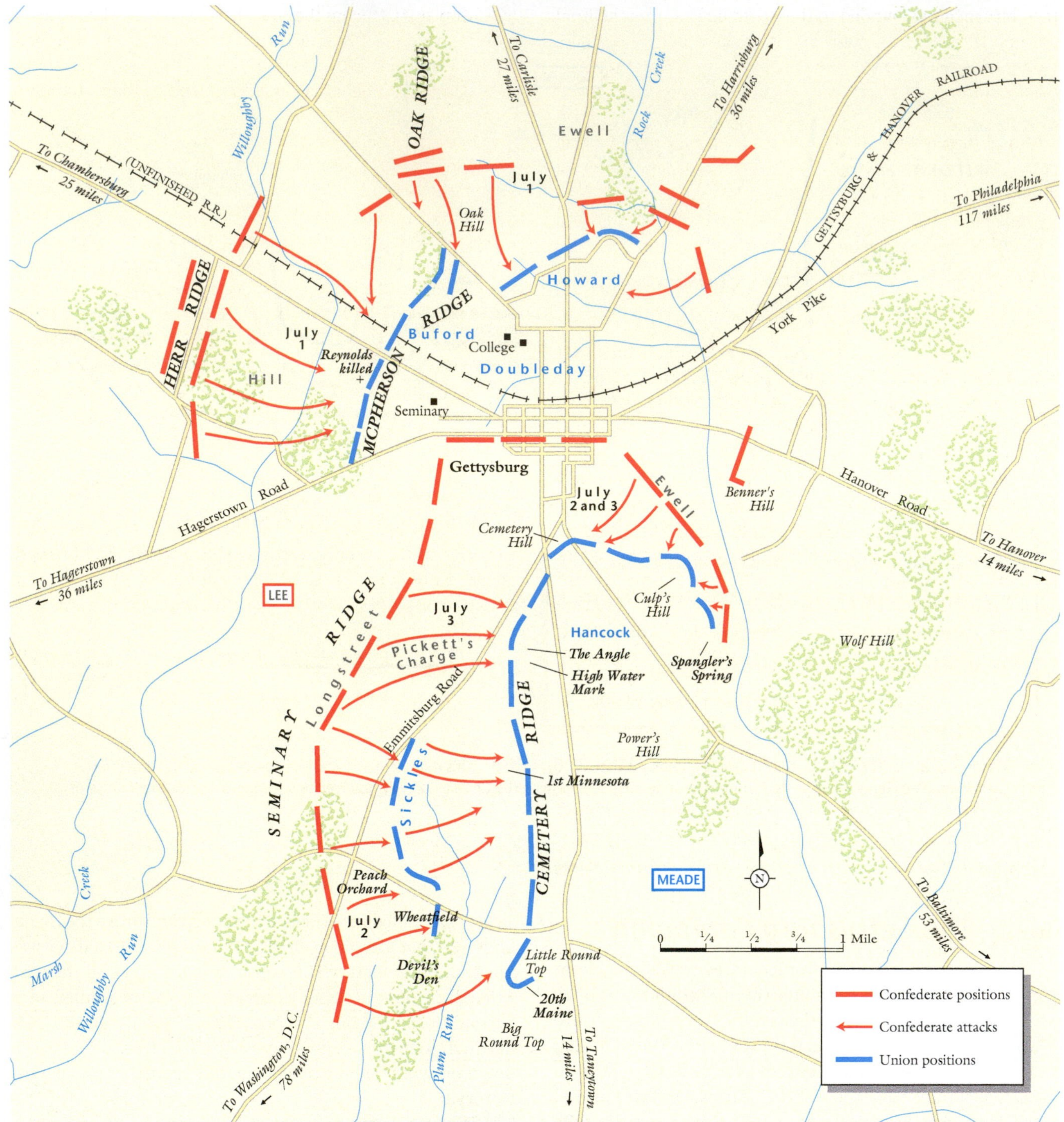

▲ **MAP 16.3 Battle of Gettysburg, July 1–3, 1863** On July 2 and 3, the Union army had the advantage of interior lines at Gettysburg, which enabled General Meade to shift reinforcements from his right on Culp's Hill to his left near Little Round Top over a much shorter distance than Confederate reinforcements from one flank to the other would have to travel.

Q *What are the main reasons for Union victory at Gettysburg?*

Q *How important was Union victory at Gettysburg to the outcome of the war?*

with names like Peach Orchard, Wheat Field, Devil's Den, and Little Round Top were turned into killing fields. By the end of the day, Confederate forces had made small gains at great cost, but the main Union line had held firm.

Lee was not yet ready to yield the offensive. Having attacked both Union flanks, he thought the center might be weak. On July 3, he ordered a frontal attack on Cemetery Ridge, led by a fresh division under George Pickett. After a two-hour artillery barrage, Pickett's 5,000 men and 8,000 additional troops moved forward on that sultry afternoon in a picture-book assault that forms our most enduring image of the Civil War. "Pickett's Charge" was shot to pieces; scarcely half of the men returned unwounded to their own lines. It was the final act in a three-day drama that left some 50,000 men killed, wounded, or captured: 23,000 Federals and 25,000 to 28,000 Confederates.

Lee limped back to Virginia, pursued by the Union troops. Lincoln was unhappy with Meade for not cutting off the Confederate retreat. Nevertheless, Gettysburg was a great northern victory, and it came at the same time as other important Union successes in Mississippi, Louisiana, and Tennessee.

16-4c *The Vicksburg Campaign*

In mid-April, Grant had begun a move that would put Vicksburg in a vise. The Union ironclad fleet ran downriver past the big guns at Vicksburg with little damage. Grant's troops marched down the Mississippi's west bank and ferried across the river 40 miles south of Vicksburg.

There they kept the Confederate defenders off balance by striking east toward Jackson instead of marching north to Vicksburg. Grant's purpose was to scatter the Confederate forces in central Mississippi and to destroy the rail network so that his rear would be secure when he turned toward Vicksburg. It was a brilliant strategy, flawlessly executed (see Map 16.4). During the first three weeks of May, Grant's troops marched 180 miles, won five battles, and trapped 32,000 Confederate troops and 3,000 civilians in Vicksburg between the Union army on land and the Union gunboats on the river.

But the Confederate army was still full of fight. Confederate soldiers threw back Union assaults against the Vicksburg trenches on May 19 and 22. Grant then settled down for a siege. Running out of supplies, the Vicksburg garrison surrendered on July 4. On July 9, the Confederate garrison at Port Hudson, 200 river miles south of Vicksburg, surrendered to a besieging Union army. Northern forces now controlled the entire length of the Mississippi River. "The Father of Waters again goes unvexed to the sea," said Lincoln. The Confederacy had been torn in two, and Lincoln knew who deserved the credit. "Grant is my man," he said, "and I am his the rest of the war."

16-4d *Chickamauga and Chattanooga*

Northerners had scarcely finished celebrating the twin victories of Gettysburg and Vicksburg when they learned of an important—and almost bloodless—triumph in Tennessee (see Map 16.5). On June 24, Union commander

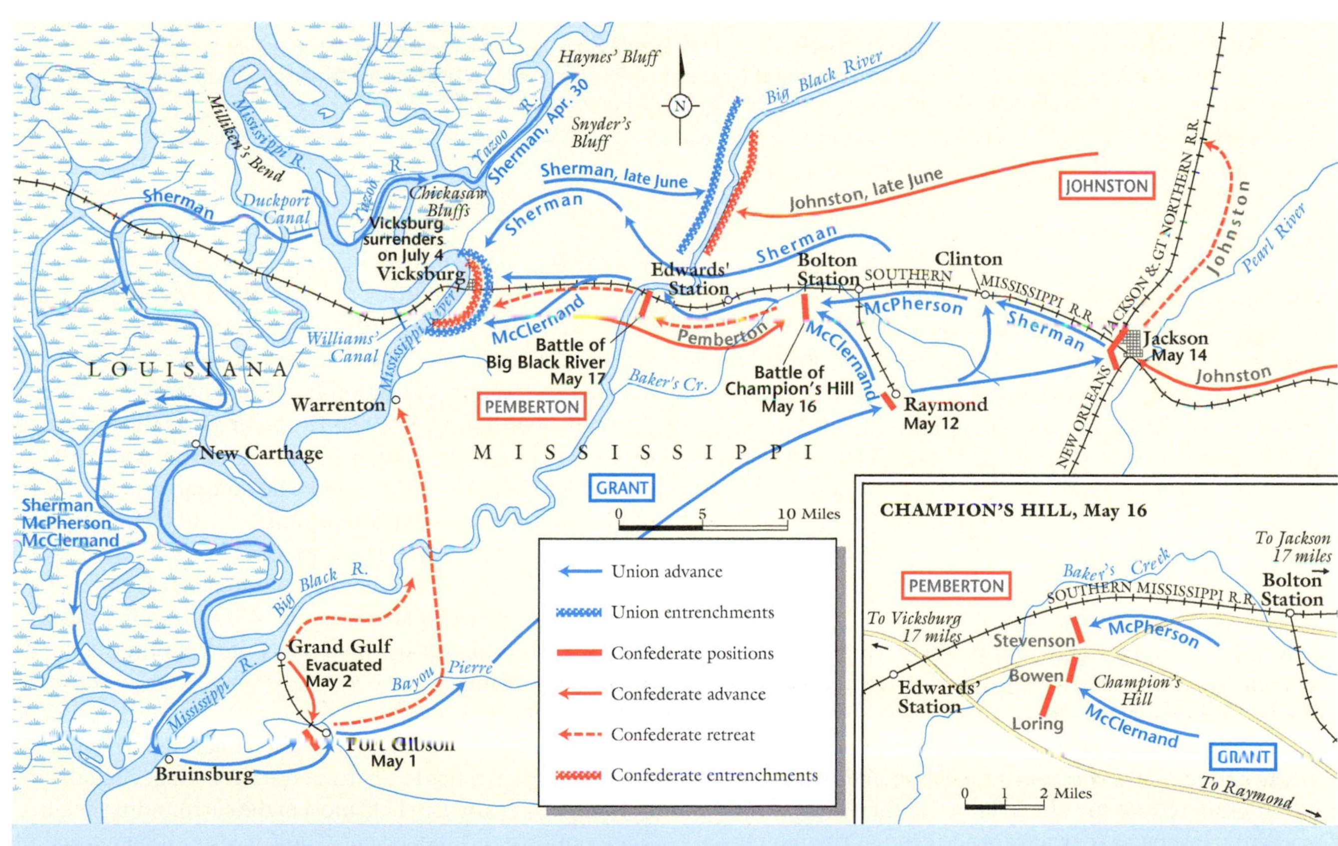

▲ **MAP 16.4 Vicksburg Campaign, April–July 1863** This map illustrates Grant's brilliant orchestration of the campaign that involved Sherman's feint at Haynes' Bluff (top of map) on April 30 while the rest of the Union forces crossed at Bruinsburg (bottom of map) and then cleared Confederate resistance out of the way eastward to Jackson before turning west to invade Vicksburg.

Q *What were Grant's chief strengths as a general?*

Q *How would you compare Lee and Grant as generals?*

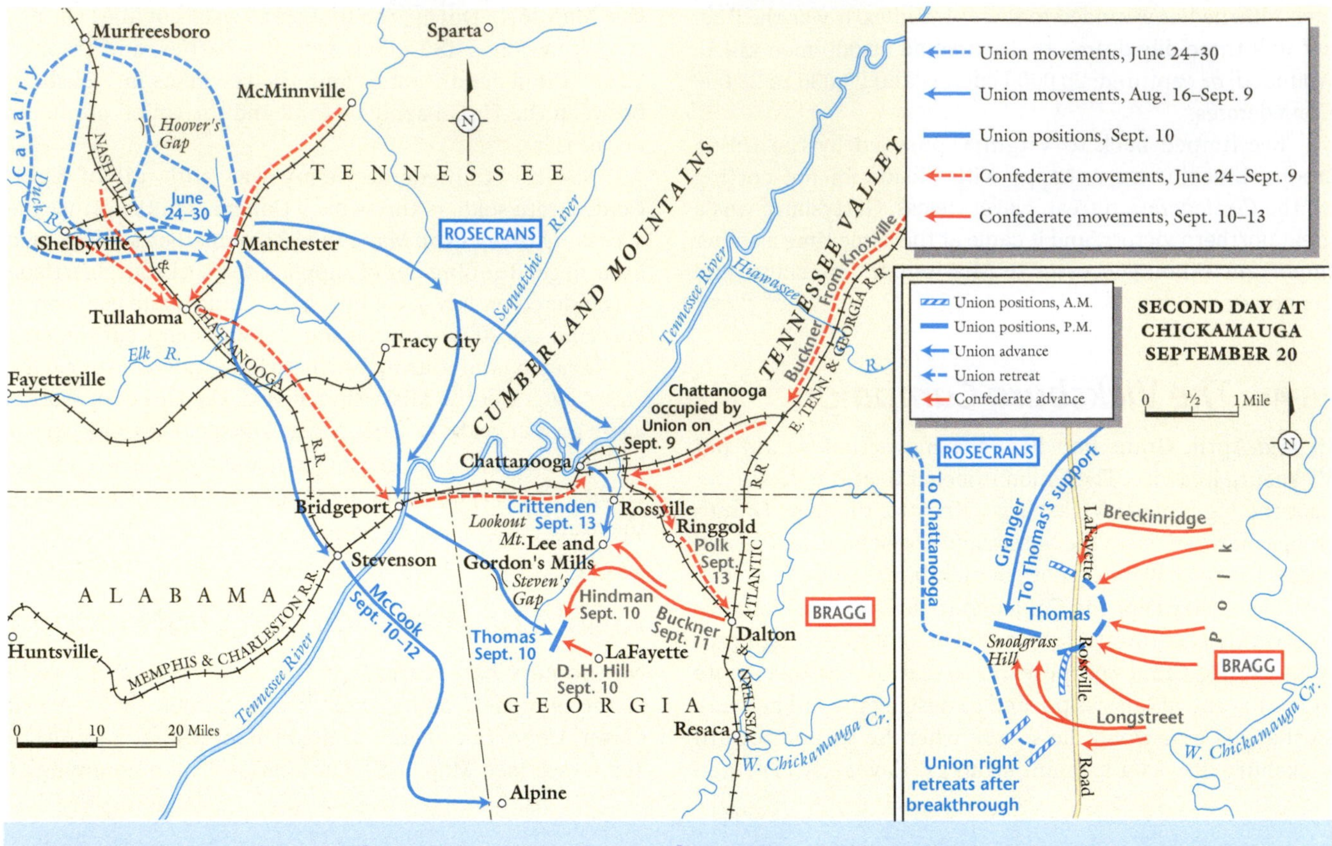

▲ MAP 16.5 Road to Chickamauga, June–September 1863 From Murfreesboro to Chattanooga, Rosecrans's campaign of maneuver on multiple fronts forced Bragg's Army of Tennessee all the way south into Georgia in a campaign with minimal casualties before Bragg counterattacked at Chickamauga.

Q *What effect did Chickamauga and Chattanooga have on Southern morale?*

Q *How did modes of fighting battles change over the course of the war?*

William S. Rosecrans assaulted the Confederate defenses in the Cumberland foothills of east-central Tennessee. In the first week of July, the Confederates retreated all the way to Chattanooga. After a pause to resupply, Rosecrans's army advanced again in August, this time in tandem with a smaller Union army in eastern Tennessee. Again the outnumbered Confederates fell back, evacuating Knoxville on September 2 and Chattanooga on September 9. This action severed the South's only direct east-west rail link. Having sliced the Confederacy in half with the capture of Vicksburg and Port Hudson, Union forces now stood poised for a campaign into Georgia that threatened to slice it into three parts. For the Confederacy, it was a stunning reversal of the situation only four months earlier, after Chancellorsville, when the Union cause had appeared hopeless.

Confederate general Braxton Bragg reached into his bag of tricks and sent fake deserters into Union lines with tales of a Confederate retreat toward Atlanta. He then laid a trap for Rosecrans's troops as they advanced through the mountain passes south of Chattanooga. To help him spring it, Jefferson Davis approved the detachment of Longstreet with two divisions from Lee's army to reinforce Bragg. On September 19, the Confederates turned and counterattacked Rosecrans's now outnumbered army in the valley of Chickamauga Creek.

On that day and the next, in ferocious fighting that produced more casualties (35,000) than any other single battle save Gettysburg, the Confederates finally scored a victory. On September 20, after a confusion of orders left a division-size gap in the Union line, Longstreet's men broke through, sending part of the Union army reeling back to Chattanooga. Only a firm stand by corps commander George H. Thomas—a Virginian who had remained loyal to the Union—prevented a Union rout. For this feat, Thomas earned the nickname "Rock of Chickamauga." Lincoln subsequently appointed Thomas commander of the Army of the Cumberland to replace Rosecrans, who was, in Lincoln's words, "confused and stunned like a duck hit on the head" after Chickamauga.

Lincoln also sent two army corps from Virginia under Hooker and two from Vicksburg under Sherman to reinforce Thomas, whose troops in Chattanooga were under virtual siege by Bragg's forces, which held most of the surrounding heights. More important, Lincoln put Grant in overall command of the beefed-up Union forces there. When Grant arrived in late October, he welded the various northern units into a new army and opened a new supply line into Chattanooga. On November 24, Hooker's troops drove Confederate besiegers off massive Lookout Mountain.

The next day, an assault on Bragg's main line at Missionary Ridge east of Chattanooga won a smashing success against seemingly greater odds than Pickett had faced at Gettysburg. The Union troops that had been routed at Chickamauga two months earlier redeemed themselves by driving the Confederates off Missionary Ridge and 20 miles south into Georgia.

These battles climaxed a string of Union victories in the second half of 1863. The southern diarist Mary Boykin Chesnut found "gloom and unspoken despondency hang[ing] like a pall everywhere." Jefferson Davis removed the discredited Bragg from command of the Army of Tennessee and reluctantly replaced him with Joseph E. Johnston, in whom Davis had little confidence. Lincoln summoned Grant to Washington and appointed him general-in-chief of all Union armies in March 1864, signifying a relentless fight to the finish.

16-5 Black Men in Blue

Q *What contribution did African Americans make to the Union war effort?*

The events of the second half of 1863 also confirmed emancipation as a Union war aim. Northerners had not greeted the Emancipation Proclamation with great enthusiasm. Democrats and border-state Unionists continued to denounce it, and many Union soldiers resented the idea that they would now be risking their lives for black freedom. The Democratic Party had hoped to capitalize on this opposition, and on Union military failures, to win important off-year elections. Northern military victories knocked one prop out from under the Democratic platform, and the performance of black soldiers fighting for the Union knocked out another.

The enlistment of black soldiers was a logical corollary of emancipation. Proposals to recruit black soldiers, Democrats said, were part of a Republican plot to establish "the equality of the black and white races." In a way, that charge was correct. One consequence of black men fighting for the Union would be to advance the black race a long way toward equal rights. "Once let the black man get upon his person the brass letters, U.S.," said Frederick Douglass, "and a musket on his shoulder and bullets in his pocket, and there is no power on earth which can deny that he has earned the right to citizenship."

But it was pragmatism more than principle that pushed the North toward black recruitment. One purpose of emancipation was to deprive the Confederacy of black laborers and to use them for the Union. Putting some of those former laborers in uniform was a compelling idea, especially as white enlistments lagged and the North had to enact conscription in 1863. Some Union commanders in occupied portions of Louisiana, South Carolina, and Missouri began to organize black regiments in 1862. The Emancipation Proclamation legitimized this policy with its proposal to enroll able-bodied male contrabands in new black regiments, although these units would serve as labor battalions, supply troops, and garrison forces rather than as combat troops. They would be paid less than white soldiers, and their officers would be white.

16-5a *Black Soldiers in Combat*

Continuing pressure from abolitionists, as well as military necessity, partly eroded this discrimination. Congress enacted equal pay in 1864. Officers worked for better treatment of their men. Above all, the regiments lobbied for the right to fight as combat soldiers. Even some previously hostile white soldiers came around to the notion that black men might just as well stop enemy bullets as white men. In May and June 1863, black regiments in Louisiana fought well in an assault on Port Hudson and in defense of a Union outpost at Milliken's Bend, near Vicksburg. "The bravery of the blacks in the battle of Milliken's Bend completely revolutionized the sentiment of the army with regard to the employment of negro troops," wrote the assistant secretary of war, who had been on the spot with Grant's army.

Even more significant was the action of the 54th Massachusetts Infantry, the first black regiment raised mainly in the North. Its officers, headed by Colonel Robert Gould Shaw, came from prominent New England antislavery families. Two sons of Frederick Douglass were in the regiment—one of them as sergeant major. Shaw worked hard to win the right for the regiment to fight. On July 18, 1863, he succeeded: The 54th was assigned to lead an assault on Fort Wagner, part of the network of Confederate defenses protecting Charleston. Although the attack failed, the 54th fought courageously, suffering 50 percent casualties, including Colonel Shaw, who was killed.

16.9 **Part of Company E, Fourth U.S. Colored Infantry**
Organized in July 1863, most of the men were former slaves from North Carolina. The Fourth fought in several actions on the Petersburg and Richmond fronts in 1864, helping to capture part of the Petersburg defenses on June 15. Of the 166 black regiments in the Union army, the Fourth suffered the fourth-largest number of combat deaths.

The battle took place just after white mobs of draft rioters in New York had lynched blacks. Abolitionist and Republican commentators drew the moral: Black men who fought for the Union deserved more respect than white men who rioted against it. Lincoln made this point eloquently in a widely published letter to a political meeting in August 1863. When final victory was achieved, he wrote, "there will be some black men who can remember that, with silent tongue, and clenched teeth, and steady eye, and well-poised bayonet, they have helped mankind on to this great consummation; while, I fear, there will be some white ones, unable to forget that, with malignant heart, and deceitful speech, they have strove to hinder it."

16-5b *Emancipation Confirmed*

Lincoln's letter set the tone for Republican campaigns in state elections that fall. The party swept them all, including Ohio, where they buried Vallandigham under a 100,000-vote margin swelled by the soldier vote, which went 94 percent for his opponent. In effect, the elections were a powerful endorsement of the administration's emancipation policy. If the Emancipation Proclamation had been submitted to a referendum a year earlier, observed a newspaper editor in November 1863, "the voice of a majority would have been against it. And yet not a year has passed before it is approved by an overwhelming majority."

Emancipation would not be assured of survival until it had been christened by the Constitution. On April 8, 1864, the Senate passed the Thirteenth Amendment to abolish slavery, but Democrats in the House blocked the required two-thirds majority there. Not until after Lincoln's reelection in 1864 would the House pass the amendment, which became part of the Constitution on December 6, 1865. In the end, though, the fate of slavery depended on the outcome of the war. And despite Confederate defeats in 1863, that outcome was by no means certain. Some of the heaviest fighting lay ahead.

16-6 The Year of Decision

Q *Why did Lincoln think he would not win reelection in 1864?*

Many southerners succumbed to defeatism in the winter of 1863–1864. "I have never actually despaired of the cause," wrote a Confederate War Department official in November, but "steadfastness is yielding to a sense of hopelessness." Desertions from Confederate armies increased. Inflation galloped out of control. According to a Richmond diarist, a merchant told a poor woman in October 1863 that the price of a barrel of flour was $70: "'My God!' exclaimed she, 'how can I pay such prices? I have seven children; what shall I do?' 'I don't know, madam,' said he, coolly, 'unless you eat your children.'"

The Davis administration, like the Lincoln administration a year earlier, had to face congressional elections during a time of public discontent, for the Confederate constitution mandated such elections in odd-numbered years. Political parties had ceased to exist in the Confederacy after Democrats and former Whigs had tacitly declared a truce in 1861 to form a united front for the war effort. Many congressmen had been elected without opposition in 1861. By 1863, however, significant hostility to Davis had emerged. Although it was not channeled through any organized party, it took on partisan trappings, as an inchoate anti-Davis faction surfaced in the Confederate Congress and in the election campaign of 1863.

Some anti-administration candidates ran on a quasi-peace platform (analogous to that of the Copperheads in the North) that called for an armistice and peace negotiations. The movement left unresolved the terms of such negotiations—reunion or independence—but any peace overture from a position of weakness was tantamount to conceding defeat. The peace movement was especially strong in North Carolina, where for a time it appeared that the next governor would be elected on a peace platform (in the end, the "peace candidate" was defeated). Still, anti-administration candidates made significant gains in the 1863 Confederate elections, although they fell about 15 seats short of a majority in the House and two seats short in the Senate.

16-6a *Out of the Wilderness*

Shortages, inflation, political discontent, military defeat, high casualties, and the loss of thousands of slaves bent but did not break the southern spirit. As spring 1864 came on, a renewed determination infused both home front and battlefront. The Confederate armies no longer had the strength to invade the North or to win the war with a knockout blow, but they could still fight a war of attrition. If they could hold out long enough and inflict enough casualties on the Union armies, they might weaken the northern will to continue fighting.

Northerners were vulnerable to this strategy. Military success in 1863 had created a mood of confidence, and people expected a quick, decisive victory in 1864. The mood grew with Grant's appointment as general-in-chief. When Grant decided to remain in Virginia with the Army of the Potomac and to leave Sherman in command of the Union forces in northern Georgia, northerners expected these two heavyweights to floor the Confederacy with a one-two punch. Lincoln was alarmed by this euphoria. "The people are too sanguine," he told a reporter. "They expect too much at once." Disappointment might trigger despair.

Lincoln was nearly proved right. Grant's strategic plan was elegant in its simplicity. While smaller Union armies in peripheral theaters carried out auxiliary campaigns, the two principal armies in Virginia and Georgia would attack the main Confederate forces under Lee and Johnston. Convinced that in years past Union armies in various theaters had "acted independently and without concert, like a balky team, no two ever pulling together," Grant ordered simultaneous offensives on all fronts, to prevent the Confederates from shifting reinforcements to one theater from another.

History Through Film Lincoln (2012)

Directed by Steven Spielberg.
Starring Daniel Day-Lewis (Abraham Lincoln), Sally Field (Mary Lincoln), David Strathairn (William H. Seward), Tommy Lee Jones (Thaddeus Stevens)

Despite its title, *Lincoln* is not a biopic, but instead tells the surprisingly gripping story of the passage of the 13th Amendment. In early 1865, as it becomes clear that the North will most likely win the Civil War in a matter of months rather than years, President Lincoln decides that he wants to make an all-out effort for passage of the 13th Amendment, in order to abolish slavery permanently from America. He meets resistance to this idea everywhere—especially from his own quarrelsome Cabinet. Why distract from the war effort? Why not wait until after the South sues for peace and the war ends? Why do this *now*? But Lincoln is clear: the Emancipation Proclamation, issued on January 1, 1863, is not enough to guarantee the *permanent* eradication of slavery. What if the next President simply overturns Lincoln's executive order for emancipation? Will slavery then return to America? No, the eradication of slavery must have a firm legal basis, Lincoln argues. It must be enshrined in the Constitution itself.

And thus begins a mad scramble to obtain enough votes in Congress to ensure the 13th Amendment's passage. Not every film can make an exciting cliffhanger out of a Congressional vote, but *Lincoln* manages this feat, in part due to the energetic direction of Steven Spielberg. In addition, the superb screenplay by the playwright Tony Kushner (*Angels in America*) brilliantly captures the horse-trading—and even corruption—involved in getting lawmakers to change their votes. Individual holdouts spring to vivid life on the screen, as they are personally cajoled and pressured by Lincoln and also by a cynical huckster hired for the task, played with gusto by a perfectly cast James Spader.

Along the way, we gain insights into the tensions in Lincoln's Cabinet, which he had composed as a "team of rivals." (The film is based in part on Doris Kearns Goodwin's excellent history *Team of Rivals: The Political Genius of Abraham Lincoln*.) We also follow the trajectory of the Radical Republican Thaddeus Stevens—played by Tommy Lee Jones—who in early 1865 would have preferred to fight for social as well as legal equality for African Americans, but is portrayed as reluctantly agreeing to postpone that larger fight out of political expediency.

Daniel Day-Lewis gives a brilliant performance, showcasing Lincoln's love of humor and off-color jokes; his canny political abilities despite his folksy style; his extraordinary intelligence, depth of knowledge, and eloquence; and his deep and abiding love of freedom and justice. The film is also good at depicting Lincoln's relationships with his family. His eldest son Robert is desperate to join the Army in the waning days of the war, chafing against his father's proscription against enlistment. The film captures both the tensions between father and son and Lincoln's tempestuous relationship with his wife Mary, played convincingly by Sally Field.

What are the faults with the film? Some viewers might object to its sentimental frame: near the opening, for instance, three earnest soldiers, fresh from the battlefield, recite the Gettysburg Address from memory to Lincoln. Is this believable for early 1865? Not really. But when the film closes with a retrospective scene of Lincoln delivering his great Second Inaugural Address, we are willing to grant the film's right to a few sentimental moments.

Critics have pointed out that the crucial story of black self-emancipation—the all-important actions of former slaves who liberated themselves from slavery by coming into Union lines, and thus *forced* the Union to deal with the issue of emancipation—receives no attention here. Obviously that important social reality deserves filmic treatment. *Lincoln* accomplishes something different: focused on the practice of politics in Washington, it ultimately makes the argument that in a democracy, we must embrace the legislative process—even if not perfect, even if exceedingly messy—as our best path forward to freedom and justice for all. ■

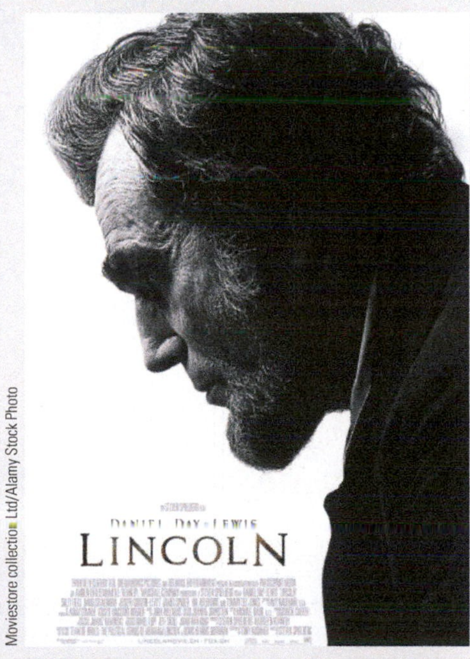

Moviestore collection Ltd/Alamy Stock Photo

16.10 An advertising poster for the film *Lincoln* that shows the actor Daniel Day-Lewis's successful physical transformation for the role of Abraham Lincoln.

Grant's offensives began the first week of May. The heaviest fighting occurred in Virginia. When the Army of the Potomac crossed the Rapidan River, Lee attacked its flank in the thick scrub forest of the Wilderness, where Union superiority in numbers and artillery would count for little (and where Lee had defeated Hooker a year earlier at Chancellorsville). Lee's action brought on two days (May 5–6) of the most confused, frenzied fighting the war had yet seen (see Map 16.6). Hundreds of wounded men burned to death in brush fires set off by exploding shells or muzzle flashes. The battle surged back and forth, with the Confederates inflicting 18,000 casualties and suffering 12,000. Having apparently halted Grant's offensive, they claimed a victory.

16-6b *Spotsylvania and Cold Harbor*

But Grant did not retreat, as other Union commanders in Virginia had done. Instead, he moved toward Spotsylvania Courthouse, a key crossroads 10 miles closer to Richmond. Skillfully, Lee pulled back to cover the road junction. Repeated Union assaults during the next 12 days (May 8–19) left another 18,000 northerners and 12,000 southerners killed, wounded, or captured. The Confederates fought from an elaborate network of trenches and log breastworks they had constructed virtually overnight. Civil War soldiers had learned the advantages of trenches, which gave the defense an enormous advantage and made frontal assaults almost suicidal.

Having achieved no better than stalemate around Spotsylvania, Grant again moved south around Lee's right flank in an effort to force the outnumbered Confederates into an open fight. Lee, however, anticipated Grant's moves and confronted him from behind formidable defenses at the North Anna River, Totopotomoy Creek, and near the crossroads inn of Cold Harbor, only 10 miles northeast of Richmond. Believing the Confederates must be exhausted and demoralized by their repeated retreats, Grant decided to attack at Cold Harbor on June 3—a costly mistake. Lee's troops were ragged and hungry but far from demoralized. Their withering fire inflicted 7,000 casualties in less than an hour. "I regret this assault more than any other one I have ordered," said Grant.

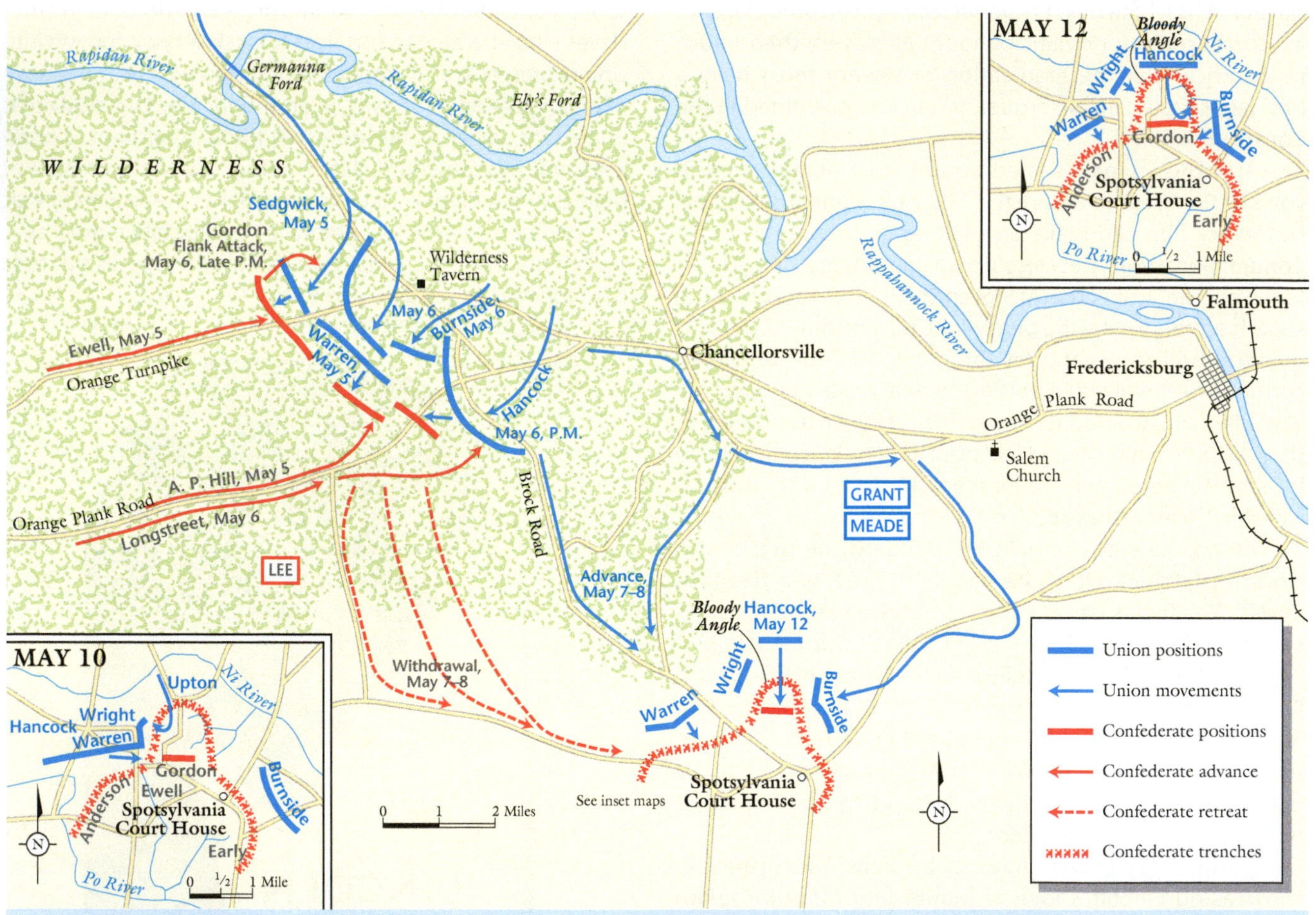

▲ **MAP 16.6 Battle of the Wilderness and Spotsylvania, May 5–12, 1864** Four major battles with a total of more than 100,000 casualties to both sides were fought within a few miles of Fredericksburg between December 1862 and May 1864. Compare this map with Map 16.2. The first battle of Fredericksburg on December 13, 1862 (described p. 444), was fought in the same vicinity as the Fredericksburg fighting on May 3, 1863, shown on the Chancellorsville map.

Q *How are these battles similar or different?*

Q *How did Union and Confederate forces employ trenches to their advantage during the war?*

16-6c *Stalemate in Virginia*

Now Grant moved all the way across the James River to strike at Petersburg, an industrial city and rail center 20 miles south of Richmond. If Petersburg fell, the Confederates could not hold Richmond. Once more Lee's troops raced southward on the inside track and blocked Grant's troops. Four days of Union assaults (June 15–18) produced another 11,000 northern casualties but no breakthrough. Such high Union losses in just six weeks—some 65,000 killed, wounded, and captured, compared with 37,000 Confederate casualties—cost the Army of the Potomac its offensive power. Grant reluctantly settled down for a siege along the Petersburg–Richmond front that would last more than nine grueling months.

Meanwhile, other Union operations in Virginia had achieved little success. Benjamin Butler bungled an attack up the James River against Richmond and was stopped by a scraped-together army under General P. G. T. Beauregard. Jubal Early, commanding Stonewall Jackson's old corps, blocked a Union thrust up the Shenandoah Valley at Lynchburg in June. Then Early led a raid all the way to the outskirts of Washington on July 11 and 12 before being driven back to Virginia. Union cavalry under Philip Sheridan inflicted considerable damage on Confederate resources in Virginia—including the mortal wounding of Jeb Stuart in the battle of Yellow Tavern on May 11—but again failed to strike a crippling blow. In the North, frustration set in over failure to win the quick, decisive victory the public had expected in April.

16-6d *The Atlanta Campaign*

In Georgia, Sherman's army seemed to have accomplished more at less cost than Grant had in Virginia, but there too Union efforts had bogged down in apparent stalemate by August. The strategy and tactics of both Sherman and Johnston in Georgia contrasted with those of Grant and Lee in Virginia. Sherman forced Johnston south toward Atlanta by constantly flanking him to the Union right, generally without bloody battles (see Map 16.7). Grant constantly forced Lee back by flanking moves to the Union left, but only after bloody battles. By the end of June, Sherman had advanced 80 miles at the cost of 17,000 casualties to Johnston's 14,000—only one-third of the combined losses of Grant and Lee.

Davis grew alarmed by Johnston's apparent willingness to yield territory without a fight. Sherman again flanked the Confederate defenses (after a failed attack) at Kennesaw Mountain in early July. He crossed the Chattahoochee River and drove Johnston back to Peachtree Creek, less than five miles from Atlanta. Fearing that Johnston would abandon the city, on July 17 Davis replaced him with John Bell Hood.

A fighting general from Lee's army who had lost a leg at Chickamauga, Hood immediately prepared to counterattack against the Yankees. He did so three times, in late July. Each time, the Confederates reeled back in defeat, suffering a total of 15,000 casualties to Sherman's 6,000. At last, Hood retreated into the formidable earthworks ringing Atlanta and launched no more attacks. But his army did manage to keep Sherman's cavalry and infantry from taking the two railroads leading into Atlanta from the south. Like Grant at Petersburg, Sherman seemed to settle down for a siege.

16-6e *Peace Overtures*

By August, the Confederate strategy of attrition seemed to be working. Union casualties on all fronts during the preceding three months totaled a staggering 110,000—double the number for any comparable period of the war. "Who shall revive the withered hopes that bloomed at the opening of Grant's campaign?" asked the leading Democratic newspaper, the *New York World*. "STOP THE WAR!" shouted Democratic headlines. "All are tired of this damnable tragedy."

Even Republicans joined the chorus of despair. "Our bleeding, bankrupt, almost dying country longs for peace," wrote Horace Greeley of the *New York Tribune*. Greeley became involved in abortive "peace negotiations" spawned by Confederate agents in Canada. Those agents convinced Greeley that they carried peace overtures from Davis, but Lincoln was skeptical. Still, given the mood of the North in midsummer 1864, Lincoln could not reject any opportunity to stop the bloodshed. He deputized Greeley to meet with the Confederate agents in Niagara Falls on the Canadian side of the border. At almost the same time (mid-July), two other northerners met under a flag of truce with Davis in Richmond. Lincoln had carefully instructed them—and Greeley—that his conditions for peace were "restoration of the Union and abandonment of slavery."

Davis would no more accept those terms than Lincoln would accept his. Although neither of the peace contacts came to anything, the Confederates gained a propaganda victory by claiming that Lincoln's terms had been the only obstacle to peace. Northern Democrats ignored the southern refusal to accept reunion and focused on the slavery issue as the sole stumbling block. "Tens of thousands of white men must yet bite the dust to allay the negro mania of the President," ran a typical Democratic editorial. By August, even staunch Republicans were convinced that "the desire for peace" and the impression that Lincoln "is fighting not for the Union but for the abolition of slavery" made his reelection "an impossibility." Lincoln thought so, too. "I am going to be beaten," he told a friend in August, "and unless some great change takes place, *badly* beaten."

Lincoln faced enormous pressure to drop emancipation as a condition of peace, but he refused to yield. He would rather lose the election than go back on the promise he had made in the Emancipation Proclamation. Some 130,000 black soldiers and sailors were fighting for the Union. They would not do so if they thought the North intended to forsake them.

> If they stake their lives for us they must be prompted by the strongest motive ... the promise of freedom. And the promise being made, must be kept... . There have been men who proposed to me to return to slavery the[se] black warriors... . I should be damned in time & eternity for so doing. The world shall know that I will keep my faith to friends and enemies, come what will.

Library of Congress, Prints and Photographs Division

16.11 **Union Supply Base at City Point, Virginia** During the Union army's siege of Petersburg from June 1864 to April 1865, the army built up a huge complex of wharfs and warehouses at City Point on the James River (today's Hopewell, Virginia) where ships unloaded supplies and trains carried them to the front. Note the boxcars of the U.S. Military Rail Road shown in the photograph.

At the end of August, the Democrats nominated McClellan for president. The platform on which he ran declared, "after four years of failure to restore the Union by the experiment of war ... [we] demand that immediate efforts be made for a cessation of hostilities." Southerners were jubilant. Democratic victory on that platform, said the *Charleston Mercury*, "must lead to peace and our independence [if] for the next two months *we hold our own and prevent military success by our foes*."

16-6f *The Prisoner-Exchange Controversy*

The Democratic platform also condemned the Lincoln administration's "shameful disregard" of prisoners of war in Confederate prison camps. This raised another contentious matter. By midsummer 1864, the plight of Union and Confederate captives had become one of the most bitter issues of the war. The upcoming presidential election and the generally worse conditions in southern prisons made it mainly a northern political issue.

In 1862, the Union and Confederate armed forces had signed a cartel for the exchange of prisoners captured in battle. The arrangement had worked reasonably well for a year, making large prison camps unnecessary. When the Union army began to organize regiments of former slaves, however, the Confederate government announced that if they were captured, they and their white officers would be put to death for the crime of fomenting slave insurrections. In practice, the Confederate government did not enforce this policy because Lincoln threatened retaliation on Confederate prisoners of war if it did so. But Confederate troops sometimes murdered black soldiers and their officers as they tried to

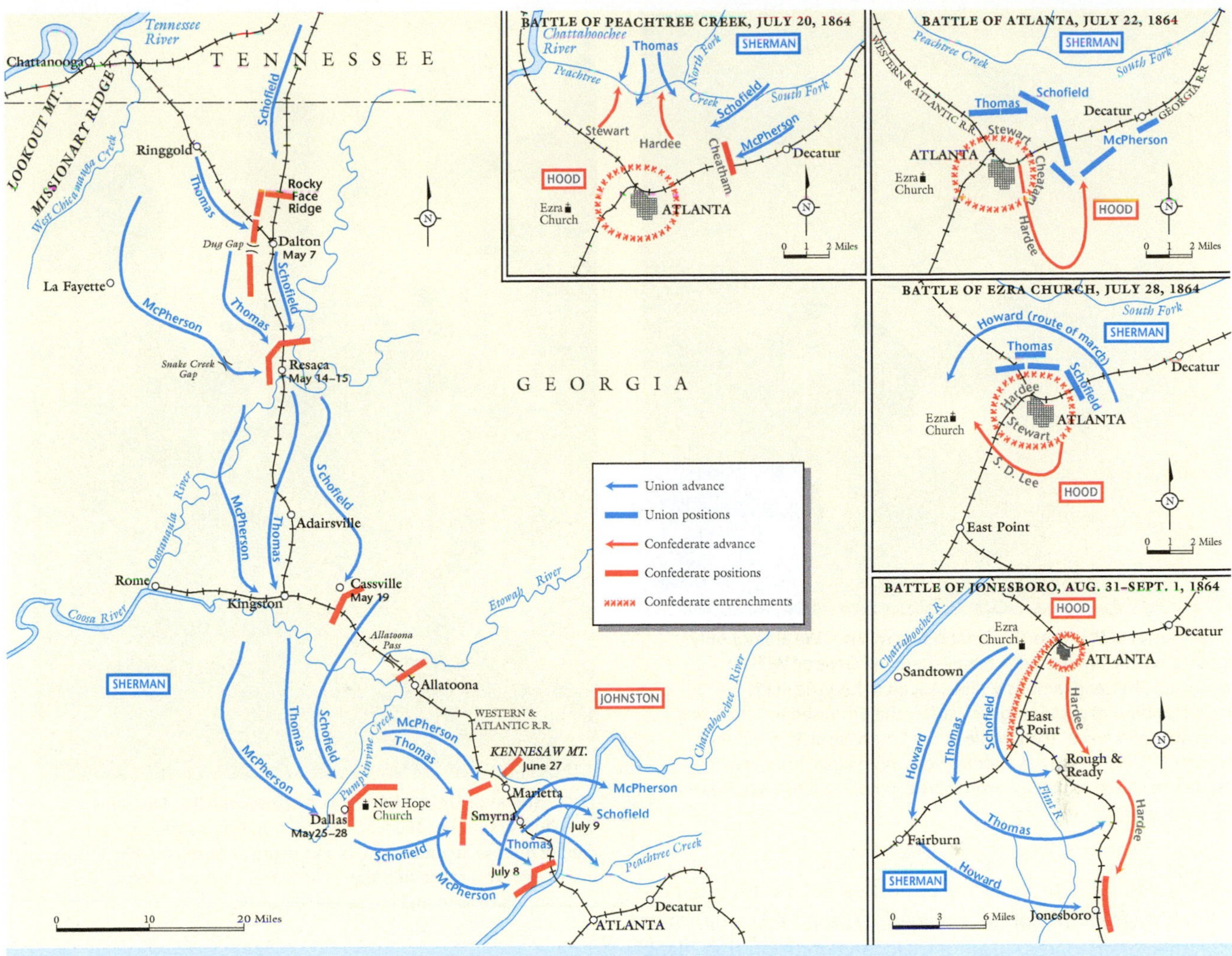

▲ **MAP 16.7 Campaign for Atlanta, May–September 1864** The main map illustrates Sherman's campaign of maneuver that forced Johnston back to Atlanta with relatively few battles. The first three inset maps show the Confederate counterattacks launched by Hood, and the fourth shows how the Union army got astride the last two railroads entering Atlanta from the south and forced Hood to evacuate the city.

Q *How important was Union victory in this campaign to Lincoln's re-election?*

Q *What were Sherman's strengths and weaknesses as a general?*

surrender—most notably at Fort Pillow, a Union garrison on the Mississippi north of Memphis, where cavalry commanded by Nathan Bedford Forrest slaughtered scores of black (and some white) prisoners on April 12, 1864.

In most cases, Confederate officers returned captured black soldiers to slavery or put them to hard labor on southern fortifications. Expressing outrage at this treatment of soldiers wearing the United States uniform, the Lincoln administration in 1863 suspended the exchange of prisoners until the Confederacy agreed to treat white and black prisoners alike. The Confederacy refused. The South would "die in the last ditch," said the Confederate exchange agent, before "giving up the right to send slaves back to slavery as property recaptured."

There matters stood as the heavy fighting of 1864 poured many thousands of captured soldiers into hastily contrived prison compounds that quickly became death camps. Prisoners were subjected to overcrowding, poor sanitation, contaminated water, scanty rations, inadequate medical facilities, and exposure to deep-South summer heat and northern winter cold. The suffering of northern prisoners was especially acute, because the deterioration of the southern economy made it hard to feed and clothe even Confederate soldiers and civilians, let alone Yankee prisoners. Nearly 16 percent of all Union soldiers held in southern prison camps died, compared with 12 percent of Confederate soldiers in northern camps. Andersonville was the most notorious hellhole. A stockade camp of 26 acres with neither huts nor tents, designed to accommodate 15,000 prisoners, it held 33,000 in August 1864. They died at the rate of more than 100 per day. Altogether, 13,000 Union soldiers died at Andersonville.

The suffering of Union prisoners brought heavy pressure on the Lincoln administration to renew exchanges, but the Confederates would not budge on the question of exchanging

Source: U.S. National Archives and Records Administration (NARA)

16.12 **General William Tecumseh Sherman** "We are not only fighting hostile armies, but a hostile people," General William Tecumseh Sherman famously said. Ahead of his time in his understanding of psychological warfare, he promised to "make war so terrible and make" the people of the South "so sick of war that generations will pass away before they would again appeal to it." Sherman's March to the Sea arguably accomplished this aim, hastening the close of war.

Library of Congress, Prints and Photographs Division

16.13 **Burial of Union POWs at Andersonville** On many days during summer 1864, at least 100 Union prisoners of war died of disease, malnutrition, or exposure at Andersonville Prison in Georgia. This scene of burial in long trenches became so commonplace as to dull the sense of horror.

black soldiers. After a series of battles on the Richmond–Petersburg front in September 1864, Lee proposed an informal exchange of prisoners. Grant agreed, on condition that black soldiers captured in the fighting be included "the same as white soldiers." Lee replied, "negroes belonging to our citizens are not considered subjects of exchange and were not included in my proposition." No exchange, then, responded Grant. The Union government was "bound to secure to all persons received into her armies the rights due to soldiers." Lincoln backed this policy. He would not sacrifice the principle of equal treatment of black prisoners, even though local Republican leaders warned that many in the North "will work and vote against the President, because they think sympathy with a few negroes, also captured, is the cause of a refusal" to exchange prisoners

16-6g *The Issue of Black Soldiers in the Confederate Army*

During the winter of 1864–1865, the Confederate government quietly abandoned its refusal to exchange black prisoners, and exchanges resumed. One reason for this reversal was a Confederate decision to recruit slaves to fight for the South. Two years earlier, Davis had denounced the North's arming of freed slaves as "the most execrable measure recorded in the history of guilty man." Ironically, a few black laborers and body servants with southern armies had taken up arms in the heat of battle and had unofficially fought alongside their masters against the Yankees. By February 1865, southern armies were desperate for manpower, and slaves constituted the only remaining reserve. Supported by Lee's powerful influence, Davis pressed the Confederate Congress to enact a bill for recruitment of black soldiers. The assumption that any slaves who fought for the South would have to be granted freedom generated bitter opposition to the measure. "What did we go to war for, if not to protect our property?" asked a Virginia senator. By three votes in the House and one in the Senate, the Confederate Congress finally passed the bill on March 13, 1865. Before any southern black regiments could be organized, however, the war ended.

16-7 Lincoln's Reelection and the End of the Confederacy

Q *Why, after doubting he would be re-elected, did Lincoln ultimately win reelection by a substantial margin?*

Despite Republican fears, battlefield events, rather than political controversies, had the strongest impact on U.S. voters in 1864. In effect, the election became a referendum on whether to continue fighting for unconditional victory. Within days after the Democratic national convention had declared the war a failure, the military situation changed dramatically.

16-7a *The Capture of Atlanta*

After a month of apparent stalemate on the Atlanta front, Sherman's army again made a large movement by the right flank to attack the last rail link into Atlanta from the south. At the battle of Jonesboro on August 31 and September 1, Sherman's men captured the railroad. Hood abandoned Atlanta to save his army. On September 3, Sherman sent a jaunty telegram to Washington: "Atlanta is ours, and fairly won."

16-7b *The Shenandoah Valley*

If Atlanta was not enough to brighten the prospects for Lincoln's reelection, events in Virginia's Shenandoah Valley were. After Early's raid through the valley all the way to Washington in July, Grant put Philip Sheridan in charge of a reinforced Army of the Shenandoah and told him to "go after Early and follow him to the death." Sheridan infused the same spirit into the three infantry corps of the Army of the Shenandoah that he had previously imbued in his cavalry. On September 19, they attacked Early's force near Winchester, and after a daylong battle sent the Confederates flying to the south. Sheridan pursued them, attacking again on September 22 at Fisher's Hill 20 miles south of Winchester. Early's line collapsed, and his routed army fled 60 more miles southward.

Early's retreat enabled Sheridan to carry out the second part of his assignment in the Shenandoah Valley, which had twice served as a Confederate route of invasion and whose farms helped feed Confederate armies. Sheridan now set about destroying the valley's crops and mills so thoroughly that "crows flying over it for the balance of the season will have to carry their provender with them." Sheridan boasted that by the time he was through, "the Valley, from Winchester up to Staunton, ninety-two miles, will have little in it for man or beast."

But Jubal Early was not yet willing to give up. Reinforced by a division from Lee, on October 19 he launched a dawn attack across Cedar Creek, 15 miles south of Winchester. He caught the Yankees by surprise and drove them back in disorder. At the time of the attack, Sheridan was at Winchester, returning to his army from Washington, where he had gone to confer on future strategy. He jumped onto his horse and sped to the battlefield in a ride that became celebrated in poetry and legend. By sundown, Sheridan's charisma and tactical leadership had turned the battle from a Union defeat into another Confederate rout. The battle of Cedar Creek ended Confederate power in the valley.

Sherman's and Sheridan's victories ensured Lincoln's reelection on November 8 by a majority of 212 to 21 in the Electoral College. Soldiers played a notable role in the balloting. Every northern state except three whose legislatures were controlled by Democrats had passed laws allowing absentee voting by soldiers. Seventy-eight percent of the military vote went to Lincoln—compared with 54 percent of the civilian vote. The men who were doing the fighting had sent a clear message that they meant to finish the job.

Library of Congress Prints and Photographs Division[LC-DIG-cwpb-03356]

16.14 Sherman's Soldiers Tearing Up the Railroad in Atlanta
One of the objectives of Sherman's march from Atlanta to the sea was to demolish the railroads so they could not transport supplies to Confederate armies. The soldiers did a thorough job. They tore up the rails and ties, made a bonfire of the ties, heated the rails in the fire, and then wrapped them around trees, creating "Sherman neckties."

16-7c *From Atlanta to the Sea*

Many southerners got the message, but not Davis. The Confederacy remained "as erect and defiant as ever," he told his Congress in November 1864. It was this last-ditch resistance that Sherman set out to break in his famous march from Atlanta to the sea.

Sherman had concluded, "We are not only fighting hostile armies, but a hostile people." Defeat of the Confederate armies was not enough to win the war; the railroads, factories, and farms that supported those armies must also be destroyed. The will of the civilians who sustained the war must be crushed. Sherman expressed more bluntly than anyone else the meaning of this strategy. He was ahead of his time in his understanding of psychological warfare. "We cannot change the hearts of those people of the South," he said, "but we can make war so terrible and make them so sick of war that generations would pass away before they would again appeal to it."

Sherman urged Grant to let him march through the heart of Georgia, living off the land and destroying all resources not needed by his army—the same policy

What They Said

The Evacuation of Atlanta: General Hood versus General Sherman on the Laws of War

Once Sherman had captured Atlanta, he ordered its citizens to evacuate the city. This famous exchange between Confederate general Hood and Sherman reveals just how swiftly the nature of warfare was changing.

HDQRS. ARMY OF TENNESSEE, *OFFICE CHIEF OF STAFF, September* 9, 1864

To Maj. Gen. W. T. SHERMAN, Commanding U.S. Forces in Georgia

GENERAL: Your letter of yesterday's date [7th] … is received. You say therein "I deem it to be to the interest of the United States that the citizens now residing in Atlanta should remove," &c. I do not consider that I have any alternative in this matter. I therefore accept your proposition to declare a truce of two days, or such time as may be necessary to accomplish the purpose mentioned, and shall render all assistance in my power to expedite the transportation of citizens in this direction. I suggest that a staff officer be appointed by you to superintend the removal from the city to Rough and Ready, while I appoint a like officer to control their removal farther south; that a guard of 100 men be sent by either party, as you propose, to maintain order at that place, and that the removal begin on Monday next. And now, sir, permit me to say that the unprecedented measure you propose transcends, in studied and ingenious cruelty, all acts ever before brought to my attention in the dark history of war. In the name of God and humanity I protest, believing that you will find that you are expelling from their homes and firesides the wives and children of a brave people.

I am, general, very respectfully, your obedient servant,
J. B. HOOD, *General.*

HDQRS. MILITARY DIVISION OF THE MISSISSIPPI
In the Field, Atlanta, Ga., September 10, 1864.

To General J. B. HOOD, *C. S. Army, Comdg. Army of Tennessee:*

GENERAL: I have the honor to acknowledge the receipt of your letter of this date [9th], at the hands of Messrs. Ball and Crew, consenting to the arrangements I had proposed to facilitate the removal south of the people of Atlanta who prefer to go in that direction. I inclose you a copy of my orders, which will, I am satisfied, accomplish my purpose perfectly. You style the measure proposed "unprecedented," and appeal to the dark history of war for a parallel as an act of "studied and ingenious cruelty." It is not unprecedented, for General Johnston himself, very wisely and properly, removed the families all the way from Dalton down, and I see no reason why Atlanta should be excepted. Nor is it necessary to appeal to the dark history of war when recent and modern examples are so handy. You, yourself, burned dwelling-houses along your parapet, and I have seen to-day fifty houses that you have rendered uninhabitable because they stood in the way of your forts and men. You defended Atlanta on a line so close to town that every cannon shot and many musket shots from our line of investment that overshot their mark went into the habitations of women and children. General Hardee did the same at Jonesborough, and General Johnston did the same last summer at Jackson, Miss. I have not accused you of heartless cruelty, but merely instance these cases of very recent occurrence, and could go on and enumerate hundreds of others and challenge any fair man to judge which of us has the heart of pity for the families of a "brave people." I say that it is kindness to these families of Atlanta to remove them now at once from scenes that women and children should not be exposed to, and the "brave people" should scorn to commit their wives and children to the rude barbarians who thus, as you say, violate the laws of war, as illustrated in the pages of its dark history. In the name of common sense I ask you not to appeal to a just God in such a sacrilegious manner; you who, in the midst of peace and prosperity, have plunged a nation into war, dark and cruel war; who dared and badgered us to battle, insulted our flag, seized our arsenals and forts that were left in the honorable custody of peaceful ordnance sergeants; seized and made "prisoners of war" the very garrisons sent to protect your people against negroes and Indians long before any overt act was committed by the, to you, hated Lincoln Government; tried to force Kentucky and Missouri into rebellion, spite of themselves; falsified the vote of Louisiana, turned loose your privateers to plunder unarmed ships; expelled Union families by the thousands; burned their houses and declared by an act of your Congress the confiscation of all debts due Northern men for goods had and received. Talk thus to the marines, but not to me, who have seen these things, and who will this day make as much sacrifice for the peace and honor of the South as the best born Southerner among you. If we must be enemies, let us be men and fight it out, as we propose to do, and not deal in such hypocritical appeals to God and humanity. God will judge us in due time, and He will pronounce whether it be more humane to fight with a town full of women, and the families of "a brave people" at our back, or to remove them in time to places of safety among their own friends and people.

W. T. SHERMAN, *Major-general, Commanding.*

Q *What are the "laws of war" General Hood accuses General Sherman of violating? Is he justified in making his complaint?*

Q *What is Sherman's response to Hood's accusation? How effective are his arguments?*

Q *How had the conduct of the Civil War changed from 1861 to 1864? Why?*

Sources: (top) General Hood's letter to Sherman, September 9, 1864. Author accessed at: http://www.civilwarhome.com/atlantaevacuation.htm. This website draws from the Official Records of the War, Series 1, Volume XXXIX/2 [S #78]; (bottom) General Sherman's letter to Hood, September 10, 1864. Author accessed at: http://www.civilwarhome.com/atlantaevacuation.htm. This website draws from the Official Records of the War, Series 1, Volume XXXIX/2 [S #78].

Sheridan was carrying out in the Shenandoah Valley. Grant and Lincoln were reluctant to authorize such a risky move, especially with Hood's army of 40,000 men still intact in northern Alabama. Sherman assured them that he would send George Thomas to take command of a force of 60,000 men in Tennessee, who would be more than a match for Hood. With another 60,000, Sherman could "move through Georgia, smashing things to the sea ... I can make the march, and make Georgia howl!"

Lincoln and Grant finally consented. On November 16, Sherman's avengers marched out of Atlanta after burning a third of the city, including some nonmilitary property. Southward they marched 280 miles to Savannah, wrecking everything in their path that could, by any stretch of the imagination, be considered of military value.

16-7d *The Battles of Franklin and Nashville*

They encountered little resistance. Instead of chasing Sherman, Hood invaded Tennessee with the hope of recovering that state for the Confederacy, a disastrous campaign that virtually destroyed his army. On November 30, the Confederates attacked part of the Union force at Franklin, 20 miles south of Nashville. The slaughter claimed no fewer than 12 Confederate generals and 54 regimental commanders as casualties. Instead of retreating, Hood moved on to Nashville, where on December 15 and 16, Thomas launched an attack that almost wiped out the Army of Tennessee. Its remnants retreated to Mississippi, where Hood resigned in January 1865 (see Map 16.8).

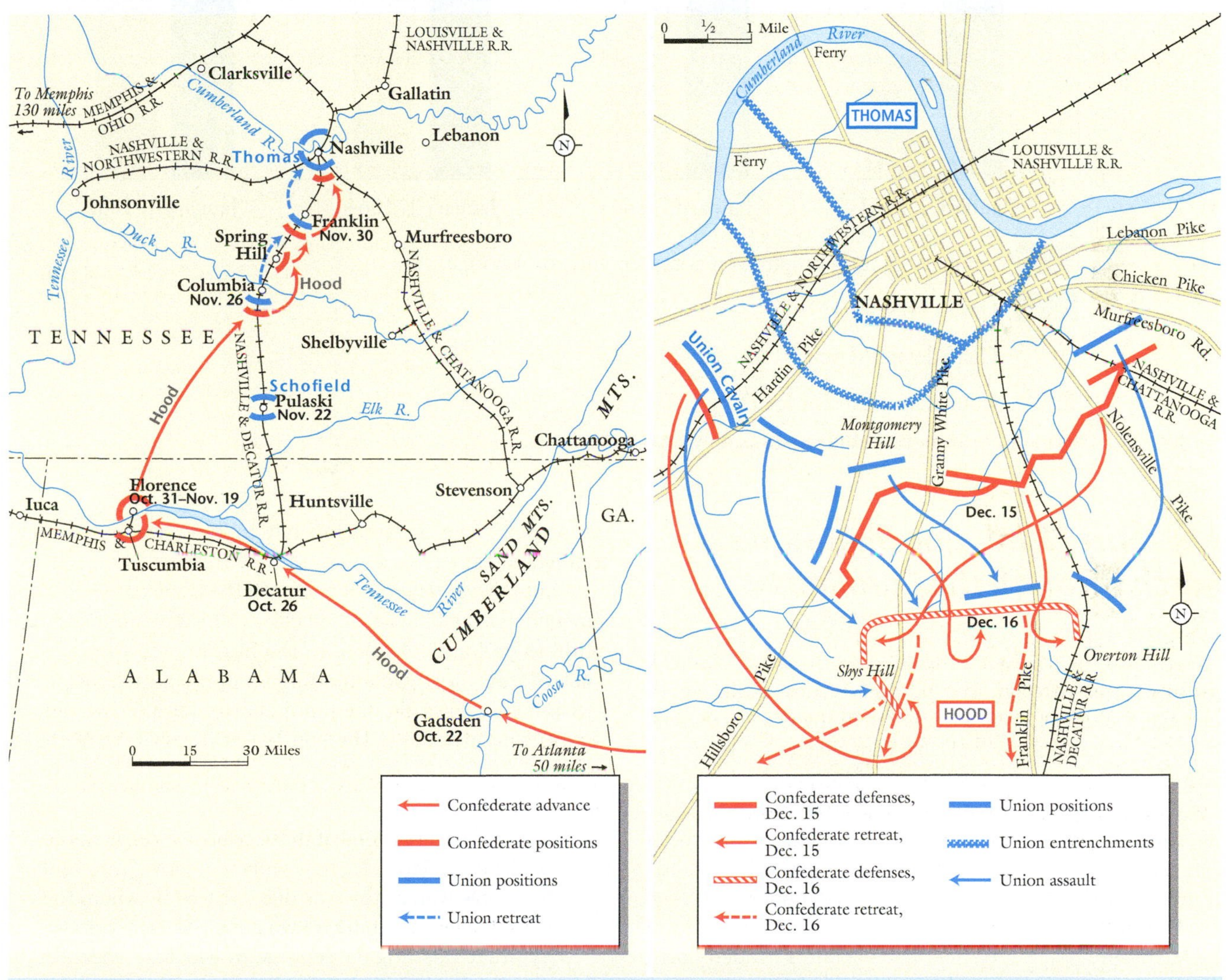

▲ **MAP 16.8 Hood's Tennessee Campaign, October–November 1864, and Nashville, December 15–16, 1864** The battle of Nashville on December 15–16, 1864, was the most carefully planned and decisive battle of the war. After Thomas's army drove the Confederates from their first line on December 15 (solid red line), it attacked again and overran the second position (striped red line) on the 16th. The Confederate army virtually disintegrated as it retreated.

Q *What led Hood to embark on this disastrous invasion of Tennessee?*

Q *What pressures led some Confederate soldiers to desert late in the war?*

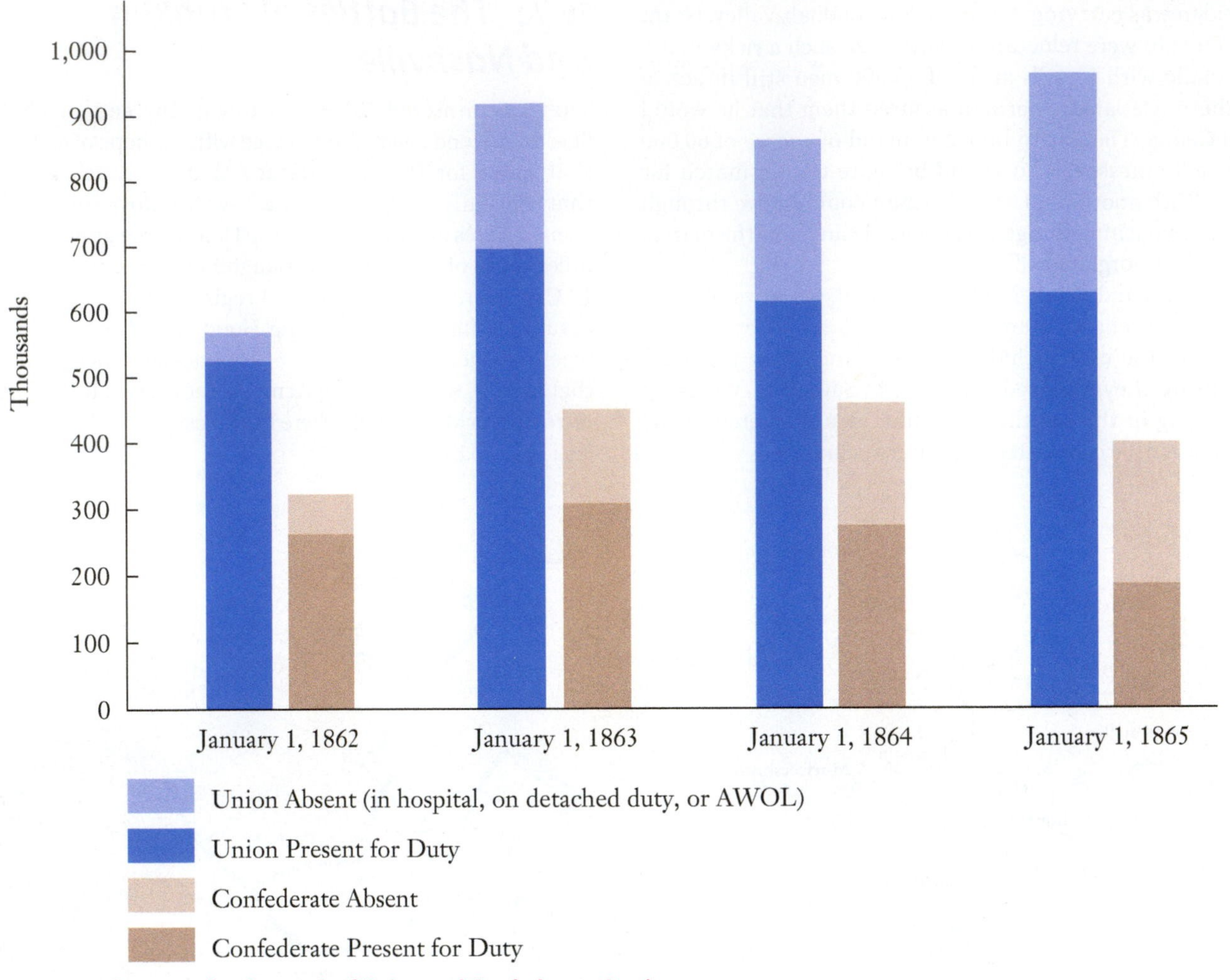

Figure 16.2 **Comparative Strength of Union and Confederate Armies**

16-7e *Fort Fisher and Sherman's March through the Carolinas*

Worse was yet to come for the Confederates. Lee's army in Virginia drew its dwindling supplies overland from the Carolinas and through the port of Wilmington, North Carolina, the only city still accessible to blockade runners. The big guns at massive Fort Fisher kept blockade ships at bay and protected the runners. In January 1865, though, the largest armada of the war—58 ships with 627 guns—pounded Fort Fisher for two days, disabling most of its big guns. Army troops captured the fort on January 15. That ended the blockade running, and Sherman soon put an end to supplies from the Carolinas as well.

At the end of January, Sherman's soldiers headed north from Savannah, eager to take revenge on South Carolina, which to their mind had started the war. Here, they made even less distinction between civilian and military property than they had in Georgia and left even less of Columbia standing than they had of Atlanta. Seemingly invincible, Sherman's army pushed into North Carolina and brushed aside the force that Joseph E. Johnston had assembled to stop them. The devastation left in their wake appalled Confederates.

But the war would not end until the Confederate armies surrendered, as Lincoln made clear in his second inaugural address on March 4, 1865. In the best-known words from that address, he urged a binding up of the nation's wounds "with malice toward none [and] charity for all." Even more significant, given that the conflict still raged, were these words:

> American Slavery is one of those offences which, in the providence of God ... He now wills to remove [through] this terrible war, as the woe due to those by whom the offence came ... . Fondly do we hope—fervently do we pray—that this mighty scourge of war may speedily pass away. Yet if God wills that it continue, until all the wealth piled by the bondman's two hundred and fifty years of unrequited toil shall be sunk, and until every drop of blood drawn with the lash, shall be paid by another drawn with the sword, as was said three thousand years ago, so still it must be said "the judgments of the Lord, are true and righteous altogether."

16-7f *The Road to Appomattox*

The Army of Northern Virginia was now the only entity that kept the Confederacy alive, but it was on the verge of disintegration. Scores of its soldiers were deserting every day (see Figure 16.2). On April 1, Sheridan's cavalry and an infantry corps smashed the right flank of Lee's line at Five Forks and cut off the last railroad into Petersburg. The next day, Grant attacked all along the line and forced Lee to abandon both Petersburg and Richmond. As the Confederate government fled its capital, its army set fire to all the military stores it could not carry. The fires spread and destroyed more of Richmond than the northern troops had destroyed of Atlanta or Columbia.

Lee's starving men limped westward, hoping to turn south and join the remnants of Johnston's army in North Carolina. Sheridan's cavalry raced ahead and cut them off at Appomattox, 90 miles from Petersburg, on April 8. When the weary Confederates tried a breakout attack the next morning, their first probe revealed solid ranks of Union infantry arrayed behind the cavalry. It was the end. "There is nothing left for me to do," said Lee, "but to go and see General Grant, and I would rather die a thousand deaths."

In an Appomattox farmhouse, the son of an Ohio tanner dictated surrender terms to a scion of one of Virginia's First Families. The terms were generous. Thirty thousand captured Confederates were allowed to go home on condition that they promise never again to take up arms against the United States. After completing the surrender formalities on April 9, Grant introduced Lee to his staff, which included Colonel Ely Parker, a Seneca Indian. As Lee shook hands with Parker, he stared for a moment at Parker's dark features and said: "I am glad to see one real American here." Parker replied solemnly: "We are all Americans." And indeed they now were.

16-7g *The Assassination of Lincoln*

Wild celebrations broke out in the North at news of the fall of Richmond, followed soon by news of Appomattox. Almost overnight, the celebrations turned to mourning. On the evening of April 14, the care-worn Abraham Lincoln sought to relax by attending a comedy at Ford's Theatre. In the middle of the play, John Wilkes Booth broke into Lincoln's box and fatally shot the president in the head. A prominent actor, Booth was a native of Maryland and a frustrated, unstable egotist who hated Lincoln for what he had done to Booth's beloved South. As he jumped from Lincoln's box to the stage and escaped out a back door, he shouted Virginia's state motto at the stunned audience: "Sic semper tyrannis" ("Thus always to tyrants").

Lincoln's death in the early morning of April 15 produced an outpouring of grief throughout the North and among newly freed slaves in the South. The martyred president did not live to see the culmination of his great achievement in leading the nation to a victory that preserved its existence and abolished

Library of Congress Prints and Photographs Division

16.15 The Fruits of War Several southern cities suffered enormous damage in the Civil War from Union shelling and from the fires caused by Confederate soldiers when they destroyed everything of military value before evacuating the cities. Such was true of Charleston, where a northern photographer who entered the city after it fell in February 1865 posed four black children amid the ruins to portray the symbolism of destruction and renewal.

Table 16.1 CASUALTIES IN CIVIL WAR ARMIES AND NAVIES

Confederate records are incomplete; the Confederate data listed here are therefore estimates. The actual Confederate totals were probably higher.

	Killed and Mortally Wounded in Combat	Died of Disease	Died in Prison	Miscellaneous Deaths*	Total Deaths	Wounded, Not Mortally	Total Casualties
Union	111,904	197,388	30,192	24,881	364,345	277,401	641,766
Confederate (estimated)	94,000	140,000	26,000	No Estimates	260,000	195,000	455,000
Both Armies (estimated)	205,904	337,388	56,192	24,881	624,365	472,401	1,096,766

*Accidents, drownings, causes not stated, etc.

Library of Congress Prints and Photographs Division [LC-DIG-ppmsca-19469]

16.16 **Abraham Lincoln in 1865** This is the last photograph of Lincoln, taken on April 10, 1865, four days before his assassination. Compare this image to the photograph of Lincoln (14.2) on page 379. Four years of war had left their mark on the 56-year-old president; note the lines of strain, fatigue, and sadness in his face.

slavery. Within 11 days of Lincoln's death, his assassin was trapped and killed in a burning barn in Virginia (April 26). The remaining Confederate armies surrendered one after another (April 26, May 4, May 26, June 23), and Union cavalry captured the fleeing Jefferson Davis in Georgia (May 10). The trauma of civil war was over, but the problems of peace and reconstruction had just begun.

Conclusion

Northern victory in the Civil War resolved two fundamental questions of liberty and power left unresolved by the Revolution of 1776 and the Constitution of 1789: (1) whether this fragile republican experiment in federalism called the United States would survive as one nation; and (2) whether that nation, founded on a charter of liberty, would continue to exist as the largest slaveholding country in the world. Before 1861, the question of whether a state could secede from the Union had remained open. Eleven states did secede, but their defeat in a war that cost 625,000 lives resolved the issue (see Table 16.1). Since 1865, no state has seriously threatened secession. And in 1865, the adoption of the Thirteenth Amendment to the Constitution confirmed the supreme power of the national government to abolish slavery and ensure the liberty of all Americans.

The Civil War also accomplished a regional transfer of power from South to North. From 1800 to 1860, the slave states had used their leverage in the Jeffersonian Republican and Jacksonian Democratic parties to control national politics most of the time. A southern slaveholder was president of the United States during two-thirds of the years from 1789 to 1861. Most congressional leaders and Supreme Court justices during that period were southerners. In the 50 years after 1861, no native of a southern state was elected president, only one served as Speaker of the House and none as president pro tem of the Senate, and only 5 of the 26 Supreme Court justices appointed during that half-century were from the South. In 1860, the South's share of the national wealth was 30 percent; in 1870, it was 12 percent.

The institutions and ideology of a plantation society and a caste system that had dominated half the country before 1861 went down with a great crash in 1865—to be replaced by the institutions and ideology of free-labor capitalism. Once feared as the gravest threat to liberty, the power of the national government sustained by a large army had achieved the greatest triumph of liberty in American history. With victory and peace in 1865, the reunited nation turned its attention to the issue of equality.

CHAPTER REVIEW

Review

1. What factors led Lincoln to his decision to issue the Emancipation Proclamation?
2. What were the sources of internal dissent and dissension in the Confederacy? In the Union?
3. How did wartime legislation transform American society? How did women contribute to the war effort?
4. How did the Union army achieve a victory at Gettysburg?
5. What contribution did African Americans make to the Union war effort?
6. Why did Lincoln think he would not win reelection in 1864?
7. What factors enabled Lincoln to win reelection by a substantial margin in 1864?

Critical Thinking

1. How did a war that began, on the part of the North, with the goal of restoring a Union in which slavery existed in half of the country, become transformed into a war to give the nation a new birth of freedom?
2. In the winter of 1862–1863, northern morale was at rock bottom and the prospects for Confederate success appeared bright. Yet two years later, the Confederacy lay in ruins and its dream of independent nationhood was doomed. How and why did this happen?

Identifications

Review your understanding of the following key terms, people, and events for this chapter (terms in bold in text are included in the Glossary).

"contraband of war," p. 438
compensated emancipation, p. 439
Copperheads, p. 440
martial law, p. 444
Twenty Negro Law, p. 445
"bounty jumpers," p. 445
commutation fee, p. 445

Suggested Readings

Several studies offer important information and insights about questions of strategy and command in military operations: **Joseph G. Glatthaar**, ***Partners in Command: The Relationships between Leaders in the Civil War*** (1993); **Richard M. McMurry**, ***Two Great Rebel Armies*** (1989); **Michael C. Adams**, ***Our Masters the Rebels: A Speculation on Union Military Defeat in the East, 1861–1865*** (1978), reissued under the title ***Fighting for Defeat*** (1992); **Mark Grimsley**, ***The Hard Hand of War: Union Military Policy toward Southern Civilians, 1861–1865*** (1995); and **Gary W. Gallagher**, ***The Confederate War*** (1997).

On the path to emancipation, see **Chandra Manning**, ***Troubled Refuge: Struggling for Freedom in the Civil War*** (2016); **James Oakes**, ***Freedom National: The Destruction of Slavery in the United States, 1861–1865*** (2012); and **Ira Berlin et al., eds.**, ***Slaves No More: Three Essays on Emancipation and the Civil War*** (1992). Excellent studies of the Emancipation Proclamation and the Thirteenth Amendment are **Allen C. Guelzo**, ***Lincoln's Emancipation Proclamation*** (2004), and **Michael Vorenberg**, ***Final Freedom: The Civil War, the Abolition of Slavery, and the Thirteenth Amendment*** (2001). On Lincoln's changing views of slavery, see **Eric Foner**, ***The Fiery Trial: Abraham Lincoln and American Slavery*** (2010).

Of the many books about black soldiers in the Union army, the most useful is **Joseph T. Glatthaar**, ***Forged in Battle: The Civil War Alliance of Black Soldiers and White Officers*** (1990). The Confederate debate about enlisting and freeing slave soldiers is chronicled in **Bruce Levine**, ***Confederate Emancipation: Southern Plans to Free and Arm Slaves During the Civil War*** (2006).

For the draft riots in New York, see **Iver Bernstein**, ***The New York City Draft Riots: Their Significance for American Society and Politics in the Age of the Civil War*** (1990). The story of the Copperheads is told by **Jennifer L. Weber**, ***Copperheads: The Rise and Fall of Lincoln's Opponents in the North*** (2006). The best study of the civil liberties issue in the North is **Mark E. Neely, Jr.**, ***The Fate of Liberty: Abraham Lincoln and Civil Liberties*** (1990), and the same author has covered the same issue in the Confederacy in ***Southern Rights: Political Prisoners and the Myth of Confederate Constitutionalism*** (1999). For Civil War medicine, see **Alfred Jay Bollet**, ***Civil War Medicine: Challenges and Triumphs*** (2002); and **Jane E. Schultz**, ***Women at the Front: Hospital Workers in Civil War America*** (2004). A succinct account of the emancipation issue is **Ira Berlin, et al.**, ***Slaves No More: Three Essays on Emancipation and the Civil War*** (1992).

The activities of women in the U.S. Sanitary Commission, as spies, and even as soldiers are covered in **Jeanie Attie**, ***Patriotic Toil: Northern Women and the Civil War*** (1998); and **Elizabeth D. Leonard**, ***All the Daring of a Soldier: Women of the Civil War Armies*** (1999).

MINDTAP is a fully online personalized learning experience built upon Cengage Learning content. MindTap® combines student learning tools—readings, multimedia, activities, and assessments—into a singular Learning Path that guides students through the course and helps students develop the critical thinking, analysis, and communication skills that are essential to academic and professional success.

17 Reconstruction, 1863–1877

17.1 **The Cotton Pickers** The great American painter Winslow Homer began his career during the Civil War as a battlefront artist for *Harper's Weekly*. After the Civil War he returned to the South, painting a number of sensitive individual portraits of African Americans during Reconstruction. This 1876 painting captures the yearning of two women who, even with the end of slavery, are still picking cotton.

FROM THE BEGINNING of the Civil War, the North fought to "reconstruct" the Union. Lincoln at first attempted to restore the Union as it had existed before 1861, but once the abolition of slavery became a northern war aim, the Union could never be reconstructed on its old foundations. Instead, it must experience a "new birth of freedom," as Lincoln had said at the dedication of the military cemetery at Gettysburg.

But precisely what did "a new birth of freedom" mean? At the very least, it meant the end of slavery. The slave states would be reconstructed on a free-labor basis. But what would liberty look like for the 4 million freed slaves? Would they become citizens equal to their former masters in the eyes of the law? Would they have the right to vote? Should Confederate leaders and soldiers be punished for treason? On what terms should the Confederate states return to the Union? What would be the powers of the states and of the national government in a reconstructed Union? ■

17-1 Wartime Reconstruction

Q *What plans for reconstruction did Lincoln consider during the war?*

Lincoln pondered these problems long and hard. At first he feared that whites in the South would never extend equal rights to the freed slaves. After all, even most northern states were denying full civil equality to the few black people within their borders. In 1862, Lincoln encouraged freedpeople to emigrate to all-black countries such as Haiti, where they would have a chance to get ahead without having to face the racism of whites. Black leaders, abolitionists, and many Republicans objected to that policy. Blacks were Americans. Why should they not have the rights of American citizens instead of being urged to leave the country?

Lincoln eventually embraced the logic and justice of that view. But in beginning the process of reconstruction, he first reached out to southern whites whose allegiance to the Confederacy was lukewarm. On December 8, 1863, Lincoln issued his Proclamation of Amnesty and Reconstruction, which offered a presidential pardon to southern whites who took an oath of allegiance to the United States and accepted the abolition of slavery. In any state where the number of white males aged 21 or older who took this oath equaled 10 percent of the number of voters in 1860, that nucleus could reestablish a state government to which Lincoln promised presidential recognition.

Because the war was still raging, this policy could be carried out only where Union troops controlled substantial portions of a Confederate state: Louisiana, Arkansas, and Tennessee in early 1864. Nevertheless, Lincoln hoped that once the process had begun in those areas, it might snowball as Union military victories convinced more and more Confederates that their cause was hopeless. But those military victories were long delayed, and in most parts of the South, reconstruction did not begin until 1865.

17-1a *Radical Republicans and Reconstruction*

Growing opposition within Lincoln's own party slowed the process as well. Many Republicans believed that white men who had fought against the Union should not be rewarded with restoration of their political rights while black men who had fought for the Union were denied those rights. Radical Republicans, led by Thaddeus Stevens in the House and Charles Sumner in the Senate, distrusted oaths of allegiance sworn by ex-Confederates. Rather than simply restoring the old ruling class to power, asked Sumner, why not give freed slaves the vote, to provide a genuinely loyal nucleus of supporters in the South? If the freedpeople were landless, some Radical Republicans said, provide them with land by confiscating the plantations of leading Confederates as punishment for treason.

These radical positions did not command a majority of Congress in 1864. Yet the experience of Louisiana, the first state to reorganize under Lincoln's more moderate policy, convinced even non-Radical Republicans to block Lincoln's program. Enough white men in the occupied portion of the state took the oath of allegiance to satisfy Lincoln's conditions. They adopted a new state constitution and formed a government that abolished slavery and provided a school system for blacks. But despite Lincoln's private appeal to the new government to grant literate blacks and black Union soldiers the right to vote, the reconstructed Louisiana legislature chose not to do so. It also authorized planters to enforce restrictive labor policies on black plantation workers. Louisiana's actions alienated a majority of congressional Republicans, who refused to admit representatives and senators from the "reconstructed" state.

At the same time, though, Congress failed to enact a reconstruction policy of its own. This was not for lack of trying. In fact, both houses passed the Wade-Davis reconstruction bill (named for Senator Benjamin Wade of Ohio and Representative Henry Winter Davis of Maryland) in July 1864. That bill did not **enfranchise** blacks, but it did impose such stringent loyalty requirements on southern whites that few of them could take the required oath. Lincoln therefore vetoed it.

Lincoln's action infuriated many Republicans, and the bitter squabble threatened for a time to destroy Lincoln's chances of being reelected. Union military success in fall 1864, however, reunited the Republicans behind Lincoln. The collapse of Confederate military resistance the following spring set the stage for compromise between the president and Congress on a policy for the postwar South. Two days after Appomattox, Lincoln promised that he would soon announce such a policy, which probably would have included voting rights for some blacks and stronger measures to protect their civil rights. But three days later, Lincoln was assassinated.

17-2 Andrew Johnson and Reconstruction

Q *What were the positions of Presidents Abraham Lincoln and Andrew Johnson and of the moderate and Radical Republicans in Congress on the issues of restoring the South to the Union and protecting the rights of freed slaves?*

In 1864, Republicans had adopted the name Union Party to attract the votes of War Democrats and border-state Unionists who could not bring themselves to vote Republican. For the same reason, they also nominated Andrew Johnson of Tennessee as Lincoln's running mate.

Of "poor white" heritage, Johnson had clawed his way up in the rough-and-tumble politics of east Tennessee. This region of small farms and few slaves held little love for the planters who controlled the state. Andrew Johnson denounced the planters as "stuck-up aristocrats" who had no empathy

CHRONOLOGY

1863	Lincoln issues Proclamation of Amnesty and Reconstruction
1864	Congress passes Wade-Davis bill; Lincoln kills it by pocket veto
1865	Congress establishes Freedmen's Bureau • Andrew Johnson becomes president, announces his reconstruction plan • Southern states enact Black Codes • Congress refuses to seat southern congressmen elected under Johnson's plan
1866	Congress passes civil rights bill and expands Freedmen's Bureau over Johnson's vetoes • Race riots in Memphis and New Orleans • Congress approves Fourteenth Amendment • Republicans increase congressional majority in fall elections
1867	Congress passes Reconstruction Acts over Johnson's vetoes • Congress passes Tenure of Office Act over Johnson's veto
1868	Most southern senators and representatives readmitted to Congress under congressional plan of Reconstruction • Andrew Johnson impeached but not convicted • Ulysses S. Grant elected president • Fourteenth Amendment is ratified
1870	Fifteenth Amendment is ratified
1871	Congress passes Ku Klux Klan Act
1872	Liberal Republicans defect from party • Grant wins reelection
1873	Economic depression begins with the Panic of 1873
1874	Democrats win control of House of Representatives
1875	Democrats implement Mississippi Plan • Congress passes Civil Rights Act
1876	Centennial celebration in Philadelphia • Disputed presidential election causes constitutional crisis
1877	Compromise of 1877 installs Rutherford B. Hayes as president • Hayes withdraws troops from South
1883	Supreme Court declares Civil Rights Act of 1875 unconstitutional

with the southern yeomen for whom Johnson became a self-appointed spokesman. Johnson, although a Democrat, was the only senator from a seceding state who refused to support the Confederacy. For this stance, the Republicans rewarded him with the vice presidential nomination, hoping to attract the votes of pro-war Democrats and upper-South Unionists.

Booth's bullet therefore elevated to the presidency a man who still thought of himself as primarily a Democrat and a southerner. The trouble this might cause in a party that was mostly Republican and northern was not immediately apparent, however. In fact, Johnson's enmity toward the "stuck-up aristocrats" whom he blamed for leading the South into secession prompted him to utter dire threats. "Traitors must be impoverished.... They must not only be punished, but their social power must be destroyed."

Radical Republicans liked the sound of this. Johnson seemed to promise the type of reconstruction they favored—one that would deny political power to ex-Confederates and would enfranchise blacks. They envisioned a coalition between these new black voters and the small minority of southern whites who had never supported the Confederacy. These men could be expected to vote Republican. Republican governments in southern states would guarantee freedom and would pass laws to provide civil rights and economic opportunity for freed slaves. They would also strengthen the Republican Party nationally.

17-2a *Johnson's Policy*

From a combination of pragmatic, partisan, and idealistic motives, therefore, Radical Republicans prepared to implement a progressive reconstruction policy. But Johnson unexpectedly refused to cooperate. Instead of calling Congress into special session, he moved ahead on his own. On May 29, 1865, Johnson issued two proclamations. The first provided a blanket **amnesty** for all but the highest-ranking Confederate officials and military officers, and those ex-Confederates with taxable property worth $20,000 or more—the "stuck-up aristocrats." The second named a provisional governor for North Carolina and directed him to call an election of delegates to frame a new state constitution. Only white men who had received amnesty and taken an oath of allegiance could vote. Similar proclamations soon followed for other former Confederate states. Johnson's policy was clear: He would exclude both blacks and upper-class whites from the reconstruction process.

Although at first many Republicans supported Johnson's policy, the radicals were dismayed. They feared that restricting the vote to whites would lead to oppression of the newly freed slaves and restoration of the old power structure in the South. They began to sense that Johnson (who had owned slaves) was as dedicated to white supremacy as any Confederate. "White men alone must govern the South," he told a Democratic senator. After a tense confrontation with a group of black men led by Frederick Douglass, who had visited the White House to urge black suffrage, Johnson told his private secretary: "I know that damned Douglass; he's just like any nigger, and he would sooner cut a white man's throat than not."

Moderate Republicans believed that black men should participate to some degree in the reconstruction process, but in 1865 they were not yet prepared to break with the president. They regarded his policy as an "experiment" that would be modified as time went on.

17-2b *Southern Defiance*

As it happened, none of the state conventions enfranchised a single black. Some of them even balked at ratifying the Thirteenth Amendment (which abolished slavery). Reports

Library of Congress, Prints and Photographs Division

Library of Congress, Prints and Photographs Division

17.2a (left) and 17.2b (right) **Andrew Johnson and Frederick Douglass** By 1866, the president and the leading black advocate for equal rights represented opposite poles in the debate about reconstruction. Johnson (left) wanted to bring the South back into the Union on the basis of white suffrage; Douglass (right) wanted black men to be granted the right to vote.

Q *How did Johnson's resistance to black voting rights become a factor in his impeachment two years later?*

from the South told of neo-Confederate violence against blacks and their white sympathizers. Johnson seemed to encourage such activities by allowing the organization of white militia units.

Then there was the matter of presidential pardons. After talking fiercely about punishing traitors, and after excluding several classes of them from his amnesty proclamation, Johnson began to issue special pardons to many ex-Confederates, restoring to them all property and political rights. Under the new state constitutions, southern voters were electing hundreds of ex-Confederates to state offices. Even more alarming to northerners, who thought they had won the war, was the election to Congress of no fewer than nine ex-Confederate congressmen, seven ex-Confederate state officials, four generals, four colonels, and even the former Confederate vice president, Alexander H. Stephens.

Somehow the aristocrats and traitors Johnson had denounced in April had taken over the reconstruction process. They did so by flattering the presidential ego. Thousands of prominent ex-Confederates applied for pardons, confessing the error of their ways and appealing for presidential mercy. Johnson reveled in his power over these once-haughty aristocrats. Johnson also received praise and support from leading northern Democrats. Although the Republicans had placed him on their presidential ticket in 1864, Johnson was after all a Democrat. That party's leaders enticed Johnson with visions of reelection as a Democrat in 1868 if he could manage to reconstruct the South in a manner that would preserve a Democratic majority there.

17-2c *The Black Codes*

That was just what the Republicans feared. In the fall of 1865, their concern that state governments devoted to white supremacy would reduce the freedpeople to a condition close to slavery was confirmed when some of those governments enacted "**Black Codes**."

One of the first tasks of the legislatures of the reconstructed states was to define the rights of 4 million former slaves. The option of treating them exactly like white citizens was scarcely considered. Instead, the states excluded black people from juries and the ballot box, did not permit them to testify against whites in court, banned interracial marriage, and punished blacks more severely than whites for certain crimes. Some states defined any unemployed black person as a vagrant and hired him out to a planter, forbade blacks to lease land, and provided for the apprenticing to whites of black youths.

These Black Codes aroused anger among northern Republicans, who saw them as a brazen attempt to reinstate a **quasi-slavery**. "We tell the white men of Mississippi," declared the *Chicago Tribune*, "that the men of the North will convert the State of Mississippi into a frog pond before they will allow such laws to disgrace one foot of the soil in which the bones of our soldiers sleep and over which the flag of freedom waves." And in fact, the Union army's occupation forces did suspend the implementation of Black Codes that discriminated on racial grounds.

17-2d *Land and Labor in the Postwar South*

The Black Codes, although discriminatory, were designed to address a genuine problem. The end of the war had left black-white relations in the South in a state of limbo. The South's economy was in a shambles. Burned-out plantations, fields growing up in weeds, and railroads without tracks, bridges, or rolling stock marked the trail of war. Nearly half of the livestock in the former Confederacy and most other tangible assets except the land had been destroyed. Law and order broke down in many areas. The war had ended early enough in the spring to allow the planting of at least some food crops. But who would cultivate them? One-quarter of the South's white farmers had been killed in the war; the slaves were slaves no more. "We have nothing left to begin anew with," lamented a South Carolina planter. "I never did a day's work in my life, and I don't know how to begin."

Despite all of this trouble, life went on. Soldiers' widows and their children plowed and planted. Slaveless planters and their wives calloused their hands for the first time. Confederate veterans drifted home and went to work. Former slave owners asked their former slaves to work the land for wages or shares of the crop, and many did so. Others refused, because for them an essential part of freedom was leaving the place where they had been in bondage.

Thus, the roads were alive with freedpeople who were on the move in summer 1865. Many of them signed on to work at farms just a few miles from their old homes. Others moved into town. Some looked for relatives who had been sold away during slavery or from whom they had been separated during the war. Some wandered aimlessly. Crime increased as people, both blacks and whites, stole food to survive, and as whites organized vigilante groups to discipline blacks and force them to work.

17-2e *The Freedmen's Bureau*

Into this vacuum stepped the U.S. Army and the **Freedmen's Bureau**. Tens of thousands of troops remained in the South as an occupation force until civil government could be restored. The Freedmen's Bureau (its official title was Bureau of Refugees, Freedmen, and Abandoned Lands), created by Congress in March 1865, became the principal agency for overseeing relations between former slaves and owners. Headed by the antislavery general Oliver O. Howard and staffed by army officers, the bureau established posts throughout the South to supervise free-labor wage contracts between landowners and freedpeople. The Freedmen's Bureau also issued food rations to 150,000 people daily during 1865, one-third of them to whites. Southern whites viewed the Freedmen's Bureau with hostility. Without it, however, the postwar chaos and devastation in the South would have been much greater—as some whites privately admitted. Bureau agents used their influence with freedpeople to encourage them to sign free-labor contracts and return to work.

In negotiating labor contracts, the bureau tried to establish minimum wages. Lack of money in the South, however, caused many contracts to call for **share wages**—that is, paying workers with shares of the crop. At first, landowners worked their laborers in large groups (called gangs). But many black workers resented this arrangement as reminiscent of slavery. Thus, a new system evolved, called **sharecropping**, whereby a black family worked a specific piece of land in return for a share of the crop produced on it.

17.3 **The Freedmen's Bureau** Created in 1865, the Freedmen's Bureau stood between freed slaves and their former masters in the postwar South, charged with the task of protecting freedpeople from injustice and repression. Staffed by officers of the Union army, the bureau symbolized the military power of the government in its efforts to keep peace in the South.

Q *How does this 1868 Harper's Weekly illustration celebrate the Freedmen's Bureau?*

17-2f *Land for the Landless*

Freedpeople, of course, would have preferred to own the land they farmed. Some black farmers did manage to save up enough money to buy small plots of land. Demobilized black soldiers purchased land with their bounty payments, sometimes pooling their money to buy an entire plantation on which several black families settled. Northern philanthropists helped some freedmen buy land. But most ex-slaves found the purchase of land impossible. Few of them had money, and even if they did, whites often refused to sell their land because it would mean losing a source of cheap labor and encouraging notions of black independence.

Several northern radicals proposed legislation to confiscate ex-Confederate land and redistribute it to freedpeople, but those proposals went nowhere. The most promising effort to put thousands of slaves on land of their own also failed. In January 1865, after his march through Georgia, General William T. Sherman had issued a military order setting aside thousands of acres of abandoned plantation land in the Georgia and South Carolina lowcountry for settlement by freed slaves. The army even turned over some of its surplus mules to black farmers. The expectation of **40 acres and a mule** excited freedpeople in 1865, but President Johnson's Amnesty Proclamation and his wholesale issuance of pardons restored most of this property to pardoned ex-Confederates. The same thing happened to white-owned land elsewhere in the South. Placed under the temporary care of the Freedmen's Bureau for subsequent possible distribution to freedpeople, by 1866 nearly all of this land had been restored to its former owners by order of President Johnson.

17-2g *Churches and Schools*

One of the success stories of Reconstruction was the founding of churches and schools by freedmen and freedwomen. Eager to move away from the control of whites, blacks founded numerous African Methodist Episcopal (AME) churches, as well as other denominations, across the South. In addition to being sites of worship, these churches became vital community centers, in which African Americans could also hone political skills. In some places churches became the sites of Republican Party convocations.

Likewise, freedmen and freedwomen were instrumental in founding schools across the South. Especially in rural areas away from towns or large plantations, black men and women had to take the initiative themselves to build schoolhouses and hire teachers. Elsewhere, the Freedmen's Bureau, hand in hand with freedpeople and Northern abolitionists, worked to set up schools.

Library of Congress, Prints and Photographs Division

17.4 A Black School during Reconstruction In the antebellum South, teaching slaves to read and write was forbidden. Thus, about 90 percent of the freedpeople were illiterate in 1865. One of their top priorities was education. At first, most of the teachers in the freedmen's schools established by northern missionary societies were northern white women, but as black teachers were trained, they took over the elementary schools, such as this one, photographed in the 1870s.

During the war, northern freedmen's aid societies and missionary societies founded by abolitionists had sent teachers to Union-occupied areas of the South to set up schools for freed slaves. Now, this effort was expanded. Two thousand northern teachers, three-quarters of them women, fanned out into every part of the South, working with freedpeople and the Freedmen's Bureau. As freedwomen in particular gained education as teachers, they staffed the mission schools and later the public schools established by Reconstruction state governments. By 1867 African Americans comprised one-third of the teachers in freedmen's schools, and their numbers continued to grow.

After 1870, the missionary societies concentrated more heavily on making higher education available to African Americans. Many of the traditionally black colleges in the South today were founded and supported by their efforts. This education crusade, which the black leader W. E. B. Du Bois described as "the most wonderful peace-battle of the nineteenth century," reduced the southern black illiteracy rate to 70 percent by 1880 and to 48 percent by 1900.

17-3 The Advent of Congressional Reconstruction

Q *What were the major accomplishments of congressional Reconstruction?*

Political reconstruction shaped the civil and political rights of freedpeople. By the time Congress met in December 1865, the Republican majority was determined to control the process by which former Confederate states would regain full representation. Congress refused to admit the representatives and senators elected by the former Confederate states under Johnson's reconstruction policy and set up a special committee to formulate new terms. The committee held hearings at which southern Unionists, freedpeople, and U.S. Army officers testified to abuse and terrorism in the South. Their testimony convinced Republicans of the need for stronger federal intervention to define and protect the civil rights of freedpeople. Many radicals wanted to go further and grant the ballot to black men.

Most Republicans realized that northern voters would not support such a radical policy, however. Racism was still strong in the North, where most states denied the right to vote to the few blacks living within their borders. Moderate Republicans feared that Democrats would exploit northern racism in the congressional elections of 1866 if Congress made black suffrage a cornerstone of Reconstruction. Instead, the special committee decided to draft a constitutional amendment that would encourage southern states to enfranchise blacks but would not require them to do so.

17-3a *Schism between President and Congress*

Meanwhile, Congress passed two laws to protect the economic and civil rights of freedpeople. The first extended the life of the Freedmen's Bureau and expanded its powers. The second defined freedpeople as citizens with equal legal rights and gave federal courts appellate jurisdiction to enforce those rights. To the dismay of moderates who were trying to heal the widening breach between the president and Congress, Johnson vetoed both measures. He followed this action with a speech to Democratic supporters in which he denounced Republican leaders as traitors who did not want to restore the Union except on terms that would degrade white southerners. Democratic newspapers applauded the president for vetoing bills that would "compound our race with niggers, gypsies, and baboons."

17-3b *The Fourteenth Amendment*

Johnson had thrown down the gauntlet to congressional Republicans, and they did not hesitate to take it up. With more than a two-thirds majority in both houses, they passed the Freedmen's Bureau and Civil Rights bills over the president's vetoes. Then on April 30, 1866, the special committee submitted to Congress its proposed Fourteenth Amendment to the Constitution. After lengthy debate, the amendment received the required two-thirds majority in Congress on June 13 and went to the states for ratification. Section 1 defined all native-born or naturalized persons, including blacks, as American citizens and prohibited the states from abridging the "privileges and immunities" of citizens, from depriving "any person of life, liberty, or property without due process of law," and from denying to any person "the equal protection of the laws." Section 2 gave states the option of either enfranchising black males or losing a proportionate number of congressional seats and electoral votes. Section 3 disqualified a significant number of ex-Confederates from holding federal or state office. Section 4 guaranteed the national debt and repudiated the Confederate debt. Section 5 empowered Congress to enforce the Fourteenth Amendment by "appropriate legislation." The Fourteenth Amendment had far-reaching consequences. Section 1 has become the most important provision in the Constitution for defining and enforcing civil rights.

17-4c *The 1866 Elections*

Republicans entered the 1866 congressional elections campaign with the Fourteenth Amendment as their platform. They made clear that any ex-Confederate state that ratified the amendment would be declared "reconstructed" and that its representatives and senators would be seated in Congress. Tennessee ratified the amendment, but Johnson counseled other southern legislatures to reject the amendment, which they did. Johnson then prepared for an all-out campaign to gain a friendly northern majority in the congressional elections.

Johnson began his campaign by creating a National Union Party made up of a few conservative Republicans who disagreed with their party, some border-state Unionists who

© Stock Montage, Inc.

"PARDON, Columbia—'Shall I Trust These Men'?"

Nast, Thomas, 1840–1902/Library of Congress Prints and Photographs Division[LC-USZ62-102257]

"FRANCHISE—'And Not This Man'?"

17.5 **Cartoons for Freedom** One of the best political cartoonists in American history, Thomas Nast drew scores of cartoons for *Harper's Weekly* in the 1860s and 1870s advocating the use of federal power to guarantee the liberty and enforce the equal rights of freed slaves. This illustration (1865) is an eloquent graphic expression of a powerful argument for giving freedmen the right to vote: Black men who fought for the Union were more deserving of this privilege than white men who fought against it. Several of the kneeling figures are recognizable Confederate leaders: Alexander Stephens and Robert E. Lee in the foreground, Jefferson Davis to Lee's left, and John C. Breckinridge, Joseph E. Johnston, and Robert Toombs behind and to Davis's left.

Q *What other visual details does Nast's illustration include to make an argument for black male enfranchisemnt?*

supported the president, and Democrats. But many northern Democrats still carried the taint of having opposed the war effort, and most northern voters did not trust them. Further, race riots in Memphis and New Orleans, with white mobs attacking blacks, bolstered Republican arguments that national power was necessary to protect "the fruits of victory" in the South. Perhaps the biggest liability of the National Union Party was Johnson. In a whistle-stop tour through the North, he traded insults with hecklers and embarrassed his supporters by comparing himself to Christ and his Republican adversaries to Judas.

Republicans swept the election: They gained a three-to-one majority in the next Congress. Having rejected the Reconstruction terms embodied in the Fourteenth Amendment, southern Democrats now faced far more stringent terms. "They would not cooperate in rebuilding what they destroyed," wrote an exasperated moderate Republican, so "we must remove the rubbish and rebuild from the bottom. Whether they are willing or not, we must compel obedience to the Union and demand protection for its humblest citizen."

17-3d *The Reconstruction Acts of 1867*

In March 1867, the new Congress enacted over Johnson's vetoes two laws prescribing new procedures for the full restoration of the former Confederate states to the Union. The Reconstruction Acts of 1867 divided the 10 southern states into five military districts, directed army officers to register voters for the election of delegates to new constitutional conventions, and enfranchised males aged 21 and older (including blacks) to vote in those elections. When a state had adopted a new constitution that granted equal civil and political rights regardless of race and had ratified the Fourteenth Amendment, it would be declared reconstructed, and its newly elected congressmen would be seated.

These measures embodied a true revolution. Just a few years earlier, southern whites had been masters of 4 million slaves and part of an independent Confederate nation. Now they were shorn of political power, with their former slaves not only free but also politically empowered.

What They Said

Black Codes versus Black Politics

At first, during Reconstruction white southerners attempted to reerect a legal and racial system as close to slavery as possible. But after the passage of the Reconstruction Acts of 1867, African Americans met in conventions throughout the South to affirm a politics of freedom. These two selections trace the differences between white and black ideas of freedom after Emancipation.

From the Mississippi Black Code, November 1865

Section 2. *Be it further enacted*, that all freedmen, free Negroes, and mulattoes in this state over the age of eighteen years found on the second Monday in January 1866, or thereafter, with no lawful employment or business, or found unlawfully assembling themselves together either in the day or nighttime, and all white persons so assembling with freedmen, free Negroes, or mulattoes, or usually associating with freedmen, free Negroes, or mulattoes on terms of equality, or living in adultery or fornication with a freedwoman, free Negro, or mulatto, shall be deemed vagrants; and, on conviction thereof, shall be fined in the sum of not exceeding, in the case of a freedman, free Negro, or mulatto, $150, and a white man, $200, and imprisoned at the discretion of the court, the free Negro not exceeding ten days, and the white man not exceeding six months.

Address of the Colored Convention to the People of Alabama, 1867

As there seems to be considerable difference of opinion concerning the "legal rights of the colored man," it will not be amiss to say that we claim exactly *the same rights, privileges and immunities as are enjoyed by white men*—we ask nothing more and will be content with nothing less. *All legal* distinctions between the races are now abolished. The word *white* is stricken from our laws. . . . So long as a park or a street is a public park or street the entire public has the right to use it; so long as a car or a steamboat is a public conveyance, it must carry all who come to it, and serve all alike who pay alike. The law no longer knows white nor black, but simply men, and consequently we are entitled to ride in public conveyances, hold office, sit on juries and do everything else which we have in the past been prevented from doing solely on the ground of our color.

Q *What white anxieties regarding post-emancipation society are expressed in Mississippi's Black Code?*

Q *How do these two documents define the legal rights of blacks differently?*

Sources: (top) Mississippi Black Code, November 1865; (middle) Address of the Colored Convention to the People of Alabama, 1867. (bottom) Excerpt from U.S. Attorney General's reply to Governor Adelbert Ames' request for troops (1875).

In 1867, the emancipation and enfranchisement of black Americans seemed, as a sympathetic French journalist described it, "one of the most radical revolutions known in history."

Like most revolutions, the reconstruction process did not go smoothly. Many Southern Democrats breathed defiance and refused to cooperate. The presence of the army minimized antiblack violence, but thousands of white southerners who were eligible to vote refused to do so, hoping that their nonparticipation would delay the process long enough for northern voters to come to their senses and elect Democrats to Congress.

Blacks and their white allies organized **Union leagues** to inform and mobilize the new black voters into the Republican Party. Democrats branded southern white Republicans as "**scalawags**" and northern settlers as "**carpetbaggers**." By September 1867, the 10 states had 735,000 black voters and only 635,000 white voters registered. At least one-third of the registered white voters were Republicans.

President Johnson did everything he could to block Reconstruction. He replaced several Republican generals in command of southern military districts with Democrats. He had his attorney general issue a ruling that interpreted the Reconstruction acts narrowly, thereby forcing a special session of Congress to pass a supplementary act in July 1867. He encouraged southern whites to obstruct the registration of voters and the election of convention delegates.

Johnson's purpose was to slow the process until 1868 in the hope that northern voters would repudiate Reconstruction in the presidential election of that year, when Johnson planned to run as the Democratic candidate. Off-year state elections in fall 1867 encouraged that hope. Republicans suffered setbacks in several northern states, especially where they endorsed referendum measures to enfranchise black men.

Library of Congress, Prints and Photographs Division

17.6 **The Burning of a Freedmen's School** Because freedpeople's education symbolized black progress, whites who resented and resisted this progress sometimes attacked and burned freedmen's schools. This dramatic *Harper's Weekly* illustration shows a white mob burning a school during antiblack riots in Memphis in May 1866.

17-4 The Impeachment of Andrew Johnson

Q *Why was Andrew Johnson impeached? Why was he acquitted?*

Johnson struck even more boldly against Reconstruction after the 1867 elections. "What does Johnson mean to do?" an exasperated Republican asked another. "I am afraid his doings will make us all favor impeachment." In February 1868, Johnson removed from office Secretary of War Edwin M. Stanton, who had administered the War Department in support of the congressional Reconstruction policy. This appeared to violate the Tenure of Office Act, passed the year before over Johnson's veto, which required Senate consent for such removals. By a vote of 126 to 47 along party lines, the House impeached Johnson on February 24. The official reason for **impeachment** was that he had violated the Tenure of Office Act (which Johnson considered unconstitutional). The real reason was Johnson's stubborn defiance of Congress on Reconstruction.

Under the U.S. Constitution, impeachment by the House does not remove an official from office. It is more like a grand jury indictment that must be tried by a petit jury—in this case, the Senate, which sat as a court to try Johnson on the impeachment charges brought by the House. If convicted by a two-thirds majority of the Senate, he would be removed from office.

The impeachment trial proved long and complicated, which worked in Johnson's favor by allowing passions to cool. The Constitution specifies the grounds on which a president can be impeached and removed: "Treason, Bribery, or other high Crimes and Misdemeanors." The issue was whether Johnson was guilty of any of these acts. His able defense counsel exposed technical ambiguities in the Tenure of Office Act that raised doubts about whether Johnson had actually violated it.

Several moderate Republicans feared that the precedent of impeachment might upset the delicate balance of powers between the executive branch, Congress, and the judiciary that was an essential element of the Constitution. Behind the scenes, Johnson strengthened his case by promising to appoint the respected general John M. Schofield as secretary of war and to stop obstructing the Reconstruction acts. In the end, seven Republican senators plus all Democrats voted for acquittal on May 16, and the final tally fell one vote short of the necessary two-thirds majority.

17-4a *The Completion of Formal Reconstruction*

The impeachment trial's end cleared the poisonous air in Washington, and Johnson quietly served out his term. Constitutional conventions met in the South during the 1867–1868 winter and the following spring (see Map 17.1). Hostile whites described them as "Bones and Banjoes Conventions" and the Republican delegates as "ragamuffins and jailbirds." In sober fact, however, the delegates were earnest advocates of a new order, and the constitutions they wrote were among the most progressive in the nation. Three-quarters of the delegates to the 10 conventions were Republicans. About 25 percent of those Republicans were northern whites who had relocated to the South after the war; 45 percent were native southern whites who braved the social ostracism of the white majority to cast their lot with the despised Republicans; and 30 percent were blacks. Only in the South Carolina convention were blacks in the majority.

The new state constitutions enacted **universal male suffrage**, putting them ahead of most northern states on that score. Some of the constitutions disfranchised certain classes of ex-Confederates for several years, but by 1872, all such disqualifications had been removed. The constitutions mandated statewide public schools for both races for the first time in the South. Most states permitted segregated schools, but schools of any kind for blacks represented a great step forward. Most of the constitutions increased the state's responsibility for social welfare beyond anything previously known in the South.

Violence in some parts of the South marred the voting on ratification of these state constitutions. The **Ku Klux Klan**, a night-riding white terrorist organization, made its first appearance during the elections. Nevertheless, voters in seven

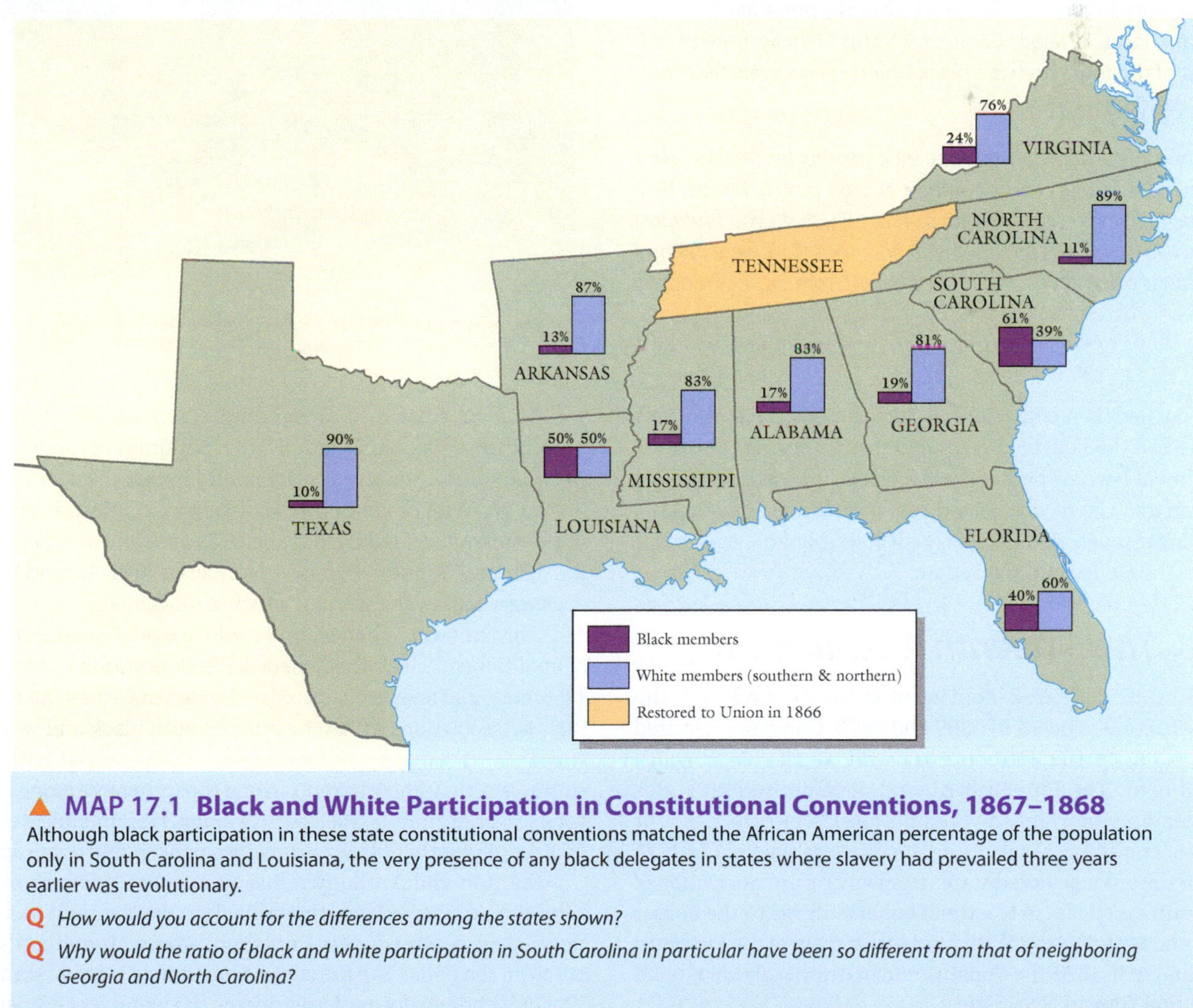

▲ **MAP 17.1 Black and White Participation in Constitutional Conventions, 1867–1868**
Although black participation in these state constitutional conventions matched the African American percentage of the population only in South Carolina and Louisiana, the very presence of any black delegates in states where slavery had prevailed three years earlier was revolutionary.

Q *How would you account for the differences among the states shown?*

Q *Why would the ratio of black and white participation in South Carolina in particular have been so different from that of neighboring Georgia and North Carolina?*

Interpreting the Visual Past

An Unholy Alliance: "This Is a White Man's Government"

This powerful allegorical cartoon by Thomas Nast, published in *Harper's Weekly* on September 5, 1868, offers a visual critique of Democrats during the 1868 elections. Nast pictures three white men, each representing a different constituency, hands clasped in an unholy alliance. On the left is an Irish American man, whose facial features are depicted in crude racist terms. His cap tells us that he is from the Five Points slum in New York City, and he carries a club labeled "A Vote" to indicate the violence he will use to ensure a white man's government. In the background we see New York's Colored Orphans Asylum in flames, as well as a black man hanged on a lamppost, to remind us that the Irish were implicated in the draft riots violence against blacks in 1863.

The central figure carries a dagger labeled "The Lost Cause" in his left hand, wears a belt buckle with the initials "CSA" (Confederate States of America), and has the initials "N.B.F" on his straw hat. He is Nathan Bedford Forrest, a founder of the Ku Klux Klan and a participant in the massacre of black soldiers at Fort Pillow (he wears a badge on the left side labeled "Fort Pillow"). The man on the right, August Belmont, is a northern financier. His badge reads "5th Avenue," and he holds a purse aloft, stuffed with banknotes, labeled "Capital for Votes." Finally, underneath the feet of the three men is a black Union veteran reaching with his left hand for a ballot box.

Q *Compare this cartoon to political cartoons by Thomas Nast elsewhere in this chapter (image 17.5 on p. 476, image 17.10 on p. 485, and image 17.11 on p. 486). Which do you find most effective visually as an argument, and why? How were political cartoons of the 1860s and 1870s different from those of today?*

Nast, Thomas, 1840–1902/Library of Congress Prints and Photographs Division[LC-USZ62-121735]

17.7 **Thomas Nast, "This Is a White Man's Government," 1868.**

states ratified their constitutions and elected new legislatures that ratified the Fourteenth Amendment in spring 1868. That amendment became part of the U.S. Constitution the following summer, and the newly elected representatives and senators from those seven states, nearly all Republicans, took their seats in the House and the Senate.

17-4b *The Fifteenth Amendment*

The remaining three southern states completed the reconstruction process in 1869 and 1870. Congress required them to ratify the Fifteenth as well as the Fourteenth Amendment. The Fifteenth Amendment prohibited states from denying the right to vote on grounds of race, color, or previous condition of servitude. Its purpose was not only to prevent the reconstructed states from any future revocation of black suffrage, but also to extend equal suffrage to the border states and to the North. With final ratification of the Fifteenth Amendment in 1870, the Constitution became truly color blind for the first time in U.S. history.

But the Fifteenth Amendment still left half of the population disfranchised. Many supporters of woman suffrage were embittered by its failure to ban discrimination on the grounds of gender as well as race. The radical wing of the suffragists, led by Elizabeth Cady Stanton and Susan B. Anthony, therefore opposed the Fifteenth Amendment, causing a split in the woman suffrage movement.

This movement had shared the ideological egalitarianism of abolitionism since the Seneca Falls Convention of 1848. In 1866, male and female abolitionists formed the American Equal Rights Association (AERA) to work for both black and woman suffrage. Although some Republicans sympathized with the suffragists, they knew that no strong constituency among male voters favored granting the vote to women. Most members of the AERA thought that black enfranchisement should come first.

Stanton and Anthony refused to accept this reasoning. Why should illiterate southern blacks have the right to vote, they asked, when educated northern women remained shut out from the polls? The Fifteenth Amendment would establish "the most odious form of aristocracy the world has ever seen:

an aristocracy of sex." When a majority of delegates at the 1869 convention of the AERA voted to endorse the Fifteenth Amendment, several women led by Stanton and Anthony walked out and founded the National Woman Suffrage Association. The remaining delegates reorganized as the American Woman Suffrage Association. For the next two decades, these rival organizations, working for the same cause, remained at odds with each other.

17-4c *The Election of 1868*

Just as the presidential election of 1864 was a referendum on Lincoln's war policies, so the election of 1868 was a referendum on the Reconstruction policy of the Republicans. The Republican nominee was General **Ulysses S. Grant**. Although he had no political experience, Grant commanded greater authority and prestige than anyone else in the country. As general-in-chief of the army, he had opposed Johnson's Reconstruction policy in 1866 and had broken openly with the president in January 1868. That spring, Grant agreed to run for the presidency in order to preserve in peace the victory he had won in war.

The Democrats turned away from Andrew Johnson, who carried too many political liabilities. They nominated Horatio Seymour, the wartime governor of New York, bestowing on him the dubious privilege of running against Grant. Hoping to put together a majority consisting of the South plus New York and two or three other northern states, the Democrats adopted a militant platform denouncing the Reconstruction acts as "a flagrant usurpation of power ... unconstitutional, revolutionary, and void." The platform also demanded "the abolition of the Freedmen's Bureau, and all political instrumentalities designed to secure negro supremacy."

The vice presidential candidate, Frank Blair of Missouri, proclaimed that Democrats sought to "allow the white people to reorganize their own governments." The only way to achieve this bold counterrevolutionary goal was to suppress Republican voters in the South. This the Ku Klux Klan tried its best to do. In Louisiana, Georgia, Arkansas, and Tennessee, the Klan or Klan-like groups committed dozens of murders and intimidated thousands of black voters. The violence helped the Democratic cause in the South, but probably hurt it in the North, where many voters perceived the Klan as an organization of neo-Confederate paramilitary guerrillas. In fact, many Klansmen were former soldiers, and such famous Confederate generals as Nathan Bedford Forrest and John B. Gordon held high positions in the Klan.

Seymour did well in the South, carrying five former slave states and coming close in others, despite the solid Republican vote of the newly enfranchised blacks. Grant, however, swept the electoral vote 214 to 80. Seymour actually won a slight majority of the white voters nationally; without black enfranchisement, Grant would have had a minority of the popular vote.

Library of Congress Prints and Photographs Division[LC-USZ62-13018]

17.8 **Ulysses S. Grant as President** Grant's administration has long been criticized for its rampant corruption. But his own reputation as president has risen in recent years due to a recognition of his continuing commitment to principles of justice and equality for all during Reconstruction.

17-5 The Grant Administration

Q *Why was there an explosion of corruption during Grant's presidency? Why was the Republican coalition unstable in the South?*

Grant is usually considered a failure as president. That indictment is only partly correct. Grant's inexperience and poor judgment betrayed him into several unwise appointments of officials, who were later convicted of corruption, and scandals that plagued his back-to-back administrations (1869–1877). His secretary of war was impeached for selling appointments to army posts and Indian reservations, and his attorney general and secretary of the interior resigned under suspicion of malfeasance in 1875.

Although he was an honest man, Grant was too trusting of subordinates. He appointed many former members of his military family, as well as several of his wife's relatives, to offices for which they were scarcely qualified. In an era notorious for corruption at all levels of government, many of the scandals were not Grant's fault. The Tammany Hall "Ring" of "Boss" William Marcy Tweed in New York City may have stolen more money from taxpayers than all of the federal agencies combined. It was said that the only thing the Standard Oil Company could not do with the Ohio legislature was to refine it. In Washington, one of the most widely publicized scandals, the **Credit Mobilier Affair**, concerned Congress rather than the Grant administration. Several congressmen had accepted stock in the Credit Mobilier, a construction company for the Union Pacific Railroad, which received loans and land grants from the government. In return, the company expected lax congressional supervision, thereby permitting its financial manipulations.

What accounted for this explosion of corruption in the postwar decade? During the war, expansion of government contracts and the bureaucracy had created new opportunities for the unscrupulous. Following the intense sacrifices of the war years came a relaxation of tensions and standards. Rapid postwar economic growth, led by an extraordinary rush of railroad construction, further encouraged greed and get-rich-quick schemes of the kind satirized by Mark Twain and Charles Dudley Warner in their 1873 novel *The Gilded Age*, which gave its name to the era.

17-5a *Civil Service Reform*

Some of the apparent increase in corruption during the Gilded Age was more a matter of perception. Reformers focused a harsh light into the dark corners of corruption, hitherto unilluminated because of the nation's preoccupation with war and reconstruction. Thus, reformers' publicity may have exaggerated the actual extent of corruption. In reality, during the Grant administration, several government agencies made real progress in eliminating abuses that had flourished in earlier administrations.

The chief target of civil service reform was the "**spoils system**." With the slogan "To the victor belongs the spoils," the victorious party in an election rewarded party workers with appointments as postmasters, customs collectors, and the like. The spoils system politicized the bureaucracy and staffed it with unqualified personnel who spent more time working for their party than for the government. It also plagued every incoming president (and other elected officials) with the "swarm of office seekers" that loom so large in contemporary accounts (including those of the humorist Orpheus C. Kerr, whose nom de plume was pronounced "Office Seeker").

Civil service reformers wanted to separate the bureaucracy from politics by requiring competitive examinations for the appointment of civil servants. This movement gathered steam during the 1870s and finally achieved success in 1883 with the passage of the Pendleton Civil Service Reform Act, which established the modern structure of the civil service. When Grant took office, he seemed to share the sentiments of civil service reformers; several of his cabinet officers inaugurated examinations for certain appointments and promotions in their departments. Grant also named a civil service commission headed by George William Curtis, a leading reformer and editor of *Harper's Weekly*. But many congressmen, senators, and other politicians resisted civil service reform because **patronage** greased the political machines that kept them in office. They managed to subvert reform, sometimes using Grant as an unwitting ally and thus turning many reformers against the president.

17-5b *Foreign Policy Issues*

A foreign policy controversy added to Grant's woes. The irregular procedures by which his private secretary had negotiated a treaty to annex Santo Domingo (now the Dominican Republic) alienated leading Republican senators, who defeated ratification of the treaty. Politically inexperienced, Grant acted like a general who needed only to give orders, rather than a president who must cultivate supporters. The fallout from the Santo Domingo affair widened the fissure in the Republican Party between "spoilsmen" and "reformers."

But, the Grant administration had some solid foreign policy achievements to its credit. Hamilton Fish, the able secretary of state, negotiated the Treaty of Washington in 1871 to settle the vexing *Alabama* claims. These were damage claims against Britain for the destruction of American shipping by the C.S.S. *Alabama* and other Confederate commerce raiders built in British shipyards. The treaty established an international tribunal to arbitrate the U.S. claims, resulting in the award of $15.5 million in damages to U.S. ship owners and a British expression of regret.

17-5c *Reconstruction in the South*

During Grant's two administrations, the "Southern Question" was the most intractable issue. A phrase in Grant's acceptance of the presidential nomination in 1868 had struck a responsive chord in the North: "Let us have peace." With the ratification of the Fifteenth Amendment, many people breathed a sigh of relief at the apparent resolution of "the last great point that remained to be settled of the issues of the war." It was time to deal with other matters that had been long neglected. Ever since the annexation of Texas a quarter-century earlier, the nation had known scarcely a moment's respite from sectional strife. "Let us have done with Reconstruction," pleaded the *New York Tribune* in 1870. "LET US HAVE PEACE." But there was no peace. Reconstruction was not over; it had hardly begun. State governments elected by black and white voters were in place in the South, but Democratic violence against Reconstruction and the instability of the Republican coalition that sustained it portended trouble (see Map 17.2).

17-5d *Blacks in Office*

About 80 percent of southern Republican voters were black. During Reconstruction there were over one hundred African American men who held statewide office, whether elected or appointed, across the South. Another eight hundred served in state legislatures. An even larger number of officeholders held local positions. By any measure, black political achievements during Reconstruction were considerable.

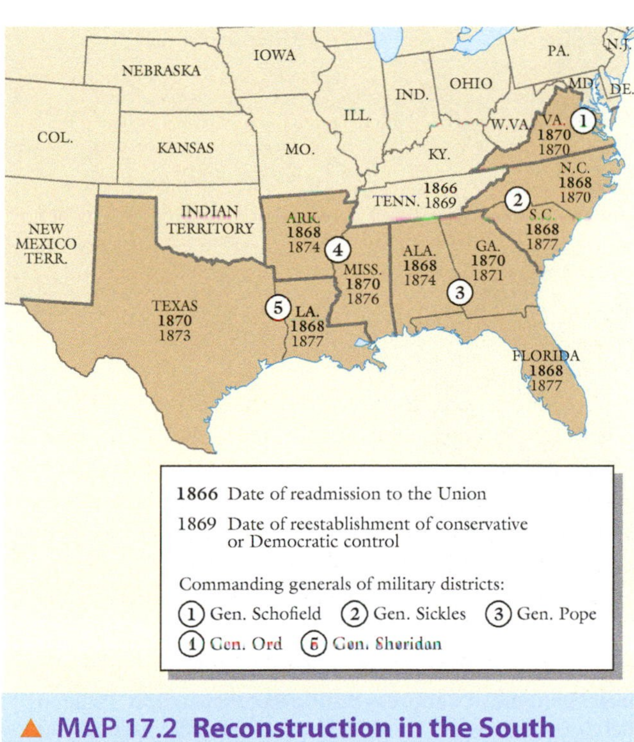

▲ MAP 17.2 Reconstruction in the South
The dates for each state listed on this map show how short-lived "Radical Reconstruction" was in most southern states.

Q *Why would the dates of Radical Reconstruction have differed among these states?*

Q *What are the main reasons for the end of Radical Reconstruction?*

But they were also fragile. Southern whites, who perceived the Republican Party as a symbol of conquest and humiliation, portrayed black voters and office-holders as illiterate, venal, incompetent, and corrupt. Yet most black leaders were educated and many had been free before the war. Of 14 black representatives and two black senators elected in the South between 1868 and 1876, all but three had attended secondary school and four had attended college. Several of the blacks elected to state offices were among the best-educated men of their day. Jonathan Gibbs, secretary of state in Florida from 1868 to 1872 and state superintendent of education from 1872 to 1874, was a graduate of Dartmouth College and Princeton Theological Seminary. Francis L. Cardozo, secretary of state in South Carolina for four years and treasurer for another four, was educated at the University of Glasgow and at theological schools in Edinburgh and London.

Unlike these black leaders, most black voters were former slaves who had been denied an education under the slave regime. But illiteracy did not preclude an understanding of political issues for black voters any more than it did for Irish American voters in the North, some of whom were also illiterate. Southern blacks thirsted for education. Participation in the Union League and the experience of voting were forms of education. Black churches and fraternal organizations proliferated during Reconstruction and tutored African Americans in their rights and responsibilities.

Still, the myth of black incompetence was longlasting in a racist society. The theme of "Negro rule" was also a staple of Democratic propaganda, as was the legend of the "Africanization" of southern governments during Reconstruction. These various myths were to be enshrined in folk memory, in generations of textbooks, and in film (see History Through Film: *The Birth of a Nation* (1915), page 488). In fact, however, blacks held only 15 to 20 percent of public offices, even at the height of Reconstruction in the early 1870s. No states had black governors (although the black lieutenant governor of Louisiana acted as governor for a month), and only one black man became a state supreme court justice. Nowhere except in South Carolina did blacks hold office in numbers anywhere near their proportion of the population; in that state, they constituted 52 percent of all state and federal elected officials from 1868 to 1876.

17-5e *"Carpetbaggers"*

Next to "Negro rule," carpetbagger corruption and scalawag rascality have been the prevailing myths of Reconstruction. Carpetbaggers did hold a disproportionate number of high political offices in southern state governments during Reconstruction. More than half of the Republican governors and nearly half of the congressmen and senators were northerners. A few did resemble the proverbial adventurer who came south with nothing but a carpetbag in which to stow the loot plundered from a helpless people. But most of the northerners were Union army officers who stayed on after the war as Freedmen's Bureau agents, teachers in black schools, or business

Library of Congress, Prints and Photographs Division

Library of Congress, Prints and Photographs Division

Robert B. Elliott, circa 1875 (litho), American Photographe, (19th century)/Schlesinger Library, Radcliffe Institute, Harvard University/The Bridgeman Art Library

17.9a (top left) 17.9b (top right) and 17.9c (bottom) **Three African American Members of Congress during Reconstruction** Pictured clockwise are Blanche K. Bruce (top left), Robert Smalls (top right), and Robert B. Elliott (bottom). Born into slavery, Bruce and Smalls became the two most prominent blacks in Congress during the 1870s. Bruce was elected to the United States Senate from Mississippi in 1875 and served his full six-year term despite the takeover of Mississippi by white-supremacist Democrats later in 1875. Smalls gained fame when he delivered the Confederate dispatch steamer *Planter* to the Union blockade fleet outside Charleston in 1862. After working as a pilot for the navy, Smalls emerged as a leader of the South Carolina Republican Party during Reconstruction and served several terms in the House. Of West Indian descent, Elliott was born in England and immigrated to South Carolina in 1867. He was elected to the House for two terms and became an eloquent spokesman for civil rights.

investors. They hoped to rebuild southern society in the image of the free-labor North. Many were college graduates at a time when fewer than 2 percent of Americans had attended college. Most brought not empty carpetbags but considerable capital, which they invested in what they hoped would become a new South. They also invested human capital—themselves—in a drive to modernize the region's social structure and democratize its politics. But they underestimated the hostility of southern whites, most of whom regarded them as agents of an alien culture and leaders of an enemy army—as indeed they had been—in a war that for many southerners was not yet over.

17-5f *"Scalawags"*

Most of the native-born whites who joined the southern Republican Party came from the upcountry Unionist areas of western North Carolina and Virginia, eastern Tennessee, and elsewhere. Others were former Whigs who saw an opportunity to rebuild the South's economy in partnership with northern Republicans. Republicans, said a North Carolina scalawag, were the "party of progress, of education, of development... . Yankees and Yankee notions are just what we want in this country. We want their capital to build factories and work shops, and railroads."

But Yankees and Yankee notions were just what most southern whites did not want. Democrats saw that the southern Republican Party they abhorred was a fragile coalition of blacks and whites, Yankees and southerners, hill-country yeomen and lowcountry entrepreneurs, illiterates and college graduates. The party was weakest along the seams where these disparate elements joined, especially the racial seam. Democrats attacked that weakness with every weapon at their command, from social ostracism of white Republicans to economic intimidation of black employees and sharecroppers. The most potent Democratic weapon was violence.

17-5g *The Ku Klux Klan*

The generic name for the secret groups that terrorized the southern countryside was the Ku Klux Klan, but some went by other names (the Knights of the White Camelia in Louisiana, for example). Part of the Klan's purpose was social control of the black population. Sharecroppers who tried to extract better terms from landowners, or black people who were considered too "uppity," were likely to receive a midnight

878 HARPER'S W

How easily wicked and treasonable organizations may gain the control over the peaceable and the industrious members of society has always been signally apparent at the South. A Tennessee, venture even to denounce the murderers or the violators of the laws; or if any Northern journal, roused to a proper indignation by the wrongs inflicted upon peaceable settlers

17.10 Thomas Nast, "The Union As It Was," 1874. This Harper's Weekly cartoon shows a White Leaguer and a hooded member of the Ku Klux Klan shaking hands on the Lost Cause. Some of their violent handiwork as white supremacists is visible in the background, with a lynched body hanging from a tree on the left, while a black schoolhouse burns on the right. In the foreground an African American family tries to protect itself. The caption on the shield reads "The Lost Cause; Worse Than Slavery."

whipping—or worse—from white-sheeted Klansmen. Scores of black schools, perceived as a particular threat to white supremacy, went up in flames.

The Klan's main purpose was political: to destroy the Republican Party by terrorizing its voters and, if necessary, by murdering its leaders. No one knows how many politically motivated killings took place—certainly hundreds, probably thousands. Nearly all of the victims were Republicans; most of them were black. In one notorious incident, the Colfax Massacre in Louisiana (April 18, 1873), a clash between black militia and armed whites left three whites and nearly 100 blacks dead. Half of the blacks were killed in cold blood after they had surrendered. In some places, notably Tennessee and Arkansas, Republican militias formed to suppress and disarm the Klan, but in most areas the militias were outgunned and outmaneuvered by ex-Confederate veteran Klansmen. Some Republican governors were reluctant to use black militia against white guerrillas for fear of sparking a racial bloodbath—as happened at Colfax.

The answer seemed to be federal troops. In 1870 and 1871, Congress enacted three laws intended to enforce the Fourteenth and Fifteenth Amendments. Interference with voting rights became a federal offense, and any attempt to deprive another person of civil or political rights became a felony. The third law, passed on April 20, 1871, and popularly called the Ku Klux Klan Act, gave the president power to suspend the writ of **habeas corpus** and send in federal troops to suppress armed resistance to federal law.

Armed with these laws, the Grant administration moved against the Klan. Because Grant was sensitive to charges of "military despotism," he used his powers with restraint. He suspended the writ of habeas corpus in only nine South Carolina counties. Nevertheless, there and elsewhere federal marshals backed by troops arrested thousands of suspected Klansmen. Federal grand juries indicted more than 3,000, and several hundred defendants pleaded guilty in return for suspended sentences. To clear clogged court dockets so that the worst offenders could be tried quickly, the Justice Department dropped charges against nearly 2,000 others. About 600 Klansmen were convicted; most of them received fines or light jail sentences, but 65 went to a federal penitentiary for terms of up to five years.

17-5h *The Election of 1872*

These measures broke the back of the Klan in time for the 1872 presidential election. A group of dissident Republicans had emerged to challenge Grant's reelection. They believed

IT IS ONLY A TRUCE TO REGAIN POWER ("PLAYING POSSUM").
H. G. "Clasp hands over the bloody chasm."
C. S. "Freely accept the hand that is offered, and reach forth thine own in friendly grasp."

17.11 **One of Thomas Nast's Anti-Greeley Cartoons** This cartoon appeared in *Harper's Weekly* during the 1872 election campaign. It shows Greeley and Charles Sumner (whose bitterness toward President Grant caused him to support Greeley) trying to get a black man to "clasp hands across the bloody chasm" with a member of the Ku Klux Klan whose hand is dripping with the blood of the man's wife, whom he has murdered. On the Klansman's left stands a Nast caricature of an Irishman, while in the background are scenes from the New York draft riots in 1863. Nast portrays this alliance as the essence of the Liberal Republican/Democratic coalition in 1872.

that conciliation of southern whites rather than continued military intervention was the only way to achieve peace in the South. Calling themselves Liberal Republicans, these dissidents nominated Horace Greeley, the famous editor of the *New York Tribune*. Under the slogan "Anything to beat Grant," the Democratic Party also endorsed Greeley's nomination, although he had long been their antagonist. On a platform denouncing "bayonet rule" in the South, Greeley urged his fellow northerners to put the issues of the Civil War behind them and to "clasp hands across the bloody chasm which has too long divided" North and South.

This phrase would come back to haunt Greeley. Most voters in the North were still not prepared to trust Democrats or southern whites. Powerful anti-Greeley cartoons by political cartoonist Thomas Nast showed Greeley shaking the hand of a Klansman dripping with the blood of a murdered black Republican. Nast's most famous cartoon portrayed Greeley as a pirate captain bringing his craft alongside the ship of state, while Confederate leaders, armed to the teeth, hid below waiting to board it.

Grant swamped Greeley on Election Day. Republicans carried every northern state and 10 of the 16 southern and border states. Blacks in the South enjoyed more freedom in voting than they would again for a century. But this apparent triumph of Republicanism and Reconstruction would soon unravel.

17-5i *The Panic of 1873*

The U.S. economy had grown at an unprecedented pace since recovering from a mild postwar recession. The first transcontinental railroad had been completed on May 10, 1869, when a golden spike was driven at Promontory Summit, Utah Territory, linking the Union Pacific and the Central Pacific. But the building of a second transcontinental line, the Northern Pacific, precipitated a Wall Street panic in 1873 and plunged the economy into a five-year depression.

Jay Cooke's banking firm, fresh from its triumphant marketing of Union war bonds, took over the Northern Pacific in 1869. Cooke pyramided every conceivable kind of equity and loan financing to raise the money to begin laying rails west from Duluth, Minnesota. Other investment firms did the same as a fever of speculative financing gripped the country. In September 1873, the pyramid of paper collapsed. Cooke's firm was the first to go bankrupt. Like dominoes, thousands of banks and businesses also collapsed. Unemployment rose to 14 percent, and hard times set in.

17-6 The Retreat from Reconstruction

Q *Why did a majority of the northern people and their political leaders turn against continued federal involvement in southern Reconstruction in the 1870s?*

It is an axiom of American politics that the voters will punish the party in power in times of economic depression. That axiom held true in the 1870s. Democrats made large gains in the congressional elections of 1874, winning a majority in the House for the first time in 18 years.

Public opinion also began to turn against Republican policies in the South. The campaign by Liberal Republicans and Democrats against "bayonet rule" and "carpetbag corruption" that left most northern voters unmoved in 1872 found a growing audience in subsequent years. Intraparty battles among Republicans in southern states enabled Democrats to regain control of several state governments. Well-publicized corruption scandals also discredited Republican leaders. Although corruption was probably no worse in southern states than in many parts of the North, southern postwar poverty made waste and extravagance seem worse. White Democrats scored propaganda points by claiming that corruption proved the incompetence of "Negro-carpetbag" regimes.

Northerners grew increasingly weary of what seemed to be the endless turmoil of southern politics. Most of them had never had a strong commitment to racial equality, and they were growing more and more willing to let white supremacy regain sway in the South. "The truth is," confessed a northern Republican, "our people are tired out with this worn out cry of 'Southern outrages'!!! Hard times & heavy taxes make them wish the 'nigger,' 'everlasting nigger,' were in hell or Africa."

By 1875, only four southern states remained under Republican control: South Carolina, Florida, Mississippi, and Louisiana. In those states, white Democrats had revived paramilitary organizations under various names: White Leagues (Louisiana), Rifle Clubs (Mississippi), and Red Shirts (South Carolina). Unlike the Klan, these groups operated openly. In Louisiana, they fought pitched battles with Republican militias in which scores were killed. When the Grant administration sent large numbers of federal troops to Louisiana, people in both North and South cried out against military rule. The protests grew even louder when soldiers marched onto the floor of the Louisiana legislature in January 1875 and expelled several Democratic legislators after a contested election. Was this America? Republican senator Carl Schurz asked in a widely publicized speech: "If this can be done in Louisiana, how long will it be before it can be done in Massachusetts and Ohio? How long before a soldier may stalk into the national House of Representatives, and, pointing to the Speaker's mace, say 'Take away that bauble!'"

17-6a *The Mississippi Election of 1875*

The backlash against the Grant administration affected the Mississippi state election of 1875. Democrats there devised a strategy called the Mississippi Plan. The first step was to "persuade" the 10 to 15 percent of white voters still calling themselves Republicans to switch to the Democrats. Only a handful of carpetbaggers could resist the economic pressures, social ostracism, and threats that made it "too damned hot for [us] to stay out," wrote one white Republican who changed parties.

History Through Film The Birth of a Nation (1915)

Directed by D. W. Griffith.
Starring Lillian Gish (Elsie Stoneman), Henry B. Walthall (Ben Cameron), Ralph Lewis (Austin Stoneman), George Siegmann (Silas Lynch).

Few if any films have had such a pernicious impact on historical understanding and race relations as *Birth of a Nation*. This movie popularized a version of Reconstruction that portrayed predatory carpetbaggers and stupid, brutish blacks plundering a prostrate South and lusting after white women. It perpetuated vicious stereotypes of rapacious black males. It glorified the Ku Klux Klan of the Reconstruction era, inspiring the founding of the "second Klan" in 1915, which became a powerful force in the 1920s (see Chapter 24).

The first half of the film offers a conventional Victorian romance of the Civil War. The two sons and daughter of Austin Stoneman (a malevolent Radical Republican who is a thinly disguised Thaddeus Stevens) become friends with the three sons and two daughters of the Cameron family of "Piedmont," South Carolina, through the friendship of Ben Cameron and Phil Stoneman at college. The Civil War tragically separates the families. The Stoneman and Cameron boys enlist in the Union and Confederate armies and—predictably—face each other on the battlefield. Two Camerons and one Stoneman are killed in the war, and Ben Cameron is badly wounded and captured, to be nursed back to health by—you guessed it—Elsie Stoneman. After the war, the younger Camerons and Stonemans renew their friendship. During the Stonemans' visit to South Carolina, Ben Cameron and Elsie Stoneman, and Phil Stoneman and Flora Cameron fall in love. If the story had stopped there, *Birth of a Nation* would have been just another Hollywood romance. But Austin Stoneman brings south with him Silas Lynch, an ambitious, leering mulatto demagogue who stirs up the animal passions of the ignorant black majority to demand "Equal Rights, Equal Politics, Equal Marriage." A "renegade Negro," Gus, stalks the youngest Cameron daughter, who saves herself from rape by jumping from a cliff to her death. Silas Lynch tries to force Elsie to marry him. "I will build a Black Empire," he tells the beautiful, virginal Elsie (Lillian Gish was the Hollywood beauty queen of silent films), "and you as my queen shall rule by my side."

Finally, provoked beyond endurance, white South Carolinians led by Ben Cameron organize the Ku Klux Klan to save "the Aryan race." Riding to the rescue of embattled whites in stirring scenes that anticipated the heroic actions of the cavalry against Indians in later Hollywood Westerns, the Klan executes Gus, saves Elsie, disperses black soldiers and mobs, and carries the next election for white rule by intimidating black voters. The film ends with a double marriage that unites the Camerons and Stonemans in a symbolic rebirth of a nation that joins whites of the North and South in a new union rightfully based on the supremacy of "the Aryan race."

The son of a Confederate lieutenant colonel, David Wark (D. W.) Griffith was the foremost director of the silent movie era. He pioneered many precedent-setting cinematic techniques and profoundly influenced filmmaking throughout the world. *Birth of a Nation* was the first real full-length feature film, technically and artistically superior to anything before it. Apart from its place in the history of cinema, though, why should anyone today watch a movie that perpetuates such wrongheaded history and noxious racist stereotypes? Precisely because it reflects and amplifies an interpretation of Reconstruction that prevailed from the 1890s to the 1950s, and thereby shaped not only historical understanding but also contemporary behavior (as in its inspiration for the Klan of the 1920s). Although *Birth of a Nation* aroused controversy in parts of the North and was picketed by the NAACP, some 200 million people saw the film in the United States and abroad from 1915 to 1946. The story, and director Griffith, demonstrated in dramatic fashion how the South, having lost the Civil War, won the battle for how the war and especially Reconstruction would be remembered for more than half a century. ■

Bettmann/Corbis

17.12 Ben Cameron (Henry B. Walthall) kissing the hand of Elsie Stoneman (Lillian Gish) in *Birth of a Nation*.

The second step in the Mississippi Plan was to intimidate black voters because, even with all whites voting Democratic, the party could still be defeated by the 55 percent black majority. Economic coercion against black sharecroppers and workers kept some of them away from the polls, but violence was the most effective method. Democratic "rifle clubs" showed up at Republican rallies, provoked riots, and shot down dozens of blacks in the ensuing melees. Governor Adelbert Ames—a native of Maine, a Union general who had won a medal of honor in the war, and one of the ablest of southern Republicans—called for federal troops to control the violence. Grant intended to comply, but Ohio Republicans warned him that if he sent troops to Mississippi, the Democrats would exploit the issue of "bayonet rule" to carry Ohio in that year's state elections. Grant yielded—in effect giving up Mississippi for Ohio. The U.S. attorney general replied to Ames's request for troops:

> The whole public are tired out with these annual autumnal outbreaks in the South, and the great majority are now ready to condemn any interference on the part of the government… . Preserve the peace by the forces in your own state, and let the country see that the citizens of Mississippi, who are … largely Republican, have the courage to fight for their rights.

Governor Ames did try to organize a loyal state militia, but that proved difficult—and in any case, he was reluctant to use a black militia for fear of provoking a race war. "No matter if they are going to carry the State," said Ames with weary resignation, "let them carry it, and let us be at peace and have no more killing." The Mississippi Plan worked like a charm. In five of the state's counties with large black majorities, the Republicans polled 12, 7, 4, 2, and 0 votes, respectively. What had been a Republican majority of 30,000 in 1874 became a Democratic majority of 30,000 in 1875.

17-6b *The Supreme Court and Reconstruction*

Even if Grant had been willing to continue intervening in southern state elections, Congress and the courts would have constricted such efforts. The new Democratic majority in the House threatened to cut any appropriations for the Justice Department and the army intended for use in the South.

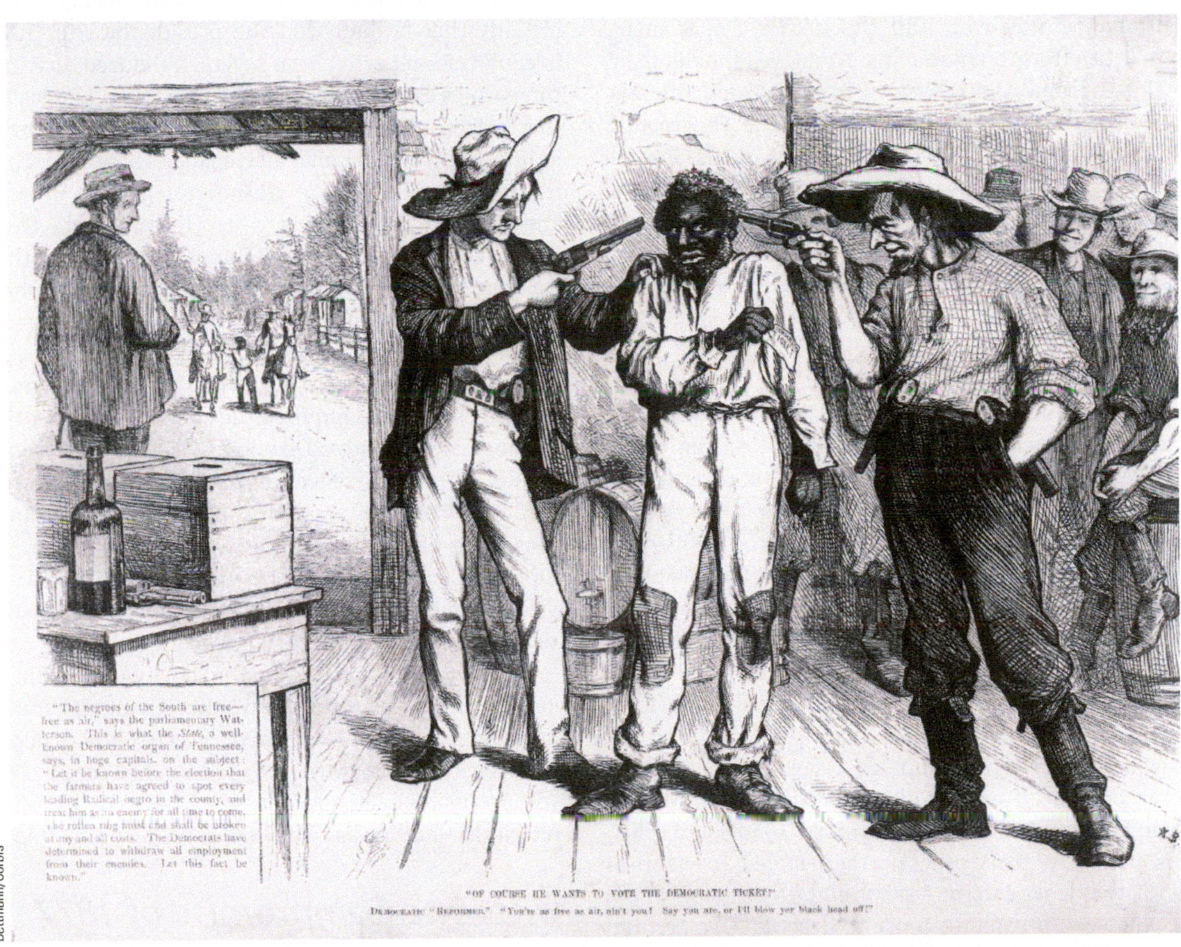

Bettmann/Corbis

17.13 How the Mississippi Plan Worked In this *Harper's Weekly* cartoon, the black voter holds a Democratic ticket while one of the white men, described in the caption as a "Democratic reformer," holds a revolver to his head and says: "You're as free as air, ain't you? Say you are, or I'll blow your black head off!"

Q *What other intimidation techniques were used against black voters in the Mississippi state election of 1875?*

In 1876, the U.S. Supreme Court handed down two decisions that declared parts of the 1870 and 1871 laws for enforcement of the Fourteenth and Fifteenth Amendments unconstitutional. In *U.S. v. Cruikshank* and *U.S. v. Reese*, the Court ruled on cases from Louisiana and Kentucky. Both cases grew out of provisions in these laws authorizing federal officials to prosecute *individuals* (not states) for violations of the civil and voting rights of blacks. But, the Court pointed out, the Fourteenth and Fifteenth Amendments apply to actions by *states*: "No State ... deprive any person of life, liberty, or property ... nor deny to any person ... equal protection of the laws" and the right to vote "shall not be denied ... by any State." Therefore, the portions of these laws that empowered the federal government to prosecute individuals were declared unconstitutional.

The Court did not say what could be done when states were controlled by white-supremacy Democrats who had no intention of enforcing equal rights. Meanwhile, in another ruling, *Civil Rights* Cases (1883), the Court declared unconstitutional a civil rights law passed by Congress in 1875. That law banned racial discrimination in all forms of public transportation and public accommodations. If enforced, it would have effected a sweeping transformation of race relations—in the North as well as in the South. Even some of the congressmen who voted for the bill doubted its constitutionality, however, and the Justice Department had made little effort to enforce it. Several cases made their way to the Supreme Court, which in 1883 ruled the law unconstitutional—again on grounds that the Fourteenth Amendment applied only to states, not to individuals. Several states—all in the North—passed their own civil rights laws in the 1870s and 1880s, but less than 10 percent of the black population resided in those states. The mass of African Americans lived a segregated existence.

17-6c *The Election of 1876*

In 1876, the remaining southern Republican state governments fell victim to the passion for "reform." The mounting revelations of corruption at all levels of government ensured that reform would be the leading issue in the presidential election. In this centennial year of the birth of the United States, marked by a great exposition in Philadelphia, Americans wanted to put their best foot forward. Both major parties gave their presidential nominations to governors who had earned reform reputations in their states: Democrat Samuel J. Tilden of New York and Republican Rutherford B. Hayes of Ohio.

Democrats entered the campaign as favorites for the first time in two decades. It seemed likely that they would be able to put together an electoral majority from a "solid South" plus New York and two or three other northern states. To ensure a solid South, they looked to the lessons of the Mississippi Plan. In 1876, a new word came into use to describe Democratic techniques of intimidation: *bulldozing*. To bulldoze black voters meant to trample them down or keep them away from the polls. In South Carolina and Louisiana, the Red Shirts and the White Leagues mobilized for an all-out bulldozing effort.

The most notorious incident, the Hamburg Massacre, occurred in the village of Hamburg, South Carolina, where a battle between a black militia unit and 200 Red Shirts resulted in the capture of several militiamen, five of whom were shot "while attempting to escape." This time Grant did send in federal troops. He pronounced the Hamburg Massacre "cruel, blood-thirsty, wanton, unprovoked ... a repetition of the course that has been pursued in other Southern States."

The federal government also put several thousand deputy marshals and election supervisors on duty in the South. Although they kept an uneasy peace at the polls, they could do little to prevent assaults, threats, and economic coercion in backcountry districts, which reduced the potential Republican tally in the former Confederate states by at least 250,000 votes.

17-6d *Disputed Results*

When the results were in, Tilden had carried four northern states, including New York with its 35 electoral votes, and all of the former slave states except—apparently—Louisiana, South Carolina, and Florida, which produced disputed returns (see Map 17.3). Because Tilden needed only one of them to win the presidency, while Hayes needed all three, and because Tilden seemed to have carried Louisiana and Florida, it appeared initially that he had won the presidency. But frauds and irregularities reported from several bulldozed districts in the three states clouded the issue. For example, a Louisiana parish that had recorded 1,688 Republican votes in 1874 reported only 1 in 1876. Many other similar discrepancies appeared. The official returns ultimately sent to Washington gave all three states—and therefore the presidency—to Hayes, but the Democrats refused to recognize the results, and they controlled the House.

The country now faced a serious constitutional crisis. Armed Democrats threatened to march on Washington. Many people feared another civil war. The Constitution offered no clear guidance on how to deal with the matter. A count of the state electoral votes required the concurrence of both houses of Congress, but with a Democratic House and a Republican Senate, such concurrence was not forthcoming. To break the deadlock, Congress created a special electoral commission consisting of five representatives, five senators, and five Supreme Court justices split evenly between the two parties, with one member, a Supreme Court justice, supposedly an independent—but in fact a Republican.

Tilden had won a national majority of 252,000 popular votes, and the raw returns gave him a majority in the three disputed states. But an estimated 250,000 southern Republicans had been bulldozed away from the polls. In a genuinely fair and free election, the Republicans might have carried Mississippi and North Carolina as well as the three disputed states.

17-6e *The Compromise of 1877*

In February 1877, three months after voters had gone to the polls, the electoral commission issued its ruling. By a partisan vote of 8 to 7—with the "independent" justice voting with the Republicans—the commission awarded all of the

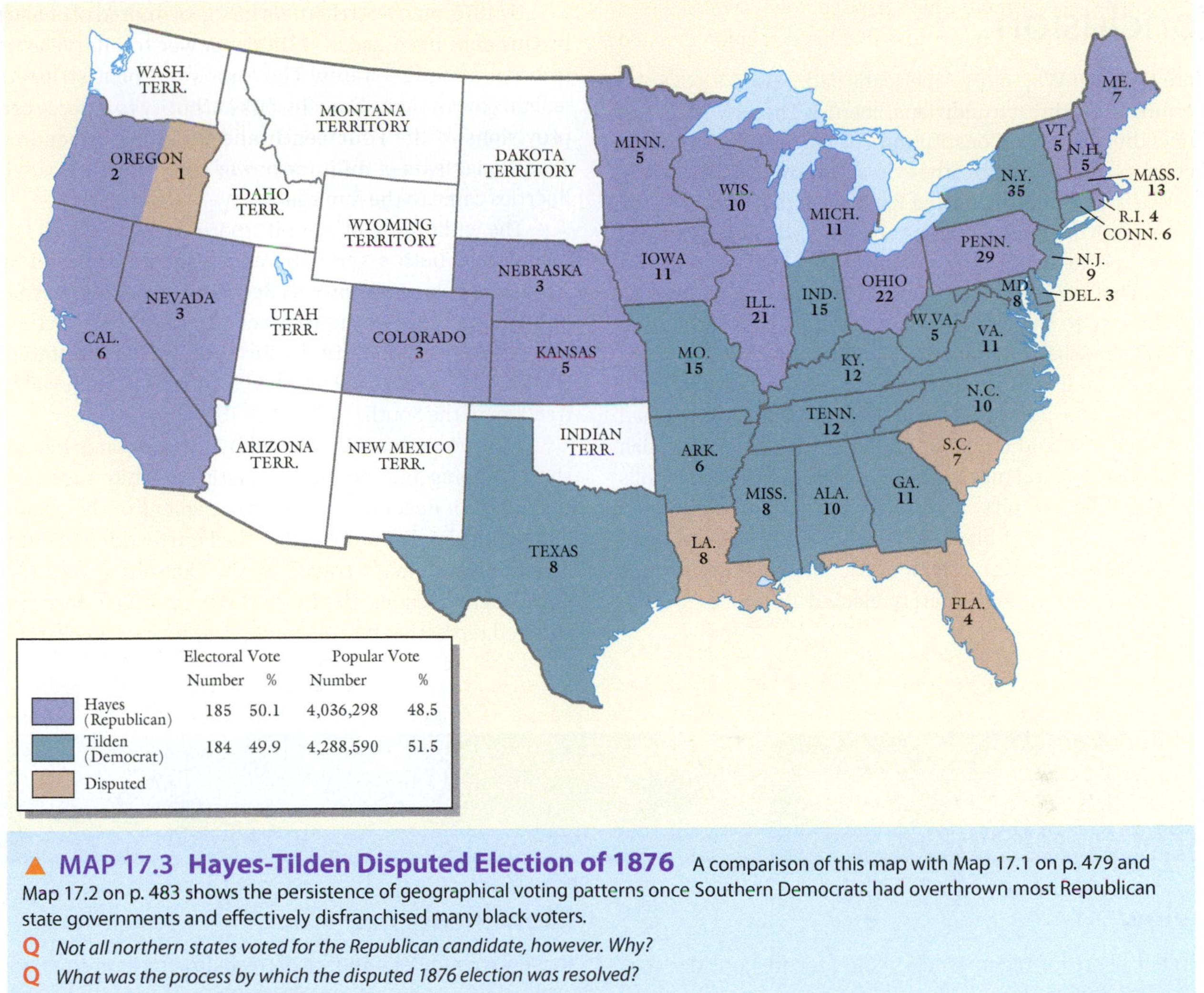

▲ **MAP 17.3 Hayes-Tilden Disputed Election of 1876** A comparison of this map with Map 17.1 on p. 479 and Map 17.2 on p. 483 shows the persistence of geographical voting patterns once Southern Democrats had overthrown most Republican state governments and effectively disfranchised many black voters.

Q *Not all northern states voted for the Republican candidate, however. Why?*

Q *What was the process by which the disputed 1876 election was resolved?*

disputed states to Hayes. The Democrats cried foul and began a **filibuster** in the House to delay the final electoral count beyond the inauguration date of March 4, to throw the election to the House of Representatives, an eventuality that threatened to bring total anarchy. But, behind the scenes, a compromise began to take shape. Both northern Republicans and Southern Democrats of Whig heritage had similar interests in liquidating the sectional rancor and in getting on with the business of economic recovery and development. To wean southern Whiggish Democrats away from a House filibuster, Hayes promised his support as president for federal appropriations to rebuild war-destroyed **levees** on the lower Mississippi and federal aid for a southern transcontinental railroad. Hayes's lieutenants also hinted at the appointment of a southerner as postmaster general, who would have a considerable amount of patronage at his disposal—the appointment of thousands of local postmasters.

Most important, southerners wanted to know what Hayes would do about Louisiana and South Carolina. Hayes signaled his intention to end "bayonet rule," which he had for some time considered a bankrupt policy. He believed that the goodwill and influence of southern moderates would offer better protection for black rights than federal troops could provide. In return for his commitment to withdraw the troops, Hayes asked for—and received—promises of fair treatment of freedpeople and respect for their constitutional rights.

17-6f *The End of Reconstruction*

Such promises were easier to make than to keep, as future years would reveal. In any case, the Democratic filibuster collapsed, and Hayes was inaugurated on March 4. He soon fulfilled his part of the Compromise of 1877: Ex-Confederate Democrat David Key of Tennessee became postmaster general; in 1878, the South received more federal money for internal improvements than ever before; and federal troops left the capitals of Louisiana and South Carolina. The last two Republican state governments collapsed. The old abolitionist and Radical Republican warhorses denounced Hayes's actions as a sellout of southern blacks.

But voices of protest could scarcely be heard above the sighs of relief that the crisis was over. Most Americans, including even most Republicans, wanted no more military intervention in state affairs.

Conclusion

Before the Civil War, most Americans had viewed a powerful government as a threat to individual liberties. That is why the first 10 amendments to the Constitution (the Bill of Rights) imposed strict limits on the powers of the federal government. During the Civil War and especially during Reconstruction, however, the national government had to exert an unprecedented amount of power to free the slaves and guarantee their equal rights as free citizens. That is why the Thirteenth, Fourteenth, and Fifteenth Amendments to the Constitution contained clauses stating that "Congress shall have power" to enforce these provisions for liberty and equal rights.

During the post–Civil War decade, Congress passed civil rights laws and enforcement legislation to accomplish this purpose. Federal marshals and troops patrolled the polls to protect black voters, arrested thousands of Klansmen and other violators of black civil rights, and even occupied state capitals to prevent Democratic paramilitary groups from overthrowing legitimately elected Republican state governments.

By 1875, many northerners had grown tired of or alarmed by this continued use of military power to intervene in the internal affairs of states. The Supreme Court stripped the federal government of much of its authority to enforce certain provisions of the Fourteenth and Fifteenth Amendments. Traditional fears of military power as a threat to individual liberties came to the fore again.

The withdrawal of federal troops from the South in 1877 constituted both a symbolic and a substantive end of the 12-year postwar era known as Reconstruction. Reconstruction had achieved the two great objectives inherited from the Civil War: (1) to reincorporate the former Confederate states into the Union and (2) to accomplish a transition from slavery to freedom in the South.

That transition was marred by the economic inequity of sharecropping and the social injustice of white supremacy. A third goal of Reconstruction, enforcement of the equal civil and political rights promised in the Fourteenth and Fifteenth Amendments, was betrayed by the Compromise of 1877. In subsequent decades, the freed slaves and their descendants suffered repression into segregated, second-class citizenship.

CHAPTER REVIEW

Review

1. What plans for reconstruction did Lincoln consider during the war?
2. What were the positions of Presidents Abraham Lincoln and Andrew Johnson and of moderate and Radical Republicans in Congress on the issues of restoring the South to the Union and protecting the rights of freed slaves?
3. What were the major accomplishments of congressional Reconstruction?
4. Why was Andrew Johnson impeached? Why was he acquitted?
5. Why was there an explosion of corruption during Grant's presidency? Why was the Republican coalition unstable in the South?
6. Why did a majority of the northern people and their political leaders turn against continued federal involvement in southern Reconstruction in the 1870s?

Critical Thinking

1. The two main goals of Reconstruction were to bring the former Confederate states back into the Union and to ensure the equal citizenship and rights of the former slaves. Why was the first goal more successfully achieved than the second?
2. Why have "carpetbaggers" and "scalawags" had such a bad historical image? Did they deserve it?

Identifications

Review your understanding of the following key terms, people, and events for this chapter (terms in bold in text are included in the Glossary).

enfranchise, p. 470
amnesty, p. 471
Black Codes, p. 472
quasi-slavery, p. 472
Freedmen's Bureau, p. 473
share wages, p. 473
sharecropping, p. 473
40 acres and a mule, p. 474
Union leagues, p. 477
scalawags, p. 477
carpetbaggers, p. 477
impeachment, p. 478
universal male suffrage, p. 479
Ku Klux Klan, p. 479
Ulysses S. Grant, p. 481
Credit Mobilier Affair, p. 482
spoils system, p. 482
patronage, p. 482
habeas corpus, p. 486
filibuster, p. 491
levees, p. 491

Suggested Readings

The most comprehensive history of Reconstruction remains **Eric Foner**, ***Reconstruction: America's Unfinished Revolution 1863–1877*** (1988). For a skillful abridgement of this book, see **Foner, *A Short History of Reconstruction*** (1990). An important history of black politics spanning Reconstruction is **Steven Hahn, *A Nation Under Our Feet: Black Political Struggles in the Rural South from Slavery to the Great Migration*** (2003). Incisive interpretations can be found in **Thomas J. Brown**, ***Reconstruction: New Perspectives on the Postbellum United States*** (2006). A classic study of the South Carolina Sea Islands as a laboratory of Reconstruction is **Willie Lee Rose**, ***Rehearsal for Reconstruction: The Port Royal Experiment*** (1964).

Two important studies of Andrew Johnson and his conflict with Congress over Reconstruction are **Hans L. Trefousse, *The Radical Republicans: Lincoln's Vanguard for Racial Justice*** (1969); and **Michael Les Benedict**, ***The Impeachment and Trial of Andrew Johnson*** (1973). Two books by **Michael Perman** connect events in the South and in Washington during Reconstruction: ***Reunion without Compromise: The South and Reconstruction, 1865–1868*** (1973) and ***The Road to Redemption: Southern Politics 1868–1879*** (1984). The emotional undertones of Reconstruction politics are analyzed in **Mark Wahlgren Summers**, ***A Dangerous Stir: Fear, Paranoia, and the Making of Reconstruction*** (2009). For counter-Reconstruction violence in the South, see **Hannah Rosen**, ***Terror in the Heart of Freedom: Citizenship, Sexual Violence, and the Meaning of Race in the Postemancipation South*** (2009); **George C. Rable**, ***But There Was No Peace: The Role of Violence in the Politics of Reconstruction*** (1984); **Nicholas Lemann**, ***Redemption: The Last Battle of the Civil War*** (2006); and **Carole Emberton**, ***Beyond Redemption: Race, Violence, and the American South After the Civil War*** (2013). The evolution of sharecropping and other aspects of the transition from slavery to freedom are treated in **Roger L. Ransom and Richard Sutch**, ***One Kind of Freedom: The Economic Consequences of Emancipation*** (1977).

Of the many books on African Americans in Reconstruction, the following are perhaps the most valuable: **Thomas Holt**, ***Black over White: Negro Political Leadership in South Carolina during Reconstruction*** (1977); and **Laura F. Edwards**, ***Gendered Strife and Confusion: The Political Culture of Reconstruction*** (1997). Both black and white churches are the subject of **Daniel Stowell**, ***Rebuilding Zion: The Religious Reconstruction of the South, 1863–1877*** (1998).

18 A Transformed Nation: The West and the New South, 1865–1900

Bettmann/Corbis

18.1 **The Golden Spike** This carefully posed scene records the merging of the Central Pacific and Union Pacific railroads at Promontory Point, Utah, on May 10, 1869, to create the nation's first transcontinental railroad. A celebration of the industrialization of the American West, the photograph includes hundreds of white laborers, but reflects the racial prejudice of the time in excluding Chinese railroad workers who also played a central role in building the railroad.

"HOW I DO WISH YOU could all come out here," the new Kansas homesteader Mary Abell wrote to her family back east in 1871. "It is such a beautiful country—I did not know there was any thing so beautiful in the whole world as the country we passed over in coming here." Just arrived from New York with her husband, Abell was excited about the prospect of a new life in the West: "Robert has got a piece of land that suits him," she told her sister. "It seems so fortunate." She knew there was much to do in the days ahead—"There is a house to be built fences to make—a well to be dug and a cow to be got." But Abell didn't seem to mind: "I should never be content to live East now," she said. "Things there would look very little."

Abell was part of a great wave of settlement in the post–Civil War era that would transform the West. From 1865 to 1890, the white population in the trans-Mississippi West increased some 400 percent to 8,628,000—a figure that includes both native-born and white immigrants. The dream of western lands also inspired many African Americans, whose cherished hopes for liberty led hundreds of thousands to leave the South for points west from 1880 to 1910. At the same time, immigrants from China, Mexico, and other countries were drawn to the economic opportunities of the West as part of a global movement of peoples in this period.

All of these men and women were driven by desires for a better life, but this motivation often conflicted with the rights and desires of the diverse peoples who already inhabited the West, including, among others, a variety of Indian cultures and societies; borderlands villages of Spanish-speaking peoples; settlements of Chinese miners and laborers; and Mexicans in California. Settlement set in motion conflict and resistance in numerous locations. Who would gain power over western lands? Whose liberty would be respected? What efforts would be made to achieve equality—or deny equality—to all of these peoples? ■

18-1 An Industrializing West

Q *How did the industrialization of the West change American lives?*

Industrialization in the West had many linked components: settlement, including the creation of farms, communities, and western cities; production of commodities such as cattle and timber that could be shipped east; creation of western consumers and thus the demand for manufactured goods; extraction of resources through mining and logging; and the shipment of commodities using a national transportation network. These western processes of resource extraction may have looked different from the factory-centered industrialization that developed in the East and Midwest at this time (see Chapter 19), but they still involved the transformation of an agrarian economy into an industrial society. Like eastern industrialization, western industrialization also had global reach, pulling immigrants from China, Peru, Chile, Hawaii, Europe, and Mexico to the already diverse West.

18-1a *The Homestead Act*

Many migrants to the West were able to become homesteaders because of legislation that took effect on January 1, 1863—the same day that the Emancipation Proclamation became law. Meant to provide free land for western settlers, the **Homestead Act** embodied a cherished American ideal that stretched back to the Jeffersonian era: the belief that individual ownership of land by farmers was at the heart of a virtuous citizenry and a sound democratic republic.

In the 1850s, many people believed that a western "safety valve" was necessary to ward off the potential evils of industrialization, urbanization, and capitalist expansion. Free land in the West would allow individual farmers to support themselves and ultimately help preserve American values of democratic individualism. Yet, settlement of the West was not so much an escape from industrialization as an important factor in the ongoing industrialization of the West.

The provisions of the Homestead Act were remarkably egalitarian for their day—up to a point. Both men and unmarried women were eligible to file for up to 160 acres of surveyed land in the public domain, as long as they were over the age of 21. (Married women were assumed to be dependents of their homesteading husbands.) Immigrants who affirmed their intention to become citizens were also eligible. As long as homesteaders lived on the land for five years, not only cultivating it but also "improving" it by building a house or barn, they could receive full title for a fee of only $10. Utilizing these provisions, white homesteaders ultimately claimed some 285 million acres of land.

Despite this surface egalitarianism, the Homestead Act privileged white farmers over African Americans and Hispanics, who rarely had the resources necessary to homestead. Even free land required tools and seed, plus costly transportation. The act also denied access to Chinese laborers, who could not become U.S. citizens and had few property rights. It made no provisions for the truly poor.

Furthermore, the Homestead Act was part of a larger process of conquest, driven by the twin pressures of industrialization and white settlement, through which Indians were irrevocably stripped of their lands. A final problem with the act was corruption in its implementation. Those who agitated for a homestead act in the antebellum period had been fueled by a sense of idealism. Ironically, however, through chicanery, outright fraud, and government giveaways, more public land actually fell into the hands of railroads, other corporations, and speculators than into the hands of individual farmers.

CHRONOLOGY

1862	Sioux uprising in Minnesota; 38 Sioux executed
1864	Colorado militia massacres Cheyenne in village at Sand Creek, Colorado
1866	Cowboys conduct first cattle drive north from Texas
1869	President Grant announces his "peace policy" toward Indians
1876	Sioux and Cheyenne defeat Custer at Little Big Horn
1880	James A. Garfield elected president
1881	Garfield assassinated; Chester A. Arthur becomes president
1883	Pendleton Act begins reform of civil service
1884	Grover Cleveland elected president
1887	Dawes Severalty Act dissolves Indian tribal units and implements individual ownership of tribal lands
1888	Benjamin Harrison elected president
1889	Government opens Indian Territory (Oklahoma) to white settlement
1890	Wounded Knee massacre • New Mississippi constitution pioneers black disfranchisement in South • Republicans try but fail to enact federal elections bill to protect black voting rights • Congress enacts McKinley Tariff
1892	Grover Cleveland again elected president
1895	Booker T. Washington makes his Atlanta Compromise address
1896	*Plessy v. Ferguson* legalizes "separate but equal" state racial segregation laws
1898	*Williams v. Mississippi* condones use of literacy tests and similar measures to restrict voting rights

18-1b *Railroads*

Nothing was more important to the industrialization of the West than the railroad. Just as free land for homesteaders was a long-held dream for many Americans, so, too, was the creation of a transcontinental railroad that would link East and West. The two dreams were connected: The settlement of the West would be greatly facilitated by the extension of the railroad into far-flung territory. Thus, it was no accident that in 1862, the year the government passed the Homestead Act, it also passed the Pacific Railroad Bill, which provided large loans and extremely generous subsidies of land to two railroad companies, the Union Pacific (working west) and the Central Pacific (working east), in order to enable them to build a transcontinental line stretching from Omaha, Nebraska, to Sacramento, California. (Railroad lines already existed from Omaha to the East.) Two years later, the government also provided a substantial monetary subsidy for each mile of track laid in the West. Ultimately, the government would give away 131 million acres of land to support transcontinental railroads.

These lavish subsidies set off a frenzy of railroad building; they also made a few individuals very rich, including the "Big Four" of the Central Pacific: Leland Stanford, Collis P. Huntington, Mark Hopkins, and Charles Crocker. Big in every way (they collectively weighed 860 pounds), the four men had come to California during the gold rush and had shrewdly sized up its entrepreneurial opportunities. They now avidly seized the historic opportunity at hand and formed a partnership that split up the work necessary in such a giant task, including the work of influencing lawmakers. Like so many others involved in the notoriously corrupt postwar railway boom, they were not shy about using bribery or graft to achieve their aims.

Having provided generous subsidies, the government expected the railroads to obtain their own financing. Various railroads sold millions of dollars of stocks or bonds, often selling as much stock as the market would bear without much relationship to the actual value of the railroads. This "watered" stock was part of the runaway corruption that surrounded financing railroads. The Big Four participated wholeheartedly in this corruption, creating construction contracts, for instance, that paid them $90 million for work that only cost them $32.2 million.

Once financing had been arranged for this complex venture, the Union Pacific and Central Pacific embarked on a daunting task that would engage some 20,000 workers at a time. From 1865 on, the two railroads raced against each other, as whoever laid the most track stood to gain in government subsidies as well as later commerce. The Union Pacific employed primarily Irish laborers, while the Central Pacific employed a workforce that was by 1867 almost 90 percent Chinese.

18-1c *Chinese Laborers and the Railroads*

A global economy had drawn thousands of Chinese laborers to California during the gold rush, beginning in 1849. Mostly peasants emigrating from the Pearl River delta of Guangdong Province in southeast China, they were pushed from home by poverty and unstable political conditions related to China's defeat in the British Opium Wars. While only a few hundred men emigrated in 1849 and 1850, by the mid-1850s, thousands of Chinese immigrants arrived annually. By 1870, there were some 63,000 Chinese in the United States, with over three-quarters settled in California.

Almost entirely men, Chinese immigrants intended to be sojourners, not permanent settlers: They planned to take their hard-earned savings home to the wives and families they had left behind. At first they worked as independent prospectors panning for gold, but as gold profits dwindled, they moved into other areas of work. In the 1860s, labor contractors in China actively recruited young men to come to America to build the transcontinental railroad, as well as to work as agricultural laborers, to develop fisheries and vineyards, and to help reclaim California swamplands. Some 12,000 Chinese

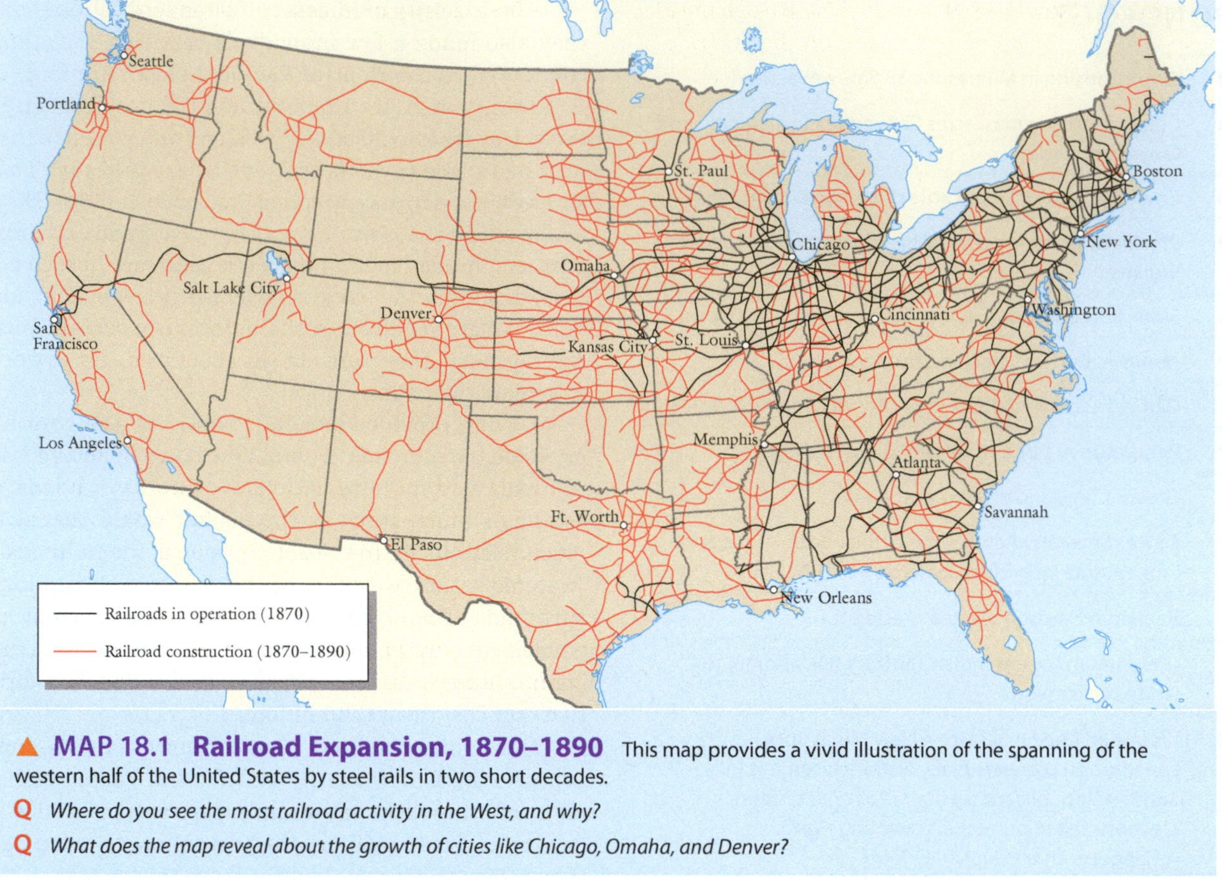

▲ **MAP 18.1 Railroad Expansion, 1870–1890** This map provides a vivid illustration of the spanning of the western half of the United States by steel rails in two short decades.

Q *Where do you see the most railroad activity in the West, and why?*

Q *What does the map reveal about the growth of cities like Chicago, Omaha, and Denver?*

laborers ultimately built the Central Pacific Railroad, often under exceptionally harsh conditions, and with substantially less pay than white laborers.

Even before they began working on the railroads, Chinese miners and laborers faced prejudice from white nativists. In 1850, the California State legislature responded to anti-foreigner agitation with a Foreign Miners' Tax aimed at all foreigners; two years later, the legislature specifically targeted Chinese immigrants. Western labor leaders, particularly Dennis Kearney of the Workingman's Party of California, inflamed nativist crowds of white workers with anti-Chinese rhetoric: In 1877, during the national Great Railway Strike (see Chapter 19), mobs of white workers rioted against Chinese workers in San Francisco's Chinatown. Violence against Chinese workers occurred in numerous places in the West during the 1870s and 1880s, including a massacre in Rock Springs, Colorado, after the Union Pacific Railroad decided to hire Chinese workers. Twenty-eight Chinese died in an attack that included burning down Chinese homes; similar attacks soon occurred throughout the West.

At the local level, Chinese immigrants faced a host of discriminatory ordinances specifically targeting them, from queue ordinances regulating the length of men's hair (forbidding the distinctive braid worn by Chinese men) to sidewalk ordinances preventing the carrying of baskets on shoulders. At the state level, California laws denied Chinese the right to own land, to testify in court, to intermarry with whites, and to immigrate. Under these conditions, Chinese workers created communities of their own against stiff odds. By 1850, a thriving Chinatown had emerged in San Francisco, and Chinese sections emerged in numerous communities throughout the West.

In 1882, the federal government weighed in with its first discriminatory law targeting a specific immigrant group. The **Chinese Exclusion Act** suspended Chinese immigration for 10 years with the exception of a few job categories. Wealthy Chinese businessmen and merchants were allowed entry because of the U.S. government's interest in trade with China. But, the law forbade Chinese laborers, who were said to endanger "the good order of certain localities." Renewed in 1892, the Chinese Exclusion Act achieved its aim: The population of Chinese declined from 105,465 in 1880 to 89,863 in 1900, during a period in which immigration swelled for other groups (for more on Chinese immigrants, see Chapter 20).

18-1d *The Golden Spike*

By the early spring of 1869, what one commentator called the "irrepressible railroad" was almost an accomplished fact. The only question was where East and West would meet. In the final stages of track-laying, the two railroads—which would receive money, after all, based on miles of track built—actually built some track parallel to one another before finally being instructed by no less than President Grant to determine a meeting point.

The result, on May 10, 1869, was the historic driving of a "golden spike" in Promontory, Utah, to mark the merging of the two lines. Present that day, we know from the historical record, were "men of every color, creed, and nationality," including the Chinese laborers who had built the railroad and laid the very last track. But official photographs of the event leave them out—a silence that speaks volumes about racial prejudice at the time.

By 1893, a total of five transcontinental railroads were in service, and track mileage west of the Mississippi had increased from 3,272 miles at the end of the Civil War to 72,473 miles (see Map 18.1). No single factor was as important to the industrialization of the West as the building of railroads, which provided an infrastructure for the western economy as well as connection to eastern markets.

18-1e *Railroads and Borderlands Communities*

The arrival of the railroads, as well as the Anglo settlers who followed swiftly in their wake, dramatically changed the borderlands communities of northern New Mexico and southern Colorado. In the 1870s, Hispanic villagers lived communally in this area, grazing sheep and cattle on the open range.

But the coming of the railroads in the 1880s put new pressure on Hispanic village life. In places like Rio Arriba County, New Mexico, Hispanic villagers who had done a thriving trade freighting—hauling goods by wagons—found themselves replaced by the railroads. Even worse, in a pattern repeated throughout the West, Hispanic villagers found that Anglo settlement and fencing of once-open lands reduced the available range for grazing their sheep.

As Anglo-owned livestock companies moved in, bringing in better breeds and buying up grazing land, they began to squeeze out the Hispanic farmers. By the 1890s villagers began to depend on credit for the first time; in the turbulent economy of that decade, many of them were unable to pay their debts. The end result was the loss of their sheep—and livelihood—to Anglo businessmen who had extended credit to them. Many ended up working for livestock companies, sometimes caring for herds they had once owned themselves. Eventually others ended up as miners, forced to become wage laborers.

Resentment became active resistance in the 1880s, when a secret organization, *Las Gorras Blancas* (The White Caps), rode mostly at night to cut fences, tear up railroad track, and burn bridges. "Our purpose is to protect the rights of the people in general and especially those of the helpless classes," the group declared in its platform. But, the group had only limited success in achieving these goals.

18-1f *Mining*

A similar process held true in mining. The California Gold Rush of 1849 and the early 1850s had drawn miners from across the United States—and from Mexico, Europe, China, Chile, and other countries, as well—to pan for gold. But by the 1870s the majority of miners had become wage laborers who worked for corporations, not for themselves. Mining was big business, with groups of investors consolidating holdings in some of the richest mines. George Hearst began by investing in 1859 in the legendary Comstock Lode in Nevada—the richest vein of silver in America. "If you're ever inclined to think that there's no such thing as luck," Hearst remarked, "just think of me." In 1877, Hearst and business partners bought the Homestake Mine in the Black Hills, and then enriched their holdings still further by buying up the claims of surrounding miners. Other financiers invested in the industries related to mining, including railroads, lumber companies, and smelters.

Gold rush prospectors had worked the surface of the earth with picks, shovels, and tin pans. But soon miners and mining companies developed new technologies to extract ore, whether on the surface of the earth or underground. Hydraulic mining, used as early as the 1850s, employed high-pressure jets of water to wash away banks of earth and even mountains in order to extract gold. By the 1880s, hydraulic mining produced 90 percent of California's gold, but it also ravaged the environment, tearing away indiscriminately at earth, boulders, and trees, and leaving desolate landscapes in its wake. The debris (tailings) from hydraulic mining clogged rivers and caused floods, ruining farms with muddy waste. Other types of mining destroyed landscapes as well: Copper mining in particular created strip-mining moonscapes.

Railroads played a central role in the development of industrial mining, not only providing access to mines but also enabling a new kind of mining late in the century. Gold discoveries had propelled the first waves of western settlement, but by the 1870s, silver eclipsed gold in volume and, some years, even in value (see Map 18.2). Copper mining became profitable because the railroads allowed the transportation of huge quantities of ore. In Butte, Montana, the 1881 arrival of the railroad made possible the extraction of a copper lode known as the "richest hill on earth." The railroad also catalyzed copper mining in southern Arizona in the 1880s. Large-scale resource extraction was at the heart of western industrialization.

Working conditions in these heavily mechanized hard-rock mines grew steadily worse. Miners sometimes worked in mines with temperatures of well over 100 degrees—sometimes as much as 150 degrees deep underground. Miners died of the heat, of poor ventilation, of the release of toxic gases, and of accidents with mining equipment. Accidents disabled one out of every 30 miners in the 1870s. By the end of the 19th century, mining was the most dangerous industry in the country.

Unions gained only a limited foothold in the 1870s and 1880s. But wage cuts in the early 1890s inspired a new burst of labor radicalism and resistance. After a violent confrontation in 1892 between miners and the National Guard at Coeur d'Alene, Idaho, mining unions met at Butte, Montana, in 1893 to form the **Western Federation of Miners (WFM)**, whose radical politics included a call to transform the American economic system. That year, a violent strike at Cripple Creek, Colorado, broke out over mine owners' attempts to move from an eight-hour to a ten-hour day. These strikes were part of nationwide labor activism and resistance in the 1890s (see Chapter 19). Ultimately the WFM would help to found the 20th-century Industrial Workers of the World (IWW) (see Chapter 21). The IWW's leader, William "Big Bill" Haywood, later remembered being approached by a WFM organizer as a young man in Idaho. "I had never heard of the need of workingmen organizing for mutual protection," Haywood said, but he soon became a leader of the WFM himself. The industrialization of the West became a radicalizing political experience for many.

18-1g *Cattle Drives and the Open Range*

A postwar boom in the range cattle industry had its beginnings in southern Texas. The Spaniards had introduced longhorn cattle there in the 18th century. This hardy breed multiplied rapidly: By the 1850s, millions of them roamed freely on the Texas plains. The market for them was limited in this sparsely settled region—the nearest railhead was usually too far distant to make shipping them north and east economically feasible.

The Civil War changed all that. With beef supplies depleted in the older states, prices rose to the unheard-of sum of $40 per head. The postwar explosion of population and railroads westward brought markets and railheads ever closer to western cattle that were free to anyone who rounded them up and branded them.

Astute Texans quickly saw that the longhorns represented a fortune on the hoof—if they could be driven northward the 800 miles to the railhead at Sedalia, Missouri. In spring 1866, cowboys hit the trail with 260,000 cattle in the first of the great drives. Disease, stampedes, bad weather, Indians, and irate farmers in Missouri (who were afraid that the Texas fever carried by some of the longhorns would infect their own stock) killed or ran off most of the cattle.

Only a few thousand head made it to Sedalia, but the prices they fetched convinced ranchers that the system would work, if only they could find a better route. By 1867, the rails of the Kansas Pacific had reached Abilene, Kansas, 150 miles closer to Texas, making it possible to drive the herds through a sparsely occupied portion of Indian Territory. About 35,000 longhorns reached Abilene that summer, where they were loaded onto cattle cars for the trip to Kansas City or Chicago. This success resulted in the interlocking institutions of the cattle drive and the Chicago stockyards. The development of refrigerated rail cars in the 1870s enabled Chicago to ship dressed beef all over the country. Abilene mushroomed overnight from a sleepy village where one bartender spent his spare time catching prairie dogs into a boomtown where 25 saloons stayed open all night.

More than a million longhorns bellowed their way north on the **Chisholm Trail** to Abilene over the next four years, while the railhead crept westward to other Kansas towns, chiefly Dodge City, which became the most wide-open and famous of the cow towns (see Figure 18.1). As buffalo and Indians disappeared from the grasslands north of Texas, ranches moved northward to take their place. Cattle drives grew shorter as railroads inched forward. Ranchers grazed their cattle for free on millions of acres of open, unfenced government land. But clashes with "grangers" (the ranchers' contemptuous term for farmers), on the one hand, and with a growing army of sheep ranchers on the other—not to mention rustlers—led to several "range wars." Most notable was the Johnson County War in Wyoming in 1892. Grangers and small ranchers there (who had sometimes gotten their start by rustling) defeated the hired guns of the Stock Growers' Association, which represented larger ranchers.

By that time, open-range grazing was already in decline. The boom years of the early 1880s had overstocked the range and driven down prices. Then came record cold and blizzards on the southern range in the winter of 1884 and 1885, followed by even worse weather on the northern plains two years later. Hundreds of thousands of cattle froze or starved to death. These catastrophes spurred reforms that ended open-range grazing. The ranchers who survived turned to growing hay and supplemental feed for the winter. They reduced the size of their herds, started buying or leasing land and fencing in their cattle, and invested in scientific breeding that crossed longhorns with higher-quality stock to produce a better grade of beef.

18-1h *The Industrialization of Ranching*

As open-range grazing declined, industrialized ranching expanded. By 1900, the California corporation Miller & Lux was one of the largest industrial enterprises in the country, having integrated raising cattle on vast landholdings together with meatpacking in San Francisco. Its two founding partners were German immigrants who had started out working as butchers in San Francisco but soon owned their own shops. Mobilizing large amounts of capital, they employed over a thousand laborers in extensive operations that tightly connected ranchlands with the city.

18-1i *Industrial Cowboys*

Some of their employees were cowboys who rode the extensive Miller & Lux landholdings. Before the 1870s, the most valuable of the firm's cowboys were ***vaqueros***, Mexican cowboys who rounded up cattle, branded them, and drove them to San Francisco. The tradition of the vaqueros had arrived in the New World with the Spanish, who introduced herding by men on horseback. By the late 19th century, the raising of cattle herds by *vaqueros* had been practiced for centuries in California. But the arrival of railroads took a toll on the positions of *vaqueros*: After the 1870s, cattle were shipped to market by rail.

18-1j *Mexican Americans*

The *vaqueros* at Miller & Lux received less pay than their white coworkers, reflecting prevalent discrimination against Mexicans. Throughout the late 19th century,

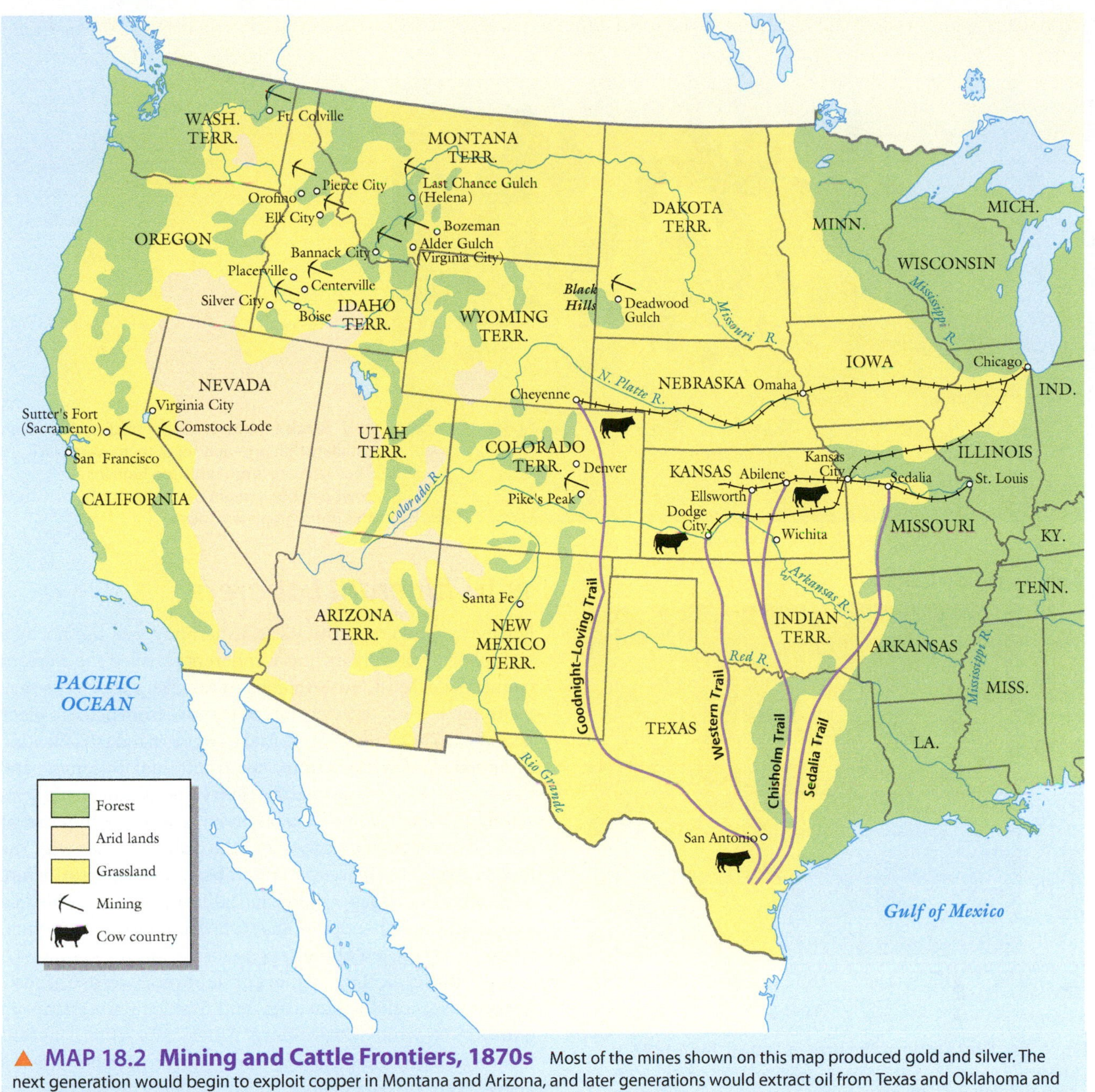

▲ **MAP 18.2 Mining and Cattle Frontiers, 1870s** Most of the mines shown on this map produced gold and silver. The next generation would begin to exploit copper in Montana and Arizona, and later generations would extract oil from Texas and Oklahoma and coal and oil from Wyoming.

Q *What do the arid lands shown on the map suggest about the future difficulties homesteaders would face?*

Q *How was the growth of the railroads (see Map 18.1) connected to the locations of these mining and cattle frontiers?*

Mexican Americans, many of whom had owned their land for generations, lost both property and political influence to incoming Anglo-American settlers. Many elite *Californios*, who were ranchers in southern California, had to sell their lands to pay outstanding debts after devastating droughts in the 1860s virtually destroyed the ranching industry. But even as early as 1849 in the northern California goldfields, resentment of "foreigners" provoked violence against Mexican American miners—and the Foreign Miners' Tax of 1850 effectively forced Mexican Americans out of the goldfields (even though they were not "foreigners"). As the 19th century progressed, hordes of Anglo-American "squatters" invaded the expansive holdings of *Californios*, who were forced to seek relief in the courts. Although their claims were generally upheld, legal proceedings often stretched on for years. After exorbitant legal fees and other expenses were taken into account, a legal triumph was often a Pyrrhic victory. In the end, most Mexican American landholders in northern California, like those in southern California, had to sell the very lands they had fought to keep in order to pay their mounting debts.

The migration of Anglos into eastern Texas had played a role in fomenting the war for Texas independence and

18.2 **Black Cowboys** Some studies of cowboys estimate that one-quarter of them were black. That estimate is probably too high for all cowboys, but it might be correct for Texas, where this photograph was taken.

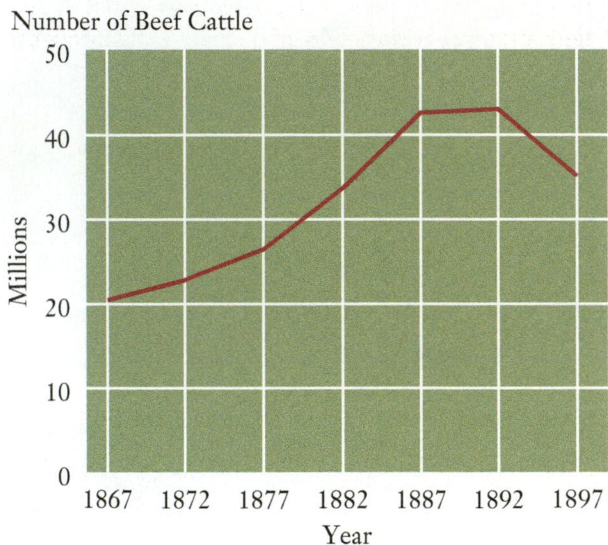

Figure 18.1 **Beef Cattle in the United States, 1867–1897**

in bringing about the war with Mexico (see Chapter 13). By the latter half of the 19th century, eastern Texas was overwhelmingly Anglo; most *Tejanos* (people of Mexican origin or descent) were concentrated in the Rio Grande Valley of southern Texas. As in California, Anglos in Texas used force and intimidation, coupled with exploitative legal maneuvering, to disenfranchise the *Tejanos*. The Texas Rangers often acted as an Anglo vigilante force that exacted retribution for the real or imagined crimes of Mexican Americans.

Similar patterns prevailed in New Mexico, but the effects were mitigated somewhat because New Mexicans continued to outnumber Anglo-American settlers. Throughout the Southwest, Spanish-speaking peoples maintained their cultural traditions in the face of Anglo settlement, with the Roman Catholic Church serving as an important center of community life. An influx of immigrants from Mexico toward the end of the century created a new basis for community as well.

18-1k *Itinerant Laborers*

For many workers in the West, itinerancy was the norm; a virtual army of workers and wanderers traveled the western countryside. Most low-level jobs in ranching were seasonal, meaning that workers were forced to move from place to place periodically in search of work. And as western industrialization uprooted many workers from their traditional lives, more and more people took to the road. As Henry George said in his best-selling 1879 book, *Progress and Poverty*, a scathing indictment of the current economic system, "the 'tramp' comes with the locomotive." For George, who had been a prospector before becoming a newspaper editor in California, the fault lay in a system of "land monopoly" that allowed control of land and resources by the few at the expense of the many.

At Miller & Lux, itinerant laborers were Chinese, Portuguese, Italian, Mexican, and Mexican American, in addition to white, native-born Americans. One itinerant laborer on an irrigation crew, Joseph Warren Matthews, was a farmer who had heavy debts. To pay his debts he had taken on a series of grueling temporary jobs, including wage labor for a lumber company in the Pacific Northwest, work in the Alaskan goldfields, pipe laying for a water company, ore smelting, and ditch digging. His situation underlined the precariousness of many lives in the industrializing West.

18-1l *Homesteading and Farming*

Homesteaders and farmers shared that precariousness. Not only were 49 percent of all homesteaders unable to "prove up" their claims, but many were ultimately forced off their homesteads by the unforgiving climate of the Great Plains.

A great wave of settlement of the Great Plains occurred during the late 1870s to the mid-1880s, when rainfall was relatively abundant, but years of drought inevitably followed. The truth was that the average normal rainfall on

History Through Film Oklahoma! (1955)

Directed by Fred Zinnemann.
Starring Gordon MacRae (Curly); Shirley Jones (Laurey); and Rod Steiger (Jud).

Only a history textbook would ask you to connect the great Rodgers & Hammerstein musical *Oklahoma!* to the range wars of the late-19th-century West. But think about it: When the cast members sing "The Farmer and the Cowman" during a square dance, right before launching into a colorful fistfight, they express the different viewpoints of farmers and cattle ranchers. One rancher says he wishes the "dirtscratchers" had stayed in Missouri; another complains that farmers are building fences right across the cattle ranges. It's up to one of the songs to suggest a solution to this dispute, by advising that cowmen and farmers be friends.

Oklahoma! isn't really about Oklahoma, even if it is set in 1907, right before the territory became a state. It's really about a mythic western space in Americans' imagination, where Americans come together in harmony at square dances and box suppers and where a cowboy like the masculine hero Curly is not a wage laborer for life, but instead is about to become a prosperous farmer. *Oklahoma!* may be set in Indian Territory, but there are no Native Americans here. It is an entirely white, native-born world except for the peddler Ali Hakim, and he is clearly just passing through. There's certainly no indication of Oklahoma's arid climate and the devastating drought of the Great Depression, which would have been in recent memory when the musical was written in 1943. In fact, some of the people associated with the musical were uneasy about the title "Oklahoma!" precisely because they were afraid it would remind audiences of the "Okies," the poverty-stricken farmers forced to flee the arid plains during the Depression. Instead, this is a world of green abundance where "the corn is as high as an elephant's eye." The only shadow in this sunlit world with its "bright golden haze on the meadow," is Jud, the hired hand.

And perhaps that's why Jud is the most interesting character in this movie musical. Played with a heavy, menacing scowl by none other than Rod Steiger, Jud is the dark side of the western dream, a man with a deep violent streak (unlike the boys-will-be-boys scuffling of the cowboys) and an unhealthy liking for "girly pictures." All of these negative qualities are loaded onto his status as the "hired hand"; he provides an uneasy reminder that class lines did exist in the West and that not everyone was on the brink of becoming prosperous. Jud is the only real problem in the mythic world of *Oklahoma!*, and the musical blithely dispatches him by having him fall on his own knife in a fight with Curly.

A huge hit right in the midst of World War II, the show's determined exuberance and confidence struck deep chords. The show's brilliant choreographer, Agnes DeMille, remembered that soldiers and sailors would stand weeping at the back of the theater, so deeply did *Oklahoma!* evoke what they considered the essence of America. "Oh, what a beautiful mornin'" sings Curly at the beginning, and it reassured Americans that having grown up on that mythic frontier, they were at the dawn of a new era. ■

18.3 Vibrant movie posters for the 1955 movie musical *Oklahoma!* emphasized the fresh-faced, homespun appeal of romantic leads Gordon MacRae (Curly) and Shirley Jones (Laurey), who began her movie career with this role.

the Great Plains was scarcely enough to support farming except in certain river valleys. Homesteaders and farmers in Minnesota, Iowa, and parts of Kansas and Nebraska were relatively lucky—those areas had rich soil and adequate rainfall. In Iowa, for instance, farmers had great success with a "corn and hog" farm economy. But other land was arid and unproductive, producing heartbreak for homesteaders and farmers. Between 1888 and 1892, half the population of Kansas and Nebraska was forced to give up and move back east to Illinois or Iowa.

18-1m *The Experience of Homesteading*

Homesteading families on the Great Plains literally built their houses from the ground up: In an environment without trees, they cut the dense prairie sod into blocks and stacked them up to form walls, providing a small window and a door in a "soddy" of around 18 by 24 feet. **Soddies** were a practical solution to a difficult problem on the plains, but they were also dark, dank, and claustrophobic.

Kansas State Historical Society/Topeka/Kansas

18.4 Destruction of the Buffalo Historians estimate that as many as 30 million bison (popularly called buffalo) once roamed the grasslands of North America. By the mid-19th century, however, expansion of the European American settlement, the demand for buffalo robes in the European and eastern U.S. markets, and competition from Indian horses for grazing lands had reduced the herds by many millions. Such pressures intensified after the Civil War—as railroads penetrated the West and new technology enabled tanners to process buffalo hides for leather. Professional hunters flocked to the range and systematically killed the bison. By the 1880s, the buffalo were almost extinct, leaving behind millions of bones, which were gathered in piles, as in this photograph of buffalo skulls, and shipped to plants that ground them into fertilizer.

Q *Do you think the industrialization of the West was the chief cause of the virtual extinction of the buffalo?*

As Kansas homesteader Mary Abell explained to her sister: "Imagine living in a place dug out of the side of a hill (one side to the weather with door and window—top covered with dirt and you have our place of abode). No one east would think of putting pigs in such a place." Abell's letters from 1871 to 1875 make clear the hard labor involved in homesteading: In addition to caring for five children, in the fall of 1873, she had been her husband's "sole help in getting up and stacking at least 25 tons of hay and oats." Less than a week later, "one of those dreadful prairie fires" swept through the Abells' land, and they lost not only their hay and oats but also chickens and farm equipment. In 1874, she faced both drought and grasshoppers, and wrote to her family that "none of you have the least conception" of "actual want, destitution." In 1875, Abell died at the age of 29.

Not all homesteaders faced dire straits. Of the 4 million immigrants who came from Germany, the Czech region of the Austro-Hungarian Empire, and the Scandinavian countries from 1865 to 1890, many settled in the upper Midwest and northern plains and became successful farmers. The northern plains region had the highest proportion of foreign-born residents in the nation during the last quarter of the century. These European immigrants formed homogeneous ethnic enclaves that maintained the distinctive culture and traditions of their homelands. Swedish immigrants in Minnesota spoke Swedish with one another and centered their lives around the Swedish Lutheran church; their children attended Swedish schools and learned to read the Swedish bible, sing Swedish songs, and recite Swedish history; and both men and women wore traditional Swedish dress on holidays. By the end of the century, there were also homogeneous ethnic communities of Germans, Czechs, Poles, Hungarians, and Norwegians dotting the northern landscape.

18-1n *Gender and Western Settlement*

The Homestead Act was unusual in allowing unmarried women to make claims; between 5 and 15 percent of homestead entries in different locales went to women in the late 19th century. Many of these women probably "proved up" only to immediately sell their land, rather than farm it themselves. Still, the existence of women homesteaders suggests just one way gender roles were different in the West than other regions.

Another difference was the overwhelmingly masculine makeup of mining camps and towns. During the gold rush, California was up to 93 percent male, and many ranches, including Miller & Lux holdings, were exclusively male as well. Mining towns were known as violent places, and many observers were anxious to establish a more respectable family life there.

Prostitutes from all over the world were drawn to mining towns throughout the late 19th century, but nowhere except in San Francisco were women systematically forced into sexual slavery. There, the situation of Chinese laborers encouraged an exploitative world trade in women. Although by the last

18.5 **A Nebraska Soddy** This young family stands proudly in front of their Nebraska soddy in 1884 or 1885, during a time when rainfall was abundant on the Great Plains. A long-term drought began in 1886, however, making us wonder whether this family was able to hang on to its homestead through the coming difficult times.

decades of the century Chinese merchants were allowed to bring their wives and daughters to America, laborers had no such rights. Furthermore, respectable single women were expected to stay home. The number of Chinese women in America never rose above 5,000 during the 19th century.

The absence of Chinese women encouraged a brutal international trade in prostitution. Chinese women who were kidnapped or purchased from poor parents were sold into indentured servitude or slavery and shipped to America to become prostitutes. In San Francisco, an estimated 85 to 97 percent of Chinese women were prostitutes in 1860; around 72 percent in 1870; and between 21 and 50 percent in 1880. They faced a harsh existence. However, a number of women managed to escape prostitution. Some married men who had saved up enough money to purchase the contracts that bound them; Protestant missionaries worked to rescue prostitutes, as well.

As these few examples show, settlement patterns of the West produced—at least for a short period of time—societies with unequal numbers of men and women, with different results in different places. The impact of these disparities continues to intrigue historians, who still puzzle, for instance, over the reasons why several western states were the first to grant woman suffrage (see Chapter 21).

18-2 Conquest and Resistance: American Indians in the Trans-Mississippi West

Q *How did the Indian peoples of the trans-Mississippi West respond to white settlement and U.S. government policies?*

The westward expansion of ranching and farming after 1865 doomed the free range of the Plains Indians and the buffalo. In the 1830s, eastern tribes had been forcibly moved to preserves west of the Mississippi so as permanently to separate whites and Indians. Yet in scarcely a decade, white settlers had penetrated these lands via the overland trails to the Pacific coast. In the 1850s, when the Kansas and Nebraska territories opened to white settlement, the government forced a dozen tribes living there to cede 15 million acres, leaving them on reservations totaling less than 1.5 million acres. Thus began what one historian has called the "policy of concentration": No longer were Indians to be pushed ever westward. Instead, they were to be concentrated onto reservations a fraction of the size of where they had formerly hunted freely.

Even before the Civil War, the nomadic Plains Indians, whose culture and economy were based on the buffalo, faced pressure not only from the advancing tide of white settlement but also from the forced migration of eastern tribes into their domain. In the aftermath of the Civil War, the process of concentrating Indian tribes on reservations accelerated. Chiefs of the five "Civilized Tribes"—Cherokees, Creeks, Choctaws, Chickasaws, and Seminoles—had signed treaties of alliance with the Confederacy. At that time, they were living in Indian Territory (most of present-day Oklahoma), where their economy was linked to the South. Many of them, especially members of the mixed-blood upper class, were slaveholders. Bitter toward the United States, the tribal leaders cast their lot with the Confederacy on the principle that "the enemy of my enemy is my friend." The Cherokee leader Stand Watie rose to brigadier general in the Confederate army and was the last Confederate commander to surrender, on June 23, 1865.

But siding with the Confederacy proved to be a costly mistake for these tribes. The U.S. government "reconstructed" Indian Territory more quickly and with less contention than it reconstructed the former Confederate states. Treaties with the five tribes in 1866 required them to grant tribal citizenship to their freed slaves and reduced tribal lands by half. The government then settled Indians who had been dispossessed from other areas on the land it had taken from these tribes. Although Reconstruction has usually been thought of as occurring only in the South, it reshaped the West as well.

18-2a *Conflict with the Dakota Sioux*

The Civil War set in motion a generation of Indian warfare that was more violent and widespread than anything since the 17th century. For years the government had largely ignored the Plains. But no more. In order to fight Confederate expansion into the West, and to maintain access to precious metals, the

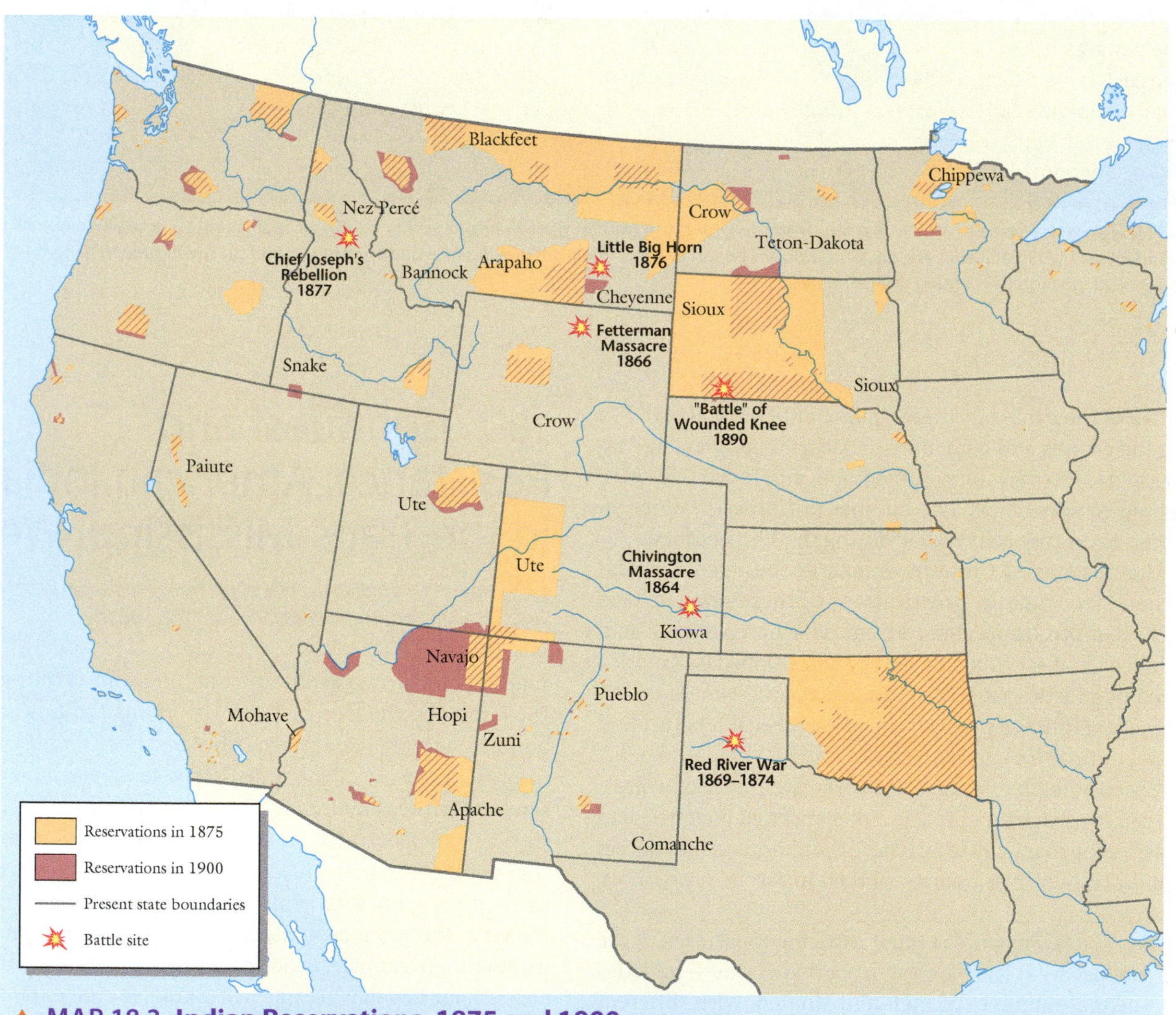

▲ **MAP 18.3 Indian Reservations, 1875 and 1900** Before the Civil War, Indians had hunted and trapped over most of this vast region. The shrinking areas on which they were confined by the reservation policy vividly illustrate that for the first Americans, the story was not "the expansion of America" but "the contraction of America."

Q *How did different Indian tribes respond to their lands being taken away?*

Q *How did government policy regarding Indians shift over the course of this period?*

Union sought to keep overland trails open and to gain access to Indian lands. At the same time, the Homestead Act of 1862, a wartime measure, set off a wave of settlement that directly threatened Indians' nomadic way of life. Conflict was virtually inevitable, not only with nomadic tribes but also with those tribes who had already been forced onto reservations and were now neglected by a government that had promised to provide for them.

The first major conflict occurred in 1862 in the northern plains. Herded onto reservations along the Minnesota River by the Treaty of Traverse des Sioux in 1851, the Dakota Sioux faced conditions of starvation in 1862. Already angry, they responded to a trader's perceived insult by openly rebelling, attacking farms, towns, and forts over several weeks and eventually massacring at least 500 white Minnesotans.

Hastily mobilized militia and army units finally suppressed the uprising. A military court convicted 319 Indians of murder and atrocities and sentenced 303 of them to death. Appalled by this ferocious retaliation, Lincoln personally reviewed the trial transcripts and reduced the number of executions to 38—the largest act of executive clemency in American history. Even so, the hanging of 38 Dakota Sioux on December 26, 1862, was the largest mass execution the country has ever witnessed. The government evicted the remaining Dakota Sioux from Minnesota to Dakota Territory.

In the meantime, the army's pursuit of fleeing Dakota Sioux provoked other Lakota Sioux farther west. By 1864, and for a decade afterward, fighting flared between the army and the Sioux across the northern plains. It reached a climax in 1874 and 1875 after gold-seekers poured into the Black Hills of western Dakota, a sacred place to the Lakota Sioux. At the **Battle of Little Bighorn** in Montana Territory on June 25, 1876, Sioux warriors led by **Sitting Bull** and Crazy Horse, along with their Cheyenne allies, wiped out George A. Custer and the 225 men with him in the Seventh Cavalry. In retaliation, General Philip Sheridan carried out a winter campaign in which the Sioux and Cheyenne were crushed.

The largest and most warlike of the Plains tribes, the Lakota Sioux were confined to a reservation in Dakota Territory where poverty, disease, and alcoholism reduced them to a desperate condition.

18-2b *Suppression of Central Plains Indians*

Just as the Dakota Sioux uprising in Minnesota had triggered war on the northern plains in 1862, a massacre of Cheyenne in Colorado in 1864 sparked a decade of conflict in the central plains. The discovery of gold near Pike's Peak set off a rush to Colorado in 1858–1859. By 1861, the government was eager to clear title to the land in Colorado Territory, and arranged a treaty with some of the Arapahos and Southern Cheyennes. They were assigned to a barren reservation at Sand Creek in southeast Colorado.

In 1864, facing desperate conditions on the reservation, some Cheyennes returned to the lands where they had long hunted. Along the way they raided white settlements. Skirmishes soon erupted into open warfare. In the fall, Cheyenne chief Black Kettle, believing that he had concluded peace with the Colorado settlers, returned to the reservation. There, at dawn on November 29, militia commanded by Colonel John Chivington surrounded and attacked Black Kettle's unsuspecting camp, killing 200 Indians, half of them women and children.

The notorious **Sand Creek massacre** set a pattern for several similar attacks on Indian villages in subsequent years. Ever since the earliest battles between colonists and Indians in the 17th century, whites had followed the strategy of burning Indian crops and villages as a means of destroying or driving off the Indians. Sherman and Sheridan had adopted a similar strategy against the Confederates and followed it again as military commanders responsible for subduing the Plains Indians. Their purpose was to corral the Indians onto the reservations that were being created throughout the West. In addition to trying to defeat the Indians in battle, which proved to be difficult against the mounted Plains Indians, the army encouraged the extermination of the buffalo herds. Professional hunters slaughtered the large, clumsy animals by the millions for their hides, thus depriving Plains Indians of both physical and spiritual sustenance. When the buffalo became nearly extinct in 1883, the Plains Indians understood that their old way of life was gone forever. "Nothing happened after that," recalled one Crow warrior. "We just lived. There were no more war parties, no capturing horses from the Piegan and the Sioux, no buffalo to hunt. There is nothing more to tell."

The Indians were left with no alternative but to come into the reservations, and by the 1880s, nearly all of them had done so (see Map 18.3). Chief Joseph of the Nez Percé pronounced the epitaph for their way of life when federal troops blocked the escape of his band from Montana to Canada in 1877:

> I am tired of fighting. Our chiefs are killed. The old men are all dead. It is cold and we have no blankets ... no food.... The little children are freezing to death.... Hear me, my chiefs; I am tired; my heart is sick and sad. From where the sun now stands, I will fight no more forever.

18-2c *The "Peace Policy"*

Many eastern reformers condemned America's suppression of the Indians. The most prominent was Helen Hunt Jackson, whose *A Century of Dishonor* (1881) was an outraged indictment of anti-Indian violence, exploitation, and broken treaties. Yet, as sympathetic as Jackson was to the Indians' plight, she was not sympathetic to Indian culture; like other white Protestant reformers of her day, she believed that Indians must be stripped of their culture in order to assimilate to American society.

In this she was in alignment with the government. In 1869 President Grant had announced a new "peace policy" toward Indians, urging "their civilization and ultimate citizenship." "Civilization" meant acceptance of white culture, including the English language, Christianity, and individual ownership of property. It also meant allegiance to the United States rather than to a tribe. In 1869, Grant established a Board of Indian Commissioners and staffed it with humanitarian reformers.

In 1871, the century-long policy of negotiating treaties with Indian "nations" came to an end. From then on, Indians became "wards of the nation," to be "civilized" and prepared for citizenship, first on reservations and eventually on individually owned parcels of land that were carved out of the reservations. Most Indians acquiesced in the "reconstruction" that offered them citizenship by the 1880s—they had little choice.

18-2d *The Dawes Severalty Act and Indian Boarding Schools*

In order to further the goal of Indian ownership of private property, Protestant reformers in the 1880s found themselves in a strange alliance with land-hungry westerners, who greedily eyed the 155 million acres of land tied up in reservations. If part of that land could be allotted directly for individual ownership by Indian families, the remainder would become available for purchase by whites. The 1887 **Dawes Severalty Act** combined these impulses toward greed and reform. This landmark legislation called for the dissolution of Indian tribes as legal entities, offered Indians the opportunity to become citizens, and allotted heads of families 160 acres of farmland or 320 acres of grazing land, as long as they were "severed" from their tribe.

For whites who were eager to seize reservation land, the Dawes Act brought a bonanza. At noon on April 22, 1889, the government threw open specified parts of the Indian Territory to "Boomers," who descended on the region like locusts and by nightfall had staked claim to nearly 2 million acres. Indians did not just lose the lands legally opened for white settlement: Many Indians who received individual land titles through the Dawes Act also lost these lands to unscrupulous whites through fraud and misrepresentation. Eventually, whites gained title to 108 million acres of former reservation land.

For Indians, the Dawes Severalty Act was a disaster. Private ownership of land was an alien concept to most tribes. Indians received little training for a transition to farming, much less the appropriate tools and supplies. Moreover, the poor quality of their land allotments made farming difficult, if not impossible. In an attempt to strip Indians of their culture, the Dawes Act forbade Indian religions and the telling of Indian myths and legends, as well as the practices of medicine men.

Indian boarding schools, established beginning in the late 1870s, were another attempt to deny Indians their culture. Children were taken from their families to the Hampton Institute in Virginia and the Carlisle Institute in Pennsylvania, among other schools. There they were forbidden to speak Indian languages or wear Indian clothing. As one 1890 set of instructions from the U.S. Bureau of Indian Affairs put it: "Pupils must be compelled to converse with each other in English, and should be properly rebuked or punished for persistent violation of this rule." The writer Zitkala-Sa, a Yankton Sioux, later remembered her life in an Indian school: "The melancholy of those black days has left so long a shadow that it darkens the path of years that have since gone by."

After graduation from an Indian boarding school, Zitkala-Sa taught at the Carlisle School and became a much-praised writer in New York. But later she would undergo a spiritual crisis: She compared herself to a "slender tree" that had been "uprooted from my mother, nature, and God," and lamented that she had "forgotten the healing in trees and brooks." Eventually she left New York, married a Sioux, and became an activist for Native American rights.

18-2e *The Ghost Dance*

At a time of despair for many Indians, a new visionary religious movement swept through Indian peoples in 1890, offering a different kind of resistance to white domination. The **Ghost Dance** began with the visions of the Paiute shaman Wovoka, who counseled Indians that if they gave up alcohol, lived a simple life, and devoted themselves to prayer, white men would disappear from the earth, Indian lands would be restored, and dead Indians would rejoin the living. This message of hope was embodied in the Ghost Dance ritual, involving days of worship expressed in part through dance.

18.6 The Ghost Dance This photograph shows a Lakota Sioux performing the Ghost Dance with a sacred whistle in 1890. This religious dance became part of a movement of resistance to white domination that ended tragically in the Wounded Knee Massacre of 1890.

Interpreting the Visual Past

Indian Children at the Hampton Institute

The goal of Indian boarding schools was assimilation to white culture. But such schools had a very narrow vision of the place Indians would hold in a white world. At the Hampton Institute, Indian girls taken from reservations led a regimented life and learned domestic skills such as cooking and sewing. Girls were educated not for college but for menial jobs as servants; many spent long hours working in school laundries as virtual servants of the schools that were supposed to teach them. Students resisted as best they could by running away, often only to be caught and returned to school again. Many adults later resisted the training they had received by returning to Indian traditions.

Take a close look at these two "before-and-after" shots. Such photographs were used by a number of educational and charitable institutions in the late 19th century in fundraising efforts aimed at potential donors. In the first photograph, the three girls, wrapped in plaid blankets, sit close together on a bare tile floor. In the second photograph, the girls are apparently at leisure. They are playing checkers and reading, with a doll prominently displayed in the small chair.

Q *What messages do you think such "before-and-after" photographs were supposed to convey? Look closely at these images, examining the girls' postures and expressions. How successful do you think these images are as signs of the girls' transformation? How contented do they look? Do their postures and expressions offer any resistance to the goals of the photographer?*

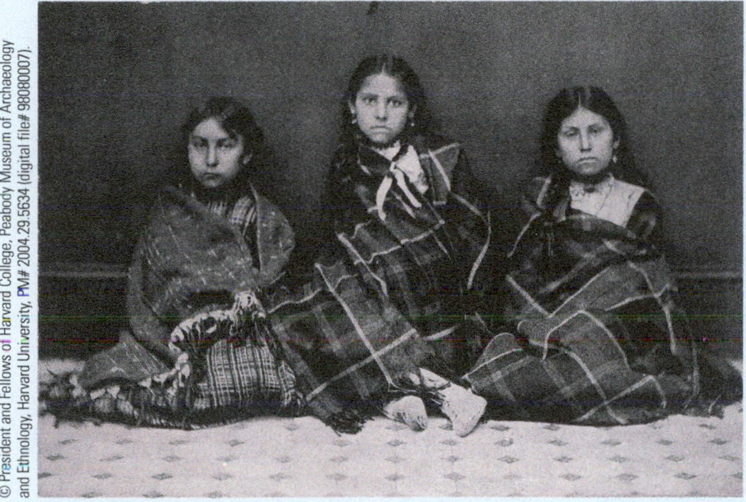

18.7 **On Arrival at Hampton, Virginia: Carrie Anderson—12 years, Annie Dawson—10 years, and Sarah Walker—13 years.**

18.8 **Fourteen Months After.**

When the Ghost Dance religion spread to those Lakotas led by Sitting Bull, and they began days of ecstatic dancing, Indian agents grew alarmed: As one agent telegraphed authorities, "Indians are dancing in the snow and are wild and crazy. *We need protection and we need it now.*" The results of the ensuing confrontations between Indians and authorities were tragic. First Sitting Bull and his grandson were killed in a skirmish with reservation authorities. A few days later, trigger-happy members of the Seventh Cavalry—Custer's old regiment—opened fire on Sioux men, women, and children at **Wounded Knee** in the Pine Ridge Reservation, killing 146 Indians, including 44 women and 18 children. Twenty-five soldiers also died. For many, the massacre at Wounded Knee symbolized the death of 19th-century Plains Indian culture.

18-2f *Sitting Bull and Buffalo Bill: Popular Myths of the West*

Only a few years before he was killed, Sitting Bull had been one of the prime attractions in the entertainment extravaganza known as Buffalo Bill Cody's Wild West Show. Sitting Bull had been a canny negotiator of fees for his appearances in 1885; he required an interpreter, several attendants, and a salary that came to half the annual salary of the typical Indian agent. He also used press interviews while on the Wild West tour to ask the U.S. government to live up to its promises to Indians. If Cody was using Sitting Bull, Sitting Bull was certainly using Cody right back.

Having "real" Indians in his show was of vital importance to Cody, who capitalized on the public's hunger for "authentic" spectacular entertainments in his popular Wild West shows. Cody was an extraordinary mix of the new industrializing West, the frontier West, and an emerging culture of mass entertainment. Having begun his career as a soldier in the Civil War, Cody then worked for one of the transcontinental railroad lines (where he gained the nickname "Buffalo Bill" for slaughtering buffalo) before becoming a scout for the Fifth Cavalry. When he became the subject of a popular dime Western novel, the most improbable turn in Cody's career occurred: He decided to dramatize his own life in a series of theatrical entertainments. By the year Sitting Bull joined Buffalo Bill's Wild West Show with its band of trick riders and sharpshooters, it required 18 railroad cars to transport

18.9 **Sitting Bull and Buffalo Bill** Before he was killed in 1890 during the Ghost Dance movement, the renowned Lakota leader Sitting Bull became an important part of Buffalo Bill's Wild West Show, negotiating shrewdly for his salary. In this remarkable 1885 staged image, the elaborately costumed Buffalo Bill and Sitting Bull both rest a hand on the same rifle.

Q *What message do you think this image is attempting to convey?*

performers (including a number of Indians), work crews, animals, and equipment.

The Wild West Show celebrated the white conquest of the West in a series of acts called "The Drama of Civilization," which showed scenes of an emigrant train crossing the prairie, Buffalo Bill rescuing a pioneer family from Indians, and a mining camp. Billed as "America's National Entertainment," these shows revealed just how tightly linked industrialization and conquest were in Americans' thinking—and even in their entertainment.

18-3 Industrialization and the New South

Q *How did industrialization shape the African American experience in the post-Reconstruction South?*

Like the West, the South underwent a surge of industrialization in the last decades of the 19th century. Boosters like the energetic and influential Henry Grady, editor of the Atlanta *Constitution*, proclaimed that a New South had emerged, one hospitable to industry and to northern investment.

Some people scoffed at such promotional talk in a world that was still decidedly rural, but in fact the pace of industrialization quickened in the last decades of the century, with textiles leading the way. In 1880, the South had only 5 percent of the country's textile-producing capacity; by 1900, it had 23 percent and was well on its way to surpassing New England a generation later. Tobacco industrialized as well, with James B. Duke of North Carolina transforming the industry (see Chapter 19).

Railroads and iron also saw a surge in growth. Between 1877 and 1900 the South built railroads faster than any other region in the country. In 1880, the former slave states produced only 9 percent of the nation's pig iron; by 1890, after a decade of extraordinary expansion for the industry nationwide, that proportion had doubled. Most of the growth was concentrated in northern Alabama, where the proximity of coal, limestone, and ore made the new city of Birmingham the "Pittsburgh of the South."

But there were limits to southern industrialization. It was difficult to catch up with well-established northern industries. Thus, southerners competed in the few areas in which they could find markets for local crops and resources: textiles produced from their own cotton; cigarettes manufactured from southern tobacco; as well as lumber, sugar, and iron.

Not all of the wealth from the new industries went into the pockets of southerners, though. Over the late 19th century, southern industry attracted more and more northern capital in a pattern that held true across industries. At first, for instance, southerners supplied most of the capital in the expansion of the textile industry. But after 1893, an increasing amount came from the North, as New England mill owners began to recognize the benefits of relocating to the low-wage, nonunion South. In the tobacco industry, too, initial southern capital gave way to northern financing, especially after James Duke moved to New York in the 1880s. But most dependent on northern capital were the railroads and iron industries. When in 1886 southern railroads switched their tracks from the regional gauge to the national standard, the symbolic domination of the North seemed complete.

Heavy northern investment in southern industry meant that the South had less control over economic decisions that affected its welfare. Some historians have referred to the South's "colonial" relationship to the North in the late 19th century. One result was that the low wages prevailing in the South made for inequitable distribution of the economic benefits of industrial growth. Average southern per capita income remained only two-fifths of the average in the rest of the country well into the 20th century.

18-3a *Race and Industrialization*

Even those low wages were unequally distributed, as the politics of race influenced the structuring of industrial jobs. Along the piedmont from Virginia to Alabama, new cotton mills sprang up for a white labor force drawn from farm families on the worn-out red clay soil of this region. About 40 percent of the workers were women, and 25 percent were children aged 16 and younger. Living in company towns, workers labored long hours for wages about half the level prevailing in New England's mills, with their cheap labor giving mill owners a competitive advantage.

At first, African Americans assumed that there would be jobs for them in this new textile industry. And why not? Blacks had worked in mills before the Civil War, and they continued to work in tobacco factories in the postwar era, albeit in the lowest-paid jobs and performing the dirtiest work. There seemed no reason why such a large and inexpensive workforce might not become a mainstay of the mills.

But industrialization did not mean progress for blacks. Instead, it went hand in hand with segregation in the increasingly white supremacist world of the 1880s and 1890s. To attract white workers, mill owners promised them segregated environments. The bargain offered was this: Mill workers might not earn very much, but they would gain what one historian has called the "wages of whiteness," a sense of racial superiority that could serve as compensation for their low economic status. Thus, the emerging industrial economy of the New South was built around the politics of race. For most African Americans, agricultural work was thus the only option.

18-3b *Southern Agriculture*

A major success story, however, was increasing black ownership of land in the post-Reconstruction period, with almost 200,000 farmers achieving that cherished goal. Most black landowners in the South were in the upper South or coastal areas; others were in the trans-Mississippi West.

Still, most blacks were tenants rather than landowners, and many blacks and whites faced lives of grinding rural poverty. Those who owned land risked sliding into tenantry; those who did not own land found it impossible to make the leap to landownership. One-crop specialization, overproduction, declining prices, and an exploitative credit system all contributed to the problem. The basic institution of the southern rural economy was the crop lien system, which came into being because of the shortage of money and credit in the war-ravaged South. Few banks had survived the war, and land values had plummeted, which left farmers unable to secure a bank loan with their land as collateral. Instead, merchants in the crossroads country stores that sprang up across the South provided farmers with supplies and groceries in return for a lien on their next crop.

This system might have worked well if the merchants had charged reasonable interest rates and if cotton and tobacco prices had remained high enough for the farmer to pay off his debts after harvest with a little left over. But the country storekeeper charged a credit price 50 or 60 percent above the cash price, and crop prices, especially for cotton, were dropping steadily. Cotton prices declined from an average of 12 cents per pound in the 1870s to 6 cents in the 1890s. As prices fell, many farmers went deeper and deeper into debt to the merchants. **Sharecroppers** and tenants incurred a double indebtedness: (1) to the landowner whose land they sharecropped or rented and (2) to the merchant who furnished them supplies on credit. Because many landowners became merchants, and vice versa, that indebtedness was often to the same man.

One reason cotton prices fell was overproduction. Britain had encouraged the expansion of cotton growing in Egypt and India during the Civil War to make up for the loss of American cotton. After the war, southern growers had to face international competition. By 1878, the southern crop had reached the output of the best antebellum year, and during the next 20 years, output doubled. This overproduction drove prices ever lower. To obtain credit, farmers had to plant every acre with the most marketable cash crop—cotton. This practice exhausted the soil and required ever-increasing amounts of expensive fertilizer, which fed the cycle of overproduction and declining prices.

It also reduced the amount of land that could be used to grow food crops. Farmers who might otherwise have produced their own cornmeal and raised their own hogs for bacon became dependent on merchants for these supplies. Before the Civil War, the cotton states had been nearly self-sufficient in food; by the 1890s, they had to import nearly half their food at a price 50 percent higher than it would have cost to grow their own. Many southerners recognized that only diversification could break this dependency, but the crop lien system locked them into dependency.

18-3c *Exodusters and Emigrationists*

Many rural African Americans dreamed of escaping these difficulties by leaving the South entirely. In the late 1870s, a movement called Exodus gained momentum among African Americans who believed that they might have to "repeat the history of the Israelites" and "seek new homes beyond the reign and rule of Pharaoh." Most pinned their hopes on internal emigration to the West, although some explored the possibility of emigration to Liberia as well. In 1875, Benjamin Singleton, a former Tennessee slave, helped a group of African Americans establish new lives in an agrarian colony in western Kansas; three years later, he circulated an advertisement picturing prairie abundance in the hopes of enticing a few hundred more settlers. Instead, in the spring of 1879, some 20,000 African Americans began an exodus to Kansas from all over the Southwest—drawn not just by the advertisement but also by rumors that there was free land available for settlers as well as free supplies from the government. The rumors were false, but many of these **Exodusters** stayed on in Kansas anyway, although not as homesteaders amidst the prairie abundance but as domestics and laborers in Kansan towns, including some they founded, such as Nicodemus.

18-3d *Race Relations in the New South*

The desire to emigrate for better jobs, autonomy, and a place where African Americans could be truly free did not end with the Exodusters. "The disposition among the colored people to migrate now is strong, and is increasing," commented a white southerner in 1889. There was a net loss of 537,000 African Americans in the South between 1880 and 1910. Economic reasons were important, but so too was the worsening world of white supremacy that arose in that period.

Adherence to the industrial ideology behind the New South, with its emphasis on racial cooperation, was shallow at best among broad classes of whites. Many refused to let go of the legacy of the defeated plantation South. They celebrated the Lost Cause by organizing fraternal and sororal organizations such as the United Daughters of the Confederacy (UDC). The UDC, like the Daughters of the American Revolution (DAR) on which it was modeled, was open only to white women who could prove their relation to the "first families" of the South. Its members decorated the graves of Confederate soldiers, funded public statues of Confederate heroes, and sought to preserve a romanticized history of the slavery era. Several white southern authors became famous writing stories about this fabled South. Thomas Nelson Page's racist sentimental story "Marse Chan" created a national craze for southern literature in the 1880s. Published in a northern magazine, the story was written in what Page claimed to be authentic black dialect, with an aging freedman telling of the glorious days before the war when slaves supposedly had little work to do. Such stories romanticized the southern plantation, cleansing it of the horrors of slavery.

The national appeal of such stories made it clear that antiblack racism was not just a southern phenomenon. Certainly, there was shockingly little northern reaction to the wave of lynchings of black men in the South in the 1890s. Lynchings rose to an all-time high, averaging 188 per year, while the viciousness of racist propaganda reached an

Everett Collection/Newscom

18.10 **Ida B. Wells** A passionate crusader for justice, the renowned journalist Ida B. Wells received death threats after she began a campaign against lynching in her Memphis, Tennessee, newspaper, *Free Speech*, in 1892. Forced to leave Memphis, Wells moved to Chicago and continued her anti-lynching crusade in pamphlets, newspaper columns, and public lectures delivered both in the United States and in England. Together with Booker T. Washington, Wells was one of the most prominent African American leaders of the 1890s.

all-time low. At a time when many middle-class blacks were steadily gaining economically even as a downward spiral in the rural economy frustrated whites, lynchings of black men were not just extraordinarily violent acts. They were also clear symbolic messages to entire black communities to keep their "place" in a white-dominated society. Ritualized expressions of white power, lynchings were not secret or furtive events, but often well-orchestrated community affairs advertised in advance and sometimes even including men, women, and children as spectators.

In 1892, three respected African American businessmen who owned a grocery store in Memphis, Tennessee, were taken from the jail where they awaited trial and lynched by a white mob. Their ostensible crime was attempted murder—firing on three white intruders who had burst into their store—but their real offense was successfully challenging the dominance of a white grocery store in their area.

In response to the lynching, the African American journalist **Ida B. Wells** embarked on an extensive anti-lynching campaign involving an economic boycott as well as a series of fiery editorials in her newspaper, *Free Speech*, that called into question the usual white rationale for lynching: the supposed rape or molestation of a white woman. Exposing this common trumped-up charge as "the old racket," Wells ignited the wrath of white Memphis residents and was forced to flee for her life to the North. But there her anti-lynching campaign met with indifference from northerners until Wells traveled to England on a speaking tour. She received widespread publicity as she called into question how civilized America could be if it tolerated a barbaric practice like lynching; she also touched a nerve back home. Upper-class white northerners indifferent to the murder of blacks but sensitive to English opinion finally sat up and began to notice her campaign. Her English travels were a brilliant strategy to shake up northern complacency and challenge northern complicity in lynching.

18-3e *The Emergence of an African American Middle Class*

Wells was part of an extensive African American middle class that came of age in the 1880s and 1890s. These men and women, educated in the emerging black colleges, became teachers, doctors, lawyers, ministers, and business owners. They formed numerous civic organizations, such as the 1896 National Association of Colored Women, which was part of the women's club movement of the late 19th century (see Chapter 19). Echoing the moral reform activities of white middle-class women, its president, Mary Church Terrell, called on middle-class black women to work with "the masses of our women" and to "uplift and claim them."

Such institution building, combined with increasing prosperity, gave middle-class blacks great optimism that "racial uplift" might reduce or even eliminate racism in

American society. "We as a race are enjoying the brightest rays of Christian civilization," wrote one bishop in the African Methodist Episcopal (AME) Church. Middle-class blacks believed that through education and self-improvement, they could become "best men" and "best women," seen as equals by middle-class whites. These were not naïve hopes as black entry into the middle class surged in the 1880s and early 1890s.

18-3f *The Rise of Jim Crow*

But these visible successes of middle-class African Americans enraged white supremacists, who denied any possibility of class solidarity across racial lines. Serious antiblack riots broke out in Wilmington, North Carolina, in 1898 and in Atlanta in 1906. Several states adopted new constitutions that disfranchised most black voters by means of literacy or property qualifications (or both), poll taxes, and other clauses implicitly aimed at black voters. The new constitutions contained "understanding clauses" or "grandfather clauses" that enabled registrars to register white voters who were unable to meet the new requirements. In *Williams v. Mississippi* (1898), the U.S. Supreme Court upheld these disfranchisement clauses on the grounds that they did not discriminate "on their face" against blacks. State Democratic parties then established primary elections in which only whites could vote.

During these same years, most southern states passed **Jim Crow laws** (the name came from blackface minstrelsy; see Chapter 10) mandating racial segregation in public facilities of all kinds. Many African Americans resisted: In 1884, Ida B. Wells, at the time a young schoolteacher, refused to give up her seat in a railway "ladies' car." The conductor "tried to drag me out of the seat," she remembered, "but the moment he caught hold of my arm I fastened my teeth in the back of his hand. I had braced my feet against the seat in front and was holding to the back, and as he had already been badly bitten he didn't try it again by himself. He went forward and got the baggageman and another man to help him and of course they succeeded in dragging me out." Wells sued the railroad, winning her case in a lower court before losing it on appeal.

In 1896 came a tremendous setback for American equality. In the landmark case of ***Plessy v. Ferguson***, the Supreme Court sanctioned Jim Crow laws so long as the separate facilities for blacks were equal to those for whites—which, in practice, they never were. At this "nadir" of the black experience in freedom, as one historian has called the 1890s, a new black leader emerged as successor of the abolitionists and Reconstruction politicians who were fading from the scene. **Booker T. Washington**, a 39-year-old educator who had founded Tuskegee Institute in Alabama, gave a speech at

Hulton Archive/Archive Photos /Getty Images

UniversalImagesGroup/Getty Images

18.11a (left) and 18.11b (right) **Booker T. Washington and W. E. B. Du Bois** The most powerful African American leader of his time, Washington (left) built an excellent secondary school and industrial training institute at Tuskegee, Alabama, and gained great influence with philanthropists and political leaders. But several prominent African American writers and activists, including W. E. B. Du Bois (right), accused Washington of acquiescing in segregation and second-class citizenship for African Americans in exchange for the crumbs of philanthropy.

What They Said

Differing Visions of Black Progress: Booker T. Washington and W. E. B. Du Bois

The most prominent black leader at the turn of the century, Booker T. Washington was not without critics. Compare the two selections below. The first is a passage from Washington's famous 1895 Atlanta Exposition Address, delivered to a primarily white audience but widely read by blacks. The second selection is a discussion of Washington's philosophy by the emerging African American leader **W. E. B. Du Bois**. The passage is taken from his masterpiece *The Souls of Black Folk*, a set of essays written between 1897 and 1903.

Booker T. Washington

Our greatest danger is that in the great leap from slavery to freedom we may overlook the fact that the masses of us are to live by the productions of our hands, and fail to keep in mind that we shall prosper in proportion as we learn to dignify and glorify common labour, and put brains and skill into the common occupations of life; shall prosper in proportion as we learn to draw the line between the superficial and the substantial, the ornamental gewgaws of life and the useful. No race can prosper till it learns that there is as much dignity in tilling a field as in writing a poem. It is at the bottom of life we must begin, and not at the top. Nor should we permit our grievances to overshadow our opportunities.

To those of the white race who look to the incoming of those of foreign birth and strange tongue and habits for the prosperity of the South, were I permitted I would repeat what I say to my own race, "Cast down your bucket where you are." Cast it down among the eight millions of Negroes whose habits you know, whose fidelity and love you have tested in days when to have proved treacherous meant the ruin of your firesides. Cast down your bucket among these people who have, without strikes and labour wars, tilled your fields, cleared your forests, builded your railroads and cities, and brought forth treasures from the bowels of the earth, and helped make possible this magnificent representation of the progress of the South. Casting down your bucket among my people, helping and encouraging them as you are doing on these grounds, and to education of head, hand, and heart, you will find that they will buy your surplus land, make blossom the waste places in your fields, and run your factories. While doing this, you can be sure in the future, as in the past, that you and your families will be surrounded by the most patient, faithful, law-abiding, and unresentful people that the world has seen. As we have proved our loyalty to you in the past, in nursing your children, watching by the sick-bed of your mothers and fathers, and often following them with tear-dimmed eyes to their graves, so in the future, in our humble way, we shall stand by you with a devotion that no foreigner can approach, ready to lay down our lives, if need be, in defense of yours, interlacing our industrial, commercial, civil, and religious life with yours in a way that shall make the interests of both races one. In all things that are purely social we can be as separate as the fingers, yet one as the hand in all things essential to mutual progress.

W. E. B. Du Bois

Mr. Washington represents in Negro thought the old attitude of adjustment and submission; but adjustment at such a peculiar time as to make his programme unique. This is an age of unusual economic development, and Mr. Washington's programme naturally takes an economic cast, becoming a gospel of Work and Money to such an extent as apparently almost completely to overshadow the higher aims of life. Moreover, this is an age when the more advanced races are coming in closer contact with the less developed races, and the race-feeling is therefore intensified; and Mr. Washington's programme practically accepts the alleged inferiority of the Negro races. Again, in our own land, the reaction from the sentiment of war time has given impetus to race-prejudice against Negroes, and Mr. Washington withdraws many of the high demands of Negroes as men and American citizens… . But so far as Mr. Washington apologizes for injustice, North or South, does not rightly value the privilege and duty of voting, belittles the emasculating effects of caste distinctions, and opposes the higher training and ambition of our brighter minds,—so far as he, the South, or the Nation, does this,—we must unceasingly and firmly oppose them.

Q *How do Washington and Du Bois differ in their vision of the place of blacks in American life? Are their aims fundamentally different, or can you find similarities in their two philosophies?*

Sources: (top) Booker T. Washington's famous *1895 Atlanta Exposition Address*. Accessed at: http://historymatters.gmu.edu/d/39/; (bottom) W. E. B. Du Bois's *The Souls of Black Folk*, 3rd. ed. (Chicago: A. C. McClurg & Co., 1903), pp. 50 & 59. Accessed at: http://books.google.com/books?id=7psUAAAAYAAJ&printsec=frontcover&dq=the+souls+of+black+folk&hl=en&sa=X&ei=Lf8VU_yzO8uE2AXd14CIBw&ved=0CCkQ6AEwAA#v=onepage&q=the%20souls%20of%20black%20folk&f=false.

the 1895 Atlanta Exposition that made him famous—and has been controversial ever since.

Speaking to a white audience at this celebration of southern industry and progress, Washington was introduced as "a representative of Negro enterprise and civilization." Assuring his audience that he wanted to "cement the friendship of the races," Washington talked of the "new era of industrial progress" and told the industrialists before him that they should hire African Americans rather than immigrants. "Cast down your bucket where you are," he told them, "among the eight million of Negroes whose habits you know." If they did so, Washington said, they would not only find people to "run your factories," but could also be assured that they would be surrounded by a "faithful, law-abiding, and unresentful" people. In the most famous sentence of the speech, Washington then promised that "in all things that are purely social we can be as separate as the fingers, yet one as the hand in all things essential to mutual progress." In effect, Washington accepted segregation as a temporary accommodation between the races in return for white support of black efforts for education, social uplift, and economic progress.

It was a complex, canny speech, much like the man himself, and Washington's listeners came away with very different impressions. Many African Americans applauded his appeal for black inclusion in the new industrial order; many white audience members simply took away the idea that Washington approved of segregation, vocational training for blacks, and a permanent, second-class status.

18-4 The Politics of Stalemate

Q *Why did politicians fail to address many of the most serious economic and social issues facing the nation in the post-Reconstruction world?*

During the 20 years between the Panic of 1873 and the Panic of 1893, serious economic and social issues beset the American polity. The strains of rapid industrialization, an inadequate monetary system, agricultural distress, and labor protest built up to a potentially explosive force. The two mainstream political parties, however, seemed indifferent to these problems. Partisan memories of the Civil War mired Americans in the politics of the past. Paralysis gripped the national government.

18-4a *Knife-Edge Electoral Balance*

The five presidential elections from 1876 through 1892, taken together, were the most closely contested elections in American history. No more than 1 percent separated the popular vote of the two major candidates in any of these contests except 1892, when the margin was 3 percent. The Democratic candidate won twice (Grover Cleveland in 1884 and 1892), and in two other elections carried a tiny plurality of popular votes (Tilden in 1876 and Cleveland in 1888) but lost narrowly in the Electoral College. During the 20 years covered by these five administrations, the Democrats controlled the House of Representatives in seven Congresses to the Republicans' three, while the Republicans controlled the Senate in eight Congresses to the Democrats' two. During only six of those 20 years did the same party control the presidency and both houses, and then by only razor-thin margins.

Divided government and the even balance between the two major parties made for political stalemate. Neither party had the power to enact a bold legislative program; both parties avoided taking firm stands on controversial issues. At election time, Republican candidates "waved the bloody shirt" to keep alive the memory of the Civil War. They castigated Democrats as former rebels or Copperheads who could not be trusted with the nation's destiny. Democrats, in turn, especially in the South, denounced racial equality and branded Republicans as the party of "Negro rule." From 1876 almost into the 20th century, scarcely anyone but a Confederate veteran could be elected governor or senator in the South.

The solid Democratic South and the rather less solid Republican North gave each party a firm bloc of electoral votes in every election. But in three large northern states—New York, Ohio, and Indiana—the two parties were so closely balanced that the shift of a few thousand votes would determine the margin of victory for one or the other party in the state's electoral votes. These three states alone represented 74 electoral votes, fully one-third of the total necessary for victory. Of 20 nominees for president and vice president by the two parties in five elections, 16 were from these three states. Only once did each party nominate a presidential candidate from outside these three states—both lost.

18-4b *Civil Service Reform*

The most salient issue of national politics in the early 1880s was civil service reform. Old-guard factions in both parties opposed it. Republicans split into three factions known in the colorful parlance of the time as Mugwumps (the reformers), Stalwarts (who opposed reform), and Half-Breeds (who supported halfway reforms). Mugwumps and Half-Breeds combined to nominate James A. Garfield for president in 1880. Stalwarts received a consolation prize with the nomination of Chester A. Arthur for vice president. Four months after Garfield took office, a man named Charles Guiteau approached the president at the railroad station in Washington and shot him. Garfield lingered for two months before dying on September 19, 1881.

Described by psychiatrists as a paranoid schizophrenic, Guiteau was viewed by the public as a symbol of the spoils system at its worst. He had been a government clerk and a supporter of the Stalwart faction of the Republican Party but had lost his job under the new administration. As he shot Garfield, he shouted, "I am a Stalwart and Arthur is president now!" This tragedy gave a final impetus to civil service reform. If the spoils system could cause the assassination of a president, it was time to get rid of it.

In 1883, Congress passed the Pendleton Act, which established a category of civil service jobs that were to be filled by competitive examinations. At first, only one-tenth of government positions fell within that category, but a succession of presidential orders gradually expanded the list to about half by 1897. State and local governments began to emulate federal civil service reform in the 1880s and 1890s.

Like the other vice presidents who had succeeded presidents who had died in office (John Tyler, Millard Fillmore, and Andrew Johnson), Arthur failed to achieve nomination for president in his own right. The Republicans turned in 1884 instead to their most charismatic figure, James G. Blaine of Maine. His 18 years in the House and Senate had included six years (1869–1875) as Speaker of the House. He had made enemies over the years, however, especially among Mugwumps, who believed that his cozy relationship with railroad lobbyists while Speaker and rumors of other shady dealings disqualified him for the presidency.

The Mugwumps were small in number but large in influence. Many were editors, authors, lawyers, college professors, or clergymen. Concentrated in the Northeast, particularly in New York, they admired the Democratic governor of that state, Grover Cleveland, who had gained a reputation as an advocate of reform and "good government." When Blaine won the Republican nomination, the Mugwumps defected to Cleveland.

In such a closely balanced state as New York, that shift could make a decisive difference. Cleveland carried New York State by 1,149 votes (a margin of one-tenth of 1 percent) and thus became the first Democrat to be elected president in 28 years.

18-4c *The Tariff Issue*

Ignoring a rising tide of farmer and labor discontent, Cleveland decided to make or break his presidency on the tariff issue. He devoted his annual State of the Union message in December 1887 entirely to the tariff, maintaining that lower duties would help all Americans by reducing the cost of consumer goods and by expanding American exports through reciprocal agreements with other nations. Republicans responded that low tariffs would flood the country with products from low-wage industries abroad, forcing American factories to close and throwing American workers out on the streets. The following year, the Republican nominee for president, Benjamin Harrison, pledged to retain the protective tariff. To reduce the budget surplus that had built up during the 1880s, the Republicans also promised more generous pensions for Union veterans.

The voters' response was ambiguous. Cleveland's popular-vote plurality actually increased from 29,000 in 1884 to 90,000 in 1888 (out of more than 10 million votes cast). Even so, a shift of six-tenths of 1 percent put New York in the Republican column and Harrison in the White House. Republicans also gained control of both houses of Congress. They promptly made good on their campaign pledges by passing legislation that almost doubled Union pensions and by enacting the McKinley Tariff of 1890. Named for Congressman William McKinley of Ohio, this law raised duties on a large range of products to an average of almost 50 percent.

The voters reacted convincingly—and negatively. They handed the Republicans a decisive defeat in midterm congressional elections, converting a House Republican majority of 6 to a Democratic majority of 147, and a Senate Republican majority of 8 to a Democratic majority of 6. Nominated for a third time in 1892, Cleveland built on this momentum to win the presidency by the largest margin in 20 years, but this outcome was deceptive. On March 4, 1893, when Cleveland took the oath of office for the second time, he stood atop a social and economic volcano that would soon erupt.

Conclusion

In 1890, the superintendent of the U.S. Census made a sober announcement of dramatic import: "Up to and including 1880 the country had a frontier of settlement, but at present the unsettled area has been so broken into by isolated bodies of settlement that there can hardly be said to be a frontier line ... any longer."

This statement prompted a young historian at the University of Wisconsin, Frederick Jackson Turner, to deliver a paper in 1893 that became the single most influential essay ever published by an American historian. For nearly 300 years, said Turner, the existence of a frontier of European American settlement advancing relentlessly westward had shaped American character. To the frontier Americans owed their upward mobility, their high standard of living, and the rough equality of opportunity that made liberty and democracy possible. "American social development has been continually beginning over again on the frontier," declared Turner. He continued:

> This perennial rebirth, this fluidity of American life, this expansion westward with its new opportunities ... furnish the forces dominating American character... . Frontier individualism has from the beginning promoted democracy [and] that restless, nervous energy, that dominant individualism ... and withal that buoyancy and exuberance which comes with freedom—these are traits of the frontier, or traits called out elsewhere because of the existence of the frontier.

For many decades, Turner's insight dominated Americans' perceptions of themselves and their history. Today, however, the Turner thesis is largely discredited as failing to explain the experiences of the great majority of people throughout most of American history who lived and worked in older cities and towns or on farms or plantations hundreds of miles from any frontier, and whose culture and institutions were molded more by their place of origin than by a frontier. The whole concept of a frontier as a line beyond which lay empty, uninhabited land has also been discredited.

The Turner thesis also ignored the environmental consequences of the westward movement. The virtual destruction of the bison, the hunting almost to extinction of other forms of wildlife, the ravaging of virgin forests by indiscriminate logging, and the plowing of semiarid grasslands on the plains drastically changed the ecological balance in the West. These ecological changes stored up trouble for the future in the form of soil erosion, dust bowls, and diminished biodiversity. Thoughtful Americans began to express concern about these problems in the 1890s, foreshadowing the launching of a conservation movement in the following decade.

For most Americans, however, the exploitation of the West was a matter of pride, not concern. The positive claims of the Turner thesis reflected beliefs shared widely among whites. They *believed* that liberty and equality were both at least partly the product of the frontier, of the chance to go west and start a new life. And now that opportunity seemed to be ending. In fact, to many Americans it seemed that a new and worrisome power had overtaken American life, threatening American liberty: the power of the corporation.

CHAPTER REVIEW

Review

1. How did the industrialization of the West change American lives?
2. How did the Indian peoples of the trans-Mississippi West respond to white settlement and U.S. government policies?
3. How did industrialization shape the African American experience in the post-Reconstruction South?
4. Why did politicians fail to address many of the most serious economic and social issues facing the nation in the post-Reconstruction world?

Critical Thinking

1. Both the South and the West industrialized in the late 19th century. What were the major differences in the industries that developed in each section, and why?
2. How were ordinary people's experiences of industrialization different in the two regions? Why? Assess the opportunities that were provided by industrialization as well as its drawbacks in the West and South.

Identifications

Review your understanding of the following key terms, people, and events for this chapter (terms in bold in text are included in the Glossary).

Homestead Act, p. 496
Chinese Exclusion Act, p. 498
Western Federation of Miners (WFM), p. 499
Chisholm Trail, p. 500
vaqueros, p. 500
soddies, p. 503
Battle of Little Bighorn, p. 507
Sitting Bull, p. 507
Sand Creek massacre, p. 507
Dawes Severalty Act, p. 508
Ghost Dance, p. 508
Wounded Knee, p. 510
sharecroppers, p. 512
Exodusters, p. 512
Ida B. Wells, p. 513
Jim Crow laws, p. 514
Plessy v. Ferguson, p. 514
Booker T. Washington, p. 514
W. E. B. Du Bois, p. 515

Suggested Readings

An excellent general history linking West and South is **Richard White, *The Republic for Which It Stands: The United States during Reconstruction and the Gilded Age, 1865–1896*** (2017). See also **Pekka Hämäläinen, *The Comanche Empire*** (2008); **Robert V. Hine and John Mack Faragher, *The American West: A New Interpretive History*** (2000); **Richard White, *"It's Your Misfortune and None of My Own": A New History of the American West*** (1991); **William Deverell, ed., *A Companion to the American West*** (2004); and **Patricia Nelson Limerick, *The Legacy of Conquest: The Unbroken Past of the American West*** (1987).

On the global nature of the Gold Rush, see **David Igler, *The Great Ocean: Pacific Worlds from Captain Cook to the Gold Rush*** (2013). On the corruption involved in the building of the railroads, see **Richard White, *Railroaded: The Transcontinentals and the Making of Modern America*** (2011). On industrial ranching, see especially **David Igler, *Industrial Cowboys: Miller & Lux and the Transformation of the Far West, 1850–1920*** (2001). Influential and useful treatments of the industrial transformation of the West are **William Cronon, *Nature's Metropolis: Chicago and the Great West*** (1991); and **William G. Robbins, *Colony and Empire: The Capitalist Transformation of the American West*** (1994).

Histories that explore the Chinese in America include **Ronald Takaki, *Strangers from a Different Shore: A History of Asian Americans*** (1989, rev. 1998); **Yong Chen, *Chinese San Francisco, 1850–1943: A Trans-Pacific Community*** (2000); **Judy Yung, *Unbound Feet: A Social History of Chinese Women in San Francisco*** (1995); **Erika Lee, *At America's Gates: Chinese Immigration during the Exclusion Era, 1882–1943*** (2003); and **Sucheng Chan, *This Bittersweet Soil: The Chinese in California Agriculture, 1860–1910*** (1986). For a discussion of Southwest borderlands, see **Sarah Deutsch, *No Separate Refuge: Culture, Class, and Gender on an Anglo-Hispanic Frontier in the American Southwest, 1880–1940*** (1987). On mining, see **Elizabeth Jameson, *All That Glitters: Class, Conflict, and Community in Cripple Creek*** (1998). On women, see **Rebecca J. Mead, *How the Vote Was Won: Woman Suffrage in the Western United States, 1868–1914*** (2004); and **Peggy Pascoe, *Relations of Rescue: The Search for Female Moral Authority in the American West, 1974–1939*** (1990).

On the 19th- and 20th-century myths of the frontier, see **Richard White and Patricia Nelson Limerick, *The Frontier in American Culture*** (1994). The Indians' response to the reservation system after the 1860s is discussed in **Frederick Hoxie, Peter C. Mancall, and James H. Merrill**, eds., ***American Nations: Encounters in Indian Country, 1850 to the Present*** (2001), and **Robert M. Utley, *The Indian Frontier of the American West, 1846–1890*** (1984).

On the New South, see especially **Edward I. Ayers, *The Promise of the New South Life after Reconstruction*** (1992). The Lost Cause ideology is examined in **Gaines M. Foster, *Ghosts of the Confederacy: Defeat, the Lost Cause, and the Emergence of the New South*** (1987). The rising tide of white racism is chronicled by **Joel Williamson, *A Rage for Order: Black-White Relations in the American South since Emancipation*** (1986). On Ida B. Wells and the campaign against lynching, see **Mia Bay, *To Tell the Truth Freely: The Life of Ida B. Wells*** (2009). See also **Crystal N. Feimster, *Southern Horrors: Women and the Politics of Rape and Lynching*** (2011).

On African American political action after the war, the best book is **Steven Hahn, *A Nation under Our Feet: Black Political Struggles in the Rural South from Slavery to the Great Migration*** (2003). On black experience after Reconstruction, see **Glenda Elizabeth Gilmore, *Gender and Jim Crow: Women and the Politics of White Supremacy in North Carolina, 1896–1920*** (1996); and **Michele Mitchell, *Righteous Propagation: African Americans and the Politics of Racial Destiny after Reconstruction*** (2004).

19 The Rise of Corporate America, 1865–1914

Everett Historical/Shutterstock.com

19.1 New England Factory Life Artist Winslow Homer's 1868 engraving, "Bell Time," shows tired workers leaving a New England textile mill at the end of the workday. Note the many children present in an era before child labor laws.

IN THE SUMMER OF 1877, the same year that President Rutherford B. Hayes withdrew federal troops from the South and effectively ended Reconstruction, he called out the military to suppress the most serious labor uprising in the nation's history. The Great Railroad Strike was a national event that ultimately involved hundreds of thousands of people across America; claimed at least 100 lives; resulted in injuries to hundreds more; and caused the destruction of millions of dollars of property. It also caught many onlookers by surprise: "Sudden as a thunder-burst from a clear sky," one journalist wrote, "the crisis came upon the country. It seemed as if the whole social and political structure was on the very brink of ruin."

But the strike was not so sudden as it seemed to shocked middle-class observers: Tensions between capital and labor had been building for years. The end of the Civil War had inaugurated an era of rapid economic expansion, but industrialization left many workers as permanent wage earners, with little hope of the independence that had been a cherished part of antebellum free-labor ideology. As a roller-coaster economy also subjected employers to boom-and-bust cycles, many resorted to periodic price-cutting and wage-cutting, even while demanding longer hours. The result was that capital and labor had never been more at odds with one another.

The Great Railroad Strike raised troubling questions that would continue to haunt Americans over the next few decades: Who held power in the emerging corporate order? How was liberty now defined, and whose liberty would the government uphold? Had America become a permanently unequal society? ■

CHRONOLOGY

1869	Knights of Labor founded
1873	Financial panic begins economic depression
1877	Railroad strikes cost 100 lives and millions of dollars in damage
1883	Railroads establish four standard time zones
1886	Knights of Labor membership crests at 700,000 • Haymarket triggers antilabor backlash • American Federation of Labor founded
1888	Edward Bellamy publishes *Looking Backward*
1890	Congress passes Sherman Antitrust Act
1892	Homestead Strike fails • Populists organize the People's Party
1893	Financial panic begins economic depression
1894	"Coxey's army" of the unemployed marches on Washington • Pullman Strike paralyzes the railroads and provokes federal intervention
1896	William McKinley defeats William Jennings Bryan for the presidency
1897	Depression ends; prosperity returns
1899	Theodore Roosevelt urges Americans to live the "strenuous life"
1901	U.S. Steel is formed from 200 separate companies • Andrew Carnegie devotes himself to philanthropic pursuits • One of every 400 railroad workers dies on the job
1909	Henry Ford unveils his Model T

19-1 A Dynamic Corporate Economy

Q *What were the main engines of American economic growth in the late 19th and early 20th centuries?*

The decades following the Civil War saw an unprecedented surge of growth in the economy. The gross national product was $9 billion for the five-year period from 1869 to 1873; it was $37 billion for the period from 1897 to 1901. In the 1880s, manufacturing began to outstrip agriculture as a source of new value added to the economy, underlining America's ongoing transformation to an industrial society (see Figure 19.1). America moved from fourth in the world in production in 1865 to first in 1900.

But this tremendous economic growth was accompanied by spectacular volatility. Cycles of overexpansion and overproduction were followed by inevitable contraction. Significant labor uprisings correlated with economic downturns, as employers and businesses sought to cut their losses by cutting wages or laying workers off. The **Great Railroad Strike of 1877** occurred during an extended depression; 1886, another depression year, saw 1,400 strikes involving half a million workers. The great Homestead Strike of 1892 followed the announcement of a wage cut of 18 percent. Another extended depression stretched from 1893 to 1897.

Still, the enormous growth of the economy in this period meant great opportunity and increased prosperity for many Americans (see Figure 19.2). Titans of industry piled up previously unimaginable fortunes. A flourishing middle class achieved new power. But the working class shared unequally in this rising prosperity.

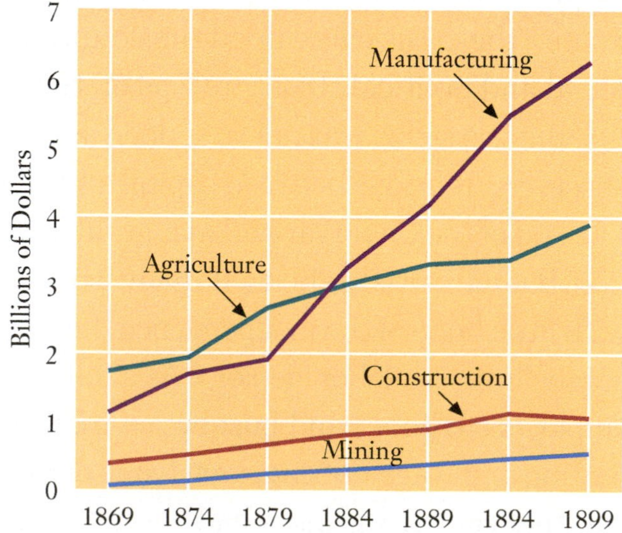

Figure 19.1 **Value Added by Economic Sector, 1869–1899 (in 1879 prices)**

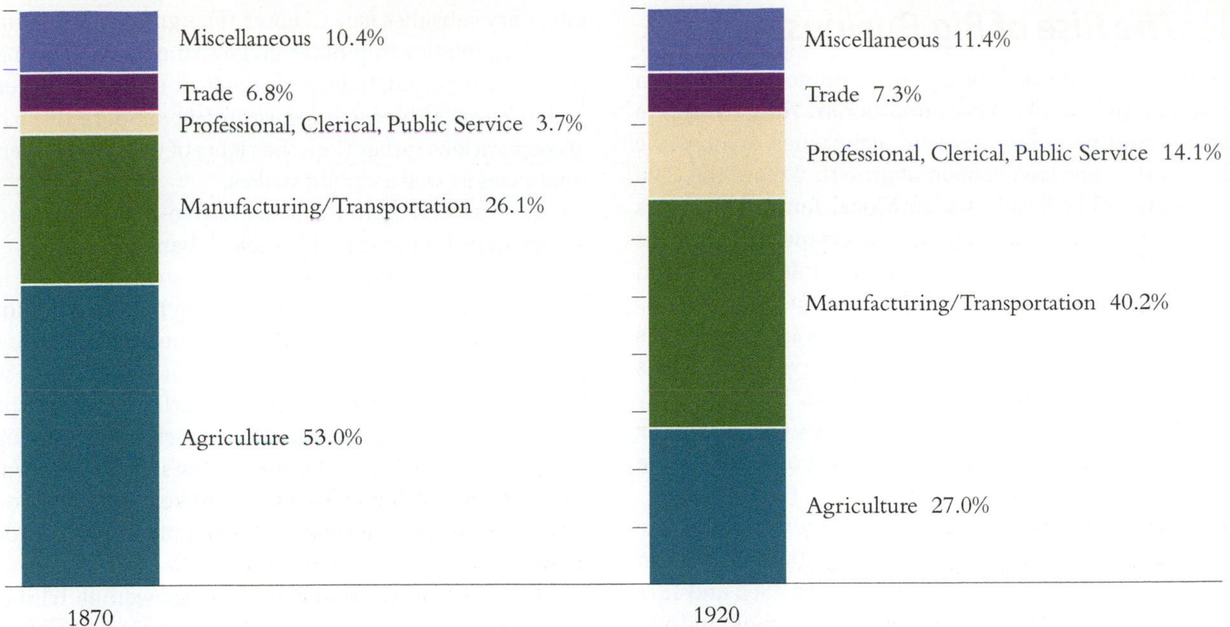

Figure 19.2 **Change in Distribution of the American Workforce, 1870–1920**

Source: Data from Alba Edwards, *Comparative Occupational Statistics for the United States 1870–1940*, U.S. Bureau of the Census, Sixteenth Census of the United States, 1940, Population (Washington, D.C., 1943).

19-1a *Engines of Economic Growth*

The railroads were the largest single employer of labor in this period. An important spur to economic growth, railroads increased in miles of track from 30,000 in 1860 to some 200,000 in 1900. Railroad expansion meant a greater need for coal and iron, and later steel, to build railroad cars and lay track: Steel production soared from 732,000 tons in 1878 to 10,188,000 tons by 1900. The steel industry in turn was a catalyst for a host of other industries, in a pattern repeated across the American industrial landscape (see Map 19.1).

As a result, manufacturing expanded dramatically in this period. In 1859, the value of American manufactured goods was $1.9 billion, but by 1899 it had risen to $13 billion.

Just before the Civil War, there were 140,000 factories and manufacturing shops across the country; by 1899, this figure had risen to 512,000 and included the rise of industrial giants such as Carnegie Steel.

Growth after 1900 was also dramatic. Employment in Chicago's International Harvester factory, where agricultural implements were built, nearly quadrupled from 4,000 in 1900 to 15,000 in 1916. Delaware's DuPont Corporation, a munitions and chemical manufacturer, employed 1,500 workers in 1902 and 31,000 workers in 1920.

19-1b *Technological Innovation*

Growth in manufacturing spurred technological innovation, while invention in turn spurred increased and more efficient manufacturing. Railroads, for instance, ran on a promise of reliability and efficiency, but poorly constructed tracks and rails were a significant hindrance to delivering on that promise. Technological advances like automatic signals and air brakes not only improved railroad efficiency, but aided railroad growth; similarly, the switch from iron to steel tracks aided the efficient production of railroad tracks and promoted the growth of the new steel industry.

No one understood the link between technological innovation and manufacturing growth better than **Thomas Alva Edison**, who invented an astonishing array of devices in this period, from a patented vote-recording machine before he was 21, to the phonograph, the incandescent light bulb, and the kinetoscope (or movie camera). "The Wizard of Menlo Park" was a savvy businessman and self-promoter who kept a sharp eye on the market. "I have always kept," he once told a reporter, "strictly within the lines of commercially useful inventions." In 1876, Edison moved a group of workers to Menlo Park, New Jersey, to set up an "invention factory" that deliberately mimicked the world of manufacturing. An inventor–entrepreneur, Edison incorporated the Edison Electric Light Company in 1878.

Scientists had long been fascinated by electricity, but only in the late 19th century did they find ways to make it practically useful. The work of Edison, George Westinghouse, and Nikola Tesla not only produced the incandescent bulb that brought electric lighting into homes and offices but also the alternating current (AC) that made electric transmission possible over long distances. From 1890 to 1920, the proportion of American industry powered by electricity rose from virtually nil to almost one-third. A host of other inventions in this period spurred economic growth as well: gasoline engines, Kodak cameras, the Otis elevator, and Alexander Graham Bell's telephone.

19-1c *The Rise of Big Business*

But technological breakthroughs alone do not fully explain the nation's spectacular economic boom. New corporate structures and new management techniques created the conditions that powered economic growth. Before the Civil War, most American businesses were local, family-run affairs that received little or no aid from the government and did not sell stock to raise capital. But railroad companies inaugurated a new era of big business that had profound effects on business practice. Many businesses after the Civil War organized as corporations rather than single proprietorships: Corporations could raise capital through selling shares in a company directly to the public. They also used boards of directors as a management tool, allowing for shared responsibility and a new scale and complexity of enterprise.

Railroads were big business in every way, requiring huge tracts of land as well as enormous amounts of capital. In order to encourage railroad building, between 1862 and 1871 the government stepped in with extremely generous land and monetary subsidies (see Chapter 18), signaling the beginning of a close relationship between government and business in the postwar period. Indeed, throughout the late 19th century and into the 20th century, government supported the rights of corporations rather than the rights of workers in a series of legal cases as well as major strikes.

19.2 **The Great Railway Strike** On August 11, 1877, *Harper's Weekly* printed this illustration with the caption, "The Great Strike—the Sixth Maryland Regiment Fighting Its Way Through Baltimore." At first glance the illustration seems sympathetic to the strikers being fired upon in the foreground. The article accompanying this illustration, however, talked of the "reign of terror inaugurated by the railroad strikers" and "scenes of riot and bloodshed," such as "we have never before witnessed in the uprising of labor against capital."

Q *How would you characterize mainstream attitudes towards labor activism and resistance in the post-Civil War era?*

Railroad companies needed often-staggering sums of money in order to build. Financiers, bankers, and a wealthy elite seized this golden opportunity to obtain power in the new industrial order. The savvy young banker **J.P. Morgan** helped finance the Albany & Susquehanna Railroad in upstate New York and joined its board in 1870. Morgan would become the most celebrated and powerful banker of the late 19th century, in large part through his shrewd investing in a variety of industries, including Edison's first electric power plant in 1882. Numerous other bankers would also gain new power through providing the finance capital needed by industry.

But there were financial losers as well as winners in the railroad-building frenzy of the post-Civil War era. The most spectacular and far-reaching downfall of the postwar years was that of Jay Cooke, the legendary financial genius behind the sale of Union bonds during the Civil War. Cooke was undone by his attempts to finance the Northern Pacific Railroad: He ran out of capital in 1873 after selling risky bonds and mortgaging government property. When the Northern Pacific went into receivership, Cooke was forced to close his powerful Philadelphia banking house. Within hours, his closure triggered the crash of the New York Stock Exchange, which in turn began the Panic of 1873. In the severe depression that followed, 18,000 businesses went under. Ordinary investors who hoped to make their fortunes by investing in the railroads often lost their shirts instead.

19-1d *Corporate Consolidation*

Corporations began looking for ways to insulate themselves from harrowing downturns in the business cycle. The railroads led the way in tackling this problem. Rather than engaging in ruinous rate wars, railroads took to sharing information on costs and profits, establishing standardized rates, and allocating discrete portions of the freight business among themselves. These cooperative arrangements rarely succeeded for long because they depended heavily on voluntary compliance. During difficult economic times, the temptation to lower rates and exceed one's market share could become too strong to resist.

Corporate efforts to restrain competition and inject order into the economic environment continued unabated, however. A number of corporate titans innovated with corporate organization, including **Andrew Carnegie**, the industrial leader who built giant Carnegie Steel after the Civil War. Carnegie steadily took control of all parts of the steelmaking process, starting with the mining of the raw material of iron ore and ending with the transportation and marketing of the final product. This vertical integration was a powerful new

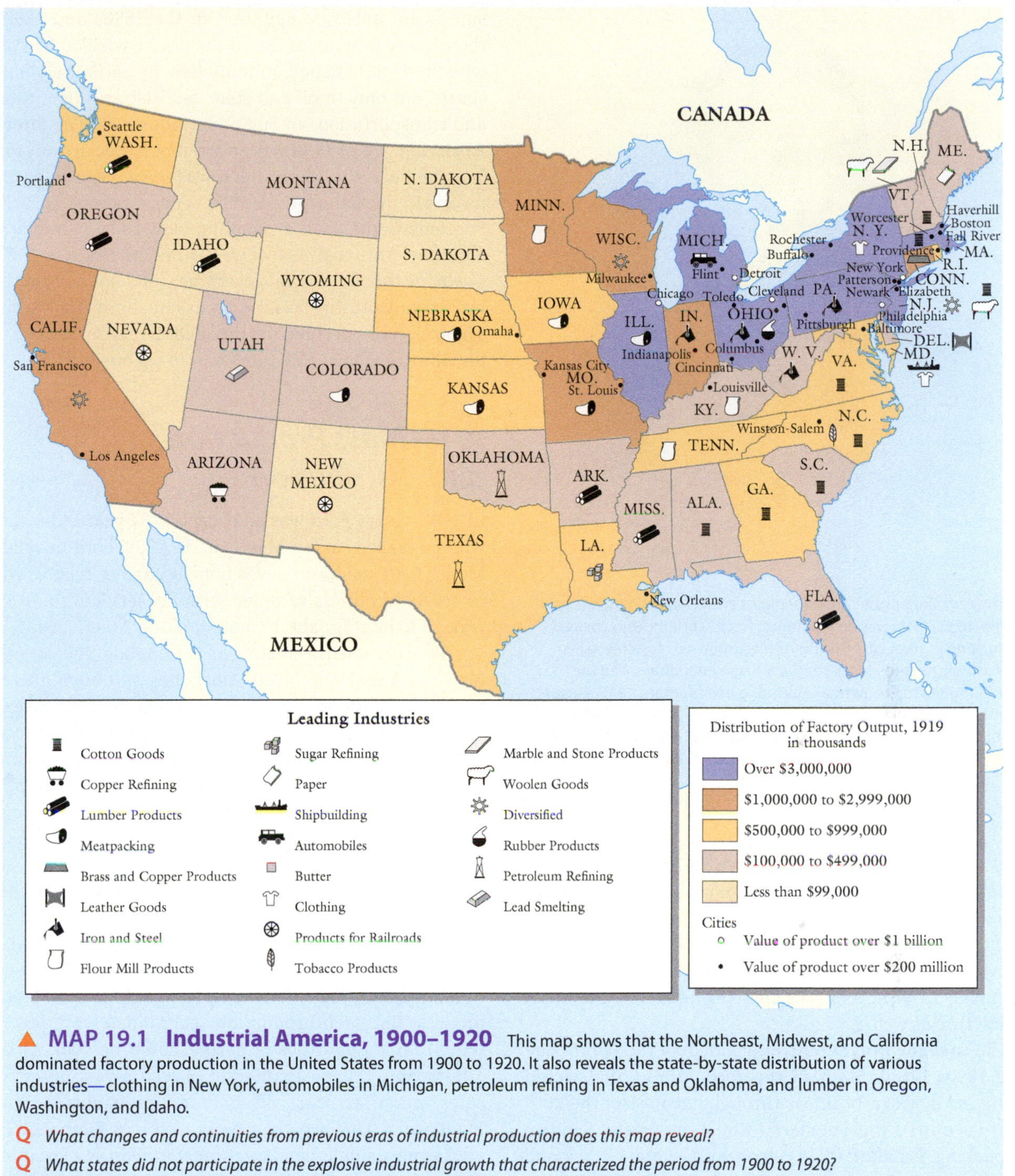

▲ **MAP 19.1 Industrial America, 1900–1920** This map shows that the Northeast, Midwest, and California dominated factory production in the United States from 1900 to 1920. It also reveals the state-by-state distribution of various industries—clothing in New York, automobiles in Michigan, petroleum refining in Texas and Oklahoma, and lumber in Oregon, Washington, and Idaho.

Q *What changes and continuities from previous eras of industrial production does this map reveal?*

Q *What states did not participate in the explosive industrial growth that characterized the period from 1900 to 1920?*

form of business organization that allowed for unprecedented consolidation and the building of business on a previously unimagined scale.

Another titan, the ruthless **John D. Rockefeller** of Standard Oil, either bought out or ruined his rivals through practices such as "predatory pricing" (selling below cost until he bankrupted a competitor) and demanding secret rebates from railroads that wanted his business. In the 1880s, he pioneered a new form of corporate structure, the trust. A vehicle for the creation of a monopoly, a trust was initially used by Rockefeller to gain control over the oil-refining industry and create the horizontal integration of one aspect of his business. Soon, he engaged in vertical integration as well in order to gain control over every aspect of the oil industry, from extraction of crude oil to marketing. By the 1890s, Rockefeller controlled 90 percent of the oil business, with Standard Oil a major force on the world stage.

Mergers also emerged as an important instrument of corporate expansion and consolidation. Smoking tobacco manufacturer James Buchanan Duke led the way in 1890 when

The Granger Collection, NYC

19.3 **Andrew Carnegie** An industrialist and business magnate, Carnegie (1835–1919) was an immigrant from Scotland who created a vast fortune in steel, often using ruthless methods to achieve his goals. A classic rags-to-riches story, Carnegie later disavowed the pursuit of money for its own sake, arguing in his famous 1889 "Gospel of Wealth" that the rich should act as "trustees" of their wealth for the public good. One of several **"robber barons"** who later became philanthropists, Carnegie was famous in his own day for providing free public library buildings around the nation.

he and four competitors merged to form the American Tobacco Company. Over the next eight years, the quantity of cigarettes produced by Duke-controlled companies quadrupled, from 1 billion to almost 4 billion per year. American Tobacco used its powerful position in cigarette manufacture to achieve dominance in pipe tobacco, chewing tobacco, and snuff manufacture as well.

The **merger movement** intensified as the depression of the 1890s lifted. Many of the corporations that would dominate American business throughout most of the 20th century acquired their modern form: Armour and Swift in meatpacking, Standard Oil in petroleum, General Electric and Westinghouse in electrical manufacture, American Telephone and Telegraph (AT&T) in communications, International Harvester in the manufacture of agricultural implements, and DuPont in munitions and chemical processing. The largest merger occurred in steel in 1901, when Andrew Carnegie and J.P. Morgan together fashioned the U.S. Steel Corporation from 200 separate iron and steel companies. U.S. Steel controlled 60 percent of the country's steelmaking capacity. Moreover, its 78 iron-ore boats and 1,000 miles of railroad gave it substantial control over procuring raw materials and distributing finished steel products.

A weak federal government and a conservative Supreme Court set few limits on corporations in this period, despite significant antitrust agitation in the 1880s and 1890s. By then, many Americans feared the power wielded by tycoons who had established monopolies or monopoly market shares not only in oil and steel, but also in sugar, tobacco, and transportation, among other industries. The **Sherman Antitrust Act of 1890** was an attempt to declare any form of "restraint of trade" illegal, but it was so vague as to be almost useless in the actual prosecution of corporations. In 1895, the Supreme Court dealt a crippling blow to the already weak Sherman Antitrust Act when it ruled in *U.S. v. E.C. Knight Company* that the federal government did not have authority over manufacturing because it was not commerce—a form of semantic hair-splitting that revealed the conservative Court's unwillingness to curtail the power of big business.

19-1e *Mass Production and Distribution*

In 1900, Henry Ford was an eccentric 37-year-old mechanic who built race cars in Michigan. In 1909, Ford unveiled his Model T: an unadorned, even homely car, but reliable enough to travel hundreds of miles without servicing and cheap enough to be affordable to most working Americans.

Ford dreamed of creating an automobile civilization with his Model T, and by the 1920s Americans were buying his car by the millions. The stimulus this insatiable demand gave to the economy can scarcely be exaggerated. Millions of cars required millions of pounds of steel alloys, glass, rubber, petroleum, and other material. Millions of jobs in coal and iron-ore mining, oil refining and rubber manufacturing, steelmaking and machine tooling, road construction, and service stations came to depend on automobile manufacturing.

Ford innovated with **mass-production** techniques that increased production speed and lowered unit costs. Mass production often meant replacing skilled workers with machines that were coordinated to permit high-speed, uninterrupted production at every stage of the manufacturing process. But such production techniques were profitable only if large quantities of output could be sold. Although a burgeoning domestic market offered a vast potential for sales, manufacturers often found distribution systems inadequate. This was the case with James Buchanan Duke, who almost single-handedly transformed the cigarette into one of the best-selling commodities in American history. In 1885, at a time when relatively few Americans smoked, Duke invested in several Bonsack cigarette machines, each of which manufactured 120,000 cigarettes per day. To create a market for the millions of cigarettes he was producing, Duke advertised his product aggressively throughout the country. He also established regional sales offices so that his sales representatives could keep in touch with local jobbers and retailers. As cigarette sales skyrocketed, more corporations sought to emulate Duke's techniques. Over the course of the next 20 years, those corporations that integrated mass production and mass distribution, as Duke did in the 1880s and 1890s, came to define American "big business."

19-1f *Revolution in Management*

The growth in the number and size of corporations revolutionized corporate management. The ranks of managers mushroomed. Increasingly, senior managers took over from owners the responsibility for long-term planning. Day-to-day operations fell to middle managers who oversaw particular departments (e.g., purchasing, research, production, labor) in corporate headquarters or who supervised regional sales offices or directed particular factories. Middle managers also managed the people—accountants, clerks, foremen, engineers, salesmen—in these departments, offices, or factories. The rapid expansion within corporate managerial ranks created a new middle class, whose members were intensely loyal to their employers but at odds both with blue-collar workers and with the older middle class of shopkeepers, small businessmen, and independent craftsmen.

As management techniques grew in importance, companies tried to make them more scientific. Firms introduced cost-accounting methods. Many corporations began requiring college or university training in science, engineering, or accounting for entry into middle management. Corporations that had built their success on a profitable invention or discovery created research departments and hired professional scientists—those with doctorates from American or European universities—to come up with new technological and scientific breakthroughs. Such departments were modeled on Thomas Edison's industrial research laboratory.

19-2 Corporations and American Culture

Q *How did the rise of corporations reshape the everyday experiences of Americans?*

New technological innovations reshaped almost all Americans' lives. Electricity, streetcars, and elevators were just a few of the industrial innovations that changed urban dwellers' everyday relationship to physical space. Even people's relationship to time changed. The world of mass-produced consumer goods provided a new standardization of experience and created a new national consumer culture.

19-2a *Standardized Time*

Before the post-Civil War boom in railroads, there was no such thing as "standard" time; instead, many localities and cities kept their own time, derived from the sun's meridian in each locality. If the clock read noon in Chicago, for instance, it read 11:50 in St. Louis, 11:38 in St. Paul, and 11:27 in Omaha, with many other local times in between. This situation played havoc with railroad timetables.

In a sign of corporations' power over American life, in 1883 a consortium of railroad companies agreed to standardize North American time with the creation of four different time zones—much as they exist today—in which all clocks would be set to exactly the same time. Some grumbling followed about the arrogance of railroad presidents changing "God's time." But "railroad time" was quickly adopted by people everywhere, although Congress did not officially sanction standard time zones until 1918.

19-2b *A National Consumer Culture*

Consumer goods also standardized American experience as manufacturers produced national brands such as Ivory soap, Quaker oats, and Jell-O. Advertising firms began working hand in hand with manufacturers to create national marketing campaigns. Expenditures on advertising increased enormously: from some $50 million in 1867 to $500 million by 1900.

Advertisements became part of a shared visual culture, as technological improvements in lithography and the half-tone process in the 1880s and 1890s allowed advertisers to create bright, colorful images that were distributed

From the General Negative Collection, North Carolina State Archives, Raleigh, NC.

19.4 **Cigarette-Making Machine** James Albert Bonsack's 1880 invention of a cigarette-making machine revolutionized the production of cigarettes. Skilled individual workers were able to produce around 200 cigarettes an hour. With the Bonsack machine, that rate soared to some 12,000 an hour.

nationally. Multicolor advertising trade cards (including baseball cards from cigarette companies) became a national fad. Technological breakthroughs in printing allowed new popular magazines and mass-circulation newspapers to reach hundreds of thousands of readers nationally, as well. The *Ladies' Home Journal*, founded in 1893, soon reached over 500,000 readers. Newspapers responded to the demands of a growing population with the first color comics, women's pages, Sunday sections, society pages, and sports pages.

Advertising revenues from department stores fueled the growth of newspapers in large cities around the country. These "palaces of consumption" dramatically changed the urban experience of buying consumer goods. In a major retailing innovation, stores such as Marshall Field & Co. in Chicago (1865) and R. H. Macy's in New York (1866) sold a wide variety of items—from perfume to shoes to hats to clothing to household goods—all under one roof in different departments, instead of in different stores. Customers strolled down carpeted aisles—arranged to mimic city streets—and gazed at a dazzling array of goods in glass cases. Ornate interiors with mirrors and lights added to a sensory experience of profusion, color, and excitement.

Outside of cities, men and women could participate in the new national culture of consumption through mail order. Mail-order catalogs were the brilliant idea of A. Montgomery Ward, who had worked at Marshall Field's firm in Chicago. Starting with a single price sheet of items in 1872, by 1884 Ward was producing a thick, 240-page catalogue that listed close to 1,000 items for sale—everything from women's underclothing to entire houses.

19-2c *Ideas of Wealth and Society*

A profusion of consumer goods reached a wide national audience in this period. But among the wealthy, some also practiced what the economist Thorstein Veblen described in *The Theory of the Leisure Class* (1899) as "conspicuous consumption." They sent agents to Europe to buy paintings and tapestries from impoverished aristocrats. In their mansions on Fifth Avenue and their summer homes at Newport, Rhode Island, they entertained lavishly. At one famous costume ball in New York in 1897, guests in satin gowns sewn with jewels impersonated aristocrats. Such aristocratic pretensions extended to marriage: Between 1874 and 1911, 72 American heiresses married British peers. The extravagant habits of a wealthy elite gave substance to Mark Twain's labeling of this era as the Gilded Age. The estimated number of *millionaires* (a word that came into use during this era) in 1860 was 300; by 1892, the number was 4,000. While this was not a large proportion of the population, it was nevertheless a highly visible group.

Many among the wealthy, and eventually among a broader middle class as well, justified their right to wealth with an emerging post-Civil War vocabulary of **Social Darwinism**. "The growth of a large business," wrote John D. Rockefeller, "is merely a survival of the fittest, the working out of a law of nature and a law of God." In assuming that market forces were in fact laws of nature, Rockefeller and other industrial titans such as Andrew Carnegie drew upon the influential work of the English author Herbert Spencer, who had coined the phrase "survival of the fittest" in applying the evolutionary theories of Charles Darwin to human society. According to the tenets of Social Darwinism, human history could be understood in terms of an ongoing struggle among races, with the strongest and fittest invariably triumphing. The wealth and power of the Anglo-Saxon race were ample testimony, in this view, to its superior fitness.

At first popular mostly among intellectuals (the social sciences took shape during these years), Social Darwinism was quickly adopted by a broader public, with "survival of the fittest" becoming a popular catchphrase. Social Darwinism provided a comfortable way of understanding the glaring social inequality of the era: Workers were doomed to be permanent wage laborers not because of some fault in the emerging corporate system, but because they were not "fit." The rich, meanwhile, were entitled to every dollar that came their way.

19-2d *Sharpened Class Distinctions*

The well-publicized activities of the wealthy sharpened a growing sense of class distinction in this era. Throughout the late 19th century, many Americans worried over the class distinctions they saw emerging around them as part of the corporate reordering of American life. Was this sharpened sense of class distinction acceptable in a republican society that promised equality for all? A source of uneasiness at first, class distinctions became a source of alarm among numerous observers in the 1880s and especially the 1890s, when widespread labor activism challenged the existing social order.

The rise of corporations produced a need for salaried managers, engineers, office workers, and retail clerks—"white-collar" workers (a reference to detachable, starched white collars for shirts). Agricultural labor dropped from 53 percent of the gainfully employed in 1870, to 35 percent in 1900, and to 21 percent in 1930; clerical work in the same period rose from less than 1 percent to over 8 percent. The profession of engineer, directly related to the expansion of manufacturing, leapt by an astonishing 586 percent between 1870 and 1900.

Many members of this new corporate middle class sought to distinguish themselves from the "lower classes." The post-Civil War suburbanization movement was one important spatial realization of this drive for distinction. As early as 1873, *Scribner's* magazine noted that "the middle class, who cannot live among the rich, and will not live among the poor ... go out of the city to find their houses." By the end of the 19th century, suburban communities of detached houses, surrounded by lawns, were markers of the middle-class status of businessmen and professionals who worked by day in cities and traveled back and forth by train or streetcar to their homes.

What They Said

Wealth and Poverty

These two selections offer sharply differing views of emerging class distinctions in the late 19th century. The industrialist Andrew Carnegie affirmed a "gospel of wealth" in this passage from an 1889 article. In contrast, Henry George puzzled over the apparent connection between industrial progress and deepening poverty in his best-selling 1879 *Progress and Poverty*.

Andrew Carnegie

The problem of our age is the proper administration of wealth, so that the ties of brotherhood may still bind together the rich and poor in harmonious relationship. The conditions of human life have not only been changed, but revolutionized, within the past few hundred years. . . . The contrast between the palace of the millionaire and the cottage of the laborer with us to-day measures the change which has come with civilization.

The change, however, is not to be deplored, but welcomed as highly beneficial. It is well, nay, essential for the progress of the race, that the houses of some should be homes for all that is highest and best in literature and the arts, and for all the refinements of civilization, rather than that none should be so. Much better this great irregularity than universal squalor. . . .

The price which society pays for the law of competition is also great; but the advantages of this law are also greater still, for it is to this law that we owe our wonderful material development, which brings improved conditions in its train. But, whether the law be benign or not, we must say of it, as we say of the change in the conditions of men to which we have referred: It is here, we cannot evade it; no substitutes for it have been found; and while the law may be sometimes hard for the individual, it is best for the race, because it insures the survival of the fittest in every department. We accept and welcome, therefore, as conditions to which we must accommodate ourselves, great inequality of environment, the concentration of business, industrial and commercial, in the hands of a few, and the law of competition between these, as being not only beneficial, but essential for the future progress of the race.

Henry George

And, unpleasant as it may be to admit it, it is at last becoming evident that the enormous increase in productive power which has marked the present century and is still going on with accelerating ratio, has no tendency to extirpate poverty or to lighten the burdens of those compelled to toil. It simply widens the gulf between Dives and Lazarus, and makes the struggle for existence more intense. The march of invention has clothed mankind with powers of which a century ago the boldest imagination could not have dreamed. But in factories where labor-saving machinery has reached its most wonderful development, little children are at work; wherever the new forces are anything like fully utilized, large classes are maintained by charity or live on the verge of recourse to it; amid the greatest accumulations of wealth, men die of starvation, and puny infants suckle dry breasts; while everywhere, the greed of gain, the worship of wealth, shows the force of the fear of want. The promised land flies before us like the mirage. . . .

This association of poverty with progress is the great enigma of our times. It is the central fact from which spring industrial, social, and political difficulties that perplex the world, and with which statesmanship and philanthropy and education grapple in vain. From it come the clouds that overhang the future of the most progressive and self-reliant nations. . . . So long as all the increased wealth which modern progress brings goes but to build up great fortunes, to increase luxury and make sharper the contrast between the House of Have and the House of Want, progress is not real and cannot be permanent.

Q *What value for society does Andrew Carnegie see in the accumulation of great wealth by a few individuals? How does he connect wealth to progress and "civilization"?*

Q *What does Henry George mean when he says that "the association of poverty with progress" is the "great enigma" of the age? What critique does he offer of the building up of fortunes by men such as Carnegie?*

Sources: (top) Andrew Carnegie, "Wealth," *North American Review* 148 (June 1889), pp. 653–654, (middle) Henry George, *The Complete Works of Henry George*, vol. 1, *Progress and Poverty*, Library ed. (Garden City, New York: Doubleday, Page, and Company, 1905), p. 12.

Theater, literature, and art were also arenas of class distinction. Before the Civil War, performances of Shakespeare had often been rowdy, participatory, cross-class events. By the end of the century, however, the middle class not only claimed Shakespeare as an icon of "high" culture, but also imposed new expectations of "genteel" silence during performances. In literary magazines, middle-class critics decried the vulgarity of "low" literature such as dime novels and westerns. *Century* and *Harper's New Monthly* published "tasteful" fiction, including literature of nostalgia for slavery with virulently

Interpreting the Visual Past Women and Bicycles

The new embrace of sports in the 1890s let to a manufacturing boom in sports equipment—including the bicycle. In 1885 there were only six cycle manufacturers in the United States, producing 11,000 bicycles. By 1895 there were 126 manufacturers producing nearly half a million bicycles each year. By 1896, production totals reached one million bicycles. A bicycling craze reached its apex that year.

What was the appeal of the bicycle? Much as today, the bicycle allowed both men and women freedom, adventure, and exercise. But arguably the bicycle had a transformative impact on women's lives. As *Munsey's Magazine* commented in 1896, "To men, the bicycle in the beginning was merely a new toy, another machine added to the long list of devices they knew in their work and play. To women, it was a steed upon which they rode into a new world." The bicycle craze encouraged a new style of dressing for women, less constrained and more sporty. It allowed women the possibility of roaming freely on their own, without supervision. And it gave many women a way of engaging in vigorous exercise for the first time. "Let me tell you what I think of bicycling," Susan B. Anthony commented. "I think it has done more to emancipate women than anything else in the world."

Q *Why did sports such as bicycling become so popular in the 1890s?*

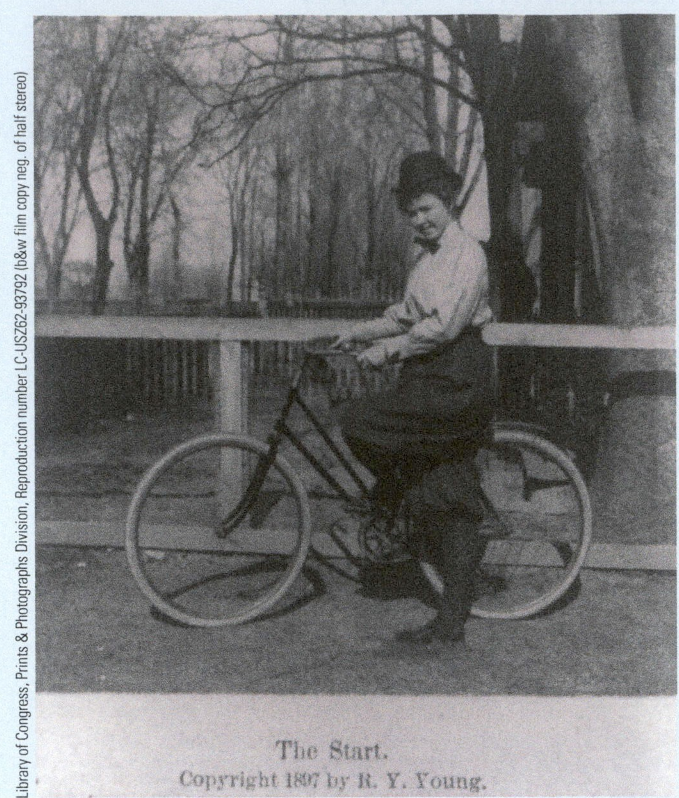
The Start.
Copyright 1897 by R. Y. Young.

19.5 **R.Y. Young, "The Start," 1897.**

racist portrayals of blacks. This white nostalgia for black subordination paralleled growing middle-class alarm over the "insubordination" of the working class in late-19th-century labor strife. A new art movement, American Impressionism, also expressed a middle-class desire for gentility. Influenced by French Impressionism, artists such as William Merrit Chase and Childe Hassam painted light-flecked landscapes or flower-filled urban parks, recording middle-class pleasures in cities strikingly devoid of workers.

Yet, increasingly over the late 19th century, mere gentility began to seem arid to some middle-class artists and writers. Painters such as Thomas Eakins and Thomas Anshutz pioneered a style that would develop into the "realism" of the early 20th century, with its grittier view of city life and less idealized vision of the human form. The dean of American letters, William Dean Howells, wrote novels exploring issues that had rarely been touched by American authors, including divorce, the moral bankruptcy of capitalism, and interracial marriage.

Alarmed by the widening gulf between the classes, Edward Bellamy, in his 1888 utopian novel, *Looking Backward*, imagined a world in the year 2000 in which "labor troubles" and social inequities had been eradicated through a form of socialism called Nationalism. Bellamy's powerful fictional indictment of Gilded Age society resonated with half a million readers, making his novel one of the most popular of the 19th century.

19-2e *Obsession with Physical and Racial Fitness*

The fractious events of the 1890s induced many middle-class and wealthy Americans to engage in what Theodore Roosevelt dubbed **"the strenuous life."** In an 1899 essay with that title, Roosevelt exhorted Americans to live vigorously, to test their physical strength and endurance in competitive athletics, and to experience nature through hiking, hunting, and mountain climbing. Other writers, too, argued that through sport and vigorous activity, men could find and express their virility.

The 1890s were a time of heightened enthusiasm for competitive sports, physical fitness, and outdoor recreation. Millions of Americans, both women and men, began riding bicycles and eating healthier foods. Young women began to engage in organized sports and other athletic activities. A passion for athletic competition also gripped American universities. The power and violence of football helped make it the sport of choice at the nation's elite campuses, and, for 20 years, Ivy League schools were the nation's football powerhouses.

In the country at large, the new enthusiasm for athletics and the outdoor life reflected a widespread dissatisfaction with the growing regimentation of industrial society. Among middle-class and wealthy Americans, the quest for physical superiority reflected a deeper and more ambiguous anxiety: their *racial* fitness. Most of them were native-born Americans whose families had lived in the United States for several generations and whose ancestors had come from the British Isles, the Netherlands, or some other region of northwestern Europe. Having embraced the principles of Social Darwinism, they liked to attribute their success and good fortune to their "racial superiority." They saw themselves as "natural" leaders, members of a noble Anglo-Saxon race endowed with uncommon intelligence, imagination, and discipline. But events of the 1890s challenged the legitimacy of the elite's wealth and authority, and the ensuing depression mocked their ability to exert economic leadership. The immigrant masses laboring in factories, despite their poverty and alleged racial inferiority, seemed to possess a vitality that the "superior" Anglo-Saxons lacked.

19-3 Workers' Resistance to Corporations

Q *How effective was workers' resistance to the new corporations? Why?*

A national culture of consumption had grown up in the last decades of the 19th century, but not everyone had equal access to it. Wages that did not keep pace with the booming economy meant less money to spend, not to mention a struggle to put food on the table.

Although the average per capita income of all Americans increased by 35 percent from 1878 to 1893, real wages advanced only 20 percent (see Figure 19.3). That advance masked sharp inequalities of wages by skill, region, race, and gender. Many unskilled and semiskilled workers made barely enough to support themselves, much less a family; many families, especially recent immigrants (who formed a large part of the blue-collar workforce), needed two or three wage earners to survive.

"Eight hours for work, eight hours for rest, eight hours for what we will" was a famous slogan of the labor movement in the post-Civil War era. In the demand for "eight hours for what we will," workers voiced their belief that they had a right to leisure time under their own control. As one worker told a Senate committee in 1883, "A workingman wants something besides food and clothes in this country... . He wants recreation. Why should not a workingman have it as well as other people?"

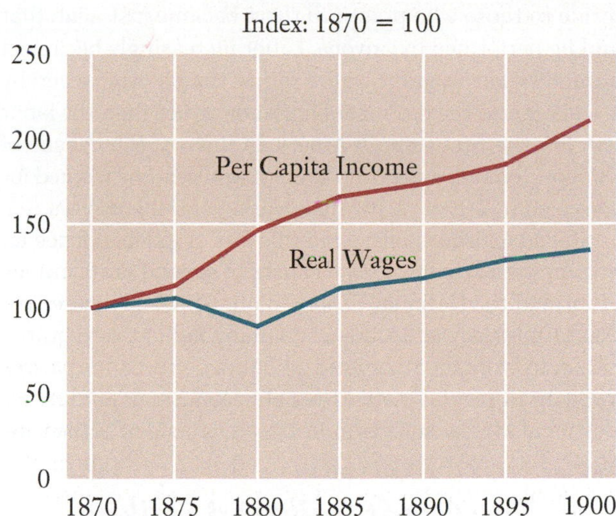

Figure 19.3 **Real Wages of Workers and Per Capita Income of All Americans, 1870–1900**

Why not indeed? While some alarmed middle-class observers believed that all workers were revolutionaries who wanted to overturn the American government, only a small percentage were political radicals, much less revolutionaries. The truth was more prosaic: Workers wanted fair wages and fair conditions in the workplace. They wanted equality in a system in which power had been systematically stripped from them, and liberty seemed to accrue more to corporations than to individuals. Broad-based workers' movements throughout the late 19th century attempted to rectify a situation in which equal opportunities no longer seemed to be available to all.

19-3a *Industrial Conditions*

One source of the rising tide of worker discontent was the dangerous conditions in the industrial workplace. The drive for even greater speed and productivity on railroads and in factories gave the United States the unhappy distinction of having the world's highest rate of industrial accidents. The railroads were particularly hazardous, with over 72,000 deaths of employees on the tracks between 1890 and 1917. What one historian has called "mechanized violence" characterized other industries as well: Coal mines threatened underground collapses, explosions, and the release of toxic gases; iron mills and steel mills required work with molten metals at open hearths; textile mills threatened mutilation and dismemberment. Yet there was little government regulation of industrial safety, and workmen's compensation did not appear until the 1930s. As a result, many families were impoverished by workplace accidents that killed or maimed their chief breadwinner.

Another source of discontent was the erosion of worker autonomy in factories, where new machinery took over tasks once performed by skilled workers and where managers made decisions about the procedures and pace of operations once made by workers. Many crafts that had once been a source of pride to those who practiced them became just a job that could be performed by anyone. Labor increasingly became a commodity bartered for wages rather than a craft whereby the worker sold the product of his labor rather than the labor itself. For the first time in American history, the census of 1870 reported that a majority of employed persons worked for wages paid by others rather than working for themselves.

Skilled artisans considered this loss of independence an alarming trend. In 1866, the leaders of several craft unions had formed the National Labor Union, which advocated for an eight-hour day at a time when many industries required workers to work for 10 or even 12 hours daily. Labor parties sprang up in several states; the Labor Reform candidate for governor of Massachusetts in 1870 won 13 percent of the vote.

19-3b *The Great Railroad Strike of 1877*

Yet the National Labor Union withered away in the depression of the 1870s, and industrial violence escalated. The worst labor violence in U.S. history up to that time, the Great Railroad Strike of 1877 underscored the deep discontent of workers nationwide. In July, the Baltimore and Ohio Railroad cut wages by 10 percent—its third recent wage reduction. When workers in Martinsburg, West Virginia, walked out in protest, workers up and down the B & O line joined them.

The strike touched a nerve nationally and spread rapidly; within a few days, what had begun as a local protest had traveled to Baltimore, Philadelphia, Pittsburgh, New York, Louisville, Chicago, St. Louis, Kansas City, and San Francisco. Women as well as men joined angry crowds in the streets; workers from a variety of industries walked out in sympathy. Strikers and militia in a number of cities fired on each other, and workers set fire to railroad cars and depots. Alarmed at the possibility of a "national insurrection," President Hayes called in the army. The strike finally ended in early August—"The strikers have been put down *by force*," Hayes noted in his diary.

But this spontaneous, unorganized labor upheaval did not produce solutions to workers' dilemmas. On the contrary, fears of a workers' "insurrection" led to a new cohesion in the middle class, which began to talk of a "war" between capital and labor. Not only did the middle class strongly support military intervention in the wake of 1877, but it also supported the construction of armories in the nation's largest cities.

19-3c *The Knights of Labor*

Many workers in the wake of 1877 looked to a new labor organization for inspiration. The **Knights of Labor** had been founded in 1869 in Philadelphia as a secret fraternal organization, one of many such artisan societies in eastern cities. Under the leadership of Terence Powderly, a machinist by trade, it became public in 1879 and then expanded rapidly in the wake of the Great Railroad Strike, finally achieving hundreds of thousands of members nationally in the 1880s.

The Knights of Labor offered workers an inspiring vision of an alternative to competitive corporate society. Rooted in the artisan republicanism of the antebellum era, with even its name suggesting a nostalgic look backward, the Knights opposed the wage labor system, declaring "an inevitable and irresistible conflict between the wage-system of labor and republican system of government." Instead it offered an inclusive vision of a "cooperative commonwealth" that would include both men and women and would not discriminate by race. In its platform it called for an eight-hour day, equal pay for women, public ownership of railroads, abolition of child labor, and a graduated income tax.

By the late 1870s, the Knights were a potent national federation of unions—or "assemblies," as they were officially known—and departed in several respects from the norm of labor organization at that time. Most of its assemblies were organized by industry rather than by craft, giving many unskilled and semiskilled workers union representation for the first time. It was also a more inclusive labor organization than most, although in local practice the Knights did not live up to its lofty ideals. Only some assemblies admitted women or blacks. Tendencies toward exclusivity of craft, gender, and race divided and weakened many assemblies.

A paradox of purpose also plagued the Knights. Most members wanted to improve their lot within the existing system through higher wages, shorter hours, better working conditions—the bread-and-butter goals of working people. This meant collective bargaining with employers; it also meant strikes. The assemblies won some strikes. Powderly and the Knights' national leadership discouraged strikes, however, partly out of practicality: A losing strike often destroyed an assembly, as employers replaced strikes with strikebreakers, or "scabs."

Another reason for Powderly's antistrike stance was philosophical. Strikes constituted a tacit recognition of the legitimacy of the wage system. In Powderly's view, wages siphoned off to capital a part of the wealth created by labor. The Knights, he said, intended "to secure to the workers the full enjoyment of the wealth they create." This was a goal grounded both in the past independence of skilled workers and in a radical vision of the future, in which workers' cooperatives would own the means of production. "There is no reason," said Powderly, "why labor cannot, through cooperation, own and operate mines, factories, and railroads."

The Knights did sponsor several modest workers' cooperatives. Their success was limited, though, partly from lack of capital and of management experience and partly because even the most skilled craftsmen found it difficult to compete with machines in a mass-production economy. Ironically, the Knights gained their greatest triumphs through strikes. In 1884 and 1885, successful strikes against the Union Pacific and Missouri Pacific railroads won prestige and a rush of new members, which by 1886 totaled 700,000. Expectations ran high, but defeat in a second strike against the Missouri Pacific in spring 1886 was a serious blow. Then came the **Haymarket** bombing in Chicago.

History Through Film *The Molly Maguires* (1970)

Directed by Martin Ritt.
Starring Richard Harris (James McParlan), Sean Connery (Jack Kehoe), Samantha Eggar (Mary Raines).

The gritty realism of *The Molly Maguires* offers a compelling portrait of labor conditions in 19th-century coal mines. Filmed on location in the anthracite region of eastern Pennsylvania, the film takes the viewer deep into the earth where Irish American miners labored long hours for a pittance at the dangerous, back-breaking, health-destroying job of bringing out the coal that heated American homes and fueled American industry.

These mining communities constituted a microcosm of ethnic and class tensions in American society. Most of the mine owners were Scots-Irish Presbyterians; many foremen, skilled workers, and police were English or Welsh Protestants; most of the unskilled workers were Irish Catholics. This was a volatile mixture, as vividly depicted in the movie. The skilled miners had formed the Workingmen's Benevolent Association, which had won modest gains for its members by 1873. Many Irish belonged to the Ancient Order of Hibernians, which aided sick miners and supported the widows and orphans of those who died—and there were many such. The inner circle of this order called itself the Molly Maguires, after an anti-landlord organization in Ireland that resisted the eviction of tenants. In Pennsylvania, the Mollies retaliated against exploitative owners, unpopular foremen, and the police with acts of sabotage, violence, intimidation, and murder.

The economic depression following the Panic of 1873 exacerbated tensions and violence. The owners hired the Pinkerton detective agency to infiltrate and gather criminal evidence against the Mollies. Detective James McParlan went to work in the mines, gained the confidence of his fellow Irish Americans, and was eventually admitted to the Molly Maguires. For more than two years, he lived a dangerous double existence (foreshortened in the movie) that would have meant instant death if the Mollies had discovered his mole role. In a series of widely publicized trials from 1875 to 1877 in which McParlan was the main witness, dozens of Molly Maguires were convicted and 20 were hanged. Richard Harris and Sean Connery are superb as McParlan and Jack Kehoe, the Mollies' leader. The real Jamie McParlan courted the sister-in-law of one of the Mollies; the film expands this into a poignant romance between McParlan and a retired miner's beautiful daughter. The love interest fits with the film's effective presentation of McParlan's conflicted conscience and the moral ambiguity of his role as the agent of justice (as defined by the ruling class), which requires him to betray the men with whom he had lived, sung, plotted, swapped stories, and carried out raids. What were McParlan's real motives? The film does not successfully answer that question, but neither does history. Most viewers, however, will take from this movie a feeling of empathy with the Mollies, whose protest against terrible conditions drove them to desperate acts of violence. ■

Bettmann/Corbis

19-6 Sean Connery (Jack Kehoe, right) and Art Lund (a fellow Molly Maguire) prepare to dynamite a coal train in *The Molly Maguires*.

19-3d Haymarket

Chicago was a center of labor activism and radicalism. In 1878, the newly formed Socialist Labor Party won 14 percent of the vote in the city, electing five aldermen and four members of the Illinois legislature. With recovery from the depression after 1878, the Socialist Labor Party fell onto lean times. Four-fifths of its members were foreign-born, mostly Germans. Internal squabbles generated several offshoots of the party in the 1880s. One of these embraced anarchism and called for the violent destruction of the capitalist system so that a new socialist order could be built on its ashes. Anarchists infiltrated some trade unions in Chicago and leaped aboard the bandwagon of a national movement centered in that city for a general strike on May 1, 1886, to achieve the eight-hour workday. Chicago police were notoriously hostile to labor organizers and strikers, so the scene was set for a violent confrontation.

The May 1 showdown coincided with a strike at the McCormick farm machinery plant in Chicago. A fight outside the gates on May 3 brought a police attack on the strikers in which four people were killed. Anarchists then organized a protest meeting at Haymarket Square on May 4. Toward the end of the meeting, when the rain-soaked crowd was already dispersing, the police suddenly arrived in force. When someone threw a bomb into their midst, the police opened fire. When the wild melee was over, 50 people lay wounded and 10 dead, 6 of them policemen.

Haymarket set off a wave of hysteria against labor radicals. Police in Chicago rounded up hundreds of labor leaders. Eight anarchists (seven of them German-born) went on trial for conspiracy to commit murder, although no evidence turned up to prove that any of them had thrown the bomb. All eight were convicted; seven were sentenced to hang. One of the men committed suicide; the governor commuted the sentences of two others to life imprisonment; the remaining four were hanged on November 11, 1887. The case became a cause célèbre that bitterly divided the country. Many workers, civil libertarians, and middle-class citizens who were troubled by the events branded the verdicts judicial murder, but most Americans applauded the summary repression of radicalism they regarded as un-American.

The Knights of Labor were caught in this antilabor backlash. Although the Knights had nothing to do with the Haymarket affair and Powderly had repeatedly denounced anarchism, his opposition to the wage system sounded to many Americans suspiciously like socialism, perhaps even anarchism. Membership in the Knights plummeted from 700,000 in spring 1886 to fewer than 100,000 by 1890.

Bettmann/Corbis

19.7 **Urban Fortresses** In the 1880s and 1890s, numerous armories were built in cities across the country to protect against a perceived threat from the "dangerous classes"—workers and the poor. This immense, castlelike 1894 armory in Brooklyn, New York, was meant to inspire awe.

19-3e *The American Federation of Labor (AFL)*

As the Knights of Labor waned, a new national labor organization waxed. Founded in 1886, the American Federation of Labor (AFL) was a loosely affiliated association of unions organized by trade or craft: cigar makers, machinists, carpenters, typographers, plumbers, painters, and so on. Most AFL members were skilled workers. The leader of the AFL, **Samuel F. Gompers**, was a onetime Marxist and cigar maker who was reelected to the AFL presidency every year from 1896 until his death in 1924.

Many workers understood that the only hope for economic improvement lay in organizing unions powerful enough to wrest wage concessions from reluctant employers. But this was no easy task. Federal and state governments had shown themselves ready to use military force to break strikes. The courts, following the lead of the U.S. Supreme Court, repeatedly found unions in violation of the Sherman Antitrust Act, even though that act had been intended to control corporations, not unions. Judges in most states usually granted employer requests for injunctions—court orders that barred striking workers from picketing their place of employment (and thus from obstructing employer efforts to hire replacement workers). Before 1916, no federal laws protected workers' right to organize or required employers to bargain with the unions to which their workers belonged.

This hostile legal environment retarded the growth of unions from the 1890s through the 1920s. It also made the AFL, the major labor organization of those years, more timid and conservative than it had been before the depression of the 1890s. Few AFL members were women and blacks. The AFL accepted capitalism and the wage system. Instead of agitating for governmental regulation of the economy and the workplace, it concentrated on the bread-and-butter issues of better conditions, higher wages, shorter hours, and occupational safety within the system—"pure and simple unionism," as Gompers called it.

The AFL had concluded that labor's powerful opponents in the legislatures and the courts would find ways to undermine whatever governmental gains organized labor managed to achieve. That conclusion was reinforced by a 1905 ruling, *Lochner v. New York,* in which the U.S. Supreme Court declared unconstitutional a seemingly innocent New York state law that limited bakery employees to a 10-hour day.

Yet, in its early years the AFL showed considerable vitality under the leadership of Gompers, with its membership quadrupling from less than a half million in 1897 to more than 2 million in 1904. Craft unions negotiated contracts, or trade agreements, with employers that stipulated the wages workers were to be paid, the hours they were to work, and the rules under which new workers would be accepted into the trade.

19.8 **Pennsylvania Militia at Carnegie's Homestead Steel Mill, 1892** After the shootout between striking workers and Pinkerton guards, the Pennsylvania militia reopened the mills and protected strikebreakers from striking workers. This photograph shows the militia using steel beams manufactured by the mill as a makeshift barricade.

These agreements were accorded the same legal protection that American law bestowed on other commercial contracts.

Still, the AFL had limited success. Its 2 million members represented only a small portion of the industrial workforce. Its concentration among craft workers, moreover, distanced it from most workers, who were not skilled. Unskilled and semiskilled workers could only be organized into an industrial union that offered membership to all workers in a particular industry. Gompers understood the importance of such unions and allowed several of them, including the United Mine Workers (UMW) and the International Ladies Garment Workers Union (ILGWU), to participate in the AFL. But AFL ranks remained dominated by skilled workers who looked down upon the unskilled, especially immigrants. AFL members demonstrated even worse prejudice toward black workers, with more than 10 AFL unions excluding African Americans from membership in the early 20th century.

19-3f *The Homestead Strike*

During the 1890s, strikes occurred with a frequency and a fierceness that made 1877 and 1886 look like mere preludes to the main event. The most dramatic confrontation took place in 1892 at the **Homestead** plant (near Pittsburgh) of the Carnegie Steel Company. Carnegie and his plant manager, Henry Clay Frick, were determined to break the power of the country's strongest union, the Amalgamated Association of Iron, Steel, and Tin Workers. Frick used a dispute over wages and work rules as an opportunity to close the plant (a "lockout"), preparatory to reopening it with nonunion workers. When the union called a strike and refused to leave the plant, Frick called in 300 Pinkerton guards to oust them. (The Pinkerton detective agency had evolved since the Civil War era into a private security force that specialized in anti-union activities.) A full-scale gun battle between strikers and Pinkertons erupted on July 6, leaving nine strikers and seven Pinkertons dead and scores wounded. Frick persuaded the governor to send in 8,000 militia to protect the strikebreakers, and the plant reopened. Public sympathy, much of it prounion at first, shifted when an anarchist tried to murder Frick on July 23. The failed Homestead Strike crippled the Amalgamated Association; another strike against U.S. Steel (successor of Carnegie Steel) in 1901 destroyed it.

19-3g *The Depression of 1893–1897*

By the 1890s, the use of state militias to protect strikebreakers had become common. Events after 1893 brought an escalation of conflict. The most serious economic crisis since the 1873–1878 depression was triggered by the Panic of 1893, a collapse of the stock market that plunged the economy into a severe four-year depression. The bankruptcy of the Reading Railroad and the National Cordage Company in early 1893 set off a process that by the end of the year had caused 491 banks and 15,000 other businesses to fail. By mid-1894, the unemployment rate had risen to more than 15 percent.

An Ohio reformer named Jacob Coxey conceived the idea of sending Congress a "living petition" of unemployed workers to press for appropriations to put them to work on road building and other public works. "Coxey's army," as the press dubbed it, inspired other groups to hit the road and ride the rails to Washington during 1894. This descent of the unemployed on the capital provoked arrests by federal marshals and troops, and ended in anticlimax when Coxey and others were arrested for trespassing on the Capitol grounds. Coxey's idea for using public works to relieve unemployment turned out to be 40 years ahead of its time.

19-3h *The Pullman Strike*

The explosive tensions between capital and labor fueled the **Pullman Strike** of 1894. George M. Pullman had made a fortune in the manufacture of sleeping cars and other rolling stock for railroads. Workers in his large factory complex lived in the company town of Pullman just south of Chicago, with paved streets, clean parks, and decent houses rented from the

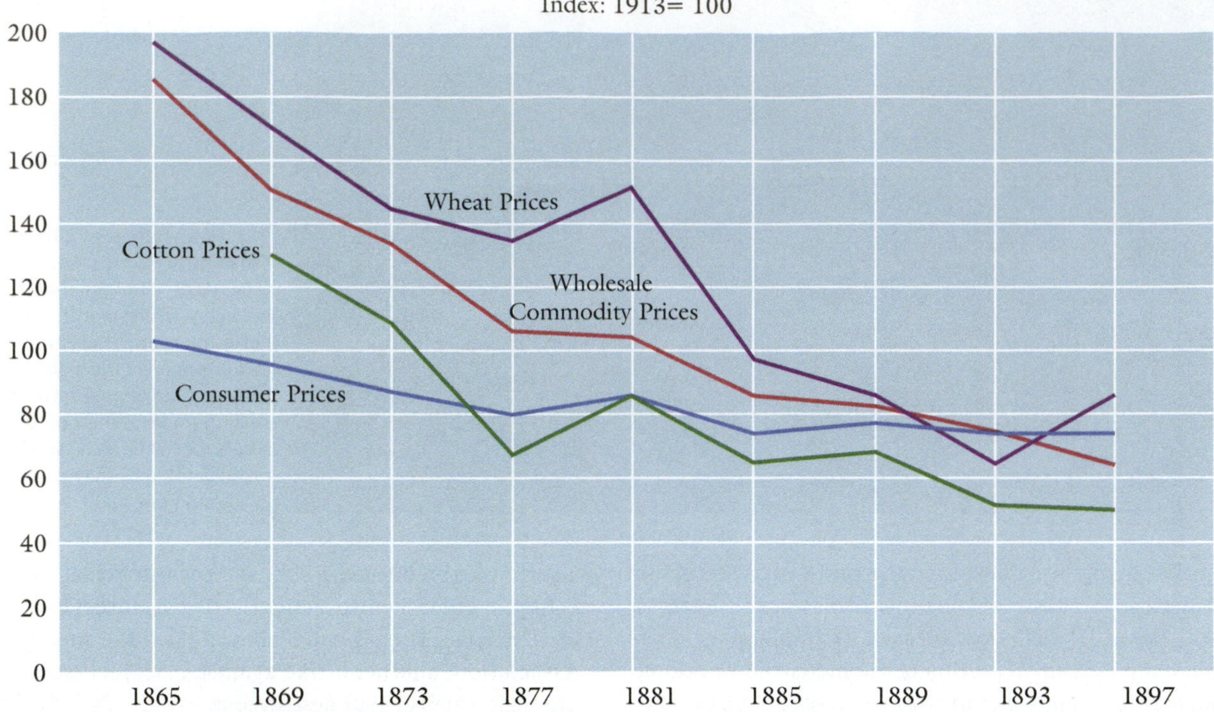

Figure 19.4 **Wholesale and Consumer Price Indexes, 1865–1897**

company. But Pullman controlled many aspects of their lives, including banning liquor from the town and punishing workers whose behavior did not suit his ideas of decorum. When the Panic of 1893 caused a sharp drop in orders for Pullman cars, the company laid off one-third of its workforce and cut wages for the rest by 30 percent but did not reduce company house rents or company store prices. Pullman refused to negotiate with a workers' committee, which called a strike and appealed to the American Railway Union (ARU) for help.

The ARU had been founded the year before by Eugene V. Debs. A native of Indiana, Debs had been elected secretary of the Brotherhood of Locomotive Firemen in 1875 at the age of 20. By 1893, he had become convinced that the conservative stance of the various craft unions in railroading (firemen, engineers, brakemen, and so forth) was divisive and contrary to the best interests of labor. He formed the ARU to include all railroad workers in one union. With 150,000 members, the union won a strike against the Great Northern Railroad in spring 1894. When George Pullman refused the ARU's offer to arbitrate the strike of Pullman workers, Debs launched a boycott by which ARU members would refuse to run any trains that included Pullman cars. When the railroads attempted to fire the ARU sympathizers, whole train crews went on strike and quickly paralyzed rail traffic.

Over the protests of Illinois governor John P. Altgeld, who sympathized with the strikers, President Grover Cleveland sent in federal troops. That action inflamed violence instead of containing it. The U.S. attorney general (a former railroad lawyer) obtained a federal injunction against Debs under the Sherman Antitrust Act on grounds that the boycott and the strike were a conspiracy in restraint of trade. This creative use of the Sherman Act was upheld by the Supreme Court in 1895 and became a powerful weapon against labor unions in the hands of conservative judges.

For a week in July 1894, the Chicago railroad yards resembled a war zone. Millions of dollars of equipment went up in smoke. Thirty-four people, mostly workers, were killed. Finally, 14,000 state militia and federal troops restored order and broke the strike. Debs went to jail (for violation of the federal injunction) for six months. He emerged from prison a socialist.

To many Americans, 1894 was the worst year of crisis since the Civil War. The Pullman Strike was only the most dramatic event of a year in which 750,000 workers went on strike and another 3 million were unemployed. But it was a surge of discontent from farmers that wrenched American politics off its foundations in the 1890s.

19-4 Farmers' Movements

Q *What provoked the farmer protest movements in the last third of the 19th century?*

Between 1870 and 1890, America's soaring grain production increased three times as fast as the American population. Only rising exports could sustain such expansion in farm production. But by the 1880s, the improved efficiency of large farms in eastern Europe brought intensifying competition and consequent price declines, especially for wheat, just as competition from Egypt and India had eroded prices for American cotton. Prices on the world market for these two staples of American agriculture—wheat and cotton—fell about 60 percent from 1870 to 1895, while the wholesale price index for all commodities (including other farm products) declined by 45 percent during the same period (see Figure 19.4). Not surprisingly, distress was greatest and protest loudest in the wheat-producing West and the cotton-producing South.

Victims of a world market largely beyond their control, farmers lashed out at targets nearer home: railroads, banks, commission merchants, and the monetary system. In truth, these institutions did victimize farmers, although not always intentionally.

19-4a *Resistance to Railroads*

The power wielded by the railroad companies inevitably aroused hostility. Companies often charged less for long hauls than for short hauls in areas with little or no competition. The rapid proliferation of tracks produced overcapacity in some areas, which led to rate-cutting wars that benefited some shippers at the expense of others—usually large shippers at the expense of small ones. To avoid "ruinous competition" (as the railroads viewed it), companies formed "pools" by which they divided traffic and fixed their rates. Some of these practices made sound economic sense, but others appeared discriminatory and exploitative. Railroads gave credence to farmers' charges of monopoly exploitation by keeping rates higher in areas with no competition (most farmers lived in areas served by only one line) than in regions with competition. Grain elevators, many of which were owned by railroad companies, came under attack for cheating farmers by rigging the classification of their grain.

Farmers responded by organizing cooperatives to sell crops and buy supplies. The umbrella organization for many of these cooperatives was the Patrons of Husbandry, known as the Grange, founded in 1867. But because farmers could not build their own railroads, they organized "antimonopoly" parties and elected state legislators who enacted "Granger laws" in several states. These laws established railroad commissions that fixed maximum freight rates and warehouse charges. Railroads challenged the laws in court. Eight challenges made their way to the U.S. Supreme Court, which in *Munn v. Illinois* (1877) ruled that states could regulate businesses clothed with a "public interest"—railroads and other common carriers, millers, innkeepers, and the like. It was a landmark decision.

The welter of different and sometimes conflicting state laws, plus rulings by the U.S. Supreme Court in the 1880s that states could not regulate interstate railroad traffic, brought a drive for federal regulation. After years of discussion, Congress passed the Interstate Commerce Act in 1887. This law, like most such laws, reflected compromise between the varying viewpoints of shippers, railroads, and other pressure groups. It outlawed pools, discriminatory rates, long-haul versus short-haul differentials, and rebates to favored shippers. It required that freight and passenger rates must be "reasonable and just." What that meant was not entirely clear, but the law created the Interstate Commerce Commission (ICC) to define the requirement on a case-by-case basis. Because the ICC had minimal enforcement powers, however, federal courts frequently refused to issue the orders the ICC requested. Staffed by men who were knowledgeable about railroading, the ICC often sympathized with the viewpoint of the industry it was supposed to regulate. Nevertheless, its powers of publicity had some effect on railroad practices, and freight rates continued to decline during this period as railroad operating efficiency improved.

The Kansas State Historical Society/Topeka/Kansas

19.9 **Returning to Illinois, 1894** This photograph shows one of the thousands of farm families who had moved into Kansas, Nebraska, and other plains states in the wet years of the 1870s and 1880s, only to give up during the dry years of the 1890s. Their plight added fuel to the fire of rural unrest and protest during those years.

19-4b The Greenback and Silver Movements

The long period of price deflation from 1865 to 1897, unique in American history, made credit even more costly for farmers. When the price of wheat or cotton declined, farmers earned even less money with which to pay back loans from country store merchants. Thus, it was not surprising that angry farmers who denounced banks or country store merchants for gouging them also attacked a monetary system that brought deflation.

The federal government's monetary policies worsened deflation problems. The 1862 emergency wartime issuance of treasury "greenback" notes (see Chapter 15) had created a dual currency—gold and greenbacks—with the greenback dollar's value relative to gold rising and falling according to Union military fortunes. After the war, the U.S. Treasury moved to bring the greenback dollar to par with gold by reducing the number of greenbacks in circulation. This limitation of the money supply produced deflationary pressures, with the South and West suffering from downward pressures on prices they received for their crops. Western farmers were particularly vociferous in their protests against this situation, which introduced a new sectional conflict into politics—not North against South, but East against West.

Many farmers in 1876 and 1880 supported the Greenback Party, whose platform called for the issuance of more U.S. Treasury notes (greenbacks). Even more popular was the movement for **"free silver."** Until 1873, government mints had coined both silver and gold dollars at a ratio of 16 to 1—that is, 16 ounces of silver were equal in value to 1 ounce of gold. However, when new discoveries of gold in the West after 1848 placed more gold in circulation relative to silver, that ratio undervalued silver, so that little was being sold for coinage.

Silver miners joined with farmers to demand a return to silver dollars. In 1878, Congress responded by passing, over President Hayes's veto, the Bland–Allison Act requiring the Treasury to purchase and coin no less than $2 million and no more than $4 million of silver monthly. Once again, silver dollars flowed from the mint. But with increased production of new silver mines, the market price of silver actually dropped to a ratio of 20 to 1.

Pressure for "free silver"—that is, for government purchase of all silver offered for sale at a price of 16 to 1 and its coinage into silver dollars—continued during the 1880s. The admission of five new western states in 1889 and 1890 contributed to the passage of the Sherman Silver Purchase Act in 1890. That act increased the amount of silver coinage, but not at the 16-to-1 ratio. Even so, it went too far to suit "gold bugs," who wanted to keep the United States on the international gold standard.

President Cleveland blamed the Panic of 1893 on the Sherman Silver Purchase Act, which caused a run on the Treasury's gold reserves triggered by uncertainty over the future of the gold standard. Cleveland called a special session of Congress in 1893 and persuaded it to repeal the Sherman Silver Purchase Act, setting the stage for the most bitter political contest in a generation.

19-4c Grangers and the Farmers' Alliance

Agrarian reformers supported the free silver movement, but many had additional grievances concerning problems of credit, railroad rates, and the exploitation of workers and farmers by the "money power." Both the Grange and the Farmers' Alliance, a new farmers' organization that expanded rapidly in the 1880s, addressed these political concerns. Both also addressed farm families' social and cultural needs, providing them with a sense of community that helped reduce rural isolation. The Grange sponsored picnics and cultural events, actively encouraging the participation of women. Local chapters were required to have female members, and women took up positions of leadership at the local level and also attended national meetings. The Grangers were not anticonsumption, but they desired to avoid middlemen; this made them a good audience for the new mail-order catalogs. Indeed, the innovative retailer Montgomery Ward first gained a foothold in the mail-order business by styling himself as the official supply house for the Grange.

Like the Grange, the Farmers' Alliance also provided a sense of community for farmers. Starting in Texas as the Southern Farmers' Alliance, it expanded into other southern states and the North. By 1890, the movement had evolved into the National Farmers' Alliance and Industrial Union, which was affiliated with the Knights of Labor. It was also affiliated with a separate Colored Farmers' Alliance, formed by African Americans who recognized the utility of the Farmers' Alliance but were not welcome in the larger whites-only organization. Reaching out to 2 million farm families, the Farmers' Alliance set up marketing cooperatives to eliminate the middlemen who profited as "parasites" on the backs of farmers. Like the Grange, the Alliance served the social needs of farm families as well as their economic needs, organizing picnics and educational institutes in addition to camp meetings. Appealing to women as well as men, the Alliance helped farmers to overcome their isolation, especially in the sparsely settled regions of the West. The Alliance also gave farmers a sense of pride and solidarity to counter the image of "hick" and "hayseed" being purveyed by an increasingly urban American culture.

The Farmers' Alliance developed a comprehensive political agenda. At a national convention in Ocala, Florida, in December 1890, it set forth these objectives: (1) a graduated income tax; (2) direct election of U.S. senators (instead of election by state legislatures); (3) free and unlimited coinage of silver at a ratio of 16 to 1; (4) effective government control and, if necessary, ownership of railroad, telegraph, and telephone companies; and the establishment of "subtreasuries" (federal warehouses) for the storage of crops, with government loans at 2 percent interest on those crops. The most important of these goals, especially for southern farmers, was the subtreasuries. Government storage would allow farmers to hold their crops until market prices were more favorable. Low-interest government loans on the value of these crops would enable farmers to pay their annual debts and thus escape the ruinous interest rates of the crop lien system in the South and bank mortgages in the West.

These were radical demands for the time. Nevertheless, most of them eventually became law: the income tax and the direct election of senators by constitutional amendments in 1913; government control of transportation and communications by various laws in the 20th century; and the subtreasuries in the form of the Commodity Credit Corporation in the 1930s.

Anticipating that the Republicans and the Democrats would resist these demands, many Alliancemen were eager to form a third party. In Kansas they had already done so, launching the People's Party, whose members were known as Populists, in summer 1890. White southerners, mostly Democrats, opposed the idea of a third party for fear that it might open the way for the return of the Republican Party, and African Americans, to power.

In 1890, farmers helped elect numerous state legislators and congressmen who pledged to support their cause, but the legislative results were thin. By 1892, many Alliance members were ready to take the third-party plunge. The two-party system seemed fossilized and unable to respond to the explosive problems of the 1890s.

19-5 The Rise and Fall of the People's Party

Q *Why did many Americans find Populism appealing in the 1890s?*

Enthusiasm for a third party was particularly strong in the plains and mountain states, five of which had been admitted since the last presidential election: North and South Dakota, Montana, Wyoming, and Idaho. The most prominent leader of the Farmers' Alliance was Leonidas L. Polk of North Carolina. A Confederate veteran, Polk commanded support in the West as well as in the South. He undoubtedly would have been nominated for president by the newly organized People's Party had not death cut short his career at the age of 55 in June 1892.

The first nominating convention of the People's Party met at Omaha a month later. The preamble of their platform expressed the grim mood of delegates. "We meet in the midst of a nation brought to the verge of moral, political, and material ruin," it declared. "The fruits of the toil of millions are boldly stolen to build up colossal fortunes for a few... . From the same prolific womb of governmental injustice we breed the two great classes—tramps and millionaires." The platform called for unlimited coinage of silver at 16 to 1; creation of the subtreasury program for crop storage and farm loans; government ownership of railroad, telegraph, and telephone companies; a graduated income tax; direct election of senators; and laws to protect labor unions against prosecution for strikes and boycotts. To ease the lingering tension between southern and western farmers, the party nominated Union veteran James B. Weaver of Iowa for president and Confederate veteran James G. Field of Virginia for vice president.

Despite winning 9 percent of the popular vote and 22 electoral votes, Populist leaders were shaken by the outcome. In the South, most of the black farmers who were allowed to vote stayed with the Republicans. Democratic bosses in several southern states dusted off the racial demagoguery and intimidation machinery of Reconstruction days to keep white farmers in line for the party of white supremacy. Only in Alabama and Texas, among southern states, did the Populists get more than 20 percent of the vote. They did even worse in the older agricultural states of the Midwest, where their share of the vote ranged from 11 percent in Minnesota down to 2 percent in Ohio. Only in distressed wheat states such as Kansas, Nebraska, and the Dakotas and in the silver states of the West did the Populists do well, carrying Kansas, Colorado, Idaho, and Nevada.

The party remained alive, however, and the anguish caused by the Panic of 1893 seemed to boost its prospects. In several western states, Populists or a Populist–Democratic coalition controlled state governments for a time, and a Populist–Republican coalition won the state elections of 1894 in North Carolina. Women as well as men campaigned for the Populists: Mary Lease, one of the few women practicing law in Kansas, became famous for her impassioned speeches against corporate power.

In 1893, President Cleveland's success in getting the Sherman Silver Purchase Act repealed drove a wedge into the Democratic Party. Southern and western Democrats turned against Cleveland. In what was surely the most abusive attack on a president ever delivered by a member of his own party, Senator Benjamin Tillman of South Carolina told his constituents in 1894: "When Judas betrayed Christ, his heart was not blacker than this scoundrel, Cleveland, in deceiving the Democracy. He is an old bag of beef and I am going to Washington with a pitchfork and prod him in his fat ribs."

19-5a *The Silver Issue*

Clearly the silver issue stirred deep emotions. For many people silver meant far more than a mere change in monetary policy: It also represented a widespread yearning for a more equitable society in which corporations and banks held less power. Thus, when Democratic dissidents stood poised to take over the party in 1896, they adopted free silver as the centerpiece of their program. This stand raised possibilities for a fusion with the Populists, who hoped the Democrats would adopt other features of their platform as well. Meanwhile, out of the West came a new and charismatic figure, a silver-tongued orator named **William Jennings Bryan**, whose shadow would loom large across the political landscape for the next generation. A one-term congressman from Nebraska, Bryan had taken up the cause of free silver. He came to the Democratic convention in 1896 as a young delegate—only 36 years old. Given the opportunity to make the closing speech in the debate on the silver plank in the party's platform, Bryan brought the house to its feet in a frenzy of cheering with his peroration: "You shall not press down upon the brow of labor this crown of thorns, you shall not crucify mankind upon a cross of gold."

Everett Collection Inc/Alamy Stock Photo

19.10 **Mary Lease, Lecturer for the Populists** Kansas lawyer Mary Lease was a popular and impassioned speaker for the Populist Party at a time when women's public speaking was still unusual in politics due to deep-seated prejudices against women in public life.

This speech catapulted Bryan into the presidential nomination. He ran on a platform that not only endorsed free silver but also embraced the idea of an income tax, condemned trusts, and opposed the use of injunctions against labor. Bryan's nomination created turmoil in the People's Party. Although some Populists wanted to continue as a third party, most of them saw fusion with silver Democrats as the road to victory. At the Populist convention, the fusionists got their way and endorsed Bryan's nomination. In effect, the Democratic whale swallowed the Populist fish in 1896.

19-5b *The Election of 1896*

The Republicans nominated William McKinley, who would have preferred to campaign on his specialty, the tariff. Bryan made that impossible. Crisscrossing the country in an unprecedented whistle-stop campaign covering 18,000 miles, Bryan gave as many as 30 speeches a day, focusing almost exclusively on the free silver issue. Republicans responded by denouncing the Democrats as irresponsible inflationists. Free silver, they said, would mean a 57-cent dollar and would demolish the workingman's gains in real wages achieved over the preceding 30 years.

Under the skillful leadership of Ohio businessman Mark Hanna, chairman of the Republican National Committee, McKinley waged a "front-porch campaign" in which various delegations visited his home in Canton, Ohio, to hear carefully crafted speeches that were widely publicized in the mostly Republican press. Hanna sent out an army of speakers and printed pamphlets in more than a dozen languages to reach immigrant voters. His propaganda portrayed Bryan as a wild man from the prairie whose monetary schemes would further wreck an economy that had been plunged into depression during a Democratic administration. McKinley's election, by contrast, would maintain the gold standard, revive business confidence, and end the depression.

The 1896 election was the most impassioned and exciting in a generation. Many Americans believed that the fate of the nation hinged on the outcome. The number of voters jumped by 15 percent over the 1892 election. The sectional pattern of South and West versus Northeast and North Central was almost as pronounced as the North–South split of 1860 (see Map 19.2). Republicans won a substantial share of the urban, immigrant, and labor vote by arousing fear about the Democratic 57-cent dollar and by inspiring hope with the slogan of McKinley as "the advance agent of prosperity." McKinley rode to a convincing victory by carrying every state in the northeast quadrant of the country. Bryan carried most of the rest. Republicans won decisive control of Congress as well as the presidency. They would maintain control for the next 14 years. The election of 1896 marked a crucial turning point in American political history away from the stalemate of the preceding two decades.

Whether by luck or by design, McKinley did prove to be the advance agent of prosperity. The economy pulled out of the depression during his first year in office and entered into a long period of growth—not because of anything the new administration did (except perhaps to encourage a revival of confidence) but because of the mysterious workings of the business cycle. With the discovery of rich new goldfields in the Yukon, in Alaska, and in South Africa, the silver issue lost potency, and a cascade of gold poured into the world economy. The long deflationary trend since 1865 reversed itself in 1897. Farmers entered a new—and unfamiliar—era of prosperity. Bryan ran against McKinley again in 1900 but lost even more emphatically. The nation seemed embarked on a placid sea of plenty. But below the surface, the currents of protest and reform that had boiled up in the 1890s still ran strong.

19-6 "Robber Barons" No More

How and why did American elites seek to alter their "robber baron" image in the late 19th and early 20th centuries?

The depression of the 1890s—along with the Populist movement and labor protests such as the Homestead and Pullman strikes—shook the confidence of members of the industrial elite. Industrialists were terrified when in 1892

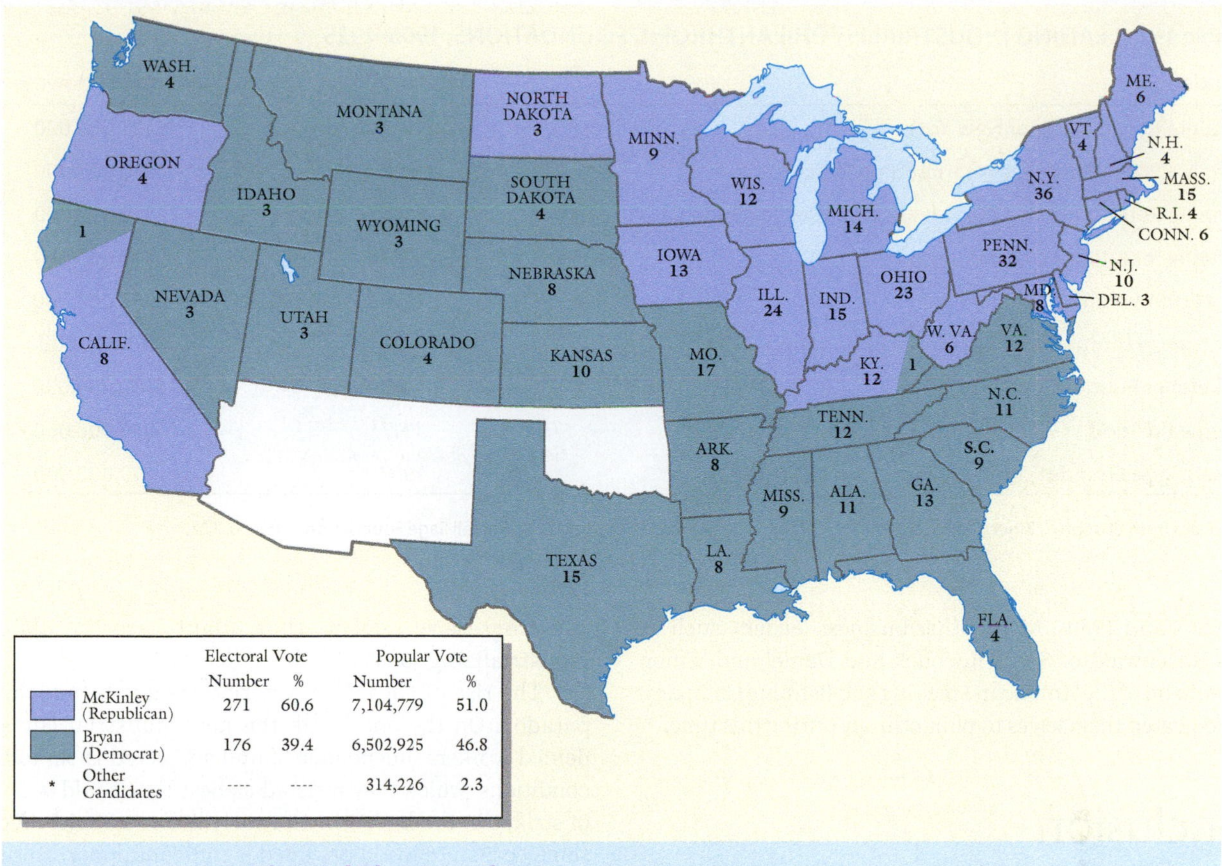

	Electoral Vote		Popular Vote	
	Number	%	Number	%
McKinley (Republican)	271	60.6	7,104,779	51.0
Bryan (Democrat)	176	39.4	6,502,925	46.8
* Other Candidates	----	----	314,226	2.3

▲ **MAP 19.2 Presidential Election of 1896** Once again, note the continuity of voting patterns over the two generations from the 1850s to the 1890s by comparing this map with the maps found on pages 388, 412, and 491.

Q *What were the chief reasons why McKinley won this hotly contested election?*

Q *Do you see any changes in voting patterns?*

anarchist Alexander Berkman marched into the office of Henry Clay Frick, Andrew Carnegie's right-hand man, and shot him at point-blank range (Frick survived). Although such physical assaults were rare, anger over ill-gotten and ill-spent wealth was widespread. In the 1890s, popular rage forced Mrs. Bradley Martin and her husband to flee to England after she spent $370,000 (roughly $3.5 million in 2007 dollars) on one evening of entertainment for her friends in New York's high society.

Industrial titans were often called "robber barons." Seeking a more favorable image, some industrialists began to restrain their displays of wealth and use their private fortunes to advance the public welfare. As early as 1889, Andrew Carnegie had advocated a "gospel of wealth." The wealthy, he believed, should consider all income in excess of their needs as a "trust fund" for their communities. In 1901, the year in which he formed U.S. Steel, Carnegie withdrew from industry and devoted himself to philanthropic pursuits, especially in art and education. By the time he died in 1919, he had given away or entrusted to several Carnegie foundations 90 percent of his fortune. Among the projects he funded were New York's Carnegie Hall, Pittsburgh's Carnegie Institute (now Carnegie Mellon University), and 2,500 public libraries throughout the country.

Other industrialists, including John D. Rockefeller, soon followed Carnegie's lead (see Table 19.1). A devout Baptist with an ascetic bent, Rockefeller had never flaunted his wealth, but his ruthless business methods in assembling the Standard Oil Company and in crushing his competition made him one of the most reviled of the robber barons. In the wake of journalist Ida Tarbell's stinging 1904 exposé of Standard Oil's business practices, and of the federal government's subsequent prosecution of Standard Oil for monopolistic practices in 1906, Rockefeller transformed himself into a public-spirited philanthropist. Between 1913 and 1919, his Rockefeller Foundation dispersed an estimated $500 million. His most significant gifts included money to establish the University of Chicago and the Rockefeller Institute for Medical Research (later renamed Rockefeller University). His charitable efforts did not escape criticism, however; many Americans interpreted them as an attempt to establish control over American universities, scientific research, and public policy. Still, Rockefeller's largesse helped build for the Rockefeller family a reputation for public-spiritedness and good works, one that grew even stronger in

Table 19.1 LEADING INDUSTRIALIST PHILANTHROPIC FOUNDATIONS, 1905–1925

Foundation	Date of Origin	Original Endowment
Carnegie Corporation of New York	1911	$125,000,000
Carnegie Endowment for International Peace	1910	$10,000,000
Carnegie Foundation for the Advancement of Teaching	1905	$10,000,000
Carnegie Institution of Washington	1902	$10,000,000
Duke Endowment	1924	$40,000,000
John Simon Guggenheim Memorial Foundation	1925	$3,000,000
Rockefeller Foundation	1913	$100,000,000
Rosenwald Fund	1917	$20,000,000
Russell Sage Foundation	1907	$10,000,000

Source: Data from Joseph C. Kiger, *Operating Principles of the Larger Foundations* (New York: Russell Sage Foundation, 1957), p. 122.

the 1920s and 1930s. Many other business leaders, such as Julius Rosenwald of Sears Roebuck and Daniel and Simon Guggenheim of the American Smelting and Refining Company, also dedicated themselves to philanthropy during this time.

Conclusion

For many Americans, the strikes and violence and third-party protests of the 1890s were a wake-up call. They realized that wrenching economic change threatened the liberty and equality they had long taken for granted as part of the American dream. Many middle-class Americans began to support greater government power to carry out progressive reforms that might cure the ills of an industrializing society.

The rise of corporate America created a fundamental paradox: On the one hand, the new industrial landscape denied workers independence and subjected them to harsh conditions, which they resisted as best they could in a series of strikes in the late 19th and early 20th centuries. Yet that same corporate world provided significant opportunities for a better life—opportunities that were especially embraced by the millions of immigrants who settled in American cities at the turn of the century. There, immigrants often found greater liberties than they had known before. But opportunity did not necessarily translate into equality: The search for a more equal society was far from finished.

CHAPTER REVIEW

Review

1. What were the main engines of American economic growth in the late 19th and early 20th centuries?
2. How did the rise of corporations reshape the everyday experiences of Americans?
3. How effective was workers' resistance to the new corporations? Why?
4. What provoked the farmer protest movements in the last third of the 19th century?
5. Why did many Americans find Populism appealing in the 1890s?
6. How and why did American elites seek to alter their "robber baron" image in the late 19th and early 20th centuries?

Critical Thinking

1. Some historians have argued that corporate power went virtually unchecked in the 19th century. Is this true? Why or why not?
2. How did the ongoing struggle between capital and labor reshape American society in the late 19th century?

Identifications

Review your understanding of the following key terms, people, and events for this chapter (terms in bold in text are included in the Glossary).

Great Railroad Strike of 1877, p. 522
Thomas Alva Edison, p. 523
J.P. Morgan, p. 524
Andrew Carnegie, p. 524
John D. Rockefeller, p. 525
"robber barons," p. 526
merger movement, p. 526
Sherman Antitrust Act of 1890, p. 526
mass-production, p. 526
Social Darwinism, p. 528
"the strenuous life," p. 530
Knights of Labor, p. 532
Haymarket, p. 532
Samuel F. Gompers, p. 534
Homestead (Strike), p. 535
Pullman Strike, p. 535
"free silver," p. 538
William Jennings Bryan, p. 539

Suggested Readings

For a general overview of the period, see **Richard White**, ***The Republic for Which It Stands: The United States during Reconstruction and the Gilded Age, 1865–1896*** (2017). See also **Alan Dawley**, ***Struggles for Justice: Social Responsibility and the Liberal State*** (1991); and **Nell Irvin Painter**, ***Standing at Armageddon: The United States, 1877–1919*** (1987). On economic growth and corporate development, see **Harold G. Vatter**, ***The Drive to Industrial Maturity: The United States Economy, 1860–1914*** (1975); and **Glenn Porter**, ***The Rise of Big Business, 1860–1910*** (1973).

On the titans of the Gilded Age, see especially **Ron Chernow**, ***Titan: The Life of John D. Rockefeller, Sr.*** (1998); **David Nasaw**, ***Andrew Carnegie*** (2006); and **Jean Strouse**, ***Morgan: American Financier*** (1999). For culture in the Gilded Age, see **Rebecca Edwards**, ***New Spirits: Americans in the Gilded Age, 1865–1905*** (2006), **Sven Beckert**, ***The Monied Metropolis: New York City and the Consolidation of the American Bourgeoisie, 1850–1896*** (2001); and **Alan Trachtenberg**, ***The Incorporation of America: Culture and Society in the Gilded Age*** (1982). On the "strenuous life" and changing ideas of masculinity and civilization, see **Gail Bederman**, ***Manliness and Civilization: A Cultural History of Gender and Race in the United States, 1880–1917*** (1995).

The labor movement is treated in **David Montgomery**, ***The Fall of the House of Labor: The Workplace, the State, and American Labor Activism*** (1987). For the Knights of Labor, see **Leon Fink**, ***Workingman's Democracy: The Knights of Labor and American Politics*** (1983). On Haymarket and Pullman, see **Carl Smith**, ***Urban Disorder and the Shape of Belief: The Great Chicago Fire, the Haymarket Bomb, and the Model Town of Pullman*** (1995).

For a fresh interpretation of Populism, see **Charles Postel**, ***The Populist Vision*** (2007); and the classic **Lawrence Goodwyn**, ***Democratic Promise: The Populist Moment in America*** (1976).

20 Cities, Peoples, Cultures, 1890–1920

Hester Street, 1905 (oil on canvas), Luks, George (1867–1933)/Brooklyn Museum of Art, New York, USA/ The Bridgeman Art Library

20.1 **Hester Street** This 1905 painting by George Luks recreates a busy corner of the Lower East Side, then home to New York City's immigrant Jewish community. Peddlers and consumers, men and women, adults and children crowd this painting, which stresses the energy, diversity, and commerce of this bustling urban district.

AMERICA'S CITIES GREW RAPIDLY in the late 19th and early 20th centuries, both to accommodate expanded production and trade and to house masses of workers who labored on the wharves and streets and in factories. Growth called forth technological advance: running water, electric lighting and trolley lines, steel suspension bridges, skyscrapers, and elevators. Immigration soared to remedy severe labor shortfalls in manufacturing and construction; foreign languages and cultures, as a result, became a more prominent feature of American urban life.

New economic elites sought to impart to their cities an architectural elegance and cultural *gravitas* that, in their minds, rivaled those of the greatest cities in history—London, Paris, Rome, Athens, and Berlin. Their plans transformed cities but also brought the rich into conflict with the poor, whose presence could not be ignored. A vigorous commercial culture had taken root in working-class and ethnic districts of the city, appearing in dance halls, **nickelodeons**, and amusement parks. Exuberance rather than refinement, adventure rather than education defined these working-class leisure pursuits. Young, working-class women pioneered a sexual revolution, and immigrants energized cities with the diversity of their communities and cultures. The interactions among the different ethnic communities, as well as between rich and poor, made American cities sites of innovation, transformation, and conflict. In them, a new America was taking shape. ■

20-1 The Rise of the City

In what ways did urban elites seek to shape the physical and cultural character of their cities in the years between 1890 and 1910?

By the late 19th century, cities were changing the face of America. Their populations, their physical size, and their capacity to transform the landscapes they inhabited dwarfed those of cities a mere 50 years earlier. The rate of urban growth was staggering. Chicago, for example, grew from 30,000 residents in 1850 to 500,000 in 1880 to 1,700,000 by 1900. The number of cities with more than 100,000 residents soared from 18 in 1870 to 38 in 1900. Chicago, along with New York and Philadelphia, surpassed 1 million.

A new kind of building, the skyscraper, symbolized the aspirations taking shape in America's expanding urban milieu. These modern towers were made possible by the use of steel rather than stone in the framework and by the invention of electric-powered elevators. Impelled upward by rising real estate values, they were intended to evoke the same sense of grandeur as Europe's Gothic cathedrals. But these monuments celebrated man, not God; material wealth, not spiritual riches; science, not faith. Reaching into the sky, dwarfing Europe's cathedrals, they were convincing embodiments of America's urban might.

If advances in construction made possible the vertical reach of America's urban areas, technological advances encouraged horizontal expansion. Most important in this regard was the application of electricity to urban transportation systems. Between 1890 and 1920, virtually every major city built electric-powered transit systems to replace horse-drawn trolleys and carriages. By 1912, some 40,000 miles of electrical railway and trolley track had been laid. In Boston, electricity made possible the construction of the first subways in 1897, and New York and Philadelphia soon followed suit.

As a result of these transportation improvements, it now became possible for urban dwellers to live miles away from where they worked. As recently as the 1870s, many of America's urban centers had been **walking cities**. They were compact entities, with residential areas abutting work districts, and different income and ethnic groups living in close proximity to each other. By the 1890s, these walking cities had given way to metropolitan entities, with core areas of work and commerce—"downtowns"—now surrounded by expanding rings of residential areas offering inhabitants their own homes and gardens and the promise of tree-lined streets. The intensifying congestion, dirt, poor air, and poverty of urban cores impelled the more affluent residents of these areas to seek homes in the quiet and healthy neighborhoods taking shape on the periphery. In some cases, these areas were jurisdictionally separate from cities, becoming prototypes of the independent 20th-century suburb: Brookline, Massachusetts, a town southwest of Boston, and Evanston, Illinois, a town north of Chicago, were two early examples of this phenomenon. In other urban centers, the new residential districts arose as part of the cities themselves. The old cores, meanwhile, increasingly became home to the poor, to immigrants, and to racial minorities.

Changes in cities below ground matched those going on above. None were more important than water and sewage systems. By 1900, Chicago was pumping 500 million gallons per day to its inhabitants through 1,900 miles of water pipes. Another 1,500 miles of sewage pipe carried used water and other waste products away from Chicagoan households. The 139 gallons that Chicago and other American cities were pumping a day for each inhabitant dwarfed the 20 to 40 gallons per capita that British and German cities were distributing to their residents. The scale and power of these water systems made flush toilets and bathtubs standard equipment in virtually every American middle-class urban home by 1900. Such improvements came more slowly to the urban poor. In cities such as Pittsburgh, for example, water supplies and water pressure were much steadier in prosperous than in poor neighborhoods. As late as the First World War, a significant percentage of working-class families still lacked running water in their homes. Still, America's urban poor had better access to running water than did their counterparts in Europe.

These water systems reflected engineering prowess. In New York City, a network of aqueducts that one historian has described as "the greatest project in water engineering since the Roman Empire" carried water in tunnels that were more than 13 feet in diameter a distance of 30 miles from upstate

CHRONOLOGY

1893	Columbia Exposition opens
1900	Chicago joins New York City and Philadelphia as the only U.S. cities with populations exceeding 1 million
1900–1914	Immigration averages more than 1 million per year
1907	Congress establishes Dillingham Commission to study immigration problems
1907–1911	An average of 73 of every 100 Italian immigrants return to Italy
1908	Israel Zangwill's play, *The Melting-Pot*, debuts
1909	Immigrants and their children constitute more than 90 percent of labor force building and maintaining railroads
1910	Black skilled tradesmen in northern cities reduced to 10 percent of total skilled trades workforce • Roughly 20,000 nickelodeons dot northern cities
1911	Triangle Shirtwaist Company fire kills 146 workers
1914	Theda Bara, movies' first sex symbol, debuts • *The Masses*, a radical journal, begins publication
1916	Randolph Bourne publishes "Trans-National America"
1919	Japanese farmers in California sell $67 million in agricultural goods, 10 percent of state's total
1920	Nation's urban population outstrips rural population for first time

reservoirs. If measured by their ability to procure, pump, and carry away huge volumes of water, these American systems were unrivalled in the world.

These waterworks impressed less when measured by efforts to control costs, to ensure the safety of workers building tunnels and aqueducts, and to enhance public health. The construction and administration of these projects occurred within political systems that were often corrupt. City and state officials expected to receive kickbacks for awarding contracts. Some regarded the size of the kickback as a more important consideration in choosing a contractor than the firm's competence or the prudent use of taxpayer monies. Those in charge of designing and building this infrastructure often did not do enough to protect laborers from the hazards of working underground, to ensure that consumers used the water efficiently, or to protect local lakes, rivers, and oceans against contamination from sewage. In Chicago in 1882, the city's polluted water triggered a typhoid fever outbreak that killed more than 20,000 people. In some cities, nonbacterial contaminants compromised water quality, limiting its use for drinking. One Philadelphia newspaper reported in 1895 that the local water tasted "like a solution of gum boots and coal tar."

By 1900, the problems caused by contaminated water had begun to recede. Urban governments were installing water filtration systems and developing safer processes for sewage disposal and treatment. Newly paved roads reduced the amount of dirt, mud, and stagnant pools of water on city streets and thus further curtailed the spread of disease. As a result, urban mortality rates began to fall.

Advances in water systems, transportation, and housing reflected a growing commitment in America's urban centers to improving the lives of urban dwellers. This commitment extended well beyond questions of physical well-being to those of education and morals. In the late 19th century, urban elites launched major campaigns for cultural improvement. Symphonies, opera companies, museums, and libraries sprouted in countless cities, often housed in imposing buildings that transformed the urban landscape. In New York, Cleveland, and Philadelphia these cultural institutions, designed in conjunction with new urban parks, anchored ambitiously conceived districts meant to be places where city dwellers might escape the struggles of daily life and cultivate their higher sensibilities. Thus in New York City, the Metropolitan Museum of Art and the American Museum of Natural History appeared in the 1870s alongside Central Park, the first landscaped public park in the United States. The park's principal designer, **Frederick Law Olmsted**, designed his 50-block-long masterpiece, with its 5 million plantings, as a refuge from the city, a place where people "may stroll for an hour, seeing, hearing, and feeling nothing of the bustle and jar of the streets." If these same people took another hour to sample the art and culture on display at the Metropolitan Museum and the American Museum of Natural History, both located at the edges of Central Park, so much the better. Olmsted's success with New York parks gave him an opportunity to replicate it in numerous other cities, including Atlanta, Boston, Brooklyn, Hartford, Detroit, Chicago, Louisville, and Washington, D.C. No other single individual exercised as large an influence on American urban landscapes.

Urban elites of the late 19th century were drawn to Beaux-Arts architecture, a Paris-based style that merged neoclassical size and scale with Italian Renaissance and Baroque decorative influences. By 1902, the Metropolitan Museum had acquired its signature Beaux-Arts façade, which defines the exterior look of the museum to this day. A few years earlier, the Boston Public Library, then the finest public library in the world, moved into magnificent new quarters, whose features included a massive reading room resembling a Roman basilica and a central courtyard modeled on a 16th-century Italian Renaissance cloister. Free and open to the public, the library was celebrated by local newspapers as a "palace of the people" and as "feeding the most careless or unconscious eye with the food of high artistic loveliness."

The scale and ornateness of these structures revealed the ambitions of the urban elites who built them. These elites imagined their museums and libraries as permanent monuments to their civic vision and influence. They were, at the same time, making a deep investment in their cities, proclaiming their concern for the well-being of the urban masses. Founders of the Metropolitan expressed this sentiment in 1880, when they talked about diffusing "knowledge of art in its higher forms of beauty" in order to "educate and refine a practical and laborious people."

The energy that they poured into these institutions, however, also revealed anxieties about their own social status. For the newly wealthy in their ranks, museums, symphonies, operas, and the like offered a form of alchemy that converted their riches into cultural prestige and authority. As one museum leader said, these institutions would "convert pork into porcelain, grain and produce into priceless pottery, the rude ores of commerce into sculptured marble, and railroad shares and mining stocks ... into the glorified canvas of the world's masters."

Elites worried, too, about plebeian resistance to their civilizing projects. What if the masses ignored these institutions? Or misused them? New York museums and Central Park both became sites of conflict in the late 19th century between administrators and the people: the former laying down sets of rules about dress and comportment for those who used these institutions, the latter repeatedly declaring their intention to be left alone or demanding a role in shaping park and museum rules to their own preferences. In the 1880s, 100 labor organizations, representing 50,000 workers, presented petitions to the Metropolitan and Natural History museums asking that these institutions open their doors to the public on Sunday, the only day that was free of work for most of New York City's inhabitants. Religious groups and pious individuals on the boards of trustees brought intense pressure on these museums to keep their doors closed on the Sabbath. By 1892, however, both institutions decided to open on Sundays, handing a victory to the city's labor movement. Privately, at least, the more visionary museum leaders had to be pleased that the demand among the city's poor for access had become so strong.

The conflicts of urban life were acutely felt in Chicago. As the fastest-growing American city, it was also one of the hardest to control. Rapid growth spurred innovation but also generated a gulf between the rich and the poor, violent labor-capital conflict (see Chapter 19), and widespread corruption. The city had also suffered from disasters such as the typhoid epidemic of 1882 and the Chicago Fire of 1871, which destroyed the homes of 100,000 residents across a four-mile stretch of land. The massive destruction caused by the fire actually accelerated urban creativity and innovation. A pioneering group of American architects, the so-called Chicago School,

Johnston, Frances Benjamin/Library of Congress Prints and Photographs Division [LC-USZ62-104795]

20.2 **The White City** This photograph captures the scale, grandeur, and classical lines of the Columbia Exposition's White City.

Q *Why build such an extravagant and temporary city that would leave no enduring mark on Chicago?*

Union Station, Washington D.C. 1928 (color litho), American School (20th century)/Private Collection/Peter Newark American Pictures/The Bridgeman Art Library

20.3 **Union Station, Washington, D.C.** The capital city's train station, which opened in 1908 and is still being used today, is an exemplary piece of City Beautiful architecture. Its lines and landscaping reveal how much it was influenced by Chicago's White City. Indeed, the two projects shared an architect, Daniel Burnham. This color lithograph dates from 1928.

Q *What civic ideals was City Beautiful architecture meant to express? Does Union Station seem to be a successful embodiment of these ideals?*

coalesced in the city a decade after the fire. It included men such as Louis Sullivan and John Wellborn Root and a young draftsman by the name of Frank Lloyd Wright. America's most daring skyscraper designs emerged from their ranks, as did buildings (mostly Sullivan's creations) that merged crisp modern lines, functionality, and wondrous ornamentation. At a later time, Wright would take what he learned as Root's and Sullivan's assistant and develop a distinctive American form of modernist architecture that made his buildings in Chicago and elsewhere among the most original and admired in 20th-century America.

Chicago's rapid ascent as a center for manufacturing, trade, and architectural innovation made it the choice for hosting the Columbia Exposition of 1893, a world's fair to celebrate the 400th anniversary of Columbus's discovery of America. The fair's two square miles of area made it three times as large as the fair in Paris four years before, and the giant Ferris wheel unveiled by exposition planners was meant to rival the Eiffel Tower as an architectural marvel wrought of iron and steel.

At the heart of this enterprise was a monumental set of gleaming buildings called the "**White City**," meant to evoke the classical grandeur of Greece and Rome and to trumpet the maturation of American civilization. One set of buildings—Agriculture, Transportation, Manufacturing, among them—devoted itself to inventorying America's achievements in various economic sectors. Other buildings celebrated American women; the histories, cultures, and peoples of the individual states; and the contributions of foreign nations to the story of human progress. The Transportation Building, designed by Sullivan, was the most innovative of the fair's structures, while the Manufactures Building was the largest, covering more than twice as much area as the Great Pyramid of Egypt and requiring 120,000 incandescent lamps to keep it lit. Steel skeletons held the buildings up; they were sheathed in perishable stucco, unlikely to survive even one Chicago winter. The stucco was easy to work with, however, and thus allowed architects to unleash their decorative instincts in their building designs.

The individual buildings were carefully laid out around a man-made lagoon created by landscape master Olmsted himself, who imparted a neoclassical unity to the entire enterprise. Broad, open courts studded with statuary and interspersed with fountains and parks connected the buildings to each other. It is remarkable that exposition planners invested so much effort in a "city" meant to exist only for a few months.

The planners nevertheless hoped that their work would endure in terms of influencing urban design, if not as an actual urban space. Indeed, the White City, an exemplar of Beaux-Art principles, gave rise to a movement of urban architectural renovation that would become known as the **City Beautiful movement**. Its carefully composed vision of urban order, its American leaders hoped, would inspire city planners across the United States to impose a similar kind of order on the urban environments in which they lived. Metaphorically, the rise of this White City out of the swamps of Jackson Park south of Chicago symbolized the city's and the nation's capacity for rebirth. A utopian dream of an ordered city and a triumphant industrial civilization, the White City embodied America's quest for and belief in perfection.

With paid admissions exceeding 21 million people (in a nation of with a population of 63 million), the Columbia Exposition was by far the most successful fair in American history. Americans from everywhere came to marvel at this reincarnation of ancient Rome and to record their impressions in special printed books that thoughtfully guided them through the fair, beginning with the page, "My first day in the 'White City.'" The White City did fill many fairgoers with pride and inspiration, much as the planners of the fair hoped it would. Visitors, however, also found their attention drawn to another part of the fair, one that focused on amusement rather than education, and on the dissonances of modern life rather than its symmetry. The **Midway Plaisance** was a long strip located at some distance from the White City, full of concessions where one could buy food and drink, engage in games, line up for rides including the Ferris wheel, and gaze upon the curiosities that countless small entrepreneurs had gathered into their traveling dime museums and freak shows. This, Daniel Burnham, the fair's head designer understood, was "the lighter and more fantastic side of the Fair." The chaotic variety of its sights and smells proved irresistible to tourists.

Part of Midway's variety was deliberately ethnographic, as numerous pavilions displayed life in areas of Africa and Asia. The accent was on the primitive and exotic: The pavilions did not emphasize the modernizing elites of these faraway places, or their achievements in manufacture or transportation, but rather native peoples supposedly barely touched by civilization. It was hard to miss the implication that civilization occurred in America and Europe, as represented in the White City, while primitivism belonged to people of color from Africa, the Middle East, and Asia.

The very structure of the fair thus embodied and reinforced a racial hierarchy that posited the superiority of white, middle-class civilization. African Americans understood how much this hierarchy organized not only America's relationship with much of the world but also life

20.4 **Midway Plaisance** Columbian Exposition fairgoers were drawn to this lively entertainment strip. They rode the giant Ferris wheel, poked their heads in shops, mounted camels, and explored the exotic cultures on display in Asian and African pavilions.

Q *What elements of the world's national, religious, and racial diversity were on display in this artistic rendering of Midway?*

Q *Might the diversity of Midway be construed as an endorsement of the diversity of America's urban centers? Why or why not?*

within the United States itself. The anti-lynching crusader Ida B. Wells (see Chapter 18) published a pamphlet, with contributions from several black leaders, titled "The Reason Why the Colored American Is Not in the World's Columbian Exposition." Exploring the intertwined histories of American slavery and racism, this pamphlet offered a detailed accounting of the refusal of fair organizers to include African Americans in their plans. "Theoretically open to all Americans, the Exposition practically is, literally and figuratively, a 'White City,'" the pamphlet asserted. Wells boycotted the fair on "Colored American Day," but former abolitionist Frederick Douglass attended in order to give a stirring speech. "Men talk of the Negro problem," he said. "There is no Negro problem. The problem is whether the American people have honesty enough, loyalty enough, honor enough, patriotism enough to live up to their own Constitution." Try as it might, the Columbia Exposition could not erase the question of race; nor could all the striving for unity and placidity in the White City erase the presence in Chicago and other major American cities of polyglot populations of diverse ethnic origins. These international populations would stake a claim to define the urban areas in which they lived as much as the elites who built the palatial museums, opera houses, and White Cities.

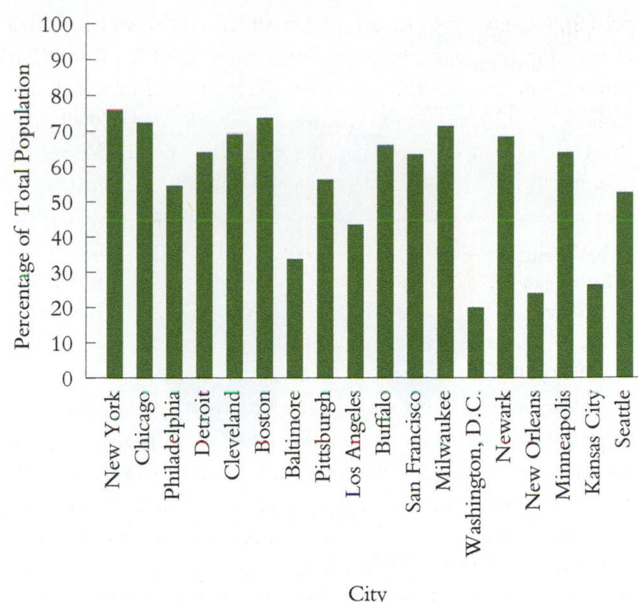

Figure 20.1 **Immigrants and Their Children as a Percentage of the Population of Selected Cities, 1920**

Source: Data from U.S. Department of Commerce, Bureau of the Census, *Fourteenth Census of the United States*, 1920, Population (Washington, D.C.).

20-2 Immigration

Q From which parts of the world did immigrants come in the years between 1880 and 1920? What caused them to migrate? What were their patterns of work and residence in the United States?

The United States had always been a nation of immigrants, but never had so many come in so short a time. Between 1880 and 1920, some 23 million immigrants came to a country that numbered only 76 million in 1900. From 1900 to 1914, an average of 1 million immigrants arrived each year. In many cities of the Northeast and Midwest, immigrants and their children constituted a majority of the population. In 1920s Boston, New York City, Chicago, and Milwaukee, immigrants accounted for more than 70 percent of the total population; in Buffalo, Detroit, and Minneapolis, more than 60 percent; and in Philadelphia, Pittsburgh, and Seattle, more than 50 percent (see Figure 20.1). Everywhere in the country, except in the South, the working class was heavily ethnic.

European immigration accounted for approximately three-fourths of the total. Some states received significant numbers of non-European immigrants—Chinese, Japanese, and Filipinos in California; Mexicans in California and the Southwest; and French Canadians in New England. Although their presence profoundly affected regional economies, politics, and culture, their numbers, relative to the number of European immigrants, were small. Immigrants from Latin America were free to enter the United States throughout this period, but few did until 1910, when the social disorder caused by the Mexican Revolution propelled a stream of refugees to southwestern parts of the United States. Half a million French Canadians had migrated to New England and the upper Midwest between 1867 and 1901. After that, the rate slowed as the pace of industrialization in Quebec quickened.

20-2a *European Immigration*

Most of the European immigrants who arrived between 1880 and 1914 came from eastern and southern Europe. Among them were 3 to 4 million Italians, 2 million Russian and Polish Jews, 2 million Hungarians, and an estimated 5 million Slavs and other peoples from eastern and southeastern Europe (Poles, Bohemians, Slovaks, Russians, Ukrainians, Lithuanians, Serbians, Croatians, Slovenians, Montenegrins, Bulgarians, Macedonians, and Greeks). Hundreds of thousands came as well from Turkey, Armenia, Lebanon, Syria, and other Near Eastern lands abutting the European continent (see Figure 20.2).

These post-1880 arrivals were called "new immigrants" to underscore the cultural gap separating them from the "old immigrants," who had come from northwestern Europe—Great Britain, Scandinavia, and Germany. Old immigrants were regarded by many native-born Americans as racially fit, culturally sophisticated, and politically mature. The new immigrants, by contrast, were often regarded as racially inferior, culturally impoverished, and incapable of assimilating American values and traditions. This negative view of the new immigrants reflected in part a fear of their alien languages, religions, and economic backgrounds. Few spoke English, and most adhered to Catholicism, Orthodoxy, or Judaism rather than Protestantism. Most, with the exception of Jewish immigrants, were peasants, unaccustomed to urban industrial life, but they were not as different from the old immigrants as the label implied. For example, many of the earlier-arriving

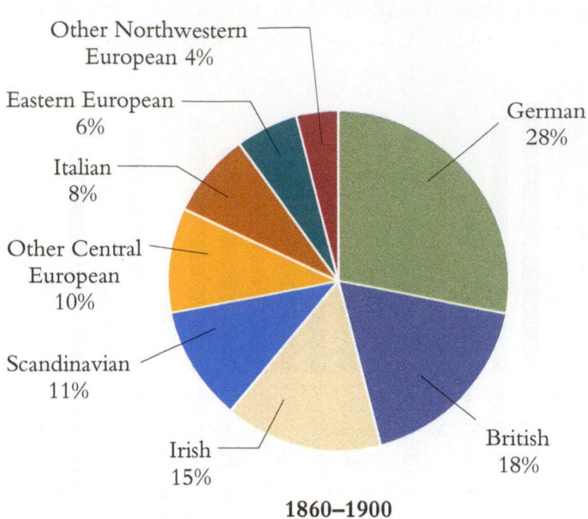

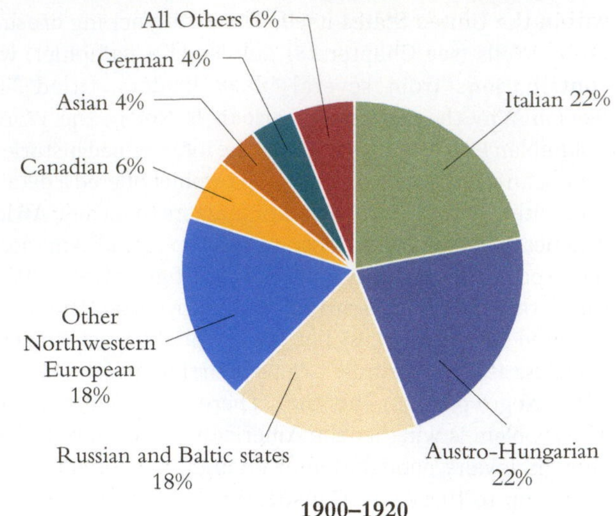

Figure 20.2 **Sources of Immigration**

Source: Data from *Historical Statistics of the United States, Colonial Times to 1970* (White Plains, NY: Kraus International, 1989), pp. 105–109.

Catholic peasants from Ireland and Germany had had no more familiarity with American values and traditions than did the Italians and Slavs who arrived later.

Most mass immigration was propelled by economic hardship. Europe's rural population was growing faster than what the land could support. An individual's or family's decision to emigrate often depended on having a contact—a family member, relative, or fellow villager—already established in an American city. These people provided immigrants with a destination, inspiration (they were examples of success in America), advice about jobs, and financial aid. Sometimes whole villages in southern Italy or western Russia—or at least all of the young men there—seemed to disappear, only to reappear in a certain section of Chicago, Pittsburgh, or New York. Villages without contacts in the United States were relatively unaffected by the emigration mania.

Most immigrants viewed their trip to the United States as a temporary sojourn. They came not in search of permanent settlement but in search of high wages that would enable them to improve their economic standing in their homeland. For them, America was a land of economic opportunity, not a land to call home. This attitude explains why men vastly outnumbered women and children in the migration stream. From 1899 to 1910, three-fourths of the immigrants from southern and eastern Europe were adult men. Some had left wives and children behind; more were single. Most wanted merely to make enough money to buy a farm in their native land. True to their dream, many did return home. For every 100 Italian immigrants who arrived in the United States between 1907 and 1911, for example, 73 returned to Italy. Before the First World War, an estimated 60 to 80 percent of all Slavic immigrants eventually returned to the land of their birth. Most immigrants looked forward to returning to Europe. Not until the First World War shut down transatlantic travel did most immigrants begin to regard their presence in the United States as permanent.

20-2b *Chinese and Japanese Immigration*

The relatively small numbers of Chinese and Japanese immigrants who came to the United States in the late 19th and early 20th centuries reflected the efforts of native-born Americans and their allies to keep them out. As many as 300,000 Chinese immigrants arrived in the United States between 1851 and 1882, and more than 200,000 Japanese immigrants journeyed to Hawaii and the western continental United States between 1891 and 1907. They contributed in major ways to the development of two of the West's major industries: railroad building and commercial agriculture. These two immigrant groups might have formed two of America's largest, each numbering in the millions, but the U.S. government began to exclude Chinese immigrant laborers in 1882 (via the Chinese Exclusion Act) and Japanese immigrant laborers in 1907 (see Chapter 22). The government also interpreted a 1790 law to mean that Chinese, Japanese, and other East Asian immigrants were ineligible for citizenship. These exclusions remained in force until the 1940s and 1950s. They expressed the racial prejudice felt by most native-born white Americans toward nonwhite Asian immigrants, and they also revealed how determined America was to remain a nation of European immigrants and their descendants.

The early streams of Chinese and Japanese migration to the United States were overwhelmingly composed of men looking for work. Similar to the European immigrants, the Chinese and Japanese sojourners tended to follow precise migratory paths—from one region or village in China or Japan to one city or region in the United States. Conditions in China were more desperate than those in Japan, where industrialization had begun to generate new wealth and absorb some of the rural population. Chinese immigrants, as a result, often suffered greater hardship than did their Japanese counterparts. In the 19th century, many were forced to sign contracts with suppliers of overseas laborers that subjected them to slavelike conditions: They were herded onto boats for the transpacific voyage, bound to particular employers for years on end, thrust into dangerous working conditions, and paid paltry wages.

Significant numbers of Chinese and Japanese immigrants continued to try to enter the United States during the period of Asian immigrant exclusion—after 1882 in the case of the Chinese and after 1907 in the case of the Japanese. Some were desperate to reunite with family members already living in the United States, while others were driven to escape deteriorating economic circumstances in their homeland. Many attempted to enter the United States with forged papers declaring them to be merchants (a permitted class of Chinese and Japanese immigrants) when they were not or stating that they had been resident in the United States before the exclusion laws had gone into effect (and were thus entitled to return). San Francisco was their principal port of entry, and Angel Island, in San Francisco Harbor, became the counterpart of Ellis Island in New York Harbor: the place where inspectors for the U.S. Bureau of Immigration interrogated them and scrutinized their documents and often sent them back to Asia.

Other East Asian immigrants attempted to come into the United States through Canada or Mexico, hoping to find a nonpatrolled part of the land border and to cross into the United States undetected. They became, in effect, America's first illegal aliens. That a certain percentage of East Asian immigrants had entered the country illegally, and were subject to deportation, generated considerable fear among the Asian immigrant populations resident in the United States, deepening tendencies within these communities to secrecy and to separation from mainstream American society. Despite these considerable hardships, Asian immigrants would prove to be resourceful and find ways to build homes and livelihoods in America.

20-2c *Immigrant Labor*

In the first decade of the 20th century, immigrant men and their male children constituted 70 percent of the workforce in 15 of the 19 leading U.S. industries. They concentrated in industries where work was the most backbreaking. Immigrants built the nation's railroads and tunnels; mined its coal, iron ore, and other minerals; stoked its hot and sometimes deadly steel furnaces; and slaughtered and packed its meat in Chicago's putrid packinghouses. In 1909, first and second-generation immigrants—especially Greeks, Italians, Japanese, and Mexicans—constituted more than 90 percent of the labor force that built and maintained the nation's railroads. Of the 750,000 Slovaks who arrived in America before 1913, at least 600,000 headed for the coal mines and steel mills of western Pennsylvania. The steel mills of Pittsburgh, Buffalo, Cleveland, and Chicago also attracted disproportionately large numbers of Poles and other Slavs.

Immigrants also performed "lighter" but no less arduous work. Jews and Italians predominated in the garment manufacturing shops of New York City, Chicago, Philadelphia, Baltimore, and Boston. In 1900, French Canadian immigrants and their children held one of every two jobs in New England's cotton textile industry. By 1920, the prosperity of California's rapidly growing agricultural industry depended primarily on Mexican and Filipino labor. In these industries, immigrant women and children, who worked for lower wages than men,

Bettmann / Corbis

20.5 Immigrant Japanese Children Arrive at Angel Island, San Francisco Harbor, 1905 Beginning in 1907, as a result of the "gentlemen's agreement" between the United States and Japanese governments, it would no longer be possible for most Japanese immigrants to come to the United States. Had they tried to enter the United States after 1907, these children might well have been turned away.

Q *What were the effects of exclusion on the Japanese and Chinese populations already in the United States at this time?*

formed a large part of the labor force. Few states restricted child labor. More than 25 percent of boys and 10 percent of girls aged 10 to 15 were "gainfully employed."

Those who worked in heavy industry, mining, or railroading were especially vulnerable to accident and injury. In 1901, for instance, 1 in every 400 railroad workers died on the job and 1 in every 26 suffered injury. Between the years 1906 and 1911, almost one-quarter of the recent immigrants employed at the U.S. Steel Corporation's South Works (Pittsburgh) were injured or killed on the job. Lax attention to safety rendered even light industry hazardous and sometimes fatal. In 1911, a fire broke out on an upper floor of the **Triangle Shirtwaist Company**, a New York City garment factory. The building had no fire escapes. The owners of the factory, moreover, had locked the entrances to each floor as a way of keeping their employees at work. A total of 146 workers, mostly young Jewish and Italian women, perished in the fire or from desperate nine-story leaps to the pavement below.

Chronic fatigue and inadequate nourishment increased the risk of accident and injury. Workweeks averaged 60 hours—10 hours every day except Sunday. Workers who were granted Saturday afternoons off, thus reducing their workweek to 55 hours, considered themselves fortunate. Steelworkers were not so lucky. They labored from 72 to 89 hours per week and were required to work one 24-hour shift every two weeks.

Most workers had to labor long hours simply to eke out a meager living. In 1900, the annual earnings of American manufacturing workers averaged only $400 to $500 per year. Skilled jobs offered immigrants far more (as much as $1,500 to $2,000 per year), but most of these jobs were held by Yankees and by Germans, Irish, Welsh, and other "old immigrant" Europeans. Through their unions, workers of northern European extraction also controlled access to new jobs that opened up and usually managed to fill them with a son, relative, or fellow countryman. Consequently, relatively few of the new immigrants rose to the prosperous ranks of skilled labor. In any case, employers were replacing many skilled workers with machines operated by cheaply paid operatives.

Most working families required two or three wage earners to survive. If a mother could not go out to work because she had small children at home, she might rent rooms to some of the many single men who had recently immigrated. But economic security was difficult to attain. In his 1904 book, *Poverty*, social investigator Robert Hunter conservatively estimated that 20 percent of the industrial population of the North lived in poverty.

Museum of the City of New York/Corbis

20.6 **Triangle Shirtwaist Company Fire** In 1911, a fire at the Triangle Shirtwaist Company in New York City claimed the lives of 146 workers, most of them young Jewish and Italian women. Many died because they could not escape the flames. The building had no fire escapes, and the employer had locked the entrances to each floor to keep workers on the job. The tragedy spurred the growth of unions and the movement for factory reform in New York.

20-2d *Living Conditions*

Strained economic circumstances confined many working-class families to cramped and dilapidated living quarters. Many of them lived in two- or three-room apartments, with several people sleeping in each room. To make ends meet, one immigrant New York City family of eight living in a two-room apartment took in six boarders. Some boarders considered themselves lucky to have their own bed. That luxury was denied the 14 Slovaks who shared eight beds in a small Pittsburgh apartment and the New York City printer who slept on a door he unhinged every night and balanced across two chairs. The lack of windows in city tenements allowed little light or air into these apartments. Crowding was endemic. The population density of New York City's Lower East Side—where most of the city's Jewish immigrants settled—reached 700 per acre in 1900, a density matching or exceeding that of the world's poorest cities. Overcrowding and poor sanitation resulted in high rates of infectious diseases, especially diphtheria, typhoid fever, and pneumonia. In the early years of the 20th century, improvements in the quality of housing and public health finally began to ease the dangers of urban life.

20-3 Building Ethnic Communities

In what ways did immigrants seek economic success and social mobility? How successful were they in their efforts?

The immigrants may have been poor, but they were not helpless. Migration had required a good deal of resourcefulness, self-help, and mutual aid—assets that survived in the new surroundings of American cities.

20-3a *A Network of Institutions*

Each ethnic group quickly established a network of institutions that supplied a sense of community and multiplied sources of communal assistance. Some immigrants simply reproduced those institutions that had been important to them in the Old Country. The devout established churches and synagogues. Lithuanian, Jewish, and Italian radicals reestablished Old World socialist and anarchist organizations. Irish nationalists set up clandestine chapters of the Clan Na Gael to keep alive the struggle to free Ireland from the English. Germans felt at home in their *Turnevereins* (athletic clubs) and musical societies.

Immigrants developed new institutions as well. In the larger cities, foreign-language newspapers disseminated news, advice, and culture. Each ethnic group created fraternal societies to bring together immigrants who had known each other in the Old Country, or who shared the same trade, or who had come from the same town or region. Most of these societies provided members with a death benefit (ranging from a few hundred to a thousand dollars) that guaranteed the deceased a decent burial and the family a bit of cash. Some fraternal societies made small loans as well. Among those ethnic groups that prized homeownership, especially the Slavic groups, the fraternal societies also provided mortgage money. And all of them served as centers of sociability—places to have a drink, play cards, or simply relax with fellow countrymen. The joy, solace, and solidarity these groups generated helped countless immigrants adjust to American life.

20-3b *The Emergence of an Ethnic Middle Class*

Within each ethnic group, a sizable minority directed their talents and ambitions toward economic gain. Some of these entrepreneurs addressed their communities' needs for basic goods and services. Immigrants preferred to buy from fellow countrymen with whom they shared a language, a history, and presumably a bond of trust. Enterprising individuals responded by opening dry-goods stores, food shops, butcher shops, and saloons in their ethnic neighborhoods. Those who could not afford to rent a store hawked their fruit, clothing, or dry goods from portable stands, wagons, or sacks carried on their backs. The work was endless and the competition tough. Men often enlisted the entire family—wife, older children, younger children—in their undertakings. Few family members were ever paid for their labor, no matter how long or hard they worked. Although many of these small businesses failed, enough survived to give some immigrants and their children a toehold in the middle class.

Other immigrants turned to small industry, particularly garment manufacture, truck farming, and construction. A clothing manufacturer needed only a few sewing machines to become competitive. Many Jewish immigrants, having been tailors in Russia and Poland, opened such facilities. If a rented space proved beyond their means, they set up shop in their own apartments. Competition among these small manufacturers was fierce, and critics condemned the work environments as "sweatshops." Workers suffered from inadequate lighting, heat, and ventilation; 12-hour workdays and 70-hour workweeks during peak seasons, with every hour spent bent over a sewing machine; and poor pay and no employment security, especially for the women and children who made up a large part of this labor force. Even at this level of exploitation, many small manufacturers failed. But over time, significant numbers of them managed to firm up their position as manufacturers and to evolve into stable, responsible employers. Their success contributed to the emergence of a Jewish middle class.

The story was much the same in urban construction, where Italians who had established themselves as labor contractors, or *padroni*, went into business for themselves to take advantage of the rapid expansion of American cities. Although few became general contractors on major downtown projects, many of them did well building family residences or serving as subcontractors on larger buildings.

In southern California, Japanese immigrants chose agriculture as their route to the middle class. Working as

Interpreting the Visual Past

The Photography of Jacob Riis and Lewis Hine

Jacob Riis and Lewis Hine were pioneering documentary photographers of the late 19th and early 20th centuries. Both men were fiercely committed to recording the lives and daily struggles of the urban poor and to bringing those lives and struggles to the attention of a broad middle-class public. Both men hoped that their work would generate political discussions and then political pressure to improve working and living conditions. For many Americans, Riis's and Hine's photographs had precisely this effect.

As much as their goals overlapped, the two photographers' styles were very different. Consider the two photographs reprinted on this page. The Riis photograph, "The Poverty and Gloom of New York Streets," drawn from Riis's 1890 book, *How the Other Half Lives*, depicts three runaway boys who have no family and no home. They are living by their wits in the streets and grabbing for their resting place whatever secluded corner of urban space they can claim. We do not get a good glimpse of the boys' faces, or of their individuality or humanity. They are a faceless heap, anonymous victims of a harsh urban environment.

Lewis Hine's photograph, "Looking for Lost Baggage, Ellis Island," is startlingly different. The photograph has a foreboding quality: The luggage of this immigrant family is already lost. Fear laces the face of every family member. Will they make their way in the strange new world called America? Or is the sense of disorientation at Ellis Island the first step toward social disintegration, to be followed by unemployment and poverty and perhaps the young boy ending up as one of Riis's anonymous runaways? And yet there is something else in this photograph: dignity and resolve in the eyes of family members, a sense that that they are not just victims but agents of their own lives. And there is unity too: Vital luggage may be gone, but the family, and its spirit, is intact.

Q *Do you "read" the photographs in a way similar to the interpretation offered in the text above? Or do you interpret their meaning differently?*

Q *Do you think that photography is a reliable technique for documenting the human condition, or does the photographer have too much opportunity to shape objective reality to a preconceived story that he or she is trying to tell?*

Jacob August Riis/Bettmann/Corbis

20.7a **Jacob Riis, "The Poverty and Gloom of New York Streets," 1890.**

akg-images/Newscom

20.7b **Lewis Hine, "Looking for Lost Baggage, Ellis Island," 1905.**

agricultural laborers in the 1890s, they began to acquire their own land in the early years of the 20th century. Their specialization in fresh vegetables and fruits (particularly strawberries), combined with their family-labor-intensive agricultural methods, was yielding $67 million in annual revenues by 1919—one-tenth of the total California agriculture revenue that year. Japanese farmers sold their produce to Japanese fruit and vegetable wholesalers in Los Angeles, who had chosen a mercantile route to middle-class status. The success of Japanese farmers was all the more impressive given that the state of California had passed the Alien Land Law in 1913, prohibiting Japanese and other Asian aliens from owning property in the state. Japanese immigrant farmers thus depended on their native-born children or friendly whites to acquire land for them, arrangements that made them more vulnerable to losing the land—or control of it—than if they had been able to own it outright themselves.

Each ethnic group created its own history of economic success and social mobility. From the emerging middle classes came leaders who would provide their ethnic groups with identity, legitimacy, and power and would lead the way toward Americanization and assimilation. Their children tended to do better in school than the children of working-class ethnics, and academic success served as a ticket to upward social mobility in a society that increasingly depended on university-trained engineers, managers, lawyers, doctors, and other professionals.

20-3c *Political Machines and Organized Crime*

The underside of this success story was the rise of government corruption and organized crime. Many ethnic entrepreneurs operated on the margins of economic failure and bankruptcy, and some accepted the help of those who promised financial assistance. Sometimes the help came from honest unions and upright government officials, but other times it did not. Unions were generally weak, and some government officials, lacking experience and economic security, were susceptible to bribery. Economic necessity became a breeding ground for government corruption and greed. A contractor who was eager to win a city contract—to build a trolley system, a sewer line, or a new city hall, for example—would find it necessary to pay off government officials who could throw the contract his way. By 1900, such payments, referred to as "graft," had become essential to the day-to-day operation of government in most large cities. Graft, in turn, made local office holding a source of economic gain. Politicians began building political organizations called machines to guarantee their success in municipal elections. The machine "bosses" used a variety of legal and illegal means to bring victory on Election Day. They won the loyalty of urban voters—especially immigrants—by providing poor neighborhoods with paved roads and sewer systems. They helped newly arrived immigrants find jobs (often on city payrolls) and occasionally provided food, fuel, or clothing to families in need. Many of their clients were grateful for these services in an age when government provided little public assistance.

The bosses who ran the **political machines**—including "King Richard" Croker in New York, James Michael Curley in Boston, Tom Pendergast in Kansas City, Martin Behrman in New Orleans, and Abe Ruef in San Francisco—served their own needs first. They saw to it that construction contracts went to those who offered the most graft, not to those who were likely to do the best job. They protected gamblers, pimps, and other purveyors of urban vice who contributed large amounts to their machine coffers. They often required city employees to contribute to their campaign chests, solicit political contributions, and get out the vote on Election Day. And they engaged in widespread election fraud by rounding up truckloads of newly arrived immigrants and paying them to vote a certain way; having their supporters vote two or three times; and stuffing ballot boxes with the votes of phantom citizens who had died, moved away, or never been born.

Big-city machines, then, were both positive and negative forces in urban life. Reformers despised them for disregarding election laws and encouraging vice, but many immigrants valued them for providing social welfare services and for creating opportunities for upward mobility.

Underworld figures, too, influenced urban life. In the early years of the 20th century, gangsterism was a scourge of Italian neighborhoods, where Sicilian immigrants had established outposts of the notorious Mafia; Irish, Jewish, Chinese, and other ethnic communities suffered from organized crime as well. Favorite targets of these gangsters were small-scale manufacturers and contractors, who were threatened with violence and economic ruin if they did not pay a gang for "protection." Gangsters imposed their demands with physical force, beating up or killing those who failed to abide by the "rules." In Chinese communities, secret societies originating in China, or *tongs*, and initially set up in America to strengthen communal life among the immigrants, occasionally crossed the line into crime. Sometimes this transition resulted from good intentions—for example, tong members might smuggle into the United States the wife and children of an immigrant Chinese man who had no legal way of reuniting his family—but other times, tongs became enmeshed in far more damaging criminal activities, such as the opium trade, prostitution, and gambling.

Eager for money, power, and fame, many immigrant and ethnic criminals considered themselves authentic entrepreneurs cut from the American mold. By the 1920s, petty extortion had escalated in urban areas, and underworld crime had become big business. **Al Capone**, the ruthless Chicago mobster who made a fortune from gambling, prostitution, and bootleg liquor during Prohibition, once quipped: "Prohibition is a business. All I do is to supply a public demand. I do it in the best and least harmful way I can." New York City's Arnold Rothstein, whose financial sophistication won him a gambling empire and the power to fix the 1919 World Series, nurtured his reputation as "the J. P. Morgan of the underworld." Mobsters like Rothstein and Capone were charismatic figures, both in their ethnic communities and in the nation at large. Few immigrants, however, followed their criminal path to economic success.

20.8 "Keeping Tammany's Boots Shined" This 1880s cartoon by Joseph Keppler declares that the real boss of New York City was not its elected mayor, Hugh Graham, here depicted as a shoeshiner, but the city's political machine, known as Tammany Hall. The loose strap underneath the boot, used to control both City Hall and Tammany, belongs to Richard Croker, Tammany's leader from 1886 to 1901.

Q *What view of New York City's government is Keppler conveying in this cartoon?*

20-4 African American Labor and Community

Q *What were the similarities and differences between the African American and immigrant experiences in the early 20th century?*

Unlike immigrants, African Americans remained a predominantly rural and southern people in the early 20th century (see Map 20.1). Most blacks were sharecroppers and tenant farmers. The markets for cotton and other southern crops had stabilized in the early 20th century, but black farmers remained vulnerable to exploitation. Landowners, most of them white, often forced sharecroppers to accept artificially low prices for their crops. At the same time, they charged high prices for seed, tools, and groceries at the local stores they controlled. Few rural areas generated enough business to support more than one store or to create a competitive climate that might force prices down. Those sharecroppers who traveled elsewhere to sell their crops or purchase their necessities risked retaliation—either physical assaults by white vigilantes or eviction from their land. Thus, most remained beholden to their landowners, mired in poverty and debt.

Some African Americans sought a better life by migrating to industrial areas of the South and the North. In the South, they worked in iron and coal mines, in furniture and cigarette manufacture, as railroad tracklayers and longshoremen, and as laborers in the steel mills of Birmingham, Alabama. By the early 20th century, their presence was growing in the urban North as well, where they worked on the fringes of industry as janitors, elevator operators, teamsters, and servants of various kinds.

In southern industries, blacks were subjected to hardships and indignities that even the newest immigrants were not expected to endure. Railroad contractors in the South, for example, treated their black tracklayers like prisoners. Armed guards marched them to work in the morning and back at night. Tracklayers were paid only once a month and forced to purchase food at the company commissary, where the high prices claimed most of what they earned. Their belongings were locked up to discourage them from running away. Although other southern employers of black workers did not engage in labor practices as harsh as those of the railroad contractors, they still confined blacks to the dirtiest and most grueling jobs. The Jim Crow laws passed by every southern state legislature in the 1890s legalized this rigid separation of the black and white races (see Chapter 18).

The nation's worsening racial climate adversely affected southern blacks who moved north, even though these migrants had moved to states that generally did not have Jim Crow laws. Northern industrialists generally refused to hire black migrants for manufacturing jobs, preferring the labor of European immigrants. Only when those immigrants went on strike did employers turn to African Americans.

African Americans who had long resided in northern urban areas also experienced intensifying discrimination in the late 19th and early 20th centuries. In 1870, about one-third of the black men in many northern cities had been skilled tradesmen: blacksmiths, painters, shoemakers, and carpenters. Serving both black and white clients, these men enjoyed steady work and good pay, but by 1910 only 10 percent of black men made a living in this way. In many cities, the number of barbershops and food catering businesses owned by blacks also declined, as did black representation in the ranks of restaurant and hotel waiters. These barbers, food caterers, and waiters had formed a black middle class whose livelihood depended on the patronage of white clients. By the early 20th century, this middle class was shrinking, the victim of growing racism. Whites were no longer willing to engage the services of blacks, preferring to have their hair cut, beards shaved, and food prepared and served by European immigrants. The residential segregation of northern blacks also rose in these years, as whites excluded them from growing numbers of urban neighborhoods.

African Americans did not lack for resourcefulness. In urban areas of settlement, they laced their communities with the same array of institutions—churches, fraternal insurance societies, political organizations—that solidified ethnic neighborhoods. A new black middle class arose consisting of ministers, professionals, and businesspeople who serviced the needs of their racial group. Black-owned real estate agencies, funeral homes, doctors' offices, newspapers, groceries, restaurants, and bars opened for business on the commercial thoroughfares of African American neighborhoods. Many businessmen had been inspired by the words of black

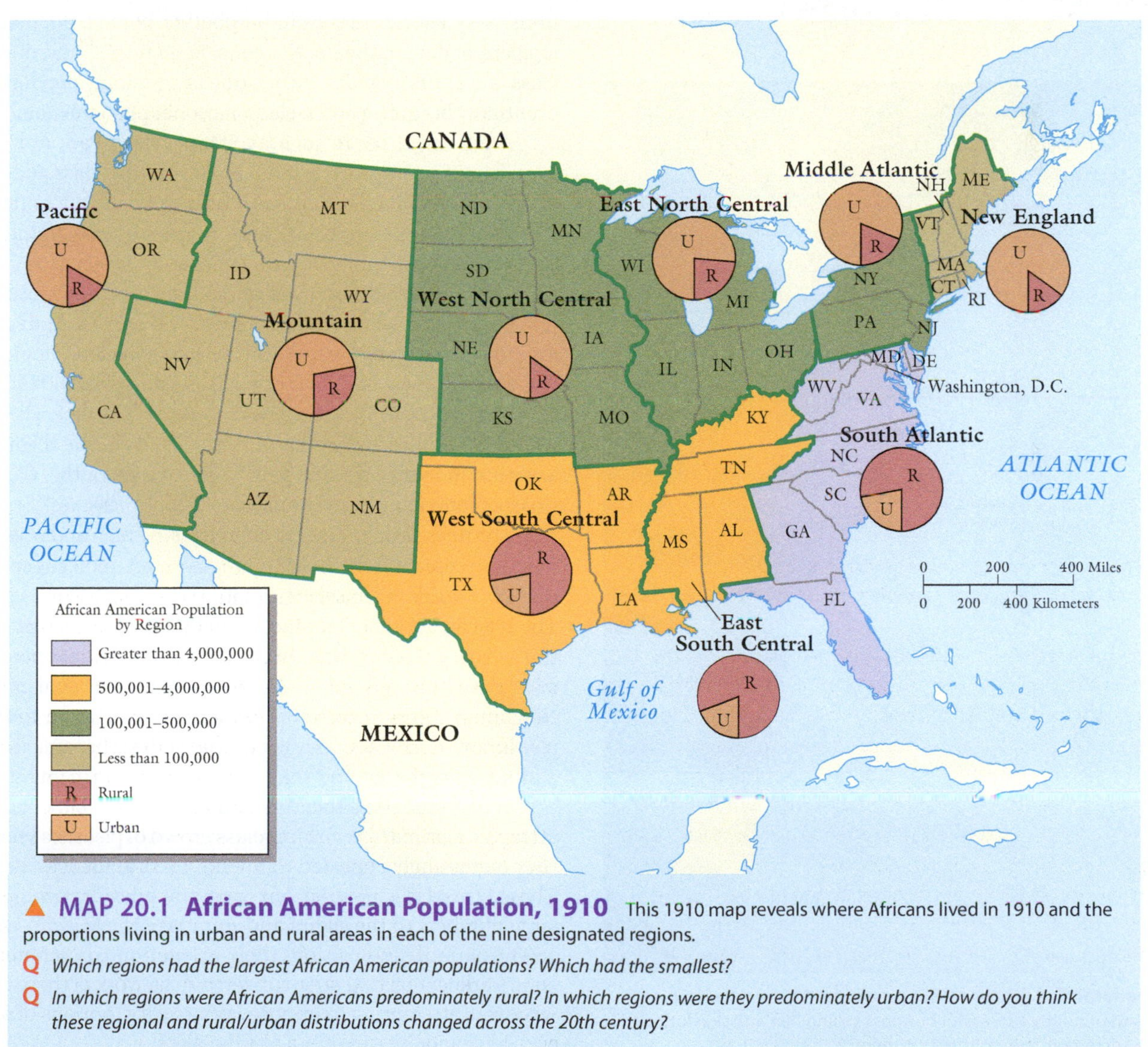

▲ **MAP 20.1 African American Population, 1910** This 1910 map reveals where Africans lived in 1910 and the proportions living in urban and rural areas in each of the nine designated regions.

Q *Which regions had the largest African American populations? Which had the smallest?*

Q *In which regions were African Americans predominately rural? In which regions were they predominately urban? How do you think these regional and rural/urban distributions changed across the 20th century?*

educator Booker T. Washington, and specifically by his argument that blacks should devote themselves to self-help and self-sufficiency. **Madame C.J. Walker** offers one example of a black woman who built a lucrative business from the hair and skin lotions she devised and sold to black customers throughout the country. In many cities, African American real estate agents achieved significant wealth and power.

Nevertheless, entrepreneurial success remained more elusive among African Americans than among immigrants. Black communities were often smaller and poorer than white ethnic ones; economic opportunities were fewer, and black businessmen found it more difficult than their white ethnic counterparts to cultivate customers outside of their core community. Racial prejudice stood as an obstacle to black business success. Meanwhile, blacks were so marginalized in politics that they had little opportunity to gain power or wealth through holding political office or controlling a political machine. Thus, the African American middle class remained smaller and more precarious than did its counterparts in ethnic communities, less able to lead the way toward affluence and assimilation.

Everett Collection/Newscom

20.9 **Madame C. J. Walker** This prominent African American entrepreneur built a successful business selling hair and skin lotions to black customers throughout the country.

20-5 Working-Class and Commercial Culture

What kinds of commercial entertainment took root among urban workers in the late 19th and early 20th century? How did this commercial culture compare to the cultural initiatives undertaken by urban elites?

As much as the white elites and their middle-class allies attempted to impose a genteel order on city life, the city's vitality escaped such bounds. Most workers shared in a new culture of commercial entertainment that included dance halls, music halls, vaudeville theaters, nickelodeons (early storefront movie theaters), amusement parks, and ballparks. Storefront vaudeville theaters, for instance, began to advertise "cheap amusements" to a broad working public in the 1880s. With roots in such antebellum entertainments as minstrelsy, circuses, and dime museums, vaudeville shows offered a variety of miscellaneous short acts for only a dime. A typical show might include sentimental ballads, acrobats, soft-shoe dances, magicians, mind readers, one-act plays, blackface minstrelsy, sports stars from baseball or boxing, puppeteers, jugglers, or dancing bears. Not considered respectable middle-class fare at first, vaudeville became increasingly popular and eventually became a cross-class, national phenomenon.

Amusement parks such as Steeplechase Park at Coney Island, built in 1895, attracted a large working-class audience of men and women while soon also appealing to middle-class youth. Older middle-class commentators found the unchaperoned mingling of young men and women in an urban public space troubling, even shocking, but that loosening of restraint was what made Coney Island so pleasurable and exciting. A new kind of institution in American life, Coney Island was a structured world promoting gaiety and play, with dozens of rides and titillating attractions such as the "Blowhole Theater," whose jets of air blew women's skirts up. "Will she throw her arms around your neck and yell?" asked a sign for the "Cannon Coaster," providing its own answer: "Well, I guess, yes!"

The rides at Coney Island offered young men and women a temporary escape from their working lives, yet ironically enough many of the rides themselves imitated the industrial workplace. The 1884 Switchback Railroad, for instance, an early precursor to the roller coaster, was directly inspired by the operation of gravity-powered coal cars in the shafts of coal mines. New innovations in technology and transportation found a pleasurable mirror at Coney Island and at the other amusement parks around the country that quickly sprang up in imitation.

While vaudeville theaters and amusement parks at first attracted a primarily working-class crowd of pleasure seekers, they increasingly appealed to middle-class audiences as well. These cross-class populations were the ones drawn in such large numbers to the sights and sounds of the Midway at the 1893 Columbia Exposition, their attraction to commercial entertainment on that strip subverting the work of those elites who were attempting to impose "White City" notions of order and demeanor on America's city dwellers.

20.10 **Surf Avenue and Luna Park, Coney Island, 1913** With its 1 million lights, Surf Avenue in Brooklyn, New York, advertised itself as the most brilliantly lit thoroughfare in the world. The avenue included the entrance to Luna Park, one of Coney Island's most popular attractions.

20-5a *Popular Literature and the Movies*

Just as in the antebellum period, urban workers read a wide variety of dime novels (paperbacks that sold for a dime; see Chapter 10) and newspapers. Beginning in the 1860s and 1870s, a flourishing cheap literature reflected the presence of working women in the new industrial order. The popular 1871 story, "Bertha the Sewing Machine Girl; or, Death at the Wheel," inspired many imitators and was staged as a popular play in New York City. Its author, Laura Jane Libbey, published more than 60 novels in the 1880s appealing to a working-class audience. Working women read a variety of romances as well, purchasing dime novels from newsstands and pushcarts in large cities. Featuring wealthy heroines or working women who discovered that by birth they were actually aristocrats, these romantic tales offered fantasies that—in imagination, at least—closed the gulf between the classes. Dime novels appealing to working-class men often told heroic stories of individuals overcoming poverty and other obstacles to become the foremen or owners of factories. Such stories allowed a form of imagined compensation for the loss of independence men actually experienced as poorly paid wage earners.

If literature gestured toward the past, another form of popular entertainment, the movies, pointed toward the future. Movies were well suited to poor city dwellers with little money, little free time, and little command of English. Initially, the movies cost only a nickel. The "nickelodeons" where they were shown were usually converted storefronts in working-class neighborhoods. Movies required little leisure time because at first, they lasted only 15 minutes, on average. Viewers with more time on their hands could stay for a cycle of two or three films (or several cycles). And even non-English-speakers could understand what was happening on the "silent screen." By 1910, approximately 20,000 nickelodeons dotted northern cities (see Table 20.1).

These early "moving pictures" were primitive by today's standards, but they were thrilling just the same. The figures appearing on the screen were "larger than life." Moviegoers could transport themselves to parts of the world they would otherwise never see, encounter people they would otherwise never meet, and watch boxing matches they could otherwise not afford to attend. The darkened theater provided a setting in which secret desires, especially sexual ones, could be explored. As one newspaper breathlessly commented in 1899: "For the first time in the history of the world it is possible to see what a kiss looks like."

No easy generalizations are possible about the content of these early films, more than half of which came from France, Germany, and Italy. American-made films tended toward slapstick comedies, adventure stories, and romances such as those generated by Buster Keaton and Fatty Arbuckle, two silent screen stars (see the *History through Film* feature, p. 563). Producers did not yet shy away, as they soon would, from the lustier or seedier sides of American life. The Hollywood formula of happy endings had yet to be worked out. In fact, the industry, centered in New York City and Fort Lee, New Jersey, had yet to locate itself in sunny southern California. In 1914, the movies' first sex symbol, Theda Bara, debuted in a movie that showed her tempting an upstanding American ambassador into infidelity and ruin. She would be the first of the big screen's vamps, so-called because the characters they portrayed, like vampires, thrived on the blood (and death) of men.

Table 20.1 NICKELODEONS IN MAJOR AMERICAN CITIES, 1910

Cities	Population	Nickelodeons (estimate)	Seating Capacity	Population per Seat
New York	4,338,322	450	150,000	29
Chicago	2,000,000	310	93,000	22
Philadelphia	1,491,082	160	57,000	26
St. Louis	824,000	142	50,410	16
Cleveland	600,000	75	22,500	27
Baltimore	600,000	83	24,900	24
San Francisco	400,000	68	32,400	12
Cincinnati	350,000	75	22,500	16
New Orleans	325,000	28	5,600	58

Source: Garth Jowett, *Film: The Democratic Art* (Boston: Little, Brown, 1976), p. 46.

20-6 The "New Woman" and the Rise of Feminism

How did women's experiences change in the late 19th and early 20th centuries and what new conceptions of womanhood arose as a result?

The appearance of the vamp was one sign of a broad struggle triggered by industrialization and urbanization over the proper place of women. By 1900, 21 percent of all women—middle class and working class—were in the workforce, as opposed to 9.7 percent of women in 1860. After the Civil War, women had moved into nursing and office work, while continuing to be a mainstay in teaching. By the end of the 19th century, middle-class women were also becoming editors, literary agents, and journalists in larger numbers, while also entering the professions of medicine and law in small numbers. Many college women moved to cities to take up work, living in apartments on their own as "bachelor girls."

The increased interest in work was reflected in literature of the period. Louisa May Alcott's 1873 novel *Work* imagined an ideal cross-class, cross-race world of supportive female workers. Elizabeth Stuart Phelps spoke for many discontented middle-class women in her 1877 novel *The Story of Avis*, in which the despairing heroine ultimately gave up being an artist for her marriage. Writer and economist Charlotte Perkins Gilman's 1892 biting novella *The Yellow Wallpaper* spoke powerfully of a new domestic claustrophobia. In that brief work, the unnamed heroine desires to write after the birth of a child but is told by her husband and doctor that she must rest instead and is virtually imprisoned in her home.

Few middle-class observers—men or women—were able to imagine women combining work with family. And yet many women had to do so: The nationally known journalist Jane Croly, for instance, who wrote columns under the name "Jenny June," supported her sick husband and four children as an editor and author during the 1880s before becoming the first female professor of journalism at Rutgers University.

Those who opposed women's new roles sometimes argued that science was on their side. Thus, Harvard Medical School professor Edward H. Clarke asserted in 1873 that intellectual work damaged women's reproductive organs. "A girl could study and learn," he warned, "but she could not do all this and retain uninjured health, and a future secure from neuralgia, uterine disease, hysteria, and other derangements of the nervous system." Clark's "science" is no longer considered credible, but in the nineteenth century it did lend authority to the notion that women should not engage in higher education, professions, and other "manly" pursuits.

Women seeking accurate knowledge about their bodies and reproductive matters often found it hard to obtain. The Comstock Law of 1872 made it illegal to send reproductive literature or devices through the mails on the grounds that they were "obscene." Yet, across the 1880s and 1890s, women increasingly challenged these efforts to keep them ignorant about their sex and to define them as vulnerable creatures who risked physical decline if they crossed into domains defined as male. When bicycle riding became popular in the 1890s, women flocked to the sport to demonstrate their vigor and independence. Frances Willard, leader of the massive Women's Christian Temperance Union, took up bicycling at age 53 because she knew her example would "help women to a wider world."

Women on bicycles styled themselves (and were styled by others) as exemplars of the **"New Woman"**: athletic, self-confident, young, and independent. These women were matriculating at colleges and universities in increasing numbers and then seeking places to deploy their learning in the world of work. They were deeply engaged with sports—golf and tennis in addition to cycling. Some were beginning to live independently from parents and family. They pioneered a new style of dress—skirts, shirtwaists, and men's style jackets and bow ties—to distinguish their aspirations from those of their mothers' generation.

History Through Film Coney Island (1917)

Directed by Roscoe "Fatty" Arbuckle (uncredited).
Starring Roscoe "Fatty" Arbuckle (Fatty), Buster Keaton (Rival), Alice Mann (Love Interest), Agnes Neilson (Fatty's Wife), and Al St. John (Old Friend).

Coney Island was one of the first silent films to feature a classic comedy duo: Roscoe "Fatty" Arbuckle and Buster Keaton. The two met through a mutual friend in New York City in 1917 and quickly struck up a silver-screen partnership. Arbuckle, already a silent movie star, and Keaton, a veteran of the vaudeville circuit, crafted a crude, slapstick tour de force of pratfalls, gags, and fights. It was the beginning of a popular style of comedy on film, the fat/skinny buddy pic, which would be recast in famous teams like Abbot and Costello, Laurel and Hardy, and to an extent, the Three Stooges.

Coney Island opens to images of Luna Park at night: brightly lit towers, luminescent avenues, mechanized roller coasters. Highlighting these modern inventions, the film showcases the technological innovations of the late 19th and early 20th centuries. Coney Island itself—its state-of-the-art rides (The Witching Waves, Chutes), its street vendors hawking ice cream and candy, its carnival-like, consumer-driven atmosphere—is one of the most prominent "characters" in the film. It is cast as having irresistible allure. Like the Midway Plaisance and in contrast to the White City, Coney Island sought to fill urban dwellers' leisure time with adventure and fun rather than with moral improvement.

At the beginning of the film, Buster Keaton's character watches a parade with his girlfriend (Alice Mann) before the two decide to enter Luna Park. When Keaton comes up short on the entry fee, his lady friend drops him for a man who has the admission cash (Al St. John). Meanwhile, Fatty sits, bored, on the beach with his dowdy wife, but he eventually sneaks away from her after burying himself in the sand to hide. For the rest of the film, Keaton, Arbuckle, and St. John vie for Mann's attention, punching and pranking each other in the process. Keaton eventually wins back Mann's affection, and Fatty and St. John swear off women altogether, until they spy another young lady and run after her.

The raucous style of physical comedy that dominates this film offers us a glimpse of the values then coursing their way through working-class commercial culture. The cinematic displays of informal association between men and women, of adventure and sexuality, had been inspired by behaviors that many young urban dwellers, including sizable numbers of immigrants, had themselves embraced. The film is notable, too, for the breadth of its attack on social conventions and authority figures. In the movie, no relationship is sacred (the primary narrative follows Fatty's attempts to cheat on his wife), no authority figure is powerful (the inadequate and often thickly mustachioed Keystone Kops end up locked in jail, knocked out cold), and no gender line is firm (Fatty cross-dresses to disguise himself from his wife). While the assault on authority in the movie is presented in a hilarious style, it carries a more serious message; namely, that working-class individuals were going to make their own way in the world. It is precisely these declarations of cultural independence that made urban elites and their middle-class allies so anxious about their ability to impose their own sense of order and morality on city life.

By the 1920s, executives in the movie industry had taken steps to expunge Arbuckle-style antics from their films, and to make these art forms more suitable for refined middle-class audiences. Once decorum in the movies became the rule of the day, lords of cinematic anarchy, like Arbuckle, lost their footing. In fact, Arbuckle's career crashed in the twenties. In 1921, actress Virginia Rappe died four days after attending a bootleg liquor party at Fatty's San Francisco apartment. Arbuckle was accused of rape and was tried three times for manslaughter. Though eventually acquitted, his career as an actor never recovered. He died in 1933 of a heart attack at age 46. Buster Keaton, however, went on to become a successful actor, sharing the Hollywood limelight with the likes of Charlie Chaplin. ■

Courtesy of Everett Collection

20.11 Fatty Arbuckle (center) getting clobbered by Buster Keaton (right) in a scene from *Coney Island*. Their love interest, played by Alice Mann, looks on.

Bettmann/Corbis

20.12 **Theda Bara as Cleopatra (1917)** Bara was the first movie actress to gain fame for her roles as a "vamp"—a woman whose irresistible sexual charm led men to ruin.

Q *How did the American public react to the frank expressions of sexual allure and danger that were becoming a prominent feature of American cinema, evident in this still from* Cleopatra *and in another 1917 movie,* Coney Island, *discussed on the previous page?*

Although most New Women were middle class, historians now recognize that some emerged from the ranks of the working class. By the early years of the twentieth century, these working-class New Women were beginning to experiment with more open expressions of sexuality. Entering the labor force in large numbers, these women were mixing at workplaces, in loosely supervised ways, with men their own age. The associations between young men and women that sprang up at work carried over into leisure. Young people of both sexes flocked to the dance halls that were opening in every major city. They rejected the stiff formality of earlier ballroom dances such as the cotillion or the waltz for the freedom and intimacy of newer forms, such as the foxtrot, tango, and bunny-hug. They went to movies and amusement parks together, and they engaged, far more than their parents had, in premarital sex. It is estimated that the proportion of women having sex before marriage rose from 10 to 25 percent in the generation that was coming of age between 1910 and 1920.

This movement toward sexual freedom expressed yet again women's dissatisfaction with restrictions that had been imposed on them by earlier generations. Amidst the ferment generated by these multiple challenges to traditional gender roles, some women began to make the case for full female freedom and equality. Charlotte Perkins Gilman called for the release of women from domestic chores through the collectivization of housekeeping. Social activist Margaret Sanger insisted in her lectures on birth control that women should be free to enjoy sexual relations without having to worry about unwanted motherhood. The anarchist Emma Goldman denounced marriage as a kind of prostitution and embraced the ideal of "free love"—love unburdened by contractual commitment. Alice Paul, founder of the National Women's Party, brought a new militancy to the campaign for woman suffrage (see Chapter 21).

These women were among the first to use the term **feminism** to describe their desire for complete equality with men. Some of them came together in Greenwich Village, a community of radical artists and writers in lower Manhattan, where they found a supportive environment in which to express and live by their feminist ideals. Crystal Eastman, a leader of the feminist **Greenwich Village** group called Heterodoxy, defined the feminist challenge as "how to arrange the world so that women can be human beings, with a chance to exercise their infinitely varied gifts in infinitely varied ways, instead of being destined by the accident of their sex to one field of activity."

The movement for sexual and gender equality aroused considerable anxiety. Parents worried about the promiscuity of their children. Conservatives were certain that sexual assertiveness among women would transform American cities into dens of iniquity. Vice commissions sprang up in every major city to clamp down on prostitution, drunkenness, and pornography. The campaign for prohibition—a ban on the sale of alcoholic beverages—gathered steam. Movie theater owners were pressured into excluding "indecent" films from their screens. Many believed lurid tales of international vice lords scouring foreign lands for innocent girls who could be delivered to American brothel owners. This "white slave trade" inspired passage of the 1910 Mann Act, which made the transportation of women across state lines for immoral purposes a federal crime (see Chapter 21).

Nor did it escape the attention of conservatives that Greenwich Village was home not only to the exponents of "free love" but also to advocates of class warfare. William "Big Bill" Haywood, leader of a newly formed radical labor organization, the Industrial Workers of the World (IWW) (see Chapter 21), frequented Greenwich Village. So, too, did IWW organizer and Heterodoxy member Elizabeth Gurley Flynn. Flynn's lover, Carlo Tresca, was an IWW theoretician. When Greenwich Village radicals began publishing an avant-garde artistic journal in 1914, they called it *The Masses;* its editor was Max Eastman, the brother of Crystal. This convergence of labor and feminist militancy intensified conservative feeling that the nation had strayed too far from its roots.

20-7 Reimagining American Nationality

Q *How did Israel Zangwill and Randolph Bourne reimagine American nationality?*

The large presence of immigrants in America also alarmed conservatives. Among the native-born middle and upper classes, the prevailing view was that immigrants should shed their ethnic backgrounds and become thoroughly American in speech, dress, and culture and in their commitment to the principles of liberty and democracy. A refusal or inability to do so was increasingly interpreted by these conservative sectors of the population as marking the inferiority of the immigrants in question or their unfitness for life in America. Such interpretations of immigrant behavior generated support for coercive Americanization campaigns and for legislation that would extend the ban on "undesirable" immigrant groups from East Asians to eastern and southern Europeans, West Asians, and Africans. In 1907, Congress established the Dillingham Commission to collect information on every immigrant group in America with an eye toward making a factual case for closing America's immigrant gates.

As these pressures mounted, others began to fight back, some insisting that all immigrants had the capacity to become fully American, others declaring that America would be a better place if it made room for at least some of the diversity that immigrants had brought to American culture. In 1908, Israel Zangwill, an Anglo-Jewish writer, debuted his play, *The Melting-Pot*, on Broadway. The play's theme was that all immigrants, even those originating from eastern Europe, could become the most successful and best of Americans. The play's protagonist, David Quixano, belongs to a Russian Jewish family that has been killed in Russian anti-Jewish riots. David alone survives and flees to New York City, where he is taken in by his uncle and his uncle's mother, both older souls who will never successfully adapt to America. But David himself has the youth, drive, and desire to succeed. A talented musician, he seizes the opportunity that America gives him, writes a successful American symphony, marries the Gentile girl of his dreams, and becomes a proud American.

20.13 **Emma Goldman, Anarchist and Feminist** Goldman was a radical who campaigned to abolish capitalism, marriage, and other practices that she regarded as inimical to human freedom.

Library of Congress Prints & Photographs Division Washington, DC

20.14 ***The Melting Pot*** This program cover of a 1916 production of Zangwill's play visually recreates the process that unfolds in the drama itself: A swirl of diverse immigrants from many parts of the world is thrown into one great pot and fused into a strong, freedom-loving people.

Q *Why is the image of a melting pot as mechanism through which American nationality was to be forged much less appealing today than in the early years of the twentieth century?*

It mattered greatly to Zangwill, the playwright, that David's success grew out of his willingness to abandon his ethnic and religious past and to embrace America. Zangwill imagined an America in which all immigrants, or at least all immigrants from Europe, would succeed in similar ways, leaving behind their Old World cultures (and grievances) and melting together to form a new and vigorous nationality. The climactic moment in the play comes when Zangwill puts these words in David's mouth: "America is God's Crucible, the great Melting-Pot where all the races of Europe are melting and re-forming!" From this time forward, the **melting pot** became a popular metaphor for how the diverse populations of America might become one people.

Zangwill attracted prominent reform figures to his point of view. President Theodore Roosevelt wrote Zangwill in 1908, after watching a performance of *The Melting-Pot:* "I do not know when I have seen a play that stirred me as much." And President Woodrow Wilson declared in 1915 that America was "the only country in the world" that experiences a "constant and repeated rebirth." Wilson credited this rebirth to immigrants and to the contributions they had made to the "glory and majesty of a great country."

Other thinkers were discomfited by the kind of melting pot that Zangwill had advocated. One of them was the native-born intellectual Randolph Bourne. Bourne located America's uniqueness in the encounters that occurred between immigrant cultures on the one hand and the nation's atmosphere of freedom and democracy on the other. This atmosphere permitted individuals from all kinds of groups, immigrant and native-born, both to preserve their own cultures and to partake of others. Bourne believed that immigrants delighted in the process of cultural exchange that America's environment of freedom encouraged. He celebrated such exchanges, and the variety of identities that arose from

What They Said

Should America Be a Melting Pot?

As the immigrant presence became prominent in America in the early 20th century, thinkers and artists began to write about the likely effect of that presence on American culture. This feature deepens this textbook's engagement with two such thinkers, Israel Zangwill and Randolph Bourne. Zangwill, an Anglo-Jewish writer who spent considerable time in the United States, debuted his play, *The Melting-Pot* in New York in 1908. The play was the first to popularize the idea of America as melting pot, as a society in which many immigrant peoples were fused into one, the resulting alloy being stronger than any of the individual cultures thrown into the mix. Bourne was a native-born Protestant American whose family had been in the United States for generations. He rejected the pursuit of a "homogeneous Americanism," whether imposed by America's powerful "Anglo-Saxons" or generated in the heat of Zangwill's melting pot. Instead, Bourne called for a "cosmopolitan America" in which ethnic groups would share their cultures with each other without losing their distinctiveness.

Israel Zangwill, *The Melting-Pot* (1908)

In the passages that follow, Zangwill's main protagonist, David Quixano, a Russian Jewish immigrant, celebrates the melting pot as the key to American greatness.

Oh, I love going to Ellis Island to watch the ships coming in from Europe, and to think that all those weary, sea-tossed wanderers are feeling what I felt when America first stretched out her great mother-hand to me… .

America is God's Crucible, the great Melting-Pot where all the races of Europe are melting and re-forming! Here you stand, good folk, think I, when I see them at Ellis Island, here you stand … in your fifty groups, with your fifty languages and histories, and your fifty blood hatreds and rivalries. But you won't be long like that, brothers, for these are the fires of God you've come to—these are the fires of God. A fig for your feuds and vendettas! Germans and Frenchmen, Irishmen and Englishmen, Jews and Russians—into the Crucible with you all! God is making the American… .

[T]he real American has not yet arrived. He is only in the Crucible, I tell you—he will be the fusion of all races, perhaps the coming superman."

Randolph S. Bourne, "Trans-National America," *The Atlantic Monthly* (1916)

The foreign cultures have not been melted down or run together, made into some homogeneous Americanism, but have remained distinct but cooperating for the greater glory and benefit, not only of themselves but of all the native 'Americanism' around them… . It is for the American of the younger generation to accept this cosmopolitanism, and carry it along with self-conscious and fruitful purpose… .

[I]t is not uncommon for the eager Anglo-Saxon who goes to a vivid American university to-day to find his true friends not among his own race but among the acclimatized German or Austrian, the acclimatized Jew, the acclimatized Scandinavian or Italian. In them he finds the cosmopolitan note… . These friends are oblivious to the repressions of that tight little society in which he so provincially grew up. He has a pleasurable sense of liberation from the stale and familiar attitudes of those whose ingrowing culture has scarcely created anything vital for America of to-day… .

His new friends have gone through a similar evolution. America has burned most of the baser metal also from them. Meeting now with this common American background, all of them may yet retain that distinctiveness of their native cultures and their national spiritual slants. They are more valuable and interesting to each other for being different, yet the difference could not be creative were it not for this new cosmopolitan outlook which America has given and which they all equally possess.

Q *What does Zangwill mean when he describes America as "God's Crucible," and how does it differ from Bourne's vision of "cosmopolitanism?"*

Q *When Bourne refers to the "eager Anglo-Saxon" attending a "vivid American university," he is writing about his own experience growing up in a sheltered community in New Jersey and then entering Columbia University. What do you think of Bourne's decision to use his college experience as the foundation on which to theorize a new conception of American nationality?*

Q *Why are nonwhite groups absent from Zangwill's imagining of the melting pot and from Bourne's depiction of a cosmopolitan America?*

Sources: (top) Israel Zangwill, *The Melting-Pot*, 1908; (bottom) Randolph S. Bourne, "Trans-National America," The *Atlantic Monthly* CXVIII (1916), 90, 93–94.

them, as essential to the American ideal. Through this process of exchange, Bourne argued, individuals would share more and more of their cultures with each other and would, as a result, learn to live in harmony. These exchanges, too, would encourage immigrants to believe that they "may have a hand in the destiny of America," thereby deepening their American patriotism. Such integration, cooperation, and patriotism would create a nationality superior, Bourne wrote, to any emerging from a "narrow 'Americanism' or forced chauvinism," or indeed from the kind of fusion imagined by Zangwill and other melting pot enthusiasts.

For Bourne, melting all Americans into one shape would yield a society of stifling homogeneity. Bourne celebrated variety and believed that America's atmosphere of freedom and commitment to democracy would allow such variety to flourish as it had in few other countries. **Cosmopolitanism** was the word he used to describe his vision of American nationality.

Zangwill and Bourne both failed to grapple sufficiently with race and with the discrimination that America imposed on groups marked as racially different, especially African Americans. Their writings did not address the perniciousness of Jim Crow, nor did they acknowledge the reality of Chinese and Japanese exclusion. Nevertheless, these thinkers' reckoning with the immigrant presence in America was innovative. They were among the first to articulate in public forums arguments that the immigrants could be a positive and dynamic force in American culture. And Bourne was one of the first to celebrate diversity and cosmopolitanism as values to be promoted in American life.

Like feminism, cosmopolitanism generated anxiety in large stretches of America, especially in farming communities and small towns, and in the South, where industrialization and urbanization were proceeding at a slower rate than elsewhere. To these Americans, it seemed as though the cultures that immigrants were creating in cities were taking the nation too far from its Anglo-Saxon and Protestant roots.

The urban elites who exercised considerable cultural power in America were also troubled by the immigrant masses and the urban cultures they were creating. Many of their members, long frustrated by the apparent immigrant preference for movies, amusement parks, and saloons over the "civilizing forces" of museums, libraries, and lectures, were not predisposed to find virtue in immigrant cultures. Nevertheless, change was beginning to occur in these elite circles, as the positive reactions of Presidents Roosevelt and Wilson to Zangwill's depiction of America as a melting pot indicate. Both Roosevelt and Wilson had begun to understand that American nationality might be strengthened by the infusion into it of new peoples and new cultures, and that the resulting hybridity might be superior to an imagined Anglo-Saxon purity. Jane Addams, an important urban reformer who increasingly traveled in Roosevelt's and Wilson's political circles, ventured beyond where these two presidents were willing to go by acknowledging the importance of "immigrant gifts"—aspects of immigrant cultures that should be preserved even as immigrants assimilated into an American nationality. Addams's concession to diversity was a small one, and she would continue to insist, across several decades of work with immigrants (see Chapter 21), on the importance of immigrant assimilation to American middle-class values and norms. Nevertheless, Addams's gesture revealed how much the immigrant presence was beginning to influence urban elites.

Conclusion

By 1920, America's urban population outstripped its rural population for the first time in the country's history. Despite a political system that was chronically vulnerable to corruption, urban leaders found ways to build housing and infrastructure that enabled cities to address the demands placed on them by rapid growth. Through the invention of skyscrapers, elevators, electrified railroad and trolley lines, and sophisticated water systems, cities became centers of technological innovation. Urban elites wanted to make their cities centers of culture, too, and embarked on grand projects of architectural and landscape renovation to disseminate culture, civilization, and refinement through the ranks of the urban masses.

The gap between the elites and their cultural projects on the one hand and the lives of the urban poor on the other remained large, however. Millions of city dwellers, many of them foreign born, suffered from job and income insecurity. Groups defined as racially different—African Americans, Chinese and Japanese immigrants, and even groups of southern and eastern European immigrants—were held back by prejudice as well. Every group could point to examples of economic success within its ranks, and, by the second decade of the 20th century, solid middle classes had emerged within them. Yet, majorities remained working class, coming up short in their quest for equality and opportunity in America.

If economic success remained elusive, the urban masses nevertheless injected creativity and dynamism into urban life. The culture emerging out of dance halls, amusement parks, and nickelodeons prized adventure rather than refinement, liberty rather than order, and diversity rather than conformity. Many urban dwellers thrived in this new environment. Working-class women discovered liberties in dress, employment, dating, and sex that they had not known and propelled feminism into existence. Social critics began to imagine forms of American nationality that not only put immigrants on the same footing as the native born, but also praised diversity as a central part of the American experience. More and more Americans looked to cities as centers of innovation and modernity.

This association of the cities with newness and difference only increased the cultural distance between them and the countryside. Within the cities, the popular culture of the immigrant masses also troubled urban elites and their middle-class allies. These cultural tensions had already begun to spill over into politics, shaping a new reform movement called progressivism.

Review

1. In what ways did urban elites seek to shape the physical and cultural character of their cities in the years between 1890 and 1910?
2. From which parts of the world did immigrants come in the years between 1880 and 1920? What caused them to migrate? What were their patterns of work and residence in the United States?
3. In what ways did immigrants seek economic success and social mobility? How successful were they in their efforts?
4. What were the similarities and differences between the African American and immigrant experiences in the early 20th century?
5. What kinds of commercial entertainment took root among urban workers in the late 19th and early 20th centuries? How did this commercial culture compare to the cultural initiatives undertaken by urban elites?
6. How did women's experiences change in the late 19th and early 20th centuries and what new conceptions of womanhood arose as a result?
7. How did Israel Zangwill and Randolph Bourne reimagine American nationality?

Critical Thinking

1. Which group had a greater influence on urban life in the early 20th century: urban elites or immigrant masses?
2. Which philosophy, do you think, offered the best recipe for incorporating immigrants into American society in the early 20th century: melting-pot assimilation, cosmopolitanism, or something else?

Identifications

Review your understanding of the following key terms, people, and events for this chapter (terms in bold in text are included in the Glossary).

nickelodeons, p. 545
walking cities, p. 546
Frederick Law Olmsted, p. 547
White City, p. 549
City Beautiful movement, p. 550
Midway Plaisance, p. 550
Triangle Shirtwaist Company, p. 554
political machines, p. 557
Al Capone, p. 557
Madame C.J. Walker, p. 560
"New Woman," p. 562
feminism, p. 564
Greenwich Village, p. 565
melting pot, p. 566
cosmopolitanism, p. 568

Suggested Readings

On the changes in American cities in the late 19th and early 20th centuries, see **Jon C. Teaford**, ***The Unheralded Triumph: City Government in America, 1870–1900*** (1984) and **Julia Guarneri**, ***Newspaper Metropolis: City Papers and the Making of Modern America*** (2017). On Chicago (in addition to Guarneri), see **William Cronon**, ***Nature's Metropolis: Chicago and the Great West*** (1991), and **Daniel Bluestone**, ***Constructing Chicago*** (1991). On New York, see **Roy Rosenzweig and Elizabeth Blackmar**, ***The Park and the People: A History of Central Park*** (1991). On the changing character of American elites during this time, see **Steve Fraser and Gary Gerstle, eds.**, ***Ruling America: Wealth and Power in a Democracy*** (2005) and **David Huyssen**, ***Progressive Inequality: Rich and Poor in New York, 1890–1920*** (2014). For an excellent overview of immigration, consult **Roger Daniels**, ***Coming to America: A History of Immigration and Ethnicity in American Life*** (2002) and **John Bodnar**, ***The Transplanted: A History of Immigration*** (1985). For an introduction to the experiences of Chinese, Japanese, and other non-European immigrants, see **Erika Lee and Judy Yung**, ***Angel Island: Immigrant Gateway to America*** (2010). For an excellent study of the early movement toward immigration restriction, see **Katherine Benton-Cohen**, ***Inventing the Immigration Problem: The Dillingham Commission and its Legacy*** (2018).

Steven P. Erie, ***Rainbow's End: Irish Americans and the Dilemmas of Urban Machine Politics, 1840–1945*** (1988), insightfully examines the benefits and costs of big city machines. **John Hope Franklin and Evelyn Brooks Higginbotham**, ***From Slavery to Freedom: A History of African Americans***, 9th ed. (2011), offers a comprehensive account of African American life, while an important account of black female workers can be found in **Jacqueline Jones**, ***Labor of Love, Labor of Sorrow: Black Women, Work and the Family from Slavery to the Present*** (1985). On the rise of mass culture, see **David Nasaw**, ***Going Out: The Rise and Fall of Public Amusements*** (1993). On the new woman and feminism, consult **Nancy F. Cott**, ***The Grounding of Modern Feminism*** (1987), and **Christine Stansell**, ***American Moderns: Bohemian New York and the Creation of a New Century*** (2000). For an introduction to debates about American nationality in which Zangwill and Bourne took part, see **Jonathan M. Hansen**, ***The Lost Promise of Patriotism: Debating American Identity, 1890–1920*** (2003).

21 Progressivism, 1900–1917

21.1 **"A New Captain in the District"** This cartoon depicts newly elected president Woodrow Wilson as a police captain who is determined to clean up Washington politics and regulate "crooked business." It illustrates a key belief shared by Wilson, Theodore Roosevelt, and most other progressives: An activist government was society's best hope for solving the nation's political and economic problems.

PROGRESSIVISM was a reform movement that took its name from individuals who left the Republican Party in 1912 to join Theodore Roosevelt's new party, the Progressive Party. The term *progressive,* however, refers to a much larger and more varied group of reformers than those who gathered around Roosevelt in 1912.

As early as 1900, these reformers had set out to cleanse and reinvigorate an America whose politics and society they considered in decline. Progressives wanted to rid politics of corruption, tame the power of corporations, and in the process inject more liberty into American life. They fought against prostitution, gambling, drinking, and other forms of vice. They first appeared in municipal politics, organizing movements to oust crooked mayors and to break up local gas or streetcar monopolies. They carried their fights to the states and finally to the nation. Two presidents, Theodore Roosevelt and Woodrow Wilson, placed themselves at the head of this movement.

Progressivism was popular among a variety of groups who brought to the movement distinct, and often conflicting, aims. On one issue, however, most progressives agreed: the need for an activist government to right political, economic, and social wrongs. Some progressives wanted government to become active only long enough to clean up the political process, root out vice, upgrade the electorate, and break up monopolies. These problems were so difficult to solve that many other progressives endorsed the notion of a permanently active government—with the power to tax income, regulate industry, protect consumers from fraud, empower workers, safeguard the environment, and provide social welfare. Many progressives, in other words, came to see the federal government as the institution best equipped to solve social problems.

Such positive attitudes toward government power marked an important change in American politics. Americans had long been suspicious of centralized government, viewing it as the enemy of liberty. The Populists had broken with that view (see Chapter 19), but they had been defeated. The progressives had to build a new case for strong government as the protector of liberty and equality. ■

21-1 Where Reform Incubated

Q *What were the similarities among the various groups spearheading reform? What were the differences?*

Progressivism emerged in the early years of the 20th century from the activities of multiple groups. Four such groups were of particular importance: young, alienated middle-class Protestants; journalists who took the name "muckrakers"; women active in the settlement house movement; and an assortment of socialists.

21-1a *Young Protestants*

Progressivism emerged first and most strongly among young, mainly Protestant, middle-class Americans who felt alienated from their society. Many had been raised in Protestant homes in which religious conviction had often been a spur to social action. They were expected to become ministers or missionaries or to serve their church in some other way. They had abandoned this path, but they never lost their zeal for righting moral wrongs and for uplifting the human spirit. They were distressed by the immorality and corruption in American politics and by the gap that separated rich from poor.

Other Protestant reformers retained their faith. This was true of William Jennings Bryan, the former Populist leader who became an ardent progressive and evangelical. Throughout his political career, Bryan insisted that Christian piety and American democracy were integrally related. Billy Sunday, a former major league baseball player who became the most theatrical evangelical preacher of his day, elevated opposition to saloons and the "liquor trust" into a righteous crusade. And Walter Rauschenbusch led a movement known as the Social Gospel, which emphasized the duty of Christians to work for the social good.

21-1b *Muckrakers*

Many disaffected Protestants found a focus for their alienation in the work of investigative journalists known as **muckrakers**, so-called because of their determination to dredge up the "muck" saturating important institutions of American life. Ida Tarbell revealed the shady practices by which John D. Rockefeller had transformed his Standard Oil Company into a monopoly. Lincoln Steffens unraveled the webs of bribery and corruption that were strangling local governments in the nation's cities. George Kibbe Turner documented the extent of prostitution and family disintegration in the ethnic ghettos of those cities. These muckrakers wanted to shock the public into recognizing the shameful state of political, economic, and social affairs and to prompt "the people" to take action.

The muckrakers were riding a wave of expanded magazine circulation. Cheap, 10-cent periodicals such as *McClure's Magazine* and *Ladies' Home Journal*, with circulations of 400,000 to 1 million, were displacing genteel and relatively expensive 35-cent publications such as *Harper's* and *The Atlantic Monthly*. The expanded readership (see Figure 21.1) brought journalists considerably more money and prestige and attracted many talented and ambitious men and women to the profession. Wider circulation also made magazine publishers more receptive to stories that might appeal to their expanded readership.

A large middle class, uneasy about the state of American society, applauded the muckrakers for exposing America's problems and began trumpeting the virtues of reform. Members of this class pressured city and state governments to send crooked government officials to jail and to stamp out the sources of corruption and vice. Between 1902 and 1916, more than 100 cities launched investigations of the prostitution trade. The federal government, meanwhile, began to raise questions about "the trusts"—large corporations that had amassed overwhelming economic power. Progressivism began to crystallize into a political movement centered on the abuses the muckrakers had exposed.

CHRONOLOGY

1889	Hull House established
1890–1904	All ex-Confederate states pass laws designed to disfranchise black voters • Virtually all states adopt the Australian (secret) ballot
1900	La Follette elected governor of Wisconsin • City commission plan introduced in Galveston, Texas
1901–1914	More than 1,000 African Americans lynched
1901	Johnson elected reform mayor of Cleveland • McKinley assassinated; Roosevelt becomes president
1902	Direct primary introduced in Mississippi • Initiative and referendum introduced in Oregon • Roosevelt sides with workers in coal strike
1903	*McClure's Magazine* publishes Standard Oil exposé • Federal court dissolves Northern Securities Company
1904	Roosevelt defeats Alton B. Parker for presidency
1905	National Forest Service established
1906	La Follette elected to U.S. Senate • Congress passes Hepburn Act • Upton Sinclair publishes *The Jungle* • Congress passes Pure Food and Drug Act and Meat Inspection Act
1908	Taft defeats Bryan for presidency
1909	Congress passes Payne–Aldrich Tariff Act
1910	Ballinger–Pinchot controversy • NAACP founded • Wilson elected governor of New Jersey
1911	National Urban League founded • City manager plan introduced in Sumter, South Carolina • Wisconsin Industrial Commission established • Frederick Winslow Taylor publishes *The Principles of Scientific Management*
1912	Roosevelt forms Progressive Party • Wilson defeats Roosevelt, Taft, and Debs for presidency
1913	Sixteenth (federal income tax) and Seventeenth (direct election of U.S. senators) Amendments ratified • Congress passes Underwood-Simmons Tariff • Congress establishes Federal Reserve
1914	Congress establishes Federal Trade Commission • Congress passes Clayton Antitrust Act
1916	Louis Brandeis appointed to Supreme Court • Kern–McGillicuddy Act, Keating–Owen Act, and Adamson Act passed • National Park Service formed • National Women's Party founded
1919	Eighteenth Amendment (prohibition) ratified
1920	Nineteenth Amendment (woman suffrage) ratified

21-1c *Settlement Houses and Clubwomen*

Progressivism also began to take shape in settlement houses, urban institutions set up by middle-class, largely Protestant women to help the urban poor cope with the harsh conditions

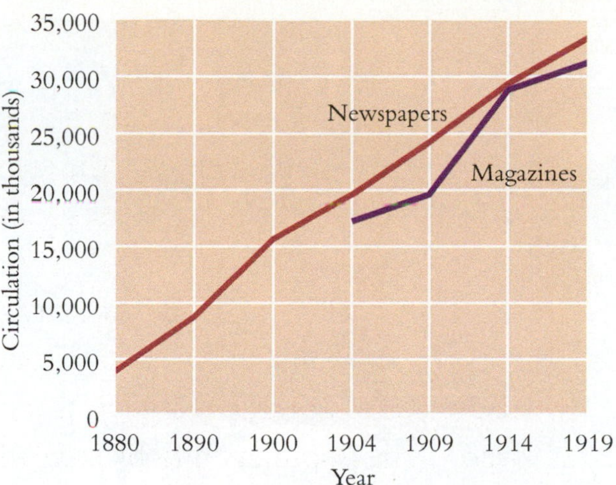

Figure 21.1 **Circulation of Daily Newspapers and Magazines, 1880–1919**

Source: Data from *Historical Statistics of the United States, Colonial Times to 1970* (White Plains, NY: Kraus International, 1989).

of city life. Jane Addams and Ellen Gates Starr established the nation's first settlement house in Chicago in 1889 when they bought a decaying mansion that had once been the country home of a prominent Chicagoan, Charles J. Hull. By 1889, **Hull House** stood amidst factories, churches, saloons, and tenements inhabited by poor, largely foreign-born working-class families.

Addams moved into the building and demanded others who worked there do the same. She, and the women such as Florence Kelley and Julia Lathrop who assisted her, set up a nursery for the children of working mothers, a penny savings bank, an employment bureau, a baby clinic, a neighborhood playground, and social clubs. Determined to minister to cultural as well as economic needs, Hull House sponsored an orchestra, reading groups, and a lecture series. Members of Chicago's widening circle of reform-minded intellectuals, artists, and politicians contributed their energies to the enterprise. John Dewey taught philosophy, and Frank Lloyd Wright lectured on architecture. Clarence Darrow, the workingman's lawyer, and Henry Demarest Lloyd, Chicago's radical muckraker, spent considerable time at Hull House. In 1893, Illinois governor John P. Altgeld named Hull House's Florence Kelley as the state's chief factory inspector. Her investigations led to Illinois's first factory law, which prohibited child labor, limited the employment of women to eight hours a day, and authorized the state to hire inspectors to enforce the law.

Julia Lathrop used her appointment to the State Board of Charities to agitate for improvements in the care of the poor, the handicapped, and the delinquent. With Edith Abbott and Sophonisba Breckinridge, she established the Department of Social Research at the University of Chicago (which would evolve into the nation's first school of social work). Alice Hamilton, who had overcome gender discrimination to become a doctor, pioneered in the field of public health.

Thousands of women across the country were inspired to build their own settlement houses on the Hull House model. Eventually more than 400 settlement houses would open

Picture History/Newscom

21.2 **Ida M. Tarbell, Muckraker** Tarbell rose to national prominence as a result of her investigative reporting on John D. Rockefeller and the Standard Oil Company, published in *McClure's Magazine* in 1903.

nationwide. By 1910, Jane Addams had become one of the nation's most famous women. She and other settlement house workers played a critical role in fashioning the progressive agenda and in drafting pieces of progressive legislation.

Settlement house workers were more sympathetic toward the poor, the illiterate, and the downtrodden than the muckrakers were. Although she disapproved of machine politics, Jane Addams saw firsthand the benefits that machine politicians delivered to their constituents. She respected the cultural inheritance of the immigrants and admired their resourcefulness. Although she wanted them to become Americans, she encouraged them to integrate their "immigrant gifts" into their new identities. Those attitudes were more liberal than those of other reformers, who considered many immigrants to be culturally, even racially, inferior.

But there were limits even to Addams's sympathy for the immigrants. She disapproved of the new working-class entertainments that gave adolescents extensive and unregulated opportunities for intimate association. She was troubled by the emerging sexual revolution (see Chapter 20), which she worried would lead many more poor women into prostitution. And she critiqued male working-class drinking habits, which she saw as encouraging alcoholism, draining away meager family resources, and increasing tensions between these men and their wives. Addams and other settlement house workers joined hands with the Women's Christian Temperance Union (245,000 members strong by 1911) and the Anti-Saloon League to push for legislation to shut down the saloons. By 1916, this anti-drinking coalition had won prohibition of the sale and manufacture of alcoholic beverages in 16 states. In 1919, its crowning achievement was the Eighteenth Amendment to the U.S. Constitution, making prohibition the law of the land (see Chapter 23).

In depicting alcohol and saloons as unmitigated evils, the prohibition movement ignored the larger role that saloons played in ethnic, working-class communities. On Chicago's South Side, for example, saloons provided food, meeting space for fraternal organizations, and camaraderie to men longing to speak in their native tongue. Saloonkeepers sometimes functioned as informal bankers, cashing checks and making small loans. Not surprisingly, many immigrants shunned the prohibition movement.

Settlement house workers comprised one part of a nationwide network of female reformers. Hundreds of thousands of women belonged to local women's clubs that sought to improve schools, build libraries and playgrounds, expand educational and vocational opportunities for girls, and secure fire and sanitation codes for tenement houses. In so doing, they made traditional female concerns—the nurturing and education of children, the care of the home—questions of public policy.

Wallace Kirkland//Time Life Pictures/Getty Images

21.3 **Jane Addams** The founder of the settlement house movement, Addams was the most famous female reformer of the Progressive Era. This photograph depicts her late in her career, sitting with a girl in the Hull House nursery school.

Q *What did Jane Addams do to support working mothers and what concerned her about the sexual revolution?*

Library of Congress Prints and Photographs Division [LC-USZ62-137950]

21.4 **Florence Kelley** A leading progressive reformer, member of Hull House, and Illinois's first chief factory inspector.

These women's clubs had first appeared in the 1860s and 1870s, when women writers and journalists in New York City, excluded on account of their gender from male press clubs, formed the club Sorosis (a name chosen to suggest sisterhood). Distinct from antebellum moral reform societies, clubs like Sorosis were secular and had a variety of different purposes, from intellectual discussion to civic reform. By the turn of the 20th century, this network was vast and increasingly drawn to the efforts of Jane Addams and other female reformers to break down the barriers that had so rigidly excluded women from the public sphere.

Frustration with such sex discrimination had risen along with the educational advancement of women in the late 19th century. The number of women enrolled in higher education institutions had increased a remarkable twelvefold between 1870 and 1900. In the 1860s and after, new public universities in the Midwest and West had opened their doors to women; simultaneously, women's colleges, beginning with the founding of Vassar in 1865, had begun to appear throughout the Northeast. Women seized upon the new educational opportunities offered them; by 1910, they constituted nearly 40 percent of all students enrolled in colleges and universities (see Table 21.1).

Yet these women discovered that their educational achievements counted for little in the professions and the public sphere, where men seemed intent on maintaining their dominance. Women had broken into medical training as early as 1849 with the admission of Elizabeth Blackwell to Geneva Medical College in upstate New York. But as separate medical colleges gave way to medical schools in the late 19th century, women lost ground. Professional organizations also excluded women. At the turn of the 20th century, the American Medical Association, a gatekeeper to the profession, was an all-white, all-male organization, as were the American Bar Association, the American Historical Association, and the American Economic Association. While these new professional organizations established much-needed uniform standards and training in a variety of professions and disciplines, they also closed ranks against women.

Professional women who joined women's clubs in these years were not content to make these institutions mere refuges from the male world that shunned them. Rather, they were determined to use their clubs to establish new channels through which they might deploy their talents and exercise influence. They constituted an enormous reserve army of activists, eager to find ways to enlarge women's voices in the public sphere. They responded with enthusiasm to the work of Jane Addams and her fellow pioneers, and sought to embark on similar experiments in their own communities. In so doing, they propelled progressivism forward.

Table 21.1 WOMEN ENROLLED IN INSTITUTIONS OF HIGHER EDUCATION, 1870–1930

Year	Women's Colleges (thousands of students)	Coed Institutions (thousands of students)	Total (thousands of students)	Percentage of All Students Enrolled
1870	6.5	4.6	11.1	21.0%
1880	15.7	23.9	39.6	33.4%
1890	16.8	39.5	56.3	35.9%
1900	24.4	61.0	85.4	36.8%
1910	34.1	106.5	140.6	39.6%
1920	52.9	230.0	282.9	39.6%
1930	82.1	398.7	480.8	43.7%

Source: Data in Mabel Newcomer, *A Century of Higher Education for American Women* (New York: Harper and Row, 1959), p. 46.

Clubwomen rose to prominence in black communities, too. Middle-class black women drew on their extensive experiences in church organizations and Republican aid societies to network with each other and to intervene in matters of pressing importance to their communities. On matters of sexuality and alcohol, they often shared the conservative sentiments of many white clubwomen. Some groups of black clubwomen ventured into community affairs even more boldly than their white counterparts, especially in southern states, where black men were being stripped of the right to vote, to serve on juries, and to hold political office. As this assault on black citizenship and manhood unfolded, southern black women stepped into the breach, providing indispensable services and leadership to their communities.

21-1d *Socialists*

In the early 20th century, **socialism** stood for the transfer of control over big businesses from the capitalists who owned them to the laboring masses who worked in them. Socialists believed that such a transfer, usually defined in terms of government ownership and operation of corporations, would make it impossible for wealthy elites to control society.

The Socialist Party of America, founded in 1901, became a political force during the first 20 years of the century, and socialist ideas influenced progressivism. In 1912, at the peak of its influence, the Socialist Party enrolled more than 115,000 members. Its presidential candidate, the charismatic **Eugene Victor Debs** of Terre Haute, Indiana, attracted almost a million votes—6 percent of the total votes cast that year. In that same year, 1,200 Socialists held elective office in 340 different municipalities. Of these, 79 were mayors of cities as geographically and demographically diverse as Schenectady, New York; Milwaukee, Wisconsin; Butte, Montana; and Berkeley, California (see Map 21.1). More than 300 newspapers and periodicals, with a combined circulation exceeding 2 million, spread the socialist gospel. The most important socialist publication was *Appeal to Reason*, published by Julius Wayland from Kansas and sent out each week to 750,000 subscribers. In 1905, Wayland published, in serial form, a novel by a muckraker named Upton Sinclair, which depicted the scandalous working conditions in Chicago's meatpacking industry. When it was later published in book form, in 1906, *The Jungle* created such an outcry that the federal government was forced to regulate the meat industry.

Socialists came in many varieties. In Milwaukee, they consisted of predominantly German working-class immigrants and their descendants; in New York City, their numbers were strongest among Jewish immigrants from eastern Europe. In the Southwest, tens of thousands of disgruntled native-born farmers who had been Populists in the 1890s now flocked to the socialist banner. In the West, socialism was popular among miners, timber cutters, and others who labored in isolated areas where industrialists possessed extraordinary power over work, politics, and community life. These westerners gravitated to the militant labor union, the Industrial Workers of the World (IWW), which found a home in the Socialist Party from 1905 to 1913.

Although the IWW's membership at any one time rarely exceeded 20,000, it acquired a national reputation by organizing the poorest and most isolated workers and leading them in strikes against employers who were unaccustomed to having their authority challenged. Violence lurked beneath the surface of these strikes and occasionally erupted in bloody skirmishes between strikers and police, National Guardsmen, or the private security forces hired by employers.

Mainstream socialists, led by Debs, shared the IWW's desire to end capitalism but believed that socialism could be achieved democratically, by electing socialists to office and ultimately to the presidency itself. Progressives often worked hand-in-hand with socialists to win economic and political reforms. Many intellectuals and reformers—including John Dewey, Richard Ely, Thorstein Veblen, and Helen Keller, the leading spokesperson for the disabled—moved back and forth between socialism and progressivism. But Debs's radicalism also scared progressives, as did his efforts to organize a working-class political movement independent of middle-class involvement or control. Although progressives wanted to tame capitalism, they stopped short of wanting to eliminate it. They wanted to improve working and living conditions for the masses but not cede political control to them. The progressives hoped to offer a political program with enough reform elements to counter the appeal of Debs's more radical movement. In this, they would be successful.

21-2 Reform of City Governments

Q *What were the benefits and costs of municipal reform?*

Progressive Era reform battles first erupted over control of municipal transportation networks and utilities. Private corporations typically owned and operated street railways and electrical and gas systems. Many of these corporations used their monopoly power to charge exorbitant fares and rates, and they often won that power by bribing city officials who belonged to one of the political machines. Corporations achieved generous reductions in real estate taxes in the same way.

The attack on private utilities and their protectors in city government gained momentum in the mid-1890s. Occasionally, a reform politician would rise to power through one of the regular political parties. But this path to power was a difficult one, especially in cities where the political parties were controlled by political machines. Consequently, progressives worked to strip the parties of their power. Two of their favorite reforms were the city commission and the city manager forms of government.

First introduced in Galveston, Texas, in 1900, in the wake of a devastating tidal wave, city commissions shifted municipal power from the mayor and his aldermen to five city commissioners, each responsible for a different department of city government. In Galveston and elsewhere, the impetus for this reform came from civic-minded businessmen who were determined to rebuild government on the principles of efficient and scientific management that had energized the private sector. The results were often impressive. The Galveston commissioners restored the city's credit after a brush with bankruptcy, improved the city's harbor, and built a massive seawall to protect the city from future floods. They accomplished all of this on budgets that had been cut by one-third. By 1913, more than 300 cities, most of them small to middling in size, had adopted the city commission plan.

The city commission system did not always work to perfection, however. Sometimes the commissioners used their position to reward electoral supporters with jobs and contracts; other times, they pursued power and prestige for their respective departments. The city manager plan was meant to overcome such problems. Under this plan, the commissioners continued to set policy, but policy implementation now rested with a "chief executive." This official, who was not elected but appointed by the commissioners, would curtail rivalries among commissioners and ensure that no outside influences interfered with the impartial, businesslike management of the city. The job of city manager was modeled after that of a corporation executive. First introduced in Sumter, South Carolina, in 1911 and then in Dayton, Ohio, in 1913, by 1919 the city manager plan had spread to 130 cities.

Although these reforms limited corruption and improved services, they were not universally popular. Poor and minority voters, in particular, saw their influence in local affairs weakened by them. Previously, candidates for municipal office (other than the mayor) competed in ward elections rather than in citywide elections. Voters in working-class wards commonly elected workingmen to represent them, and voters in immigrant wards made sure that fellow ethnics represented their interests on city councils. Citywide elections diluted the strength of these constituencies. Candidates from poor districts often lacked the money needed to mount a citywide campaign, and they were further hampered by the nonpartisan nature of such elections. Denied the support of a political party or platform, they had to make themselves personally known to voters throughout the city. That was a much easier task for the city's "leading citizens"—manufacturers, merchants, and lawyers—than it was for workingmen. In Dayton, the percentage of citizens voting Socialist rose from 25 to 44 percent in the years following the introduction of the commission manager system, but the number of Socialists elected to office declined from five to zero. Progressive political reforms thus sometimes reduced the influence of radicals, minorities, and the poor in elections.

21-3 Reform in the States

Q *What were the results of progressive efforts to create a "responsible" and "virtuous" electorate?*

As at the local level, political parties at the state level were often dominated by corrupt politicians who did the bidding of powerful private lobbies. In New Jersey in 1903, for example, industrial and financial interests, working through the Republican Party machine, controlled numerous appointments to state government, including the chief justice of the state supreme court, the attorney general, and the commissioner of banking and insurance. Such webs of influence ensured that New Jersey would provide large corporations such as the railroads with favorable political and economic legislation.

21-3a *Overhauling Election Laws and the Electorate*

Progressives introduced reforms designed to undermine the power of party bosses, restore sovereignty to "the people," and encourage honest, talented individuals to enter politics.

Keystone/Hulton Archive/Getty Images

21.5 **Eugene V. Debs** This photograph captures the energy and charisma of Debs as he addresses a working-class audience in New York during his 1912 presidential campaign.

Q *On which political issues did Debs's beliefs overlap with those of progressives? On which issues did they diverge?*

▲ **MAP 21.1 Cities and Towns Electing Socialist Mayors or Other Major Municipal Officers, 1911–1920** This map reveals the strength of socialist electoral support in some unexpected areas: western Pennsylvania; Ohio; Illinois; Minnesota; a cluster of towns where Oklahoma, Missouri, and Kansas meet; Colorado; and Utah.

Q *What might explain the concentration of socialist mayors in western Pennsylvania and Ohio in 1912?*

Q *Why were there so few socialist mayors and other elected officeholders in the South in 1912?*

One such reform was the direct primary, a mechanism that enabled voters, rather than party bosses, to choose party candidates. Mississippi introduced this reform in 1902 and Wisconsin in 1903. By 1916, all but three states had adopted the direct primary. Closely related was a movement to strip state legislatures of their power to choose U.S. senators. State after state enacted legislation that permitted voters to choose Senate candidates in primary elections. In 1912, a reluctant U.S. Senate was obliged to approve the Seventeenth Amendment to the Constitution, mandating the direct election of senators. The state legislatures ratified this amendment in 1913.

Populists had first proposed direct election of U.S. senators in the 1890s; they also proposed the **initiative** and the **referendum**, both of which were adopted first by Oregon in 1902 and then by 18 other states between 1902 and 1915. The initiative allowed reformers to put legislative proposals before voters in general elections without having to wait for state legislatures to act. The referendum gave voters the right in general elections to repeal an unpopular act that a state legislature had passed. Less widely adopted but important nevertheless was the **recall**, a device that allowed voters to remove from office public servants who had betrayed their trust. As a further control over the behavior of elected officials, numerous states enacted laws that regulated corporate campaign contributions and restricted lobbying activities in state legislatures. These laws neither eliminated corporate privilege nor destroyed the power of machine politicians. Nevertheless, they made politics more honest and strengthened the influence of ordinary voters.

Progressive reformers focused as well on creating a responsible electorate that understood the importance of the vote and that resisted efforts to manipulate elections. To create this ideal electorate, reformers had to see to it that all of those citizens who were deemed virtuous could cast their votes free of coercion and intimidation. At the same time, reformers sought to disfranchise citizens who were considered irresponsible and corruptible. In pursuing these goals, progressives substantially altered the composition of the electorate and strengthened

Bettmann/Corbis

21.6 **Helen Keller, Labor Activist** Best known for her work in calling attention to the rights and needs of disabled Americans, Keller also agitated on behalf of America's workers. Here she stiffens the resolve of actors on strike against a New York City opera house. Her companion, Anne Sullivan Macy, stands to her right, serving as Keller's interpreter.

government regulation of voting. Progressives enlarged the electorate by extending the right to vote to women; but they also either initiated or tolerated laws that barred large numbers of minority and poor voters from the polls.

Government regulation of voting had begun in the 1890s, when virtually every state adopted the **Australian ballot (secret ballot)**. This reform required voters to vote in private rather than in public. It also required the government, rather than political parties, to print the ballots and supervise the voting. Before this time, each political party had printed its own ballot with only its candidates listed. At election time, each party mobilized its loyal supporters. Party workers offered liquor, free meals, and other bribes to entice voters to the polls and to "persuade" them to cast the party ballot. Because the ballots were cast in public, few voters who had accepted gifts of liquor and food dared to cross watchful party officials. Critics argued that the system corrupted the electoral process. They also pointed out that it made "ticket splitting"—dividing one's vote between candidates of two or more parties—virtually impossible.

The Australian ballot solved these problems. Although it predated progressivism, it embodied the progressives' determination to use government power to encourage citizens to cast their votes responsibly and wisely.

That same determination was apparent in the progressives' support for the personal registration laws that virtually every state passed between 1890 and 1920. These laws allowed prospective voters to register to vote only if they appeared at a designated government office with proper identification. Frequently, these laws also mandated a certain period of residence in the state before registration and a certain interval between registration and actual voting.

Personal registration laws were meant to disfranchise citizens who showed no interest in voting until Election Day, when a party worker arrived with a few dollars and offered a free ride to the polls. However, they also excluded many hardworking, responsible, poor people who wanted to vote but had failed to register, either because their work schedules made it impossible or because they were intimidated by the complex regulations. The laws were particularly frustrating for immigrants with limited knowledge of English.

Science History Images/Alamy Stock Photo

21.7 **W.E.B. Du Bois, Scholar and Civil Rights Activist** This photograph depicts Du Bois at his desk at Atlanta University, where he was professor of economics, history, and sociology from 1897 to 1909. In 1910, Du Bois became a founding member of the NAACP and the editor of its newspaper, *The Crisis*.

Progressives also promoted election laws expressly designed to keep noncitizen immigrants from voting. In the 1880s, 18 states had passed laws allowing immigrants to vote without first becoming citizens. Progressives reversed this trend. At the same time, the newly formed Bureau of Immigration and Naturalization (1906) made it more difficult to become a citizen. Most progressives defended the added rigor of the naturalization process. U.S. citizenship, they believed, carried responsibilities; it was not to be bestowed lightly. In many cities and towns where immigrants dominated the workforce, the numbers of registered voters fell steeply.

Laws excluding voters from the electorate affected the South more than any other region (see Figure 21.2). Between 1890 and 1904, every ex-Confederate state passed laws designed to strip blacks of their right to vote. Because laws explicitly barring blacks from voting would have violated the Fifteenth Amendment, this exclusion had to be accomplished indirectly—through literacy tests, property qualifications, and poll taxes mandated by the legislatures of the ex-Confederate states. Any citizen who failed a reading test, or who could not sign his name, or who did not own a minimum amount of property, or who could not pay a poll tax, lost his right to vote. The citizens who failed these tests most frequently were blacks—who formed the poorest and least educated segment of the southern population—but a large segment of the region's poor whites also failed the tests. The effects of **disfranchisement** were stark. In 1900, only 1,300 blacks voted in Mississippi elections, down from 130,000 in the 1870s. Virginia's voter turnout dropped from 60 percent of adult men (white and black) in 1900 to 28 percent in 1904.

Many progressives in the North, such as Governor Robert La Follette of Wisconsin, criticized southern disfranchisement. Some, including Jane Addams and John Dewey, joined in 1910 with W. E. B. Du Bois and other black reformers to found the **National Association for the Advancement of Colored People (NAACP)**, an interracial political organization that made black equality its primary goal. In the South, however, white progressives rarely challenged disfranchisement.

In the process of identifying particular groups as "unfit" to hold the franchise, some progressives soured on the electoral process altogether. The more they looked for rational and virtuous voters, the fewer they found. The growing disillusionment with the electorate, in combination with intensifying restrictions on the franchise, created an environment in which fewer and fewer Americans actually went to the polls. Voter participation rates fell from 79 percent in 1896 to only 49 percent in 1920 (see Figure 21.3).

21-3b *Woman Suffrage*

The major exception to this trend was the enfranchisement of women. This momentous reform was adopted by several states during the 1890s and the first two decades of the 20th century and became federal law with the ratification of the Nineteenth Amendment to the Constitution in 1920.

Wyoming, which attained statehood in 1890, became the first state to grant women the right to vote, followed in 1893

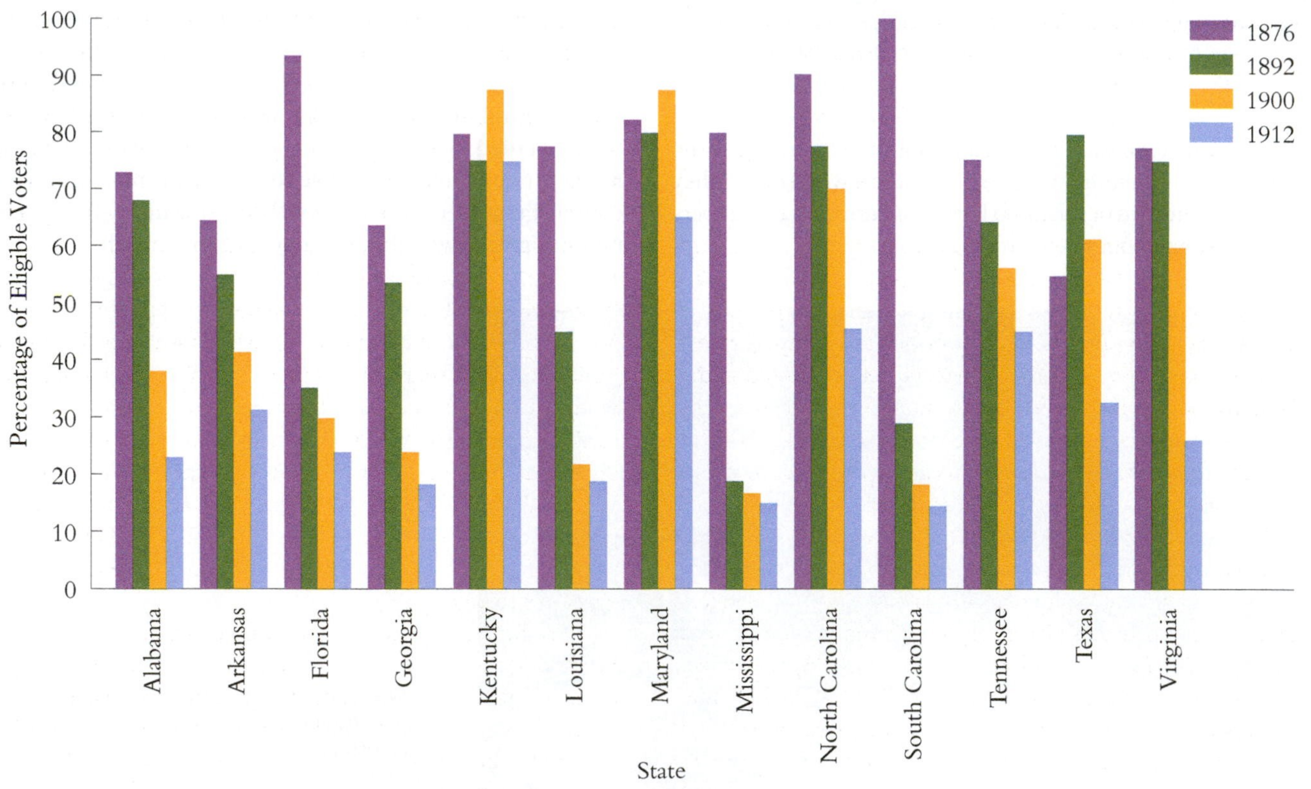

Figure 21.2 **Voter Participation in 13 Southern States, 1876, 1892, 1900, 1912**

Source: Data from *Historical Statistics of the United States, Colonial Times to 1970* (White Plains, NY: Kraus International, 1989).

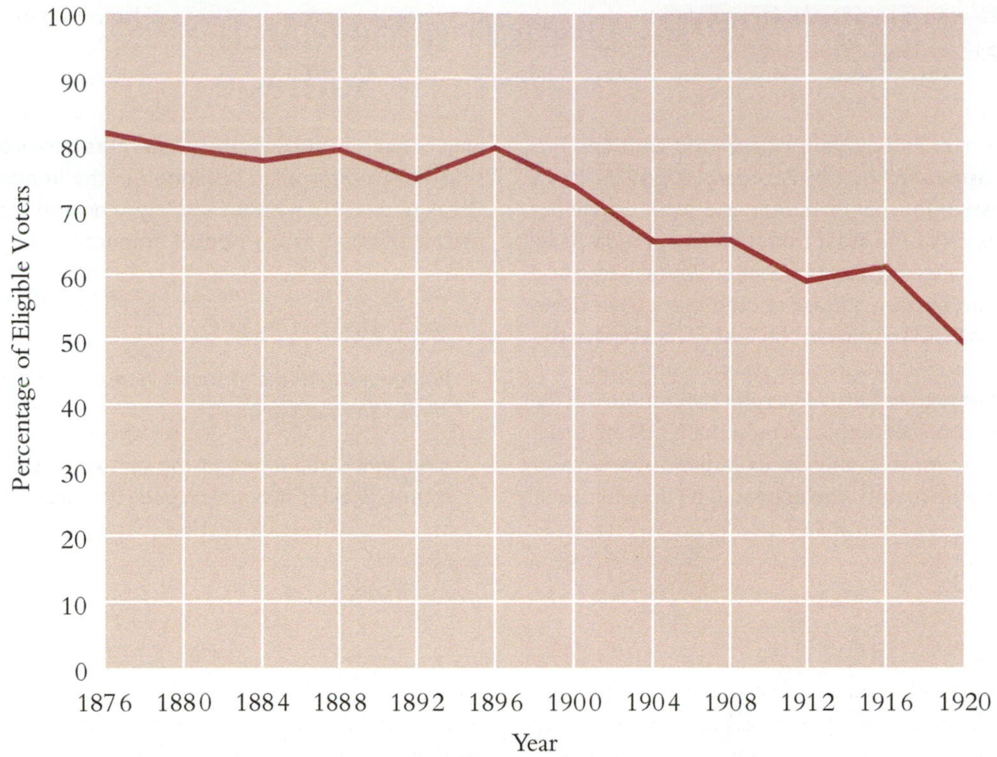

Figure 21.3 **Voter Participation in Presidential Elections, 1876–1920**

Source: Data from *Historical Statistics of the United States, Colonial Times to 1970* (White Plains, NY: Kraus International, 1989).

by Colorado and in 1896 by Idaho and Utah (see Map 21.2). The main reason for success in these sparsely populated western states was not egalitarianism but rather the conviction that women's supposedly gentler and more nurturing nature would tame and civilize the men who had populated the frontier.

In the mid-19th century, supporters of women's suffrage (those who wanted to give women the vote) had insisted that women were fundamentally equal to men. In the Progressive Era, however, many suffragists did not base their argument for enfranchisement on male-female equality. Women, they stressed, were different than men, possessing a moral sense and a nurturing quality that men lacked. Consequently, they could be trusted to vote virtuously and thereby advance the progressive aim of cleansing politics of corruption. Their experience as mothers and household managers, moreover, would enable them to guide local and state governments in efforts to improve education, sanitation, family wholesomeness, and the condition of women and children in the workforce. In other words, the enfranchisement of women would enhance the quality of both public and private life without obligating anyone to think that members of the female sex were the equals of men in all respects.

Suffragists were slow to ally themselves with blacks, Asians, and other disfranchised groups. In fact, many suffragists, especially those in the South and West, opposed the franchise for Americans of color. They, like their male counterparts, believed that members of these groups lacked moral strength and thus did not deserve the right to vote. Unlike the suffrage pioneers of the 1840s and 1850s, many Progressive Era suffragists were little troubled by racial discrimination and injustice.

Washington, California, Kansas, Oregon, and Arizona followed the lead of the other western states by enfranchising women between 1910 and 1912. After a series of setbacks in eastern and midwestern states, the movement regained momentum under the leadership of the strategically astute Carrie Chapman Catt, who became president of the **National American Woman Suffrage Association (NAWSA)** in 1915 and successfully coordinated myriad grassroots campaigns. Equally important was Alice Paul, a radical who founded the Congressional Union in 1913 and later renamed it the National Woman's Party. Paul and her supporters focused their attention on the White House, picketing President Wilson's home 24 hours a day, brandishing large posters that chastised him for abandoning his democratic principles, and daring the police to arrest them. When several suffrage demonstrators were jailed, they continued their protests by going on hunger strikes (refusing to eat). Aided by a heightened enthusiasm for democracy generated by America's participation in the First World War (see Chapter 23), which generated a more positive popular response to Paul's tactics than might otherwise have been the case, the suffragists achieved their goal of universal woman suffrage in 1920.

Predictions that suffrage for women would radically alter politics turned out to be false. The political system was neither cleansed of corruption, nor did the government rush headlong to address the private needs of women and their families. Although the numbers of voters increased after 1920, voter participation rates continued to decline. Still, the extension of the vote to women, 144 years after the founding of the nation, was a major political achievement.

Interpreting the Visual Past

Depicting the March of Women's Suffrage

This map/cartoon, drawn by Henry Mayer and entitled "The Awakening," appeared in the February 20, 1915, issue of *Puck*, a progressive journal of humor and satire. It vividly shows the divergence of the West from the East in regards to woman suffrage. Only western states (colored white) had given women the vote; no eastern states (colored black) had done so. Many Americans liked to think of the East as incubating the country's most advanced, progressive thought and gradually conquering the West with eastern ideals and civilization. But for women's suffrage to succeed, this cartoon makes clear, ideals and civilization had to move from West to East and awaken and uplift the women in the region who appear to be drowning in a kind of hell. Fortunately, the westerners have Columbia on their side—a strong woman fashioned in the image of Athena, the Greek goddess of wisdom and law, who was increasingly being used at this time as a symbol of America's noblest ideals.

Q *Why do you think women's suffrage had advanced in the West and had failed in the East?*

Q *Why do you think the cartoonist here enlisted Athena in the cause of women's suffrage?*

Q *How would you interpret the cartoonist's decision to depict women in the East as having been dragged down into hell?*

21.8 **Henry Mayer, "The Awakening," 1915.**

21-3c *Wisconsin and New York: State Laboratories of Reform*

In some states, progressives extended reform efforts well beyond election law and the electorate. Progressives also fought to limit corporate power, strengthen organized labor, and offer social welfare protection to the weak. Many state governments were pressured into passing such legislation by progressive alliances of middle-class and working-class reformers and by dynamic state governors.

Nowhere did the progressives' campaign for social reform flourish as it did in Wisconsin. The movement arose first in the 1890s, in hundreds of Wisconsin cities and towns, as citizens began to mobilize against the state's corrupt Republican Party and the special privileges the party had granted to private utilities and railroads. In 1897, Robert La Follette assumed leadership of this movement.

La Follette was born into a prosperous farming family in 1855. Elected governor in 1900, he secured for Wisconsin both a direct primary and a law that stripped the railroad corporations of tax exemptions they had long enjoyed.

A tireless campaigner and a spellbinding speaker, "Fighting Bob" won election to the U.S. Senate in 1906. Meanwhile, Wisconsin's labor and socialist movements pressured

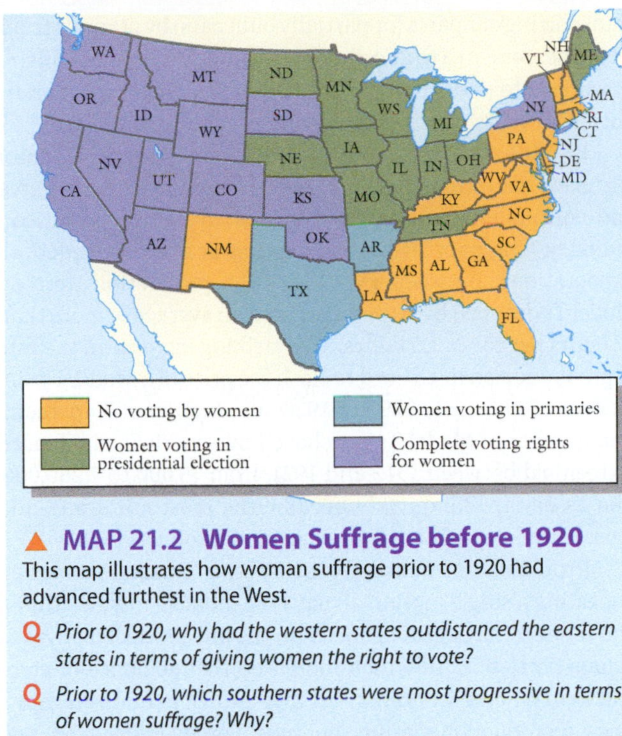

▲ **MAP 21.2 Women Suffrage before 1920**
This map illustrates how woman suffrage prior to 1920 had advanced furthest in the West.

Q *Prior to 1920, why had the western states outdistanced the eastern states in terms of giving women the right to vote?*

Q *Prior to 1920, which southern states were most progressive in terms of women suffrage? Why?*

progressive reformers to shrink corporate profits and expand social welfare. By 1910, reformers had passed state laws that regulated railroad and utility rates, instituted the nation's first state income tax, and provided workers with compensation for injuries, limitations on work hours, restrictions on child labor, and minimum wages for women.

Many of these laws were written by social scientists at the University of Wisconsin. In the first decade of the 20th century, John R. Commons, University of Wisconsin economist, drafted Wisconsin's civil service and public utilities laws. In 1911, Commons designed and won legislative approval for the Wisconsin Industrial Commission, which brought together employers, trade unionists, and professionals and gave them broad powers to investigate and regulate relations between industry and labor throughout the state. For the first time, a state government had put the rights of labor on par with those of industry. Equally important was the responsibility the commission delegated to nonelected professionals: social scientists, lawyers, engineers, and others. Commission professionals, Wisconsin reformers believed, would resolve disputes between capital and labor with their expertise, impartiality, and good judgment.

Ohio, Indiana, New York, and Colorado quickly adopted this "**Wisconsin Idea.**" In 1913, the federal government established its own Industrial Relations Commission and hired Commons to direct its investigative staff. In other areas, too, reformers began urging state and federal governments to shift the policy-making initiative away from political parties and toward administrative agencies staffed by professionals.

New York was second only to Wisconsin in the vigor and breadth of its progressive movement. As in Wisconsin, New York progressives focused first on fighting political corruption, establishing several public service commissions to regulate railroads and utility companies. Also as in Wisconsin, the labor movement exercised clout. New York City garment workers struck and forced state legislators to regulate working conditions. With the establishment of the Factory Investigating Committee, New York, like Wisconsin, became a pioneer in labor and social welfare policy.

New York's state legislators faced pressure from middle-class reformers—settlement house workers such as Lillian Wald of the Henry Street Settlement and lawyers such as Louis Brandeis—who had become convinced of the need for new laws to protect the disadvantaged. This combined pressure from working-class and middle-class constituencies persuaded some state Democrats, including Assemblyman Alfred E. Smith and Senator Robert F. Wagner, to convert from machine to reform politics. Their appearance in the progressive ranks represented the arrival of a new reform sensibility. Wagner and Smith were both ethnic Catholics (Wagner was born in Germany, and Smith was the grandchild of Irish immigrants). Though they opposed city commissions, voter registration laws, and other legislative initiatives whose intent seemed anti-immigrant or anti-Catholic, they supported reforms meant to improve the working and living conditions of New York's urban poor. They fought for a minimum wage, factory safety, workmen's compensation, the

21.9 **Robert La Follette, Wisconsin Progressive** La Follette was one of the country's most important progressives. This portrait conveys something about the personal intensity that drew many reform-minded men and women to him.

Q *What contributions did Wisconsin, under La Follette's leadership, make to progressive reform?*

right of workers to join unions, and the regulation of excessively powerful corporations. Their participation in progressivism accelerated the movement's national shift away from a preoccupation with political parties and electorates and toward questions of economic justice and social welfare.

21-4 Scientific Management and the Reform of Work

Q *How was scientific management applied to the factory floor? How successful a reform was it?*

Progressivism drew support, too, from businessmen who saw in it an opportunity to introduce efficiency, science, and harmony into industrial relations. Just as business-oriented progressives in Galveston and elsewhere drew on the principles of scientific management to reform local government, so, too, some businessmen attempted to use those principles to create more productive and cohesive workplaces.

Scientific management had developed in the last two decades of the 19th century among managers and engineers who were looking to develop arrangements of machines and workers that would achieve the highest speed in production with the fewest human or mechanical interruptions. Their leader was **Frederick Winslow Taylor**, who, as chief engineer at Philadelphia's Midvale Steel Company in the 1880s, had examined every human task and mechanical movement involved in his company's production process. Taylor pioneered the "time-and-motion study," the technique through which managers recorded every distinct movement a worker made in performing his or her job, how long it took, and how often it was performed. Taylor hoped thereby to identify and eliminate wasted human energy. His goal was to make human labor emulate the smooth and apparently effortless operation of an automatic, perfectly calibrated piece of machinery.

Taylor's program of "scientific management" fired the imagination of the business- and efficiency-oriented sectors of the progressive movement. By the time he published in 1911 his popular treatise, *The Principles of Scientific Management*, Taylor himself had been influenced by the spirit of progressive reform. He now offered his program as a way of achieving industrial peace. Scientific management, Taylor claimed, would allow each worker to be matched with a job well suited to his or her abilities. Efficiency and wages would rise; so, too, would worker satisfaction. Most, if not all, workplace antagonisms would then dissolve.

Henry Ford, the pioneer in automobile manufacturing, was a Taylor disciple. By 1910, Ford's engineers had broken down the production of its main car, the "Model T," into a series of simple, sequential tasks. Each worker performed only one task: installing an engine, bolting in seats, mounting tires onto axles. Then, in 1913, Ford's engineers introduced the first moving assembly line, a continuously moving conveyor belt that carried cars in production through each workstation. This innovation eliminated precious time previously wasted in transporting car parts (or partially built cars) by crane or truck from one work area to another. It also limited the time available to workers to perform their assigned tasks. Only the foreman, not the workers, could stop the line or change its speed.

By 1913, the continuous assembly line made Ford Motor Company's new Highland Park plant the most tightly integrated and continuously moving production system in American industry. The pace of car production at Ford exceeded all expectations. Between 1910 and 1914, production time on Model Ts dropped by 90 percent, from an average of more than 12 hours per car to 1.5 hours. This striking increase in the rate of production enabled Ford to slash the price of a Model T from $950 in 1909 to only $295 in 1923, a reduction of 70 percent. The number of Model Ts purchased by Americans increased sixteenfold between 1912 and 1921, from 79,000 to 1,250,000. The assembly line quickly became the most admired—and most feared—symbol of American mass production.

Problems immediately beset the system, however. Repeating a single motion all day long induced mental stupor, and managerial efforts to speed up the line produced physical exhaustion—both of which increased the incidence of error and injury. Some workers tried to organize a union to gain a voice in production matters, but most Ford workers expressed their dissatisfaction simply by quitting. By 1913, employee turnover at Highland Park had reached the astounding rate of

Bettman/CORBIS

21.10 Frederick W. Taylor Taylor's ideas for revolutionizing production techniques and worker management attracted many supporters in the early 20th century.

Q *Taylor was admired, as was Henry Ford, one of his principal disciples. Why, then, did not more businessmen follow Taylor's and Ford's lead and implement the principles of scientific management at their workplaces?*

370 percent per year. At that rate, Ford had to hire about 52,000 workers every year just to keep his factory fully staffed at 14,000.

A problem of that magnitude demanded a dramatic solution. Ford provided it in 1914 by raising the wage he paid his assembly-line workers to $5 per day, double the average manufacturing wage then prevalent in American industry. The result: Workers, especially young and single men, flocked to Detroit. The high productivity rates of Ford's factories permitted him to absorb the wage increase without cutting substantially into profits.

Taylor had believed that improved efficiency would lead to dramatic wage gains. Ford's ability to double his wage payout, in this respect, proved Taylor right. But Taylor's theory of human psychology remained primitive, inadequate to the task of comprehending the range of emotions that employees brought to the workplace and the multiple sources of employee–employer conflict. Ford recognized that workers were more complex than Taylor had allowed, which is why his innovations went well beyond what Taylor himself had contemplated. Thus, Ford set up a sociology department, forerunner of the personnel department, to collect job, family, and other information about his employees. He sent social workers into workers' homes to inquire into their personal lives. For the foreign-born, he instituted Americanization classes. He offered his employees housing subsidies, medical care, and other benefits. Ford's success was widely admired; nevertheless, it would take another generation or two for significant sectors of the corporate world to follow his lead. And thus throughout the first two decades of the 20th century, American industry remained more the target than the ally of progressive reform.

21-5 A New Campaign for Racial Equality

Q *How did W. E. B. Du Bois's approach to reforms for African Americans differ from that of Booker T. Washington?*

The reform energy unleashed by the progressives inspired a new generation of African American activists to insist that the nation grapple again with issues of racial inequality. Indeed, the modern civil rights movement can be said to have started in the early years of the 20th century.

Booker T. Washington's message—that blacks should accept segregation and disfranchisement as unavoidable and focus their energies instead on self-help and self-improvement—faced increasing criticism from young black activists such as **W. E. B. Du Bois**, Ida B. Wells, Monroe Trotter, and others. Washington's accommodationist leadership (see Chapter 18), in their eyes, had brought southern blacks no reprieve from racism. More than 100 blacks had been lynched in 1900 alone; between 1901 and 1914, at least 1,000 others would be hanged.

Increasingly, unsubstantiated rumors of black assaults on whites became occasions for white mobs to rampage through black neighborhoods and destroy life and property. In 1908, a mob in Springfield, Illinois, attacked black businesses and individuals; a force of 5,000 state militia was required to restore order. The troops were too late, however, to stop the lynching of two innocent black men, one a successful barber and the other an 84-year-old man who had been married to a white woman for more than 30 years.

Booker T. Washington had long believed that blacks who educated themselves or who succeeded in business would be accepted as equals by whites. As Du Bois and other black militants observed, however, white rioters made no distinction between rich blacks and poor, or between solid citizens and petty criminals. All that had seemed to matter was the color of one's skin. Similarly, many black militants knew from personal experience that individual accomplishment was not enough to overcome racial prejudice. Du Bois was a brilliant scholar who became, in 1899, the first African American to receive a doctorate from Harvard University. Had he been white, Du Bois would have been asked to teach at Harvard or another elite academic institution, but no prestigious white university made him an offer.

Seeing no future in accommodation, Du Bois and other young black activists came together at Niagara Falls in 1905 to fashion a more militant political agenda. They demanded that African Americans regain the right to vote in states that had taken it away, that segregation be abolished, and that the many discriminatory barriers to black advancement be removed. They declared their commitment to freedom of speech, the brotherhood of all men, and respect for the workingman. Although their numbers were small, the members of the so-called Niagara movement were inspired by the example of the antebellum abolitionists. Meeting in Boston, Oberlin, and Harpers Ferry—all places of special significance to the abolitionist cause—they hoped to rekindle the militant, uncompromising spirit of that earlier crusade (see Chapters 12 and 14).

The 1908 Springfield riot had shaken many whites. Some, especially those already working for social and economic reform, now joined in common cause with the Niagara movement. Together, black and white activists planned a conference for Lincoln's birthday in 1909 to revive, in the words of author William English Walling, "the spirit of the abolitionists" and to "treat the Negro on a plane of absolute political and social equality." The conference brought together distinguished progressives, white and black, including Mary White Ovington, Jane Addams, Oswald Garrison Villard, John Dewey, William Dean Howells, Ida B. Wells, and W. E. B. Du Bois. They drew up plans to establish an organization dedicated to fighting racial discrimination and prejudice. In May 1910, the National Association for the Advancement of Colored People (NAACP) was launched, with Moorfield Storey of Boston as president, Walling as chairman of the executive committee, and Du Bois as the director of publicity and research.

The formation of the NAACP marked the beginning of the modern civil rights movement. The organization launched a magazine, *The Crisis*, edited by Du Bois, to publicize and protest the lynchings, riots, and other abuses directed against black citizens. Equally important was the Legal Redress Committee, which initiated lawsuits against city and state governments for violating the constitutional

History Through Film The Great White Hope (1970)

Directed by Martin Ritt.
Starring James Earl Jones (Jack Jefferson) and Jane Alexander (Eleanor Backman).

This movie is a fictional retelling of the life of Jack Johnson, the first black world heavyweight boxing champion, and of the furor that his dominance over white boxers, his outspokenness, and his relationships with white women generated in early 20th-century America. The movie opens with white boxing promoters persuading a former white champion (James Bradley) to come out of retirement to battle the black champion, here called Jack Jefferson (rather than Johnson). In a subsequent scene, Jefferson destroys Bradley in the ring and reacts with defiant cheeriness to the boos and racial epithets that rain down upon him from the predominantly white crowd.

Jefferson refuses to accept the limitations that white society placed on black men at the time. He is neither submissive nor deferential toward whites, and he openly dates white women. Whites fear him for defying the era's racial conventions. One evening, federal agents burst in on Jefferson and his white lover, Eleanor Backman (Jane Alexander), and accuse Jefferson of violating the Mann Act, a 1910 law that made it illegal to transport women across state lines for sexual purposes. At Jefferson's trial, prosecutors expected to convince a jury that Backman was coerced into sex, for no white woman, they intended to argue, would have freely chosen to consort with a black man in this way.

20TH Century Fox/The Kobal Collection

21.11 James Earl Jones as Jack Jefferson.

Jefferson manages to evade the authorities and flee to Europe, where Backman joins him. The early months abroad are invigorating for both, as Jefferson is celebrated for his fighting prowess and the couple's love for each other flourishes. Soon, however, the boxing opponents disappear, money stops coming in, and a sense of despair grows between the two lovers. Their exile ends disastrously in Mexico, where Backman kills herself after an argument with Jefferson. Jefferson, his spirit finally broken, agrees to throw a fight against the newest Great White Hope, Jess Willard, in return for an opportunity to end his fugitive status and return to the United States.

Made in 1970, *The Great White Hope* was inspired by the brash heavyweight champion of the 1960s, Muhammad Ali. The film is quite faithful to the story of the real Jack Johnson, who dated white women, was arrested for allegedly violating the Mann Act, fled the country rather than submit to jail, and ultimately lost a heavyweight bout to Jess Willard. The film endows Backman, a fictional character, with more "class" and refinement than the real women who associated with Johnson usually possessed. The film also fictionalizes Johnson's fight against Willard by suggesting that Johnson could have won the fight had he not been required to throw it. Despite these changes, the film successfully re-creates the racial climate of the early 20th century and the white hostility imperiling a black man who dared to assert his pride and independence. ■

rights of African Americans. The committee scored its first major success in 1915, when the U.S. Supreme Court ruled that the so-called grandfather clauses of the Oklahoma and Maryland constitutions violated the Fifteenth Amendment. (These clauses extended the right to vote to whites who had failed to pay their state's poll tax or to pass its literacy test while denying the same right to blacks.) NAACP lawyers won again in 1917 when the Supreme Court declared unconstitutional a Louisville, Kentucky, law that required all blacks to reside in predetermined parts of the city.

By 1914, the NAACP had enrolled thousands of members in scores of branches throughout the United States. The organization's success generated other civil rights groups. The National Urban League, founded in 1911, worked to improve the economic and social conditions of blacks in cities.

Progress toward racial equality remained slow. Attacking segregation and discrimination through lawsuits was, by its nature, a strategy that would take decades to complete. The growing membership of the NAACP, although impressive, was not large enough to qualify it as a mass movement, and its interracial character made the organization seem dangerously radical to millions of whites. White NAACP leaders responded to this hostility by limiting the number and power of African Americans who worked for the organization. This policy, in turn, angered black militants who argued that no civil rights organization should be in the business of appeasing white racists.

The Granger Collection, NYC

21.12 **Lynching** This grim photo records the deaths of five of the approximately 1,000 African Americans who were lynched between 1901 and 1914. The increase in lynching was one measure of the virulence of white racism in the early years of the 20th century.

Despite its limitations, the NAACP made significant strides. It gave Du Bois the security and visibility he needed to carry on his fight against Booker T. Washington's accommodationist philosophy. The NAACP, more than any other organization, helped resurrect the issue of racial equality at a time when many white Americans had accepted as normal the practices of racial segregation and discrimination.

21-6 The Roosevelt Presidency

What would you identify as Roosevelt's three most important contributions to progressive reform?

Progressives increasingly sought to increase their influence in national politics. State-level regulations seemed inadequate to the task of curtailing the power of the trusts, protecting workers, or monitoring the quality of consumer goods. The courts repeatedly struck down as unconstitutional state laws regulating working hours or setting minimum wages, on the grounds that they impinged on the freedom of contract and trade. A national progressive movement could force passage of federal laws that were less vulnerable to judicial veto or elect a president who could overhaul the federal judiciary with progressive-minded judges.

National leadership was slow to emerge from Congress. The Populist challenge of the 1890s had left the Democratic Party divided between radical Bryanites and the conservative followers of Grover Cleveland. An "Old Guard" controlled the Republican Party in Congress. The impetus for innovation and reform thus shifted from the legislative to the executive branch, and to one chief executive in particular, Theodore Roosevelt.

When the Republican bosses chose Theodore Roosevelt as William McKinley's running mate in 1900, their purpose was more to remove this headstrong, unpredictable character from New York State politics than to groom him for national leadership. As governor of New York, Roosevelt had been a moderate reformer, but even his modest efforts to rid the state's Republican Party of corruption and patronage were too much for the state party machine. Consigning Roosevelt to the vice presidency seemed a safe solution. McKinley was a young, vigorous politician, fully in control of his party and his presidency. Less than a year into his second term, in September 1901, McKinley was shot by an anarchist assassin. The president clung to life for nine days, and then died. Upon succeeding McKinley, Theodore Roosevelt, age 42, became the youngest chief executive in the nation's history.

Although born to an elite and moneyed New York City family, Roosevelt developed an uncommon affection for "the people." Asthmatic, sickly, and nearsighted as a boy, he remade himself into a vigorous adult. With an insatiable appetite for high-risk adventure—everything from "dude ranching" in the Dakota Territory, to big-game hunting in Africa, to wartime combat—he was also a voracious reader and an accomplished writer. Aggressive and swaggering in his public rhetoric, he was in private a skilled, patient negotiator. A believer in the superiority of the English-speaking peoples, he nevertheless assembled an administration that was diverse by the standards of the time. Rarely has a president's personality so enthralled the American public. He is the only 20th-century president immortalized on Mount Rushmore.

21-6a *Regulating the Economy*

Roosevelt quickly revealed his flair for the dramatic. In 1902, he ordered the Justice Department to prosecute the Northern Securities Company, a $400 million monopoly that controlled all railroad lines and traffic in the Northwest from Chicago to Washington State. Never before had an American president sought to use the Sherman Antitrust Act to break up a business monopoly. The news shocked the banker J. P. Morgan, who had brokered the deal that had created Northern Securities. Morgan rushed to the White House, where he is said to have told Roosevelt: "If we have done anything wrong, send your man to my man and they can fix it up." Roosevelt would have none of this "fixing." In 1903, a federal court ordered Northern Securities dissolved, and the U.S. Supreme Court upheld the decision the next year. Roosevelt was hailed as the nation's "trust-buster."

Roosevelt, however, did not believe in breaking up all, or even most, large corporations. Industrial concentration, he believed, brought the United States wealth, productivity, and a rising standard of living. Rather than bust them up, Roosevelt argued, government should regulate the industrial giants and punish those that used their power improperly. This new role would require the federal government to expand its powers. A newly fortified government—the centerpiece of a political program that Roosevelt would later call the **New Nationalism**—was to be led by a forceful president, who was willing to use his power to achieve prosperity and justice.

Roosevelt had displayed his willingness to use government power to protect the economically weak in a 1902 coal miners' strike. Miners in the anthracite fields of eastern Pennsylvania

21.13 **Theodore Roosevelt** The youthful and animated president addresses a crowd in Evanston, Illinois (a suburb of Chicago), in 1903.

Q *Is Roosevelt better understood as a "trust-buster" or as someone seeking to impose a regime of regulation on large corporations?*

wanted recognition for their union, the United Mine Workers (UMW). They also wanted a 10 to 20 percent increase in wages and an eight-hour day. When their employers, led by George F. Baer of the Reading Railroad, refused to negotiate, they went on strike. In October, the fifth month of the strike, Roosevelt summoned the mine owners and John Mitchell, the UMW president, to the White House. Baer expected Roosevelt to threaten the striking workers with arrest by federal troops if they failed to return to work. Instead, Roosevelt supported Mitchell's request for arbitration and warned the mine owners that if they refused to go along, 10,000 federal troops would seize their property. Stunned, the mine owners agreed to submit the dispute to arbitrators, who awarded the unionists a 10 percent wage increase and a nine-hour day.

The mere fact that the federal government had ordered employers to compromise with their workers carried great symbolic weight. Roosevelt enjoyed a surge of support from Americans convinced that he shared their dislike for ill-gotten wealth and privilege. He also raised the hopes of African Americans when, only a month into his presidency, he dined with Booker T. Washington at the White House and then shrugged off the protests of white southerners.

In his 1904 election campaign, Roosevelt promised that, if reelected, he would offer every American a "square deal." The slogan resonated with voters and helped carry Roosevelt to a victory (57 percent of the popular vote) over the conservative Democrat Alton B. Parker. To the surprise of many, Roosevelt had aligned the Republican Party with the cause of reform.

Emboldened by his victory, the president intensified his efforts to extend government regulation of economic affairs. In 1906, he persuaded Congress to pass the Hepburn Act, which significantly increased the Interstate Commerce Commission's ability to set railroad shipping rates and thereby to eliminate the industry's discriminatory marketing practices. Roosevelt supported the Pure Food and Drug Act, passed by Congress that same year, which protected the public from fraudulently marketed and dangerous foods and medications. He also campaigned for the Meat Inspection Act (1906), which obligated the government to monitor the quality and safety of meat being sold to American consumers.

21-6b *Conserving the Environment*

Roosevelt also did more than any previous president to extend federal control over the nation's physical environment. He was not a "preservationist" in the manner of John Muir, founder of the Sierra Club, who insisted that the beauty of the land and the well-being of its wildlife should be protected from all human interference. Instead, Roosevelt viewed the wilderness as a place to live strenuously, to test oneself against the rough outdoors, and to match wits against strong and clever game. He further believed that in the West—that land of ancient forests, lofty mountain peaks, and magnificent canyons—Americans could learn something important about their nation's roots and destiny. To preserve this West, Roosevelt oversaw the creation of 5 new national parks, 16 national monuments, and 53 wildlife reserves. The work of his administration led directly to the formation of the National Park Service in 1916.

Roosevelt also emerged a strong supporter of the **conservationist** movement. Conservationists cared little for national parks or grand canyons. They wanted to manage the environment scientifically so as to ensure that the nation's resources were put to the most efficient economic use. Roosevelt shared the conservationists' belief that the plundering of western timberlands, grazing areas, water resources, and minerals had reached crisis proportions. They sought to deploy in environmental policy a version of the scientific management model then being applied both to city government and private industry.

Roosevelt therefore appointed a Public Lands Commission in 1903 to survey public lands, inventory them, and establish permit systems to regulate the kinds and numbers of users. Soon after, the Departments of the Interior and Agriculture placed certain western lands rich in natural resources and waterpower off-limits to agricultural users. Government officials also limited waterpower development by requiring companies to acquire permits and pay fees for the right to generate electricity on public land. When political favoritism and corruption within the Departments of the Interior and Agriculture threatened these efforts at regulation, Roosevelt authorized the hiring of university-trained experts to replace state and local politicians. Scientific expertise, rather than political connections, would now determine the distribution and use of western territory.

Gifford Pinchot, a specialist in forestry management, and Roosevelt's close friend, led the drive for scientific management of natural resources. In 1905, he persuaded Roosevelt to relocate jurisdiction for the national forests from the Department of the Interior to the Department of Agriculture, which, Pinchot argued, was the most appropriate department to oversee the efficient "harvest" of the nation's forest crop. The newly created National Forest Service, under Pinchot's control, quickly instituted a system of competitive bidding for the right to harvest timber on national forest lands. Pinchot and his expanding staff of college-educated foresters also exacted user fees from livestock ranchers who had previously used national forest grazing lands for free. Armed with new legislation and authority, Pinchot and fellow conservationists in the Roosevelt administration declared vast stretches of federal land in the West off-limits to mining and dam construction.

The Republican Old Guard disliked these initiatives. When Roosevelt recommended prosecution of cattlemen and lumbermen who were illegally using federal land for private gain, congressional conservatives struck back with legislation (in 1907) that curtailed the president's power to create new government land reserves. Roosevelt responded by seizing another 17 million acres for national forest reserves before the new law went into effect. To his conservative opponents, excluding commercial activity from public land was bad enough, but flouting the will of Congress with a last minute 17-million-acre land grab violated constitutional principles governing the separation of powers. Yet, among millions of American voters, Roosevelt's willingness to defy western cattle barons, mining tycoons, and other "malefactors of great wealth" increased his popularity.

21-6c *Progressivism: A Movement for the People?*

Historians have long debated how much Roosevelt's economic and environmental reforms altered the balance of power between the "interests" and the people. Some have argued that many corporations were eager for federal government regulation—that railroad corporations wanted relief from the rate wars that were driving them into bankruptcy, for example, and that the larger meat packers believed that the costs of government food inspections would drive smaller meat packers out of business. So, too, historians have shown that agribusinesses, timber companies, and mining corporations in the West believed that government regulation would aid them and hurt smaller competitors. According to this view, government regulation benefited sectors of corporate America more than it benefited workers, consumers, and small businessmen.

Indeed, these early reforms often curtailed corporate power only to a limited extent. But in 1907, the progressive program was still evolving. Popular anger over corporate power and political corruption remained a driving force of progressivism. The presence in the Senate of La Follette, Albert Beveridge of Indiana, and other anticorporate Republicans gave that anger an influential national voice. Whether the corporations or the people would benefit most from progressive reforms had yet to be determined.

21-7 The Taft Presidency: Progressive Disappointment and Resurgence

Q *What were the sources of tension between Taft and the progressives?*

Deepening fissures between Roosevelt and Old Guard conservatives in the Republican Party influenced Roosevelt's decision not to seek reelection in 1908. Sensing that he might fail to win his party's nomination, and mindful of a rash promise he had made in 1904 not to run again in 1908, Roosevelt announced his retirement from politics. It was a decision he would soon regret. Barely 50 years old, he was too young and energetic to end his political career.

Roosevelt thought he had found in William Howard Taft, his secretary of war, an ideal successor. But Taft was very different from Roosevelt. He had held only one elected office, and a minor one. He was by nature a cautious and conservative man. Taft won the election of 1908, defeating Democrat William Jennings Bryan with 52 percent of the vote. His conservatism soon revealed itself in his choice of corporation lawyers, rather than reformers, for cabinet positions.

21-7a *Battling Progressives*

Taft's troubles began when he appeared to side against progressives in an acrimonious congressional battle over tariff legislation. The Payne–Aldrich Tariff Act that Taft signed into law in 1909 did little to effect the tariff reductions that progressives had deemed so important as a way of reducing an average workingman's cost of living. A bruising fight over

Private Collection/Photo © Christie's Images/The Bridgeman Art Library

21.14 **Index Peak, Yellowstone National Park, 1914** An environmental movement emerged during the Progressive Era to protect beautiful areas of the American West such as those located in Yellowstone Park, the country's first national park. Thomas Moran painted this image of Index Peak.

Taft's conservation policies brought relations between Taft and the insurgent Republicans to the breaking point.

Secretary of the Interior Richard A. Ballinger had aroused progressives' suspicions by reopening for private commercial use 1 million acres of land that the Roosevelt administration had previously brought under federal protection. Gifford Pinchot, still head of the National Forest Service, accused Ballinger of bowing to corporate interests and of profiting personally from the leases of this land. When Taft defended Ballinger, Pinchot went public with his charges. Whatever hope Taft may have had of escaping political damage disappeared when Roosevelt, returning from an African hunting trip by way of Europe in spring 1910, staged a public rendezvous with Pinchot in England. In so doing, Roosevelt signaled his continuing support for his old friend Pinchot and his displeasure with Taft.

21-7b *Roosevelt's Return*

Roosevelt had barely returned to the United States in summer 1910 when he dove back into politics. In September, Roosevelt embarked on a speaking tour, the high point of which was his elaboration at Osawatomie, Kansas, of his New Nationalism, an ambitious reform program that called for the federal government to stabilize the economy, protect the weak, and restore social harmony.

The 1910 congressional elections confirmed the popularity of Roosevelt's positions. Insurgent Republicans trounced conservative Republicans in primary after primary, and the Democrats' embrace of reform brought them a majority in the House of Representatives for the first time since 1894. When Robert La Follette, who was challenging Taft for the Republican presidential nomination, seemed to suffer a nervous breakdown in February 1912, Roosevelt announced his own candidacy. In the 13 states sponsoring preferential primaries, Roosevelt won nearly 75 percent of the delegates, but the party's national leadership remained in the hands of the Old Guard, and they were determined to deny Roosevelt the Republican nomination. At the Republican convention in Chicago, Taft won renomination on the first ballot.

Roosevelt had expected this outcome. The night before the convention opened, he had told an assembly of 5,000 supporters that the party leaders would not succeed in derailing their movement. "We stand at Armageddon," he declared, and "we battle for the Lord." The next day, Roosevelt and his supporters withdrew from the convention and from the Republican Party. In August, the reformers reassembled as the new **Progressive Party**, nominated Roosevelt for president and California governor Hiram W. Johnson for vice president, and hammered out the reform platform they had long envisioned: sweeping regulation of the corporations, extensive protections for workers, a sharply graduated income tax, and woman suffrage. "I am as strong as a bull moose," Roosevelt roared as he readied for combat; his proud followers took to calling themselves "Bull Moosers."

Some of them, however, probably including Roosevelt, knew that their mission was likely futile. Not enough Republicans had subscribed to Roosevelt's third-party cause to force Taft out of the race. A split in Republican votes between Roosevelt and Taft would likely open the door to a Democratic challenger, a rising star from New Jersey, Woodrow Wilson.

21-7c *The Rise of Woodrow Wilson and the Election of 1912*

Few would have predicted in 1908 that the distinguished president of Princeton University, Woodrow Wilson, would be the 1912 Democratic nominee for president of the United States. Before 1910, Wilson had never run for elective office, nor had he ever held an appointed post in a local, state, or federal administration. The son of a Presbyterian minister from Virginia, Wilson had practiced law for a short time after graduating from Princeton (then the College of New Jersey) in 1879 before settling on an academic career. Earning his doctorate in political science from Johns Hopkins in 1886, he taught history and political science at Bryn Mawr and Wesleyan (Connecticut) before returning to Princeton in 1890. He became president of Princeton in 1902, a post he held until he successfully ran for the governorship of New Jersey in 1910.

Identifying himself with the anti-Bryan wing of the Democratic Party, Wilson attracted the attention of wealthy conservatives, who saw him as a potential presidential candidate. They convinced the bosses of the New Jersey Democratic machine to nominate Wilson for governor in 1910. Wilson accepted the nomination and won the governorship handily. He then shocked his conservative backers by declaring his independence from the state's Democratic machine and moving New Jersey into the forefront of reform.

At the Democratic convention of 1912, Wilson was something of a dark horse, running a distant second to House Speaker Champ Clark of Missouri. When the New York delegation gave Clark a simple majority of delegates, virtually everyone assumed that Clark would soon command the two-thirds majority needed to win the nomination. But Wilson's managers held on to Wilson's delegates and began

Historical/Corbis

21.15 **William Howard Taft** Roosevelt's handpicked successor, Taft, turned out to be much less of a progressive than his predecessor.

Q *The split between Taft and Roosevelt opened the door to a Democratic victory in 1912. Could Republicans have avoided their internal split? If they had remained united, and won the election of 1912, might the history of progressivism from 1912 unfolded in a different way?*

What They Said

Regulate the Trusts or Break Them Up? Roosevelt and Wilson Square Off

One of the biggest issues of the early 20th century was what to do about the trusts—private corporations of such size and power that they seemed to threaten opportunity and democracy in America. As they faced off against each other in the 1912 presidential election, Theodore Roosevelt and Woodrow Wilson gave very different answers to that question. Roosevelt, drawing on the New Nationalist program that he had laid out in a speech at Osawatomie, Kansas, in 1910, wanted to regulate the trusts in the public interest. Wilson did not think that government had the capacity to regulate these behemoth institutions, which he called monopolies, and he criticized the plank in the 1912 Progressive Party platform for asserting that such regulation was a worthy goal. Wilson wanted to break up existing monopolies, and to use the law to prevent new ones from developing in the future.

Theodore Roosevelt

We have come here to-day to commemorate one of the epoch-making events of the long struggle for the rights of man—the long struggle for the uplift of humanity. Our country—this great republic—means nothing unless it means the triumph of a real democracy, the triumph of popular government, and, in the long run, of an economic system under which each man shall be guaranteed the opportunity to show the best that there is in him… .

The true friend of property, the true conservative, is he who insists that property shall be the servant and not the master of the commonwealth; who insists that the creature of man's making shall be the servant and not the master of the man who made it. The citizens of the United States must effectively control the mighty commercial forces which they have themselves called into being… .

Combinations in industry are the result of an imperative economic law which cannot be repealed by political legislation. The effort at prohibiting all combination has substantially failed. The way out lies, not in attempting to prevent such combinations, but in completely controlling them in the interest of the public welfare… . This, I know, implies a policy of a far more active governmental interference with social and economic conditions in this country than we have yet had, but I think we have got to face the fact that such an increase in governmental control is now necessary… .

The man who wrongly holds that every human right is secondary to this profit must now give way to the advocate of human welfare, who rightly maintains that every man holds his property subject to the general right of the community to regulate its use to whatever degree the public welfare may require it.

Woodrow Wilson

Mr. Roosevelt attached to his platform some very splendid suggestions as to noble enterprises which we ought to undertake for the uplift of the human race; but when I hear an ambitious platform put forth, I am very much more interested in the dynamics of it than in the rhetoric of it… . If you have read the trust plank in that platform as often as I have read it, you have found it very long, but very tolerant. It did not anywhere condemn monopoly, except in words; its essential meaning was that the trusts have been bad and must be made to be good… . All that it is proposed to do is to take them under control and regulation… .

I have read and reread that plank, so as to be sure that I get it right… . There will be an avowed partnership between the government and the trusts. I take it that the [government-trust] firm will be ostensibly controlled by the senior member. For I take it that the government of the United States is at least the senior member, though the younger member has all along been running the business. But when all the momentum, when all the energy, when a great deal of the genius, as so often happens in partnerships the world over, is with the junior partner, I don't think that the superintendence of the senior partner is going to amount to very much. And I don't believe that benevolence can be read into the hearts of the trusts by the superintendence and suggestions of the federal government; because the government has never within my recollection had its suggestions accepted by the trusts. On the contrary, the suggestions of the trusts have been accepted by the government… .

There is no hope to be seen for the people of the United States until the partnership is dissolved. And the business of the party now entrusted with power [the Democrats] is going to be to dissolve it… .

We purpose to prevent private monopoly by law, to see to it that the methods by which monopolies have been built up are legally made impossible.

Q *What is Roosevelt's approach to the question of the trusts? What is Wilson's?*

Q *Why is Wilson critical of Roosevelt?*

Q *Roosevelt presents himself as the "true conservative." In this debate, who was the conservative and who was the progressive?*

Q *Which approach, the New Nationalism or the New Freedom, stood a greater chance of success?*

Sources: (top) Theodore Roosevelt, "The New Nationalism," in *Roosevelt, The New Nationalism* (New York: The Outlook Company, 1910), pp. 3, 13, 15, 18, 23–24; (bottom) Woodrow Wilson, *The New Freedom: A Call for the Emancipation of the Generous Energies of a People* (New York: Doubleday, Page & Co., 1913), pp. 193–194, 195, 202–203, 222.

Historical/Corbis

21.16 **Woodrow Wilson** The Democratic presidential candidate campaigning from the back of a train in 1912, pledging to fulfill progressivism's promise.

Q *Why, during the years of Wilson's presidency, did the Republicans cede their reputation as the party of reform to the Democrats?*

chipping away at Clark's lead. On the fourth day, on the 46th ballot, Wilson won the nomination.

Given the split in Republican ranks, Democrats had their best chance in 20 years of regaining the White House. A Wilson victory, moreover, would give the country its first southern-born president in almost 50 years. Finally, whatever its outcome, the election promised to deliver a vote for reform. Both Roosevelt and Wilson were running on reform platforms, and the Socialist Party candidate, Eugene V. Debs, was attracting larger crowds and generating greater enthusiasm than had been expected. Taft was so certain of defeat that he barely campaigned.

Debate among the candidates focused on the trusts. All three reform candidates—Roosevelt, Wilson, and Debs—agreed that corporations had acquired too much economic power. Debs argued that the only way to ensure popular control of that power was for the federal government to assume ownership of the trusts. Roosevelt called for the establishment of a strong government that would regulate and, if necessary, curb the power of the trusts. This was the essence of his New Nationalism, the program he had been advocating since 1910.

Rather than regulate the trusts, Wilson declared his intention to break them up. He wanted to reverse the tendency toward economic concentration and thus restore opportunity to the people. This philosophy, which Wilson labeled the **New Freedom**, called for a temporary concentration of governmental power in order to dismantle the trusts. But once that was accomplished, Wilson promised, the government would relinquish its power.

Wilson won the November election with 42 percent of the popular vote to Roosevelt's 27 percent and Taft's 23 percent; Debs made a strong showing with 6 percent, the largest in his party's history (see Map 21.3).

21-8 The Wilson Presidency

Q *What were the key similarities and differences in the progressive politics of Theodore Roosevelt and Woodrow Wilson?*

Wilson quickly assembled a cabinet of talented men who could be counted on for wise counsel, loyalty, and influence over vital Democratic constituencies. He cultivated a public image of himself as a president firmly in charge of his party and as a faithful tribune of the people. Wilson first turned his attention to tariff reform. The House passed a tariff-reduction bill within a month, and Wilson used his leadership skills to push the bill through a reluctant Senate. The resulting Underwood Simmons Tariff Act of 1913 reduced tariff barriers from approximately 40 to 25 percent. To make up for revenue lost to tariff reductions, Congress then passed an income tax law. The Sixteenth Amendment to the Constitution, ratified by the states in 1913, had already given the government the right to impose an income tax. The law passed by Congress made good on the progressive pledge to reduce the power and privileges of wealthy Americans by requiring them to pay taxes on a greater percentage of their income than the poor.

21-8a *The Rise and Fall of the New Freedom*

Wilson then asked Congress to overhaul the nation's financial system. The banking interests and their congressional supporters wanted the government to give the authority to regulate credit and currency flows either to a single bank or to several regional banks. Progressives opposed the vesting of so much financial power in private hands and insisted that any

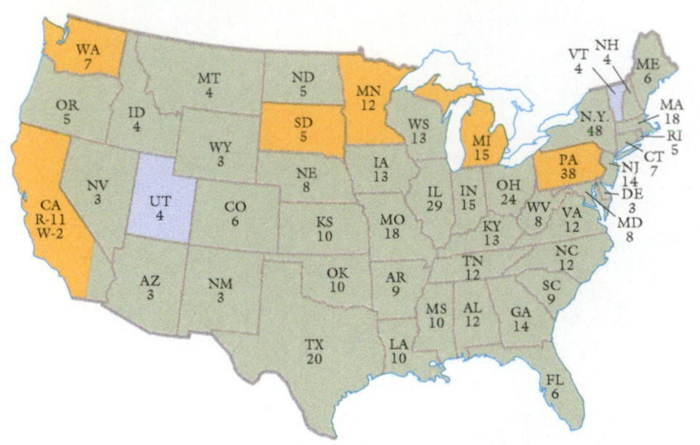

	Electoral Vote		Popular Vote	
	Number	%	Number	%
Wilson (Democrat)	435	82.0	6,296,547	42.5
Taft (Republican)	8	1.5	3,486,720	23.6
Roosevelt (Progressive)	88	16.5	4,118,571	27.8
Debs (Socialist)	----	----	900,672	6.1

▲ **MAP 21.3 Presidential Election, 1912**

Taft and Roosevelt split the Republican vote, allowing Wilson to win with a plurality of the popular vote (42 percent) and a big majority (82 percent) of the electoral vote.

Q *How was it possible for a candidate like Wilson to win less than a majority of the popular vote but more than 80 percent of the electoral vote?*

Q *Which areas of the country possessed the greatest concentration of electoral votes during the Progressive era? Did this distribution affect how the parties chose their candidates for the presidency?*

reformed financial system must be publicly controlled. Wilson worked out a compromise plan that included both private and public controls, and he marshaled the votes to push it through both the House and the Senate. By the end of 1913, Wilson had signed the **Federal Reserve Act**, the most important law passed in his first administration.

The Federal Reserve Act established 12 regional banks, each controlled by the private banks in its region (see Map 21.4). Every private bank in the country was required to deposit an average of 6 percent of its assets into its regional Federal Reserve bank. The reserve would be used to make loans to member banks and to issue paper currency (Federal Reserve notes) to facilitate financial transactions. The regional banks were also instructed to use their funds to shore up member banks in distress and to respond to sudden changes in credit demands by easing or tightening the flow of credit. A Federal Reserve Board appointed by the president and responsible to the public rather than to private bankers would set policy and oversee activities within the 12 reserve banks.

The Federal Reserve system strengthened the nation's financial structure and was in most respects an impressive political achievement for Wilson. In its final form, however, it revealed that Wilson was retreating from his New Freedom pledge. The Federal Reserve Board was a less powerful and less centralized federal authority than a national bank would have been, but it nevertheless represented a substantial increase in the central government's control of banking. Moreover, the bill authorizing the system made no attempt to break up private financial institutions that had grown too powerful or to prohibit the interlocking directorates that large banks used to augment their power. Because it sought to work with large banks rather than to break them up, the Federal Reserve system seemed more consonant with the principles of Roosevelt's New Nationalism than with those of Wilson's New Freedom.

Wilson's failure to mount a vigorous antitrust campaign confirmed his drift toward the New Nationalism. For example, in 1914, Wilson supported the Federal Trade Commission Act, which created a government agency by that name to regulate business practices. The Federal Trade Commission (FTC) had wide powers to collect information on corporate pricing policies and on cooperation and competition among businesses. The FTC might have attacked trusts for "unfair trade practices," but the Senate stripped the FTC Act's companion legislation, the Clayton Antitrust Act, of most provisions that would have allowed the government to prosecute the trusts. Wilson supported this weakening of the Clayton Act, having decided that the breakup of large-scale industry was no longer practical or preferable. The FTC, in Wilson's eyes, would help businesses, large and small, to regulate themselves in ways that contributed to national well-being. In accepting giant industry as an inescapable feature of modern life and in seeking to regulate industrial behavior by means of government agencies such as the FTC, Wilson had become, in effect, a New Nationalist.

At first, Wilson's shift to New Nationalist policies led him to support business interests. His nominations to the Federal Reserve Board, for example, were generally men who had worked for Wall Street firms and large industrial corporations. At the same time, he usually refused to use government powers to aid organized groups of workers and farmers. Court rulings had made worker and farmer organizations vulnerable to prosecution under the terms of the Sherman Antitrust Act of 1890. AFL president Samuel Gompers and other labor leaders tried but failed to convince Wilson to insert into the Clayton Antitrust Act a clause that would unambiguously grant labor and farmer organizations immunity from further antitrust prosecutions.

Nor did Wilson, at this time, view with any greater sympathy the campaign for African American political equality. He supported efforts by white southerners in his cabinet, such as Postmaster General Albert Burleson and Treasury Secretary William McAdoo, to segregate their government departments, and he largely ignored pleas from the NAACP to involve the federal government in a campaign against lynching.

21-8b *Progressivism for the People*

In late 1915, however, Wilson moved to the left, in part because he feared losing his reelection in 1916. The Bull Moosers of 1912 were retreating back to the Republican Party. Wilson

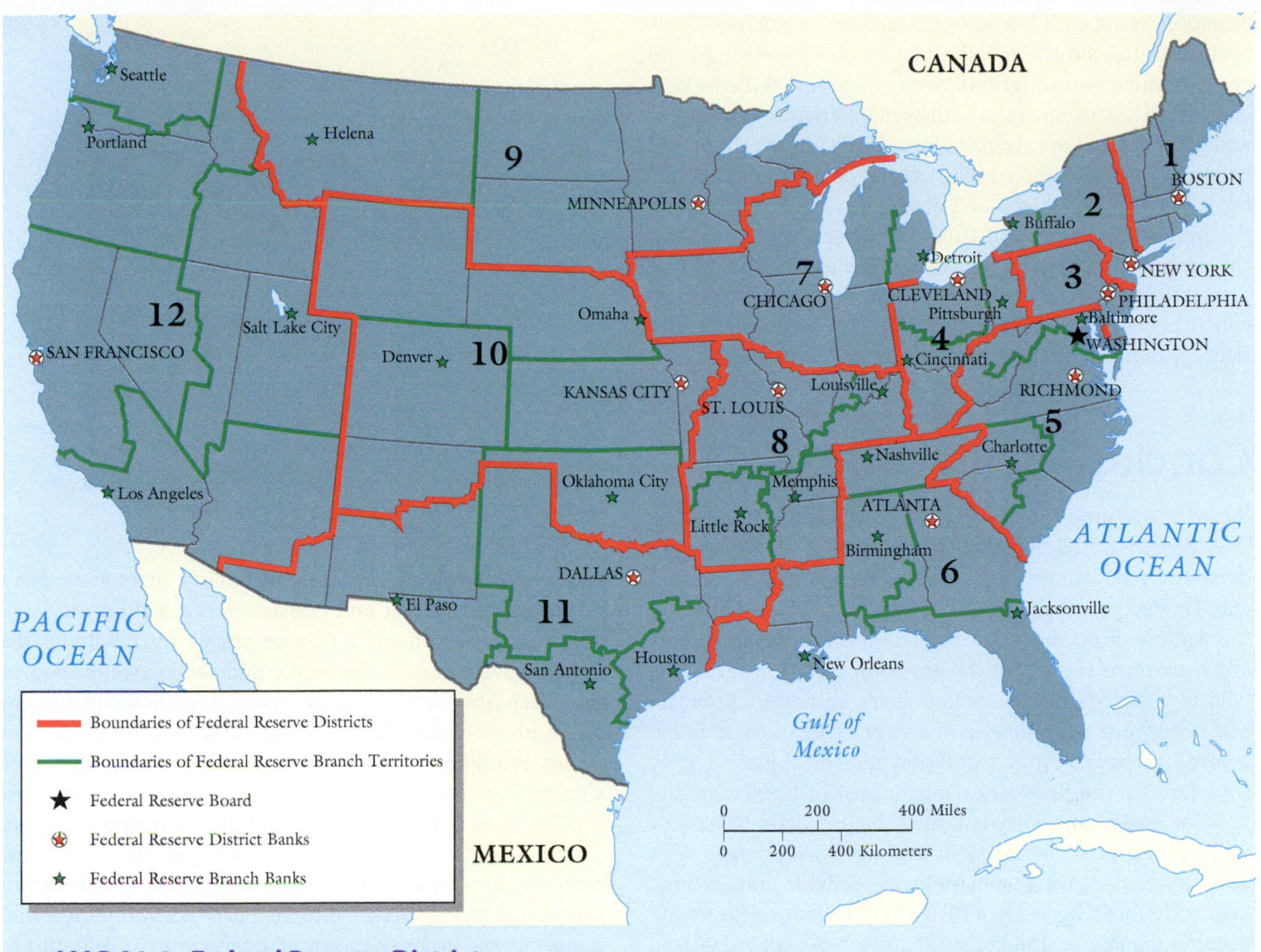

▲ **MAP 21.4 Federal Reserve Districts** This map demonstrates in visual terms how the Federal Reserve (FR) attempted to impose order on the nation's financial system: via 12 districts, each with an FR district bank. Most of the districts were subdivided into branches, in which the FR also established a banking presence.

Q *Why were early 20th-century Federal Reserve Districts so much smaller in the East than in the West?*

Q *Does this map provide a clue as to where the banking power of the United States was concentrated in the early 20th century?*

remembered how much his 1912 victory, based on only 42 percent of the popular vote, had depended on the Republican split. To halt the progressives' rapprochement with the GOP, he made a bid for their support. In January 1916, he nominated Louis Brandeis to the Supreme Court. Not only was Brandeis one of the country's most respected progressives, but he was also the first Jew nominated to serve on the country's highest court. Congressional conservatives did everything they could to block the confirmation of a man they regarded as dangerously radical, but Wilson, as usual, was better organized, and by June his forces in the Senate had emerged victorious.

Wilson followed up this victory by pushing through Congress the first federal workmen's compensation law (the Kern–McGillicuddy Act, which covered federal employees), the first federal law outlawing child labor (the Keating–Owen Act), and the first federal law guaranteeing workers an eight-hour day (the Adamson Act, which covered the nation's 400,000 railway workers). The number of Americans affected by these acts was relatively small. Nevertheless, Wilson had reoriented the Democratic Party to a New Nationalism that cared as much about the interests of the powerless as the interests of the powerful.

Trade unionists flocked to Wilson, as did most of the prominent progressives who had followed the Bull Moose in 1912. Meanwhile, Wilson had appealed to the supporters of William Jennings Bryan by supporting legislation that made federal credit available to farmers in need. He had put together a reform coalition capable of winning a majority at the polls. In the process, he had transformed the Democratic Party. From 1916 on, the Democrats, rather than the Republicans, became the chief guardians of the American reform tradition.

That Wilson did so underscores the strength of the reform and radical forces in American society. By 1916, the ranks of middle-class progressives had grown broad and deep. Working-class protest had also accelerated in scope and intensity. In Lawrence, Massachusetts, in 1912, and in Paterson, New Jersey, in 1913, for example, the IWW organized strikes of textile workers that drew national attention, as did a 1914 strike by Colorado mine workers. These protests reflected the mobilization of those working-class constituencies—immigrants, women, the unskilled—long considered inconsequential both by mainstream labor leaders and party politicians. Assisted by radicals, these groups had begun to fashion a more inclusive and politically ambitious labor movement. Wilson and other Democrats understood the potential strength of this new labor insurgency, and the president's pro-labor legislative agenda in 1916 can be understood, in part, as an effort to channel labor's new constituents into the Democratic Party. It was a successful strategy that contributed to Wilson's reelection in 1916.

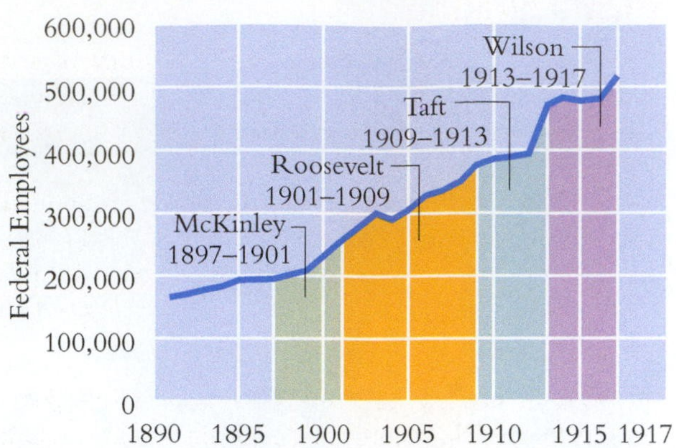

Figure 21.4 **Growth in Federal Employment, 1891–1917**

Source: Adapted from *The Federal Government Service*, ed. W. S. Sayre (Upper Saddle River, NJ: Prentice-Hall, 1965), p. 41, The American Assembly.

Conclusion

By 1916, the progressives had accomplished a great deal. They demonstrated that traditional American concerns with democracy and liberty could be adapted to an industrial age. They exposed and curbed some of the worst abuses of the American political system. They enfranchised women and took steps to protect the environment. They broke the hold of laissez-faire economic policies on national politics and replaced it with the idea of a strong federal government committed to economic regulation and social justice. They transformed the presidency into a post of legislative and popular leadership. They enlarged the executive branch by establishing new commissions and agencies charged with administering government policies. Federal employment nearly doubled between 1901, when Theodore Roosevelt became president, and early 1917, when Woodrow Wilson completed his first term (see Figure 21.4).

The progressives, in short, had begun to create a strong national government, one in which power increasingly flowed away from municipalities and states and toward Washington. This reorientation followed a compelling logic: A national government stood a better chance of solving the problems of growing economic inequality, mismanagement of natural resources, and consumer fraud than did local and state governments. This emphasis on involving the federal government in economic and social affairs became progressivism's most enduring legacy. It made the movement a forerunner of the liberalism and "New Deal" that emerged under Franklin Roosevelt's leadership in the 1930s (see Chapter 25).

The rise of progressivism had also revealed, however, that powerful economic interests could themselves become quite comfortable with government regulation, believing that they would be able to turn it to their own advantage. Another danger lurked in the claims by new government regulators to a special authority deriving from their expertise in science and management. Would they truly be disinterested civil servants, capable of discerning and implementing democratic wishes? In 1916, progressivism remained a work in progress, its accomplishments still partial, its character not yet fully formed.

CHAPTER REVIEW

Review

1. What were the similarities among the various groups spearheading reform? What were the differences?
2. What were the benefits and costs of municipal reform?
3. What were the results of progressive efforts to create a "responsible" and "virtuous" electorate?
4. How was scientific management applied to the factory floor? How successful a reform was it?
5. How did W. E. B. Du Bois's approach to reforms for African Americans differ from that of Booker T. Washington?
6. What would you identify as Roosevelt's three most important contributions to progressive reform?
7. What were the sources of tension between Taft and the progressives?
8. What were the key similarities and differences in the progressive politics of Theodore Roosevelt and Woodrow Wilson?

Critical Thinking

1. Progressivism sought to reform all of American society—politics, economy, and culture. What were the most important reforms in each of these realms? Were these reforms successful in achieving their aims?
2. When the progressive reform movement peaked during the first Wilson administration (1913–1917), did it result in greater liberty and equality for ordinary Americans?

Identifications

Review your understanding of the following key terms, people, and events for this chapter (terms in bold in text are included in the Glossary).

muckrakers, p. 574
Hull House, p. 575
socialism, p. 578
Eugene Victor Debs, p. 578
initiative, p. 580
referendum, p. 580
recall, p. 580
Australian ballot (secret ballot), p. 581
disfranchisement, p. 582
National Association for the Advancement of Colored People (NAACP), p. 582
National American Woman Suffrage Association (NAWSA), p. 583
Wisconsin Idea, p. 585
Frederick Winslow Taylor, p. 586
W. E. B. Du Bois, p. 587
New Nationalism, p. 589
conservationist, p. 590
Progressive Party, p. 592
New Freedom, p. 595
Federal Reserve Act, p. 596

Suggested Readings

No topic in 20th-century American history has generated as large and rapidly changing a scholarship as has progressivism. In ***The Age of Reform: From Bryan to FDR*** (1955), **Richard Hofstadter** argues that progressivism was the expression of a declining Protestant middle class at odds with the new industrial order. In ***The Search for Order, 1877–1920*** (1967), **Robert Wiebe** finds the movement's core in a rising middle class, closely allied to the corporations and bureaucratic imperatives that were defining this new order. **James Weinstein**, ***The Corporate Ideal in the Liberal State, 1900–1918*** (1969), argues that progressivism was the work of businessmen, who were eager to ensure corporate stability and profitability in a dangerously unstable capitalist economy.

Without denying the importance of this corporate search for order, **Alan Dawley**, ***Struggles for Justice: Social Responsibility and the Liberal State*** (1991), insists on the role of the working class, men and women, whites and blacks, in shaping the progressive agenda. **James T. Kloppenberg**, ***Uncertain Victory: Social Democracy and Progressivism in European and American Thought, 1870–1920*** (1986), emphasizes the influence of socialism on progressive thought, while **Martin J. Sklar**, ***The Corporate Reconstruction of American Capitalism, 1900–1916: The Market, the Law and Politics*** (1988), stresses the role of progressivism in "containing" or taming socialism. **Michael McGerr**, ***A Fierce Discontent: The Rise and Fall of the Progressive Movement in America, 1870–1920*** (2003), is the most recent effort to comprehend the whole of the progressive movement.

Daniel T. Rodgers reconstructs the international networks of reform that nourished progressivism in ***Atlantic Crossings: Social Politics in a Progressive Age*** (1998). **Nick Salvatore** captures the charisma and enigma of Debs in his ***Eugene V. Debs: Citizen and Socialist*** (1982). **Paul Boyer**, ***Urban Masses and Moral Order in America, 1820–1920*** (1978), treats progressivism as a cultural movement to enforce middle-class norms on unruly urban and immigrant populations. **Theda Skocpol**, ***Protecting Soldiers and Mothers: The Political Origins of Social Policy in the United States*** (1992), and **Robyn Muncy**, ***Creating a Female Dominion in American Reform, 1890–1935*** (1991), reconstruct the central role of middle-class Protestant women in shaping progressive social policy, while **Robert M. Crunden**, ***Ministers of Reform: The Progressives' Achievement in American Civilization, 1889–1920*** (1982), stresses the religious roots of progressive reform. **Michael Kazin**, ***A Godly Hero: The Life of William Jennings Bryan*** (2006), is indispensable on the religious dimensions of progressivism, while **Alexander Keyssar**, ***The Right to Vote: The Contested History of Democracy in the United States*** (2000), is an essential guide to political reform during this period. **Eric Yellin**, ***Racism in the Nation's Service: Government Workers and the Color Line in Woodrow Wilson's America*** (2013), is the most probing study of how the Woodrow Wilson administration resegregated government work in Washington, D.C., in the 1910s. **Benjamin Heber Johnson**, ***Escaping the Dark, Gray City: Fear and Hope in Progressive-Era Conservation*** (2017), ably situates the conservation movement within the broader context of progressive reform.

22 Becoming a World Power, 1898–1917

22.1 **Uncle Sam Gets Cocky, 1901** From 1898 to 1917, the United States broadened its influence in world affairs and especially sought to establish its dominance in Latin America. This cartoon illustrates that dominance through the figure of a giant Uncle Sam rooster that dwarfs both the European chickens (locked up in a coop) and the diminutive Latin American republics.

FOR MUCH OF THE 19TH CENTURY, most Americans were preoccupied by continental expansion. Elections rarely turned on international events, and presidents rarely made their reputations as statesmen in the world arena. The diplomatic corps, like most agencies of the federal government, was small and inexperienced. The government projected its limited military power westward and possessed virtually no capacity or desire for involvement overseas.

The nation's rapid industrial growth in the late 19th century forced a turn away from such continentalism. Technological advances, especially the laying of transoceanic cables and the introduction of steamship travel, diminished America's physical isolation. The babble of languages one could hear in American cities testified to how much the Old World had penetrated the New. Then, too, Americans watched anxiously as England, Germany, Russia, Japan, and other industrial powers intensified their competition for overseas markets and colonies. Some believed America also needed to enter this contest.

A war with Spain in 1898 gave the United States an opportunity to upgrade its military and acquire colonies and influence in the Western Hemisphere and Asia. Under Presidents William McKinley and Theodore Roosevelt, the United States pursued these initiatives and established a small but strategically important empire. Not all Americans supported this imperial project, and many protested the subjugation of the peoples of Cuba, Puerto Rico, and the Philippines that imperial expansion seemed to entail. In the eyes of anti-imperialists, the United States seemed to be becoming the kind of nation that many Americans had long despised—one that valued power more than liberty.

Roosevelt brushed aside these objections and set about creating an international system in which a handful of industrial nations pursued their global economic interests, dominated world trade, and kept the world at peace. Woodrow Wilson, however, was more troubled by America's imperial turn. His doubts became apparent in his efforts to devise a policy toward post-revolutionary Mexico that restrained American might and respected Mexican desires for liberty. It was a worthy ambition but one that proved difficult to achieve. ■

22-1 The United States Looks Abroad

Which groups in American society were most interested in expanding U.S. influence abroad?

By the late 19th century, sizable numbers of Americans had become interested in extending their country's influence abroad. The most important groups were Protestant missionaries, businessmen, and imperialists.

22-1a *Protestant Missionaries*

Protestant missionaries were among the most active promoters of American interests abroad. Overseas missionary activity grew quickly between 1870 and 1900, most of it directed toward China. Between 1880 and 1900, the number of women's missionary societies doubled, from 20 to 40; by 1915, these societies enrolled 3 million women. Convinced of the superiority of the Anglo-Saxon race, Protestant missionaries considered it their Christian duty to teach the Gospel to the "ignorant" Asian masses and save their souls. Missionaries also believed that their conversion efforts would free those masses from their racial destiny, enabling them to become "civilized."

22-1b *Businessmen*

Industrialists, traders, and investors also began to look overseas, sensing that they could make fortunes in foreign lands. Exports of American manufactured goods rose substantially after 1880 (see Figure 22.1). By 1914, American foreign investment equaled a sizable 7 percent of the nation's gross national product. Companies such as Eastman Kodak (film and cameras), Singer Sewing Machine, Standard Oil, American Tobacco, and International Harvester had become multinational corporations with overseas branch offices.

Some industrialists became entranced by the prospect of clothing, feeding, housing, and transporting the 400 million people of China. James B. Duke, who headed American Tobacco, was selling 1 billion cigarettes per year in East Asian markets. Looking for ways to fill empty boxcars heading west from Minnesota to Tacoma, Washington, the railroad tycoon James J. Hill imagined stuffing them with wheat and steel destined for China and Japan. He actually distributed wheat cookbooks throughout East Asia to convince Asians to shift from a rice-based to a bread-based diet (so that there would be a market there for U.S. flour exports). Although export trade with East Asia during this period never fulfilled the expectations of Hill and other industrialists, their talk about the "wealth of the Orient" impressed on politicians its importance to American economic health.

Events of the 1890s only intensified the appeal of foreign markets. First, the 1890 U.S. census announced that the frontier had disappeared and that America had completed the task of westward expansion. Then, in 1893, a young historian named Frederick Jackson Turner published an essay, "The Significance of the Frontier in American History," articulating what many Americans feared: that the frontier had been essential to the growth of the economy and to the cultivation of democracy.

Living on the frontier, Turner argued, had transformed the Europeans who settled the New World into Americans. They shed their European clothing styles, social customs, and political beliefs, and acquired distinctively American characteristics—rugged individualism, egalitarianism, and

CHRONOLOGY

1893	Frederick Jackson Turner publishes an essay announcing the end of the frontier
1898	Spanish-American War (April 14–August 12) • Treaty of Paris signed (December 10), giving United States control of Philippines, Guam, and Puerto Rico • United States annexes Hawaii
1900	United States annexes Puerto Rico • United States and other imperial powers put down Chinese Boxer Rebellion
1899–1902	American-Filipino War
1901	United States forces Cuba to adopt constitution favorable to U.S. interests
1903	Hay–Bunau-Varilla Treaty signed, giving United States control of Panama Canal Zone
1904	"Roosevelt Corollary" to Monroe Doctrine proclaimed
1905	Roosevelt negotiates end to Russo-Japanese War
1906–1917	United States intervenes in Cuba, Nicaragua, Haiti, Dominican Republic, and Mexico
1907	Roosevelt and Japanese government reach a "gentlemen's agreement" restricting Japanese immigration and ending the segregation of Japanese schoolchildren in California
1907–1909	Great White Fleet circles the world
1909–1913	Taft conducts "dollar diplomacy"
1910	Mexican Revolution begins
1914	Panama Canal opens
1914–1917	Wilson struggles to develop a policy toward Mexico
1917	United States purchases Virgin Islands from Denmark

a democratic faith. How, Turner wondered, could the nation continue to prosper now that the frontier had gone?

In recent years, historians of the American West have criticized **Turner's "frontier thesis."** They have argued that the very idea of the frontier as uninhabited wilderness overlooked the tens of thousands of Indians who occupied the region and that much else of what Americans believed about the West was based more on myth than on reality. They have also pointed out that it makes little sense to view the 1890s as a decade in which opportunities for economic gain disappeared in the West. Yet, Turner's essay is still relevant for the way in which it expressed a fear that America had lost its way. As the depression of the 1890s settled on the nation, Americans began to ask what the republic could do to regain its economic prosperity and political stability. Where would it find its new frontiers? One answer to these questions focused on the pursuit of overseas expansion.

22-1c *Imperialists*

Eager to assist in the drive for overseas expansion was a group of politicians, intellectuals, and military strategists who viewed such expansion as essential to the pursuit of world power. They wanted the United States to join Britain, France, Germany, and Russia as a great imperial nation. They believed that the United States should build a strong navy, solidify a sphere of influence in the Caribbean, and extend markets into Asia. Their desire to control ports and territories beyond the continental borders of their own country made them **imperialists**.

One of the era's best-known imperialists was **Alfred Thayer Mahan**. In an influential book, *The Influence of Sea Power upon History, 1660–1783* (1890), Mahan argued that past empires, beginning with Rome, had relied on their capacity to control the seas. Mahan called for the construction of a U.S. navy with enough ships and firepower to make its presence felt across the world. To be effective, that global fleet would require a canal across Central America through which U.S. warships could pass swiftly from the Atlantic to the Pacific oceans. It would also require a string of far-flung service bases from the Caribbean to the southwestern Pacific. Mahan recommended that the U.S. government take possession of Hawaii and other strategically located Pacific islands with superior harbor facilities.

Presidents William McKinley and Theodore Roosevelt would eventually make almost the whole of Mahan's vision a reality, but in the early 1890s, Mahan doubted that Americans would accept the responsibility and costs of empire. Many Americans still insisted that the United States should not acquire overseas bases and colonize foreign peoples.

Mahan underestimated, however, the government's alarm over the scramble of Europeans to extend their imperial control. Every U.S. administration from the 1880s on committed to a "big navy" policy. By 1898, the U.S. Navy ranked fifth in the world, and by 1900, it ranked third (see Table 22.1). Already in 1878, the United States had secured rights to Pago Pago, a superb deep-water harbor in Samoa (a collection of islands in the southwest Pacific inhabited by Polynesians), and in 1885, it had leased Pearl Harbor from the Hawaiians. Both harbors were expected to serve as fueling stations for the growing U.S. fleet.

These attempts to project U.S. power overseas had already deepened the government's involvement in the affairs of distant lands. In 1889, the United States established a protectorate over part of Samoa, a move meant to forestall German and British efforts to weaken American influence on the islands. In the early 1890s, President Grover Cleveland's administration was increasingly drawn into Hawaiian affairs, as tensions between American sugar plantation owners there and native Hawaiians upset the islands' economic and political stability. In 1891, U.S. plantation owners succeeded in deposing the Hawaiian king and putting into power Queen Liliuokalani. But when Liliuokalani strove to establish her independence from American interests, the planters, assisted by U.S. sailors, overthrew her regime, too. Cleveland declared Hawaii a protectorate in 1893, but he resisted the imperialists in Congress who wanted to annex the islands.

22.2 **Singer Sewing Machine Advertisement** The Singer Sewing Machine Company was one of the first American multinational corporations. This advertisement, with its maps of the Western Hemisphere and its description of Singer as "the universal sewing machine," stresses Singer's global orientation.

Q *Why did the Singer Sewing Machine Company choose to represent its international influence through the figure of Columbia, herself modeled on Athena, the Greek Goddess of wisdom and law? Compare and contrast this representation of Columbia/Athena with the one appearing on p. 584 of Chapter 21.*

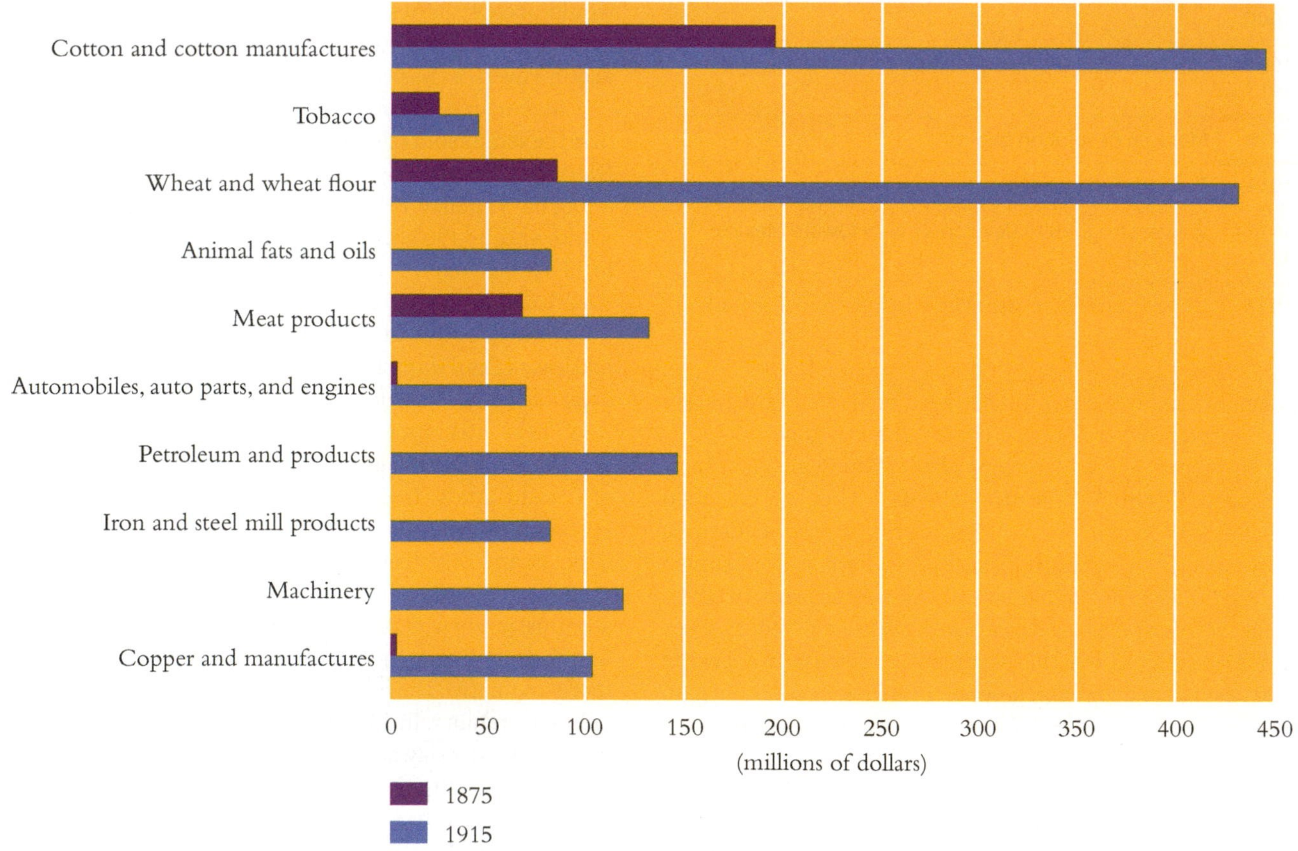

Figure 22.1 **Leading U.S. Exports, 1875 and 1915**

Source: Data from *Historical Statistics of the United States, Colonial Times to 1970* (White Plains, NY: Kraus International, 1989).

Still, imperialist sentiment in Congress and across the nation continued to grow, fueled by "jingoism." Jingoists were nationalists who thought that a swaggering foreign policy and a willingness to go to war would enhance their nation's glory. The anti-imperialist editor of *The Nation*, E. L. Godkin, exclaimed in 1894: "The number of men and officials of this country who are now mad to fight somebody is appalling." Recent feminist scholarship has emphasized the degree to which men of the 1890s saw war as an opportunity to revive frontier-like notions of masculinity—of men as warriors and conquerors—that were proving difficult to sustain in industrializing and bureaucratizing America. Spain's behavior in Cuba in the 1890s gave those men the war they sought.

22-2 The Spanish–American War

Q *In going to war against Spain in 1898, was the United States impelled more by imperialist or anti-imperialist motives?*

Relations between the Cubans and their Spanish rulers had long been deteriorating. The Spanish had taken 10 years to subdue a revolt begun in 1868. In 1895, the Cubans staged another revolt, sparked by their continuing resentment of Spanish control and by a depressed economy. The fighting was brutal. Cuban forces destroyed large areas of the island to make it uninhabitable by the Spanish. The Spanish army, led by General Valeriano Weyler, responded in kind, forcing large numbers of Cubans into concentration camps. Denied adequate food, shelter, and sanitation, an estimated 200,000 Cubans—one-eighth of the island's population—died of starvation and disease.

Such tactics, especially those ascribed to "Butcher" Weyler (as he was known in much of the U.S. press), inflamed American opinion. Many Americans sympathized with the Cubans, who seemed to be fighting the kind of anticolonial war Americans had waged more than 100 years earlier. Americans stayed informed about Cuban–Spanish struggles by reading the *New York Journal*, owned by William Randolph Hearst, and the *New York World*, owned by Joseph Pulitzer. Hearst and Pulitzer were transforming newspaper publishing in much the same way that *McClure's Magazine* and *Ladies' Home Journal* had revolutionized the magazine business (see Chapter 21). To boost circulation, Hearst and Pulitzer sought out sensational and shocking stories and described them in lurid detail. They were accused of engaging in **yellow journalism**—embellishing stories with titillating details when the true reports did not seem dramatic enough.

The sensationalism of the yellow press and its frequently jingoistic accounts failed to bring about American intervention in Cuba, however. In the final days of his administration, President Cleveland resisted mounting pressure to intervene. William McKinley, who succeeded him in 1897, denounced the Spanish harshly, with the aim of forcing Spain into concessions that would satisfy the Cuban rebels and end the conflict. Initially, this strategy seemed to work: Spain relieved "Butcher" Weyler of his command, released some incarcerated Cubans from concentration camps, and granted Cuba limited autonomy. But these concessions did not satisfy Cuban rebels, who were demanding full independence. Late in 1897, when riots broke out in Havana, McKinley ordered the battleship *Maine* into Havana Harbor to protect U.S. citizens and their property. Then, two unexpected events set off a war.

The first was the February 9, 1898, publication in Hearst's *New York Journal* of a letter stolen from Enrique Dupuy de Lôme, the Spanish minister to Washington, in which he described McKinley as "a cheap politician" and a "bidder for the admiration of the crowd." The de Lôme letter also implied that the Spanish cared little about resolving the Cuban crisis through negotiation and reform. The news embarrassed Spanish officials and outraged many in the United States. Then, only six days later, the *Maine* exploded in Havana Harbor, killing 260 American sailors. Although subsequent investigations indicated that the most probable cause of the explosion was a malfunctioning boiler, Americans were certain that it had been the work of Spanish saboteurs. "Remember the *Maine!*" screamed the headlines in the yellow press. On March 8, Congress responded to the clamor for war by authorizing $50 million to mobilize U.S. forces. In the meantime, McKinley notified Spain of his conditions for avoiding war: Spain would pay an indemnity for the *Maine*,

Table 22.1 THE U.S. NAVY, 1890–1914: EXPENDITURES AND BATTLESHIP SIZE

Fiscal Year	Total Federal Expenditures	Naval Expenditures	Naval Expenditures as Percentage of Total Federal Expenditures	Size of Battleships (average tons displaced)
1890	$318,040,711	$ 22,006,206	6.9%	11,000
1900	520,860,847	55,953,078	10.7	12,000
1901	524,616,925	60,506,978	11.5	16,000
1905	657,278,914	117,550,308	20.7	16,000
1909	693,743,885	115,546,011	16.7	27,000 (1910)
1914	735,081,431	139,682,186	19.0	32,000

Sources: (for expenditures) E. B. Potter, *Sea Power: A Naval History* (Annapolis: Naval Institute Press, 1982), p. 187; (for size of ships) Harold Sprout, *Toward a New Order of Sea Power* (New York: Greenwood Press, 1976), p. 52.

22.3 **Uncle Sam Gives Spain More Than It Can Handle** By going to war in 1898, this poster suggests, the United States would topple Spain and the remnants of its empire.

Q *What does this cartoon reveal about American attitudes toward its rival, Spain?*

abandon its concentration camps, end the fighting with the rebels, and commit to Cuban independence. On April 9, Spain accepted the first three demands but not the last. Thus, on April 11, McKinley asked Congress for authority to go to war. Three days later, Congress approved a war resolution, which included a declaration (spelled out in the Teller Amendment) that the United States would not use the war as an opportunity to acquire territory in Cuba. On April 24, Spain responded with a formal declaration of war against the United States.

22-2a *"A Splendid Little War"*

Secretary of State John Hay called the fight with Spain "a splendid little war." Begun in April, it ended in August. More than 1 million men volunteered to fight, and fewer than 500 were killed or wounded in combat. The American victory over Spain was complete, not just in Cuba but in the neighboring island of Puerto Rico and in the Philippines, Spain's strategic possession in the Pacific.

Actually, the war was more complicated than it seemed. The main reason for the easy victory was U.S. naval superiority. In the war's first major battle, a naval engagement in Manila's harbor in the Philippines on May 1, a U.S. fleet commanded by Commodore George Dewey destroyed an entire Spanish fleet and lost only one sailor (to heat stroke). On land, the story was different. On the eve of war, the U.S. Army consisted of only 26,000 troops. These soldiers were skilled at skirmishing with Indians but ill-prepared and ill-equipped for all-out war. A force of 80,000 Spanish regulars awaited them in Cuba, with another 50,000 in reserve in Spain. Congress immediately increased the army to 62,000 and called for an additional 125,000 volunteers. The response to this call was astounding, but outfitting, training, and transporting the new recruits overwhelmed the army's capacities. Its standard-issue, blue flannel uniforms proved too heavy for fighting in tropical Cuba. Rations were so poor that soldiers referred to one common item as "embalmed beef." Most of the volunteers had to make do with ancient Civil War rifles that still used black, rather than smokeless, powder. The army as a whole was unprepared for the effects of malaria and other tropical diseases.

That the Cuban revolutionaries were predominantly black also came as a shock to the U.S. forces. In their attempts to arouse support for the Cuban cause, U.S. newspapers had portrayed Cuban rebels as similar to white Americans. They were described as intelligent, civilized, and democratic, possessing an "Anglo-Saxon tenacity of purpose." And they were "fully nine-tenths" white, according to one report. The Spanish oppressors, by contrast, were depicted as dark-complexioned—"dark cruel eyes, dark swaggering men" wrote author Sherwood Anderson—and as possessing the characteristics of their "dark race": barbarism, cruelty, and indolence. The U.S. troops' first encounters with Cuban and Spanish forces challenged these stereotypes. Their Cuban allies appeared poorly outfitted, rough mannered, and largely black. The Spanish soldiers appeared well disciplined, tough in battle, and light-complexioned.

The Cuban rebels were skilled guerrilla fighters, but racial prejudice prevented most U.S. soldiers and reporters from crediting their military expertise. Instead, they judged the Cubans harshly—as primitive, savage, and incapable of self-control or self-government. White U.S. troops preferred not to fight alongside the Cubans; increasingly, they refused to coordinate strategy with them.

At first, the U.S. Army's logistical unpreparedness and its racial misconceptions did little to diminish the soldiers' hunger for a good fight. No one was more eager for battle than Theodore Roosevelt, who, along with Colonel Leonard Wood, led a motley volunteer cavalry unit composed of Ivy League graduates, western cowboys, sheriffs, prospectors, Indians, and small numbers of Hispanics and ethnic European Americans. Roosevelt's **Rough Riders**, as the unit came to be known, landed with the invasion force and played an active role in the three battles fought in the hills surrounding Santiago. Their most famous action, the one on which Roosevelt would build his lifelong reputation as a military hero, was a furious charge up Kettle Hill into the teeth of Spanish defenses. Roosevelt's bravery was stunning, although his judgment was faulty. Nearly 100 men were killed or wounded. Reports of Roosevelt's bravery overshadowed the equally brave performance of other troops, notably the **Ninth and Tenth Negro Cavalries**, which played a pivotal role in clearing away Spanish fortifications on Kettle Hill and allowing Roosevelt's Rough Riders to make

Chicago History Museum

22.4 **"Remember the *Maine*!"** The explosion of the battleship *Maine* in Havana Harbor on February 15, 1898, killed 260 American sailors and helped drive the United States into war with Spain.

Q *Can you identify ways in which this painting partook of the "yellow journalism" of the early 20th century (see p. 605)? Was yellow journalism "embellishment" justified in this instance because of the large number of deaths caused by the explosion?*

their charge. One Rough Rider commented: "If it had not been for the Negro cavalry, the Rough Riders would have been exterminated." The Twenty-fourth and Twenty-fifth Negro Infantry Regiments performed equally vital tasks in the U.S. Army's conquest of the adjacent San Juan Hill.

Theodore Roosevelt saw the Rough Rider regiment that he commanded in the Spanish–American War as a melting pot of different groups of white Americans. Combat, he further believed, would forge these many groups into one, as war had always done in the American past. African Americans were the group most conspicuously absent from the Rough Rider mix. Yet the fury of the fighting on Kettle Hill and San Juan Hill so scrambled the white and black regiments that by the time the troops reached the San Juan summit, they were racially intermixed. Combat had brought blacks into the great American melting pot. The black troops, Roosevelt declared, were "an excellent breed of Yankee," and no "Rough Rider will ever forget," he added, "the tie that binds us to the Ninth and Tenth Cavalry."

But Roosevelt did not truly believe that blacks were the equals of whites or that they could be absorbed into the American nation. So, a few months after returning home, Roosevelt downplayed the role of black troops and questioned their ability to fight. The attack on black fighting abilities would become so widespread that by the start of the First World War, the U.S. military had largely excluded black troops from combat. Thus, an episode that had first demonstrated the possibility of interracial cooperation in America ended in the hardening of racial boundaries.

The taking of Kettle Hill, San Juan Hill, and other high ground surrounding Santiago gave the U.S. forces a substantial advantage over the Spanish defenders in Santiago. Nevertheless, the troops were short of food, ammunition, and medical facilities. Their ranks were devastated by malaria, typhoid, and dysentery: more than 5,000 soldiers died from disease. Fortunately, the Spanish had lost the will to fight. On July 3, a Spanish fleet fleeing Santiago Harbor ran into a U.S. naval blockade and was promptly destroyed by U.S. warships (see Map 22.1). The Spanish army in Santiago surrendered on July 16; on July 18, the Spanish government asked for peace. While negotiations for an armistice proceeded, U.S. forces overran the neighboring island of Puerto Rico. On August 12, the U.S. and Spanish governments agreed to an armistice; before this news reached the Philippines, the United States had captured Manila and had taken prisoner 13,000 Spanish soldiers.

The armistice required Spain to relinquish its claim to Cuba, cede Puerto Rico and the Pacific island of Guam to the United States, and tolerate the American occupation of Manila until a peace conference could be convened in Paris on October 1, 1898. At that conference, American diplomats startled their Spanish counterparts by demanding that Spain also cede the Philippines to the United States. After two months of stalling, the Spanish government agreed to relinquish its coveted Pacific colony for $20 million. The transaction was sealed by the Treaty of Paris on December 10, 1898.

Interpreting the Visual Past White and Black Soldiers in Cuba, 1898

These photographs depict two of the major groups involved in the successful U.S. assaults on Kettle Hill and San Juan Hill, Cuba, in 1898 (see Map 22.1 for locations of these battles). The Rough Riders were a white volunteer cavalry group led by Theodore Roosevelt (standing in the center of the Rough Rider photo, with no one sitting in front of him), who took leave from his position as assistant secretary of the navy to lead this regiment in Cuba. The Tenth Cavalry was a black regular regiment in the U.S. Army, and one of the army's most experienced fighting units. The racially homogeneous character of both these units highlights the U.S. military's determination to prevent white and black soldiers from mingling in battle or behind the lines, when they were at rest. That these white and black soldiers became intermixed in the battles on Kettle and San Juan hills came to be seen in the United States as a violation of the segregationist policies that the American South in particular had embraced.

The Granger Collection, NYC

22.5a **Photographer Unknown, Segregated Company of U.S. Soldiers, 1898.**

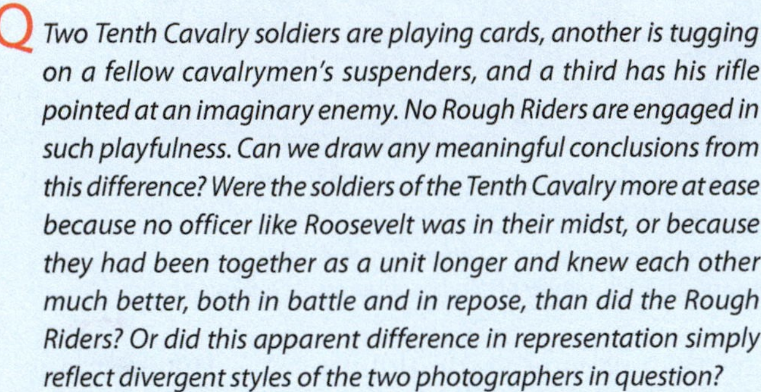

Q *Two Tenth Cavalry soldiers are playing cards, another is tugging on a fellow cavalrymen's suspenders, and a third has his rifle pointed at an imaginary enemy. No Rough Riders are engaged in such playfulness. Can we draw any meaningful conclusions from this difference? Were the soldiers of the Tenth Cavalry more at ease because no officer like Roosevelt was in their midst, or because they had been together as a unit longer and knew each other much better, both in battle and in repose, than did the Rough Riders? Or did this apparent difference in representation simply reflect divergent styles of the two photographers in question?*

Q *At the turn of the 20th century, photographs were often thought to be a truer representation of "reality" then paintings or journalistic reports. What, then is the significance of black soldiers being excluded from the Rough Riders' victory photograph atop San Juan Hill?*

Bettmann/Corbis

22.5b **Photographer Unknown, Theodore Roosevelt and Rough Riders on San Juan Hill, Cuba, 1898.**

22-3 The United States Becomes a World Power

Q *What different mechanisms of control did the United States use to achieve its aims in Hawaii, Cuba, the Philippines, Puerto Rico, and China?*

America's initial war aim had been to oust the Spanish from Cuba—an aim that both imperialists and anti-imperialists supported, but for different reasons. Imperialists hoped to incorporate Cuba into a new American empire; anti-imperialists hoped to see the Cubans gain their independence. But only the imperialists condoned the U.S. acquisition of Puerto Rico, Guam, and particularly the Philippines, which they viewed as integral to the extension of U.S. interests into Asia. Soon after the war began, President McKinley had cast his lot with the imperialists. First, he annexed Hawaii, giving the United States permanent control of Pearl Harbor. Next, he established a U.S. naval base at Manila. Never before had the United States sought such a large military presence outside the Western Hemisphere (see Map 22.2).

In a departure of equal importance, McKinley announced his intent to administer much of this newly acquired territory as U.S. colonies. Virtually all territory the United States had obtained in the 19th century had been part of the North American continent. These lands had been settled by Americans, who were quick to petition Congress for statehood. Of these new territories, however, only Hawaii would be put on the path toward statehood. There, the powerful U.S. sugar plantation owners prevailed on Congress to pass an act in 1900 extending U.S. citizenship to all Hawaiian citizens and making their islands eligible for statehood. No such influential group of Americans resided in the Philippines. The country was made a U.S. colony and placed under a U.S. administration that took its orders from Washington rather than from the Filipino people. Such colonization was necessary, in the eyes of American imperialists, to prevent other powers, such as Japan and Germany, from gaining a foothold somewhere in the 400-island archipelago and launching attacks on the U.S. naval base in Manila.

The United States might have negotiated an arrangement with **Emilio Aguinaldo**, the leader of an anticolonial movement in the Philippines, that would have given the Philippines independence in exchange for a U.S. naval base at Manila. An American fleet stationed there would have been able to protect both American interests and the fledgling Philippine nation from assaults by Japan, Germany, or Britain. Alternatively, the United States might have annexed the Philippines outright and offered Filipinos U.S. citizenship as the first step toward statehood. McKinley and his supporters, however, believed that the "inferior" Filipino people lacked the capacity for self-government. The United States would undertake a solemn mission to "civilize" the Filipinos and thereby prepare them for independence, but until that mission was complete, the Philippines would submit to rule by presidentially appointed U.S. governors.

22-3a *The Debate over the Treaty of Paris*

The proposed acquisition of the Philippines aroused opposition both in the United States and in the Philippines. The Anti-Imperialist League, strong in the Northeast, enlisted the support of Carl Schurz, former senator from Missouri, and other elder statesmen in McKinley's own party, as well as the former Democratic president Grover Cleveland, the industrialist Andrew Carnegie, and the labor leader Samuel Gompers. William Jennings Bryan, meanwhile, marshaled a vigorous anti-imperialist protest among Democrats in the South and West, while Mark Twain, William James, William Dean Howells, and other men of letters lent the cause their prestige. Some anti-imperialists believed that subjugating the Filipinos would violate the nation's most precious principle: the right of all people to independence and self-government. Moreover, they feared that the military and diplomatic establishment needed in Washington to administer the colony would threaten political liberties at home.

Other anti-imperialists were motivated more by self-interest than by democratic ideals. U.S. sugar producers, for example, feared competition from Filipino producers. Trade unionists worried that poor Filipino workers would flood the U.S. labor market and depress wage rates. Still other anti-imperialists feared the contaminating effects of contact with "inferior" Asian races.

Despite their contrasting motivations, the anti-imperialists almost dealt McKinley and his fellow imperialists a defeat in the U.S. Senate. On February 6, 1899, the Senate voted 57 to 27 in favor of the Treaty of Paris, only one vote beyond the minimum two-thirds majority required for ratification.

22.6 **Leaders of the Cuban Struggle for Independence**
By 1898, Cubans had been fighting to free their country from Spain for 30 years. This lithograph, a souvenir of the Grand Cuban-American Fair held in New York in 1896, depicts five leaders of the Cuban struggle: Máximo Gómez (upper left), Antonio Maceo (upper right), Calixto García (bottom right), and Salvador Cisneros (bottom left). At the center is José Martí, the "Father of the Revolution," killed in battle in 1895.

22-3b *The American-Filipino War*

The acquisition of the Philippines embroiled the United States in a long, brutal war to subdue the Filipino rebels. In four years of fighting, more than 120,000 American soldiers served in the Philippines and more than 4,200 of them died. The war cost $160 million, or eight times what the United States had paid Spain to acquire the archipelago. The war brought Americans face-to-face with an unpleasant truth: American actions in the Philippines were virtually indistinguishable from Spain's actions in Cuba. Like Spain, the United States refused to acknowledge a people's aspiration for self-rule. Like "Butcher" Weyler, American generals permitted the use of savage tactics. Whole communities suspected of harboring guerrillas were driven into concentration camps, and their houses, farms, and livestock were destroyed. One New York infantryman wrote home that his unit had killed 1,000 Filipinos—men, women, and children—in retaliation for the murder of a single American soldier. A total of 15,000 Filipino soldiers died in the fighting. Estimates of total Filipino deaths from gunfire, starvation, and disease range from 50,000 to 200,000.

The United States finally gained the upper hand in the war after General Arthur MacArthur (father of Douglas) was appointed commander of the islands in 1900. MacArthur did not lessen the war's ferocity, but he understood that it could not be won by guns alone. He offered amnesty to Filipino guerrillas who agreed to surrender, and he cultivated close relations with the islands' economic elites. McKinley, meanwhile, sent William Howard Taft to the islands in 1900

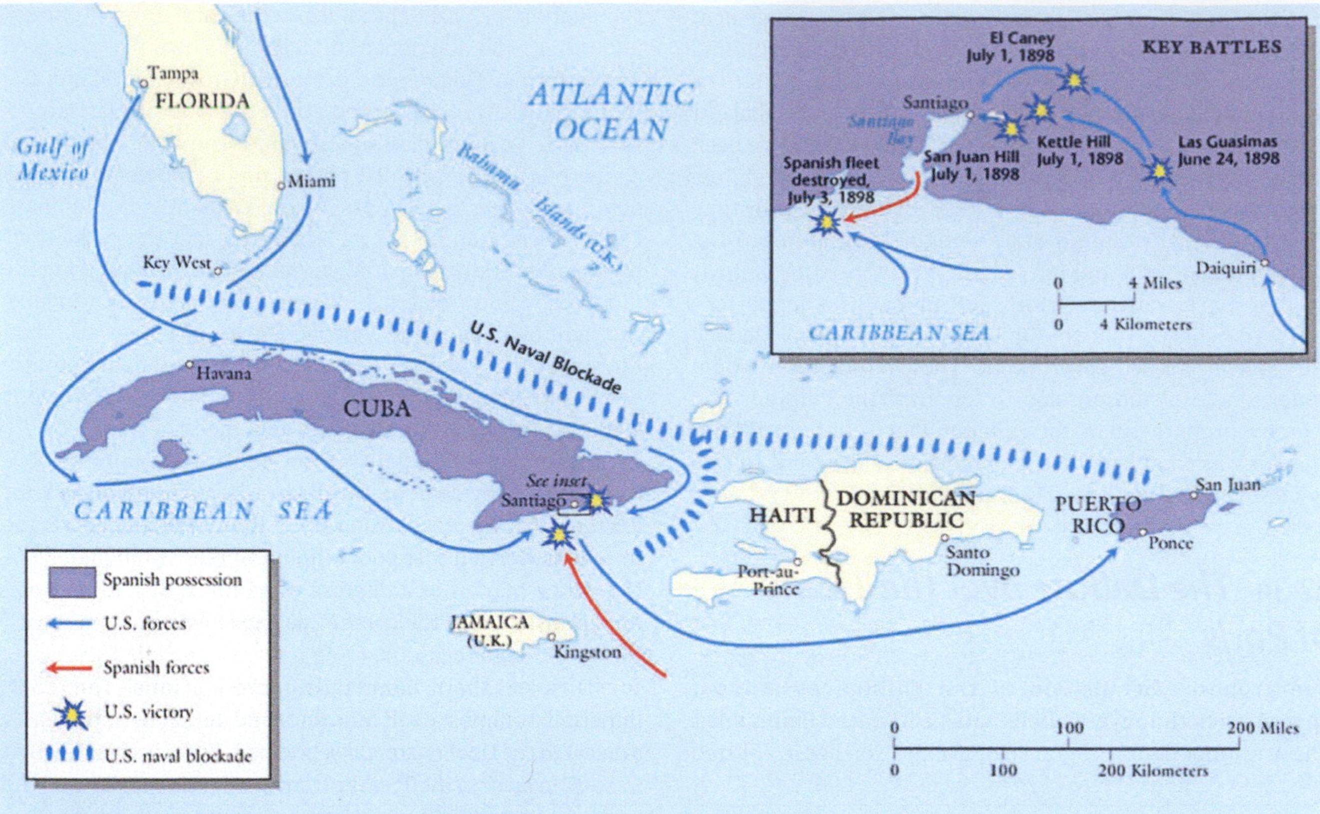

▲ **MAP 22.1 Spanish-American War in Cuba, 1898** This map shows the following: the routes taken by U.S. ships transporting troops from Florida to Cuba; the concentration of troop landings and battles around Santiago, Cuba; and a U.S. naval blockade, stretching hundreds of miles from Puerto Rico to Cuba, that attempted to keep the Spanish troops in Cuba and Puerto Rico from being reinforced.

Q *Why do you think the fighting in Cuba between the U.S. and Spain was so brief and so concentrated in such a small part of the island?*

Q *What does this map suggest about the size and effectiveness of the U.S. Navy?*

to establish a civilian government. In 1901, Taft became the colony's first "governor-general" and declared that he intended to prepare the Filipinos for independence. He transferred many governmental functions to Filipino control and launched a program of public works (roads, bridges, schools) that would give the Philippines the infrastructure necessary for economic development and political independence. By 1902, this dual strategy of ruthless war against those who had taken up arms and concessions to those who were willing to live under benevolent American rule crushed the revolt. Though sporadic fighting continued until 1913, Americans had secured control of the Philippines. The explicit commitment of the United States to Philippine independence (a promise that was deferred until 1946), together with an extensive program of internal improvements, eased America's conscience.

22-3c *Controlling Cuba and Puerto Rico*

Helping the Cubans achieve independence had been a major rationale for the war against Spain. In 1900, the United States seemed to be delivering on this pledge when General Leonard Wood, commander of U.S. forces in Cuba, authorized a constitutional convention to write the laws for a Cuban republic. Yet, at the same time, the McKinley administration made clear it would not easily relinquish control of the island. At McKinley's urging, the U.S. Congress attached to a 1901 army appropriations bill the **Platt Amendment**, delineating three conditions for Cuban independence: (1) Cuba would not be permitted to make treaties with foreign powers; (2) the United States would have broad authority to intervene in Cuban political and economic affairs; and (3) Cuba would sell or lease land to the United States for naval stations. The delegates to Cuba's constitutional convention were outraged, but the dependence of Cuba's vital sugar industry on the U.S. market and the continuing presence of the U.S. Army on Cuban soil rendered resistance futile. In 1901, by a vote of 15 to 11, the delegates reluctantly wrote the Platt conditions into their constitution. "There is, of course, little or no independence left Cuba under the Platt Amendment," Wood candidly admitted to his friend Theodore Roosevelt, who had recently succeeded the assassinated McKinley as president.

Cuba's status, in truth, differed little from that of the Philippines. Both were colonies of the United States. In the case of Cuba, economic dependence closely followed political subjugation. Between 1898 and 1914, U.S. trade with Cuba increased more than tenfold (from $27 million to $300 million),

What They Said

Should America Become an Imperial Nation?

After the Spanish–American War of 1898, the McKinley administration proposed to make two of the territories it had taken from Spain, Puerto Rico and the Philippines, into American colonies. This proposal sparked furious debate both within Congress and in the country at large, for it marked the first time (outside the realm of Indian land) that the United States was proposing to rule new territory indefinitely without the consent of the people who lived in those lands, and without intending to grant these people the rights and institutions of self-government as set forth in the Constitution. Was it legitimate for America to expand its rule in this way? The Democratic senator from Indiana, Albert Beveridge, believed it was. For Carl Schurz, former Republican senator from Missouri and a leading figure in the American Anti-Imperialist League, it was not.

Albert Beveridge, "The March of the Flag," September 1898

Have we no mission to perform, no duty to discharge to our fellow-man? Has God endowed us with gifts beyond our deserts and marked us as the people of His peculiar favor, merely to rot in our own selfishness. . . . [S]hall we reap the reward that waits on our discharge of our high duty; shall we occupy new markets for what our farmers raise, our factories make, our merchants sell—aye, and please God, new markets for what our ships shall carry?

Hawaii is ours; Porto Rico is to be ours; at the prayer of her people Cuba finally will be ours ... the flag of liberal government is to float over the Philippines. . . .

The Opposition tells us that we ought not to govern a people without their consent. I answer: The rule of liberty that all just government derives its authority from the consent of the governed, applies only to those who are capable of self-government. We govern the Indians without their consent, we govern our territories without their consent, we govern our children without their consent. How do they know what our government would be without their consent? Would not the people of the Philippines prefer the just, humane, civilizing government of the Republic to the savage, bloody rule of pillage and extortion from which we have rescued them? ... Shall we turn these peoples back to the reeking hands from which we have taken them? Shall we abandon them, with Germany, England, Japan, hungering for them? Shall we save them from those nations, to give them a self-rule of tragedy?

Carl Schurz, "American Imperialism," January 4, 1899

It is proposed to embark this Republic in a course of imperialistic policy by permanently annexing to it certain islands taken, from Spain in the late war. . . . If we adopt such a system, then we shall, for the first time since the abolition of slavery, again have two kinds of Americans: Americans of the first class, who enjoy the privilege of taking part in the government in accordance with our old constitutional principles, and Americans of the second class, who are to be ruled in a substantially arbitrary fashion by the Americans of the first class. . . .

This will be a difference no better—nay, rather somewhat worse—than that which a century and a quarter ago still existed between Englishmen of the first and Englishmen of the second class, the first represented by King George and the British Parliament, and the second by the American colonists. This difference called forth that great paean of human liberty, the American Declaration of Independence,—a document which, I regret to say, seems, owing to the intoxication of conquest, to have lost much of its charm among some of our fellow citizens. Its fundamental principle was that "governments derive their just powers from the consent of the governed." We are now told that we have never fully lived up to that principle, and that, therefore, in our new policy we may cast it aside altogether. But I say to you that, if we are true believers in democratic government, it is our duty to move in the direction toward the full realization of that principle and not in the direction away from it. If you tell me that we cannot govern the people of those new possessions in accordance with that principle, then I answer that this is a good reason why this democracy should not attempt to govern them at all.

Q *What are Beveridge's arguments for making Puerto Rico and the Philippines into colonies? What are Schurz's arguments against doing so?*

Q *Both men invoke self-government, or what Schurz calls democratic government, as a key American ideal, but they draw different lessons regarding its relevance to the territories acquired by the United States in its war against Spain. What are the different lessons the two men draw about democratic government in these territories?*

Sources: (top) Albert Beveridge, "The March of the Flag: Speech Opening the Indiana Republican Campaign at Tomlinson Hall, Indianapolis, September 16, 1898," in Albert J. Beveridge, *The Meaning of the Times, and Other Speeches* (Indianapolis: Bobbs-Merrill, 1908), 47–57; (bottom) Carl Schurz, *American Imperialism: The Convocation Address Delivered on the Occasion of the Twenty-Seventh Convocation of the University of Chicago, January 4, 1899* (Boston: Dana Estes and Company, 1899), 3–31.

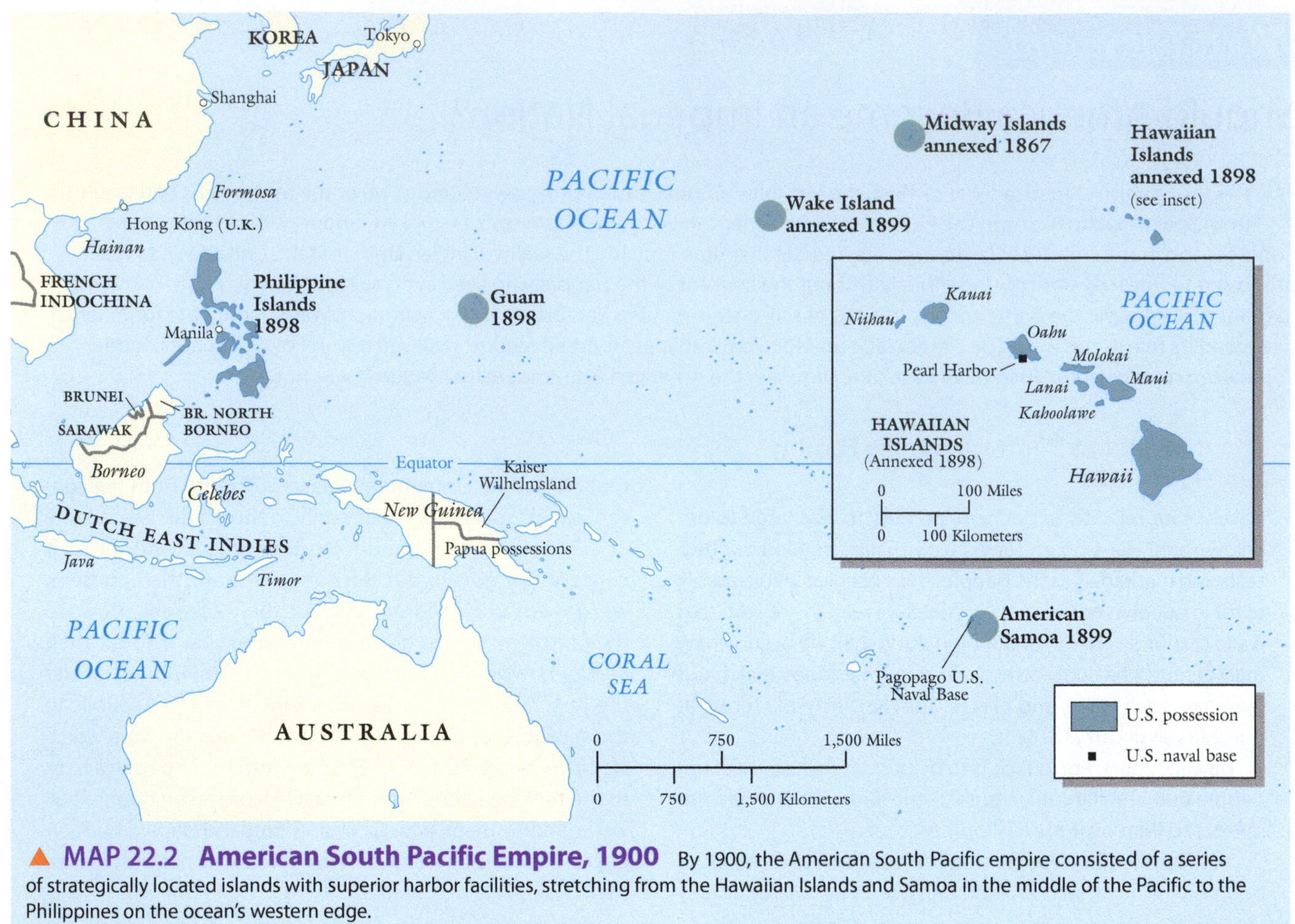

▲ **MAP 22.2 American South Pacific Empire, 1900** By 1900, the American South Pacific empire consisted of a series of strategically located islands with superior harbor facilities, stretching from the Hawaiian Islands and Samoa in the middle of the Pacific to the Philippines on the ocean's western edge.

Q *America's acquisition of an island empire in the South Pacific was the result of a deliberate strategy pursued by the U.S. government. What was the purpose of focusing on islands? Was it a successful strategy?*

while investments more than quadrupled (from $50 million to $220 million). In 1903, the United States compelled Cuba to lease it 45 square miles of land and water on the island nation's southeast coast. There the United States built the U.S. Naval Station at Guantanamo Bay, a facility that it maintains to this day. The United States also intervened in Cuban political affairs five times between 1906 and 1921 to protect its economic interests and those of the indigenous ruling class with whom it had become closely allied. The economic, political, and military control that the United States imposed on Cuba would fuel anti-American sentiment there for years to come.

Puerto Rico received somewhat different treatment. The United States annexed the island outright with the Foraker Act (1900). Unlike every previous annexation authorized by Congress since 1788, this act contained no provision for making the inhabitants of Puerto Rico citizens of the United States. Instead, Puerto Rico was designated an "unincorporated" territory, which meant that Congress would dictate the island's government and specify the rights of its inhabitants. Puerto Ricans were allowed no role in designing their government, nor was their consent to its establishment sought. With the Foraker Act, Congress had, in effect, invented a new imperial mechanism for ensuring sovereignty over lands deemed vital to U.S. economic and military security. The U.S. Supreme Court upheld the constitutionality of this mechanism in a series of historic decisions, known as the Insular Cases, in the years from 1901 to 1904.

In some respects, Puerto Rico fared better than "independent" Cuba. Puerto Ricans were granted U.S. citizenship in 1917 and won the right to elect their own governor in 1947. Still, Puerto Ricans enjoyed fewer political rights than Americans in the 48 states. Moreover, throughout the 20th century, they endured a poverty rate far exceeding that of the mainland. In its skewed distribution of wealth and its lack of industrial development, Puerto Rico resembled the poorly developed nations of Central and South America more than it did the affluent country that took over its government in 1900.

The subjugation of Cuba and the annexation of Puerto Rico troubled Americans far less than the U.S. takeover in the Philippines. Since the first articulation of the Monroe Doctrine in 1823, the United States had, in effect, claimed the Western Hemisphere as its sphere of influence. Within that sphere, many Americans believed, the United States possessed the right to act unilaterally to protect its interests. Before 1900, most of its actions (with the exception of the Mexican War) had been designed to limit the influence of European powers—Britain, France, Russia, and Spain—on the countries of the hemisphere. After 1900, however, the United States assumed

Keystone-France/Getty Images

22.7 **General Emilio Aguinaldo, Leader of Filipino Independence Struggle.** Aguinaldo was a key figure in the post-1898 struggle to resist a U.S. takeover of the Philippines. Here he speaks to his countrymen in Manila about the future of the Philippines at a moment (1903) when hopes for Filipino independence were fading.

a more aggressive role, seizing land, overturning governments it did not like, and forcing its economic and political policies on weaker neighbors in order to turn the Caribbean Sea into what policymakers called (with the example of ancient Rome in mind) an American Mediterranean.

22-3d *China and the "Open Door"*

Except for Hawaii, the Philippines, and Guam, the United States made no effort to take control of Asian lands. Such a policy might well have triggered war with other world powers that were already well established in the area. The United States opted for a diplomatic rather than a military strategy to achieve its foreign policy objectives. For China, in 1899 and 1900, it proposed the policy of the "open door."

The United States was concerned that the actions of the other world powers in China would block its own efforts to open up China's markets to American goods. Britain, Germany, Japan, Russia, and France each coveted a chunk of China, where they could monopolize trade, exploit cheap labor, and establish military bases. By the 1890s, each of these powers was building a sphere of influence, either by wringing economic and territorial concessions from the weak Chinese government or by seizing outright the land and trading privileges it desired.

To prevent China's breakup and to preserve U.S. economic access to the whole of China, McKinley's secretary of state, John Hay, sent "open door" notes to the major world powers. The notes asked each power to open its Chinese sphere of influence to the merchants of other nations and to grant them reasonable harbor fees and railroad rates. Hay also asked each power to respect China's sovereignty by enforcing Chinese tariff duties in the territory it controlled.

None of the world powers embraced either of Hay's requests, although Britain and Japan gave provisional assent. France, Germany, Russia, and Italy responded evasively, indicating their support for the **Open Door policy** in theory but insisting that they could not implement it until all of the other powers had done so. Hay put the best face on their responses by declaring that all of the powers had agreed to observe his Open Door principles and that he regarded their assent as "final and definitive." The rivals may have been

JT Vintage/Glasshouse Images/Alamy Stock Photo

22.8 **U.S. Soldiers in the Philippines, c. 1900** This photograph, taken near Manila, captures the denseness of the wooded terrain in which American soldiers often had to fight.

Q *The Filipino rebels were an unconventional military force, especially in their guerrilla tactic of blending in with the civilian population. How did the U.S. military respond to the difficulty it had in distinguishing between Filipino rebels and civilians?*

Library of Congress Prints and Photograph Division

22.9 **New Americans?** The terms of Puerto Rico's 1900 annexation did not permit the island's inhabitants, such as those depicted in this 1900 photograph, to become citizens of the United States. Instead they became a colonized people.

Q *Why did the United States refuse to grant American citizenship to Puerto Ricans in the years immediately following the island's annexation?*

impressed by Hay's diplomacy, but whether they intended to uphold the United States' Open Door policy was not at all clear.

The first challenge to Hay's policy came from the Chinese. In May 1900, a Chinese organization colloquially known as the **"Boxers"** sparked an uprising to rid China of all "foreign devils" and foreign influences. Hundreds of Europeans were killed, as were many Chinese men and women who had converted to Christianity. When the Boxers laid siege to the foreign legations in Beijing and cut off communication between that city and the outside world, the imperial powers raised an expeditionary force to rescue the diplomats and punish the Chinese rebels. The force, which included 5,000 U.S. soldiers, put down the Boxer Rebellion by September.

Hay feared that other major powers would use the rebellion as a reason to demand greater control over Chinese territory. He sent out a second round of Open Door notes, now asking each power to respect China's political independence and territorial integrity, in addition to guaranteeing unrestricted access to its markets. Now, Britain, France, and Germany endorsed Hay's policy outright. With that support, Hay was able to check Russian and Japanese designs on Chinese territory. Significantly, when the powers decided that the Chinese government should pay them reparations for their property and personnel losses during the Boxer Rebellion, Hay convinced them to accept payment in cash rather than in territory. By keeping China intact and open to free trade, the United States had achieved a major foreign policy victory.

22-4 Theodore Roosevelt, Geopolitician

Q *What were the similarities and differences between Theodore Roosevelt's foreign policies in Latin America and East Asia? What explains the differences?*

Roosevelt had been a driving force in the transformation of U.S. foreign policy during the McKinley administration. As assistant secretary of the navy, as a military hero, as a speaker and writer, and then as vice president, Roosevelt worked tirelessly to vault the country into the ranks of the world's great powers. He believed that Americans were a racially superior people destined for supremacy in economic and political affairs. He did not assume, however, that international supremacy would automatically accrue to the United States. A nation, like an individual, had to strive for greatness and cultivate physical and mental fitness; it had to build a military force that could convincingly project power overseas; and it had to be prepared to fight. All great nations, Roosevelt declared, ultimately depended on the skill and dedication of their warriors.

Roosevelt's appetite for a good fight caused many people to rue the ascension of this "cowboy" to the White House after McKinley's assassination in 1901. But Roosevelt was also a shrewd analyst of international relations. As much as he craved power for himself and the nation, he understood that the United States could not rule every portion of the globe through military or economic means. Consequently, he sought a balance of power among the industrial nations through negotiation rather than war. Such a balance would enable each imperial power to safeguard its key interests and contribute to world peace and progress.

The Granger Collection, NYC

22.10 **Restoring Order in China** This 1900 photograph depicts the international nature of the expeditionary force raised to defeat the Chinese rebels known as Boxers. The soldiers/marines depicted in this photo represented these nations (left to right): Great Britain, the United States, Russia, India, Germany, France, Austria-Hungary, Italy, and Japan.

Q *It was rare for so many nations to cooperate with each other in putting down an anti-colonial rebellion. Why were nine nations willing to put aside their differences to crush the Chinese Boxers?*

Roosevelt had little patience with the claims to sovereignty of small countries or the human rights of weak peoples. In his eyes, the peoples of Latin America, Asia (with the exception of Japan), and Africa were racially inferior and thus incapable of self-government or industrial progress.

22-4a *The Roosevelt Corollary*

Ensuring U.S. dominance in the Western Hemisphere ranked high on Roosevelt's list of foreign policy objectives. In 1904, he issued a "corollary" to the Monroe Doctrine, which had asserted the right of the United States to keep European powers from meddling in hemispheric affairs. In his corollary, Roosevelt declared that the United States possessed a further right: to intervene in the domestic affairs of nations in the Western Hemisphere to quell disorder and forestall European intervention. The **Roosevelt Corollary** formalized a policy that the United States had already deployed against Cuba and Puerto Rico in 1900 and 1901. A few years later, the United States took over the Dominican Republic's customs collections and refinanced the country's national debt as a way of dissuading European powers from invading this island nation to collect on loans that Dominicans had not repaid (see Map 22.3).

22-4b *The Panama Canal*

Roosevelt had long believed, along with Alfred Mahan, that the nation needed a way of moving its ships swiftly between the Pacific and Atlantic oceans. Central America's narrow width, especially in its southern half, made it the logical place to build a canal (see Map 22.4). In fact, a French company had obtained land rights and had begun construction of a canal across the Colombian province of Panama in the 1880s. But even though a "mere" 40 miles of land separated the two oceans, the French were stymied by technological difficulties and by the financial costs of literally moving mountains. Moreover, French doctors found they were unable to check the spread of malaria and yellow fever among canal workers. By the time Roosevelt entered the White House in 1901, the French Panama Company had gone bankrupt.

Roosevelt was not deterred by the French failure. He presided over the signing of the Hay–Pauncefote Treaty with Great Britain in 1901, releasing the United States from an 1850 agreement that prohibited either country from building a Central American canal without the other's participation. By threatening to build a canal from scratch across Nicaragua, Roosevelt persuaded the French company to lower the price on its half-finished Panamanian canal from $109 to $40 million. Secretary of State Hay quickly negotiated an agreement with Tomas Herran, the Colombian chargé d'affaires in Washington, which gave the

▲ **MAP 22.3 United States Presence in Latin America, 1895–1934** The United States possessed few colonies in Latin America but intervened often in Mexico, Cuba, Nicaragua, Panama, Haiti, the Dominican Republic, and Venezuela to secure its economic and political interests.

Q *Count the number of times that the United States intervened in Latin America between 1895 and 1934. Are the large number of interventions a sign of foreign policy success or failure?*

Q *Would it not have been simpler for the U.S. to have extended its formal rule over the countries in question, as it did with Puerto Rico in 1898? Why did it not pursue a policy of formal rule throughout Central America and the northern areas of South America?*

▲ **MAP 22.4 Panama Canal Zone, 1914** This map shows the route of the completed canal through Panama and the 10-mile-wide zone surrounding it that the United States controlled. The inset map locates the Canal Zone in the context of Central and South America.

Q *Study the map inset. The narrowness of the land in Panama made this location especially attractive to canal builders. Was Roosevelt's threat to build a canal from scratch across Nicaragua a credible one?*

Q *Study the larger map: does it reveal a geographical feature other than the land's narrow width that made this site appealing?*

United States a six-mile-wide strip across Panama on which to finish the canal started by the French. Colombia was to receive a one-time $10 million payment and annual rent of $250,000.

The Colombian legislature, however, rejected the proposed payment as insufficient and sent a new ambassador to the United States with instructions to ask for better terms. Roosevelt, in response, encouraged the Panamanians to revolt against Colombian rule. Panamanians had staged several rebellions in the previous 25 years, all of which had failed. The 1903 rebellion succeeded, mainly because a U.S. naval force prevented the Colombian government from landing troops in its Panama province. Meanwhile, the USS *Nashville* put U.S. troops ashore to help the new nation secure its independence. The United States formally recognized Panama as a sovereign state only two days after the rebellion against Colombia began.

Philippe Bunau-Varilla, a director of the French company from which the United States had bought the rights to the canal, declared himself Panama's diplomatic representative, even though he was a French citizen operating out of a Wall Street law firm and hadn't set foot in Panama in 15 years. Before the true Panamanian delegation (appointed by the new Panamanian government) even reached the United States for negotiations over the canal, Bunau-Varilla and Secretary of State Hay signed the Hay–Bunau-Varilla Treaty (1903). The treaty granted the United States a 10-mile-wide canal zone in Panama in return for the package Colombia had rejected—$10 million down and $250,000 annually. Thus, the United States secured its canal by dealing with Bunau-Varilla's French company rather than with the newly installed Panamanian government. The instrument through which the United States secured the Canal Zone is known in Panamanian history as "the treaty which no Panamanian signed," and it bedeviled relations between the two countries for much of the 20th century.

Roosevelt turned the building of the **Panama Canal** into a test of American ingenuity and willpower. The canal remains a testament to the labor of some 30,000 workers, imported mainly from the West Indies, who, over a 10-year period, labored 10 hours a day, six days a week, for 10 cents an hour. Roosevelt visited the canal site in 1906, becoming the first American president to travel overseas while in office. When the canal was triumphantly opened to shipping in 1914, the British ambassador James Bryce described it as "the greatest liberty Man has ever taken with Nature." The canal shortened the voyage from San Francisco to New York by more than 8,000 miles and significantly enhanced the international prestige of the United States. The strategic importance of the canal, in turn, made the United States even more determined to preserve political order in Central America and the Caribbean.

In 1921, the United States paid the Colombian government $25 million as compensation for its loss of Panama. Panama waited more than 70 years, however, to regain control of the 10-mile-wide strip of land that Bunau-Varilla, in connivance with the U.S. government, had bargained away in 1903. President Jimmy Carter signed a treaty in 1977 providing for the reintegration of the Canal Zone into Panama, and the canal was transferred to Panama in 2000.

22-4c *Keeping the Peace in East Asia*

Roosevelt strove to preserve the Open Door policy in China and the balance of power throughout the region. The chief threats came from Russia and Japan, both of whom wanted large chunks of China. At first, Russian expansion into Manchuria and Korea prompted Roosevelt to support Japan's 1904 attack on the Russian Pacific fleet anchored at Port Arthur, China. Once the ruinous effects of the war on Russia became clear, however, Roosevelt entered into secret negotiations to arrange a peace. He invited representatives of Japan and Russia to Portsmouth, New Hampshire, and prevailed on them to negotiate a compromise. The settlement favored Japan by perpetuating its control over most of the territories, including Korea, it had won during the brief **Russo-Japanese War**. Russia, however, avoided paying Japan a huge indemnity, and it retained Siberia, thus preserving its role as an East Asian power. Finally, Roosevelt protected China's territorial integrity by inducing the armies of both Russia and Japan to leave Manchuria. Roosevelt's success in ending the Russo-Japanese War won him the Nobel Peace Prize in 1906; he was the first American to win that award.

Although Roosevelt succeeded in negotiating a peace between these two world powers, he subsequently ignored, and sometimes encouraged, challenges to the sovereignty of

National Archives/Historical/Corbis

22.11 **Building the Canal with West Indian Labor** A ship delivers 1,500 Barbadian laborers to Panama in 1909 to work on the canal.

© TopFoto/The Image Works

22.12 **"The 13th Labor of Hercules"** This illustration, derived from a poster designed by Perham W. Nahl for the 1915 Panama Pacific International Exposition in San Francisco, graced the back cover of Frank Morton Todd's 1921 book, *The Story of The Exposition*. The drawing celebrates the building of the Panama Canal as a work on the scale of Hercules, among the greatest—and the strongest—of Greco-Roman heroes.

Q *Why did the United States succeed in building a canal across Panama where France had failed?*

weaker Asian nations. In a secret agreement with Japan (the Taft–Katsura Agreement of 1905), for example, the United States agreed that Japan could dominate Korea in return for a Japanese promise not to attack the Philippines. And in the Root–Takahira Agreement of 1908, the United States tacitly reversed its earlier stand on the inviolability of Chinese borders by recognizing Japanese expansion into southern Manchuria.

In Roosevelt's eyes, the overriding need to maintain peace with Japan justified ignoring the claims of Korea and, increasingly, of China. The task of American diplomacy, he believed, was first to allow the Japanese to build a secure sphere of influence in East Asia (much as the United States had done in Central America and the Caribbean), and second to encourage them to join the United States in pursuing peace rather than war. This was a delicate diplomatic task that required both sensitivity and strength, especially when anti-Japanese agitation broke out in California in 1906.

White Californians had long feared the presence of East Asian immigrants (see Chapter 20). They had pressured Congress into passing the Chinese Exclusion Act of 1882, which ended most Chinese immigration to the United States. They next turned their racism on Japanese immigrants, whose numbers in California had reached 24,000. In 1906, the San Francisco school board ordered the segregation of Asian schoolchildren so that they would not "contaminate" white children. In 1907, the California legislature debated a law to end Japanese immigration to the state. Anti-Asian riots erupted in San Francisco and Los Angeles, encouraged in part by hysterical stories in the press about the "Yellow Peril."

Outraged militarists in Japan began talking of a possible war with the United States. Roosevelt assured the Japanese government that he, too, was appalled by the Californians' behavior. In 1907, he reached a **gentlemen's agreement** with the Japanese, by which the Tokyo government promised to halt the immigration of Japanese adult male laborers to the United States in return for Roosevelt's pledge to end anti-Japanese discrimination in California. Roosevelt did his part by persuading the San Francisco school board to rescind its segregation ordinance.

At the same time, Roosevelt worried that the Tokyo government would interpret his sensitivity to Japanese honor as weakness. So he ordered the main part of the U.S. fleet, consisting of 16 battleships, to embark on a 45,000-mile world tour, including a splashy stop in Tokyo Bay (see Map 22.5). Many Americans deplored the cost of the tour and feared that the appearance of the U.S. Navy in a Japanese port would provoke military retaliation. Roosevelt brushed his critics aside, and, true to his prediction, the Japanese were impressed by the **Great White Fleet**. Their response seemed to lend validity to the African proverb Roosevelt often invoked: "Speak softly and carry a big stick."

Roosevelt's handling of Japan was arguably the most impressive aspect of his foreign policy. Unlike many other Americans, he refused to let racist attitudes cloud his

History Through Film *Tarzan, the Ape Man* (1932)

Directed by W. S. Van Dyke.
Starring Johnny Weissmuller (Tarzan), Maureen O'Sullivan (Jane Parker), Neil Hamilton (Harry Holt), C. Aubrey Smith (James Parker), and Cheeta the Chimp.

This movie introduced Americans to Tarzan, one of the most popular screen figures of the 1930s, 1940s, and 1950s. Based on the best-selling novels of Edgar Rice Burroughs, this Tarzan movie, like the ones that followed, was meant to puncture the civilized complacency in which Americans and other Westernized, imperial peoples had enveloped themselves. The movie opens with an American woman, Jane Parker, arriving in Africa to join her father, James, and the crew he has assembled to search for the mythic elephant graveyard thought to contain untold riches in ivory tusks. Jane is depicted as bright, energetic, attractive, and defiant of female gender conventions. The rest of the white adventurers are portrayed as greedy, haughty, contemptuous of the African environment, or just ignorant. The Africans who act as their servants and guides are presented as primitive and superstitious, more like animals than humans. This expedition in search of ivory is destined for disaster, and the movie provides thrills by showing expedition members succumbing to attacks by wild animals and "wild humans" who inhabit the "dark continent" of Africa.

During one such attack by hippos and pygmies, Tarzan, played by handsome Olympic swimming champion Johnny Weissmuller, comes to the rescue, scaring off the attackers by mobilizing a stampede of elephants with his piercing, high-pitched, and unforgettable jungle cry. He takes Jane, who has become separated from the group, to his tree house. Thus begins one of the more unusual and famous screen romances.

Tarzan's origins are not explained in the movie, although one intuits that he somehow lost his white family and was raised by apes. He has none of the refining features of civilization—decent clothes, language, manners—but he possesses strength, honesty, and virtue. As Jane falls in love with Tarzan and decides to share a jungle life with him, we, the viewers, are asked to contemplate, with Jane, the benefits of peeling off the layers of civilized life (which seem to drop away from Jane along with many of her clothes) and returning to a simpler, more wholesome, and more natural form of existence.

The movie critiques and lampoons the imperial pretensions and smugness of the West, but it never asks viewers to see the indigenous African peoples as anything other than savage. Tarzan may have been ignorant of civilized customs, but he was white and, as such, equipped with the "native" intelligence and character of his race. The Africans depicted in the movie show no such intelligence or character. They are presented as weak and superstitious or as brutally aggressive and indifferent to human life. Thus *Tarzan, the Ape Man* manages to critique the West without asking Western viewers to challenge the racism that justified the West's domination of non-Western peoples and territories. ■

Bettmann/Corbis

22.13 Johnny Weissmuller and Maureen O'Sullivan as Tarzan and Jane.

thinking. He knew when to make concessions and when to stand firm. His policies lessened the prospect of a war with Japan while preserving a strong U.S. presence in East Asia.

22-5 William Howard Taft, Dollar Diplomat

Q *What was "dollar diplomacy," and how effective was it as a foreign policy tool for the United States under William Howard Taft?*

William Howard Taft brought impressive foreign policy credentials to the job of president. He had gained valuable experience in colonial administration as the first governor-general of the Philippines. As Roosevelt's secretary of war and chief negotiator for the Taft–Katsura agreement of 1905, he had learned a great deal about conducting diplomacy with imperialist rivals. Yet Taft lacked Roosevelt's grasp of balance-of-power politics and capacity for leadership in foreign affairs. Furthermore, Taft's secretary of state, Philander C. Knox, a corporation lawyer from Pittsburgh, was short on diplomatic expertise. Knox's conduct of foreign policy seemed directed almost entirely toward expanding opportunities for corporate

North Wind/North Wind Picture Archives

22.14 **Anti-Asian Hysteria in San Francisco** In 1906, in the midst of a wave of anti-Asian prejudice in California, the San Francisco school board ordered the segregation of all Asian schoolchildren. Here, a nine-year-old Japanese student submits an application for admission to a public primary school and is refused by the principal, Miss M. E. Dean.

investment overseas, a disposition that prompted critics to deride his policies as **dollar diplomacy.**

Taft and Knox believed that U.S. investments would effectively substitute "dollars for bullets," and thus offer a more peaceful and less coercive way of maintaining stability and order. Taking a swipe at Roosevelt's "big stick" policy, Taft announced that "modern diplomacy is commercial."

The inability of Taft and Knox to grasp the complexities of power politics, however, led to a diplomatic reversal in East Asia. Prodded by banker associates, Knox sought to expand

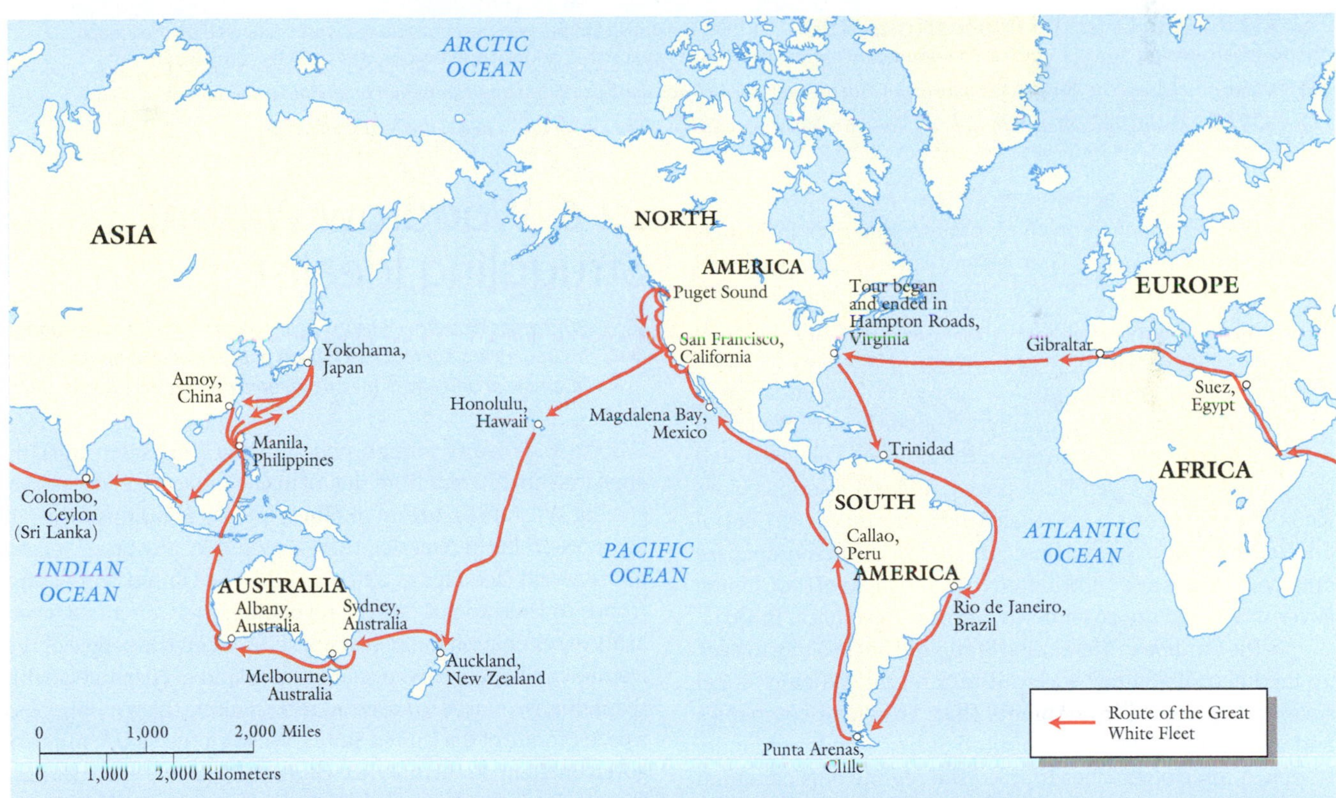

▲ **MAP 22.5 Route of the Great White Fleet, 1907–1909** A 16-battleship-strong U.S. fleet left Virginia in 1907 for a 45,000-mile world tour, whose most important stop was Japan.

Q *Locate on this map the narrow junction in Central America where the U.S. would soon build the Panama Canal. By what percentage (roughly) would such a canal, had it existed in 1907, have reduced the distance that Roosevelt's Great White Fleet needed to travel to complete its world tour?*

Q *A second crucial canal, in operation since the middle of the 19th century, did shorten the Great White Fleet's journey by a significant amount. Can you identify this other canal? Which country controlled it?*

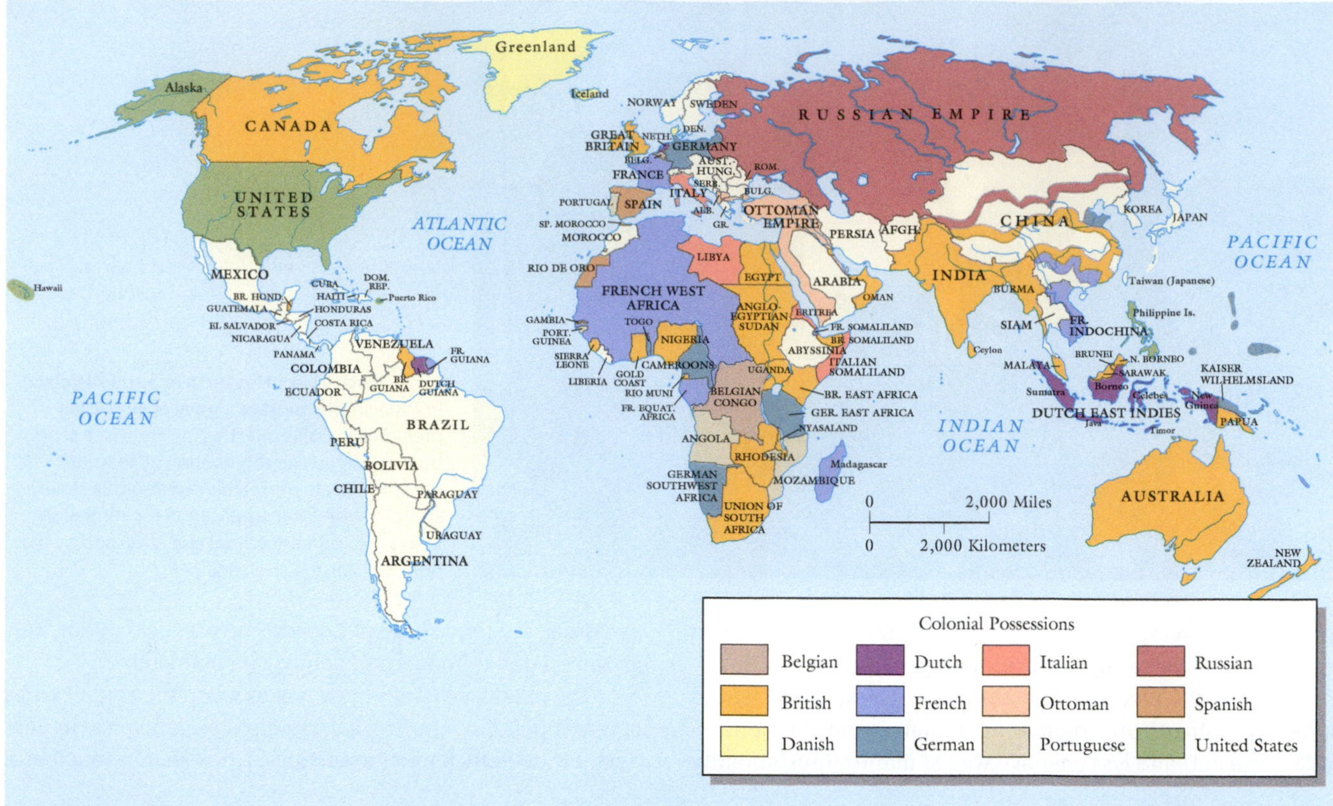

▲ **MAP 22.6 Colonial Possessions, 1900** In 1900, the British Empire was the largest in the world, followed by the French and Russian empires. The U.S. empire, if measured by the square miles of land held as colonial possessions, was small by comparison.

Q *Did the small size of the American empire mean that the United States was significantly less imperialist than Great Britain or France?*

Q *Latin America was the continent most free of formal colonial rule. Did this make the continent free of imperialist influence?*

American economic activities in China—even in Manchuria, where they encroached on the Japanese sphere of influence. In 1911, Knox proposed that a syndicate of European and American bankers buy the Japanese-controlled South Manchurian Railroad to open up North China to international trade. Japan reacted by signing a friendship treaty with Russia, its former enemy, which signaled their joint determination to exclude American, British, and French goods from Manchurian markets. Knox's plan to purchase the railroad collapsed, and the United States' Open Door policy suffered a serious blow. Knox's further efforts to increase American trade with Central and South China triggered hostile responses from the Japanese and the Russians and contributed to the collapse of the Chinese government and the onset of the Chinese Revolution in 1911.

In the Caribbean, the United States did not hesitate to back up its dollar diplomacy with military might. When political turmoil threatened investments that American companies had made in the region, the United States simply sent in its troops. A force of marines toppled the regime of Nicaraguan dictator José Santos Zelaya in 1910 after he reportedly began negotiating with a European country to build a second trans-Isthmian canal. Marines landed again in 1912 when Zelaya's successor, Adolfo Diaz, angered Nicaraguans with his pro-American policies. This time the marines were instructed to keep the Diaz regime in power, which they did by staying in Nicaragua almost continuously until 1933.

22-6 Woodrow Wilson, Struggling Idealist

Q *What does Woodrow Wilson's policy toward Mexico reveal about his underlying approach to foreign policy? How did his approach resemble or differ from the one favored by Theodore Roosevelt?*

Woodrow Wilson's foreign policy in the Caribbean initially appeared no different from that of his Republican predecessors. During Wilson's first term in office, U.S. corporations invested far more in Latin America than they did in any other region of the world (see Figure 22.2). In 1915, the United States sent troops to Haiti to put down a revolution; they remained as an army of occupation for 21 years. In 1916, when the people of the Dominican Republic (who shared the island of Hispaniola with the Haitians) refused to accept a treaty making them more or less a protectorate of the United States, Wilson forced a U.S. military government upon them. When German influence in the Danish West Indies began to expand, Wilson purchased the islands from Denmark, renamed them the Virgin Islands, and added them to the U.S. Caribbean empire. By the time Wilson left office in 1921, he had intervened militarily in the Caribbean more often than any American president before him.

Wilson's relationship with Mexico in the wake of its revolution, however, reveals that he was troubled by a foreign

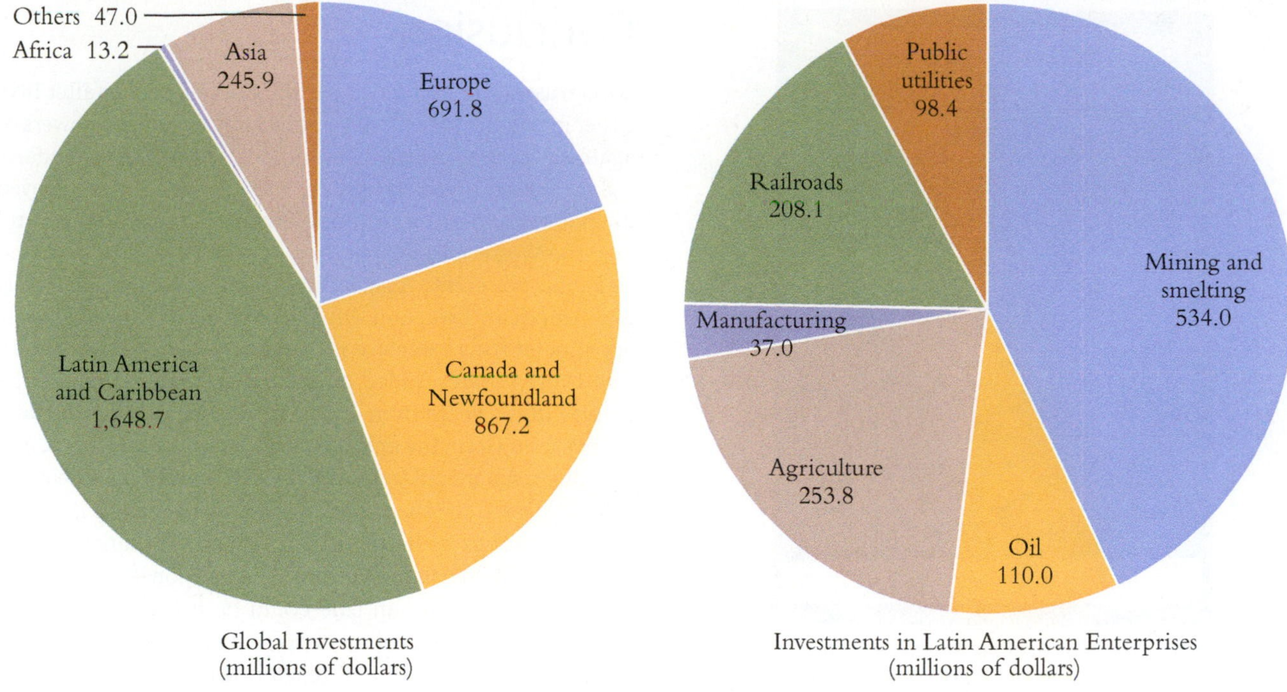

Figure 22.2 **U.S. Global Investments and Investments in Latin America, 1914**

Source: From Cleona Lewis, *America's Stake in International Investments* (Washington, D.C.: The Brookings Institute, 1938), pp. 576–606.

policy that ignored a less powerful nation's right to determine its own future. He deemed Mexicans capable of making democracy work and, in general, showed a concern for morality and justice in foreign affairs—matters to which Roosevelt and Taft had paid scant attention. Wilson wanted U.S. foreign policy to advance democratic ideals and institutions in Mexico.

Another motivation in Wilson's Mexican dealings was a fear that political unrest in Mexico could lead to violence, social disorder, and a revolutionary government hostile to U.S. economic interests. With a U.S.-style democratic government in Mexico, Wilson believed, property rights would be respected and U.S. investments would remain secure. Wilson's desire both to encourage democracy and to limit the extent of social change made it difficult to devise a consistent foreign policy toward Mexico.

The Mexican Revolution broke out in 1910 when dictator Porfirio Diaz, who had ruled for 34 years, was overthrown by democratic forces led by Francisco Madero. Madero's talk of democratic reform frightened many foreign investors, especially those in the United States and Great Britain, who owned more than half of Mexico's real estate, 90 percent of the country's oil reserves, and practically all of its railroads. Thus, when Madero was overthrown early in 1913 by Victoriano Huerta, a conservative general who promised to protect foreign investments, the dollar diplomatists in the Taft administration and in Great Britain breathed a sigh of relief. Henry Lane Wilson, the U.S. ambassador to Mexico, had helped engineer Huerta's coup. Before close relations between the United States and Huerta could be worked out, however, Huerta's men murdered Madero.

Woodrow Wilson, who became president shortly after Madero's assassination in 1913, refused to recognize Huerta's "government of butchers" and demanded that Mexico hold democratic elections. Wilson favored Venustiano Carranza and **Francisco ("Pancho") Villa**, two enemies of Huerta who commanded rebel armies and who claimed to be democrats. In April 1914, Wilson used the arrest of several U.S. sailors by Huerta's troops as a reason to send a fleet into Mexican waters and to order the U.S. Marines to go ashore at the Mexican port city of Veracruz. In the resulting battle between U.S. and Mexican forces, 19 Americans and 126 Mexicans were killed. The battle brought the two countries dangerously close to war. American control over Veracruz weakened Huerta's regime to the point where Carranza was able to take power.

Carranza did not behave as Wilson had expected, however. Carranza proposed a bold land reform program that would redistribute property from the rich to the poor and that would transfer developmental rights on oil lands from foreign corporations, including U.S. petroleum companies, to the Mexican government. An angry Wilson now threw his support to Pancho Villa, who seemed more willing than Carranza to protect U.S. oil interests. When Carranza's forces defeated Villa's forces in 1915, Wilson reluctantly withdrew his support of Villa and prepared to recognize the Carranza government.

Furious that Wilson had abandoned him, Villa and his soldiers pulled 18 U.S. citizens from a train in northern Mexico and murdered them, along with another 17 in an attack on Columbus, New Mexico. Determined to punish Villa, Wilson received permission from Carranza to send a U.S. expeditionary force under General John J. Pershing into Mexico to hunt down Villa's "bandits." Pershing's troops pursued Villa's forces 300 miles into Mexico but failed to catch

Library of Congress Prints and Photographs Division [LC-DIG-npcc-19554]

22.15 **Francisco "Pancho" Villa, Mexican Revolutionary** Angered by President Wilson's policies toward Mexico, Villa attacked U.S. civilians and soldiers in 1916 and brought the two countries dangerously close to war.

them. The U.S. troops did, however, clash twice with Mexican troops under Carranza's command, once again bringing the countries to the brink of war. The United States, about to enter the First World War, could not afford a fight with Mexico; in 1917, Wilson quietly ordered Pershing's troops home and grudgingly recognized the Carranza government.

Wilson's policies toward Mexico from 1913 to 1917 seemed to have produced few concrete results, except to reinforce an already deep antagonism among Mexicans toward the United States. His repeated changes in strategy, moreover, seemed to indicate a lack of skill and decisiveness in foreign affairs. Actually, however, Wilson recognized something that Roosevelt and Taft had not: that more and more peoples of the world were determined to control their own destinies. The United States, under Wilson, was looking for a way to support their democratic aspirations while also safeguarding its own economic interests. The First World War would make this quest for a balance between democratic principles and national self-interest all the more urgent.

Conclusion

We can assess the dramatic turn in U.S. foreign policy after 1898 either in relation to the foreign policies of rival world powers or against America's own democratic ideals. By the first standard, U.S. foreign policy looks impressive. The United States achieved its major objectives in world affairs: It tightened its control over the Western Hemisphere and projected its military and economic power into Asia. It did so while sacrificing relatively few American lives and while constraining the jingoistic appetite for truly extensive military adventure and conquest. The United States added only 125,000 square miles to its empire in the years from 1870 to 1900, while Great Britain, France, and Germany enlarged their empires by 4.7, 3.5, and 1.0 million square miles, respectively. Relatively, few foreigners were subjected to U.S. colonial rule. By contrast, in 1900, the British Empire extended more than 12 million square miles and embraced one-fourth of the world's population (see Map 22.6).

At times, American rule could be brutal, as it was to Filipino soldiers and civilians alike, but on the whole it was no more severe than British or French rule and significantly less severe than that of German, Belgian, or Japanese imperialists. McKinley, Roosevelt, Taft, and Wilson all placed limits on American expansion and avoided, until 1917, extensive foreign entanglements and wars.

If measured against the standard of America's own democratic ideals, however, U.S. foreign policy after 1898 must be judged more harshly. It demeaned the peoples of the Philippines, Puerto Rico, Guam, Cuba, and Colombia as inferior and primitive and denied them the right to govern themselves. In choosing to behave like the imperialist powers of Europe, the United States abandoned its longstanding claim to being a different kind of nation—one that valued liberty more than power.

Many Americans of the time judged their nation by both standards and thus faced a dilemma that would extend throughout the 20th century. On the one hand, they believed with Roosevelt that the size, economic strength, and honor of the United States required it to accept the role of world power and policeman. On the other hand, they continued to believe with Wilson that they had a mission to spread the democratic values of 1776 to the farthest reaches of the earth. The Mexico example demonstrates how hard it was for the United States to reconcile these two very different approaches to world affairs.

CHAPTER REVIEW

Review Questions

1. Which groups in American society were most interested in expanding U.S. influence abroad?
2. In going to war against Spain in 1898, was the United States impelled more by imperialist or anti-imperialist motives?
3. What different mechanisms of control did the United States use to achieve its aims in Hawaii, Cuba, the Philippines, Puerto Rico, and China?
4. What were the similarities and differences between Theodore Roosevelt's foreign policies in Latin America and East Asia? What explains the differences?

5. What was "dollar diplomacy," and how effective was it as a foreign policy tool for the United States under William Howard Taft?
6. What does Woodrow Wilson's policy toward Mexico reveal about his underlying approach to foreign policy? How did his approach resemble or differ from the one favored by Theodore Roosevelt?

Critical Thinking Questions

1. What is the appropriate standard for judging the 1898 turn in U.S. foreign policy: the policies of rival world powers or America's own democratic ideals?
2. If you had been a president, secretary of state, or leading senator in the period from 1898 to 1917, with the power to alter U.S. foreign policy, what, if anything, would you have changed? What leads you to believe that your changes in policy would have been not only desirable but successful in achieving their aims?

Identifications

Review your understanding of the following key terms, people, and events for this chapter (terms in bold in text are included in the Glossary).

Turner's "frontier thesis," p. 603
imperialists, p. 603
Alfred Thayer Mahan, p. 603
yellow journalism, p. 605
Rough Riders, p. 606
Ninth and Tenth Negro Cavalries, p. 606
Emilio Aguinaldo, p. 609
Platt Amendment, p. 610
Open Door policy, p. 613
"Boxers," p. 614
Roosevelt Corollary, p. 615
Panama Canal, p. 616
Russo-Japanese War, p. 616
gentlemen's agreement, p. 617
Great White Fleet, p. 617
dollar diplomacy, p. 619
Francisco ("Pancho") Villa, p. 621

Suggested Readings

General works on America's imperialist turn in the 1890s and early years of the 20th century include **Walter LaFeber**, ***The Cambridge History of Foreign Relations: The Search for Opportunity, 1865–1913*** (1993); **A. G. Hopkins**, ***American Empire: A Global History*** (2018); and **Emily Rosenberg**, ***Spreading the American Dream: American Economic and Cultural Expansion, 1890–1945*** (1982). **David F. Trask**, ***The War with Spain in 1898*** (1981) is a comprehensive study of the Spanish-American War. **Gerald F. Linderman**, ***The Mirror of War: American Society and the Spanish-American War*** (1974), brilliantly recaptures the shock that overtook Americans who discovered that their Cuban allies were black and the Spanish enemies were white. The role of gender in the Spanish–American War is explored in **Kristin L. Hoganson**, ***Fighting for American Manhood: How Gender Politics Provoked the Spanish–American and Philippine–American Wars*** (1998). On missionaries, see **Ian Tyrrell**, ***Reforming the World: The Creation of America's Moral Empire*** (2010); and **David A. Hollinger**, ***Protestants Abroad: How Missionaries Tried to Change the World but Changed America*** (2017).

Paul A. Kramer, ***The Blood of Government: Race, Empire, the United States, and the Philippines*** (2006), analyzes the effects of U.S. colonialism on the Philippines and America. **Louis A. Perez**, ***Cuba under the Platt Amendment, 1902–1934*** (1986), explores the extension of U.S. control over Cuba, while **Marilyn B. Young**, ***The Rhetoric of Empire: American China Policy, 1895–1901*** (1968), examines the unfolding Open Door policy. The history of Puerto Rico following its annexation by the United States is explored in **Raymond Carr**, ***Puerto Rico: A Colonial Experiment*** (1984). On U.S. interventions in Central America, see **Walter LaFeber**, ***Inevitable Revolutions: The United States in Central America, Second Edition*** (1993).

Howard K. Beale, ***Theodore Roosevelt and the Rise of America to World Power*** (1956), is still a crucial work on Roosevelt's foreign policy. On the Panama Canal, see **Julie Greene**, ***The Canal Builders: Making America's Empire at the Panama Canal*** (2009). Consult **Emily Rosenberg**, ***Financial Missionaries to the World: The Politics and Culture of Dollar Diplomacy, 1900–1930*** (1999), on the "dollar diplomacy" that emerged during the Taft administration. On Wilson's foreign policy, see **Thomas J. Knock**, ***To End All Wars: Woodrow Wilson and the Quest for a New World Order*** (1992); **Lloyd C. Gardner**, ***Safe for Democracy: The Anglo-American Response to Revolution, 1913–1923*** (1984); and **Mary A. Renda**, ***Taking Haiti: Military Occupation and the Culture of U.S. Imperialism, 1915–1940*** (2001).

23 War and Society, 1914–1920

Mary Evans Picture Library/The Image Works

23.1 **The Sinking of the *Lusitania*** On May 7, 1915, a German U-boat torpedoed and sank the British passenger liner *Lusitania*, killing 1,198 people, 128 of them Americans. The event turned U.S. opinion sharply against the Germans, especially because the civilians on board had been given no chance to escape or surrender.

THE FIRST WORLD WAR broke out in Europe in August 1914. The **Triple Alliance** of Germany, Austria-Hungary, and the Ottoman Empire squared off against the **Triple Entente** of Great Britain, France, and Russia. The United States entered the war on the side of the Entente (the Allies, or Allied Powers, as they came to be called) in 1917. Over the next year and a half, the United States converted its large, sprawling economy into a disciplined war production machine, raised a 5-million-man army, and provided both the war matériel and troops that helped propel the Allies to victory.

The war also convulsed American society more deeply than any event since the Civil War. This was the first "total" war, meaning that combatants devoted virtually all of their resources to the fight. The U.S. government had no choice but to pursue a degree of industrial control and social regimentation that was unprecedented in American history. This level of government control was controversial in a society that had long distrusted state power. Moreover, significant numbers of Americans from a variety of constituencies opposed the war. To overcome this opposition, Wilson couched American war aims in disinterested and idealistic terms: The United States, he claimed, wanted a **"peace without victory,"** a "war for democracy," and liberty for the world's oppressed peoples.

Although many people in the United States and abroad responded enthusiastically to Wilson's ideals, Wilson needed England and France's support to deliver peace without victory, and this support never came. In America, protests spread among groups who believed that war was undermining liberty, equality, and economic opportunity for the poor. Wilson supported repressive policies to silence these rebels and to enforce unity and conformity on the American people. In the process, he tarnished the ideals for which America had been fighting. ■

CHRONOLOGY

1914	First World War breaks out (July–August)
1915	German submarine sinks the *Lusitania* (May 7)
1916	Woodrow Wilson unveils peace initiative • Wilson reelected as "peace president"
1917	Germany resumes unrestricted submarine warfare (February) • Tsar Nicholas II overthrown in Russia (March) • United States enters the war (April 6) • Committee on Public Information established • Congress passes Selective Service Act and Espionage Act • War Industries Board established • Lenin's Bolsheviks come to power in Russia (November)
1918	Lenin signs treaty with Germany, pulls Russia out of war (March) • Germany launches offensive on Western Front (March–April) • Congress passes Sabotage Act and Sedition Act • Allied Powers and United States advance toward Germany (April–October) • Eugene V. Debs jailed for antiwar speech • Germany signs armistice (November 11)
1919	Treaty of Versailles signed (June 28) • Chicago race riot (July) • Wilson suffers stroke (October 2) • Police strike in Boston • Eighteenth Amendment (Prohibition) ratified
1919–1920	Steelworkers strike in Midwest • Red Scare prompts "Palmer raids" • Senate refuses to ratify Treaty of Versailles • Universal Negro Improvement Association grows under Marcus Garvey's leadership
1920	Anarchists Sacco and Vanzetti convicted of murder

23-1 Europe's Descent into War

What caused World War I?

Europe's descent into war began on June 28, 1914, in Sarajevo, Bosnia, when a Bosnian nationalist assassinated Archduke Franz Ferdinand, heir to the Austro-Hungarian throne. This act was meant to protest the Austro-Hungarian imperial presence in the Balkans and to encourage the Bosnians, Croatians, and other Balkan peoples to join the Serbs in establishing independent nations. Austria-Hungary responded to this provocation on July 28 by declaring war on Serbia, holding it responsible for the archduke's murder.

The conflict might have remained local if an intricate series of treaties had not divided Europe into two hostile camps. Germany, Austria-Hungary, and Italy, the so-called Triple Alliance, had promised to come to each other's aid if attacked. Italy would soon opt out of this alliance, to be replaced by the Ottoman Empire. Arrayed against the nations of the Triple Alliance were Britain, France, and Russia in the Triple Entente. Russia was obligated by another treaty to defend Serbia against Austria-Hungary, and consequently on July 30, it mobilized its armed forces to go to Serbia's aid. That brought Germany into the conflict to protect Austria-Hungary from Russian attack. On August 3, German troops struck not at Russia but at France, Russia's western ally. To reach France, German troops had marched through neutral Belgium. On August 4, Britain reacted by declaring war on Germany. Within the space of only a few weeks, Europe was engulfed in war.

Complicated alliances and defense treaties of the European nations undoubtedly hastened the rush toward war. But equally important was the competition among the European powers to build the strongest economies, the largest armies and navies, and the grandest colonial empires. Britain and Germany, in particular, were engaged in a bitter struggle for European and world supremacy. Few Europeans had any idea that these military buildups might lead to a terrible war that would kill millions and expose the barbarity lurking in their civilization. Historians now believe that several advisers close to the German emperor, Kaiser Wilhelm II, were eager to engage Russia and France in a fight for supremacy on the European continent. They expected that a European war would be swift and decisive—in Germany's favor.

Victory was not swift for any of the combatants. The first wartime use of machine guns and barbed wire made defense against attack easier than staging an offensive. (Both tanks and airplanes had been invented, but military strategists were slow to put them to offensive use.) On the western front, after the initial German attack narrowly failed to take Paris in 1914, the two opposing armies confronted each other along a battle line stretching from Belgium in the north to the Swiss border in the south (see Map 23.1). Troops dug trenches to protect themselves from artillery bombardment and poison gas attacks. Commanders on both sides mounted suicidal ground assaults on the enemy by

▲ **MAP 23.1 Europe Goes to War** In the First World War, Great Britain, France, and Russia squared off against Germany, Austria-Hungary, and the Ottoman Empire. Most of the fighting occurred in Europe along the western front in France (purple line) or the eastern front in Russia (red line). This map also shows Britain's blockade of German ports. British armies based in Egypt (then a British colony) clashed with Ottoman armies in Arabia and other parts of the Ottoman Empire.

Q *What does this map reveal about why Germany pursued its U-Boat strategy with such determination?*

Q *Note how close Paris was to the Western Front. Had the Germans been successful in taking Paris in 1914, might the course and outcome of the war have been different?*

sending tens of thousands of infantry, armed only with rifles, bayonets, and grenades, out of the trenches and directly into enemy fire. Barbed wire further retarded forward progress, enabling enemy artillery and machine guns to cut down appalling numbers of men. Many of those who were not killed in combat succumbed to disease that spread rapidly in cold, wet, and rat-infested trenches. In eastern Europe, the armies of Germany and Austria-Hungary squared off against those of Russia and Serbia. Although that front did not employ trench warfare, the combat was no less lethal. By the time the First World War ended, an estimated 8.5 million soldiers had died, and more than twice that number had been wounded. Total casualties, both military and civilian, had reached 37 million.

23-2 American Neutrality

Q *Why did the U.S. policy of neutrality fail, and why did America get drawn into war?*

Soon after the fighting began, Woodrow Wilson told Americans that this was a European war; neither side was threatening a vital American interest. The United States would therefore proclaim its neutrality and maintain normal relations with both sides while seeking to secure peace. Normal relations meant that the United States would continue trading with both camps. Wilson's neutrality policy met with opposition, especially from Theodore Roosevelt, who was convinced that the United States should join the Entente to check German power and expansionism. A majority of Americans, however, applauded Wilson's determination to keep the country out of war.

Neutrality was easier to proclaim than to achieve, however. Many Americans, especially those with economic and political power, identified culturally more with Britain than with Germany. They shared with the English a language, a common ancestry, and a commitment to liberty. Meanwhile, Germany's acceptance of monarchical rule, the prominence of militarists in German politics, and its lack of democratic traditions inclined U.S. officials to judge Germany harshly.

The United States had strong economic ties to Great Britain as well. In 1914, the United States exported more than $800 million in goods to Britain and its allies, compared with $170 million to Germany and Austria-Hungary (which came to be known as the Central Powers). As soon as the war began, the British and then the French turned to the United States for food, clothing, munitions, and other war supplies. The U.S. economy, which had been languishing in 1914, enjoyed a boom as a result. Meanwhile, the British navy was blockading German ports, shrinking the United States' already limited trade with Germany. By 1916, U.S. exports to the Central Powers had plummeted to barely $1 million, a fall of more than 99 percent in two years.

The Wilson administration protested the British navy's search and occasional seizure of American merchant ships, but it never retaliated by suspending loans or exports to Great Britain. In failing to protect its right to trade with Germany, the United States compromised its neutrality and allowed itself to be drawn into war.

23-2a *Submarine Warfare*

To combat British control of the seas and to check the flow of U.S. goods to the Allies, Germany unveiled a terrifying new weapon, the *Unterseeboot*, or U-boat, the first militarily effective submarine. Early in 1915, Germany announced its intent to use its U-boats to sink on sight enemy ships en route to the British Isles. On May 7, 1915, without warning, a German U-boat torpedoed the British passenger liner *Lusitania*, en route from New York to London. The ship sank in 22 minutes, killing 1,198 men, women, and children, 128 of them U.S. citizens. Shocked by the loss of life, the United States accused Germany of a barbaric act. The circumstances surrounding the sinking of the *Lusitania*, however, were more complicated than most Americans realized.

Before its sailing, the Germans had alleged that the *Lusitania* was secretly carrying a large store of munitions to Great Britain (a charge that proved true), and that it therefore was subject to U-boat attack. Germany had warned American passengers not to travel on British passenger ships that carried munitions. Germany also claimed that the purpose of the U-boat attacks—the disruption of Allied supply lines—was no different from Britain's purpose in blockading German ports. If a submarine attack seemed more reprehensible than a conventional sea battle, the Germans argued, it was no more so than the British attempt to starve the German people into submission with a blockade.

American political leaders might have used the *Lusitania* incident to denounce both Germany's U-boat strategy and Britain's blockade. Only Secretary of State Bryan did so, however, and his stand proved so unpopular in Washington that he resigned from office; Wilson chose the pro-British Robert Lansing to take his place. Wilson denounced the sinking of the *Lusitania* and demanded that Germany pledge never to launch another attack on the citizens of neutral nations. Germany temporarily acquiesced to Wilson's demand.

In March 1916, however, a German submarine torpedoed the French passenger liner *Sussex*, causing a heavy loss of life and injuring several Americans. Such attacks strengthened the hand of Theodore Roosevelt and others who had been arguing that war with Germany was inevitable and that the United States must prepare to fight. Wilson in response sought and won congressional approval for bills to increase the size of the army and navy, tighten federal control over National Guard forces, and authorize the building of a merchant fleet. Still not ready to concede the inevitability of war, however, Wilson intensified his diplomatic initiatives to secure a peace, angering the British with his insistence on an impartial, negotiated settlement in which the claims of the Allies and Central Powers would be treated with respect.

Topham/The Image Works

23.2 ***Gassed* by John Singer Sargent** An artist renders the horror of a poison gas attack in the First World War. The Germans were the first to use this new and brutal weapon, which contributed greatly to the terror of war.

23-2b *The Peace Movement*

Underlying Wilson's 1916 peace initiative was a vision of a new world order in which relations between nations would be governed by negotiation rather than war and in which justice would replace power as the fundamental principle of diplomacy. On May 27, 1916, Wilson formally declared his support for what he would later call the League of Nations, an international parliament dedicated to the pursuit of peace, security, and justice for all the world's peoples.

Many Americans supported Wilson's efforts to commit national prestige to the cause of international peace. Carrie Chapman Catt, president of the National American Woman Suffrage Association, and Jane Addams, founder of the Women's Peace Party, opposed the war. A substantial pacifist group emerged among the nation's Protestant clergy. Midwestern progressives such as Robert La Follette, William Jennings Bryan, and George Norris urged the United States to steer clear of this European conflict, as did leading socialists such as Eugene V. Debs. In April 1916, many of the country's most prominent progressives and socialists joined hands in the American Union Against Militarism, pressuring Wilson to continue pursuing the path of peace. The country's sizable Irish and German ethnic populations, who wanted to block a formal military alliance with Great Britain, also supported Wilson's peace campaign. Wilson embraced the portrait of himself as the "peace president" and rode the slogan "He kept us out of war" to victory over Republican Charles Evans Hughes in the 1916 presidential race.

On December 16, 1916, Wilson sent a peace note to the belligerent governments on both sides, entreating them to consider ending the conflict. Appearing before the Senate on January 22, 1917, Wilson reaffirmed his commitment to the League of Nations. For such a league to succeed, Wilson argued, it would have to be handed a sturdy peace settlement. This entailed a "peace without victory," one that refused to crown a victor or humiliate a loser. Only such a peace, Wilson argued, would last.

Wilson listed the crucial principles of a lasting peace: freedom of the seas; disarmament; and the right of every people to self-determination, democratic self-government, and security against aggression. Wilson was proposing to allow all of the world's peoples, regardless of their country's size or strength, to achieve political independence and to participate as equals in world affairs. These views, rarely expressed by the leader of a world power, stirred the masses of Europe and elsewhere caught in deadly conflict.

23-2c *German Escalation*

The German military responded to Wilson's entreaties for peace by preparing to throw its full military might at France and Britain. On February 25, 1917, the British intercepted and passed on to the president a telegram from Germany's foreign secretary, Arthur Zimmermann, to the German minister in Mexico. The infamous **Zimmermann telegram** instructed the minister to ask the Mexican government to attack the United States in the event of war between Germany and the United States. In return, Germany would pay the Mexicans a large fee and regain for them the "lost provinces" of Texas, New Mexico, and Arizona. Wilson, Congress, and the American public were outraged by this proposed deal.

In March, news arrived that Tsar Nicholas II's autocratic regime in Russia had collapsed and had been replaced by a liberal-democratic government under the leadership of Alexander Kerensky. As long as the tsar ruled Russia and stood to benefit from the Central Powers' defeat, Wilson could not honestly claim that America's going to war against Germany would bring democracy to Europe. The fall of the tsar and Russia's fledgling democratic government's need for assistance gave Wilson the rationale he needed to justify American intervention.

Appearing before a joint session of Congress on April 2, Wilson declared that the United States must enter the war

Library of Congress, Prints and Photographs Division [Bain News Service/LC-DIG-ggbain-18848]

23.3 **Women Peace Delegates** This photograph depicts female American peace activists aboard the ocean liner *Noordam* on their way to the Hague, the Netherlands, to attend the 1915 International Congress of Women. These activists, Jane Addams among them (faintly visible on the stairs in the rear), were determined to keep the United States out of war and to find a way to bring the European conflict to a quick end.

Q *Why did these anti-war activists insist on having an exclusively female peace organization? How widespread was anti-war sentiment in American society?*

because "the world must be made safe for democracy." He continued:

> We shall fight for the things which we have always carried nearest our hearts—for democracy, for the right of those who submit to authority to have a voice in their own Governments, for the rights and liberties of small nations, for a universal dominion of right by such a concert of free peoples as shall bring peace and safety to all nations and make the world itself at last free. To such a task we dedicate our lives and our fortunes.

After a few days of debate, Congress voted 373–50 in the House and 82–6 in the Senate to declare war on the Central Powers. Wilson understood all too well the risks of his undertaking. A few days before his speech to Congress, he had confided to a journalist his worry that the American people, once at war, will "forget there ever was such a thing as tolerance. To fight you must be brutal and ruthless, and the spirit of ruthless brutality will enter into the very fiber of our national life, infecting Congress, the courts, the policeman on the beat, the man in the street." Still, Wilson was hopeful that America could make this struggle "a war to end all wars" and use it as an occasion to strengthen liberty and democracy in countries where these principles were weak.

23-3 American Intervention

Q *What contribution did the U.S. make to the Allied Powers' victory?*

The entry of the United States into the war gave the Allies the muscle they needed to defeat the Central Powers, but it almost came too late. Germany's resumption of unrestricted submarine warfare took a frightful toll on Allied shipping. From February through July 1917, German subs sank almost 4 million tons of shipping, more than one-third of Britain's entire merchant fleet. One of every four large freighters departing Britain in those months never returned; at one point, the British Isles were down to a mere four weeks of provisions. American intervention ended Britain's vulnerability in dramatic fashion. U.S. and British naval commanders now grouped merchant ships into convoys and provided them with warship escorts through the most dangerous stretches of the North Atlantic. Destroyers armed with depth charges were particularly effective as escorts. Their shallow draft made them invulnerable to torpedoes, and their acceleration and speed allowed them to pursue slow-moving U-boats. The U.S. and British navies had begun to use sound waves (later called "sonar") to pinpoint the location of underwater craft, and

The Granger Collection, New York

23.4 ***The Rock of the Marne*** Mal Thompson's painting shows infantry units of the U.S. 30th and 38th regiments from the Third Division of the American Expeditionary Force engaging German troops in France in July 1918. Although he shows them under fire and operating in terrain desolated by war, Thompson depicts the soldiers as focused and calm.

this new technology increased the effectiveness of destroyer attacks. By the end of 1917, the tonnage of Allied shipping lost each month to U-boat attacks had declined by two-thirds, from almost 1 million tons in April to 350,000 tons in December.

The French and British armies had bled themselves white by taking the offensive in 1916 and 1917 and had scarcely budged the trench lines. The Germans had been content in those years simply to hold their trench position in the West until they defeated the Russians in the East. This they did in late 1917 when a second Russian revolution overthrew Kerensky's liberal-democratic government and brought to power a revolutionary socialist government under Vladimir Lenin and his Bolshevik Party. Lenin pulled Russia out of the war on the grounds that the war did not serve the best interests of the working classes, that it was a conflict between rival capitalist elites interested only in wealth and power (and indifferent to the slaughter of soldiers in the trenches).

Lenin also published the texts of secret Allied treaties showing that Britain and France, like Germany, had plotted to enlarge their nations and empires through war. The revelation that the Allies were fighting for land and riches rather than democratic principles outraged large numbers of people in France and Great Britain, demoralized Allied troops, and threw the French and British governments into disarray. The treaties also embarrassed Wilson, who had brought America into the war to fight for democracy, not territory. Wilson quickly moved to restore the Allies' credibility by unveiling, in January 1918, a concrete program for peace. His **Fourteen Points** reaffirmed America's commitment to an international system governed by laws rather than by might and renounced territorial aggrandizement as a legitimate war aim. This document provided the ideological cement that held the Allies together at a critical moment. (The Fourteen Points are discussed more fully in a subsequent section of the chapter, "Failure of the International Peace.")

The Allies needed every bit of fortitude they could muster. In March and April 1918, Germany sent British and French troops reeling by launching a huge offensive against Allied positions. German troops advanced 10 miles a day—a faster pace than any on the western front since the earliest days of the war—until they reached the Marne River, within striking distance of Paris (see Map 23.2). The French government prepared to evacuate the city. At this perilous moment, a large American army—fresh, well equipped, and oblivious to the horrors of trench warfare—arrived to reinforce what remained of the French lines.

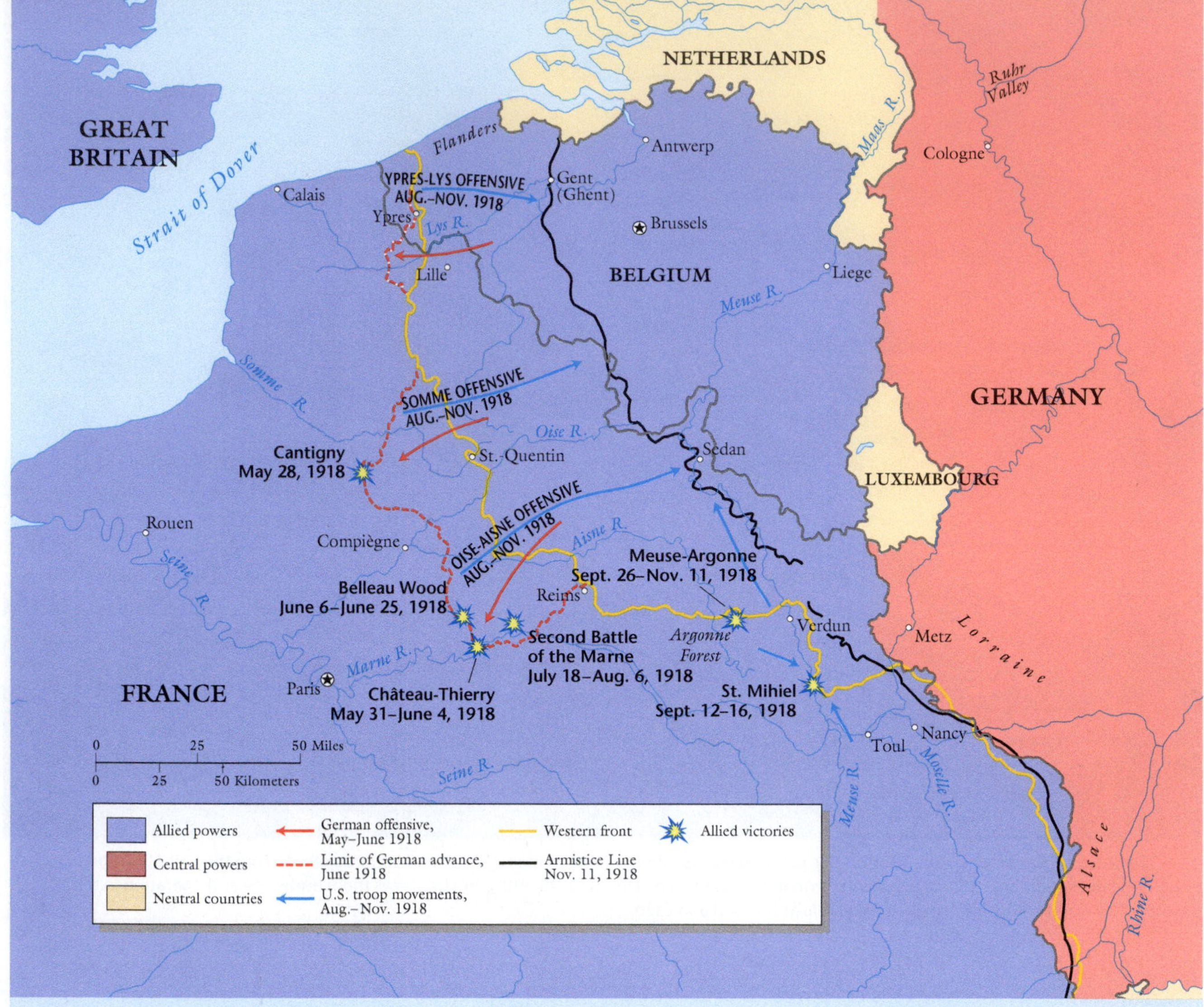

▲ **MAP 23.2 America in the First World War: Western Front, 1918** In 1918, American forces joined the Allied forces in the climactic battles of the war. The red arrows show the major offensive by the Germans in the spring of 1918, and the blue arrows the decisive counteroffensive by the Allies in the fall of 1918. The fighting stopped along the black armistice line on November 11, 1918, after German capitulation. As in 1914, the course of the war turned on the Allied forces' ability to keep the Germans from entering Paris.

Q *Why was Paris so important?*

Q *Were the Germans right in calculating that their best chance of winning the war was to overwhelm the Allied defenses on the Western Front before the American troops were ready to fight?*

These American troops, part of the American Expeditionary Force (AEF) commanded by General **John J. Pershing**, had begun landing in France almost a year earlier. The United States had had to create a modern army from scratch, because its existing force was so small, ranking only 17th in the world. Men had to be drafted, trained, and supplied with food and equipment; ships for transporting them to Europe had to be found or built. In France, Pershing put his troops through additional training before committing them to battle. He was determined that the American soldiers—or "doughboys," as they were called—should acquit themselves well on the battlefield. The army he ordered into battle to counter the German spring offensive of 1918 fought well. Many American soldiers fell, but the German offensive ground to a halt. Paris was saved, and Germany's best chance for victory slipped from its grasp.

Buttressed by this show of AEF strength, the Allied troops staged a major offensive of their own in late September. Millions of Allied troops (including more than a million from the AEF) advanced across the 200-mile-wide Argonne Forest in France, cutting German supply lines. By late October, they had reached the German border. Faced with an invasion of their homeland and with rapidly mounting popular dissatisfaction toward the war, German leaders asked for an armistice, to be followed by peace negotiations based on Wilson's Fourteen Points. Having forced the Germans to agree to numerous concessions, the Allies ended the war on November 11, 1918.

23-4 Mobilizing for "Total" War

Q *What problems did the U.S. encounter in mobilizing for total war, and how successfully were those problems overcome?*

Compared to Europe, the United States suffered little from the war. The deaths of 112,000 American soldiers paled in comparison to European losses of 900,000 by Great Britain, 1.2 million by Austria-Hungary, 1.4 million by France, 1.7 million by Russia, and 2 million by Germany. The U.S. civilian population was spared most of the war's ravages—the destruction of homes and industries, the shortages of food and medicine, the spread of disease—that afflicted millions of Europeans. Only with the flu epidemic that swept across the Atlantic from Europe in 1919 to claim approximately 500,000 lives did Americans briefly experience wholesale suffering and death.

Still, the war had a profound effect on American society. Every military engagement the United States had fought since the Civil War—the Indian wars, the Spanish-American War, the American-Filipino War, the Boxer Rebellion, the Latin American interventions—had been limited in scope. Even the troop mobilizations that seemed large at the time—the more than 100,000 needed to fight the Spanish and then the Filipinos—did not overwhelm American resources.

The First World War was different. It was a "total" war for which every nation involved in the conflict had to mobilize virtually all its manpower and economic resources. The scale of the effort in the United States became apparent early in 1917 when Wilson asked Congress for a conscription law that would permit the federal government to raise a multimillion-man army. The United States would also have to devote much of its agricultural, transportation, industrial, and population resources to the war effort if it wished to end the European stalemate. Who would organize this massive effort? Who would pay for it? Would Americans accept the sacrifice and regimentation it would demand? These were vexing questions for a nation long committed to individual liberty, small government, and a weak military.

23-4a *Organizing Industry*

At first, Wilson pursued a decentralized approach to mobilization, delegating tasks to local defense councils throughout the country. When that effort failed, Wilson created centralized federal agencies, each charged with supervising nationwide activity in its assigned economic sector.

The success of these agencies varied. The Food Administration, headed by mining engineer and executive Herbert Hoover, substantially increased production of basic foodstuffs and put in place an efficient distribution system that delivered food to millions of troops and European civilians. Treasury Secretary William McAdoo, head of the U.S. Railroad Administration, also performed well in shifting the rail system from private to public control, coordinating dense train traffic, and making capital improvements that allowed goods to move rapidly to eastern ports, where they were loaded onto ships and sent to Europe. At the other extreme, the Aircraft Production Board and Emergency Fleet Corporation did a poor job of supplying the Allies with combat aircraft and merchant vessels. On balance, the U.S. economy performed wonders in supplying troops with uniforms, food, rifles, munitions, and other basic items; it did much less well in producing sophisticated weapons and machines such as artillery, aircraft, and ships.

Most of the new government agencies were more powerful on paper than in fact. Consider, for example, the **War Industries Board (WIB)**, an administrative body established by Wilson in July 1917 to harness manufacturing might to military needs. The WIB floundered for its first nine months, lacking the statutory authority to force manufacturers and the military to adopt its plans. Only the appointment of Wall Street investment banker Bernard Baruch as WIB chairman in March 1918 turned the agency around. Rather than force manufacturers to do the government's bidding, Baruch permitted industrialists to charge high prices for their products. He won exemptions from antitrust laws for corporations that complied with his requests. In general, he made war production too lucrative an activity to resist; however, he did not hesitate to unleash his wrath on corporations that resisted WIB enticements.

Baruch's forceful leadership worked reasonably well throughout his nine months in office. War production increased, and manufacturers discovered the financial benefits of cooperation between the public and private sectors. But Baruch's favoritism toward large corporations hurt smaller competitors. Moreover, the cozy relationship between government and corporations that he encouraged violated the progressive pledge to protect the people from the "interests." Achieving cooperation by boosting corporate profits, finally, was an expensive way for the government to do business. The costs of the war soared to $33 billion, a figure more than three times expectations.

23-4b *Securing Labor*

War increased the demand for industrial labor while cutting the supply. European immigrants had long been the most important source of new labor for American industry, and during the war they stopped coming. Meanwhile, millions of workers already in America were conscripted into the military and thus lost to industry.

Manufacturers responded to the labor shortage by recruiting new sources of labor from the rural South; 500,000 African Americans migrated to northern cities between 1916 and 1920 (see Map 23.3). Another half-million white southerners followed the same path during that period. Hundreds of thousands of Mexicans fled their revolution-ridden homeland for the American Southwest and Midwest. Tens of thousands of northern women found work as streetcar conductors, railroad workers, metalworkers, munitions makers, and in other jobs customarily reserved for men. The

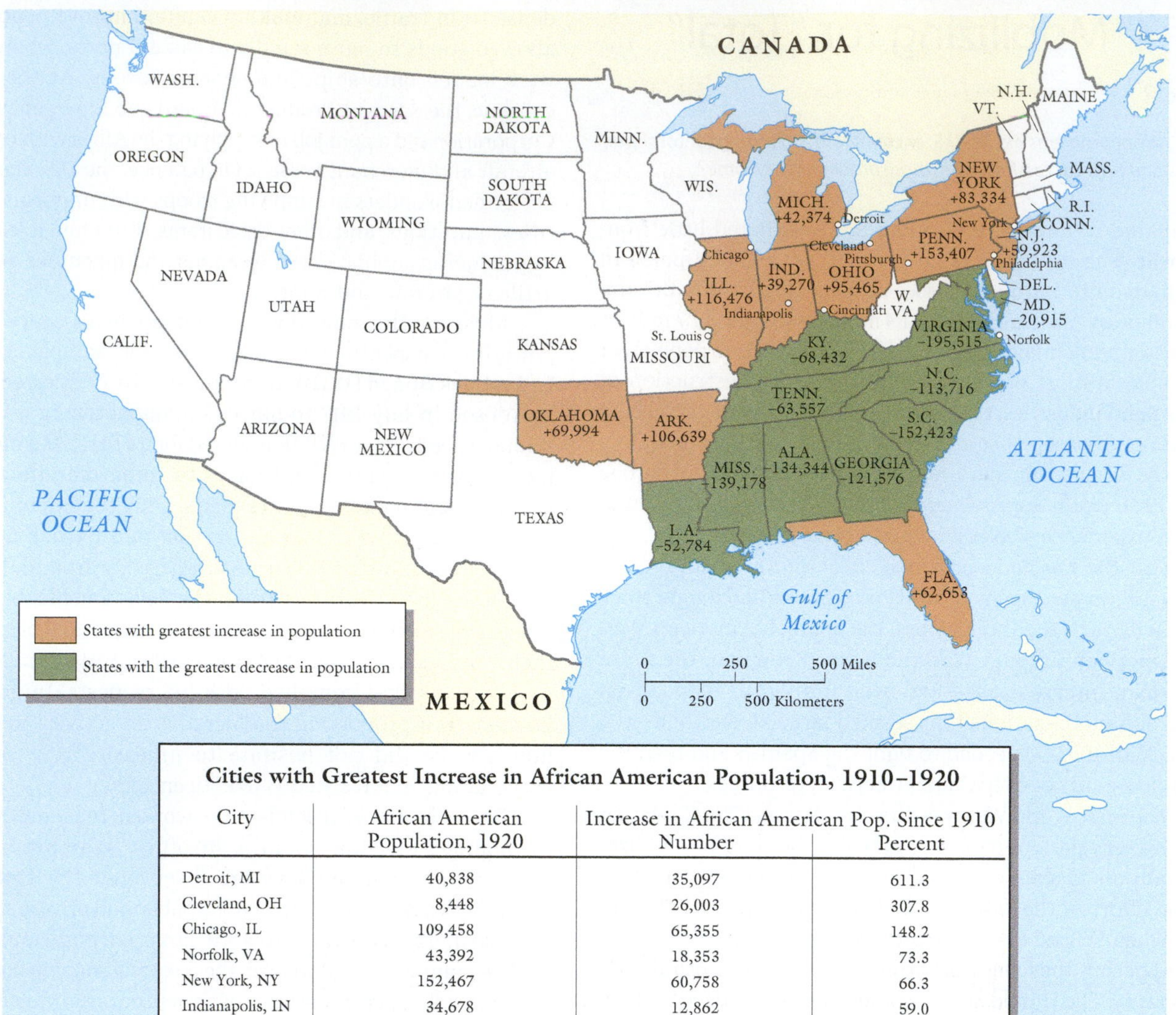

Cities with Greatest Increase in African American Population, 1910–1920

City	African American Population, 1920	Increase in African American Pop. Since 1910 Number	Percent
Detroit, MI	40,838	35,097	611.3
Cleveland, OH	8,448	26,003	307.8
Chicago, IL	109,458	65,355	148.2
Norfolk, VA	43,392	18,353	73.3
New York, NY	152,467	60,758	66.3
Indianapolis, IN	34,678	12,862	59.0
Philadelphia, PA	134,229	49,770	58.9
St. Louis, MO	69,854	25,894	58.9
Cincinnati, OH	30,079	10,440	53.2
Pittsburgh, PA	37,725	12,102	47.2

▲ **MAP 23.3 African American Migration, 1910–1920** Most southern states each lost 50,000 to 200,000 African Americans during the years of the Great Migration, while many northern states, in the industrial belt stretching from Illinois through New York, gained 40,000 to 150,000 apiece. The table inset on the map shows the cities posting the biggest gains.

Q *Why did the northern migration of African Americans focus so heavily on six states: Illinois, Indiana, Michigan, Ohio, Pennsylvania, and New York?*

Q *Virginia lost the greatest number of African Americans in absolute terms. But the black population of Norfolk, Virginia, increased by nearly 75 percent. Why?*

number of female clerical workers doubled between 1910 and 1920, with many of these women finding work in government war bureaucracies. Altogether, a million women toiled in war-related industries (see Figure 23.1).

These workers alleviated but did not eliminate the nation's labor shortage. Unemployment, which had hovered around 8.5 percent in 1915, plunged to 1.2 percent in 1918. Quick to recognize the benefits of the tight labor market, workers quit jobs they did not like and took part in strikes and other collective actions in large numbers. From 1916 to 1920, more than 1 million workers went on strike every year. Union membership almost doubled, from 2.6 million in 1915 to 5.1 million in 1920. Workers commonly sought higher wages and shorter hours through strikes and unionization. Wages rose an average of 137 percent from 1915 to 1920, although inflation largely negated these gains. The average workweek declined in that same period from 55 to 51 hours. Workers also struck in response to managerial attempts to speed up production and tighten discipline. As time passed, increasing numbers of workers began to wonder why the war

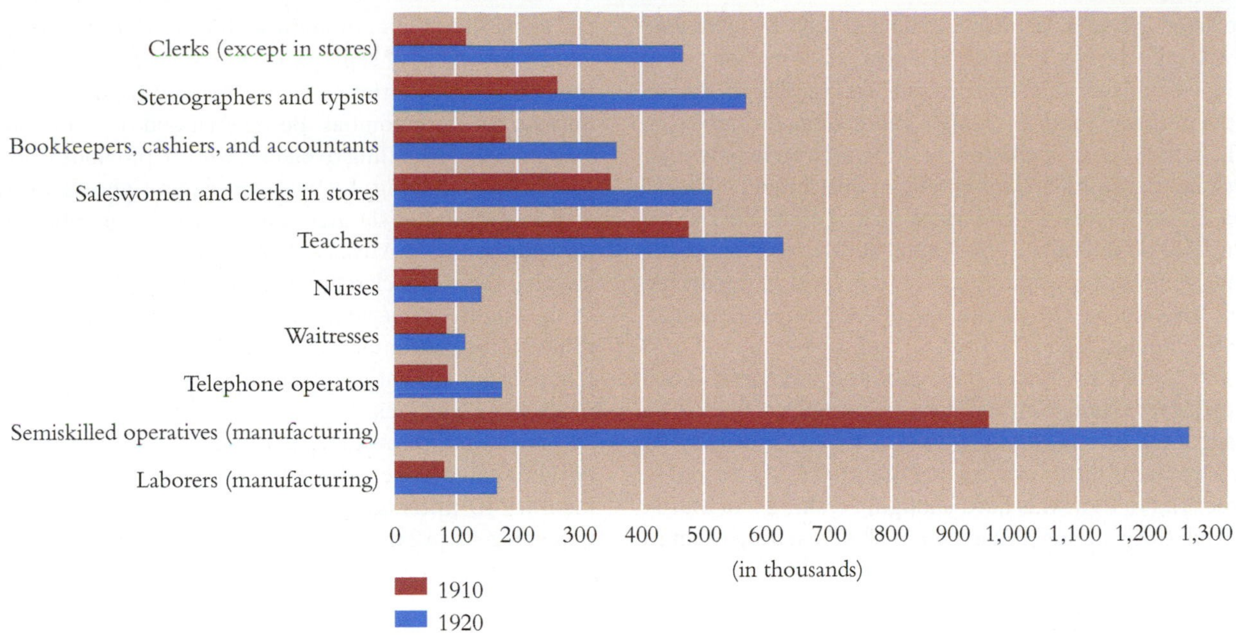

Figure 23.1 **Occupations with Largest Increase in Women, 1910–1920**

Source: Joseph A. Hill, *Women in Gainful Occupations*, 1870–1920, U.S. Bureau of the Census, Monograph no. 9 (Washington, D.C.: Government Printing Office, 1929), p. 33.

Chicago History Museum/Getty Images

23.5 **Mexicans Migrate to Chicago** Labor shortages caused by the war opened up new opportunities for Mexican immigrant laborers. In this 1917 photograph, a group of such laborers cuts grass alongside a road near Chicago.

Q *What other populations in America found labor opportunities opened to them as a result of the war?*

for democracy in Europe had no counterpart in their factories at home. Democratizing the workplace—a campaign known as "industrial democracy"—became the battle cry of an awakened labor movement.

Wilson's willingness to include labor in his 1916 progressive coalition reflected his awareness of labor's potential power (see Chapter 21). In 1918, he bestowed prestige on the newly formed **National War Labor Board (NWLB)** by appointing former president William Howard Taft to be co-chair alongside Samuel Gompers, president of the American Federation of Labor. The NWLB brought together representatives of labor, industry, and the public to resolve labor disputes.

23-4c *Raising an Army*

To raise an army, the Wilson administration committed itself to conscription—the drafting of most men of a certain age, irrespective of their family's wealth, ethnic background, or social standing. The Selective Service Act of May 1917 empowered the administration to do just that. By war's end, local Selective Service boards had registered 24 million young men age 18 and older and had drafted nearly 3 million of them into the military; another 2 million volunteered for service.

Relatively few men resisted the draft, even among recently arrived immigrants. Foreign-born men constituted 18 percent of the armed forces—a percentage greater than their share of the total population. Almost 400,000 African Americans served, representing approximately 10 percent of the armed forces, the same as the percentage of African Americans in the total population.

The U.S. Army, under the command of Chief of Staff Peyton March and General John J. Pershing, faced the difficult task of fashioning these ethnically and racially diverse millions into a professional fighting force. Teaching raw recruits to fight was hard enough, Pershing and March observed; the generals refused the task of teaching them to put aside their racial prejudices. Rather than integrate the armed forces, they segregated black soldiers from white. Most African Americans were assigned to all-black units and barred from combat. Being stripped of a combat role was particularly galling to blacks, who, in previous wars, had proven to be among the best American fighters. Pershing was fully aware of the African American contribution. He had commanded African American troops in the Tenth Cavalry, the all-black regiment that had distinguished itself in the Spanish-American War (see Chapter 22). Pershing's military reputation had depended so heavily on the black troops who fought for him that he had acquired the nickname Black Jack.

For a time, the military justified its intensified discrimination against blacks by referring to the results of rudimentary IQ (intelligence quotient) tests administered by psychologists to 2 million AEF soldiers. These tests allegedly

23.6 **The 369th Returns to New York** Denied the opportunity to fight in the U.S. Army, this unit fought for the French. For the length and distinction of its service in the front lines, this entire unit was awarded the *Croix de Guerre* (War Cross) by the French government.

Q *Why was the U.S. government so intent on excluding African Americans soldiers from combat, especially in view of their strong performance record as fighters in past wars, including in the Spanish-American War of 1898 (see Chapter 22).*

"proved" that native-born Americans and immigrants from the British Isles, Germany, and Scandinavia were well endowed with intelligence, whereas African Americans and immigrants from southern and eastern Europe were poorly endowed. The tests were scientifically so ill conceived, however, that their findings revealed nothing about the true distribution of intelligence in the soldier population. Their most sensational revelation was that more than half of the soldiers in the AEF—white and black—were "morons," men who had failed to reach the mental age of 13. After trying to absorb the apparent news that most U.S. soldiers were feebleminded, the military sensibly rejected the pseudoscience on which these intelligence findings were based. In 1919, it discontinued the IQ testing program.

Given the racial and ethnic differences among American troops and the short time Pershing and his staff had to train recruits, the AEF's performance was impressive. The United States increased the army from a mere 100,000 to 5 million in little more than a year. The Germans sank no troop ships, nor were any soldiers killed during the dangerous Atlantic crossing. In combat, U.S. troops became known for their sharp-shooting skills. The most decorated soldier in the AEF was Sergeant Alvin C. York of Tennessee, who captured 35 machine guns, took 132 prisoners, and killed 17 German soldiers with 17 bullets. One of the most decorated AEF units was **New York's 369th Regiment**, a black unit recruited in Harlem. Bowing to pressure from civil rights groups to allow some black troops to fight, Pershing had offered the 369th to the French army. The 369th served in forward Allied trenches along with French troops for 191 days (longer than any other U.S. regiment), and scored several major successes. In gratitude for its service, the French government decorated the unit with one of its highest honors—the *Croix de Guerre* (War Cross).

23-4d *Paying the Bills*

The government incurred large debts buying food, uniforms, munitions, weapons, vehicles, and sundry other items for the U.S. military. To help pay its bills, the government slapped the rich with a 67 percent income tax and a 25 percent inheritance tax. Corporations were ordered to pay an "excess profits" tax. Progressives wanted to make sure that all Americans would sacrifice something for the war and that monied interests would not be able to use the war to enrich themselves.

Tax revenues, however, provided only about one-third of the $33 billion that the government ultimately spent on the war. The rest came from the sale of **Liberty Bonds**. These 30-year government bonds offered individual purchasers a return of 3.5 percent in annual interest. The government offered five bond issues between 1917 and 1920 and all quickly sold out, thanks, in no small measure, to the high-powered sales pitch orchestrated by Treasury Secretary William G. McAdoo that equated bond purchases with patriotic duty.

23-4e *Arousing Patriotic Ardor*

The Treasury's bond campaign was only one aspect of a wide-ranging government effort to arouse public support for the war. In 1917, Wilson set up a new agency, the **Committee on Public Information (CPI)**, to popularize the war. Under the chairmanship of George Creel, a midwestern progressive and a muckraker, the CPI distributed 75 million copies of pamphlets explaining U.S. war aims in several languages. It trained a force of 75,000 "Four-Minute Men" to deliver succinct, uplifting war speeches to numerous groups in their home cities and towns. It papered the walls of virtually every public institution (and many private ones) with posters, placed advertisements in

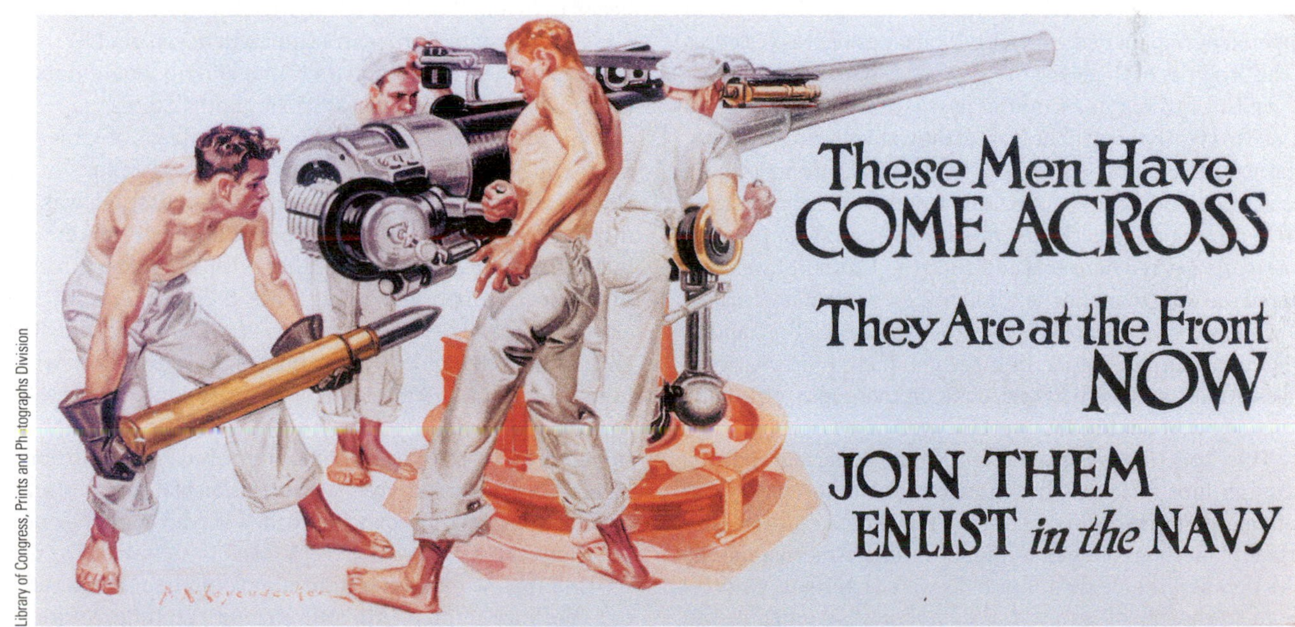

Library of Congress, Prints and Photographs Division

23.7 **Recruiting Poster, First World War, 1917** The government plastered public institutions with recruiting posters. This one represents navy work as glamorous, masculine, and brave.

National Archives and Records Administration

23.8 **Women Doing "Men's Work"** Labor shortages during the war allowed thousands of women to take industrial jobs customarily reserved for men. Here women operate pneumatic hammers at the Midvale Steel and Ordnance Company, Nicetown, Pennsylvania, 1918.

Q *After looking at this photograph, study Figure 23.1. Were the greatest gains in women's employment between 1910 and 1920 in domains traditionally allocated to men (manufacturing), or in the new white-collar sectors (clerks, typists, cashiers, saleswomen, etc.)?*

mass-circulation magazines, sponsored exhibitions, and peppered newspaper editors with thousands of press releases on the progress of the war.

Faithful to his muckraking past (see Chapter 21), Creel wanted to give the people the facts of the war, believing that well-informed citizens would see the wisdom of Wilson's policies. He also saw his work as an opportunity to achieve the progressive goal of uniting all Americans into a single moral community. Americans everywhere learned that the United States had entered the war "to make the world safe for democracy," to help the world's weaker peoples achieve self-determination, and to bring a measure of justice into the conduct of international affairs. Americans were asked to affirm those ideals by doing everything they could to support the war.

This uplifting message affected the American people, although not necessarily in ways anticipated by CPI propagandists. Workers, women, European ethnics, and African Americans began demanding that America live up to its democratic ideals at home as well as abroad. Workers rallied to the cry of "industrial democracy." Women seized on the democratic fervor to bring their fight for suffrage to a successful conclusion (see Chapter 21). African Americans began to dream that the war might deliver them from second-class citizenship. European ethnics believed that Wilson's support of their countrymen's rights abroad would improve their own chances for success in the United States.

Although the CPI had helped to unleash it, this new democratic enthusiasm troubled Creel and others in the Wilson administration. The United States, after all, was still divided along class, ethnic, and racial lines. Workers and industrialists regarded each other with suspicion. Cultural differences compounded this class division: The working class was heavily ethnic in composition, and the industrial and political elites consisted mainly of the native-born whose families had been Americans for generations. Progressives had fought hard to overcome these divisions. They had tamed the power of capitalists, improved the condition of workers, encouraged the Americanization of immigrants, and articulated a new, more inclusive idea of who could belong to the American nation.

But their work was far from complete when the war broke out. German immigrants still formed the largest foreign-born population group at 2.3 million. Another 2.3 million immigrants came from some part of the Austro-Hungarian

Empire, and more than 1 million Americans—native-born and immigrants—supported the Socialist Party and the Industrial Workers of the World (IWW), both of which opposed the war. The decision to authorize the CPI's comprehensive unity campaign indicates that the progressives understood how widespread the discord was. Still, they had not anticipated that the promotion of democratic ideals at home would exacerbate, rather than lessen, the nation's social and cultural divisions.

23-4f *Wartime Repression*

By early 1918, the CPI's campaign had developed a darker, more coercive side. Inflammatory advertisements called on patriots to report on neighbors, coworkers, and ethnics they suspected of subverting the war effort. Propagandists called on all immigrants, especially those from central, southern, and eastern Europe, to pledge themselves to "100 percent Americanism" and to repudiate all ties to their homeland, native language, and ethnic customs. The CPI aroused hostility toward Germans by spreading tales of German atrocities and encouraging the public to see movies such as *The Prussian Cur* and *The Beast of Berlin*. The Justice Department arrested thousands of German and Austrian immigrants suspected of subversive activities. Congress passed the Trading with the Enemy Act, which required foreign-language publications to submit all war-related stories to post office censors for approval.

German Americans became the objects of popular hatred. In Boston, performances of Beethoven's symphonies were banned, and the German-born conductor of the Boston Symphony Orchestra was forced to resign. Although Americans would not give up the German foods they had grown to love, they would no longer call them by their German names (see Table 23.1). Libraries removed works of German literature from their shelves, and Theodore Roosevelt and others urged school districts to prohibit the teaching of the German language. Patriotic school boards in Lima, Ohio, and elsewhere burned the German books in their districts.

German Americans risked being fired from work, losing their businesses, and being assaulted on the street. A St. Louis mob lynched an innocent German immigrant they suspected of subversion. After only 25 minutes of deliberation, a St. Louis jury acquitted the mob leaders, who had brazenly defended their crime as an act of patriotism. German Americans began hiding their ethnic identity, changing their names, speaking German only in the privacy of their homes, and celebrating their holidays only with trusted friends.

The anti-German campaign escalated into a general anti-immigrant crusade. Congress passed the Immigration Restriction Act of 1917, over Wilson's veto, which declared that all adult immigrants who failed a reading test would be denied admission to the United States. The act also banned the immigration of laborers from India, Indochina, Afghanistan, Arabia, the East Indies, and other countries located within an "Asiatic Barred Zone."

Table 23.1 ELIMINATING GERMAN WORDS AND NAMES

German Word or Name	Replacement Word or Name
hamburger	salisbury steak, liberty steak, liberty sandwich
Sauerkraut	liberty cabbage
Hamburg Avenue, Brooklyn, New York	Wilson Avenue, Brooklyn, New York
Germantown, Nebraska	Garland, Nebraska
East Germantown, Indiana	Pershing, Indiana
Berlin, Iowa	Lincoln, Iowa
pinochle	Liberty
German shepherd	Alsatian shepherd
Deutsches Haus of Indianapolis	Athenaeum of Indiana
Germania Maennerchor of Chicago	Lincoln Club
Kaiser Street	Maine Way

Source: From La Vern J. Rippley, *The German Americans* (Boston: Twayne, 1976), p. 186; and Robert H. Ferrell, *Woodrow Wilson and World War I, 1917–1921* (New York: Harper and Row, 1985), pp. 205–6.

Congress also passed the Eighteenth Amendment to the Constitution, which prohibited the manufacture and distribution of alcoholic beverages (see Chapter 21). The campaign for prohibition was not new, but anti-immigrant feelings generated by the war gave it added impetus. Prohibitionists pictured the nation's urban ethnic ghettos as scenes of drunkenness, immorality, and disloyalty. They also accused German American brewers of operating a "liquor trust" to sap people's will to fight. The states quickly ratified the Eighteenth Amendment, and in 1919, Prohibition became the law of the land.

In the **Espionage, Sabotage, and Sedition Acts** passed in 1917 and 1918, Congress gave the administration sweeping powers to silence and imprison dissenters. These acts went beyond outlawing behavior that no nation at war could be expected to tolerate, such as spying for the enemy, sabotaging war production, and calling for the enemy's victory. Now citizens could be prosecuted for writing or uttering any statement that could be construed as profaning the flag, the Constitution, or the military. These acts constituted the most drastic restrictions of free speech at the national level since the Alien and Sedition Acts of 1798 (see Chapter 7).

Government repression fell most heavily on the IWW and the Socialist Party. Both groups had opposed intervention. Although they subsequently muted their opposition, they continued to insist that the true enemies of American workers were to be found in the ranks of American employers, not in Germany or Austria-Hungary. The government responded by banning many socialist materials from the mails and by disrupting socialist and IWW meetings. By spring 1918, government agents had raided countless IWW offices and had

Interpreting the Visual Past

Turning the German Enemy into a Beast

By 1918, the government's campaign to engender support for the war focused as much on fear as on hope. In this poster, the German enemy is represented as a terrifying brute who violates Columbia—the Athena-like woman who was thought to embody America's highest aspirations to liberty, fairness, and wisdom. Many Americans had long admired Germany for the quality of its culture and of the immigrants it had sent to America. But Germany's lack of democracy and perceived militarism had also generated suspicions that pro-war propagandists now sought to use to strengthen sentiment in America for war.

The poster is notable, too, for its imagery of sexual violence. Fantasies of black brutes using their force to overpower and deflower chaste white women were common in America at this time; they became part of the rationale for segregating blacks from whites and for justifying the lynching of African American men. Here these fantasies are being deployed for foreign rather than domestic purposes.

Q *Compare this depiction of Columbia with the one in the Interpreting the Visual Past feature in Chapter 21 (see Image 21.8). What are the similarities? What are the differences? Why did Columbia become such a popular symbol of America?*

Q *Do you think that the artist who created this poster was correct in thinking that the sexualized images at the heart of this design would be effective in influencing attitudes toward Germany?*

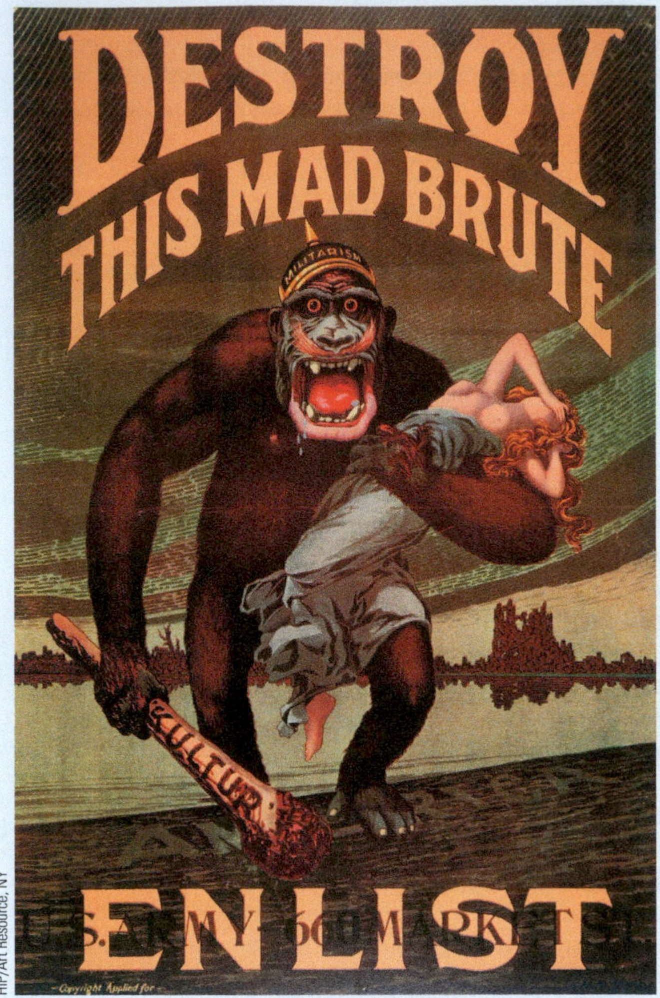

HIP/Art Resource, NY

23.9 **Harry R. Hopps, *Destroy This Mad Brute, Enlist*, 1918.**

arrested 2,000 IWW members, including the organization's entire executive board. William Haywood, the IWW president, fled to Europe and then to the Soviet Union rather than go to jail. In summer 1918, Eugene V. Debs, the 62-year-old head of the Socialist Party, received a 10-year jail term for making an antiwar speech in Canton, Ohio.

This federal repression, carried out in an atmosphere of supercharged patriotism, encouraged local governments and private citizens to initiate their own antiradical crusades. In the mining town of Bisbee, Arizona, a sheriff with a force of 2,000 deputized citizens kidnapped 1,200 IWW members, herded them into cattle cars, and dumped them in the New Mexico desert with little food or water. Vigilantes in Butte, Montana, chained an IWW organizer to a car and let his body scrape the pavement as they drove the vehicle through city streets. Next, they strung him up to a railroad trestle, castrated him, and left him to die. The 250,000 members of the American Protective League, most of them businessmen and professionals, routinely spied on fellow workers and neighbors. They opened mail and tapped phones and otherwise harassed those suspected of disloyalty. Attorney General Thomas Gregory publicly endorsed the group and sought federal funds to support its "police" work.

The spirit of coercion even infected institutions that had long prided themselves on tolerance. In July 1917, Columbia University fired two professors for speaking out against U.S. intervention in the war. The National Americanization Committee, which before 1917 had pioneered a humane approach to the problem of integrating immigrants into American life, now supported surveillance, internment, and deportation of aliens suspected of anti-American sentiments.

Wilson did attempt to block certain pieces of repressive legislation but did little to halt Attorney General Gregory's prosecution of radicals or Postmaster General Burleson's campaign to exclude Socialist Party publications from the mail. His acquiescence in these matters cost him support among progressives. Wilson believed, however, that once the Allies, with U.S. support, won the war and arranged a just peace in accordance with the Fourteen Points, his administration's wartime actions would be forgiven and the progressive coalition would be restored.

23-5 The Failure of the International Peace

Q *What were Woodrow Wilson's peace proposals, and how did they fare?*

In the month following Germany's surrender on November 11, 1918, Wilson was confident about the prospects of achieving a just peace. Both Germany and the Allies had publicly accepted the Fourteen Points as the basis for negotiations. Wilson's international prestige had grown. Poles, Lithuanians, and other eastern Europeans whose pursuit of nationhood had been frustrated for 100 years or more now believed that independence might be within their reach. Zionist Jews in Europe and the United States dared to dream of a Jewish homeland in Palestine within their lifetimes. Countless African and Asian peoples imagined achieving their freedom from colonial domination.

When Wilson arrived in France for the peace conference in January 1919, some 2 million French citizens—the largest throng ever assembled on French soil—lined the parade route in Paris to see him. In Rome, Milan, and La Scala, Italians acclaimed him "The Savior of Humanity" and "The Moses from Across the Atlantic."

In the Fourteen Points, Wilson had translated his principles for a new world order into specific proposals for international peace and justice. The first group of points called for all nations to abide by a code of conduct that embraced free trade, freedom of the seas, open diplomacy, disarmament, and the resolution of disputes through mediation. A second group, based on the principle of self-determination, proposed redrawing the map of Europe to give national sovereignty to the subjugated peoples of the Austro-Hungarian, Ottoman, and Russian empires. The last point called for establishing the League of Nations, an assembly in which all nations would be represented and in which international disputes would be given a fair hearing and an opportunity for peaceful solutions.

New York Times

23.10 **"The Savior of Humanity"** Wherever he went in Europe, Woodrow Wilson was greeted by huge crowds eager to thank him for ending Europe's terrible war and to endorse his vision of a peaceful, democratic world. Here millions of Italians greet Wilson's arrival in Milan.

Q *Why do you think the outpouring of emotion and support for Wilson in Europe occurred on such a vast scale?*

23-5a *The Paris Peace Conference and the Treaty of Versailles*

Although representatives of 27 nations began meeting in Paris on January 12, 1919, to discuss Wilson's Fourteen Points, negotiations were controlled by the "Big Four": Wilson, Prime Minister David Lloyd George of Great Britain, Premier Georges Clemenceau of France, and Prime Minister Vittorio Orlando of Italy. When Orlando quit the conference after a dispute with Wilson, the Big Four became the Big Three. Wilson quickly learned that his negotiating partners' support for the Fourteen Points was much weaker than he had believed. Clemenceau and Lloyd George refused to include most of Wilson's points in the peace treaty. The points having to do with freedom of the seas and free trade were omitted, as were the proposals for open diplomacy and Allied disarmament. Wilson won partial endorsement of the principle of self-determination: Belgian sovereignty was restored, Poland's status as a nation was affirmed, and the nations of Czechoslovakia, Yugoslavia, Finland, Lithuania, Latvia, and Estonia were created or re-formed. In addition, some lands of the former Ottoman Empire—Armenia, Palestine, Mesopotamia, and Syria—were to be placed under League of Nations' trusteeships with the understanding that they would someday gain their independence (see Map 23.4). Wilson failed in his efforts to block a British plan to transfer former German colonies in Asia to Japanese control, an Italian plan to annex territory inhabited by 200,000 Austrians, and a French plan to take from Germany its valuable Saar coal mines (see Table 23.2).

Nor could Wilson blunt the drive to punish Germany for its wartime aggression. In addition to awarding the Saar basin to France, the Allies gave portions of northern Germany to Denmark and portions of eastern Germany to Poland and Czechoslovakia. Germany was stripped of virtually its entire navy and air force, and forbidden to place soldiers or fortifications in western Germany along the Rhine. It was allowed to keep an army of only 100,000 men. In addition, Germany was forced to admit its responsibility for the war. In accepting this "war guilt," Germany was, in effect, agreeing to compensate the victors in cash (reparations) for the pain and suffering it had inflicted on them.

Lloyd George and Clemenceau brushed off the protests of those who viewed this desire to prostrate Germany as a cruel and vengeful act. That the German people, after their nation's 1918 defeat, had overthrown the monarch (Kaiser Wilhelm II) who had taken them to war, and had reconstituted their nation as a democratic republic—the first in their country's history—won them no leniency. On June 28, 1919, Great Britain, France, the United States, Germany, and other European nations signed the Treaty of Versailles. In 1921, an Allied commission notified the Germans that they were to pay the victors $33 billion, a sum well beyond the resources of a defeated and economically ruined Germany.

23-5b *The League of Nations*

The Allies' single-minded pursuit of self-interest disillusioned many liberals and socialists in the United States, but Wilson seemed undismayed. He had won approval of the most important of his Fourteen Points—that which called for the creation of the League of Nations. The League, whose structure and responsibilities were set forth in the Covenant attached to the peace treaty, would usher in Wilson's new world order. Drawing its membership from the signatories to the Treaty of Versailles (except, for the time being, Germany), the League would function as an international parliament and judiciary, establishing rules of international behavior and resolving disputes between nations through rational and peaceful means. A nine-member executive council—the United States, Britain, France, Italy, and Japan would have permanent seats on the council, while the other four seats would rotate among the smaller powers—was charged with administering decisions.

Wilson believed that the League would redeem the failures of the Paris Peace Conference. Under its auspices, free trade and freedom of the seas would be achieved, reparations against Germany would be reduced or eliminated, disarmament of the Allies would proceed, and the principle of self-determination would be extended to peoples outside Europe. Moreover, **Article X of the Covenant** would endow the League with the power to punish aggressor nations through economic isolation and military retaliation.

23-5c *Wilson versus Lodge: The Fight over Ratification*

The League's success, however, depended on Wilson's ability to convince the U.S. Senate to ratify the Treaty of Versailles. Wilson knew that this would not be easy. The Republicans had gained a majority in the Senate in 1918, and two groups within their ranks were determined to frustrate Wilson's ambitions. One group was a caucus of 14 midwesterners and westerners known as the **irreconcilables**. Most of them were conservative isolationists who wanted the United States to preserve its separation from Europe, but a few were prominent progressives—Robert La Follette, William Borah, and Hiram Johnson—who had voted against the declaration of war in 1917. The self-interest displayed by England and France at the peace conference convinced this group that the Europeans were incapable of decent behavior in international matters.

Senator **Henry Cabot Lodge** of Massachusetts led the second opposition group. Its members subscribed to Theodore Roosevelt's vision of a world controlled by a few great nations, each militarily strong, secure in its sphere of influence, and determined to avoid war through a carefully negotiated balance of power. These Republicans preferred to let Europe return to the power politics that had prevailed before the war rather than experiment with a new world order that would recognize the rights of numerous new and weak nations and that might constrain and compromise U.S. power and autonomy.

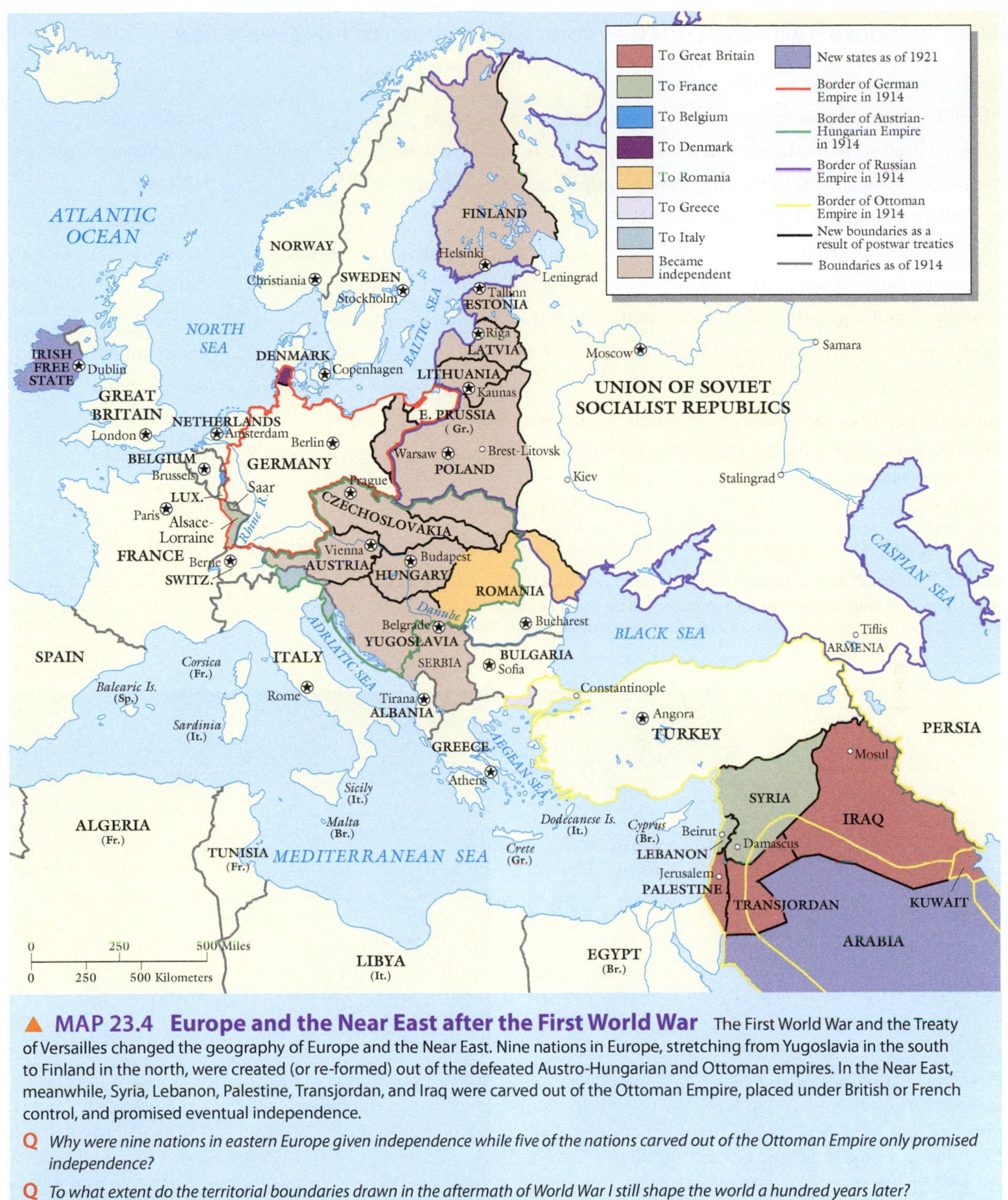

▲ **MAP 23.4 Europe and the Near East after the First World War** The First World War and the Treaty of Versailles changed the geography of Europe and the Near East. Nine nations in Europe, stretching from Yugoslavia in the south to Finland in the north, were created (or re-formed) out of the defeated Austro-Hungarian and Ottoman empires. In the Near East, meanwhile, Syria, Lebanon, Palestine, Transjordan, and Iraq were carved out of the Ottoman Empire, placed under British or French control, and promised eventual independence.

Q *Why were nine nations in eastern Europe given independence while five of the nations carved out of the Ottoman Empire only promised independence?*

Q *To what extent do the territorial boundaries drawn in the aftermath of World War I still shape the world a hundred years later?*

This Republican critique was a cogent one that merited extended discussion. Particularly important were questions that Republicans raised about Article X, which gave the League the right to undertake military actions against aggressor nations. Did Americans want to authorize an international organization to decide when the United States would go to war? Was this not a violation of the Constitution, which vested war-making power solely in Congress? Even if the constitutional problem could be solved, how could the United States ensure that it would not be forced into a military action that might damage its national interest?

It soon became clear, however, that several Republicans, including Lodge, were as interested in humiliating Wilson as they were in developing an alternative approach to foreign policy. They accused Wilson of promoting socialism through his wartime expansion of government power. They were angry

Table 23.2 WOODROW WILSON'S FOURTEEN POINTS, 1918: RECORD OF IMPLEMENTATION

1. Open covenants of peace openly arrived at	Not fulfilled
2. Absolute freedom of navigation upon the seas in peace and war	Not fulfilled
3. Removal of all economic barriers to the equality of trade among nations	Not fulfilled
4. Reduction of armaments to the level needed only for domestic safety	Not fulfilled
5. Impartial adjustments of colonial claims	Not fulfilled
6. Evacuation of all Russian territory; Russia to be welcomed into the society of free nations	Not fulfilled
7. Evacuation and restoration of Belgium	Fulfilled
8. Evacuation and restoration of all French lands; return of Alsace-Lorraine to France	Fulfilled
9. Readjustment of Italy's frontiers along lines of Italian nationality	Compromised
10. Self-determination for the former subjects of the Austro-Hungarian Empire	Compromised
11. Evacuation of Romania, Serbia, and Montenegro; free access to the sea for Serbia	Compromised
12. Self-determination for the former subjects of the Ottoman Empire; secure sovereignty for Turkish portion	Compromised
13. Establishment of an independent Poland with free and secure access to the sea	Fulfilled
14. Establishment of the League of Nations to secure mutual guarantees of independence and territorial integrity	Compromised

Source: From G. M. Gathorne-Hardy, The *Fourteen Points and the Treaty of Versailles, Oxford Pamphlets on World Affairs*, no. 6 (1939), pp. 8–34; and Thomas G. Paterson et al., *American Foreign Policy: A History*, 2nd ed. (Lexington, MA: Heath, 1983), vol. 2, pp. 282–93.

Bettmann/Corbis

23.11 **Wilson in Paris, 1919** This photograph shows President Wilson (on right), recently arrived in Paris to negotiate the Treaty of Versailles, striding confidently and comfortably alongside his two allies, British Prime Minister Lloyd George (on left) and French Premier Clemenceau (in center).

Q *How did Lloyd George's and Clemenceau's ambitions for the peace conference diverge from those of Wilson? Whose ambitions prevailed?*

Library of Congress Prints and Photographs Division [LC-USZ62-36185]

23.12 **Henry Cabot Lodge, Wilson's Adversary** Republican Senator Lodge led the fight in the Senate against ratifying the Treaty of Versailles. This photograph dates from about 1916.

Q *Was Lodge's opposition to Wilson principled or opportunistic?*

that he had failed to include any prominent Republicans, such as Lodge, Elihu Root, or William Howard Taft, in the Paris peace delegation. And they were still bitter about the 1918 congressional elections, when Wilson had argued that a Republican victory would embarrass the nation abroad.

As chairman of the Senate Foreign Relations Committee, charged with considering the treaty before reporting it to the Senate floor, Lodge did everything possible to obstruct ratification. He packed the committee with senators who were likely to oppose the treaty. He delayed action by reading every one of the treaty's 300 pages aloud and by subjecting it to endless criticism in six long weeks of public hearings. When his committee finally reported the treaty to the full Senate, it came encumbered with nearly 50 amendments whose adoption Lodge made a precondition of his support. Some of the amendments expressed reasonable concerns—namely, that participation in the League not diminish the role of Congress in determining foreign policy, compromise American sovereignty, or involve the United States in an unjust or ill-advised war—but many were meant only to complicate the task of ratification.

Despite Lodge's obstructionism, the treaty's chances for ratification by the required two-thirds majority of the Senate remained good. Many Republicans were prepared to vote for ratification if Wilson indicated his willingness to accept some of the proposed amendments. Wilson could have salvaged the treaty and, along with it, U.S. participation in the League of Nations, but he refused to compromise with the Republicans and announced that he would carry his case directly to the American people instead. In September 1919, Wilson undertook a whirlwind cross-country tour that covered more than 8,000 miles with 37 stops. He addressed as many crowds as he could reach, sometimes speaking for an hour at a time, four times a day.

On September 25, after giving a speech at Pueblo, Colorado, Wilson suffered excruciating headaches. His physician ordered him back to Washington, where on October 2 he suffered a near-fatal stroke. Wilson hovered near death for two weeks and remained seriously disabled for another six. His condition improved somewhat in November, but his left side remained paralyzed, his speech was slurred, his energy level low, and his emotions unstable. Wilson's wife, Edith Bolling Wilson, and his doctor isolated him from Congress and the press, withholding news they thought might upset him and preventing the public from learning how much his body and mind had deteriorated.

Many historians believe that the stroke impaired Wilson's political judgment. He refused to consider any of the Republican amendments to the treaty, even after it had become clear that compromise offered the only chance of winning U.S. participation in the League of Nations. When Lodge presented an amended treaty for a ratification vote on November 19, Wilson ordered Senate Democrats to vote against it; 42 of 47 Democratic senators complied, and with the aid of 13 Republican irreconcilables, the Lodge version was defeated. Only moments later, the unamended version of the treaty—Wilson's version—received only 38 votes.

23-5d *The Treaty's Final Defeat*

As the magnitude of the calamity became apparent, supporters of the League in Congress, the nation, and the world urged the Senate and the president to reconsider. Wilson would not budge. A last-ditch effort at ratification failed on March 8, 1920, by a margin of seven votes. Wilson's dream of a new world order died that day. The crumpled figure in the White House seemed to bear little resemblance to the hero who, barely 15 months before, had been greeted in Europe as the world's savior. Wilson filled out his remaining 12 months in office as an invalid, presiding over the interment of progressivism. He died in 1924.

The judgment of history lies heavily on these events, for many believe that the flawed treaty and the failure of the League contributed to Adolf Hitler's rise in Germany and the outbreak of a second world war more devastating than the first. It is necessary to ask, then, whether American participation in the League would have significantly altered the course of world history.

The mere fact of U.S. membership in the League would not have magically solved Europe's postwar problems. The U.S. government was inexperienced in diplomacy and prone to mistakes. Its freedom to negotiate solutions to international disputes would have been limited by the large number of American voters who remained strongly opposed to U.S. entanglement in European affairs. Even if such opposition could have been overcome, the United States would still have confronted European countries determined to go their own way.

Nevertheless, one thing is clear: No stable international order could have arisen after the First World War without the full involvement of the United States. The League of Nations required American authority and prestige in order to operate effectively as an international parliament. We cannot know whether the League, with American involvement, would have offered the Germans a less-humiliating peace, allowing them to rehabilitate their economy and salvage their national pride; nor whether an American-led League would have stopped Hitler's expansionism before it escalated into full-scale war in 1939. Still, it seems fair to suggest that American participation would have strengthened the League and improved its ability to bring a lasting peace to Europe.

23-6 Postwar: A Society in Convulsion

Q *What issues convulsed American society in the immediate aftermath of war, and how were they resolved?*

The end of the war brought no respite from the forces convulsing American society. Workers were determined to regain the purchasing power they had lost to inflation. Employers were determined to halt or reverse the wartime gains labor had made. Radicals saw in this conflict between capital and labor

What They Said

Should the United States Join the League of Nations?

The most prominent advocate of U.S. membership in the League was President Woodrow Wilson, who believed that U.S. participation would help prevent future wars. Opponents of the League, including Senators Henry Cabot Lodge and William Borah, argued that U.S. membership would embroil the United States in European affairs and, through Article X (see pages 642–643), deprive Congress of the ability to have the final say on when the United States ought to go to war.

Woodrow Wilson, Address at Pueblo, Colorado, September 25, 1919

Reflect, my fellow citizens, that the membership of this great league is going to include all the great fighting nations of the world, as well as the weak ones. . . .

And what do they unite for? They enter into a solemn promise to one another that they will never use their power against one another for aggression; that they never will impair the territorial integrity of a neighbor; that they never will interfere with the political independence of a neighbor; that they will abide by the principle that great populations are entitled to determine their own destiny and that they will not interfere with that destiny; and that no matter what differences arise amongst them they will never resort to war without first having done one or other of two things—either submitted the matter of controversy to arbitration, in which case they agree to abide by the result without question, or submitted it to the consideration of the council of the league of nations, laying before that council all the documents, all the facts, agreeing that the council can publish the documents, all the facts, agreeing that the council can publish the documents and the facts to the whole world, agreeing that there shall be six months allowed for the mature consideration of those facts by the council, and agreeing that at the expiration of the six months, even if they are not then ready to accept the advice of the council with regard to the settlement of the dispute, they will still not go to war for another three months. . . .

I am dwelling upon these points, my fellow citizens, in spite of the fact that I dare say to most of you they are perfectly well known, because in order to meet the present situation we have got to know what we are dealing with. We are not dealing with the kind of document which this is represented by some gentlemen to be; and inasmuch as we are dealing with a document simon-pure in respect of the very principles we have professed and lived up to, we have got to do one or other of two things—we have got to adopt it or reject it. There is no middle course. You can not go in on a special-privilege basis of your own. . . . We go in upon equal terms [with other nations] or we do not go in at all; and if we do not go in, my fellow citizens, think of the tragedy of that result—the only sufficient guaranty to the peace of the world withheld!

Senator William Borah, Speech to Congress, November 19, 1919

We have said, Mr. President, that we would not send our troops abroad without the consent of Congress [should the League invoke Article X and call up troops from member nations to punish an aggressor]. What will the Congress of the United States do [if U.S. troops were to be requisitioned by the League in this way]? What right will it have left, except the bare technical right to refuse, which as a moral proposition it will not dare to exercise. . . .

[Were we to join the League of Nations, we would be] sending to the council one man. That man represents 110,000,000 [Americans]... . Here, sitting in the Senate, we have two from every State in the Union, and over in the other House we have Representatives in accordance with population, and the responsibility is spread out in accordance with our obligations to our constituency. But now we are transferring to one man the stupendous power of representing the sentiment and convictions of 110,000,000 people in tremendous questions which may involve the peace or may involve the war of the world. . . .

What is the result of all this? We are in the midst of all of the affairs of Europe. We have entangled ourselves with all European concerns. We have joined in alliance with all the European nations which have thus far joined the league, and all nations which may be admitted to the league. We are sitting there dabbling in their affairs and intermeddling in their concerns. In other words, Mr. President—and this comes to the question which is fundamental with me—we have forfeited and surrendered, once and for all, the great policy of "no entangling alliances" upon which the strength of this Republic has been founded for 150 years. . . .

This league of nations ... whatever else it does or does not do, does surrender and sacrifice that policy, and once having surrendered and become a part of the European concerns, where, my friends, are you going to stop?

Q *What reasons does Wilson give for why the United States ought to join the League of Nations?*

Q *What reasons does Borah give for why the United States should not join the League?*

Q *Imagine that you are a senator in 1919. Would you support United States membership in the League? Why or why not?*

Sources: (top) Woodrow Wilson, "Address at Pueblo, Colo., September 25, 1919," reprinted in *Cong. Rec.*, October 7, 1919, 66th Cong., 1st sess., 7606 S.doc.120, 1919, 359-370; (bottom) Senator William Borah, Speech to Congress, November 19, 1919, *Cong. Rec.*, 66th Cong., 1st sess., 8781–8784.

the possibility of a socialist revolution. Conservatives were certain that the revolution had already begun. Returning white servicemen were nervous about regaining their civilian jobs and looked suspiciously at black, Hispanic, and female workers recruited to take their places. Black veterans were in no mood to return to segregation and subordination. The federal government, meanwhile, uneasy over how much it had centralized power during the war, quickly dismantled much of its wartime bureaucratic infrastructure.

23-6a *Labor–Capital Conflict*

Nowhere was the escalation of conflict more evident than in the workplace. In 1919, 4 million workers—one-fifth of the nation's manufacturing workforce—went on strike. In January 1919, a general strike paralyzed the city of Seattle when 60,000 workers walked off their jobs. By August, walkouts had been staged by 400,000 eastern and midwestern coal miners, 120,000 New England textile workers, and 50,000 New York City garment workers. Then came two strikes that turned public opinion sharply against labor. In September, Boston policemen walked off their jobs after the police commissioner refused to negotiate with their newly formed union. Rioting and looting soon broke out. Massachusetts governor Calvin Coolidge, outraged by the policemen's betrayal of their sworn public duty, fired the entire police force. His tough stand would bring him national fame and the Republican vice presidential nomination in 1920.

Hard on the heels of the policemen's strike came a strike by more than 300,000 steelworkers in the Midwest. No union had established a footing in the steel industry since the 1890s, when Andrew Carnegie had ousted the ironworkers' union from his mills in Homestead, Pennsylvania. Most steelworkers labored long hours (the 12-hour shift was still standard) for low wages in dangerous workplaces. The organizers of the 1919 Steel Strike had persuaded steelworkers with varied skill levels and ethnic backgrounds to put aside their differences and demand an eight-hour day and union recognition. When the employers rejected those demands, the workers walked off their jobs. Employers responded by hiring nonunion labor to keep the plants running and by portraying strike leaders as dangerous radicals. In many areas, local and state police prohibited union meetings, ran strikers out of town, and opened fire on those who disobeyed orders. In these circumstances, public opinion turned against the steelworkers; their strike collapsed in January 1920.

23-6b *Radicals and the Red Scare*

The steel companies fanned the public's fear that revolutionary sentiment was spreading among workers. Radical sentiment was indeed on the rise. Mine workers and railroad workers had begun calling for the permanent nationalization of coal mines and railroads. Longshoremen in San Francisco and Seattle refused to load ships carrying supplies to the White Russians who had taken up arms against Lenin's Bolshevik government in Russia. Socialist trade unionists mounted the most serious challenge to Gompers's control of the AFL in 25 years. In 1920, nearly a million Americans voted for socialist presidential candidate Debs, who ran his campaign from the Atlanta Federal Penitentiary.

23.13 **Bartolomeo Vanzetti and Nicola Sacco, Anarchists** Vanzetti and Sacco were executed for murder in 1927. Many in 1920s America believed that the fear of radicalism and foreigners had made it impossible for these two immigrant anarchists to receive a fair trial. The artist, Ben Shahn, portrays them sympathetically in this 1931-32 painting.

This radical surge did not mean, however, that leftists had fashioned themselves into a single movement or political party. On the contrary, the Russian Revolution had split the American Socialist Party. One faction, which would keep the "Socialist" name and would continue under Debs's leadership, insisted that radicals follow a democratic path to socialism. The other group, which would take the name "Communist," wanted to establish a Lenin-style "dictatorship of the proletariat." Small groups of anarchists, some of whom advocated campaigns of terror to speed the revolution, represented yet a third radical tendency.

Few Americans noticed the disarray in the radical camp. Most assumed that radicalism was a single, coordinated movement bent on establishing a communist government on American soil. They saw the nation's immigrant communities as breeding grounds for Bolshevism. Beginning in 1919, this perceived **Red Scare** prompted government officials and private citizens to embark on yet another campaign of repression.

The postwar repression of radicalism closely resembled the wartime repression of dissent. Thirty states passed sedition laws to punish those who advocated revolution. Numerous public and private groups intensified Americanization campaigns designed to strip foreigners of their subversive ways and remake them into loyal citizens. Universities fired radical professors, and vigilante groups broke into the offices of socialists and assaulted IWW agitators. A newly formed veterans' organization, the American Legion, took on the American Protective League's role of identifying seditious individuals and organizations and ensuring the public's devotion to "100 percent Americanism."

The Red Scare reached its climax on New Year's Day 1920, when federal agents broke into the homes and meeting places of thousands of suspected revolutionaries in 33 cities. Directed by Attorney General A. Mitchell Palmer, these widely publicized "Palmer raids" were meant to expose the extent of revolutionary activity. Palmer's agents uncovered three pistols, no rifles, and no explosives. Nevertheless, they arrested more than 4,000 people and kept many of them in jail for weeks without formally charging them with a crime. Finally, those who were not citizens (approximately 600) were deported and the rest were released.

Palmer's failure to expose a revolutionary plot blunted support for him in official circles. Undeterred, Palmer then alleged that revolutionaries were planning a series of assaults on government officials and government buildings for May 1, 1920. In this atmosphere, two Italian-born anarchists, Nicola Sacco and Bartolomeo Vanzetti, were arrested in Brockton, Massachusetts, and charged with armed robbery and murder. Both men proclaimed their innocence and insisted that they were being punished for their political beliefs. Their foreign accents and their defiant espousal of anarchist doctrines in the courtroom inclined many Americans, including the judge who presided at their trial, to view them harshly. Despite the weak case against them, they were convicted of first-degree murder and sentenced to death. Their lawyers attempted numerous appeals, all of which failed. Anger over the verdicts in the **Sacco-Vanzetti case** began to build among Italian Americans, radicals, and liberal intellectuals. Protests compelled the governor of Massachusetts to appoint a commission to review the case, but no new trial was ordered. On August 23, 1927, Sacco and Vanzetti were executed, still insisting they were innocent.

23-6c *Racial Conflict and the Rise of Black Nationalism*

The more than 400,000 blacks who served in the armed forces believed that a victory for democracy abroad would help them achieve democracy for their people at home. At first, despite the discrimination they encountered in the military, they maintained their conviction that they would be treated as full-fledged citizens upon their return. Many began to talk about the birth of a New Negro—independent and proud. Thousands joined the National Association for the Advancement of Colored People (NAACP), an organization at the forefront of the fight for racial equality. By 1918, 100,000 African Americans subscribed to the NAACP's magazine, *The Crisis*, whose editor, W. E. B. Du Bois, had urged them to support the war.

This wartime optimism made the postwar discrimination and hatred African Americans encountered difficult to endure. Many black workers who had found jobs in the North were fired to make way for returning white veterans. Returning black servicemen, meanwhile, had to scrounge for poorly paid jobs as unskilled laborers. In the South, lynch mobs targeted black veterans who refused to tolerate the usual insults and indignities; 10 of the 70 blacks lynched in the South in 1919 were veterans.

The worst antiblack violence that year occurred in the North, however. Crowded city conditions during the war had forced black and ethnic white city dwellers into close proximity. Many white ethnics resented having to share neighborhoods, trolleys, parks, streets, and workplaces with blacks. Many also wanted African Americans barred from unions, seeing them as threats to their job security.

Racial tensions escalated into race riots. The deadliest explosion occurred in Chicago in July 1919, when a black teenager who had been swimming in Lake Michigan was killed by whites after coming too close to a whites-only beach. Rioting soon broke out, with white mobs invading black neighborhoods, torching homes and stores, and attacking innocent residents. Led by war veterans, some armed, blacks fought back, turning the border areas between white and black neighborhoods into battle zones. Fighting raged for five days, leaving 38 dead (23 black, 15 white) and more than 500 injured. Race riots in other cities pushed the death toll to 120 before summer's end.

The riots made it clear to blacks that the North was not the Promised Land. Confined to unskilled jobs and segregated neighborhoods with substandard housing and exorbitant rents, black migrants in Chicago, New York, and other northern cities suffered economic hardship throughout the 1920s. The NAACP carried on its campaign for civil rights and racial equality, but many blacks no longer shared its belief that they would one day be accepted as first-class citizens. They turned instead to a leader from Jamaica, **Marcus Garvey**, who gave voice to their bitterness: "The first dying that is to be done by the black man in the future," Garvey declared in 1918, "will be done to make himself free. And then when we are finished, if we have any charity to bestow, we may die for the white man. But as for me, I think I have stopped dying for him."

Garvey called on blacks to give up their hopes for integration and to set about forging a separate black nation. He reminded blacks that they possessed a rich culture stretching back over the centuries that would enable them to achieve greatness as a nation. Garvey's ambition was to build a black nation in Africa that would bring together all of the world's people of African descent. In the short term, he wanted to help American and Caribbean blacks to achieve economic and cultural independence.

Garvey's call for black separatism and self-sufficiency—or black nationalism, as it came to be known—elicited a favorable response among African Americans. In the early 1920s, the Universal Negro Improvement Association (UNIA), which Garvey had founded, enrolled millions of members in 700 branches in 38 states. His newspaper, the *Negro World*, reached a circulation of 200,000. The New York chapter of UNIA undertook an economic development program that included the establishment of grocery stores, restaurants, and factories. Garvey's most visible economic venture was the Black Star Line, a shipping company with three ships flying the UNIA flag from their masts.

This black nationalist movement did not last long. Garvey entered into bitter disputes with other black leaders, including W. E. B. Du Bois, who regarded him as a flamboyant, self-serving demagogue. Garvey sometimes showed poor judgment, as when he expressed support for the Ku Klux Klan on the grounds that it shared his pessimism about the possibility of racial integration. Inexperienced in economic

History Through Film Reds (1981)

Directed by Warren Beatty.
Starring Warren Beatty (John Reed), Diane Keaton (Louise Bryant), Edward Herrmann (Max Eastman), Jerzy Kosinski (Grigory Zinoviev), Jack Nicholson (Eugene O'Neill), and Maureen Stapleton (Emma Goldman).

In this epic film, Warren Beatty, producer, director, and screenplay co-writer, attempts to interweave the history of the American Left in the early 20th century with a love story about two radicals of that era, John "Jack" Reed and Louise Bryant. Reed was a well-known radical journalist whose dispatches from Russia during its 1917 revolution, *Ten Days That Shook the World*, brought him international notice. Though never acquiring Reed's fame, Bryant was an integral member of the radical circles that gathered in apartments and cafés in New York's Bohemian Greenwich Village before and during the First World War.

The movie successfully conveys an important and historically accurate message about the American Left, especially before the First World War—namely, that its participants wanted to revolutionize the personal as well as the political. Radicals not only debated how to build a socialist future but also whether men and women should be equal and whether women should enjoy the same sexual freedom as men. (See the section entitled: "The 'New Woman' and the Rise of Feminism" in Chapter 20.)

Reds is also an exceptionally serious film about politics. The film follows the arc of Reed's and Bryant's lives from their prewar days as discontented members of the Portland, Oregon, social elite, through their flight to the freedom and radicalism of Greenwich Village, to the hardening of their radicalism as a result of repression during the First World War at home and the Bolshevik triumph in November 1917. Beatty has recreated detailed and complex stories about internal fights within the Left both in the United States and Russia, through which he seeks to show how hopes for social transformation went awry. To give this film added historical weight, Beatty introduces "witnesses," individuals who actually knew the real Reed and Bryant and who appear on screen periodically to share their memories, both serious and whimsical, about the storied couple and the times in which they lived. ■

23.14 Diane Keaton as Louise Bryant and Warren Beatty as John Reed, together in Russia in the midst of that country's socialist revolution.

Library of Congress, Prints and Photographs Division

23.15 **Marcus Garvey, Black Nationalist** This portrait was taken in 1924, after Garvey's conviction on mail fraud charges.

Q *Why did Garvey worry the U.S. government so much?*

matters, Garvey squandered UNIA money on abortive business ventures. The U.S. government regarded his rhetoric as inflammatory and sought to silence him. In 1923, he was convicted of mail fraud involving the sale of Black Star stocks and was sentenced to five years in jail. In 1927, he was deported to Jamaica, and the UNIA folded. Garvey's philosophy of black nationalism, however, endured.

Conclusion

The resurgence of racism in 1919 was a sign that the high hopes of the war years had been dashed. Industrial workers, immigrants, and radicals also found their pursuit of liberty and equality interrupted by the fear, intolerance, and repression unleashed by the war. They came to understand as well that Wilson's commitment to these ideals counted for less than did his administration's and Congress's determination to discipline a people whom they regarded as dangerously heterogeneous and unstable. Of the reform groups, only woman suffragists made enduring gains—especially the right to vote. For feminists, however, these steps forward failed to compensate for the collapse of the progressive movement and with it, their program of achieving equal rights for women across the board.

A similar disappointment engulfed those who had embraced and fought for Wilson's dream of creating a new and democratic world order. The world in 1919 appeared as volatile as it had been in 1914. More and more Americans—perhaps even a majority—were coming to believe that U.S. intervention had been a mistake.

In other ways, the United States benefited a great deal from the war. By 1919, the American economy was by far the world's strongest. Many of the nation's leading corporations had flourished during the war. U.S. banks were poised to supplant those of London as the most influential in international finance. The nation's economic strength triggered impressive growth in the 1920s, and millions of Americans rushed to take advantage of the prosperity that a "people's capitalism" had put within their grasp. But even 1920s affluence would fail to dissolve the class, ethnic, and racial tensions that the war had exposed. And the failure of the peace process added to Europe's problems, delayed the emergence of the United States as a leader in world affairs, and created the preconditions for another world war.

CHAPTER REVIEW

Review

1. What caused World War I?
2. Why did the U.S. policy of neutrality fail, and why did America get drawn into war?
3. What contribution did the U.S. make to the Allied Powers' victory?
4. What problems did the U.S. encounter in mobilizing for total war, and how successfully were those problems overcome?
5. What were Woodrow Wilson's peace proposals, and how did they fare?
6. What issues convulsed American society in the immediate aftermath of war, and how were they resolved?

Critical Thinking

1. Did the First World War do more to enhance or interrupt the pursuit of liberty and equality on the home front?
2. Do you think that the chances of a second world war breaking out in Europe in the late 1930s would have been substantially lessened had Woodrow Wilson prevailed on the U.S. Senate to ratify the Treaty of Versailles in 1919, thereby bringing the United States into the League of Nations?

Identifications

Review your understanding of the following key terms, people, and events for this chapter (terms in bold in text are included in the Glossary).

Triple Alliance, p. 625
Triple Entente, p. 625
"peace without victory," p. 625
Zimmermann telegram, p. 629
Fourteen Points, p. 631
John J. Pershing, p. 632
War Industries Board (WIB), p. 633
National War Labor Board (NWLB), p. 635
New York's 369th Regiment, p. 637
Liberty Bonds, p. 637
Committee on Public Information (CPI), p. 637
Espionage, Sabotage, and Sedition Acts, p. 639
Article X of the Covenant, p. 642
irreconcilables, p. 642
Henry Cabot Lodge, p. 642
Red Scare, p. 647
Sacco-Vanzetti case, p. 648
Marcus Garvey, p. 648

Suggested Readings

On the origins of World War I, see **Christopher Clark**, ***The Sleepwalkers: How Europe Went to War in 1914*** (2012). On America's neutrality and road to war, consult **John Milton Cooper**, ***Woodrow Wilson: A Biography*** (2009); and **Michael Kazin**, ***War Against War: The American Fight for Peace, 1914–1918*** (2017). On the effects of war on American society, consult **David Kennedy**, ***Over Here: The First World War and American Society*** (1980); **Christopher Capozzola**, ***Uncle Sam Wants You: World War I and the Making of the Modern American Citizen*** (2008); and **Gary Gerstle**, ***Liberty and Coercion: The Paradox of American Government from the Founding to the Present*** (2015). For industrial mobilization and labor-management relations, see **Robert D. Cuff**, ***The War Industries Board: Business-Government Relations during World War I*** (1973); and **Joseph A. McCartin**, ***Labor's Great War: The Struggle for Industrial Democracy and the Origins of Modern Labor Relations, 1912–1921*** (1997).

For efforts to situate the U.S. during the war and postwar in an international context, see **Alan Dawley**, ***Changing the World: American Progressives in War and Revolution*** (2003); and **Adam Tooze**: ***The Deluge: The Great War and the Remaking of Global Order, 1916–1931*** (2014). On the migration of African Americans to northern industrial centers and the movement of women into war production, see **Joe William Trotter Jr., ed.**, ***The Great Migration in Historical Perspective: New Dimensions of Race, Class, and Gender*** (1991); and **Maurine W. Greenwald**, ***Women, War and Work*** (1980). **Stephen Vaughn**, ***Holding Fast the Inner Lines: Democracy, Nationalism, and the Committee on Public Information*** (1980), is an important account of the CPI. **Geoffrey R. Stone**, ***Perilous Times: Free Speech in War Time from the Sedition Act of 1798 to the War on Terrorism*** (2004), analyzes the repression of dissent.

On Wilson, Versailles, and the League of Nations, consult **Thomas J. Knock**, ***To End All Wars: Woodrow Wilson and the Quest for a New World Order*** (1992); **Margaret MacMillan**, ***Peacemakers: the Paris Peace Conference of 1919 and its Attempt to End the War*** (2001); **Arno Mayer**, ***The Politics and Diplomacy of Peacemaking: Containment and Counterrevolution at Versailles, 1918–1919*** (1967); and **Susan Pederson**, ***The Guardians: The League of Nations and the Crisis of Empire*** (2015). On Republican opposition to the League of Nations, see **William C. Widenor**, ***Henry Cabot Lodge and the Search for an American Foreign Policy*** (1980).

Beverly Gage, ***The Day Wall Street Exploded: A Story of America in Its First Age of Terror*** (2009), offers a fresh analysis of the Red Scare. On Sacco and Vanzetti, see **Moshe Temkin**, ***America on Trial: The Sacco-Vanzetti Affair*** (2011). **Steven Hahn**, ***The Political Worlds of Slavery and Freedom*** (2009), places Garveyism in its American historical context while **Adam Ewing**, ***The Age of Garvey: How a Jamaican Activist Created a Mass Movement and Changed Global Black Politics*** (2014) situates the movement in its international context.

24 The 1920s

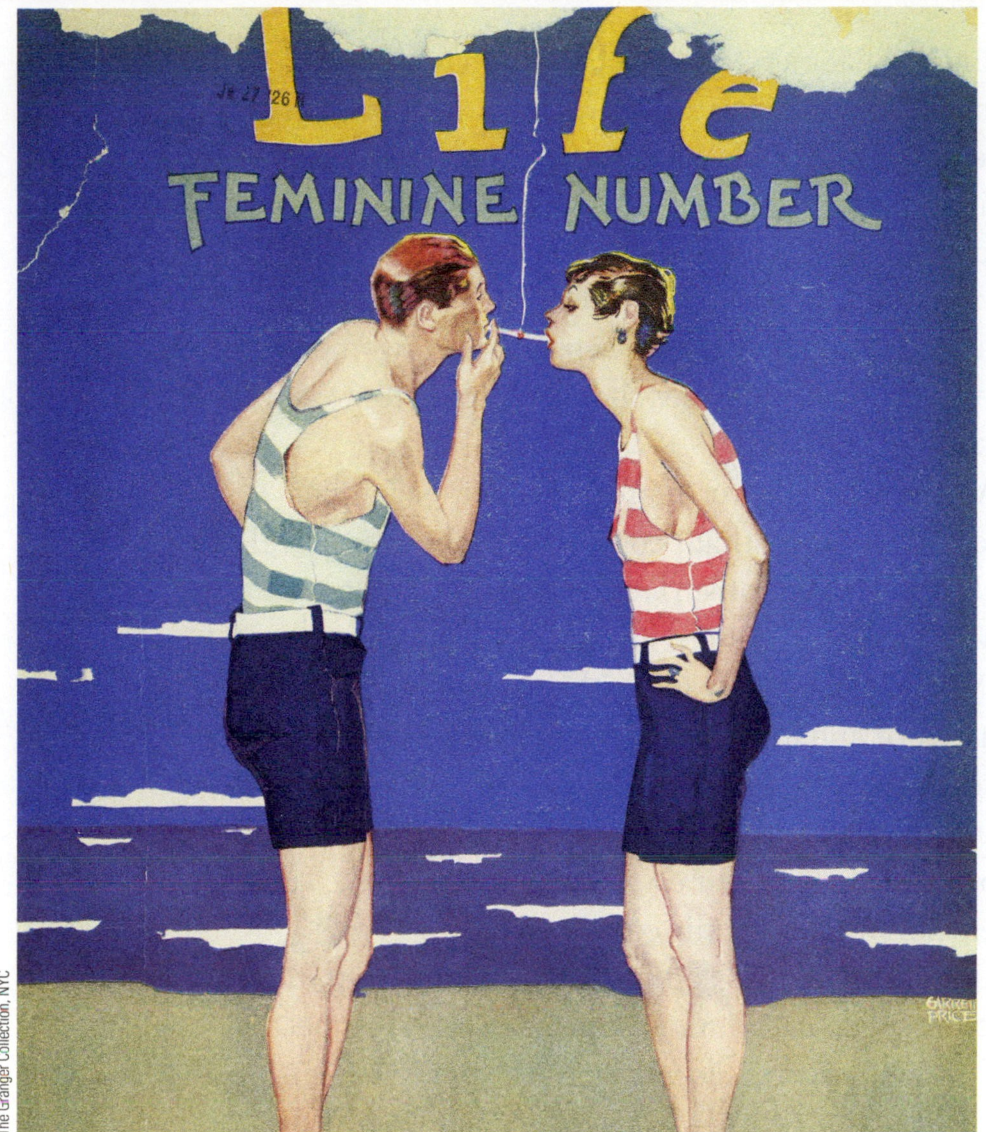

24.1 **The Age of the Flapper** The 1920s witnessed the emergence of the "flapper," the name given to single women who deliberately flouted social rules governing female life. On this cover of *Life*, we see "Jill" sporting the same short hair and form-fitting bathing suit as her male friend, "Jack." Not only was she smoking in public, but she was also getting her light directly from a cigarette in Jack's mouth. Could a public kiss between Jack and Jill have been far behind?

IN 1920, AMERICANS ELECTED AS PRESIDENT Warren G. Harding, a man who could not have been more different from his predecessor, Woodrow Wilson. A Republican, Harding presented himself as a common man with common desires. In his 1920 campaign, he called for a "return to normalcy." Although he died in office in 1923, his carefree spirit is thought to characterize the 1920s.

To many Americans, the decade was one of fun rather than reform, of good times rather than high ideals. It was, in the words of novelist F. Scott Fitzgerald, the "Jazz Age," a time when the search for personal gratification seemed to replace the quest for public welfare.

Despite Harding's call for a return to a familiar past, America seemed to be rushing headlong into the future. The word *modern* began appearing everywhere: modern times, modern women, modern technology, the modern home, modern marriage. Although the word was rarely defined, it connoted certain beliefs: that science was a better guide to life than religion; that people should be free to choose their own lifestyles; that sex should be a source of pleasure for women as well as men; that women and minorities should be equal to white men and enjoy the same rights.

Many other Americans, however, reaffirmed their belief that God's word transcended science; that people should obey the moral code set forth in the Bible; that women were not equal to men; and that blacks, Mexicans, and eastern European immigrants were inferior to Anglo-Saxon whites. They made their voices heard in a resurgent **Ku Klux Klan** and in the fundamentalist movement, and on issues such as evolution and immigration. In seeking to restore an older America, some in their ranks were prepared to deny individual Americans the liberty to choose their own ways of living and to insist that all people were not fundamentally equal.

Modernists and traditionalists confronted each other in party politics, in legislatures, in courtrooms, and in the press. Their battles belie the vision of the 1920s merely as a time for the pursuit of leisure. ■

24-1 Prosperity

What were the achievements and limitations of "people's capitalism" in the 1920s?

On balance, the First World War had been good for the American economy. American industries had emerged intact from, even strengthened by, the war. Manufacturers and bankers had exported so many goods and extended so many loans to the Allies that, by war's end, the United States was the world's leading creditor nation. New York City challenged London as the hub of world finance.

From 1919 to 1921, the country struggled to redirect industry from wartime to civilian production, a process slowed by the government's hasty withdrawal from its wartime role as economic regulator and stabilizer. Workers went on strike to protest wage reductions or increases in the workweek. Farmers were hit by a depression as the overseas demand for American foodstuffs fell from its 1918–1919 peak. Disgruntled workers and farmers joined forces to form statewide farmer-labor parties, which for a time threatened to disrupt the country's two-party system in the upper Midwest. In 1924, the two groups formed a national Farmer-Labor Party. Robert La Follette, their presidential candidate, received an impressive 16 percent of the vote that year, but then the third-party movement fell apart.

Its collapse reflected a rising public awareness of how vigorous and productive the economy had become. From 1922 to 1929, the gross national product grew at an annual rate of 5.5 percent, rising from $149 billion to $227 billion. The unemployment rate never exceeded 5 percent, and real wages rose about 15 percent.

24-1a *A Consumer Society*

In the 19th century, economic growth had rested primarily on the production of capital goods, such as factory machinery and railroad tracks. In the 1920s, however, growth rested

CHRONOLOGY

1920	Prohibition goes into effect • Warren G. Harding defeats James M. Cox for presidency • Census reveals that a majority of Americans live in urban areas • Eight million cars on roads
1921	Sheppard–Towner Act passed
1922	United States, Britain, Japan, France, and Italy sign Five-Power Treaty, agreeing to reduce size of their navies
1923	Teapot Dome scandal lands Secretary of the Interior Albert Fall in jail • Harding dies in office • Calvin Coolidge becomes president
1924	Dawes Plan to restructure Germany's war debt put into effect • Coolidge defeats John W. Davis for presidency • Ku Klux Klan membership approaches 4 million • Johnson–Reed Immigration Restriction Act cuts immigration by 80 percent
1925	Scopes trial upholds right of Tennessee to ban teaching of evolution in public schools • *Survey Graphic* issues a special issue on the Harlem Renaissance • F. Scott Fitzgerald publishes *The Great Gatsby* • United States withdraws marines from Nicaragua
1926	Revenue Act cuts income and estate taxes • United States sends marines back to Nicaragua to end civil war and protect U.S. property
1927	Coolidge vetoes high tariffs legislation (McNary–Haugen bill) • Babe Ruth hits 60 home runs • Charles Lindbergh flies across the Atlantic
1928	Fifteen nations sign Kellogg–Briand Pact, pledging to avoid war • Coolidge vetoes McNary–Haugen bill again • Herbert Hoover defeats Alfred E. Smith for presidency
1929	Union membership drops to 3 million • Twenty-seven million cars on roads • William Faulkner publishes *The Sound and the Fury* • Josh Gibson joins the National Negro League
1930	Los Angeles's Mexican population reaches 100,000

more on consumer goods. Some products, such as cars and telephones, had been available since the early 1900s, but in the 1920s their sales reached new levels. In 1920, just 12 years after Ford introduced the Model T, 8 million cars were on the road. By 1929, there were 27 million—one for every five Americans. Other consumer goods became available for the first time: tractors, washing machines, refrigerators, electric irons, radios, and vacuum cleaners. The term "consumer durable" was coined to describe such goods, which, unlike food, clothing, and other perishables, were meant to last. Even perishables took on new allure. Scientists had discovered the importance of vitamins in the diet and began urging Americans to consume more fresh fruits and vegetables. The agricultural economy of southern California grew rapidly as urban demand for its products skyrocketed. Improvements in refrigeration and in packaging, meanwhile, allowed fresh produce to travel long distances and extended its shelf life in grocery stores. And more stores were being operated by large grocery chains that could afford the latest refrigeration and packaging technology (see Figure 24.1).

The public responded to these innovations with excitement. American industry had made fresh food and stylish clothes available to the masses. Refrigerators, vacuum cleaners, and washing machines would spare women the drudgery of housework. Radios would expand the public's cultural horizons. Cars, asphalt roads, service stations, hot dog stands, "tourist cabins" (the forerunners of motels), and traffic lights seemed to herald a wholly new automobile civilization. By the middle of the decade, the country possessed a network of paved roads (see Map 24.1). City dwellers now had easy access to rural areas and made a ritual of daylong excursions. Camping trips and long-distance vacations became routine. Farmers and their families could now hop into their cars and head for the nearest town to take advantage of its stores, movie theater, amusement park, and sporting events. Suburbs proliferated, billed as the perfect mix of urban and rural life. Young men and women everywhere discovered that cars were a place where they could "make out," and even make love, without fear of being found out by prudish parents or prying neighbors.

In the 1920s, some Americans also discovered the benefits of owning stocks. By 1929, as many as 7 million Americans possessed stock, most of them people of middle- or upper-class means. The New York Stock Exchange, first organized in 1792, assisted in processing complicated transactions. Capitalists boasted that they had created a **"people's capitalism"** in which virtually all Americans could participate. Everyone could own a piece of corporate America and afford amenities. Poverty, capitalists claimed, was banished, and the gap between rich and poor would soon close.

Actually, although wages were rising, millions of Americans still earned too little to partake fully of the marketplace. The percentage of Americans owning stocks

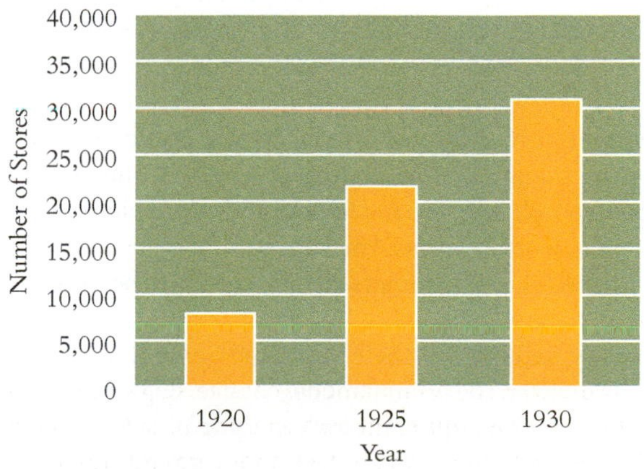

Figure 24.1 **Growth of Six Leading Grocery Chains by Number of Stores, 1920–1930**

Source: From Godfrey M. Labhar, *Chain Stores in America, 1859–1962* (New York: Chain Store Publishing, 1963).

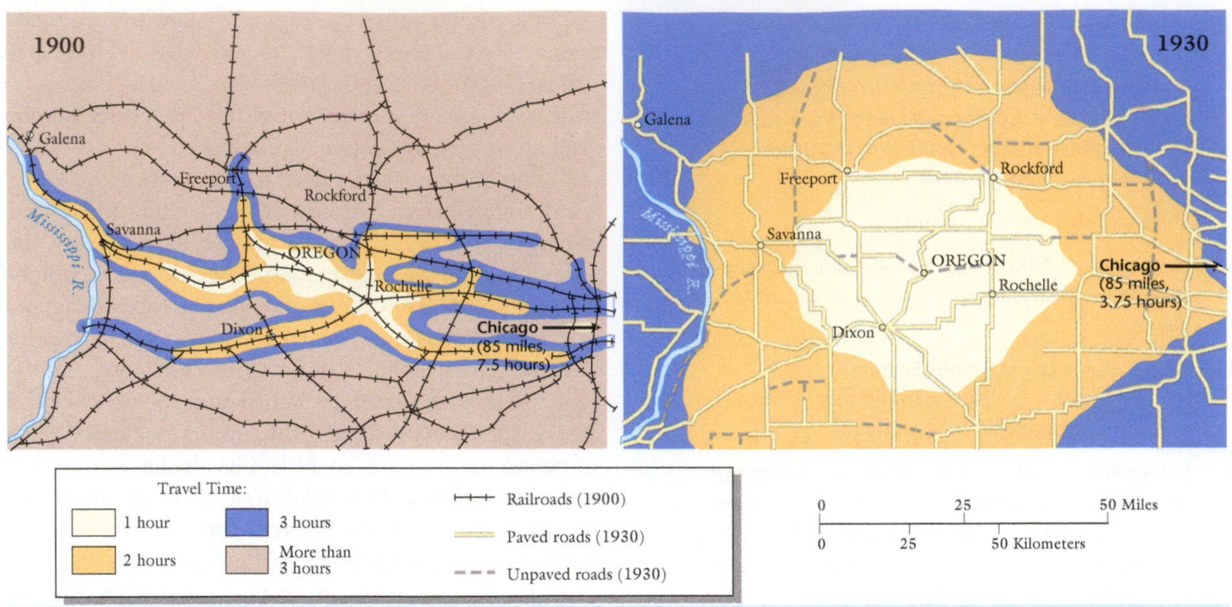

▲ MAP 24.1 Automobile Civilization: Cars, Roads, and the Expansion of Travel Horizons in Oregon, Illinois In 1900, someone wanting to travel outside Oregon, Illinois, could not get very far in an hour or two, unless his or her destination lay exactly on the major train line running through town. By 1930, the distances people could travel and the variety of destinations they could reach in two hours—signified on the right-hand map by the white and tan circles surrounding Oregon—had expanded dramatically.

Q *How did these changing travel horizons reshape American life in the 1920s? Do you think this new car mobility did more to revitalize rural areas or to drain Americans away from them?*

remained small. Social scientists Robert and Helen Lynd discovered, in their celebrated 1929 study of Muncie, Indiana, that working-class families who bought a car often lacked money for other goods. One housewife admitted: "We don't have no fancy clothes when we have the car to pay for... . The car is the only pleasure we have." Many industrialists resisted pressure to increase wages, and workers lacked the organizational strength to force them to pay more.

One solution came with the introduction of consumer credit. Car dealers, home appliance salesmen, and other merchants began to offer installment plans that enabled consumers to purchase a product by making a down payment and promising to pay the rest in installments. By 1930, 15 percent of all purchases were made on the installment plan.

Even so, many poor Americans benefited little from the consumer revolution. Middle-class Americans acquired a disproportionate share of consumer durables. They also could afford to purchase more fresh fruits and vegetables and stocks than most working-class Americans.

Middle-class consumers themselves had to be wooed. How could they be persuaded to buy another car only a few years after they had bought their first one? General Motors (GM) had the answer: the annual model change. Beginning in 1926, GM cars took on a different look every year as GM engineers modified headlights and chassis colors, streamlined bodies, and added new features. The strategy worked. GM leaped past Ford and became the world's largest car manufacturer.

Henry Ford reluctantly introduced his Model A in 1927 to provide customers with a colorful alternative to the black Model T. Having spent his lifetime selling a product renowned for its utility and reliability, Ford rejected the idea that sales could be increased by appealing to the intangible hopes and fears of consumers. He was wrong. The desire to be beautiful, handsome, or sexually attractive; to exercise power and control; to demonstrate competence and success; to escape anonymity, loneliness, and boredom; to experience pleasure—all such desires, once activated, could motivate a consumer to buy a new car even when the old one was still serviceable, or to spend money on goods that might have once seemed frivolous.

Arousing such desires required more than bright colors, sleek lines, and attractive packaging. It called for advertising campaigns intended to make a product seem to be the answer to the consumer's desires. To create those campaigns, corporations turned to a new kind of company: professional advertising firms. Advertising entrepreneurs, people such as Edward Bernays, Doris Fleischmann, and Bruce Barton, tended to be well educated, sensitive to public taste, and knowledgeable about human psychology. In their campaigns, advertisers played on the emotions and vulnerabilities of their target audiences. A perfume manufacturer's ad pronounced: "The first duty of woman is to attract... . It does not matter how clever or independent you may be, if you fail to influence the men you meet, consciously or unconsciously, you are not fulfilling your fundamental duty as a woman." A tobacco ad matter-of-factly declared: "Men at the top are apt to be pipe-smokers... . It's no coincidence—pipe-smoking is a calm and deliberate habit—restful, stimulating. His pipe helps a man think straight. A pipe is back of most big ideas."

Advertising professionals believed they were helping people to manage their lives in ways that would increase their satisfaction and pleasure. Expenditures on advertising more than doubled between 1915 and 1929 (see Figure 24.2). American consumers responded enthusiastically. The most enthusiastic of all were middle-class Americans, who could afford to buy what the advertisers were selling. Many of them were newcomers to middle-class ranks, searching for ways to affirm—or even create—their new identity.

As male wage earners moved into the new middle class, their wives were freed from the necessity of working outside the home. Advertisers appealed to the new middle-class woman, too, as she refocused her attention toward dressing in the latest fashion, managing the household, and raising children. Vacuum cleaners and other consumer durables would make her more efficient, and books on child rearing, many imbued with a popularized Freudianism, would enable her to mold her children for future success in work and marriage. Cosmetics would aid women in their "first duty"—to be beautiful and sexual for their husbands and boyfriends.

24-1b *Marriage, Sexuality, Celebrity*

That husbands and wives were encouraged to pursue sexual satisfaction together was one sign of how prescriptions for married life had changed since the 19th century, when women were thought to lack sexual passion and men were tacitly expected to satisfy their drives through extramarital liaisons. Modern husbands and wives were expected to share other leisure activities as well—dining out, playing cards with friends, going to the movies, attending concerts, and discussing the latest selection from the newly formed Book-of-the-Month Club. Husbands and wives now aspired to a new ideal—to be best friends, full partners in the pursuit of happiness.

The public pursuit of pleasure was also noticeable among young and single middle-class women. The so-called **flappers** of the 1920s set out to break the informal rules governing young women's lives: They donned short dresses, rolled their stockings down, wore red lipstick, and smoked in public. Flappers were signaling their desire for independence and equality, but they had little thought of achieving those

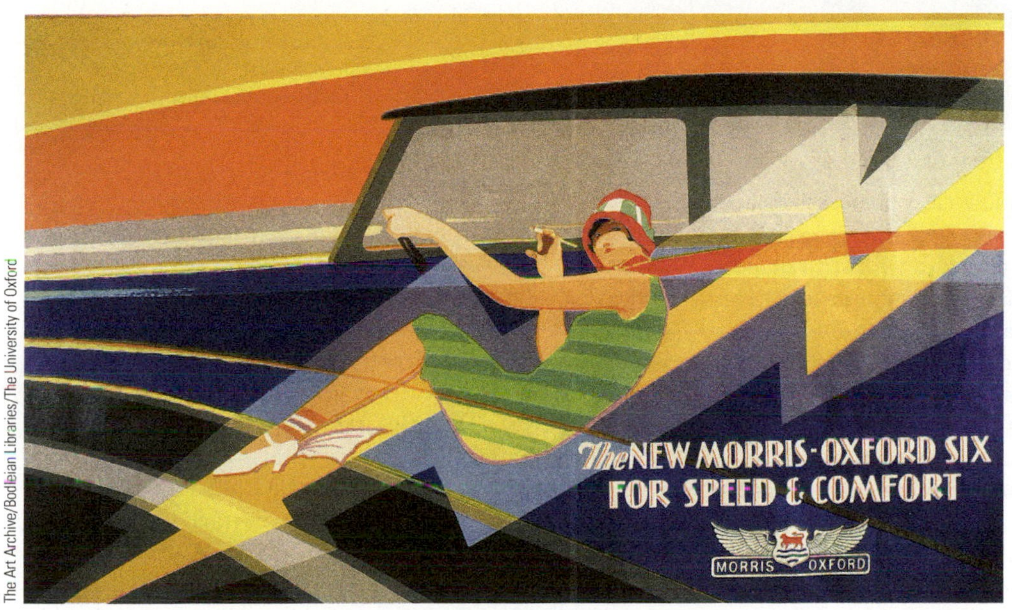

The Art Archive/Bodleian Libraries/The University of Oxford

24.2 **The Art of Selling Cars**
The creators of this dazzling advertisement mixed female sexuality, bold colors, and the power and speed of lightning bolts to generate consumer interest in the "New Morris-Oxford Six" automobile.

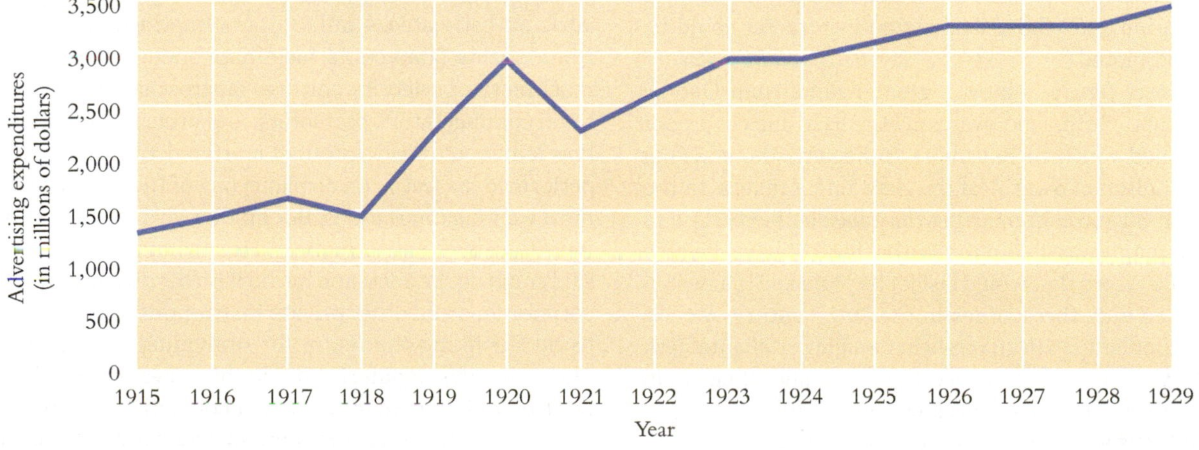

Figure 24.2 **Expenditures on Advertising, 1915–1929**
Source: Data from *Historical Statistics of the United States, Colonial Times to 1970* (White Plains, NY: Kraus International, 1989), p. 856.

Bettmann/Corbis

24.3 **Babe Ruth at the Plate** The "Sultan of Swat" watches one of his towering shots soar toward the stadium fence.

goals through politics as their middle-class predecessors had in the woman's suffrage movement. Rather, they aimed to create a new female personality endowed with self-reliance, outspokenness, and a new appreciation for the pleasures of life.

The pursuit of pleasure became both an individual and a group endeavor. Mass marketers began to understand that they could make money by staging mega-events, mostly connected to sports, that tens of thousands would attend and that radio announcers would broadcast to a virtual audience of millions. When Yankee Stadium opened in New York City in 1923, it set a new standard for the scale and magnificence of sports amphitheaters. Boxing matches began drawing audiences that would have been unimaginable 20 years earlier. To succeed on this scale, these sports required not just stirring athletic competitions but also individual athletes who seemed larger than life and whose exploits and character could be endlessly promoted.

No sports figure achieved greater fame than George Herman "Babe" Ruth, who overcame the hardships of a poor and orphaned youth in Baltimore to become the slugging star—the "Sultan of Swat"—of the New York Yankees. In the 1920s, Ruth hit more home runs than baseball experts had thought humanly possible, culminating in 1927, when he hit a magical 60, a record that would last for 34 years and that would be surpassed only three times in the 20th century. A close second in popularity to Ruth was heavyweight prizefighter Jack Dempsey, whose combination of ruthlessness and efficiency in the ring with gentleness outside it enthralled millions.

Americans also drew their celebrities from the movies, where stars such as comedian Charlie Chaplin and the exotically handsome Rudolph Valentino stirred laughter and sexual longings, respectively, in audiences. These and other figures became so familiar on the silver screen that they created an insatiable appetite among movie fans for news about their private lives as well, an interest that the movie industry was only too eager to exploit.

Perhaps no one in the 1920s attracted as much adulation as was bestowed on **Charles A. Lindbergh**, the young airman who, in 1927, became the first individual to cross the Atlantic in a solo flight. Piloting his single-engine white monoplane, *The Spirit of St. Louis*, Lindbergh flew nonstop (and without sleep) for 34 hours from the time he took off from Long Island until he landed at Le Bourget Airport in Paris. Thousands of Parisians were waiting for him at the airfield and began charging his plane as soon as it landed. When Lindbergh returned to New York, an estimated 4 million fans lined the parade route. None of this fame could have happened without the new machinery of celebrity culture—aggressive journalists and radio commentators, promoters, and others who understood how fame could yield a profit. It mattered, too, that Lindbergh performed his feat in an airplane, one of the era's newest and most exciting innovations. But Lindbergh's celebrity involved more than hype and technology: He accomplished what others said could not be done, and he did it on his own in a time when corporations and other private institutions of power seemed to be shrinking the realm for individual initiative. Some of Lindbergh's popularity no doubt rested on his ability to demonstrate that an individual of conviction and skill could still make a difference in an increasingly industrialized and bureaucratized world.

24-1c Business Promises, Work Realities

Industrialists, advertisers, and merchandisers in the 1920s began to claim that their accomplishments lay at the heart of American civilization. Business, they argued, made America great, and businessmen provided the nation with its wisest, most vigorous leadership. In 1924, President Calvin Coolidge declared, "The business of America is business." Even religion became a business. Bruce Barton, in his best seller *The Man Nobody Knows* (1925), depicted Jesus as a business executive "who picked up twelve men from the bottom ranks of business and forged them into an organization that conquered the world." Elsewhere, Barton hailed Jesus as an early "national advertiser," and proclaimed that Peter and Paul were really not so different from Americans who sold vacuum cleaners.

Some corporate leaders adopted benevolent attitudes toward their employees. They set up workplace cafeterias, hired doctors and nurses to staff on-site medical clinics, and engaged psychologists to counsel troubled workers. They built ball fields and encouraged employees to join industry-sponsored leagues. They published employee newsletters and gave awards to employees who did their jobs well and with good spirit.

The real purpose of these measures—collectively known as welfare capitalism—was to encourage employees to be loyal to their firm and to convince them (contrary to what labor unions had been arguing) that industry did have the best interests of its employees at heart. As the decade proceeded and prosperity rolled on, welfare capitalism reflected the confidence that capitalism had become more responsive to employee concerns and thus more humane.

Many industrial workers benefited from the nation's prosperity. A majority enjoyed rising wages and a reasonably steady income. Skilled craftsmen in the older industries of construction, railroad transportation, and printing fared especially well. Their real wages rose by 30 to 50 percent over the decade. The several million workers employed in the large mass-production industries (such as automobile and electrical equipment manufacture) also did well. Their wages were relatively high, and some of them enjoyed good benefits—paid sick leave, paid vacations, life insurance, stock options, and retirement pensions. Although all workers in companies with these programs were eligible for such benefits, skilled workers were in the best position to claim them.

Semiskilled and unskilled industrial workers had to contend with a labor surplus throughout the decade. As employers replaced workers with machines, the aggregate demand for industrial labor increased at a lower rate than it had in the preceding 20 years. Despite a weakening demand for labor, rural whites, rural blacks, and Mexicans continued their migration to the cities, stiffening the competition for factory jobs. Employers could hire and fire as they saw fit and could therefore keep wage increases lagging behind increases in productivity.

This softening demand for labor helps explain why many working-class families benefited little from the decade's

The Library of Congress Prints and Photographs Division Washington, D.C. [LC-USZ62-93443]

24.4 **Charles A. Lindbergh and the *Spirit of St. Louis*** Lindbergh poses before the plane that will carry him from Long Island to Paris in the first solo flight across the Atlantic.

Q *What explains Lindbergh's extraordinary popularity in the 1920s?*

prosperity or from its consumer revolution. An estimated 40 percent of workers remained poor, unable to afford a healthy diet or adequate housing, much less any of the more costly consumer goods.

The million or more workers who labored in the nation's two largest industries, coal and textiles, suffered the most during the 1920s. Throughout the decade, both industries experienced severe overcapacity. By 1926, only half of the coal mined each year was being sold. Many New England textile cities experienced levels of unemployment that sometimes approached 50 percent. One reason was that many textile industrialists had shifted their operations to the South, where taxes and wages were lower (see Figure 24.3). But the southern textile industry also suffered from excess capacity. Plant managers North and South pressured their workers to speed up production. Workers loathed the frequent "speed-ups" of machines and the "stretch-outs" in the number of spinning or weaving machines each worker was expected to tend. By the late 1920s, labor strife and calls for unionization were rising among disgruntled workers.

Unionization of textiles and coal, and of more prosperous industries as well, would have brought workers a larger share of the decade's prosperity. Some labor leaders, such as Sidney Hillman of the Amalgamated Clothing Workers, argued that unionization would actually increase corporate profits by compelling employers to observe uniform wage and hour schedules that would restrain ruinous competition. Hillman pointed out—as Henry Ford had in the preceding decade

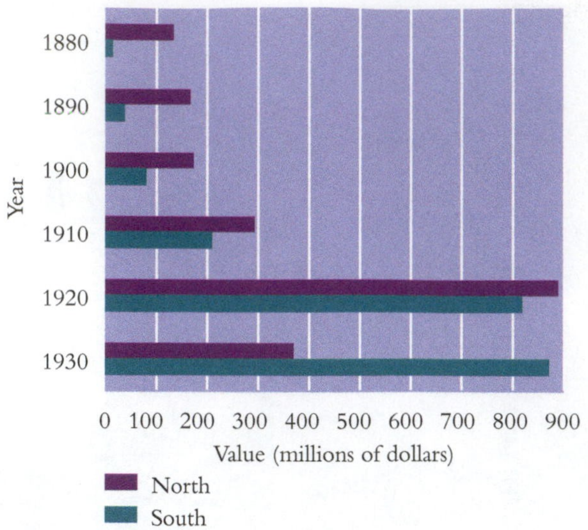

Figure 24.3 **Value of Regional Cotton Textile Output, 1880–1930**

Source: Data from Nancy F. Kane, *Textiles in Transition: Technology, Wages, and Industry Relocation in the U.S. Textile Industry, 1880–1939* (New York: Greenwood Press, 1988), p. 29.

(see Chapter 21)—that rising wages would enable workers to purchase more consumer goods and thus increase corporate sales and revenues. Hillman's views, however, were largely ignored outside the garment industry.

In most industries, unions lost ground in the 1920s, as business and government, backed by middle-class opinion, remained hostile to labor organization. Employers attacked unions as un-American. A conservative Supreme Court whittled away at labor's legal protections, which made it more difficult to organize unions. Trade union membership fell from a high of 5 million in 1920 to less than 3 million in 1929, a mere 10 percent of the nation's industrial workforce. Other forces contributed to the decline, too. Many workers, especially those benefiting from welfare capitalist programs, decided they no longer needed unions. And the labor movement hurt itself by moving too slowly to open its ranks to semiskilled and unskilled factory workers.

Women workers experienced the same hardships as men in the industrial workforce and fewer of the benefits. They were largely excluded from the ranks of the skilled craftsmen and thus missed out on the substantial wage increases that the men in those positions enjoyed. Women also had trouble finding work in the automobile industry, the highest paying of the mass-production industries. They had better access to the electrical equipment and meatpacking industries, although they were often kept in departments given over to "women's work." Where women were allowed to compete for the same jobs as men, they usually earned less. Thus, a female trimmer in a meatpacking plant typically made only two-thirds of what a male trimmer earned. The textile industry had long been a major source of employment for women, but in the 1920s, women and men alike in this ailing manufacturing sector suffered high rates of unemployment and declining wages.

White-collar work established itself, in the 1920s, as a magnet for women. Discrimination generally prevented women from becoming managers, accountants, or supervisors, but they did dominate the lower-level ranks of secretaries, typists, filing assistants, bank tellers, and department store sales clerks. By the 1930s, 2 million women, or 20 percent of the female workforce, labored in these and related occupations. Initially, these positions had a glamour that factory work

Hulton-Deutsch Collection/Historical/Corbis

24.5 **Amelia Earhart, Aviation Pioneer** Earhart strikes a flapper pose in front of the biplane that she was preparing to fly across the Atlantic.

Library of Congress Prints and Photographs Division [Harris Ewing/LC-DIG-hec-12348]

24.6 **Alice Paul** Paul was a leading proponent of women's suffrage in the 1910s. In the 1920s, she led the unsuccessful struggle for an Equal Rights Amendment to the Constitution.

Q *Why did the women's movement drift in the 1920s?*

lacked. Work environments were cleaner and brighter, and women had the opportunity—indeed, were expected—to dress well. But wages were low and managerial authority was absolute. Unions had virtually no presence in white-collar places of employment, and workers had difficulty finding alternative ways of protesting unfair managers or difficult working conditions.

Women with ambitious work aspirations most often pursued the "female" professions, such as teaching, nursing, social work, and librarianship. Opportunities in several of these fields, especially teaching and social work, were growing, and women responded by enrolling in college in large numbers. The number of female college students increased by 50 percent during the 1920s. Some of these college graduates used their skills in new fields, such as writing for women's magazines. A few, drawing strength from their feminist forebears during the Progressive Era, managed to crack such male bastions of work as mainstream journalism and university research and teaching. In every field of endeavor, even such exotic ones as airplane flying, at least one woman arose to demonstrate that her sex had the necessary talent and drive to match or exceed what men had done.

Thus, in 1932, Amelia Earhart became the first woman to fly the Atlantic solo, matching Lindbergh's feat and inspiring women everywhere. Even so, Earhart's feat failed to improve substantial opportunities for women who wanted to work as pilots in the airline industry. In this industry, as in most lines of work, gender prejudices remained too entrenched, and the women who had broken the gender line remained, by and large, solitary figures.

24-1d *The Women's Movement Adrift*

Many supporters of the Nineteenth Amendment to the Constitution, which in 1920 gave women the right to vote, expected it to transform American politics. Women voters would reverse the decline in voter participation, cleanse politics of corruption, and launch a variety of reform initiatives that would improve the quality of life for women and men alike. This female-inspired transformation, however, failed to materialize. The women's movement, instead, seemed to succumb to the same exhaustion and frustration as had the more general progressive movement from which it had emerged 20 years earlier. Younger women searching for independence and equality (such as the flappers discussed earlier in this chapter) often turned away from reform altogether, preferring a lifestyle that emphasized private achievement and personal freedom to a political career devoted to improving the collective status of America's women. Those who continued to agitate for reform found progress more difficult to achieve once the conservative Republican administrations of Harding and Coolidge took office.

Nevertheless, some female reformers made significant strides in the 1920s. In 1921, one group succeeded in getting Congress to pass the **Sheppard–Towner Act**, a social welfare program that provided federal funds for prenatal and child health-care centers throughout the United States. It remained in effect until 1929. In 1923, Alice Paul, still head of the National Woman's Party (NWP, see Chapter 21), and her allies prevailed on Congress to consider an Equal Rights Amendment (ERA) to the Constitution, phrased as follows: "Men and women shall have equal rights throughout the United States and every place subject to its jurisdiction." And in 1920, the National American Woman Suffrage Association, the major force behind the struggle for suffrage, transformed into the **League of Women Voters (LWV)**. During the next decade, the LWV launched numerous initiatives to encourage women to run for elective office, to educate voters about the issues before them, and to improve the condition of those Americans—the poor, female and child laborers, the mentally ill—who needed assistance.

Sometimes the women's movement was stymied not just by external opposition but also by internal division—as it was over the ERA. The NWP and other supporters of the ERA insisted that there could be no compromise with the proposition that women were the equals of men in every respect. But, the LWV countered, child-rearing and mothering duties did render women different from men in key respects and thus, in some instances, in need of special treatment by Congress and other lawmaking bodies.

The question of female difference crystallized around the issue of protective labor legislation for women. Should women, on account of their sex, be given protections at the workplace—limitations on the hours of labor, prohibitions on overnight work, and other such measures—that men did not have? The League of Women Voters said yes; Alice Paul and supporters of the Equal Rights Amendment said no, arguing that women and men should be treated the same in all respects.

This issue of whether women should be treated somewhat differently than men was a genuinely complicated one, and women activists would continue to argue about it with each other for decades. In the 1920s, their inability to speak with a single voice on this matter weakened their cause in the eyes of their adversaries.

24-2 The Politics of Business

Q *What were the similarities and differences in the politics of Harding, Coolidge, and Hoover?*

Republican presidents governed the country from 1921 to 1933. In the beginning, this transition engulfed national politics in scandal, as Warren Harding, the first of the decade's three Republican presidents, allowed high-ranking members of his administration to indulge in spectacular acts of corruption. But his successor, Calvin Coolidge, restored virtue and honor to the presidency while carrying out his 1924 campaign pledge to overturn the legacy of progressivism and reduce the role of the government in economic affairs. The most significant challenge to Coolidge's small-government program came from his own secretary of commerce and then his successor as president, Herbert Hoover, who sought to sustain the spirit of activist government that Theodore Roosevelt had introduced to Republican politics, albeit in a somewhat altered form.

24-2a *Harding and the Politics of Personal Gain*

Warren Gamaliel Harding defeated Democrat James M. Cox for the presidency in 1920. From modest origins as a newspaper editor in the small town of Marion, Ohio, Harding had risen to the U.S. Senate chiefly because the powerful Ohio Republican machine knew it could count on him to do its bidding. He gained the presidency for the same reason. The Republican Party bosses believed that almost anyone they nominated in 1920 could defeat the Democratic opponent. They chose Harding because they could control him. Harding's good looks and geniality made him a favorite with voters, and he swept into office with 61 percent of the popular vote, the greatest landslide since 1820.

To his credit, Harding released the aging Socialist Party leader Eugene V. Debs from jail and took other measures to cool the passions unleashed by the Red Scare. He also included talented men in his cabinet. His choices of Herbert Hoover as secretary of commerce, Charles Evans Hughes as secretary of state, and Andrew Mellon as secretary of the treasury were impressive. Still, Harding lacked the will to alter his ingrained political habits. He had built his political career on a willingness to please the lobbyists who came to his Senate office asking for favors and deals. He had long followed Ohio boss Harry M. Daugherty's advice and would continue to do so now that he had appointed Daugherty attorney general. Harding regarded Daugherty as his friend; they had been together since the beginning of Harding's career. Many a night Harding could be found drinking (despite **Prohibition**), gambling, and womanizing with Daugherty and other members of the "Ohio Gang" at its K Street hangout. Sometimes the gang even convened in the White House.

The K Street house was more than a place to carouse. It was a place of business where the Ohio Gang became rich selling government appointments, judicial pardons, and police protection to bootleggers. By 1923, the corruption could no longer be concealed. Journalists and senators began to focus attention on Secretary of the Interior Albert Fall, who had persuaded Harding to transfer control of large government oil reserves at **Teapot Dome**, Wyoming, and Elk Hills, California, from the navy to the Department of the Interior. Fall had immediately leased the deposits to two oil tycoons, Harry F. Sinclair and Edward L. Doheny, who pumped oil from the wells in exchange for providing the navy with a system of fuel tank reserves. Fall had issued the leases secretly, without allowing other oil corporations to compete for them, and he had accepted almost $400,000 from Sinclair and Doheny.

Fall would pay for this shady deal with a year in jail. Charles R. Forbes, head of the Veterans' Bureau, would go to Leavenworth Prison for swindling the government out of $200 million in hospital supplies. The exposure of Forbes's theft prompted his lawyer, Charles Cramer, to commit suicide; Jesse Smith, Attorney General Daugherty's close friend and housemate, also killed himself, apparently to avoid being indicted and brought to trial. Daugherty managed to escape conviction and incarceration for bribery by burning incriminating documents held by his brother's Ohio bank. Still, Daugherty left government service in disgrace.

Harding could only keep himself blind to this widespread use of public office for private gain for so long. In summer 1923, in poor spirits, he left Washington for a West Coast tour. He fell ill in Seattle and died from a heart attack in San Francisco. The train returning his body to Washington attracted crowds of grief-stricken mourners who little suspected the web of corruption and bribery in which Harding had been caught. Even as the revelations poured forth in 1924 and 1925, few Americans seemed to care. Some of this insouciance reflected the carefree atmosphere of the 1920s, but much of it had to do with the character of the man who succeeded Harding.

24-2b *Coolidge and Laissez-Faire Politics*

Calvin Coolidge rarely smiled. Silence was his public creed, much to the chagrin of Washington's socialites. He was never enticed into carousing with the "boys," nor did he ever stand by as liquor was being served. He believed that the best government was the government that governed least, and that the welfare of the country hinged not on politicians but on the people—their willingness to work hard, to be honest, and to live within their means.

Born in Vermont and raised in Massachusetts, Calvin Coolidge gained national visibility in September 1919, when as governor of Massachusetts he took a firm stand against Boston's striking policemen (see Chapter 23). His reputation as a man who battled labor radicals earned him a place on the 1920 national Republican ticket. His image as an ordinary man helped convince voters in 1920 that the Republican Party would return the country to its commonsensical ways after a decade or more of progressive reform. Coolidge won his party's presidential nomination handily in 1924 and easily defeated his Democratic opponent, John W. Davis. Coolidge's popularity remained strong throughout his first full term, and he probably would have been renominated and reelected in 1928, but he chose not to run.

Coolidge took greatest pride in those measures that reduced the government's control over the economy. The

Library of Congress Prints and Photographs Division Washington, D.C. 20540 USA

24.7 **President Warren G. Harding and Attorney General Harry M. Daugherty** Daugherty was also a long-time friend of Harding, the boss of the Ohio Republican machine, and a source of corruption in the Harding administration.

Revenue Act of 1926 slashed the high income and estate taxes that progressives had pushed through Congress during the First World War. Coolidge curtailed the power of the Federal Trade Commission to regulate business affairs and endorsed Supreme Court decisions invalidating Progressive Era laws that had strengthened organized labor and improved the conditions of children and women at workplaces.

24-2c *Hoover and the Politics of Associationalism*

Some Republicans in the 1920s conceived of government as having a more dynamic role than Coolidge favored. Their leader was Secretary of Commerce Herbert Hoover, who envisioned an economy built on the principle of association. Industrialists, wholesalers, retailers, operators of railroad and shipping lines, small businessmen, farmers, workers, doctors: Hoover wanted each of these groups to form a trade association whose members would share economic information, discuss problems of production and distribution, and seek ways of achieving greater efficiency and profit. Hoover believed that the very act of associating in this way—an approach that historian Ellis Hawley has called **"associationalism"**—would convince participants of the superiority of cooperation over competition, of negotiation over conflict, of public service over selfishness.

A graduate of Stanford University, Hoover had worked first as a mining engineer and then as an executive in multinational mining corporations. During the war, he had directed the government's Food Administration. From that experience, he had come to appreciate the role that government could play in coordinating the activities of thousands of producers and distributors scattered across the country. As commerce secretary, he persuaded farmers to join together in marketing cooperatives, steel executives to abandon the 12-hour day for their employees, and some groups of bankers in the South to organize their institutions into regional associations with adequate resources and expertise. Hoover's dynamic conception of government did not endear him to Coolidge, who declared in 1927: "That man has offered me unsolicited advice for six years, all of it bad."

24-2d *The Politics of Business Abroad*

Republican domestic policy disagreements over whether to pursue laissez-faire or associationalism spilled over into foreign policy as well. Hoover wanted the world's leading nations to meet regularly in conferences, to limit military buildups, and to foster an international environment in which capitalism could flourish. Aware that the United States must help to create such an environment, Hoover hoped to persuade American bankers to adopt investment and loan policies that would aid European recovery from the First World War. If they refused to do so, he was prepared to urge the government to take an activist, supervisory role in foreign investment.

Bettmann/Corbis

24.8 **A Stern Yankee** In contrast to Harding, President Calvin Coolidge did not enjoy informality, banter, or carousing. Here he seems to take little satisfaction in performing what most would have regarded as a pleasurable task: throwing out the first ball of the 1924 baseball season.

Q *Why did Coolidge's stern demeanor appeal to voting Americans during the Jazz Age?*

In 1921 and 1922, Hoover helped to design the Washington Conference on the Limitation of Armaments. Although he did not serve as a negotiator at the conference—Secretary of State Charles Evans Hughes reserved that role for himself and his subordinates—Hoover did supply Hughes's team with a wealth of economic information that became the basis for bold, detailed proposals for disarmament. Those proposals gave U.S. negotiators a decided advantage over their European and Asian counterparts and helped them win an impressive accord, the Five-Power Treaty, by which the United States, Britain, Japan, France, and Italy agreed to scrap more than 2 million tons of warships. Hughes also obtained pledges from all of the signatories that they would respect the "Open Door" in China, long a U.S. foreign policy objective (see Chapter 22).

These triumphs redounded to Hughes's credit but not to Hoover's, and Hughes used them to consolidate his control over foreign policy. He rebuffed Hoover's efforts to put international economic affairs under the direction of the

Commerce Department and rejected Hoover's suggestion to intervene in the international activities of U.S. banks.

Hughes's approach was not entirely laissez-faire, as he demonstrated in his 1923 reaction to a crisis in Franco-German relations. The victorious Allies had imposed on Germany an obligation to pay $33 billion in war reparations (see Chapter 23). When the impoverished German government suspended its payments in 1923, France sent troops to occupy the Ruhr Valley, whose industry was vital to the German economy. German workers retaliated by going on strike. The crisis threatened to undermine Europe's precarious economic recovery. Hughes responded by intensifying American financial pressure on the French and by compelling them to attend a U.S.-sponsored conference in 1924 to restructure Germany's debt obligation.

The conference produced the **Dawes Plan** (after the Chicago banker and chief negotiator, Charles G. Dawes), which reduced German reparations from $542 million to $250 million annually and called on U.S. and foreign banks to stimulate the German economy with a quick infusion of $200 million in loans. Within a matter of days, banker J. P. Morgan, Jr., raised more than $1 billion from American investors. Money poured into German financial markets, and the German economy appeared to stabilize.

The Dawes Plan won applause on both sides of the Atlantic, but soon the U.S. money flooding into Germany created its own problems. American investors were so eager to lend to Germany that their investments became speculative and unsound. At this point, a stronger U.S. government effort to direct loans to sound investments, a strategy that Hoover supported, might have helped. But neither Hughes nor his successor as secretary of state, Frank Kellogg, was interested in such initiatives, and neither was Secretary of the Treasury Mellon. The laissez-faire approach had reasserted itself, and Hoover's plan to involve the U.S. government directly in international economic matters had been sidetracked.

Republican initiatives to ensure world peace continued, however. Secretary of State Kellogg drew up a treaty with Aristide Briand, the French foreign minister, outlawing war as a tool of national policy. In 1928, representatives of the United States, France, and 13 other nations met in Paris to sign the Kellogg–Briand Pact, an agreement that soon attracted the support of 48 other nations. Coolidge viewed Kellogg–Briand as a way of reducing American military commitments abroad and thereby further shrinking the size of the U.S. government at home. With the threat of war removed, the United States could scale back its military forces and eliminate much of the bureaucracy needed to support a large standing army and navy. The celebrated pact contained no enforcement mechanism, however, rendering itself largely ineffective as a foreign policy tool.

Republican administrations attempted to curtail American military involvement in the Caribbean and Central America as well. Thus, the Coolidge administration pulled U.S. troops out of the Dominican Republic in 1924 and Nicaragua in 1925. But U.S. investments in the region, which more than doubled from 1917 to 1929, proved too important for the U.S. government to ignore. Coolidge sent the marines back into Nicaragua in 1926 to end a war between liberals and conservatives there and to protect American property; this time they stayed until 1934. U.S. troops, meanwhile, occupied Haiti continuously between 1919 and 1934, keeping in power governments friendly to U.S. interests.

Bettmann/Corbis

24.9 **Herbert Hoover, Secretary of Commerce** Hoover used his cabinet position to encourage innovation in American industry. In 1927, he participated in the nation's first television broadcast. In this photograph, Hoover and his associates in Washington converse with men in an ATT broadcast studio in New York.

Q *In what ways was Hoover's conception of government's role more dynamic than that of Harding and Coolidge?*

24-3 Farmers, Small-Town Protestants, and Moral Traditionalists

Q *What concerned farmers and conservative white Protestants in the 1920s, and what policies did they support?*

Although many Americans benefited from the prosperity of the 1920s, others did not. Overproduction was impoverishing substantial numbers of farmers. Beyond these economic hardships, many white Protestants, especially those in rural areas and small towns, feared the new economy and new culture that were taking shape in the cities. Increasingly, these Americans made their voices heard in politics.

24-3a *Agricultural Depression*

During the war, domestic demand for farm products had risen steadily and foreign demand had exploded as the war disrupted agricultural production in France, Ukraine, and other European food-producing regions. Soon after the war, however, Europe's farmers quickly reestablished customary levels of production. Foreign demand for American foodstuffs fell precipitously, leaving U.S. farmers with an oversupply and depressed prices (see Figure 24.4).

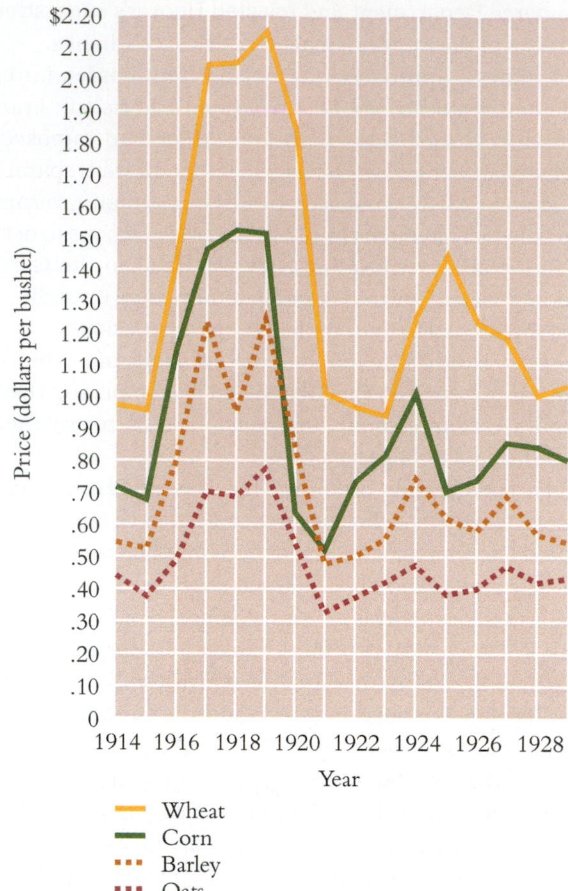

Figure 24.4 **Price of Major Crops, 1914–1929**

Source: Data from *Historical Statistics of the United States, Colonial Times to 1970* (White Plains, NY: Kraus International, 1989), pp. 511–12.

A rise in agricultural productivity made possible by the tractor also worsened the plight of farmers. The number of tractors in use almost quadrupled in the 1920s, and 35 million new acres came under cultivation. Produce flooded the market. Prices fell even further, as did farm incomes. By 1929, the annual per capita income of rural Americans was only $223, one-quarter that of the nonfarm population. Hundreds of thousands had to sell their farms and scrape together a living as tenants or abandon farming altogether. Many chose to abandon farm life and headed for the city.

Those who stayed on the land grew increasingly assertive in their demands. Early in the decade, radical farmers led the movement, working through such organizations as the Nonpartisan League of North Dakota and farmer-labor parties in Minnesota, Wisconsin, and other midwestern states. By the second half of the decade, however, leadership had passed from farming radicals to farming moderates, and from small farmers in danger of dispossession to larger farmers and agribusinesses seeking to extend their holdings. Lobbying through such organizations as the American Farm Bureau Federation, the more powerful agricultural interests pressured Congress to set up economic controls that would protect them from failure. Their proposals passed Congress twice, only to be vetoed by President Coolidge.

24-3b *Cultural Dislocation*

Added to the economic plight of the farmers was a sense of cultural dislocation among the majority who were white, Protestant, and of northern European descent. These farmers had long perceived themselves as the backbone of the nation—hardworking, honest, God-fearing yeomen, guardians of independence and liberty.

The 1920 census challenged the validity of that view. For the first time, a slight majority of Americans now lived in urban areas. That finding in itself signified little because the census classified as "urban" those towns with a population as small as 2,500. But the census figures did reinforce the widespread perception that both the economic and cultural vitality of the nation had shifted from the countryside to the city (see Map 24.2). Industry, the chief engine of prosperity, was an urban phenomenon. Commercialized leisure—the world of amusement parks, department stores, professional sports, movies, cabarets, and theaters—was to be enjoyed in cities; so too were flashy fashions and open sexuality. Catholics, Jews, and African Americans, who together outnumbered white Protestants in many cities, seemed to be the principal creators of this new world. They were also thought to be the purveyors of Bolshevism and other kinds of radicalism. Cities, finally, were the home of secular intellectuals who had scrapped their belief in scripture and in God and embraced science as their new authority.

Throughout the Progressive Era, rural white Americans believed that the cities could be redeemed, that city dwellers could be reformed, and that the Protestant values of rural

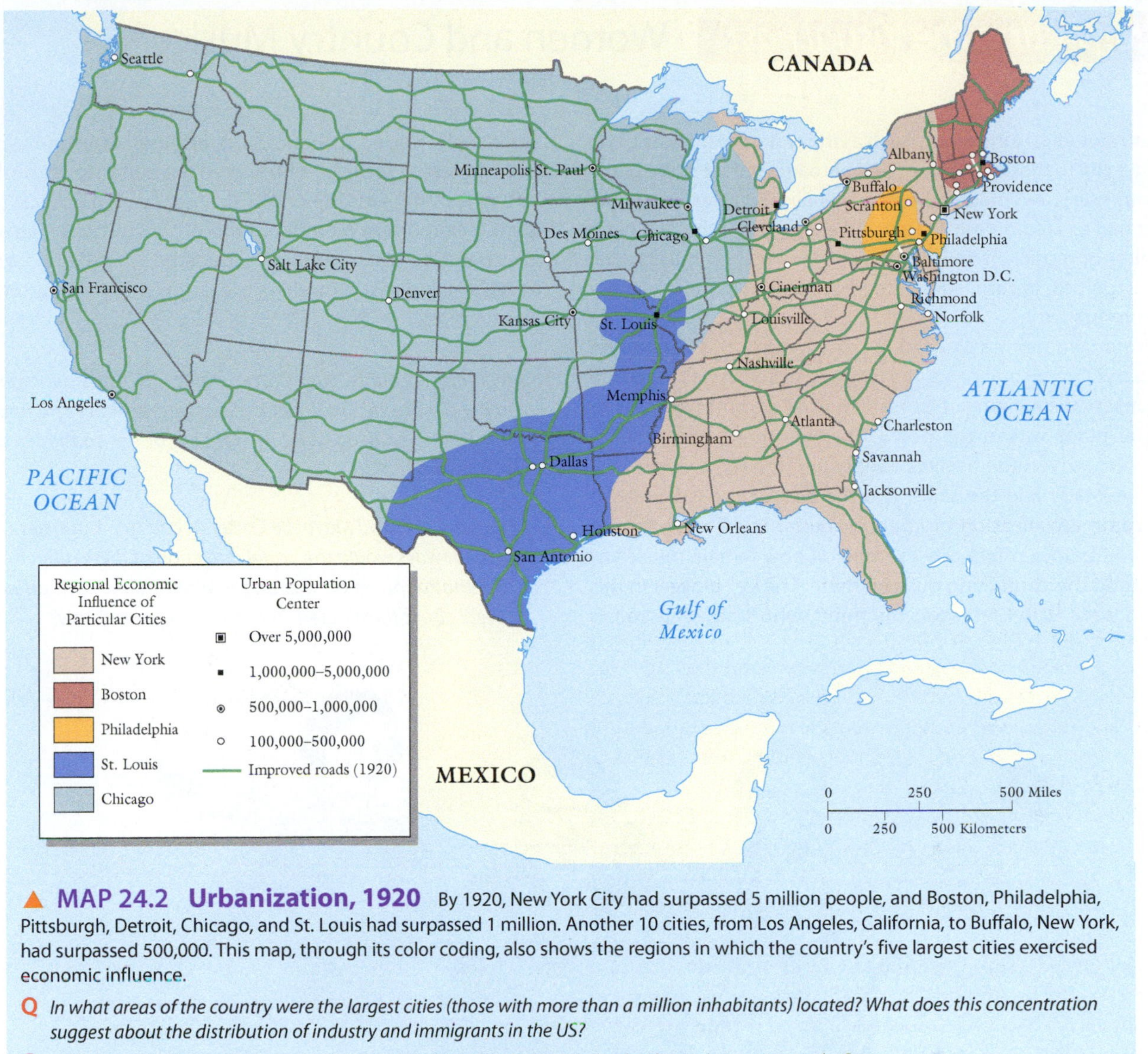

▲ **MAP 24.2 Urbanization, 1920** By 1920, New York City had surpassed 5 million people, and Boston, Philadelphia, Pittsburgh, Detroit, Chicago, and St. Louis had surpassed 1 million. Another 10 cities, from Los Angeles, California, to Buffalo, New York, had surpassed 500,000. This map, through its color coding, also shows the regions in which the country's five largest cities exercised economic influence.

Q *In what areas of the country were the largest cities (those with more than a million inhabitants) located? What does this concentration suggest about the distribution of industry and immigrants in the US?*

Q *Which cities with a million plus residents in the 1920s are still regarded as leading urban centers today?*

America would triumph. War had undermined that confidence and replaced it with the fear that urban culture and urban people might swamp the "superior" values of rural America.

These fears grew more intense as consumer culture and its commodities entered the countryside. Even small towns now sported movie theaters and automobile dealerships. Radio waves carried news of city life into isolated farmhouses. The growth in the circulation of national magazines also broke down the wall separating country from city. Mail-order catalogs invited farmers to fantasize that they too could fill their homes with refrigerators, RCA Victrola phonographs, and Hoover vacuum cleaners.

Rural white Americans showed ambivalence toward this cultural invasion. On the one hand, most country dwellers were eager to participate in the consumer marketplace. On the other hand, many worried that doing so would expose the countryside to atheism, immorality, and radicalism. They expressed their determination to protect their imperiled way of life in their support for Prohibition, the Ku Klux Klan, immigration restriction, and religious fundamentalism.

24-3c *Prohibition*

The Eighteenth Amendment to the Constitution, which prohibited the manufacture and sale of alcohol, went into effect in January 1920. Initially it drew support from large and varied constituencies including farmers, middle-class city dwellers, feminists, and progressive reformers who loathed the powerful "liquor trust" and who saw firsthand the deleterious effects of drink on the urban poor. It soon became apparent, however, that Prohibition was doing as much to encourage lawbreaking as abstinence. With only 1,500 federal agents to enforce the law, the government could not possibly police the drinking habits of 110 million people. With little fear of punishment, those who wanted to drink did so, either brewing liquor at home or buying it from speakeasies and bootleggers.

Interpreting the Visual Past Women and Country Music

Technological innovation, such as the radio, did not just bring the city to the countryside. It also broadcast the culture of the countryside to regional, and even national, publics far larger than what had existed before. Bigger audiences meant that a greater number of musicians could make a living via their music; such opportunities, in turn, stimulated a surge in musical creativity and productivity.

Would women be allowed to participate in this expanding industry? On the one hand, the white rural South was a bastion of conservatism; many of its residents insisted that a woman's proper place was in the home. On the other hand, women had long woven themselves deeply into the region's musical culture. Many had the skills, and the desire, to participate in the commercialization of country music. The Carter Family, pictured below, offers one example of how female musicians managed the conflicting pulls on them. The key players in this group were Sara Carter (on the right), who sang lead vocals and usually played the Autoharp, and her sister-in-law, Maybelle Carter (on the left), who played the guitar. Sara's husband, A.P., who dominates the photo's center, was, in musical terms, the least important member of this group. But as a man and as a husband, he lent an aura of respectability to the two women musicians and cast himself as the catalyst for the Carter Family's success.

Q *By many accounts, Sara Carter was a "liberated" woman who, in her private life, wore slacks, shot game, wrote and arranged music, and smoked. Why is that side of her so hidden in this photograph?*

Q *Imagine Sara and Maybelle Carter as country music stars today: In what ways would the visual depiction of them differ from the one that appears on this page? What might such differences reveal about the differences between then and now?*

Michael Ochs Archives/Corbis

24.10 **Photographer Unknown, The Carter Family (Maybelle, A.P., Sara, left to right), 1937.**

Because the law prevented legitimate businesses from manufacturing liquor, organized crime added alcohol to its portfolio. Mobsters procured much of their liquor from Canadian manufacturers, smuggled it across the border, protected it in warehouses, and distributed it to speakeasies. Al Capone's Chicago-based mob alone employed 1,000 men to protect its liquor trafficking, which was so lucrative that Capone became the richest (and most feared) gangster in America. Blood flowed in the streets of Chicago and other northern cities as rival mobs fought one another to enlarge their share of the market.

These unexpected consequences caused many early advocates of Prohibition, especially in the cities, to withdraw their support. Many rural white Protestants, however, became more, not less, determined to rid the country of liquor once and for all. The violence spawned by liquor trafficking confirmed their view of alcohol as evil. The high-profile participation of Italian, Irish, and Jewish gangsters in the bootleg trade caused many rural Protestant Americans to view Catholics and Jews as threats to law and morality.

24-3d *The Ku Klux Klan*

The original Ku Klux Klan, formed in the South in the late 1860s, had died out with the defeat of Reconstruction and the reestablishment of white supremacy (see Chapter 17). A new Klan had been created in 1915 by William Simmons, a white southerner who had been inspired by D. W. Griffith's racist film, *Birth of a Nation* (For a discussion of the film, see the History through Film feature in Chapter 17, p. 488.). By the 1920s, Hiram Evans, a Texas dentist, had replaced Simmons as head of the Klan, and the groups on its hate list had expanded to include Jews and Catholics, in addition to blacks. Evans's Klan propagated a nativist message that the country should limit—or better yet, eliminate—the influence of Jews and Catholics and restore "Anglo-Saxon" racial purity, Protestant supremacy, and traditional morality to national life.

By 1924, as many as 4 million Americans are thought to have belonged to the Klan, including the half million members of its female auxiliary, Women of the Ku Klux Klan. Not only was the Klan strong in states of the former Confederacy, such as Louisiana and Texas, and in border states such as Oklahoma and Kansas, but it thrived, too, in such northern states as Indiana, Pennsylvania, Washington, and Oregon. It even drew significant membership from the cities of those states. Indiana, for example, was home to 500,000 Klansmen and women, many of them in the Indianapolis area. In 1924, Indiana voters elected a Klansman to the governorship and sent several other Klan members to the statehouse.

The Klan offered its members friendship networks, social services, and conviviality. Its rituals, regalia, and mock-medieval language (the Imperial Wizard, Exalted Cyclops, Grand Dragons, and such) gave initiates a sense of superiority, valor, and mystery similar to what other fraternal societies—from the Masons to the Knights of Columbus—imparted to their members.

But the Klan also thrived on hate, much of it directed against blacks, Jews, and Catholics. The KKK saw itself as the enforcer of white supremacy and was proud of its reputation for using force to punish blacks who dared to cross color lines or in other ways offend white sensibilities. Jews stood accused of international banking conspiracies on the one hand and of fomenting communist revolution on the other. And the presence of Catholics in America, the Klan alleged, would allow authoritarian popes to meddle in the affairs of American democracy.

24.11 **Al Capone, Chicago Mob Leader** Capone built a liquor distribution empire during Prohibition. This 1920s photograph is a mug shot of Capone taken by police during one of his arrests. The government would jail him for tax evasion, but not until 1932.

Q *Why did the government have so much difficulty enforcing Prohibition?*

24-3e *Immigration Restriction*

Although most white Protestants never joined the Klan, many of them did respond to the Klan's nativist argument that the country and its values would best be served by limiting the entry of outsiders who were thought to threaten America. That was the purpose of the **Johnson–Reed Immigration Restriction Act of 1924**.

By the early 1920s, most Americans believed that the country could no longer accommodate the million immigrants who had been arriving each year before the war and the more than 800,000 who arrived in 1921. Industrialists no longer needed unskilled European laborers to operate their factories, their places having been taken either by machines or by African American, Mexican, or Filipino workers. Most labor movement leaders were convinced that the influx of workers unfamiliar with English and with trade unions had weakened labor solidarity. Progressive reformers no longer believed that immigrants could be easily Americanized or that harmony between the native-born and the foreign-born could be readily achieved. Congress responded to constituents' concerns by passing an immigration restriction act in 1921. In 1924, the more comprehensive Johnson–Reed Act imposed a yearly quota of 165,000 immigrants from countries outside the Western Hemisphere, effectively reducing total immigration to only 20 percent of the prewar annual average.

The sponsors of the 1924 act believed that certain groups—British, Germans, and Scandinavians, in particular—were racially superior and that, consequently, these groups should be allowed to enter the United States in greater numbers; however, because the Constitution prohibited the enactment of explicitly racist laws, Congress had to achieve this racist aim through subterfuge. Lawmakers established a formula to determine the annual immigrant quota for each foreign country, which was to be computed at 2 percent of the total number of immigrants from that country already resident in the United States in the year 1890. In 1890, immigrant ranks had been dominated by the British, Germans, and Scandinavians, so the new quotas would thus allow for a relatively larger cohort of immigrants from those countries. Immigrant groups that were poorly represented in the 1890 population—Italians, Greeks, Poles, Slavs, and eastern European Jews—were effectively locked out.

The Johnson–Reed Act also reaffirmed the longstanding policy of excluding Chinese immigrants, and it added Japanese and other groups of East and South Asians to the list of groups that were barred from entry. The act did not officially limit immigration from nations in the Western Hemisphere, chiefly because agribusiness interests in Texas and California had convinced Congress that cheap Mexican labor was indispensable to their industry's prosperity. Still, the establishment of a Border Patrol along the U.S.-Mexican border and the imposition of a $10 head tax on all prospective Mexican immigrants made entry into the United States more difficult than it had been.

The Johnson–Reed Act accomplished Congress's underlying goal. Annual immigration from transoceanic nations fell by 80 percent. The large number of available slots for English and German immigrants regularly went unfilled, while the smaller number of available slots for Italians, Poles, Russian Jews, and others prevented hundreds of thousands of them from entering the country. A "national origins" system put in place in 1927 further reduced the total annual quota to 150,000 and reserved more than 120,000 of these slots for immigrants from northwestern Europe (see Table 24.1). Except for minor modifications in 1952, the Johnson–Reed Act would govern U.S. immigration policy until 1965.

Remarkably few Americans, outside of the ethnic groups being discriminated against, objected to these laws at the time they were passed—an indication of how broadly acceptable racism and nativism had become. In fact, racism and religious bigotry enjoyed resurgences during the Jazz Age. The pseudoscience of eugenics, based on the idea that a nation could improve the racial quality of its population by expanding its stronger racial strains and shrinking its weaker ones, found supporters not only in Congress but among the ranks of scientists as well. Universities such as

Table 24.1 ANNUAL IMMIGRANT QUOTAS UNDER THE JOHNSON–REED ACT, 1925–1927

Northwest Europe and Scandinavia		Eastern and Southern Europe		Other Countries	
Country	**Quota**	**Country**	**Quota**	**Country**	**Quota**
Germany	51,227	Poland	5,982	Africa (other than Egypt)	1,100
Great Britain and Northern Ireland	34,007	Italy	3,845	Armenia	124
Irish Free State (Ireland)	28,567	Czechoslovakia	3,073	Australia	121
Sweden	9,561	Russia	2,248	Palestine	100
Norway	6,453	Yugoslavia	671	Syria	100
France	3,954	Romania	603	Turkey	100
Denmark	2,789	Portugal	503	New Zealand and Pacific Islands	100
Switzerland	2,081	Hungary	473	All others	1,900
Netherlands	1,648	Lithuania	344		
Austria	785	Latvia	142		
Belgium	512	Spain	131		
Finland	471	Estonia	124		
Free City of Danzig	228	Albania	100		
Iceland	100	Bulgaria	100		
Luxembourg	100	Greece	100		
Total (number)	142,483	Total (number)	18,439	Total (number)	3,745
Total (%)	86.5%	Total (%)	11.2%	Total (%)	2.3%

Note: Total annual immigrant quota was 164,667.

Source: From *Statistical Abstract of the United States* (Washington, D.C.: Government Printing Office, 1929), p. 100.

Harvard and Columbia set quotas similar to those of the Johnson–Reed Act to reduce the proportion of Jews among their undergraduates.

24-3f *Fundamentalism versus Liberal Protestantism*

Of all the movements protesting against the modern elements of urban life in the 1920s, Protestant fundamentalism was perhaps the most enduring. **Fundamentalists** regarded the Bible as God's word and thus the source of all "fundamental" truth. They believed that every event depicted in the Bible, from the creation of the world in six days to the resurrection of Christ, happened exactly as the Bible described it. For fundamentalists, God was a deity who intervened directly in the lives of individuals and communities and who made known both his pleasure and his wrath to those who acknowledged his divinity. Sin had to be actively purged, and salvation actively sought.

The rise of the fundamentalist movement from the 1870s through the 1920s roughly paralleled the rise of urban-industrial society. Fundamentalists recoiled from the "evils" of the city—from what they perceived as its poverty, its moral degeneracy, its irreligion, and its crass materialism. Fundamentalism took shape in reaction against two additional aspects of urban society: the growth of liberal Protestantism and the revelations of science.

Liberal Protestants believed that religion had to be adapted to the skeptical and scientific temper of the modern age. The Bible was to be mined for its ethical values rather than for its literal truth. Liberal Protestants removed God from his active role in history and refashioned him into a distant and benign deity who watched over the world but did not intervene to punish or to redeem. They turned religion away from the quest for salvation and toward the pursuit of good deeds, social conscience, and love for one's neighbor. Although those with a liberal bent constituted only a minority of Protestants, they were articulate, visible, and influential in social reform movements. Fundamentalism arose in part to counter the "heretical" claims of the liberal Protestants.

Liberal Protestants and fundamentalists both understood that science was the source of most challenges to Christianity. Scientists believed that rational inquiry was a better guide to the past and to the future than prayer and revelation. Scientists even challenged the ideas that God had created the world and had fashioned humankind in his own image. These were assertions that many religious peoples, particularly fundamentalists, simply could not accept. Conflict was inevitable. It came in 1925, in Dayton, Tennessee.

24-3g *The Scopes Trial*

No aspect of science aroused more anger among fundamentalists than Charles Darwin's theory of evolution. There was no greater blasphemy than to suggest that man emerged from lower forms of life instead of being created by God. In Tennessee in 1925, fundamentalists succeeded in passing a law that forbade teaching "any theory that denies the story of the divine creation of man as taught in the Bible."

For Americans who accepted the authority of science, denying the truth of evolution was as ludicrous as insisting that the sun revolved around the earth. They ridiculed the fundamentalists, but they worried that the passage of the Tennessee law might signal the onset of a campaign to undermine First Amendment guarantees of free speech. The American Civil Liberties Union (ACLU), founded by liberals during the Red Scare of 1919 and 1920, began searching for a teacher who would be willing to challenge the constitutionality of the Tennessee law. The ACLU found its man in John T. Scopes, a 24-year-old biology teacher in Dayton, Tennessee. After confessing that he had taught evolution to his students, Scopes was arrested. The case quickly attracted national attention. William Jennings Bryan, the former Populist, progressive, and secretary of state, announced that he would help prosecute Scopes, and the famous liberal trial lawyer Clarence Darrow

The Granger Collection, New York

24.12 **"Spoiling the Broth"** This anti-immigrant cartoon, appearing in 1921, shows America's fabled melting pot being forced to accommodate far more immigrants from Europe and Asia than it could handle. The result was hundreds of thousands, even millions, of immigrants being disgorged from the pot as "unassimilated aliens."

Q *Why did America lose faith in its capacity to absorb immigrants?*

Bettmann/Corbis

24.13 **Aimee Semple McPherson** A famous 1920s evangelist, McPherson pioneered the use of modern media to broadcast a religious message. In Los Angeles, McPherson built one of the country's first mega-churches, the Angelus Temple. This photograph shows her in Washington, D.C., in 1927, where a crowd of 7,000 stormed the stage after her sermon to draw close to this charismatic woman.

rushed to Dayton to lead Scopes's defense. That Bryan and Darrow had once been allies in the progressive movement only heightened the drama. A small army of journalists descended on Dayton, led by H. L. Mencken, a Baltimore-based journalist famous for his savage critiques of the alleged stupidity and prudishness of small-town Americans.

Most observers expected Scopes to be convicted, and he was. But the hearing took an unexpected turn when Darrow persuaded the judge to let Bryan testify as an "expert on the Bible." Darrow knew that Bryan's testimony would have no bearing on the question of Scopes's innocence or guilt. The jury was not even allowed to hear it. His aim was to expose Bryan as a fool for believing that the Bible was a source of literal truth and thus to embarrass the fundamentalists. In a riveting confrontation, Darrow made Bryan's defense of the Bible look problematic and led Bryan to admit that the "truth" of the Bible was not always easy to determine. But Darrow could not shake Bryan's belief that the Bible was God's word and thus the source of all truth.

In his account of the trial, Mencken portrayed Bryan as a pathetic figure devastated by his humiliating experience on the witness stand, a view popularized in the 1960 movie about the trial, *Inherit the Wind*. When Bryan died only a week after the trial ended, Mencken claimed that the trial had broken Bryan's heart. Bryan deserved a better epitaph than the one Mencken had given him. Diabetes caused his death, not a broken heart. Nor was Bryan the innocent fool that Mencken made him out to be. He remembered when social conservatives had used Darwin's phrase "survival of the fittest" to argue that the wealthy and politically powerful were racially superior to the poor and powerless. His rejection of Darwinism evidenced his democratic faith that all human beings were creatures of God and thus capable of striving for perfection and equality.

The public ridicule attendant on the Scopes trial took its toll on fundamentalists. Many of them retreated from politics and refocused their attention on purging sin from their own hearts rather than from the hearts of others. In the end, the fundamentalists prevailed on three more states to prohibit the teaching of evolution, but the controversy had even more far-reaching effects. Worried about losing sales, publishers quietly removed references to Darwin from their science textbooks, a policy that would remain in force until the 1960s. In this respect, the fundamentalists had scored a significant victory.

24-4 Ethnic and Racial Communities

Q *How were the experiences of ethnic and racial groups in 1920s America similar and how were they different?*

The 1920s were a decade of change for ethnic and racial minorities. Some minorities benefited from the prosperity of the decade; others created and sustained vibrant subcultures. All, however, experienced a surge in religious and racial discrimination that made them uneasy in Jazz Age America.

24-4a *European American Ethnics*

European American ethnics—and especially the southern and eastern European majority among them—were concentrated in the cities of the Northeast and Midwest. Many were semiskilled and unskilled industrial laborers with little economic security. In addition, they faced cultural discrimination. Catholics and Jews were targets of the Klan. Catholics generally opposed Prohibition, viewing it as a crude attempt by Protestants to control their behavior. Southern and eastern Europeans, particularly Jews and Italians, resented

Everett Collection Inc/Alamy stock Photo

24.14 **Darrow vs. Bryan, 1925** In this photograph of the extraordinary gathering outside the Court House in Dayton, Tennessee, Clarence Darrow (standing, at center of image) interrogates William Jennings Bryan (seated with bow tie, facing Darrow) regarding the literal truth of the Bible.

Q *What were the consequences of the Scopes Trial for fundamentalists and for America?*

immigration restriction and the implication that they were inferior to Anglo-Saxon whites. Many Italians were outraged by the execution of Nicola Sacco and Bartolomeo Vanzetti in 1927 (see Chapter 23). If the two men had been native-born white Protestants, many Italian Americans argued, their lives would have been spared.

Southern and eastern Europeans everywhere endured intensive Americanization campaigns. State after state passed laws requiring public schools to instruct children in the essentials of citizenship. Several states, including Rhode Island, extended these laws to private schools as well, convinced that the children of immigrants who were attending Catholic parochial schools were spending too much time learning about their native religion, language, and country. An Oregon law tried to eliminate Catholic schools altogether by ordering all children aged 8 to 16 to enroll in public schools. But attending a public school was no guarantee of acceptance, either—a lesson learned by Jewish children who had excelled in urban public high schools only to be barred from Harvard, Columbia, and other elite universities.

Southern and eastern Europeans responded to these insults and attacks by strengthening the very institutions and customs Americanizers sought to undermine. Ethnic associations flourished in the 1920s—Catholic churches and Jewish synagogues, fraternal and mutual benefit societies, banks and charitable organizations, athletic leagues and youth groups. Children learned their native languages and customs at home and at church if not at school, and they joined with their parents to celebrate their ethnic heritage. Among Italians and French Canadians, saints' days were occasions for parades, speeches, band concerts, games, and feasts, all serving to solidify ethnic bonds and affirm ethnic identity.

Many of these immigrants and their children, however, also embraced the new consumer culture. They flocked to movies and amusement parks, to baseball games and boxing matches. Children usually entered more enthusiastically into the world of American mass culture than did their immigrant parents, a behavior that often set off family conflicts. For a time, however, many ethnics found it possible to reconcile their own culture with American culture.

European American ethnics also resolved to develop sufficient political muscle to defeat the forces of nativism and to turn government policy in a more favorable direction. One sign of this determination was a sharp rise in the number of immigrants who became U.S. citizens. The percentage of immigrant Poles, Slavs, Italians, Lithuanians, and Hungarians who became naturalized citizens nearly doubled during the decade; the percentage of naturalized Greeks almost tripled. Armed with the vote, ethnics turned out on election days to defeat unsympathetic city councilmen, mayors, state representatives, and even an occasional governor (see Table 24.2). Their growing national strength first became apparent at the Democratic National Convention of 1924, when urban-ethnic delegates almost won approval of planks calling for the repeal of Prohibition and condemnation of the Klan. After denying the presidential nomination to William G. McAdoo—Woodrow Wilson's treasury secretary, son-in-law, and heir apparent—they nearly secured it for their candidate, **Alfred E. Smith**, the Irish American governor of New York. McAdoo represented the rural and southern constituencies of the Democratic Party. His forces ended up battling Smith's urban-ethnic forces for 103 ballots, until both men gave up, and supporters from each camp switched their votes to a compromise candidate, the corporate lawyer John W. Davis.

The nomination fight damaged the Democratic Party in the short term, and popular Calvin Coolidge easily defeated the little-known Davis. The split between the party's rural Protestant and urban-ethnic constituencies would keep the Democrats from the White House for nearly a decade, but the convention upheaval of 1924 also marked an important

What They Said

The Debate over Immigration

In 1924, Congress debated the virtues and defects of the proposed Johnson–Reed Immigration Reform Act. In the first excerpt below, Representative Henry Purnell, a Republican from Indiana, justifies the legislation as a necessary defense of America against immigrants from southern and eastern Europe who, in his eyes, constituted a "stream of broken and irresponsible wreckage" contaminating America with the "social and political diseases of the Old World." In the second excerpt below, Representative Emmanuel Celler, a Democrat from New York, calls on his colleagues to stop demonizing the new immigrants and to desist from heaping the blame for America's ills on them. He reminds his colleagues that, in the 1840s and 1850s, nativists subjected German and Irish immigrants to similar hatred and slurs. "We were mistaken then," he declares. Germans and Italians became good Americans, Celler argues, and so would eastern and southern Europeans, if given the chance.

Representative Henry Purnell (Republican, Indiana)

If we fail to enact any new law upon this subject [immigration restriction], our failure will be equivalent to opening the gates to the greatest and most dangerous horde of foreigners any nation has ever seen. . . .

It has been urged by those who favor less restriction that this is the great "melting pot" into which has been poured for a hundred years the people of many races and from which has sprung the hardy, red-blooded, liberty-loving American of whom we love to boast. But those who take this view forget that there is little or no similarity between the clear-thinking, self-governing stocks that sired the American people and this stream of broken and irresponsible wreckage that is pouring into the lifeblood of America the social and political diseases of the Old World. . . .

Once within our borders they herd together in the congested centers, seeking out their own countrymen where they read and speak their native language, and soon become the easy prey of those whose highest ambition in life is to destroy the only Government that offers them life, hope, and opportunity. . . . They did not come over here to work on the farms where they are really needed. In fact … they did not come to work at all. . . . It is not work but easy money that inspires the modern immigrant. . . .

I am anxious that Americans rather than aliens shall inherit the land of our fathers.

Representative Emanuel Celler (Democrat, New York)

[I]mmigration started in 1850 in large and goodly numbers, and from 1850 on that was the inception of our real prosperity and the opening up of the West, the opening up of the mines of the Appalachian Ranges and of the Rocky Mountains, and the building of the railroads and the development of our great industries, and all of it paralleled the great numbers of immigrants who came to our shores, and they have done yeoman service in reference to the development of the country and in giving our large and prosperous [economic sectors] … everything that makes for the material welfare of the country. . . .

Let us … be truthful. . . . It is as clear as the sun that the majority of the Immigration Committee [in 1924] and most proponents of this measure … do not want the "wops," "dagoes," "Hebrews," "hunkies," "bulls," and others known by similar epithets. Just so, in 1840, 1850, and 1860 you did not want the "beery Germans" and "dirty Irish." The Germans and the Irish were [then seen as] mongrels, self-seekers, disreputable, and would not assimilate. We know now how good a citizenry they have become.

In those turbulent days the Irish were called "paddies" and "clodhoppers," and although they spoke English, their convents were destroyed in New York, Massachusetts, Maryland, Kentucky, and Alabama. Astounding to relate, entire Irish quarters in those States were pillaged and burned. We might call these outrages "Irish pogroms." Although the German immigrants were Protestants, they likewise suffered and were ostracized for their attempts to make Sunday a day of pleasure. We were mistaken then. Let us not make any more mistakes. Let us profit by our previous experience.

Q *According to Purnell, what were the dangers posed by southern and eastern European immigrants in the 1920s?*

Q *What kind of argument does Celler make to defend the immigrants whose reputation, in the 1920s, was under assault?*

Q *Celler's argument for why America's immigrant gates should remain open did not prevail in the 1920s. Can you imagine an argument that would have persuaded Congressmen inclined toward immigration restriction to change their minds?*

Sources: (top) From congressional speech by Representative Henry Purnell (Republican, Indiana), *Congressional Record* 65 (March 17, 1924) pp. 4389–4391; (bottom) From congressional speech by Representative Emanuel Celler (Democrat, New York), *Congressional Record* 65 (April 8, 1924) p. 5912.

Table 24.2 DEMOCRATIC PRESIDENTIAL VOTING IN CHICAGO BY ETHNIC GROUPS, 1924 AND 1928

	Percent Democratic	
	1924	1928
Czechoslovaks	40%	73%
Poles	35	71
Lithuanians	48	77
Yugoslavs	20	54
Italians	31	63
Germans	14	58
Jews	19	60

Source: From John M. Allswang, *A House for All Peoples: Ethnic Politics in Chicago, 1890–1936* (Lexington: University Press of Kentucky), p. 42.

milestone in the bid by European American ethnics for political power. They would achieve a second milestone at the Democratic National Convention of 1928 when, after another bitter nomination struggle, they secured the presidential nomination for Al Smith. Never before had a major political party nominated a Catholic for president. Herbert Hoover crushed Smith in the general election, as nativists stirred up anti-Catholic prejudice yet again and as large numbers of southern Democrats either stayed home or voted Republican (see Map 24.3). Even so, the campaign offered encouraging signs, not the least of which was Smith beating Hoover in the nation's 12 largest cities.

24-4b *African Americans*

Despite the urban race riots of 1919 (see Chapter 23), African Americans continued to leave their rural homes for the industrial centers of the South and the North. In the 1920s alone, nearly a million blacks traveled north. In New York City and Chicago, their numbers grew so large—300,000 in New York and 230,000 in Chicago—that they formed cities unto themselves. When word of the size and vigor of New York City's urban black enclave reached the Caribbean, thousands of West Indian blacks set off for Harlem. Complex societies emerged within these black metropolises consisting of workers, businessmen, professionals, intellectuals, artists, and entertainers. Social differentiation intensified as various groups—long-resident northerners and newly arrived southerners, religious conservatives and cultural radicals, African Americans and African Caribbeans—found reason to disapprove of one another's ways. Still, the diversity and complexity of urban black America were thrilling, nowhere more so than in Harlem, the "Negro capital." Black writer James Weldon Johnson described Harlem in the 1920s:

> Throughout colored America Harlem is the recognized Negro capital. Indeed, it is Mecca for the sightseer, the pleasure-seeker, the curious, the adventurous, the enterprising, the ambitious, and the talented of the entire Negro world... . Not merely a colony or a community or a settlement—not at all a "quarter" or a slum or a fringe—[Harlem is] ... a black city, located in the heart of white Manhattan, and containing more Negroes to the square mile than any other spot on earth. It strikes the uninformed observer as a phenomenon, a miracle straight out of the skies.

Not even the glamour of Harlem could erase the reality of racial discrimination, however. Most African Americans could find work only in New York City's least-desired and lowest-paying jobs. Because they could rent apartments only in areas that real estate agents and banks had designated as "colored," African Americans suffered the highest rate of residential segregation of any minority group. Although Harlem had its fashionable districts where affluent blacks lived, much of the area's housing stock was poor and rents were high. Harlem became a black ghetto, an area set apart from the rest of the city by the skin color of its inhabitants, its higher population density and poverty rate, its higher incidence of infectious diseases, and the lower life expectancy of its people (see Table 24.3).

Blacks did enjoy some important economic breakthroughs in the 1920s. Henry Ford, for example, hired large numbers of African Americans to work in his Detroit auto factories. Even here, however, a racist logic was operating, for Ford believed that automobile workers divided along racial lines would not challenge his authority. Until the 1940s, in fact, unions made less headway at Ford plants than at the plants of other major automobile manufacturers.

Racial divisions carried over from work to play. African Americans loved baseball as much as white Americans did, and Babe Ruth enjoyed a large black following, but black baseball players were barred from playing in the lily-white major leagues. In response, they formed their own Negro Leagues in the United States and also played professional ball in Mexico and the Caribbean, where they earned extra income and escaped some of the prejudice that trailed them everywhere in the United States.

The greatest black baseball player of the time was probably Josh Gibson, who joined the Homestead Grays of the National Negro League in 1929 at the age of 18. In his 17-year career, he compiled statistics that surpassed those of any professional ballplayer of his era, white or black, including those of the legendary Ruth. Gibson slugged 962 career home runs, hit 84 home runs in a single season, and compiled a .373 lifetime batting average. Because he died in 1947, at the age of 35, just months before the integration of major league baseball, Gibson rarely was able to test his skills against the best white ballplayers.

In the 1920s, African Americans grew pessimistic about achieving racial equality. After Marcus Garvey's black-nationalist movement collapsed in the mid-1920s (see Chapter 23), no comparable organization arose to take its place. The NAACP continued to fight racial discrimination, and the Urban League carried on quiet negotiations with industrial elites to secure jobs for African Americans. Black socialists led by A. Philip Randolph built a strong all-black

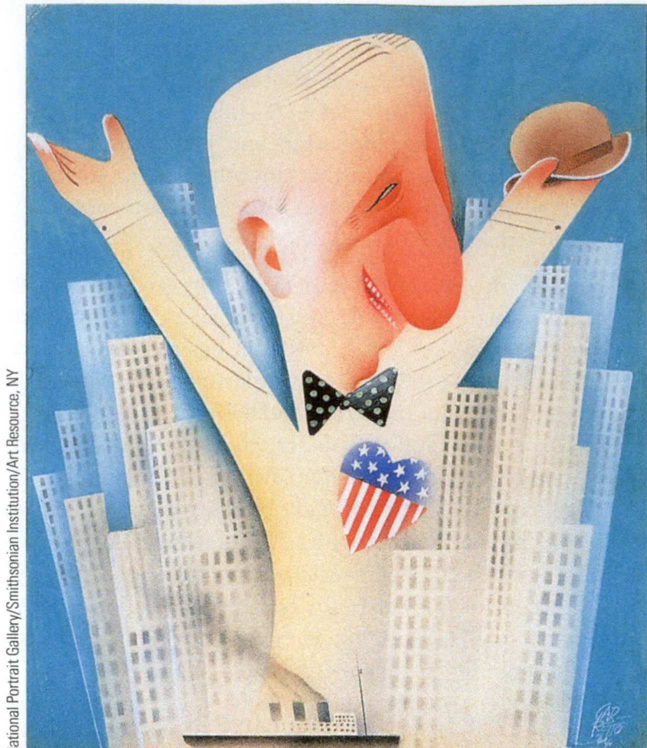

National Portrait Gallery/Smithsonian Institution/Art Resource, NY

24.15 Alfred E. Smith, New York Democrat This portrait of Al Smith, the New York–born Irish American politician who became the first Catholic to be nominated for the presidency by one of the two major parties, originally appeared in the *New Yorker* magazine in 1934. It suggests that his spirit was as buoyant and irrepressible as that of New York City, but there is a touch of sadness etched in his eyes and smile, a reflection perhaps of the defeats he had suffered, first in the 1928 presidential election and then in 1932, when the presidential nomination that he hoped would come his way again went instead to his rival (and successor as governor of New York), Franklin D. Roosevelt.

union, the Brotherhood of Sleeping Car Porters, but the victories were small and white allies were scarce. The political initiatives emerging among European American ethnics had few counterparts in the African American community.

In terms of black culture, however, the 1920s were vigorous and productive. Black musicians coming north to Chicago and New York brought with them their distinctive musical styles, most notably the blues and ragtime. Influenced by the harmonies and techniques of European classical music, which black musicians learned from European American ethnic counterparts, these southern styles metamorphosed into jazz. Urban audiences, first black and then white, found this new music alluring. They responded to its melodies, its sensuality, its creativity, its savvy. In Chicago, Detroit, New York, New Orleans, and elsewhere, jazz musicians came together in cramped apartments, cabarets, and nightclubs to jam, compete, and entertain. Willie Smith, Charles P. Johnson, Count Basie, Fats Waller, Duke Ellington, and Louis Armstrong were among the most famous musicians of the day. By the late 1920s, they were being hailed in Europe as well.

Jazz seemed to express something quintessentially modern. Jazz musicians broke free of convention: They improvised and produced new sounds that created new sensations. Both blacks and whites found in jazz an escape from the routine, the predictable, and the conventions of their everyday lives.

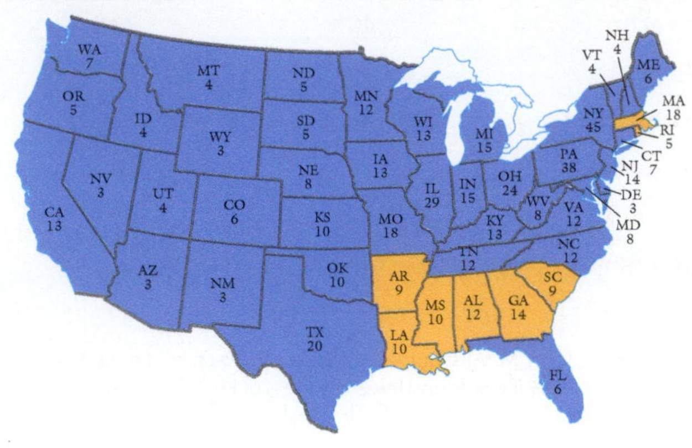

	Electoral Vote		Popular Vote	
	Number	%	Number	%
Smith (Democrat)	87	16.4	15,016,169	40.9
Hoover (Republican)	444	83.6	21,391,993	58.2

▲ **MAP 24.3 Presidential Election, 1928** This map shows Hoover's landslide victory in 1928, as he carried all but eight states and won almost 84 percent of the electoral vote.

Q *Why did Al Smith do so poorly in the South, traditionally thought to be united in its support for the Democratic Party?*

Q *What do you think accounts for his failure to win his home state of New York?*

Table 24.3 DEATH RATES FROM SELECTED CAUSES FOR NEW YORK CITY RESIDENTS, 1925

Cause of Death	Total Population	African American Population
General death rate (per 1,000 population)	11.4	16.5
Pneumonia	132.8	282.4
Pulmonary tuberculosis	75.5	258.4
Infant mortality (per 1,000 live births)	64.6	118.4
Maternal mortality (per 1,000 total births)	5.3	10.2
Stillbirths (per 1,000 births)	47.6	82.7
Homicide	5.3	19.5
Suicide	14.8	9.7

Note: Death rates are per 100,000, unless noted otherwise.
Source: Cheryl Lynn Greenberg, *"Or Does It Explode?" Black Harlem in the Great Depression* (New York: Oxford University Press, 1991), p. 32.

History Through Film The Immigrant (2013)

Directed by James Gray
Starring Marion Cotillard (Ewa Cybulska), Joaquin Phoenix (Bruno Weiss), and Jeremy Renner (Emil).

The opening shot of *The Immigrant* sets the tone for the entire movie: The Statue of Liberty looms in the background as a ship bearing immigrants arrives in New York Harbor. This is not an iconic shot of Lady Liberty, however, gazing benevolently on masses huddled in ships, or of the faces of the new arrivals etched with hope that America would become their promised land. Here we see only the back of the statue, as though Lady Liberty is utterly indifferent to the arrival of immigrants. The New World, this image tells us, is like the Old World, a cruel place all too ready to crush the hopes and aspirations of newcomers.

The year is 1921: America has yet to impose immigration restriction, but that policy is in the works and hostility to immigrants is manifest on Ellis Island, where all those entering the country through New York Harbor were to be scrutinized by doctors and government officials for disease, poverty, and low morals. Those failing one or more tests were to be quarantined for an indefinite period (if sick) or sent back to Europe on the next available boat. This is the fate that awaits two sisters, Ewa and Magda Cybulska, fleeing Poland after Cossacks killed their parents in the violence that followed the First World War. Madga is diagnosed with tuberculosis and quarantined, while Ewa (Marion Cotillard) is designated for return to Europe after fellow passengers accused her of being a woman of "low morals."

The director, James Gray, has meticulously recreated the cavernous arrivals building at Ellis Island and the long lines in which immigrants had to await their inspection. Gray casts the doctors and immigration officials not as overtly cruel, but as overworked and indifferent. They have encountered too many desperate people and heard too many humanitarian appeals to care about new ones. They do, however, accept bribes from pimps and other hustlers seeking to admit vulnerable single women who can then be coerced into prostitution and other aspects of the vice trade. This is the fate that awaits Ewa, "saved" from deportation by Bruno Weiss, a representative of the "Immigrant Aid Society." Bruno grooms the unsuspecting Ewa for prostitution; once Ewa discovers Bruno's true intent, she cannot escape, for prostitution is the only way that she can accumulate enough money to free her sister Magda from Ellis Island detention. Bruno clearly intends to make it impossible for Ewa ever to assemble adequate funds to allow either her or her sister to escape their fates.

AF archive/Alamy Stock Photo

24.16 In this dark saga, immigrant Ewa Cybulska (Marion Cotillard) struggles to free herself from pimp Bruno Weiss (Joaquin Phoenix) on the left, and his fabulist cousin, Emil (Jeremy Renner) on the right.

A virtue of the movie is the matter-of-factness with which Gray renders Bruno's world of petty crime and exploitation. Gray's recreations of the Lower East Side are finely crafted but they have none of the allure that other movies about New York City immigrants, such as *The Godfather Part II* (1974) and *Hester Street* (1975), imparted to this once legendary urban neighborhood. Gray offers his viewers no images of bustling marketplaces, or of loving families gathered on stoops, or of children playing baseball. Nowhere in his movie does he suggest that immigrants might have been invigorating New York with their youthful energy and inventiveness. Almost all of Gray's shots, exterior and interior, are bleak. The characters who populate the screen are notable for their limited horizons. They are without ambition, or their ambitions are overwhelmed by circumstance, or they are hobbled by lack of inner strength or conviction. Bruno's cousin Emil (Jeremy Renner), whose appearance in the film seems to offer Ewa a path toward salvation, is exposed as a weak-willed fabulist. Even Bruno Weiss, the would-be vice king, is ultimately rendered a pathetic figure. Ewa is the only individual who gains stature as the film unfolds, drawing strength in equal parts from her dedication to her sister and her Catholic faith. She is something of a feminist heroine, never ceasing in her efforts to find a way to free herself from men determined to prey upon her. The movie ends with another unforgettable shot of a boat in New York Harbor. Ewa and Magda have gained a second chance, however slim, of achieving freedom.

To make its points, this movie exaggerates the bleakness of the immigrant experience (for an alternative view of immigrants in 1920s America, see pp. 672–674). Nevertheless, it usefully reminds us how difficult migration from one country to another could be. And it compels us to contemplate how immigrants coped with circumstances in America that were harsh and sometimes morally compromising. ■

24-4c The Harlem Renaissance

Paralleling the emergence of jazz was a black literary and artistic awakening known as the **Harlem Renaissance**. Black novelists, poets, painters, sculptors, and playwrights set about creating works rooted in their own culture instead of imitating the styles of white Europeans and Americans. The movement had begun during the war, when blacks sensed that they might at last be advancing to full equality. It was symbolized by the image of the "New Negro," a black man or woman who would no longer be deferential to whites and who would display his or her independence through talent and determination.

Langston Hughes, a young black poet, said of the Harlem Renaissance: "We younger Negro artists who create now intend to express our individual dark-skinned selves without fear or shame. If white people are pleased, we are glad. If they are not, it doesn't matter. We know we are beautiful. And ugly, too." Writers Claude McKay, Jean Toomer, and Zora Neale Hurston; poet Countee Cullen; painter Aaron Douglas; and philosopher and cultural critic Alain Locke were other prominent Renaissance participants. The appearance in 1925 of a special issue of *Survey Graphic,* a white liberal magazine, devoted entirely to "Harlem—the Mecca of the New Negro," announced the Renaissance's arrival.

Even these cultural advances, however, failed to escape white prejudice. The most popular jazz nightclubs in Harlem, most of which were owned and operated by whites, often refused to admit black customers; only African American jazz musicians, singers and dancers, prostitutes, and kitchen help were permitted inside. Moreover, the black musicians often had to perform what the white patrons wanted to hear. Some black entertainers, such as Josephine Baker, the legendary dancer, left America for Europe in the 1920s, in the hope that they would find in Paris and elsewhere the artistic and personal freedom denied them in the land of their birth.

Black writers experienced similar pressures. Many depended for their sustenance on the support of white patrons, who often wanted a return on their investment. Charlotte Mason, the New York City matron who supported Hughes and Hurston, for example, expected them to entertain her friends by demonstrating "authentic Negritude" in their work. Hurston accepted this role, but for Hughes it became unbearable. Both Hughes and Hurston paid a price for their patron's support, including the collapse of their once-close friendship with each other.

24-4d Mexican Americans

After the Johnson–Reed Act passed Congress in 1924, Mexicans became the country's chief source of immigrant labor. A total of 500,000 Mexicans came to the United States in the 1920s. Some headed for the steel, auto, and meatpacking plants of the Midwest, but most settled in the Southwest, where they worked on railroads and in construction, agriculture, and manufacturing (see Map 24.4). In Texas,

24.17 **"Into Bondage"** In this modernist painting, Aaron Douglas, a leading figure in the arts movement known as Harlem Renaissance, conveys both the pride and pain of Africans being sold into slavery and marched to a slave ship that would deliver them to New World plantations.

three of four construction workers and eight of every ten migrant farmworkers were Mexicans. In California, Mexican immigrants made up 75 percent of the state's agricultural workforce.

Mexican farm laborers in Texas worked long hours for little money. As a rule, they earned 50 cents to a dollar less per day than Anglo workers. Forced to follow the crops, they had little opportunity to develop settled homes and communities. They depended for shelter on whatever facilities farm owners offered. Because farm owners rarely required the services of Mexican workers for more than several days or weeks, few were willing to spend the money required to provide decent homes and schools. Houses typically lacked even wooden floors or indoor plumbing. Mexican laborers found it difficult to protest these conditions. Their knowledge of English was limited. Many were in debt to employers who had advanced them money and who threatened them with jail if they failed to fulfill the terms of their contract. Others feared deportation; they lacked visas, having slipped into the United States illegally rather than pay the immigrant tax or endure harassment from the Border Patrol.

Increasing numbers of Mexican immigrants found their way to California, where, on the whole, wages exceeded those in Texas. Some men escaped agricultural labor altogether for construction and manufacturing jobs. Others worked in the city's large railroad yards, at the city's numerous construction sites, and as unskilled workers in local factories. Mexican women labored in the city's garment shops, fish canneries, and food-processing plants. By 1930, Los Angeles had become the largest area of settlement for Mexicans in the United States.

By the mid-1920s, the Los Angeles Mexican American community included a sizable professional class, a proud group of ***Californios*** (Spanish speakers who had been resident in California for generations), many musicians and entertainers, a small but energetic band of entrepreneurs and businessmen, conservative priests and intellectuals who had fled or been expelled from revolutionary Mexico, and Mexican government officials who had been sent to counter the influence of the conservative exiles and to strengthen the ties of the immigrants to their homeland. This diverse mix created much internal conflict, but it also generated considerable cultural vitality. Los Angeles became a magnet for Mexican Americans similar to what Harlem had become for African Americans.

Mexican musicians flocked to Los Angeles, as did Mexican playwrights. The city supported a vigorous Spanish-language theater. Mexican musicians performed on street corners, at ethnic festivals and weddings, at cabarets, and on the radio. Especially popular were folk ballads, called *corridos*, that spoke to the experiences of Mexican immigrants. Although different in form and melody from the African American blues, *corridos* resembled the blues in their emphasis on the suffering, hope, and frustrations of ordinary people.

This flowering of Mexican American culture in Los Angeles could not erase the low wages, high rates of infant mortality, racial discrimination, and other hardships Mexicans faced; nor did it encourage Mexicans, in Los Angeles or elsewhere, to mobilize as a political force. Unlike European immigrants, Mexican immigrants showed little interest in becoming American citizens and acquiring the vote. Yet, the cultural vibrancy of the Mexican immigrant community did sustain many individuals who were struggling to survive in a strange, often hostile, environment.

24-5 The "Lost Generation" and Disillusioned Intellectuals

Q *To whom did the phrase "Lost Generation" refer, and what caused these individuals to become disillusioned?*

Before the First World War, American intellectuals and artists had been deeply engaged with "the people." Although they were critical of many aspects of American society, they believed they could help bring about a new politics and improve social conditions. The war, however, shook their confidence in Americans' capacity for reform. The wartime push for consensus generated intolerance of radicals, immigrants, and blacks. Intellectuals had been further dismayed by Prohibition, the rebirth of the Ku Klux Klan, the rise of fundamentalism, and the execution of Sacco and Vanzetti. To many it seemed as though ordinary middle-class Americans had embraced conformity for themselves and now sought to impose it on others. In 1921, the young critic Harold Stearns wrote that "the most moving and pathetic fact in the social life of America today is emotional and aesthetic starvation." Before these words were published, Stearns had sailed for France. So many alienated young men like Stearns showed up in Paris that Gertrude Stein, an American writer whose Paris apartment became a gathering place for them, took to calling them the **"Lost Generation."**

Their indictment of America was harsh. Most of these white writers possessed little knowledge of how most Americans lived. Still, they managed to convert their disillusionment into a rich literary sensibility. The finest works of the decade focused on the psychological toll of living in what the poet T. S. Eliot referred to as *The Waste Land* (1922). F. Scott Fitzgerald's novel *The Great Gatsby* (1925) told of a man destroyed by his desire to be accepted into a world of wealth, fancy cars, and fast women. In the novel *A Farewell to Arms* (1929), Ernest Hemingway wrote of an American soldier overwhelmed by the senselessness and brutality of war who deserts the army for the company of a woman he loves. Playwright Eugene O'Neill created characters haunted by despair, loneliness, and unfulfilled longing. Writers innovated in style as well as in content. Sherwood Anderson, in his novel *Winesburg, Ohio* (1919), blended fiction and autobiography. John Dos Passos, in *Manhattan Transfer* (1925), mixed journalism with more traditional literary methods. Hemingway wrote in an understated, laconic prose that somehow drew attention to his characters' rage and vulnerability.

White southern writers found a tragic sensibility surviving from the South's defeat in the Civil War that spoke to their own loss of hope. One group of such writers, calling themselves the Agrarians, argued that the enduring agricultural character of their region offered a more hopeful path to the future than did the mass-production and mass-consumption regime that had overtaken the North. In 1929, William Faulkner published *The Sound and the Fury,* the first in a series of novels set in northern Mississippi's fictional Yoknapatawpha County. Faulkner explored the violence and terror that marked relationships among family members and townspeople, while maintaining compassion and understanding. Faulkner, Lewis, Hemingway, O'Neill, and Eliot would each receive the Nobel Prize for Literature.

24-5a *Democracy on the Defensive*

Disdain for the masses led many intellectuals to question democracy. Although few intellectuals were as frank as Mencken, who dismissed democracy as "the worship of jackals by jackasses," their distrust of democracy ran deep. Walter Lippmann, a former radical and progressive, declared that modern society had rendered democracy obsolete. In his view, average citizens, buffeted by propaganda emanating from powerful opinion makers, could no longer make the kind of informed, rational judgments needed to make democracy work. They were vulnerable to demagogues who played on their emotions and fears. Lippmann's solution, and that of many other political commentators, was to shift government power from the people to educated elites. Those elites, who would be appointed rather than elected, would conduct foreign and domestic policy in an informed, intelligent way. Only then, in Lippmann's view, could government be effective and just.

Mencken's and Lippmann's antidemocratic views did not go uncontested. The philosopher **John Dewey**, who taught at Columbia University but whose reputation and influence extended well beyond academia, was the most articulate spokesman for the "pro-democracy" position. He acknowledged that the concentration of power in giant organizations had eroded the authority of Congress, the presidency, and other

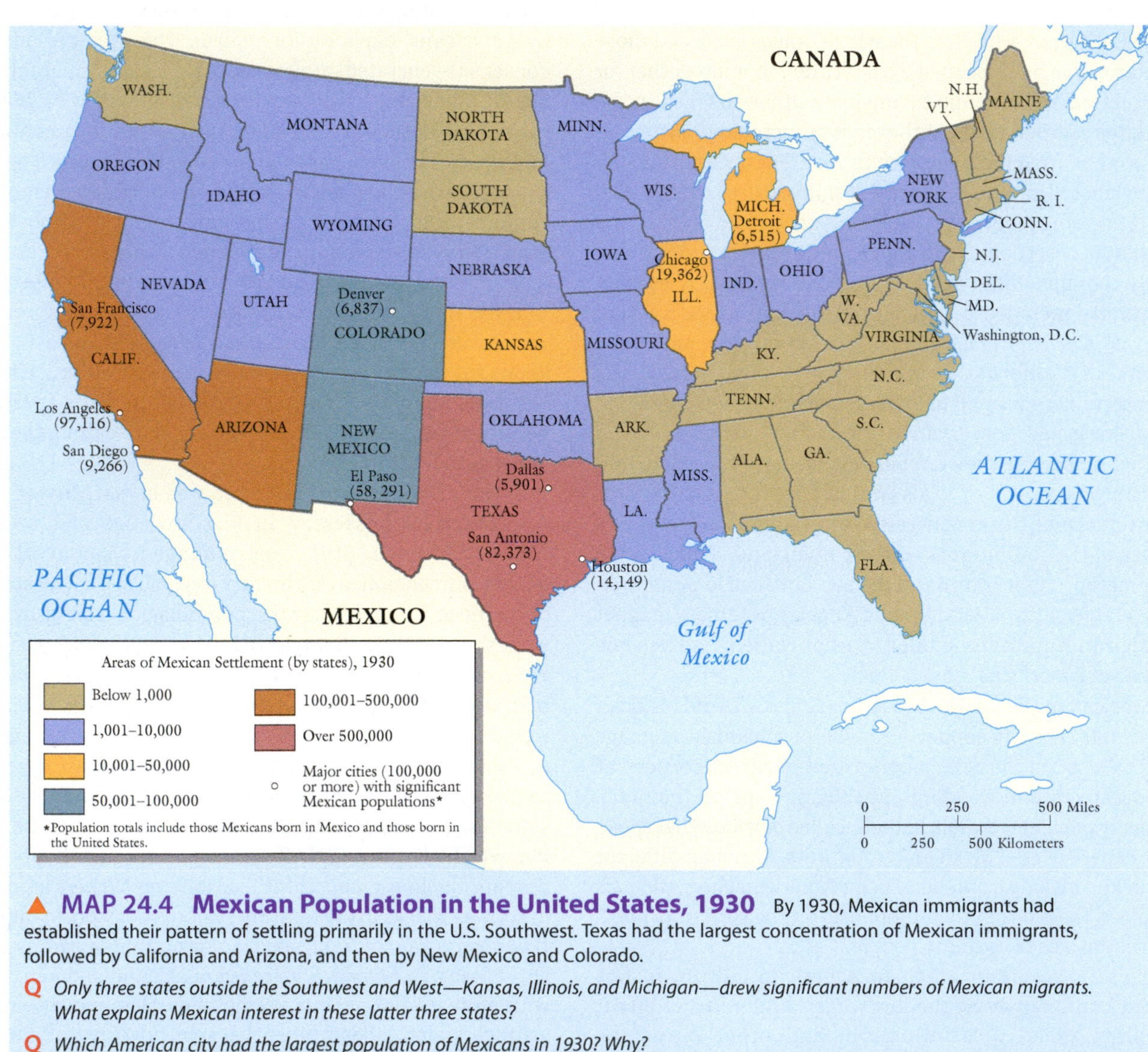

▲ **MAP 24.4 Mexican Population in the United States, 1930** By 1930, Mexican immigrants had established their pattern of settling primarily in the U.S. Southwest. Texas had the largest concentration of Mexican immigrants, followed by California and Arizona, and then by New Mexico and Colorado.

Q *Only three states outside the Southwest and West—Kansas, Illinois, and Michigan—drew significant numbers of Mexican migrants. What explains Mexican interest in these latter three states?*

Q *Which American city had the largest population of Mexicans in 1930? Why?*

24.18 **Mexican-American Women Workers, 1920s** These women were employed in a newspaper recycling facility in Los Angeles. The used paper was being prepared for shipment to China where the ink would be extracted and the paper reused for packaging.

Q *In what other California industries did Mexican women work?*

democratic institutions, but democracy, he insisted, was not doomed. Government could use its power to democratize corporations and regulate the communications industry to ensure that every citizen had access to the facts needed to make reasonable, informed political decisions.

Dewey's views attracted the support of a wide range of liberal intellectuals and reformers, including Robert and Helen Lynd; Rexford Tugwell, professor of economics at Columbia; and Felix Frankfurter, a rising star at Harvard's law school. Some of these activists had ties to labor leaders and to New York governor Franklin D. Roosevelt. They formed the vanguard of a new liberal movement committed to taking up the work the progressives had left unfinished.

These reformers had little influence in the 1920s, however. Moreover, Hoover's smashing victory in 1928 suggested that the trends of the 1920s—the dominance of the Republicans, the centrality of Prohibition to political debate, the paralysis of the Democrats, the growing economic might of capitalism, and the pervasive influence of consumer culture—would continue unabated.

Conclusion

Signs abounded in the 1920s that Americans were creating a new and bountiful society. The increased accessibility of cars, radios, vacuum cleaners, and other consumer durables; rising real wages, low unemployment, and installment buying; the widening circle of stock owners; the spread of welfare capitalism—all of these developments pointed to an economy that had become more prosperous, more consumer oriented, even somewhat more egalitarian. Moves to greater equality within marriage and to enhanced liberty for single women suggested that economic change was propelling social change as well.

Even so, many working-class and rural Americans benefited little from the decade's prosperity. Moreover, the decade's social changes aroused resistance, especially from white farmers and small-town Americans, who feared that the rapid growth of cities and the large urban settlements of European and Mexican Catholics, Jews, and African Americans were rendering their white Protestant America unrecognizable.

In the Democratic Party, farmers, small-town Americans, and moral traditionalists fought bitterly against the growing power of urban, ethnic constituencies. Elsewhere, the traditionalists battled hard to protect religion's authority against the inroads of science and to purge the nation of "inferior" population streams. In the process they arrayed themselves against American traditions of liberty and equality, even as they posed as the defenders of the best that America had to offer.

Their resistance to change caused many of the nation's most talented artists and writers to turn away from their fellow Americans. Meanwhile, although ethnic and racial minorities experienced high levels of discrimination, they nevertheless found enough freedom to create vibrant ethnic and racial communities and to launch projects—as in the case of African Americans in Harlem and Mexican Americans in Los Angeles—of cultural renaissance.

The Republican Party, having largely shed its reputation for reform, took credit for engineering the new economy of consumer plenty. It looked forward to years of political dominance. A steep and unexpected economic depression, however, would soon dash that expectation, revive the Democratic Party, and destroy Republican political power for a generation.

CHAPTER REVIEW

Review

1. What were the achievements and limitations of "people's capitalism" in the 1920s?
2. What were the similarities and differences in the politics of Harding, Coolidge, and Hoover?
3. What concerned farmers and conservative white Protestants in the 1920s, and what policies did they support?
4. How were the experiences of ethnic and racial groups in 1920s America similar and how were they different?
5. To whom did the phrase "Lost Generation" refer, and what caused these individuals to become disillusioned?

Critical Thinking

1. Can the deep cultural differences that divided Americans in the 1920s best be explained by where people lived (country versus city), where they were born (in the United States or abroad), their race (white or not), their class, or something else?
2. A great depression was the farthest thing from Americans' minds in the 1920s. Reviewing carefully what you have learned about the economy in these years, can you locate areas of economic trouble that contemporaries may have overlooked?

Identifications

Review your understanding of the following key terms, people, and events for this chapter (terms in bold in text are included in the Glossary).

Ku Klux Klan, p. 654
"people's capitalism," p. 655
flappers, p. 657
Charles A. Lindbergh, p. 658
Sheppard-Towner Act, p. 662
League of Women Voters (LWV), p. 662
Prohibition, p. 662
Teapot Dome, p. 663
"associationalism," p. 664
Dawes Plan, p. 665
Johnson–Reed Immigration Restriction Act of 1924, p. 669
fundamentalists, p. 671
liberal Protestants, p. 671
Alfred E. Smith, p. 673
Harlem Renaissance, p. 678
Californios, p. 679
"Lost Generation," p. 679
John Dewey, p. 680

Suggested Readings

William Leuchtenberg, ***The Perils of Prosperity, 1914–1932*** (1958); and **Ellis Hawley,** ***The Great War and the Search for a Modern Order: A History of the American People and Their Institutions, 1917–1933*** (1979), offer useful overviews of the 1920s. Important works on consumer culture include **Roland Marchand,** ***Advertising the American Dream: Making Way for Modernity, 1920–1940*** (1985); and **Kathy Lee Peiss,** ***Hope in a Jar: The Making of America's Beauty Culture*** (1998). For a penetrating look at U.S. imperialism in the Caribbean in the 1920s, see **Mary A. Renda,** ***Taking Haiti: Military Occupation and the Culture of U.S. Imperialism*** (2001). For a revisionist view of the Kellogg-Briande Pact, see **Oona A. Hathaway and Scott J. Shapiro,** ***The Internationalists: How a Radical Plan to Outlaw War Remade the World*** (2017).

On agricultural distress and protest, see **Theodore Saloutos and John D. Hicks,** ***Twentieth Century Populism: Agricultural Discontent in the Middle West, 1900–1939*** (1951). For an examination of the economic and social effects of Prohibition, see **Lisa McGirr,** ***The War on Alcohol: Prohibition and the Rise of the American State*** (2015). The best treatment of the Scopes trial can be found in **Michael Kazin,** ***A Godly Hero: The Life of William Jennings Bryan*** (2006). **John Higham,** ***Strangers in the Land: Patterns of American Nativism, 1865–1925*** (1955); and **Mae Ngai,** ***Impossible Subjects: Illegal Aliens and the Making of Modern America*** (2004), are excellent works on the spirit of intolerance that gripped America in the 1920s. For new work on KKK, see **Linda Gordon,** ***The Second Coming of the KKK: The Ku Klux Klan of the 1920s and the American Political Tradition*** (2017). On the emergence of liberal Protestantism, see **David A. Hollinger,** ***After Cloven Tongues of Fire: Protestant Liberalism in Modern American History*** (2013).

On ethnic communities, Americanization, and political mobilization in the 1920s, see **Gary Gerstle,** ***Working-Class Americanism: The Politics of Labor in a Textile City, 1914–1960*** (1989); and **George J. Sánchez,** ***Becoming Mexican American: Ethnicity, Culture and Identity in Chicano Los Angeles, 1900–1945*** (1993). On the Harlem Renaissance, see **Nathan Huggins,** ***Harlem Renaissance*** (1971); and **Jeffrey C. Stewart,** ***The New Negro: The Life of Alain Locke*** (2018). **Malcolm Cowley,** ***Exiles Return*** (1934), is a marvelous account of the writers and artists who comprised the "Lost Generation." For a provocative interpretation of the intertwined character of white and black literary cultures in 1920s New York, see **Ann Douglas,** ***Terrible Honesty: Mongrel Manhattan in the 1920s*** (1995).

MINDTAP is a fully online personalized learning experience built upon Cengage Learning content. MindTap® combines student learning tools—readings, multimedia, activities, and assessments—into a singular Learning Path that guides students through the course and helps students develop the critical thinking, analysis, and communication skills that are essential to academic and professional success.

25 The Great Depression and the New Deal, 1929–1939

Marmaduke St. John/Alamy stock photo

25.1 **Humbling America's Manufacturing Might**
This Diego Rivera 1933 fresco, painted on the South Wall of the Detroit Institute of Art, portrays automobile workers in Henry Ford's River Rouge plant in Dearborn, Michigan, then considered one of the largest and best integrated production facilities in the world. Contemporary viewers of this fresco may have wondered how it was that manufacturing plants of such ambition and ingenuity could have been humbled for so long by the America's Great Depression.

THE GREAT DEPRESSION began on Tuesday, October 29, 1929, with a spectacular stock market crash. On that one day, stock values plummeted $14 billion. By the end of that year, stock prices had fallen 50 percent from their September highs. By 1932, the worst year of the Depression, they had fallen another 30 percent. In three years, $74 billion of wealth had simply vanished. Meanwhile, the unemployment rate had soared to 25 percent.

Many Americans who lived through the Great Depression could never forget the scenes of misery they saw everywhere. In cities, the poor meekly awaited their turn for a piece of stale bread and thin gruel at charity soup kitchens. Scavengers poked through garbage cans for food, scoured railroad tracks for coal that had fallen from trains, and sometimes ripped up railroad ties for fuel. Hundreds of thousands of Americans built makeshift shelters out of cardboard, scrap metal, and whatever else they could find in the city dump. They called their towns "Hoovervilles," after the president they despised for his apparent refusal to help them.

The Great Depression brought cultural crisis as well as economic crisis. In the 1920s, American business leaders had successfully redefined the national culture in business terms, as Americans' values became synonymous with those that entrepreneurs espoused: economic growth, freedom of enterprise, and acquisitiveness.

But the swagger of American businessmen during the 1920s made them vulnerable to attack in the 1930s, as jobs, incomes, and growth all disappeared. With the prestige of business and business values in decline, how would Americans regain their hope and recover their confidence in the future? The first years of the 1930s held no convincing answers.

The gloom broke in early 1933 when **Franklin Delano Roosevelt** became president and unleashed the power of government to regulate capitalist enterprises, to restore the economy to health, and to guarantee social welfare for Americans unable to help themselves. Roosevelt called his pro-government program a "new deal for the American people," and it would dominate national politics for the next 40 years. Hailed as a hero, Roosevelt became (and remains) the only president to be elected more than two times. In the short term, the New Deal failed to restore prosperity to America, but the **liberalism** it championed found acceptance among millions who agreed with Roosevelt that only a large and powerful government could guarantee Americans their liberty. ■

25-1 Causes of the Great Depression

What caused the crash of 1929, and why did the ensuing depression last so long?

America had experienced other depressions, or "panics," and no one would have been surprised if the boom of the 1920s had been followed by a one- or two-year economic downturn. No one was prepared, however, for the economic catastrophe of the 1930s.

25-1a *Stock Market Speculation*

In 1928 and 1929, stock values had doubled. Money had poured into the market, but many investors were buying on 10 percent "margin," putting up only 10 percent of the price of a stock and borrowing the rest from brokers or banks. Few thought they would ever have to repay these loans with money out of their own pockets. Instead, investors expected to resell their shares within a few months at dramatically higher prices, pay back their loans from the proceeds, and still clear a handsome profit. And, for a while, that is exactly what they did.

The possibility of making a fortune by investing a few thousand dollars only intensified investors' greed. As speculation became rampant, money flowed indiscriminately into all kinds of risky enterprises. The stock market spiraled upward, out of control. When, in October 1929, confidence in future earnings faltered, creditors began demanding that investors who had bought stocks on margin repay their loans. The market crashed from its dizzying heights.

The crash by itself fails to explain why the Great Depression lasted as long as it did. Poor decision making by the Federal Reserve Board, an ill-advised tariff that took effect soon after the Depression hit, and excessive concentration of wealth in the hands of the rich deepened the economic collapse and made recovery more difficult.

25-1b *Mistakes by the Federal Reserve Board*

In 1930 and 1931, the Federal Reserve curtailed the amount of money in circulation and raised interest rates, thereby making credit more difficult for the public to secure. Employing a

CHRONOLOGY

1929	Herbert Hoover assumes the presidency • Stock market crashes on "Black Tuesday"
1930	Tariff Act (Hawley–Smoot) raises tariffs
1931	More than 2,000 U.S. banks fail
1932	Unemployment rate reaches 25 percent • Reconstruction Finance Corporation established • Bonus Army marches on Washington • Roosevelt defeats Hoover for presidency
1933	Roosevelt assumes presidency • Hundred Days legislation defines First New Deal (March–June) • Roosevelt administration recognizes the Soviet Union • Good Neighbor Policy toward Latin America launched
1934	Father Charles Coughlin and Huey Long challenge conservatism of First New Deal • Two thousand strikes occur across country • Democrats overwhelm Republicans in off-year election • Radical political movements emerge in several states • Indian Reorganization Act grants limited right of self-government to American Indians • Reciprocal Trade Agreement lowers tariffs
1935	Committee for Industrial Organization (CIO) formed • Supreme Court declares National Recovery Administration (NRA) unconstitutional • Roosevelt unveils his Second New Deal • Congress passes Social Security Act and National Labor Relations Act (Wagner Act) • Holding Company Act breaks up utilities' near-monopoly • Congress passes Wealth Tax Act • Works Progress Administration established • Rural Electrification Administration launched • Number of Mexican immigrants returning to Mexico reaches 500,000
1936	Roosevelt defeats Alf Landon for second term • Supreme Court declares Agricultural Adjustment Act (AAA) unconstitutional • Congress passes Soil Conservation and Domestic Allotment Act to replace AAA • Farm Security Administration established
1937	United Auto Workers defeats General Motors in sit-down strike • Roosevelt attempts to "pack" the Supreme Court • Supreme Court upholds constitutionality of Social Security Act and National Labor Relations Act • Severe recession hits
1938	Conservative opponents of New Deal do well in off-year election • Superman comic debuts
1939	Crowd of 75,000 gathers to hear Marian Anderson sing at Lincoln Memorial

tight money policy during the boom years of 1928 and 1929 might have restrained the stock market while ensuring that economic growth rested on a solid foundation. Deploying such a policy once the market had crashed was a disastrous decision. What the economy needed in 1930 and 1931 was an expanded money supply, lower interest rates, and easier credit. Such a course would have made it easier for debtors to pay their creditors. Instead, by choosing the opposite course, the Federal Reserve plunged an economy starved for credit deeper into depression. Higher interest rates also triggered an international crisis, as the banks of Germany and Austria, heavily dependent on U.S. loans, went bankrupt. The German-Austrian collapse, in turn, spread financial panic throughout Europe and hurt U.S. manufacturers and banks specializing in European trade and investment.

25-1c *An Ill-Advised Tariff*

The Tariff Act of 1930, also known as the Hawley–Smoot Tariff Act, accelerated economic decline abroad and at home. Throughout the 1920s, agricultural interests had sought higher tariffs to protect American farmers against foreign competition. But Hawley–Smoot not only raised tariffs on 75 agricultural goods from 32 to 40 percent (the highest rate in American history), it also raised tariffs by a similar percentage on 925 manufactured products. Angry foreign governments retaliated by raising their own tariff rates to keep out American goods. International trade, already weakened by the tight credit policies of the Federal Reserve, declined even further.

25-1d *A Maldistribution of Wealth*

A maldistribution in the nation's wealth that had developed in the 1920s also stymied economic recovery. Although average income rose in the 1920s, the incomes of the wealthiest families rose higher than the rest. Between 1918 and 1929, the share of the national income that went to the wealthiest 20 percent of the population rose by more than 10 percent, while the share that went to the poorest 60 percent fell by almost 13 percent (see Figure 25.1). The Coolidge administration contributed to this maldistribution by lowering taxes on the wealthy, thereby allowing a higher proportion of national wealth to remain in their hands. The deepening inequality of income distribution slowed consumption and held back the growth of consumer-oriented industries (cars, household appliances, processed and packaged foods, recreation), the most dynamic elements of the U.S. economy. Even when the rich spent their money lavishly—building huge mansions, buying expensive cars, vacationing on the French Riviera—they still spent a smaller proportion of their total incomes on consumption than wage earners did. The average 1920s wage earner, for example, might spend one-quarter to one-half of his annual earnings to buy a car.

Putting more of the total increase in national income into the pockets of average Americans during the 1920s would have strengthened the newer consumer industries. Such an economy might have recovered relatively quickly from the stock market crash of 1929. Instead, recovery from the Great Depression lagged until 1941, more than a decade later.

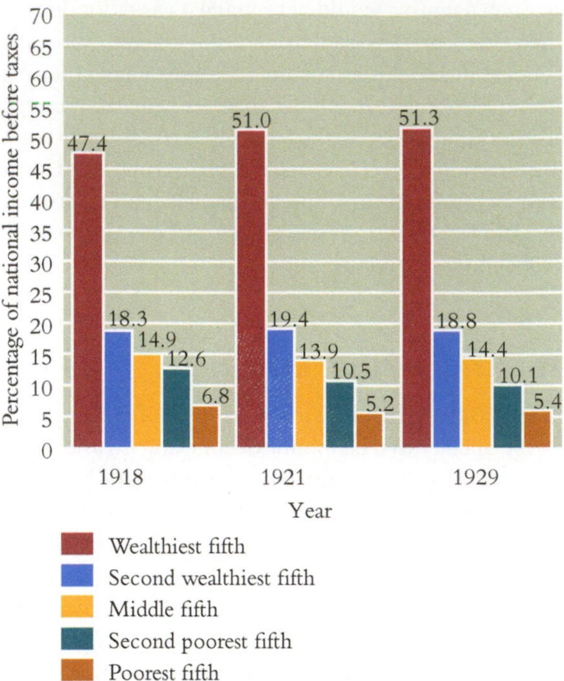

Figure 25.1 **Income Distribution before the Great Depression**

Source: From Gabriel Kolko, *Wealth and Power in America: An Analysis of Social Class and Income Distribution* (New York: Praeger, 1962), p. 14.

25.2 **Unemployed Men in New York City, 1931** The thousands of men waiting to register at the Emergency Unemployment Relief office became so frustrated that they rioted. Police reserves arrived to restore order.

25-2 Crisis and Hope, 1929–1933

Q *Why did Herbert Hoover become a reviled political figure? How did political pessimism influence American culture? What transformed Franklin Roosevelt into a focused politician and reformer?*

The magnitude of the economic collapse overwhelmed the newly elected Republican president, Herbert Hoover. Cultural gloom settled on the country as the Depression stretched into its third year.

25-2a *The Fall of a Self-Made Man*

In 1928, Herbert Hoover seemed to embody the American dream. From modest beginnings, Hoover had parlayed his intelligence and drive into gaining admission to Stanford University, becoming a mining engineer, and then rising rapidly to top management positions in globe-spanning mining companies. A talented and tireless administrator, Hoover won an international reputation in the First World War for his success, as head of the U.S. Food Administration, in feeding millions of European soldiers and civilians. Then, in the 1920s, he became an active and influential secretary of commerce (see Chapters 23 and 24). As the decade wound down, no American seemed better qualified to become president of the United States, an office that Hoover assumed in March 1929. Hoover was certain he could make prosperity a permanent feature of American life. "We in America today are nearer to the final triumph over poverty than ever before in the history of any land," he declared in August 1928. A little more than a year later, the Great Depression struck.

To cope with the crisis, Hoover encouraged organizations of farmers, industrialists, and bankers to share information, bolster one another's spirits, and devise policies to aid economic recovery. He urged farmers to restrict output, industrialists to hold wages at predepression levels, and bankers to help each other remain solvent. The federal government would provide them with information, strategies of mutual aid, occasional loans, and morale-boosting speeches.

Hoover also secured a one-year moratorium on loan payments that European governments owed American banks. He steered through Congress the Glass–Steagall Act of 1932, which was intended to help American banks meet the demands of European depositors who wished to convert their dollars to gold. And to ease the crisis at home, he created the Reconstruction Finance Corporation (RFC) to make $2 billion available in loans to ailing banks and to corporations willing to build low-cost housing, bridges, and other public works. The RFC was the biggest federal peacetime intervention in the economy up to that point in American history. The Home Loan Bank Board, set up that same year, offered funds to savings and loans, mortgage companies, and other financial institutions that lent money for home construction and mortgages.

Despite this new government activism, Hoover was uncomfortable with the idea of high levels of government spending. When 1932 RFC expenditures created the largest peacetime deficit in U.S. history, Hoover tried to balance the federal budget. He also insisted that the RFC issue loans only to relatively healthy institutions that were capable of repaying them and that it favor public works, such as toll bridges, that were likely to become self-financing. Hoover was especially reluctant to engage the government in providing relief to unemployed and homeless Americans. To give money to the poor, he insisted, would destroy their desire to work and undermine their sense of self-worth.

Hoover saw no similar peril in extending government assistance to ailing banks and businesses. Critics pointed to the seeming hypocrisy of Hoover's policies. For example, in 1930, Hoover refused a request of $25 million to help feed Arkansas farmers and their families but approved $45 million to feed the same farmers' livestock. In 1932, shortly after rejecting an urgent request from the city of Chicago for aid to help pay its teachers and municipal workers, Hoover approved a $90 million loan to rescue that city's Central Republic Bank.

In spring 1932, a group of army veterans mounted a particularly emotional challenge to Hoover's policies. In 1924, Congress had authorized a $1,000 bonus for First World War veterans in the form of compensation certificates that would mature in 1945. Impoverished veterans were now demanding immediate payment. A group of Portland, Oregon, veterans, calling themselves the Bonus Expeditionary Force, hopped onto empty boxcars of freight trains heading east. As this "army" moved, its ranks multiplied, so that by the time it reached Washington its numbers had swelled to 20,000, including wives and children. The so-called **Bonus Army** set up camp in the Anacostia Flats, southeast of the Capitol, and petitioned Congress for early payment of the bonus. The House of Representatives agreed, but the Senate turned them down. Hoover refused to meet with the veterans. In July, federal troops led by Army Chief of Staff Douglas MacArthur and Third Cavalry Commander George Patton entered the veterans' Anacostia encampment, set the tents and shacks ablaze, and dispersed the protestors. In the process, more than 100 veterans were wounded and one infant died.

News that veterans and their families had been attacked in the nation's capital served only to harden anti-Hoover opinion. In the 1932 elections, the Republicans were voted out of office after having dominated national politics (excepting Woodrow Wilson's two terms) for 36 years. Hoover received only 39.6 percent of the popular vote and just 59 (of 531) electoral votes (see Map 25.1). He left the presidency in 1933 a bewildered man, reviled by Americans for his seeming indifference to suffering and his ineptitude in dealing with the crisis.

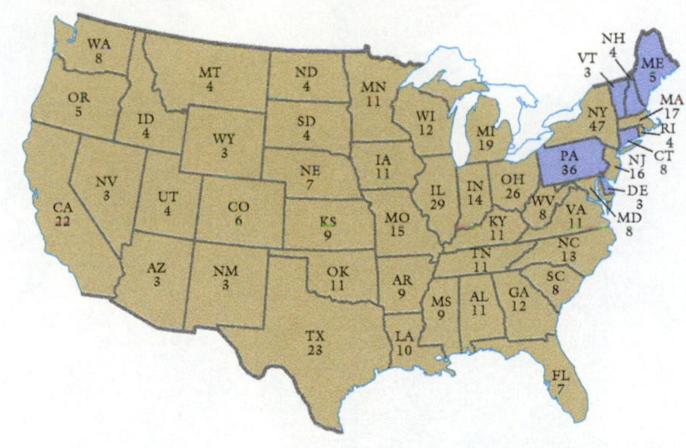

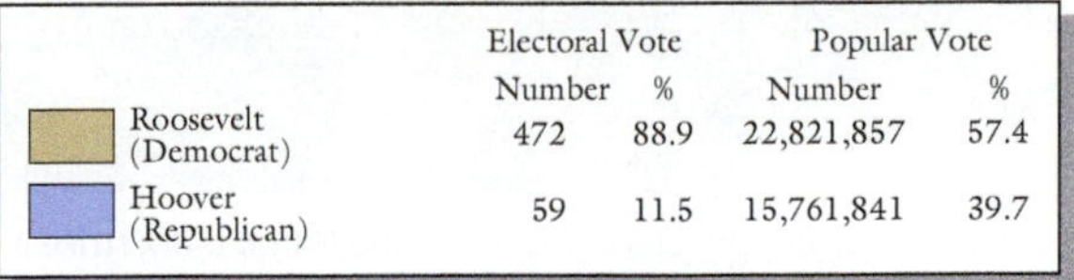

	Electoral Vote		Popular Vote	
	Number	%	Number	%
Roosevelt (Democrat)	472	88.9	22,821,857	57.4
Hoover (Republican)	59	11.5	15,761,841	39.7

▲ **MAP 25.1 Presidential Election, 1932** In 1928, Hoover had won 444 electoral votes and carried forty states (see Map 24.3, p. 676). In 1932, by contrast, he won only 59 electoral votes and carried only six states—Delaware, Pennsylvania, Connecticut, Vermont, New Hampshire, and Maine. His Democratic opponent, Franklin D. Roosevelt, was the big winner.

Q *What caused such a massive shift in the electorate?*

Q *Why was the Northeast the only region of the country to continue to show support for Hoover?*

25-2b *Cultural Distress*

The economic crisis of the early 1930s expressed itself not just in politics but also in the literature and cinema of the time. The journalist and literary critic Edmund Wilson found mostly economic misery and spiritual depression during his journey across America. A sense of aimlessness characterized one of the major literary works of the early 1930s, the Studs Lonigan trilogy (1932–1935) written by the Chicago-born writer James T. Farrell. Farrell's scrappy Irish American protagonist, Studs, lacks focus and is repeatedly overcome by the harshness of his environment. He dies poor and alone, not yet 30. Meanwhile, the popular writer Nathaniel West was publishing *Miss Lonelyhearts* (1933) and *A Cool Million* (1934), novels similarly built around central characters succumbing to failure, drift, even insanity.

One can detect parallel themes of despair in the period's cinema, especially in movies such as the Academy Award Winner *I Am a Fugitive from a Chain Gang* (1932), in which an industrious and honorable man, James Allen, is unfairly sentenced to 10 years on a Georgia chain gang. Allen escapes his penitentiary but is condemned to being a man on the run, unable to prove his innocence, earn a decent living, or build enduring relationships. Less grim but still sobering were the gangster movies of the early 1930s, especially *Little Caesar* (1930) and *The Public Enemy* (1931), which told stories of hard-nosed and violent men who became wealthy and influential by living outside the law and bending people to their will.

Lawlessness also surfaced in the wild comedy of Groucho, Chico, Harpo, and Zeppo Marx, vaudevillians who, in the 1920s and 1930s, made the transition to the silver screen. The Marx Brothers ridiculed figures of authority, broke every rule of etiquette, smacked around their antagonists (and each other), and deliberately and delightfully mangled the English language. Anarchy ruled their world. While hilarious to watch, Marx Brothers movies sometimes carried serious political messages. *Duck Soup* (1933) made fun of the fictional nation of Fredonia, where leaders were pompous, the legal system a fraud, and clueless citizens easily misled. In this 90-minute movie, the Marx Brothers emptied politics of all meaning and honesty. This cinematic sentiment paralleled the conviction held by many Americans in 1932 and early 1933 that their own politicians had failed them in a time of need.

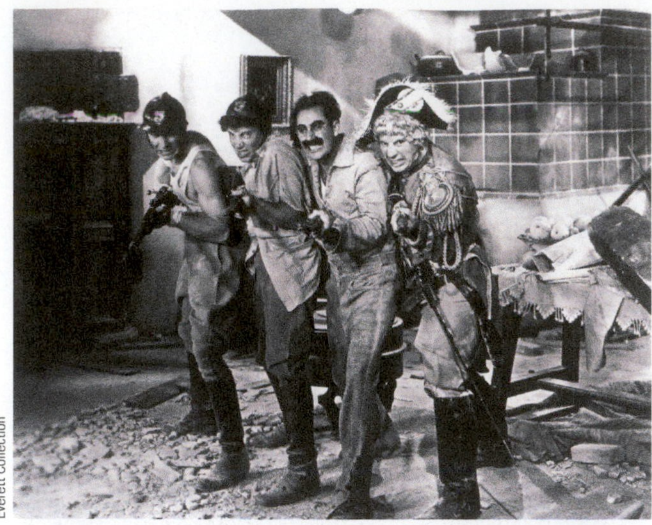
Everett Collection

25.3 **Duck Soup** Zeppo, Chico, Groucho, and Harpo Marx strike a comic pose for the camera during the movie's final, and satirical, war scenes. Though filled with laughs, the movie delivered the dispiriting early 1930s message that politics lacked purpose.

Q *Did audiences grasp the political commentary imbedded in movies such as* Duck Soup*? Or were they simply drawn to the Marx Brothers by the diverting nature of their comedy?*

25-2c *A Democratic Roosevelt*

Franklin D. Roosevelt was born in 1882 into a patrician family descended, on his father's side, from Dutch gentry in New York. By the 1880s, the Hyde Park manor where Roosevelt grew up had been in the family for more than 200 years. His mother's family—the Delanos—traced its ancestry back to the *Mayflower*. Roosevelt's education at Groton, Harvard College, and Columbia Law School was typical of the path followed by the sons of America's elite.

Young Franklin at first found it hard to fill the shoes of his famous cousin, Theodore. Franklin distinguished himself neither at school nor at law. Prior to the 1920s, he could point to few significant political achievements. He was charming, gregarious, and fun loving, always eager to sail, party, and enjoy the company of women other than his wife, Eleanor. Then, in 1921, at the age of 39, Roosevelt was both stricken and transformed by a devastating illness, polio, which paralyzed him from the waist down for the rest of his life.

During the two years Roosevelt spent bedridden, he seemed to acquire a new determination and focus. He developed a compassion for those suffering misfortune that would later enable him to reach out to the millions caught in the Great Depression. Roosevelt's physical debilitation also transformed his relationship with Eleanor, whose dedication to nursing him back to health forged a new bond between them. More conscious of his dependence on others, he now welcomed her as a partner in his career. Eleanor soon displayed a talent for political organization and public speaking that surprised those who knew her only as a shy, awkward woman. She was an indispensable player in the revival of Franklin's political fortunes, which began in 1928 with his election to the governorship of New York State. Eleanor would also become an active, eloquent First Lady, her husband's trusted ally, and an architect of American liberalism.

As governor of New York for four years (1929–1933), Roosevelt had initiated various reform programs. He surrounded himself with men and women who embraced a reform movement that began to call itself "liberal." Frances Perkins, Harry Hopkins, Raymond Moley, Rexford Tugwell, Adolph Berle, Samuel Rosenman—all were interventionist in economic matters and libertarian on questions of personal behavior. In other words, they believed that the government had an active role to play in regulating the economy, but that the government should refrain from telling people how to live their lives. How much Roosevelt had himself embraced this liberalism before 1932 is not clear. But during his acceptance speech at the Democratic National Convention that year, he declared: "Ours must be the party of liberal thought, of planned action, of enlightened international outlook, and of the greatest good for the greatest number of citizens." He promised "a new deal for the American people."

25-3 The First New Deal, 1933–1935

Q *What do you consider to be the three or four most important pieces of legislation in the First New Deal? Why?*

By the time Roosevelt assumed office in March 1933, the economy lay in shambles. From 1929 to 1932, industrial production had fallen by 50 percent, while new investment had declined from $16 billion to less than $1 billion. In those same years, more than 100,000 businesses went bankrupt, including thousands of banks (see Figure 25.2). In early 1933, with the nation's banking system on the verge of collapse, 34 states

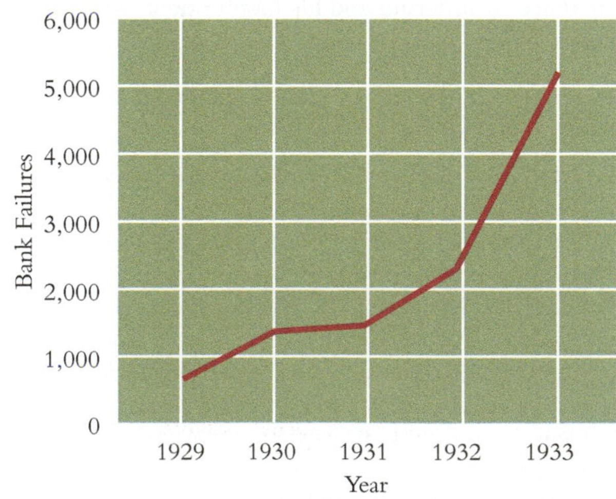

Figure 25.2 **Bank Failures, 1929–1933**

Source: From C. D. Bremer, *American Bank Failures* (New York: Columbia University Press, 1935), p. 42.

ordered all the banks in their jurisdictions to close their doors. No one seemed to be able to bring the unemployment rate under control. Some Americans feared that the opportunity for reform had already passed.

Not Roosevelt. "This nation asks for action, and action now," Roosevelt declared in his inaugural address. Roosevelt was true to his word. In his first Hundred Days, from early March through early June 1933, Roosevelt persuaded Congress to pass 15 major pieces of legislation to help bankers, farmers, industrialists, workers, homeowners, the unemployed, and the hungry. He also prevailed on Congress to repeal Prohibition (see Table 25.1). Not all of the new laws helped relieve distress and promote recovery, but in the short term that seemed to matter little. Roosevelt had brought excitement and hope to the nation. He was confident, decisive, and defiantly cheery. "The only thing we have to fear is fear itself," he declared.

On the second Sunday after his inauguration, he launched a series of radio addresses known as "fireside chats," speaking in a plain, direct voice to the forlorn and discouraged. In his first chat, he explained the banking crisis in simple terms but without condescension. "I want to take a few minutes to talk with the people of the United States about banking," he began. An estimated 20 million Americans listened.

To hear the president speaking as though he were actually there in the room was riveting. An estimated 500,000 Americans wrote letters to Roosevelt in the early weeks after he assumed office. Millions more would write to him and to **Eleanor Roosevelt** over the next few years. Many of the letters were simply addressed to "Mr. or Mrs. Roosevelt, Washington, D.C." Democrats began to hang portraits of Franklin Roosevelt in their homes, often next to a picture of Jesus or the Madonna.

Underwood Archives/Archive Photos/Getty Images

25.4 **Connecting with Ordinary Americans** In 1933, FDR began broadcasting "Fireside Chats," frank and accessible radio addresses about the problems confronting the nation and how Americans might solve them. Millions listened to these chats in their homes.

Q *Why did these broadcasts have such a big impact on the popular mood?*

Table 25.1 LEGISLATION ENACTED DURING THE "HUNDRED DAYS," MARCH 9–JUNE 16, 1933

Date	Legislation	Purpose
March 9	Emergency Banking Act	Provide federal loans to private bankers
March 20	Economy Act	Balance the federal budget
March 22	Beer–Wine Revenue Act	Repeal Prohibition
March 31	Unemployment Relief Act	Create the Civilian Conservation Corps
May 12	Agricultural Adjustment Act	Establish a national agricultural policy
May 12	Emergency Farm Mortgage Act	Provide refinancing of farm mortgages
May 12	Federal Emergency Relief Act	Establish a national relief system, including the Civil Works Administration
May 18	Tennessee Valley Authority Act	Promote economic development of the Tennessee Valley
May 27	Securities Act	Regulate the purchase and sale of new securities
June 5	Gold Repeal Joint Resolution	Cancel the gold clause in public and private contracts
June 13	Home Owners Loan Act	Provide refinancing of home mortgages
June 16	National Industrial Recovery Act	Set up a national system of industrial self-government and establish the Public Works Administration
June 16	Glass–Steagall Banking Act	Create Federal Deposit Insurance Corporation; separate commercial and investment banking
June 16	Farm Credit Act	Reorganize agricultural credit programs
June 16	Railroad Coordination Act	Appoint federal coordinator of transportation

Source: Arthur M. Schlesinger, Jr., *The Coming of the New Deal* (Boston: Houghton Mifflin, 1959), pp. 20–21.

25-3a *Saving the Banks*

By Inauguration Day, many of the nation's banks had shut their doors. Roosevelt immediately ordered all the nation's banks closed—a bold move he brazenly called a "bank holiday." At his request, Congress rushed through the Emergency Banking Act, which made federal loans available to private bankers, and the Economy Act, which committed the government to balancing the budget. Both were fiscally conservative programs that Hoover had proposed.

After the financial crisis eased, Roosevelt turned to the structural reform of banking. A second Glass–Steagall Act (1933) separated commercial banking from investment banking. It also created the Federal Deposit Insurance Corporation (FDIC), which assured depositors that the government would protect up to $5,000 of their savings. The Securities Act (1933) and the Securities Exchange Act (1934) imposed long-overdue regulation on the New York Stock Exchange, both by reining in buying on the margin and by establishing the Securities and Exchange Commission (SEC) to enforce federal law.

25-3b *Economic Relief*

Roosevelt understood the need to temper financial prudence with compassion. Congress responded swiftly in 1933 to Roosevelt's request to establish the Federal Emergency Relief Administration (FERA), granting it $500 million for relief to the poor. To head FERA, Roosevelt appointed a brash young reformer, Harry Hopkins, who disbursed $2 million during his first two hours on the job. Roosevelt next won congressional approval for the Civilian Conservation Corps (CCC), which assembled more than 2 million single young men to plant trees, halt erosion, and otherwise improve the environment. The following winter, Roosevelt launched the Civil Works Administration (CWA), an ambitious work-relief program, also under the direction of Harry Hopkins, which hired 4 million unemployed people at $15 per week and put them to work on 400,000 small-scale government projects. For middle-class Americans threatened with the loss of their homes, Roosevelt won congressional approval for the Homeowners' Loan Corporation (1933) to refinance mortgages. These direct subsidies to millions of jobless and homeowning Americans lent credibility to Roosevelt's claim that the New Deal would set the country on a new course.

25-3c *Agricultural Reform*

In 1933, Roosevelt expected economic recovery to come not from relief, but through agricultural and industrial cooperation. He regarded the Agricultural Adjustment Act, passed in May, and the National Industrial Recovery Act (NIRA), passed in June, as the most important legislation of his Hundred Days. Both were based on the idea that curtailing production would trigger economic recovery. By shrinking the supply of agricultural and manufactured goods, Roosevelt's economists reasoned, they could restore the balance of normal market forces. As demand for scarce goods exceeded supply, prices would rise and revenues would climb. Farmers and industrialists, earning a profit once again, would increase their investment in new technology and hire more workers, and prosperity and full employment would be the final result.

To curtail farm production, the **Agricultural Adjustment Administration (AAA),** which was set up by the Agricultural Adjustment Act, began paying farmers to keep a portion of their land out of cultivation and to reduce the size of their herds. The program was controversial. Many farmers were skeptical of a government offer to pay more money for working less land and husbanding fewer livestock, but few refused to accept payments. As one young Kansas farmer reported:

> There were mouthy individuals who seized every opportunity to run down the entire program ... condemning it as useless, crooked, revolutionary, or dictatorial; but ... when the first AAA payments were made available, shortly before Christmas, these same wordy critics made a beeline for the courthouse. They jostled and fell over each other in their mad scramble to be the first in line to receive allotment money.

The AAA had made no provision for the tenant farmers and farm laborers who would be thrown out of work by the reduction in acreage. In the South, the victims were disproportionately black. A Georgia sharecropper wrote Harry Hopkins of his misery: "I have Bin farming all my life But the man I live with Has Turned me loose taking my mule [and] all my feed... . I can't get a Job so Some one said Rite you." New Dealers within the Department of Agriculture, such as Rexford Tugwell and Jerome Frank, were sympathetic to the plight of sharecroppers, but they failed during the First New Deal to extend to them the government's helping hand.

The programs of the AAA also proved inadequate to Great Plains farmers, whose economic problems had been compounded by ecological crisis. Just as the Depression rolled in, the rain stopped falling on the plains, and the land, stripped of its native grasses by decades of excessive plowing, dried up and turned to dust. And then the dust began to blow, sometimes traveling 1,000 miles across open prairie. The worst dust storm occurred on April 14, 1935, when a great mass of dust, moving at speeds of 45 to 70 miles per hour, roared through Colorado, Kansas, and Oklahoma, blackening the sky, suffocating cattle, and dumping thousands of tons of topsoil and red clay on homes and streets (see Map 25.2).

The government responded to this calamity by establishing the Soil Conservation Service (SCS) in 1935, which assisted plains farmers in planting soil-conserving grasses and legumes in place of wheat. The SCS also taught farmers how to plow along contour lines and how to build terraces—techniques that had been proven effective in slowing the run-off of rainwater and improving its absorption into the soil. With this assistance, plains agriculture began to recover.

In 1936, the Supreme Court ruled that AAA-mandated limits on farm production constituted an illegal restraint of

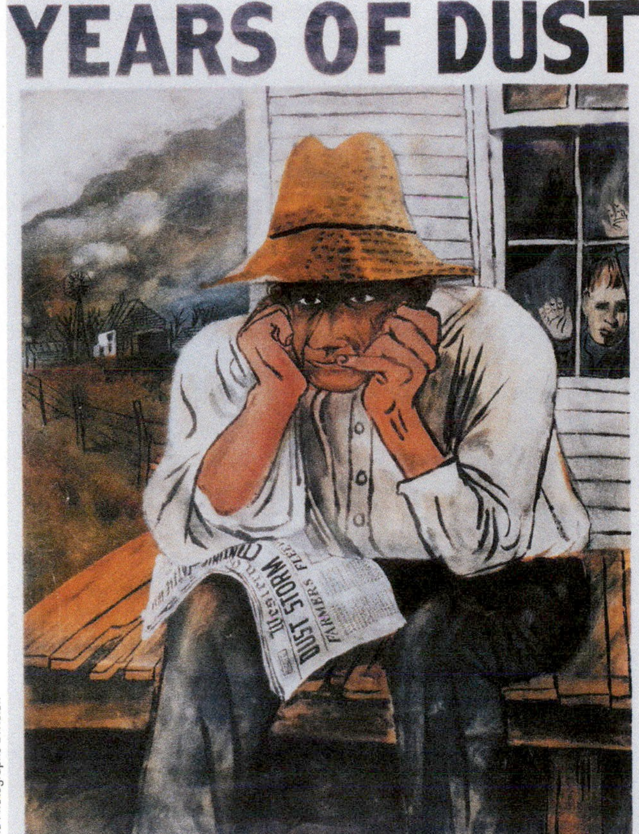

25.5 **Helping Dust Bowl Victims** This poster by pro-New Deal artist Ben Shahn dramatizes the plight of an American farmer and his family caught up in the Dust Bowl.

Q *How does Shahn portray the farmer?*

Q *Who will come to the rescue?*

Q *Would an artist sympathetic to Herbert Hoover's politics have rendered this farmer and his plight differently?*

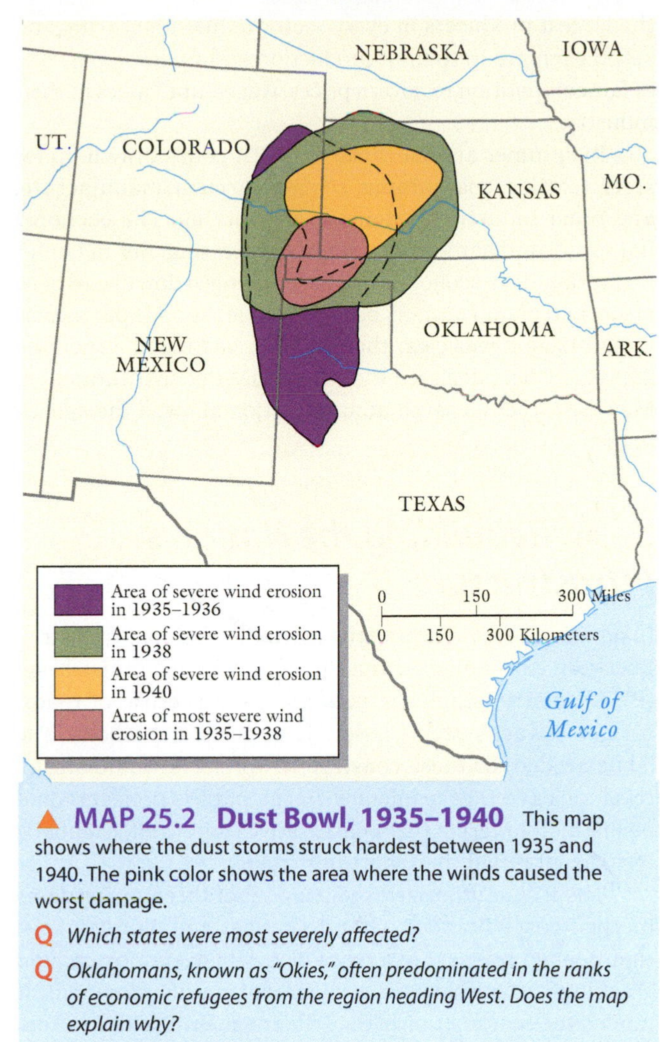

▲ **MAP 25.2 Dust Bowl, 1935–1940** This map shows where the dust storms struck hardest between 1935 and 1940. The pink color shows the area where the winds caused the worst damage.

Q *Which states were most severely affected?*

Q *Oklahomans, known as "Okies," often predominated in the ranks of economic refugees from the region heading West. Does the map explain why?*

trade. Congress responded by passing the Soil Conservation and Domestic Allotment Act, which justified the removal of land from cultivation for reasons of conservation rather than economics. This new act also called on landowners to share their government subsidies with sharecroppers and tenant farmers, although many landowners managed to evade this requirement.

The use of subsidies, begun by the AAA, did eventually bring stability and prosperity to agriculture, but at high cost. Agriculture became the most heavily subsidized sector of the U.S. economy, and the Department of Agriculture grew into one of the government's largest bureaucracies. The rural poor, black and white, never received a fair share of federal benefits. Beginning in the 1930s, and continuing in the 1940s and 1950s, millions would be forced off the land and into the cities of the North and West.

25-3d *Industrial Reform*

American industry was so vast that Roosevelt's administration never contemplated paying individual manufacturers direct subsidies to reduce, or even halt, production. Instead, the government decided to limit production through persuasion and association—techniques that Hoover had also favored. The first task of the **National Recovery Administration (NRA),** authorized under the National Industrial Recovery Act, was to persuade industrialists and businessmen to agree to raise employee wages to a minimum of 30 to 40 cents per hour and to limit employee hours to a maximum of 30 to 40 hours per week. The limitation on hours was meant to reduce the quantity of goods that any factory or business could produce.

The NRA undertook a high-powered publicity campaign, distributing pamphlets and pins throughout the country, promoting its goals on the radio, and urging employers to place a "blue eagle"—the logo of the NRA—on storefronts, at factory entrances, and on company stationery. Blue eagles began sprouting up everywhere, usually accompanied by the slogan "We Do Our Part." The NRA also brought together the largest producers in every sector of manufacturing and asked each group to limit production and to develop a code of fair competition to govern prices, wages, and hours in their industry.

In summer and fall 1933, the NRA codes drawn up for steel, textiles, coal mining, rubber, garment manufacture, and other industries seemed to be working. The economy improved, and hard times seemed to be easing. But in winter and spring 1934, economic indicators plunged downward once again, and manufacturers began to evade the code provisions. By fall 1934, it was clear that the NRA had failed. When the Supreme Court declared the NRA codes unconstitutional in May 1935, the Roosevelt administration allowed the agency to die.

25-3e *Rebuilding the Nation's Infrastructure*

In addition to establishing the NRA, the National Industrial Recovery Act launched the Public Works Administration (PWA) to strengthen the nation's infrastructure of roads, bridges, sewage systems, hospitals, airports, and schools. The labor needed for these construction projects would shrink relief rolls and reduce unemployment, but the projects could be justified in terms that conservatives approved: economic investment rather than short-term relief.

The PWA authorized the building of three major dams in the West—Boulder, Grand Coulee, and Bonneville—that opened up large stretches of Arizona, California, and Washington to industrial and agricultural development. It funded the construction of the Triborough Bridge in New York City and the 100-mile causeway linking Florida to Key West.

25.6 **Selling the NRA through Sex and Sunburn** Americans were asked to display their support for the NRA by pasting eagles onto their factory entrances, storefronts, and even clothes. The young women in this photo dispensed with pasting, choosing instead to allow the sun to burn their bare backs around a stenciled blue eagle and NRA lettering, which were being applied by the woman in the white gown.

It also appropriated money for the construction of thousands of new schools.

25-3f *The TVA Alternative*

One piece of legislation passed during Roosevelt's First New Deal specified a strategy for economic recovery significantly different from the one promoted by the NIRA. The Tennessee Valley Authority Act (1933) called for the government—rather than private corporations—to promote economic development throughout the Tennessee Valley, a vast river basin winding through parts of Kentucky, Tennessee, Mississippi, Alabama, Georgia, and North Carolina. The act created the **Tennessee Valley Authority (TVA)** to control flooding on the Tennessee River, harness its waterpower to generate electricity, develop local industry (such as fertilizer production), improve river navigability, and ease the poverty and isolation of the area's inhabitants. In some respects, the TVA's mandate resembled that of the PWA, but the TVA enjoyed even greater authority. Its establishment reflected the influence of Rexford Tugwell and other New Dealers who were committed to a government-planned and government-operated economy. Although they rarely said so, these reformers were drawn to socialism.

The accomplishments of the TVA were many. It built, completed, or improved more than 20 dams, including the huge Wheeler Dam near Muscle Shoals in Alabama (see Map 25.3). At several of the dam sites, the TVA built hydroelectric generators and soon became the nation's largest producer of electricity. Its low electric rates compelled private utility companies to reduce their rates. The TVA also constructed waterways to bypass nonnavigable stretches of the river, reduced the danger of flooding, and taught farmers how to prevent soil erosion and use fertilizers.

Although the TVA was one of the New Deal's most celebrated successes, it generated little support for more ambitious experiments in national planning. For the government to have assumed control of established industries and banks would have been quite a different matter from bringing prosperity to an impoverished region. Like Roosevelt, few members of Congress or the public favored the radical growth of governmental power that such programs would have entailed. Thus, the thought of replacing the NRA with a nationwide TVA, for instance, made little headway. The New Deal never embraced the idea of the federal government as a substitute for private enterprise.

25-3g *The New Deal and Western Development*

As the TVA showed, New Deal programs could powerfully influence a particular region's welfare. Other regional beneficiaries of the New Deal included the New York

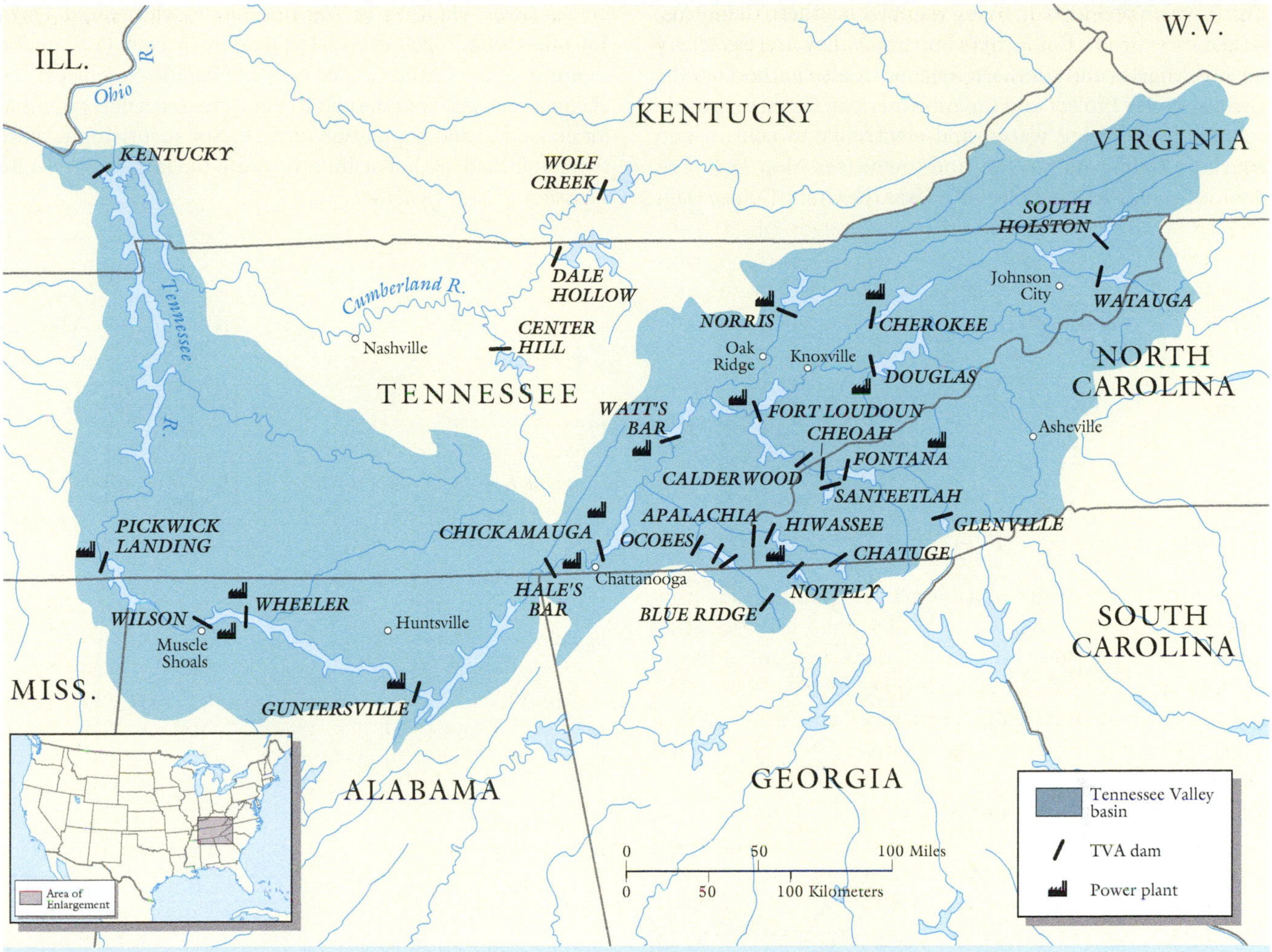

▲ **MAP 25.3 Tennessee Valley Authority** This map shows the vast scale of the TVA.

Q *Through how many states did the Tennessee River wind? How many dams did the TVA build? How many power plants?*

Q *Why do you think Washington chose this area for its most ambitious government-sponsored and -managed initiative?*

City area, which prospered from the close links of local politicians to the Roosevelt administration. The region that benefited most from the New Deal, however, was the West. Between 1933 and 1939, per capita payments for public works projects, welfare, and federal loans in the Rocky Mountain and Pacific Coast states outstripped those of any other region.

Dam building was central to this western focus. Western real estate and agricultural interests wanted to dam the West's major rivers to provide water and electricity for urban and agricultural development, but the costs were prohibitive, even to the largest capitalists, until the New Deal offered to defray the expenses with federal dollars. Western interests found a government ally in the Bureau of Reclamation, a hitherto small federal agency (in existence since 1902) that became, under the New Deal, a prime dispenser of funds for dam construction, reservoir creation, and the provision of water to western cities and farms. Drawing on PWA monies, the bureau oversaw the building of the Boulder Dam (later renamed the Hoover

25.7 **The Hoover Dam** This was a massive government-funded project undertaken in the 1930s (when it was known as the Boulder Dam) to harness the Colorado River to irrigate, electrify, and provide drinking water for the Southwest.

Dam), which provided drinking water for southern California, irrigation water for California's Imperial Valley, and electricity for Los Angeles and southern Arizona. It also authorized the Central Valley Project and the All-American Canal to provide irrigation, drinking water, and electricity to central and southern California farmers and towns (see Map 25.4). The greatest construction project of all was the Grand Coulee Dam on the Columbia River in Washington, which created a lake 150 miles long. Together with the Bonneville Dam (also on the Columbia), the Grand Coulee gave the Pacific Northwest the cheapest electricity in the country and created a new potential for economic and population growth. Not surprisingly, these two dams also made Washington State the largest per capita recipient of New Deal aid.

▲ **MAP 25.4 Federal Water Projects in California Built or Authorized by the New Deal** These water projects—dams, canals, aqueducts, pumping stations, and power plants—extended from the Shasta Dam in the north to the Colorado River Aqueduct (which carried drinking water to Los Angeles) and the All American Canal that traversed the Imperial Valley in the south.

Q *What were the principal aims of this vast investment in California's water infrastructure?*

Q *Where did the drinking water for Los Angeles originate? How many miles did it have to traverse before Angelenos could get access to it?*

These developments attracted less attention in the 1930s than the TVA because their benefits did not fully materialize until after the Second World War. Also, dam building in the West was not seen as a radical experiment in government planning and management. Unlike the TVA, the Bureau of Reclamation hired private contractors to do the work. Moreover, the benefits of these dams were intended to flow first to large agricultural and real estate interests, not to the poor; they were intended to aid private enterprise, rather than bypass it. In political terms, dam building in the West was more conservative than it was in the Tennessee Valley. Even so, this activity made the federal government a key architect of the modern American West.

25-4 Political Mobilization, Political Unrest, 1934–1935

Q *What forms did political unrest take in 1934 and 1935?*

Although Roosevelt and the New Dealers dismantled the NRA in 1935, they could not stop the political forces it had set in motion. Ordinary Americans now believed they could make a difference. If the New Dealers could not achieve economic recovery, then the people would find others who could.

25-4a *Populist Critics of the New Deal*

Some critics were disturbed by what they perceived as the conservative character of New Deal programs. Banking reforms, the AAA, and the NRA, they alleged, all seemed to favor large economic interests. Ordinary people had been ignored.

In the South and Midwest, millions listened regularly to the radio addresses of Louisiana senator **Huey Long**, a former governor of that state and an accomplished orator. In attacks on New Deal programs, he alleged that "not a single thin dime of concentrated, bloated, pompous wealth, massed in the hands of a few people has been raked down to relieve the masses." Long offered a simple alternative: "Break up the swollen fortunes of America and ... spread the wealth among all our people." He called for a redistribution of wealth that would guarantee each American family a $5,000 estate.

Long's rhetoric inspired hundreds of thousands of Americans to join the Share the Wealth clubs his supporters organized. Most came from middle-class ranks or from the ranks of skilled workers. By 1935, Roosevelt regarded Long as the man most likely to unseat him in the presidential election of 1936. Before that campaign began, however, Long was assassinated.

Meanwhile, in the Midwest, **Father Charles Coughlin**, the "radio priest," delivered a message similar to Long's. Like Long, Coughlin appealed to anxious middle-class Americans and to once-privileged groups of workers who believed that security and respectability were slipping from their grasp. A former Roosevelt supporter, Coughlin had become a critic. The New Deal was run by bankers, he claimed. The NRA was a program to resuscitate corporate profits. Coughlin called for a strong government to compel capital, labor, agriculture, professionals, and other interest groups to do its bidding. He founded the National Union of Social Justice (NUSJ) in 1934 as a precursor to a political party that would challenge the Democrats in 1936.

As Coughlin's disillusionment with the New Deal deepened, a strain of anti-Semitism became apparent in his radio talks, as in his accusation that Jewish bankers were masterminding a world conspiracy to dispossess the toiling masses. Although Coughlin was a compelling speaker, he failed to build the NUSJ into an effective political force. Its successor, the Union Party, attracted only a small percentage of voters in 1936. Embittered, Coughlin moved further to the political right. By 1939, his denunciations of democracy and Jews had become so extreme that some radio stations refused to carry his addresses. Still, millions of Americans continued to put their faith in the "radio priest."

Another popular figure was Francis E. Townsend, a California doctor who claimed that the way to end the Depression was to give every senior citizen $200 a month. The Townsend Plan briefly garnered the support of an estimated 20 million Americans.

25-4b *Labor Protests*

The attacks by Long, Coughlin, and Townsend on New Deal programs deepened popular discontent and helped to legitimate other insurgencies. The most important was the labor movement. Workers began joining unions in response to the National Industrial Recovery Act, and especially its clause granting them the right to join labor organizations of their own choosing and obligating employers to bargain with them in good faith. Union members' demands were modest at first: They wanted to be treated fairly by their foremen, and they wanted employers to observe the provisions of the NRA codes and to recognize their unions. But few employers were willing to grant workers any say in their working conditions. Many ignored the NRA's wage and hour guidelines altogether and even used their influence with NRA code authorities to get worker requests for wage increases and union recognition rejected.

Workers flooded Washington with letters of protest and then began to take matters into their own hands. In 1934 they staged 2,000 strikes in virtually every industry and region of the country. A few of these strikes escalated into armed confrontations between workers and police that shocked the nation. In Toledo, Ohio, in May, 10,000 workers surrounded the Electric Auto-Lite plant, declaring that they would block all exits and entrances until the company agreed to shut down operations and negotiate a union contract. Two strikers were killed in an exchange of gunfire. In Minneapolis, unionized truck drivers and warehousemen fought police, private security forces, and the National Guard in a series of street battles from

Bettmann/Corbis

25.8 **Huey Long, Populist** A spellbinding speaker, Long called on government to transfer a good deal of wealth from the rich to the poor.

Q *Why did Roosevelt fear Long so much?*

May through July that left four dead and hundreds wounded. In San Francisco in July, skirmishes between longshoremen and employers killed two and wounded scores of strikers. This violence provoked a general strike in San Francisco that shut down the city's transportation, construction, and service industries for two weeks. In September, 400,000 textile workers at mills from Maine to Alabama walked off their jobs. Attempts by employers to bring in replacement workers triggered violent confrontations that caused several deaths, hundreds of injuries, and millions of dollars in property damages.

25-4c *Anger at the Polls*

In the fall of 1934, workers took their anger to the polls. In Rhode Island, they broke the Republican Party's 30-year domination of state politics. In the South Carolina gubernatorial race, working-class voters rejected a conservative Democrat, Coleman Blease, and chose instead Olin T. Johnston, a former mill worker and an ardent New Dealer. In the country as a whole, Democrats won 70 percent of the contested seats in the Senate and House. The Democrats increased their majority, from 310 to 319 (out of 432) in the House, and from 60 to 69 (out of 96) in the Senate. No sitting president's party had ever done so well in an off-year election.

The victory was not an unqualified one for Roosevelt and the First New Deal, however. The 74th Congress would include the largest contingent of radicals ever sent to Washington: Tom Amlie of Wisconsin, Ernest Lundeen of Minnesota, Maury Maverick of Texas, Vito Marcantonio of New York, and some 30 others. Their support for the New Deal depended on whether Roosevelt delivered more relief, more income security, and more political power to farmers, workers, the unemployed, and the poor.

25-4d *Radical Third Parties*

Radical critics of the New Deal also made an impressive showing in state politics in 1934 and 1936. In Wisconsin, Philip La Follette, the son of Robert La Follette (see Chapter 21), was elected governor in 1934 and 1936 as the candidate of the radical Wisconsin Progressive Party. In Minnesota, discontented agrarians and urban workers organized the Minnesota Farmer-Labor (MFL) Party and elected their candidate to the governorship in 1930, 1932, 1934, and 1936. In Washington, yet another radical third party, the Commonwealth Builders, elected both senators and almost half the state legislators in 1932 and 1934. And in California in 1934, the socialist and novelist Upton Sinclair and his organization, End Poverty in California (EPIC), came close to winning the governorship.

A widespread movement to form local labor parties offered further evidence of voter volatility, as did the growing appeal of the **Communist Party**. The American Communist Party (CP) had emerged in the early 1920s with the support of radicals who wanted to adopt the Soviet Union's path to socialism (see Chapter 23). In the early 1930s, CP organizers spread out among the poorest and most vulnerable populations in America—homeless urban blacks in the North, black and white sharecroppers in the South, Chicano and Filipino agricultural workers in the West—and mobilized them into unions and unemployment leagues. CP members also played significant roles in strikes described earlier, and they were influential in the Minnesota Farmer-Labor Party and in Washington's Commonwealth Builders. Once they stopped preaching world revolution in 1935 and began calling instead for a "popular front" of democratic forces against fascism (a term used to describe the new kinds of dictatorships appearing in Hitler's Germany and Mussolini's Italy), their ranks grew even more. By 1938, approximately 80,000 Americans are thought to have been members of the Communist Party.

Although the Communist Party proclaimed its allegiance to democratic principles beginning in 1935, it nevertheless remained a dictatorial organization that took its orders from the Soviet Union. Many Americans feared the growing strength of the CP and began to call for its suppression. The CP, however, was never strong enough to gain power for itself. Its chief role in 1930s politics was to channel popular discontent into unions and political parties that would, in turn, force New Dealers to respond to the demands of the nation's poor.

Detroit Industry, north wall, 1933 (fresco) (detail), Rivera, Diego (1886-1957)/The Detroit Institute of Arts, USA /The Bridgeman Art Library

25.9 **Men at Work** This is a detail from one of the 27 frescoes of the Ford Motor Company that the Mexican artist Diego Rivera painted on the walls of the Detroit Art Museum in 1932–1933.

Q *Compare Rivera's portrait of Ford's workers with Ben Shahn's image of the Dust Bowl farmer (25.5) appearing in this chapter on p. 693. How are the two portraits of working men similar? How are they different?*

25-5 The Second New Deal, 1935–1937

Q *How was the Second New Deal different from the First New Deal?*

For a time, Roosevelt kept his distance from the masses mobilizing in his name, but in spring 1935, with the 1936 presidential election looming, he decided to place himself at their head. He called for the "abolition of evil holding companies," attacked the wealthy for their profligate ways, and called for new programs to aid the poor and downtrodden. Rather than becoming a socialist, as his critics charged, Roosevelt sought to reinvigorate his appeal among poorer Americans and turn them away from radical solutions.

25-5a *Philosophical Underpinnings*

To point the New Deal in a more populist direction, Roosevelt turned increasingly to a relatively new economic theory, **underconsumptionism**. Advocates of this theory held that a chronic weakness in consumer demand had caused the Great Depression. The path to recovery lay, therefore, not in restricting production, as the architects of the First New Deal had tried to do, but in boosting consumer expenditures through government support for strong labor unions (to force up wages), higher social welfare expenditures (to put more money in the hands of the poor), and ambitious public works projects (to create millions of new jobs).

Underconsumptionists did not worry that new welfare and public works programs might strain the federal budget. If the government found itself short of revenue, it could always borrow additional funds from private sources. These reformers, in fact, viewed government borrowing as a useful antidepression tool. Those who lent the government money would receive a return on their investment; those who received government assistance would have additional income to spend on consumer goods; and manufacturers would profit from increases in consumer spending. Government borrowing, in short, would stimulate the circulation of money through the economy, increase consumer demand, and end the Depression. This fiscal policy, a reversal of the conventional wisdom that government should always balance its budget, would in the 1940s come to be known as Keynesianism, after John Maynard Keynes, the British economist who had been its architect.

As the nation entered its sixth year of the Depression, Roosevelt was willing to give these new ideas a try. Reform-minded members of the 1934 Congress were eager for a new round of legislation directed more to the needs of ordinary Americans than to the needs of big business.

25-5b *Legislation*

Congress passed much of that legislation in January to June 1935, a period that came to be known as the Second New Deal. Two of the acts were of historic importance: the **Social Security Act** and the National Labor Relations Act. The Social Security Act, passed in May, required the states to set up welfare funds from which money would be disbursed to the elderly poor, the unemployed, unmarried mothers with dependent children, and the disabled. It also enrolled a majority of working Americans in a pension program that guaranteed them a steady income upon retirement. A federal system of employer and employee taxation was set up to fund the pensions. Despite limitations on coverage and inadequate pension levels, the Social Security Act of 1935 provided a foundation on which future presidents and congresses would erect the American welfare state.

Equally historic was the passage, in June, of the National Labor Relations Act (NLRA). This act delivered what the NRA had only promised: the right of every worker to join a union of his or her own choosing and the obligation of employers to bargain with that union in good faith. The **NLRA**, also called the **Wagner Act** after its Senate sponsor, Robert Wagner of New York, set up a National Labor Relations Board (NLRB) to supervise union elections and to investigate claims of unfair labor practices. The NLRB was to be staffed by federal

Interpreting the Visual Past Monopoly

Monopoly's precursor was The Landlord's Game, a board game invented in 1903 by Lizzie Magie to promote reformer Henry George's economic ideas (see Chapter 19). Magie's game was meant to teach Americans about the evils of concentrated property ownership: Winning the game involved gouging renters and bankrupting rival property owners. Groups of radical economists played the game, but it did not catch on with the public until the 1930s, when Charles Darrow, an unemployed Philadelphia salesman, refashioned it with clever artwork and rules changes and retitled it Monopoly. He then succeeded where Magie had failed: He persuaded a major games manufacturer to acquire and distribute it. Parker Brothers purchased the rights in 1935 and marketed it in 1936. In one year, Monopoly became the country's best-selling board game. The game both drew players closer to and distanced them from economic realities of the 1930s. On the one hand, it gave players a taste of the financial vulnerability that, for many, defined the decade. Material well-being could vanish in a flash, with a simple role of the dice; defeat resulted from a rival person of wealth using ruthless means to drive the competition out of business. On the other hand, the Monopoly board offered players a view of the American economy far removed from 1930s realities. No industries, farms, mines, or stock exchanges had a role in the game. Railroads comprised the only means of transportation, and political institutions were represented exclusively by the quaint "Community Chest."

Q *Imagine that an archaeologist a thousand years in the future found an intact version of Monopoly in the ruins of an American city. What, if anything, could he or she learn from it about the economy, or real estate, or attitudes toward money and risk in Depression–era America?*

Q *As anti-monopoly sentiment declined in the 1930s, anti-corporate sentiment surged. How were anti-monopoly and anti-corporate sentiments similar? How were they different?*

Q *Did the popularity of anti-corporate sentiment in 1930s America contribute to Monopoly's success? Or did this game succeed primarily because it offered an engrossing diversion from the decade's hardships?*

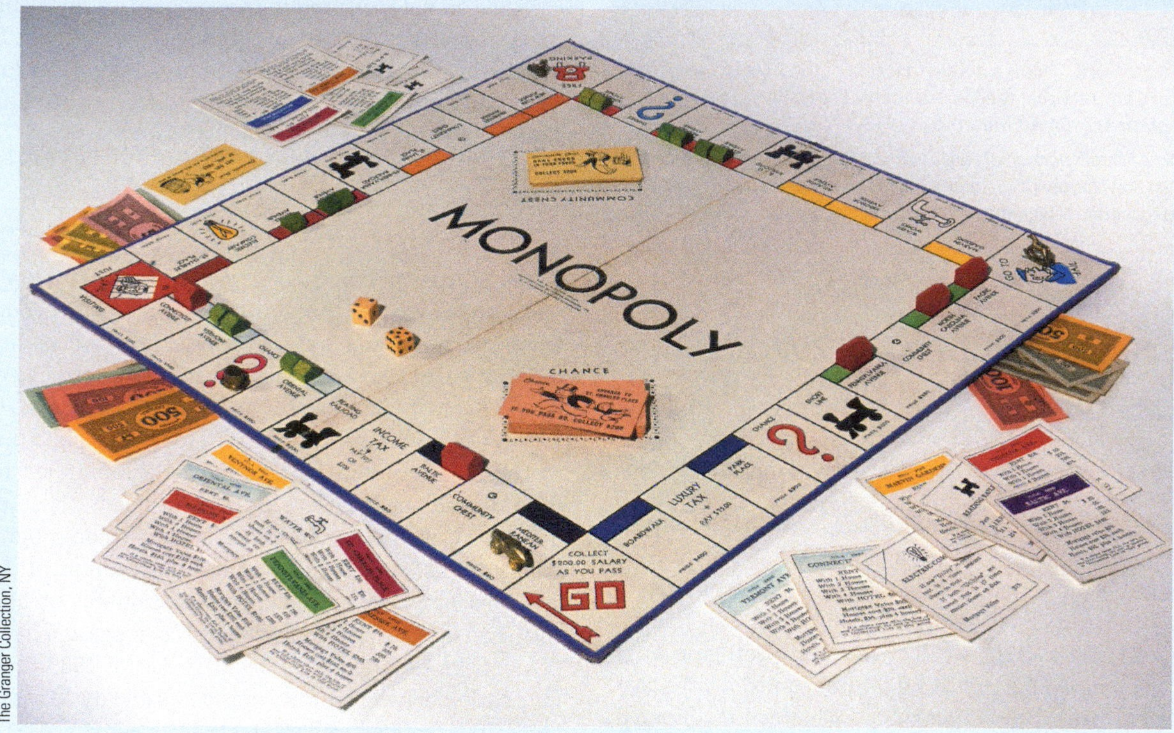

The Granger Collection, NY

25.10 **Parker Brothers, Monopoly Boardgame, 1935.**

appointees with power to impose fines on employers who violated the law. Union leaders hailed the act as their Magna Carta.

Congress also passed the Holding Company Act to break up the 13 utility companies that controlled 75 percent of the nation's electric power. It passed the Wealth Tax Act, which increased tax rates on the wealthy from 59 to 75 percent, and on corporations from 13.75 to 15 percent; and it passed the Banking Act, which strengthened the power of the Federal Reserve Board over its member banks. It created the Rural Electrification Administration (REA) to bring electric power to rural households. Finally, it

Table 25.2 SELECTED WPA PROJECTS IN NEW YORK CITY, 1938

Construction and Renovation	Education, Health, and Art	Research and Records
East River Drive	Adult education: homemaking, trade and technical skills, and art and culture	Sewage treatment, community health, labor relations, and employment trends surveys
Henry Hudson Parkway	Children's education: remedial reading, lip reading, and field trips	Museum and library catalogs and exhibits
Bronx sewers	Prisoners' vocational training, recreation, and nutrition	Municipal office clerical support
Glendale and Queens public libraries	Dental clinics	Government forms standardization
King's County Hospital	Tuberculosis examination clinics	
Williamsburg housing project	Syphilis and gonorrhea treatment clinics	
School buildings, prisons, and firehouses	City hospital kitchen help, orderlies, laboratory technicians, nurses, doctors	
Coney Island and Brighton Beach boardwalks	Subsistence gardens	
Orchard Beach	Sewing rooms	
Swimming pools, playgrounds, parks, drinking fountains	Central Park sculpture shop	

Source: John David Millet, *The Works Progress Administration in New York City* (Chicago: Public Administration Service, 1938), pp. 95–126.

passed the huge $5 billion Emergency Relief Appropriation Act. Roosevelt funneled part of this sum to the PWA, the CCC, and the newly created National Youth Administration (NYA), which provided work and guidance to the nation's youth.

Roosevelt directed most of the new relief money, however, to the **Works Progress Administration (WPA)** under the direction of Harry Hopkins, now known as the New Deal's "minister of relief." The WPA built or improved thousands of schools, playgrounds, airports, and hospitals. WPA crews raked leaves, cleaned streets, and landscaped cities. In the process, the WPA provided jobs to approximately 30 percent of the nation's jobless (see Table 25.2).

By the time the decade ended, the WPA, in association with an expanded Reconstruction Finance Corporation, the PWA, and other agencies, had built 500,000 miles of roads, 100,000 bridges, 100,000 public buildings, and 600 airports. The New Deal had transformed America's urban and rural landscapes. The awe generated by these public works projects helped Roosevelt retain popular support at a time when the success of the New Deal's economic policies was uncertain. The WPA also funded a vast program of public art, supporting the work of thousands of painters, architects, writers, playwrights, actors, and intellectuals. Beyond extending relief to struggling artists, it fostered the creation of art that spoke to the concerns of ordinary Americans, adorned public buildings with colorful murals, and boosted public morale.

25-5c *Victory in 1936: The New Democratic Coalition*

In his 1936 reelection campaign, Roosevelt excoriated the corporations as "economic royalists" who had "concentrated into their own hands an almost complete control over other people's property, other people's money, other people's labor—other people's lives." He called on voters to strip the corporations of their power and "save a great and precious form of government for ourselves and the world." American voters responded by handing Roosevelt the greatest victory in the history of American presidential politics. He received 61 percent of the popular vote; Alf Landon of Kansas, his Republican opponent, received only 37 percent. Only two states, Maine and Vermont, representing a mere eight electoral votes, went for Landon (see Map 25.5).

The 1936 election won the Democratic Party its reputation as the party of reform and the party of the "forgotten American." Of the 6 million Americans who went to the polls for the first time (see Figure 25.3), many of them European ethnics, 5 million voted for Roosevelt. Among the poorest Americans, Roosevelt received 80 percent of the vote. Black voters in the North left the Republican Party—the "Party of Lincoln"—calculating that their interests would be served better by the "Party of the Common Man." Roosevelt also did well among white middle-class voters, many of whom stood to benefit from the Social Security Act. These constituencies

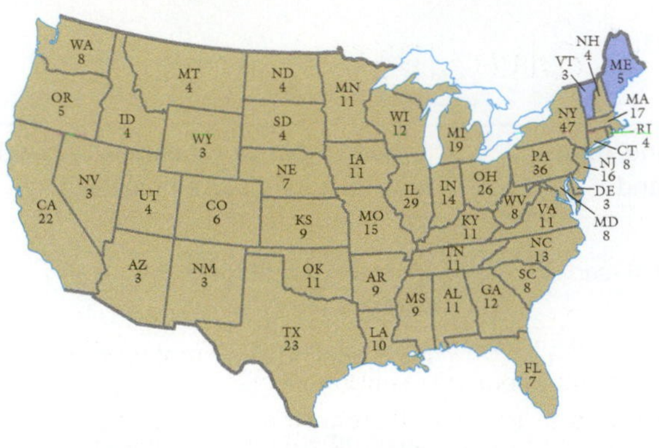

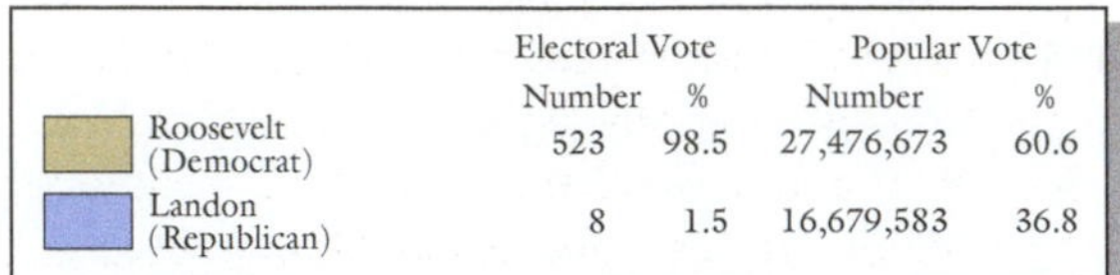

	Electoral Vote		Popular Vote	
	Number	%	Number	%
Roosevelt (Democrat)	523	98.5	27,476,673	60.6
Landon (Republican)	8	1.5	16,679,583	36.8

▲ **MAP 25.5 Presidential Election, 1936** Franklin D. Roosevelt's reelection numbers were overwhelming: 98 percent of the electoral vote and more than 60 percent of the popular vote.

Q *Can you find an example in this textbook of a previous or subsequent election that was as one-sided as this one? What explains Roosevelt's landslide?*

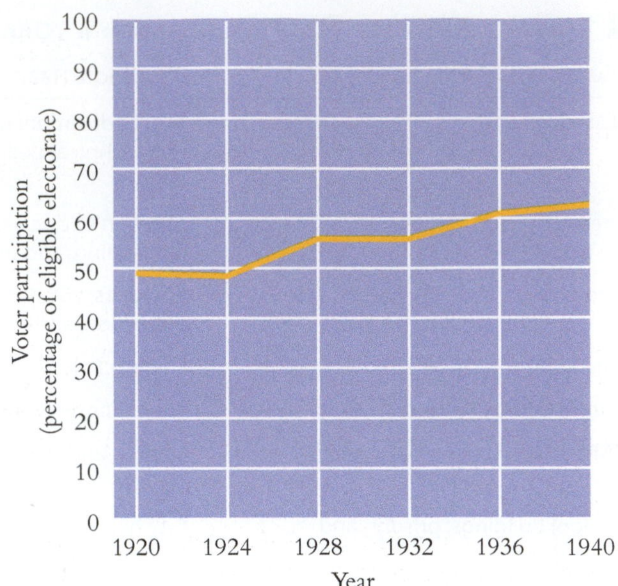

Figure 25.3 **Voter Participation in Presidential Elections, 1920–1940**

Source: Data from *Historical Statistics of the United States, Colonial Times to 1970* (White Plains, NY: Kraus International, 1989), p. 1071.

would constitute the "Roosevelt coalition" for most of the next 40 years, helping to solidify the Democratic Party as the new majority party in American politics.

25-5d *Rhetoric versus Reality*

Roosevelt's 1935–1936 anticorporate rhetoric was more radical than the laws he supported. The Wealth Tax Act took considerably less out of wealthy incomes and estates than was advertised, and the utility companies that the Holding Company Act was meant to break up remained largely intact. Moreover, Roosevelt promised more than he delivered to the nation's poor. Farmworkers, for example, were not covered by the Social Security Act or by the National Labor Relations Act. Consequently, thousands of African American sharecroppers in the South, along with substantial numbers of Mexican American and Filipino farmworkers in the Southwest and West, missed out on protections and benefits brought by these laws. The sharecroppers were shut out because southern Democrats would not have voted for an act that was seen as improving the economic or social condition of southern blacks. For the same reason, the New Deal made little effort to restore voting rights to southern blacks or to protect their basic civil rights. White supremacy lived on in New Deal democracy.

Roosevelt's 1935–1936 populist stance also obscured the support that some capitalists were giving the Second New Deal. In the West, Henry J. Kaiser headed a consortium of six companies that built the Hoover, Bonneville, and Grand Coulee dams. In Texas, building contractors Herman and George Brown were bankrolling a group of elected officials that included a young Democratic congressman named Lyndon Johnson. In the Midwest and the East, Roosevelt's corporate supporters included real estate developers, mass merchandisers (such as Bambergers and Sears, Roebuck), clothing manufacturers, and the like. These firms, in turn, had financial connections with recently established investment banks such as Lehman Brothers and Goldman Sachs, competitors of the House of Morgan and its allies in the Republican banking establishment, and with consumer-oriented banks such as the Bank of America and the Bowery Savings Bank. They tolerated strong labor unions, welfare programs, and high levels of government spending in the belief that these developments would strengthen consumer spending, but they had no intention of surrendering their own wealth or power. The Democratic Party had become, in effect, the party of the masses and one section of big business. The conflicting interests of these two constituencies would create tensions within the Democratic Party throughout the years of its political domination.

25-5e *Men, Women, and Reform*

The years 1936 and 1937 were exciting ones for academics, policymakers, and bureaucrats who designed and administered the rapidly growing roster of New Deal programs and agencies. Fueled by idealism and dedication, they were confident they could make the New Deal work. They planned and won congressional approval for the Farm Security Administration (FSA), an agency designed to improve the economic lot of tenant farmers, sharecroppers, and farm laborers. They drafted and passed legislation that outlawed child labor, set minimum wages and maximum hours for adult

History Through Film Mr. Deeds Goes to Town (1936)

Directed by Frank Capra.
Starring Gary Cooper (Longfellow Deeds), Jean Arthur (Babe Bennett), Lionel Stander (Cornelius Cobb), George Bancroft (McWade), and H. B. Warner (Judge Walker).

Mr. Deeds Goes to Town was one of several films made by Frank Capra, the most popular director of the 1930s, in which he charmed audiences with fables of simple, small-town heroes vanquishing the evil forces of wealth and decadence. The protagonist in *Mr. Deeds* is Longfellow Deeds from Mandrake Falls, Vermont, who goes to New York City to claim a fortune left to him by a deceased uncle. Deciding to give the fortune away, he becomes the laughingstock of slick city lawyers, hard-boiled newspaper reporters, cynical literati, and self-styled aristocrats. He also becomes a hero to the unemployed and downtrodden to whom he wishes to give the money. By making the conflict between the wealthy and ordinary Americans central to this story, Capra illuminated convictions that were popular in 1930s politics, as expressed by the New Deal.

The movie delivers its serious message, however, in an entertaining and often hilarious style. Capra was a master of what became known as "screwball" comedy. Longfellow Deeds slides down banisters, locks his bodyguards in a closet, uses the main hall of his inherited mansion as an echo chamber, punches a famous intellectual in the "kisser" (face), and turns his own trial for insanity into a delightful attack on the pretensions and peculiarities of corporate lawyers, judges, and psychiatrists. Central to the story, too, is an alternately amusing and serious love story between Deeds and a newspaperwoman, Babe Bennett (Jean Arthur). Bennett insinuates herself into Deeds's life by pretending to be a destitute woman without work, shelter, family, or friends. Deeds has long dreamed about rescuing a "lady in distress," and he falls for the beautiful Bennett. Bennett, in turn, uses her privileged access to Deeds to learn about his foibles and to mock them (and him) in newspaper stories written for a ruthless and scandal-hungry public. But Deeds's idealism, honesty, and virtue overwhelm Bennett's cynicism and cause her to fall in love with him. By movie's end, she has proclaimed her love and seems ready to return with Deeds to Mandrake Falls, where she will become his devoted wife and the nurturing mother of his children.

In Babe Bennett's conversion from tough reporter to female romantic, we can detect the gender conservatism of 1930s culture. The movie suggests that Bennett's early cruelty toward Deeds arose as a consequence of her inappropriate involvement in the rough, male realm of newspaper work. Only by abandoning this realm and returning to the "natural" female realm of hearth and home can she recover her true and soft womanly soul. Thus this movie is as rich a document for exploring attitudes toward male and female behavior as for examining relations between the rich and poor. ■

The Granger Collection, NY

25.11 Gary Cooper as Longfellow Deeds (center of photo with hand on cheek) during his hilarious insanity trial. Cooper's bodyguard, Lionel Stander (Cobb), sits to the left of Cooper, and Cooper is looking at H. B. Warner (Judge Walker), who is presiding at the trial.

workers, and committed the federal government to building low-cost housing. They investigated and tried to regulate concentrations of corporate power.

Although they worked on behalf of "the people," the New Dealers constituted a new class of technocrats. The prospect of building a strong state committed to prosperity and justice fired their imaginations. They delighted in the intellectual challenge and the technical complexity of social policy.

Many of the male New Dealers had earned advanced degrees in law and economics at elite universities such as Harvard, Columbia, and Wisconsin. Not all had been raised among wealth and privilege, however. To his credit, Franklin Roosevelt was the first president since his cousin Theodore Roosevelt to welcome Jews and Catholics into his administration. Some became members of Roosevelt's inner circle of advisers—men such as Thomas "Tommy the Cork" Corcoran, Jim Farley, Ben Cohen, and Samuel Rosenman.

These men had struggled to make their way, first on the streets and then in school and at work. They brought to the New Deal intellectual aggressiveness, quick minds, and mental toughness.

The profile of New Deal women was different. Although a few, notably Eleanor Roosevelt and Secretary of Labor Frances Perkins (the first woman to be appointed to the U.S. cabinet), were more visible than women in previous administrations had been, many of the female New Dealers worked in relative obscurity, in agencies such as the Women's Bureau or the Children's Bureau (both in the Department of Labor). Women who worked on major legislation, as did Mary Van Kleeck on the Social Security Act, or who directed major programs, as did Jane Hoey, chief of the Social Security's Bureau of Public Assistance, received less credit than men in comparable positions. Moreover, female New Dealers tended to be a generation older than their male colleagues and were more likely to be Protestant than Catholic or Jewish. Many of them had known each other since the days of Progressive Era reform and women's suffrage (see Chapter 21).

The New Deal offered these female reformers little opportunity to advance the cause of women's equality. Demands for greater economic opportunity, sexual freedom, and full equality for women were put forward less often in the 1930s than they had been in the preceding two decades. One reason was that the women's movement had lost momentum after achieving the vote in 1920 (see Chapter 24). Another was that prominent New Deal women, rather than vigorously pursuing a campaign for equal rights, chose to concentrate instead on "protective legislation"—laws that safeguarded female workers. Those who insisted that women needed special protections could not easily argue that women were equal to men in all respects.

Feminism was also hemmed in on all sides by a male hostility that the Depression had intensified. Many men had built their male identities on the value of hard work and the ability to provide economic security for their families. For them, the loss of work unleashed feelings of inadequacy. Male vulnerability increased as unemployment rates of men—most of whom labored in blue-collar industries—rose higher than those of women, many of whom worked in white-collar occupations less affected by job cutbacks (see Table 25.3). Many fathers and husbands resented wives and daughters who had taken on breadwinning roles.

This male anxiety had political and social consequences. Several states passed laws outlawing the hiring of married women. New Deal relief agencies were reluctant to authorize aid for unemployed women. The labor movement made protection of the male wage earner one of its principal goals. The Social Security pension system left out waitresses, domestic servants, and other largely female occupations. Norman Cousins of the *Saturday Evening Post* suggested that the Depression could be ended simply by firing 10 million working women and giving their jobs to men. "Presto!" he declared. "No unemployment, no relief rolls. No Depression."

Many artists introduced a strident masculinism into their painting and sculpture. Mighty *Superman*, the new comic-strip hero of 1938, reflected the spirit of the times. Superman was depicted as a working-class hero, who on several occasions saved workers from coal mine explosions and other disasters caused by the greed and negligence of villainous employers.

Superman's greatest vulnerability, however, other than kryptonite, was his attraction to the *working* woman Lois Lane. He could never resolve his dilemma by marrying Lois and tucking her away in a safe domestic sphere, because the

Table 25.3 RATES OF UNEMPLOYMENT IN SELECTED MALE AND FEMALE OCCUPATIONS, 1930

Male Occupations	Percentage Male	Percentage Unemployed
Iron and steel	96%	13%
Forestry and fishing	99	10
Mining	99	18
Heavy manufacturing	86	13
Carpentry	100	19
Laborers (road and street)	100	13
Female Occupations	**Percentage Female**	**Percentage Unemployed**
Stenographers and typists	96%	5%
Laundresses	99	3
Trained nurses	98	4
Housekeepers	92	3
Telephone operators	95	3
Dressmakers	100	4

Source: U.S. Department of Commerce, Bureau of the Census, *Fifteenth Census of the United States, 1930, Population* (Washington, D.C.: Government Printing Office, 1931).

What They Said

Government's Proper Role

The 1936 presidential election between Franklin Delano Roosevelt and his Republican challenger, Alf Landon, served as a referendum on the New Deal philosophy of using the power of the federal government to increase the economic security and general welfare of ordinary Americans. Roosevelt and his supporters argued that changing times required the federal government to play a more active role than it had done in the past. Opponents of the New Deal, such as Landon and former president Herbert Hoover, argued that the Democrats' desire to expand the federal government posed a serious threat to the American ideals of individual liberty, hard work, and self-reliance. For this reason, Hoover described the 1936 election as "more than a contest between two men. It is a contest between two philosophies of government."

Franklin D. Roosevelt, Inaugural Address, January 20, 1937

When four years ago we met to inaugurate a President, the Republic, single-minded in anxiety, stood in spirit here. We dedicated ourselves to the fulfillment of a vision—to speed the time when there would be for all the people that security and peace essential to the pursuit of happiness. . . .

Our covenant with ourselves did not stop there. Instinctively we recognized a deeper need—the need to find through government the instrument of our united purpose to solve for the individual the ever-rising problems of a complex civilization. Repeated attempts at their solution without the aid of government had left us baffled and bewildered. . . .

We of the Republic sensed the truth that democratic government has innate capacity to protect its people against disasters once considered inevitable, to solve problems once considered unsolvable. . . . We refused to leave the problems of our common welfare to be solved by the winds of chance and the hurricanes of disaster.

This year marks the one hundred and fiftieth anniversary of the Constitutional Convention which made us a nation. At that Convention our forefathers found the way out of the chaos which followed the Revolutionary War; they created a strong government with powers of united action sufficient then and now to solve problems utterly beyond individual or local solution. A century and a half ago they established the Federal Government in order to promote the general welfare and secure the blessings of liberty to the American people.

Today we invoke those same powers of government to achieve the same objectives. . . .

Nearly all of us recognize that as intricacies of human relationships increase, so [the] power to govern them also must increase–power to stop evil; power to do good. The essential democracy of our Nation and the safety of our people depend not upon the absence of power, but upon lodging it with those whom the people can change or continue at stated intervals through an honest and free system of elections.

Herbert Hoover, "The Challenge to Liberty," October 30, 1936

We are near the end of this debate. More than in any election for two generations we are voting on the direction which American civilization will take.

Many of the problems discussed in this campaign concern our material welfare. That is right. But there are things far more important to a nation than material welfare. It is possible to have a prosperous country under a dictatorship. It is not possible to have a free country. . . . What is the nation profited if it shall gain the whole world and lose its own soul?

The transcendent issue before us today is free men and women. How do we test freedom? It is not a catalogue of political rights. It is a thing of the spirit. Men must be free to worship, to think, to hold opinions, to speak without fear. They must be free to challenge wrong and oppression with surety of justice. Freedom conceives that the mind and spirit of man can be free only if he be free to pattern his own life, to develop his own talents, free to earn, to spend, to save, to acquire property as the security of his old age and his family.

Freedom demands that these rights and ideals shall be protected from infringement by others, whether men or groups, corporations or governments.

The conviction of our fathers was that all these freedoms come from the Creator and that they can be denied by no man or no government or no New Deal. They were spiritual rights of men. The prime purpose of liberal government is to enlarge and not to destroy these freedoms. It was for that purpose that the Constitution of the United States was enacted. For that reason we demand that the safeguards of freedom shall be upheld. It is for this reason that we demand that this country should turn its direction from a system of personal centralized government to the ideals of liberty.

And again I repeat that statement of four years ago–"This campaign is more than a contest between two men. It is a contest between two philosophies of government."

Q *What are the major differences between the approaches toward government outlined by Roosevelt and Hoover?*

Q *Hoover argues that "the prime purpose of liberal government" was to safeguard American liberties from an overreaching central government. Yet Roosevelt imagined that his big government New Deal approach was itself liberal. How can we explain how these two men imbued the word liberal with such different meanings?*

Q *In the 1930s and 1940s, Roosevelt's meaning would triumph, forcing Hoover and his ideological descendants to find a different term for their philosophy. Which term did they choose?*

Sources: (top) From President Franklin D. Roosevelt, "The Second Inaugural Address," January 20, 1937, in ed. Samuel I. Rosenman, *The Public Papers and Addresses of Franklin D. Roosevelt, with a Special Introduction and Explanatory Notes by President Roosevelt*, vol. 6 (New York: Macmillan, 1941), 1–5; (bottom) Herbert Hoover, "The Challenge to Liberty," October 30, 1936, in Hoover, *Addresses Upon the American Road, 1933–1938* (New York: Charles Scribner's Sons, 1938), 216–227.

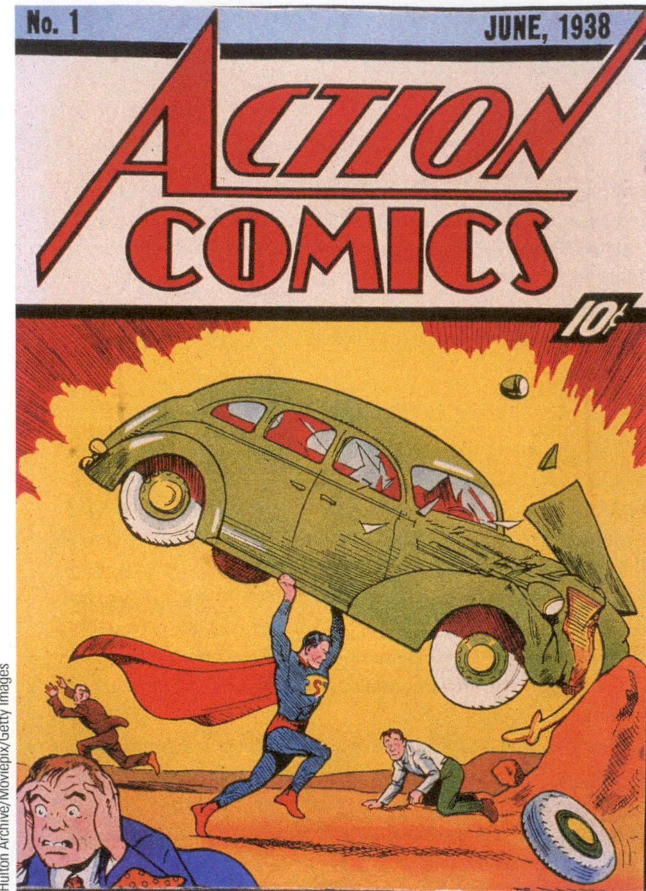

Hulton Archive/Moviepix/Getty Images

25.12 **Man of Steel** The comic book *Superman* debuted in 1938, with the cover that appears in this reproduction. The character Superman partook of the New Deal's commitment to help ordinary Americans in need while offering men a fantasy about unconquerable male power.

continuation of the comic strip demanded that Superman be repeatedly exposed to kryptonite and female danger. But the producers of male and female images in other mass media, such as the movies, faced no such technical obstacles. Anxious men could take comfort from the conclusion of the movie *Woman of the Year*, in which Spencer Tracy persuades the ambitious Katharine Hepburn to exchange her successful newspaper career for the bliss of motherhood and homemaking. From a thousand different points, 1930s politics and culture made it clear that a woman's proper place was in the home. Faced with such obstacles, it is not surprising that women activists failed to make feminism a major part of New Deal reform.

25-5f *Labor in Politics and Culture*

In 1935, John L. Lewis of the United Mine Workers, Sidney Hillman of the Amalgamated Clothing Workers, and the leaders of six other unions that had seceded from the American Federation of Labor (AFL) cobbled together a new labor organization. The Committee for Industrial Organization (**CIO**)—later renamed the Congress of Industrial Organizations—aspired to organize millions of unskilled and semiskilled workers whom the AFL had largely ignored. In 1936, Lewis and Hillman created a second organization, Labor's Non-Partisan League (LNPL), to channel labor's money, energy, and talent into Roosevelt's reelection campaign. Roosevelt welcomed the league's help, and labor would become a key constituency of the new Democratic coalition. The passage of the Wagner Act and the creation of the NLRB in 1935 enhanced the labor movement's status and credibility. Membership in labor unions climbed steadily, and in short order union members began flexing their muscles (see Figure 25.4).

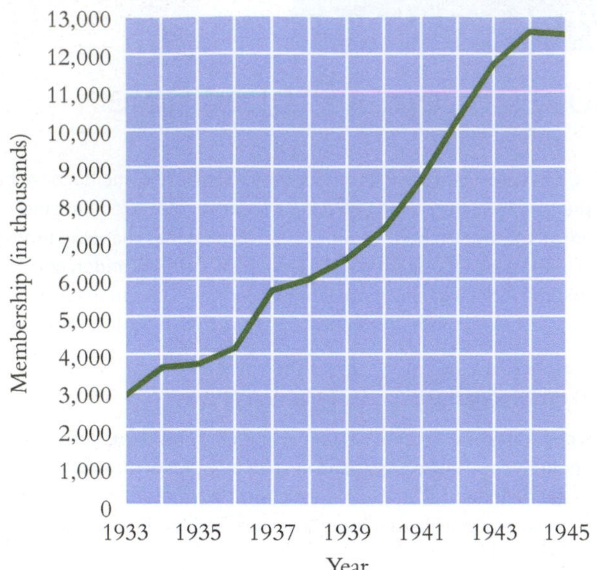

Figure 25.4 **Labor Union Membership, 1933–1945**

Source: From Christopher Tomlins, "AFL Unions in the 1930s," in Melvyn Dubofsky and Stephen Burwood, eds., *Labor* (New York: Garland, 1990), p. 1023.

In late 1936, the United Auto Workers (UAW) took on General Motors, widely regarded as the most powerful corporation in the world. Workers occupied key GM factories in Flint, Michigan, declaring that their **sit-down strike** would continue until GM agreed to recognize the UAW and negotiate a collective bargaining agreement. Frank Murphy, the pro-labor governor of Michigan, refused to use National Guard troops to evict the strikers, and Roosevelt declined to send federal troops. A 50-year-old practice of the government using soldiers to break strikes ended, and General Motors capitulated after a month of resistance. Soon, the U.S. Steel Corporation, which had defeated unionists in the bloody strike of 1919 (see Chapter 23), announced that it was ready to negotiate a contract with the newly formed CIO steelworkers union.

The labor movement's public stature grew along with its size. Many writers and artists, funded through the WPA, depicted the labor movement as the voice of the people and the embodiment of the nation's values. Murals sprang up in post offices and other public buildings featuring portraits of blue-collar Americans at work. Broadway's most celebrated play in

AP images

25.13 **An Activist First Lady** This 1935 photograph depicts Eleanor Roosevelt mixing with miners in the Willow Grove Mine in Bellaire, Ohio.

Q *What does Roosevelt's apparent ease amidst the throng that surrounds her suggest about her ability to interact with ordinary Americans?*

Q *Note the women in coveralls and hardhats on the right side of the photograph. Does their presence suggest anything unusual about this place of employment?*

Library of Congress, Prints and Photographs Division

25.14 **Woody Guthrie** A bard from Okemah, Oklahoma, Guthrie was embraced by millions for his homespun melodies and lyrics and for his hopeful message that Americans could survive the Depression with their dignity and sense of humor intact.

1935 was Clifford Odets's *Waiting for Lefty*, a raw drama about taxi drivers who confront their bosses and organize an honest union. *Pins and Needles*, a 1937 musical about the hopes and dreams of garment workers, performed by actual members of the International Ladies Garment Workers Union, became the longest-running play in Broadway history (until *Oklahoma!* broke its record of 1,108 performances in 1943).

Similarly, many of the most popular novels and movies of the 1930s celebrated the decency, honesty, and patriotism of ordinary Americans. In *Mr. Deeds Goes to Town* (1936) and *Mr. Smith Goes to Washington* (1939), Frank Capra delighted movie audiences with fables of simple, small-town heroes vanquishing the evil forces of wealth and decadence. Likewise, in *The Grapes of Wrath*, the best-selling novel of 1939, John Steinbeck told an epic tale of an Oklahoma family's fortitude in surviving eviction from their land, migrating westward, and suffering exploitation in the "promised land" of California. In 1940, John Ford turned Steinbeck's novel into one of that year's highest-grossing and most acclaimed movies. Moviegoers found special meaning in the declaration of one of the story's main characters, Ma Joad: "We'll go on forever ... cause we're the people."

The Okie migrants to California included a writer and musician named Woody Guthrie. Born in 1913 in Okemah, Oklahoma, Woody Guthrie grew up in nearby Pampa, Texas. He wasn't born poor—his father was a small businessman and a local politician—but by the time he reached his twenties, Guthrie had known a great deal of hardship: His father's business failed, three family homes burned down, and one sister died from burns. Then the drought and dust storms struck. In the 1930s, Guthrie joined the migration of Okies to California. There, his musical gifts were discovered, chiefly because radio stations, in particular, were keen to put "singing cowboys" on the air. Guthrie had emerged from a country music tradition in Texas and Oklahoma and found an audience among the many people from those states who had gone to California.

Guthrie also developed a broader appeal as he cast himself as the bard of ordinary Americans everywhere. He loved America for the beauty of its landscape and its people, sentiments he expressed in one of his most popular songs, "This Land Is Your Land," which he wrote in 1940 in response to Irving Berlin's "God Bless America" (a song Guthrie did not like because of the false sense of complacency he thought it induced). Guthrie did not possess a refined singing voice, but his "hillbilly" lyrics, melodies, and humor were inventive and often inspiring. He would become a powerful influence on subsequent generations of musicians, including such major figures as Bob Dylan and Bruce Springsteen.

Guthrie traveled extensively in the 1930s. The more he learned about the hardships of individual Americans, the angrier and more politically active he became. He drew close to the labor movement and to the Communist Party, and increasingly, in his writings and songs, he criticized the industrialists, financiers, and their political agents who, he believed, had brought the Depression on America. But Guthrie always associated his criticism with the hope that the working people of America, if united, could take back their land—which is the message he meant to convey when he sang "This Land Is Your Land"—and restore its greatness. The optimism of his message underscored how much the cultural mood had changed since the early 1930s. In his focus on ordinary working Americans, in his hope for the future, and in his fusion of dissent and patriotism, Guthrie was emblematic of a major stream of culture and politics in the late 1930s.

25-6 America's Minorities and the New Deal

Q Which minority groups in American society benefited the most from the New Deal, and which benefited the least?

Reformers in the 1930s generally believed that issues of capitalism's viability, economic recovery, and the inequality of wealth and power outweighed problems of racial and ethnic discrimination; only in the case of American Indians did New Dealers pass legislation specifically designed to improve a minority's social and economic position. Because they were disproportionately poor, most minority groups did profit from the populist and pro-labor character of New Deal reforms, but the gains were distributed unevenly. Eastern and southern European ethnics benefited the most, and African Americans and Mexican Americans advanced the least.

25-6a *Eastern and Southern European Ethnics*

Eastern and southern European immigrants and their children had begun mobilizing politically in the 1920s in response to religious and racial discrimination (see Chapter 24). Roosevelt understood their political importance well, for he was a product of New York Democratic politics, where men such as Robert Wagner and Al Smith had begun to organize the ethnic vote even before 1920 (see Chapter 21). He made sure that a significant portion of New Deal monies for welfare, building and road construction, and unemployment relief reached the urban areas where most European ethnics lived. As a result, Jewish and Catholic Americans, especially those descended from eastern and southern European immigrants, voted for Roosevelt in overwhelming numbers. The New Deal did not eliminate anti-Semitism and anti-Catholicism from American society, but it did allow millions of European ethnics to believe, for the first time, that they would overcome the second-class status they had long endured.

Eastern and southern European ethnics also benefited from their sizable presence in the mass-production industries of the Northeast, Midwest, and West Coast and in the new labor unions. Roosevelt understood and feared the power they wielded through their labor organizations.

25-6b *African Americans*

The New Deal did more to reproduce patterns of racial discrimination than to advance the cause of racial equality. African Americans who belonged to CIO unions or who lived in northern cities benefited from New Deal programs, but most blacks lived in the rural South, where they were barred from voting, largely excluded from AAA programs, and denied federal protection in their efforts to form agricultural unions. The CCC ran separate camps for black and white youth. The TVA hired few blacks. Those enrolled in the CWA and other work-relief programs frequently received less pay than whites for doing the same jobs. Roosevelt consistently refused to support legislation to make lynching a federal crime.

This failure to push a strong civil rights agenda did not mean that New Dealers were oblivious to concerns about race. Eleanor Roosevelt spoke out frequently against racial injustice. In 1939, she resigned from the Daughters of the American Revolution when the organization refused to allow black opera singer **Marian Anderson** to perform in its concert hall. She then pressured the federal government into granting Anderson permission to sing from the steps

Hulton Archive/Archive Photos/Getty Images

25.15 **Marian Anderson and Abraham Lincoln** The opera star Marian Anderson performs in 1939 at one of America's most sacred sites, the Lincoln Memorial, after having been denied the opportunity to sing at the Washington DC hall owned by the Daughters of the American Revolution.

Q Why did the New Deal do little to advance the cause of racial equality?

of the Lincoln Memorial. On Easter Sunday, 75,000 people gathered to hear Anderson and to demonstrate their support for racial equality. The president did not attend.

Franklin Roosevelt did eliminate segregationist practices in the federal government that had been in place since Woodrow Wilson's presidency. He appointed Mary McLeod Bethune, Robert Weaver, William Hastie, and other African Americans to important second-level posts in his administration. Working closely with each other in what came to be known as the Black Cabinet, these officials fought hard to end discrimination in New Deal programs.

Roosevelt, however, refused to support the Black Cabinet if it meant alienating white southern senators who controlled key congressional committees. He believed that pushing for civil rights too much would cost him the support of the white South. Meanwhile, African Americans and their supporters were not yet strong enough as an electoral constituency or as a reform movement to compel Roosevelt to support a civil rights agenda.

25-6c *Mexican Americans*

The Mexican American experience in the Great Depression was particularly harsh. In 1931, Hoover's secretary of labor, William N. Doak, announced a plan for repatriating illegal aliens (returning them to their land of origin) and giving their jobs to American citizens. The federal campaign quickly focused on Mexican immigrants in California and the Southwest. The U.S. Immigration Service rounded up large numbers of Mexicans and Mexican Americans and demanded that each detainee prove his or her legal status. Those who failed to produce the necessary documentation were deported. Local and state governments pressured many more Mexicans into leaving. The combined efforts of federal, state, and local governments created a climate of fear in Mexican communities that prompted 500,000 to return to Mexico by 1935. This total equaled the number of Mexicans who had come to the United States in the 1920s. Los Angeles lost one-third of its Mexican population. Included in repatriate ranks were a significant number of legal immigrants who were unable to produce their immigration papers, the American-born children of illegals, and some Mexican Americans who had lived in the Southwest for generations.

The advent of the New Deal in 1933 eased but did not eliminate pressure on Mexican communities. New Deal agencies made money available for relief; Mexican Americans who worked in urban, blue-collar industries joined unions in large numbers. Most Mexicans, however, lived in rural areas and labored in agricultural jobs, and the New Deal offered them little help. The National Labor Relations Act did not protect their right to organize unions, and the Social Security Act excluded them from the new federal welfare system. Where Mexicans gained access to relief rolls, they often received payments lower than those given to "Anglos" (whites). New Dealers also did not do much to dissuade local officials from continuing their campaign to deport Mexican immigrants.

Life grew harder for immigrant Mexicans who stayed behind. The Mexican cultural renaissance that had emerged in 1920s Los Angeles (see Chapter 24) stalled. Mexicans in the city retreated into the separate community of East Los Angeles. To many, they became the "invisible minority."

25-6d *American Indians*

From the 1880s until the early 1930s, federal policy had contributed to the elimination of American Indians as a distinctive population. The Dawes Act of 1887 (see Chapter 18) had called for tribal lands to be broken up and allotted to individual owners in the hope that Indians would adopt the work habits and lifestyles of white farmers. But American Indians had proved stubbornly loyal to their languages, religions, and cultures. Few of them succeeded as farmers, and many lost land to white speculators. By 1933, nearly half the American Indians living on reservations where communal land had been allotted (distributed as private property to individual Indians) were landless. Many who retained allotments held largely desert or semidesert land.

The shrinking land base in combination with a growing population deepened American Indian poverty. The assimilationist pressures on American Indians, meanwhile, reached a climax in the 1920s, when the Bureau of Indian Affairs (BIA) outlawed Indian religious ceremonies, forced

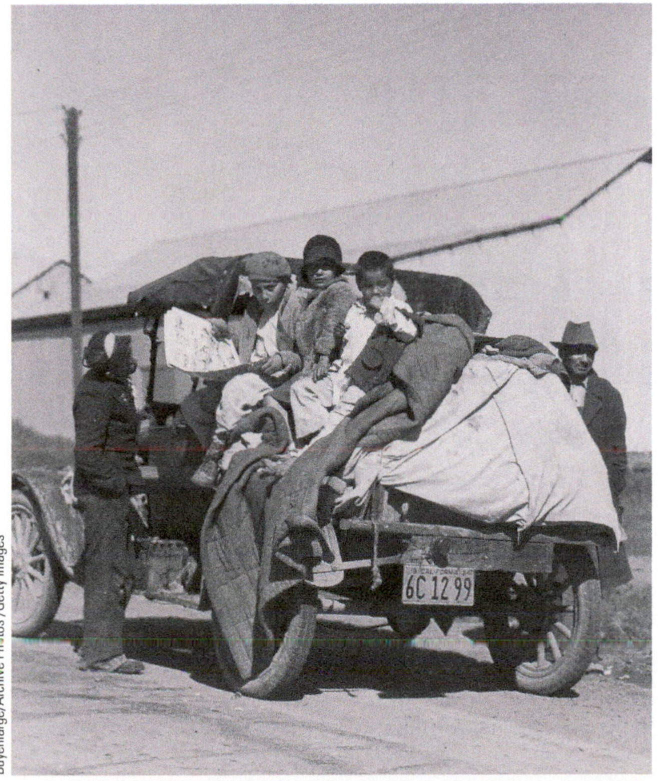

Buyenlarge/Archive Photos/Getty Images

25.16 Mexican Hardship The Great Depression made it difficult for Mexican agricultural workers in California to find adequate work. Many suffered additional injury when state and local authorities pressured them into returning to Mexico.

children from tribal communities into federal boarding schools, banned polygamy, and imposed limits on the length of men's hair.

Government officials working in the Hoover administration began to question this assimilationist policy, but its reversal had to await the New Deal and Roosevelt's appointment of **John Collier** as the commissioner of the BIA. Collier pressured the CCC, AAA, and other New Deal agencies to employ Indians on projects that improved reservation land and trained Indians in land conservation methods. He prevailed on Congress to pass the Pueblo Relief Act of 1933, which compensated Pueblos for land taken from them in the 1920s, and the Johnson-O'Malley Act of 1934, which provided funds to the states for Indian health care, welfare, and education. As part of his campaign to make the BIA more responsive to American Indian needs, Collier increased the number of Indian BIA employees from a few hundred in 1933 to 4,600 in 1940.

Collier also took steps to abolish federal boarding schools, encourage enrollment in local public schools, and establish community day schools. He insisted that American Indians be allowed to practice their traditional religions, and he created the Indian Arts and Crafts Board in 1935 to nurture traditional Indian artists and to help them market their work.

The centerpiece of Collier's reform strategy was the Indian Reorganization Act (IRA, also known as the Wheeler-Howard Act) of 1934, which revoked the allotment provisions of the Dawes Act. This landmark act recognized the rights of Native American tribes to chart their own political, cultural, and economic futures. It reflected Collier's commitment to "cultural pluralism," a doctrine that celebrated the diversity of peoples and cultures in American society and sought to protect that diversity against the pressures of assimilation. Specifically, the IRA restored land to tribes, granted Indians the right to establish constitutions and bylaws for self-government, and provided support for new tribal corporations that would regulate the use of communal lands.

Collier encountered opposition everywhere: from Protestant missionaries and cultural conservatives who wanted to continue an assimilationist policy; from white farmers and businessmen who feared that the new legislation would restrict their access to Native American land; and even from a sizable number of Indian groups that had either embraced assimilation or would not be persuaded that this latest attempt by the federal government to impose "the white man's will" would benefit them. This opposition made the IRA a more modest bill than the one Collier had originally championed.

A vocal minority of Indians continued to oppose the act even after its passage. The Navajo, the nation's largest tribe, voted to reject its terms, as did 76 other tribes. Still, 181 tribes, nearly 70 percent of the total, supported Collier's reform and began organizing new governments under the IRA. Although their quest for independence would suffer setbacks, these tribes gained significant measures of freedom and autonomy during the New Deal.

Library of Congress, Prints and Photographs Division

25.17 **Indian Children** An Arnold Rothstein photograph depicting three Indian children on the Mescalero Reservation in New Mexico in 1936.

Q *A New Deal for Indians took shape in the 1930s. How successful was it?*

25-7 The New Deal Abroad

Q *What were the achievements and limitations of the New Deal's turn toward internationalism?*

When he first entered office, Roosevelt favored a nationalist approach to international relations. The United States, he believed, should pursue foreign policies to benefit its domestic affairs, without regard for the effects of those policies on world trade and international stability. Thus, in June 1933, Roosevelt pulled the United States out of the World Economic Conference in London, a meeting called by leading nations to strengthen the gold standard and thereby stabilize the value of their currencies. Roosevelt feared that the United States would be forced into an agreement designed to keep the gold content of the dollar high and U.S. commodity prices low, which would frustrate New Deal efforts to inflate the prices of agricultural and industrial goods.

Soon after his withdrawal from the London conference, however, Roosevelt put the United States on a more internationalist course. In November 1933, he became the first president to recognize the Soviet Union and to establish diplomatic ties with its communist rulers. In December 1933, he inaugurated a **Good Neighbor Policy** toward Latin

America by formally renouncing U.S. rights to intervene in the affairs of Latin American nations. To back up his pledge, Roosevelt ordered home the U.S. Marines stationed in Haiti and Nicaragua; scuttled the Platt Amendment that had given the United States control over the Cuban government since 1901; and granted Panama more political autonomy and a greater administrative role in operating the Panama Canal (see Chapter 22).

None of this, however, meant that the United States had given up its influence over Latin America. When a 1934 revolution brought a radical government to power in Cuba, the U.S. ambassador there worked with conservative Cubans to replace the government with a regime more favorable to U.S. interests. The United States did refrain from sending troops to Cuba. It also kept its troops at home in 1936 when Mexico nationalized several U.S. and British owned petroleum companies. Instead, the United States demanded that Mexico compensate the oil companies for their lost property, which Mexico eventually did. In such ways, the United States exercised restraint while remaining the dominant force in hemispheric affairs.

The Roosevelt administration's internationalism also reflected its interest in stimulating trade. American businessmen wanted access to the Soviet Union's domestic market. Latin America was already a major market for the United States, but one in need of greater stability. To win the support of American traders and investors, Roosevelt stressed how the Good Neighbor Policy would improve the region's business climate.

Roosevelt further expressed his commitment to international trade through his support for the Reciprocal Trade Agreement, passed by Congress in 1934. This act allowed the United States to lower its tariffs by as much as 50 percent in exchange for similar reductions by other nations. By the end of 1935, the United States had negotiated reciprocal trade agreements with 14 countries. Roosevelt's emphasis on international trade—a move consonant with the Second New Deal's program of increasing the circulation of goods and money through the economy—further solidified support for the New Deal in parts of the business community, especially among those firms, such as United Fruit and Coca-Cola, with large overseas investments.

25-8 Stalemate, 1937–1940

Why did the New Deal lose momentum in 1937 and 1938?

By 1937 and 1938, the New Deal had begun to lose momentum. One reason was an emerging split between working-class and middle-class Democrats. After the UAW's victory over General Motors in 1937, other workers began to imitate the successful tactics of the Flint, Michigan, militants. Sit-down strikes spread to many industries and regions, a development that worried many middle-class Americans.

25-8a *The Court-Packing Fiasco*

The president's proposal on February 5, 1937, to alter the makeup of the Supreme Court exacerbated middle-class fears. Roosevelt asked Congress to give him the power to appoint one new Supreme Court justice for every member of the Court who was older than age 70 and had served at least 10 years. His stated reason was that the current justices were too old to handle the large volume of cases coming before them, but his real purpose was to prevent the conservative justices on the court—most had been appointed by Republican presidents—from dismantling his New Deal. His proposal, if accepted, would have given him the authority to appoint six additional justices, thereby securing a pro-New Deal majority.

The president seemed genuinely surprised by the indignation that greeted his **"court-packing"** proposal. Although working-class support for Roosevelt remained strong, many middle-class voters turned away from the New Deal. In 1937 and 1938, a conservative opposition took shape, uniting Republicans and conservative Democrats (many of them southerners) who believed that the changes unleashed by the New Deal had gone too far.

Ironically, Roosevelt's court-packing scheme may have been unnecessary. In March 1937, just one month after he proposed his plan, Supreme Court Justice Owen J. Roberts, a former opponent of New Deal programs, decided to support them. In April and May, the Court upheld the constitutionality of the Wagner Act and Social Security Act, both by a 5-to-4 margin. The principal reforms of the New Deal would endure. Roosevelt allowed his court-reform proposal to die in Congress that summer. Within three years, five of the aging justices had retired, giving Roosevelt the opportunity to fashion a court more to his liking. Nonetheless, Roosevelt's reputation had suffered.

25-8b *The Recession of 1937–1938*

Whatever hope Roosevelt may have had for a quick recovery from his attempt at court-packing was dashed by a sharp recession that struck the country in late 1937 and 1938. The New Deal programs of 1935 had stimulated the economy, prompting Roosevelt to scale back relief programs. Meanwhile, new payroll taxes took $2 billion from wage earners' salaries to finance the Social Security pension fund even though the government did not intend to begin paying benefits until 1941. Thus, the government shrank the volume of dollars it was putting into circulation. Starved for money, the economy and stock market crashed once again. Unemployment, which had fallen to 14 percent, shot back up to 20 percent (see Figure 25.5). In the 1938 elections, voters vented their frustration by electing many conservative Democrats and Republicans who were opposed to the New Deal. These conservatives could not dismantle the New Deal reforms already in place, but they did block the passage of new programs.

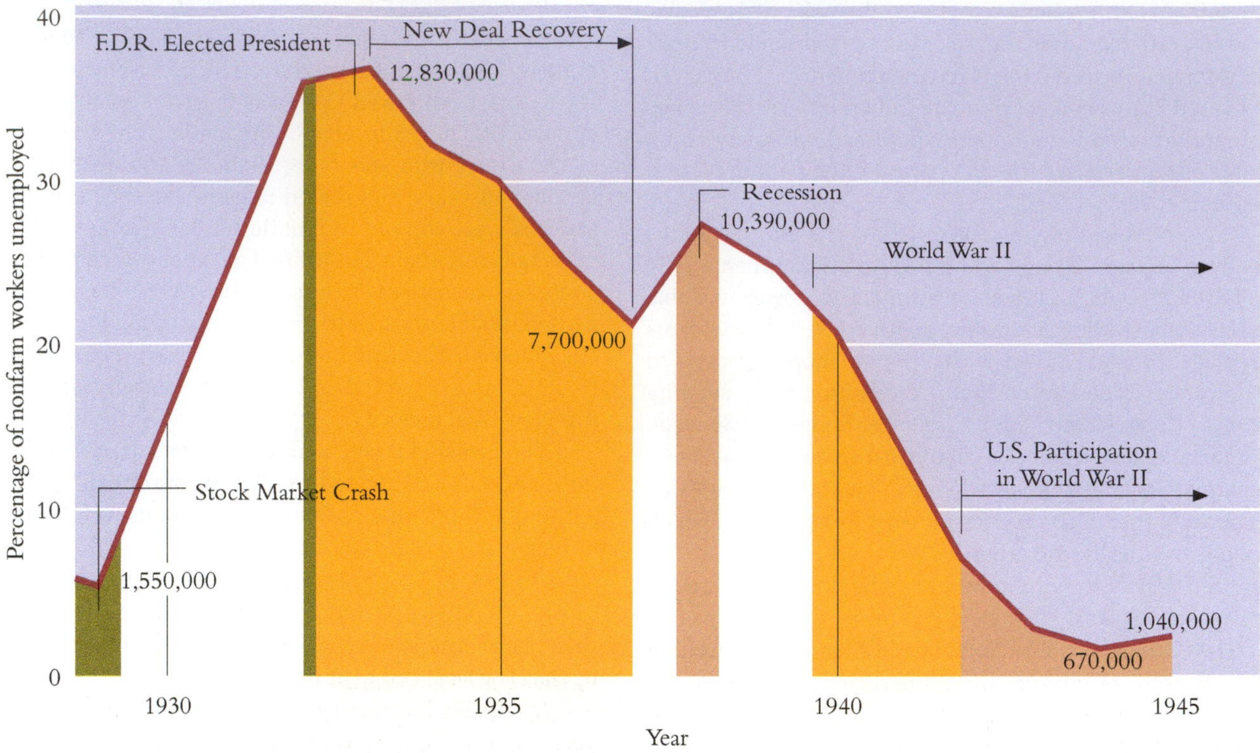

Figure 25.5 **Unemployment in the Nonfarm Labor Force, 1929–1945**

Source: Data from *Historical Statistics of the United States, Colonial Times to 1970* (White Plains, NY: Kraus International, 1989), p. 126.

Conclusion

Roosevelt first assumed the presidency in the same week that Adolf Hitler established a Nazi dictatorship in Germany. Some feared that Roosevelt, by accumulating more power into the hands of the federal government than had ever been held in peacetime, aspired to autocratic rule. Nothing of the sort happened. Roosevelt and the New Dealers not only strengthened democracy, they also inspired millions of Americans who had never before voted to go to the polls. Groups that had been marginalized—eastern and southern European ethnics, unskilled workers, American Indians—now believed that their political activism could make a difference.

Not everyone benefited to the same degree from the broadening of American democracy. Northern factory workers, farm owners, European American ethnics, and middle-class consumers (especially homeowners) were among the groups who benefited most. In contrast, the socialist and communist elements of the labor movement failed to achieve their radical aims. Unionization proceeded far more slowly among southern industrial workers, black and white, than in the North. Sizable occupational groups, such as farm laborers and domestic servants, were denied Social Security benefits. Feminists made little headway. African Americans and Mexican Americans gained meager influence over public policy.

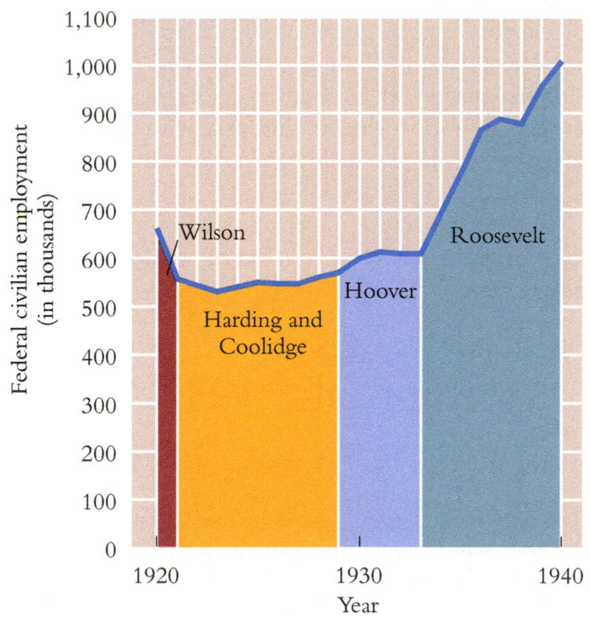

Figure 25.6 **Growth in Federal Civilian Employment, 1920–1940**

Source: Data from *Historical Statistics of the United States, Colonial Times to 1970* (White Plains, NY: Kraus International, 1989), p. 1105.

New Deal reforms might not have mattered to any group if the Second World War had not rescued the New Deal economic program. With government war orders flooding factories from 1941 on, the economy grew vigorously, unemployment vanished, and prosperity finally returned. The architects of the Second New Deal, who had argued that large government expenditures would stimulate consumer demand and trigger economic recovery, were vindicated.

The war also solidified the political reforms of the 1930s: an increased role for the government in regulating the economy and in ensuring the social welfare of those unable to help themselves; strong state support of unionization, agricultural subsidies, and progressive tax policies; the use of government power and money to develop the West and Southwest. All this central state activity required a substantial increase in government employment. Indeed, federal civilian employment nearly doubled from its 1920s levels (see Figure 25.6).

In contrast to progressivism, the reforms of the New Deal endured. Voters returned Roosevelt to office for unprecedented third and fourth terms, and these same voters remained wedded for the next 40 years to Roosevelt's central idea: that a powerful state would enhance the pursuit of liberty and equality.

CHAPTER REVIEW

Review

1. What caused the crash of 1929, and why did the ensuing depression last so long?
2. Why did Hoover become a reviled political figure? How did political pessimism influence American culture? What transformed Roosevelt into a focused politician and reformer?
3. What do you consider to be the three or four most important pieces of legislation in the First New Deal? Why?
4. What forms did political unrest take in 1934 and 1935?
5. How was the Second New Deal different from the First New Deal?
6. Which minority groups in American society benefited the most from the New Deal, and which benefited least?
7. What were the achievements and limitations of the New Deal's turn toward internationalism?
8. Why did the New Deal lose momentum in 1937 and 1938?

Critical Thinking

1. How did the Great Depression and New Deal shape the literature and art of the 1930s?
2. Why did the New Deal prove so popular given that, in the 1930s, it failed to solve the problem of unemployment?

Identifications

Review your understanding of the following key terms, people, and events for this chapter (terms in bold in text are included in the Glossary).

Franklin Delano Roosevelt, p. 686
liberalism, p. 686
Bonus Army, p. 689
Eleanor Roosevelt, p. 691
Agricultural Adjustment Administration (AAA), p. 692
National Recovery Administration (NRA), p. 693
Tennessee Valley Authority (TVA), p. 694
Huey Long, p. 697
Father Charles Coughlin, p. 697
Communist Party, p. 698
underconsumptionism, p. 699
Social Security Act, p. 699
NLRA/Wagner Act, p. 699
Works Progress Administration (WPA), p. 701
CIO, p. 706
sit-down strike, p. 706
Marian Anderson, p. 708
John Collier, p. 710
Good Neighbor Policy, p. 710
"court-packing," p. 711

Suggested Readings

T. H. Watkins, ***The Great Depression: America in the 1930s*** (1993), provides a broad overview of society and politics during the 1930s. **Ira Katznelson, *Fear Itself: The New Deal and the Origins of Our Time*** (2013); and **David M. Kennedy, *Freedom from Fear: The American People in Depression and War, 1929–1945*** (1999) are masterful accounts of the origins and development of the New Deal.

Kenneth S. Davis, *FDR* (1972–1993), in four volumes, is the most complete biography of FDR, and one that is remarkably good at balancing Roosevelt's life and times. **Anthony J. Badger, *FDR: The First Hundred Days*** (2007) offers an excellent account of the early months of the first Roosevelt administration. On Eleanor Roosevelt, see **Blanche Wiesen Cook, *Eleanor Roosevelt***, vol. 1 (1992) and vol. 2 (1999). On the New Deal as a political order that would dominate American politics for forty years, see **Steve Fraser and Gary Gerstle, eds., *The Rise and Fall of the New Deal Order, 1930–1980*** (1989). For a sharply critical view of the New Deal, consult

Amity Shlaes, ***The Forgotten Man: A New History of the Great Depression*** (2007).

Michael Denning, ***The Cultural Front: The Laboring of American Culture in the Twentieth Century*** (1996), is essential reading on the centrality of labor and the "common man" to literary and popular culture in the 1930s. For the economic and cultural ties between the New Deal and the rebirth of the labor movement, see **Lizabeth Cohen**, ***Making a New Deal: Industrial Workers in Chicago, 1919–1939*** (1990). On the gendered nature of New Deal reform, consult **Alice Kessler-Harris**, ***In Pursuit of Equity: Women, Men, and the Quest for Economic Citizenship in Twentieth-Century America*** (2001). On limits of labor and agricultural reform during the New Deal, see **Gary Gerstle**, ***Liberty and Coercion: The Paradox of American Government from the Founding to the Present*** (2015).

Harvard Sitkoff, ***A New Deal for Blacks*** (1978), is a wide-ranging examination of the place of African Americans in New Deal reform. On the precarious situation of Mexicans in the 1930s, see **Abraham Hoffman**, ***Unwanted Mexican Americans in the Great Depression: Repatriation Pressures, 1929–1939*** (1974); and **Kelly Lytle Hernandez**, ***Migra! A history of the U.S. Border Patrol*** (2010). The importance of John Collier and the Indian Reorganization Act are treated well in **Lawrence C. Kelly**, ***The Assault on Assimilation: John Collier and the Origins of Indian Policy Reform*** (1983). **James T. Patterson**, ***Congressional Conservatism and the New Deal*** (1967), analyzes the growing opposition to the New Deal in the late 1930s, while **Alan Brinkley**, ***The End of Reform: New Deal Liberalism in Recession and War*** (1995), provocatively examines the efforts of New Dealers to adjust their beliefs and programs as they lost support, momentum, and confidence in the late 1930s. On the international ramifications of the New Deal, see **Kiran Klaus Patel**, ***The New Deal: A Global History*** (2016).

26 America during the Second World War, 1939–1945

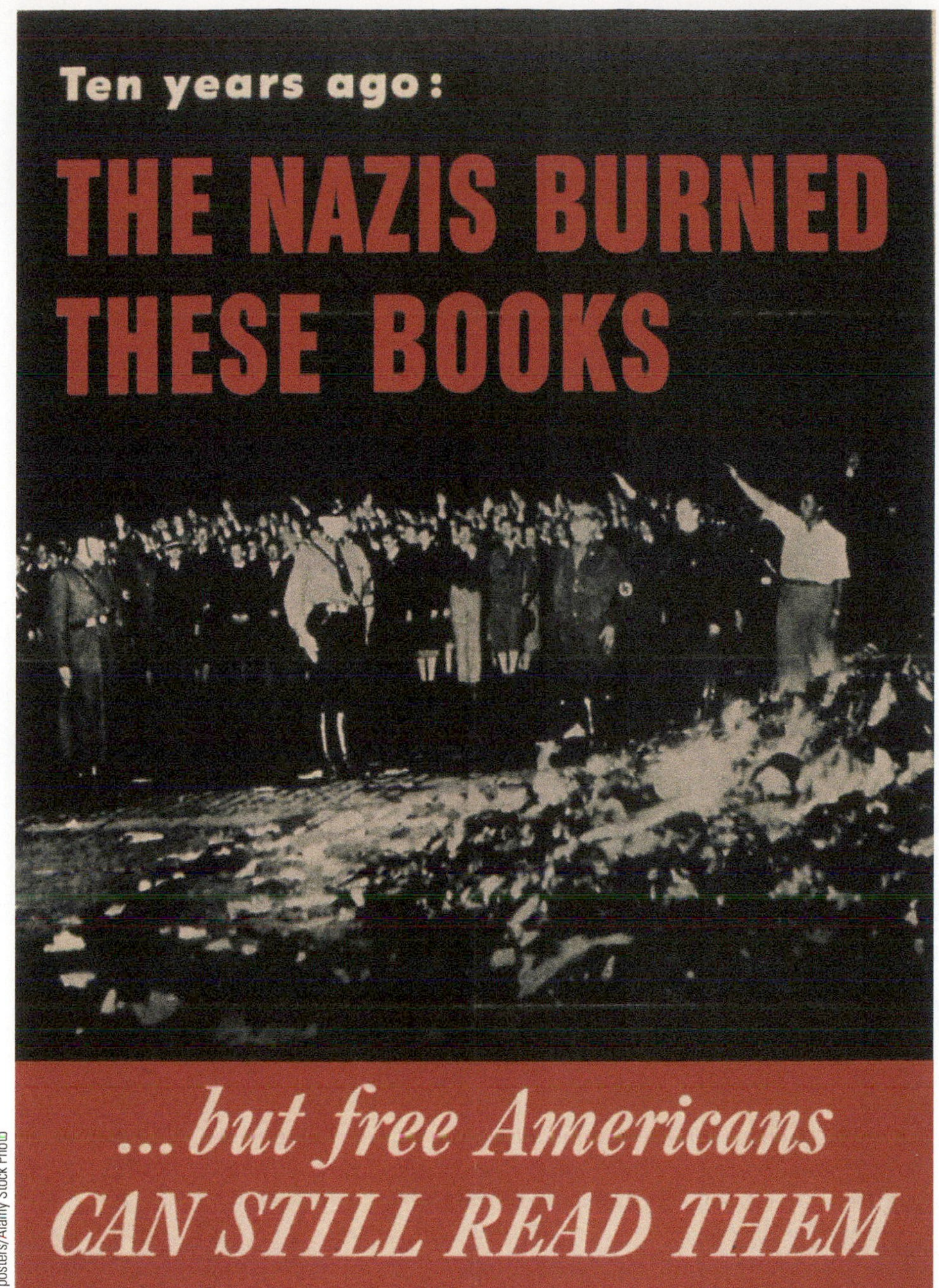
Ten years ago:
THE NAZIS BURNED THESE BOOKS
...but free Americans
CAN STILL READ THEM

war posters/Alamy Stock Photo

26.1 **U.S. Government War Poster** The governmental agencies charged with promoting support for U.S. participation in the Second World War often employed images from Nazi Germany as a way of dramatizing how we were fighting to preserve "the American way of life."

Q *What specific value in the "American way" is being endorsed here?*

THE SECOND WORLD WAR vastly changed American life. The United States abandoned isolationism, moved toward military engagement on the side of the Allies, and emerged triumphant in a global war. The nation's productive capacity—spurred by innovative technologies and by a new working relationship among government, business, labor, and scientific researchers—dwarfed that of all other nations and provided the economic basis for military victory. The mobilization for war finally lifted the economy out of the Great Depression.

The war also raised questions about the meanings of liberty and equality in America. How would the nation, while striving for victory, reorder its economy, its politics, and the cultural and social patterns that had shaped racial, ethnic, and gender relationships during the 1930s? What processes of reconstruction, at home and abroad, might be required to build a prosperous and lasting peace? ■

26-1 The Road to War: Aggression and Response

Q *Why did events in Asia and in Europe prompt debate within the United States over whether or not to embrace more interventionist policies overseas?*

The road to the Second World War began at least a decade before U.S. entry in 1941. In Japan, Italy, and Germany, economic stagnation created political conditions that nurtured ultranationalist movements bent on territorial expansion. Elsewhere in Europe and in the United States, economic problems led governments to concentrate on domestic recovery and avoid foreign entanglements.

26-1a *The Rise of Aggressor States*

On September 18, 1931, Japanese military forces seized Manchuria and created Manchukuo, a puppet state of Japan. This action violated the League of Nations charter, the Washington Naval Treaties, and the Kellogg-Briand Pact (see Chapter 24). Focused on domestic matters, the international community hesitated to oppose Japan's move. The Hoover-Stimson Doctrine (1931) announced a U.S. policy of "nonrecognition" toward Manchukuo, and the League of Nations condemned Japan's action. Japan simply ignored these rebukes.

Meanwhile, ultranationalist states in Europe also sought to alleviate domestic ills through military aggression. **Adolf Hitler's** National Socialist (Nazi) Party came to power in Germany in 1933 and instituted a fascist regime, a one-party dictatorial state. Hitler denounced the Versailles peace settlement of 1919, blamed Germany's problems on a Jewish conspiracy, claimed a genetic superiority for the "Aryan race" of German-speaking peoples, and promised a new Germanic empire, the **Third Reich**. His regime withdrew from the League of Nations in 1933 and, in a blatant violation of the Versailles Treaty, dramatically boosted Germany's military budget. Another fascist government, in Italy, headed by Benito Mussolini, also launched a military buildup and dreamed of empire. In October 1935, Mussolini's armies took over Ethiopia, an independent nation in Africa.

26-1b *U.S. Neutrality*

Many Americans wished to isolate their nation from these foreign troubles. Antiwar movies, such as *All Quiet on the Western Front* (1931), implicitly portrayed the First World War as a power game played by business and governmental elites, who used appeals to nationalism to dupe young soldiers into serving as cannon fodder. During the mid-1930s a Senate investigating committee headed by Republican Gerald P. Nye of North Dakota held well-publicized hearings and concluded that the United States had been maneuvered into the First World War to preserve the profits of bankers and munitions makers. By 1935, opinion polls suggested that Americans overwhelmingly opposed involvement in foreign conflicts.

To prevent a repetition of the circumstances that had supposedly drawn the United States into the First World War, Congress enacted neutrality legislation. The **Neutrality Acts** of 1935 and 1936 mandated an arms embargo against belligerents, prohibited loans to them, and curtailed travel by Americans on ships belonging to nations at war. The Neutrality Act of 1937 extended the embargo to include all trade with any belligerent, unless the nation paid in cash and carried the purchases away in its own ships.

Critics charged that forswearing U.S. intervention actively aided expansionist powers. In March 1936, Nazi troops seized the Rhineland, a German area from which the 1919 peace settlement had barred military installations. A few months later, Hitler and Mussolini began assisting General Francisco Franco, a fellow fascist seeking to overthrow Spain's republican government. Republicans in Spain appealed to nonfascist nations for assistance, but only the Soviet Union responded. Britain, France, and the United States, fearing that the conflict would flare into world war if more nations took sides, remained uninvolved.

Although the United States remained officially aloof, the **Spanish Civil War** precipitated a major debate. Conservative groups generally hailed Franco as a staunch anticommunist who supported the Catholic Church and social traditionalism in Spain. In contrast, the political left championed republican Spain and denounced fascism. Cadres of Americans, including the famed "Abraham Lincoln Brigade," crossed the Atlantic to fight alongside republican forces in Spain. American peace groups

CHRONOLOGY

1931	Japanese forces seize Manchuria
1933	Hitler takes power in Germany
1936	Spanish Civil War begins • Germany and Italy agree to cooperate as the Axis powers
1937	Neutrality Act broadens provisions of Neutrality Acts of 1935 and 1936 • Roosevelt makes "Quarantine" speech • Japan invades China
1938	France and Britain appease Hitler at Munich
1939	Hitler invades Poland; war breaks out in Europe • Congress amends Neutrality Act to assist Allies
1940	Paris falls after German *blitzkreig* • Roosevelt makes "destroyers-for-bases" deal with Britain • Selective Service Act passed • Roosevelt wins third term
1941	Lend-Lease established • Roosevelt creates Fair Employment Practices Commission • Roosevelt and Churchill proclaim the Atlantic Charter • Congress narrowly repeals Neutrality Act • Japanese forces attack Pearl Harbor (December 7)
1942	President signs Executive Order 9066 for internment of Japanese Americans • General MacArthur driven from Philippines • United States victorious in Battle of Midway • German army defeated at Battle of Stalingrad • Operation TORCH begins
1943	Axis armies in North Africa surrender • Allies invade Sicily and Italy • "Zoot suit" incidents in Los Angeles; racial violence in Detroit • Allies begin drive toward Japan through South Pacific islands
1944	Allies land at Normandy (D-Day, June 6) • Roosevelt reelected to fourth term • Bretton Woods Conference creates IMF and World Bank • Dumbarton Oaks Conference establishes plan for United Nations
1945	United States firebombs Japan • Yalta Conference • Roosevelt dies; Truman becomes president • Germany surrenders • Hiroshima and Nagasaki hit with atomic bombs • Japan surrenders • United Nations established

splintered: Some continued to advocate neutrality and isolation, but others argued for intervention against the spread of fascism.

In October 1937, Franklin D. Roosevelt called for international cooperation to "quarantine" aggressor nations and suggested that Congress should modify its earlier neutrality measures. Still suspicious of foreign entanglements, a majority in Congress refused to budge, even when this meant a victory by Franco in Spain's civil war.

26-1c *The Mounting Crisis*

As Americans debated how to deal with foreign aggression, Japan invaded China. In summer 1937, after an exchange of gunfire between Japanese and Chinese troops at the Marco Polo Bridge near Beijing, Japanese armies captured Shanghai, Nanjing, Shandong, and Beijing. Japan demanded that China become subservient to Tokyo. It also proposed an **East Asian Co-Prosperity Sphere** that would supposedly liberate Asian nations from Western colonialism and create a self-sufficient economic zone under Japanese leadership. Later that year Japanese planes sank the American gunboat *Panay* as it evacuated Americans from Nanjing. Japan's quick apology defused a potential crisis, but the *Panay* incident and Japan's brutal occupation of Nanjing—where perhaps 300,000 Chinese civilians were killed—alarmed Roosevelt.

In Europe, Germany continued on the march. In March 1938, Hitler annexed Austria to the Third Reich and announced his intention to seize the Sudetenland, a portion of Czechoslovakia inhabited by 3.5 million people of German descent. In May, FDR began a program of naval rearmament. French and British leaders, still hoping to avoid war, met with Hitler at the **Munich Conference** in September. They acquiesced to Germany's seizure of the Sudetenland in return for Hitler's promise to seek no more territory. Hailed by Britain's prime minister as a guarantee of "peace in our time," the arrangement soon became a symbol of what interventionists called the "appeasement" of aggression.

In March 1939, Germans marched into Prague and, within a few months, annexed the rest of Czechoslovakia. In August, Hitler signed a nonaggression pact with the Soviet Union, previously his bitter enemy. In a secret protocol, Hitler and Soviet leader Joseph Stalin agreed on a plan to divide up Poland and permit Soviet annexation of the Baltic states (Latvia, Lithuania, and Estonia).

26-1d *The Outbreak of War in Europe*

When Hitler's armies stormed into Poland on September 1, 1939, the Second World War officially began in Europe. Britain and France declared war against Germany, but these Allied powers could not mobilize in time to help Poland, which fell within weeks. Then an eerie calm settled over Europe during the winter.

In April 1940, a full-scale German *blitzkrieg*, or "lightning war," began moving swiftly, shocking Allied leaders and overrunning Denmark, Norway, the Netherlands, Belgium, Luxembourg, and France. Early in June, Italy and Germany—which had earlier formed the Axis powers—declared war on the Allies. Later in June, France fell, and Hitler installed a pro-Nazi government at Vichy in southern France. In only six weeks, Hitler's army had seized complete control of Europe's Atlantic coastline, from the North Sea south to Spain, where Franco remained officially neutral but decidedly pro-Axis. The Axis gained another member in September 1940, when Japan joined Germany and Italy in a Tripartite Pact.

26-1e *The U.S. Response to War in Europe*

Alarmed at the Nazi surge, Roosevelt pressured Congress to modify its neutrality legislation and called for other measures, "short of war," to help Britain and France. Late in 1939, Congress lifted the ban on selling military armaments to belligerents and substituted a cash-and-carry provision that permitted arms sales to belligerents who could pay cash and use their own ships for transport. This arrangement minimized risks to American exporters. Because its naval forces dominated the Atlantic sea-lanes, Britain primarily benefited from this policy change. Congress also boosted military funding and passed the Selective Training and Service Act of 1940, the first peacetime draft in U.S. history. Abandoning any pretense of neutrality, the United States also facilitated Britain's direct acquisition of U.S. "surplus" war materiel. In an attempt to broaden bipartisan support for these controversial measures, Roosevelt added pro-interventionist Republicans to his cabinet.

Meanwhile, from August through October 1940, Germany's *Luftwaffe* (air force) conducted daily raids on British air bases and nearly knocked out its Royal Air Force (RAF). On the verge of a knockout, however, Hitler suddenly changed strategy and ordered, instead, the bombing of London and other cities. The use of airpower against civilians in the Battle of Britain, as it was called, steeled Britain's resolve and aroused sympathy among Americans who heard of events during dramatic radio broadcasts from London. CBS's Edward R. Murrow, observed one American writer, "skillfully burned the city of London in our homes, and we felt the flames (see Map 26.1)."

▲ **MAP 26.1 German Expansion at Its Height** This map shows the expansion of German power from 1938 through 1942.

Q *Which countries fell to German control? Why might Americans have differed over whether these moves by Germany represented a strategic threat to U.S. national security?*

In September 1940, Roosevelt agreed to transfer 50 First World War–era naval destroyers to the British navy. In return, the United States gained the right to build eight naval bases in British territories in the Western Hemisphere. This "destroyers-for-bases" deal infuriated those who favored staying out of the war. The America First Committee, organized by General Robert E. Wood, head of Sears, Roebuck, and Company, launched a campaign to sway public opinion. The aviator hero Charles A. Lindbergh, America First's most famous member, flew around the country rallying opposition to aiding Britain.

Those who favored staying out of the war were generally lumped together as **"isolationists,"** but this single term obscures their diversity. Pacifists opposed all wars as immoral. Some political progressives detested fascism but feared even more the centralization of governmental power that conducting a war would require in the United States. And some conservatives sympathized with the anticommunism of fascist states.

An undercurrent of anti-Jewish sentiment also existed in the United States. In 1939, congressional leaders had quashed the Wagner-Rogers bill, which would have boosted immigration quotas in order to allow for the entry of 20,000 Jewish children otherwise slated for Hitler's concentration camps. Bowing to anti-Semitic prejudices, the United States adopted a restrictive refugee policy. The consequences of these policies became especially grave after June 1941, when Hitler established the death camps that would systematically exterminate millions of Jews, gypsies, homosexuals, communists, and anyone else whom the Nazis deemed unfit for life in the Third Reich. In September 1941, Senator Burton K. Wheeler created a Senate committee to investigate whether Jewish producers in Hollywood were using movies to promote pro-interventionist views. Some isolationists expressed blatantly anti-Semitic views.

Those who favored supporting the Allies also organized. The Committee to Defend America by Aiding the Allies, headed by a well-known Republican newspaper editor, organized more than 300 local chapters in just a few weeks. Similar to the isolationists, interventionist organizations mobilized a diverse group of supporters. All, however, sounded alarms that fascist aggressors might overrun Europe and thus threaten American security.

Electoral politics in 1940 forced Roosevelt, nominated for a third term, to tone down his pro-Allied rhetoric. He promised not to send American troops to fight in "foreign wars." Once he had won an unprecedented third term against Republican nominee Wendell Willkie, however, Roosevelt unveiled his most ambitious plan yet to support Britain's war effort.

26-1f *An "Arsenal of Democracy"*

Britain was nearly out of money, so the president proposed that the United States would now "lend-lease," or loan rather than sell, munitions to the Allies. Making the United States a "great arsenal of democracy," Roosevelt claimed, would "keep war away from our country and our people." After bitter congressional debate, the **Lend-Lease Act** passed on March 11, 1941. When Germany turned away from Britain and suddenly attacked its recent ally, the Soviet Union, in June, Roosevelt extended Lend-Lease assistance to the communist regime of Joseph Stalin.

Roosevelt next began coordinating military strategy with Britain. He secretly pledged to follow a Europe-first approach if the United States were drawn into a two-front war against both Germany and Japan. Publicly, Roosevelt deployed U.S. Marines to Greenland and Iceland to free up the British forces. In August 1941, Roosevelt and British prime minister Winston Churchill met on the high seas off the coast of Newfoundland to forge a formal wartime alliance.

They agreed to an eight-point Atlantic Charter that disavowed territorial expansion, endorsed protection of human rights and self-determination, and pledged the postwar creation of a new world organization that would ensure "general security." Roosevelt also agreed to Churchill's request that the U.S. Navy convoy American goods as far as Iceland. Soon, in an undeclared naval war, Germany's formidable submarine packs began attacking U.S. ships.

By this time Roosevelt believed that defeating Hitler would require U.S. entry into the war, but public support still lagged. Privately, the president likely hoped that Germany would commit some provocative act in the North Atlantic that would jar public opinion. The October 1941 sinking of the U.S. destroyer *Reuben James* did just that. Congress repealed its earlier neutrality legislation, but the vote was so close and debate so bitter that Roosevelt could not yet seek a formal declaration of war.

26-1g *Pearl Harbor*

As it turned out, Japan, rather than Germany, sparked America's involvement. In response to Japan's 1937 invasion of China, the United States extended credit to China and curtailed sales of equipment to Japan. In 1939, the United States abrogated its Treaty of Commerce and Navigation with Japan, an action that further restricted U.S. exports to the island nation. A 1940 ban on the sale of aviation fuel and high-grade scrap iron was also intended to slow Japan's military advances.

These measures did not halt Japanese expansion, but made it seem even more imperative to Japan's leaders. As the European war sapped the strength of France, the Netherlands, and Great Britain, Japanese militarists hoped to grab Europe's Asian colonies and incorporate them into Japan's own East Asian Co-Prosperity Sphere. Japan therefore pushed deep into French Indochina, seeking the raw materials it could no longer buy from the United States, and prepared to launch attacks on Singapore, the Netherlands East Indies (Indonesia), and the Philippines.

Roosevelt expanded the trade embargo against Japan, promised further assistance to China, accelerated a U.S. military buildup in the Pacific, and in mid-1941 froze all Japanese assets in the United States. Faced with impending economic strangulation, Japanese leaders did not reassess their plan to create an East Asian empire. Instead, they began planning a preemptive attack on the United States. With limited supplies of raw materials, especially oil, Japan had little

The Granger Collection, NYC

26.2 **The Fight against Interventionism** The effort to keep the United States out of the Second World War mobilized powerful personalities, impassioned rhetoric, and colorful imagery. What nationalistic and patriotic themes does this emblem invoke in the cause of avoiding, rather than engaging in, war?

hope of winning a prolonged war. Japanese military strategists gambled that a surprise, crippling blow would force U.S. concessions. General Hideki Tojo, who became Japan's prime minister, knew the risks but remarked that "sometimes a man has to jump with his eyes closed."

On December 7, 1941, Japanese bombers swooped down on **Pearl Harbor**, Hawaii, and destroyed much of the U.S. Pacific Fleet. Altogether, 19 ships were sunk or severely damaged; nearly 200 aircraft were destroyed or disabled; and 2,200 Americans were killed. The attack could have been worse. U.S. aircraft carriers, out to sea at the time, were spared, as were the base's fuel storage tanks and repair facilities. In a dramatic message broadcast by radio on December 8, Roosevelt decried the attack and labeled December 7 as "a date which will live in infamy," a phrase that served as a battle cry throughout the war. Japan had rallied Americans, not brought them to terms.

A few Americans charged that Roosevelt had intentionally provoked Japan in order to open a "back door" to war. They asked why the fleet at Pearl Harbor lay vulnerable, not even in a state of full alert. The actions and inactions of leaders, however, were more confused than devious. Intelligence experts, who had broken Japanese diplomatic but not military code, expected Japan to move toward Singapore or other British or Dutch possessions in Asia. Intercepted messages, along with visual sightings of Japanese ships, seemed to confirm preparations for a strike in Southeast Asia (which did occur). American leaders doubted that Japan would risk a direct attack or that its military planners had the skill to mount an air assault of such distance.

On December 8, 1941, Congress declared war against Japan. Japan's allies, Germany and Italy, declared war on the United States three days later. Hitler mistakenly assumed that the fight against Japan would keep the United States preoccupied in the Pacific. The three Axis powers drastically underestimated America's ability to mobilize swiftly and effectively.

26-2 Fighting the War in Europe and the Pacific

Q *Why, after initial military setbacks in Europe and Asia, did the Allies ultimately defeat the Axis powers?*

Initially, the war went badly for the Allies. German forces controlled most of Europe, from Norway to Greece, and had pushed eastward into the Soviet Union. Now they rolled across

North Africa, and German submarines endangered Allied supply lines in the Atlantic. Japan seemed unstoppable in the Pacific, overrunning Malaya, the Netherlands East Indies, and the Philippines and moving against the British in Burma and the Australians in New Guinea.

The United States had been unprepared for war, but new bureaucracies and technologies quickly guided a crash program for mobilization. The newly formed Joint Chiefs of Staff, consisting of representatives from each of the armed services, directed strategy. The War Department's **Pentagon** complex, a giant, five-story, five-sided building, was completed in January 1943 after 16 months of around-the-clock work. In 1942, aircraft equipped with radar, a new technology developed in collaboration with Britain, proved effective against submarines, and during 1943 Germany's U-boat threat faded "from menace to problem," in the words of one U.S. naval commander. Perhaps most critical, a massive Allied code-breaking operation perfected decryption techniques for use against Germany's supposedly inviolable encoding machine. Decrypted German messages, called "Ultra" for "ultrasecret," gave the Allies a crucial advantage. Throughout the war, the Germans never discovered that many of their decoded radio communications were being forwarded to Allied commanders—sometimes even before they had reached their German recipients. In the postwar world, the code-breaking effort would contribute to the development of computer technology.

26-2a *Campaigns in North Africa and Italy*

The Allies differed over military strategy. Stalin pleaded with Roosevelt and Churchill to open a second front in western Europe, by way of an invasion across the English Channel into France, to relieve pressure on the Soviet Union. Many of Roosevelt's advisers agreed: If German troops succeeded in knocking the Soviet Union out of the war, Hitler could turn his full attention toward Britain. Churchill urged instead the invasion of French North Africa, which German forces now controlled, in order to nibble away at the edges of enemy power.

At a meeting in Casablanca, Morocco, in January 1943, Roosevelt sided with Churchill. He argued that a cross-Channel invasion of France carried too many risks at that time. To assuage Stalin's fear that his allies might sign a separate peace with Hitler, however, Roosevelt and Churchill promised to remain in the fight until Germany agreed to an "unconditional surrender."

The North African operation, code-named TORCH, began with Anglo-American landings in Morocco and Algeria in November 1942. As TORCH progressed, the Soviets turned the tide of battle on the eastern front with a decisive victory at Stalingrad. The Battle of Stalingrad, which lasted nearly six months and killed over 1 million people, was perhaps the bloodiest in modern history.

Hitler poured reinforcements into North Africa but could stop neither TORCH nor the British drive westward from Egypt. In summer 1943, the Allies followed up their successful North African campaign by overrunning the island of Sicily and then fighting their way, slowly, northward through Italy's mountains.

Some U.S officials worried about the postwar implications of wartime strategy. Secretary of War Henry Stimson warned that the Allied campaigns through Africa and Italy might leave the Soviets dominant in most of Europe. Acting on this advice, Roosevelt finally agreed to set a date for the cross-Channel invasion that Stalin had long been promised.

26-2b *Operation OVERLORD*

Operation **OVERLORD**, directed by General Dwight D. Eisenhower, began on June 6, 1944, D-Day. During the preceding months, probably the largest invasion force in history had assembled in England. Disinformation and diversionary tactics fooled the Germans into expecting a landing at the narrowest part of the English Channel rather than in the Normandy region. After several weather-related delays, nervous commanders finally ordered the daring plan to begin. The night before, as naval guns pounded the Normandy shore, three divisions of paratroopers dropped behind enemy lines to disrupt German communications. Then at dawn, more than 4,000 Allied ships landed troops and supplies on Normandy's beaches. The first American forces to come ashore at Omaha Beach took enormous casualties, but the waves of invading troops continued. Only three weeks after D-Day, more than a million Allied personnel controlled the French coast and opened the long-awaited Second Front.

Just as the 1943 Battle of Stalingrad had reversed the course of the war in the East, so OVERLORD changed the momentum in the West. Within three months, U.S., British, and Free French troops entered Paris. After repulsing a desperate German counteroffensive in Belgium, at the Battle of the Bulge in December and January, Allied armies swept eastward, crossing the Rhine, and headed toward Berlin to meet up with westward-advancing Soviet troops (see Map 26.2).

As the war in Europe drew to a close, the horrors perpetrated by the Third Reich became fully visible. Hitler's campaign of extermination, now called the Holocaust, killed more than 5 million Jews out of Europe's prewar population of 10 million. Hundreds of thousands more from various other groups were also murdered. Although only a military victory put an end to German death camps, the Allies might have saved thousands of Jews before and during the war by helping them escape and emigrate. Allied leaders, however, had worried about how to deal with large numbers of Jewish refugees, and they also claimed that, during the war, they could not spare scarce ships to transport refugees to sanctuary. The Allies would, in 1945 and 1946, bring 24 German high officials to trial at Nuremberg for "crimes against humanity." Large quantities of money, gold, and jewelry that Nazi leaders stole from victims of the Holocaust and deposited in Swiss banks, however, remained concealed for more than 50 years. Not

▲ **MAP 26.2 Allied Military Strategy in North Africa, Italy, and France** This map shows the European theater of war from 1942 through 1944.

Q *How did the crucial Battle of Stalingrad and the North African campaign begin a rollback of German power?*

Q *Why was June 1944 such a critical month for the Allied effort?*

until 1997 did Jewish groups and the U.S. government force an investigation of the Swiss banking industry's holdings of stolen "Nazi gold," an inquiry that finally prompted some monetary restitution for victims' families.

With Hitler's suicide in April and Germany's surrender on May 8, 1945, the military foundations for peace in Europe were complete. Soviet armies controlled Eastern Europe; British and U.S. forces predominated in Italy and the rest of the Mediterranean; Germany and Austria fell under divided occupation. Governmental leaders now needed to work out a plan for transforming these military arrangements into a comprehensive political settlement for the postwar era (see Map 26.3).

26-2c *Seizing the Offensive in the Pacific*

Meanwhile, the war in the Pacific was far from over. During the six months following Pearl Harbor, Japan's forces steadily advanced. Singapore fell. Japan overwhelmed U.S. naval garrisons in the Philippines and the islands of Guam

▲ **MAP 26.3 Allied Advances and Collapse of German Power** This map depicts the final Allied advances and the end of the war in Germany.

Q *Through what countries did Soviet armies move, and how might their advance have affected the postwar situation?*

Q *How might the division of Germany by occupying powers have been expected to affect postwar politics?*

and Wake. Filipino and American troops surrendered at Bataan and Corregidor in the Philippines. Other Japanese forces headed southward to menace Australia and New Zealand.

When Japan finally suffered its first naval setback at the Battle of the Coral Sea in May 1942, Japanese naval commanders decided to hit back hard. They amassed 200 ships and 600 planes to destroy what remained of the U.S. Pacific Fleet and to take Midway Island, from which they could assault Hawaii. U.S. naval intelligence, however, was monitoring Japanese codes and warned Admiral Chester W. Nimitz of the plan. Surprising the Japanese armada in the Battle of Midway, U.S. planes sank four Japanese carriers and destroyed a total of 322 planes (see Map 26.4).

History Through Film *Saving Private Ryan* (1998)

Directed by Steven Spielberg.
Starring Tom Hanks (Captain John Miller), Matt Damon (Private James Ryan), and Harve Presnell (General George Marshall).

Hollywood marked the 50th anniversary of the Allied effort in the Second World War with a series of films about "the good war." Although Saving Private Ryan invited comparison with The Longest Day (1962) because of its depiction of the D-Day invasion, Steven Spielberg's battlefield sequences represented a considerable advance in the art of waging war on film. His production team employed sophisticated computer graphics and nearly deafening Dolby sound to mount battle scenes so realistic that reviewers cautioned veterans susceptible to post-traumatic stress syndrome about watching the film.

The film also suggested the kind of family-centered melodrama that Spielberg had grafted onto the sci-fi genre in *E.T.: The Extra-Terrestrial* (1982). A heroic squad led by Captain John Miller is trying to locate a single U.S. soldier, Private James Ryan, whose mother has already lost her three other sons to the war. The film poses the question of whether such a family-related mission legitimates and sanctifies the sacrifices of the Second World War. *Private Ryan* answers yes to this question.

The major body of the film carefully justifies the rescue mission. Although Captain Miller wonders if his dangerous assignment is simply a public relations stunt, he quickly drops this idea and pursues his mission with the gallantry required of a Hollywood-commissioned officer. Later, his platoon members debate the morality of risking eight lives to save one, but the cause of Ryan's mother always seems overriding. General George Marshall cuts off debate over the appropriateness of the Ryan mission by invoking an earlier war leader, Abraham Lincoln, who once faced a similar dilemma. When Miller's troops finally locate Private Ryan, the film's audience discovers that he is the kind of clean-cut Iowa farm boy who will stay with his would-be saviors rather than retreat to safety. Ryan survives, although most of his comrades perish. Captain Miller, dying, implores young Ryan to lead a "good" life to justify the sacrifice of so many others.

The film *Saving Private Ryan*, in contrast to its characters, takes few risks. It secures its emotional investment in the rescue effort by bracketing the Second World War segments with two brief framing sequences in which an aging Ryan, along with his own family, returns to Normandy and visits the grave of Captain Miller. In the final segment, Ryan's wife provides the additional reassurance that the trauma of the Second World War served a good cause, because Private Ryan's own family life has justified Miller's sacrifice. "Tell me I've led a good life. Tell me I'm a good man," he implores his wife. After nearly three hours of this Spielberg epic, the answer to this question seems self-evident. ■

Screen Prod/Photononstop/Glowimages

26.3 *Saving Private Ryan*, which garnered four Academy Award nominations, celebrated the heroism of what popular historians called America's "greatest generation."

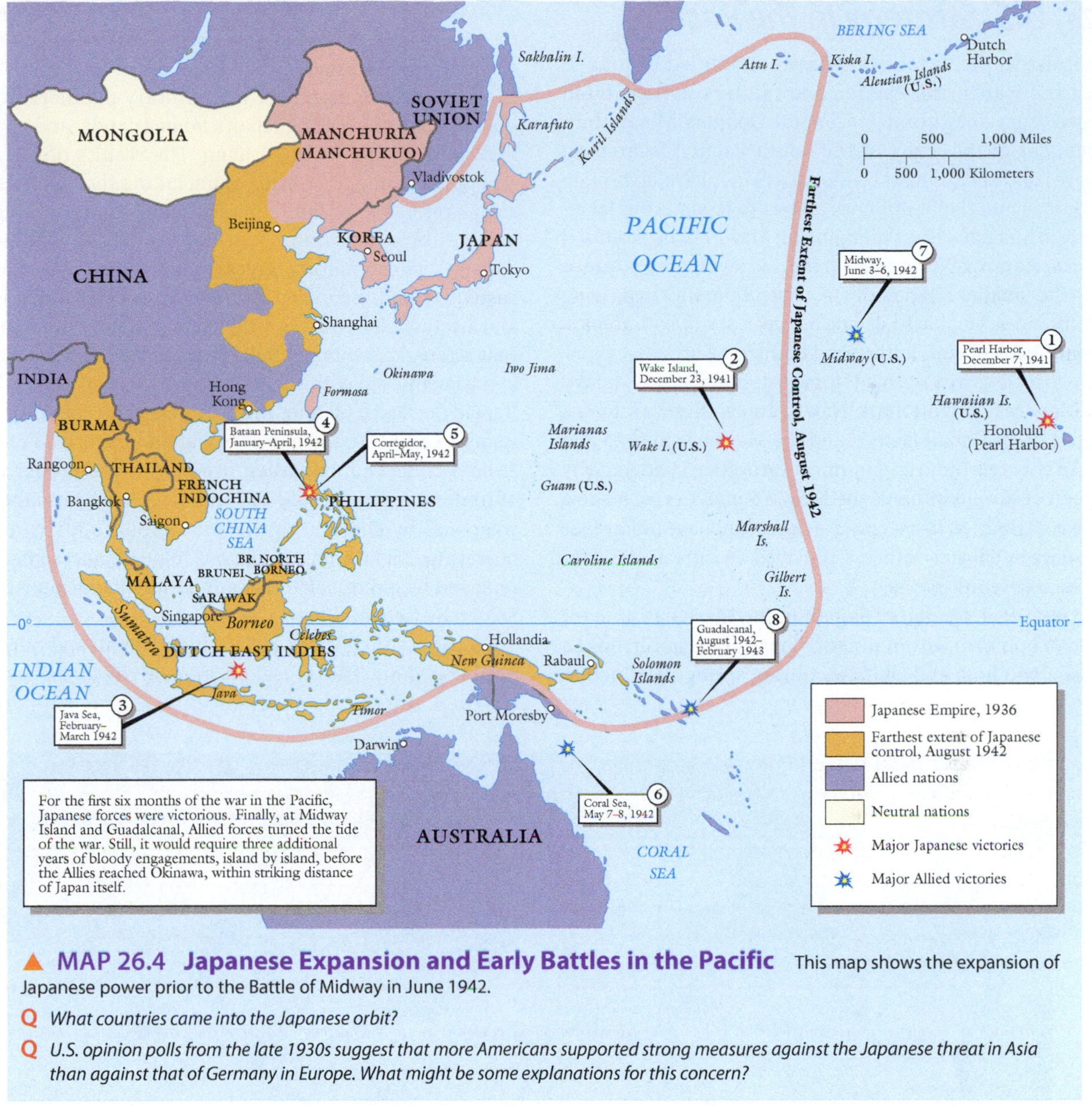

▲ **MAP 26.4 Japanese Expansion and Early Battles in the Pacific** This map shows the expansion of Japanese power prior to the Battle of Midway in June 1942.

Q *What countries came into the Japanese orbit?*

Q *U.S. opinion polls from the late 1930s suggest that more Americans supported strong measures against the Japanese threat in Asia than against that of Germany in Europe. What might be some explanations for this concern?*

Two months later, American forces splashed ashore at Guadalcanal in the Solomon Islands. The bloody engagements in the Solomons continued for months on both land and sea, but they accomplished one major objective: seizing the military initiative in the Pacific. According to prewar plans, the war in Europe was to have received highest priority, but by 1943 the two theaters were receiving roughly equal resources.

The bloody Pacific engagements reinforced racial prejudices and brutality on both sides. Japanese leaders hoped the war would confirm the superiority of their divine Yamato race. Prisoners taken by the Japanese, particularly on the Asian mainland, were brutalized in almost unimaginable ways. The Japanese Army's Unit 731 tested bacteriological weapons in China and conducted horrifying medical experiments on live subjects. American propaganda images played on themes of racial superiority, portraying the Japanese people as animalistic subhumans. American troops often rivaled Japan's forces in their disrespect for the enemy dead and sometimes killed the enemy rather than take prisoners.

26-2d *China Policy*

U.S. policymakers hoped that China would fight effectively against Japan and emerge from the war as a strong, united nation. Neither hope seemed realistic. China was beset by civil war.

Jiang Jieshi's Nationalist government was incompetent and unpopular. It avoided engaging the Japanese invaders and still made extravagant demands for U.S. assistance. A growing communist movement led by Mao Zedong fought more effectively against the Japanese invaders, but U.S. policy continued to support Jiang as China's future leader. All the while, Japan's advance continued, and in 1944 its forces captured seven key U.S. air bases in China.

26-2e U.S. Strategy in the Pacific

In contrast to the European theater, no unified command guided the war in the Pacific, and military actions often emerged from compromise. General Douglas MacArthur, commander of the army in the South Pacific, favored an offensive launched from his headquarters in Australia through New Guinea and the Philippines and on to Japan. After Japan had driven him out of the Philippines in May 1942, he promised to return. Admiral Nimitz disagreed. He favored an advance across the smaller islands of the central Pacific, bypassing the Philippines. Unable to decide between the two strategies, the Joint Chiefs of Staff authorized both.

Both offensives moved forward, marked by heavy casualties. MacArthur took New Guinea. Nimitz's forces liberated the Marshall Islands and the Marianas in 1943 and 1944. An effective radio communication system conducted by a platoon of Navajo Indians, the Navajo Signal Corps, made a unique contribution to success. Navajo, a language unfamiliar to Japanese intelligence officers, provided a secure medium for sensitive communications.

In late 1944, the fall of Saipan in the Marianas brought American bombers within range of Japan. The capture of the islands of Iwo Jima and Okinawa during spring 1945 further shortened that distance. Okinawa illustrated the ferocity of the campaigns: An estimated 120,000 Japanese and 48,000 American soldiers died.

Given these numbers, U.S. military planners dreaded the prospect of invading Japan's home islands, and airpower looked more and more enticing. The results of the Allies' strategic bombing of Germany, including the destruction of such large cities as Hamburg and Dresden, were ambiguous, and military historians continue to debate whether the damage against military targets really offset the huge civilian casualties and the unsustainable losses of American pilots and aircraft. Nonetheless, U.S. strategists continued to claim that strategic bombing might provide the crucial advantage in the Pacific. In February 1944, General Henry Harley ("Hap") Arnold devised a plan for firebombing major Japanese cities. Bombers added to the horror of war and terrorized civilians, Arnold conceded, but when used "with the proper degree of understanding" could become "the most humane of all weapons" by shortening the war. Arnold's air campaign, operating from China, turned out to be cumbersome. It was replaced by a more effective and lethal operation run from Saipan by General Curtis LeMay.

LeMay summarized his strategy: "Bomb and burn them until they quit." The official position on the incendiary raids

Corbis

26.4 **Navajo Signal Corps** Sending messages in their native language, which neither the Japanese nor the Germans could decipher, Navajo Indians in the Signal Corps made a unique contribution to preserving the secrecy of U.S. intelligence.

against Japanese cities was that they constituted "precision" rather than "area" bombing. In actuality, the success of a mission was measured by the number of square miles it left scorched. Air attacks on Tokyo during the night of March 9–10, 1945, leveled nearly a quarter of the city and incinerated more than 100,000 people.

By the winter of 1944–1945, a combined sea and air strategy had emerged: The United States sought "unconditional surrender" by blockading Japan's seaports, bombarding its cities from the air, and invading if necessary. Critics of the policy of unconditional surrender, which most Japanese assumed meant the death of their emperor, later suggested that it might have hardened Japan's determination to fight even after defeat had become inevitable. Defenders of the policy suggest that any softening of U.S. terms would have encouraged Japanese resistance. Whatever the case, American leaders decided that victory would only come through massive destruction (see Map 26.5).

26-2f A New President, the Atomic Bomb, and Japan's Surrender

On April 12, 1945, Franklin Roosevelt died of a cerebral hemorrhage. Sorrow and shock spread throughout a nation in which many young men and women had hardly known any other president. Through diplomatic conference halls, Roosevelt's personal magnetism had often brought unity, if not always clarity. To be sure, he had accumulated critics and enemies, and his support had waned. He

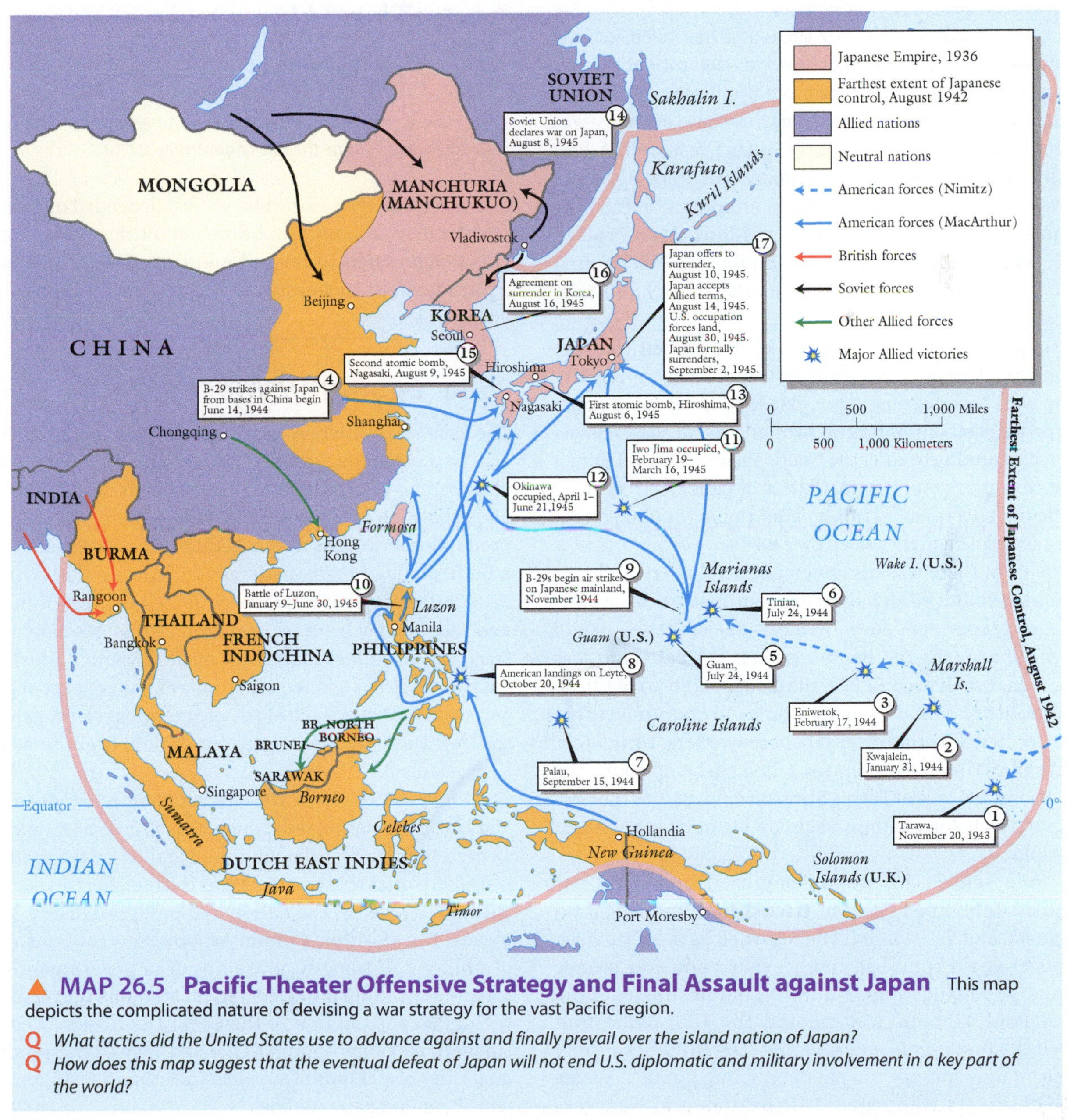

▲ **MAP 26.5 Pacific Theater Offensive Strategy and Final Assault against Japan** This map depicts the complicated nature of devising a war strategy for the vast Pacific region.

Q *What tactics did the United States use to advance against and finally prevail over the island nation of Japan?*

Q *How does this map suggest that the eventual defeat of Japan will not end U.S. diplomatic and military involvement in a key part of the world?*

had defeated Republican Thomas E. Dewey in the 1944 presidential election by the smallest popular-vote margin in nearly 30 years, and Republicans had further cut into the Democrat's majorities in the House and Senate. But among his supporters, he had symbolized optimism through depression and war.

Emerging from Roosevelt's shadow, Vice President Harry S Truman seemed an unimposing presence in the White House. Born on a farm near Independence, Missouri, Truman served in France during the First World War, became a U.S. senator in 1934, and was tabbed as Roosevelt's running mate in 1944. Roosevelt offered an upper-class image of well-practiced and worldly charm. In contrast, Truman came from a middle-class background, and he knew little about international affairs and virtually nothing about any informal understandings that Roosevelt may have had with foreign leaders.

Only after succeeding Roosevelt did Truman learn about events at Los Alamos, New Mexico. There, since the late 1930s, scientists from all across the world had been secretly working on a new weapon. Advances in theoretical physics had suggested that splitting the atom (fission) would release a tremendous amount of energy. Fearful that Germany was racing ahead of the United States in this research, Albert Einstein, a Jewish refugee from Germany, had urged Roosevelt to launch a secret program to build an atomic bomb. The government enlisted top scientists in the **Manhattan Project**, a huge, secret military operation. On July 16, 1945, the first atomic weapon was successfully tested at Trinity Site, near Alamogordo, New Mexico.

Truman and his top policymakers assumed that the weapon would be put to immediate use. They were eager to end the war, both because a possible land invasion of Japan might prove costly in American lives and because the Soviet Union was planning to enter the Pacific theater, where Truman wished to limit Soviet power. Churchill called the bomb a "miracle of deliverance." Truman later publicly claimed that he had never lost a night's sleep over its use.

Privately, there was disagreement over where and how the bomb should be deployed. A commission of atomic scientists recommended a "demonstration" that would impress Japan with the bomb's power, yet cause no loss of life. General George C. Marshall suggested using it on purely military installations or only on manufacturing sites, after first warning away Japanese workers. Ultimately, the Truman administration discarded these options. The bomb, Secretary of War Henry Stimson said, had to make "a profound psychological impression on as many inhabitants as possible."

In one sense, the atomic bombs dropped on the previously unbombed cities of **Hiroshima** and Nagasaki on August 6 and 9, 1945, could be regarded as merely bigger, more effective firebombs. In another sense, however, atomic weapons produced almost unimaginable destruction. Colonel Paul Tibbets, who piloted the U.S. plane that dropped the first bomb, reported that "the shimmering city became an ugly smudge ... a pot of bubbling hot tar." Teams of U.S. observers who entered Hiroshima and Nagasaki in the aftermath were stunned at the instantaneous incineration of both human beings and manmade structures and shocked to contemplate the longer-lasting horror of radiation disease.

The mushroom clouds over Hiroshima and Nagasaki inaugurated a new "atomic age" in which dreams of peace mingled with nightmares of global destruction. Shortly after the bombing, Stimson wrote to Truman that atomic weapons represented "a new control by man over the forces of nature too revolutionary and dangerous to fit into old concepts." But in those late summer days of 1945, most Americans sighed with relief. News reports of August 15 proclaimed Japan's surrender, V-J Day. All across the nation people spontaneously flooded into the streets to celebrate the end of the Second World War.

26-3 The War at Home: The Economy

Q *How did mobilizing for war change American economic conditions and enlarge the role of government?*

The success of the U.S. military effort depended on economic mobilization at home. Mobilization ultimately brought the Great Depression to an end and transformed the nation's government, its business and financial institutions, and its labor force.

26-3a *Economic Mobilization*

The federal bureaucracy nearly quadrupled in size during the war. New economic agencies proliferated. The most powerful of these, the War Production Board, oversaw the conversion and expansion of factories, allocated resources, and enforced production priorities and schedules. The War Labor Board adjudicated labor-management disputes. The Office of Price Administration regulated prices to control inflation and rationed such scarce commodities as gasoline, rubber, steel, shoes, coffee, sugar, and meat. Although most of the controls were abandoned after the war, the concept of greater governmental oversight of the economy survived, extending the New Deal's activist legacy that would begin to be called Keynesianism.

From 1940 to 1945, the U.S. economy expanded rapidly, and the gross national product (GNP) rose, year by year, by 15 percent or more. When Roosevelt called for the production of 60,000 planes shortly after Pearl Harbor, skeptics jeered. Yet within a few years, the nation had produced nearly 300,000 planes. The Maritime Commission oversaw the construction of millions of tons of new ships. The government's huge wartime spending provided a fiscal stimulus that eradicated the underconsumption of the Great Depression. The once-stagnant economy sprang to life and spewed out prodigious quantities of all kinds of supplies, including 2.5 million trucks and 50 million pairs of shoes.

Striving to increase production, industry entered into a close relationship with government to promote scientific and technological research and development (R&D). Government money subsidized new industries, such as electronics, and transformed others, such as rubber and chemicals. Eventually, an Office of Scientific Research and Development contracted with universities and scientists. Under this program, radar and penicillin (both British discoveries), rocket engines, and other new products were perfected for wartime use. The Manhattan Project, of course, provided the most dramatic example of the government's new involvement in military research. Refugees from Nazi tyranny contributed significantly to this scientific innovation.

26-3b *Business and Finance*

To finance the war effort, government spending rose from $9 billion in 1940 to $98 billion in 1944. In 1941, the national debt stood at $48 billion; by V-J Day, it was $280 billion.

Bettmann/Corbis

UPI-Bettmann/Corbis

26.5a (top) and 26.5b (bottom) **Total War: Dresden and Hiroshima** These photographs graphically illustrate the effects of "total war." The top photo shows the devastation of Dresden, Germany, by the British Bomber Command and the U.S. Eighth Air Force on February 13 and 14, 1945. The bottom photo shows the destruction of Hiroshima, Japan, by the U.S. 509th Composite Group on August 6, 1945. During the initial attack on Dresden, 786 aircraft dropped 5,824,000 pounds (2,600 long tons) of bombs on the city, killing an estimated 60,000 people and injuring another 30,000. An area of more than 2.5 square miles in the city center was demolished, and some 37,000 buildings were destroyed. To critics, the bombing of Dresden, a target that seemed of little strategic value, exemplified the excessive use of airpower.

In sobering comparison, a single atomic bomb weighing only 10,000 pounds and dropped from one aircraft devastated Hiroshima. The U-235 bomb killed 68,000 people outright, injured another 30,000, and left 10,000 missing. (These figures do not include those who later developed diseases from deadly gamma rays.) The atomic bomb obliterated almost five square miles of the city's center and destroyed 40,653 buildings. Many hailed dropping the atomic bomb as a necessary step toward military victory; others worried about what the dawn of the "nuclear age" portended.

As production shifted from autos to tanks, and from refrigerators to guns, consumer goods became scarce. With few goods to buy, Americans put money in their savings accounts and invested in war bonds. Essentials such as food, fabrics, and gasoline were rationed and, consequently, were shared more equitably than before the war. Higher taxes on wealthier Americans redistributed income and narrowed the gap in wealth between the well-to-do and other citizens. War bonds, rationing, and progressive taxation encouraged a sense of shared sacrifice.

The war fostered personal savings and lessened income inequality, but it also facilitated the dismantling of some New Deal agencies most concerned with the poor. A Republican surge in the midterm elections of 1942 helped strengthen an anti-New Deal coalition in Congress. In 1943, legislators abolished the job-creation programs of the Works Progress Administration (WPA), the Civilian Conservation Corps (CCC), and the National Youth Administration (NYA) (see Chapter 25). They also shut down the Rural Electrification Administration (REA) and Farm Security Administration (FSA), agencies that had assisted rural areas.

As business executives flocked to Washington, D.C., to run the new wartime agencies, the Roosevelt administration adopted a cooperative stance toward big business, and corporations considered essential to wartime victory flourished under governmental subsidies. What was essential became a matter of definition. Coca-Cola and Wrigley's chewing gum won precious sugar allotments by arguing that GIs overseas "needed" to enjoy these products. The California-based Kaiser Corporation, whose spectacular growth during the 1930s had been spurred by federal dam contracts, now turned its attention to building ships, aircraft, and military

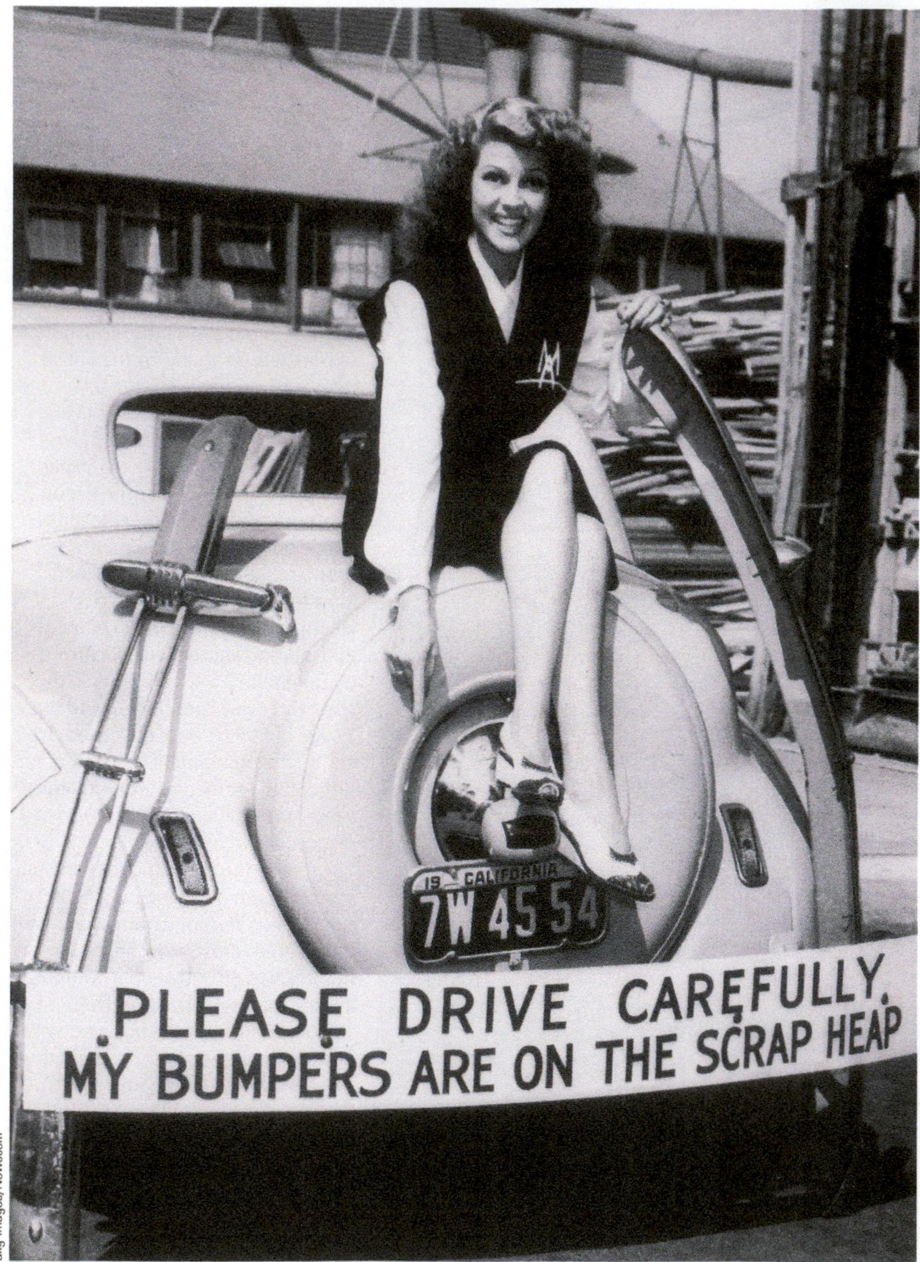
19 CALIFORNIA
7W 45 54
PLEASE DRIVE CAREFULLY.
MY BUMPERS ARE ON THE SCRAP HEAP

akg-images/Newscom

26.6 **Rita Hayworth Scraps Her Bumpers** Movie stars aided the war effort by promoting the sale of war bonds and urging shared sacrifice.

Q *Why does this photo invoke a glamorous Hollywood star to highlight the campaign to collect scrap metal?*

vehicles. By 1943, Kaiser controlled nearly a third of the nation's military construction business and helped bring an economic boom to coastal California and Washington State. New manufacturing transformed cities particularly in the South and West, areas previously dominated mostly by agricultural production.

The war concentrated power in the largest corporations. Roosevelt ordered his justice department to postpone enforcement of antitrust laws. Congressional efforts to investigate possible collusion in the awarding of large government contracts and to increase assistance to small businesses made little headway. The top 100 companies, which had provided 30 percent of the nation's total manufacturing output in 1940, provided 70 percent by 1943.

26-3c *The Workforce*

During the early years of the military buildup, people who had scrounged for jobs during the Great Depression found work. Employment in heavy industry invariably went to men, and most of the skilled jobs went to whites. But as military service depleted the ranks of white males, both private employers and public officials began encouraging women to join the paid labor force, southern African Americans to seek jobs in northern and western industrial cities, and Mexicans to enter the United States under the *bracero* guest farmworker program.

Hired for jobs never before open to them, women became welders, shipbuilders, lumberjacks, and miners. They won places in prestigious symphony orchestras, and one Major League Baseball owner financed the creation of a women's league to give new life to the national pastime. Many employers hired married women, who before the war would have been lucky to obtain a position even in traditionally female occupations such as teaching. Minority women moved into clerical and sales jobs, where they had not previously been welcome. Most workplaces, however, continued to be segregated by sex.

The scope of unpaid labor, long provided primarily by women, also expanded. Volunteer activities such as Red Cross projects, civil defense work, and recycling drives claimed the time of women, children, and older people. Government publications exhorted homemakers: "Wear it out, use it up, make it do, or do without." In both home and workplace, women's responsibilities and workloads increased.

The new labor market improved the general economic position of African Americans. By executive order in June 1942, Roosevelt created the Fair Employment Practices Commission (FEPC), which aimed to ban discrimination in hiring. In 1943 his administration announced that it would not recognize as collective bargaining agents any unions that discriminated on the basis of race. The War Labor Board outlawed the practice of paying different wages to whites and nonwhites doing the same job. Before the war, the African American population had been mainly southern, rural, and agricultural; within a few years, a substantial percentage of African Americans had become northern, urban, and industrial. Although employment discrimination was hardly eliminated, twice as many African Americans held skilled jobs at the end of the war as at the beginning.

For both men and women, the war brought higher wages and longer work hours. During the war, average weekly earnings for industrial workers rose nearly 70 percent. Farmers, who had suffered through many years of low prices and overproduction, doubled their income and then doubled it again.

26-3d *The Labor Front*

The scarcity of labor during the war strengthened the union movement. Union membership rose by 50 percent. Although women and workers of color joined unions in unprecedented numbers, the main beneficiaries of labor's new clout were the white males who still comprised the bulk of unionized workers.

Especially on the national level, the commitment of organized labor to female workers was weak. Not a single woman served on the executive boards of either the American Federation of Labor (AFL) or the Congress of Industrial Organizations (CIO). The International Brotherhood of Teamsters even required women to sign a statement that their union membership could be revoked when the war was over. Unions did fight for contracts stipulating equal pay for men and women who worked in the same job, but these benefited women only as long as they held "male" jobs. The unions' primary purpose in advocating equal pay was to maintain wage levels for the men who would return to their jobs after the war. During the first year of peace, as employers trimmed their workforces, both businesses and unions gave special preference to returning veterans and eased women and minority workers out of their wartime positions. Unions based their policies on seniority and their wage demands on the goal of securing male workers a "family wage," one sufficient to support an entire family.

Some union leaders feared that hiring traditionally lower-paid workers (women and minorities) would jeopardize the wage gains and recognition that unions had won during the 1930s. As growing numbers of African Americans were hired, racial tensions in the workplace increased. At some plants white workers walked off the job to protest the hiring of African Americans, fearing that management might use the war as an excuse to erode union power.

The labor militancy of the 1930s, although muted by a wartime no-strike pledge, persisted into the 1940s. Wildcat strikes erupted among St. Louis bus drivers, Detroit assembly-line workers, and Philadelphia streetcar conductors. The United Mine Workers called a walkout in the bituminous coal fields in 1943. When the War Labor Board took a hard line against the union's demands, the strike was prolonged. The increasingly conservative Congress responded with the Smith-Connally Act of 1943, which empowered the president to seize plants or mines if strikes interrupted war production. Even so, the war helped to strengthen organized labor's place in American life.

26.7 **Women Join the War Effort** Women workers at a Douglas Aircraft plant in Long Beach, California, perform jobs traditionally filled only by men.

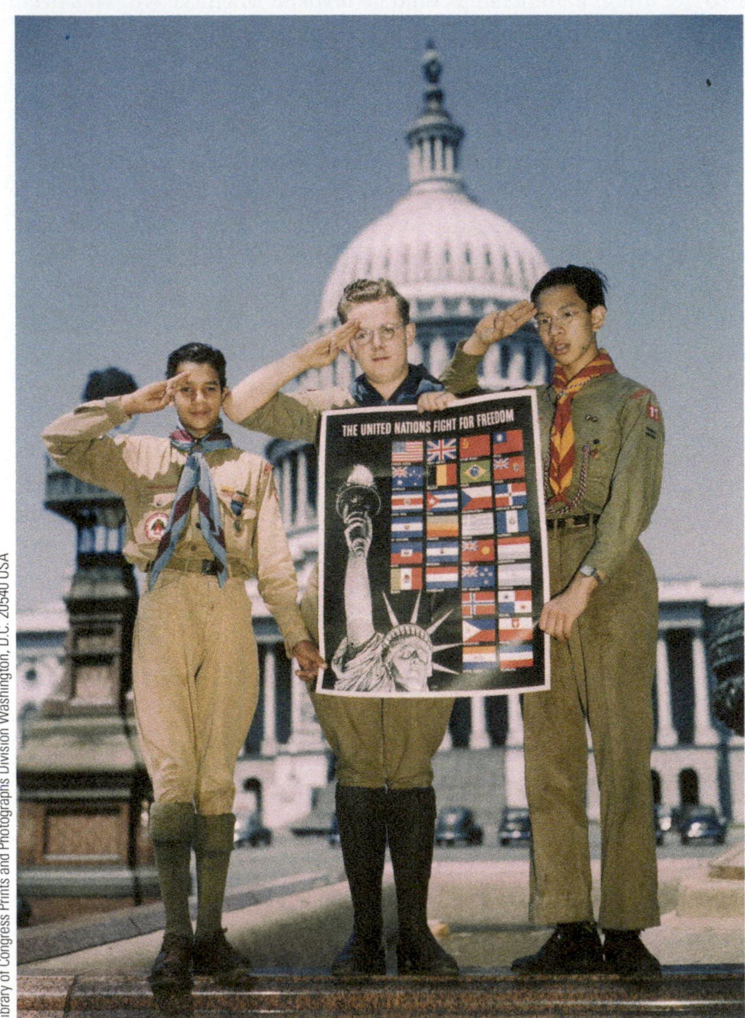

26.8 **United Nations Fight for Freedom** Three Boy Scouts, standing in front of the U.S. Capitol, support the war effort by delivering a poster celebrating the international coalition of nations fighting fascism.

Q *How does this image carry out the wartime themes of inter-ethnic and international cooperation?*

26-3e *Enlarging the Role of Government*

The growth of governmental power during the war years prompted debate over what the role of government should be in a postwar world. As military victory began to seem likely, President Roosevelt and his advisers talked of harnessing the national government's power behind expanded efforts to enhance personal security in everyday life. Some favored extending wartime health care and day-care programs into a more comprehensive social welfare system.

In 1944, Roosevelt introduced his ideas for a **"Second Bill of Rights,"** advocating measures to ensure that Americans could enjoy the "rights" to regular employment, adequate food and shelter, appropriate educational opportunities, and guaranteed health care. Translating this vision into reality, its proponents assumed, would require the government to continue playing a large role in economic and social planning.

Large insurance companies and some private businesses, recognizing the popularity of such proposals, advanced private alternatives to governmental programs. Insurers expanded their earlier efforts to market individual policies that would pay in cases of sickness, disability, and unexpected death. At the same time, insurance companies worked with large corporations to develop group insurance plans that would make expansion of government programs less attractive and provide supplements for existing New Deal-era programs such as Social Security. Questions about what should be the proper role for government in providing social safety nets would roil American life in the postwar era.

26-4 The War at Home: Social Issues

Q *Why did the war propel movements for greater equality in American life?*

The war demanded sacrifice from all, and most Americans willingly obliged. The war effort unsettled established patterns, and wartime ideals spotlighted everyday inequalities.

26-4a *Selling the War*

Hollywood answered the government's call to mobilize the country for war. The film factories produced both commercial movies with military themes, such as *Destination Tokyo* (1943), and documentaries, such as the *Why We Fight* series, directed by Frank Capra. Capra contrasted images of wholesome and diverse Americans with harrowing portrayals of the tightly regimented lifestyles in the dictatorships of Germany, Italy, and Japan. Walt Disney's animation teams produced war-themed cartoons. Hollywood personalities sold war bonds, entertained the troops, and worked on documentaries for the Army's Pictorial Division.

The advertising industry, lacking many consumer products to sell, also contributed. Roosevelt encouraged advertisers to sell the benefits of freedom. "Freedom" often appeared in the form of new washing machines, streamlined automobiles, a wider range of lipstick hues, and other consumer products. As soon as the fighting ended, wartime ads promised, technological know-how would transform the United States into a consumer's paradise.

In spring 1942, Roosevelt created the **Office of War Information (OWI)** to coordinate propaganda and censorship. Many New Deal Democrats viewed the OWI as catering more to advertisers who preferred imagery extolling the future joys of consumerism than to ones promoting broader visions of liberty and equality. Republicans, by contrast, blasted the agency for cranking out political appeals for causes favored by New Dealers. Despite criticism from both left and right, the OWI established branch offices throughout the world and produced hundreds of films, posters, and radio broadcasts.

26-4b *Gender Issues*

The changes sweeping American life became apparent in a range of social issues affecting women.

The wartime United States called on women to serve their country as more than wives and mothers. Some 350,000 women volunteered for military duty during the war, and more than a thousand became pilots for the Women Airforce Service Pilots (WASPs). Not everyone approved. One member of Congress asked: "What has become of the manhood of America?" Most in Congress, however, supported the creation of a women's corps in each branch of the military.

Even as the war brought larger numbers of women into the paid labor force, widespread imagery frequently portrayed this change as a short-term sacrifice intended, ultimately, to preserve and protect women's "natural" sphere in the home. Stereotypes abounded. A typical ad suggesting that women take on farmwork declared: "A woman can do anything if she knows she looks beautiful doing it."

An Equal Rights Amendment (ERA) to the Constitution continued to be debated both within Congress and around the country. Should the Constitution guarantee women "equal" status with men, or should the law continue to allow women some kind of "protected" status in view of their special vulnerability to exploitation? The war raised but did not settle this issue, over which even women's advocates were split.

In some ways, the war may have even widened the symbolic gap between notions of femininity and masculinity. Military culture fostered a "pinup" mentality toward women. Tanks and planes were decorated with images of female sexuality, and the home-front entertainment industry promoted its glamorous female stars as anxious to "please" their "boys" in the military.

Public policy-making sometimes worked to reinforce gender divisions. The military assigned most of the women who joined the armed services to stateside clerical and supply jobs. Day-care programs for mothers working outside their homes received reluctant and inadequate funding. The thousands of child-care centers set up during the conflict filled only a fraction of the need and were swiftly shut down after the war. Social scientists oftentimes blamed mothers for an apparent spike in rates of juvenile delinquency and divorce during the war years.

26-4c *Racial Issues*

Messages about race were as ambiguous as those related to gender. President Roosevelt refused to abandon the policy of segregation in the armed forces despite pressure from the NAACP and others. Although the army integrated Latino and American Indian soldiers, along with those from various European ethnic groups, into its combat units, military leaders did not do the same for people of African and Japanese ancestry. Desegregation of the armed forces drew determined opposition from politically powerful white Democrats in the South, who feared it might lead to broader demands for desegregation at home. The army even adopted the scientifically absurd practice of segregating donated blood into separate stores of "white" and "black" plasma. African Americans were relegated to inferior, often highly dangerous, jobs and excluded from combat duty. Toward the end of the war, when troop shortages finally forced the administration to put African American units into combat, they performed with distinction.

On the home front, volatile social issues continued to simmer. As the wartime production system created more jobs, vast numbers of people from the rural South, including several hundred thousand African Americans, moved to cities such as Los Angles and Detroit. People already living in these areas often chafed at the influx of newcomers, who competed with them for jobs and housing and placed greater demands on public services such as transportation, education, and recreational facilities.

Social strains sometimes flared into violence. This escalation most often occurred in overcrowded urban spaces, where diverse populations and cultures already competed and clashed. In Detroit, in June 1943, conflict between white and black youth at an amusement park rapidly spiraled into a multiple-day riot. The violence left nearly 40 people, most of them African American, dead, injured hundreds, and inflicted millions of dollars worth of damage to property.

Racial disturbances were not restricted to confrontations between whites and blacks. In Los Angeles, complicated and long-standing ethnic tensions erupted in the "Zoot Suit Riots" of 1943. Soldiers and sailors from nearby military bases attacked young Mexican American and African American men wearing zoot suits—flamboyant outfits featuring oversized coats and trousers. Violence only escalated as the city's police force entered the fray, often beating and arresting Mexican Americans. A military order restricting servicemen to their bases finally helped quell the disorder.

Even when wartime tensions did not produce the level of violence seen in Detroit and Los Angeles, the Second World War highlighted long-standing social divisions. For many Native Americans, for instance, the wartime years increased the pressures associated with longer-term patterns of migration and assimilation. Approximately 25,000 Indian men and several hundred Indian women served in the armed forces. Tens of thousands of other American Indians, many leaving their reservations for the first time, found wartime work in urban areas such as Rapid City, Minneapolis, Flagstaff, and Billings. Many Indians moved back and forth between city and reservation, seeking to live in two significantly different worlds.

26-4d *Internment of Japanese Americans*

People of Japanese descent faced a unique situation. Shortly after the attack on Pearl Harbor, fear of sabotage by pro-Japanese residents engulfed West Coast communities. One military report claimed that a "large, unassimilated, tightly knit racial group, bound to an enemy nation by strong ties of race, culture, custom, and religion ... constituted a menace" that justified extraordinary action.

Although lacking evidence of disloyalty, the president in February 1942 issued Executive Order 9066, directing the relocation and **internment** of first- and second-generation Japanese Americans (called Issei and Nisei, respectively) at inland camps. Nearly 130,000 people were affected. Significantly, in Hawaii, where the presumed danger of subversion might have seemed much greater, no internment took place. There, people of Japanese ancestry constituted nearly 40 percent of the population and were essential to the economy. The government also closely watched foreign-born Germans and Italians who lived in the United States and detained roughly 10,000 Germans and several hundred Italians.

Forced to abandon their possessions or sell them for a pittance, Japanese American evacuees were confined in flimsy barracks, enclosed by barbed wire and under armed guard. These camps, often in remote locations such as Heart Mountain, Wyoming, offered only the barest accommodations: cots for beds, a meager daily ration of food, overcrowded rooms. Two-thirds of the detainees were native-born U.S. citizens, and many gave up thriving agricultural enterprises that they had built in California over generations. Some evacuated so quickly that they arrived at their camps with little more than the clothes they wore.

Internment was controversial. In December 1944, a divided U.S. Supreme Court upheld the constitutionality of Japanese relocation in *Korematsu* v. *United States* (1944). In 1988, Congress officially apologized for the internment, revealed that military investigators at the time had reported no cases of subversion, and authorized a cash indemnity for anyone who had been confined in the camps.

Interpreting the Visual Past Government Mobilization of the Home Front

The Office of War Information (OWI) flooded wartime America with millions of pictures. Colorful posters sought to shore up emotional support for the war and encourage everyday activities that aided the military effort overseas. Some imagery drew from the advertising industry's familiarity with "soft-sell" techniques. Other pictures used a far more directive tone in their appeals.

These two widely distributed posters, FOOD IS A WEAPON and WHEN YOU RIDE ALONE YOU RIDE WITH HITLER, show differing persuasive techniques in both their words and their visual imagery.

Q *What precise wartime behaviors are both posters seeking to encourage among ordinary Americans?*

Q *What are the various strategies of persuasion in these posters? Which poster do you see as more directive? Which do you see as employing a "softer-sell" strategy?*

Q *How might some people have feared that allowing such pictorial power to the OWI set a dangerous precedent? Why might the practice of public officials using governmental power to mount sophisticated, well-funded campaigns aimed at influencing the private behavior of a democratic citizenry raise potentially troubling issues? Why might this practice seem legitimate and necessary?*

PF/NA/Alamy Stock Photo

26.9a **Weimer Pursell for Office of Price Administration, When Your Ride Alone You Ride with Hitler, 1943.**

War posters/Alamy Stock Photo

26.9b **Anonymous Artist for Office of War Information, Food Is a Weapon, 1943.**

26-4e *Challenging Racial Inequality*

The global fight against fascism proved helpful to movements working for greater racial equality in America. Nazism, based on the idea of racial inequality, exposed the racist underpinnings of older social science research. The view that racial difference was not the result of biology gained wider acceptance during the war. "The Huns have wrecked the theory of the master race," stated an Alabama politician. The idea that a democracy could bridge cultural and social differences provided a basis for the postwar struggle against discrimination.

The *Amsterdam News*, a Harlem newspaper, called for a **"Double V" campaign**—victory at home as well as abroad.

Bettmann/Corbis

26.10 **A Segregated Military** This photo of an African American regiment eating in a mess hall during the Second World War illustrates racial segregation in the armed forces.

In January 1941, the labor leader A. Philip Randolph promised to lead tens of thousands of black workers in a march on Washington to demand more defense jobs and integration of the military forces. President Roosevelt feared the event would embarrass his administration and urged that it be canceled. Randolph's persistence ultimately forced Roosevelt to create the FEPC. Although this new agency gained little effective power, its very existence helped advance the ideal of nondiscrimination.

Northward migration of African Americans accelerated demands for equality. Drawn by the promise of wartime jobs, nearly 750,000 African Americans relocated to northern cities, where many sensed the possibility of political power for the first time in their lives. They found an outspoken advocate of civil rights in First Lady Eleanor Roosevelt, who antagonized southern white Democrats and members of her husband's administration by her advocacy of civil rights and her participation in integrated social functions.

Particularly in urban areas, civil rights groups emerged from the wartime years with a strong base from which to fight for jobs and political power. Founded in 1942, the interracial Committee (later, Congress) on Racial Equality (CORE) devised new ways of opposing discrimination. CORE activists staged sit-ins to integrate restaurants, theaters, and other public facilities, especially in Washington, D.C.

In California and throughout the Southwest during the war years, Latino organizations, too, highlighted the irony of fighting overseas for a nation that denied equality at home. They challenged the United States to live up to its democratic rhetoric. Approximately 500,000 Mexican Americans served, often with great distinction, in the military. Not wishing to anger this constituency, the Roosevelt administration also feared discrimination might harm the credibility of its Good Neighbor Policy in Latin America (see Chapter 25). The president's coordinator of Inter-American affairs allocated federal money to train Spanish-speaking workers for wartime employment, improve education in the *barrios*, and provide high school graduates with new opportunities to enter college.

Although legal precedents in California and other southwestern states classified Latinos as "white," actual practices, especially in public schools, usually discriminated against people of Mexican descent. Organizations such as the League of United Latin American Citizens (LULAC) mounted several drives against such discrimination during the war, and they prepared for greater challenges in the postwar period.

People of Japanese descent, despite their internment, also laid the basis for postwar campaigns for equality. The courage and sacrifice of Japanese American soldiers became legendary. The 100th Battalion and the 442nd Regimental Combat Team, segregated units, suffered stunning casualties, often while undertaking extremely dangerous combat missions in Europe. Moreover, in the Pacific theater, 6,000 Japanese American members of the Military Intelligence Service provided invaluable service.

In the face of divisive issues and calls for greater equality, wartime propaganda stressed national unity and contrasted America's "melting pot" ethos with German and Japanese obsessions about racial "purity." Movies, plays, radio dramas, and music fostered a sense of national community by celebrating cultural diversity. As members of each of America's racial and ethnic groups distinguished themselves in the military, the claim of equality—"Americans All," in the words of a wartime slogan—took on greater moral force. Imagery extolling social solidarity and freedom provided a foundation for the antidiscrimination movements of the decades ahead.

AP Images

26.11 **Zoot Suit, June 7, 1943** A deputy sheriff inspects the haircut and clothing styles of a young man arrested during disturbances in East Los Angeles.

Q *Why did hairstyles and zoot suit attire become highly contested symbols during the war?*

26-5 Shaping the Peace

Q *How did major new institutions and policies, adopted at the end of the war, attempt to promote reconstruction and build a more lasting peace?*

Even before the war ended, U.S. policymakers began considering postwar peace arrangements. The Truman administration built on Roosevelt's wartime conferences and agreements to shape the framework of international relations for the next half-century.

26-5a *International Organizations*

In the Atlantic Charter of 1941, and at a conference in Moscow in October 1943, the Allied powers had pledged to create a replacement for the defunct League of Nations. Internationalist-minded Americans hoped the new **United Nations (UN)** would offer a more realistic version of Woodrow Wilson's vision for a world body that could deter aggressor nations and promote peaceful political change. At the Dumbarton Oaks Conference in Washington in August 1944, and at a subsequent meeting in San Francisco in April 1945, the Allies worked out the UN's organizational structure. It included a General Assembly, in which each member nation would be represented and cast one vote. A smaller body, the Security Council, would include five permanent members from the Allied coalition—the United States, Great Britain, the Soviet Union, France, and Nationalist China—and six rotating members. The Security Council would have primary responsibility for maintaining peace, but permanent members could veto any council decision. A UN Secretariat, headed by a secretary general, would handle day-to-day business, and an Economic and Social Council would sponsor measures to improve living conditions throughout the world.

Source: huffingtonpost.com

26.12 **Heart Mountain Japanese Internment Camp near Cody, Wyoming** Photos of the internment camps were usually in black and white, so this color photo is a rarity. It was taken by a camp internee, Bill Manbo and shows the forbidding terrain and isolated nature of the camps.

Q *Why were camps established in places such as Heart Mountain?*

The U.S. Senate, with only two dissenting votes, approved joining the UN in July 1945. This victory for internationalism contrasted sharply with the Senate's 1919 rejection of membership in the League of Nations. Opponents of Wilson's dream had worried that internationalist policies might limit the ability of the United States to pursue its own interests, but following the Second World War a newly powerful United States appeared able to dominate international organizations such as the UN. In addition, most U.S. leaders recognized that the war had partly resulted from the lack of a coordinated, international response to aggression during the 1930s.

Eleanor Roosevelt played a prominent role in building the new postwar internationalist ethos. A delegate to the first meeting of the UN's General Assembly, she chaired its Commission on Human Rights and guided the drafting of a **Universal Declaration of Human Rights**, adopted by the UN in 1948. The document set forth "inalienable" human rights and freedoms as cornerstones of international law.

Economic agreements also illustrated a growing acceptance of international organizations. They sought to remedy some of the causes of international instability that had touched off the Great Depression and the war. At the Bretton Woods (New Hampshire) Conference of 1944, assembled nations created the International Monetary Fund (IMF), which was designed to maintain stable currency exchange rates by ensuring that each nation's currency could be converted into any other national currency at a fixed rate. The International Bank for Reconstruction and Development, later renamed the World Bank, was also created to provide loans to war-battered countries and promote the resumption of world trade. In 1948 the General Agreement on Tariffs and Trade (GATT) established the institutional groundwork for breaking up closed trading blocs and implementing free and fair trade agreements.

26-5b *Spheres of Interest and Postwar Settlements*

In wartime negotiations, Stalin, Churchill, and Roosevelt had assumed that powerful nations—their own—would enjoy special "spheres of influence" in the postwar world. As early as January 1942, the Soviet ambassador to the United States reported to Stalin that Roosevelt had tacitly assented to Soviet postwar control over the Baltic states of Lithuania, Latvia, and Estonia. In 1944 Stalin and Churchill agreed, informally and secretly, that Britain would continue its sway over Greece and that the Soviets could control Romania and Bulgaria. U.S. leaders assumed that Latin America would remain within their sphere of influence. Roosevelt expressed contradictory positions on the Soviet Union. He

What They Said

Civil Liberties in Wartime: *Korematsu v. United States*

Fred Korematsu, an American of Japanese background, was born in Oakland, California, and had been a law-abiding citizen. In his early 20s, when the order to relocate Japanese Americans to internment camps was announced, he challenged the legality of the measure. Ultimately, the Supreme Court heard his case. In a controversial 1944 decision, a divided court upheld the constitutionality of internment. The following selections suggest some of the arguments made in both the majority and minority opinions. Nearly 45 years later, after an exhaustive examination of military records, Congress took a stand on the issue. Officially apologizing for internment, Congress stated that it was "not justified by military necessity, and … not driven by analysis of military conditions.

Justice Hugo Black

from the majority opinion of the Supreme Court in *Korematsu* v. *United States* (1944), upholding the constitutionality of Executive Order 9066

Exclusion of those of Japanese origin was deemed necessary because of the presence of an unascertained number of disloyal members of the group, most of whom we have no doubt were loyal to this country. It was because we could not reject the finding of the military authorities that it was impossible to bring about an immediate segregation of the disloyal from the loyal… .

Compulsory exclusion of large groups of citizens from their homes, except under circumstances of direct emergency and peril, is inconsistent with our basic governmental institutions. But when under conditions of modern warfare our shores are threatened by hostile forces, the power to protect must be commensurate with the threatened danger… . To cast this case into outlines of racial prejudice, without reference to the real military dangers which were presented, merely confuses the issue.

Justice Frank Murphy

from the dissenting opinion in *Korematsu* v. *United States*

We must accord great respect and consideration to the judgments of the military authorities who are on the scene and who have full knowledge of the military facts… . At the same time, however, it is essential that there be definite limits to military discretion, especially where martial law has not been declared. Individuals must not be left impoverished of their constitutional rights on a plea of military necessity that has neither substance nor support… .

In support of this blanket condemnation of all persons of Japanese descent, however, no reliable evidence is cited to show that such individuals were generally disloyal, or had … furnished reasonable ground for their exclusion as a group… . No adequate reason is given for the failure to treat these Japanese Americans on an individual basis by holding investigations and hearings to separate the loyal from the disloyal, as was done in the case of persons of German and Italian ancestry… . I dissent, therefore, from this legalization of racism.

Q *What circumstances, according to Justice Black, might constitutionally permit detention of citizens on the basis of their nationality or ethnic background?*

Q *How does Justice Murphy frame the constitutional issues when countering Justice Black's claims?*

Q *What might explain Congress's later decision to issue an apology?*

Sources: (top) From the majority opinion by Justice Hugo Black in the Supreme Court case *Korematsu* v. *U.S.* (1944), upholding the constitutionality of Executive Order 9066. (bottom) From the dissenting opinion by Justice Frank Murphy in the Supreme Court case *Korematsu* v. *U.S.* (1944).

sometimes seemed to imply that he accepted Stalin's goal of having states friendly to the USSR on his vulnerable western border, but at the Tehran Conference of November 1943 he also told Stalin that U.S. voters of Eastern European descent expected their homelands to be independent after the war. After Roosevelt's death, the Soviets' powerful position in Eastern Europe became a focus of tensions with the United States.

Early in the war, both the United States and the Soviet Union had urged the dismemberment and deindustrialization of a defeated Nazi Germany. At a conference held at Yalta, in Ukraine, in February 1945, the three Allied powers agreed to divide Germany into four zones of occupation (with France as the fourth occupying force). Later, as relations among the victors worsened, this temporary division of Germany hardened into a Soviet-dominated zone in the east and the other three zones to its west. Berlin, the German capital, also was divided, even though the city itself lay totally within the Soviet zone.

The future of Poland also posed difficult issues. At Yalta, the Soviets agreed to permit free elections in postwar

Poland, but Stalin believed that the other Allied leaders had tacitly accepted Soviet dominance over Poland's government. The agreement at Yalta was ambiguous at best; the war was still at a critical stage, and the western Allies chose to sacrifice clarity in order to encourage cooperation from the Soviets. After Yalta, the Soviets assumed that Poland would be in their sphere of influence, but many Americans charged the Soviets with bad faith for failing to hold free elections and for not relinquishing control.

In Asia, military realities likewise influenced postwar settlements. At Tehran and again at Yalta, Stalin pledged to send troops to fight Japan as soon as Germany surrendered. The first U.S. atomic bomb fell on Hiroshima, however, just one day before the Soviets were to enter the Pacific war, and the United States assumed total charge of the occupation and postwar reorganization of Japan. The Soviet Union and the United States divided Korea, which had been controlled by Japan, into separate zones of occupation. Here, as in Germany, these zones would later emerge as two antagonistic states (see Chapter 27).

The fate of the European colonies seized by Japan in Southeast Asia was another contentious issue. Most U.S. officials preferred to see the former British and French colonies become independent nations, but they also worried about the left-leaning politics of many anticolonial nationalist movements. As the United States developed an anticommunist foreign policy after the end of the war, it moved to support British and French efforts to reassemble their colonial empires.

In the Philippines, the United States honored its long-standing pledge to grant independence. A friendly government that agreed to respect American economic interests and military bases took power in 1946 and enlisted American advisers to help suppress leftist rebels. In 1947 the United Nations designated the Mariana, Caroline, and Marshall Islands as the "Trust Territories of the Pacific" and authorized the United States to administer their affairs.

Although the nations of Latin America had been only indirectly involved in military conflict and peace negotiations, the war directly affected U.S. relations with them. Roosevelt's Good Neighbor Policy and a new Office of Inter-American Affairs (OIAA), created in 1937, expanded cultural and economic ties, and Latin American leaders stood nearly united behind the Allies. After U.S. entry into the war, at a conference in Rio de Janeiro in January 1942, every Latin American country except Chile and Argentina broke diplomatic ties with the Axis governments. When naval warfare in the Atlantic severed commercial connections between Latin America and Europe, Latin American countries became critical suppliers of raw materials to the United States.

Wartime conferences avoided clear decisions about creating a Jewish homeland in the Middle East. The Second World War prompted survivors of the Holocaust and Jews from around the world to take direct action. Zionism, the movement to found a Jewish state in Palestine, which Jews claimed to be their ancient homeland, fueled a mass migration of Jews. They began to carve out, against the resistance from Palestinians and other Arab people, the new nation of Israel.

Conclusion

The world changed dramatically during the Second World War. For the United States, wartime mobilization ended the Great Depression and focused attention on international concerns. A more powerful national government, concerned with preserving national security, assumed nearly complete control over the economy. Government, business, and scientific researchers worked together to provide the seemingly miraculous growth in productivity that ultimately won the war.

The 1940s also sharpened debates over liberty and equality. Many Americans saw the Second World War as a struggle to protect and preserve liberties they already enjoyed. Others, inspired by a struggle against racism and injustice abroad, insisted that a war for freedom overseas should help redress inequalities at home.

The war brought victory over dictatorial, expansionist regimes, and the United States emerged as the world's preeminent power. Still, Americans remained uncertain about postwar policies. As the dislocations of war gave way to the uncertainties of peace, they worried about the recovery of Europe and relations with their wartime ally, the Soviet Union. And the nation now faced the future without the charismatic leadership of Franklin D. Roosevelt.

CHAPTER REVIEW

Review

1. Why did events in Asia and in Europe prompt debate within the United States over whether or not to embrace more interventionist policies overseas?
2. Why, after initial military setbacks in Europe and Asia, did the Allies ultimately defeat the Axis powers?
3. How did mobilizing for war change American economic conditions and enlarge the role of government?
4. Why did the war propel movements for greater equality in American life?
5. How did major new institutions and policies, adopted at the end of the war, attempt to promote reconstruction and build a more lasting peace?

Critical Thinking

1. In what ways had the United States already moved, even before the attack on Pearl Harbor, toward intervention in the Second World War?
2. How might Franklin Roosevelt's domestic policies during the Second World War be seen to retreat from the aspirations of his New Deal?

Identifications

Review your understanding of the following key terms, people, and events for this chapter (terms in bold in text are included in the Glossary).

Adolf Hitler, p. 718
Third Reich, p. 718
Neutrality Acts, p. 718
Spanish Civil War, p. 718
East Asian Co-Prosperity Sphere, p. 719
Munich Conference, p. 719
"isolationists," p. 721
Lend-Lease Act, p. 721
Pearl Harbor, p. 722
Pentagon, p. 723
OVERLORD, p. 723
Manhattan Project, p. 730
Hiroshima, p. 730
"Second Bill of Rights," p. 735
Office of War Information (OWI), p. 735
internment, p. 736
"Double V" campaign, p. 737
United Nations (UN), p. 739
Universal Declaration of Human Rights, p. 740

Suggested Readings

On the U.S. entry into the war, see **David Kaiser**, ***No End Save Victory: How FDR Led the Nation Into War*** (2014). The many excellent accounts of the Second World War include **Max Hastings**, ***Inferno: The World at War, 1939–1945*** (2012). **J. Samuel Walker**, ***Prompt and Utter Destruction: Truman and the Use of the Atomic Bombs against Japan*** (2005), examines the war's end; and **John Dower**, ***War without Mercy: Race and Power in the Pacific War*** (1987), is a superb analysis of the culture of violence.

On the home front, see **David Kennedy**, ***The American People in World War II: Freedom from Fear*** (2003); **Alan Winkler**, ***Home Front U.S.A: America during World War II*** (3rd ed., 2012); and **Gerald D. Nash**, ***The American West Transformed: The Impact of the Second World War*** (1990).

Maury Klein, ***A Call to Arms: Mobilizing America for World War II*** (2013), is a lengthy economic history (2013). **Thomas Patrick Doherty**, ***Projections of War: Hollywood, American Culture, and World War II*** (1993), examines wartime films. **Melissa A. McEuen**, ***Making Women: Femininity and Duty on the American Home Front, 1941–1945*** (2011) provides an overview.

Ronald Takaki, ***Double Victory: A Multicultural History of America in World War II*** (2000), examines issues of race and ethnicity. More specialized studies include **Kevin Kruse and Stephen Tuck, eds.**, ***Fog of War: The Second World War and the Civil Rights Movement*** (2012); and **Luis Alvarez**, ***The Power of the Zoot: Youth Culture and Resistance during World War II*** (2008).

27 The Age of Containment, 1946–1953

HER BEAUTY served a mob of terror whose one mission is to destroy!
RKO
I MARRIED a Communist
LARAINE DAY · ROBERT RYAN · JOHN AGAR
THOMAS GOMEZ · JANIS CARTER

Everett Collection

27.1 **Hollywood in the Service of the Anticommunist Crusade** Fears about communist infiltration of the motion picture industry prompted Hollywood studios to display their anticommunist credentials by blacklisting left-leaning employees and by making films such as RKO's *I Married a Communist*. These anticommunist films, with their simplistic political messages, generally bombed at the box office. This particular film did better when rebranded as a *film noir* and rereleased as *The Woman on Pier 13*.

THE SECOND WORLD WAR, popularly portrayed as a struggle to preserve the "American way of life," ended up transforming it. The fight against fascism propelled foreign policy issues to the forefront of American politics, and postwar tensions kept them there. As combat operations gave way to friction between the United States and the Soviet Union, U.S. leaders overhauled military strategy. They claimed broad powers for the executive branch and called for a global stand against communism. The effort to shore up "national security" soon translated into an ever-larger military establishment and an economic system that could supply its needs.

At home, debate over increased governmental power generated immediate controversy. Wartime production, overseen by government bureaucracies in Washington, had finally ended the economic downturn of the 1930s. Should Washington help organize a postwar economy that satisfied household as well as military consumption? Should a more powerful and active government in Washington assist movements seeking greater equality? Could such a government limit security threats at home without endangering liberty? Questions such as these enlivened, and embittered, public debate in the aftermath of the Second World War. ■

CHRONOLOGY

1946	Employment Act passed • Republicans gain control of Congress
1947	Truman Doctrine announced • George Kennan's "Mr. X" article published • National Security Act passed • Marshall Plan proposed • Taft–Hartley Act passed
1948	Marshall Plan adopted • Berlin Airlift begins • Truman wins reelection
1949	NATO established • Soviet Union explodes atomic device • Truman unveils his Fair Deal
1950	NSC-68 adopted • Korean War begins
1951	Truman removes General MacArthur as commander in Korea • *Dennis* decision in Supreme Court
1952	National Security Agency (NSA) created • Republican Dwight Eisenhower elected president

27-1 Creating a National Security State, 1945–1949

Q *How did disputes between the United States and the Soviet Union shape the cold war and prompt a focus on national security?*

The wartime alliance between the United States and the Soviet Union proved little more than a brief marriage of convenience. Defeating the Axis had forced the two nations to cooperate, but collaboration began unraveling even before war's end. Relations deteriorated into a **cold war** of mutual suspicions and massive military buildups but few direct confrontations between the superpowers.

27-1a *Onset of the Cold War*

Historians have dissected the onset of the cold war from different perspectives. A familiar view focuses on Soviet expansionism, stressing a historically rooted appetite for new territory, an ideological zeal to spread communism, or some interplay between the two. According to this interpretation, the United States needed to adopt firm anti-Soviet policies. Other historians—generally called revisionists—see the Soviet Union's desire to secure its borders as an understandable response to the invasion of its territory during both world wars. The United States, in this view, should have tried to reassure the Soviet Union (USSR), pursuing conciliatory measures instead of ones that intensified Soviet fears. Still other scholars maintain that assigning blame obscures how clashing interests and differing political cultures made postwar conflict between the two superpowers unavoidable.

In almost every view, President Harry Truman's role was central. Truman initially hoped to bargain productively with the Soviet Union and its premier, Joseph Stalin. As differences between the former allies sharpened, however, Truman came to distrust Stalin and to listen to hard-line anti-Soviet advisers.

The atomic bomb became an important source of friction. At the Potsdam Conference of July 1945, Truman had casually told Stalin, without mentioning the bomb, about a new U.S. weapon of "unusual destructive force." Well informed by Soviet intelligence operations about the Manhattan Project, Stalin calmly advised Truman to make "good use" of this weapon. Stalin also ordered Soviet scientists, with far less calm, to intensify their nuclear weapons program. Truman likely hoped that the bomb would scare the Soviets—and it did. Historians debate whether it frightened Moscow into more cautious behavior or made it a more aggressive cold war adversary.

As atomic warfare against Japan gave way to atomic diplomacy with the Soviet Union, U.S. leaders differed over how to proceed. One group, recognizing that the Soviets would soon possess atomic weapons, urged Truman to share technology with the USSR in hopes of forestalling a future arms race. Hard-liners, fearing Soviet intentions and underestimating their nuclear knowledge, rejected this approach.

In 1946, Truman authorized Bernard Baruch, his special representative at the United Nations, to explore ways of controlling atomic power. The Baruch Plan proposed that the United States abandon its atomic weapons if the USSR agreed to outside monitoring of its weapons program and surrendering its veto power in the UN on atomic issues. Soviet leaders counter-proposed that the United States destroy its atomic weapons as the first step toward any bargain. The United States rejected this idea. Both nations used the deadlock to justify a stepped-up arms race.

Other sources of friction involved U.S. loan policy and Soviet domination of Eastern Europe. Truman ended Lend-Lease assistance to the Soviet Union at the end of the war and linked any new loans for postwar reconstruction to Soviet cooperation with the United States over the future of Europe. This linkage strategy failed. Lack of capital and suspicions about the intentions of the United States and its allies provided the Soviets with excuses for their own hard-line stance. A repressive Soviet sphere of influence, which Stalin called defensive and Truman labeled expansionist, spread over Eastern Europe.

By 1946, the former allies seemed ready to become bitter adversaries. Early that year, Winston Churchill famously declared that an "Iron Curtain," with free nations on one side and communist ones on the other, had descended across Europe. The communist countries to the east, under the control of the Soviet Union, threatened the security of Western Europe, the British leader proclaimed. Truman agreed and pledged to stop any communist aggression. His anticommunist initiatives, in both foreign and domestic affairs, extended the power of the executive branch and laid the basis for a national security state.

27-1b *The Truman Doctrine and Containment Abroad*

In March 1947, the president announced what soon became known as the **Truman Doctrine** when speaking to Congress about a civil war in Greece, where communist-led insurgents

The Granger Collection, NYC

27.2 **Testing the Atomic Bomb at Bikini Atoll** This atomic test, one of 23 detonations at Bikini Atoll in the Marshall Islands during the late 1940s, raised a column of water 5,000 feet high. Although Bikini islanders were evacuated from the blast sites, the radiation still affected nearby people, including U.S. service personnel, and the area's ecology for years to come. As nuclear-related imagery spread through cold war culture, new "bikini" swimsuits for "bombshell" women became a fashion rage.

threatened to topple a pro-Western government. In private, London had informed Washington that it lacked the economic and military resources to act in Greece, long within Great Britain's sphere of influence. Truman's advisers feared a leftist victory in Greece would expose Turkey, a nation critical to the U.S. strategic position, to Soviet expansionism. In publicly justifying U.S. aid to Greece and Turkey, Truman asserted that U.S. security interests now spanned the globe and that the fate of "free peoples" everywhere hung in the balance. Unless the United States aided people "resisting attempted subversion by armed minorities or by outside pressures," totalitarian communism would spread and ultimately threaten the United States.

The Truman Doctrine's global vision of national security encountered some skepticism. Henry A. Wallace, the most visible Democratic critic, chided Truman for exaggerating the Soviet threat and urged a more conciliatory approach toward Moscow. Conservative Republicans, though fervently anticommunist, feared the increase in presidential power and the vast expenditures that implementing the Truman Doctrine would seemingly entail. If Truman wanted broad support for his position, Republican senator Arthur Vandenberg had already advised, he should "scare hell" out of people, something Truman proved quite willing to do when justifying his new doctrine. With votes from Republicans and Democrats, the president gained congressional approval for $400 million in assistance to Greece and Turkey, most of it for military aid, in the spring of 1947. This vote signaled broad, bipartisan support for a national security policy that came to be called **containment**.

The term *containment* first appeared in a 1947 article in the journal *Foreign Affairs* by George Kennan, the State Department's leading Soviet expert. Writing under the pseudonym "X," Kennan argued that the "main element" in U.S. policy "must be that of a long-term, patient but firm and vigilant containment of Russian expansive tendencies." The measured and limited containment policy, which Kennan later claimed he had outlined in this article, soon became associated with the urgent tone and expansive approach of the Truman Doctrine.

Containment thus became a catchphrase for a global, anticommunist national security policy. As popularly articulated, containment linked all leftist insurgencies, wherever they occurred, to a totalitarian movement controlled from Moscow that directly threatened American security. Even a small gain for the Soviets in one part of the world could encourage communist aggression elsewhere. Although foreign policy debates included sharp disagreement over precisely how to pursue containment, most American leaders came to support an activist, anticommunist foreign policy that spanned the globe.

27-1c *Truman's Loyalty Program and Containment at Home*

Nine days after proclaiming the Truman Doctrine, the president issued Executive Order 9835. It authorized a system of government loyalty boards empowered to gather evidence in order to determine if there were "reasonable grounds" for concluding that a federal employee belonged to a subversive organization or espoused ideas that might endanger national security. Persons found to pose a "security risk" would lose their government jobs. The Truman administration also empowered the Justice Department to identify political organizations it deemed subversive and place them on a new Attorney General's List. The Loyalty Program, partly intended to show that Truman's administration considered communism a serious domestic threat, suggested that containing communist activities at home would require the type of aggressive measures being adopted overseas.

The Truman administration thus embarked on what became a controversial approach to containing communism, including Soviet espionage, at home. Although few people ever doubted that the Soviets were conducting spy operations inside the United States, there has long been sharp disagreement over their scope and effectiveness. Such debates now take place in light of declassified evidence from Soviet and U.S. surveillance files revealing that both nations conducted a wide range of intelligence activity. By 1943, the United States had begun intercepting transmissions between Moscow and certain American groups and individuals. Collected as the VENONA files and finally released in 1995, these intercepted messages show that the Soviet Union had helped finance America's Communist Party, placed informants in governmental agencies, and obtained secret information about U.S. atomic work. Uncovering Soviet espionage, in short, was a legitimate objective. Historians remain divided, however, over the reliability and relevance of specific pieces of the evidence collected by the VENONA project—and also over how much of the intercepted information became immediately available to the Truman administration.

Truman's loyalty policy worried a diverse group of critics. The president claimed that the existence of even a few security risks demanded an unprecedented response. Truman's position, however, angered more fervent anticommunists, particularly Republicans, who accused the president of doing too little to fight subversion at home. Civil libertarians, in contrast, charged Truman with whipping up fear about communism that far exceeded any actual threat. They called for a carefully targeted approach. Internal security policy, for example, should treat an atomic scientist with links to the Soviet Union differently from an outspoken clerical worker in a nonsensitive governmental position.

27-1d *The National Security Act, the Marshall Plan, and the Berlin Crisis*

Shaking off criticism, the Truman administration continued to extend its containment initiative. It secured congressional approval of the **National Security Act of 1947**, which created several new government bureaucracies. The old Navy and War Departments, by 1949, would combine into the Department of Defense. An entirely new addition to the executive branch, the National Security Council, obtained broad authority over planning the new containment policy. The air force became a separate service equal to the army and navy. The National

27.3 **The Marshall Plan** Showing the colors of many flags, this promotional poster for the Marshall Plan uses the image of a water-pumping windmill to advocate cooperation in promoting economic development.

Q *How does this poster carry out themes of unity already familiar from the wartime period? Can you name which countries were symbolized by these emblems?*

Security Act also created the Central Intelligence Agency (CIA) to gather information about communist threats and conduct covert activities outside the United States.

The CIA quickly became the most flexible arm of this new national security apparatus. A series of secret presidential directives expanded the CIA's role, while its activities and budget remained shrouded from public scrutiny. Soon, the CIA's covert operations crisscrossed the globe. CIA operatives cultivated ties with anti-Soviet groups in Eastern Europe and within the Soviet Union. The agency helped finance pro-U.S. labor unions in Western Europe to curtail the influence of leftist organizations. It orchestrated covert campaigns to prevent the Italian Communist Party from winning an electoral victory in 1948 and to bolster anticommunist political parties in France, Japan, and elsewhere.

The Truman administration also linked economic initiatives in Western Europe to its overall containment policy. Fearing that Europe's economic problems might create opportunities for local communist movements, Secretary of State General George C. Marshall sought to strengthen the region's economies. Under his 1947 proposal, known as the European Recovery Program or simply the Marshall Plan, U.S. funds would help postwar governments in Europe to coordinate programs of economic reconstruction. Although invited to participate, the Soviet Union quickly denounced the Marshall Plan as the economic component of a larger U.S. effort to dominate all of Europe.

The Marshall Plan, enacted by Congress in early 1948, ultimately achieved the hopes of its architects. It helped brighten the economic picture in Western Europe, where industrial production rebounded. Improved standards of living enhanced political stability and helped undercut the appeal of leftist movements. Between 1946 and 1951, the United States provided nearly $13 billion in assistance to 17 Western European nations. When critics in the United States condemned the Marshall Plan as an expensive "giveaway" scheme, supporters stressed how it would expand both overseas markets and investment opportunities for American businesses. They also hailed it for contributing to the larger containment strategy for safeguarding national security.

While lobbying for the Marshall Plan, the Truman administration also sought to expand U.S. military forces. The Soviet Union helped install a pro-Moscow government in Czechoslovakia in early 1948, and some U.S. officials warned of a Soviet military strike into Western Europe. Truman declared that "moral God-fearing peoples ... must save the world from atheism" and Soviet totalitarianism. As a brief war scare gripped Washington, national security planners successfully implored Congress to increase defense spending, largely for new aircraft, and reinstate a military draft.

Policymakers in the United States viewed the future of Germany, initially divided into four zones of occupation, as crucial. In June 1948, the United States, Great Britain, and France announced currency reform as the first step toward integrating their separate sectors into a Federal Republic of Germany or West Germany. Having been invaded by German forces in both world wars, however, the Soviets feared a resurgent Germany. Hoping to sidetrack Western plans, the Soviets cut off all highways, railroads, and water routes into West Berlin, which was located within their zone of military occupation.

The Soviet's **Berlin Blockade** failed. American and British aircraft, in what became known as the **Berlin Airlift**, delivered the supplies West Berliners needed. Truman, hinting at a military response, dispatched to Great Britain two squadrons of B-29 bombers, reportedly able to deliver atomic bombs to Soviet territory. Unable to seal off West Berlin, Stalin abandoned his blockade in May 1949. The Soviets then created the German Democratic Republic, or East Germany, out of their military sector. West Berlin, which survived as an anticommunist enclave inside East Germany, would remain a focus of cold war tensions.

27-1e *The Election of 1948*

Meanwhile, national security issues helped Harry Truman win the 1948 presidential election. For several years, the president had been losing support among those Democrats—led by his secretary of commerce, Henry A. Wallace—who considered Truman's containment policies overly confrontational. When Wallace continued to criticize these initiatives, the president had ousted him from the cabinet. Two months later, in the midterm national elections of November 1946, voters had given the Republicans control of Congress for the first time since 1928. Although Truman's political fortunes had improved by late 1947, few political handicappers liked his chances in 1948.

Truman faced three other presidential hopefuls. Challenged from the left by a new Progressive Party, which nominated Wallace, and from the right by Thomas E. Dewey, the Republican nominee, and J. Strom Thurmond, the pro-segregationist candidate of the new States' Rights Party, or Dixiecrats, the president waged a vigorous campaign. Only months before Election Day, Truman called the GOP-controlled Congress into special session and presented it with a list of domestic programs, including a plan for national health care, abhorrent to most Republicans. Then he denounced "that do-nothing, good-for-nothing, worst Congress" for failing to enact his agenda.

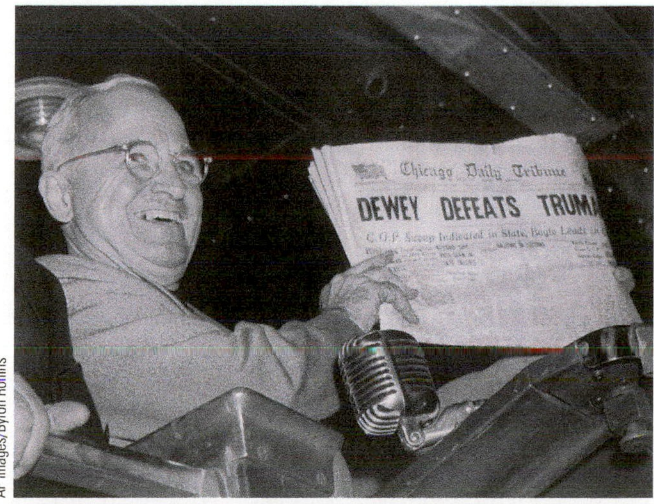

AP Images/Byron Rollins

27.4 **Dewey Defeats Truman?** President Harry S. Truman holds up an Election Day edition of the *Chicago Daily Tribune*, which embarrassingly announced "Dewey Defeats Truman" in the 1948 presidential election. The president told well-wishers "That is one for the books!".

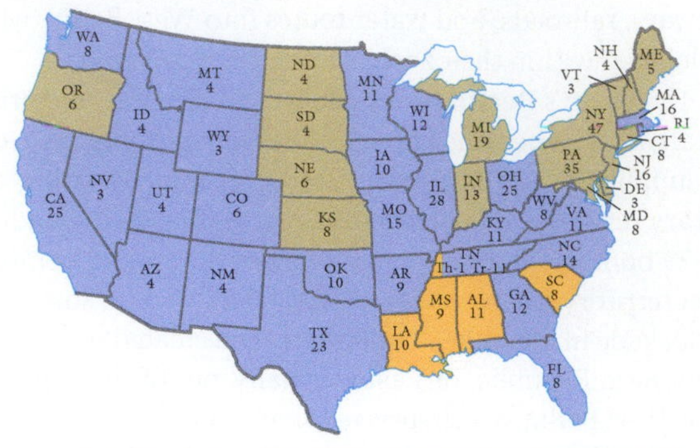

	Electoral Vote		Popular Vote	
	Number	%	Number	%
Truman (Democrat)	303	57.1	24,105,812	49.9
Dewey (Republican)	189	35.6	21,970,065	45.3
Thurmond (States' Rights)	39	7.3	1,169,021	2.4
Wallace (Progressive)	----	-----	1,157,172	2.4

▲ MAP 27.1 Presidential Election, 1948

Q *How does this electoral map help show how Truman won the presidency with less than 50 percent of the popular vote?*

Q *How does it provide important clues to future electoral changes that will affect the Democratic Party after 1948?*

Truman's victory now seems less surprising to historians than it did to analysts in 1948. Despite the GOP's electoral successes in 1946, the Democratic Party was hardly enfeebled. Loyalty to the memory of Roosevelt and his New Deal programs helped bring Truman's triumph. Moreover, although Thurmond's Dixiecrat movement portended a political shift among southern whites, who had voted overwhelmingly Democratic since the late 19th century, Truman carried all but four states of the old Confederacy in 1948. Finally, Truman's staunch anticommunism helped bury Henry Wallace's challenge. Hampered by his Progressive Party's refusal to reject support from the U.S. Communist Party, Wallace received less than 3 percent of the popular tally and no electoral votes. The 1948 election suggested a blueprint for winning elections to come: Successful presidential candidates must never appear "soft" on national security issues (see Map 27.1).

27-2 The Era of the Korean War, 1949–1952

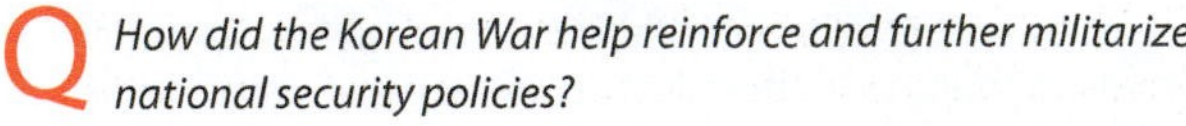

Q *How did the Korean War help reinforce and further militarize national security policies?*

A series of cold war crises in 1949 and the outbreak of war on the Korean peninsula in 1950, which heightened anticommunist fervor in the United States, boosted support for funding a vastly expanded national security state.

27-2a *NATO, China, and Nuclear Weaponry*

In April 1949, the United States, Canada, and 10 European nations formed the **North Atlantic Treaty Organization (NATO)**. They pledged that an attack against one nation would automatically be treated as a strike against all. Republican senator Robert Taft called NATO a provocation to the Soviet Union, an "entangling alliance" in violation of settled foreign policy principles, and a threat to Congress's constitutional power to declare war. Still, the NATO concept prevailed (see Map 27.2).

Events in China heightened cold war tensions. Although the United States had extended Jiang Jieshi's struggling Nationalist Party–led government billions in military aid and economic assistance, Jiang's forces had steadily lost ground to those of Mao Zedong's communist movement. Experienced U.S. diplomats privately predicted that incompetence and corruption would speed Jiang's downfall, but the Truman administration publicly portrayed Jiang as the respected leader of an embattled but "free" China. In 1949, Mao's armies forced Jiang off the mainland to the nearby island of Formosa (Taiwan).

Mao's triumph shocked most Americans. Financed by conservative business leaders, the powerful "China lobby" blamed Truman and his new secretary of state, Dean Acheson, for having "lost" China to communism. This domestic political pressure and new international tensions quickly convinced the Truman administration to embrace Jiang's fledgling government on Taiwan and to refuse diplomatic recognition for Mao's "Red China."

The communist challenge grew more alarming when, in 1949, the Soviets exploded a crude atomic device, marking the end of the U.S. monopoly. Besieged by critics who saw recent history marked by Soviet gains and U.S. losses, Truman authorized U.S. scientists to develop a deadly new weapon, the hydrogen bomb, or "superbomb."

27-2b *NSC-68 and the Korean War*

The Truman administration also reviewed its core assumptions about foreign policy. The task of coordinating this review fell to Paul Nitze, a hard-liner who shaped a top-secret policy paper, **NSC-68** (National Security Council Document 68). It opened with a dramatic account of a global clash between "freedom," spread by U.S. power, and "slavery," promoted by the Soviet Union, the center of an international communist movement. Despairing of fruitful negotiations with the Soviets, NSC-68 urged a dramatic upgrade of U.S. national security capabilities. The United States should "find every weak spot in the enemy's armor" and "hit him with anything that comes to hand," one of NSC-68's architects insisted. NSC-68 thus endorsed covert action, economic pressure, propaganda campaigns, and a massive military buildup. Because Americans might oppose larger military spending and budget deficits, the report cautioned, U.S. actions should be labeled as "defensive" and

▲ **MAP 27.2 Divided Germany and the NATO Alliance** This map provides a snapshot of the geopolitics of the cold war. Note how Berlin became a divided city, even though it was located within East Germany.

Q *Which countries aligned with the United States through NATO? Which aligned with the Soviet Union through the Warsaw Pact?*

spending increases presented as a stimulus to the economy rather than as a drain on national resources. The details of NSC-68 remained secret until 1975, but the Truman administration immediately invoked its assumptions and rhetoric when framing specific policies and shaping public opinion.

The alarmist tone of NSC-68 seemed to be confirmed in June 1950 when communist North Korea invaded South Korea. Truman characterized the invasion, which U.S. intelligence agencies had failed to anticipate, as a simple case of Soviet-inspired aggression and invoked the rhetoric of containment: "If aggression is successful in Korea, we can expect it to spread through Asia and Europe to this hemisphere," the president declared.

The Korean situation, however, defied a one-dimensional analysis. Japanese military forces had occupied Korea between 1905 and 1945, and after Japan's defeat in the Second World

What They Said

Civil Rights Divide the Democratic Party, 1948

Although national party conventions have become scripted affairs designed for prime-time television viewing, earlier gatherings featured free-ranging, unpredictable debates. These included heated clashes over the "convention platforms," which were composed of the various "planks" or statements of the principles and programs for which the party stood—and on which its candidates would campaign. After particularly acrimonious debate, the 1948 Democratic National Convention voted a series of planks favoring national action to advance civil rights. This prompted some leading southern Democrats to form a rival States' Rights (or "Dixiecrat") Democratic Party with a platform offering very different civil rights planks.

1948 Democratic Party Platform

The Democratic Party is responsible for the great civil rights gains made in recent years in eliminating unfair and illegal discrimination based on race, creed or color.

The Democratic Party commits itself to continuing its efforts to eradicate all racial, religious and economic discrimination. . . .

We highly commend President Harry S. Truman for his courageous stand on the issue of civil rights.

We call upon the Congress to support our President in guaranteeing these basic and fundamental American Principles: (1) the right of full and equal political participation; (2) the right to equal opportunity of employment; (3) the right of security of person; and the right of equal treatment in the service and defense of our nation.

1948 Platform of the States' Rights Democratic (or "Dixiecrat") Party

We stand for the segregation of the races and the racial integrity of each race; the constitutional right to choose one's associates; to accept private employment without governmental interference, and to earn one's living in any lawful way. We oppose the elimination of segregation, the repeal of miscegenation statutes, the control of private employment by Federal bureaucrats called for by the misnamed civil rights program. We favor home-rule, local self-government and a minimum interference with individual rights.

We oppose and condemn the action of the Democratic Convention in sponsoring a civil rights program calling for the elimination of segregation, social equality by Federal fiat, regulations of private employment practices, voting, and local law enforcement.

We affirm that the effective enforcement of such a program would be utterly destructive of the social, economic and political life of the Southern people, and of other localities in which there may be differences in race, creed or national origin in appreciable numbers. We demand that there be returned to the people to whom of right they belong, those powers needed for the preservation of human rights and the discharge of our responsibility as democrats for human welfare. We oppose a denial of those by political parties, a barter or sale of those rights by a political convention, as well as any invasion or violation of those rights by the Federal Government. We call upon all Democrats and upon all other loyal Americans who are opposed to totalitarianism at home and abroad to unite with us in ignominiously defeating Harry S. Truman... and every other candidate for public office who would establish a Police Nation in the United States of America.

Q *How do the 1948 civil rights planks of the Democratic Party envision civil rights policy that is broader than ending racial segregation?*

Q *What are the different grounds on which the Dixiecrat platform opposed the civil rights planks of the Democratic Party? What rights claims do the southern Democrats invoke? Which of these rights claims, over time, largely disappeared from political rhetoric? Which ones continue to be invoked against using federal power to extend civil rights?*

Sources: (top) 1948 Democratic Party Platform. Authors accessed at: http://www.presidency.ucsb.edu/ws/?pid=29599; (bottom) 1948 Platform of the States Rights Democratic (or "Dixiecrat") Party. Authors accessed at: http://www.presidency.ucsb.edu/ws/?pid=25851.

War, Koreans had expected their country to reemerge as one independent nation. Instead, the Soviet and U.S. zones of occupation resulting from the war became the basis for two separate states, artificially divided at the 38th parallel. The Soviet Union backed a communist government in North Korea, headed by the dictatorial Kim Il-sung. The United States supported Syngman Rhee, the leader of an unsteady and autocratic, but anticommunist, government in South Korea.

On June 25, 1950, after receiving tacit approval from Soviet and Chinese leaders, Kim Il-sung moved troops across the 38th parallel in an attempt to reunify Korea. Rhee appealed to the United States for military assistance, and Truman responded without consulting Congress. Events quickly escalated into an international conflict, the **Korean War**. The Soviets, unaware of the details of Kim's plans, were boycotting the UN when North Korea's military action began and could not veto a U.S. proposal to send a UN peacekeeping force to Korea. Acting under UN auspices, the United States rushed assistance to Rhee, who moved to quell dissent in the South as well as to repel the armies of the North.

The United States confronted several options in Korea. It could simply contain communism by driving North Korea's forces back across the 38th parallel. It could risk a wider war and seek to reunify Korea under Rhee's leadership. This option seemed somewhat fanciful when North Korean forces pushed rapidly southward. Within three months, they captured Seoul, the capital of South Korea, and approached the southern tip of the Korean Peninsula. UN troops, most of them from the United States, seemed initially unprepared. American firepower, however, gradually took its toll on North Korea's elite troops and on the ill-trained recruits sent to replace them.

General Douglas MacArthur, the U.S. Army commander who led UN forces in Korea, then devised a plan that most other strategists considered crazy: an amphibious landing behind enemy lines. Those stunned by his audacious proposal were even more astounded by its results. On September 15, 1950, General MacArthur's troops landed at Inchon, suffered minimal casualties, and quickly recaptured Seoul.

The shifting tide of battle devastated Korea. The Korean War is called a "limited" war because it never spread off the Korean Peninsula or involved nuclear weapons, but its impact was hardly narrow. Intense bombing preceded every military move, and neither side seemed particularly concerned about civilian casualties. The number of estimated dead and wounded reached perhaps one-tenth of North and South Korea's combined population. While rival armies battled for

Time & Life Pictures/Getty Images

27.5 **Devastation during Korean War** In the wake of back-and-forth military campaigns by rival armies, Korean women and children search through the rubble of Seoul, South Korea's capital city, for anything that might be useful for survival.

Q *Despite such destruction, how could the Korean conflict nevertheless be considered a "limited war"?*

Seoul, the city became rubble, with only the capitol building and a train station left standing.

As MacArthur's troops drove northward, Truman faced a crucial decision. Emboldened by success, MacArthur urged moving beyond containment to an all-out war of "liberation" and reunification. Other U.S. military strategists warned that China would retaliate if MacArthur's forces approached its border. Truman did allow the general to carry the war into the North but cautioned against provoking intervention by China or the Soviet Union.

When MacArthur pushed near to the Chinese–Korean border, however, China sent at least 400,000 troops into North Korea and forced MacArthur back across the 38th parallel. China's Mao Zedong envisioned helping unite Korea under communist control. With China now in the war and MacArthur seeking authority to use nuclear weapons, the Truman administration hastily reassessed U.S. priorities. "I could not bring myself to order the slaughter of 25,000,000 non-combatants" by using the atomic bomb, the president later claimed. Although Truman maintained a "limited" war, MacArthur's troops eventually regrouped and regained the initiative. As they moved back northward, Truman ordered the general to negotiate a truce at the 38th parallel. MacArthur, challenging the president, argued for a victory over North Korea—and over China, too. Truman thereupon relieved MacArthur of his command in April 1951. The Constitution made military officers subordinate to the president, the nation's commander in chief, Truman declared.

MacArthur returned to the United States a war hero. Yet, during Senate hearings on MacArthur's dismissal, strategists dismissed his scenario for Korea as the "wrong war in the wrong place." Expanding and securing American power elsewhere around the world, particularly in Europe, should remain the central objective of U.S. policy. This broader goal dictated merely the containment, not a rollback, of communism in Korea, they successfully argued. MacArthur's once luminous image, along with his political ambitions, soon faded.

As negotiations for a peace settlement for Korea stalled, another military hero, Dwight Eisenhower, became the 1952 Republican nominee for president. He promised to go to Korea if elected and accelerate the peace process. Harry Truman would leave office in 1953 without formally ending the Korean War (see Map 27.3).

27-2c Korea and Containment

The Korean War bolstered support for the global anticommunist vision of NSC-68. The United States formulated plans to rearm West Germany, scarcely five years after the defeat of the Third Reich, and to expand NATO's military forces throughout Western Europe. A proposal for direct military aid to Latin American governments, which had been rejected in the past, now slid through Congress. In the Philippines, the United States stepped up military and CIA assistance to the government of Ramón Magsaysay so it could suppress the leftist Hukbalahap (or Huk) movement. In 1951, Washington finally signed a formal peace treaty with Japan and secured a security pact that granted the United States a sprawling military base on the island of Okinawa. The United States acquired similar bases in the Middle East, bolstering its strategic position in that oil-rich area.

In addition, the Truman administration made important moves in French Indochina. It greatly expanded economic assistance for the effort to retain France's colonial possession against the challenge from communist Ho Chi Minh's Democratic Republic of Vietnam. Policymakers in Washington had hardly favored a communist-led government in Indochina but worries about identifying the United States too closely with French colonialism in Southeast Asia had initially limited U.S. support for France's military effort against Ho's forces. The outbreak of the Korean conflict, however, elevated preventing a communist victory in Indochina into a major policy goal.

Warning of potential communist gains, U.S. policymakers became increasingly insistent about opposing overseas movements that seemed to lean toward the political left. The U.S. occupation government in Japan, for example, restricted the activities of labor unions, suspended an antitrust program that American officials had earlier implemented, and barred communists from posts in Japan's government and universities. As in Germany, the United States tried to contain communism elsewhere by strengthening pro-U.S. elites and by promoting economic growth through marketplace rather than state-directed mechanisms.

Containment considerations also prompted the United States to ally with South Africa. In 1949, the all-white (and militantly anticommunist) Nationalist Party instituted a legal-social system called apartheid, based on elaborate rules of racial separation and subordination of blacks. Some State Department officials warned that a close relationship with South Africa, by implying support for apartheid, would damage America's international reputation, but the Truman administration nonetheless supported South Africa's white supremacist regime.

Most importantly, the elaboration of containment during the Korean War era featured the military buildup proposed in NSC-68. By early 1953, U.S. military production totaled seven times what it had been before the North Korean attack. The United States also continued to expand its worldwide system of military bases. And economic pressure, CIA covert activities, and propaganda campaigns helped further implement containment objectives. A global "Campaign of Truth," a sustained informational and psychological offensive, countered Soviet propaganda with mass media and cultural exchanges sponsored by Washington. A rhetoric organized around the concept of "national security" took hold: The Defense Department replaced the War Department, and the new phrase *national security* supplanted the older, more limited language of gauging the best *national interest*.

NSC-68 provided a master plan for using military, economic, and covert action to advance a worldwide national security policy. It also facilitated what the historian Michael Sherry has called "the militarization of American life." By 1951, two-thirds of the federal budget went for military-related spending, with continued bipartisan support. Congress granted a new Atomic Energy Commission broad authority to oversee development of a U.S. nuclear

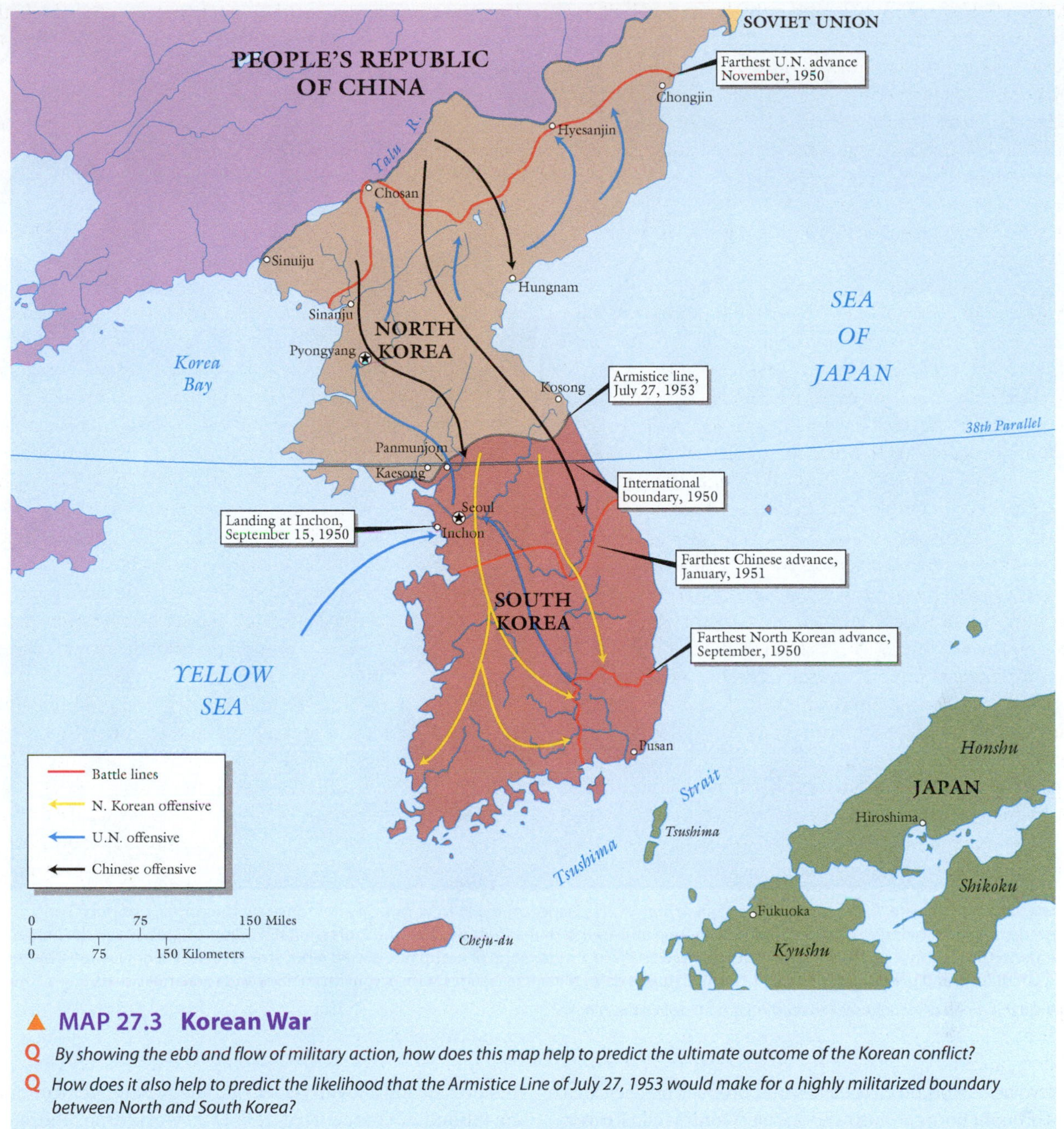

▲ **MAP 27.3 Korean War**

Q *By showing the ebb and flow of military action, how does this map help to predict the ultimate outcome of the Korean conflict?*

Q *How does it also help to predict the likelihood that the Armistice Line of July 27, 1953 would make for a highly militarized boundary between North and South Korea?*

power industry. The prospect of creating military jobs in congressional districts muted opposition from cost-conscious members of Congress.

27-3 Pursuing National Security at Home

Q *How did the emphasis on national security spread throughout American culture?*

Although containment abroad generally gained bipartisan support, debate flared over programs for containing subversive influences at home. Civil libertarians complained about "witch hunts" against people who merely expressed dissent. Militant anticommunists leveled alarming allegations about internal communist subversion being left unchecked, while even firm anticommunists worried that exaggerated charges and wild goose chases after unlikely subversives harmed the effort to identify authentic Soviet agents. The search for supposed threats to national security eventually touched many areas of postwar life.

27-3a *Anticommunism and the U.S. Labor Movement*

The politics of anticommunism came to affect the U.S. labor movement. After the end of the Second World War, many workers struck for increased wages and benefits and for a

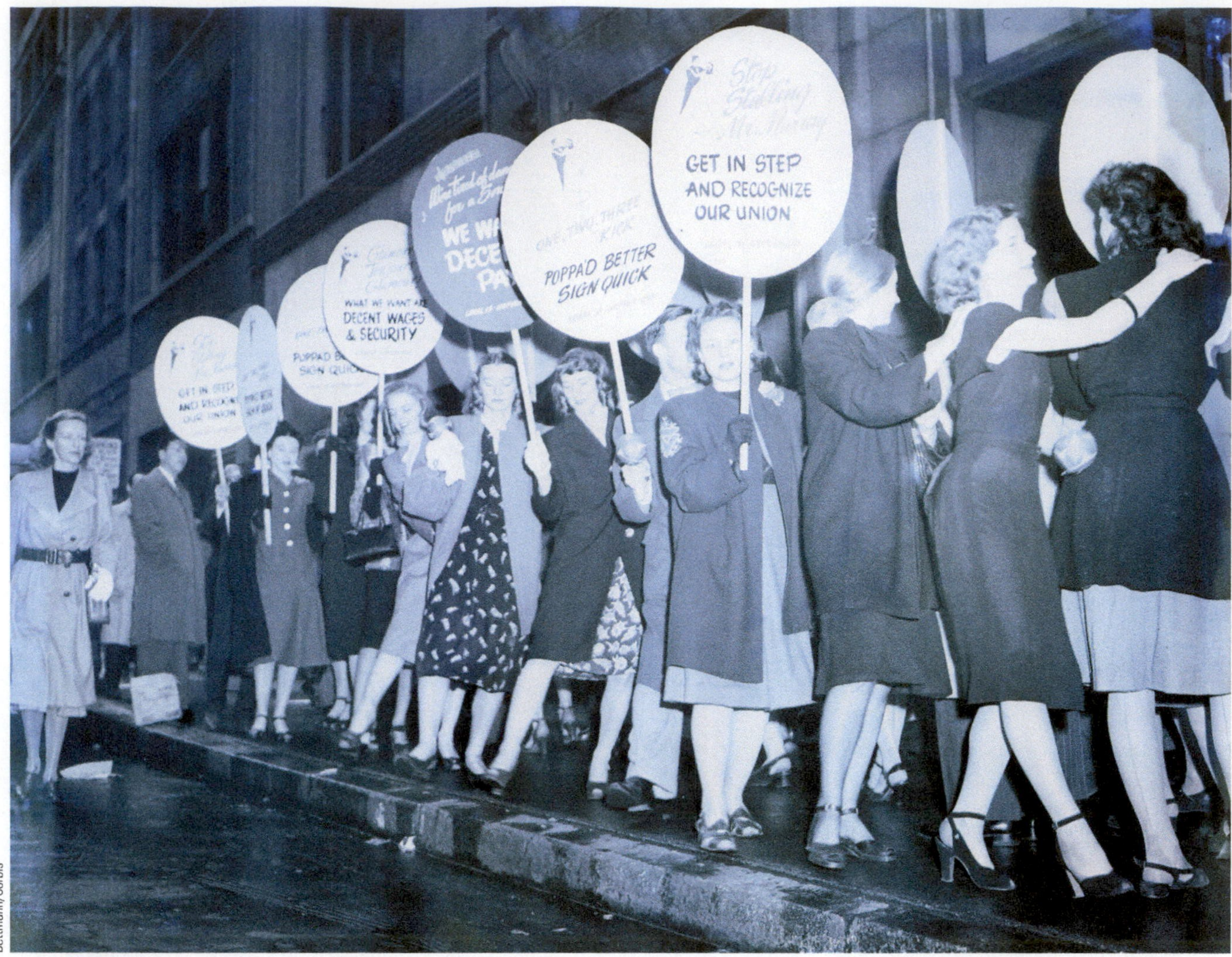

Bettmann/Corbis

27.6 **Instructors on Strike, 1947** Employees of an Arthur Murray Dance Studio in New York City demonstrate the conga, a popular Latin American dance—and their determination to form a union affiliated with the United Office and Professional Workers of America. In the immediate postwar period, in response to unionization campaigns, workers in a wide range of occupations used labor strikes to seek higher wages, better working conditions, and greater job security. After 1947, union gains met increased resistance from businesses and some politicians.

Q *How did this group of workers seek to dramatize and explain their cause?*

greater voice in workplace routines and production decisions. Strikes brought both the auto and the electronics industries to a standstill. After President Truman threatened to seize mines and railroads that had been shut down by work stoppages and to order strikers back to work, labor militancy began to subside.

In 1947, a Republican-controlled Congress tapped anticommunist sentiment to help pass the Labor-Management Relations Act, popularly known as the **Taft–Hartley Act**. The law negated gains made by organized labor during the 1930s. It limited a union's power to conduct boycotts, to compel employers to accept "closed shops" in which only union members could be hired, and to continue a strike that the president judged harmful to national security. In addition, the measure required union officials to pledge that they did not belong to the Communist Party or any other "subversive" organization. A union that refused to comply was denied protections under national labor laws. Congress overrode Truman's veto of Taft–Hartley, and by the end of his presidency a loyalty-security check had been conducted on about 20 percent of the U.S. workforce, more than 13 million people. The Congress of Industrial Organizations (CIO) expelled 13 unions—a full third of its membership—as anticommunism also influenced internal labor politics. Many workers found that their political commitments could put their own jobs at risk.

27-3b *Containing Communism at Home*

Anticommunists scrutinized workers in the entertainment industry with special zeal. In 1947, the House Un-American Activities Committee (HUAC) opened hearings into communist influences in Hollywood. Basking in the glare of newsreel cameras, members of this committee seized on the refusal of ten screenwriters, producers, and directors—all current or former members of the American Communist Party—to testify about political allegiances within the film community. "The Hollywood Ten" claimed that the First Amendment barred HUAC from scrutinizing their political activities. The federal courts upheld HUAC's investigative powers, however, and the Hollywood Ten eventually went to prison for contempt of Congress.

Hollywood studios as well as radio and television networks enforced their own internal "blacklists" of workers, allegedly subversives, whom they agreed not to hire. Blacklists affected not only prominent performers but many anonymous labor union members who worked behind the scenes in technical and support positions. Many entertainment workers were unable to find jobs unless they agreed to become "friendly witnesses" before HUAC or other investigative committees and to provide the names of people they had seen at some "communist meeting" in the past. Some of those called to testify, such as the screenwriter Lillian Hellman, refused to answer any questions. Others, such as the movie director Elia Kazan and the writer Budd Schulberg, cooperated. Decisions over whether or not to "name names" would divide people in the entertainment industry and the labor union movement for decades.

The search for subversives created anticommunist celebrities. Ronald Reagan, president of the Screen Actors Guild and a secret informant for the FBI (identified as "T-10"), testified about communist influence in Hollywood. Richard Nixon, an obscure member of Congress from California, began his political ascent in 1948 when Whittaker Chambers, a journalist formerly active in communist circles, came before HUAC. Chambers charged Alger Hiss, a prominent Democrat, with having been a party member and with passing classified information to Soviet agents during the late 1930s.

The Hiss–Chambers–Nixon affair still sparks controversy. Legal considerations barred an indictment of Hiss for espionage, but the government charged him with perjury for allegedly lying to Congress. Ultimately convicted on two counts, Hiss spent nearly four years in prison. To Nixon and his supporters, the case of Alger Hiss, who had advised Franklin Roosevelt during the Yalta Conference (see Chapter 26), demonstrated how deeply rooted communist subversion had become. To his supporters, Hiss appeared the victim of a frame-up. In the mid-1990s, newly declassified documents revived the Hiss controversy. A few scholars continued to defend Hiss. The vast majority, however, concluded that Hiss (along with several other high-ranking government officials) had likely passed information to the Soviets during the 1930s and 1940s. Historians continue to differ, however, over the precise nature of this material and its value to Moscow.

Meanwhile, the Truman administration pursued its own anticommunist course at home. It dismissed hundreds of federal employees under its loyalty program. Truman's attorney general, Tom Clark, secretly authorized J. Edgar Hoover, head of the FBI, to compile a list of alleged subversives the government could detain during any national emergency without any legal hearing.

Fear that subversives might immigrate to the United States helped shape several provisions of the **McCarran-Walter Act**. Also known as the Immigration and Nationality Act of 1952, this law authorized denial of immigrant status to anyone who might compromise national security by bringing dangerous ideas into the country. It also allowed the deportation of immigrants, even naturalized citizens, who belonged to organizations on the Attorney General's List. Calling these measures "un-American," Truman rejected McCarran-Walter, but Congress overrode his veto.

Hoover's FBI also undertook an extensive campaign of surveillance. It compiled confidential dossiers on artists and intellectuals suspected of radical views. Some of its targets, including the writers Ernest Hemingway and John Steinbeck, had no links to the Communist Party. The FBI often singled out prominent African Americans, including civil rights activist Bayard Rustin, Richard Wright (author of the acclaimed novel *Native Son*), and W. E. B. Du Bois (a celebrated African American historian). Paul Robeson (a well-known entertainer-activist) encountered trouble from the State Department and immigration officials. His association with the U.S. Communist Party and identification with anti-imperialist and antiracist organizations throughout the world curtailed his ability to travel overseas. In addition, suspicions of homosexuality could make people, including the nominally closeted Rustin, targets for governmental surveillance and discrimination.

27-3c *Targeting Sexual Difference*

Public focus on homosexual behavior increased. During the Second World War, very visible gay and lesbian subcultures had emerged, particularly in larger cities such as New York and San Francisco. After the war, Dr. Alfred Kinsey's research on sexual behavior—his first volume, on male sexuality, appeared in 1948—claimed to find homosexuality throughout American life and a wide range of sexual behaviors from exclusively heterosexual to exclusively homosexual. In 1952, transsexuality hit the headlines when the press revealed that, after a series of "sex-change" operations in Europe, George W. Jorgensen, Jr., had become a "blonde beauty," Christine Jorgensen.

By this time, a small "homophile" movement had emerged to challenge the most egregious forms of discrimination. Gay men formed the Mattachine Society (in 1950), and lesbians later founded the Daughters of Bilitis, organizations that sought legal protection for the basic constitutional rights of homosexuals. They condemned police departments for singling out businesses catering to gays and lesbians when making raids for "disorderly conduct" and the post office for banning homosexual publications on the basis of "decency" requirements.

The homophile movement of the 1950s, however, confronted a newly aggressive effort to restrict the visibility of homosexuality. The Kinsey Report's implicit claim that homosexuality was simply another form of sexuality, alongside the emergence of new gay and lesbian organizations, helped fuel this campaign. The fact that several founders of the Mattachine Society had also been members of the Communist Party, coupled with the claim that Soviet agents could blackmail homosexuals more easily than heterosexuals, helped link homosexuality with the communist threat to national security. "One homosexual can pollute a Government office," a U.S. Senate report claimed.

Today, historians of sexuality see a "Lavender Scare" about homosexuality accompanying the "Red Scare" about communism. Popular imagery portrayed both homosexuality and communism as subversive "diseases" that could spread throughout the body politic. Suspicion of "sexual deviance" became an acceptable basis for subjecting government employees to loyalty board hearings and, ultimately, denying them legal and constitutional protections enjoyed by heterosexuals.

27-3d *The "Great Fear"*

The postwar search for subversion unfolded within an atmosphere of anxiety that some cultural historians call the "Great Fear." Genuine threats, such as the atomic program of the Soviets, heightened the impact of spurious claims about communist agents roaming military bases or gay subversives shaping foreign policy. A growing sense of cultural and social insecurity, in turn, intensified efforts to safeguard national security.

As this atmosphere of fear was settling over American life, the Justice Department announced the arrests, in 1950, of several members of a spy ring alleged to have been channeling nuclear secrets to Moscow. Two of the arrested, Julius and Ethel Rosenberg, the parents of two young children and members of the Communist Party, became the central characters in a legal-cultural controversy.

The Rosenberg spy case became a cold war melodrama. The couple's trial, the guilty verdicts, the death sentences, the numerous legal appeals, the worldwide protests, and their 1953 executions for having committed atomic espionage captured media attention. To their supporters, the Rosenbergs (who died maintaining their innocence) had fallen victim to anticommunist hysteria. Federal officials, according to the couple's defenders, seemed primarily interested in finding scapegoats. To others, however, solid evidence pointed toward their involvement in an extensive operation, which included a confessed British spy. Documents released after the fall of the Soviet Union in 1989 now clearly confirm Julius Rosenberg's spying activities. Ethel Rosenberg likely knew about his work, but evidence of her direct involvement in passing information to the Soviets remains ambiguous.

The performance of the nation's criminal justice system in this cultural drama helps to complicate the historical picture. Federal prosecutors never moved, for example, against people who almost certainly were atomic spies. Theodore Hall, a physicist who worked on America's bomb and whose expertise about nuclear matters obviously exceeded that of Julius or Ethel Rosenberg, was among them. Officials likely feared revealing valuable counter-intelligence operations—or perhaps illegal surveillance activities. In any case, only the Rosenbergs, of all those who were identified or prosecuted, faced a charge that carried the death penalty.

The courts' response to the Great Fear has been a matter of sustained debate. During a 1949 prosecution of leaders of the American Communist Party, the trial judge accepted the Justice Department's plea that the 11 defendants be considered participants in an international conspiracy. Their Marxist ideas and publications, even without any proof of subversive acts, could justify convicting them of the crime of sedition. Civil libertarians insisted that the government never showed how Communist Party publications and speeches, by themselves, posed a "clear and present danger" to national security. In this view, *political expression* should enjoy the protection of the First Amendment and only *illegal activity* could be put on trial. In *Dennis* v. *U.S.* (1951), the Supreme Court upheld the convictions of the Communist Party leaders. The Soviet threat was so serious, the Court ruled, that pro-communist expression, in the absence of any overt criminal activity, could constitute sedition.

Meanwhile, the Truman administration continued to incur the ire of more zealous red-hunters. In Congress, Republicans and conservative Democrats denounced Truman's anticommunist initiatives as too limited and passed, over Truman's veto, the Subversive Activities Control Act of 1950. It created a Subversive Activities Control Board (SACB) to oversee the registration of groups allegedly controlled or infiltrated by communists. It barred communists from working in the defense industry, holding a labor union office, and acquiring a passport. Unaware of J. Edgar Hoover's secret detention program, Congress also authorized the confinement of alleged subversives during any national emergency.

27-3e *Joseph McCarthy*

Joseph McCarthy, a Republican senator from Wisconsin, became the Truman administration's prime accuser. An intelligence officer during the Second World War, McCarthy had entered politics as a battle-tested combat vet, "Tailgunner Joe." Elected to the U.S. Senate in 1946, McCarthy showed little interest in legislative matters, but he emerged as a two-fisted investigator of communist subversion during the Great Fear.

McCarthy became a celebrity when he claimed, during a 1950 speech in Wheeling, West Virginia, to have compiled a list of 205 communists then working in the State Department. Americans rightly feared the future, according to McCarthy, "not because our only powerful potential enemy has sent men to invade our shores, but rather because of the traitorous actions of those who have been treated so well by this Nation." Although McCarthy quickly shrank his number of subversives to 57, he also expanded his attacks. Secretary of State Dean Acheson and his predecessor, General George C. Marshall, soon came into range.

Adept at using political imagery and sexual innuendo, McCarthy linked the Lavender Scare and Red Scare. He portrayed key members of Truman's administration as both overly privileged and insufficiently manly. People like Acheson who had been "born with silver spoons in their mouths," represented effete "enemies from within." McCarthy derided the smartly dressed Acheson as the "Red Dean of fashion" and as the leader of the "lace handkerchief crowd."

Interpreting the Visual Past "It's Okay—We're Hunting Communists"

Herbert Block (1909–2001), who published editorial cartoons under the name "Herblock," began his career in Chicago at the end of the 1920s. He published his last cartoon 72 years later, shortly before his death. It appeared in the paper for which he had worked since 1946, the *Washington Post*. His work garnered numerous awards, including three Pulitzer Prizes.

Developing his political perspective during the era of Franklin Roosevelt's New Deal, Block favored the national government playing an active role in both domestic and foreign policy. His cartoons thus supported anticommunist cold war policies such as the Marshall Plan. At the same time, however, Block's work satirized governmental measures that he saw threatening personal liberties, especially constitutionally protected political expression.

During the era of the "Great Fear," Herblock cartoons portrayed the anticommunism of Richard Nixon, Joseph McCarthy, and the House Committee on Un-American Activities (HUAC) as a grave threat to constitutionally protected liberties.

This 1947 cartoon for the *Washington Post* addresses HUAC's approach to investigating communist subversion.

Q *How is this cartoon critical of the overall effort to contain communism at home?*

Q *What, specifically, does "Herblock" find objectionable in HUAC's brand of anticommunism?*

Q *How can an analysis of cartoons from the past illuminate the linkage between politics and culture?*

Library of Congress, Prints and Photographs Division

27.7 Herbert Block, "It's Okay—We're Hunting Communists," 1947.

Initially, McCarthy seemed unstoppable. He substantiated none of his more sensational claims but lacked neither imagination nor targets. In the summer of 1950 a Senate subcommittee, after examining government files, concluded that McCarthy's charges against the State Department amounted to "the most nefarious campaign of half-truths and untruths in the history of this republic." McCarthy responded that the files had been "raped," and he went after Millard Tydings, the Democratic senator who had chaired the subcommittee. In the November 1950 elections, Tydings went down to defeat, in part because of a fabricated photograph that linked him to communist activities.

Despite McCarthy's erratic course, influential people initially tolerated, even encouraged, him. Conservative anticommunist leaders of the Roman Catholic Church embraced McCarthy, himself a Catholic. Leading Republicans welcomed McCarthy's assaults on their Democratic rivals. Others insisted the senator's commitment to the cause of anticommunism outweighed complaints about his slapdash investigations and overzealous methods. In contrast, critics charged that the senator personified a reckless form of demagogic "attack politics," and they called his careless, flamboyant style "McCarthyism."

27-3f *A National Security Constitution and the Structure of Governance*

Focusing on the furor over McCarthyism, however, can obscure fundamental changes in constitutional governance that generated relatively little controversy. Except for the Twenty-Second Amendment, adopted in 1951, which barred presidents from following Franklin Roosevelt's example and being elected to more than two terms, there were no formal modifications to the written Constitution during the era of the Great Fear. But congressional legislation shaped a new national security constitutional framework during the early postwar years.

The view that the office of the president possessed only limited powers gave way to the idea that protecting national security justified extending the reach of the executive branch. Truman encountered no constitutional roadblocks to an undeclared war in Korea, and in 1952, he issued a secret executive order that created the super-secret **National Security Agency (NSA)**. Using sophisticated technology, the NSA began collecting any information, from communications networks around the globe, which might affect the nation's safety. Covert eavesdropping on a massive scale became part of a new, partially unwritten and secret, national security framework.

The specter of constitutional limitations on presidential power did arise in 1952, however, when Truman ordered his commerce secretary to seize control of the U.S. steel industry in order to prevent a threatened strike. Although Truman could have invoked a 60-day "cooling off" period under the Taft–Hartley Act, he sought to justify this action with a more fundamental, novel, and controversial constitutional claim: The president, as commander in chief, possessed extraordinary power whenever emergency action was required to safeguard national security.

The steel companies challenged this assertion in court. When *Youngstown Sheet & Tube Company v. Sawyer* (1952) reached the Supreme Court, three justices who had been nominated by Truman supported his claim of executive power. Six others, for differing reasons, rejected Truman's position in this particular instance, but all supported a broad view of presidential authority whenever national security seemed more clearly at stake. Constitutional scholars would come to see this case as a short-term defeat for Truman but a long-term victory for the idea of an expansive "National Security Constitution."

27-4 Postwar Social and Economic Policy-Making

Q *Why did some of President Truman's policy proposals gain congressional and public approval while others did not?*

Truman embraced Franklin Roosevelt's domestic agenda, and many supporters of FDR's New Deal still championed his Second Bill of Rights of 1944 (see Chapter 26). But proposals for government planning and for new social welfare measures stalled during Truman's presidency. Any attempt to build on the New Deal and wartime arrangements, insisted most Republicans and some Democrats, would threaten unconstitutional intrusions into people's liberties and undermine individual initiative and responsibility. Dixiecrat Democrats from the South joined conservative Republicans to block any legislation that they believed might dismantle white supremacy in their region. The National Association of Manufacturers (NAM) denounced the Truman administration as a menace to the nation's free-enterprise system.

27-4a *The Employment Act of 1946 and Economic Growth*

The 1946 debate over the Full Employment Bill provided a new template for domestic policy-making. This measure, as conceived, would have empowered Washington to ensure employment for all citizens seeking work. To the bill's opponents, the emphasis on "full employment" implied a step toward a European-style welfare state, even socialism.

As the effort to enact this measure stalled, a scaled-back approach emerged. The law that Congress finally passed, the **Employment Act of 1946**, called for "maximum" (rather than full) employment and specifically declared that private enterprise, not government, bore primary responsibility for economic decision making. The measure nonetheless created a new executive branch body, the Council of Economic Advisers, to formulate long-range policy recommendations, and it signaled that government would assume considerable responsibility for the performance of the economy.

The Employment Act of 1946 underscored a growing faith that *advice* to public officials from economic experts, as an alternative to government *planning*, could guarantee a constantly expanding economy. An influential group of economists, disciples of Britain's John Maynard Keynes, insisted that their expertise could temper boom-and-bust cycles.

The promise of economic expansion dazzled postwar leaders. Using the relatively new measure of gross national product (GNP)—defined as the total dollar value of all goods and services produced in the nation during a given year—economists could calculate the nation's growing economic bounty. Corporate executives, who had feared that the end of the war would bring long-term labor unrest and trigger a deep recession, viewed a rising GNP as a guarantor of social stability. The Truman administration welcomed the prospect of an expanding economy, which would increase federal tax revenues and, in turn, finance governmental programs at home and abroad.

Truman and his advisers spread the gospel of economic growth. This new faith nicely dovetailed with their national security plans. Spending for the cold war could serve as a "pump primer" for the U.S. economy. Sharp increases in military rearmament signaled a tilt in economic policy that critical observers began calling "military Keynesianism." Moreover, cold war assistance programs such as the Marshall Plan could create markets and investment opportunities for Americans overseas. Economic growth at home was linked to development in the world at large—and to the all-pervasive concern with national security.

27-4b *Truman's Fair Deal*

In 1949, Truman unveiled his "**Fair Deal**." He proposed extending popular New Deal programs such as Social Security and minimum wage laws; enacting legislation dealing with civil rights, national health care, and federal aid for education; and repealing the Taft–Hartley Act. The Fair Deal also envisioned substantial spending on public housing projects and a complicated plan to support farm prices. The Fair Deal's faith that sustained economic growth could finance new government programs came to focus the Truman administration's policy planning.

Two prominent programs illustrate the background assumptions that shaped domestic social policy. The **GI Bill** (officially titled the Serviceman's Readjustment Act of 1944) had been passed during the war to provide comprehensive benefits for those who served in the armed forces. The bill offered veterans financial assistance for college and job-training programs. By 1947, the year of peak enrollment, roughly half of the students enrolled at colleges and universities were receiving aid under the GI Bill. Veterans also received preferential treatment when applying for government jobs; favorable financial terms when purchasing homes or businesses; and, eventually, comprehensive medical care in veterans' hospitals. The Veterans Readjustment Assistance Act of 1952, popularly known as the "GI Bill of Rights," extended these programs to veterans of the Korean War. Although the Truman administration never enacted FDR's Second Bill of Rights, the GI Bills did extend some of its key promises to veterans.

The Social Security program also expanded. Rebutting attacks from conservatives, Social Security's supporters defended its provisions for the disabled and the blind and argued that older people had earned its "income security" through years of work and monetary contributions withheld from their paychecks. Under the Social Security Act of 1950, the level of benefits increased significantly; the retirement portions of the program expanded; and coverage was extended to more than 10 million people, including agricultural workers.

More expansive (and expensive) Fair Deal proposals, however, either failed or were scaled back. Truman's plan for a comprehensive national health insurance program faced opposition from several different quarters. Consumer groups and labor unions, intent on creating nonprofit community-run health plans, feared that a centralized system would unnecessarily bureaucratize medical care. The American Medical Association (AMA) and the American Hospital Association (AHA) opposed any governmental intervention in the traditional fee-for-service medical system. Large insurance companies, which were continuing to push their own private plans, also opposed the Truman initiative.

The Fair Deal's housing proposals made some headway. Continued shortage of affordable housing in urban areas stirred support for home-building programs. Even some conservatives supported the Housing Act of 1949. This law

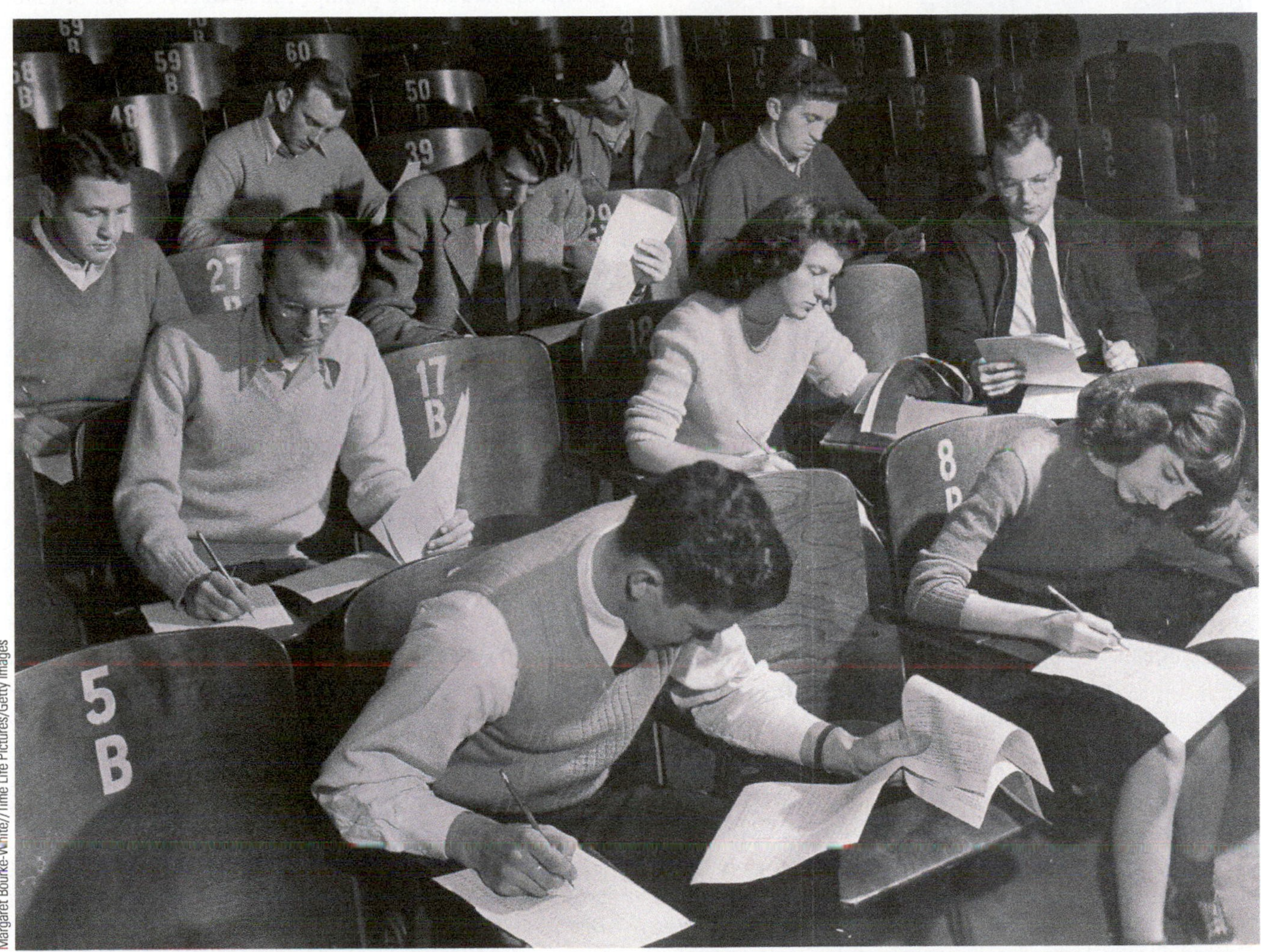

Margaret Bourke-White/Time Life Pictures/Getty Images

27.8 The Postwar College Scene This picture by the famed photojournalist Margaret Bourke-White shows a cold war era classroom at the University of Iowa. Tapping financial support offered under the 1944 GI Bill, more than 600 veterans enrolled in 1946 at Iowa. The flood of returning servicemen, some of whom struggled with disabilities incurred during the war, taxed existing facilities. Much the same pattern emerged at other colleges, universities, and technical schools throughout the country.

Q *How did the postwar GI Bill affect the gender dynamics in higher education?*

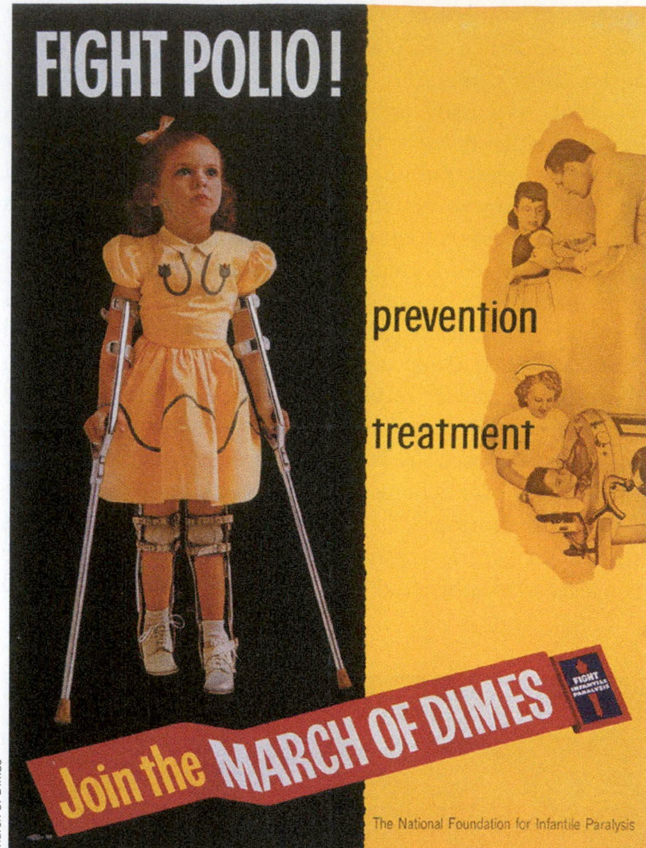

27.9 **Polio Scare** Mary Kosloski, a young polio victim from Tennessee, was often pictured in posters for the March of Dimes, an organization that conducted fundraising throughout the country in an ultimately successful effort to find and distribute a vaccination against the often-crippling disease. In 1952 nearly 58,000 cases of polio were reported and nearly half of those afflicted either died or experienced disabling paralysis.

Q *How might words like "fight" and "join" seem useful for mobilizing this postwar generation of Americans?*

authorized construction of 810,000 public housing units and provided federal funds for "urban renewal" zones, areas to be cleared of run-down dwellings and rebuilt with new construction. The Housing Act proclaimed ambitious goals but provided relatively modest funding, especially for its public-housing component. Private construction firms and real estate agents welcomed funding for federal home loan guarantee programs—such as those established under the GI Bill—but they lobbied effectively against publicly financed housing projects.

Fair Deal policy-making thus ultimately focused on specific groups, such as veterans and older Americans, rather than on more extensive programs such as national health care or a national housing program. With opponents of the Fair Deal continually charging that it would move the United States toward a European-style "welfare state," the White House found it easier to defend more narrowly targeted programs that it could present as economic security measures for specific recipients who merited government assistance.

27-4c *Civil Rights*

The Truman administration also struggled to place the national government's power behind a growing civil rights movement. After returning home, veterans of African, Latino, and American Indian descent increasingly refused to remain passive bystanders when laws and discriminatory practices reduced them to second-class citizens. Moreover, the people of color who had moved to cities seeking wartime employment wanted to build on the gains they had made. Drives to translate their visions of liberty and equality into reality animated grassroots activists in the postwar period.

During his 1948 presidential campaign, Truman endorsed the proposals of his new civil rights committee. Its report, entitled "To Secure These Rights," called for federal legislation against lynching; a special civil rights division within the Department of Justice; antidiscrimination initiatives in employment, housing, and public facilities; and desegregation of the military. These proposals had helped prompt the Dixiecrat revolt of 1948, but they also gained Truman significant support from civil rights groups.

Civil rights became an increasingly important concern. After successive Congresses failed to enact any civil rights legislation—including a law against lynching and a ban on poll taxes—leaders of the movement turned to the White House and to the federal courts. A plan by labor leader A. Philip Randolph to organize a protest campaign prompted Truman to issue Executive Order 9981 (1948), which called for gradual desegregation of the armed forces. Truman understood how segregation tarnished America's image in a cold war world "which is 90 percent colored." Although cold war politics could help justify harassment of African American leaders allegedly linked to subversive causes, the crusade against communism on behalf of the "free world" also made racial discrimination into a foreign policy liability.

Truman's Justice Department thus appeared in court to support litigants who contested government-backed "restrictive covenants" (legal agreements that prevented racial or religious minorities from acquiring real estate) and segregated education. In 1946, the Supreme Court declared restrictive covenants unconstitutional and began chipping away at the "separate-but-equal" principle used since *Plessy v. Ferguson* (1896) to justify segregated schools. A federal court in California, ruling on a case brought the previous year in Orange County by a coalition of Mexican American and African American activists, held that segregating students of Mexican descent in separate, and unequal, schools violated their constitutional rights. In 1948, a second federal court— with the case now entitled *Westminster School District v. Mendez*—agreed with the first. In 1950, the Supreme Court ruled that, under the Fourteenth Amendment, racial segregation in state-financed graduate and law schools was unconstitutional. The familiar arguments used to legitimize racial segregation in public education seemed ripe for a successful challenge.

27-5 Signs of a Changing Culture

Q *Why were significant cultural changes of the postwar years both welcomed and feared?*

The pace of cultural change accelerated during the postwar years. Encouraged by the advertising industry, Americans seemed, in one sense, to view anything new as "progress." Yet, in another, the speed and scope of change appeared to accentuate feelings of uneasiness and anxiety. As a result, the impulse toward containment affected postwar culture as well as foreign and domestic policy-making.

27-5a *The "Color Line" and the National Pastime*

The interplay between celebrating and containing change could be seen in the integration of organized baseball during the 1940s and early 1950s. In 1947, Jackie Robinson finally cracked Major League Baseball's policy of racial segregation. A graduate of UCLA who had battled segregation while serving in the U.S. Army during the Second World War, Robinson had also played semiprofessional football and in the Negro National Baseball League before joining the Brooklyn Dodgers. Some ballplayers opposed to integration, including several on Robinson's own team, considered a boycott. Baseball's leadership, seeking new sources of players and more African American fans coming through the turnstiles, threatened to suspend any player who would not play with or against Robinson.

Officially, organized baseball desegregated. The Cleveland Indians signed Larry Doby, and other stars began abandoning the Negro leagues for clubs in the American and National circuits. Eventually, the skills of Robinson—named Rookie of the Year in 1947 and the National League's Most Valuable Player in 1949—and other players of African descent carried the day. Although light-skinned Latinos had long passed through the racial barrier, Orestes ("Minnie") Minoso, a Cuban-born veteran of the Negro circuits, became the first Afro-Latino to break into the big leagues in 1949. Major League teams began fielding greater numbers of African American and Latino players, and some accelerated recruitment efforts in Mexico and the Caribbean.

Yet, baseball's leadership had unofficially limited its own desegregation effort. Several teams waited years before integrating their rosters, claiming that they could find no talented African American or Latino prospects. More commonly, clubs restricted the number of nonwhite players they would take on and hired only whites as managers, coaches, and front-office personnel.

African American and Latino players who followed in Robinson's footsteps confronted continuing obstacles. They encountered overt, off-the-field discrimination during spring training in the South and Southwest and in many small towns elsewhere when playing in the minor leagues. Spanish-speaking players struggled to convince managers, sportswriters, and teammates that they could "understand" the subtleties of either baseball or North American culture.

Highsmith, Carol M/Library of Congress Prints and Photographs Division Washington, D.C. [LC-DIG-highsm-24443]

27.10 **Remembering Jackie Robinson** In 1947, Robinson joined the Brooklyn Dodgers and became the first African American since the 19th century to play baseball in the major leagues. Racial integration of the national pastime became a powerful symbol of progress in race relations. This bust of Robinson is located in Pasadena, California, and appears next to a similar statue of his brother, a silver medalist in the 1936 Olympics.

Q *How can memorials to prominent people reflect changing cultural circumstances?*

27-5b *The New Suburbia*

In suburbia, too, change was simultaneously celebrated and feared—and thus subject to various strategies for limiting the impact of the new.

Suburban living had long been a feature of the "American dream." The new Long Island town of Levittown, New York, which welcomed its first residents in October 1947, seemed to make that dream an affordable reality for middle-income families. Similar developments, such as Lakewood and Panorama City in California, soon began springing up in other parts of the country. For years, however, developers and officials at all levels of government vigorously enforced policies designed to maintain these new suburbs as spaces that excluded non-whites and upheld racial segregation.

Nearly everything about Levittown and its counterparts seemed unprecedented. Levitt & Sons, a construction company that had mass-produced military barracks during the Second World War, claimed to be completing a five-room bungalow every 15 minutes. Architectural and cultural critics sneered at these "little boxes," but potential buyers stood in long lines for the chance to purchase one. By 1950, Levittown contained more than 10,000 homes and 40,000 residents. At the same time, bulldozers and construction crews were sweeping through other suburban developments across the country.

To assist potential buyers, the national government offered an extensive set of programs. The Federal Housing Administration (FHA), a government agency, underwrote an elaborate lending system through long-term, government-insured mortgages. Veterans enjoyed favorable terms under the GI loan program. These government programs made it cheaper to purchase a suburban house than to rent an apartment in most cities. Moreover, the law provided suburban homeowners with an additional subsidy: They could deduct the interest payments on their mortgages from their federal income tax.

The new suburbs quickly gained a reputation for being ideal places for nurturing a **baby boom generation**. Sheer numbers helped identify "baby boomers," people born between 1946 and 1964, as a unique social and cultural force. The Great Depression and the Second World War had deflated the U.S. birth rate, but it began to soar even before war's end. A number of factors, including earlier marriages and rising incomes, fueled a continuing boom in babies. More than 75 million babies were born in the United States during the baby boom era (see Figure 27.1).

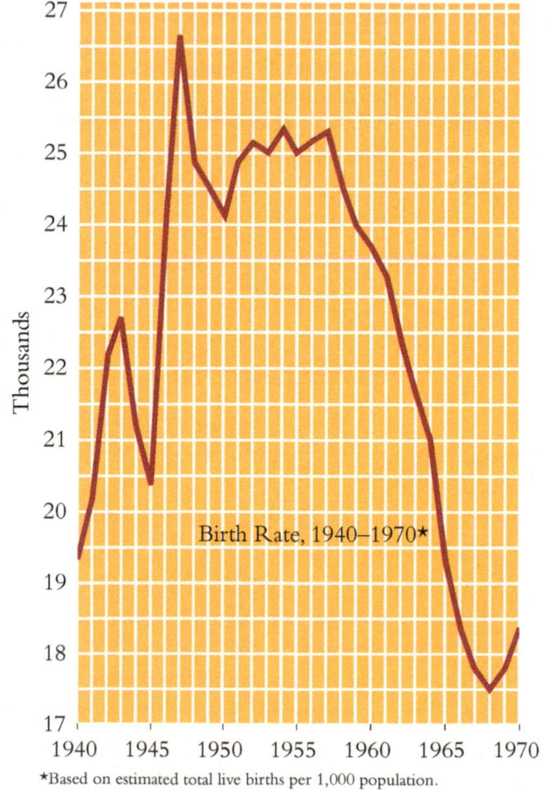

Figure 27.1 **The Baby Boom**

Although baby boomers lived everywhere, they became closely identified with the new suburbia. With houses occupying only about 15 percent of new suburban lots, large lawns served as private playgrounds. Suburban schools were as new as the homes, and their well-appointed facilities attracted both skilled and enthusiastic teachers. In many respects, suburbia symbolized new possibilities, confidence in the future, and embrace of change.

As contemporary observers noted, however, suburbia also appeared to offer a material and psychological refuge. Buying a suburban home seemed a way of containing the impact of the social and cultural changes of the cold war era. As African American families continued to migrate to northern and western cities in search of jobs and greater opportunity, for example, whites began to see a move to the new suburbs as a way to avoid living in racially integrated neighborhoods. Governmental policies contributed to this trend through the financial incentives provided to homebuyers. Even after the Supreme Court declared restrictive covenants unconstitutional, local officials often successfully undercut the ruling's immediate impact. Various informal and extralegal arrangements prevented, until well into the 1960s, any African American from buying a home in most new suburbs such as Levittown.

Other policies and practices helped to limit diversity. Local governments could veto public housing projects in their communities. Although land and building costs would have been cheaper in the suburbs, public housing remained concentrated on relatively expensive, high-density urban sites. At the same time, the lending industry channeled government-guaranteed loans away from most urban neighborhoods, and private lenders routinely denied credit to African Americans and Latinos seeking to buy new suburban housing.

Leaders of the postwar housing industry denied any discriminatory intent. William Levitt could identify his private housing projects with the public crusade against communism. "No man who owns his house and lot can be a Communist," he remarked in 1948. "He has too much to do." Even as Levitt claimed he could help solve the problem of housing—and perhaps even that of communist subversion—he also resisted any suggestion that the private decisions of his construction business had anything to do with race. Architects of postwar suburbia similarly saw nothing problematic with postwar gender patterns. The private financial industry extended the vast majority of its loan guarantees to white men. Only rarely could single women obtain loans. The FHA justified a similar policy on the grounds that men were the family breadwinners and women seldom qualified as good credit risks. Analogous justifications often kept men of non-European background from obtaining loans for housing in the new suburbs.

27-5c *Postwar Hollywood*

Hollywood turned out movies filled with powerful symbols of the cold war era's fascination with—and containment of—change. The motion picture industry still commanded the nation's entertainment dollars at the start of the postwar period. As overseas markets reopened and Hollywood's male

Grey Villet/Getty Images

27.11 **Southdale Center in Edina, Minnesota** Opened in 1956, this first climate controlled, indoor mall, anchored by two major department stores, symbolized a suburban lifestyle dominated by cars and shopping. Notice how people are dressed and are using space. Malls based on this model proliferated in cities large and small for several decades.

Q *Why did the Southdale model prove attractive for so long?*

Q *Why are many malls now closing or undergoing radical redevelopment?*

stars returned from military service, the U.S. film industry expected to prosper and prepared to cheer the nation through the cold war much as it had through the Depression and the Second World War. The familiar musical genre, filled with lively stars, upbeat tunes, and flashy dance sequences, provided a ready formula for expressing postwar optimism. Attendance at movie theaters reached an all-time high in 1948.

Hollywood's fortunes, however, began changing. In 1948, the Supreme Court ruled that antitrust laws required the major studios to give up their highly profitable ownership of local movie theaters. This decision rocked Hollywood just as it faced labor strife, internal conflict over blacklisting, and soaring production costs. The challenge of television delivered yet another blow to an industry already reeling backward. Attendance figures—along with profits—began to plummet in 1949.

Hollywood had already begun to release a cycle of motion pictures that came to be called *film noir*, or "dark cinema." Almost always filmed in black and white and generally set in large cities, *film noir* peeked into the dark corners of postwar America and expressed the anxiety, even dread, associated with the Great Fear. *Noir* characters still pursued their dreams and hopes, but with little chance of fulfilling them. Failure and loss seemed to be the rule rather than the exception in these movies.

Film noir invariably featured alluring *femmes fatales*. These beautiful but dangerous female characters challenged the prevailing order, particularly its gender relationships. Hollywood's *femmes fatales* disdained the confinement that came with being faithful, nurturing wives and mothers. Usually unmarried and childless, their continual scheming to escape their containment threatened both men and women. The postwar era's leading female stars—including Barbara Stanwyck, Joan Crawford, Rita Hayworth, and Lana Turner—achieved both popular and critical acclaim playing *femmes fatales*.

27-6 The Election of 1952

Q *How did Dwight Eisenhower's appeal bring the Republican Party back into the White House for the first time since 1933?*

Harry Truman, his popular approval rating ultimately falling to near 20 percent, declined to run for another term in 1952. His presidency had put his Democratic Party on the defensive, while denunciations of communism and of Truman's outgoing administration animated Republicans.

History Through Film High Noon (1952)

Directed by Fred Zinnemann.
Starring Gary Cooper (Will Kane), Grace Kelly (Amy Fowler Kane), and Katy Jurado (Helen Ramirez).

During the early cold war era, few Hollywood movies gained as much popular and critical acclaim—and created as much controversy—as *High Noon*.

Montana-born Gary Cooper, while starring in movies such as *Mr. Deeds Goes to Town* (1936), had come to embody Hollywood's idealized version of "everyman." *High Noon* cast him as Will Kane, a veteran Old West lawman who retires as Hadleyville's marshal, marries a young woman (played by Grace Kelly), and prepares to become a storekeeper. Kane's plans are suddenly shattered when news arrives that Frank Miller, a vicious outlaw who had once controlled the town, has been released from prison. Slated to return on the noontime train, Miller has pledged to kill Kane and regain power. Will the marshal strap on his gun and defend Hadleyville against Miller and his henchmen? Or will he respect his new wife's Quaker pacifism, renounce violence, and flee from harm's way with her at his side?

Although the rules of the western genre require Kane to stand his ground, *High Noon's* script greatly complicated his course. Although Kane had earlier saved the townspeople from Miller, they now refuse to help him defend their community. If Kane will simply leave, they hope to cut a deal with the returning outlaw. As images of clocks ticking toward high noon fill the screen, Kane prepares for a showdown with Miller and his gang.

Reviewers at the time invariably agreed that *High Noon* offered a parable about the cold war era but disagreed about its meaning. While critics of extreme anticommunism viewed the movie as a commentary about how McCarthyism generated a fear that paralyzed American communities, including that of Hollywood, other commentators saw this view as too parochial. They considered *High Noon* a tale about the choices the United States faced in the postwar world. From this perspective, the movie's climactic gunfight—during which Kane, with unexpected assistance from his wife, dispatches the Miller gang—could be seen as a symbolic affirmation of the U.S. policy of containing, rather than negotiating with, communist aggressors.

High Noon's final sequence further complicated the debate: In it, a triumphant Will Kane throws down his marshal's badge and rides out of town on a buckboard with his wife. Was he expressing his disgust over the townspeople's refusal to help? Was he suggesting that he had dispatched Miller to uphold his personal code of honor rather than to defend Hadleyville or vindicate the rule of law?

Hollywood executives could hardly miss *High Noon's* most obvious message. The movie, which won four Academy Awards, showed that the venerable western genre still resonated, for many reasons, with cold war audiences. Hollywood and television stations began deluging audiences with westerns that generally ended, as had *High Noon*, with a showdown between two well-armed, well-defined adversaries. By the end of the 1950s, prime-time TV featured more than 25 different series set in the Old West, and westerns remained reliable moneymakers for the motion picture industry. ■

27.12 Gary Cooper as Marshall Will Kane.

27-6a Continuing Containment

Both major political parties embraced the policy of containment in 1952. Adlai Stevenson of Illinois, the Democratic presidential candidate, warned that "Soviet secret agents and their dupes" had "burrowed like moles" into governments throughout the world. "We cannot let our guard drop for even a moment," he claimed. A solidly anticommunist stance, however, could not save Stevenson or his party. The Republicans linked Stevenson to the unpopular Truman presidency and highlighted several scandals that featured administration figures receiving kickbacks for granting government contracts. The GOP's vice presidential nominee, Senator Richard Nixon of California, called Stevenson "Adlai the appeaser." The Republican formula for electoral victory could be expressed in a simple equation, "K1C2": "Korea, corruption, and communism."

27-6b *A Soldier-Politician*

For a presidential candidate, Republicans ultimately turned to a hero of the Second World War, General Dwight David Eisenhower, popularly known as "Ike." Eisenhower grew up in Kansas; graduated from West Point; ascended through the army ranks; and, as Supreme Allied Commander, directed the Normandy invasion of 1944. He served as Army Chief of Staff from 1945 to 1948 and, after an interim period as president of Columbia University, became the commander of NATO. Eisenhower had never before sought elective office, but a half-century of military service had honed his political instincts and administrative skills. Still vigorous at 62 years of age, Eisenhower seemed much younger than the departing Truman, only six years his senior.

Eisenhower's personal appeal dazzled political insiders, media commentators, and ordinary voters. Although his partisan affiliations seemed hazy enough that Democrats (as well as Republicans) had courted him as their presidential choice in 1948, Eisenhower eventually emerged as the standard-bearer of the GOP in 1952.

The crucial political battle of that year took place, before the general election, within Republican ranks. The more conservative of the party stalwarts rallied behind Senator Robert Taft of Ohio and his goals of reversing the New Deal and tempering Truman's global foreign policy. Marketed as a middle-of-the-road candidate, Eisenhower had broader appeal and appeared ready to direct the nation through a cold war as skillfully as he had led it through a hot one. The Republican campaign, the first to feature televised appeals, downplayed Eisenhower's uncertain grasp of complicated policy issues in favor of highlighting his winning personality. A special TV address helped Senator Richard M. Nixon of California, Ike's vice-presidential running mate, rescue his political career after allegations of having received illegal campaign funds threatened his place on the ticket.

The first military leader to gain the presidency since Ulysses S. Grant (1869–1877), Eisenhower could claim a great personal victory. The Eisenhower–Nixon ticket rolled up almost 7 million more popular votes than did the Democrats and carried the Electoral College ballots by a nearly five-to-one margin. The Republican Party, however, made only modest gains. It managed a single-vote majority in the Senate and an eight-vote edge in the House of Representatives. The New Deal political coalition still survived, even if it showed increasing signs of fraying in the South. There, some of the segregationist vote that had gone to the Dixiecrats in 1948 began moving toward the Republicans, and Eisenhower carried four states in the Democratic Party's once "Solid South" in 1952 (see Map 27.4).

27.13 **General Dwight Eisenhower Campaigning in Lubbock, Texas**

Q *How does this carefully composed photo, taken in the state in which Eisenhower was born, illustrate his campaign's emphasis on personal appeal rather than political ideology.*

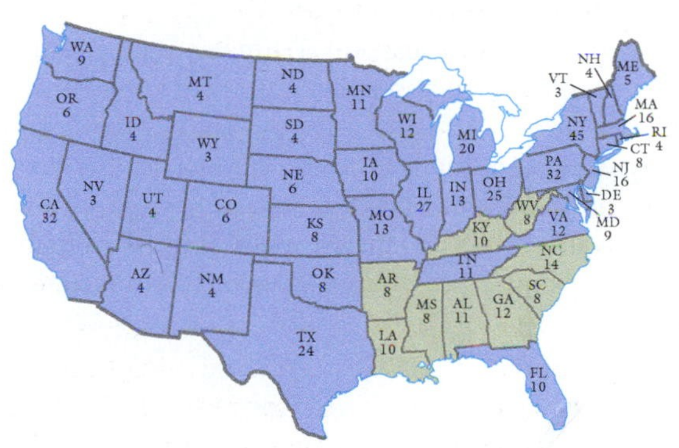

	Electoral Vote		Popular Vote	
	Number	%	Number	%
Stevenson (Democrat)	89	16.8	27,314,992	44.4
Eisenhower (Republican)	442	83.3	33,936,234	55.1

▲ **MAP 27.4 Presidential Election, 1952** An overwhelming victory for Dwight Eisenhower, this election saw Adlai Stevenson carrying a handful of states.

Q *How did the absence of a third, southern-based party, similar to the States' Rights Party of 1948 (review Map 27.1), inflate the Democratic Party's totals in the Electoral vote of 1952? What key states in the South, carried by the Democrats in 1948, were carried in 1952 by the Republicans?*

Conclusion

An emphasis on safeguarding national security reshaped national life during the immediate postwar years. As worsening relations between the United States and the Soviet Union produced a cold war, the Truman administration pursued anti-communist initiatives that expanded the power of the government, particularly the executive branch. The militarization of foreign policy intensified when the United States, after going to war in Korea in 1950, began implementing the assumptions laid out in NSC-68.

Americans also debated how best to safeguard security and calm cultural anxieties on the home front. The New Deal vision faded, but Truman's Fair Deal promised that new economic wisdom would guarantee economic growth and thereby provide tax revenues to expand domestic programs. The Truman administration also expressed support, even when it alienated many white southerners, for a civil rights agenda. Cultural change added to national security concerns in contributing to the Great Fear.

Although the 1952 election of Dwight Eisenhower gave the Republicans the presidency for the first time in two decades, Eisenhower's personal appeal did not signal an end to the Democratic coalition that had held sway since the 1930s.

CHAPTER REVIEW

Review

1. How did disputes between the United States and the Soviet Union shape the cold war and prompt a focus on national security?
2. How did the Korean War help reinforce and further militarize national security policies?
3. How did the emphasis on national security spread throughout American culture?
4. Why did some of President Truman's policy proposals gain congressional and public approval while others did not?
5. Why were significant cultural changes of the postwar years both welcomed and feared?
6. Why did Dwight Eisenhower's appeal bring the Republican Party back into the White House for the first time since 1933?

Critical Thinking

1. How did the postwar preoccupation with national security prompt important changes in the nation's system of constitutional governance? How did U.S. intervention in Korea help to underscore these changes?
2. How did domestic postwar policy-making follow—and also depart from—the vision of Franklin Roosevelt's New Deal?

Identifications

Review your understanding of the following key terms, people, and events for this chapter (terms in bold in text are included in the Glossary).

cold war, p. 746
Truman Doctrine, p. 746
containment, p. 747
National Security Act of 1947, p. 748
Berlin Blockade, p. 749
Berlin Airlift, p. 749
North Atlantic Treaty Organization (NATO), p. 750
NSC-68, p. 750
Korean War, p. 753
General Douglas MacArthur, p. 753
Taft–Hartley Act, p. 756
McCarran-Walter Act, p. 757
Joseph McCarthy, p. 758
National Security Agency (NSA), p. 759
Employment Act of 1946, p. 760
"Fair Deal," p. 760
GI Bill, p. 760
baby boom generation, p. 764

Suggested Readings

Melvyn P. Leffler and Odd Arne Westad, eds., ***The Cambridge History of the Cold War*** **(2 vols., 2010)** contain outstanding essays on every aspect of the cold war. **Melvyn P. Leffler,** ***For the Soul of Mankind: The United States, the Soviet Union and the Cold War*** (2008); **Frank Costigliola,** ***Roosevelt's Lost Alliances: How Personal Politics Helped Start the Cold War*** (2012); and **Odd Arne Westad,** ***The Global Cold War: Third World Interventions and the Making of Our Times*** (2005) offer excellent views of foreign policy. **Bruce Cumings,** ***Dominion from Sea to Sea: Pacific Ascendancy and American Power*** (2009), resituates its author's specialized studies of the Korean War in a broader framework.

The domestic consequences of national security policies are analyzed critically in **Garry Wills,** ***Bomb Power: The Modern Presidency and the National Security State*** (2010), and the relevant chapters of **Athan Theoharis,** ***Chasing Spies: How the FBI Failed in Counter-Intelligence But Helped Promote the Politics of McCarthyism in the Cold War Years*** (2002). ***Spies: The Rise and Fall of the KGB in***

America **(2010), by John Earl Haynes, Harvey Klehr, and Alexander Vassiliev, offers a different perspective. See also Landon R. Y. Storrs,** ***The Second Red Scare and the Unmaking of the New Deal Left*** (2013); and **David Oshinsky,** ***A Conspiracy So Immense: The World of Joe McCarthy*** (2005).

The essays in ***Rethinking Cold War Culture*****, Peter J. Kuznick and James Gilbert, eds.**, can be supplemented with **Thomas Doherty,** ***Cold War, Cool Medium: Television, McCarthyism, and American Culture*** (2005); and **Glenn Frankel,** ***High Noon: The Hollywood Black List and the Making of an American Classic*** (2017). **Robert Weintraub,** ***The Victory Season: The End of World War II and the Birth of Baseball's Golden Age*** (2013), places the desegregation of the national pastime in the context of the emerging cold war.

Important social histories include **Elaine Tyler May,** ***Homeward Bound: American Families in the Cold War Era*** (rev. ed., 2008); **Lisabeth Cohen,** ***A Consumer's Republic: Mass Consumption in Cold War America*** (2003); and **Susan L. Carruthers,** ***Cold War Captives: Imprisonment, Escape, and Brainwashing*** (2009). On civil rights, see **Thomas J. Sugrue,** ***Sweet Land of Liberty: The Forgotten Struggle for Civil Rights in the North*** (2008); and **Risa L. Goluboff,** ***The Lost Promise of Civil Rights*** (2007).

28 America at Midcentury, 1953–1963

28-1 **Reorienting Containment, 1953–1960**

Learning Objective: *Detail the ways in which the Eisenhower administration both retained and also reoriented the foreign policy of containment.*

Eisenhower Takes Command
The New Look, Global Alliances, and Summitry
Policies toward the Third World

28-2 **Affluence—A "People of Plenty"**

Learning Objective: *Evaluate how steady economic growth changed American life during the post-1953 decade by considering governmental policies, business and labor practices, and the dominant faith in political and religious pluralism.*

Economic Growth
Highways and Waterways
Labor-Management Accord
Political Pluralism
A Religious People

28-3 **Discontents of Affluence**

Learning Objective: *Explain why an affluent society generated social criticism during the 1950s and early 1960s.*

Conformity in an Affluent Society
Restive Youth
The Critique of Mass Culture

28-4 **Debating the Role of Government**

Learning Objective: *Identify the major contending arguments over the role of government in the 1950s.*

The New Conservative Critique
The Case for a More Active Government

28-5 **New Frontiers, 1960–1963**

Learning Objective: *Describe how the administration of John F. Kennedy both continued and refashioned the policies of the Eisenhower administration.*

The Election of 1960
Foreign Policy, 1960–1963
Cuba and Berlin
Southeast Asia and Flexible Response
Domestic Policy, 1960–1963

28-6 **The Politics of Gender**

Learning Objective: *Analyze the social, economic, and cultural forces that worked to change gender roles during the 1950s and early 1960s.*

The New Suburbs and Gender Politics
Signs of Women's Changing Roles
A New Women's Movement

28-7 **The Expanding Civil Rights Movements, 1953–1963**

Learning Objective: *Trace how new movements to expand and enforce civil rights became a central part of domestic politics in the 1950s and 1960s.*

The *Brown* Cases, 1954–1955
The Montgomery Bus Boycott
The Politics of Civil Rights: From the Local to the Global
The Politics of American Indian Policy
Spanish-Speaking Communities and Civil Rights
Urban-Suburban Issues
New Forms of Direct Action, 1960–1963

28-8 **November 1963**

Learning Objective: *Understand the range of important issues that were left unsettled at Kennedy's death and would shape the rest of the 1960s.*

Policy Choices
The Assassination of John F. Kennedy

THE FINAL FROST BARRIER!
IT'S HERE!
A FROST-PROOF
FOOD FREEZER!
NO FROST!
NO FROST-LOCKED
FOODS!
NO DEFROSTING!
You'll feel like a queen . . .
• Trim Upright Freezer with award-winning Sheer Look and embossed white-bright Lacework Styling.
• Takes so little floor space—only 32 inches wide—yet this 16 cu. ft. Frost-Proof Imperial Freezer shown, stores 560 lbs. of food.
• Serve family meals in minutes. Be always ready for guests.
• Shop once a week. Enjoy bulk buying that cuts food bills.
• Cook and bake in quantity. Enjoy "free" days.
• Freeze leftovers, like stew, turkey, cake, enjoy them weeks later.
• Have fun freezing your own fruits and vegetables; fish and game, too.
UFPI-160-59
DESIGNED WITH YOU IN MIND!
GM
Built and Backed by General Motors

The Granger Collection, NYC

28.1 **The Queen of Abundance** The double-store, frost-free refrigerator offered consumers an elegant display case for the new prepackaged and frozen food products that became available during the 1950s.

Q *How does this advertisement illustrate the idea that Americans had become a "people of plenty?"*

Q *How does it link gender roles for women to the new mass consumer society?*

CONTAINMENT OF COMMUNISM continued to dominate American foreign policy between 1953 and 1963. Republican President Dwight David Eisenhower toned down the pitch of the anticommunist rhetoric, but both he and his Democratic successor, John F. Kennedy, pursued new ways to fight the cold war.

At home, Ike and JFK supported, with differing degrees of enthusiasm, social and economic programs that had been initiated during the 1930s and 1940s. Eisenhower's administration accepted the key elements of the New Deal: the economic regulatory structure, the safety net of Social Security, the ability of labor to bargain collectively, and the building of infrastructure projects. Calling Eisenhower's policies too cautious, Kennedy came to the presidency promising more vigorous governmental action at home and, especially, overseas.

Sustained economic growth encouraged talk about an age of "affluence." Economic data bolstered optimism. Between 1941 and 1950, the real income of the bottom 50 percent of the population grew by more than one-third. The bottom 20 percent saw its income rise by a higher percentage than the top 20 percent. Economic growth simultaneously generated discontent, particularly over conformity, restive young people, and commercial mass culture. At the same time, continued economic disparities and racial discrimination sparked debate over greater use of governmental power—and the meanings of liberty and equality. ■

28-1 Reorienting Containment, 1953–1960

Q *How did the Eisenhower administration retain but also reorient the foreign policy of containment?*

The U.S. strategy for safeguarding national security by containing communism shifted emphasis during the 1950s. Bipolar confrontation between the United States and the Soviet Union over European issues gave way to greater reliance on nuclear weaponry and on power plays in the so-called Third World: the Middle East, Asia, Latin America, and Africa.

28-1a *Eisenhower Takes Command*

Eisenhower honored his campaign pledge to visit Korea and help end the military conflict there. Anxious to conclude matters, Eisenhower even began to hint about using nuclear weapons if diplomacy moved too slowly. In July 1953, the warring parties signed a truce, and a conflict that claimed the lives of more than 2 million Asians, mostly noncombatants, and 53,000 Americans finally ended. A formal peace treaty remained unsigned, however, and the heavily fortified 38th parallel divided the two Koreas.

At home, Ike patiently wrested control of the national security issue from more militant anticommunists. Congress exceeded the wishes of the Eisenhower administration when enacting the Communist Control Act of 1954, which barred the American Communist Party from running candidates in elections and extended the provisions of the Subversive Activities Control Act of 1950. With a GOP president in the White House, however, Republicans began turning away from the confrontational styles of anticommunist politics associated with Joe McCarthy.

McCarthy finally careened out of control. He railed against the Eisenhower administration and about supposed subversives in the U.S. Army. He denounced as "unfit to wear the uniform" a well-respected general who had denied his charges. A special Senate committee began investigating the sensational allegations, and these "Army–McCarthy Hearings" turned into a television miniseries that began in April of 1954. Under the glare of TV lights, McCarthy seemed a crude bully, hurling slanders in every direction. And his habit of interrupting the proceedings with a "point of order" made for tiresome television. In late 1954, McCarthy's colleagues in the Senate, including half of his fellow Republicans, voted to "condemn" him for "unbecoming" conduct. Three years later, McCarthy died, still in office but exiled from the national spotlight. Eisenhower's decision to allow McCarthy to self-destruct, rather than to confront him head-on, seemed vindicated.

Indeed, presidential historians now generally see Eisenhower as a skilled chief executive. By expanding the

CHRONOLOGY

1953	Eisenhower becomes president • Korean War ends
1954	New Look in foreign policy unveiled • *Brown* cases decided • Geneva Peace Accords for Indochina signed
1955	Montgomery bus boycott begins • *National Review* founded
1956	Federal Highway Act passed • Eisenhower reelected
1957	Eisenhower sends troops to Little Rock • Congress passes a Civil Rights Act • Soviet Union sends *Sputniks* into orbit
1958	National Defense Education Act passes
1959	Khrushchev visits United States • Castro overthrows Batista in Cuba
1960	Kennedy elected president
1961	Bay of Pigs invasion fails • Berlin Wall goes up
1962	Cuban Missile Crisis endangers world
1963	Civil rights groups hold March on Washington • Kennedy assassinated

White House staff, he could employ the power of the presidency while seeming to do relatively little. Eisenhower, in the words of one scholar, conducted a "hidden hand presidency." Ike encouraged the idea that his aides directed domestic matters. Recognizing the importance of regular TV appearances, Ike honed his folksy image and became a capable television performer.

28-1b *The New Look, Global Alliances, and Summitry*

Working behind the scenes, Eisenhower collaborated with his national security advisers to reinforce executive branch leadership in foreign policy. He allowed Secretary of State John Foster Dulles to warn, repeatedly, that a new administration might seek to "roll back," rather than simply to contain, communism. The excesses of legislators like McCarthy helped the White House justify its claims for a constitutional privilege to withhold national security materials from Congress and to beat back a proposed constitutional amendment to limit presidential power in foreign affairs. Eisenhower also extended Harry Truman's earlier programs of domestic surveillance and continued a secret initiative to develop new aerial surveillance reconnaissance.

The Eisenhower administration also secretly reviewed overall military policy. It initially decided to rein in military spending by introducing a **New Look**, which emphasized nuclear weaponry and airpower as a way to halt spiraling expenditures. The former general and his allies in the military recognized that the cold war would not end any time soon and that they needed a national security policy that would be affordable over the long haul.

Eisenhower's New Look became associated with the doctrine of **massive retaliation**. In early 1954, John Foster Dulles announced that the United States reserved the right to respond to military aggression "with means of our own choosing." This thinly veiled threat to unleash U.S. nuclear weaponry was aimed at keeping the Soviets in check. To widen the U.S. nuclear umbrella, Eisenhower expanded NATO to include West Germany and added other mutual defense pacts with noncommunist nations in Central and Southeast Asia.

The Eisenhower administration soon began augmenting the New Look and massive retaliation by emphasizing more flexible approaches to national security policy. It embraced covert action and economic pressure as useful strategies. The administration also elevated psychological warfare and informational programs into additional weapons of the cold war. The government-run Voice of America extended its radio broadcasts globally. Washington secretly funded Radio Free Europe, Radio Liberty (beamed to the Soviet Union), and Radio Asia. In 1953, Eisenhower persuaded Congress to create the United States Information Agency (USIA) to coordinate anticommunist propaganda campaigns.

One piece of this cultural offensive fought the cold war with jazz. Beginning in 1955, Willis Conover hosted a program that hailed jazz as "music of freedom" and reached more than 100 million listeners around the globe. After Conover's death in 1996, an admiring obituary quipped that his show would "bombard Budapest with Billy Taylor, strafe Poland with Oscar Peterson and drop John Coltrane on Moscow." American mass culture in all its forms circled the globe.

The United States and the USSR, hoping to improve relations, began holding high-level "summit meetings" in 1955. In May, U.S. and Soviet leaders agreed to end the occupation of Austria and to transform it into a neutral nation. Two months later, the United States, the Soviet Union, Britain, and France met in Geneva, Switzerland, and inaugurated cultural exchanges. During fall 1959, hoping to heal a rift over the future of divided Berlin, Khrushchev travelled to the United States. He called on a farm family in Iowa, visited Hollywood, and toured Disneyland. Although a 1960 summit meeting in Paris fell apart after the Soviets shot down an American U-2 spy plane over their territory, the tone of cold war rhetoric became somewhat less strident during Eisenhower's two-term presidency.

The United States and the Soviet Union also began negotiations over their already vast stockpiles of nuclear weapons. Eisenhower's "Open Skies" initiative of 1955 proposed mutual reconnaissance flights over each other's territory to verify efforts at reduction. The Soviets balked, but some progress was made in limiting atomic testing. Responding to the health hazards of radioactive fallout, both nations slowed above-ground testing and discussed a broader test-ban agreement.

For some Americans, these efforts came too late. Documents finally declassified in the 1980s confirmed that people who had lived or worked downwind from nuclear test sites during the 1940s and 1950s suffered a number of atomic-related illnesses. More than one-third of the crew that worked on the Hollywood movie *The Conqueror* (1956), shot in a downwind area of Utah, contracted or died of cancer. Subsequent revelations also showed that the government had secretly experimented with radioactive materials on unsuspecting citizens.

Meanwhile, events in Eastern Europe tested the likelihood of the United States and the Soviet Union clashing militarily in this region. Dissidents within the Soviet-dominated "satellite" countries resented their badly managed communist economies and detested their police-state regimes. Insurgents in Poland, seizing on hints that the Soviet Union might relax its heavy hand, staged a rebellion in June 1956. They forced the Soviets to accept an old foe of Moscow as Poland's head of state.

Hungarians then rallied in support of Imre Nagy, a communist–nationalist who promised a multiparty political system for his country. Soviet military forces moved against the new government, and Hungarian insurgents appealed to the United States for assistance. Despite Secretary of State Dulles's rhetoric about "rolling back" Soviet power in Eastern Europe, strategists at the Pentagon recognized the danger of mounting any military operation so close to Soviet territory. Soviet armies brutally crushed the uprising in Hungary and killed thousands, including Nagy.

28-1c *Policies toward the Third World*

The U.S. campaign to contain communism increasingly shifted toward what came to be called the Third World (emerging nations in decolonizing areas of the world in which U.S. and Soviet interest increasingly clashed). Here, the Eisenhower administration employed covert action and economic pressure as primary tools. These approaches, less visible and less expensive than military deployments, seemed less likely to provoke political controversy at home or overt showdowns with the Soviets abroad.

The CIA, headed by Allen Dulles, brother of the secretary of state, played a key role. In 1953 the CIA helped engineer the election of the anticommunist Ramón Magsaysay as president of the Philippines. That same year, the CIA facilitated a coup in Iran, overthrowing Mohammed Mossadegh's constitutional (and left-leaning) government and restoring Shah (emperor) Reza Pahlavi to power. The increasingly dictatorial leader ensured that Iran would remain allied with Washington and supportive of American oil interests. In 1954 the CIA spearheaded a successful plot to topple President Jacobo Arbenz Guzmán's elected government in Guatemala. Officials in Washington and executives of the United Fruit Company desired the ouster of Arbenz, whose broad support included that of Guatemala's communist party. The CIA strategy included a full-scale propaganda offensive that helped undermine Arbenz's popular appeal among Guatemalans.

Impressed by these covert operations, the National Security Council widened the CIA's mandate. By 1961 the CIA

Source: Wisconsin Historical Society

28.2 **Ribbon-Cutting Ceremony, 1958** Opening the new interstate highway 94 near Waukesha, Wisconsin.

Q *How could the new interstate highway system be justified as a national security measure?*

Q *How did this new highway system affect the economy and change the character of small and large cities?*

deployed approximately 15,000 agents, as compared to about 6,000 only eight years earlier, around the world.

Eisenhower also employed economic strategies—trade and aid—to contain communism and win allies. Governmental initiatives sought to open new opportunities for American enterprises overseas, discourage other countries from adopting state-directed economic systems, and encourage expanded trade ties. Supporters of these efforts credited U.S. policy with promoting greater stability in recipient countries. U.S. military aid to the Third World nations also rose sharply between 1953 and 1963. This buildup of armaments provided the United States with stronger anticommunist allies but also contributed to the development of military dictatorships.

In Latin America, the Eisenhower White House gravitated toward dictatorial regimes that welcomed U.S. economic investment and opposed leftist movements. Such policies encouraged anti-American sentiment, and events in Cuba dramatized the growing hostility. In late 1959, a revolutionary movement led by Fidel Castro toppled dictator Fulgencio Batista's pro-U.S. regime and pledged to reduce Cuba's dependence on the United States. The Eisenhower administration responded with an economic boycott. Castro turned to the Soviet Union, openly embraced communism, squashed dissent at home, and pledged to support Cuban-style insurgencies throughout Latin America. The CIA pondered how best to hamstring, and then eliminate, Castro.

In the Middle East, distrust of nationalism and neutralism shaped U.S. policy. In 1954, when Colonel Gamal Abdel Nasser led a successful military coup in Egypt against a corrupt monarchy, he promised to rescue other Arab nations from European domination and guide them toward "positive neutralism" in the cold war. Nasser denounced Israel; boosted Egypt's economic and military power; extended diplomatic recognition to the People's Republic of China; and purchased advanced weapons from communist Czechoslovakia.

The Eisenhower administration viewed Nasser's policies as neither positive nor neutral. It cancelled loans for building the Aswan Dam, a project designed to improve agriculture along the Nile River and provide power for new Egyptian industries. Nasser responded, in July 1956, by seizing the British-controlled Suez Canal. British forces, joined by those of France and Israel, attacked Egypt in October and took back the canal (see Map 28.1).

Eisenhower distrusted Nasser but also opposed Britain's attempt to retain its imperial position. Denouncing the Anglo-French-Israeli action, he threatened to destabilize Britain's currency unless the invasion ended. Eventually, a plan supported by the United States and the UN gave Egypt control over the canal and defused this Suez Crisis, but U.S. influence in the area suffered as the Soviet Union underwrote construction of the Aswan Dam.

The Eisenhower administration feared the spread of "Nasserism" throughout the energy-rich Middle East. In spring 1957, the **Eisenhower Doctrine** pledged that the United States would defend Middle Eastern countries "against overt armed aggression from any nation controlled by international communism." When governments in Lebanon and Jordan faced revolts by domestic forces friendly to Nasser, Eisenhower dispatched U.S. Marines to Lebanon, and Britain helped Jordan's King Hussein retain his throne.

Eisenhower's effort to thwart communism and neutralism in the Third World set the stage for his most substantial commitment—in Indochina. During the Korean War, the Truman administration had increased economic aid for France's war to retain its colony in Indochina against a communist-nationalist movement led by Ho Chi Minh (see Chapter 27). Eisenhower continued Truman's policy.

During the early spring of 1954, Ho's forces surrounded French troops in the valley of Dien Bien Phu. France surrendered and abandoned the colony it had created in 1887. The **Geneva Peace Accords of 1954**, which the Eisenhower administration refused to sign, divided French Indochina into three new nations: Laos, Cambodia, and Vietnam. The accords temporarily split Vietnam, at the 17th parallel, into two jurisdictions—North Vietnam and South Vietnam—until a subsequent election could unify the country under a single government. Ho Chi Minh and his communist allies in China and the Soviet Union accepted this settlement, confident that Ho would win the election, scheduled for 1956.

▲ **MAP 28.1 Israel, the Middle East, and the Suez Crisis, 1956** The creation of Israel in 1948 and the Suez Crisis of 1956 shaped international politics in the Middle East during the postwar era.

Q *How does this map suggest some reasons why the establishment of Israel sharpened Arab nationalism and why the Suez Canal continued to be seen as an important strategic location?*

What They Said

Eisenhower and Kennedy on Military Spending

Dwight Eisenhower's presidency extended the scope of the cold war. It also expanded the stakes with its New Look emphasis on airpower and nuclear weapons. His administration introduced the construction of new missile systems to deliver nuclear bombs; sophisticated aerial surveillance techniques; and innovative tracking facilities for better coordination of the nation's military might. Yet, when leaving office, Eisenhower issued a carefully prepared farewell address that, in its most noted section, warned against the growth of what he called the military industrial complex.

While a U.S. senator during the Eisenhower presidency, John F. Kennedy seldom involved himself in the process of fashioning domestic legislation but did gain a reputation for criticizing the foreign and military policies of Eisenhower's administration. The United States, Kennedy insisted, needed more assertive policies and greater spending on its missile program. Kennedy aligned his critique with those who claimed that Eisenhower had allowed a "missile gap" to develop between the United States and its adversary, the Soviet Union. These themes, prominently on display during Kennedy's campaigns for the Democratic nomination and, then, for the presidency, reappeared in his inaugural address, delivered with the outgoing president, Dwight Eisenhower, in attendance.

President Dwight Eisenhower, Farewell Address, 1961

We annually spend on military security more than the net income of all United States corporations.

This conjunction of an immense military establishment and a large arms industry is new in the American experience. The total influence—economic, political, even spiritual—is felt in every city, every Statehouse, every office of the Federal government. We recognize the imperative need for this development. Yet we must not fail to comprehend its grave implications. Our toil, resources and livelihood are all involved; so is the very structure of our society.

In the councils of government, we must guard against the acquisition of unwarranted influence, whether sought or unsought, by the military–industrial complex. The potential for the disastrous rise of misplaced power exists and will persist.

We must never let the weight of this combination endanger our liberties or democratic processes.

President John F. Kennedy, Inaugural Address, 1961

Let the word go forth from this time and place, to friend and foe alike, that the torch has been passed to a new generation of Americans—born in this century, tempered by war, disciplined by a hard and bitter peace, proud of our ancient heritage—and unwilling to witness or permit the slow undoing of those human rights to which this nation has always been committed, and to which we are committed today at home and around the world.

Let every nation know, whether it wishes us well or ill, that we shall pay any price, bear any burden, meet any hardship, support any friend, oppose any foe to assure the survival and the success of liberty.

This much we pledge—and more. . . .

We dare not tempt [those nations who would make themselves our adversary] with weakness. For only when our arms are sufficient beyond doubt can we be certain beyond doubt that they will never be employed.

Q *Why, according to Eisenhower, does the "military–industrial complex" threaten American democracy? How does Kennedy's inaugural speech implicitly, reject the warning of his predecessor?*

Q *How does the inaugural address of Kennedy (born in 1917) seem to offer a generational break from how Eisenhower (born in 1890) had been waging the cold war?*

Q *More than half a century after these two presidents set forth their differing visions of national security policy, how would you evaluate their rhetoric?*

Sources: (top) From speech, President Dwight Eisenhower, Farewell Address, 1961; (bottom) From speech, President John F. Kennedy, Inaugural Address, 1961.

Eisenhower's advisers feared that a communist electoral victory in Vietnam might set off a geopolitical chain reaction that could "endanger the stability and security" of noncommunist nations throughout Asia, a formulation known as the **domino theory**. After Ho Chi Minh's communist government consolidated control over the Democratic Republic of Vietnam (North Vietnam), Eisenhower ordered covert operations and economic programs to forestall Ho from assuming control of a unified Vietnam. The CIA staged a rigged 1955 election that installed Ngo Dinh Diem as the first president of the Republic of Vietnam (South Vietnam).

An anticommunist Catholic, Ngo Dinh Diem renounced the Geneva Peace Accords and the election intended to create a unified government. He consolidated his political support, augmented his military forces, and cracked down on his opponents. Diem's policies cost him support inside South Vietnam, especially among the sizable Buddhist population, and he became increasingly dependent on the United States. Although Eisenhower feared that direct U.S. military involvement in South Vietnam would be a "tragedy," he increased aid, dispatched military advisers, and tied America's policy to Diem's shaky political fortunes.

The Eisenhower administration sent billions of dollars and hundreds of military advisers to prop up Diem's government. Meanwhile, in early 1959, North Vietnam finally decided to send troops as well as supplies into the South. They traveled along a shifting route of highways and roads that became known as the "Ho Chi Minh Trail." Any decision about whether Eisenhower's commitments would ever lead the United States to intervene with its own military forces would fall to his successors.

28-2 Affluence—A "People of Plenty"

Q *In what ways did economic growth change American life during the post-1953 decade considering governmental policies, business and labor practices, and the dominant faith in political and religious pluralism?*

In his farewell address of 1961, Dwight Eisenhower warned that the greatest danger to the United States was not communism but the nation's own **military–industrial complex**. This term signified an informal relationship among military, political, and economic elites committed to expanding national security capabilities. This complex, the former general warned, threatened to so accelerate the costs of cold war containment that the burden of military expenditures could eventually harm the U.S. domestic economy.

Eisenhower's speech masked certain ironies. Most obviously, his administration, while trying to contain costs, failed to prevent ever-larger sums of money from flowing to the military. Moreover, Ike's selection of corporate executives to head the Department of Defense seemingly dramatized the very same linkage his farewell address would later decry.

In 1940, the United States had still teetered on the brink of economic depression. Twenty years later, it could claim a GNP more than five times that of Great Britain and roughly 10 times that of Japan. National security policies facilitated U.S. access to raw materials and energy. Government spending for these same policies, what economists sometimes called "military Keynesianism," also pumped money into the economy. By 1955, military expenditures accounted for about 10 percent of the GNP.

28-2a *Economic Growth*

The post-1953 decade, despite three brief recessions, would mark the midpoint of a period of steady economic growth that would eventually stretch from the Second World War to the early 1970s. Corporations turned out vast quantities of consumer goods and enjoyed rising profits. The label "Made in America" announced both the quality of particular products and the economic power of the United States (see Figure 28.1).

Newer American-based industries, such as those involving chemicals and electronics, dominated world

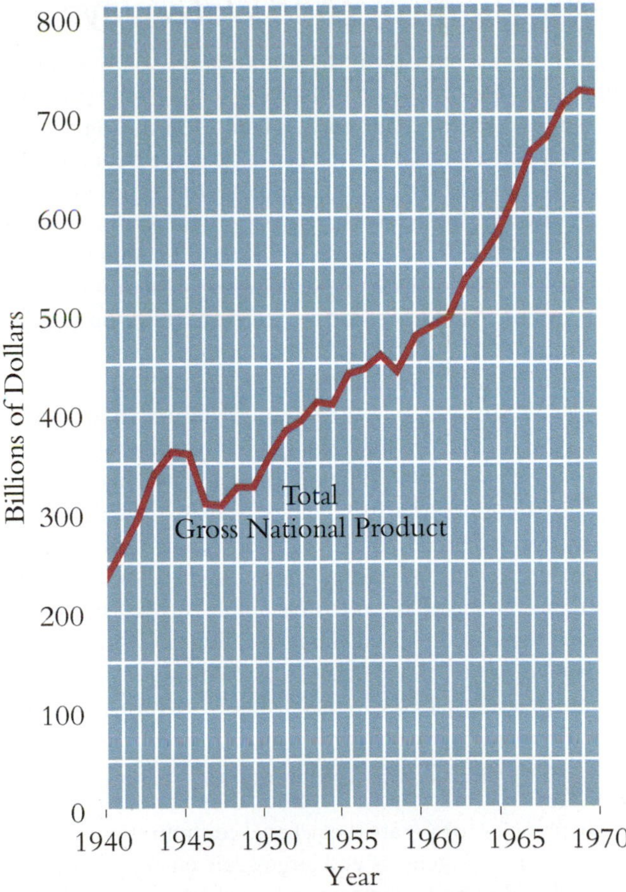

Figure 28.1 **Steady Growth of Gross National Product, 1940–1970**

markets. Corning Glass reported that most of its sales in the mid-1950s came from products that had been unknown in 1940. General Electric proclaimed, "Progress is our most important product."

The new suburbs highlighted the fruits of this booming economy. Because these outlying areas invariably lacked adequate mass transit, life revolved around the automobile. Car buying expanded during the 1950s as the two-car family and new suburban shopping malls, surrounded by acres of free parking, became tangible symbols of economic growth. Kitchen appliances, television sets, and automobiles supported the claim that Americans were, in the words of historian David Potter, a "people of plenty." *Fortune* magazine celebrated "The Rich Middle-Income Class." Harvard economist John Kenneth Galbraith reached the best-seller lists with a book entitled *The Affluent Society* (1958).

The term *affluence* nicely captured the dominant vision that celebrated constant economic growth and steady improvement of living standards as a uniquely American way of life. The gulf between rich and poor no longer seemed to be between people with cars and those without them, but between people with Cadillacs and Lincolns and those with Fords and Chevrolets. "Luxury has reached the masses," proclaimed *Fortune*.

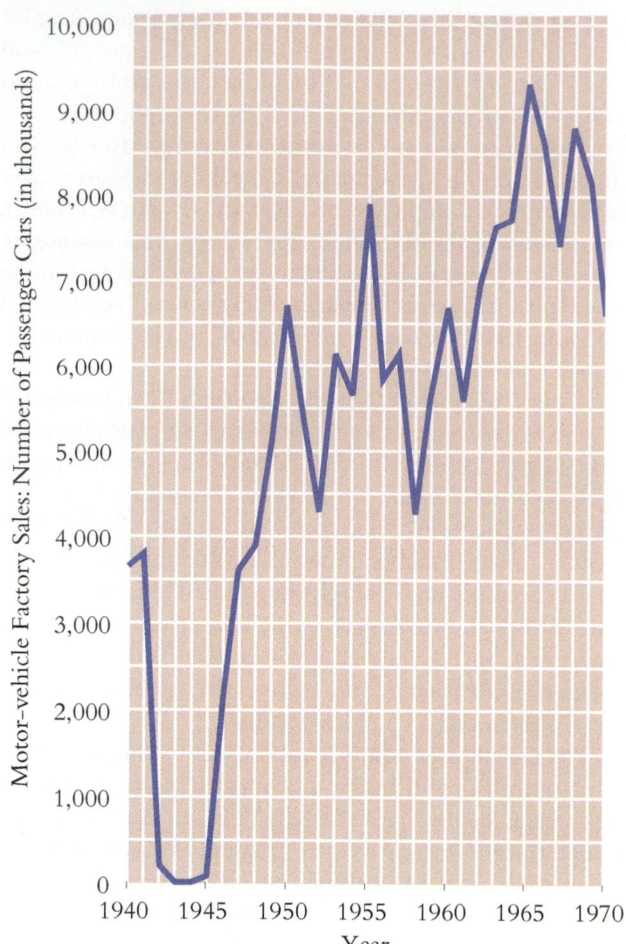

Figure 28.2 **Auto Sales, 1940–1970**

28-2b *Highways and Waterways*

Eisenhower advocated the importance of a balanced federal budget but endorsed several costly new programs. He supported the **Highway Act of 1956**, citing national security considerations. Financed largely by a national tax on gasoline, the act funded a nationwide system of limited-access expressways. Touted as the largest public works project in world history, this program delighted the oil, concrete, and tire industries; provided steady work for construction firms and labor unions; and boosted the interstate trucking business. It confirmed the victory of the automobile over competing modes of surface transportation (see Figure 28.2).

The White House also supported expensive water-diversion projects in the West. The Army Corps of Engineers and the Bureau of Reclamation, governmental agencies with powerful supporters in business and in Congress, spent billions of dollars on dams, irrigation canals, and reservoirs. Irrigation turned desert into cropland, and elaborate pumping systems even forced rivers to flow uphill. By 1960, much of the West enjoyed access to trillions of gallons of water per year, and governmental expenditures encouraged substantial economic growth in the "Sun Belt states" of Texas, California, and Arizona.

These water projects came at a price. Technologically complicated and costly to build, they spawned complex bureaucracies to operate them. Local communities lost power to government agencies and large-scale entrepreneurs, who pushed aside smaller farmers and ranchers. American Indian tribes found sections of their land being flooded for reservoirs or purchased by agribusinesses. These vast projects—which diverted surface waters, tapped into groundwater tables, and dotted the West with dams and reservoirs—also produced ecological problems. They degraded habitats and contributed to the buildup of salt by-products in the water and the soil. Some scientists began to warn about the overuse of toxic pesticides.

Eisenhower took a personal interest in agricultural policy. Although the number of farms plummeted during the 1950s, new machines, corporate-style operations, and hybrid seeds spurred greater production. As overproduction drove down commodity prices, government support programs propped up farm incomes. The idea that Washington should guarantee farmers "parity," or a fair price for their labor, remained the centerpiece of federal agricultural policy. The Eisenhower administration also tried to increase agricultural exports and began the "Soil Bank Program," which paid farmers for taking land out of production.

28-2c *Labor-Management Accord*

Labor leaders were coming to believe that cooperation with corporate management could promote union stability and political influence. Roughly 35 percent of nonagricultural

Interpreting the Visual Past A Car for Suburbia

Marketing experts in the 1950s claimed that women made about 80 percent of the decisions about purchasing consumer items. Consequently, the advertising industry, which boomed during this decade, directed its appeals especially to women. This ad for a 1958 Buick suggests an interrelationship between advertising and social behavior. Critically examine the ad and its messages by considering the following questions.

Q *Advertisers have carefully chosen the people, the words, the use of color, and the layout of this advertisement to sell this 1958 Buick. To whom and how are its appeals directed?*

Q *Compare this ad to print automobile ads from today. How have cars, families, and advertising techniques changed?*

The Advertising Archives

28.3 **General Motors Advertisement for New Buick, 1958.**

workers belonged to a union during the 1950s. Taking its cue from the United Auto Workers (UAW), one of the most militant unions back in the 1930s, organized labor agreed to bargain aggressively on wages and fringe benefits but to defer to management on broader issues and to disavow militant tactics such as wildcat strikes. To oversee this new labor-management accord, both sides looked to the federal government's National Labor Relations Board (NLRB). Meanwhile, in 1955, the American Federation of Labor (AFL) and the Congress of Industrial Organizations (CIO), long at odds, merged. The 1950s thus seemed to signal an end to the kind of labor-capital conflict that had marked the 1930s and late 1940s.

Business leaders generally applauded the new direction. *Fortune* magazine noted that corporations paid a price in more costly employee benefits and higher wages, but that they "got a bargain" on the larger issues of labor peace and managerial power. The labor-management accord also divided the industrial workforce because workers in more profitable sectors could bargain more effectively than those in sectors with smaller profit margins.

Some nonunionized businesses voluntarily expanded benefits for their workers. Companies such as Sears and Eastman Kodak encouraged a cooperative corporate culture, which included health and pension plans, profit-sharing arrangements, and social programs. Some firms created private recreational parks for exclusive use by their employees. Satisfying workers, corporate executives reasoned, would reduce the appeal of both unionization and governmental regulatory measures.

During the 1950s and early 1960s real wages (what workers make after adjusting their paychecks for inflation) rose steadily, and jobs were plentiful. The frequency of industrial accidents dropped; fringe benefits (health insurance, paid vacation time, and retirement plans) improved; and job security was generally high. Still, most unionized workers lived in only 10 states and companies in some areas of union strength, such as the Northeast, were moving jobs to states in the South, where unions were weak.

28-2d *Political Pluralism*

Economic growth also gained credit for producing political stability. After the conflicts of the 1930s, the disruptions during the Second World War, and the Great Fear of the early

Joe Munroe/Science Source

28.4 Turning Deserts into Cropland
California's 153-mile-long Friant-Kern Canal, one of many projects of the Army Corps of Engineers, allowed farmers to cultivate water-intensive fruit and other crops. Huge irrigation projects, financed by the federal government, turned dry western lands into farming areas but also carried long-term environmental implications for water tables and soil quality.

cold war period, the 1950s seemed an era of relative tranquility. An increasingly prosperous nation, most observers agreed, would effectively mute social conflict and eventually help solve major problems. The future, according to one prominent sociologist, would see the end of clashing political ideologies.

According to this dominant viewpoint, which political scientists called "pluralism" (or "interest-group pluralism"), American politics featured a roughly equal bargaining process among well-organized interest groups. John Kenneth Galbraith coined the term "countervailing power" when claiming that labor unions, consumer lobbies, farm organizations, and other groups could check the desires of giant corporations. No single group could dictate terms to the others, celebrants of political pluralism claimed, because so many interests felt so securely empowered. Pluralists shrugged off signs of decline in political participation, clearly evident in how few people cast ballots on election days, by arguing that voter behavior showed widespread satisfaction with how well the process of political pluralism worked.

In addition to praising the process, pluralists praised the results. Short-term conflicts over specific issues would never disappear, but America's growing economy would continue to help moderate political passions and point warring interests toward agreement on fundamental arrangements. As a professor at Harvard Law School put it, constant economic growth meant that "in any conflict of interest," it was "always possible to work out a solution" because an expanding economy guaranteed that any settlement would leave all interests "better off than before."

28-2e A Religious People

Most observers professed an analogous faith in religious pluralism. Congress, as part of the crusade against "atheistic communism," constructed a nondenominational prayer room on Capitol Hill; added the phrase "under God" to the Pledge of Allegiance; and declared the phrase "In God We Trust" as the nation's official motto. In the view of pluralists, intense religious allegiances no longer divided people as much as in the past. President Eisenhower declared that "our government makes no sense unless it is founded in a deeply felt religious faith—and I don't care what it is."

Religious leaders echoed the theme of pluralism. Will Herberg's *Protestant–Catholic–Jew* (1955) argued that these three faiths were really "saying the same thing" in affirming the "spiritual ideals" and "moral values" of the American way of life. The rabbi who headed the Jewish Chaplain's Organization reassured Protestants and Catholics that they and their Jewish neighbors shared "the same rich heritage of the Old Testament... the sanctity of the Ten Commandments, the wisdom of the prophets, and the brotherhood of man." A 1954 survey claimed that more than 95 percent of the population identified with one of the three major faiths, and religious commentators praised how the "Judeo-Christian tradition" enriched American life.

This tradition could also produce religious celebrities. The Baptist evangelist Billy Graham achieved superstar status during the 1950s. Norman Vincent Peale, a minister in the Reformed Church of America, sold millions of books which declared that belief in a higher power could bring "health, happiness, and goodness" to daily life. His most famous volume, *The Power of Positive Thinking* (1952), remained a best seller throughout the 1950s. The Catholic bishop Fulton J. Sheen moved from radio to TV during the 1950s, and won an Emmy Award for hosting a prime-time program entitled *Life Is Worth Living*.

Peale, Sheen, and Graham generally identified their religious ideals with conservative, anticommunist causes, but an emphasis on religious faith could be found all across the political spectrum. Dorothy Day, a Catholic who had been involved in community activism since the early 1930s,

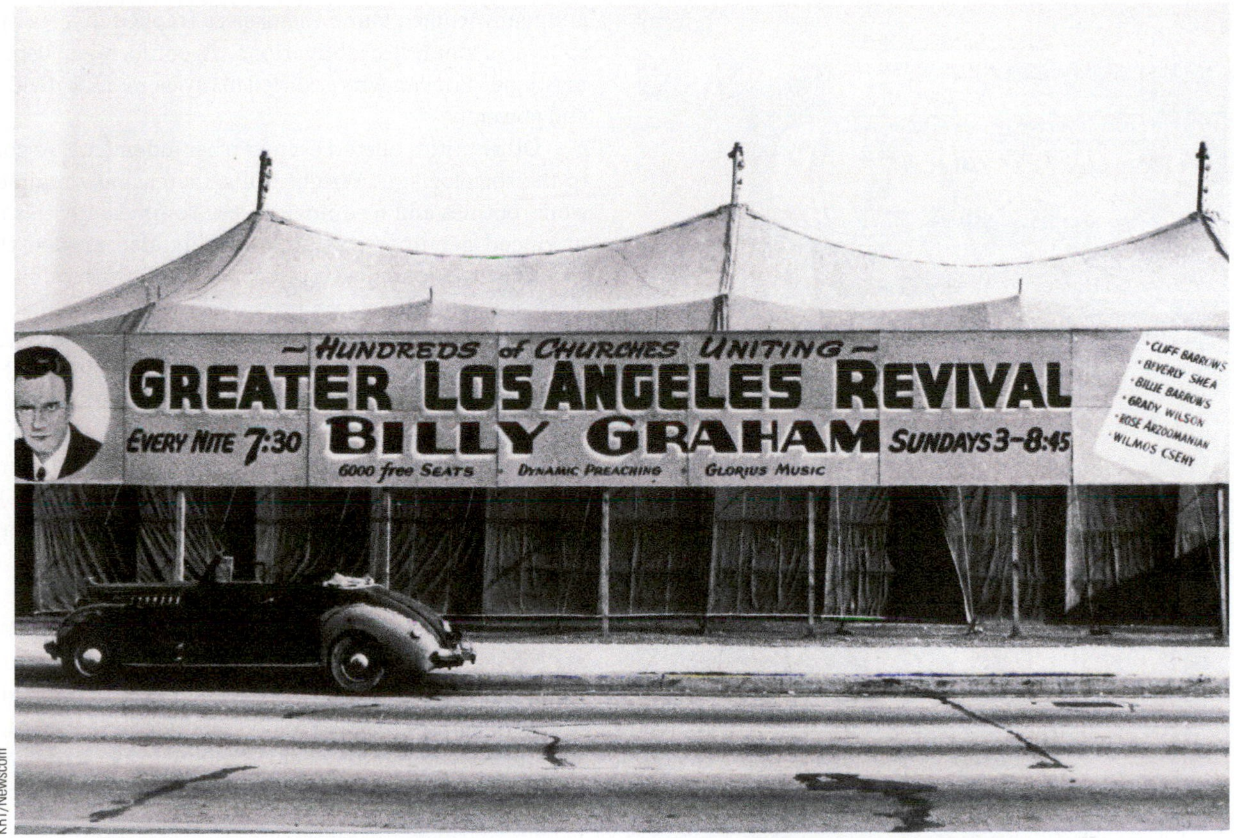

KRT/Newscom

28.5 **Southern Baptist Evangelist** Billy Graham's 1949 revival debut in Los Angeles attracted such large crowds that it gained Graham nationwide attention and launched his career as America's leading evangelical minister and adviser to presidents.

continued to crusade for world peace and for domestic programs aimed at redistributing wealth. Leaders from all three major religions supported civil rights efforts. Billy Graham, for example, refused to preach to racially segregated audiences.

28-3 Discontents of Affluence

Q *Why did an affluent society generate social criticism during the 1950s and early 1960s?*

Alongside the celebration of economic growth, there were widely expressed fears about the impact of the new material bounty and about the celebration of economic growth, political pluralism, and religious faith. Much of the discontent revolved around several interrelated issues: the alleged threats posed by conformity, restive young people, and mass culture; the persistence of discrimination; and the effects of socioeconomic inequality.

28-3a *Conformity in an Affluent Society*

The least tangible concern involved "conformity." Affluence appeared to be undermining the nation's tradition of individualism, a peril most evident in the new suburbs. Suburbanites, according to a popular protest song, lived in "little boxes" that all "looked just the same." Working in the same satirical vein, the comedian Mort Sahl pioneered a form of stand-up comedy that lampooned people who were filling their "little boxes" with piles of consumer goods. Hi-fi speakers were becoming so large, according to one of his routines, that people might soon be living inside them and converting their house into part of their sound system.

Male social comics such as Mort Sahl implicitly identified their routines with other cultural critics. J. D. Salinger's iconic novel *Catcher in the Rye* (1951) takes a tragicomic look at Holden Caulfield, a rebellious high school student, who decries the conformists and "phonies" that he feels crush his spirit. *Rebel without a Cause* (1955) featured James Dean as another high school rebel who challenges a conformist adult world that is "trying to kill me," at least emotionally. The movie sympathetically portrays how growing up in the new suburbia of the 1950s could produce an understandable restiveness that adults too often mistook for "juvenile delinquency."

In *The Organization Man* (1956), the sociologist William H. Whyte, Jr., indicted corporate culture for also contributing to conformity. Whyte saw corporate employees deferring to the dictates of their bosses at the expense of their own wishes and values. Journalist Vance Packard's best-selling *The Hidden Persuaders* (1957) criticized the advertising industry's calculated appeals to the insecurities of consumers for encouraging conformist behavior. David Riesman, another

28.6 **Split-Level Living** This 1960 cartoon, by the *Washington Post's* "Herblock" (Herbert Block), illustrates the growing critique of Eisenhower era social policy. While suburbanites enjoy new affluence in a split-level home, public services and distressed people remain underfunded.

Q *How does Herblock use suburban affluence to critique rather than celebrate the era?*

Q *How might political cartoons be useful to those studying the past?*

sociologist, offered a broader critique of conformity in *The Lonely Crowd* (1950). This book envisioned a shift from an "inner-directed" culture, in which people looked to themselves and their immediate families for their sense of identity and self-worth, to an "other-directed" one, in which people looked to others for approval and increasingly measured their worth against mass cultural imagery. *The Lonely Crowd* claimed that *Tootle the Engine*, a popular children's book, was part of the mass culture that taught baby boomers conformist values. After Tootle shows a preference for jumping the rails and frolicking in the fields, intense pressure from his community gets him "back on the tracks." If he remains on the straight and narrow, following lines laid down by others, a bright future seems assured.

Critics such as Whyte, Packard, and Riesman highlighted signs of conformity among middle-class white men, but Betty Friedan warned about an analogous malaise among white women. Top business executives expected middle-class wives to help their husbands deal with the demands of corporate life, and many women found themselves trapped in a stultifying sphere of domestic obligations. A conformist "feminine mystique," Friedan wrote, stifled many women's individuality and power.

Other critics offered even harsher judgments. According to the sociologist C. Wright Mills, increasingly regimented work routines and meaningless leisure-time activities rarely produced genuine satisfaction. Mills also argued that a "power elite"—composed of corporate executives, military planners, political leaders, prominent academics, and media celebrities—set the agenda for public policy discussions. This undemocratic group dominated decisions about national security matters and domestic spending priorities.

The "Beat movement," a loosely connected group of writers and poets, denied that either affluence or conventional spiritual ideals of the 1950s provided fulfillment. The Beats claimed that consumer goods and technology condemned most people to wander through alienated lives feeling oppressed, emotionally crippled, or just plain bored. Beat writers such as Jack Kerouac, author of *On the Road* (1957), praised nonconformists for challenging settled routines and seeking more instinctual and sensual ways of living. Beat poet Allen Ginsberg's *Howl* (1956) decried soulless materialism and puritanical moral codes. Ginsberg celebrated the kind of personal freedom that he found in drugs, mysticism, and same-sex love affairs.

28-3b *Restive Youth*

The restiveness among many young people drew attention. *Seduction of the Innocent* (1954), by the psychologist Frederick Wertham, blamed comic books featuring images of sex and violent crime for stimulating social unrest and juvenile delinquency. Responding to legislation by some U.S. cities and to calls for federal regulation, the comic book industry drafted its own self-censorship code. Publishers who followed the code's guidelines for portraying violence and deviant behavior could display a seal of approval. The "great comic book scare" soon faded away.

Other worrisome signs persisted, however. In 1954, Elvis Presley, a former truck driver from Memphis, enjoyed a string of "rock 'n' roll" hits on the tiny Sun record label. Presley's sensual, electric stage presence thrilled his young admirers and outraged critics. Presley and other youthful exponents of fifties rock—including Buddy Holly from West Texas, Richard Valenzuela (Richie Valens) from East Los Angeles, Frankie Lymon from Spanish Harlem, and "Little Richard" (Penniman) from Georgia—leaped over cultural and ethnic barriers. They reshaped older musical forms, especially African American rhythm and blues and the "hillbilly" music of southern whites, into new sounds. Rock 'n' rollers claimed to sing about the hopes and fears of the millions of their young fans. They celebrated the joy of "having a ball tonight"; decried the pain of the "summertime blues"; complained about the torment of being "a teenager in love"; and preached the promise of deliverance, through the power of rock, from "the days of old."

Songs such as "Roll over Beethoven" by Chuck Berry became powerful teen anthems.

Guardians of more genteel cultural forms denounced rock 'n' roll as an assault on the very idea of music. Even its name, these critics complained, brazenly appealed to raging teenage hormones. Religious groups denounced rock as the "Devil's music"; anticommunists detected a covert Red strategy to corrupt youth; and segregationists saw rock as part of a plot to encourage "race-mixing." The dangers of rock 'n' roll seemed on display in *The Blackboard Jungle* (1955), a movie about a racially mixed group of sexually active students who defy adult authority and terrorize high school classrooms. Rock 'n' roll music spoke, however, to the concerns of its young fans. Chuck Berry's "School Days" challenged pieties about the benefits of schooling, as he sang of bored teenagers riding around "with no particular place to go." This kind of social criticism in songs anticipated the more overtly rebellious music of the 1960s.

At the same time, rock music and the larger youth culture of the 1950s merged into that era's general affluence. Sun Records, lacking sufficient capital to distribute Presley's hits and promote his image, sold his contract to RCA. Colonel Tom Parker, his personal promoter, soon had the Elvis brand affixed to everything from 45 rpm records to Hollywood musicals. Record companies and the new Top 40 radio stations saw teenagers, with their part-time jobs and their own allowances, as a market segment worth targeting. They promoted performers who exalted the pursuit of "fun, fun, fun," which apparently required the latest in "cool" clothes, late-model automobiles, and rock 'n' roll records.

Bettmann/Corbis

28.7 **Elvis Presley** Raised in interracial neighborhoods in the South, Elvis Presley drew on his familiarity with blues, gospel, hillbilly, and pop music traditions to become the premier rock 'n' roll star of the 1950s.

Q *How might this glamour photo of young Elvis have stoked fears among adults already inclined to dread the arrival of rock 'n' roll's raucous sound? How might he look threatening?*

28-3c *The Critique of Mass Culture*

Concern about conformity and youth culture figured in the broader **mass-culture critique** of the 1950s. Anxiety about the decline of individualism and the rise of disruptive young people became linked to fears that the "hidden persuaders" of the commercial culture industry could reach millions of people with standardized imagery and messages. Critics worried that "bad" art—seemingly evident in comics and rock 'n' roll—would eventually purge anything "good" from the cultural marketplace. They further warned that the superficial imagery manufactured for a "mass" national audience could wipe out vibrant local and regional traditions.

Network television, dominated by three large corporations (NBC, CBS, and ABC) and sustained by advertising revenue, provided a prominent target for this mass-culture critique. Picturing millions of passive viewers gathered around "the boob tube," critics decried both the quality and the presumed impact of mass-produced TV programming. By the late 1950s, the television networks were stocking their prime-time hours with western-themed series (about a mythical Old West) and staged quiz programs (whose contestants had been supplied the answers that they pretended to be puzzling over). Independent stations without network ties programmed the cultural leftovers: ancient B movies from Hollywood's vaults, cheaply produced adventure series, and amateurish local programming. The head of the Federal Communications Commission (FCC) would soon denounce TV as a "vast wasteland."

Critics also disliked how the "boob tube" changed the fabric of everyday life. Architects rearranged living space so that the TV set could become the focal point of home life. New products—such as the frozen TV dinner, the TV tray, the recliner chair, and *TV Guide* magazine—became extensions of television culture.

The mass culture that critics decried, however, was embedded within the economic system and the pluralist political process they celebrated. If, for example, Congress legislated against "dangerous" comic books, its censorship might end up curtailing free expression. If local communities were to step in, the results might be even worse. The prospect of southern segregationists confiscating civil rights literature, or local censorship boards banning books by celebrated authors or "art films" from Europe, hardly appealed to the cosmopolitan critics of mass culture. Their extensive critique seemed short on solutions and offered nothing to halt the flood of consumer products and forms of entertainment aimed at an never-expanding popular audience.

28-4 Debating the Role of Government

Q *What were the major contending arguments over the proper role of government in the 1950s?*

Although Eisenhower occasionally hinted that he favored rolling back the New and Fair Deals, he actually presided over a modest expansion of earlier initiatives: a broader Social Security system, a higher minimum wage, better unemployment benefits, and a new Department of Health, Education, and Welfare (HEW). Eisenhower liked to call his approach "modern Republicanism."

28-4a *The New Conservative Critique*

Eisenhower's brand of Republicanism angered members of a political movement eventually called the "new conservatism." It drew its energy from Republicans who conceded Eisenhower's popularity but questioned his commitment to core GOP principles. Eisenhower appeared to be allowing too many congressional Republicans to cross the aisle and support Democratic-backed spending programs.

Arizona's Senator Barry Goldwater emerged as the key political spokesperson for the new conservatism. After he won a second term in the U.S. Senate in 1958, a year when several other prominent GOP conservatives lost, a national magazine hailed him as "The Glittering Mr. Goldwater." A slim, ghostwritten book, *The Conscience of a Conservative* (1960), summarized Goldwater's critique. By refusing to take stronger military measures against the Soviet Union and by not making "victory the goal" of U.S. policy, Eisenhower was endangering the nation's security. Goldwater portrayed most domestic programs, including those supported by Eisenhower, as threats to individual liberty and as steps toward national bankruptcy. The GOP needed a clean break from the Democratic Party's "New Deal antics" and Ike's "dime store New Deal," the senator charged.

For economic ideas, the new conservatism looked to Europeans, such as Friedrich von Hayek, and to their American disciples, particularly Milton Friedman. Once a Keynesian, the quick-witted, fast-talking Friedman had later reoriented his economic ideas in a libertarian direction. Governmental action, he argued, generally interfered with self-correcting marketplace forces and thus generated additional problems rather than genuine solutions. When government absolutely needed to act, as it should have done more forcefully during the Great Depression, its touch must be as light as possible. Friedman's impressive list of popular and scholarly publications showed that he could write as clearly, and as quickly, as he spoke. Headquartered at the University of Chicago, he helped symbolize a persistent pattern: Economists generally sympathetic to Keynesianism tended to migrate to institutions on either coast, while those embracing more free market approaches generally gravitated toward the heartland.

Meanwhile, Friedman's eventual ally, the author-publisher William F. Buckley, Jr., was framing a broad ideological platform for the new conservatism. In *God and Man at Yale* (1952), the devoutly Roman Catholic Buckley attacked what he saw as a "collectivist" and anti-religious tilt in higher education. A second book, *McCarthy and His Enemies* (1954), defended the controversial senator. Then, in 1955, Buckley began his most ambitious enterprise: a new conservative magazine, the **National Review**. This publication avoided the anti-Semitism of some old-line conservatives and adopted an organizational strategy for the long run. To this end, Buckley joined other conservatives in establishing Young Americans for Freedom (YAF) in 1960, several years before similar college-based political organizations emerged on the political left.

Buckley's group adopted another long-term approach to building a conservative movement, "fusionism." The *National Review* featured a creative tension that fused three broad constituencies: "traditionalist" conservatives, who insisted that social stability depended on the educated, talented few, such as themselves, dominating the nation's institutions; "libertarians," who favored drastically limiting the power of government; and staunch anticommunists who endorsed unleashing U.S. military power against the Soviets.

The *National Review* attracted an eclectic group of writers who collaborated on developing ideas that could shape the new conservatism. Any program for coexistence with communism, according to the magazine's manifesto, was "neither desirable nor possible, nor honorable." Excessive "bipartisanship" was robbing politics of necessary conflict, while "Big Brother government" and "union monopolies" were threatening economic freedom. The *National Review* also sought to cover cultural affairs from a conservative perspective that made "excellence (rather than 'newness')" and "honest intellectual combat (rather than conformity)" its watchwords.

A zest for cultural combat animated other conservative projects. The writer Ayn Rand's fierce brand of secular libertarianism and commitment to sexual experimentation made her unwelcome at the staid *National Review.* Her novel *Atlas Shrugged* (1957), however, confirmed Rand's iconic status among libertarians, who endorsed her call for ignoring any "public good" and for advancing, instead, one's own self-interest. A number of conservative groups spread the religious ideals that Rand ridiculed. The Campus Crusade for Christ urged college students to live according to traditional religious ideals and to preach this message among their peers. Clarence Manion, a prominent Catholic Democrat, developed a forceful conservative presence on the radio dial, *The Manion Forum,* and helped spearhead an effort to draft Barry Goldwater to run as Eisenhower's successor in 1960.

Goldwater's western brand of conservatism spread across the new suburbs of the Sun Belt states. Many suburban conservatives derived their family incomes from high-tech jobs in the military-related sector and called for increased federal spending on national defense. On domestic issues, however, these "suburban warriors" championed a vision of more limited government and denounced "outside" authorities, both state and national, for infringing on the liberty and power of their local communities.

28-4b *The Case for a More Active Government*

While the new conservatism argued for scaling back the domestic role of government, a diverse group urged expanding the national government's reach, at home as well as overseas. When unemployment shot up during an economic downturn in 1958–1959, Keynesian economists ridiculed Eisenhower's commitment to a balanced budget. They called for greater government spending, even a temporary deficit, to stimulate economic activity. Even after economic conditions improved, Keynesians such as John Kenneth Galbraith and Paul Samuelson urged significant deficit spending as a spur to greater growth. During the 1950s, Samuelson's textbook (or a less-demanding knockoff) became the standard choice for younger college professors who taught introductory economics.

Other members of this group also criticized Eisenhower's national security policies for their timidity. The **Gaither Report** urged an immediate increase of about 25 percent in the Pentagon's budget. Prepared by analysts with ties to the defense industry and links to NSC-68 (see Chapter 27), the Gaither Report also endorsed building fallout shelters, developing intercontinental ballistic missiles (ICBMs), and expanding conventional military forces.

Eisenhower reacted cautiously. Keeping his defense budget well below the levels critics proposed, he even reduced the size of several army and air force units. As a consequence of super-secret U-2 surveillance flights over the Soviet Union, Eisenhower knew that the Soviets were lagging behind, rather than outpacing, the United States in military capability. Their missile program, he also learned, featured a few well-publicized successes but many unreported problems.

Concerns about national security and calls for greater government spending also affected U.S. educational policies. Throughout the 1950s critics complained about schools imparting "life-adjustment" skills instead of teaching traditional academic subjects. The best-selling *Why Johnny Can't Read* (1956) anticipated books that asked why Johnny and his classmates couldn't add or subtract very well either, and why they lagged behind their counterparts in the Soviet Union in science. These critics urged more funding for public schools. Simultaneously, the nation's leading research universities sought greater federal aid for higher education, and prominent scientists urged expanded government funding for basic scientific research. The case for increased spending suddenly became more compelling when, in October 1957, the Soviets launched the world's first artificial satellite—a 22-inch sphere called *Sputnik* (Russian for "satellite") that circled the earth, initially accompanied by a "beep beep" soundtrack, for nearly three months.

A ***Sputnik* crisis** gripped Washington when a second Soviet satellite, carrying a dog, went into orbit in early November. The missile technology that lifted up the *Sputniks*, argued Eisenhower's critics, could eventually rain down nuclear weapons on U.S cities. The United States needed, therefore, to expand its military arsenal, educational resources, and research capabilities.

After the *Sputniks*, new appeals to "national security" and "national defense" cleared the way for federal money to flow more freely to educational institutions. The National Defense Education Act of 1958 funneled financial aid to university programs in science, engineering, foreign languages, and the social sciences. This act marked a milestone in overcoming congressional opposition to federal funding of education, especially from southerners who feared that economic aid could increase pressure for racial integration.

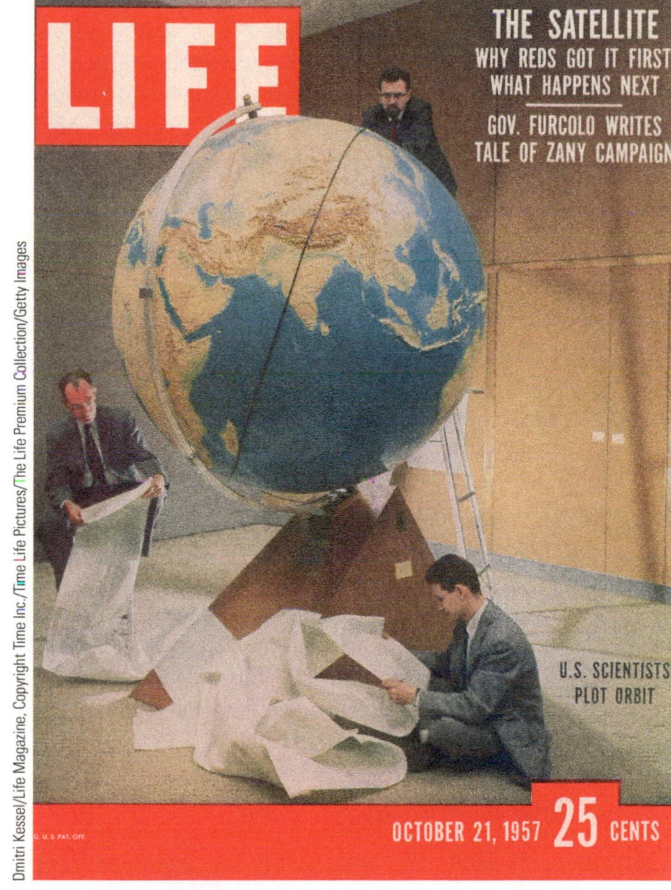

28.8 **U.S. Scientists Plot Orbit** In October 1957, the Soviets launched *Sputnik*, the first satellite to orbit the earth and a major achievement for the Soviet Union. U.S. scientists took measure of the achievement; popular magazines featured stories about how the "Reds got it first"; and Americans scanned the nighttime skies for a glimpse of the light refracted by the large Soviet rocket that had propelled *Sputnik* into space.

Q *How might the fear that the United States could lose the "space race" have influenced the debate over the proper role of government in the 1950s and early 1960s?*

The Soviets' apparent superiority in satellite technology also fueled an ambitious R&D effort overseen by a new National Aeronautics and Space Administration (NASA).

John Kenneth Galbraith spoke for those who hoped that domestic social welfare programs would become similar beneficiaries of increased federal spending. He saw a dangerous tilt in the "social balance" away from "public goods." Affluent families could vacation in their new automobiles, but they needed to pass through shabby cities along litter-filled roadsides. The researcher who improved automobile performance was well rewarded. But anyone "who dreams up a new public service" is accused of wasting tax dollars, Galbraith's book sardonically noted.

Galbraith's critique seemed mild when compared to that of the socialist writer Michael Harrington. His passionate writings about economic inequality, especially *The Other America* (1962), recalled the radical literature of the 1930s and his own apprenticeship at Dorothy Day's *Catholic Worker* during the early 1950s. At least one-third of the nation's people—living in rural areas, small towns, and cities—barely subsisted in a land of supposed abundance. Avoiding detached economic analysis, Harrington crafted dramatic stories about how poverty ravaged the health and spirit of people whose lives had been largely untouched by the economic growth of the post-Depression era. Americans and their politicians who celebrated affluence, Harrington charged, should be ashamed of ignoring such glaring economic inequalities. During the early 1960s, when addressing social and economic issues became a legislative priority, Galbraith and Harrington would become political celebrities. They had first entered the public arena, however, through the critical culture of the 1950s.

28-5 New Frontiers, 1960–1963

Q *How did the administration of John F. Kennedy both continue and refashion the policies of the Eisenhower administration?*

By 1960, the chance to revive the spirit of New Deal liberalism seemed at hand. The elections of 1958 had deposed some conservative Republican stalwarts and emboldened politicians sympathetic to more energetic government. One of these was John Fitzgerald Kennedy.

28-5a *The Election of 1960*

A wealthy, politically ambitious father had groomed John Fitzgerald Kennedy for the White House. The young Kennedy graduated from Harvard University, won military honors as a naval officer during the Second World War, became a representative from Massachusetts in 1946, and captured a Senate seat in 1952. Kennedy became better known for his social life than his command of legislative details, but he parlayed charm and youthful good looks into political stardom. His 1953 marriage to Jacqueline Bouvier added another dash of glamour. A favorite of the media herself, Jackie won plaudits for her cultural taste, stylish dress, and fluency in several languages.

Often accompanied by his family, John F. Kennedy (JFK) began barnstorming the country. His presidential campaigning, along with a talented staff and his family's vast wealth, helped Kennedy overwhelm two Democratic challengers, Senators Hubert Humphrey of Minnesota and Lyndon Johnson of Texas, two stalwarts of New Deal liberalism. By pledging to separate his Catholic religion from his politics and by directly confronting those who appealed to anti-Catholic prejudice, Kennedy defused the religious issue that had doomed the candidacy of Al Smith in 1928 (see Chapter 24). Despite chronic and severe health problems, which his entourage concealed, Kennedy projected personal vigor and energy, if not much experience in directing affairs of state.

Vice President Richard Nixon, running for the Republicans, defied easy labeling. The new conservatives hardly needed to be reminded of Nixon's anticommunist credentials, but his record during the Eisenhower administration, particularly on civil rights, appeared that of a modern Republican. Indeed, Democrats with suspicions about Kennedy's priorities could arguably insist that Nixon's stand on policy issues hardly differed from that of JFK.

Nixon spent much of the 1960 presidential campaign on the defensive. Eisenhower would likely have run for a third term were it not for the Twenty-second Amendment, and he appeared unenthusiastic about Nixon's candidacy. Nixon himself seemed notably off-balance during the first of several televised debates in which a tanned, relaxed Kennedy emerged, according to surveys of TV viewers, with a clear victory over a pale, nervous Nixon. Radio listeners, in contrast, awarded Nixon no worse than a draw.

Kennedy's 1960 campaign highlighted issues from the 1950s that, taken together, became the agenda for his **New Frontier**. Although Senator Kennedy's civil rights record had been mixed, candidate Kennedy declared support for new legislation and, in an important symbolic act, dispatched aides to Georgia to assist the civil rights leader Martin Luther King, Jr., who was facing jail time for a minor traffic violation. Kennedy also endorsed new social programs to rebuild rural communities, increase educational opportunities, and improve urban conditions.

Kennedy's New Frontier included two other concerns rooted in the critical culture of the 1950s—promoting greater economic growth and conducting a more aggressive foreign policy. Kennedy suggested using tax cuts and deficit spending to juice the economy. He also criticized Eisenhower for failing to rid the hemisphere of Castro in Cuba and for allowing a "missile gap" to develop in the arms race with the Soviet Union. By spending more on national security, Kennedy claimed, he could create a more "flexible response" against communism, especially in the Third World. "Flexible response" became the umbrella term to cover a wide range of military and nonmilitary strategies for use overseas. The "American people are tired of the drift in our national course ... and ... they are ready to move again," Kennedy proclaimed.

Kennedy defeated Nixon by only about 100,000 popular votes, and his victory in the Electoral College rested on razor-thin margins in several states, including Illinois. Republicans urged their candidate to challenge Kennedy's suspicious vote total there, but Nixon chose to accept the disputed result. JFK's triumph owed a considerable debt to his vice presidential running mate, Lyndon Baines Johnson, whose regional appeal helped the Democratic ticket carry the Deep South and his home state of Texas. The Democratic Party, however, failed to duplicate its successes of 1958 and lost 20 seats in the House of Representatives and 1 in the Senate (see Map 28.2).

Supporters of the new president forgot about the closeness of his election, as JFK and Jackie, already first name celebrities, riveted media attention on the White House. The couple hobnobbed with movie stars and hosted prominent intellectuals. Kennedy's inauguration featured designer clothing, a poignant appearance by the aged poet Robert Frost, and an oft-quoted speech in which JFK challenged people to "ask not what your country can do for you; ask what you can do for your country."

28-5b *Foreign Policy, 1960–1963*

Implementing flexible response gained Kennedy's immediate attention. Although Secretary of Defense Robert McNamara found that the missile gap never existed, the Kennedy administration boosted the defense budget anyway. It

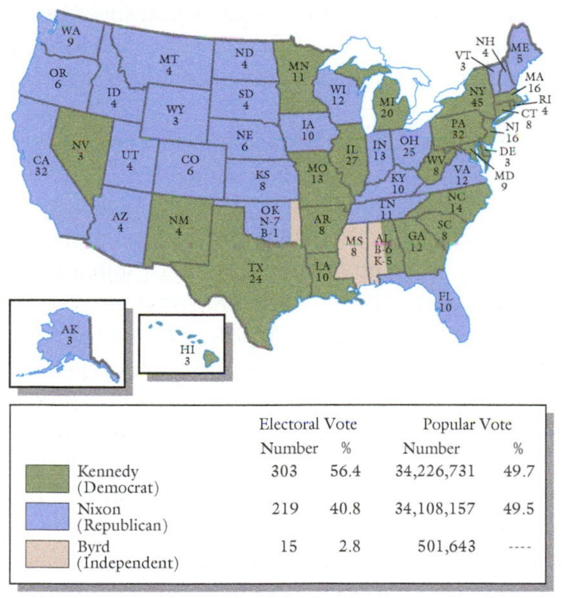

	Electoral Vote		Popular Vote	
	Number	%	Number	%
Kennedy (Democrat)	303	56.4	34,226,731	49.7
Nixon (Republican)	219	40.8	34,108,157	49.5
Byrd (Independent)	15	2.8	501,643	----

▲ **MAP 28.2 Presidential Election, 1960** In one of the closest elections in American history in terms of the popular vote, Kennedy only narrowly outpolled Nixon.

Q *How might Kennedy's commanding victory in the electoral vote help supporters claim that his presidency represented an important turning point in U.S. history? At the same time, how did this victory also generate debate about the consequences of the Electoral College one day producing a president who had failed to carry the popular vote, a situation that did happen in 2000 and 2016?*

supported military assistance programs, propaganda agencies, and covert-action plans. In one of his most popular initiatives, the president created the Peace Corps, a volunteer program that sent Americans, especially young people, to nations around the world to work on development projects that might undercut communism's appeal.

Eisenhower's effort to reorient U.S.–Latin American policy away from dictators and toward socioeconomic programs was repackaged as Kennedy's "Alliance for Progress." Unveiled in spring 1961 in hopes of checking the spread of insurgencies that looked to Fidel Castro for inspiration, the Alliance promised $20 billion in loans over a 10-year period to Latin American countries that would undertake land reform and economic development.

28-5c *Cuba and Berlin*

The first misstep of the Kennedy presidency, an ill-conceived 1961 CIA mission against Cuba, also had its roots in the Eisenhower administration. The CIA had been secretly planning an invasion to oust Fidel Castro. Overriding the doubts of key advisers, Kennedy approved this Eisenhower-era plan. On April 17, 1961, however, when U.S.-trained forces (mainly anticommunist Cuban exiles) landed at the Bahia de Cochinas (Bay of Pigs) on the southern coast of Cuba, the expected popular uprising against Castro failed to materialize. Instead, forces loyal to the Cuban revolution quickly surrounded and captured members of the mission. Kennedy rejected any additional steps, including the air strikes that the Cuban exiles had expected, and initially denied any U.S. involvement in this **Bay of Pigs invasion**. The CIA's role quickly became public knowledge, however, and anti-U.S. sentiment swept across Latin America. Castro tightened his grip over Cuban life and strengthened his ties to the Soviet Union.

Kennedy responded by calling the Bay of Pigs invasion a mistake—and by devising a new, covert program called "Operation Mongoose." It abandoned the idea of an invasion in favor of destabilizing Cuba's economy and, in concert with organized crime figures, trying to assassinate the Cuban leader.

Tensions between the United States and the Soviet Union increased as well. In June 1961, Nikita Khrushchev and Kennedy met in Vienna, Austria, where the Soviets proposed ending the Western presence in Berlin and reuniting the city as part of East Germany. Kennedy refused to abandon West Berlin, but in August 1961 the communist regime began to erect a barbed wire fence and then a concrete barrier to separate East from West Berlin. This Berlin Wall became a symbol of communist repression. Kennedy's assertion in a 1963 speech, "*Ich bin ein Berliner* (I am a Berliner)," delivered in front of the wall to a cheering crowd of West Berliners, provided a memorable image of JFK's presidency.

Superpower confrontation, however, had already escalated to a potentially lethal level during the **Cuban Missile Crisis** of October 1962. The Soviet Union, responding to pleas from Castro, sent sophisticated armaments to Cuba. After U-2 spy planes revealed missile-launching sites in Cuba, the Kennedy administration declared it would never allow the Soviet Union to place nuclear warheads so close to U.S. soil. It demanded that the Soviets dismantle the missile silos and turn back supply ships heading for Cuba. After tense strategizing sessions with his top advisers, Kennedy rejected a military strike against Cuba, fearing it might lead to war with the Soviet Union. Instead, he ordered the navy to "quarantine" Cuba. The Strategic Air Command went on full alert for a possible nuclear conflict. Both sides also began frantic, secret diplomatic maneuvers to forestall such a catastrophe.

The showdown ended after 13 anxious days. On October 28, 1962, Khrushchev ordered the Soviet missiles in Cuba dismantled and the supply ships brought home; Kennedy promised not to invade Cuba and secretly assured Khrushchev that he would complete a previously planned withdrawal of U.S. missiles from Turkey. When Soviet archives were opened in the mid-1990s, people learned that the Cuban Missile Crisis had been even more dangerous than earlier imagined. Unknown to the Kennedy administration in 1962, the Soviets had already placed tactical nuclear weapons, which could have reached U.S. targets, inside Cuba. Some historical evidence suggests Castro favored atomic conflict over diplomatic concessions.

The Cuban Missile Crisis underscored the peril of nuclear conflict and made the two superpowers more cautious. To prevent a future confrontation or an accident, they established a direct telephone hot-line between Moscow and Washington, D.C.

28-5d *Southeast Asia and Flexible Response*

In Southeast Asia, Kennedy retained the goal of preserving a noncommunist state in South Vietnam. After the Bay of Pigs debacle, in which the overthrow of an already established communist government had failed, JFK became determined to prevent any communist-led "war of national liberation" from toppling a noncommunist regime.

Even so, the odds against nurturing a pro-U.S. government in South Vietnam seemed to grow longer as Kennedy's own presidency lengthened. Opposition to the regime of Ngo Dinh Diem, in power since the mid-1950s, had now coalesced in the National Liberation Front (NLF). Formed in December 1960, the NLF included noncommunist groups that resented Diem's dependence on the United States; communists who demanded more extensive land reform; an array of political leaders fed up with Diem's corruption and cronyism; and groups directly beholden to Ho Chi Minh's communist government in the North. North Vietnam continued sending supplies and troops to the South in support of the anti-Diem coalition.

The Kennedy administration saw Vietnam as the crucial test case for flexible response. It dispatched the Green Berets, elite U.S. troops who were trained in "counterinsurgency" tactics, to aid the South Vietnamese government. It also sent teams of social scientists, charged with "nation building," to consult on socioeconomic reforms and internal security. Finally, JFK dispatched U.S. combat troops. These forces, numbering nearly 24,000 by late 1963, would supposedly only advise, but were soon actively fighting alongside South Vietnam's forces.

South Vietnam still lacked a credible government. Diem's decision, in May 1963, to fire on Buddhist demonstrators in the city of Hue prompted confrontations between protestors and his government. In support of the anti-government effort, several Buddhist monks committed suicide by setting fire to their robes. The Kennedy administration recognized these self-immolations as a sign of the deep-seated opposition to Diem—and as a public relations disaster. The Kennedy administration signaled to South Vietnam's powerful military that U.S. support for Diem was nearing its end.

28-5e *Domestic Policy, 1960–1963*

Kennedy's domestic agenda initially received far less attention than his foreign policy initiatives. Conservative Republicans and southern Democrats retained enough clout in Congress to stall or vote down proposals with which they disagreed. Despite his lengthy service in Congress, Kennedy seemed uncertain about how to deal with its old-line leadership and sided with advisers who urged a go-slow approach. This strategy meant that Kennedy did not press for the government-spending measures he had promised would speed economic growth. He feared any action that might unbalance the federal budget and thus alienate fiscal conservatives and business leaders.

In 1962, the White House finally asked Congress to lower tax rates as a means of stimulating economic growth. Kennedy argued that lower tax rates, along with special deductions for businesses that invested in new plants and equipment, would produce more jobs and greater growth. Despite opposition from fiscal conservatives and from Keynesians who thought Kennedy's proposal tilted toward corporations and the wealthy, the president's tax bill slowly moved through Congress.

On social welfare issues, the Kennedy administration proposed a higher minimum wage and new urban rebuilding programs. It also supported directing federal grants and loans to impoverished areas such as Appalachia, the 13-state region running along the Appalachian Mountain chain from southern New York to northern Mississippi.

28-6 The Politics of Gender

Q *How did social, economic, and cultural forces work to change gender roles during the 1950s and early 1960s?*

The 1950s and early 1960s saw significant changes in how and where people lived and worked. This era produced especially important changes in the everyday politics of gender.

28-6a *The New Suburbs and Gender Politics*

In middle-class homes, especially in the new suburbs, women discovered the ambiguous impact of technological change. The time that women spent on domestic duties was not reduced so much as shifted to new activities requiring new household gadgets like automatic clothes washers and more powerful electric vacuum cleaners.

Life in the new suburbs, moreover, was structured by a broad pattern of "separate spheres": a public sphere of paid work and politics dominated by men, and a private one of unpaid housework and child care reserved for women. Because relatively few businesses initially located in the new suburbs, men commuted from home to work, while women found employment opportunities about as scarce as professional child-care facilities. Mothers thus spent considerable time tending to their baby boomer children. In contrast to the urban neighborhoods or small-town communities where many suburban housewives had grown up, newly constructed suburbs contained few older relatives or single women who could help with household and child-care duties.

Without mothers or grandmothers living close by, young suburban mothers often turned to child-care manuals for advice. The various editions of *Baby and Child Care* (1946), written by Dr. Benjamin Spock, sold millions of copies. Like earlier advice books, Spock's assigned virtually all child-care duties to women and implied that the family and the nation itself depended on how well mothers looked after the baby boom generation.

An alarmist tone in these books reflected—and helped generate—a widespread concern about juvenile delinquency. A problem teen, according to one study, sprang from a "family atmosphere not conducive to development of emotionally well-integrated, happy youngsters, conditioned to obey legitimate authority." The ideal mother devoted herself to rearing her children. Women who sought careers outside of the home and marriage risked being labeled as maladjusted and deviant—real-life versions of the *femmes fatales* who populated *film noirs* (see Chapter 27).

Variations on this message appeared nearly everywhere. Even the nation's prestigious women's colleges assumed their graduates would pursue men and marriage. In a 1955 commencement address at Smith College, Adlai Stevenson, the Democratic Party's urbane presidential aspirant, reminded graduates of their "duty" to keep a husband "truly purposeful, to keep him whole." Popular magazines, psychological literature, and pop-culture imagery suggested that wives and mothers held the keys to social stability. This meant that women who desired alternative arrangements, either in their work or their sexual preferences, needed to be pressured, much as in *Tootle the Engine*, to return to the straight and narrow.

Competing portraits, however, painted a somewhat more complicated picture of gender arrangements. Most men told researchers that they preferred an "active partner" to a "submissive, stay-at-home" wife. Popular TV shows, such as *Father Knows Best* and *Leave It to Beaver*, suggested that fathers should be more engaged in family life than they seemed to be. Parenting literature, while envisioning suburban husbands earning their family's entire income, increasingly urged them to be "real fathers" at home and emphasized family togetherness. Institutions such as the Young Men's Christian Association (YMCA) offered courses on how to achieve it.

This call for family togetherness was partly in response to what cultural historians now see as an incipient "male revolt" against the "male breadwinner role." Hugh Hefner's *Playboy* magazine, which debuted in 1953, epitomized this trend. It ridiculed men who neglected their own happiness in order to support a wife and children as suckers rather than saints. *Playboy*'s first issue proclaimed: "We aren't a 'family magazine.'" In Hefner's version of the good life, a man rented a "pad" rather than owned a home, drove a sports car rather than a station wagon, and admired the Playmate of the Month rather than the Mother of the Year.

28-6b *Signs of Women's Changing Roles*

Meanwhile, greater numbers of women were working outside the house. Female employment, even among married women, rose steadily as jobs expanded in the clerical and service sectors. In 1948, about 25 percent of married mothers worked outside the home; at the end of the 1950s, nearly 40 percent did. With the 1960 introduction of a new method of oral contraception, the birth control pill, women could exercise greater control over family planning and career decisions—and over decisions about their own sexual behavior. By 1964, one-quarter of the couples that used contraception relied on "The Pill." At the same time, activists began to press for an end to state antiabortion laws that restricted the ability of women to find legal and relatively safe ways to terminate pregnancies.

Employment opportunities still remained circumscribed. Virtually all of the nation's nurses, telephone operators, secretaries, and elementary school teachers were women. Historically, pay scales in these areas lagged behind those for men in occupations that required comparable training. Jobs for women in the unionized job sectors remained rare. And chances for advancement in the corporate field were similarly limited. As the number of low-paying jobs for women expanded during the 1950s, better-paying professional opportunities actually narrowed. Medical, law, and other professional schools admitted lower percentages of women than in the past. When Sandra Day (who would later become the U.S. Supreme Court Justice Sandra Day O'Connor) graduated with honors from a prestigious law school during the 1950s, not a single private firm offered her a job. She worked, without pay, in the public sector. The number of women on college faculties shrank even from the low levels of earlier decades.

Although employers still invoked the "family wage" ideal to justify higher pay for men, more women than ever before were trying to support a family on their own paychecks. This was especially true for women of color. Recognizing that images of domesticity hardly fit the lives of many African American women, *Ebony* magazine celebrated black women who combined success in parenting and at work.

Mass-circulation magazines aimed at women of European descent also carried increasingly mixed messages about gender roles. Although social commentators commonly labeled a woman's pursuit of activities outside the home as "unnatural," popular magazines increasingly featured stories about women in public life and in business. The 1950s, in short, saw growing diversity in both the social roles that women were assuming and the ways in which mass culture represented them.

28-6c *A New Women's Movement*

The seeds of a resurgent **women's movement** were also being sown between 1953 and 1963. All across the political spectrum, women began speaking out on contemporary issues. The energy of women such as Phyllis Schlafly, whose book *A Choice, Not an Echo* (1964) became a leading manifesto from the political right, helped fuel the new conservatism. African American activists such as Bernice Johnson Reagon (whose work with the Freedom Singers combined music and social activism) and Fannie Lou Hamer (who spearheaded the organization of a racially integrated Freedom Democratic Party in Mississippi) fought discrimination based on both race and gender. Women union leaders pushed for greater employment opportunities and more equitable work environments. Chicana farmworkers became key figures in union-organizing efforts in California. Women also played a central role in protests, through organizations such as the Committee for a Sane Nuclear Policy (SANE) and the Women's Strike for Peace, against the U.S.–Soviet arms race. During Kennedy's final year in office, Betty Friedan published *The Feminine Mystique*. Widely credited with helping to revive organized feminist activity in the United States, Friedan's book drew on her own social criticism from the late 1950s and articulated the dissatisfaction that many middle-class women felt about the narrow confines of domestic life and the lack of public roles available to them.

To address women's concerns, Kennedy appointed a Presidential Commission on the Status of Women, chaired by Eleanor Roosevelt. After negotiating differences between moderate and more militant members, the commission issued a report that documented discrimination against women in employment and wages. Kennedy responded with a presidential order to eliminate gender discrimination within the federal civil service. He also supported the Equal Pay Act of 1963, which made it a federal crime for employers to pay lower wages to women who did the same work as men.

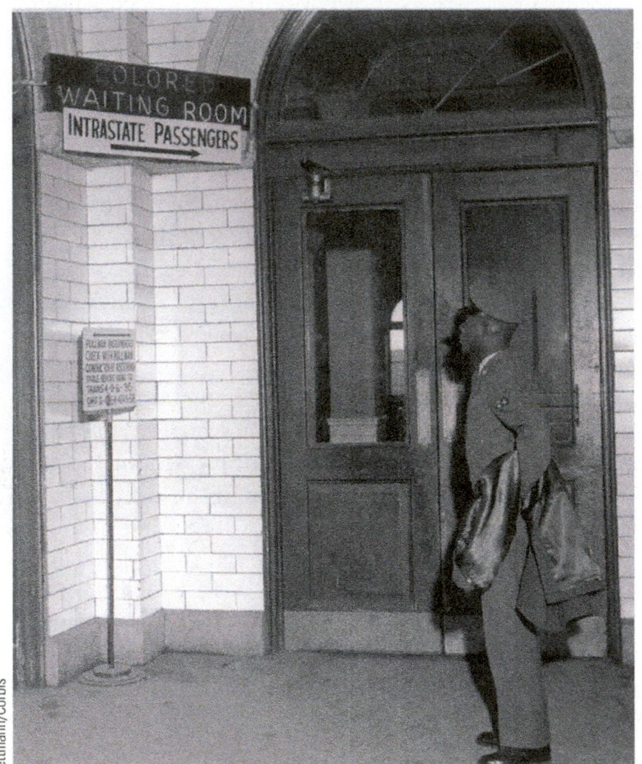

Bettmann/Corbis

28.9 Segregation Dressed in his air force uniform, a young man from New York City confronts a "colored waiting room" in an Atlanta bus terminal in 1956. Before the civil rights revolution of the 1960s, southern states maintained legally enforced segregation in most public facilities, the practice popularly called Jim Crow (see Chapter 18).

Q *How did America's increasingly global role help undermine the policy of legal segregation at home?*

28-7 The Expanding Civil Rights Movements, 1953–1963

Q *Why did the new movements to expand and enforce civil rights become such a central part of politics in the 1950s and 1960s?*

When Dwight Eisenhower took office in 1953, the U.S. Supreme Court was preparing to rehear a legal challenge to racially segregated educational systems. The NAACP and its chief legal strategist, Thurgood Marshall, spearheaded this effort. Before the rehearing took place, Eisenhower appointed Earl Warren, a former Republican governor of California, as chief justice. The Supreme Court, with Warren in its center chair, became a crucial force in the expanding civil rights struggle.

28-7a *The Brown Cases, 1954–1955*

The Supreme Court litigation popularly known as "the *Brown* decision" actually included a series of constitutional rulings, the ***Brown* cases**. In 1954, Chief Justice Warren wrote a unanimous opinion (in *Brown* v. *Board of Education of Topeka*) declaring that states could not segregate their public schools on the basis of race without violating the constitutional right of African American students to equal protection of the law. A companion case decided the same day (*Bolling* v. *Sharpe*) outlawed racially segregated schools in the District of Columbia. Although the *Brown* and *Bolling* decisions technically applied only to schools, they suggested that other segregated public facilities could no longer survive constitutional challenge. In 1955, though, a follow-up Supreme Court decision, known as "*Brown II*," decreed that the process of dismantling illegally segregated school systems should not go into effect immediately; desegregation could, instead, move forward "with all deliberate speed."

Implementing the *Brown* cases challenged the nation's political, social, and cultural institutions. The politics of civil rights sometimes seemed focused on the 16 states that the Census Bureau officially called "the South," but demographic changes helped make civil rights more than a regional phenomenon.

During the 1950s the South was becoming more like the rest of the country. Network television penetrated the region. Machines were displacing the region's fieldworkers, most of whom were black. The absence of strong labor unions and the presence of favorable tax laws encouraged northern-based businesses to move south. National chain stores, unaccustomed to state segregation laws elsewhere in the country, extended throughout the South.

Meanwhile, the racial composition of cities in the West, Midwest, and Northeast became more like that of the South. In 1940, more than three-quarters of the nation's African Americans lived in the South, many on farms and in small towns. During and after the Second World War, much of this population left the rural South and became important to political life in northern urban areas, where Republicans joined Democrats in generally supporting efforts to end racial discrimination. As more African Americans voted Democratic, however, the GOP gained ground among white voters in the South and in the new suburban neighborhoods, especially in the Middle and Far West.

The most familiar stories about civil rights activities during the 1950s have long concentrated on the South, but recent histories emphasize how the struggle increasingly became nationwide in scope. Efforts to end segregation and racial discrimination emerged in virtually every northern and western city. These urban-based movements employed a variety of tactics, such as "shop where you can work" campaigns, which urged black consumers to patronize only businesses that would employ them. They tried to bring more workers from non-European backgrounds into the union movement and the public service sector, enlarging jobs in police and fire departments as well as in all of the agencies of state and local government. Increasingly, though, gaining legal-constitutional leverage seemed crucial to future successes.

As African Americans mounted new attacks on segregation and discrimination in the South, white segregationists pledged "massive resistance" to the *Brown* decisions and went to court with delaying tactics. One hundred members of Congress signed a "Southern Manifesto" in 1956 that condemned the Supreme Court's desegregation rulings as a "clear abuse of judicial power" and pledged support for any state that intended "to resist forced integration by any lawful means."

Bettmann/Getty Images

28.10 **A Bus Left Empty by the Montgomery Bus Boycott, 1955-56** This boycott proved to be a galvanizing moment in the fight against state enforced racial segregation.

Q *How does this iconic photograph dramatize the everyday dynamic of this ultimately successful local movement?*

Defiance went beyond the courtroom. White vigilantes unfurled the banners of the Ku Klux Klan and formed new racist organizations, such as the White Citizens Council. People who worked in the civil rights cause constantly risked injury and death. Racial tensions escalated. In August 1955, two white Mississippians murdered 14-year-old Emmett Till, a visitor from Chicago, because they thought he had been "disrespectful" toward a white woman. Mamie Till Bradley insisted that her son's death not remain a private incident. She demanded that his maimed corpse be displayed for "the whole world to see" and that his killers be punished. When their case came to trial, an all-white Mississippi jury quickly found the two men—who would subsequently confess their crime to a magazine reporter—not guilty.

28-7b *The Montgomery Bus Boycott*

The southern civil rights movement increasingly supplemented legal maneuvering with direct action. Following an earlier, partially successful 1953 campaign to desegregate the transportation system in Baton Rouge, Louisiana, activists in Montgomery, Alabama, raised their sights. After police arrested Rosa Parks for defying a segregation ordinance that required segregated seating on municipal buses, Montgomery's black community came to demand complete desegregation, boycotted public transportation, and organized carpools as alternative transit. Joining with Rosa Parks, a longtime bastion of the local NAACP chapter, many other black women in Montgomery helped coordinate the complicated, months-long boycott. Responding to events in Montgomery, the Supreme Court extended the premise of the *Brown* decisions on education and specifically declared segregation of public buses to be unconstitutional.

The year-long Montgomery bus boycott ended in victory. City officials, saddled with financial losses and legal defeats, agreed to end Montgomery's separatist transit policy. Events in Montgomery suggested that black activists, even in the segregated South, could effectively mobilize—and then organize—community resources to fight racial discrimination.

The bus boycott vaulted **Dr. Martin Luther King, Jr.**, one of its leaders, into the national spotlight. Born and educated in Atlanta, with a doctorate in theology from Boston University, King and other black ministers followed up the victory in Montgomery by forming the Southern Christian Leadership Conference (SCLC). In addition to demanding desegregated public facilities, the SCLC sought to organize an ongoing sociopolitical movement that would work for other changes.

The young, male ministers in the SCLC sought assistance across generational and gender divides. Tapping the strategic wisdom of Bayard Rustin, who had been involved in civil rights activism since the 1940s, and the tactical skills of Ella Baker, another veteran organizer, Dr. King led the SCLC's effort to register African American voters throughout the South.

King and the SCLC relied on civil disobedience to obtain change. Nonviolent direct action would dramatize, through both word and deed, the evil of racial discrimination. King's powerful presence and religiously rooted rhetoric carried the message of civil rights to most parts of the United States and the world.

28-7c *The Politics of Civil Rights: From the Local to the Global*

All across the country, civil rights activities went forward. Shortly after the conclusion of the Montgomery bus boycott, New York City passed the nation's first "open housing" ordinance, a model for other local and state measures aimed at ending racial discrimination in the sale and rental of homes and apartments. Efforts to change housing patterns faced tough going, however. Typically, white homeowners in those urban and older suburban neighborhoods where African Americans or Latinos might hope to buy or rent adopted the exclusionary strategies used so effectively by their counterparts in the new suburbs.

Outside the South, civil rights groups also sought legislation to outlaw racial discrimination in hiring. In 1958, for example, a labor union–civil rights coalition in California, joining under slogans such as "Fight Sharecropper Wages," defeated an anti-union right-to-work proposal it said threatened to drive down pay rates for all workers. Buoyed by this success, the same coalition began lobbying members of the California legislature to enact a statewide open housing measure (see Map 28.3).

Political institutions in Washington, D.C., felt similar pressure to act on civil rights. With southern segregationists, all members of the Democratic majority, holding key posts on Capitol Hill, antidiscrimination measures faced formidable obstacles. Nevertheless, Congress did pass its first civil rights measures in more than 80 years. The **Civil Rights Act of 1957** expedited lawsuits by African Americans who claimed that southern states were systematically abridging their right to vote. The law also created a Commission on Civil Rights, an advisory body empowered to study alleged violations and recommend remedies. In 1960, with the crucial support of Lyndon Johnson of Texas, the Democratic leader in the Senate, a second civil rights act added more procedures to safeguard voting rights. These civil rights measures became law against fierce opposition from southern Democrats and conservative Republicans such as Barry Goldwater.

President Eisenhower initially hesitated to use his executive powers to aid civil rights efforts. He did support the Civil Rights Act of 1957 but held back when some Republicans urged a dramatic presidential step—such as barring racial discrimination on all construction projects financed by federal funds. Eisenhower saw ending racial segregation as a slow process, viewed desegregation as primarily a local matter, and doubted that federal power could change the attitudes of people opposed to integration.

In 1957, however, events in Little Rock, Arkansas, left Eisenhower no choice but to enforce a federal court decree

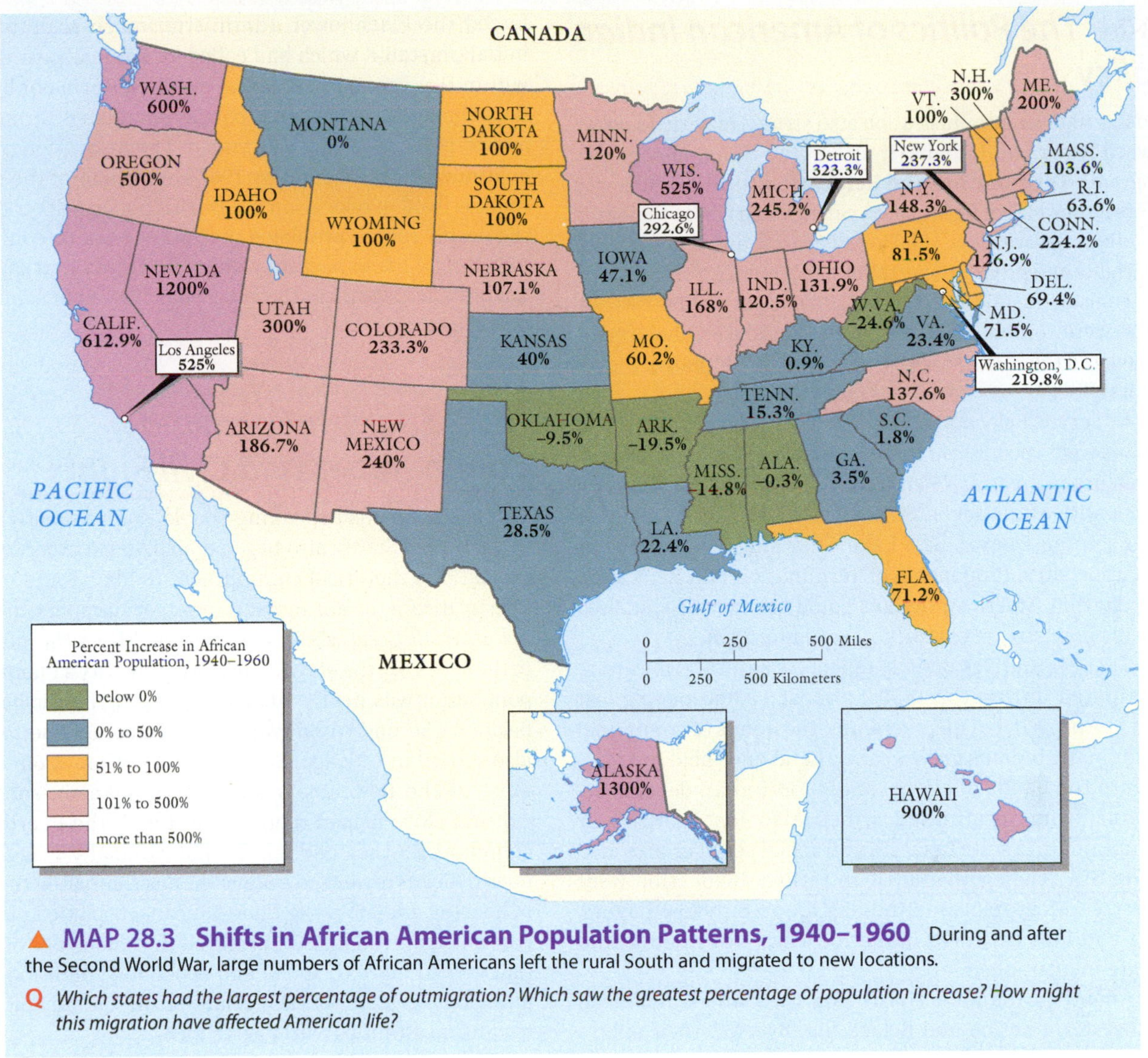

▲ **MAP 28.3 Shifts in African American Population Patterns, 1940–1960** During and after the Second World War, large numbers of African Americans left the rural South and migrated to new locations.

Q *Which states had the largest percentage of outmigration? Which saw the greatest percentage of population increase? How might this migration have affected American life?*

ordering the desegregation of the city's Central High School. Orval Faubus, the state's segregationist governor, promised to prevent black students from entering the school building and deployed his state's National Guard to block them. Confronting this direct challenge to national authority, Eisenhower took command of the Arkansas National Guard and augmented it with members of the U.S. Army. Black students, protected by armed troops, finally entered Central High. The primary issue at stake, Eisenhower insisted, was a state's defiance of a federal court order rather than school desegregation.

The confrontation in Little Rock also underscored the international dimension of civil rights politics in the United States. Washington often found itself on the defensive when foreign critics pointed to the U.S. record on civil rights. The Soviet Union delighted in telling people, particularly in the Third World, how racial discrimination showed "the façade of the so-called 'American democracy.'" When the U.S. Supreme Court, in *Cooper* v. *Aaron* (1958), unanimously invalidated an Arkansas law intended to block school integration, the Eisenhower administration's global informational campaign stressed this decision as a good example of America's support for liberty and equality.

During the 1950s the State Department sent Dizzy Gillespie, Louis Armstrong, Duke Ellington, and many other African American jazz musicians as "goodwill ambassadors" to build more cordial relationships with new states in Africa and Asia. These tours presented jazz as a uniquely American art form that symbolized freedom, and sought to counter Soviet charges by highlighting the accomplishments of African Americans. America's cultural diplomacy, in fact, encouraged racially integrated musical acts to perform abroad—even though they might have been unwelcome in many venues at home. Racial discrimination and conflict, warned Secretary of State Dulles, was "not helpful to the influence of the United States abroad." The cold war's battle for hearts and minds throughout the world provided yet another kind of pressure on behalf of civil rights efforts.

28-7d The Politics of American Indian Policy

The Eisenhower administration also struggled with its policy toward American Indians. It attempted to implement two programs, **Termination and Relocation**, already under way before it took office. Termination called for an end to the status of Indians as "wards of the United States" and a grant of all the "rights and privileges pertaining to American citizenship." The goals of Termination, to be pursued on a tribe-by-tribe basis, were to abolish reservations, liquidate tribal assets, and curtail the social services offered by the Bureau of Indian Affairs (BIA).

Under the Relocation program, which had begun in 1951, Indians were encouraged to leave rural reservations and seek jobs in urban areas. In 1954, the BIA intensified its relocation efforts, with Minneapolis, St. Louis, Dallas, and several other cities joining Denver, Salt Lake City, and Los Angeles as relocation sites. Proponents of Termination and Relocation insisted that American Indians could easily be assimilated into the mainstream of U.S. life (see Figure 28.3).

These initiatives quickly failed. As several tribes were terminated during the 1950s, almost 12,000 people lost their status as tribal members, and the bonds of communal life for many Indians grew weaker. Land once held by tribes fell into the hands of commercial, non-Indian developers. Indians from terminated tribes also lost both their exemption from state taxation and social services provided by the BIA. They gained little in return. Relocation went no better. Most relocated Indians found only low-paying, dead-end jobs and discrimination from both public and private institutions.

American Indian activists and their allies mobilized against Termination and Relocation. By 1957, their efforts forced the Eisenhower administration to scale back the initial timetable, which had called for liquidating every tribe within five years. In 1960, the party platforms of both the Republican and Democratic parties repudiated Termination, and in 1962 the policy was ended. The Relocation program continued, however, and by 1967 almost half of the nation's Indians lived in relocation cities. This policy neither touched the deeply rooted problems that many Indians confronted, including a life expectancy only two-thirds that of whites, nor provided significantly better employment or educational opportunities.

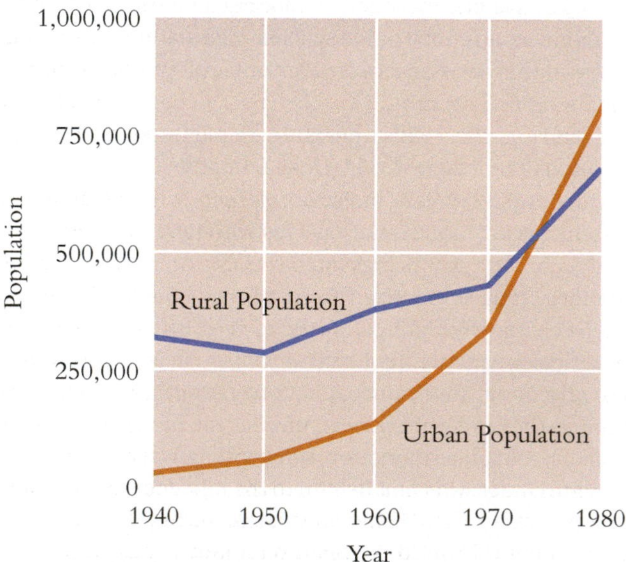

Figure 28.3 **Total Urban and Rural Indian Population in the United States, 1940–1980**

28-7e Spanish-Speaking Communities and Civil Rights

Millions of Spanish-speaking people, many recently arrived in the United States, also began mobilizing in order to realize the nation's rhetorical commitment to liberty and equality. Puerto Ricans began moving in larger numbers than ever before from their island commonwealth to the mainland in the 1950s. By the early 1960s, New York City's Puerto Rican population was nearly 100 times greater than it had been before the Second World War. Large numbers of Puerto Ricans also settled in Chicago, Boston, and Hartford, Connecticut. Most of the newcomers spoke only Spanish; social and cultural clubs helped them connect with the Puerto Rican communities they had left behind. Officially U.S. citizens, Puerto Ricans organized against the discrimination they faced in housing and jobs. The Puerto Rican–Hispanic Leadership Forum, organized in 1957, presaged the emergence of groups that looked more to social and economic conditions—and, ultimately, greater political clout—in the United States than to cultural affinities with Puerto Rico.

Spanish-speaking people from Mexico were continuing to move to California and states in the Southwest, where they joined long-established Mexican American communities. In 1940, Mexican Americans had been the most rural of all the major ethnic groups; by 1950, in contrast, more than 65 percent of Mexican Americans were living in urban areas, a figure that would climb to 85 percent during the 1960s. Mexican Americans were becoming a political force in many southwestern cities and an important constituency for the national Democratic Party.

Beginning in 1942 and continuing until 1967, the U.S. government sponsored the *bracero* (or farmhand) program, which brought nearly 5 million Mexicans northward to fill agricultural jobs. Many *braceros* and their families remained in the United States after their work contracts expired. Legal immigrants from Mexico joined them, as did undocumented immigrants, who became targets of a government dragnet called "Operation Wetback." ("Wetback" was a term of derision, implying a person of Mexican descent had illegally crossed the Rio Grande River to reach the United States.) During a five-year period the government claimed to have rounded up and deported to Mexico nearly 4 million undocumented immigrants. This operation, critics charged, helped stigmatize U.S. citizens of Mexican heritage and justify further discriminatory treatment.

As a result, civil rights groups representing Mexican Americans intensified earlier mobilization efforts. Labor organizers sought higher wages and better working conditions in the factories, fields, and mines, even as the FBI labeled their efforts "communist inspired" and harassed unions with large Mexican American memberships, such as the United Cannery, Agricultural, Packing, and Allied Workers of America (UCAPAWA). A lengthy mining strike in New Mexico became the subject of the independent motion picture *Salt of the Earth* (1954). Pressure from Washington, the film industry, and anticommunist labor unions throughout the 1950s prevented distribution of this collaboration among blacklisted filmmakers, striking miners (many of whom were Mexican American), and their families.

Civil rights organizations such as the League of United Latin American Citizens (LULAC) and the Unity League sought to desegregate schools and other public facilities throughout California and the Southwest. Lawyers for these groups faced a strategic dilemma, since most states classified persons whose ancestors came from Mexico as legally "white." As earlier cases such as *Westminster* had shown (see Chapter 27), school officials in states such as California and Texas cited language deficiencies, rather than race, as justification for segregating students of Mexican descent. The "other white" legal status of Mexican Americans, in other words, complicated the ability of organizations such as LULAC to frame court challenges that could rely on legal precedents involving white-against-black discrimination.

28-7f *Urban–Suburban Issues*

The growth of suburbia during the 1950s helped to highlight urban issues, many of them related to changing racial patterns. Throughout this period, both public and private institutions began shifting their financial resources away from cities, especially away from neighborhoods in which Latinos and African Americans lived. Adopting a policy called **redlining**, banks and other lending institutions generally denied loans for homebuyers and businesses in areas that were labeled "decaying" or "marginal" because they contained aging buildings, dense populations, and growing numbers of people of non-European descent. The Federal Housing Administration (FHA) and other governmental agencies channeled most of their lending activities toward the newer suburbs. In 1960, for example, the FHA failed to put up a single dollar for home loan guarantees in Camden or Paterson, New Jersey—cities in which minority populations were growing—while it poured millions of dollars into surrounding, largely all-white suburbs.

Urban renewal programs, authorized by the Housing Act of 1949 (see Chapter 27), often seemed aimed at "urban removal." Although the law called for "a feasible method for the temporary relocation" of persons displaced, developers generally ignored the requirement. For several decades, the person who directed New York City's vast construction projects, Robert Moses, consistently understated the number of people dislocated by his urban renewal and highway building programs. Defenders of Robert Moses insisted that he pursued a progressive vision that ultimately benefited all New Yorkers, but the costs of progress—and perhaps its benefits—hardly seemed equally shared.

Plans for federally built public housing faltered. Although suburban areas, where land was abundant and inexpensive, seemed the obvious place to locate affordable housing, white homeowners used their political clout and local zoning laws to freeze out government-sponsored housing projects. Private housing interests lobbied to limit the number of public units actually constructed in urban areas and to ensure that they offered tenants fewer amenities, including closets with doors, than could be found in private units. Originally conceived as short-term alternatives for families who would soon move to their own homes, publicly built facilities became stigmatized as "the projects," permanent housing of last resort for people with chronically low incomes.

The urban–suburban policies came under bipartisan criticism. In 1960, both the Democratic and Republican parties pledged to create a new cabinet office for urban affairs and to reconsider how Washington could better address the cycle of continued suburban growth and onrushing urban decay.

28-7g *New Forms of Direct Action, 1960–1963*

Although John F. Kennedy had talked about new civil rights legislation, his administration initially tried to placate the segregationist wing of his Democratic Party. The president and his brother, Robert Kennedy, who had become attorney general, listened sympathetically when J. Edgar Hoover, director of the FBI, falsely warned of continuing ties between Martin Luther King, Jr., and members of the Communist Party. To monitor King's activities, the FBI illegally recorded many of his private conversations and clamped a tight web of surveillance around his every move. King's SCLC also faced another challenge: that from more militant civil rights organizations that favored new forms of direct action.

In early 1960, African American students at North Carolina A & T College in Greensboro sat down at a segregated lunch counter and politely asked to be served in the same manner as white customers. This was the beginning of the **sit-in movement**, a new phase of civil rights activism. In both the South and the North, young demonstrators staged nonviolent sit-ins at restaurants, bus and train stations, and other public facilities. Singing civil rights anthems such as "We Shall Overcome" to inspire solidarity, the sit-in movement encouraged further activism. In 1961, an interracial group from CORE and the Student Nonviolent Coordinating Committee (SNCC), a student-dominated organization that emerged from the sit-in movement, risked racist retaliation by reviving a form of direct action that CORE had first tried

28.11 **The Freedom Singers** Formed in 1962 members of this a capella group took the lead in singing songs, such as "We Shall Overcome," to help boost the spirits of beleaguered young activists and link their generation's activities with the musical culture of the black church. With encouragement from the veteran protest singer Pete Seeger, The Freedom Singers appeared before predominately white audiences at colleges throughout the North and West. The group encouraged students to support the struggle in the South and raised a significant part of SNCC's budget from older sympathizers. Black civil rights leaders in the North sometimes worried that concerts to aid the movement in the South drained attention—and funds—away from their own work in the North.

Q *What role can music play in social movements?*

in the 1940s: "freedom rides" across the segregated South. The new **freedom riders** were challenging the Kennedy administration to enforce federal court decisions that had declared state laws requiring segregation on interstate buses (and in bus stations) to be unconstitutional.

The new grassroots activism forced the Kennedy administration into action of its own. It dispatched U.S. marshals and National Guard troops to protect the freedom riders. It also deployed federal power to help integrate educational institutions in the Deep South, including the University of Mississippi and University of Alabama. In November 1962, Kennedy issued a long-promised executive order that banned racial discrimination in federally financed housing. The following February he sent Congress a civil rights bill that called for speedier trials in cases involving challenges to racial discrimination in voting.

Nearly 1,500 civil rights demonstrations took place across the country the following spring. Protests in the urban Northeast and Midwest generally focused on improving educational opportunities. Most of these called for accelerating school integration plans, but a "Walk to Freedom March" in Detroit attracted more than 125,000 people on behalf of a broad agenda that included job creation and open housing legislation.

Events in the South, however, attracted the most attention. Beginning in the spring of 1963, violent conflict convulsed Birmingham, Alabama. Direct action in this Alabama industrial center, according to Dr. King, was to create a situation "so crisis packed that it will inevitably open the door to negotiation" over desegregation of public facilities. White police officers unleashed dogs and turned high-pressure water hoses on demonstrators, including children. Four young girls were later murdered (and 20 people injured) when white supremacists bombed Birmingham's Sixteenth Street Baptist Church, a center of the local civil rights campaign. After thousands of African Americans rallied in protest—and two more children were killed, this time by police officers—the Kennedy administration could no longer remain outside the struggle. It conceded that images from Birmingham played badly in the international media and among African American communities outside of Alabama.

The determination of Birmingham's civil rights activists created a real-life drama that played to the entire world on television. Kennedy had already used the same medium when pleading for a national commitment to the battle against discrimination. Recent events had raised "a moral issue ... as old as Scriptures and ... as clear as the Constitution." Racial violence was "weakening the respect with which the rest of

28.12 **Racial Conflict in Birmingham** Images such as this 1963 photograph of a confrontation in Birmingham, Alabama, in which segregationists turned dogs on youthful demonstrators, helped rally popular support outside the white South for civil rights legislation. Events in Birmingham also presaged the increasingly violent clashes that would punctuate the efforts to end racial discrimination.

the world regards us," the president insisted in a June televised address.

The White House still hoped to influence the direction and pace of change. It crafted additional civil rights legislation designed to dampen enthusiasm for demonstrations and other forms of direct action. It now called for a ban against racial discrimination in public facilities and housing and for new measures to protect the voting rights of African Americans in the South. The administration soon recognized that its legislative proposals would not derail a **March on Washington for Jobs and Freedom** scheduled for the late summer of 1963, modeled after the earlier march in Detroit and sponsored by a coalition of civil rights and labor organizations. It belatedly endorsed the demonstration.

On August 28, 1963, an integrated group of more than 200,000 people marched through the nation's capital to the Lincoln Memorial. There, Dr. Martin Luther King, Jr., delivered his famous "I Have a Dream" speech. Speakers on that day generally applauded Kennedy's latest initiatives but urged a far broader agenda, including a higher minimum wage and a federal program to guarantee new jobs. Well organized and smoothly run, the event received overwhelmingly favorable coverage from the national media and put additional pressure on the White House and Congress to lend a hand to civil rights efforts.

28-8 November 1963

What important issues were left unsettled at Kennedy's death and would shape the rest of the 1960s?

As fall turned to winter in 1963, the United States confronted major policy issues. They had deep historical roots but now carried special urgency.

28-8a *Policy Choices*

The Kennedy administration continued to puzzle over how to recast Eisenhower's containment policy and execute its own flexible-response approach in Vietnam. U.S. officials gave disgruntled South Vietnamese military officers the green light to orchestrate the overthrow of Diem's regime. On November 2, 1963, Diem was routed from his presidential palace and—despite assurances to the contrary from the coup's leaders—murdered. This coup, which brought a military regime to power in Saigon, bred even greater political instability throughout South Vietnam. The NLF and North Vietnam ratcheted up their military activities.

There were also domestic political dilemmas. Kennedy's tax bill was languishing in Congress. On the civil rights front, the administration renewed efforts to mobilize its political resources on behalf of long-promised congressional legislation. Recognizing that provisions to lessen discrimination in housing would never pass, White House strategists pondered how best to use federal power to eliminate state-sanctioned segregation in the South and to advance a "fair employment" agenda everywhere.

28-8b *The Assassination of John F. Kennedy*

On November 22, 1963, the president was shot dead as his presidential motorcade moved through Dallas, Texas. Vice President Lyndon Johnson, who had accompanied Kennedy to Texas, took the oath of office and rushed back to Washington. Equally quickly, the Dallas police arrested Lee Harvey Oswald and pegged him as JFK's assassin. Oswald had vague ties to organized crime; had once lived in the Soviet Union; and had

History Through Film *JFK* (1991)

Directed by Oliver Stone.
Starring Kevin Costner (Jim Garrison), Tommy Lee Jones (Clay Shaw), Donald Sutherland ("Mr. X"), and Joe Pesci (David Ferrie)

JFK addressed two questions that have intrigued the historical profession and the general public: Did John F. Kennedy fall victim to a lone assassin or a larger conspiracy? How might the course of U.S. history, including the nation's involvement in Vietnam, have been different if Kennedy's presidency had not ended in November 1963?

This movie restages the 1967 criminal prosecution by Jim Garrison, then the district attorney of New Orleans, against Clay Shaw, a local business leader. This real-life court case provides the vehicle for speculating that a shadowy conspiracy—involving government officials, military officers, and business executives—killed Kennedy because of fears he would end the U.S. commitment in South Vietnam.

To dramatize its claims, *JFK* employs numerous cinematic techniques. When showing the famous "Zapruder film," the home movie that provides the most important visual record of Kennedy's shooting, *JFK* inserts simulated, black-and-white images of sharpshooters catching the president in a deadly cross fire. Later, the movie shows a mysterious figure planting the "magic bullet," a nearly pristine projectile the Warren Commission insisted came from the rifle of Lee Harvey Oswald and passed through Kennedy's body, on a hospital gurney.

JFK is vintage Oliver Stone. This controversial filmmaker-historian delights in disrupting dominant narratives about the past. His most successful historical movies—*JFK*, *Platoon* (1986), *Born on the Fourth of July* (1989), *The Doors* (1991), and *Nixon* (1995)—all feature disjuncture and uncertainty. When the Garrison character in *JFK* decides to challenge the official story of the Kennedy assassination, he warns his staff that "we're through the looking glass ... white is black, and black is white."

Warner Bros/The Kobal Collection

28.13 Kevin Costner portrays New Orleans District Attorney Jim Garrison in *JFK*.

Resembling Stone's equally controversial *Natural Born Killers* (1994), *JFK* focuses less on telling a coherent tale than using the film format to suggest tangled relationships between visual imagery and popular perception. The opening sequence of his Kennedy movie bombards the screen with quick-moving, seemingly disconnected imagery. Viewers, as if they themselves are passing "through the looking glass," immediately must struggle to connect the disjointed visual pieces contained in the cinematic puzzle that is *JFK*.

The movie, in this sense, seems more interested in posing, rather than settling, historical questions. Viewers might compare and contrast, for example, how *JFK* uses two very differently composed sequences, featuring performances by two very different character actors (Donald Sutherland and Joe Pesci), to speculate about Kennedy's death. Sutherland's "Mr. X," supposedly an employee in the national security bureaucracy, sees Kennedy's assassination as only one in a long line of "dirty tricks" orchestrated by a military-industrial complex. During a scene shot against the iconography of the nation's capital, Sutherland calmly offers Garrison (and film viewers) a logically ordered, tightly packaged account of Kennedy's assassination. In contrast, the brief sequence featuring Joe Pesci's frenetic David Ferrie—a foot soldier in organized crime and Cuban-exile circles—lacks any coherent center. This real-life character, in contrast to Sutherland's fictional one, warns Garrison that he will never puzzle out Kennedy's death.

JFK, the movie, prompted a massive, congressionally ordered project to safeguard any evidence that might relate to Kennedy's assassination. Will the preservation of these sources ever bring historians any closer to solving, beyond reasonable doubts, Kennedy's assassination? Or, as Joe Pesci's character warns in *JFK*, will historians still confront "a mystery, inside a riddle, wrapped in an enigma"? ■

Photograph by Cecil Stoughton, White House, in the John F. Kennedy Presidential Library and Museum, Boston.

28.14 **JFK and Jackie Arrive at Love Field, November 22, 1963** President Kennedy and the First Lady, often treated in the manner of Hollywood movie stars, carefully orchestrated their public appearances. During Kennedy's final political trip to Texas, he and the First Lady traveled the short distance from Ft. Worth to Dallas by airplane, rather than automobile, as a way of making their arrival, marked by roses for the First Lady, appear more dramatic. Within hours, subsequent photographs of Jacqueline Kennedy would famously show her French-designed pink suit stained with the blood of the slain president, shot down while the presidential limousine passed through Dallas Dealey Plaza.

a bizarre set of political affiliations, including shadowy ones with groups interested in Cuba. He declared his innocence but never faced trial. Jack Ruby, a Dallas nightclub owner, killed Oswald on national television, while the alleged gunman was in police custody. An investigation by a special commission headed by Chief Justice Earl Warren concluded that both Oswald and Ruby had acted alone.

Kennedy's life and presidency remain topics of historical debate and tabloid-style speculation. His assassination still provokes conspiracy theories and controversies. Researchers have provided new details about his poor health, reliance on exotic medications, and dalliances with women—all of which were kept from the public at the time. Historians continue to debate what JFK might have done in Vietnam and on the domestic front had he won the 1964 presidential election.

Conclusion

Tensions with the Soviet Union, which brought the superpowers to the brink of nuclear war during the Cuban Missile Crisis of 1962, dominated national security calculations between 1953 and 1963. The United States stockpiled nuclear weapons, employed new forms of economic pressure, and expanded covert activities. Left-leaning movements in the Third World, particularly in Cuba and Southeast Asia, became of growing concern to policymakers.

At home, the post-1953 decade brought economic growth. New consumer products encouraged talk about an age of affluence but also produced apprehension about conformity, unruly youth, and mass culture. At the same time, the millions of people whom economic prosperity bypassed, and those who faced racial and ethnic discrimination, worked to bring their causes to the center of public debate over the role of government. Critics charged the Eisenhower administration with failing to use governmental power to support civil rights and to promote faster, more equitably distributed economic growth. Although Kennedy also hesitated, the press of domestic events, particularly those associated with civil rights movements, forced him to consider how best to advance the issues of liberty and equality at home. More quietly, a new conservative movement with ideas different from those of Kennedy, and even Eisenhower, was also taking shape.

The years that immediately followed Kennedy's assassination would continue to highlight questions about liberty, equality, and power at home and abroad during an increasingly divisive war.

CHAPTER REVIEW

Review

1. How did the Eisenhower administration retain but also reorient the foreign policy of containment?
2. In what ways did economic growth change American life during the post-1953 decade considering governmental policies, business and labor practices, and the dominant faith in political and religious pluralism?
3. Why did an affluent society generate social criticism during the 1950s and early 1960s?
4. What were the major contending arguments over the proper role of government in the 1950s?
5. How did the administration of John F. Kennedy both continue and refashion the policies of the Eisenhower administration?
6. How did social, economic, and cultural forces work to change gender roles during the 1950s and early 1960s?
7. Why did the new movements to expand and enforce civil rights become such a central part of politics in the 1950s and 1960s?
8. What important issues were left unsettled at Kennedy's death and would shape the rest of the 1960s?

Critical Thinking

1. How did the policies of the Eisenhower and the Kennedy administrations toward the cold war, economic growth, and civil rights show both differences and similarities?
2. Why did rising material well-being (affluence) produce both a celebration of American life and a broad range of critiques?
3. Why does the relatively brief presidency of JFK loom so large in popular memory?

Identifications

Review your understanding of the following key terms, people, and events for this chapter (terms in bold in text are included in the Glossary).

New Look, p. 773
massive retaliation, p. 773
Eisenhower Doctrine, p. 775
Geneva Peace Accords of 1954, p. 775
domino theory, p. 777
military–industrial complex, p. 777
Highway Act of 1956, p. 778
mass-culture critique, p. 783
***National Review*,** p. 784
Gaither Report, p. 785
***Sputnik* crisis**, p. 785
New Frontier, p. 786
Bay of Pigs invasion, p. 787
Cuban Missile Crisis, p. 787
women's movement, p. 790
***Brown* cases**, p. 790
Dr. Martin Luther King, Jr., p. 792
Civil Rights Act of 1957, p. 792
Termination and Relocation, p. 794
redlining, p. 795
sit-in movement, p. 795
freedom riders, p. 796
March on Washington for Jobs and Freedom, p. 797

Suggested Readings

Peter G. Boyle, *Eisenhower* (2005), is a brief biography that can lead readers to the lengthier ones. **Kenneth Osgood, *Total Cold War: Eisenhower's Secret Propaganda Battle at Home and Abroad*** (2006); **Lawrence Friedman, *Kennedy's Wars: Berlin, Cuba, Laos, and Vietnam*** (2002); **Mark Bradley, *Vietnam at War*** (2009); **Nick Turse, *Kill Anything That Moves*** (2013); **Jason Parker, *Hearts, Minds, Voices: U.S. Cold War Diplomacy and the Formation of the Third World*** (2016), and **William J. Rust, *Eisenhower and Cambodia: Diplomacy, Covert Action and the Origins of the Second Indochina War*** (2016) examine foreign policy. **Robert Dallek, *An Unfinished Life: John F. Kennedy, 1917–1963*** (2003), remains the best biography of JFK.

Major trends in economic and social policy-making can be found in the relevant chapters of **G. Calvin Mackenzie and Robert Weisbrot, *The Liberal Hour: Washington and the Politics of Change in the 1960s*** (2008).

On cultural themes, see **Karal Ann Marling, *As Seen on TV: The Visual Culture of Everyday Life in the 1950s*** (1994); **Thomas Doherty, *Cold War, Cool Medium: Television, McCarthyism, and American Culture*** (2003); and **George Marsden, *The Twilight of the American Enlightenment: The 1950s and the Crisis of Liberal Belief*** (2014). On the new conservatism, see **Rick Perlstein, *Before the Storm: Barry Goldwater and the Unmaking of the American Consensus*** (2001); and **Kim Phillips-Fein, *Invisible Hands: The Making of the Conservative Movement from the New Deal to Reagan*** (2009).

For major trends in cultural and gender politics, see **Elaine Tyler May, *Homeward Bound: American Families in the Cold War Era*** (rev. ed., 2008) and **Andrea Carosso, *Cold War Narratives: American Culture in the 1950s*** (rev. ed., 2013). On civil rights, **Taylor Branch, *The King Years*** (2010), distills the author's three-volume study; see also **Matt Garcia, *A World of Its Own: Race, Labor, and Citrus in the Making of Greater Los Angeles*** (2001); **Edward Charles Valandra, *Not Without Our Consent: Lakota Resistance to Termination 1953–59*,** (2006); **Thomas J. Sugrue, *Sweet Land of Liberty: The Forgotten Struggle for Civil Rights in the North*** (2008); and **Brett Gadsden, *Between North and South: Delaware, Desegregation, and the Myth of American Sectionalism*** (2013), a superb local study.

MINDTAP is a fully online personalized learning experience built upon Cengage Learning content. MindTap® combines student learning tools—readings, multimedia, activities, and assessments—into a singular Learning Path that guides students through the course and helps students develop the critical thinking, analysis, and communication skills that are essential to academic and professional success.

29 America during a Divisive War, 1963–1974

29-1 The Great Society

Learning Objective: *Identify the major goals and programs of Lyndon Johnson's Great Society, and assess why they were controversial.*

29-2 Escalation in Vietnam

Learning Objective: *Trace the process by which Lyndon Johnson's decision to enlarge America's military role in Vietnam, although initially popular, came to produce widening dissent.*

29-3 Activism at Home

Learning Objective: *Describe the social movements that emerged during the divisive war in Vietnam. Examine how they sought to change U.S. politics and culture. Assess the relationships between mass media and these movements.*

29-4 1968

Learning Objective: *Outline why historians see the events of a single year, 1968, as pivotal in the larger history of the era of the Vietnam War.*

29-5 Continued Polarization, 1969–1974

Learning Objective: *Trace the sources of the political and cultural turmoil during the late 1960s and early 1970s. Consider President Nixon's law and order stance, social policies, environmentalism, rights-related claims, and economic issues.*

29-6 Foreign Policy in a Time of Turmoil, 1969–1974

Learning Objective: *Explain the Nixon administration's major foreign policy aims, and assess how successful it was in implementing its policies.*

29-7 A Crisis of Governance, 1972–1974

Learning Objective: *Analyze the factors in the early 1970s that prompted a crisis of governance, undermined Richard Nixon's presidency, and forced his resignation.*

Joseph Sohm/Encyclopedia/Visions of America/Corbis

29.1 **The Vietnam War Memorial** This memorial, a kind of "wailing wall" bearing the names of all Americans who died in the Vietnam War, was dedicated on the Mall in Washington, D.C., in 1982.

Q *How does this memorial differ from more traditional war memorials?*

Q *Why might these differences initially have sparked controversy?*

WHAT HAPPENED DURING the years between 1963 and 1974 profoundly affected how Americans viewed most public, and even personal, matters during the next half-century of U.S. history. This tumultuous era, often called "the long Sixties," included a divisive, ultimately failed military intervention in Southeast Asia; a flood of social and regulatory legislation by Washington; sudden reversals in partisan political fortunes that included a Democratic and then a Republican president leaving office less than four years after both had gained overwhelming electoral victories; and new forms of citizen mobilization—including movements on behalf of Black Power, grassroots democracy, and conservatism—that changed the forms and meaning of political activism. Economic signals from this period suggested that the widely shared affluence of the immediate post-World War II era might not continue. Cultural disputes began expanding into heated clashes over the nation's core values. And rising levels of violence, including more assassinations of prominent public leaders, prompted anxiety and different responses.

By 1974, the nation's politics, social fabric, economic health, and culture looked very different from how they had appeared in 1963. ■

CHRONOLOGY

1964	Civil Rights Act of 1964 passes • Congress approves Gulf of Tonkin Resolution • Johnson defeats Barry Goldwater
1965	Congress passes Voting Rights Act • Violence convulses the Watts area of Los Angeles • U.S. role in Vietnam dramatically expands
1966	Supreme Court decides *Miranda v. Arizona* • United States begins massive air strikes against North Vietnam
1967	Mass antiwar demonstrations begin
1968	Tet Offensive begins • Martin Luther King, Jr., and Robert Kennedy assassinated • Civil Rights Act passed • Richard Nixon wins presidency
1969	Nixon announces "Vietnamization" policy • My Lai massacre becomes public
1970	U.S. troops enter Cambodia • Congress creates Environmental Protection Agency • Activists stage first Earth Day
1971	Stagflation upsets U.S. economy • U.S. dollar begins to "float" on world currency markets
1972	Watergate burglars caught inside Democratic headquarters • Nixon crushes George McGovern in presidential election
1973	OPEC oil embargo begins • Paris Peace Accords signed • Supreme Court decides *Roe* v. *Wade* • Special Senate committee begins hearings into "Watergate"
1974	House votes for impeachment and Nixon resigns • Gerald Ford assumes presidency
1975	Saigon falls to North Vietnamese forces

29-1 The Great Society

What were the major goals and programs of the Johnson administration's Great Society and why did these become controversial?

Lyndon Johnson lacked John Kennedy's charisma, but during his long career in Congress he had learned to flatter, cajole, or threaten people until they lent him support. Johnson's skill in gaining congressional funding for building projects boosted Texas cities such as Dallas and Houston, along with much of the Southwest. LBJ himself acquired a personal fortune.

Kennedy's death gave Johnson the opportunity to display his political skills on the presidential stage. Although eager to enact a bold social-economic program, Johnson began cautiously. He asked Congress to honor JFK's memory by addressing three legislative issues proposed by Kennedy's administration: tax cutting, economic inequality, and civil rights.

29-1a *Closing the New Frontier*

Working behind the scenes, Johnson easily secured passage of the Kennedy tax cut. Although analysts still differ in their assessment of the contribution this legislation made to the economic boom of the mid-1960s, it appeared to work. GNP rose 7 percent in 1964 and 8 percent the following year, unemployment dropped, and inflation remained low.

In his January 1964 State of the Union address, Johnson upped the ante on Kennedy's cautious effort to address economic inequality by calling for "an unconditional war on poverty in America." Relentlessly prodded by the White House, Congress soon passed the Economic Opportunity Act of 1964. It created the Office of Economic Opportunity (OEO) to coordinate a multipart program for "eliminating the paradox of poverty in the midst of plenty." The act mandated loans for rural and small-business development; established a work-training program called the Jobs Corps; created Volunteers in Service to America (VISTA), a domestic version of the Peace Corps; provided low-wage, public service jobs for young people; began a "work-study program" to assist college students; and authorized the creation of federally funded social programs to be planned in concert with local community groups.

Johnson also helped push an expanded version of Kennedy's civil rights proposal through Congress. Although championing the measure as a memorial to JFK, LBJ knew that southerners in his own Democratic Party would try to block it. Consequently, he successfully sought Republican support to curtail a southern-led filibuster. Johnson also helped hammer out compromises on several key provisions and reconcile the differing bills enacted by the House and Senate.

The **Civil Rights Act of 1964**, passed in July, strengthened federal remedies, monitored by a new Equal Employment Opportunity Commission (EEOC), against racially inspired job discrimination. The act also prohibited racial discrimination in all public accommodations connected to interstate commerce, such as motels and restaurants. Moreover, Title VII, a provision added during congressional debate, barred discrimination based on sex and became an important legal tool for the reviving women's movement. Although opponents of the 1964 act argued that its extension of federal power violated the Constitution, the Supreme Court, effectively a political ally of Lyndon Johnson during his presidency, curtly rejected the claim.

That same summer, a coalition of civil rights groups recruited nearly a thousand young volunteers for **Freedom Summer**, an effort to register African American voters in Mississippi. During a tension-filled summer, at least six civil rights workers met violent deaths. In the most notorious incident, a conspiracy among Ku Klux Klan (KKK) leaders and law enforcement officers from Neshoba County, Mississippi, led to the brutal murders of three volunteers—James Chaney, Michael Schwerner, and Andrew Goodman. No one was convicted of any crime until 2005, when a Mississippi jury convicted a former KKK leader, by then in his 80s, of manslaughter for participating in the triple killing of 1964.

The New York Times Photo Archives/Redux

The New York Times Photo Archives/Redux Pictures

29.2a (left) and 29.2b (right) **The Presence of Lyndon B. Johnson** Not even the aged and famously loyal Democratic Senator Theodore F. Green of Rhode Island, who headed the Senate Foreign Relations Committee (pictured on the right), could escape the "Johnson Treatment" when President Lyndon Baines Johnson (on the left) decided to apply the pressure through body language.

Q *What might be the advantages and possible limits of this approach to presidential leadership?*

Meanwhile, supporters of Freedom Summer pressed forward, only to see the national Democratic Party reject their grassroots political work. Pressured by LBJ, the 1964 Democratic convention voted to seat Mississippi's "regular" all-white delegates rather than members of a new, racially diverse Mississippi Freedom Democratic Party (MFDP). The regulars had made clear their intention to support the GOP's presidential candidate, but Johnson declined to support the MFDP in hopes of keeping some other southern states in the Democratic camp in the fall election. LBJ's rebuff of the MFDP prompted its leaders, such as Fannie Lou Hamer, to question the president's commitment to their cause.

29-1b *The Election of 1964*

After a bruising battle within GOP ranks, the Republicans nominated Senator **Barry Goldwater** of Arizona, hero of the new conservatism, to challenge Johnson. Goldwater's strategists claimed that a stoutly conservative GOP campaign would attract the vast number of voters who supposedly rejected both Democratic policies and Dwight Eisenhower's "modern Republicanism." Goldwater denounced Johnson's foreign policy for tolerating communist expansion and attacked his domestic agenda, including civil rights, for destroying individual liberties. One of only eight Republican senators who had opposed the 1964 Civil Rights Act, Goldwater condemned the measure as an unconstitutional extension of national power on behalf of the laudable goal of combating discrimination, a matter for state and local governments to address.

The Goldwater campaign quickly fizzled. The Democratic campaign savaged the candidate's policies, his grasp of issues, and even his mental stability. A tendency to make ill-considered remarks already haunted Goldwater. He had suggested that people who feared nuclear war were "silly and sissified." He had wondered out loud if participation in the Social Security program should become voluntary. And his proclamation at the 1964 Republican convention that "extremism in the pursuit of liberty is no vice" and "moderation in the pursuit of justice is no virtue" fed Democratic claims that "extremist" forces on the "radical right" would dominate a Goldwater presidency.

Many modern Republicans deserted Goldwater, who led the GOP to a spectacular defeat in November. Johnson carried 44 states and won more than 60 percent of the popular vote; Democrats also gained 38 seats in Congress.

Vote for
President Johnson
on November 3

Lyndon B. Johnson Presidential Library/Picture Research Consultants & Archives

29.3 **LBJ's 1964 Campaign against Barry Goldwater** In this controversial television ad from the 1964 campaign (available for viewing on the internet), Lyndon Johnson's supporters exploited Republican Barry Goldwater's image as a far-right "extremist" who might take the nation into a nuclear war.

Q *How might historians use political advertising to help understand the dynamics of a particular election—or the mood of a particular era?*

Although the 1964 election boosted support for Johnson's agenda, it also foreshadowed significant political changes. Indeed, during the Democratic primaries of 1964, Alabama's segregationist governor, George Wallace, had run strongly against the president in several states by denouncing any "meddling" by Washington in local affairs. The 1964 election proved the last, until that of 2008, in which the Democratic Party would capture the White House by proposing an expansion in the power of the national government.

Goldwater's defeat invigorated rather than discouraged supporters of the new conservatism. His staff pioneered innovative campaign tactics, such as direct-mail fundraising. By refining these techniques during future campaigns, conservative strategists helped make 1964 the beginning, not the end, of their plan to push the Republican Party, and the country, to the right. Goldwater's continued criticism of the Civil Rights Act of 1964 helped him carry five southern states. These victories—along with Wallace's earlier appeal to "white backlash" voters—suggested that the new conservatism could woo southern whites away from the Democratic Party.

An important electoral issue in California gave conservatives further hope. The Democratic national ticket easily carried the state, but real-estate interests joined with suburban conservatives to sponsor a referendum measure that repealed a recently enacted law prohibiting racial discrimination in the sale or rental of housing. Opponents of this "open housing" measure adopted a political strategy that conservatives would increasingly embrace: downplay racial issues and, instead, denounce governmental regulations for violating the principles of equal rights and individual liberties.

The Goldwater campaign also introduced a new corps of conservative celebrities, many of them from the Sunbelt, to national politics. Ronald Reagan championed the new conservatism so effectively that Goldwater Republicans in California began grooming the former movie and TV actor for a political career. Younger conservatives, such as William Rehnquist and Newt Gingrich, entered the national arena as supporters of Goldwater's vision. Goldwater also enlisted Milton Friedman, the staunchly conservative economist and a critic of Keynesian policies, as an adviser. Historians now credit the Goldwater effort of 1964 with helping to spearhead the overhaul of American conservatism—and the Republican Party.

29-1c *Lyndon Johnson's Great Society*

Lyndon Johnson rushed to capitalize on his electoral victory. Enjoying broad support in Congress, Johnson unveiled plans for a **Great Society**, an array of federal programs designed to "enrich and elevate our national life." Some of the programs fulfilled the dreams of his Democratic predecessors. Nationally funded medical coverage for the elderly (Medicare) and for low-income citizens (Medicaid) grew out of health-care proposals from the New Deal and Fair Deal eras. Similarly, a new cabinet office, the Department of Housing and Urban Development (HUD), built on earlier plans for coordinating urban revitalization programs.

The **Voting Rights Act of 1965**, which created mechanisms for national oversight of state and local elections in the South, capped the long-term effort to eliminate racial and ethnic discrimination, especially sham "literacy tests," from political life. The measure gave the Justice Department broad authority to monitor electoral procedures in jurisdictions with a history of discriminating against African American voters. Modified and extended over the years, the Voting Rights Act came to require ballots printed in languages other than English.

Congress also enacted another milestone measure that addressed matters long discussed—and long avoided. The **Immigration and Nationality Act of 1965** finally abolished the discriminatory "national origins" quota system established in 1924 (see Chapter 24). Henceforth, roughly the same set of rules would apply to people wishing to immigrate to the United States from any part of the world. This change, in practice, would allow the entry of far more people from Asia and Africa than had previously been allowed.

Many of the Great Society's other proposals rested on the midcentury "affluence" that the Johnson administration expected to continue for years to come. Ongoing economic growth could provide the tax dollars to underwrite a bold expansion of national power without any overhaul of fundamental political and economic arrangements.

The array of Great Society initiatives that rolled through Congress during the mid-1960s heartened LBJ's supporters and appalled his critics. The Model Cities Program (1966) offered smaller-scale alternatives to urban renewal efforts. Rent supplements and an expanded food stamp program went to help low-income families. The Head Start Program (1965) provided help for children considered educationally unprepared for kindergarten. Other new federal educational programs aimed to upgrade classroom instruction, especially in low-income neighborhoods, and a legal services initiative provided lawyers to clients who could not afford to hire an attorney. These measures aimed at providing low-income people with the kind of professional expertise, routinely available to the more affluent, that could help them fight their way out of social and economic distress. The Great Society's service-based approach, Johnson insisted, would give people a "hand up" rather than a "handout."

The Community Action Program (CAP) promised a different tack. It authorized local activists, working through neighborhood organizations, to design community-based projects that could gain funding from Washington. By promoting "maximum feasible participation" by ordinary citizens rather than relying on planning experts, the architects of CAP proposed to nurture a grassroots democracy that could revitalize American politics from the bottom up.

29-1d *Evaluating the Great Society*

How did the Great Society become so controversial? Most obviously, the extension of Washington's reach rekindled old debates about the proper use of the power of the national government. In addition, Johnson announced ambitious objectives, such as an "unconditional" victory over poverty, which failed to survive the short-term rhythms of partisan politics. Republicans picked up 47 seats in Congress in the midterm elections of 1966, and the Great Society ideal could never again gain the overwhelming congressional support that it had enjoyed when first announced.

The expectation that continued economic growth would generate tax revenues sufficient to finance new social programs faded. Uncertain economic conditions, exacerbated by the escalating cost of the war in Vietnam, made social welfare measures politically vulnerable. Facing financial worries of their own, people who had been initially supportive of the Great Society became receptive to the claim, first championed by George Wallace and the Goldwater campaign in 1964, that bureaucrats in Washington would waste their hard-earned tax dollars on flawed social experiments.

Historians disagree about the impact of Johnson's programs. Charles Murray's *Losing Ground* (1984) reframed the welfare policy debate by charging that the Great Society encouraged too many people, lured by welfare payments, to abandon the goals of marrying, settling down, and seeking jobs. Money spent on Johnson's programs, moreover, allegedly created government deficits that slowed economic growth. A central text of the new conservatism, Murray's book saw Johnson's Great Society as a cause of, not a solution for, economic distress.

Other analysts rejected this view, especially the claim that most people preferred welfare to meaningful work. Funds actually spent on Great Society programs neither matched Johnson's promises nor reached the lavish levels claimed by the new conservatism. The charge that government expenditures choked off growth ignored the systemic economic problems that emerged in the early 1970s. The data also point toward some successes for Great Society initiatives. Poverty rates fell from 19 percent in 1962 to 10 percent by 1969.

Still, antipoverty activists complained that the Johnson administration failed to challenge the prevailing distribution of political and economic power and favored large-scale bureaucratic solutions forged by power brokers in Washington. The administration jettisoned the CAP model of grassroots empowerment when local politicians began complaining about having to compete for federal funding. The assumption that economic growth would fund the Great Society precluded any serious attempt, such as a revision of the tax code, to redistribute income and wealth.

Washington's financial outlay for domestic programs did increase more than 10 percent during every year of LBJ's presidency. In 1960, federal spending on social welfare constituted 28 percent of total governmental outlays; by 1970, this figure had risen to more than 40 percent. Moreover, Great

Society programs such as Medicaid, legal assistance, and job training gave low-income families access to social services and slightly narrowed the disparity between rich and poor.

From the crucial perspective of political viability, though, the Great Society proved a failure. Opposition to the assumptions and goals of Johnson's Great Society gave new energy to the conservative movement. As support for domestic spending programs waned, even most Democrats hesitated to defend Lyndon Johnson's vision.

29-2 Escalation in Vietnam

Q *Why did Lyndon Johnson's decision to enlarge America's military role in Vietnam, although initially popular, produce widening dissent?*

Lyndon Johnson's divisive crusade to build a Great Society at home found its counterpart abroad. His pledge to protect South Vietnam from communism demanded ever more of the nation's resources, diminished the country's international standing, further polarized its domestic politics, and strained its economy.

29-2a *Implementing the Gulf of Tonkin Resolution*

Immediately after John Kennedy's assassination, Johnson resisted additional support for South Vietnam. His fears of appearing soft on communism, however, soon led him to side with advisers who recommended air strikes against North Vietnam as the necessary first step. Johnson prepared a congressional resolution authorizing this escalation of hostilities.

Events in the Gulf of Tonkin, off the coast of North Vietnam, provided the rationale for taking the resolution to Capitol Hill. On August 1, 1964, the U.S. destroyer *Maddox*, while on an intelligence-gathering mission, exchanged gunfire with North Vietnamese ships. Three days later, the *Maddox* returned with the *Turner Joy* and, during severe weather, reported what seemed to be signs of a failed torpedo attack. Although the *Maddox*'s commander advised that the episode needed further analysis, Johnson immediately denounced "unprovoked aggression" by North Vietnam against the United States. (A later study concluded that there had never been a North Vietnamese attack.) With only two dissenting votes in the Senate, Congress passed the **Gulf of Tonkin Resolution**, which authorized Johnson to take "all necessary measures to repel armed attack."

Johnson immediately began bombing strikes against North Vietnam and used the Gulf of Tonkin Resolution as tantamount to a congressional declaration of war. The congressional resolution also helped Johnson position himself as a tough but cautious moderate during the presidential campaign of 1964. Barry Goldwater demanded stronger measures against North Vietnam and even hinted at possible use of tactical nuclear weapons. Johnson's campaign managers portrayed Goldwater as a threat to the survival of civilization, and the president seemingly promised not to commit U.S. troops to any land war in Southeast Asia.

Soon after the November election of 1964, however, Johnson faced a complicated decision. More than a year after the 1963 coup against Diem (see Chapter 28), South Vietnam still faced political disarray, and South Vietnamese troops were deserting at an alarming rate. North Vietnam continued expanding its military aid to the National Liberation Front (NLF) and began sending more of its own troops into South Vietnam. By the beginning of 1965, the NLF controlled much of the countryside. In January, another government in Saigon collapsed, and factionalism stalled the emergence of any viable alternative.

National Security Adviser McGeorge Bundy predicted South Vietnam's collapse unless the United States greatly increased its military role. Another key aide, Walt W. Rostow, assured Johnson that North Vietnam would give up its aggressive plans if the United States clearly showed its determination to oppose them. Undersecretary of State George Ball, by contrast, warned that "no one has demonstrated that a white ground force of whatever size can win a guerrilla war—which is at the same time a civil war between Asians—in jungle terrain in the midst of a population that refuses cooperation to the white forces." Senate Majority Leader Mike Mansfield, an expert in Asian history, urged finding some way of reuniting Vietnam as a neutral country. Top military officials, beset by interservice rivalries, provided differing assessments and no clear guidance.

Although Johnson privately doubted the chances for a successful U.S. intervention, he seemed incapable of translating these doubts into a decision to alter the U.S. commitment to containing communism in Vietnam. Johnson became obsessed about the adverse political and diplomatic consequences of a U.S. pullout or compromise. He feared that domestic criticism of anything looking like a communist victory in Vietnam would endanger his Great Society programs and embolden the new conservatives.

Johnson also embraced the familiar domino theory, the claim that a U.S. withdrawal could lead to further communist aggression in Asia, encourage communist-leaning insurgencies in Latin America, increase Soviet pressure on West Berlin, and damage U.S. credibility around the world. Both Eisenhower and Kennedy had staked U.S. prestige on a noncommunist South Vietnam. Johnson either had to revise that commitment or chart an uncertain course by ordering the direct infusion of U.S. combat troops.

Ultimately, Johnson greatly expanded U.S. military involvement. A deadly attack on the U.S. military outpost at Pleiku in early 1965 prompted retaliatory bombing against North Vietnam. Within a month, the United States inaugurated a sustained campaign of bombing, code-named Rolling Thunder. Washington also began deploying U.S. ground forces to regain lost territory in the South, expanding covert operations, and boosting economic aid to the beleaguered South Vietnamese government. Only six months after the 1964 election, with his advisers still divided, Johnson had decisively committed the United States to a wider war (see Map 29.1).

▲ **MAP 29.1 U.S. Involvement in Indochina (1964–1975)** The war in Vietnam spread into neighboring countries of Indochina as the United States sought to prevent North Vietnam from bringing supplies and troops southward along a network called the Ho Chi Minh Trail. Unlike the Korean War (see Map 27.3), the guerrilla-style war in Indochina had few conventional battle fronts.

Q *How does this map vividly illustrate the difficulties of keeping the war against North Vietnam geographically limited in scope?*

Q *How does this map emphasize that the commonly used term "Vietnam War" fails to represent the geographical extent of this conflict?*

29-2b *The War Continues to Widen*

Combat operations in Vietnam grew steadily more intense. Hoping to break the enemy's spirit, U.S. military commanders sought to inflict massive casualties. The Johnson administration authorized the use of napalm, an incendiary and toxic chemical that charred both foliage and people, and allowed the air force to bomb new targets. Additional U.S. combat troops arrived, but every escalation seemed to require a further one. After North Vietnam rejected a Johnson peace plan that Hanoi viewed as tantamount to its surrender, the United States again escalated. North Vietnam's leadership, pursuing a long-term strategy of attrition in South Vietnam, became convinced that Johnson would eventually lose public and congressional support for continuing the costly intervention.

In April 1965, Johnson applied his cold war, anticommunist principles in Latin America. Responding to exaggerated reports about a communist threat in the Dominican Republic, Johnson sent U.S. troops to unseat a left-leaning, elected president and to install a government supportive of U.S. interests. This incursion violated a long-standing "good neighbor" pledge not to intervene militarily in the Western Hemisphere. Although angering critics of the United States throughout Latin America, the overthrow of a leftist government in the Dominican Republic seemed to steel Johnson's determination to hold the line against communism in Vietnam.

Later that spring, as another South Vietnamese government was forming in Saigon, **General William Westmoreland**, who directed the U.S. effort, recommended using "search-and-destroy" missions against communist forces. By relying on helicopters to deploy U.S. forces quickly, Westmoreland envisioned that U.S. troops would engage enemy units, inflict as many casualties as possible, and withdraw without trying to secure the battleground. "Body count"—the number of enemy forces killed or disabled—became the key measure of success for these missions. In July 1965, Johnson publicly agreed to send 50,000 additional military personnel to Vietnam. Privately, he pledged to send another 50,000 and left open the possibility of deploying even more. LBJ also approved saturation bombing in the South Vietnamese countryside and intensified bombardment of the North.

Some advisers urged Johnson to inform the public candidly about the expanded U.S. military effort. They recommended seeking an outright declaration of war from Congress or at least legislation allowing the president to wield the economic and informational controls that previous administrations had used during wartime. Worried about provoking antiwar members of Congress and expanding a still-small antiwar movement, however, Johnson decided to stress the administration's willingness to negotiate and to act as if the war he was expanding was not really a war. The Johnson administration talked of seeing "light at the end of the tunnel" and apparently hoped that most people in the United States would remain largely in the dark about events in Vietnam.

Over the next three years, U.S. involvement steadily increased. The number of U.S. troops in Vietnam grew to 535,000. Operation Ranch Hand scorched South Vietnam's croplands and defoliated half its forests in an effort to eliminate the natural cover for enemy troop movements. Operation Rolling Thunder, despite several brief pauses, continued until the Pentagon finally declared it a strategic failure in late 1968. Overall, U.S. planes dropped approximately 1.5 million tons of bombs—more than all the tonnage dropped during the Second World War—that pounded North Vietnamese cities and pummeled the villages and hamlets of the South.

Despite this level of violence, Vietnam remained a "limited" war. The United States avoided bombing close to the Chinese border. China had stationed more than 300,000 troops in North Vietnam, and Johnson feared provoking their entry, or possibly even that of the Soviet Union. The strategy remained one of containing the NLF and North Vietnam by steadily escalating the cost they would pay in lost lives and bombed-out infrastructure. Estimates that a kill ratio of 10 to 1 would force North Vietnam and the NLF to pull back encouraged the U.S. military command to unleash more firepower and further inflate enemy casualty figures. Whenever the number of enemy forces seemed to increase, the Pentagon requested more U.S. troops to maintain the desired kill ratio.

Johnson, whose notorious temper flared at the first hint of bad news, used body count numbers to justify public claims of victory being "just around the corner." Privately, though, a different picture began to emerge. Enjoying material assistance from the Soviet Union and China, North Vietnam could match every U.S. escalation. The North Vietnamese funneled troops and supplies into the South through the shifting network of roads and paths, primarily through Laos, called the Ho Chi Minh Trail. By the end of 1967, several of Johnson's key aides, most notably Secretary of Defense Robert McNamara, decided that the United States could not sustain its commitment to South Vietnam. The price for containing North Vietnam had become far too steep. The majority of Johnson's advisers, however, refused to accept McNamara's assessment.

Johnson continued to lack an effective ally in Saigon. The devastation of the countryside from the U.S. military strategy, the economic destabilization from the flood of U.S. dollars, and the political corruption of Saigon officials took their toll. The "pacification" and "strategic hamlet" programs, which gathered Vietnamese farmers into tightly guarded villages, sounded viable in Washington but created greater instability by uprooting many South Vietnamese from their villages and ancestral lands. Buddhist priests persistently demonstrated against foreign influence. In 1967, Generals Nguyen Van Thieu and Nguyen Cao Ky, having sustained a military regime in Saigon longer than any of their predecessors, tried to legitimate their rule by holding a new election. But a voting process shot through with corruption only highlighted their precarious political position and their dependence on aid from Washington.

29-2c *The Media and the War*

The destruction wreaked by U.S. forces was giving the NLF, North Vietnamese, Chinese, and Soviet leaders a propaganda advantage in what had become an international war of imagery. Pictures from Southeast Asia allowed critics around the world to condemn the U.S. bombardments and its search-and-destroy strategy. In Western Europe, demonstrations against the United States became prominent features of political life. Antiwar protesters at home constantly hounded the president and members of his administration, and Johnson eventually complained of being a prisoner in his own White House.

Interpreting the Visual Past Incident on a Saigon Street, 1968

The Vietnam War was the first major war in which TV's moving images became part of the conflict. It was also the last one in which print publications, such as *LIFE* magazine, sent skilled photojournalists into the field with no restrictions on their movement or the images they sent back home.

Many photos from Vietnam came to provide iconic images, but few have as fascinating a backstory as does this Pulitzer Prize-winning one by Eddie Adams (1933–2004). A combat photographer for the U.S. Marines during the Korean conflict, Adams was working for the Associated Press (AP) when he snapped this picture of an execution carried out by a South Vietnamese general during the communist Tet Offensive of 1968.

The photo, which became known as "Saigon Execution," was shocking to many Americans because it seemed to summarize, in a single visual image, the falsity of the argument from President Lyndon Johnson and his generals that the United States was fighting for democracy and winning.

Other subsequent developments, however, added crucial context to the photo. The prisoner in the photo was not a civilian, as it appeared, but a military officer in the NLF (Viet Cong) who was directing combat operations in Saigon. Minutes before this picture was taken, subsequent evidence verified, he had been overseeing the killing of South Vietnamese civilians. The war had come to the streets of Saigon. Adams came to regret how the photo affected public debate—and how it destroyed the reputation and career of a distinguished South Vietnamese military leader. "The general killed the Viet Cong. I killed the general with my camera," Adams mused.

Q *Why might a viewer in 1968, who knew little more about events in Vietnam than what is shown in "Execution in Saigon," have reacted with such shock to this image? What does it suggest about the impact of the Tet Offensive? Do you think this image would be as shockingly memorable today?*

Q *How might this photo, without its complicated backstory, have helped to bolster the antiwar movement in the United States?*

Q *How does "Saigon Execution" underscore the argument that visual images, even when the photographer is acting as if "a fly on the wall," always do more than simply hold up a mirror to reality? How might the history of this photo affect your own approach to visual evidence from and about the past?*

29.4 **Eddie Adams, Saigon Execution, 1968.**

In previous wars, Washington had restricted media coverage. Hoping to avoid the controversy that overt censorship would surely cause, the Johnson administration tried to employ informal ways of managing information. With television making Vietnam a "living room war"—one that people could watch in their own homes—Johnson kept three TV sets playing in his office in order to monitor what viewers were seeing. Most of what he saw, early on, he liked. *Time* magazine initially praised General Westmoreland's leadership and named him its "Man of the Year" for 1965. In time, however, media coverage changed. Images of unrelenting destruction coming across TV screens undercut the optimistic words coming from the White House. After gazing at his TV sets, LBJ started telephoning network executives, castigating them for broadcasts to which he objected. More and more journalists, following the lead of Pulitzer Prize winning reporter David Halberstam, challenged reassuring claims by U.S. officials. Younger journalists who traveled alongside U.S. troops, such as Michael Herr, came to represent the American mission as a drug-drenched trip into the surreal.

As the conflict dragged on, the media began to talk about a "war at home." Initially, commentators generally adopted a stark, bipolar story frame. It pitted the "hawks," people who wanted to fight in Vietnam until the United States "won," against the "doves," those who desired to end U.S. involvement as quickly as possible. Johnson claimed to be following the time-tested policy of containment, and Secretary of State Dean Rusk warned of the dangers of "appeasement." But influential U.S. politicians—led by J. William Fulbright of Arkansas, chair of the Senate Foreign Relations Committee—complained of misplaced priorities in Vietnam and of an American "arrogance of power." Gradually, it seemed as if the fundamental structures of domestic politics, society, and culture might unravel.

29-3 Activism at Home

How did the social movements that emerged during the divisive war in Vietnam seek to change U.S. politics and culture? What role did mass media play?

Even as Lyndon Johnson's policy in Southeast Asia was coming under attack from antiwar activists, a broader culture of dissent emerged. Growing tensions produced a political landscape marked by bitterness, confrontation, polarization, and violence on a scale not seen in the United States for many years.

29-3a *The Movement of Movements*

No single group can lay exclusive claim to "the Sixties," the period from roughly 1963 to 1974 that coincided with the war in Vietnam. Still, those on the political and cultural left, especially when gaining recruits from the huge baby boom generation, initially dominated media accounts and the earliest histories of the era. Iconic images from the 1960s provide a kaleidoscopic panorama of what can be called a "movement of movements" that generally rejected a dominant ideal of the 1950s and early 1960s: the faith that political pluralism would almost always unite the nation (see Chapter 28).

Activists increasingly questioned the existing political system. At the same time, disparate movements based on deeply held values—involving issues such as war and peace, race relations, gender politics, the environment, and sexuality—took shape. Many activists sought the media spotlight to attract support for their visions of change. Four of the earliest and most prominent of the movements involved a New Left, a counterculture, Black Power, and an antiwar insurgency.

29-3b *A New Left*

While relatively few college students actually joined left-leaning movements, the activities of a **New Left** dominated politics on many campuses, attracted media attention, and in time generated popular controversy.

In 1962, two years after the new conservatism had formed Young Americans for Freedom (see Chapter 28), the left-leaning Students for a Democratic Society (SDS) emerged on the opposite end of the political spectrum. Although SDS advocated familiar causes, especially civil rights, it also called for a new style of personal politics. SDS's *Port Huron Statement* (1962) pledged to fight the "loneliness, estrangement, isolation" that supposedly afflicted many people. Charging that the dominant political culture valued bureaucratic expertise over citizen engagement and economic growth over meaningful work, SDS spoke for alternative visions. In politics, it called for "participatory democracy"—grassroots activism and institutions responsive to local needs.

The 1964 Freedom Summer in Mississippi provided a tangible example of participatory democracy as volunteers from the North joined local activists in registering African American voters and organizing for political action. Some volunteers remained in the South, working for civil rights, but others joined neighborhood-based political projects elsewhere in the country. Small-scale movements promised young people and their older allies the chance to reenergize political life from the ground up.

New Left activists constantly expanded their view of what counted as "politics." Although voter registration drives remained important in the South, for example, local movements came to place greater emphasis on alternative political forms, such as sit-ins and demonstrations. Their generation's vast size and its educational attainments made

Larry Mulvehill/Science Source

29.5 **Antiwar Demonstration in Washington, D.C.** Mass rallies against U.S. involvement in the Vietnam War became an important part of antiwar politics during the late 1960s and early 1970s. Earlier chapters indicate that large street demonstrations have a long history in America.

Q *How might such protests both boost and deplete the energy needed to sustain a dissenting movement?*

these insurgents ideally suited to confront a political system dominated by powerful and entrenched interests.

On campus, discontent simmered. Many restive students chafed at classes that seemed irrelevant to the issues of the day and at college bureaucracies that imposed restrictions on their living arrangements and lifestyle choices. They challenged whether deans of students should be able to establish dress codes and restrict visiting hours in dorms for students who, while off campus, qualified as adults. Far worse, according to New Left activists, giant universities compromised their independence and integrity by welcoming funding from the military-industrial complex and by seeming oblivious to the social and moral implications of war-related research.

During the "Berkeley Revolt" of 1964 and 1965, students and sympathetic faculty expanded their activism. They first protested how the University of California restricted political activity on campus and then began speaking out against its complicity in the Vietnam War and in racial discrimination. Protests rocked most other campuses during the Sixties, but the long-running drama at Berkeley, which disrupted classes and polarized one of the world's most prestigious universities, remained the preeminent symbol of the broader turmoil that the media began calling "the war on campus."

29-3c *The Counterculture*

Berkeley also hosted some of the earliest encounters between the political movements of the New Left and the free-wheeling energies of a youth-dominated **counterculture**.

The counterculture of the mid-1960s remains a difficult "movement" to identify. Embracing the slogan "Do Your Own Thing," the counterculture elected no officers, held no formal meetings, and maintained no central office to issue manifestos. It burst into view in low-income neighborhoods, such as San Francisco's Haight-Ashbury area, and along the streets bordering college campuses, such as Berkeley's Telegraph Avenue. Its self-appointed spokespeople embraced values, lifestyles, and institutions hailed as alternatives to those of the dominant culture.

People drawn to this counterculture looked to earlier models, especially the Beats of the 1950s, but they eventually left their own imprint on a wide range of social and cultural movements, including the creation of cooperatives, radical feminism, environmentalism, and the fight against legal restrictions on lifestyle choices. The counterculture also affected mainstream consumer culture. The mass media, for example, invariably highlighted the flamboyant clothing, hairstyles, and uninhibited sexuality among younger devotees of the counterculture. They liked to portray countercultural "hippies" as being on the cutting edge of a massive, fun-filled "youth rebellion" and focused on use of drugs, such as marijuana and LSD, communal living arrangements, and new forms of music, such as the folk-rock of the Byrds and the acid rock of the Grateful Dead.

The counterculture developed its own soundtrack and created its own media. Music-oriented publications such as *Rolling Stone* magazine (founded in 1967) celebrated singer-songwriters, such as Bob Dylan and Joni Mitchell, as the counterculture's prophet laureates. Radio stations began featuring folk-rock and other sounds associated with the counterculture. In a pre-Internet age, these stations provided audio billboards for promoting musical and political events. Some stations joined print publications, such as the *Berkeley Barb*, in dispatching youthful journalists to report on—and participate in—the countercultural scene.

Images and products from the counterculture soon found a market among otherwise conventional consumers. The ad agency for Chrysler Motors urged car buyers to break from older patterns, purchase a youthful-looking 1965 model, and thereby join the "Dodge Rebellion." Recognizing the appeal of bands such as San Francisco's Jefferson Airplane, the music industry, too, saw profits to be made. An early countercultural happening, the "Human Be-In," organized by community activists from San Francisco in early 1967, provided a model for subsequent, commercially dominated music festivals such as Monterrey Pop (later in 1967) and Woodstock (in 1969).

Some of the students and faculty attracted to New Left politics worried that the counterculture would deflect young people from the hard work of political activism. The novelist Ken Kesey implicitly mocked a 1965 political demonstration at Berkeley with a style of politics indebted to the counterculture. Accompanied by veterans from the Beat movement and youthful members of his communal group, "the Merry Pranksters," Kesey alternated between singing choruses of "Home on the Range" and suggesting students ignore more traditional forms of politics and refashion, especially through drugs such as LSD, the personal politics of their own lives.

29-3d *Civil Rights and Black Power*

The media played an important and controversial role in efforts to achieve liberty and equality for African Americans. Civil rights leaders, of course, had long recognized the value of media coverage. TV images of the violence in Selma, Alabama, in 1965 had helped Dr. King's Southern Christian Leadership Conference (SCLC) galvanize support for federal voting rights legislation. At one point, ABC television interrupted a special showing of the anti-Nazi film *Judgment at Nuremberg* to show white Alabama state troopers beating peaceful, mostly African American, voting rights marchers. Lyndon Johnson went on television to proclaim that "we shall overcome" the nation's "crippling legacy of bigotry and injustice."

The violence associated with the civil rights campaigns prompted different views. Segregationists and their allies insisted that media coverage of activism encouraged lawbreaking and violence and that only a renewed commitment to law and order would ease social tensions. Movement activists who looked to Dr. King replied that racism, lack of opportunity, and inadequate government remedies produced the frustration that spawned violence. Other more militant voices within the broad movement of movements argued that governments in the United States could not be relied upon to address race-related issues effectively and that aggrieved groups needed to mobilize themselves.

What They Said

Dissent and Surveillance

The student demonstrations at the University of California, Berkeley, during the mid-1960s came to symbolize a number of controversies. University regulations limited political activity on campus, and protesting students initially waged a fight for free speech. They advocated the freedom to discuss or leaflet for any cause, including opposition to the war in Vietnam and to racial discrimination.

As tensions between dissenting students and university administrators began to grow, the issues began to expand. Mario Savio, an undergraduate deeply committed to civil rights work, became the voice of the movement. During a December 1964 address on the steps of Berkeley's Sproul Hall, sometimes known as "The End of History Speech," Savio framed the struggle on campus as a microcosm of a more fundamental clash over values and over the kind of world that his generation must oppose.

At the same time that Savio was urging students to confront the vast bureaucratic machinery that was allegedly attempting to control their lives, the FBI bureaucracy was conducting extensive secret surveillance on him and other dissenting students. His FBI file was not declassified until 1999.

Mario Savio, Bureaucracy and "The End of History"

In our free-speech fight at the University of California, we have come up against what may emerge as the greatest problem of our nation—depersonalized, unresponsive bureaucracy... . We find functionaries who cannot make policy but can only hide behind the rules... . As a bureaucrat, an administrator believes that nothing new happens... . The conception that bureaucrats have is that history has come to an end.

Students have begun not only to question but, having arrived at answers, to act on those answers. This is part of a growing understanding among many people in America that history has not ended, that a better society is possible, and that it is worth dying for.

Many students here at the university, many people in society, are wandering aimlessly about. Strangers in their own lives, there is no place for them. They are people who have not learned to compromise, who for example have come to the university to learn to question, to grow, to learn—all the standard things that sound like cliches because no one takes them seriously. And they find at one point or other that for them to become part of society, to become lawyers, ministers, businessmen, people in government, that very often they must compromise those principles which were most dear to them. They must suppress the most creative impulses that they have; this is a prior condition for being part of the system. The university is well structured, well tooled, to turn out people with all the sharp edges worn off, the well-rounded person. The university is well equipped to produce that sort of person, and this means that the best among the people who enter must for four years wander aimlessly much of the time questioning why they are on campus at all, doubting whether there is any point in what they are doing, and looking toward a very bleak existence afterward in a game in which all of the rules have been made up, which one cannot really amend.

It is a bleak scene, but it is all a lot of us have to look forward to. Society provides no challenge. American society in the standard conception it has of itself is simply no longer exciting. The most exciting things going on in America today are movements to change America. America is becoming ever more the utopia of sterilized, automated contentment. The "futures" and "careers" for which American students now prepare are for the most part intellectual and moral wastelands. This chrome-plated consumers' paradise would have us grow up to be well-behaved children. But an important minority of men and women coming to the front today have shown that they will die rather than be standardized, replaceable and irrelevant.

The FBI Bureaucracy Secretly Responds

FBI Memo, December 11, 1964

Mario Savio is the leader of the recent lawless demonstration at the University of California Berkeley ... and is also chief spokesman for the Free Speech Movement... . Investigation of Savio to date has not developed any information indicating affiliation on his part with a subversive group. However, he has been extremely close and in frequent company of Bettina Aptheker, a current active leader in the Community Party in San Francisco... .

All offices have been instructed to intensify their coverage of the activities of Savio... .

FBI Memo, February 13, 1967

It is noted that subject ... has been the leader of student rebellions at the University of California at Berkeley, and has actively participated in numerous demonstrations against United States policy in Vietnam.

In view of the foregoing the Bureau is of the opinion that subject's activities warrant the inclusion of his name in the Security Index.

FBI Memo, May 17, 1968

A review of Savio's file has been completed at the Bureau... . It may well be that the subject is maturing politically and may no longer be categorized as a key Activist... . Some key activists have travelled extensively both nationally and abroad in the past. You should remain alert to this in order that you might promptly advise the bureau of any travel planned by the subject.

In evaluating this case, you should bear in mind that one of the prime objectives should be to neutralize him in the new left movement... .

You should be expected to pursue this investigation aggressively and with imagination. Delays in reporting important developments will not be tolerated.

NOTE: Savio was designated a Key Activist by [code name] based upon his activities in the New Left movement. His file has been reviewed as a result of recent campus unrest and the San Francisco office is being furnished with certain observations in order that a more aggressive investigation might be instituted.

Q *Mario Savio's critics claimed the fears expressed in "The End of History" were largely baseless. How might the revelations of widespread FBI surveillance, about which Savio did not know in 1964, affect an assessment of his speech? Was surveillance of people who acted and spoke in the manner of Mario Savio justified?*

Q *Do you think there was a possible threat to democratic politics from college and university campuses during the 1960s? Do you think there was a threat to democratic politics from FBI surveillance?*

Q *What issues related to surveillance are in the news recently, and how might your views on surveillance today affect how you judge Savio's "The End of History" and other examples of dissent during the 1960s?*

Sources: (top) Mario Savio, Bureaucracy and "The End of History" [commonly referred to as "The End of History" speech]. Originally delivered in 1964 on the campus of U.C. Berkeley; it has been widely reprinted. Authors accessed it at: www.historyisaweapon.com. (bottom) From three FBI memos dated Dec. 11, 1964; Feb. 13, 1967; and May 17, 1968. All from FBI file on Mario Savio, declassified in 1999. Authors accessed at: vault.fbi.gov/mario-savio

In 1965, this debate intensified in the wake of conflict in Los Angeles. An altercation between a white highway patrol officer and a black motorist escalated into six days of violence, centered in the largely African American community of Watts in the South-Central area of Los Angeles. Thirty-four people died; hundreds of businesses and homes were burned; heavily armed National Guard troops patrolled the streets; and television carried images of the destruction to the nation and the world. What provoked this conflagration? Had TV cameras and radio reports helped to fan the flames?

A stunned Lyndon Johnson called for new social welfare resources for Watts. "Let's move in—money, marbles, and chalk," LBJ reportedly ordered. The mayor and police chief of Los Angeles, conversely, blamed civil rights "agitators" and sought new resources for law enforcement. Local activist leaders created new organizations, such as the Watts Writers Workshop, and argued that only a determined strategy of local empowerment could produce access to more equitable policing practices, higher-paying jobs, and better housing.

The basic structure of the post-Watts debate would change relatively little as violence continued to move through, usually during the summer, other urban neighborhoods. According to one estimate, there were more than 300 cases of serious urban conflict between 1965 and 1969. Property damage reached into the billions of dollars, and hundreds of people lost their lives. Significant portions of major cities—but almost never the more affluent areas or nearby suburbs—became battlegrounds that would bear the scars of the Sixties for years to come. Commentators from different political camps applied their own value-soaked labels, including "riot," "rebellion," and "insurrection." The major outbreaks produced investigative commissions that debated these labels, parsed increasingly familiar arguments about causation, and pondered recommendations for change.

How do these "long, hot summers" fit into a history of the 1960s? The earliest narrative saw escalating violence and militant **Black Power** groups as splintering a previously united civil rights cause. A competing story about a movement of movements, however, suggests that there was never a single *movement* that could have been splintered. Long before Watts, a variety of black activist movements were advocating different ways to gain greater power for black communities.

Many Black Power efforts during the late 1950s and early 1960s looked to **Malcolm X**. He had initially gained attention as a minister in the Nation of Islam, a North American-based group popularly known as the "Black Muslims." Malcolm X oftentimes criticized Dr. King's gradual, nonviolent approach as largely irrelevant to the everyday problems of most African Americans and questioned the desirability or feasibility of racial integration. Malcolm X never advocated initiating confrontation, but he did endorse self-defense "by any means necessary."

Portrayed as a dangerous subversive by the FBI and most mainstream media, Malcolm X urged African Americans to "recapture our heritage and identity" and "launch a cultural revolution to unbrainwash an entire people." Seeking to extend his movement, Malcolm X eventually broke from the Black Muslims and established his own Organization of Afro-American Unity. Murdered in 1965 by enemies from the Nation of Islam, Malcolm X remained, especially after the posthumous publication of his *Autobiography* (1965), a powerful symbol for black-centered political and cultural visions of the future.

These visions increasingly diverged from those of LBJ's program for expanding civil rights legislation, and the president privately struggled to understand movements with goals that differed from his. During a "racial summit" at the White House in 1965, A. Philip Randolph, Bayard Rustin, and others lobbied for a Freedom Budget, an overt criticism of their host's

Henry Diltz/Historical/Corbis

29.6 **San Francisco's Counterculture Gathers** Beat poet Allen Ginsberg performs at the 1967 Human Be-In with singers backing him up in Golden Gate Park.

Q *How might countercultural displays such as this one unnerve more traditional activists and outrage supporters of the war in Vietnam?*

Bettmann/Corbis

29.7 **Violence in Detroit, 1967** Violence swept through many U.S. cities between 1965 and 1969. The 1967 upheaval in Detroit, which federal troops quelled, left 43 dead and many African American neighborhoods in ruin.

Q *When is federal intervention justified in dealing with mass protest?*

spending priorities. They called for allocating $100 billion on infrastructure projects in low-income neighborhoods. Johnson privately denounced these veteran civil rights leaders and the Freedom Budget for "raising un-shirted hell" at *his* summit.

Events in the South highlighted other differences among the movements. In June 1966, a KKK gunman shot James Meredith, who had integrated the University of Mississippi several years earlier and was now conducting a one-person March against Fear from Tennessee to Jackson, Mississippi. A coalition of civil rights groups quickly organized an expanded March against Fear that would complete Meredith's walk. This was the first large-scale movement project—in contrast to the 1963 March on Washington and the 1965 voting rights campaign in Alabama—that did not seek new civil rights legislation. It sought, instead, to demonstrate that movements for liberty and equality could advance everyday struggles for safety, dignity, pride, and empowerment. The march also tried to capitalize on the national media coverage that Meredith's shooting had already attracted.

During the march, Stokely Carmichael played to the omnipresent TV cameras. Carmichael's rise to prominence had begun the previous year, when he organized a third-party political movement, bearing the striking logo of a coiled black panther, in Lowndes County, Alabama. In Mississippi, he questioned an unwavering commitment to nonviolence and urged that the civil rights struggle not remain just one for "Freedom," the byword of the SCLC, but for "Black Power." As Carmichael later explained, Black Power was "a call for black people in this country to unite, to recognize their heritage, to build a sense of community." They should "define their own goals" and "lead their own organizations."

Black Power came to provide a sometimes inflammatory label for an often pragmatic set of claims that local civil rights groups had been making for some time. They sought greater on-the-ground power both in and for their own communities. Operating from this perspective, in 1966, several college students from Oakland announced a new Black Power organization that borrowed its name and logo from Carmichael's earlier movement in Lowndes County. This Black Panther Party's platform employed militant rhetoric on behalf of 10 objectives, including greater opportunities for housing, education, and employment; legal protections, especially against police misconduct; and improved health and nutrition initiatives in low-income black neighborhoods.

The Panther's trio of media-savvy young members—Huey Newton, Bobby Seale, and Eldridge Cleaver—adapted symbolism and rhetoric from Third World revolutionary movements. A 1967 rally in Sacramento, California, on behalf of the Second Amendment right to use firearms for self-defense attracted the notice of J. Edgar Hoover. He made destroying the Black Panther Party a key goal of his FBI.

Less flamboyant groups and movements were also invoking the Black Power approach. Fully embracing the word *black* and a political-cultural agenda based on racial identity, they sought the power to pursue separate, African American-directed routes not just toward liberty and equality but also toward "liberation" from the prevailing political culture. "Black Is Beautiful" became a watchword. James Brown, the "Godfather of Soul," captured this new spirit with his song, "Say It Loud, I'm Black and I'm Proud" (1968).

Within this volatile context, Congress passed the **Civil Rights Act of 1968**. One provision of this omnibus measure, popularly known as the "Fair Housing Act," followed in the wake of earlier state-level measures and aimed at eliminating racial discrimination in the national real estate market. The act, however, contained ambiguous language that eventually enfeebled its enforcement. Another section in the law declared it a crime to cross state lines in order to incite a "riot." Supporters hailed this provision as a victory for law and order, while critics countered that it targeted political activists, especially those in the Black Power movement.

History Through Film Malcolm X (1992)

Directed by Spike Lee.
Starring Denzel Washington (Malcolm X), Angela Bassett (Betty Shabbaz), and Al Freeman, Jr. (Elijah Muhammad).

For more than 25 years, Hollywood tried to make a movie portraying Malcolm X, whose *Autobiography* (1965) is a literary classic. Problems always stymied production plans. Finally, in 1992, Spike Lee's independent production company (named Forty Acres and a Mule, after the land distribution program for former slaves advocated after the Civil War) released a movie that argues for Malcolm X's continuing relevance.

The montage sequences that begin and end the movie underscore the film director's outlook. Against the backdrop of the Warner Brothers logo, the soundtrack introduces the actual voice of Malcolm X decrying the nature of racial politics over the course of U.S. history. Malcolm X's accusations continue as a giant American flag appears on screen and is cut into pieces by jagged images from an amateur video of Los Angeles police officers beating Rodney King, a notorious instance of police misconduct that took place in 1991. Next, the flag begins to burn until, revealed behind it, a giant "X," adorned with remnants of the flag, fills the frame. Some three hours later, the ending of the movie presents archival footage of Malcolm X, along with images of South African freedom fighter Nelson Mandela, while the voice of Ozzie Davis, the celebrated African American actor, gives a eulogy.

When first released, the film opened to packed movie houses. Despite a multimedia publicity blitz, box office revenues steadily declined. Viewers reported that the lengthy, episodic movie taxed their patience and attention spans.

Being able to watch a digital version of *Malcolm X* today, however, allows viewers to concentrate on its best sequences, speeding by ones that seem to drag, and returning to those that initially might seem muddled. *Malcolm X* offers a complex account of the early Black Power movement, its foremost spokesperson, and the social ferment that gripped the nation during the 1960s. ■

AF archive/Alamy Stock Photo

29.8 Denzel Washington stars as Malcolm X.

29-3e *The Antiwar Movement*

Meanwhile, another of these multifaceted movements was coming to overshadow all others: the one to end the war in Vietnam.

The antiwar movement, like its counterparts, never fell into neat categories. Some of the strongest "antiwar" sentiment, for example, blamed LBJ for not prosecuting the war *aggressively enough*. At the other end of the spectrum, several small movements called for a North Vietnam–NLF victory. The chant, "Ho, Ho, Ho Chi Minh/NLF Is Gonna Win" enraged Johnson and distressed most others in the antiwar coalition.

The antiwar effort faced the same questions as the other movements of the Sixties. What kind of politics best expressed its ethical and spiritual values? How might it reach out to people not already in the movement? Could it mobilize enough support to change public policy?

The antiwar movement gradually expanded the scope of its activism. On college campuses, supporters and opponents of the war initially debated at "teach-ins," academic-style events that soon gave way to demonstrations and sit-ins. A draft-resistance effort emerged, often symbolized by the burning of draft cards, which urged young men to refuse to serve in the military. This effort gained its most celebrated member when the heavyweight boxing champion Muhammad Ali refused induction into the military. Campus protests passed into a new phase when a pitched, bloody battle broke out between antiwar demonstrators and police at the University of Wisconsin in Madison in 1967.

Dr. Martin Luther King, Jr., now faced pressure from other antiwar clergy to proclaim publicly his opposition to the war, connect this conflict overseas to the civil rights cause at home, and elaborate his vision of the moral–spiritual issues at stake. Speaking at New York's Riverside Church in April 1967, Dr. King highlighted a black-and-white truth. African American troops, mostly from low-income communities, served and died in numbers far greater than their proportion of the U.S. population "for a nation that has been unable to seat them together in the same schools." The immoral "madness" in Vietnam "must cease," Dr. King concluded. Voices from the political-media mainstream condemned his antiwar address, and as Dr. King continued to broaden his political agenda, criticism from onetime supporters commonly followed.

Meanwhile, a massive 1967 antiwar demonstration in Washington suggested how the politics of the New Left and the spirit of the counterculture could march together, at least when opposing LBJ's policies in Vietnam. Noting the visual media's voracious appetite for pictures of colorful dissenters, a small group of activists had invented a kind of "non-movement movement" that bypassed mobilization and organization in favor of making the media its primary constituency. Two members of this group, Abbie Hoffman and Jerry Rubin, proclaimed themselves leaders of a (nonexistent) Youth International Party (or YIPPIE!) and waited for media coverage to surround their activities, as they knew it would.

Hoffman and Rubin raised the curtain on a new style of countercultural-political performance. In one incident, they mocked the symbolic value of stocks on the New York Exchange by tossing real dollar bills onto the trading floor. Invoking the sit-in movement, they joked about staging department store "loot-ins." Their contribution to the 1967 antiwar march in Washington would be to lead a separate trek to the Pentagon, where marchers would chant mystical incantations and try to levitate the building.

Although the Pentagon remained firmly planted, the march against it did generate eye-catching media imagery. The event also gained the novelist and antiwar activist Norman Mailer a National Book Award for *Armies of the Night* (1968). Mailer's book, which wove together personal impressions and journalistic observation, helped to reinvent political reporting. Cultural observers identified accounts such as Mailer's as a "new journalism" and saw this form of reportage paralleling how political activists were creating a "new politics" that expanded ideas about what counted as political involvement.

29-4 1968

What helped to make the single year of 1968 seem a pivotal time in the larger history of the era of the Vietnam War?

The relationship between this new politics and the media seemed uncertain. Might not images of colorful quipsters such as Hoffman and Rubin help fuel cultural polarization rather than political action? Was the media's taste for spectacular demonstrations trivializing underlying issues? Such questions became even more pressing during the tumultuous 12 months of 1968.

29-4a *Turmoil in Vietnam, 1968*

At the end of January 1968, during a supposed truce in observance of Tet, the Vietnamese lunar New Year celebration, NLF and North Vietnamese forces suddenly went on the attack throughout South Vietnam. A small NLF force even temporarily seized the grounds of the U.S. embassy in Saigon. Militarily, this **Tet Offensive** gained the NLF and the North relatively little territory at a very high cost. The NLF lost three-quarters of its military forces and much of its civilian support structure. But in the United States, the Tet Offensive was a turning point. It discredited General Westmoreland's pre-Tet forecasts about seeing "light at the end of the tunnel." Even after rolling back the communist onslaught, the U.S. military command appeared ill prepared to pursue the badly mauled enemy forces.

Most importantly, the mere fact of a Tet Offensive undercut the optimistic story that the Johnson administration had been spinning (see Figure 29.1). After CBS-TV news anchor Walter Cronkite returned from a post-Tet trip to Vietnam, he told a national audience that the United States would never prevail militarily. Lyndon Johnson reportedly lamented that if he had lost "the most trusted person in America," as Cronkite was then known, he had lost the rest of the country.

Johnson received more bad news after summoning his most trusted advisers and a select group of senior outsiders, including Dean Acheson, for advice on General Westmoreland's request for an additional 206,000 U.S. troops. Most rejected Westmoreland's call and insisted that South Vietnamese troops shoulder more of the military burden. The views of the senior members, the so-called "Wise Men," proved especially sobering since they had formulated America's anticommunist containment policy following the Second World War (see Chapter 27). Dean Acheson now advised the president that the United States "could no longer do the job we set out to do" in Vietnam "in the time we have left, and we must begin to take steps to disengage."

Other factors weighed on Johnson as well. Any plan for using additional U.S. military power to crush North Vietnam carried an unthinkable risk: a larger conflict with China and/or the Soviet Union. Sobered by public opinion polls showing rapidly declining confidence in U.S. policy and pressured by his new secretary of defense, Clark Clifford, another early architect of cold war containment, Johnson changed his guiding assumption about Vietnam. The cost of continuing the U.S. intervention vastly outweighed whatever benefit might accrue. Johnson continued to prosecute the war but simultaneously moved toward negotiation.

29-4b *Turmoil at Home*

The Tet Offensive also destroyed Lyndon Johnson's political plans. The antiwar wing of the Democratic Party was already trying to do what seasoned political pundits had declared impossible: deny Johnson renomination. The dissidents backed **Senator Eugene McCarthy** of Minnesota, still the only prominent Democrat willing to challenge LBJ. The McCarthy

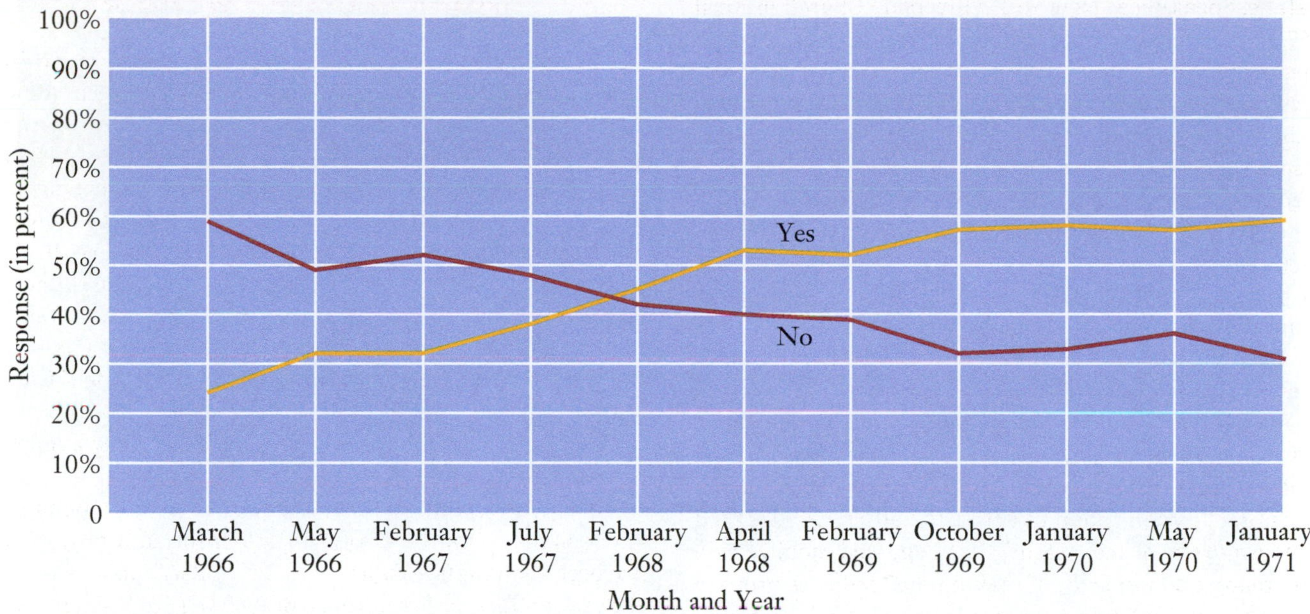

Figure 29.1 **American Attitudes toward the Vietnam War** Responses to the question: "Do you think that the United States made a mistake in sending troops to fight?"

movement's version of new politics relied on the wisdom of a few seasoned political strategists and the energy of thousands of college students. Young people packed away grubby campus attire, donned fresh clothing to "come clean for Gene," and stumped New Hampshire in the initial primary of 1968. Because Johnson refused to campaign personally, this "Dump Johnson" effort enjoyed unexpected media coverage. Johnson's forces actually won the New Hampshire primary, but McCarthy came close enough to claim a symbolic victory. Polls predicted he would easily beat Johnson, head-to-head, in the upcoming Wisconsin primary.

Even before the Wisconsin contest, Senator Robert Kennedy of New York, brother of the slain president, jumped into the race. He had refused earlier entreaties to challenge Johnson but now declared that the nation's "perilous course" impelled him to seek the presidency. Facing two Democratic challengers, President Johnson surprised all but his closest confidants when, during a live TV address in late March about Vietnam, he suddenly announced that he would not seek reelection. He also limited U.S. bombing of North Vietnam and signaled a readiness to begin peace negotiations in Paris.

Johnson's withdrawal created a three-way race for the Democratic nomination. McCarthy now faced Robert Kennedy and Johnson's ever-loyal vice president, Hubert H. Humphrey, who had entered the fray after LBJ's surprise announcement. Humphrey, however, steered clear of the remaining primaries, leaving the two senators to fight a series of brass-knuckled contests that pitted McCarthy's new politics against Kennedy's blend of the new and the old. Kennedy once quipped that the "'A' students may have already flocked to McCarthy," but that he was "locking up those receiving 'Bs.'" The Democratic Party's A-level celebrities generally divided their support between the two, while Humphrey courted the Democratic power brokers who had been allied with LBJ.

Martin Luther King, Jr., welcomed LBJ's withdrawal and hoped that an antiwar candidate, ideally Kennedy, would head the Democratic ticket in November. On April 4, 1968, however, Dr. King took a break from planning an upcoming "Poor People's March" on Washington and visited Memphis, Tennessee, in support of a strike by African American sanitation workers. There, he was assassinated while standing on the balcony of his motel. Law enforcement officials identified James Earl Ray, a career criminal, as the lone killer. Ray was eventually captured and charged with King's murder. He waived a jury trial, pleaded guilty, and received a 99-year prison sentence. Subsequently, Ray recanted and claimed to have been a pawn in a conspiracy directed by white supremacists. He died in prison still insisting on his innocence, but few people credit his claims.

As news of Dr. King's murder spread, violence swept through more than 100 cities and towns; 39 people died; 75,000 regular and National Guard troops were called to duty. When President Johnson proclaimed Sunday, April 7, as a day of national mourning for the slain civil rights leader, parts of the nation's capital city remained ablaze.

Following Dr. King's memorial service, Gene McCarthy and Robert Kennedy returned to campaigning. Kennedy sought to demonstrate that popular opinion favored his candidacy. He also hoped to convince the insiders now backing Humphrey that only a Democrat without ties to Lyndon Johnson, especially another Kennedy, could capture the White House in November.

On June 5, an ebullient Kennedy defeated McCarthy in California's Democratic primary. While preparing to leave the hotel that had hosted his victory celebration, Kennedy was slain by yet another political assassin. Bystanders grabbed Sirhan Sirhan, a Palestinian immigrant, who was later convicted of the killing. Nonstop network television coverage

Bettmann/Corbis

29.9 **The Funeral Procession of Dr. Martin Luther King, Jr., April 9, 1968** A vast crowd of mourners, including ordinary people and dignitaries, accompanied the body of Dr. King through the streets of Atlanta, Georgia. The simple, horse-drawn wagon had become the symbol of one of his final efforts, a Poor People's Campaign, that was to include a march on the nation's capital. After Dr. King's assassination in Memphis, a wagon would bear his body through the streets of the city in which he had grown up and gone to college.

of Kennedy's body being returned by train to Washington and his state funeral were reminders of Dr. King's recent murder and of the 1963 assassination of RFK's own brother. Bowing to the reality of Humphrey's delegate total, McCarthy effectively closed down his campaign.

Questions abounded. Was some "sickness" plaguing American political culture? Did "government by gunplay," rather than political pluralism, best describe the current system? Could the presidential election of 1968 possibly produce a legitimate victor?

The violence of 1968 continued. That summer, thousands of antiwar demonstrators converged on Chicago, site of the Democratic Party's convention, to protest the nomination of Hubert Humphrey, still supporting Johnson's policy in Vietnam. Responding to provocative acts by some demonstrators, including Abbie Hoffman and Jerry Rubin, police officers attacked antiwar protestors and some nearby journalists. Opinion polls showed that most people supported the use of force against the demonstrators, a judgment subsequently challenged by a special commission, whose report assessed the violence in Chicago as a "police riot." Tensions from this "Siege of Chicago" filtered into the convention hall, as antiwar delegates and supporters of the vice president denounced one another. Humphrey easily captured the Democratic presidential nod, but bitter feelings over Johnson's Vietnam policy and the conduct of Chicago's police force left his party deeply divided.

29-4c *The Election of 1968*

Both Humphrey and the Republican nominee, former vice president Richard Nixon, worried about Alabama's George Wallace, who was running for president as a third-party candidate on the American Independent ticket. His opposition to civil rights well established, Wallace concentrated his fire on the counterculture and the antiwar movement. If any "hippie" protestor ever blocked his motorcade, he once announced, it would "be the last car he'll ever lay down in front of." Although Wallace had generally supported the Democratic Party's domestic spending programs, he now courted voters who saw themselves the captives of "tax-and-spend" bureaucracies in Washington.

Wallace never expected to gain the presidency. If a candidate from the two major parties failed to win a majority in the Electoral College vote, however, the Constitution required that the president be selected by the House of Representatives, where Wallace hoped to play the power-broker role by winning a sizable number of electoral votes.

Humphrey struggled with antiwar Democrats over his inability, until late in the campaign, to break from the Vietnam

29.10 **Robert F. Kennedy's Funeral** An elaborately staged funeral followed the 1968 assassination of Robert F. Kennedy. The shootings of the two leaders—Dr. King and Senator Kennedy—within such a short space of time prompted widespread concern about the stability of America's social and political fabric.

policies of Lyndon Johnson, his political patron. Conservative Republicans who favored Ronald Reagan as the GOP's 1968 nominee still suspected Nixon to be an Eisenhower moderate. They also recognized, however, that Nixon clearly stood to Humphrey's political right and that he appeared a safer guardian of conservative values than the mercurial Wallace. Nixon promised to restore order at home and hinted at a secret plan for ending U.S. involvement in Vietnam.

Nixon narrowly prevailed in November. Although he won 56 percent of the electoral vote, Nixon outpolled Humphrey in the popular vote by less than 1 percent. George Wallace's plan collapsed when he picked up only 46 electoral votes, all from the Deep South, and just 13.5 percent of the popular vote nationwide. Nixon won five crucial southern states and attracted, all across the country, votes from people he called "the forgotten Americans, the non-shouters, the non-demonstrators."

The results in several states, however, were so close that relatively small shifts could have produced a victory for Humphrey or the scenario that Wallace had envisioned playing out in the House of Representatives. Humphrey's campaign suddenly gained momentum when Lyndon Johnson temporarily halted all bombing of North Vietnam and sought to accelerate the peace talks in Paris. Nixon's forces responded with back-channel overtures to South Vietnamese leaders about getting a better deal if they stalled peace negotiations until a Nixon presidency. Illegal wiretaps informed Johnson of Nixon's maneuver, but LBJ never intervened on Humphrey's behalf (see Map 29.2).

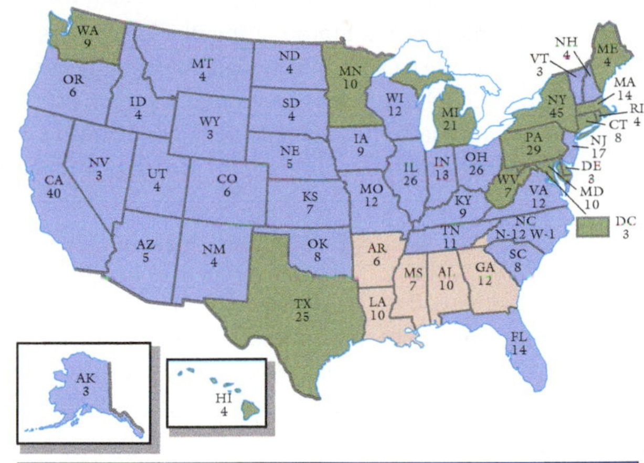

	Electoral Vote		Popular Vote	
	Number	%	Number	%
Humphrey (Democrat)	191	35.5	31,275,166	42.9
Nixon (Republican)	301	56.0	31,785,480	43.6
Wallace (American Independent)	46	8.5	9,906,473	13.5

▲ **MAP 29.2 Presidential Election, 1968**

George Wallace sought to throw the 1968 presidential election into the House of Representatives with his independent, third-party candidacy.

Q *What does this map suggest about the political changes already sweeping through the once solidly Democratic South?*

Q *Why might Republican strategists, after studying electoral maps such as this, have felt optimistic about their party's chances in the presidential race of 1972?*

29-5 Continued Polarization, 1969–1974

Q *What were the sources of the political and cultural turmoil during the late 1960s and early 1970s? Consider President Nixon's law and order stance, social policies, environmentalism, rights-related claims, and economic issues.*

Raised a Quaker, **Richard Milhous Nixon** campaigned as someone able to restore the kind of tranquility he had known when growing up in Yorba Linda, California. His presidency, however, failed to calm the troubled waters.

29-5a *Lawbreaking, Violence, and a New President*

A handful of people on the leftist fringe embraced violence, generally through bomb attacks. There were nearly 200 actual and attempted bombings on college campuses during the 1969–1970 academic year; an explosion at the University of Wisconsin claimed the life of a graduate student. Nonlethal attacks rocked several large banks and the U.S. Capitol building. In 1970, three members of a small faction that had broken with SDS, "the Weather Underground," blew themselves apart when their bomb factory in New York City exploded.

At the same time, government officials stepped up their use of violent force. Fred Hampton of the Black Panthers and prison activist George Jackson died under circumstances their supporters called political assassination and public officials considered normal law enforcement. J. Edgar Hoover's FBI harassed activists, planted damaging rumors, and even dispatched *agent provocateurs* who incited protestors to undertake actions that officials could later prosecute as crimes.

State and local officials redoubled their efforts to bring order. During the fall of 1971, New York governor Nelson Rockefeller broke off negotiations with inmates at Attica State Prison, who had seized several cell blocks and taken guards hostage in a protest over living conditions. He then ordered heavily armed state troopers and National Guard forces into the complex. When this "Attica Uprising" finally ended, 29 prisoners and 11 guards lay dead. On college campuses, too, local officials were increasingly ready to employ force against demonstrators.

Richard Nixon insisted that his vast public experience made him the ideal leader for such turbulent times. After graduating from Whittier College in California, Nixon studied law at Duke University and served in the navy during the Second World War. He then began a political career that took him from a small-town law practice to the House of Representatives in 1946, the Senate in 1950, and the vice presidency in 1952.

Nixon claimed that he excelled at confronting personal and political challenges. He entitled an early memoir *Six Crises*. Nixon had announced his own retirement from politics in 1962, but campaigned loyally for Barry Goldwater in 1964 and for Republican candidates in 1966. The GOP's comeback that year boosted Nixon's stature, and supporters talked about a "New Nixon." Detractors complained of seeing "the same Old Nixon, now just a little older."

29-5b *Social Policy*

Although Nixon considered foreign policy his specialty, he initially crafted an ambitious domestic agenda. At the urging of Democrat Daniel Patrick Moynihan, a special presidential adviser, Nixon decided he could push through bolder programs than any Democratic president. Moynihan encouraged Nixon to think of himself as a conservative who could bring about progressive change. In 1969, Nixon thus proposed his **Family Assistance Plan (FAP)**, a dramatic overhaul of welfare policy. FAP proposed replacing most existing welfare measures, including the controversial Aid to Families with Dependent Children (AFDC). AFDC provided government payments to cover the basic costs of care for low-income children who had lost the support of a breadwinning parent.

Under the FAP proposal, *every* low-income family would be guaranteed an annual income of $1,600. Moynihan and Nixon touted FAP as advancing equality since it replaced existing arrangements that assisted only those with special circumstances. Nixon liked the measure because it promised to cut out the layers of bureaucracy needed to administer the requirements of a complicated program such as AFDC.

Nixon's FAP proposal debuted to tepid reviews. Conservatives complained about income supplements for families with regularly employed, albeit low-paid, wage earners. Proponents of more generous governmental assistance programs argued that FAP's income guarantee was too miserly. The House of Representatives approved a modified version of FAP in 1970, but a curious alliance of senators who opposed Nixon's proposal for very different reasons blocked its passage. Nixon quickly abandoned FAP, and the nation's welfare system would not be overhauled until the 1990s.

Congress did pass Nixon's revenue-sharing plan, part of his "new federalism," which returned a portion of federal tax dollars to state and local governments in the form of block grants. Instead of Washington specifying how these funds could be used, the block grant concept allowed state and local officials, within general guidelines, to spend the funds as they saw fit.

A Democratic-controlled Congress and a Republican White House also agreed to continue and even increase funding for many Great Society initiatives: Medicare, Medicaid, rent subsidies for low-income people, and Supplementary Security Insurance (SSI) payments to those who were elderly, blind, or disabled. In 1972, Social Security benefits were "indexed," which meant they would increase along with the inflation rate (see Figure 29.2).

Nixon had adopted a complicated approach to civil rights during his campaign. He commonly criticized existing policies, such as the busing of children to advance school integration, but carefully distinguished his stance from that of George

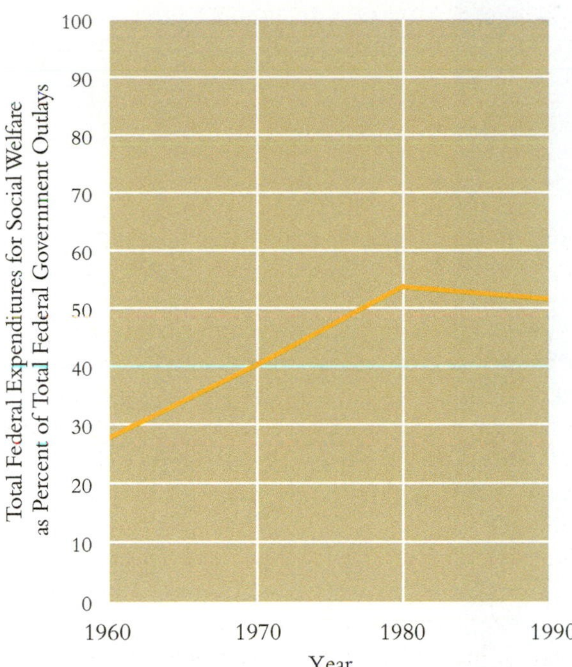

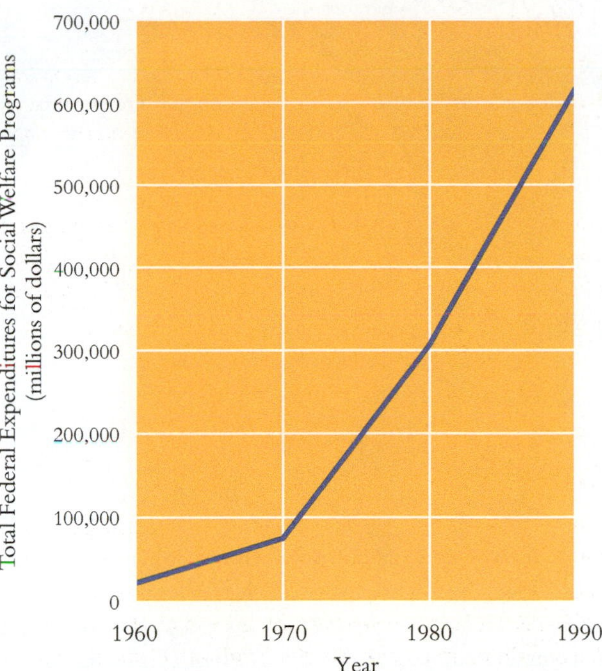

Figure 29.2 **Social Welfare Spending, 1960–1990** These charts seem to present two very different views of social welfare spending in the 1970s and 1980s.

Q *What is the basis on which these different measurements rest? Which measure seems most useful to critics of the Great Society? Which appears most useful to its defenders?*

Wallace. The new Nixon administration included Republicans anxious to aid civil rights causes, and the White House allowed, and sometimes even urged, federal bureaucracies to extend the reach of civil rights measures passed during the Great Society. In line with candidate Nixon's call for supporting "black capitalism" through small-business loans, the new president helped extend the plan to other minority entrepreneurs, particularly Hispanics. His administration also helped implement the bilingual education programs that had been authorized in 1968 legislation. Indeed, many federal social welfare programs expanded during Nixon's first term, and the percentage of people living below the poverty line declined.

29-5c *Environmentalism*

Nixon also worked with the new environmental movement that became a significant political force during his presidency. Landmark legislation of the 1960s—such as the Wilderness Act of 1964, the National Wild and Scenic Rivers Act of 1968, and the National Trails Act of 1968—had already protected large areas of the country from commercial development. In the 1970s, a broader environmental movement focused on people's health and on ecological balance. Accounts such as *The Silent Spring* (1962) by Rachel Carson raised concerns that the pesticides used in agriculture, especially DDT, threatened bird populations. Air pollution (smog) in cities such as Los Angeles had become so toxic that simply breathing became equivalent to smoking several packs of cigarettes per day. Industrial processes, atomic weapons testing, and nuclear power plants prompted fear of cancer-causing materials. The Environmental Defense Fund, a private organization formed in 1967, went to court to try to limit DDT and other dangerous toxins. Earth Day, a festival first held in 1970, aimed to raise awareness about the many newly publicized hazards of environmental degradation.

The Nixon administration, although remaining aloof from Earth Day, took environmental issues seriously. The president supported creation of the Environmental Protection Agency (EPA) and signed major pieces of congressional legislation: the Resources Recovery Act of 1970 (dealing with waste management), the Clean Air Act of 1970, the Water Pollution Control Act of 1972, the Pesticides Control Act of 1972, and the Endangered Species Act of 1973. National parks and wilderness areas were expanded, and a new law required that "environmental impact statements" be prepared in advance of any major government project.

The new environmental standards brought both unanticipated problems and significant improvements. The Clean Air Act's requirement for taller factory smokestacks, for example, moved pollutants higher into the atmosphere, where they produced a dangerous by-product, "acid rain." Still, the act's restrictions on auto and smokestack emissions cleared smog out of city skies and helped people with respiratory ailments. The law reduced six major airborne pollutants by one-third in a single decade. Lead emissions into the atmosphere declined by 95 percent.

Julian Wasser/Getty Images

29.11 **Students at Cerritos College in Norwalk, California Mark Earth Day, 1970** The first Earth Day signaled a rising environmental consciousness in which college students initially played major public roles.

Q *How did these large balloons, used in many Earth Day gatherings, seem an apt symbol for the environmental movement?*

Q *How is concern for the health of the environment currently represented on campuses and schools?*

29-5d *Controversies over Rights*

Activism on social and environmental concerns accompanied fierce debate over the federal government's responsibility to protect the rights and liberties of citizens. The struggle to locate and define these rights soon embroiled the nation's constitutional culture in controversy.

A majority of the justices on the Supreme Court of the Sixties had supported the Great Society's political vision and sought to bring an expanding list of rights under constitutional protection. As this group charted the Court's path, two Eisenhower appointees, Chief Justice Earl Warren and Associate Justice William Brennan, often led the way. Although many of the Warren Court's decisions involving rights issues drew critical fire, the case that raised the most public controversy involved handling criminal suspects. *Miranda v. Arizona* (1966) famously held that the Constitution required police officers to advise persons suspected of having committed a felony offense of their constitutional right to remain silent and to consult an attorney, which would be provided to indigents by the government. Amid rising public concern over crime, political conservatives made decisions such as *Miranda* symbols of what they alleged were the judicial "coddling" of criminals and the Warren Court "inventing" rights not found in the Constitution.

Richard Nixon had campaigned for president as an opponent of the Warren Court and promised to appoint federal judges who would "apply" rather than "invent" the law on matters such as criminal rights and court-ordered school busing. As candidate Nixon continued to assail the Warren Court, the chief justice announced his retirement, and Lyndon Johnson's plan to anoint his close confidant, Associate Justice Abe Fortas, as Warren's successor stalled. Consequently, the victorious Nixon appointed a Republican loyalist, Warren Burger, as chief justice. Subsequent vacancies allowed Nixon to appoint three other Republicans to the High Court.

This new Burger Court immediately faced controversial rights-related cases. Lawyers sympathetic to the Great Society vision of social welfare advanced the argument that access to adequate economic assistance from the federal government was a constitutionally protected right. The Burger Court, however, narrowly rejected this claim in 1970 (*Dandridge v. Williams*), holding that payments to welfare recipients could vary from state to state without violating the constitutional requirement of equal protection of the law.

Other rights-related claims generally fared better. After vetoing two earlier versions, because of his opposition to funding levels, President Nixon signed the Rehabilitation Act of 1973. This civil rights law, pressed by a broadly based activist movement, not only helped people with disabilities fight against various forms of public and private discrimination but assisted them in gaining access to a wide range of governmental services. A vigorous consumer movement, which had initially drawn inspiration from Ralph Nader's exposé about auto safety (*Unsafe at Any Speed*, 1965), joined with environmentalists to bolster new rights claims in the context of workplace safety, consumer protection, and a nontoxic environment. Their efforts found expression in such legislation as the Occupational Safety Act of 1973 and stronger consumer and environmental protection laws. The Burger Court invariably supported the constitutionality of these measures.

At the same time, the newly energized women's rights movement pressed another set of issues. An **Equal Rights Amendment (ERA)**, initially proposed during the 1920s, would explicitly guarantee women the same legal rights as men. Easily passed by Congress in 1972 and quickly ratified by more than half the states, the ERA suddenly stalled. Conservative women's groups, such as Phyllis Schlafly's "Stop ERA," charged that this constitutional amendment would undermine traditional "family values" and expose women to new dangers such as military service. The ERA failed to attain approval from the three-quarters of states needed for ratification. Ultimately, women's groups abandoned the ERA effort in favor of using the courts to adjudicate equal rights claims on a case-by-case, issue-by-issue basis.

One of these issues, whether a woman possessed a constitutional right to terminate a pregnancy, became far more controversial than the ERA. The abortion issue, in contrast to controversies over busing and criminal procedure, had never played a prominent role in Nixon's 1968 campaign, and his administration thus paid little attention to this rights-related question when nominating federal judges. In ***Roe v. Wade* (1973)**, the Burger Supreme Court ruled, in a 7–2 decision, that a state law making abortion a criminal offense violated a woman's "right to privacy." Two of the three justices appointed by Nixon voted with the majority. The *Roe* decision outraged antiabortion groups, who rallied under the "Right-to-Life" banner on behalf of the unborn fetus and provided new support for the already expanding conservative wing of the Republican Party. On the other side, feminist groups made the issue of individual choice in reproductive decisions a central rallying point.

Meanwhile, with little controversy, President Nixon signed an extension of the Voting Rights Act of 1965, and in 1972 approved another civil rights measure popularly known as "Title IX." It banned sexual discrimination in higher education and became the legal basis for requiring colleges and universities to adopt "gender equity" in all areas, including intercollegiate athletics. The Nixon administration also refined the "affirmative action" concept, which had surfaced during Lyndon Johnson's presidency, and required that all hiring and contracting that depended on federal funding take "affirmative" steps to enroll greater numbers of people from underrepresented groups as union apprentices.

29-5e *Economic Woes*

The Nixon administration eventually confronted economic problems that had been unthinkable only a decade earlier. No single cause can account for them, but most analyses begin with the war in Vietnam. This expensive military commitment, along with increased domestic spending and a volatile international economy, began to curtail economic growth. Lyndon Johnson had been determined to contain communism in Indochina without cutting Great Society programs or raising taxes, and thus he had concealed the true costs of the war. Nixon inherited a deteriorating (although still favorable) balance of trade and rising rate of inflation. Nixon never expected to grapple with a faltering economy. One of his economic advisers conceded that the president had "an almost pathological block about considering economic issues."

By 1971, though, the unemployment rate topped 6 percent. According to conventional wisdom, expressed in an economic concept called "the Phillips curve," when unemployment rises, prices should remain constant or even decline. Yet *both* unemployment and inflation numbers were going up simultaneously. Economists coined the term ***stagflation*** to describe this puzzling convergence of economic stagnation and price inflation. Along with stagflation, U.S. exports were becoming less competitive in international markets and in 1971, for the first time in the 20th century, the United States ran a trade deficit, importing more products than it exported.

Although long critical of economic regulation, Nixon now needed a quick governmental cure for the nation's economic ills. His narrow victory in 1968 and GOP setbacks in the midterm elections of 1970 left him fearful of the political fallout from stagflation and trade imbalances. In January 1971 he suddenly, and surprisingly, announced, "I am now a Keynesian in economics" and began proclaiming his faith in governmental remedies. In August, he unveiled a "New Economic Policy" that included a 90-day freeze on any increases in wages and prices, to be followed by government monitoring to detect "excessive" increases in either.

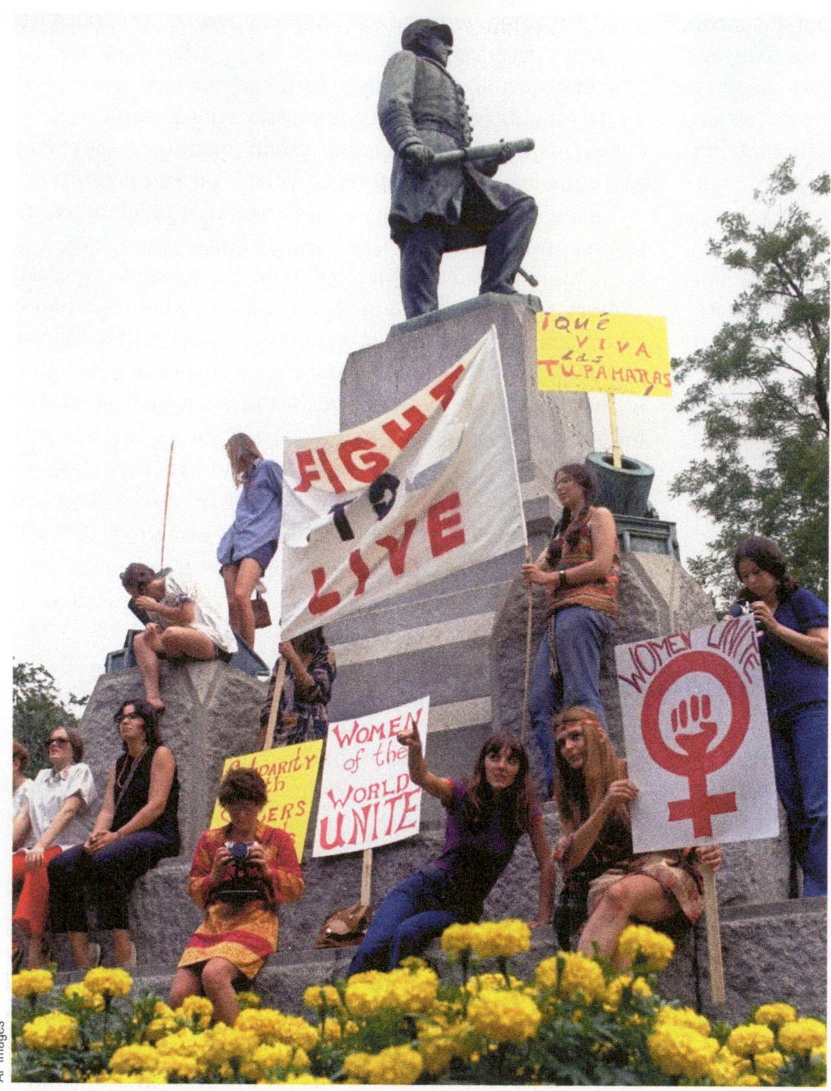

AP Images

29.12 **Women's Rights Demonstrators, August 16, 1970** Activists, who gathered in Washington, D.C. to demonstrate on behalf of women's rights, take time to rest.

Q *Why might they have chosen to "occupy" a statue erected in honor of a 19th-century military hero, Admiral David G. Farragut?*

Nixon simultaneously took an even more daring step. Dating from the 1944 Bretton Woods agreement (see Chapter 26), the value of the U.S. dollar had been tied to the value of gold—at $35 for every ounce. This meant that the United States would exchange its dollars for gold at that rate whenever any other nation's central bank requested it to do so. Other countries had fixed their own currency exchange rate in relation to the value of the U.S. dollar. But U.S. trade deficits were undermining the dollar and allowing foreign banks to exchange U.S. dollars for gold at rates far more favorable than $35 per ounce. In response, the Nixon administration abandoned the fixed gold-to-dollar ratio. Henceforth, the U.S. dollar would "float" in value against the prevailing market price for gold and against all other currencies in the world. This change would devalue the dollar and hopefully make American exports more competitive in the global marketplace. The strategy fundamentally altered the international economic order by allowing the value of all currencies to float and fluctuate.

In October 1973, oil-producing nations in the Middle East further changed international economic arrangements. Citing the declining U.S. dollar and falling oil revenues as justifications, petroleum producers began curtailing exports as a means of raising prices. About a week later, in response to U.S. military aid for Israel, then engaged in the Yom Kippur War with Egypt and Syria, Arab nations temporarily embargoed oil shipments to the United States. Nixon and Congress responded with a series of measures that included rationing, lower speed limits, and the naming of a new "energy czar." The days of "cheap oil" were coming to an end in the United States.

29-6 Foreign Policy in a Time of Turmoil, 1969–1974

Q *What were the Nixon administration's major foreign policy aims and how successful was it in implementing its policies?*

Even as it wrestled with divisive domestic concerns, the Nixon administration was far more interested in international affairs. Henry Kissinger, Nixon's national security adviser and later his secretary of state, laid out a grand strategy: ***détente*** with the Soviet Union, normalization of relations with China, and disengagement from direct military involvement in South Vietnam.

29-6a *Détente*

Although Nixon had built his early political career on hard-line anticommunism, he and Kissinger worked to ease tensions with the two major communist nations: the Soviet Union and China. The Nixon-Kissinger team expected that improved relations might lead these nations to reduce their support for North Vietnam, increasing chances for a successful pullback of U.S. combat troops.

Arms control talks took top priority in U.S.–Soviet relations. In 1969, the two superpowers opened the Strategic Arms Limitation Talks (SALT); after several years of high-level diplomacy, they signed an agreement (SALT I) that limited further development of both antiballistic missiles (ABMs) and offensive intercontinental ballistic missiles (ICBMs). SALT I's impact on the arms race was limited because it said nothing about the number of nuclear warheads that a single missile might carry. Still, the ability to conclude any arms-control pact signaled improving relations.

Nixon's overtures toward the People's Republic of China brought an even more dramatic break with the cold war past. Secret negotiations, often conducted personally by Kissinger, led to a slight easing of U.S. trade restrictions and then to an invitation from China for Americans to compete in a table tennis match. This celebrated "Ping-Pong diplomacy" presaged more significant diplomatic exchanges. Most spectacularly, Nixon visited China in 1972, posing for photos with Mao Zedong and strolling along the Great Wall. A few months later, the UN admitted the People's Republic as the sole representative of China, and in 1973 the United States and China exchanged informal diplomatic missions.

29-6b *Vietnamization and the Nixon Doctrine*

In Vietnam, the Nixon administration decided to speed withdrawal of U.S. ground forces by embracing a policy called "Vietnamization," which had already informally begun during Lyndon Johnson's administration. Put simply, this meant that South Vietnamese, rather than U.S. troops, should bear the burden of ground combat operations. In July 1969, the **Nixon Doctrine** announced a broader version of this approach. It pledged that the United States would extend military assistance to anticommunist governments in Asia but would require them to supply their own combat forces. From the outset, the Nixon Doctrine for Vietnam envisioned the eventual removal of U.S. ground troops without accepting compromise or defeat. While officially adhering to Johnson's 1968 bombing halt over the North, Nixon and Kissinger accelerated both the ground and air wars by launching new offensives and by approving a military "incursion" into Cambodia, an ostensibly neutral country. The 1970 operation into Cambodia, which targeted North Vietnamese there, aimed at shortening U.S. military engagement in Southeast Asia by temporarily expanding it.

The invasion of Cambodia set off a new wave of protests in the United States and around the world. U.S. campuses exploded in angry demonstrations against this obvious widening of the war, and a number of institutions began the summer vacation early. White police officers fatally shot two students at the all-black Jackson State College in Mississippi, and National Guard troops at Kent State University in Ohio fired on unarmed protesters, killing four students. As antiwar demonstrators descended on Washington, D.C., Nixon seemed personally unnerved by the furor, especially during an unscheduled, late-night meeting with protesting students.

A continuing controversy over the **My Lai Incident** further polarized sentiment over the war. Shortly after the 1968 Tet Offensive, U.S. troops had entered the small South Vietnamese hamlet of My Lai and murdered more than 200 civilians, most of them women and children. This massacre only became public in 1969. Military courts convicted only one officer, Lieutenant William Calley, of any offense. Critics charged that the military was using Calley as a scapegoat for

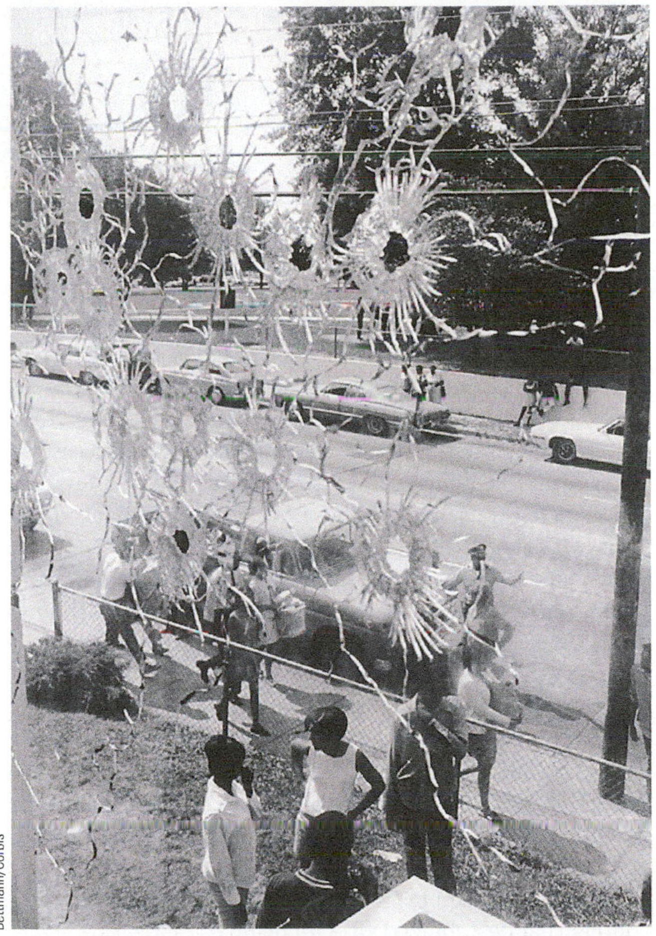
Bettmann/Corbis

29.13 **Jackson State** The era of America's divisive war was a time of violence overseas and at home. In May 1970, police gunfire killed two students and wounded 15 others at Jackson State University in Mississippi. This picture was taken through a bullet-riddled window in a women's dorm.

29.14 **Henry Kissinger** As the U.S. intervention in Vietnam dragged on, prowar and anti-war factions came to be known respectively as "hawks" and "doves."

Q *How does this 1973 caricature draw on this terminology to challenge Secretary of State Kissinger's reputation as a peacemaker who won a Nobel Peace Prize that year?*

a failed strategy that emphasized body counts and lax rules of engagement. Injecting the White House into this controversy, Nixon ordered that the young lieutenant be confined to his officer's quarters, rather than prison, pending the results of his appeal. Ultimately, Calley was ordered released based on procedural irregularities. Controversy over the Calley case inflamed tensions between those Americans who backed and those who opposed the war.

Meanwhile, the Nixon administration widened military operations to include Laos as well as Cambodia. Although it denied waging any such campaign, large areas of those agricultural countries were ravaged. As the number of refugees inside Cambodia swelled and food supplies dwindled, the communist guerrilla force there—the Khmer Rouge—came to power and in a murderous attempt to eliminate dissent turned Cambodia into a "killing field." It slaughtered more than 1 million Cambodians. While Nixon continued to plan U.S. troop withdrawals and conduct peace negotiations with North Vietnam in Paris, the Vietnam War had become a conflict that destabilized all of Indochina.

Even greater violence was yet to come. During the spring of 1972, North Vietnam's "Easter Offensive" approached within 30 miles of Saigon before falling back. The surge showed the limits of Vietnamization and swelled South Vietnam's refugee population. Nixon responded with an escalation as great as that by Lyndon Johnson in 1965. He ordered the systematic bombing of North Vietnam, the mining of its harbors, and the institution of a naval blockade. Just weeks before the November 1972 elections in the United States, Henry Kissinger declared that "peace is at hand" and announced a cease-fire. After Nixon's reelection, however, the impending peace deal fell apart in Paris, and the United States unleashed even greater firepower over North Vietnam. During the "Christmas bombing" of December 1972, the heaviest bombardment in history, B-52 planes pounded military and civilian targets in North Vietnam around the clock. North Vietnam, which was also feeling diplomatic pressure from the Soviet Union and China, decided to conclude peace negotiations with Washington and Saigon.

29-6c *The United States Leaves Vietnam*

Much of the U.S. media, Congress, and the public were also calling for an end to the war. Many were tired of the violence in Asia and of the administration's effort to stem dissent at home. In addition, sagging morale among U.S. troops hindered the missions that the U.S. command was still conducting. Soldiers questioned the purpose of their sacrifices; some refused to engage the enemy; and a few openly defied their superiors. At home, Vietnam Veterans Against the War (VVAW), a new organization, joined the antiwar coalition. Running out of nonbombing options, Nixon proceeded with full-scale Vietnamization.

In January 1973, the warring parties signed peace accords in Paris that provided for the withdrawal of U.S. troops. The actual terms closely resembled those in the preelection deal that Kissinger had celebrated but which had later fallen apart. By allowing North Vietnamese troops to remain in the South, the Paris accords left Nguyen Van Thieu's government in a precarious position, and Nixon may have anticipated preserving it by future bombing campaigns. As U.S. ground forces departed, the South Vietnamese army continued to fight. In spring 1975, nearly two years after the Paris accords, South Vietnam's army and Thieu's government would collapse as North Vietnamese armies entered the capital of Saigon (see Chapter 30). America's increasingly divisive war ended with its objective of maintaining a noncommunist South Vietnam unfulfilled.

Between 1960 and 1973, approximately 3.5 million American men and women served in Vietnam; 58,000 died, 150,000 were wounded, and 2,000 were classified as missing. War-related disabilities, both physical and mental, would continue to affect veterans and to challenge the nation's medical and social services. In this aftermath, Americans struggled to understand why their country failed to defeat a small, barely industrialized nation. Those still supporting the war argued that it had been lost on the home front. They blamed an irresponsible media, a disloyal antiwar movement, and a Congress afflicted by a "failure of will." The war, they insisted, had been for a laudable cause. Politicians, setting unrealistic limits on the Pentagon, had prevented strategists from attaining victory. By contrast, those who had come to oppose the war stressed the overextension of U.S. power, the misguided belief in national omnipotence, the dangers of touching off a wider war with China, and the strategic miscalculations of decision makers. For them, the United States had waged a war in the wrong place for the wrong reasons. The human costs in both the United States and Indochina outweighed any possible gain.

Regardless of their position on the war, most Americans seemed to agree on a single proposition: "no more Vietnams." The United States should never undertake another military operation unless it involved clear and compelling political objectives, sustained public support, and realistic means to accomplish its goals. Eventually, people who wanted to reassert U.S. power in the world dismissed this caution as "the Vietnam syndrome." The legacy of these divisions would continue far beyond the end of the war.

29-6d *Expanding the Nixon Doctrine*

Although the Nixon Doctrine initially only applied to the Vietnamization of the war in Indochina, Nixon and Kissinger extended its premise to the entire world. The White House made clear that the United States would not dispatch its troops to quash insurgencies but would generously aid anticommunist regimes or factions willing to fight their own battles.

During the early 1970s, U.S. cold war strategy came to rely on supporting staunchly anticommunist regional powers. These included nations such as Iran under Shah Reza Pahlavi, South Africa with its apartheid regime, and Brazil with its military dictatorship. All of these countries built large, U.S.-trained military establishments. U.S. military assistance, together with covert CIA operations, also incubated and protected anticommunist dictatorships in South Korea, the Philippines, and much of Latin America. U.S. arms sales to the rest of the world skyrocketed. In one of its most controversial foreign policies, the Nixon administration employed covert action against the elected socialist government of Salvador Allende Gossens in Chile in 1970. After Allende took office, Kissinger pressed for the destabilization of his government. On September 11, 1973, the Chilean military overthrew Allende, immediately suspended democratic rule, and announced that Allende had committed suicide.

Critics charged that the United States, in the name of anticommunism, too often linked its diplomatic fortunes to questionable covert actions and unpopular military governments. In 1973, Democratic senator Frank Church conducted Senate hearings into abuses of power by the executive branch, especially the CIA's actions in Chile. Supporters of Nixon and Kissinger, however, gave the pair high marks for a pragmatic foreign policy that combined détente toward the communist giants with containment directed against the spread of revolutionary regimes.

29-7 A Crisis of Governance, 1972–1974

Q *What were the factors in the early 1970s that prompted a crisis of governance, undermined Richard Nixon's presidency, and forced his resignation?*

A political loner who ruminated about taking revenge against his enemies, Nixon often seemed his own greatest foe. He ordered the Internal Revenue Service (IRS) to harass prominent Democrats with expensive audits; placed antiwar and Black Power activists under surveillance; and conducted risky covert activities on the domestic front that even rattled the constitutional sensibilities of an old ally, J. Edgar Hoover. Isolated with a close-knit group of advisers, Nixon eventually created his own secret intelligence unit, "the Plumbers," which set up shop in the White House.

During the summer of 1971, Daniel Ellsberg, an antiwar activist who had once worked in the national security bureaucracy, leaked to the press a top-secret, highly critical history of U.S. involvement in the Vietnam War, subsequently known as the "Pentagon Papers." Nixon responded by seeking, unsuccessfully, a court injunction to stop publication and, more ominously, by unleashing his Plumbers unit to stop leaks to the media. Seeking something that might discredit Ellsberg, the Plumbers burglarized his psychiatrist's office. Thus began a series of secretive political "dirty tricks" and clear-cut crimes, sometimes financed by funds solicited for Nixon's 1972 reelection campaign.

29-7a *The Election of 1972*

Nixon's political strategists worried that domestic troubles and the war in Vietnam might deny the president another term. Creating a campaign organization separate from that of the Republican Party, with the ironic acronym of CREEP (Committee to Re-elect the President), they secretly raised millions of dollars, much of it from illegal contributions.

As the 1972 campaign took shape, Nixon's chances for reelection dramatically improved. An assassin's bullet crippled George Wallace and kept him from playing the spoiler's role in November. Senator Edmund Muskie of Maine, initially Nixon's leading Democratic challenger, made a series of blunders (some of them, perhaps, precipitated by Republican "dirty tricksters") that derailed his campaign. Eventually, Senator George McGovern of South Dakota, an outspoken opponent of the Vietnam War but a lackluster campaigner, won the Democratic nomination.

McGovern never seriously challenged Nixon. The Democratic candidate called for higher taxes on the wealthy, a guaranteed minimum income for all Americans, amnesty for Vietnam War draft resisters, and the decriminalization of marijuana. In foreign policy, he urged deep cuts in defense spending and peace in Vietnam—proposals that Nixon successfully portrayed as signs of "weakness." Nixon won an easy victory in November, receiving the Electoral College votes of all but one state and the District of Columbia. Although the Twenty-sixth Amendment, ratified one year before the election, had lowered the voting age to 18, relatively few of the newly enfranchised voters cast ballots (see Map 29.3).

While helping achieve this victory, the president's supporters left a trail of crime and corruption that eventually led to a crisis of governance. In June 1972, a surveillance team with links to both CREEP and the White House had been arrested while fine-tuning eavesdropping equipment in the Democratic Party's headquarters in Washington's Watergate office complex. In public, Nixon's spokespeople dismissed the Watergate break-in as a "third-rate burglary." In private, the president and his inner circle launched a cover-up. They paid hush money to the Watergate burglars and ordered CIA officials to misinform the FBI that any investigation into the episode would jeopardize national security. Nixon contained the political damage through the 1972 election, but events associated with **Watergate** soon overtook him.

29-7b *The Watergate Investigations*

While reporters from the *Washington Post* pursued the taint of scandal coming from the election, Congress, the federal courts, and government prosecutors also sought evidence of lawbreaking. Federal District Judge John Sirica, a Republican appointee presiding over the trial of the Watergate burglars, suspected a cover-up and pressed the defendants before his court for additional information. In May 1973, U.S. Senate leaders convened a special, bipartisan Watergate Committee, headed by North Carolina's conservative Democratic senator Sam Ervin, to investigate. Federal prosecutors uncovered evidence that seemed to link key administration figures, including John Mitchell, Nixon's former attorney general and later the head of CREEP, to illegal activities.

The Ervin hearings, carried live on TV, eventually became a daily political drama that much of the country watched. Testimony from John Dean, who had been the president's chief legal counsel, linked Nixon himself to attempts to cover up Watergate and to other illegal activities. The president steadfastly denied Dean's charges.

Along the way, though, Senate investigators discovered that a voice-activated taping system had recorded conversations between Nixon and his aides in the Oval Office. These tapes made it possible to determine whether the president or Dean, Nixon's primary accuser, was lying. While contending he was not "a crook," Nixon also claimed an "executive privilege" to keep the tapes from being released, but Judge Sirica, Archibald Cox (a special, independent prosecutor in the Watergate case), and Congress all demanded access to them.

If Nixon's Watergate-related problems were not enough, his vice president, Spiro Agnew, suddenly resigned in October 1973 after pleading no contest to income tax evasion. Agnew agreed to a plea-bargain arrangement to avoid prosecution for having accepted illegal kickbacks while in Maryland politics. Acting under the Twenty-fifth Amendment (ratified in 1967), Nixon appointed—and both houses of Congress confirmed—Republican representative Gerald R. Ford of Michigan as the new vice president.

29-7c *Nixon's Resignation*

Nixon's clumsy efforts to protect himself backfired. During the fall of 1973, Nixon had abruptly fired Archibald Cox, hoping to prevent him from gaining access to the tapes. Nixon's own release of edited transcripts of some Watergate-related conversations, including one key transcript containing an 18-minute gap in the tape, merely strengthened demand for the original recordings. Finally, by proclaiming that he would obey only a "definitive" Supreme Court decision, Nixon all but invited the justices to deliver a unanimous ruling against his withholding of the tapes in a criminal investigation. In July 1974, the Burger Court did just that in the case of *U.S. v. Nixon*. After televised deliberations, a bipartisan majority of the House Judiciary Committee voted three formal articles of impeachment against the president for obstruction of justice, violation of constitutional liberties, and refusal to produce evidence.

Nixon promised to rebut these accusations during a trial by the Senate, but his aides were already orchestrating his departure. One of his own attorneys had discovered

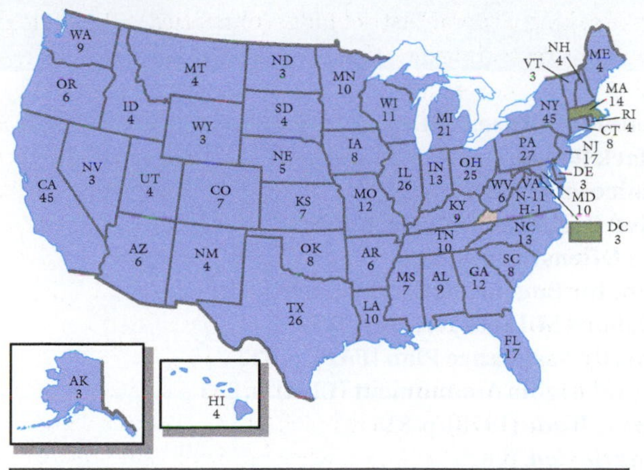

	Electoral Vote		Popular Vote	
	Number	%	Number	%
McGovern (Democrat)	17	3.1	29,170,383	37.5
Nixon (Republican)	520	96.7	47,169,911	60.7
Hospers (Libertarian)	1	0.2	3,673	----
Schmitz (American)	----	----	1,099,482	1.4

▲ **MAP 29.3 Presidential Election, 1972**

In contrast to the closely contested election of 1968, the 1972 election produced a landslide victory for Richard Nixon.

Q *What helps explain the stark difference between these two elections?*

Q *What events would force Richard Nixon, in 1974, to leave an office to which he had been overwhelmingly returned?*

that a tape Nixon had been withholding contained the long-sought "smoking gun," clear evidence of a criminal offense. It confirmed that during a 1972 conversation, Nixon had helped hatch a plan by which the CIA would advance the fraudulent claim of national security in order to stop the FBI from investigating the Watergate break-in. Nixon's own secretary of defense now ordered military commanders to ignore any order from the president, unless the secretary had countersigned it. Abandoned by most prominent Republicans and confronted by a Senate prepared to vote him guilty on the impeachment charges, Nixon went on television on August 8, 1974, to announce his resignation. On August 9, Gerald Ford became the nation's 38th chief executive. He assumed the post never having been elected president or vice president.

In 1974, most people told pollsters that the string of abuses collectively known as "Watergate" was one of the gravest crises in the history of the republic and that the Nixon administration had posed a serious threat to constitutional governance. Opinion polls conducted on the 20th anniversary of Nixon's resignation, however, suggested that Americans by then only dimly recalled the crisis of governance associated with the Nixon administration.

What might account for this change? First, nearly a dozen members of Nixon's administration—including its chief law enforcement officer, John Mitchell—were convicted of criminal activities, but the president avoided prosecution. Gerald Ford granted Nixon an unconditional pardon. The nation was spared the spectacle of a former president undergoing trial, but it was also denied an authoritative accounting, in a court of law, of Nixon's misdeeds.

Another reason for fading memories may be the media's habit of attaching the Watergate label to nearly every political scandal of the post-Nixon era. The suffix "gate" became affixed to grave constitutional episodes and to obviously trivial political events. Over time, then, "Watergate" became almost a synonym for "politics as usual." Finally, images of what the historian Stanley Kutler calls the "Wars of Watergate" have tended to blend into the broader picture of political, social, economic, and cultural turmoil that characterized the era.

Conclusion

The years from 1963 to 1974 brought fundamental changes to American life. At home, the first significant wave of domestic legislation since the New Deal stretched the reach of national programs (and that of the bureaucracies that administered them), thus igniting fierce debate over the proper power of Washington in American life. Legislative acts, court decisions, and administrative rulings aimed at addressing racial and gender discrimination helped produce the sectional realignment of the two major parties, as conservative white southerners dramatically accelerated their move from the Democratic into the Republican Party. The civil rights movements of the earlier post-World War II period broadened into an array of insurgencies that sought to mobilize and empower people according to group identities that included race, ethnicity, gender, sexual preference, and spiritual belief. These mobilizations sparked controversies over redefinitions of basic rights of citizenship.

Overseas, what began as a limited cold war era intervention against communism in Asia morphed into a brutal and divisive conflict that ended with the United States being forced to abandon its effort to maintain a noncommunist regime in South Vietnam. In trying to blunt domestic dissent against this Vietnam War and to shield foreign policy activities from public scrutiny, the executive branch, especially during Richard Nixon's administration, widened the gaze of surveillance bureaucracies. By 1974, most Americans, including a bipartisan majority of political leaders, judged the Nixon presidency so threatening to constitutional governance that they forced, through informal pressures as well as the impeachment process, the first presidential resignation in the nation's history.

During the rest of the 20th and the early years of the 21st centuries, debates over governance, fundamental rights, social-economic policy, and America's role in the world took place within frameworks constructed between 1963 and 1974. Decisions made and directions chosen, as one recent history puts it, initiated an important "realignment of American democracy."

CHAPTER REVIEW

Review

1. What were the major goals and programs of the Johnson administration's Great Society, and why did these become controversial?
2. Why did Lyndon Johnson's decision to enlarge America's military role in Vietnam, although initially popular, produce widening dissent?
3. How did the social movements that emerged during the divisive war in Vietnam seek to change U.S. politics and culture? What role did mass media play?
4. What helped to make the single year of 1968 seem a pivotal time in the larger history of the era of the Vietnam War?
5. What were the sources of the political and cultural turmoil during the late 1960s and early 1970s? Consider President Nixon's law and order stance, social policies, environmentalism, rights-related claims, and economic issues.
6. What were the Nixon administration's major foreign policy aims and how successful was it in implementing its policies?
7. What were the factors in the early 1970s that prompted a crisis of governance, undermined Richard Nixon's presidency, and forced his resignation?

Critical Thinking

1. What were the long-term repercussions of the war in Vietnam on America's economy, social fabric, culture, and foreign policy?
2. Great Society proposals deepened long-term debates over the extension of government power and over definitions of civil and personal liberties. How did issues of race, gender, and the distribution of wealth and income figure in these debates?
3. How did the polarization and civic turmoil of the Vietnam War era affect how different people and groups saw the history and future of the United States? Does this era still affect U.S. politics and culture?

Identifications

Review your understanding of the following key terms, people, and events for this chapter (terms in bold in text are included in the Glossary).

Civil Rights Act of 1964, p. 804
Freedom Summer, p. 804
Barry Goldwater, p. 805
Great Society, p. 806
Voting Rights Act of 1965, p. 807
Immigration and Nationality Act of 1965, p. 807
Gulf of Tonkin Resolution, p. 808
General William Westmoreland, p. 810
New Left, p. 812
counterculture, p. 813
Black Power, p. 815
Malcolm X, p. 815
Civil Rights Act of 1968, p. 816
Tet Offensive, p. 818
Senator Eugene McCarthy, p. 818
Richard Milhous Nixon, p. 822
Family Assistance Plan (FAP), p. 822
Equal Rights Amendment (ERA), p. 825
***Roe v. Wade* (1973)**, p. 825
stagflation, p. 825
détente, p.826
Nixon Doctrine, p. 827
My Lai Incident, p. 827
Watergate, p. 830

Suggested Readings

On policy-making in the 1960s, see **C. Calvin Mackenzie and Robert Weisbrot**, ***The Liberal Hour: Washington and the Politics of Change in the 1960s*** (2008). The best biographies of Lyndon Johnson include **Robert J. Dallek**, ***Flawed Giant: Lyndon Johnson and His Times, 1961–1973*** (1998); and **Randall B. Woods**, ***LBJ: Architect of American Ambition*** (2006). **Robert Caro**, ***The Years of Lyndon Johnson: The Passage of Power*** (2012), details the transition from the New Frontier to the Great Society, including the passage of the Civil Rights Act of 1964. **Clay Risen**, ***The Bill of the Century: The Epic Battle for the Civil Rights Act*** (2014) disputes some of Caro's claims about LBJ's role.

The many outstanding histories of U.S. involvement in Vietnam include **Mark Philip Bradley**, ***Vietnam at War*** (2009); **Mark Atwood Lawrence**, ***The Vietnam War: A Concise International History***, (2008); and **Nick Turse**, ***Kill Anything That Moves: The Real American War in Vietnam*** (2013); and **Christian Appy**, ***American Reckoning: The Vietnam War and Our National Identity*** (2015).

The following books offer introductions to the "movement of movements" during the 1960s: **Terry Anderson**, ***The Movement and the Sixties: Protest in America From Greensboro to Wounded Knee*** (1996); **Robert Self**, ***American Babylon: Race and the Struggle for Postwar Oakland*** (2003); **Peniel E. Joseph**, ***Waiting 'Til the Midnight Hour: A Narrative History of Black Power in America*** (2007); and **Joseph's** biography of Stokely Carmichael, ***Stokely: A Life*** (2014). The year 1965 is highlighted in **James T. Patterson**, ***The Eve of Destruction: How 1965 Transformed America*** (2012), as is 1968 in **Mark Kurlansky**, ***1968: The Year that Rocked the World*** (2003). On student movements, see **Seth Rosenfeld**, ***Subversives: The FBI's War on Student Radicals and Reagan's Rise to Power*** (2013). On prisoner rights movements, see **Heather A. Thompson**, ***Blood in the Water: The Attica Prison Uprising of 1971 and Its Legacy*** (2016).

On the transition from the late 1960s to the early 1970s, see **Andreas Hillen**, ***1973 Nervous Breakdown: Watergate, Warhol, and the Birth of Post-Sixties America*** (2006). On the riddle that was Richard Nixon, see **David Greenberg**, ***Nixon's Shadow: The History of an Image*** (2003). **Stanley I. Kutler, ed.**, ***Abuse of Power: The New Nixon Tapes*** (1997), provides evidence, in the president's own words, of Nixon's approach to politics and constitutional limitations. Other constitutional and legal issues can be followed in **Bruce Ackerman**, ***We the People, Volume 3: The Civil Rights Revolution*** (2014); and **Lucas A. Powe, Jr.**, ***The Warren Court and American Politics*** (2000).

30 Uncertain Times, 1974–1992

MCA/Universal Pictures/Everett Collection.

30.1 **Back to the Future** As president, Ronald Reagan seemed as fluent with the movie culture of the 1980s as with that from his own Hollywood past. His 1986 State of the Union Address invoked a line from *Back to the Future* (1985)—"Where we're going, we don't need roads"—to underscore his faith that reliance on the nation's past history of technological innovation would ensure its future. Several quips from this movie, which featured time travel between 1985 and 1955, also played on Reagan's own unorthodox path from the silver screen to the White House.

Q *How can images of cars and roads be employed in political rhetoric?*

EVENTS OF THE 1960s AND EARLY 1970s, particularly Vietnam and Watergate, shook popular faith in government. Secrecy, corruption, and economic problems bred further disillusionment. During the 1970s and 1980s, Americans debated how to respond to an aging industrial economy, a growing federal deficit, and a beleaguered social welfare system. Did the country need new governmental programs, or might conditions improve if Washington reduced its role in daily life?

Disagreement extended to foreign policy. Should the United States minimize anticommunism to pursue other goals, as Democratic president Jimmy Carter (1977–1981) initially urged, or should it wage the cold war even more vigorously, as his successor, Republican Ronald Reagan (1981–1989), advocated? After 1989, when the cold war ended unexpectedly, the United States needed to find a foreign policy for a post-cold war world.

Meanwhile, the "movement of movements," a legacy of the 1960s, refused to fade away. Social movements associated with women's rights, gay rights, and racial and ethnic identities affected how Americans saw themselves and their nation's future. Some of the goals of these movements, however, met strident opposition from the New Right that had helped build Reagan's popularity. During these years, the polarization of American politics that had become so evident during the Vietnam War and Watergate eras deepened and broadened, sparking new controversies over issues such as abortion, taxation, affirmative action, and environmental regulations. ■

CHRONOLOGY

1974	Nixon resigns and Ford becomes president • Ford soon pardons Nixon
1975	South Vietnam falls to North Vietnam • Ford asserts U.S. power in *Mayaguez* incident
1976	Jimmy Carter elected president
1978	Carter helps negotiate Camp David peace accords on Middle East • OPEC announces it will sharply raise oil prices
1979	Soviet Union invades Afghanistan • *Sandinistas* come to power in Nicaragua • U.S. hostages seized in Iran
1980	Reagan elected president • U.S. hostages in Iran released
1981	Reagan tax cut passed
1983	U.S. troops removed from Lebanon • Reagan announces SDI ("Star Wars") program
1984	Reagan defeats Walter Mondale
1986	Reagan administration rocked by revelation of Iran–contra affair
1988	George H. W. Bush defeats Michael Dukakis in presidential election • Congress enacts Indian Gaming Regulation Act
1989	Communist regimes in Eastern Europe collapse • Berlin Wall falls • Cold war, in effect, ends
1990	Bush angers conservative Republicans by agreeing to a tax increase
1991	Bush orchestrates Persian Gulf War against Iraq
1992	Bill Clinton defeats Bush

30-1 Searching for Direction, 1974–1980

Q *How did the legacies of the Vietnam War and Watergate help shape U.S. politics in the years that immediately followed?*

When Richard Nixon resigned in August 1974, **Gerald R. Ford**, his vice president, moved from one office to which voters had never elected him to another, the presidency. Ford promised to "heal the land," but he achieved little success. A genial, unpretentious former college football star, Ford preferred that his public appearances be accompanied by the fight song of his alma mater, the University of Michigan, rather than "Hail to the Chief." His attempt to present his administration as an updated version of the "modern Republicanism" of the 1950s quickly foundered. His appointment of Nelson Rockefeller as vice president infuriated GOP conservatives, and his pardoning of former president Nixon, in September 1974, angered almost everyone. Ford's approval rating skidded downward, and he nearly lost the GOP's 1976 presidential nomination to Ronald Reagan, who campaigned as a "true conservative" owing nothing to Washington insiders.

The Democrats did turn to an outsider, **James Earl (Jimmy) Carter**. A retired naval officer, engineer, peanut farmer, and former governor of Georgia, Carter campaigned by stressing personal character. He highlighted his smalltown roots and his Southern Baptist faith. To balance the ticket, he picked Senator Walter Mondale of Minnesota as his running mate. In November of 1976 Carter won a narrow victory over Ford (see Map 30.1).

Carter's election rested on a transitory coalition. He carried every southern state except Virginia, running well among both whites who belonged to fundamentalist and evangelical churches and African Americans. Carter also courted former antiwar activists by promising to pardon most Vietnam-era draft resisters. Walter Mondale's appeal helped capture the Democratic strongholds of New York, Pennsylvania, and Ohio. The election was close, however, and voter turnout hit its lowest mark (54 percent) since the end of the Second World War.

Jimmy Carter's lack of a popular mandate and his outsider status proved serious handicaps. After leaving government, Carter reflected on his difficulties: "I had a different way of governing... . I was a southerner, a born-again Christian, a Baptist, a newcomer." Moreover, Carter was caught between advisers who, on the one hand, claimed that the national government exercised too much power and, on the other, argued that Washington did too little to address domestic and foreign problems.

The 865-day presidency of Ford and the one-term administration of Carter reflected the political uncertainties of post-Vietnam and post-Watergate America. The sense of national crisis seemed unrelenting, as politicians and citizens alike attempted to cope with a staggering economy, disruptive energy shortages, and sensationalized foreign challenges.

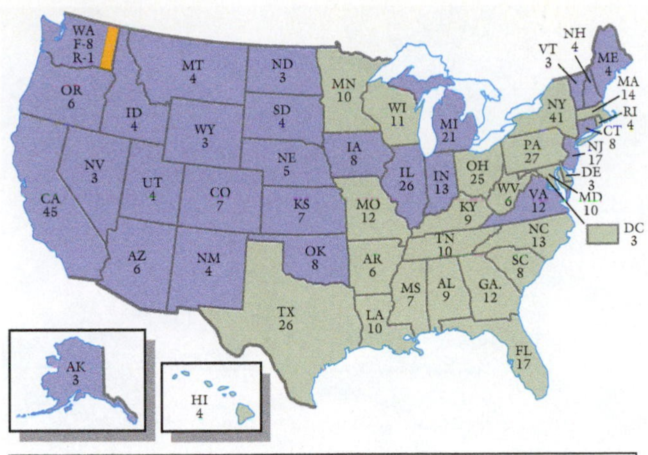

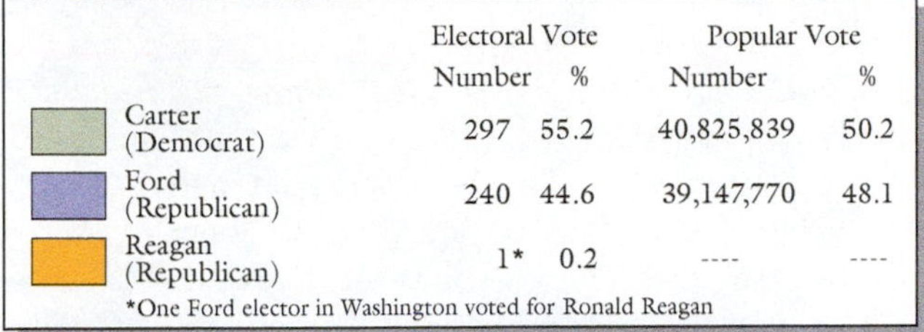

	Electoral Vote		Popular Vote	
	Number	%	Number	%
Carter (Democrat)	297	55.2	40,825,839	50.2
Ford (Republican)	240	44.6	39,147,770	48.1
Reagan (Republican)	1*	0.2	----	----

*One Ford elector in Washington voted for Ronald Reagan

▲ **MAP 30.1 Presidential Election, 1976** This map shows the low voter turnout and the very close election that made Jimmy Carter president.

Q *How did Carter, from Georgia, provide a broad regional appeal for the Democratic party?*

Q *In which states, later to become Democratic strongholds, did the Republicans gain substantial electoral votes?*

30-1a *Debating Economic Policies*

Economic problems dominated the domestic side of Ford's caretaker presidency. Ford first touted a program called "Whip Inflation Now" (WIN), which included a temporary increase in income taxes and cuts in federal spending. WIN proved to be a loser. During 1975 unemployment reached 8.5 percent and the inflation rate topped 9 percent. Ford also clashed with the Democratic-controlled Congress over how to deal with the ever-rising price of oil and with stagflation, which combined economic stagnation with price inflation. Democrats tended to favor programs that might stimulate employment and economic growth; most Republicans urged policies that cut government spending. Ford, who vetoed nearly 40 spending bills while in office, finally agreed to a congressional economic package forged from an uneasy compromise of diverse goals. It included a tax cut, an increase in unemployment benefits, an unbalanced federal budget, and limited controls on oil prices. Democrats charged that Ford could not implement coherent programs. Many Republicans complained that he could not stand up to congressional Democrats.

Although the rate of job creation during Jimmy Carter's presidency initially topped that of administrations that followed, economic problems persisted. Carter pushed for tax cuts, increased public works spending, and pro-growth Federal Reserve Board policies. These measures failed to bring the sustained economic recovery that had also eluded Carter's Republican predecessors. By 1980 the economy had virtually stopped expanding; unemployment was on the rise; and the rate of inflation reached double digits. Most voters told pollsters that their economic fortunes had deteriorated while Carter was in office.

Economic distress spread beyond individuals. Bankruptcy threatened New York City until private bankers and public officials secured congressional "bailout" legislation that granted special loan guarantees to America's largest city. Chicago lost 200,000 manufacturing jobs during the 1970s. Bricks from demolished buildings in St. Louis became one of that city's leading products. Rising unemployment, soaring crime rates, deteriorating downtowns, and shrinking tax revenues afflicted most urban areas, even as inflation further eroded the buying power of city budgets.

Conservative economists and business interests charged that domestic programs favored by most congressional Democrats contributed to economic distress. Increasing the minimum wage and enforcing stringent safety and antipollution regulations, they argued, drove up the cost of doing business and forced companies to raise prices to consumers. During his last two years in office, Carter seemed to tilt toward this analysis. Defying many Democrats in Congress, he cut spending for social programs, sought to reduce capital gains taxes to encourage investment, and inaugurated the process of "deregulating" key industries, beginning with the financial and transportation sectors. This policy of deregulation would become a major emphasis that Republican administrations would pursue after 1980.

30-1b *Debating Welfare and Energy Policies*

Carter puzzled over how to respond to economic and social issues. His staff differed over whether to propose increasing monetary assistance to low-income families or to advocate increased federal spending to create several million public service jobs. A proposed compromise failed in Congress. Similarly, efforts to overhaul the nation's social welfare system went nowhere. Republicans tended to argue for reduced government spending on welfare programs; Democrats generally favored increasing federal assistance.

The president pushed the hardest on energy issues. The United States obtained 90 percent of its energy from fossil fuels, much of it from imported petroleum. In 1978, as in 1973, the Organization of Petroleum Exporting Countries (OPEC), a cartel dominated by oil-rich nations in the Middle East, dramatically raised the price of crude oil and precipitated acute worldwide shortages. As gasoline became expensive and scarce, drivers faced higher prices and long lines at the gas pumps around the country. Carter, in response, promised to make the United States less dependent on imported fossil fuel and charged James Schlesinger, head of a new Department of Energy, with developing a plan.

Neither Carter nor Schlesinger consulted Congress or even some key members of the president's own administration. Instead, in early 1977, Carter announced that the **energy crisis** represented "the moral equivalent of war,"

Bill Pierce/The LIFE Images Collection/Getty Images

30.2 **Partial Meltdown at Three Mile Island Nuclear Power Facility, 1979** The most serious nuclear accident in U.S. history, near Harrisburg, Pennsylvania, called into question the safety and commercial viability of nuclear power generation. The clean-up at this site took nearly fifteen years, cost over a billion dollars, and began a long decline in the industry.

Q *How did this accident affect long-term energy policies in the United States?*

Q *How have the cooling towers, once a symbol of progress, become a more ambiguous icon of modern times?*

and he abruptly advanced a complex plan that included more than 100 interrelated provisions including increased taxation, deregulation, and promotion of coal and nuclear power. Congress quickly rejected it. Gas and oil interests opposed higher taxes. Consumer activists blocked deregulation. Environmentalists emphasized that greater use of coal would increase air pollution.

The nuclear option generated especially sharp controversy. In theory, nuclear reactors could provide inexpensive, almost limitless amounts of energy. The cost of building and maintaining them, however, far exceeded original estimates and posed safety risks. In 1979 a serious reactor malfunction at **Three Mile Island**, Pennsylvania, along with a popular movie about a similar event (*The China Syndrome*), heightened fears of a nuclear reactor meltdown. Responding to growing concerns, power companies canceled orders for new reactors, and the nuclear power industry's expansion halted.

Meanwhile, OPEC oil prices continued to rise, from about $3.60 a barrel in 1971 to nearly $36 a decade later, at the end of Carter's presidency. Such dramatic price increases in a commodity that fueled the American economy helped drive the damaging stagflation of the 1970s. Although few Americans agreed on how to solve this oil crisis and America's broader energy problems, many lost confidence in Carter's domestic leadership.

30-1c *Negotiation and Confrontation in Foreign Policy*

Foreign policy lurched along a similarly uncertain course. Upon assuming office in late 1974, President Ford pledged renewal of U.S. military support to the government in South Vietnam, if North Vietnam ever directly threatened its survival. The antiwar mood in the United States and battlefield conditions in Vietnam, however, made fulfilling this commitment impossible. North Vietnam's armies stormed across the South in March 1975, and Congress, relieved that U.S. troops had finally been withdrawn after the 1973 Paris Peace Accords, refused to support any new American involvement. Conducting their last mission in Vietnam, U.S. helicopters scrambled to airlift U.S. officials and top-ranking South Vietnamese officers off the American embassy's rooftop.

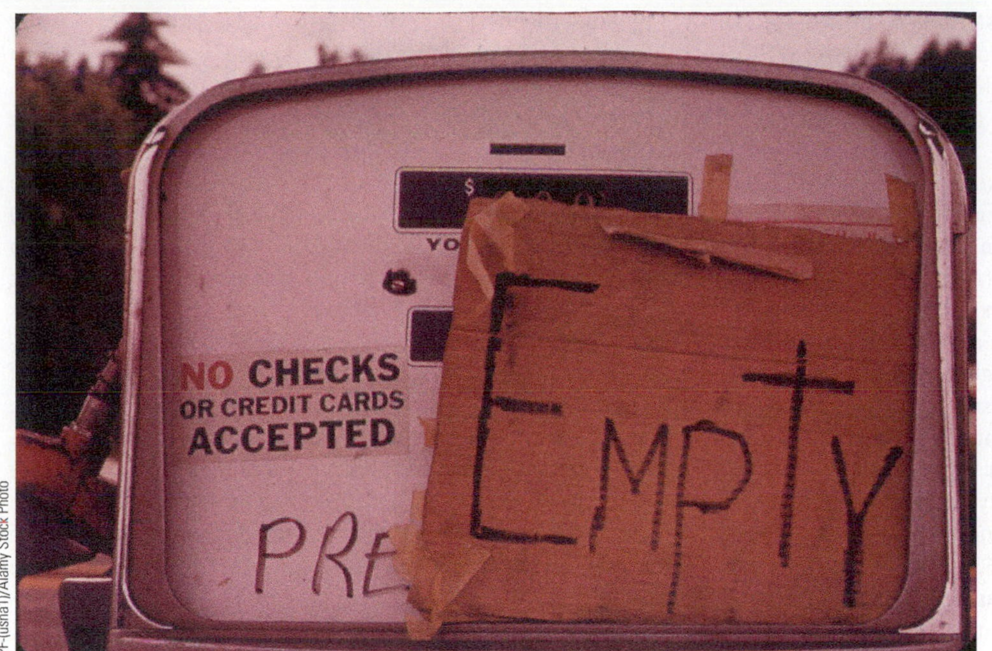

PF-(usna1)/Alamy Stock Photo

30.3 **Gasoline Shortages, 1973** An embargo by oil-producing nations hit American gas stations and consumers. Drivers waited in long lines to fill their tanks but often encountered signs such as this one. This "energy crisis" of the early 1970s contributed to rapid inflation, political discontents, and resentment against the oil-producing cartel.

Q *What impact might rising gas prices have on politics? What policies might address price rises at the pump?*

Spring 1975 brought new communist victories in Indochina. In early April, Khmer Rouge forces in Cambodia drove a U.S.-backed government from the capital of Phnom Penh, and on April 30, 1975, North Vietnamese troops overran the South Vietnamese capital of Saigon, renaming it Ho Chi Minh City. Debate over U.S. policy in Indochina became especially heated in the months that followed.

Within this charged atmosphere, Ford tried to demonstrate U.S. military power. In May 1975 a contingent of Khmer Rouge boarded a U.S. ship, the *Mayaguez*, taking its crew hostage. Secretary of State Henry Kissinger declared that it was time to "look ferocious" and convinced Ford to order bombing strikes against Cambodia and a rescue operation for the crew. This military response, coupled with Chinese pressure on the Khmer Rouge, secured the release of the *Mayaguez* and its crew. Although the *Mayaguez* rescue cost more lives than it saved, Ford's approval ratings briefly shot up. His other foreign policy initiatives, which included extending Nixon's policy of détente with the Soviet Union and pursuing peace negotiations in the Middle East, achieved little.

Carter promised new directions. On his first day in office, he granted amnesty to most Vietnam-era draft resisters. He soon declared that he would not display an "inordinate fear of Communism" and would endorse human-rights initiatives. After four years, however, Carter's foreign policy initiatives seemed in as much disarray as were his economic and energy policies.

Carter had little background in foreign policy, and his top aides advanced contradictory agendas. Secretary of State Cyrus Vance preferred quiet diplomacy and avoidance of confrontations, while National Security Adviser Zbigniew Brzezinski favored a hard-line anti-Soviet policy with an emphasis on military muscle. Pulled in divergent directions, Carter's foreign policy seemed to waffle.

Still, Carter's faith in his own skills as a facilitator and negotiator yielded some successes. On the issue of the Panama Canal, the object of diplomatic negotiations for 13 years, Carter secured treaties that granted Panama increasing authority over the waterway and full control in 2000. Carter convinced skeptical senators, whose votes he needed in order to ratify any treaty, that the canal was no longer an economic or strategic necessity.

Carter's personal touch also emerged during the **Camp David Peace Talks of 1978**. Relations between Egypt and Israel had been strained since the Yom Kippur War of 1973, when Israel repelled an Egyptian attack and seized the Sinai Peninsula and territory along the West Bank (of the Jordan River). Reviving earlier Republican efforts to broker a peace settlement, Carter brought Menachem Begin and Anwar Sadat, leaders of Israel and Egypt, respectively, to the presidential retreat at Camp David. After 13 days of difficult bargaining, the three leaders announced a framework for further negotiations and a peace treaty. Middle East tensions hardly vanished, but the accords reached at Camp David kept alive high-level discussions, lowered the level of acrimony between Egypt and Israel, and bound both nations to the United States through Carter's promises of economic aid.

In Asia, the Carter administration built on Nixon's initiative, expanding economic and cultural relations with the communist government in China. The United States finally established formal diplomatic ties with the People's Republic on New Year's Day 1979.

Carter's foreign agenda emphasized a **human rights policy**. Carter argued that alliances with repressive dictatorships, even in the name of anticommunism, undermined U.S. influence in the world. The policy, however, proved difficult to orchestrate. His administration continued to support some harsh dictators, such as Ferdinand Marcos in the Philippines. Moreover, rhetoric about human rights helped justify uprisings against long-standing dictator-allies in Nicaragua and Iran. Revolutions in these countries, fueled by resentment against the United States, brought anti-American regimes to power and presented Carter with difficult choices.

In Nicaragua, the *Sandinista* movement toppled the dictatorship of Anastasio Somoza, which the United States had long supported. The Sandinistas, initially a coalition of moderate democrats and leftists, soon tilted toward a militant Marxism and began to expropriate private property. Republican critics charged that Carter's policies had given a green light to communism throughout Central America, and some pledged to oust the Sandinistas.

If events in Nicaragua brought dilemmas to Carter, those in Iran and Afghanistan all but shattered his presidency. The United States had steadfastly supported the dictatorial Shah Reza Pahlavi, who had reigned in oil-rich Iran since an American-supported coup in 1953. The shah's overthrow in the **Iranian Revolution of January 1979**, by a movement dominated by Islamic fundamentalists, signaled a massive repudiation of U.S. influence. When the White House allowed the deposed shah to enter the United States for medical treatment in November 1979, Iranians seized the U.S. embassy in Tehran and 66 American hostages. Iran demanded the return of the shah in exchange for the hostages' release.

In response, Carter turned to tough talk, levied economic sanctions against Iran, and—over the objections of Cyrus Vance (who subsequently resigned)—sent a combat team to rescue the hostages. This military effort ended in an embarrassing failure. Carter's critics cited this "hostage crisis" as conclusive proof of his incompetence and used the issue relentlessly in the next presidential campaign. After Carter's defeat in the 1980 election, diplomatic efforts finally freed the hostages, but the United States and Iran remained at odds.

Criticism of Carter also focused on the Soviet Union's 1979 invasion of Afghanistan, a move primarily sparked by Soviet leaders' fear of the growing influence of Islamic fundamentalists along their borders. Carter halted grain exports to the Soviet Union (angering American farmers), organized a boycott of the 1980 Summer Olympic Games in Moscow, withdrew a new Strategic Arms Limitation Treaty (SALT) from the Senate, and revived registration for the military draft. Still, Republicans (along with some Democrats) charged Carter with allowing U.S. power and prestige to decline while the Soviet Union was embarking on a new campaign of expanding communism.

For a time, after Senator Edward Kennedy of Massachusetts entered the 1980 presidential primaries, it seemed as if Carter's own Democratic Party might deny him a second term. Although Kennedy's challenge eventually fizzled, it popularized anti-Carter themes that Republicans would embrace in the election of 1980. "It's time to say no more hostages, no more high interest rates, no more high inflation, and no more Jimmy Carter," was Kennedy's standard stump speech.

30-1d *The New Right*

By 1976, the idea of preventing another Carter or another Kennedy presidency animated a diverse coalition of conservatives: a **New Right**. This broadly based movement succeeded in holding together several different constituencies. One was the already disparate group that had initially gathered around William F. Buckley's *National Review* during the 1950s. Buckley reached out to new converts through television. His long-running interview show, *Firing Line*, debuted on PBS in 1971 (and ran for another 28 years). The economist Milton Friedman—a frequent Buckley guest, 1976 Nobel laureate, and creator of a PBS series touting free-market economic principles—provided another important link between the conservatism of the 1950s and 1970s. In addition, many of the then-youthful conservatives who had energized Barry Goldwater's 1964 presidential campaign, such as Patrick

Bettmann / Corbis

30.4 American Hostages in Iran The Iranian government presents American hostages to the press under a banner protesting Carter's decision to admit the shah into the United States to obtain medical treatment.

Q *How could the "hostage crisis" of 1979 and images such as this one fuel partisan political passions? Would these passions complicate efforts to resolve issues diplomatically?*

Buchanan, came to the New Right after having worked in Richard Nixon's administration.

In contrast, the "neoconservative" (or "neocon") wing of the New Right of the 1970s had generally identified with Democrats, rather than Republicans, during the 1950s and the early 1960s. Anticommunist writers and academics such as Norman Podhoretz and Jeane Kirkpatrick feared that the Democratic Party might abandon a strong anticommunist stance, and neoconservatives viewed the movement of movements as threatening the social stability and intellectual values they admired. This initial generation of neoconservatives, many the offspring of European Jewish immigrants, also complained that U.S. foreign policy, even under Richard Nixon and Henry Kissinger, failed to support Israel strongly enough.

Conservative business leaders provided another important New Right constituency. In their view, new regulatory legislation accepted by the Nixon administration, especially measures dealing with workplace safety and environmental concerns, threatened "economic freedom" and "entrepreneurial liberty." Convinced that anticorporate faculties dominated most colleges and universities, conservative business leaders and their philanthropic foundations generously funded conservative-leaning research institutions, such as the American Enterprise Institute (founded in 1943), and created new ones, such as The Heritage Foundation (established in 1973) and the Cato Institute (founded in 1977).

Money from New Right businesspeople also financed lobbying efforts, such as those mounted by the Business Roundtable (created in 1973) and The Committee on the Present Danger (CPD), which argued that foreign policymakers, including the CIA, underestimated the threat that the Soviet Union still posed. In 1975, activists who had worked for Goldwater's 1964 campaign formed the National Conservative Political Action Committee (NCPAC), the first of many similar organizations aimed at grassroots organizing. The NCPAC backed conservative political candidates and supported a wide range of initiatives opposing feminism, legalized abortion, and LGBT (lesbian, gay, bisexual, and transgender) lifestyles.

The New Right of the 1970s also attracted support from Protestants in fundamentalist and evangelical churches. People from these religious groups had generally stayed clear of overtly partisan politics since the 1920s but continued to express concern about public issues that involved spiritual and social matters. Already angered by Supreme Court decisions that seemed to eliminate religious prayers from public schools, many expressed greater outrage over *Roe v. Wade* (1973), the landmark abortion ruling. Reaching out to antiabortion Catholics, people whom most members of southern Protestant congregations would have shunned a generation earlier, a "Religious Right" slowly took shape. The Reverend Jerry Falwell of the Thomas Road Baptist Church and *The Old Time Gospel Hour* television ministry declared that *Roe* showed the necessity of political action. Anti-religious elites in Washington "have been imposing morality on us for the last 50 years," Falwell proclaimed.

Leaders of the Religious Right insisted that sacred values should actively shape political policy-making. They viewed a clear separation between church and state, a guiding principle of constitutionalism during the era of Earl Warren's Supreme Court, as a violation of a right specifically mentioned in the First Amendment: the "free exercise of religion." Particularly in the South, conservatives embarked on a lengthy legal struggle to prevent the Internal Revenue Service from denying tax-exempt status to the private Christian colleges and academies that opposed racial integration. They also urged that government should use tax dollars to help fund church-centered education and "faith-based" social programming. Most spokespeople for the Religious Right championed foreign policies that maximized the use of U.S. military power, especially on behalf of Israel. Protestants who embraced "dispensational premillennialism," the belief that the Second Coming of Christ would occur in their lifetimes, saw the survival of a Jewish state in the Middle East as crucial to the future they expected to unfold according to biblical prophecy.

In 1976, most evangelicals and fundamentalists from the South, including Falwell, supported Jimmy Carter. His religious values made him seem less committed to the *Roe* decision than Gerald Ford, whose spouse, Betty Ford, often identified herself with women's issues. Very soon, however, Falwell and others on the Religious Right began realigning their politics with those of the GOP's conservative bloc, placing their growing movement behind a refashioned Republican party under the leadership of Ronald Reagan.

30-2 The Reagan Revolution, 1981–1992

Q *To what extent did Ronald Reagan's presidency represent a victory for the New Right agenda in both domestic and foreign policy?*

Ronald Reagan courted the New Right on national security, economic, and social issues. He used the hostage crisis with Iran as a symbol of Carter's failures, while his militantly anticommunist rhetoric included calls for a stronger military posture and greater defense spending. A taxpayer revolt that had swept through California politics during the late 1970s provided a model for Reagan's attack on "tax-and-spend" policy-making at the federal level. (The situation was ironic, since California's tax revolt had emerged in response to tax increases adopted while Reagan was the state's governor.) Reagan also opposed abortion rights, advocated prayer in school, and extolled conservative "family values."

30-2a *The Election of 1980*

Easily capturing the Republican nomination, and anointing one of his defeated rivals, George H. W. Bush, as a running mate, Ronald Reagan advanced an optimistic vision of a rejuvenated America. Punctuating his speeches with quips inspired by Hollywood movies, he stressed his opposition to domestic social spending and high taxes while promising support for a stronger national defense. To underscore the nation's economic problems under Carter, Reagan asked repeatedly, "Are you better off now than you were four years ago?" Quickly offering his own answer, Reagan cited the "misery index," an economic measure that added the rate of inflation to the rate of unemployment and that Jimmy Carter had used during his 1976 presidential campaign against Gerald Ford.

Reagan also seized issues that the Democratic Party had long regarded its own: economic growth and increased personal consumption. In 1979, one of Jimmy Carter's advisers had gloomily portrayed the nation's economic and energy problems as so severe that there was "no way we can avoid a decline in our standard of living. All we can do is adapt to it." In contrast, Reagan promised that sharp tax cuts and policies to increase the supply of oil would restore robust economic expansion.

The Reagan-Bush team swept to victory. Although it gained only slightly more than 50 percent of the popular vote (John Anderson, a middle-of-the-road Republican who ran as an independent, won about 7 percent), the GOP ticket captured the Electoral College tally by a 489 to 49 margin. Republicans also took away 12 Democratic Senate seats, gaining control of the Senate, though not the House of Representatives (see Map 30.2).

The Reagan administration focused on three major priorities: cutting federal taxes, reorienting the national government's relationship to economic matters, and boosting national security capabilities.

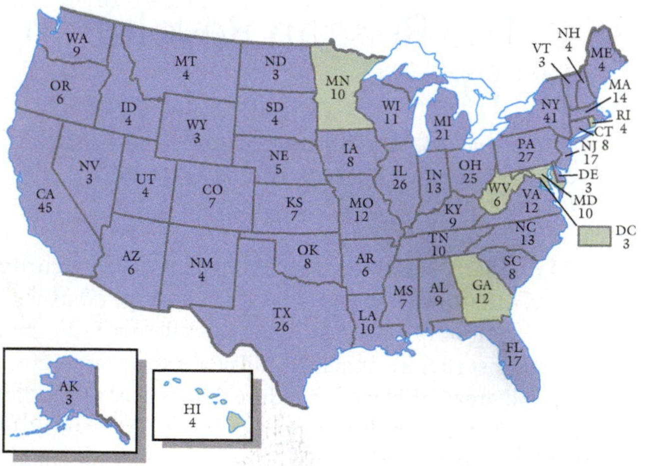

	Electoral Vote		Popular Vote	
	Number	%	Number	%
Carter (Democrat)	49	9.1	35,480,948	41.2
Reagan (Republican)	489	90.9	43,642,639	50.6
Anderson (Independent)	----	----	5,719,437	6.6

▲ **MAP 30.2 Presidential Election, 1980**

Compare this map with the one showing the election of Jimmy Carter four years earlier.

Q *How much in your view did the movie star aura of Ronald Reagan contribute to such a landslide?*

Q *What factors might explain such a sudden downturn in Democratic fortunes?*

30-2b *Supply-Side Economics*

To justify cutting taxes, Reagan touted **supply-side economics**. This economic theory held that tax reductions targeted toward investors and businesses would stimulate production, create jobs, and brighten the general economic picture. Reagan pushed a tax-reduction plan, endorsed by many Democrats, through Congress in 1981. At the same time, the Federal Reserve Board under Paul Volker, a Carter appointee, kept interest rates high to drive down inflation.

In the short run, high interest rates continued to choke off growth, and economic conditions deteriorated. A severe economic downturn in 1981 and 1982 sent Reagan's approval ratings diving below 40 percent, and the Republican Party experienced losses in the off-year election of 1982. Slowly, however, inflation moderated, and the economy rebounded to enter a period of noninflationary growth. According to one study, the economy added nearly 17 million new jobs and inflation dropped from double digits to around 2 percent. Although unemployment figures did not fall as sharply, Reagan's supporters hailed a "Reagan revolution" that had rescued the country from stagflation.

This revival and its causes remain controversial. Reagan had not matched tax cuts with sufficient spending reductions, and budget deficits soared. Reagan constantly inveighed against deficits and "big spenders," but his eight years in Washington, even after some of the early tax reductions were rolled back, saw annual deficits triple to nearly $300 billion. To finance such deficit spending, the United States borrowed abroad and piled up the largest foreign debt of any nation in the world at that time.

Although partisans of the Reagan revolution promised that its effects would ultimately "trickle down" and benefit everyone, its detractors countered that the country was developing a "Swiss-cheese" economy in which many groups were falling through the holes. The tax cuts of 1981 benefited the richest 1 percent and made little difference for everyone else. Farmers in the Midwest watched falling crop prices hamper their repayment of high-interest loans they had contracted during the inflation-ridden 1970s. Mortgage foreclosures, reminiscent of the 1930s, hit the farm states, and the ripple effect decimated the economies of small towns across the country. Urban areas saw a decline in federal spending for such things as public transit, housing, and job training, even as they tried to cope with growing unemployment, population loss, and falling tax revenues. One historian estimates that urban America bore two-thirds of the cost of Reagan-era budget cuts. The minimum wage, when adjusted for inflation, also declined in value during Reagan's presidency.

This mixed economic picture certainly applied to African Americans. The number of African American families earning a solid middle-class income, for example, more than doubled between 1970 and 1990. People with educational credentials and marketable skills made significant economic gains, and African American college graduates could expect incomes comparable to those of their white classmates. Partly as a result of affirmative action hiring plans put in place by the

Nixon and Carter administrations, many could afford to leave problem-plagued inner-city neighborhoods. The situation looked different, however, for those who remained persistently unemployed, perhaps trapped in declining urban centers. At the end of the 1980s one-third of all African American families lived in poverty, and the number earning less than $15,000 per year had doubled since 1970. In inner cities, fewer than half of African American children were completing high school, and more than 60 percent were unemployed. The gap between the well off and the disadvantaged widened during the 1980s.

30-2c *Curtailing Unions, Regulations, and Welfare*

Meanwhile, Reagan pursued his second major goal: reorienting Washington's economic role.

In 1981 Reagan fired the nation's air traffic controllers after their union refused to halt a nationwide strike. The action portended more aggressive anti-union strategies that both his administration and business interests would pursue during the 1980s. The percentage of unionized workers fell to just 16 percent by the end of Reagan's presidency. Recognizing the balance of power tilting against them, workers increasingly turned away from strikes as an economic weapon.

Eve Arnold/Magnum Photos

30.5 Selling off the Farm Hard times during the early 1980s forced the liquidation of many small, family-run farms. Here, neighbors gather at a farm where everything, including a well-used pitchfork, is headed to the auction block.

Q *What might be the economic and social consequences of the decline of family farms?*

Reagan had entered office promising to tame OPEC by encouraging the development of new sources of oil. Rejecting environmentalists' calls to decrease U.S. dependence on fossil fuels by promotion of renewable sources, Reagan and his successor, George H. W. Bush, pursued a "cheap oil" policy. The tapping of new oil fields at home and abroad, together with rivalries among OPEC's members, weakened the cartel's hold on the world market and reduced energy prices worldwide. Lower energy costs, in turn, helped moderate the inflationary pressures.

To oversee environmental issues, Reagan appointed James Watt, an outspoken critic of governmental regulation, as secretary of the interior. Watt supported the so-called "sagebrush rebellion," in which western states demanded fewer federal restrictions on the use of natural resources from public lands within their borders. Reagan's first two appointees to the Department of Energy actually proposed eliminating the cabinet office they headed—an idea that Congress blocked. Both the Energy and Interior departments relaxed enforcement of federal safety and environmental regulations.

Reagan's agenda for **deregulation** singled out the financial system. His economic advisers insisted that financial markets were largely self-regulating and self-correcting. Minimal governmental interference in the marketplace, they argued, would bring greater economic efficiencies and therefore greater prosperity overall. The Carter administration had previously pursued programs of deregulation especially in the transportation sector, and many Democrats in Congress now joined Republicans in crafting a looser regulatory environment for financial institutions. Before the 1980s, state usury laws limited the interest rates that lending institutions could charge their clients, and "Savings and Loan" (S&L) institutions issued home mortgages under carefully controlled rules. Several pieces of legislation in the 1980s, however, wiped away these and other regulations. More credit became available to more people, as a new "sub-prime loan" industry boomed.

But there were hazards. During Reagan's second term, corruption and mismanagement in the financial industry increasingly appeared as toxic by-products of deregulation. S&L companies had ventured into risky loans, particularly in real estate. Regulators and politicians ignored forecasts of an impending meltdown until bankruptcies began to cascade through the S&L industry, eventually forcing the closure of 747 institutions. Finally, in 1989, Congress created a bailout plan designed to save some S&Ls and to transfer assets from already failed institutions to solvent ones. The plan proved astronomically expensive, and taxpayers footed costs that eventually reached around $125 billion. Meanwhile, the process by which large, well-connected commercial banks purchased the remaining assets of bankrupt S&Ls at bargain-basement prices reeked of corruption and scandal. As a result of the S&L debacle of the 1980s, the banking industry went through a sudden, unplanned consolidation. Many people lost savings.

The Reagan administration also sought to limit social welfare spending. It decreased funding for various public-benefit programs, particularly Aid to Families with Dependent Children (AFDC). The Family Support Act of 1988 pressured states to inaugurate work-training programs and to begin moving people, including mothers receiving AFDC payments, off the welfare rolls. Reductions in food stamps and other programs increased poverty rates and fell disproportionately on female-headed households and on children. By the end of the 1980s, one of every five children was growing up in a household where the income fell below the official poverty line.

The president nevertheless rejected calls for eliminating the basic set of New Deal–Great Society programs, such as Social Security and Medicare, which he called a "social safety net." During the 1970s Social Security payments had been "indexed" to automatically increase along with the rate of inflation. Larger Social Security checks, along with Medicare benefits, enabled millions of Americans over 65 to do relatively well during the Reagan years.

The Reagan administration also seized the opportunity to move the federal legal system in a more conservative direction. Reagan nominated a Supreme Court justice, Sandra Day O'Connor (the first woman to sit on the Court), who appeared to be a conservative. With the Republican Party controlling the Senate until 1986, he also named prominent conservative jurists, such as Robert Bork and Antonin Scalia, to lower federal courts. Conservatives who had decried the "rights revolution" of the Warren Supreme Court welcomed the influx of conservative judges, but civil libertarians complained that the federal courts were becoming less hospitable to the legal-constitutional arguments of criminal defendants, labor unions, and political dissenters.

In 1986, the resignation of Warren Burger allowed Reagan to elevate **William Rehnquist** to the position of chief justice and appoint Scalia to replace Rehnquist as an associate justice. In 1987, however, the Senate, now with a Democratic majority following the 1986 elections, rebuffed Reagan's attempt to place Bork, a particular favorite of the New Right, on the High Court. Bork's rejection enraged conservatives, some blaming Reagan for not working hard enough on Bork's behalf. Still, by 1990, a flood of retirements meant that about half of all federal judges had reached the bench during Ronald Reagan's presidency. Reagan also staffed the Justice Department with young attorneys, such as John Roberts and Samuel Alito, who expressed a desire to help conservative judges whittle back Warren-era judicial precedents.

No matter what problems beset his administration, criticism rarely stuck to Reagan, whom one frustrated Democrat dubbed the "Teflon president." His genial optimism seemed unshakable. His smile, jokes, and confident air disarmed and inspired many. He even appeared to rebound quickly—although close observers noted a clear decline in his energies—after being shot by a would-be assassin in March 1981.

30-2d *Reagan to Bush*

Democrats continually underestimated Reagan's appeal—a miscalculation that doomed their 1984 presidential effort. Walter Mondale, Jimmy Carter's vice president, ran on a platform calling for an expansion of social welfare programs. Mondale proposed higher taxes to fund this agenda and chose as his running mate Representative Geraldine Ferraro of New York, the first woman to run for president or vice president on a major party ticket.

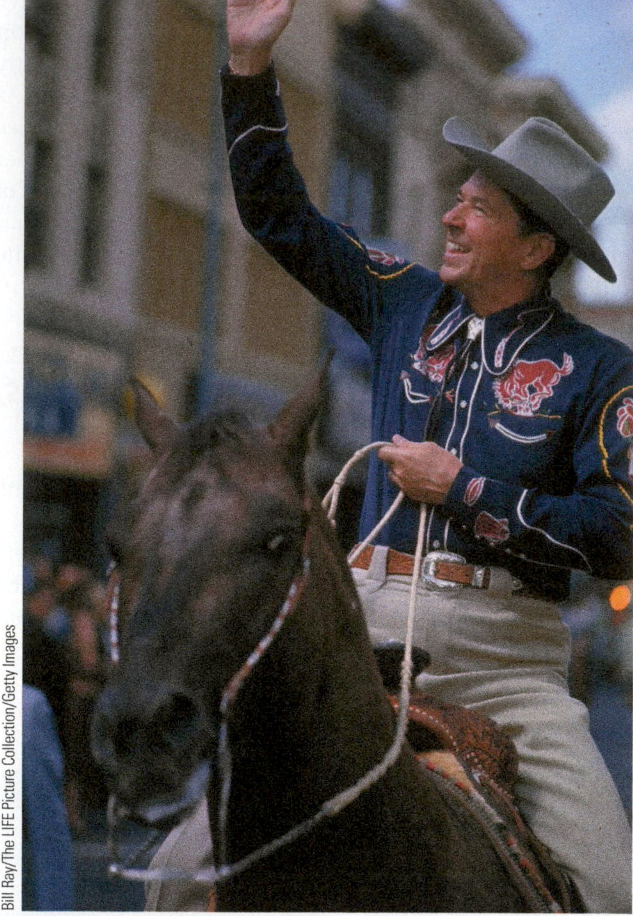

Bill Ray/The LIFE Picture Collection/Getty Images

30.6 **Riding the Presidential Range** Ronald Reagan in cowboy attire.

Q *How did Reagan's political image draw from his earlier movie roles, particularly in Western films?*

Republican campaign ads—often framed by the slogan "It's Morning Again in America"—portrayed a glowing landscape of bustling small towns and lush farmlands. They attacked Mondale's support from labor unions and civil rights groups as a vestige of the "old politics" of "special interests" and his tax proposal as a return to the policies popularly associated with the stagflation of the 1970s. The 1984 presidential election ended with Mondale carrying only his home state of Minnesota and the District of Columbia.

The election suggested how the Reagan revolution had changed the nation's political vocabulary. Democrats had once invoked "liberalism" to stand for governmental initiatives to stimulate the economy, promote greater equality, and advance liberty for all. Republicans recast the term "liberal" as a code word for wasteful social programs devised by a bloated federal government that gouged hardworking people and squandered their tax dollars. The term "conservative," as used by New Right Republicans, came to stand for economic growth through the curtailment of governmental power and support for traditional sociocultural values. The once-dominant Democratic Party of the New Deal, Fair Deal, and Great Society seemingly confronted an uncertain future.

In the election of 1988, the Reagan legacy fell to the president's heir apparent, Vice President **George H. W. Bush**. Born into a wealthy Republican family and educated at Yale, Bush had prospered in the oil business, served in the House of Representatives, and headed the CIA. To court the New Right, decidedly lukewarm to his candidacy, he pledged "no new taxes" and chose Senator J. Danforth (Dan) Quayle, a youthful conservative from Indiana, as a running mate. Quayle would soon delight political comedians who highlighted his verbal blunders.

Governor Michael Dukakis of Massachusetts emerged as the Democratic presidential candidate. Dukakis avoided talk of new domestic programs and higher taxes. Instead, he pledged to bring competence and honesty to the White House.

Although Bush emerged the winner, Democrats retained control of both houses of Congress. The turnout was the lowest for any national election since 1924, and polls suggested that many voters remained unimpressed with either Bush or Dukakis.

Once in the White House, Bush began to lose crucial support. He angered New Right Republicans by agreeing to an increase in the minimum wage and by failing to veto a law that allowed for some affirmative action in the hiring of women and people of color into occupations where they were underrepresented. The Religious Right detected tepid support from the president in its campaigns against abortion and in favor of religious prayers in public schools. Most important, in 1990 Bush broke his "no new taxes" pledge in an attempt to curb the still-rising federal deficit. Taxation had emerged as one of the New Right's central issues, even though Reagan himself had raised taxes during his second term, and the New Right bitterly denounced Bush's tax policy. Worse for the president's political future, the economic growth of the Reagan years began slowing while the budget deficit continued to grow.

Millions of Americans remember Bush's presidency for its support for the last landmark civil rights act of the 20th century, the **Americans with Disabilities Act (ADA)**, passed in 1990. Activists supportive of disability rights, who employed the strategies and tactics of other movements, provided the long-term impetus for this legislation. In addition, officials within the Bush administration and members of congress offered timely support. Building on earlier laws to assist people with disabilities, the ADA fully embraced the legal-constitutional framework of the Civil Rights Act of 1964. It banned discrimination against disabled persons—such as those with limitations of hearing, sight, and mobility—seeking educational advancement, gainful employment, housing, recreational opportunities, and access to other areas of daily life. The ADA empowered the Equal Employment Opportunities Commission (EEOC), the Civil Rights Division of the federal justice department, and the national judicial system to implement and enforce its guarantees.

30-3 Renewing and Ending the Cold War

Q *Why did cold war tensions mount during the 1980s, and how can the sudden end of the cold war be explained?*

In foreign policy, Reagan promised to reverse what he derided as Carter's passivity. He declared that the Vietnam War had been a "noble cause" that politicians had refused to win. Renewing the rhetoric of strident anticommunism, Reagan denounced the Soviet Union as an "evil empire" and promised a military buildup to confront communism. This renewal of the cold war, however, proved short lived. By the late 1980s, a variety of internal and external circumstances brought communist regimes under unsustainable pressure. Reagan had begun his presidency by renewing the cold war, but he and his successor, George H. W. Bush, also presided over its end.

30-3a *The Defense Buildup*

In response to his campaign promises, Reagan led off with dramatic increases in military spending, even as tax cuts reduced federal revenues. The Pentagon enlarged the navy and expanded strategic nuclear forces, deploying new missiles throughout Western Europe. At the height of Reagan's military buildup, which produced gaping budget deficits, the Pentagon was purchasing about 20 percent of the nation's manufacturing output.

In 1983 Reagan proposed the most expensive defense system in history: a space-based shield against incoming missiles. This **Strategic Defense Initiative (SDI)** soon had its own Pentagon agency, which sought $26 billion, over five years, for research costs alone. Controversy swirled around SDI. Skeptics dubbed it "Star Wars" and shuddered at its astronomical costs. Although most scientists dismissed the plan as too speculative, Congress voted appropriations for SDI. Reagan insisted that a defensive missile shield could work and also suggested that the Soviet Union might collapse under the economic strain of competing in an accelerating arms race.

Reagan's foreign policy agenda included numerous nonmilitary initiatives. A new "informational" offensive funded conservative media groups around the world and established Radio Martí, a Florida station beamed at Cuba and designed to discredit Fidel Castro's communist government. When the United Nations Educational, Scientific, and Cultural Organization (UNESCO) adopted an allegedly anti-American tone, Reagan cut off U.S. contributions to this agency. The White House also championed free markets, pressing other nations to minimize tariffs and restrictions on foreign investment. The Caribbean Basin Initiative, for example, rewarded with aid small nations in the Caribbean region that adhered to free-market principles.

History Through Film The First Movie-Star President

Ronald Reagan began his presidency in Hollywood. The political career of the "Great Communicator" built on, rather than broke away from, his days in the entertainment industry. His media advisers could count on directing a seasoned professional who always knew where to stand; how to deliver lines effectively; how to convey emotions through both body language and dialogue; and when to melt into the background so that other players in the cast of his presidency might carry a crucial scene.

Several of Reagan's movies provided rehearsals for roles he would play in the White House. Efforts to cheer on the nation during the 1980s consciously invoked Reagan's favorite film role, that of 1920s Notre Dame football star George Gipp in *Knute Rockne, All American* (1940). Similarly, when tilting with a Democratic-controlled Congress over tax policy, Reagan invoked Clint Eastwood's famous screen character "Dirty Harry," promising to shoot down any tax increase. "Go ahead, make my day," he taunted. On another occasion, he cited *Rambo* (1982), an action thriller set in post-1975 Vietnam, as a possible blueprint for dealing with countries that had seized U.S. hostages. Occasionally, Reagan seemed unable to separate "reel" from "real" life. During one session with reporters, he incorrectly referred to his own dog as "Lassie," the canine performer who had once been his Hollywood contemporary.

Life in Hollywood also provided a prologue to President Reagan's conservative policies. Early in his film career, Reagan appeared in four films as the same character, a government agent named "Brass Bancroft." In these B-grade thrillers, Reagan developed an image that he later deployed in politics: the action-oriented character who could distinguish (good) friends from (evil) foes. *Murder in the Air* (1940) even featured a science fiction-style "death ray" that resembled the SDI ("Star Wars") armaments that President Reagan would champion more than 40 years later.

Bettmann/Corbis

30.7 Ronald Reagan as the "Gipper" in *Knute Rockne, All American.*

Poor eyesight kept Reagan out of combat during the Second World War, but he served long hours as an Army Air Corps officer, producing movies in support of the war effort. He appeared in several films, such as *For God and Country* (1943), and more often provided upbeat voiceovers, once even sharing a soundtrack with President Franklin Roosevelt. He also starred, on loan from the Air Corps, in *This Is the Army* (1943), one of the most successful of wartime Hollywood's military-oriented musicals. After the war, Reagan increasingly directed his energies toward cold war politics in the film capital. His tenure as the anticommunist president of the Screen Actors Guild—and as a secret FBI informant—likely speeded his conversion from New Deal Democrat to right-leaning Republican. In his final onscreen roles Reagan usually portrayed the kind of independent, rugged individualist—often in westerns such as *Law and Order* (1953)—that he would later invoke during his presidency.

Nancy Reagan, who costarred with her husband in *Hellcats of the Navy* (1957) and later as the nation's First Lady, offered her close-up view of the relationship between Reagan the actor and Reagan the politician: "There are not two Ronald Reagans." ■

The CIA, headed by William Casey, stepped up its covert activities. Some became so obvious they hardly qualified as covert. It was no secret, for instance, that the United States sent aid to anticommunist forces in Afghanistan, many of them radical Islamic fundamentalist groups. The CIA also helped train and support the *contras* in Nicaragua, a military force fighting to topple the Sandinista government. To contain the power of Iran, assistance went to its bitter enemy, Saddam Hussein in Iraq.

30-3b Deploying Military Power

In renewing the global cold war, Reagan promised military support to "democratic" revolutions anywhere, a move designed to contain the Soviet Union's sphere of influence. Reagan's UN ambassador, Jeane Kirkpatrick, wrote that "democratic" forces included almost any movement, no matter how autocratic, that was anticommunist. The United States thus funded opposition forces in countries aligned with the

Soviet Union: Ethiopia, Angola, South Yemen, Cambodia, Guatemala, Grenada, Afghanistan, and Nicaragua. Reagan called the participants in such anticommunist insurgencies "freedom fighters," although few displayed any visible commitment to democratic values or institutions.

The Reagan administration also deployed U.S. military power, initially in southern Lebanon in 1982. Here, Israeli troops faced off against Islamic groups supported by Syria and Iran. Fearing loss of influence within Lebanon, the Reagan administration convinced Israel to withdraw and sent 1,600 U.S. Marines as part of an international "peacekeeping force." Islamic militias, however, turned against the U.S. forces. After a massive truck bomb attack against a military compound killed 241 U.S. troops, mostly marines, in April 1983, Reagan decided to end this ill-defined undertaking. In February 1984 he ordered the withdrawal of U.S. troops.

Another military intervention seemed more successful. In October 1983 Reagan sent 2,000 U.S. troops to the tiny Caribbean island of Grenada, whose socialist leader was forging ties with Castro's Cuba. U.S. troops swept aside Grenada's government and installed one friendlier to U.S. policies.

Buoyed by Grenada, the Reagan administration fixed its sights on Nicaragua, where the Marxist-leaning Sandinista government was trying to break Nicaragua's dependence on the United States. The administration responded with economic pressure, a propaganda campaign, and greater assistance to the contras—initiatives that stirred controversy because of mounting evidence of the contras' corruption and brutality. Finally, Democrats in Congress barred additional military aid to the contras.

Meanwhile, violence continued to escalate throughout the Middle East. Militant Islamic groups increased attacks against Israel and Western powers. Bombings and kidnappings of westerners became more frequent. Apparently, Libya's Muammar al-Qaddafi and Iranian leaders encouraged such activities. In the spring of 1986, the United States launched an air strike into Qaddafi's personal compound. It killed his young daughter, but Qaddafi and his government survived. Despite what looked like a long-range assassination attempt against a foreign leader—an action outlawed by Congress—Americans generally approved of using strong measures against sponsors of terrorism and hostage taking.

30-3c *The Iran–Contra Controversy*

In November 1986 a magazine in Lebanon reported that the Reagan administration was selling arms to Iran in order to secure the release of Americans being held hostage by Islamic militants. These alleged deals violated the Reagan administration's own pledges against selling arms to Iran or rewarding hostage taking by negotiating for the release of captives. During the 1980 campaign Reagan had made hostages in Iran a symbol of U.S. weakness under Carter. When Iranian-backed groups continued to kidnap Americans during Reagan's own presidency, it seemed that Reagan had sought clandestine ways to recover hostages and avoid such charges being leveled at him.

As Congress began to investigate, the story became more bizarre. It appeared that the Reagan administration had not only secretly sold arms to Iran but had funneled profits from these back-channel deals to the contra forces in Nicaragua, thereby circumventing the congressional ban on U.S. military aid. Oliver North, an aide to the national security adviser, had directed the effort, working with international arms dealers and private go-betweens. North's covert activities seemingly violated both the official policy of the White House and an act of Congress.

This **Iran–contra affair** never reached the proportions of the Watergate scandal. Ronald Reagan stepped forward and testified, through a deposition, that he could not recall any details about either the release of hostages or the funding of the contras. His management skills might deserve criticism, Reagan admitted, but he had never intended to break any laws or violate any presidential promise. Vice President George H. W. Bush also claimed ignorance. Several officials in the Reagan administration were convicted of felonies, including falsifying documents and lying to Congress, but appellate courts later overturned these verdicts. North destroyed so many documents and left so many false paper trails that congressional investigators struggled even to compile a simple narrative of his activities. Finally, in 1992, just a few days before the end of his presidency, George H. W. Bush pardoned six former Reagan-era officials connected to the Iran–contra controversy.

30-3d *The Cold War Eases—and Ends*

After six years of renewed cold war confrontation, Reagan's last two years saw a sudden thaw in U.S.–Soviet relations. The economic cost of superpower rivalry was burdening both nations, and political changes sweeping the Soviet Union eliminated reasons for confrontation. **Mikhail Gorbachev**, who became general secretary of the Communist Party in 1985, understood that his nation faced economic stagnation and environmental problems brought on by decades of poorly planned industrial development. To redirect the Soviet Union's course, he withdrew troops from Afghanistan, reduced commitments to Cuba and Nicaragua, proclaimed a policy *of glasnost* ("openness"), and began to implement *perestroika* ("economic liberalization") at home.

Gorbachev's policies gained him acclaim throughout the West, and summit meetings with the United States yielded breakthroughs in arms control. At Reykjavik, Iceland, in October 1986, Reagan shocked both Gorbachev and his own advisers by proposing a wholesale ban on nuclear weapons. Although negotiations at Reykjavik stumbled over Soviet insistence that the United States abandon SDI, Gorbachev later dropped that condition. In December 1987, Reagan and Gorbachev signed a major arms treaty that reduced each nation's supply of intermediate-range missiles and allowed for on-site verification, which the Soviets had never before permitted. The next year, Gorbachev scrapped the policy that forbade nations under Soviet influence from renouncing communism. In effect, he declared an end to the cold war.

Owen Franken/Historical/Corbis

30.8 **Berlin Wall, 1989** Berliners celebrated the end of the cold war by chiseling away at the Berlin Wall, which the communist East German state had erected in 1962 to prevent the flow of refugees to West Berlin. Pieces of the Berlin Wall became coveted symbols of the fall of communism.

Q *Why did the Berlin Wall become and remain such a powerful symbol throughout the second half of the twentieth century?*

Within the next few years, communist states began to topple like dominoes. In 1989, the first year of George H. W. Bush's presidency, Poland's anticommunist labor movement, Solidarity, ousted a pro-Soviet regime. The pro-Moscow government in East Germany fell in November 1989. West and East Germans hacked down the Berlin Wall and then began the process of reunifying Germany as a single nation. Popular movements similarly forced out communist governments throughout Eastern Europe. Yugoslavia quickly disintegrated, and warfare ensued as rival ethnic groups recreated separate states in Slovenia, Serbia, Bosnia, and Croatia. Latvia, Lithuania, and Estonia, which had been under Soviet control since the Second World War, declared their independence. In December 1991 Boris Yeltsin, the president of the new state of Russia, brokered a plan to abolish the Soviet Union and replace it with 11 separate republics, loosely joined in a commonwealth arrangement (see Map 30.3).

30-3e *Post-Cold War Policy and the Persian Gulf War*

The Bush administration set about redefining U.S. national security in a post-cold war era. The collapse of the Soviet Union weakened support for the leftist insurgencies in Central America that had so preoccupied the Reagan administration. Nicaraguans voted out the Sandinistas, who became just another political party in a multiparty system. The Pentagon pondered new military missions, imagining rapid, sharply targeted strikes rather than lengthy, conventional campaigns. The armed forces assessed, for example, how they might serve in the "war against drugs," an effort that Bush had suggested during his 1988 presidential campaign.

General Manuel Noriega, the president of Panama, was deeply involved in the drug trade, and the Reagan administration had secured an indictment against him for international narcotics trafficking. Confronting Noriega posed a potentially embarrassing problem for Bush. The anticommunist general had been recruited as a CIA "asset" during the mid-1970s, when Bush had headed the agency. Nevertheless, the United States needed a friendly and stable government in Panama in order to complete the transfer of the Panama Canal to Panamanian sovereignty in 2000, and Bush decided to topple Noriega. During "Operation Just Cause," U.S. Marines landed in Panama in December 1989 and laid siege to the president's headquarters. Noriega soon surrendered, was extradited to Florida, and went to prison after a 1992 conviction for trafficking in cocaine.

Deposing the leader of a foreign government by unilateral military action raised questions of international law, but the Panamanian operation, which involved 25,000 U.S. troops and few casualties, provided a model for the post-cold war era. The Pentagon firmed up plans for creating highly mobile, rapid deployment forces. A test of its new strategy came during the Persian Gulf War of 1991.

On August 2, 1990, Iraq's Saddam Hussein ordered his troops to occupy the neighboring oil-rich emirate of Kuwait. U.S. intelligence analysts had been caught off guard, and they now warned that Iraq's next target might be Saudi Arabia, the largest oil exporter in the Middle East and a longtime U.S. ally.

Moving swiftly, Bush orchestrated a multilateral, international response. Four days after Iraq's invasion of Kuwait, he launched Operation Desert Shield by sending several hundred thousand U.S. troops to Saudi Arabia. Bush convinced the Saudi government, concerned about allowing Western troops on sacred Islamic soil, to accept a U.S. military presence in Saudi Arabia. After consulting with European leaders, Bush approached the UN, which denounced Iraqi aggression, ordered economic sanctions against Iraq, and authorized the United States to lead an international force into the Gulf region if Saddam Hussein's troops did not withdraw from Kuwait.

Bush assembled a massive coalition force, ultimately nearly 500,000 troops from the United States and some 200,000 from other countries. He claimed a moral obligation to rescue Kuwait, and his policymakers also spoke frankly about the economic threat that Hussein's aggression posed for the

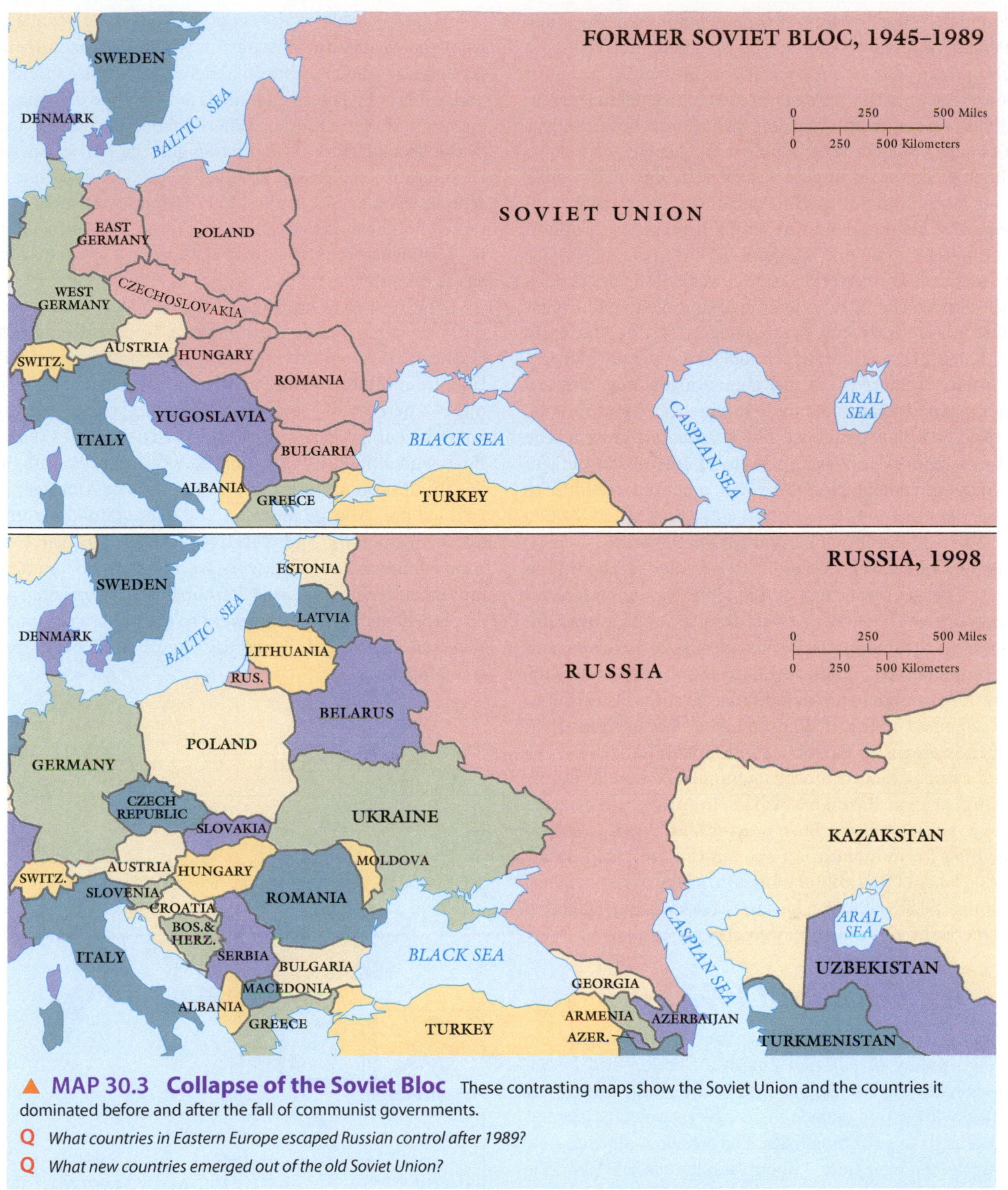

▲ **MAP 30.3 Collapse of the Soviet Bloc** These contrasting maps show the Soviet Union and the countries it dominated before and after the fall of communist governments.

Q *What countries in Eastern Europe escaped Russian control after 1989?*

Q *What new countries emerged out of the old Soviet Union?*

oil-dependent economies of the United States and its allies. These arguments persuaded Congress to approve a resolution backing the use of force.

In mid-January 1991 the United States launched an air war against Iraq and, after a period of devastating aerial bombardment, began a ground offensive in late February. Coalition forces, enjoying air supremacy, decimated Saddam Hussein's armies in a matter of days. U.S. casualties were relatively light (148 combat deaths). Estimates of Iraqi casualties ranged from 25,000 to 100,000 deaths. Although this **Persian Gulf War** lasted scarcely six weeks, it took an enormous toll on highways, bridges, communications, and other infrastructure facilities in both Iraq and Kuwait.

In a controversial decision, Bush stopped short of ousting Saddam Hussein, a goal that the UN had never approved and that U.S. military planners considered too costly and risky. Instead, the United States, backed by the UN, maintained its economic pressure, ordered the dismantling of Iraq's capability to produce nuclear and bacteriological weapons, and enforced "no-fly" zones over northern and southern Iraq to help protect the

Kurds and Shi'a Muslims from Hussein's continued persecution. The Persian Gulf War temporarily boosted George H. W. Bush's popularity. An increasingly vocal and influential group of neoconservative critics, however, argued that Saddam Hussein should have been overthrown. Ten years later, with President Bush's son as president, they would get another chance.

Bush's economic foreign policy, although less visible than his leadership during the Persian Gulf War, comprised a key part of his post-cold war vision. It pressed a program of international economic integration. During the mid-1980s, huge debts that Third World nations owed to U.S. institutions had threatened the international banking system, but most of these obligations had been renegotiated by the early 1990s. Market economies, which replaced centrally planned ones, began to emerge in former communist states. Western Europe moved toward economic integration. Most nations of the Pacific Rim experienced steady economic growth. The president supported (but was unable to pass) a North American Free Trade Agreement (NAFTA), which proposed to eliminate tariff barriers and join Canada, the United States, and Mexico together in the largest free-market zone in the world.

Voters ultimately judged the president's record on foreign affairs as something of a muddle. He had organized an international coalition against Iraq, assisted a peaceful post-cold war transition in Russia and Eastern Europe, and embraced global economic integration. Despite this leadership, the president publicly projected indecisiveness. The United States remained on the sidelines as full-scale warfare erupted among the states of the former Yugoslavia, with Serbs launching a brutal campaign of territorial aggrandizement and "ethnic cleansing" against Bosnian Muslims. In Africa, when severe famine wracked Somalia, Bush ordered U.S. troops to secure supply lines for humanitarian aid, but the American public remained wary of this military mission. As the old objective of containing the Soviet Union became irrelevant, Bush failed to rally Americans around any new foreign policy goal.

30-3f *The Election of 1992*

The inability to project a coherent vision for either domestic or foreign policy threatened Bush's reelection and forced concessions to the New Right. Dan Quayle, although clearly a liability with voters outside his conservative constituency, returned as Bush's running mate. The president allowed New Right activists, who talked about "a religious war" for "the soul of America," to dominate the 1992 Republican National Convention. Conservative Democrats and independents, who had supported Reagan and Bush in the previous three presidential elections, found this rhetoric unsettling.

Bush's Democratic challenger, Governor William Jefferson Clinton of Arkansas, stressed economic issues. Campaigning as a "New Democrat," Bill Clinton promised job creation, deficit reduction, and an overhaul of the nation's health-care system. Sounding almost like a moderate Republican, Clinton pledged to shrink the size of government and to "end this [welfare] system as we know it." This platform made it difficult for Bush to label Clinton as a "big-government liberal."

Clinton's focus on the economy helped deflect attention from the sociocultural issues on which he was vulnerable. As a college student, Clinton had avoided service in Vietnam and, while in England as a Rhodes Scholar, had demonstrated against the Vietnam War. When Bush, a decorated veteran of the Second World War, challenged the patriotism of his Democratic challenger, Clinton emphasized, rather than repudiated, his roots in the 1960s. He appeared on MTV and touted his devotion to (relatively soft) rock music. In addition, he chose Senator Albert Gore of Tennessee, a Vietnam veteran, as his running mate.

The 1992 election brought Clinton a clear victory. The quixotic campaign of Ross Perot, a Texas billionaire who financed his own third-party run, took more votes from Bush than from Clinton. With Perot in the race, Clinton garnered only 43 percent of the popular vote but won 370 electoral votes by carrying 32 states and the District of Columbia. Bush won a majority only among white Protestants in the South. Clinton carried the Jewish, African American, and Latino vote by large margins and even gained a plurality among people who had served in the Vietnam War. He also ran well among independents who had supported Reagan and Bush during the 1980s. Perhaps most surprising, about 55 percent of eligible voters went to the polls, a turnout that reversed 32 years of steady decline in voter participation (see Map 30.4).

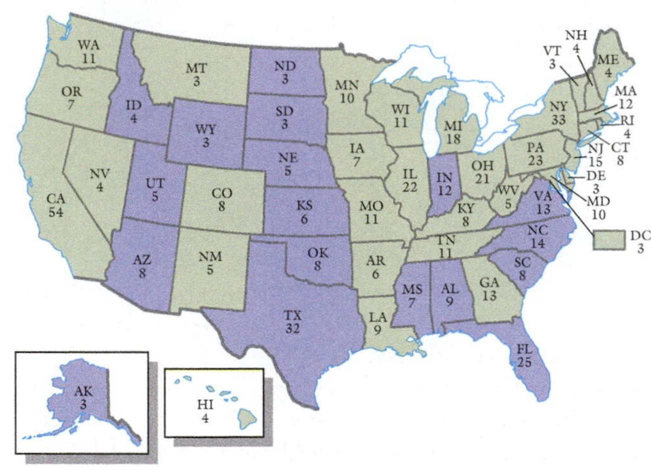

	Electoral Vote Number	Electoral Vote %	Popular Vote Number	Popular Vote %
Clinton (Democrat)	370	68.8	44,909,889	43
Bush (Republican)	168	31.2	39,104,545	37.5
Perot (Independent)	----	----	19,742,267	18.9

▲ MAP 30.4 Presidential Election, 1992

Q *Is a political system based on the consent of the people consistent with one in which a presidential candidate won nearly 20 percent of the popular vote but gained literally nothing in the crucial electoral balloting?*

Q *What role do third party efforts, such as that mounted by Ross Perot in 1992, play in modern American politics?*

30-4 The Politics of Social Movements

Q How did social movements of the post-1960s era affect American public life and the ways people saw their own personal identities?

The activism associated with the 1960s became firmly embedded in most areas of American life during the decades that followed. Mass demonstrations reminiscent of those against the Vietnam War remained one tool of advocacy and protest. Both antiabortion and pro-choice forces, for example, regularly demonstrated in Washington, D.C. During the 1980s, the Clamshell Alliance conducted a campaign of civil disobedience against a nuclear reactor being built in Seabrook, New Hampshire, and a coalition of West Coast activists waged a lengthy, unsuccessful struggle to close the University of California's Lawrence Livermore National Laboratory, which was developing nuclear weapons. In nearly every major city and many smaller towns, women's groups staged annual Take Back the Night rallies to call attention to the issue of sexual assault.

The media increasingly ignored most mass demonstrations, however, unless they sparked violent conflict. In 1991, for example, 30,000 Korean Americans staged a march for racial peace in Los Angeles. Although it was the largest demonstration ever conducted by any Asian American group, even the local media failed to cover it. Only C-Span, a niche network devoted to public affairs programming, provided minimal coverage of events of social and political protest. Social activism from all parts of the political spectrum and all sections of the country, in short, did not go away during the 1980s, but it did become less reliant on media spectacles.

30-4a *Women's Issues*

In this political environment, women's groups adopted a range of methods to rally new supporters and reenergize their core constituencies. Struggles over gender-related issues had emerged within the labor movement and the civil rights and antiwar movements of the 1960s. Initially, many of the men involved in these causes complained that issues of gender equality interfered with broader fights to redirect labor, racial, or foreign policies. Women, however, insisted on calling attention to their second-class status in movements that claimed to be egalitarian. The spread of the birth control pill during the 1960s gave women greater control over reproductive choices but also complicated the meaning of "sexual freedom." Throughout the 1970s women promoted "consciousness-raising" sessions to discuss how *political* empowerment was inseparable from *personal* power relationships involving housework, child rearing, sexuality, and economic independence. "The personal is political" became a watchword for the new women's movement.

The number of groups addressing issues of concern to women continually expanded. The National Organization for Women (NOW) became generally identified with the rights-based agenda of the mainstream of the Democratic Party. African American women often formed separate organizations that emphasized issues of cultural and ethnic identity. Chicana groups coalesced within the United Farm Workers (UFW) movement and other Mexican American organizations. Lesbians organized their own groups, often allying with an emerging gay rights movement. Many U.S. feminist organizations joined with groups in other nations on behalf of international women's rights. Although never embracing the word "feminism," conservative women also played leadership roles in causes associated with the New Right.

With agendas often varying along lines of class, race, ethnicity, and religion, the women's movement remained highly diverse, but women from different backgrounds often cooperated to build new institutions and networks. Their efforts included battered-women's shelters; health and birthing clinics specializing in women's medicine; rape crisis centers; economic development counseling for women-owned businesses; union-organizing efforts led by women; organizations of women in specific businesses or professions; women's and gender studies programs in colleges and universities; and academic journals and popular magazines devoted to women's issues. Pressure for gender equity also affected existing institutions. Country clubs and service organizations began admitting women members. Many Protestant denominations came to accept women into the ministry, and Reform Judaism placed women in its pulpits. Educational institutions adopted "gender-fair" hiring practices and instructional material. American women by the beginning of the 21st century lived in an environment significantly different from that of their mothers.

Economic self-sufficiency became an especially pressing issue. Reagan-era budget cuts for social programs took their toll, especially in urban centers. Homeless shelters, which once catered almost exclusively to single men, began taking in growing numbers of women and children. As this feminization of poverty gained attention, proposals on the state and federal levels called for reshaping patterns of public support by limiting direct governmental payments and emphasizing strategies to move women, even those with young children, into the workforce.

The job market, however, remained laced with inequalities. Women constituted 30 percent of the labor force in 1950 and more than 45 percent in 2001. Although women increasingly entered the professions and gained unionized positions (by 2000 nearly 45 percent of union members were women, compared with 18 percent in 1960), the average female worker still earned around 75 cents for every dollar taken home by men. "Glass ceilings" limited women's chances for promotion, and childcare expenses often fell disproportionately on women who worked outside the home.

Sexual harassment in the workplace became a controversial issue. Most women's groups pressed government and private employers to curtail sexually charged behaviors that they saw as demeaning women and exploiting their lack of power vis-à-vis male supervisors and coworkers. In 1986,

Interpreting the Visual Past

Launching a New Forum for Women's Issues

Initially an offshoot of *New York Magazine*, an important outlet for writers associated with the "New Journalism," *Ms.* debuted as a separate publication in January 1972 under the editorship of Gloria Steinem, who had long linked her journalism to the feminist movement. Its cover featured the comic book character Wonder Woman as a candidate for president. As the feature articles suggested, *Ms.* saw its mission as being "More than a Magazine." Despite predictions that *Ms.* would be a niche publication and soon fade away, the magazine, now published by a feminist foundation, celebrated its 40th anniversary in 2012.

Perhaps inspired by images of multiple-armed Hindu deities, the artist Miriam Mosk produced a surrealistic cover for the December 1971 preview issue of *Ms.* Ironically, much of Mosk's earlier work had consisted of fashion illustrations for major women's fashion magazines, publications whose treatment of women's issues and reliance on glamorous imagery had drawn fire from feminists. She did several other covers for *Ms.* before moving to the West Coast, where she abandoned illustration in favor of other kinds of artistic work. Mosk became best known for complex collages that offered what she called the "overload of sensory materials."

Mosk's cover for the preview issue provided a template for several of her other *Ms.* illustrations depicting multitasking women.

Q *On this preview cover, what tasks does Mosk show the woman doing, and how do all of these images relate to feminist themes?*

Q *What do you think the name of the magazine was intended to convey?*

Q *Why might a cover featuring the comic book character Wonder Woman be an appropriate follow-up to the preview-issue cover by Miriam Mosk?*

30.9 **Miriam Mosk, First Issue Cover Art, 1972.**

the U.S. Supreme Court ruled that sexual harassment constituted a form of discrimination covered by the Civil Rights Act of 1964.

In 1991, the issue gained national attention when Anita Hill, an African American law professor, accused Clarence Thomas, an African American nominee for the U.S. Supreme Court, of having sexually harassed her when both worked for the federal government. Feminists denounced the all-male Senate Judiciary Committee, which was responsible for considering Thomas's nomination, for failing even to understand, let alone investigate seriously, the issue of sexual harassment. Although the Senate narrowly approved Thomas for the High Court, women's groups mobilized female voters and elected four women as U.S. senators in 1992.

Sexual harassment also became of concern to the U.S. military, which began to recruit women more actively. The service academies accepted female cadets, and women found places within the military hierarchy. Soon, however, revelations about harassment and even sexual assaults against female naval officers by male comrades revealed problems. Attempts by navy officials to cover up sexual harassment during the 1991 Tailhook convention provoked outrage, and several high-ranking officers were forced to step down.

30-4b *Sexual Politics*

Issues involving gays and lesbians also became more public and political. In 1969, New York City police raided the Stonewall Inn, a bar in Greenwich Village with a largely homosexual clientele. Patrons resisted arrest, and the resultant confrontations pitted the neighborhood's gay and lesbian activists, who claimed to be the victims of police harassment, against law enforcement officials.

What They Said

Cultural Disagreements: Equality for Women?

The changing role of women in America dramatically altered family and civic life during this era. Many of the cultural and political disputes of these years revolved around issues related to gender. Advocates of "full equality" for women, such as the National Organization for Women (NOW), clashed with New Right activists, who opposed gender equality as an affront to the "natural" order.

National Organization For Women (NOW)

Statement of Purpose, 1966

The purpose of NOW is to take action to bring women into full participation in the mainstream of American society now, exercising all the privileges and responsibilities thereof in truly equal partnership with men... . We reject the current assumptions that a man must carry the sole burden of supporting himself, his wife, and family, and that a woman is automatically entitled to lifelong support by a man upon her marriage, or that marriage, home and family are primarily woman's world and responsibility... . We believe that a true partnership between the sexes demands a different concept of marriage, an equitable sharing of the responsibilities of home and children and of the economic burdens of their support... .

We will strive to ensure that no party, candidate, president, senator, governor, congressman, or any public official who betrays or ignores the principle of full equality between the sexes is elected or appointed to office.

Reverend Jerry Falwell

(calling for a "moral majority" in his 1980 book *Listen America!*)

I believe that at the foundation of the women's liberation movement there is a minority core of women who were once bored with life, whose real problems are spiritual problems. Many women have never accepted their God-given roles... . God Almighty created men and women biologically different and with differing needs and roles.

He made men and women to complement each other and to love each other. Not all the women involved in the feminist movement are radicals. Some are misinformed, and some are lonely... . I believe that women deserve more than equal rights... . Men and women have differing strengths... . Because a woman is weaker does not mean that she is less important.

Q *How does Reverend Falwell counter NOW's claim that women are entitled to full equality with men?*

Q *On what differing assumptions about proper gender roles do the arguments of NOW and Falwell turn? How might these differing assumptions play into other public policy disputes, especially in areas related to military service, families and reproduction, and labor rights?*

Q *How does this equal rights debate about women seem similar to, and different from, other rights debates, especially those featured in Chapters 26 and 27?*

Sources: (top) From the National Organization for Women (NOW) Statement of Purpose, 1966, mimeographed handout, Washington, D.C., p. 1; (bottom) Jerry Falwell, *Listen America!* (New York: Doubleday, 1980), pp. 150–151.

Historians of sexuality have come to criticize what they call "the Stonewall Narrative," in which events at a single Greenwich Village bar ignited what would become known as the LGBT (lesbian, gay, bisexual, and transgender) movement. Recent studies emphasize that LGBT activism did not suddenly emerge in 1969 but instead grew out of earlier movements, such as the Mattachine Society, and cultural communities such as the Beats (see Chapter 28).

Still, the 1969 events at the Stonewall Inn, because of the prominence they received in mainstream and alternative media, marked an important benchmark in sexual politics. Gay and lesbian activism became an important part of the larger movement of movements that continued during the 1970s and 1980s. Thousands of advocacy and support groups, such as New York City's Gay Activist Alliance (GAA), sprang up. As many individuals "came out of the closet," newspapers, theaters, nightspots, and religious groups proudly identified themselves as activists. LGBT communities emerged particularly in larger cities and benefited from a general relaxation of legal and cultural controls over the portrayal and practice of sexuality. They demanded that law enforcement officials treat attacks against them no less seriously than attacks against all other communities. They also asserted constitutional claims to equal access to housing, jobs, and benefits for domestic partners.

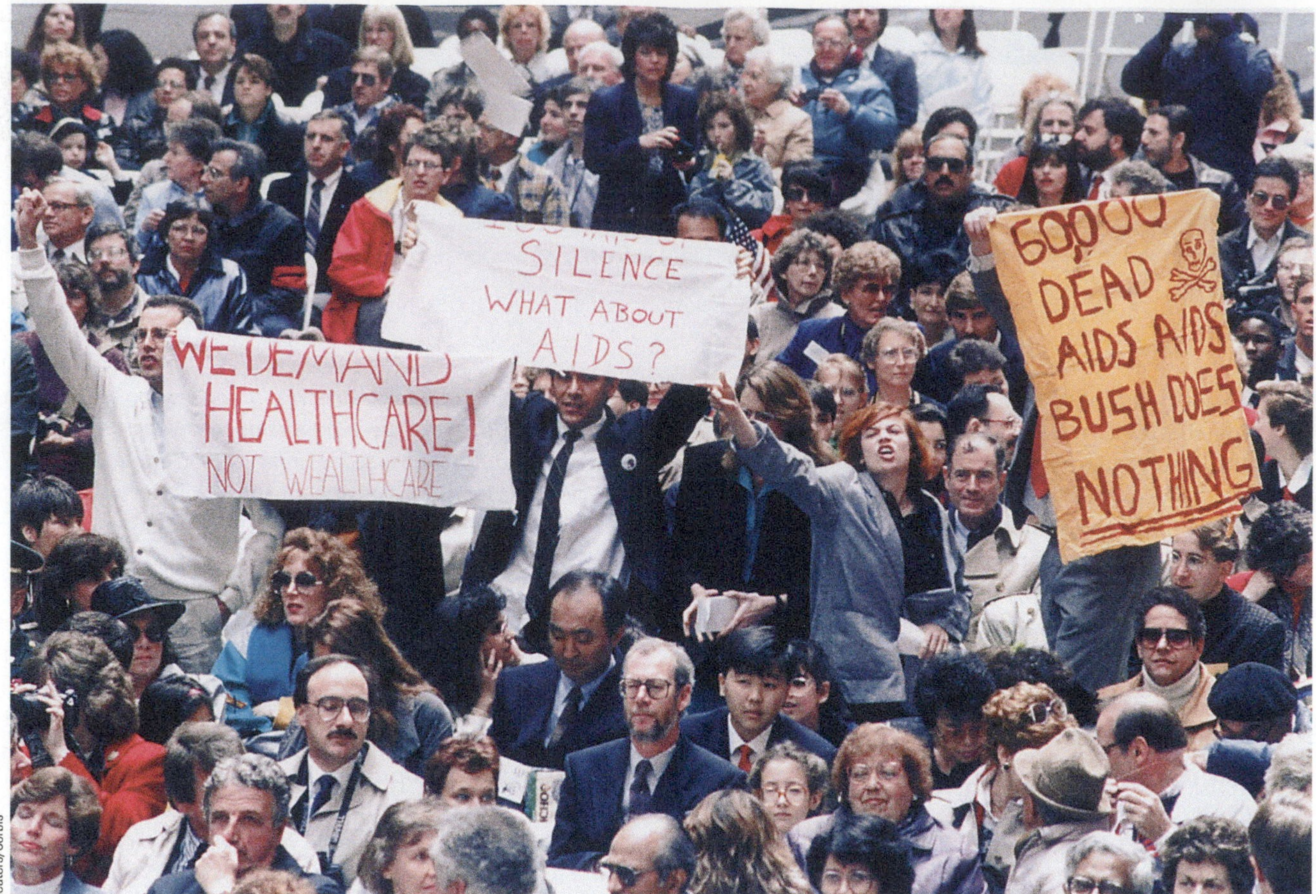

Reuters/Corbis

30.10 **Aids "ACT UP" Campaign** Health-care issues increasingly galvanized grassroots activists. In 1989, members of ACT UP, a group that embraced direct action, protested what they saw as the federal government's inattention to the issue of AIDS during the 1980s.

Q *How do organizations such as ACT UP illustrate the links between public policy and personal identity?*

Q *Are mass demonstrations an effective way of reaching out to people beyond those already committed to a specific movement?*

One issue, with international implications, was especially urgent. A human immunodeficiency virus produced an immune deficiency syndrome, HIV-AIDS, a contagious disease for which medical science offered virtually nothing in the way of cure. The disease could be transmitted through the careless use of intravenous drugs, tainted blood supplies, and unprotected sexual intercourse. At first, the incidence of HIV-AIDS in the United States was primarily limited to gay men, and activists charged that, as a consequence, cultural and religious conservatives placed a low priority on medical efforts to understand its causes, check its spread, or devise a cure. The resultant controversy over medical funding galvanized empowerment efforts among LGBT organizations, such as the Aids Coalition to Unleash Power, or ACT UP. With the development of prevention programs and drugs that could combat HIV-AIDS, however, most public figures came to support new efforts both at home and overseas, particularly in Africa, to address HIV-AIDS. It has remained a modern health threat in many parts of the world, but its specific identification with LGBT rights has faded.

30-4c *Activism among African Americans*

The emphasis on group identity as the fulcrum for social activism became especially strong among racial and ethnic communities. Extending the movement of movements of the 1960s, groups emphasized pride in their distinctive cultural traditions and insisted that differences should be affirmed rather than feared.

Having accomplished many of the legislative goals of the 1960s, African American activists, one observed, were "heading into a completely new era, and we don't know what to make of it." Mobilization to promote political and cultural change proceeded along many fronts.

African American leaders became increasingly prominent in national and local politics. One media spotlight fell on the Reverend Jesse Jackson. Jackson had spent the late 1960s in Chicago directing a local effort sponsored by Dr. Martin Luther King, Jr.'s, Southern Christian Leadership Conference (SCLC). After Dr. King's 1968 assassination, Jackson created his own Chicago-based organization, Operation PUSH, which pressured public officials and corporations to create jobs and promote community development projects. Abundant media coverage made Reverend Jackson best known for addressing a wide range of national and international issues, including the status of the Palestinians and apartheid in South Africa. During the 1980s, he formed the Rainbow Coalition to provide a national umbrella for his movement and to facilitate his campaigns for the Democratic Party's presidential nomination in 1984 and 1988. Jackson's efforts garnered several primary victories and helped shape Democratic Party politics.

Other types of political activism also left a significant imprint on electoral politics during the 1970s and 1980s. The civil rights movement of the 1960s (see Chapter 29) provided the legal-constitutional basis for greater political participation by African Americans, and change came rapidly. In 1970, 13 African American members of Congress established the Congressional Black Caucus (CBC) to form a common front on a wide range of foreign and domestic issues. Picking up the mantle of A. Philip Randolph and Bayard Rustin's "Freedom Budget" of the 1960s, the CBC regularly issued a hypothetical "Alternative Budget," which proposed more money for social initiatives. The caucus also campaigned on behalf of better relations between the United States and African nations and took stands on issues that particularly affected African Americans, such as inequities in drug sentencing.

By the end of the 1980s, more than 7,000 African Americans (including nearly 1,500 women) held political office. The year the Voting Rights Act passed, 1965, there had been fewer than 200. Urban centers with significant African American populations, such as Gary and Detroit, elected black mayors, but so did cities such as Denver, where African American candidates successfully formed cross-ethnic alliances. The new direction pursued by the Republican Party during the 1970s and 1980s meant that virtually all of this political activity occurred within Democratic ranks.

This form of black political activism confronted clear limits. Few mayors, whatever their ethnic identity, could mobilize the economic resources that large cities required to deal with rising crime rates, decaying infrastructures, and galloping inflation. The stagnant economy under Carter and the urban budget cutting that characterized the Reagan years hit African Americans in inner cities with severity.

In addition to political activism, a diverse set of cultural movements emerged. The hyper-violent 1970s cycle of "Blaxploitation movies," such as *Shaft* (1971) and *Coffy* (1973), prompted heated debate over whether representing urban black life "like it [supposedly] was," rather than "like it [supposedly] should be," advanced African American interests. The 1980s movies of Spike Lee also created controversy by tackling issues such as the politics of gender and "light skin" in African American life. *Do the Right Thing* (1989), arguably an even more ambitious movie—though smaller budgeted—than the epic *Malcolm X* (1991), provided a complex meditation about African American heroes, multiculturalism, law enforcement patterns, and personal activism amidst the uncertainties of urban life.

Prominent academics such as **Henry Louis Gates, Jr.**, worked in another venue to expand the study of the African American experience and to challenge a movement that advocated creating an "Afrocentric" school curriculum. African American culture, in the view of Gates, was not "a thing apart, separate from the whole, having no influence on the shape and shaping of American culture." Gates insisted on viewing African American authors, such as Toni Morrison and Alice Walker, as writers who take "the blackness of the culture for granted" and use this as "a springboard to write about those human emotions that we share with everyone else." The cultural works of African Americans should simultaneously be seen as unique and different, *and also* be viewed in relationship to broader cultural traditions, he believed.

30-4d *Activism among American Indians*

American Indians, of course, had long-standing identities based on their tribal affiliation, and many issues, particularly those involving land and treaty disputes, turned on specific, tribal-based claims. Other questions, which seemed to require strategies that extended beyond a single tribe or band, became identified as "pan-Indian" in nature.

In 1969, people from several tribes began a two-year sit-in designed to dramatize a history of broken treaty promises, at the former federal prison on Alcatraz Island in San Francisco harbor. Expanding on this tactic, the American Indian Movement (AIM), created in 1968 by young activists from several Northern Plains tribes, adopted even more confrontational approaches. Clashes with both federal officials and older American Indian leaders erupted in 1973 on the Pine Ridge Reservation in South Dakota. In response, federal officials targeted members of AIM with illegal surveillance and a series of controversial criminal prosecutions.

Meanwhile, important social and legal changes were taking place. In the Civil Rights Act of 1968, which contained several sections that became known as the "Indian Bill of Rights," Congress extended most of the provisions of the constitutional Bill of Rights to Native Americans living on reservations, while reconfirming the legitimacy of tribal laws. Federal legislation and several Supreme Court decisions in the 1970s subsequently reinforced the principle of "tribal self-determination." Tribal identification itself required legal action. By the early 21st century, the federal government officially recognized nearly 600 separate tribes and bands. After 1978 Congress also provided funds for educational institutions that would teach job skills and preserve tribal cultures.

Tapping the expertise of the Native American Rights Fund (NARF), tribes pressed demands that derived from old treaties with the U.S. government. Some campaigns sought recognition of fishing and agricultural rights and often provoked resentment among non-Indians who argued that these claims, based on federal authority, should not take precedence over state and local laws.

30.11 **Gaming at Potawatomi Casino** During the 1980s, casino-style gaming became one of the nation's leading entertainment enterprises. Native Americans embraced casinos, such as this one located in Milwaukee, Wisconsin, as important sources of jobs and capital on Indian reservations.

Q *How does this Potawatomi complex, which opened in 1991, juxtapose traditionally styled sculptures and an Indian heritage center with an imaginatively designed building, rooms of slot machines, and a Las Vegas-style dinner theatre?*

American Indians also sued to protect tribal water rights and traditional religious ceremonies, some of which included the ritualistic use of drugs such as peyote. In 1990, Congress passed the Native American Graves Protection and Repatriation Act, which required universities and museums to return human remains and sacred objects to tribes that requested them.

Claiming exemption from state gaming laws, Native Americans began to open bingo halls and then full-blown casinos. In 1988 the U.S. Supreme Court ruled that states could not prohibit gambling operations on tribal land, and Congress responded with the Indian Gaming Regulatory Act. Gambling emerged as one of the most lucrative sectors of the nation's entertainment business, and many Indian-owned casinos thrived. Ironically, the glitzy, tribal-owned casinos often financed tribal powwows and other efforts to nurture traditional cultural practices. Sometimes the competition to establish casinos in prime locations prompted intertribal political and legal conflicts.

To forestall the disappearance of native languages and cultures, American Indian activists urged bilingualism and renewed attention to tribal rituals. Indian groups also denounced the use of stereotypical nicknames, such as "Chiefs" and "Redskins," and Indian-related logos in sports. The federal government assisted this cultural-pride movement by funding two National Museums of the American Indian, one in New York and the other in Washington, D.C. The National Park Service changed the name of "Custer Battlefield" in Montana to "Little Bighorn Battlefield," redesigning its exhibits to honor American Indian culture.

30-4e *Activism in Spanish-Speaking Communities*

Spanish-speaking Americans, who constituted the fastest-growing ethnic group in the United States, highlighted the diversity and complexity of identity. Many Spanish-speaking people, especially in the Southwest, preferred the umbrella term "Latino," whereas others, particularly in Florida, used the term "Hispanic." At the same time, people the U.S. Census began (in 1980) labeling "Hispanic" most frequently identified themselves according to the specific Spanish-speaking country or commonwealth from which they or their ancestors had immigrated.

Mexican Americans, members of the oldest and most numerous Spanish-speaking group, could tap a long tradition of social activism. The late 1960s saw an emerging spirit of **Chicanismo**, a populist-style pride in a heritage that could be traced back to the ancient civilizations of Middle America. Young activists made the words *Chicano* and *Chicana*, terms of derision that most Mexican Americans had generally avoided in the past, into a rallying cry.

In cities in the Southwest during the 1970s, advocates of Chicanismo gained cultural influence. Members of La Raza Unida, a political party founded in 1967, began to win local elections. At the same time, Mexican American communities experienced a cultural flowering. New Spanish-language newspapers and journals reinforced a growing sense of pride, and many churches sponsored festivals with ethnic dancing, mural painting, poetry, and literature. Mexican Americans successfully pushed for programs in Chicano/a studies at colleges and universities.

Mexican Americans also organized politically. In San Antonio, Texas, in the 1970s Ernesto Cortes, Jr., took the lead in founding Communities Organized for Public Service (COPS), a group that brought the energy and talents of Mexican Americans, particularly women, into the city's public arena for the first time. Mexican American activists worked with Anglo business leaders and Democratic politicians such as Henry Cisneros, who became the city's mayor in 1981. Other locally based organizations formed on the model of COPS, such as United Neighborhood Organization (UNO) in Los Angeles, also worked on community concerns.

On the national level, the Mexican American Legal Defense and Education Fund (MALDEF), established in 1968, emerged as a highly visible advocacy group ready to lobby or litigate. Professional groups, such as the National Network of Hispanic Women, also proliferated. Mexican American activists, however, became especially well known for their labor-organizing efforts, particularly among farmworkers and in the rapidly expanding service sector.

Efforts to organize agricultural workers, who were largely of Mexican and Filipino descent, dramatized both the successes and the difficulties of expanding the union movement to largely immigrant workers. **Dolores Huerta and Cesar Chavez**, charismatic leaders who emulated the nonviolent tactics of Martin Luther King, Jr., vaulted the United Farm Workers (UFW) into public attention during the 1970s. Chavez undertook personal hunger strikes, and Huerta helped organize well-publicized consumer boycotts of lettuce and grapes to pressure growers into collective bargaining agreements with the UFW. Despite some successes, the UFW steadily lost ground during the later 1970s and the 1980s. Strong anti-union stands by growers and the continued influx of new immigrants eager for work undercut the UFW's efforts.

Social activism among Puerto Ricans in the United States emerged more slowly. Some stateside Puerto Ricans focused their political energy on the persistent "status" question—that is, whether Puerto Rico should seek independence, strive for statehood, or retain a commonwealth connection to the mainland. New York City's Puerto Rican Day Parade became the city's largest ethnic celebration and an important focus of cultural pride. A 1976 report by the U.S. Commission on Civil Rights, however, concluded that Puerto Ricans remained "the last in line" for government-funded benefits and opportunity programs. Over time, the Puerto Rican Legal Defense and Education Fund and allied groups helped Puerto Ricans surmount obstacles to the ballot box, gain political office, and achieve social and economic gains.

Cuban Americans, who had begun immigrating in large numbers to south Florida after Fidel Castro came to power, generally enjoyed greater access to education and higher incomes. They also tended to be politically conservative, generally voted Republican, and lobbied for a hard line toward Castro's communist government. Cuban Americans developed a dense network of institutions that leveraged them into positions of power in Florida politics and civic affairs.

Beneath a common Spanish language, then, lay great diversity in terms of economic status, national and cultural identification, political affiliation, and activist goals and organizations. Established communities that identified with Mexico, Puerto Rico, and Cuba developed a wide range of mobilizing and organizing styles. More recent immigrants from the Dominican Republic and Central America, who were among the most economically deprived and the least organized, also began to add their voices and concerns.

30-4f *Activism among Asian Americans*

Americans of Chinese, Japanese, Korean, Filipino, and other backgrounds began to create an Asian American movement in the 1970s. Organizations such as the Asian Pacific Planning Council (APPCON), founded in 1976, lobbied to obtain government funding for projects that benefited Asian American communities. The Asian Law Caucus, founded during the early 1970s by opponents of U.S. intervention in Vietnam, and the Committee against Anti-Asian Violence, created a decade later in response to a wave of racially motivated attacks, mobilized for a wide range of legal battles. During the 1970s Asian American studies programs also took shape at colleges and universities, particularly on the West Coast. By the early 1980s, Asian American political activists enjoyed growing influence, especially within the Democratic Party, and began gaining public office.

Emphasizing a broad, Asian American identity raised questions of inclusion, exclusion, and rivalry. Filipino American activists, members of the second largest Asian American group in the United States in 2000, often resisted the Asian American label because they believed that Chinese Americans or Japanese Americans dominated groups such as APPCON. Many people of Filipino descent focused on specific goals, particularly an effort to obtain citizenship and veterans' benefits for former soldiers of the Second World War who had

Ralf-Finn Hestoft/Encyclopedia/Corbis

30.12 **Mural Art in Chicago** Wall murals appeared in Mexican American communities throughout the country.

Q *How do these murals reflect themes in Mexican history and culture and build on styles inspired by the great Mexican muralists?*

fought against Japan. Japanese American groups also lobbied on behalf of specific issues, and in 1988 Congress formally apologized and voted to approve a reparations payment of $20,000 to every living Japanese American who had been confined in internment camps during the Second World War (see Chapter 26). Similarly, Hmong and Vietnamese groups pursued their own concerns related to the aftermath of the struggles in Indochina.

Socioeconomic differences made it difficult to frame a single Asian American agenda. Although many groups showed remarkable upward educational and economic mobility during the late 1980s and early 1990s, immigrants who were especially recent or impoverished often struggled to find jobs that paid more than the minimum wage.

As a result of combined pressure from different ethnic groups, the federal government finally designated "Asian or Pacific Islanders" (API) as a single pan-ethnic category in the censuses from 1990 on. It also provided nine specifically enumerated subcategories (such as Native Hawaiian or Filipino) and allowed other API groups (such as Hmong or Samoan) to write in their respective ethnic identifications. Thus, the term "Asian American"—which by the second decade of the 21st century applied to more than 16 million people and dozens of different ethnicities—both reflected, and was challenged by, the new emphasis on ethnic identity.

30-4g *Anti-Government Activism*

Ronald Reagan's first inaugural address of 1981 declared that "government is not the solution to our problem; government is the problem." As president, Reagan exempted national security institutions from this principle and rarely applied it literally to basic safety-net programs such as Social Security and Medicare. In the face of budget deficits, Reagan proved willing to raise taxes to support government's expenditures. His claim that government action was almost always harmful, however, did appeal to the increasingly important New Right segment of the larger Reagan coalition. During the 1980s, denunciations of federal power spread throughout the culture, propelled especially by controversies over affirmative action and various regulatory rules.

Affirmative action programs had grown from bipartisan roots in the administrations of Lyndon Johnson and Richard Nixon. Public officials, proponents argued, should act affirmatively to help people who belonged to groups with a shared history of discrimination—especially African Americans, Latinos, and women—obtain an equitable share of the nation's jobs, public spending, and educational programs. Affirmative action would help compensate for past discrimination and for continued, sometimes hidden, prejudice that laws merely guaranteeing formal equality failed to rectify. Advocates of affirmative action emphasized

Nik Wheeler/Corbis

30.13 **Vietnamese American Businesses in Los Angeles**
New Asian immigrants, especially from Southeast Asia, established a growing economic presence in many U.S. cities and suburbs.

Q *How has this new wave of immigration helped to revitalize older neighborhoods?*

that *any* process of selection inevitably "affirmed" some qualities, such as family or old school lineages, at the expense of others. Efforts at undoing years of discrimination against entire groups of people, in this view, required a complicated, seemingly paradoxical view of what counted as "equal" treatment by government.

Critics of affirmative action began to identify it as one of the most dangerous examples of increased governmental power. They noted that until the mid-1960s even supporters of civil rights had opposed government officials categorizing individuals according to group identities based on race or ethnicity. They often quoted Dr. King's words about judging people by the "content of their character" rather than the "color of their skin" and argued that government should remain "blind" to color and gender. They rejected the claim that policymakers needed to craft special rules or programs in order to eliminate discriminatory barriers to individual opportunity. Even some beneficiaries of these programs, such as Supreme Court Justice Clarence Thomas, charged that the derogatory label of "affirmative action applicant" threw into question the talents and capabilities of individuals. More broadly, critics of affirmative action programs denounced "set-aside" job programs and special educational admission procedures for previously disadvantaged groups as examples of illegal quotas, violations of constitutional guarantees, and even harbingers of totalitarianism. Did not affirmative action *on behalf* of people in some groups always constitute "reverse discrimination" *against* those in others?

In the midst of this controversy, federal courts initially managed to square affirmative action programs with older antidiscrimination precedents. They struck down affirmative action plans that contained inflexible quotas but upheld ones that made group identity only one of several criteria for making hiring or educational decisions. In the celebrated Supreme Court decision popularly known as the *Bakke* case (1978), a majority of justices ruled that affirmative action programs in educational settings could pass constitutional muster because they aimed at redressing past discrimination *and* because they contributed to "diversity," an intangible social and psychological quality important in any social, educational, or business environment. Many leaders of corporations, educational establishments, and the military came to endorse this *Bakke* principle: Diversity benefited not just applicants from historically discriminated groups but *all* people who worked within those environments as well as *all* those who relied on their services and expertise.

Opposition to affirmative action programs mobilized anti-government activists who found a close ally in New Right radio. During the 1970s, the FM dial had become dominated by musical programming, and many AM radio stations switched to an all-talk format. One of the personalities who made the switch was Rush Hudson Limbaugh III. Raised in a staunchly conservative Republican family, Limbaugh broke into AM as a radio host in several different markets under (as was the custom) several different names. Then, in 1984, Limbaugh took over an already-prominent New Right talk show in California. Limbaugh's ability to galvanize anti-government listeners gained him a spot in New York City and propelled him to the top ranks of a rapidly expanding, informal radio network that fueled anti-government activism.

New Right radio also thrived by attacking federal environmental regulations in the name of defending property rights. During the 1970s, western entrepreneurs associated with the sagebrush rebellion advocated transferring to state and private hands some of the vast amount of land held by the federal government for recreational parks and environmental purposes. Freed of restrictions from Washington, the rebels argued, westerners could make productive use of lands that lay within their states. A parallel effort, the "property rights movement," emerged across much of the country, particularly in areas of scenic beauty and where plans of suburban developers encountered environmental restrictions. Private builders denounced government for insisting on environmental impact assessments that might limit the ability of property owners to use land as they wished. In this movement, anti-government activists fought not only regulations from Washington but from any governmental body that claimed the power to regulate the use of private property in the name of some larger public purpose.

Denunciations of government regulations also flourished within a freshly deregulated communications industry. Beginning in 1949, the Federal Communications Commission (FCC), the government agency that regulated broadcasting, had required stations to represent a diversity of viewpoints. This "Fairness Doctrine" had survived constitutional challenge in the courts. Anti-government activists in the legal community, however, worked to overturn the doctrine, and in 1986, two conservative jurists, Antonin Scalia and Robert Bork, issued a federal court opinion ruling that Congress had never given the FCC any authority to mandate fairness. One year later, this decision prompted an FCC dominated by members appointed by Ronald Reagan to eliminate the Fairness Doctrine. New Right radio now enjoyed freedom to further ramp up its rhetoric against governmental power.

The overturning of the Fairness Doctrine dovetailed with the central tenet of the new anti-government activism: "Free markets," not government, provided the best structures for enhancing individual freedom and ensuring social-economic progress. The faith that markets served people better than governments, an idea older than the U.S. Constitution, had taken a considerable hit during the economic disarray of the 1930s. As a consequence, New Dealers had built on a very different conviction popularized under the label of Keynesianism: that government regulation must tame market excesses and prevent them from unleashing irrational and self-destructive forces into the larger political economy (see Chapter 25). In the 1950s and 1960s, conservative academics such as Milton Friedman had fired away at the Keynesian underpinnings of the New Deal–Great Society governmental structure, but during the 1970s and 1980s, conservatives rolled out much heavier weaponry.

Academics in the fields of law and economics at the University of Chicago took the lead. The economists crafted highly technical, mathematically complex arguments for ideas that soon became the new economic orthodoxy. Government regulators could never understand the risks from economic activities such as trading stocks or lending money as well as the people who actually worked in the marketplace. Markets almost always got things right, at least in the long run, while government regulators invariably got them wrong. Moreover, governmental bureaucracies such as the Securities and Exchange Commission (SEC) and the Federal Reserve Board were not really regulating markets in the public interest. Government bureaucrats were just another "special interest" looking out for themselves or for some other interest groups. They seldom acted as honest brokers between contending interests, as the interest-group pluralist model of the 1950s had claimed. Most importantly, the argument went, bureaucrats armed with the power of government invariably interfered with the most magical quality of free markets—their ability to provide self-correcting mechanisms.

A widening circle of academic and legal proponents of these anti-government ideas pressed this case. New economic textbooks challenged the Keynesian-oriented ones that had once dominated college and university classrooms. A new legal field, called "law and economics," attracted lawyers and judges (including Bork and Scalia) who crafted doctrines that accorded with free-market assumptions rather than the pro-regulatory ones that had guided New Deal–Great Society jurisprudence. Economist-activists carried the case against government regulation into the conservative think tanks, such as the Heritage Foundation, which were helping to shape public policy discussions. Taking advantage of loosened regulations, the business and financial world began to test the theories of self-regulating markets on Wall Street by devising new investment and creative financial instruments.

Ralf-Finn Hestoft/CORBIS

30.14 **Antiabortion Protest, 1989** Legalized abortions became a major political issue after the 1973 Supreme Court decision in *Roe v. Wade*. Here, on the 16th anniversary of *Roe*, protesters assemble in front of the Supreme Court building.

Q *Why did the steps in front of the Supreme Court increasingly become a site for political protest?*

By the end of the 1980s, opposition to government had become a prominent feature of American political culture. Although the left-leaning movements still argued for an activist government to promote social equality and economic fairness, they found a significant challenge in those who claimed that reducing the power of government would be the best way to solve social-economic problems and preserve liberty. Within this debate, anti-government activists, like other activists, hardly moved in lockstep. Some cared deeply about opposing new rules for affirmative action; others placed greater priority on economic or environmental deregulation. While remaining a coalition of disparate parts, however, anti-government activism (always linked to antitax sentiment) became a powerful force. It drew populist strength from the expertly crafted speeches of Ronald Reagan, the bombast of New Right radio, and the political mobilization of the religious right. It found justification within the mathematically informed papers of Nobel Prize winners and top-rung law professors. Successfully challenging the once-dominant political agendas of the Democratic Party, it propelled the mainstream of the Republican Party decidedly rightward, established a strong foothold in public policy and media discussions, and succeeded in remapping the nation's cultural and informational landscape.

Conclusion

The "Reagan revolution" of the 1980s rested on a conservative movement that had been taking shape for several decades. New Right Republicans distrusted extending federal government power, advocated sharp tax cuts with deregulation, and stressed a sociocultural agenda emphasizing "traditional" values. The dozen years of Republican dominance of the White House, from 1980 to 1992, helped shift the terms of political debate in the United States. The "liberal" label became one that most Democrats sought to avoid. In the international realm, the Reagan and Bush presidencies facilitated the end of the cold war, a struggle that had defined U.S. foreign policy since the end of the Second World War.

Meanwhile, American society seemed to fragment into specialized identifications. Social activism increasingly organized around sexual, racial, ethnic, and ideological identities. The New Right's stress on limiting the power of government and promoting conservative values reconfigured discussions about how government power could best promote liberty and equality.

CHAPTER REVIEW

Review

1. How did the legacies of the Vietnam War and Watergate help shape U.S. politics in the years that immediately followed?
2. To what extent did Ronald Reagan's presidency represent a victory for the New Right agenda in both domestic and foreign policy?
3. Why did cold war tensions mount during the 1980s, and how can the sudden end of the cold war be explained?
4. How did social movements of the post-1960s era affect American public life and the ways people saw their own personal identities?

Critical Thinking

1. In domestic policy, the Reagan presidency sought a decisive swing away from the Democratic agenda that had dated from the New Deal of the 1930s. Critically evaluate this proposition.
2. Discuss the many ways in which social activism continued to play an important role in politics and culture during the 1970s and 1980s.

Identifications

Review your understanding of the following key terms, people, and events for this chapter (terms in bold in text are included in the Glossary).

Gerald R. Ford, p. 836
James Earl (Jimmy) Carter, p. 836
energy crisis, p. 837
Three Mile Island, p. 838
Camp David Peace Talks of 1978, p. 839
human rights policy, p. 839
Iranian Revolution of January 1979, p. 840
New Right, p. 840
Ronald Reagan, p. 841
supply-side economics, p. 842
deregulation, p. 843
William Rehnquist, p. 844
George H. W. Bush, p. 845
American Disabilities Act (ADA), p. 845
Strategic Defense Initiative (SDI), p. 845
Iran-contra affair, p. 847
Mikhail Gorbachev, p. 847

Persian Gulf War, p. 849
Henry Louis Gates, Jr., p. 855
Chicanismo, p. 857
Dolores Huerta and Cesar Chavez, p. 857

Suggested Readings

For differing perspectives on political trends that came together during the 1980s and early 1990s, see **Robert O. Self, *All in the Family: The Realignment of American Democracy since the 1960s*** (2013); **Douglas Brinkley, *The Unfinished Presidency: Jimmy Carter's Journey to the Nobel Peace Prize*** (1998); **Steven F. Hayward, *The Age of Reagan: Conservative Counterrevolution, 1980–1989*** (2009); **Betty Glad, *An Outsider in the White House: Jimmy Carter, His Advisors, and the Making of American Foreign Policy*** (2010); and **Rick Perlstein, *The Invisible Bridge: The Fall of Nixon and the Rise of Reagan*** (2014).

See also **Sean Wilentz, *The Age of Reagan: A History, 1974–2008*** (2008); **Donald T. Critchlow, *The Conservative Ascendancy: How the Republican Right Rose to Power in Modern America*** (rev. ed., 2011); and **Kim Phillips-Fein, *Fear City: New York's Fiscal Crisis and the Rise of Austerity Politics*** (2017). On foreign policy see **Odd Arne Westad, *The Cold War: A World History*** (2017); and **Jeffrey A. Engel, *When the World Seemed New: George W. Bush and the End of the Cold War*** (2017).

Suggestive studies about social and cultural activism include **Juan P. Garcia, ed., *Mexican Americans in the 1990s*** (1997); **Lisa McGirr, *Suburban Warriors: The Origins of the New American Right*** (2001); **Matthew D. Lassiter, *The Silent Majority: Suburban Politics in the Sunbelt South*** (2007); **Frank Wu, *Yellow: Race in America Beyond Black and White*** (2002); **Larry Nesper, *The Walleye War: The Struggle for Ojibwe Spear-fishing and Treaty Rights*** (2002); **Sara Evans, *Tidal Wave: How Women Changed America at Century's End*** (2003); **David Carter, *Stonewall: The Riots that Sparked the Gay Revolution*** (2004); **Marjorie J. Spruill, *Divided We Stand: The Battle Over Women's Rights and Family Values that Polarized America*** (2017); **Miriam Pawel, *The Crusades of Caesar Chavez: A Biography*** (2014); the relevant portions of **Kim E. Nielson, *A Disability History of the United States*** (2012); and **Allan J. Lichtman, *White Protestant Nation: The Rise of the American Conservative Movement*** (2008).

Economic, Social, and Cultural Change at the Dawn of the 21st Century

David R. Frazier Photolibrary, Inc./Alamy Stock Photo

31.1 **Container Ship Revolution**
The busy sea port of Los Angeles highlights the globalization that accompanied the expanded use of steel cargo containers, which brought flexibility, automation, and lower costs to national and international commerce.

Q *How, specifically, might the spreading use of such steel boxes have affected corporate profits, wages, labor unions, and consumer prices?*

THE DAWN OF THE TWENTY-FIRST CENTURY saw sweeping changes in American life. A dramatic increase in immigration, along with movements of people throughout metropolitan areas and into states of the West and South, altered the demographic landscape. Business operations became more global, more high-tech, and more intertwined with a burgeoning financial sector. The continuing decline of employment in the manufacturing sector changed labor patterns. A constantly transforming digital environment revolutionized how people and institutions communicated. The entertainment-informational complex, with an emphasis on big-time sports, steadily expanded. At the same time, religious life became more diverse and more closely intertwined with the nation's politics. ■

CHRONOLOGY

1971	Starbucks Coffee opens first store
1972	Congress passes Title IX (Patsy Mink Equal Opportunity in Education Act)
1973	Federal Express (FedEx) opens for business
1977	Congress passes Community Reinvestment Act
1978	Supreme Court decision frees banks to relocate credit-card operations
1979	ESPN joins the cable TV lineup
1981	MTV and CNN debut on cable TV
1982	Congress relaxes regulations on S&Ls
1986	Congress passes Immigration Reform and Control Act (Simpson-Mazzoli Act)
1987	Prices crash on New York Stock Exchange and then rebound
1988	Fox television network begins
1989	Congress enacts bailout plan for recently deregulated Savings and Loan industry
1990	Congress passes The Immigration Act of 1990
1991	First McDonald's opens in Moscow
1995	Amazon.com begins selling books online
1996	Fox News Network debuts
2000	Human Genome Project issues preliminary draft

31-1 A Changing People

Q *What were the major demographic changes that affected American life in this period?*

America's population was becoming older, more metropolitan, and more ethnically and racially diverse. Moreover, the nation's centers of power continued shifting away from the Northeast and toward the South and West.

31-1a *An Aging, Mobile Population*

During the 1950s, the height of the baby boom, the population had grown by 1.8 percent per year; after 1970, even with new waves of immigration and longer life expectancies, the growth rate slowed to about 1 percent per year. Younger people often delayed marriage until well into their 20s; most raised smaller families than had their parents; and many adults remained unmarried for much of their lives. The number of households with at least one child under 18 continually shrank. In 1960, nearly half fell into this category; by 1999, only about a third of U.S. households contained even one person under the age of 18. Consequently, at the turn of the 21st century, people in the 35 through 55 age categories (the baby boom generation) constituted a larger slice of the U.S. population than any other, and the number in their teens to early 20s was relatively small (see Figure 31.1).

The steady rise of the median age of the population brought public policy, as well as personal, dilemmas. As aging baby boomers pondered retirement, policymakers began debating how to cover projected Social Security and Medicare payouts. Trend watchers of the 1960s had talked of a "youth revolt." By the end of the 20th century, their counterparts discussed the "graying of America."

The changing geographical distribution of population restructured political and economic life (see Map 31.1). After 1970, most of the population growth occurred in the South and the West. Nevada, California, Florida, and Arizona became the fastest-growing states, and by 2000 more than 1 in 10 Americans lived in California. Western and southern states gained seats in the U.S. House of Representatives, while northeastern states shed them (see Map 31.2). Many reasons helped account for this demographic shift: affordable air-conditioning; the expansion of tourism and new retirement communities; and for businesses, the attraction of lower labor costs and the absence of strong unions.

The development of high-tech industries connected to military spending and the computer revolution also played an important role. Fox example, California's Santa Clara County, a once rural area near San Francisco, benefited from spectacular growth in its semiconductor industry and its network of computer-related enterprises and became

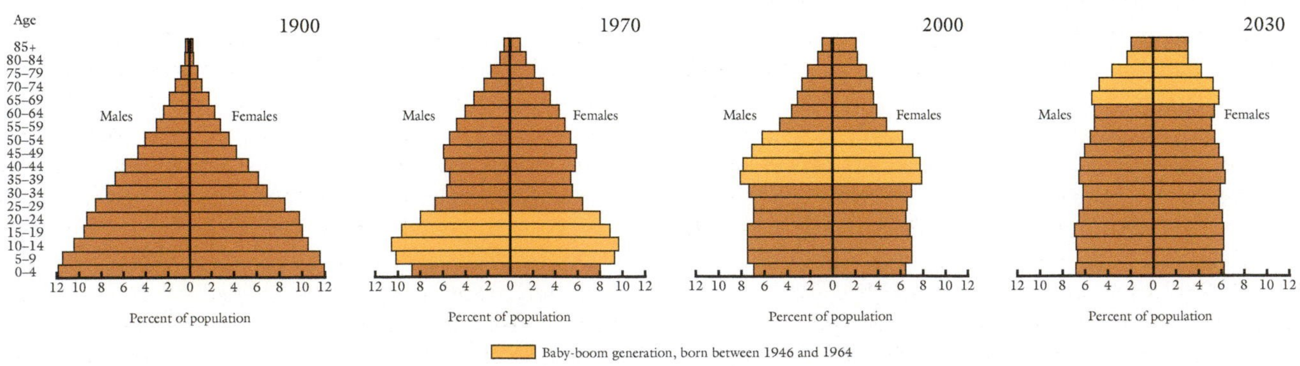

Figure 31.1 **The Aging of America.**

Source: U.S. Census Bureau. Adapted from C. L. Himes, "Elderly Americans," *Population Bulletin*, 2002, 56(4), p. 4.

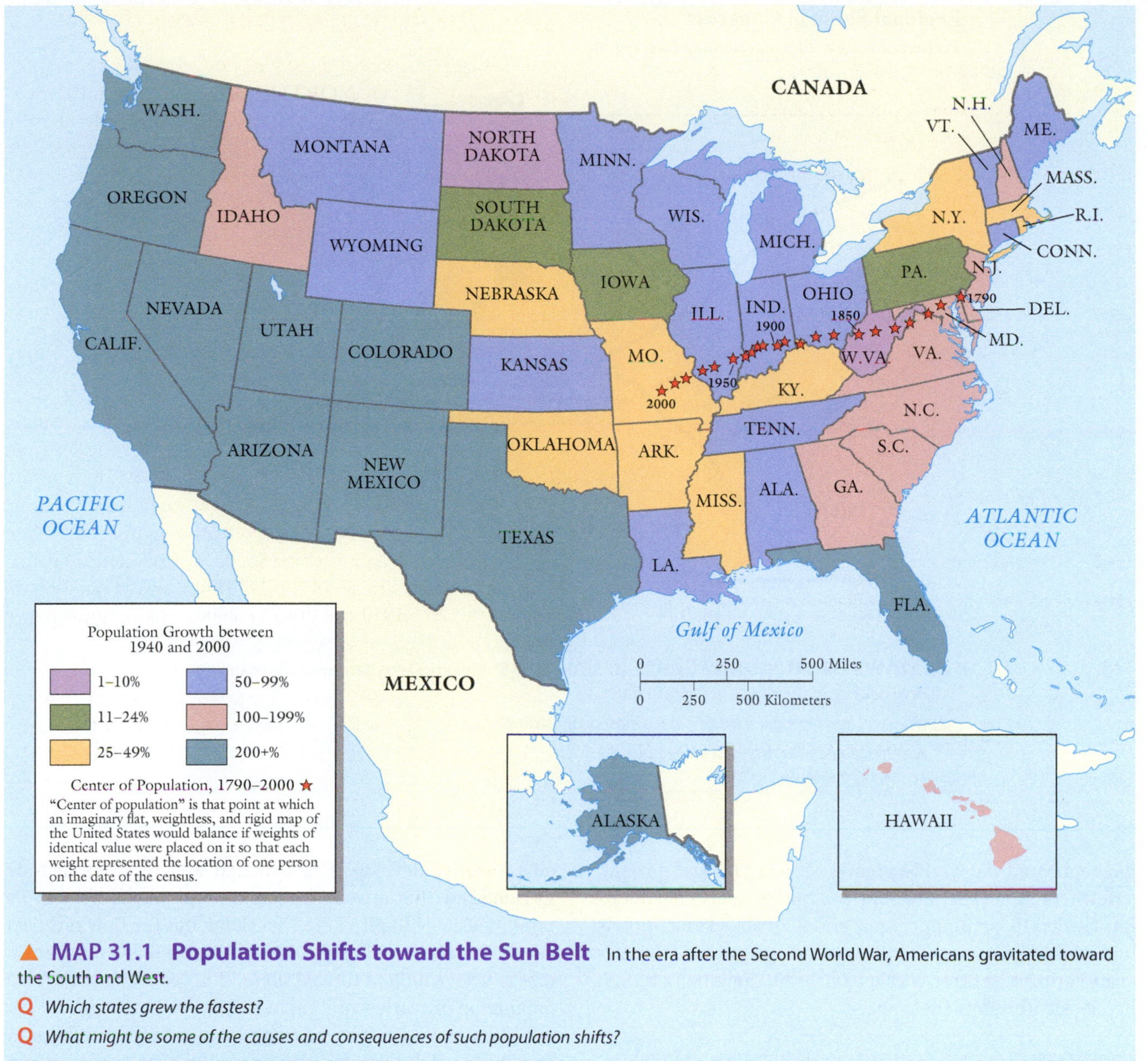

▲ **MAP 31.1 Population Shifts toward the Sun Belt** In the era after the Second World War, Americans gravitated toward the South and West.

Q *Which states grew the fastest?*

Q *What might be some of the causes and consequences of such population shifts?*

known as "Silicon Valley" during the 1970s. It spawned companies such as Google and Yahoo!

The governmentally financed space program, directed by the National Aeronautics and Space Administration (NASA) from installations in Texas and Florida, propelled the shift of research and technology to the Sun Belt. In 1961, President Kennedy had announced plans for the manned Apollo program, and in July 1969, astronaut Neil Armstrong had walked on the lunar surface. Apollo flights continued until 1972, when NASA began to develop a space station. In the 1980s, NASA started operating space shuttles, manned craft that served as scientific laboratories in outer space and could be flown back to earth for reuse. In early 1986, the program suffered a tragic setback when the *Challenger* shuttle exploded shortly after liftoff. After a hiatus of more than two years, the program resumed its operations, with new safety procedures in place.

Individual entrepreneurs and giant corporations also migrated to the Sun Belt and crafted multiple versions of a single product: *entertainment.* The Sun Belt featured a host of "magical" places such as Disneyland and Las Vegas. These tourist destinations predated the 1970s, but they boomed during the final decades of the 20th century as they constantly expanded their offerings in search of ever-larger crowds and ever-greater profits. An enlarged version of Disneyland in Florida, Walt Disney World, opened in 1971. Las Vegas morphed from an underworld-controlled outpost for sin, a jungle with green felt gaming tables, into an entertainment magnet that added family-oriented attractions to the mix. A spectacle itself, Las Vegas hosted other spectacles: architecture

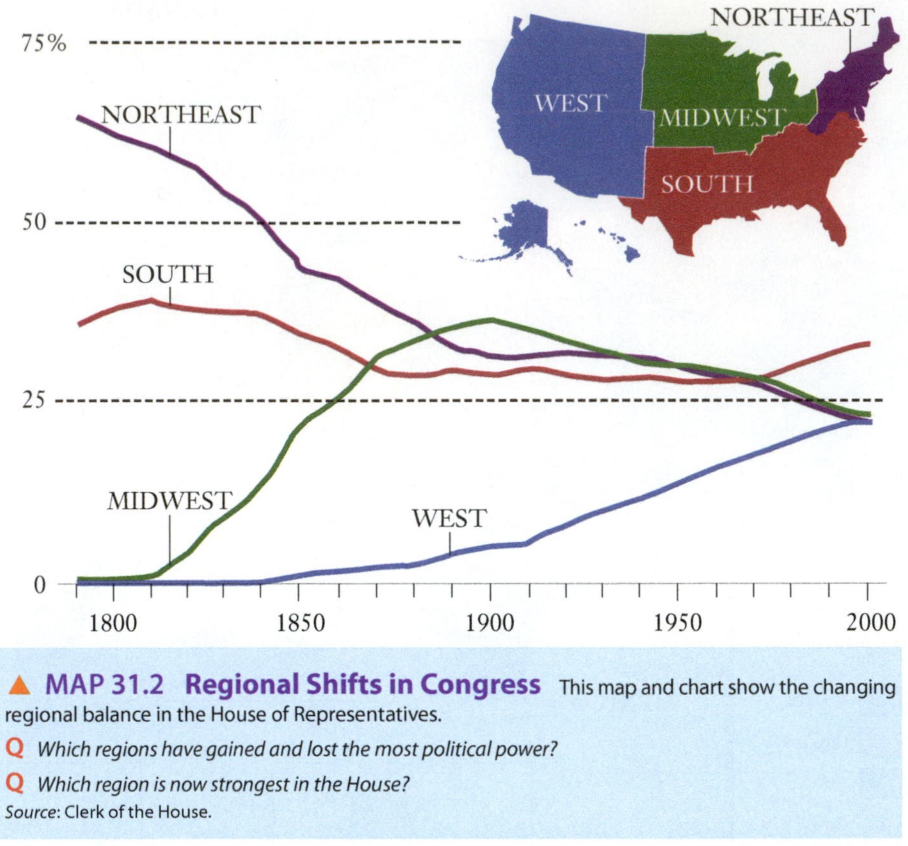

▲ **MAP 31.2 Regional Shifts in Congress** This map and chart show the changing regional balance in the House of Representatives.

Q *Which regions have gained and lost the most political power?*

Q *Which region is now strongest in the House?*

Source: Clerk of the House.

that replicated the world's greatest cities, past and present; performers from every area of show business; art collections that rivaled those in museums; and luxurious resort-hotels that could house and feed thousands of guests. The Las Vegas "strip," retrofitted with mass transit, remained a round-the-clock entertainment venue.

31-1b *New Immigration*

A dramatic increase in immigration from countries mostly to the south and west of the United States accounted for much of the U.S. population growth in the late 20th century. The vast bulk of post-1970 immigration came from Asia, Oceania, Latin America, Africa, and the Middle East rather than from Europe, which had previously been the primary source of immigrants. In 2000, roughly 12 percent of the U.S. population had been born outside the United States, compared to the all-time high of 15 percent in 1890 (see Map 31.3).

The largest number of non-European immigrants came from Mexico. Responding to labor shortages in the United States and poor economic prospects at home, immigration from Mexico rose substantially in every decade. Ninety percent of all Mexican Americans lived in the Southwest, primarily Texas and California.

Most people moving from Puerto Rico to the mainland settled around New York City, but sizable Puerto Rican communities developed in Chicago and in cities in New England and Ohio as well. The economic problems of the 1970s prompted some to return to the island, but the flow reversed again after about 1980. By 2000, the Puerto Rican population on the U.S. mainland totaled about 3 million, compared to a population of nearly 4 million in Puerto Rico.

Cubans had begun immigrating in large numbers in response to Fidel Castro's revolution. In 1962, Congress had designated people fleeing from Castro's Cuba as refugees eligible for admittance, and during the next 20 years, more than 800,000 Cubans from every strata of society came to the United States. They gradually moved northward into many major American cities, but the greatest impact was in south Florida. An agreement with Castro in 1995 brought the first U.S. restrictions on the flow of immigrants from Cuba, but about half of all Miamians were of Cuban descent by 2000.

The number of Spanish-speaking people in the United States at the turn of the 21st century exceeded that of all but four countries of Latin America. Los Angeles became the second largest "Mexican city" in the world, trailing only Mexico City, and its Salvadoran population just about equaled that of San Salvador. More Puerto Ricans lived in New York City than in San Juan, and the Big Apple's Dominican population rivaled that of Santo Domingo.

These changes in immigration patterns began with the landmark **Immigration and Nationality Act of 1965**, which

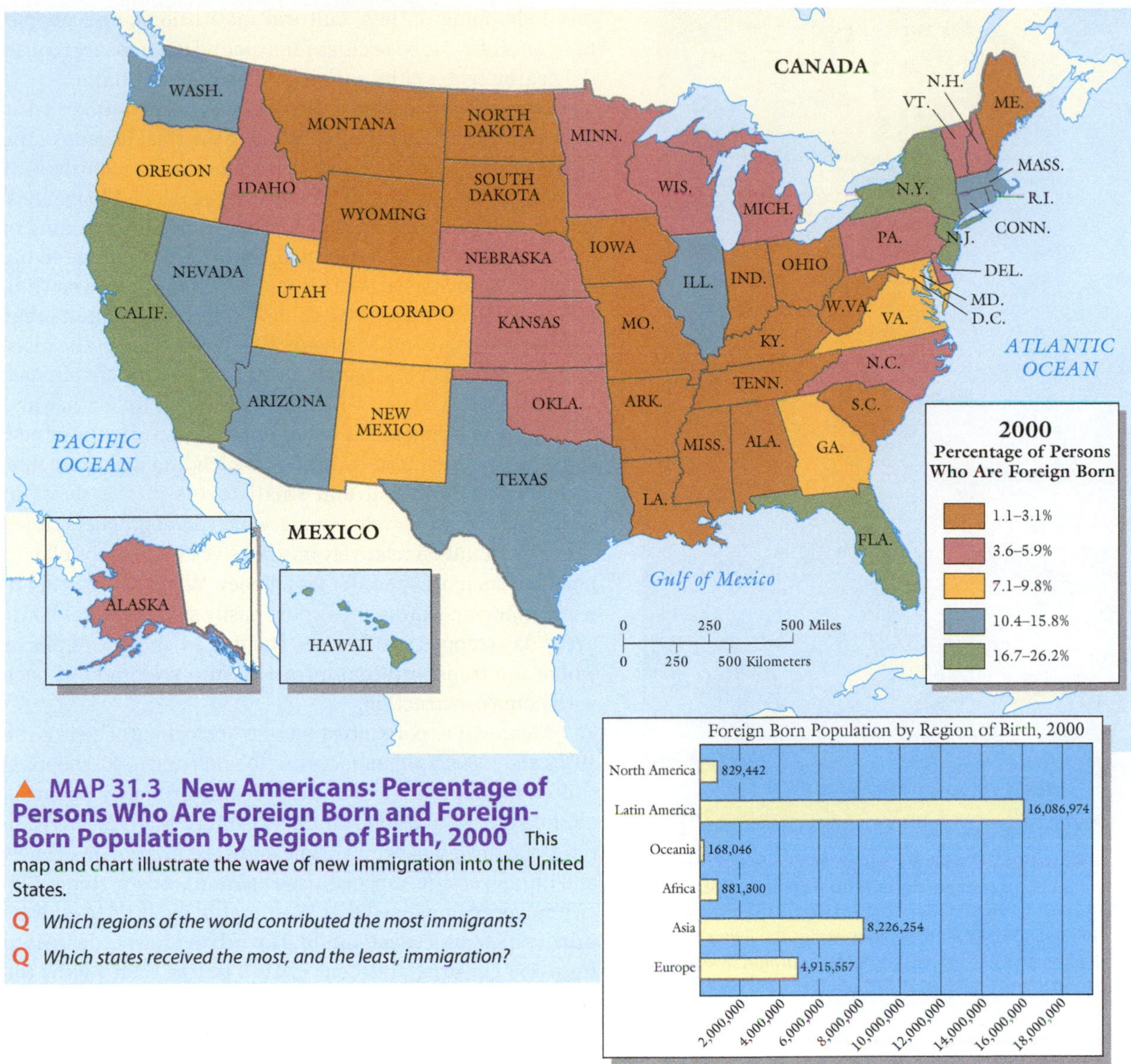

▲ **MAP 31.3 New Americans: Percentage of Persons Who Are Foreign Born and Foreign-Born Population by Region of Birth, 2000** This map and chart illustrate the wave of new immigration into the United States.

Q *Which regions of the world contributed the most immigrants?*

Q *Which states received the most, and the least, immigration?*

abolished quotas based on national origin (see Chapter 24). Instead, it placed a ceiling of 20,000 immigrants for every country, gave preference to people with close family ties in the United States, and accorded priority to those with special skills and those classified as "refugees." Although largely unforeseen at the time, this legislation laid the basis for not only a resumption of high-volume immigration but also a substantial shift in region of origin.

International events also affected U.S. immigration policy. Following the American withdrawal from Vietnam, for example, U.S. officials facilitated the admittance of many Vietnamese, Cambodians, Laotians, and Hmong (an ethnically distinct people who inhabited lands extending across the borders of these three Asian countries). The goal was to resettle some of the people who had allied with the United States during the Vietnam War and whose families were consequently in peril.

In response to the growing number of people seeking admission to the United States, Congress passed the Refugee Act of 1980. It favored political refugees, "those fleeing overt persecution," over people seeking simply to improve their economic circumstances. In practice, U.S. officials interpreted the terms "political" and "economic" so that people leaving communist regimes were generally admitted but those fleeing right-wing dictatorships were usually turned away or deported. For example, Cubans and Soviet Jews were admitted, but most Guatemalans and Salvadorans, hoping to escape repressive military governments backed by the United States during the 1980s, stood little chance of legal entry as refugees.

Immigration policy sparked political controversies. The **Immigration Reform and Control Act of 1986 (or the Simpson-Mazzoli Act)** imposed stricter penalties on businesses employing undocumented workers, increased border security, and granted permanent residency to people with proof they had been living in the United States since 1982. Immigration continued to soar as the economic upturn during the 1990s acted as a magnet for newcomers. The Immigration Act of 1990 increased the number of people who could be

AP Images/Jim Mone

31.2 **Somalis in Minneapolis** Minnesota hosted the largest concentration in the United States of immigrants from Somalia, who were overwhelmingly Sunni Muslims. Many settled in high-rise apartments near downtown Minneapolis. Several decades earlier, the Riverside Plaza high-rises had been celebrated as the latest in progressive urban design and were used in the opening of TV's popular *Mary Tyler Moore Show* (1970–1977).

Q *What economic, social, and political consequences might flow from the demographic shift illustrated in this photo?*

admitted on the basis of special job skills or the investment capital they could bring into the United States. Those favoring continued high levels of immigration saw potential benefits for the entire nation, but proponents of greater restrictions decried the economic, social, and cultural burdens that newcomers supposedly posed. Starkly conflicting perspectives stalemated new congressional legislation on immigration policy for decades.

31-1c *A Metropolitan Nation*

Relationships between urban centers and outlying areas, too, were in a state of flux. At the turn of the 21st century, more than 80 percent of Americans lived in sprawling metropolitan corridors, strips of suburbs that ran between older cities such as Seattle and Tacoma or Washington D.C. and Baltimore. In some cases, "edge cities" such as Irvine in California or Boca Raton in Florida sprouted up in these corridors and competed with older urban centers for businesses, job opportunities, retail shopping outlets, cultural institutions, and people. Residents of these edge cities rarely found it necessary to visit the nearby center cities such as Los Angeles or Miami.

Demographic patterns within urban and suburban areas were also changing. Especially during the final decade of the 20th century, minority groups began moving to suburbs, just as more affluent white suburbanites were relocating in cities. As a result, the percentage of African Americans residing in urban centers steadily declined, and the percentage living in suburbia increased. With some new immigrants settling outside central cities, some suburbs—in metropolitan areas such as Chicago and Minneapolis—came to contain more foreign-born residents than the central cities they surrounded.

Moreover, the newest suburbs sprouted up farther and farther away from either core or edge cities. A frenzy of new construction, financed by innovative lending arrangements, transformed farmland and small towns into a series of sprawling housing developments, which demographers called **"exurbs."** Built on relatively inexpensive land, exurbs offered homebuyers more space for less money. When commuting to work, however, exurbanites could easily spend several hours every day trapped inside a car, inching in and out of places where the transportation infrastructure seldom kept pace with home construction.

Meanwhile, core cities were transformed. During the 1970s and 1980s, as manufacturing jobs left and retail shopping shifted to suburban malls, cities became primarily financial, administrative, and entertainment centers. Many faced rising rates of homelessness and crime and deterioration in schools and infrastructure, especially sewage and water systems. Big-city mayors complained that Washington did little to address urban problems. Federal funding for urban projects decreased from $64 per urban resident in 1980 to less than $30 by the early 1990s.

In time, though, certain areas within most central cities underwent stunning revivals. Building booms brought new office towers, residential buildings, arts complexes, and sports facilities to many downtowns across the country. People with cash or credit to spend on housing, restaurants, and entertainment began flocking to select areas, which became labeled as "gentrified."

This urban growth, which gained momentum throughout the 1990s, sprang from many sources (see Map 31.4). A brighter economic picture and improvements in air quality helped. Innovations in urban design integrated diverse architectural styles with new green spaces and revitalized riverbanks and lakefronts. Community development corporations (CDCs), grassroots efforts indebted to movement cultures of the 1960s, supported initiatives for affordable housing, better child-care facilities, and expanded employment opportunities. The **Community Reinvestment Act of 1977**, which obliged banks to finance more home buying in low-income neighborhoods, provided a stimulus. Community policing, a trend toward harsher sentencing, and an aging population lowered urban crime rates. Affluent suburban commuters realized that they could save both time and money by moving to the revitalizing downtowns. In addition, some new immigrants repopulated

Interpreting the Visual Past Mapping the Future

Road maps, a form of cartography that can claim a history extending to ancient times, became an essential automobile accessory almost as soon as people began to drive cars. The American Automobile Association (AAA) began preparing maps for its motoring members in 1905, at about the same time that a commercial company, Rand McNally, also started producing road maps. By the middle of the 20th century, the thousands of service stations connected to the major oil companies were distributing millions of free maps in order to help drivers find or stay on the right road. Although, by the 1970s, complimentary maps became harder and harder to find at gas stations, states often continued distributing free road maps as a public service and, as with the California maps excerpted here, to complement tourism promotion campaigns.

The California Division of Highways produced and distributed the maps pictured here in 1940 and 1990. These maps were especially intended to help drivers navigate the rapidly changing geography of Southern California. Today, although outdated and nearly useless as travel guides, such maps can still serve as important visual evidence to help illuminate the changing history of this Southern California locale and of urban-suburban change more generally.

Q *What are the most obvious changes in Southern California between 1940 and 1990 that can be seen by looking at the basic cartographic elements these road maps employ—lines signifying major roads and highways and dots showing cities and towns?*

Q *What kinds of cartographic elements and techniques used in the 1990 map are not present in the map from 1940? What historical changes—beyond simply the existence of more highways—are suggested by these new elements and techniques?*

Q *How does a comparison of these two maps illustrate the changing relationship between Los Angeles and San Diego—and the changes in the area between these two urban centers—from 1940 and 1990? How might areas of the country with which you are familiar have experienced similar trends over this period of time?*

Q *Do maps such as these have any future in an era of GPS?*

California Department of Transportation

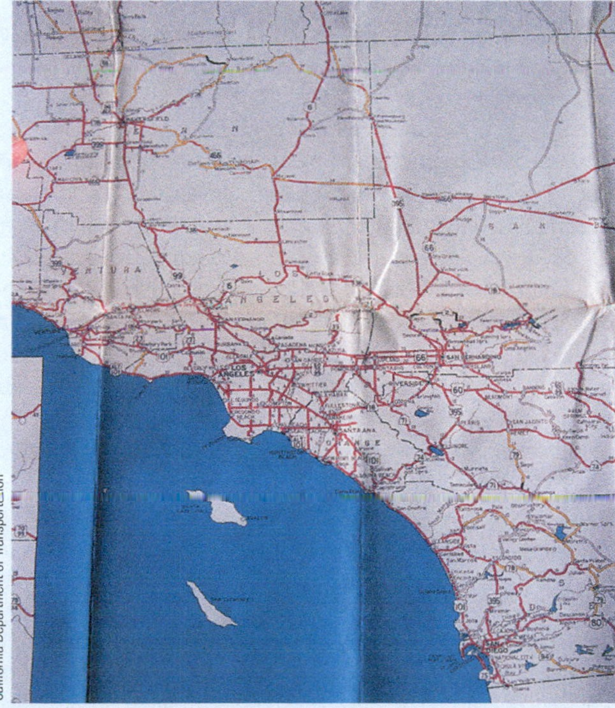

California Department of Transportation

California Department of Transportation

31.3a (top), 31.3b (bottom left), and 31.3c (bottom right) **State of California Road Maps, 1940 and 1990.**

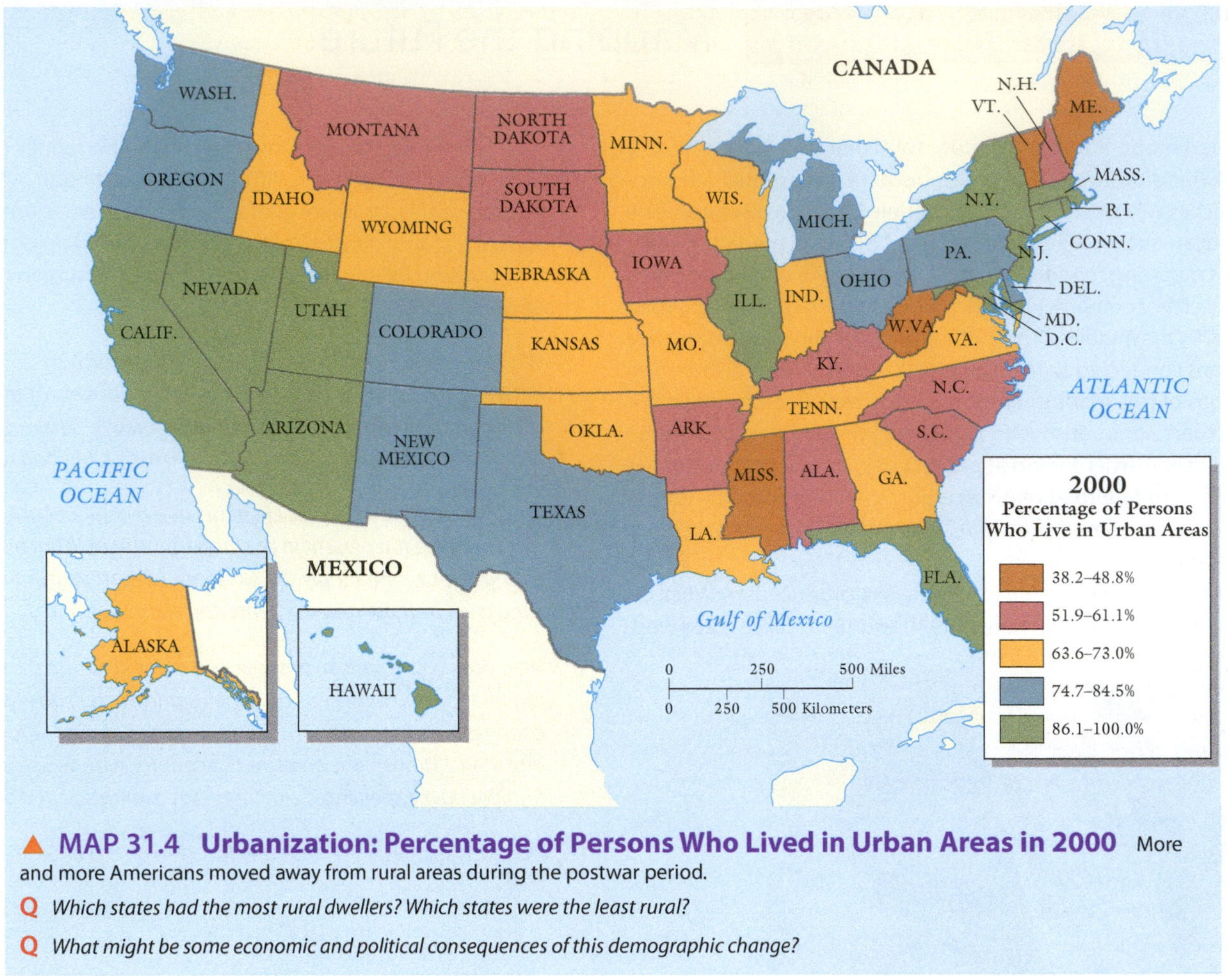

▲ **MAP 31.4 Urbanization: Percentage of Persons Who Lived in Urban Areas in 2000** More and more Americans moved away from rural areas during the postwar period.

Q *Which states had the most rural dwellers? Which states were the least rural?*

Q *What might be some economic and political consequences of this demographic change?*

once-declining neighborhoods, refurbishing the housing stock and reviving the commercial zones. By 2000, many U.S. cities featured vibrant, transnational spaces.

These transformed urban areas especially appealed to college-educated professionals who had benefited from the dramatic expansion of higher education. During the 1960s, colleges and universities had doubled their enrollment. The boom continued as the federal government's Pell Grant program (which provides financial assistance to students from low-income families) and various loan arrangements softened the immediate economic burden of attending college. More students of non-European ancestry and increasing numbers of women enrolled. Gaining a college degree could produce a costly debt burden but would generally increase a person's income and occupational mobility.

The ability to live and play in the new metropolitan spaces, of course, ultimately depended on household income. During the two decades after 1980, households in the top 10 percent of the income pyramid saw a substantial increase. The incomes of those at the very top, the superwealthy 1 percent, fared even better. The vast majority of individuals and families, by contrast, saw far more modest, if any, gains. An important part of this story of widening income inequality involved the transformations that were occurring throughout the U.S. and international economies.

31-2 Economic Transformations

Q *What were the major elements of post-1970 economic change and how did each one generate both new problems and new possibilities for Americans?*

A latter-day Rip van Winkle, awakening from a lengthy sleep in the early 21st century, would have marvelled at the consumer products in daily use. People could awaken to sounds from a digital device, stream an on-line version of the morning news, use a personal computer to work from home, or to watch sports or entertainment programs. They could also enter a fantasy world through a video game or catch up with the world and friends via the social networking applications on their mobile phone. If one looked past large pockets of persistent poverty, it could seem as if new technologies and innovative businesses were transforming America into a consumer paradise.

31-2a *New Technologies*

The computer revolution, which had begun during the 1940s, entered a new phase after 1970. Microchips increased hardware capacity and reduced the size and cost of computers. Microsoft and Apple, two companies founded during the 1970s, challenged mighty IBM for supremacy in the personal computer market and introduced competing operating systems and Web browsers. Their celebrity CEOs, Bill Gates and Steve Jobs, became two of the wealthiest and most influential people in the world—and came to symbolize key differences between these cyber-era giants. Although Microsoft quickly beat out Apple for domination in the war over lucrative operating systems, the companies continued to battle over virtually everything else, including that all-important intangible: the loyalty of customers who saw their computers, especially if they owned a Mac, as part of their personal identity.

Changes in the speed and accessibility of informational systems rearranged how people interacted with the larger economy and lived their daily lives. Enhanced memory capacity and parallel processors, which allow many computer operations to run simultaneously, rapidly transformed the handling of words and images. Enhanced by new communications technologies, such as fiber-optic networks and then satellite transmission, successive generations of computers fueled an **information revolution**. Libraries replaced card catalogs with networked computer databases; screens replaced paper. Voicemail, fax transmissions, e-mail, and text messaging came to supplement or substitute for posted mail and telephone conversations. The use of cellular phones spread rapidly during the 1990s and, along with improved computer access, made telecommuting from home to work an attractive option.

Innovation in other fields such as biotechnology promised to produce similarly dramatic effects. Beginning in 1990, for example, the **Human Genome Project** sought to map the genetic code. This international effort, which unveiled a preliminary draft of the human genome in 2000, sought to provide techniques for gene transfer, embryo manipulation, tissue regeneration, and even cloning. Other biotechnological research portended new approaches to the treatment of cancer and other diseases. Breakthroughs in genetic manipulation promised to revolutionize waste conversion and toxic cleanup. Large food producers heralded the use of genetically modified crops as an extension of the earlier "green revolution," which had boosted agricultural yields. Foods that had been modified, beginning with those derived from soybeans and corn, first reached consumers during the early 1990s. A genetically modified tomato, which would ripen without softening, debuted in 1994.

These new technologies raised legal and ethical questions. How would the computer revolution, for example, affect traditional ideas and laws about privacy? Biotechnological research also generated controversial questions. Almost immediately after the Supreme Court decided the abortion case of *Roe* v. *Wade*, for instance, Congress banned federal funding for research involving fetal tissue. Fears that experimentation with embryonic stem cells would increase abortions blocked federal support for research, but scientific work with other kinds of stem cells began to show benefits in regenerating human tissue. Controversy, more gradually, came to swirl around genetically modified (GM) foods. Critics asked how GM foods might affect individuals with allergies and, more ominously, harm biodiversity across the entire planet.

31-2b *Changes in the Structure and Operation of Business*

Computerization encouraged businesses to change their modes of operation. Computer networks helped lower costs and boost productivity (the output of goods per labor hour). Companies increasingly abandoned paperwork in favor of computerized tracking systems. The resulting improvement in information processing helped businesses more accurately

Keren Su/Encyclopedia/Corbis

31.4 **Lattes in Shanghai** American chain businesses spread throughout the world, part of the process known as globalization.

Q *How did new technologies facilitate globalization and create both opportunities and challenges for U.S. businesses?*

calculate the relationship between what they produced (or ordered from suppliers) and sales projections. Computers thus enabled "just in time production," or JIT. This streamlined process eliminated waste throughout the production-consumption loop and permitted the downscaling of warehousing operations for unsold products and unused supplies.

The computer revolution also speeded the continued expansion of chain and franchise businesses. McDonald's and Holiday Inn had pioneered nationwide standardization in the fast-food and travel industries during the late 1950s. Other businesses adapted this model. Starbucks Coffee Company began as a local operation in 1971, rapidly expanded beyond Seattle during the 1980s, and opened a new store somewhere in the world every day during the 1990s. Starbucks helped to add a new term to the labor lexicon, *barista*, and to elevate a once-simple beverage into a pricey designer commodity.

The Walmart chain prospered by moving in the opposite direction: The company promised customers it was constantly rolling back prices. Walmart initially avoided the upscale metropolitan areas where Starbucks was thriving, focusing instead on small towns and exurban areas, places where someone other than a *barista* was likely serving coffee. Here, the company could find workers, called "associates," willing to work part-time at relatively low pay. Walmart's labor force thus contained many married women and retirees who could not find or did not desire full-time employment. Walmart became the largest private employer in the United States; by the turn of the 21st century, nearly 1 of every 120 workers, and 1 of every 20 in the retail sector, worked for the company. Communities were often divided over the arrival of a Walmart. The retailing giant did offer consumers a wide array of merchandise at lower prices, but it also crushed local, independent businesses in thousands of midsized and small towns.

U.S.-owned chain and franchise businesses also expanded overseas, especially after the end of the cold war. In 1991, McDonald's opened to great fanfare in Moscow, and its Pushkin Square restaurant immediately claimed the title of the world's busiest "Mickey D's." U.S.-based hotel chains opened competing, luxury facilities in the former Soviet Union and throughout Eastern Europe. The demise of the Soviet Union also allowed Pepsi and Coke to carry their ongoing "cola wars" into new territory. During the 1970s, Pepsi had struck a special deal with the Kremlin that allowed its cola to be the first American product sold in the Soviet Union. During the 1990s, Coca-Cola debuted and quickly challenged its rival for cola supremacy in post-cold war Russia's newly competitive soft-drink market.

Launched in 1995, Amazon.com led a different kind of retailing revolution—e-commerce, or the practice of selling over the Internet. It began with books and soon added other products. Toward the very end of the 1990s, a wave of new "dot-com" businesses flooded the Internet and set off a short-term bubble in dot-com stocks that Amazon.com managed to survive. Buying and selling over the Internet quickly became central to consumer culture. Amazon and the online auction site eBay became models for doing business in cyberspace.

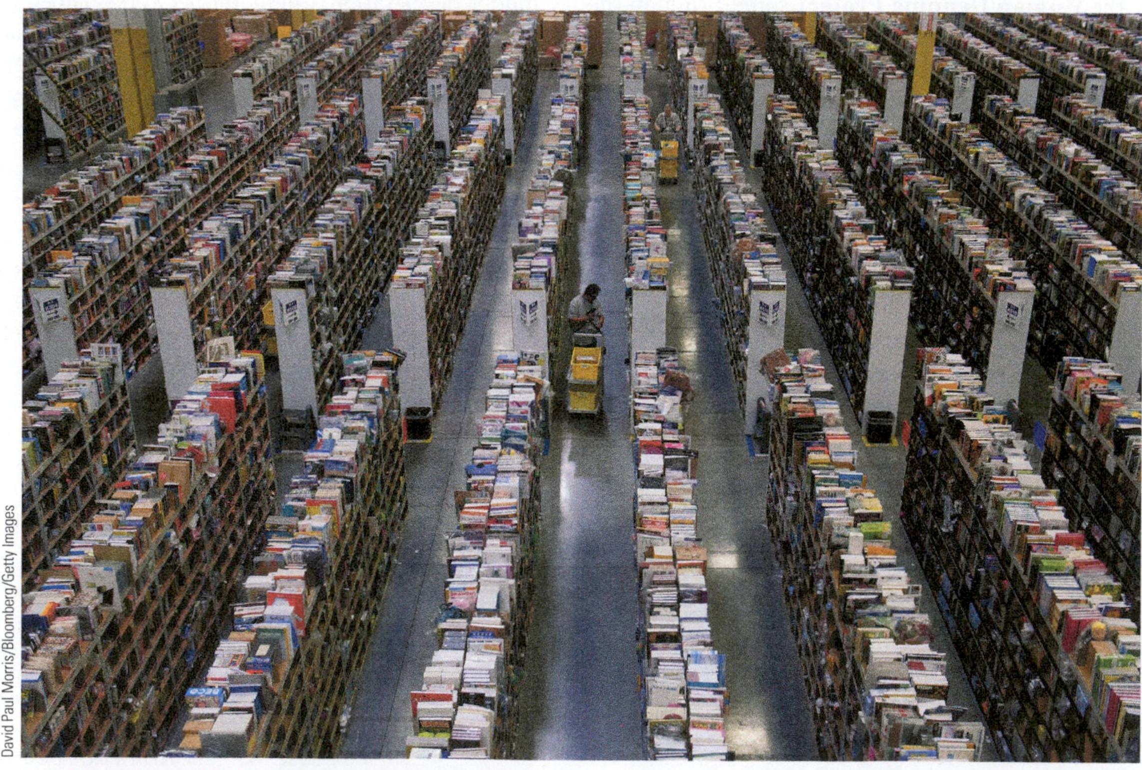

David Paul Morris/Bloomberg/Getty Images

31.5 **Cyber-Assembly Line** In this massive center in Phoenix, workers assembled for shipment the computerized orders that consumers had placed on Amazon.com.

Q *How did e-commerce transform retailing, distribution, and labor arrangements?*

Changes in the transportation of products, when joined to the computer revolution, transformed the global economic marketplace—and America's place within it. Air cargo service improved dramatically, and the Federal Express Corporation (or FedEx) could claim annual revenues of $1 billion only a decade after its debut in 1973. The greatly expanded use of **steel cargo containers**, which dramatically lowered the cost of transporting finished goods and raw materials over long distances, similarly facilitated national and international commerce. Containers could be easily stacked, refrigerated, unloaded from a cargo ship or plane, and trucked to their final destination.

As suppliers and markets increasingly gave businesses worldwide scope, commercial publications began to refer to the process as **globalization**. U.S. automakers, for example, increasingly looked outside the United States to procure parts and even to assemble automobiles and trucks. The trend toward privatization (the sale of government-owned industries to private business) in many overseas economies provided firms based in the United States with new opportunities for acquisitions. Conversely, foreign buyers purchased companies and real estate holdings inside the United States. So many industrial giants had become globalized that it became difficult to define what constituted a U.S. company or a foreign one.

New technologies and globalization interacted to change the basic structure of American businesses and their workforces. Citing pressure from declining profits and international competitors, which often paid workers a fraction of the U.S. wage rate, many industrial companies cut back their labor pools and trimmed their management staffs. This process became known as **"downsizing."** The U.S. auto industry, for example, began to lay off thousands of workers.

Business restructuring, encouraged by globalization and generous interpretations of antitrust laws by both Republican and Democratic administrations, touched off a merger boom. During the late 1990s, huge mergers, with acquisitions totaling more than $1.6 trillion per year, brought a concentration in production unseen since the 1890s.

As employment in traditional manufacturing and extractive sectors (such as mining) declined, jobs in service, high-tech, and information and entertainment sectors increased. Positions in financial services, computing, and other high-tech industries offered high salaries—astronomical ones for top management—but most jobs in the rapidly expanding service sector, such as clerical and janitorial jobs, remained low paying, part-time, and nonunionized (see Figure 31.2). Walmart's enormous nonunion workforce, for example, earned an average of $7 to $8 per hour and most employees had limited, or no, health benefits. U.S. manufacturers wanting to lower costs moved plants to countries with cheap labor environments, further contributing to the decline of relatively better-paid manufacturing jobs in the United States.

The impact of these changes became a matter of bitter debate. Celebrants of change insisted that globalization and corporate downsizing would temporarily mean lost jobs, but that gains in productivity would soon translate into lower consumer prices and a rise in living standards for everyone.

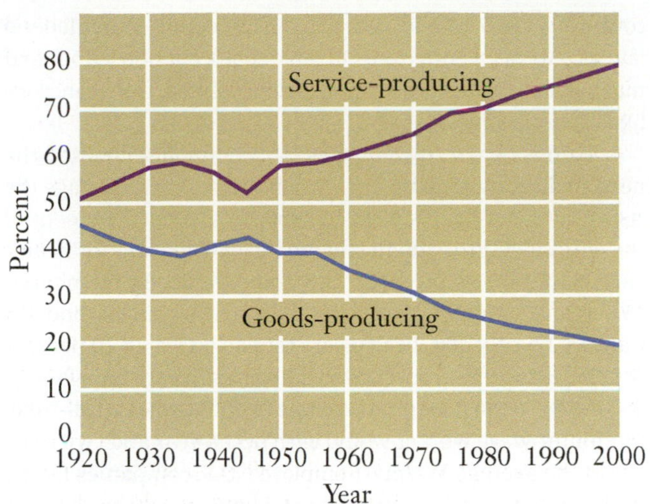

Figure 31.2 **Growth of Service Sector Jobs, 1920–2000.**

Source: U.S. Census Bureau.

They also highlighted the success stories, especially in high-tech industries, where constant technological innovation paved a broad avenue of upward economic mobility for people with skills in post-industrial areas such as computing. Real wages did rise slightly for a brief period during the late 1990s, especially for women.

Critics worried that this shift toward a service economy could permanently change the wage structure, "de-skill" the American labor force, and erode the standard of living in the United States. They warned that the widening gulf between highly paid skilled positions and minimum-wage jobs with few benefits was undermining the middle-class nature of American society.

The labor market changed in other ways. Skilled workers during the middle of the 20th century, for example, had generally stuck to one profession and even the same place of employment throughout their working life. By the end of the century, however, both blue- and white-collar workers were likely to switch employers several times before retiring. The need for training and retraining programs that served people of all ages transformed ideas about the relationship between education and work.

There was also a dramatic drop in labor union membership. During the 1950s, more than 30 percent of American workers belonged to a union. By the end of the 20th century, the figure stood at only 13 percent. Although the labor movement mounted organizing drives among clerical, restaurant, and hotel workers, it struggled to make significant inroads into these sectors of the economy. The major growth for organized labor came among government employees and health-care workers.

Most businesses adamantly fought unionization, and the health and retirement benefits that American companies had once proudly offered began to disappear. During the 1940s and 1950s, a generous benefit package had helped employers attract workers without having to pay dramatically high wages and salaries. Moreover, the amount of money a company paid toward its share of a health plan did not count, under federal law, as part of an employee's taxable compensation. Labor and management both stood to gain, it had seemed, from generous benefit programs.

Things began to change as U.S. companies claimed the need to meet increasing foreign competition and manage the rising costs for health care. In 1960, only about 7 percent of the entire U.S. gross domestic product (GDP) went for health care; some 40 years later, the comparable figure neared 15 percent, a greater percentage than people paid for food. (In Canada, by contrast, health care totaled less than 10 percent of GDP.) The annual cost of providing health care for a family, according to most estimates, came to about what a full-time, minimum-wage worker would earn over a year and twice the pay of the average Walmart employee. U.S. companies facing foreign competition complained about extensive benefit packages that included health care for their aging workforces.

Individuals and families increasingly maintained their lifestyles by incurring rising levels of debt. Economists began to analyze this **household deficit**—the difference between what U.S. households earned and what they spent. As late as 1980, the rate of household indebtedness, though higher than that during the 1950s, still remained lower than it had been during the 1920s. The 1980s, however, inaugurated a trend that would accelerate into the next century. As more people shouldered greater debt, the number of personal bankruptcies increased, and the rate of personal savings in the United States fell to the lowest level in the industrialized world (see Figure 31.3).

31-2c *The Financial Sector*

The household deficit became intertwined with one of the most dramatic post-1970 economic changes: the expansion of a vast, constantly innovating financial industry. A wide range of financial institutions—from international superbanks such as Citigroup, to payday loan institutions like Moneytree, to pawnshop chains such as Pawn America, right on down to illegal loan-sharking operations—profited from people unable to balance their personal books. By the end of the century, loans to homebuyers who lacked the resources to repay them were helping to sustain the financial industry. The industry also thrived, however, on wealthy investors who appeared awash in assets to invest. By 2000, according to one estimate, more than 40 percent of U.S. corporate profits came from the financial services sector while only about 10 percent derived from manufacturing.

The computer revolution helped the financial industry expand and changed its relationship to customers. Use of bank-issued credit cards, monitored through computerized systems, vastly expanded, and extending credit via "plastic" became a highly lucrative enterprise, especially after a 1978 U.S. Supreme Court decision declared that national banks headquartered in one state could move their card operations to any other. This ruling effectively eliminated anti-usury laws, which had traditionally limited interest rates, as states competed to attract the credit-card operations of giant banks. These institutions deluged potential cardholders, particularly college students, with competing enticements. "Free" credit cards, once interest and service charges began piling up, proved anything but free to most people who used them. Other innovations—automated teller machines (ATMs), automatic deposits, debit cards, and electronic bill payment—moved Americans ever closer to a cashless economy.

The financial system increasingly shed the regulatory restrictions crafted earlier in the century, particularly during the New Deal (see Chapter 25). Free-market economists and the financial industry argued that deregulation would speed the flow of investment capital, and Congress initially responded by lifting many of the restrictions on the operation of Savings and Loan institutions (S&Ls) in 1982. The S&L industry boomed, but too many institutions enjoyed deregulation far too much. They made risky loans, speculated in real estate, or simply cooked their books. The entire industry eventually required a massively expensive governmental bailout (see Chapter 30), but problems elsewhere in the financial sector seemed limited to individual firms and to specific times, such as the meltdown on the New York Stock Market in October 1987. A rapid rebound of stock prices seemed to bolster ultimately false claims that all markets, including the larger financial ones, were self-correcting, even self-regulating. The warning signs signaled by the S&L debacle were ignored.

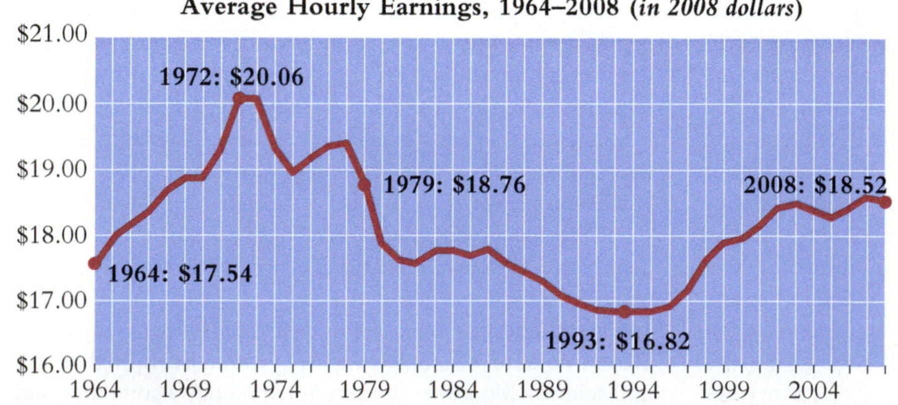

Figure 31.3 **Hourly Wages** Between 1972 and 1993, the average hourly wage dropped from $20.06 to $16.82, measured in 2008 dollars. Since 1993, the real average hourly wage has regained only a part of the ground lost, rising to $18.52 in 2008 before dropping again.

Meanwhile, celebrants of the financial sector continued to present it as a model for how deregulation led to dynamic growth. Wall Street investment firms, such as Lehman Brothers, and large banks, such as Chase Manhattan, did well. Newer types of financial ventures, such as "hedge fund" operations, which managed complicated investment portfolios for a limited number of affluent clients, performed *very* well. These funds, which took in vast pools of money and paid out sizable profits to their investors, came to make up a "shadow banking system"—one whose financial dealings were not covered by the regulatory system that oversaw more traditional banking institutions. Financial investments—whether in real estate, individual stocks, corporate bonds, or hedge funds—still risked losing money, but a new generation of managers claimed the ability to forecast and thus *manage* risk.

The financial sector could also create, and then trade, new forms of investment that carried the generic name of "derivatives," because they had been "derived" from other financial transactions. Entrepreneurs in the financial sector, for example, began purchasing individual home-loan contracts. Combining those of dubious value with sounder ones, they would market the resultant package of loan contracts as a new form of investment called a "collateralized debt obligation" (CDO). Complex mathematical calculations, which relatively few people in the financial industry fully understood, supposedly proved that a CDO carried little risk to the financial firm that had created it or to investors who purchased it. Financial analysts argued that the chance of so many different loan contracts defaulting at the same time was so slim that a CDO was comparatively safe.

CDOs based on home loans were only one of many different types of new securities derived from other kinds of financial transactions. This part of the larger financial system produced huge profits. It also provided similarly outsized payouts, in bonuses and stock options, to the people who worked in this largely unregulated, little-understood enterprise. Economists and public officials, including those at the Treasury Department and the Federal Reserve System, cheered the creation of new types of securities. Governmental regulation of them, according to Alan Greenspan, chairman of the Federal Reserve Board from 1987 to 2006, would discourage innovation and prevent the financial system from delivering an ever-increasing array of secure investments to clients all over the world. The deregulation and globalization of the financial industry echoed other economic transformations that began during the last three decades of the 20th century. The hazards would become all too apparent in 2008, when a massive financial crisis would hit (see Chapter 31).

31-2d *The Booming Sports-Entertainment Industry*

The sports-entertainment industry also grew exponentially during this era. Metropolitan areas competed to obtain—or retain—professional teams. TV contracts and tax write-offs tempted tycoons such as George Steinbrenner of the New York Yankees to run a sporting empire.

Baseball led off this expansionist era. Seeking a better fit with emerging economic, demographic, and social forces, the leadership of Major League Baseball (MLB) realigned the "national pastime." During a single decade, the 1970s, MLB shuffled teams in and out of Milwaukee, Seattle, and Washington, D.C. By relocating franchises from struggling to thriving metropolitan areas, MLB acquired new ticket buyers, advantageous TV deals, and stadiums financed by public money. If moving existing franchises made sense, creating new ones seemed an even shrewder option. During the mid-1950s, there had been only 16 Big League teams, none located west of Chicago; by 2000, 30 MLB franchises stretched across the United States and into Canada.

Other sports followed baseball's lead. The National Football League (NFL), noting how surveys showed fans shifting their allegiances from baseball to faster-paced sports, also expanded into new metropolitan areas. Just in time for the 1970 season, the NFL merged with the rival American Football League (AFL), with which it had been playing a "Super Bowl" since 1967. In contrast to the economic philosophy of MLB, that of the revamped NFL helped small-market teams such as the Green Bay Packers remain competitive with larger-market franchises. During the 1970s, ABC began televising an NFL game during primetime hours, and the success of *Monday Night Football* signaled the growing importance of football to TV and to the nation's popular culture.

Basketball's small court made National Basketball Association (NBA) games extremely TV-friendly, and entrepreneurs easily gained television contracts to underwrite new professional franchises. As a result, the NBA faced a lengthy off-the-court rivalry with the upstart American Basketball Association (ABA). When the two leagues finally merged in 1976, the NBA jettisoned the ABA's garish, multicolored basketball but retained its three-point shot and emphasis on marketing African American stars like Julius ("Dr. J") Irving. After joining the league in 1984, Michael Jordan soon became the preeminent symbol for marketing the NBA and anchored the "Dream Team" of professionals that captured basketball's Gold Medal at the 1992 Olympic Games. The NBA also elevated African Americans into coaching and management positions far more quickly than did the NFL and MLB.

Virtually all sports-entertainment operations flourished. By the end of the 20th century, the National Hockey League (NHL) supported 28 franchises. Professional play in tennis, aided by TV coverage, featured tours for both men and women. Professional golf for men—tightly controlled by the Professional Golfers' Association (PGA)—continually grew in popularity, especially after it found its own version of Michael Jordan, Eldrick (Tiger) Woods. During the early 1990s, Woods became *the* brand name for a sports business that attracted corporate sponsors, sold a vast array of high-end products, and sustained a media presence that included a separate Golf Channel (1995–) on cable TV. The economic and cultural impact of the Ladies Professional Golf Association (LPGA)

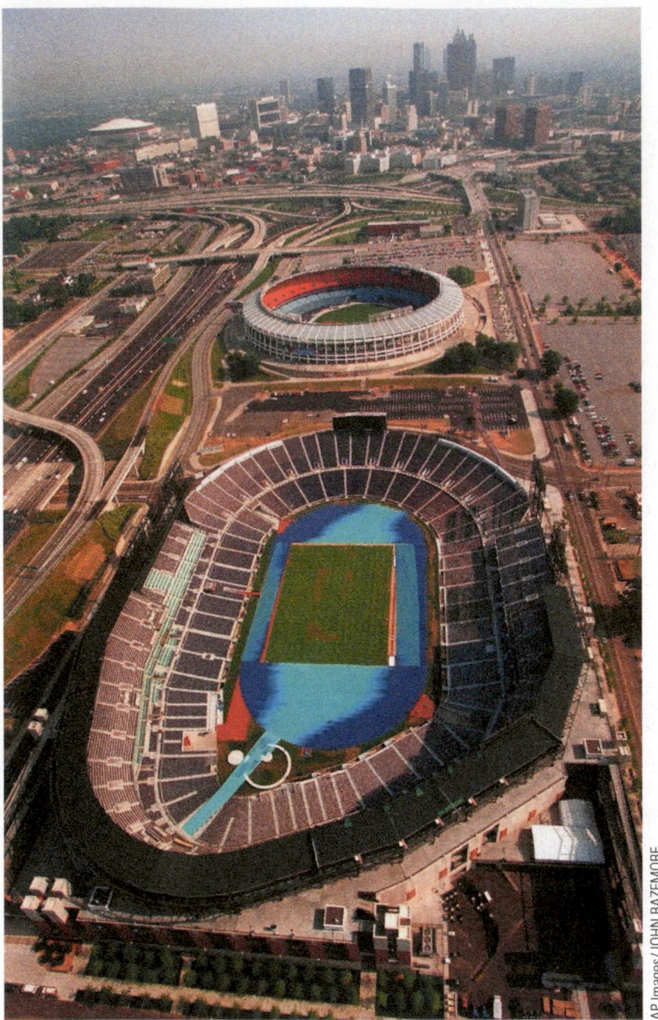

AP Images/JOHN BAZEMORE

31.6 **Sports Stadium Shuffle** Centennial Olympic Stadium, shown in the foreground, was built for the 1996 Summer Olympics in Atlanta, Georgia. It was then re-constructed as Turner Field for MLB's Atlanta Braves, who once shared Fulton County Stadium, shown in the background, with the NFL's Atlanta Falcons. In 2013, the Braves announced they would not only leave Turner Field, but Atlanta, whose downtown appears in the far background, for a new stadium, financed in part by public funds, in suburban Cobb County. Turner Field avoided the fate of Fulton County Stadium (demolished in 1997) and was redesigned for college football.

lagged behind that of the men's, but the women's tour still prospered and added a number of players from outside the United States to its ranks.

The national romance with automobiles helped to speed the growth of auto racing. The Indianapolis 500 initially vied with the Super Bowl for recognition as the most spectacular one-day event in sports, but events sponsored by the National Association for Stock Car Racing (NASCAR) eventually overtook those of Indy-style racing. As new technologies brought TV viewers onto the track and even into the cars, NASCAR moved beyond its traditional base in the South. Its signature event, the Daytona 500, replaced the Indy 500 as the nation's premier automobile race.

College sports grew in similar fashion. Television coverage mushroomed, especially after TV entrepreneurs created **ESPN** (1979–), a cable network devoted entirely to sports. ESPN initially helped so-called minor collegiate sports, such as gymnastics and lacrosse, gain TV time, but college football and basketball, with their highly popular postseason contests, ultimately benefited the most. The vast revenues from television allowed the National Collegiate Athletic Association (NCAA) to create more lucrative bowl games and build the playoff arrangement in basketball into an extended extravaganza that became marketed as "March Madness." University administrators insisted that success on their playing fields and in their arenas, which became ever larger and more luxurious, translated into visibility and prestige, and into increased donations that helped support the educational mission of their institutions.

The glamour and excitement generated by the sports-entertainment industry increasingly merged with political culture. Candidates competed to sign up prominent athletes for their campaign squads, and some retired players, including football's Jack Kemp and Hall of Fame baseball hurler Jim Bunning, made the transition from the sports to the political field. In addition to tapping his family connections, George W. Bush parlayed his family name and partial ownership of the Texas Rangers baseball team into an entrée into electoral politics, first as governor of Texas and then as the first president of the 21st century.

With the business of sports booming, its legal foundations inevitably shifted. MLB's star players, armed with union advisers and their own attorneys, successfully spearheaded new legal challenges to old doctrines that contractually bound them to a single franchise year after year. Court rulings eventually brought differing versions of "free agency" to the major team sports. These systems soon produced powerful new players in the sporting world: sports agents who could help professional athletes auction their athletic talents and celebrity status to the highest bidder. Although some fans and sportswriters grumbled when highly paid players seemed to underperform, owners discovered that steadily rising TV revenues, tax breaks, and favorable stadium deals allowed them to adjust to the new salary structures and strong union movements. The truly knowledgeable sports fan became as conversant in contract law and labor-management relations as in more traditional matters such as batting averages and yards-per-carry statistics.

Sports and legal disputes also became intertwined with social issues. Women's rights advocates saw big-time sports promoting gender stereotypes—pointing, for example, to *Sports Illustrated*'s swimsuit issue and to NFL cheerleading squads that resembled Las Vegas chorus lines—and urged equality for women athletes. One result of this pressure was **Title IX** of a 1972 congressional measure, which was later retitled the **Patsy Mink Equal Opportunity in Education Act**. By mandating gender equity in intercollegiate sports activities, Title IX required colleges and universities to upgrade the financing and promotion of women's sports. A much-hyped 1973 exhibition tennis match between Billy Jean King, the leading women's player of the day, and an aging male star from the 1940s, Bobby Riggs, helped dramatize the gender-equity issues that Title IX addressed. (Billy Jean King

Bob Harmeyer/Getty Images

31.7 **NASCAR's 1993 Daytona 500** Fabled driver Dale Earnhardt (1951–2001) temporarily leads the field before a crowd of 135,000, during the 35th running of racing's premier spectacle. By the 1990s, events sponsored by the National Association for Stock Car Racing (NASCAR) were drawing huge crowds and attracting a massive following, especially in the South and among fans that identified as political conservatives. NASCAR would later expand its brand beyond stock cars and its appeal beyond the borders of the United States.

Q *Sports and politics often intertwine; can you think of examples in addition to stock car racing?*

won the match.) Over time, professional tennis surpassed every other sport in narrowing the gender gap in prize money, endorsement contracts, and media coverage. And it also was the first major sport to feature LGBT stars.

While the sports-entertainment complex was growing in visibility and profitability, traditionalists detected signs of corruption. The familiar complaint about intercollegiate athletics debasing educational standards gained new force. Critics also found too many sporting enterprises awash in hypercommercialism, financial double-dealing, and on-field cheating. The success of MLB, for example, seemingly owed much to the prodigious feats of home run hitters who, it ultimately became apparent, were using performance-enhancing drugs—and perhaps also benefiting from souped-up baseballs. The popularity of football, neurologists warned, put greater numbers of players at risk for brain damage.

31-3 Culture and Media

Q *How did new forms of media change the ways in which people received entertainment, information, and religion? Why were new media forms controversial?*

New technologies significantly altered how people received and used books, movies, TV, music, and other sources of information and entertainment. By the beginning of the 21st century, virtually every home or apartment had at least one television and an accompanying recording device. About 80 percent had a personal computer. People began looking to the Internet for access to print publications, music, television programming, and movies. E-mail and then text messaging became the first choice for contacting friends. The omnipresent video screen seemed the preeminent symbol of American popular culture.

31-3a *Television*

At the beginning of the 1970s, three broadcast networks could promise advertisers that a rough cross section of the American public would be watching their nighttime programs and the accompanying commercials. During that decade, however, changes in the viewing habits of Americans increasingly led the networks to embrace the strategy called **"narrowcasting,"** in which TV programmers acknowledged that the viewing audience was fragmenting into different demographic segments. CBS replaced several highly watched programs, such as *The Beverly Hillbillies*, with "edgier" shows aimed at viewers under the age of 40, who were coveted by advertisers because they were most likely to purchase products and services. *All in the Family*, a sitcom about intergenerational conflict within a blue-collar family, made its proudly bigoted protagonist, "Archie Bunker," a lightning rod for issues involving race and gender. Although *The Mary*

What They Said

The Sports Construction Boom: Who Pays, Who Gains?

During the 1990s, the growing importance of the sports-entertainment industry brought a boom in the construction of expensive facilities in which baseball, football, and basketball teams competed. New sports complexes appeared in Baltimore, Charlotte, Chicago, Cincinnati, Cleveland, Milwaukee, Nashville, San Francisco, St. Louis, Seattle, Tampa, and Washington, D.C. Other cities, including New York and Dallas, began planning for new construction.

Funding almost always came from public sources as well as from the privately owned teams and leagues that benefited most directly. Some localities used their own taxing authority to help foot the bill, but the national government played an important role as well. The Tax Reform Act of 1986 supposedly barred the federal government from the game, but sports attorneys found a loophole that enabled state and local governments to help finance new complexes by issuing revenue bonds that enjoyed the same exemption from federal taxation as did bonds issued for school construction and other public projects. Tax experts differed on how much potential revenue this loophole cost the federal government but agreed it was considerable. Critics such as Senator Daniel Patrick Moynihan of New York argued that the bulk of the economic benefits from this subsidy accrued to the wealthy owners of sports franchises and to the relatively small group of similarly well-heeled investors who purchased the tax-exempt bonds.

Senator Moynihan made several attempts during the 1990s to pass new legislation that would end this federal tax subsidy for the construction of sports facilities. All of his efforts failed. Meanwhile, proponents of public financing continued to extoll the benefits that flowed from constructing new sports facilities.

Senator Daniel Patrick Moynihan (June 6 and September 20, 1996) explains his bill entitled "The Stop Tax Exempt Arena Debt Issuance Act"

This legislation will close a big loophole, a loophole that ultimately injures State and local governments and other issuers of tax-exempt bonds, that provides an unintended Federal subsidy (in fact, contravenes congressional intent), and that contributes to the enrichment of persons who need no Federal assistance whatsoever.

I refer to the large number of professional sports facilities subsidized in recent years through the issuance of tax-exempt bonds. It seems that nearly every day, another professional sports franchise owner demands a new stadium, one subsidized by Federal, State and local taxpayers.

Why do owners want new stadiums? Our existing stock of stadiums is not functionally obsolete. Many stadiums are new, and our older ones generally can and will continue to serve, and serve well, for the exhibition of professional sports for years to come. In fact many older, historic stadiums are beloved by fans. The reason for new stadiums is economics—the team owners' bottom line. The owner can generate more revenues with a new stadium replete with luxury skyboxes and other amenities.

Building new professional sports facilities is fine by me. Let the new stadiums be built. But, please, do not ask the American taxpayer to pay for them.

In the last 6 years alone, over $4 billion has been spent to build 30 new professional sports stadiums. According to Prof. Robert Baade, an economist at Lake Forest College in Illinois and an expert in stadium financing, that amount could "completely refurbish the physical plants of the Nation's public elementary and secondary schools." An additional $7 billion of stadiums are in the planning stages, and there is no end in sight. This is why I recently introduced S. 1880—the Stop Tax-exempt Arena Debt Issuance Act—or STADIA for short—to end the Federal tax subsidy for these stadium deals. Only the team owners and players profit, while taxpayers and fans pick up the tab.

Rick Horrow, president of a Miami-based sports consulting firm, makes the case for public financing in a U.S. Senate committee hearing held on June 22, 1999.

There are a number of quantifiable and intangible benefits that have been accepted by over 100 regions that have successfully implemented major and minor league sports and entertainment facilities during this decade.

First, the facilities have been perceived to generate substantial economic impact during construction… .

Second, successful projects have also generated substantial retail sales and development activities surrounding these facilities. As Jacobs Field opened in Cleveland in 1995, more than 20 restaurants or retail establishments have opened after that. And more than 85 store fronts have been renovated, at a cost of $1.2 million. The downtown development-oriented Gateway Project has created 6,200 permanent jobs since 1994, generating $6.5 million in payroll taxes.

The third major impact involves the major and special events that will occasionally be attracted to a new facility. Recent Super Bowls in San Diego, Arizona, New Orleans and Miami have each generated over $250 million of new spending to their respective local economies.

Fourth, many communities will identify the intangible impact of a sports franchise and corresponding facility on its marketability and potential to attract new business. The Jacksonville Chamber of Commerce spoke about the Jacksonville Jaguars and Alltel Stadium as being indirectly responsible for creation of upwards of 50,000 new jobs by virtue of companies expanding or relocating to Jacksonville as a consequence of a successful marketing campaign.

And, finally, although more difficult to quantify, many community leaders have advocated a franchise facility as a critical component of image enhancement and community pride.

Once these facilities are developed, they provide substantial economic, tangible and psychological benefits for the entire region for years to come.

Q *What were the major arguments for and against public tax subsidies (federal or state) for sports facilities during the 1990s? Have these arguments changed during the years since then?*

Q *How do these arguments flow from differing views about how to build strong, vibrant communities?*

Q *How might the boom in the construction of expensive sports facilities be related to the development of metropolitan corridors?*

Sources: (top) Senator Daniel Patrick Moynihan statement (June 6 and September 20, 1996), accessed at: http://capitolwords.org/date/1996/09/20/S11103_s-1880-the-stop-tax-exempt-arena-debt-issuance-act/http://capitolwords.org/date/1996/06/14/S6305-3_statements-on-introduced-bills-and- joint-resolutio/; (bottom) Rick Horrow statement (June 22, 1999), accessed at: http://www.gpo.gov/fdsys/ pkg/CHRG-106shrg63000/pdf/CHRG-106shrg63000.pdf

Tyler Moore Show rarely took overtly feminist positions, it did address the personal politics of working women. In 1980, 9 of every 10 television sets were still tuned to a network program during primetime viewing hours.

The narrowcasting strategy helped the entire TV industry prosper until the 1990s, when programmers began to struggle as viewers began deserting network offerings. The networks responded by slashing budgets and staff, especially in their news divisions. Local stations without any network affiliation, which had been limping along, began picking up viewers by carrying older Hollywood movies, sporting events, and reruns of canceled primetime shows now being syndicated to individual stations. Several hundred of these independent television stations debuted during the 1980s.

Capitalizing on this trend, the media mogul Rupert Murdoch introduced the first new network in decades, Fox TV, in 1988. Using a pattern later adopted by far less-successful imitators, Fox's operation began by offering a limited schedule to previously nonaffiliated stations. Fox's first big hit, *The Simpsons* (1989–), an animated send-up of the standard family sitcom, became a pop culture phenomenon and mass-marketing bonanza. In 1993 Fox outbid CBS for the TV rights to carry NFL games. Throughout the 1990s, Fox and the other fledgling networks introduced programs—such as *In Living Color* and *Buffy the Vampire Slayer*—for audiences that contained more minority, young, and urban viewers than those of the three older networks.

New technologies, which promised viewers greater choice, challenged all of the broadcast networks. The remote control, an innovation introduced during the 1960s that finally clicked during the 1980s, created a television aesthetic called "channel surfing," in which viewers flip rapidly from program to program. Videocassette recorders (VCRs), introduced during the 1970s, became the first of the record-and-view-later technologies that allowed viewers to create their own TV schedules.

The initial threat to the broadcast networks came from cable television, which had wired nearly three-quarters of the nation's homes by 2000. The expansion of cable accentuated audience fragmentation and narrowcasting. Atlanta's Ted Turner led the way by introducing the Cable News Network (CNN), several movie channels, and an all-cartoon network before his communication empire merged with that of Time-Warner in 1996. Challenging both the networks and cable, companies selling direct satellite transmission and companies offering streaming services over the internet began gaining an important share of the increasingly fragmented viewing audience. By the beginning of the 21st century, the share of viewers watching primetime network programs had fallen to under 60 percent, and non-network shows were beginning to compete for the television industry's annual Emmy Awards.

31-3b *Hollywood*

Hollywood also adapted to changing business arrangements and new technologies. With movie attendance in 1970 about the same as it had been in 1960, the movie industry began raising ticket prices, betting on a few blockbuster films such as the highly profitable *Star Wars* series (1977–2017), and hoping for a surprise hit such as *The Blair Witch Project* (1999). Although Hollywood endured super-expensive flops such as *Heaven's Gate* (1980) and *Peter Pan* (2013), motion pictures survived through adaptation.

Volatility in the movie market encouraged most filmmakers to play it safe, recycling many titles and special effects that had made money in the past. They transferred popular stories, such as *How the Grinch Stole Christmas* (2000), and TV shows, such as *The Brady Bunch* (1995), to the big screen and produced sequels for any movie, such as *Jaws* (1975), that had even approached blockbuster status. In addition, Hollywood expanded the older practice of targeting younger viewers with movies such as *Ferris Bueller's Day Off* (1986). Meanwhile, dramatic stories that tapped themes in popular history, such as *Braveheart* (1995) and *Titanic* (1997), impressed both ticket buyers and industry insiders.

At the same time, a cultural complex that nurtured "independent" films emerged. Wes Anderson became one of the most prominent U.S. filmmakers committed to independent movies with quirky story lines and detailed attention to style. In 1981, Robert Redford launched the Sundance Film Institute in hopes of encouraging innovative screenwriting and direction. Its annual Sundance Festival, held in Park City, Utah, began attracting Hollywood moguls. They sought the next small movie, such as *Pulp Fiction* (1994), that might find a large audience. Sundance supported the work of African American, Latino, and Asian American directors by showcasing movies like *Hoop Dreams* (1994), *El Mariachi* (1993), and *Picture Bride* (1995). It also celebrated women directors such as Lizzie Borden (*Working Girls*, 1986) and Barbara Kopple (*American Dream*, 1990). The Landmark movie chain led the way in screening independent films unlikely to find space in any of the growing number of suburban multiplexes. Major studios even created special divisions, such as Fox Searchlight Pictures, which specialized in so-called independent films.

Hollywood became increasingly intertwined with the emerging home-viewing industries. It gained badly needed revenue by licensing its offerings to TV and for distribution on videocassettes and digital video disks (DVDs). For a brief time during the early 1990s, the United States could claim more video rental outlets than movie theaters. Advances in DVD technology provided improved visual imagery, bonus attractions (such as footage cut from the theatrical release), widescreen prints, and expert commentary by a movie's director. As Hollywood discovered new sources of revenue beyond theatrical distribution, it came to favor action movies with elaborate special effects that promised to sell well in the home-viewing and international markets. Filmmakers also confronted "pirating" technologies that meant movies might appear in bootlegged editions at virtually the same time they debuted in theaters.

31-3c *Pop Music Media*

New business ventures and technologies also transformed the relationship between the media and the lucrative pop music industry. A Music Television channel (MTV) debuted

History Through Film Star Wars (1977)

Directed by George Lucas

Starring Mark Hamill (Luke Skywalker), Alec Guinness (Obi-Wan Kenobi), Harrison Ford (Han Solo), Carrie Fisher (Princess Leia), and James Earl Jones (voice of Darth Vader).

Star Wars: Episode IV—A New Hope (1977), which took three years and the then-astronomical sum of $30 million to produce, generated a similarly outsized popular response. Within three years, it returned nearly a 2,000 percent profit, gained 10 Academy Award nominations, seven Oscars, and three Grammies. The movie also financed a private media empire for its creator, George Lucas—Lucasfilm Ltd.; introduced six-track Dolby stereo sound to movie theaters; helped to make viewers in their teens and early 20s Hollywood's primary target audience; and pioneered computerized breakthroughs in the use of graphic imagery and camera movement. Hollywood increasingly depended less on producing a steady supply of successful films and more on releasing a few "blockbusters" modeled on *Star Wars*.

The initial *Star Wars* entry of 1977, eventually the fourth installment in a multipart series, arguably tells an allegorical story that works against the cynicism and divisions of the Vietnam era. Young Luke Skywalker, aided by the wizened Obi-Wan Kenobi and Han Solo, joins the fight to defeat the "Empire" and to rescue Princess Leia from the villainous Darth Vader. The movie embellishes this sparse tale with imagery borrowed from various Hollywood genres, including science fiction, combat films, westerns, and the Saturday-morning serials of the 1930s and 1940s.

The film's major event, Luke Skywalker's destruction of the "Death Star," can seem to be a set of combat sequences that might replace the traumatic history of U.S. involvement in Southeast Asia with a heroic folktale about triumph over evil. Similarly, the alliance between the youthful Skywalker and the aging Obi-Wan Kenobi might seem a parable about the need to move beyond the generational conflict of the 1960s.

Seen another way, though, an entertainment product such as *Star Wars* seemed to rest less on crafting the kind of political-historical allegory found in a cold war-era movie such as *High Noon* (1952) than on complex market calculations. Blockbusters aimed at attracting a huge initial audience to theaters, creating an expectation of sequels, doing well overseas, and selling briskly in formats aimed at the home viewing market. Those modeled on the *Star Wars* series also became vehicles for creating eye-popping special effects (often portraying considerable violence and mayhem) and images (such as those of cute robots and various cuddly creatures) intended to support the sale of movie merchandise. Marketing campaigns for *Star Wars* began in the era of low-tech products, such as Luke Skywalker lunch boxes, and extended into the age of interactive computer video games. George Lucas earned more money from licensing images from *Star Wars* for various product tie-ins than he garnered from the movie's unprecedented box-office receipts. In this sense, blockbuster spectacles such as *Star Wars* merit historical attention primarily as windows into new marketing techniques and the economic health of the Hollywood film industry. By 2017, the Star Wars franchise included eight intricately related movies.■

31.8 *Star Wars'* C-3PO and R2-D2, a 'droid and a robot with personalities, generated considerable nonfilm revenue from product tie-ins.

in 1981 and subsequently adjusted to changes in the cable TV and music industries. Initially offering a 24-hour supply of rock videos, MTV came under fire for portraying women as sex objects and excluding artists of color. The network eventually defused complaints, especially after featuring Michael Jackson's 29-minute video based on his hit single "Thriller" (1983). By the turn of the 21st century, MTV and other cable channels programmed videos that represented the increasingly multiethnic nature of the music industry.

MTV also seemed on the cutting edge of changes in media programming. Its stars of the 1980s such as Jackson and Madonna used MTV to forge a new relationship between music and visual imagery: the **"MTV aesthetic."** This fast-paced visual style played with traditional ideas about time and space, recycled images from earlier movies and TV programs, and often carried a sharply satirical edge. During the 1990s, MTV introduced a wide range of youth-oriented programming such as *The Real World* (1992–). MTV's longest-running program, *The Real World* popularized the "reality TV" genre that spread to other cable channels and the broadcast networks. *The Apprentice* (2004–2017) enhanced the celebrity status of Donald Trump.

Entertainment conglomerates began marketing music in ever-newer formats. The 45-rpm record and the long-play album (LP), associated with the musical revolutions of the 1950s and 1960s, all but disappeared. Analog cassette tapes, which could be played through a variety of portable stereo devices including Sony's Walkman, arrived during the 1970s. The compact discs (CDs) of the early 1980s changed not only the technology for delivering pop music but also, eventually, the nature of the product and the listening experience. The now-classic rock LPs of the 1960s and early 1970s, such as The Beatles' *Magical Mystery Tour* (1967), had featured 10 to 12 songs, split between the two sides and often organized around a core concept. By the late 1990s, however, CD offerings and other new digital technologies were beginning to feature unusual musical mixes that generally lacked any unifying theme.

Changing formats enabled listeners to obtain, preserve, and exchange music in entirely new ways. FM radio stations began to stream their programs over the Internet during the early 1990s, and one of rock's most venerable bands, The Rolling Stones, was the first to simulcast a live concert in 1994. After several years in which Internet users experimented with exchanging musical files, in 1999 a college student introduced Napster. This short-lived venture provided a technology by which users could freely share music gleaned from commercially produced CDs. Artists as well as corporate executives confronted a serious threat to CD sales—and the future of their industry. They charged Internet technologies with facilitating the "pirating" of copyrighted material. Technological innovation would continue to reshape the soundscape on which music was made, stored, and distributed.

31-3d *New Mass Culture Debates*

New trends in mass commercial culture generated other controversies. In 1975, the Federal Communications Commission (FCC) ordered the television networks to dedicate the first 60 minutes of primetime each evening to "family" programming free of violence and "mature" themes. Federal courts struck down this family-hour requirement as a violation of the First Amendment. Demands that Congress regulate rock lyrics and album covers soon ran afoul of predictions that this kind of legislation would be unconstitutional. TV programmers, record producers, and new Internet gaming ventures responded by following the example of the Hollywood film industry and using "warning labels" that supposedly informed parents about products with violent and sexually explicit imagery.

Commercial pop culture also produced new aesthetic disputes. Unlike the cultural critics of the 1950s, who had dismissed mass fare as trivial and degenerate (see Chapter 28), analysts from the new academic field of "cultural studies" often seemed unabashed fans of the commercial products they studied. They jettisoned any bright-line distinction between lowbrow and highbrow as untenable. The music of The Beatles could be studied along with that of Beethoven, the lyrics of Bob Dylan alongside classic poetry. Rejecting the elitist-themed criticism of the 1950s, which had seen consumers as cultural dupes who passively soaked up junk, cultural studies stressed people's creative interaction with commercial culture. Scholarly accounts of *Star Trek*, for example, examined how, through self-produced magazines (called "fanzines"), conventions, and the Internet, Trekkies created a grassroots subculture that used the original TV series and its spinoffs to launch serious discussions about social and political issues. The cultural studies approach also tended to embrace multiculturalism, highlighting works produced by women, political outsiders, and non-Western writers and artists. It encouraged students to see traditional texts within their political and historical contexts rather than as timeless works. Traditionalists condemned this "cultural turn" as a legacy of the counterculture of the 1960s and blamed it for eroding settled ideas about the quality and value of artistic expression.

Some of the fiercest debates over popular culture involved the impact of an "infotainment" complex. An imprecise cultural category, infotainment signaled that the always-delicate balance between actually informing and merely amusing audiences had tilted decisively toward the latter.

Cable TV's news operations embraced infotainment in ways that the major broadcast networks had long avoided. While maintaining a 24/7 schedule, CNN initially followed the networks in pursuing a "hard-news" agenda from camera crews and correspondents stationed around the globe, claiming "News is the star." It also introduced, however, programs such as *Crossfire*, which featured the in-studio pyrotechnics of verbally dueling pundits. CNN's eventual rival, the Fox News Channel (FNC), which debuted in 1996, retrofitted the *Crossfire* model to much of its programming. FNC featured verbally nimble personalities who covered the news from studio sets and emphasized, despite labels such as "fair and balanced," opinions that tilted toward those of political conservatives and the Republican Party.

Public affairs broadcasting on cable TV increasingly adopted a narrowcasting strategy. FNC made clear, for example, that its idea of "balance" would attract viewers who saw the major networks and CNN as "biased." CNN and MSNBC, in response, began positioning their coverage toward people uncomfortable with FNC. This approach, critics charged, featured news programming that reinforced rather than broadened the perspectives of core constituencies. A fake news program, *The Daily Show*, satirized the narrowness of its cable TV counterparts. It also arguably produced—or simply attracted—viewers who were more broadly informed about issues than were the aficionados of "real" newscasts.

31-3e *The Religious Landscape*

A pervasive religiosity differentiated the United States from most European nations. Attention commonly focused on Americans drawn to the Religious Right, but a propensity to see daily life and world events through religious teachings spanned the political and cultural spectrums. Polls taken at the turn of the 21st century suggested that more than three-quarters of Americans believed in a divine being that performed miracles on earth.

The nation's religious landscape showed greater diversity than ever before (see Figure 31.4). During the 1950s, Will Herberg could see his book entitled *Protestant-Catholic-Jew* (1955) as adequately covering the religious dimension of the "American way of life." A half-century later, however, these three faiths represented only some of the religious denominations in the United States.

After about 1970, cultural and social change helped produce this religious diversity. Movements such as the Jesus People loosely affiliated with the counterculture. A few other countercultural groups withdrew to communal retreats structured by religious teachings. Many people drawn to alternative cultures also embraced spiritual impulses outside the Protestant-Catholic-Jewish triad. Asian-inspired traditions, such as Transcendental Meditation and Buddhism, proved particularly appealing. New Age spiritual movements, which stressed individual insights over group doctrines, also traced their most immediate origins back to the early 1970s.

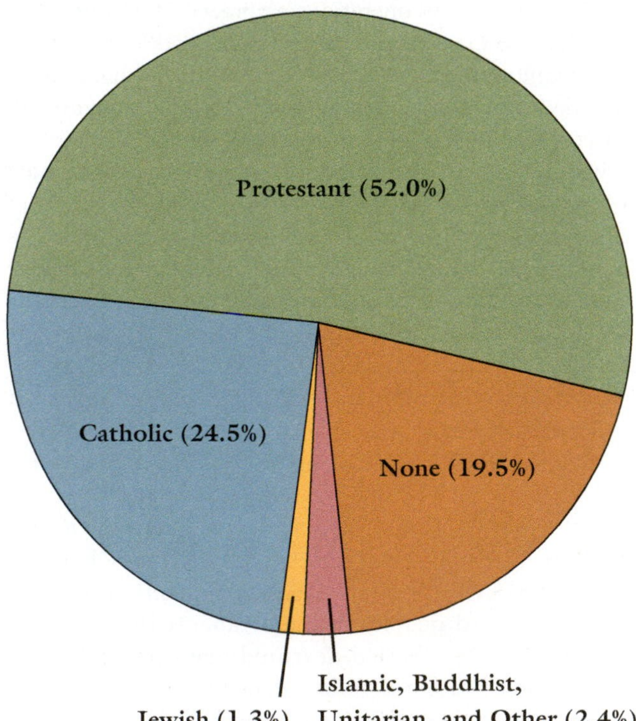

Figure 31.4 **Religion in America, 2001** This chart shows the self-described religious affiliations of the American people compiled through sampling techniques.

Source: Data adapted from *The American Religious Identification Survey*, Graduate Center, City University of New York.

Immigration swelled the numbers in various faiths, especially Islam, which had held a minimal presence in the United States prior to 1970. The Black Power movement had attracted new converts to the homegrown Nation of Islam (NOI) during the 1960s, and post-1970 immigration from countries with large Islamic populations brought millions of people who practiced more orthodox versions to the United States. The dynamic and outspoken Louis Farrakhan, once a rival to Malcolm X, revived the NOI during the 1980s, but it attracted far fewer members than other versions of Islam. According to some estimates (the official U.S. Census does not track religious affiliations), the number of residents practicing Islam by the year 2000 surpassed the number practicing Judaism—and even the number identifying with several mainline Protestant denominations, including Presbyterian and Episcopalian. Adapting to American cultural practices, mosques began making Sunday, rather than the traditional Friday, the week's major Islamic holy day. The faith's leading institutions, such as the Islamic Center of Southern California, provided a variety of religious and nonreligious services for their congregations. They also sought to inform non-Muslims about Islam, which claimed more followers worldwide than any other religion.

Other religions experienced similar growth. The number of Protestant evangelicals, for a time, grew faster than the U.S. population. Between 1970 and the late 1990s, the Southern Baptist Convention expanded beyond its traditional regional base and added 6 million new members. The Church of Jesus Christ of Latter-day Saints (the Mormon faith) gained more than half that many. Along with augmenting their membership rolls at home, many of these groups greatly expanded their international missionary activities.

Religious faith did not determine political belief. Most fundamentalists and evangelicals favored the politics of the New Right, but there were evangelical groups, such as the Sojourners, that espoused political-social positions identified with the political left. Moreover, some evangelicals joined mainline religious movements in espousing environmental causes opposed by conservatives. In 1991, the United States Conference of Catholic Bishops issued a lengthy document focused on the relationship between Church teachings and environmental movements for the "planetary common good."

Most organized religious groups also struggled with the relationship between their spiritual faiths and other social and cultural causes. Religious communities offered very different responses, for example, to the emergence of lesbian, gay, bisexual, and transgender (LGBT) movements. Most leaders of the Religious Right, such as Jerry Falwell and Pat Robertson, mobilized against what they saw as the "moral decay" posed by LGBT activism. Orthodox Judaism, Islam, and Catholicism, without mobilizing on the scale of the Religious Right, still labeled same-sex relationships as sinful. In stark contrast, a minority of churches, synagogues, and temples—especially in larger cities—welcomed LGBT members. A few denominations accepted gays and lesbians as ministers and rabbis, and recognizable bodies of "gay theology," grounded in specific biblical passages and on more general principles of tolerance,

Rebecca Cook/Reuters/Corbis

31.9 The Islamic Center of America, Dearborn, Michigan This 70,000-square-foot facility dramatizes the growing presence of Islam in the United States. It features building materials imported from all over the world, a gold dome, twin minarets, and a prayer hall that accommodates a thousand worshipers.

Q *How has the growing visibility of Islam affected life in the United States?*

began to emerge. Churches also faced, along with the nation at large, growing pressure to address the legality of gay marriages (see Chapter 32).

Religious divisions emerged over foreign policy questions. The movement to contain the spread of nuclear weaponry attracted a number of religious groups. After prolonged internal debate, the Conference of Catholic Bishops issued a pastoral letter entitled "The Challenge of Peace" (1983). It joined statements by several Protestant groups and, in effect, declared U.S. nuclear policy in conflict with religious teachings. At about the same time, some Catholic priests joined dissident Protestant congregations in offering sanctuary to undocumented refugees from Latin America, particularly El Salvador and Guatemala, who were fleeing U.S.-supported military regimes and, once they reached the United States, American immigration authorities. On the other hand, many spiritual leaders and laypeople, particularly those associated with evangelical churches, gravitated toward the fervent anticommunist initiatives supported by the New Right and the Reagan administration.

Three prominent religious figures who entered the partisan arena exemplified the diversity of organized religion's relationship to political action. Father Robert F. Drinan, a member of the U.S. House of Representatives from 1971 to 1981, often embraced positions on issues, such as abortion, contrary to the pronouncements of his own Roman Catholic Church. Eventually, the Church hierarchy decreed that no priest should hold a political office, and Father Drinan resigned from the House. The presidential bids, in 1984 and 1988, of the Reverend Jesse Jackson, a Baptist, recalled movement-style politics that looked back to the religious fervor of the civil rights crusade but also moved in step with the largely secular multiculturalism of the 1980s. Pat Robertson, in contrast, used his firm identification with the Religious Right to unsuccessfully challenge Vice President George H. W. Bush for the 1988 GOP presidential nomination.

Although his presidential bid failed, Robertson did shore up his religious empire at a time when several other media-enabled religious movements were being swamped by controversy. Jim and Tammy Faye Bakker of the "Praise the Lord" (PTL) movement and Jimmy Lee Swaggart saw their multimillion-dollar operations collapse when they violated the moral values their ministries preached. After being convicted on multiple counts of fraud, Jim Bakker landed in jail. Swaggart's dalliances with prostitutes left his ministry, which had once claimed a worldwide media audience of more than 500 million people, relegated to cable TV's public access channels.

Others religious ministries, however, prospered in the manner of Pat Robertson's. The Billy Graham Evangelistic Association's crusade (created in 1950) avoided even the hint of financial or moral malfeasance, and Graham himself remained one of the nation's most admired—and officially nonpartisan—citizens. Another charismatic Baptist minister, Rick Warren, gradually established a thriving "mega-church" in Southern California; in 2000, his Saddleback Church ranked among the 10 largest congregations in the country.

Successful movements on the Religious Right, such as Falwell's and Warren's, became cultural conglomerates. They included publishing enterprises, bookstores, radio and TV outlets, Christian academies and other "charter" schools, religiously affiliated colleges and seminaries, and even schools of law and of public policy. Apocalyptic novels from this religious milieu, including the *Left Behind* series by Tim LaHaye and Jerry Jenkins, and Christian-themed movies, including *A Thief in the Night* (1972), found large audiences. The Christian music industry easily surpassed the classical and jazz genres in sales by the turn of the 21st century.

The Religious Right also advanced several influential cultural narratives about the nation's past and the role that people of faith should play in shaping its future. The influential historian-theologian Francis Schaeffer, a committed evangelical, argued that the "secularist humanist" ideas on

Shawn Kashou/Shutterstock.com

31.10 **The Crystal Cathedral, Garden Grove, Orange County, California, 1981** Designed by the celebrated modernist architect Philip Johnson, the cathedral seated nearly 3,000 worshipers. It was reputedly the largest glass building in the world and home to the Reformed Church in America, an evangelical ministry founded by Robert Schuller in 1955. Schuller's congregation of mostly white Protestant suburbanites encountered tough times as the demography of Orange County changed. In 2010, a bankruptcy court put the Crystal Cathedral up for bids. The Roman Catholic Diocese of Orange in California secured ownership, renamed the renovated building Christ Cathedral, and began serving ethnically diverse Catholic worshippers.

Q *How have the varying architectural styles for houses of worship reflected the new religious diversity in America?*

which the United States had been founded bequeathed an insufficiently solid religious base. According to an alternative history that slowly gained ascendancy over that of Schaeffer, however, the original intent of the Founding Fathers was to create a Christian nation. The subsequent movement toward secularism, grounded in claims about a "separation between church and state," lacked both historical and legal-constitutional grounding. Both of these historical narratives pointed toward forging a new politics devoted to joining the sacred with the secular.

The Republican Party remained the primary political vehicle for this project. The Religious Right, in addition to gravitating to the GOP at the national level, became a vital force in state and local politics, steadily pressing Republican organizations toward its perspective on issues such as school curricula and textbook selection. It also placed supporters on officially nonpartisan bodies such as local school boards.

Conclusion

Sweeping changes occurred in demographics, economics, culture, and society during the last quarter of the 20th century. The nation aged, and more of its people gravitated to the Sun Belt. Sprawling urban corridors challenged older central cities as sites for development. Technological change fueled the growth of globalized industries and the restructuring of the American labor force.

The most prominent developments in American popular culture involved the proliferation of video screens and digital technologies (see also Chapter 32). Television, motion pictures, the Internet, and even services for phones increasingly targeted specific audiences, and the fragmentation of cultural reception—exemplified by the rise of new, particularistic media ventures—affected entertainment, politics, and religion.

CHAPTER REVIEW

Review

1. What were the major demographic changes that affected American life in this period?
2. What were the major elements of post-1970 economic change and how did each one generate both new problems and new possibilities for Americans?
3. How did new forms of media change the ways in which people received entertainment, information, and religion? Why were new media forms controversial?

Critical Thinking

1. How did fundamental demographic changes around the turn of the 21st century help shape economic restructuring?
2. How did the spread of video screens affect so many areas of American life?

Identifications

Review your understanding of the following key terms, people, and events for this chapter (terms in bold in text are included in the Glossary).

Immigration and Nationality Act of 1965 , p. 868
Immigration Reform and Control Act of 1986 (Simpson-Mazzoli Act), p. 869
"exurbs," p. 870
Community Reinvestment Act of 1977, p. 870
information revolution, p. 873
Human Genome Project, p. 873
steel cargo containers, p. 875
globalization, p. 875
"downsizing," p. 875
household deficit, p. 876
ESPN, p. 878
Title IX, or Patsy Mink Equal Opportunity in Education Act, p. 878
"narrowcasting," p. 879
"MTV aesthetic," p. 882

Suggested Readings

An overview of the demographic landscape at the end of the 20th century can be found in **Robert E. Lang and Bruce Katz, eds.**, ***Redefining Urban and Suburban America: Evidence from Census 2000*** (2006). See also by **Jon Teaford**, ***The Metropolitan Revolution: The Rise of Post-Urban America*** (2006), and **Edward Glaeser**, ***The Triumph of the City*** (2012).

The economic ferment can be surveyed in **Justin Fox**, ***The Myth of the Rational Market: A History of Risk, Reward, and Delusion on Wall Street*** (2009); **Joseph Stiglitz**, ***Free Fall: America, Free Markets, and the Sinking of the World Economy*** (2009); and ***Michael Lewis, Liar's Poker*** (rev. ed., 2014). On the transportation and biotech revolutions, see **Marc Levinson**, ***The Box: How the Shipping Container Made the World Smaller and the World Economy Bigger*** (2010), and **Sally Smith Hughes**, ***Genentech: The Beginnings of Biotech*** (2011).

On the sports-entertainment complex, see **Walter LaFeber**, ***Michael Jordan and the New Global Capitalism*** (2002); **Karen Blumenthal**, ***Let Me Play: Title IX—The Law that Changed the Future of Girls in America*** (2005); **Michael Oriard**, ***Brand NFL: Making and Selling America's Favorite Sport*** (2007); and ***Pamela Grundy*** and **Benjamin G. Rader**, ***American Sports: From the Age of Folk Games to the Age of Televised Sports*** (7th ed., 2016).

The cultural scene comes into view in **Robert G. Kolker**, ***The Cinema of Loneliness: Penn, Kubrick, Scorsese, Spielberg, Altman*** (rev ed., 2000); **Alan Wolfe**, ***The Transformation of American Religion: How We Actually Live Our Faith*** (2005); **David Bordwell**, ***The Way Hollywood Tells It: Story and Style in Modern Movies*** (2006); **Thomas Hine**, ***The Great Funk: Falling Apart and Coming Together (On a Shag Rug) in the Seventies*** (2007); **Jason Mittell**, ***Television and American Culture*** (2012); **Elijah Wald**, ***How the Beatles Destroyed Rock n' Roll: An Alternative History of American Popular Music*** (2011); **Stephen Witt**, ***How Music Got Free: A Story of Obsession and Invention*** (2016); **John Wisser**, ***PTL: The Rise and Fall of Jim and Tammy Faye Bakker's Evangelical Empire*** (2017); **Nadia Marzouki**, ***Islam: An American Religion*** (2017); and **Frances Fitzgerald**, ***The Evangelicals: The Struggle to Shape America*** (2017).

32 A Time of Hope and Fear, 1993–2018

Lee Snider/Photo Images/Corbis News/Corbis

32.1 **Ground Zero, September 11, 2001** The South Tower of the World Trade Center collapses as the North Tower burns after terrorists commandeered two airliners and used them as deadly missiles.

Q *How did this deadly, surprise attack change America's approach to national security and leave profound effects on American life?*

A TENSION between hope and fear marked American life during the decades that directly preceded and followed the turn of the 21st century. With the collapse of the Soviet Union in 1991, America's military and institutions seemed to have emerged triumphant from the cold war challenge of communism. The Pentagon operated thousands of military installations around the globe; American consumers enjoyed an expanding array of products and services; and stock market prices reached record highs in early 2000; in 2007; and, once again, in 2018.

Hopes for the future, however, found their match in new fears. Could the nation's economy cope with the challenges of a rapidly changing financial sector, growing inequality in wages and wealth, and a digital revolution? Would its polarized political structure meet demands for better governance? Could the nation's vast military power and surveillance tools effectively counter threats from potentially hostile nations and terrorist networks? The attacks in New York City and Washington on September 11, 2001 added new fears to the mix. Would unleashing new forms of power to fight terrorism endanger liberty and equality at home?

Meanwhile, national political life became increasingly volatile. The presidencies of Democrat **William Jefferson (Bill) Clinton**, Republican **George W. Bush**, and Democrat **Barack Hussein Obama** ran their full, two-term limits. Each, in different ways, tried to use the presidency to redesign the political landscape and generated controversy. Partisan polarization further increased as the severe economic meltdown called the **Great Recession** rippled through the economy and tepid recovery measures rescued the financial sector while leaving many Americans with lost homes, depleted savings, and uncertain employment. Most Democrats hoped for a governmental response that bore some resemblance to that undertaken in reaction to the Great Depression of the 1930s. Republican leaders and members of congress, however, feared spending measures and new economic regulations. Political turbulence only intensified with the unusual 2016 election in which **Donald J. Trump**, a celebrity business person with no experience in either government or politics, captured the Republican presidential nomination and then the White House. ■

32-1 The Politics of Polarization, 1993–2008

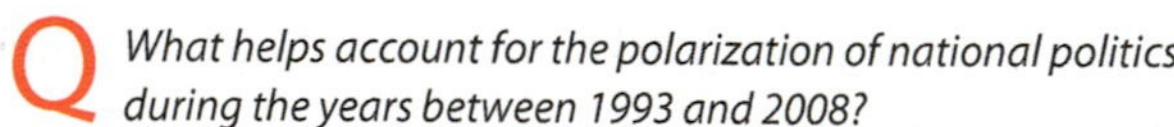

Q *What helps account for the polarization of national politics during the years between 1993 and 2008?*

Bill Clinton—the first Democratic president since another southerner, Jimmy Carter—brought images of youth, vitality, and cultural diversity to Washington. Events at his inauguration included separate parties for different musical tastes, including one broadcast on MTV. His initial cabinet included three African Americans and two Latinos; three cabinet posts went to women. Ruth Bader Ginsburg, his first nominee to the Supreme Court, became only the second woman to sit on the High Court. As ambassador to the United Nations, Clinton named Madeleine Albright, who, during his second term, would become the country's first female secretary of state.

32-1a *A New Democrat*

The Clinton administration achieved several of its domestic goals. It steered through Congress the Family Medical Leave Act, which allowed most working parents to take unpaid leaves in times of emergency; helped establish AmeriCorps, a program that allowed students to repay college loans through community service; and secured passage of the Brady Bill, which instituted restrictions on handgun purchases that the Supreme Court subsequently declared unconstitutional. An executive order ended, for the duration of Clinton's presidency, the Reagan era's ban on federal funding for abortion counseling.

Vice President Al Gore's tiebreaking vote in the Senate allowed passage of Clinton's 1993 economic package. It featured a modest tax increase and cuts in spending aimed at reducing the federal deficit and lowering interest rates to stimulate economic growth. The plan also expanded an existing governmental program, the **Earned Income Tax Credit (EITC)**, for low- and moderate-income households

CHRONOLOGY

1993	Congress approves North American Free Trade Agreement (NAFTA)
1994	Republicans gain control of Congress • O. J. Simpson saga begins
1996	Congress overhauls national welfare system • Clinton reelected president • FOX News debuts
1997	Congress and White House agree on deficit reduction plan
1998	House of Representatives impeaches Clinton
1999	Senate trial ends with Clinton's acquittal
2000	*Bush* v. *Gore* decision clears way for George W. Bush to become president
2001	Congress passes Bush tax cut • Terrorists from al-Qaeda destroy World Trade Center and attack Pentagon • Congress passes Patriot Act • U.S. forces invade Afghanistan
2002	*National Security Strategy of 2002* reasserts the Bush Doctrine
2003	Bush secures another tax cut • U.S. invades Iraq to topple Saddam Hussein government
2004	Bush defeats Kerry in the presidential race • Facebook debuts at Harvard
2005	Hurricane Katrina hits Gulf Coast • YouTube goes online • Insurgency in Iraq continues as permanent Iraqi government debuts
2006	Democrats gain control of Congress • Housing "bubble" reaches its peak
2007	New U.S. strategy adopted in Iraq • Housing "bubble" bursts
2008	Bush administration and Federal Reserve Board respond to financial meltdown • Great Recession, worst since 1930s, begins • Barack Obama wins presidential race
2009	Obama administration passes economic stimulus plan • U.S. devotes more resources to war in Afghanistan while withdrawing from Iraq
2010	Republicans surge at national, state, and local levels in elections of 2010
2011	A White House–ordered, CIA-directed raid into Pakistan by U.S. Navy SEALs kills Osama bin Laden in early May
2012	Facebook begins offering stock shares to the public • Barack Obama reelected president
2013	Affordable Care Act (ACA), passed in 2010, takes effect and launches its website • 16-day government shutdown in congressional dispute over raising debt ceiling
2014	Republicans control Congress after taking Senate in midterm elections
2015	Supreme Court's *Obergefell* v. *Hodges* decision rules in favor of marriage equality • Nuclear weapons agreement with Iran
2016	Donald Trump wins presidency • Major tax overhaul reduces corporate and individual tax rates and augers larger deficits

with children. This measure, which lowered tax bills and increased refunds for those who qualified, provided millions of people with another safety-net program.

Identifying himself as a **"New Democrat"** (see also Chapter 30), Clinton broke with his party's recent stance on criminal justice issues. He backed a 1994 law that provided funding for more police officers and more prisons. Its controversial "three strikes" provision required a life sentence for a third felony conviction in federal courts.

The Clinton administration calculated its positions on social–cultural issues. While endorsing a woman's right to a legal abortion, the president also stressed that the procedure should be a "rare" occurrence. Clinton arrived in Washington as a supporter of ending the military's prohibition against gay men and lesbians being open about their sexuality, but he conceded that ending this ban would spark "discomfort" among heterosexual service personnel and possibly harm morale within military ranks. His administration's compromise policy based on silence and denial—popularly known as "don't ask, don't tell"—had little effect on discrimination against gays and lesbians in the military.

The administration's effort to revamp the nation's health-care system ended in failure. A task force chaired by Hillary Rodham Clinton, the First Lady, tried to extend coverage to the tens of millions who lacked insurance and to contain the rising cost of care. The plan that emerged included complex mechanisms for financing and delivering health care. Republicans denounced it, extolled the existing system, and assailed Clinton as a proponent of "big government." Sick on arrival, the health-care proposal died in Congress during early 1994.

The November 1994 elections proved a stunning triumph for the GOP. An aggressive campaign spearheaded by Representative Newt Gingrich of Georgia produced Republican majorities in both houses of Congress for the first time in 40 years. Republicans also won several new governorships, gained ground in most state legislatures, and made significant headway in many city and county elections, particularly across the South. There, for the first time since the 19th century, the number of Republicans sitting in Congress topped the number of Democrats. Gingrich claimed a mandate for what he labeled a **Contract with America**. It drew from Ronald Reagan's 1985 State of the Union address and included calls for overhauling the welfare system, enacting additional anticrime legislation, streamlining federal legal procedures, requiring a three-fifths majority for any increase in taxation, and reducing the nation's role in the UN.

Gingrich downplayed polls that showed few voters knew much about the contract and overplayed his new role as Speaker of the House by continually challenging Clinton's policies. A deadlock between a Democratic president and a GOP Congress over federal spending produced two brief shutdowns of federal agencies in late 1995 and early 1996. Most people blamed Gingrich and the Republicans rather than the White House for interrupting the delivery of government services.

A continually improving economy sustained Clinton's approval ratings. Economic growth spurred millions of new jobs, decreased the federal deficit, boosted corporate profits, propelled stock and bond markets to new heights, and enabled an astronomical boom in the financial industry. The fruits of economic expansion, however, were distributed unequally, as the income gulf between the wealthiest 1 percent of households and the other 99 percent deepened. Still, most people saw their economic fortunes improve, however slightly. Unemployment fell during the 1990s, averaging less than 2 percent a year, and real income inched upward for the first time in nearly 15 years.

Clinton's 1996 State of the Union address declared that the era of "big government" was at an end. The Personal Responsibility and Work Opportunity Reconciliation Act of 1996 incorporated compromises between the Republican-dominated Congress and Clinton, who had vetoed two earlier welfare-related measures. The new law replaced the controversial AFDC program, which provided funds and services to poor families headed by single, unemployed women, with **Temporary Assistance to Needy Families (TANF)**. This measure allowed individual states to design, under general federal guidelines, programs aimed at getting people off welfare and into paying jobs.

TANF worried many Democrats. Provisions limiting governmental assistance over a person's lifetime to five years and authorizing states to suspend benefits if recipients failed to find employment within two years ignored the difficulties faced by people without job skills. TANF's opponents also feared its impact on children, particularly in states with already minimal child-care, nutrition, and medical care programs. Senator Daniel Patrick Moynihan, who had earlier devised Richard Nixon's FAP program (see Chapter 29), denounced TANF as "the most brutal act of social policy" since the 19th century.

New Democrats such as Clinton, however, saw a necessary merger of policy innovation with electoral reality. TANF could assuage conservatives by embracing their call for a smaller federal government; acknowledging critiques of the existing system of social support; and affirming the idea that wages, rather than welfare, should provide the primary source of personal income. TANF's Democratic supporters echoed Republicans who predicted the new arrangement would encourage states to devise programs that both reduced welfare costs and created jobs. TANF immediately assisted Clinton's reelection prospects by eliminating the welfare issue from partisan debate and bolstering the president's claim that he was reducing the size and cost of government.

In the 1996 election, the Clinton-Gore team defeated Republicans Robert Dole and Jack Kemp by about the same margin as it had beaten George H. W. Bush and Dan Quayle four years earlier. Although another presidential run by Ross Perot again denied the Democratic ticket a popular majority, a low-key campaign effort gained Perot's third-party candidacy less than 10 percent of the vote. Clinton became the first Democratic president since Franklin D. Roosevelt to win back-to-back terms. A reelected president and a Congress still controlled by Republicans then agreed on a timetable for eradicating the federal deficit, which the president accurately predicted would soon disappear. But any hope for further accommodations disappeared as the nation's political culture began revolving around a legal-constitutional debate over the future of Bill Clinton's presidency rather than his policy initiatives.

32-1b *The Investigation and Trial of a President*

Intensive legal inquiries into Clinton's public and private life capped a decade of popular fascination with investigations and trials. Americans, of course, had long been drawn to legal spectacles, such as the Scopes trial of the 1920s (see Chapter 24). During the 1990s, however, investigative and courtroom dramas inundated popular culture. Coverage of real trials, a staple of media culture, entered a new phase when Court TV (renamed truTV in 2008) arrived in 1991. The legal thrillers of John Grisham made this author-attorney the best-selling fiction writer of the 1990s, and six of his novels became feature motion pictures. The year 1990 marked the debut of what would become one of TV's longest-running drama series, *Law & Order* (1990–2010).

Meanwhile, groups on the New Right started bankrolling private investigations into supposed crimes in Bill Clinton's past. One concerned a scandal-plagued real estate venture called "Whitewater," to which Hillary and Bill Clinton had been financially connected. Confident of rebutting all allegations, the Clinton administration asked for the appointment of a special independent prosecutor to investigate Whitewater. The president also faced a civil suit for monetary damages by Paula Jones, who claimed that Clinton, while governor of Arkansas, had sexually harassed her. The U.S. Supreme Court ruled that this private lawsuit could proceed while Clinton still held public office, and it became entangled with the Whitewater inquiry when Kenneth Starr replaced the initial special prosecutor. A religious conservative, Starr allowed his staff to extend the Whitewater investigation into allegations that Clinton was concealing a series of sexually charged encounters.

Clinton's denials crumbled in early 1998 after conservative activists helped Starr obtain irrefutable evidence of White House trysts between Clinton and a young intern, Monica Lewinsky. Republican leaders in the House of Representatives claimed that Clinton's conduct justified his removal from office. Democrats condemned Clinton's behavior but insisted that private failings did not qualify as the kind of "high crimes and misdemeanors" the Constitution required for impeachment, let alone conviction, of a president.

At Newt Gingrich's insistence, Republicans made Clinton's character their major issue during the midterm elections of 1998, but the president won this electoral trial. Republicans, surprisingly, lost five seats in the House of Representatives. Even worse for Gingrich, public revelation of a long-term extramarital affair forced him to resign from the House. Kenneth Starr conceded that the original Whitewater charges lacked merit, but his official report detailed Clinton's dalliances with Monica Lewinsky and the president's effort to conceal them when testifying under oath. Using evidence gathered by Starr's investigators, the Republican majority in the lame-duck House of Representatives mobilized enough votes, in mid-December 1998, for two articles of impeachment (one for perjury and another for obstruction of justice) against Clinton. The subsequent Senate trial generated surprisingly little drama and concluded (on February 12, 1999) with both articles of impeachment gaining nowhere near the 67 votes that the Constitution required for conviction.

Although Clinton remained president, he hardly escaped unscathed. His presidency remained under sustained GOP attack, highlighting the Lewinsky affair, and the evolution of Fox News on cable TV added a spicy new ingredient to the media recipe book. Initially, Fox's partisan Republican slant was less important than its popularization of an adversarial format for political coverage on cable TV. Fox perfected a cost-cutting technique by which its camera crews gathered eye-catching imagery and brief interviews that its producers could, employing new digital technologies, archive, quickly retrieve, and re-edit for endless recycling. On-air commentators became ever more skillful in using fleeting imagery and brief sound bites as the basis for trading opinions and speculation without leaving the studio or doing any actual reporting.

A medium newer and even more adversarial than cable TV—political sites on the Internet—came online at a critical point during the Clinton presidency. Other outlets eventually might have reported rumors about the president's personal life, but there was a long tradition (most evident for John F. Kennedy) of burying such stories as purely private matters. The first news of the Clinton-Lewinsky relationship surfaced on *The Drudge Report,* a conservative opinion-gossip site that other media had previously disdained. Over the course of the 1990s, in short, discussions of the president's private affairs increasingly preoccupied new communications formats and helped to slow—indeed, almost paralyze—the Clinton administration's efforts to do the actual work of governance.

32-1c *The Long Election and Trials of 2000*

The lengthy presidential election of 2000 eventually featured a legal drama that attracted this sound-bite style of coverage, especially on cable TV news. Al Gore, Clinton's vice president for eight years, ran as the Democratic presidential nominee and selected Senator Joseph Lieberman of Connecticut as his running mate. The Republican ballot, for the fifth time in the last six elections, bore the name of Bush. George W. Bush chose **Richard (Dick) Cheney**—a conservative Republican stalwart who had served in the administration of George H. W. Bush (1989–1993)—to be his vice-presidential running mate.

The campaign of 2000 energized the Republican Party's base but stirred less passion elsewhere. Bush, the son of the former president Bush, claimed his record as governor of Texas showed he could work with Democrats, appeal to African Americans and Hispanics, and pursue a "compassionate conservatism." Gore's disorganized campaign struggled to articulate coherent themes. By distancing himself from Clinton, the vice president likely squandered his primary asset—eight years of relative prosperity with a Democratic administration in the White House. Barely 50 percent of eligible voters went to the polls in 2000. Following recent patterns, the vote highlighted the gender, racial, and ethnic differences between the two major parties. Bush attracted 54 percent of the ballots cast by men but only 43 percent of those from women. He received 38 percent of the votes from Latinos, 37 percent from Asian Americans, and 9 percent from African Americans.

The election ended in a dead heat. Republicans narrowly maintained control of the House of Representatives, and the Senate ended up evenly split between the two parties. Al Gore carried the popular vote by about 500,000 ballots, but the only tally that mattered, the one in the Electoral College, turned on the 25 electoral votes from Florida. Only about 1,000 popular votes from the Sunshine State initially separated the two candidates. As other media outlets held back, Fox News declared that the Republican ticket had carried Florida—and thus had secured its electoral votes and the presidency.

When it became evident that no clear winner had emerged, cable TV news shifted to an "All Election, All the Time" focus on Florida, where Bush's brother Jeb was governor and the GOP dominated the state legislature. Republican officials declared Bush the victor in Florida by a margin of 930 votes. Democrats charged that numerous irregularities—including antiquated voting machines, deliberately confusing ballots, and an apparent effort to suppress the African American vote—had distorted the count. A torrent of lawsuits, by Democrats and Republicans alike, quickly ensued. Both parties, especially the GOP, flooded Florida with cadres of lawyers and party activists who performed for the benefit of TV cameras. Florida's highest court finally ordered hand recounts in several counties where Gore's totals seemed suspiciously low. When early results began reducing Bush's slim lead, Republicans charged Democrats with "stealing" his victory and appealed to the U.S. Supreme Court.

With media coverage approaching a near-frenzied state, the Supreme Court handed down its final decision, ***Bush* v. *Gore***, on December 12, 2000. Five conservative Republican justices (over the dissents of two other Republicans and two Democrats) ruled that no more Florida ballots could be recounted. Outvoted in court, Gore conceded political defeat, and George W. Bush became the 43rd president of the United States (see Map 32.1).

32-1d *A Conservative Washington, 2001–2008*

The Bush presidency's program for tax cuts, educational reform, and expanding oil drilling got off to a fast start. In contrast to Clinton, who had preferred lengthy, loosely structured, intellectual give-and-take sessions, Bush favored brief, tightly controlled meetings that moved toward clearly

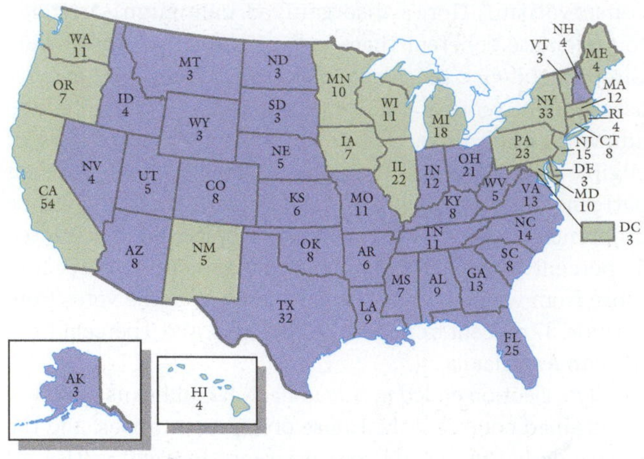

	Electoral Vote		Popular Vote	
	Number	%	Number	%
Gore (Democrat)	267	49.6	50,996,582	48.4
Bush (Republican)	271	50.4	50,456,062	47.8
Nader (Green)	----	----	2,858,843	2.7
Buchanan (Reform)	----	----	483,760	.4

▲ MAP 32.1 Presidential Election, 2000

Although Gore won the popular vote, Bush won the electoral vote after a bitter fight over disputed ballots in Florida.

Q *Why do some say that the Supreme Court elected the president in this election?*

Q *Which key states, closely identified with President Bill Clinton and candidate Al Gore, did George W. Bush carry in 2000?*

delineated decisions. He initially allowed Vice President Cheney and Donald Rumsfeld, the secretary of defense, wide latitude to set policy directions. Bush also proclaimed that religious faith directly shaped his political outlook.

Several divisive issues immediately emerged. An economic downturn accompanied by an early 2001 plunge in U.S stock markets—a consequence of a bubble in high-tech stocks and fraudulent activities by several large corporations—signaled trouble ahead. Revenue surpluses at the national and state levels began dwindling and then turning to deficits. Consumer confidence slumped. The Bush administration responded by urging a tax cut to provide an economic stimulus.

The White House pressed two other proposals. First, Cheney put together an ambitious energy plan, focused on easing restrictions on oil drilling and regulations on pricing. Critics complained that it primarily benefited large oil and gas firms—many headquartered in Texas—and did little to develop alternative sources of energy. Second, the president personally championed an educational initiative called "No Child Left Behind" that would employ nationwide testing to determine which schools were teaching students effectively.

Bush's proposals seemed bolder than either his campaign rhetoric or his loss of the popular vote might have suggested. A revised tax plan, which phased in the substantial cuts that tilted toward the wealthiest 1 percent of Americans, became law in June 2001. "No Child Left Behind" also passed. Opponents of the pro-oil and pro-gas energy bill blocked its passage, but only until 2005. In 2003 the administration narrowly passed a costly addition (the first in 35 years) to the Medicare system. **The Medicare Prescription Drug Improvement and Modernization Act** created complex arrangements by which federal funds would pay for some, but not all, of the drug costs of Medicare recipients. Benefiting drug companies as well as patients, this measure helped further increase the federal deficit.

The president's approval ratings, which had hovered under 50 percent, soared after the attacks on the World Trade Center and the Pentagon on September 11, 2001. (For the foreign policy implications of 9/11, especially in the Middle East, see pp. 898-899.) The midterm elections of 2002 left the GOP with secure control of the U.S. Senate and an even larger margin in the House of Representatives.

Downplaying the rapidly growing federal deficit, largely the result of Bush's earlier tax reductions, the White House secured yet another tax cut in 2003. It again insisted that this measure would spur economic growth. Democrats condemned these cuts for tilting toward the already wealthy in an economy that had shed nearly 3 million jobs and had shown a widening income gap.

The White House's political strategy for the 2004 elections stressed Bush's role in combating terrorism. The Democratic nominee, Senator John Kerry of Massachusetts, had served in Vietnam during the 1960s before becoming an antiwar activist. Kerry endorsed the rationale for the Bush administration's national security initiatives, while criticizing its strategy and tactics for combating the terrorist threat and keeping his distance from a movement that opposed the Iraq War.

A fiercely partisan campaign ensued. Some Bush supporters falsely disparaged Kerry's Vietnam War record and portrayed a Kerry presidency as a danger to national security. Democrats charged Bush with bumbling leadership, an escalating burden of debt, and a tax policy favoring the wealthiest Americans. The GOP's mobilization effort produced a large Republican turnout. Bush defeated Kerry by about 3 percent of the popular vote and only 15 electoral ballots. As in 2000, Bush did best in suburbia and small towns, among men, and with people who attended church regularly. Kerry failed to do as well as had Al Gore in 2000 among white voters—still more than three-quarters of the electorate—or to win enough middle-income voters, people whom Democrats claimed were suffering from Bush's economic policies.

Bush claimed an electoral mandate and announced an ambitious second-term agenda that featured substantial overhauls of the Social Security system and the tax code. He barnstormed the country on behalf of these initiatives, but most people appeared wary in light of a shaky economy, a yawning federal deficit, and warfare overseas. Moreover, a Republican-controlled Congress became a depreciating asset to the White House after revelations of illegal contributions from lobbyists and personal misconduct forced the resignation of several GOP leaders. Congress's approval rating skidded below that of President Bush.

WEDNESDAY

SYRACUSE
HERALD-JOURNAL

ELECTION SPECIAL
NOVEMBER 8, 2000

RECOUNT!

GORE LEADS THE POPULAR VOTE, ELECTORAL UNDECIDED

48,601,697 GORE — Bush 48% Gore 48% — 48,347,466 BUSH

CLINTON CLOBBERS LAZIO
STORIES BELOW, PAGE A7

GOP KEEPS SLIM HOLD OF CONGRESS

Giuliani blamed

'A world leader'

Walsh re-elected

Boehlert returns

McHugh re-elected

Houghton wins again

Bond act fails

Magnarelli victorious

Hoffmann wins

Easy win for DeFrancisco

Christensen wins

TODD VERSTEEGH, right, vents his frustration while waiting for presidential election results to be announced over television as Mark Sanda looks on at a Republican Party gathering early today in Iowa City, Iowa.

As the nation waits, Florida will decide race for president

▶ Cliffhanger election comes down to a few votes. Recount could be finished by the end of the day Thursday.

Gore retracts concession call to Bush

SENATOR-ELECT Hillary Rodham Clinton laughs after she is introduced by retiring Sen. Daniel Patrick Moynihan, left, as she appears at a New York City victory rally.

First lady makes history with election to Senate

Clinton 55% Lazio 43%

GOOD EVENING

Syracuse Newspapers/The Image Works

ESYR0606273 Syracuse, NY: November 8, 2000. Historic front pages. Syracuse Herald Journal - Recount! ©Syracuse Newspapers / The Image Works NOTE: The copyright notice must include "The Image Works" DO NOT SHORTEN THE NAME OF THE COMPANY ©Syracuse Newspapers / The Image Works

32.2 **The Contested Presidential Election of 2000** The inconclusive popular vote in Florida extended the 2000 presidential election process. Partisan activists, especially on the Republican side, rushed to Florida and onto TV. GOP demonstrators insisted that George W. Bush had carried the Sunshine State and that the hand counting of ballots was meant to steal his victory. The Supreme Court halted the recount.

Q *How does this photo demonstrate the polarized politics of this era?*

AP Images/Pablo Martinez Monsivais

32.3 **George W. Bush Shows Texas Style** The 43rd president, in contrast to his father, George H. W. Bush, always emphasized his Texas roots. Here, he steps out at an inaugural ball.

Q *Why might Bush have wanted to downplay his elite family roots in the Northeast section of the country?*

32-1e *Politics and Social–Cultural Issues*

With the major political parties locked in partisan stalemate, a variety of movement groups tried to seize the initiative on specific issues. Immigration policy emerged as one of the most contentious. Entering the United States in near-record numbers, immigrants were now seeking jobs throughout the country, particularly in the South. Organizations opposed to immigration demanded new legislative restrictions, tighter border security, and stronger penalties for employers of undocumented immigrants.

Pro-immigration organizations responded, particularly in California and other states with large Mexican American populations. Tapping the power of Spanish-language radio and TV, they staged temporary work stoppages and street demonstrations to show the economic importance of immigrant workers and the political clout of their movement. They refuted claims that undocumented immigrants "took away" jobs from American citizens and depressed wage levels.

Political leaders moved cautiously. House Republicans from districts with strong anti-immigration sentiment favored new restrictions, but enough Republicans in the Senate joined Democrats to block any such measure. The Bush administration promised a more vigorous effort to police the U.S.–Mexican border but angered congressional Republicans by endorsing a "guest worker" arrangement, an option favored by most business interests. Uncertain about how immigration legislation might affect electoral results in 2008, Republicans backed off from taking action at the national level.

Differences also sharpened over the role the government should play in public health regulations. Business interests joined prominent Republicans in supporting continued deregulation. The free market, they contended, would self-correct to protect the public, and regulators would stifle business growth. In response, environmentalist groups argued that hazardous wastes, though a potential threat to everyone, most directly affected people with low incomes who lacked the political power to keep toxic by-products out of their neighborhoods. Activists further charged that the relatively few corporations that dominated the global production and sale of food brutalized animals, overused antibiotics, depleted soil quality and vital rain forests, and polluted the environment with toxic waste. New governmental regulations, they argued, were needed to safeguard the health of people—and of the entire planet. Environmentalists spearheaded a "buy local" movement that sparked demand for organic products, farmers' markets, and well-prepared "slow food."

The issue of gay rights also emerged as a major political-cultural flashpoint, as LGBT movements sought legal recognition of long-term partnerships. When the U.S. Supreme Court struck down state anti-sodomy laws (in *Lawrence* v. *Texas*, 2003), the constitutional rationale for this decision seemingly suggested that bans against same-sex marriage could not withstand legal scrutiny either. In several states, courts held that the bedrock principle of legal-constitutional equality guaranteed gays and lesbians a "right to marry," a liberty that some state legislatures also began to affirm.

Conservative activists joined the Bush administration in seeking an amendment to the U.S. Constitution that specifically declared marriage as a "union between a man and a woman." Opponents of the amendment narrowly turned back a congressional effort to send such a measure to the states for ratification in 2006. In response, conservatives mobilized to overturn, by constitutional amendment or referendum, legislative and court actions that legalized gay marriage in a number of states.

Mobilization on the political right also highlighted conflict between some religious beliefs and scientific research and medical practice. In July 2006, after Congress passed a law in support of stem cell research, President Bush responded by issuing, on live television, the first veto of his presidency, rejecting this measure on "culture-of-life" grounds.

Many of these religious-cultural issues became entangled in judicial politics. The conservative legal movement continued its successful campaign to staff the lower federal courts with rightward-tilting judges and even blocked a Bush nominee for the Supreme Court, Harriet Myers, because of her seemingly moderate stance on abortion and gay rights. The White House easily obtained Senate confirmations for two staunchly conservative Supreme Court nominees: John Roberts to replace William Rehnquist as Chief Justice of the United States, and Samuel Alito (rather than Harriet Myers) to succeed the retiring Sandra Day O'Connor as an associate justice.

The **Roberts Court** generally converted the arguments of the conservative legal movement into constitutional law. In one of several key decisions breaking 5–4—with Justice Anthony Kennedy replacing Justice O'Connor as the swing vote—the Supreme Court limited women's access to abortion. It rebuffed traditional civil rights groups with a similarly restrictive view of the ability of local school districts to use racial identification in pursuit of desegregation strategies. In another 5–4 decision that Second Amendment activists applauded, the Roberts Court ruled that the right to bear arms included that of individual citizens to possess firearms and thus struck down an ordinance regulating gun ownership in Washington, D.C. Moreover, the logic of this 2008 decision, *District of Columbia* v. *Heller*, pointed toward the subsequent invalidation of similar regulations at the state and local levels. The Court also invariably upheld claims made by corporations that were fighting government regulations.

32-2 Foreign Policies of Hope and Terror: 1993–2008

Why are the Clinton administration's foreign policies generally regarded as "internationalist"? How did the administration of George W. Bush, especially after September 11, 2001, seek to reorient Clinton's approach?

For nearly half a century, the goal of containing Soviet communism had shaped U.S. foreign policy. After the collapse of the Soviet Union, George H. W. Bush's attempt to fashion new goals for a post–cold war world had failed to impress either his Democratic or Republican critics (see Chapter 30). Bill Clinton came to the White House with a more ambitious foreign policy agenda. A committed internationalist, he assigned top priority to devising guidelines for military intervention, improving relations with the UN, promoting free-market policies that supported economic globalization, addressing environmental concerns that were both global and local in nature, and reducing threats from nuclear materials. After Clinton's internationalist approach, his successor, George W. Bush, assumed a more unilateralist tone, especially after the terrorist attacks of September 11, 2001.

32-2a *Clinton's Internationalist Agenda*

One of the most perplexing foreign policy issues involved decisions about when to employ U.S. military power in localized conflicts that no longer could be traced back to the now-defunct Soviet Union. No consistent guidelines for intervention ever emerged. In Somalia, U.S. troops, under the umbrella of a UN mission since May 1992, had been assisting a humanitarian effort. After a battle in Mogadishu (subsequently portrayed in the book and movie *Black Hawk Down*) took the lives of 18 U.S. service personnel in the fall of 1993, however, domestic criticism mounted. Clinton ordered a pullout the following spring. Recalling the criticism of involvement in Somalia, Clinton withheld support from a UN peacekeeping effort in Rwanda, where 500,000 Tutsis died during a genocidal civil war. In Haiti, though, Clinton dispatched U.S. troops, in cooperation with the UN, to reinstall an elected president who had been ousted in a coup. The White House, in cooperation with NATO, also deployed 20,000 U.S. troops in the former Yugoslavia to prevent Bosnian Serbs from massacring Bosnian Muslims. U.S. forces remained in Bosnia to oversee a ceasefire and peace-building process that resulted from the U.S.-brokered Dayton (Ohio) Peace Accords of 1995.

In March 1999 Clinton supported a NATO bombing campaign to protect Muslims from Serbia's "ethnic cleansing" program in its province of Kosovo. After heavy bombardment, the Serbian government withdrew its forces from Kosovo; Serbs soon elected a new president supportive of multiethnic democracy and the West, and former Serbian officials faced trial before an international human rights court in the Netherlands. U.S. and NATO troops remained in Kosovo as peacekeepers.

Clinton's military moves in Haiti, Bosnia, and Kosovo provoked controversy. Republican critics accused the president of lacking clear guidelines about when, where, and how to employ U.S. force. Suspicious of cooperating with the UN, they denounced peacekeeping and "nation-building" programs and demanded clear-cut exit strategies to prevent the United States from getting bogged down in lengthy occupations. Defenders of intervention insisted that Clinton's flexibility and willingness to work with NATO and the UN were strengths, not weaknesses, in a post–cold war world. Such debates about when and where to intervene in trouble spots would increase over the coming years.

32-2b *Globalization*

In addition, the Clinton administration placed great emphasis on lowering barriers to trade and expanding global markets to advance the international economic process called "globalization" (see Chapter 31). His stance angered many labor leaders, who claimed that globalization was contributing to the loss of industrial jobs in the United States. It also sparked a highly visible anti-globalization movement that emerged in most nations to challenge the political power of corporate elites.

In pursuit of globalization, Clinton pushed the stalled North American Free Trade Agreement (NAFTA) among the United States, Canada, and Mexico through Congress in a close vote that depended on Republican support and faced fierce opposition from labor unions. Then, in early 1995, a severe debt crisis and currency devaluation in Mexico prompted the Clinton administration to extend a $20 billion loan. Unprecedented and controversial, the loan stabilized the Mexican economy and, within a few years, had been repaid with $1 billion in interest. When Asian economies later faltered, Clinton lobbied the International Monetary Fund (IMF) to provide emergency credits to shore up financial systems from Korea to Indonesia.

Promising that expanded trade ties would benefit all nations, the Clinton administration supported creation of the **World Trade Organization (WTO)** in 1995. It also signed more than 300 bilateral trade agreements with other nations. Anxious to move China toward a market economy, Clinton backed China's entry into the WTO, in exchange for its promise to relax trade restrictions. Similarly, the United States ended its 19-year-old trade embargo against Vietnam. Clinton continually extolled the coming of a "New Century" in which freer trade would expand prosperity, and "liberty will spread by cell phone and cable modem."

32-2c *Protecting the Planet*

International environmental issues were another area of major concern. Clinton's secretary of the interior set aside 16 new national monuments and blocked road construction and logging in nearly 60 million acres of wild areas in national forests. Building on decisions by his Republican predecessors, Clinton placed almost 6 million new surface and underwater acres under federal protection.

The Clinton administration also revealed how, during the cold war past, actions by the U.S. government had contributed to environmental degradation. Governmental nuclear facilities had spewed toxic wastes, and workers had been inadequately warned about the dangers of radiation. In 1993, Clinton's energy secretary released long-secret medical records relating to radiation poisoning and promised programs to inform and compensate victims. The legacy of other military-related pollutants also became evident after many of the nation's military bases were shut down during the post–cold war 1990s.

Most importantly, Clinton supported the environmental movement's increasing focus on international ecological dangers. Environmentalists warned of holes in the ozone layer caused by chlorofluorocarbons (CFCs), potentially catastrophic climate change associated with deforestation and desertification, pollution of the world's oceans, and the decline of biodiversity in plant and animal species. Solutions to global environmental problems seemingly required worldwide cooperation toward "sustainable development." An "Earth Summit" was held in Brazil in 1992. International conventions signed in Kyoto in 1997 and at The Hague in 2000 pointed toward establishing international standards on emissions of CFCs and gases that contributed to global climate changes.

Clinton's post–cold war agenda also included nonproliferation of nuclear weapons. His administration dismantled some of the U.S. nuclear arsenal and increased economic aid to Ukraine, then the third greatest nuclear power in the world, in exchange for a pledge to disarm its 1,600 Soviet-era warheads. The White House successfully pressed for a new Nuclear Nonproliferation Treaty in the spring of 1995, and three years later neared the brink of war with Iraq to maintain international inspections of its weapons programs. After enduring punishing air strikes, Iraq still expelled the investigators and left analysts wondering if Iraq had resumed building weapons of mass destruction (WMDs).

32-2d *September 11, 2001 and the Bush Doctrine*

During the 1990s, intelligence experts highlighted a growing concern about attacks by a foreign terrorist network called al-Qaeda. Its operatives bombed the World Trade Center in New York City in 1993; U.S. embassies in Kenya and Tanzania in 1998; and a U.S. battleship, the *Cole*, in 2000. These bombings prompted heightened security efforts and special efforts to track al-Qaeda's leaders. As the Clinton administration left office, national security officers warned about what al-Qaeda's Osama bin Laden, an Islamic fundamentalist from Saudi Arabia, might be plotting. The Bush administration rejected their sense of urgency.

On September 11, 2001, 19 suicide terrorists, organized in separate squads, seized four jetliners, already airborne and loaded with flammable jet fuel, for use as high-octane, human-guided missiles. Two planes toppled the Twin Towers of New York's World Trade Center; another ripped into the Pentagon building; and only the courageous action of passengers on a fourth plane, which crashed in Pennsylvania, prevented an attack against the United States Capitol in Washington, D.C. Nearly 3,000 people, including several hundred plane passengers and an even larger number of police officers and firefighters in New York City, perished.

George W. Bush, donning the mantle of a wartime president, declared a war on terrorism. Tracing the attacks to Osama bin Laden and al-Qaeda operating out of Afghanistan, the Bush administration organized a multinational invasion force. In December 2001, U.S.-led troops toppled the Taliban regime that had been dominating Afghanistan with bin Laden's help and installed a pro-U.S. government in Afghanistan's capital city of Kabul. The effort failed, however, to secure that nation's countryside or to capture bin Laden and his top aides.

Meanwhile, the president proclaimed what became known as the **Bush Doctrine**. As fully expressed in the **National Security Strategy of 2002**, it denounced not only terrorist networks but any nation sponsoring terrorism or accumulating WMDs that terrorists might use. The Bush Doctrine additionally proclaimed that the United States possessed the unilateral authority to wage preemptive war against any force, including any foreign nation, threatening American security.

Congressional legislation bolstered the Bush Doctrine. Many Democrats joined Republicans in passing the USA Patriot Act, which gave the executive branch broad latitude to watch over and detain people it considered threats to national security. A newly created agency, the Department of Homeland Security, launched an array of new measures including screenings for all airline passengers. Fear of more terrorist attacks, heightened by mysterious mailings of deadly anthrax bacteria to several public officials, strengthened the case for extending the power of the executive branch.

32-2e *Unilateralism and the Iraq War*

After Osama bin Laden dropped from sight, the White House invoked the Bush Doctrine against Iraq and Saddam Hussein, the old nemesis of the president's father, who controlled some of the richest oil reserves in the world. The Bush administration contended that Iraq posed a clear and immediate danger to the United States. Claiming that intelligence reports showed that Saddam Hussein possessed WMDs and had ties to al-Qaeda, the Bush administration asked the UN and other nations to support a military strike to remove Saddam from power.

The Bush administration, which preferred taking unilateral action rather than working with international bodies, included a group of **neoconservatives** who had been calling for such an approach to foreign affairs since the 1990s. According to neoconservative advisers to Vice President Dick Cheney and Secretary of Defense Donald Rumsfeld, the United States should use its enormous military power to go on the offensive and clear away threatening, repressive regimes, beginning with that in Iraq. International organizations and agreements should not hamper efforts to enhance U.S. influence, especially in the Middle East. In contrast to his father, an internationalist who had carefully courted UN backing for the Persian Gulf War in 1991, George W. Bush endorsed a policy of overthrowing Saddam regardless of the UN's position.

Acting without UN support, in early 2003 the Bush administration assembled its own "coalition of the willing"—troops from the United States and Great Britain plus small contingents from several other countries. On March 20, this coalition launched an air and ground assault against Iraq. Overriding military planners who recommended at least 300,000 U.S. troops, the White House's Operation Iraqi Freedom deployed only one-third that many. Saddam Hussein's regime did fall in less than two months, and on May 1 President Bush proclaimed, during a celebration staged on the deck of the aircraft carrier *Abraham Lincoln*, that "significant combat" had ended in Iraq.

This carefully crafted media event quickly rebounded against the president, however, as resistance flared against the ill-planned, American-led occupation of Iraq, which aimed at creating a pro-U.S. government and a new economic order closely tied to U.S. companies. Terrorist groups from outside Iraq, particularly those claiming connections to al-Qaeda, joined the fight, while internal divisions among religious, ethnic, and political factions inside Iraq fueled an insurgency that soon overlapped with a civil war. The military warned that the Iraq War was stretching resources so thin that the United States might not be able to respond in other areas of the globe. As U.S. casualties in Iraq mounted, so did the monetary costs. The lack of international support for U.S. action meant that, unlike in the 1991 Persian Gulf War, U.S. taxpayers directly bore the costs, and the Bush administration repeatedly asked Congress for billions of dollars, but no increase in taxes, to fund the lengthening engagement in Iraq. Meanwhile, the war in Afghanistan stalled, the Taliban regrouped, and the al-Qaeda leaders who had attacked on September 11, 2001, hid in mountainous safe havens and in Pakistan.

AP Images/Khakid Mohammed

32.4 **Baghdad, Iraq, 2006** Bombings aimed at both Iraqis and U.S. personnel followed the fall of Saddam Hussein. In May 2006, a bomb attack hit a news crew from CBS, underscoring the danger that journalists, as well as troops, confronted whenever they left the relative safety of the U.S.-controlled "Green Zone" in central Baghdad.

Q *How do images such as this seem at odds with the U.S. efforts at nation-building in Iraq?*

As the Iraqi operation faltered, the Bush administration's public rationale for having undertaken it fell apart. The White House could never document any connection between al-Qaeda and Saddam Hussein, and an exhaustive official report concluded that Iraq had possessed no biological or nuclear WMDs at the time of the invasion. Later evidence suggested that the Bush administration had used bogus intelligence information to bolster its justification for war. In response, Congress in December 2004 placed existing intelligence-gathering and assessment efforts under a new umbrella agency, headed by a new coordinating official, the Director of National Intelligence.

As the initial case for war came under fire, so did its conduct. Photographs showing abuse of detained Iraqis, especially at Baghdad's Abu Ghraib prison, and stories of a few U.S. troops deliberately killing civilians cast doubt on the wisdom of U.S. forces occupying a country about which they knew relatively little. Controversy also developed over whether what the Bush administration called "enhanced interrogation" of prisoners was a euphemism for what others called "torture."

Contrary to the premise of the Bush Doctrine and neoconservative claims, regime change in Iraq produced neither a stable nor a pro-American Middle East. Ever-growing Iranian influence within Iraq especially irked neoconservatives who had hoped the Iraqi invasion would be the first step toward a similar operation against Iran. In addition, the backlash against U.S. interventionism inflamed passions across the Middle East and made the policy of Israel, a U.S. ally, toward Palestinians more complicated than ever.

32-2f *National Security and Presidential Power*

Hurricane Katrina, slamming into the U.S. Gulf Coast region in late August 2005, prompted an intense controversy over national security on the home front. Local and state officials bumbled through the first serious post–9/11 emergency when the area around New Orleans experienced severe flooding and devastation. The Department of Homeland Security, presumably created to deal efficiently with threats, seemed unprepared. Although the White House would claim no one had "anticipated the breach of levees" intended to protect New Orleans from floodwaters churned up by hurricanes, videotapes later showed the president receiving precisely such a warning. Katrina exacted an especially heavy toll, including several thousand deaths, on the Gulf Coast's oldest, poorest, and African American residents.

What They Said

Debating Torture

In the wake of the 9/11 attacks by operatives of al-Qaeda, attorneys working in President George W. Bush's Department of Justice issued a series of advisory opinions that supported the legality of certain antiterrorist measures. One of the most controversial issues involved whether the use of various tactics for interrogating terrorists, especially "waterboarding," would violate a specific U.S. criminal statute that prohibited "torture." The Bush Justice Department, relying on a memorandum of March 14, 2003, drafted by John Yoo, a law professor at the University of California, Berkeley, offered a very narrow definition of what constituted torture.

> March 14, 2003
>
> Memorandum from John Yoo for William J. Haynes, General Counsel of the Department of Defense
>
> Re: Military Interrogation of Alien Unlawful Combatants Held Outside the United States
>
> [According to this legal analysis, torture] is not the mere infliction of pain or suffering on another, but is instead a step well removed. The victim must experience intense pain or suffering of the kind that is equivalent to the pain that would be associated with serious physical injury so severe that death, organ failure, or permanent damage resulting in a loss of significant body function will likely result.... In addition, these acts must cause long-term mental harm.
>
> Indeed, this view of the criminal act of torture is consistent with the term's common meaning. Torture is generally understood to involve "intense pain" or "excruciating pain," or put another way, "extreme anguish of body or mind." *Black's Law Dictionary* at 1498 (7th Ed. 1999); *Random House Webster's Unabridged Dictionary* 1999 (1999); *Webster's New International Dictionary* 2674 (2d ed. 1935). In short, reading the definition of torture as a whole, it is plain that the term encompasses only extreme acts.

In April 2005, Professor Yoo engaged in a debate over his views at Columbia University Law School. There, law professor Jeremy Waldron of Columbia directly challenged Yoo's position.

> [T]he restriction on torture is absolute, even in times of emergency. To sneakily mess with the definition seems to me a terrible mistake, and flies directly in the face of the absoluteness of the prohibition. There is a danger of turning the word torture into a technical, legalistic term. If someone is being half drowned, and we say it is not torture, torture becomes a legal term like "certiorari." The ordinary [U.S.] soldiers understand that they benefit from a convention framed in ordinary language terms. When we laid down an absolute prohibition on torture in human rights instruments, we didn't do so as an academic exercise. We laid down this law specifically to constrain us in the circumstances where torture would be a temptation, not in peacetime academia. Apart from the disgraceful discussion in Yoo's memo, you undermine the legal and military culture by changing the meaning of torture.

Professor Yoo stuck to the basic position he had outlined in his memorandum.

> The federal criminal statute prohibits torture abroad, but not cruel, unusual inhuman treatment. In a traditional war, we may not need intelligence information from captures because we can survey troop movements, but when we're fighting a non-state actor, probably the only way to pre-emptively stop an attack is to gain intelligence from captured operatives.

Professor Waldron, again, disputed such a view, especially in response to a question from the debate's moderator about the legitimacy of using any means necessary to obtain information from someone who knows about the whereabouts of a "ticking time bomb," the explosion of which would cause extensive loss of life. This often-used hypothetical question, Professor Waldron argued, was ... corrupt [as a matter of fact because it] supposes that torture is capable of getting accurate information. The war on terror is a war of information and intelligence. To think primarily in terms of TV scenarios of massively important pieces of information that we know are there is not realistic. The nature of the relationship between torturer and victim means that the victim will tell the torturer what the torturer thinks he wants to know.

> Also, the question assumes that somehow we have the people who are trained to torture, yet who will do it only in this one case. There will be a cadre of torturers sitting around looking for work. There will be a culture of torture developed, changing the politics, training and discipline of the CIA and FBI. Everything we know about torture from the 20th century is that it grows out of control. We unleash everything depraved and sadistic in human affairs. We need to think about the trauma to the legal system, of having it be known that we have concocted room for torture. Everything that's had its reference on respect for human dignity begins to totter and crumble under this response.

Q *What strategy does the Justice Department memorandum, as framed by Professor Yoo, employ to claim it is not endorsing torture?*

Q *How does Professor Waldron counter this strategy?*

Q *In the debate at Columbia Law School, how does Professor Yoo invoke the "realities" of the war on terror to defend the position outlined in his memorandum?*

Q *What, according to Professor Waldron, will be the real-world consequences of using interrogation methods that, by any use of ordinary language, amount to "torture"?*

Sources: (top) From March 14, 2003 Memorandum by John Yoo for William J. Haynes, General Counsel of the Department of Defense Re: Military Interrogation of Alien Unlawful Combatants Held Outside the United States. This is a public document, accessed at: https://www.aclu.org/sites/default/files/pdfs/safefree/ yoo_army_torture_memo.pdf (pp. 44–45); (bottom) From April 2005 debate at Columbia University between law professor Jeremy Waldron of Columbia and law professor John Yoo of the University of California, Berkeley on the definition of torture. Accessed at: http://expost.blogspot.com/2005/04/waldron-yoodebate-on-torture.html.

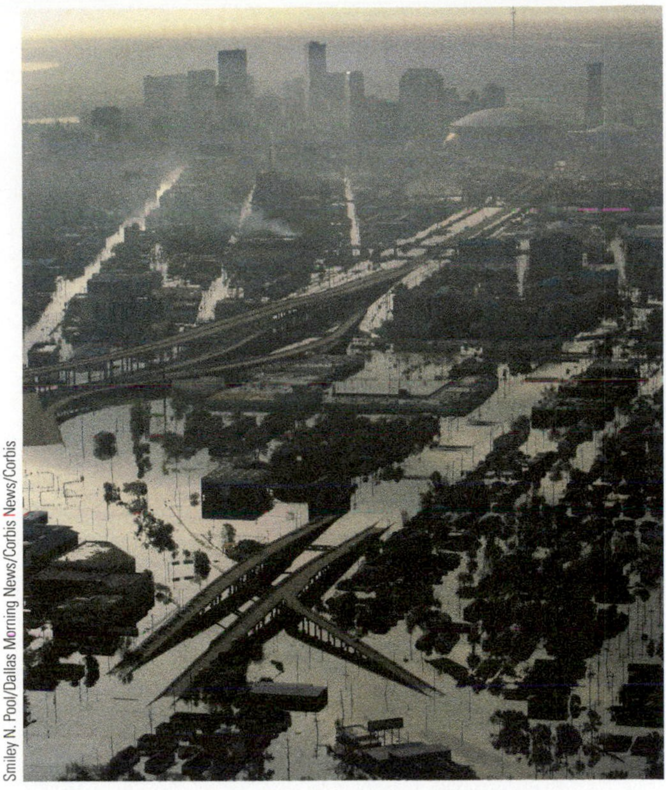

Smiley N. Pool/Dallas Morning News/Corbis News/Corbis

Jason Reed/Reuters/Corbis

32.5a (left), and 32.5b (right) **Hurricane Katrina Hits New Orleans, 2005** These photos provide bird's-eye and ground-level views of New Orleans after Hurricane Katrina made landfall, and they highlight the domestic dimensions of "homeland security."

Q *How do the photos dramatize the devastation that befell the Crescent City and the challenges faced by those charged with devising an effective response?*

The Bush administration's limited response to Katrina departed from its usual preference for expanding the reach of the executive branch. Vice President Cheney and Secretary of Defense Rumsfeld, who had served in Republican administrations during the immediate post-Watergate era of the 1970s, pressed Bush to challenge congressional and judicial restrictions put in place in response to executive-branch overreach by Richard Nixon. Initially, when dealing with alleged terrorists captured overseas, especially in Afghanistan, the Bush administration chose to operate outside both domestic and international precedents and detain captives at a new facility in the U.S. enclave at Guantanamo Bay, Cuba. Later, it devised special legal procedures for trying detainees, which the U.S. Supreme Court, on three separate occasions, declared unconstitutional. The Bush administration bypassed the Foreign Intelligence Surveillance Act of 1978 (FISA), which mandated special procedures before undertaking domestic wiretaps, until it and Congress agreed on revisions to FISA that granted surveillance agencies broader power to monitor communication networks in the name of safeguarding national security. The Bush administration also convinced Congress to renew the Patriot Act, which otherwise would have automatically expired in 2006.

Personnel changes in Washington drained some of the discord from the issues of war and presidential power during the final years of the Bush presidency. In late 2006, Bush named Robert Gates, a resourceful bureaucratic manager, to replace the mercurial Donald Rumsfeld as head of the Department of Defense. Gates helped design a new strategy for Iraq: **the surge**. It temporarily increased U.S. troop levels and placed in command General David Petraeus, an expert on counterinsurgency warfare. Deploying U.S. troops more selectively, General Petraeus also stepped up training for Iraqi forces and ramped up payments to tribal leaders in exchange for their political cooperation. The surge strategy reduced the level of civil violence and decreased political tension within Iraq as Bush prepared to leave office and began drawing down U.S. troop levels.

32-2g *Divisions over Foreign Policy Direction*

By the end of Bush's presidency, the wars in Afghanistan and Iraq had claimed the lives of nearly 5,000 U.S. troops. Iraqi civilian casualties numbered, by the most conservative estimates, in the tens of thousands. The war against terrorism also took a toll on the physical and mental health of U.S. service personnel who survived. By the end of 2013, roughly half of those who had served in Iraq and Afghanistan had filed for permanent disability status. By 2008, the ongoing occupation of Iraq was costing the United States $6 billion per month. George W. Bush, once a critic of "nation-building" projects, had embarked in Iraq on just such an effort, the largest in the history of the United States. With Americans deeply divided over the justification for the invasion and the conduct of the occupation, popular approval of Bush dropped below 30 percent. This backlash against Bush helped the Democratic Party capture control of Congress in the midterm elections of November 2006.

Democratic critics, looking toward the election of 2008, articulated a foreign policy agenda that repudiated the Bush administration's neoconservative blueprint in favor of new approaches. They advocated a timetable for removing U.S. combat troops from Iraq, a renewed military and diplomatic effort to stabilize Afghanistan, and a clearer focus on al-Qaeda, which seemed increasingly entrenched in remote areas of Pakistan and Yemen. Critics also urged moving away from the military emphasis of the Bush years. In their view, Bush's unilateralism had neglected threats to national security that required international cooperation, such as securing loose stockpiles of nuclear material before they fell into the hands of terrorists.

Another threat, according to most scientists, involved human-made climate change. Republican neoconservatives opposed the Kyoto Protocol, under which nations would agree to curb emissions that contributed to global warming. Members of the Bush administration joined most other Republicans in rejecting the scientific case for climate change, and they objected to emission-reduction targets that did not apply evenhandedly to developed and developing nations. After a Republican-dominated Senate rejected the Kyoto Protocol, prominent Democrats, such as the former vice president, Al Gore, continued to highlight the dangers of climate change and advocate rejoining the international forums working on the issue. They also pressed for development of "green energy" sources that would both lessen U.S. reliance on supplies of oil from the Middle East and help reduce carbon output.

32-3 Toward the Great Recession: The Economy, 1993–2008

What forces fueled the various economic bubbles from the late 1990s to 2008? How did governmental officials respond to the financial meltdown of 2008 and the Great Recession?

In 2003, the Nobel Prize–winning economist Robert Lucas credited his generation with effectively mastering the "central problem of depression-prevention." He spoke for those who believed that the U.S. economy was enjoying "The Great Moderation," an economy that was shedding burdensome governmental regulation and would no longer face the extremes of boom and bust. At times, the economy might not perform to its optimum level, but downturns would be temporary—and moderate. This conviction dominated economic thought and policy-making during the 1990s and the early years of the 21st century. Then, beginning in 2006, the American economy reached the high point of what, in retrospect, was an economic-financial bubble that helped conceal other, dismal economic trends. During the Bush presidency, for example, the economy gained only about 3 million new jobs, a fraction of the total added during the 1990s. The Great Recession of 2008 loomed on the horizon.

32-3a *Financial Deregulation during the 1990s*

The financial sector had remained the most dynamic and exciting part of the economy throughout the 1990s (see Chapter 31). It produced roughly 30 percent of all domestic profits by the mid-1990s, and the people who worked in it gained a special aura. Talented college graduates, primarily but not exclusively men, increasingly sought the rewards and excitement associated with a financial career.

Robert Rubin, who accepted a huge pay cut when leaving Wall Street, assumed responsibility for coordinating the Clinton administration's economic policy-making. He recruited talented theorists and technicians and became secretary of the treasury in 1995. Clinton's economic brain trust concluded that the economy had outgrown the New Deal regulatory structure but still saw a limited economic role for government. If the economy were to continue growing, these New Democrats argued, Washington occasionally needed to mount activist rescue efforts both at home and abroad to ensure that problems remained moderate. They touted the 1995 effort that restored Mexico's financial and economic stability and one in 1998 that bailed out a shoddily run financial venture at home known as Long-Term Capital Management as examples of their preference for government rescuing rather than regulating.

The Clinton administration and the Federal Reserve Board under Republican Alan Greenspan disdained the financial regulations from the New Deal era. In 1999, Rubin supported Republican senator Phil Gramm's successful effort to repeal the Glass–Steagall Act (see Chapter 25). "We have learned government is not the answer," said Gramm. "We have learned that freedom and competition are the answers" in the financial world.

The Clinton administration also resisted regulation of new financial products for fear of hampering innovation. Using regulatory ideas of the 1930s, a Clinton adviser once quipped, would be akin to forcing modern tennis pros to play with wooden rackets. Advocates of "Rubinomics" thus sided with financial interests outside the administration that wanted to translate the faith in minimal regulation into congressional legislation. The Commodities Futures Modernization Act of 2000 prohibited Washington from regulating the new financial inventions called "derivatives" (see Chapter 31).

32-3b *Economics for a New Century, 2000–2006*

The administration of Republican George W. Bush surpassed that of New Democrat Bill Clinton in its enthusiasm for supporting deregulation and promoting financial innovation. Henry (Hank) Paulson, who became secretary of the treasury in 2006, was another alumnus of Wall Street. Just before joining the Bush administration, Paulson had successfully pressed federal regulators to exempt the five largest investment houses, including his own Goldman Sachs, from a rule that required investment firms to reserve a specific amount of capital to cover their debt obligations. This move dramatically increased the capacity of these five firms to borrow money and, consequently, to speculate in risky investments.

Critics of deregulation noted early signs of trouble. During 2002, several fraud-plagued firms fell into bankruptcy. The most spectacular case involved Enron, a Texas-based energy firm with close ties to members of the Bush administration. The absence of effective regulation had allowed the company to engage in legally suspect speculation and in clearly illegal bookkeeping that lifted its profits to fictional heights. Congress responded with the Sarbanes-Oxley Act of 2002, designed to prevent publicly traded companies from fraudulently reporting their financial condition as Enron and others had done.

Systemic problems also plagued the real estate sector. The Bush administration had quickly abandoned its predecessor's commitment to a small federal deficit, but it doubled down on promoting homeownership. Owning a home supposedly increased people's ties to their communities and provided a rock-solid financial investment. Bush touted the importance of an "ownership society," and his administration encouraged financial institutions to help low- and moderate-income homebuyers. By 2006, nearly 70 percent of households lived in their own homes, an all-time high.

The nation, however, became increasingly caught up in an unsustainable **housing bubble**. Why? First, as more buyers entered the housing market, home prices moved upward and then skyrocketed. Many people who desired—and were being urged—to become homeowners simply lacked household incomes that could handle a conventional mortgage.

Second, the home lending industry devised an array of "nonconventional" mortgages for people whose incomes or credit histories disqualified them from obtaining a fixed rate loan. By 2006, far too many new loans involved **subprime mortgages**, meaning that they carried a high risk of default. In 2001, less than 10 percent of home mortgages qualified as less than prime quality. In contrast, 40 percent of the new loans processed between 2001 and 2006 fell into this category.

Third, problems extended beyond subprime mortgages. People with houses whose market value had dramatically increased could refinance their existing mortgage at a lower interest rate. As if by magic, refinancing on the basis of the higher valuation gave them more money to spend. Mortgage refinancing helped stimulate overall economic activity but also created mortgage holders who would, if the economy faltered, be unable to meet their payments.

Fourth, people at the commanding heights of the financial system worked overtime to boost the residential housing market. They recognized that the home-buying and homebuilding industries were the primary engines driving the U.S., and even much of the world, economy. The Federal Reserve Board, under Alan Greenspan (who began a fifth term in 2002) and his successor Ben Bernanke (who took over in 2006), pegged interest rates at historic lows. This kept relatively "cheap money" flowing through the financial sector—and kept the residential housing market bubbling. Greenspan and Bernanke insisted, however, that economic "fundamentals" remained sound.

Finally, the giant firms at the top of the financial structure kept their optimistic risk assessments in place. Compliant investing services such as Moody's provided "low-risk" ratings for the mortgage-backed collateralized debt obligations (CDOs) that investment firms such as Goldman Sachs and Lehman Brothers were marketing as top-grade securities (see Chapter 31).

By 2006, knowledgeable observers detected a bubble about to burst. Lenders privately joked about offering "pick-a-payment loans" and dealing with "zombie buyers," whose newly minted mortgages were virtually certain to default. The fabled investor Warren Buffett of Berkshire Hathaway called mortgage-backed CDOs "financial weapons of mass destruction" and forecast trouble for the home loan industry: "Dumb lending always has its consequences."

32-3c *The Bubble Bursts, 2006–2008*

Buffett, long-hailed as "the Oracle of Omaha," proved prophetic. Beginning in late 2006, the rise in housing prices first slowed and, then, home prices headed rapidly downward. The financial industry soon fell victim to the housing bubble it had helped inflate. As loans went into default, the ripple effect cascaded into financial institutions overloaded with mortgage-derived securities. Credit stopped flowing, and economies throughout the world began to contract. As economic growth halted in most places in the world, future factory orders declined, and unemployment figures rose.

The Bush administration and the Federal Reserve's Bernanke sought to respond. First, the Fed extended massive financial assistance to the banking industry. Then, during spring 2008, Bernanke and the Treasury Department's Hank Paulson helped J. P. Morgan Chase acquire a rival Wall Street firm headed for bankruptcy but later allowed Lehman Brothers, another Wall Street stalwart, to collapse. The Bush administration and the Fed appeared to be signaling that a short-lived era of governmental rescue was over.

Almost instantaneously, a complete global financial meltdown loomed. In a massive sell-off, the Dow Jones stock average plummeted nearly 20 percent during a single week in early October 2008. People began draining cash from their savings and money market accounts. The world's financial system seized up, as it had done at the start of the Great Depression of the 1930s. The Great Recession had begun.

Bush's Treasury Department and the Federal Reserve responded to the immediate financial crisis. Paulson hastily designed a rescue plan, and Congress passed a revised version as the Emergency Economic Stabilization Act of 2008, enacted with greater support from Democrats than from Republicans. It included the **Troubled Assets Relief Program (TARP)**. Implicitly based on the principle that financial giants were "too big to fail" or to go through normal bankruptcy procedures, TARP empowered the Treasury Department, guided only by loosely defined rules, to spread $700 billion throughout the financial system to rescue Wall Street institutions.

32-3d The Politics of the Great Recession: The 2008 Election

Differences over how to respond to the downward spiral of the Great Recession dominated the 2008 political season. The presidential contest pitted septuagenarian Republican senator John McCain of Arizona against his much-younger senatorial colleague, Democrat Barack Obama, the first African American to run for the nation's highest office. The Democratic effort capitalized on a media-savvy campaign staff, an innovative fundraising operation, Obama's skills at oratory, and the unpopularity of the outgoing Bush administration. The Obama campaign also energized many of the movements, such as those opposing immigration restriction and favoring gay rights, which had become active during the early years of the 21st century. Many voters blamed Bush for the economic morass and viewed McCain, who admitted to knowing little about the economy, as lagging behind Obama in economic sagacity. Obama's campaign featured two words: "hope" and "change."

McCain's zigzag effort undercut his always-slim chances for victory. He distanced his campaign from the false claims that Obama had not been born in the United States (and therefore was ineligible for the presidency) and secretly practiced Islam. McCain's gamble in selecting Alaska's half-term governor, Sarah Palin, as a running mate mollified conservative Republicans, but her lack of experience proved an embarrassment, especially when compared to Obama's experienced running mate, Joe Biden.

Veteran pundits who personally admired McCain expected a close finish, but younger, Internet-based forecasters correctly predicted a fairly substantial Obama victory. Youthful voters turned out in record numbers. Voting by Latinos and Asian Americans also reached all-time highs. In contrast, the percentage of white Americans casting ballots fell slightly from that of 2004. Forty-three percent of this vote, a slight increase from what Kerry had gained four years prior, went to Obama. In addition to the presidency, the Democratic Party picked up seats in both branches of Congress and in many state and local races, especially outside the South (see Map 32.2).

32-4 Political Volatility in the Age of the Great Recession

Q *How did earlier political polarization continue to feed both hopes and fears during the administration of Barack Obama?*

With the economy suffering, Barack Obama entered the White House surrounded by conflicting sets of hopes and fears. His most fervent supporters foresaw a presidency that would respond to the Great Recession in much the same way that Franklin Delano Roosevelt had tackled the Great Depression of the 1930s. Obama, however, soon stumbled over what political scientists call the "Green Lantern Theory of the Presidency." According to this concept, presidential aspirants such as Obama, whose campaign had ambitiously promised "Change We Can Believe In," confronted the stark reality that presidents, unlike fictional Super Heroes such as the Green Lantern, cannot possibly translate their many promises into policies. Could a biracial leader, whose soaring rhetoric claimed there were not Democratic and Republican states but only "the United States," realistically hope to transcend the deep political polarization? Might a president who self-identified as African American significantly ameliorate the economic challenges afflicting other African Americans even as he was inundated by an outpouring of racialized fears about his own values and political agenda?

Some critics circulated preposterous charges. For example, his ultimate successor in the White House, Donald

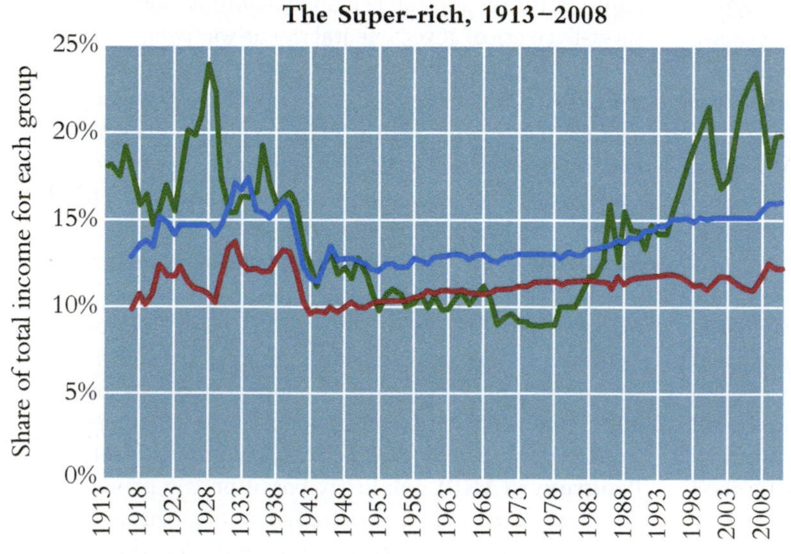

Figure 32.1 **Rising Income Inequality** Even before the financial crisis and Great Recession that began in 2008, income inequality had been on the rise. In 2007 the top 1 percent took in 23.5 percent of total pretax income, the highest level since 1928, while income even for the nearly wealthy, within the top 10%, stagnated.

Source: Thomas Piketty and Emmanuel Saez, "Income Inequality in the United States, 1913–1998," *Quarterly Journal of Economics* 118(1), 2003. Updated to 2011 at http://emlab.berkeley.edu/users/saez.

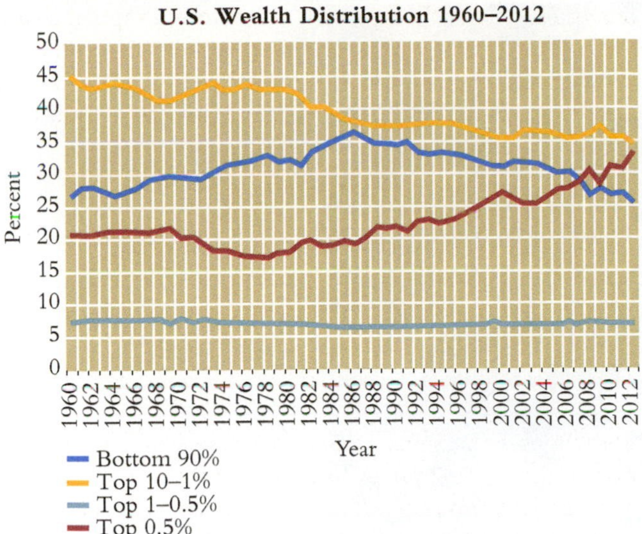

Figure 32.2 **U.S. Wealth Distribution 1960–2012** Economic changes since the mid-1970s rapidly increased the share of wealth owned by the top one-half of 1 percent of the population. As the share of wealth owned by middle-class and poor Americans stagnated or dropped sharply after the Great Recession of 2008, the share of wealth owned by the super-rich soared to Gilded Age levels.

Source: Saze and Zucman 2014

Trump, joined a chorus that continued to challenge Obama's citizenship and even insisted that he "show his records" to prove he had "deserved" entry to two Ivy League universities. Some extremists spread the view that the president was secretly practicing Islam and plotting to bring Sharia law to America. In such an atmosphere, President Obama invariably became cautious when trying to negotiate bipartisan public policy deals with Republicans in Congress. He also generally found it expedient to temper his rhetoric when addressing racial issues. His most eloquent speeches, for example, memorialized events from the past, such as the Civil Rights Act of 1964 and the "Bloody Sunday" attack in 1965 that led to the Voting Rights Act, the enforcement of which a Republican-dominated Supreme Court was seeking to hamstring.

32-4a *A Volatile Political Culture*

Barack Obama's administrative team displayed even greater diversity—and more star power—than had those of Clinton and Bush. The key position of secretary of state went to Hillary Clinton. Steven Chu, a Nobel Prize winner, became secretary of energy. Perhaps most crucially, Robert Gates, a Republican who had been a calming presence toward the end of Bush's presidency, agreed to remain as secretary of defense. The president's inaugural address urged the nation to tackle the current crises with "hope and virtue."

Obama's inclination to reach out to Republicans disappointed Democrats hoping for fundamental changes. The new administration's stance on counterterrorism, for instance, initially resembled that employed during the final years of the Bush presidency. After fierce opposition from Republicans in Congress, Obama set aside his earlier pledge to close the detention facility at Guantanamo and try terrorist suspects in U.S. courts. Civil libertarians found only minor differences between the broad legal-constitutional claims for executive power made by the Bush and Obama administrations. On the crucial economic front, Timothy Geithner, a Federal Reserve official who had helped devise the Bush administration's financial bailout of 2008, became Obama's treasury secretary, and the new president reappointed Ben Bernanke to lead the Federal Reserve Board.

In the Middle East, the Obama administration brought modest changes of emphasis. In Afghanistan and along that nation's border with Pakistan, it upped troop levels, placed increased reliance on air attacks by unmanned drones, and budgeted additional financial resources. It authorized an ambitious counterinsurgency effort against the Taliban modeled on the surge in Iraq, pressed the Afghani government to rein in corruption, and pressured Pakistani officials to move more determinedly against Taliban supporters in their own country. The administration, however, promised to withdraw troops by 2014 and continued Bush's troop withdrawal from Iraq.

In domestic policy, the Obama administration could claim some early victories: Senate confirmation of two Supreme Court nominees (Sonia Sotomayor and Elena Kagan), a law regulating tobacco products, an expansion of Bush's effort to bail out auto manufacturers, a measure extending land conservation policies, and yet another creating a "bill of

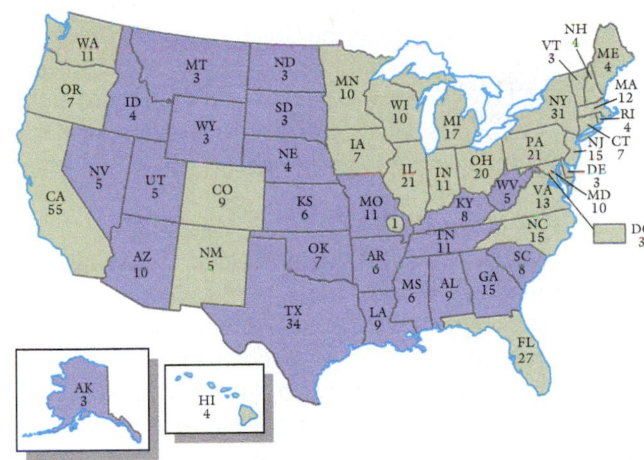

	Electoral Vote Number	Electoral Vote %	Popular Vote Number	Popular Vote %
Obama (Democrat)	332	67.8	69,456,000	52.9
McCain (Republican)	173	32.2	59,934,000	45.7

▲ **MAP 32.2 Presidential Election, 2008** The victory of Barack Obama over John McCain is illustrated in this state-by-state tally of votes in the Electoral College.

Q *How did the 2008 presidential election break from the regional pattern that had boosted George W. Bush to the White House (see Map 32.1 on page 894)?*

Q *What states did Obama carry that Al Gore had failed to win in 2000?*

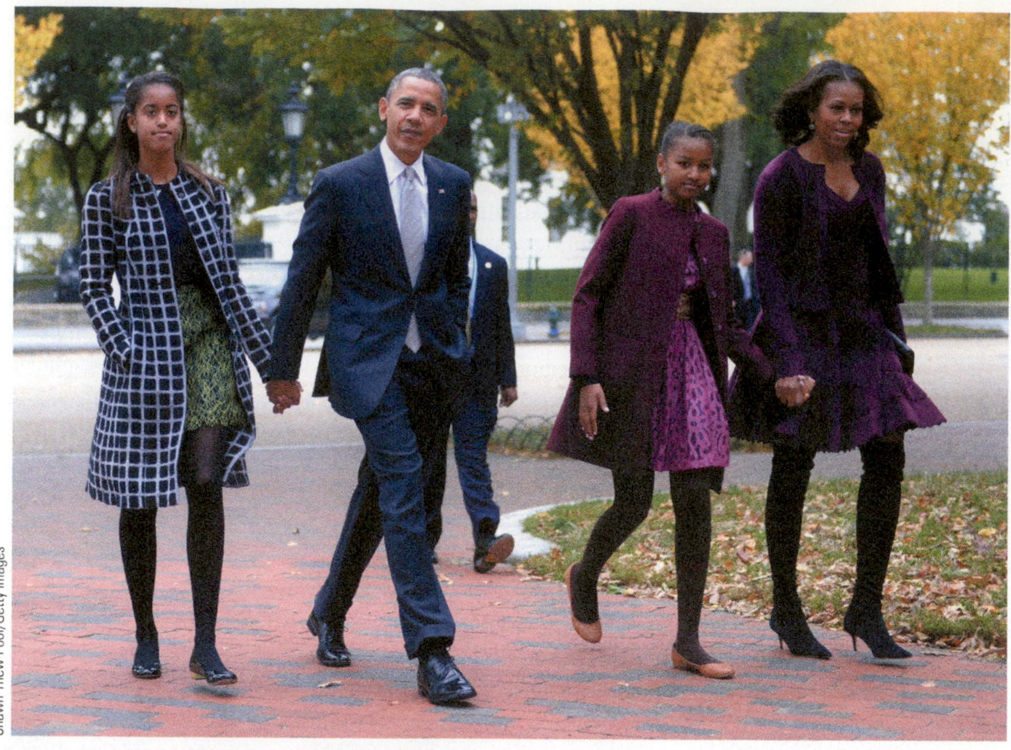

Shawn Thew-Pool/Getty Images

32.6 **The First Family, 2013** President Barack Obama walks with his wife, Michelle (right), and two daughters, Malia (left) and Sasha (second from right), through Lafayette Park to St. John's Church in Washington, D.C.

rights" for credit card holders. The American Recovery and Reinvestment Act of 2009, popularly known as "the Stimulus," provided $212 billion in tax cuts and $575 billion in new federal spending to combat the Great Recession. Only three Republican senators (and no Republican representatives in the House), however, supported this plan to stimulate the economy. A congressional measure to re-regulate parts of the financial industry also passed in the face of Republican opposition.

Months of negotiation between the White House and congressional Democrats finally yielded the **Affordable Health Care for America Act** of 2010 (ACA). Republicans revived the strategy used to derail the Clinton health-care plan 16 years earlier and unanimously opposed the measure. ACA's proponents, however, rounded up just enough Democratic votes to pass the law designed to extend, over time, coverage to some 30 million people. The ACA also expanded the Medicaid system, created mechanisms (called "exchanges") for increasing competition among insurance companies, and prohibited insurers from denying coverage to people with preexisting health conditions. Its most controversial provision required every American to carry health insurance. Critics charged that the ACA would surely cost much more than official estimates, endanger the Medicare program, kill off jobs, and create uncertainty throughout the health-care system. The administration countered with studies showing it would save money and make health care available to all.

Taken together, these initiatives to curb abusive practices from Wall Street, generate new spending to reverse the economic crisis, and reform the health-care system slowed, but hardly stopped, the rippling effects of the financial meltdown and Great Recession. Unemployment continued to spread on Main Streets across America, inequality of income and wealth worsened, and anger grew that banks and mortgage lenders had received bailouts while many ordinary people lost homes, savings, and livelihoods (see Figures 32.1 and 32.2). The resentments simmering from the Great Recession would provide a backdrop to the increasingly volatile political scene.

The GOP's most conservative factions rebranded themselves as part of a "Tea Party" movement and threatened primary challenges to any Republican incumbent tempted to support White House initiatives. Pressed by Tea Party activists, the GOP increasingly portrayed Obama as a danger to fundamental liberties and accelerated the party's decades-long movement toward the political right. To the horror of economists supportive of Keynesian policies, Republicans rejected additional federal spending to stimulate a still-sputtering economy and insisted that cutting governmental programs and lowering the federal deficit should take precedence over programs for creating jobs and assisting unemployed workers. A familiar question resurfaced: Was government action the core cause of economic problems or a necessary part of their solutions?

An explosion in April 2010, of a BP pumping rig in the Gulf of Mexico—which took 11 lives and sent 62,000 barrels of oil a day spilling into the water and fragile coastal habitats—focused further debate over this contentious question. The White House immediately joined BP in devising a response effort, but environmental groups criticized Obama for having failed to change the regulatory approach of his predecessor quickly enough and for permitting BP to direct the cleanup. Republicans simultaneously criticized the president for overmanaging the federal government's response and for pressuring BP and the oil industry to change their drilling practices. The BP disaster exemplified how opposing narratives about the proper role of government played out in particular crisis situations.

The GOP ran squarely against Obama and his policies in the midterm elections of 2010. Tea Party leaders denounced Democrats as well as Republican "RINOS" (Republicans In Name Only), whom they considered insufficiently oppositional. GOP primary contests eliminated a number of Republican stalwarts in favor of Tea Party activists. Democratic candidates, especially those who had benefited in 2006 and 2008 from economic turmoil and an unpopular Republican president, found themselves burdened by a tepid economic recovery and their own embattled president. In contrast to 2008, many younger voters stayed home in 2010 while older ones, who tended to favor Republican candidates, turned out in higher numbers. Republicans linked Obama to continued high unemployment and federal budget deficits, legacies of the Great Recession that had begun before his presidency. As a result, the 2010 midterm elections followed a long-familiar pattern: The party controlling the White House and Congress almost always loses legislative seats.

The results of the GOP's well-funded electoral effort, however, exceeded the historical average. Republicans took control of the House of Representatives, cut into the Democrats' majority in the Senate, and gained more than 600 legislative seats and 20 gubernatorial offices in states throughout the country. A national political culture marked by extreme volatility would continue into a new decade.

32-4b *The Election of 2012*

The 2012 election season began almost immediately. As the Republican Party continued to move rightward, W. Mitt Romney struggled to gain its presidential nomination. The GOP's conservative stalwarts had long distrusted Romney's commitment to their views on issues such as abortion, taxes, immigration, and health care. Romney—a wealthy venture capitalist from a devout Mormon family with a long record of governmental service—sought to win them over by pledging a presidency that would scale back government regulations, slash taxes, expand the military, and erase the federal budget deficit through spending cuts. Seeking to mobilize the Republican base, Romney also advocated the immediate repeal of the ACA (what the Republicans derisively called "Obamacare"), termination of federal funding for Planned Parenthood, and elimination or reduction of the disaster relief programs of the Federal Emergency Management Agency (FEMA). He ultimately selected U.S. Representative Paul Ryan of Wisconsin, a conservative favorite, as his running mate. Republicans denounced Obama's presidency as "socialistic," and its fiercest anti-Obama spokespeople continued to fuel suspicions grounded in the president's racial heritage and to spread misinformation about his religious faith. The Romney campaign enjoyed lavish funding as a consequence of the Supreme Court's decision to strike down previous limits on political contributions in its *Citizens United v. Federal Election Commission* decision (2010).

The Obama campaign, which also garnered sizable donations, focused on several central themes. In addition to highlighting Obama's first term domestic achievements, it touted the killing of Osama bin Laden and the winding down of the unpopular wars in Iraq and Afghanistan. Democrats went on the attack, assailing Romney as beholden to ultraconservatives on social issues, such as abortion and contraception, and to the very wealthy on tax policy. Moreover, Democrats backed legislation favored by pro-immigration groups.

Republican strategists ridiculed statistical data that showed Obama was maintaining a solid lead and expected a Romney victory, but the president dominated the Electoral College vote and captured the popular one as well (see Map 32.3). The Romney campaign did best among white voters, especially men over the age of 50, while Obama won overwhelming majorities among African Americans, Hispanics, and Asian Americans. About 55 percent of women voters broke for Obama, and people between the ages of 18 and 29, who voted in record numbers, strongly supported the president. Prognosticators foresaw only more political turbulence in the days ahead.

32-4c *Contentious Times*

Indeed, seemingly unbridgeable differences affected a wide range of issues. When matters such as climate change, gun laws, or personal sexuality entered the political arena, disagreement over both underlying values and specific policies tracked "blue" (Democratic) versus "red" (Republican) divisions at the state, county, city, and even neighborhood levels. Increasingly, Republicans tended to live near other Republicans and Democrats near other Democrats, and people seemed inclined to discuss public issues mainly with those whose partisan preferences and sources of information approximated their own.

Similarly, Congress became more partisan than at any time since the 19th century. The GOP's commitment to scuttling the ACA, for example, prompted the Republican-controlled House of Representatives to take more than 50 votes on bills to repeal it, even though there was no chance the Democratic-controlled Senate would have concurred. Republicans in the Senate made the filibuster, once a relatively rare parliamentary maneuver, central to a larger strategy of blocking Democratic legislative initiatives and presidential appointments. House Speaker John Boehner, who sometimes seemed willing to bargain with the Democrats over various issues, including immigration policy, clashed with the Tea Party wing of his own Republican caucus. Even solidly conservative Republican senators and representatives now feared primary challenges from their political right more than general-election contests against Democrats. For their part, Democratic congressional candidates generally saw little to be gained from appealing to voters unlikely to vote a crossover ticket, a situation that only ratcheted up the polarization.

Win McNamee/Getty Images News/Getty Images

32.7 Presidential Candidates Debate, 2016 Donald J. Trump and Hillary R. Clinton face off, displaying vivid contrasts in themes and styles.

Q *What role have presidential debates come to play in the electoral system?*

Q *What roles have visual and social media come to play in shaping the images of candidates for popular consumption?*

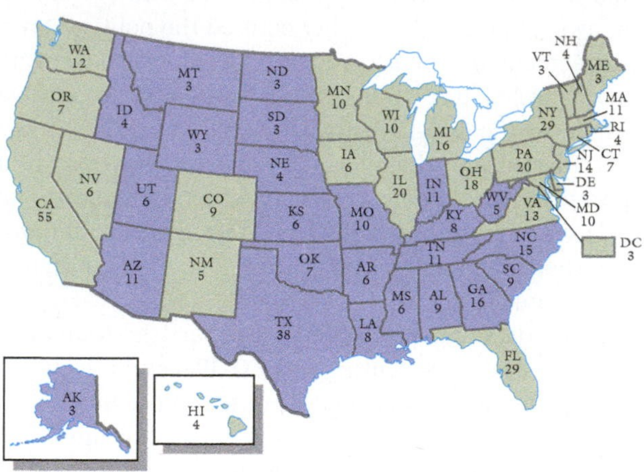

	Electoral Vote Number	Electoral Vote %	Popular Vote Number	Popular Vote %
Obama (Democrat)	332	61.7	62,085,892	50.6
Romney (Republican)	206	38.3	58,777,012	47.9

▲ MAP 32.3 Presidential Election, 2012

President Barack Obama won a second term by dominating the Electoral College vote. He also captured the popular vote.

Q *Why did many conservative Republicans, after looking at the results of the 2008 and 2012 elections, conclude that John McCain and Mitt Romney seemed identically flawed candidates (review Map 32.2 on page 905)?*

Q *Why might many have believed that their party's next presidential nominee should be an entirely different kind of candidate?*

Judicial politics followed the broader pattern of polarization. A 2013 Supreme Court decision that broke 5–4 declared a key section of the Voting Rights Act of 1965 (see Chapter 29) to be unconstitutional. This decision, rolling back an iconic Civil Rights measure, meant that nine states, eight of them in the now Republican-dominated South and all with a pre-1965 history of overtly discriminating against non-Caucasian voters, could now revise their electoral procedures without prior approval from the Justice Department. Chief Justice John Roberts argued that the forms of racial discrimination against which Congress had legislated in 1965 no longer existed, and Republican activists promoted the idea that states needed greater power to prevent people who were ineligible to vote from casting ballots. Democrats, by contrast, warned that racial discrimination at the ballot box could reemerge in new and less visible ways, and they refuted claims that voter fraud had become a serious problem.

Social and cultural conservatives also hoped for favorable rulings from the federal court system. In 2013, the U.S. Supreme Court disappointed conservatives when Justice Anthony Kennedy wrote a 5-4 majority opinion (*U.S.* v. *Windsor*) that struck down, as a violation of equal protection of the law, a key provision of the federal Defense of Marriage Act (DOMA, 1996) that had defined marriage as being between a man and a woman. This ruling cleared the way for the Obama administration to grant same-sex couples government benefits, including Medicare and Medicaid, on the same basis as traditional couples. By this same time, a majority of states were issuing marriage licenses to same-sex couples, and transgendered people were seeking equal access to public facilities in many cities and states. When the validity of a complete state ban against recognizing same-sex marriage came before the Supreme Court, though, conservatives anticipated that a 5-4 vote that would halt the LGBT momentum. Instead, Justice Kennedy wrote a 5-4 opinion (*Obergefell* v. *Hodges*, 2015) that declared, building on the principle of equality, the legality of same-sex marriage throughout the United States. The same egalitarian reasoning, legal analysts observed, would seemingly apply to any restriction of state and local laws that discriminated against LGBT people.

Legal controversies raged on, however, when the discrimination involved private citizens who resisted interacting with LGBT citizens in their daily lives. Here, the immediate legal-constitutional controversy focused on a Colorado baker who had refused, even after an order from his state's civil rights commission, to craft a cake for a gay couple's wedding celebration. Using his talents to honor LGBT people would force him, as an opponent of same-sex marriage, to violate his First Amendment Rights of religious freedom and free expression. LGBT advocates and most civil liberties groups supported the gay couple, fearing the long-term consequences for the cause of equality if this kind of discrimination, even when grounded in religious belief, could be leveled against a social–cultural group.

Debate over economic policies became another partisan flashpoint, especially after studies conclusively showed that the slow economic recovery from the Great Recession had been far more beneficial to stock prices on Wall Street and to the wealthiest 1 percent of the population than to the 99 percent of Americans below the super-rich category. Claims that such inequality represented the consequences of post-1970 economic policy (see Chapters 30 and 31) and merited redress, however, sparked debate that recalled—and also went beyond—that over the war on poverty of the 1960s (see Chapter 29). Were governmental policies the cause or the cure for some people falling behind economically? Were people without work or stuck in low-paying jobs deserving of taxpayer assistance, or were their own failings the primary cause of their situation?

Such questions prompted highly partisan controversy on unemployment insurance and the minimum wage rate. In 2014, for example, when Democrats in the Senate finally found enough Republican votes to break a filibuster against a bill extending payments to the long-term unemployed, the Republican leadership in the House declared it would not even consider such a measure. Similarly, calls for raising the federal minimum wage to $10.10 (the current rate of $7.25 had declined to less than $5 per hour when measured in constant dollars) won widespread support from Democrats but virtually none from Republicans. Neo-Keynesian economists cited models showing that a hike in the minimum wage would both benefit low-paid workers and, by boosting demand for goods and services, stimulate economic growth. Free-market economists countered with models depicting how a higher minimum wage would increase unemployment and generate renewed inflation; they continued to call for new tax cuts and reduction of the federal deficit as the path toward improving both workers' pay and the economy's overall health. The dynamics of hyperpolarization continued to revolve around the ACA. It had passed through Congress without a single Republican vote and had remained the object of constant partisan wrangling.

Controversies filtered down to state governments. Although the Supreme Court had upheld the constitutionality of the ACA's requirement that everyone be required to purchase insurance, the justices also ruled that the national government lacked the constitutional power to require states to participate in the act's expansion of Medicaid. Consequently, solidly Republican states, particularly in the South, refused to expand their Medicaid rolls. Some red state activists tried to leverage the broader constitutional logic of this ruling against federal power into claims that states could openly nullify federal mandates, especially those related to Second Amendment rights, gay marriage, and access to federal land. In addition, conservative constitutional lawyers pressed arguments that the First Amendment's free exercise of religion clause should bar the enforcement of the ACA's requirements for covering birth control and abortions on groups and corporations who asserted religiously based objections.

Partisan conflict spread to issues on which there had long been grounds for bipartisan votes. Republicans in the House, for example, threatened to revolt against the long-standing, across-the-aisle practice of preserving the nation's credit rating by raising the debt ceiling unless the White House backtracked on implementing the ACA. In the fall of 2013 they orchestrated a 16-day shutdown of many federal government operations in an effort to delay or suspend the health-care program. The parties finally reached an agreement on budget deficit reduction, but hopes for a "grand bargain" involving both spending cuts and revenue enhancements failed to materialize. The legislative machinery in Washington slowed down and, then, ground to a virtual halt. The 113th Congress passed fewer than 60 bills during 2013, and many Republicans hailed this record-low number as a positive sign.

Foreign policy issues added to controversy. Obama had rejected the Bush administration's controversial methods of "enhanced interrogation" that were tantamount to torture (see "What They Said"), but his national security team enhanced other Bush-era developments such as broad data sweeps to gather information about potential terrorism and remotely controlled drones to kill people designated as enemies. The "war on terrorism" continued to expand globally.

The post-9/11 increase in data collection by the CIA and the National Security Agency (NSA) became especially contested after Edward Snowden, a former NSA civilian contract employee, revealed a massive surveillance operation that extended from collecting the phone call data of ordinary American citizens to monitoring the communications of foreign leaders. In the wake of Snowden's 2013 release of classified documents, which recalled but dwarfed that by Daniel Ellsberg in the 1970s (see Chapter 29), investigators uncovered controversial practices of data collection and data mining. The Obama administration rejected arguments that

US Air Force Photo/Alamy Stock Photo

32.8 **A Revolution in Warfare** A remotely controlled Predator drone takes off from Balad Air Base, Iraq.

Q *The military vastly expanded drone capabilities. How might such new remote-controlled technologies change the nature of warfare?*

Snowden merited protection as a whistleblower, indicted him for espionage, and convened a presidential task force to recommend new rules for safeguarding privacy while still collecting massive amounts of information on the grounds of national security. Senators, however, learned that secretive CIA surveillance even extended into the halls of government; they discovered that the CIA had covertly monitored a Senate investigation into possible CIA involvement in the torture of suspected terrorists between 2002 and 2006.

Although the Obama administration continued to promise to withdraw military forces from Afghanistan, it also greatly expanded the use of drones, often directed from computer terminals in the United States, against suspected terrorists. Indeed, drones became favored weapons, and a special group within the Obama White House approved which people, including American citizens living abroad and deemed terrorists, merited inclusion on a "kill list." The administration defended drone operations as carefully targeted, while critics charged that the casualties often impacting innocent people near a drone strike might ultimately create more enemies. Opinion polls, however, showed overwhelming popular support in the United States for the use of drones as a substitute for American "boots on the ground."

Obama's foreign policy faced challenges on several specific issues. Republicans had been charging the Obama administration, particularly Secretary of State Hillary Clinton, with serious misconduct surrounding two September 11, 2012 attacks by Islamic terrorists in Benghazi, Libya, that took the lives of 4 Americans. Libya, however, was not the only country descending into chaos. A civil war raged in Syria, and as religious rivalries among different Islamic groups spread throughout the region, Iraq fell apart. A militant Sunni group gained control of Iraq's western regions even as regional Kurdish leaders assumed greater sovereignty in its northeast. Meanwhile, civil strife surged in Ukraine, where factions allied with Western Europe and with Russia faced off against each other and threatened to re-ignite the rivalries of the cold war. While some people called for greater assertion of U.S. power in such troubled regions, others argued that the complexities of multipolar alliances necessitated a measured assessment and response.

Uncertainty over the international situation rippled through an already bitterly partisan political season, one in which billions of dollars financed especially nasty campaigns. The midterm election of November 2014 suggested that a majority of voters were confused about contested issues or simply disgruntled by politics in general. The turnout fell under 40 percent, the lowest since 1940. People inclined to vote Democratic, especially younger people, sat out the election in far greater numbers than older, Republican stalwarts, reinforcing the pattern in which any party holding the White House stood to lose seats in midterm balloting. A wave of Republican victories resulted. The GOP took control of the U.S. Senate and padded its majority in the House of Representatives.

Debates over foreign policies, especially the U.S. role in the Middle East, only grew more heated after the midterm election. A group calling itself the Islamic State, a violent fundamentalist Sunni coalition, declared formation of a new Islamic "caliphate" based in eastern Syria and parts of northern Iraq. While the Islamic State seized more and more Iraqi territory, the Shia-dominated armies of the central government proved ineffective. Moreover, the Islamic State released videos showing the gruesome beheadings, including of western journalists, which shocked the world. President Obama announced an expanded air war led by the United States, more arms and additional training to local groups fighting against the Islamic State, and mobilization of international allies including those in the Arab world. Although he ruled out any formal re-introduction of U.S. ground forces into Iraq, he dispatched several hundred troops to "advise and assist" the Iraqi military and the Kurdish Peshmerga forces who were engaging fighters from the Islamic State. As this new war spread and grew more violent, partisan disagreements over Obama's Middle Eastern policies became more heated.

A framework for a nuclear deal struck between Iran and six world powers (the US, UK, Russia, France, China, and Germany), reached in April 2015, became what many policymakers considered the signature foreign policy achievement of Obama's presidency. The agreement lifted crippling economic sanctions on Iran in return for limits on Iran's nuclear energy program, which international powers feared was close to producing a nuclear weapon. Many Republicans attacked the agreement as tilting too far toward Iran, while supporters of the deal hailed it as proof that negotiation, rather than the kind of destabilizing war waged against Iraq in 2003, could stem nuclear threats. The wisdom of the Iran agreement would become a debating point in the 2016 presidential election.

32-4d *The Digital Domain of Liberty, Equality, Power*

Life during the early 21st century increasingly unfolded within a digitalized environment. Any institution, movement, or individual hoping to make a mark on the world did so by leaving digital footprints. The Internet, for example, increasingly influenced politics. One of the creators of the **social networking** service Facebook joined the Obama team early on and helped build the Internet-assisted operations that outperformed the digital campaigns of John McCain and Mitt Romney in 2008 and 2012. Similarly, the blueprint for health-care reform rested on a vision of creating a series of Web sites, headed by healthcare.gov, for enrolling people in new insurance plans; of digitizing all patient records; and of monitoring and sharing these records to facilitate greater efficiency and better patient care.

Celebrants of a digital future proclaimed that new technologies could forge networks that transcended the boundaries of time and space far more quickly and effectively than the best machinery from the old analog world. Undergraduates at Harvard University had created Facebook in 2004 to facilitate "linking up" with other students, and this venture quickly attracted wealthy investors from Silicon Valley and tapped sufficient advertising revenue to make its operations profitable by 2009. YouTube, developed by Silicon Valley entrepreneurs in 2005, offered a different social networking model. Its rate of growth, a measure of the popular desire to produce as well as consume visual imagery, was phenomenal, and Google eventually incorporated it into its empire. *Time* magazine, seeing the handwriting (or imagery) on the wall, selected You—all of the millions of people using networking sites—as its Person of the Year for 2008. By this time, well over a billion people were using the Internet to facilitate both their social and workplace lives.

The specter of a digitalized world worried some observers. They feared that Internet news and commentary only expanded the adversarial framework that had come to dominate cable TV news. They saw Internet "bloggers" preying on the legwork of journalists from print publications rather than doing original reporting. At the same time, online sites were luring readers from print publications and thus diminishing their value to potential advertisers. Losing readership and revenue, magazines and newspapers struggled to survive. Frequent Internet postings, moreover, seemed to be accelerating the already frenetic 24/7 news cycle. American politics was becoming "an almost minute-by-minute spectacle," growled an editor at one embattled newspaper. While voicing analogous concerns about the cultural impact of social networking sites, critics also feared that linking up digitally would obliterate traditional notions of privacy and threaten the safety of the young and vulnerable.

Champions of the Internet, however, praised it—and the larger digital environment—for creating new networks that could help people reimagine liberty, equality, and power. Freely shared and communally developed software might help liberate communication from corporate control. Interactive Internet sites might empower people and challenge hierarchical arrangements. Political activists as well as ordinary users might employ Web sites and networking services such as Facebook to evade traditional media gatekeepers. Internet journalists sometimes effectively took on traditional media commentators and spinmeisters for special interests. Networking sites helped reconfigure restaurant, TV, and motion picture reviews by aggregating responses from diners and audiences without special expertise in culinary or cultural artistry, a form of populist criticism that bypassed reviewing elites. Wikipedia supplanted hard-copy encyclopedias with a collaboratively written, ever-changing, and controversial source on virtually everything. Even history textbooks began to devise more participatory digital formats.

The most ebullient digital enthusiasts heralded the arrival of a new epoch in which older institutions and routines seemed outdated. The collapse—and extraordinarily expensive rescue—of much of the world's banking system in 2008–2009 encouraged digital visionaries to introduce "bitcoin." This digitized monetary system, operated independently of governmental regulators, brought concern and ridicule from financial experts who saw the theoretical and practical pitfalls of this peer-to-peer medium of exchange as insolvable. Bitcoin's libertarian-leaning supporters, though, argued that virtually every earlier digital enterprise, including Amazon and Facebook, had once faced similar scorn.

Digital outreach became an increasingly central—and controversial—part of political action. After a number of African Americans died at the hands of police officers across the country, for example, activists assigned social media a crucial role in creating a new national movement, Black Lives Matter (BLM). For BLM's youthful founders, creating a Twitter hashtag—#BlackLivesMatter—seemed the most obvious way to begin organizing a new movement against racial violence. Use of this hashtag exploded during the fall of 2015 after a grand jury in Ferguson, Missouri, declined to indict a white police officer who had shot and killed Michael Brown, an unarmed young black man. Social media became central to bringing activists across the country to protests in Ferguson, and "#Ferguson" ultimately became the most used social-issue hashtag during the first

Interpreting the Visual Past The Future of Print Media

This final edition of Denver's *Rocky Mountain News*—which appeared on February 27, 2009—offered a poignant and perceptive look at the past and present of newspaper publishing. This tabloid source of news and opinion, which had garnered four coveted Pulitzer Prizes during its final decade of publishing, accompanied many other newspapers around the country into oblivion.

As the arrival of the Internet transformed how people communicated with one another, the familiar medium of the newspaper lost its economic viability. People who wanted to obtain the day's news, sample political opinion, or survey evening entertainment options began firing up their computers rather than glancing at the printed page. Sports fans, especially, found that the morning sports page, long a major incentive for opening up a newspaper, seemed a pale imitation of what they could find on ESPN and its constantly expanding Web site.

Sources of revenue for newspapers steadily shrank. As print papers began developing their own sites in cyberspace, they found that they were "giving away" material that they were still asking print readers to purchase. Moreover, with fewer readers, newspaper publishers saw advertising revenues, the lifeblood of their business, dry up. The economics of publishing meant that most cities, even ones as large as Denver, could no longer support several newspapers.

Q *Look carefully at this page from the final day in the life of the Rocky Mountain News. How do the paper's publishers seek to tell, in prose, the story of a nearly 150-year relationship with Denver?*

Q *How does the visual composition of this page, which harkens back to a time when Denver was not yet a city and Colorado not a state, show that the Rocky Mountain News and the citizens of Denver were now living in a different era? What, for example, do you see running down the left-hand side of this re-creation of a mid-19th-century newspaper that you might see sprinkled through an early 21st-century Web site?*

ROCKY MOUNTAIN NEWS.

VOL. 1. CHERRY CREEK, K. T., SATURDAY, APRIL 23 1859. NO. 1.

1859 FINAL EDITION 2009

Goodbye, Colorado

IT IS WITH GREAT SADNESS THAT WE SAY GOODBYE TO YOU TODAY. Our time chronicling the life of Denver and Colorado, the nation and the world, is over. Thousands of men and women have worked at this newspaper since William Byers produced its first edition on the banks of Cherry Creek on April 23, 1859. We speak, we believe, for all of them, when we say that it has been an honor to serve you. To have reached this day, the final edition of the *Rocky Mountain News*, just 55 days shy of its 150th birthday, is painful. We will scatter. And all that will be left are the stories we have told, captured on microfilm or in digital archives, devices unimaginable in those first days. But what was present in the paper then and has remained to this day is a belief in this community and the people who make it what it has become and what it will be. We part in sorrow because we know so much lies ahead that will be worth telling, and we will not be there to do so. We have celebrated life in Colorado, praising its ways, but we have warned, too, against steps we thought were mistaken. We have always been a part of this special place, striving to reflect it accurately and with compassion. We hope Coloradans will remember this newspaper fondly from generation to generation, a reminder of Denver's history — the ambitions, foibles and virtues of its settlers and those who followed. We are confident that you will build on their dreams and find new ways to tell your story. Farewell — and thank you for so many memorable years together.

Rocky Mountain News

AFP/Getty Images/Newscom

32.9 **Final Edition, *Rocky Mountain News*, 2009.**

History Through Film *Selma* (2014)

Directed by Ava DuVernay
Starring David Oyelowo (Martin Luther King, Jr); Carmen Ejogo (Coretta Scott King); Tom Wilkinson (Lyndon Baines Johnson); Steven James (John Lewis).

Selma, which looks back to the grass-roots struggle for the landmark Voting Rights Act of 1965 (p. 807), took shape amidst the civil rights activism of 2013–2014. Oprah Winfrey, the famed African American performer-producer, joined forces with younger black artists, especially Ava DuVernay, to bring the project to fruition.

The first African American woman to win the best director prize at the Sundance Film Festival, for *Middle of Nowhere* (2012), DuVernay turned screenwriter for *Selma* and expanded an existing script that had concentrated on Dr. King's relationship with President Lyndon Johnson. DuVernay's revision featured a broad range of activists and sought to portray Dr. King as a "leader among leaders" rather than a larger-than-life hero. *Selma* forthrightly acknowledges Dr. King's personal shortcomings, especially those involving his wife, Coretta Scott King. And since Dr. King's family had licensed use of his speeches to another film project, DuVernay's *Selma* had to skillfully mimic his words while avoiding verbatim quotes.

A drama about events from the past, *Selma* bears the imprint of its own time. The very fact that a major motion picture was directed by a black woman with an extensive cast of African American actors spoke to the ongoing campaign to bring more women and people of color into the Hollywood system. In addition, work on this historical movie proceeded against the backdrop of a surge in civil rights activism. A movie about voting rights legislation, released in 2014, implicitly addressed the fact that a 5-4 Supreme Court decision, only the year before, had declared unconstitutional a key provision of the Voting Rights Act of 1965 (*Shelby County* v. *Holder*). And just as Selma was debuting in theaters, the killings of young African Americans at the hands of police officers in Ferguson, Missouri and New York City sparked protests and the Black Lives Matter movement. "Glory," the song that plays over the closing credits of *Selma*, pointedly links protests in Selma in 1965 with those in Ferguson in 2014.

Opening at a brisk pace, *Selma* immediately shows the major public obstacle to any progress on guaranteeing voting rights in the South—murderous opposition from white segregationist forces. The movie begins by depicting the 1963 bombing at Birmingham, Alabama's all-black 16th Avenue Baptist Church by members of the local Ku Klux Klan (KKK), an act that killed four young girls. After a longer second sequence in Oslo, Norway, where Dr. King receives the 1964 Noble Peace Prize, *Selma* transports viewers to its titled locale in 1965. Here in Selma, a third deliberately paced sequence shows a middle-aged woman, Anna Lee Cooper (played by Oprah Winfrey), patiently trying to become the first black voter in Selma. A white registrar scours her application form for trivial errors and then administers an impossible-to-pass "quiz" about public affairs. Mrs. Cooper can only watch as her humiliation ritual ends with a well-worn but freshly inked stamp rejecting her paperwork with a single word: "**DENIED**."

These three opening sequences establish the narrative structure of the movie. It proceeds to interweave sequences depicting the daily grind of civil rights activities with ones that show segregationists suddenly unleashing various forms of power in hopes of blocking efforts to achieve greater liberty and equality for African Americans. Most dramatically, *Selma* recreates the now-iconic clash at the Edmund Pettis Bridge ("Bloody Sunday"), a turning point in both the voting rights drive and this movie. A heavily armed force composed of white policing officials and KKK recruits brutally assault an inter-racial group trying to march from Selma to take their cause to the state capitol in Montgomery.

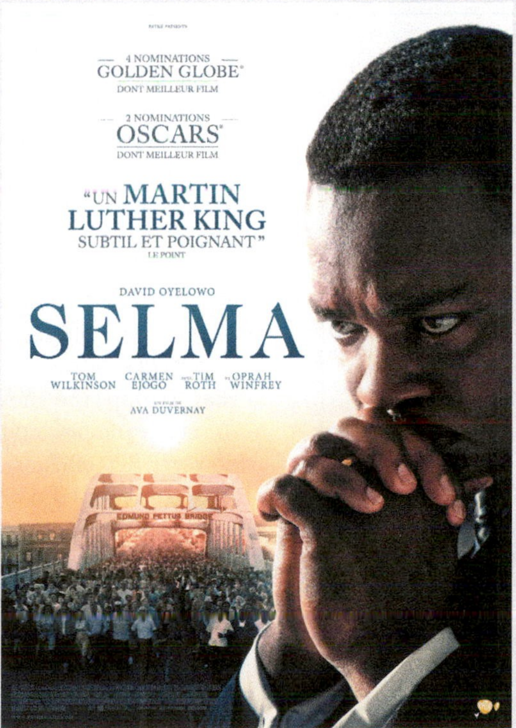

32.10 This poster highlights a major theme of *Selma* (2014): The reciprocal relationship between Dr. Martin Luther King (played by David Oyelowo) and the civil rights activists who joined him in March of 1965 at the Edmund Pettus Bridge.

Although memorializing Dr. King and the passage of the Voting Rights Act of 1965, *Selma* never descends into simple celebration. Partisans of Lyndon Johnson, for example, have criticized how the movie portrays a political leader who ultimately did provide crucial support for the civil rights movement. In declining to cast the historic Johnson as a heroic figure, however, *Selma* treats the president no differently than its primary protagonist, a civil rights martyr. This is a movie that offers a complex narrative in which everyone makes history within tangled webs of contending pressures and a complex mix of competing motivations. ■

ten years of Twitter's existence. The new visibility afforded by digital media brought other cases of police shootings under scrutiny and sparked a nationwide conversation about police practices, especially in communities of color.

For almost everyone, online connectivity through increasingly smaller devices and screens became ever more integral to daily life. Most people, especially those who had grown up in the digital world, seemed inclined to accept the collection, storage, and dissemination of digitized data on a massive scale as inevitable. What some called "Big Data" seemed a new and powerful source that could generate innovation but could also foster centralized control and threaten privacy and personal security. How might the digital domain remake the meanings of liberty and equality?

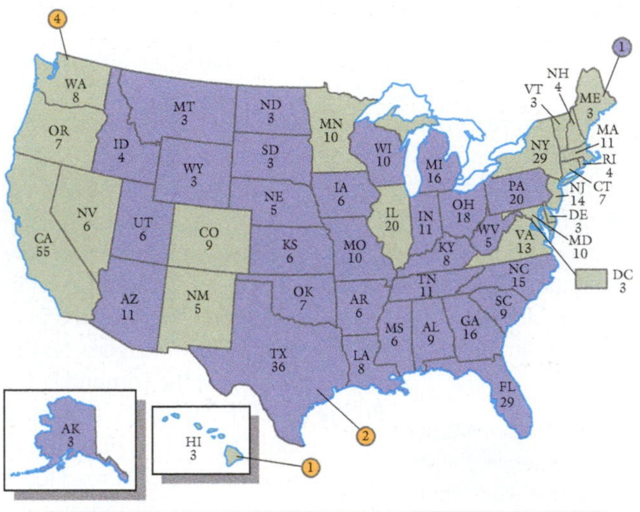

	Electoral Vote Number	Electoral Vote %	Popular Vote Number	Popular Vote %
Clinton (Democrat)	227	42.1	65,844,610	48.1
Trump (Republican)	304	56.5	62,979,636	46.0
Johnson (Libertarian)	----	----	4,489,221	3.2
Stein (Green)	----	----	1,457,216	1.0
Other* [Colin Powell (3), Faith Spotted Eagle (1), WA; Ron Paul (1), John Kasich (1), TX; Bernie Sanders (1) HI]	7	1.3	------------	----

*Seven electors defected and voted against the candidate they were pledged to vote for.

▲ MAP 32.4 Presidential Election, 2016

Democratic candidate Hillary Clinton won the popular vote by a solid margin, but Donald Trump became president because he gained the majority of electoral ballots.

Q *Compare this map with map 32.3 from the election of 2012. Which states did Donald Trump win that Barack Obama had carried four years earlier?*

Q *How did Trump's early presidential record compare to that of George W. Bush, another president who also failed to gain a majority of the popular vote? Consider both similarities and differences.*

32-4e *The 2016 Election of Donald Trump*

Social media increasingly intersected with the volatile political realm during the election season of 2016.

Hillary Rodham Clinton gained the Democratic nomination. She was a candidate with long experience in public life but also one with negatives that accompanied her high visibility as the spouse of a former President and as Secretary of State in the Obama administration. Clinton's march through the Democratic primaries and caucuses rankled critics who saw her as too cozy with large corporations and the financial industry. Many of these people rallied behind the presidential bid of Senator Bernie Sanders of Vermont, an independent who caucused with Senate Democrats. Sanders pressed an agenda that included government-funded health care and education for all. Clinton enjoyed strong support across the party spectrum, especially from women, but the challenge from Sanders and his "Bernie-ites" highlighted divisions within the Democratic Party that never quite healed.

Most political observers, who viewed Clinton's candidacy as a triumph of the inevitable, initially foresaw a similarly familiar candidate gaining the Republican presidential nomination: Jeb Bush, son of one former president and brother of another. Few imagined that Donald J. Trump, a real estate mogul and reality TV star without any electoral experience, would emerge from a crowded field. The entertainment-savvy Trump dominated center stage during raucous rallies at which he denounced "crooked Hillary," capitalizing on an FBI investigation into Clinton's emails that ultimately produced no indictments, and decried virtually every policy of the outgoing Obama administration. He promised to put "America First," particularly on matters such as immigrant restriction and trade policy. He dismissed critical media accounts of his personal and business past as either irrelevant or "fake news." Trump's campaign, featuring the slogan Make America Great Again (MAGA), largely bypassed the expensive TV-driven electoral strategy used by Clinton and, instead, hired digital companies with the expertise to gather data with which to target individual groups of voters through social media, especially Facebook and Twitter.

As the electoral season wore on, few pollsters recognized that Trump, the most unpopular presidential candidate in recent history, could possibly prevail. On Election Day, however, Republicans—especially whites living in rural areas, small towns, and outer-ring suburbs—turned out. Returns from crucial precincts in the key states of Michigan and Pennsylvania, which Obama had carried in 2008 and 2012, favored Trump and tipped the national contest in his favor. Despite Clinton winning the overall popular vote, Trump went over the top where it really mattered—the Electoral College tally (see Map 32.4). Republicans retained dominance in the House of Representatives and narrow control of the Senate.

In the aftermath of the 2016 election, evidence publicly emerged that Russia had undertaken a major covert operation, largely through social media platforms, to influence American politics. U.S. intelligence agencies and the Senate Intelligence Committee both issued reports concluding that Russian propaganda and cyberwarfare efforts, likely ordered by Soviet leader Vladimir Putin himself, aimed at dividing American voters particularly along ethnic and racial lines; undermining the U.S. alliance with Western Europe; and hurting Hillary Clinton, Putin's longtime foe. Meanwhile, cyber experts revealed exactly how fake Russian social media accounts, masquerading as American, had propelled targeted messages into circulation. Facebook ultimately made public thousands of Russian-originated postings designed to help Trump and promised future efforts to identify and disable fake accounts.

Russian involvement in the 2016 election begged a crucial question. Had the Trump campaign cooperated with Putin's effort to defeat Clinton? This question roiled the political world on almost a daily basis. In mid-May of 2017, Rod Rosenstein, a deputy attorney general in the Department of Justice who had been appointed by Trump, tapped Robert Mueller, a former FBI head, to lead a probe into the Trump campaign's possible collusion and into President Trump's possible subsequent attempts to undermine the investigation. During the first half of 2018, Mueller and the Southern District Court in New York charged 25 Russians with tampering in the 2016 election. They also leveled various kinds of related and unrelated charges against several of Trump's top campaign officials. These probes, gathering information through subpoenas served on people in the Trump network, widened to include possible election law violations and potentially illegal financial dealings involving Trump's family and friends and foreign interests. Explosive allegations of Trump campaign-related payoffs to silence women who were threatening to go public with charges of sexual affairs added to the legal drama associated with the 2016 election. People who hoped for a rapid end to the investigation headed by Mueller—both Democrats who sought clear-cut proof of presidential wrongdoing and Republicans who sought to terminate it—had to live with Mueller's cautious, deliberative pace. The political implications of Russian meddling and of possible financial shenanigans remained unclear as the midterm elections of 2018 approached.

During his first year and one-half in office, President Donald Trump's manner of governing proved as controversial as his election. Chaotic and dominated by the president's own seemingly unquenchable need for constant publicity, the Trump administration saw a dizzying rate of turnover in top advisory and cabinet offices. The president set forth policies through social media that often surprised even his closest aides. His tweets became famous for convoluted wording, contradictory assertions, and easily demonstrable falsehoods. Critics warned that the president's prevarications were undermining normal governing processes and fact-based policies, while his supporters applauded Trump's in-your-face volatility and barrages of anger directed against Democrats and what he called "fake news" from members of the media.

The president seemed to channel the anger of his Republican base especially on social issues related to race, feminism, LGBT recognition, and immigration. On these issues, which had been at the center of cultural politics for decades, Trump embraced a hard-right stance. At various levels of government Trump's appointees challenged rights-based agendas favoring voter registration, gender parity, LGBT equality, access to safe and legal abortions, and affirmative action—agendas that had changed American life since the 1960s and 1970s. Conservative legal strategists turned rights-based arguments away from concern for the less powerful and used them instead to bolster the rights claimed by religious conservatives and already powerful corporations and property holders. Meanwhile, Trump, a wealthy New Yorker who assembled a cabinet of millionaires and billionaires, continued to claim he was "draining the swamp" of special privilege. The president's opportunity to fill two new vacancies on the Supreme Court suggested that the nation's highest tribunal would support the conservatives' long-term social goals.

On two issues during Trump's first years in office, grassroots movements generally aligned with Democratic Party priorities became especially active. First, with many people outraged by the president's history of sexual improprieties, women who had experienced sexual harassment became emboldened. A movement using the hashtag MeToo quickly called out many prominent offenders in media, politics, and business. The range of MeToo charges and the resultant high-profile resignations heightened awareness of how the persistent sexual exploitation by powerful men afflicted women's livelihoods. Secondly, continued mass shootings—especially one in a public school in Parkland, Florida—raised grassroots concerns over the lax regulation of military style weapons and the power that the National Rifle Association (NRA) exerted in American political life. Activist mobilization and marches on these two issues—women's rights and stricter gun control—reached a scale not seen since the early 1970s, but the overall political impact remained uncertain.

On most domestic economic issues, President Trump generally followed the Republican Party playbook. He and congressional Republicans tried to repeal the Affordable Care Act, a signature program of the Obama administration, but the effort failed when Republicans could not agree on a replacement measure. They did, however, enact a bill providing a huge tax cut—primarily benefiting corporations and wealthy Americans. Other measures favored by the Trump administration boosted government spending on the military, began rolling back regulations on financial institutions and fossil fuel companies, and eased environmental restrictions and other governmental oversight functions. The anti-regulatory agenda and the large economic stimulus provided by the tax cut, coupled with the spending increases, further juiced the economy, which had remained strong during the transition from a Democratic to a Republican administration. Unemployment dropped to its lowest level since 2008, while the federal deficit grew.

Appealing to people who opposed the growing ethnic and religious diversity of American life (see Chapter 31), the Trump administration launched a series of efforts to "protect the nation's borders." In addition to seeking funding for a wall on the Mexican border, Trump banned entry of individuals from a group of mostly Muslim countries; ended the refugee status of particular groups, especially El Salvadorans whom the administration of George W. Bush had admitted after two devastating earthquakes in 2001; and stepped up deportation of people who lacked official documentation, even those who had been residents and taxpayers for decades. President Obama had created a special dispensation for so-called "Dreamers," who had arrived involuntarily as children, grown up in the United States, and showed no criminal record. President Trump threatened even the Dreamers with deportation. Their status, along with that of refugees, remained a highly charged but unresolved political and personal issue as the country headed toward the 2018 midterm election.

Trump's anti-immigrant nationalism fit seamlessly with his America First agenda, one that cast internationalism as a harm rather than a benefit. Trump met one-on-one with the leader of North Korea, Kim Jong Un, and with Vladimir Putin. The president also repudiated some of the key international agreements that Obama's administration had hammered into place. He withdrew the U.S. from creation of a Trans-Pacific Partnership, which had envisioned a zone of freer trade between the United States and nations of the Pacific Rim; from the Paris Agreement of 2016 on climate change, which had set targets for carbon reduction; and from the 2015 nuclear deal with Iran. He insisted that NAFTA be renegotiated or scrapped. And his administration also undermined bodies designed to stabilize and free up global trade by imposing selective tariffs on imported products. These actions, which unsettled a variety of multilateral frameworks including NATO, sparked tensions with traditional allies and shook the global order, which since World War II had been anchored by U.S. leadership based on the principles of internationalism and freer trade.

Conclusion

Three presidents, two of them Democrats and one a Republican, dominated national politics at the end of the 20th and the beginning of the 21st centuries. Bill Clinton's administration pressed a modest domestic agenda that moved the Democratic Party away from its "big government" image. It worked with Republicans to pare back the welfare system and supported economic policies that eliminated the federal deficit. As partisan polarization escalated during the late 1990s, however, Clinton's personal behavior ensnared him in legal investigations that led to an impeachment trial (but not a conviction) in 1999. The Bush administration's conservative agenda featured tax cuts, deregulation, overhaul of education practices, and an expensive prescription drug subsidy. It also converted the budget surplus left by Clinton into a rising federal deficit.

The U.S. economy enjoyed a lengthy period of sustained growth during the 1990s, but the early years of the 21st century produced a mixed picture. The financial industry continued to reap phenomenal profits, aided by a spectacular bubble in the residential housing market. In 2007, declining home prices and a wave of mortgage foreclosures rocked the financial sector, and the impact rippled quickly throughout the entire global economy. Although the Bush administration and the Federal Reserve Board, with more Democratic than Republican support, rescued the financial industry, the larger economy slid into the Great Recession, the worst since the 1930s.

Both Clinton and Bush tried to chart foreign policies for a post–cold war world. Clinton's internationalist policy deployed military power selectively and concentrated on measures fostering the globalization of economic relationships. After the terrorist attacks of 9/11, the Bush administration focused its unilateralist foreign policy on fighting a global "war on terror." The United States first invaded Afghanistan and then attacked Iraq, where it began the kind of expensive "nation-building" project that Republicans had once opposed.

The country's expanding economic distress and the growing unpopularity of the war in Iraq helped the Democratic Party regain control of Congress in 2006 and lifted its standard-bearer, Barack Obama, to the presidency in 2008 and again in 2012. While seeking to help end the Great Recession, the Obama administration began a phased withdrawal of U.S. forces from Iraq and then Afghanistan, revamped the domestic health-care system, and returned some greater degree of regulation to the financial system. But these moves were hotly contested and helped a Republican surge in the elections of 2014 and 2016. Political volatility grew, as Americans debated social policy, international relations, economic recovery, immigration, and race relations. Arguments became magnified by the rapidly changing forms of digital networks. The election of 2016, which brought President Donald Trump to the presidency, promised renewed and reconfigured debates over the meanings of liberty, equality, and power.

CHAPTER REVIEW

Review

1. What helps account for the polarization of national politics during the years between 1993 and 2008?
2. Why are the Clinton administration's foreign policies generally regarded as "internationalist"? How did the administration of George W. Bush, especially after September 11, 2001, seek to reorient Clinton's approach?
3. What forces fueled the various economic bubbles from the late 1990s to 2008? How did governmental officials respond to the financial meltdown of 2008 and the Great Recession?

4. How did earlier political polarization continue to feed both hopes and fears during the administration of Barack Obama?

Critical Thinking

1. Before the 1980s, Republicans had generally opposed expensive domestic programs and large deficits, which they identified with Democratic administrations. What factors help explain how, between 1980 and 2000, Republican administrations created large government deficits, while New Democrats offered their party as the guarantor of fiscal prudence? How did both the war in Iraq and the Great Recession of 2008 affect the situation?
2. How did Bill Clinton and George W. Bush, who espoused differing visions of government power and social policy, generate different popular followings? Why could Bush, who generally lacked the strong approval ratings of Clinton, greatly expand the authority of the presidency?

Identifications

Review your understanding of the following key terms, people, and events for this chapter (terms in bold in text are included in the Glossary).

William Jefferson (Bill) Clinton, p. 890
George W. Bush, p. 890
Barack Hussein Obama, p. 890
Great Recession, p. 890
Donald J. Trump, p. 890
Earned Income Tax Credit (EITC), p. 890
New Democrat, p. 891
Contract with America, p. 891
Temporary Assistance to Needy Families (TANF), p. 892
Richard (Dick) Cheney, p. 893
Bush* v. *Gore, p. 893
Medicare Prescription Drug Improvement and Modernization Act, p. 894
Roberts Court, p. 896
World Trade Organization (WTO), p. 897
Bush Doctrine, p. 898
National Security Strategy of 2002, p. 898
neoconservatives, p. 898
the surge, p. 901
housing bubble, p. 903
subprime mortgages, p. 903
Troubled Assets Relief Program (TARP), p. 903
Affordable Health Care for America Act, p. 906
social networking, p. 911

Suggested Readings

William L. O'Neill, ***A Bubble in Time: America during the Interwar Years, 1989–2001*** (2009), is a popular study by an academic historian. **Taylor Branch,** ***The Clinton Tapes: Wrestling with the President*** (2009), is a unique collaboration between a president and a designated historian-chronicler. On the "long election," see **Jeffrey Toobin,** ***Too Close to Call: The Thirty-Six-Day Battle to Decide the 2000 Election*** (2002). On George W. Bush, see **Peter Baker,** ***Days of Fire: Bush and Cheney in the White House*** (2013); and **Jean Edward Smith,** ***Bush*** (2016).

On the political stalemate of this era, see **Thomas E. Mann and Norman J. Orenstein,** ***It's Even Worse Than It Was: How the American Constitutional System Collided with the New Politics of Extremism*** (2016), and **Christopher H. Achen and Larry Bartels,** ***Democracy for Realists: Why Elections Do Not Produce Responsive Government*** (2016). On Bush's foreign policy, especially in Iraq, consult two books by **Thomas Ricks,** ***Fiasco: The American Military Adventure in Iraq, 2003–2005*** (2006), and ***The Gamble: General David Petraeus and the American Military Adventure in Iraq, 2006–2008*** (2009).

The story of the fiscal-economic crack-up can be followed in **John Cassidy,** ***How Markets Fail: The Logic of Economic Calamities*** (2009); **Simon Johnson** and **James Kwak,** ***13 Bankers: The Wall Street Takeover and the Next Financial Meltdown*** (2010); and **Andrew Ross Sorkin,** ***Too Big to Fail: The Inside Story of How Washington and Wall Street Sought to Save the Financial System—And Themselves*** (2010). **Michael Grunwald,** ***The New New Deal: The Hidden Story of Change in the Obama Era*** (2012), and **Michael Eric Dyson,** ***The Black Presidency: Barack Obama and the Politics of Race in America*** (2016) are early efforts at understanding the 44th president and his 2008 victory. A first-cut on the Trump presidency is **Michael Nelson,** ***Trump's First Year*** (2018).

Contrasting views of social media include **Tim Wu,** ***The Master Switch: The Rise and Fall of Information Empires*** (2010), and **Evgeny Morozov,** ***To Save Everything, Click Here*** (2013).

Appendix

The Declaration of Independence

The Unanimous Declaration of the Thirteen United States of America

When in the Course of human events it becomes necessary for one people to dissolve the political bands which have connected them with another, and to assume among the Powers of the earth, the separate and equal station to which the Laws of Nature and of Nature's God entitle them, a decent respect to the opinions of mankind requires that they should declare the causes which impel them to the separation.

We hold these truths to be self-evident, that all men are created equal, that they are endowed by their Creator with certain unalienable Rights, that among these are Life, Liberty and the pursuit of Happiness. That to secure these rights, Governments are instituted among Men, deriving their just Powers from the consent of the governed. That whenever any Form of Government becomes destructive of these ends, it is the Right of the People to alter or to abolish it, and to institute new Government, laying its foundation on such principles and organizing its Powers in such form, as to them shall seem most likely to effect their Safety and Happiness. Prudence, indeed, will dictate that Governments long established should not be changed for light and transient causes; and accordingly all experience hath shewn, that mankind are more disposed to suffer, while evils are sufferable, than to right themselves by abolishing the forms to which they are accustomed. But when a long train of abuses and usurpations, pursuing invariably the same Object evinces a design to reduce them under absolute Despotism, it is their right, it is their duty, to throw off such Government, and to provide new Guards for their future security. Such has been the patient sufferance of these Colonies; and such is now the necessity which constrains them to alter their former Systems of Government. The history of the present King of Great Britain is a history of repeated injuries and usurpations, all having in direct object the establishment of an absolute Tyranny over these States. To prove this, let Facts be submitted to a candid world.

He has refused his Assent to Laws, the most wholesome and necessary for the public good.

He has forbidden his Governors to pass Laws of immediate and pressing importance, unless suspended in their operation till his Assent should be obtained; and when so suspended, he has utterly neglected to attend to them.

Text is reprinted from the facsimile of the engrossed copy in the National Archives. The original spelling, capitalization, and punctuation have been retained. Paragraphing has been added.

He has refused to pass other Laws for the accommodation of large districts of people, unless those people would relinquish the right of Representation in the Legislature, a right inestimable to them and formidable to tyrants only.

He has called together legislative bodies at places unusual, uncomfortable, and distant from the depository of their Public Records, for the sole Purpose of fatiguing them into compliance with his measures.

He has dissolved Representative Houses repeatedly, for opposing with manly firmness his invasions on the rights of the People.

He has refused for a long time, after such dissolutions, to cause others to be elected; whereby the Legislative Powers, incapable of Annihilation, have returned to the People at large for their exercise; the State remaining in the mean time exposed to all the dangers of invasion from without, and convulsions within.

He has endeavoured to prevent the Population of these States; for that purpose obstructing the Laws for Naturalization of Foreigners; refusing to pass others to encourage their migrations hither, and raising the conditions of new Appropriations of Lands.

He has obstructed the Administration of Justice, by refusing his Assent to Laws for establishing Judiciary Powers.

He has made Judges dependent on his Will alone, for the tenure of their offices, and the amount and payment of their salaries.

He has erected a multitude of New Offices, and sent hither swarms of Officers to harass our People, and eat out their substance.

He has kept among us, in times of peace, Standing Armies without the Consent of our legislatures.

He has affected to render the Military independent of and superior to the Civil Power.

He has combined with others to subject us to a jurisdiction foreign to our constitution, and unacknowledged by our laws; giving his Assent to their Acts of pretended Legislation: For Quartering large bodies of armed troops among us: For protecting them, by a mock Trial, from Punishment for any Murders which they should commit on the Inhabitants of these States: For cutting off our Trade with all parts of the world: For imposing Taxes on us without our Consent: For depriving us in many cases, of the benefits of Trial by Jury: For transporting us beyond Seas to be tried for pretended offences: For abolishing the free System of English Laws in a neighbouring

Province, establishing therein an Arbitrary government, and enlarging its Boundaries so as to render it at once an example and fit instrument for introducing the same absolute rule into these Colonies: For taking away our Charters, abolishing our most valuable Laws, and altering fundamentally the Forms of our Governments: For suspending our own Legislatures, and declaring themselves invested with Power to legislate for us in all cases whatsoever.

He has abdicated Government here, by declaring us out of his Protection, and waging War against us.

He has plundered our seas, ravaged our Coasts, burnt our towns, and destroyed the lives of our people.

He is at this time transporting large Armies of foreign Mercenaries to compleat the works of death, desolation and tyranny, already begun with circumstances of Cruelty and perfidy scarcely paralleled in the most barbarous ages, and totally unworthy the Head of a civilized nation.

He has constrained our fellow Citizens taken Captive on the high Seas to bear Arms against their Country, to become the executioners of their friends and Brethren, or to fall themselves by their Hands.

He has excited domestic insurrections amongst us, and has endeavoured to bring on the inhabitants of our frontiers, the merciless Indian Savages, whose known rule of warfare, is an undistinguished destruction of all ages, sexes and conditions.

In every stage of these Oppressions We have Petitioned for Redress in the most humble terms: Our repeated Petitions have been answered only by repeated injury. A Prince, whose character is thus marked by every act which may define a Tyrant, is unfit to be the ruler of a free People.

Nor have We been wanting in attentions to our British brethren. We have warned them from time to time of attempts by their legislature to extend an unwarrantable jurisdiction over us. We have reminded them of the circumstances of our emigration and settlement here. We have appealed to their native justice and magnanimity, and we have conjured them by the ties of our common kindred to disavow these usurpations, which, would inevitably interrupt our connections and correspondence. They too have been deaf to the voice of justice and of consanguinity. We must, therefore, acquiesce in the necessity, which denounces our Separation, and hold them, as we hold the rest of mankind, Enemies in War, in Peace Friends.

We, therefore, the Representatives of the United States of America, in General Congress, Assembled, appealing to the Supreme Judge of the world for the rectitude of our intentions, do, in the Name, and by Authority of the good People of these Colonies, solemnly publish and declare, That these United Colonies are, and of Right ought to be Free and Independent States; that they are Absolved from all Allegiance to the British Crown, and that all political connection between them and the State of Great Britain, is and ought to be totally dissolved; and that, as Free and Independent States, they have full Power to levy War, conclude Peace, contract Alliances, establish Commerce, and to do all other Acts and Things which Independent States may of right do. And for the support of this Declaration, with a firm reliance on the protection of divine Providence, we mutually pledge to each other our Lives, our Fortunes and our sacred Honor.

The Constitution of the United States of America

We the People of the United States, in Order to form a more perfect Union, establish Justice, insure domestic Tranquility, provide for the common defence, promote the general Welfare, and secure the Blessings of Liberty to ourselves and our Posterity, do ordain and establish this Constitution for the United States of America.

Article I

SECTION 1. All legislative Powers herein granted shall be vested in a Congress of the United States, which shall consist of a Senate and House of Representatives.

SECTION 2. The House of Representatives shall be composed of Members chosen every second Year by the People of the several States, and the Electors in each State shall have the Qualifications requisite for Electors of the most numerous Branch of the State Legislature.

No Person shall be a Representative who shall not have attained to the Age of twenty five Years, and been seven Years a Citizen of the United States, and who shall not, when elected, be an Inhabitant of that State in which he shall be chosen.

Representatives and direct Taxes[1] shall be apportioned among the several States which may be included within this Union, according to their respective Numbers, which shall be determined by adding to the whole Number of free Persons, including those bound to Service for a Term of Years, and excluding Indians not taxed, three fifths of all other Persons.[2]

The actual Enumeration shall be made within three Years after the first Meeting of the Congress of the United States, and within every subsequent Term of ten Years, in such Manner as they shall by Law direct. The Number of Representatives shall not exceed one for every thirty Thousand, but each State shall have at Least one Representative; and until such enumeration shall be made, the State of New Hampshire shall be entitled to chuse three; Massachusetts eight; Rhode Island and Providence Plantations one; Connecticut five; New York six; New Jersey four; Pennsylvania eight; Delaware one; Maryland six; Virginia ten; North Carolina five; South Carolina five; and Georgia three.

When vacancies happen in the Representation from any State, the Executive Authority thereof shall issue Writs of Election to fill such Vacancies.

The House of Representatives shall chuse their Speaker and other Officers; and shall have the sole Power of Impeachment.

SECTION 3. The Senate of the United States shall be composed of two Senators from each State, chosen by the Legislature thereof, for six Years; and each Senator shall have one Vote.[3]

Immediately after they shall be assembled in Consequence of the first Election, they shall be divided as equally as may be into three Classes. The Seats of the Senators of the first Class shall be vacated at the Expiration of the second Year, of the second Class at the Expiration of the fourth Year, and of the third Class at the Expiration of the sixth Year, so that one third may be chosen every second Year; and if Vacancies happen by Resignation, or otherwise, during the Recess of the Legislature of any State, the Executive thereof may make temporary Appointments until the next Meeting of the Legislature, which shall then fill such Vacancies.[4]

No Person shall be a Senator who shall not have attained to the Age of thirty Years, and been nine Years a Citizen of the United States, and who shall not, when elected, be an Inhabitant of that State for which he shall be chosen.

The Vice President of the United States shall be President of the Senate, but shall have no Vote, unless they be equally divided.

The Senate shall chuse their other Officers, and also a President pro tempore, in the Absence of the Vice President, or when he shall exercise the Office of President of the United States.

The Senate shall have the sole Power to try all Impeachments. When sitting for that Purpose, they shall be on Oath or Affirmation. When the President of the United States is tried, the Chief Justice shall preside: And no Person shall be convicted without the Concurrence of two thirds of the Members present.

Judgment in Cases of Impeachment shall not extend further than to removal from Office, and disqualification to hold and enjoy any Office of honor, Trust or Profit under the United States: but the Party convicted shall nevertheless be liable and subject to Indictment, Trial, Judgment and Punishment, according to Law.

Text is from the engrossed copy in the National Archives. Original spelling, capitalization, and punctuation have been retained.

1 Modified by the Sixteenth Amendment.

2 Replaced by the Fourteenth Amendment.

3 Superseded by the Seventeenth Amendment.

4 Modified by the Seventeenth Amendment.

SECTION 4. The Times, Places and Manner of holding Elections for Senators and Representatives, shall be prescribed in each State by the Legislature thereof, but the Congress may at any time by Law make or alter such Regulation, except as to the Places of chusing Senators.

The Congress shall assemble at least once in every Year, and such Meeting shall be on the first Monday in December, unless they shall by Law appoint a different Day.[5]

SECTION 5. Each House shall be the Judge of the Elections, Returns and Qualifications of its own Members, and a Majority of each shall constitute a Quorum to do Business; but a smaller Number may adjourn from day to day, and may be authorized to compel the Attendance of absent Members, in such Manner, and under such Penalties as each House may provide.

Each House may determine the Rules of its Proceedings, punish its Members for disorderly Behaviour, and, with the Concurrence of two thirds, expel a Member.

Each House shall keep a Journal of its Proceedings, and from time to time publish the same, excepting such Parts as may in their Judgment require Secrecy; and the Yeas and Nays of the Members of either House on any question shall, at the Desire of one fifth of those Present, be entered on the Journal.

Neither House, during the Session of Congress, shall, without the Consent of the other, adjourn for more than three days, nor to any other Place than that in which the two Houses shall be sitting.

SECTION 6. The Senators and Representatives shall receive a Compensation for their Services, to be ascertained by Law, and paid out of the Treasury of the United States. They shall in all Cases, except Treason, Felony and Breach of the Peace, be privileged from Arrest during their Attendance at the Session of their respective Houses, and in going to and returning from the same; and for any Speech or Debate in either House, they shall not be questioned in any other Place.

No Senator or Representative shall, during the Time for which he was elected, be appointed to any civil Office under the Authority of the United States, which shall have been created, or the Emoluments whereof shall have been encreased during such time; and no Person holding any Office under the United States, shall be a Member of either House during his Continuance in Office.

SECTION 7. All Bills for raising Revenue shall originate in the House of Representatives; but the Senate may propose or concur with Amendments as on other Bills.

Every Bill which shall have passed the House of Representatives and the Senate shall, before it become a Law, be presented to the President of the United States; If he approve he shall sign it, but if not he shall return it, with his Objections to that House in which it shall have originated, who shall enter the Objections at large on their Journal, and proceed to reconsider it. If after such Reconsideration two thirds of that House shall agree to pass the Bill, it shall be sent, together with the Objections, to the other House, by which it shall likewise be reconsidered, and if approved by two thirds of that House, it shall become a Law. But in all such Cases the Votes of both Houses shall be determined by yeas and Nays, and the Names of the Persons voting for and against the Bill shall be entered on the Journal of each House respectively. If any Bill shall not be returned by the President within ten Days (Sundays excepted) after it shall have been presented to him, the Same shall be a Law, in like Manner as if he had signed it, unless the Congress by their Adjournment prevent its Return, in which Case it shall not be a Law.

Every Order, Resolution, or Vote to which the Concurrence of the Senate and House of Representatives may be necessary (except on a question of Adjournment) shall be presented to the President of the United States; and before the Same shall take Effect, shall be approved by him, or being disapproved by him shall be repassed by two thirds of the Senate and House of Representatives, according to the Rules and Limitations prescribed in the Case of a Bill.

SECTION 8. The Congress shall have power To lay and collect Taxes, Duties, Imposts and Excises, to pay the Debts and provide for the common Defence and general Welfare of the United States; but all Duties, Imposts and Excises shall be uniform throughout the United States; To borrow Money on the credit of the United States; To regulate Commerce with foreign Nations, and among the several States, and with the Indian Tribes; To establish an uniform Rule of Naturalization, and uniform Laws on the subject of Bankruptcies throughout the United States; To coin Money, regulate the Value thereof, and of foreign Coin, and fix the Standard of Weights and Measures; To provide for the Punishment of counterfeiting the Securities and current Coin of the United States; To establish Post Offices and post Roads; To promote the Progress of Science and useful Arts, by securing for limited Times to Authors and Inventors the exclusive Right to their respective Writings and Discoveries; To constitute Tribunals inferior to the supreme Court; To define and punish Piracies and Felonies committed on the high Seas, and Offences against the Law of Nations;

To declare War, grant Letters of Marque and Reprisal, and make Rules concerning Captures on Land and Water; To raise and support Armies, but no Appropriation of Money to that Use shall be for a longer Term than two Years; To provide and maintain a Navy; To make Rules for the Government and Regulation of the land and naval Forces; To provide for calling forth the Militia to execute the Laws of the Union, suppress Insurrections and repel Invasions; To provide for organizing, arming, and disciplining, the Militia, and for governing such Part of them as may be employed in the Service of the United States, reserving to the States respectively, the Appointment of the Officers, and the Authority of training the Militia according to the discipline prescribed by Congress; To exercise exclusive Legislation in all Cases whatsoever, over such District (not exceeding ten Miles square) as may, by Cession of particular States, and the Acceptance of Congress, become the Seat of the Government of the United States, and to exercise like Authority over all Places purchased by the Consent of the Legislature of the State in which the Same shall be, for the Erection of Forts, Magazines, Arsenals, dock-Yards, and other needful

5 Superseded by the Twentieth Amendment.

Buildings;—And To make all Laws which shall be necessary and proper for carrying into Execution the foregoing Powers, and all other Powers vested by this Constitution in the Government of the United States, or in any Department or Officer thereof.

SECTION 9. The Migration or Importation of such Persons as any of the States now existing shall think proper to admit, shall not be prohibited by the Congress prior to the Year one thousand eight hundred and eight, but a Tax or duty may be imposed on such Importation, not exceeding ten dollars for each Person.

The Privilege of the Writ of Habeas Corpus shall not be suspended, unless when in Cases of Rebellion or Invasion the public Safety may require it.

No Bill of Attainder or ex post facto Law shall be passed. No Capitation, or other direct, Tax shall be laid, unless in Proportion to the Census or Enumeration herein before directed to be taken.

No Tax or Duty shall be laid on Articles exported from any State.

No Preference shall be given by any Regulation of Commerce or Revenue to the Ports of one State over those of another: nor shall Vessels bound to, or from, one State, be obliged to enter, clear, or pay Duties in another.

No Money shall be drawn from the Treasury, but in Consequence of Appropriations made by Law, and a regular Statement and Account of the Receipts and Expenditures of all public Money shall be published from time to time.

No Title of Nobility shall be granted by the United States: And no Person holding any Office of Profit or Trust under them, shall, without the Consent of the Congress, accept of any present, Emolument, Office, or Title, of any kind whatever, from any King, Prince, or foreign State.

SECTION 10. No State shall enter into any Treaty, Alliance, or Confederation; grant Letters of Marque and Reprisal; coin Money; emit Bills of Credit; make any Thing but gold and silver Coin a Tender in Payment of Debts; pass any Bill of Attainder, ex post facto Law, or Law impairing the Obligation of Contracts, or grant any Title of Nobility.

No State shall, without the Consent of the Congress, lay any Imposts or Duties on Imports or Exports, except what may be absolutely necessary for executing its inspection Laws: and the net Produce of all Duties and Imposts, laid by any State on Imports or Exports, shall be for the Use of the Treasury of the United States; and all such Laws shall be subject to the Revision and Controul of the Congress.

No State shall, without the Consent of Congress, lay any Duty of Tonnage, keep Troops, or Ships of War in time of Peace, enter into any Agreement or Compact with another State, or with a foreign Power, or engage in War, unless actually invaded, or in such imminent Danger as will not admit of delay.

Article II

SECTION 1. The executive Power shall be vested in a President of the United States of America. He shall hold his Office during the Term of four Years, and, together with the Vice President, chosen for the same Term, be elected, as follows: Each State shall appoint, in such Manner as the Legislature thereof may direct, a Number of Electors, equal to the whole Number of Senators and Representatives to which the State may be entitled in the Congress: but no Senator or Representative, or Person holding an Office of Trust or Profit under the United States, shall be appointed an Elector.

The Electors shall meet in their respective States, and vote by Ballot for two Persons, of whom one at least shall not be an Inhabitant of the same State with themselves. And they shall make a List of all the Persons voted for, and of the Number of Votes for each; which List they shall sign and certify, and transmit sealed to the Seat of the Government of the United States, directed to the President of the Senate. The President of the Senate shall, in the Presence of the Senate and House of Representatives, open all the Certificates, and the Votes shall then be counted. The Person having the greatest Number of Votes shall be the President, if such Number be a Majority of the whole Number of Electors appointed; and if there be more than one who have such Majority, and have an equal Number of Votes, then the House of Representatives shall immediately chuse by Ballot one of them for President; and if no Person have a Majority, then from the five highest on the List the said House shall in like Manner chuse the President. But in chusing the President, the Votes shall be taken by States, the Representation from each State having one Vote; A quorum for this Purpose shall consist of a Member or Members from two thirds of the States, and a Majority of all the States shall be necessary to a Choice. In every Case, after the Choice of the President, the Person having the greatest Number of Votes of the Electors shall be the Vice President. But if there should remain two or more who have equal Votes, the Senate shall chuse from them by Ballot the Vice President.[6]

The Congress may determine the Time of chusing the Electors, and the Day on which they shall give their Votes; which Day shall be the same throughout the United States.

No Person except a natural born Citizen, or a Citizen of the United States, at the time of the Adoption of this Constitution, shall be eligible to the Office of President, neither shall any Person be eligible to that Office who shall not have attained to the Age of thirty five Years, and been fourteen Years a Resident within the United States.

In Case of the Removal of the President from Office, or of his Death, Resignation, or Inability to discharge the Powers and Duties of the said Office, the Same shall devolve on the Vice President, and the Congress may by Law provide for the Case of Removal, Death, Resignation or Inability, both of the President and Vice President, declaring what Officer shall then act as President, and such Officer shall act accordingly, until the Disability be removed, or a President shall be elected.[7]

The President shall, at stated Times, receive for his Services, a Compensation, which shall neither be encreased nor diminished during the Period for which he shall have been

6 Superseded by the Twelfth Amendment.

7 Modified by the Twenty-fifth Amendment.

elected, and he shall not receive within that Period any other Emolument from the United States, or any of them.

Before he enter on the Execution of his Office, he shall take the following Oath or Affirmation:—"I do solemnly swear (or affirm) that I will faithfully execute the Office of President of the United States, and will to the best of my Ability, preserve, protect and defend the Constitution of the United States."

SECTION 2. The President shall be Commander in Chief of the Army and Navy of the United States, and of the Militia of the several States, when called into the actual Service of the United States; he may require the Opinion, in writing, of the principal Officer in each of the executive Departments, upon any Subject relating to the Duties of their respective Offices, and he shall have Power to grant Reprieves and Pardons for Offences against the United States, except in Cases of Impeachment.

He shall have Power, by and with the Advice and Consent of the Senate, to make Treaties, provided two thirds of the Senators present concur; and he shall nominate, and by and with the Advice and Consent of the Senate, shall appoint Ambassadors, other public Ministers and Consuls, Judges of the supreme Court, and all other Officers of the United States, whose Appointments are not herein otherwise provided for, and which shall be established by Law; but the Congress may by Law vest the Appointment of such inferior Officers, as they think proper, in the President alone, in the Courts of Law, or in the Heads of Departments.

The President shall have Power to fill up all Vacancies that may happen during the Recess of the Senate, by granting Commissions which shall expire at the End of their next Session.

SECTION 3. He shall from time to time give the Congress Information of the State of the Union, and recommend to their Consideration such Measures as he shall judge necessary and expedient; he may, on extraordinary Occasions, convene both Houses, or either of them, and in Case of Disagreement between them, with Respect to the Time of Adjournment, he may adjourn them to such Time as he shall think proper; he shall receive Ambassadors and other public Ministers; he shall take Care that the Laws be faithfully executed, and shall Commission all the Officers of the United States.

SECTION 4. The President, Vice President and all civil Officers of the United States, shall be removed from Office on Impeachment for, and Conviction of, Treason, Bribery, or other high Crimes and Misdemeanors.

Article III

SECTION 1. The judicial Power of the United States, shall be vested in one supreme Court, and in such inferior Courts as the Congress may from time to time ordain and establish.

The Judges, both of the supreme and inferior Courts, shall hold their Offices during good Behaviour, and shall, at stated Times, receive for their Services, a Compensation, which shall not be diminished during their Continuance in Office.

SECTION 2. The judicial Power shall extend to all Cases, in Law and Equity, arising under this Constitution, the Laws of the United States, and Treaties made, or which shall be made, under their Authority;—to all Cases affecting Ambassadors, other public Ministers and Consuls;—to all Cases of admiralty and maritime Jurisdiction;—to Controversies to which the United States shall be a Party;—to Controversies between two or more States;—between a State and Citizens of another State;[8]—between Citizens of different States,—between Citizens of the same State claiming Lands under Grants of different States, and between a State, or the Citizens thereof, and foreign States, Citizens or Subjects.

In all Cases affecting Ambassadors, other public Ministers and Consuls, and those in which a State shall be Party, the supreme Court shall have original Jurisdiction. In all the other Cases before mentioned, the supreme Court shall have appellate Jurisdiction, both as to Law and Fact, with such Exceptions, and under such Regulations as the Congress shall make.

The Trial of all Crimes, except in Cases of Impeachment, shall be by Jury; and such Trial shall be held in the State where the said Crimes shall have been committed; but when not committed within any State, the Trial shall be at such Place or Places as the Congress may by Law have directed.

SECTION 3. Treason against the United States, shall consist only in levying War against them, or in adhering to their Enemies, giving them Aid and Comfort. No Person shall be convicted of Treason unless on the Testimony of two Witnesses to the same overt Act, or on Confession in open Court.

The Congress shall have Power to declare the Punishment of Treason, but no Attainder of Treason shall work Corruption of Blood, or Forfeiture except during the Life of the Person attainted.

Article IV

SECTION 1. Full Faith and Credit shall be given in each State to the public Acts, Records, and judicial Proceedings of every other State. And the Congress may by general Laws prescribe the Manner in which such Acts, Records and Proceedings shall be proved, and the Effect thereof.

SECTION 2. The Citizens of each State shall be entitled to all Privileges and Immunities of Citizens in the several States.

A Person charged in any State with Treason, Felony, or other Crime, who shall flee from Justice, and be found in another State, shall on Demand of the executive Authority of the State from which he fled, be delivered up, to be removed to the State having Jurisdiction of the Crime.

No Person held to Service or Labour in one State, under the Laws thereof, escaping into another, shall, in Consequence of any Law or Regulation therein, be discharged from such Service or Labour, but shall be delivered up on Claim of the Party to whom such Service or Labour may be due.

SECTION 3. New States may be admitted by the Congress into this Union; but no new State shall be formed or erected within the Jurisdiction of any other State, nor any State be formed by the Junction of two or more States, or Parts of States, without the Consent of the Legislatures of the States concerned as well as of the Congress.

8 Modified by the Eleventh Amendment.

The Congress shall have Power to dispose of and make all needful Rules and Regulations respecting the Territory or other Property belonging to the United States; and nothing in this Constitution shall be so construed as to Prejudice any Claims of the United States, or of any particular State.

SECTION 4. The United States shall guarantee to every State in this Union a Republican Form of Government, and shall protect each of them against Invasion; and on Application of the Legislature, or of the Executive (when the Legislature cannot be convened) against domestic Violence.

Article V

The Congress, whenever two thirds of both Houses shall deem it necessary, shall propose Amendments to this Constitution, or, on the Application of the Legislatures of two thirds of the several States, shall call a Convention for proposing Amendments, which, in either Case, shall be valid to all Intents and Purposes, as Part of this Constitution, when ratified by the Legislatures of three fourths of the several States, or by Conventions in three fourths thereof, as the one or the other Mode of Ratification may be proposed by the Congress; Provided that no Amendment which may be made prior to the Year One thousand eight hundred and eight shall in any Manner affect the first and fourth Clauses in the Ninth Section of the first Article; and that no State, without its Consent, shall be deprived of its equal Suffrage in the Senate.

Article VI

All Debts contracted and Engagements entered into, before the Adoption of this Constitution, shall be as valid against the United States under this Constitution, as under the Confederation.

This Constitution, and the Laws of the United States which shall be made in Pursuance thereof; and all Treaties made, or which shall be made, under the Authority of the United States, shall be the supreme Law of the Land; and the Judges in every State shall be bound thereby, any Thing in the Constitution or Laws of any State to the Contrary notwithstanding.

The Senators and Representatives before mentioned, and the Members of the several State Legislatures, and all executive and judicial Officers, both of the United States and of the several States, shall be bound by Oath or Affirmation, to support this Constitution; but no religious Test shall ever be required as a Qualification to any Office or public Trust under the United States.

Article VII

The Ratification of the Conventions of nine States, shall be sufficient for the Establishment of this Constitution between the States so ratifying the Same.

Done in Convention by the Unanimous Consent of the States present the Seventeenth Day of September in the Year of our Lord one thousand seven hundred and Eighty seven and of the Independence of the United States of America the Twelfth. In witness whereof We have hereunto subscribed our Names,

Articles in Addition to, and Amendment of, the Constitution of the United States of America, Proposed by Congress, and Ratified by the Legislatures of the Several States, Pursuant to the Fifth Article of the Original Constitution.

Amendment I[9]

Congress shall make no law respecting an establishment of religion, or prohibiting the free exercise thereof; or abridging the freedom of speech, or of the press; or the right of the people peaceably to assemble, and to petition the Government for a redress of grievances.

Amendment II

A well regulated Militia, being necessary to the security of a free State, the right of the people to keep and bear Arms shall not be infringed.

Amendment III

No Soldier shall, in time of peace, be quartered in any house, without the consent of the Owner, nor in time of war, but in a manner to be prescribed by law.

Amendment IV

The right of the people to be secure in their persons, houses, papers, and effects, against unreasonable searches and seizures, shall not be violated, and no Warrants shall issue, but upon probable cause, supported by Oath or affirmation, and particularly describing the place to be searched, and the persons or things to be seized.

Amendment V

No person shall be held to answer for a capital or otherwise infamous crime, unless on a presentment or indictment of a Grand Jury, except in cases arising in the land or naval forces, or in the Militia, when in actual service in time of War or public danger; nor shall any person be subject for the same offence to be twice put in jeopardy of life or limb; nor shall be compelled in any criminal case to be a witness against himself, nor be deprived of life, liberty, or property, without due process of law; nor shall private property be taken for public use, without just compensation.

Amendment VI

In all criminal prosecutions, the accused shall enjoy the right to a speedy and public trial, by an impartial jury of the State and district wherein the crime shall have been committed, which district shall have been previously ascertained by law,

9 The first ten amendments were passed by Congress September 25, 1789. They were ratified by three-fourths of the states December 15, 1791.

and to be informed of the nature and cause of the accusation; to be confronted with the witnesses against him; to have compulsory process for obtaining witnesses in his favor, and to have the Assistance of Counsel for his defence.

Amendment VII

In suits at common law, where the value in controversy shall exceed twenty dollars, the right of trial by jury shall be preserved, and no fact tried by a jury, shall be otherwise reexamined in any Court of the United States, than according to the rules of the common law.

Amendment VIII

Excessive bail shall not be required, nor excessive fines imposed, nor cruel and unusual punishments inflicted.

Amendment IX

The enumeration in the Constitution, of certain rights, shall not be construed to deny or disparage others retained by the people.

Amendment X

The powers not delegated to the United States by the Constitution; nor prohibited by it to the States, are reserved to the States respectively, or to the people.

Amendment XI[10]

The Judicial power of the United States shall not be construed to extend to any suit in law or equity, commenced or prosecuted against one of the United States by Citizens of another State, or by Citizens or Subjects of any Foreign State.

Amendment XII[11]

The Electors shall meet in their respective States and vote by ballot for President and Vice-President, one of whom, at least, shall not be an inhabitant of the same State with themselves; they shall name in their ballots the person voted for as President, and in distinct ballots the person voted for as VicePresident, and they shall make distinct lists of all persons voted for as President, and of all persons voted for as VicePresident, and of the number of votes for each, which lists they shall sign and certify, and transmit sealed to the seat of the government of the United States, directed to the President of the Senate;—The President of the Senate shall, in the presence of the Senate and House of Representatives, open all the certificates and the votes shall then be counted;—The person having the greatest number of votes for President, shall be the President, if such number be a majority of the whole number of Electors appointed; and if no person have such majority, then from the persons having the highest numbers not exceeding three on the list of those voted for as President, the House of Representatives shall choose immediately, by ballot, the President.

But in choosing the President, the votes shall be taken by states, the representation from each state having one vote; a quorum for this purpose shall consist of a member or members from two-thirds of the states, and a majority of all the states shall be necessary to a choice. And if the House of Representatives shall not choose a President whenever the right of choice shall devolve upon them, before the fourth day of March next following, then the Vice-President shall act as President, as in the case of the death or other constitutional disability of the President.—The person having the greatest number of votes as Vice-President, shall be the Vice-President, if such number be a majority of the whole number of Electors appointed, and if no person have a majority, then from the two highest numbers on the list, the Senate shall choose the Vice-President; a quorum for the purpose shall consist of two-thirds of the whole number of Senators, and a majority of the whole number shall be necessary to a choice. But no person constitutionally ineligible to the office of President shall be eligible to that of Vice-President of the United States.

Amendment XIII[12]

SECTION 1. Neither slavery nor involuntary servitude, except as a punishment for crime whereof the party shall have been duly convicted, shall exist within the United States, or any place subject to their jurisdiction.

SECTION 2. Congress shall have power to enforce this article by appropriate legislation.

Amendment XIV[13]

SECTION 1. All persons born or naturalized in the United States, and subject to the jurisdiction thereof, are citizens of the United States and of the State wherein they reside. No State shall make or enforce any law which shall abridge the privileges or immunities of citizens of the United States; nor shall any State deprive any person of life, liberty, or property, without due process of law; nor deny to any person within its jurisdiction the equal protection of the laws.

SECTION 2. Representatives shall be apportioned among the several States according to their respective numbers, counting the whole number of persons in each State, excluding Indians not taxed. But when the right to vote at any election for the choice of electors for President and VicePresident of the United States, Representatives in Congress, the Executive and Judicial officers of a State, or the members of the Legislature thereof, is denied to any of the male inhabitants of such State,

10 Passed March 4, 1794. Ratified January 23, 1795.

11 Passed December 9, 1803. Ratified June 15, 1804.

12 Passed January 31, 1865. Ratified December 6, 1865.

13 Passed June 13, 1866. Ratified July 9, 1868.

being twenty-one years of age, and citizens of the United States, or in any way abridged, except for participation in rebellion, or other crime, the basis of representation therein shall be reduced in the proportion which the number of such male citizens shall bear to the whole number of male citizens twenty-one years of age in such State.

SECTION 3. No person shall be a Senator or Representative in Congress, or elector of President and Vice-President, or hold any office, civil or military, under the United States, or under any State, who, having previously taken an oath, as a member of Congress, or as an officer of the United States, or as a member of any State legislature, or as an executive or judicial officer of any State, to support the Constitution of the United States, shall have engaged in insurrection or rebellion against the same, or given aid or comfort to the enemies thereof. But Congress may by a vote of two-thirds of each House, remove such disability.

SECTION 4. The validity of the public debt of the United States, authorized by law, including debts incurred for payment of pensions and bounties for services in suppressing insurrection or rebellion, shall not be questioned. But neither the United States nor any State shall assume or pay any debt or obligation incurred in aid of insurrection or rebellion against the United States, or any claim for the loss or emancipation of any slave; but all such debts, obligations, and claims shall be held illegal and void.

SECTION 5. The Congress shall have the power to enforce, by appropriate legislation, the provisions of this article.

Amendment XV[14]

SECTION 1. The right of citizens of the United States to vote shall not be denied or abridged by the United States or by any State on account of race, color, or previous conditions of servitude—

SECTION 2. The Congress shall have power to enforce this article by appropriate legislation.

Amendment XVI[15]

The Congress shall have power to lay and collect taxes on incomes, from whatever source derived, without apportionment among the several States, and without regard to any census or enumeration.

Amendment XVII[16]

The Senate of the United States shall be composed of two Senators from each State, elected by the people thereof, for six years; and each Senator shall have one vote. The electors in each State shall have the qualifications requisite for electors of the most numerous branch of the State legislatures.

When vacancies happen in the representation of any State in the Senate, the executive authority of such State shall issue writs of election to fill such vacancies: Provided, That the legislature of any State may empower the executive thereof to make temporary appointments until the people fill the vacancies by election as the legislature may direct.

This amendment shall not be so construed as to affect the election or term of any Senator chosen before it becomes valid as part of the Constitution.

Amendment XVIII[17]

SECTION 1. After one year from the ratification of this article the manufacture, sale, or transportation of intoxicating liquors within, the importation thereof into, or the exportation thereof from the United States and all territory subject to the jurisdiction thereof for beverage purposes is hereby prohibited.

SECTION 2. The Congress and the several States shall have concurrent power to enforce this article by appropriate legislation.

SECTION 3. This article shall be inoperative unless it shall have been ratified as an amendment to the Constitution by the legislatures of the several States, as provided in the Constitution, within seven years from the date of the submission hereof to the States by the Congress.

Amendment XIX[18]

The right of citizens of the United States to vote shall not be denied or abridged by the United States or by any State on account of sex.

Congress shall have power to enforce this article by appropriate legislation.

Amendment XX[19]

SECTION 1. The terms of the President and VicePresident shall end at noon on the 20th day of January, and the terms of Senators and Representatives at noon on the 3d day of January, of the years in which such terms would have ended if this article had not been ratified; and the terms of their successors shall then begin.

SECTION 2. The Congress shall assemble at least once in every year, and such meeting shall begin at noon on the 3d day of January, unless they shall by law appoint a different day.

SECTION 3. If, at the time fixed for the beginning of the term of the President, the President elect shall have died, the Vice-President elect shall become President. If a President shall not have been chosen before the time fixed for the beginning of his term, or if the President elect shall have failed to qualify, then the Vice-President elect shall act as President until a President shall have qualified; and the Congress may by law provide for the case wherein neither a President elect

14 Passed February 26, 1869. Ratified February 2, 1870.
15 Passed July 12, 1909. Ratified February 3, 1913.
16 Passed May 13, 1912. Ratified April 8, 1913.
17 Passed December 18, 1917. Ratified January 16, 1919.
18 Passed June 4, 1919. Ratified August 18, 1920.
19 Passed March 2, 1932. Ratified January 23, 1933.

nor a Vice-President elect shall have qualified, declaring who shall then act as President, or the manner in which one who is to act shall be selected, and such person shall act accordingly until a President or Vice-President shall have qualified.

SECTION 4. The Congress may by law provide for the case of the death of any of the persons from whom the House of Representatives may choose a President whenever the right of choice shall have devolved upon them, and for the case of the death of any of the persons from whom the Senate may choose a Vice-President whenever the right of choice shall have devolved upon them.

SECTION 5. Sections 1 and 2 shall take effect on the 15th day of October following the ratification of this article.

SECTION 6. This article shall be inoperative unless it shall have been ratified as an amendment to the Constitution by the legislatures of three-fourths of the several States within seven years from the date of its submission.

Amendment XXI[20]

SECTION 1. The eighteenth article of amendment to the Constitution of the United States is hereby repealed.

SECTION 2. The transportation or importation into any State, Territory, or possession of the United States for delivery or use therein of intoxicating liquors, in violation of the laws thereof, is hereby prohibited.

SECTION 3. This article shall be inoperative unless it shall have been ratified as an amendment to the Constitution by conventions in the several States, as provided in the Constitution, within seven years from the date of the submission hereof to the States by the Congress.

Amendment XXII[21]

No person shall be elected to the office of the President more than twice, and no person who has held the office of President, or acted as President, for more than two years of a term to which some other person was elected President shall be elected to the office of the President more than once.

But this Article shall not apply to any person holding the office of President when this Article was proposed by the Congress, and shall not prevent any person who may be holding the office of President, or acting as President, during the term within which this Article becomes operative from holding the office of President or acting as President during the remainder of such term.

Amendment XXIII[22]

SECTION 1. The District constituting the seat of Government of the United States shall appoint in such manner as the Congress may direct: A number of electors of President and Vice President equal to the whole number of Senators and Representatives in Congress to which the District would be entitled if it were a State, but in no event more than the least populous State; they shall be in addition to those appointed by the States, but they shall be considered, for the purposes of the election of President and Vice President, to be electors appointed by the State; and they shall meet in the District and perform such duties as provided by the twelfth article of amendment.

SECTION 2. The Congress shall have power to enforce this article by appropriate legislation.

Amendment XXIV[23]

SECTION 1. The right of citizens of the United States to vote in any primary or other election for President or Vice President, or for Senator or Representative in Congress, shall not be denied or abridged by the United States or any State by reason of failure to pay any poll tax or other tax.

SECTION 2. The Congress shall have power to enforce this article by appropriate legislation.

Amendment XXV[24]

SECTION 1. In case of the removal of the President from office or of his death or resignation, the Vice President shall become President.

SECTION 2. Whenever there is a vacancy in the office of the Vice President, the President shall nominate a Vice President who shall take office upon confirmation by a majority vote of both Houses of Congress.

SECTION 3. Whenever the President transmits to the President pro tempore of the Senate and the Speaker of the House of Representatives his written declaration that he is unable to discharge the powers and duties of his office, and until he transmits them a written declaration to the contrary, such powers and duties shall be discharged by the Vice President as Acting President.

SECTION 4. Whenever the Vice President and a majority of either the principal officers of the executive department or of such other body as Congress may by law provide, transmit to the President pro tempore of the Senate and the Speaker of the House of Representatives their written declaration that the President is unable to discharge the powers and duties of his office, the Vice President shall immediately assume the powers and duties of the office of Acting President.

Thereafter, when the President transmits to the President pro tempore of the Senate and the Speaker of the House of Representatives his written declaration that no inability exists, he shall resume the powers and duties of his office unless the Vice President and a majority of either

20 Passed February 20, 1933. Ratified December 5, 1933.

21 Passed March 12, 1947. Ratified March 1, 1951.

22 Passed June 16, 1960. Ratified April 3, 1961.

23 Passed August 27, 1962. Ratified January 23, 1964.

24 Passed July 6, 1965. Ratified February 11, 1967.

the principal officers of the executive department or of such other body as Congress may by law provide, transmit within four days to the President pro tempore of the Senate and the Speaker of the House of Representatives their written declaration that the President is unable to discharge the powers and duties of his office. Thereupon Congress shall decide the issue, assembling within forty-eight hours for that purpose if not in session. If the Congress, within twenty-one days after receipt of the latter written declaration, or, if Congress is not in session, within twenty-one days after Congress is required to assemble, determines by two-thirds vote of both Houses that the President is unable to discharge the powers and duties of his office, the Vice President shall continue to discharge the same as Acting President; otherwise, the President shall resume the powers and duties of his office.

Amendment XXVI[25]

SECTION 1 The right of citizens of the United States, who are eighteen years of age or older, to vote shall not be denied or abridged by the United States or by any State on account of age.

SECTION 2. The Congress shall have power to enforce this article by appropriate legislation.

Amendment XXVII[26]

No law, varying the compensation for the service of the Senators and Representatives, shall take effect, until an election of Representatives shall have intervened.

---

25 Passed March 23, 1971. Ratified July 5, 1971.

26 Passed September 25, 1789. Ratified May 7, 1992.

ADMISSION OF STATES

Order of admission	State	Date of admission	Order of admission	State	Date of admission
1	Delaware	December 7, 1787	26	Michigan	January 26, 1837
2	Pennsylvania	December 12, 1787	27	Florida	March 3, 1845
3	New Jersey	December 18, 1787	28	Texas	December 29, 1845
4	Georgia	January 2, 1788	29	Iowa	December 28, 1846
5	Connecticut	January 9, 1788	30	Wisconsin	May 29, 1848
6	Massachusetts	February 6, 1788	31	California	September 9, 1850
7	Maryland	April 28, 1788	32	Minnesota	May 11, 1858
8	South Carolina	May 23, 1788	33	Oregon	February 14, 1859
9	New Hampshire	June 21, 1788	34	Kansas	January 29, 1861
10	Virginia	June 25, 1788	35	West Virginia	June 20, 1863
11	New York	July 26, 1788	36	Nevada	October 31, 1864
12	North Carolina	November 21, 1789	37	Nebraska	March 1, 1867
13	Rhode Island	May 29, 1790	38	Colorado	August 1, 1876
14	Vermont	March 4, 1791	39	North Dakota	November 2, 1889
15	Kentucky	June 1, 1792	40	South Dakota	November 2, 1889
16	Tennessee	June 1, 1796	41	Montana	November 8, 1889
17	Ohio	March 1, 1803	42	Washington	November 11, 1889
18	Louisiana	April 30, 1812	43	Idaho	July 3, 1890
19	Indiana	December 11, 1816	44	Wyoming	July 10, 1890
20	Mississippi	December 10, 1817	45	Utah	January 4, 1896
21	Illinois	December 3, 1818	46	Oklahoma	November 16, 1907
22	Alabama	December 14, 1819	47	New Mexico	January 6, 1912
23	Maine	March 15, 1820	48	Arizona	February 14, 1912
24	Missouri	August 10, 1821	49	Alaska	January 3, 1959
25	Arkansas	June 15, 1836	50	Hawaii	August 21, 1959

POPULATION OF THE UNITED STATES

Year	Total population	Number per square mile	Year	Total population	Number per square mile	Year	Total population	Number per square mile
1790	3,929	4.5	1830	12,901	7.4	1870	39,905	13.4
1791	4,056		1831	13,321		1871	40,938	
1792	4,194		1832	13,742		1872	41,972	
1793	4,332		1833	14,162		1873	43,006	
1794	4,469		1834	14,582		1874	44,040	
1795	4,607		1835	15,003		1875	45,073	
1796	4,745		1836	15,423		1876	46,107	
1797	4,883		1837	15,843		1877	47,141	
1798	5,021		1838	16,264		1878	48,174	
1799	5,159		1839	16,684		1879	49,208	
1800	5,297	6.1	1840	17,120	9.8	1880	50,262	16.9
1801	5,486		1841	17,733		1881	51,542	
1802	5,679		1842	18,345		1882	52,821	
1803	5,872		1843	18,957		1883	54,100	
1804	5,065		1844	19,569		1884	55,379	
1805	6,258		1845	20,182		1885	56,658	
1806	6,451		1846	20,794		1886	57,938	
1807	6,644		1847	21,406		1887	59,217	
1808	6,838		1848	22,018		1888	60,496	
1809	7,031		1849	22,631		1889	61,775	
1810	7,224	4.3	1850	23,261	7.9	1890	63,056	21.2
1811	7,460		1851	24,086		1891	64,361	
1812	7,700		1852	24,911		1892	65,666	
1813	7,939		1853	25,736		1893	66,970	
1814	8,179		1854	26,561		1894	68,275	
1815	8,419		1855	27,386		1895	69,580	
1816	8,659		1856	28,212		1896	70,885	
1817	8,899		1857	29,037		1897	72,189	
1818	9,139		1858	29,862		1898	73,494	
1819	9,379		1859	30,687		1899	74,799	
1820	9,618	5.6	1860	31,513	10.6	1900	76,094	25.6
1821	9,939		1861	32,351		1901	77,585	
1822	10,268		1862	33,188		1902	79,160	
1823	10,596		1863	34,026		1903	80,632	
1824	10,924		1864	34,863		1904	82,165	
1825	11,252		1865	35,701		1905	83,820	
1826	11,580		1866	36,538		1906	85,437	
1827	11,909		1867	37,376		1907	87,000	
1828	12,237		1868	38,213		1908	88,709	
1829	12,565		1869	39,051		1909	90,492	

POPULATION OF THE UNITED STATES, CONTINUED

Year	Total population	Number per square mile	Year	Total population	Number per square mile	Year	Total population	Number per square mile
1910	92,407	31.0	1946	141,936		1982	232,520	
1911	93,868		1947	144,698		1983	234,799	
1912	95,331		1948	147,208		1984	237,001	
1913	97,227		1949	149,767		1985	239,283	
1914	99,118		1950	150,697	50.7	1986	241,596	
1915	100,549		1951	154,878		1987	234,773	
1916	101,966		1952	157,553		1988	245,051	
1917	103,414		1953	160,184		1989	247,350	
1918	104,550		1954	163,026		1990	250,122	70.3
1919	105,063		1955	165,931		1991	254,521	
1920	106,466	35.6	1956	168,903		1992	245,908	
1921	108,541		1957	171,984		1993	257,908	
1922	110,055		1958	174,882		1994	261,875	
1923	111,950		1959	177,830		1995	263,434	
1924	114,113		1960	178,464	60.1	1996	266,096	
1925	115,832		1961	183,642		1997	267,901	
1926	117,399		1962	186,504		1998	269,501	
1927	119,038		1963	189,197		1999	272,700	
1928	120,501		1964	191,833		2000	282,172	80.0
1929	121,700		1965	194,237		2001	285,082	
1930	122,775	41.2	1966	196,485		2002	287,804	
1931	124,040		1967	198,629		2003	290,326	
1932	124,840		1968	200,619		2004	293,046	
1933	125,579		1969	202,599		2005	295,753	
1934	126,374		1970	203,875	57.5[1]	2006	298,593	
1935	127,250		1971	207,045		2007	301,580	
1936	128,053		1972	208,842		2008	304,375	
1937	128,825		1973	210,396		2009	307,007	
1938	129,825		1974	211,894		2010	308,746	87.4
1939	130,880		1975	213,631		2011	311,588	
1940	131,669	44.2	1976	215,152		2012	313,914	
1941	133,894		1977	216,880		2013	316,439	
1942	135,361		1978	218,717		2014	318,563	
1943	137,250		1979	220,584		2015	320,987	
1944	138,916		1980	226,546	64.0	2016	323,128	
1945	140,468		1981	230,138		2017	325,719	

Numbers are from *Historical Statistics of the United States, Colonial Times to 1957* (1961), pp. 7, 8; *Statistical Abstract of the United States: 1974*, p. 5, Census Bureau for 1974 and 1975; *Statistical Abstract of the United States: 1988*, p. 7; https://data.worldbank.org/country/united-states data.worldbank.org for 2014-2016; and https://www.census.gov/quickfacts/fact/table/US/PST045216 for 2017.

Note: Population numbers are in thousands. Thus the number 325,719 appearing in the box alongside the year 2017 is actually 325,719,000. Numbers after 1940 represent total population including armed forces abroad, except in official census years. Density figures are for land area of continental United States.

PRESIDENTIAL ELECTIONS

Year	Number of states	Candidates[1]	Parties	Popular vote	Electoral vote	Percentage of popular vote[2]
1789	11	**George Washington**	No party designations		69	
		John Adams			34	
		Minor Candidates			35	
1792	15	**George Washington**	No party designations		132	
		John Adams			77	
		George Clinton			50	
		Minor Candidates			5	
1796	16	**John Adams**	Federalist		71	
		Thomas Jefferson	Democratic-Republican		68	
		Thomas Pinckney	Federalist		59	
		Aaron Burr	Democratic-Republican		30	
		Minor Candidates			48	
1800	16	**Thomas Jefferson**	Democratic-Republican		73	
		Aaron Burr	Democratic-Republican		73	
		John Adams	Federalist		65	
		Charles C. Pinckney	Federalist		64	
		John Jay	Federalist		1	
1804	17	**Thomas Jefferson**	Democratic-Republican		162	
		Charles C. Pinckney	Federalist		14	
1808	17	**James Madison**	Democratic-Republican		122	
		Charles C. Pinckney	Federalist		47	
		George Clinton	Democratic-Republican		6	
1812	18	**James Madison**	Democratic-Republican		128	
		DeWitt Clinton	Federalist		89	
1816	19	**James Monroe**	Democratic-Republican		183	
		Rufus King	Federalist		34	
1820	24	**James Monroe**	Democratic-Republican		231	
		John Quincy Adams	Independent Republican		1	
1824	24	**John Quincy Adams**	Democratic-Republican	108,740	84	30.5
		Andrew Jackson	Democratic-Republican	153,544	99	43.1
		William H. Crawford	Democratic-Republican	46,618	41	13.1
		Henry Clay	Democratic-Republican	47,136	37	13.2
1828	24	**Andrew Jackson**	Democratic	647,286	178	56.0
		John Quincy Adams	National Republican	508,064	83	44.0

Numbers are from *Historical Statistics of the United States, Colonial Times to 1957* (1961), pp. 682–83; the U.S. Department of Justice; and the Federal Election Commission (FEC).

[1]Before the passage of the Twelfth Amendment in 1804, the Electoral College voted for two presidential candidates; the runner-up became vice president.

[2]Candidates receiving less than 1 percent of the popular vote have been omitted. For that reason the percentage of popular vote given for any election year may not total 100 percent.

PRESIDENTIAL ELECTIONS, CONTINUED

Year	Number of states	Candidates	Parties	Popular vote	Electoral vote	Percentage of popular vote
1832	24	**Andrew Jackson**	Democratic	687,502	219	55.0
		Henry Clay	National Republican	530,189	49	42.4
		William Wirt	Anti-Masonic		7	
		John Floyd	National Republican	33,108	11	2.6
1836	26	**Martin Van Buren**	Democratic	765,483	170	50.9
		William H. Harrison	Whig		73	
		Hugh L. White	Whig	739,795	26	
		Daniel Webster	Whig		14	
		W. P. Mangum	Whig		11	
1840	26	**William H. Harrison**	Whig	1,274,624	234	53.1
		Martin Van Buren	Democratic	1,127,781	60	46.9
1844	26	**James K. Polk**	Democratic	1,338,464	170	49.6
		Henry Clay	Whig	1,300,097	105	48.1
		James G. Birney	Liberty	62,300		2.3
1848	30	**Zachary Taylor**	Whig	1,360,967	163	47.4
		Lewis Cass	Democratic	1,222,342	127	42.5
		Martin Van Buren	Free Soil	291,263		10.1
1852	31	**Franklin Pierce**	Democratic	1,601,117	254	50.9
		Winfield Scott	Whig	1,385,453	42	44.1
		John P. Hale	Free Soil	155,825		5.0
1856	31	**James Buchanan**	Democratic	1,832,955	174	45.3
		John C. Frémont	Republican	1,339,932	114	33.1
		Millard Fillmore	American	871,731	8	21.6
1860	33	**Abraham Lincoln**	Republican	1,865,593	180	39.8
		Stephen A. Douglas	Democratic	1,382,713	12	29.5
		John C. Breckinridge	Democratic	848,356	72	18.1
		John Bell	Constitutional Union	592,906	39	12.6
1864	36	**Abraham Lincoln**	Republican	2,206,938	212	55.0
		George B. McClellan	Democratic	1,803,787	21	45.0
1868	37	**Ulysses S. Grant**	Republican	3,013,421	214	52.7
		Horatio Seymour	Democratic	2,706,829	80	47.3
1872	37	**Ulysses S. Grant**	Republican	3,596,745	286	55.6
		Horace Greeley	Democratic	2,843,446	[3]	43.9
1876	38	**Rutherford B. Hayes**	Republican	4,036,572	185	48.0
		Samuel J. Tilden	Democratic	4,284,020	184	51.0

[3]Greeley died shortly after the election; the electors supporting him then divided their votes among other candidates.

(Continued)

PRESIDENTIAL ELECTIONS, CONTINUED

Year	Number of states	Candidates	Parties	Popular vote	Electoral vote	Percentage of popular vote
1880	38	**James A. Garfield**	Republican	4,453,295	214	48.5
		Winfield S. Hancock	Democratic	4,414,082	155	48.1
		James B. Weaver	Greenback-Labor	308,578		3.4
1884	38	**Grover Cleveland**	Democratic	4,879,507	219	48.5
		James G. Blaine	Republican	4,850,293	182	48.2
		Benjamin F. Butler	Greenback-Labor	175,370		1.8
		John P. St. John	Prohibition	150,369		1.5
1888	38	**Benjamin Harrison**	Republican	5,477,129	233	47.9
		Grover Cleveland	Democratic	5,537,857	168	48.6
		Clinton B. Fisk	Prohibition	249,506		2.2
		Anson J. Streeter	Union Labor	146,935		1.3
1892	44	**Grover Cleveland**	Democratic	5,555,426	277	46.1
		Benjamin Harrison	Republican	5,182,690	145	43.0
		James B. Weaver	People's	1,029,846	22	8.5
		John Bidwell	Prohibition	264,133		2.2
1896	45	**William McKinley**	Republican	7,102,246	271	51.1
		William J. Bryan	Democratic	6,492,559	176	47.7
1900	45	**William McKinley**	Republican	7,218,491	292	51.7
		William J. Bryan	Democratic; Populist	6,356,734	155	45.5
		John C. Wooley	Prohibition	208,914		1.5
1904	45	**Theodore Roosevelt**	Republican	7,628,461	336	57.4
		Alton B. Parker	Democratic	5,084,223	140	37.6
		Eugene V. Debs	Socialist	402,283		3.0
		Silas C. Swallow	Prohibition	258,536		1.9
1908	46	**William H. Taft**	Republican	7,675,320	321	51.6
		William J. Bryan	Democratic	6,412,294	162	43.1
		Eugene V. Debs	Socialist	420,793		2.8
		Eugene W. Chafin	Prohibition	253,840		1.7
1912	48	**Woodrow Wilson**	Democratic	6,296,547	435	41.9
		Theodore Roosevelt	Progressive	4,118,571	88	27.4
		William H. Taft	Republican	3,486,720	8	23.2
		Eugene V. Debs	Socialist	900,672		6.0
		Eugene W. Chafin	Prohibition	206,275		1.4
1916	48	**Woodrow Wilson**	Democratic	9,127,695	277	49.4
		Charles E. Hughes	Republican	8,533,507	254	46.2
		A. L. Benson	Socialist	585,113		3.2
		J. Frank Hanly	Prohibition	220,506		1.2

PRESIDENTIAL ELECTIONS, CONTINUED

Year	Number of states	Candidates	Parties	Popular vote	Electoral vote	Percentage of popular vote
1920	48	**Warren G. Harding**	Republican	16,143,407	404	60.4
		James N. Cox	Democratic	9,130,328	127	34.2
		Eugene V. Debs	Socialist	919,799		3.4
		P. P. Christensen	Farmer-Labor	265,411		1.0
1924	48	**Calvin Coolidge**	Republican	15,718,211	382	54.0
		John W. Davis	Democratic	8,385,283	136	28.8
		Robert M. La Follette	Progressive	4,831,289	13	16.6
1928	48	**Herbert C. Hoover**	Republican	21,391,993	444	58.2
		Alfred E. Smith	Democratic	15,016,169	87	40.9
1932	48	**Franklin D. Roosevelt**	Democratic	22,809,638	472	57.4
		Herbert C. Hoover	Republican	15,758,901	59	39.7
		Norman Thomas	Socialist	881,951		2.2
1936	48	**Franklin D. Roosevelt**	Democratic	27,752,869	523	60.8
		Alfred M. Landon	Republican	16,674,665	8	36.5
		William Lemke	Union	882,479		1.9
1940	48	**Franklin D. Roosevelt**	Democratic	27,307,819	449	54.8
		Wendell L. Willkie	Republican	22,321,018	82	44.8
1944	48	**Franklin D. Roosevelt**	Democratic	25,606,585	432	53.5
		Thomas E. Dewey	Republican	22,014,745	99	46.0
1948	48	**Harry S. Truman**	Democratic	24,105,812	303	49.5
		Thomas E. Dewey	Republican	21,970,065	189	45.1
		J. Strom Thurmond	States' Rights	1,169,063	39	2.4
		Henry A. Wallace	Progressive	1,157,172		2.4
1952	48	**Dwight D. Eisenhower**	Republican	33,936,234	442	55.1
		Adlai E. Stevenson	Democratic	27,314,992	89	44.4
1956	48	**Dwight D. Eisenhower**	Republican	35,590,472	457	57.6
		Adlai E. Stevenson	Democratic	26,022,752	73	42.1
1960	50	**John F. Kennedy**	Democratic	34,227,096	303	49.9
		Richard M. Nixon	Republican	34,108,546	219	49.6
1964	50	**Lyndon B. Johnson**	Democratic	43,126,506	486	61.1
		Barry M. Goldwater	Republican	27,176,799	52	38.5
1968	50	**Richard M. Nixon**	Republican	31,785,480	301	43.4
		Hubert H. Humphrey	Democratic	31,275,165	191	42.7
		George C. Wallace	American Independent	9,906,473	46	13.5
1972	50	**Richard M. Nixon**	Republican	47,169,911	520	60.7
		George S. McGovern	Democratic	29,170,383	17	37.5

(Continued)

PRESIDENTIAL ELECTIONS, CONTINUED

Year	Number of states	Candidates	Parties	Popular vote	Electoral vote	Percentage of popular vote
1976	50	**Jimmy Carter**	Democratic	40,827,394	297	50.0
		Gerald R. Ford	Republican	39,145,977	240	47.9
1980	50	**Ronald W. Reagan**	Republican	43,899,248	489	50.8
		Jimmy Carter	Democratic	35,481,435	49	41.0
		John B. Anderson	Independent	5,719,437		6.6
		Ed Clark	Libertarian	920,859		1.0
1984	50	**Ronald W. Reagan**	Republican	54,281,858	525	59.2
		Walter F. Mondale	Democratic	37,457,215	13	40.8
1988	50	**George H. Bush**	Republican	47,917,341	426	54
		Michael Dukakis	Democratic	41,013,030	112	46
1992	50	**William Clinton**	Democratic	44,908,254	370	43.0
		George H. Bush	Republican	39,102,343	168	37.4
		Ross Perot	Independent	19,741,065		18.9
1996	50	**William Clinton**	Democratic	45,628,667	379	49.2
		Robert Dole	Republican	37,869,435	159	40.8
		Ross Perot	Reform	7,874,283		8.5
2000	50	**George W. Bush**	Republican	50,456,062	271	47.9
		Albert Gore	Democratic	50,996,582	266	48.4
		Ralph Nader	Green	2,858,843		2.7
2004	50	**George W. Bush**	Republican	62,040,606	286	51
		John F. Kerry	Democratic	59,028,109	252	48
		Ralph Nader	Green/Independent	411,304		1
2008	50	**Barack Obama**	Democratic	66,882,230	365	53
		John McCain	Republican	58,343,671	173	46
2012	50	**Barack Obama**	Democratic	65,917,258	332	51
		Mitt Romney	Republican	60,932,235	206	47
2016	50	**Donald J. Trump**	Republican	62,984,825	304	46.1
		Hillary Clinton	Democrat	65,853,516	227	48.2
		Gary Johnson	Libertarian	4,489,221		3.3
		Jill Stein	Green	1,457,216		1.1

PRESIDENTS AND VICE PRESIDENTS

Term	President	Vice President
1789–1793	George Washington	John Adams
1793–1797	George Washington	John Adams
1797–1801	John Adams	Thomas Jefferson
1801–1805	Thomas Jefferson	Aaron Burr
1805–1809	Thomas Jefferson	George Clinton
1809–1813	James Madison	George Clinton (d. 1812)
1813–1817	James Madison	Elbridge Gerry (d. 1814)
1817–1821	James Monroe	Daniel D. Tompkins
1821–1825	James Monroe	Daniel D. Tompkins
1825–1829	John Quincy Adams	John C. Calhoun
1829–1833	Andrew Jackson	John C. Calhoun (resigned 1832)
1833–1837	Andrew Jackson	Martin Van Buren
1837–1841	Martin Van Buren	Richard M. Johnson
1841–1845	William H. Harrison (d. 1841) John Tyler	John Tyler
1845–1849	James K. Polk	George M. Dallas
1849–1853	Zachary Taylor (d. 1850) Millard Fillmore (d. 1850)	Millard Fillmore
1853–1857	Franklin Pierce	William R. D. King (d. 1853)
1857–1861	James Buchanan	John C. Breckinridge
1861–1865	Abraham Lincoln	Hannibal Hamlin
1865–1869	Abraham Lincoln (d. 1865) Andrew Johnson	Andrew Johnson
1869 -1873	1873 Ulysses S. Grant	Schuyler Colfax
1873–1877	Ulysses S. Grant	Henry Wilson (d. 1875)
1877–1881	Rutherford B. Hayes	William A. Wheeler
1881–1885	James A. Garfield (d. 1881) Chester A. Arthur	Chester A. Arthur
1885–1889	Grover Cleveland	Thomas A. Hendricks (d. 1885)
1889–1893	Benjamin Harrison	Levi P. Morton
1893–1897	Grover Cleveland	Adlai E. Stevenson
1897–1901	William McKinley	Garret A. Hobart (d. 1899)
1901–1905	William McKinley (d. 1901) Theodore Roosevelt	Theodore Roosevelt
1905–1909	Theodore Roosevelt	Charles W. Fairbanks
1909–1913	William H. Taft	James S. Sherman (d. 1912)
1913–1917	Woodrow Wilson	Thomas R. Marshall
1917–1921	Woodrow Wilson	Thomas R. Marshall
1921–1925	Warren G. Harding (d. 1923) Calvin Coolidge	Calvin Coolidge
1925–1929	Calvin Coolidge	Charles G. Dawes
1929–1933	Herbert Hoover	Charles Curtis
1933–1937	Franklin D. Roosevelt	John N. Garner
1937–1941	Franklin D. Roosevelt	John N. Garner
1941–1945	Franklin D. Roosevelt	Henry A. Wallace
1945–1949	Franklin D. Roosevelt (d. 1945) Harry S Truman	Harry S Truman
1949–1953	Harry S Truman	Alben W. Barkley
1953–1957	Dwight D.Eisenhower	Richard M. Nixon
1957–1961	Dwight D. Eisenhower	Richard M. Nixon
1961–1965	John F. Kennedy (d. 1963) Lyndon B. Johnson	Lyndon B. Johnson
1965–1969	Lyndon B. Johnson	Hubert H. Humphrey, Jr.Spiro T.
1969–1974	Richard M. Nixon (resigned 1974) Gerald R. Ford	Agnew (resigned 1973)
1981–1985	Ronald Reagan	George H. W. Bush
1985–1989	Ronald Reagan	George H. W. Bush
1989–1993	George H. W. Bush	J. Danforth Quayle III
1993–1997	William Clinton	Albert Gore, Jr.
1997–2001	William Clinton	Albert Gore, Jr.
2001–2005	George W. Bush	Richard Cheney
2005–2009	George W. Bush	Richard Cheney
2009–2013	Barack Obama	Joseph Biden
2013–2017	Barack Obama	Joseph Biden
2017–	Donald J. Trump	Michael Pence

JUSTICES OF THE U.S. SUPREME COURT

Name	Term of service	Years of service	Appointed by	Name	Term of service	Years of service	Appointed by
John Jay	1789–1795	5	Washington	Samuel F. Miller	1862–1890	28	Lincoln
John Rutledge	1789–1791	1	Washington	David Davis	1862–1877	14	Lincoln
William Cushing	1789–1810	20	Washington	Stephen J. Field	1863–1897	34	Lincoln
James Wilson	1789–1798	8	Washington	Salmon P. Chase	1864–1873	8	Lincoln
John Blair	1789–1796	6	Washington	William Strong	1870–1880	10	Grant
Robert H. Harrison	1789–1790	—	Washington	Joseph P. Bradley	1870–1892	22	Grant
James Iredell	1790–1799	9	Washington	Ward Hunt	1873–1882	9	Grant
Thomas Johnson	1791–1793	1	Washington	Morrison R. Waite	1874–1888	14	Grant
William Paterson	1793–1806	13	Washington	John M. Harlan	1877–1911	34	Hayes
John Rutledge[1]	1795	—	Washington	William B. Woods	1880–1887	7	Hayes
Samuel Chase	1796–1811	15	Washington	Stanley Matthews	1881–1889	7	Garfield
Oliver Ellsworth	1796–1800	4	Washington	Horace Gray	1882–1902	20	Arthur
Bushrod Washington	1798–1829	31	J. Adams	Samuel Blatchford	1882–1893	11	Arthur
Alfred Moore	1799–1804	4	J. Adams	Lucius Q. C. Lamar	1888–1893	5	Cleveland
John Marshall	1801–1835	34	J. Adams	Melville W. Fuller	1888–1910	21	Cleveland
William Johnson	1804–1834	30	Jefferson	David J. Brewer	1890–1910	20	B. Harrison
H. Brockholst Livingston	1806–1823	16	Jefferson	Henry B. Brown	1890–1906	16	B. Harrison
Thomas Todd	1807–1826	18	Jefferson	George Shiras, Jr.	1892–1903	10	B. Harrison
Joseph Story	1811–1845	33	Madison	Howell E. Jackson	1893–1895	2	B. Harrison
Gabriel Duval	1811–1835	24	Madison	Edward D. White	1894–1910	16	Cleveland
Smith Thompson	1823–1843	20	Monroe	Rufus W. Peckham	1895–1909	14	Cleveland
Robert Trimble	1826–1828	2	J. Q. Adams	Joseph McKenna	1898–1925	26	McKinley
John McLean	1829–1861	32	Jackson	Oliver W. Holmes, Jr.	1902–1932	30	T. Roosevelt
Henry Baldwin	1830–1844	14	Jackson	William R. Day	1903–1922	19	T. Roosevelt
James M. Wayne	1835–1867	32	Jackson	William H. Moody	1906–1910	3	T. Roosevelt
Roger B. Taney	1836–1864	28	Jackson	Horace H. Lurton	1910–1914	4	Taft
Philip P. Barbour	1836–1841	4	Jackson	Charles E. Hughes	1910–1916	5	Taft
John Catron	1837–1865	28	Van Buren	Willis Van Devanter	1911–1937	26	Taft
John McKinley	1837–1852	15	Van Buren	Joseph R. Lamar	1911–1916	5	Taft
Peter V. Daniel	1841–1860	19	Van Buren	Edward D. White	1910–1921	11	Taft
Samuel Nelson	1845–1872	27	Tyler	Mahlon Pitney	1912–1922	10	Taft
Levi Woodbury	1845–1851	5	Polk	James C. McReynolds	1914–1941	26	Wilson
Robert C. Grier	1846–1870	23	Polk	Louis D. Brandeis	1916–1939	22	Wilson
Benjamin R. Curtis	1851–1857	6	Fillmore	John H. Clarke	1916–1922	6	Wilson
John A. Campbell	1853–1861	8	Pierce	William H. Taft	1921–1930	8	Harding
Nathan Clifford	1858–1881	23	Buchanan	George Sutherland	1922–1938	15	Harding
Noah H. Swayne	1862–1881	18	Lincoln	Pierce Butler	1922–1939	16	Harding

JUSTICES OF THE U.S. SUPREME COURT, CONTINUED

Name	Term of service	Years of service	Appointed by	Name	Term of service	Years of service	Appointed by
Edward T. Sanford	1923–1930	7	Harding	Potter Stewart	1958–1981	23	Eisenhower
Harlan F. Stone	1925–1941	16	Coolidge	Byron R. White	1962–1993	31	Kennedy
Charles E. Hughes	1930–1941	11	Hoover	Arthur J. Goldberg	1962–1965	3	Kennedy
Owen J. Roberts	1930–1945	15	Hoover	Abe Fortas	1965–1969	4	Johnson
Benjamin N. Cardozo	1932–1938	6	Hoover	Thurgood Marshall	1967–1994	24	Johnson
Hugo L. Black	1937–1971	34	F. Roosevelt	Warren E. Burger	1969–1986	18	Nixon
Stanley F. Reed	1938–1957	19	F. Roosevelt	Harry A. Blackmun	1970–1994	24	Nixon
Felix Frankfurter	1939–1962	23	F. Roosevelt	Lewis F. Powell, Jr.	1971–1987	15	Nixon
William O. Douglas	1939–1975	36	F. Roosevelt	William H. Rehnquist [2]	1971–2005	34	Nixon
Frank Murphy	1940–1949	9	F. Roosevelt	John P. Stevens III	1975–2010	35	Ford
Harlan F. Stone	1941–1946	5	F. Roosevelt	Sandra Day O'Connor	1981–2006	25	Reagan
James F. Byrnes	1941–1942	1	F. Roosevelt	Antonin Scalia	1986–2016	29	Reagan
Robert H. Jackson	1941–1954	13	F. Roosevelt	Anthony M. Kennedy	1988–2018	30	Reagan
Wiley B. Rutledge	1943–1949	6	F. Roosevelt	David Souter	1990–2009	19	G. H. W. Bush
Harold H. Burton	1945–1958	13	Truman	Clarence Thomas	1991–	—	G. H. W. Bush
Fred M. Vinson	1946–1953	7	Truman	Ruth Bader Ginsburg	1993–	—	Clinton
Tom C. Clark	1949–1967	18	Truman	Stephen G. Breyer	1994–	—	Clinton
Sherman Minton	1949–1956	7	Truman	John G. Roberts, Jr.	2005–	—	G. W. Bush
Earl Warren	1953–1969	16	Eisenhower	Samuel Anthony Alito, Jr.	2006–	—	G. W. Bush
John Marshall Harlan	1955–1971	16	Eisenhower	Sonia Sotomayor	2009–	—	Obama
William J. Brennan, Jr.	1956–1990	34	Eisenhower	Elena Kagan	2010–	—	Obama
Charles E. Whittaker	1957–1962	5	Eisenhower	Neil M. Gorsuch	2017–	—	Trump

[1]Acting chief justice; Senate refused to confirm appointment.

[2]Chief justice from 1986 on (Reagan administration).

Glossary

40 acres and a mule Largely unfulfilled hope of many former slaves that they would receive free land from the confiscated property of ex-Confederates.

abolitionism Movement begun in the North about 1830 to abolish slavery immediately and without compensation to owners.

Affordable Health Care for America Act Designed to extend healthcare to some 30 million people, expand the Medicaid system, create mechanisms for increasing competition among insurance companies, prohibit the use of pre-existing health conditions do deny coverage, and provide every American health insurance.

Agricultural Adjustment Administration (AAA) 1933 attempt to promote economic recovery by reducing supply of crops, dairy, and meat produced by American farmers.

Aguinaldo, Emilio Anti-colonial leader who fought for independence of the Philippines first from Spain and then from the United States.

Alamo Battle between Texas revolutionaries and the Mexican army at the San Antonio mission called the Alamo on March 6, 1836, in which all 187 Texans were killed.

Albany Congress An inter-colonial congress that met in Albany, New York, in June 1754. The delegates urged the Crown to assume direct control of Indian relations beyond the settled boundaries of the colonies, and they drafted a plan of confederation for the continental colonies. No colony ratified it, nor did the Crown or Parliament accept it.

Alien and Sedition Acts Four laws passed by a Federalist-controlled Congress and signed by President John Adams in 1798 during military hostilities with France. The first three laws, directed at immigrants, extended the naturalization period to become citizens from 5 to 14 years and empowered the president to detain enemy aliens during wartime and to deport those he deemed dangerous to the United States. The fourth law—the Sedition Act—set jail terms and fines for persons who advocated disobedience to federal law or publicly criticized the government.

American Colonization Society Established by elite gentlemen of the middle and upper-south states in 1816, this organization encouraged voluntary emancipation of slaves, to be followed by their emigration to the West African colony of Liberia.

American System Program proposed by Henry Clay and others to foster national economic growth and interdependence among the geographical sections. It included a protective tariff, a national bank, and internal improvements.

American Temperance Society Society established in 1826 by northeastern evangelicals that headed the crusade for alcohol temperance.

Americans with Disabilities Act (ADA) Measure that made it illegal to discriminate against people with disabilities in employment, transportation, and other key areas of public life. The law, revised in 2008, assigned enforcement responsibilities to several federal agencies.

amnesty General pardon granted to a large group of people.

Anasazi An advanced pre-Columbian cliff-dwelling culture that flourished for two centuries in what are now the states of Arizona, New Mexico, Utah, and Colorado before abandoning these sites in the late 13th century A.D.

Anderson, Marian Black opera singer who broke a color barrier in 1939 when she sang to an interracial audience of 75,000 from the steps of the Lincoln Memorial.

anglicization Process during the 18th century in which the American colonies reverted to British cultural forms, including in politics, law, fashion, religion, and consumption patterns.

anxious bench Bench at or near the front of a religious revival meeting where the most likely converts were seated.

Article X of the Covenant Addendum to the Treaty of Versailles that empowered the League of Nations to undertake military actions against aggressor nations.

(the) Association Groups created by the First Continental Congress in local committees to enforce its trade sanctions against Britain. The creation of these groups was an important sign that Congress was beginning to act as a central government.

associationalism Herbert Hoover's approach to managing the economy. Firms and organizations in each economic sector would be asked to cooperate with each other in the pursuit of efficiency, profit, and the public good.

Atlantic slave trade A European commerce that led to the enslavement of millions of people who were shipped from their African homelands to European colonies in the Americas.

Auburn system Prison system designed to reform criminals and reduce expenses through the sale of items produced in workshops. Prisoners slept in solitary cells, marched in military formation to meals and workshops, and were forbidden to speak to one another at any time.

Australian ballot (secret ballot) Practice that required citizens to vote in private rather than in public and required the government (rather than political parties) to supervise the voting process.

Aztecs The last pre-Columbian high culture in the Valley of Mexico. It was conquered by the Spaniards in 1519–1521.

baby boom generation People born between 1946 and 1964; more than 75 million babies were born in the U.S. during this time.

balance of trade The relationship between imports and exports. The difference between exports and imports is the balance between the two. A healthy nation should export more than it imports. This is known as a favorable balance of trade.

banknotes Paper money, issued by banks, that circulated as currency.

Barack Hussein Obama 44th President of the United States and the first president of African descent; voted into office in 2008 with a campaign for "hope" and "change."

Battle of Little Big Horn A battle in eastern Montana Territory on the bluffs above Little Big Horn River on June 25, 1876.

Bay of Pigs invasion Site of an ill-fated 1961 invasion of Cuba by a U.S.-trained force that attempted to overthrow the government of Fidel Castro.

Berlin Airlift American and British aircraft that provided all of the items needed in West Berlin during the Berlin Blockade.

Berlin Blockade Soviet Union cut off all highways, railroads, and water routes into West Berlin, Germany in attempt to weaken the nation.

Bill of Rights First ten amendments to the Constitution, which protect the rights of individuals from abuses by the federal government.

Black Codes Laws passed by southern states that restricted the rights and liberties of former slaves.

Black Power Mid-1960s movement that called for modifying integrationist goals in favor of gaining political and economic power for separate black-directed institutions and emphasized pride in AfricanAmerican heritage.

Black Republicans Label coined by the Democratic Party to attack the Republican Party as believers in racial equality. The Democrats used this fear to convince many whites to remain loyal to them.

blockade runner A ship designed to run through a blockade.

blockade The closing of a country's harbors by enemy ships to prevent trade and commerce, especially to prevent traffic in military supplies.

blood sports Sporting activities emphasizing bloodiness that were favored by working-class men of the cities. The most popular in the early 19th century were cockfighting, ratting, dogfights, and various types of violence between animals.

Bonus Army Army veterans who marched on Washington, D.C., in 1932 to lobby for economic relief but who were rebuffed by Hoover.

border ruffians Term used to describe proslavery Missourians who streamed into Kansas in 1854, determined to vote as many times as necessary to install a proslavery government there.

Boston Brahmins Protestant families in Boston, many of whom descended from New England's first English settlers, who constituted the city's upper class by the early 19th century.

Boston Massacre The colonial term for the confrontation between colonial protestors and British soldiers in front of the customs house on March 5, 1770. Five colonists were killed and six wounded.

Boston Tea Party In December 1773, Boston's Sons of Liberty threw 342 chests of East India Company tea into Boston harbor rather than allow them to be landed and pay the hated tea duty.

bounty jumpers Men who enlisted in the Union army to collect the bounties offered by some districts to fill military quotas; these men would enlist and then desert as soon as they got their money.

Boxers Chinese nationalist organization that instigated an uprising in 1900 to rid China of all foreign influence.

Brandt, Joseph Mohawk Indian who served as one of Britain' s most effective commanders of loyalist and Indian forces in the American Revolutionary War. After the war, he led most of the Six Nations to Canada for resettlement.

Brown cases Refers to several Supreme Court cases that challenged the nation's political, social and cultural institutions by outlawing racial segregation in public schools and public facilities.

Brown, John Prominent abolitionist who fought for the antislavery cause in Kansas (1856) and led a raid to seize the Harpers Ferry arsenal in 1859.

Bryan, William Jennings A two-term Democratic congressman from Nebraska who won the party's presidential nomination in 1896 after electrifying delegates with his "Cross of Gold" speech. Bryan was twice more nominated for president (1900 and 1908); he lost all three times.

Burr, Aaron Vice President under Thomas Jefferson who killed Alexander Hamilton in a duel and eventually hatched schemes to detach parts of the west from the United States.

Bush Doctrine Denounced terrorist networks and proclaimed that the U.S. had the right to wage war against any force that endangered American as expressed in the National Security Strategy of 2002.

Bush v. Gore Court case over the 2000 election between George W. Bush and Al Gore; the courts ceased the recounting of ballots in Florida and ruled George W. Bush the 43rd President of the United States.

Bush, George H. W. Republican President (1989–1993) who directed an international coalition against Iraq in the Persian Gulf War.

Bush, George W. Republican President (2001–2009) whose two terms were defined by the September 11, 2001, attacks on the World Trade Center and the Pentagon, the resulting wars in Afghanistan and Iraq, and the financial crash of 2008. Bush did achieve tax cuts, educational reform, and medicare expansion, but much of his 'compassionate conservatism' program failed to take hold.

bushwhackers Confederate guerrilla raiders especially active in Missouri. Jayhawkers were the Union version of the same type of people. Both groups did a tremendous amount of damage with raids, arson, ambush, and murder.

Cahokia The largest city created by Mississippian mound builders. Located in Illinois near modern St. Louis, it thrived from A.D. 900 to 1250 and then declined.

Californios Spanish-speaking people whose families had resided in California for generations.

Camp David Peace Talks of 1978 President Carter negotiated a peace treaty with Menachem Begin and Anwar Sadat, leaders of Israel and Egypt.

camp meeting Outdoor revival often lasting for days; a principal means of spreading evangelical Christianity in the United States.

Capone, Al Chicago mobster who made a fortune from gambling, prostitution, and bootleg liquor during Prohibition.

caravel A new type of oceangoing vessel that could sail closer to a head wind than any other sailing ship and make speeds of from three to twelve knots per hour.

Carnegie, Andrew A Scottish immigrant who became the most efficient entrepreneur in the U.S. steel industry and earned a great fortune.

carpetbaggers Northerners who settled in the South during Reconstruction.

Carter, James Earl (Jimmy) Democratic president (1977–1981) whose single term in office was marked by inflation, fuel shortages, and a hostage crisis.

changing system Elaborate system of neighborhood debts and bartering used primarily in the South and West where little cash money was available.

Cheney, Richard (Dick) Conservative republican who served as vice president to George W. Bush.

Chicanismo Populistic pride in the Mexican American heritage that emerged in the late 1960s. Chicano, once a term of derision, became a rallying cry among activists.

Chinese Exclusion Act Suspended Chinese immigration for 10 years with the exception of a few job categories.

Chisholm Trail Trail used to get longhorn cattle from Texas to Abilene, Kansas where they were loaded into railcars and shipped to Kansas City or Chicago.

CIO The Committee (and then Congress) for Industrial Organization, founded in 1935 to organize the unskilled and semiskilled workers ignored by the AFL. The CIO reinvigorated the labor movement.

circuit court Court that meets at different places within a district.

circuit-riding preachers Methodist ministers who traveled from church to church, usually in rural areas.

City Beautiful movement A movement of urban architectural renovation.

Civil Rights Act of 1957 First civilrights act since Reconstruction, aimed at securing voting rights for African Americans in the South.

Civil Rights Act of 1964 A historic act that denied federal funding to segregated schools and barred discrimination by race and sex in employment, public accommodations, and labor unions.

Civil Rights Act of 1968 Measure that banned racial discrimination in housing and made interference with a person's civil rights a federal crime. It also stipulated that crossing state lines to incite a riot was a federal crime.

Civilized Tribes 60,000 Cherokees, Creeks, Choctaws, Chickasaws, and Seminoles who remained on their ancestral lands in the Old Southwest and were considered sovereign peoples.

Clinton, William Jefferson (Bill) Democratic president (1993–2001) whose two-term presidency witnessed rapid economic growth but also a sexual scandal that fueled an impeachment effort, which he survived.

Clovis tip A superior spear point developed before 9000 B.C. It was in use nearly everywhere in North and South America and produced such an improvement in hunting ability that it contributed to the extinction of most large mammals.

Coercive Acts Four statutes passed by Parliament in response to the Boston Tea Party, including one that closed the port of Boston until the tea was paid for, and another that overturned the Massachusetts Charter of 1691. The colonists called them the Intolerable Acts and included the Quebec Act under that label.

cold war The political, military, cultural, and economic rivalry between the United States and the Soviet Union that developed after the Second World War and lasted until the disintegration of the Soviet State after 1989.

Collier, John Activist head of the Bureau of Indian Affairs who improved U.S. policy toward Native Americans and guided the landmark Indian Reorganization Act through Congress.

colonial economy Economy based on the export of agricultural products and the import of manufactured goods; sometimes used to describe the dependence of the South on the North.

Columbian Exchange A term coined by Alfred W. Crosby to describe the exchange of plants, animals, diseases, culture, and people between the American and European continents following the Spanish discovery of the New World.

Committee on Public Information (CPI) U.S. Government agency established in 1917 to arouse support for the war and, later, to generate suspicion of war dissenters.

committees of correspondence Bodies formed on both the local and colonial levels that played an important role in exchanging ideas and information. They spread primarily anti-British material and were an important step in the first tentative unity of people in different colonies.

common schools Tax-supported public schools built by state and local governments.

Communist Party Radical group that wanted America to follow the Soviet Union's path to socialism. The CP organized some of the country's poorest workers into unions and pushed the New Deal leftward, but was never popular enough to bid for power itself.

Community Reinvestment Act of 1977 Forced banks to finance home buying in low-income neighborhoods to stimulate economic activity.

commutation fee $300 fee that could be paid by a man drafted into the Union army to exempt him from the current draft call.

compensated emancipation Idea that the federal government would offer compensation or money to states that voluntarily abolished slavery.

competence Understood in the early republic as the ability to live up to neighborhood economic standards while protecting the long-term independence of the household.

Compromise of 1850 Series of laws enacted in 1850 intended to settle all outstanding slavery issues.

congressional caucus In the early republic, the group of congressmen who traditionally chose the party's presidential candidates. By the 1820s, the American public distrusted the caucus as undemocratic because only one party contested for power. The caucus was replaced by the national nominating convention.

Connecticut Compromise Deal forged at the Constitutional Convention of 1787 by delegates from Connecticut, led by Roger Sherman, between supporters of the Virginia Plan and the New Jersey Plan. Under the compromise, one house of Congress adopted proportional representation (House of Representatives), while the other kept state equality (Senate).

conquistadores The Spanish word for conquerors.

Conscience Whigs A group of anti-slavery members of the Whig Party.

conservationist Scientific environmentalists who were concerned with making sure the nation's resources were not being wasted.

consumer society A society in which a large percentage of people buy goods and value material possessions. America first became a consumer society in the early 18th century, when British goods, including cloth, ceramics, glassware, paper, and cutlery, flooded into the colonies.

containment Label used to describe the global anticommunist nationalsecurity policies adopted by the United States to stop the expansion of communism during the late 1940s.

contraband of war Term used to describe slaves who came within the Union lines.

Contract with America 1994 Republican campaign document, largely devised by Representative Newt Gingrich, that called for overhauling the welfare system, enacting new anti-crime legislation, making it more difficult to raise federal taxes, and other measures attractive to conservative voters.

Copperheads Term used by some Republicans to describe Peace Democrats to imply that they were traitors to the Union.

Corrupt Bargain Following the election of 1824, Andrew Jackson and his supporters alleged that, in a "corrupt bargain," Henry Clay sold his support during the House vote in the disputed election of 1824 of John Quincy Adams in exchange for appointment as Secretary of State.

Cortés, Hernán Spanish conquistador who in 1519 led an expedition that defeated the Aztec empire and established Spanish imperial presence in mainland Mexico.

cosmopolitanism Ideal of American nationality developed by Randolph Bourne that encouraged creating new cultural forms from the combinations of peoples and cultures.

Cotton Belt Region stretching from South Carolina to eastern Texas and south into Florida that specialized in cotton production by the mid-19th century.

cotton gin Machine, or "engine," that used metal pins fitted into rollers to comb the seeds from short-staple cotton. Invented by Eli Whitney in 1793, it opened the way for the mass production of cotton and the expansion of slavery in the Deep South.

Coughlin, Father Charles The "radio priest" from the Midwest who alleged that the New Deal was being run by bankers. His growing antiSemitism discredited him by 1939.

counterculture Antiestablishment movement that symbolized the youthful social upheaval of the 1960s. Ridiculing traditional attitudes toward such matters as clothing, hair styles, and sexuality, the counterculture urged a more open and less regimented approach to daily life.

coureurs de bois In Canada and the northern US, a woodsman or trader of French origin.

court-packing 1937 attempt by Roosevelt to appoint one new Supreme Court justice for every sitting justice over the age of 70 and who had sat for at least 10 years. Roosevelt's purpose was to prevent conservative justices from dismantling the New Deal, but the plan died in Congress and inflamed opponents of the New Deal.

Covenant Chain of Peace An agreement negotiated by Governor Edmund Andros in 1677 that linked the colony of New York to the Iroquois Five Nations and was later expanded to include other colonies and Indian peoples.

coverture A common-law doctrine under which the legal personality of the husband covered the wife, and he made all legally binding decisions.

Credit Mobilier Affair Construction company for the Union Pacific Railroad that gave shares of stock to some congressmen in return for favors.

crisis conversion Understood in evangelical churches as a personal transformation that resulted from directly experiencing the Holy Spirit.

Cuban Missile Crisis Serious Cold War confrontation between the United States and the Soviet Union over the installation of Soviet missiles in Cuba.

Dartmouth College v. Woodward 1816 Supreme Court case that showcased one of many important decisions made by John Marshall to protect the sanctity of contracts and corporate charters against state legislatures.

Davis, Jefferson Mississippi planter and prominent leader of the Southern Democrats in the 1850s, who later served as president of the Confederacy.

Dawes Plan 1924 U.S.-backed agreement to reduce German reparation payments by more than half. The plan also called on banks to invest $200 million in the German economy.

Dawes Severalty Act 1887 legislation that called for the dissolution of Indian tribes as legal entities, offered Indians citizenship, and allotted each head of family 160 acres of farmland or 320 acres of grazing land.

Debs, Eugene Victor Leader of the Socialist Party who received almost a million votes in the election of 1912.

Denmark Vesey Leader of a slave conspiracy in and around Charleston, South Carolina, in 1822.

deregulation To reduce or remove government rules or policies; Reagan's deregulation agenda focused on the financial system.

détente An easing of tensions, particularly between the United States and the Soviet Union.

Dewey, John Philosopher who believed that American technological and industrial power could be made to serve the people and democracy.

disfranchisement Process of barring groups of adult citizens from voting.

Dix, Dorothea Boston reformer who traveled throughout the country campaigning for humane, state-supported asylums for the insane.

dollar diplomacy Diplomatic strategy formulated under President Taft that focused on expanding American investments abroad, especially in Latin America and East Asia.

Dolores Huerta and Cesar Chavez Political activists, leaders of the United Farm Workers of America, and the most influential Mexican American leaders during the 1970s.

domestic fiction Sentimental literature that centered on household and domestic themes that emphasized the toil and travails of women and children who overcame adversity through religious faith and strength of character.

domino theory Idea that if a communist movement toppled one country that surrounding nations would also fall, as if a row of dominoes, to a communist assault. Supporters of the need to preserve a non-communist government in South Vietnam often cited this cold war theory as justification for their policy choices.

Double V campaign An effort by African-American leaders to use the Second World War as the occasion for campaigns against racial discrimination at home as well as against fascism overseas.

dower rights The right of a widow to a portion of her deceased husband's estate (usually one-third of the value of the estate). It was passed to their children upon her death.

downsizing Process of cutting back in labor pools and management staffs by businesses usually due to declining profits.

dowry The cash or goods a woman received from her father when she married.

Du Bois, W. E. B. Leader of the NAACP, the editor of its newspaper, The Crisis, and an outspoken critic of Booker T. Washington and his accomodationist approach to race relations.

Dunmore's Proclamation Edict released in November 1775 by Lord Dunmore, governor of Virginia, offering freedom to slaves who left their American masters and joined British military forces. The offer, while popular with slaves, helped to push southern planters toward supporting American independence.

Earned Income Tax Credit (EITC) Assisted lower and moderate income households with children.

East Asian Co-Prosperity Sphere Proposition from Japan to China that would liberate Asian nations from Western colonialism and create a self-sufficient economic zone under Japanese leadership.

Edison, Thomas Alva Inventor of the 1800s who developed an array of devices including the phonograph, incandescent light bulb, and movie camera.

Eisenhower Doctrine Policy that stated that the United States would use armed force to respond to imminent or actual communist aggression in the Middle East.

Electoral College The group that elects the president. Each state receives as many electors as it has congressmen and senators combined and can decide how to choose its electors. Every elector votes for two candidates, one of whom has to be from another state.

Embargo Act Law passed in late 1807 and signed by President Thomas Jefferson that prohibited the movement of merchant ships and goods in and out of American ports. Enacted to punish Britain for depredations on the high seas, the act instead crippled American commerce and was revoked in 1809.

Employment Act of 1946 Called for maximum employment and declared private enterprises responsible for economic decision making.

encomienda A system of labor introduced into the Western Hemisphere by the Spanish.

It permitted the holder, or encomendero, to claim labor from Indians in a district for a stated period of time.

energy crisis OPEC raised the price of crude oil and precipitated acute worldwide shortages in 1978; gasoline became expensive and scarce.

enfranchise To grant the right to vote.

Enlightenment The new learning in science and philosophy that took hold, at least in England, between 1660 and the American Revolution. Nearly all of its spokesmen were religious moderates who were more interested in science than religious doctrine and who favored broad religious toleration.

entail A legal device that required a landowner to keep his estate intact and pass it on to his heir.

enumerated commodities A group of colonial products that had to be shipped from the colony of origin to England or another English colony. The most important commodities were sugar and tobacco.

Equal Rights Amendment (ERA) Proposed amendment to the Constitution providing that equal rights could not be abridged on account of sex. It won congressional approval in 1972 but failed to gain ratification by the states.

Erie Canal Canal linking the Hudson River at Albany with the Great Lakes at Buffalo that helped commercialize the farms of the Great Lakes watershed and channel that commerce into New York City.

Espionage, Sabotage, and Sedition Acts Laws passed in 1917 and 1918 that gave the federal government sweeping powers to silence and even imprison dissenters.

ESPN Cable network devoted entirely to sports.

evangelical A style of Christian ministry that includes much zeal and enthusiasm. Evangelical ministers emphasized personal conversion and faith rather than religious ritual.

excise tax Internal tax on goods or services.

Exodusters Name given to the 20,000 African Americans who moved to Kansas believing rumors of free land for settlers and supplies from the government in 1879.

exurbs Housing developments that expanded further away from larger cities into farmlands and small towns.

factories A term used to describe small posts established for the early slave trade along the coast of Africa or on small offshore islands.

Fair Deal Proposed in 1949 by President Truman to extend New Deal programs, enact legislation dealing with civil rights, national health care, and federal aid for education, provide funds for public housing, and support farm prices.

fall line A geographical landmark defined by the first waterfalls encountered when going upriver from the sea. These waterfalls prevented oceangoing ships from sailing further inland and thus made the fall line a significant early barrier. Land between the falls and the ocean was called the tidewater. Land above the falls but below the mountains was called the piedmont.

Family Assistance Plan (FAP) Proposed by Nixon in 1969 to replace the existing welfare policy; it called to provide every low-income family an annual income of $1,600.

Federal Reserve Act Act that brought private banks and public authority together to regulate and strengthen the nation's financial system.

Federalists Supporters of the Constitution during the ratification process. Anti-Federalists resisted ratification.

feminism Desire for complete equality between men and women.

feudal revival The reliance on old feudal charters for all of the profits that could be extracted from them. It took hold in several colonies in the mid-18th century and caused serious problems between many landowners and tenants.

fiat money Paper money backed only by the promise of the government to accept it in payment of taxes. It originated in Massachusetts after a military emergency in 1690.

filibuster Congressional delaying tactic involving lengthy speeches that prevent legislation from being enacted.

filibustering A term used to describe several groups that invaded or attempted to invade various Latin American areas to attempt to add them to the slaveholding regions of the United States. The word originated from filibustero, meaning a freebooter or pirate.

First Continental Congress This intercolonial body met in Philadelphia in September and October 1774 to organize resistance against the Coercive Acts by defining American rights, petitioning the king, and appealing to the British and American people. It created the Association, local committees in each community to enforce nonimportation.

flappers Rebellious middle-class young women who signaled their desire for independence and equality through style and personality rather than through politics.

Ford, Gerald R. A GOP member of the House of Representatives, Gerald Ford became the first person to be appointed Vice President of the United States. When Richard Nixon resigned in 1974, Ford became President.

Fort Sumter Fort in Charleston's harbor occupied by United States troops after the secession of South Carolina.

Fourteen Points Plan laid out by Woodrow Wilson in January 1918 to give concrete form to his dream of a "peace without victory" and a new world order.

free silver Idea that the government would purchase all silver offered for sale and coin it into silver dollars at the preferred ratio between silver and gold of 16 to 1.

free-labor ideology Belief that all work in a free society is honorable and that manual labor is degraded when it is equated with slavery or bondage.

Free-Soilers A term used to describe people who opposed the expansion of slavery into the territories. It came from the name of a small political party in the election of 1848.

Freedmen's Bureau Federal agency created in 1865 to supervise newly freed people. It oversaw relations between whites and blacks in the South, issued food rations, and supervised labor contracts.

freedom riders Members of interracial groups who traveled the South on buses to test a series of federal court decisions declaring segregation on buses and in waiting rooms to be unconstitutional.

Freedom Summer Summer of 1964 when nearly a thousand white volunteers went to Mississippi to aid in voter registration and other civilrights projects.

Freemasons A religion of manliness, complete with mysterious rituals that extolled sobriety, industry, brotherhood, benevolence, and citizenship.

frontier An area on the advancing edge of American civilization.

fugitive slaves Runaway slaves who escaped to a free state.

Fulton, Robert Post-2005 Supreme Court, headed by Chief Justice John Roberts, in which conservatives used their five-justice majority to issue a number of rulings that tracked the theories of legal-constitutional conservatives.

fundamentalists Religious groups that preached the necessity of fidelity to a strict moral code, individual commitment to Christ, and faith in the literal truth of the Bible.

funded national debt The state agreed to pay the interest due to its creditors before all other obligations.

Gabriel's Rebellion Carefully planned but unsuccessful rebellion of slaves in Richmond, Virginia, and the surrounding area in 1800.

gag rule Procedure in which Congress voted at each session from 1836 to 1844 to table antislavery petitions without reading them in order avoid any debate.

Gaither Report Report that encouraged President Eisenhower to increase national security and government spending in 1957.

gang system A system where planters organized their field slaves into gangs, supervised them closely, and kept them working in the fields all day. This type of labor was used on tobacco plantations.

Garrison, William Lloyd Abolitionist and publisher of the first issue of the Liberator.

Garvey, Marcus Jamaican-born black nationalist who attracted millions of African Americans in the early

Gates, Henry Lewis, Jr. Activist for the academics of African American's in the 1990s.

General William Westmoreland Recommended the "search and destroy" method in North Vietnam to incapacitate NLF and North Vietnamese forces and to allow Saigon government time to develop.

Geneva Peace Accords of 1954 Divided French Indochina into three new nations: Laos, Cambodia, and Vietnam; Vietnam was also split into two jurisdiction at the 17th parallel until an election could unify the country.

gentlemen's agreement (1907) Agreement by which the Japanese government promised to halt the immigration of its adult male laborers to the United States in return for President Theodore Roosevelt's pledge to end the discriminatory treatment of Japanese immigrant children in California's public schools.

Ghost Dance Indian ritual involving days of worship expressed in part through dance.

GI Bill Officially called the Serviceman's Readjustment Act of 1944. It provided veterans with college and job-training assistance, preferential treatment in hiring, and subsidized home loans, and was later extended to Korean War veterans in 1952.

globalization Spread of businesses throughout world.

Goldwater, Barry Republican candidate defeated by Lyndon B. Johnson in the 1964 presidential election.

Gompers, Samuel F. America's most famous trade unionist while serving as president of the AFL (1896–1924). He achieved his greatest success in organizing skilled workers.

Good Neighbor Policy Roosevelt's foreign policy initiative that formally renounced the right of the United States to intervene in Latin American affairs, leading to improved relations between the United States and Latin American countries.

Gorbachev, Mikhail Reform-minded Soviet leader whose policies helped to set the stage for the end of the Cold War in 1989-90 and the demise of the Soviet Union itself.

gradual emancipation Process in the northern states in the American revolutionary era whereby slaves gained freedom. Rather than free slaves immediately, most states set up systems in which slaves became free gradually over a number of years.

Grant, Ulysses S. General-in-chief of Union armies who led those armies to victory in the Civil War.

Great American Desert The treeless area in the plains that most Americans considered unsuitable for settlement. It generally was passed over by settlers going to the Pacific Coast areas.

Great Railroad Strike of 1877 Strike that occurred during a time of depression that caused employers to cut wages and lay off workers.

Great Recession A severe downturn in the global economy that began with the financial crash of 2008. The ensuing recovery was weak, marked by low wages and slow job creation. Wealth disparities between the rich and the poor widened, sharpening political discontent.

Great Society Series of domestic initiatives announced in 1964 by President Lyndon Johnson to "end poverty and racial injustice." They included the Voting Rights Act of 1965; the establishment of the Department of Housing and Urban Development, Head Start, and jobtraining programs; Medicare and Medicaid expansion; and various community action programs.

Great White Fleet Naval ships sent on a 45,000-mile world tour by

President Roosevelt (1907–1909) to showcase American military power.

Greene, Nathanael Mohawk Indian who served as one of Britain's most effective commanders of loyalist and Indian forces in the American Revolutionary War. After the war, he led most of the Six Nations to Canada for resettlement.

Greenwich Village Community of radical artists and writers in lower Manhattan that provided a supportive environment for various kinds of radical ideals.

Grimke, Sarah Along with her sister Angelina, this elite South Carolina woman moved north and campaigned against slavery and for temperance and women's rights.

Gulf of Tonkin Resolution Measure passed by Congress in August 1964 that provided authorization for an air war against North Vietnam after U.S. destroyers were allegedly attacked by North Vietnamese torpedoes. Johnson invoked it as authority for expanding the Vietnam War.

Gullah A language spoken by newly imported African slaves. Originally, it was a simple second language for everyone who spoke it, but it gradually evolved into modern black English.

habeas corpus Right of an individual to obtain a legal document as protection against illegal imprisonment.

hacienda A large landed estate established by wealthy Spanish colonists in the Americas for farming, ranching, manufacturing, and mining. In many parts of South America, the hacienda system survived the end of the colonial period in the early 19th century.

Hale, Sarah Josepha Editor of Godey's Ladies Book and an important arbiter of domesticity and taste for middleclass housewives.

Harlem Renaissance 1920s African-American literary and artistic awakening that sought to create works rooted in black culture instead of imitating white styles.

Harpers Ferry Site of John Brown's 1859 raid on a U.S. armory and arsenal for the manufacture and storage of military rifles.

Haymarket Bombing at an Anarchist protest meeting at Haymarket Square in Chicago on May 4 resulting in 10 deaths, 6 of them policemen.

headright A colonist received 50 acres of land for every person whose passage to America he financed, including himself. This system was introduced in Virginia.

Hessians A term used by Americans to describe the 17,000 mercenary troops hired by Britain from various German states, especially Hesse.

High Federalists A term used to describe Alexander Hamilton and some of his less-moderate supporters. They wanted the naval war with France to continue and also wanted to severely limit the rights of an opposition party.

Highway Act of 1956 Act that appropriated $25 billion for the construction of more than 40,000 miles of interstate highways over a 10-year period.

Hiroshima Japanese city destroyed by an atomic bomb on August 6, 1945.

Hitler, Adolf German fascist dictator whose aggressive policies touched off the Second World War.

Homestead (Strike) Carnegie Steel Company closed its Homestead plant planning to reopen with nonunion workers; the union went on strike refusing to leave the building, which led to a gun battle and several deaths.

Homestead Act Legislation that took effect on January 1, 1863 to provide free land for western settlers.

House of Burgesses The assembly of early Virginia that settlers were allowed to elect. Members met with the governor and his council and enacted local laws. It first met in 1619.

household deficit Difference between what U.S. households earned and what they spent.

housing bubble Refers to people who became home owners but lacked the incomes to handle a conventional mortgage.

Huguenots French Protestants who followed the beliefs of John Calvin.

Hull House First American settlement house established in Chicago in 1889 by Jane Addams and Ellen Gates Starr.

Human Genome Project Program launched in 1985 to map all genetic material in the 24 human chromosomes. It sparked ongoing debate over the potential consequences of genetic research and manipulation.

human rights policy The effort by President Jimmy Carter (1977-81) to craft a foreign policy, intended to advance both American national security and global progress, that emphasized basic political, social, and economic rights.

Hutchinson, Anne A religious radical who attracted a large following in Massachusetts, especially in Boston. She warned that nearly all of the ministers were preaching a covenant of works instead of the covenant of grace. Convicted of the Antinomian heresy after claiming that she received direct messages from God, she and her most loyal followers were banished to Rhode Island in 1638.

Immigration and Nationality Act of 1965 Law eliminating the nationalorigins quota system for immigration and substituting preferences for people with certain skills or with relatives in the United States.

Immigration Reform and Control Act of 1986 (Simpson-Mazzoli Act) Created stricter penalties for employing undocumented workers and provided residency for people that had lived in the U.S. since 1982.

impeachment Act of charging a public official with misconduct in office.

imperialists Those who wanted to expand their nation's world power through military prowess, economic strength, and control of foreign territory (often organized into colonies).

impressment Removal of sailors from American ships by British naval officers.

Incas The last and most extensive pre-Columbian empire in the Andes and along the Pacific coast of South America.

Independent Treasury Bill 1840 bill that permitted the federal government to hold and dispense money without depositing it in banks and required that customs and land purchases be paid in gold and silver coins or notes from specie-paying banks.

Indian Removal Act (1830) Legislation that offered the native peoples of the lower South the option of removal to federal lands west of the Mississippi. Those who did not take the offer were removed by force in 1838.

information revolution Acceleration of the speed and availability of information resulting from use of computer and satellite systems.

initiative Reform that gave voters the right to propose and pass a law independently of their state legislature.

intendant The officer who administered the system of justice in New France.

interchangeable parts Industrial technique using machine tools to cut and shape a large number of similar parts that can be fitted together with other parts to make an entire item such as a gun.

internal improvements 19th-century term for transportation facilities such as roads, canals, and railroads.

internment U.S. policy, justified on the basis of national security, of detaining about 130,000 people, including citizens, of Japanese descent and far fewer of German and Italian ancestry in special "internment camps" during the Second World War.

interstate slave trade The trade for slaves within the domestic United States, which expanded dramatically after the end of the international slave trade in 1808. By 1860, around 1 million slaves were moved westward from old slaveholding regions, particularly the Chesapeake.

Iran-contra affair Reagan administration scandal in which the U.S. secretly sold arms to Iran, a country implicated in holding American hostages, and diverted the money to finance the attempt by the contras to overthrow the Sandinista government of Nicaragua. Both transactions violated acts of Congress, which had prohibited funding the contra and selling weapons to Iran.

Iranian Revolution of January 1979 Islamic fundamentalists overthrew Iranian dictator Shah Reza Pahlavi; the rebellion led to 66 Americans taken hostage when Carter allowed the shah into the U.S. for medical assistance.

Iroquois League A confederation of five Indian nations centered around the Mohawk Valley who were very active in the fur trade. They first worked with the Dutch and then the English. They were especially successful in using adoption as a means of remaining strong.

irreconcilables Group of 14 midwestern and western senators who opposed the Treaty of Versailles.

isolationists Name given to people who were not in favor of war during World War II.

itinerant preachers Ministers who lacked their own parishes and who traveled from place to place.

Jackson, Thomas J. ("Stonewall") A native of Virginia, he emerged as one of the Confederacy's best generals in 1861–1862.

Jim Crow laws Laws passed by southern states mandating racial segregation in public facilities of all kinds.

Johnson-Reed Immigration Restriction Act of 1924 Limited immigration to the United States to 165,000 per year, shrank immigration from southern and eastern Europe to insignificance, and banned immigration from East and South Asia.

joint-stock company A form of business organization that resembled a modern corporation. Individuals invested in the company through the purchase of shares. One major difference between then and today was that each stockholder had one vote regardless of how many shares he owned. The first permanent English colonies in North America were established by joint-stock companies.

journeyman Wage-earning craftsman who completed an apprenticeship but had not yet become a master, or owner of his own business.

judicial review Supreme Court's power to rule on the constitutionality of congressional acts.

Kansas-Nebraska Act Law enacted in 1854 to organize the new territories of Kansas and Nebraska that effectively repealed the provision of the 1820 Missouri Compromise by leaving the question of slavery to the territories' settlers.

King, Martin Luther, Jr. African American clergyman who advocated nonviolent social change and shaped the civil-rights movement of the 1950s and 1960s.

Knights of Labor Secret fraternal organization founded in 1869 in Philadelphia.

Know-Nothings Adherents of nativist organizations and of the American party who wanted to restrict the political rights of immigrants.

Korean War Conflict lasting from 1950 to 1953 between communist North Korea, aided by China, and South Korea, aided by United Nations forces consisting primarily of U.S. troops.

Ku Klux Klan White terrorist organization in the South originally founded as a fraternal society in 1866. Reborn in 1915, it achieved popularity in the 1920s through its calls for AngloSaxon purity, Protestant supremacy, and the subordination of blacks, Catholics, and Jews.

League of Women Voters (LWV) Successor to the National American Woman Suffrage Association, it promoted women's role in politics and dedicated itself to educating voters.

Lee, Robert E. U.S. army officer until his resignation to join the Confederacy as general-in-chief.

legal tender Any type of money that the government requires everyone to accept at face value.

Lend-Lease Act A 1941 act by which the United States "loaned" munitions to the Allies, hoping to avoid war by becoming an "arsenal" for the Allied cause.

levees Earthen dike or mound, usually along the banks of rivers, used to prevent flooding.

liberal Protestants Those who believed that religion had to be adapted to science and that the Bible was to be mined for its ethical values rather than for its literal meaning.

liberalism New reform movement that took shape under Franklin Roosevelt and the New Deal in the 1930s. It sought to regulate capitalism in the public interest but not the morals or behavior of private citizens.

Liberty Bonds Thirty-year government bonds with an annual interest rate of 3.5 percent sold to fund the war effort.

limited liability Liability that protected directors and stockholders of corporations from corporate debts by separating those debts from personal liabilities.

Lincoln-Douglas debates Series of seven debates between Abraham Lincoln and Stephen Douglas in their contest for election to the U.S. Senate in 1858.

Lincoln, Abraham Prominent abolitionist who fought for the antislavery cause in Kansas (1856) and led a raid to seize the Harpers Ferry arsenal in 1859.

Lindbergh, Charles A. First individual to fly solo across the Atlantic (1927) and the greatest celebrity of the 1920s.

Lodge, Henry Cabot Republican Senator from Massachusetts who led the campaign to reject the Treaty of Versailles.

Long, Huey Democratic senator and former governor of Louisiana who used the radio to attack the New Deal as too conservative. FDR regarded him as a major rival.

Lost Generation Term used by Gertrude Stein to describe U.S. writers and artists who fled to Paris in the 1920s after becoming disillusioned with America.

Louisiana Purchase Land purchased from France in 1803 that doubled the size of the United States.

Lowell mill girls Single, young farm women in New England who worked as wage laborers in mills owned by Francis Cabot Lowell's Boston Manufacturing Company, including at Lowell, Massachusetts. The company provided boardinghouses for the women and enforced strict rules of conduct.

loyalists People in the 13 colonies who remained loyal to Britain during the Revolution.

MacArthur, General Douglas Supreme commander of Allied forces in the southwest Pacific during the Second World War; leader of the occupation forces in the reconstruction of Japan; and head of United Nations forces during the Korean War.

Mahan, Alfred Thayer Influential imperialist who advocated construction of a large navy as crucial to the successful pursuit of world power.

Malcolm X Charismatic African American leader who criticized integration and urged the creation of separate black economic and cultural institutions. He became a hero to members of the Black Power movement.

Manhattan Project Major secret military operation that involved the development of the first atomic weapon.

Manifest Destiny The belief that the United States was destined to grow from the Atlantic to the Pacific and from the Arctic to the tropics. Providence supposedly intended for Americans to have this area for a great experiment in liberty.

manumission The act of freeing a slave, done at the will of the owner.

Marbury v. Madison 1803 case involving the disputed appointment of a federal justice of the peace in which Chief Justice John Marshall expanded the Supreme Court's authority to review legislation.

March on Washington for Jobs and Freedom On August 28, 1960, 200,000 people marched through Washington D.C. to the Lincoln Memorial for the rights of African Americans; Dr. Martin Luther King Jr. delivered his famous "I Have a Dream" speech on this day.

Market Revolution Term used to describe the transformation of the United States, particularly in the North, between 1815 and 1850 from a largely subsistence economy to a market society in which farmers and other business owners produced surplus goods to sell to growing regional, national, and international markets.

martial law Government by military force rather than by citizens.

mass production High-speed and high-volume production.

mass-culture critique Fear that the cultural traditions of the 1950s would be drastically altered due to the influences of art, music, and TV.

massive retaliation Assertion by the Eisenhower administration that the threat of U.S. atomic weaponry would hold Communist powers in check.

matrilineal A society that determines inheritance and roles in life based on the female or maternal line.

Mayan Indigenous people and culture of what today are southeast Mexico, Granada, and Belize.

McCarran-Walter Act Authorized the denial of immigrant status to anyone who might compromise national security by bringing dangerous ideas into the country; it also allowed the deportation of immigrants who belonged to organizations on the Attorney General's List.

McCarthy, Joseph 1946 U.S. Senator who unfairly accused numerous people of being Communists.

McCarthy, Senator Eugene Anti-war Democrat who dared to challenge Lyndon Johnson in the party's primaries and who helped prompt LBJ's decision to forgo another presidential run in 1968.

McClellan, George B. One of the most promising young officers in the U.S. army, he became the principal commander of Union armies in 1861–1862.

McCulloch v. Maryland Supreme Court case in which the Bank of the United States Baltimore branch challenged the Maryland legislature's attempt to tax the bank; lead by John Marshall, the Court decided in favor of the Bank and denied Maryland's right to tax the Bank or any other federal agency.

melting pot Term first used in the early 1900s that referred to the fusing of immigrants' culture with American culture as a continuous rebirth of the nation.

Menéndez de Avilé, Pedro The Spanish Admiral charged with Havana's protection after it was sacked by the Huguenots. Forces under Aviles' command expanded Spanish influence in the region, attacking and conquering settlements on Florida's Atlantic coast in 1565.

mercantilism An economic theory that stresses a direct relationship between a nation's wealth and its power. Mercantilist nations in the 17th century sought to increase their wealth and power through aggressive trade expansion within their colonies.

merger movement Late-19th and early 20th-century effort to integrate different enterprises into single, giant corporations able to eliminate competition, achieve economic order, and boost profits.

middle class Social group that developed in the early 19th century comprised of urban and country merchants, master craftsmen who had turned themselves into manufacturers, and market-oriented farmers—small-scale entrepreneurs who rose within market society.

Middle Passage The forced voyage taken by enslaved Africans across the Atlantic Ocean between Africa and destinations in the Western Hemisphere. More than 1 million slaves died during the journey due to the subhuman conditions aboard slave ships.

midnight judges Federal judicial officials appointed under the Judiciary Act of 1801, in the last days of John Adams's presidency.

Midway Plaisance A section of the Columbia Exposition of 1893 that included concessions, games, the Ferris Wheel, traveling museums, and freak shows.

military–industrial complex Refers to the relationship between military, political, and economic elites committed to expanding national security capabilities.

Millerites Followers of the Baptist leader William Miller, who preached that God would destroy the world during the year following March 1843. They later formed the SeventhDay Adventist Church.

minstrel show Popular form of theater among working men of the northern cities in which white men in blackface portrayed African Americans in song and dance.

missions Outposts established by the Spanish along the northern frontier to aid in Christianizing the native peoples. They also were used to exploit these peoples' labor.

Missouri Compromise Compromise that maintained sectional balance in Congress by admitting Missouri as a slave state and Maine as a free state and by drawing a line west from the 368 309 parallel separating future slave and free states.

Monroe Doctrine Foreign policy doctrine proposed by Secretary of State John Quincy Adams in 1823 that denied the right of European powers to establish new colonies in the Americas while maintaining the United States' right to annex new territory.

Morgan, J. P. Most celebrated and powerful banker of the late 19th century.

Mormons Members of the Church of Jesus Christ of Latter-Day Saints, founded by Joseph Smith in 1830; the Book of Mormon is their Bible.

Mourning Wars An Indian war often initiated by a widow or bereaved relative who insisted that her male relatives provide captives to repair the loss.

MTV aesthetic Created a relationship between music and visual imagery.

muckrakers Investigative journalists who propelled Progressivism by exposing corruption, economic monopolies, and moral decay in American society.

Munich Conference French and British leaders met with Adolf Hitler in 1938 to avoid war.

My Lai Incident U.S. troops murdered more than 200 civilians, most of them women and children, in the small South Vietnamese village of My Lai in 1968.

narrowcasting Tactic used by TV programmers to target specific audiences with corresponding shows.

National American Women Suffrage Association (NAWSA) Organization established in 1890 to promote woman suffrage; stressed that women's special virtue made them indispensable to politics.

National Association for the Advancement of Colored People (NAACP) Organization launched in 1910 to fight racial discrimination and prejudice and to promote civil rights for blacks.

National Recovery Administration (NRA) 1933 attempt to promote economic recovery by persuading private groups of industrialists to decrease production, limit hours of work per employee, and standardize minimum wages.

National Review Magazine started in 1955 by William F. Buckley Jr. that represents conservative opinions and commentary about current events and politics.

National Road A road that attempted to link west and east through the Chesapeake by connecting the Potomac River with the Ohio River at Wheeling, Virginia in 1818.

National Security Act of 1947 Reorganized the U.S. military forces within a new Department of Defense, and established the National Security Council and the Central Intelligence Agency.

National Security Agency (NSA) Super-secret agency created in 1952 that came to enjoy broad power to monitor and archive global communications in the name of protecting national security.

National Security Strategy of 2002 Denounced terrorist networks and proclaimed that the U.S. had the right to wage war against any force that endangered Americans.

National War Labor Board (NWLB) U.S. government agency that brought together representatives of labor, industry, and the public to resolve labor disputes.

nativism Hostility of native-born Americans toward immigrants.

neoconservatives Group of intellectuals, many of whom had been anticommunist Democrats during the 1950s and 1960s, who came to emphasize hard-line foreign policies and conservative social stances.

Neolithic The period known also as the late Stone Age. Agriculture developed, and stone, rather than metal, tools were used.

Neutrality Acts Legislation that restricted loans, trade, and travel with belligerent nations in an attempt to avoid the entanglements that had brought the United States into the First World War.

New Democrat A member of the Democratic Party, such as Bill Clinton, who urged policies – such as deregulating business and financial activities, cutting federal welfare expenditures, and embracing strict crime control measures – which Democrats from the New Deal, Fair Deal, and Great Society eras had generally opposed.

New Freedom Wilson's reform program of 1912 that called for temporarily concentrating government power so as to dismantle the trusts and return America to 19thcentury conditions of competitive capitalism.

New Frontier Term used by John F. Kennedy in his 1960 campaign as a reference to what lied ahead for the country. Kennedy spoke of new social programs to rebuild rural communities, increase educational opportunities and improve urban conditions; he also promoted economic growth and more aggressive foreign policy.

New Jersey Plan Proposal by William Patterson of New Jersey at the Constitutional Convention of 1787 to maintain the existing system of representation under the Articles of Confederation in which each state had one vote in Congress. Also known as the "small state" plan.

New Left 1960s movement that sought to re-orient politics; people were urged to expand their minds and seek alternative ways of living.

New Lights Term used to describe prorevival Congregationalists.

New Look President Eisenhower's attempt to minimize the military budget by focusing on nuclear weaponry and air power.

New Nationalism Roosevelt's reform program between 1910 and 1912, which called for establishing a strong federal government to regulate corporations, stabilize the economy, protect the weak, and restore social harmony.

New Right A diverse coalition of conservatives that focused on social issues and national sovereignty; they supported the Republican party under the leadership of Ronald Reagan.

New Sides Term used to describe evangelical Presbyterians.

New Woman A term used to describe the emergence of a new style of middle-class womanhood in the late nineteenth century, as young women attended college, engaged in sports, and entered a variety of professions.

New York Magdalen Society Female established society whose mission was to separate prostitutes from male power, pray with them, and convert them to middle-class morality.

New York's 369th Regiment Black army unit recruited in Harlem that served under French command and was decorated with the Croix de Guerre for its valor.

nickelodeons Converted storefronts in working-class neighborhoods that showed early short silent films usually lasting 15 minutes, requiring little comprehension of English, and costing only a nickel to view.

Ninth and Tenth Negro Cavalries African-American army units that played a pivotal role in the Spanish-American War.

Nixon Doctrine Pledged that the U.S. would extend military assistance to anticommunist governments in Asia but would require them to supply their own combat forces.

Nixon, Richard Milhous President of the United States (1969–1974) during the final years of the Vietnam War. He resigned the presidency when he faced impeachment for the Watergate scandals.

Non-Separatists English Puritans who insisted that they were faithful members of the Church of England while demanding that it purge itself of its surviving Catholic rituals and vestments.

nonimportation agreements Agreements not to import goods from Great Britain. They were designed to put pressure on the British economy and force the repeal of unpopular parliamentary acts.

normal schools State colleges established to train teachers.

North Atlantic Treaty Organization (NATO) Established by treaty in 1949 to provide for the collective defense of noncommunist European and North American nations against possible aggression from the Soviet Union and to encourage political, economic, and social cooperation.

Northwest Ordinance Established the Northwest Territory between the Ohio River and the Great Lakes. Adopted by the Confederation Congress in 1787, it abolished slavery in the territory and provided that it be divided into three to five states that would eventually be admitted to the Union as full equals of the original thirteen.

NSC-68 National Security Council Document number 68 (1950) that provided the rationale and comprehensive strategic vision for U.S. policy during the Cold War.

nullification Beginning in the late 1820s, John C. Calhoun and others argued that the Union was a voluntary compact between sovereign states, that states were the ultimate judges of the constitutionality of federal law, that states could nullify federal laws within their borders, and that they had the right to secede from the Union.

Office of War Information (OWI) Created in 1942 by President Roosevelt to coordinate propaganda and censorship.

Old Lights Antirevival Congregationalists.

Old Sides Antirevival Presbyterians.

Olmecs The oldest pre-Columbian high culture to appear in what is now Mexico.

Olmsted, Frederick Law Principal designer of Central Park in New York City.

Onontio An Algonquian word that means "great mountain" and that was used by Indians of the Middle Ground to designate the governor of New France.

Open Door policy The policy through which the United States sought to keep China open to American merchants and American goods in the late 19th and early 20th centuries. The policy entailed preventing European powers from establishing exclusive control over parts of China and China itself from shutting down its trade with foreign nations.

OVERLORD Massive invasion of Germany that began on June 6, 1944, known as D-Day; this event was the beginning of the end to the war in Europe.

Panama Canal An engineering marvel completed in 1914 across the new Central American nation of Panama. Connecting the Atlantic and Pacific oceans, it shortened ship travel between New York and San Francisco by 8,000 miles.

patronage The act of appointing people to government jobs or awarding them government contracts, often based on political favoritism rather than on abilities.

patroonship Vast estates along the Hudson River that were established by the Dutch. They had difficulty attracting peasant labor, and most were not successful.

Patsy Mink Equal Opportunity in Education Act Required colleges and universities to improve the financing and promotion of women's sports in 1972.

peace without victory Woodrow Wilson's 1917 pledge to work for a peace settlement that did not favor one side over the other but ensured an equality among combatants.

Pearl Harbor Japan's December 7, 1941 attack on a U.S. base in Hawaii that brought the United States into the Second World War.

Pentagon Completed in January of 1943, this five-story, five-sided building houses the United States' War Department.

people's capitalism An egalitarian capitalism in which all Americans could participate and enjoy the consumer goods that U.S. industry had made available.

Pershing, John J. Commander of the American Expeditionary Force that began landing in Europe in 1917 and that entered battle in the spring and summer of 1918.

Persian Gulf War Conflict that lasted six weeks in 1991 between the U.S. and Iraq; Bush ordered aid to Kuwait when Saddam Hussein and his armies invaded their land.

personal liberty laws Laws enacted by nine northern states to prohibit the use of state law facilities such as jails or law officers in the recapture of fugitive slaves.

placemen Appointed office holders who sat in the British Parliament. The Country party in 18th century England lobbied to ban placemen, whom they saw as a threat to the natural balance of the British system of government.

Platt Amendment Clause that the U.S. forced Cuba to insert into its constitution giving the U.S. broad control over Cuba's foreign and domestic policies.

Plessy v. Ferguson 1896 Supreme Court case that sanctioned Jim Crow laws as long as the separate facilities for black and whites were equal.

political machines Organizations that controlled local political parties and municipal governments through bribery, election fraud, and support of urban vice while providing some municipal services to the urban poor.

politics of harmony A system in which the governor and the colonial assembly worked together through persuasion rather than through patronage or bullying.

Pontiac's War A large group of Indians, including Seneca, Mingo, Delaware, Shawnee, Wyandot, Miami, Ottawa, and other warriors, joined forces in 1763, attacking 13 British posts in the West in hopes to drive British settlers back to the Eastern seaboard.

popular sovereignty The concept that settlers of each territory would decide for themselves whether to allow slavery.

Postal Campaign Abolitionist tactic to force the nation to confront the slavery question by flooding the mails, both North and South, with antislavery literature. Their hope was to raise controversy within an area that was the province of the federal government.

postmillennialists Middle-class evangelicals that believed that Christ's Second Coming would occur at the end of 1,000 years of social perfection brought about by the missionary conversion of the world.

praying Indians The Christian Indians of New England.

predestination A theory that states that God has decreed, even before he created the world, who will be saved and who will be damned.

premillennialists Christians (usually ordinary Baptists, Methodists, and Disciples of Christ) who assumed that the millennium would arrive with world-destroying violence, followed by 1,000 years of Christ's rule on Earth.

Presbytery An intermediate level of organization in the Presbyterian church, above individual congregations but below the synod. One of its primary responsibilities was the ordination and placement of ministers.

presidios Military posts constructed by the Spanish to protect the settlers from hostile Indians. They also were used to keep non-Spanish settlers from the area.

press gangs Small groups within the British navy, or hired by the service, to force seamen into British naval service. Press gangs operated in the American colonies during the late 17th and 18th centuries and continued to seize U.S. citizens in the years leading to the War of 1812.

primogeniture The right, by law or custom, of the first-born to inherit the entire estate, to the exclusion of younger siblings.

private fields Farms of up to five acres on which slaves working under the task system were permitted to produce items for their own use and sale in a nearby market.

privateer Privately owned ships that were authorized by a government to attack enemy ships during times of war. The owners of the ships got to claim a portion of whatever was captured. This practice damaged any enemy country that could not dramatically increase naval protection for its merchant ships.

Proclamation of 1763 Issued by the Privy Council, it tried to prevent the colonists from encroaching upon Indian lands by prohibiting settlement west of the Appalachian watershed unless the government first purchased those lands by treaty.

Progressive Party Political party formed by Theodore Roosevelt in 1912 when the Republicans refused to nominate him for president. The party adopted a sweeping reform program.

Prohibition Constitutional ban on the manufacture and sale of alcohol in the United States (1920–1933).

proprietary colonies Territories with legal titles and full governing rights granted to individuals or groups by British monarchs. Several proprietary colonies were established in North America in the late 17th century; three survived until the independence of the United States.

provincial congress A type of convention elected by the colonists to organize resistance. They tended to be larger than the legal assemblies they displaced, and they played a major role in politicizing the countryside.

public Friends The men and women who spoke most frequently and effectively for the Society of Friends. They were as close as the Quakers came to having a clergy. They occupied special elevated seats in some meetinghouses.

public virtue Meant, to the revolutionary generation, patriotism and the willingness of a free and independent people to subordinate their interests to the common good and even to die for their country.

Pullman Strike 1894 Labor strike that became the first nationwide workers' strike against the railroad.

putting-out system Production system in the early Industrial Revolution in which employers "put out" materials to workers, especially women, to make finished products, such as clothing and shoes. Also known as "cottage industry" because the work was done in homes or small workshops.

quasi-slavery Position that resembled slavery, such as that created by the Black Codes.

quitrent A relic of feudalism, a quitrent was a small required annual fee attached to a piece of land. British colonial governments used it as a way of distributing land to settlers while creating a stream of revenue for themselves.

Reagan, Ronald Republican president (1981–1989) who steered domestic politics in a conservative direction and sponsored a huge military buildup.

recall Reform that gave voters the right to remove from office a public servant who had betrayed their trust.

Red Scare Widespread fear in 1919–1920 that radicals had coalesced to establish a communist government on American soil. In response, U.S. government and private citizens undertook a campaign to identify, silence, and, in some cases, imprison radicals.

redemptioners Servants with an indentured contract that allowed them to find masters after they arrived in the colonies. Many German immigrant families were redemptioners and thus were able to stay together while they served their terms.

redlining Refusal by banks and loan associations to grant loans for home buying and business expansion in neighborhoods that contained aging buildings, dense populations, and growing numbers of nonwhites.

referendum Procedure that allows the electorate to decide an issue through a direct vote.

Rehnquist, William Appointed to Chief Justice of the Supreme Court by Reagan in 1986.

republican wife/mother New status gained by women in the American Revolution that entrusted them to educating their sons and ensuring that their sons and husbands were upstanding citizens.

republics Independent Indian villages that were willing to trade with the British teapotand remained outside the French system of Indian alliances.

Restorationism Belief that all theological and institutional changes since the end of biblical times were manmade mistakes and that religious organizations must restore themselves to the purity and simplicity of the apostolic church.

revival A series of emotional religious meetings that led to numerous public conversions.

revolving turret A low structure, often round, on a ship that moved horizontally and contained mounted guns.

Rhode Island System Factory system founded by Samuel Slater and centered on the Arkwright spinning mill at Pawtucket, Rhode Island, in the late 18th century. The system, later imitated by other mill owners, featured factory villages in the countryside where owners could exert better control over their operations and their workers.

rifling Process of cutting spiral grooves in a gun's barrel to impart a spin to the bullet. Perfected in the 1850s, it produced greater accuracy and longer range.

robber barons Industrial leaders who began to restrain their displays of wealth and make significant philanthropic contributions to the public.

Roberts Court Post-2005 Supreme Court, headed by Chief Justice John Roberts, in which conservatives used their five-justice majority to issue a number of rulings that tracked the theories of legal-constitutional conservatives.

Rockefeller, John D. Founder of the Standard Oil Company, whose aggressive practices drove many competitors out of business and made him one of the richest men in America.

Roe v. Wade Supreme Court decision in 1973 that ruled that a blanket prohibition against abortion violated a woman's right to privacy and prompted decades of political controversy.

Roosevelt Corollary 1904 corollary to the Monroe Doctrine, stating that the United States had the right to intervene in domestic affairs of hemispheric nations to quell disorder and forestall European intervention.

Roosevelt, Eleanor A politically engaged and effective First Lady, and an architect of American liberalism.

Roosevelt, Franklin Delano President from 1933 to 1945 and the creator of the New Deal.

Rough Riders Much-decorated volunteer cavalry unit organized by Theodore Roosevelt and Leonard Wood to fight in Cuba in 1898.

Russo-Japanese War Territorial conflict between imperial Japan and Russia mediated by Theodore Roosevelt at Portsmouth, New Hampshire. The peace agreement gave Korea and other territories to Japan, ensured Russia's continuing control over Siberia, and protected China's territorial integrity.

Sacco-Vanzetti Case (1920) Controversial conviction of two Italian-born anarchists accused of armed robbery and murder.

sachem An Algonquian word that means "chief."

Sand Creek massacre Attack led by Colonel John Chivington that killed 200 Cheyenne Indians that returned in peace to their Colorado reservation.

Santa María The flagship and the largest of the three ships used by Christopher Columbus during his first voyage to the Americas. The three-masted vessel ran aground off the northern coast of Haiti.

Saratoga A major turning point in the Revolutionary War. American forces prevented John Burgoyne's army from reaching Albany, cut off its retreat, and forced it to surrender in October 1777. This victory helped bring France into the war.

scalawags Term used by southern Democrats to describe southern whites who worked with the Republicans.

Scott, Dred Missouri slave who sued for freedom on grounds of prolonged residence in a free state and free territory; in 1857, the Supreme Court found against his case, declaring the Missouri Compromise unconstitutional.

secession The act of a state withdrawing from the Union. South Carolina was the first state to attempt to do this in 1860.

Second Bill of Rights 1944 Proposal by President Roosevelt advocating governmental action to ensure that Americans could enjoy a wide range of guaranteed rights, including those of regular employment, adequate food and shelter, appropriate educational opportunities, and health care.

Second Continental Congress The intercolonial body that met in Philadelphia in May 1775 a few weeks after the Battles of Lexington and Concord. It organized the Continental Army, appointed George Washington commander-in-chief, and simultaneously pursued policies of military resistance and conciliation. When conciliation failed, it chose independence in July 1776 and in 1777 drafted the Articles of Confederation, which finally went into force in March 1781.

Second Great Awakening Religious revival that spread across the United States between the 1790s and 1850s, with greatest intensity among the emerging northern middle class from the mid-1820s into the 1830s.

Seneca Falls Convention (1848) First national convention of women's rights activists.

separation of powers The theory that a free government, especially in a republic, should have three independent branches capable of checking or balancing one another: the executive, the legislative (usually bicameral), and the judicial.

Separatists One of the most extreme English Protestant groups that were followers of John Calvin. They began to separate from the Church of England and form their own congregations.

serfdom Early medieval Europe's predominant labor system, which tied peasants to their lords and the land. They were not slaves because they could not be sold from the land.

share wages Payment of workers' wages with a share of the crop rather than with cash.

sharecroppers Tenant farmers who gave up a portion of their crops, primarily as rent to the owners of the land they worked.

sharecropping Working land in return for a share of the crops produced instead of paying cash rent.

Shays's Rebellion An uprising of farmers in western Massachusetts in the winter of 1786–1787. They objected to high taxes and foreclosures for unpaid debts.

Militia from eastern Massachusetts suppressed the rebels.

Sheppard-Towner Act Major social welfare program providing federal funds for prenatal and child health care, 1921–1929.

Sherman Antitrust Act of 1890 Intended to declare any form of trade restraint illegal, but proved to be useless in prosecution of corporations.

sickle cell A crescentor sickle-shaped red blood cell sometimes found in African Americans. It helped protect them from malaria but exposed some children to the dangerous and painful condition of sickle cell anemia.

sit-down strike Labor strike strategy in which workers occupied their factory but refused to do any work until the employer agreed to recognize the workers' union. This strategy succeeded against General Motors in 1937.

sit-in movement Activity that challenged legal segregation by demanding that blacks have the same access to public facilities as whites. These nonviolent demonstrations were staged at restaurants, bus and train stations, and other public places.

Sitting Bull Hunkapapa Lakota (Sioux) chief and holy man who led warriors against the U.S. Army in Montana Territory in 1876, culminating in the Battle of Little Big Horn.

slave labor Coerced involuntary work performed by people under the threat of violence or hardship. Historically, slave labor has taken many forms from chattel slavery, in which people are treated as legally owned personal property, to debt bondage where a person pledges his or her labor to pay off a loan.

Smith, Alfred E. Irish American, Democratic governor of New York who became in 1928 the first Catholic ever nominated for the presidency by a major party.

Smith, Joseph Poor New York farm boy whose visions led him to translate the Book of Mormon in late 1820s. He became the founder and the prophet of the Church of Jesus Christ of Latter-day Saints (Mormons).

Social Darwinism Set of beliefs explaining human history as an ongoing evolutionary struggle between different groups of people for survival and supremacy that was used to justify inequalities between races, classes, and nations.

social networking The process by which people socialize with one another through sites on the Internet.

Social Security Act Centerpiece of the welfare state (1935) that instituted the first federal pension system and set up funds to take care of groups (such as the disabled and unmarried mothers with children) that were unable to support themselves.

socialism Political movement that called for the transfer of industry from private to public control, and the transfer of political power from elites to the laboring masses.

soddies Houses built by Great Plains settlers made from prairie sod that was cut into blocks and stacked to form walls.

sovereign power A term used to describe supreme or final power.

Spanish Civil War Conflict between Spain's republican government and nationalist rebels led by General Francisco Franco.

specie Also called "hard money" as against paper money. In colonial times, it usually meant silver, but it could also include gold coins.

Specie Circular Provision added to the Deposit Act in 1836 that required speculators to pay in silver and gold coins when buying large parcels of public land.

spoils system A postelection practice where a victorious political party awards loyal supporters with appointive public offices.

Sputnik crisis Following Russia's second successful satellite launch, the possibility of nuclear weapons development forced President Eisenhower to expand military arsenal, educational resources, and research capabilities.

stagflation Condition of simultaneous economic stagnation and price inflation.

Stanton, Elizabeth Cady Feminist abolitionist who organized the Seneca Falls Convention.

staple crop A crop grown for commercial sale. It usually was produced in a colonial area and was sold in Europe. The first staple crops were sugar and tobacco.

stay laws A law that delays or postpones something. During the 1780s, many states passed stay laws to delay the due date on debts because of the serious economic problems of the times.

steel cargo containers Made shipping goods and raw materials long distances easier and less expensive.

Strategic Defense Initiative (SDI) Popularly termed "Star Wars," a proposal to develop technology for creation of a space-based defensive missile shield around the United States.

subprime mortgages Mortgages extended to homebuyers who have a poor credit history or whose financial situation suggests a high likelihood of defaulting on their housing loan.

supply-side economics Economic theory that tax reductions targeted toward investors and businesses would stimulate production and eventually create jobs.

Synod The governing body of the Presbyterian church. A synod was a meeting of Presbyterian ministers and prominent laymen to set policies for the whole church.

Taft-Hartley Act Limited a union's power to conduct boycotts, force employers to hire only union members, and to continue a strike harmful to national security; it also required union officials to sign affidavits stating that they did not belong to the Communist Party.

Tallmadge Amendments Two amendments proposed by James Tallmadge Jr. to be added to the Missouri statehood bill before

Missouri's admission to the union; the first barred slaved from being brought into Missouri and the second emancipated Missouri slaves born after admission once they reached their 25th birthday.

tariff A tax on imports.

Tariff of Abominations A 1828 tariff passed by Congress to protect the manufacturers of the northern states by setting high duties on imported goods. Southern opponents denounced the tariff, arguing that it was unconstitutional and harmful to the South's agrarian interests and cotton trade.

task system A system of slave labor under which slaves had to complete specific assignments each day. After these assignments were finished, their time was their own. It was used primarily on rice plantations. Slaves often preferred this system over gang labor because it gave them more autonomy and free time.

Taylor, Frederick Winslow Chief engineer at Philadelphia's Midvale Steel Company whose goal was to make human labor mimic the efficiency of a piece of machinery.

Teapot Dome Political scandal by which Secretary of Interior Albert Fall allowed oil tycoons access to government oil reserves in exchange for $400,000 in bribes.

tejanos Spanish-speaking settlers of Texas. The term comes from the Spanish word Tejas for Texas.

Temporary Assistance to Needy Families (TANF) Program that allowed each state to design its own welfare-to-work programs under general federal guidelines.

tenancy System under which farmers worked land that they did not own.

Tennessee Valley Authority (TVA) Ambitious and successful use of government resources and power to promote economic development throughout the Tennessee Valley.

Tenochtitlán The huge Aztec capital city destroyed by Cortés.

Termination and Relocation Policies designed to assimilate American Indians by terminating tribal status and relocating individuals off reservations.

Tet Offensive Surprise National Liberation Front (NLF) attack during the lunar new year holiday in early 1968 that brought high casualties to the NLF but fueled pessimism about the war's outcome in the United States.

The Medicare Prescription Drug Improvement and Modernization Act 2003 act that created Medicare Part D, a new program that would provide prescription drug benefits for Medicare recipients. The law was controversial because of its enormous cost and because the Federal government was prohibited from negotiating discounts with drug companies.

the strenuous life A phrase coined by Theodore Roosevelt to describe his ideal of a vigorous, athletic new approach to life at the turn of the century.

the surge 2007 effort by the Bush administration, and credited to General David Petraus, that temporarily helped to stabilize Iraq by the short-term deployment of additional U.S. troops and by payments to Sunni tribes in exchange for tempering their opposition to the Shitedominated government in Baghdad.

Third Reich New empire that Adolf Hitler promised the German people would bring glory and unity to the nation.

Three Mile Island Housed a nuclear power plant in Pennsylvania that experienced a major reactor malfunction in 1979; the industry stopped development following this event.

Tories A term for Irish Catholic peasants who murdered Protestant landlords. It was used to describe the followers of Charles II and became one of the names of the two major political parties in England.

transportation revolution New forms of transportation following the War of 1812, including improved roads, canals, and railroads, which made the transition to a market society physically possible by drastically reducing the cost of shipping surplus crops and goods.

treasury notes Paper money used by the Union to help finance the Civil War. One type of treasury note was known as a greenback because of its color.

Treaty of Guadalupe Hidalgo Treaty that authorized the purchase of California, New Mexico, and a Texas border on the Rio Grande from Mexico for 15 million dollars.

Triangle Shirtwaist Company New York City site of a tragic 1911 industrial fire that killed 146 workers who were unable to find their way to safety.

Triple Alliance One set of combatants in World War I, consisting of Germany, Austria-Hungary, and Italy. When Italy left the alliance, this side became known as the Central Powers.

Triple Entente One set of combatants in World War I, consisting of Britain, France, and Russia. As the war went on, this side came to be known as the Allies or Allied Powers.

Troubled Assets Relief Program (TARP) Section of the Emergency Economic Stabilization act of 2008 that authorized the Treasury Department to spread $700 billing throughout the financial system.

Truman Doctrine Policy established by President Truman in 1947 to aid Greece and Turkey in order to prevent Soviet expansionism and the spread of communism.

Trump, Donald J. Republican president who overcame long odds in the 2016 election to win the White House. Though a real estate billionaire, Trump ran as a champion of poor white Americans. He promised them that he would "make America great again."

Tsenacommacah Powhatan Indians' name for their homeland. It may be translated to mean "our land" or "densely inhabited land." Extending from the James River in the south to the Potomac River in the north and from the Eastern Shore of Virginia to the fall line, Tsenacommacah covered all of Tidewater Virginia.

Turner, Nat Baptist lay preacher whose religious visions encouraged him to lead a slave revolt in southern Virginia in 1831 in which 55 whites were killed—more than any other American slave revolt.

Turner's frontier thesis Theory developed by historian Frederick Jackson Turner, who argued that the frontier had been central to the shaping of American character and the success of the U.S. economy and democracy.

Twenty Negro Law Confederate conscription law that exempted from the draft one white man on every plantation owning 20 or more slaves. The law's purpose was to exempt overseers or owners who would ensure discipline over the slaves and keep up production but was regarded as discrimination by nonslaveholding families.

Uncle Tom's Cabin Published by Harriet Beecher Stowe in 1852, this sentimental novel told the story of the Christian slave Uncle Tom and became a best seller and the most powerful antislavery tract of the antebellum years.

underconsumptionism Theory that underconsumption, or a chronic weakness in consumer demand, had caused the depression. This theory guided the Second New Deal, leading to the passage of laws designed to stimulate consumer demand.

underground railroad A small group who helped slaves escape bondage in the South. It took on legendary status, and its role was much exaggerated.

unicameral legislature A legislature with only one chamber or house.

Union leagues Organizations that informed African American voters of, and mobilized them to, support the Republican Party.

Unionists Southerners who remained loyal to the Union during the Civil War.

United Nations (UN) An international organization of Allied powers formed in 1945 to promote peaceful political change and to deter aggressive nations.

Universal Declaration of Human Rights Document adopted by the United Nations in 1948 that established human rights and freedoms as cornerstones of international law.

universal male suffrage System that allowed all adult males to vote without regard to property, religious, or race qualifications or limitations.

vaqueros Mexican cowboys who rounded up cattle, branded them, and drove them to San Francisco.

Villa, Francisco ("Pancho") Favored by Woodrow Wilson to be elected Mexico's leader in 1913.

Virginia and Kentucky Resolves Resolutions authored by James Madison and Thomas Jefferson and passed by the Virginia and Kentucky legislatures in 1798 and 1799 in protest of the Alien and Sedition Acts. Jefferson's Kentucky Resolves claimed that states could nullify laws that they deemed unconstitutional, an argument that states'rights southerners would use after 1830.

Virginia Plan Drafted by James Madison for the Constitutional Convention of 1787, it proposed a bicameral legislature, with representation in both houses apportioned according to population. Also known as the "large state" plan.

virtual representation The English concept that Members of Parliament represented the entire empire, not just a local constituency and its voters. According to this theory, settlers were represented in Parliament in the same way that nonvoting subjects in Britain were represented. The colonists accepted virtual representation for nonvoting settlers within their colonies but denied that the term could describe their relationship with Parliament.

Voting Rights Act of 1965 Law that provided new federal mechanisms to help guarantee African Americans the right to vote.

Wagner Act (NLRA) Named after its sponsor Senator Robert Wagner (D-NY), this 1935 act gave every worker the right to join a union and compelled employers to bargain with unions in good faith.

Walker, Madame C. J. Black entrepreneur who built a lucrative business from the hair and skin lotions she devised and sold to black customers throughout the country.

walking cities Compact residential areas near working districts with different income and ethnic groups living in close proximity.

Waltham-Lowell System Factory system founded by Francis Cabot Lowell's Boston Manufacturing Company, which established its first mill at Waltham, Massachusetts, in 1813. The system built on the earlier Rhode Island factory model by using heavier machinery to produce finished cloth and by employing single, young farm women in New England.

War Hawks Members of the 12th Congress, most of them young nationalists from southern and western areas, who promoted war with Britain.

War Industries Board (WIB) U.S. government agency responsible for mobilizing American industry for war

Washington Temperance Society Society established in 1840 by reformed drinkers of the laboring classes who operated separate from the church and converted drinkers through compassion and persuasion.

Washington, Booker T. Founder of Tuskegee Institute and most famous for his controversial speech at the 1895 Atlanta Exposition.

Watergate Business and residential complex in Washington, D.C., that came to stand for the political espionage and cover-ups directed by the Nixon administration. The complicated web of Watergate scandals brought about Nixon's resignation in 1974.

Wells, Ida B. Anti-lynching activist who wrote and spoke in protest, gaining the attention of the North only after taking her campaign to England.

Western Federation of Miners (WFM) Association of union mine workers established in 1893 to protect their rights.

Wheatley, Phillis Eight-year-old Phillis Wheatley arrived in Boston from Africa in 1761 and was sold as a slave to wealthy John and Susannah Wheatley. Susannah taught her to read and write, and in 1767 she published her first poem in Boston. In 1773, she visited London to celebrate the publication there of a volume of her poetry, an event that made her a transatlantic sensation. On her return to Boston, the Wheatleys emancipated her.

Whigs The name of an obscure sect of Scottish religious extremists who favored the assassination of Charles and James of England. The term was used to denote one of the two leading political parties of late 17th-century England.

Whiskey Rebellion Revolt in Western Pennsylvania against the federal excise tax on whiskey.

White City Monument created for the Columbia Exposition of 1893 in Chicago.

Whitney, Eli The Connecticut-born tutor who invented the cotton gin.

Wilmot Proviso Famous proviso made by Congressman David Wilmot regarding an amendment to an army appropriations bill that framed the national debate over slavery for the next 15 years.

Wisconsin Idea Refers to a policy, first adopted in Wisconsin in the early years of the 20th century, to bring together employers, trade unionists and professionals to discuss and shape relations between industry and labor in the state; a number of other states would adopt this policy.

women's movement Took place between 1953 and 1963; women began speaking out about their political rights, race and gender discrimination, employment opportunities and equitable working environments, and the lack of public roles available to them.

Works Progress Administration (WPA) Federal relief agency established in 1935 that disbursed billions to pay for infrastructural improvements and funded a vast program of public art.

World Trade Organization (WTO) Established in 1995 to head international trade between nations.

Wounded Knee Site of a shootout between Indians and Army troops at the Pine Ridge Indian reservation in southwestern South Dakota.

XYZ Affair Incident that precipitated an undeclared war with France when three French officials (identified as X, Y, and Z) demanded that American emissaries pay a bribe before negotiating disputes between the two countries.

Yankees A Dutch word for New Englanders that originally meant something like "land pirate."

yellow journalism Newspaper stories embellished with sensational or titillating details when the true reports did not seem dramatic enough.

Yorktown The last major engagement of the Revolutionary War. Washington's army, two French armies, and a French fleet trapped Lord Cornwallis at Yorktown and forced his army to surrender in October 1781.

Young America movement A group of men affiliated with the Democratic Party in the 1840s who sought the expansion of the United States across the continent.

Zenger, John Peter Printer of the New York Weekly Journal who was acquitted in 1735 by a jury of the crime of seditious libel after his paper sharply criticized Governor William Cosby.

Zimmerman telegram Telegram from Germany's foreign secretary instructing the German minister in Mexico to ask that country's government to attack the United States in return for German assistance in regaining Mexico's "lost provinces" (Texas, New Mexico, and Arizona).

Index

Page numbers in italics refer to illustrations.

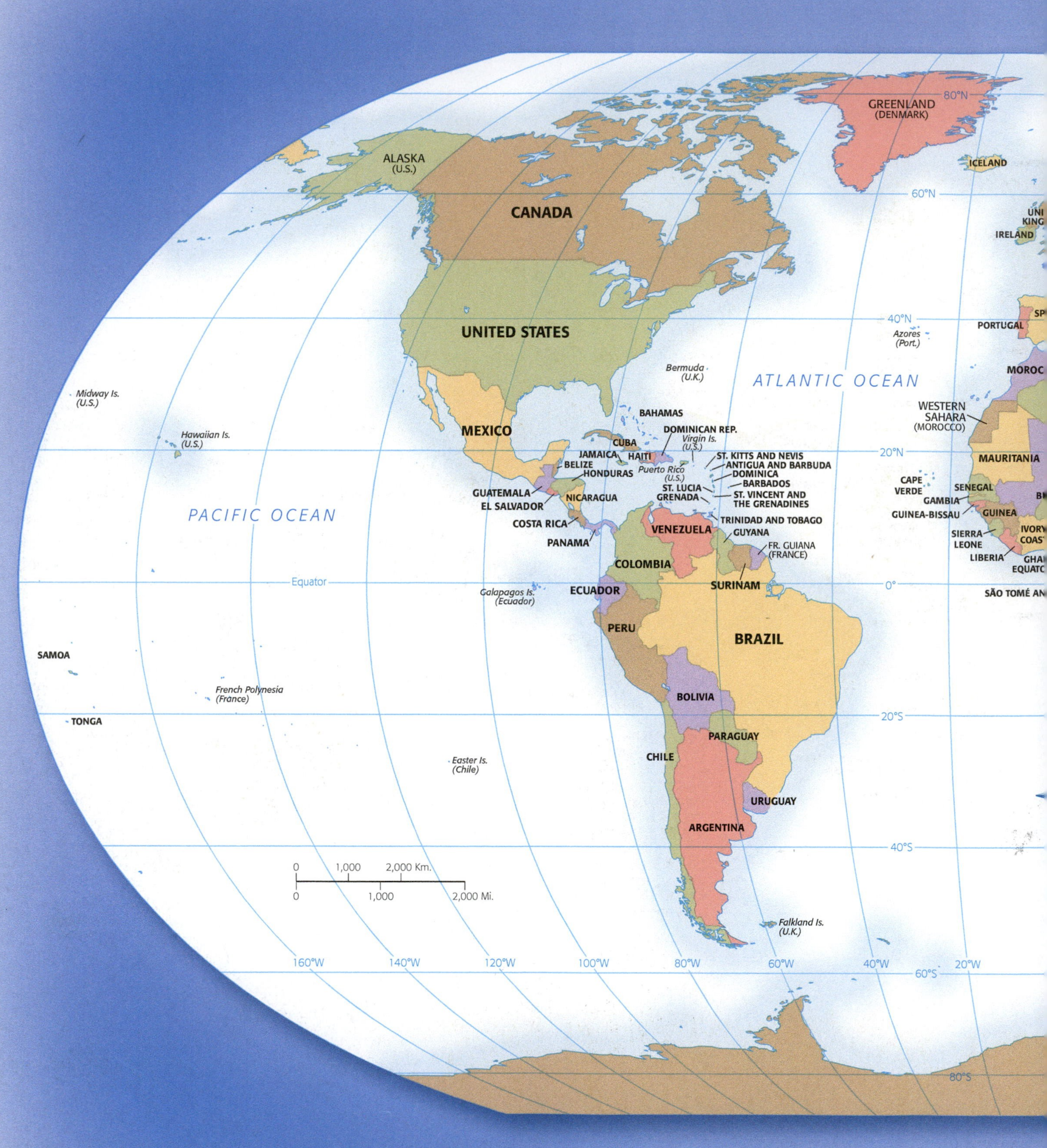

GREENLAND
(DENMARK)
ICELAND
ALASKA
(U.S.)
CANADA
UNITED STATES
MEXICO
ATLANTIC OCEAN
PACIFIC OCEAN
Midway Is.
(U.S.)
Hawaiian Is.
(U.S.)
Bermuda
(U.K.)
Azores
(Port.)
PORTUGAL
IRELAND
WESTERN
SAHARA
(MOROCCO)
MAURITANIA
CAPE
VERDE
SENEGAL
GAMBIA
GUINEA-BISSAU
GUINEA
SIERRA
LEONE
LIBERIA
BAHAMAS
DOMINICAN REP.
Virgin Is.
(U.S.)
CUBA
JAMAICA
HAITI
BELIZE
HONDURAS
Puerto Rico
(U.S.)
ST. KITTS AND NEVIS
ANTIGUA AND BARBUDA
DOMINICA
BARBADOS
ST. LUCIA
GRENADA
ST. VINCENT AND
THE GRENADINES
GUATEMALA
EL SALVADOR
NICARAGUA
COSTA RICA
PANAMA
TRINIDAD AND TOBAGO
VENEZUELA
GUYANA
FR. GUIANA
(FRANCE)
COLOMBIA
SURINAM
ECUADOR
Galapagos Is.
(Ecuador)
PERU
BRAZIL
BOLIVIA
PARAGUAY
CHILE
URUGUAY
ARGENTINA
Falkland Is.
(U.K.)
SAMOA
TONGA
French Polynesia
(France)
Easter Is.
(Chile)
Equator
80°N
60°N
40°N
20°N
0°
20°S
40°S
60°S
80°S
160°W
140°W
120°W
100°W
80°W
60°W
40°W
20°W
0
1,000
2,000 Km.
0
1,000
2,000 Mi.

ABBREVIATIONS

AUS.	AUSTRIA
BEL.	BELGIUM
B. H.	BOSNIA AND HERZEGOVINA
CR.	CROATIA
CZ.	CZECH REPUBLIC
DEN.	DENMARK
HUNG.	HUNGARY
K.	KOSOVO
LUX.	LUXEMBOURG
MAC.	MACEDONIA
MO.	MONTENEGRO
NETH.	NETHERLANDS
SE.	SERBIA
SLK.	SLOVAKIA
SLN.	SLOVENIA
SWITZ.	SWITZERLAND

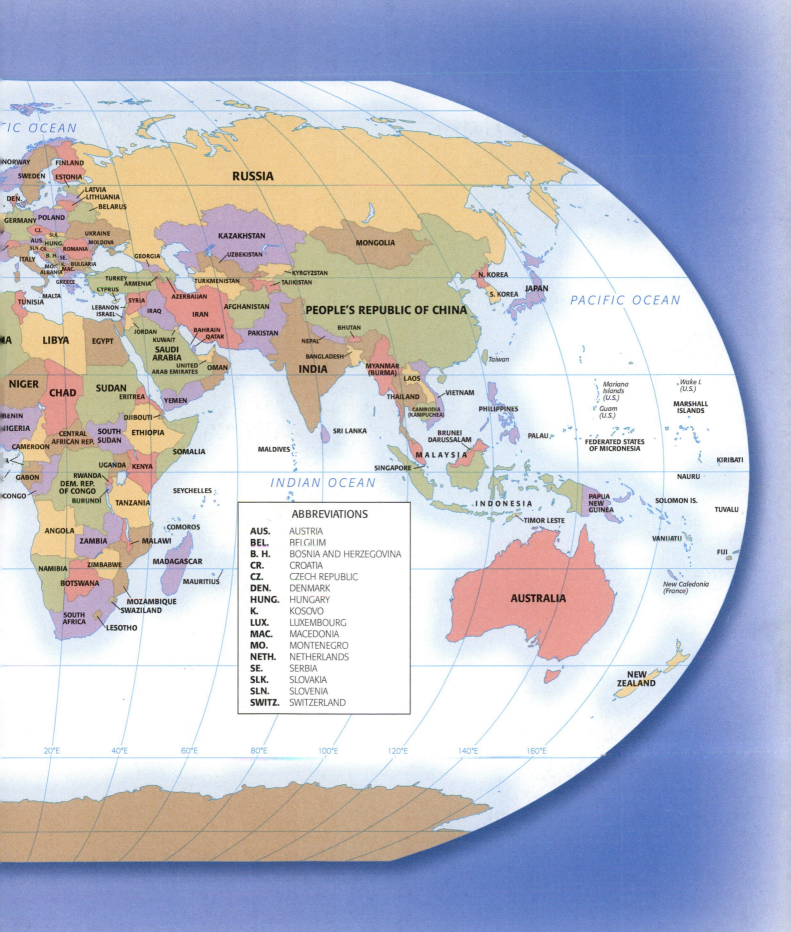